The Norton Introduction to

LITERATURE

FIFTH EDITION

The Norton Introduction to LITERATURE

FIFTH EDITION

Carl E. Bain

Jerome Beaty

J. Paul Hunter

W · W · NORTON & COMPANY · NEW YORK · LONDON

Printed in the United States of America.

The text of this book is composed in Electra,
with the display set in Kabel.
Composition by Maple-Vail Book Mfg Group.
Manufacturing by R. R. Donnelley.
Book design by Jack Meserole.

ISBN 0-393-95938-4
W. W. Norton & Company, Inc., 500 Fifth Avenue, New York, N.Y. 10110
W. W. Norton & Company, Ltd., 10 Coptic Street, London WC1A 1PU

4 5 6 7 8 9 0

CONTENTS

FICTION

POETRY

Reading Poetry 611

Understanding the Text 639

DRAMA

WRITING ABOUT LITERATURE

FOREWORD TO THE FIFTH EDITION

Reading is action. Even though it is often done quietly and alone, reading is a profoundly social activity, and a vigorous and demanding one. There is nothing passive about reading; it requires attention, energy, an act of will. Texts have the potential for meaning, implication, response, and result; but the reader must activate them, give them life, and turn them from quiet print into a lively interplay of ideas and feelings. Reading makes things happen, usually in the mind and imagination, but sometimes in the larger world as well, for the process of reading involves not just the consciousness of the self but an awareness of the other—what is beyond the self. Reading doesn't just happen to you; you have to **do** it, and doing it involves decision, reaching out, discovery, awareness. Reading is an act of power, and learning how to get the most out of its possibilities can be an invigorating activity. For all its association with quietness, solitude, and the sedentary life, reading involves—at its deepest level—action and interaction.

Through five editions, *The Norton Introduction to Literature* has been committed to these principles. This edition, like those before it, offers many different ways of building and reinforcing the skills of reading; it emphasizes the power and importance of historical and cultural contexts. In this edition, we have added an introductory chapter on each major literary genre—*Reading Fiction*, *Reading Poetry*, *Reading Drama*—and we have also added chapters on evaluating each genre and on how the many different elements in any text add up to a whole. And we have retained the popular section on writing about literature, added paper topics and analytical questions, and provided many, many new selections.

The Norton Introduction to Literature offers in a single volume a complete course in reading and writing about literature. It is both an anthology and a textbook—a "teaching anthology"—for the indispensable course in which college student and college teacher begin to read literature seriously together.

But *The Norton Introduction to Literature* remains more than a grab-bag of good things to read. The works are arranged in order to introduce a reader to the serious study of literature. Each genre—fiction, poetry, drama—is approached in three logical steps. Fiction, for example, is introduced by *Reading Fiction*, which treats the purpose and nature of fiction and the reading experience generally. This is followed by the seven-chapter section called *Understanding the Text*, in which stories are analyzed by questions of craft, the so-called elements of fiction; this section ends with a chapter entitled *The Whole Text*, which makes use of all or most of the analytical aids offered in the previous chapters, putting them together to see the work as a whole. *Exploring Contexts* suggests some ways of seeing a work of literature interacting with its temporal and cultural contexts and reaching out beyond the page.

The sections on reading, analyzing, and placing the work in context are followed, in each genre, by guidance in taking that final and extremely difficult step—evaluation. *Evaluating Poetry*, for example, discusses how one would go about assessing the merits of two poems, not to offer definitive judgments, a litmus test, or even a checklist or formula, but to show how one goes about bringing to consciousness, defining, modifying, articulating, and negotiating one's judgments about a work of literature.

Ending each genre, *Reading More* —— is a reservoir of additional examples, for independent study or a different approach. The book's arrangement seeks to facilitate the reader's movement from narrower to broader questions, mirroring the way people read—wanting to learn more as they experience more.

We offer a full section on *Writing about Literature*. In it we deal both with the writing process as applied to literary works—choosing a topic, gathering evidence, developing an argument, and so forth—and with the varieties of a reader's written responses, from copying and paraphrasing to analysis and interpretation: we explore not merely the hows, but the whats and whys as well.

In the 90s it is no longer enough, either for reading or writing about literature, to be familiar only with the methods of formal analysis. New to this edition is a discussion of critical approaches, designed to provide the student with a basic overview of contemporary critical theory, as well as an introduction to its terminology.

The Fifth Edition includes 48 stories, 16 of which are new; over 400 poems, 88 of which are new; and 18 plays, 8 of which are new.

The drama section, especially, has been reinvigorated. New selections include Susan Glaspell's *Trifles*, Lillian Hellman's *The Little Foxes*, Molière's *The Doctor in Spite of Himself*, Sharon Pollock's *Blood Relations*, August Wilson's *Fences*, Aristophanes's *Lysistrata*, Margaret Duras's screenplay for *Hiroshima Mon Amour*, and David Henry Hwang's *M. Butterfly*.

In fiction, we have added stories by Margaret Atwood, Ann Beattie, Louise Erdrich, Richard Ford, Charlotte Perkins Gilman, Nadine Gordimer, Ernest Hemingway, Jamaica Kincaid, Bharati Mukherjee, Flannery O'Connor, Katherine Anne Porter, Elizabeth Tallent, Amy Tan, Leo Tolstoy, and Luisa Valenzuela.

The poetry section has been similarly infused with selections familiar and fresh, with newly included works by Dannie Abse, Diane Ackerman, Agha Shahid Ali, John Ashbery, Margaret Atwood, Aphra Behn, Robert Bringhurst, Marilyn Chin, Amy Clampitt, Robert Creeley, Nora Dauenhauer, Peter De Vries, Rita Dove, Alan Dugan, Stephen Dunn, David Ferry, Robert Francis, Tess Gallagher, Robert Hass, David Helwig, Elizabeth Jennings, D. G. Jones, Donald Justice, Galway Kinnell, Irving Layton, Li-Young Lee, Dorothy Livesay, Douglas Lochhead, Heather McHugh, Claude McKay, Eli Mandel, Harry Mathews, William Matthews, Pat Mora, Sharon Olds, Michael Ondaatje, Eric Ormsby, P. K. Page, Linda Pastan, Sylvia Plath, Katha Pollitt, Jim Powell, Ishmael Reed, Adrienne Rich, Alberto Ríos, Pattiann Rogers, Mary Jo Salter, Anne Sexton, Alan Shapiro, Stevie Smith, William Stafford, Ruth Stone, Miriam Waddington, David Wagoner, and Judith Wright.

Certain editorial procedures that proved their usefulness in earlier editions have been retained. First of all, the works are annotated, as is customary in Norton anthologies; the notes are informational and not interpretative, for the aim is to help readers understand and appreciate the work, not to dictate a meaning or a response. In order to avoid giving the impression that all literature was written at the same time, we have noted at the right margin after each selection the date of first book publication (or, when preceded by a *p*, first periodical publication or, when the date appears at the left margin, the year of composition).

In all our work on this edition we have been guided by teachers in other English departments and in our own, by students who wrote us as the authors of the textbook they were using, and by those who were able to approach us after class as their teachers: we hope that with such help we have been able to offer you a solid and stimulating introduction to the experience of literature.

Acknowledgments We would like to thank our teachers, for their example in the love of literature and in the art of sharing that love; our students, for their patience as we are learning from them to be better teachers of literature; our wives and children, for their understanding when the work of preparing this text made us seem less than perfectly loving husbands and fathers.

We would also like to thank our colleagues, many of whom have taught our book and evaluated our efforts, for their constant encouragement and enlightenment. Of our colleagues at Emory University and the University of Chicago, we would like especially to thank Michaelyn Burnette, William B. Dillingham, Ron Schuchard, John Sitter, Floyd C. Watkins, and Sally Wolff (Emory) and Marianne Conroy, Timothy Dykstal, Marianne Eismann, Nancy Henry, Jonathan Martin, Robert von Hallberg, and John Wright (Chicago). And we thank also Clark Blaise (University of Iowa); T. E. Blom (University of British Columbia); Patricia Brocker; Thomas R. Carper (University of Maine); Frank W. Childrey (Northwest Mississippi Junior College); Claudia Citkowitz; Randy R. Conine (El Centro College); Michael P. Dean (University of Mississippi); Stephen F. Evans (University of Kansas); Norman Feltes (York University); Lila F. Fink (Pepperdine University); Frederick Goldberg (Clayton Junior College); Larry Gray (Southeastern Louisiana University); Alan Grob (Rice University); Daniel A. Harris (Rutgers University); Christopher Hudgins (University of Nevada); Kathryn Hunter (Northwestern University School of Medicine); Kristin Hunter (University of Pennsylvania); Lisa Hunter (SUNY Buffalo Medical School); William Kinsley (Université de Montréal); Stuart Kurland (Muhlenberg College); Vincent J. Liesenfeld (University of Oklahoma); Gayla McGlamery (Loyola College in Maryland); Wallace Martin (University of Toledo); William Morgan (Illinois State University); Nils Peterson (San José State University); Linda Ray Pratt (University of Nebraska); Richard Quaintance (Douglass College); Joseph N. Riddell (University of California at Los Angeles); Ronald Schleifer (University of Oklahoma); John Shaw (Florida State University); John R. Shriver (Wayne State University); Irwin Simpkins (DeKalb College); John M. Slatin (University of Texas at Austin); Frederick Stocking (Williams College); Kristina Straub (Carnegie-Mellon University); Anna Taruschio; Rae Thompson (University of Guelph); Dennis

Todd (Georgetown University); Richard Turner (Indiana University—Purdue University at Indianapolis); Patricia Vicari (Scarborough College of the University of Toronto); Melissa Walker; Arthur Williams (Louisiana School for Mathematics, Science and the Arts): Dorothy A. Winsor (Wayne State University); and Curt R. Zimansky (University of Colorado).

We would like to thank our friends at W. W. Norton & Company, especially the late John Benedict, to whom we dedicate this revision, and also John Mardirosian, Fred McFarland, Diane O'Connor, Nancy Palmquist, Candace Watt, and last (and most) Barry Wade.

J.B., J.P.H.

The Norton Introduction to

LITERATURE

FIFTH EDITION

FICTION

Reading Fiction

SPENCER HOLST

The Zebra Storyteller

Once upon a time there was a Siamese cat who pretended to be a lion and spoke inappropriate Zebraic.

That language is whinnied by the race of striped horses in Africa.

Here now: An innocent zebra is walking in a jungle and approaching from another direction is the little cat; they meet.

"Hello there!" says the Siamese cat in perfectly pronounced Zebraic. "It certainly is a pleasant day, isn't it? The sun is shining, the birds are singing, isn't the world a lovely place to live today!"

The zebra is so astonished at hearing a Siamese cat speaking like a zebra, 5
why—he's just fit to be tied.

So the little cat quickly ties him up, kills him, and drags the better parts of the carcass back to his den.

The cat successfully hunted zebras many months in this manner, dining on filet mignon of zebra every night, and from the better hides he made bow neckties and wide belts after the fashion of the decadent princes of the Old Siamese court.

He began boasting to his friends he was a lion, and he gave them as proof the fact that he hunted zebras.

The delicate noses of the zebras told them there was really no lion in the neighborhood. The zebra deaths caused many to avoid the region. Superstitious, they decided the woods were haunted by the ghost of a lion.

One day the storyteller of the zebras was ambling, and through his mind ran 10
plots for stories to amuse the other zebras, when suddenly his eyes brightened, and he said, "That's it! I'll tell a story about a Siamese cat who learns to speak our language! What an idea! That'll make 'em laugh!"

Just then the Siamese cat appeared before him, and said, "Hello there! Pleasant day today, isn't it!"

The zebra storyteller wasn't fit to be tied at hearing a cat speaking his language, because he'd been thinking about that very thing.

He took a good look at the cat, and he didn't know why, but there was something about his looks he didn't like, so he kicked him with a hoof and killed him.

That is the function of the storyteller.

1971

"The Zebra Storyteller" suggests that the purpose of stories is to prepare us for the unexpected. Though the storyteller thinks he is just spinning stories out of his own imagination, in order to amuse, his stories prove to be practical. When the extraordinary occurs—like a Siamese cat speaking Zebraic—the storyteller is prepared because he has already imagined it, and he alone is able to protect his tribe against the unheard-of.

Other storytellers make the function of fiction less extraordinary. According to them, fiction enables readers to avoid projecting false hopes and fears (such as the zebras' superstitious belief that they are being preyed on by the ghost of a lion) and shows them what they can actually expect in their everyday lives, so that they can prepare themselves. In George Eliot's novel *Adam Bede,* Hetty Sorrel is being paid admiring attention by the young squire, and she dreams of elopement, marriage, all sorts of vague pleasures. She does not dream that she will be seduced, made pregnant, abandoned. Her imagination has not been trained to project any "narrative" other than her dreams: "Hetty had never read a novel," George Eliot tells us, "[so] how could she find a shape for her expectations?"

We are all storytellers, then, of one stripe or another. Whenever we plan the future or ponder a decision, we are telling stories—projecting expectations through narrative. Whether we tell stories or read them, we are educating our imaginations, either extending our mental experience in the actual, as Hetty might have done by reading novels, or preparing ourselves for the extraordinary and unexpected, like the zebra storyteller.

The actual and the extraordinary suggest two different uses readers make of fiction. Sometimes we want to read about people like ourselves, or about places, experiences, and ideas that are familiar and agreeable. Most of us initially prefer American literature and twentieth-century literature to literature remote in time or place. Indeed, stories must somehow be related to our own lives before we can find them intellectually or emotionally meaningful. No matter what our literary experience and taste, most of us relate in a special way to stories about people like us, experiences like our own, and especially to a story that mentions our hometown or neighborhood or the name of the street that we used to walk along on our way to school. No one would deny that one of the many things that fiction may be "for" is learning about ourselves and the world around us.

But at other times the last thing we want is a story about people like ourselves, experiences like those of our everyday lives, and places and times like here and now. At such times we want (or are accused of wanting) to escape. If fiction must be relevant enough to relate meaningfully to us, it must also be "irrelevant," different, strange—as strange, perhaps, as a Siamese cat speaking Zebraic. It must take us out of ourselves, out of the confining vision of our own eyes, which is conditioned by our own background and experience, and show us that there are ways of looking at the world other than our own. So, in addition to many stories about approximately our own time and place, this collection includes a sprinkling of stories written in the last century, a few written in vastly different cultures, and a fair number written about worlds that have not existed or do not (yet) exist.

What a story shows us or teaches us we may call its **message**—an objective, universal truth that we were unaware of before reading the story. We gradually learn, however, that stories tell us not so much what life means as what it's like. Rather than abstract or "objective" truths, stories deal with perceptions. These perceptions may be translated into messages, but we soon discover that the messages boil down to things like "There's good and bad in everybody," "Hurting people is wrong," and "Everything is not what it seems"—messages that Western Union, much less Western literature, might not find too urgent or startlingly illuminating. Indeed, we do not have to agree with what a story says or shows so long as we are convinced that if we had *those* eyes and were *there*, this is what we might see.

Whenever we can say yes, we are convinced, then we have been able to go beyond the limitations of our own vision, our own past and conditions. We are able to see a new world, or the same old world in a new way. And by recognizing that we can see things differently, we realize that things we used to think were fixed, objective entities "out there" were fixed only in our perceptions. Or, as is too often the case, we realize that we have been accepting things at face value; we have been perceiving what habit and convention have told us is "really there." This, then, may awaken us to look at things for ourselves. For example, we "know" a table top is square, but in a story we may be told it is diamond-shaped. We understand that if we were to look at the table top from a certain angle it would look diamond-shaped. But doesn't that mean that the table top is square only when we look from a certain angle? How often do we look at it from that angle? We look again, and we recognize that though we've always "known" a table top is a square, we've never really *seen* it as one. The story has not only allowed us to see reality from another angle, but it has helped us to sharpen our own vision, our own experience.

In the story that follows, both the eighteen-year-old narrator and Jack are storytellers: each projects a future. The story, however, remains in the present, so we cannot tell which projection is right. Like the characters, we are more or less in the same position as we are in the middle of our own lives. Though they may not get to know the future, both Jack and the narrator learn through their storytelling that more than one scenario of the future can be projected. Even if we think the narrator as naive as George Eliot's Hetty, projecting a dream rather than a possible reality, she has now at least "read Jack's novel," so she knows there are alternative futures. And so do we.

Since Jack and the narrator are not zebras but people, people you might think of as real, maybe even people somewhat like yourself, you may feel in a position to take sides. You may be surprised to find that some of your classmates do not agree with you. But in discussion or argument you may discover not only that there are reasonable differences of opinion, but that what one believes about the future of the story tells you something about that person (and that what they believe about their future tells you something about the characters of Jack and the narrator). And it tells you more, perhaps, than just what they think about love. If the storytelling of others tells you something about them, then your own storytelling (opinions, expectations, guesses) tells them and yourself something about you. You may realize too that you, your classmates, Jack, and the narrator may all become increasingly aware of differences and possibilities.

ELIZABETH TALLENT

No One's a Mystery

For my eighteenth birthday Jack gave me a five-year diary with a latch and a little key, light as a dime. I was sitting beside him scratching at the lock, which didn't seem to want to work, when he thought he saw his wife's Cadillac in the distance, coming toward us. He pushed me down onto the dirty floor of the pickup and kept one hand on my head while I inhaled the musk of his cigarettes in the dashboard ashtray and sang along with Rosanne Cash on the tape deck. We'd been drinking tequila and the bottle was between his legs, resting up against his crotch, where the seam of his Levi's was bleached linen-white, though the Levi's were nearly new. I don't know why his Levi's always bleached like that, along the seams and at the knees. In a curve of cloth his zipper glinted, gold.

"It's her," he said. "She keeps the lights on in the daytime. I can't think of a single habit in a woman that irritates me more than that." When he saw that I was going to stay still he took his hand from my head and ran it through his own dark hair.

"Why does she?" I said.

"She thinks it's safer. Why does she need to be safer? She's driving exactly fifty-five miles an hour. She believes in those signs: 'Speed Monitored by Aircraft.' It doesn't matter that you can look up and see that the sky is empty."

"She'll see your lips move, Jack. She'll know you're talking to someone."

"She'll think I'm singing along with the radio."

He didn't lift his head, just raised the fingers in salute while the pressure of his palm steadied the wheel, and I heard the Cadillac honk twice, musically; he was driving easily eighty miles an hour. I studied his boots. The elk heads stitched into the leather were bearded with frayed thread, the toes were scuffed, and there was a compact wedge of muddy manure between the heel and the sole—the same boots he'd been wearing for the two years I'd known him. On the tape deck Rosanne Cash sang, "Nobody's into me, no one's a mystery."

"Do you think she's getting famous because of who her daddy is or for herself?" Jack said.

"There are about a hundred pop tops on the floor, did you know that? Some little kid could cut a bare foot on one of these, Jack."

"No little kids get into this truck except for you."

"How come you let it get so dirty?"

" 'How come,' " he mocked. "You even sound like a kid. You can get back into the seat now, if you want. She's not going to look over her shoulder and see you."

"How do you know?"

"I just know," he said. "Like I know I'm going to get meat loaf for supper. It's in the air. Like I know what you'll be writing in that diary."

"What will I be writing?" I knelt on my side of the seat and craned around to look at the butterfly of dust printed on my jeans. Outside the window Wyoming was dazzling in the heat. The wheat was fawn and yellow and parted smoothly by the thin dirt road. I could smell the water in the irrigation ditches hidden in the wheat.

"Tonight you'll write, 'I love Jack. This is my birthday present from him. I can't imagine anybody loving anybody more than I love Jack.' "

"I can't."

"In a year you'll write, 'I wonder what I ever really saw in Jack. I wonder why I spent so many days just riding around in his pickup. It's true he taught me something about sex. It's true there wasn't ever much else to do in Cheyenne.' "

"I won't write that."

"In two years you'll write, 'I wonder what that old guy's name was, the one with the curly hair and the filthy dirty pickup truck and time on his hands.' "

"I won't write that."

"No?"

"Tonight I'll write, 'I love Jack. This is my birthday present from him. I can't imagine anybody loving anybody more than I love Jack.' "

"No, you can't," he said. "You can't imagine it."

25 “In a year I’ll write, ‘Jack should be home any minute now. The table’s set—my grandmother’s linen and her old silver and the yellow candles left over from the wedding—but I don’t know if I can wait until after the trout à la Navarra to make love to him.’ ”

“It must have been a fast divorce.”

“In two years I’ll write, ‘Jack should be home by now. Little Jack is hungry for his supper. He said his first word today besides “Mama” and “Papa.” He said “kaka.” ’ ”

Jack laughed. “He was probably trying to finger-paint with kaka on the bathroom wall when you heard him say it.”

“In three years I’ll write, ‘My nipples are a little sore from nursing Eliza Rosamund.’ ”

30 “Rosamund. Every little girl should have a middle name she hates.”

“ ‘Her breath smells like vanilla and her eyes are just Jack’s color of blue.’ ”

“That’s nice,” Jack said.

“So, which one do you like?”

“I like yours,” he said. “But I believe mine.”

35 “It doesn’t matter. I believe mine.”

“Not in your heart of hearts, you don’t.”

“You’re wrong.”

“I’m not wrong,” he said. “And her breath would smell like your milk, and it’s kind of a bittersweet smell, if you want to know the truth.”

1985

Reading fiction may ultimately contribute significantly to the way we understand and experience our own lives, but what kind of an experience is reading fiction itself? What is going on inside us while we are reading? What are we thinking? What are we feeling?

One way to find out is by an act of mental contortion: try looking over your own shoulder while you read. Try it with the next story, Guy de Maupassant’s “The Jewelry,” paying more attention than you usually do not just to the story but to your own thoughts and responses while you are reading it. You may want to pause a few extra heartbeats after each sentence, fifteen to thirty extra seconds after each paragraph, and two or three minutes after you finish reading the whole thing.

Consider the title first. “The Jewelry”—Will it be lost? Will it be stolen? Inherited? Something else? What will happen? What kind of story will it be? Read the one-sentence first paragraph: nothing about jewelry! But we have a young man and a young woman and love. M. (for Monsieur) Lantin is “enveloped in love as in a net.” This does not sound very promising, does it? What are these people like? What is their situation? As you read along how do your expectations change? How does your view of the characters change? As you get into the story notice what you remember of the early portions and any details in mid-story that remind you of earlier ones. There are other questions, but they can wait until after you have watched yourself read the story.

GUY DE MAUPASSANT

The Jewelry[1]

Having met the girl one evening, at the house of the office-superintendent, M. Lantin became enveloped in love as in a net.

She was the daughter of a country-tutor, who had been dead for several years. Afterward she had come to Paris with her mother, who made regular visits to several bourgeois families of the neighborhood, in hopes of being able to get her daughter married. They were poor and respectable, quiet and gentle. The young girl seemed to be the very ideal of that pure good woman to whom every young man dreams of entrusting his future. Her modest beauty had a charm of angelic shyness; and the slight smile that always dwelt about her lips seemed a reflection of her heart.

Everybody sang her praises; all who knew her kept saying: "The man who gets her will be lucky. No one could find a nicer girl than that."

M. Lantin, who was then chief clerk in the office of the Minister of the Interior, with a salary of 3,500 francs a year,[2] demanded her hand, and married her.

He was unutterably happy with her. She ruled his home with an economy 5
so adroit that they really seemed to live in luxury. It would be impossible to conceive of any attentions, tendernesses, playful caresses which she did not lavish upon her husband; and such was the charm of her person that, six years after he married her, he loved her even more than he did the first day.

There were only two points upon which he ever found fault with her—her love of the theater, and her passion for false jewelry.

Her lady-friends (she was acquainted with the wives of several small office holders) were always bringing her tickets for the theaters; whenever there was a performance that made a sensation, she always had her *loge* secured, even for first performances; and she would drag her husband with her to all these entertainments, which used to tire him horribly after his day's work. So at last he begged her to go to the theater with some lady-acquaintances who would consent to see her home afterward. She refused for quite a while—thinking it would not look very well to go out thus unaccompanied by her husband. But finally she yielded, just to please him; and he felt infinitely grateful to her therefor.

Now this passion for the theater at last evoked in her the desire of dress. It was true that her toilette remained simple, always in good taste, but modest; and

1. Translated by Lafcadio Hearn.
2. A mid-level bureaucratic wage, perhaps about $25,000–$30,000 today.

her sweet grace, her irresistible grace, ever smiling and shy, seemed to take fresh charm from the simplicity of her robes. But she got into the habit of suspending in her pretty ears two big cut pebbles, fashioned in imitation of diamonds; and she wore necklaces of false pearls, bracelets of false gold, and haircombs studded with paste-imitations of precious stones.

Her husband, who felt shocked by this love of tinsel and show, would often say—"My dear, when one has not the means to afford real jewelry, one should appear adorned with one's natural beauty and grace only—and these gifts are the rarest of jewels."

But she would smile sweetly and answer: "What does it matter? I like those things—that is my little whim. I know you are right; but one can't make oneself over again. I've always loved jewelry so much!"

And then she would roll the pearls of the necklaces between her fingers, and make the facets of the cut crystals flash in the light, repeating: "Now look at them—see how well the work is done. You would swear it was real jewelry."

He would then smile in his turn, and declare to her: "You have the tastes of a regular Gypsy."

Sometimes, in the evening, when they were having a chat by the fire, she would rise and fetch the morocco box in which she kept her "stock" (as M. Lantin called it)—would put it on the tea-table, and begin to examine the false jewelry with passionate delight, as if she experienced some secret and mysterious sensations of pleasure in their contemplation; and she would insist on putting one of the necklaces round her husband's neck, and laugh till she couldn't laugh any more, crying out: "Oh! how funny you look!" Then she would rush into his arms, and kiss him furiously.

One winter's night, after she had been to the Opera, she came home chilled through, and trembling. Next day she had a bad cough. Eight days after that, she died of pneumonia.

Lantin was very nearly following her into the tomb. His despair was so frightful that in one single month his hair turned white. He wept from morning till night, feeling his heart torn by inexpressible suffering—ever haunted by the memory of her, by the smile, by the voice, by all the charm of the dead woman.

Time did not assuage his grief. Often during office hours his fellow-clerks went off to a corner to chat about this or that topic of the day—his cheeks might have been seen to swell up all of a sudden, his nose wrinkle, his eyes fill with water—he would pull a frightful face, and begin to sob.

He had kept his dead companion's room just in the order she had left it, and he used to lock himself up in it every evening to think about her—all the furniture, and even all her dresses, remained in the same place they had been on the last day of her life.

But life became hard for him. His salary, which, in his wife's hands, had amply sufficed for all household needs, now proved scarcely sufficient to supply his own few wants. And he asked himself in astonishment how she had managed always to furnish him with excellent wines and with delicate eating which he could not now afford at all with his scanty means.

He got a little into debt, like men obliged to live by their wits. At last one morning that he happened to find himself without a cent in his pocket, and a whole week to wait before he could draw his monthly salary, he thought of selling something; and almost immediately it occurred to him to sell his wife's "stock"—for he had always borne a secret grudge against the flash-jewelry that used to annoy him so much in former days. The mere sight of it, day after day, somewhat spoiled the sad pleasure of thinking of his darling.

He tried a long time to make a choice among the heap of trinkets she had left behind her—for up to the very last day of her life she had kept obstinately buying them, bringing home some new thing almost every night—and finally he resolved to take the big pearl necklace which she used to like the best of all, and which he thought ought certainly to be worth six or eight francs, as it was really very nicely mounted for an imitation necklace.

He put it in his pocket, and walked toward the office, following the boulevards, and looking for some jewelry-store on the way, where he could enter with confidence.

Finally he saw a place and went in; feeling a little ashamed of thus exposing his misery, and of trying to sell such a trifling object.

"Sir," he said to the jeweler, "please tell me what this is worth."

The jeweler took the necklace, examined it, weighed it, took up a magnifying glass, called his clerk, talked to him in whispers, put down the necklace on the counter, and drew back a little bit to judge of its effect at a distance.

M. Lantin, feeling very much embarrassed by all these ceremonies, opened his mouth and began to declare—"Oh! I know it can't be worth much" . . . when the jeweler interrupted him saying:

"Well, sir, that is worth between twelve and fifteen thousand francs; but I cannot buy it unless you can let me know exactly how you came by it."

The widower's eyes opened enormously, and he stood gaping—unable to understand. Then after a while he stammered out: "You said? . . . Are you sure?" The jeweler, misconstruing the cause of this astonishment, replied in a dry tone—"Go elsewhere if you like, and see if you can get any more for it. The very most I would give for it is fifteen thousand. Come back and see me again, if you can't do better."

M. Lantin, feeling perfectly idiotic, took his necklace and departed; obeying a confused desire to find himself alone and to get a chance to think.

But the moment he found himself in the street again, he began to laugh, and he muttered to himself: "The fool!—oh! what a fool; If I had only taken him at his word. Well, well!—a jeweler who can't tell paste from real jewelry!"

And he entered another jewelry-store, at the corner of the Rue de la Paix. The moment the jeweler set eyes on the necklace, he examined—"Hello! I know that necklace well—it was sold here!"

M. Lantin, very nervous, asked:

"What's it worth?"

"Sir, I sold it for twenty-five thousand francs. I am willing to buy it back again for eighteen thousand—if you can prove to me satisfactorily, according to legal presciptions, how you came into possession of it"—This time, M. Lantin was simply paralyzed with astonishment. He said: "Well . . . but please look at it again, sir. I always thought until now that it was . . . was false."

The jeweler said:

"Will you give me your name, sir?"

"Certainly. My name is Lantin; I am employed at the office of the Minister of the Interior. I live at No. 16, Rue des Martyrs."

The merchant opened the register, looked, and said: "Yes; this necklace was sent to the address of Madame Lantin, 16 Rue des Martyrs, on July 20th, 1876."

And the two men looked into each other's eyes—the clerk wild with surprise; the jeweler suspecting he had a thief before him.

The jeweler resumed:

"Will you be kind enough to leave this article here for twenty-four hours only—I'll give you a receipt."

M. Lantin stuttered: "Yes-ah! certainly." And he went out folding up the receipt, which he put in his pocket.

Then he crossed the street, went the wrong way, found out his mistake, returned by way of the Tuileries, crossed the Seine, found out he had taken the wrong road again, and went back to the Champs-Elysées without being able to get one clear idea into his head. He tried to reason, to understand. His wife could never have bought so valuable an object as that. Certainly not. But then, it must have been a present! . . . A present from whom? What for?

He stopped and stood stock-still in the middle of the avenue.

A horrible suspicion swept across his mind. . . . She? . . . But then all those other pieces of jewelry must have been presents also! . . . Then it seemed to him that the ground was heaving under his feet; that a tree, right in front of him, was falling toward him; he thrust out his arms instinctively, and fell senseless.

He recovered his consciousness again in a drug-store to which some bystanders had carried him. He had them lead him home, and he locked himself into his room.

Until nightfall he cried without stopping, biting his handkerchief to keep himself from screaming out. Then, completely worn out with grief and fatigue, he went to bed, and slept a leaden sleep.

A ray of sunshine awakened him, and he rose and dressed himself slowly to go to the office. It was hard to have to work after such a shock. Then he reflected that he might be able to excuse himself to the superintendent, and he wrote to him. Then he remembered he would have to go back to the jeweler's; and shame made his face purple. He remained thinking a long time. Still he could not leave the necklace there; he put on his coat and went out.

It was a fine day; the sky extended all blue over the city, and seemed to make it smile. Strollers were walking aimlessly about, with their hands in their pockets.

Lantin thought as he watched them passing: "How lucky the men are who have fortunes! With money a man can even shake off grief—you can go where you please—travel—amuse yourself! Oh! if I were only rich!"

He suddenly discovered he was hungry—not having eaten anything since the evening before. But his pockets were empty; and he remembered the necklace. Eighteen thousand francs! Eighteen thousand francs!—that was a sum—that was!

He made his way to the Rue de la Paix and began to walk backward and forward on the sidewalk in front of the store. Eighteen thousand francs! Twenty times he started to go in; but shame always kept him back.

Still he was hungry—very hungry—and had not a cent. He made one brusque resolve, and crossed the street almost at a run, so as not to let himself have time to think over the matter; and he rushed into the jeweler's.

As soon as he saw him, the merchant hurried forward, and offered him a chair with smiling politeness. Even the clerks came forward to stare at Lantin, with gaiety in their eyes and smiles about their lips.

The jeweler said: "Sir, I made inquiries; and if you are still so disposed, I am ready to pay you down the price I offered you."

The clerk stammered: "Why, yes—sir, certainly."

The jeweler took from a drawer eighteen big bills,[3] counted them, and held them out to Lantin, who signed a little receipt, and thrust the money feverishly into his pocket.

Then, as he was on the point of leaving, he turned to the ever-smiling merchant, and said, lowering his eyes: "I have some—I have some other jewelry, which came to me in the same—from the same inheritance. Would you purchase them also from me?"

The merchant bowed, and answered: "Why, certainly, sir—certainly. . . ." One of the clerks rushed out to laugh at his ease; another kept blowing his nose as hard as he could.

Lantin, impassive, flushed and serious, said: "I will bring them to you."

And he hired a cab to get the jewelry.

When he returned to the store, an hour later, he had not yet breakfasted. They examined the jewelry—piece by piece—putting a value on each. Nearly all had been purchased from that very house.

Lantin, now, disputed estimates made, got angry, insisted on seeing the books, and talked louder and louder the higher the estimates grew.

The big diamond earrings were worth 20,000 francs; the bracelets, 35,000; the brooches, rings and medallions, 16,000; a set of emeralds and sapphires, 14,000; solitaire, suspended to a gold neckchain, 40,000; the total value being estimated at 196,000 francs.

The merchant observed with mischievous good nature: "The person who owned these must have put all her savings into jewelry."

Lantin answered with gravity: "Perhaps that is as good a way of saving money as any other." And he went off, after having agreed with the merchant that an expert should make a counter-estimate for him the next day.

When he found himself in the street again, he looked at the Column Vendôme[4] with the desire to climb it, as if it were a May pole. He felt jolly enough to play leapfrog over the Emperor's head—up there in the blue sky.

He breakfasted at Voisin's[5] restaurant, and ordered wine at 20 francs a bottle.

Then he hired a cab and drove out to the Bois.[6] He looked at the carriages

3. French paper money varies in size; the larger the bill, the larger the denomination. 4. Famous column with a statue of Napoleon at the top. 5. Like the Café Anglais below, a well-known and high-priced restaurant. 6. Large Parisian park where the rich took their outings.

passing with a sort of contempt, and a wild desire to yell out to the passers-by: "I am rich, too—I am! I have 200,000 francs!"

The recollection of the office suddenly came back to him. He drove there, walked right into the superintendent's private room, and said: "Sir, I come to give you my resignation. I have just come into a fortune of *three* hundred thousand francs." Then he shook hands all round with his fellow-clerks; and told them all about his plans for a new career. Then he went to dinner at the Café Anglais.

Finding himself seated at the same table with a man who seemed to him quite genteel, he could not resist the itching desire to tell him, with a certain air of coquetry, that he had just inherited a fortune of *four* hundred thousand francs.

For the first time in his life he went to the theater without feeling bored by the performance; and he passed the night in revelry and debauch.

Six months after he married again. His second wife was the most upright of spouses, but had a terrible temper. She made his life very miserable.

1883

QUESTIONS

1. What specific words or phrases in the first two paragraphs of "The Jewelry" alert you to the possibility that all may not be as it seems? How are these expectations or fears allayed in the next few paragraphs? What new fears or expectations are aroused very soon thereafter?

2. Since the story is called "The Jewelry" and life does not come wrapped in such convenient titles, you may come to suspect the truth before M. Lantin. How does your attitude toward him change?

WRITING SUGGESTIONS

1. Copy "The Zebra Storyteller." Exchange papers with a classmate. Carefully proofread each other's papers. Can you believe you could have made errors in simple copying?

2. Write a parody or imitation of "No One's a Mystery" using "I'm Bad" or a more recent song as the title.

Understanding the Text

1 PLOT

In "The Zebra Storyteller" you can see the skeleton of the typical short story **plot** or **plot structure.** Plot simply means the arrangement of the **action**, an imagined event or a series of such events.

Action usually involves **conflict**, a struggle between opposing forces, and it often falls into something like the same five parts that we find in a play: exposition, rising action, turning point (or climax), falling action, conclusion. The conflict in this little tale is between the Siamese cat and the zebras, especially the zebra storyteller. The first part of the action, called the **exposition**, introduces the characters, situation, and, usually, time and place. The exposition here is achieved in three sentences: the time is "once upon a," the place Africa, the characters a Siamese cat who speaks Zebraic and an innocent zebra, and the situation their meeting. We then enter the second part of the plot, the **rising action**: events that complicate the situation and intensify or complicate the conflict or introduce new ones. The first event here is the meeting between an innocent zebra and the Zebraic-speaking cat. That initial conflict of zebra and cat is over in a hurry—the zebra who is "fit to be tied" is tied up and eaten. Complications build with the cat's continuing success in killing zebras, and the zebras' growing fears and consequent superstitious belief that the ghost of a lion haunts the region preying on zebras. The **turning point** or **climax** of the action is the third part of the story, the appearance of the zebra storyteller: until now the cat has had it all his way, but his luck is about to change. From this point on the complications that grew in the first part of the story are untangled—the zebra storyteller, for example, is not surprised when he meets a Siamese cat speaking Zebraic, "because he'd been thinking about that very thing"; this is the fourth part of the story, the reverse movement or **falling action**. The story ends at the fifth part, the **conclusion**: the point at which the situation that was destablized at the beginning of the story (when the Zebraic-speaking cat appeared) becomes stable once more: Africa is once again free of cats speaking the language of zebras.

Before an author can arrange the parts of the action he or she must select them. Writers leave out some things that seem at first to be important to the story and include others that do not seem very important. **Selection** of events and details is a significant element of storytelling.

But what do we mean when we say an author selects events? Selects from where? It is not as if these events exist somewhere, as historical events do. Like scientists with their hypotheses and philosophers with their premises, many of us who talk or write about fiction begin with a fiction: we speak as if the people and places exist and the events of a story take place in a world of the author's imagination, a world from which he or she chooses the story elements, a world we can understand and almost re-create in terms of our own. We call this world the **history** behind the story.

The opening passage of "The Cask of Amontillado" suggests some of the issues involved in selection. "The thousand injuries of Fortunato I had borne as I best could, but when he ventured upon insult I vowed revenge." What kind of injuries? Were there actually so many? Were they real injuries or is the narrator overly sensitive or paranoid and the injuries exaggerated or merely imagined? What was the insult? How could an insult be worse than a thousand injuries? Poe could have invented answers for these questions—perhaps he did—but he chose not to present them to the reader. He chose or selected what he was to present.

The exciting action of Margaret Atwood's "The Whirlpool Rapids" takes place in just four paragraphs in the middle of the story and the details of the event itself are rather vague, filtered through Emma's rather uninformed recollection. The exposition and rising action leading up to the main event, beginning with the fifth paragraph of the story, seem functional and justified. But why are the first four paragraphs here? How about the final six paragraphs?

Once events have been selected, they must be connected. In the history behind the story, events take place in simple chronological sequence: "The king died and then the queen died," to use one critic's example. This sequential narrative of events, the critic says, is not a plot, for it has not been "tampered with" by an author. But if we connect the events, if we structure the history—"The king died and then the queen died of grief"—we have a plot, a **structuring** of the action.

Many of us are used to thinking of cause and effect as a natural part of an event, as somehow *in* the event, rather than as an interpretation of a relationship between two sequential events, so a simple statement of a cause-effect relationship ("died of grief") may not seem like authorial structuring. Many authors seem to like to hide their structuring, to make it seem as if the events in a story are just naturally or inevitably *there*. Montresor's scheme of revenge against Fortunato in "The Cask of Amontillado" is not the author's plot, Poe leads us to believe, but Montresor's; and, while reading, we probably accept that it is Montresor who, interpreting Fortunato's insult as cause for revenge, generates the events that follow. Only later, putting the story down, do we bother to realize that it is Poe who invented and arranged the events, created the plot.

Sometimes, when the characters do not turn sequence into cause or make any of the connections that turn history into plot, the author makes the reader do it. Though the first-person narrator of "Sonny's Blues" seems to be interpreting all the events for us, making the connections, he says he does not know why he always gives money to the young addict who is a friend of Sonny's (par. 9). It is up to us to make the connection. Some readers will conclude that it is because the boy reminds the narrator of Sonny, so in "helping" him, he is helping Sonny. Other readers will see a different connection.

In the history, events exist in chronological sequence, and they can be reported that way in the story: "The king died and then the queen died." But the events in the story can be ordered differently: "The queen died after the King died" recounts the same history, but the order in which the events are reported has been changed. The history has been structured. The reader of the first sentence focuses on the king first, the reader of the second sentence on the queen. The "same thing" has been said, but the structure has been changed, and the difference in focus, emphasis, effect, and thus in the full meaning of the statement can be significant.

In some stories, such as "The Cask of Amontillado," the events seem to come unstructured from the history: Montresor meets Fortunato, tempts him into the vaults, they walk to the end, and so on. The events are presented one after another in the same order as in the history. The reader finds out moment by moment what happens next. In other stories—detective stories, for example—the major action (the crime) has taken place before the story begins, and the forward action of the story is the detective's attempt to re-create the past and figure out what happened. The reader does not ask, "What will happen?" but "What has happened?" In some other stories, like Faulkner's "A Rose for Emily" in the next chapter, readers may not feel compelled to ask what has happened until the end, when a sudden revelation from the fictional past forces them to reconsider all that has gone before. In such stories it is obvious that the author has created a plot, ordered the events in the story in a sequence different from that in which they occurred. But just as Poe disguised his plot as his narrator's, so Faulkner disguises his reordering of events as the order of the narrator's recollections followed by that narrator's learning a new fact about the past at the end of the story.

Though the sequence of events in the detective story is reordered in terms of the reader's knowledge of events—we learn "who done it" in the past only long after the story begins—the past is not usually replayed: we do not "see" the crime reenacted before us (although detectives often describe the crime when they give their solutions). The story simply begins in the middle of the history—after the crime—and moves forward as the detective figures out what happened. In "Sonny's Blues," however, there is a replay or **flashback** (or rather a series of flashbacks). There is a very brief scene from the past triggered by the word "safe" (par. 79), the narrator recalling his father's words, which then leads to a specific dramatized scene—the last time the narrator talked to his mother. This is followed by another scene—the narrator's conversation with Sonny after their mother's funeral. This scene of course follows the previous one but in terms of where the story began (the fictional present) it is in the past, and therefore is in fact a flashback. Nor does the story return to the fictional present for some time—"I read about Sonny's trouble in the spring. Little Grace died in the fall . . ." (par. 177)—when Sonny has been living with the narrator for two weeks, and it proceeds from that point to the end.

One reason for structuring the history into plot is to engage the reader's attention, to make the reader read on. This can be done not only by arousing the reader's expectations of what will happen next but also by generating **curiosity**—the desire to know what is happening or has happened. It is the sheer power of curiosity, for example, that keeps us reading intensely when we know as little as Watson or Sherlock Holmes himself at the beginning of a story or "case." Nor is it only the detective story that plays upon our curiosity. "Sonny's Blues" begins, "I read about it in the paper . . . ," and that "it" without antecedent is repeated seven times in the first paragraph and first two sentences of the second paragraph. Read those first two paragraphs and stop. If you try at this point to examine what is going on in your mind, you more than likely will find that you are asking yourself what "it" might refer to, and you will more than likely have framed for yourself several possible answers. It may be in part for this reason that Baldwin begins how and where he does, getting you engaged in the story, so that you will read on. Even a title, such as "The Zebra Storyteller," "A Very Old Man with Enormous Wings," or "The Rocking

Horse Winner," can make us curious enough to pick up a story; after that, it's up to the story to keep us engaged.

Perhaps stronger than curiosity is **suspense**—that particular kind of expectation involving anticipation of and doubt about what is going to happen next (as differentiated from expectations about what a character is like, what the theme is or how it will develop, and so on). Even in reading a little fable like "The Zebra Storyteller" our minds are—or should be—at work: a cat speaking Zebraic is killing zebras; the zebra storyteller thinking of plots comes up with the idea of a story in which a cat speaking Zebraic is killing zebras: "What an idea! That'll make 'em laugh!" he tells himself. Then he meets the cat—what will happen next? How many possibilities did you or can you anticipate?

Sometimes the suspense is generated and defined not so much by what happens within the story as it is by what we expect from stories. In "The Jewelry," for example, when Lantin's wife dies so early in the story, we know this is not the end; something is going to happen or be revealed because there are several pages left and stories do not go on unless something is going to happen. But what? Lantin grieves so intensely, locks himself in her room . . . will her ghost return? He is going bankrupt, he looks over his wife's jewelry, and when he goes to sell a piece he finds it is not mere costume jewelry, but real. How much sooner than Lantin himself do you realize the source of the jewelry? There is a certain satisfaction in seeing the truth before he does. But *then* what do you expect to happen next? Do you anticipate his debauching? How did you expect the story to end?

If you were to pause just before reading the final paragraph of the Maupassant story and consciously explore your expectations, you would see that these are based on fictional and actual conventions—indeed, most of us would probably assume the story could have ended with the word "debauch," without the final brief paragraph, and that the story would end with the irony of Lantin's getting pleasure out of his having been betrayed. We can accept this even within our conventional moral terms—he may get bitter pleasures for a time, but he will soon tire of such pleasures or be undone by them.

The final paragraph, however, if it does not contradict, deepens the irony: now he has a truly "upright" wife—and he is miserable. Our conventional expectations that morality brings happiness, that infidelity and debauchery lead to various kinds of ruin, are wrenched into question. He has tired of debauchery, but is he better off leading a moral life? Is the world amoral—or even immoral? Do good guys finish last? We do not have to believe this, but to read the story fully we need to call our perhaps more optimistic and conventional views into question.

In order to keep you engaged and alert, a story must make you ask questions about what will happen or what will be revealed next. To respond fully to a story you must be alert to the signals and guess along with the author. One way of seeing whether and how your mind is engaged in your reading is to pause at crucial points in your reading and consciously explore what you think is coming. In "No One's a Mystery" the story does the pausing and the conscious specification of what might happen next for you—it gives two versions of what might happen and then the story ends, without resolution. (Though not without point; for to suggest that both naivete and cynicism are merely attitudes, and that neither is an infallible clue to the future, is an insight and a challenge, even if it is not, strictly speaking, a resolution.) At least in one aspect, fiction is a guessing game.

Like all guessing games, from quiz show to philosophy, the plot game in fiction has certain guidelines. A well-structured plot will play fair with you, offering at appropriate points all the necessary indications or clues to what will happen next, not just springing new and essential information on you at the last minute ("Meanwhile, unknown to our hero, the Marines were just on the other side of the hill . . ."). It is this playing fair that makes the ending of a well-structured story satisfying or, when you look back on it, inevitable. Most stories also offer a number of reasonable but false signals (red herrings) to get you off the scent, so that in a well-structured story the ending, though inevitable, is also surprising. And though there is usually an overarching action from beginning to end, in many stories there are layers of expectation or suspense, so that as soon as one question is answered another comes forth to replace it, keeping you in doubt and suspense as to the final outcome.

Unlike most guessing games, however, the reward is not for the right guess—anticipating the outcome before the final paragraph—but for the number of guesses, right *and* wrong, that you make, the number of signals you respond to. If you are misled by none of the false signals in the early pages of a story—by Sonny's friend saying, " 'Listen. They'll let him out and then it'll just start all over again' " (par. 36), for example—you may be closer to being "right," but you have missed many of the implications of the story. But, more important, you have missed the pleasure of learning the "truth" offered by the story for yourself, and you know how much less meaningful it is to be told something than it is to learn it for yourself, through your own experience. Fiction is a way of transmitting not just perception but experience.

Though plot is the structuring of events, an event can be an outcome or consequence as well as a happening, and the expectation, surprise, and perception surrounding plot structure can involve meaning as well as action. So, in

"The Whirlpool Rapids," the results of Emma's adventure are somewhat surprising, modifying our conventional expectations of what it means to survive death and become fearless. Though such conventional expectations are not so consciously aroused as are those aroused by action and adventure—the kind of expectation described by the term "suspense"—their fulfillment, modification, or contradiction is a significant aim and effect of many stories. For though fiction is in part a guessing game, it is not merely a game. Many stories seek to give new insights into human perception, experience, meaning, or at least to challenge our more or less unconsciously held beliefs. They strive to tell truths—new, subjective truths, but truths—even though they "lie" about the actuality of the people and events represented. But first they have to get your attention, and one way is by arousing your curiosity and exciting your anticipation. That is one of the primary functions of plot.

Alertness to signals, anticipating what is to come next, and remembering what has been said and signaled earlier are essential to fully appreciating and understanding stories and their structures. How, for example, do you react in "The Cask of Amontillado" to Montresor's concern for Fortunato's coughing? What do you anticipate? What is it that you later discover? By the time you finish the Poe story, you may know why insult is more important to Montresor than injury; you may even be able to suggest why Poe did not recount the thousand injuries or the fatal insult.

▽ ▽ ▽

PLOT A Glossary

action: an imagined event or series of events (an event may be verbal as well as physical, so that saying something or telling a story within the story may be an event)

climax: see *turning point*

conclusion: the fifth part of the structure, the point at which the situation that was destabilized at the beginning of the story becomes stable once more

conflict: a struggle between opposing forces, such as between two people, a person and something in nature or society, or even between two drives, impulses, or parts of the self

curiosity: the desire to know what is happening or has happened

expectation: the anticipation of what is to happen next (see *suspense*), what a character is like or how he or she will develop, what the theme or meaning of the story will prove to be, and so on

exposition: that part of the structure which sets the scene, introduces and identifies characters, establishes the situation at the beginning of the narrative, though additional exposition is often scattered throughout the story

flashback: that structuring device whereby a scene from the fictional past is inserted into the fictional present or dramatized out of order

history: the imaginary people, places, chronologically arranged events that we assume exist in the world of the author's imagination, a world from which he or she chooses and arranges or re-arranges the story elements

plot/plot structure: the arrangement of the action

red herring: a false lead, something that misdirects expectations

rising action: the second of the five parts of plot structure, in which events are introduced complicating the situation that existed at the beginning of a work and intensifying or complicating the conflict or introducing new ones

selection: the process by which authors leave out some things that seem to be important to the story and include some things that do not seem very important

structuring: the arrangement or rearrangement of the elements in the history

suspense: the expectation of and doubt about what is going to happen next

turning point or **climax:** the third part of plot structure, the point at which the action stops rising and begins falling or reversing

EDGAR ALLAN POE

The Cask of Amontillado

The thousand injuries of Fortunato I had borne as I best could, but when he ventured upon insult I vowed revenge. You, who so well know the nature of my soul, will not suppose, however, that I gave utterance to a threat. *At length* I would be avenged; this was a point definitively settled—but the very definitiveness with which it was resolved precluded the idea of risk. I must not only punish but punish with impunity. A wrong is unredressed when retribution overtakes its redresser. It is equally unredressed when the avenger fails to make himself felt as such to him who has done the wrong.

It must be understood that neither by word nor deed had I given Fortunato cause to doubt my good will. I continued, as was my wont, to smile in his face, and he did not perceive that my smile *now* was at the thought of his immolation.

He had a weak point—this Fortunato—although in other regards he was a man to be respected and even feared. He prided himself upon his connoisseurship in wine. Few Italians have the true virtuoso spirit. For the most part their enthusiasm is adopted to suit the time and opportunity, to practice imposture upon the British and Austrian *millionaires*. In painting and gemmary, Fortunato, like his countrymen, was a quack, but in the matter of old wines he was sincere. In this respect I did not differ from him materially;—I was skilful in the Italian vintages myself, and bought largely whenever I could.

It was about dusk, one evening during the supreme madness of the carnival season, that I encountered my friend. He accosted me with excessive warmth, for he had been drinking much. The man wore motley. He had on a tight-fitting parti-striped dress, and his head was surmounted by the conical cap and bells. I was so pleased to see him that I should never have done wringing his hand.

I said to him—"My dear Fortunato, you are luckily met. How remarkably 5
well you are looking to-day. But I have received a pipe[1] of what passes for Amontillado, and I have my doubts."

"How?" said he. "Amontillado? A pipe? Impossible! And in the middle of the carnival!"

"I have my doubts," I replied; "and I was silly enough to pay the full Amontillado price without consulting you in the matter. You were not to be found, and I was fearful of losing a bargain."

"Amontillado!"

"I have my doubts."

"Amontillado!" 10

"And I must satisfy them."

"Amontillado!"

"As you are engaged, I am on my way to Luchresi. If any one has a critical turn it is he. He will tell me——"

1. A cask holding 126 gallons.

"Luchresi cannot tell Amontillado from Sherry."

"And yet some fools will have it that his taste is a match for your own."

"Come, let us go."

"Whither?"

"To your vaults."

"My friend, no; I will not impose upon your good nature. I perceive you have an engagement. Luchresi——"

"I have no engagement;—come."

"My friend, no. It is not the engagement, but the severe cold with which I perceive you are afflicted. The vaults are insufferably damp. They are encrusted with nitre."

"Let us go, nevertheless. The cold is merely nothing. Amontillado! You have been imposed upon. And as for Luchresi, he cannot distinguish Sherry from Amontillado."

Thus speaking, Fortunato possessed himself of my arm; and putting on a mask of black silk and drawing a *roquelaire*[2] closely about my person, I suffered him to hurry me to my palazzo.

There were no attendants at home; they had absconded to make merry in honour of the time. I had told them that I should not return until the morning, and had given them explicit orders not to stir from the house. These orders were sufficient, I well knew, to insure their immediate disappearance, one and all, as soon as my back was turned.

I took from their sconces two flambeaux, and giving one to Fortunato, bowed him through several suites of rooms to the archway that led into the vaults. I passed down a long and winding staircase, requesting him to be cautious as he followed. We came at length to the foot of the descent, and stood together upon the damp ground of the catacombs of the Montresors.

The gait of my friend was unsteady, and the bells upon his cap jingled as he strode.

"The pipe," said he.

"It is farther on," said I; "but observe the white web-work which gleams from these cavern walls."

He turned towards me, and looked into my eyes with two filmy orbs that distilled the rheum of intoxication.

"Nitre?" he asked, at length.

"Nitre," I replied. "How long have you had that cough?"

"Ugh! ugh! ugh!—ugh! ugh! ugh!—ugh! ugh! ugh!—ugh! ugh! ugh!—ugh! ugh! ugh!"

My poor friend found it impossible to reply for many minutes.

"It is nothing," he said, at last.

"Come," I said, with decision, "we will go back; your health is precious. You are rich, respected, admired, beloved; you are happy, as once I was. You are a man to be missed. For me it is no matter. We will go back; you will be ill, and I cannot be responsible. Besides, there is Luchresi——"

2. Roquelaure: man's heavy, knee-length cloak.

"Enough," he said; "the cough is a mere nothing; it will not kill me. I shall not die of a cough."

"True—true," I replied; "and, indeed, I had no intention of alarming you unneccessarily—but you should use all proper caution. A draught of this Medoc[3] will defend us from the damps."

Here I knocked off the neck of a bottle which I drew from a long row of its fellows that lay upon the mould.

"Drink," I said, presenting him the wine.

He raised it to his lips with a leer. He paused and nodded to me familiarly, while his bells jingled.

"I drink," he said, "to the buried that repose around us."

"And I to your long life."

He again took my arm, and we proceeded.

"These vaults," he said, "are extensive."

"The Montresors," I replied, "were a great and numerous family."

"I forget your arms."

"A huge human foot d'or,[4] in a field azure; the foot crushes a serpent rampant whose fangs are imbedded in the heel."

"And the motto?"

"*Nemo me impune lacessit*."[5]

"Good!" he said.

The wine sparkled in his eyes and the bells jingled. My own fancy grew warm with the Medoc. We had passed through long walls of piled skeletons, with casks and puncheons intermingling, into the inmost recesses of the catacombs. I paused again, and this time I made bold to seize Fortunato by an arm above the elbow.

"The nitre!" I said; "see, it increases. It hangs like moss upon the vaults. We are below the river's bed. The drops of moisture trickle among the bones. Come, we will go back ere it is too late. Your cough——"

"It is nothing," he said; "let us go on. But first, another draught of the Medoc."

I broke and reached him a flaçon of De Grâve. He emptied it at a breath. His eyes flashed with a fierce light. He laughed and threw the bottle upwards with a gesticulation I did not understand.

I looked at him in surprise. He repeated the movement—a grotesque one.

"You do not comprehend?" he said.

"Not I," I replied.

"Then you are not of the brotherhood."

"How?"

"You are not of the masons."[6]

"Yes, yes," I said; "yes, yes."

"You? Impossible! A mason?"

"A mason," I replied.

"A sign," he said, "a sign."

3. Like De Grâve (below), a French wine. 4. Of gold. 5. No one provokes me with impunity. 6. Masons or Freemasons, an international secret society condemned by the Catholic Church. Montresor means by mason one who builds with stone, brick, etc.

"It is this," I answered producing from beneath the folds of my *roquelaire* a trowel.

"You jest," he exclaimed, recoiling a few paces. "But let us proceed to the Amontillado."

"Be it so," I said, replacing the tool beneath the cloak and again offering him my arm. He leaned upon it heavily. We continued our route in search of the Amontillado. We passed through a range of low arches, descended, passed on, and descending again, arrived at a deep crypt, in which the foulness of the air caused our flambeaux rather to glow than flame.

At the most remote end of the crypt there appeared another less spacious. Its walls had been lined with human remains, piled to the vault overhead, in the fashion of the great catacombs of Paris. Three sides of this interior crypt were still ornamented in this manner. From the fourth side the bones had been thrown down, and lay promiscuously upon the earth, forming at one point a mound of some size. Within the wall thus exposed by the displacing of the bones, we perceived a still interior crypt or recess, in depth about four feet, in width three, in height six or seven. It seemed to have been constructed for no especial use within itself, but formed merely the interval between two of the colossal supports of the roof of the catacombs, and was backed by one of their circumscribing walls of solid granite.

It was in vain that Fortunato, uplifting his dull torch, endeavoured to pry into the depth of the recess. Its termination the feeble light did not enable us to see.

"Proceed," I said; "herein is the Amontillado. As for Luchresi——"

"He is an ignoramus," interrupted my friend, as he stepped unsteadily forward, while I followed immediately at his heels. In an instant he had reached the extremity of the niche, and finding his progress arrested by the rock, stood stupidly bewildered. A moment more and I had fettered him to the granite. In its surface were two iron staples, distant from each other about two feet, horizontally. From one of these depended a short chain, from the other a padlock. Throwing the links about his waist, it was but the work of a few seconds to secure it. He was too much astounded to resist. Withdrawing the key I stepped back from the recess.

"Pass your hand," I said, "over the wall; you cannot help feeling the nitre. Indeed, it is *very* damp. Once more let me *implore* you to return. No? Then I must positively leave you. But I will first render you all the little attentions in my power."

"The Amontillado!" ejaculated my friend, not yet recovered from his astonishment.

"True," I replied; "the Amontillado."

As I said these words I busied myself among the pile of bones of which I have before spoken. Throwing them aside, I soon uncovered a quantity of building stone and mortar. With these materials and with the aid of my trowel, I began vigorously to wall up the entrance of the niche.

I had scarcely laid the first tier of the masonry when I discovered that the intoxication of Fortunato had in great measure worn off. The earliest indication I had of this was a low moaning cry from the depth of the recess. It was *not* the cry of a drunken man. There was then a long and obstinate silence. I laid the second tier, and the third, and the fourth; and then I heard the furious vibration of the chain. The noise lasted for several minutes, during which, that I might hearken to it with the more satisfaction, I ceased my labours and sat down upon the bones. When at last the clanking subsided, I resumed the trowel, and finished without interruption the fifth, the sixth, and the seventh tier. The wall was now nearly upon a level with my breast. I again paused, and holding the flambeaux over the mason-work, threw a few feeble rays upon the figure within.

A succession of loud and shrill screams, bursting suddenly from the throat of the chained form, seemed to thrust me violently back. For a brief moment I hesitated, I trembled. Unsheathing my rapier, I began to grope with it about the recess; but the thought of an instant reassured me. I placed my hand upon the solid fabric of the catacombs and felt satisfied. I reapproached the wall. I replied to the yells of him who clamoured. I reechoed, I aided, I surpassed them in volume and in strength. I did this, and the clamourer grew still.

It was now midnight, and my task was drawing to a close. I had completed the eighth, the ninth and the tenth tier. I had finished a portion of the last and the eleventh; there remained but a single stone to be fitted and plastered in. I struggled with its weight; I placed it partially in its destined position. But now there came from out the niche a low laugh that erected the hairs upon my head. It was succeeded by a sad voice, which I had difficulty in recognizing as that of the noble Fortunato. The voice said—

"Ha! ha! ha!—he! he! he!—a very good joke, indeed—an excellent jest. We will have many a rich laugh about it at the palazzo—he! he! he!—over our wine—he! he! he!"

"The Amontillado!" I said.

"He! he! he!—he! he! he!—yes, the Amontillado. But is it not getting late? Will not they be awaiting us at the palazzo—the Lady Fortunato and the rest? Let us be gone."

"Yes," I said, "let us be gone."

"*For the love of God, Montresor!*"

"Yes," I said, "for the love of God!"

But to these words I hearkened in vain for a reply. I grew impatient. I called aloud—

"Fortunato!"

No answer. I called again—

"Fortunato!"

No answer still. I thrust a torch through the remaining aperture and let it fall within. There came forth in return only a jingling of the bells. My heart grew sick; it was the dampness of the catacombs that made it so. I hastened to make an end of my labour. I forced the last stone into its position; I plastered it up. Against the new masonry I re-erected the old rampart of bones. For the half of a century no mortal has disturbed them. *In pace requiescat!*[7]

1846

7. May he rest in peace.

JAMES BALDWIN

Sonny's Blues

I read about it in the paper, in the subway, on my way to work. I read it, and I couldn't believe it, and I read it again. Then perhaps I just stared at it, at the newsprint spelling out his name, spelling out the story. I stared at it in the swinging lights of the subway car, and in the faces and bodies of the people, and in my own face, trapped in the darkness which roared outside.

It was not to be believed and I kept telling myself that, as I walked from the subway station to the high school. And at the same time I couldn't doubt it. I was scared, scared for Sonny. He became real to me again. A great block of ice got settled in my belly and kept melting there slowly all day long, while I taught my classes algebra. It was a special kind of ice. It kept melting, sending trickles of ice water all up and down my veins, but it never got less. Sometimes it hardened and seemed to expand until I felt my guts were going to come spilling out or that I was going to choke or scream. This would always be at a moment when I was remembering some specific thing Sonny had once said or done.

When he was about as old as the boys in my classes his face had been bright and open, there was a lot of copper in it; and he'd had wonderfully direct brown eyes, and great gentleness and privacy. I wondered what he looked like now. He had been picked up, the evening before, in a raid on an apartment downtown, for peddling and using heroin.

I couldn't believe it: but what I mean by that is that I couldn't find any room for it anywhere inside me. I had kept it outside me for a long time. I hadn't wanted to know. I had had suspicions, but I didn't name them, I kept putting them away. I told myself that Sonny was wild, but he wasn't crazy. And he'd always been a good boy, he hadn't ever turned hard or evil or disrespectful, the way kids can, so quick, so quick, especially in Harlem. I didn't want to believe that I'd ever see my brother going down, coming to nothing, all that light in his face gone out, in the condition I'd already seen so many others. Yet it had happened and here I was, talking about algebra to a lot of boys who might, every one of them for all I knew, be popping off needles every time they went to the head.[1] Maybe it did more for them than algebra could.

5 I was sure that the first time Sonny had ever had horse,[2] he couldn't have been much older than these boys were now. These boys, now, were living as we'd been living then, they were growing up with a rush and their heads bumped abruptly against the low ceiling of their actual possibilities. They were filled with rage. All they really knew were two darknesses, the darkness of their lives, which was now closing in on them, and the darkness of the movies, which had blinded them to that other darkness, and in which they now, vindictively, dreamed, at once more together than they were at any other time, and more alone.

When the last bell rang, the last class ended, I let out my breath. It seemed

1. Lavatory. 2. Heroin.

I'd been holding it for all that time. My clothes were wet—I may have looked as though I'd been sitting in a steam bath, all dressed up, all afternoon. I sat alone in the classroom a long time. I listened to the boys outside, downstairs, shouting and cursing and laughing. Their laughter struck me for perhaps the first time. It was not the joyous laughter which—God knows why—one associates with children. It was mocking and insular, its intent was to denigrate. It was disenchanted, and in this, also, lay the authority of their curses. Perhaps I was listening to them because I was thinking about my brother and in them I heard my brother. And myself.

One boy was whistling a tune, at once very complicated and very simple, it seemed to be pouring out of him as though he were a bird, and it sounded very cool and moving through all that harsh, bright air, only just holding its own through all those other sounds.

I stood up and walked over to the window and looked down into the courtyard. It was the beginning of the spring and the sap was rising in the boys. A teacher passed through them every now and again, quickly, as though he or she couldn't wait to get out of that courtyard, to get those boys out of their sight and off their minds. I started collecting my stuff. I thought I'd better get home and talk to Isabel.

The courtyard was almost deserted by the time I got downstairs. I saw this boy standing in the shadow of a doorway, looking just like Sonny. I almost called his name. Then I saw that it wasn't Sonny, but somebody we used to know, a boy from around our block. He'd been Sonny's friend. He'd never been mine, having been too young for me, and, anyway, I'd never liked him. And now, even though he was a grown-up man, he still hung around that block, still spent hours on the street corners, was always high and raggy. I used to run into him from time to time and he'd often work around to asking me for a quarter or fifty cents. He always had some real good excuse, too, and I always gave it to him. I don't know why.

But now, abruptly, I hated him. I couldn't stand the way he looked at me, partly like a dog, partly like a cunning child. I wanted to ask him what the hell he was doing in the school courtyard.

He sort of shuffled over to me, and he said, "I see you got the papers. So you already know about it."

"You mean about Sonny? Yes, I already know about it. How come they didn't get you?"

He grinned. It made him repulsive and it also brought to mind what he'd looked like as a kid. "I wasn't there. I stay away from them people."

"Good for you." I offered him a cigarette and I watched him through the smoke. "You come all the way down here just to tell me about Sonny?"

"That's right." He was sort of shaking his head and his eyes looked strange, as though they were about to cross. The bright sun deadened his damp dark brown skin and it made his eyes look yellow and showed up the dirt in his kinked hair. He smelled funky. I moved a little away from him and I said, "Well, thanks. But I already know about it and I got to get home."

"I'll walk you a little ways," he said. We started walking. There were a couple of kids still loitering in the courtyard and one of them said goodnight to me and looked strangely at the boy beside me.

"What're you going to do?" he asked me. "I mean, about Sonny?"

"Look. I haven't seen Sonny for over a year, I'm not sure I'm going to do anything. Anyway, what the hell *can* I do?"

"That's right," he said quickly, "ain't nothing you can do. Can't much help old Sonny no more, I guess."

It was what I was thinking and so it seemed to me he had no right to say it.

"I'm surprised at Sonny, though," he went on—he had a funny way of talking, he looked straight ahead as though he were talking to himself—"I thought Sonny was a smart boy, I thought he was too smart to get hung."

"I guess he thought so too," I said sharply, "and that's how he got hung. And how about you? You're pretty goddamn smart, I bet."

Then he looked directly at me, just for a minute. "I ain't smart," he said. "If I was smart, I'd have reached for a pistol a long time ago."

"Look. Don't tell *me* your sad story, if it was up to me, I'd give you one." Then I felt guilty—guilty, probably, for never having supposed that the poor bastard *had* a story of his own, much less a sad one, and I asked, quickly, "What's going to happen to him now?"

He didn't answer this. He was off by himself some place.

"Funny thing," he said, and from his tone we might have been discussing the quickest way to get to Brooklyn, "when I saw the papers this morning, the first thing I asked myself was if I had anything to do with it. I felt sort of responsible."

I began to listen more carefully. The subway station was on the corner, just before us, and I stopped. He stopped, too. We were in front of a bar and he ducked slightly, peering in, but whoever he was looking for didn't seem to be there. The juke box was blasting away with something black and bouncy and I half watched the barmaid as she danced her way from the juke box to her place behind the bar. And I watched her face as she laughingly responded to something someone said to her, still keeping time to the music. When she smiled one saw the little girl, one sensed the doomed, still-struggling woman beneath the battered face of the semi-whore.

"I never *give* Sonny nothing," the boy said finally, "but a long time ago I come to school high and Sonny asked me how it felt." He paused, I couldn't bear to watch him, I watched the barmaid, and I listened to the music which seemed to be causing the pavement to shake. "I told him it felt great." The music stopped, the barmaid paused and watched the juke box until the music began again. "It did."

All this was carrying me some place I didn't want to go. I certainly didn't want to know how it felt. It filled everything, the people, the houses, the music, the dark, quicksilver barmaid, with menace; and this menace was their reality.

"What's going to happen to him now?" I asked again.

"They'll send him away some place and they'll try to cure him." He shook his head. "Maybe he'll even think he's kicked the habit. Then they'll let him loose"—he gestured, throwing his cigarette into the gutter. "That's all."

"What do you mean, that's *all?*"

But I knew what he meant.

"I *mean*, that's *all*." He turned his head and looked at me, pulling down the corners of his mouth. "Don't you know what I mean?" he asked, softly.

"How the hell *would* I know what you mean?" I almost whispered it, I don't know why.

"That's right," he said to the air, "how would *he* know what I mean?" He turned toward me again, patient and calm, and yet I somehow felt him shaking, shaking as though he were going to fall apart. I felt that ice in my guts again, the dread I'd felt all afternoon; and again I watched the barmaid, moving about the bar, washing glasses, and singing. "Listen. They'll let him out and then it'll just start all over again. That's what I mean."

"You mean—they'll let him out. And then he'll just start working his way back in again. You mean he'll never kick the habit. Is that what you mean?"

"That's right," he said, cheerfully. "*You* see what I mean."

"Tell me," I said at last, "why does he want to die? He must want to die, he's killing himself, why does he want to die?"

He looked at me in surprise. He licked his lips. "He don't want to die. He wants to live. Don't nobody want to die, ever."

Then I wanted to ask him—too many things. He could not have answered, or if he had, I could not have borne the answers. I started walking. "Well, I guess it's none of my business."

"It's going to be rough on old Sonny," he said. We reached the subway station. "This is your station?" he asked. I nodded. I took one step down. "Damn!" he said, suddenly. I looked up at him. He grinned again. "Damn it if I didn't leave all my money home. You ain't got a dollar on you, have you? Just for a couple of days, is all."

All at once something inside gave and threatened to come pouring out of me. I didn't hate him any more. I felt that in another moment I'd start crying like a child.

"Sure," I said. "Don't sweat." I looked in my wallet and didn't have a dollar, I only had a five. "Here," I said. "That hold you?"

He didn't look at it—he didn't want to look at it. A terrible, closed look came over his face, as though he were keeping the number on the bill a secret from him and me. "Thanks," he said, and now he was dying to see me go. "Don't worry about Sonny. Maybe I'll write him or something."

"Sure," I said. "You do that. So long."

"Be seeing you," he said. I went on down the steps.

And I didn't write Sonny or send him anything for a long time. When I finally did, it was just after my little girl died, and he wrote me back a letter which made me feel like a bastard.

Here's what he said:

Dear brother,

You don't know how much I needed to hear from you. I wanted to write you many a time but I dug how much I must have hurt you and so I didn't write. But now I feel like a man who's been trying to climb up out of some deep, real deep and funky hole and just saw the sun up there, outside. I got to get outside.

I can't tell you much about how I got here. I mean I don't know how to tell you. I guess I was afraid of something or I was trying to escape from something and you know I have never been very strong in the head (smile). I'm glad Mama and Daddy are dead and can't see what's happened to their son and I swear if I'd known what I was doing I would never have hurt you so, you and a lot of other fine people who were nice to me and who believed in me.

I don't want you to think it had anything to do with me being a musician. It's more than that. Or maybe less than that. I can't get anything straight in my head down here and I try not to think about what's going to happen to me when I get outside again. Sometime I think I'm going to flip and *never* get outside and sometime I think I'll come straight back. I tell you one thing, though, I'd rather blow my brains out than go through this again. But that's what they all say, so they tell me. If I tell you when I'm coming to New York and if you could meet me, I sure would appreciate it. Give my love to Isabel and the kids and I was sure sorry to hear about little Gracie. I wish I could be like Mama and say the Lord's will be done, but I don't know it seems to me that trouble is the one thing that never does get stopped and I don't know what good it does to blame it on the Lord. But maybe it does some good if you believe it.

Your brother,
Sonny

Then I kept in constant touch with him and I sent him whatever I could and I went to meet him when he came back to New York. When I saw him many things I thought I had forgotten came flooding back to me. This was because I had begun, finally, to wonder about Sonny, about the life that Sonny lived inside. This life, whatever it was, had made him older and thinner and it had deepened the distant stillness in which he had always moved. He looked very unlike my baby brother. Yet, when he smiled, when we shook hands, the baby brother I'd never known looked out from the depths of his private life, like an animal waiting to be coaxed into the light.

"How you been keeping?" he asked me.

"All right. And you?"

"Just fine." He was smiling all over his face. "It's good to see you again."

"It's good to see you."

The seven years' difference in our ages lay between us like a chasm: I wondered if these years would ever operate between us as a bridge. I was remembering, and it made it hard to catch my breath, that I had been there when he was born; and I had heard the first words he had ever spoken. When he started to walk, he walked from our mother straight to me. I caught him just before he fell when he took the first steps he ever took in this world.

"How's Isabel?"

"Just fine. She's dying to see you."

"And the boys?"

"They're fine, too. They're anxious to see their uncle."

"Oh, come on. You know they don't remember me."

"Are you kidding? Of course they remember you."

He grinned again. We got into a taxi. We had a lot to say to each other, far too much to know how to begin.

As the taxi began to move, I asked, "You still want to go to India?"

He laughed. "You still remember that. Hell, no. This place is Indian enough for me."

"It used to belong to them," I said.

And he laughed again. "They damn sure knew what they were doing when they got rid of it."

Years ago, when he was around fourteen, he'd been all hipped on the idea 70
of going to India. He read books about people sitting on rocks, naked, in all kinds of weather, but mostly bad, naturally, and walking barefoot through hot coals and arriving at wisdom. I used to say that it sounded to me as though they were getting away from wisdom as fast as they could. I think he sort of looked down on me for that.

"Do you mind," he asked, "if we have the driver drive alongside the park? On the west side—I haven't seen the city in so long."

"Of course not," I said. I was afraid that I might sound as though I were humoring him, but I hoped he wouldn't take it that way.

So we drove along, between the green of the park and the stony, lifeless elegance of hotels and apartment buildings, toward the vivid, killing streets of our childhood. These streets hadn't changed, though housing projects jutted up out of them now like rocks in the middle of a boiling sea. Most of the houses in which we had grown up had vanished, as had the stores from which we had stolen, the basements in which we had first tried sex, the rooftops from which we had hurled tin cans and bricks. But houses exactly like the houses of our past yet dominated the landscape, boys exactly like the boys we once had been found themselves smothering in these houses, came down into the streets for light and air and found themselves encircled by disaster. Some escaped the trap, most didn't. Those who got out always left something of themselves behind, as some animals amputate a leg and leave it in the trap. It might be said, perhaps, that I had escaped, after all, I was a school teacher; or that Sonny had, he hadn't lived in Harlem for years. Yet, as the cab moved uptown through streets which seemed, with a rush, to darken with dark people, and as I covertly studied Sonny's face, it came to me that what we both were seeking through our separate cab windows was that part of ourselves which had been left behind. It's always at the hour of trouble and confrontation that the missing member aches.

We hit 110th Street and started rolling up Lenox Avenue. And I'd known this avenue all my life, but it seemed to me again, as it had seemed on the day I'd first heard about Sonny's trouble, filled with a hidden menace which was its very breath of life.

"We almost there," said Sonny. 75

"Almost." We were both too nervous to say anything more.

We live in a housing project. It hasn't been up long. A few days after it was up it seemed uninhabitably new, now, of course, it's already rundown. It looks like a parody of the good, clean, faceless life—God knows the people who live in it do their best to make it a parody. The beat-looking grass lying around isn't enough to make their lives green, the hedges will never hold out the streets, and they know it. The big windows fool no one, they aren't big enough to make space out of no space. They don't bother with the windows, they watch the TV screen instead. The playground is most popular with the children who don't play at jacks, or skip rope, or roller skate, or swing, and they can be found in it after dark. We moved in partly because it's not too far from where I teach, and partly for the kids; but it's really just like the houses in which Sonny and I grew up. The same things happen, they'll have the same things to remember. The moment Sonny and I started into the house I had the feeling that I was simply bringing him back into the danger he had almost died trying to escape.

Sonny has never been talkative. So I don't know why I was sure he'd be dying to talk to me when supper was over the first night. Everything went fine, the oldest boy remembered him, and the youngest boy liked him, and Sonny had remembered to bring something for each of them; and Isabel, who is really much nicer than I am, more open and giving, had gone to a lot of trouble about dinner and was genuinely glad to see him. And she's always been able to tease Sonny in a way that I haven't. It was nice to see her face so vivid again and to hear her laugh and watch her make Sonny laugh. She wasn't, or, anyway, she didn't seem to be, at all uneasy or embarrassed. She chatted as though there were no subject which had to be avoided and she got Sonny past his first, faint stiffness. And thank God she was there, for I was filled with that icy dread again. Everything I did seemed awkward to me, and everything I said sounded freighted with hidden meaning. I was trying to remember everything I'd heard about dope addiction and I couldn't help watching Sonny for signs. I wasn't doing it out of malice. I was trying to find out something about my brother. I was dying to hear him tell me he was safe.

"Safe!" my father grunted, whenever Mama suggested trying to move to a neighborhood which might be safer for children. "Safe, hell! Ain't no place safe for kids, nor nobody."

80 He always went on like this, but he wasn't, ever, really as bad as he sounded, not even on weekends, when he got drunk. As a matter of fact, he was always on the lookout for "something a little better," but he died before he found it. He died suddenly, during a drunken weekend in the middle of the war, when Sonny was fifteen. He and Sonny hadn't ever got on too well. And this was partly because Sonny was the apple of his father's eye. It was because he loved Sonny so much and was frightened for him, that he was always fighting with him. It doesn't do any good to fight with Sonny. Sonny just moves back, inside himself, where he can't be reached. But the principal reason that they never hit it off is that they were so much alike. Daddy was big and rough and loud-talking, just the opposite of Sonny, but they both had—that same privacy.

Mama tried to tell me something about this, just after Daddy died. I was home on leave from the army.

This was the last time I ever saw my mother alive. Just the same, this picture gets all mixed up in my mind with pictures I had of her when she was younger. The way I always see her is the way she used to be on a Sunday afternoon, say, when the old folks were talking after the big Sunday dinner. I always see her wearing pale blue. She'd be sitting on the sofa. And my father would be sitting in the easy chair, not far from her. And the living room would be full of church folks and relatives. There they sit, in chairs all around the living room, and the night is creeping up outside, but nobody knows it yet. You can see the darkness growing against the windowpanes and you hear the street noises every now and again, or maybe the jangling beat of a tambourine from one of the churches close by, but it's real quiet in the room. For a moment nobody's talking, but every face looks darkening, like the sky outside. And my mother rocks a little from the waist, and my father's eyes are closed. Everyone is looking at something a child can't see. For a minute they've forgotten the children. Maybe a kid is lying on the rug, half asleep. Maybe somebody's got a kid in his lap and is absent-mindedly stroking the kid's head. Maybe there's a kid, quiet and big-eyed, curled up in a big chair in the corner. The silence, the darkness coming, and the darkness in the faces frighten the child obscurely. He hopes that the hand which strokes his forehead will never stop—will never die. He hopes that there will never come a time when the old folks won't be sitting around the living room, talking about where they've come from, and what they've seen, and what's happened to them and their kinfolk.

But something deep and watchful in the child knows that this is bound to end, is already ending. In a moment someone will get up and turn on the light. Then the old folks will remember the children and they won't talk any more that day. And when light fills the room, the child is filled with darkness. He knows that every time this happens he's moved just a little closer to that darkness outside. The darkness outside is what the old folks have been talking about. It's what they've come from. It's what they endure. The child knows that they won't talk any more because if he knows too much about what's happened to *them*, he'll know too much too soon, about what's going to happen to *him*.

The last time I talked to my mother, I remember I was restless. I wanted to get out and see Isabel. We weren't married then and we had a lot to straighten out between us.

There Mama sat, in black, by the window. She was humming an old church 85
song, *Lord, you brought me from a long ways off*. Sonny was out somewhere. Mama kept watching the streets.

"I don't know," she said, "if I'll ever see you again, after you go off from here. But I hope you'll remember the things I tried to teach you."

"Don't talk like that," I said, and smiled. "You'll be here a long time yet."

She smiled, too, but she said nothing. She was quiet for a long time. And I said, "Mama, don't you worry about nothing. I'll be writing all the time, and you be getting the checks. . . ."

"I want to talk to you about your brother," she said, suddenly. "If anything happens to me he ain't going to have nobody to look out for him."

"Mama," I said, "ain't nothing going to happen to you *or* Sonny. Sonny's 90
all right. He's a good boy and he's got good sense."

"It ain't a question of his being a good boy," Mama said, "nor of his having good sense. It ain't only the bad ones, nor yet the dumb ones that gets sucked under." She stopped, looking at me. "Your Daddy once had a brother," she said, and she smiled in a way that made me feel she was in pain. "You didn't never know that, did you?"

"No," I said, "I never knew that," and I watched her face.

"Oh, yes," she said, "your Daddy had a brother." She looked out of the window again. "I know you never saw your Daddy cry. But *I* did—many a time, through all these years."

I asked her, "What happened to his brother? How come nobody's ever talked about him?"

95 This was the first time I ever saw my mother look old.

"His brother got killed," she said, "when he was just a little younger than you are now. I knew him. He was a fine boy. He was maybe a little full of the devil, but he didn't mean nobody no harm."

Then she stopped and the room was silent, exactly as it had sometimes been on those Sunday afternoons. Mama kept looking out into the streets.

"He used to have a job in the mill," she said, "and, like all young folks, he just liked to perform on Saturday nights. Saturday nights, him and your father would drift around to different places, go to dances and things like that, or just sit around with people they knew, and your father's brother would sing, he had a fine voice, and play along with himself on his guitar. Well, this particular Saturday night, him and your father was coming home from some place, and they were both a little drunk and there was a moon that night, it was bright like day. Your father's brother was feeling kind of good, and he was whistling to himself, and he had his guitar slung over his shoulder. They was coming down a hill and beneath them was a road that turned off from the highway. Well, your father's brother, being always kind of frisky, decided to run down this hill, and he did, with that guitar banging and clanging behind him, and he ran across the road, and he was making water behind a tree. And your father was sort of amused at him and he was still coming down the hill, kind of slow. Then he heard a car motor and that same minute his brother stepped from behind the tree, into the road, in the moonlight. And he started to cross the road. And your father started to run down the hill, he says he don't know why. This car was full of white men. They was all drunk, and when they seen your father's brother they let out a great whoop and holler and they aimed the car straight at him. They was having fun, they just wanted to scare him, the way they do sometimes, you know. But they was drunk. And I guess the boy, being drunk, too, and scared, kind of lost his head. By the time he jumped it was too late. Your father says he heard his brother scream when the car rolled over him, and he heard the wood of that guitar when it give, and he heard them strings go flying, and he heard them white men shouting, and the car kept on a-going and it ain't stopped till this day. And, time your father got down the hill, his brother weren't nothing but blood and pulp."

Tears were gleaming on my mother's face. There wasn't anything I could say.

100 "He never mentioned it," she said, "because I never let him mention it before you children. Your Daddy was like a crazy man that night and for many

a night thereafter. He says he never in his life seen anything as dark as that road after the lights of that car had gone away. Weren't nothing, weren't nobody on that road, just your Daddy and his brother and that busted guitar. Oh, yes. Your Daddy never did really get right again. Till the day he died he weren't sure but that every white man he saw was the man that killed his brother."

She stopped and took out her handkerchief and dried her eyes and looked at me.

"I ain't telling you all this," she said, "to make you scared or bitter or to make you hate nobody. I'm telling you this because you got a brother. And the world ain't changed."

I guess I didn't want to believe this. I guess she saw this in my face. She turned away from me, toward the window again, searching those streets.

"But I praise my Redeemer," she said at last, "that He called your Daddy home before me. I ain't saying it to throw no flowers at myself, but, I declare, it keeps me from feeling too cast down to know I helped your father get safely through this world. Your father always acted like he was the roughest, strongest man on earth. And everybody took him to be like that. But if he hadn't had me there—to see his tears!"

She was crying again. Still, I couldn't move. I said, "Lord, Lord, Mama, I 105
didn't know it was like that."

"Oh, honey," she said, "there's a lot that you don't know. But you are going to find out." She stood up from the window and came over to me. "You got to hold on to your brother," she said, "and don't let him fall, no matter what it looks like is happening to him and no matter how evil you gets with him. You going to be evil with him many a time. But don't you forget what I told you, you hear?"

"I won't forget," I said. "Don't you worry, I won't forget. I won't let nothing happen to Sonny."

My mother smiled as though she was amused at something she saw in my face. Then, "You may not be able to stop nothing from happening. But you got to let him know you's *there*."

Two days later I was married, and then I was gone. And I had a lot of things on my mind and I pretty well forgot my promise to Mama until I got shipped home on a special furlough for her funeral.

And, after the funeral, with just Sonny and me alone in the empty kitchen, 110
I tried to find out something about him.

"What do you want to do?" I asked him.

"I'm going to be a musician," he said.

For he had graduated, in the time I had been away, from dancing to the juke box to finding out who was playing what, and what they were doing with it, and he had bought himself a set of drums.

"You mean, you want to be a drummer?" I somehow had the feeling that being a drummer might be all right for other people but not for my brother Sonny.

"I don't think," he said, looking at me very gravely, "that I'll ever be a good 115
drummer. But I think I can play a piano."

I frowned. I'd never played the role of the oldest brother quite so seriously before, had scarcely ever, in fact, *asked* Sonny a damn thing. I sensed myself in the presence of something I didn't really know how to handle, didn't understand. So I made my frown a little deeper as I asked: "What kind of musician do you want to be?"

He grinned. "How many kinds do you think there are?"

"Be *serious*," I said.

He laughed, throwing his head back, and then looked at me. "I *am* serious."

120 "Well, then, for Christ's sake, stop kidding around and answer a serious question. I mean, do you want to be a concert pianist, you want to play classical music and all that, or—or what?" Long before I finished he was laughing again. "For Christ's *sake*, Sonny!"

He sobered, but with difficulty. "I'm sorry. But you sound so—*scared!*" and he was off again.

"Well, you may think it's funny now, baby, but it's not going to be so funny when you have to make your living at it, let me tell you *that*." I was furious because I knew he was laughing at me and I didn't know why.

"No," he said, very sober now, and afraid, perhaps, that he'd hurt me, "I don't want to be a classical pianist. That isn't what interests me. I mean"—he paused, looking hard at me, as though his eyes would help me to understand, and then gestured helplessly, as though perhaps his hand would help—"I mean, I'll have a lot of studying to do, and I'll have to study *everything*, but, I mean, I want to play *with*—jazz musicians." He stopped. "I want to play jazz," he said.

Well, the word had never before sounded as heavy, as real, as it sounded that afternoon in Sonny's mouth. I just looked at him and I was probably frowning a real frown by this time. I simply couldn't see why on earth he'd want to spend his time hanging around nightclubs, clowning around on bandstands, while people pushed each other around a dance floor. It seemed—beneath him, somehow. I had never thought about it before, had never been forced to, but I suppose I had always put jazz musicians in a class with what Daddy called "good-time people."

125 "Are you *serious?*"

"Hell, *yes*, I'm serious."

He looked more helpless than ever, and annoyed, and deeply hurt.

I suggested, helpfully: "You mean—like Louis Armstrong?"

His face closed as though I'd struck him. "No. I'm not talking about none of that old-time, down home crap."

130 "Well, look, Sonny, I'm sorry, don't get mad. I just don't altogether get it, that's all. Name somebody—you know, a jazz musician you admire."

"Bird."

"Who?"

"Bird! Charlie Parker![3] Don't they teach you nothing in the goddamn army?"

3. Charlie ("Bird") Parker (1920–1955), perhaps the greatest saxophonist and innovator of jazz; cofounder, with Dizzy Gillespie, of the new jazz, once called "bebop." He was a narcotics addict.

I lit a cigarette. I was surprised and then a little amused to discover that I was trembling. "I've been out of touch," I said. "You'll have to be patient with me. Now. Who's this Parker character?"

"He's just one of the greatest jazz musicians alive," said Sonny, sullenly, his 135
hands in his pockets, his back to me. "Maybe *the* greatest," he added, bitterly, "that's probably why *you* never heard of him."

"All right," I said, "I'm ignorant. I'm sorry. I'll go out and buy all the cat's records right away, all right?"

"It don't," said Sonny, with dignity, "make any difference to me. I don't care what you listen to. Don't do me no favors."

I was beginning to realize that I'd never seen him so upset before. With another part of my mind I was thinking that this would probably turn out to be one of those things kids go through and that I shouldn't make it seem important by pushing it too hard. Still, I didn't think it would do any harm to ask: "Doesn't all this take a lot of time? Can you make a living at it?"

He turned back to me and half leaned, half sat, on the kitchen table. "Everything takes time," he said, "and—well, yes, sure, I can make a living at it. But what I don't seem to be able to make you understand is that it's the only thing I want to do."

"Well, Sonny," I said gently, "you know people can't always do exactly what 140
they *want* to do—"

"*No*, I don't know that," said Sonny, surprising me. "I think people *ought* to do what they want to do, what else are they alive for?"

"You getting to be a big boy," I said desperately, "it's time you started thinking about your future."

"I'm thinking about my future," said Sonny, grimly. "I think about it all the time."

I gave up. I decided, if he didn't change his mind, that we could always talk about it later. "In the meantime," I said, "you got to finish school." We had already decided that he'd have to move in with Isabel and her folks. I knew this wasn't the ideal arrangement because Isabel's folks are inclined to be dicty[4] and they hadn't especially wanted Isabel to marry me. But I didn't know what else to do. "And we have to get you fixed up at Isabel's."

There was a long silence. He moved from the kitchen table to the window. 145
"That's a terrible idea. You know it yourself."

"Do you have a *better* idea?"

He just walked up and down the kitchen for a minute. He was as tall as I was. He had started to shave. I suddenly had the feeling that I didn't know him at all.

He stopped at the kitchen table and picked up my cigarettes. Looking at me with a kind of mocking, amused defiance, he put one between his lips. "You mind?"

"You smoking already?"

He lit the cigarette and nodded, watching me through the smoke. "I just 150

4. Snobbish, bossy.

wanted to see if I'd have the courage to smoke in front of you." He grinned and blew a great cloud of smoke to the ceiling. "It was easy." He looked at my face. "Come on, now. I bet you was smoking at my age, tell the truth."

I didn't say anything but the truth was on my face, and he laughed. But now there was something very strained in his laugh. "Sure. And I bet that ain't all you was doing."

He was frightening me a little. "Cut the crap," I said. "We already decided that you was going to go and live at Isabel's. Now what's got into you all of a sudden?"

"*You* decided it," he pointed out. "*I* didn't decide nothing." He stopped in front of me, leaning against the stove, arms loosely folded. "Look, brother. I don't want to stay in Harlem no more, I really don't." He was very earnest. He looked at me, then over toward the kitchen window. There was something in his eyes I'd never seen before, some thoughtfulness, some worry all his own. He rubbed the muscle of one arm. "It's time I was getting out of here."

"Where do you want to *go*, Sonny?"

"I want to join the army. Or the navy, I don't care. If I say I'm old enough, they'll believe me."

Then I got mad. It was because I was so scared. "You must be crazy. You goddamn fool, what the hell do you want to go and join the *army* for?"

"I just told you. To get out of Harlem."

"Sonny, you haven't even finished *school*. And if you really want to be a musician, how do you expect to study if you're in the *army*?"

He looked at me, trapped, and in anguish. "There's ways. I might be able to work out some kind of deal. Anyway, I'll have the G.I. Bill when I come out."

"*If* you come out." We stared at each other. "Sonny, please. Be reasonable. I know the setup is far from perfect. But we got to do the best we can."

"I ain't learning nothing in school," he said. "Even when I go." He turned away from me and opened the window and threw his cigarette out into the narrow alley. I watched his back. "At least, I ain't learning nothing you'd want me to learn." He slammed the window so hard I thought the glass would fly out, and turned back to me. "And I'm sick of the stink of these garbage cans!"

"Sonny," I said, "I know how you feel. But if you don't finish school now, you're going to be sorry later that you didn't." I grabbed him by the shoulders. "And you only got another year. It ain't so bad. And I'll come back and I swear I'll help you do *whatever* you want to do. Just try to put up with it till I come back. Will you please do that? For me?"

He didn't answer and he wouldn't look at me.

"Sonny. You hear me?"

He pulled away. "I hear you. But you never hear anything *I* say."

I didn't know what to say to that. He looked out of the window and then back at me. "OK," he said, and sighed. "I'll try."

Then I said, trying to cheer him up a little, "They got a piano at Isabel's. You can practice on it."

And as a matter of fact, it did cheer him up for a minute. "That's right," he said to himself. "I forgot that." His face relaxed a little. But the worry, the thoughtfulness, played on it still, the way shadows play on a face which is staring into the fire.

But I thought I'd never hear the end of that piano. At first, Isabel would write me, saying how nice it was that Sonny was so serious about his music and how, as soon as he came in from school, or wherever he had been when he was supposed to be at school, he went straight to that piano and stayed there until suppertime. And, after supper, he went back to that piano and stayed there until everybody went to bed. He was at the piano all day Saturday and all day Sunday. Then he bought a record player and started playing records. He'd play one record over and over again, all day long sometimes, and he'd improvise along with it on the piano. Or he'd play one section of the record, one chord, one change, one progression, then he'd do it on the piano. Then back to the record. Then back to the piano.

Well, I really don't know how they stood it. Isabel finally confessed that it 170
wasn't like living with a person at all, it was like living with sound. And the sound didn't make any sense to her, didn't make any sense to any of them—naturally. They began, in a way, to be afflicted by this presence that was living in their home. It was as though Sonny were some sort of god, or monster. He moved in an atmosphere which wasn't like theirs at all. They fed him and he ate, he washed himself, he walked in and out of their door; he certainly wasn't nasty or unpleasant or rude, Sonny isn't any of those things; but it was as though he were all wrapped up in some cloud, some fire, some vision all his own; and there wasn't any way to reach him.

At the same time, he wasn't really a man yet, he was still a child, and they had to watch out for him in all kinds of ways. They certainly couldn't throw him out. Neither did they dare to make a great scene about that piano because even they dimly sensed, as I sensed, from so many thousands of miles away, that Sonny was at that piano playing for his life.

But he hadn't been going to school. One day a letter came from the school board and Isabel's mother got it—there had, apparently, been other letters but Sonny had torn them up. This day, when Sonny came in, Isabel's mother showed him the letter and asked where he'd been spending his time. And she finally got it out of him that he'd been down in Greenwich Village, with musicians and other characters, in a white girl's apartment. And this scared her and she started to scream at him and what came up, once she began—though she denies it to this day—was what sacrifices they were making to give Sonny a decent home and how little he appreciated it.

Sonny didn't play the piano that day. By evening, Isabel's mother had calmed down but then there was the old man to deal with, and Isabel herself. Isabel says she did her best to be calm but she broke down and started crying. She says she just watched Sonny's face. She could tell, by watching him, what was happening with him. And what was happening was that they penetrated his cloud, they had reached him. Even if their fingers had been a thousand times more gentle than human fingers ever are, he could hardly help feeling that they had stripped him naked and were spitting on that nakedness. For he also had to see that his presence, that music, which was life or death to him, had been torture for them and that they had endured it, not at all for his sake, but only for mine. And Sonny couldn't take that. He can take it a little better today than he could then but he's still not very good at it and, frankly, I don't know anybody who is.

The silence of the next few days must have been louder than the sound of all the music ever played since time began. One morning, before she went to work, Isabel was in his room for something and she suddenly realized that all of his records were gone. And she knew for certain that he was gone. And he was. He went as far as the navy would carry him. He finally sent me a postcard from some place in Greece and that was the first I knew that Sonny was still alive. I didn't see him any more until we were both back in New York and the war had long been over.

175 He was a man by then, of course, but I wasn't willing to see it. He came by the house from time to time, but we fought almost every time we met. I didn't like the way he carried himself, loose and dreamlike all the time, and I didn't like his friends, and his music seemed to be merely an excuse for the life he led. It sounded just that weird and disordered.

Then we had a fight, a pretty awful fight, and I didn't see him for months. By and by I looked him up, where he was living, in a furnished room in the Village, and I tried to make it up. But there were lots of other people in the room and Sonny just lay on his bed, and he wouldn't come downstairs with me, and he treated these other people as though they were his family and I weren't. So I got mad and then he got mad, and then I told him that he might just as well be dead as live the way he was living. Then he stood up and he told me not to worry about him any more in life, that he *was* dead as far as I was concerned. Then he pushed me to the door and the other people looked on as though nothing were happening, and he slammed the door behind me. I stood in the hallway, staring at the door. I heard somebody laugh in the room and then the tears came to my eyes. I started down the steps, whistling to keep from crying, I kept whistling to myself, *You going to need me, baby, one of these cold, rainy days*.

I read about Sonny's trouble in the spring. Little Grace died in the fall. She was a beautiful little girl. But she only lived a little over two years. She died of polio and she suffered. She had a slight fever for a couple of days, but it didn't seem like anything and we just kept her in bed. And we would certainly have called the doctor, but the fever dropped, she seemed to be all right. So we thought it had just been a cold. Then, one day, she was up, playing, Isabel was in the kitchen fixing lunch for the two boys when they'd come in from school, and she heard Grace fall down in the living room. When you have a lot of children you don't always start running when one of them falls, unless they start screaming or something. And, this time, Gracie was quiet. Yet, Isabel says that when she heard that *thump* and then that silence, something happened to her to make her afraid. And she ran to the living room and there was little Grace on the floor, all twisted up, and the reason she hadn't screamed was that she couldn't get her breath. And when she did scream, it was the worst sound, Isabel says, that she'd ever heard in all her life, and she still hears it sometimes in her dreams. Isabel will sometimes wake me up with a low, moaning, strangling sound and I have to be quick to awaken her and hold her to me and where Isabel is weeping against me seems a mortal wound.

I think I may have written Sonny the very day that little Grace was buried. I was sitting in the living room in the dark, by myself, and I suddenly thought of Sonny. My trouble made his real.

One Saturday afternoon, when Sonny had been living with us, or anyway, been in our house, for nearly two weeks, I found myself wandering aimlessly about the living room, drinking from a can of beer, and trying to work up courage to search Sonny's room. He was out, he was usually out whenever I was home, and Isabel had taken the children to see their grandparents. Suddenly I was standing still in front of the living room window, watching Seventh Avenue. The idea of searching Sonny's room made me still. I scarcely dared to admit to myself what I'd be searching for. I didn't know what I'd do if I found it. Or if I didn't.

On the sidewalk across from me, near the entrance to a barbecue joint, some people were holding an old-fashioned revival meeting. The barbecue cook, wearing a dirty white apron, his conked[5] hair reddish and metallic in the pale sun, and a cigarette between his lips, stood in the doorway, watching them. Kids and older people paused in their errands and stood there, along with some older men and a couple of very tough-looking women who watched everything that happened on the avenue, as though they owned it, or were maybe owned by it. Well, they were watching this, too. The revival was being carried on by three sisters in black, and a brother. All they had were their voices and their Bibles and a tambourine. The brother was testifying[6] and while he testified two of the sisters stood together, seeming to say, amen, and the third sister walked around with the tambourine outstretched and a couple of people dropped coins into it. Then the brother's testimony ended and the sister who had been taking up the collection dumped the coins into her palm and transferred them to the pocket of her long black robe. Then she raised both hands, striking the tambourine against the air, and then against one hand, and she started to sing. And the two other sisters and the brother joined in.

It was strange, suddenly, to watch, though I had been seeing these meetings all my life. So, of course, had everybody else down there. Yet, they paused and watched and listened and I stood still at the window. "*'Tis the old ship of Zion,*" they sang, and the sister with the tambourine kept a steady, jangling beat, "*it has rescued many a thousand!*" Not a soul under the sound of their voices was hearing this song for the first time, not one of them had been rescued. Nor had they seen much in the way of rescue work being done around them. Neither did they especially believe in the holiness of the three sisters and the brother, they knew too much about them, knew where they lived, and how. The woman with the tambourine, whose voice dominated the air, whose face was bright with joy, was divided by very little from the woman who stood watching her, a cigarette between her heavy, chapped lips, her hair a cuckoo's nest, her face scarred and swollen

5. Processed: straightened and greased. 6. Publicly professing belief.

from many beatings, and her black eyes glittering like coal. Perhaps they both knew this, which was why, when, as rarely, they addressed each other, they addressed each other as Sister. As the singing filled the air the watching, listening faces underwent a change, the eyes focusing on something within; the music seemed to soothe a poison out of them; and time seemed, nearly, to fall away from the sullen, belligerent, battered faces, as though they were fleeing back to their first condition, while dreaming of their last. The barbecue cook half shook his head and smiled, and dropped his cigarette and disappeared into his joint. A man fumbled in his pockets for change and stood holding it in his hand impatiently, as though he had just remembered a pressing appointment further up the avenue. He looked furious. Then I saw Sonny, standing on the edge of the crowd. He was carrying a wide, flat notebook with a green cover, and it made him look, from where I was standing, almost like a schoolboy. The coppery sun brought out the copper in his skin, he was very faintly smiling, standing very still. Then the singing stopped, the tambourine turned into a collection plate again. The furious man dropped in his coins and vanished, so did a couple of the women, and Sonny dropped some change in the plate, looking directly at the woman with a little smile. He started across the avenue, toward the house. He has a slow, loping walk, something like the way Harlem hipsters walk, only he's imposed on this his own half-beat. I had never really noticed it before.

I stayed at the window, both relieved and apprehensive. As Sonny disappeared from my sight, they began singing again. And they were still singing when his key turned in the lock.

"Hey," he said.

"Hey, yourself. You want some beer?"

"No. Well, maybe." But he came up to the window and stood beside me, looking out. "What a warm voice," he said.

They were singing *If I could only hear my mother pray again!*

"Yes," I said, "and she can sure beat that tambourine."

"But what a terrible song," he said, and laughed. He dropped his notebook on the sofa and disappeared into the kitchen. "Where's Isabel and the kids?"

"I think they went to see their grandparents. You hungry?"

"No." He came back into the living room with his can of beer. "You want to come some place with me tonight?"

I sensed, I don't know how, that I couldn't possibly say no. "Sure. Where?"

He sat down on the sofa and picked up his notebook and started leafing through it. "I'm going to sit in with some fellows in a joint in the Village."

"You mean, you're going to play, tonight?"

"That's right." He took a swallow of his beer and moved back to the window. He gave me a sidelong look. "If you can stand it."

"I'll try," I said.

He smiled to himself and we both watched as the meeting across the way broke up. The three sisters and the brother, heads bowed, were singing *God be with you till we meet again*. The faces around them were very quiet. Then the song ended. The small crowd dispersed. We watched the three women and the lone man walk slowly up the avenue.

"When she was singing before," said Sonny, abruptly, "her voice reminded me for a minute of what heroin feels like sometimes—when it's in your veins. It makes you feel sort of warm and cool at the same time. And distant. And—and sure." He sipped his beer, very deliberately not looking at me. I watched his face. "It makes you feel—in control. Sometimes you've got to have that feeling."

"Do you?" I sat down slowly in the easy chair.

"Sometimes." He went to the sofa and picked up his notebook again. "Some people do."

"In order," I asked, "to play?" And my voice was very ugly, full of contempt and anger.

"Well"—he looked at me with great, troubled eyes, as though, in fact, he hoped his eyes would tell me things he could never otherwise say—"they *think* so. And *if* they think so—!"

"And what do *you* think?" I asked.

He sat on the sofa and put his can of beer on the floor. "I don't know," he said, and I couldn't be sure if he were answering my question or pursuing his thoughts. His face didn't tell me. "It's not so much to *play*. It's to *stand* it, to be able to make it at all. On any level." He frowned and smiled: "In order to keep from shaking to pieces."

"But these friends of yours," I said, "they seem to shake themselves to pieces pretty goddamn fast."

"Maybe." He played with the notebook. And something told me that I should curb my tongue, that Sonny was doing his best to talk, that I should listen. "But of course you only know the ones that've gone to pieces. Some don't—or at least they haven't *yet* and that's just about all *any* of us can say." He paused. "And then there are some who just live, really, in hell, and they know it and they see what's happening and they go right on. I don't know." He sighed, dropped the notebook, folded his arms. "Some guys, you can tell from the way they play, they on something *all* the time. And you can see that, well, it makes something real for them. But of course," he picked up his beer from the floor and sipped it and put the can down again, "they *want* to, too, you've got to see that. Even some of them that say they don't—*some*, not all."

"And what about you?" I asked—I couldn't help it. "What about you? Do *you* want to?"

He stood up and walked to the window and I remained silent for a long time. Then he sighed. "Me," he said. Then: "While I was downstairs before, on my way here, listening to that woman sing, it struck me all of a sudden how much suffering she must have had to go through—to sing like that. It's *repulsive* to think you have to suffer that much."

I said: "But there's no way not to suffer—is there, Sonny?"

"I believe not," he said and smiled, "but that's never stopped anyone from trying." He looked at me. "Has it?" I realized, with this mocking look, that there stood between us, forever, beyond the power of time or forgiveness, the fact that I had held silence—so long!—when he had needed human speech to help him. He turned back to the window. "No, there's no way not to suffer. But you try all kinds of ways to keep from drowning in it, to keep on top of it, and to make it seem—well, like *you*. Like you did something, all right, and now you're suffering for it. You know?" I said nothing. "Well you know," he said, impatiently, "why *do* people suffer? Maybe it's better to do something to give it a reason, *any* reason."

"But we just agreed," I said, "that there's no way not to suffer. Isn't it better, then, just to—take it?"

"But nobody just takes it," Sonny cried, "that's what I'm telling you! *Everybody* tries not to. You're just hung up on the *way* some people try—it's not *your* way!"

The hair on my face began to itch, my face felt wet. "That's not true," I said, "that's not true. I don't give a damn what other people do, I don't even care how they suffer. I just care how *you* suffer." And he looked at me. "Please believe me," I said, "I don't want to see you—die—trying not to suffer."

"I won't," he said flatly, "die trying not to suffer. At least, not any faster than anybody else."

"But there's no need," I said, trying to laugh, "is there? in killing yourself."

I wanted to say more, but I couldn't. I wanted to talk about will power and how life could be—well, beautiful. I wanted to say that it was all within; but was it? or, rather, wasn't that exactly the trouble? And I wanted to promise that I would never fail him again. But it would all have sounded—empty words and lies.

So I made the promise to myself and prayed that I would keep it.

"It's terrible sometimes, inside," he said, "that's what's the trouble. You walk these streets, black and funky and cold, and there's not really a living ass to talk to, and there's nothing shaking, and there's no way of getting it out—that storm inside. You can't talk it and you can't make love with it, and when you finally try to get with it and play it, you realize *nobody's* listening. So *you've* got to listen. You got to find a way to listen."

And then he walked away from the window and sat on the sofa again, as though all the wind had suddenly been knocked out of him. "Sometimes you'll do *anything* to play, even cut your mother's throat." He laughed and looked at me. "Or your brother's." Then he sobered. "Or your own." Then: "Don't worry. I'm all right now and I think I'll *be* all right. But I can't forget—where I've been. I don't mean just the physical place I've been, I mean where I've *been*. And *what* I've been."

"What have you been, Sonny?" I asked.

He smiled—but sat sideways on the sofa, his elbow resting on the back, his fingers playing with his mouth and chin, not looking at me. "I've been something I didn't recognize, didn't know I could be. Didn't know anybody could be." He stopped, looking inward, looking helplessly young, looking old. "I'm not talking about it now because I feel *guilty* or anything like that—maybe it would be better if I did, I don't know. Anyway, I can't really talk about it. Not to you, not to anybody," and now he turned and faced me. "Sometimes, you know, and it was actually when I was most *out* of the world, I felt that I was in it, that I was *with* it, really, and I could play or I didn't really have to *play*, it just came out of me, it was there. And I don't know how I played, thinking about it now, but I know I did awful things, those times, sometimes, to people. Or it wasn't that I *did* anything to them—it was that they weren't real." He picked up the beer can; it was empty; he rolled it between his palms: "And other times—well, I needed a fix, I needed to find a place to lean, I needed to clear a space to *listen*—and I couldn't find it, and I—went crazy, I did terrible things to *me*, I was terrible *for* me." He began pressing the beer can between his hands, I watched the metal begin to give. It glittered, as he played with it like a knife, and I was afraid he would cut himself, but I said nothing. "Oh well. I can never tell you. I was all by myself at the bottom of something, stinking and sweating and crying and shaking, and I smelled it, you know? *my* stink, and I thought I'd die if I couldn't get away from it and yet, all the same, I knew that everything I was doing was just locking me in with it. And I didn't know," he paused, still flattening the beer can, "I didn't know, I still *don't* know, something kept telling me that maybe it was good to smell your own stink, but I didn't think that *that* was what I'd been trying to do—and—who can stand it?" and he abruptly dropped the ruined beer can, looking at me with a small, still smile, and then rose, walking to the window as though it were the lodestone rock. I watched his face, he watched the avenue. "I couldn't tell you when Mama died—but the reason I wanted to leave Harlem so bad was to get away from drugs. And then, when I ran away, that's what I was running from—really. When I came back, nothing had changed, *I* hadn't changed, I was just—older." And he stopped, drumming with his fingers on the windowpane. The sun had vanished, soon darkness would fall. I watched his face. "It can come again," he said, almost as though speaking to himself. Then he turned to me. "It can come again," he repeated. "I just want you to know that."

"All right," I said, at last. "So it can come again. All right."

He smiled, but the smile was sorrowful. "I had to try to tell you," he said.

"Yes," I said. "I understand that."

"You're my brother," he said, looking straight at me, and not smiling at all.

"Yes," I repeated, "yes. I understand that."

He turned back to the window, looking out. "All that hatred down there," he said, "all that hatred and misery and love. It's a wonder it doesn't blow the avenue apart."

We went to the only nightclub on a short, dark street, downtown. We squeezed through the narrow, chattering, jampacked bar to the entrance of the big room, where the bandstand was. And we stood there for a moment, for the lights were very dim in this room and we couldn't see. Then, "Hello, boy," said the voice and an enormous black man, much older than Sonny or myself, erupted out of all that atmospheric lighting and put an arm around Sonny's shoulder. "I been sitting right here," he said, "waiting for you."

He had a big voice, too, and heads in the darkness turned toward us.

Sonny grinned and pulled a little away, and said, "Creole, this is my brother. I told you about him."

Creole shook my hand. "I'm glad to meet you, son," he said, and it was clear that he was glad to meet me *there*, for Sonny's sake. And he smiled, "You got a real musician in *your* family," and he took his arm from Sonny's shoulder and slapped him, lightly, affectionately, with the back of his hand.

"Well. Now I've heard it all," said a voice behind us. This was another musician, and a friend of Sonny's, a coal-black, cheerful-looking man, built close to the ground. He immediately began confiding to me, at the top of his lungs, the most terrible things about Sonny, his teeth gleaming like a lighthouse and his laugh coming up out of him like the beginning of an earthquake. And it turned out that everyone at the bar knew Sonny, or almost everyone; some were musicians, working there, or nearby, or not working, some were simply hangers-on, and some were there to hear Sonny play. I was introduced to all of them and they were all very polite to me. Yet, it was clear that, for them, I was only Sonny's brother. Here, I was in Sonny's world. Or, rather: his kingdom. Here, it was not even a question that his veins bore royal blood.

They were going to play soon and Creole installed me, by myself, at a table in a dark corner. Then I watched them, Creole, and the little black man, and Sonny, and the others, while they horsed around, standing just below the bandstand. The light from the bandstand spilled just a little short of them and, watching them laughing and gesturing and moving about, I had the feeling that they, nevertheless, were being most careful not to step into that circle of light too suddenly; that if they moved into the light too suddenly, without thinking, they would perish in flame. Then, while I watched, one of them, the small black man, moved into the light and crossed the bandstand and started fooling around with his drums. Then—being funny and being, also, extremely ceremonious—Creole took Sonny by the arm and led him to the piano. A woman's voice called Sonny's name and a few hands started clapping. And Sonny, also being funny and being ceremonious, and so touched, I think, that he could have cried, but neither hiding it nor showing it, riding it like a man, grinned, and put both hands to his heart and bowed from the waist.

Creole then went to the bass fiddle and a lean, very bright-skinned brown man jumped up on the bandstand and picked up his horn. So there they were, and the atmosphere on the bandstand and in the room began to change and tighten. Someone stepped up to the microphone and announced them. Then there were all kinds of murmurs. Some people at the bar shushed others. The waitress ran around, frantically getting in the last orders, guys and chicks got closer to each other, and the lights on the bandstand, on the quartet, turned to a kind of indigo. Then they all looked different there. Creole looked about him for the last time, as though he were making certain that all his chickens were in the coop, and then he—jumped and struck the fiddle. And there they were.

All I know about music is that not many people ever really hear it. And even then, on the rare occasions when something opens within, and the music enters, what we mainly hear, or hear corroborated, are personal, private, vanishing evocations. But the man who creates the music is hearing something else, is dealing with the roar rising from the void and imposing order on it as it hits the air. What is evoked in him, then, is of another order, more terrible because it has no words, and triumphant, too, for that same reason. And his triumph, when he triumphs, is ours. I just watched Sonny's face. His face was troubled, he was working hard, but he wasn't with it. And I had the feeling that, in a way, everyone on the bandstand was waiting for him, both waiting for him and pushing him along. But as I began to watch Creole, I realized that it was Creole who held them all back. He had them on a short rein. Up there, keeping the beat with his whole body, wailing on the fiddle, with his eyes half closed, he was listening to everything, but he was listening to Sonny. He was having a dialogue with Sonny. He wanted Sonny to leave the shoreline and strike out for the deep water. He was Sonny's witness that deep water and drowning were not the same thing—he had been there, and he knew. And he wanted Sonny to know. He was waiting for Sonny to do the things on the keys which would let Creole know that Sonny was in the water.

And, while Creole listened, Sonny moved, deep within, exactly like some- 235
one in torment. I had never before thought of how awful the relationship must be between the musician and his instrument. He has to fill it, this instrument, with the breath of life, his own. He has to make it do what he wants it to do. And a piano is just a piano. It's made out of so much wood and wires and little hammers and big ones, and ivory. While there's only so much you can do with it, the only way to find this out is to try; to try and make it do everything.

And Sonny hadn't been near a piano for over a year. And he wasn't on much better terms with his life, not the life that stretched before him now. He and the piano stammered, started one way, got scared, stopped; started another way, panicked, marked time, started again; then seemed to have found a direction, panicked again, got stuck. And the face I saw on Sonny I'd never seen before. Everything had been burned out of it, and, at the same time, things usually hidden were being burned in, by the fire and fury of the battle which was occurring in him up there.

Yet, watching Creole's face as they neared the end of the first set, I had the feeling that something had happened, something I hadn't heard. Then they finished, there was scattered applause, and then, without an instant's warning, Creole started into something else, it was almost sardonic, it was *Am I Blue.*[7] And, as though he commanded, Sonny began to play. Something began to happen. And Creole let out the reins. The dry, low, black man said something awful on the drums, Creole answered, and the drums talked back. Then the horn insisted, sweet and high, slightly detached perhaps, and Creole listened, commenting now and then, dry, and driving, beautiful and calm and old. Then they all came together again, and Sonny was part of the family again. I could tell this from his face. He seemed to have found, right there beneath his fingers, a damn brand-new piano. It seemed that he couldn't get over it. Then, for a while, just being happy with Sonny, they seemed to be agreeing with him that brand-new pianos certainly were a gas.

Then Creole stepped forward to remind them that what they were playing was the blues. He hit something in all of them, he hit something in me, myself, and the music tightened and deepened, apprehension began to beat the air. Creole began to tell us what the blues were all about. They were not about anything very new. He and his boys up there were keeping it new, at the risk of ruin, destruction, madness, and death, in order to find new ways to make us

7. A favorite blues piece, brilliantly recorded by Billie Holiday.

listen. For, while the tale of how we suffer, and how we are delighted, and how we may triumph is never new, it always must be heard. There isn't any other tale to tell, it's the only light we've got in all this darkness.

And this tale, according to that face, that body, those strong hands on those strings, has another aspect in every country, and a new depth in every generation. Listen, Creole seemed to be saying, listen. Now these are Sonny's blues. He made the little black man on the drums know it, and the bright, brown man on the horn. Creole wasn't trying any longer to get Sonny in the water. He was wishing him Godspeed. Then he stepped back, very slowly, filling the air with the immense suggestion that Sonny speak for himself.

Then they all gathered around Sonny and Sonny played. Every now and again one of them seemed to say, amen. Sonny's fingers filled the air with life, his life. But that life contained so many others. And Sonny went all the way back, he really began with the spare, flat statement of the opening phrase of the song. Then he began to make it his. It was very beautiful because it wasn't hurried and it was no longer a lament. I seemed to hear with what burning he had made it his, and what burning we had yet to make it ours, how we could cease lamenting. Freedom lurked around us and I understood, at last, that he could help us to be free if we would listen, that he would never be free until we did. Yet, there was no battle in his face now, I heard what he had gone through, and would continue to go through until he came to rest in earth. He had made it his: that long line, of which we knew only Mama and Daddy. And he was giving it back, as everything must be given back, so that, passing through death, it can live forever. I saw my mother's face again, and felt, for the first time, how the stones of the road she had walked on must have bruised her feet. I saw the moonlit road where my father's brother died. And it brought something else back to me, and carried me past it, I saw my little girl again and felt Isabel's tears again, and I felt my own tears begin to rise. And I was yet aware that this was only a moment, that the world waited outside, as hungry as a tiger, and that trouble stretched above us, longer than the sky.

Then it was over. Creole and Sonny let out their breath, both soaking wet, and grinning. There was a lot of applause and some of it was real. In the dark, the girl came by and I asked her to take drinks to the bandstand. There was a long pause, while they talked up there in the indigo light and after awhile I saw the girl put a Scotch and milk on top of the piano for Sonny. He didn't seem to notice it, but just before they started playing again, he sipped from it and looked toward me, and nodded. Then he put it back on top of the piano. For me, then, as they began to play again, it glowed and shook above my brother's head like the very cup of trembling.[8]

1957

8. See Isaiah 51:17, 22–23: "Awake, awake, stand up, O Jerusalem, which hast drunk at the hand of the Lord the cup of his fury; thou hast drunken the dregs of the cup of trembling, and wrung them out. . . . Behold, I have taken out of thine hand the cup of trembling, even the dregs of the cup of my fury; thou shalt no more drink it again: But I will put it into the hands of them that afflict thee; . . ."

MARGARET ATWOOD

The Whirlpool Rapids

There are some women who seem to be born without fear, just as there are people who are born without the ability to feel pain. The painless ones go around putting their hands on hot stoves, freezing their feet to the point of gangrene, scalding the lining from their throats with boiling coffee, because there is no warning anguish. Evolution does not favor them. So too perhaps with the fearless women, because there aren't very many of them around. I myself have known only two. One was a maker of television documentaries, and was one of the first to shoot footage in Vietnam. There would be the beach and then the line of jungle with the soldiers advancing toward it, and in front of them, walking backward, would be this woman. Providence appears to protect such women, maybe out of astonishment. Or else, sooner or later, it doesn't.

I'm told the fearlessness goes away when these women have babies. Then they become cowards, like the rest of us. If the baby is threatened they become ferocious, of course, but that is not out of the ordinary.

The other woman I knew, and still know—her luck has held—is Emma, who has always intrigued me. I think of Emma as a woman who will do anything, though that isn't how she thinks of herself. The truly fearless think of themselves as normal.

This, as far as I've been able to tell, is how she got like that.

When she was twenty-one, Emma nearly died. Or so she was told, and since 5
four of those with her actually did die, she had to believe it. At the time she hadn't felt anywhere near dead.

It was a freak accident, and the fact that she was there at all was an accident too, the result of a whim and of knowing someone. Emma always knows a lot of people. The person she knew for this occasion was a man, a boy really, about her own age. He didn't qualify as a boyfriend; he was just one of the group she'd hung out with the previous year, at the university. In the summers he worked for a travel agency, a good one that specialized in organizing out-of-the-ordinary tours: bicycle trips through France, African game parks, that sort of thing. This boy, whose name was Bill, was one of the tour leaders. Because of his prowess with bicycles he had well-developed leg muscles, clearly visible that day, as he was wearing shorts and a T-shirt. It may have been these bicycle muscles that saved him, in the event.

Emma did not have bicycle muscles. At that time she had good biceps, though, the result of lifting heavy trays. She was working as a waitress in the coffee shop of a tourist motel in Niagara Falls. The motel had a neon sign outside that showed two entwined hearts, and even had a bridal suite, wallpapered in red.

This place reflected the vulgarity of the town itself, its transience, its tinsel-and-waxworks tawdriness, fitting contrast to the notion of Eternal Love, which, despite the jokes she's made about it at various times in her life, Emma has never ceased to believe in.

At that point she wasn't thinking of love, but of making enough money to get her through her last year at the university. Niagara Falls was a good place for that: The satiated tip well. If she had been elsewhere, none of this would have happened.

There was nothing remarkable about Bill; he was merely one of those agents of Fate who have intruded on Emma's life from time to time and then departed from it, mission accomplished. Like many fearless people, Emma believes in Fate.

Bill was a nice boy; nice enough so that when he ambled into Emma's coffee shop one day and told her that he wanted her body, Emma took it as a joke and did not resent it. Really he wanted her to come on a test run, he said. The travel agency he was working for was doing a pilot project on a new kind of tour: down the Whirlpool Rapids below Niagara Falls, on a big rubber raft. They'd done the run nine times so far, and it was perfectly safe, but they weren't ready to open the tour to the public until they'd had one more test. It was only travel agency people and their friends going, he said, and they were short of bodies: There had to be a full contingent for the thing to work; they needed forty people for the weight and balance. It struck him as the kind of thing that might appeal to Emma.

Emma was flattered by this image of herself, and readily accepted it as a true one: a physically brave young woman, a bit of a daredevil, willing to put on a life jacket at a moment's notice and sit on a large inflated platform of rubber and swirl down the dangerous Niagara Whirlpool Rapids. It would be like roller coasters, which she'd always found compelling. She would join the ranks of those who had, in the past, wished to challenge Niagara Falls: the tightrope walkers, and those who'd had themselves bolted into padded barrels and flung into the river above the drop; even the suicides, whom Emma lumped in with the challengers, because if you were not in some way gambling, why not just use a gun? In all of these attempts, it seemed to Emma, there was an element of religious trial. All of these people were flinging themselves on the mercy of something or other. Certainly not just a river. *Save me, Lord; show me I'm important enough to deserve it.* This, Emma thought, looking back on it afterward, was what had prompted her: a desire to risk the self that was really a form of arrogance.

Emma said yes at once, and arranged for her next day off to coincide with the tenth rubber-raft test run. On the morning of the day, which was a Monday, Bill picked her up from the run-down frame house she rented with three other girls and drove her across the Rainbow Bridge to the launching site which was on the American side. It turned out afterward—some reporter dug it up—that the Canadian officials had refused permission to launch the raft on their side, considering the enterprise too hazardous. But even if Emma had known this it probably wouldn't have stopped her.

The raft was black and enormous, and seemed, resting at its moorings, very stable. Emma was given an orange life jacket, and buckled herself into it, helped by Bill. Then they scrambled on board and found seats at the front end. They were among the first to arrive, and had to wait for the others. Emma began to feel slightly let down and to wonder why she'd come. The raft was too big, too solid; it was like a floating parking lot.

But once they'd moved out into the current, the rubber surface under her began to ripple, in large waves of contraction, like a giant throat swallowing, and spray came in upon them; and Emma knew that the rapids, which had looked so decorative, so much like cake frosting from a distance, were actual after all. There were some dutiful thrilled noises from the other passengers, and then some genuine noises, less thrilled. Emma found herself clutching Bill's arm, a thing she wouldn't ordinarily have done. The sky was an unnatural blue, and the shore—dotted with the white-clad or pastel figures of tourists, which appeared static and painted, like a design on wallpaper—was very far away.

There was a lot of talk later about why the tenth run should have failed so badly, after the other nine had gone without a hitch. Some attempts were made to pin it on the design of the raft; others said that, owing to an unseasonable amount of rain during the preceding week, the water level had been too high and the current far swifter than usual. Emma could not remember wondering why, at the time. All she saw was the front of the raft tipping down into a trough deeper than any they'd yet hit, while a foaming wall of water rose above them. The raft should have curved sinuously, sliding up the wave. Instead it buckled across the middle, the front half snapping toward the back, like the beak of a bird closing. Emma and Bill and the other people in the front row shot backward over the heads of the rest who were jumbling in a heap at the bottom of the V, now submerging. (Emma didn't exactly see this at the time; she deduced it later. Her impressions were of her own movement only, and of course it was all very fast.)

Something struck her on the side of the head—a foot in a boot, perhaps—and she was underwater. Later she learned that the raft had flipped and a man had been trapped underneath it and drowned, so it was just as well that she had been flung clear. But underwater she did not think. Something else made her hold her breath and struggle toward the surface, which she could see above her, white and silver—so her eyes must have been open. Her head rose up, she gasped air and was sucked under.

The water tumbled and boiled and Emma fought it. She was filled almost to bursting with an energy that came from anger: *I refuse to die in such a stupid way* was how she formulated this afterward. She thinks she shouted, at least once: *No.* Which was a waste of breath, as there was nobody around to hear her. There were rocks, and she collided with several and was bruised and scraped, but nothing more hit her head. After what seemed like an hour but was really only ten minutes, the current slowed and she found she could keep her head above the water and actually swim. It was hard to move her arms. She propelled herself toward the shore, and, finally, dragged herself up onto a a small rocky beach. Her running shoes were gone. She must have kicked them off, though she couldn't remember doing it; or maybe they had been torn off. She wondered how she was going to get over the rocks without shoes.

The sky was even bluer than it had been before. There were some blue flowers also, weeds of some kind, cornflowers, growing among the rocks. Emma looked at them and did not feel anything. She must have been cut; her clothes were certainly ripped and there was a lump on the side of her forehead, but she didn't notice any of this at the time. Two people, a man and a woman, in summery clothes, came sauntering toward her along a path.

"What country am I in?" Emma asked them.

"Canada," said the man.

They walked past her and continued their stroll, as if they did not notice anything unusual about her. Probably they didn't. The news of the accident had not yet reached them, so they didn't realize there had been one.

Emma, in her turn, did not find their behavior out of place. That's good then, she thought to herself. She wouldn't have to go back over the bridge and through Immigration, which was lucky, because her purse had been swept away. She began to walk upstream, slowly, because of her bare feet. There was an unusual number of helicopters around. She thumbed a lift to the motel—she doesn't know why she elected to go there instead of to her house—and by the time she got there, the accident had been on the news and everyone thought she was dead.

She was taken to the hospital and treated for shock, and interviewed on television. Her picture was, briefly, in the papers. Bill came to see her and described his own experience to her. He had reached a point, under the water, at which he had given up, and the water had become very peaceful and very beautiful. This was how Emma realized that she herself hadn't been at all close to death. But Bill's bicycle-muscled legs had kicked by themselves, like a wounded frog's, and brought him back.

For a while Emma felt closer to Bill than she did to anyone, but this feeling passed, although they still send each other Christmas cards. There was never any possibility of a romance: They were, after the accident, too much like twins, and then too much like strangers. Intimacy brought about by shared catastrophe can only go so far.

Emma has told me that she learned several things from this experience. One of them was that many more people than she'd thought would have known about her death, had it occurred, and been affected by it in some way; but they wouldn't have been affected very deeply or very long. Soon she would have become just a name, the name of a woman who had died young, in a tragic accident, some years ago. It was for this reason, perhaps, that Emma never had any of those wistful longings for death, those flirtations with the pale horseman, that afflict so many women in their twenties. She never thought to herself, a little hopefully, a little melodramatically, that maybe she wouldn't see thirty, that some unspecified but graceful disease would carry her off. Not her. She was determined to live no matter what.

Nor was she ever tempted, after that, to give up anything—a man, an apartment, a job, even a vacation—in the mistaken conviction that by doing so she would be helping along the happiness of others. Because she found out early how very little difference she makes in the general scheme of things, she has clenched her teeth, ignored whimpers and even threats, and done what she liked, almost always. For instance, none of her friends will go to auctions or bargain sales with Emma anymore: She tends to get what you wanted. And at least four marriages have been trashed by Emma, who has decided in every case that the man wasn't right for her after all. Women who believe in Eternal Love develop such habits.

As you might expect, Emma has frequently been called selfish and unfeeling. I think it has been to her credit that on these occasions she has not trotted out the story of her near-death by drowning as a justification for her dubious behavior.

But the most obvious effect of the accident on Emma was her strong subsequent belief—it amounted to an article of religious faith—that she was invulnerable. She didn't merely feel this, she knew it, as firmly as she knew that her hand was her hand. She had been thrown into the Whirlpool Rapids of Niagara Falls and had lived; therefore nothing could touch her. She walked in a bubble of charmed air, which at times she imagined she could almost see, shimmering around her like mist; like, in fact, the mist that rose from the Falls themselves.

Little by little this belief faded. It was strongest right after the accident, but 30
evaporated year by year, until by now nothing is left of it but a faint phosphorescence. Her friends call it optimism, this conviction of hers that everything will work out for her somehow.

What Emma has become, finally and after many false starts, is an insurance investigator for an airline company, a job that takes her to some strange locales and is more hazardous than you might think. Emma is always getting free cases of champagne, which she returns, or death threats, which she doesn't. I myself keep up with her through the postcards she sends, from places like Zaire. When I see her, once or twice a year, I find myself looking at her skin. The rest of us are beginning to wrinkle, but for some reason Emma is not. It must be that small injection of death, that early dose of mortality, that has rendered her immune.

1983

QUESTIONS

1. Who is the "you" addressed in the first paragraph of "The Cask of Amontillado"? (You may want to wait until you have finished the last sentence in the story before answering this.)

2. Has Emma's experience in "The Whirlpool Rapids" been good or bad for her? made her a better or a worse person?

3. In "Sonny's Blues" how is the first-person narrator, the person telling the story, identified or characterized in the first sentence? in the first paragraph? in the first couple of pages? in the story as a whole?

4. Is Sonny or the narrator the protagonist of "Sonny's Blues"? Why?

WRITING SUGGESTIONS

1. Rearrange the episodes in "Sonny's Blues" as they would appear in the hypothetical history—that is, in chronological order. Pick the three or four changes that seem to you most important. Describe the difference in significance and effect that is achieved by the structuring or rearrangement.

2. Rewrite the action portion of "The Whirlpool Rapids" (pars. 13–20) as if it were the entire story. You may want to add a very brief new beginning and ending. Then write a paragraph of perhaps 250 words explaining the major ways in which your new story differs from the original.

2 POINT OF VIEW

Structuring involves more than plot, more than the ordering of events; selection involves more than the choosing or inventing of incidents. What would "Sonny's Blues" be like seen through the eyes of Sonny? What incidents might he choose to tell? In what order might he arrange them? And what does it do to "The Cask of Amontillado" when we realize, at the end, that it is being told by Montresor fifty years after the event and that his last—probably dying—words, referring to Fortunato, are, "*In pace requiescat*"? Why is he telling the story now? What additional resonance do his final words have?

Who is telling us the story—whose words are we reading? Where does this person stand in relation to what is going on in the story? In drama, events appear before us directly. In narrative, someone is always *between* us and the events—a viewer, a speaker, or both. Narrative, unlike drama, is always mediated. The way a story is mediated is a key element in fictional structure. This mediation involves both the angle of vision—the point from which the people, events, and other details are viewed—and also the words of the story lying between us and the history. The viewing aspect is called the **focus,** and the verbal aspect the **voice.** Both are generally lumped together in the term **point of view.**

Focus acts much as a movie camera does, choosing what we can look at and the angle at which we can view it, framing, proportioning, emphasizing—even distorting. Plot is a structure that places us in a time relationship to the history; focus places us in a spatial relationship.

We must pay careful attention to the focus at any given point in a story. Is it fixed or mobile? Does it stay at more or less the same angle to, and at the same distance from, the characters and action, or does it move around or in and out? In the first three and a half paragraphs of "An Occurrence at Owl Creek Bridge," for example, we seem to be seeing through the lens of a camera that can swing left or right, up or down, but that stays pretty much at the same angle and distance from the bridge. By the middle of the fourth paragraph, however, we're inside the mind of the man who's about to be hanged: "The arrangement commended itself to his judgment . . . He looked a moment . . . A piece of dancing driftwood caught his attention . . . How slowly it appeared to move!" From now on we are inside the condemned man's head. The focus is more limited in scope—for almost all the rest of the story we can see and hear only what he sees and hears. But because the focus is internal as well as limited, we can also know what he thinks. This limited, internal focus is usually called the **centered** or **central consciousness.**

The centered consciousness has been perhaps the most popular focus in fiction for the past hundred years—through most of the history of the modern short story, in fact—and its tightly controlled range and concentration on a single individual seem particularly suited for the short form. During much of this period, fiction, both long and short, has been in one sense realistic—that is, treating the everyday and the natural. It has become increasingly clear, however, that the apparently real is not necessarily what "is" but what is *perceived by* the senses and mind of the individual. (This is sometimes called **psychological realism.**) The centered consciousness, in which things, people, and events are narrated as if they have been perceived through the filter of an individual character's consciousness, has therefore seemed the more realistic way to tell a story. It is a comfortable focus for readers, too. On the one hand, they can identify with someone whose thoughts and perception they share, even if the character is fallible, like Lantin in "The Jewelry," or reprehensible, like Montresor. We can identify with point of view in a story told in the first person ("I"), too, but we are too close at times. We cannot escape. The camera cannot pull back as it can in a third-person story.

First-person stories, like "The Summer My Grandmother Was Supposed to Die," are always limited too, and almost all the time are internal as well (though Montresor in "The Cask of Amontillado" hides his plans from us). While they cannot retract spatially from the narrator, they almost always are withdrawn temporally: that is, the "I" telling the story is older than the "I" experiencing the events of the story, as in "The Summer My Grandmother Was Supposed to Die," where the narrator is clearly older than the boy he was when the action of the story took place.

The psychological realism gained by having a limited narrator exacts a price from the reader. If we don't hold the author (or the story) responsible for the absolute truth, validity, accuracy, and opinions of the focal character—if he or she is just telling us what he or she thinks, feels, sees—we must accept the possibility that the narrator's vision may be **unreliable.** At a significant point in "Owl Creek Bridge," for example, you will find that the camera pulls back from Peyton Farquhar and we are made to recognize to what extent his consciousness is a reliable witness to what has been going on. The history here is only an occurrence; the limited point of view structures the mere occurrence into a story.

When the point of view is limited, whether to a first-person narrator or to a centered consciousness, it is tied to that individual. When he or she leaves the room, the camera must go too, and if we are to know what happens in the room when the focal character is gone, some means of bringing the information to that character must be devised, such as a letter or a report by another character. The camera may pull back out of the character's mind or even, as in "Owl Creek Bridge," above and away from the character, but it does not generally jump around. The somewhat unusual first-person plural point of view of "A Rose for Emily" is not limited to a single individual; anything the town of Jefferson in general can know of past or present, the narrative can know. But neither is it an unlimited focus; "we" could not get into Emily's house before she dies and could never get into her mind.

An unlimited point of view permits such freedom. In "The Zebra Storyteller" we are with the first zebra (who is killed) when he meets a cat speaking Zebraic and are told he is "astonished." We learn that the zebras can smell no lion and so "decided the woods were haunted by the ghost of a lion," and we get inside the mind of the storyteller and "hear" him speaking to himself. Throughout, the story seems free to see matter from one focus or another and even to dip inside a character's mind.

There are no laws governing point of view in fiction, but there is a general feeling that once a point of view is chosen that ought to be the law for that story. The movement of the focus at the beginning of "An Occurrence at Owl Creek Bridge" is not a jump but a narrowing down: the panorama at the beginning of the story, apparently from the point of view and in the voice of a distant observer, is adjusted and then we settle in, which is not an uncommon device (note how many movies used to begin with a panoramic shot of a town and gradually focused on a house or room). When toward the end of the story the "camera" moves back and away from Peyton Farquhar, we find there has been another reason for the panoramic shot at the beginning. There has been no jumping around and the narrowing and widening seem to be justifiable and meaningful. There are stories in this anthology—"The Most Dangerous Game," "Barn Burning," and "The Lame Shall Enter First," for example—in which the point of view does shift—or jump—from a previously established centered consciousness. Whether these are "flaws" must be judged in each case in terms of function: is the shift merely a narrative convenience or manipulation or is it consistent with or does it contribute to the significance or vision of the story?

Focus and voice often coincide; that is why they are commonly lumped together as point of view. There is no discrepancy that I can see (or hear) between the viewing and the telling in "The Cask of Amontillado," for example. But in "The Summer My Grandmother Was Supposed to Die," the

"I" telling the story is older than the "I" experiencing the events of the story, and that is why it is useful to have at hand the terms and concepts of focus and voice as two different aspects of point of view. Notice in the Richler story how many phrases there are like "years later I was shown the telegram" and "in those days . . ." So, too, the language of the story is clearly not that of a young boy: "She arrived punctually at noon"; "I've been told that to study Talmud with him had been a rare pleasure"; "lots of slender volumes of sermons, chassidic tales, and rabbinical commentaries." Such expressions may deal with incidents and information within the boy's perception, but the language in which they are expressed is clearly beyond him.

Like the focus, the voice in "Owl Creek Bridge" at the beginning of the story is not centered in Peyton Farquhar, but even when the focus narrows on him the voice telling the story is not his; note, for example, "As these thoughts, *which have here to be set down in words,* were flashed into the doomed man's brain" (emphasis added). The discrepancy may prepare a careful reader for later developments in the story.

I have used the common term **narrator** in the usual way—to mean the person who tells the story. You will have noticed that often the narrator really is a person in the story, like Muttel, the narrator in "The Summer My Grandmother Was Supposed to Die." But how about the narrator in "Owl Creek Bridge"? Who is it who sets down Farquhar's words and can say things like this: "Death is a dignitary who, when he comes announced, is to be received with formal manifestations of respect, even by those most familiar with him. In the code of military etiquette silence and fixity are forms of deference" (par. 2). Where is he or she standing? What kind of person is this narrator? We might ask the same question of the elusive, unnamed spokesman for the town of Jefferson in "A Rose for Emily." Close attention to the language and chronology of the story, to the references to race and gender, to the use of "they" and "we," reveals that the narrator is an educated white male who at the time of Emily's death is probably a boy or very young man.

Is he Faulkner? Where the narrator plays some role in the story we are less likely to identify him or her with the author; where the narrator is an unidentified voice we often tend to do so. We call the narrator of "Owl Creek Bridge" "Bierce." This is not necessarily wrong, but it can be misleading. We can dig up a few facts about the author's life and read them into the story, or, worse, read the character or detail of the story into the author's life. It is more prudent, therefore, especially on the basis of a single story, not to speak of the author but of the author's **persona,** the voice or figure of the author who tells and structures the story, who may or may not resemble in nature or values the actual person of the author. Mary Anne Evans wrote novels under the name of George Eliot; her first-person narrator speaks of "himself." That male narrator may be a good example of the persona or representative that most authors construct to "write" their stories.

We say *write* the stories. The narrator of "Owl Creek Bridge" has to "set down in words" what Farquhar is thinking. But just as poets write of singing their songs (poems), so we often speak of telling a story, and we speak of a narrator, which means a teller. There are stories, usually with first-person narrators, that make much of the convention of oral storytelling—"My Man Bovanne," for example.

We are used to thinking of a story in terms of its plot, so that to summarize a story usually means giving a plot summary. But if you shift focus and voice you will often find that though the history has not changed, the story has. You might want to test this out by rewriting "The Summer My Grandmother Was Supposed to Die" with the focus and perhaps with the voice of Muttel's mother or "A Rose for Emily" in Emily's voice and focus.

▽ ▽ ▽

POINT OF VIEW A Glossary

centered (central) consciousness: a limited point of view, one tied to a single character throughout the story, often with access to his or her inner thoughts (but not to the thoughts of others)

focus: the point from which the people, events, and other details in a story are viewed. See *point of view*

limited point of view or **limited focus:** a perspective pinned to a single character, whether first-person or a third-person centered consciousness, so that we cannot know for sure what is going on in the minds of other characters; when the focal character leaves the room in a story we must go too and cannot know what is going on while our "eyes" or "camera" is gone. A variation on this, which generally has no name and is often lumped with the *omniscient point of view,* is the point of view that can wander like a camera from one character to another and close in or move back but cannot (or at least does not) get inside anyone's head, does not present from the inside any character's thoughts.

omniscient point of view: see *unlimited point of view*

point of view: focus; the point from which the people, events, and other details in a story are viewed. This term is sometimes used to include both focus and voice.

psychological realism: a modification of the concept of realism, or telling it like it is, which recognizes that what is real to the individual is that which he or she perceives. It is the ground for the use of the centered consciousness, or the first-person narrator, since both of these present reality only as something perceived by the focal character.

unlimited focus or **omniscient point of view:** a perspective that can be that seen from one character's view, then another's, then another's, or can be moved in or out of any character at any time

unreliable narrator: a speaker or voice whose vision or version of the details of the story are consciously or unconsciously deceiving; such a narrator's version is usually subtly undermined by details in the story or the reader's general knowledge of facts outside the story; if, for example, the narrator were to tell you that Columbus was Spanish, and that he discovered America in the fourteenth century when his ship *The Golden Hind* landed on the coast of Florida near present-day Gainesville, you might not trust other things he tells you.

voice: the acknowledged or unacknowledged source of the words of the story; the "speaker;" the "person" telling the story

AMBROSE BIERCE

An Occurrence at Owl Creek Bridge

I

A man stood upon a railroad bridge in Northern Alabama, looking down into the swift waters twenty feet below. The man's hands were behind his back, the wrists bound with a cord. A rope loosely encircled his neck. It was attached to a stout cross-timber above his head, and the slack fell to the level of his knees. Some loose boards laid upon the sleepers supporting the metals of the railway supplied a footing for him and his executioners—two private soldiers of the Federal army, directed by a sergeant, who in civil life may have been a deputy sheriff. At a short remove upon the same temporary platform was an officer in the uniform of his rank, armed. He was a captain. A sentinel at each end of the bridge stood with his rifle in the position known as "support," that is to say, vertical in front of the left shoulder, the hammer resting on the forearm thrown straight across the chest—a formal and unnatural position, enforcing an erect carriage of the body. It did not appear to be the duty of these two men to know what was occurring at the centre of the bridge; they merely blockaded the two ends of the foot plank which traversed it.

Beyond one of the sentinels nobody was in sight; the railroad ran straight away into a forest for a hundred yards, then, curving, was lost to view. Doubtless there was an outpost further along. The other bank of the stream was open ground—a gentle acclivity crowned with a stockade of vertical tree trunks, loopholed for rifles, with a single embrasure through which protruded the muzzle of a brass cannon commanding the bridge. Midway of the slope between bridge and fort were the spectators—a single company of infantry in line, at "parade rest," the butts of the rifles on the ground, the barrels inclining slightly backward against the right shoulder, the hands crossed upon the stock. A lieutenant stood at the right of the line, the point of his sword upon the ground, his left hand resting upon his right. Excepting the group of four at the centre of the bridge not a man moved. The company faced the bridge, staring stonily, motionless. The sentinels, facing the banks of the stream, might have been statues to adorn the bridge. The captain stood with folded arms, silent, observing the work of his subordinates but making no sign. Death is a dignitary who, when he comes announced, is to be received with formal manifestations of respect, even by those most familiar with him. In the code of military etiquette silence and fixity are forms of deference.

The man who was engaged in being hanged was apparently about thirty-five years of age. He was a civilian, if one might judge from his dress, which was that of a planter. His features were good—a straight nose, firm mouth, broad forehead, from which his long, dark hair was combed straight back, falling behind his ears to the collar of his well-fitting frock coat. He wore a moustache and pointed beard, but no whiskers; his eyes were large and dark grey and had a kindly expression which one would hardly have expected in one whose neck was in the hemp. Evidently this was no vulgar assassin. The liberal military code makes provision for hanging many kinds of people, and gentlemen are not excluded.

The preparations being complete, the two private soldiers stepped aside and each drew away the plank upon which he had been standing. The sergeant turned to the captain, saluted and placed himself immediately behind that officer, who in turn moved apart one pace. These movements left the condemned man and the sergeant standing on the two ends of the same plank, which spanned three of the cross-ties of the bridge. The end upon which the civilian stood almost, but not quite, reached a fourth. This plank had been held in place by the weight of the captain; it was now held by that of the sergeant. At a signal from the former, the latter would step aside, the plank would tilt and the condemned man go down between two ties. The arrangement commended itself to his judgment as simple and effective. His face had not been covered nor his eyes bandaged. He looked a moment at his "unsteadfast footing," then let his gaze wander to the swirling water of the stream racing madly beneath his feet. A piece of dancing driftwood caught his attention and his eyes followed it down the current. How slowly it appeared to move! What a sluggish stream!

5 He closed his eyes in order to fix his last thoughts upon his wife and children. The water, touched to gold by the early sun, the brooding mists under the banks at some distance down the stream, the fort, the soldiers, the piece of drift—all had distracted him. And now he became conscious of a new disturbance. Striking through the thought of his dear ones was a sound which he could neither ignore nor understand, a sharp, distinct, metallic percussion like the stroke of a blacksmith's hammer upon the anvil; it had the same ringing quality. He wondered what it was, and whether immeasurably distant or near by—it seemed both. Its recurrence was regular, but as slow as the tolling of a death knell. He awaited each stroke with impatience and—he knew not why—apprehension. The intervals of silence grew progressively longer, the delays became maddening. With their greater infrequency the sounds increased in strength and sharpness. They hurt his ear like the thrust of a knife; he feared he would shriek. What he heard was the ticking of his watch.

He unclosed his eyes and saw again the water below him. "If I could free my hands," he thought, "I might throw off the noose and spring into the stream. By diving I could evade the bullets, and, swimming vigorously, reach the bank, take to the woods, and get away home. My home, thank God, is as yet outside their lines; my wife and little ones are still beyond the invader's farthest advance."

As these thoughts, which have here to be set down in words, were flashed into the doomed man's brain rather than evolved from it, the captain nodded to the sergeant. The sergeant stepped aside.

II

Peyton Farquhar was a well-to-do planter, of an old and highly-respected Alabama family. Being a slave owner, and, like other slave owners, a politician, he was naturally an original secessionist and ardently devoted to the Southern cause. Circumstances of an imperious nature which it is unnecessary to relate here, had prevented him from taking service with the gallant army which had fought the disastrous campaigns ending with the fall of Corinth,[1] and he chafed under the inglorious restraint, longing for the release of his energies, the larger life of the soldier, the opportunity for distinction. That opportunity, he felt, would come, as it comes to all in war time. Meanwhile he did what he could. No service was too humble for him to perform in aid of the South, no adventure too perilous for him to undertake if consistent with the character of a civilian who was at heart a soldier, and who in good faith and without too much qualification assented to at least a part of the frankly villainous dictum that all is fair in love and war.

One evening while Farquhar and his wife were sitting on a rustic bench near the entrance to his grounds, a grey-clad soldier rode up to the gate and asked for a drink of water. Mrs. Farquhar was only too happy to serve him with her own white hands. While she was gone to fetch the water, her husband approached the dusty horseman and inquired eagerly for news from the front.

"The Yanks are repairing the railroads," said the man, "and are getting ready for another advance. They have reached the Owl Creek bridge, put it in order, and built a stockade on the other bank. The commandant has issued an order, which is posted everywhere, declaring that any civilian caught interfering with the railroad, its bridges, tunnels, or trains, will be summarily hanged. I saw the order."

"How far is it to the Owl Creek bridge?" Farquhar asked.

"About thirty miles."

"Is there no force on this side the creek?"

"Only a picket post half a mile out, on the railroad, and a single sentinel at this end of the bridge."

"Suppose a man—a civilian and student of hanging—should elude the picket post and perhaps get the better of the sentinel," said Farquhar, smiling, "what could he accomplish?"

The soldier reflected. "I was there a month ago," he replied. "I observed that the flood of last winter had lodged a great quantity of driftwood against the wooden pier at this end of the bridge. It is now dry and would burn like tow."

The lady had now brought the water, which the soldier drank. He thanked her ceremoniously, bowed to her husband, and rode away. An hour later, after nightfall, he repassed the plantation, going northward in the direction from which he had come. He was a Federal scout.

III

As Peyton Farquhar fell straight downward through the bridge, he lost consciousness and was as one already dead. From this state he was awakened—ages later, it seemed to him—by the pain of a sharp pressure upon his throat, followed by

1. Corinth, Mississippi, captured by General Grant in April 1862.

a sense of suffocation. Keen, poignant agonies seemed to shoot from his neck downward through every fibre of his body and limbs. These pains appeared to flash along well-defined lines of ramification, and to beat with an inconceivably rapid periodicity. They seemed like streams of pulsating fire heating him to an intolerable temperature. As to his head, he was conscious of nothing but a feeling of fullness—of congestion. These sensations were unaccompanied by thought. The intellectual part of his nature was already effaced; he had power only to feel, and feeling was torment. He was conscious of motion. Encompassed in a luminous cloud, of which he was now merely the fiery heart, without material substance, he swung through unthinkable arcs of oscillation, like a vast pendulum. Then all at once, with terrible suddenness, the light about him shot upward with the noise of a loud plash; a frightful roaring was in his ears, and all was cold and dark. The power of thought was restored; he knew that the rope had broken and he had fallen into the stream. There was no additional strangulation; the noose about his neck was already suffocating him, and kept the water from his lungs. To die of hanging at the bottom of a river!—the idea seemed to him ludicrous. He opened his eyes in the blackness and saw above him a gleam of light, but how distant, how inaccessible! He was still sinking, for the light became fainter and fainter until it was a mere glimmer. Then it began to grow and brighten, and he knew that he was rising toward the surface—knew it with reluctance, for he was now very comfortable. "To be hanged and drowned," he thought, "that is not so bad; but I do not wish to be shot. No; I will not be shot; that is not fair."

He was not conscious of an effort, but a sharp pain in his wrist apprised him that he was trying to free his hands. He gave the struggle his attention, as an idler might observe the feat of a juggler, without interest in the outcome. What splendid effort!—what magnificent, what superhuman strength! Ah, that was a fine endeavour! Bravo! The cord fell away; his arms parted and floated upward, the hands dimly seen on each side in the growing light. He watched them with a new interest as first one and then the other pounced upon the noose at his neck. They tore it away and thrust it fiercely aside, its undulations resembling those of a water-snake. "Put it back, put it back!" He thought he shouted these words to his hands, for the undoing of the noose had been succeeded by the direst pang which he had yet experienced. His neck ached horribly; his brain was on fire; his heart, which had been fluttering faintly, gave a great leap, trying to force itself out at his mouth. His whole body was racked and wrenched with an insupportable anguish! But his disobedient hands gave no heed to the command. They beat the water vigorously with quick, downward strokes, forcing him to the surface. He felt his head emerge; his eyes were blinded by the sunlight; his chest expanded convulsively, and with a supreme and crowning agony his lungs engulfed a great draught of air, which instantly he expelled in a shriek!

He was now in full possession of his physical senses. They were, indeed, preternaturally keen and alert. Something in the awful disturbance of his organic system had so exalted and refined them that they made record of things never before perceived. He felt the ripples upon his face and heard their separate sounds as they struck. He looked at the forest on the bank of the stream, saw the individual trees, the leaves and the veining of each leaf—the very insects upon them, the locusts, the brilliant-bodied flies, the grey spiders stretching their webs from twig to twig. He noted the prismatic colors in all the dewdrops upon a million blades of grass. The humming of the gnats that danced above the eddies of the stream, the beating of the dragon flies' wings, the strokes of the water spiders' legs, like oars which had lifted their boat—all these made audible music. A fish slid along beneath his eyes and he heard the rush of its body parting the water.

He had come to the surface facing down the stream; in a moment the visible world seemed to wheel slowly round, himself the pivotal point, and he saw the bridge, the fort, the soldiers upon the bridge, the captain, the sergeant, the two privates, his executioners. They were in silhouette against the blue sky. They shouted and gesticulated, pointing at him; the captain had drawn his pistol, but did not fire; the others were unarmed. Their movements were grotesque and horrible, their forms gigantic.

Suddenly he heard a sharp report and something struck the water smartly within a few inches of his head, spattering his face with spray. He heard a second report, and saw one of the sentinels with his rifle at his shoulder, a light cloud of blue smoke rising from the muzzle. The man in the water saw the eye of the man on the bridge gazing into his own through the sights of the rifle. He observed that it was a grey eye, and remembered having read that grey eyes were keenest and that all famous marksmen had them. Nevertheless, this one had missed.

A counter swirl had caught Farquhar and turned him half round; he was again looking into the forest on the bank opposite the fort. The sound of a clear, high voice in a monotonous singsong now rang out behind him and came across the water with a distinctness that pierced and subdued all other sounds, even the beating of the ripples in his ears. Although no soldier, he had frequented camps enough to know the dread significance of that deliberate, drawling, aspirated chant; the lieutenant on shore was taking a part in the morning's work. How coldly and pitilessly—with what an even, calm intonation, presaging and enforcing tranquillity in the men—with what accurately-measured intervals fell those cruel words:

"Attention, company. . . . Shoulder arms. . . . Ready. . . . Aim. . . . Fire."

Farquhar dived—dived as deeply as he could. The water roared in his ears 25
like the voice of Niagara, yet he heard the dulled thunder of the volley, and rising again toward the surface, met shining bits of metal, singularly flattened, oscillating slowly downward. Some of them touched him on the face and hands, then fell away, continuing their descent. One lodged between his collar and neck; it was uncomfortably warm, and he snatched it out.

As he rose to the surface, gasping for breath, he saw that he had been a long time under water; he was perceptibly farther down stream—nearer to safety. The soldiers had almost finished reloading; the metal ramrods flashed all at once in the sunshine as they were drawn from the barrels, turned in the air, and thrust into their sockets. The two sentinels fired again, independently and ineffectually.

The hunted man saw all this over his shoulder; he was now swimming vigorously with the current. His brain was as energetic as his arms and legs; he thought with the rapidity of lightning.

"The officer," he reasoned, "will not make that martinet's error a second time. It is as easy to dodge a volley as a single shot. He has probably already given the command to fire at will. God help me, I cannot dodge them all!"

An appalling plash within two yards of him, followed by a loud rushing sound, *diminuendo,* which seemed to travel back through the air to the fort and died in an explosion which stirred the very river to its deeps! A rising sheet of water, which curved over him, fell down upon him, blinded him, strangled him! The cannon had taken a hand in the game. As he shook his head free from the commotion of the smitten water, he heard the deflected shot humming through the air ahead, and in an instant it was cracking and smashing the branches in the forest beyond.

"They will not do that again," he thought; "the next time they will use a charge of grape. I must keep my eye upon the gun; the smoke will apprise me—the report arrives too late; it lags behind the missile. It is a good gun."

Suddenly he felt himself whirled round and round—spinning like a top. The water, the banks, the forest, the now distant bridge, fort and men—all were commingled and blurred. Objects were represented by their colors only; circular horizontal streaks of color—that was all he saw. He had been caught in a vortex and was being whirled on with a velocity of advance and gyration which made him giddy and sick. In a few moments he was flung upon the gravel at the foot of the left bank of the stream—the southern bank—and behind a projecting point which concealed him from his enemies. The sudden arrest of his motion, the abrasion of one of his hands on the gravel, restored him and he wept with delight. He dug his fingers into the sand, threw it over himself in handfuls and audibly blessed it. It looked like gold, like diamonds, rubies, emeralds; he could think of nothing beautiful which it did not resemble. The trees upon the bank were giant garden plants; he noted a definite order in their arrangement, inhaled the fragrance of their blooms. A strange, roseate light shone through the spaces among their trunks, and the wind made in their branches the music of æolian harps. He had no wish to perfect his escape, was content to remain in that enchanting spot until retaken.

A whizz and rattle of grapeshot among the branches high above his head roused him from his dream. The baffled cannoneer had fired him a random farewell. He sprang to his feet, rushed up the sloping bank, and plunged into the forest.

All that day he travelled, laying his course by the rounding sun. The forest seemed interminable; nowhere did he discover a break in it, not even a woodman's road. He had not known that he lived in so wild a region. There was something uncanny in the revelation.

By nightfall he was fatigued, footsore, famishing. The thought of his wife and children urged him on. At last he found a road which led him in what he knew to be the right direction. It was as wide and straight as a city street, yet it seemed untravelled. No fields bordered it, no dwelling anywhere. Not so much as the barking of a dog suggested human habitation. The black bodies of the great trees formed a straight wall on both sides, terminating on the horizon in a point, like a diagram in a lesson in perspective. Overhead, as he looked up through this rift in the wood, shone great golden stars looking unfamiliar and grouped in strange constellations. He was sure they were arranged in some order which had a secret and malign significance. The wood on either side was full of singular noises, among which—once, twice, and again—he distinctly heard whispers in an unknown tongue.

His neck was in pain, and, lifting his hand to it, he found it horribly swollen. 35
He knew that it had a circle of black where the rope had bruised it. His eyes felt congested; he could no longer close them. His tongue was swollen with thirst; he relieved its fever by thrusting it forward from between his teeth into the cool air. How softly the turf had carpeted the untravelled avenue! He could no longer feel the roadway beneath his feet!

Doubtless, despite his suffering, he fell asleep while walking, for now he sees another scene—perhaps he has merely recovered from a delirium. He stands at the gate of his own home. All is as he left it, and all bright and beautiful in the morning sunshine. He must have travelled the entire night. As he pushes open the gate and passes up the wide white walk, he sees a flutter of female garments; his wife, looking fresh and cool and sweet, steps down from the verandah to meet him. At the bottom of the steps she stands waiting, with a smile of ineffable joy, an attitude of matchless grace and dignity. Ah, how beautiful she is! He springs forward with extended arms. As he is about to clasp her, he feels a stunning blow upon the back of the neck; a blinding white light blazes all about him, with a sound like the shock of a cannon—then all is darkness and silence!

Peyton Farquhar was dead; his body, with a broken neck, swung gently from side to side beneath the timbers of the Owl Creek bridge.

1891

WILLIAM FAULKNER

A Rose for Emily

I

When Miss Emily Grierson died, our whole town went to her funeral: the men through a sort of respectful affection for a fallen monument, the women mostly out of curiosity to see the inside of her house, which no one save an old manservant—a combined gardener and cook—had seen in at least ten years.

It was a big, squarish frame house that had once been white, decorated with cupolas and spires and scrolled balconies in the heavily lightsome style of the seventies, set on what had once been our most select street. But garages and cotton gins had encroached and obliterated even the august names of that neighborhood; only Miss Emily's house was left, lifting its stubborn and coquettish decay above the cotton wagons and the gasoline pumps—an eyesore among eyesores. And now Miss Emily had gone to join the representatives of those august names where they lay in the cedar-bemused cemetery among the ranked and anonymous graves of Union and Confederate soldiers who fell at the battle of Jefferson.

Alive, Miss Emily had been a tradition, a duty, and a care; a sort of hereditary obligation upon the town, dating from that day in 1894 when Colonel Sartoris, the mayor—he who fathered the edict that no Negro woman should appear on the streets without an apron—remitted her taxes, the dispensation dating from the death of her father on into perpetuity. Not that Miss Emily would have accepted charity. Colonel Sartoris invented an involved tale to the effect that Miss Emily's father had loaned money to the town, which the town, as a matter of business, preferred this way of repaying. Only a man of Colonel Sartoris' generation and thought could have invented it, and only a woman could have believed it.

When the next generation, with its more modern ideas, became mayors and aldermen, this arrangement created some little dissatisfaction. On the first of the year they mailed her a tax notice. February came, and there was no reply. They wrote her a formal letter, asking her to call at the sheriff's office at her convenience. A week later the mayor wrote her himself, offering to call or to send his car for her, and received in reply a note on paper of an archaic shape, in a thin, flowing calligraphy in faded ink, to the effect that she no longer went out at all. The tax notice was also enclosed, without comment.

They called a special meeting of the Board of Aldermen. A deputation waited upon her, knocked at the door through which no visitor had passed since she ceased giving china-painting lessons eight or ten years earlier. They were admitted by the old Negro into a dim hall from which a stairway mounted into still more shadow. It smelled of dust and disuse—a close, dank smell. The Negro led them into the parlor. It was furnished in heavy, leather-covered furniture. When the Negro opened the blinds of one window, a faint dust rose sluggishly about their thighs, spinning with slow motes in the single sun-ray. On a tarnished gilt easel before the fireplace stood a crayon portrait of Miss Emily's father.

They rose when she entered—a small, fat woman in black, with a thin gold chain descending to her waist and vanishing into her belt, leaning on an ebony cane with a tarnished gold head. Her skeleton was small and spare; perhaps that was why what would have been merely plumpness in another was obesity in her. She looked bloated, like a body long submerged in motionless water, and of that pallid hue. Her eyes, lost in the fatty ridges of her face, looked like two small pieces of coal pressed into a lump of dough as they moved from one face to another while the visitors stated their errand.

She did not ask them to sit. She just stood in the door and listened quietly until the spokesman came to a stumbling halt. Then they could hear the invisible watch ticking at the end of the gold chain.

Her voice was dry and cold. "I have no taxes in Jefferson. Colonel Sartoris explained it to me. Perhaps one of you can gain access to the city records and satisfy yourselves."

"But we have. We are the city authorities, Miss Emily. Didn't you get a notice from the sheriff, signed by him?"

"I received a paper, yes," Miss Emily said. "Perhaps he considers himself the sheriff. . . . I have no taxes in Jefferson."

"But there is nothing on the books to show that, you see. We must go by the—"

"See Colonel Sartoris. I have no taxes in Jefferson."

"But, Miss Emily—"

"See Colonel Sartoris." (Colonel Sartoris had been dead almost ten years.) "I have no taxes in Jefferson. Tobe!" The Negro appeared. "Show these gentlemen out."

II

So she vanquished them, horse and foot, just as she had vanquished their fathers thirty years before about the smell. That was two years after her father's death and a short time after her sweetheart—the one we believed would marry her—had deserted her. After her father's death she went out very little; after her sweetheart went away, people hardly saw her at all. A few of the ladies had the temerity to call, but were not received, and the only sign of life about the place was the Negro man—a young man then—going in and out with a market basket.

"Just as if a man—any man—could keep a kitchen properly," the ladies said; so they were not surprised when the smell developed. It was another link between the gross, teeming world and the high and mighty Griersons.

A neighbor, a woman, complained to the mayor, Judge Stevens, eighty years old.

"But what will you have me do about it, madam?" he said.

"Why, send her word to stop it," the woman said. "Isn't there a law?"

"I'm sure that won't be necessary," Judge Stevens said. "It's probably just a snake or a rat that nigger of hers killed in the yard. I'll speak to him about it."

The next day he received two more complaints, one from a man who came in diffident deprecation. "We really must do something about it, Judge. I'd be the last one in the world to bother Miss Emily, but we've got to do something." That night the Board of Aldermen met—three gray-beards and one younger man, a member of the rising generation.

"It's simple enough," he said. "Send her word to have her place cleaned up. Give her a certain time to do it in, and if she don't . . ."

"Dammit, sir," Judge Stevens said, "will you accuse a lady to her face of smelling bad?"

So the next night, after midnight, four men crossed Miss Emily's lawn and slunk about the house like burglars, sniffing along the base of the brickwork and at the cellar openings while one of them performed a regular sowing motion with his hand out of a sack slung from his shoulder. They broke open the cellar door and sprinkled lime there, and in all the outbuildings. As they recrossed the lawn, a window that had been dark was lighted and Miss Emily sat in it, the light behind her, and her upright torso motionless as that of an idol. They crept quietly across the lawn and into the shadow of the locusts that lined the street. After a week or two the smell went away.

That was when people had begun to feel really sorry for her. People in our town, remembering how old lady Wyatt, her great-aunt, had gone completely crazy at last, believed that the Griersons held themselves a little too high for what they really were. None of the young men were quite good enough for Miss Emily and such. We had long thought of them as a tableau; Miss Emily a slender figure in white in the background, her father a spraddled silhouette in the foreground, his back to her and clutching a horsewhip, the two of them framed by the back-flung front door. So when she got to be thirty and was still single, we were not pleased exactly, but vindicated; even with insanity in the family she wouldn't have turned down all of her chances if they had really materialized.

When her father died, it got about that the house was all that was left to her; and in a way, people were glad. At last they could pity Miss Emily. Being left alone, and a pauper, she had become humanized. Now she too would know the old thrill and the old despair of a penny more or less.

The day after his death all the ladies prepared to call at the house and offer condolence and aid, as is our custom. Miss Emily met them at the door, dressed as usual and with no trace of grief on her face. She told them that her father was not dead. She did that for three days, with the ministers calling on her, and the doctors, trying to persuade her to let them dispose of the body. Just as they were about to resort to law and force, she broke down, and they buried her father quickly.

We did not say she was crazy then. We believed she had to do that. We remembered all the young men her father had driven away, and we knew that with nothing left, she would have to cling to that which had robbed her, as people will.

III

She was sick for a long time. When we saw her again, her hair was cut short, making her look like a girl, with a vague resemblance to those angels in colored church windows—sort of tragic and serene.

The town had just let the contracts for paving the sidewalks, and in the summer after her father's death they began to work. The construction company came with niggers and mules and machinery, and a foreman named Homer Barron, a Yankee—a big, dark, ready man, with a big voice and eyes lighter than his face. The little boys would follow in groups to hear him cuss the niggers, and the niggers singing in time to the rise and fall of picks. Pretty soon he knew everybody in town. Whenever you heard a lot of laughing anywhere about the square, Homer Barron would be in the center of the group. Presently we began to see him and Miss Emily on Sunday afternoons driving in the yellow-wheeled buggy and the matched team of bays from the livery stable.

At first we were glad that Miss Emily would have an interest, because the ladies all said, "Of course a Grierson would not think seriously of a Northerner, a day laborer." But there were still others, older people, who said that even grief could not cause a real lady to forget *noblesse oblige*—without calling it *noblesse oblige*. They just said, "Poor Emily. Her kinsfolk should come to her." She had some kin in Alabama; but years ago her father had fallen out with them over the estate of old lady Wyatt, the crazy woman, and there was no communication between the two families. They had not even been represented at the funeral.

And as soon as the old people said, "Poor Emily," the whispering began. "Do you suppose it's really so?" they said to one another. "Of course it is. What else could . . . " This behind their hands; rustling of craned silk and satin behind jalousies closed upon the sun of Sunday afternoon as the thin, swift clop-clop-clop of the matched team passed: "Poor Emily."

She carried her head high enough—even when we believed that she was fallen. It was as if she demanded more than ever the recognition of her dignity as the last Grierson; as if it had wanted that touch of earthiness to reaffirm her imperviousness. Like when she bought the rat poison, the arsenic. That was over a year after they had begun to say "Poor Emily," and while the two female cousins were visiting her.

"I want some poison," she said to the druggist. She was over thirty then, still a slight woman, though thinner than usual, with cold, haughty black eyes in a face the flesh of which was strained across the temples and about the eyesockets as you imagine a lighthouse-keeper's face ought to look. "I want some poison," she said.

"Yes, Miss Emily. What kind? For rats and such? I'd recom—"

"I want the best you have. I don't care what kind."

The druggist named several. "They'll kill anything up to an elephant. But what you want is—"

"Arsenic," Miss Emily said. "Is that a good one?"

"Is . . . arsenic? Yes ma'am. But what you want—"

"I want arsenic."

The druggist looked down at her. She looked back at him, erect, her face like a strained flag. "Why, of course," the druggist said. "If that's what you want. But the law requires you to tell what you are going to use it for."

Miss Emily just stared at him, her head tilted back in order to look him eye for eye, until he looked away and went and got the arsenic and wrapped it up. The Negro delivery boy brought her the package; the druggist didn't come back. When she opened the package at home there was written on the box, under the skull and bones: "For rats."

IV

So the next day we all said, "She will kill herself"; and we said it would be the best thing. When she had first begun to be seen with Homer Barron, we had said, "She will marry him." Then we said, "She will persuade him yet," because Homer himself had remarked—he liked men, and it was known that he drank with the younger men in the Elk's Club—that he was not a marrying man. Later we said, "Poor Emily," behind the jalousies as they passed on Sunday afternoon in the glittering buggy, Miss Emily with her head high and Homer Barron with his hat cocked and a cigar in his teeth, reins and whip in a yellow glove.

Then some of the ladies began to say that it was a disgrace to the town and a bad example to the young people. The men did not want to interfere, but at last the ladies forced the Baptist minister—Miss Emily's people were Episcopal—to call upon her. He would never divulge what happened during that interview, but he refused to go back again. The next Sunday they again drove about the streets, and the following day the minister's wife wrote to Miss Emily's relations in Alabama.

So she had blood-kin under her roof again and we sat back to watch developments. At first nothing happened. Then we were sure that they were to be married. We learned that Miss Emily had been to the jeweler's and ordered a man's toilet set in silver, with the letters H. B. on each piece. Two days later we learned that she had bought a complete outfit of men's clothing, including a nightshirt, and we said, "They are married." We were really glad. We were glad because the two female cousins were even more Grierson than Miss Emily had ever been.

So we were not surprised when Homer Barron—the streets had been finished some time since—was gone. We were a little disappointed that there was not a public blowing-off, but we believed that he had gone on to prepare for Miss Emily's coming, or to give her a chance to get rid of the cousins. (By that time it was a cabal, and we were all Miss Emily's allies to help circumvent the cousins.) Sure enough, after another week they departed. And, as we had expected all along, within three days Homer Barron was back in town. A neighbor saw the Negro man admit him at the kitchen door at dusk one evening.

And that was the last we saw of Homer Barron. And of Miss Emily for some time. The Negro man went in and out with the market basket, but the front door remained closed. Now and then we would see her at a window for a moment, as the men did that night when they sprinkled the lime, but for almost six months she did not appear on the streets. Then we knew that this was to be expected too; as if that quality of her father which had thwarted her woman's life so many times had been too virulent and too furious to die.

When we next saw Miss Emily, she had grown fat and her hair was turning gray. During the next few years it grew grayer and grayer until it attained an even pepper-and-salt iron-gray, when it ceased turning. Up to the day of her death at seventy-four it was still that vigorous iron-gray, like the hair of an active man.

From that time on her front door remained closed, save for a period of six or seven years, when she was about forty, during which she gave lessons in china-painting. She fitted up a studio in one of the downstairs rooms, where the daughters and grand-daughters of Colonel Sartoris' contemporaries were sent to her with the same regularity and in the same spirit that they were sent on Sundays with a twenty-five cent piece for the collection plate. Meanwhile her taxes had been remitted.

Then the newer generation became the backbone and the spirit of the town, and the painting pupils grew up and fell away and did not send their children to her with boxes of color and tedious brushes and pictures cut from the ladies' magazines. The front door closed upon the last one and remained closed for good. When the town got free postal delivery Miss Emily alone refused to let them fasten the metal numbers above her door and attach a mailbox to it. She would not listen to them.

Daily, monthly, yearly we watched the Negro grow grayer and more stooped, going in and out with the market basket. Each December we sent her a tax notice, which would be returned by the post office a week later, unclaimed. Now and then we would see her in one of the downstairs windows—she had evidently shut up the top floor of the house—like the carven torso of an idol in a niche, looking or not looking at us, we could never tell which. Thus she passed from generation to generation—dear, inescapable, impervious, tranquil, and perverse.

And so she died. Fell ill in the house filled with dust and shadows, with only a doddering Negro man to wait on her. We did not even know she was sick; we had long since given up trying to get any information from the Negro. He talked to no one, probably not even to her, for his voice had grown harsh and rusty, as if from disuse.

She died in one of the downstairs rooms, in a heavy walnut bed with a curtain, her gray head propped on a pillow yellow and moldy with age and lack of sunlight.

V

The Negro met the first of the ladies at the front door and let them in, with their hushed, sibilant voices and their quick, curious glances, and then he disappeared. He walked right through the house and out the back and was not seen again.

The two female cousins came at once. They held the funeral on the second 55
day, with the town coming to look at Miss Emily beneath a mass of bought flowers, with the crayon face of her father musing profoundly above the bier and the ladies sibilant and macabre; and the very old men—some in their brushed Confederate uniforms—on the porch and the lawn, talking of Miss Emily as if she had been a contemporary of theirs, believing that they had danced with her and courted her perhaps, confusing time with its mathematical progression, as the old do, to whom all the past is not a diminishing road, but, instead, a huge meadow which no winter ever quite touches, divided from them now by the narrow bottleneck of the most recent decade of years.

Already we knew that there was one room in that region above stairs which no one had seen in forty years, and which would have to be forced. They waited until Miss Emily was decently in the ground before they opened it.

The violence of breaking down the door seemed to fill this room with pervading dust. A thin, acrid pall as of the tomb seemed to lie everywhere upon this room decked and furnished as for a bridal: upon the valance curtains of faded rose color, upon the rose-shaded lights, upon the dressing table, upon the delicate array of crystal and the man's toilet things backed with tarnished silver, silver so tarnished that the monogram was obscured. Among them lay a collar and tie, as if they had just been removed, which, lifted, left upon the surface a pale crescent in the dust. Upon a chair hung the suit, carefully folded; beneath it the two mute shoes and the discarded socks.

The man himself lay in the bed.

For a long while we just stood there, looking down at the profound and fleshless grin. The body had apparently once lain in the attitude of an embrace, but now the long sleep that outlasts love, that conquers even the grimace of love, had cuckolded him. What was left of him, rotted beneath what was left of the nightshirt, had become inextricable from the bed in which he lay; and upon him and upon the pillow beside him lay that even coating of the patient and biding dust.

Then we noticed that in the second pillow was the indentation of a head. One of us lifted something from it, and leaning forward, that faint and invisible dust dry and acrid in the nostrils, we saw a long strand of iron-gray hair.

1931

MORDECAI RICHLER

The Summer My Grandmother Was Supposed to Die

Dr. Katzman discovered the gangrene on one of his monthly visits. "She won't last a month," he said.

He repeated that the second month, the third, and the fourth, and now she lay dying in the heat of the back bedroom.

"If only she'd die," my mother said. "Oh, God, why doesn't she die? God in heaven, what's she holding on for?"

The summer my grandmother was supposed to die we did not chip in with the Breenbaums to take a cottage in the Laurentians.[1] It wouldn't have been practical. The old lady couldn't be moved, the nurse came daily and the doctor twice a week, and so it seemed best to stay in the city and wait for her to die or, as my mother said, pass away. It was a hot summer, her bedroom was just behind the kitchen, and when we sat down to eat we could smell her. The dressings on my grandmother's left leg had to be changed several times a day and, according to Dr. Katzman, her condition was hopeless. "It's in the hands of the Almighty," he said.

"It won't be long now," my father said, "and she'll be better off, if you know what I mean."

"Please," my mother said.

A nurse came every day from the Royal Victorian Order. She arrived punctually at noon and at five to twelve I'd join the rest of the boys under the outside staircase to look up her dress as she climbed to our second-story flat. Miss Monohan favored lacy pink panties and that was better than waiting under the stairs for Cousin Bessie, for instance. She wore enormous cotton bloomers, rain or shine.

I was sent out to play as often as possible, because my mother felt it was not

1. Mountains in eastern Canada between Hudson Bay and the St. Lawrence River.

good for me to see somebody dying. Usually I'd just roam the scorched streets shooting the breeze. There was Arty, Gas sometimes, Hershey, Stan, and me. We talked about everything from A to Z.

"Why is it," Arty wanted to know, "that Tarzan never shits?"

"Dick Tracy too."

"Or Wonder Woman."

"She's a dame."

"So?"

"Jees, wouldn't it be something if Superman crapped in the sky? He could just be flying over Waverly Street when, whamo, Mr. Rabinovitch catches it right in the kisser."

Mr. Rabinovitch was our Hebrew teacher.

"But there's Tarzan," Arty insisted, "in the jungle, week in and week out, and never once does he need to go to the toilet. It's not real, that's all."

Arty told me, "Before your grandma dies she's going to roll her eyes and gurgle. That's what they call the death-rattle."

"Aw, you know everything. Big shot."

"I *read* it, you jerk," Arty said, whacking me one, "in Perry Mason."

Home again I'd find my mother weeping.

"She's dying by inches," she said to my father one stifling night, "and none of them even come to see her. Oh, such children! They should only rot in hell."

"They're not behaving right. It's certainly not according to Hoyle," my father said.

"When I think of all the money and effort that went into making a rabbi out of Israel—the way Mother doted on him—and for what? Oh, what's the world coming to? God."

"It's not right."

Dr. Katzman was amazed. "I never believed she'd last this long. Really, it must be will-power alone that keeps her going. And your excellent care."

"I want her to die, Doctor. That's not my mother in the back room. It's an animal. I want her to please please die."

"Hush. You don't mean it. You're tired." And Dr. Katzman gave my father some pills for my mother to take. "A remarkable woman," he said. "A born nurse."

At night in bed my brother Harvey and I used to talk about our grandmother. "After she dies," I said, "her hair will go on growing for another twenty-four hours."

"Sez who?"

"Arty. It's a scientific fact. Do you think Uncle Lou will come from New York for the funeral?"

"Sure."

"Boy, that means another fiver for me. You too."

"You shouldn't say things like that, kiddo, or *her ghost will come back to haunt you*."

"Well," I said, "I'll be able to go to her funeral, anyway. I'm not too young any more."

35 I was only six years old when my grandfather died, and I wasn't allowed to go to his funeral.

I have only one memory of my grandfather. Once he called me into his study, set me down on his lap, and made a drawing of a horse for me. On the horse he drew a rider. While I watched and giggled he gave the rider a beard and the round fur-trimmed cap of a rabbi.

My grandfather was a Zaddik,[2] one of the Righteous, and I've been told that to study Talmud with him had been a rare pleasure. I wasn't allowed to go to his funeral, but years after I was shown the telegrams of condolence that had come from Eire and Poland and Israel and even Japan. My grandfather had written many books: a translation of the Zohar into modern Hebrew—some twenty years' work—and lots of slender volumes of sermons, chassidic tales, and rabbinical commentaries. His books had been published in Warsaw and later in New York. He had been famous.

"At the funeral," my mother told me, "they had to have six motorcycle policemen to control the crowds. It was such a heat that twelve women fainted—and I'm *not* counting Mrs. Waxman from upstairs. With her, you know, *anything* to fall into a man's arms. Even Pinsky's. And did I tell you that there was even a French-Canadian priest there?"

"No kidding?"

40 "The priest was a real big *knacker*.[3] A bishop maybe. He used to study with the *zeyda*.[4] The *zeyda* was some personality, you know. Spiritual and worldly-wise at the same time. Such personalities they don't make any more. Today, rabbis and peanuts are the same size."

But, according to my father, the *zeyda* (his father-in-law) hadn't been as famous as all that. "There are things I could say," he told me. "There was another side to him."

My grandfather had come from generations and generations of rabbis, his youngest son was a rabbi, but none of his grandchildren would be one. My brother Harvey was going to be a dentist and at the time, 1937, I was interested in flying and my cousin Jerry was already a communist. I once heard Jerry say, "Our grandpappy wasn't all he was cracked up to be." When the men at the kosher bakeries went out on strike he spoke up against them on the streets where they were picketing and in the *shule*.[5] It was of no consequence to him that they were grossly underpaid. His superstitious followers had to have bread. "Grandpappy," Jerry said, "was a prize reactionary."

A week after my grandfather died my grandmother suffered a stroke. Her right side was completely paralyzed. She couldn't speak. At first, it's true, my grandmother could say a few words and move her right hand enough to write her name in Hebrew. Her name was Malka. But her condition soon began to deteriorate.

My grandmother had six children and seven stepchildren, for my grandfather had been married before. His first wife had died in the old country. Two years

2. "Righteous man" in Hebrew. 3. Big shot. 4. Grandfather. 5. Synagogue.

later he had married my grandmother, the only daughter of the richest man in the village, and their marriage had been a singularly happy one. My grandmother had been a beautiful girl. She had also been a wise, resourceful, and patient wife. Qualities, I fear, indispensable to life with a Zaddik. For the synagogue had paid my grandfather no stipulated salary and much of the money he had picked up here and there he had habitually distributed among rabbinical students, needy immigrants, and widows. A vice, and such it was to his hard-pressed family, which made him as unreliable a provider as a drunkard. And indeed, to carry the analogy further, my grandmother had had to make many hurried trips to the pawnbroker with her jewelry. Not all of it had been redeemed, either. But her children had been looked after. The youngest, her favorite, was a rabbi in Boston, the eldest was the actor-manager of a Yiddish theater in New York, and another was a lawyer. One daughter lived in Toronto, two in Montreal. My mother was the youngest daughter, and when my grandmother had her stroke there was a family meeting and it was decided that my mother would take care of her. This was my father's fault. All the other husbands spoke up—they protested their wives had too much work, they could never manage it—but my father detested quarrels, and he was silent. So my grandmother came to stay with us.

Her bedroom, the back bedroom, had actually been promised to me for my 45
seventh birthday. But all that was forgotten now, and I had to go on sharing a bedroom with my brother Harvey. So naturally I was resentful when each morning before I left for school my mother said, "Go in and kiss the *baba*[6] good-bye."

All the same I'd go into the bedroom and kiss my grandmother hastily. She'd say "Bouyo-bouyo," for that was the only sound she could make. And after school it was, "Go in and tell the *baba* you're home."

"I'm home, *baba*."

"Bouyo-bouyo."

During those first hopeful months—"Twenty years ago who would have thought there'd be a cure for diabetes?" my father asked; "where there's life there's hope, you know"—she'd smile at me and try to speak, her eyes charged with effort. And even later there were times when she pressed my head urgently to her bosom with her surprisingly strong left arm. But as her illness dragged on and on and she became a condition in the house, something beyond hope or reproach, like the leaky icebox, there was less recognition and more ritual in those kisses. I came to dread her room. A clutter of sticky medicine bottles and the cracked toilet chair beside the bed; glazed but imploring eyes and a feeble smile, the wet slap of her lips against my cheeks. I flinched from her touch. After two years of it I protested to my mother. "Look what's the use of telling her I'm going or I'm here. She doesn't even recognize me any more."

"Don't be fresh. She's your grandmother." 50

My uncle who was in the theater in New York sent money regularly to help support my grandmother and, for the first few months, so did the other children. But once the initial and sustaining excitement had passed and it became likely

6. Grandma.

that my grandmother might linger in her invalid condition for two or maybe even three more years, the checks began to drop off, and the children seldom came to our house any more. Anxious weekly visits—"and how is she today, poor lamb?"—quickly dwindled to a dutiful monthly looking in, then a semiannual visit, and these always on the way to somewhere.

"The way they act," my father said, "you'd think that if they stayed long enough to take off their coats we'd make them take the *baba* home with them."

When the children did come to visit, my mother made it difficult for them.

"It's killing me," she said. "I have to lift her onto that chair three times a day maybe. Have you any idea how heavy she is? And what makes you think I always catch her in time? Sometimes I have to change her bed twice a day. That's a job I'd like to see your wife do," she said to my uncle, the rabbi.

"We could send her to the Old People's Home," the rabbi said.

"Now there's an idea," my father said.

But my mother began to sob. "Not as long as I'm alive," she said. And she gave my father a stony look. "Say something."

"It wouldn't be according to Hoyle."

"You want to be able to complain to everybody in town about all the other children," the rabbi said. "You've got a martyr complex."

"Everybody has a point of view, you know. You know what I mean?" my father said. "So what's the use of fighting?"

Meanwhile, Dr. Katzman came once a month to examine my grandmother. "It's remarkable, astonishing," he'd say each time. "She's as strong as a horse."

"Some life for a person," my father said. "She can't speak—she doesn't recognize anybody—what is there for her?"

The doctor was a cultivated man; he spoke often for women's clubs, sometimes on Yiddish literature and other times, his rubicund face hot with impatience, the voice taking on a doomsday tone, on the cancer threat.

"Who are we to judge?" he asked.

Every evening, during the first months of my grandmother's illness, my mother read her a story by Sholem Aleichem.[7] "Tonight she smiled," my mother would say. "She understood. I can tell." And my father, my brother, and I would not comment. Once a week my mother used to give the old lady a manicure. Sunny afternoons she'd lift her into a wheelchair and put her out in the sun. Somebody always had to stay in the house in case my grandmother called. Often, during the night, she would begin to wail unaccountably, and my mother would get up and rock the old lady in her arms for hours. But in the fourth year of my grandmother's illness the strain and fatigue began to tell on my mother. Besides looking after my grandmother—"and believe you me," the doctor assured her with a clap on the back, "it would be a full-time job for a professional nurse"—she had to keep house for a husband and two sons. She began to quarrel with my father and she became sharp with Harvey and me. My father started to spend his evenings playing pinochle at Tansky's Cigar & Soda. Weekends he took Harvey and

7. "Peace be with you," pen name of Yiddish author and humorist Shalom Rabinovitz (1859–1916).

me to visit his brothers and sisters. And everywhere he went people had little bits of advice for him.

"Sam, you might as well be a bachelor. You're just going to have to put your foot down for once."

"Yeah, in your face maybe."

My cousin Libby, who was at McGill,[8] said, "This could have a very damaging effect on the development of your boys. These are their formative years, Uncle Samuel, and the omnipresence of death in the house . . ."

"What you need," my father said, "is a boy friend. *And how.*"

At Tansky's Cigar & Soda it was, "Come clean, Sam. It's no hardship. If I know you, the old lady's got a big insurance policy and when the time comes . . ."

My mother lost lots of weight. After dinner she'd fall asleep in her chair in the middle of Lux Radio Theater.[9] One minute she'd be sewing a patch on my breeches or be making a list of girls to call for a bingo party (proceeds for the Talmud Torah),[1] and the next she'd be snoring. Then, one morning, she just couldn't get out of bed, and Dr. Katzman came round a week before his regular visit. "Well, well, this won't do, will it?" He sat in the kitchen with my father and the two men drank apricot brandy out of small glasses.

"Your wife is a remarkable woman," Dr. Katzman said.

"You don't say?"

"She's got a gallstone condition."

My father shrugged. "Have another one for the road," he said.

"Thank you, but I have several more calls to make." Dr. Katzman rose, sighing. "There she lies in that back room, poor old woman," he said, "hanging desperately onto life. There's food for thought there."

My grandmother's children met again, and the five of them sat around my mother's bed embarrassed, irritated, and quick to take insult. All except my uncle who was in the theater. He sucked a cigar and drank whisky. He teased my mother, the rabbi, and my aunts, and if not for him I think they would have been at each other's throats. It was decided, over my mother's protests, to send my grandmother to the Old People's Home on Esplanade Street. An ambulance came to take my grandmother away and Dr. Katzman said, "It's for the best." But my father had been in the back bedroom when the old lady had held on tenaciously to the bedpost, not wanting to be moved by the two men in white—"Easy does it, granny," the younger one had said—and afterwards he could not go in to see my mother. He went out for a walk.

"She looked at me with such a funny expression," he told my brother. "Is it my fault?"

My mother stayed in bed for another two weeks. My father cooked for us and we hired a woman to do the housework. My mother put on weight quickly, her cheeks regained their normal pinkish hue and, for the first time in months, she actually joked with Harvey and me. She became increasingly curious about our schools and whether or not we shined our shoes regularly. She began to cook

8. University in Montreal. 9. Weekly radio drama sponsored by Lux soap. 1. Orthodox Jewish school for boys.

again, special dishes for my father, and she resumed old friendships with women on the parochial school board. The change reflected on my father. Not only did his temper improve, but he stopped going to Tansky's every other night, and began to come home early from work. Life at home had never been so rich. But my grandmother's name was never mentioned. The back bedroom remained empty and I continued to share a room with Harvey. I couldn't see the point and so one evening I said, "Look, why don't I move into the back bedroom?"

My father glared at me across the table.

"But it's empty like."

My mother left the table. And the next afternoon she put on her best dress and coat and new spring hat.

"Where are you going?" my father asked.

"To see my mother."

"Don't go looking for trouble."

"It's been a month. Maybe they're not treating her right."

"They're experts."

"Did you think I was never going to visit her? I'm not inhuman, you know."

"All right, go," he said.

But after she'd gone my father went to the window and said, "Son-of-a-bitch."

Harvey and I sat outside on the steps watching the cars go by. My father sat on the balcony above, cracking peanuts. It was six o'clock, maybe later, when the ambulance turned the corner, slowed down, and parked right in front of the house.

"Son-of-a-bitch," my father said. "I knew it."

My mother got out first, her eyes red and swollen, and hurried upstairs to make my grandmother's bed.

"I'm sorry, Sam, I had to do it."

"You'll get sick again, that's what."

"You think she doesn't recognize people. From the moment she saw me she cried and cried. Oh, it was terrible."

"They're experts there. They know how to handle her better than you do."

"Experts? Expert murderers you mean. She's got bedsores, Sam. Those dirty little Irish nurses they don't change her linen often enough, they hate her. She must have lost twenty pounds there."

"Another month and you'll be flat on your back again."

"Sam, what could I do? Please Sam."

"She'll outlive all of us. Even Muttel.[2] I'm going out for a walk."

She was back and I was to blame.

My father became a regular at Tansky's Cigar & Soda again and every morning I had to go in and kiss my grandmother. She began to look like a man. Little hairs had sprouted on her chin, she had a spiky gray mustache and, of course, she was practically bald. This near-baldness, I guess, sprang from the fact that

2. The narrator's Yiddish name; could be the equivalent of Mordecai.

she had been shaving her head ever since she had married my grandfather the rabbi.[3] My grandmother had four different wigs, but she had not worn one since the first year of her illness. She wore a little pink cap instead. And so, as before, she said, "bouyo-bouyo," to everything.

Once more uncles and aunts sent five-dollar bills, though erratically, to help pay for my grandmother's support. Elderly people, former followers of my grandfather, came to inquire after the old lady's health. They sat in the back bedroom with her for hours, leaning on their canes, talking to themselves, rocking, always rocking to and fro. "The Holy Shakers," my father called them, and Harvey and I avoided them, because they always wanted to pinch our cheeks, give us a dash of snuff and laugh when we sneezed, or offer us a sticky old candy from a little brown bag with innumerable creases in it. When the visit was done the old people would unfailingly sit in the kitchen with my mother for another hour, watching her make lockshen[4] or bake bread. My mother always served them lemon tea and they would talk about my grandfather, recalling his books, his sayings, and his charitable deeds.

And so another two years passed, with no significant change in my grandmother's condition. But fatigue, bed temper, and even morbidity enveloped my mother again. She fought with her brothers and sisters and once, when I stepped into the living room, I found her sitting with her head in her hands, and she looked up at me with such anguish that I was frightened.

"What did I do now?" I asked.

"If, God forbid, I had a stroke, would you send me to the Old People's Home?"

"Don't be a joke. Of course not."

"I hope that never in my life do I have to count on my children for anything."

The summer my grandmother was supposed to die, the seventh year of her illness, my brother took a job as a shipper and he kept me awake at night with stories about the factory. "What we do, see, is clear out the middle of a huge pile of lengths of material. That makes for a kind of secret cave. A hideout. Well, then you coax one of the *shiksas*[5] inside and hi-diddle-diddle."

One night Harvey waited until I had fallen asleep and then he wrapped himself in a white sheet, crept up to my bed, and shouted, "Bouyo-bouyo."

I hit him. He shouted.

"Children. Children, please," my mother called. "I must get some rest."

As my grandmother's condition worsened—from day to day we didn't know when she'd die—I was often sent out to eat at my aunt's or at my other grandmother's house. I was hardly ever at home. On Saturday mornings I'd get together with the other guys and we'd walk all the way past the mountain to Eaton's, which was our favorite department store for riding up and down escalators and stealing.

3. Married Orthodox Jewish women customarily either shave their heads or cover their hair.
4. Noodles. 5. Gentile girls.

In those days they let boys into the left-field bleachers free during the week and we spent many an afternoon at the ball park. The Montreal Royals, part of the Dodger farm system, was some ball club too. There was Jackie Robinson and Roy Campanella, Honest John Gabbard, Chuck Connors, and Kermit Kitman was our hero. It used to kill us to see that crafty little hebe[6] running around there with all those tall dumb *goyim.*[7] "Hey, Kitman," we'd yell. "Hey, hey, sho-head,[8] if your father knew you played ball on *shabus*—[9] Kitman, unfortunately, was all field and no hit. He never made the majors. "There goes Kermit Kitman," we'd yell, after he'd gone down swinging again, "the first Jewish strike-out king of the International League." This we usually followed up by bellowing some choice imprecations in Yiddish.

It was after one of these games, on a Friday afternoon, that I came home to find a small crowd gathered in front of the house.

"That's the grandson."

"Poor kid."

Old people stood silent and expressionless across the street staring at our front door. A taxi pulled up and my aunt hurried out, hiding her face in her hands.

"After so many years," somebody said.

"And probably next year they'll discover a cure. Isn't that *always* the case?"

I took the stairs two at a time. The flat was full. Uncles and aunts from my father's side of the family, odd old people, Dr. Katzman, Harvey, neighbors, were all standing around and talking in hushed voices in the living room. I found my father in the kitchen, getting out the apricot brandy. "Your grandmother's dead," he said.

"She didn't suffer," somebody said. "She passed away in her sleep."

"A merciful death."

"Where's Maw?"

"In the bedroom with . . . you'd better not go in," my father said.

"I want to see her."

My mother's face was long with grief. She wore a black shawl, and glared down at a knot of handkerchief clutched in a fist that had been cracked by washing soda. "Don't come in here," she said.

Several bearded, round-shouldered men in black shiny coats stood round the bed. I couldn't see my grandmother.

"Your grandmother's dead."

"Daddy told me."

"Go and wash your face and comb your hair. You'll have to get your own supper."

"O.K."

"One minute. The *baba* left some jewelry. The ring is for Harvey's wife and the necklace is for yours."

"Who's getting married?"

"Better go and wash your face. And remember behind the ears, Muttel."

6. Hebrew, Jew. 7. Gentiles. 8. Possibly *shorn-head* (?), referring to short hair or crew cut of athlete, in contrast to traditional long locks of Orthodox Jews (?). 9. Sabbath.

Telegrams were sent, long-distance calls were made, and all through the evening relatives and neighbors came and went like swarms of fish when crumbs have been dropped into the water.

"When my father died," my mother said, "they had to have *six* motorcycle policemen to control the crowds. Twelve people fainted, such a heat . . ."

The man from the funeral parlor came.

"There goes the only Jewish businessman in town," my Uncle Harry said, "who wishes all his customers were Germans."

"This is no time for jokes."

"Listen, life goes on."

My cousin Jerry had begun to use a cigarette holder. "Everyone's going to be sickeningly sentimental," he said. "Soon the religious mumbo-jumbo starts. I can hardly wait."

Tomorrow was the Sabbath and so, according to the law, my grandmother couldn't be buried until Sunday. She would have to lie on the floor all night. Two old grizzly women in white came to move and wash the body and a professional mourner arrived to sit up and pray for her.

"I don't trust his face," my mother said. "He'll fall asleep., You watch him, Sam."

"A fat lot of good prayers will do her now."

"Will you just watch him, please."

"I'll watch him, I'll watch him." My father was livid about my Uncle Harry. "The way he's gone after that apricot brandy you'd think that guy never saw a bottle in his life before."

Harvey and I were sent to bed, but we couldn't sleep. My aunt was sobbing over the body in the living room—"That dirty hypocrite," my mother said—there was the old man praying, coughing, and spitting into his handkerchief each time he woke; and hushed voices and whimpering from the kitchen, where my father and mother sat. Harvey was in a good mood, he let me have a few puffs of his cigarette.

"Well, kiddo, this is our last night together. Tomorrow you can take over the back bedroom."

"*Are you crazy?*"

"You always wanted it for yourself."

"She died in there, bud. You think I'm going to sleep in there?"

"Good night. Happy dreams, kiddo."

"Hey, let's talk some more."

Harvey told me a ghost story. "Did you know that when they hang a man," he said, "the last thing that happens is that he has an orgasm?"

"A what?"

"Forget it. I forgot you were still in kindergarten."

"I know plenty. Don't worry."

"At the funeral they're going to open her coffin to throw dirt in her face. It's supposed to be earth from Eretz.[1] They open it and you're going to have to

1. Eretz Yisrael, the Land of Israel.

look." Harvey stood up on his bed, holding his hands over his head like claws. He made a hideious face. "Bouyo-bouyo. Who's that sleeping in my bed? Woo-woo."

My uncle who was in the theater, the rabbi, and my aunt from Toronto, all came to Montreal for the funeral. Dr. Katzman came too.

"As long as she was alive," my mother said, "he couldn't even send five dollars a month. Some son! What a rabbi! I don't want him in my house, Sam. I can't bear the sight of him."

"You don't mean a word of that and you know it," Dr. Katzman said.

"Maybe you'd better give her a sedative," the rabbi said.

"Sam. Sam, will you say something, please."

My father stepped up to the rabbi, his face flushed. "I'll tell you this straight to your face, Israel," he said. "You've gone down in my estimation."

"Really," the rabbi said, smiling a little.

My father's face burned a deeper red. "Year by year," he said, "your stock has gone down with me."

And my mother began to weep bitterly, helplessly, without control. She was led unwillingly to bed. While my father tried his best to comfort her, as he said consoling things, Dr. Katzman plunged a needle into her arm. "There we are," he said.

I went to sit in the sun on the outside stairs with Arty. "I'm going to the funeral," I said.

"I couldn't go anyway."

Arty was descended from the tribe of high priests and so was not allowed to be in the presence of a dead body. I was descended from the Yisroelis.[2]

"The lowest of the low," Arty said.

"Aw."

My uncle, the rabbi, and Dr. Katzman stepped into the sun to light cigarettes.

"It's remarkable that she held out for so long," Dr. Katzman said.

"Remarkable?" my uncle said. "It's written that if a man has been married twice he will spend as much time with his first wife in heaven as he did on earth. My father, may he rest in peace, was married to his first wife for seven years and my mother, may she rest in peace, has managed to keep alive for seven years. Today in heaven she will be able to join my father, may he rest in peace."

Dr. Katzman shook his head, he pursed his lips. "It's amazing," he said. "The mysteries of the human heart. Astonishing."

My father hurried outside. "Dr. Katzman, please. It's my wife. Maybe the injection wasn't strong enough? She just doesn't stop crying. It's like a tap. Could you come please?"

"Excuse me," Dr. Katzman said to my uncle.

"Of course."

My uncle approached Arty and me.

"Well, boys," he said, "what would you like to be when you grow up?"

1961

2. The lowest of the three categories into which the Jewish people are traditionally divided.

QUESTIONS

1. Looking back over "An Occurrence at Owl Creek Bridge," how many of Peyton Farquhar's sensory perceptions can you reinterpret in terms of what must have really been happening?

2. What are the effects, both emotional and in interpretation, of the manipulation of chronology in "A Rose for Emily"?

3. What is there in the second paragraph of "A Rose for Emily" that suggests that the speaker is not just casually spinning a yarn about a weird lady but sees some more general meaning in the tale?

4. What does "supposed to die" mean in the title of the Richler story?

5. What is the effect of having such details in Richler's story as those involving baseball, Miss Monohan's lacy pink panties, and the humor in this rather serious story?

WRITING SUGGESTIONS

1. Write an outline of "A Rose for Emily" arranging the events in chronological order and dating them as precisely as possible. Then write a three-paragraph analysis of why the story is structured—the chronology rearranged—as it is.

2. Write a brief personal narrative (1000–1500 words), preferably (but not necessarily) based on a real episode, that is in some way comparable to "The Summer My Grandmother Was Supposed to Die."

3 CHARACTERIZATION

In a good many stories the narrator is a disembodied offstage voice, without an identity or a personal history, without influence on the action, without qualities other than those that a voice and style may suggest. So it is in some of the earlier stories in this volume—"The Zebra Storyteller," "No One's a Mystery," "The Jewelry," "An Occurrence at Owl Creek Bridge." Poe's narrator, however, not only tells us the story but acts out the action; without him we not only would not know the story, there just would not be any. Richler's narrator looks back into his past; he is there in the story, speaking, listening, reacting. In addition to being the narrator, he is a **character**: someone who acts, appears, or is referred to in a work.

The most common term for the character with the leading male role is **hero,** the "good guy" who opposes the **villain,** or "bad guy." The leading female character is the **heroine.** Heroes and heroines are usually larger than life, stronger or better than most human beings, almost godlike (and there's even a brand of heroes nowadays so close to being godlike that they are called superheroes). In most modern fiction, however, the leading character is much more ordinary, more like the rest of us. Such a character is called the **antihero,** not because he opposes the hero but because he is not like a hero in stature or perfection. An older and more neutral term than hero for the leading character, a term that does not imply either the presence or absence of outstanding virtue (and with the added advantage of referring equally to male and female), is **protagonist,** whose opponent is the **antagonist.** You might get into long and pointless arguments by calling Lantin or Montresor a hero, but either is his story's protagonist.

The **major characters** are those we see more of over a longer period of time; we learn more about them, and we think of them as more complex and frequently therefore more "realistic" than the **minor characters,** the figures who fill out the story. These major characters can grow and change, as Lantin does and as Judith does in Doris Lessing's "Our Friend Judith"; by the end of these stories both protagonists have acted in a way not predictable from what we learned about them and their past actions earlier in the story. Characters who can thus "surprise convincingly," an influential critic says, are **round characters.** Tallent's and Poe's characters are not very complex and they do not change in surprising ways; they are therefore called **flat.** But we must be careful not to let terms like *flat* and *round* turn into value judgments. Because flat characters are less complex than round ones it is easy to assume they are artistically inferior; we need only to think of the characters of Charles Dickens, almost all of whom are flat, to realize that this is not always true.

The terms *flat* and *round*, like the terms *hero* and *antihero*, are not absolute or precise. They designate extremes or tendencies, not pigeonholes. Is Poe's Montresor entirely flat? Is Shakespeare's Falstaff? Charlie Chaplin's Little Tramp? Little Orphan Annie? Are all these characters equally flat? We will probably agree that Baldwin's Sonny is a round character, but what about Faulkner's Emily? Atwood's Emma? Are they all equally round? Our answers are less important than our looking carefully at these characters to see what we know about each of them, to what degree they can be summed up in a phrase or a sentence; to discover how we learned what we know about them and how our judgment has been controlled by the story; to think about and perhaps judge the assumptions about human motivation, behavior, and nature that underlie the character and his or her characterization. Flat and round are useful as categories but are even more useful as tools of investigation, ways of focusing our attention and sharpening our perception.

Though most of Dickens's flat characters are highly individualized, not to say unique, some, like Fagin, the avaricious Jewish moneylender, are **stereotypes:** characters based on conscious or unconscious cultural assumptions that sex, age, ethnic or national identification, occupation, marital status, and so on are predictably accompanied by certain character traits, actions, even values.

The stereotype may be very useful in creating a round character, one who can surprise convincingly: Judith, according to a Canadian woman, is "one of your typical English spinsters." Judith, however, acts in ways that deny the limitations of the stereotype. A stereotype is, after all, only a quick—and somewhat superficial—form of classification, and classification is a common first step in definitions. One of the chief ways we have of describing or defining is by placing the thing to be defined in a category or class and then distinguishing it from the other members of that class. A good deal of **characterization**—the art, craft, method of presentation, or creation of fictional personages—involves a similar process. Characters are almost inevitably identified by category—by sex, age, nationality, occupation, and so on. We soon learn that the narrator of "My Man Bovanne" is a middle-aged urban black woman, that Major Monarch is a middle-aged English gentleman, and, as we have seen, that Judith is an English spinster.

You may have noticed something that may seem odd at first: putting a character in more than one general group does not make that character more generalized or stereotyped, but more individual. The category *middle-aged* includes the narrator of "My Man Bovanne," Major and Mrs. Monarch, and Judith.

That Major Monarch is male separates him from the other three; that the narrator of "Bovanne" is American and black separates her from the others, though she is, like Mrs. Monarch and Judith, a woman. So Hazel is to some degree particularized by being identified as a member of three general categories.

Not all generalizations involve cultural stereotypes, of course. Some may involve generalized character traits that the story or narrator defines for us (and that we must accept unless events in the story prove otherwise). Bovanne is said to be "just a nice old gent from the block," the kind of man whose conversation is "comfy and cheery." Physical characteristics also serve as categories. Bovanne is blind. Before we are introduced to him, we are told that blind people hum, and that a blind man called Shakey Bee hums. Only then are we told that there is a blind man named Bovanne who also has the habit of humming. As physical characteristics are multiplied, the result is more and more particularizing or individualizing. The detailed physical description of Judith makes it possible to visualize her rather fully, almost to recognize her as an individual:

> Judith is tall, small-breasted, slender. Her light brown hair is parted in the center and cut straight around her neck. A high straight forehead, straight nose, and full grave mouth are setting for her eyes, which are green, large and prominent. Her lids are very white, fringed with gold, and molded close over the eyeball. . . . (Par. 7)

There are many other ways in which a character is characterized and individualized besides stereotyping and "de-stereotyping," and besides classifying and particularizing by physical description. In most cases we see what characters do and hear what they say; we sometimes learn what they think, and what other people think or say about them; we often know what kind of clothes they wear, what and how much they own, treasure, or covet; we may be told about their childhood, parents, or some parts of their past. We learn a bit about Hazel, the narrator of "My Man Bovanne," from her age, sex, and ethnic identification. We learn a great deal more from the way she talks to her children and they to her, from the fact that men call her "long distance and in the middle of the night for a little Mama comfort," the fact that she carried her baby daughter strapped to her chest until the baby was nearly two years old, and from her short, low-cut dress. We even know what she is thinking.

No matter how many methods of characterization are employed, however, at some point the particularization of the individual stops. No matter how individualized the character may be, he or she remains a member of a number of groups, and we make certain assumptions about the character based on our fixed or stereotyped notions of the groups. To destroy a stereotype, a story must introduce a stereotype to destroy. And somehow the de-stereotyped character, no matter how particularized, remains to some degree representative. If Judith turns out to be not as prudish and prissy as the stereotype of the English spinster has led us to believe, we may well conclude that the stereotype is false and Judith is more representative of the real English spinster than the stereotype is. Indeed, this tendency to generalize from the particulars of a story extends beyond cultural groups, sometimes to human character at large: if Sonny can change his ways after years of habitual conduct, then human character, the story might seem to say, is not permanently fixed at birth, in infancy, childhood, ever.

One of the reasons it is so difficult to discuss character is precisely that the principles of definition and evaluation of fictional characters (not of their characterization, the way they are presented) are the same as those we use for real people, an area of violent controversy and confusion. The very term *character* itself, when it refers not to a fictional personage but to a combination of qualities in a human being, is somewhat ambiguous. It usually has moral overtones, often favorable (a man of character); it is sometimes neutral but evaluative (character reference). Judgment about character (not characterization, remember) usually involves moral terms like *good* and *bad* and *strong* and *weak*. **Personality** usually implies that which distinguishes or individualizes a person, and the judgment called for is not so much moral as social—*pleasing* or *displeasing*. An older term, **nature** (it is his nature to be so or do such), usually implies something inherent or inborn, something fixed and thus predictable. The **existential character** implies the opposite; that is, whatever our past, our conditioning, our pattern or previous behavior, we can, by choice, by free will, change all that right this minute, as Sonny does.

Fictional characters thus frequently seem to be part of the history that lies behind the story or beyond the story as part of our own world, to exist in a reality that is detachable from the words and events of the story in which they appear. We feel we might recognize Tom Jones, Jane Eyre, or Sherlock Holmes on the street, and we might be able to anticipate what they might say or do in *our* world, outside the story. Fictional characters are neither real nor detachable, of course, and they exist only in the words of the works in which they are presented. We must not forget the distinction between the character and the characterization, the method by which he or she is presented; so we must be careful to distinguish the *good character*, meaning someone whom, if real, we would consider virtuous, and the *good characterization*, meaning a fictional person who, no matter what his or her morality or behavior, is well presented.

Henry James's story "The Real Thing" is about the difference between reality and art, character and characterization. Major Monarch is described as a "gentleman, a man of fifty, very high and very straight, with a moustache slightly grizzled and a dark grey walking-coat admirably fitted . . ." (par. 1). He looks like the stereotype of a celebrity. The painter-narrator of "The Real Thing," however, immediately recognizes that because of a "paradoxical law," Major Monarch's appearance means that he is *not* a celebrity: celebrities are not often so "striking." It does not take the narrator long to recognize the Major's real type. Just by the Major's appearance, the painter can "see" the Major's whole gentlemanly life: his hunting, his clothes, his umbrellas, his luggage, his servants, and he can see as well Mrs. Monarch's lady's life, clothes, and so on. They are "the real thing," a real gentleman and a real lady. They are therefore useless as models for the artist. Not only are they so much *one* real thing that they can pose only for that type and no other, but even as a lady and gentleman they are so stereotypical they are useful only for illustrations of bad, stereotyped novels. James seems to be distinguishing *character* and *characterization:* the first is "the real thing" which will not do for art or the *representation* of the real; the second, "the alchemy of art," offers not a copy of reality but an *illusion* of reality, an illusion that seems more real in its representation than the real thing would.

Even if we entirely agree with Henry James—and not all readers do—his distinction between reality and representation does not mean that we cannot learn from one about the other. We must recognize that characters are not finally detachable—that they have roles, functions, limitations, and their very existence in the context of other elements of the story; we must not confuse fictional characters with real people, or character with characterization. This is not to say, however, that we may not learn about real people from characters in fiction or learn to understand fictional characters in part from what we know about real people. For real people too exist in a context of other people and other elements, their history and geography and their "narrator," the one who is representing them—that is, *you*. Indeed, it may be worth paying particular attention to how stories create the images of people and what those images assume about human character precisely because this process and these assumptions are so similar to the way we get to know and understand real people. For we are all artists representing reality to ourselves. If we study the art of characterization we may become better artists, able to enrich both our reading and our lives.

▽ ▽ ▽

CHARACTERIZATION A Glossary

antagonist: a neutral term for a character who opposes the leading male or female character; see *hero / ine* and *antagonist*

antihero: a leading character who is not, like a "hero," perfect or even outstanding but is rather ordinary and representative of the more or less average person

character: (1) a fictional personage; (2) a combination of a person's qualities, especially moral qualities, so that such terms as "good" and "bad," "strong" and "weak," often apply. See *personality* and *nature*

characterization: the fictional or artistic presentation of a fictional personage; terms like "a good character" can, then, be ambiguous—they may mean that the personage is virtuous, or that he or she is well presented whatever his or her characteristics or moral qualities.

existential character: a person real or fictional who, whatever his or her past or conditioning, can change by an act of will

flat character: fictional character, often but not always a minor character, who is relatively simple, who is presented as having rather few, though sometimes dominant, traits, and who thus does not change much in the course of a story. See *round character*

hero / heroine: the leading male / female character, usually larger than life, sometimes almost godlike. See *antihero, protagonist*, and *villain*

nature: as it refers to a person—"it is his [or her] nature"—a rather old term suggesting something inborn, inherent, fixed, and thus predictable. See *character, personality*

personality: that which distinguishes or individualizes a person; its qualities are judged not so much in terms of their moral value, as in "character," but as to whether they are "pleasing" or "unpleasing."

protagonist: the main character in a work, who may be male or female, heroic or not heroic; thus the most neutral term. See *hero / ine, antihero*, and *antagonist*

round character: a complex character, often a major character, who can grow and change and "surprise convincingly"—that is, act in a way that you did not expect from what had gone before but now accept as possible, even probable, and "realistic."

stereotype: a characterization based on conscious or unconscious assumptions that some one aspect, such as gender, age, ethnic or national identity, religion, occupation, marital status, determines what humans are like, and so is accompanied by certain traits, actions, and even value.

villain: the one who opposes the hero and heroine, the "bad guy"; see *antagonist* and *hero*

TONI CADE BAMBARA

My Man Bovanne

Blind people got a hummin jones[1] if you notice. Which is understandable completely once you been around one and notice what no eyes will force you into to see people, and you get past the first time, which seems to come out of nowhere, and it's like you in church again with fat-chest ladies and old gents gruntin a hum low in the throat to whatever the preacher be saying. Shakey Bee bottom lip all swole up with Sweet Peach[2] and me explaining how come the sweet-potato bread was a dollar-quarter this time stead of dollar regular and he say uh hunh he understand, then he break into this *thizzin* kind of hum which is quiet, but fiercesome just the same, if you ain't ready for it. Which I wasn't. But I got used to it and the onliest time I had to say somethin bout it was when he was playin checkers on the stoop one time and he commenst to hummin quite churchy seem to me. So I says, "Look here Shakey Bee, I can't beat you and Jesus too." He stop.

So that's how come I asked My Man Bovanne to dance. He ain't my man mind you, just a nice ole gent from the block that we all know cause he fixes things and the kids like him. Or used to fore Black Power got hold their minds and mess em around till they can't be civil to ole folks. So we at this benefit for my niece's cousin who's runnin for somethin with this Black party somethin or other behind her. And I press up close to dance with Bovanne who blind and I'm hummin and he hummin, chest to chest like talkin. Not jammin my breasts into the man. Wasn't bout tits. Was bout vibrations. And he dug it and asked me what color dress I had on and how my hair was fixed and how I was doin without a man, not nosy but nice-like, and who was at this affair and was the canapés dainty-stingy or healthy enough to get hold of proper. Comfy and cheery is what I'm tryin to get across. Touch talkin like the heel of the hand on the tambourine or on a drum.

But right away Joe Lee come up on us and frown for dancin so close to the man. My own son who knows what kind of warm I am about; and don't grown men call me long distance and in the middle of the night for a little Mama comfort? But he frown. Which ain't right since Bovanne can't see and defend himself. Just a nice old man who fixes toasters and busted irons and bicycles and things and changes the lock on my door when my men friends get messy. Nice man. Which is not why they invited him. Grass roots you see. Me and Sister Taylor and the woman who does heads at Mamies and the man from the barber shop, we all there on account of we grass roots. And I ain't never been souther than Brooklyn Battery and no more country than the window box on my fire escape. And just yesterday my kids tellin me to take them countrified rags off my head and be cool. And now can't get Black enough to suit em. So everybody passin sayin My Man Bovanne. Big deal, keep steppin and don't even stop a minute to get the man a drink or one of them cute sandwiches or tell him what's

1. Compelling need. 2. A brand of dipping snuff.

goin on. And him standin there with a smile ready case someone do speak he want to be ready. So that's how come I pull him on the dance floor and we dance squeezin past the tables and chairs and all them coats and people standin round up in each other face talkin bout this and that but got no use for this blind man who mostly fixed skates and skooters for all these folks when they was just kids. So I'm pressed up close and we touch talkin with the hum. And here come my daughter cuttin her eye[3] at me like she do when she tell me about my "apolitical" self like I got hoof and mouf disease and there ain't no hope at all. And I don't pay her no mind and just look up in Bovanne shadow face and tell him his stomach like a drum and he laugh. Laugh real loud. And here come my youngest, Task, with a tap on my elbow like he the third grade monitor and I'm cuttin up on the line to assembly.

"I was just talkin on the drums," I explained when they hauled me into the kitchen. I figured drums was my best defense. They can get ready for drums what with all this heritage business. And Bovanne stomach just like that drum Task give me when he come back from Africa. You just touch it and it hum thizzm, thizzm. So I stuck to the drum story. "Just drummin that's all."

"Mama, what are you talkin about?"

"She had too much to drink," say Elo to Task cause she don't hardly say nuthin to me direct no more since that ugly argument about my wigs.

"Look here Mama," say Task, the gentle one. "We just tryin to pull your coat. You were makin a spectacle of yourself out there dancing like that."

"Dancin like what?"

Task run a hand over his left ear like his father for the world and his father before that.

"Like a bitch in heat," say Elo.

"Well uhh, I was goin to say like one of them sex-starved ladies gettin on in years and not too discriminating. Know what I mean?"

I don't answer cause I'll cry. Terrible thing when your own children talk to you like that. Pullin me out the party and hustlin me into some stranger's kitchen in the back of a bar just like the damn police. And ain't like I'm old old. I can still wear me some sleeveless dresses without the meat hangin off my arm. And I keep up with some thangs through my kids. Who ain't kids no more. To hear them tell it. So I don't say nuthin.

"Dancin with that tom," say Elo to Joe Lee, who leanin on the folks' freezer. "His feet can smell a cracker a mile away and go into their shuffle number post haste. And them eyes. He could be a little considerate and put on some shades. Who wants to look into them blown-out fuses that—"

"Is this what they call the generation gap?" I say.

"Generation gap," spits Elo, like I suggested castor oil and fricassee possum in the milk-shakes or somethin. "That's a white concept for a white phenomenon. There's no generation gap among Black people. We are a col—"

"Yeh, well never mind," says Joe Lee. "The point is Mama . . . well, it's pride. You embarrass yourself and us too dancin like that."

"I wasn't shame." Then nobody say nuthin. Them standin there in they

3. Giving a sharp look.

pretty clothes with drinks in they hands and gangin up on me, and me in the third-degree chair and nary a olive to my name. Felt just like the police got hold to me.

"First of all," Task say, holdin up his hand and tickin off the offenses, "the dress. Now that dress is too short, Mama, and too low-cut for a woman your age. And Tamu's going to make a speech tonight to kick off the campaign and will be introducin you and expecting you to organize the council of elders—"

"Me? Didn nobody ask me nuthin. You mean Nisi? She change her name?"

"Well, Norton was supposed to tell you about it. Nisi wants to introduce you and then encourage the older folks to form a Council of the Elders to act as an advisory—"

"And you going to be standing there with your boobs out and that wig on your head and that hem up to your ass. And people'll say, 'Ain't that the horny bitch that was grindin with the blind dude?' "

"Elo, be cool a minute," say Task, gettin to the next finger. "And then there's the drinkin. Mama, you know you can't drink cause next thing you know you be laughin loud and carryin on," and he grab another finger for the loudness. "And then there's the dancin. You been tattooed on the man for four records straight and slow draggin even on the fast numbers. How you think that look for a woman your age?"

"What's my age?"

"What?"

"I'm axin you all a simple question. You keep talkin bout what's proper for a woman my age. How old am I anyhow?" And Joe Lee slams his eyes shut and squinches up his face to figure. And Task run a hand over his ear and stare into his glass like the ice cubes goin calculate for him. And Elo just starin at the top of my head like she goin rip the wig off any minute now.

"Is your hair braided up under that thing? If so, why don't you take it off? You always did do a neat cornroll."[4]

"Uh huh," cause I'm thinkin how she couldn't undo her hair fast enough talking bout cornroll so countrified. None of which was the subject. "How old, I say?"

"Sixtee-one or—"

"You a damn lie Joe Lee Peoples."

"And that's another thing," say Task on the fingers.

"You know what you all can kiss," I say, gettin up and brushin the wrinkles out my lap.

"Oh, Mama," Elo say, puttin a hand on my shoulder like she hasn't done since she left home and the hand landin light and not sure it supposed to be there. Which hurt me to my heart. Cause this was the child in our happiness fore Mr. Peoples die. And I carried that child strapped to my chest till she was nearly two. We was close is what I'm tryin to tell you. Cause it was more me in the child than the others. And even after Task it was the girlchild I covered in the night and wept over for no reason at all less it was she was a chub-chub like

4. Cornrow, a hairstyle in which all the hair is interwoven from the scalp into small braids.

me and not very pretty, but a warm child. And how did things get to this, that she can't put a sure hand on me and say Mama we love you and care about you and you entitled to enjoy yourself cause you a good woman?

"And then there's Reverend Trent," say Task, glancin from left to right like they hatchin a plot and just now lettin me in on it. "You were suppose to be talking with him tonight, Mama, about giving us his basement for campaign headquarters and—"

"Didn nobody tell me nuthin. If grass roots mean you kept in the dark I can't use it. I really can't. And Reven Trent a fool anyway the way he tore into the widow man up there on Edgecomb cause he wouldn't take in three of them foster children and the woman not even comfy in the ground yet and the man's mind messed up and—"

"Look here," say Task. "What we need is a family conference so we can get all this stuff cleared up and laid out on the table. In the meantime I think we better get back into the other room and tend to business. And in the meantime, Mama, see if you can't get to Reverend Trent and—"

"You want me to belly rub with the Reven, that it?"

"Oh damn," Elo say and go through the swingin door.

"We'll talk about all this at dinner. How's tomorrow night, Joe Lee?" While Joe Lee being self-important I'm wonderin who's doin the cookin and how come no body ax me if I'm free and do I get a corsage and things like that. Then Joe nod that it's O.K. and he go through the swingin door and just a little hubbub come through from the other room. Then Task smile his smile, lookin just like his daddy and he leave. And it just me in this stranger's kitchen, which was a mess I wouldn't never let my kitchen look like. Poison you just to look at the pots. Then the door swing the other way and it's My Man Bovanne standin there sayin Miss Hazel but lookin at the deep fry and then at the steam table, and most surprised when I come up on him from the other direction and take him on out of there. Pass the folks pushin up towards the stage where Nisi and some other people settin and ready to talk, and folks gettin to the last of the sandwiches and the booze fore they settle down in one spot and listen serious. And I'm thinkin bout tellin Bovanne what a lovely long dress Nisi got on and the earrings and her hair piled up in a cone and the people bout to hear how we all getting screwed and gotta form our own party and everybody there listenin and lookin. But instead I just haul the man on out of there, and Joe Lee and his wife look at me like I'm terrible, but they ain't said boo to the man yet. Cause he blind and old and don't nobody there need him since they grown up and don't need they skates fixed no more.

"Where we goin, Miss Hazel?" Him knowin all the time.

"First we gonna buy you some dark sunglasses. Then you comin with me to the supermarket so I can pick up tomorrow's dinner, which is goin to be a grand thing proper and you invited. Then we goin to my house."

"That be fine. I surely would like to rest my feet." Bein cute, but you got to let men play out they little show, blind or not. So he chat on bout how tired he is and how he appreciate me takin him in hand this way. And I'm thinkin I'll have him change the lock on my door first thing. Then I'll give the man a nice warm bath with jasmine leaves in the water and a little Epsom salt on the sponge to do his back. And then a good rubdown with rose water and olive oil. Then a cup of lemon tea with a taste in it. And a little talcum, some of that fancy stuff Nisi mother sent over last Christmas. And then a massage, a good face massage round the forehead which is the worryin part. Cause you gots to take care of the older folks. And let them know they still needed to run the mimeo machine and keep the spark plugs clean and fix the mailboxes for folks who might help us get the breakfast program goin, and the school for the little kids and the campaign and all. Cause old folks is the nation. That what Nisi was sayin and I mean to do my part.

"I imagine you are a very pretty woman, Miss Hazel."

"I surely am," I say just like the hussy my daughter always say I was.

1972

HENRY JAMES

The Real Thing

I

When the porter's wife, who used to answer the house-bell, announced "A gentleman and a lady, sir" I had, as I often had in those days—the wish being father to the thought—an immediate vision of sitters. Sitters my visitors in this case proved to be; but not in the sense I should have preferred. There was nothing at first however to indicate that they mightn't have come for a portrait. The gentleman, a man of fifty, very high and very straight, with a moustache slightly grizzled and a dark grey walking-coat admirably fitted, both of which I noted professionally—I don't mean as a barber or yet as a tailor—would have struck me as a celebrity if celebrities often were striking. It was a truth of which I had for some time been conscious that a figure with a good deal of frontage was, as one might say, almost never a public institution. A glance at the lady helped to remind me of this paradoxical law: she also looked too distinguished to be a "personality." Moreover one would scarcely come across two variations together.

Neither of the pair immediately spoke—they only prolonged the preliminary gaze suggesting that each wished to give the other a chance. They were visibly shy; they stood there letting me take them in—which, as I afterwards perceived, was the most practical thing they could have done. In this way their embarrassment served their cause. I had seen people painfully reluctant to mention that they desired anything so gross as to be represented on canvas; but the scruples of my new friends appeared almost insurmountable. Yet the gentleman might have said "I should like a portrait of my wife," and the lady might have said "I should like a portrait of my husband." Perhaps they weren't husband and wife—this naturally would make the matter more delicate. Perhaps they wished to be done together—in which case they ought to have brought a third person to break the news.

"We come from Mr. Rivet," the lady finally said with a dim smile that had the effect of a moist sponge passed over a "sunk"[1] piece of painting, as well as of a vague allusion to vanished beauty. She was as tall and straight, in her degree, as her companion, and with ten years less to carry. She looked as sad as a woman could look whose face was not charged with expression; that is her tinted oval mask showed waste as an exposed surface shows friction. The hand of time had played over her freely, but to an effect of elimination. She was slim and stiff, and so well-dressed, in dark blue cloth, with lappets and pockets and buttons, that it was clear she employed the same tailor as her husband. The couple had an indefinable air of prosperous thrift—they evidently got a good deal of luxury for their money. If I was to be one of their luxuries it would behove me to consider my terms.

"Ah, Claude Rivet recommended me?" I echoed; and I added that it was very kind of him, though I could reflect that, as he only painted landscape, this wasn't a sacrifice.

The lady looked very hard at the gentleman, and the gentleman looked round the room. Then staring at the floor a moment and stroking his moustache, he rested his pleasant eyes on me with the remark: "He said you were the right one."

"I try to be, when people want to sit."

"Yes, we should like to," said the lady anxiously.

"Do you mean together?"

My visitors exchanged a glance. "If you could do anything with *me* I suppose it would be double," the gentleman stammered.

"Oh yes, there's naturally a higher charge for two figures than for one."

"We should like to make it pay," the husband confessed.

"That's very good of you," I returned, appreciating so unwonted a sympathy—for I supposed he meant pay the artist.

A sense of strangeness seemed to draw on the lady.

"We mean for the illustrations—Mr. Rivet said you might put one in."

"Put in—an illustration?" I was equally confused.

"Sketch her off, you know," said the gentleman, colouring.

It was only then that I understood the service Claude Rivet had rendered me; he had told them how I worked in black-and-white, for magazines, for storybooks, for sketches of contemporary life, and consequently had copious employment for models. These things were true, but it was not less true—I may confess it now; whether because the aspiration was to lead to everything or to nothing I leave the reader to guess—that I couldn't get the honours, to say nothing of the emoluments, of a great painter of portraits out of my head. My "illustrations" were my pot-boilers; I looked to a different branch of art—far and away the most interesting it had always seemed to me—to perpetuate my fame. There was no shame in looking to it also to make my fortune; but that fortune was by so much further from being made from the moment my visitors wished to be "done" for nothing. I was disappointed; for in the pictorial sense I had immediately *seen* them. I had seized their type—I had already settled what I would do with it.

1. When colors lose their brilliance after they have dried on the canvas, they have "sunk in."

Something that wouldn't absolutely have pleased them, I afterwards reflected.

"Ah you're—you're—a—?" I began as soon as I had mastered my surprise. I couldn't bring out the dingy word "models": it seemed so little to fit the case.

"We haven't had much practice," said the lady.

"We've got to *do* something, and we've thought that an artist in your line might perhaps make something of us," her husband threw off. He further mentioned that they didn't know many artists and that they had gone first, on the off-chance—he painted views of course, but sometimes put in figures; perhaps I remembered—to Mr. Rivet, whom they had met a few years before at a place in Norfolk where he was sketching.

"We used to sketch a little ourselves," the lady hinted.

"It's very awkward, but we absolutely *must* do something," her husband went on.

"Of course we're not so *very* young," she admitted with a wan smile.

With the remark that I might as well know something more about them the husband had handed me a card extracted from a neat new pocket-book—their appurtenances were all of the freshest—and inscribed with the words "Major Monarch." Impressive as these words were they didn't carry my knowledge much further; but my visitor presently added: "I've left the army and we've had the misfortune to lose our money. In fact our means are dreadfully small."

"It's awfully trying—a regular strain," said Mrs. Monarch.

They evidently wished to be discreet—to take care not to swagger because they were gentlefolk. I felt them willing to recognise this as something of a drawback, at the same time that I guessed at an underlying sense—their consolation in adversity—that they *had* their points. They certainly had; but these advantages struck me as preponderantly social; such for instance as would help to make a drawing-room look well. However, a drawing-room was always, or ought to be, a picture.

In consequence of his wife's allusion to their age Major Monarch observed: "Naturally it's more for the figure that we thought of going in. We can still hold ourselves up." On the instant I saw that the figure was indeed their strong point. His "naturally" didn't sound vain, but it lighted up the question. "*She* has the best one," he continued, nodding at his wife with a pleasant after-dinner absence of circumlocution. I could only reply, as if we were in fact sitting over our wine, that this didn't prevent his own from being very good; which led him in turn to make answer: "We thought that if you ever have to do people like us we might be something like it. *She* particularly—for a lady in a book, you know."

I was so amused by them that, to get more of it, I did my best to take their point of view; and though it was an embarrassment to find myself appraising physically, as if they were animals on hire or useful blacks, a pair whom I should have expected to meet only in one of the relations in which criticism is tacit, I looked at Mrs. Monarch judicially enough to be able to exclaim after a moment with conviction: "Oh yes, a lady in a book!" She was singularly like a bad illustration.

"We'll stand up, if you like," said the Major; and he raised himself before me with a really grand air.

I could take his measure at a glance—he was six feet two and a perfect gentleman. It would have paid any club in process of formation and in want of a stamp to engage him at a salary to stand in the principal window. What struck me at once was that in coming to me they had rather missed their vocation; they could surely have been turned to better account for advertising purposes. I couldn't of course see the thing in detail, but I could see them make somebody's fortune—I don't mean their own. There was something in them for a waistcoat-maker, an hotel-keeper or a soap-vendor. I could imagine "We always use it" pinned on their bosoms with the greatest effect; I had a vision of the brilliancy with which they would launch a table d'hôte.

Mrs. Monarch sat still, not from pride but from shyness, and presently her husband said to her; "Get up, my dear, and show how smart you are." She obeyed, but she had no need to get up to show it. She walked to the end of the studio and then came back blushing, her fluttered eyes on the partner of her appeal. I was reminded of an incident I had accidentally had a glimpse of in Paris being with a friend there, a dramatist about to produce a play, when an actress came to him to ask to be entrusted with a part. She went through her paces before him, walked up and down as Mrs. Monarch was doing. Mrs. Monarch did it quite as well, but I abstained from applauding. It was very odd to see such people apply for such poor pay. She looked as if she had ten thousand a year. Her husband had used the word that described her: she was in the London current jargon essentially and typically "smart." Her figure was, in the same order of ideas, conspicuously and irreproachably "good." For a woman of her age her waist was surprisingly small; her elbow moreover had the orthodox crook. She held her head at the conventional angle, but why did she come to *me*? She ought to have tried on jackets at a big shop. I feared my visitors were not only destitute but "artistic"—which would be a great complication. When she sat down again I thanked her, observing that what a draughtsman most valued in his model was the faculty of keeping quiet.

"Oh *she* can keep quiet," said Major Monarch. Then he added jocosely: "I've always kept her quiet."

"I'm not a nasty fidget, am I?" It was going to wring tears from me, I felt, the way she hid her head, ostrich-like, in the other's broad bosom.

The owner of this expanse addressed his answer to me. "Perhaps it isn't out of place to mention—because we ought to be quite business-like, oughtn't we?—that when I married her she was known as the Beautiful Statue."

"Oh dear!" said Mrs. Monarch ruefully.

"Of course I should want a certain amount of expression," I rejoined.

"Of *course*!"—and I had never heard such unanimity.

"And then I suppose you know that you'll get awfully tired."

"Oh we *never* get tired!" they eagerly cried.

"Have you had any kind of practice?"

They hesitated—they looked at each other. "We've been photographed—*immensely*," said Mrs. Monarch.

"She means the fellows have asked us themselves," added the Major.

"I see—because you're so good-looking."

"I don't know what they thought, but they were always after us."

"We always got our photographs for nothing," smiled Mrs. Monarch.

"We might have brought some, my dear," her husband remarked.

"I'm not sure we have any left. We've given quantities away," she explained to me.

"With our autographs and that sort of thing," said the Major.

"Are they to be got in the shops?" I enquired as a harmless pleasantry.

"Oh yes, *hers*—they used to be."

"Not now," said Mrs. Monarch with her eyes on the floor.

II

I could fancy the "sort of thing" they put on the presentation copies of their photographs, and I was sure they wrote a beautiful hand. It was odd how quickly I was sure of everything that concerned them. If they were now so poor as to have to earn shillings and pence they could never have had much of a margin. Their good looks had been their capital, and they had good-humouredly made the most of the career that this resource marked out for them. It was in their faces, the blankness, the deep intellectual repose of the twenty years of country-house visiting that had given them pleasant intonations. I could see the sunny drawing-rooms, sprinkled with periodicals she didn't read, in which Mrs. Monarch had continuously sat; I could see the wet shrubberies in which she had walked, equipped to admiration for either exercise. I could see the rich covers[2] the Major had helped to shoot and the wonderful garments in which, late at night, he repaired to the smoking-room to talk about them. I could imagine their leggings and waterproofs, their knowing tweeds and rugs, their rolls of sticks and cases of tackle and neat umbrellas; and I could evoke the exact appearance of their servants and the compact variety of their luggage on the platforms of country stations.

They gave small tips, but they were liked; they didn't do anything themselves, but they were welcome. They looked so well everywhere; they gratified the general relish for stature, complexion and "form." They knew it without fatuity or vulgarity, and they respected themselves in consequence. They weren't superficial; they were thorough and kept themselves up—it had been their line. People with such a taste for activity had to have some line. I could feel how even in a dull house they could have been counted on for the joy of life. At present something had happened—it didn't matter what, their little income had grown less, it had grown least—and they had to do something for pocket-money. Their friends could like them, I made out, without liking to support them. There was something about them that represented credit—their clothes, their manners, their type; but if credit is a large empty pocket in which an occasional chink reverberates, the chink at least must be audible. What they wanted of me was to help to make it so. Fortunately they had no children—I soon divined that. They would also perhaps wish our relations to be kept secret: this was why it was "for the

2. Flocks of game birds.

figure"— the reproduction of the face would betray them.

I liked them—I felt, quite as their friends must have done—they were so simple; and I had no objection to them if they would suit. But somehow with all their perfections I didn't easily believe in them. After all they were amateurs, and the ruling passion of my life was the detestation of the amateur. Combined with this was another perversity—an innate preference for the represented subject over the real one: the defect of the real one was so apt to be a lack of representation. I liked things that appeared; then one was sure. Whether they *were* or not was a subordinate and almost always a profitless question. There were other considerations, the first of which was that I already had two or three recruits in use, notably a young person with big feet, in alpaca, from Kilburn, who for a couple of years had come to me regularly for my illustrations and with whom I was still—perhaps ignobly—satisfied. I frankly explained to my visitors how the case stood, but they had taken more precautions than I supposed. They had reasoned out their opportunity, for Claude Rivet had told them of the projected *édition de luxe* of one of the writers of our day—the rarest of the novelists—who, long neglected by the multitudinous vulgar and dearly prized by the attentive (need I mention Philip Vincent?) had had the happy fortune of seeing, late in life, the dawn and then the full light of a higher criticism; an estimate in which on the part of the public there was something really of expiation. The edition preparing, planned by a publisher of taste, was practically an act of high reparation; the wood-cuts with which it was to be enriched were the homage of English art to one of the most independent representatives of English letters. Major and Mrs. Monarch confessed to me they had hoped I might be able to work *them* into my branch of the enterprise. They knew I was to do the first of the books, "Rutland Ramsay," but I had to make clear to them that my participation in the rest of the affair—this first book was to be a test—must depend on the satisfaction I should give. If this should be limited my employers would drop me with scarce common forms. It was therefore a crisis for me, and naturally I was making special preparations, looking about for new people, should they be necessary, and securing the best types. I admitted however that I should like to settle down to two or three good models who would do for everything.

"Should we have often to—a—put on special clothes?" Mrs. Monarch timidly demanded.

"Dear yes—that's half the business."

"And should we be expected to supply our own costumes?"

"Oh no; I've got a lot of things. A painter's models put on—or put off—anything he likes."

"And you mean—a—the same?"

"The same?"

Mrs. Monarch looked at her husband again.

"Oh she was just wondering," he explained, "if the costumes are in *general* use." I had to confess that they were, and I mentioned further that some of them—I had a lot of genuine greasy last-century things—had served their time, a hundred years ago, on living world-stained men and women; on figures not perhaps so far removed, in that vanished world, from *their* type, the Monarchs', *quoi!*[3] of a breeched and bewigged age. "We'll put on anything that *fits*," said the Major.

"Oh I arrange that—they fit in the pictures."

"I'm afraid I should do better for the modern books. I'd come as you like," said Mrs. Monarch.

"She has got a lot of clothes at home: they might do for contemporary life," her husband continued.

"Oh I can fancy scenes in which you'd be quite natural." And indeed I could see the slipshod rearrangements of stale properties—the stories I tried to produce pictures for without the exasperation of reading them—whose sandy tracts the good lady might help to people. But I had to return to the fact that for this sort of work—the daily mechanical grind—I was already equipped: the people I was working with were fully adequate.

"We only thought we might be more like *some* characters," said Mrs. Monarch mildly, getting up.

Her husband also rose; he stood looking at me with a dim wistfulness that was touching in so fine a man.

"Wouldn't it be rather a pull sometimes to have—a—to have—?" He hung fire; he wanted me to help him by phrasing what he meant. But I couldn't—I didn't know. So he brought it out awkwardly: "The *real* thing; a gentleman, you know, or a lady." I was quite ready to give a general assent—I admitted that there was a great deal in that. This encouraged Major Monarch to say, following up his appeal with an unacted gulp: "It's awfully hard—we've tried everything." The gulp was communicative; it proved too much for his wife. Before I knew it Mrs. Monarch had dropped again upon a divan and burst into tears. Her husband sat down beside her, holding one of her hands; whereupon she quickly dried her eyes with the other, while I felt embarrassed as she looked up at me. "There isn't a confounded job I haven't applied for—waited for—prayed for. You can fancy we'd be pretty bad first. Secretaryships and that sort of thing? You might as well ask for a peerage. I'd be *anything*—I'm strong; a messenger or a coalheaver. I'd put on a gold-laced cap and open carriage-doors in front of the haberdasher's; I'd hang about a station to carry portmanteaux; I'd be a postman. But they won't *look* at you; there are thousands as good as yourself already on the ground. *Gentlemen*, poor beggars, who've drunk their wine, who've kept their hunters!"

I was as reassuring as I knew how to be, and my visitors were presently on their feet again while, for the experiment, we agreed on an hour. We were discussing it when the door opened and Miss Churm came in with a wet umbrella. Miss Churm had to take the omnibus to Maida Vale and then walk half a mile. She looked a trifle blowsy and slightly splashed. I scarcely ever saw her come in without thinking fresh how odd it was that, being so little in herself, she should yet be so much in others. She was a meagre little Miss Churm, but was such an ample heroine of romance. She was only a freckled cockney, but she could represent everything, from a fine lady to a shepherdess; she had the faculty as she might have had a fine voice or long hair. She couldn't spell and she loved

3. Whatever.

beer, but she had two or three "points," and practice, and a knack, and mother-wit, and a whimsical sensibility, and a love of the theatre, and seven sisters, and not an ounce of respect, especially for the *h*.[4] The first thing my visitors saw was that her umbrella was wet, and in their spotless perfection they visibly winced at it. The rain had come on since their arrival.

"I'm all in a soak; there *was* a mess of people in the 'bus. I wish you lived near a stytion," said Miss Churm. I requested her to get ready as quickly as possible, and she passed into the room in which she always changed her dress. But before going out she asked me what she was to get into this time.

"It's the Russian princess, don't you know?" I answered; "the one with the 'golden eyes,' in black velvet, for the long thing in the *Cheapside*."

"Golden eyes? I *say!*" cried Miss Churm, while my companions watched her with intensity as she withdrew. She always arranged herself, when she was late, before I could turn around; and I kept my visitors a little on purpose, so that they might get an idea, from seeing her, what would be expected of themselves. I mentioned that she was quite my notion of an excellent model—she was really very clever.

"Do you think she looks like a Russian princess?" Major Monarch asked with lurking alarm.

"When I make her, yes."

"Oh if you have to *make* her—!" he reasoned, not without point.

"That's the most you can ask. There are so many who are not makeable."

"Well now, *here's* a lady"—and with a persuasive smile he passed his arm into his wife's—"who's already made!"

"Oh I'm not a Russian princess," Mrs. Monarch protested a little coldly. I could see she had known some and didn't like them. There at once was a complication of a kind I never had to fear with Miss Churm.

This young lady came back in black velvet—the gown was rather rusty and very low on her lean shoulders—and with a Japanese fan in her red hands. I reminded her that in the scene I was doing she had to look over some one's head. "I forget whose it is; but it doesn't matter. Just look over a head."

"I'd rather look over a stove," said Miss Churm; and she took her station near the fire. She fell into position, settled herself into a tall attitude, gave a certain backward inclination to her head and a certain forward droop to her fan, and looked, at least to my prejudiced sense, distinguished and charming, foreign and dangerous. We left her looking so while I went downstairs with Major and Mrs. Monarch.

"I believe I could come about as near it as that," said Mrs. Monarch.

"Oh, you think she's shabby, but you must allow for the alchemy of art."

However, they went off with an evident increase of comfort founded on their demonstrable advantage in being the real thing. I could fancy them shuddering over Miss Churm. She was very droll about them when I went back, for I told her what they wanted.

"Well, if *she* can sit I'll tyke to bookkeeping," said my model.

4. Working-class Londoners, especially in the East End (cockneys), drop *h*'s 'orribly.

"She's very ladylike," I replied as an innocent form of aggravation.

"So much the worse for *you*. That means she can't turn round."

"She'll do for the fashionable novels."

"Oh yes, she'll *do* for them!" my model humorously declared. "Ain't they bad enough without her?" I had often sociably denounced them to Miss Churm.

III

It was for the elucidation of a mystery in one of these works that I first tried Mrs. Monarch. Her husband came with her, to be useful if necessary—it was sufficiently clear that as a general thing he would prefer to come with her. At first I wondered if this were for "propriety's" sake—if he were going to be jealous and meddling. The idea was too tiresome, and if it had been confirmed it would speedily have brought our acquaintance to a close. But I soon saw there was nothing in it and that if he accompanied Mrs. Monarch it was—in addition to the chance of being wanted—simply because he had nothing else to do. When they were separate his occupation was gone and they never *had* been separate. I judged rightly that in their awkward situation their close union was their main comfort and that this union had no weak spot. It was a real marriage, an encouragement to the hesitating, a nut for pessimists to crack. Their address was humble—I remember afterwards thinking it had been the only thing about them that was really professional—and I could fancy the lamentable lodgings in which the Major would have been left alone. He could sit there more or less grimly with his wife—he couldn't sit there anyhow without her.

He had too much tact to try and make himself agreeable when he couldn't be useful; so when I was too absorbed in my work to talk he simply sat and waited. But I liked to hear him talk—it made my work, when not interrupting it, less mechanical, less special. To listen to him was to combine the excitement of going out with the economy of staying at home. There was only one hindrance—that I seemed not to know any of the people this brilliant couple had known. I think he wondered extremely, during the term of our intercourse, whom the deuce I *did* know. He hadn't a stray sixpence of an idea to fumble for, so we didn't spin it very fine; we confined ourselves to questions of leather and even of liquor—saddlers and breeches-makers and how to get excellent claret cheap—and matters like "good trains" and the habits of small game. His lore on these last subjects was astonishing—he managed to interweave the station-master with the ornithologist. When he couldn't talk about greater things he could talk cheerfully about smaller, and since I couldn't accompany him into reminiscences of the fashionable world he could lower the conversation without a visible effort to my level.

So earnest a desire to please was touching in a man who could so easily have knocked one down. He looked after the fire and had an opinion on the draught of the stove without my asking him, and I could see that he thought many of my arrangements not half knowing. I remember telling him that if I were only rich I'd offer him a salary to come and teach me how to live. Sometimes he gave a random sigh of which the essence might have been: "Give me even such a bare old barrack as *this*, and I'd do something with it!" When I wanted to use him he came alone; which was an illustration of the superior courage of women. His wife could bear her solitary second floor, and she was in general more discreet; showing by various small reserves that she was alive to the propriety of keeping our relations markedly professional—not letting them slide into sociability. She wished it to remain clear that she and the Major were employed, not cultivated, and if she approved of me as a superior, who could be kept in his place, she never thought me quite good enough for an equal.

She sat with great intensity, giving the whole of her mind to it, and was capable of remaining for an hour almost as motionless as before a photographer's lens. I could see she had been photographed often, but somehow the very habit that made her good for that purpose unfitted her for mine. At first I was extremely pleased with her ladylike air, and it was a satisfaction, on coming to follow her lines, to see how good they were and how far they could lead the pencil. But after a little skirmishing I began to find her too insurmountably stiff; do what I would with it my drawing looked like a photograph or a copy of a photograph. Her figure had no variety of expression—she herself had no sense of variety. You may say that this was my business and was only a question of placing her. Yet I placed her in every conceivable position and she managed to obliterate their differences. She was always a lady certainly, and into the bargain was always the same lady. She was the real thing, but always the same thing. There were moments when I rather writhed under the serenity of her confidence that she *was* the real thing. All her dealings with me and all her husband's were an implication that this was lucky for *me*. Meanwhile I found myself trying to invent types that approached her own, instead of making her own transform itself—in the clever way that was not impossible for instance to poor Miss Churm. Arrange as I would and take the precautions I would, she always came out, in my pictures, too tall—landing me in the dilemma of having represented a fascinating woman as seven feet high, which (out of respect perhaps to my own very much scantier inches) was far from my idea of such personage.

The case was worse with the Major—nothing I could do would keep *him* down, so that he became useful only for representation of brawny giants. I adored variety and range, I cherished human accidents, the illustrative note; I wanted to characterise closely, and the thing in the world I most hated was the danger of being ridden by a type. I had quarrelled with some of my friends about it; I had parted company with them for maintaining that one *had* to be, and that if the type was beautiful—witness Raphael and Leonardo[5]—the servitude was only a gain. I was neither Leonardo nor Raphael—I might only be a presumptuous young modern searcher; but I held that everything was to be sacrificed sooner than character. When they claimed that the obsessional form could easily *be* character I retorted, perhaps superficially, "Whose?" It couldn't be everybody's—it might end in being nobody's.

After I had drawn Mrs. Monarch a dozen times I felt surer even than before 95

5. Raffaello Sanzio (1483–1520), Leonardo da Vinci (1452–1519), famous Italian Renaissance painters. Leonardo, of course, was also an inventor, military engineer, architect, sculptor, anatomist, etc.

that the value of such a model as Miss Churm resided precisely in the fact that she had no positive stamp, combined of course with the other fact that what she did have was a curious and inexplicable talent for imitation. Her usual appearance was like a curtain which she could draw up at request for a capital performance. This performance was simply suggestive; but it was a word to the wise—it was vivid and pretty. Sometimes even I thought it, though she was plain herself, too insipidly pretty; I made it a reproach to her that the figures drawn from her were monotonously (*bêtement*,[6] as we used to say) graceful. Nothing made her more angry: it was so much of her pride to feel she could sit for characters that had nothing in common with each other. She would accuse me at such moments of taking away her "reputytion."

It suffered a certain shrinkage, this queer quantity, from the repeated visits of my new friends. Miss Churm was greatly in demand, never in want of employment, so I had no scruple in putting her off occasionally, to try them more at my ease. It was certainly amusing at first to do the real thing—it was amusing to do Major Monarch's trousers. They *were* the real thing, even if he did come out colossal. It was amusing to do his wife's back hair—it was so mathematically neat—and the particular "smart" tension of her tight stays. She lent herself especially to positions in which the face was somewhat averted or blurred; she abounded in ladylike back views and *profils perdus*.[7] When she stood erect she took naturally one of the attitudes in which court-painters represent queens and princesses; so that I found myself wondering whether, to draw out this accomplishment, I couldn't get the editor of the *Cheapside* to publish a really royal romance, "A Tale of Buckingham Palace." Sometimes however the real thing and the make-believe came into contact; by which I mean that Miss Churm, keeping an appointment or coming to make one on days when I had much work in hand, encountered her invidious rivals. The encounter was not on their part, for they noticed her no more than if she had been the housemaid; not from intentional loftiness, but simply because as yet, professionally, they didn't know how to fraternise, as I could imagine they would have liked—or at least that the Major would. They couldn't talk about the omnibus—they always walked; and they didn't know what else to try—she wasn't interested in good trains or cheap claret. Besides, they must have felt—in the air—that she was amused at them, secretly derisive of their ever knowing how. She wasn't a person to conceal the limits of her faith if she had had a chance to show them. On the other hand Mrs. Monarch didn't think her tidy; for why else did she take pains to say to me—it was going out of the way, for Mrs. Monarch—that she didn't like dirty women?

One day when my young lady happened to be present with my other sitters—she even dropped in, when it was convenient, for a chat—I asked her to be so good as to lend a hand in getting tea, a service with which she was familiar and which was one of a class that, living as I did in a small way, with slender domestic resources, I often appealed to my models to render. They liked to lay hands on my property, to break the sitting, and sometimes the china—it made them

6. Foolishly. 7. Incomplete profile, showing more of the back of the head and less of the face.

feel Bohemian. The next time I saw Miss Churm after this incident she surprised me greatly by making a scene about it—she accused me of having wished to humiliate her. She hadn't resented the outrage at the time, but had seemed obliging and amused, enjoying the comedy of asking Mrs. Monarch, who sat vague and silent, whether she would have cream and sugar, and putting an exaggerated simper into the question. She had tried intonations—as if she too wished to pass for the real thing—till I was afraid my other visitors would take offence.

Oh they were determined not to do this, and their touching patience was the measure of their great need. They would sit by the hour, uncomplaining, till I was ready to use them; they would come back on the chance of being wanted and would walk away cheerfully if it failed. I used to go to the door with them to see in what magnificent order they retreated. I tried to find other employment for them—I introduced them to several artists. But they didn't "take," for reasons I could appreciate, and I became rather anxiously aware that after such disappointments they fell back upon me with a heavier weight. They did me the honor to think me most *their* form. They weren't romantic enough for the painters, and in those days there were few serious workers in black-and-white. Besides, they had an eye to the great job I had mentioned to them—they had secretly set their hearts on supplying the right essence for my pictorial vindication of our fine novelist. They knew that for this undertaking I should want no costume-effects, none of the frippery of past ages—that it was a case in which everything would be contemporary and satirical and presumably genteel. If I could work them into it their future would be assured, for the labour would of course be long and the occupation steady.

One day Mrs. Monarch came without her husband—she explained his absence by his having had to go to the City.[8] While she sat there in her usual relaxed majesty there came at the door a knock which I immediately recognised as the subdued appeal of a model out of work. It was followed by the entrance of a young man whom I at once saw to be a foreigner and who proved in fact an Italian acquainted with no English word but my name, which he uttered in a way that made it seem to include all others. I hadn't then visited his country, nor was I proficient in his tongue; but as he was not so meanly constituted—what Italian is?—as to depend only on that member for expression he conveyed to me, in familiar but graceful mimicry, that he was in search of exactly the employment in which the lady before me was engaged. I was not struck with him at first, and while I continued to draw I dropped few signs of interest or encouragement. He stood his ground however—not importunately, but with a dumb dog-like fidelity in his eyes that amounted to innocent impudence, the manner of a devoted servant—he might have been in the house for years—unjustly suspected. Suddenly it struck me that this very attitude and expression made a picture; whereupon I told him to sit down and wait till I should be free. There was another picture in the way he obeyed me, and I observed as I worked that there were others still in the way he looked wonderingly, with his head

8. Financial and legal center of London.

thrown back, about the high studio. He might have been crossing himself in Saint Peter's. Before I finished I said to myself "The fellow's a bankrupt orange-monger, but a treasure."

100 When Mrs. Monarch withdrew he passed across the room like a flash to open the door for her, standing there with the rapt pure gaze of the young Dante spellbound by the young Beatrice.[9] As I never insisted, in such situations, on the blankness of the British domestic, I reflected that he had the making of a servant—and I needed one, but couldn't pay him to be only that—as well as of a model; in short I resolved to adopt my bright adventurer if he would agree to officiate in the double capacity. He jumped at my offer, and in the event my rashness—for I had really known nothing about him—wasn't brought home to me. He proved a sympathetic though a desultory ministrant, and had in a wonderful degree the *sentiment de la pose*.[1] It was uncultivated, instinctive, a part of the happy instinct that had guided him to my door and helped him to spell out my name on the card nailed to it. He had had no other introduction to me than a guess, from the shape of my high north window, seen outside, that my place was a studio and that as a studio it would contain an artist. He had wandered to England in search of fortune, like other itinerants, and had embarked, with a partner and a small green hand-cart, on the sale of penny ices. The ices had melted away and the partner had dissolved in their train. My young man wore tight yellow trousers with reddish stripes and his name was Oronte. He was sallow but fair, and when I put him into some old clothes of my own he looked like an Englishman. He was as good as Miss Churm, who could look, when requested, like an Italian.

IV

I thought Mrs. Monarch's face slightly convulsed when, on her coming back with her husband, she found Oronte installed. It was strange to have to recognise in a scrap of a lazzarone[2] a competitor to her magnificent Major. It was she who scented danger first, for the Major was anecdotically unconscious. But Oronte gave us tea, with a hundred eager confusions—he had never been concerned in so queer a process—and I think she thought better of me for having at last an "establishment." They saw a couple of drawings that I had made of the establishment, and Mrs. Monarch hinted that it never would have struck her he had sat for them. "Now the drawings you make from *us*, they look exactly like us," she reminded me, smiling in triumph; and I recognized that this was indeed just their defect. When I drew the Monarchs I couldn't anyhow get away from them—get into the character I wanted to represent; and I hadn't the least desire my model should be discoverable in my picture. Miss Churm never was, and Mrs. Monarch thought I hid her, very properly, because she was vulgar; whereas if

9. Dante Alighieri (1265–1321), Italian poet, author of *The Divine Comedy*, was inspired for his whole lifetime poetically and spiritually by Beatrice Portinari whom he first saw when they were children and saw only infrequently thereafter. 1. Instinct for striking poses. 2. Street-person.

she was lost it was only as the dead who go to heaven are lost—in the gain of an angel the more.

By this time I had got a certain start with "Rutland Ramsay," the first novel in the great projected series; that is I had produced a dozen drawings, several with the help of the Major and his wife, and I had sent them in for approval. My understanding with the publishers, as I have already hinted, had been that I was to be left to do my work, in this particular case, as I liked, with the whole book committed to me; but my connexion with the rest of the series was only contingent. There were moments when, frankly, it *was* a comfort to have the real thing under one's hand; for there were characters in "Rutland Ramsay" that were very much like it. There were people presumably as erect as the Major and women of as good a fashion as Mrs. Monarch. There was a great deal of country-house life—treated, it is true, in a fine fanciful ironical generalised way—and there was a considerable implication of knickerbockers and kilts. There were certain things I had to settle at the outset; such things for instance as the exact appearance of the hero and the particular bloom and figure of the heroine. The author of course gave me a lead, but there was a margin for interpretation. I took the Monarchs into my confidence, I told them frankly what I was about, I mentioned my embarrassments and alternatives. "Oh take *him!*" Mrs. Monarch murmured sweetly, looking at her husband; and "What could you want better than my wife?" the Major enquired with the comfortable candour that now prevailed between us.

I wasn't obliged to answer these remarks—I was only obliged to place my sitters. I wasn't easy in mind, and I postponed a little timidly perhaps the solving of my question. The book was a large canvas, the other figures were numerous, and I worked off at first some of the episodes in which the hero and the heroine were not concerned. When once I had set *them* up I should have to stick to them—I couldn't make my young man seven feet high in one place and five feet nine in another. I inclined on the whole to the latter measurement, though the Major more than once reminded me that *he* looked about as young as any one. It was indeed quite possible to arrange him, for the figure, so that it would have been difficult to detect his age. After the spontaneous Oronte had been with me a month, and after I had given him to understand several times over that his native exuberance would presently constitute an insurmountable barrier to our further intercourse, I waked to a sense of his heroic capacity. He was only five feet seven, but the remaining inches were latent. I tried him almost secretly at first, for I was really rather afraid of the judgment my other models would pass on such a choice. If they regarded Miss Churm as little better than a snare what would they think of the representation by a person so little the real thing as an Italian street-vendor of a protagonist formed by a public school?

If I went a little in fear of them it wasn't because they bullied me, because they had got an oppressive foothold, but because in their really pathetic decorum and mysteriously permanent newness they counted on me so intensely. I was therefore very glad when Jack Hawley came home: he was always of such good counsel. He painted badly himself, but there was no one like him for putting his finger on the place. He had been absent from England for a year; he had been somewhere—I don't remember where—to get a fresh eye. I was in a good deal of dread of any such organ, but we were old friends; he had been away for months and a sense of emptiness was creeping into my life. I hadn't dodged a missile for a year.

He came back with a fresh eye, but with the same old black velvet blouse, and the first evening he spent in my studio we smoked cigarettes till the small hours. He had done no work himself, he had only got the eye; so the field was clear for the production of my little things. He wanted to see what I had produced for the *Cheapside*, but he was disappointed in the exhibition. That at least seemed the meaning of two or three comprehensive groans which, as he lounged on my big divan, his leg folded under him, looking at my latest drawings, issued from his lips with the smoke of the cigarette.

"What's the matter with you?" I asked.

"What's the matter with *you?*"

"Nothing save that I'm mystified."

"You are indeed. You're quite off the hinge. What's the meaning of this new fad?" And he tossed me, with visible irreverence, a drawing in which I happened to have depicted both my elegant models. I asked if he didn't think it good, and he replied that it struck him as execrable, given the sort of thing I had always represented myself to him as wishing to arrive at; but I let that pass—I was so anxious to see exactly what he meant. The two figures in the picture looked colossal, but I supposed this was *not* what he meant, inasmuch as, for aught he knew the contrary, I might have been trying for some such effect. I maintained that I was working exactly in the same way as when he last had done me the honour to tell me I might do something some day. "Well, there's a screw loose somewhere," he answered; "wait a bit and I'll discover it." I depended upon him to do so: where else was the fresh eye? But he produced at last nothing more luminous than "I don't know—I don't like your types." This was lame for a critic who had never consented to discuss with me anything but the question of execution, the direction of strokes and the mystery of values.

"In the drawings you've been looking at I think my types are very handsome."

"Oh they won't do!"

"I've been working with new models."

"I see you have. *They* won't do."

"Are you very sure of that?"

"Absolutely—they're stupid."

"You mean *I* am—for I ought to get round that."

"You *can't*—with such people. Who are they?"

I told him, so far as was necessary, and he concluded heartlessly: "Ce sont des gens qu'il faut mettre à la porte."[3]

"You've never seen them; they're awfully good"—I flew to their defence.

"Not seen them? Why all this recent work of yours drops to pieces with them. It's all I want to see of them."

"No one else has said anything against it—the *Cheapside* people are pleased."

3. That kind of person should be shown the door.

"Everyone else is an ass, and the *Cheapside* people the biggest asses of all. Come, don't pretend at this time of day to have pretty illusions about the public, especially about publishers and editors. It's not for *such* animals you work—it's for those who know, *coloro che sanno;*[4] so keep straight for *me* if you can't keep straight for yourself. There was a certain sort of thing you used to try for—and a very good thing it was. But this twaddle isn't *in* it." When I talked with Hawley later about "Rutland Ramsay" and its possible successors he declared that I must get back into my boat again or I should go to the bottom. His voice in short was the voice of warning.

I noted the warning, but I didn't turn my friends out of doors. They bored me a good deal; but the very fact that they bored me admonished me not to sacrifice them—if there was anything to be done with them—simply to irritation. As I look back at this phase they seem to me to have pervaded my life not a little. I have a vision of them as most of the time in my studio, seated against the wall on an old velvet bench to be out of the way, and resembling the while a pair of patient courtiers in a royal ante-chamber. I'm convinced that during the coldest weeks of the winter they held their ground because it saved them fire. Their newness was losing its gloss, and it was impossible not to feel them objects of charity. Whenever Miss Churm arrived they went away, and after I was fairly launched in "Rutland Ramsay" Miss Churm arrived pretty often. They managed to express to me tacitly that they supposed I wanted her for the low life of the book, and I let them suppose it, since they had attempted to study the work—it was lying about the studio—without discovering that it dealt only with the highest circles. They had dipped into the most brilliant of our novelists without deciphering many passages. I still took an hour from them, now and again, in spite of Jack Hawley's warning: it would be time enough to dismiss them, if dismissal should be necessary, when the rigour of the season was over. Hawley had made their acquaintance—he had met them at my fireside—and thought them a ridiculous pair. Learning that he was a painter they tried to approach him, to show him too that they were the real thing; but he looked at them, across the big room, as if they were miles away: they were a compendium of everything he most objected to in the social system of his country. Such people as that, all convention and patent-leather, with ejaculations that stopped conversation, had no business in a studio. A studio was a place to learn to see, and how could you see through a pair of feather-beds?

The main inconvenience I suffered at their hands was that at first I was shy of letting it break upon them that my artful little servant had begun to sit to me for "Rutland Ramsay." They knew I had been odd enough—they were prepared by this time to allow oddity to artists—to pick a foreign vagabond out of the streets when I might have had a person with whiskers and credentials, but it was some time before they learned how high I rated his accomplishments. They found him in an attitude more than once, but they never doubted I was doing him as an organ-grinder. There were several things they never guessed, and one of them was that for a striking scene in the novel, in which a footman briefly

4. Dante, *The Divine Comedy*, "The Inferno," 4:131: actually, *color che sanno*—"those who know."

figured, it occurred to me to make use of Major Monarch as the menial. I kept putting this off, I didn't like to ask him to don the livery—besides the difficulty of finding a livery to fit him. At last, one day late in the winter, when I was at work on the despised Oronte, who caught one's idea on the wing, and was in the glow of feeling myself go very straight, they came in, the Major and his wife, with their society laugh about nothing (there was less and less to laugh at); came on like country-callers—they always reminded me of that—who have walked across the park after church and are presently persuaded to stay to luncheon. Luncheon was over, but they could stay to tea—I knew they wanted it. The fit was on me, however, and I couldn't let my ardour cool and my work wait, with the fading daylight, while my model prepared it. So I asked Mrs. Monarch if she would mind laying it out—a request which for an instant brought all the blood to her face. Her eyes were on her husband's for a second, and some mute telegraphy passed between them. Their folly was over the next instant; his cheerful shrewdness put an end to it. So far from pitying their wounded pride, I must add, I was moved to give it as complete a lesson as I could. They bustled about together and got out the cups and saucers and made the kettle boil. I know they felt as if they were waiting on my servant, and when the tea was prepared I said: "He'll have a cup, please—he's tired." Mrs. Monarch brought him one where he stood, and he took it from her, as if he had been a gentleman at a party squeezing a crush-hat with an elbow.

125 Then it came over me that she had made a great effort for me—made it with a kind of nobleness—and that I owed her a compensation. Each time I saw her after this I wondered what the compensation could be. I couldn't go on doing the wrong thing to oblige them. Oh it *was* the wrong thing, the stamp of the work for which they sat—Hawley was not the only person to say it now. I sent in a large number of the drawings I had made for "Rutland Ramsay," and I received a warning that was more to the point than Hawley's. The artistic adviser of the house for which I was working was of opinion that many of my illustrations were not what had been looked for. Most of these illustrations were the subjects in which the Monarchs had figured. Without going into the question of what *had* been looked for, I had to face the fact that at this rate I shouldn't get the other books to do. I hurled myself in despair on Miss Churm—I put her through all her paces. I not only adopted Oronte publicly as my hero, but one morning when the Major looked in to see if I didn't require him to finish a *Cheapside* figure for which he had begun to sit the week before, I told him I had changed my mind—I'd do the drawing from my man. At this my visitor turned pale and stood looking at me. "Is *he* your idea of an English gentleman?" he asked.

I was disappointed, I was nervous, I wanted to get on with my work; so I replied with irritation: "Oh my dear Major—I can't be ruined for *you!*" . . .

It was a horrid speech, but he stood another moment—after which, without a word, he quitted the studio. I drew a long breath, for I said to myself that I shouldn't see him again. I hadn't told him definitely that I was in danger of having my work rejected, but I was vexed at his not having felt the catastrophe in the air, read with me the moral of our fruitless collaboration, the lesson that in the deceptive atmosphere of art even the highest respectability may fail of being plastic.

I didn't owe my friends money, but I did see them again. They reappeared together three days later, and, given all the other facts, there was something tragic in that one. It was a clear proof they could find nothing else in life to do. They had threshed the matter out in a dismal conference—they had digested the bad news that they were not in for the series. If they weren't useful to me even for the *Cheapside* their function seemed difficult to determine, and I could only judge at first that they had come, forgivingly, decorously, to take a last leave. This made me rejoice in secret that I had little leisure for a scene; for I had placed both my other models in position together and I was pegging away at a drawing from which I hoped to derive glory. It had been suggested by the passage in which Rutland Ramsay, drawing up a chair to Artemisia's piano-stool, says extraordinary things to her while she ostensibly fingers out a difficult piece of music. I had done Miss Churm at the piano before—it was an attitude in which she knew how to take on an absolutely poetic grace. I wished the two figures to "compose" together with intensity, and my little Italian had entered perfectly into my conception. The pair were vividly before me, the piano had been pulled out; it was a charming show of blended youth and murmured love, which I had only to catch and keep. My visitors stood and looked at it, and I was friendly to them over my shoulder.

They made no response, but I was used to silent company and went on with my work, only a little disconcerted—even though exhilarated by the sense that *this* was at least the ideal thing—at not having got rid of them after all. Presently I heard Mrs. Monarch's sweet voice beside or rather above me: "I wish her hair were a little better done." I looked up and she was staring with a strange fixedness at Miss Churm, whose back was turned to her. "Do you mind my just touching it?" she went on—a question which made me spring up for an instant as with the instinctive fear that she might do the young lady a harm. But she quieted me with a glance I shall never forget—I confess I should like to have been able to paint *that*—and went for a moment to my model. She spoke to her softly, laying a hand on her shoulder and bending over her; and as the girl, understanding, gratefully assented, she disposed her rough curls, with a few quick passes, in such a way as to make Miss Churm's head twice as charming. It was one of the most heroic personal services I've ever seen rendered. Then Mrs. Monarch turned away with a low sigh and, looking about her as if for something to do, stooped to the floor with a noble humility and picked up a dirty rag that had dropped out of my paint-box.

The Major meanwhile had also been looking for something to do, and, wan- 130
dering to the other end of the studio, saw before him my breakfast-things neglected, unremoved. "I say, can't I be useful *here?*" he called out to me with an irrepressible quaver. I assented with a laugh that I fear was awkward, and for the next ten minutes, while I worked, I heard the light clatter of china and the tinkle of spoons and glass. Mrs. Monarch assisted her husband—they washed up my crockery, they put it away. They wandered off into my little scullery, and I afterwards found that they had cleaned my knives and that my slender stock of plate had an unprecedented surface. When it came over me, the latent eloquence of what they were doing, I confess that my drawing was blurred for a moment—the picture swam. They had accepted their failure, but they couldn't

accept their fate. They had bowed their heads in bewilderment to the perverse and cruel law in virtue of which the real thing could be so much less precious than the unreal; but they didn't want to starve. If my servants were my models; then my models might be my servants. They would reverse the parts—the others would sit for the ladies and gentlemen and *they* would do the work. They would still be in the studio—it was an intense dumb appeal to me not to turn them out. "Take us on," they wanted to say—"we'll do *anything*."

My pencil dropped from my hand; my sitting was spoiled and I got rid of my sitters, who were also evidently rather mystified and awestruck. Then, alone with the Major and his wife I had a most uncomfortable moment. He put their prayer into a single sentence: "I say, you know—just let *us* do for you, can't you?" I couldn't—it was dreadful to see them emptying my slops; but I pretended I could, to oblige them, for about a week. Then I gave them a sum of money to go away, and I never saw them again. I obtained the remaining books, but my friend Hawley repeats that Major and Mrs. Monarch did me a permanent harm, got me into false ways. If it be true I'm content to have paid the price—for the memory.

1892, 1909

DORIS LESSING

Our Friend Judith

I stopped inviting Judith to meet people when a Canadian woman remarked, with the satisfied fervour of one who has at last pinned a label on a rare specimen: "She is, of course, one of your typical English spinsters."

This was a few weeks after an American sociologist, having elicited from Judith the facts that she was fortyish, unmarried, and living alone, had enquired of me: "I suppose she has given up?" "Given up what?" I asked; and the subsequent discussion was unrewarding.

Judith did not easily come to parties. She would come after pressure, not so much—one felt—to do one a favour, but in order to correct what she believed to be a defect in her character. "I really ought to enjoy meeting new people more than I do," she said once. We reverted to an earlier pattern of our friendship: odd evenings together, an occasional visit to the cinema, or she would telephone to say: "I'm on my way past you to the British Museum. Would you care for a cup of coffee with me? I have twenty minutes to spare."

It is characteristic of Judith that the word "spinster," used of her, provoked fascinated speculation about other people. There are my aunts, for instance: aged seventy-odd, both unmarried, one an ex-missionary from China, one a retired matron of a famous London hospital. These two old ladies live together under the shadow of the cathedral in a country town. They devote much time to the Church, to good causes, to letter writing with friends all over the world, to the grandchildren and the great-grandchildren of relatives. It would be a mistake, however, on entering a house in which nothing has been moved for fifty years, to diagnose a condition of fossilised late-Victorian integrity. They read every book review in the *Observer* or the *Times*,[1] so that I recently got a letter from Aunt Rose enquiring whether I did not think that the author of *On the Road*[2] was not—perhaps?—exaggerating his difficulties. They know a good deal about music, and write letters of encouragement to young composers they feel are being neglected—"You must understand that anything new and original takes time to be understood." Well-informed and critical Tories, they are as likely to dispatch telegrams of protest to the Home Secretary[3] as letters of support. These ladies, my aunts Emily and Rose, are surely what is meant by the phrase "English spinster." And yet, once the connection has been pointed out, there is no doubt that Judith and they are spiritual cousins, if not sisters. Therefore it follows that one's pitying admiration for women who have supported manless and uncomforted lives needs a certain modification?

One will, of course, never know; and I feel now that it is entirely my fault 5
that I shall never know. I had been Judith's friend for upward of five years before the incident occurred which I involuntarily thought of—stupidly enough—as the first time Judith's mask slipped.

A mutual friend, Betty, had been given a cast-off Dior[4] dress. She was too short for it. Also she said: "It's not a dress for a married woman with three children and a talent for cooking. I don't know why not, but it isn't." Judith was the right build. Therefore one evening the three of us met by appointment in Judith's bedroom, with the dress. Neither Betty nor I was surprised at the renewed discovery that Judith was beautiful. We had both often caught each other, and ourselves, in moments of envy when Judith's calm and severe face, her undemonstratively perfect body, succeeded in making everyone else in a room or a street look cheap.

Judith is tall, small-breasted, slender. Her light brown hair is parted in the centre and cut straight around her neck. A high straight forehead, straight nose, a full grave mouth are setting for her eyes, which are green, large and prominent. Her lids are very white, fringed with gold, and moulded close over the eyeball, so that in profile she has the look of a staring gilded mask. The dress was of dark green glistening stuff, cut straight, with a sort of loose tunic. It opened simply at the throat. In it Judith could of course evoke nothing but classical images. Diana, perhaps, back from the hunt, in a relaxed moment? A rather intellectual wood nymph who had opted for an afternoon in the British Museum Reading Room? Something like that. Neither Betty nor I said a word, since Judith was examining herself in a long mirror, and must know she looked magnificent.

Slowly she drew off the dress and laid it aside. Slowly she put on the old cord skirt and woollen blouse she had taken off. She must have surprised a resigned glance between us, for she then remarked, with the smallest of mocking smiles:

1. Prestigious London newspapers representing roughly the younger more liberal establishment and the Establishment proper respectively. 2. Jack Kerouac (1922–69), leader of the beatniks, 1950s forerunners of the hippies. Kerouac heroes felt themselves completely cut off from and victimized by American society. 3. Head of the British government department responsible for domestic matters. 4. Famous French designer of high fashions.

"One surely ought to stay in character, wouldn't you say?" She added, reading the words out of some invisible book, written not by her, since it was a very vulgar book, but perhaps by one of us: "It does everything *for* me, I must admit."

"After seeing you in it," Betty cried out, defying her, "I can't bear for anyone else to have it. I shall simply put it away." Judith shrugged, rather irritated. In the shapeless skirt and blouse, and without makeup, she stood smiling at us, a woman at whom forty-nine out of fifty people would not look twice.

A second revelatory incident occurred soon after. Betty telephoned me to say that Judith had a kitten. Did I know that Judith adored cats? "No, but of course she would," I said.

Betty lived in the same street as Judith and saw more of her than I did. I was kept posted about the growth and habits of the cat and its effect on Judith's life. She remarked for instance that she felt it was good for her to have a tie and some responsibility. But no sooner was the cat out of kittenhood than all the neighbours complained. It was a tomcat, ungelded, and making every night hideous. Finally the landlord said that either the cat or Judith must go, unless she was prepared to have the cat "fixed."[5] Judith wore herself out trying to find some person, anywhere in Britain, who would be prepared to take the cat. This person would, however, have to sign a written statement not to have the cat "fixed." When Judith took the cat to the vet to be killed, Betty told me she cried for twenty-four hours.

"She didn't think of compromising? After all, perhaps the cat might have preferred to live, if given the choice?"

"Is it likely I'd have the nerve to say anything so sloppy to Judith? It's the nature of a male cat to rampage lustfully about, and therefore it would be morally wrong for Judith to have the cat fixed, simply to suit her own convenience."

"She said that?"

"She wouldn't have to *say* it, surely?"

A third incident was when she allowed a visiting young American, living in Paris, the friend of a friend and scarcely known to her, to use her flat while she visited her parents over Christmas. The young man and his friends lived it up for ten days of alcohol and sex and marijuana, and when Judith came back it took a week to get the place clean again and the furniture mended. She telephoned twice to Paris, the first time to say that he was a disgusting young thug and if he knew what was good for him he would keep out of her way in the future; the second time to apologise for losing her temper. "I had a choice either to let someone use my flat, or to leave it empty. But having chosen that you should have it, it was clearly an unwarrantable infringement of your liberty to make any conditions at all. I do most sincerely ask your pardon." The moral aspects of the matter having been made clear, she was irritated rather than not to receive letters of apology from him—fulsome, embarrassed, but above all, baffled.

It was the note of curiosity in the letters—he even suggested coming over to get to know her better—that irritated her most. "What do you suppose he means?"

5. Gelded, castrated.

she said to me. "He lived in my flat for ten days. One would have thought that should be enough, wouldn't you?"

The facts about Judith, then, are all in the open, unconcealed, and plain to anyone who cares to study them; or, as it became plain she feels, to anyone with the intelligence to interpret them.

She has lived for the last twenty years in a small two-roomed flat high over a busy West London street. The flat is shabby and badly heated. The furniture is old, was never anything but ugly, is now frankly rickety and fraying. She has an income of two hundred pounds[6] a year from a dead uncle. She lives on this and what she earns from her poetry, and from lecturing on poetry to night classes and extramural university classes.

She does not smoke or drink, and eats very little, from preference, not self-discipline.

She studied poetry and biology at Oxford, with distinction.

She is a Castlewell. That is, she is a member of one of the academic upper-middleclass families, which have been producing for centuries a steady supply of brilliant but sound men and women who are the backbone of the arts and sciences in Britain. She is on cool good terms with her family, who respect her and leave her alone.

She goes on long walking tours, by herself, in such places as Exmoor or West Scotland.

Every three or four years she publishes a volume of poems.

The walls of her flat are completely lined with books. They are scientific, classical and historical; there is a great deal of poetry and some drama. There is not one novel. When Judith says: "Of course I don't read novels," this does not mean that novels have no place, or a small place, in literature; or that people should not read novels; but that it must be obvious she can't be expected to read novels.

I had been visiting her flat for years before I noticed two long shelves of books, under a window, each shelf filled with the works of a single writer. The two writers are not, to put it at the mildest, the kind one would associate with Judith. They are mild, reminiscent, vague and whimsical. Typical English *belles-lettres*, in fact, and by definition abhorrent to her. Not one of the books in the two shelves has been read; some of the pages are still uncut. Yet each book is inscribed or dedicated to her: gratefully, admiringly, sentimentally and, more than once, amorously. In short, it is open to anyone who cares to examine these two shelves, and to work out dates, to conclude that Judith from the age of fifteen to twenty-five had been the beloved young companion of one elderly literary gentleman, and from twenty-five to thirty-five the inspiration of another.

During all that time she had produced her own poetry, and the sort of poetry, it is quite safe to deduce, not at all likely to be admired by her two admirers. Her poems are always cool and intellectual; that is their form, which is contradicted or supported by a gravely sensuous texture. They are poems to read often; one has to, to understand them.

6. About one-third or even one-half of a subsistence income.

I did not ask Judith a direct question about these two eminent but rather fusty lovers. Not because she would not have answered, or because she would have found the question impertinent, but because such questions are clearly unnecessary. Having those two shelves of books where they are, and books she could not conceivably care for, for their own sake, is publicly giving credit where credit is due. I can imagine her thinking the thing over, and deciding it was only fair, or perhaps honest, to place the books there; and this despite the fact that she would not care at all for the same attention be paid to her. There is something almost contemptuous in it. For she certainly despises people who feel they need attention.

For instance, more than once a new emerging wave of "modern" young poets have discovered her as the only "modern" poet among their despised and well-credited elders. This is because, since she began writing at fifteen, her poems have been full of scientific, mechanical and chemical imagery. This is how she thinks, or feels.

More than once has a young poet hastened to her flat, to claim her as an ally, only to find her totally and by instinct unmoved by words like "modern," "new," "contemporary." He has been outraged and wounded by her principle, so deeply rooted as to be unconscious, and to need no expression but a contemptuous shrug of the shoulders, that publicity seeking or to want critical attention is despicable. It goes without saying that there is perhaps one critic in the world she has any time for. He has sulked off, leaving her on her shelf, which she takes it for granted is her proper place, to be read by an appreciative minority.

Meanwhile she gives her lectures, walks alone through London, writes her poems, and is seen sometimes at a concert or a play with a middleaged professor of Greek, who has a wife and two children.

Betty and I had speculated about this professor, with such remarks as: Surely she must sometimes be lonely? Hasn't she ever wanted to marry? What about that awful moment when one comes in from somewhere at night to an empty flat?

It happened recently that Betty's husband was on a business trip, her children visiting, and she was unable to stand the empty house. She asked Judith for a refuge until her own home filled again.

Afterwards Betty rang me up to report: "Four of the five nights Professor Adams came in about ten or so."

"Was Judith embarrassed?"

"Would you expect her to be?"

"Well, if not embarrassed, at least conscious there was a situation?"

"No, not at all. But I must say I don't think he's good enough for her. He can't possibly understand her. He calls her Judy."

"Good God."

"Yes. But I was wondering. Suppose the other two called her Judy—'little Judy'—imagine it! Isn't it awful? But it does rather throw a light on Judith?"

"It's rather touching."

"I suppose it's touching. But *I* was embarrassed—oh, not because of the situation. Because of how she was, with him. 'Judy, is there another cup of tea in that pot?' And she, rather daughterly and demure, pouring him one."

"Well yes, I can see how you felt."

"Three of the nights he went to her bedroom with her—very casual about it, because she was being. But he was not there in the mornings. So I asked her. You know how it is when you ask her a question. As if you've been having long conversations on that very subject for years and years, and she is merely continuing where you left off last. So when she says something surprising, one feels such a fool to be surprised?"

"Yes. And then?"

"I asked her if she was sorry not to have children. She said yes, but one couldn't have everything."

"One can't have everything, she said?"

"Quite clearly feeling she *has* nearly everything. She said she thought it was a pity, because she would have brought up children very well."

"When you come to think of it, she would, too."

"I asked about marriage, but she said on the whole the role of a mistress suited her better."

"She used the word 'mistress'?"

"You must admit it's the accurate word."

"I suppose so."

"And then she said that while she liked intimacy and sex and everything, she enjoyed waking up in the morning alone and *her own person*."

"Yes, *of course*."

"Of course. But now she's bothered because the professor would like to marry her. Or he feels he ought. At least, he's getting all guilty and obsessive about it. She says she doesn't see the point of divorce, and anyway, surely it would be very hard on his poor old wife after all these years, particularly after bringing up two children so satisfactorily. She talks about his wife as if she's a kind of nice old charwoman, and it wouldn't be *fair* to sack her, you know. Anyway. What with one thing and another. Judith's going off to Italy soon in order *to collect herself*."

"But how's she going to pay for it?"

"Luckily the Third Programme's[7] commissioning her to do some arty programmes. They offered her a choice of The Cid—El Thid[8] you know—and the Borgias. Well, the Borghese, then. And Judith settled for the Borgias."

"The Borgias," I said, "*Judith?*"

"Yes, quite. I said that too, in that tone of voice. She saw my point. She says the epic is right up her street, whereas the Renaissance has never been on her wave length. Obviously it couldn't be, all the magnificence and cruelty and *dirt*. But of course chivalry and a high moral code and all those idiotically noble goings-on are right on her wave length."

"Is the money the same?"

7. British Broadcasting Corporation public radio service (and now also television channel) specializing in classical music, literature and plays, lectures, etc. 8. Castilian, standard Spanish, pronunciation of El Cid, the title of an eleventh-century soldier-hero and hero of many works of literature.

"Yes. But is it likely Judith would let money decide? No, she said that one should always choose something new, that isn't up one's street. Well, because it's better for her character, and so on, to get herself unsettled by the Renaissance. She didn't say *that*, of course."

"Of course not."

Judith went to Florence; and for some months postcards informed us tersely of her doings. Then Betty decided she must go by herself for a holiday. She had been appalled by the discovery that if her husband was away for a night she couldn't sleep; and when he went to Australia for three weeks, she stopped living until he came back. She had discussed this with him, and he had agreed that if she really felt the situation to be serious, he would despatch her by air, to Italy, in order to recover her self-respect. As she put it.

I got this letter from her: "It's no use, I'm coming home. I might have known. Better face it, once you're really married you're not fit for man nor beast. And if you remember what I used to be like! *Well!* I moped around Milan. I sunbathed in Venice, then I thought my tan was surely worth something, so I was on the point of starting an affair with another lonely soul, but I lost heart, and went to Florence to see Judith. She wasn't there. She'd gone to the Italian Riviera. I had nothing better to do, so I followed her. When I saw the place I wanted to laugh, it's so much not Judith, you know, all those palms and umbrellas and gaiety at all costs and ever such an ornamental blue sea. Judith is in an enormous stone room up on the hillside above the sea, with grape vines all over the place. You should see her, she's got beautiful. It seems for the last fifteen years she's been going to Soho[9] every Saturday morning to buy food at an Italian shop. I must have looked surprised, because she explained she liked Soho. I suppose because all that dreary vice and nudes and prostitutes and everything prove how right she is to be as she is? She told the people in the shop she was going to Italy, and the *signora*[1] said, what a coincidence, she was going back to Italy too, and she did hope an old friend like Miss Castlewell would visit her there. Judith said to me: 'I felt lacking, when she used the word friend. Our relations have always been formal. Can you understand it?' she said to me. 'For fifteen years,' I said to her. She said: 'I think I must feel it's a kind of imposition, don't you know, expecting people to feel friendship for one.' *Well.* I said: 'You ought to understand it, because you're like that yourself.' 'Am I?' she said. 'Well, think about it,' I said. But I could see she didn't want to think about it. Anyway, she's here, and I've spent a week with her. The widow Maria Rineiri inherited her mother's house, so she came home, from Soho. On the ground floor is a tatty little *rosticceria*[2] patronised by the neighbours. They are all working people. This isn't tourist country, up on the hill. The widow lives above the shop with her little boy, a nasty little brat of about ten. Say what you like, the English are the only people who know how to bring up children, I don't care if that's insular. Judith's room is at the back, with a balcony. Underneath her room is the barber's shop, and the barber is Luigi Rineiri, the widow's younger brother. Yes, I was keeping him

9. A section of London roughly equivalent to Greenwich Village in New York—foreign restaurants and groceries, haunt of writers, painters, etc.—but in recent years increasingly known for prostitutes and pornography. 1. Proprietress. 2. Grill.

until the last. He is about forty, tall dark handsome, a great *bull*, but rather a sweet fatherly bull. He has cut Judith's hair and made it lighter. Now it looks like a sort of gold helmet. Judith is all brown. The widow Rineiri has made her a white dress and a green dress. They fit, for a change. When Judith walks down the street to the lower town, all the Italian males take one look at the golden girl and melt in their own oil like ice cream. Judith takes all this in her stride. She sort of acknowledges the homage. Then she strolls into the sea and vanishes into the foam. She swims five miles every day. *Naturally*. I haven't asked Judith whether she has collected herself, because you can see she hasn't. The widow Rineiri is matchmaking. When I noticed this I wanted to laugh, but luckily I didn't because Judith asked me, really wanting to know: 'Can you see me married to an Italian barber?' (Not being snobbish, but stating the position, so to speak.) 'Well yes,' I said, 'you're the only women I know who I can see married to an Italian barber.' Because it wouldn't matter who she married, she'd always be her *own person*. 'At any rate, for a time,' I said. At which she said, asperously[3]. 'You can use phrases like for a time in England but not in Italy.' Did you ever see England, at least London, as the home of licence, liberty and free love? No, neither did I, but of course she's right. Married to Luigi it would be the family, the neighbours, the church and the *bambini*.[4] All the same she's thinking about it, believe it or not. Here she's quite different, all relaxed and free. She's melting in the attention she gets. The widow mothers her and makes her coffee all the time, and listens to a lot of good advice about how to bring up that nasty brat of hers. Unluckily she doesn't take it. Luigi is crazy for her. At mealtimes she goes to the *trattoria*[5] in the upper square and all the workmen treat her like a goddess. Well, a film star then. I said to her, you're mad to come home. For one thing her rent is ten bob[6] a week, and you eat *pasta* and drink red wine till you bust for about one and sixpence. No, she said, it would be nothing but self-indulgence to stay. Why? I said. She said, she's got nothing to stay for. (Ho ho.) And besides, she's done her research on the Borghese, though so far she can't see her way to an honest presentation of the facts. What made these people tick? she wants to know. And so she's only staying because of the cat. I forgot to mention the cat. This is a town of cats. The Italians here love their cats. I wanted to feed a stray cat at the table, but the waiter said no; and after lunch, all the waiters came with trays crammed with leftover food and stray cats came from everywhere to eat. And at dark when the tourists go in to feed and the beach is empty—you know how empty and forlorn a beach is at dusk?—well cats appear from everywhere. The beach seems to move, then you see it's cats. They go stalking along the thin inch of grey water at the edge of the sea, shaking their paws crossly at each step, snatching at the dead little fish, and throwing them with their mouths up on to the dry stand. Then they scamper after them. You've never seen such a snarling and fighting. At dawn when the fishing boats come in to the empty beach, the cats are there in dozens. The fisherman throw them bits of fish. The cats snarl and fight over it. Judith gets up early and goes down to watch. Some-

3. Sharply, harshly. 4. Children. 5. Inexpensive restaurant. 6. Shillings. There are twenty shillings to the pound; *one and sixpence* below is one and a half shillings.

times Luigi goes too, being tolerant. Because what he really likes is to join the evening promenade with Judith on his arm around and around the square of the upper town. Showing her off. Can you *see* Judith? But she does it. Being tolerant. But she smiles and enjoys the attention she gets, there's no doubt about it.

"She has a cat in her room. It's a kitten really, but it's pregnant. Judith says she can't leave until the kittens are born. The cat is too young to have kittens. Imagine Judith. She sits on her bed in that great stone room, with her bare feet on the stone floor, and watches the cat, and tries to work out why a healthy uninhibited Italian cat always fed on the best from the *rosticceria* should be neurotic. Because it is. When it sees Judith watching it gets nervous and starts licking at the roots of its tail. But Judith goes on watching, and says about Italy that the reason why the English love the Italians is because the Italians make the English feel superior. They have no discipline. And that's a despicable reason for one nation to love another. Then she talks about Luigi and says he has no sense of guilt, but a sense of sin; whereas she has no sense of sin but she has guilt. I haven't asked her if this has been an insuperable barrier, because judging from how she looks, it hasn't. She says she would rather have a sense of sin, because sin can be atoned for, and if she understood sin, perhaps she would be more at home with the Renaissance. Luigi is very healthy, she says, and not neurotic. He is a Catholic of course. He doesn't mind that she's an atheist. His mother has explained to him that the English are all pagans, but good people at heart. I suppose he thinks a few smart sessions with the local priest would set Judith on the right path for good and all. Meanwhile the cat walks nervously around the room, stopping to lick, and when it can't stand Judith watching it another second, it rolls over on the floor, with its paws tucked up, and rolls up its eyes, and Judith scratches its lumpy pregnant stomach and tells it to relax. It makes *me* nervous to see her, it's not like her, I don't know why. Then Luigi shouts up from the barber's shop, then he comes up and stands at the door laughing, and Judith laughs, and the widow says: Children, enjoy yourselves. And off they go, walking down to the town eating ice cream. The cat follows them. It won't let Judith out of its sight, like a dog. When she swims miles out to sea, the cat hides under a beach hut until she comes back. Then she carries it back up the hill, because that nasty little boy chases it. *Well.* I'm coming home tomorrow thank God, to my dear old Billy, I was mad ever to leave him. There is something about Judith and Italy that has upset me, I don't know what. The point is, what on earth can Judith and Luigi *talk* about? Nothing. How can they? And of course it doesn't matter. So I turn out to be a prude as well. See you next week."

It was my turn for a dose of the sun, so I didn't see Betty. On my way back from Rome I stopped off in Judith's resort and walked up through narrow streets to the upper town, where, in the square with the vine-covered *trattoria* at the corner, was a house with ROSTICCERIA written in black paint on a cracked wooden board over a low door. There was a door curtain of red beads, and flies settled on the beads. I opened the beads with my hands and looked into a small dark room with a stone counter. Loops of salami hung from metal hooks. A glass bell covered some plates of cooked meats. There were flies on the salami and on the glass bell. A few tins on the wooden shelves, a couple of pale loaves, some wine casks and an open case of sticky pale green grapes covered with fruit flies seemed to be the only stock. A single wooden table with two chairs stood in a corner, and two workmen sat there, eating lumps of sausage and bread. Through another bead curtain at the back came a short, smoothly fat, slender-limbed woman with greying hair. I asked for Miss Castlewell, and her face changed. She said in an offended, offhand way: "Miss Castlewell left last week." She took a white cloth from under the counter, and flicked at the flies on the glass bell. "I'm a friend of hers," I said, and she said: *Si*,[7] and put her hands palm down on the counter and looked at me, expressionless. The workmen got up, gulped down the last of their wine, nodded and went. She *ciao*'d[8] them; and looked back at me. Then, since I didn't go, she called: "Luigi!" A shout came from the back room, there was a rattle of beads, and in came first a wiry sharp-faced boy, and then Luigi. He was tall, heavy-shouldered, and his black rough hair was like a cap, pulled low over his brows. He looked good-natured, but at the moment uneasy. His sister said something, and he stood beside her, an ally, and confirmed: "Miss Castlewell went away." I was on the point of giving up, when through the bead curtain that screened off a dazzling light eased a thin tabby cat. It was ugly and it walked uncomfortably, with its back quarters bunched up. The child suddenly let out a "Ssssss" through his teeth, and the cat froze. Luigi said something sharp to the child, and something encouraging to the cat, which sat down, looked straight in front of it, then began frantically licking at its flanks. "Miss Castlewell was offended with us," said Mrs. Rineiri suddenly, and with dignity. "She left early one morning. We did not expect her to go." I said: "Perhaps she had to go home and finish some work."

Mrs. Rineiri shrugged, then sighed. Then she exchanged a hard look with her brother. Clearly the subject had been discussed, and closed forever.

"I've known Judith a long time," I said, trying to find the right note. "She's a remarkable woman. She's a poet." But there was no response to this at all. Meanwhile the child, with a fixed bared-teeth grin, was staring at the cat, narrowing his eyes. Suddenly he let out another "Sssssss" and added a short high yelp. The cat shot backwards, hit the wall, tried desperately to claw its way up the wall, came to its senses and again sat down and began its urgent, undirected licking at its fur. This time Luigi cuffed the child, who yelped in earnest, and then ran out into the street past the cat. Now that the way was clear the cat shot across the floor, up onto the counter, and bounded past Luigi's shoulder and straight through the bead curtain into the barber's shop, where it landed with a thud.

"Judith was sorry when she left us," said Mrs. Rineiri uncertainly. "She was crying."

"I'm sure she was."

"And so," said Mrs. Rineiri, with finality, laying her hands down again, and looking past me at the bead curtain. That was the end. Luigi nodded brusquely at me, and went into the back. I said goodbye to Mrs. Rineiri and walked back

7. "Yes." 8. Said goodbye to.

to the lower town. In the square I saw the child, sitting on the running board of a lorry[9] parked outside the *trattoria*, drawing in the dust with his bare toes, and directing in front of him a blank, unhappy stare.

I had to go through Florence, so I went to the address Judith had been at. No, Miss Castlewell had not been back. Her papers and books were still here. Would I take them back with me to England? I made a great parcel and brought them back to England.

I telephoned Judith and she said she had already written for the papers to be sent, but it was kind of me to bring them. There had seemed to be no point, she said, in returning to Florence.

"Shall I bring them over?"

"I would be very grateful, of course."

Judith's flat was chilly, and she wore a bunchy sage-green woollen dress. Her hair was still a soft gold helmet, but she looked pale and rather pinched. She stood with her back to a single bar of electric fire—lit because I demanded it—with her legs apart and her arms folded. She contemplated me.

"I went to the Rineiris' house."

"Oh. Did you?"

"They seemed to miss you."

She said nothing.

"I saw the cat too."

"Oh. Oh, I suppose you and Betty discussed it?" This was with a small unfriendly smile.

"Well, Judith, you must see we were likely to?"

She gave this her consideration and said: "I don't understand why people discuss other people. Oh—I'm not criticising you. But I don't see why you are so interested. I don't understand human behaviour and I'm not particularly interested."

"I think you should write to the Rineiris."

"I wrote and thanked them, of course."

"I don't mean that."

"You and Betty have worked it out?"

"Yes, we talked about it. We thought we should talk to you, so you should write to the Rineiris."

"Why?"

"For one thing, they are both very fond of you."

"Fond," she said smiling.

"Judith, I've never in my life felt such an atmosphere of being let down."

Judith considered this. "When something happens that shows one there is really a complete gulf in understanding, what is there to say?"

"It could scarcely have been a complete gulf in understanding. I suppose you are going to say we are being interfering?"

Judith showed distaste. "That is a very stupid word. And it's a stupid idea. No one can interfere with me if I don't let them. No, it's that I don't understand

9. Truck.

people. I don't understand why you or Betty should care. Or why the Rineiris should, for that matter," she added with the small tight smile.

"Judith!"

"If you've behaved stupidly, there's no point in going on. You put an end to it."

"What happened? Was it the cat?"

"Yes, I suppose so. But it's not important." She looked at me, saw my ironical face, and said: "The cat was too young to have kittens. That is all there was to it."

"Have it your way. But that is obviously not all there is to it."

"What upsets me is that I don't understand at all why I was so upset then."

"What happened? Or don't you want to talk about it?"

"I don't give a damn whether I talk about it or not. You really do say the most extraordinary things, you and Betty. If you want to know, I'll tell you. What does it matter?"

"I would like to know, of course."

"*Of course!*" she said. "In your place I wouldn't care. Well, I think the essence of the thing was that I must have had the wrong attitude to that cat. Cats are supposed to be independent. They are supposed to go off by themselves to have their kittens. This one didn't. It was climbing up on to my bed all one night and crying for attention. I don't like cats on my bed. In the morning I saw she was in pain. I stayed with her all that day. Then Luigi—he's the brother, you know."

"Yes."

"Did Betty mention him? Luigi came up to say it was time I went for a swim. He said the cat should look after itself. I blame myself very much. That's what happens when you submerge yourself in somebody else."

Her look at me was now defiant; and her body showed both defensiveness and aggression. "Yes. It's true. I've always been afraid of it. And in the last few weeks I've behaved badly. It's because I let it happen."

"Well, go on."

"I left the cat and swam. It was late, so it was only for a few minutes. When I came out of the sea the cat had followed me and had had a kitten on the beach. That little beast Michele—the son, you know?—well, he always teased the poor thing, and now he had frightened her off the kitten. It was dead, though. He held it up by the tail and waved it at me as I came out of the sea. I told him to bury it. He scooped two inches of sand away and pushed the kitten in—on the beach, where people are all day. So I buried it properly. He had run off. He was chasing the poor cat. She was terrified and running up the town. I ran too. I caught Michele and I was so angry I hit him. I don't believe in hitting children. I've been feeling beastly about it ever since."

"You were angry."

"It's no excuse. I would never have believed myself capable of hitting a child. I hit him very hard. He went off, crying. The poor cat had got under a big lorry parked in the square. Then she screamed. And then a most remarkable thing happened. She screamed just once, and all at once cats just materialised. One minute there was just one cat, lying under a lorry, and the next, dozens of cats.

They sat in a big circle around the lorry, all quite still, and watched my poor cat."

"Rather moving," I said.

"Why?"

"There is no evidence one way or the other," I said in inverted commas, "that the cats were there out of concern for a friend in trouble."

"No," she said energetically. "There isn't. It might have been curiosity. Or anything. How do we know? However, I crawled under the lorry. There were two paws sticking out of the cat's back end. The kitten was the wrong way round. It was stuck. I held the cat down with one hand and I pulled the kitten out with the other." She held out her long white hands. They were still covered with fading scars and scratches. "She bit and yelled, but the kitten was alive. She left the kitten and crawled across the square into the house. Then all the cats got up and walked away. It was the most extraordinary thing I've ever seen. They vanished again. One minute they were all there, and then they had vanished. I went after the cat, with the kitten. Poor little thing, it was covered with dust—being wet, don't you know. The cat was on my bed. There was another kitten coming, but it got stuck too. So when she screamed and screamed I just pulled it out. The kittens began to suck. One kitten was very big. It was a nice fat black kitten. It must have hurt her. But she suddenly bit out—snapped, don't you know, like a reflex action, at the back of the kitten's head. It died, just like that. Extraordinary, isn't it?" she said, blinking hard, her lips quivering. "She was its mother, but she killed it. Then she ran off the bed and went downstairs into the shop under the counter. I called to Luigi. You know, he's Mrs. Rineiri's brother."

"Yes, I know."

"He said she was too young, and she was badly frightened and very hurt. He took the alive kitten to her but she got up and walked away. She didn't want it. Then Luigi told me not to look. But I followed him. He held the kitten by the tail and he banged it against the wall twice. Then he dropped it into the rubbish heap. He moved aside some rubbish with his toe, and put the kitten there and pushed rubbish over it. Then Luigi said the cat should be destroyed. He said she was badly hurt and it would always hurt her to have kittens."

"He hasn't destroyed her. She's still alive. But it looks to me as if he were right."

"Yes, I expect he was."

"What upset you—that he killed the kitten?"

"Oh no, I expect the cat would if he hadn't. But that isn't the point, is it?"

"What is the point?"

"I don't think I really know." She had been speaking breathlessly, and fast. Now she said slowly: "It's not a question of right or wrong, is it? Why should it be? It's a question of what one is. That night Luigi wanted to go promenading with me. For him, that was *that*. Something had to be done, and he'd done it. But I felt ill. He was very nice to me. He's a very good person," she said, defiantly.

"Yes, he looks it."

"That night I couldn't sleep. I was blaming myself. I should never have left the cat to go swimming. Well, and then I decided to leave the next day. And I did. And that's all. The whole thing was a mistake, from start to finish."

"Going to Italy at all?"

"Oh, to go for a holiday would have been all right."

"You've done all that work for nothing? You mean you aren't going to make use of all that research?"

"No. It was a mistake."

"Why don't you leave it a few weeks and see how thing are then?"

"Why?"

"You might feel differently about it."

"What an extraordinary thing to say. Why should I? Oh, you mean, time passing, healing wounds—that sort of thing? What an extraordinary idea. It's always seemed to me an extraordinary idea. No, right from the beginning I've felt ill at ease with the whole business, not myself at all."

"Rather irrationally, I should have said."

Judith considered this, very seriously. She frowned while she thought it over. Then she said: "But if one cannot rely on what one feels, what can one rely on?"

"On what one thinks, I should have expected you to say."

"Should you? Why? Really, you people are all very strange. I don't understand you." She turned off the electric fire, and her face closed up. She smiled, friendly and distant, and said: "I don't really see any point at all in discussing it."

1963

QUESTIONS

1. At the end of "The Real Thing," the narrator says that though it may have done his art some harm, he is glad of his experience with the Monarchs "for the memory." What is so valuable about the memory? Did it not seem a rather painful experience?

2. Because we are told the story of "Our Friend Judith" by a friend, we never get to know Judith from the inside and are never very close to the action. This seems to have the effect of lessening the suspense and perhaps even our interest in or feelings for Judith. What is gained by this focus and voice? How does it change the meaning of the story?

3. The friend says she blundered and lost her opportunity to find out what Judith and her life were really like. How did she lose the opportunity? Was it really a blunder? Could she have found out what she wanted to know if she had not "blundered"?

4. What is the friend "really" like?

WRITING SUGGESTIONS

1. Write a 1000–1500 word scene from "My Man Bovanne" using an omniscient or unlimited point of view or using the focus and voice of one of Hazel's children.

2. Do you agree with Henry James that "real people" do not look like the popular stereotypes of their class, occupation, status, and so on? Write a personal essay describing your own experience of meeting someone who did or did not look like the stereotype: a president, congressman, mayor; an author, a poet; a woman lawyer; a major league baseball / football / basketball player; an actor or actress.

3. Write an analysis of the character of the narrator of "Our Friend Judith." Base your interpretation solidly on specific passages, incidents, and attitudes in the story.

4. Write for or against one of these two interpretations of Judith's character. Or show why neither is satisfactory:

   a. Judith seems to be cool, intellectual, and respectable, but she's really fiery and passionate; she's hypocritical, since she lives one kind of life in the open and another in secret.
   b. Judith is her own woman. She does not need a man to lean on or depend on, but has her own full life, her profession, and does her own thing in her own way, the way men are praised for doing but women often condemned for doing.

4 SETTING

All stories, like all individuals, are embedded in a context or setting—a time, a place, and a culture. The time can be contemporary ("No One's a Mystery") or historical ("The Cask of Amontillado") or even mythically vague ("The Zebra Storyteller"). It can be very limited, only a few minutes elapsing ("No One's a Mystery") or some years ("Sonny's Blues"). The place can be rather fixed and interior ("The Real Thing") or varied ("Our Friend Judith"). It can be foreign ("The Cask of Amontillado") or American ("My Man Bovanne") or tied to a region ("A Rose for Emily" and the South) or a locale ("Sonny's Blues" and Harlem). The individuals in the stories are embedded in the specific context, and the more we know of the setting, and of the relationship of the character to the setting, the more likely we are to understand the character and the story.

Even in a spare story like "No One's a Mystery" the interaction or interrelation of setting, character, and plot are important and revealing. The eighteen-year-old narrator and Jack, her lover, are in his dirty pickup truck on the highway. His wife approaches in her Cadillac—with the lights on even though it's daytime, a habit he hates. The vehicles they drive and their condition tell you a good deal about Jack, his wife, and their relationship. The significance of Jack's driving a pickup (and of the muddy manure on his boots) is modulated by the almost casually dropped information that they are in Wyoming, in or near Cheyenne.

Place or setting is seldom insignificant or unrelated to a larger cultural context. "The Jewelry" is set in Paris in the late 1870s. Quite naturally, you might say, since it was written by a Frenchman in the early 1880s; he's just writing about his own time and place. True enough, but the cynicism, the somewhat bitter irony of the story set among the bourgeoisie and the bureaucracy, owes a good deal of its tone to the recent (1870–71) defeat of France and the siege and occupation of Paris by the Prussian Bismarck. (France paid Germany a billion dollars in reparations, an unheard-of amount in those days, and did so, to the world's astonishment, in just three years; might this have something to do with the emphasis on money in the story?) The interaction of tone and times, setting and situation, are fused in this story in a way that would scarcely be possible in another context. Money, adultery, and high living are not unknown in our society, but try rewriting this story by setting it in New York.

John Cheever's "The Country Husband" is set in the early to middle 1950s, in my time and close enough to yours so that you know the important things about the period—Elvis, Marilyn, all that. World War II seems distant, but not too distant: a man in a mid-life crisis served in the army during that time. It is set in suburban New York, not too remote or exotic a setting, since it has many of the qualities of the suburbs of any medium-sized to large city in the 1990s. Yet the story is still somewhat of a period piece. The myth of the calm, undisturbed, comfortable good life—peace and plenty in the suburbs after the decades of Depression and war, the milieu of "Leave It to Beaver" and "Father Knows Best"—still prevailed. Airplane accidents and alcoholic fathers and memories of war were banned. And it seemed, at certain times, boring, almost unbearably so. All the excitement, all the romance of life, was gone, kept away by rows of white picket fences. Yes, we have suburbs like Shady Hill, but not many of the wives stay at home like Julia Weed and we no longer believe they are fenced off from the problems and promises of the Big City. The setting of this 1958 story makes of Francis a "weed" and though there are still crabgrass and dandelions in some of our finest neighborhoods, he and history would be difficult to transplant.

"The Country Husband" is, despite its relative modernity, an historical story. Its time, place, and cultural setting interact with its narrative. Some stories are more overtly historical, and their cultural milieu—or the stereotypes associated with it—are more obviously significant than those in Cheever's tale. The protagonist and the plot of "The Cask of Amontillado" are Machiavellian (characterized by subtle or unscrupulous cunning; after the Italian Renaissance politician and writer Niccolò Machiavelli, 1460–1527), and the story is set in Italy during the Renaissance. The Puritan Goodman Brown lives in the reign of King William (1689–1702) in Salem, Massachusetts, where in 1692 the famous witch trials were held—what better place and time for a story whose subject is a witches' meeting and whose theme has to do with man's natural depravity? An *English* "spinster" seems (or seemed) much more prudish and virginal than just any old spinster, Italian lovers more sensual than Anglo-Saxon ones, and in "Our Friend Judith" testing that cultural convention is, virtually, the story.

In some stories setting, even when appropriate and natural, can symbolize whole ways of life or value systems. In "The Lady with the Dog," Yalta with its fruit, seashore, and semi-tropical climate exemplifies a more passionate, pleasurable, exciting life than the cold and cloudy, bureaucratic, intellectually rarefied air and routine of Moscow.

Jing-Mei Woo, the narrator of "A Pair of Tickets," explores the relation of place, cultural heritage, and ethnic identity. Living in San Francisco she had, at fifteen, "vigorously denied that I had any Chinese whatsoever below my skin" (par. 2), but at thirty-six, as she crosses the border from Hong Kong into China, she finds that she is "becoming Chinese." In Guangzhou, however, she discovers that within the vast change of place and cultures, in the modern world, at least among the privileged, there is a homogeneity: though men and women are working without safety belts or helmets on a scaffold made of bamboo held together with plastic strips, the hotel she is taken to "looks like a grander version of the Hyatt Regency." There are "shopping arcades and restaurants all encased in granite and glass," and in the rooms color television sets, a wet bar, Coke Classic, M & M's, Johnnie Walker Red, and so on. Her father's family circumvents her plan to have a Chinese feast and they dine on hamburgers, french fries, apple pie à la mode, delivered by room service. In the modern city of Shanghai, meeting her twin half-sisters for the first time, she finds she is Chinese not because of place or face, but because of "blood." But within this story is another story, her mother's story, with another setting in time and conditions. Fleeing from Kweilin and the advance of the Japanese army in 1944, Jing-Mei's mother was forced by overwhelming circumstances to abandon her twin babies. Jing-Mei can now explain a good deal about her own past, about her mother and their relationship, from the story of her actions and the historical circumstances of the war.

If one of the functions of literature is to engender the sympathetic understanding of others and of other subjective visions of the world, setting—the time, place, and culture in which the fictional characters and action are embedded—is an essential element.

JOHN CHEEVER

The Country Husband

To begin at the beginning, the airplane from Minneapolis in which Francis Weed was traveling East ran into heavy weather. The sky had been a hazy blue, with the clouds below the plane lying so close together that nothing could be seen of the earth. The mist began to form outside the windows, and they flew into a white cloud of such density that it reflected the exhaust fires. The color of the cloud darkened to gray, and the plane began to rock. Francis had been in heavy weather before, but he had never been shaken up so much. The man in the seat beside him pulled a flask out of his pocket and took a drink. Francis smiled at his neighbor, but the man looked away; he wasn't sharing his pain killer with anyone. The plane began to drop and flounder wildly. A child was crying. The air in the cabin was overheated and stale, and Francis' left foot went to sleep. He read a little from a paper book that he had bought at the airport, but the violence of the storm divided his attention. It was black outside the ports. The exhaust fires blazed and shed sparks in the dark, and, inside, the shaded lights, the stuffiness, and the window curtains gave the cabin an atmosphere of intense and misplaced domesticity. Then the light flickered and went out. "You know what I've always wanted to do?" the man beside Francis said suddenly. "I've always wanted to buy a farm in New Hampshire and raise beef cattle." The stewardess announced that they were going to make an emergency landing. All but the children saw in their minds the spreading wings of the Angel of Death. The pilot could be heard singing faintly, "I've got sixpence, jolly, jolly sixpence. I've got sixpence to last me all my life . . ."[1] There was no other sound.

The loud groaning of the hydraulic valves swallowed up the pilot's song, and there was a shrieking high in the air, like automobile brakes, and the plane hit flat on its belly in a cornfield and shook them so violently that an old man up forward howled, "Me kidneys! Me kidneys!" The stewardess flung open the door, and someone opened an emergency door at the back, letting in the sweet noise of their continuing mortality—the idle splash and smell of a heavy rain. Anxious for their lives, they filed out of the doors and scattered over the cornfield in all directions, praying that the thread would hold. It did. Nothing happened. When it was clear that the plane would not burn or explode, the crew and the stewardess gathered the passengers together and led them to the shelter of a barn. They were not far from Philadelphia, and in a little while a string of taxis took them into the city. "It's just like the Marne,"[2] someone said, but there was surprisingly little relaxation of that suspiciousness with which many Americans regard their fellow travelers.

In Philadelphia, Francis Weed got a train to New York. At the end of that journey, he crossed the city and caught just as it was about to pull out the commuting train that he took five nights a week to his home in Shady Hill.

He sat with Trace Bearden. "You know, I was in that plane that just crashed outside Philadelphia," he said. "We came down in a field . . ." He had traveled faster than the newspapers or the rain, and the weather in New York was sunny and mild. It was a day in late September, as fragrant and shapely as an apple. Trace listened to the story, but how could he get excited? Francis had no powers that would let him re-create a brush with death—particularly in the atmosphere of a commuting train, journeying through a sunny countryside where already, in the slum gardens, there were signs of harvest. Trace picked up his newspaper, and Francis was left alone with his thoughts. He said good night to Trace on the platform at Shady Hill and drove in his secondhand Volkswagen up to the Blenhollow neighborhood, where he lived.

The Weeds' Dutch Colonial house was larger than it appeared to be from the driveway. The living room was spacious and divided like Gaul,[3] into three parts. Around an ell to the left as one entered from the vestibule was the long table, laid for six, with candles and a bowl of fruit in the center. The sounds and

1. Song popular with Allied troops in World War II. 2. On September 8, 1914, over 1000 Paris taxicabs were requisitioned to move troops to the Marne River to halt the encircling Germans. 3. Ancient France (Gaul) is so described by Julius Caesar in *The Gallic War*.

smells that came from the open kitchen door were appetizing, for Julia Weed was a good cook. The largest part of the living room centered on a fireplace. On the right were some bookshelves and a piano. The room was polished and tranquil, and from the windows that opened to the west there was some late-summer sunlight, brilliant and as clear as water. Nothing here was neglected; nothing had not been burnished. It was not the kind of household where, after prying open a stuck cigarette box, you would find an old shirt button and a tarnished nickel. The hearth was swept, the roses on the piano were reflected in the polish of the broad top, and there was an album of Schubert waltzes on the rack. Louisa Weed, a pretty girl of nine, was looking out the western windows. Her young brother Henry was standing beside her. Her still younger brother, Toby, was studying the figures of some tonsured monks drinking beer on the polished brass of the woodbox. Francis, taking off his hat and putting down his paper, was not consciously pleased with the scene; he was not that reflective. It was his element, his creation, and he returned to it with that sense of lightness and strength with which any creature returns to his home. "Hi, everybody," he said. "The plane from Minneapolis . . ."

Nine times out of ten, Francis would be greeted with affection, but tonight the children are absorbed in their own antagonisms. Francis had not finished his sentence about the plane crash before Henry plants a kick in Louisa's behind. Louisa swings around, saying, "*Damn you*!" Francis makes the mistake of scolding Louisa for bad language before he punishes Henry. Now Louisa turns on her father and accuses him of favoritism. Henry is always right; she is persecuted and lonely; her lot is hopeless. Francis turns to his son, but the son has justification for the kick—she hit him first; she hit him on the ear, which is dangerous. Louisa agrees with this passionately. She hit him on the ear, and she *meant* to hit him on the ear, because he messed up her china collection. Henry says that this is a lie. Little Toby turns away from the woodbox to throw in some evidence for Louisa. Henry claps his hand over little Toby's mouth. Francis separates the two boys but accidentally pushes Toby into the woodbox. Toby begins to cry. Louisa is already crying. Just then, Julia Weed comes into that part of the room where the table is laid. She is a pretty, intelligent woman, and the white in her hair is premature. She does not seem to notice the fracas. "Hello, darling," she says serenely to Francis. "Wash your hands, everyone. Dinner is ready." She strikes a match and lights the six candles in this vale of tears.[4]

This simple announcement, like the war cries of the Scottish chieftains, only refreshes the ferocity of the combatants. Louisa gives Henry a blow on the shoulder. Henry, although he seldom cries, has pitched nine innings and is tired. He bursts into tears. Little Toby discovers a splinter in his hand and begins to howl. Francis says loudly that he has been in a plane crash and that he is tired. Julia appears again from the kitchen and, still ignoring the chaos, asks Francis to go upstairs and tell Helen that everything is ready. Francis is happy to go; it is like getting back to headquarters company.[5] He is planning to tell his oldest daughter about the airplane crash, but Helen is lying on her bed reading a *True Romance*

4. Common figurative reference to earthly life (vale is valley), though here the tears are literal.
5. That is, like escaping from combat to relative safety behind the lines.

magazine, and the first thing Francis does is to take the magazine from her hand and remind Helen that he has forbidden her to buy it. She did not buy it, Helen replies. It was given to her by her best friend, Bessie Black. Everybody reads *True Romance*. Bessie Black's father reads *True Romance*. There isn't a girl in Helen's class who doesn't read *True Romance*. Francis expresses his detestation of the magazine and then tells her that dinner is ready—although from the sounds downstairs it doesn't seem so. Helen follows him down the stairs. Julia has seated herself in the candlelight and spread a napkin over her lap. Neither Louisa nor Henry has come to the table. Little Toby is still howling, lying face down on the floor. Francis speaks to him gently: "Daddy was in a plane crash this afternoon, Toby. Don't you want to hear about it?" Toby goes on crying. "If you don't come to the table now, Toby," Francis says, "I'll have to send you to bed without any supper." The little boy rises, gives him a cutting look, flies up the stairs to his bedroom, and slams the door. "Oh, dear," Julia says, and starts to go after him. Francis says that she will spoil him. Julia says that Toby is ten pounds underweight and has to be encouraged to eat. Winter is coming, and he will spend the cold months in bed unless he has his dinner. Julia goes upstairs. Francis sits down at the table with Helen. Helen is suffering from the dismal feeling of having read too intently on a fine day, and she gives her father and the room a jaded look. She doesn't understand about the plane crash, because there wasn't a drop of rain in Shady Hill.

Julia returns with Toby, and they all sit down and are served. "Do I have to look at that big, fat slob?" Henry says, of Louisa. Everybody but Toby enters into this skirmish, and it rages up and down the table for five minutes. Toward the end, Henry puts his napkin over his head and, trying to eat that way, spills spinach all over his shirt. Francis asks Julia if the children couldn't have their dinner earlier. Julia's guns are loaded for this. She can't cook two dinners and lay two tables. She paints with lightning strokes that panorama of drudgery in which her youth, her beauty, and her wit have been lost. Francis says that he must be understood; he was nearly killed in an airplane crash, and he doesn't like to come home every night to a battlefield. Now Julia is deeply concerned. Her voice trembles. He doesn't come home every night to a battlefield. The accusation is stupid and mean. Everything was tranquil until he arrived. She stops speaking, puts down her knife and fork, and looks into her plate as if it is a gulf. She begins to cry. "Poor Mummy!" Toby says, and when Julia gets up from the table, drying her tears with a napkin, Toby goes to her side. "Poor Mummy," he says. "Poor Mummy!" And they climb the stairs together. The other children drift away from the battlefield, and Francis goes into the back garden for a cigarette and some air.

It was a pleasant garden, with walks and flower beds and places to sit. The sunset had nearly burned out, but there was still plenty of light. Put into a thoughtful mood by the crash and the battle, Francis listened to the evening sounds of Shady Hill. "Varmints! Rascals!" old Mr. Nixon shouted to the squirrels in his bird-feeding station. "Avaunt and quit my sight!" A door slammed. Someone was cutting grass. Then Donald Goslin, who lived at the corner, began to play the "Moonlight Sonata."[6] He did this nearly every night. He threw the tempo out the window and played it *rubato*[7] from beginning to end, like an outpouring of tearful petulance, lonesomeness, and self-pity—of everything it was Beethoven's greatness not to know. The music rang up and down the street beneath the trees like an appeal for love, for tenderness, aimed at some lovely housemaid—some fresh-faced, homesick girl from Galway, looking at old snapshots in her third-floor room. "Here, Jupiter, here, Jupiter," Francis called to the Mercers' retriever. Jupiter crashed through the tomato vines with the remains of a felt hat in his mouth.

Jupiter was an anomaly. His retrieving instincts and his high spirits were out of place in Shady Hill. He was as black as coal, with a long, alert, intelligent, rakehell face. His eyes gleamed with mischief, and he held his head high. It was the fierce, heavily collared dog's head that appears in heraldry, in tapestry, and that used to appear on umbrella handles and walking sticks. Jupiter went where he pleased, ransacking wastebaskets, clotheslines, garbage pails, and shoe bags. He broke up garden parties and tennis matches, and got mixed up in the processional at Christ Church on Sunday, barking at the men in red dresses.[8] He crashed through old Mr. Nixon's rose garden two or three times a day, cutting a wide swath through the Condesa de Sastagos,[9] and as soon as Donald Goslin lighted his barbecue fire on Thursday nights, Jupiter would get the scent. Nothing the Goslins did could drive him away. Sticks and stones and rude commands only moved him to the edge of the terrace, where he remained, with his gallant and heraldic muzzle, waiting for Donald Goslin to turn his back and reach for the salt. Then he would spring onto the terrace, lift the steak lightly off the fire, and run away with the Goslins' dinner. Jupiter's days were numbered. The Wrightsons' German gardener or the Farquarsons' cook would soon poison him. Even old Mr. Nixon might put some arsenic in the garbage that Jupiter loved. "Here, Jupiter, Jupiter!" Francis called, but the dog pranced off, shaking the hat in his white teeth. Looking at the windows of his house, Francis saw that Julia had come down and was blowing out the candles.

Julia and Francis Weed went out a great deal. Julia was well liked and gregarious, and her love of parties sprang from a most natural dread of chaos and loneliness. She went through the morning mail with real anxiety, looking for invitations, and she usually found some, but she was insatiable, and if she had gone out seven nights a week, it would not have cured her of a reflective look—the look of someone who hears distant music—for she would always suppose that there was a more brilliant party somewhere else. Francis limited her to two week-night parties, putting a flexible interpretation on Friday, and rode through the weekend like a dory in a gale. The day after the airplane crash, the Weeds were to have dinner with the Farquarsons.

Francis got home late from town, and Julia got the sitter while he dressed, and then hurried him out of the house. The party was small and pleasant, and Francis settled down to enjoy himself. A new maid passed the drinks. Her hair

6. Beethoven's *Sonata Quasi una Fantasia* (1802), a famous and frequently sentimentalized piano composition. 7. With intentional deviations from strict tempo. 8. Probably the choir. 9. Rather uncommon yellow and red roses difficult to grow.

was dark, and her face was round and pale and seemed familiar to Francis. He had not developed his memory as a sentimental faculty. Wood smoke, lilac, and other such perfumes did not stir him, and his memory was something like his appendix—a vestigial repository. It was not his limitation at all to be unable to escape the past; it was perhaps his limitation that he had escaped it so successfully. He might have seen the maid at other parties, he might have seen her taking a walk on Sunday afternoons, but in either case he would not be searching his memory now. Her face was, in a wonderful way, a moon face—Norman or Irish—but it was not beautiful enough to account for his feeling that he had seen her before, in circumstances that he ought to be able to remember. He asked Nellie Farquarson who she was. Nellie said that the maid had come through an agency, and that her home was Trénon, in Normandy—a small place with a church and a restaurant that Nellie had once visited. While Nellie talked on about her travels abroad, Francis realized where he had seen the woman before. It had been at the end of the war. He had left a replacement depot with some other men and taken a three-day pass in Trénon. On their second day, they had walked out to a crossroads to see the public chastisement of a young woman who had lived with the German commandant during the Occupation.

It was a cool morning in the fall. The sky was overcast, and poured down onto the dirt crossroads a very discouraging light. They were on high land and could see how like one another the shapes of the clouds and the hills were as they stretched off toward the sea. The prisoner arrived sitting on a three-legged stool in a farm cart. She stood by the cart while the Mayor read the accusation and the sentence. Her head was bent and her face was set in that empty half smile behind which the whipped soul is suspended. When the Mayor was finished, she undid her hair and let it fall across her back. A little man with a gray mustache cut off her hair with shears and dropped it on the ground. Then, with a bowl of soapy water and a straight razor, he shaved her skull clean. A woman approached and began to undo the fastenings of her clothes, but the prisoner pushed her aside and undressed herself. When she pulled her chemise over her head and threw it on the ground, she was naked. The women jeered; the men were still. There was no change in the falseness or the plaintiveness of the prisoner's smile. The cold wind made her white skin rough and hardened the nipples of her breasts. The jeering ended gradually, put down by the recognition of their common humanity. One woman spat on her, but some inviolable grandeur in her nakedness lasted through the ordeal. When the crowd was quiet, she turned—she had begun to cry—and, with nothing on but a pair of worn black shoes and stockings, walked down the dirt road alone away from the village. The round white face had aged a little, but there was no question but that the maid who passed his cocktails and later served Francis his dinner was the woman who had been punished at the crossroads.

The war seemed now so distant and that world where the cost of partisanship had been death or torture so long ago. Francis had lost track of the men who had been with him in Vésey. He could not count on Julia's discretion. He could not tell anyone. And if he had told the story now, at the dinner table, it would have been a social as well as a human error. The people in the Farquarsons' living room seemed united in their tacit claim that there had been no past, no war—that there was no danger or trouble in the world. In the recorded history of human arrangements, this extraordinary meeting would have fallen into place, but the atmosphere of Shady Hill made the memory unseemly and impolite. The prisoner withdrew after passing the coffee, but the encounter left Francis feeling languid; it had opened his memory and his senses, and left them dilated. Julia went into the house. Francis stayed in the car to take the sitter home.

Expecting to see Mrs. Henlein, the old lady who usually stayed with the children, he was surprised when a young girl opened the door and came out onto the lighted stoop. She stayed in the light to count her textbooks. She was frowning and beautiful. Now, the world is full of beautiful young girls, but Francis saw here the difference between beauty and perfection. All those endearing flaws, moles, birthmarks, and healed wounds were missing, and he experienced in his consciousness that moment when music breaks glass, and felt a pang of recognition as strange, deep and wonderful as anything in his life. It hung from her frown, from an impalpable darkness in her face—a look that impressed him as a direct appeal for love. When she had counted her books, she came down the steps and opened the car door. In the light, he saw that her cheeks were wet. She got in and shut the door.

"You're new," Francis said.

"Yes. Mrs. Henlein is sick. I'm Anne Murchison."

"Did the children give you any trouble?"

"Oh, no, no." She turned and smiled at him unhappily in the dim dashboard light. Her light hair caught on the collar of her jacket, and she shook her head to set it loose.

"You've been crying."

"Yes."

"I hope it was nothing that happened in our house."

"No, no, it was nothing that happened in your house." Her voice was bleak. "It's no secret. Everybody in the village knows. Daddy's an alcoholic, and he just called me from some saloon and gave me a piece of his mind. He thinks I'm immoral. He called just before Mrs. Weed came back."

"I'm sorry."

"Oh, *Lord*!" She gasped and began to cry. She turned toward Francis, and he took her in his arms and let her cry on his shoulder. She shook in his embrace, and this movement accentuated his sense of the fineness of her flesh and bone. The layers of their clothing felt thin, and when her shuddering began to diminish, it was so much like a paroxysm of love that Francis lost his head and pulled her roughly against him. She drew away. "I live on Belleview Avenue," she said. "You go down Lansing Street to the railroad bridge."

"All right." He started the car.

"You turn left at that traffic light. . . . Now you turn right here and go straight on toward the tracks."

The road Francis took brought him out of his own neighborhood, across the tracks, and toward the river, to a street where the near-poor lived, in houses whose peaked gables and trimmings of wooden lace conveyed the purest feelings of pride and romance, although the houses themselves could not have offered much privacy or comfort, they were all so small. The street was dark, and, stirred by the grace and beauty of the troubled girl, he seemed, in turning into it, to have come into the deepest part of some submerged memory. In the distance, he saw a porch light burning. It was the only one, and she said that the house with the light was where she lived. When he stopped the car, he could see beyond the porch light into a dimly lighted hallway with an old-fashioned clothes tree. "Well, here we are," he said, conscious that a young man would have said something different.

She did not move her hands from the books, where they were folded, and she turned and faced him. There were tears of lust in his eyes. Determinedly—not sadly—he opened the door on his side and walked around to open hers. He took her free hand, letting his fingers in between hers, climbed at her side the two concrete steps, and went up a narrow walk through a front garden where dahlias, marigolds, and roses—things that had withstood the light frosts—still bloomed, and made a bittersweet smell in the night air. At the steps, she freed her hand and then turned and kissed him swiftly. Then she crossed the porch and shut the door. The porch light went out, then the light in the hall. A second later, a light went on upstairs at the side of the house, shining into a tree that was still covered with leaves. It took her only a few minutes to undress and get into bed, and then the house was dark.

Julia was asleep when Francis got home. He opened a second window and got into bed to shut his eyes on that night, but as soon as they were shut—as soon as he had dropped off to sleep—the girl entered his mind, moving with perfect freedom through its shut doors and filling chamber after chamber with her light, her perfume, and the music of her voice. He was crossing the Atlantic with her on the old *Mauretania*[1] and, later, living with her in Paris. When he woke from his dream, he got up and smoked a cigarette at the open window. Getting back into bed, he cast around in his mind for something he desired to do that would injure no one, and he thought of skiing. Up through the dimness in his mind rose the image of a mountain deep in snow. It was late in the day. Wherever his eyes looked, he saw broad and heartening things. Over his shoulder, there was a snow-filled valley, rising into wooded hills where the trees dimmed the whiteness like a sparse coat of hair. The cold deadened all sound but the loud, iron clanking of the lift machinery. The light on the trails was blue, and it was harder than it had been a minute or two earlier to pick the turns, harder to judge—now that the snow was all deep blue—the crust, the ice, the bare spots, and the deep piles of dry powder. Down the mountain he swung, matching his speed against the contours of a slope that had been formed in the first ice age, seeking with ardor some simplicity of feeling and circumstance. Night fell then, and he drank a Martini with some old friend in a dirty country bar.

In the morning, Francis' snow-covered mountain was gone, and he was left with his vivid memories of Paris and the *Mauretania*. He had been bitten gravely.

1. The original *Mauretania* (1907–1935), sister ship of the *Lusitania*, which was sunk by the Germans in 1915, was the most famous transatlantic liner of its day.

He washed his body, shaved his jaws, drank his coffee, and missed the seventy-thirty-one. The train pulled out just as he brought his car to the station, and the longing he felt for the coaches as they drew stubbornly away from him reminded him of the humors of love. He waited for the eight-two, on what was now an empty platform. It was a clear morning; the morning seemed thrown like a gleaming bridge of light over his mixed affairs. His spirits were feverish and high. The image of the girl seemed to put him into a relationship to the world that was mysterious and enthralling. Cars were beginning to fill up the parking lot, and he noticed that those that had driven down from the high land above Shady Hill were white with hoarfrost. This first clear sign of autumn thrilled him. An express train—a night train from Buffalo or Albany—came down the tracks between the platforms, and he saw that the roofs of the foremost cars were covered with a skin of ice. Struck by the miraculous physicalness of everything, he smiled at the passengers in the dining car, who could be seen eating eggs and wiping their mouths with napkins as they traveled. The sleeping-car compartments, with their soiled bed linen, trailed through the fresh morning like a string of rooming-house windows. Then he saw an extraordinary thing; at one of the bedroom windows sat an unclothed woman of exceptional beauty, combing her golden hair. She passed like an apparition through Shady Hill, combing and combing her hair, and Francis followed her with his eyes until she was out of sight. Then old Mrs. Wrightson joined him on the platform and began to talk.

"Well, I guess you must be surprised to see me here the third morning in a row," she said, "but because of my window curtains I'm becoming a regular commuter. The curtains I bought on Monday I returned on Tuesday, and the curtains I bought Tuesday I'm returning today. On Monday, I got exactly what I wanted—it's a wool tapestry with roses and birds—but when I got them home, I found they were the wrong length. Well, I exchanged them yesterday, and when I got them home, I found they were still the wrong length. Now I'm praying to high heaven that the decorator will have them in the right length, because you know my house, you *know* my living-room windows, and you can imagine what a problem they present. I don't know what to do with them."

"I know what to do with them," Francis said.

"What?"

"Paint them black on the inside, and shut up." 35

There was a gasp from Mrs. Wrightson, and Francis looked down at her to be sure that she knew he meant to be rude. She turned and walked away from him, so damaged in spirit that she limped. A wonderful feeling enveloped him, as if light were being shaken about him, and he thought again of Venus combing and combing her hair as she drifted through the Bronx. The realization of how many years had passed since he had enjoyed being deliberately impolite sobered him. Among his friends and neighbors, there were brilliant and gifted people—he saw that—but many of them, also, were bores and fools, and he had made the mistake of listening to them all with equal attention. He had confused a lack of discrimination with Christian love, and the confusion seemed general and destructive. He was grateful to the girl for this bracing sensation of independence. Birds were singing—cardinals and the last of the robins. The sky shone like enamel. Even the smell of ink from his morning paper honed his appetite for life, and the world that was spread out around him was plainly a paradise.

If Francis had believed in some hierarchy of love—in spirits armed with hunting bows, in the capriciousness of Venus and Eros[2]—or even in magical potions, philters, and stews, in scapulae and quarters of the moon,[3] it might have explained his susceptibility and his feverish high spirits. The autumnal loves of middle age are well publicized, and he guessed that he was face to face with one of these, but there was not a trace of autumn in what he felt. He wanted to sport in the green woods, scratch where he itched, and drink from the same cup.

His secretary, Miss Rainey, was late that morning—she went to a psychiatrist three mornings a week—and when she came in, Francis wondered what advice a psychiatrist would have for him. But the girl promised to bring back into his life something like the sound of music. The realization that this music might lead him straight to a trial for statutory rape at the country courthouse collapsed his happiness. The photograph of his four children laughing into the camera on the beach at Gay Head reproached him. On the letterhead of his firm there was a drawing of the Laocoön,[4] and the figure of the priest and his sons in the coils of the snake appeared to him to have the deepest meaning.

He had lunch with Pinky Trabert. At a conversational level, the mores of his friends were robust and elastic, but he knew that the moral card house would come down on them all—on Julia and the children as well—if he got caught taking advantage of a baby-sitter. Looking back over the recent history of Shady Hill for some precedent, he found there was none. There was no turpitude; there had not been a divorce since he lived there; there had not even been a breath of scandal. Things seemed arranged with more propriety even than in the Kingdom of Heaven. After leaving Pinky, Francis went to a jeweler's and bought the girl a bracelet. How happy this clandestine purchase made him, how stuffy and comical the jeweler's clerks seemed, how sweet the women who passed at his back smelled! On Fifth Avenue, passing Atlas with his shoulders bent under the weight of the world,[5] Francis thought of the strenuousness of containing his physicalness within the patterns he had chosen.

He did not know when he would see the girl next. He had the bracelet in his inside pocket when he got home. Opening the door of his house, he found her in the hall. Her back was to him, and she turned when she heard the door close. Her smile was open and loving. Her perfection stunned him like a fine day—a day after a thunderstorm. He seized her and covered her lips with his, and she struggled but she did not have to struggle for long, because just then little Gertrude Flannery appeared from somewhere and said, "Oh, Mr. Weed . . ."

Gertrude was a stray. She had been born with a taste for exploration, and she

2. The Roman name for the goddess of love (Greek *Aphrodite*) and the Greek name for her son (Roman *Cupid*). 3. Love-inducing and predictive magic; *scapulae* are shoulderblades or bones of the back. 4. Famous Greek statue, described here, now in the Vatican museum; the "meaning" for Weed seems to reside in the physical struggle, not in the legend (in which the priest and his sons were punished for warning the Trojans about the wooden horse). 5. In Greek legend the Titan Atlas supported the heavens on his shoulders but has come to be depicted as bearing the globe; the statue is at Rockefeller Center.

did not have it in her to center her life with her affectionate parents. People who did not know the Flannerys concluded from Gertrude's behavior that she was the child of a bitterly divided family, where drunken quarrels were the rule. This was not true. The fact that little Gertrude's clothing was ragged and thin was her own triumph over her mother's struggle to dress her warmly and neatly. Garrulous, skinny, and unwashed, she drifted from house to house around the Blenhollow neighborhood, forming and breaking alliances based on an attachment to babies, animals, children her own age, adolescents, and sometimes adults. Opening your front door in the morning, you would find Gertrude sitting on your stoop. Going into the bathroom to shave, you would find Gertrude using the toilet. Looking into your son's crib, you would find it empty, and, looking further, you would find that Gertrude had pushed him in his baby carriage into the next village. She was helpful, pervasive, honest, hungry, and loyal. She never went home of her own choice. When the time to go arrived, she was indifferent to all its signs. "Go home, Gertrude," people could be heard saying in one house or another, night after night. "Go home, Gertrude. It's time for you to go home now, Gertrude." "You had better go home and get your supper, Gertrude." "I told you to go home twenty minutes ago, Gertrude." "Your mother will be worrying about you, Gertrude." "Go home, Gertrude, go home."

There are times when the lines around the human eye seem like shelves of eroded stone and when the staring eye itself strikes us with such a wilderness of animal feeling that we are at a loss. The look Francis gave the little girl was ugly and queer, and it frightened her. He reached into his pockets—his hands were shaking—and took out a quarter. "Go home, Gertrude, go home, and don't tell anyone, Gertrude. Don't—" He choked and ran into the living room as Julia called down to him from upstairs to hurry and dress.

The thought that he would drive Anne Murchison home later that night ran like a golden thread through the events of the party that Francis and Julia went to, and he laughed uproariously at dull jokes, dried a tear when Mabel Mercer told him about the death of her kitten, and stretched, yawned, sighed, and grunted like any other man with a rendezvous at the back of his mind. The bracelet was in his pocket. As he sat talking, the smell of grass was in his nose, and he was wondering where he would park the car. Nobody lived in the old Parker mansion, and the driveway was used as a lovers' lane. Townsend Street was a dead end, and he could park there, beyond the last house. The old lane that used to connect Elm Street to the riverbanks was overgrown, but he had walked there with his children, and he could drive his car deep enough into the brushwoods to be concealed.

The Weeds were the last to leave the party, and their host and hostess spoke of their own married happiness while they all four stood in the hallway saying good night. "She's my girl," their host said, squeezing his wife. "She's my blue sky. After sixteen years, I still bite her shoulders. She makes me feel like Hannibal crossing the Alps."[6]

The Weeds drove home in silence. Francis brought the car up the driveway 45

6. The Carthaginian general (274–183 B.C.) attacked the Romans from the rear by crossing the Alps, considered impregnable, with the use of elephants.

and sat still, with the motor running. "You can put the car in the garage," Julia said as she got out. "I told the Murchison girl she could leave at eleven. Someone drove her home." She shut the door, and Francis sat in the dark. He would be spared nothing then, it seemed, that a fool was not spared: ravening lewdness, jealousy, this hurt to his feelings that put tears in his eyes, even scorn—for he could see clearly the image he now presented, his arms spread over the steering wheel and his head buried in them for love.

Francis had been a dedicated Boy Scout when he was young, and, remembering the precepts of his youth, he left his office early the next afternoon and played some round-robin squash, but, with his body toned up by exercise and a shower, he realized that he might better have stayed at his desk. It was a frosty night when he got home. The air smelled sharply of change. When he stepped into the house, he sensed an unusual stir. The children were in their best clothes, and when Julia came down, she was wearing a lavender dress and her diamond sunburst. She explained the stir: Mr. Hubber was coming at seven to take their photograph for the Christmas card. She had put out Francis' blue suit and a tie with some color in it, because the picture was going to be in color this year. Julia was lighthearted at the thought of being photographed for Christmas. It was the kind of ceremony she enjoyed.

Francis went upstairs to change his clothes. He was tired from the day's work and tired with longing, and sitting on the edge of the bed had the effect of deepening his weariness. He thought of Anne Murchison, and the physical need to express himself, instead of being restrained by the pink lamps of Julia's dressing table, engulfed him. He went to Julia's desk, took a piece of writing paper, and began to write on it. "Dear Anne, I love you, I love you, I love you . . ." No one would see the letter, and he used no restraint. He used phrases like "heavenly bliss," and "love nest." He salivated, sighed, and trembled. When Julia called him to come down, the abyss between his fantasy and the practical world opened so wide that he felt it affected the muscles of his heart.

Julia and the children were on the stoop, and the photographer and his assistant had set up a double battery of floodlights to show the family and the architectural beauty of the entrance to their house. People who had come home on a late train slowed their cars to see the Weeds being photographed for their Christmas card. A few waved and called to the family. It took half an hour of smiling and wetting their lips before Mr. Hubber was satisfied. The heat of the lights made an unfresh smell in the frosty air, and when they were turned off, they lingered on the retina of Francis' eyes.

Later that night, while Francis and Julia were drinking their coffee in the living room, the doorbell rang. Julia answered the door and let in Clayton Thomas. He had come to pay for some theatre tickets that she had given his mother some time ago, and that Helen Thomas had scrupulously insisted on paying for, though Julia had asked her not to. Julia invited him in to have a cup of coffee. "I won't have any coffee," Clayton said, "but I will come in for a minute." He followed her into the living room, said good evening to Francis, and sat awkwardly in a chair.

Clayton's father had been killed in the war, and the young man's fatherlessness surrounded him like an element. This may have been conspicuous in Shady Hill because the Thomases were the only family that lacked a piece; all the other marriages were intact and productive. Clayton was in his second or third year of college, and he and his mother lived alone in a large house, which she hoped to sell. Clayton had once made some trouble. Years ago, he had stolen some money and run away; he had got to California before they caught up with him. He was tall and homely, wore hornrimmed glasses, and spoke in a deep voice.

"When do you go back to college, Clayton?" Francis asked.

"I'm not going back," Clayton said. "Mother doesn't have the money, and there's no sense in all this pretense. I'm going to get a job, and if we sell the house, we'll take an apartment in New York."

"Won't you miss Shady Hill?" Julia asked.

"No," Clayton said. "I don't like it."

"Why not?" Francis asked.

"Well, there's a lot here I don't approve of," Clayton said gravely. "Things like the club dances. Last Saturday night, I looked in toward the end and saw Mr. Granner trying to put Mrs. Minot into the trophy case. They were both drunk. I disapprove of so much drinking."

"It was Saturday night," Francis said.

"And all the dovecotes are phony," Clayton said. "And the way people clutter up their lives. I've thought about it a lot, and what seems to me to be really wrong with Shady Hill is that it doesn't have any future. So much energy is spent in perpetuating the place—in keeping out undesirables, and so forth—that the only idea of the future anyone has is just more and more commuting trains and more parties. I don't think that's healthy. I think people ought to be able to dream big dreams about the future. I think people ought to be able to dream great dreams."

"It's too bad you couldn't continue with college," Julia said.

"I want to go to divinity school," Clayton said.

"What's your church?" Francis asked.

"Unitarian, Theosophist, Transcendentalist, Humanist,"[7] Clayton said.

"Wasn't Emerson a transcendentalist?" Julia asked.

"I mean the English transcendentalists," Clayton said. "All the American transcendentalists were goops."

"What kind of job do you expect to get?" Francis asked.

"Well, I'd like to work for a publisher," Clayton said, "but everyone tells me there's nothing doing. But it's the kind of thing I'm interested in. I'm writing a long verse play about good and evil. Uncle Charlie might get me into a bank, and that would be good for me. I need the discipline. I have a long way to go in forming my character. I have some terrible habits. I talk too much. I think I ought to take vows of silence. I ought to try not to speak for a week, and discipline

7. All are deviations from orthodox Christianity and tend to be more man- than God-oriented, though their differences hardly seem reconcilable; the American Transcendentalists (see below) tended to change the emphasis from the study of thought to belief in "intuition."

myself. I've thought of making a retreat at one of the Episcopalian monasteries, but I don't like Trinitarianism."

"Do you have any girl friends?" Francis asked.

"I'm engaged to be married," Clayton said. "Of course, I'm not old enough or rich enough to have my engagement observed or respected or anything, but I bought a simulated emerald for Anne Murchison with the money I made cutting lawns this summer. We're going to be married as soon as she finishes school."

Francis recoiled at the mention of the girl's name. Then a dingy light seemed to emanate from his spirit, showing everything—Julia, the boy, the chairs—in their true colorlessness. It was like a bitter turn of the weather.

"We're going to have a large family," Clayton said. "Her father's a terrible rummy, and I've had my hard times, and we want to have lots of children. Oh, she's wonderful, Mr. and Mrs. Weed, and we have so much in common. We like all the same things. We sent out the same Christmas card last year without planning it, and we both have an allergy to tomatoes, and our eyebrows grow together in the middle. Well, goodnight."

Julia went to the door with him. When she returned, Francis said that Clayton was lazy, irresponsible, affected, and smelly. Julia said that Francis seemed to be getting intolerant; the Thomas boy was young and should be given a chance. Julia had noticed other cases where Francis had been short-tempered. "Mrs. Wrightson has asked everyone in Shady Hill to her anniversary party but us," she said.

"I'm sorry, Julia."

"Do you know why they didn't ask us?"

"Why?"

"Because you insulted Mrs. Wrightson."

"Then you know about it?"

"June Masterson told me. She was standing behind you."

Julia walked in front of the sofa with a small step that expressed, Francis knew, a feeling of anger.

"I did insult Mrs. Wrightson, Julia, and I meant to. I've never liked her parties, and I'm glad she's dropped us."

"What about Helen?"

"How does Helen come into this?"

"Mrs. Wrightson's the one who decides who goes to the assemblies."

"You mean she can keep Helen from going to the dances?"

"Yes."

"I hadn't thought of that."

"Oh. I knew you hadn't thought of it," Julia cried, thrusting hiltdeep into this chink of his armor. "And it makes me furious to see this kind of stupid thoughtlessness wreck everyone's happiness."

"I don't think I've wrecked anyone's happiness."

"Mrs. Wrightson runs Shady Hill and has run it for the last forty years. I don't know what makes you think that in a community like this you can indulge every impulse you have to be insulting, vulgar, and offensive."

"I have very good manners," Francis said, trying to give the evening a turn toward the light.

"Damn you, Francis Weed!" Julia cried, and the spit of her words struck him in the face. "I've worked hard for the social position we enjoy in this place, and I won't stand by and see you wreck it. You must have understood when you settled here that you couldn't expect to live like a bear in a cave."

"I've got to express my likes and dislikes."

"You can conceal your dislikes. You don't have to meet everything head on, like a child. Unless you're anxious to be a social leper. It's no accident that we get asked out a great deal! It's no accident that Helen has so many friends. How would you like to spend your Saturday nights at the movies? How would you like to spend your Sunday raking up dead leaves? How would you like it if your daughter spent the assembly nights sitting at her window, listening to the music from the club? How would you like it—" He did something then that was, after all, not so unaccountable, since her words seemed to raise up between them a wall so deadening that he gagged. He struck her full in the face. She staggered and then, a moment later, seemed composed. She went up the stairs to their room. She didn't slam the door. When Francis followed, a few minutes later, he found her packing a suitcase.

"Julia, I'm very sorry."

"It doesn't matter," she said. She was crying.

"Where do you think you're going?"

"I don't know. I just looked at a timetable. There's an eleven-sixteen into New York. I'll take that."

"You can't go, Julia."

"I can't stay. I know that."

"I'm sorry about Mrs. Wrightson, Julia, and I'm—"

"It doesn't matter about Mrs. Wrightson. That isn't the trouble."

"What is the trouble?"

"You don't love me."

"I do love you, Julia."

"No, you don't."

"Julia, I do love you, and I would like to be as we were—sweet and bawdy and dark—but now there are so many people."

"You hate me."

"I don't hate you, Julia."

"You have no idea of how much you hate me. I think it's subconscious. You don't realize the cruel things you've done."

"What cruel things, Julia?"

"The cruel acts your subconscious drives you to in order to express your hatred of me."

"What, Julia?"

"I've never complained."

"Tell me."

"You don't know what you're doing."

"Tell me."

"Your clothes."

"What do you mean?"

"I mean the way you leave your dirty clothes around in order to express your subconscious hatred of me."

"I don't understand."

"I mean your dirty socks and your dirty pajamas and your dirty underwear and your dirty shirts!" She rose from kneeling by the suitcase and faced him, her eyes blazing and her voice ringing with emotion. "I'm talking about the fact that you've never learned to hang up anything. You just leave your clothes all over the floor where they drop, in order to humiliate me. You do it on purpose!" She fell on the bed, sobbing.

"Julia, darling!" he said, but when she felt his hand on her shoulder she got up.

"Leave me alone," she said. "I have to go." She brushed past him to the closet and came back with a dress. "I'm not taking any of the things you've given me," she said. "I'm leaving my pearls and the fur jacket."

"Oh, Julia!" Her figure, so helpless in its self-deceptions, bent over the suitcase made him nearly sick with pity. She did not understand how desolate her life would be without him. She didn't understand the hours that working women have to keep. She didn't understand that most of her friendships existed within the framework of their marriage, and that without this she would find herself alone. She didn't understand about travel, about hotels, about money. "Julia, I can't let you go! What you don't understand, Julia, is that you've come to be dependent on me."

She tossed her head back and covered her face with her hands. "Did you say that *I* was dependent on *you?*" she asked. "Is that what you said? And who is it that tells you what time to get up in the morning and when to go to bed at night? Who is it that prepares your meals and picks up your dirty clothes and invites your friends to dinner? If it weren't for me, your neckties would be greasy and your clothing would be full of moth holes. You were alone when I met you, Francis Weed, and you'll be alone when I leave. When Mother asked you for a list to send out invitations to our wedding, how many names did you have to give her? Fourteen!"

"Cleveland wasn't my home, Julia."

"And how many of your friends came to the church? Two!"

"Cleveland wasn't my home, Julia."

"Since I'm not taking the fur jacket," she said quietly, "you'd better put it back into storage. There's an insurance policy on the pearls that comes due in January. The name of the laundry and maid's telephone number—all those things are in my desk. I hope you won't drink too much, Francis. I hope that nothing bad will happen to you. If you do get into serious trouble, you can call me."

"Oh, my darling, I can't let you go!" Francis said. "I can't let you go, Julia!" He took her in his arms.

"I guess I'd better stay and take care of you for a little while longer," she said.

Riding to work in the morning, Francis saw the girl walk down the aisle of the coach. He was surprised; he hadn't realized that the school she went to was in the city, but she was carrying books, she seemed to be going to school. His surprise delayed his reaction, but then he got up clumsily and stepped into the aisle. Several people had come between them, but he could see her ahead of him, waiting for someone to open the car door, and then, as the train swerved, putting out her hand to support herself as she crossed the platform into the next car. He followed her through that car and halfway through another before calling her name—"Anne! Anne!"—but she didn't turn. He followed her into still another car, and she sat down in an aisle seat. Coming up to her, all his feelings warm and bent in her direction, he put his hand on the back of her seat—even this touch warmed him—and leaning down to speak to her, he saw that it was not Anne. It was an older woman wearing glasses. He went on deliberately into another car, his face red with embarrassment and the much deeper feeling of having his good sense challenged; for if he couldn't tell one person from another, what evidence was there that his life with Julia and the children had as much reality as his dreams of iniquity in Paris or the litter, the grass smell, and the cave-shaped trees in Lovers' Lane.

Late that afternoon, Julia called to remind Francis that they were going out for dinner. A few minutes later, Trace Bearden called. "Look, fellar," Trace said. "I'm calling for Mrs. Thomas. You know? Clayton, that boy of hers, doesn't seem able to get a job, and I wondered if you could help. If you'd call Charlie Bell—I know he's indebted to you—and say a good word for the kid, I think Charlie would—"

"Trace, I hate to say this," Francis said, "but I don't feel that I can do anything for that boy. The kid's worthless. I know it's a harsh thing to say, but it's a fact. Any kindness done for him would backfire in everybody's face. He's just a worthless kid, Trace, and there's nothing else to be done about it. Even if we got him a job, he wouldn't be able to keep it for a week. I know that to be a fact. It's an awful thing, Trace, and I know it is, but instead of recommending that kid, I'd feel obligated to warn people against him—people who knew his father and would naturally want to step in and do something. I'd feel obliged to warn them. He's a thief . . ."

The moment this conversation was finished, Miss Rainey came in and stood by his desk. "I'm not going to be able to work for you any more, Mr. Weed," she said. "I can stay until the seventeenth if you need me, but I've been offered a whirlwind of a job, and I'd like to leave as soon as possible."

She went out, leaving him to face alone the wickedness of what he had done 135
to the Thomas boy. His children in their photograph laughed and laughed, glazed with all the bright colors of summer, and he remembered that they had met a bagpiper on the beach that day and he had paid the piper a dollar to play them a battle song of the Black Watch.[8] The girl would be at the house when he got home. He would spend another evening among his kind neighbors, pick-

8. Originally a British Highland regiment that became a line regiment and distinguished itself in battle.

ing and choosing dead-end streets, cart tracks, and the driveways of abandoned houses. There was nothing to mitigate his feeling—nothing that laughter or a game of softball with the children would change—and, thinking back over the plane crash, the Farquarsons' new maid, and Anne Murchison's difficulties with her drunken father, he wondered how he could have avoided arriving at just where he was. He was in trouble. He had been lost once in his life, coming back from a trout stream in the north woods, and he had now the same bleak realization that no amount of cheerfulness or hopefulness or valor or perseverance could help him find, in the gathering dark, the path that he'd lost. He smelled the forest. The feeling of bleakness was intolerable, and he saw clearly that he had reached the point where he would have to make a choice.

He could go to a psychiatrist, like Miss Rainey; he could go to church and confess his lusts; he could go to a Danish-massage parlor[9] in the West Seventies that had been recommended by a salesman; he could rape the girl or trust that he would somehow be prevented from doing this; or he could get drunk. It was his life, his boat, and, like every other man, he was made to be the father of thousands, and what harm could there be in a tryst that would make them both feel more kindly toward the world? This was the wrong train of thought, and he came back to the first, the psychiatrist. He had the telephone number of Miss Rainey's doctor, and he called and asked for an immediate appointment. He was insistent with the doctor's secretary—it was his manner in business—and when she said that the doctor's schedule was full for the next few weeks, Francis demanded an appointment that day and was told to come at five.

The psychiatrist's office was in a building that was used mostly by doctors and dentists, and the hallways were filled with the candy smell of mouthwash and memories of pain. Francis' character had been formed upon a series of private resolves—resolves about cleanliness, about going off the high diving board or repeating any other feat that challenged his courage, about punctuality, honesty, and virtue. To abdicate the perfect loneliness in which he had made his most vital decisions shattered his concept of character and left him now in a condition that felt like shock. He was stupefied. The scene for his *miserere mei Deus*[1] was, like the waiting room of so many doctor's offices, a crude token gesture toward the sweets of domestic bliss: a place arranged with antiques, coffee tables, potted plants, and etchings of snow-covered bridges and geese in flight, although there were no children, no marriage bed, no stove, even, in this travesty of a house, where no one had ever spent the night and where the curtained windows looked straight onto a dark air shaft. Francis gave his name and address to a secretary and then saw, at the side of the room, a policeman moving toward him. "Hold it, hold it," the policeman said. "Don't move. Keep your hands where they are."

"I think it's all right, Officer," the secretary began. "I think it will be—"

"Let's make sure," the policeman said, and he began to slap Francis' clothes, looking for what—pistols, knives, an icepick? Finding nothing, he went off and

9. Sometimes "fronts" for houses of prosititution.

1. "Have mercy upon me, O God"; first words of 51st Psalm.

the secretary began a nervous apology: "When you called on the telephone, Mr. Weed, you seemed very excited, and one of the doctor's patients has been threatening his life, and we have to be careful. If you want to go in now?" Francis pushed open a door connected to an electrical chime, and in the doctor's lair sat down heavily, blew his nose into a handkerchief, searched in his pockets for cigarettes, for matches, for something, and said hoarsely, with tears in his eyes, "I'm in love, Dr. Herzog."

It is a week or ten days later in Shady Hill. The seven-fourteen has come 140
and gone, and here and there dinner is finished and the dishes are in the dishwashing machine. The village hangs, morally and economically, from a thread; but it hangs by its thread in the evening light. Donald Goslin has begun to worry the "Moonlight Sonata" again. *Marcato ma sempre pianissimo!*[2] He seems to be wringing out a wet bath towel, but the housemaid does not heed him. She is writing a letter to Arthur Godfrey.[3] In the cellar of his house, Francis Weed is building a coffee table. Dr. Herzog recommends woodwork as a therapy, and Francis finds some true consolation in the simple arithmetic involved and in the holy smell of new wood. Francis is happy. Upstairs, little Toby is crying, because he is tired. He puts off his cowboy hat, gloves, and fringed jacket, unbuckles the belt studded with gold and rubies, the silver bullets and holsters, slips off his suspenders, his checked shirt, and Levi's, and sits on the edge of his bed to pull off his high boots. Leaving this equipment in a heap, he goes to the closet and takes his space suit off a nail. It is a struggle for him to get into the long tights, but he succeeds. He loops the magic cape over his shoulders and, climbing onto the footboard of his bed, he spreads his arms and flies the short distance to the floor, landing with a thump that is audible to everyone in the house but himself.

"Go home, Gertrude, go home," Mrs. Masterson says. "I told you to go home an hour ago, Gertrude. It's way past your suppertime, and your mother will be worried. Go home!" A door on the Babcocks' terrace flies open, and out comes Mrs. Babcock without any clothes on, pursued by a naked husband. (Their children are away at boarding school, and their terrace is screened by a hedge.) Over the terrace they go and in at the kitchen door, as passionate and handsome a nymph and satyr as you will find on any wall in Venice. Cutting the last of the roses in her garden, Julia hears old Mr. Nixon shouting at the squirrels in his bird-feeding station. "Rapscallions! Varmints! Avaunt and quit my sight!" A miserable cat wanders into the garden, sunk in spiritual and physical discomfort. Tied to its head is a small straw hat—a doll's hat—and it is securely buttoned into a doll's dress, from the skirts of which protrudes its long, hairy tail. As it walks, it shakes its feet, as if it had fallen into water.

"Here, pussy, pussy, pussy!" Julia calls.

"Here, pussy, here, poor pussy!" But the cat gives her a skeptical look and stumbles away in its skirts. The last to come is Jupiter. He prances through the tomato vines, holding in his generous mouth the remains of an evening slipper.

2. "Stressed but always very softly." 3. At the time of the story, host of a daytime radio program especially popular with housewives.

Then it is dark; it is a night where kings in golden suits ride elephants over the mountains.

1958

AMY TAN

A Pair of Tickets

The minute our train leaves the Hong Kong border and enters Shenzhen, China, I feel different. I can feel the skin on my forehead tingling, my blood rushing through a new course, my bones aching with a familiar old pain. And I think, My mother was right. I am becoming Chinese.

"Cannot be helped," my mother said when I was fifteen and had vigorously denied that I had any Chinese whatsoever below my skin. I was a sophomore at Galileo High in San Francisco, and all my Caucasian friends agreed: I was about as Chinese as they were. But my mother had studied at a famous nursing school in Shanghai, and she said she knew all about genetics. So there was no doubt in her mind, whether I agreed or not: Once you are born Chinese, you cannot help but feel and think Chinese.

"Someday you will see," said my mother. "It's in your blood, waiting to be let go."

And when she said this, I saw myself transforming like a werewolf, a mutant tag of DNA suddenly triggered, replicating itself insidiously into a *syndrome,* a cluster of telltale Chinese behaviors, all those things my mother did to embarrass me—haggling with store owners, pecking her mouth with a toothpick in public, being color-blind to the fact that lemon yellow and pale pink are not good combinations for winter clothes.

5 But today I realize I've never really known what it means to be Chinese. I am thirty-six years old. My mother is dead and I am on a train, carrying with me her dreams of coming home. I am going to China.

We are going to Guangzhou, my seventy-two-year-old father, Canning Woo, and I, where we will visit his aunt, whom he has not seen since he was ten years old. And I don't know whether it's the prospect of seeing his aunt or if it's because he's back in China, but now he looks like he's a young boy, so innocent and happy I want to button his sweater and pat his head. We are sitting across from each other, separated by a little table with two cold cups of tea. For the first time I can ever remember, my father has tears in his eyes, and all he is seeing out the train window is a sectioned field of yellow, green, and brown, a narrow canal flanking the tracks, low rising hills, and three people in blue jackets riding an ox-driven cart on this early October morning. And I can't help myself. I also have misty eyes, as if I had seen this a long, long time ago, and had almost forgotten.

In less than three hours, we will be in Guangzhou, which my guidebook tells me is how one properly refers to Canton these days. It seems all the cities I have heard of, except Shanghai, have changed their spellings. I think they are saying China has changed in other ways as well. Chungking is Chongqing. And Kweilin is Guilin. I have looked these names up, because after we see my father's aunt in Guangzhou, we will catch a plane to Shanghai, where I will meet my two half-sisters for the first time.

They are my mother's twin daughters from her first marriage, little babies she was forced to abandon on a road as she was fleeing Kweilin for Chungking in 1944. That was all my mother had told me about these daughters, so they had remained babies in my mind, all these years, sitting on the side of a road, listening to bombs whistling in the distance while sucking their patient red thumbs.

And it was only this year that someone found them and wrote with this joyful news. A letter came from Shanghai, addressed to my mother. When I first heard about this, that they were alive, I imagined my identical sisters transforming from little babies into six-year-old girls. In my mind, they were seated next to each other at a table, taking turns with the fountain pen. One would write a neat row of characters: *Dearest Mama. We are alive.* She would brush back her wispy bangs and hand the other sister the pen, and she would write: *Come get us. Please hurry.*

Of course they could not know that my mother had died three months before, 10
suddenly, when a blood vessel in her brain burst. One minute she was talking to my father, complaining about the tenants upstairs, scheming how to evict them under the pretense that relatives from China were moving in. The next minute she was holding her head, her eyes squeezed shut, groping for the sofa, and then crumpling softly to the floor with fluttering hands.

So my father had been the first one to open the letter, a long letter it turned out. And they did call her Mama. They said they always revered her as their true mother. They kept a framed picture of her. They told her about their life, from the time my mother last saw them on the road leaving Kweilin to when they were finally found.

And the letter had broken my father's heart so much—these daughters calling my mother from another life he never knew—that he gave the letter to my mother's old friend Auntie Lindo and asked her to write back and tell my sisters, in the gentlest way possible, that my mother was dead.

But instead Auntie Lindo took the letter to the Joy Luck Club and discussed with Auntie Ying and Auntie An-mei what should be done, because they had known for many years about my mother's search for her twin daughters, her endless hope. Auntie Lindo and the others cried over this double tragedy, of losing my mother three months before, and now again. And so they couldn't help but think of some miracle, some possible way of reviving her from the dead, so my mother could fulfill her dream.

So this is what they wrote to my sisters in Shanghai: "Dearest Daughters, I too have never forgotten you in my memory or in my heart. I never gave up hope that we would see each other again in a joyous reunion. I am only sorry it has been too long. I want to tell you everything about my life since I last saw you. I want to tell you this when our family comes to see you in China. . . ." They signed it with my mother's name.

It wasn't until all this had been done that they first told me about my sisters, the letter they received, the one they wrote back.

"They'll think she's coming, then," I murmured. And I had imagined my sisters now being ten or eleven, jumping up and down, holding hands, their pigtails bouncing, excited that their mother—*their* mother—was coming, whereas my mother was dead.

"How can you say she is not coming in a letter?" said Auntie Lindo. "She is their mother. She is your mother. You must be the one to tell them. All these years, they have been dreaming of her." And I thought she was right.

But then I started dreaming, too, of my mother and my sisters and how it would be if I arrived in Shanghai. All these years, while they waited to be found, I had lived with my mother and then had lost her. I imagined seeing my sisters at the airport. They would be standing on their tiptoes, looking anxiously, scanning from one dark head to another as we got off the plane. And I would recognize them instantly, their faces with the identical worried look.

"*Jyejye, Jyejye*. Sister, Sister. We are here," I saw myself saying in my poor version of Chinese.

"Where is Mama?" they would say, and look around, still smiling, two flushed and eager faces. "Is she hiding?" And this would have been like my mother, to stand behind just a bit, to tease a little and make people's patience pull a little on their hearts. I would shake my head and tell my sisters she was not hiding.

"Oh, that must be Mama, no?" one of my sisters would whisper excitedly, pointing to another small woman completely engulfed in a tower of presents. And that, too, would have been like my mother, to bring mountains of gifts, food, and toys for children—all bought on sale—shunning thanks, saying the gifts were nothing, and later turning the labels over to show my sisters, "Calvin Klein, 100% wool."

I imagined myself starting to say, "Sisters, I am sorry, I have come alone . . ." and before I could tell them—they could see it in my face—they were wailing, pulling their hair, their lips twisted in pain, as they ran away from me. And then I saw myself getting back on the plane and coming home.

After I had dreamed this scene many times—watching their despair turn from horror into anger—I begged Auntie Lindo to write another letter. And at first she refused.

"How can I say she is dead? I cannot write this," said Auntie Lindo with a stubborn look.

"But it's cruel to have them believe she's coming on the plane," I said. "When they see it's just me, they'll hate me."

"Hate you? Cannot be." She was scowling. "You are their own sister, their only family."

"You don't understand," I protested.

"What I don't understand?" she said.

And I whispered. "They'll think I'm responsible, that she died because I didn't appreciate her."

And Auntie Lindo looked satisfied and sad at the same time, as if this were true and I had finally realized it. She sat down for an hour, and when she stood up she handed me a two-page letter. She had tears in her eyes. I realized that the very thing I had feared, she had done. So even if she had written the news of my mother's death in English, I wouldn't have had the heart to read it.

"Thank you," I whispered.

The landscape has become gray, filled with low flat cement buildings, old factories, and then tracks and more tracks filled with trains like ours passing by in the opposite direction. I see platforms crowded with people wearing drab Western clothes, with spots of bright colors: little children wearing pink and yellow, red and peach. And there are soldiers in olive green and red, and old ladies in gray tops and pants that stop mid-calf. We are in Guangzhou.

Before the train even comes to a stop, people are bringing down their belongings from above their seats. For a moment there is a dangerous shower of heavy suitcases laden with gifts to relatives, half-broken boxes wrapped in miles of string to keep the contents from spilling out, plastic bags filled with yarn and vegetables and packages of dried mushrooms, and camera cases. And then we are caught in a stream of people rushing, shoving, pushing us along, until we find ourselves in one of a dozen lines waiting to go through customs. I feel as if I were getting on a number 30 Stockton bus in San Francisco. I am in China, I remind myself. And somehow the crowds don't bother me. It feels right. I start pushing too.

I take out the declaration forms and my passport. "Woo," it says at the top, and below that, "June May," who was born in "California, U.S.A.," in 1951. I wonder if the customs people will question whether I'm the same person as in the passport photo. In this picture, my chin-length hair is swept back and artfully styled. I am wearing false eyelashes, eye shadow, and lip liner. My cheeks are hollowed out by bronze blusher. But I had not expected the heat in October. And now my hair hangs limp with the humidity. I wear no makeup; in Hong Kong my mascara had melted into dark circles and everything else had felt like layers of grease. So today my face is plain, unadorned except for a thin mist of shiny sweat on my forehead and nose.

Even without makeup, I could never pass for true Chinese. I stand five-foot-six, and my head pokes above the crowd so that I am eye level only with other tourists. My mother once told me my height came from my grandfather, who was a northerner, and may have even had some Mongol blood. "This is what your grandmother once told me," explained my mother. "But now it is too late to ask her. They are all dead, your grandparents, your uncles, and their wives and children, all killed in the war, when a bomb fell on our house. So many generations in one instant."

She had said this so matter-of-factly that I thought she had long since gotten over any grief she had. And then I wondered how she knew they were all dead.

"Maybe they left the house before the bomb fell," I suggested.

"No," said my mother. "Our whole family is gone. It is just you and I."

"But how do you know? Some of them could have escaped."

"Cannot be," said my mother, this time almost angrily. And then her frown was washed over by a puzzled blank look, and she began to talk as if she were trying to remember where she had misplaced something. "I went back to that house. I kept looking up to where the house used to be. And it wasn't a house, just the sky. And below, underneath my feet, were four stories of burnt bricks and wood, all the life of our house. Then off to the side I saw things blown into the yard, nothing valuable. There was a bed someone used to sleep in, really just a metal frame twisted up at one corner. And a book, I don't know what kind, because every page had turned black. And I saw a teacup which was unbroken but filled with ashes. And then I found my doll, with her hands and legs broken, her hair burned off. . . . When I was a little girl, I had cried for that doll, seeing it all alone in the store window, and my mother had bought it for me. It was an American doll with yellow hair. It could turn its legs and arms. The eyes moved up and down. And when I married and left my family home, I gave the doll to my youngest niece, because she was like me. She cried if that doll was not with her always. Do you see? If she was in the house with that doll, her parents were there, and so everybody was there, waiting together, because that's how our family was."

The woman in the customs booth stares at my documents, then glances at me briefly, and with two quick movements stamps everything and sternly nods me along. And soon my father and I find ourselves in a large area filled with thousands of people and suitcases. I feel lost and my father looks helpless.

"Excuse me," I say to a man who looks like an American. "Can you tell me where I can get a taxi?" He mumbles something that sounds Swedish or Dutch.

"Syau Yen! Syau Yen!" I hear a piercing voice shout from behind me. An old woman in a yellow knit beret is holding up a pink plastic bag filled with wrapped trinkets. I guess she is trying to sell us something. But my father is staring down at this tiny sparrow of a woman, squinting into her eyes. And then his eyes widen, his face opens up and he smiles like a pleased little boy.

"*Aiyi! Aiyi!*"—Auntie Auntie!—he says softly.

45 "Syau Yen!" coos my great-aunt. I think it's funny she has just called my father "Little Wild Goose." It must be his baby milk name, the name used to discourage ghosts from stealing children.

They clasp each other's hands—they do not hug—and hold on like this, taking turns saying, "Look at you! You are so old. Look how old you've become!" They are both crying openly, laughing at the same time, and I bite my lip, trying not to cry. I'm afraid to feel their joy. Because I am thinking how different our arrival in Shanghai will be tomorrow, how awkward it will feel.

Now Aiyi beams and points to a Polaroid picture of my father. My father had wisely sent pictures when he wrote and said we were coming. See how smart she was, she seems to intone as she compares the picture to my father. In the letter, my father had said we would call her from the hotel once we arrived, so this is a surprise, that they've come to meet us. I wonder if my sisters will be at the airport.

It is only then that I remember the camera. I had meant to take a picture of my father and his aunt the moment they met. It's not too late.

"Here, stand together over here," I say, holding up the Polaroid. The camera flashes and I hand them the snapshot. Aiyi and my father still stand close together, each of them holding a corner of the picture, watching as their images begin to form. They are almost reverentially quiet. Aiyi is only five years older than my father, which makes her around seventy-seven. But she looks ancient, shrunken, a mummified relic. Her thin hair is pure white, her teeth are brown with decay. So much for stories of Chinese women looking young forever, I think to myself.

Now Aiyi is crooning to me: "*Jandale.*" So big already. She looks up at me, 50
at my full height, and then peers into her pink plastic bag—her gifts to us, I have figured out—as if she is wondering what she will give to me, now that I am so old and big. And then she grabs my elbow with her sharp pincerlike grasp and turns me around. A man and a woman in their fifties are shaking hands with my father, everybody smiling and saying, "Ah! Ah!" They are Aiyi's oldest son and his wife, and standing next to them are four other people, around my age, and a little girl who's around ten. The introductions go by so fast, all I know is that one of them is Aiyi's grandson, with his wife, and the other is her granddaughter, with her husband. And the little girl is Lili, Aiyi's great-granddaughter.

Aiyi and my father speak the Mandarin dialect from their childhood, but the rest of the family speaks only the Cantonese of their village. I understand only Mandarin but can't speak it that well. So Aiyi and my father gossip unrestrained in Mandarin, exchanging news about people from their old village. And they stop only occasionally to talk to the rest of us, sometimes in Cantonese, sometimes in English.

"Oh, it is as I suspected," says my father, turning to me. "He died last summer." And I already understood this. I just don't know who this person, Li Gong, is. I feel as if I were in the United Nations and the translators had run amok.

"Hello," I say to the little girl. "My name is Jing-mei." But the little girl squirms to look away, causing her parents to laugh with embarrassment. I try to think of Cantonese words I can say to her, stuff I learned from friends in Chinatown, but all I can think of are swear words, terms for bodily functions, and short phrases like "tastes good," "tastes like garbage," and "she's really ugly." And then I have another plan: I hold up the Polaroid camera, beckoning Lili with my finger. She immediately jumps forward, places one hand on her hip in the manner of a fashion model, juts out her chest, and flashes me a toothy smile. As soon as I take the picture she is standing next to me, jumping and giggling every few seconds as she watches herself appear on the greenish film.

By the time we hail taxis for the ride to the hotel, Lili is holding tight onto my hand, pulling me along.

In the taxi, Aiyi talks nonstop, so I have no chance to ask her about the 55
different sights we are passing by.

"You wrote and said you would come only for one day," says Aiyi to my father in an agitated tone. "One day! How can you see your family in one day! Toishan is many hours' drive from Guangzhou. And this idea to call us when you arrive. This is nonsense. We have no telephone."

My heart races a little. I wonder if Auntie Lindo told my sisters we would call from the hotel in Shanghai?

Aiyi continues to scold my father. "I was so beside myself, ask my son, almost turned heaven and earth upside down trying to think of a way! So we decided the best was for us to take the bus from Toishan and come into Guangzhou—meet you right from the start."

And now I am holding my breath as the taxi driver dodges between trucks and buses, honking his horn constantly. We seem to be on some sort of long freeway overpass, like a bridge above the city. I can see row after row of apartments, each floor cluttered with laundry hanging out to dry on the balcony. We pass a public bus, with people jammed in so tight their faces are nearly wedged against the window. Then I see the skyline of what must be downtown Guangzhou. From a distance, it looks like a major American city, with highrises and construction going on everywhere. As we slow down in the more congested part of the city, I see scores of little shops, dark inside, lined with counters and shelves. And then there is a building, its front laced with scaffolding made of bamboo poles held together with plastic strips. Men and women are standing on narrow platforms, scraping the sides, working without safety straps or helmets. Oh, would OSHA[1] have a field day here, I think.

60 Aiyi's shrill voice rises up again: "So it is a shame you can't see our village, our house. My sons have been quite successful, selling our vegetables in the free market. We had enough these last few years to build a big house, three stories, all of new brick, big enough for our whole family and then some. And every year, the money is even better. You Americans aren't the only ones who know how to get rich!"

The taxi stops and I assume we've arrived, but then I peer out at what looks like a grander version of the Hyatt Regency. "This is communist China?" I wonder out loud. And then I shake my head toward my father. "This must be the wrong hotel." I quickly pull out our itinerary, travel tickets, and reservations. I had explicitly instructed my travel agent to choose something inexpensive, in the thirty-to-forty-dollar range. I'm sure of this. And there it says on our itinerary: Garden Hotel, Huanshi Dong Lu. Well, our travel agent had better be prepared to eat the extra, that's all I have to say.

The hotel is magnificent. A bellboy complete with uniform and sharp-creased cap jumps forward and begins to carry our bags into the lobby. Inside, the hotel looks like an orgy of shopping arcades and restaurants all encased in granite and glass. And rather than be impressed, I am worried about the expense, as well as the appearance it must give Aiyi, that we rich Americans cannot be without our luxuries even for one night.

But when I step up to the reservation desk, ready to haggle over this booking mistake, it is confirmed. Our rooms are prepaid, thirty-four dollars each. I feel sheepish, and Aiyi and the others seem delighted by our temporary surroundings. Lili is looking wide-eyed at an arcade filled with video games.

Our whole family crowds into one elevator, and the bellboy waves, saying he will meet us on the eighteenth floor. As soon as the elevator door shuts, everybody becomes very quiet, and when the door finally opens again, everybody talks at once in what sounds like relieved voices. I have the feeling Aiyi and the others have never been on such a long elevator ride.

1. Occupational Safety and Health Administration.

Our rooms are next to each other and are identical. The rugs, drapes, bedspreads are all in shades of taupe. There's a color television with remote-control panels built into the lamp table between the two twin beds. The bathroom has marble walls and floors. I find a built-in wet bar with a small refrigerator stocked with Heineken beer, Coke Classic, and Seven-Up, mini-bottles of Johnnie Walker Red, Bacardi rum, and Smirnoff vodka, and packets of M & M's, honey-roasted cashews, and Cadbury chocolate bars. And again I say out loud, "This is communist China?" 65

My father comes into my room. "They decided we should just stay here and visit," he says, shrugging his shoulders. "They say, Less trouble that way. More time to talk."

"What about dinner?" I ask. I have been envisioning my first real Chinese feast for many days already, a big banquet with one of those soups steaming out carved winter melon, chicken wrapped in clay, Peking duck, the works.

My father walks over and picks up a room service book next to a *Travel & Leisure* magazine. He flips through the pages quickly and then points to the menu. "This is what they want," says my father.

So it's decided. We are going to dine tonight in our rooms, with our family, sharing hamburgers, french fries, and apple pie à la mode.

Aiyi and her family are browsing the shops while we clean up. After a hot ride on the train, I'm eager for a shower and cooler clothes. 70

The hotel has provided little packets of shampoo which, upon opening, I discover is the consistency and color of hoisin sauce.[2] This is more like it, I think. This is China. And I rub some in my damp hair.

Standing in the shower, I realize this is the first time I've been by myself in what seems like days. But instead of feeling relieved, I feel forlorn. I think about what my mother said, about activating my genes and becoming Chinese. And I wonder what she meant.

Right after my mother died, I asked myself a lot of things, things that couldn't be answered, to force myself to grieve more. It seemed as if I wanted to sustain my grief, to assure myself that I had cared deeply enough.

But now I ask the questions mostly because I want to know the answers. What was that pork stuff she used to make that had the texture of sawdust? What were the names of the uncles who died in Shanghai? What had she dreamt all these years about her other daughters? All the times when she got mad at me, was she really thinking about them? Did she wish I were they? Did she regret that I wasn't?

▽ ▽ ▽

At one o'clock in the morning, I awake to tapping sounds on the window. I must have dozed off and now I feel my body uncramping itself. I'm sitting on the floor, leaning against one of the twin beds. Lili is lying next to me. The others are asleep, too, sprawled out on the beds and floor. Aiyi is seated at a little table, 75

2. Sweet brownish-red sauce made from soybeans, flour, sugar, water, spices, garlic, and chili.

looking very sleepy. And my father is staring out the window, tapping his fingers on the glass. The last time I listened my father was telling Aiyi about his life since he last saw her. How he had gone to Yenching University, later got a post with a newspaper in Chungking, met my mother there, a young widow. How they later fled together to Shanghai to try to find my mother's family house, but there was nothing there. And then they traveled eventually to Canton and then to Hong Kong, then Haiphong and finally to San Francisco. . . .

"Suyuan didn't tell me she was trying all these years to find her daughters," he is now saying in a quiet voice. "Naturally, I did not discuss her daughters with her. I thought she was ashamed she had left them behind."

"Where did she leave them?" asks Aiyi. "How were they found?"

I am wide awake now. Although I have heard parts of this story from my mother's friends.

"It happened when the Japanese took over Kweilin," says my father.

"Japanese in Kweilin?" says Aiyi. "That was never the case. Couldn't be. The Japanese never came to Kweilin."

"Yes, that is what the newspapers reported. I know this because I was working for the news bureau at the time. The Kuomintang[3] often told us what we could say and could not say. But we knew the Japanese had come into Kwangsi Province. We had sources who told us how they had captured the Wuchang-Canton railway. How they were coming overland, making very fast progress, marching toward the provincial capital."

Aiyi looks astonished. "If people did not know this, how could Suyuan know the Japanese were coming?"

"An officer of the Kuomintang secretly warned her," explains my father. "Suyuan's husband also was an officer and everybody knew that officers and their families would be the first to be killed. So she gathered a few possessions and, in the middle of the night, she picked up her daughters and fled on foot. The babies were not even one year old."

"How could she give up those babies!" sighs Aiyi. "Twin girls. We have never had such luck in our family." And then she yawns again.

"What were they named?" she asks. I listen carefully. I had been planning on using just the familiar "Sister" to address them both. But now I want to know how to pronounce their names.

"They have their father's surname, Wang," says my father. "And their given names are Chwun Yu and Chwun Hwa."

"What do the names mean?" I ask.

"Ah." My father draws imaginary characters on the window. "One means 'Spring Rain,' the other 'Spring Flower,' " he explains in English, "because they born in the spring, and of course rain come before flower, same order these girls are born. Your mother like a poet, don't you think?"

I nod my head. I see Aiyi nod her head forward, too. But it falls forward and stays there. She is breathing deeply, noisily. She is asleep.

"And what does Ma's name mean?" I whisper.

3. "National People's Party" led by General Chiang Kai-shek (1887–1975).

" 'Suyuan,' " he says, writing more invisible characters on the glass. "The way she write it in Chinese, it mean 'Long-Cherished Wish.' Quite a fancy name, not so ordinary like flower name. See this first character, it means something like 'Forever Never Forgotten.' But there is another way to write 'Suyuan.' Sound exactly the same, but the meaning is opposite." His finger creates the brushstrokes of another character. "The first part look the same: 'Never Forgotten.' But the last part add to first part make the whole word mean 'Long-Held Grudge.' Your mother get angry with me, I tell her her name should be Grudge."

My father is looking at me, moist-eyed. "See, I pretty clever, too, hah?"

I nod, wishing I could find some way to comfort him. "And what about my name," I ask, "what does 'Jing-mei' mean?"

"Your name also special," he says. I wonder if any name in Chinese is not something special. " 'Jing' like excellent *jing*. Not just good, it's something pure, essential, the best quality. *Jing* is good leftover stuff when you take impurities out of something like gold, or rice, or salt. So what is left—just pure essence. And 'Mei,' this is common *mei*, as in *meimei*, 'younger sister.' "

I think about this. My mother's long-cherished wish. Me, the younger sister who was supposed to be the essence of the others. I feed myself with the old grief, wondering how disappointed my mother must have been. Tiny Aiyi stirs suddenly, her head rolls and then falls back, her mouth opens as if to answer my question. She grunts in her sleep, tucking her body more closely into the chair.

"So why did she abandon those babies on the road?" I need to know, because now I feel abandoned too.

"Long time I wondered this myself," says my father. "But then I read that letter from her daughters in Shanghai now, and I talk to Auntie Lindo, all the others. And then I knew. No shame in what she done. None."

"What happened?"

"Your mother running away—" begins my father.

"No, tell me in Chinese," I interrupt. "Really, I can understand."

He begins to talk, still standing at the window, looking into the night.

▽ ▽ ▽

After fleeing Kweilin, your mother walked for several days trying to find a main road. Her thought was to catch a ride on a truck or wagon, to catch enough rides until she reached Chungking, where her husband was stationed.

She had sewn money and jewelry into the lining of her dress, enough, she thought, to barter rides all the way. If I am lucky, she thought, I will not have to trade the heavy gold bracelet and jade ring. These were things from her mother, your grandmother.

By the third day, she had traded nothing. The roads were filled with people, everybody running and begging for rides from passing trucks. The trucks rushed by, afraid to stop. So your mother found no rides, only the start of dysentery pains in her stomach.

Her shoulders ached from the two babies swinging from scarf slings. Blisters grew on the palms from holding two leather suitcases. And then the blisters burst and began to bleed. After a while, she left the suitcases behind, keeping only the food and a few clothes. And later she also dropped the bags of wheat flour and rice and kept walking like this for many miles, singing songs to her little girls, until she was delirious with pain and fever.

Finally, there was not one more step left in her body. She didn't have the strength to carry those babies any further. She slumped to the ground. She knew she would die of her sickness, or perhaps from thirst, from starvation, or from the Japanese, who she was sure were marching right behind her.

She took the babies out of the slings and sat them on the side of the road, then lay down next to them. You babies are so good, she said, so quiet. They smiled back, reaching their chubby hands for her, wanting to be picked up again. And then she knew she could not bear to watch her babies die with her.

She saw a family with three young children in a cart going by. "Take my babies, I beg you," she cried to them. But they stared back with empty eyes and never stopped.

She saw another person pass and called out again. This time a man turned around, and he had such a terrible expression—your mother said it looked like death itself—she shivered and looked away.

When the road grew quiet, she tore open the lining of her dress, and stuffed jewelry under the shirt of one baby and money under the other. She reached into her pocket and drew out the photos of her family, the picture of her father and mother, the picture of herself and her husband on their wedding day. And she wrote on the back of each the names of the babies and this same message: "Please care for these babies with the money and valuables provided. When it is safe to come, if you bring them to Shanghai, 9 Weichang Lu, the Li family will be glad to give you a generous reward. Li Suyuan and Wang Fuchi."

And then she touched each baby's cheek and told her not to cry. She would go down the road to find them some food and would be back. And without looking back, she walked down the road, stumbling and crying, thinking only of this last hope, that her daughters would be found by a kindhearted person who would care for them. She would not allow herself to imagine anything else.

She did not remember how far she walked, which direction she went, when she fainted, or how she was found. When she awoke, she was in the back of a bouncing truck with several other sick people, all moaning. And she began to scream, thinking she was now on a journey to Buddhist hell. But the face of an American missionary lady bent over her and smiled, talking to her in a soothing language she did not understand. And yet she could somehow understand. She had been saved for no good reason, and it was now too late to go back and save her babies.

When she arrived in Chungking, she learned her husband had died two weeks before. She told me later she laughed when the officers told her this news, she was so delirious with madness and disease. To come so far, to lose so much and to find nothing.

I met her in a hospital. She was lying on a cot, hardly able to move, her dysentery had drained her so thin. I had come in for my foot, my missing toe, which was cut off by a piece of falling rubble. She was talking to herself, mumbling.

"Look at these clothes," she said, and I saw she had on a rather unusual dress 115
for wartime. It was silk satin, quite dirty, but there was no doubt it was a beautiful dress.

"Look at this face," she said, and I saw her dusty face and hollow cheeks, her eyes shining black. "Do you see my foolish hope?"

"I thought I had lost everything, except these two things," she murmured. "And I wondered which I would lose next. Clothes or hope? Hope or clothes?"

"But now, see here, look what is happening," she said, laughing, as if all her prayers had been answered. And she was pulling hair out of her head as easily as one lifts new wheat from wet soil.

It was an old peasant woman who found them. "How could I resist?" the peasant woman later told your sisters when they were older. They were still sitting obediently near where your mother had left them, looking like little fairy queens waiting for their sedan to arrive.

The woman, Mei Ching, and her husband, Mei Han, lived in a stone cave. 120
There were thousands of hidden caves like that in and around Kweilin so secret that the people remained hidden even after the war ended. The Meis would come out of their cave every few days and forage for food supplies left on the road, and sometimes they would see something that they both agreed was a tragedy to leave behind. So one day they took back to their cave a delicately painted set of rice bowls, another day a little footstool with a velvet cushion and two new wedding blankets. And once, it was your sisters.

They were pious people, Muslims, who believed the twin babies were a sign of double luck, and they were sure of this when, later in the evening, they discovered how valuable the babies were. She and her husband had never seen rings and bracelets like those. And while they admired the pictures, knowing the babies came from a good family, neither of them could read or write. It was not until many months later that Mei Ching found someone who could read the writing on the back. By then, she loved these baby girls like her own.

In 1952 Mei Han, the husband, died. The twins were already eight years old, and Mei Ching now decided it was time to find your sisters' true family.

She showed the girls the picture of their mother and told them they had been born into a great family and she would take them back to see their true mother and grandparents. Mei Ching told them about the reward, but she swore she would refuse it. She loved these girls so much, she only wanted them to have what they were entitled to—a better life, a fine house, educated ways. Maybe the family would let her stay on as the girls' amah. Yes, she was certain they would insist.

Of course, when she found the place at 9 Weichang Lu, in the old French Concession, it was something completely different. It was the site of a factory building, recently constructed, and none of the workers knew what had become of the family whose house had burned down on that spot.

Mei Ching could not have known, of course, that your mother and I, her 125
new husband, had already returned to that same place in 1945 in hopes of finding both her family and her daughters.

Your mother and I stayed in China until 1947. We went to many different cities—back to Kweilin, to Changsha, as far south as Kunming. She was always looking out of one corner of her eye for twin babies, then little girls. Later we went to Hong Kong, and when we finally left in 1949 for the United States, I think she was even looking for them on the boat. But when we arrived, she no longer talked about them. I thought, At last, they have died in her heart.

When letters could be openly exchanged between China and the United States, she wrote immediately to old friends in Shanghai and Kweilin. I did not know she did this. Auntie Lindo told me. But of course, by then, all the street names had changed. Some people had died, others had moved away. So it took many years to find a contact. And when she did find an old schoolmate's address and wrote asking her to look for her daughters, her friend wrote back and said this was impossible, like looking for a needle on the bottom of the ocean. How did she know her daughters were in Shanghai and not somewhere else in China? The friend, of course, did not ask, How do you know your daughters are still alive?

So her schoolmate did not look. Finding babies lost during the war was a matter of foolish imagination, and she had no time for that.

But every year, your mother wrote to different people. And this last year, I think she got a big idea in her head, to go to China and find them herself. I remember she told me, "Canning, we should go, before it is too late, before we are too old." And I told her we were already too old, it was already too late.

I just thought she wanted to be a tourist! I didn't know she wanted to go and look for her daughters. So when I said it was too late, that must have put a terrible thought in her head that her daughters might be dead. And I think this possibility grew bigger and bigger in her head, until it killed her.

Maybe it was your mother's dead spirit who guided her Shanghai schoolmate to find her daughters. Because after your mother died, the schoolmate saw your sisters, by chance, while shopping for shoes at the Number One Department Store on Nanjing Dong Road. She said it was like a dream, seeing these two women who looked so much alike, moving down the stairs together. There was something about their facial expressions that reminded the schoolmate of your mother.

She quickly walked over to them and called their names, which of course, they did not recognize at first, because Mei Ching had changed their names. But your mother's friend was so sure, she persisted. "Are you not Wang Chwun Yu and Wang Chwun Hwa?" she asked them. And then these double-image women became very excited, because they remembered the names written on the back of an old photo, a photo of a young man and woman they still honored, as their much-loved first parents, who had died and become spirit ghosts still roaming the earth looking for them.

▽ ▽ ▽

At the airport, I am exhausted. I could not sleep last night. Aiyi had followed me into my room at three in the morning, and she instantly fell asleep on one of the twin beds, snoring with the might of a lumberjack. I lay awake thinking about my mother's story, realizing how much I have never known about her, grieving that my sisters and I had both lost her.

And now at the airport, after shaking hands with everybody, waving good-bye, I think about all the different ways we leave people in this world. Cheerily waving good-bye to some at airports, knowing we'll never see each other again. Leaving others on the side of the road, hoping that we will. Finding my mother in my father's story and saying good-bye before I have a chance to know her better.

Aiyi smiles at me as we wait for our gate to be called. She is so old. I put one 135
arm around her and one arm around Lili. They are the same size, it seems. And then it's time. As we wave good-bye one more time and enter the waiting area, I get the sense I am going from one funeral to another. In my hand I'm clutching a pair of tickets to Shanghai. In two hours we'll be there.

The plane takes off. I close my eyes. How can I describe to them in my broken Chinese about our mother's life? Where should I begin?

"Wake up, we're here," says my father. And I awake with my heart pounding in my throat. I look out the window and we're already on the runway. It's gray outside.

And now I'm walking down the steps of the plane, onto the tarmac and toward the building. If only, I think, if only my mother had lived long enough to be the one walking toward them. I am so nervous I cannot feel my feet. I am just moving somehow.

Somebody shouts, "She's arrived!" And then I see her. Her short hair. Her small body. And that same look on her face. She has the back of her hand pressed hard against her mouth. She is crying as though she had gone through a terrible ordeal and were happy it is over.

And I know it's not my mother, yet it is the same look she had when I was 140
five and had disappeared all afternoon, for such a long time, that she was convinced I was dead. And when I miraculously appeared, sleepy-eyed, crawling from underneath my bed, she wept and laughed, biting the back of her hand to make sure it was true.

And now I see her again, two of her, waving, and in one hand there is a photo, the Polaroid I sent them. As soon as I get beyond the gate, we run toward each other, all three of us embracing, all hesitations and expectations forgotten.

"Mama, Mama," we all murmur, as if she is among us.

My sisters look at me, proudly. "*Meimei jandale*," says one sister proudly to the other. "Little Sister has grown up." I look at their faces again and I see no trace of my mother in them. Yet they still look familiar. And now I also see what part of me is Chinese. It is so obvious. It is my family. It is in our blood. After all these years, it can finally be let go.

My sisters and I stand, arms around each other, laughing and wiping the tears from each other's eyes. The flash of the Polaroid goes off and my father hands me the snapshot. My sisters and I watch quietly together, eager to see what develops.

145 The gray-green surface changes to the bright colors of our three images, sharpening and deepening all at once. And although we don't speak, I know we all see it: Together we look like our mother. Her same eyes, her same mouth, open in surprise to see, at last, her long-cherished wish.

1989

ANTON CHEKHOV

The Lady with the Dog

I

People were telling one another that a newcomer had been seen on the promenade—a lady with a dog. Dmitry Dmitrich Gurov had been a fortnight in Yalta,[1] and was accustomed to its ways, and he, too, had begun to take an interest in fresh arrivals. From his seat in Vernet's outdoor café, he caught sight of a young woman in a toque, passing along the promenade; she was fair and not very tall; after her trotted a white Pomeranian.

Later he encountered her in the municipal park and in the square several times a day. She was always alone, wearing the same toque, and the Pomeranian always trotted at her side. Nobody knew who she was, and people referred to her simply as "the lady with the dog."

"If she's here without her husband, and without any friends," thought Gurov, "it wouldn't be a bad idea to make her acquaintance."

He was not yet forty but had a twelve-year-old daughter and two sons in high school. He had been talked into marrying in his third year at college, and his wife now looked nearly twice as old as he did. She was a tall woman with dark eyebrows, erect, dignified, imposing, and, as she said of herself, a "thinker." She was a great reader, omitted the "hard sign"[2] at the end of words in her letters, and called her husband "Dimitry" instead of Dmitry; and though he secretly considered her shallow, narrow-minded, and dowdy, he stood in awe of her, and disliked being at home. He had first begun deceiving her long ago and he was now constantly unfaithful to her, and this was no doubt why he spoke slightingly of women, to whom he referred as *the lower race.*

5 He considered that the ample lessons he had received from bitter experience entitled him to call them whatever he liked, but without this "lower race" he could not have existed a single day. He was bored and ill-at-ease in the company of men, with whom he was always cold and reserved, but felt quite at home among women, and knew exactly what to say to them, and how to behave; he

1. Russian city on the Black Sea; a resort for southern vacations. 2. Conventional sign that was used following consonants; to omit it was then "progressive."

could even be silent in their company without feeling the slightest awkwardness. There was an elusive charm in his appearance and disposition which attracted women and caught their sympathies. He knew this and was himself attracted to them by some invisible force.

Repeated and bitter experience had taught him that every fresh intimacy, while at first introducing such pleasant variety into everyday life, and offering itself as a charming, light adventure, inevitably developed, among decent people (especially in Moscow, where they are so irresolute and slow to move), into a problem of excessive complication leading to an intolerably irksome situation. But every time he encountered an attractive woman he forgot all about this experience, the desire for life surged up in him, and everything suddenly seemed simple and amusing.

One evening, then, while he was dining at the restaurant in the park, the lady in the toque came strolling up and took a seat at a neighboring table. Her expression, gait, dress, coiffure, all told him that she was from the upper classes, that she was married, that she was in Yalta for the first time, alone and bored. . . . The accounts of the laxity of morals among visitors to Yalta are greatly exaggerated, and he paid no heed to them, knowing that for the most part they were invented by people who would gladly have transgressed themselves, had they known how to set about it. But when the lady sat down at a neighboring table a few yards away from him, these stories of easy conquests, of excursions to the mountains, came back to him, and the seductive idea of a brisk transitory liaison, an affair with a woman whose very name he did not know, suddenly took possession of his mind.

He snapped his fingers at the Pomeranian and, when it trotted up to him, shook his forefinger at it. The Pomeranian growled. Gurov shook his finger again.

The lady glanced at him and instantly lowered her eyes.

"He doesn't bite," she said, and blushed.

"May I give him a bone?" he asked, and on her nod of consent added in friendly tones: "Have you been long in Yalta?"

"About five days."

"And I am dragging out my second week here."

Neither spoke for a few minutes.

"The days pass quickly, and yet one is so bored here," she said, not looking at him.

"It's the thing to say it's boring here. People never complain of boredom in godforsaken holes like Belyev or Zhizdra, but when they get here it's: 'Oh, the dullness! Oh, the dust!' You'd think they'd come from Granada[3] to say the least."

She laughed. Then they both went on eating in silence, like complete strangers. But after dinner they left the restaurant together, and embarked upon the light, jesting talk of people free and contented, for whom it is all the same where they go, or what they talk about. They strolled along, remarking on the strange light over the sea. The water was a warm, tender purple, the moonlight lay on its

3. Romantic city in southern Spain.

surface in a golden strip. They said how close it was, after the hot day. Gurov told her he was from Moscow, had a degree in literature but worked in a bank; that he had at one time trained himself to sing in a private opera company, but had given up the idea; that he owned two houses in Moscow. . . . And from her he learned that she had grown up in Petersburg, but had gotten married in the town of S., where she had been living two years, that she would stay another month in Yalta, and that perhaps her husband, who also needed a rest, would join her. She was quite unable to explain whether her husband was a member of the province council, or on the board of the *zemstvo*,[4] and was greatly amused at herself for this. Further, Gurov learned that her name was Anna Sergeyevna.

Back in his own room he thought about her, and felt sure he would meet her the next day. It was inevitable. As he went to bed he reminded himself that only a very short time ago she had been a schoolgirl, like his own daughter, learning her lessons; he remembered how much there was of shyness and constraint in her laughter, in her way of conversing with a stranger—it was probably the first time in her life that she found herself alone, and in a situation in which men could follow her and watch her, and speak to her, all the time with a secret aim she could not fail to divine. He recalled her slender, delicate neck, her fine gray eyes.

"And yet there's something pathetic about her," he thought to himself as he fell asleep.

II

A week had passed since the beginning of their acquaintance. It was a holiday. Indoors it was stuffy, but the dust rose in clouds out of doors, and people's hats blew off. It was a parching day and Gurov kept going to the outdoor café for fruit drinks and ices to offer Anna Sergeyevna. The heat was overpowering.

In the evening, when the wind had dropped, they walked to the pier to see the steamer come in. There were a great many people strolling about the landing-place; some, bunches of flowers in their hands, were meeting friends. Two peculiarities of the smart Yalta crowd stood out distinctly—the elderly ladies all tried to dress very youthfully, and there seemed to be an inordinate number of generals about.

Owing to the roughness of the sea the steamer arrived late, after the sun had gone down, and it had to maneuver for some time before it could get alongside the pier. Anna Sergeyevna scanned the steamer and passengers through her lorgnette, as if looking for someone she knew, and when she turned to Gurov her eyes were glistening. She talked a great deal, firing off abrupt questions and forgetting immediately what it was she had wanted to know. Then she lost her lorgnette in the crush.

The smart crowd began dispersing, features could no longer be made out, the wind had quite dropped, and Gurov and Anna Sergeyevna stood there as if waiting for someone else to come off the steamer. Anna Sergeyevna had fallen

4. An elective provincial council.

silent, every now and then smelling her flowers, but not looking at Gurov.

"It's turning out a fine evening," he said. "What shall we do? We might go for a drive."

She made no reply.

He looked steadily at her and suddenly took her in his arms and kissed her lips, and the fragrance and dampness of the flowers closed round him, but the next moment he looked behind him in alarm—had anyone seen them?

"Let's go to your room," he murmured.

And they walked off together, very quickly.

Her room was stuffy and smelt of some scent she had bought in the Japanese shop. Gurov looked at her, thinking to himself: "How full of strange encounters life is!" He could remember carefree, good-natured women who were exhilarated by love-making and grateful to him for the happiness he gave them, however short-lived; and there had been others—his wife among them—whose caresses were insincere, affected, hysterical, mixed up with a great deal of quite unnecessary talk, and whose expression seemed to say that all this was not just love-making or passion, but something much more significant; then there had been two or three beautiful, cold women, over whose features flitted a predatory expression, betraying a determination to wring from life more than it could give, women no longer in their first youth, capricious, irrational, despotic, brainless, and when Gurov had cooled to these, their beauty aroused in him nothing but repulsion, and the lace trimming on their underclothes reminded him of fish-scales.

But here the timidity and awkwardness of youth and inexperience were still apparent; and there was a feeling of embarrassment in the atmosphere, as if someone had just knocked at the door. Anna Sergeyevna, "the lady with the dog," seemed to regard the affair as something very special, very serious, as if she had become a fallen woman, an attitude he found odd and disconcerting. Her features lengthened and drooped, and her long hair hung mournfully on either side of her face. She assumed a pose of dismal meditation, like a repentant sinner in some classical painting.

"It isn't right," she said. "You will never respect me anymore."

On the table was a watermelon. Gurov cut himself a slice from it and began slowly eating it. At least half an hour passed in silence.

Anna Sergeyevna was very touching, revealing the purity of a decent, naïve woman who had seen very little of life. The solitary candle burning on the table scarcely lit up her face, but it was obvious that her heart was heavy.

"Why should I stop respecting you?" asked Gurov. "You don't know what you're saying."

"May God forgive me!" she exclaimed, and her eyes filled with tears. "It's terrible."

"No need to seek to justify yourself."

"How can I justify myself? I'm a wicked, fallen woman, I despise myself and have not the least thought of self-justification. It isn't my husband I have deceived, it's myself. And not only now, I have been deceiving myself for ever so long. My husband is no doubt an honest, worthy man, but he's a flunky. I don't know what it is he does at his office, but I know he's a flunky. I was only twenty when I married him, and I was devoured by curiosity, I wanted something higher. I told myself that there must be a different kind of life I wanted to live, to live. . . . I was burning with curiosity . . . you'll never understand that, but I swear to God I could no longer control myself, nothing could hold me back, I told my husband I was ill, and I came here. . . . And I started going about like one possessed, like a madwoman . . . and now I have become an ordinary, worthless woman, and everyone has a right to despise me."

Gurov listened to her, bored to death. The naïve accents, the remorse, all was so unexpected, so out of place. But for the tears in her eyes, she might have been jesting or play-acting.

"I don't understand," he said gently. "What is it you want?"

She hid her face against his breast and pressed closer to him.

"Do believe me, I implore you to believe me," she said. "I love all that is honest and pure in life, vice is revolting to me, I don't know what I'm doing. The common people say they are snared by the Devil. And now I can say that I have been snared by the Devil, too."

"Come, come," he murmured.

He gazed into her fixed, terrified eyes, kissed her, and soothed her with gentle affectionate words, and gradually she calmed down and regained her cheerfulness. Soon they were laughing together again.

When, a little later, they went out, there was not a soul on the promenade, the town and its cypresses looked dead, but the sea was still roaring as it dashed against the beach. A solitary fishing-boat tossed on the waves, its lamp blinking sleepily.

They found a carriage and drove to Oreanda.

"I discovered your name in the hall, just now," said Gurov, "written up on the board. Von Diederitz. Is your husband a German?"

"No. His grandfather was, I think, but he belongs to the Orthodox Church himself."

When they got out of the carriage at Oreanda they sat down on a bench not far from the church, and looked down at the sea, without talking. Yalta could be dimly discerned through the morning mist, and white clouds rested motionless on the summits of the mountains. Not a leaf stirred, the grasshoppers chirruped, and the monotonous hollow roar of the sea came up to them, speaking of peace, of the eternal sleep lying in wait for us all. The sea had roared like this long before there was any Yalta or Oreanda, it was roaring now, and it would go on roaring, just as indifferently and hollowly, when we had passed away. And it may be that in this continuity, this utter indifference to the life and death of each of us lies hidden the pledge of our eternal salvation, of the continuous movement of life on earth, of the continuous movement toward perfection.

Side by side with a young woman, who looked so exquisite in the early light, soothed and enchanted by the sight of all this magical beauty—sea, mountains, clouds and the vast expanse of the sky—Gurov told himself that, when you came to think of it, everything in the world is beautiful really, everything but our own thoughts and actions, when we lose sight of the higher aims of life, and of our dignity as human beings.

Someone approached them—a watchman, probably—looked at them and went away. And there was something mysterious and beautiful even in this. The steamer from Feodosia could be seen coming towards the pier, lit up by the dawn, its lamps out. 50

"There's dew on the grass," said Anna Sergeyevna, breaking the silence.

"Yes. Time to go home."

They went back to the town.

After this they met every day at noon on the promenade, lunching and dining together, going for walks, and admiring the sea. She complained of sleeplessness, of palpitations, asked the same questions over and over again, alternately surrendering to jealousy and the fear that he did not really respect her. And often, when there was nobody in sight in the square or the park, he would draw her to him and kiss her passionately. The utter idleness, these kisses in broad daylight, accompanied by furtive glances and the fear of discovery, the heat, the smell of the sea, and the idle, smart, well-fed people continually crossing their field of vision, seemed to have given him a new lease on life. He told Anna Sergeyevna she was beautiful and seductive, made love to her with impetuous passion, and never left her side, while she was always pensive, always trying to force from him the admission that he did not respect her, that he did not love her a bit, and considered her just an ordinary woman. Almost every night they drove out of town, to Oreanda, the waterfall, or some other beauty-spot. And these excursions were invariably a success, each contributing fresh impressions of majestic beauty.

All this time they kept expecting her husband to arrive. But a letter came in which he told his wife that he was having trouble with his eyes, and implored her to come home as soon as possible. Anna Sergeyevna made hasty preparations for leaving. 55

"It's a good thing I'm going," she said to Gurov. "It's the intervention of fate."

She left Yalta in a carriage, and he went with her as far as the railway station. The drive took nearly a whole day. When she got into the express train, after the second bell had been rung, she said:

"Let me have one more look at you. . . . One last look. That's right."

She did not weep, but was mournful, and seemed ill, the muscles of her cheeks twitching.

"I shall think of you . . . I shall think of you all the time," she said. "God bless you! Think kindly of me. We are parting forever, it must be so, because we ought never to have met. Good-bye—God bless you." 60

The train steamed rapidly out of the station, its lights soon disappearing, and a minute later even the sound it made was silenced, as if everything were conspiring to bring this sweet oblivion, this madness, to an end as quickly as possible. And Gurov, standing alone on the platform and gazing into the dark distance, listened to the shrilling of the grasshoppers and the humming of the telegraph wires, with a feeling that he had only just awakened. And he told himself that this had been just one more of the many adventures in his life, and that it, too, was over, leaving nothing but a memory. . . . He was moved and sad, and felt a slight remorse. After all, this young woman whom he would never again see had not been really happy with him. He had been friendly and affectionate with her, but in his whole behaviour, in the tones of his voice, in his very caresses, there had been a shade of irony, the insulting indulgence of the fortunate male, who was, moreover, almost twice her age. She had insisted in calling him good, remarkable, high-minded. Evidently he had appeared to her different from his real self, in a word he had involuntarily deceived her. . . .

There was an autumnal feeling in the air, and the evening was chilly.

"It's time for me to be going north, too," thought Gurov, as he walked away from the platform. "High time!"

III

When he got back to Moscow it was beginning to look like winter; the stoves were heated every day, and it was still dark when the children got up to go to school and drank their tea, so that the nurse had to light the lamp for a short time. Frost had set in. When the first snow falls, and one goes for one's first sleigh-ride, it is pleasant to see the white ground, the white roofs; one breathes freely and lightly, and remembers the days of one's youth. The ancient lime-trees and birches, white with hoarfrost, have a good-natured look, they are closer to the heart than cypresses and palms, and beneath their branches one is no longer haunted by the memory of mountains and the sea.

65 Gurov had always lived in Moscow, and he returned to Moscow on a fine frosty day, and when he put on his fur-lined overcoat and thick gloves, and sauntered down Petrovka Street, and when, on Saturday evening, he heard the church bells ringing, his recent journey and the places he had visited lost their charm for him. He became gradually immersed in Moscow life, reading with avidity three newspapers a day, while declaring he never read Moscow newspapers on principle. Once more he was caught up in a whirl of restaurants, clubs, banquets, and celebrations, once more glowed with the flattering consciousness that well-known lawyers and actors came to his house, that he played cards in the Medical Club opposite a professor. He could once again eat a whole serving of Moscow Fish Stew served in a pan.

He had believed that in a month's time Anna Sergeyevna would be nothing but a vague memory, and that hereafter, with her wistful smile, she would only occasionally appear to him in dreams, like others before her. But the month was now well over and winter was in full swing, and all was as clear in his memory as if he had parted with Anna Sergeyevna only the day before. And his recollections grew ever more insistent. When the voices of his children at their lessons reached him in his study through the evening stillness, when he heard a song, or the sounds of a music-box in a restaurant, when the wind howled in the chimney, it all came back to him: early morning on the pier, the misty mountains, the steamer from Feodosia, the kisses. He would pace up and down his room for a long time, smiling at his memories, and then memory turned into dreaming, and what had happened mingled in his imagination with what was going to happen. Anna Sergeyevna did not come to him in his dreams, she accompanied him everywhere, like his shadow, following him everywhere he went. When he closed his eyes, she seemed to stand before him in the flesh, still lovelier, younger, tenderer than she had really been, and looking back, he saw himself, too, as better than he had been in Yalta. In the evenings she looked out at him from the bookshelves, the fireplace, the corner, he could hear her breathing, the sweet rustle of her skirts. In the streets he followed women with his eyes, to see if there were any like her. . . .

He began to feel an overwhelming desire to share his memories with someone. But he could not speak of his love at home, and outside his home who was there for him to confide in? Not the tenants living in his house, and certainly not his colleagues at the bank. And what was there to tell? Was it love that he had felt? Had there been anything exquisite, poetic, anything instructive or even amusing about his relations with Anna Sergeyevna? He had to content himself with uttering vague generalizations about love and women, and nobody guessed what he meant, though his wife's dark eyebrows twitched as she said:

"The role of a coxcomb doesn't suit you a bit, Dimitry."

One evening, leaving the Medical Club with one of his card-partners, a government official, he could not refrain from remarking:

"If you only knew what a charming woman I met in Yalta!"

The official got into his sleigh, and just before driving off, turned and called out:

"Dmitry Dmitrich!"

"Yes?"

"You were quite right, you know—the sturgeon was just a *leetle* off."

These words, in themselves so commonplace, for some reason infuriated Gurov, seemed to him humiliating, gross. What savage manners, what people! What wasted evenings, what tedious, empty days! Frantic card-playing, gluttony, drunkenness, perpetual talk always about the same thing. The greater part of one's time and energy went on business that was no use to anyone, and on discussing the same thing over and over again, and there was nothing to show for it all but a stunted wingless existence and a round of trivialities, and there was nowhere to escape to, you might as well be in a madhouse or a convict settlement.

Gurov lay awake all night, raging, and went about the whole of the next day with a headache. He slept badly on the succeeding nights, too, sitting up in bed, thinking, or pacing the floor of his room. He was sick of his children, sick of the bank, felt not the slightest desire to go anywhere or talk about anything.

When the Christmas holidays came, he packed his things, telling his wife he had to go to Petersburg in the interests of a certain young man, and set off for the town of S. To what end? He hardly knew himself. He only knew that he must see Anna Sergeyevna, must speak to her, arrange a meeting, if possible.

He arrived at S. in the morning and engaged the best suite in the hotel, which had a carpet of gray military frieze, and a dusty ink-pot on the table, surmounted by a headless rider, holding his hat in his raised hand. The hall porter told him what he wanted to know: von Diederitz had a house of his own in Staro-Goncharnaya Street. It wasn't far from the hotel, he lived on a grand scale, luxuriously, kept carriage-horses, the whole town knew him. The hall porter pronounced the name "Drideritz."

Gurov strolled over to Staro-Goncharnaya Street and discovered the house. In front of it was a long gray fence with inverted nails hammered into the tops of the palings.

"A fence like that is enough to make anyone want to run away," thought Gurov, looking at the windows of the house and the fence.

He reasoned that since it was a holiday, Anna's husband would probably be at home. In any case it would be tactless to embarrass her by calling at the house. And a note might fall into the hands of the husband, and bring about catastrophe. The best thing would be to wait about on the chance of seeing her. And he walked up and down the street, hovering in the vicinity of the fence, watching for his chance. A beggar entered the gate, only to be attacked by dogs, then, an hour later, the faint, vague sounds of a piano reached his ears. That would be Anna Sergeyevna playing. Suddenly the front door opened and an old woman came out, followed by a familiar white Pomeranian. Gurov tried to call to it, but his heart beat violently, and in his agitation he could not remember its name.

He walked on, hating the gray fence more and more, and now ready to tell himself irately that Anna Sergeyevna had forgotten him, had already, perhaps, found distraction in another—what could be more natural in a young woman who had to look at this accursed fence from morning to night? He went back to his hotel and sat on the sofa in his suite for some time, not knowing what to do, then he ordered dinner, and after dinner, had a long sleep.

"What a foolish, restless business," he thought, waking up and looking towards the dark windowpanes. It was evening by now. "Well, I've had my sleep out. And what am I to do in the night?"

He sat up in bed, covered by the cheap gray quilt, which reminded him of a hospital blanket, and in his vexation he fell to taunting himself.

"You and your lady with a dog . . . there's adventure for you! See what you get for your pains."

On his arrival at the station that morning he had noticed a poster announcing in enormous letters the first performance at the local theatre of *The Geisha*.[5] Remembering this, he got up and made for the theatre.

"It's highly probable that she goes to first nights," he told himself.

The theatre was full. It was a typical provincial theatre, with a mist collecting over the chandeliers, and the crowd in the gallery fidgeting noisily. In the first row of the stalls[6] the local dandies stood waiting for the curtain to go up, their hands clasped behind them. There, in the front seat of the governor's box, sat the governor's daughter, wearing a boa, the governor himself hiding modestly behind the drapes, so that only his hands were visible. The curtain stirred, the

5. Operetta by Sidney Jones (1861–1946) which toured Eastern Europe in 1898–99. 6. Seats at the front of a theater, near the stage and separated from nearby seats by a railing.

orchestra took a long time tuning up their instruments. Gurov's eyes roamed eagerly over the audience as they filed in and occupied their seats.

Anna Sergeyevna came in, too. She seated herself in the third row of the stalls, and when Gurov's glance fell on her, his heart seemed to stop, and he knew in a flash that the whole world contained no one nearer or dearer to him, no one more important to his happiness. This little woman, lost in the provincial crowd, in no way remarkable, holding a silly lorgnette in her hand, now filled his whole life, was his grief, his joy, all that he desired. Lulled by the sounds coming from the wretched orchestra, with its feeble, amateurish violinists, he thought how beautiful she was . . . thought and dreamed. . . .

Anna Sergeyevna was accompanied by a tall, round-shouldered young man with small whiskers, who nodded at every step before taking the seat beside her and seemed to be continually bowing to someone. This must be her husband, whom, in a fit of bitterness, at Yalta, she had called a "flunky." And there really was something of a lackey's servility in his lanky figure, his side-whiskers, and the little bald spot on the top of his head. And he smiled sweetly, and the badge of some scientific society gleaming in his buttonhole was like the number on a footman's livery.

The husband went out to smoke in the first interval, and she was left alone in her seat. Gurov, who had taken a seat in the stalls, went up to her and said in a trembling voice, with a forced smile: "How d'you do?"

She glanced up at him and turned pale, then looked at him again in alarm, unable to believe her eyes, squeezing her fan and lorgnette in one hand, evidently struggling to overcome a feeling of faintness. Neither of them said a word. She sat there, and he stood beside her, disconcerted by her embarrassment, and not daring to sit down. The violins and flutes sang out as they were tuned, and there was a tense sensation in the atmosphere, as if they were being watched from all the boxes. At last she got up and moved rapidly towards one of the exits. He followed her and they wandered aimlessly along corridors, up and down stairs; figures flashed by in the uniforms of legal officials, high-school teachers and civil servants, all wearing badges; ladies, coats hanging from pegs flashed by; there was a sharp draft, bringing with it an odor of cigarette butts. And Gurov, whose heart was beating violently, thought:

"What on earth are all these people, this orchestra for? . . ."

The next minute he suddenly remembered how, after seeing Anna Sergeyevna off that evening at the station, he had told himself that all was over, and they would never meet again. And how far away the end seemed to be now!

She stopped on a dark narrow staircase over which was a notice bearing the inscription "To the upper circle."

"How you frightened me!" she said, breathing heavily, still pale and half-stunned. "Oh, how you frightened me! I'm almost dead! Why did you come? Oh, why?"

"But, Anna," he said, in low, hasty tones. "But, Anna. . . . Try to understand . . . do try. . . ."

She cast him a glance of fear, entreaty, love, and then gazed at him steadily, as if to fix his features firmly in her memory.

"I've been so unhappy," she continued, taking no notice of his words. "I could think of nothing but you the whole time, I lived on the thoughts of you. I tried to forget—why, oh, why did you come?"

On the landing above them were two schoolboys, smoking and looking down, but Gurov did not care, and, drawing Anna Sergeyevna towards him, began kissing her face, her lips, her hands.

"What are you doing, oh, what are you doing?" she said in horror, drawing back. "We have both gone mad. Go away this very night, this moment. . . . By all that is sacred, I implore you. . . . Somebody is coming."

Someone was ascending the stairs.

"You must go away," went on Anna Sergeyevna in a whisper. "D'you hear me, Dmitry Dmitrich? I'll come to you in Moscow. I have never been happy, I am unhappy now, and I shall never be happy—never! Do not make me suffer still more! I will come to you in Moscow, I swear it! And now we must part! My dear one, my kind one, my darling, we must part."

She pressed his hand and hurried down the stairs, looking back at him continually, and her eyes showed that she was in truth unhappy. Gurov stood where he was for a short time, listening, and when all was quiet, went to look for his coat, and left the theatre.

IV

And Anna Sergeyevna began going to Moscow to see him. Every two or three months she left the town of S., telling her husband that she was going to consult a specialist on female diseases, and her husband believed her and did not believe her. In Moscow she always stayed at the Slavyanski Bazaar, sending a man in a red cap to Gurov the moment she arrived. Gurov went to her, and no one in Moscow knew anything about it.

One winter morning he went to see her as usual (the messenger had been to him the evening before, but had not found him at home). His daughter was with him, for her school was on the way and he thought he might as well see her to it.

"It is forty degrees," said Gurov to his daughter, "and yet it is snowing. You see it is only above freezing close to the ground, the temperature in the upper layers of the atmosphere is quite different."

"Why doesn't it ever thunder in winter, Papa?"

He explained this, too. As he was speaking, he kept reminding himself that he was going to a rendezvous and that not a living soul knew about it, or, probably, ever would. He led a double life—one in public, in the sight of all whom it concerned, full of conventional truth and conventional deception, exactly like the lives of his friends and acquaintances, and another which flowed in secret. And, owing to some strange, possibly quite accidental chain of circumstances, everything that was important, interesting, essential, everything about which he was sincere and never deceived himself, everything that composed the kernel of his life, went on in secret, while everything that was false in him, everything that composed the husk in which he hid himself and the truth which was in him—his work at the bank, discussions at the club, his "lower race," his attendance at anniversary celebrations with his wife—was on the surface. He began to judge others by himself, no longer believing what he saw, and always assuming that the real, the only interesting life of every individual goes on as under cover of night, secretly. Every individual existence revolves around mystery, and perhaps that is the chief reason that all cultivated individuals insisted so strongly on the respect due to personal secrets.

After leaving his daughter at the door of her school Gurov set off for the 110
Slavyanski Bazaar. Taking off his overcoat in the lobby, he went upstairs and knocked softly on the door. Anna Sergeyevna, wearing the gray dress he liked most, exhausted by her journey and by suspense, had been expecting him since the evening before. She was pale and looked at him without smiling, but was in his arms almost before he was fairly in the room. Their kiss was lingering, prolonged, as if they had not met for years.

"Well, how are you?" he asked. "Anything new?"

"Wait, I'll tell you in a minute. . . . . I can't. . . ."

She could not speak, because she was crying. Turning away, she held her handkerchief to her eyes.

"I'll wait till she's had her cry out," he thought, and sank into a chair.

He rang for tea, and a little later, while he was drinking it, she was still 115
standing there, her face to the window. She wept from emotion, from her bitter consciousness of the sadness of their life; they could only see one another in secret, hiding from people, as if they were thieves. Was not their life a broken one?

"Don't cry," he said.

It was quite obvious to him that this love of theirs would not soon come to an end, and that no one could say when this end would be. Anna Sergeyevna loved him ever more fondly, worshipped him, and there would have been no point in telling her that one day it must end. Indeed, she would not have believed him.

He moved over and took her by the shoulders, intending to caress her, to make a joke, but suddenly he caught sight of himself in the looking-glass.

His hair was already beginning to turn gray. It struck him as strange that he should have aged so much in the last few years, have lost so much of his looks. The shoulders on which his hands lay were warm and quivering. He felt a pity for this life, still so warm and exquisite, but probably soon to fade and droop like his own. Why did she love him so? Women had always believed him different from what he really was, had loved in him not himself but the man their imagination pictured him, a man they had sought for eagerly all their lives. And afterwards when they discovered their mistake, they went on loving him just the same. And not one of them had ever been happy with him. Time had passed, he had met one woman after another, become intimate with each, parted with each, but had never loved. There had been all sorts of things between them, but never love.

And only now, when he was gray-haired, had he fallen in love properly, 120
thoroughly, for the first time in his life.

He and Anna Sergeyevna loved one another as people who are very close and intimate, as husband and wife, as dear friends love one another. It seemd to them that fate had intended them for one another, and they could not understand why she should have a husband, and he a wife. They were like two migrating birds, the male and the female, who had been caught and put into separate cages. They forgave one another all that they were ashamed of in the past and in the present, and felt that this love of theirs had changed them both.

Formerly, in moments of melancholy, he had consoled himself by the first argument that came into his head, but now arguments were nothing to him, he felt profound pity, desired to be sincere, tender.

"Stop crying, my dearest," he said. "You've had your cry, now stop. . . . Now let us have a talk, let us try and think what we are to do."

Then they discussed their situation for a long time, trying to think how they could get rid of the necessity for hiding, deception, living in different towns, being so long without meeting. How were they to shake off these intolerable fetters?

125 "How? How?" he repeated, clutching his head. "How?"

And it seemed to them that they were within an inch of arriving at a decision, and that then a new, beautiful life would begin. And they both realized that the end was still far, far away, and that the hardest, the most complicated part was only just beginning.

1899

QUESTIONS

1. Describe the location, appearance, and socio-economic make-up of Shady Hill in John Cheever's "The Country Husband." Why is the dog Jupiter "an anomaly" (par. 10)? Why do Clayton Thomas and Anne also not "belong"? You might look at the story as a struggle between Francis Weed (weeds do not belong on suburban lawns) and Shady Hill; who wins? The story begins, "To begin at the beginning . . ." and tells about the near-crash of Francis's plane; why is that the beginning? what is it the beginning of?

2. "The Country Husband" is set in the 1950s; how would the story differ if set in a similar environment but in the 1990s?

3. The mother of Jing-Mei Woo, in "A Pair of Tickets," told her that being Chinese is a matter of genetics and she finds that that is true. What is the role of place and time (history), then, in this story?

4. Yalta, where "The Lady with the Dog" opens, is a resort on the Black Sea; Moscow, where Gurov lives, is described at the beginning of section III. To what extent do the settings relate to the events and emotions of the story? How do other details—such as the watermelon in II (Yalta) and the slightly "off"

sturgeon in III (Moscow)—relate to the settings and the attitudes and feelings associated with the places? Which are conventionally assumed to be more real, the feelings we have on holiday or those in our everyday lives? How is this convention related to our expectations about the outcome of the story? to the meaning of the story?

WRITING SUGGESTIONS

1. Re-tell "The Country Husband," or a portion of it, from Julia Weed's point of view (or from Anne's).

2. Compare the use of episodes from World War II in "The Country Husband" and "A Pair of Tickets."

3. Write a personal narrative about a visit to a place important in your family history that you had never visited before and how you felt about your relation to that place; or about an episode that made you recognize or affirm your ethnic identity or heritage.

4. Compare the treatment of infidelity in Cheever and Chekhov.

5. Write a fifth section of "The Lady with the Dog."

5 SYMBOLS

One of the chief devices for bridging the gap between the writer's vision and the reader's is the **symbol,** commonly defined as something that stands for something else: a flower, for example, may be seen as a symbol of a particular state. Symbols are generally **figurative**; that is, they compare or put together two *unlike* things. While a senator may represent a state, he represents it *literally*: the state is a governmental unit, and the senator is a member of the government. But the flower has little to do with governing the state, and so represents it only figuratively.

But why speak of anything in terms of something else? Why should snakes commonly be symbolic of evil? Sure, some snakes are poisonous, but for some people so are bees, and a lot of snakes are not only harmless but actually helpful ecologically. (In Kipling's *The Jungle Book* the python Ka, while frightening, is on the side of Law and Order.) Through repeated use over the centuries, the snake has become a traditional symbol of Evil—not just danger, sneakiness, repulsiveness, but theological, absolute Evil. Had Peyton Farquhar, in "An Occurrence at Owl Creek Bridge," been confronted by a snake when he was thrown ashore, we would not necessarily have said, "Aha—snake, symbol of Evil," though that potential meaning might have hovered around the incident and sent us looking backward and forward in the story for supporting evidence that this snake was being used symbolically. However, when we discover that the stranger in "Young Goodman Brown" has a walking stick upon which is carved the image of a snake, we are much more likely to find it such a symbol because of other, related potential symbols or meanings in the context: the term *Goodman* in the title of the story sets up the distinct possibility that Brown (how common a name) stands for more than a "mere" individual young man. Brown's bride is named Faith—a common name among the early Puritans, but together with *Goodman* suggesting symbolic possibilities. Then, just before the stranger with the walking stick appears, Brown says, "What if the devil himself should be at my very elbow!"

A single item, even something as traditionally fraught with meaning as a snake or a rose, becomes a symbol only when its potentially symbolic meaning is confirmed by something else in the story, just as a point needs a second point to define a line. Multiple symbols, potential symbols, direct and indirect hints such as Brown's mention of the devil: these are among the ways in which details may be identified as symbols (for interpreting symbols is relatively easy once you know what is and what is probably not a symbol).

One form of what may be called an indirect hint is repetition. That an "old maid" like Judith should have a cat seems so ordinary it borders on the trite. But when she chooses to have her male cat put to death rather than neutered, it is likely to make some of us sit up and take notice. This choice may suggest something about the unconventional in her character, but we probably don't think of the cat in itself representing anything. What happens, though, when there appears another cat, a female this time, whose sex life calls forth strange behavior on Judith's part? And when the killing of a kitten interrupts Judith's affair with Luigi? It is difficult to say when or if the literal cats shade off into symbols, for they remain so solidly cats in the story. All we can say for sure is that cats become more important in reading and understanding this story than, say, the cask of Amontillado does in the Poe story. The cask remains a thing pure and simple. Repetition, then, calls attention to details and may alert us to potential symbolic overtones, but it does not necessarily turn a thing into a symbol; so long as we get the suggestions of significance, however, agreeing on exactly what—or when—something can be called a symbol is not important.

Direct hints may take the form of explicit statements. (Authors are not so anxious to hide their meanings as some readers are prone to believe.) We also may be alerted to the fact that something is standing for something else when the something does not seem to make literal sense in itself. It does not take us long to realize that "Young Goodman Brown" is not entirely as realistic a story as "My Man Bovanne" or "The Whirlpool Rapids." When things do not seem explicable in terms of everyday reality, we often look beyond them for some meaning. Roses are real enough, but neither Faulkner's narrator nor anyone else in the story gives Emily a real rose. What, then, does the rose in the title "A Rose for Emily" suggest?

We must remember, however, that symbols do not exist solely for the transmission of a meaning we can paraphrase; they do not disappear from the story, our memory, or our response once their "meaning" has been sucked out of them, any more than Emily ceases to exist as an individual after we recognize her representative or universal nature. Faith's pink ribbons and Judith's cats are objects in their stories, whatever meanings or suggestions of meanings they have given rise to.

As I have often implied and occasionally said, few symbols can be exhausted, translated into an abstract phrase or equivalent: the "something else" that the "something" stands for is ultimately elusive. After you have read Ann Beattie's "Janus" try to paraphrase just what the bowl stands for. Or explain with certainty what Faith's pink ribbon symbolizes in "Young Goodman

Brown." It is not that the bowl and the ribbon mean nothing but that they mean so many things that no single equivalence will do; even an abstract statement seems to reduce rather than fully explain the significance to the reader.

When a figure is expressed as an explicit comparison, often signaled by *like* or *as*, it is called a **simile:** "eyes as blue as the sky"; "the baby brother I'd never known looked out from the depths of his private life, like an animal waiting to be coaxed into the light" ("Sonny's Blues"). An implicit comparison or identification of one thing with another unlike itself, without a verbal signal but just seeming to say "A *is* B," is called a **metaphor:** "the grass was a green carpet"; "there was a boiling wave of dogs about them" ("The Old People"). Sometimes all figures are loosely referred to as metaphors.

An **allegory** is like a metaphor in that one thing (usually non-rational, abstract, religious) is implicitly spoken of in terms of something that is concrete and usually sensuous (perceptible by the senses), but the comparison in allegory is extended to include a whole work or a large portion of a work. *The Pilgrim's Progress* is probably the most famous prose allegory in English; its central character is named Christian; he was born in the City of Destruction and sets out for the Celestial City, passes through the Slough of Despond and Vanity Fair, meets men named Pliable and Obstinate, and so on.

When an entire story, like "Young Goodman Brown," is symbolic, it is sometimes called a **myth.** *Myth* originally meant a story of communal origin that provided an explanation or religious interpretation of man, nature, the universe, and the relation between them. From the vantage point of another culture or set of beliefs, the word usually implied that the story was false: we speak of classical myths, but Christians do not speak of Christian myth. We also apply the term *myth* now to stories by individuals, sophisticated authors, but often there is still the implication that the mythic story relates to a communal or group experience, whereas a symbolic story may be more personal or private. It is hard to draw the line firmly: "Young Goodman Brown" seems to have clearly national, American implications, while "The Rocking-Horse Winner" may be a private Lawrencian symbol or a myth of modern bourgeois society. A plot or character element that recurs in cultural or cross-cultural myths, such as images of the devil, as in "Young Goodman Brown," is now widely called an **archetype.**

A symbol can be as brief and local as a metaphor or as extended as an allegory. Like an allegory it usually speaks in concrete terms of the non- or superrational, the abstract, that which is not immediately perceived by the senses. Though some allegories can be complex, with paraphrasable equivalences, allegory usually refers to a one-to-one relationship (as the names from *The Pil-*

grim's Progress imply), and literary symbols usually have high complex or even inexpressible equivalences, as in "Janus." "The Termitary" is a rather simple symbolic story. It gets the effect of complexity by masking the symbol until the final sentence, compelling us to think back over the story and construct or reconstruct the parallels, and it gets its power from the surprise and the complex bitterness of the ending. "Janus" is somewhat more complexly symbolic in that there are areas of meaning or implication that cannot be rendered in other terms or conveniently separated from the particulars of the story. The ultimate unparaphrasable nature of most symbolic images or stories is not vagueness but richness, not disorder but complexity.

▽ ▽ ▽

SYMBOLS A Glossary

allegory: as in *metaphor*, one thing (usually non-rational, abstract, religious) is implicitly spoken of in terms of something concrete, usually sensuous, but in an allegory the comparison is extended to include an entire work or large portion of a work.

archetype: a plot or character element that recurs in cultural or cross-cultural myths

figurative: non-literal; implicitly or explicitly representative of something in terms of some other unlike thing that seems to be similar or analogous

metaphor: an implicit comparison or identification of one thing with another unlike itself without the use of a verbal signal

myth: like allegory, myth usually is symbolic and extensive, including an entire work or story; though it no longer is necessarily specific to a single culture and pervasive in that culture—individual authors may now be said to create myths—there is still a sense that myth is communal or cultural, while the symbolic can often be private or personal.

simile: a figure that explicitly expresses the comparison, often signaled by *like* or *as*

symbol: a person, place, thing, event, or pattern in a literary work that designates itself and at the same time figuratively represents or "stands for" something else. Often the thing or idea represented is more abstract, general, non- or super-rational; the symbol more concrete and particular.

NATHANIEL HAWTHORNE

Young Goodman Brown

Young goodman Brown came forth, at sunset, into the street of Salem village,[1] but put his head back, after crossing the threshold, to exchange a parting kiss with his young wife. And Faith, as the wife was aptly named, thrust her own pretty head into the street, letting the wind play with the pink ribbons of her cap, while she called to goodman Brown.

"Dearest heart," whispered she, softly and rather sadly, when her lips were close to his ear, "pr'y thee, put off your journey until sunrise, and sleep in your own bed to-night. A lone woman is troubled with such dreams and such thoughts, that she's afeard of herself, sometimes. Pray, tarry with me this night, dear husband, of all nights in the year!"

"My love and my Faith," replied young goodman Brown, "of all nights in the year, this one night must I tarry away from thee. My journey, as thou callest it, forth and back again, must needs be done 'twixt now and sunrise. What, my sweet, pretty wife, dost thou doubt me already, and we but three months married!"

"Then, God bless you!" said Faith, with the pink ribbons, "and may you find all well, when you come back."

5 "Amen!" cried goodman Brown. "Say thy prayers, dear Faith, and go to bed at dusk, and no harm will come to thee."

So they parted; and the young man pursued his way, until, being about to turn the corner by the meeting-house, he looked back, and saw the head of Faith still peeping after him, with a melancholy air, in spite of her pink ribbons.

"Poor little Faith!" thought he, for his heart smote him. "What a wretch am I, to leave her on such an errand! She talks of dreams, too. Methought, as she spoke, there was trouble in her face, as if a dream had warned her what work is to be done to-night. But, no, no! 't would kill her to think it. Well; she's a blessed angel on earth; and after this one night, I'll cling to her skirts and follow her to Heaven."

With this excellent resolve for the future, goodman Brown felt himself justified in making more haste on his present evil purpose. He had taken a dreary road, darkened by all the gloomiest trees of the forest, which barely stood aside to let the narrow path creep through, and closed immediately behind. It was all as lonely as could be; and there is this peculiarity in such a solitude, that the traveler knows not who may be concealed by the innumerable trunks and the thick boughs overhead; so that, with lonely footsteps, he may yet be passing through an unseen multitude.

"There may be a devilish Indian behind every tree," said goodman Brown,

1. Salem, Massachusetts, Hawthorne's birthplace (1804) was the scene of the famous witch trials of 1692; *goodman*: husband, master of household.

to himself; and he glanced fearfully behind him, as he added, "What if the devil himself should be at my very elbow!"

His head being turned back, he passed a crook of the road, and looking 10
forward again, beheld the figure of a man, in grave and decent attire, seated at the foot of an old tree. He arose, at goodman Brown's approach, and walked onward, side by side with him.

"You are late, goodman Brown," said he. "The clock of the Old South was striking as I came through Boston; and that is full fifteen minutes agone."

"Faith kept me back awhile," replied the young man, with a tremor in his voice, caused by the sudden appearance of his companion, though not wholly unexpected.

It was now deep dusk in the forest, and deepest in that part of it where these two were journeying. As nearly as could be discerned, the second traveler was about fifty years old, apparently in the same rank of life as goodman Brown, and bearing a considerable resemblance to him, though perhaps more in expression than features. Still, they might have been taken for father and son. And yet, though the elder person was as simply clad as the younger, and as simple in manner too, he had an indescribable air of one who knew the world, and would not have felt abashed at the governor's dinner-table, or in king William's[2] court, were it possible that his affairs should call him thither. But the only thing about him, that could be fixed upon as remarkable, was his staff, which bore the likeness of a great black snake, so curiously wrought, that it might almost be seen to twist and wriggle itself, like a living serpent. This, of course, must have been an ocular deception, assisted by the uncertain light.

"Come, goodman Brown!" cried his fellow-traveler, "this is a dull pace for the beginning of a journey. Take my staff, if you are so soon weary."

"Friend," said the other, exchanging his slow pace for a full stop, "having 15
kept covenant by meeting thee here, it is my purpose now to return whence I came. I have scruples, touching the matter thou wot'st of."

"Sayest thou so?" replied he of the serpent, smiling apart. "Let us walk on, nevertheless, reasoning as we go, and if I convince thee not, thou shalt turn back. We are but a little way in the forest, yet."

"Too far, too far!" exclaimed the goodman, unconsciously resuming his walk. "My father never went into the woods on such an errand, nor his father before him. We have been a race of honest men and good Christians, since the days of the martyrs. And shall I be the first of the name of Brown, that ever took this path, and kept"—

"Such company, thou wouldst say," observed the elder person, interpreting his pause. "Good, goodman Brown! I have been as well acquainted with your family as with ever a one among the Puritans; and that's no trifle to say. I helped your grandfather, the constable, when he lashed the Quaker woman so smartly through the streets of Salem. And it was I that brought your father a pitch-pine

2. William III 1650–1702, ruled England from 1689 to 1702, until 1694 jointly with his wife, Mary II.

knot, kindled at my own hearth, to set fire to an Indian village, in king Philip's[3] war. They were my good friends, both; and many a pleasant walk have we had along this path, and returned merrily after midnight. I would fain be friends with you, for their sake."

"If it be as thou sayest," replied goodman Brown, "I marvel they never spoke of these matters. Or, verily, I marvel not, seeing that the least rumor of the sort would have driven them from New-England. We are a people of prayer, and good works, to boot, and abide no such wickedness."

"Wickedness or not," said the traveler with the twisted staff, "I have a very general acquaintance here in New-England. The deacons of many a church have drunk the communion wine with me; the selectmen, of divers towns, make me their chairman; and a majority of the Great and General Court are firm supporters of my interest. The governor and I, too—but these are state-secrets."

"Can this be so!" cried goodman Brown, with a stare of amazement at his undisturbed companion. "Howbeit, I have nothing to do with the governor and council; they have their own ways, and are no rule for a simple husbandman, like me. But, were I to go on with thee, how should I meet the eye of that good old man, our minister, at Salem village? Oh, his voice would make me tremble, both Sabbath-day and lecture-day!"[4]

Thus far, the elder traveler had listened with due gravity, but now burst into a fit of irrepressible mirth, shaking himself so violently, that his snake-like staff actually seemed to wriggle in sympathy.

"Ha! ha! ha!" shouted he, again and again; then composing himself, "Well, go on, goodman Brown, go on; but, pr'y thee, don't kill me with laughing!"

"Well, then, to end the matter at once," said goodman Brown, considerably nettled, "there is my wife, Faith. It would break her dear little heart; and I'd rather break my own!"

"Nay, if that be the case," answered the other, "e'en[5] go thy ways, goodman Brown. I would not, for twenty old women like the one hobbling before us, that Faith should come to any harm."

As he spoke, he pointed his staff at a female figure on the path, in whom goodman Brown recognized a very pious and exemplary dame, who had taught him his catechism, in youth, and was still his moral and spiritual adviser, jointly with the minister and deacon Gookin.

"A marvel, truly, that goody[6] Cloyse should be so far in the wilderness, at night-fall!" said he. "But, with your leave, friend, I shall take a cut through the woods, until we have left this Christian woman behind. Being a stranger to you, she might ask whom I was consorting with, and whither I was going."

"Be it so," said his fellow-traveler. "Betake you to the woods, and let me keep the path."

Accordingly, the young man turned aside, but took care to watch his com-

3. Metacom or Metacomet, chief of the Wampanoag Indians, known as King Philip, led a war against the New England colonists in 1675–76 which devastated many frontier communities.
4. The day—in the New England colonies usually a Thursday—appointed for an informal sermon.
5. Just. 6. Short for "goodwife" or housewife.

panion, who advanced softly along the road, until he had come within a staff's length of the old dame. She, meanwhile, was making the best of her way, with singular speed for so aged a woman, and mumbling some indistinct words, a prayer, doubtless, as she went. The traveler put forth his staff, and touched her withered neck with what seemed the serpent's tail.

"The devil!" screamed the pious old lady.

"Then goody Cloyse knows her old friend?" observed the traveler, confronting her, and leaning on his writhing stick.

"Ah, forsooth, and is it your worship, indeed?" cried the good dame. "Yea, truly is it, and in the very image of my old gossip, goodman Brown, the grandfather of the silly fellow that now is. But, would your worship believe it? my broomstick hath strangely disappeared, stolen, as I suspect, by that unhanged witch, goody Cory, and that, too, when I was all anointed with the juice of smallage and cinque-foil and wolf's-bane"—[7]

"Mingled with fine wheat and the fat of a new-born babe," said the shape of old goodman Brown.

"Ah, your worship knows the receipt," cried the old lady, cackling aloud. "So, as I was saying, being all ready for the meeting, and no horse to ride on, I made up my mind to foot it; for they tell me, there is a nice young man to be taken into communion to-night. But now your good worship will lend me your arm, and we shall be there in a twinkling."

"That can hardly be," answered her friend. "I may not spare you my arm, goody Cloyse, but here is my staff, if you will."

So saying, he threw it down at her feet, where, perhaps, it assumed life, being one of the rods which its owner had formerly lent to the Egyptian Magi.[8] Of this fact, however, goodman Brown could not take cognizance. He had cast up his eyes in astonishment, and looking down again, beheld neither goody Cloyse nor the serpentine staff, but his fellow-traveler alone, who waited for him as calmly as if nothing had happened.

"That old woman taught me my catechism!" said the young man; and there was a world of meaning in this simple comment.

They continued to walk onward, while the elder traveler exhorted his companion to make good speed and persevere in the path, discoursing so aptly, that his arguments seemed rather to spring up in the bosom of his auditor, than to be suggested by himself. As they went, he plucked a branch of maple, to serve for a walking-stick, and began to strip it of the twigs and little boughs, which were wet with evening dew. The moment his fingers touched them, they became strangely withered and dried up, as with a week's sunshine. Thus the pair proceeded, at a good free pace, until suddenly, in a gloomy hollow of the road, goodman Brown sat himself down on the stump of a tree, and refused to go any farther.

7. Plants traditionally associated with witchcraft. 8. Exodus 7:9–12. The Lord instructs Moses to have his prophet Aaron throw down his rod before the Pharaoh, whereupon it will be turned into a serpent, and by which miracle the Pharaoh will be persuaded to let the Jews go into the wilderness to sacrifice to God. The Pharaoh has his magicians (Magi) do likewise, "but Aaron's rod swallowed up their rods."

"Friend," said he, stubbornly, "my mind is made up. Not another step will I budge on this errand. What if a wretched old woman do choose to go to the devil, when I thought she was going to Heaven! Is that any reason why I should quit my dear Faith, and go after her?"

"You will think better of this, by-and-by," said his acquaintance, composedly. "Sit here and rest yourself awhile; and when you feel like moving again, there is my staff to help you along."

Without more words, he threw his companion the maple stick, and was as speedily out of sight, as if he had vanished into the deepening gloom. The young man sat a few moments, by the roadside, applauding himself greatly, and thinking with how clear a conscience he should meet the minister, in his morning-walk, nor shrink from the eye of good old deacon Gookin. And what calm sleep would be his, that very night, which was to have been spent so wickedly, but purely and sweetly now, in the arms of Faith! Amidst these pleasant and praiseworthy meditations, goodman Brown heard the tramp of horses along the road, and deemed it advisable to conceal himself within the verge of the forest, conscious of the guilty purpose that had brought him thither, though now so happily turned from it.

On came the hoof-tramps and the voices of the riders, two grave old voices, conversing soberly as they drew near. These mingled sounds appeared to pass along the road, within a few yards of the young man's hiding-place; but owing, doubtless, to the depth of the gloom, at that particular spot, neither the travelers nor their steeds were visible. Though their figures brushed the small boughs by the way-side, it could not be seen that they intercepted, even for a moment, the faint gleam from the strip of bright sky, athwart which they must have passed. Goodman Brown alternately crouched and stood on tip-toe, pulling aside the branches, and thrusting forth his head as far as he durst, without discerning so much as a shadow. It vexed him the more, because he could have sworn, were such a thing possible, that he recognized the voices of the minister and deacon Gookin, jogging along quietly, as they were wont to do, when bound to some ordination or ecclesiastical council. While yet within hearing, one of the riders stopped to pluck a switch.

"Of the two, reverend Sir," said the voice like the deacon's, "I had rather miss an ordination-dinner than to-night's meeting. They tell me that some of our community are to be here from Falmouth[9] and beyond, and others from Connecticut and Rhode-Island; besides several of the Indian powows, who, after their fashion, know almost as much deviltry as the best of us. Moreover, there is a goodly young woman to be taken into communion."

"Mighty well, deacon Gookin!" replied the solemn old tones of the minister. "Spur up, or we shall be late. Nothing can be done, you know, until I get on the ground."

The hoofs clattered again, and the voices, talking so strangely in the empty air, passed on through the forest, where no church had ever been gathered, nor solitary Christian prayed. Whither, then, could these holy men be journeying,

9. A port in extreme southern Massachusetts; Salem is in northern Massachusetts.

so deep into the heathen wilderness? Young goodman Brown caught hold of a tree, for support, being ready to sink down on the ground, faint and overburthened with the heavy sickness of his heart. He looked up to the sky, doubting whether there really was a Heaven above him. Yet, there was the blue arch, and the stars brightening in it.

"With Heaven above, and Faith below, I will yet stand firm against the devil!" cried goodman Brown.

While he still gazed upward, into the deep arch of the firmament, and had lifted his hands to pray, a cloud, though no wind was stirring, hurried across the zenith, and hid the brightening stars. The blue sky was still visible, except directly overhead, where this black mass of cloud was sweeping swiftly northward. Aloft in the air, as if from the depths of the cloud, came a confused and doubtful sound of voices. Once, the listener fancied that he could distinguish the accents of town's-people of his own, men and women, both pious and ungodly, many of whom he had met at the communion-table, and had seen others rioting at the tavern. The next moment, so indistinct were the sounds, he doubted whether he had heard aught but the murmur of the old forest, whispering without a wind. Then came a stronger swell of those familiar tones, heard daily in the sunshine, at Salem village, but never, until now, from a cloud of night. There was one voice, of a young woman, uttering lamentations, yet with an uncertain sorrow, and entreating for some favor, which, perhaps, it would grieve her to obtain. And all the unseen multitude, both saints and sinners, seemed to encourage her onward.

"Faith!" shouted goodman Brown, in a voice of agony and desperation; and the echoes of the forest mocked him, crying—"Faith! Faith!" as if bewildered wretches were seeking her, all through the wilderness.

The cry of grief, rage, and terror, was yet piercing the night, when the unhappy husband held his breath for a response. There was a scream, drowned immediately in a louder murmur of voices, fading into far-off laughter, as the dark cloud swept away, leaving the clear and silent sky above goodman Brown. But something fluttered lightly down through the air, and caught on the branch of a tree. The young man seized it, and beheld a pink ribbon.

"My Faith is gone!" cried he, after one stupefied moment. "There is no good 50
on earth; and sin is but a name. Come, devil! for to thee is this world given."

And maddened with despair, so that he laughed loud and long, did goodman Brown grasp his staff and set forth again, at such a rate, that he seemed to fly along the forest-path, rather than to walk or run. The road grew wilder and drearier, and more faintly traced, and vanished at length, leaving him in the heart of the dark wilderness, still rushing onward, with the instinct that guides mortal man to evil. The whole forest was peopled with frightful sounds; the creaking of the trees, the howling of wild beasts, and the yell of Indians; while, sometimes, the wind tolled like a distant church-bell, and sometimes gave a broad roar around the traveler, as if all Nature were laughing him to scorn. But he was himself the chief horror of the scene, and shrank not from its other horrors.

"Ha! ha! ha!" roared goodman Brown, when the wind laughed at him. "Let us hear which will laugh loudest! Think not to frighten me with your deviltry! Come witch, come wizard, come Indian powow, come devil himself! and here come goodman Brown. You may as well fear him as he fear you!"

In truth, all through the haunted forest, there could be nothing more frightful than the figure of goodman Brown. On he flew, among the black pines, brandishing his staff with frenzied gestures, now giving vent to an inspiration of horrid blasphemy, and now shouting forth such laughter, as set all the echoes of the forest laughing like demons around him. The fiend in his own shape is less hideous, than when he rages in the breast of man. Thus sped the demoniac on his course, until, quivering among the trees, he saw a red light before him, as when the felled trunks and branches of a clearing have been set on fire, and throw up their lurid blaze against the sky, at the hour of midnight. He paused, in a lull of the tempest that had driven him onward, and heard the swell of what seemed a hymn, rolling solemnly from a distance, with the weight of many voices. He knew the tune; it was a familiar one in the choir of the village meeting-house. The verse died heavily away, and was lengthened by a chorus, not of human voices, but of all the sounds of the benighted wilderness, pealing in awful harmony together. Goodman Brown cried out; and his cry was lost to his own ear, by its unison with the cry of the desert.

In the interval of silence, he stole forward, until the light glared full upon his eyes. At one extremity of an open space, hemmed in by the dark wall of the forest, arose a rock, bearing some rude, natural resemblance either to an altar or a pulpit, and surrounded by four blazing pines, their tops a flame, their stems untouched, like candles at an evening meeting. The mass of foliage, that had overgrown the summit of the rock, was all on fire, blazing high into the night, and fitfully illuminating the whole field. Each pendent twig and leafy festoon was in a blaze. As the red light arose and fell, a numerous congregation alternately shone forth, then disappeared in shadow, and again grew, as it were, out of the darkness, peopling the heart of the solitary woods at once.

55 "A grave and dark-clad company!" quoth goodman Brown.

In truth, they were such. Among them, quivering to-and-fro, between gloom and splendor, appeared faces that would be seen, next day, at the council-board of the province, and others which, Sabbath after Sabbath, looked devoutly heavenward, and benignantly over the crowded pews, from the holiest pulpits in the land. Some affirm, that the lady of the governor was there. At least, there were high dames well known to her, and wives of honored husbands, and widows, a great multitude, and ancient maidens, all of excellent repute, and fair young girls, who trembled, lest their mothers should espy them. Either the sudden gleams of light, flashing over the obscure field, bedazzled goodman Brown, or he recognized a score of the church-members of Salem village, famous for their especial sanctity. Good old deacon Gookin had arrived, and waited at the skirts of that venerable saint, his revered pastor. But, irreverently consorting with these grave, reputable, and pious people, these elders of the church, these chaste dames and dewy virgins, there were men of dissolute lives and women of spotted fame, wretches given over to all mean and filthy vice, and suspected even of horrid crimes. It was strange to see, that the good shrank not from the wicked, nor were the sinners abashed by the saints. Scattered, also, among their pale-faced enemies, were the Indian priests, or powows, who had often scared their native forest with more hideous incantations than any known to English witchcraft.

"But, where is Faith?" thought goodman Brown; and, as hope came into his heart, he trembled.

Another verse of the hymn arose, a slow and solemn strain, such as the pious love, but joined to words which expressed all that our nature can conceive of sin, and darkly hinted at far more. Unfathomable to mere mortals is the lore of fiends. Verse after verse was sung, and still the chorus of the desert swelled between, like the deepest tone of a mighty organ. And, with the final peal of that dreadful anthem, there came a sound, as if the roaring wind, the rushing streams, the howling beasts, and every other voice of the unconverted wilderness, were mingling and according with the voice of guilty man, in homage to the prince of all. The four blazing pines threw up a loftier flame, and obscurely discovered shapes and visages of horror on the smoke-wreaths, above the impious assembly. At the same moment, the fire on the rock shot redly forth, and formed a glowing arch above its base, where now appeared a figure. With reverence be it spoken, the apparition bore no slight similitude, both in garb and manner, to some grave divine of the New-England churches.

"Bring forth the converts!" cried a voice, that echoed through the field and rolled into the forest.

At the word, goodman Brown stept forth from the shadow of the trees, and 60
approached the congregation, with whom he felt a loathful brotherhood, by the sympathy of all that was wicked in his heart. He could have well nigh sworn, that the shape of his own dead father beckoned him to advance, looking downward from a smoke-wreath, while a woman, with dim features of despair, threw out her hand to warn him back. Was it his mother? But he had no power to retreat one step, nor to resist, even in thought, when the minister and good old deacon Gookin, seized his arms, and led him to the blazing rock. Thither came also the slender form of a veiled female, led between Goody Cloyse, that pious teacher of the catechism, and Martha Carrier, who had received the devil's promise to be queen of hell. A rampant hag was she! And there stood the proselytes, beneath the canopy of fire.

"Welcome, my children," said the dark figure, "to the communion of your race! Ye have found, thus young, your nature and your destiny. My children, look behind you!"

They turned; and flashing forth, as it were, in a sheet of flame, the fiend-worshippers were seen; the smile of welcome gleamed darkly on every visage.

"There," resumed the sable form, "are all whom ye have reverenced from youth. Ye deemed them holier than yourselves, and shrank from your own sin, contrasting it with their lives of righteousness, and prayerful aspirations heavenward. Yet, here are they all, in my worshipping assembly! This night it shall be granted you to know their secret deeds; how hoary-bearded elders of the church have whispered wanton words to the young maids of their households; how many a woman, eager for widow's weeds, has given her husband a drink at bed-time, and let him sleep his last sleep in her bosom; how beardless youths have made haste to inherit their fathers' wealth; and how fair damsels—blush not, sweet ones!—have dug little graves in the garden, and bidden me, the sole guest, to an infant's funeral. By the sympathy of your human hearts for sin, ye shall scent out all the places—whether in church, bed-chamber, street, field, or forest—where crime has been committed, and shall exult to behold the whole earth one stain of guilt, one mighty blood-spot. Far more than this! It shall be yours to penetrate, in every bosom, the deep mystery of sin, the fountain of all wicked arts, and which, inexhaustibly supplies more evil impulses than human power—than my power, at its utmost!—can make manifest in deeds. And now, my children, look upon each other."

They did so; and, by the blaze of the hell-kindled torches, the wretched man beheld his Faith, and the wife her husband, trembling before that unhallowed altar.

"Lo! there ye stand, my children," said the figure, in a deep and solemn tone, almost sad, with its despairing awfulness, as if his once angelic nature could yet mourn for our miserable race. "Depending upon one another's hearts, ye had still hoped, that virtue were not all a dream. Now are ye undeceived! Evil is the nature of mankind. Evil must be your only happiness. Welcome, again, my children, to the communion of your race!"

"Welcome!" repeated the fiend-worshippers, in one cry of despair and triumph.

And there they stood, the only pair, as it seemed, who were yet hesitating on the verge of wickedness, in this dark world. A basin was hollowed, naturally, in the rock. Did it contain water, reddened by the lurid light? or was it blood? or, perchance, a liquid flame? Herein did the Shape of Evil dip his hand, and prepare to lay the mark of baptism upon their foreheads, that they might be partakers of the mystery of sin, more conscious of the secret guilt of others, both in deed and thought, than they could now be of their own. The husband cast one look at his pale wife, and Faith at him. What polluted wretches would the next glance shew them to each other, shuddering alike at what they disclosed and what they saw!

"Faith! Faith!" cried the husband. "Look up to Heaven, and resist the Wicked One!"

Whether Faith obeyed, he knew not. Hardly had he spoken, when he found himself amid calm night and solitude, listening to a roar of the wind, which died heavily away through the forest. He staggered against the rock and felt it chill and damp, while a hanging twig, that had been all on fire, besprinkled his cheek with the coldest dew.

The next morning, young goodman Brown came slowly into the street of Salem village, staring around him like a bewildered man. The good old minister was taking a walk along the graveyard, to get an appetite for breakfast and meditate his sermon, and bestowed a blessing, as he passed, on goodman Brown. He shrank from the venerable saint, as if to avoid an anathema. Old deacon Gookin was at domestic worship, and the holy words of his prayer were heard through the open window. "What God doth the wizard pray to?" quoth goodman Brown. Goody Cloyse, that excellent old Christian, stood in the early sunshine, at her own lattice, catechising a little girl, who had brought her a pint of morning's milk. Goodman Brown snatched away the child, as from the grasp of the fiend himself. Turning the corner by the meeting-house, he spied the head of Faith, with the pink ribbons, gazing anxiously forth, and bursting into such joy at sight of him, that she skipt along the street, and almost kissed her husband before the whole village. But, goodman Brown looked sternly and sadly into her face, and passed on without a greeting.

Had goodman Brown fallen asleep in the forest, and only dreamed a wild dream of a witch-meeting?

Be it so, if you will. But, alas! it was a dream of evil omen for young goodman Brown. A stern, a sad, a darkly meditative, a distrustful, if not a desperate man, did he become, from the night of that fearful dream. On the Sabbath-day, when the congregation were singing a holy psalm, he could not listen, because an anthem of sin rushed loudly upon his ear, and drowned all the blessed strain. When the minister spoke from the pulpit, with power and fervid eloquence, and, with his hand on the open bible, of the sacred truths of our religion, and of saint-like lives and triumphant deaths, and of future bliss or misery unutterable, then did goodman Brown turn pale, dreading, lest the roof should thunder down upon the gray blasphemer and his hearers. Often, awakening suddenly at midnight, he shrank from the bosom of Faith, and at morning or eventide, when the family knelt down at prayer, he scowled, and muttered to himself, and gazed sternly at his wife, and turned away. And when he had lived long, and was borne to his grave, a hoary corpse, followed by Faith, an aged woman, and children and grandchildren, a goodly procession, besides neighbors, not a few, they carved no hopeful verse upon his tomb-stone; for his dying hour was gloom.

1835

NADINE GORDIMER

The Termitary

When you live in a small town far from the world you read about in municipal library books, the advent of repair men in the house is a festival. Daily life is gaily broken open, improvisation takes over. The living-room masquerades as a bedroom while the smell of paint in the bedroom makes it uninhabitable. The secret backs of confident objects (matchwood draped with cobwebs thickened by dust) are given away when furniture is piled to the centre of the room. Meals are picnics at which table manners are suspended because the first principle of deportment drummed into children by their mother—sitting down at table—is missing: there is nowhere to sit. People are excused eccentricities of dress because no one can find anything in its place.

A doctor is also a kind of repair man. When he is expected the sheets are changed and the dog chased off the patient's bed. If a child is sick, she doesn't have to go to school, she is on holiday, with presents into the bargain—a whole roll of comics tied with newsagent's string, and crayons or card games. The mother is alone in the house, except for the patient out of earshot in the sick-room; the other children are at school. Her husband is away at work. She takes off her apron, combs her hair and puts on a bit of lipstick to make herself decent for the doctor, setting ready a tea-tray for two in the quiet privacy of the deserted living-room as for a secret morning visit from the lover she does not have. After she and the doctor, who smells intoxicating, coldly sweet because he has just come from the operating theatre, have stood together looking down at the patient and making jolly remarks, he is glad to accept a cup of tea in his busy morning round and their voices are a murmur and an occasional rise of laughter from behind the closed living-room door.

Plumber, painter, doctor; with their arrival something has happened where nothing ever happens; at home: a house with a bungalow face made of two bow-window eyes on either side of a front-door mouth, in a street in a gold-mining town of twenty-five thousand people in South Africa in the 1930s.

Once the upright Steinway piano stood alone on the few remaining boards of a room from which the floor had been ripped. I burst in to look at the time on the chiming clock that should have been standing on the mantelpiece and instead flew through the air and found myself jolted down into a subterranean smell of an earth I'd never smelt before, the earth buried by our house. I was nine years old and the drop broke no bones; the shock excited me, the thought of that hollow, earth-breaking dark always beneath our Axminster[1] thrilled me; the importance I gained in my mother's accounts of how I might so easily have injured myself added to the sense of occasion usual in the family when there were workmen in.

5 This time it was not the painters, Mr. Strydom and his boys, over whom my mother raised a quarrel every few years. *I'm not like any other woman. I haven't got a husband like other women's. The state this house is in. You'd see the place fall to pieces before you'd lift a finger. Too mean to pay for a lick of paint, and then when you do you expect it to last ten years. I haven't got a home like other women.* Workmen were treated as the house-guests we never had; my mother's friends were neighbors, my father had none, and she wouldn't give house-room to a spare bed, anyway, because she didn't want his relatives coming. Mr. Strydom was served sweet strong tea to his taste many times a day, while my mother stood by to chat and I followed his skills with the brush, particularly fascinated when he was doing something he called, in his Afrikaner's English, "pulling the line." This was the free-hand deftness with which he could make a narrow black stripe dividing the lower half of our passage, painted dark against dirty finger-prints, from the cream upper half. *Yust a sec while I first pull the line, ay.*

Then he would drain his cup so completely that the tea leaves swirled up and stuck to the sides. This workmanlike thirst, for me, was a foreign custom, sign of the difference between being Afrikaans and English, as we were, just as I accepted that it must be in accordance with *their* custom that the black "boys" drank their tea from jam tins in the yard. But Mr. Strydom, like the doctor, like deaf dapper Mr. Waite the electrician, who had drinking bouts because he had

1. Type of carpet.

been through something called Ypres,[2] and Mr. Hartman who sang to himself in a sad soprano while he tuned the Steinway upright my mother had brought from her own mother's house, was a recurrent event. The state the house was in, this time, was one without precedent; the men who were in were not repair men. They had been sent for to exterminate what we called white ants—termites who were eating our house away under our feet. A million jaws were devouring steadily night and day the timber that supported our unchanging routines: one day (if my mother hadn't done something about it you may be sure no one else would) that heavy Steinway in its real rosewood case would have crashed through the floor-boards.

For years my mother had efficiently kicked apart the finely-granulated earth, forming cones perfect as the shape taken by sand that has trickled through an egg-timer, that was piled in our garden by ordinary black ants. My father never did a hand's turn; she herself poured a tar-smelling disinfectant down the ant-holes and emptied into them kettles of boiling water that made the ground break out in a sweat of gleaming, struggling, pin-head creatures in paroxysm. Yet (it was another event) on certain summer evenings after rain we would rush out into the garden to be in the tropical snowfall of millions of transparent wings from what we called flying ants, who appeared from nowhere. We watched while frogs bold with greed hopped onto the verandah to fill their pouched throats with these apparently harmless insects, and our cat ate steadily but with more self-control, spitting out with a shake of her whiskers any fragment of wing she might have taken up by mistake. We did not know that when these creatures shed their four delicate dragon-fly wings (some seemed to struggle like people getting out of coats) and became drab terrestrials, and some idiotically lifted their hindquarters in the air as if they were reacting to injury, they were enacting a nuptial ceremony that, one summer night or another, had ended in one out of these millions being fertilized and making her way under our house to become queen of a whole colony generated and given birth to by herself. Somewhere under our house she was in an endless parturition that would go on until she was found and killed.

The men had been sent for to search out the queen. No evil-smelling poisons, no opening-up of the tunnels more skilfully constructed than the London Underground, the Paris Metro or the New York subway I'd read about, no fumigation such as might do for cockroaches or moles or wood-borer beetles, could eradicate termites. No matter how many thousands were killed by my mother, as, in the course of the excavations that tore up the floor-boards of her house, the brittle passages made of grains of earth cemented by a secretion carried in the termites' own bodies were broken, and the inhabitants poured out in a pus of white moving droplets with yellow heads—no matter how many she cast into death agony with her Flit spray, the termitary would at once be repopulated so long as the queen remained, alive, hidden in that inner chamber where her subjects who were also her progeny had walled her in and guarded and tended her.

2. Belgian town, site of heavy fighting in World War I.

The three exterminators were one white and two black. All had the red earth of underground clinging to their clothes and skin and hair; their eyes were bloodshot; the nails of their hands, black or white, were outlined in red, their ears rimmed. The long hairs in the nostrils of the white man were coated with red as a bee's legs area yellow with pollen. These men themselves appeared to have been dug up, raw from that clinging earth entombed beneath buildings. Bloodied by their life-long medieval quest, they were ready to take it up once more: the search for a queen. They were said to be very good; my mother was sceptical as she was about the powers of water-diviners with bent twigs or people who got the dead to spell out messages by moving a glass to letters of the alphabet. But what else could she do? My father left it all to her, she had the responsibility.

She didn't like the look of these men. They were so filthy with earth; hands like exposed roots reaching for the tea she brought. She served even the white man with a tin mug.

It was she who insisted they leave a few boards intact under the piano; she knew better than to trust them to move it without damage to the rosewood case. They didn't speak while children watched them at work. The only sound was the pick stopped by the density of the earth under our living-room, and the gasp of the black man who wielded the pick, pulling it free and hurling it back into the earth again. Held off by silence, we children would not go away. We stolidly spent all our free time in witness. Yet in spite of our vigilance, when it happened, when they found her, at last—the queen—we were not there.

My mother was mixing a cake and we had been attracted away to her by that substance of her alchemy that was not the beaten eggs and butter and sugar that went into it; even the lightest stroke of a quick forefinger into the bowl conveyed a coating of fragrant creamy sweetness to the mouth which already had foreknowledge of its utter satisfaction through the scent of vanilla that came not only from the bowl, but from her clothes, her hair, her very skin. Suddenly my mother's dog lifted his twitching lip back over his long teeth and began to bounce towards and back away from the screen door as he did when any stranger approached her. We looked up; the three men had come to the back steps. The white gestured his ochre hand brusquely at one of the blacks, who tramped forward with a child's cardboard shoe-box offered. The lid was on and there were rough air-holes punched in it here and there, just as in the boxes where we had kept silk worms until my mother thought they smelled too musty and threw them away. The white man gestured again; he and my mother for a moment held their hands the same way, his covered with earth, hers with flour. The black man took off the lid.

And there she was, the queen. The smallest child swallowed as if about to retch and ran away to the far end of the kitchen. The rest of us crowded nearer, but my mother made us make way, she wasn't going to be fobbed off with anything but complete satisfaction for her husband's money. We all gazed at an obese, helpless white creature, five inches long, with the tiny, shiny-visored head of an ant at one end. The body was a sort of dropsical sac attached to this head; it had no legs that could be seen, neither could it propel itself by peristaltic action, like a slug or worm. The queen. The queen whose domain, we had seen for ourselves in the galleries and passages that had been uncovered beneath our house, was as big as ours.

The white man spoke, "That's 'er, missus."

"You're sure you've got the queen?" 15

"We got it. That's it." He gave a professional snigger at ignorance.

Was she alive? —But again the silence of the red-eyed, red-earthed men kept us back; they wouldn't let us daringly put out a finger to touch that body that seemed blown up in sections, like certain party balloons, and that had at once the suggestion of tactile attraction and repugnance—if a finger were to be stroked testingly along that perhaps faintly downy body, sweet creamy stuff might be expected to ooze from it. And in fact, when I found a book in the library called *The Soul of the White Ant*, by Eugène Marais, an Afrikaner like the white man who had found the queen's secret chamber, I read that the children-subjects at certain times draw nourishment from a queen's great body by stroking it so that she exudes her own rich maternal elixir.

"Ughh. Why's she so fat?" The smallest child had come close enough to force himself to look again.

"S'es full of ecks," the white man said. "They lays about a million ecks a day."

"Is it dead?"

But the man only laughed, now that his job was done, and like the show- 20
man's helper at the conclusion of an act, the black man knew to clap the lid back on the shoe-box. There was no way for us to tell; the queen cannot move, she is blind; whether she is underground, the tyrannical prisoner of her subjects who would not have been born and cannot live without her, or whether she is captured and borne away in a show-box, she is helpless to evade the consequences of her power.

My mother paid the men out of her housekeeping allowance (but she would have to speak to our father about that) and they nailed back the living-room floor-boards and went away, taking the cardboard box with them. My mother had heard that the whole thing was a hoax; these men went from house to house, made the terrible mess they'd left hers in, and produced the same queen time and again, carrying it around with them.

Yet the termites left our house. We never had to have those particular workmen in again. The Axminster carpet was laid once more, the furniture put back in its place, and I had to do the daily half-hour practice on the Steinway that I had been freed of for a week. I read in the book from the library that when the queen dies or is taken away all the termites leave their posts and desert the termitary; some find their way to other communities, thousands die. The termitary with its fungus-gardens for food, its tunnels for conveying water from as much as forty feet underground, its elaborate defence and communications system, is abandoned.

We lived on, above the ruin. The children grew up and left the town; coming back from the war after 1946 and later from visits to Europe and America and the Far East, it bored them to hear the same old stories, to be asked: "D'you remember Mr. Hartman who used to come in to tune the piano? He was asking after you the other day—poor thing, he's crippled with arthritis." "D'you remember old Strydom, 'pulling the line' . . . how you kids used to laugh, I was quite ashamed . . ." "D'you remember the time the white ant men were in, and you nearly broke your leg?" Were these events the sum of my mother's life? Why should I remember? I, who—shuddering to look back at those five rooms behind the bow-window eyes and the front-door mouth—have oceans, continents, snowed-in capitals, islands where turtles swim, cathedrals, theatres, palace gardens where people kiss and tramps drink wine—all these to remember. My father grew senile and she put him in a home for his last years. She stayed on, although she said she didn't want to; the house was a burden to her, she had carried the whole responsibility for him, for all of us, all her life. Now she is dead and although I suppose someone else lives in her house, the secret passages, the inner chamber in which she was our queen and our prisoner are sealed up, empty.

1980

ANN BEATTIE

Janus

The bowl was perfect. Perhaps it was not what you'd select if you faced a shelf of bowls, and not the sort of thing that would inevitably attract a lot of attention at a crafts fair, yet it had real presence. It was as predictably admired as a mutt who has no reason to suspect he might be funny. Just such a dog, in fact, was often brought out (and in) along with the bowl.

Andrea was a real estate agent, and when she thought that some prospective buyers might be dog lovers, she would drop off her dog at the same time she placed the bowl in the house that was up for sale. She would put a dish of water in the kitchen for Mondo, take his squeaking plastic frog out of her purse and drop it on the floor. He would pounce delightedly, just as he did every day at home, batting around his favorite toy. The bowl usually sat on a coffee table, though recently she had displayed it on top of a pine blanket chest and on a lacquered table. It was once placed on a cherry table beneath a Bonnard[1] still life, where it held its own.

Everyone who has purchased a house or who has wanted to sell a house must be familiar with some of the tricks used to convince a buyer that the house is quite special: a fire in the fireplace in early evening; jonquils in a pitcher on the kitchen counter, where no one ordinarily has space to put flowers; perhaps the slight aroma of spring, made by a single drop of scent vaporizing from a lamp bulb.

The wonderful thing about the bowl, Andrea thought, was that it was both subtle and noticeable—a paradox of a bowl. Its glaze was the color of cream and seemed to glow no matter what light it was placed in. There were a few bits of

1. Pierre Bonnard (1867–1947), French painter.

color in it—tiny geometric flashes—and some of these were tinged with flecks of silver. They were as mysterious as cells seen under a microscope; it was difficult not to study them, because they shimmered, flashing for a split second, and then resumed their shape. Something about the colors and their random placement suggested motion. People who liked country furniture always commented on the bowl, but then it turned out that people who felt comfortable with Biedermeier[2] loved it just as much. But the bowl was not at all ostentatious, or even so noticeable that anyone would suspect that it had been put in place deliberately. They might notice the height of the ceiling on first entering a room, and only when their eye moved down from that, or away from the refraction of sunlight on a pale wall, would they see the bowl. Then they would go immediately to it and comment. Yet they always faltered when they tried to say something. Perhaps it was because they were in the house for a serious reason, not to notice some object.

Once, Andrea got a call from a woman who had not put in an offer on a 5
house she had shown her. That bowl, she said—would it be possible to find out where the owners had bought that beautiful bowl? Andrea pretended that she did not know what the woman was referring to. A bowl, somewhere in the house? Oh, on a table under the window. Yes, she would ask, of course. She let a couple of days pass, then called back to say that the bowl had been a present and the people did not know where it had been purchased.

When the bowl was not being taken from house to house, it sat on Andrea's coffee table at home. She didn't keep it carefully wrapped (although she transported it that way, in a box); she kept it on the table, because she liked to see it. It was large enough so that it didn't seem fragile, or particularly vulnerable if anyone sideswiped the table or Mondo blundered into it at play. She had asked her husband to please not drop his house key in it. It was meant to be empty.

When her husband first noticed the bowl, he had peered into it and smiled briefly. He always urged her to buy things she liked. In recent years, both of them had acquired many things to make up for all the lean years when they were graduate students, but now that they had been comfortable for quite a while, the pleasure of new possessions dwindled. Her husband had pronounced the bowl "pretty," and he had turned away without picking it up to examine it. He had no more interest in the bowl than she had in his new Leica.[3]

She was sure that the bowl brought her luck. Bids were often put in on houses where she had displayed the bowl. Sometimes the owners, who were always asked to be away or to step outside when the house was being shown, didn't even know that the bowl had been in their house. Once—she could not imagine how—she left it behind, and then she was so afraid that something might have happened to it that she rushed back to the house and sighed with relief when the woman owner opened the door. The bowl, Andrea explained—she had purchased a bowl and set it on the chest for safekeeping while she toured the house with the prospective buyers, and she . . . She felt like rushing past the frowning woman and seizing her bowl. The owner stepped aside, and it was only

2. Mid-19th-century heavy, stuffed German furniture.

3. An expensive German camera.

when Andrea ran to the chest that the lady glanced at her a little strangely. In the few seconds before Andrea picked up the bowl, she realized that the owner must have just seen that it had been perfectly placed, that the sunlight struck the bluer part of it. Her pitcher had been moved to the far side of the chest, and the bowl predominated. All the way home, Andrea wondered how she could have left the bowl behind. It was like leaving a friend at an outing—just walking off. Sometimes there were stories in the paper about families forgetting a child somewhere and driving to the next city. Andrea had only gone a mile down the road before she remembered.

In time, she dreamed of the bowl. Twice, in a waking dream—early in the morning, between sleep and a last nap before rising—she had a clear vision of it. It came into sharp focus and startled her for a moment—the same bowl she looked at every day.

10 She had a very profitable year selling real estate. Word spread, and she had more clients than she felt comfortable with. She had the foolish thought that if only the bowl were an animate object she could thank it. There were times when she wanted to talk to her husband about the bowl. He was a stockbroker, and sometimes told people that he was fortunate to be married to a woman who had such a fine aesthetic sense and yet could also function in the real world. They were a lot alike, really—they had agreed on that. They were both quiet people—reflective, slow to make value judgments, but almost intractable once they had come to a conclusion. They both liked details, but while ironies attracted her, he was more impatient and dismissive when matters became many sided or unclear. But they both knew this; it was the kind of thing they could talk about when they were alone in the car together, coming home from a party or after a weekend with friends. But she never talked to him about the bowl. When they were at dinner, exchanging their news of the day, or while they lay in bed at night listening to the stereo and murmuring sleepy disconnections, she was often tempted to come right out and say that she thought that the bowl in the living room, the cream-colored bowl, was responsible for her success. But she didn't say it. She couldn't begin to explain it. Sometimes in the morning, she would look at him and feel guilty that she had such a constant secret.

Could it be that she had some deeper connection with the bowl—a relationship of some kind? She corrected her thinking: how could she imagine such a thing, when she was a human being and it was a bowl? It was ridiculous. Just think of how people lived together and loved each other . . . But was that always so clear, always a relationship? She was confused by these thoughts, but they remained in her mind. There was something within her now, something real, that she never talked about.

The bowl was a mystery, even to her. It was frustrating, because her involvement with the bowl contained a steady sense of unrequited good fortune; it would have been easier to respond if some sort of demand were made in return. But that only happened in fairy tales. The bowl was just a bowl. She did not believe that for one second. What she believed was that it was something she loved.

In the past, she had sometimes talked to her husband about a new property she was about to buy or sell—confiding some clever strategy she had devised to persuade owners who seemed ready to sell. Now she stopped doing that, for all her strategies involved the bowl. She became more deliberate with the bowl, and more possessive. She put it in houses only when no one was there, and removed it when she left the house. Instead of just moving a pitcher or a dish, she would remove all the other objects from a table. She had to force herself to handle them carefully, because she didn't really care about them. She just wanted them out of sight.

She wondered how the situation would end. As with a lover, there was no exact scenario of how matters would come to a close. Anxiety became the operative force. It would be irrelevant if the lover rushed into someone else's arms, or wrote her a note and departed to another city. The horror was the possibility of the disappearance. That was what mattered.

She would get up at night and look at the bowl. It never occurred to her that she might break it. She washed and dried it without anxiety, and she moved it often, from coffee table to mahogany corner table or wherever, without fearing an accident. It was clear that she would not be the one who would do anything to the bowl. The bowl was only handled by her, set safely on one surface or another; it was not very likely that anyone would break it. A bowl was a poor conductor of electricity: it would not be hit by lightning. Yet the idea of damage persisted. She did not think beyond that—to what her life would be without the bowl. She only continued to fear that some accident would happen. Why not, in a world where people set plants where they did not belong, so that visitors touring a house would be fooled into thinking that dark corners got sunlight—a world full of tricks?

She had first seen the bowl several years earlier, at a crafts fair she had visited half in secret, with her lover. He had urged her to buy the bowl. She didn't *need* any more things, she told him. But she had been drawn to the bowl, and they had lingered near it. Then she went on to the next booth, and he came up behind her, tapping the rim against her shoulder as she ran her fingers over a wood carving. "You're still insisting that I buy that?" she said. "No," he said. "I bought it for you." He had bought her other things before this—things she liked more, at first—the child's ebony-and-turquoise ring that fitted her little finger; the wooden box, long and thin, beautifully dovetailed, that she used to hold paper clips; the soft gray sweater with a pouch pocket. It was his idea that when he could not be there to hold her hand she could hold her own—clasp her hands inside the lone pocket that stretched across the front. But in time she became more attached to the bowl than to any of his other presents. She tried to talk herself out of it. She owned other things that were more striking or valuable. It wasn't an object whose beauty jumped out at you; a lot of people must have passed it by before the two of them saw it that day.

Her lover had said that she was always too slow to know what she really loved. Why continue with her life the way it was? Why be two-faced, he asked her. He had made the first move toward her. When she would not decide in his favor, would not change her life and come to him, he asked her what made her think she could have it both ways. And then he made the last move and left. It was a decision meant to break her will, to shatter her intransigent ideas about honoring previous commitments.

Time passed. Alone in the living room at night, she often looked at the bowl sitting on the table, still and safe, unilluminated. In its way, it was perfect: the world cut in half, deep and smoothly empty. Near the rim, even in dim light, the eye moved toward one small flash of blue, a vanishing point on the horizon.

1986

QUESTIONS

1. Why does goodman Brown go to a witches' meeting?

2. Why does Faith Brown, his wife, wear pink ribbons?

3. Who speaks the first passage of italicized words of "The Termitary" (par. 5)? To whom are they addressed?

4. When do you first begin to anticipate the symbolic function of the termite queen?

5. Why is the centered consciousness, the female protagonist, in "Janus" never referred to by name?

WRITING SUGGESTIONS

1. Write a parody of "Young Goodman Brown" or an imitation, perhaps in the style of Stephen King or Anne Rice.

2. Write an analysis of the symbolism in one of the stories in Reading Fiction or in one of the first three chapters in Text.

3. Write an essay on the characterization of the mother *and father* in "The Termitary" and discuss their function as symbols.

4. Analyze the character of the centered consciousness, the female protagonist, of "Janus."

6 THEME

If you ask what a story is "about," an author is likely to answer by telling you the **subject.** Indeed, many authors tell you the subject in their titles: "An Occurrence at Owl Creek Bridge," "The Termitary," "Her First Ball." Though a subject is always concrete, it may be stated at somewhat greater length than the few words of a title: "a man's thoughts as he faces execution for spying during the Civil War" ("Owl Creek Bridge"); "a young girl's excitement at her first grown-up dance and an incident that temporarily depresses her" ("Her First Ball").

A friend might be more likely to tell you what a story is about by giving you a summary of the action: "This weird Southern lady is jilted by a Yankee. She kills him and sleeps with his corpse. There's a smell around the house before too long, but nobody knows about the murder until she dies." (We sometimes call this a **plot summary,** but you will notice that this summary is of the history, of the events in more or less chronological order, while the plot is an arrangement or structuring of that history; in "A Rose for Emily," remember, we do not figure out there's been a murder and certainly don't know about Emily's sleeping with him until the end of the story, though of course the jilting, murder, and so on happen in the order described in the summary of the history.)

Your teacher may well tell you what a story is about by summarizing its **theme.** Some refer to the central idea, the thesis, or even the message of the story, and that is roughly what we mean by theme: a generalization or abstraction from the story.

The subject of "Young Goodman Brown" may be said to be a coven (witches' meeting) or, more fully, "a young colonial New England husband is driven mad by finding everyone he thought good and pure attending a witches' meeting." The theme may be "everyone partakes of evil," or, more succinctly, "the Fall." There are, as you can see, degrees of generalization and abstraction; subject (a young man finds that everyone is evil) shades off into theme, which itself can be more or less general and abstract.

Discussions of literature in or out of class sometimes seem to suggest that stories exist for their themes, that we read only to get the "point" or message. But most themes, you must admit, are somewhat less than earth-shattering. That all men and women are evil may be debatable, but it certainly isn't news. That not all unmarried women (even English women) of a certain age are prudish, dried up, and repressed—an apparent theme of "Our Friend Judith"—is rather widely recognized, something we scarcely need a dozen or so pages of fiction to find out. No wonder, then, that some of our more skeptical friends contend that stories are only elaborate ways of "saying something simple," that literature is a game in which authors hide their meanings under shells of words.

Of course, reading a dozen or so pages of a story like "Our Friend Judith" can be enjoyable. Could it be that we really read fiction for fun, and all our talk about themes is just hiding from our Puritan natures the fact that we are goofing off?

I don't believe that articulating the theme of a story is either the purpose of or the excuse for reading fiction, or that authors hide their meanings like Easter eggs. In order to relate his or her unique vision of reality to an absent and unknown reader, a writer must find a way of communicating—some common ground on which to meet the various unique individuals who will read the story. Common experiences, common assumptions, common language, and commonplaces offer such ground. Readers reach out from their own subjective worlds toward that new and different vision of the author with the help of the common elements (the general), and especially through the commonplaces of theme, bringing back the particulars and generalizations of the story to their own reading and living experience. In "Janus," the reader sees a successful suburban real estate agent who is married to a stockbroker but who has lost her lover, a man she truly loved, because she could not or would not decide to leave her husband; a woman whose world is "perfect," but cut in half and empty, like the beloved bowl her lover picked out for her and gave her. Generalizing, the reader may conclude that what the story says (its theme) is that life, or a full or happy life, is more than convention and material success, that love is more important than comfort and "perfection." Though the reader's own situation and choices may be considerably different from those of the protagonist in Beattie's story, he or she may be led by the story to ponder what is truly important and valuable in life, what "the perfect life" consists in, thereby coming to a greater understanding of the story—and, whether he or she agrees with the conclusions of the story or not, to a fuller understanding of the issues and theme of the story.

The significance of any story is modified to some extent by the reader's experience of books and life. You should not reduce every story to the dimensions of what you already know and feel, but you should reach out to the story and bring it back to your own experience as an addition and modification. If you're going to make a story yours, and if you are going to make it more than a yarn about a woman who sells real estate and has been unfaithful to her stockbroker husband and was left by her lover because she would not get a divorce, you will translate it somehow into terms that, while not necessarily psychological or moral precepts, alter or broaden to some degree your own vision of yourself, others, life in general.

When I discussed symbols, I said that even while a symbol suggests the meaning beyond the particulars of the fiction, it remains a detail in the fictional world—the snakelike staff of the stranger in "Young Goodman Brown" remains a staff, Judith's cats remain cats. Some critics would say that this is true also of theme and that theme is related to the story as integrally as symbolic meaning is to detail; that is, rather than "Young Goodman Brown" telling us something we did not know before, its theme and its story modify each other. The theme as I've stated it relates to spiritual evil, the kind of evil suggested by the snake and Satan figures. But this theme is not entirely portable—it cannot be taken out of the story and used as substitute for what the story "means"—nor can it, without qualification, be used to explain all the significant details in the story: the facts that Brown is a newlywed, that Faith wears pink (coquettish?) ribbons, and that she, whom Brown thought so pure and innocent, shows up at the meeting of witches and sinners, suggest a more specific kind of evil than the spiritual or theological evil suggested by the snake and Satan: moral or, even more specifically, sexual evil. This means we must modify our definition of the theme. But how? What does the story imply about the relationship of sex and evil? Is all sex evil? Is original sin sexual? Some details—the snake, the Satanic guide—suggest a theme, other details modify it; still others—Brown's behavior after the night of the witches' meeting—may modify it further, so that the theme, though an approximate version of it may be abstracted from the story, remains embedded in it, ultimately inseparable from the details of plot, character, setting, and symbol.

A statement that can do justice to all the complexity and all the particulars of the story is not likely to take the simple form of a **message.** Indeed, it is the complex particularity of literature, its ultimate irreducibility, that makes critics and teachers reject "message" (which suggests a simple packaged statement) as a suitable term even for the paraphrasable thematic content of a story.

"Young Goodman Brown" is an allegorical story whose details do function as symbols with paraphrasable meanings, yet even its theme refuses to be reduced to a simple statement. "How Much Land Does a Man Need?" is a **parable,** a short fiction that illustrates an explicit moral lesson. That lesson, the theme, is implied by the title. (And here the devil appears not only, at times, in disguise, but also in his proper person.) Even so, Tolstoy's story is not without complexity. How do you account for the first section of the story? Does your paraphrase of the theme accommodate the conversation between the sisters there?

"Her First Ball" is not allegorical and neither is it parabolic. Though realistic, however, it is a short, rather simple story that seems to have a simple theme overtly enunciated by one of the characters: Leila's elderly partner. But the scene with the elderly partner is not the end of the story. Leila goes on to dance with a young partner and seems to forget the man's "message." What is the story "saying"? Is her forgetting "bad"? Or "sad"? Or "good"? The specifics of the story modify and enrich all the generalizations we can abstract from it, while these themes and questions, if we recognize them, modify and enrich our reading, our experience of the story.

I realize I may have been talking as if a theme or themes spring out at the reader, while to some of you my inference of themes may seem like pulling rabbits out of hats. "How Much Land Does a Man Need?" does not involve much of a trick: the title asks the question that, once answered, suggests the theme. But there isn't even too much conjuring in "Young Goodman Brown": I derived the theme of theological evil from the symbols (the snake-staff, Satan figure, names) and I tested physical details—like pink ribbons and the narrative situation (the three-month marriage)—which had sexual implications against the theme to see if I would have to modify my paraphrase. In "Her First Ball" a character raises a general issue that is tested by subsequent events in the story and modified by them. The title "Beyond the Pale" hints at a theme but too faintly and obliquely to signify until one of the characters brings it to the surface toward the end of the story.

There are, of course, other means by which details suggest generalizations or meaning or by which meaning may be abstracted from detail. Aided by footnotes, perhaps, you likely noticed the historical and biblical **allusions**—references to history, the Bible, sometimes literature, paintings, and so on—in "Young Goodman Brown." The scene is Salem in the time of King William—that is, about the time of the Salem witch trials—and the stranger's serpentine staff is related to Exodus (where the staff of the Egyptian Magi does not turn into a snake). So allusion as well as symbols, plot, focus and voice, and character are elements that contribute to and must be accounted for in paraphrasing a theme. That is why theme is important, and why it comes last in a discussion of the elements of fiction.

But remember, the theme is an inadequate abstraction from the story; the story and its details do not disappear or lose significance once distilled into theme, nor could you reconstruct a story merely from its paraphrased theme.

Indeed, theme and story, history and structure, do not so much interact, are not so much interrelated, as they are fused, inseparable.

▽ ▽ ▽

THEME A Glossary

allusion: reference in a story to history, the Bible, literature, painting, music, and so on, that suggests the meaning or generalized relevance of details in the story

message: a misleading term for *theme*, or the central idea or statement of a story, misleading because it suggests a simple, packaged statement that pre-exists and for the simple communication of which the story is written

parable: a short fiction that illustrates an explicit moral lesson

plot summary: a description of the arrangement of the action in the order in which it actually appears in a story; the term is popularly used to mean the description of the history, or chronological order, of the action as it would have appeared in reality. It is important to indicate exactly in which sense you are using the term.

subject: the concrete and literal description of what a story is about

theme: a generalized, abstract paraphrase of the inferred central or dominant idea of a story

LEO TOLSTOY

How Much Land Does a Man Need?[1]

I

An elder sister came to visit her younger sister in the country. The elder was married to a tradesman in town, the younger to a peasant in the village. As the sisters sat over their tea talking, the elder began to boast of the advantages of town life: saying how comfortably they lived there, how well they dressed, what fine clothes her children wore, what good things they ate and drank, and how she went to the theatre, promenades, and entertainments.

The younger sister was piqued, and in turn disparaged the life of a tradesman, and stood up for that of a peasant.

"I would not change my way of life for yours," said she. "We may live roughly, but at least we are free from anxiety. You live in better style than we do, but though you often earn more than you need, you are very likely to lose all you have. You know the proverb, 'Loss and gain are brothers twain.' It often happens that people who are wealthy one day are begging their bread the next. Our way is safer. Though a peasant's life is not a fat one, it is a long one. We shall never grow rich, but we shall always have enough to eat."

The elder sister said sneeringly:

"Enough? Yes, if you like to share with the pigs and the calves! What do you know of elegance or manners! However much your goodman may slave, you will die as you are living—on a dung heap—and your children the same."

"Well, what of that?" replied the younger. "Of course our work is rough and coarse. But, on the other hand, it is sure, and we need not bow to anyone. But you, in your towns, are surrounded by temptations; to-day all may be right, but to-morrow the Evil One may tempt your husband with cards, wine, or women, and all will go to ruin. Don't such things happen often enough?"

Pahóm, the master of the house, was lying on the top of the stove and he listened to the women's chatter.

"It is perfectly true," thought he. "Busy as we are from childhood tilling mother earth, we peasants have no time to let any nonsense settle in our heads. Our only trouble is that we haven't land enough. If I had plenty of land, I shouldn't fear the Devil himself!"

The women finished their tea, chatted a while about dress, and then cleared away the tea-things and lay down to sleep.

But the Devil had been sitting behind the stove, and had heard all that was said. He was pleased that the peasant's wife had led her husband into boasting, and that he had said that if he had plenty of land he would not fear the Devil himself.

1. Translated by Louise and Aylmer Maude.

"All right," thought the Devil. "We will have a tussle. I'll give you land enough; and by means of that land I will get you into my power."

II

Close to the village there lived a lady, a small landowner who had an estate of about three hundred acres. She had always lived on good terms with the peasants until she engaged as her steward an old soldier, who took to burdening the people with fines. However careful Pahóm tried to be, it happened again and again that now a horse of his got among the lady's oats, now a cow strayed into her garden, now his calves found their way into her meadows—and he always had to pay a fine.

Pahóm paid up, but grumbled and, going home in a temper, was rough with his family. All through that summer, Pahóm had much trouble because of this steward, and he was even glad when winter came and the cattle had to be stabled. Though he grudged the fodder when they could no longer graze on the pasture-land, at least he was free from anxiety about them.

In the winter the news got about that the lady was going to sell her land and that the keeper of the inn on the high road was bargaining for it. When the peasants heard this they were very much alarmed.

"Well," thought they, "if the innkeeper gets the land, he will worry us with fines worse than the lady's steward. We all depend on that estate."

So the peasants went on behalf of their Commune, and asked the lady not to sell the land to the innkeeper, offering her a better price for it themselves. The lady agreed to let them have it. Then the peasants tried to arrange for the Commune to buy the whole estate, so that it might be held by them all in common. They met twice to discuss it, but could not settle the matter; the Evil One sowed discord among them and they could not agree. So they decided to buy the land individually, each according to his means; and the lady agreed to this plan as she had to the other.

Presently Pahóm heard that a neighbor of his was buying fifty acres, and that the lady had consented to accept one half in cash and to wait a year for the other half. Pahóm felt envious.

"Look at that," thought he, "the land is all being sold, and I shall get none of it." So he spoke to his wife.

"Other people are buying," said he, "and we must also buy twenty acres or so. Life is becoming impossible. That steward is simply crushing us with his fines."

So they put their heads together and considered how they could manage to buy it. They had one hundred rúbles laid by. They sold a colt and one half of their bees, hired out one of their sons as a laborer and took his wages in advance; borrowed the rest from a brother-in-law, and so scraped together half the purchase money.

Having done this, Pahóm chose out a farm of forty acres, some of it wooded, and went to the lady to bargain for it. They came to an agreement, and he shook hands with her upon it and paid her a deposit in advance. Then they went to town and signed the deeds; he paying half the price down, and undertaking to pay the remainder within two years.

So now Pahóm had land of his own. He borrowed seed, and sowed it on the land he had bought. The harvest was a good one, and within a year he had managed to pay off his debts both to the lady and to his brother-in-law. So he became a landowner, ploughing and sowing his own land, making hay on his own land, cutting his own trees, and feeding his cattle on his own pasture. When he went out to plough his fields, or to look at his growing corn, or at his grass-meadows, his heart would fill with joy. The grass that grew and the flowers that bloomed there seemed to him unlike any that grew elsewhere. Formerly, when he had passed by that land, it had appeared the same as any other land, but now it seemed quite different.

III

So Pahóm was well-contented, and everything would have been right if the neighboring peasants would only not have trespassed on his corn-fields and meadows. He appealed to them most civilly, but they still went on: now the Communal herdsmen would let the village cows stray into his meadows, then horses from the night pasture would get among his corn. Pahóm turned them out again, and forgave their owners, and for a long time he forbore to prosecute any one. But at last he lost patience and complained to the District Court. He knew it was the peasants' want of land, and no evil intent on their part, that caused the trouble, but he thought:

"I cannot go on overlooking it or they will destroy all I have. They must be taught a lesson."

So he had them up, gave them one lesson, and then another, and two or three of the peasants were fined. After a time Pahóm's neighbors began to bear him a grudge for this, and would now and then let their cattle on to his land on purpose. One peasant even got into Pahóm's wood at night and cut down five young lime trees for their bark. Pahóm passing through the wood one day noticed something white. He came nearer and saw the stripped trunks lying on the ground, and close by stood the stumps where the trees had been. Pahóm was furious.

"If he had only cut one here and there it would have been bad enough," thought Pahóm, "but the rascal has actually cut down a whole clump. If I could only find out who did this, I would pay him out."

He racked his brain as to who it could be. Finally he decided: "It must be Simon—no one else could have done it." So he went to Simon's homestead to have a look round, but he found nothing, and only had an angry scene. However, he now felt more certain than ever that Simon had done it, and he lodged a complaint. Simon was summoned. The case was tried, and retried, and at the end of it all Simon was acquitted, there being no evidence against him. Pahóm felt still more aggrieved, and let his anger loose upon the Elder and the Judges. "You let thieves grease your palms," said he. "If you were honest folk yourselves you would not let a thief go free."

So Pahóm quarrelled with the Judges and with his neighbors. Threats to burn his building began to be uttered. So though Pahóm had more land, his place in the Commune was much worse than before.

About this time a rumor got about that many people were moving to new parts.

"There's no need for me to leave my land," thought Pahóm. "But some of the others might leave our village and then there would be more room for us. I would take over their land myself and make my estate a bit bigger. I could then live more at ease. As it is, I am still too cramped to be comfortable."

One day Pahóm was sitting at home when a peasant, passing through the village, happened to call in. He was allowed to stay the night, and supper was given him. Pahóm had a talk with this peasant and asked him where he came from. The stranger answered that he came from beyond the Vólga, where he had been working. One word led to another, and the man went on to say that many people were settling in those parts. He told how some people from his village had settled there. They had joined the Commune, and had had twenty-five acres per man granted them. The land was so good, he said, that the rye sown on it grew as high as a horse, and so thick that five cuts of a sickle made a sheaf. One peasant, he said, had brought nothing with him but his bare hands, and now he had six horses and two cows of his own.

Pahóm's heart kindled with desire. He thought:

"Why should I suffer in this narrow hole, if one can live so well elsewhere? I will sell my land and my homestead here, and with the money I will start afresh over there and get everything new. In this crowded place one is always having trouble. But I must first go and find out all about it myself."

Towards summer he got ready and started. He went down the Vólga on a steamer to Samára, then walked another three hundred miles on foot, and at last reached the place. It was just as the stranger had said. The peasants had plenty of land: every man had twenty-five acres of Communal land given him for his use, and any one who had money could buy, besides, at a rúble an acre as much good freehold land as he wanted.

Having found out all he wished to know, Pahóm returned home as autumn came on, and began selling off his belongings. He sold his land at a profit, sold his homestead and all his cattle, and withdrew from membership in the Commune. He only waited till the spring, and then started with his family for the new settlement.

IV

As soon as Pahóm and his family reached their new abode, he applied for admission into the Commune of a large village. He stood treat to the Elders and obtained the necessary documents. Five shares of Communal land were given him for his own and his sons' use: that is to say—125 acres (not all together, but in different fields) besides the use of the Communal pasture. Pahóm put up the buildings he needed, and bought cattle. Of the Communal land alone he had three times as much as at his former home, and the land was good corn-land.

He was ten times better off than he had been. He had plenty of arable land and pasturage, and could keep as many head of cattle as he liked.

At first, in the bustle of building and settling down, Pahóm was pleased with it all, but when he got used to it he began to think that even here he had not enough land. The first year, he sowed wheat on his share of the Communal land and had a good crop. He wanted to go on sowing wheat, but had not enough Communal land for the purpose, and what he had already used was not available; for in those parts wheat is only sown on virgin soil or on fallow land. It is sown for one or two years, and then the land lies fallow till it is again overgrown with prairie grass. There were many who wanted such land and there was not enough for all; so that people quarreled about it. Those who were better off wanted it for growing wheat, and those who were poor wanted it to let to dealers, so that they might raise money to pay their taxes. Pahóm wanted to sow more wheat, so he rented land from a dealer for a year. He sowed much wheat and had a fine crop, but the land was too far from the village—the wheat had to be carted more than ten miles. After a time Pahóm noticed that some peasant-dealers were living on separate farms and were growing wealthy; and he thought:

"If I were to buy some freehold land and have a homestead on it, it would be a different thing altogether. Then it would all be nice and compact."

The question of buying freehold land recurred to him again and again.

He went on in the same way for three years, renting land and sowing wheat. The seasons turned out well and the crops were good, so that he began to lay money by. He might have gone on living contentedly, but he grew tired of having to rent other people's land every year, and having to scramble for it. Wherever there was good land to be had, the peasants would rush for it and it was taken up at once, so that unless you were sharp about it you got none. It happened in the third year that he and a dealer together rented a piece of pasture-land from some peasants; and they had already ploughed it up, when there was some dispute and the peasants went to law about it, and things fell out so that the labor was all lost.

"If it were my own land," thought Pahóm, "I should be independent, and there would not be all this unpleasantness."

So Pahóm began looking out for land which he could buy; and he came across a peasant who had bought thirteen hundred acres, but having got into difficulties was willing to sell again cheap. Pahóm bargained and haggled with him, and at last they settled the price at 1,500 rúbles, part in cash and part to be paid later. They had all but clinched the matter when a passing dealer happened to stop at Pahóm's one day to get a feed for his horses. He drank tea with Pahóm and they had a talk. The dealer said that he was just returning from the land of the Bashkírs,[2] far away, where he had bought thirteen thousand acres of land, all for 1,000 rúbles. Pahóm questioned him further, and the tradesman said:

"All one need do is to make friends with the chiefs. I gave away one hundred

2. Extreme eastern European Russia, extending southwest from the Ural mountains; the land is chiefly steppes with fertile meadows in the valleys.

rúbles' worth of silk robes and carpets, besides a case of tea, and I gave wine to those who would drink it; and I got the land for less than a penny an acre." And he showed Pahóm the title-deeds, saying:

"The land lies near a river, and the whole prairie is virgin soil."

Pahóm plied him with questions, and the tradesman said:

"There is more land there than you could cover if you walked a year, and it all belongs to the Bashkírs. They are as simple as sheep, and land can be got almost for nothing."

"There now," thought Pahóm, "with my one thousand rúbles, why should I get only thirteen hundred acres, and saddle myself with a debt besides? If I take it out there, I can get more than ten times as much for the money."

V

Pahóm inquired how to get to the place, and as soon as the tradesman had left him, he prepared to go there himself. He left his wife to look after the homestead, and started on his journey taking his man with him. They stopped at a town on their way and bought a case of tea, some wine, and other presents, as the tradesman had advised. On and on they went until they had gone more than three hundred miles, and on the seventh day they came to a place where the Bashkírs had pitched their tents. It was all just as the tradesman had said. The people lived on the steppes, by a river, in felt-covered tents. They neither tilled the ground, nor ate bread. Their cattle and horses grazed in herds on the steppe. The colts were tethered behind the tents, and the mares were driven to them twice a day. The mares were milked, and from the milk kumiss was made. It was the women who prepared kumiss, and they also made cheese. As far as the men were concerned, drinking kumiss and tea, eating mutton, and playing on their pipes, was all they cared about. They were all stout and merry, and all the summer long they never thought of doing any work. They were quite ignorant, and knew no Russian, but were good-natured enough.

As soon as they saw Pahóm, they came out of their tents and gathered round their visitor. An interpreter was found, and Pahóm told them he had come about some land. The Bashkírs seemed very glad; they took Pahóm and led him into one of the best tents, where they made him sit on some down cushions placed on a carpet, while they sat around him. They gave him some tea and kumiss, and had a sheep killed, and gave him mutton to eat. Pahóm took presents out of his cart and distributed them among the Bashkírs, and divided the tea amongst them. The Bashkírs were delighted. They talked a great deal among themselves, and then told the interpreter to translate.

"They wish to tell you," said the interpreter, "that they like you, and that it is our custom to do all we can to please a guest and to repay him for his gifts. You have given us presents, now tell us which of the things we possess please you best, that we may present them to you."

"What pleases me best here," answered Pahóm, "is your land. Our land is crowded and the soil is exhausted; but you have plenty of land and it is good land. I never saw the like of it."

The interpreter translated. The Bashkírs talked among themselves for a while. Pahóm could not understand what they were saying, but saw that they were much amused and that they shouted and laughed. Then they were silent and looked at Pahóm while the interpreter said:

"They wish me to tell you that in return for your presents they will gladly give you as much land as you want. You have only to point it out with your hand and it is yours."

The Bashkírs talked again for a while and began to dispute. Pahóm asked what they were disputing about, and the interpreter told him that some of them thought they ought to ask their Chief about the land and not act in his absence, while others thought there was no need to wait for his return.

VI

While the Bashkírs were disputing, a man in a large fox-fur cap appeared on the scene. They all became silent and rose to their feet. The interpreter said, "This is our Chief himself."

Pahóm immediately fetched the best dressing-gown and five pounds of tea, and offered these to the Chief. The Chief accepted them, and seated himself in the place of honor. The Bashkírs at once began telling him something. The Chief listened for a while, then made a sign with his head for them to be silent, and addressing himself to Pahóm, said in Russian:

"Well, let it be so. Choose whatever piece of land you like; we have plenty of it."

"How can I take as much as I like?" thought Pahóm. "I must get a deed to make it secure, or else they may say, 'It is yours,' and afterwards may take it away again."

"Thank you for your kind words," he said aloud. "You have much land, and I only want a little. But I should like to be sure which bit is mine. Could it not be measured and made over to me? Life and death are in God's hands. You good people give it to me, but your children might wish to take it away again."

"You are quite right," said the Chief. "We will make it over to you."

"I heard that a dealer had been here," continued Pahóm, "and that you gave him a little land, too, and signed title-deeds to that effect. I should like to have it done in the same way."

The Chief understood.

"Yes," replied he, "that can be done quite easily. We have a scribe, and we will go to town with you and have the deed properly sealed."

"And what will be the price?" asked Pahóm.

"Our price is always the same: one thousand rúbles a day."

Pahóm did not understand.

"A day? What measure is that? How many acres would that be?"

"We do not know how to reckon it out," said the Chief. "We sell it by the day. As much as you can go round on your feet in a day is yours, and the price is one thousand rúbles a day."

Pahóm was surprised.

"But in a day you can get round a large tract of land," he said.

The Chief laughed.

"It will all be yours!" said he. "But there is one condition: If you don't return on the same day to the spot whence you started, your money is lost."

"But how am I to mark the way that I have gone?"

"Why, we shall go to any spot you like, and stay there. You must start from that spot and make your round, taking a spade with you. Wherever you think necessary, make a mark. At every turning, dig a hole and pile up the turf; then afterwards we will go round with a plough from hole to hole. You may make as large a circuit as you please, but before the sun sets you must return to the place you started from. All the land you cover will be yours."

Pahóm was delighted. It was decided to start early next morning. They talked a while, and after drinking some more kumiss and eating some more mutton, they had tea again, and then the night came on. They gave Pahóm a feather-bed to sleep on, and the Bashkírs dispersed for the night, promising to assemble the next morning at daybreak and ride out before sunrise to the appointed spot.

VII

Pahóm lay on the feather-bed, but could not sleep. He kept thinking about the land.

"What a large tract I will mark off!" thought he. "I can easily do thirty-five miles in a day. The days are long now, and within a circuit of thirty-five miles what a lot of land there will be! I will sell the poorer land, or let it to peasants, but I'll pick out the best and farm it. I will buy two oxteams, and hire two more laborers. About a hundred and fifty acres shall be plough-land, and I will pasture cattle on the rest."

Pahóm lay awake all night, and dozed off only just before dawn. Hardly were his eyes closed when he had a dream. He thought he was lying in that same tent and heard somebody chuckling outside. He wondered who it could be, and rose and went out, and he saw the Bashkír Chief sitting in front of the tent holding his sides and rolling about with laughter. Going nearer to the Chief, Pahóm asked: "What are you laughing at?" But he saw that it was no longer the Chief, but the dealer who had recently stopped at his house and had told him about the land. Just as Pahóm was going to ask, "Have you been here long?" he saw that it was not the dealer, but the peasant who had come up from the Vólga, long ago, to Pahóm's old home. Then he saw that it was not the peasant either, but the Devil himself with hoofs and horns, sitting there and chuckling, and before him lay a man barefoot, prostrate on the ground, with only trousers and a shirt on. And Pahóm dreamt that he looked more attentively to see what sort of a man it was that was lying there, and he saw that the man was dead, and that it was himself! He awoke horror-struck.

"What things one does dream," thought he.

Looking round he saw through the open door that the dawn was breaking.

"It's time to wake them up," thought he. "We ought to be starting."

He got up, roused his man (who was sleeping in his cart), bade him harness; and went to call the Bashkírs.

"It's time to go to the steppe to measure the land," he said.

The Bashkírs rose and assembled, and the Chief came too. Then they began drinking kumiss again, and offered Pahóm some tea, but he would not wait.

"If we are to go, let us go. It is high time," said he.

VIII

The Bashkírs got ready and they all started: some mounted on horses, and some in carts. Pahóm drove in his own small cart with his servant and took a spade with him. When they reached the steppe, the morning red was beginning to kindle. They ascended a hillock (called by the Bashkírs a *shikhan*) and dismounting from their carts and their horses, gathered in one spot. The Chief came up to Pahóm and stretching out his arms towards the plain:

"See," said he, "all this, as far as your eye can reach, is ours. You may have any part of it you like."

Pahóm's eyes glistened: it was all virgin soil, as flat as the palm of your hand, as black as the seed of a poppy, and in the hollows different kinds of grasses grew breast high.

The Chief took off his fox-fur cap, placed it on the ground and said:

"This will be the mark. Start from here, and return here again. All the land you go round shall be yours."

Pahóm took out his money and put it on the cap. Then he took off his outer coat, remaining in his sleeveless under-coat. He unfastened his girdle and tied it tight below his stomach, put a little bag of bread into the breast of his coat, and tying a flask of water to his girdle, he drew up the tops of his boots, took the spade from his man, and stood ready to start. He considered for some moments which way he had better go—it was tempting everywhere.

"No matter," he concluded, "I will go towards the rising sun."

He turned his face to the east, stretched himself, and waited for the sun to appear above the rim.

"I must lose no time," he thought, "and it is easier walking while it is still cool."

The sun's rays had hardly flashed above the horizon, before Pahóm, carrying the spade over his shoulder, went down into the steppe.

Pahóm started walking neither slowly nor quickly. After having gone a thousand yards he stopped, dug a hole, and placed pieces of turf one on another to make it more visible. Then he went on; and now that he had walked off his stiffness he quickened his pace. After a while he dug another hole.

Pahóm looked back. The hillock could be distinctly seen in the sunlight, with the people on it, and the glittering tires of the cart-wheels. At a rough guess Pahóm concluded that he had walked three miles. It was growing warmer; he took off his under-coat, flung it across his shoulder, and went on again. It had grown quite warm now; he looked at the sun, it was time to think of breakfast.

"The first shift is done, but there are four in a day, and it is too soon yet to turn. but I will just take off my boots," said he to himself.

He sat down, took off his boots, stuck them into his girdle, and went on. It 100
was easy walking now.

"I will go on for another three miles," thought he, "and then turn to the left. This spot is so fine, that it would be a pity to lose it. The further one goes, the better the land seems."

He went straight on for a while, and when he looked round, the hillock was scarcely visible and the people on it looked like black ants, and he could just see something glistening there in the sun.

"Ah," thought Pahóm, "I have gone far enough in this direction, it is time to turn. Besides I am in a regular sweat, and very thirsty."

He stopped, dug a large hole, and heaped up pieces of turf. Next he untied his flask, had a drink, and then turned sharply to the left. He went on and on; the grass was high, and it was very hot.

Pahóm began to grow tired: he looked at the sun and saw that it was noon. 105

"Well," he thought, "I must have a rest."

He sat down, and ate some bread and drank some water; but he did not lie down, thinking that if he did he might fall asleep. After sitting a little while, he went on again. At first he walked easily: the food had strengthened him; but it had become terribly hot and he felt sleepy, still he went on, thinking: "An hour to suffer, a life-time to live."

He went a long way in this direction also, and was about to turn to the left again, when he perceived a damp hollow: "It would be a pity to leave that out," he thought. "Flax would do well there." So he went on past the hollow, and dug a hole on the other side of it before he turned the corner. Pahóm looked towards the hillock. The heat made the air hazy: it seemed to be quivering, and through the haze the people on the hillock could scarcely be seen.

"Ah!" thought Pahóm, "I have made the sides too long; I must make this one shorter." And he went along the third side, stepping faster. He looked at the sun: it was nearly half-way to the horizon, and he had not yet done two miles of the third side of the square. He was still ten miles from the goal.

"No," he thought, "though it will make my land lop-sided, I must hurry 110
back in a straight line now. I might go too far, and as it is I have a great deal of land."

So Pahóm hurriedly dug a hole, and turned straight towards the hillock.

IX

Pahóm went straight towards the hillock, but he now walked with difficulty. He was done up with the heat, his bare feet were cut and bruised, and his legs began to fail. He longed to rest, but it was impossible if he meant to get back before sunset. The sun waits for no man, and it was sinking lower and lower.

"Oh dear," he thought, "if only I have not blundered trying for too much! What if I am too late?"

He looked towards the hillock and at the sun. He was still far from his goal, and the sun was already near the rim.

Pahóm walked on and on; it was very hard walking but he went quicker and quicker. He pressed on, but was still far from the place. He began running, threw away his coat, his boots, his flask, and his cap, and kept only the spade which he used as a support.

"What shall I do," he thought again, "I have grasped too much and ruined the whole affair. I can't get there before the sun sets."

And this fear made him still more breathless. Pahóm went on running, his soaking shirt and trousers stuck to him and his mouth was parched. His breast was working like a blacksmith's bellows, his heart was beating like a hammer, and his legs were giving way as if they did not belong to him. Pahóm was seized with terror lest he should die of the strain.

Though afraid of death, he could not stop. "After having run all that way they will call me a fool if I stop now," thought he. And he ran on and on, and drew near and heard the Bashkírs yelling and shouting to him, and their cries inflamed his heart still more. He gathered his last strength and ran on.

The sun was close to the rim, and cloaked in mist looked large, and red as blood. Now, yes now, it was about to set! The sun was quite low, but he was also quite near his aim. Pahóm could already see the people on the hillock waving their arms to hurry him up. He could see the fox-fur cap on the ground and the money on it, and the Chief sitting on the ground holding his sides. And Pahóm remembered his dream.

"There is plenty of land," thought he, "but will God let me live on it? I have lost my life, I have lost my life! I shall never reach that spot!"

Pahóm looked at the sun, which had reached the earth: one side of it had already disappeared. With all his remaining strength he rushed on, bending his body forward so that his legs could hardly follow fast enough to keep him from falling. Just as he reached the hillock it suddenly grew dark. He looked up—the sun had already set! He gave a cry: "All my labor has been in vain," thought he, and was about to stop, but he heard the Bashkírs still shouting, and remembered that though to him, from below, the sun seemed to have set, they on the hillock could still see it. He took a long breath and ran up the hillock. It was still light there. He reached the top and saw the cap. Before it sat the Chief laughing and holding his sides. Again Pahóm remembered his dream, and he uttered a cry: his legs gave way beneath him, he fell forward and reached the cap with his hands.

"Ah, that's a fine fellow!" exclaimed the Chief. "He has gained much land!"

Pahóm's servant came running up and tried to raise him, but he saw that blood was flowing from his mouth. Pahóm was dead!

The Bashkírs clicked their tongues to show their pity.

His servant picked up the spade and dug a grave long enough for Pahóm to lie in, and buried him in it. Six feet from his head to his heels was all he needed.

1886

KATHERINE MANSFIELD

Her First Ball

Exactly when the ball began Leila would have found it hard to say. Perhaps her first real partner was the cab. It did not matter that she shared the cab with the Sheridan girls and their brother. She sat back in her own little corner of it, and the bolster on which her hand rested felt like the sleeve of an unknown young man's dress suit; and away they bowled, past waltzing lampposts and houses and fences and trees.

"Have you really never been to a ball before, Leila? But, my child, how too weird—" cried the Sheridan girls.

"Our nearest neighbor was fifteen miles," said Leila softly, gently opening and shutting her fan.

Oh, dear, how hard it was to be indifferent like the others! She tried not to smile too much; she tried not to care. But every single thing was so new and exciting . . . Meg's tuberoses, Jose's long loop of amber, Laura's little dark head, pushing above her white fur like a flower through snow. She would remember for ever. It even gave her a pang to see her cousin Laurie throw away the wisps of tissue paper he pulled from the fastening of his new gloves. She would like to have kept those wisps as a keepsake, as a remembrance. Laurie leaned forward and put his hand on Laura's knee.

5 "Look here, darling," he said. "The third and the ninth as usual, Twig?"

Oh, how marvellous to have a brother! In her excitement Leila felt that if there had been time, if it hadn't been impossible, she couldn't have helped crying because she was an only child, and no brother had ever said "Twig?" to her; no sister would ever say, as Meg said to Jose that moment, "I've never known your hair go up more successfully than it has tonight!"

But, of course, there was no time. They were at the drill hall already; there were cabs in front of them and cabs behind. The road was bright on either side with moving fan-like lights, and on the pavement gay couples seemed to float through the air; little satin shoes chased each other like birds.

"Hold on to me, Leila; you'll get lost," said Laura.

"Come on, girls, let's make a dash for it," said Laurie.

10 Leila put two fingers on Laura's pink velvet cloak, and they were somehow lifted past the big gold lantern, carried along the passage, and pushed into the little room marked "Ladies." Here the crowd was so great there was hardly space to take off their things; the noise was deafening. Two benches on either side were stacked high with wraps. Two old women in white aprons ran up and down tossing fresh armfuls. And everybody was pressing forward trying to get at the little dressing table and mirror at the far end.

A great quivering jet of gas lighted the ladies' room. It couldn't wait; it was dancing already. When the door opened again and there came a burst of tuning from the drill hall, it leaped almost to the ceiling.

Dark girls, fair girls were patting their hair, tying ribbons again, tucking handkerchiefs down the front of their bodices, smoothing marble-white gloves. And because they were all laughing it seemed to Leila that they were all lovely.

"Aren't there any invisible hairpins?" cried a voice. "How most extraordinary! I can't see a single invisible hairpin."

"Powder my back, there's a darling," cried some one else.

"But I must have a needle and cotton. I've torn simply miles and miles of the frill," wailed a third.

Then, "Pass them along, pass them along!" The straw basket of programs was tossed from arm to arm. Darling little pink-and-silver programs, with pink pencils and fluffy tassels. Leila's fingers shook as she took one out of the basket. She wanted to ask someone, "Am I meant to have one too?" but she had just time to read: "Waltz 3. *Two, Two in a Canoe*. Polka 4. *Making the Feathers Fly*," when Meg cried, "Ready, Leila?" and they pressed their way through the crush in the passage towards the big double doors of the drill hall.

Dancing had not begun yet, but the band had stopped tuning, and the noise was so great it seemed that when it did begin to play it would never be heard. Leila, pressing close to Meg, looking over Meg's shoulder, felt that even the little quivering colored flags strung across the ceiling were talking. She quite forgot to be shy; she forgot how in the middle of dressing she had sat down on the bed with one shoe off and one shoe on and begged her mother to ring up her cousins and say she couldn't go after all. And the rush of longing she had had to be sitting on the veranda of their forsaken upcountry home, listening to the baby owls crying "More pork" in the moonlight, was changed to a rush of joy so sweet that it was hard to bear alone. She clutched her fan, and, gazing at the gleaming, golden floor, the azaleas, the lanterns, the stage at one end with its red carpet and gilt chairs and the band in a corner, she thought breathlessly, "How heavenly; how simply heavenly!"

All the girls stood grouped together at one side of the doors, the men at the other, and the chaperones in dark dresses, smiling rather foolishly, walked with little careful steps over the polished floor towards the stage.

"This is my little country cousin Leila. Be nice to her. Find her partners; she's under my wing," said Meg, going up to one girl after another.

Strange faces smiled at Leila—sweetly, vaguely. Strange voices answered, "Of course, my dear." But Leila felt the girls didn't really see her. They were looking towards the men. Why didn't the men begin? What were they waiting for? There they stood, smoothing their gloves, patting their glossy hair and smiling among themselves. Then, quite suddenly, as if they had only just made up their minds that that was what they had to do, the men came gliding over the parquet. There was a joyful flutter among the girls. A tall, fair man flew up to Meg, seized her program, scribbled something; Meg passed him on to Leila. "May I have the pleasure?" He ducked and smiled. There came a dark man wearing an eyeglass, then cousin Laurie with a friend, and Laura with a little freckled fellow whose tie was crooked. Then quite an old man—fat, with a big bald patch on his head—took her program and murmured, "Let me see, let me see!" And he was a long time comparing his program, which looked black with names, with hers. It seemed to give him so much trouble that Leila was ashamed. "Oh, please don't bother," she said eagerly. But instead of replying the fat man wrote something, glanced at her again. "Do I remember this bright little face?" he said softly. "Is it known to me of yore?" At that moment the band began playing; the fat man disappeared. He was tossed away on a great wave of music that came flying over the gleaming floor, breaking the groups up into couples, scattering them, sending them spinning. . . .

Leila had learned to dance at boarding school. Every Saturday afternoon the boarders were hurried off to a little corrugated iron mission hall where Miss Eccles (of London) held her "select" classes. But the difference between that dusty-smelling hall—with calico texts on the walls, the poor terrified little woman in a brown velvet toque with rabbit's ears thumping the cold piano, Miss Eccles poking the girls' feet with her long white wand—and this was so tremendous that Leila was sure if her partner didn't come and she had to listen to that marvelous music and to watch the others sliding, gliding over the golden floor, she would die at least, or faint, or lift her arms and fly out of one of those dark windows that showed the stars.

"Ours, I think—" Some one bowed, smiled, and offered her his arm; she hadn't to die after all. Some one's hand pressed her waist, and she floated away like a flower that is tossed into a pool.

"Quite a good floor, isn't it?" drawled a faint voice close to her ear.

"I think it's most beautifully slippery," said Leila.

"Pardon!" The faint voice sounded surprised. Leila said it again. And there was a tiny pause before the voice echoed. "Oh, quite!" and she was swung round again.

He steered so beautifully. That was the great difference between dancing with girls and men, Leila decided. Girls banged into each other, and stamped on each other's feet; the girl who was gentleman always clutched you so.

The azaleas were separate flowers no longer; they were pink and white flags streaming by.

"Were you at the Bells' last week?" the voice came again. It sounded tired. Leila wondered whether she ought to ask him if he would like to stop.

"No, this is my first dance," said she.

Her partner gave a little gasping laugh. "Oh, I say," he protested.

"Yes, it is really the first dance I've ever been to." Leila was most fervent. It was such a relief to be able to tell somebody. "You see, I've lived in the country all my life up until now. . . ."

At that moment the music stopped, and they went to sit on two chairs against the wall. Leila tucked her pink satin feet under and fanned herself, while she blissfully watched the other couples passing and disappearing through the swing doors.

"Enjoying yourself, Leila?" asked Jose, nodding her golden head.

Laura passed and gave her the faintest little wink; it made Leila wonder for a moment whether she was quite grown up after all. Certainly her partner did not say very much. He coughed, tucked his handkerchief away, pulled down his waistcoat, took a minute thread off his sleeve. But it didn't matter. Almost immediately the band started, and her second partner seemed to spring from the ceiling.

35 "Floor's not bad," said the new voice. Did one always begin with the floor? And then, "Were you at the Neaves' on Tuesday?" And again Leila explained. Perhaps it was a little strange that her partners were not more interested. For it was thrilling. Her first ball! she was only at the beginning of everything. It seemed to her that she had never known what the night was like before. Up till now it had been dark, silent, beautiful very often—oh, yes—but mournful somehow. Solemn. And now it would never be like that again—it had opened dazzling bright.

"Care for an ice?" said her partner. And they went through the swing doors, down the passage, to the supper room. Her cheeks burned, she was fearfully thirsty. How sweet the ices looked on little glass plates, and how cold the frosted spoon was, iced too! And when they came back to the hall there was the fat man waiting for her by the door. It gave her quite a shock again to see how old he was; he ought to have been on the stage with the fathers and mothers. And when Leila compared him with her other partners he looked shabby. His waistcoat was creased, there was a button off his glove, his coat looked as if it was dusty with French chalk.

"Come along, little lady," said the fat man. He scarcely troubled to clasp her, and they moved away so gently, it was more like walking than dancing. But he said not a word about the floor. "Your first dance, isn't it?" he murmured.

"How *did* you know?"

"Ah," said the fat man, "that's what it is to be old!" He wheezed faintly as he steered her past an awkward couple. "You see, I've been doing this kind of thing for the last thirty years."

40 "Thirty years?" cried Leila. Twelve years before she was born!

"It hardly bears thinking about, does it?" said the fat man gloomily. Leila looked at his bald head, and she felt quite sorry for him.

"I think it's marvelous to be still going on," she said kindly.

"Kind little lady," said the fat man, and he pressed her a little closer, and hummed a bar of the waltz. "Of course," he said, "you can't hope to last anything like as long as that. No-o," said the fat man, "long before that you'll be sitting up there on the stage, looking on, in your nice black velvet. And these pretty arms will have turned into little short fat ones, and you'll beat time with such a different kind of fan—a black bony one." The fat man seemed to shudder. "And you'll smile away like the poor old dears up there, and point to your daughter, and tell the elderly lady next to you how some dreadful man tried to kiss her at the club ball. And your heart will ache, ache"—the fat man squeezed her closer still, as if he really was sorry for that poor heart—"because no one wants to kiss you now. And you'll say how unpleasant these polished floors are to walk on, how dangerous they are. Eh, Mademoiselle Twinkletoes?" said the fat man softly.

Leila gave a light little laugh, but she did not feel like laughing. Was it—could it all be true? It sounded terribly true. Was this first ball only the beginning of her last ball after all? At that the music seemed to change; it sounded sad, sad it rose upon a great sigh. Oh, how quickly things changed! Why didn't happiness last for ever? For ever wasn't a bit too long.

"I want to stop," she said in a breathless voice. The fat man led her to the door.

"No," she said. "I won't go outside. I won't sit down. I'll just stand here, thank you." She leaned against the wall, tapping with her foot, pulling up her gloves and trying to smile. But deep inside her a little girl threw her pinafore over her head and sobbed. Why had he spoiled it all?

"I say, you know," said the fat man, "you mustn't take me seriously, little lady."

"As if I should!" said Leila, tossing her small dark head and sucking her underlip. . . .

Again the couples paraded. The swing doors opened and shut. Now new music was given out by the bandmaster. But Leila didn't want to dance any more. She wanted to be home, or sitting on the veranda listening to those baby owls. When she looked through the dark windows at the stars, they had long beams like wings. . . .

But presently a soft, melting, ravishing tune began, and a young man with curly hair bowed before her. She would have to dance, out of politeness, until she could find Meg. Very stiffly she walked into the middle; very haughtily she put her hand on his sleeve. But in one minute, in one turn, her feet glided, glided. The lights, the azaleas, the dresses, the pink faces, the velvet chairs, all became one beautiful flying wheel. And when her next partner bumped her into the fat man and he said, "Par*don*," she smiled at him more radiantly than ever. She didn't even recognize him again.

1922

WILLIAM TREVOR

Beyond the Pale

We always went to Ireland in June.

Ever since the four of us began to go on holidays together, in 1965 it must have been, we had spent the first fortnight of the month at Glencorn Lodge in Co. Antrim.[1] Perfection, as Dekko put it once, and none of us disagreed. It's a Georgian house by the sea, not far from the village of Ardbeag. It's quite majestic in its rather elegant way, a garden running to the very edge of a cliff, its long rhododendron drive—or avenue, as they say in Ireland. The English couple who bought the house in the early sixties, the Malseeds, have had to build on quite a bit but it's all been discreetly done, the Georgian style preserved throughout. Figs grow in the sheltered gardens, and apricots, and peaches in the greenhouses

1. County in Northern Ireland containing the national capital, Belfast.

which old Mr. Saxton presides over. He's Mrs. Malseed's father actually. They brought him with them from Surrey, and their Dalmatians, Charger and Snooze.

It was Strafe who found Glencorn for us. He'd come across an advertisement in the *Lady* in the days when the Malseeds still felt the need to advertise. "How about this?" he said one evening at the end of the second rubber, and then read out the details. We had gone away together the summer before, to a hotel that had been recommended on the Costa del Sol, but it hadn't been a success because the food was so appalling. "We could try this Irish one," Dekko suggested cautiously, which is what eventually we did.

The four of us have been playing bridge together for ages, Dekko, Strafe, Cynthia and myself. They call me Milly, though strictly speaking my name is Dorothy Milson. Dekko picked up his nickname at school, Dekko Deakin sounding rather good, I dare say. He and Strafe were in fact at school together, which must be why we all call Strafe by his surname: Major R. B. Strafe he is, the initials standing for Robert Buchanan. We're of an age, the four of us, all in the early fifties: the prime of life, so Dekko insists. We live quite close to Leatherhead, where the Malseeds were before they decided to make the change from Surrey to Co. Antrim. Quite a coincidence, we always think.

5 "How *very* nice," Mrs. Malseed said, smiling her welcome again this year. Some instinct seems to tell her when guests are about to arrive, for she's rarely not waiting in the large low-ceilinged hall that always smells of flowers. She dresses beautifully, differently every day, and changing of course in the evening. Her blouse on this occasion was scarlet and silver, in stripes, her skirt black. This choice gave her a brisk look, which was fitting because being so busy she often has to be a little on the brisk side. She has smooth grey hair which she once told me she entirely looks after herself, and she almost always wears a black velvet band in it. Her face is well made up, and for one who arranges so many vases of flowers and otherwise has to use her hands she manages to keep them marvellously in condition. Her fingernails are varnished a soft pink, and a small gold bangle always adorns her right wrist, a wedding present from her husband.

"Arthur, take the party's luggage," she commanded the old porter, who doubles as odd-job man. "Rose, Geranium, Hydrangea, Fuchsia." She referred to the titles of the rooms reserved for us: in winter, when no one much comes to Glencorn Lodge, pleasant little details like that are seen to. Mrs Malseed herself painted the flower-plaques that are attached to the doors of the hotel instead of numbers; her husband sees to redecoration and repairs.

"Well, well, well," Mr. Malseed said now, entering the hall through the door that leads to the kitchen regions. "A hundred thousand welcomes," he greeted us in the Irish manner. He's rather shorter than Mrs. Malseed, who's handsomely tall. He wears Donegal[2] tweed suits and is brown as a berry, including his head, which is bald. His dark brown eyes twinkle at you, making you feel rather more than just another hotel guest. They run the place like a country house, really.

2. County in the northern portion of the Irish Republic.

"Good trip?" Mr. Malseed enquired.

"Super," Dekko said. "Not a worry all the way."

"Splendid."

"The wretched boat sailed an hour early one day last week," Mrs. Malseed said. "Quite a little band were left stranded at Stranraer."

Strafe laughed. Typical of that steamship company, he said. "Catching the tide, I dare say?"

"They caught a rocket from me," Mrs. Malseed replied good-humouredly. "A couple of old dears were due with us on Tuesday and had to spend the night in some awful Scottish lodging-house. It nearly finished them."

Everyone laughed, and I could feel the others thinking that our holiday had truly begun. Nothing had changed in Glencorn Lodge, all was well with its Irish world. Kitty from the dining-room came out to greet us, spotless in her uniform. "Ach, you're looking younger," she said, paying the compliment to all four of us, causing everyone in the hall to laugh again. Kitty's a bit of a card.

Arthur led the way to the rooms called Rose, Geranium, Hydrangea and Fuchsia, carrying as much of our luggage as he could manage and returning for the remainder. Arthur has a beaten, fisherman's face and short grey hair. He wears a green baize apron, and a white shirt with an imitation-silk scarf tucked into it at the neck. The scarf, in different swirling greens which blend nicely with the green of his apron, is an idea of Mrs. Malseed's and one appreciates the effort, if not at a uniform, at least at tidiness.

"Thank you very much," I said to Arthur in my room, smiling and finding him a coin.

We played a couple of rubbers after dinner as usual, but not of course going on for as long as we might have because we were still quite tired after the journey. In the lounge there was a French family, two girls and their parents, and a honeymoon couple—or so we had speculated during dinner—and a man on his own. There had been other people at dinner of course, because in June Glencorn Lodge is always full: from where we sat in the window we could see some of them strolling about the lawns, a few taking the cliff path down to the seashore. In the morning we'd do the same: we'd walk along the sands to Ardbeag and have coffee in the hotel there, back in time for lunch. In the afternoon we'd drive somewhere.

I knew all that because over the years this kind of pattern had developed. We had our walks and our drives, tweed to buy in Cushendall, Strafe's and Dekko's fishing day when Cynthia and I just sat on the beach, our visit to the Giant's Causeway[3] and one to Donegal perhaps, though that meant an early start and taking pot-luck for dinner somewhere. We'd come to adore Co. Antrim, its glens and coastline, Rathlin Island and Tievebulliagh. Since first we got to know it, in 1965, we'd all four fallen hopelessly in love with every variation of this

3. A formation of basalt cliffs projecting several hundred feet into the sea on the north coast of Antrim.

remarkable landscape. People in England thought us mad of course: they see so much of the troubles[4] on television that it's naturally difficult for them to realize that most places are just as they've always been. Yet coming as we did, taking the road along the coast, dawdling through Ballygally, it was impossible to believe that somewhere else the unpleasantness was going on. We'd never seen a thing, nor even heard people talking about incidents that might have taken place. It's true that after a particularly nasty carry-on a few winters ago we did consider finding somewhere else, in Scotland perhaps, or Wales. But as Strafe put it at the time, we felt we owed a certain loyalty to the Malseeds and indeed to everyone we'd come to know round about, people who'd always been glad to welcome us back. It seemed silly to lose our heads, and when we returned the following summer we knew immediately we'd been right. Dekko said that nothing could be further away from all the violence than Glencorn Lodge, and though his remark could hardly be taken literally I think we all knew what he meant.

"Cynthia's tired," I said because she'd been stifling yawns. "I think we should call it a day."

"Oh, not at all," Cynthia protested. "No, please."

But Dekko agreed with me that she was tired, and Strafe said he didn't mind stopping now. He suggested a nightcap, as he always does, and as we always do also, Cynthia and I declined. Dekko said he'd like a Cointreau.

The conversation drifted about. Dekko told us an Irish joke about a drunk who couldn't find his way out of a telephone box, and then Strafe remembered an incident at school concerning his and Dekko's housemaster, A. D. Cowley-Stubbs, and the house wag, Thrive Major. A. D. Cowley-Stubbs had been known as Cows and often featured in our after-bridge reminiscing. So did Thrive Major.

"Perhaps I *am* sleepy," Cynthia said. "I don't think I closed my eyes once last night."

She never does on a sea crossing. Personally I'm out like a light the moment my head touches the pillow; I often think it must be the salt in the air because normally I'm an uneasy sleeper at the best of times.

"You run along, old girl," Strafe advised.

"Brekky at nine," Dekko said.

Cynthia said good-night and went, and we didn't remark on her tiredness because as a kind of unwritten rule we never comment on one another. We're four people who play bridge. The companionship it offers, and the holidays we have together, are all part of that. We share everything: the cost of petrol, the cups of coffee or drinks we have; we even each make a contribution towards the use of Strafe's car because it's always his we go on holiday in, a Rover it was on this occasion.

"Funny, being here on your own," Strafe said, glancing across what the Malseeds call the After-Dinner Lounge at the man who didn't have a compan-

4. Since the 1960s there have been agitation and considerable violence in Northern Ireland. Catholics, led chiefly by the underground Irish Republican Army, want the three counties of Ulster (Northern Ireland) united with the (Catholic) Republic of Ireland.

ion. He was a red-haired man of about thirty, not wearing a tie, his collar open at the neck and folded back over the jacket of his blue serge suit. He was uncouth-looking, though it's a hard thing to say, not at all the kind of person one usually sees at Glencorn Lodge. He sat in the After-Dinner Lounge as he had in the dining-room, lost in some concentration of his own, as if calculating sums in his mind. There had been a folded newspaper on his table in the dining-room. It now reposed tidily on the arm of his chair, still unopened.

"Commercial gent," Dekko said. "Fertilizers."

"Good heavens, never. You wouldn't get a rep in here." 30

I took no part in the argument. The lone man didn't much interest me, but I felt that Strafe was probably right: if there was anything dubious about the man's credentials he might have found it difficult to secure a room. In the hall of Glencorn Lodge there's a notice which reads: *We prefer not to feature in hotel guides, and we would be grateful to our guests if they did not seek to include Glencorn Lodge in the Good Food Guide, the Good Hotel Guide, the Michelin, Egon Ronay or any others. We have not advertised Glencorn since our early days, and prefer our recommendations to be by word of mouth.*

"Ah, thank you," Strafe said when Kitty brought his whisky and Dekko's Cointreau. "Sure you won't have something?" he said to me, although he knew I never did.

Strafe is on the stout side, I suppose you could say, with a gingery moustache and gingery hair, hardly touched at all by grey. He left the Army years ago, I suppose because of me in a sense, because he didn't want to be posted abroad again. He's in the Ministry of Defence now.

I'm still quite pretty in my way, though nothing like as striking as Mrs. Malseed, for I've never been that kind of woman. I've put on weight, and wouldn't have allowed myself to do so if Strafe hadn't kept saying he can't stand a bag of bones. I'm careful about my hair and, unlike Mrs. Malseed, I have it very regularly seen to because if I don't it gets a salt and pepper look, which I hate. My husband, Ralph, who died of food-poisoning when we were still quite young, used to say I wouldn't lose a single look in middle age, and to some extent that's true. We were still putting off having children when he died, which is why I haven't any. Then I met Strafe, which meant I didn't marry again.

Strafe is married himself, to Cynthia. She's small and ineffectual, I suppose 35
you'd say without being untruthful or unkind. Not that Cynthia and I don't get on or anything like that, in fact we get on extremely well. It's Strafe and Cynthia who don't seem quite to hit it off, and I often think how much happier all round it would have been if Cynthia had married someone completely different, someone like Dekko in a way, except that that mightn't quite have worked out either. The Strafes have two sons, both very like their father, both of them in the Army. And the very sad thing is they think nothing of poor Cynthia.

"Who's that chap?" Dekko asked Mr. Malseed, who'd come over to wish us good-night.

"Awfully sorry about that, Mr. Deakin. My fault entirely, a booking that came over the phone."

"Good heavens, not at all," Strafe protested, and Dekko looked horrified in case it should be thought he was objecting to the locals. "Splendid-looking fellow," he said, overdoing it.

Mr. Malseed murmured that the man had only booked in for a single night, and I smiled the whole thing away, reassuring him with a nod. It's one of the pleasantest of the traditions at Glencorn Lodge that every evening Mr. Malseed makes the rounds of his guests just to say good-night. It's because of little touches like that that I, too, wished Dekko hadn't questioned Mr. Malseed about the man because it's the kind of thing one doesn't do at Glencorn Lodge. But Dekko is a law unto himself, very tall and gangling, always immaculately suited, a beaky face beneath mousy hair in which flecks of grey add a certain distinction. Dekko has money of his own and though he takes out girls who are half his age he has never managed to get around to marriage. The uncharitable might say he has a rather gormless laugh; certainly it's sometimes on the loud side.

We watched while Mr. Malseed bade the lone man good-night. The man didn't respond, but just sat gazing. It was ill-mannered, but this lack of courtesy didn't appear to be intentional: the man was clearly in a mood of some kind, miles away.

"Well, I'll go up," I said. "Good-night, you two."

"Cheery-bye, Milly," Dekko said. "Brekky at nine, remember."

"Good-night, Milly," Strafe said.

The Strafes always occupy different rooms on holidays, and at home also. This time he was in Geranium and she in Fuchsia. I was in Rose, and in a little while Strafe would come to see me. He stays with her out of kindness, because he fears for her on her own. He's a sentimental, good-hearted man, easily moved to tears: he simply cannot bear the thought of Cynthia with no one to talk to in the evenings, with no one to make her life around. "And besides," he often says when he's being jocular, "it would break up our bridge four." Naturally we never discuss her shortcomings or in any way analyse the marriage. The unwritten rule that exists among the four of us seems to extend as far as that.

He slipped into my room after he'd had another drink or two, and I was waiting for him as he likes me to wait, in bed but not quite undressed. He has never said so, but I know that that is something Cynthia would not understand in him, or ever attempt to comply with. Ralph, of course, would not have understood either; poor old Ralph would have been shocked. Actually it's all rather sweet, Strafe and his little ways.

"I love you dear," I whispered to him in the darkness, but just then he didn't wish to speak of love and referred instead to my body.

If Cynthia hadn't decided to remain in the hotel the next morning instead of accompanying us on our walk to Ardbeag everything might have been different. As it happened, when she said at breakfast she thought she'd just potter about the garden and sit with her book out of the wind somewhere, I can't say I was displeased. For a moment I hoped Dekko might say he'd stay with her, allowing Strafe and myself to go off on our own, but Dekko—who doesn't go in for saying what you want him to say—didn't. "Poor old sausage,"[5] he said instead, examining Cynthia with a solicitude that suggested she was close to the grave, rather than just a little lowered by the change of life or whatever it was.

"I'll be perfectly all right," Cynthia assured him. "Honestly."

"Cynthia likes to mooch,[6] you know," Strafe pointed out, which of course is only the truth. She reads too much, I always think. You often see her putting down a book with the most melancholy look in her eyes, which can't be good for her. She's an imaginative woman, I suppose you would say, and of course her habit of reading so much is often useful on our holidays: over the years she has read her way through dozens of Irish guide-books. "That's where the garrison pushed the natives over the cliffs," she once remarked on a drive. "Those rocks are known as the Maidens," she remarked on another occasion. She has led us to places of interest which we had no idea existed: Garron Tower on Garron Point, the mausoleum at Bonamargy, the Devil's Backbone. As well as which, Cynthia is extremely knowledgeable about all matters relating to Irish history. Again she has read endlessly: biographies and autobiographies, long accounts of the centuries of battling and politics there've been. There's hardly a town or village we ever pass through that hasn't some significance for Cynthia, although I'm afraid her impressive fund of information doesn't always receive the attention it deserves. Not that Cynthia ever minds; it doesn't seem to worry her when no one listens. My own opinion is that she'd have made a much better job of her relationship with Strafe and her sons if she could have somehow developed a bit more character.

We left her in the garden and proceeded down the cliff path to the shingle beneath. I was wearing slacks and a blouse, with the arms of a cardigan looped round my neck in case it turned chilly: the outfit was new, specially bought for the holiday, in shades of tangerine. Strafe never cares how he dresses and of course she doesn't keep him up to the mark: that morning, as far as I remember, he wore rather shapeless corduroy trousers, the kind men sometimes garden in, and a navy-blue fisherman's jersey. Dekko as usual was a fashion plate: a pale green linen suit with pleated jacket pockets, a maroon shirt open at the neck, revealing a medallion on a fine gold chain. We didn't converse as we crossed the rather difficult shingle, but when we reached the sand Dekko began to talk about some girl or other, someone called Juliet who had apparently proposed marriage to him just before we'd left Surrey. He'd told her, so he said, that he'd think about it while on holiday and he wondered now about dispatching a telegram from Ardbeag saying, *Still thinking*. Strafe, who has a simple sense of humour, considered this hugely funny and spent most of the walk persuading Dekko that the telegram must certainly be sent, and other telegrams later on, all with the same message. Dekko kept laughing, throwing his head back in a way that always reminds me of an Australian bird I once saw in a nature film on television. I could see this was going to become one of those jokes that would accompany us all through the holiday, a man's thing really, but of course I didn't mind. The

5. Soul. (Cockney rhyming slang: "sausage [roll]" = soul.) 6. Wander about.

girl called Juliet was nearly thirty years younger than Dekko. I supposed she knew what she was doing.

Since the subject of telegrams had come up, Strafe recalled the occasion when Thrive Major had sent one to A. D. Cowley-Stubbs: *Darling regret three months gone love Rowena*. Carefully timed, it had arrived during one of Cows' Thursday evening coffee sessions. Rowena was a maid, known as the Bicycle, who had been sacked the previous term, and old Cows had something of a reputation as a misogynist. When he read the message he apparently went white and collapsed into an armchair. Warrington P. J. managed to read it too, and after that the fat was in the fire. The consequences went on rather, but I never minded listening when Strafe and Dekko drifted back to their schooldays. I just wish I'd known Strafe then, before either of us had gone and got married.

We had our coffee at Ardbeag, the telegram was sent off, and then Strafe and Dekko wanted to see a man called Henry O'Reilly whom we'd met on previous holidays, who organizes mackerel-fishing trips. I waited on my own, picking out postcards in the village shop that sells almost everything, and then I wandered down towards the shore. I knew that they would be having a drink with the boatman because a year had passed since they'd seen him last. They joined me after about twenty minutes, Dekko apologizing but Strafe not seeming to be aware that I'd had to wait because Strafe is not a man who notices little things. It was almost one o'clock when we reached Glencorn Lodge and were told by Mr. Malseed that Cynthia needed looking after.

The hotel, in fact, was in a turmoil. I have never seen anyone as ashen-faced as Mr. Malseed; his wife, in a forget-me-not[7] dress, was limp. It wasn't explained to us immediately what had happened, because in the middle of telling us that Cynthia needed looking after Mr. Malseed was summoned to the telephone. I could see through the half-open door of their little office a glass of whisky or brandy on the desk and Mrs. Malseed's bangled arm reaching out for it. Not for ages did we realize that it all had to do with the lone man whom we'd speculated about the night before.

"He just wanted to talk to me," Cynthia kept repeating hysterically in the hall. "He sat with me by the magnolias."

I made her lie down. Strafe and I stood on either side of her bed as she lay there with her shoes off, her rather unattractively cut plain pink dress crumpled and actually damp from her tears. I wanted to make her take it off and to slip under the bed-clothes in her petticoat but somehow it seemed all wrong, in the circumstances, for Strafe's wife to do anything so intimate in my presence.

"I couldn't stop him," Cynthia said, the rims of her eyes crimson by now, her nose beginning to run again. "From half past ten till well after twelve. He had to talk to someone, he said."

I could sense that Strafe was thinking precisely the same as I was: that the red-haired man had insinuated himself into Cynthia's company by talking about himself and had then put a hand on her knee. Instead of simply standing up and

7. Blue.

going away Cynthia would have stayed where she was, embarrassed or tongue-tied, at any rate unable to cope. And when the moment came she would have turned hysterical. I could picture her screaming in the garden, running across the lawn to the hotel, and then the pandemonium in the hall. I could sense Strafe picturing that also.

"My God, it's terrible," Cynthia said.

"I think she should sleep," I said quietly to Strafe. "Try to sleep, dear," I said to her, but she shook her head, tossing her jumble of hair about on the pillow.

"Milly's right," Strafe urged. "You'll feel much better after a little rest. We'll bring you a cup of tea later on."

"My God!" she cried again. "My God, how could I sleep?"

I went away to borrow a couple of mild sleeping pills from Dekko, who is never without them, relying on the things too much in my opinion. He was tidying himself in his room, but found the pills immediately. Strangely enough, Dekko's always sound in a crisis.

I gave them to her with water and she took them without asking what they were. She was in a kind of daze, one moment making a fuss and weeping, the next just peering ahead of her, as if frightened. In a way she was like someone who'd just had a bad nightmare and hadn't yet completely returned to reality. I remarked as much to Strafe while we made our way down to lunch, and he said he quite agreed.

"Poor old Cynth!" Dekko said when we'd all ordered lobster bisque and entrecôte béarnaise.[8] "Poor old sausage."

You could see that the waitress, a new girl this year, was bubbling over with excitement; but Kitty, serving the other half of the dining-room, was grim, which was most unusual. Everyone was talking in hushed tones and when Dekko said, "Poor old Cynth!" a couple of heads were turned in our direction because he can never keep his voice down. The little vases of roses with which Mrs. Malseed must have decorated each table before the fracas had occurred seemed strangely out of place in the atmosphere which had developed.

The waitress had just taken away our soup-plates when Mr. Malseed hurried into the dining-room and came straight to our table. The lobster bisque surprisingly hadn't been quite up to scratch, and in passing I couldn't help wondering if the fuss had caused the kitchen to go to pieces also.

"I wonder if I might have a word, Major Strafe." Mr. Malseed said, and Strafe rose at once and accompanied him from the dining-room. A total silence had fallen, everyone in the dining-room pretending to be intent on eating. I had an odd feeling that we had perhaps got it all wrong, that because we'd been out for our walk when it had happened all the other guests knew more of the details than Strafe and Dekko and I did. I began to wonder if poor Cynthia had been raped.

Afterwards Strafe told us what occurred in the Malseeds' office, how Mrs. Malseed had been sitting there, slumped, as he put it, and how two policemen

8. Steak cut from between ribs, with sauce of egg and butter.

had questioned him. "Look, what on earth's all this about!" he had demanded rather sharply.

"It concerns this incident that's taken place, sir," one of the policemen explained in an unhurried voice. "On account of your wife—"

"My wife's lying down. She must not be questioned or in any way disturbed."

"Ach, we'd never do that, sir."

Strafe does a good Co. Antrim brogue and in relating all this to us he couldn't resist making full use of it. The two policemen were in uniform and their natural slowness of intellect was rendered more noticeable by the lugubrious air the tragedy had inspired in the hotel. For tragedy was what it was; after talking to Cynthia for nearly two hours the lone man had walked down to the rocks and been drowned.

When Strafe finished speaking I placed my knife and fork together on my plate, unable to eat another mouthful. The facts appeared to be that the man, having left Cynthia by the magnolias, had clambered down the cliff to a place no one ever went to, on the other side of the hotel from the sands we had walked along to Ardbeag. No one had seen him except Cynthia, who from the cliff-top had apparently witnessed his battering by the treacherous waves. The tide had been coming in, but by the time old Arthur and Mr. Malseed reached the rocks it had begun to turn, leaving behind it the fully dressed corpse. Mr. Malseed's impression was that the man had lost his footing on the seaweed and accidentally stumbled into the depths, for the rocks were so slippery it was difficult to carry the corpse more than a matter of yards. But at least it had been placed out of view, while Mr. Malseed hurried back to the hotel to telephone for assistance. He told Strafe that Cynthia had been most confused, insisting that the man had walked out among the rocks and then into the sea, knowing what he was doing.

Listening to it all, I no longer felt sorry for Cynthia. It was typical of her that she should so sillily have involved us in all this. Why on earth had she sat in the garden with a man of that kind instead of standing up and making a fuss the moment he'd begun to paw her? If she'd acted intelligently the whole unfortunate episode could clearly have been avoided. Since it hadn't, there was no point whatsoever in insisting that the man had committed suicide when at that distance no one could possibly be sure.

"It really does astonish me," I said at the lunch table, unable to prevent myself from breaking our unwritten rule. "Whatever came over her?"

"It can't be good for the hotel," Dekko commented, and I was glad to see Strafe giving him a little glance of irritation.

"It's hardly the point," I said coolly.

"What I meant was, hotels occasionally hush things like this up."

"Well, they haven't this time." It seemed an age since I had waited for them at Ardbeag, since we had been so happily laughing over the effect of Dekko's telegram. He'd included his address in it so that the girl could send a message back, and as we'd returned to the hotel along the seashore there'd been much speculation between the two men about the form this would take.

"I suppose what Cynthia's thinking," Strafe said, "is that after he'd tried 80
something on with her he became depressed."

"Oh, but he could just as easily have lost his footing. He'd have been on edge anyway, worried in case she reported him."

"Dreadful kind of death," Dekko said. His tone suggested that that was that, that the subject should now be closed, and so it was.

After lunch we went to our rooms, as we always do at Glencorn Lodge, to rest for an hour. I took my slacks and blouse off, hoping that Strafe would knock on my door, but he didn't and of course that was understandable. Oddly enough I found myself thinking of Dekko, picturing his long form stretched out in the room called Hydrangea, his beaky face in profile on his pillow. The precise nature of Dekko's relationship with these girls he picks up has always privately intrigued me: was it really possible that somewhere in London there was a girl called Juliet who was prepared to marry him for his not inconsiderable money?

I slept and briefly dreamed. Thrive Major and Warrington P. J. were running the post office in Ardbeag, sending telegrams to everyone they could think of, including Dekko's friend Juliet. Cynthia had been found dead beside the magnolias and people were waiting for Hercule Poirot[9] to arrive. "Promise me you didn't do it," I whispered to Strafe, but when Strafe replied it was to say that Cynthia's body reminded him of a bag of old chicken bones.

Strafe and Dekko and I met for tea in the tea-lounge. Strafe had looked in to
see if Cynthia had woken, but apparently she hadn't. The police officers had left 85
the hotel, Dekko said, because he'd noticed their car wasn't parked at the front any more. None of the three of us said, but I think we presumed, that the man's body had been removed from the rocks during the quietness of the afternoon. From where we sat I caught a glimpse of Mrs. Malseed passing quite briskly through the hall, seeming almost herself again. Certainly our holiday would be affected, but it might not be totally ruined. All that remained to hope for was Cynthia's recovery, and then everyone could set about forgetting the unpleasantness. The nicest thing would be if a jolly young couple turned up and occupied the man's room, exorcising the incident, as newcomers would.

The family from France—the two little girls and their parents—were chattering away in the tea-lounge, and an elderly trio who'd arrived that morning were speaking in American accents. The honeymoon couple appeared, looking rather shy, and began to whisper and giggle in a corner. People who occupied the table next to ours in the dining-room, a Wing-Commander Orfell and his wife, from Guildford,[1] nodded and smiled as they passed. Everyone was making an effort, and I knew it would help matters further if Cynthia felt up to a rubber or two before dinner. That life should continue as normally as possible was essential for Glencorn Lodge, the example already set by Mrs. Malseed.

Because of our interrupted lunch I felt quite hungry, and the Malseeds pride themselves on their teas. The chef, Mr. McBride, whom of course we've met,

9. Detective in many of Agatha Christie's murder mysteries.

1. In Surrey, southern England.

has the lightest touch I know with sponge cakes and little curranty scones. I was, in fact, buttering a scone when Strafe said:

"Here she is."

And there indeed she was. By the look of her she had simply pushed herself off her bed and come straight down. Her pink dress was even more crumpled than it had been. She hadn't so much as run a comb through her hair, her face was puffy and unpowdered. For a moment I really thought she was walking in her sleep.

Strafe and Dekko stood up. "Feeling better, dear?" Strafe said, but she didn't answer.

"Sit down, Cynth," Dekko urged, pushing back a chair to make room for her.

"He told me a story I can never forget. I've dreamed about it all over again." Cynthia swayed in front of us, not even attempting to sit down. To tell the truth, she sounded inane.

"Story, dear?" Strafe enquired, humouring her.

She said it was the story of two children who had apparently ridden bicycles through the streets of Belfast, out into Co. Antrim. The bicycles were dilapidated, she said; she didn't know if they were stolen or not. She didn't know about the children's homes because the man hadn't spoken of them, but she claimed to know instinctively that they had ridden away from poverty and unhappiness. "From the clatter and the quarrelling," Cynthia said, "Two children who later fell in love."

"Horrid old dream," Strafe said. "Horrid for you, dear."

She shook her head, and then sat down. I poured another cup of tea. "I had the oddest dream myself," I said. "Thrive Major was running the post office in Ardbeag."

Strafe smiled and Dekko gave his laugh, but Cynthia didn't in any way acknowledge what I'd said.

"A fragile thing the girl was, with depths of mystery in her wide brown eyes. Red-haired of course he was himself, thin as a rake in those days. Glencorn Lodge was derelict then."

"You've had a bit of a shock, old thing," Dekko said.

Strafe agreed, kindly adding, "Look, dear, if the chap actually interfered with you—"

"Why on earth should he do that?" Her voice was shrill in the tea-lounge, edged with a note of hysteria. I glanced at Strafe, who was frowning into his teacup. Dekko began to say something, but broke off before his meaning emerged. Rather more calmly Cynthia said:

"It was summer when they came here. Honeysuckle he described. And mother of thyme.[2] He didn't know the name of either."

No one attempted any kind of reply, not that it was necessary, for Cynthia just continued.

"At school there were the facts of geography and arithmetic. And the legends

2. A low-growing, wide-spreading variety of the aromatic thyme.

of scholars and of heroes, of Queen Maeve and Finn MacCool. There was the coming of St. Patrick[3] to a heathen people. History was full of kings and high-kings, and Silken Thomas and Wolfe Tone, the Flight of the Earls, the Siege of Limerick."[4]

When Cynthia said that, it was impossible not to believe that the unfortunate 105
events of the morning had touched her with some kind of madness. It seemed astonishing that she had walked into the tea-lounge without having combed her hair, and that she'd stood there swaying before sitting down, that out of the blue she had started on about two children. None of it made an iota of sense, and surely she could see that the nasty experience she'd suffered should not be dwelt upon? I offered her the plate of scones, hoping that if she began to eat she would stop talking, but she took no notice of my gesture.

"Look, dear," Strafe said, "there's not one of us who knows what you're talking about."

"I'm talking about a children's story, I'm talking about a girl and a boy who visited this place we visit also. He hadn't been here for years, but he returned last night, making one final effort to understand. And then he walked out into the sea."

She had taken a piece of her dress and was agitatedly crumpling it between the finger and thumb of her left hand. It was dreadful really, having her so grubby-looking. For some odd reason I suddenly thought of her cooking, how she wasn't in the least interested in it or in anything about the house. She certainly hadn't succeeded in making a home for Strafe.

"They rode those worn-out bicycles through a hot afternoon. Can you feel all that? A newly surfaced road, the snap of chippings beneath their tyres, the smell of tar? Dust from a passing car, the city they left behind?"

"Cynthia dear," I said, "drink your tea, and why not have a scone?" 110

"They swam and sunbathed on the beach you walked along today. They went to a spring for water. There were no magnolias then. There was no garden, no neat little cliff paths to the beach. Surely you can see it clearly?"

"No," Strafe said. "No, we really cannot, dear."

"This place that is an idyll for us was an idyll for them too: the trees, the ferns, the wild roses near the water spring, the very sea and sun they shared. There was a cottage lost in the middle of the woods: they sometimes looked for that. They played a game, a kind of hide and seek. People in a white farmhouse gave them milk."

3. Patrick converted the Irish to Catholicism. *Maeve:* First-century ruler of Connaught who reputedly invaded Ulster and in folk tradition is queen of the fairies. *Finn MacCumhaill:* Third-century chieftain who reputedly possessed gifts of poetry, second sight, and healing. 4. The town of Limerick in southwest Ireland was, in 1791, besieged by troops of King William, and the Irish Army, loyal to the Catholic James II who had been forced off the British throne, was defeated. *Silken Thomas:* Thomas Fitzgerald, tenth Earl of Kildare, rebelled against Henry VIII when he heard his father had been executed, and adorned his helmet and those of his supporters with silken fringe. *Wolfe Tone:* A founder and leader of the United Irishmen, supported religious toleration, separation from England, and the French Revolution and was sentenced to death as a traitor. *The Flight of the Earls:* In 1607 almost a hundred leaders ("Earls") of the North fled rather than serve England and James I, a flight that some believe permanently damaged the Irish cause.

For the second time I offered Cynthia the plate of scones and for the second time she pointedly ignored me. Her cup of tea hadn't been touched. Dekko took a scone and cheerfully said:

"All's well that's over."

But Cynthia appeared to have drifted back into a daze, and I wondered again if it could really be possible that the experience had unhinged her. Unable to help myself, I saw her being led away from the hotel, helped into the back of a blue van, something like an ambulance. She was talking about the children again, how they had planned to marry and keep a sweetshop.

"Take it easy, dear," Strafe said, which I followed up by suggesting for the second time that she should make an effort to drink her tea.

"Has it to do with the streets they came from? Or the history they learnt, he from his Christian Brothers, she from her nuns? History is unfinished in this island; long since it has come to a stop in Surrey."

Dekko said, and I really had to hand it to him:

"Cynth, we have to put it behind us."

It didn't do any good. Cynthia just went rambling on, speaking again of the girl being taught by nuns, and the boy by Christian Brothers. She began to recite the history they might have learnt, the way she sometimes did when we were driving through an area that had historical connections. "Can you imagine," she embarrassingly asked, "our very favourite places bitter with disaffection, with plotting and revenge? Can you imagine the treacherous murder of Shane O'Neill the Proud?"[5]

Dekko made a little sideways gesture of his head, politely marvelling. Strafe seemed about to say something, but changed his mind. Confusion ran through Irish history, Cynthia said, like convolvulus in a hedgerow. On May 24th, 1487, a boy of ten called Lambert Simnel, brought to Dublin by a priest from Oxford, was declared Edward VI of all England and Ireland, crowned with a golden circlet taken from a statue of the Virgin Mary. On May 24th, 1798, here in Antrim, Presbyterian farmers fought for a common cause with their Catholic labourers.[6] She paused and looked at Strafe. Chaos and contradiction, she informed him, were hidden everywhere beneath nice-sounding names. "The Battle of the Yellow Ford," she suddenly chanted in a sing-song way that sounded thoroughly peculiar, "the Statutes of Kilkenny. The Battle of Glenmama, the Convention of Drumceat.[7] The Act of Settlement, the Renunciation Act. The Act of Union,

5. Sixteenth-century leader who tried to take control of Ulster from England (Elizabeth); when the O'Donnells, egged on by the government, defeated Shane (1567), he fled to Scotland, where, though received peacefully, he was murdered. 6. "Edward VI's" rebel forces were defeated by Henry VII and he and the priest were jailed; Antrim was one of the sites of the uprising of the United Irishmen. 7. At the Battle of Yellow Ford, 1598, Hugh O'Neill, nephew of Shane, Earl of Tyrone, in his struggle to prevent the anglicization of Ireland, defeated the English. The statutes, 1366, ordered English (Norman) settlers not to intermarry with the Irish, speak their language, or adopt their customs. At Glenmama, near Dublin, in 999, the Irish defeated the Danes. Dalriada was a kingdom, partly in northeastern Ireland, partly in southwestern Scotland, and in 590 a convention was called at Drumceat County, Londonderry, to see if Scots should give allegiance to the Irish "high king."

the Toleration Act.[8] Just so much history it sounds like now, yet people starved or died while other people watched. A language was lost,[9] a faith forbidden. Famine followed revolt, plantation followed that. But it was people who were struck into the soil of other people's land, not forests of new trees; and it was greed and treachery that spread as a disease among them all. No wonder unease clings to these shreds of history and shots ring out in answer to the mockery of drums. No wonder the air is nervy with suspicion."

There was an extremely awkward silence when she ceased to speak. Dekko nodded, doing his best to be companionable. Strafe nodded also. I simpy examined the pattern of roses on our tea-time china, not knowing what else to do. Eventually Dekko said:

"What an awful lot you know, Cynth!"

"Cynthia's always been interested," Strafe said. "Always had a first-rate memory."

"Those children of the streets are part of the battles and the Acts," she went on, seeming quite unaware that her talk was literally almost crazy. "They're part of the blood that flowed around those nice-sounding names." She paused, and for a moment seemed disinclined to continue. Then she said:

"The second time they came here the house was being rebuilt. There were concrete-mixers, and lorries drawn up on the grass, noise and scaffolding everywhere. They watched all through another afternoon and then they went their different ways: their childhood was over, lost with their idyll. He became a dockyard clerk. She went to London, to work in a betting shop."

"My dear," Strafe said very gently, "it's interesting, everything you say, but it really hardly concerns us."

"No, of course not." Quite emphatically Cynthia shook her head, appearing wholly to agree. "They were degenerate, awful creatures. They must have been."

"No one's saying that, my dear."

"Their story should have ended there, he in the docklands of Belfast, she recording bets. Their complicated childhood love should just have dissipated, as such love often does. But somehow nothing was as neat as that."

Dekko, in an effort to lighten the conversation, mentioned a boy called Gollsol who'd been at school with Strafe and himself, who'd formed a romantic attachment for the daughter of one of the groundsmen and had later actually married her. There was a silence for a moment, then Cynthia, without emotion, said:

"You none of you care. You sit there not caring that two people are dead."

8. Under the Act of Settlement of 1652, those not friendly to Cromwell's Puritan English government could forfeit part or all of their property. In 1783 the English Parliament recognized Irish independence, rights of Irish courts, and as valid for Ireland only those laws enacted by English king *and* Irish Parliament. Not much later, 1800, the Act of Union united the parliament and kingdoms (thus the United Kingdom or U.K.). Earlier, 1719, the Toleration Act, forced on the Irish Parliament, allowed the Irish freedom to worship and to serve in parish offices if they would swear civil allegiance and renounce "popish," i.e. Roman Catholic, doctrines.

9. The British forbade the Irish to speak or teach their own language and anglicized all place names. *Plantation* (below): the expropriation of Irish land, which was then given to English settlers; it began under Mary I in the 1500s and continued for centuries.

"Two people, Cynthia?" I said.

"For God's sake, I'm telling you!" she cried. "That girl was murdered in a room in Maida Vale."[1]

Although there is something between Strafe and myself, I do try my best to be at peace about it. I go to church and take communion, and I know Strafe occasionally does too, although not as often as perhaps he might. Cynthia has no interest in that side of life, and it rankled with me now to hear her blaspheming so casually, and so casually speaking about death in Maida Vale on top of all this stuff about history and children. Strafe was shaking his head, clearly believing that Cynthia didn't know what she was talking about.

"Cynthia dear," I began, "are you sure you're not muddling something up here? You've been upset, you've had a nightmare: don't you think your imagination, or something you've been reading—"

"Bombs don't go off on their own. Death doesn't just happen to occur in Derry and Belfast, in London and Amsterdam and Dublin, in Berlin and Jerusalem. There are people who are murderers: that is what this children's story is about."

A silence fell, no one knowing what to say. It didn't matter of course because without any prompting Cynthia continued.

"We drink our gin with Angostura bitters, there's lamb or chicken Kiev. Old Kitty's kind to us in the dining-room and old Arthur in the hall. Flowers are everywhere, we have our special table."

"Please let us take you to your room now," Strafe begged, and as he spoke I reached out a hand in friendship and placed it on her arm. "Come on, old thing," Dekko said.

"The limbless are left on the streets, blood spatters the car-parks. *Brits Out* it says on a rockface, but we know it doesn't mean us."

I spoke quietly then, measuring my words, measuring the pause between each so that its effect might be registered. I felt the statement had to be made, whether it was my place to make it or not. I said:

"You are very confused, Cynthia."

The French family left the tea-lounge. The two Dalmatians, Charger and Snooze, ambled in and sniffed and went away again. Kitty came to clear the French family's tea things. I could hear her speaking to the honeymoon couple, saying the weather forecast was good.

"Cynthia," Strafe said, standing up, "we've been very patient with you but this is now becoming silly."

I nodded just a little. "I really think," I softly said, but Cynthia didn't permit me to go on.

"Someone told him about her. Someone mentioned her name, and he couldn't believe it. She sat alone in Maida Vale, putting together the mechanisms of her bombs: this girl who had laughed on the seashore, whom he had loved."

"Cynthia," Strafe began, but he wasn't permitted to continue either. Hopelessly, he just sat down again.

1. Section of London with many foreign transients and rooming houses.

"Whenever he heard of bombs exploding he thought of her, and couldn't understand. He wept he said that; her violence haunted him, he said. He couldn't work, he couldn't sleep at night. His mind filled up with images of her, their awkward childhood kisses, her fingers working neatly now. He saw her with a carrier-bag, hurrying it through a crowd, leaving it where it could cause most death. In front of the mouldering old house that had once been Glencorn Lodge they'd made a fire and cooked their food. They'd lain for ages on the grass. They'd cycled home to their city streets." 150

It suddenly dawned on me that Cynthia was knitting this whole fantasy out of nothing. It all worked backwards from the moment when she'd had the misfortune to witness the man's death in the sea. A few minutes before he'd been chatting quite normally to her, he'd probably even mentioned a holiday in his childhood and some girl there'd been: all of it would have been natural in the circumstances, possibly even the holiday had taken place at Glencorn. He'd said good-bye and then unfortunately he'd had his accident. As she watched from the cliff edge, something had cracked in poor Cynthia's brain, she having always been a prey to melancholy. I suppose it must be hard having two sons who don't think much of you, and a marriage and offering you a great deal, bridge and holidays probably the best part of it. For some odd reason of her own she'd created her fantasy about a child turning into a terrorist. The violence of the man's death had clearly filled her imagination with Irish violence, so regularly seen on television. If we'd been on holiday in Suffolk I wondered how it would have seemed to the poor creature.

I could feel Strafe and Dekko beginning to put all that together also, beginning to realize that the whole story of the red-haired man and the girl was clearly Cynthia's invention. "Poor creature," I wanted to say, but did not do so.

"For months he searched for her, pushing his way among the people of London, the people who were her victims. When he found her she just looked at him, as if the past hadn't even existed. She didn't smile, as if incapable of smiling. He wanted to take her away, back to where they came from, but she didn't reply when he suggested that. Bitterness was like a disease in her, and when he left her he felt the bitterness in himself."

Again Strafe and Dekko nodded, and I could feel Strafe thinking that there really was no point in protesting further. All we could hope for was that the end of the saga was in sight.

"He remained in London, working on the railways. But in the same way as before he was haunted by the person she'd become, and the haunting was more awful now. He bought a gun from a man he'd been told about and kept it hidden in a shoe-box in his rented room. Now and again he took it out and looked at it, then put back. He hated the violence that possessed her, yet he was full of it himself: he knew he couldn't betray her with anything but death. Humanity had left both of them when he visited her again in Maida Vale." 155

To my enormous relief and, I could feel, to Strafe's and Dekko's too, Mr. and Mrs. Malseed appeared beside us. Like his wife, Mr. Malseed had considerably recovered. He spoke in an even voice, clearly wishing to dispose of the matter. It was just the diversion we needed.

"I must apologize, Mrs. Strafe," he said. "I cannot say how sorry we are that you were bothered by that man."

"My wife is still a little dicky,[2] Strafe explained, "but after a decent night's rest I think we can say she'll be as right as rain again."

"I only wish, Mrs. Strafe, you had made contact with my wife or myself when he first approached you." There was a spark of irritation in Mr. Malseed's eyes, but his voice was still controlled. "I mean, the unpleasantness you suffered might just have been averted."

"Nothing would have been averted, Mr. Malseed, and certainly not the horror we are left with. Can you see her as the girl she became, seated at a chipped white table, her wires and fuses spread around her? What were her thoughts in that room, Mr. Malseed? What happens in the mind of anyone who wishes to destroy? In a back street he bought his gun for too much money. When did it first occur to him to kill her?"

"We really are a bit at sea," Mr. Malseed replied without the slightest hesitation. He humoured Cynthia by displaying no surprise, by speaking very quietly.

"All I am saying, Mr. Malseed, is that we should root our heads out of the sand and wonder about two people who are beyond the pale."

"My dear," Strafe said, "Mr. Malseed is a busy man."

Still quietly, still perfectly in control of every intonation, without a single glance around the tea-lounge to ascertain where his guests' attention was, Mr. Malseed said:

"There is unrest here, Mrs. Strafe, but we do our best to live with it."

"All I am saying is that perhaps there can be regret when two children end like this."

Mr. Malseed did not reply. His wife did her best to smile away the awkwardness. Strafe murmured privately to Cynthia, no doubt beseeching her to come to her senses. Again I imagined a blue van drawn up in front of Glencorn Lodge, for it was quite understandable now that an imaginative woman should go mad, affected by the ugliness of death. The garbled speculation about the man and the girl, the jumble in the poor thing's mind—a children's story as she called it—all somehow hung together when you realized they didn't have to make any sense whatsoever.

"Murderers are beyond the pale, Mr. Malseed, and England has always had its pales. The one in Ireland began in 1395."[3]

"Dear," I said, "what has happened has nothing whatsoever to do with calling people murderers and placing them beyond some pale or other. You witnessed a most unpleasant accident, dear, and it's only to be expected that you've become just a little lost. The man had a chat with you when you were sitting by the magnolias and then the shock of seeing him slip on the seaweed—"

"He didn't slip on the seaweed," she suddenly screamed. "My God, he didn't slip on the seaweed."

2. Shaky. 3. Richard II visited Ireland 1394–95 to bolster royal authority and (unsuccessfully) to extend English control over lands. The small area around Dublin controlled by England at the time was the "pale," which by extension now refers to areas of British control and influence.

Strafe closed his eyes. The other guests in the tea-lounge had fallen silent ages ago, openly listening. Arthur was standing near the door and was listening also. Kitty was waiting to clear away our tea things, but didn't like to because of what was happening.

"I must request you to take Mrs. Strafe to her room, Major," Mr. Malseed said. "And I must make it clear that we cannot tolerate further upset in Glencorn Lodge."

Strafe reached for her arm, but Cynthia took no notice.

"An Irish joke," she said, and then she stared at Mr. and Mrs. Malseed, her eyes passing over each feature of their faces. She stared at Dekko and Strafe, and last of all at me. She said eventually:

"An Irish joke, an unbecoming tale: of course it can't be true. Ridiculous, that a man returned here. Ridiculous, that he walked again by the seashore and through the woods, hoping to understand where a woman's cruelty had come from."

"This talk is most offensive," Mr. Malseed protested, his calmness slipping just a little. The ashen look that had earlier been in his face returned. I could see he was beside himself with rage. "You are trying to bring something to our doorstep which most certainly does not belong there."

"On your doorstep they talked about a sweetshop: Cadbury's bars and different-flavoured creams, nut-milk toffee, Aero and Crunchie."

"For God's sake pull yourself together," I clearly heard Strafe whispering, and Mrs. Malseed attempted to smile. "Come along now, Mrs. Strafe," she said, making a gesture. "Just to please us, dear. Kitty wants to clear away the dishes. Kitty!" she called out, endeavouring to bring matters down to earth.

Kitty crossed the lounge with her tray and gathered up the cups and saucers. The Malseeds, naturally still anxious, hovered. No one was surprised when Cynthia began all over again, by crazily asking Kitty what she thought of us.

"I think, dear," Mrs. Malseed began, "Kitty's quite busy really."

"Stop this at once," Strafe quietly ordered.

"For fourteen years, Kitty, you've served us with food and cleared away the tea-cups we've drunk from. For fourteen years we've played our bridge and walked about the garden. We've gone for drives, we've bought our tweed, we've bathed as those children did."

"Stop it," Strafe said again, a little louder. Bewildered and getting red in the face, Kitty hastily bundled china on to her tray. I made a sign at Strafe because for some reason I felt that the end was really in sight. I wanted him to retain his patience, but what Cynthia said next was almost unbelievable.

"In Surrey we while away the time, we clip our hedges. On a bridge night there's coffee at nine o'clock, with macaroons or *petits fours*. Last thing of all we watch the late-night News, packing away our cards and scoring-pads, our sharpened pencils. There's been an incident in Armagh, one soldier's had his head shot off, another's run amok. Our lovely Glens of Antrim, we all four think, our coastal drives: we hope that nothing disturbs the peace. We think of Mr. Malseed, still busy in Glencorn Lodge, and Mrs. Malseed finishing her flower-plaques for the rooms of the completed annexe."

"Will you for God's sake shut up?" Strafe suddenly shouted. I could see him struggling with himself, but it didn't do any good. He called Cynthia a bloody spectacle, sitting there talking rubbish. I don't believe she even heard him.

"Through honey-tinted glasses we love you and we love your island, Kitty. We love the lilt of your racy history, we love your earls and heroes. Yet we made a sensible pale here once, as civilized people create a garden, pretty as a picture."

Strafe's outburst had been quite noisy and I could sense him being ashamed of it. He muttered that he was sorry, but Cynthia simply took advantage of his generosity, continuing about a pale.

"Beyond it lie the bleak untouchables, best kept as dots on the horizon, too terrible to contemplate. How can we be blamed if we make neither head nor tail of anything, Kitty, your past and your present, those battles and Acts of Parliament? We people of Surrey: how can we know? Yet I stupidly thought, you see, that the tragedy of two children could at least be understood. He didn't discover where her cruelty had come from because perhaps you never can: evil breeds evil in a mysterious way. That's the story the red-haired stranger passed on to me, the story you huddle away from."

Poor Strafe was pulling at Cynthia, pleading with her, still saying he was sorry.

"Mrs. Strafe," Mr. Malseed tried to say, but got no further. To my horror Cynthia abruptly pointed at me.

"That woman," she said, "is my husband's mistress, a fact I am supposed to be unaware of, Kitty."

"My God!" Strafe said.

"My husband is perverted in his sexual desires. His friend, who shared his schooldays, has never quite recovered from that time. I myself am a pathetic creature who has closed her eyes to a husband's infidelity and his mistress's viciousness. I am dragged into the days of Thrive Major and A. D. Cowley-Stubbs: mechanically I smile. I hardly exist, Kitty."

There was a most unpleasant silence, and then Strafe said:

"None of that's true. For God's sake, Cynthia," he suddenly shouted, "go and rest yourself."

Cynthia shook her head and continued to address the waitress. She'd had a rest, she told her. "But it didn't do any good, Kitty, because hell has invaded the paradise of Glencorn, as so often it has invaded your island. And we, who have so often brought it, pretend it isn't there. Who cares about children made into murderers?"

Strafe shouted again. "You fleshless ugly bitch!" he cried. "You bloody old fool!" He was on his feet, trying to get her to hers. The blood was thumping in his bronzed face, his eyes had a fury in them I'd never seen before. "Fleshless!" he shouted at her, not caring that so many people were listening. He closed his eyes in misery and in shame again, and I wanted to reach out and take his hand but of course I could not. You could see the Malseeds didn't blame him, you could see them thinking that everything was ruined for us. I wanted to shout at Cynthia too, to batter the silliness out of her, but of course I could not do that. I could feel the tears behind my eyes, and I couldn't help noticing that Dekko's hands were shaking. He's quite sensitive behind his joky manner, and had quite obviously taken to heart her statement that he had never recovered from his schooldays. Nor had it been pleasant, hearing myself described as vicious.

"No one cares," Cynthia said in the same unbalanced way, as if she hadn't just been called ugly and a bitch. "No one cares, and on our journey home we shall all four be silent. Yet is the truth about ourselves at least a beginning? Will we wonder in the end about the hell that frightens us?"

Strafe still looked wretched, his face deliberately turned away from us. Mrs. Malseed gave a little sigh and raised the fingers of her left hand to her cheek, as if something tickled it. Her husband breathed heavily. Dekko seemed on the point of tears.

Cynthia stumbled off, leaving a silence behind her. Before it was broken I knew she was right when she said we would just go home, away from this country we had come to love. And I knew as well that neither here nor at home would she be led to a blue van that was not quite an ambulance. Strafe would stay with her because Strafe is made like that, honourable in his own particular way. I felt a pain where perhaps my heart is, and again I wanted to cry. Why couldn't it have been she who had gone down to the rocks and slipped on the seaweed or just walked into the sea, it didn't matter which? Her awful rigmarole hung about us as the last of the tea things were gathered up—the earls who'd fled, the famine and the people planted. The children were there too, grown up into murdering riff-raff.

1981

QUESTIONS

1. How much land *does* a man—or woman—need? What do you mean by "need"?

2. Leila, in "Her First Ball," soon shakes off the gloomy thoughts offered her by her older partner. Is she just an empty-headed girl too shallow to think of serious things, or is she just young and healthy, enjoying life?

3. What does "pale" in the title of the Trevor story mean? How is it significant in the story?

WRITING SUGGESTIONS

1. Compare Hawthorne's and Tolstoy's devils, their disguises, and how they function, and analyze what these figures imply about God and virtue in the two stories.

2. Land works well as a symbol of material wealth and as a symbol of the vanity of human wishes, the inevitable end of life, and therefore of the need for spiritual values. "How Many BMWs Does a Man Need" does not quite make it (but you could try a parody along those lines). Can you find a contemporary symbol that can work the way land does for Tolstoy? If you can, write an imitation or parody, calling it, perhaps, "How Much —— Does a Person Need?"

3. Rewrite "Her First Ball" using another focus and voice.

7 THE WHOLE TEXT

I feel that discussing story-writing in terms of plot, character, and theme is like trying to describe the expression on a face by saying where the eyes, nose, and mouth are.

—FLANNERY O'CONNOR, "Writing Short Stories"

Plot, point of view, character, symbol, and theme are useful concepts. But they do not really exist as discrete parts or constituents of a finished work. In "Beyond the Pale," for example, the connection between the private lives of the vacationing English couples and the Irish "troubles" is both part of the story's plot and part of its theme; and what the English vacationers do, say, and think—their contributions to plot and theme—is inextricably related to their individual characters. Similarly, in "How Much Land Does a Man Need?" Pahóm's greed is a constituent both of his character and of the story's theme.

Analyzing a story means breaking it down into pieces we can handle. Analyzing may require talking or writing about a story in terms of its "elements," but we must remain aware of the arbitrariness of those distinctions and of the inextricable, organic integrity of the story itself. As you read the stories that follow in this chapter, apply all that you have learned about the history, the structure, and the elements of fiction, but be especially alert as to how the elements interact. Notice how after taking it apart in order to analyze it, we can put the story back together.

JOSEPH CONRAD

The Secret Sharer

I

On my right hand there were lines of fishing-stakes resembling a mysterious system of half-submerged bamboo fences, incomprehensible in its division of the domain of tropical fishes, and crazy[1] of aspect as if abandoned for ever by some nomad tribe of fishermen now gone to the other end of the ocean; for there was no sign of human habitation as far as the eye could reach. To the left a group of barren islets, suggesting ruins of stone walls, towers, and blockhouses, had its foundations set in a blue sea that itself looked solid, so still and stable did it lie

1. Irregular, rickety.

below my feet; even the track of light from the westering sun shone smoothly, without that animated glitter which tells of an imperceptible ripple. And when I turned my head to take a parting glance at the tug which had just left us anchored outside the bar, I saw the straight line of the flat shore joined to the stable sea, edge to edge, with a perfect and unmarked closeness, in one leveled floor half brown, half blue under the enormous dome of the sky. Corresponding in their insignificance to the islets of the sea, two small clumps of trees, one on each side of the only fault in the impeccable joint, marked the mouth of the river Meinam[2] we had just left on the first preparatory stage of our homeward journey; and, far back on the inland level, a larger and loftier mass, the grove surrounding the great Paknam pagoda, was the only thing on which the eye could rest from the vain task of exploring the monotonous sweep of the horizon. Here and there gleams as of a few scattered pieces of silver marked the windings of the great river; and on the nearest of them, just within the bar, the tug steaming right into the land became lost to my sight, hull and funnel and masts, as though the impassive earth had swallowed her up without an effort, without a tremor. My eye followed the light cloud of her smoke, now here, now there, above the plain, according to the devious curves of the stream, but always fainter and farther away, till I lost it at last behind the mitre-shaped hill of the great pagoda. And then I was left alone with my ship, anchored at the head of the Gulf of Siam.

She floated at the starting-point of a long journey, very still in an immense stillness, the shadows of her spars flung far to the eastward by the setting sun. At that moment I was alone on her decks. There was not a sound in her—and around us nothing moved, nothing lived, not a canoe on the water, not a bird in the air, not a cloud in the sky. In this breathless pause at the threshold of a long passage we seemed to be measuring our fitness for a long and arduous enterprise, the appointed task of both our existences to be carried out, far from all human eyes, with only sky and sea for spectators and for judges.

There must have been some glare in the air to interfere with one's sight, because it was only just before the sun left us that my roaming eyes made out beyond the highest ridge of the principal islet of the group something which did away with the solemnity of perfect solitude. The tide of darkness flowed on swiftly; and with tropical suddenness a swarm of stars came out above the shadowy earth, while I lingered yet, my hand resting lightly on my ship's rail as if on the shoulder of a trusted friend. But, with all that multitude of celestial bodies staring down at one, the comfort of quiet communion with her was gone for good. And there were also disturbing sounds by this time—voices, footsteps forward; the steward flitted along the main deck, a busily ministering spirit; a hand-bell tinkled urgently under the poop deck. . . .

I found my two officers waiting for me near the supper table, in the lighted cuddy. We sat down at once, and as I helped the chief mate, I said:

"Are you aware that there is a ship anchored inside the islands? I saw her mast-heads above the ridge as the sun went down."

2. The Menan (Chao Phraya) runs through Bangkok, Thailand, into the Gulf of Siam. The Paknam Pagoda stands at the mouth of the river.

He raised sharply his simple face, overcharged by a terrible growth of whisker, and emitted his usual ejaculations, "Bless my soul, sir! You don't say so!"

My second mate was a round-cheeked, silent young man, grave beyond his years, I thought; but as our eyes happened to meet I detected a slight quiver on his lips. I looked down at once. It was not my part to encourage sneering on board my ship. It must be said, too, that I knew very little of my officers. In consequence of certain events of no particular significance, except to myself, I had been appointed to the command only a fortnight before. Neither did I know much of the hands forward. All these people had been together for eighteen months or so, and my position was that of the only stranger on board. I mention this because it has some bearing on what is to follow. But what I felt most was my being a stranger to the ship; and if all the truth must be told, I was somewhat of a stranger to myself. The youngest man on board (barring the second mate), and untried as yet by a position of the fullest responsibility, I was willing to take the adequacy of the others for granted. They had simply to be equal to their tasks; but I wondered how far I should turn out faithful to that ideal conception of one's own personality every man sets up for himself secretly.

Meantime the chief mate, with an almost visible effect of collaboration on the part of his round eyes and frightful whiskers, was trying to evolve a theory of the anchored ship. His dominant trait was to take all things into earnest consideration. He was of a painstaking turn of mind. As he used to say, he "liked to account to himself" for practically everything that came in his way, down to a miserable scorpion he had found in his cabin a week before. The why and the wherefore of that scorpion—how it got on board and came to select his room rather than the pantry (which was a dark place and more what a scorpion would be partial to), and how on earth it managed to drown itself in the inkwell of his writing-desk—had exercised him infinitely. The ship within the islands was much more easily accounted for; and just as we were about to rise from table he made his pronouncement. She was, he doubted not, a ship from home lately arrived. Probably she drew too much water to cross the bar except at the top of spring tides. Therefore she went into that natural harbor to wait for a few days in preference to remaining in an open roadstead.

"That's so," confirmed the second mate suddenly, in his slightly hoarse voice. "She draws over twenty feet. She's the Liverpool ship *Sephora* with a cargo of coal. Hundred and twenty-three days from Cardiff."

We looked at him in surprise. 10

"The tugboat skipper told me when he come on board for your letters, sir," explained the young man. "He expects to take her up the river the day after tomorrow."

After thus overwhelming us with the extent of his information he slipped out of the cabin. The mate observed regretfully that he "could not account for that young fellow's whims." What prevented him telling us all about it at once, he wanted to know.

I detained him as he was making a move. For the last two days the crew had had plenty of hard work, and the night before they had very little sleep. I felt painfully that I—a stranger—was doing something unusual when I directed him to let all hands turn in without setting an anchor-watch.[3] I proposed to keep on deck myself till one o'clock or thereabouts. I would get the second mate to relieve me at that hour.

"He will turn out the cook and the steward at four," I concluded, "and then give you a call. Of course at the slightest sign of any sort of wind we'll have the hands up and make a start at once."

He concealed his astonishment. "Very well, sir." Outside the cuddy he put his head in the second mate's door to inform him of my unheard-of caprice to take a five hours' anchor-watch on myself. I heard the other raise his voice incredulously—"What? The captain himself?" Then a few more murmurs, a door closed, then another. A few moments later I went on deck.

My strangeness, which had made me sleepless, had prompted that unconventional arrangement, as if I had expected in those solitary hours of the night to get on terms with the ship of which I knew nothing, manned by men of whom I knew very little more. Fast alongside a wharf, littered like any ship in port with a tangle of unrelated things, invaded by unrelated shore people, I had hardly seen her yet properly. Now, as she lay cleared for sea, the stretch of her main deck seemed to me very fine under the stars. Very fine, very roomy for her size, and very inviting. I descended the poop and paced the waist, my mind picturing to myself the coming passage through the Malay Archipelago, down the Indian Ocean, and up the Atlantic. All its phases were familiar enough to me, every characteristic, all the alternatives which were likely to face me on the high seas—everything! . . . except the novel responsibility of command. But I took heart from the reasonable thought that the ship was like other ships, the men like other men, and that the sea was not likely to keep any special surprises expressly for my discomfiture.

Arrived at that comforting conclusion, I bethought myself of a cigar and went below to get it. All was still down there. Everybody at the after end of the ship was sleeping profoundly. I came out again on the quarter-deck, agreeably at ease in my sleeping suit on that warm, breathless night, barefooted, a glowing cigar in my teeth, and, going forward, I was met by the profound silence of the fore end of the ship. Only as I passed the door of the forecastle I heard a deep, quiet, trustful sigh of some sleeper inside. And suddenly I rejoiced in the great security of the sea as compared with the unrest of the land, in my choice of that untempted life presenting no disquieting problems, invested with an elementary moral beauty by the absolute straightforwardness of its appeal and by the singleness of its purpose.

The riding-light[4] in the fore-rigging burned with a clear, untroubled, as if symbolic, flame, confident and bright in the mysterious shades of the night. Passing on my way aft along the other side of the ship, I observed that the rope side-ladder, put over, no doubt, for the master of the tug when he came to fetch away our letters, had not been hauled in as it should have been. I became annoyed

3. A detachment of seamen kept on deck while the ship lies at anchor. 4. Special light displayed by ship while ("riding") at anchor.

at this, for exactitude in small matters is the very soul of discipline. Then I reflected that I had myself peremptorily dismissed my officers from duty, and by my own act had prevented the anchor-watch being formally set and things properly attended to. I asked myself whether it was wise ever to interfere with the established routine of duties even from the kindest of motives. My action might have made me appear eccentric. Goodness only knew how that absurdly whiskered mate would "account" for my conduct, and what the whole ship thought of that informality of their new captain. I was vexed with myself.

Not from compunction certainly, but, as it were mechanically, I proceeded to get the ladder in myself. Now a side-ladder of that sort is a light affair and comes in easily, yet my vigorous tug, which should have brought it flying on board, merely recoiled upon my body in a totally unexpected jerk. What the devil! . . . I was so astounded by the immovableness of that ladder that I remained stockstill, trying to account for it to myself like that imbecile mate of mine. In the end, of course, I put my head over the rail.

The side of the ship made an opaque belt of shadow on the darkling glassy shimmer of the sea. But I saw at once something elongated and pale floating very close to the ladder. Before I could form a guess a faint flash of phosphorescent light, which seemed to issue suddenly from the naked body of a man, flickered in the sleeping water with the elusive, silent play of summer lightning in a night sky. With a gasp I saw revealed to my stare a pair of feet, the long legs, a broad livid back immersed right up to the neck in a greenish cadaverous glow. One hand, awash, clutched the bottom rung of the ladder. He was complete but for the head. A headless corpse! The cigar dropped out of my gaping mouth with a tiny plop and a short hiss quite audible in the absolute stillness of all things under heaven. At that I suppose he raised up his face, a dimly pale oval in the shadow of the ship's side. But even then I could only barely make out down there the shape of his black-haired head. However, it was enough for the horrid, frost-bound sensation which had gripped me about the chest to pass off. The moment of vain exclamations was past too. I only climbed on the spare spar and leaned over the rail as far as I could, to bring my eyes nearer to that mystery floating alongside.

As he hung by the ladder, like a resting swimmer, the sea-lightning played about his limbs at every stir; and he appeared in it ghastly, silvery, fish-like. He remained as mute as a fish, too. He made no motion to get out of the water, either. It was inconceivable that he should not attempt to come on board, and strangely troubling to suspect that perhaps he did not want to. And my first words were prompted by just that troubled incertitude.

"What's the matter?" I asked in my ordinary tone, speaking down to the face upturned exactly under mine.

"Cramp," it answered, no louder. Then slightly anxious, "I say, no need to call any one."

"I was not going to," I said.

"Are you alone on deck?"

"Yes."

I had somehow the impression that he was on the point of letting go the ladder to swim away beyond my ken—mysterious as he came. But, for the moment, this being appearing as if he had risen from the bottom of the sea (it was certainly the nearest land to the ship) wanted only to know the time. I told him. And he, down there, tentatively:

"I suppose your captain's turned in?"

"I am sure he isn't," I said.

He seemed to struggle with himself, for I heard something like the low, bitter murmur of doubt. "What's the good?" His next words came out with a hesitating effort.

"Look here, my man. Could you call him out quietly?"

I thought the time had come to declare myself.

"*I* am the captain."

I heard a "By Jove!" whispered at the level of the water. The phosphorescence flashed in the swirl of the water all about his limbs, his other hand seized the ladder.

"My name's Leggatt."

The voice was calm and resolute. A good voice. The self-possession of that man had somehow induced a corresponding state in myself. It was very quietly that I remarked:

"You must be a good swimmer."

"Yes. I've been in the water practically since nine o'clock. The question for me now is whether I am to let go this ladder and go on swimming till I sink from exhaustion or—to come on board here."

I felt this was no mere formula of desperate speech, but a real alternative in the view of a strong soul. I should have gathered from this that he was young; indeed, it is only the young who are ever confronted by such clear issues. But at the time it was pure intuition on my part. A mysterious communication was established already between us two—in the face of that silent, darkened tropical sea. I was young, too; young enough to make no comment. The man in the water began suddenly to climb up the ladder, and I hastened away from the rail to fetch some clothes.

Before entering the cabin I stood still, listening in the lobby at the foot of the stairs. A faint snore came through the closed door of the chief mate's room. The second mate's door was on the hook, but the darkness in there was absolutely soundless. He, too, was young and could sleep like a stone. Remained the steward, but he was not likely to wake up before he was called. I got a sleeping suit out of my room, and, coming back on deck, saw the naked man from the sea sitting on the main-hatch, glimmering white in the darkness, his elbows on his knees and his head in his hands. In a moment he had concealed his damp body in a sleeping suit of the same gray-stripe pattern as the one I was wearing, and followed me like my double on the poop. Together we moved right aft, barefooted, silent.

"What is it?" I asked in a deadened voice, taking the lighted lamp out of the binnacle, and raising it to his face.

"An ugly business."

He had rather regular features; a good mouth; light eyes under somewhat heavy, dark eyebrows; a smooth, square forehead; no growth on his cheeks; a small, brown mustache, and a well-shaped, round chin. His expression was concentrated, meditative, under the inspecting light of the lamp I held up to his face; such as a man thinking hard in solitude might wear. My sleeping suit was just right for his size. A well-knit young fellow of twenty-five at most. He caught his lower lip with the edge of white, even teeth.

"Yes," I said, replacing the lamp in the binnacle. The warm, heavy tropical night closed upon his head again.

"There's a ship over there," he murmured.

"Yes, I know. The *Sephora*. Did you know of us?"

"Hadn't the slightest idea. I am the mate of her—" He paused and corrected himself. "I should say I *was*."

"Aha! Something wrong?"

"Yes. Very wrong indeed. I've killed a man."

"What do you mean? Just now?"

"No, on the passage. Weeks ago. Thirty-nine south. When I say a man—"

"Fit of temper," I suggested confidently.

The shadowy, dark head, like mine, seemed to nod imperceptibly above the ghostly gray of my sleeping suit. It was, in the night, as though I had been faced by my own reflection in the depths of a sombre and immense mirror.

"A pretty thing to have to own up to for a Conway[5] boy," murmured my double distinctly.

"You're a Conway boy?"

"I am," he said, as if startled. Then, slowly . . . "Perhaps you too . . ."

It was so; but being a couple of years older I had left before he joined. After a quick interchange of dates a silence fell; and I thought suddenly of my absurd mate with his terrific whiskers and the "Bless my soul—you don't say so" type of intellect. My double gave me an inkling of his thoughts by saying:

"My father's a parson in Norfolk. Do you see me before a judge and jury on that charge? For myself I can't see the necessity. There are fellows that an angel from heaven—And I am not that. He was one of those creatures that are just simmering all the time with a silly sort of wickedness. Miserable devils that have no business to live at all. He wouldn't do his duty and wouldn't let anybody else do theirs. But what's the good of talking! You know well enough the sort of ill-conditioned snarling cur . . ."

He appealed to me as if our experiences had been as identical as our clothes. And I knew well enough the pestiferous danger of such a character where there are no means of legal repression. And I knew well enough also that my double there was no homicidal ruffian. I did not think of asking him for details, and he told me the story roughly in brusque, disconnected sentences. I needed no more. I saw it all going on as though I were myself inside that other sleeping suit.

5. The wooden battleship *Conway*, which was used to train young officers for the Royal Navy and merchant service.

"It happened while we were setting a reefed foresail, at dusk. Reefed foresail! You understand the sort of weather. The only sail we had left to keep the ship running; so you may guess what it had been like for days. Anxious sort of job, that. He gave me some of his cursed insolence at the sheet.[6] I tell you I was overdone with this terrific weather that seemed to have no end to it. Terrific, I tell you—and a deep ship. I believe the fellow himself was half crazed with funk. It was no time for gentlemanly reproof, so I turned round and felled him like an ox. He up and at me. We closed just as an awful sea made for the ship. All hands saw it coming and took to the rigging, but I had him by the throat, and went on shaking him like a rat, the men above us yelling. 'Look out! Look out!' Then a crash as if the sky had fallen on my head. They say that for over ten minutes hardly anything was to be seen of the ship—just the three masts and a bit of the forecastle head and of the poop all awash driving along in a smother of foam. It was a miracle that they found us, jammed together behind the forebits. It's clear that I meant business, because I was holding him by the throat still when they picked us up. He was black in the face. It was too much for them. It seems they rushed us aft together, gripped as we were, screaming 'Murder!' like a lot of lunatics, and broke into the cuddy. And the ship running for her life, touch and go all the time, any minute her last in a sea fit to turn your hair gray only a-looking at it. I understand that the skipper, too, started raving like the rest of them. The man had been deprived of sleep for more than a week, and to have this spring on him at the height of a furious gale nearly drove him out of his mind. I wonder they didn't fling me overboard after getting the carcass of their precious shipmate out of my fingers. They had rather a job to separate us, I've been told. A sufficiently fierce story to make an old judge and a respectable jury sit up a bit. The first thing I heard when I came to myself was the maddening howling of that endless gale, and on that the voice of the old man. He was hanging on to my bunk, staring into my face out of his sou'wester.

" 'Mr. Leggatt, you have killed a man. You can act no longer as chief mate of this ship.' "

His care to subdue his voice made it sound monotonous. He rested a hand on the end of the skylight to steady himself with, and all that time did not stir a limb, so far as I could see. "Nice little tale for a quiet tea party," he concluded in the same tone.

One of my hands, too, rested on the end of the skylight; neither did I stir a limb, so far as I knew. We stood less than a foot from each other. It occurred to me that if old "Bless my soul—you don't say so" were to put his head up the companion and catch sight of us, he would think he was seeing double, or imagine himself come upon a scene of weird witchcraft: the strange captain having a quiet confabulation by the wheel with his own gray ghost. I became very much concerned to prevent anything of the sort. I heard the other's soothing undertone:

"My father's a parson in Norfolk," it said. Evidently he had forgotten he had

6. Rope or chain attached to lower corner of sail used for shortening or slackening it.

told me this important fact before. Truly a nice little tale.

"You had better slip down into my stateroom now," I said, moving off stealthily. My double followed my movements; our bare feet made no sound; I let him in, closed the door with care, and, after giving a call to the second mate, returned on deck for my relief.

"Not much sign of any wind yet," I remarked when he approached.

"No, sir. Not much," he assented sleepily in his hoarse voice, with just enough deference, no more, and barely suppressing a yawn.

"Well, that's all you have to look out for. You have got your orders."

"Yes, sir."

I paced a turn or two on the poop and saw him take up his position face forward with his elbow in the ratlines of the mizzen-rigging before I went below. The mate's faint snoring was still going on peacefully. The cuddy lamp was burning over the table on which stood a vase with flowers, a polite attention from the ship's provision merchant—the last flowers we should see for the next three months at the very least. Two bunches of bananas hung from the beam symmetrically, one on each side of the rudder-casing. Everything was as before in the ship—except that two of her captain's sleeping suits were simultaneously in use, one motionless in the cuddy, the other keeping very still in the captain's stateroom.

It must be explained here that my cabin had the form of the capital letter L, the door being within the angle and opening into the short part of the letter. A couch was to the left, the bedplace to the right; my writing-desk and the chronometers' table faced the door. But any one opening it, unless he stepped right inside, had no view of what I call the long (or vertical) part of the letter. It contained some lockers surmounted by a bookcase; and a few clothes, a thick jacket or two, caps, oilskin coat, and such-like, hung on hooks. There was at the bottom of that part a door opening into my bathroom, which could be entered also directly from the saloon. But that way was never used.

The mysterious arrival had discovered the advantage of this particular shape. Entering my room, lighted strongly by a big bulkhead lamp swung on gimbals above my writing-desk, I did not see him anywhere till he stepped out quietly from behind the coats hung in the recessed part.

"I heard somebody moving about, and went in there at once," he whispered.

I, too, spoke under my breath.

"Nobody is likely to come in here without knocking and getting permission."

He nodded. His face was thin and the sunburn faded, as though he had been ill. And no wonder. He had been, I heard presently, kept under arrest in his cabin for nearly nine weeks. But there was nothing sickly in his eyes or in his expression. He was not a bit like me, really; yet, as we stood leaning over my bedplace, whispering side by side, with our dark heads together and our backs to the door, anybody bold enough to open it stealthily would have been treated to the uncanny sight of a double captain busy talking in whispers with his other self.

"But all this doesn't tell me how you came to hang on to our sideladder," I inquired, in the hardly audible murmurs we used, after he had told me something more of the proceedings on board the *Sephora* once the bad weather was over.

"When we sighted Java Head[7] I had had time to think all those matters out several times over. I had six weeks of doing nothing else, and with only an hour or so every evening for a tramp on the quarterdeck."

He whispered, his arms folded on the side of my bedplace, staring through the open port. And I could imagine perfectly the manner of this thinking out—a stubborn if not a steadfast operation; something of which I should have been perfectly incapable.

"I reckoned it would be dark before we closed with the land," he continued, so low that I had to strain my hearing, near as we were to each other, shoulder touching shoulder almost. "So I asked to speak to the old man. He always seemed very sick when he came to see me—as if he could not look me in the face. You know, that foresail saved the ship. She was too deep to have run long under bare poles. And it was I that managed to set it for him. Anyway, he came. When I had him in my cabin—he stood by the door looking at me as if I had the halter round my neck already—I asked him right away to leave my cabin door unlocked at night while the ship was going through Sunda Straits. There would be the Java coast within two or three miles, off Anjer Point. I wanted nothing more. I've had a prize for swimming my second year in the Conway."

"I can believe it," I breathed out.

"God only knows why they locked me in every night. To see some of their faces you'd have thought they were afraid I'd go about at night strangling people. Am I a murdering brute? Do I look it? By Jove! if I had been he wouldn't have trusted himself like that into my room. You'll say I might have chucked him aside and bolted out, there and then—it was dark already. Well, no. And for the same reason I wouldn't think of trying to smash the door. There would have been a rush to stop me at the noise, and I did not mean to get into a confounded scrimmage. Somebody else might have got killed—for I would not have broken out only to get chucked back, and I did not want any more of that work. He refused, looking more sick than ever. He was afraid of the men, and also of that old second mate of his who had been sailing with him for years—a gray-headed old humbug; and his steward, too, had been with him devil knows how long—seventeen years or more—a dogmatic sort of loafer who hated me like poison, just because I was the chief mate. No chief mate ever made more than one voyage in the *Sephora*, you know. Those two old chaps ran the ship. Devil only knows what the skipper wasn't afraid of (all his nerve went to pieces altogether in that hellish spell of bad weather we had)—of what the law would do to him—of his wife, perhaps. Oh yes! she's on board. Though I don't think she would have meddled. She would have been only too glad to have me out of the ship in any way. The 'brand of Cain'[8] business, don't you see? That's all right. I was ready

7. A famous landmark for clipper ships engaged in the China trade on the western end of Java, the southern entrance to the Sunda Straits mentioned below; the killing thus took place some 1,500 miles south of the present scene. 8. Genesis 4:14–15.

enough to go off wandering on the face of the earth—and that was price enough to pay for an Abel of that sort. Anyhow, he wouldn't listen to me. 'This thing must take its course. I represent the law here.' He was shaking like a leaf. 'So you won't?' 'No!' 'Then I hope you will be able to sleep on that," I said, and turned my back on him. 'I wonder that *you* can,' cries he, and locks the door.

"Well, after that, I couldn't. Not very well. That was three weeks ago. We have had a slow passage through the Java Sea; drifted about Carimata[9] for ten days. When we anchored here they thought, I suppose, it was all right. The nearest land (and that's five miles) is the ship's destination; the consul would soon set about catching me; and there would have been no object in bolting to these islets there. I don't suppose there's a drop of water on them. I don't know how it was, but tonight that steward, after bringing me my supper, went out to let me eat it, and left the door unlocked. And I ate it—all there was, too. After I had finished I strolled out on the quarterdeck. I don't know that I meant to do anything. A breath of fresh air was all I wanted, I believe. Then a sudden temptation came over me. I kicked off my slippers and was in the water before I had made up my mind fairly. Somebody heard the splash and they raised an awful hullabaloo. 'He's gone! Lower the boats! He's committed suicide! No, he's swimming.' Certainly I was swimming. It's not easy for a swimmer like me to commit suicide by drowning. I landed on the nearest islet before the boat left the ship's side. I heard them pulling about in the dark, hailing, and so on, but after a bit they gave up. Everything quieted down and the anchorage became as still as death. I sat down on a stone and began to think. I felt certain they would start searching for me at daylight. There was no place to hide on those stony things—and if there had been, what would have been the good? But now I was clear of that ship I was not going back. So after a while I took off all my clothes, tied them up in a bundle with a stone inside, and dropped them in the deep water on the outer side of that islet. That was suicide enough for me. Let them think what they liked, but I didn't mean to drown myself. I meant to swim till I sank—but that's not the same thing. I struck out for another of these little islands, and it was from that one that I first saw your riding-light. Something to swim for. I went on easily, and on the way I came upon a flat rock a foot or two above water. In the daytime, I dare say, you might make it out with a glass from your poop. I scrambled up on it and rested myself for a bit. Then I made another start. That last spell must have been over a mile."

His whisper was getting fainter and fainter, and all the time he stared straight 85
out through the porthole, in which there was not even a star to be seen. I had not interrupted him. There was something that made comment impossible, in his narrative, or perhaps in himself; a sort of feeling, a quality, which I can't find a name for. And when he ceased, all I found was a futile whisper, "So you swam for our light?"

"Yes—straight for it. It was something to swim for. I couldn't see any stars low down because the coast was in the way, and I couldn't see the land, either.

9. The Karimata Islands in the straits between Borneo and Sumatra, some three hundred miles northeast of the Sunda Straits.

The water was like glass. One might have been swimming in a confounded thousand feet deep cistern with no place for scrambling out anywhere; but what I didn't like was the notion of swimming round and round like a crazed bullock before I gave out; and as I didn't mean to go back . . . No. Do you see me being hauled back, stark naked, off one of these little islands by the scruff of the neck and fighting like a wild beast? Somebody would have got killed for certain, and I did not want any of that. So I went on. Then your ladder—"

"Why didn't you hail the ship?" I asked, a little louder.

He touched my shoulder lightly. Lazy footsteps came right over our heads and stopped. The second mate had crossed from the other side of the poop and might have been hanging over the rail, for all we knew.

"He couldn't hear us talking—could he?" My double breathed into my very ear anxiously.

90 His anxiety was an answer, a sufficient answer, to the question I had put to him. An answer containing all the difficulty of that situation. I closed the porthole quietly, to make sure. A louder word might have been overheard.

"Who's that?" he whispered then.

"My second mate. But I don't know much more of the fellow than you do."

And I told him a little about myself. I had been appointed to take charge while I least expected anything of the sort, not quite a fortnight ago. I didn't know either the ship or the people. Hadn't had the time in port to look about me or size anybody up. And as to the crew, all they knew was that I was appointed to take the ship home. For the rest, I was almost as much of a stranger on board as himself, I said. And at the moment I felt it most acutely. I felt that it would take very little to make me a suspect person in the eyes of the ship's company.

He had turned about meantime; and we, the two strangers in the ship, faced each other in identical attitudes.

95 "Your ladder—" he murmured, after a silence. "Who'd have thought of finding a ladder hanging over at night in a ship anchored out here! I felt just then a very unpleasant faintness. After the life I've been leading for nine weeks, anybody would have got out of condition. I wasn't capable of swimming round as far as your rudder-chains. And, lo and behold! there was a ladder to get hold of. After I gripped it I said to myself, 'What's the good?' When I saw a man's head looking over I thought I would swim away presently and leave him shouting—in whatever language it was. I didn't mind being looked at. I—I liked it. And then you speaking to me so quietly—as if you had expected me—made me hold on a little longer. It had been a confounded lonely time—I don't mean while swimming. I was glad to talk a little to somebody that didn't belong to the *Sephora*. As to asking for the captain, that was a mere impulse. It could have been no use, with all the ship knowing about me and the other people pretty certain to be round here in the morning. I don't know—I wanted to be seen, to talk with somebody, before I went on. I don't know what I would have said. . . . 'Fine night, isn't it?' or something of the sort."

"Do you think they will be round here presently?" I asked, with some incredulity.

"Quite likely," he said faintly.

He looked extremely haggard all of a sudden. His head rolled on his shoulders.

"H'm. We shall see then. Meantime get into that bed," I whispered. "Want help? There."

It was a rather high bedplace with a set of drawers underneath. This amazing swimmer really needed the lift I gave him by seizing his leg. He tumbled in, rolled over on his back, and flung one arm across his eyes. And then, with his face nearly hidden, he must have looked exactly as I used to look in that bed. I gazed upon my other self for a while before drawing across carefully the two green serge curtains which ran on a brass rod. I thought for a moment of pinning them together for greater safety, but I sat down on the couch, and once there I felt unwilling to rise and hunt for a pin. I would do it in a moment. I was extremely tired, in a peculiarly intimate way, by the strain of stealthiness, by the effort of whispering, and the general secrecy of this excitement. It was three o'clock by now, and I had been on my feet since nine, but I was not sleepy; I could not have gone to sleep. I sat there, fagged out, looking at the curtains, trying to clear my mind of the confused sensation of being in two places at once, and greatly bothered by an exasperating knocking in my head. It was a relief to discover suddenly that it was not in my head at all, but on the outside of the door. Before I could collect myself, the words "Come in" were out of my mouth, and the steward entered with a tray, bringing in my morning coffee. I had slept, after all, and I was so frightened that I shouted, "This way! I am here, steward," as though he had been miles away. He put down the tray on the table next the couch and only then said, very quietly, "I can see you are here, sir." I felt him give me a keen look, but I dared not meet his eyes just then. He must have wondered why I had drawn the curtains of my bed before going to sleep on the couch. He went out, hooking the door open as usual.

I heard the crew washing decks above me. I knew I would have been told at once if there had been any wind. Calm, I thought, and I was doubly vexed. Indeed, I felt dual more than ever. The steward reappeared suddenly in the doorway. I jumped up from the couch so quickly that he gave a start.

"What do you want here?"

"Close your port, sir—they are washing decks."

"It is closed," I said, reddening.

"Very well, sir." But he did not move from the doorway and returned my stare in an extraordinary, equivocal manner for a time. Then his eyes, wavered, all his expression changed, and in a voice unusually gentle, almost coaxingly.

"May I come in to take the empty cup away, sir?"

"Of course!" I turned my back on him while he popped in and out. Then I unhooked and closed the door and even pushed the bolt. This sort of thing could not go on very long. The cabin was as hot as an oven, too. I took a peep at my double, and discovered that he had not moved; his arm was still over his eyes; but his chest heaved, his hair was wet, his chin glistened with perspiration. I reached over him and opened the port.

"I must show myself on deck," I reflected.

Of course, theoretically, I could do what I liked, with no one to say nay to me within the whole circle of the horizon; but to lock my cabin door and take the key away I did not dare. Directly I put my head out of the companion I saw the group of my two officers, the second mate barefooted, the chief mate in long india-rubber boots, near the break of the poop, and the steward half-way down the poop ladder talking to them eagerly. He happened to catch sight of me and dived, the second ran down on the main deck shouting some order or other, and the chief mate came to meet me, touching his cap.

110 There was a sort of curiosity in his eye that I did not like. I don't know whether the steward had told them that I was "queer" only, or downright drunk, but I know the man meant to have a good look at me. I watched him coming with a smile which, as he got into point-blank range, took effect and froze his very whiskers. I did not give him time to open his lips.

"Square the yards by lifts and braces before the hands go to breakfast."

It was the first particular order I had given on board that ship; and I stayed on deck to see it executed too. I had felt the need of asserting myself without loss of time. That sneering young cub got taken down a peg or two on that occasion, and I also seized the opportunity of having a good look at the face of every foremast man as they filed past me to go to the after braces. At breakfast time, eating nothing myself, I presided with such frigid dignity that the two mates were only too glad to escape from the cabin as soon as decency permitted; and all the time the dual working of my mind distracted me almost to the point of insanity. I was constantly watching myself, my secret self, as dependent on my actions as my own personality, sleeping in that bed, behind that door which faced me as I sat at the head of the table. It was very much like being mad, only it was worse, because one was aware of it.

I had to shake him for a solid minute, but when at last he opened his eyes it was in the full possession of his senses, with an inquiring look.

"All's well so far," I whispered. "Now you must vanish into the bathroom."

115 He did so, as noiseless as a ghost, and I then rang for the steward, and facing him boldly, directed him to tidy up my stateroom while I was having my bath—"and be quick about it." As my tone admitted of no excuses, he said, "Yes, sir," and ran off to fetch his dustpan and brushes. I took a bath and did most of my dressing, splashing, and whistling softly for the steward's edification, while the secret sharer of my life stood drawn bolt upright in that little space, his face looking very sunken in daylight, his eyelids lowered under the stern, dark line of his eyebrows drawn together by a slight frown.

When I left him there to go back to my room the steward was finishing dusting. I sent for the mate and engaged him in some insignificant conversation. It was, as it were, trifling with the terrific character of his whiskers; but my object was to give him an opportunity for a good look at my cabin. And then I could at last shut, with a clear conscience, the door of my stateroom and get my double back into the recessed part. There was nothing else for it. He had to sit still on a small folding stool, half smothered by the heavy coats hanging there. We listened to the steward going into the bathroom out of the saloon, filling the water-bottles there, scrubbing the bath, setting things to rights, whisk, bang, clatter—out again into the saloon—turn the key—click. Such was my scheme for keeping my second self invisible. Nothing better could be contrived under the circumstances. And there we sat: I at my writing-desk ready to appear busy with some papers, he behind me, out of sight of the door. It would not have been prudent to talk in daytime; and I could not have stood the excitement of that queer sense of whispering to myself. Now and then, glancing over my shoulder, I saw him far back there, sitting rigidly on the low stool, his bare feet close together, his arms folded, his head hanging on his breast—and perfectly still. Anybody would have taken him for me.

I was fascinated by it myself. Every moment I had to glance over my shoulder. I was looking at him when a voice outside the door said:

"Beg pardon, sir."

"Well!" . . . I kept my eyes on him, and so when the voice outside the door announced, "There's a ship's boat coming our way, sir," I saw him give a start—the first movement he had made for hours. But he did not raise his bowed head.

"All right. Get the ladder over." 120

I hesitated. Should I whisper something to him? But what? His immobility seemed to have been never disturbed. What could I tell him he did not know already? . . . Finally I went on deck.

II

The skipper of the *Spehora* had a thin, red whisker all round his face, and the sort of complexion that goes with hair of that color; also the particular, rather smeary shade of blue in the eyes. He was not exactly a showy figure; his shoulders were high, his stature but middling—one leg slightly more bandy than the other. He shook hands, looking vaguely around. A spiritless tenacity was his main characteristic, I judged. I behaved with a politeness which seemed to disconcert him. Perhaps he was shy. He mumbled to me as if he were ashamed of what he was saying; gave his name (it was something like Archbold—but at this distance of years I hardly am sure), his ship's name, and a few other particulars of that sort, in the manner of a criminal making a reluctant and doleful confession. He had had terrible weather on the passage out—terrible—terrible—wife aboard, too.

By this time we were seated in the cabin and the steward brought in a tray with a bottle and glasses. "Thanks! No." Never took liquor. Would have some water, though. He drank two tumblerfuls. Terrible thirsty work. Ever since daylight had been exploring the islands round his ship.

"What was that for—fun?" I asked with an appearance of polite interest.

"No!" He sighed. "Painful duty." 125

As he persisted in his mumbling and I wanted my double to hear every word, I hit upon the notion of informing him that I regretted to say I was hard of hearing.

"Such a young man too!" he nodded, keeping his smeary, blue, unintelligent eyes fastened upon me. "What was the cause of it—some disease?" he inquired, without the least sympathy and as if he thought that, if so, I'd got no more than I deserved.

"Yes; disease," I admitted in a cheerful tone which seemed to shock him.

But my point was gained, because he had to raise his voice to give me his tale. It is not worth while to record that version. It was just over two months since all this had happened, and he had thought so much about it that he seemed completely muddled as to its bearings, but still immensely impressed.

"What would you think of such a thing happening on board your own ship? I've had the *Sephora* for these fifteen years. I am a well-known shipmaster."

130 He was densely distressed—and perhaps I should have sympathized with him if I had been able to detach my mental vision from the unsuspected sharer of my cabin as though he were my second self. There he was on the other side of the bulkhead, four or five feet from us, no more, as we sat in the saloon. I looked politely at Captain Archbold (if that was his name), but it was the other I saw, in a gray sleeping suit, seated on a low stool, his bare feet close together, his arms folded, and every word said between us falling into the ears of his dark head bowed on his chest.

"I have been at sea now, man and boy, for seven and thirty years, and I've never heard of such a thing happening in an English ship. And that it should be my ship. Wife on board, too."

I was hardly listening to him.

"Don't you think," I said, "that the heavy sea which, you told me, came aboard just then might have killed the man? I have seen the sheer weight of a sea kill a man very neatly, by simply breaking his neck."

"Good God!" he uttered impressively, fixing his smeary blue eyes on me. "The sea! No man killed by the sea ever looked like that." He seemed positively scandalized at my suggestion. And as I gazed at him, certainly not prepared for anything original on his part, he advanced his head close to mine and thrust his tongue out at me so suddenly that I couldn't help starting back.

135 After scoring over my calmness in this graphic way he nodded wisely. If I had seen the sight, he assured me, I would never forget it as long as I lived. The weather was too bad to give the corpse a proper sea burial. So next day at dawn they took it up on the poop, covering its face with a bit of bunting; he read a short prayer, and then, just as it was, in its oilskins and long boots, they launched it amongst those mountainous seas that seemed ready every moment to swallow up the ship herself and the terrified lives on board of her.

"That reefed foresail saved you," I threw in.

"Under God—it did," he exclaimed fervently. "It was by a special mercy, I firmly believe, that it stood some of those hurricane squalls."

"It was the setting of that sail which—" I began.

"God's own hand in it," he interrupted me. "Nothing less could have done it. I don't mind telling you that I hardly dared give the order. It seemed impossible that we could touch anything without losing it, and then our last hope would have been gone."

140 The terror of that gale was on him yet. I let him go on for a bit, then said casually—as if returning to a minor subject:

"You were very anxious to give up your mate to the shore people, I believe?"

He was. To the law. His obscure tenacity on that point had in it something incomprehensible and a little awful; something, as it were, mystical, quite apart from his anxiety that he should not be suspected of "countenancing any doings of that sort." Seven and thirty virtuous years at sea, of which over twenty of immaculate command, and the last fifteen in the *Sephora*, seemed to have laid him under some pitiless obligation.

"And you know," he went on, groping shamefacedly amongst his feelings, "I did not engage that young fellow. His people had some interest with my owners. I was in a way forced to take him on. He looked very smart, very gentlemanly, and all that. But do you know—I never liked him, somehow. I am a plain man. You see, he wasn't exactly the sort for the chief mate of a ship like the *Sephora*."

I had become so connected in thoughts and impressions with the secret sharer of my cabin that I felt as if I, personally, were being given to understand that I, too, was not the sort that would have done for the chief mate of a ship like the *Sephora*. I had no doubt of it in my mind.

"Not at all the style of man. You understand," he insisted superfluously, looking hard at me.

I smiled urbanely. He seemed at a loss for a while.

"I suppose I must report a suicide."

"Beg pardon?"

"Sui-cide! That's what I'll have to write to my owners directly I get in."

"Unless you manage to recover him before tomorrow," I assented dispassionately. . . . "I mean, alive."

He mumbled something which I really did not catch, and I turned my ear to him in a puzzled manner. He fairly bawled:

"The land—I say, the mainland is at least seven miles off my anchorage."

"About that."

My lack of excitement, of curiosity, of surprise, of any sort of pronounced interest, began to arouse his distrust. But except for the felicitous pretense of deafness I had not tried to pretend anything. I had felt utterly incapable of playing the part of ignorance properly, and therefore was afraid to try. It is also certain that he had brought some ready-made suspicions with him, and that he viewed my politeness as a strange and unnatural phenomenon. And yet how else could I have received him? Not heartily! That was impossible for psychological reasons, which I need not state here. My only object was to keep off his inquiries. Surlily? Yes, but surliness might have provoked a point-blank question. From its novelty to him and from its nature, punctilious courtesy was the manner best calculated to restrain the man. But there was the danger of his breaking through my defense bluntly. I could not, I think, have met him by a direct lie, also for psychological (not moral) reasons. If he had only known how afraid I was of his putting my feeling of identity with the other to the test! But, strangely enough (I thought of it only afterward), I believe that he was not a little disconcerted by the reverse side of that weird situation, by something in me that reminded him of the man he was seeking—suggested a mysterious similitude to the young fellow he had distrusted and disliked from the first.

However that might have been the silence was not very prolonged. He took another oblique step.

"I reckon I had no more than a two-mile pull to your ship. Not a bit more."

"And quite enough, too, in this awful heat," I said.

Another pause full of mistrust followed. Necessity, they say, is mother of invention, but fear, too, is not barren of ingenious suggestions. And I was afraid he would ask me point-blank for news of my other self.

"Nice little saloon, isn't it?" I remarked, as if noticing for the first time the way his eyes roamed from one closed door to the other. "And very well fitted out, too. Here, for instance," I continued, reaching over the back of my seat negligently and flinging the door open, "is my bathroom."

He made an eager movement, but hardly gave it a glance. I got up, shut the door of the bathroom, and invited him to have a look round, as if I were very proud of my accommodation. He had to rise and be shown round, but he went through the business without any raptures whatever.

"And now we'll have a look at my stateroom," I declared, in a voice as loud as I dared to make it, crossing the cabin to the starboard side with purposely heavy steps.

He followed me in and gazed around. My intelligent double had vanished. I played my part.

"Very convenient—isn't it?"

"Very nice. Very comf . . ." He didn't finish, and went out brusquely as if to escape from some unrighteous wiles of mine. But it was not to be. I had been too frightened not to feel vengeful; I felt I had him on the run, and I meant to keep him on the run. My polite insistence must have had something menacing in it, because he gave in suddenly. And I did not let him off a single item: mates' rooms, pantry, storerooms, the very sail-locker, which was also under the poop—he had to look into them all. When at last I showed him out on the quarter-deck he drew a long, spiritless sigh, and mumbled dismally that he must really be going back to his ship now. I desired my mate, who had joined us, to see to the captain's boat.

The man of whiskers gave a blast on the whistle which he used to wear hanging round his neck, and yelled, "*Sephora's* away!" My double down there in my cabin must have heard, and certainly could not feel more relieved than I. Four fellows came running out from somewhere forward and went over the side, while my own men, appearing on deck too, lined the rail. I escorted my visitor to the gangway ceremoniously, and nearly overdid it. He was a tenacious beast. On the very ladder he lingered, and in that unique, guiltily conscientious manner of sticking to the point:

"I say . . . you . . . you don't think that—"

I covered his voice loudly.

"Certainly not. . . . I am delighted. Goodbye."

I had an idea of what he meant to say, and just saved myself by the privilege of defective hearing. He was too shaken generally to insist, but my mate, close witness of that parting, looked mystified and his face took on a thoughtful cast. As I did not want to appear as if I wished to avoid all communication with my officers, he had the opportunity to address me.

"Seems a very nice man. His boat's crew told our chaps a very extraordinary story, if what I am told by the steward is true. I suppose you had it from the captain, sir?"

"Yes. I had a story from the captain."

"A very horrible affair—isn't it, sir?"

"It is."

"Beats all these tales we hear about murders in Yankee ships."

"I don't think it beats them. I don't think it resembles them in the least."

"Bless my soul—you don't say so! But of course I've no acquaintance whatever with American ships, not I, so I couldn't go against your knowledge. It's horrible enough for me. . . . But the queerest part is that those fellows seemed to have some idea the man was hidden aboard here. They had really. Did you ever hear of such a thing?"

"Preposterous—isn't it?"

We were walking to and fro athwart the quarter-deck. No one of the crew forward could be seen (the day was Sunday), and the mate pursued:

"There was some little dispute about it. Our chaps took offense. 'As if we would harbor a thing like that,' they said. 'Wouldn't you like to look for him in our coal-hole?' Quite a tiff. But they made it up in the end. I suppose he did drown himself. Don't you, sir?"

"I don't suppose anything."

"You have no doubt in the matter, sir?"

"None whatever."

I left him suddenly. I felt I was producing a bad impression, but with my double down there it was most trying to be on deck. And it was almost as trying to be below. Altogether a nerve-trying situation. But on the whole I felt less torn in two when I was with him. There was no one in the whole ship whom I dared take into my confidence. Since the hands had got to know his story, it would have been impossible to pass him off for any one else, and an accidental discovery was to be dreaded now more than ever. . . .

The steward being engaged in laying the table for dinner, we could talk only with our eyes when I first went down. Later in the afternoon we had a cautious try at whispering. The Sunday quietness of the ship was against us; the stillness of air and water around her was against us; the elements, the men were against us—everything was against us in our secret partnership; time itself—for this could not go on for ever. The very trust in Providence was, I supposed, denied to his guilt. Shall I confess that this thought cast me down very much? And as to the chapter of accidents which counts for so much in the book of success, I could only hope that it was closed. For what favorable accident could be expected?

"Did you hear everything?" were my first words as soon as we took up our position side by side, leaning over my bedplace.

He had. And the proof of it was his earnest whisper, "The man told you he hardly dared to give the order."

I understood the reference to be to that saving foresail.

"Yes. He was afraid of it being lost in the setting."

"I assure you he never gave the order. He may think he did, but he never gave it. He stood there with me on the break of the poop after the maintopsail blew away, and whimpered about our last hope—positively whimpered about it and nothing else—and the night coming on! To hear one's skipper go on like that in such weather was enough to drive any fellow out of his mind. It worked me up into a sort of desperation. I just took it into my own hands and went away from him, boiling, and—But what's the use telling you? *You* know! . . . Do you think that if I had not been pretty fierce with them I should have got the men to do anything? Not it! The boss'en[1] perhaps? Perhaps! It wasn't a heavy sea—it was a sea gone mad! I suppose the end of the world will be something like that; and a man may have the heart to see it coming once and be done with it—but to have to face it day after day . . . I don't blame anybody. I was precious little better than the rest. Only—I was an officer of that old coal-wagon, anyhow. . . ."

"I quite understand," I conveyed that sincere assurance into his ear. He was out of breath with whispering; I could hear him pant slightly. It was all very simple. The same strung-up force which had given twenty-four men a chance, at least, for their lives had, in a sort of recoil, crushed an unworthy mutinous existence.

But I had no leisure to weigh the merits of the matter—footsteps in the saloon, a heavy knock. "There's enough wind to get under way with, sir." Here was the call of a new claim upon my thoughts and even upon my feelings.

"Turn the hands up," I cried through the door. "I'll be on deck directly."

I was going out to make the acquaintance of my ship. Before I left the cabin our eyes met—the eyes of the only two strangers on board. I pointed to the recessed part where the little camp-stool awaited him and laid my finger on my lips. He made a gesture—somewhat vague—a little mysterious, accompanied by a faint smile, as if of regret.

This is not the place to enlarge upon the sensations of a man who feels for the first time a ship move under his feet to his own independent word. In my case they were not unalloyed. I was not wholly alone with my command; for there was that stranger in my cabin. Or, rather, I was not completely and wholly with her. Part of me was absent. That mental feeling of being in two places at once affected me physically as if the mood of secrecy had penetrated my very soul. Before an hour had elapsed since the ship had begun to move, having occasion to ask the mate (he stood by my side) to take a compass bearing of the Pagoda, I caught myself reaching up to his ear in whispers. I say I caught myself, but enough had escaped to startle the man. I can't describe it otherwise than by saying that he shied. A grave, preoccupied manner, as though he were in possession of some perplexing intelligence, did not leave him henceforth. A little later I moved away from the rail to look at the compass with such a stealthy gait that the helmsman noticed it—and I could not help noticing the unusual roundness of his eyes. These are trifling instances, though it's to no commander's advantage to be suspected of ludicrous eccentricities. But I was also more seriously affected. There are to a seaman certain words, gestures, that should in given conditions come as naturally, as instinctively, as the winking of a menaced

1. *Bosun* or *boatswain*, petty officer in charge of deck crew and of rigging.

eye. A certain order should spring on to his lips without thinking; a certain sign should get itself made, so to speak, without reflection. But all unconscious alertness had abandoned me. I had to make an effort of will to recall myself back (from the cabin) to the conditions of the moment. I felt that I was appearing an irresolute commander to those people who were watching me more or less critically.

And, besides, there were the scares. On the second day out, for instance, coming off the deck in the afternoon (I had straw slippers on my bare feet) I stopped at the open pantry door and spoke to the steward. He was doing something there with his back to me. At the sound of my voice he nearly jumped out of his skin, as the saying is, and incidentally broke a cup.

"What on earth's the matter with you?" I asked, astonished.

He was extremely confused. "Beg your pardon, sir. I made sure you were in your cabin."

"You see I wasn't."

"No, sir. I could have sworn I had heard you moving in there not a moment ago. It's most extraordinary . . . very sorry, sir."

I passed on with an inward shudder. I was so identified with my secret double that I did not even mention the fact in those scanty, fearful whispers we exchanged. I suppose he had made some slight noise of some kind or other. It would have been miraculous if he hadn't at one time or another. And yet, haggard as he appeared, he looked always perfectly self-controlled, more than calm—almost invulnerable. On my suggestion he remained almost entirely in the bathroom, which, upon the whole, was the safest place. There could be really no shadow of an excuse for any one ever wanting to go in there, once the steward had done with it. It was a very tiny place. Sometimes he reclined on the floor, his legs bent, his head sustained on one elbow. At others I would find him on the campstool, sitting in his gray sleeping suit and with his cropped dark hair like a patient, unmoved convict. At night I would smuggle him into my bedplace, and we would whisper together, with the regular footfalls of the officer of the watch passing and repassing over our heads. It was an infinitely miserable time. It was lucky that some tins of fine preserves were stowed in a locker in my stateroom; hard bread I could always get hold of; and so he lived on stewed chicken, pâté de foie gras, asparagus, cooked oysters, sardines—on all sorts of abominable sham-delicacies out of tins. My early morning coffee he always drank; and it was all I dared do for him in that respect.

Every day there was the horrible maneuvering to go through so that my room and then the bathroom should be done in the usual way. I came to hate the sight of the steward, to abhor the voice of that harmless man. I felt that it was he who would bring on the disaster of discovery. It hung like a sword over our heads.

The fourth day out, I think (we were then working down the east side of the Gulf of Siam, tack for tack,[2] in light winds and smooth water)—the fourth day, I say, of this miserable juggling with the unavoidable, as we sat at our evening

2. By a series of shiftings back and forth of sails.

meal, that man, whose slightest movement I dreaded, after putting down the dishes ran up on deck busily. This could not be dangerous. Presently he came down again; and then it appeared that he had remembered a coat of mine which I had thrown over a rail to dry after having been wetted in a shower which had passed over the ship in the afternoon. Sitting stolidly at the head of the table I became terrified at the sight of the garment on his arm. Of course he made for my door. There was no time to lose.

"Steward!" I thundered. My nerves were so shaken that I could not govern my voice and conceal my agitation. This was the sort of thing that made my terrifically whiskered mate tap his forehead with his forefinger. I had detected him using that gesture while talking on deck with a confidential air to the carpenter. It was too far to hear a word, but I had no doubt that this pantomime could only refer to the strange new captain.

"Yes, sir," the pale-faced steward turned resignedly to me. It was this maddening course of being shouted at, checked without rhyme or reason, arbitrarily chased out of my cabin, suddenly called into it, sent flying out of his pantry on incomprehensible errands, that accounted for the growing wretchedness of his expression.

"Where are you going with that coat?"

"To your room, sir."

"Is there another shower coming?"

"I'm sure I don't know, sir. Shall I go up again and see, sir?"

"No! never mind."

My object was attained, as of course my other self in there would have heard everything that passed. During this interlude my two officers never raised their eyes off their respective plates; but the lip of that confounded cub, the second mate, quivered visibly.

I expected the steward to hook my coat on and come out at once. He was very slow about it; but I dominated my nervousness sufficiently not to shout after him. Suddenly I became aware (it could be heard plainly enough) that the fellow for some reason or other was opening the door of the bathroom. It was the end. The place was literally not big enough to swing a cat in. My voice died in my throat and I went stony all over. I expected to hear a yell of surprise and terror, and made a movement, but had not the strength to get on my legs. Everything remained still. Had my second self taken the poor wretch by the throat? I don't know what I could have done next moment if I had not seen the steward come out of my room, close the door, and then stand quietly by the sideboard.

"Saved," I thought. "But, no! Lost! Gone! He was gone!"

I laid my knife and fork down and leaned back in my chair. My head swam. After a while, when sufficiently recovered to speak in a steady voice, I instructed my mate to put the ship round at eight o'clock himself.

"I won't come on deck," I went on. "I think I'll turn in, and unless the wind shifts I don't want to be disturbed before midnight. I feel a bit seedy."

"You did look middling bad a little while ago," the chief mate remarked without showing any great concern.

They both went out, and I stared at the steward clearing the table. There was nothing to be read on that wretched man's face. But why did he avoid my eyes?

I asked myself. Then I thought I should like to hear the sound of his voice.

"Steward!"

"Sir!" Startled as usual.

"Where did you hang up that coat?"

"In the bathroom, sir." The usual anxious tone. "It's not quite dry yet, sir."

For some time longer I sat in the cuddy. Had my double vanished as he had come? But of his coming there was an explanation, whereas his disappearance would be inexplicable. . . . I went slowly into my dark room, shut the door, lighted the lamp, and for a time dared not turn round. When at last I did I saw him standing bolt upright in the narrow recessed part. It would not be true to say I had a shock, but an irresistible doubt of his bodily existence flitted through my mind. Can it be, I asked myself, that he is not visible to other eyes than mine? It was like being haunted. Motionless, with a grave face, he raised his hands slightly at me in a gesture which meant clearly, "Heavens! what a narrow escape!" Narrow indeed. I think I had come creeping quietly as near insanity as any man who has not actually gone over the border. That gesture restrained me, so to speak.

The mate with the terrific whiskers was now putting the ship on the other tack. In the moment of profound silence which follows upon the hands going to their stations I heard on the poop his raised voice: "Hard alee!"[3] and the distant shout of the order repeated on the main deck. The sails, in that light breeze, made but a faint fluttering noise. It ceased. The ship was coming round slowly; I held my breath in the renewed stillness of expectation; one wouldn't have thought that there was a single living soul on her decks. A sudden brisk shout, "Mainsail haul!" broke the spell, and in the noisy cries and rush overhead of the men running away with the main brace we two, down in my cabin, came together in our usual position by the bedplace.

He did not wait for my question. "I heard him fumbling here and just managed to squat myself down in the bath," he whispered to me. "The fellow only opened the door and put his arm in to hang the coat up. All the same. . . ."

"I never thought of that," I whispered back, even more appalled than before at the closeness of the shave, and marveling at that something unyielding in his character which was carrying him through so finely. There was no agitation in his whisper. Whoever was being driven distracted, it was not he. He was sane. And the proof of his sanity was continued when he took up the whispering again.

"It would never do for me to come to life again."

It was something that a ghost might have said. But what he was alluding to was his old captain's reluctant admission of the theory of suicide. It would obviously serve his turn—if I had understood at all the view which seemed to govern the unalterable purpose of his action.

"You must maroon me as soon as ever you can get amongst these islands off the Cambodje[4] shore," he went on.

"Maroon you! We are not living in a boy's adventure tale," I protested. His scornful whispering took me up.

"We aren't indeed! There's nothing of a boy's tale in this. But there's nothing

3. Put the helm all the way over to the side away from the wind.
4. Cambodian.

else for it. I want no more. You don't suppose I am afraid of what can be done to me? Prison or gallows or whatever they may please. But you don't see me coming back to explain such things to an old fellow in a wig and twelve respectable tradesmen, do you? What can they know whether I am guilty or not—or of *what* I am guilty, either? That's my affair. What does the Bible say? 'Driven off the face of the earth.'[5] Very well. I am off the face of the earth now. As I came at night so I shall go."

"Impossible!" I murmured. "You can't."

"Can't? . . . . Not naked like a soul on the Day of Judgment. I shall freeze on to this sleeping suit. The Last Day is not yet—and . . . you have understood thoroughly. Didn't you?"

I felt suddenly ashamed of myself. I may say truly that I understood—and my hesitation in letting that man swim away from my ship's side had been a mere sham sentiment, a sort of cowardice.

"It can't be done now till next night," I breathed out. "The ship is on the offshore tack and the wind may fail us."

"As long as I know that you understand," he whispered. "But of course you do. It's a great satisfaction to have got somebody to understand. You seem to have been there on purpose." And in the same whisper, as if we two whenever we talked had to say things to each other which were not fit for the world to hear, he added, "It's very wonderful."

We remained side by side talking in our secret way—but sometimes silent or just exchanging a whispered word or two at long intervals. And as usual he stared through the port. A breath of wind came now and again into our faces. The ship might have been moored in dock, so gently and on an even keel she slipped through the water, that did not murmur even at our passage, shadowy and silent like a phantom sea.

At midnight I went on deck, and to my mate's great surprise put the ship round on the other tack. His terrible whiskers flitted round me in silent criticism. I certainly should not have done it if it had been only a question of getting out of that sleepy gulf as quickly as possible. I believe he told the second mate, who relieved him, that it was a great want of judgment. The other only yawned. That intolerable cub shuffled about so sleepily and lolled against the rails in such a slack, improper fashion that I came down on him sharply.

"Aren't you properly awake yet?"

"Yes, sir! I am awake."

"Well, then, be good enough to hold yourself as if you were. And keep a look out. If there's any current we'll be closing with some islands long before daylight."

The east side of the gulf is fringed with islands, some solitary, others in groups. On the blue background of the high coast they seem to float on silvery patches of calm water, arid and gray, or dark green and rounded like clumps of evergreen bushes, with the larger ones, a mile or two long, showing the outlines of ridges, ribs of gray rock under the dank mantle of matted leafage. Unknown

5. Genesis 4:14.

to trade, to travel, almost to geography, the manner of life they harbor is an unsolved secret. There must be villages—settlements of fishermen at least—on the largest of them, and some communication with the world is probably kept up by native craft. But all that forenoon, as we headed for them, fanned along by the faintest of breezes, I saw no sign of man or canoe in the field of the telescope I kept on pointing at the scattered group.

At noon I gave no orders for a change of course, and the mate's whiskers became much concerned and seemed to be offering themselves unduly to my notice. At last I said:

"I am going to stand right in. Quite in—as far as I can take her."

The stare of extreme surprise imparted an air of ferocity also to his eyes, and he looked truly terrific for a moment.

"We're not doing well in the middle of the gulf," I continued casually. "I am going to look for the land breezes tonight."

"Bless my soul! Do you mean, sir, in the dark amongst the lot of all them islands and reefs and shoals?"

"Well, if there are any regular land breezes at all on this coast one must get close inshore to find them—mustn't one?"

"Bless my soul!" he exclaimed again under his breath. All that afternoon he wore a dreamy, comtemplative appearance which in him was a mark of perplexity. After dinner I went into my stateroom as if I meant to take some rest. There we two bent our dark heads over a half-unrolled chart lying on my bed.

"There," I said. "It's got to be Koh-ring.[6] I've been looking at it ever since sunrise. It has got two hills and a low point. It must be inhabited. And on the coast opposite there is what looks like the mouth of a biggish river—with some town, no doubt, not far up. It's the best chance for you that I can see."

"Anything. Koh-ring let it be."

He looked thoughtfully at the chart as if surveying chances and distances from a lofty height—and following with his eyes his own figure wandering on the blank land of Cochin-China, and then passing off that piece of paper clean out of sight into uncharted regions. And it was as if the ship had two captains to plan her course for her. I had been so worried and restless running up and down that I had not had the patience to dress that day. I had remained in my sleeping suit, with straw slippers and a soft floppy hat. The closeness of the heat in the gulf had been most oppressive, and the crew were used to see me wandering in that airy attire.

"She will clear the south point as she heads now," I whispered into his ear. "Goodness only knows when, though—but certainly after dark. I'll edge her in to half a mile, as far as I may be able to judge in the dark . . ."

"Be careful," he murmured warningly—and I realized suddenly that all my future, the only future for which I was fit, would perhaps go irretrievably to pieces in any mishap to my first command.

I could not stop a moment longer in the room. I motioned him to get out of

6. *Koh* or *Ko* means *island;* there are a large number of islands with that prefix at the head of the Gulf of Siam, but not, apparently, a Koh-ring.

sight and made my way on the poop. That unplayful cub had the watch. I walked up and down for a while thinking things out, then beckoned him over.

"Send a couple of hands to open the two quarter-deck ports," I said mildly.

He actually had the impudence, or else so forgot himself in his wonder at such an incomprehensible order, as to repeat:

"Open the quarter-deck ports! What for, sir?"

"The only reason you need concern yourself about is because I tell you to do so. Have them opened wide and fastened properly."

He reddened and went off, but I believe made some jeering remark to the carpenter as to the sensible practice of ventilating a ship's quarter-deck. I know he popped into the mate's cabin to impart the fact to him, because the whiskers came on deck, as it were by chance, and stole glances at me from below—for signs of lunacy or drunkenness, I suppose.

A little before supper, feeling more restless than ever, I rejoined, for a moment, my second self. And to find him sitting so quietly was surprising, like something against nature, inhuman.

I developed my plan in a hurried whisper.

"I shall stand in as close as I dare and then put her round. I shall presently find means to smuggle you out of here into the sail-locker, which communicates with the lobby. But there is an opening, a sort of square for hauling the sails out, which gives straight on the quarterdeck and which is never closed in fine weather, so as to give air to the sails. When the ship's way is deadened in stays[7] and all the hands are aft at the main braces you shall have a clear road to slip out and get overboard through the open quarter-deck port. I've had them both fastened up. Use a rope's end to lower yourself into the water so as to avoid a splash—you know. It could be heard and cause some beastly complication."

He kept silent for a while, then whispered, "I understand."

"I won't be there to see you go," I began with an effort. "The rest . . . I only hope I have understood too."

"You have. From first to last"—and for the first time there seemed to be a faltering, something strained in his whisper. He caught hold of my arm, but the ringing of the supper bell made me start. He didn't though; he only released his grip.

After supper I didn't come below again till well past eight o'clock. The faint, steady breeze was loaded with dew; and the wet, darkened sails held all there was of propelling power in it. The night, clear and starry, sparkled darkly, and the opaque, lightless patches shifting slowly amongst the low stars were the drifting islets. On the port bow there was a big one more distant and shadowily imposing by the great space of sky it eclipsed.

On opening the door I had a back view of my very own self looking at a chart. He had come out of the recess and was standing near the table.

"Quite dark enough," I whispered.

He stepped back and leaned against my bed with a level, quiet glance. I sat

7. When the ship's forward motion is slowed or stopped while its head is being turned toward the wind for the purpose of shifting the sail.

on the couch. We had nothing to say to each other. Over our heads the officer of the watch moved here and there. Then I heard him move quickly. I knew what that meant. He was making for the companion; and presently his voice was outside my door.

"We are drawing in pretty fast, sir. Land looks rather close."

"Very well," I answered. "I am coming on deck directly."

I waited till he was gone out of the cuddy, then rose. My double moved too. The time had come to exchange our last whispers, for neither of us was ever to hear each other's natural voice.

"Look here!" I opened a drawer and took out three sovereigns. "Take this, anyhow. I've got six and I'd give you the lot, only I must keep a little money to buy some fruit and vegetables for the crew from native boats as we go through Sunda Straits."

He shook his head.

"Take it," I urged him, whispering desperately. "No one can tell what . . ."

He smiled and slapped meaningly the only pocket of the sleeping jacket. It was not safe, certainly. But I produced a large old silk handkerchief of mine, and tying the three pieces of gold in a corner, pressed it on him. He was touched, I suppose, because he took it at last and tied it quickly round his waist under the jacket, on his bare skin.

Our eyes met; several seconds elapsed, till, our glances still mingled, I extended my hand and turned the lamp out. Then I passed through the cuddy, leaving the door of my room wide open. . . . "Steward!"

He was still lingering in the pantry in the greatness of his zeal, giving a rub-up to a plated cruet stand the last thing before going to bed. Being careful not to wake up the mate, whose room was opposite, I spoke in an undertone.

He looked round anxiously. "Sir!"

"Can you get me a little hot water from the galley?"

"I am afraid, sir, the galley fire's been out for some time now."

"Go and see."

He fled up the stairs.

"Now," I whispered loudly into the saloon—too loudly, perhaps, but I was afraid I couldn't make a sound. He was by my side in an instant—the double captain slipped past the stairs—through a tiny dark passage . . . a sliding door. We were in the sail-locker, scrambling on our knees over the sails. A sudden thought struck me. I saw myself wandering barefooted, bareheaded, the sun beating on my dark poll. I snatched off my floppy hat and tried hurriedly in the dark to ram it on my other self. He dodged and fended off silently. I wonder what he thought had come to me before he understood and suddenly desisted. Our hands met gropingly, lingered united in a steady, motionless clasp for a second. . . . No word was breathed by either of us when they separated.

I was standing quietly by the pantry door when the steward returned.

"Sorry, sir. Kettle barely warm. Shall I light the spirit-lamp?"

"Never mind."

I came out on deck slowly. It was now a matter of conscience to shave the land as close as possible—for now he must go overboard whenever the ship was put in stays. Must! There could be no going back for him. After a moment I walked over to leeward and my heart flew into my mouth at the nearness of the land on the bow. Under any other circumstances I would not have held on a minute longer. The second mate had followed me anxiously.

I looked on till I felt I could command my voice.

"She will weather," I said then in a quiet tone.

"Are you going to try that, sir?" he stammered out incredulously.

I took no notice of him and raised my tone just enough to be heard by the helmsman.

"Keep her good full."[8]

"Good full, sir."

The wind fanned my cheek, the sails slept, the world was silent. The strain of watching the dark loom of the land grow bigger and denser was too much for me. I had to shut my eyes—because the ship must go closer. She must! The stillness was intolerable. Were we standing still?"

When I opened my eyes the second view started my heart with a thump. The black southern hill of Koh-ring seemed to hang right over the ship like a towering fragment of the everlasting night. On that enormous mass of blackness there was not a gleam to be seen, not a sound to be heard. It was gliding irresistibly towards us and yet seemed already within reach of the hand. I saw the vague figures of the watch grouped in the waist, gazing in awed silence.

"Are you going on, sir?" inquired an unsteady voice at my elbow.

I ignored it. I had to go on.

"Keep her full. Don't check her way. That won't do now," I said warningly.

"I can't see the sails very well," the helmsman answered me, in strange, quavering tones.

Was she close enough? Already she was, I won't say in the shadow of the land, but in the very blackness of it, already swallowed up as it were, gone too close to be recalled, gone from me altogether.

"Give the mate a call," I said to the young man who stood at my elbow as still as death. "And turn all hands up."

My tone had a borrowed loudness reverberated from the height of the land. Several voices cried out together, "We are all on deck, sir."

Then stillness again, with the great shadow gliding closer, towering higher, without a light, without a sound. Such a hush had fallen on the ship that she might have been a bark of the dead floating in slowly under the very gate of Erebus.

"My God! Where are we?"

It was the mate moaning at my elbow. He was thunderstruck, and as it were deprived of the moral support of his whiskers. He clapped his hands and absolutely cried out, "Lost!"

"Be quiet," I said sternly.

He lowered his tone, but I saw the shadowy gesture of his despair. "What are we doing here?"

8. Keep the ship's sails filled with wind.

"Looking for the land wind."

He made as if to tear his hair, and addressed me recklessly.

"She will never get out. You have done it, sir. I knew it'd end in something like this. She will never weather, and you are too close now to stay. She'll drift ashore before she's round. O my God!"

I caught his arm as he was raising it to batter his poor devoted head, and shook it violently.

"She's ashore already," he wailed, trying to tear himself away.

"Is she? . . . Keep good full there!"

"Good full, sir," cried the helmsman in a frightened, thin, childlike voice.

I hadn't let go the mate's arm and went on shaking it. "Ready about,[9] do you hear? You go forward"—shake—"and stop there"—shake—"and hold your noise"—shake—"and see these head-sheets properly overhauled"—shake, shake—shake.

And all the time I dared not look towards the land lest my heart should fail me. I released my grip at last and he ran forward as if fleeing for dear life.

I wondered what my double there in the sail-locker thought of this commotion. He was able to hear everything—and perhaps he was able to understand why, on my conscience, it had to be thus close—no less. My first order "Hard alee!" re-echoed ominously under the towering shadow of Koh-ring as if I had shouted in a mountain gorge. And then I watched the land intently. In that smooth water and light wind it was impossible to feel the ship coming-to.[1] No! I could not feel her. And my second self was making now ready to slip out and lower himself overboard. Perhaps he was gone already. . . ?

The great black mass brooding over our very mast-heads began to pivot away from the ship's side silently. And now I forgot the secret stranger ready to depart, and remembered only that I was a total stranger to the ship. I did not know her. Would she do it? How was she to be handled?

I swung the mainyard and waited helplessly. She was perhaps stopped, and her very fate hung in the balance, with the black mass of Koh-ring like the gate of the everlasting night towering over her taffrail. What would she do now? Had she way on her[2] yet? I stepped to the side swiftly, and on the shadowy water I could see nothing except a faint phosphorescent flash revealing the glassy smoothness of the sleeping surface. It was impossible to tell—and I had not learned yet the feel of my ship. Was she moving? What I needed was something easily seen, a piece of paper, which I could throw overboard and watch. I had nothing on me. To run down for it I didn't dare. There was no time. All at once my strained, yearning stare distinguished a white object floating within a yard of the ship's side—white, on the black water. A phosphorescent flash passed under it. What was that thing? . . . I recognized my own floppy hat. It must have fallen off his head . . . and he didn't bother. Now I had what I wanted—the saving mark for my eyes. But I hardly thought of my other self, now gone from

9. Be ready to shift the sails (tack). The head-sheets, below, are the lines attached to the sails of the forward mast, and to overhaul is to slacken a rope by pulling it in the opposite direction to that used in hoisting a sail and thus loosening the blocks. 1. Coming to a standstill. 2. Was she moving?

the ship, to be hidden for ever from all friendly faces, to be a fugitive and a vagabond on the earth, with no brand of the curse on his sane forehead to stay a slaying hand . . . too proud to explain.

And I watched the hat—the expression of my sudden pity for his mere flesh. It had been meant to save his homeless head from the dangers of the sun. And now—behold—it was saving the ship, by serving me for a mark to help out the ignorance of my strangeness. Ha! It was drifting forward, warning me just in time that the ship had gathered sternway.

"Shift the helm," I said in a low voice to the seaman standing still like a statue.

The man's eyes glistened wildly in the binnacle light as he jumped round to the other side and spun round the wheel.

I walked to the break of the poop. On the overshadowed deck all hands stood by the forebraces waiting for my order. The stars ahead seemed to be gliding from right to left. And all was so still in the world that I heard the quiet remark, "She's round," passed in a tone of intense relief between two seamen.

"Let go and haul."

The foreyards ran round with a great noise, amidst cheery cries. And now the frightful whiskers made themselves heard giving various orders. Already the ship was drawing ahead. And I was alone with her. Nothing! no one in the world should stand now between us, throwing a shadow on the way of silent knowledge and mute affection; the perfect communion of a seaman with his first command.

Walking to the taffrail, I was in time to make out, on the very edge of a darkness thrown by a towering black mass like the very gateway of Erebus—yes, I was in time to catch an evanescent glimpse of my white hat left behind to mark the spot where the secret sharer of my cabin and of my thoughts, as though he were my second self, had lowered himself into the water to take his punishment: a free man, a proud swimmer striking out for a new destiny.

1912

The first paragraph of the story clearly functions as exposition, especially in describing the setting, the place and time of day. Its last sentence suggests something of the situation—the speaker is alone with *his* ship. It also establishes the focus and voice. In the description of the scene in the Gulf of Siam, there are some words that, though appropriate, are not necessarily inevitable. These are words that might not be used by just any narrator or in just any circumstances and so may characterize the speaker or his situation. In the first sentence alone you may notice "mysterious," "incomprehensible," even "crazy," which, though it deals with the physical irregularity of the fences, also suggests the irrational. These words arouse suspense and so further the plot, but they may also suggest something of the theme. And, since another speaker would be likely to see things somewhat differently and use different words, his choices may also characterize the speaker. Some of the details of the paragraph may also be symbolic.

1. How does the second paragraph further advance the description of setting, of situation, of theme? Are any of the details here symbolic or potentially symbolic? The last sentence of this paragraph seems to relate directly to theme, though it may also help characterize the narrator. There are many such sentences in the story—an example might be "And suddenly I rejoiced in the great security of the sea . . ." (par. 17). Collect five or six such sentences and see how they relate not only to theme but to other elements.

2. How does par. 7 characterize the second mate, explain the narrator's situation, and further arouse suspense and further define the theme?

3. How does the description of the episode with the scorpion (par. 8) characterize the chief mate, and, when looked back upon later, further the plot and suspense? How does the chief mate's propensity for logical explanations relate to the theme?

4. How does the "unconventional arrangement" of the narrator-captain's standing the first anchor-watch relate to his character? to the plot? to the theme(s)?

5. When the narrator notices that the rope side-ladder has not been hauled in, he blames himself for having disturbed the ship's routine, "the very soul of discipline," and conjectures about how he will look in the eyes of the officers and crew and how his conduct will be "accounted" for by the chief mate. All this relates to the characters of the two men, the plot or suspense, and the theme. It is just then that "the secret sharer" appears at the very end of that same ladder. Is he, then, in some way symbolic? If so, how? In the light of all that follows, is it good or bad to break the rules? Does following or breaking rules seem to have anything to do with being a captain? Explain.

6. What is the effect of par. 20, in which "something elongated and pale" appears at the bottom of the ladder? How many elements are involved in that description (including the first sentence of the next paragraph)?

7. When Leggatt comes aboard and is dressed in the captain's sleeping suit, he is described as looking like the captain's "double." That, plus Leggatt's arriving from the sea naked, looking like a fish, being phosphorescent and oblong, plus the title of the story, and the narrator's seeing his first command as a test, has led a substantial number of critics and other readers to see these details as Freudian symbols and to see in this story a Freudian, or at least a psychological, theme. Make out the best case you can for such a reading of the story. What happens to the specifics of the situation, the characters, the plot? Which details are symbolic in your version and which are not? Now make out

the best case *against* such a reading. If you are so committed to one position or the other that you cannot see how there can be another side, pair yourself off with someone else in the class who has made the best counter-argument.

8. When Leggatt tells his story there is a shift in the focus and voice. How does this story within a story function in the plot of "The Secret Sharer"? How does it help define the character of Leggatt? How does it relate to the theme of "the double" in the larger story?

9. Why does the captain hide Leggatt rather than turn him in? How do all the elements of the story contribute to your answering this question?

10. The captain of the *Sephora* tells his version of Leggatt's crime, but the narrator says, "It is not worth while to record that version. It was just over two months since all this had happened, and . . . he seemed completely muddled . . ." (par. 128). Yet the narrator is telling his and Leggatt's story at a "distance of years," and there is a bit of Archbold's story in the page that follows. Write a fuller (two- or three-page) version of how the *Sephora* captain would tell the story. How does this shift in focus and voice affect the plot? the characterization of the captain of the *Sephora?* of Leggatt? of the narrator of "The Secret Sharer"? the theme?

11. Archbold believes Leggatt was too gentlemanly to be chief mate of the *Sephora*, and the narrator, so identified now with Leggatt, thinks Archbold would not consider the narrator himself a suitable chief mate (much less captain). How would you analyze this notion in terms of focus? character? symbol? theme?

12. There seems to be a turn in the story after Archbold leaves: ironically, Leggatt seems more of a burden to the narrator, who now seems to see himself in his role as captain: "I was not wholly alone with my command; for there was that stranger in my cabin. . . . Part of me was absent" (par. 194). What is the effect of this feeling of split identity on the plot? How does it relate to focus? The whole story can be read as the initiation of the narrator into leadership or captaincy. How does Leggatt figure in that initiation theme? How does his character relate to it? Is he a symbol? If you think he is, of what is he a symbol? How do the final episode and final two paragraphs of the story relate to this portion of the plot, this view of Leggatt, this theme? Can you imagine this story—the story of a new captain taking over command of a strange ship, with mates not of his own choosing and not of his own "kind," of the strained relations between the new captain and the other officers, of his routine and unroutine orders, of his emotional state, and of his first daring act of seamanship, of all this—without any mention of, or presence of, or story of, a Leggatt, a secret sharer? Write a brief synopsis of such a story. Is there some way in which you

might still call it "The Secret Sharer"? Who has the secret and with whom does he share it?

13. How does the captain's giving Leggatt his hat figure in the plot? What does it suggest about the narrator's character and feelings? Of what, if anything, might it be a symbol?

14. Write a sequel to "The Secret Sharer" about what happens to Leggatt after he leaves the ship, using as much evidence as you can from the elements and details of Conrad's story but with a new focus and voice.

The story that follows is funnier than, but just as serious as, "The Secret Sharer." It is the title story, or chapter, of a work that calls itself a novel but can also be seen as a collection of related but separable stories (indeed, many of the chapters were first published separately as stories). Reading the whole novel or collection may enrich your understanding and enjoyment of the parts but this story is, as you will see, quite wonderful, enjoyable, and understandable by itself. It is a somewhat unfamiliar world you will be entering; though nearer to us in time and space, it is perhaps even stranger than the world of "The Secret Sharer." Stop reading after paragraph 18, look at item 1 below (p. 293), and get your bearings.

LOUISE ERDRICH

Love Medicine

I never really done much with my life, I suppose. I never had a television. Grandma Kashpaw had one inside her apartment at the Senior Citizens, so I used to go there and watch my favorite shows. For a while she used to call me the biggest waste on the reservation and hark back to how she saved me from my own mother, who wanted to tie me in a potato sack and throw me in a slough. Sure, I was grateful to Grandma Kashpaw for saving me like that, for raising me, but gratitude gets old. After a while, stale. I had to stop thanking her. One day I told her I had paid her back in full by staying at her beck and call. I'd do anything for Grandma. She knew that. Besides, I took care of Grandpa like nobody else could, on account of what a handful he'd gotten to be.

But that was nothing. I know the tricks of mind and body inside out without ever having trained for it, because I got the touch. It's a thing you got to be born with. I got secrets in my hands that nobody ever knew to ask. Take Grandma Kashpaw with her tired veins all knotted up in her legs like clumps of blue snails. I take my fingers and I snap them on the knots. The medicine flows out of me. The touch. I run my fingers up the maps of those rivers of veins or I knock very gentle above their hearts or I make a circling motion on their stomachs, and it helps them. They feel much better. Some women pay me five dollars.

I couldn't do the touch for Grandpa, though. He was a hard nut. You know, some people fall right through the hole in their lives. It's invisible, but they come to it after time, never knowing where. There is this woman here, Lulu Lamartine, who always had a thing for Grandpa. She loved him since she was a girl and always said he was a genius. Now she says that his mind got so full it exploded.

How can I doubt that? I know the feeling when your mental power builds up too far. I always used to say that's why the Indians got drunk. Even statistically we're the smartest people on the earth. Anyhow with Grandpa I couldn't hardly believe it, because all my youth he stood out as a hero to me. When he started getting toward second childhood he went through different moods. He would stand in the woods and cry at the top of his shirt. It scared me, scared everyone, Grandma worst of all.

Yet he was so smart—do you believe it?—that he *knew* he was getting foolish.

He said so. He told me that December I failed school and come back on the train to Hoopdance. I didn't have nowhere else to go. He picked me up there and he said it straight out: "I'm getting into my second childhood." And then he said something else I still remember: "I been chosen for it. I couldn't say no." So I figure that a man so smart all his life—tribal chairman and the star of movies and even pictured in the statehouse and on cans of snuff—would know what he's doing by saying yes. I think he was called to second childhood like anybody else gets a call for the priesthood or the army or whatever. So I really did not listen too hard when the doctor said this was some kind of disease old people got eating too much sugar. You just can't tell me that a man who went to Washington and gave them bureaucrats what for could lose his mind from eating too much Milky Way. No, he put second childhood on himself.

Behind those songs he sings out in the middle of Mass, and back of those stories that everybody knows by heart, Grandpa is thinking hard about life. I know the feeling. Sometimes I'll throw up a smokescreen to think behind. I'll hitch up to Winnipeg and play the Space Invaders for six hours, but all the time there and back I will be thinking some fairly deep thoughts that surprise even me, and I'm used to it. As for him, if it was just the thoughts there wouldn't be no problem. Smokescreen is what irritates the social structure, see, and Grandpa has done things that just distract people to the point they want to throw him in the cookie jar where they keep the mentally insane. He's far from that, I know for sure, but even Grandma had trouble keeping her patience once he started sneaking off to Lamartine's place. He's not supposed to have his candy, and Lulu feeds it to him. That's *one* of the reasons why he goes.

Grandma tried to get me to put the touch on Grandpa soon after he began stepping out. I didn't want to, but before Grandma started telling me again what a bad state my bare behind was in when she first took me home, I thought I should at least pretend.

I put my hands on either side of Grandpa's head. You wouldn't look at him and say he was crazy. He's a fine figure of a man, as Lamartine would say, with all his hair and half his teeth, a beak like a hawk, and cheeks like the blades of a hatchet. They put his picture on all the tourist guides to North Dakota and even copied his face for artistic paintings. I guess you could call him a monument all of himself. He started grinning when I put my hands on his templates, and I knew right then he knew how come I touched him. I knew the smokescreen was going to fall.

And I was right: just for a moment it fell.

"Let's pitch whoopee," he said across my shoulder to Grandma.

They don't use that expression much around here anymore, but for damn sure it must have meant something. It got her goat right quick.

She threw my hands off his head herself and stood in front of him, overmatching him pound for pound, and taller too, for she had a growth spurt in middle age while he had shrunk, so now the length and breadth of her surpassed him. She glared up and spoke her piece into his face about how he was off at all hours tomcatting and chasing Lamartine again and making a damn old fool of himself.

"And you got no more whoopee to pitch anymore anyhow!" she yelled at last, surprising me so my jaw just dropped, for us kids all had pretended for so long that those rustling sounds we heard from their side of the room at night never happened. She sure had pretended it, up till now, anyway. I saw that tears were in her eyes. And that's when I saw how much grief and love she felt for him. And it gave me a real shock to the system. You see I thought love got easier over the years so it didn't hurt so bad when it hurt, or feel so good when it felt good. I thought it smoothed out and old people hardly noticed it. I thought it curled up and died, I guess. Now I saw it rear up like a whip and lash.

She loved him. She was jealous. She mourned him like the dead.

And he just smiled into the air, trapped in the seams of his mind.

So I didn't know what to do. I was in a laundry then. They was like parents to me, the way they had took me home and reared me. I could see her point for wanting to get him back the way he was so at least she could argue with him, sleep with him, not be shamed out by Lamartine. She'd always love him. That hit me like a ton of bricks. For one whole day I felt this odd feeling that cramped my hands. When you have the touch, that's where longing gets you. I never loved like that. It made me feel all inspired to see them fight, and I wanted to go out and find a woman who I would love until one of us died or went crazy. But I'm not like that really. From time to time I heal a person all up good inside, however when it comes to the long shot I doubt that I got staying power.

And you need that, staying power, going out to love somebody. I knew this quality was not going to jump on me with no effort. So I turned my thoughts back to Grandma and Grandpa. I felt her side of it with my hands and my tangled guts, and I felt his side of it within the stretch of my mentality. He had gone out to lunch one day and never came back. He was fishing in the middle of Lake Turcot. And there was big thoughts on his line, and he kept throwing them back for even bigger ones that would explain to him, say, the meaning of how we got here and why we have to leave so soon. All in all, I could not see myself treating Grandpa with the touch, bringing him back, when the real part of him had chose to be off thinking somewhere. It was only the rest of him that stayed around causing trouble, after all, and we could handle most of it without any problem.

Besides, it was hard to argue with his reasons for doing some things. Take Holy Mass. I used to go there just every so often, when I got frustrated mostly, because even though I know the Higher Power dwells everyplace, there's something very calming about the cool greenish inside of our mission. Or so I thought, anyway. Grandpa was the one who stripped off my delusions in this matter, for it was he who busted right through what Father Upsala calls the sacred serenity of the place.

We filed in that time. Me and Grandpa. We sat down in our pews. Then the rosary got started up pre-Mass and that's when Grandpa filled up his chest and opened his mouth and belted out them words.

HAIL MARIE FULL OF GRACE.

He had a powerful set of lungs.

And he kept on like that. He did not let up. He hollered and he yelled them prayers, and I guess people was used to him by now, because they only muttered theirs and did not quit and gawk like I did. I was getting red-faced, I admit. I give him the elbow once or twice, but that wasn't nothing to him. He kept on. He shrieked to heaven and he pleaded like a movie actor and he pounded his chest like Tarzan in the Lord I Am Not Worthies. I thought he might hurt himself. Then after a while I guess I got used to it, and that's when I wondered: how come?

So afterwards I out and asked him. "How come? How come you yelled?"

"God don't hear me otherwise," said Grandpa Kashpaw.

I sweat. I broke right into a little cold sweat at my hairline because I knew this was perfectly right and for years not one damn other person had noticed it. God's been going deaf. Since the Old Testament, God's been deafening up on us. I read, see. Besides the dictionary, which I'm constantly in use of, I had this Bible once. I read it. I found there was discrepancies between then and now. It struck me. Here God used to raineth bread from clouds, smite the Phillipines, sling fire down on red-light districts where people got stabbed. He even appeared in person every once in a while. God used to pay attention, is what I'm saying.

Now there's your God in the Old Testament and there is Chippewa Gods as well. Indian Gods, good and bad, like tricky Nanabozho or the water monster, Missepeshu, who lives over in Lake Turcot. That water monster was the last God I ever heard to appear. It had a weakness for young girls and grabbed one of the Blues off her rowboat. She got to shore all right, but only after this monster had its way with her. She's an old lady now. Old Lady Blue. She still won't let her family fish that lake.

Our Gods aren't perfect, is what I'm saying, but at least they come around. They'll do a favor if you ask them right. You don't have to yell. But you do have to know, like I said, how to ask in the right way. That makes problems, because to ask proper was an art that was lost to the Chippewas once the Catholics gained ground. Even now, I have to wonder if Higher Power turned it back, if we got to yell, or if we just don't speak its language.

I looked around me. How else could I explain what all I had seen in my short life—King smashing his fist in things, Gordie drinking himself down to the Bismarck hospitals, or Aunt June left by a white man to wander off in the snow. How else to explain the times my touch don't work, and farther back, to the oldtime Indians who was swept away in the outright germ warfare and dirty-dog killing of the whites. In those times, us Indians was so much kindlier than now.

We took them in.

Oh yes, I'm bitter as an old cutworm just thinking of how they done to us and doing still.

So Grandpa Kashpaw just opened my eyes a little there. Was there any sense relying on a God whose ears was stopped? Just like the government? I says then, right off, maybe we got nothing but ourselves. And that's not much, just personally speaking. I know I don't got the cold hard potatoes it takes to understand everything. Still, there's things I'd like to do. For instance, I'd like to help some people like my Grandpa and Grandma Kashpaw get back some happiness within the tail ends of their lives.

I told you once before I couldn't see my way clear to putting the direct touch on Grandpa's mind, and I kept my moral there, but something soon happened to make me think a little bit of mental adjustment wouldn't do him and the rest of us no harm.

It was after we saw him one afternoon in the sunshine courtyard of the Senior Citizens with Lulu Lamartine. Grandpa used to like to dig there. He had his little dandelion fork out, and he was prying up them dandelions right and left while Lamartine watched him.

"He's scratching up the dirt, all right," said Grandma, watching Lamartine watch Grandpa out the window.

Now Lamartine was about half the considerable size of Grandma, but you would never think of sizes anyway. They were different in an even more noticeable way. It was the difference between a house fixed up with paint and picky fence, and a house left to weather away into the soft earth, is what I'm saying. Lamartine was jacked up, latticed, shuttered, and vinyl sided, while Grandma sagged and bulged on her slipped foundations and let her hair go the silver gray of rain-dried lumber. Right now, she eyed the Lamartine's pert flowery dress with such a look it despaired me. I knew what this could lead to with Grandma. Alternating tongue storms and rock-hard silences was hard on a man, even one who didn't notice, like Grandpa. So I went fetching him.

But he was gone when I popped through the little screen door that led out on the courtyard. There was nobody out there either, to point which way they went. Just the dandelion fork quibbling upright in the ground. That gave me an idea. I snookered over to the Lamartine's door and I listened in first, then knocked. But nobody. So I went walking through the lounges and around the card tables. Still nobody. Finally it was my touch that led me to the laundry room. I cracked the door. I went in. There they were. And he was really loving her up good, boy, and she was going hell for leather. Sheets was flapping on the lines above, and washcloths, pillowcases, shirts was also flying through the air, for they was trying to clear out a place for themselves in a high-heaped but shallow laundry cart. The washers and dryers was all on, chock full of quarters, shaking and moaning. I couldn't hear what Grandpa and the Lamartine was billing and cooing, and they couldn't hear me.

I didn't know what to do, so I went inside and shut the door.

The Lamartine wore a big curly light-brown wig. Looked like one of them squeaky little white-people dogs. Poodles they call them. Anyway, that wig is what saved us from the worse. For I could hardly shout and tell them I was in there, no more could I try and grab him. I was trapped where I was. There was nothing I could really do but hold the door shut. I was scared of somebody else upsetting in and really getting an eyeful. Turned out though, in the heat of the clinch, as I was trying to avert my eyes you see, the Lamartine's curly wig jumped off her head. And if you ever been in the midst of something and had a big change like that occur in the someone, you can't help know how it devastates your basic urges. Not only that, but her wig was almost with a life of its own. Grandpa's eyes were bugging at the change already, and swear to God if the thing didn't rear up and pop him in the face like it was going to start something. He scrambled up, Grandpa did, and the Lamartine jumped up after him all addled looking. They just stared at each other, huffing and puffing, with quizzical expression. The surprise seemed to drive all sense completely out of Grandpa's mind.

"The letter was what started the fire," he said. "I never would have done it."

"What letter?" said the Lamartine. She was stiff-necked now, and elegant, even bald, like some alien queen. I gave her back the wig. The Lamartine replaced it on her head, and whenever I saw her after that, I couldn't help thinking of her bald, with special powers, as if from another planet.

"That was a close call," I said to Grandpa after she had left.

But I think he had already forgot the incident. He just stood there all quiet and thoughtful. You really wouldn't think he was crazy. He looked like he was just about to say something important, explaining himself. He said something, all right, but it didn't have nothing to do with anything that made sense.

He wondered where the heck he put his dandelion fork. That's when I decided about the mental adjustment.

Now what was mostly our problem was not so much that he was not all there, but that what was there of him often hankered after Lamartine. If we could put a stop to that, I thought, we might be getting someplace. But here, see, my touch was of no use. For what could I snap my fingers at to make him faithful to Grandma? Like the quality of staying power, this faithfulness was invisible. I know it's something that you got to acquire, but I never known where from. Maybe there's no rhyme or reason to it, like my getting the touch, and then again maybe it's a kind of magic.

It was Grandma Kashpaw who thought of it in the end. She knows things. Although she will not admit she has a scrap of Indian blood in her, there's no doubt in my mind she's got some Chippewa. How else would you explain the way she'll be sitting there, in front of her TV story, rocking in her armchair and suddenly she turns on me, her brown eyes hard as lake-bed flint.

"Lipsha Morrissey," she'll say, "you went out last night and got drunk."

How did she know that? I'll hardly remember it myself. Then she'll say she just had a feeling or ache in the scar of her hand or a creak in her shoulder. She is constantly being told things by little aggravations in her joints or by her household appliances. One time she told Gordie never to ride with a crazy Lamartine boy. She had seen something in the polished-up tin of her bread toaster. So he didn't. Sure enough, the time came we heard how Lyman and Henry went out of control in their car, ending up in the river. Lyman swam to the top, but Henry never made it.

Thanks to Grandma's toaster, Gordie was probably spared.

Someplace in the blood Grandma Kashpaw knows things. She also remem- 50
bers things, I found. She keeps things filed away. She's got a memory like them video games that don't forget your score. One reason she remembers so many details about the trouble I gave her in early life is so she can flash back her total when she needs to.

Like now. Take the love medicine. I don't know where she remembered that from. It came tumbling from her mind like an asteroid off the corner of the screen.

Of course she starts out by mentioning the time I had this accident in church and did she leave me there with wet overhalls? No she didn't. And ain't I glad? Yes I am. Now what you want now, Grandma?

But when she mentions them love medicines, I feel my back prickle at the danger. These love medicines is something of an old Chippewa specialty. No other tribe has got them down so well. But love medicines is not for the layman to handle. You don't just go out and get one without paying for it. Before you get one, even, you should go through one hell of a lot of mental condensation. You got to think it over. Choose the right one. You could really mess up your life grinding up the wrong little thing.

So anyhow, I said to Grandma I'd give this love medicine some thought. I knew the best thing was to go ask a specialist like Old Man Pillager, who lives up in a tangle of bush and never shows himself. But the truth is I was afraid of him, like everyone else. He was known for putting the twisted mouth on people, seizing up their hearts. Old Man Pillager was serious business, and I have always thought it best to steer clear of that whenever I could. That's why I took the powers in my own hands. That's why I did what I could.

I put my whole mentality to it, nothing held back. After a while I started to 55
remember things I'd heard gossiped over.

I heard of this person once who carried a charm of seeds that looked like baby pearls. They was attracted to a metal knife, which made them powerful. But I didn't know where them seeds grew. Another love charm I heard about I couldn't go along with, because how was I suppose to catch frogs in the act, which it required. Them little creatures is slippery and fast. And then the powerfullest of all, the most extreme, involved nail clips and such. I wasn't anywhere near asking Grandma to provide me all the little body bits that this last love recipe called for. I went walking around for days just trying to think up something that would work.

Well I got it. If it hadn't been the early fall of the year, I never would have got it. But I was sitting underneath a tree one day down near the school just watching people's feet go by when something tells me, look up! Look up! So I look up, and I see two honkers, Canada geese, the kind with little masks on their faces, a bird what mates for life. I see them flying right over my head naturally preparing to land in some slough on the reservation, which they certainly won't get off of alive.

It hits me, anyway. Them geese, they mate for life. And I think to myself, just what if I went out and got a pair? And just what if I fed some part—say the goose heart—of the female to Grandma and Grandpa ate the other heart? Wouldn't that work? Maybe it's all invisible, and then maybe again it's magic. Love is a stony road. We know that for sure. If it's true that the higher feelings of devotion get lodged in the heart like people say, then we'd be home free. If not, eating goose heart couldn't harm nobody anyway. I thought it was worth my effort, and Grandma Kashpaw thought so, too. She had always known a good idea when she heard one. She borrowed me Grandpa's gun.

So I went out to this particular slough, maybe the exact same slough I never got thrown in by my mother, thanks to Grandma Kashpaw, and I hunched down in a good comfortable pile of rushes. I got my gun loaded up. I ate a few of these soft baloney sandwiches Grandma made me for lunch. And then I waited. The cattails blown back and forth above my head. Them stringy blue herons was spearing up their prey. The thing I know how to do best in this world, the thing I been training for all my life, is to wait. Sitting there and sitting there was no hardship on me. I got to thinking about some funny things that happened. There was this one time that Lulu Lamartine's little blue tweety bird, a paraclete, I guess you'd call it, flown up inside her dress and got lost within there. I recalled her running out into the hallway trying to yell something, shaking. She was doing a right good jig there, cutting the rug for sure, and the thing is it *never* flown out. To this day people speculate where it went. They fear she might perhaps of crushed it in her corsets. It sure hasn't ever yet been seen alive. I thought of funny things for a while, but then I used them up, and strange things that happened started weaseling their way into my mind.

I got to thinking quite naturally of the Lamartine's cousin named Wristwatch. I never knew what his real name was. They called him Wristwatch because he got his father's broken wristwatch as a young boy when his father passed on. Never in his whole life did Wristwatch take his father's watch off. He didn't care if it worked, although after a while he got sensitive when people asked what time it was, teasing him. He often put it to his ear like he was listening to the tick. But it was broken for good and forever, people said so, at least that's what they thought.

Well I saw Wristwatch smoking in his pickup one afternoon and by nine that evening he was dead.

He died sitting at the Lamartine's table, too. As she told it, Wristwatch had just eaten himself a good-size dinner and she said would he take seconds on the hot dish when he fell over to the floor. They turnt him over. He was gone. But here's the strange thing: when the Senior Citizen's orderly took the pulse he noticed that the wristwatch Wristwatch wore was now working. The moment he died the wristwatch started keeping perfect time. They buried him with the watch still ticking on his arm.

I got to thinking. What if some gravediggers dug up Wristwatch's casket in two hundred years and that watch was still going? I thought what question they would ask and it was this: Whose hand wound it?

I started shaking like a piece of grass at just the thought.

Not to get off the subject or nothing. I was still hunkered in the slough. It was passing late into the afternoon and still no honkers had touched down. Now I don't need to tell you that the waiting did not get to me, it was the chill. The rushes was very soft, but damp. I was getting cold and debating to leave, when they landed. Two geese swimming here and there as big as life, looking deep into each other's little pinhole eyes. Just the ones I was looking for. So I lifted Grandpa's gun to my shoulder and I aimed perfectly, and *blam! Blam!* I delivered two accurate shots. But the thing is, them shots missed. I couldn't hardly believe it. Whether it was that the stock had warped or the barrel got bent someways, I don't quite know, but anyway them geese flown off into the dim sky, and Lipsha Morrissey was left there in the rushes with evening fallen and his two cold hands empty. He had before him just the prospect of another day of bone-cracking chill in them rushes, and the thought of it got him depressed.

Now it isn't my style, in no way, to get depressed.

So I said to myself, Lipsha Morrissey, you're a happy S.O.B. who could be covered up with weeds by now down at the bottom of this slough, but instead you're alive to tell the tale. You might have problems in life, but you still got the touch. You got the power, Lipsha Morrissey. Can't argue that. So put your mind to it and figure out how not to be depressed.

I took my advice. I put my mind to it. But I never saw at the time how my thoughts led me astray toward a tragic outcome none could have known. I ignored all the danger, all the limits, for I was tired of sitting in the slough and my feet were numb. My face was aching. I was chilled, so I played with fire. I told myself love medicine was simple. I told myself the old superstitions was just that—strange beliefs. I told myself to take the ten dollars Mary MacDonald had paid me for putting the touch on her arthritis joint, and the other five I hadn't spent yet from winning bingo last Thursday. I told myself to go down to the Red Owl store.

And here is what I did that made the medicine backfire. I took an evil shortcut. I looked at birds that was dead and froze.

All right. So now I guess you will say, "Slap a malpractice suit on Lipsha Morrissey."

I heard of those suits. I used to think it was a color clothing quack doctors had to wear so you could tell them from the good ones. Now I know better that it's law.

As I walked back from the Red Owl with the rock-hard, heavy turkeys, I argued to myself about malpractice. I thought of faith. I thought to myself that faith could be called belief against the odds and whether or not there's any proof.

How does that sound? I thought how we might have to yell to be heard by Higher Power, but that's not saying it's not *there*. And that is faith for you. It's belief even when the goods don't deliver. Higher Power makes promises we all know they can't back up, but anybody ever go and slap an old malpractice suit on God? Or the U.S. government? No they don't. Faith might be stupid, but it gets us through. So what I'm heading at is this. I finally convinced myself that the real actual power to the love medicine was not the goose heart itself but the faith in the cure.

I didn't believe it, I knew it was wrong, but by then I had waded so far into my lie I was stuck there. And then I went one step further.

The next day, I cleaned the hearts away from the paper packages of gizzards inside the turkeys. Then I wrapped them hearts with a clean hankie and brung them both to get blessed up at the mission. I wanted to get official blessings from the priest, but when Father answered the door to the rectory, wiping his hands on a little towel, I could tell he was a busy man.

"Booshoo,[1] Father," I said. "I got a slight request to make of you this afternoon."

"What is it?" he said.

"Would you bless this package?" I held out the hankie with the hearts tied inside it.

He looked at the package, questioning it.

"It's turkey hearts," I honestly had to reply.

A look of annoyance crossed his face.

"Why don't you bring this matter over to Sister Martin," he said. "I have duties."

And so, although the blessing wouldn't be as powerful, I went over to the Sisters with the package.

I rung the bell, and they brought Sister Martin to the door. I had her as a music teacher, but I was always so shy then. I never talked out loud. Now, I had grown taller than Sister Martin. Looking down, I saw that she was not feeling up to snuff. Brown circles hung under her eyes.

"What's the matter?" she said, not noticing who I was.

"Remember me, Sister?"

She squinted up at me.

"Oh yes," she said after a moment. "I'm sorry, you're the youngest of the Kashpaws. Gordie's brother."

Her face warmed up.

"Lipsha," I said, "that's my name."

"Well, Lipsha," she said, smiling broad at me now, "what can I do for you?"

They always said she was the kindest-hearted of the Sisters up the hill, and she was. She brought me back into their own kitchen and made me take a big yellow wedge of cake and a glass of milk.

"Now tell me," she said, nodding at my package. "What have you got wrapped up so carefully in those handkerchiefs?"

Like before, I answered honestly.

1. *Bonjour*, French for "good day."

"Ah," said Sister Martin. "Turkey hearts." She waited.

"I hoped you could bless them."

She waited some more, smiling with her eyes. Kindhearted though she was, I began to sweat. A person could not pull the wool down over Sister Martin. I stumbled through my mind for an explanation, quick, that wouldn't scare her off.

"They're a present," I said, "for Saint Kateri's statue."

"She's not a saint yet."

"I know," I stuttered on, "in the hopes they will crown her."

"Lipsha," she said, "I never heard of such a thing."

So I told her. "Well the truth is," I said, "it's a kind of medicine."

"For what?"

"Love."

"Oh Lipsha," she said after a moment, "you don't need any medicine. I'm sure any girl would like you exactly the way you are."

I just sat there. I felt miserable, caught in my pack of lies.

"Tell you what," she said, seeing how bad I felt, "my blessing won't make any difference anyway. But there is something you can do."

I looked up at her hopeless.

"Just be yourself."

I looked down at my plate. I knew I wasn't much to brag about right then, and I shortly became even less. For as I walked out the door I stuck my fingers in the cup of holy water that was sacred from their touches. I put my fingers in and blessed the hearts, quick, with my own hand.

I went back to Grandma and sat down in her little kitchen at the Senior Citizens. I unwrapped them hearts on the table, and her hard agate eyes went soft. She said she wasn't even going to cook those hearts up but eat them raw so their power would go down strong as possible.

I couldn't hardly watch when she munched hers. Now that's true love. I was worried about how she would get Grandpa to eat his, but she told me she'd think of something and don't worry. So I did not. I was supposed to hide off in her bedroom while she put dinner on a plate for Grandpa and fixed up the heart so he'd eat it. I caught a glint of the plate she was making for him. She put that heart smack on a piece of lettuce like in a restaurant and then attached to it a little heap of boiled peas.

He sat down. I was listening in the next room.

She said, "Why don't you have some mash potato?" So he had some mash potato. Then she gave him a little piece of boiled meat. He ate that. Then she said, "Why you didn't never touch your salad yet. See that heart? I'm feeding you it because the doctor said your blood needs building up."

I couldn't help it, at that point I peeked through a crack in the door.

I saw Grandpa picking at that heart on his plate with a certain look. He didn't look appetized at all, is what I'm saying. I doubted our plan was going to work. Grandma was getting worried, too. She told him one more time, loudly, that he had to eat that heart.

"Swallow it down," she said. "You'll hardly notice it."

He just looked at her straight on. The way he looked at her made me think I was going to see the smokescreen drop a second time, and sure enough it happened.

"What you want me to eat this for so bad?" he asked her uncannily.

Now Grandma knew the jig was up. She knew that he knew she was working medicine. He put his fork down. He rolled the heart around his saucer plate.

"I don't want to eat this," he said to Grandma. "It don't look good."

"Why it's fresh grade-A," she told him. "One hundred percent."

He didn't ask percent what, but his eyes took on an even more warier look.

"Just go on and try it," she said, taking the salt shaker up in her hand. She was getting annoyed. "Not tasty enough? You want me to salt it for you?" She waved the shaker over his plate.

"All right, skinny white girl!" She had got Grandpa mad. Oopsy-daisy, he popped the heart into his mouth. I was about to yawn loudly and come out of the bedroom. I was about ready for this crash of wills to be over, when I saw he was still up to his old tricks. First he rolled it into one side of his cheek. "Mmmmm," he said. Then he rolled it into the other side of his cheek. "Mmmmmmm," again. Then he stuck his tongue out with the heart on it and put it back, and there was no time to react. He had pulled Grandma's leg once too far. Her goat was got. She was so mad she hopped up quick as a wink and slugged him between the shoulderblades to make him swallow.

Only thing is, he choked.

He choked real bad. A person can choke to death. You ever sit down at a restaurant table and up above you there is a list of instructions what to do if something slides down the wrong pipe? It sure makes you chew slow, that's for damn sure. When Grandpa fell off his chair better believe me that little graphic illustrated poster fled into my mind. I jumped out the bedroom. I done everything within my power that I could do to unlodge what was choking him. I squeezed underneath his ribcage. I socked him in the back. I was desperate. But here's the factor of decision: he wasn't choking on the heart alone. There was more to it than that. It was other things that choked him as well. It didn't seem like he wanted to struggle or fight. Death came and tapped his chest, so he went just like that. I'm sorry all through my body at what I done to him with that heart, and there's those who will say Lipsha Morrissey is just excusing himself off the hook by giving song and dance about how Grandpa gave up.

Maybe I can't admit what I did. My touch had gone worthless, that is true. But here is what I seen while he lay in my arms.

You hear a person's life will flash before their eyes when they're in danger. It was him in danger, not me, but it was *his* life come over me. I saw him dying, and it was like someone pulled the shade down in a room. His eyes clouded over and squeezed shut, but just before that I looked in. He was still fishing in the middle of Lake Turcot. Big thoughts was on his line and he had half a case of beer in the boat. He waved at me, grinned, and then the bobber went under.

Grandma had gone out of the room crying for help. I bunched my force up in my hands and I held him. I was so wound up I couldn't even breathe. All the moments he had spent with me, all the times he had hoisted me on his shoulders or pointed into the leaves was concentrated in that moment. Time was flashing back and forth like a pinball machine. Lights blinked and balls hopped and rubber bands chirped, until suddenly I realized the last ball had gone down the drain and there was nothing. I felt his force leaving him, flowing out of Grandpa never to return. I felt his mind weakening. The bobber going under in the lake. And I felt the touch retreat back into the darkness inside my body, from where it came.

One time, long ago, both of us were fishing together. We caught a big old 130
snapper what started towing us around like it was a motor. "This here fishline is pretty damn good," Grandpa said. "Let's keep this turtle on and see where he takes us." So we rode along behind that turtle, watching as from time to time it surfaced. The thing was just about the size of a washtub. It took us all around the lake twice, and as it was traveling, Grandpa said something as a joke. "Lipsha," he said, "we are glad your mother didn't want you because we was always looking for a boy like you who would tow us around the lake."

"I ain't no snapper. Snappers is so stupid they stay alive when their head's chopped off," I said.

"That ain't stupidity," said Grandpa. "Their brain's just in their heart, like yours is."

When I looked up, I knew the fuse had blown between my heart and my mind and that a terrible understanding was to be given.

Grandma got back into the room and I saw her stumble. And then she went down too. It was like a house you can't hardly believe has stood so long, through years of record weather, suddenly goes down in the worst yet. It makes sense, is what I'm saying, but you still can't hardly believe it. You think a person you know has got through death and illness and being broke and living on commodity rice will get through anything. Then they fold and you see how fragile were the stones that underpinned them. You see how instantly the ground can shift you thought was solid. You see the stop signs and the yellow dividing markers of roads you traveled and all the instructions you had played according to vanish. You see how all the everyday things you counted on was just a dream you had been having by which you run your whole life. She had been over me, like a sheer overhang of rock dividing Lipsha Morrissey from outer space. And now she went underneath. It was as though the banks gave way on the shores of Lake Turcot, and where Grandpa's passing was just the bobber swallowed under by his biggest thought, her fall was the house and the rock under it sliding after, sending half the lake splashing up to the clouds.

Where there was nothing. 135

You play them games never knowing what you see. When I fell into the dream alongside of both of them I saw that the dominions I had defended myself from anciently was but delusions of the screen. Blips of light. And I was scot-free now, whistling through space.

I don't know how I come back. I don't know from where. They was slapping my face when I arrived back at Senior Citizens and they was oxygenating her. I saw her chest move, almost unwilling. She sighed the way she would when somebody bothered her in the middle of a row of beads she was counting. I think it irritated her to no end that they brought her back. I knew from the way she looked after they took the mask off, she was not going to forgive them disturbing her restful peace. Nor was she forgiving Lipsha Morrissey. She had been stepping out onto the road of death, she told the children later at the funeral. I asked was there any stop signs or dividing markers on that road, but she clamped her lips in a vise the way she always done when she was mad.

Which didn't bother me. I knew when things had cleared out she wouldn't have no choice. I was not going to speculate where the blame was put for Grandpa's death. We was in it together. She had slugged him between the shoulders. My touch had failed him, never to return.

All the blood children and the took-ins, like me, came home from Minneapolis and Chicago, where they had relocated years ago. They stayed with friends on the reservation or with Aurelia or slept on Grandma's floor. They were struck down with grief and bereavement to be sure, every one of them. At the funeral I sat down in the back of the church with Albertine. She had gotten all skinny and ragged haired from cramming all her years of study into two or three. She had decided that to be a nurse was not enough for her so she was going to be a doctor. But the way she was straining her mind didn't look too hopeful. Her eyes were bloodshot from driving and crying. She took my hand. From the back we watched all the children and the mourners as they hunched over their prayers, their hands stuffed full of Kleenex. It was someplace in that long sad service that my vision shifted. I began to see things different, more clear. The family kneeling down turned to rocks in a field. It struck me how strong and reliable grief was, and death. Until the end of time, death would be our rock.

So I had perspective on it all, for death gives you that. All the Kashpaw children had done various things to me in their lives—shared their folks with me, loaned me cash, beat me up in secret—and I decided, because of death, then and there I'd call it quits. If I ever saw King again, I'd shake his hand. Forgiving somebody else made the whole thing easier to bear.

Everybody saw Grandpa off into the next world. And then the Kashpaws had to get back to their jobs, which was numerous and impressive. I had a few beers with them and I went back to Grandma, who had sort of got lost in the shuffle of everybody being sad about Grandpa and glad to see one another.

Zelda had sat beside her the whole time and was sitting with her now. I wanted to talk to Grandma, say how sorry I was, that it wasn't her fault, but only mine. I would have, but Zelda gave me one of her looks of strict warning as if to say, "I'll take care of Grandma. Don't horn in on the women."

If only Zelda knew, I thought, the sad realities would change her. But of course I couldn't tell the dark truth.

It was evening, late. Grandma's light was on underneath a crack in the door. About a week had passed since we buried Grandpa. I knocked first but there wasn't no answer, so I went right in. The door was unlocked. She was there but she didn't notice me at first. Her hands were tied up in her rosary, and her gaze was fully absorbed in the easy chair opposite her, the one that had always been Grandpa's favorite. I stood there, staring with her, at the little green nubs in the cloth and plastic armrest covers and the sad little hair-tonic stain he had made on the white doily where he laid his head. For the life of me I couldn't figure what she was staring at. Thin space. Then she turned.

"He ain't gone yet,' she said. 145

Remember that chill I luckily didn't get from waiting in the slough? I got it now. I felt it start from the very center of me, where fear hides, waiting to attack. It spiraled outward so that in minutes my fingers and teeth were shaking and clattering. I knew she told the truth. She seen Grandpa. Whether or not he had been there is not the point. She had *seen* him, and that meant anybody else could see him, too. Not only that but, as is usually the case with these here ghosts, he had a certain uneasy reason to come back. And of course Grandma Kashpaw had scanned it out.

I sat down. We sat together on the couch watching his chair out of the corner of our eyes. She had found him sitting in his chair when she walked in the door.

"It's the love medicine, my Lipsha," she said. "It was stronger than we thought. He came back even after death to claim me to his side."

I was afraid. "We shouldn't have tampered with it," I said. She agreed. For a while we sat still. I don't know what she thought, but my head felt screwed on backward. I couldn't accurately consider the situation, so I told Grandma to go to bed. I would sleep on the couch keeping my eye on Grandpa's chair. Maybe he would come back and maybe he wouldn't. I guess I feared the one as much as the other, but I got to thinking, see, as I lay there in darkness, that perhaps even through my terrible mistakes some good might come. If Grandpa did come back, I thought he'd return in his right mind. I could talk with him. I could tell him it was all my fault for playing with power I did not understand. Maybe he'd forgive me and rest in peace. I hoped this. I calmed myself and waited for him all night.

He fooled me though. He knew what I was waiting for, and it wasn't what 150
he was looking to hear. Come dawn I heard a blood-splitting cry from the bedroom and I rushed in there. Grandma turnt the lights on. She was sitting on the edge of the bed and her face looked harsh, pinched-up, gray.

"He was here," she said. "He came and laid down next to me in bed. And he touched me."

Her heart broke down. She cried. His touch was so cold. She laid back in bed after a while, as it was morning, and I went to the couch. As I lay there, falling asleep, I suddenly felt Grandpa's presence and the barrier between us like a swollen river. I felt how I had wronged him. How awful was the place where I had sent him. Behind the wall of death, he'd watched the living eat and cry and get drunk. He was lonesome, but I understood he meant no harm.

"Go back," I said to the dark, afraid and yet full of pity. "You got to be with your own kind now," I said. I felt him retreating, like a sigh, growing less. I felt his spirit as it shrunk back through the walls, the blinds, the brick courtyard of Senior Citizens. "Look up Aunt June," I whispered as he left.

I slept late the next morning, a good hard sleep allowing the sun to rise and warm the earth. It was past noon when I awoke. There is nothing, to my mind, like a long sleep to make those hard decisions that you neglect under stress of wakefulness. Soon as I woke up that morning, I saw exactly what I'd say to Grandma. I had gotten humble in the past week, not just losing the touch but getting jolted into the understanding that would prey on me from here on out. Your life feels different on you, once you greet death and understand your heart's position. You wear your life like a garment from the mission bundle sale ever after—lightly because you realize you never paid nothing for it, cherishing because you know you won't ever come by such a bargain again. Also you have the feeling someone wore it before you and someone will after. I can't explain that, not yet, but I'm putting my mind to it.

155 "Grandma," I said, "I got to be honest about the love medicine."

She listened. I knew from then on she would be listening to me the way I had listened to her before. I told her about the turkey hearts and how I had them blessed. I told her what I used as love medicine was purely a fake, and then I said to her what my understanding brought me.

"Love medicine ain't what brings him back to you, Grandma. No, it's something else. He loved you over time and distance, but he went off so quick he never got the chance to tell you how he loves you, how he doesn't blame you, how he understands. It's true feeling, not no magic. No supermarket heart could have brung him back."

She looked at me. She was seeing the years and days I had no way of knowing, and she didn't believe me. I could tell this. Yet a look came on her face. It was like the look of mothers drinking sweetness from their children's eyes. It was tenderness.

"Lipsha," she said, "you was always my favorite."

160 She took the beads off the bedpost, where she kept them to say at night, and she told me to put out my hand. When I did this, she shut the beads inside of my fist and held them there a long minute, tight, so my hand hurt. I almost cried when she did this. I don't really know why. Tears shot up behind my eyelids, and yet it was nothing. I didn't understand, except her hand was so strong, squeezing mine.

The earth was full of life and there were dandelions growing out the window, thick as thieves, already seeded, fat as big yellow plungers. She let my hand go. I got up. "I'll go out and dig a few dandelions," I told her.

Outside, the sun was hot and heavy as a hand on my back. I felt it flow down my arms, out my fingers, arrowing through the ends of the fork into the earth. With every root I prized up there was return, as if I was kin to its secret lesson. The touch got stronger as I worked through the grassy afternoon. Uncurling from me like a seed out of the blackness where I was lost, the touch spread. The spiked leaves full of bitter mother's milk. A buried root. A nuisance people dig up and throw in the sun to wither. A globe of frail seeds that's indestructible.

1982

1. In the first dramatized scene, Lipsha, the narrator, at Grandma Kashpaw's request, tries to "put the touch" on Grandpa. By this time, some seventeen or eighteen paragraphs, focus and voice and the setting and situation have been established; you should be getting a good idea of Lipsha's character, and you should be forming some fairly definite expectations about the plot, and, with the help of the title, you should have some glimmers about the developing theme. Write down what you have observed of the structure and elements of the story and what you expect to happen. As you read on, note how your expectations are fulfilled or modified: in what ways are these surprises or changes in expectations related to plot? character? theme? how do they define the world of the fiction? differ from your prior view of the world? To what extent are they convincing?

2. Voice is a dominant element in this story, and it is in large measure through Lipsha's voice that we infer his character. His language is ungrammatical—the story opens with "I never really *done* much . . ." and his narration is full of colloquial phrases like "I don't got"—and his malapropisms (ludicrous misuse of words)—"templates" for "temples," "laundry" for "quandary," and "Phillipines" for "Philistines"—tend to undercut his apparent confidence in his literary skills ("Besides the dictionary, which I'm constantly in use of, I had this Bible once. I read it." [par. 26]). His limitations, skillfully indicated, extend to his somewhat naive view of reality—or causality: for example, his version of why Grandpa has symptoms of senility, his "thoughtful" acceptance of Grandpa's illuminating insight that God is going deaf. These errors, attitudes, and views, however, are endearing and often quite funny. Some of them will turn out, in strange ways, to seem almost wise. His kindness and good nature show through the errors and naivete, and he is capable of insights that, though naive and tender still, are not ludicrous: "I thought love got easier over the years so it didn't hurt so bad when it hurt, or feel so good when it felt good' (par. 14); "From time to time I heal a person all up good inside, however when it comes to the long shot I doubt I got staying power. / And you need that, staying power, going out to love somebody" (par. 18). His voice reveals character and theme, and his character is instrumental in this plot. A challenging topic for a paper might be to show not only how the theme is presented in this story through a character who is not well educated or intellectually profound, but how the character's very limitations contribute meaning and force to that theme.

3. How is "love medicine" related to the plot? to Grandma's and Lipsha's character? to theme? In what way(s) may it be considered a symbol?

4. Lipsha tells the story of Lulu's "tweety bird" that disappeared up her

dress and of Wristwatch, whose broken watch started keeping time after its owner dropped dead. He then says, "Not to get off the subject or nothing" (par. 65). Are these stories off the subject? How do they arouse expectations? How do they function in the plot? What do they tell you of Lipsha's character? of the nature of the people on the reservation? Are they related to the theme? if so, how? When he thinks of Wristwatch's grave being dug up in 200 years, the watch still running, and the diggers asking, "Whose hand wound it?" he says he "started shaking like a piece of grass at just the thought" (par. 64). Is it with awe and fear or with laughter? Do you find it awesome or funny? If there is a difference between how you feel and how you believe Lipsha feels, what is the effect? What is the relationship of this difference to plot, character, voice, and the other elements of the story? How is this episode related to the "subject" he does not mean to be getting off of when the story continues: for example, he says he fires two "accurate" shots at the geese but the shots miss; how does this affect your view of his "reliability" and thus your reading of character? plot? theme? How does it affect your reading of his glance forward, "I never saw at the time how my thoughts led me astray toward a tragic outcome none could have known" (par. 68)? There is a death involved. Is it "tragic"? How do you respond to it? He says he took "an evil shortcut" in practicing love medicine: does that mean that he has discovered that the old beliefs are not "superstitions" or "strange" as he thought at the time?

5. Toward the end of the story, Lipsha tells Grandma that it was not "love medicine" that brought Grandpa's ghost back to her but love itself, not magic but feeling. Grandma looks at him tenderly and says, " 'Lipsha, . . . you was always my favorite' " (par. 159). Explain this passage in terms of the plot (but be sure to remember Lulu); in terms of Lipsha's character; in terms of Grandma's; in terms of theme (and you might even want to think of "love medicine" as symbol).

Exploring Contexts

8 THE AUTHOR'S WORK

Even if it were desirable to read a story as a thing in itself, separate from everything else we had ever read or seen and from everything else the author had written, this is in practice impossible. We can *first* look into Chapman's Homer or Faulkner's fiction only once. After we read a second and then a third story by an author, we recognize the voice and have a sense of familiarity, as we would with a growing acquaintance. Each story is part of the author's entire body of work—the **canon**—which, taken together, forms something like a huge single entity, a vision, a world, a "superwork."

The author's voice and vision soon create in us certain expectations—of action, structure, characterization, world view, language. We come to expect short sentences from Hemingway, long ones from Faulkner, a certain amount of violence from both. We are not surprised if a Conrad story is set in Africa or Asia or aboard ship, but we are surprised if a Faulkner story takes place outside Mississippi (his portion of which, we soon learn, he calls Yoknapatawpha). We expect indirection, irony, and uncertainty (as well as long sentences with lots of commas) from Henry James, so we watch his characters for signs of subtlety or unreliability, and his narrator for careful qualifications and qualifications of qualifications. After reading a significant amount of Faulkner, we will bring our reading of "The Old People" and other stories to our understanding of "blood" in "Barn Burning."

When we find an author's vision attractive or challenging, we naturally want to find out more about it, reading not only the literary works in the canon but the author's nonfictional prose—essays, letters, anything we can find that promises a fuller or clearer view of that unique way of looking at the world.

Such knowledge is helpful—within limits. D. H. Lawrence warned us to trust the tale and not the teller. A statement of beliefs or of intentions is not necessarily the same as what a given work may show or achieve; and, on the other hand, writers often embody in their art what they cannot articulate, what indeed may not be expressible, in discursive prose.

In this chapter we will look closely at the work of two writers, D. H. Lawrence and Flannery O'Connor. We will look both at differences between works by the same writer and at similarities.

The two short stories and brief selections from Lawrence's letters and criticism in this chapter are meant to make you feel more at home (and interested) in Lawrence's world and to raise questions about the relationship of the individual work to an author's work as a whole. Of course, a couple of short stories and a few pages of nonfiction alone cannot adequately represent the career of a writer who was a novelist, poet, critic, and essayist as well as short-story writer, nor can two stories represent the richness and variety of the fifty or more that he published. However, as the stories come from different decades, they do represent somewhat the continuities and changes during his career. "Odour of Chrysanthemums" is characteristically set in the coal-mining region of his native English Midlands, the scene of many of his novels, including three of the most famous, which also span his career—*Sons and Lovers* (1913), *The Rainbow* (1915), and *Lady Chatterly's Lover* (1928). There is no way in so few selections to represent both Lawrence's emphasis on the Midlands and the scope of his settings—his stories take place all over Western Europe, in the Americas, and in Australia. The London setting of "The Rocking-Horse Winner" only faintly indicates Lawrence's growing cosmopolitanism socially as well as geographically. It also suggests, though superficially, his developing interest in the superreal and the mythic—concerns most fully developed in *The Plumed Serpent* (1926) and *The Man Who Died* (1929)—and his movement in content and style away from nineteenth-century notions of realism.

It may be useful to see the first story here (one of Lawrence's very first stories) through the eyes of its first "professional" reader as he remembers the experience. Not long before World War I, a young woman sent to Ford Madox Ford, then editor of *The English Review*, three poems and a short story written by a schoolmaster friend of hers, the then unknown D. H. Lawrence. Ford read the story first and, he recalls, knew immediately that he had a genius on his hands, "a big one." The very title, "Odour of Chrysanthemums," Ford noted, "makes an impact on the mind," indicates that the writer is observant (not many people realize that chrysanthemums have an odor), and sets the dark autumnal tone of the story. From the very first sentence, Ford goes on to say,

> . . . you know that this fellow with the power of observation is going to write whatever he writes about from the inside. The "Number 4" shows that. He will be the sort of fellow who knows that for the sort of people who work about engines, engines have a sort of individuality. He had to give the engine the personality of a number. . . . "With seven full wagons". . . . The "seven" is good. The ordinary careless writer would say "some small wagons." This man knows what he wants. He sees the scene of his story exactly. He has an authoritative mind.
>
> "It appeared round the corner with loud threats of speed." . . . Good writing; slightly, but not *too* arresting. . . . "But the colt that it startled from among the gorse . . . out-distanced it at a canter." Good again. This fellow does not "state." He doesn't say: "It was coming slowly," or—what would have been a little better—"at seven miles an hour." Because even "seven miles an hour" means nothing definite for the untrained mind. It might mean something for a trainer or pedestrian racers. The imaginative writer writes for all humanity; he does not limit his desired readers to specialists. . . . But anyone knows that an engine that makes a great deal of noise and yet cannot overtake a colt at a canter must be a ludicrously ineffective machine. We know then that this fellow knows his job.
>
> . . . . [T]his man knows. He knows how to open a story with a sentence of the right cadence for holding the attention. He knows how to construct a paragraph. He knows the life he is writing about. . . . You can trust him for the rest. . . .
>
> —from "Before the Wars," *Selected Memories, The Bodley Head Ford Madox Ford* (London, 1962), I, 322–323

You will find the same precision of detail suggesting the author's "inside view" in that strange and strangely different story "The Rocking-Horse Winner," in the first description of Paul's riding the horse, for example; in the description of the horse's "lowered face" ("Its red mouth was slightly open, its big eye was wide and glassy-bright" [par. 42]); and in the precise accounting of the races, the odds, the money.

Ford read "Odour of Chrysanthemums" outside the context available to us. He did not know anything of the author and had read nothing else by him. Ford was an excellent editor (as well as writer) and to his credit spotted Lawrence's genius, a genius quite different from his own. Lawrence's mastery of detail made Ford trust him, but what he trusted him for seems to have been knowledge of the "other ninety-nine hundredths" of the population, the working class. An English writer of genius with knowledge of the working class was no doubt rare and notable in those pre-war days, and Lawrence's early works are full of details of the lives of miners and their families. But Lawrence, we now know, considered not class but the man-woman relationship the "great relationship of humanity," all others being subsidiary. Because we know that, know of Lawrence's notoriety for describing sexual relations, know his later works in which sexual relations are the major or basic concern—and perhaps because of the emphasis on sex in our own time—in reading "Odour of Chrysanthemums" we focus our attention less on the picture of the working class than on the strange relationship between the Bateses. The class element is still in the story, but the context of Lawrence's other works and utterances highlights this other human relationship.

Though Ford stressed Lawrence's power of observation in terms of the outside of things, he does say that "this fellow . . . is going to write whatever he writes about from the inside." It is not just Lawrence's powers of observation but his penetration to the inside of his characters' beings, to the shockingly original but convincing motives and feelings he finds there, and his insight into relationships, particularly love relationships, that mark his best work. Unfortunately, there is not space here to represent his more positive, fully developed, and explicit incarnations of man-woman love, found particularly in his novels *Women in Love* (1920) and *Lady Chatterley's Lover*. We can briefly indicate, however, what woman-man love is not in "Odour of Chrysanthemums" and what parent-child love is not in "The Rocking-Horse Winner":

> . . . when her children were present, she always felt the center of her heart go hard. This troubled her, and in her manner she was all the more gentle and anxious for her children, as if she loved them very much. Only she herself knew that at the center of her heart was a hard little place that could not feel love, no, not for anybody. Everybody else said of her: "She is such a good mother. She adores her children." Only she herself, and her children themselves, knew it was not so.
>
> (Par. 1)

In this chapter we have also included two of Flannery O'Connor's stories, both from her posthumous volume, *Everything That Rises Must Converge*, and so representative at least of the final years of her brief career. (She died at thirty-nine, having published some thirty-one stories, two novels, essays, and reviews.) The title story of that final volume is perhaps the more characteristic, for O'Connor frequently turned her piercingly accurate vision on the middle-aged and elderly, especially women, and on the Southern. Both these stories center, as many of her others do, on a sudden revelation of a truth about the self, shedding a new and unflattering light on one's attitudes, behaviors, beliefs. The exposure often involves snobbery, racism, or self-righteousness, often in false religious or falsely humanistic form. The first two are exemplified in "Everything That Rises Must Converge," self-righteousness and the falsely humanistic in "The Lame Shall Enter First." Like Lawrence, O'Connor has a keen eye for realistic detail and for her characters' self-deception. Violence is often in or near the surface of her fiction; as in Faulkner, it is used to shake up the reader and make him or her look beyond the conventional and the ordinary into a kind of truth, often an uncomfortable truth that lies within. Though O'Connor is a deeply religious and serious writer, her stories are replete with irony and wit, and are sometimes downright funny. Indeed, as you will see, she is not above using comic pratfalls seriously.

The central, sometimes obsessive concerns and assumptions that permeate an author's work not only relate the individual stories to each other, mutually illuminating and enriching them, but they also serve as the author's trademark. It is not difficult to recognize or even parody a story by Lawrence or O'Connor.

Embodying these larger concerns and underlying such larger structures as plot, focus, and voice are the basic characteristics of the author's language, such as **diction,** the choice and use of words; sentence structure; **rhetorical tropes,** figures of thought and speech; **imagery;** and **rhythm**—in other words, the author's **style.**

Perhaps because of the uniqueness of style, the vocabulary for discussing stylistic elements is not very precise or accessible. We can broadly characterize diction as **formal** ("The Cask of Amontillado") or **informal** (most of the stories in this collection), and within the broad term **informal** we can identify a level of language that approximates the speech of ordinary people and call it **colloquial** ("My Man Bovanne"). But to characterize precisely an author's diction so that it adequately describes his or her work and marks it off from the works of contemporaries is a very difficult task indeed. We can note Henry James's long sentences, but it is hard to get much definition in the stylistic fingerprint of an author merely by measuring the lengths of sentences or tabulating connectives (though these qualities no doubt do subliminally contribute to the effect of the works on readers and do help them identify an author's work).

Diction and sentence structure contribute to the **tone** of a work, or the implied attitude or stance of the author toward the characters and events, an aspect somewhat analogous to tone of voice. When what is being said and the tone are consistent, it is difficult to separate one from the other; when there seems to be a discrepancy, we have some words that are useful to describe the difference. If the language seems exaggerated, we call it **overstatement.** Sometimes it will be the narrator, sometimes a character, who uses language so intensive or exaggerated that we must read it at a discount, as it were, and judge the speaker's accuracy or honesty in the process. When Julian's mother, in "Everything That Rises Must Converge," says, " 'I've always had a great deal of respect for my colored friends. . . . I'd do anything in the world for them . . .' " (par. 32), we know she is protesting too much, exaggerating, and we see her racism through or underneath her language. When Hazel, in "My Man Bovanne," says that Bovanne "changes the lock on my door when my men friends get messy" (par. 3), we know that "messy" does not quite cover the actions of the men friends. She is indulging in a bit of obvious **understatement.** When a word or expression carries not only its literal meaning, but for the speaker has a different meaning we have an example of **verbal irony.** When Fortunato says, "I shall not die of a cough," Montresor's "True—true" may seem reassuring but we learn later in the story why it is both accurate and ominous. There are also nonverbal forms of irony, the most common of which is **dramatic irony,** in which a character holds a position or has an expectation that is reversed or fulfilled in an unexpected way. Knowing her husband's habit of drinking himself into unconsciousness, Elizabeth Bates expects him to be brought home like a log. How is her expectation fulfilled? She had also said bitterly, "But he needn't come rolling in here in his pit-dirt, for *I* won't wash him," and yet she does. Why is her determination altered? As you read through, or look back over this story, watch for other reversed or unexpectedly fulfilled expectations.

Another, highly emphasized element of style is **imagery.** In its broadest sense imagery includes any sensory detail or evocation in a work. Note how much more imagery in that sense we find in "The Old People" than in, say, "The Zebra Storyteller". Imagery in this broad sense, however, is so prevalent in literature that it would take exhaustive statistics to differentiate styles by counting the number of sensory elements per hundred or thousand words, categorizing the images as primarily visual, tactile, etc. In a more restricted sense imagery refers to figurative language (see Chapter 5 on symbols), particularly that which defines an abstraction or any emotional or psychological state with a sensory comparison. The opening paragraph of "Odour of Chrysanthemums" illustrates the broader definition of imagery, and this passage from later in the same story may represent the figurative sense: "Life with its smoky burning gone from him, had left him apart. . . . In her womb was ice of fear. . . ."

We might say that if an author's vision gives us his or her profile, the style gives us a fingerprint—though the fingerprint is unique and definitive, it is also harder to come by than a glimpse of a profile. Ultimately, however, vision and style are less distinguishable from each other than the profile-fingerprint image suggests. For vision and style, just like history and structure, do more than interact: they are inextricably fused or compounded. Let us look back at the Ford passage. He says this of "the gorse, which still flickered indistinctly in the raw afternoon" (though he misquotes it slightly and rather loosely calls it a phrase):

> . . .Good too, distinctly good. This is the just-sufficient observation of Nature that gives you, in a single phrase, landscape, time of day, weather, season.

Is this vision or style? The observation of Nature is clearly vision, but expressing that vision economically, tautly, is style. The two merge.

Whatever else this passage is, it is vintage, typical Lawrence. Perhaps it would take more than just these ten words, but surely in a paragraph or two we know we're in the fictional world that he perceived and that he embodied in his stories, novels, and poems in a language of his own created out of that language we share.

▽ ▽ ▽

THE AUTHOR'S WORK A Glossary

colloquial diction: level of language or vocabulary that is *informal* in that it is the language of ordinary people but tends to imitate or suggest ordinary spoken rather than written language.

diction: choice of words; often generally characterized as *formal, informal,* or *colloquial;* an aspect of *style*

dramatic irony: the unexpected fulfillment or reversal of a character's expectations

formal diction: large, sophisticated, and traditional vocabulary

imagery: broadly thought of, the visual descriptions, or even any sensory impressions generated, in a work, but more narrowly and usually, the figurative language, including *metaphors, similes, analogies* (see *Symbols: A Glossary,* p. 183); an aspect of *style*

informal diction: level of language or vocabulary that characterizes the written language of ordinary people

overstatement: language that is so intense or exaggerated it must be read "at a discount," as meaning less than it literally states

rhetorical tropes: figures of thought or speech; part of *style*

rhythm: the pattern of sound pulsations in the voice as one reads (or as the sound is imagined in the mind); an aspect of *style*

style: the basic characteristics of the language of an author (or an age); while sometimes considered the manner as opposed to the matter, as "ornament," it is now more often seen as organic or fused, with the substance, manner, and matter being as closely related as body and soul; indeed, much recent criticism suggests that there is no "meaning" prior to language, that to think or mean is to think or mean in language itself.

tone: the implied attitude or stance of the author toward the characters and events, somewhat like "tone of voice"

understatement: language that obviously underrates something or portrays it as lesser than it is usually thought to be

verbal irony: a word or expression that carries not only its literal meaning but for the speaker has a different, sometimes even an opposite, meaning

D. H. LAWRENCE

Odour of Chrysanthemums

I

The small locomotive engine, Number 4, came clanking, stumbling down from Selston with seven full waggons. It appeared round the corner with loud threats of speed, but the colt that it startled from among the gorse, which still flickered indistinctly in the raw afternoon, outdistanced it at a canter. A woman, walking up the railway line to Underwood, drew back into the hedge, held her basket aside, and watched the footplate of the engine advancing. The trucks thumped heavily past, one by one, with slow inevitable movement, as she stood insignificantly trapped between the jolting black waggons and the hedge; then they curved away towards the coppice where the withered oak leaves dropped noiselessly, while the birds, pulling at the scarlet hips beside the track, made off into the dusk that had already crept into the spinney. In the open, the smoke from the engine sank and cleaved to the rough grass. The fields were dreary and forsaken, and in the marshy strip that led to the whimsey, a reedy pit-pond, the fowls had already abandoned their run among the alders, to roost in the tarred fowl-house. The pit-bank loomed up beyond the pond, flames like red sores licking its ashy sides, in the afternoon's stagnant light. Just beyond rose the tapering chimneys and the clumsy black headstocks of Brinsley Colliery. The two wheels were spinning fast up against the sky, and the winding-engine rapped out its little spasms. The miners were being turned up.

The engine whistled as it came into the wide bay of railway lines beside the colliery, where rows of trucks stood in harbour.

Miners, single, trailing and in groups, passed like shadows diverging home. At the edge of the ribbed level of sidings squat a low cottage, three steps down from the cinder track. A large bony vine clutched at the house, as if to claw down the tiled roof. Round the bricked yard grew a few wintry primroses. Beyond, the long garden sloped down to a bush-covered brook course. There were some twiggy apple trees, winter-crack trees, and ragged cabbages. Beside the path hung dishevelled pink chrysanthemums, like pink cloths hung on bushes. A woman came stooping out of the felt-covered fowl-house, half-way down the garden. She closed and padlocked the door, then drew herself erect, having brushed some bits from her white apron.

She was a tall woman of imperious mien, handsome, with definite black eyebrows. Her smooth black hair was parted exactly. For a few moments she stood steadily watching the miners as they passed along the railway: then she turned towards the brook course. Her face was calm and set, her mouth was closed with disillusionment. After a moment she called:

"John!" There was no answer. She waited, and then said distinctly: 5

"Where are you?"

"Here!" replied a child's sulky voice from among the bushes. The woman looked piercingly through the dusk.

"Are you at that brook?" she asked sternly.

For answer the child showed himself before the raspberry-canes that rose like whips. He was a small, sturdy boy of five. He stood quite still, defiantly.

"Oh!" said the mother, conciliated. "I thought you were down at that wet brook—and you remember what I told you—"

The boy did not move or answer.

"Come, come on in," she said more gently, "it's getting dark. There's your grandfather's engine coming down the line!"

The lad advanced slowly, with resentful, taciturn movement. He was dressed in trousers and waistcoat of cloth that was too thick and hard for the size of the garments. They were evidently cut down from a man's clothes.

As they went slowly towards the house he tore at the ragged wisps of chrysanthemums and dropped the petals in handfuls along the path.

"Don't do that—it does look nasty," said his mother. He refrained, and she, suddenly pitiful, broke off a twig with three or four wan flowers and held them against her face. When mother and son reached the yard her hand hesitated, and instead of laying the flower aside, she pushed it in her apron-band. The mother and son stood at the foot of the three steps looking across the bay of lines at the passing home of the miners. The trundle of the small train was imminent. Suddenly the engine loomed past the house and came to a stop opposite the gate.

The engine-driver, a short man with round grey beard, leaned out of the cab high above the woman.

"Have you got a cup of tea?" he said in a cheery, hearty fashion.

It was her father. She went in, saying she would mash.[1] Directly, she returned.

"I didn't come to see you on Sunday," began the little grey-bearded man.

"I didn't expect you," said his daughter.

The engine-driver winced; then, reassuming his cheery, airy manner, he said:

"Oh, have you heard then? Well, and what do you think——?"

"I think it is soon enough," she replied.

At her brief censure the little man made an impatient gesture, and said coaxingly, yet with dangerous coldness:

"Well, what's a man to do? It's no sort of life for a man of my years, to sit at my own hearth like a stranger. And if I'm going to marry again it may as well be soon as late—what does it matter to anybody?"

The woman did not reply, but turned and went into the house. The man in the engine-cab stood assertive, till she returned with a cup of tea and a piece of bread and butter on a plate. She went up the steps and stood near the footplate of the hissing engine.

"You needn't 'a' brought me bread an' butter," said her father. "But a cup of tea"—he sipped appreciatively—"it's very nice." He sipped for a moment or two,

1. Prepare (tea).

then: "I hear as Walter's got another bout on," he said.

"When hasn't he?" said the woman bitterly.

"I heered tell of him in the 'Lord Nelson'[2] braggin' as he was going to spend that b—— afore he went: half a sovereign[3] that was."

"When?" asked the woman.

"A' Sat'day night—I know that's true."

"Very likely," she laughed bitterly. "He gives me twenty-three shillings."

"Aye, it's a nice thing, when a man can do nothing with his money but make a beast of himself!" said the grey-whiskered man. The woman turned her head away. Her father swallowed the last of his tea and handed her the cup.

"Aye," he sighed, wiping his mouth. "It's a settler, it is——"

He put his hand on the lever. The little engine strained and groaned, and the train rumbled towards the crossing. The woman again looked across the metals. Darkness was settling over the spaces of the railway and trucks: the miners, in grey sombre groups, were still passing home. The winding-engine pulsed hurriedly, with brief pauses. Elizabeth Bates looked at the dreary flow of men, then she went indoors. Her husband did not come.

The kitchen was small and full of firelight; red coals piled glowing up the chimney mouth. All the life of the room seemed in the white, warm hearth and the steel fender reflecting the red fire. The cloth was laid for tea; cups glinted in the shadows. At the back, where the lowest stairs protruded into the room, the boy sat struggling with a knife and a piece of white wood. He was almost hidden in the shadow. It was half-past four. They had but to await the father's coming to begin tea. As the mother watched her son's sullen little struggle with the wood, she saw herself in his silence and pertinacity; she saw the father in her child's indifference to all but himself. She seemed to be occupied by her husband. He had probably gone past his home, slunk past his own door, to drink before he came in, while his dinner spoiled and wasted in waiting. She glanced at the clock, then took the potatoes to strain them in the yard. The garden and fields beyond the brook were closed in uncertain darkness. When she rose with the saucepan, leaving the drain steaming into the night behind her, she saw the yellow lamps were lit along the high road that went up the hill away beyond the space of the railway lines and the field.

Then again she watched the men trooping home, fewer now and fewer.

Indoors the fire was sinking and the room was dark red. The woman put her saucepan on the hob, and set a batter pudding near the mouth of the oven. Then she stood unmoving. Directly, gratefully, came quick young steps to the door. Someone hung on the latch a moment, then a little girl entered and began pulling off her outdoor things, dragging a mass of curls, just ripening from gold to brown, over her eyes with her hat.

Her mother chid her for coming late from school, and said she would have to keep her at home the dark winter days.

2. A public house, pub.

3. A sovereign was about half a week's wage; there are 20 shillings (see below) to the pound.

"Why, mother, it's hardly a bit dark yet. The lamp's not lighted, and my father's not home."

"No, he isn't. But it's a quarter to five! Did you see anything of him?"

The child became serious. She looked at her mother with large, wistful blue eyes.

"No, mother, I've never seen him. Why? Has he come up an' gone past, to Old Brinsley? He hasn't, mother, 'cos I never saw him."

"He'd watch that," said the mother bitterly, "he'd take care as you didn't see him. But you may depend upon it, he's seated in the 'Prince o' Wales.' He wouldn't be this late."

The girl looked at her mother piteously.

"Let's have our teas, mother, should we?" said she.

The mother called John to table. She opened the door once more and looked out across the darkness of the lines. All was deserted: she could not hear the winding-engines.

"Perhaps," she said to herself, "he's stopped to get some ripping[4] done."

They sat down to tea. John, at the end of the table near the door, was almost lost in the darkness. Their faces were hidden from each other. The girl crouched against the fender slowly moving a thick piece of bread before the fire. The lad, his face a dusky mark on the shadow, sat watching her who was transfigured in the red glow.

"I do think it's beautiful to look in the fire," said the child.

"Do you?" said her mother. "Why?"

"It's so red, and full of little caves—and it feels so nice, and you can fair smell it."

"It'll want mending directly," replied her mother, "and then if your father comes he'll carry on and say there never is a fire when a man comes home sweating from the pit.—A public-house is always warm enough."

There was silence till the boy said complainingly: "Make haste, our Annie."

"Well, I am doing! I can't make the fire do it no faster, can I?"

"She keeps wafflin'[5] it about so's to make 'er slow," grumbled the boy.

"Don't have such an evil imagination, child," replied the mother.

Soon the room was busy in the darkness with the crisp sound of crunching. The mother ate very little. She drank her tea determinedly, and sat thinking. When she rose her anger was evident in the stern unbending of her head. She looked at the pudding in the fender, and broke out:

"It is a scandalous thing as a man can't even come home to his dinner! If it's crozzled[6] up to a cinder I don't see why I should care. Past his very door he goes to get to a public-house, and here I sit with his dinner waiting for him——"

She went out. As she dropped piece after piece of coal on the red fire, the shadows fell on the walls, till the room was almost in total darkness.

"I canna see," grumbled the invisible John. In spite of herself, the mother laughed.

4. Coal-mining term for taking down the roof of an underground road in order to make it higher. 5. Waving. 6. Shriveled.

"You know the way to your mouth," she said. She set the dustpan outside the door. When she came again like a shadow on the hearth, the lad repeated, complaining sulkily:

"I canna see."

"Good gracious!" cried the mother irritably, "you're as bad as your father if it's a bit dusk!"

Nevertheless she took a paper spill from a sheaf on the mantelpiece and proceeded to light the lamp that hung from the ceiling in the middle of the room. As she reached up, her figure displayed itself just rounding with maternity.

"Oh, mother——!" exclaimed the girl.

"What?" said the woman, suspended in the act of putting the lamp-glass over the flame. The copper reflector shone handsomely on her, as she stood with uplifted arm, turning to face her daughter:

"You've got a flower in your apron!" said the child, in a little rapture at this unusual event.

"Goodness me!" exclaimed the woman, relieved. "One would think the house was afire." She replaced the glass and waited a moment before turning up the wick. A pale shadow was seen floating vaguely on the floor.

"Let me smell!" said the child, still rapturously, coming forward and putting her face to her mother's waist.

"Go along, silly!" said the mother, turning up the lamp. The light revealed their suspense so that the woman felt it almost unbearable. Annie was still bending at her waist. Irritably, the mother took the flowers out from her apron-band.

"Oh, mother—don't take them out!" Annie cried, catching her hand and trying to replace the sprig.

"Such nonsense!" said the mother, turning away. The child put the pale chrysanthemums to her lips, murmuring:

"Don't they smell beautiful!"

Her mother gave a short laugh.

"No," she said, "not to me. It was chrysanthemums when I married him, and chrysanthemums when you were born, and the first time they ever brought him home drunk, he'd got brown chrysanthemums in his button-hole."

She looked at the children. Their eyes and their parted lips were wondering. The mother sat rocking in silence for some time. Then she looked at the clock.

"Twenty minutes to six!" In a tone of fine bitter carelessness she continued: "Eh, he'll not come now till they bring him. There he'll stick! But he needn't come rolling in here in his pit-dirt, for *I* won't wash him. He can lie on the floor——Eh, what a fool I've been, what a fool! And this is what I came here for, to this dirty hole, rats and all, for him to slink past his very door. Twice last week—he's begun now——"

She silenced herself, and rose to clear the table.

While for an hour or more the children played, subduedly intent, fertile of imagination, united in fear of the mother's wrath, and in dread of their father's home-coming, Mrs. Bates sat in her rocking-chair making a "singlet" of thick cream-coloured flannel, which gave a dull wounded sound as she tore off the grey edge. She worked at her sewing with energy, listening to the children, and her anger wearied itself, lay down to rest, opening its eyes from time to time and steadily watching, its ears raised to listen. Sometimes even her anger quailed and shrank, and the mother suspended her sewing, tracing the footsteps that thudded along the sleepers outside; she would lift her head sharply to bid the children "hush," but she recovered herself in time, and the footsteps went past the gate, and the children were not flung out of their playworld.

But at last Annie sighed, and gave in. She glanced at her waggon of slippers, and loathed the game. She turned plaintively to her mother.

"Mother!"—but she was inarticulate.

John crept out like a frog from under the sofa. His mother glanced up.

"Yes," she said, "just look at those shirtsleeves!"

The boy held them out to survey them, saying nothing. Then somebody called in a hoarse voice away down the line, and suspense bristled in the room, till two people had gone by outside, talking.

"It is time for bed," said the mother.

"My father hasn't come," wailed Annie plaintively. But her mother was primed with courage.

"Never mind. They'll bring him when he does come—like a log." She meant there would be no scene. "And he may sleep on the floor till he wakes himself. I know he'll not go to work tomorrow after this!"

The children had their hands and faces wiped with a flannel.[7] They were very quiet. When they had put on their nightdresses, they said their prayers, the boy mumbling. The mother looked down at them, at the brown silken bush of intertwining curls in the nape of the girl's neck, at the little black head of the lad, and her heart burst with anger at their father who caused all three such distress. The children hid their faces in her skirts for comfort.

When Mrs. Bates came down, the room was strangely empty, with a tension of expectancy. She took up her sewing and stitched for some time without raising her head. Meantime her anger was tinged with fear.

II

The clock struck eight and she rose suddenly, dropping her sewing on her chair. She went to the stairfoot door, opened it, listening. Then she went out, locking the door behind her.

Something scuffled in the yard, and she started though she knew it was only the rats with which the place was overrun. The night was very dark. In the great bay of railway lines, bulked with trucks, there was no trace of light, only away back she could see a few yellow lamps at the pit-top, and the red smear of the burning pit-bank on the night. She hurried along the edge of the track, then, crossing the converging lines, came to the stile by the white gates, whence she emerged on the road. Then the fear which had led her shrank. People were walking up to New Brinsley; she saw the lights in the houses; twenty yards further

7. Washrag.

on were the broad windows of the "Prince of Wales," very warm and bright, and the loud voices of men could be heard distinctly. What a fool she had been to imagine that anything had happened to him! He was merely drinking over there at the "Prince of Wales." She faltered. She had never yet been to fetch him, and she never would go. So she continued her walk towards the long straggling line of houses, standing blank on the highway. She entered a passage between the dwellings.

"Mr. Rigley?—Yes! Did you want him? No, he's not in at this minute."

The raw-boned woman leaned forward from her dark scullery and peered at the other, upon whom fell a dim light through the blind of the kitchen window.

"Is it Mrs. Bates?" she asked in a tone tinged with respect.

"Yes. I wondered if your Master was at home. Mine hasn't come yet."

" 'Asn't 'e! Oh, Jack's been 'ome an 'ad 'is dinner an' gone out. 'E's just gone for 'alf an hour afore bedtime. Did you call at the 'Prince of Wales'?"

"No——"

"No, you didn't like——! It's not very nice." The other woman was indulgent. There was an awkward pause. "Jack never said nothink about—about your Mester," she said.

"No!—I expect he's stuck in there!"

Elizabeth Bates said this bitterly, and with recklessness. She knew that the woman across the yard was standing at her door listening, but she did not care. As she turned:

"Stop a minute! I'll just go an' ask Jack if 'e knows anythink," said Mrs. Rigley.

"Oh, no—I wouldn't like to put—!"

"Yes, I will, if you will just step inside an' see as th' childer doesn't come downstairs and set theirselves afire."

Elizabeth Bates, murmuring a remonstrance, stepped inside. The other woman apologized for the state of the room.

The kitchen needed apology. There were little frocks and trousers and childish undergarments on the squab[8] and on the floor, and a litter of playthings everywhere. On the black American cloth[9] of the table were pieces of bread and cake, crusts, slops, and a teapot with cold tea.

"Eh, ours is just as bad," said Elizabeth Bates, looking at the woman, not at the house. Mrs. Rigley put a shawl over her head and hurried out, saying:

"I shanna be a minute."

The other sat, noting with faint disapproval the general untidiness of the room. Then she fell to counting the shoes of various sizes scattered over the floor. There were twelve. She sighed and said to herself, "No wonder!"—glancing at the litter. There came the scratching of two pairs of feet on the yard, and the Rigleys entered. Elizabeth Bates rose. Rigley was a big man, with very large bones. His head looked particularly bony. Across his temple was a blue scar, caused by a wound got in the pit, a wound in which the coal-dust remained blue like tattooing.

8. Sofa. 9. Enameled oilcloth.

" 'Asna 'e come whoam yit?" asked the man, without any form of greeting, but with deference and sympathy. "I couldna say wheer he is—'e's non ower theer!"—he jerked his head to signify the "Prince of Wales."

" 'E's 'appen[1] gone up to th' 'Yew,' " said Mrs. Rigley.

There was another pause. Rigley had evidently something to get off his mind: "Ah left 'im finishin' a stint," he began. "Loose-all[2] 'ad bin gone about ten minutes when we com'n away, an' I shouted, 'Are ter comin', Walt?' an' 'e said 'Go on, Ah shanna be but a 'ef a minnit,' so we com'n ter th' bottom, me an' Browers, thinkin' as 'e wor just behint, an' 'ud come up i' th' next bantle[3]——"

He stood perplexed, as if answering a charge of deserting his mate. Elizabeth Bates, now again certain of disaster, hastened to reassure him:

"I expect 'e's gone up to th' 'Yew Tree,' as you say. It's not the first time. I've fretted myself into a fever before now. He'll come home when they carry him."

"Ay, isn't it too bad!" deplored the other woman.

"I'll just step up to Dick's an' see if 'e *is* theer," offered the man, afraid of appearing alarmed, afraid of taking liberties.

"Oh, I wouldn't think of bothering you that far," said Elizabeth Bates, with emphasis, but he knew she was glad of his offer.

As they stumbled up the entry, Elizabeth Bates heard Rigley's wife run across the yard and open her neighbour's door. At this, suddenly all the blood in her body seemed to switch away from her heart.

"Mind!" warned Rigley. "Ah've said many a time as Ah'd fill up them ruts in this entry, sumb'dy 'll be breakin' their legs yit."

She recovered herself and walked quickly along with the miner.

"I don't like leaving the children in bed, and nobody in the house," she said.

"No, you dunna!" he replied courteously. They were soon at the gate of the cottage.

"Well, I shanna be many minnits. Dunna you be frettin' now, 'e'll be all right," said the butty.[4]

"Thank you very much, Mr. Rigley," she replied.

"You're welcome!" he stammered, moving away. "I shanna be many minnits."

The house was quiet. Elizabeth Bates took off her hat and shawl, and rolled back the rug. When she had finished, she sat down. It was a few minutes past nine. She was startled by the rapid chuff of the winding-engine at the pit, and the sharp whirr of the brakes on the rope as it descended. Again she felt the painful sweep of her blood, and she put her hand to her side, saying aloud, "Good gracious!—it's only the nine o'clock deputy going down," rebuking herself.

She sat still, listening. Half an hour of this, and she was wearied out.

"What am I working up like this for?" she said pitiably to herself, "I s'll only be doing myself some damage."

1. Perhaps. 2. Signal to quit work and come to the surface. 3. An open seat or car of the lift or elevator that takes the miners to the surface. 4. Buddy, fellow worker.

She took out her sewing again.

At a quarter to ten there were footsteps. One person! She watched for the door to open. It was an elderly woman, in a black bonnet and a black woollen shawl—his mother. She was about sixty years old, pale, with blue eyes, and her face all wrinkled and lamentable. She shut the door and turned to her daughter-in-law peevishly.

"Eh, Lizzie, whatever shall we do, whatever shall we do!" she cried.

Elizabeth drew back a little, sharply.

"What is it, mother?" she said.

The elder woman seated herself on the sofa.

"I don't know, child, I can't tell you!"—she shook her head slowly. Elizabeth sat watching her, anxious and vexed.

"I don't know," replied the grandmother, sighing very deeply. "There's no end to my troubles, there isn't. The things I've gone through, I'm sure it's enough——!" She wept without wiping her eyes, the tears running.

"But, mother," interrupted Elizabeth, "what do you mean? What is it?"

The grandmother slowly wiped her eyes. The fountains of her tears were stopped by Elizabeth's directness. She wiped her eyes slowly.

"Poor child! Eh, you poor thing!" she moaned. "I don't know what we're going to do, I don't—and you as you are—it's a thing, it is indeed!"

Elizabeth waited.

"Is he dead?" she asked, and at the words her heart swung violently, though she felt a slight flush of shame at the ultimate extravagance of the question. Her words sufficiently frightened the old lady, almost brought her to herself.

"Don't say so, Elizabeth! We'll hope it's not as bad as that; no, may the Lord spare us that, Elizabeth. Jack Rigley came just as I was sittin' down to a glass afore going to bed, an' 'e said, ''Appen you'll go down th' line, Mrs. Bates. Walt's had an accident. 'Appen you'll go an' sit wi' 'er till we can get him home.' I hadn't time to ask him a word afore he was gone. An' I put my bonnet on an' come straight down, Lizzie. I thought to myself, 'Eh, that poor blessed child, if anybody should come an' tell her of a sudden, there's no knowin'; what'll 'appen to 'er.' You mustn't let it upset you, Lizzie—or you know what to expect. How long is it, six months—or is it five, Lizzie? Ay!"—the old woman shook her head—"time slips on, it slips on! Ay!"

Elizabeth's thoughts were busy elsewhere. If he was killed—would she be able to manage on the little pension and what she could earn?—she counted up rapidly. If he was hurt—they wouldn't take him to the hospital—how tiresome he would be to nurse!—but perhaps she'd be able to get him away from the drink and his hateful ways. She would—while he was ill. The tears offered to come to her eyes at the picture. But what sentimental luxury was this she was beginning?—She turned to consider the children. At any rate she was absolutely necessary for them. They were her business.

"Ay!" repeated the old woman, "it seems but a week or two since he brought me his first wages. Ay—he was a good lad, Elizabeth, he was, in his way. I don't know why he got to be such a trouble, I don't. He was a happy lad at home, only full of spirits. But there's no mistake he's been a handful of trouble, he has! I hope the Lord'll spare him to mend his ways. I hope so, I hope so. You've had a sight o' trouble with him, Elizabeth, you have indeed. But he was a jolly enough lad wi' me, he was, I can assure you. I don't know how it is. . . ."

The old woman continued to muse aloud, a monotonous irritating sound, while Elizabeth thought concentratedly, startled once, when she heard the winding-engine chuff quickly, and the brakes skirr with a shriek. Then she heard the engine more slowly, and the brakes made no sound. The old woman did not notice. Elizabeth waited in suspense. The mother-in-law talked, with lapses into silence.

"But he wasn't your son, Lizzie, an' it makes a difference. Whatever he was, I remember him when he was little, an' I learned to understand him and to make allowances. You've got to make allowances for them—"

It was half-past ten, and the old woman was saying: "But it's trouble from beginning to end; you're never too old for trouble, never too old for that——" when the gate banged back, and there were heavy feet on the steps.

"I'll go, Lizzie, let me go," cried the old woman, rising. But Elizabeth was at the door. It was a man in pit-clothes.

"They're bringin' 'im, Missis," he said. Elizabeth's heart halted a moment. Then it surged on again, almost suffocating her.

"Is he—is it bad?" she asked.

The man turned away, looking at the darkness:

"The doctor says 'e'd been dead hours. 'E saw 'im i' th' lamp-cabin."

The old woman, who stood just behind Elizabeth, dropped into a chair and folded her hands, crying: "Oh, my boy, my boy!"

"Hush!" said Elizabeth, with a sharp twitch of a frown. "Be still, mother, don't waken th' children: I wouldn't have them down for anything!"

The old woman moaned softly, rocking herself. The man was drawing away. Elizabeth took a step forward.

"How was it?" she asked.

"Well, I couldn't say for sure," the man replied, very ill at ease. " 'E wor finishin' a stint an' th' butties 'ad gone, an' a lot o' stuff come down atop 'n 'im."

"And crushed him?" cried the widow, with a shudder.

"No," said the man, "it fell at th' back of 'im. 'E wor under th' face, an' it niver touched 'im. It shut 'im in. It seems 'e wor smothered."

Elizabeth shrank back. She heard the old woman behind her cry:

"What?—what did 'e say it was?"

The man replied, more loudly: "'E wor smothered!"

Then the old woman wailed aloud, and this relieved Elizabeth.

"Oh, mother," she said, putting her hands on the old woman, "don't waken th' children, don't waken th' children."

She wept a little, unknowing, while the old mother rocked herself and moaned. Elizabeth remembered that they were bringing him home, and she must be ready. "They'll lay him in the parlour," she said to herself, standing a moment pale and perplexed.

Then she lighted a candle and went into the tiny room. The air was cold and damp, but she could not make a fire, there was no fireplace. She set down the candle and looked round. The candlelight glittered on the lustre-glasses,[5] on the two vases that held some of the pink chrysanthemums, and on the dark mahogany. There was a cold, deathly smell of chrysanthemums in the room. Elizabeth stood looking at the flowers. She turned away, and calculated whether there would be room to lay him on the floor, between the couch and the chiffonier. She pushed the chairs aside. There would be room to lay him down and to step round him. Then she fetched the old red tablecloth, and another old cloth, spreading them down to save her bit of carpet. She shivered on leaving the parlour; so, from the dresser-drawer she took a clean shirt and put it at the fire to air. All the time her mother-in-law was rocking herself in the chair and moaning.

"You'll have to move from there, mother," said Elizabeth. "They'll be bringing him in. Come in the rocker."

The old mother rose mechanically, and seated herself by the fire, continuing to lament. Elizabeth went into the pantry for another candle, and there, in the little penthouse[6] under the naked tiles, she heard them coming. She stood still in the pantry doorway, listening. She heard them pass the end of the house, and come awkwardly down the three steps, a jumble of shuffling footsteps and muttering voices. The old woman was silent. The men were in the yard.

Then Elizabeth heard Matthews, the manager of the pit, say: "You go in first, Jim. Mind!"

The door came open, and the two women saw a collier backing into the room, holding one end of a stretcher, on which they could see the nailed pit-boots of the dead man. The two carriers halted, the man at the head stooping to the lintel of the door.

"Wheer will you have him?" asked the manager, a short, white-bearded man.

Elizabeth roused herself and came from the pantry carrying the unlighted candle.

"In the parlour," she said.

"In there, Jim!" pointed the manager, and the carriers backed round into the tiny room. The coat with which they had covered the body fell off as they awkwardly turned through the two doorways, and the women saw their man, naked to the waist, lying stripped for work. The old woman began to moan in a low voice of horror.

"Lay th' stretcher at th' side," snapped the manager, "an' put 'im on th' cloths. Mind now, mind! Look you now——!"

One of the men had knocked off a vase of chrysanthemums. He stared awkwardly, then they set down the stretcher. Elizabeth did not look at her husband. As soon as she could get in the room, she went and picked up the broken vase and the flowers.

5. Glass pendants around the edge of an ornamental vase.
6. Structure, usually with a sloping roof, attached to house.

"Wait a minute!" she said.

The three men waited in silence while she mopped up the water with a duster.

"Eh, what a job, what a job, to be sure!" the manager was saying, rubbing his brow with trouble and perplexity. "Never knew such a thing in my life, never! He'd no business to ha' been left. I never knew such a thing in my life! Fell over him clean as a whistle, an' shut him in. Not four foot of space, there wasn't—yet it scarce bruised him."

He looked down at the dead man, lying prone, half naked, all grimed with coal-dust.

"'Sphyxiated,' the doctor said. It *is* the most terrible job I've ever known. Seems as if it was done o' purpose. Clean over him, an' shut 'im in, like a mouse-trap"—he made a sharp, descending gesture with his hand.

The colliers standing by jerked aside their heads in hopeless comment.

The horror of the thing bristled upon them all.

Then they heard the girl's voice upstairs calling shrilly: "Mother, mother—who is it? Mother, who is it?"

Elizabeth hurried to the foot of the stairs and opened the door:

"Go to sleep!" she commanded sharply. "What are you shouting about? Go to sleep at once—there's nothing—"

Then she began to mount the stairs. They could hear her on the boards, and on the plaster floor of the little bedroom. They could hear her distinctly:

"What's the matter now?—what's the matter with you, silly thing?"—her voice was much agitated, with an unreal gentleness.

"I thought it was some men come," said the plaintive voice of the child. "Has he come?"

"Yes, they've brought him. There's nothing to make a fuss about. Go to sleep now, like a good child."

They could hear her voice in the bedroom, they waited whilst she covered the children under the bedclothes.

"Is he drunk?" asked the girl, timidly, faintly.

"No! No—he's not! He's—he's asleep."

"Is he asleep downstairs?"

"Yes—and don't make a noise."

There was silence for a moment, then the men heard the frightened child again:

"What's that noise?"

"It's nothing, I tell you, what are you bothering for?"

The noise was the grandmother moaning. She was oblivious of everything, sitting on her chair rocking and moaning. The manager put his hand on her arm and bade her "Sh-sh!!"

The old woman opened her eyes and looked at him. She was shocked by this interruption, and seemed to wonder.

"What time is it?"—the plaintive thin voice of the child, sinking back unhappily into sleep, asked this last question.

"Ten o'clock," answered the mother more softly. Then she must have bent down and kissed the children.

Matthews beckoned to the men to come away. They put on their caps, and took up the stretcher. Stepping over the body, they tiptoed out of the house. None of them spoke till they were far from the wakeful children.

When Elizabeth came down she found her mother alone on the parlour floor, leaning over the dead man, the tears dropping on him.

"We must lay him out," the wife said. She put on the kettle, then returning knelt at the feet, and began to unfasten the knotted leather laces. The room was clammy and dim with only one candle, so that she had to bend her face almost to the floor. At last she got off the heavy boots and put them away.

"You must help me now," she whispered to the old woman. Together they stripped the man.

When they arose, saw him lying in the naïve dignity of death, the women stood arrested in fear and respect. For a few moments they remained still, looking down, the old mother whimpering. Elizabeth felt countermanded. She saw him, how utterly inviolable he lay in himself. She had nothing to do with him. She could not accept it. Stooping, she laid her hand on him, in claim. He was still warm, for the mine was hot where he had died. His mother had his face between her hands, and was murmuring incoherently. The old tears fell in succession as drops from wet leaves; the mother was not weeping, merely her tears flowed. Elizabeth embraced the body of her husband, with cheek and lips. She seemed to be listening, inquiring, trying to get some connection. But she could not. She was driven away. He was impregnable.

She rose, went into the kitchen, where she poured warm water into a bowl, brought soap and flannel and a soft towel.

"I must wash him," she said.

Then the old mother rose stiffly, and watched Elizabeth as she carefully washed his face, carefully brushing the big blonde moustache from his mouth with the flannel. She was afraid with a bottomless fear, so she ministered to him. The old woman, jealous, said:

"Let me wipe him!"—and she kneeled on the other side drying slowly as Elizabeth washed, her big black bonnet sometimes brushing the dark head of her daughter. They worked thus in silence for a long time. They never forgot it was death, and the touch of the man's dead body gave them strange emotions, different in each of the women; a great dread possessed them both, the mother felt the lie was given to her womb, she was denied; the wife felt the utter isolation of the human soul, the child within her was a weight apart from her.

At last it was finished. He was a man of handsome body, and his face showed no traces of drink. He was blonde, full-fleshed, with fine limbs. But he was dead.

"Bless him," whispered his mother, looking always at his face, and speaking out of sheer terror. "Dear lad—bless him!" She spoke in a faint sibilant ecstasy of fear and mother love.

Elizabeth sank down again to the floor, and put her face against his neck, and trembled and shuddered. But she had to draw away again. He was dead, and her living flesh had no place against his. A great dread and weariness held her: she was so unavailing. Her life was gone like this.

"White as milk he is, clear as a twelve-month baby, bless him, the darling!" the old mother murmured to herself. "Not a mark on him, clear and clean and white, beautiful as ever a child was made," she murmured with pride. Elizabeth kept her face hidden.

"He went peaceful, Lizzie—peaceful as sleep. Isn't he beautiful, the lamb? Ay—he must ha' made his peace, Lizzie. 'Appen he made it all right, Lizzie, shut in there. He'd have time. He wouldn't look like this if he hadn't made his peace. The lamb, the dear lamb. Eh, but he had a hearty laugh. I loved to hear it. He had the heartiest laugh, Lizzie, as a lad——"

Elizabeth looked up. The man's mouth was fallen back, slightly open under the cover of the moustache. The eyes, half shut, did not show glazed in the obscurity. Life with its smoky burning gone from him, had left him apart and utterly alien to her. And she knew what a stranger he was to her. In her womb was ice of fear, because of this separate stranger with whom she had been living as one flesh. Was this what it all meant—utter, intact separateness, obscured by heat of living? In dread she turned her face away. The fact was too deadly. There had been nothing between them, and yet they had come together, exchanging their nakedness repeatedly. Each time he had taken her, they had been two isolated beings, far apart as now. He was no more responsible than she. The child was like ice in her womb. For as she looked at the dead man, her mind, cold and detached, said clearly: "Who am I? What have I been doing? I have been fighting a husband who did not exist. *He* existed all the time. What wrong have I done? What was that I have been living with? There lies the reality, this man."—And her soul died in her for fear: she knew she had never seen him, he had never seen her, they had met in the dark and had fought in the dark, not knowing whom they met nor whom they fought. And now she saw, and turned silent in seeing. For she had been wrong. She had said he was something he was not; she had felt familiar with him. Whereas he was apart all the while, living as she never lived, feeling as she never felt.

In fear and shame she looked at his naked body, that she had known falsely. And he was the father of her children. Her soul was torn from her body and stood apart. She looked at his naked body and was ashamed, as if she had denied it. After all, it was itself. It seemed awful to her. She looked at his face, and she turned her own face to the wall. For his look was other than hers, his way was not her way. She had denied him what he was—she saw it now. She had refused him as himself.—And this had been her life, and his life.—She was grateful to death, which restored the truth. And she knew she was not dead.

And all the while her heart was bursting with grief and pity for him. What had he suffered? What stretch of horror for this helpless man! She was rigid with agony. She had not been able to help him. He had been cruelly injured, this naked man, this other being, and she could make no reparation. There were the children—but the children belonged to life. This dead man had nothing to do with them. He and she were only channels through which life had flowed to issue in the children. She was a mother—but how awful she knew it now to have been a wife. And he, dead now, how awful he must have felt it to be a husband. She felt that in her next world he would be a stranger to her. If they met there, in the beyond, they would only be ashamed of what had been before. The children had come, for some mysterious reason, out of both of them. But the children did not unite them. Now he was dead, she knew how eternally he was apart from her, how eternally he had nothing more to do with her. She saw this episode of her life closed. They had denied each other in life. Now he had withdrawn. An anguish came over her. It was finished then: it had become hopeless between them long before he died. Yet he had been her husband. But how little!

"Have you got his shirt, 'Lizabeth?"

Elizabeth turned without answering, though she strove to weep and behave as her mother-in-law expected. But she could not, she was silenced. She went into the kitchen and returned with the garment.

"It is aired," she said, grasping the cotton shirt here and there to try. She was almost ashamed to handle him; what right had she or anyone to lay hands on him; but her touch was humble on his body. It was hard work to clothe him. He was so heavy and inert. A terrible dread gripped her all the while: that he could be so heavy and utterly inert, unresponsive, apart. The horror of the distance between them was almost too much for her—it was so infinite a gap she must look across.

At last it was finished. They covered him with a sheet and left him lying, with his face bound. And she fastened the door of the little parlour, lest the children should see what was lying there. Then, with peace sunk heavy on her heart, she went about making tidy the kitchen. She knew she submitted to life, which was her immediate master. But from death, her ultimate master, she winced with fear and shame.

1914

D. H. LAWRENCE

The Rocking-Horse Winner

There was a woman who was beautiful, who started with all the advantages, yet she had no luck. She married for love, and the love turned to dust. She had bonny children, yet she felt they had been thrust upon her, and she could not love them. They looked at her coldly, as if they were finding fault with her. And hurriedly she felt she must cover up some fault in herself. Yet what it was that she must cover up she never knew. Nevertheless, when her children were present, she always felt the centre of her heart go hard. This troubled her, and in her manner she was all the more gentle and anxious for her children, as if she loved them very much. Only she herself knew that at the centre of her heart was a hard little place that could not feel love, no, not for anybody. Everybody else said of her: "She is such a good mother. She adores her children." Only she herself, and her children themselves, knew it was not so. They read it in each other's eyes.

There were a boy and two little girls. They lived in a pleasant house, with a garden, and they had discreet servants, and felt themselves superior to anyone in the neighbourhood.

Although they lived in style, they felt always an anxiety in the house. There was never enough money. The mother had a small income, and the father had a small income, but not nearly enough for the social position which they had to keep up. The father went in to town to some office. But though he had good prospects, these prospects never materialized. There was always the grinding sense of the shortage of money, though the style was always kept up.

At last the mother said: "I will see if *I* can't make something." But she did not know where to begin. She racked her brains, and tried this thing and the other, but could not find anything successful. The failure made deep lines come into her face. Her children were growing up, they would have to go to school. There must be more money, there must be more money. The father, who was always very handsome and expensive in his tastes, seemed as if he never *would* be able to do anything worth doing. And the mother, who had a great belief in herself, did not succeed any better, and her tastes were just as expensive.

And so the house came to be haunted by the unspoken phrase: *There must be more money! There must be more money!* The children could hear it all the time, though nobody said it aloud. They heard it at Christmas, when the expensive and splendid toys filled the nursery. Behind the shining modern rocking-horse, behind the smart doll's-house, a voice would start whispering: "There *must* be more money! There *must* be more money!" And the children would stop playing, to listen for a moment. They would look into each other's eyes, to see if they had all heard. And each one saw in the eyes of the other two that they too had heard. "There *must* be more money! There *must* be more money!"

It came whispering from the springs of the still-swaying rocking-horse, and even the horse, bending his wooden, champing head, heard it. The big doll, sitting so pink and smirking in her new pram,[1] could hear it quite plainly, and seemed to be smirking all the more self-consciously because of it. The foolish puppy, too, that took the place of the teddy-bear, he was looking so extraordinarily foolish for no other reason but that he heard the secret whisper all over the house: "There *must* be more money!"

Yet nobody ever said it aloud. The whisper was everywhere, and therefore no one spoke it. Just as no one ever says: "We are breathing!" in spite of the fact that breath is coming and going all the time.

"Mother," said the boy Paul one day, "why don't we keep a car of our own? Why do we always use uncle's, or else a taxi?"

"Because we're the poor members of the family," said the mother.

"But why *are* we, mother?"

"Well—I suppose," she said slowly and bitterly, "it's because your father has no luck."

1. Baby carriage.

The boy was silent for some time.

"Is luck money, mother?" he asked rather timidly.

"No, Paul. Not quite. It's what causes you to have money."

"Oh!" said Paul vaguely. "I thought when Uncle Oscar said *filthy lucker*, it meant money."

"*Filthy lucre* does mean money," said the mother. "But it's lucre, not luck."

"Oh!" said the boy. "Then what *is* luck, mother?"

"It's what causes you to have money. If you're lucky you have money. That's why it's better to be born lucky than rich. If you're rich, you may lose your money. But if you're lucky, you will always get more money."

"Oh! Will you? And is father not lucky?"

"Very unlucky, I should say," she said bitterly.

The boy watched her with unsure eyes.

"Why?" he asked.

"I don't know. Nobody ever knows why one person is lucky and another unlucky."

"Don't they? Nobody at all? Does *nobody* know?"

"Perhaps God. But He never tells."

"He ought to, then. And aren't you lucky either, mother?"

"I can't be, if I married an unlucky husband."

"But by yourself, aren't you?"

"I used to think I was, before I married. Now I think I am very unlucky indeed."

"Why?"

"Well—never mind! Perhaps I'm not really," she said.

The child looked at her, to see if she meant it. But he saw, by the lines of her mouth, that she was only trying to hide something from him.

"Well, anyhow," he said stoutly, "I'm a lucky person."

"Why?" said his mother, with a sudden laugh.

He stared at her. He didn't even know why he had said it.

"God told me," he asserted, brazening it out.

"I hope He did, dear!" she said, again with a laugh, but rather bitter.

"He did, mother!"

"Excellent!" said the mother, using one of her husband's exclamations.

The boy saw she did not believe him; or, rather, that she paid no attention to his assertion. This angered him somewhat, and made him want to compel her attention.

He went off by himself, vaguely, in a childish way, seeking for the clue to "luck." Absorbed, taking no heed of other people, he went about with a sort of stealth, seeking inwardly for luck. He wanted luck, he wanted it, he wanted it. When the two girls were playing dolls in the nursery, he would sit on his big rocking-horse, charging madly into space, with a frenzy that made the little girls peer at him uneasily. Wildly the horse careered, the waving dark hair of the boy tossed, his eyes had a strange glare in them. The little girls dared not speak to him.

When he had ridden to the end of his mad little journey, he climbed down and stood in front of his rocking-horse, staring fixedly into its lowered face. Its red mouth was slightly open, its big eye was wide and glassy-bright.

"Now!" he would silently command the snorting steed. "Now, take me to where there is luck! Now take me!"

And he would slash the horse on the neck with the little whip he had asked Uncle Oscar for. He *knew* the horse could take him to where there was luck, if only he forced it. So he would mount again, and start on his furious ride, hoping at last to get there. He knew he could get there.

"You'll break your horse, Paul!" said the nurse.

"He's always riding like that! I wish he'd leave off!" said his elder sister Joan.

But he only glared down on them in silence. Nurse gave him up. She could make nothing of him. Anyhow he was growing beyond her.

One day his mother and his Uncle Oscar came in when he was on one of his furious rides. He did not speak to them.

"Hallo, you young jockey! Riding a winner?" said his uncle.

"Aren't you growing too big for a rocking-horse? You're not a very little boy any longer, you know," said his mother.

But Paul only gave a blue glare from his big, rather close-set eyes. He would speak to nobody when he was in full tilt. His mother watched him with an anxious expression on her face.

At last he suddenly stopped forcing his horse into the mechanical gallop, and slid down.

"Well, I got there!" he announced fiercely, his blue eyes still flaring, and his sturdy long legs straddling apart.

"Where did you get to?" asked his mother.

"Where I wanted to go," he flared back at her.

"That's right, son!" said Uncle Oscar. "Don't you stop till you get there. What's the horse's name?"

"He doesn't have a name," said the boy.

"Gets on without all right?" asked the uncle.

"Well, he has different names. He was called Sansovino last week."

"Sansovino, eh? Won the Ascot.[2] How did you know his name?"

"He always talks about horse-races with Bassett," said Joan.

The uncle was delighted to find that his small nephew was posted with all the racing news. Bassett, the young gardener, who had been wounded in the left foot in the war[3] and had got his present job through Oscar Cresswell, whose batman he had been, was a perfect blade of the "turf."[4] He lived in the racing events, and the small boy lived with him.

Oscar Cresswell got it all from Bassett.

"Master Paul comes and asks me, so I can't do more than tell him, sir," said

2. A race run at a course of that name in Berkshire. Other races mentioned in the story are Lincolnshire Handicap, then run at Lincoln Downs; the St. Leger Stakes, run at Doncaster; the Grand National Steeplechase, run at Aintree, the most famous steeplechase in the world; the famous Derby, a mile-and-a-half race for three-year-olds run at Epsom Downs. 3. World War I, 1914–1918. 4. Dashing young horseplayer. *Batman:* British officer's orderly.

Bassett, his face terribly serious, as if he were speaking of religious matters.

"And does he ever put anything on a horse he fancies?"

"Well—I don't want to give him away—he's a young sport, a fine sport, sir. Would you mind asking him himself? He sort of takes a pleasure in it, and perhaps he'd feel I was giving him away, sir, if you don't mind."

Bassett was serious as a church.

The uncle went back to his nephew and took him off for a ride in the car.

"Say, Paul, old man, do you ever put anything on a horse?" the uncle asked.

The boy watched the handsome man closely.

"Why, do you think I oughtn't to?" he parried.

"Not a bit of it! I thought perhaps you might give me a tip for the Lincoln."

The car sped on into the country, going down to Uncle Oscar's place in Hampshire.

"Honour bright?" said the nephew.

"Honour bright, son!" said the uncle.

"Well, then, Daffodil."

"Daffodil! I doubt it, sonny. What about Mirza?"

"I only know the winner," said the boy. "That's Daffodil."

"Daffodil, eh?"

There was a pause. Daffodil was an obscure horse comparatively.

"Uncle!"

"Yes, son?"

"You won't let it go any further, will you? I promised Bassett."

"Bassett be damned, old man! What's he got to do with it?"

"We're partners. We've been partners from the first. Uncle, he lent me my first five shillings, which I lost. I promised him, honour bright, it was only between me and him; only you gave me that ten-shilling note I started winning with, so I thought you were lucky. You won't let it go any further, will you?"

The boy gazed at his uncle from those big, hot, blue eyes, set rather close together. The uncle stirred and laughed uneasily.

"Right you are, son! I'll keep your tip private. Daffodil, eh? How much are you putting on him?"

"All except twenty pounds," said the boy. "I keep that in reserve."

The uncle thought it a good joke.

"You keep twenty pounds in reserve, do you, you young romancer? What are you betting, then?"

"I'm betting three hundred," said the boy, gravely. "But it's between you and me, Uncle Oscar! Honour bright?"

The uncle burst into a roar of laughter.

"It's between you and me all right, you young Nat Gould,"[5] he said, laughing. "But where's your three hundred?"

"Bassett keeps it for me. We're partners."

5. Nathaniel Gould (1857–1919) novelist and journalist whose writings in both genres concerned horse-racing.

"You are, are you! And what is Bassett putting on Daffodil?"

"He won't go quite as high as I do, I expect. Perhaps he'll go a hundred and fifty."

"What, pennies?" laughed the uncle.

"Pounds," said the child, with a surprised look at his uncle. "Bassett keeps a bigger reserve than I do."

Between wonder and amusement Uncle Oscar was silent. He pursued the matter no further, but he determined to take his nephew with him to the Lincoln races.

"Now, son," he said, "I'm putting twenty on Mirza, and I'll put five for you on any horse you fancy. What's your pick?"

"Daffodil, uncle."

"No, not the fiver on Daffodil!"

"I should if it was my own fiver," said the child.

"Good! Good! Right you are! A fiver for me and a fiver for you on Daffodil."

The child had never been to a race-meeting before, and his eyes were blue fire. He pursed his mouth tight, and watched. A Frenchman just in front had put his money on Lancelot. Wild with excitement, he flayed his arms up and down, yelling "*Lancelot! Lancelot!*" in his French accent.

Daffodil came in first, Lancelot second, Mirza third. The child, flushed and with eyes blazing, was curiously serene. His uncle brought him four five-pound notes, four to one.

"What am I to do with these?" he cried, waving them before the boy's eyes.

"I suppose we'll talk to Bassett," said the boy. "I expect I have fifteen hundred now; and twenty in reserve; and this twenty."

His uncle studied him for some moments.

"Look here, son!" he said. "You're not serious about Bassett and that fifteen hundred, are you?"

"Yes, I am. But it's between you and me, uncle. Honour bright!"

"Honour bright all right, son! But I must talk to Bassett."

"If you'd like to be a partner, uncle, with Bassett and me, we could all be partners. Only, you'd have to promise, honour bright, uncle, not to let it go beyond us three. Bassett and I are lucky, and you must be lucky, because it was your ten shillings I started winning with. . . ."

Uncle Oscar took both Bassett and Paul into Richmond Park for an afternoon, and there they talked.

"It's like this, you see, sir," Bassett said. "Master Paul would get me talking about racing events, spinning yarns, you know, sir. And he was always keen on knowing if I'd made or if I'd lost. It's about a year since, now, that I put five shillings on Blush of Dawn for him—and we lost. Then the luck turned, with the ten shillings he had from you, that we put on Singhalese. And since that time, it's been pretty steady, all things considering. What do you say, Master Paul?"

"We're all right when we're sure," said Paul. "It's when we're not quite sure that we go down."

"Oh, but we're careful then," said Bassett.

"But when are you *sure?*" smiled Uncle Oscar.

"It's Master Paul, sir," said Bassett, in a secret, religious voice. "It's as if he had it from heaven. Like Daffodil, now, for the Lincoln. That was as sure as eggs."

"Did you put anything on Daffodil?" asked Oscar Cresswell.

"Yes, sir. I made my bit."

"And my nephew?"

Bassett was obstinately silent, looking at Paul.

"I made twelve hundred, didn't I, Bassett? I told uncle I was putting three hundred on Daffodil."

"That's right," said Bassett, nodding.

"But where's the money?" asked the uncle.

"I keep it safe locked up, sir. Master Paul he can have it any minute he likes to ask for it."

"What, fifteen hundred pounds?"

"And twenty! And *forty,* that is, with the twenty he made on the course."

"It's amazing!" said the uncle.

"If Master Paul offers you to be partners, sir, I would, if I were you; if you'll excuse me," said Bassett.

Oscar Cresswell thought about it.

"I'll see the money," he said.

They drove home again, and sure enough, Bassett came round to the garden-house with fifteen hundred pounds in notes. The twenty pounds reserve was left with Joe Glee, in the Turf Commission deposit.

"You see, it's all right, uncle, when I'm *sure!* Then we go strong, for all we're worth. Don't we, Bassett?"

"We do that, Master Paul"

"And when are you sure?" said the uncle, laughing.

"Oh, well, sometimes I'm *absolutely* sure, like about Daffodil," said the boy; "and sometimes I have an idea; and sometimes I haven't even an idea, have I, Bassett? Then we're careful, because we mostly go down."

"You do, do you! And when you're sure, like about Daffodil, what makes you sure, sonny?"

"Oh, well, I don't know," said the boy uneasily. "I'm sure, you know, uncle; that's all."

"It's as if he had it from heaven, sir," Bassett reiterated.

"I should say so!" said the uncle.

But he became a partner. And when the Leger was coming on, Paul was "sure" about Lively Spark, which was a quite inconsiderable horse. The boy insisted on putting a thousand on the horse, Bassett went for five hundred, and Oscar Cresswell two hundred. Lively Spark came in first, and the betting had been ten to one against him. Paul had made ten thousand.

"You see," he said, "I was absolutely sure of him."

Even Oscar Cresswell had cleared two thousand.

"Look here, son," he said, "this sort of thing makes me nervous."

"It needn't, uncle! Perhaps I shan't be sure again for a long time."

"But what are you going to do with your money?" asked the uncle.

"Of course," said the boy, "I started it for mother. She said she had no luck, because father is unlucky, so I thought if *I* was lucky, it might stop whispering."

"What might stop whispering?"

"Our house. I *hate* our house for whispering."

"What does it whisper?"

"Why—why"—the boy fidgeted—"why, I don't know. But it's always short of money, you know, uncle."

"I know it, son, I know it."

"You know people send mother writs, don't you, uncle?"

"I'm afraid I do," said the uncle.

"And then the house whispers, like people laughing at you behind your back. It's awful, that is! I thought if I was lucky . . ."

"You might stop it," added the uncle.

The boy watched him with big blue eyes, that had an uncanny cold fire in them, and he said never a word.

"Well, then!" said the uncle. "What are we doing?"

"I shouldn't like mother to know I was lucky," said the boy.

"Why not, son?"

"She'd stop me."

"I don't think she would."

"Oh!"—and the boy writhed in an odd way—"I *don't* want her to know, uncle."

"All right, son! We'll manage it without her knowing."

They managed it very easily. Paul, at the other's suggestion, handed over five thousand pounds to his uncle, who deposited it with the family lawyer, who was then to inform Paul's mother that a relative had put five thousand pounds into his hands, which sum was to be paid out a thousand pounds at a time, on the mother's birthday, for the next five years.

"So she'll have a birthday present of a thousand pounds for five successive years," said Uncle Oscar. "I hope it won't make it all the harder for her later."

Paul's mother had her birthday in November. The house had been "whispering" worse than ever lately, and, even in spite of his luck, Paul could not bear up against it. He was very anxious to see the effect of the birthday letter, telling his mother about the thousand pounds.

When there were no visitors, Paul now took his meals with his parents, as he was beyond the nursery control. His mother went into town nearly every day. She had discovered that she had an odd knack of sketching furs and dress materials, so she worked secretly in the studio of a friend who was the chief "artist" for the leading drapers. She drew the figures of ladies in furs and ladies in silk and sequins for the newspaper advertisements. This young woman artist earned several thousand pounds a year, but Paul's mother only made several hundreds, and she was again dissatisfied. She so wanted to be first in something, and she did not succeed, even in making sketches for drapery advertisements.

She was down to breakfast on the morning of her birthday. Paul watched her face as she read her letters. He knew the lawyer's letter. As his mother read it, her face hardened and became more expressionless. Than a cold, determined look came on her mouth. She hid the letter under the pile of others, and said not a word about it.

"Didn't you have anything nice in the post for your birthday, mother?" said Paul.

"Quite moderately nice," she said, her voice cold and absent.

She went away to town without saying more.

But in the afternoon Uncle Oscar appeared. He said Paul's mother had had a long interview with the lawyer, asking if the whole five thousand could not be advanced at once, as she was in debt.

"What do you think, uncle?" said the boy.

"I leave it to you, son."

"Oh, let her have it, then! We can get some more with the other," said the boy.

"A bird in the hand is worth two in the bush, laddie!" said Uncle Oscar.

"But I'm sure to *know* for the Grand National; or the Lincolnshire; or else the Derby. I'm sure to know for *one* of them," said Paul.

So Uncle Oscar signed the agreement, and Paul's mother touched the whole five thousand. Then something very curious happened. The voices in the house suddenly went mad, like a chorus of frogs on a spring evening. There were certain new furnishings, and Paul had a tutor. He was *really* going to Eton, his father's school, in the following autumn. There were flowers in the winter, and a blossoming of the luxury Paul's mother had been used to. And yet the voices in the house, behind the sprays of mimosa and almond blossom, and from under the piles of iridescent cushions, simply trilled and screamed in a sort of ecstasy: "There *must* be more money! Oh-h-h; there *must* be more money Oh, now, now-w! Now-w-w—there *must* be more money!—more than ever! More than ever!"

It frightened Paul terribly. He studied away at his Latin and Greek with his tutors. But his intense hours were spent with Bassett. The Grand National had gone by: he had not "known," and had lost a hundred pounds. Summer was at hand. He was in agony for the Lincoln. But even for the Lincoln he didn't "know," and he lost fifty pounds. He became wild-eyed and strange, as if something were going to explode in him.

"Let it alone, son! Don't you bother about it!" urged Uncle Oscar. But it was as if the boy couldn't really hear what his uncle was saying.

"I've got to know for the Derby! I've got to know for the Derby!" the child reiterated, his big blue eyes blazing with a sort of madness.

His mother noticed how overwrought he was.

"You'd better go to the seaside. Wouldn't you like to go now to the seaside, instead of waiting? I think you'd better," she said, looking down at him anxiously, her heart curiously heavy because of him.

But the child lifted his uncanny blue eyes.

"I couldn't possibly go before the Derby, mother!" he said. "I couldn't possibly!"

"Why not?" she said, her voice becoming heavy when she was opposed.

"Why not? You can still go from the seaside to see the Derby with your Uncle Oscar, if that's what you wish. No need for you to wait here. Besides, I think you care too much about these races. It's a bad sign. My family has been a gambling family, and you won't know till you grow up how much damage it has done. But it has done damage. I shall have to send Bassett away, and ask Uncle Oscar not to talk racing to you, unless you promise to be reasonable about it; go away to the seaside and forget it. You're all nerves!"

"I'll do what you like, mother, so long as you don't send me away till after the Derby," the boy said.

"Send you away from where? Just from this house?"

"Yes," he said, gazing at her.

"Why, you curious child, what makes you care about this house so much, suddenly? I never knew you loved it."

He gazed at her without speaking. He had a secret within a secret, something he had not divulged, even to Bassett or to his Uncle Oscar.

But his mother, after standing undecided and a little bit sullen for some moments, said:

"Very well, then! Don't go to the seaside till after the Derby, if you don't wish it. But promise me you won't let your nerves go to pieces. Promise you won't think so much about horse-racing and events, as you call them!"

"Oh, no," said the boy casually. "I won't think much about them, mother. You needn't worry. I wouldn't worry, mother, if I were you."

"If you were me and I were you," said his mother, "I wonder what we *should* do!"

"But you know you needn't worry, mother, don't you?" the boy repeated.

"I should be awfully glad to know it," she said wearily.

"Oh, well, you *can*, you know. I mean, you *ought* to know you needn't worry," he insisted.

"Ought I? Then I'll see about it," she said.

Paul's secret of secrets was his wooden horse, that which had no name. Since he was emancipated from a nurse and a nursery-governess, he had had his rocking-horse removed to his own bedroom at the top of the house.

"Surely, you're too big for a rocking-horse!" his mother had remonstrated.

"Well, you see, mother, till I can have a *real* horse, I like to have *some* sort of animal about," had been his quaint answer.

"Do you feel he keeps you company?" she laughed.

"Oh, yes! He's very good, he always keeps me company, when I'm there," said Paul.

So the horse, rather shabby, stood in an arrested prance in the boy's bedroom.

The Derby was drawing near, and the boy grew more and more tense. He hardly heard what was spoken to him, he was very frail, and his eyes were really uncanny. His mother had sudden strange seizures of uneasiness about him. Sometimes, for half-an-hour, she would feel a sudden anxiety about him that was almost anguish. She wanted to rush to him at once, and know he was safe.

Two nights before the Derby, she was at a big party in town, when one of her rushes of anxiety about her boy, her first-born, gripped her heart till she could hardly speak. She fought with the feeling, might and main, for she believed in common-sense. But it was too strong. She had to leave the dance and go downstairs to telephone to the country. The children's nursery-governess was terribly surprised and startled at being rung up in the night.

"Are the children all right, Miss Wilmot?"

"Oh, yes, they are quite all right."

"Master Paul? Is he all right?"

"He went to bed as right as a trivet. Shall I run up and look at him?"

"No," said Paul's mother reluctantly. "No! Don't trouble. It's all right. Don't sit up. We shall be home fairly soon." She did not want her son's privacy intruded upon.

"Very good," said the governess.

It was about one o'clock when Paul's mother and father drove up to their house. All was still. Paul's mother went to her room and slipped off her white fur cloak. She had told her maid not to wait up for her. She heard her husband downstairs, mixing a whisky-and-soda.

And then, because of the strange anxiety at her heart, she stole upstairs to her son's room. Noiselessly she went along the upper corridor. Was there a faint noise? What was it?

She stood, with arrested muscles, outside his door, listening. There was a strange, heavy, and yet not loud noise. Her heart stood still. It was a soundless noise, yet rushing and powerful. Something huge, in violent, hushed motion. What was it? What in God's name was it? She ought to know. She felt that she knew the noise. She knew what it was.

Yet she could not place it. She couldn't say what it was. And on and on it went, like a madness.

Softly, frozen with anxiety and fear, she turned the door-handle.

The room was dark. Yet in the space near the window, she heard and saw something plunging to and fro. She gazed in fear and amazement.

Then suddenly she switched on the light, and saw her son, in his green pyjamas, madly surging on the rocking-horse. The blaze of light suddenly lit him up, as he urged the wooden horse, and lit her up, as she stood, blonde, in her dress of pale green and crystal, in the doorway.

"Paul!" she cried. "Whatever are you doing?"

"It's Malabar!" he screamed, in a powerful, strange voice. "It's Malabar!"

His eyes blazed at her for one strange and senseless second, as he ceased urging his wooden horse. Then he fell with a crash to the ground, and she, all her tormented motherhood flooding upon her, rushed to gather him up.

But he was unconscious, and unconscious he remained, with some brain-fever. He talked and tossed, and his mother sat stonily by his side.

"Malabar! It's Malabar! Bassett, Bassett, I *know!* It's Malabar!"

So the child cried, trying to get up and urge the rocking-horse that gave him his inspiration.

"What does he mean by Malabar?" asked the heart-frozen mother.

"I don't know," said the father stonily.

"What does he mean by Malabar?" she asked her brother Oscar.

"It's one of the horses running for the Derby," was the answer.

And, in spite of himself, Oscar Cresswell spoke to Bassett, and himself put a thousand on Malabar: at fourteen to one.

The third day of the illness was critical: they were waiting for a change. The boy, with his rather long, curly hair, was tossing ceaselessly on the pillow. He neither slept nor regained consciousness, and his eyes were like blue stones. His mother sat, feeling her heart had gone, turned actually into a stone.

In the evening, Oscar Cresswell did not come, but Bassett sent a message, saying could he come up for one moment, just one moment? Paul's mother was very angry at the intrusion, but on second thought she agreed. The boy was the same. Perhaps Bassett might bring him to consciousness.

The gardener, a shortish fellow with a little brown moustache, and sharp little brown eyes, tip-toed into the room, touched his imaginary cap to Paul's mother, and stole to the bedside, staring with glittering, smallish eyes, at the tossing, dying child.

"Master Paul!" he whispered. "Master Paul! Malabar came in first all right, a clean win. I did as you told me. You've made over seventy thousand pounds, you have; you've got over eighty thousand. Malabar came in all right, Master Paul."

"Malabar! Malabar! Did I say Malabar, mother? Did I say Malabar? Do you think I'm lucky, mother? I knew Malabar, didn't I? Over eighty thousand pounds! I call that lucky, don't you, mother? Over eighty thousand pounds! I knew, didn't I know I knew! Malabar came in all right. If I ride my horse till I'm sure, then I tell you, Bassett, you can go as high as you like. Did you go for all you were worth, Bassett?"

"I went a thousand on it, Master Paul."

"I never told you, mother, that if I can ride my horse, and *get there*, then I'm absolutely sure—oh absolutely! Mother, did I ever tell you? I *am* lucky!"

"No, you never did," said the mother.

But the boy died in the night.

And even as he lay dead, his mother heard her brother's voice saying to her: "My God, Hester, you're eighty-odd thousand to the good, and a poor devil of a son to the bad. But, poor devil, poor devil, he's best gone out of a life where he rides his rocking-horse to find a winner."

1932

D. H. LAWRENCE

Passages from Essays and Letters

from "Nottingham and the Mining Countryside"

I was born . . . in Eastwood, a mining village of some three thousand souls, about eight miles from Nottingham. . . . It is hilly country. . . . To me it seemed, and still seems, an extremely beautiful countryside, just between the red sandstone and the oak-trees of Nottingham, and the cold limestone, the ash-trees, the stone fences of Derbyshire. To me, as a child and a young man, it was still the old England of the forest and agricultural past; there were no motorcars, the mines were, in a sense, an accident in the landscape, and Robin Hood and his merry men were not very far away.

. . . The people lived almost entirely by instinct, men of my father's age could not really read. And the pit did not mechanize men. . . . My father loved the pit. He was hurt badly, more than once, but he would never stay away. He loved the contact, the intimacy, as men in the war loved the intense male comradeship of the dark days.

Now the colliers had also an instinct for beauty. The colliers' wives had not. The colliers were deeply alive, instinctively. But they had no daytime ambition, and no daytime intellect. They avoided, really, the rational aspect of life. . . . They didn't even care very profoundly about wages. It was the women, naturally, who nagged on this score. . . . The collier went to the pub and drank in order to continue the intimacy with his mates.

. . . Life for him did not consist of facts, but in a flow. Very often he loved his garden. And very often he had a genuine love of the beauty of flowers. . . .

. . . Most women love flowers as possessions, and as trimmings. They can't look at a flower, and wonder a moment, and pass on. If they see a flower that arrests their attention, they must at once pick it, pluck it. Possession! A possession! Something added on to *me!*

from "Love"

. . . the love between a man and a woman . . . is dual. It is the melting into pure communion, and it is the friction of sheer sensuality, both. In pure communion I become whole in love. And in pure, fierce passion of sensuality, I am burned into essentiality. I am driven from the matrix unto sheer separate distinction. I become my single self, inviolable and unique, as the gems were perhaps once driven into themselves out of the confusion of earths. . . .

from "Women Are So Cocksure"

. . . [My mother] was convinced . . . that a man ought not to drink beer. This conviction developed from the fact, naturally, that my father drank beer.

He sometimes drank too much. He sometimes boozed away the money necessary for the young family. When my father came in tipsy, she saw scarlet.

from "Art and Morality"

Apples are always apples! says Vox Populi, Vox Dei.[1]

Sometimes they're sin, sometimes they're a knock on the head, sometimes they're a bellyache, sometimes they're part of a pie, sometimes they're sauce for a goose.

What art has got to do, and will go on doing, is to reveal things in their different relationships. That is to say, you've got to see in the apples the bellyache. Sir Isaac's knock on the cranium, the vast, moist wall through which the insect bores to lay her eggs in the middle, and the untasted, unknown quality which Eve saw hanging on a tree.

from "Morality and the Novel"

The business of art is to reveal the relation between man and his circumambient universe, at the living moment. As mankind is always struggling in the toils of old relationships, art is always ahead of the "times," which themselves are always far in the rear of the living moment.

When van Gogh paints sunflowers, he reveals, or achieves, the vivid relation between himself, as man, and the sunflowers, as sunflower, at that quick moment of time. His painting does not represent the sunflower itself. We shall never know what the sunflower itself is. And the camera will *visualize* the sunflower far more perfectly than van Gogh can.

The vision on the canvas is a third thing, utterly intangible and inexplicable, the offspring of the sunflower itself and van Gogh himself. . . .

. . . The novel is the highest example of subtle interrelatedness that man has discovered. Everything is true in its own time, place, and circumstance, and untrue outside of its own place, time, circumstance. If you try to nail anything down, in the novel, either it kills the novel, or the novel gets up and walks away with the nail.

. . . Love is a great emotion. But if you set out to write a novel, and you yourself are in the throes of the great predilection for love, love as the supreme, the only emotion worth living for, then you will write an immoral novel.

Because *no* emotion is supreme, or exclusively worth living for. *All* emotions go to the achieving of a living relationship between a human being and the other human being or creature or thing he becomes purely related to. All emotions, including love and hate, and rage and tenderness, go to the adjusting of the oscillating, unestablished balance between two people who amount to anything.

A new relation, a new relatedness hurts somewhat in the attaining; and will always hurt. So life will always hurt. . . .

1. The voice of the people [is] the voice of God.

Each time we strive to a new relation, with anyone or anything, it is bound to hurt somewhat. Because it means the struggle with and the displacing of old connections, and this is never pleasant. And, moreover, between living things at least, an adjustment means also a fight, for each party, inevitably, must "seek its own" in the other, and be denied. When, in the two parties, each of them seeks his own, her own, absolutely, then it is a fight to the death. And this is true of the thing called "passion."

The great relationship for humanity will always be the relation between man and woman. The relation between man and man, woman and woman, parent and child, will always be subsidiary.

And the relation between man and woman will change forever, and will forever be the new central clue to human life. It is the *relation itself* which is the quick and the central clue to life, not the man, nor the woman, nor the children that result from the relationship, as a contingency.

from "Why the Novel Matters"

We have curious ideas of ourselves. We think of ourselves as a body with a spirit in it, or a body with a soul in it, or a body with a mind in it. . . .

It is a funny sort of superstition. Why should I look at my hand, as it so cleverly writes these words, and decide that it is a mere nothing compared to the mind that directs it? Why should I imagine that there is a *me* which is more *me* than my hand is? Since my hand is absolutely alive, me alive.

And that's what you learn, when you're a novelist. And that's what you are liable *not* to know, if you're a parson, or a philosopher, or a scientist, or a stupid person.

Now I absolutely flatly deny that I am a soul, or a body, or a mind, or an intelligence, or a brain, or a nervous system, or a bunch of glands, or any of the rest of these bits of me. The whole is greater than the part. And therefore, I, who am man alive, am greater than my soul, or spirit, or body, or mind, or consciousness, or anything else that is merely a part of me. I am man a man, and alive. I am man alive, and as long as I can, I intend to go on being man alive.

For this reason I am a novelist. And being a novelist, I consider myself superior to the saint, the scientist, the philosopher, and the poet, who are all great masters of different bits of man alive, but never get the whole thing.

We should ask for no absolutes, or absolute. . . . There is no absolute good, there is nothing absolutely right. All things flow and change, and even change is not absolute. . . .

. . . If the one I love remains unchanged and unchanging, I shall cease to love her. It is only because she changes and startles me into change and defies my inertia, and is herself staggered in her inertia by my changing, that I can continue to love her. If she stayed put, I might as well love the pepper-pot.

In life, there is right and wrong, good and bad, all the time. But what is right in one case is wrong in another. And in the novel you see one man becoming a corpse, because of his so-called goodness, another going dead because of his so-called wickedness. Right and wrong is an instinct: but an instinct of the whole consciousness in a man, bodily, mental, spiritual at once. And only in the novel are *all* things given full play, or at least, they may be given full play, when we realize that life itself, and not inert safety, is the reason for living. For out of the full play of all things emerges the only thing that is anything, the wholeness of a man, the wholeness of a woman, man alive, and live woman.

from Autobiographical Sketch

They ask me; "Did you find it very hard to get on and to become a success?" And I have to admit that if I can be said to have got on, and if I can be called a success, then I *did not* find it hard.

I never starved in a garret, nor waited in anguish for the post to bring me an answer from editor or publisher, nor did I struggle in sweat and blood to bring forth mighty works, nor did I ever wake up and find myself famous.

. . . My father was a collier, and only a collier, nothing praise-worthy about him. He wasn't even respectable, in so far as he got drunk rather frequently, never went near a chapel, and was usually rather rude to his little immediate bosses at the pit.

My mother was, I suppose, superior. She came from town, and belonged really to the lower bourgeoisie. She spoke King's English, without an accent, and never in her life could even imitate a sentence of the dialect which my father spoke, and which we children spoke out of doors.

I have *wanted* to feel truly friendly with some, at least, of my fellow-men. Yet I have never quite succeeded. Whether I got on *in* the world is a question; but I certainly don't get on very well *with* the world. And whether I am a worldly success or not I really don't know. But I feel, somehow, not much of a human success.

By which I mean that I don't feel there is any very cordial or fundamental contact between me and society, or me and other people. There is a breach. And my contact is with something that is nonhuman, nonvocal.

[Why?] The answer, as far as I can see, has something to do with class. Class makes a gulf, across which all the best human flow is lost. It is not exactly the triumph of the middle classes that has made the deadness, but the triumph of the middle-class *thing*.

As a man from the working class, I feel that the middle class cut off some of my vital vibration when I am with them. I admit them charming and educated and good people often enough. *But they just stop some part of me from working.* . . .

Then why don't I live with my working people? Because their vibration is limited in another direction. They are narrow, but still fairly deep and passionate, whereas the middle class is broad and shallow and passionless.

I cannot make the transfer from my own class into the middle class. I cannot, not for anything in the world, forfeit my passional consciousness and my old blood-affinity with my fellow-men and the animals and the land, for that other thin, spurious mental conceit which is all that is left of the mental consciousness once it has made itself exclusive.

from the Letters

TO A. W. MCLEOD, 26 APRIL 1913

I am so sure that only through a readjustment between men and women, and a making free and healthy of this sex, will she [England] get out of her present atrophy. Oh, Lord, and if I don't "subdue my art to a metaphysic," as somebody very beautifully said of Hardy, I do write because I want folk—English folk—to alter, and have more sense.

TO A. W. MCLEOD, 2 JUNE 1914

I think the only re-sourcing of art, revivifying it, is to make it more the joint work of man and woman. I think *the* one thing to do, is for men to have courage to draw nearer to women, expose themselves to them, and be altered by them; and for women to accept and admit men. That is the start—by bringing themselves together, men and women—revealing themselves to each other, gaining great blind knowledge and suffering and joy, which it will take a big further lapse of civilization to exploit and work out. Because the source of all life and knowledge is in man and woman, and the source of all living is in the interchange and the meeting and mingling of these two: man-life and woman-life, man-knowledge and woman-knowledge, man-being and woman-being.

TO J. B. PINKER, 16 DECEMBER 1915

. . . Tell Arnold Bennett[2] that all rules of construction hold good only for novels which are copies of other novels. A book which is not a copy of other books has its own construction, and what he calls faults, he being an old imitator, I call characteristics.

TO ROLF GARDINER, 9 AUGUST 1924

What we need is to smash a few big holes in European suburbanity, let in a little real fresh air.

2. An early twentieth-century novelist (1867–1931) whose major works—*The Old Wives' Tale* (1908) and *The Clayhanger Trilogy* (1910–15)—treat the middle classes in the pottery country of the English Midlands in a naturalistic manner (usually criticizing the money-grubbing, social-climbing selfishness of the society). In his later years he more or less turned into a hack, though a clever one, and it is to Bennett as a very popular, successful hack that Lawrence is referring.

To Lady Ottoline Morrell, 5 February 1929

. . . Don't you think it's nonsense when Murry says that my world is not the ordinary man's world and that I am a sort of animal with a sixth sense? Seems to me more likely he's a sort of animal with only four senses—the real sense of touch missing. They all seem determined to make a freak of me—to save their own short-failings, and make them "normal."

FLANNERY O'CONNOR

The Lame Shall Enter First

Sheppard sat on a stool at the bar that divided the kitchen in half, eating his cereal out of the individual pasteboard box it came in. He ate mechanically, his eyes on the child, who was wandering from cabinet to cabinet in the panelled kitchen, collecting the ingredients for his breakfast. He was a stocky blond boy of ten. Sheppard kept his intense blue eyes fixed on him. The boy's future was written in his face. He would be a banker. No, worse. He would operate a small loan company. All he wanted for the child was that he be good and unselfish and neither seemed likely. Sheppard was a young man whose hair was already white. It stood up like a narrow brush halo over his pink sensitive face.

The boy approached the bar with the jar of peanut butter under his arm, a plate with a quarter of a small chocolate cake on it in one hand and the ketchup bottle in the other. He did not appear to notice his father. He climbed up on the stool and began to spread peanut butter on the cake. He had very large round ears that leaned away from his head and seemed to pull his eyes slightly too far apart. His shirt was green but so faded that the cowboy charging across the front of it was only a shadow.

"Norton," Sheppard said, "I saw Rufus Johnson yesterday. Do you know what he was doing?"

The child looked at him with a kind of half attention, his eyes forward but not yet engaged. They were a paler blue than his father's as if they might have faded like the shirt; one of them listed, almost imperceptibly, toward the outer rim.

5 "He was in an alley," Sheppard said, "and he had his hand in a garbage can. He was trying to get something to eat out of it." He paused to let this soak in. "He was hungry," he finished, and tried to pierce the child's conscience with his gaze.

The boy picked up the piece of chocolate cake and began to gnaw it from one corner.

"Norton," Sheppard said, "do you have any idea what it means to share?"

A flicker of attention. "Some of it's yours," Norton said

"Some of it's *his*," Sheppard said heavily. It was hopeless. Almost any fault would have been preferable to selfishness—a violent temper, even a tendency to lie.

The child turned the bottle of ketchup upside down and began thumping ketchup onto the cake.

Sheppard's look of pain increased. "You are ten and Rufus Johnson is fourteen," he said. "Yet I'm sure your shirts would fit Rufus." Rufus Johnson was a boy he had been trying to help at the reformatory for the past year. He had been released two months ago. "When he was in the reformatory, he looked pretty good, but when I saw him yesterday, he was skin and bones. He hasn't been eating cake with peanut butter on it for breakfast."

The child paused. "It's stale," he said. "That's why I have to put stuff on it."

Sheppard turned his face to the window at the end of the bar. The side lawn, green and even, sloped fifty feet or so down to a small suburban wood. When his wife was living, they had often eaten outside, even breakfast, on the grass. He had never noticed then that the child was selfish. "Listen to me," he said, turning back to him, "look at me and listen."

The boy looked at him. At least his eyes were forward.

"I gave Rufus a key to this house when he left the reformatory—to show my confidence in him and so he would have a place he could come to and feel welcome any time. He didn't use it, but I think he'll use it now because he's seen me and he's hungry. And if he doesn't use it, I'm going out and find him and bring him here. I can't see a child eating out of garbage cans."

The boy frowned. It was dawning upon him that something of his was threatened.

Sheppard's mouth stretched in disgust. "Rufus's father died before he was born," he said. "His mother is in the state penitentiary. He was raised by his grandfather in a shack without water or electricity and the old man beat him every day. How would you like to belong to a family like that?"

"I don't know," the child said lamely.

"Well, you might think about it sometime," Sheppard said.

Sheppard was City Recreational Director. On Saturdays he worked at the reformatory as a counselor, receiving nothing for it but the satisfaction of knowing he was helping boys no one else cared about. Johnson was the most intelligent boy he had worked with and the most deprived.

Norton turned what was left of the cake over as if he no longer wanted it.

"Maybe he won't come," the child said and his eyes brightened slightly.

"Think of everything you have that he doesn't!" Sheppard said. "Suppose you had to root in garbage cans for food? Suppose you had a huge swollen foot and one side of you dropped lower than the other when you walked?"

The boy looked blank, obviously unable to imagine such a thing.

"You have a healthy body," Sheppard said, "a good home. You've never been taught anything but the truth. Your daddy gives you everything you need and want. You don't have a grandfather who beats you. And your mother is not in the state penitentiary."

The child pushed his plate away. Sheppard groaned aloud.

A knot of flesh appeared below the boy's suddenly distorted mouth. His face became a mass of lumps with slits for eyes. "If she was in the penitentiary," he began in a kind of racking bellow, "I could go to seeeeee her." Tears rolled down his face and the ketchup dribbled on his chin. He looked as if he had been hit in the mouth. He abandoned himself and howled.

Sheppard sat helpless and miserable, like a man lashed by some elemental force of nature. This was not a normal grief. It was all part of his selfishness. She had been dead for over a year and a child's grief should not last so long. "You're going on eleven years old," he said reproachfully.

The child began an agonizing high-pitched heaving noise.

"If you stop thinking about yourself and think what you can do for somebody else," Sheppard said, "then you'll stop missing your mother."

The boy was silent but his shoulders continued to shake. Then his face collapsed and he began to howl again.

"Don't you think I'm lonely without her too?" Sheppard said. "Don't you think I miss her at all? I do, but I'm not sitting around moping. I'm busy helping other people. When do you see me just sitting around thinking about my troubles?"

The boy slumped as if he were exhausted but fresh tears streaked his face.

"What are you going to do today?" Sheppard asked, to get his mind on something else.

The child ran his arm across his eyes. "Sell seeds," he mumbled.

Always selling something. He had four quart jars full of nickels and dimes he had saved and he took them out of his closet every few days and counted them. "What are you selling seeds for?"

"To win a prize."

"What's the prize?"

"A thousand dollars."

"And what would you do if you had a thousand dollars?"

"Keep it," the child said and wiped his nose on his shoulder.

"I feel sure you would," Sheppard said. "Listen," he said and lowered his voice to an almost pleading tone, "suppose by some chance you did win a thousand dollars. Wouldn't you like to spend it on children less fortunate than yourself? Wouldn't you like to give some swings and trapezes to the orphanage? Wouldn't you like to buy poor Rufus Johnson a new shoe?"

The boy began to back away from the bar. Then suddenly he leaned forward and hung with his mouth open over his plate. Sheppard groaned again. Everything came up, the cake, the peanut butter, the ketchup—a limp sweet batter. He hung over it gagging, more came, and he waited with his mouth open over the plate as if he expected his heart to come up next.

"It's all right," Sheppard said, "it's all right. You couldn't help it. Wipe your mouth and go lie down."

The child hung there a moment longer. Then he raised his face and looked blindly at his father.

"Go on," Sheppard said. "Go on and lie down."

The boy pulled up the end of his t-shirt and smeared his mouth with it. Then he climbed down off the stool and wandered out of the kitchen.

Sheppard sat there staring at the puddle of half-digested food. The sour odor reached him and he drew back. His gorge rose. He got up and carried the plate to the sink and turned the water on it and watched grimly as the mess ran down the drain. Johnson's sad thin hand rooted in garbage cans for food while his own child, selfish, unresponsive, greedy, had so much that he threw it up. He cut off the faucet with a thrust of his fist. Johnson had a capacity for real response and had been deprived of everything from birth; Norton was average or below and had had every advantage.

He went back to the bar to finish his breakfast. The cereal was soggy in the cardboard box but he paid no attention to what he was eating. Johnson was worth any amount of effort because he had the potential. He had seen it from the time the boy had limped in for his first interview.

Sheppard's office at the reformatory was a narrow closet with one window and a small table and two chairs in it. He had never been inside a confessional but he thought it must be the same kind of operation he had here, except that he explained, he did not absolve. His credentials were less dubious than a priest's; he had been trained for what he was doing.

When Johnson came in for his first interview, he had been reading over the boy's record—senseless destruction, windows smashed, city trash boxes set afire, tires slashed—the kind of thing he found where boys had been transplanted abruptly from the country to the city as this one had. He came to Johnson's I. Q. score. It was 140. He raised his eyes eagerly.

The boy sat slumped on the edge of his chair, his arms hanging between his thighs. The light from the window fell on his face. His eyes, steel-colored and very still, were trained narrowly forward. His thin dark hair hung in a flat forelock across the side of his forehead, not carelessly like a boy's, but fiercely like an old man's. A kind of fanatic intelligence was palpable in his face.

Sheppard smiled to diminish the distance between them.

The boy's expression did not soften. He leaned back in his chair and lifted a monstrous club foot to his knee. The foot was in a heavy black battered shoe with a sole four or five inches thick. The leather parted from it in one place and the end of an empty sock protruded like a gray tongue from a severed head. The case was clear to Sheppard instantly. His mischief was compensation for the foot.

"Well Rufus," he said, "I see by the record here that you don't have but a year to serve. What do you plan to do when you get out?"

"I don't make no plans," the boy said. His eyes shifted indifferently to something outside the window behind Sheppard in the far distance.

"Maybe you ought to," Sheppard said and smiled.

Johnson continued to gaze beyond him.

"I want to see you make the most of your intelligence," Sheppard said. "What's most important to you? Let's talk about what's important to *you*." His eyes dropped involuntarily to the foot.

"Study it and git your fill," the boy drawled.

Sheppard reddened. The black deformed mass swelled before his eyes. He ignored the remark and the leer the boy was giving him. "Rufus," he said, "you've got into a lot of senseless trouble but I think when you understand why you do these things, you'll be less inclined to do them." He smiled. They had so few friends, saw so few pleasant faces, that half his effectiveness came from nothing more than smiling at them. "There are a lot of things about yourself that I think I can explain to you," he said.

Johnson looked at him stonily. "I ain't asked for no explanation," he said. "I already know why I do what I do."

"Well good!" Sheppard said. "Suppose you tell me what's made you do the things you've done?"

A black sheen appeared in the boy's eyes. "Satan," he said. "He has me in his power."

65 Sheppard looked at him steadily. There was no indication on the boy's face that he had said this to be funny. The line of his thin mouth was set with pride. Sheppard's eyes hardened. He felt a momentary dull despair as if he were faced with some elemental warping of nature that had happened too long ago to be corrected now. This boy's questions about life had been answered by signs nailed on the pine trees: DOES SATAN HAVE YOU IN HIS POWER? REPENT OR BURN IN HELL. JESUS SAVES. He would know the Bible with or without reading it. His despair gave way to outrage. "Rubbish!" he snorted. "We're living in the space age! You're too smart to give me an answer like that."

Johnson's mouth twisted slightly. His look was contemptuous but amused. There was a glint of challenge in his eyes.

Sheppard scrutinized his face. Where there was intelligence anything was possible. He smiled again, a smile that was like an invitation to the boy to come into a school room with all its windows thrown open to the light. "Rufus," he said, "I'm going to arrange for you to have a conference with me once a week. Maybe there's an explanation for your explanation. Maybe I can explain your devil to you."

After that he had talked to Johnson every Saturday for the rest of the year. He talked at random, the kind of talk the boy would never have heard before. He talked a little above him to give him something to reach for. He roamed from simple psychology and the dodges of the human mind to astronomy and the space capsules that were whirling around the earth faster than the speed of sound and would soon encircle the stars. Instinctively he concentrated on the stars. He wanted to give the boy something to reach for besides his neighbor's goods. He wanted to stretch his horizons. He wanted him to *see* the universe, to see that the darkest parts of it could be penetrated. He would have given anything to be able to put a telescope in Johnson's hands.

Johnson said little and what he did say, for the sake of his pride, was in dissent or senseless contradiction, with the clubfoot raised always to his knee like a weapon ready for use, but Sheppard was not deceived. He watched his eyes and every week he saw something in them crumble. From the boy's face, hard but shocked, braced against the light that was ravaging him, he could see that he was hitting dead center.

70 Johnson was free now to live out of garbage cans and rediscover his old ignorance. The injustice of it was infuriating. He had been sent back to the grandfather; the old man's imbecility could only be imagined. Perhaps the boy had by now run away from him. The idea of getting custody of Johnson had occurred to Sheppard before, but the fact of the grandfather had stood in the

way. Nothing excited him so much as thinking what he could do for such a boy. First he would have him fitted for a new orthopedic shoe. His back was thrown out of line every time he took a step. Then he would encourage him in some particular intellectual interest. He thought of the telescope. He could buy a second-hand one and they could set it up in the attic window. He sat for almost ten minutes thinking what he could do if he had Johnson here with him. What was wasted on Norton would cause Johnson to flourish. Yesterday when he had seen him with his hand in the garbage can, he had waved and started forward. Johnson had seen him, paused a split-second, then vanished with the swiftness of a rat, but not before Sheppard had seen his expression change. Something had kindled in the boy's eyes, he was sure of it, some memory of the lost light.

He got up and threw the cereal box in the garbage. Before he left the house, he looked into Norton's room to be sure he was not still sick. The child was sitting cross-legged on his bed. He had emptied the quart jars of change into one large pile in front of him, and was sorting it out by nickels and dimes and quarters.

That afternoon Norton was alone in the house, squatting on the floor of his room arranging packages of flower seeds in rows around himself. Rain slashed against the window panes and rattled in the gutters. The room had grown dark but every few minutes it was lit by silent lightning and the seed packages showed up gaily on the floor. He squatted motionless like a large pale frog in the midst of this potential garden. All at once his eyes became alert. Without warning the rain had stopped. The silence was heavy as if the downpour had been hushed by violence. He remained motionless, only his eyes turning.

Into the silence came the distinct click of a key turning in the front door lock. The sound was a very deliberate one. It drew attention to itself and held it as if it were controlled more by a mind than by a hand. The child leapt up and got into the closet.

The footsteps began to move in the hall. They were deliberate and irregular, a light and then a heavy one, then a silence as if the visitor had paused to listen himself or to examine something. In a minute the kitchen door screeked. The footsteps crossed the kitchen to the refrigerator. The closet wall and the kitchen wall were the same. Norton stood with his ear pressed against it. The refrigerator door opened. There was a prolonged silence.

He took off his shoes and then tiptoed out of the closet and stepped over the 75
seed packages. In the middle of the room, he stopped and remained where he was, rigid. A thin bony-face boy in a wet black suit stood in his door, blocking his escape. His hair was flattened to his skull by the rain. He stood there like an irate drenched crow. His look went through the child like a pin and paralyzed him. Then his eyes began to move over everything in the room—the unmade bed, the dirty curtains on the one large window, a photograph of a wide-faced young woman that stood up in the clutter on top of the dresser.

The child's tongue suddenly went wild. "He's been expecting you, he's going to give you a new shoe because you have to eat out of garbage cans!" he said in a kind of mouse-like shriek.

"I eat out of garbage cans," the boy said slowly with a beady stare, "because I like to eat out of garbage cans. See?"

The child nodded.

"And I got ways of getting my own shoe. See?"

80 The child nodded, mesmerized.

The boy limped in and sat down on the bed. He arranged a pillow behind him and stretched his short leg out so that the big black shoe rested conspicuously on a fold of the sheet.

Norton's gaze settled on it and remained immobile. The sole was as thick as a brick.

Johnson wiggled it slightly and smiled. "If I kick somebody *once* with this," he said, "it learns them not to mess with me."

The child nodded.

85 "Go in the kitchen," Johnson said, "and make me a sandwich with some of that rye bread and ham and bring me a glass of milk."

Norton went off like a mechanical toy, pushed in the right direction. He made a large greasy sandwich with ham hanging out the sides of it and poured out a glass of milk. Then he returned to the room with the glass of milk in one hand and the sandwich in the other.

Johnson was leaning back regally against the pillow. "Thanks, waiter," he said and took the sandwich.

Norton stood by the side of the bed, holding the glass.

The boy tore into the sandwich and ate steadily until he finished it. Then he took the glass of milk. He held it with both hands like a child and when he lowered it for breath, there was a rim of milk around his mouth. He handed Norton the empty glass. "Go get me one of them oranges in there, waiter," he said hoarsely.

90 Norton went to the kitchen and returned with the orange. Johnson peeled it with his fingers and let the peeling drop in the bed. He ate it slowly, spitting the seeds out in front of him. When he finished, he wiped his hands on the sheet and gave Norton a long appraising stare. He appeared to have been softened by the service. "You're his kid all right," he said. "You got the same stupid face."

The child stood there stolidly as if he had not heard.

"He don't know his left hand from his right," Johnson said with a hoarse pleasure in his voice.

The child cast his eyes a little to the side of the boy's face and looked fixedly at the wall.

"Yaketty yaketty yak," Johnson said, "and never says a thing."

95 The child's upper lip lifted slightly but he didn't say anything.

"Gas," Johnson said. "Gas."

The child's face began to have a wary look of belligerence. He backed away slightly as if he were prepared to retreat instantly. "He's good," he mumbled. "He helps people."

"Good!" Johnson said savagely. He thrust his head forward. "Listen here," he hissed, "I don't care if he's good or not. He ain't *right!*"

Norton looked stunned.

The screen door in the kitchen banged and someone entered. Johnson sat 100
forward instantly. "Is that him?" he said.

"It's the cook," Norton said. "She comes in the afternoon."

Johnson got up and limped into the hall and stood in the kitchen door and Norton followed him.

The colored girl was at the closet taking off a bright red raincoat. She was a tall light-yellow girl with a mouth like a large rose that had darkened and wilted. Her hair was dressed in tiers on top of her head and leaned to the side like the Tower of Pisa.

Johnson made a noise through his teeth. "Well look at Aunt Jemima," he said.

The girl paused and trained an insolent gaze on them. They might have 105
been dust on the floor.

"Come on," Johnson said, "let's see what all you got besides a nigger." He opened the first door to his right in the hall and looked into a pink-tiled bathroom. "A pink can!" he murmured.

He turned a comical face to the child. "Does he sit on that?"

"It's for company," Norton said, "but he sits on it sometimes."

"He ought to empty his head in it," Johnson said.

The door was open to the next room. It was the room Sheppard had slept in 110
since his wife died. An ascetic-looking iron bed stood on the bare floor. A heap of Little League baseball uniforms was piled in one corner. Papers were scattered over a large roll-top desk and held down in various places by his pipes. Johnson stood looking into the room silently. He wrinkled his nose. "Guess who?" he said.

The door to the next room was closed but Johnson opened it and thrust his head into the semi-darkness within. The shades were down and the air was close with a faint scent of perfume in it. There was a wide antique bed and a mammoth dresser whose mirror glinted in the half light. Johnson snapped the light switch by the door and crossed the room to the mirror and peered into it. A silver comb and brush lay on the linen runner. He picked up the comb and began to run it through his hair. He combed it straight down on his forehead. Then he swept it to the side, Hitler fashion.

"Leave her comb alone!" the child said. He stood in the door, pale and breathing heavily as if he were watching sacrilege in a holy place.

Johnson put the comb down and picked up the brush and gave his hair a swipe with it.

"She's dead," the child said.

"I ain't afraid of dead people's things," Johnson said. He opened the top 115
drawer and slid his hand in.

"Take your big fat dirty hands off my mother's clothes!" the child said in a high suffocated voice.

"Keep your shirt on, sweetheart," Johnson murmured. He pulled up a wrinkled red polka dot blouse and dropped it back. Then he pulled out a green silk kerchief and whirled it over his head and let it float to the floor. His hand continued to plow deep into the drawer. After a moment it came up gripping a faded corset with four dangling metal supporters. "Thisyer must be her saddle," he observed.

He lifted it gingerly and shook it. Then he fastened it around his waist and jumped up and down, making the metal supporters dance. He began to snap his fingers and turn his hips from side to side. "Gonter rock, rattle and roll," he sang. "Gonter rock, rattle and roll. Can't please that woman, to save my doggone soul." He began to move around, stamping the good foot down and slinging the heavy one to the side. He danced out the door, past the stricken child and down the hall toward the kitchen.

A half hour later Sheppard came home. He dropped his raincoat on a chair in the hall and came as far as the parlor door and stopped. His face was suddenly transformed. It shone with pleasure. Johnson sat, a dark figure, in a high-backed pink upholstered chair. The wall behind him was lined with books from floor to ceiling. He was reading one. Sheppard's eyes narrowed. It was a volume of the Encyclopedia Britannica. He was so engrossed in it that he did not look up. Sheppard held his breath. This was the perfect setting for the boy. He had to keep him here. He had to manage it somehow.

"Rufus!" he said, "it's good to see you boy!" and he bounded forward with his arm outstretched.

Johnson looked up, his face blank. "Oh hello," he said. He ignored the hand as long as he was able but when Sheppard did not withdraw it, he grudgingly shook it.

Sheppard was prepared for this kind of reaction. It was part of Johnson's make-up never to show enthusiasm.

"How are things?" he said. "How's your grandfather treating you?" He sat down on the edge of the sofa.

"He dropped dead," the boy said indifferently.

"You don't mean it!" Sheppard cried. He got up and sat down on the coffee table nearer the boy.

"Naw," Johnson said, "he ain't dropped dead. I wisht he had."

"Well where is he?" Sheppard muttered.

"He's gone with a remnant to the hills," Johnson said. "Him and some others. They're going to bury some Bibles in a cave and take two of different kinds of animals and all like that. Like Noah. Only this time it's going to be fire, not flood."

Sheppard's mouth stretched wryly. "I see," he said. Then he said, "In other words the old fool has abandoned you?"

"He ain't no fool," the boy said in an indignant tone.

"Has he abandoned you or not?" Sheppard asked impatiently.

The boy shrugged.

"Where's your probation officer?"

"I ain't supposed to keep up with him," Johnson said. "He's supposed to keep up with me."

Sheppard laughed. "Wait a minute," he said. He got up and went into the hall and got his raincoat off the chair and took it to the hall closet to hang it up.

He had to give himself time to think, to decide how he could ask the boy so that he would stay. He couldn't force him to stay. It would have to be voluntary. Johnson pretended not to like him. That was only to uphold his pride, but he would have to ask him in such a way that his pride could still be upheld. He opened the closet door and took out a hanger. An old gray winter coat of his wife's still hung there. He pushed it aside but it didn't move. He pulled it open roughly and winced as if he had seen the larva inside a cocoon. Norton stood in it, his face swollen and pale, with a drugged look of misery on it. Sheppard stared at him. Suddenly he was confronted with a possibility. "Get out of there," he said. He caught him by the shoulder and propelled him firmly into the parlor and over to the pink chair where Johnson was sitting with the encyclopedia in his lap. He was going to risk everything in one blow.

"Rufus," he said, "I've got a problem. I need your help."

Johnson looked up suspiciously.

"Listen," Sheppard said, "we need another boy in the house." There was a genuine desperation in his voice. "Norton here has never had to divide anything in his life. He doesn't know what it means to share. And I need somebody to teach him. How about helping me out? Stay here for a while with us, Rufus. I need your help." The excitement in his voice made it thin.

The child suddenly came to life. His face swelled with fury. "He went in her room and used her comb!" he screamed, yanking Sheppard's arm. "He put on her corset and danced with Leola, he . . ."

"Stop this!" Sheppard said sharply. "Is tattling all you're capable of? I'm not asking you for a report on Rufus's conduct. I'm asking you to make him welcome here. Do you understand?

"You see how it is?" he asked, turning to Johnson.

Norton kicked the leg of the pink chair viciously, just missing Johnson's swollen foot. Sheppard yanked him back.

"He said you weren't nothing but gas!" the child shrieked.

A sly look of pleasure crossed Johnson's face.

Sheppard was not put back. These insults were part of the boy's defensive mechanism. "What about it, Rufus?" he said. "Will you stay with us for a while?"

Johnson looked straight in front of him and said nothing. He smiled slightly and appeared to gaze upon some vision of the future that pleased him.

"I don't care," he said and turned a page of the encyclopedia. "I can stand anywhere."

"Wonderful." Sheppard said. "Wonderful."

"He said," the child said in a throaty whisper, "you didn't know your left hand from your right."

There was a silence.

Johnson wet his finger and turned another page of the encyclopedia.

"I have something to say to both of you," Sheppard said in a voice without inflection. His eyes moved from one to the other of them and he spoke slowly as if what he was saying he would say only once and it behooved them to listen. "If it made any difference to me what Rufus thinks of me," he said, "then I wouldn't be asking him here. Rufus is going to help me out and I'm going to help him out and we're both going to help you out. I'd simply be selfish if I let what Rufus thinks of me interfere with what I can do for Rufus. If I can help a person, all I want is to do it. I'm above and beyond simple pettiness."

Neither of them made a sound. Norton stared at the chair cushion. Johnson peered closer at some fine print in the encyclopedia. Sheppard was looking at the tops of their heads. He smiled. After all, he had won. The boy was staying. He reached out and ruffled Norton's hair and slapped Johnson on the shoulder. "Now you fellows sit here and get acquainted," he said gaily and started toward the door. "I'm going to see what Leola left us for supper."

When he was gone, Johnson raised his head and looked at Norton. The child looked back at him bleakly. "God, kid," Johnson said in a cracked voice, "how do you stand it?" His face was stiff with outrage. "He thinks he's Jesus Christ!"

II

Sheppard's attic was a large unfinished room with exposed beams and no electric light. They had set the telescope up on a tripod in one of the dormer windows. It pointed now toward the dark sky where a sliver of moon, as fragile as an egg shell, had just emerged from behind a cloud with a brilliant silver edge. Inside, a kerosene lantern set on a trunk cast their shadows upward and tangled them, wavering slightly, in the joints overhead. Sheppard was sitting on a packing box, looking through the telescope, and Johnson was at his elbow, waiting to get at it. Sheppard had bought it for fifteen dollars two days before at a pawn shop.

"Quit hoggin it," Johnson said.

Sheppard got up and Johnson slid onto the box and put his eye to the instrument.

Sheppard sat down on a straight chair a few feet away. His face was flushed with pleasure. This much of his dream was a reality. Within a week he had made it possible for this boy's vision to pass through a slender channel to the stars. He looked at Johnson's bent back with complete satisfaction. The boy had on one of Norton's plaid shirts and some new khaki trousers he had bought him. The shoe would be ready next week. He had taken him to the brace shop the day after he came and had him fitted for a new shoe. Johnson was as touchy about the foot as if it were a sacred object. His face had been glum while the clerk, a young man with a bright pink bald head, measured the foot with his profane hands. The shoe was going to make the greatest difference in the boy's attitude. Even a child with normal feet was in love with the world after he had got a new pair of shoes. When Norton got a new pair, he walked around for days with his eyes on his feet.

Sheppard glanced across the room at the child. He was sitting on the floor against a trunk, trussed up in a rope he had found and wound around his legs from his ankles to his knees. He appeared so far away that Sheppard might have been looking at him through the wrong end of the telescope. He had had to whip him only once since Johnson had been with them—the first night when Norton had realized that Johnson was going to sleep in his mother's bed. He did not believe in whipping children, particularly in anger. In this case, he had done both and with good results. He had had no more trouble with Norton.

The child hadn't shown any positive generosity toward Johnson but what he 160
couldn't help, he appeared to be resigned to. In the mornings Sheppard sent the two of them to the Y swimming pool, gave them money to get their lunch at the cafeteria and instructed them to meet him in the park in the afternoon to watch his Little League baseball practice. Every afternoon they had arrived at the park, shambling, silent, their faces closed each on his own thoughts as if neither were aware of the other's existence. At least he could be thankful there were no fights.

Norton showed no interest in the telescope. "Don't you want to get up and look through the telescope, Norton?" he said. It irritated him that the child showed no intellectual curiosity whatsoever. "Rufus is going to be way ahead of you."

Norton leaned forward absently and looked at Johnson's back.

Johnson turned around from the instrument. His face had begun to fill out again. The look of outrage had retreated from his hollow cheeks and was shored up now in the caves of his eyes, like a fugitive from Sheppard's kindness. "Don't waste your valuable time, kid," he said. "You seen the moon once, you seen it."

Sheppard was amused by these sudden turns of perversity. The boy resisted whatever he suspected was meant for his improvement and contrived when he was vitally interested in something to leave the impression he was bored. Sheppard was not deceived. Secretly Johnson was learning what he wanted him to learn—that his benefactor was impervious to insult and that there were no cracks in his armor of kindness and patience where a successful shaft could be driven. "Some day you may go to the moon," he said. "In ten years men will probably be making round trips there on schedule. Why you boys may be spacemen. Astronauts!"

"Astro-nuts," Johnson said.

"Nuts or nauts," Sheppard said, "it's perfectly possible that you, Rufus John- 165
son, will go to the moon."

Something in the depths of Johnson's eyes stirred. All day his humor had been glum. "I ain't going to the moon and get there alive," he said, "and when I die I'm going to hell."

"It's at least possible to get to the moon," Sheppard said dryly. The best way to handle this kind of thing was with gentle ridicule. "We can see it. We know it's there. Nobody has given any reliable evidence there's a hell."

"The Bible has give the evidence," Johnson said darkly, "and if you die and go there you burn forever."

The child leaned forward. 170

"Whoever says it ain't a hell," Johnson said, "is contradicting Jesus. The dead are judged and the wicked are damned. They weep and gnash their teeth while they burn," he continued, "and it's everlasting darkness."

The child's mouth opened. His eyes appeared to grow hollow.

"Satan runs it," Johnson said.

Norton lurched up and took a hobbled step toward Sheppard. "Is she there?"

he said in a loud voice. "Is she there burning up?" He kicked the rope off his feet. "Is she on fire?"

175 "Oh my God," Sheppard muttered. "No no," he said, "of course she isn't. Rufus is mistaken. Your mother isn't anywhere. She's not unhappy. She just isn't." His lot would have been easier if when his wife died he had told Norton she had gone to heaven and that some day he would see her again, but he could not allow himself to bring him up on a lie.

Norton's face began to twist. A knot formed in his chin.

"Listen," Sheppard said quickly and pulled the child to him, "your mother's spirit lives on in other people and it'll live on in you if you're good and generous like she was."

The child's pale eyes hardened in disbelief.

Sheppard's pity turned to revulsion. The boy would rather she be in hell than nowhere. "Do you understand?" he said. "She doesn't exist." He put his hand on the child's shoulder. "That's all I have to give you," he said in a softer, exasperated tone, "the truth."

180 Instead of howling, the boy wrenched himself away and caught Johnson by the sleeve. "Is she there, Rufus?" he said "Is she there, burning up?"

Johnson's eyes glittered. "Well," he said, "she is if she was evil. Was she a whore?"

"Your mother was not a whore," Sheppard said sharply. He had the sensation of driving a car without brakes. "Now let's have no more of this foolishness. We were talking about the moon."

"Did she believe in Jesus?" Johnson asked.

Norton looked blank. After a second he said, "Yes," as if he saw that this was necessary. "She did," he said. "All the time."

185 "She did not," Sheppard muttered.

"She did all the time," Norton said. "I heard her say she did all the time."

"She's saved," Johnson said.

The child still looked puzzled. "Where?" he said. "Where is she at?"

"On high," Johnson said.

"Where's that?" Norton gasped.

"It's in the sky somewhere," Johnson said, "but you got to be dead to get there. You can't go in no space ship." There was a narrow gleam in his eyes now like a beam holding steady on its target.

"Man's going to the moon," Sheppard said grimly, "is very much like the first fish crawling out of the water onto land billions and billions of years ago. He didn't have an earth suit. He had to grow his adjustments inside. He developed lungs."

"When I'm dead will I go to hell or where she is?" Norton asked.

"Right now you'd go where she is," Johnson said, "but if you live long enough, you'll go to hell."

Sheppard rose abruptly and picked up the lantern. "Close the window, Rufus," he said. "It's time we went to bed."

On the way down the attic stairs he heard Johnson say in a loud whisper behind him, "I'll tell you all about it tomorrow, kid, when Himself has cleared out."

The next day when the boys came to the ball park, he watched them as they came from behind the bleachers and around the edge of the field. Johnson's hand was on Norton's shoulder, his head bent toward the younger boy's ear, and on the child's face there was a look of complete confidence, of dawning light. Sheppard's grimace hardened. This would be Johnson's way of trying to annoy him. But he would not be annoyed. Norton was not bright enough to be damaged much. He gazed at the child's dull absorbed little face. Why try to make him superior? Heaven and hell were for the mediocre, and he was that if he was anything.

The two boys came into the bleachers and sat down about ten feet away, facing him, but neither gave him any sign of recognition. He cast a glance behind him where the Little Leaguers were spread out in the field. Then he started for the bleachers. The hiss of Johnson's voice stopped as he approached.

"What have you fellows been doing today?" he asked genially.

"He's been telling me . . ." Norton started.

Johnson pushed the child in the ribs with his elbow. "We ain't been doing nothing," he said. His face appeared to be covered with a blank glaze but through it a look of complicity was blazoned forth insolently.

Sheppard felt his face grow warm, but he said nothing. A child in a Little League uniform had followed him and was nudging him in the back of the leg with a bat. He turned and put his arm around the boy's neck and went with him back to the game.

That night when he went to the attic to join the boys at the telescope, he found Norton there alone. He was sitting on the packing box, hunched over, looking intently through the instrument. Johnson was not there.

"Where's Rufus?" Sheppard asked.

"I said where's Rufus?" he said louder.

"Gone somewhere," the child said without turning around.

"Gone where?" Sheppard asked.

"He just said he was going somewhere. He said he was fed up looking at stars."

"I see," Sheppard said glumly. He turned and went back down the stairs. He searched the house without finding Johnson. Then he went to the living room and sat down. Yesterday he had been convinced of his success with the boy. Today he faced the possibility that he was failing with him. He had been over-lenient, too concerned to have Johnson like him. He felt a twinge of guilt. What difference did it make if Johnson liked him or not? What was that to him? When the boy came in, they would have a few things understood. As long as you stay here there'll be no going out at night by yourself, do you understand?

I don't have to stay here. It ain't nothing to me staying here.

Oh my God, he thought. He could not bring it to that. He would have to be firm but not make an issue of it. He picked up the evening paper. Kindness and patience were always called for but he had not been firm enough. He sat holding the paper but not reading it. The boy would not respect him unless he showed firmness. The doorbell rang and he went to answer it. He opened it and stepped back, with a pained disappointed face.

A large dour policeman stood on the stoop, holding Johnson by the elbow. At the curb a patrol car waited. Johnson looked very white. His jaw was thrust forward as if to keep from trembling.

"We brought him here first because he raised such a fit," the policeman said, "but now that you've seen him, we're going to take him to the station and ask him a few questions."

"What happened?" Sheppard muttered.

"A house around the corner from here," the policeman said. "A real smash job, dishes broken all over the floor, furniture turned upside down . . ."

"I didn't have a thing to do with it!" Johnson said. "I was walking along minding my own bidnis when this cop came up and grabbed me."

Sheppard looked at the boy grimly. He made no effort to soften his expression.

Johnson flushed. "I was just walking along," he muttered, but with no conviction in his voice.

"Come on, bud," the policeman said.

"You ain't going to let him take me, are you?" Johnson said. "You believe me, don't you?" There was an appeal in his voice that Sheppard had not heard there before.

This was crucial. The boy would have to learn that he could not be protected when he was guilty. "You'll have to go with him, Rufus," he said.

"You're going to let him take me and I tell you I ain't done a thing?" Johnson said shrilly.

Sheppard's face became harder as his sense of injury grew. The boy had failed him even before he had had a chance to give him the shoe. They were to have got it tomorrow. All his regret turned suddenly on the shoe; his irritation at the sight of Johnson doubled.

"You made out like you had all this confidence in me," the boy mumbled.

"I did have," Sheppard said. His face was wooden.

Johnson turned away with the policeman but before he moved, a gleam of pure hatred flashed toward Sheppard from the pits of his eyes.

Sheppard stood in the door and watched them get into the patrol car and drive away. He summoned his compassion. He would go to the station tomorrow and see what he could do about getting him out of trouble. The night in jail would not hurt him and the experience would teach him that he could not treat with impunity someone who had shown him nothing but kindness. Then they would go get the shoe and perhaps after a night in jail it would mean even more to the boy.

The next morning at eight o'clock the police sergeant called and told him he could come pick Johnson up. "We booked a nigger on that charge," he said. "Your boy didn't have nothing to do with it."

Sheppard was at the station in ten minutes, his face hot with shame. Johnson sat slouched on a bench in a drab outer office, reading a police magazine. There was no one else in the room. Sheppard sat down beside him and put his hand tentatively on his shoulder.

The boy glanced up—his lip curled—and back to the magazine.

Sheppard felt physically sick. The ugliness of what he had done bore in upon him with a sudden dull intensity. He had failed him at just the point where he might have turned him once and for all in the right direction. "Rufus," he said, "I apologize. I was wrong and you were right. I misjudged you."

The boy continued to read.

"I'm sorry."

The boy wet his finger and turned a page.

Sheppard braced himself. "I was a fool, Rufus," he said.

Johnson's mouth slid slightly to the side. He shrugged without raising his head from the magazine.

"Will you forget it, this time?" Sheppard said. "It won't happen again."

The boy looked up. His eyes were bright and unfriendly. "I'll forget it," he said, "but you better remember it." He got up and stalked toward the door. In the middle of the room he turned and jerked his arm at Sheppard and Sheppard jumped up and followed him as if the boy had yanked an invisible leash.

"Your shoe," he said eagerly, "today is the day to get your shoe!" Thank God for the shoe!

But when they went to the brace shop, they found that the shoe had been made two sizes too small and a new one would not be ready for another ten days. Johnson's temper improved at once. The clerk had obviously made a mistake in the measurements but the boy insisted the foot had grown. He left the shop with a pleased expression, as if, in expanding, the foot had acted on some inspiration of its own. Sheppard's face was haggard.

After this he redoubled his efforts. Since Johnson had lost interest in the telescope, he bought a microscope and a box of prepared slides. If he couldn't impress the boy with immensity, he would try the infinitesimal. For two nights Johnson appeared absorbed in the new instrument, then he abruptly lost interest in it, but he seemed content to sit in the living room in the evening and read the encyclopedia. He devoured the encyclopedia as he devoured his dinner, steadily and without dint to his appetite. Each subject appeared to enter his head, be ravaged, and thrown out. Nothing pleased Sheppard more than to see the boy slouched on the sofa, his mouth shut, reading. After they had spent two or three evenings like this, he began to recover his vision. His confidence returned. He knew that some day he would be proud of Johnson.

On Thursday night Sheppard attended a city council meeting. He dropped the boys off at a movie on his way and picked them up on his way back. When they reached home, an automobile with a single red eye above its windshield was waiting in front of the house. Sheppard's lights as he turned into the driveway illuminated two dour faces in the car.

"The cops!" Johnson said. "Some nigger has broke in somewhere and they've come for me again."

"We'll see about that," Sheppard muttered. He stopped the car in the driveway and switched off the lights. "You boys go in the house and go to bed," he said. "I'll handle this."

He got out and strode toward the squad car. He thrust his head in the window. The two policemen were looking at him with silent knowledgeable faces. "A house on the corner of Shelton and Mills," the one in the driver's seat said. "It looks like a train run through it."

"He was in the picture show downtown," Sheppard said. "My boy was with him. He had nothing to do with the other one and he had nothing to do with this one. I'll be responsible."

"If I was you," the one nearest him said, "I wouldn't be responsible for any little bastard like him."

"I said I'd be responsible," Sheppard repeated coldly. "You people made a mistake the last time. Don't make another."

The policemen looked at each other. "It ain't our funeral," the one in the driver's seat said, and turned the key in the ignition.

Sheppard went in the house and sat down in the living room in the dark. He did not suspect Johnson and he did not want the boy to think he did. If Johnson thought he suspected him again, he would lose everything. But he wanted to know if his alibi was airtight. He thought of going to Norton's room and asking him if Johnson had left the movie. But that would be worse. Johnson would know what he was doing and would be incensed. He decided to ask Johnson himself. He would be direct. He went over in his mind what he was going to say and then he got up and went to the boy's door.

It was open as if he had been expected but Johnson was in bed. Just enough light came in from the hall for Sheppard to see his shape under the sheet. He came in and stood at the foot of the bed. "They've gone," he said. "I told them you had nothing to do with it and that I'd be responsible."

There was a muttered "Yeah," from the pillow.

Sheppard hesitated. "Rufus," he said, "you didn't leave the movie for anything at all, did you?"

"You make out like you got all this confidence in me!" a sudden outraged voice cried, "and you ain't got any! You don't trust me no more now than you did then!" The voice, disembodied, seemed to come more surely from the depths of Johnson than when his face was visible. It was a cry of reproach, edged slightly with contempt.

"I do have confidence in you," Sheppard said intensely. "I have every confidence in you. I believe in you and I trust you completely."

"You got your eye on me all the time," the voice said sullenly. "When you get through asking me a bunch of questions, you're going across the hall and ask Norton a bunch of them."

"I have no intention of asking Norton anything and never did," Sheppard said gently. "And I don't suspect you at all. You could hardly have got from the picture show downtown and out here to break in a house and back to the picture show in the time you had."

"That's why you believe me!" the boy cried, "—because you think I couldn't have done it."

"No, no!" Sheppard said. "I believe you because I believe you've got the brains and the guts not to get in trouble again. I believe you know yourself well enough now to know that you don't have to do such things. I believe that you can make anything of yourself that you set your mind to."

Johnson sat up. A faint light shone on his forehead but the rest of his face was invisible. "And I could have broke in there if I'd wanted to in the time I had," he said.

"But I know you didn't," Sheppard said. "There's not the least trace of doubt in my mind."

There was a silence. Johnson lay back down. Then the voice, low and hoarse, as if it were being forced out with difficulty, said, "You don't want to steal and smash up things when you've got everything you want already."

Sheppard caught his breath. The boy was thanking him! He was thanking him! There was gratitude in his voice. There was appreciation. He stood there, smiling foolishly in the dark, trying to hold the moment in suspension. Involuntarily he took a step toward the pillow and stretched out his hand and touched Johnson's forehead. It was cold and dry like rusty iron.

"I understand. Good night, son," he said and turned quickly and left the room. He closed the door behind him and stood there, overcome with emotion.

Across the hall Norton's door was open. The child lay on the bed on his side, looking into the light from the hall.

After this, the road with Johnson would be smooth.

Norton sat up and beckoned to him.

He saw the child but after the first instant, he did not let his eyes focus directly on him. He could not go in and talk to Norton without breaking Johnson's trust. He hesitated, but remained where he was a moment as if he saw nothing. Tomorrow was the day they were to go back for the shoe. It would be a climax to the good feeling between them. He turned quickly and went back into his own room.

The child sat for some time looking at the spot where his father had stood. Finally his gaze became aimless and he lay back down.

The next day Johnson was glum and silent as if he were ashamed that he had revealed himself. His eyes had a hooded look. He seemed to have retired within himself and there to be going through some crisis of determination. Sheppard could not get to the brace shop quickly enough. He left Norton at home because he did not want his attention divided. He wanted to be free to observe Johnson's reaction minutely. The boy did not seem pleased or even interested in the prospect of the shoe, but when it became an actuality, certainly then he would be moved.

The brace shop was a small concrete warehouse lined and stacked with the equipment of affliction. Wheel chairs and walkers covered most of the floor. The walls were hung with every kind of crutch and brace. Artificial limbs were stacked on the shelves, legs and arms and hands, claws and hooks, straps and human harnesses and unidentifiable instruments for unnamed deformities. In a small clearing in the middle of the room there was a row of yellow plastic-cushioned chairs and a shoe-fitting stool. Johnson slouched down in one of the chairs and set his foot up on the stool and sat with his eyes on it moodily. What was roughly the toe had broken open again and he had patched it with a piece of canvas; another place he had patched with what appeared to be the tongue of the original shoe. The two sides were laced with twine.

There was an excited flush on Sheppard's face; his heart was beating unnaturally fast.

The clerk appeared from the back of the shop with the new shoe under his arm. "Got her right this time!" he said. He straddled the shoe-fitting stool and held the shoe up, smiling as if he had produced it by magic.

It was a black slick shapeless object, shining hideously. It looked like a blunt weapon, highly polished.

Johnson gazed at it darkly.

"With this shoe," the clerk said, "you won't know you're walking. You'll think you're riding!" He bent his bright pink bald head and began gingerly to unlace the twine. He removed the old shoe as if he were skinning an animal still half alive. His expression was strained. The unsheathed mass of foot in the dirty sock made Sheppard feel queasy. He turned his eyes away until the new shoe was on. The clerk laced it up rapidly. "Now stand up and walk around," he said, "and see if that ain't power glide." He winked at Sheppard. "In that shoe," he said, "he won't know he don't have a normal foot."

Sheppard's face was bright with pleasure.

Johnson stood up and walked a few yards away. He walked stiffly with almost no dip in his short side. He stood for a moment, rigid, with his back to them.

"Wonderful!" Sheppard said. "Wonderful." It was as if he had given the boy a new spine.

Johnson turned around. His mouth was set in a thin icy line. He came back to the seat and removed the shoe. He put his foot in the old one and began lacing it up.

"You want to take it home and see if it suits you first?" the clerk murmured.

"No," Johnson said. "I ain't going to wear it at all."

"What's wrong with it?" Sheppard said, his voice rising.

"I don't need no new shoe," Johnson said. "And when I do, I got ways of getting my own." His face was stony but there was a glint of triumph in his eyes.

"Boy," the clerk said, "is your trouble in your foot or in your head?"

"Go soak your skull," Johnson said. "Your brains are on fire."

The clerk rose glumly but with dignity and asked Sheppard what he wanted done with the shoe, which he dangled dispiritedly by the lace.

Sheppard's face was a dark angry red. He was staring straight in front of him at a leather corset with an artificial arm attached.

The clerk asked him again.

"Wrap it up," Sheppard muttered. He turned his eyes to Johnson. "He's not mature enough for it yet," he said. "I had thought he was less of a child."

The boy leered. "You been wrong before," he said.

That night they sat in the living room and read as usual. Sheppard kept himself glumly entrenched behind the Sunday New York *Times*. He wanted to recover his good humor, but every time he thought of the rejected shoe, he felt a new charge of irritation. He did not trust himself even to look at Johnson. He realized that the boy had refused the shoe because he was insecure. Johnson had been frightened by his own gratitude. He didn't know what to make of the new self he was becoming conscious of. He understood that something he had been was threatened and he was facing himself and his possibilities for the first time. He was questioning his identity. Grudgingly, Sheppard felt a slight return of sympathy for the boy. In a few minutes, he lowered his paper and looked at him.

Johnson was sitting on the sofa, gazing over the top of the encyclopedia. His expression was trancelike. He might have been listening to something far away. Sheppard watched him intently but the boy continued to listen, and did not turn his head. The poor kid is lost, Sheppard thought. Here he had sat all evening, sullenly reading the paper, and had not said a word to break the tension. "Rufus," he said.

Johnson continued to sit, stock-still, listening.

"Rufus," Sheppard said in a slow hypnotic voice, "you can be anything in 295
the world you want to be. You can be a scientist or an architect or an engineer or whatever you set your mind to, and whatever you set your mind to be, you can be the best of its kind." He imagined his voice penetrating to the boy in the black caverns of his psyche. Johnson leaned forward but his eyes did not turn. On the street a car door closed. There was a silence. Then a sudden blast from the door bell.

Sheppard jumped up and went to the door and opened it. The same policeman who had come before stood there. The patrol car waited at the curb.

"Lemme see that boy," he said.

Sheppard scowled and stood aside. "He's been here all evening," he said. "I can vouch for it."

The policeman walked into the living room. Johnson appeared engrossed in his book. After a second he looked up with an annoyed expression, like a great man interrupted at his work.

"What was that you were looking at in that kitchen window over on Winter 300
Avenue about a half hour ago, bud?" the policeman asked.

"Stop persecuting this boy!" Sheppard said. "I'll vouch for the fact he was here. I was here with him."

"You heard him," Johnson said. "I been here all the time."

"It ain't everybody makes tracks like you," the policeman said and eyed the clubfoot.

"They couldn't be his tracks," Sheppard growled, infuriated. "He's been here all the time. You're wasting your own time and you're wasting ours." He felt the *ours* seal his solidarity with the boy. "I'm sick of this," he said. "You people are too damn lazy to go out and find whoever is doing these things. You come here automatically."

The policeman ignored this and continued looking through Johnson. His 305
eyes were small and alert in his fleshy face. Finally he turned toward the door.

"We'll get him sooner or later," he said, "with his head in a window and his tail out."

Sheppard followed him to the door and slammed it behind him. His spirits were soaring. This was exactly what he had needed. He returned with an expectant face.

Johnson had put the book down and was sitting there, looking at him slyly. "Thanks," he said.

Sheppard stopped. The boy's expression was predatory. He was openly leering.

"You ain't such a bad liar yourself," he said.

"Liar?" Sheppard murmured. Could the boy have left and come back? He felt himself sicken. Then a rush of anger sent him forward. "Did you leave?" he said furiously. "I didn't see you leave."

The boy only smiled.

"You went up in the attic to see Norton," Sheppard said.

"Naw," Johnson said, "that kid is crazy. He don't want to do nothing but look through that stinking telescope."

"I don't want to hear about Norton," Sheppard said harshly. "Where were you?"

"I was sitting on that pink can by my ownself," Johnson said. "There wasn't no witnesses."

Sheppard took out his handkerchief and wiped his forehead. He managed to smile.

Johnson rolled his eyes. "You don't believe in me," he said. His voice was cracked the way it had been in the dark room two nights before. "You make out like you got all this confidence in me but you ain't got any. When things get hot, you'll fade like the rest of them." The crack became exaggerated, comic. The mockery in it was blatant. "You don't believe in me. You ain't got no confidence," he wailed. "And you ain't any smarter than that cop. All that about tracks—that was a trap. There wasn't any tracks. That whole place is concreted in the back and my feet were dry."

Sheppard slowly put the handkerchief back in his pocket. He dropped down on the sofa and gazed at the rug beneath his feet. The boy's clubfoot was set within the circle of his vision. The pieced-together shoe appeared to grin at him with Johnson's own face. He caught hold of the edge of the sofa cushion and his knuckles turned white. A chill of hatred shook him. He hated the shoe, hated the foot, hated the boy. His face paled. Hatred choked him. He was aghast at himself.

He caught the boy's shoulder and gripped it fiercely as if to keep himself from falling. "Listen," he said, "you looked in that window to embarrass me. That was all you wanted—to shake my resolve to help you, but my resolve isn't shaken. I'm stronger than you are. I'm stronger than you are and I'm going to save you. The good will triumph."

"Not when it ain't true," the boy said. "Not when it ain't right."

"My resolve isn't shaken," Sheppard repeated. "I'm going to save you."

Johnson's look became sly again. "You ain't going to save me," he said.

"You're going to tell me to leave this house. I did those other two jobs too—the first one as well as the one I done when I was supposed to be in the picture show."

"I'm not going to tell you to leave," Sheppard said. His voice was toneless, mechanical. "I'm going to save you."

Johnson thrust his head forward. "Save yourself," he hissed. "Nobody can save me but Jesus."

Sheppard laughed curtly. "You don't deceive me," he said. "I flushed that 325
out of your head in the reformatory. I saved you from that, at least."

The muscles in Johnson's face stiffened. A look of such repulsion hardened on his face that Sheppard drew back. The boy's eyes were like distorting mirrors in which he saw himself made hideous and grotesque. "I'll show you," Johnson whispered. He rose abruptly and started headlong for the door as if he could not get out of Sheppard's sight quick enough, but it was the door to the back hall he went through, not the front door. Sheppard turned on the sofa and looked behind him where the boy had disappeared. He heard the door to his room slam. He was not leaving. The intensity had gone out of Sheppard's eyes. They looked flat and lifeless as if the shock of the boy's revelation were only now reaching the center of his consciousness. "If he would only leave," he murmured. "If he would only leave now of his own accord."

The next morning Johnson appeared at the breakfast table in the grandfather's suit he had come in. Sheppard pretended not to notice but one look told him what he already knew, that he was trapped, that there could be nothing now but a battle of nerves and that Johnson would win it. He wished he had never laid eyes on the boy. The failure of his compassion numbed him. He got out of the house as soon as he could and all day he dreaded to go home in the evening. He had a faint hope that the boy might be gone when he returned. The grandfather's suit might have meant he was leaving. The hope grew in the afternoon. When he came home and opened the front door, his heart was pounding.

He stopped in the hall and looked silently into the living room. His expectant expression faded. His face seemed suddenly as old as his white hair. The two boys were sitting close together on the sofa, reading the same book. Norton's cheek rested against the sleeve of Johnson's black suit. Johnson's finger moved under the lines they were reading. The elder brother and the younger. Sheppard looked woodenly at this scene for almost a minute. Then he walked into the room and took off his coat and dropped it on a chair. Neither boy noticed him. He went on to the kitchen.

Leola left the supper on the stove every afternoon before she left and he put it on the table. His head ached and his nerves were taut. He sat down on the kitchen stool and remained there, sunk in his depression. He wondered if he could infuriate Johnson enough to make him leave of his own accord. Last night what had enraged him was the Jesus business. It might enrage Johnson, but it depressed him. Why not simply tell the boy to go? Admit defeat. The thought of facing Johnson again sickened him. The boy looked at him as if he were the guilty one, as if he were a moral leper. He knew without conceit that he was a good man, that he had nothing to reproach himself with. His feelings about Johnson now were involuntary. He would like to feel compassion for him. He would like to be able to help him. He longed for the time when there would be no one but himself and Norton in the house, when the child's simple selfishness would be all he had to contend with, and his own loneliness.

He got up and took three serving dishes off the shelf and took them to the stove. Absently he began pouring the butterbeans and the hash into the dishes. When the food was on the table, he called them in.

They brought the book with them. Norton pushed his place setting around to the same side of the table as Johnson's and moved his chair next to Johnson's chair. They sat down and put the book between them. It was a black book with red edges.

"What's that you're reading?" Sheppard asked, sitting down.

"The Holy Bible," Johnson said.

God give me strength, Sheppard said under his breath.

"We lifted it from a ten cent store," Johnson said.

"We?" Sheppard muttered. He turned and glared at Norton. The child's face was bright and there was an excited sheen to his eyes. The change that had come over the boy struck him for the first time. He looked alert. He had on a blue plaid shirt and his eyes were a brighter blue than he had ever seen them before. There was a strange new life in him, the sign of new and more rugged vices. "So now you steal?" he said, glowering. "You haven't learned to be generous but you have learned to steal."

"No he ain't," Johnson said. "I was the one lifted it. He only watched. He can't sully himself. It don't make any difference about me. I'm going to hell anyway."

Sheppard held his tongue.

"Unless," Johnson said, "I repent."

"Repent, Rufus," Norton said in a pleading voice. "Repent, hear? You don't want to go to hell."

"Stop talking this nonsense," Sheppard said, looking sharply at the child.

"If I do repent, I'll be a preacher," Johnson said. "If you're going to do it, it's no sense in doing it halfway."

"What are you going to be, Norton," Sheppard asked in a brittle voice, "a preacher too?"

There was a glitter of wild pleasure in the child's eyes. "A space man!" he shouted.

"Wonderful," Sheppard said bitterly.

"Those space ships ain't going to do you any good unless you believe in Jesus," Johnson said. He wet his finger and began to leaf through the pages of the Bible. "I'll read you where it says so," he said.

Sheppard leaned forward and said in a low furious voice, "Put that Bible up, Rufus, and eat your dinner."

Johnson continued searching for the passage.

"Put that Bible up!" Sheppard shouted.

The boy stopped and looked up. His expression was startled but pleased.

"That book is something for you to hide behind," Sheppard said. "It's for cowards, people who are afraid to stand on their own feet and figure things out for themselves."

Johnson's eyes snapped. He backed his chair a little way from the table. "Satan has you in his power," he said. "Not only me. You too."

Sheppard reached across the table to grab the book but Johnson snatched it and put it in his lap.

Sheppard laughed. "You don't believe in that book and you know you don't believe in it!"

"I believe it!" Johnson said. "You don't know what I believe and what I don't."

Sheppard shook his head. "You don't believe it. You're too intelligent."

"I ain't too intelligent," the boy muttered. "You don't know nothing about me. Even if I didn't believe it, it would still be true."

"You don't believe it!" Sheppard said. His face was a taunt.

"I believe it!" Johnson said breathlessly. "I'll show you I believe it!" He opened the book in his lap and tore out a page of it and thrust it into his mouth. He fixed his eyes on Sheppard. His jaws worked furiously and the paper crackled as he chewed it.

"Stop this," Sheppard said in a dry, burnt-out voice. "Stop it."

The boy raised the Bible and tore out a page with his teeth and began grinding it in his mouth, his eyes burning.

Sheppard reached across the table and knocked the book out of his hand. "Leave the table," he said coldly.

Johnson swallowed what was in his mouth. His eyes widened as if a vision of splendor were opening up before him. "I've eaten it!" he breathed. "I've eaten it like Ezekiel and it was honey to my mouth!"[1]

"Leave this table," Sheppard said. His hands were clenched beside his plate.

"I've eaten it!" the boy cried. Wonder transformed his face. "I've eaten it like Ezekiel and I don't want none of your food after it nor no more ever."

"Go then," Sheppard said softly. "Go. Go."

The boy rose and picked up the Bible and started toward the hall with it. At the door he paused, a small black figure on the threshold of some dark apocalypse. "The devil has you in his power," he said in a jubilant voice and disappeared.

After supper Sheppard sat in the living room alone. Johnson had left the house but he could not believe that the boy had simply gone. The first feeling of release had passed. He felt dull and cold as at the onset of an illness and dread had settled in him like a fog. Just to leave would be too anticlimactic an end for Johnson's taste; he would return and try to prove something. He might come back a week later and set fire to the place. Nothing seemed too outrageous now.

He picked up the paper and tried to read. In a moment he threw it down and

1. Ezekiel 3:1–3. The Lord in a vision told Ezekiel to eat a roll and go speak to the captive Israelites; when he ate "it was in my mouth as honey for sweetness."

got up and went into the hall and listened. He might be hiding in the attic. He went to the attic door and opened it.

The lantern was lit, casting a dim light on the stairs. He didn't hear anything. "Norton," he called, "are you up there?" There was no answer. He mounted the narrow stairs to see.

Amid the strange vine-like shadows cast by the lantern, Norton sat with his eye to the telescope. "Norton," Sheppard said, "do you know where Rufus went?"

The child's back was to him. He was sitting hunched, intent, his large ears directly above his shoulders. Suddenly he waved his hand and crouched closer to the telescope as if he could not get near enough to what he saw.

"Norton!" Sheppard said in a loud voice.

The child didn't move.

"Norton!" Sheppard shouted.

Norton started. He turned around. There was an unnatural brightness about his eyes. After a moment he seemed to see that it was Sheppard. "I've found her!" he said breathlessly.

"Found who?" Sheppard said.

"Mamma!"

Sheppard steadied himself in the door way. The jungle of shadows around the child thickened.

"Come and look!" he cried. He wiped his sweaty face on the tail of his plaid shirt and then put his eye back to the telescope. His back became fixed in a rigid intensity. All at once he waved again.

"Norton," Sheppard said, "you don't see anything in the telescope but star clusters. Now you've had enough of that for one night. You'd better go to bed. Do you know where Rufus is?"

"She's there!" he cried, not turning around from the telescope. "She waved at me!"

"I want you in bed in fifteen minutes," Sheppard said. After a moment he said, "Do you hear me, Norton?"

The child began to wave frantically.

"I mean what I say," Sheppard said. "I'm going to call in fifteen minutes and see if you're in bed."

He went down the steps again and returned to the parlor. He went to the front door and cast a cursory glance out. The sky was crowded with the stars he had been fool enough to think Johnson could reach. Somewhere in the small wood behind the house, a bull frog sounded a low hollow note. He went back to his chair and sat a few minutes. He decided to go to bed. He put his hands on the arms of the chair and leaned forward and heard, like the first shrill note of a disaster warning, the siren of a police car, moving slowly into the neighborhood and nearer until it subsided with a moan outside the house.

He felt a cold weight on his shoulders as if an icy cloak had been thrown about him. He went to the door and opened it.

Two policemen were coming up the walk with a dark snarling Johnson between them, handcuffed to each. A reporter jogged alongside and another policeman waited in the patrol car.

"Here's your boy," the dourest of the policemen said. "Didn't I tell you we'd get him?"

Johnson jerked his arm down savagely. "I was waitin for you!" he said. "You wouldn't have got me if I hadn't of wanted to get caught. It was my idea." He was addressing the policemen but leering at Sheppard.

Sheppard looked at him coldly.

"Why did you want to get caught?" the reporter asked, running around to get beside Johnson. "Why did you deliberately want to get caught?"

The question and the sight of Sheppard seemed to throw the boy into a fury. "To show up that big tin Jesus!" he hissed and kicked his leg out at Sheppard. "He thinks he's God. I'd rather be in the reformatory than in his house, I'd rather be in the pen! The Devil has him in his power. He don't know his left hand from his right, he don't have as much sense as his crazy kid!" He paused and then swept on to his fantastic conclusion. "He made suggestions to me!"

Sheppard's face blanched. He caught hold of the door facing.

"Suggestions?" the reporter said eagerly, "what kind of suggestion?"

"Immor'l suggestions!" Johnson said. "What kind of suggestions do you think? But I ain't having none of it, I'm a Christian, I'm . . ."

Sheppard's face was tight with pain. "He knows that's not true," he said in a shaken voice. "He knows he's lying. I did everything I knew how for him. I did more for him than I did for my own child. I hoped to save him and I failed, but it was an honorable failure. I have nothing to reproach myself with. I made no suggestions to him."

"Do you remember the suggestions?" the reporter asked. "Can you tell us exactly what he said?"

"He's a dirty atheist," Johnson said. "He said there wasn't no hell."

"Well, they seen each other now," one of the policemen said with a knowing sigh. "Let's us go."

"Wait," Sheppard said. He came down one step and fixed his eyes on Johnson's eyes in a last desperate effort to save himself. "Tell the truth, Rufus," he said. "You don't want to perpetrate this lie. You're not evil, you're mortally confused. You don't have to make up for that foot, you don't have to . . ."

Johnson hurled himself forward. "Listen at him!" he screamed. "I lie and steal because I'm good at it! My foot don't have a thing to do with it! The lame shall enter first! The halt'll be gathered together. When I get ready to be saved, Jesus'll save me, not that lying stinking atheist, not that . . ."

"That'll be enough out of you," the policeman said and yanked him back. "We just wanted you to see we got him," he said to Sheppard, and the two of them turned around and dragged Johnson away, half turned and screaming back at Sheppard.

"The lame'll carry off the prey!" he screeched, but his voice was muffled inside the car. The reporter scrambled into the front seat with the driver and slammed the door and the siren wailed into the darkness.

Sheppard remained there, bent slightly like a man who has been shot but continues to stand. After a minute he turned and went back in the house and sat down in the chair he had left. He closed his eyes on a picture of Johnson in a circle of reporters at the police station, elaborating his lies. "I have nothing to reproach myself with," he murmured. His every action had been selfless, his one aim had been to save Johnson for some decent kind of service, he had not spared himself, he had sacrificed his reputation, he had done more for Johnson than he had done for his own child. Foulness hung about him like an odor in the air, so close that it seemed to come from his own breath. "I have nothing to reproach myself with," he repeated. His voice sounded dry and harsh. "I did more for him than I did for my own child." He was swept with a sudden panic. He heard the boy's jubilant voice. Satan has you in his power.

"I have nothing to reproach myself with," he began again. "I did more for him than I did for my own child." He heard his voice as if it were the voice of his accuser. He repeated the sentence silently.

Slowly his face drained of color. It became almost gray beneath the white halo of his hair. The sentence echoed in his mind, each syllable like a dull blow. His mouth twisted and he closed his eyes against the revelation. Norton's face rose before him, empty, forlorn, his left eye listing almost imperceptibly toward the outer rim as if it could not bear a full view of grief. His heart constricted with a repulsion for himself so clear and intense that he gasped for breath. He had stuffed his own emptiness with good works like a glutton. He had ignored his own child to feed his vision of himself. He saw the clear-eyed Devil, the sounder of hearts, leering at him from the eyes of Johnson. His image of himself shrivelled until everything was black before him. He sat there paralyzed, aghast.

He saw Norton at the telescope, all back and ears, saw his arm shoot up and wave frantically. A rush of agonizing love for the child rushed over him like a transfusion of life. The little boy's face appeared to him transformed; the image of his salvation; all light. He groaned with joy. He would make everything up to him. He would never let him suffer again. He would be mother and father. He jumped up and ran to his room, to kiss him, to tell him that he loved him, that he would never fail him again.

The light was on in Norton's room but the bed was empty. He turned and dashed up the attic stairs and at the top reeled back like a man on the edge of a pit. The tripod had fallen and the telescope lay on the floor. A few feet over it, the child hung in the jungle of shadows, just below the beam from which he had launched his flight into space.

1965

FLANNERY O'CONNOR

Everything That Rises Must Converge

Her doctor had told Julian's mother that she must lose twenty pounds on account of her blood pressure, so on Wednesday nights Julian had to take her downtown on the bus for a reducing class at the Y. The reducing class was designed for working girls over fifty, who weighed from 165 to 200 pounds. His mother was one of the slimmer ones, but she said ladies did not tell their age or weight. She would not ride the buses by herself at night since they had been integrated, and because the reducing class was one of her few pleasures, necessary for her health, and *free*, she said Julian could at least put himself out to take her, considering all she did for him. Julian did not like to consider all she did for him, but every Wednesday night he braced himself and took her.

She was almost ready to go, standing before the hall mirror, putting on her hat, while he, his hands behind him, appeared pinned to the door frame, waiting like Saint Sebastian for the arrows to begin piercing him.[1] The hat was new and had cost her seven dollars and a half. She kept saying, "Maybe I shouldn't have paid that for it. No, I shouldn't have. I'll take it off and return it tomorrow. I shouldn't have bought it."

Julian raised his eyes to heaven. "Yes, you should have bought it," he said. "Put it on and let's go." It was a hideous hat. A purple velvet flap came down on one side of it and stood up on the other; the rest of it was green and looked like a cushion with the stuffing out. He decided it was less comical than jaunty and pathetic. Everything that gave her pleasure was small and depressed him.

She lifted the hat one more time and set it down slowly on top of her head. Two wings of gray hair protruded on either side of her florid face, but her eyes, sky-blue, were as innocent and untouched by experience as they must have been when she was ten. Were it not that she was a widow who had struggled fiercely to feed and clothe and put him through school and who was supporting him still, "until he got on his feet," she might have been a little girl that he had to take to town.

"It's all right, it's all right," he said. "Let's go." He opened the door himself 5
and started down the walk to get her going. The sky was a dying violet and the houses stood out darkly against it, bulbous liver-colored monstrosities of a uniform ugliness though no two were alike. Since this had been a fashionable neighborhood forty years ago, his mother persisted in thinking they did well to have an apartment in it. Each house had a narrow collar of dirt around it in which sat, usually, a grubby child. Julian walked with his hands in his pockets, his head down and thrust forward and his eyes glazed with the determination to make himself completely numb during the time he would be sacrificed to her pleasure.

The door closed and he turned to find the dumpy figure, surmounted by the atrocious hat, coming toward him. "Well," she said, "you only live once and paying a little more for it, I at least won't meet myself coming and going."

"Some day I'll start making money," Julian said gloomily—he knew he never would—"and you can have one of those jokes whenever you take the fit." But first they would move. He visualized a place where the nearest neighbors would be three miles away on either side.

"I think you're doing fine," she said, drawing on her gloves. "You've only been out of school a year. Rome wasn't built in a day."

1. Discovered to be a Christian, Sebastian, Roman commander in Milan, was tied to a tree, shot with arrows, and left for dead. (He recovered but reasserted his faith and was clubbed to death.)

She was one of the few members of the Y reducing class who arrived in hat and gloves and who had a son who had been to college. "It takes time," she said, "and the world is in such a mess. This hat looked better on me than any of the others, though when she brought it out I said, 'Take that thing back. I wouldn't have it on my head,' and she said, 'Now wait till you see it on,' and when she put it on me, I said, 'We-ull,' and she said, 'If you ask me, that hat does something for you and you do something for the hat, and besides,' she said, 'with that hat, you won't meet yourself coming and going.' "

Julian thought he could have stood his lot better if she had been selfish, if she had been an old hag who drank and screamed at him. He walked along, saturated in depression, as if in the midst of his martyrdom he had lost his faith. Catching sight of his long, hopeless, irritated face, she stopped suddenly with a grief-stricken look, and pulled back on his arm. "Wait on me," she said. "I'm going back to the house and take this thing off and tomorrow I'm going to return it. I was out of my head. I can pay the gas bill with that seven-fifty."

He caught her arm in a vicious grip. "You are not going to take it back," he said. "I like it."

"Well," she said, "I don't think I ought . . ."

"Shut up and enjoy it," he muttered, more depressed than ever.

"With the world in the mess it's in," she said, "it's a wonder we can enjoy anything. I tell you, the bottom rail is on the top."

Julian sighed.

"Of course," she said, "if you know who are you, you can go anywhere." She said this every time he took her to the reducing class. "Most of them in it are not our kind of people," she said, "but I can be gracious to anybody. I know who I am."

"They don't give a damn for your graciousness," Julian said savagely. "Knowing who you are is good for one generation only. You haven't the foggiest idea where you stand now or who you are."

She stopped and allowed her eyes to flash at him. "I most certainly do know who I am," she said, "and if you don't know who you are, I'm ashamed of you."

"Oh hell," Julian said.

"Your great-grandfather was a former governor of this state," she said. "Your grandfather was a prosperous land-owner. Your grandmother was a Godhigh."

"Will you look around you," he said tensely, "and see where you are now?" and he swept his arm jerkily out to indicate the neighborhood, which the growing darkness at least made less dingy.

"You remain what you are," she said. "Your great-grandfather had a plantation and two hundred slaves."

"There are no more slaves," he said irritably.

"They were better off when they were," she said. He groaned to see that she was off on that topic. She rolled onto it every few days like a train on an open track. He knew every stop, every junction, every swamp along the way, and knew the exact point at which her conclusion would roll majestically into the station: "It's ridiculous. It's simply not realistic. They should rise, yes, but on their own side of the fence."

"Let's skip it," Julian said.

"The ones I feel sorry for," she said, "are the ones that are half white. They're tragic."

"Will you skip it?"

"Suppose we were half white. We would certainly have mixed feelings."

"I have mixed feelings now," he groaned.

"Well let's talk about something pleasant," she said. "I remember going to Grandpa's when I was a little girl. Then the house had double stairways that went up to what was really the second floor—all the cooking was done on the first. I used to like to stay down in the kitchen on account of the way the walls smelled. I would sit with my nose pressed against the plaster and take deep breaths. Actually the place belonged to the Godhighs but your grandfather Chestny paid the mortgage and saved it for them. They were in reduced circumstances," she said, "but reduced or not, they never forgot who they were."

"Doubtless that decayed mansion reminded them," Julian muttered. He never spoke of it without contempt or thought of it without longing. He had seen it once when he was a child before it had been sold. The double stairways had rotted and been torn down. Negroes were living in it. But it remained in his mind as his mother had known it. It appeared in his dreams regularly. He would stand on the wide porch, listening to the rustle of oak leaves, then wander through the high-ceilinged hall into the parlor that opened onto it and gaze at the worn rugs and faded draperies. It occurred to him that it was he, not she, who could have appreciated it. He preferred its threadbare elegance to anything he could name and it was because of it that all the neighborhoods they had lived in had been a torment to him—whereas she had hardly known the difference. She called her insensitivity "being adjustable."

"And I remember the old darky who was my nurse, Caroline. There was no better person in the world. I've always had a great respect for my colored friends," she said. "I'd do anything in the world for them and they'd . . ."

"Will you for God's sake get off that subject?" Julian said. When he got on a bus by himself, he made it a point to sit down beside a Negro, in reparation as it were for his mother's sins.

"You're mighty touchy tonight," she said. "Do you feel all right?"

"Yes I feel all right," he said. "Now lay off."

She pursed her lips. "Well, you certainly are in a vile humor," she observed. "I just won't speak to you at all."

They had reached the bus stop. There was no bus in sight and Julian, his hands still jammed in his pockets and his head thrust forward, scowled down the empty street. The frustration of having to wait on the bus as well as ride on it began to creep up his neck like a hot hand. The presence of his mother was borne in upon him as she gave a pained sigh. He looked at her bleakly. She was holding herself very erect under the preposterous hat, wearing it like a banner of her imaginary dignity. There was in him an evil urge to break her spirit. He suddenly unloosened his tie and pulled it off and put it in his pocket.

She stiffened. "Why must you look like *that* when you take me to town?" she said. "Why must you deliberately embarrass me?"

"If you'll never learn where you are," he said, "you can at least learn where I am."

"You look like a—thug," she said.

"Then I must be one," he murmured.

"I'll just go home," she said. "I will not bother you. If you can't do a little thing like that for me . . ."

Rolling his eyes upward, he put his tie back on. "Restored to my class," he muttered. He thrust his face toward her and hissed, "True culture is in the mind, the *mind*," he said, and tapped his head, "the mind."

"It's in the heart," she said, "and in how you do things and how you do things is because of who you *are*."

"Nobody in the damn bus cares who you are."

"I care who I am," she said icily.

The lighted bus appeared on top of the next hill and as it approached, they moved out into the street to meet it. He put his hand under her elbow and hoisted her up on the creaking step. She entered with a little smile, as if she were going into a drawing room where everyone had been waiting for her. While he put in the tokens, she sat down on one of the broad front seats for three which faced the aisle. A thin woman with protruding teeth and long yellow hair was sitting on the end of it. His mother moved up beside her and left room for Julian beside herself. He sat down and looked at the floor across the aisle where a pair of thin feet in red and white canvas sandals were planted.

His mother immediately began a general conversation meant to attract anyone who felt like talking. "Can it get any hotter?" she said and removed from her purse a folding fan, black with a Japanese scene on it, which she began to flutter before her.

"I reckon it might could," the woman with the protruding teeth said, "but I know for a fact my apartment couldn't get no hotter."

"It must get the afternoon sun," his mother said. She sat forward and looked up and down the bus. It was half filled. Everybody was white. "I see we have the bus to ourselves," she said. Julian cringed.

"For a change," said the woman across the aisle, the owner of the red and white canvas sandals. "I come on one the other day and they were thick as fleas—up front and all through."

"The world is in a mess everywhere," his mother said. "I don't know how we've let it get in this fix."

"What gets my goat is all those boys from good families stealing automobile tires," the woman with the protruding teeth said. "I told my boy, I said you may not be rich but you been raised right and if I ever catch you in any such mess, they can send you on to the reformatory. Be exactly where you belong."

"Training tells," his mother said. "Is your boy in high school?"

"Ninth grade," the woman said.

"My son just finished college last year. He wants to write but he's selling typewriters until he gets started," his mother said.

The woman leaned forward and peered at Julian. He threw her such a malevolent look that she subsided against the seat. On the floor across the aisle there was an abandoned newspaper. He got up and got it and opened it out in front of him. His mother discreetly continued the conversation in a lower tone but the woman across the aisle said in a loud voice, "Well that's nice. Selling typewriters is close to writing. He can go right from one to the other."

"I tell him," his mother said, "that Rome wasn't built in a day."

Behind the newspaper Julian was withdrawing into the inner compartment of his mind where he spent most of his time. This was a kind of mental bubble in which he established himself when he could not bear to be a part of what was going on around him. From it he could see out and judge but in it he was safe from any kind of penetration from without. It was the only place where he felt free of the general idiocy of his fellows. His mother had never entered it but from it he could see her with absolute clarity.

The old lady was clever enough and he thought that if she had started from any of the right premises, more might have been expected of her. She lived according to the laws of her own fantasy world, outside of which he had never seen her set foot. The law of it was to sacrifice herself for him after she had first created the necessity to do so by making a mess of things. If he had permitted her sacrifices, it was only because her lack of foresight had made them necessary. All of her life had been a struggle to act like a Chestny without the Chestny goods, and to give him everything she thought a Chestny ought to have; but since, said she, it was fun to struggle, why complain? And when you had won, as she had won, what fun to look back on the hard times! He could not forgive her that she had enjoyed the struggle and that she thought *she* had won.

What she meant when she said she had won was that she had brought him up successfully and had sent him to college and that he had turned out so well—good looking (her teeth had gone unfilled so that his could be straightened), intelligent (he realized he was too intelligent to be a success), and with a future ahead of him (there was of course no future ahead of him). She excused his gloominess on the grounds that he was still growing up and his radical ideas on his lack of practical experience. She said he didn't yet know a thing about "life," that he hadn't even entered the real world—when already he was as disenchanted with it as a man of fifty.

The further irony of all this was that in spite of her, he had turned out so well. In spite of going to only a third-rate college, he had, on his own initiative, come out with a first-rate education; in spite of growing up dominated by a small mind, he had ended up with a large one; in spite of all her foolish views, he was free of prejudice and unafraid to face facts. Most miraculous of all, instead of being blinded by love for her as she was for him, he had cut himself emotionally free of her and could see her with complete objectivity. He was not dominated by his mother.

The bus stopped with a sudden jerk and shook him from his meditation. A woman from the back lurched forward with little steps and barely escaped falling in his newspaper as she righted herself. She got off and a large Negro got on. Julian kept his paper lowered to watch. It gave him a certain satisfaction to see injustice in daily operation. It confirmed his view that with a few exceptions there was no one worth knowing within a radius of three hundred miles. The

Negro was well dressed and carried a briefcase. He looked around and then sat down on the other end of the seat where the woman with the red and white canvas sandals was sitting. He immediately unfolded a newspaper and obscured himself behind it. Julian's mother's elbow at once prodded insistently into his ribs. "Now you see why I won't ride on these buses by myself," she whispered.

The woman with the red and white canvas sandals had risen at the same time the Negro sat down and had gone further back in the bus and taken the seat of the woman who had got off. His mother leaned forward and cast her an approving look.

Julian rose, crossed the aisle, and sat down in the place of the woman with the canvas sandals. From this position, he looked serenely across at his mother. Her face had turned an angry red. He stared at her, making his eyes the eyes of a stranger. He felt his tension suddenly lift as if he had openly declared war on her.

He would have liked to get in conversation with the Negro and to talk with him about art or politics or any subject that would be above the comprehension of those around them, but the man remained entrenched behind his paper. He was either ignoring the change of seating or had never noticed it. There was no way for Julian to convey his sympathy.

His mother kept her eyes fixed reproachfully on his face. The woman with the protruding teeth was looking at him avidly as if he were a type of monster new to her.

"Do you have a light?" he asked the Negro.

Without looking away from his paper, the man reached in his pocket and handed him a packet of matches.

"Thanks," Julian said. For a moment he held the matches foolishly. A NO SMOKING sign looked down upon him from over the door. This alone would not have deterred him; he had no cigarettes. He had quit smoking some months before because he could not afford it. "Sorry," he muttered and handed back the matches. The Negro lowered the paper and gave him an annoyed look. He took the matches and raised the paper again.

His mother continued to gaze at him but she did not take advantage of his momentary discomfort. Her eyes retained their battered look. Her face seemed to be unnaturally red, as if her blood pressure had risen. Julian allowed no glimmer of sympathy to show on his face. Having got the advantage, he wanted desperately to keep it and carry it through. He would have liked to teach her a lesson that would last her a while, but there seemed no way to continue the point. The Negro refused to come out from behind his paper.

Julian folded his arms and looked stolidly before him, facing her but as if he did not see her, as if he had ceased to recognize her existence. He visualized a scene in which, the bus having reached their stop, he would remain in his seat and when she said, "Aren't you going to get off?" he would look at her as a stranger who had rashly addressed him. The corner they got off on was usually deserted, but it was well lighted and it would not hurt her to walk by herself the four blocks to the Y. He decided to wait until the time came and then decide whether or not he would let her get off by herself. He would have to be at the Y at ten to bring her back, but he could leave her wondering if he was going to show up. There was no reason for her to think she could always depend on him.

He retired again into the high-ceilinged room sparsely settled with large pieces of antique furniture. His soul expanded momentarily but then he became aware of his mother across from him and the vision shriveled. He studied her coldly. Her feet in little pumps dangled like a child's and did not quite reach the floor. She was training on him an exaggerated look of reproach. He felt completely detached from her. At that moment he could with pleasure have slapped her as he would have slapped a particularly obnoxious child in his charge.

He began to imagine various unlikely ways by which he could teach her a lesson. He might make friends with some distinguished Negro professor or lawyer and bring him home to spend the evening. He would be entirely justified but her blood pressure would rise to 300. He could not push her to the extent of making her have a stroke, and moreover, he had never been successful at making any Negro friends. He had tried to strike up an acquaintance on the bus with some of the better types, with ones that looked like professors or ministers or lawyers. One morning he had sat down next to a distinguished-looking dark brown man who had answered his questions with a sonorous solemnity but who had turned out to be an undertaker. Another day he had sat down beside a cigar-smoking Negro with a diamond ring on his finger, but after a few stilted pleasantries, the Negro had rung the buzzer and risen, slipping two lottery tickets into Julian's hand as he climbed over him to leave.

He imagined his mother lying desperately ill and his being able to secure only a Negro doctor for her. He toyed with that idea for a few minutes and then dropped it for a momentary vision of himself participating as a sympathizer in a sit-in demonstration. This was possible but he did not linger with it. Instead, he approached the ultimate horror. He brought home a beautiful suspiciously Negroid woman. Prepare yourself, he said. There is nothing you can do about it. This is the woman I've chosen. She's intelligent, dignified, even good, and she's suffered and she hasn't thought it *fun*. Now persecute us, go ahead and persecute us. Drive her out of here, but remember, you're driving me too. His eyes were narrowed and through the indignation he had generated, he saw his mother across the aisle, purple-faced, shrunken to the dwarf-like proportions of her moral nature, sitting like a mummy beneath the ridiculous banner of her hat.

He was tilted out of his fantasy again as the bus stopped. The door opened with a sucking hiss and out of the dark a large, gaily dressed, sullen-looking colored woman got on with a little boy. The child, who might have been four, had on a short plaid suit and a Tyrolean hat with a blue feather in it. Julian hoped that he would sit down beside him and that the woman would push in beside his mother. He could think of no better arrangement.

As she waited for her tokens, the woman was surveying the seating possibilities—he hoped with the idea of sitting where she was least wanted. There was something familiar-looking about her but Julian could not place what it was. She was a giant of a woman. Her face was set not only to meet opposition but to seek it out. The downward tilt of her large lower lip was like a warning sign: DON'T TAMPER WITH ME. Her bulging figure was encased in a green crepe dress and her feet overflowed in red shoes. She had on a hideous hat. A purple velvet flap came down on one side of it and stood up on the other; the rest of it was green and looked like a cushion with the stuffing out. She carried a mammoth red pocketbook that bulged throughout as if it were stuffed with rocks.

To Julian's disappointment, the little boy climbed up on the empty seat beside his mother. His mother lumped all children, black and white, into the common category, "cute," and she thought little Negroes were on the whole cuter than little white children. She smiled at the little boy as he climbed on the seat.

Meanwhile the woman was bearing down upon the empty seat beside Julian. To his annoyance, she squeezed herself into it. He saw his mother's face change as the woman settled herself next to him and he realized with satisfaction that this was more objectionable to her than it was to him. Her face seemed almost gray and there was a look of dull recognition in her eyes, as if suddenly she had sickened at some awful confrontation. Julian saw that it was because she and the woman had, in a sense, swapped sons. Though his mother would not realize the symbolic significance of this, she would feel it. His amusement showed plainly on his face.

80 The woman next to him muttered something unintelligible to herself. He was conscious of a kind of bristling next to him, a muted growling like that of an angry cat. He could not see anything but the red pocketbook upright on the bulging green thighs. He visualized the woman as she had stood waiting for her tokens—the ponderous figure, rising from the red shoes upward over the solid hips, the mammoth bosom, the haughty face, to the green and purple hat.

His eyes widened.

The vision of the two hats, identical, broke upon him with the radiance of a brilliant sunrise. His face was suddenly lit with joy. He could not believe that Fate had thrust upon his mother such a lesson. He gave a loud chuckle so that she would look at him and see that he saw. She turned her eyes on him slowly. The blue in them seemed to have turned a bruised purple. For a moment he had an uncomfortable sense of her innocence, but it lasted only a second before principle rescued him. Justice entitled him to laugh. His grin hardened until it said to her as plainly as if he were saying aloud: Your punishment exactly fits your pettiness. This should teach you a permanent lesson.

Her eyes shifted to the woman. She seemed unable to bear looking at him and to find the woman preferable. He became conscious again of the bristling presence at his side. The woman was rumbling like a volcano about to become active. His mother's mouth began to twitch slightly at one corner. With a sinking heart, he saw incipient signs of recovery on her face and realized that this was going to strike her suddenly as funny and was going to be no lesson at all. She kept her eyes on the woman and an amused smile came over her face as if the woman were a monkey that had stolen her hat. The little Negro was looking up at her with large fascinated eyes. He had been trying to attract her attention for some time.

"Carver!" the woman said suddenly. "Come heah!"

85 When he saw that the spotlight was on him at last, Carver drew his feet up and turned himself toward Julian's mother and giggled.

"Carver!" the woman said. "You heah me? Come heah!"

Carver slid down from the seat but remained squatting with his back against the base of it, his head turned slyly around toward Julian's mother, who was smiling at him. The woman reached a hand across the aisle and snatched him to her. He righted himself and hung backwards on her knees, grinning at Julian's mother. "Isn't he cute?" Julian's mother said to the woman with the protruding teeth.

"I reckon he is," the woman said without conviction.

The Negress yanked him upright but he eased out of her grip and shot across the aisle and scrambled, giggling wildly, onto the seat beside his love.

"I think he likes me," Julian's mother said, and smiled at the woman. It was 90
the smile she used when she was being particularly gracious to an inferior. Julian saw everything was lost. The lesson had rolled off her like rain on a roof.

The woman stood up and yanked the little boy off the seat as if she were snatching him from contagion. Julian could feel the rage in her at having no weapon like his mother's smile. She gave the child a sharp slap across his leg. He howled once and then thrust his head into her stomach and kicked his feet against her shins. "Behave," she said vehemently.

The bus stopped and the Negro who had been reading the newspaper got off. The woman moved over and set the little boy down with a thump between herself and Julian. She held him firmly by the knee. In a moment he put his hands in front of his face and peeped at Julian's mother through his fingers.

"I see yoooooooo!" she said and put her hand in front of her face and peeped at him.

The woman slapped his hand down. "Quit yo' foolishness," she said, "before I knock the living Jesus out of you!"

Julian was thankful that the next stop was theirs. He reached up and pulled 95
the cord. The woman reached up and pulled it at the same time. Oh my God, he thought. He had the terrible intuition that when they got off the bus together, his mother would open her purse and give the little boy a nickel. The gesture would be as natural to her as breathing. The bus stopped and the woman got up and lunged to the front, dragging the child, who wished to stay on, after her. Julian and his mother got up and followed. As they neared the door, Julian tried to relieve her of her pocketbook.

"No," she murmured, "I want to give the little boy a nickel."

"No!" Julian hissed. "No!"

She smiled down at the child and opened her bag. The bus door opened and the woman picked him up by the arm and descended with him, hanging at her hip. Once in the street she set him down and shook him.

Julian's mother had to close her purse while she got down the bus step but as soon as her feet were on the ground, she opened it again and began to rummage inside. "I can't find but a penny," she whispered, "but it looks like a new one."

"Don't do it!" Julian said fiercely between his teeth. There was a streetlight 100
on the corner and she hurried to get under it so that she could better see into her pocketbook. The woman was heading off rapidly down the street with the child still hanging backward on her hand.

"Oh little boy!" Julian's mother called and took a few quick steps and caught up with them just beyond the lamppost. "Here's a bright new penny for you," and she held out the coin, which shone bronze in the dim light.

The huge woman turned and for a moment stood, her shoulders lifted and her face frozen with frustrated rage, and stared at Julian's mother. Then all at once she seemed to explode like a piece of machinery that had been given one ounce of pressure too much. Julian saw the black fist swing out with the red pocketbook. He shut his eyes and cringed as he heard the woman shout, "He don't take nobody's pennies!" When he opened his eyes, the woman was disappearing down the street with the little boy staring wide-eyed over her shoulder. Julian's mother was sitting on the sidewalk.

"I told you not to do that," Julian said angrily. "I told you not to do that!"

He stood over her for a minute, gritting his teeth. Her legs were stretched out in front of her and her hat was on her lap. He squatted down and looked her in the face. It was totally expressionless. "You got exactly what you deserved," he said. "Now get up."

105 He picked up her pocketbook and put what had fallen out back in it. He picked the hat up off her lap. The penny caught his eye on the sidewalk and he picked that up and let it drop before her eyes into the purse. Then he stood up and leaned over and held his hands out to pull her up. She remained immobile. He sighed. Rising above them on either side were black apartment buildings, marked with irregular rectangles of light. At the end of the block a man came out of a door and walked off in the opposite direction. "All right," he said, "suppose somebody happens by and wants to know why you're sitting on the sidewalk?"

She took the hand and, breathing hard, pulled heavily up on it and then stood for a moment, swaying slightly as if the spots of light in the darkness were circling around her. Her eyes, shadowed and confused, finally settled on his face. He did not try to conceal his irritation. "I hope this teaches you a lesson," he said. She leaned forward and her eyes raked his face. She seemed trying to determine his identity. Then, as if she found nothing familiar about him, she started off with a headlong movement in the wrong direction.

"Aren't you going on to the Y?" he asked.

"Home," she muttered.

"Well, are we walking?"

110 For answer she kept going. Julian followed along, his hands behind him. He saw no reason to let the lesson she had had go without backing it up with an explanation of its meaning. She might as well be made to understand what had happened to her. "Don't think that was just an uppity Negro woman," he said. "That was the whole colored race which will no longer take your condescending pennies. That was your black double. She can wear the same hat as you, and to be sure," he added gratuitously (because he thought it was funny), "it looked better on her than it did on you. What all this means," he said, "is that the old world is gone. The old manners are obsolete and your graciousness is not worth a damn." He thought bitterly of the house that had been lost for him. "You aren't who you think you are," he said.

She continued to plow ahead, paying no attention to him. Her hair had come undone on one side. She dropped her pocketbook and took no notice. He stooped and picked it up and handed it to her but she did not take it.

"You needn't act as if the world had come to an end," he said, "because it hasn't. From now on you've got to live in a new world and face a few realities for a change. Buck up," he said, "it won't kill you."

She was breathing fast.

"Let's wait on the bus," he said.

"Home," she said thickly.

"I hate to see you behave like this," he said. "Just like a child. I should be able to expect more of you." He decided to stop where he was and make her stop and wait for a bus. "I'm not going any farther," he said stopping. "We're going on the bus."

She continued to go on as if she had not heard him. He took a few steps and caught her arm and stopped her. He looked into her face and caught his breath. He was looking into a face he had never seen before. "Tell Grandpa to come get me," she said.

He stared, stricken.

"Tell Caroline to come get me," she said.

Stunned, he let her go and she lurched forward again, walking as if one leg were shorter than the other. A tide of darkness seemed to be sweeping her from him. "Mother!" he cried. "Darling, sweetheart, wait!" Crumpling, she fell to the pavement. He dashed forward and fell at her side, crying, "Mamma, Mamma!" He turned her over. Her face was fiercely distorted. One eye, large and staring, moved slightly to the left as if it had become unmoored. The other remained fixed on him, raked his face again, found nothing and closed.

"Wait here, wait here!" he cried and jumped up and began to run for help toward a cluster of lights he saw in the distance ahead of him. "Help, help!" he shouted, but his voice was thin, scarcely a thread of sound. The lights drifted farther away the faster he ran and his feet moved numbly as if they carried him nowhere. The tide of darkness seemed to sweep him back to her, postponing from moment to moment his entry into the world of guilt and sorrow.

1965

FLANNERY O'CONNOR

Passages from Essays and Letters

from "The Fiction Writer and His Country"

. . . when I look at stories I have written I find that they are, for the most part, about people who are poor, who are afflicted in both mind and body, who have little—or at best a distorted—sense of spiritual purpose, and whose actions do not apparently give the reader a great assurance of the joy of life.

Yet how is this? For I am no disbeliever in spiritual purpose and no vague believer. I see from the standpoint of Christian orthodoxy. This means that for me the meaning of life is centered in our Redemption by Christ and what I see in the world I see in its relation to that.

Some may blame preoccupation with the grotesque on the fact that here we have a Southern writer and that this is just the type of imagination that Southern life fosters. . . . I find it hard to believe that what is observable behavior in one section can be entirely without parallel in another. At least, of late, Southern writers have had the opportunity of pointing out that none of us invented Elvis Presley and that that youth is himself probably less an occasion for concern than his popularity, which is not restricted to the Southern part of the country.

When you can assume that your audience holds the same beliefs you do, you can relax a little and use more normal means of talking to it; when you have to assume that it does not, then you have to make your vision apparent by shock—to the hard of hearing you shout, and for the almost-blind you draw large and startling figures.

from "The Grotesque in Southern Fiction"

All novelists are fundamentally seekers and describers of the real, but the realism of each novelist will depend on his view of the ultimate reaches of reality. . . . If the novelist is in tune with this [modern scientific] spirit, if he believes that actions are predetermined by psychic make-up or the economic situation or some other determinable factor, then he will be concerned above all with an accurate reproduction of the things that most immediately concern man, with the natural forces that he feels control his destiny. . . .

On the other hand, if the writer believes that our life is and will remain essentially mysterious, . . . then what he sees on the surface will be of interest to him only as he can go through it into an experience of mystery itself. . . . [F]or this kind of writer, the meaning of a story does not begin except at a depth where adequate motivation and adequate psychology and the various determinations have been exhausted. Such a writer will be interested in what we don't understand rather than in what we do.

from "The Nature and Aim of Fiction"

. . . The beginning of human knowledge is through the senses, and the fiction writer begins where human perception begins. He appeals through the senses, and you cannot appeal to the senses with abstractions. . . . [F]iction is so very much an incarnational art.

Now the word *symbol* scares a good many people off, just as the word *art* does. They seem to feel that a symbol is some mysterious thing put in arbitrarily by the writer to frighten the common reader—sort of a literary Masonic grip that is only for the initiated. They seem to think that it is a way of saying something that you aren't actually saying, and so . . . they approach it as if it were a problem in algebra. Find *x*. And when they do find or think they find this abstraction, *x*, then they go off with an elaborate sense of satisfaction and the notion that they have "understood" the story. . . .

I think for the fiction writer himself, symbols are something he uses simply as a matter of course. You might say that these are details that, while having their essential place in the literal level of the story, operate in depth as well as on the surface, increasing the story in every direction.

People have a habit of saying, "What is the theme of your story?" and they expect you to give them a statement. . . . And when they've got a statement . . . , they go off happy and feel it is no longer necessary to read the story. . . . , but for the fiction writer himself the whole story is the meaning, because it is an experience, not an abstraction.

*from "Writing Short Stories"**

. . . A story is a complete dramatic action—and in good stories, the characters are shown through the action and the action is controlled through the characters, and the result of this is meaning that derives from the whole presented experience.

. . . Nothing essential to the main experience can be left out of a short story. All the action has to be satisfactorily accounted for in terms of motivation, and there has to be a beginning, a middle, and an end, though not necessarily in that order.

. . . I prefer to talk about the meaning in a story rather than the theme of a story. People talk about the theme of a story as if the theme were like the string that a sack of chicken feed is tied with. They think that if you can pick out the theme, the way you pick the right thread in the chicken-feed sack, you can rip the story open and feed the chickens. But this is not the way meaning works in fiction.

When you can state the theme of a story, when you can separate it from the story itself, then you can be sure the story is not a very good one. The meaning of a story has to be embodied in it, has to be made concrete in it. A story is a way to say something that can't be said any other way, and it takes every word in the story to say what the meaning is. You tell a story because a statement would be inadequate.

An idiom characterizes a society, and when you ignore the idiom, you are very likely ignoring the whole social fabric that could make a meaningful char-

* "The Nature and Aim of Fiction" and "Writing Short Stories" are composites, edited from O'Connor manuscripts by Sally and Robert Fitzgerald in *Mystery and Manners*.

acter. You can't cut characters off from their society and say much about them as individuals. You can't say anything meaningful about the mystery of a personality unless you put that personality in a believable and significant social context.

from "On Her Own Work"

In most English classes the short story has become a kind of literary specimen to be dissected. Every time a story of mine appears in a Freshman anthology, I have a vision of it, with its little organs laid open, like a frog in a bottle.

I realize that a certain amount of this what-is-the-significance has to go on, but I think something has gone wrong in the process when, for so many students, the story becomes simply a problem to be solved, something which you evaporate to get Instant Enlightenment.

A story isn't any good unless it successfully resists paraphrase, unless it hangs on and expands in the mind. Properly, you analyze to enjoy, but it's equally true that to analyze with any discrimination, you have to have enjoyed already, and I think that the best reason to hear a story read is that it should stimulate that primary enjoyment.

I often ask myself what makes a story work, and what makes it hold up as a story, and I have decided that it is probably some action, some gesture of a character that is unlike any other in the story, one which indicates where the real heart of the story lies. This would have to be an action or a gesture which was both totally right and totally unexpected; it would have to be one that was both in character and beyond character; it would have to suggest both the world and eternity. The action or gesture I'm talking about would have to be on the anagogical level, that is, the level which has to do with the Divine life and our participation in it. It would be a gesture that transcended any neat allegory that might have been intended or any pat moral categories a reader could make. It would be a gesture which somehow made contact with mystery.

. . . in my own stories I have found that violence is strangely capable of returning my characters to reality and preparing them to accept their moment of grace . . .

We hear many complaints about the prevalence of violence in modern fiction, and it is always assumed that this violence is a bad thing and meant to be an end in itself. With the serious writer, violence is never an end in itself. It is the extreme situation that best reveals what we are essentially . . .

from "Novelist and Believer"

. . . Great fiction . . . is not simply an imitation of feeling. The good novelist not only finds a symbol for feeling, he finds a symbol and a way of lodging it which tells the intelligent reader whether this feeling is adequate or inadequate, whether it is moral or immoral, whether it is good or evil. And his theology, even in its most remote reaches, will have a direct bearing on this.

. . . The artist penetrates the concrete world in order to find at its depths the image of its source, the image of ultimate reality. This in no way hinders his perception of evil but rather sharpens it, for only when the natural world is seen as good does evil become intelligible as a destructive force and a necessary result of our freedom.

From the Letters

TO A PROFESSOR OF ENGLISH, 28 MARCH 1961

The meaning of a story should go on expanding for the reader the more he thinks about it, but meaning cannot be captured in an interpretation. If teachers are in the habit of approaching a story as if it were a research problem for which any answer is believable so long as it is not obvious, then I think students will never learn to enjoy fiction. Too much interpretation is certainly worse than too little, and where feeling for a story is absent, theory will not supply it.

TO LOUISE AND TOM GOSSETT, 10 APRIL 1961

I have just read a review of my book *[The Violent Bear It Away]*, long and damming [sic], which says it don't give us hope and courage and that all novels should give us hope and courage. I think if the novel is to give us virtue the selection of hope and courage is rather arbitrary—why not charity, peace, patience, joy, benignity, long-suffering and fear of the Lord? Or faith? The fact of the matter is that the modern mind opposes courage to faith. It also demands that the novel provide us with gifts that only religion can give. I don't think the novel can offend against the truth, but I think its truths are more particular than general. But this is a large subject and I ain't no aesthetician.

TO ROSLYN BARNES, 17 JUNE 1961

Can you tell me if the statement: "everything that rises must converge" is a true proposition in physics? I can easily see its moral, historical and evolutionary significance, but I want to know if it is also a correct physical statement.

TO "A", 22 JULY 1961

I had a story that I had written a first draft sort of on and Caroline thought as usual that it wasn't dramatic enough (and she was right) and told me all the things that I tell you when I read one of yours. She did think the structure was good and the situation. All I got to do is write the story. This one is called "The Lame Shall Enter First."

TO "A", 16 SEPTEMBER 1961

The thing I am writing now is surely going to convince Jack [the author John Hawkes] that I am of the Devil's party. It is out of hand right now but I am hoping I can bring it into line. It is a composite of all the eccentricities of my writing and for this reason may not be any good, maybe almost a parody. But what you start, you ought to carry through and if it is no good, I don't have to publish it. I am thinking of changing the title to "The Lame Will Carry Off the Prey."

TO JOHN HAWKES, 28 NOVEMBER 1961

You haven't convinced me that I write with the Devil's will or belong in the romantic tradition and I'm prepared to argue some more with you on this if I can remember where we left off at. I think the reason we can't agree on this is because there is a difference in our two devils. My Devil has a name, a history and a definite plan. His name is Lucifer, he's a fallen angel, his sin is pride, and his aim is the destruction of the Divine plan. Now I judge that your Devil is co-equal to God, not his creature: that pride is his virtue not his sin; and that his aim is not to destroy the Divine plan because there isn't any Divine plan to destroy. My Devil is objective and yours is subjective. You say one becomes "evil" when one leaves the herd. I say that depends entirely on what the herd is doing.

TO "A", 9 DECEMBER 1961

Some friends of mine in Texas wrote me that a friend of theirs went into a bookstore looking for a paperback copy of A *Good Man*. The clerk said, "We don't have that one but we have another by that author, called *The Bear That Ran Away With It*. I foresee the trouble I am going to have with "Everything That Rises Must Converge"—"Every Rabbit That Rises Is a Sage."

TO CECIL DAWKINS, 6 SEPTEMBER 1962

About the story ["The Lame Shall Enter First"] I certainly agree that it don't work and have never felt that it did, but in heaven's name where do you get the idea that Sheppard represents Freud? Freud never entered my mind and looking back over it, I can't make him fit now. The story is about a man who thought he was good and thought he was doing good when he wasn't. Freud was a great one, wasn't he, for bringing home to people the fact that they weren't what they thought they were, so if Freud were in this, which he is not, he would certainly be on the other side of the fence from Shepp. The story doesn't work because I don't know, don't sympathize, don't like Mr. Sheppard in the way that I know and like most of my other characters. This is a story, not a statement. I think you ought to look for simpler explanations of why things don't work and not mess around with philosophical ideas where they haven't been intended or don't apply. There's nothing in the story that could possibly suggest that Sheppard represents Freud. This is some theory of which you are possessed. I am wondering if this kind of theorizing could be what is interfering with your getting going on some writing. Don't mix up thought-knowledge with felt-knowledge. If Sheppard represents anything here, it is, as he realizes at the end of the story, the empty man who fills up his emptiness with good works.

TO "A", 3 NOVEMBER 1962

. . . In that story of mine ["The Lame Shall Enter First"] . . . the little boy wouldn't have been looking for his mother if she hadn't been a good one when she was alive. This of course could be debated, but it's nowhere suggested in the story that she wasn't a good one.

TO MARION MONTGOMERY, 16 JUNE 1963

I never wrote and thanked you for innerducing me at Georgia or for the copy of *The Sermon of Introduction*, but I liked them. They made up for my present lack of popularity with the *Atlanta Journal-Constitution* book page, that alert sheet of Sunday criticism. Did you ever see their mention of "Everything That Rises Must Converge"? Unsigned. I suspect somebody from Atlanta U. did it.

TO "A", 1 SEPTEMBER 1963

The topical is poison. I got away with it in "Everything That Rises" but only because I say a plague on everybody's house as far as the race business goes.

QUESTIONS

1. What sensory details do you find in the opening paragraph of "Odour of Chrysanthemums"? later in the story? What expectations are aroused by the opening paragraph? When do you first begin to suspect that Walter Bates is not off drinking somewhere?

2. In what ways might the opening of "The Rocking-Horse Winner" prepare you for the surreal or supernatural events later in the story?

3. If you did not know that "Odour of Chrysanthemums" and "The Rocking-Horse Winner" were by the same author, what internal evidence (elements, views, language within the story) might suggest it? How does "The Rocking-Horse Winner" of 1932 differ from the early story "Odour of Chrysanthemums"?

4. How does Sheppard explain why Norton throws up ("The Lame Shall Enter First," par. 48)? Why do you think he does (other than his putting peanut butter and ketchup on his cake!)?

5. What internal evidence is there that "The Lame Shall Enter First" and "Everything That Rises Must converge" are by the same author?

WRITING SUGGESTIONS

1. Describe the continuity and the change or development in Lawrence's work, assuming those two stories are typical of that work and time of publication.

2. Briefly retell the story of "Everything That Rises Must Converge" from the point of view, perhaps even in the voice, of the African-American woman who is wearing "THE hat."

3. Compare the function of money in "The Rocking-Horse Winner" and "The Lame Shall Enter First."

9 A KIND: INITIATION

Themes are useful for grouping stories together for comparison, both to highlight similarities and to reveal differences in history and structure and so to discover the uniqueness of the work. Types of characters—stereotypes—are useful for the same purpose: to show both the common qualities and the unique combination of qualities in a particular character in a story. Though all grouping and classification, used poorly, can blur distinctions and make all members of a group seem the same, when used well they do not blur but bring into focus the individuality of the individual thing or being.

Literary criticism lacks the specific and agreed-on system of classification of biology, so that its terms are not so fixed as *phylum*, *genus*, *species*. In general, we use the term **genre** for the largest commonly agreed-on categories: fiction, poetry, drama. When I'm trying to be consistent, I use the term **subgenre** for the divisions of fiction—novel, novella, short story, and so on. A **kind** is a species or subcategory within a subgenre.

There is one kind of short story that is so common that there are those who maintain it is not a kind but is equivalent to the subgenre short story itself. That pervasive kind is the **initiation** story, in which a character—often but not always a child or young person—first learns a significant truth about the universe, reality, society, people, himself or herself. Such a subject tends to dictate the main outlines of the story's action: it begins with the protagonist in a state of innocence or mistaken belief (exposition); it leads up to the moment of illumination or the discovery of the truth (rising action to climax or turning point), and ends usually with some indication of the result of that discovery (falling action to conclusion). This kind is particularly suitable to a short story because it lends itself to brief treatment: the illumination is more or less sudden—there is no need for lengthy development, for multiple scenes or settings, for much time to pass, for too many complications of action or a large cast of characters—yet it can encapsulate a whole life or important segment of a life and wide-ranging, significant themes.

If you've been reading this anthology from the beginning, you have already run into a number of initiation stories, and you may have some idea of what kinds of truths their protagonists discover. Young goodman Brown discovers the universality of evil in human beings. The captain in "The Secret Sharer" discovers that someone very much like him, virtually his double and therefore probably he himself, is not only capable of murder but may, under certain circumstances and in his capacity as a captain or leader, consciously choose murder as the lesser of evils. Leila ("Her First Ball") comes across the truth that youth is fleeting (you cannot say she really learns it, since by the end of that very short story she has forgotten it). We have also seen that one may retreat from the truth physically or psychologically, as does Brown, or remain unchanged or revert to one's former state, as Leila does.

Since to the young all things seem possible—one can be a doctor, novelist, tennis star, saint, and swinger, serially or simultaneously—many of the truths learned in initiation stories have to do with limitation. The girl in "Boys and Girls" learns that she is "only a girl." Fortunately, growing up is not just loss, and there are positive or "happy" initiation stories. The boy in "The Old People" is initiated first into "manhood," and takes his place among "the hunters," and then into a more exclusive, privileged fraternity, that of the owners or, as Faulkner would no doubt prefer it, "custodians" of the land.

Sometimes, the initiation takes place as an unscheduled event, as in "Araby." At other times there is a ritual or **rite of passage,** such as a formal entry into society ("Her First Ball"). What do we usually think of as the purpose of a debut? How does the society intend to induct its new member? As you read "Her First Ball," think about these questions and watch how Leila's debut fulfills its ritual role, how it differs from it, and how it may induct Leila into society more truly than intended. The ritual in "The Old People" is formal, communal, and ceremonial. The formalities of the rite in this story may bring to the surface elements in the pattern that lie beneath the surface in other stories.

By the time you finish this chapter you should have some idea of the variations possible within the initiation story, and as you look back to such stories as "Sonny's Blues," "The Country Husband," "How Much Land Does a Man Need?" "Her First Ball," "Odour of Chrysanthemums," and many of the others, you should have a still better idea of the range of stories in this kind. Adults may be initiated as well as children and adolescents; the truths may be bitter or pleasing, cosmic, social, psychological; the initiates may change forever, retreat, shrug off what they have learned. By seeing all these stories as part of the large group of initiation stories you may the more readily notice the differences in the protagonists, in the learning experience, in the results of the initiation on the protagonists and whether they are permanent or temporary, life-denying or life-enhancing. You may, in other words, have gone a long way toward defining the unique vision of the story, its precise and individual illumination of reality. And that's the function of classification in the first place.

▽ ▽ ▽

KIND A Glossary

genre: the largest category for classifying literature—fiction, poetry, drama

initiation story: a *kind* of short story in which a character—often but not always a child or young person—first learns a significant, usually life-changing truth about the universe, society, people, himself or herself

kind: a species or subcategory within a *subgenre; initiation stories* are a subcategory of the subgenre short story

rite of passage: a ritual or ceremony marking an individual's passing from one stage or state to a more advance one, or an event in one's life which seems to have such significance; a formal initiation

subgenre: division within the category of a *genre*; novel, novella, and short story are subgenres of the genre fiction

JAMES JOYCE

Araby

North Richmond Street, being blind,[1] was a quiet street except at the hour when the Christian Brothers' School set the boys free. An uninhabited house of two storeys stood at the blind end, detached from its neighbours in a square ground. The other houses of the street, conscious of decent lives within them, gazed at one another with brown imperturbable faces.

The former tenant of our house, a priest, had died in the back drawing-room. Air, musty from having been long enclosed, hung in all the rooms, and the waste room behind the kitchen was littered with old useless papers. Among these I found a few paper-covered books, the pages of which were curled and damp: *The Abbot*, by Walter Scott, *The Devout Communicant* and *The Memoirs of Vidocq*.[2] I liked the last best because its leaves were yellow. The wild garden behind the house contained a central apple tree and a few straggling bushes, under one of which I found the late tenant's rusty bicycle-pump. He had been a very charitable priest; in his will he had left all his money to institutions and the furniture of his house to his sister.

When the short days of winter came, dusk fell before we had well eaten our dinners. When we met in the street the houses had grown sombre. The space of sky above us was the colour of ever-changing violet and towards it the lamps of the street lifted their feeble lanterns. The cold air stung us and we played till our bodies glowed. Our shouts echoed in the silent street. The career of our play brought us through the dark muddy lanes behind the houses, where we ran the gauntlet of the rough tribes from the cottages, to the back doors of the dark dripping gardens where odours arose from the ashpits,[3] to the dark odorous stables where a coachman smoothed and combed the horse or shook music from the buckled harness. When we returned to the street, light from the kitchen windows had filled the areas. If my uncle was seen turning the corner, we hid in the shadow until we had seen him safely housed. Or if Mangan's sister came out on the doorstep to call her brother in to his tea, we watched her from our shadow peer up and down the street. We waited to see whether she would remain or go in and, if she remained, we left our shadow and walked up to Mangan's steps resignedly. She was waiting for us, her figure defined by the light from the half-opened door. Her brother always teased her before he obeyed, and I stood by the railings looking at her. Her dress swung as she moved her body, and the soft rope of her hair tossed from side to side.

Every morning I lay on the floor in the front parlour watching her door. The

1. Dead-end street. 2. The 1820 novel by Sir Walter Scott (1771–1834) is a romance about the Catholic Mary Queen of Scots (1542–87), who was beheaded; a Catholic religious tract: *The Devout Communicant: or Pious Meditations and Aspirations for the Three Days Before and Three Days After Receiving the Holy Eucharist* (1813); the "memoirs" were probably *not* written by François Vidocq (1775–1857), a French criminal who became chief of detectives and who died poor and disgraced for his part in a crime that he solved. 3. Where fireplace ashes were dumped.

blind was pulled down to within an inch of the sash so that I could not be seen. When she came out on the doorstep my heart leaped. I ran to the hall, seized my books and followed her. I kept her brown figure always in my eye and, when we came near the point at which our ways diverged, I quickened my pace and passed her. This happened morning after morning. I had never spoken to her, except for a few casual words, and yet her name was like a summons to all my foolish blood.

Her image accompanied me even in places the most hostile to romance. On 5
Saturday evenings when my aunt went marketing I had to go to carry some of the parcels. We walked through the flaring streets, jostled by drunken men and bargaining women, amid the curses of labourers, the shrill litanies of shop-boys who stood on guard by the barrels of pigs' cheeks, the nasal chanting of street-singers, who sang a *come-all-you* about O'Donovan Rossa,[4] or a ballad about the troubles in our native land. These noises converged in a single sensation of life for me: I imagined that I bore my chalice safely through a throng of foes. Her name sprang to my lips at moments in strange prayers and praises which I myself did not understand. My eyes were often full of tears (I could not tell why) and at times a flood from my heart seemed to pour itself out into my bosom. I thought little of the future. I did not know whether I would ever speak to her or not or, if I spoke to her, how I would tell her of my confused adoration. But my body was like a harp and her words and gestures were like fingers running upon the wires.

One evening I went into the back drawing-room in which the priest had died. It was a dark rainy evening and there was no sound in the house. Through one of the broken panes I heard the rain impinge upon the earth, the fine incessant needles of water playing in the sodden beds. Some distant lamp or lighted window gleamed below me. I was thankful that I could see so little. All my senses seemed to desire to veil themselves and, feeling that I was about to slip from them, I pressed the palms of my hands together until they trembled, murmuring: "*O love! O love!*" many times.

At last she spoke to me. When she addressed the first words to me I was so confused that I did not know what to answer. She asked me was I going to *Araby*.[5] I forgot whether I answered yes or no. It would be a splendid bazaar, she said; she would love to go.

"And why can't you?" I asked.

While she spoke she turned a silver bracelet round and round her wrist. She could not go, she said, because there would be a retreat that week in her convent. Her brother and two other boys were fighting for their caps and I was alone at the railings. She held one of the spikes, bowing her head towards me. The light from the lamp opposite our door caught the white curve of her neck, lit up her hair that rested there and, falling, lit up the hand upon the railing. It fell over one side of her dress and caught the white border of a petticoat, just visible as she stood at ease.

4. Jeremiah O'Donovan (1831–1915) was a militant Irish nationalist who fought on despite terms in prison and banishment. *Come-all-you:* A song, of which there were many, which began "Come, all you Irishmen."

5. A bazaar billed as a "Grand Oriental Fête," Dublin, May 1894.

"It's well for you," she said.

"If I go," I said. "I will bring you something."

What innumerable follies laid waste my waking and sleeping thoughts after that evening! I wished to annihilate the tedious intervening days. I chafed against the work of school. At night in my bedroom and by day in the classroom her image came between me and the page I strove to read. The syllables of the word *Araby* were called to me through the silence in which my soul luxuriated and cast an Eastern enchantment over me. I asked for leave to go to the bazaar on Saturday night. My aunt was surprised and hoped it was not some Freemason[6] affair. I answered few questions in class. I watched my master's face pass from amiability to sternness; he hoped I was not beginning to idle. I could not call my wandering thoughts together. I had hardly any patience with the serious work of life which, now that it stood between me and my desire, seemed to me child's play, ugly monotonous child's play.

On Saturday morning I reminded my uncle that I wished to go to the bazaar in the evening. He was fussing at the hallstand, looking for the hat-brush, and answered me curtly:

"Yes, boy, I know."

As he was in the hall I could not go into the front parlour and lie at the window. I left the house in bad humour and walked slowly towards the school. The air was pitilessly raw and already my heart misgave me.

When I came home to dinner my uncle had not yet been home. Still it was early. I sat staring at the clock for some time and, when its ticking began to irritate me, I left the room. I mounted the staircase and gained the upper part of the house. The high, cold, empty, gloomy rooms liberated me and I went from room to room singing. From the front window I saw my companions playing below in the street. Their cries reached me weakened and indistinct and, leaning my forehead against the cool glass, I looked over at the dark house where she lived. I may have stood there for an hour, seeing nothing but a brown-clad figure cast by my imagination, touched discreetly by the lamplight at the curved neck, at the hand upon the railings and at the border below the dress.

When I came downstairs again I found Mrs. Mercer sitting at the fire. She was an old, garrulous woman, a pawnbroker's widow, who collected used stamps for some pious purpose. I had to endure the gossip of the tea-table. The meal was prolonged beyond an hour and still my uncle did not come. Mrs. Mercer stood up to go: she was sorry she couldn't wait any longer, but it was after eight o'clock and she did not like to be out late, as the night air was bad for her. When she had gone I began to walk up and down the room, clenching my fists. My aunt said:

"I'm afraid you may put off your bazaar for this night of Our Lord."

At nine o'clock I heard my uncle's latchkey in the hall door. I heard him talking to himself and heard the hallstand rocking when it had received the weight of his overcoat. I could interpret these signs. When he was midway through his dinner I asked him to give me the money to go to the bazaar. He had forgotten.

6. The Masons, or Freemasons, were considered enemies of the Catholics.

"The people are in bed and after their first sleep now," he said.

I did not smile. My aunt said to him energetically:

"Can't you give him the money and let him go? You've kept him late enough as it is."

My uncle said he was very sorry he had forgotten. He said he believed in the old saying: "All work and no play makes Jack a dull boy." He asked me where I was going and, when I had told him a second time, he asked me did I know *The Arab's Farewell to his Steed.*[7] When I left the kitchen he was about to recite the opening lines of the piece to my aunt.

I held a florin[8] tightly in my hand as I strode down Buckingham Street towards the station. The sight of the streets thronged with buyers and glaring with gas recalled to me the purpose of my journey. I took my seat in a third-class carriage of a deserted train. After an intolerable delay the train moved out of the station slowly. It crept onward among ruinous houses and over the twinkling river. At Westland Row Station a crowd of people pressed to the carriage doors; but the porters moved them back, saying that it was a special train for the bazaar. I remained alone in the bare carriage. In a few minutes the train drew up beside an improvised wooden platform. I passed out on to the road and saw by the lighted dial of a clock that it was ten minutes to ten. In front of me was a large building which displayed the magical name.

I could not find any sixpenny entrance and, fearing that the bazaar would be closed, I passed in quickly through a turnstile, handing a shilling to a weary-looking man. I found myself in a big hall girdled at half its height by a gallery. Nearly all the stalls were closed and the greater part of the hall was in darkness. I recognized a silence like that which pervades a church after a service. I walked into the centre of the bazaar timidly. A few people were gathered about the stalls which were still open. Before a curtain, over which the words *Café Chantant*[9] were written in coloured lamps, two men were counting money on a salver. I listened to the fall of the coins.

Remembering with difficulty why I had come I went over to one of the stalls and examined porcelain vases and flowered tea-sets. At the door of the stall a young lady was talking and laughing with two young gentlemen. I remarked their English accents and listened vaguely to their conversation.

"O, I never said such a thing!"

"O, but you did!"

"O, but I didn't!"

"Didn't she say that?"

"Yes. I heard her."

"O, there's a . . . fib!"

Observing me, the young lady came over and asked me did I wish to buy anything. The tone of her voice was not encouraging; she seemed to have spoken to me out of a sense of duty. I looked humbly at the great jars that stood like eastern guards at either side of the dark entrance to the stall and murmured:

7. Or *The Arab's Farewell to His Horse,* sentimental nineteenth-century poem by Caroline Norton. The speaker has sold the horse. 8. Two-shilling piece; thus four times the "sixpenny entrance" fee. 9. Café with music.

"No, thank you."

35 The young lady changed the position of one of the vases and went back to the two young men. They began to talk of the same subject. Once or twice the young lady glanced at me over her shoulder.

I lingered before her stall, though I knew my stay was useless, to make my interest in her wares seem the more real. Then I turned away slowly and walked down the middle of the bazaar. I allowed the two pennies to fall against the sixpence in my pocket. I heard a voice call from one end of the gallery that the light was out. The upper part of the hall was now completely dark.

Gazing up into the darkness I saw myself as a creature driven and derided by vanity; and my eyes burned with anguish and anger.

1914

ALICE MUNRO

Boys and Girls

My father was a fox farmer. That is, he raised silver foxes, in pens; and in the fall and early winter, when their fur was prime, he killed them and skinned them and sold their pelts to the Hudson's Bay Company or the Montreal Fur Traders. These companies supplied us with heroic calendars to hang, one on each side of the kitchen door. Against a background of cold blue sky and black pine forests and treacherous northern rivers, plumed adventurers planted the flags of England or of France; magnificent savages bent their backs to the portage.

For several weeks before Christmas, my father worked after supper in the cellar of our house. The cellar was white-washed, and lit by a hundred-watt bulb over the worktable. My brother Laird and I sat on the top step and watched. My father removed the pelt inside-out from the body of the fox, which looked surprisingly small, mean and rat-like, deprived of its arrogant weight of fur. The naked, slippery bodies were collected in a sack and buried at the dump. One time the hired man, Henry Bailey, had taken a swipe at me with this sack, saying, "Christmas present!" My mother thought that was not funny. In fact she disliked the whole pelting operation—that was what the killing, skinning, and preparation of the furs was called—and wished it did not have to take place in the house. There was the smell. After the pelt had been stretched inside-out on a long board my father scraped away delicately, removing the little clotted webs of blood vessels, the bubbles of fat; the smell of blood and animal fat, with the strong primitive odour of the fox itself, penetrated all parts of the house. I found it reassuringly seasonal, like the smell of oranges and pine needles.

Henry Bailey suffered from bronchial troubles. He would cough and cough until his narrow face turned scarlet, and his light blue, derisive eyes filled up with tears; then he took the lid off the stove, and, standing well back, shot out a great clot of phlegm—hsss—straight into the heart of the flames. We admired him for this performance and for his ability to make his stomach growl at will, and for his laughter, which was full of high whistlings and gurglings and involved the whole faulty machinery of his chest. It was sometimes hard to tell what he was laughing at, and always possible that it might be us.

After we had been sent to bed we could still smell fox and still hear Henry's laugh, but these things, reminders of the warm, safe, brightly lit downstairs world, seemed lost and diminished, floating on the stale cold air upstairs. We were afraid at night in the winter. We were not afraid of *outside* though this was the time of year when snowdrifts curled around our house like sleeping whales and the wind harassed us all night, coming up from the buried fields, the frozen swamp, with its old bugbear chorus of threats and misery. We were afraid of *inside*, the room where we slept. At this time the upstairs of our house was not finished. A brick chimney went up one wall. In the middle of the floor was a square hole, with a wooden railing around it; that was where the stairs came up. On the other side of the stairwell were the things that nobody had any use for any more—a soldiery roll of linoleum, standing on end, a wicker baby carriage, a fern basket, china jugs and basins with cracks in them, a picture of the Battle of Balaclava,[1] very sad to look at. I had told Laird, as soon as he was old enough to understand such things, that bats and skeletons lived over there; whenever a man escaped from the county jail, twenty miles away, I imagined that he had somehow let himself in the window and was hiding behind the linoleum. But we had rules to keep us safe. When the light was on, we were safe as long as we did not step off the square of worn carpet which defined our bedroom-space; when the light was off no place was safe but the beds themselves. I had to turn out the light kneeling on the end of my bed, and stretching as far as I could to reach the cord.

In the dark we lay on our beds, our narrow life rafts, and fixed our eyes on 5
the faint light coming up the stairwell, and sang songs. Laird sang "Jingle Bells," which he would sing any time, whether it was Christmas or not, and I sang "Danny Boy." I loved the sound of my own voice, frail and supplicating, rising in the dark. We could make out the tall frosted shapes of the windows now, gloomy and white. When I came to the part, *When I am dead, as dead I well may be*—a fit of shivering caused not by the cold sheets but by pleasurable emotion almost silenced me. *You'll kneel and say, an Ave there above me*—What was an Ave? Every day I forgot to find out.

Laird went straight from singing to sleep. I could hear his long, satisfied, bubbly breaths. Now for the time that remained to me, the most perfectly private and perhaps the best time of the whole day, I arranged myself tightly under the covers and went on with one of the stories I was telling myself from night to night. These stories were about myself, when I had grown a little older; they took place in a world that was recognizably mine, yet one that presented opportunities for courage, boldness and self-sacrifice, as mine never did. I rescued people from a bombed building (it discouraged me that the real war had gone on so far away from Jubilee). I shot two rabid wolves who were menacing the schoolyard (the teachers cowered terrified at my back). I rode a fine horse spiritedly down the

1. An indecisive Crimean War battle fought on October 25, 1854.

main street of Jubilee, acknowledging the townspeople's gratitude for some yet-to-be-worked-out piece of heroism (nobody ever rode a horse there, except King Billy in the Orangemen's Day[2] parade). There was always riding and shooting in these stories, though I had only been on a horse twice—bareback because we did not own a saddle—and the second time I had slid right around and dropped under the horse's feet; it had stepped placidly over me. I really was learning to shoot, but I could not hit anything yet, not even tin cans on fence posts.

Alive, the foxes inhabited a world my father made for them. It was surrounded by a high guard fence, like a medieval town, with a gate that was padlocked at night. Along the streets of this town were ranged large, sturdy pens. Each of them had a real door that a man could go through, a wooden ramp along the wire, for the foxes to run up and down on, and a kennel—something like a clothes chest with airholes—where they slept and stayed in winter and had their young. There were feeding and watering dishes attached to the wire in such a way that they could be emptied and cleaned from the outside. The dishes were made of old tin cans, and the ramps and kennels of odds and ends of old lumber. Everything was tidy and ingenious; my father was tirelessly inventive and his favourite book in the world was Robinson Crusoe.[3] He had fitted a tin drum on a wheelbarrow, for bringing water down to the pens. This was my job in summer, when the foxes had to have water twice a day. Between nine and ten o'clock in the morning, and again after supper, I filled the drum at the pump and trundled it down through the barnyard to the pens, where I parked it, and filled my watering can and went along the streets. Laird came too, with his little cream and green gardening can, filled too full and knocking against his legs and slopping water on his canvas shoes. I had the real watering can, my father's, though I could only carry it three-quarters full.

The foxes all had names, which were printed on a tin plate and hung beside their doors. They were not named when they were born, but when they survived the first year's pelting and were added to the breeding stock. Those my father had named were called names like Prince, Bob, Wally and Betty. Those I had named were called Star or Turk, or Maureen or Diana. Laird named one Maud after a hired girl we had when he was little, one Harold after a boy at school, and one Mexico, he did not say why.

Naming them did not make pets out of them, or anything like it. Nobody but my father ever went into the pens, and he had twice had blood-poisoning from bites. When I was bringing them their water they prowled up and down on the paths they had made inside their pens, barking seldom—they saved that for nighttime, when they might get up a chorus of community frenzy—but always watching me, their eyes burning, clear gold, in their pointed, malevolent faces. They were beautiful for their delicate legs and heavy, aristocratic tails and the

2. The Orange Society is an Irish Protestant group named after William of Orange, who, as King William III of England, defeated the Catholic James II. The Society sponsors an annual procession on July 12 to commemorate the victory of William III at the Battle of the Boyne (1690).

3. Novel (1719) by Daniel Defoe about a man shipwrecked on a desert island; it goes into great detail about his ingenious contraptions.

bright fur sprinkled on dark down their backs—which gave them their name—but especially for their faces, drawn exquisitely sharp in pure hostility, and their golden eyes.

Besides carrying water I helped my father when he cut the long grass, and the lamb's quarter and flowering money-musk, that grew between the pens. He cut with the scythe and I raked into piles. Then he took a pitchfork and threw fresh-cut grass all over the top of the pens, to keep the foxes cooler and shade their coats, which were browned by too much sun. My father did not talk to me unless it was about the job we were doing. In this he was quite different from my mother, who, if she was feeling cheerful, would tell me all sorts of things—the name of a dog she had had when she was a little girl, the names of boys she had gone out with later on when she was grown up, and what certain dresses of hers had looked like—she could not imagine now what had become of them. Whatever thoughts and stories my father had were private, and I was shy of him and would never ask him questions. Nevertheless I worked willingly under his eyes, and with a feeling of pride. One time a feed salesman came down into the pens to talk to him and my father said, "Like to have you meet my new hired man." I turned away and raked furiously, red in the face with pleasure.

"Could of fooled me," said the salesman. "I thought it was only a girl."

After the grass was cut, it seemed suddenly much later in the year. I walked on stubble in the earlier evening, aware of the reddening skies, the entering silences, of fall. When I wheeled the tank out of the gate and put the padlock on, it was almost dark. One night at this time I saw my mother and father standing talking on the little rise of ground we called the gangway, in front of the barn. My father had just come from the meathouse; he had his stiff bloody apron on, and a pail of cut-up meat in his hand.

It was an odd thing to see my mother down at the barn. She did not often come out of the house unless it was to do something—hang out the wash or dig potatoes in the garden. She looked out of place, with her bare lumpy legs, not touched by the sun, her apron still on and damp across the stomach from the supper dishes. Her hair was tied up in a kerchief, wisps of it falling out. She would tie her hair up like this in the morning, saying she did not have time to do it properly, and it would stay tied up all day. It was true, too; she really did not have time. These days our back porch was piled with baskets of peaches and grapes and pears, bought in town, and onions and tomatoes and cucumbers grown at home, all waiting to be made into jelly and jam and preserves, pickles and chili sauce. In the kitchen there was a fire in the stove all day, jars clinked in boiling water, sometimes a cheesecloth bag was strung on a pole between two chairs, straining blue-black grape pulp for jelly. I was given jobs to do and I would sit at the table peeling peaches that had been soaked in the hot water, or cutting up onions, my eyes smarting and streaming. As soon as I was done I ran out of the house, trying to get out of earshot before my mother thought of what she wanted me to do next. I hated the hot dark kitchen in summer, the green blinds and the flypapers, the same old oilcloth table and wavy mirror and bumpy linoleum. My mother was too tired and preoccupied to talk to me, she had no heart to tell about the Normal School Graduation Dance; sweat trickled over her face and she was always counting under her breath, pointing at jars, dumping cups of sugar. It seemed to me that work in the house was endless, dreary and peculiarly depressing; work done out of doors, and in my father's service, was ritualistically important.

I wheeled the tank up to the barn, where it was kept, and I heard my mother saying, "Wait till Laird gets a little bigger, then you'll have a real help."

What my father said I did not hear. I was pleased by the way he stood listening, politely as he would to a salesman or a stranger, but with an air of wanting to get on with his real work. I felt my mother had no business down here and I wanted him to feel the same way. What did she mean about Laird? He was no help to anybody. Where was he now? Swinging himself sick on the swing, going around in circles, or trying to catch caterpillars. He never once stayed with me till I was finished.

"And then I can use her more in the house," I heard my mother say. She had a dead-quiet, regretful way of talking about me that always made me uneasy. "I just get my back turned and she runs off. It's not like I had a girl in the family at all."

I went and sat on a feed bag in the corner of the barn, not wanting to appear when this conversation was going on. My mother, I felt, was not to be trusted. She was kinder than my father and more easily fooled, but you could not depend on her, and the real reasons for the things she said and did were not to be known. She loved me, and she sat up late at night making a dress of the difficult style I wanted, for me to wear when school started, but she was also my enemy. She was always plotting. She was plotting now to get me to stay in the house more, although she knew I hated it (*because* she knew I hated it) and keep me from working for my father. It seemed to me she would do this simply out of perversity, and to try her power. It did not occur to me that she could be lonely, or jealous. No grown-up could be; they were too fortunate. I sat and kicked my heels monotonously against a feedbag, raising dust, and did not come out till she was gone.

At any rate, I did not expect my father to pay any attention to what she said. Who could imagine Laird doing my work—Laird remembering the padlock and cleaning out the watering-dishes with a leaf on the end of a stick, or even wheeling the tank without it tumbling over? It showed how little my mother knew about the way things really were.

I have forgotten to say what the foxes were fed. My father's bloody apron reminded me. They were fed horsemeat. At this time most farmers still kept horses, and when a horse got too old to work, or broke a leg or got down and would not get up, as they sometimes did, the owner would call my father, and he and Henry went out to the farm in the truck. Usually they shot and butchered the horse there, paying the farmer from five to twelve dollars. If they had already too much meat on hand, they would bring the horse back alive, and keep it for a few days or weeks in our stable, until the meat was needed. After the war the farmers were buying tractors and gradually getting rid of horses altogether, so it sometimes happened that we got a good healthy horse, that there was just no use for any more. If this happened in the winter we might keep the horse in our stable till spring, for we had plenty of hay and if there was a lot of snow—and the plow did not always get our road cleared—it was convenient to be able to go to town with a horse and cutter.[4]

The winter I was eleven years old we had two horses in the stable. We did 20
not know what names they had had before, so we called them Mack and Flora. Mack was an old black workhorse, sooty and indifferent. Flora was a sorrel mare, a driver. We took them both out in the cutter. Mack was slow and easy to handle. Flora was given to fits of violent alarm, veering at cars and even at other horses, but we loved her speed and high-stepping, her general air of gallantry and abandon. On Saturdays we went down to the stable and as soon as we opened the door on its cosy, animal-smelling darkness Flora threw up her head, rolled her eyes, whinnied despairingly and pulled herself through a crisis of nerves on the spot. It was not safe to go into her stall; she would kick.

This winter also I began to hear a great deal more on the theme my mother had sounded when she had been talking in front of the barn. I no longer felt safe. It seemed that in the minds of the people around me there was a steady undercurrent of thought, not to be deflected, on this one subject. The word *girl* had formerly seemed to me innocent and unburdened, like the world *child;* now it appeared that it was no such thing. A girl was not, as I had supposed, simply what I was; it was what I had to become. It was a definition, always touched with emphasis, with reproach and disappointment. Also it was a joke on me. Once Laird and I were fighting, and for the first time ever I had to use all my strength against him; even so, he caught and pinned my arm for a moment, really hurting me. Henry saw this, and laughed, saying, "Oh, that there Laird's gonna show you, one of these days!" Laird was getting a lot bigger. But I was getting bigger too.

My grandmother came to stay with us for a few weeks and I heard other things. "Girls don't slam doors like that." "Girls keep their knees together when they sit down." And worse still, when I asked some questions, "That's none of girls' business." I continued to slam the doors and sit as awkwardly as possible, thinking that by such measures I kept myself free.

When spring came, the horses were let out in the barnyard. Mack stood against the barn wall trying to scratch his neck and haunches, but Flora trotted up and down and reared at the fences, clattering her hooves against the rails. Snow drifts dwindled quickly, revealing the hard grey and brown earth, the familiar rise and fall of the ground, plain and bare after the fantastic landscape of winter. There was a great feeling of opening-out, of release. We just wore rubbers now, over our shoes; our feet felt ridiculously light. One Saturday we went out to the stable and found all the doors open, letting in the unaccustomed sunlight and fresh air. Henry was there, just idling around looking at his collection of calendars which were tacked up behind the stalls in a part of the stable my mother had probably never seen.

"Come to say goodbye to your old friend Mack?" Henry said. "Here, you

4. A small, light sleigh.

give him a taste of oats." He poured some oats into Laird's cupped hands and Laird went to feed Mack. Mack's teeth were in bad shape. He ate very slowly, patiently shifting the oats around in his mouth, trying to find a stump of a molar to grind it on. "Poor old Mack," said Henry mournfully. "When a horse's teeth's gone, he's gone. That's about the way."

"Are you going to shoot him today?" I said. Mack and Flora had been in the stable so long I had almost forgotten they were going to be shot.

Henry didn't answer me. Instead he started to sing in a high, trembly, mocking-sorrowful voice, *Oh, there's no more work, for poor Uncle Ned, he's gone where the good darkies go.*[5] Mack's thick, blackish tongue worked diligently at Laird's hand. I went out before the song was ended and sat down on the gangway.

I had never seen them shoot a horse, but I knew where it was done. Last summer Laird and I had come upon a horse's entrails before they were buried. We had thought it was a big black snake, coiled up in the sun. That was around in the field that ran up beside the barn. I thought that if we went inside the barn, and found a wide crack or knothole to look through we would be able to see them do it. It was not something I wanted to see; just the same, if a thing really happened, it was better to see it, and know.

My father came down from the house, carrying the gun.

"What are you doing here?" he said.

"Nothing."

"Go on up and play around the house."

He sent Laird out of the stable. I said to Laird, "Do you want to see them shoot Mack?" and without waiting for an answer led him around to the front door of the barn, opened it carefully, and went in. "Be quiet or they'll hear us," I said. We could hear Henry and my father talking in the stable, then the heavy, shuffling steps of Mack being backed out of his stall.

In the loft it was cold and dark. Thin, crisscrossed beams of sunlight fell through the cracks. The hay was low. It was a rolling country, hills and hollows, slipping under our feet. About four feet up was a beam going around the walls. We piled hay up in one corner and I boosted Laird up and hoisted myself. The beam was not very wide; we crept along it with our hands flat on the barn walls. There were plenty of knotholes, and I found one that gave me the view I wanted—a corner of the barnyard, the gate, part of the field. Laird did not have a knothole and began to complain.

I showed him a widened crack between two boards. "Be quiet and wait. If they hear you you'll get us in trouble."

My father came in sight carrying the gun. Henry was leading Mack by the halter. He dropped it and took out his cigarette papers and tobacco; he rolled cigarettes for my father and himself. While this was going on Mack nosed around in the old, dead grass along the fence. Then my father opened the gate and they took Mack through. Henry led Mack way from the path to a patch of ground and they talked together, not loud enough for us to hear. Mack again began searching for a mouthful of fresh grass, which was not to be found. My father

5. Lines from the Stephen Foster song "Old Uncle Ned."

walked away in a straight line, and stopped short at a distance which seemed to suit him. Henry was walking away from Mack too, but sideways, still negligently holding on to the halter. My father raised the gun and Mack looked up as if he had noticed something and my father shot him.

Mack did not collapse at once but swayed, lurched sideways and fell, first on his side; then he rolled over on his back and, amazingly, kicked his legs for a few seconds in the air. At this Henry laughed, as if Mack had done a trick for him. Laird, who had drawn a long, groaning breath of surprise when the shot was fired, said out loud, "He's not dead." And it seemed to me it might be true. But his legs stopped, he rolled on his side again, his muscles quivered and sank. The two men walked over and looked at him in a businesslike way; they bent down and examined his forehead where the bullet had gone in, and now I saw his blood on the brown grass.

"Now they just skin him and cut him up," I said. "Let's go." My legs were a little shaky and I jumped gratefully down into the hay. "Now you've seen how they shoot a horse," I said in a congratulatory way, as if I had seen it many times before. "Let's see if any barn cat's had kittens in the hay." Laird jumped. He seemed young and obedient again. Suddenly I remembered how, when he was little, I had brought him into the barn and told him to climb the ladder to the top beam. That was in the spring, too, when the hay was low. I had done it out of a need for excitement, a desire for something to happen so that I could tell about it. He was wearing a little bulky brown and white checked coat, made down from one of mine. He went all the way up, just as I told him, and sat down on the top beam with the hay far below him on one side, and the barn floor and some old machinery on the other. Then I ran screaming to my father, "Laird's up on the top beam!" My father came, my mother came, my father went up the ladder talking very quietly and brought Laird down under his arm, at which my mother leaned against the ladder and began to cry. They said to me, "Why weren't you watching him?" but nobody ever knew the truth. Laird did not know enough to tell. But whenever I saw the brown and white checked coat hanging in the closet, or at the bottom of the rag bag, which was where it ended up, I felt a weight in my stomach, the sadness of unexorcized guilt.

I looked at Laird who did not even remember this, and I did not like the look on this thin, winter-pale face. His expression was not frightened or upset, but remote, concentrating. "Listen," I said, in an unusually bright and friendly voice, "you aren't going to tell, are you?"

"No," he said absently.

"Promise." 40

"Promise," he said. I grabbed the hand behind his back to make sure he was not crossing his fingers. Even so, he might have a nightmare; it might come out that way. I decided I had better work hard to get all thoughts of what he had seen out of his mind—which, it seemed to me, could not hold very many things at a time. I got some money I had saved and that afternoon we went into Jubilee and saw a show, with Judy Canova,[6] at which we both laughed a great deal. After that I thought it would be all right.

6. American comedian best known for her yodeling in hillbilly movies of the 1940s.

Two weeks later I knew they were going to shoot Flora. I knew from the night before, when I heard my mother ask if the hay was holding out all right, and my father said, "Well, after to-morrow there'll just be the cow, and we should be able to put her out to grass in another week." So I knew it was Flora's turn in the morning.

This time I didn't think of watching it. That was something to see just one time. I had not thought about it very often since, but sometimes when I was busy, working at school, or standing in front of the mirror combing my hair and wondering if I would be pretty when I grew up, the whole scene would flash into my mind: I would see the easy, practised way my father raised the gun, and hear Henry laughing when Mack kicked his legs in the air. I did not have any great feeling of horror and opposition, such as a city child might have had; I was too used to seeing the death of animals as a necessity by which we lived. Yet I felt a little ashamed, and there was a new wariness, a sense of holding-off, in my attitude to my father and his work.

It was a fine day, and we were going around the yard picking up tree branches that had been torn off in winter storms. This was something we had been told to do, and also we wanted to use them to make a teepee. We heard Flora whinny, and then my father's voice and Henry's shouting, and we ran down to the barnyard to see what was going on.

The stable door was open. Henry had just brought Flora out, and she had broken away from him. She was running free in the barnyard, from one end to the other. We climbed up on the fence. It was exciting to see her running, whinnying, going up on her hind legs, prancing and threatening like a horse in a Western movie, an unbroken ranch horse, though she was just an old driver, an old sorrel mare. My father and Henry ran after her and tried to grab the dangling halter. They tried to work her into a corner, and they had almost succeeded when she made a run between them, wild-eyed, and disappeared around the corner of the barn. We heard the rails clatter down as she got over the fence, and Henry yelled, "She's into the field now!"

That meant she was in the long L-shaped field that ran up by the house. If she got around the center, heading towards the lane, the gate was open; the truck had been driven into the field this morning. My father shouted to me, because I was on the other side of the fence, nearest the lane, "Go shut the gate!"

I could run very fast. I ran across the garden, past the tree where our swing was hung, and jumped across a ditch into the lane. There was the open gate. She had not got out, I could not see her up on the road; she must have run to the other end of the field. The gate was heavy. I lifted it out of the gravel and carried it across the roadway. I had it half-way across when she came in sight, galloping straight towards me. There was just time to get the chain on. Laird came scrambling through the ditch to help me.

Instead of shutting the gate, I opened it as wide as I could. I did not make any decision to do this, it was just what I did. Flora never slowed down; she galloped straight past me, and Laird jumped up and down, yelling, "Shut it, shut it!" even after it was too late. My father and Henry appeared in the field a moment too late to see what I had done. They only saw Flora heading for the township road. They would think I had not got there in time.

They did not waste any time asking about it. They went back to the barn and got the gun and the knives they used, and put these in the truck; then they turned the truck around and came bouncing up the field toward us. Laird called to them, "Let me go too, let me go too!" and Henry stopped the truck and they took him in. I shut the gate after they were all gone.

I supposed Laird would tell. I wondered what would happen to me. I had 50
never disobeyed my father before, and I could not understand why I had done it. Flora would not really get away. They would catch up with her in the truck. Or if they did not catch her this morning somebody would see her and telephone us this afternoon or tomorrow. There was no wild country here for her to run to, only farms. What was more, my father had paid for her, we needed the meat to feed the foxes, we needed the foxes to make our living. All I had done was make more work for my father who worked hard enough already. And when my father found out about it he was not going to trust me any more; he would know that I was not entirely on his side. I was on Flora's side, and that made me no use to anybody, not even to her. Just the same, I did not regret it; when she came running at me and I held the gate open, that was the only thing I could do.

I went back to the house, and my mother said, "What's all the commotion?" I told her that Flora had kicked down the fence and got away. "Your poor father," she said, "now he'll have to go chasing over the countryside. Well, there isn't any use planning dinner before one." She put up the ironing board. I wanted to tell her, but thought better of it and went upstairs and sat on my bed.

Lately I had been trying to make my part of the room fancy, spreading the bed with old lace curtains, and fixing myself a dressing-table with some leftovers of cretonne for a skirt. I planned to put up some kind of barricade between my bed and Laird's, to keep my section separate from his. In the sunlight, the lace curtains were just dusty rags. We did not sing at night any more. One night when I was singing Laird said, "You sound silly," and I went right on but the next night I did not start. There was not so much need to anyway, we were no longer afraid. We knew it was just old furniture over there, old jumble and confusion. We did not keep to the rules. I still stayed awake after Laird was asleep and told myself stories, but even in these stories something different was happening, mysterious alterations took place. A story might start off in the old way, with a spectacular danger, a fire or wild animals, and for a while I might rescue people; then things would change around, and instead, somebody would be rescuing me. It might be a boy from our class at school, or even Mr. Campbell, our teacher, who tickled girls under the arms. And at this point the story concerned itself at great length with what I looked like—how long my hair was, and what kind of dress I had on; by the time I had these details worked out the real excitement of the story was lost.

It was later than one o'clock when the truck came back. The tarpaulin was over the back, which meant there was meat in it. My mother had to heat dinner up all over again. Henry and my father had changed from their bloody overalls into ordinary working overalls in the barn, and they washed their arms and necks and faces at the sink, and splashed water on their hair and combed it. Laird lifted his arm to show off a streak of blood. "We shot old Flora," he said, "and cut her up in fifty pieces."

"Well I don't want to hear about it," my mother said. "And don't come to my table like that."

My father made him go and wash the blood off.

We sat down and my father said grace and Henry pasted his chewing-gum on the end of his fork, the way he always did; when he took it off he would have us admire the pattern. We began to pass the bowls of steaming, overcooked vegetables. Laird looked across the table at me and said proudly, distinctly, "Anyway it was her fault Flora got away."

"What?" my father said.

"She could of shut the gate and she didn't. She just open' it up and Flora run out."

"Is that right?" my father said.

Everybody at the table was looking at me. I nodded, swallowing food with great difficulty. To my shame, tears flooded my eyes.

My father made a curt sound of disgust. "What did you do that for?"

I did not answer. I put down my fork and waited to be sent from the table, still not looking up.

But this did not happen. For some time nobody said anything, then Laird said matter-of-factly, "She's crying."

"Never mind," my father said. He spoke with resignation, even good humour, the words which absolved and dismissed me for good. "She's only a girl," he said.

I didn't protest that, even in my heart. Maybe it was true.

1968

WILLIAM FAULKNER

The Old People

I

At first there was nothing. There was the faint, cold, steady rain, the gray and constant light of the late November dawn, with the voices of the hounds converging somewhere in it and toward them. Then Sam Fathers, standing just behind the boy as he had been standing when the boy shot his first running rabbit with his first gun and almost with the first load it ever carried, touched his shoulder and he began to shake, not with any cold. Then the buck was there. He did not come into sight; he was just there, looking not like a ghost but as if all of light were condensed in him and he were the source of it, not only moving in it but disseminating it, already running, seen first as you always see the deer, in that split second after he has already seen you, already slanting away in that first soaring bound, the antlers even in that dim light looking like a small rocking-chair balanced on his head.

"Now," Sam Fathers said, "shoot quick, and slow."

The boy did not remember the shot at all. He would live to be eighty, as his father and his father's twin brother and their father in his turn had lived to be, but he would never hear that shot nor remember even the shock of the gun-butt. He didn't even remember what he did with the gun afterward. He was running. Then he was standing over the buck where it lay on the wet earth still in the attitude of speed and not looking at all dead, standing over it shaking and jerking, with Sam Fathers beside him again, extending the knife. "Dont walk up to him in front," Sam said. "If he aint dead, he will cut you all to pieces with his feet. Walk up to him from behind and take him by the horn first, so you can hold his head down until you can jump away. Then slip your other hand down and hook your fingers in his nostrils."

The boy did that—drew the head back and the throat taut and drew Sam Fathers' knife across the throat and Sam stooped and dipped his hands in the hot smoking blood and wiped them back and forth across the boy's face. Then Sam's horn rang in the wet gray woods and again and again; there was a boiling wave of dogs about them, with Tennie's Jim and Boon Hogganbeck whipping them back after each had had a taste of the blood, then the men, the true hunters—Walter Ewell whose rifle never missed, and Major de Spain and old General Compson and the boy's cousin, McCaslin Edmonds, grandson of his father's sister, sixteen years his senior and, since both he and McCaslin were only children and the boy's father had been nearing seventy when he was born, more his brother than his cousin and more his father than either—sitting their horses and looking down at them: at the old man of seventy who had been a negro for two generations now but whose face and bearing were still those of the Chickasaw chief who had been his father; and the white boy of twelve with the prints of the bloody hands on his face, who had nothing to do now but stand straight and not let the trembling show.

"Did he do all right, Sam?" his cousin McCaslin said.

"He done all right," Sam Fathers said.

They were the white boy, marked forever, and the old dark man sired on both sides by savage kings, who had marked him, whose bloody hands had merely formally consecrated him to that which, under the man's tutelage, he had already accepted, humbly and joyfully, with abnegation and with pride too; the hands, the touch, the first worthy blood which he had been found at last worthy to draw, joining him and the man forever, so that the man would continue to live past the boy's seventy years and then eighty years, long after the man himself had entered the earth as chiefs and kings entered it;—the child, not yet a man, whose grandfather had lived in the same country and in almost the same manner as the boy himself would grow up to live, leaving his descendants in the land in his turn as his grandfather had done, and the old man past seventy whose grandfathers had owned the land long before the white men ever saw it and who had vanished from it now with all their kind, what of blood they left behind them running now in another race and for a while even in bondage and now drawing toward the end of its alien and irrevocable course, barren, since Sam Fathers had no children.

His father was Ikkemotubbe himself, who had named himself Doom. Sam told the boy about that—how Ikkemotubbe, old Issetibbeha's sister's son, had run away to New Orleans in his youth and returned seven years later with a French companion calling himself the Chevalier Soeur-Blonde de Vitry, who must have been the Ikkemotubbe of his family too and who was already addressing Ikkemotubbe as *Du Homme*[1]—returned, came home again, with his foreign Aramis[2] and the quadroon slave woman who was to be Sam's mother, and a gold-laced hat and coat and a wicker wine-hamper containing a litter of month-old puppies and a gold snuff-box filled with a white powder resembling fine sugar. And how he was met at the River landing by three or four companions of his bachelor youth, and while the light of a smoking torch gleamed on the glittering braid of the hat and coat Doom squatted in the mud of the land and took one of the puppies from the hamper and put a pinch of the white powder on its tongue and the puppy died before the one who was holding it could cast it away. And how they returned to the Plantation where Issetibbeha, dead now, had been succeeded by his son, Doom's fat cousin Moketubbe, and the next day Moketubbe's eight-year-old son died suddenly and that afternoon, in the presence of Moketubbe and most of the others (the People, Sam Fathers called them) Doom produced another puppy from the wine-hamper and put a pinch of the white powder on its tongue and Moketubbe abdicated and Doom became in fact The Man which his French friend already called him. And how on the day after that, during the ceremony of accession, Doom pronounced a marriage between the pregnant quadroon and one of the slave men which he had just inherited (that was how Sam Fathers got his name, which in Chickasaw had been Had-Two-Fathers) and two years later sold the man and woman and the child who was his own son to his white neighbor, Carothers McCaslin.

That was seventy years ago. The Sam Fathers whom the boy knew was already sixty—a man not tall, squat rather, almost sedentary, flabby-looking though he actually was not, with hair like a horse's mane which even at seventy showed no trace of white and a face which showed no age until he smiled, whose only visible trace of negro blood was a slight dullness of the hair and the fingernails, and something else which you did notice about the eyes, which you noticed because it was not always there, only in repose and not always then—something not in their shape nor pigment but in their expression, and the boy's cousin McCaslin told him what that was: not the heritage of Ham, not the mark of servitude but of bondage; the knowledge that for a while that part of his blood had been the blood of slaves. "Like an old lion or a bear in a cage," McCaslin said. "He was born in the cage and has been in it all his life; he knows nothing else. Then he smells something. It might be anything, any breeze blowing past anything and then into his nostrils. But there for a second was the hot sand or the cane-brake that he never even saw himself, might not even know if he did

1. Mistaken or provincialized French for "The Man," with overtones of nobility. **2.** One of Alexandre Dumas' three musketeers.

see it and probably does know he couldn't hold his own with it if he got back to it. But that's not what he smells then. It was the cage he smelled. He hadn't smelled the cage until that minute. Then the hot sand or the brake blew into his nostrils and blew away, and all he could smell was the cage. That's what makes his eyes look like that."

"Then let him go!" the boy cried. "Let him go!"

His cousin laughed shortly. Then he stopped laughing, making the sound that is. It had never been laughing. "His cage aint McCaslins," he said. "He was a wild man. When he was born, all his blood on both sides, except the little white part, knew things that had been tamed out of our blood so long ago that we have not only forgotten them, we have to live together in herds to protect ourselves from our own sources. He was the direct son not only of a warrior but of a chief. Then he grew up and began to learn things, and all of a sudden one day he found out that he had been betrayed, the blood of the warriors and chiefs had been betrayed. Not by his father," he added quickly. "He probably never held it against old Doom for selling him and his mother into slavery, because he probably believed the damage was already done before then and it was the same warriors' and chiefs' blood in him and Doom both that was betrayed through the black blood which his mother gave him. Not betrayed by the black blood and not wilfully betrayed by his mother, but betrayed by her all the same, who had bequeathed him not only the blood of slaves but even a little of the very blood which had enslaved it; himself his own battleground, the scene of his own vanquishment and the mausoleum of his defeat. His cage aint us," McCaslin said. "Did you ever know anybody yet, even your father and Uncle Buddy, that ever told him to do or not do anything that he ever paid any attention to?"

That was true. The boy first remembered him as sitting in the door of the plantation blacksmith-shop, where he sharpened plow-points and mended tools and even did rough carpenter-work when he was not in the woods. And sometimes, even when the woods had not drawn him, even with the shop cluttered with work which the farm waited on, Sam would sit there, doing nothing at all for half a day or a whole one, and no man, neither the boy's father and twin uncle in their day nor his cousin McCaslin after he became practical though not yet titular master, ever to say to him, "I want this finished by sundown" or "why wasn't this done yesterday?" And once each year, in the late fall, in November, the boy would watch the wagon, the hooped canvas top erected now, being loaded—the food, hams and sausage from the smokehouse, coffee and flour and molasses from the commissary, a whole beef killed just last night for the dogs until there would be meat in camp, the crate containing the dogs themselves, then the bedding, the guns, the horns and lanterns and axes, and his cousin McCaslin and Sam Fathers in their hunting clothes would mount to the seat and with Tennie's Jim sitting on the dog-crate they would drive away to Jefferson, to join Major de Spain and General Compson and Boon Hogganbeck and Walter Ewell and go on into the big bottom of the Tallahatchie where the deer and bear were, to be gone two weeks. But before the wagon was even loaded the boy would find that he could watch no longer. He would go away, running almost, to stand behind the corner where he could not see the wagon and nobody could see him, not crying, holding himself rigid except for the trembling, whispering to himself: "Soon now. Soon now. Just three more years" (or two more or one more) "and I will be ten. Then Cass said I can go."

White man's work, when Sam did work. Because he did nothing else: farmed no alloted acres of his own, as the other ex-slaves of old Carothers McCaslin did, performed no field-work for daily wages as the younger and newer negroes did—and the boy never knew just how that had been settled between Sam and old Carothers, or perhaps with old Carothers' twin sons after him. For, although Sam lived among the negroes, in a cabin among the other cabins in the quarters, and consorted with negroes (what of consorting with anyone Sam did after the boy got big enough to walk alone from the house to the blacksmith-shop and then to carry a gun) and dressed like them and talked like them and even went with them to the negro church now and then, he was still the son of that Chickasaw chief and the negroes knew it. And, it seemed to the boy, not only negroes. Boon Hogganbeck's grandmother had been a Chickasaw woman too, and although the blood had run white since and Boon was a white man, it was not chief's blood. To the boy at least, the difference was apparent immediately you saw Boon and Sam together, and even Boon seemed to know it was there—even Boon, to whom in his tradition it had never occurred that anyone might be better born than himself. A man might be smarter, he admitted that, or richer (luckier, he called it) but not better born. Boon was a mastiff, absolutely faithful, dividing his fidelity equally between Major de Spain and the boy's cousin McCaslin, absolutely dependent for his very bread and dividing that impartially too between Major de Spain and McCaslin, hardy, generous, courageous enough, a slave to all the appetites and almost unratiocinative. In the boy's eyes at least it was Sam Fathers, the negro, who bore himself not only toward his cousin McCaslin and Major de Spain but toward all white men, with gravity and dignity and without servility or recourse to that impenetrable wall of ready and easy mirth which negroes sustain between themselves and white men, bearing himself toward his cousin McCaslin not only as one man to another but as an older man to a younger.

He taught the boy the woods, to hunt, when to shoot and when not to shoot, when to kill and when not to kill, and better, what to do with it afterward. Then he would talk to the boy, the two of them sitting beneath the close fierce stars on a summer hilltop while they waited for the hounds to bring the fox back within hearing, or beside a fire in the November or December woods while the dogs worked out a coon's trail along the creek, or fireless in the pitch dark and heavy dew of April mornings while they squatted beneath a turkey-roost. The boy would never question him; Sam did not react to questions. The boy would just wait and then listen and Sam would begin, talking about the old days and the People whom he had not had time ever to know and so could not remember (he did not remember ever having seen his father's face), and in place of whom the other race into which his blood had run supplied him with no substitute.

15 And as he talked about those old times and those dead and vanished men of another race from either that the boy knew, gradually to the boy those old times would cease to be old times and would become a part of the boy's present, not

only as if they had happened yesterday but as if they were still happening, the men who walked through them actually walking in breath and air and casting an actual shadow on the earth they had not quitted. And more: as if some of them had not happened yet but would occur tomorrow, until at last it would seem to the boy that he himself had not come into existence yet, that none of his race nor the other subject race which his people had brought with them into the land had come here yet; that although it had been his grandfather's and then his father's and uncle's and was now his cousin's and someday would be his own land which he and Sam hunted over, their hold upon it actually was as trivial and without reality as the now faded and archaic script in the chancery book[3] in Jefferson which allocated it to them and that it was he, the boy, who was the guest here and Sam Father's voice the mouthpiece of the host.

Until three years ago there had been two of them, the other a full-blood Chickasaw, in a sense even more incredibly lost than Sam Fathers. He called himself Jobaker, as if it were one word. Nobody knew his history at all. He was a hermit, living in a foul little shack at the forks of the creek five miles from the plantation and about that far from any other habitation. He was a market hunter and fisherman and he consorted with nobody, black or white; no negro would even cross his path and no man dared approach his hut except Sam. And perhaps once a month the boy would find them in Sam's shop—two old men squatting on their heels on the dirt floor, talking in a mixture of negroid English and flat hill dialect and now and then a phrase of that old tongue which as time went on and the boy squatted there too listening, he began to learn. Then Jobaker died. That is, nobody had seen him in some time. Then one morning Sam was missing, nobody, not even the boy, knew when nor where, until that night when some negroes hunting in the creek bottom saw the sudden burst of flame and approached. It was Jobaker's hut, but before they got anywhere near it, someone shot at them from the shadows beyond it. It was Sam who fired, but nobody ever found Jobaker's grave.

The next morning, sitting at breakfast with his cousin, the boy saw Sam pass the dining-room window and he remembered then that never in his life before had he seen Sam nearer the house than the blacksmith-shop. He stopped eating even; he sat there and he and his cousin both heard the voices from beyond the pantry door, then the door opened and Sam entered, carrying his hat in his hand but without knocking as anyone else on the place except a house servant would have done, entered just far enough for the door to close behind him and stood looking at neither of them—the Indian face above the nigger clothes, looking at something over their heads or at something not even in the room.

"I want to go," he said. "I want to go to the Big Bottom to live."

"To live?" the boy's cousin said.

"At Major de Spain's and your camp, where you go to hunt," Sam said. "I 20
could take care of it for you all while you aint there. I will build me a little house in the woods, if you rather I didn't stay in the big one."

"What about Isaac here?" his cousin said. "How will you get away from him?

3. Public records or archives.

Are you going to take him with you?" But still Sam looked at neither of them, standing just inside the room with that face which showed nothing, which showed that he was an old man only when it smiled.

"I want to go," he said. "Let me go."

"Yes," the cousin said quietly. "Of course. I'll fix it with Major de Spain. You want to go soon?"

"I'm going now," Sam said. He went out. And that was all. The boy was nine then; it seemed perfectly natural that nobody, not even his cousin McCaslin, should argue with Sam. Also, since he was nine now, he could understand that Sam could leave him and their days and nights in the woods together without any wrench. He believed that he and Sam both knew that this was not only temporary but that the exigencies of his maturing, of that for which Sam had been training him all his life some day to dedicate himself, required it. They had settled that one night last summer while they listened to the hounds bringing a fox back up the creek valley; now the boy discerned in that very talk under the high, fierce August stars a presage, a warning, of this moment today. "I done taught you all there is of this settled country," Sam said. "You can hunt it good as I can now. You are ready for the Big Bottom now, for bear and deer. Hunter's meat," he said. "Next year you will be ten. You will write your age in two numbers and you will be ready to become a man. Your pa" (Sam always referred to the boy's cousin as his father, establishing even before the boy's orphanhood did that relation between them not of the ward to his guardian and kinsman and chief and head of his blood, but of the child to the man who sired his flesh and his thinking too.) "promised you can go with us then." So the boy could understand Sam's going. But he couldn't understand why now, in March, six months before the moon for hunting.

"If Jobaker's dead like they say," he said, "and Sam hasn't got anybody but us at all kin to him, why does he want to go to the Big Bottom now, when it will be six months before we get there?"

"Maybe that's what he wants," McCaslin said. "Maybe he wants to get away from you a little while."

But that was all right. McCaslin and other grown people often said things like that and he paid no attention to them, just as he paid no attention to Sam saying he wanted to go to the Big Bottom to live. After all, he would have to live there for six months, because there would be no use in going at all if he was going to turn right around and come back. And, as Sam himself had told him, he already knew all about hunting in this settled country that Sam or anybody else could teach him. So it would be all right. Summer, then the bright days after the first frost, then the cold and himself on the wagon with McCaslin this time and the moment would come and he would draw the blood, the big blood which would make him a man, a hunter, and Sam would come back home with them and he too would have outgrown the child's pursuit of rabbits and 'possums. Then he too would make one before the winter fire, talking of the old hunts and the hunts to come as hunters talked.

So Sam departed. He owned so little that he could carry it. He walked. He would neither let McCaslin send him in the wagon, nor take a mule to ride. No one saw him go even. He was just gone one morning, the cabin which had never had very much in it, vacant and empty, the shop in which there never had been very much done, standing idle. Then November came at last, and now the boy made one—himself and his cousin McCaslin and Tennie's Jim, and Major de Spain and General Compson and Walter Ewell and Boon and old Uncle Ash to do the cooking, waiting for them in Jefferson with the other wagon, and the surrey in which he and McCaslin and General Compson and Major de Spain would ride.

Sam was waiting at the camp to meet them. If he was glad to see them, he did not show it. And if, when they broke camp two weeks later to return home, he was sorry to see them go, he did not show that either. Because he did not come back with them. It was only the boy who returned, returning solitary and alone to the settled familiar land, to follow for eleven months the childish business of rabbits and such while he waited to go back, having brought with him, even from his brief first sojourn, an unforgettable sense of the big woods—not a quality dangerous or particularly inimical, but profound, sentient, gigantic and brooding, amid which he had been permitted to go to and fro at will, unscathed, why he knew not, but dwarfed and, until he had drawn honorably blood worthy of being drawn, alien.

Then November, and they would come back. Each morning Sam would take the boy out to the stand allotted him. It would be one of the poorer stands of course, since he was only ten and eleven and twelve and he had never even seen a deer running yet. But they would stand there, Sam a little behind him and without a gun himself, as he had been standing when the boy shot the running rabbit when he was eight years old. They would stand there in the November dawns, and after a while they would hear the dogs. Sometimes the chase would sweep up and past quite close, belling and invisible; once they heard the two heavy reports of Boon Hogganbeck's old gun with which he had never killed anything larger than a squirrel and that sitting, and twice they heard the flat unreverberant clap of Walter Ewell's rifle, following which you did not even wait to hear his horn.

"I'll never get a shot," the boy said. "I'll never kill one."

"Yes you will," Sam said. "You wait. You'll be a hunter. You'll be a man."

But Sam wouldn't come out. They would leave him there. He would come as far as the road where the surrey waited, to take the riding horses back, and that was all. The men would ride the horses and Uncle Ash and Tennie's Jim and the boy would follow in the wagon with Sam, with the camp equipment and the trophies, the meat, the heads, the antlers, the good ones, the wagon winding on among the tremendous gums and cypresses and oaks where no axe save that of the hunter had ever sounded, between the impenetrable walls of cane and brier—the two changing yet constant walls just beyond which the wilderness whose mark he had brought away forever on his spirit even from that first two weeks seemed to lean, stooping a little, watching them and listening, not quite inimical because they were too small, even those such as Walter and Major de Spain and old General Compson who had killed many deer and bear, their sojourn too brief and too harmless to excite to that, but just brooding, secret, tremendous, almost inattentive.

Then they would emerge, they would be out of it, the line as sharp as the demarcation of a doored wall. Suddenly skeleton cotton- and corn-fields would flow away on either hand, gaunt and motionless beneath the gray rain; there would be a house, barns, fences, where the hand of man had clawed for an instant, holding, the wall of the wilderness behind them now, tremendous and still and seemingly impenetrable in the gray and fading light, the very tiny orifice through which they had emerged apparently swallowed up. The surrey would be waiting, his cousin McCaslin and Major de Spain and General Compson and Walter and Boon dismounted beside it. Then Sam would get down from the wagon and mount one of the horses and, with the others on a rope behind him, he would turn back. The boy would watch him for a while against that tall and secret wall, growing smaller and smaller against it, never looking back. Then he would enter it, returning to what the boy believed, and thought that his cousin McCaslin believed, was his loneliness and solitude.

II

So the instant came. He pulled trigger and Sam Fathers marked his face with the hot blood which he had spilled and he ceased to be a child and became a hunter and a man. It was the last day. They broke camp that afternoon and went out, his cousin and Major de Spain and General Compson and Boon on the horses, Walter Ewell and the negroes in the wagon with him and Sam and his hide and antlers. There could have been (and were) other trophies in the wagon. But for him they did not exist, just as for all practical purposes he and Sam Fathers were still alone together as they had been that morning. The wagon wound and jolted between the slow and shifting yet constant walls from beyond and above which the wilderness watched them pass, less than inimical now and never to be inimical again since the buck still and forever leaped, the shaking gun-barrels coming constantly and forever steady at last, crashing, and still out of his instant of immortality the buck sprang, forever immortal;—the wagon jolting and bouncing on, the moment of the buck, the shot, Sam Fathers and himself and the blood with which Sam had marked him forever one with the wilderness which had accepted him since Sam said that he had done all right, when suddenly Sam reined back and stopped the wagon and they all heard the unmistakable and unforgettable sound of a deer breaking cover.

Then Boon shouted from beyond the bend of the trail and while they sat motionless in the halted wagon, Walter and the boy already reaching for their guns, Boon came galloping back, flogging his mule with his hat, his face wild and amazed as he shouted down at them. Then the other riders came around the bend, also spurring.

"Get the dogs!" Boon cried. "Get the dogs! If he had a nub on his head, he had fourteen points! Laying right there by the road in that pawpaw[4] thicket! If I'd a knowed he was there, I could have cut his throat with my pocket knife!"

"Maybe that's why he run," Walter said. "He saw you never had your gun." He was already out of the wagon with his rifle. Then the boy was out too with

4. Papaw, tree of custard apple family.

his gun, and the other riders came up and Boon got off his mule somehow and was scrabbling and clawing among the duffel in the wagon, still shouting, "Get the dogs! Get the dogs!" And it seemed to the boy too that it would take them forever to decide what to do—the old men in whom the blood ran cold and slow, in whom during the intervening years between them and himself the blood had become a different and colder substance from that which ran in him and even in Boon and Walter.

"What about it, Sam?" Major de Spain said. "Could the dogs bring him back?"

"We wont need the dogs," Sam said. "If he dont hear the dogs behind him, he will circle back in here about sundown to bed."

"All right," Major de Spain said. "You boys take the horses. We'll go on out to the road in the wagon and wait there." He and General Compson and McCaslin got into the wagon and Boon and Walter and Sam and the boy mounted the horses and turned back and out of the trail. Sam led them for an hour through the gray and unmarked afternoon whose light was little different from what it had been at dawn and which would become darkness without any graduation between. Then Sam stopped them.

"This is far enough," he said. "He'll be coming upwind, and he dont want to smell the mules." They tied the mounts in a thicket. Sam led them on foot now, unpathed through the markless afternoon, the boy pressing close behind him, the two others, or so it seemed to the boy, on his heels. But they were not. Twice Sam turned his head slightly and spoke back to him across his shoulder, still walking: "You got time. We'll get there fore he does."

So he tried to go slower. He tried deliberately to decelerate the dizzy rushing of time in which the buck which he had not even seen was moving, which it seemed to him must be carrying the buck farther and farther and more and more irretrievably away from them even though there were no dogs behind him now to make him run, even though, according to Sam, he must have completed his circle now and was heading back toward them. They went on; it could have been another hour or twice that or less than half, the boy could not have said. Then they were on a ridge. He had never been in here before and he could not see that it was a ridge. He just knew that the earth had risen slightly because the underbrush had thinned a little, the ground sloping invisibly away toward a dense wall of cane. Sam stopped. "This is it," he said. He spoke to Walter and Boon: "Follow this ridge and you will come to two crossings. You will see the tracks. If he crosses, it will be at one of these three."

Walter looked about for a moment. "I know it," he said. "I've even seen your deer. I was in here last Monday. He aint nothing but a yearling."

"A yearling?" Boon said. He was panting from the walking. His face still looked a little wild. "If the one I saw was any yearling, I'm still in kindergarden."

"Then I must have seen a rabbit," Walter said. "I always heard you quit school altogether two years before the first grade."

Boon glared at Walter. "If you dont want to shoot him, get out of the way," he said. "Set down somewhere. By God, I ——"

"Aint nobody going to shoot him standing here," Sam said quietly.

"Sam's right," Walter said. He moved, slanting the worn, silver-colored barrel of his rifle downward to walk with it again. "A little more moving and a little more quiet too. Five miles is still Hogganbeck range, even if we wasn't downwind." They went on. The boy could still hear Boon talking, though presently that ceased too. Then once more he and Sam stood motionless together against a tremendous pin oak in a little thicket, and again there was nothing. There was only the soaring and sombre solitude in the dim light, there was the thin murmur of the faint cold rain which had not ceased all day. Then, as if it had waited for them to find their positions and become still, the wilderness breathed again. It seemed to lean inward above them, above himself and Sam and Walter and Boon in their separate lurking-places, tremendous, attentive, impartial and omniscient, the buck moving in it somewhere, not running yet since he had not been pursued, not frightened yet and never fearsome but just alert also as they were alert, perhaps already circling back, perhaps quite near, perhaps conscious also of the eye of the ancient immortal Umpire. Because he was just twelve then, and that morning something had happened to him: in less than a second he had ceased forever to be the child he was yesterday. Or perhaps that made no difference, perhaps even a city-bred man, let alone a child, could not have understood it; perhaps only a country-bred one could comprehend loving the life he spills. He began to shake again.

"I'm glad it's started now," he whispered. He did not move to speak; only his lips shaped the expiring words: "Then it will be gone when I raise the gun ——"

Nor did Sam. "Hush," he said.

"Is he that near?" the boy whispered. "Do you think ——"

"Hush," Sam said. So he hushed. But he could not stop the shaking. He did not try, because he knew it would go away when he needed the steadiness—had not Sam Fathers already consecrated and absolved him from weakness and regret too?—not from love and pity for all which lived and ran and then ceased to live in a second in the very midst of splendor and speed, but from weakness and regret. So they stood motionless, breathing deep and quiet and steady. If there had been any sun, it would be near to setting now; there was a condensing, a densifying, of what he had thought was the gray and unchanging light until he realised suddenly that it was his own breathing, his heart, his blood—something, all things, and that Sam Fathers had marked him indeed, not as a mere hunter, but with something Sam had had in his turn of his vanished and forgotten people. He stopped breathing then; there was only his heart, his blood, and in the following silence the wilderness ceased to breathe also, leaning, stooping overhead with its breath held, tremendous and impartial and waiting. Then the shaking stopped too, as he had known it would, and he drew back the two heavy hammers of the gun.

Then it had passed. It was over. The solitude did not breathe again yet; it had merely stopped watching him and was looking somewhere else, even turning its back on him, looking on away up the ridge at another point, and the boy knew as well as if he had seen him that the buck had come to the edge of the cane and had either seen or scented them and faded back into it. But the solitude did not breathe again. It should have suspired again then but it did not. It was still facing, watching, what it had been watching and it was not here, not where he and Sam stood; rigid, not breathing himself, he thought, cried *No! No!*, knowing already that it was too late, thinking with the old despair of two and three years ago: *I'll never get a shot*. Then he heard it—the flat single clap of Walter Ewell's rifle which never missed. Then the mellow sound of the horn came down the ridge and something went out of him and he knew then he had never expected to get the shot at all.

"I reckon that's it," he said. "Walter got him." He had raised the gun slightly 55
without knowing it. He lowered it again and had lowered one of the hammers and was already moving out of the thicket when Sam spoke.

"Wait."

"Wait?" the boy cried. And he would remember that—how he turned upon Sam in the truculence of a boy's grief over the missed opportunity, the missed luck. "What for? Dont you hear that horn?"

And he would remember how Sam was standing. Sam had not moved. He was not tall, squat rather and broad, and the boy had been growing fast for the past year or so and there was not much difference between them in height, yet Sam was looking over the boy's head and up the ridge toward the sound of the horn and the boy knew that Sam did not even see him; that Sam knew he was still there beside him but he did not see the boy. Then the boy saw the buck. It was coming down the ridge, as if it were walking out of the very sound of the horn which related its death. It was not running, it was walking, tremendous, unhurried, slanting and tilting its head to pass the antlers through the undergrowth, and the boy standing with Sam beside him now instead of behind him as Sam always stood, and the gun still partly aimed and one of the hammers still cocked.

Then it saw them. And still it did not begin to run. It just stopped for an instant, taller than any man, looking at them; then its muscles suppled, gathered. It did not even alter its course, not fleeing, not even running, just moving with that winged and effortless ease with which deer move, passing within twenty feet of them, its head high and the eye not proud and not haughty but just full and wild and unafraid, and Sam standing beside the boy now, his right arm raised at full length, palm-outward, speaking in that tongue which the boy had learned from listening to him and Joe Baker in the blacksmith shop, while up the ridge Walter Ewell's horn was still blowing them in to a dead buck.

"Oleh, Chief," Sam said. "Grandfather." 60

When they reached Walter, he was standing with his back toward them, quite still, bemused almost, looking down at his feet. He didn't look up at all.

"Come here, Sam," he said quietly. When they reached him he still did not look up, standing above a little spike buck which had still been a fawn last spring. "He was so little I pretty near let him go," Walter said. "But just look at the track he was making. It's pretty near big as a cow's. If there were any more tracks here besides the ones he is laying in, I would swear there was another buck here that I never even saw."

III

It was dark when they reached the road where the surrey waited. It was turning cold, the rain had stopped, and the sky was beginning to blow clear. His cousin and Major de Spain and General Compson had a fire going. "Did you get him?" Major de Spain said.

"Got a good-sized swamp-rabbit with spike horns," Walter said. He slid the little buck down from his mule. The boy's cousin McCaslin looked at it.

"Nobody saw the big one?" he said.

"I dont even believe Boon saw it," Walter said. "He probably jumped somebody's straw cow in that thicket." Boon started cursing, swearing at Walter and at Sam for not getting the dogs in the first place and at the buck and all.

"Never mind," Major de Spain said. "He'll be here for us next fall. Let's get started home."

It was after midnight when they let Walter out at his gate two miles from Jefferson and later still when they took General Compson to his house and then returned to Major de Spain's, where he and McCaslin would spend the rest of the night, since it was still seventeen miles home. It was cold, the sky was clear now; there would be a heavy frost by sunup and the ground was already frozen beneath the horses' feet and the wheels and beneath their own feet as they crossed Major de Spain's yard and entered the house, the warm dark house, feeling their way up the dark stairs until Major de Spain found a candle and lit it, and into the strange room and the big deep bed, the still cold sheets until they began to warm to their bodies and at last the shaking stopped and suddenly he was telling McCaslin about it while McCaslin listened, quietly until he had finished. "You dont believe it," the boy said. "I know you dont——"

"Why not?" McCaslin said. "Think of all that has happened here, on this earth. All the blood hot and strong for living, pleasuring, that has soaked back into it. For grieving and suffering too, of course, but still getting something out of it for all that, getting a lot out of it, because after all you dont have to continue to bear what you believe is suffering; you can always choose to stop that, put an end to that. And even suffering and grieving is better than nothing; there is only one thing worse than not being alive, and that's shame. But you cant be alive forever, and you always wear out life long before you have exhausted the possibilities of living. And all that must be somewhere; all that could not have been invented and created just to be thrown away. And the earth is shallow; there is not a great deal of it before you come to the rock. And the earth dont want to just keep things, hoard them; it wants to use them again. Look at the seed, the acorns, at what happens even to carrion when you try to bury it: it refuses too, seethes and struggles too until it reaches light and air again, hunting the sun still. And they—" the boy saw his hand in silhouette for a moment against the window beyond which, accustomed to the darkness now, he could see sky where the scoured and icy stars glittered "—they dont want it, need it. Besides, what would it want, itself, knocking around out there, when it never had enough time about the earth as it was, when there is plenty of room about the earth, plenty of places still unchanged from what they were when the blood used and pleasured in them while it was still blood?"

"But we want them," the boy said. "We want them too. There is plenty of 70
room for us and them too."

"That's right," McCaslin said. "Suppose they dont have substance, cant cast a shadow ——"

"But I saw it!" the boy cried. "I saw him!"

"Steady," McCaslin said. For an instant his hand touched the boy's flank beneath the covers. "Steady. I know you did. So did I. Sam took me in there once after I killed my first deer."

1942

QUESTIONS

1. What does the title literally denote in the story "Araby"? What does it suggest? How do both its denotative and connotative meanings function in the story?

2. What is the point of view (focus) in "Araby"? Are the words of the story the boy's? How does the difference between focus and voice define the nature of the initiation in the story?

3. What is the nature of the initiation in "Boys and Girls"?

4. The phrase "only a girl" appears twice in Alice Munro's story. How do the contexts differ? How do the implications of the phrase differ on its two appearances (that.is, what does it mean or suggest each time)?

5. What is the point of view or focus of narration in "The Old People"? Can you rearrange the events directly or indirectly narrated into the story to their chronological order (that is, their history)? Sam tells Ike about "the People," and "gradually to the boy those old times . . . would become a part of the boy's present . . . as if they were still happening . . . as if some of them . . . would occur tomorrow" (par. 15). How does this relate to the handling of the time element? to the structure of the story? to the theme?

6. What significance do you find in the fact that the initiating act in "Boys and Girls" is the liberating of an animal, while that in "The Old People" is the killing of a gentle animal?

WRITING SUGGESTIONS

1. Compare the use of the theme of romance-of-childhood versus realism-of-maturity in "Araby" and "Boys and Girls."

2. Compare or relate the use of "blood" in "The Old People" and "Barn Burning." (You may want to consider the advantages, disadvantages, validity of using one story by an author to explain or expand your reading of another story by that same author.)

10 A MODE: FANTASY

There is a looser and wider-ranging system of literary classification than genres and kinds, one that looks at works (or even parts of works) not as organisms but in terms of **modes,** ways of perceiving or presenting experience. If we call the conventional literary genres poetry, drama, fiction, we call the conventional modes the *poetic* (or *lyric*), the *dramatic*, and the *narrative*. A work that is classified in the subgenre short story, within the genre fiction, may have passages in the poetic mode—passages marked by heightened and highly figurative language, intensification of rhythms and emotions, often focusing on the ideal or spiritual. Gurov standing by the sea or contemplating the nails in the gray fence around Anna's home in "The Lady with the Dog" and the boy wandering through the Dublin streets full of frustration and shame in "Araby" are examples of poetic passages. Some portion of a story, even a whole story, may be in the dramatic mode, like a play, with unmediated or unnarrated dialogue or action. The conversation between Clayton, Julia, and Francis in "The Country Husband" and the one between Julia and Francis that follows seem like scenes from a play; they could be transferred to the stage almost without change. Except for the first and seventh paragraphs (and the latter seems little more than a stage direction), "No One's a Mystery" comes about as close as a short story can to being fully dramatic.

Befitting the looseness of the term, modes do not descend in an orderly way through subheadings, as do genres through subgenres and kinds. **Fantasy,** for example, a literary mode involving the consciously unreal—places, societies, or beings that never existed, do not exist, or do not yet exist, or with qualities that are beyond or counter to the ordinary or commonsensical—can be found in fiction, poetry, or drama.

Fantastic fiction sometimes signals its fictionality immediately or very soon: "Once upon a time . . ." At other times, it goes to some lengths to establish its "reality": many eighteenth-century novels about medieval castles and ghosts (Gothic novels) pretend to be editions of some monk's dusty manuscript, for example. Still other stories, such as "A Very Old Man with Enormous Wings," simply treat the incredible as perfectly natural, if not perfectly common.

Much fantasy has as its aim to stretch or expand our consciousness, our perception and conception of reality. Some stories seek to open us up to possibilities by disorienting us, alternating or mixing the realistic, the fictional, the fantastic in dizzying patterns. "The Garden of Forking Paths" begins realistically, with documentation and an essay-like manner that makes it seem not like a story at all. Then the confession begins, and we recognize that we are in the midst of a common fictional kind, the spy story or thriller. The shift does not bother us too much—it's like the dusty-manuscript device, and the fictional kind we've entered on is so familiar that we're reasonably comfortable. Suddenly the spy story shifts once again, toward fantasy, and just as we're getting used to fantasy, to mysterious Chinese gardens and riddles. The fantasy is used to question whether it is the fantastic that is incredible, or whether our assumption that time is uniform and absolute is merely arbitrary and too restrictive—itself a fantasy. Given eternity, we must admit that everything that might possibly happen *will* happen. So when we make a choice, the choice we did not make but might have made will yet be made; its potential must be realized; it must exist somewhere in the vastness of eternity in a world of events parallel to our own. No wonder, then, when we return to the world of the spy story—which, though fictional, operates within the same notions of uniform, absolute time—it seems credible that the writer of the confession is not concerned with whether he lives or dies, realities that are now "unreal, insignificant."

I don't think what I have told you about "The Garden of Forking Paths" will destroy your interest in the story—indeed, everyone can probably do with a little help in reading this fascinating story for the first time. Its questioning of our assumptions about reality is not too different from what's going on in modern thought. It is precisely because history, psychology, science, philosophy—almost all the intellectual disciplines—have in recent years most urgently called into question our longstanding assumptions about reality that fantasy seems so congenial a mode for us today.

From the middle of the nineteenth century to the middle of ours, the rise of the novel and the rise of realism were assumed to be the same thing, and we looked back on literary history as progress toward the literal, the factual, the ordinary (just as some art historians saw the Renaissance and what followed as demonstrating progress in man's ability to represent things "as they really are"). Long narratives that dwelled on the extraordinary, unusual, bizarre, or supernatural were called **romances**, as opposed to the more realistic **novel**. The early modern short story leaned more heavily toward romance. In the middle of the nineteenth century Poe was perhaps our most widely respected writer, and you can see that "The Cask of Amontillado" is not exactly a story of everyday life. Late in the century, with Maupassant in France (see "The Jewelry") and Chekhov in Russia (see "The Lady with the Dog"), the realistic short story seemed to have caught up with the novel. But already in the nineteenth century "common sense" notions of realism were beginning to give way before the discovery of worlds beyond our unaided senses, observable through microscope and telescope. Darwin, with his notion that species themselves were not fixed but moving and changing in time, made the solid earth under our feet a little less solid. With the rise of psychology, which too was meant to capture more realms for consciousness and science, we became more and more aware that there were realities only dreamed of in our philosophies. When physics, the most advanced and scientific of the sciences, began to tell us that all our knowledge is, if not subjective, at least limited to what the human brain and its instruments can perceive, and is altered by our perception, we were not so sure anymore that reality was what existed "out there" or that we were contained between our hat and boots.

When they first appeared, *Rosemary's Baby* or *The Exorcist* could have had only one ending—a rational explanation for the appearance of the supernatural. Few viewers or readers then would take seriously a work that was not embedded in a world of more or less everyday reality. The supernatural or fantastic in such a world had to be explained away as a dream, hallucination, or other psychological aberration, or as a hoax of some sort, set up to take in the foolish or credulous. Similarly, we would have had to explain away stories like García Márquez's "A Very Old Man with Enormous Wings" and, in "Reading More Fiction," Franz Kafka's "A Hunger Artist" by treating them as allegories. Now we can accept them as symbolic, as experiences that cannot be explained away or reduced to everyday terms, but that exist on their own terms, explaining in fantasy more than we might in our discursive prose, our scientific formulas, graphs, and charts.

The fantasy land of science fiction is usually the future—not so much never-never as never-yet land—which does not necessarily undermine or question conventional reality but projects potential consequences of present knowledge. There are those who maintain that for this very reason it is a mistake to call sci-fi fantasy. Fantasy, they say, involves the incredible or impossible. Science fiction, while it may take place in the future or outside earthly reality, is neither incredible nor impossible but wholly logical, often based on real scientific principles. Others say that's exactly why it's fantasy: historical reality is never predictable, and certainly not by that fantasy called logic.

Science-fiction people are passionate, dedicated, and argumentative, so if it's risky to suggest that science fiction is in the mode of fantasy, it's even riskier to try to define science fiction as a kind, even though everyone will grant that generic definitions are at best only loose approximations. Approximately, **science fiction** is a narrative about events outside the bounds of Earth history, in which science or advanced technology is often centrally important. The term

Earth history allows for both space travel (to imaginary life on real or imaginary planets) in the present and time travel to prehistory. Science and technology in the stories can be merely a plot device or be important as a means of trans-historical travel, or in the operation or perception of that imaginary world, as in "The Eye Altering." I'm sure this loose baggy monster of a definition leaves something out or includes too much, but at least it separates "The Eye Altering" from the other two fantasy stories here, and from "The Rocking-Horse Winner" and, in "Reading More Fiction," from "The Kugelmass Episode" and "A Hunger Artist."

▽ ▽ ▽

MODE A Glossary

fantasy: a literary mode involving the consciously unreal—places, societies, or beings that never existed, do not exist, or do not yet exist, or with qualities that are beyond or counter to the ordinary, everyday, or commonsensical

mode: a loose system of classifying works or even passages from works of literature according to the way experience is perceived or presented; the conventional modes, then, are the *poetic* (or *lyric*), the *dramatic*, and the *narrative*

novel: a subgenre of fiction; a long, more or less realistic narrative

romance: a narrative mode characterized by the extraordinary, unusual, bizarre, or supernatural; also used to characterize a subgenre of long fiction with these qualities as distinguished from the more realistic *novel*

science fiction: a narrative about events spatially or temporally outside the bounds of earth history in which science or advanced technology is often centrally important

GABRIEL GARCÍA MÁRQUEZ

A Very Old Man with Enormous Wings[1]

A TALE FOR CHILDREN

On the third day of rain they had killed so many crabs inside the house that Pelayo had to cross his drenched courtyard and throw them into the sea, because the newborn child had a temperature all night and they thought it was due to the stench. The world had been sad since Tuesday. Sea and sky were a single ash-gray thing and the sands of the beach, which on March nights glimmered like powdered light, had become a stew of mud and rotten shellfish. The light was so weak at noon that when Pelayo was coming back to the house after throwing away the crabs, it was hard for him to see what it was that was moving and groaning in the rear of the courtyard. He had to go very close to see that it was an old man, a very old man, lying face down in the mud, who, in spite of his tremendous efforts, couldn't get up, impeded by his enormous wings.

Frightened by that nightmare, Pelayo ran to get Elisenda, his wife, who was putting compresses on the sick child, and he took her to the rear of the courtyard. They both looked at the fallen body with mute stupor. He was dressed like a ragpicker. There were only a few faded hairs left on his bald skull and very few teeth in his mouth, and his pitiful condition of a drenched great-grandfather had taken away any sense of grandeur he might have had. His huge buzzard wings, dirty and half-plucked, were forever entangled in the mud. They looked at him so long and so closely that Pelayo and Elisenda very soon overcame their surprise and in the end found him familiar. Then they dared speak to him, and he answered in an incomprehensible dialect with a strong sailor's voice. That was how they skipped over the inconvenience of the wings and quite intelligently concluded that he was a lonely castaway from some foreign ship wrecked by the storm. And yet, they called in a neighbor woman who knew everything about life and death to see him, and all she needed was one look to show them their mistake.

"He's an angel," she told them. "He must have been coming for the child, but the poor fellow is so old that the rain knocked him down."

On the following day everyone knew that a flesh-and-blood angel was held captive in Pelayo's house. Against the judgment of the wise neighbor woman, for whom angels in those times were the fugitive survivors of a celestial conspiracy, they did not have the heart to club him to death. Pelayo watched over him all afternoon from the kitchen, armed with his bailiff's club, and before going to bed he dragged him out of the mud and locked him up with the hens in the wire chicken coop. In the middle of the night, when the rain stopped, Pelayo and Elisenda were still killing crabs. A short time afterward the child woke up without a fever and with a desire to eat. Then they felt magnanimous and decided to

1. Translated by Gregory Rabassa.

put the angel on a raft with fresh water and provisions for three days and leave him to his fate on the high seas. But when they went out into the courtyard with the first light of dawn, they found the whole neighborhood in front of the chicken coop having fun with the angel, without the slightest reverence, tossing him things to eat through the openings in the wire as if he weren't a supernatural creature but a circus animal.

5 Father Gonzaga arrived before seven o'clock, alarmed at the strange news. By that time onlookers less frivolous than those at dawn had already arrived and they were making all kinds of conjectures concerning the captive's future. The simplest among them thought that he should be named mayor of the world. Others of sterner mind felt that he should be promoted to the rank of five-star general in order to win all wars. Some visionaries hoped that he could be put to stud in order to implant on earth a race of winged wise men who could take charge of the universe. But Father Gonzaga, before becoming a priest, had been a robust woodcutter. Standing by the wire, he reviewed his catechism in an instant and asked them to open the door so that he could take a close look at that pitiful man who looked more like a huge decrepit hen among the fascinated chickens. He was lying in a corner drying his open wings in the sunlight among the fruit peels and breakfast leftovers that the early risers had thrown him. Alien to the impertinences of the world, he only lifted his antiquarian eyes and murmured something in his dialect when Father Gonzaga went into the chicken coop and said good morning to him in Latin. The parish priest had his first suspicion of an imposter when he saw that he did not understand the language of God or know how to greet His ministers. Then he noticed that seen close up he was much too human: he had an unbearable smell of the outdoors, the back side of his wings was strewn with parasites and his main feathers had been mistreated by terrestrial winds, and nothing about him measured up to the proud dignity of angels. Then he came out of the chicken coop and in a brief sermon warned the curious against the risks of being ingenuous. He reminded them that the devil had the bad habit of making use of carnival tricks in order to confuse the unwary. He argued that if wings were not the essential element in determining the difference between a hawk and an airplane, they were even less so in the recognition of angels. Nevertheless, he promised to write a letter to his bishop so that the latter would write to his primate so that the latter would write to the Supreme Pontiff in order to get the final verdict from the highest courts.

His prudence fell on sterile hearts. The news of the captive angel spread with such rapidity that after a few hours the courtyard had the bustle of a marketplace and they had to call in troops with fixed bayonets to disperse the mob that was about to knock the house down. Elisenda, her spine all twisted from sweeping up so much marketplace trash, then got the idea of fencing in the yard and charging five cents admission to see the angel.

The curious came from far away. A traveling carnival arrived with a flying acrobat who buzzed over the crowd several times, but no one paid any attention to him because his wings were not those of an angel but, rather, those of a sidereal bat. The most unfortunate invalids on earth came in search of health: a poor woman who since childhood had been counting her heartbeats and had run out of numbers; a Portuguese man who couldn't sleep because the noise of the stars disturbed him; a sleepwalker who got up at night to undo the things he had done while awake; and many others with less serious ailments. In the midst of that shipwreck disorder that made the earth tremble, Pelayo and Elisenda were happy with fatigue, for in less than a week they had crammed their rooms with money and the line of pilgrims waiting their turn to enter still reached beyond the horizon.

The angel was the only one who took no part in his own act. He spent his time trying to get comfortable in his borrowed nest, befuddled by the hellish heat of the oil lamps and sacramental candles that had been placed along the wire. At first they tried to make him eat some mothballs, which, according to the wisdom of the wise neighbor woman, were the food prescribed for angels. But he turned them down, just as he turned down the papal lunches[2] that the penitents brought him, and they never found out whether it was because he was an angel or because he was an old man that in the end he ate nothing but eggplant mush. His only supernatural virtue seemed to be patience. Especially during the first days, when the hens pecked at him, searching for the stellar parasites that proliferated in his wings, and the cripples pulled out feathers to touch their defective parts with, and even the most merciful threw stones at him, trying to get him to rise so they could see him standing. The only time they succeeded in arousing him was when they burned his side with an iron for branding steers, for he had been motionless for so many hours that they thought he was dead. He awoke with a start, ranting in his hermetic language and with tears in his eyes, and he flapped his wings a couple of times, which brought on a whirlwind of chicken dung and lunar dust and a gale of panic that did not seem to be of this world. Although many thought that his reaction had been one not of rage but of pain, from then on they were careful not to annoy him, because the majority understood that his passivity was not that of a hero taking his ease but that of a cataclysm in repose.

Father Gonzaga held back the crowd's frivolity with formulas of maidservant inspiration while awaiting the arrival of a final judgment on the nature of the captive. But the mail from Rome showed no sense of urgency. They spent their time finding out if the prisoner had a navel, if his dialect had any connection with Aramaic, how many times he could fit on the head of a pin, or whether he wasn't just a Norwegian with wings. Those meager letters might have come and gone until the end of time if a providential event had not put an end to the priest's tribulations.

It so happened that during those days, among so many other carnival attractions, there arrived in town the traveling show of the woman who had been changed into a spider for having disobeyed her parents. The admission to see her was not only less than the admission to see the angel, but people were permitted to ask her all manner of questions about her absurd state and to examine her up and down so that no one would ever doubt the truth of her horror. She was a frightful tarantula the size of a ram and with the head of a sad maiden. What

2. Choice, extremely expensive meals.

was most heart-rending, however, was not her outlandish shape but the sincere affliction with which she recounted the details of her misfortune. While still practically a child she had sneaked out of her parents' house to go to a dance, and while she was coming back through the woods after having danced all night without permission, a fearful thunderclap rent the sky in two and through the crack came the lightning bolt of brimstone that changed her into a spider. Her only nourishment came from the meatballs that charitable souls chose to toss into her mouth. A spectacle like that, full of so much human truth and with such a fearful lesson, was bound to defeat without even trying that of a haughty angel who scarcely deigned to look at mortals. Besides, the few miracles attributed to the angel showed a certain mental disorder, like the blind man who didn't recover his sight but grew three new teeth, or the paralytic who didn't get to walk but almost won the lottery, and the leper whose sores sprouted sunflowers. Those consolation miracles, which were more like mocking fun, had already ruined the angel's reputation when the women who had been changed into a spider finally crushed him completely. That was how Father Gonzaga was cured forever of his insomnia and Pelayo's courtyard went back to being as empty as during the time it had rained for three days and crabs walked through the bedrooms.

The owners of the house had no reason to lament. With the money they saved they built a two-story mansion with balconies and gardens and high netting so that crabs wouldn't get in during the winter, and with iron bars on the windows so that angels wouldn't get in. Pelayo also set up a rabbit warren close to town and gave up his job as bailiff for good, and Elisenda bought some satin pumps with high heels and many dresses of iridescent silk, the kind worn on Sunday by the most desirable women in those times. The chicken coop was the only thing that didn't receive any attention. If they washed it down with creolin[3] and burned tears of myrrh inside it every so often, it was not in homage to the angel but to drive away the dungheap stench that still hung everywhere like a ghost and was turning the new house into an old one. At first, when the child learned to walk, they were careful that he not get too close to the chicken coop. But then they began to lose their fears and got used to the smell, and before the child got his second teeth he'd gone inside the chicken coop to play, where the wires were falling apart. The angel was no less standoffish with him than with other mortals, but he tolerated the most ingenious infamies with the patience of a dog who had no illusions. They both came down with chicken pox at the same time. The doctor who took care of the child couldn't resist the temptation to listen to the angel's heart, and he found so much whistling in the heart and so many sounds in his kidneys that it seemed impossible for him to be alive. What surprised him most, however, was the logic of his wings. They seemed so natural on that completely human organism that he couldn't understand why other men didn't have them too.

When the child began school it had been some time since the sun and rain had caused the collapse of the chicken coop. The angel went dragging himself about here and there like a stray dying man. They would drive him out of the

3. A disinfectant.

bedroom with a broom and a moment later find him in the kitchen. He seemed to be in so many places at the same time that they grew to think that he'd been duplicated, that he was reproducing himself all through the house, and the exasperated and unhinged Elisenda shouted that it was awful living in that hell full of angels. He could scarcely eat and his antiquarian eyes had also become so foggy that he went about bumping into posts. All he had left were the bare cannulae of his last feathers. Pelayo threw a blanket over him and extended him the charity of letting him sleep in the shed, and only then did they notice that he had a temperature at night, and was delirious with the tongue twisters of an old Norwegian. That was one of the few times they became alarmed, for they thought he was going to die and not even the wise neighbor woman had been able to tell them what to do with dead angels.

And yet he not only survived his worst winter, but seemed improved with the first sunny days. He remained motionless for several days in the farthest corner of the courtyard, where no one would see him, and at the beginning of December some large, stiff feathers began to grow on his wings, the feathers of a scarecrow, which looked more like another misfortune of decrepitude. But he must have known the reason for those changes, for he was quite careful that no one should notice them, that no one should hear the sea chanteys that he sometimes sang under the stars. One morning Elisenda was cutting some bunches of onions for lunch when a wind that seemed to come from the high seas blew into the kitchen. Then she went to the window and caught the angel in his first attempts at flight. They were so clumsy that his fingernails opened a furrow in the vegetable patch and he was on the point of knocking the shed down with the ungainly flapping that slipped on the light and couldn't get a grip on the air. But he did manage to gain altitude. Elisenda let out a sign of relief, for herself and for him, when she saw him pass over the last houses, holding himself up in some way with the risky flapping of a senile vulture. She kept watching him even when she was through cutting the onions and she kept on watching until it was no longer possible for her to see him, because then he was no longer an annoyance in her life but an imaginary dot on the horizon of the sea.

1968

URSULA K. LE GUIN

The Eye Altering

Miriam stood at the big window of the infirmary ward and looked out at the view and thought, For twenty-five years I have been standing at this window and looking out at this view. And never once have I seen what I wanted to see.

If I forget thee, O Jerusalem—[1]

1. ". . . let my right hand forget her cunning," Psalm 137:5; the psalm begins, "By the rivers of Babylon, there we sat down, yea, we wept, when we remembered Zion," Zion being both another name for Jerusalem and for the Jewish people.

The pain was forgotten, yes. The hatred and the fear, forgotten. In exile you don't remember the grey days and the black years. You remember the sunlight, the orchards, the white cities. Even when you try to forget it you remember that Jerusalem was golden.

The sky outside the ward window was dulled with haze. Over the low ridge called Ararat[2] the sun was setting; setting slowly, for New Zion had a slower spin than Old Earth, and a twenty-eight-hour day; settling, rather than setting, dully down onto the dull horizon. There were no clouds to gather the colors of sunset. There were seldom any clouds. When the haze thickened there might be a misty, smothering rain; when the haze was thin, as now, it hung high and vague, formless. It never quite cleared. You never saw the color of the sky. You never saw the stars. And through the haze the sun, no, not the sun, but NSC 641 (Class G)[3] burned swollen and vaporous, warty as an orange—remember oranges? the sweet juice on the tongue? the orchards of Haifa?—NSC 641 stared, like a bleary eye. You could stare back at it. No glory of gold to blind you. Two imbeciles staring at each other.

5 Shadows stretched across the valley towards the buildings of the Settlement. In shadows the fields and woods were black; in the light they were brown, purplish, and dark red. Dirty colors, the colors you got when you scrubbed your watercolors too much and the teacher came by and said, You'd better use some fresh water, Mimi, it's getting muddy. Because the teacher had been too kind to say to a ten-year-old, That picture's a total loss, Mimi, throw it away and start fresh.

She had thought of that before—she had thought all her thoughts before, standing at this window—but this time it reminded her of Genya, because of the painting, and she turned to see how he was doing. The shock symptoms were almost gone, his face was no longer so pale and his pulse had steadied. While she held his wrist he sighed a bit and opened his eyes. Lovely eyes he had, grey in the thin face. He had never been much but eyes, poor Genya. Her oldest patient. Twenty-four years he had been her patient, right from the moment of his birth, five pounds, purplish-blue like a fetal rat, a month premature and half dead of cyanosis: the fifth child born on New Zion, the first in Ararat Settlement. A native. A feeble and unpromising native. He hadn't even had the strength, or the sense, to cry at his first breath of this alien air. Sofia's other children had been full-term and healthy, two girls, both married and mothers now, and fat Leon who could hoist a seventy-kilo sack of grain when he was fifteen. Good young colonists, strong stock. But Miriam had always loved Genya, and all the more after her own years of miscarriages and stillbirths, and the last birth, the girl who had lived two hours, whose eyes had been clear grey like Genya's. Babies never have grey eyes, the eyes of the newborn are blue, that was all sentimental rubbish. But how could you ever make sure of what color things were under this damned warty-orange sun? Nothing ever looked right. "So there you are, Gennady Borisovich," she said, "back home, eh?"

2. The mountain, in present-day Turkey, where Noah's ark landed after the Flood. **3.** I.e., the same kind of star as our sun. *NSC 641*: The catalogue number of a fictional star.

It had been their joke when he was a child; he had spent so much time in the infirmary that whenever he came in with one of his fevers or fainting spells or gasping asthma he would say, "Here I am, back home, Auntie Doctor. . . ."

"What happened?" he asked.

"You collapsed. Hoeing down in the South Field. Aaron and Tina brought you up here on the tractor. Touch of sunstroke, maybe? You've been doing all right, haven't you?"

He shrugged and nodded.

"Dizzy? Short of breath?"

"On and off."

"Why didn't you come to the clinic?"

"It's no good, Miriam."

Since he was grown he had called her Miriam. She missed "Auntie Doctor." He had grown away from her, these last few years, withdrawn from her into his painting. He had always sketched and painted, but now, all his free time and whatever energy he had left when his Settlement duties were done, he spent in the loft of the generator building where he'd made a kind of studio, grinding colors from rocks and mixing dyes from native plants, making brushes by begging pigtail ends off little girls, and painting—painting on scraps from the lumber mill, on bits of rag, on precious scraps of paper, on smooth slabs of slate from the quarry on Ararat if nothing better was at hand. Painting portraits, scenes of Settlement life, buildings, machinery, still-lifes, plants, landscapes, inner visions. Painting anything, everything. His portraits had been much in demand—people were always kind to Genya and the other sicklies—but lately he had not done any portraits; he had gone in for queer muddy jumbles of forms and lines all in a dark haze, like worlds half created. Nobody liked those paintings, but nobody ever told Genya he was wasting his time. He was a sickly; he was an artist; O.K. Healthy people had no time to be artists. There was too much work to do. But it was good to have an artist. It was human. It was like Earth. Wasn't it?

They were kind to Toby, too, whose stomach troubles were so bad that at sixteen he weighed eighty-four pounds; kind to little Shura, who was just learning to talk at six, and whose eyes wept and wept all day long, even when she was smiling; kind to all their sicklies, the ones whose bodies could not adjust to this alien world, whose stomachs could not digest the native proteins even with the help of the metabolising pills which every colonist must take twice a day every day of his life on New Zion. Hard as life was in the Twenty Settlements, much as they needed every hand to work, they were gentle with their useless ones, their afflicted. In affliction the hand of God is visible. They remembered the words civilisation, humanity. They remembered Jerusalem.

"Genya, my dear, what do you mean, it's no good?"

His quiet voice had frightened her. "It's no good," he had said, smiling. And the grey eyes not clear but veiled, hazy.

"Medicine," he said. "Pills. Cures."

"Of course you know more about medicine than I do," Miriam said. "You're a much better doctor than I am. Or are you giving up? Is that it, Genya? Giving up?" Anger had come upon her so suddenly, from so deep within, from anxiety so long and deeply hidden, that it shook her body and cracked her voice.

"I'm giving up one thing. The metas."

"Metas? Giving them up. What are you talking about?"

"I haven't taken any for two weeks."

The despairing rage swelled in her. She felt her face go hot, so that it felt twice its normal size. "Two weeks! And so, and so, and so you're here! Where did you think you'd end up, you terrible fool? Lucky you're not dead!"

"I haven't been any worse since I stopped taking them, Miriam. Better, this whole last week. Until today. It can't be that. It must have been heatstroke. I forgot to wear a hat. . . . He too flushed faintly, in the eagerness of his pleading, or with shame. It was stupid to work in the fields bareheaded; for all its dull look NSC 641 could hit the unsheltered human head quite as hard as fiery Sol, and Genya was apologetic about his carelessness. "You see, I was feeling fine this morning, really good, I kept right up with the others hoeing. Then I felt a bit dizzy, but I didn't want to stop, it was so good to be able to work right with the others, I never thought about heatstroke."

Miriam found that there were tears in her eyes, and this made her so ultimately and absolutely angry that she couldn't speak at all. She got up off Genya's bed and strode down the ward between the rows of beds, four on one side, four on the other. She strode back and stood staring out the window at the mud-colored shapeless ugly world.

Genya was saying something—"Miriam, honestly, couldn't it be that the metas are worse for me than the native proteins are?"—but she did not listen; the grief and wrath and fear swelled in her and swelled in her, and broke, and she cried out, "Oh, Genya, Genya, how could you? Not you, to give up now, after fighting so long—I can't bear it! I can't bear it!" But she did not cry it out aloud. Not one word of it. Never. She cried out in her mind, and some tears came out and ran down her cheeks, but her back was turned to the patient. She looked through distorting tears at the flat valley and the dull sun and said to them, silent, "I hate you." Then after a while she could turn around and say aloud, "Lie down,"—for he had sat up, distressed by her long silence—"lie down, be quiet. You'll take two metas before dinner. If you need anything, Geza's in the nurse's station." And she walked out.

As she left the infirmary she saw Tina climbing up the back path from the fields, coming to see how Genya was, no doubt. For all his wheezes and fevers Genya had never wanted for girl friends. Tina, and Shoshanna, and Bella, and Rachel, he could have had his pick. But last year when he and Rachel were living together, they had got contraceptives from the clinic regularly, and then they had separated; they hadn't married, though by his age, twenty-four, Settlement kids were married and parents. He hadn't married Rachel, and Miriam knew why. Moral genetics. Bad genes. Shouldn't pass them on to the next generation. Weed out the sicklies. No procreation for him, and therefore no marriage; he couldn't ask Rachel to live barren for the love of him. What the Settlements needed was children, plenty of healthy young natives who, with the help of the meta pills, could survive on this planet.

Rachel hadn't taken up with anybody else. But she was only eighteen. She'd get over it. Marry a boy from another Settlement, most likely, and move away, away from Genya's big grey eyes. It would be best for her. And for him.

No wonder Genya was suicidal! Miriam thought, and put the thought away from her fiercely, wearily. She was very weary. She had meant to go to her room and wash, change her clothes, change her mood, before dinner; but the room was so lonesome with Leonid away at Salem Settlement and not due back for at least another month, she couldn't stand it. She went straight across the dusty central square of the Settlement to the refectory building, and into the Living Room. To get away, clear away, from the windless haze and the grey sky and the ugly sun.

Nobody was in the Living Room but Commander Marca, fast asleep on one of the padded wooden couches, and Reine, reading. The two oldest members of the Settlement. Commander Marca was in fact the oldest person in the world. He had been forty-four when he piloted the Exile Fleet from Old Earth to New Zion; he was seventy now, and very frail. People didn't wear well here. They aged early, died at fifty, sixty. Reine, the biochemist, was forty-five now but looked twenty years older. It's a damned geriatric club, Miriam thought sourly; and it was true that the young, the Zionborn, seldom used the Living Room. They came here to read, as it held the Settlement's library of books and tapes and microfilm, but not many of them read much, or had much time to read. And maybe the April light and the pictures made them a little uneasy. They were such moral, severe, serious young people; there was no leisure in their lives, no beauty in their world; how could they approve of this luxury their elders needed, this one haven, this one place like home. . . .

The Living Room had no windows. Avram, a wizard with anything electrical, had done the indirect lighting, deliberately reproducing the color and quality of sunlight—not NSC 641 light, but sunlight—so that to enter the Living Room was to enter a room in a house on Earth on a warm sunny day of April or early May, to see all things in that clear, clean, lovely light. Avram and several others had worked on the pictures, enlarging colored photos to a meter or so square: scenes of Earth, photographs and paintings brought by the colonists—Venice, the Negev, the domes of the Kremlin, a farm in Portugal, the Dead Sea, Hampstead Heath, a beach in Oregon, a meadow in Poland, cities, forests, mountains, Van Gogh's cypresses, Bierstadt's Rocky Mountains, Monet's water-lilies, Leonardo's blue mysterious caves.[4] Every wall of the room was covered with pictures, dozens of pictures, all the beauty of the Earth. So that the Earthborn could see and remember, so that the Zionborn could see and know.

There had been some discussion about the pictures, twenty years ago when Avram had started putting them up: Was it really wise? Should we look back? And so on. But then Commander Marca had come by on a visit, seen the Living Room of Ararat Settlement, and said, "This is where I'll stay." With every Set-

4. I.e., familiar scenes from their homes on earth, including those in the paintings of the Dutch Vincent Van Gogh (1853–90), the German-born American Albert Bierstadt (1830–1902), the French Claude Monet (1840–1926), and the Italian Leonardo da Vinci (1452–1519).

tlement vying to have him, he had chosen Ararat. Because of the pictures of Earth, because of the light of Earth in that room, shining on the green fields, the snowy peaks, the golden forests of autumn, the flight of gulls above the sea, the white and red and rose of waterlilies on blue pools—clear colors, true, pure, the colors of the Earth.

He slept there now, a handsome old man. Outside, in the hard, dull, orange daylight, he would look sick and old, his cheeks veined and muddy. Here you could see what he looked like.

Miriam sat down near him, facing her favorite picture, a quiet landscape by Corot, trees over a silvery stream.[5] She was so tired that for once she was willing to just sit, in a mild stupor. Through the stupor, faintly, idly, words came floating. Couldn't it be . . . honestly, couldn't it be that the metas are worse . . . Miriam, honestly, couldn't it be . . .

"Do you think I never thought of that?" she retorted in silence. "Idiot! Do you think I don't know the metas are hard on your guts? Didn't I try fifty different combinations while you were a kid, trying to get rid of the side effects? But it's not as bad as being allergic to the whole damn planet! You know better than the doctor, do you? Don't give me that. You're trying to—" But she broke off the silent dialogue abruptly. Genya was not trying to kill himself. He was not. He would not. He had courage, that one. And brains.

"All right," she said to the quiet young man in her mind. "All right! If you'll stay in the infirmary, under observation—for two weeks, and do exactly what I say—all right, I'll try it!"

Because, said another, even quieter voice deep in her, it doesn't really matter. Whatever you do or don't do, he will die. This year; next year. Two hours; twenty-four years. The sicklies can't adjust to this world. And neither can we, neither can we. We weren't meant to live here, Genya my dear. We weren't made for this world, nor it for us. We were made of Earth, by Earth, to live on Earth, under the blue sky and the golden sun.

The dinner gong began to ring. Going into the refectory she met little Shura. The child carried a bunch of the repulsive blackish-purple native weeds, as a child at home would carry a bunch of white daisies, red poppies picked in the fields. Shura's eyes were teary as usual, but she smiled up at Auntie Doctor. Her lips looked pallid in the red-orange light of sunset through the windows. Everybody's lips looked pallid. Everybody's face looked tired, set, stoical, after the long day's work, as they went into the Settlement dining hall, all together, the three hundred exiles of Ararat on Zion, the eleventh lost tribe.[6]

He was doing very well. She had to admit it. "You're doing well," she said, and he, with his grin, "I told you so!"

"It could be because you're not doing anything else," she said, "smart ass."

"Not doing anything? I filed health records for Geza all morning, I played

5. I.e., a typical work by French painter Jean-Baptiste-Camille Corot (1796–1875). 6. In popular legend, the ten northern Hebrew tribes captured by the Assyrians in the eighth century B.C. have reappeared at various times and places.

games with Rosie and Moishe for two hours, I've been grinding colors all afternoon—say, I need more mineral oil, can I have another litre? It's a much better pigment vehicle than the vegetable oil."

"Sure. But listen. I have something for you better than that. Little Tel Aviv has got their pulp mill going full time. They sent a truck over yesterday with paper—"

"Paper?"

"Half a ton of it! I took two hundred sheets for you. It's in the office." He was off like a shot, and was into the bundle of paper before she even got there. "Oh, God," he said, holding up a sheet, "beautiful, it's beautiful!" And she thought how often she had heard him say that, "beautiful!" of one drab useful thing or another. He didn't know what beauty was; he'd never seen any. The paper was thick, substantial, greyish, in big sheets, intended to be cut small and used sparingly, of course; but let him have it for his painting. There was little enough else she could give him.

"When you let me out of here," Genya said, hugging the unwieldy bundle with both arms, "I'll go over to Tel Aviv and paint their pulp mill, I'll immortalise their pulp mill!"

"You'd better go lie down."

"No, listen, I promised Moishe I'd beat him at chess. What's wrong with him, anyhow?"

"Rashes, edema."

"He's like me?"

Miriam shrugged. "He was fine till this year. Puberty triggered something. Not unusual with allergic symptoms."

"What is allergy, anyhow?"

"Well, call it a failure of adaptation. Back home, people used to feed babies cows' milk, from bottles. Some of the babies could adapt to it, but some got rashes, breathing trouble, colic. The cow's key didn't fit their metabolic lock. Well, New Zion's protein keys don't fit our locks; so we have to change our metabolism with the metas."

"Would Moishe or I have been an allergic on Earth?"

"I don't know. Prematures often are. Irving, he died, oh, twenty years ago, he was allergic to this terrible list of things on Earth, they should never have let him come, poor thing, he spends his life on Earth half suffocated and comes here and starves to death even on a quadruple dose of metas."

"Aha," said Genya, "you shouldn't have given him metas at all. Just Zion mush."

"Zion mush?" Only one of the native grains yielded enough to be worth harvesting, and it produced a gluey meal which could not be baked.

"I ate three bowls of it for lunch."

"He lies around the hospital all day complaining," Miriam said, "and then stuffs his belly with that slop. How can an artistic soul eat something that tastes like jellied bilge?"

"You feed it to your helpless child patients in your own hospital! I just ate the leftovers."

"Oh, get along with you."

"I am. I want to paint while the sun's still up. On a piece of new paper, a whole piece of new paper. . . ."

It had been a long day at the clinic, but there were no inpatients. She had sent Osip home last night in a cast with a good scolding for being so careless as to tip his tractor over, endangering not only his life but the tractor, which was even harder to replace. And young Moishe had gone back to the children's house, though she didn't like the way his rash kept coming back. And Rosie was over her asthma, and the Commander's heart was doing as well as could be expected; so the ward was empty, except for her permanent inmate of the past two weeks, Genya.

He was sprawled out on his bed under the window, so lax and still that she had a moment of alarm; but his color was good, he breathed evenly, he was simply asleep, deeply asleep, the way people slept after a hard day in the fields, exhausted.

He had been painting. He had cleaned up the rags and brushes, he always cleaned up promptly and thoroughly, but the picture stood on his makeshift easel. Usually these days he was secretive about his paintings, hid them, since people had stopped admiring them. The Commander had murmured to her, "What ugly stuff, poor boy!" But she had heard young Moishe, watching Genya paint, say, "How do you do it, Genya, how do you make it so pretty?" and Genya answer, "Beauty's in the eye, Moishe."

Well, that was true, and she went closer to look at the painting in the dull afternoon light. Genya had painted the view out the big window of the ward. Nothing vague and half created this time: realistic, all too realistic. Hideously recognisable. There was the flat ridge of Ararat, the mud-colored trees and fields, the hazy sky, the storage barn and a corner of the school building in the foreground. Her eyes went from the painted scene to the real one. To spend hours, days, painting that! What a waste, what a waste.

It was hard on Genya, it was sad, the way he hid his paintings now, knowing that nobody would want to see them, except maybe a child like Moishe fascinated with the mere skill of the hand, the craftsman's dexterity.

That night as Genya helped her straighten up the injection cabinets—he was a good deal of help around the infirmary these days—she said, "I like the picture you painted today."

"I finished it today," he corrected her. "Damn thing took all week. I'm just beginning to learn to see."

"Can I put it up in the Living Room?"

He looked at her across a tray of hypodermic needles, his eyes quiet and a little quizzical. "In the Living Room? But that's all pictures of Home."

"It's time maybe we had some pictures of our new home there."

"A moral gesture, eh? Sure. If you like it."

"I like it very much," she lied blandly.

"It isn't bad," he said. "I'll do better, though, when I've learned how to fit myself to the pattern."

"What pattern?"

"Well, you know, you have to look until you *see* the pattern, till it makes sense, and then you have to get that into your hand, too." He made large, vague, shaping gestures with a bottle of absolute alcohol.

"Anybody who asks a painter a question in words deserves what they get, I guess," said Miriam. "Babble, babble. You take the picture over tomorrow and put it up. Artists are so temperamental about where they get their pictures hung, and the lighting. Besides, it's time you were getting out. A little. An hour or two a day. No more."

"Can I eat dinner in the dining hall, then?"

"All right. It'll keep Tina from coming here to keep you from being lonely and eating up all the infirmary rations. That girl eats like a vacuum pump. Listen, if you go out in the middle of the day, will you kindly take the trouble to wear a hat?"

"You think I'm right, then."

"Right?"

"That it was sunstroke."

"That was *my* diagnosis, if you will recall."

"All right: but my addition was that I do better without metas."

"I have no idea. You've got along fine before for weeks, and then poof, down again. Nothing whatever has been proved."

"But a pattern has been established! I've lived a month without metas, and gained six pounds."

"And edema of the head, Mr. Know It All?"

She saw him the next day sitting with Rachel, just before dinnertime, on the slope below the storage barn. Rachel had not come to see him in the infirmary. They sat side by side, very close together, motionless, not talking.

Miriam went on to the Living Room. A half hour there before dinner had become a habit with her lately. It seemed to rest her from the weariness of the day. But the room was less peaceful than usual this evening; the Commander was awake, and talking with Reine and Avram. "Well, where did it come from then?" he was saying in his heavy Italian accent—he had not learned Hebrew till he was forty, in the Transit Camp. "Who put it there?" Then seeing Miriam he greeted her as always with a grand cordiality of voice and gesture. "Ah, Doctor! Please join us, come, solve our mystery for us. You know each picture in this room as well as I do. Where, do you think, and when did we acquire the new one? You see?"

It's Genya's, Miriam was about to say, when she saw the new picture. It wasn't Genya's. It was a painting, all right, a landscape, but a landscape of the Earth: a wide valley, the fields green and green-gold, orchards coming into flower, the sweeping slope of a mountain in the distance, a tower, perhaps a castle or medieval farm building, in the foreground, and over all the pure, subtle, sunlit sky. It was a complex and happy painting, a celebration of the spring, an act of praise.

"How beautiful," she said, her voice catching. "Didn't you put it up, Avram?"

"Me? I can photograph, I can't paint. Look at it, it's no reproduction. Some kind of tempera or oils, see?"

"Somebody brought it from Home. Had it in their baggage," Reine suggested.

"For twenty-five years?" said the Commander. "Why? And who? We all know what all the others have!"

"No. I think"—Miriam was confused, and stammered—"I think it's something Genya did. I asked him to put up one of his paintings here. Not this one. How did he do this?"

"Copied from a photograph," Avram suggested.

"No no no no, impossible," old Marca said, outraged. "That is a painting, not a copy! That is a work of art, that was seen, seen with the eyes and the heart!"

With the eyes and the heart.

Miriam looked, and she saw. She saw what the light of NSC 641 had hidden from her, what the artificial Earth daylight of the room revealed to her. She saw what Genya saw: the beauty of the world.

"I think it must be in Central France, the Auvergne," Reine was saying wistfully, and the Commander, "Oh no no no, it's near Lake Como, I am certain," and Avram, "Well it looks to me like where I grew up in the Caucasus," when they all turned to look at Miriam. She had made a strange noise, a gasp or laugh or sob. "It's here," she said. "Here. That's Ararat. The mountain. That's the fields, our fields, our trees. That's the corner of the school, that tower. See it? It's here. Zion. It's how Genya sees it. With the eyes and the heart."

"But look, the trees are green, look at the colors, Miriam. It's Earth—"

"Yes! It is Earth. Genya's Earth!"

"But he can't—"

"How do we know? How do we know what a child of Zion sees? We can see the picture in this light that's like Home. Take it outside, into the daylight, and you'll see what we always see, the ugly colors, the ugly planet where we're not at home. But he is at home! He is! It's we," Miriam said, laughing in tears, looking at them all, the anxious, tired, elderly faces, "*we* who lack the key. We with our—with our—" she stumbled and leapt at the idea like a horse at a high wall, "with our meta pills!"

They all stared at her.

"With our meta pills, we can survive here, just barely, right? But don't you see, he *lives* here! We were all perfectly adjusted to Earth, too well, we can't fit anywhere else—he wasn't, wouldn't have been; allergic, a misfit—the pattern a little wrong, see? The pattern. But there are many patterns, infinite patterns, he fits this one a little better than we do—"

Avram and the Commander continued to stare. Reine shot an alarmed glance at the picture, but asked gamely, "You're saying that Genya's allergies—"

"Not just Genya! All the sicklies, maybe! For twenty-five years I've been feeding them metas, and they're allergic to *Earth* proteins, the metas just foul them up, they're a different pattern, oh, idiot! Idiot! Oh, my God, he and Rachel can get married. They've got to marry, he should have kids. What about Rachel taking metas while she's pregnant, the foetus. I can work it out, I can work it out. I must call Leonid. And Moishe, thank God! maybe he's another one! Listen, I must go talk to Genya and Rachel, immediately. Excuse me!" She left, a short, grey woman moving like a lightning bolt.

Marca, Avram, and Reine stood staring after her, at each other, and finally back at Genya's painting.

It hung there before them, serene and joyful, full of light.

"I don't understand," said Avram.

"Patterns," Reine said thoughtfully.

"It is very beautiful," said the old Commander of the Exile Fleet. "Only, it makes me homesick."

1982

JORGE LUIS BORGES

The Garden of Forking Paths[1]

FOR *Victoria Ocampo*

On page 22 of Liddell Hart's *History of World War I* you will read that an attack against the Serre-Montauban[2] line by thirteen British divisions (supported by 1,400 artillery pieces), planned for the 24th of July, 1916, had to be postponed until the morning of the 29th. The torrential rains, Captain Liddell Hart comments, caused this delay, an insignificant one, to be sure.

The following statement, dictated, reread and signed by Dr. Yu Tsun, former professor of English at the *Hochschule* at Tsingtao,[3] throws an unsuspected light over the whole affair. The first two pages of the document are missing.

". . . and I hung up the receiver. Immediately afterwards, I recognized the voice that had answered in German. It was that of Captain Richard Madden. Madden's presence in Viktor Runeberg's apartment meant the end of our anxieties and—but this seemed, *or should have seemed,* very secondary to me—also the end of our lives. It meant that Runeberg had been arrested or murdered.[4] Before the sun set on that day, I would encounter the same fate. Madden was implacable. Or rather, he was obliged to be so. An Irishman at the service of

1. Translated by Donald A. Yates. 2. Liddell Hart's work is entitled *The Real War, 1914–1918* (1930) and *A History of the World War, 1914–1918* in the enlarged English-language edition (1934). The events of July 1916 do not appear on page 22 in the first and are unlikely to appear so early in any edition. A line between Serre and Montauban forms a defensive position about a hundred miles north-northeast of Paris, north of the Somme River. There is a dizzying mixture of factual references and fiction in this story, the most unlikely often being the factual. 3. The high school in what was the capital of the German colonial enclave in China until the First World War. 4. An hypothesis both hateful and odd, The Prussian spy Hans Rabener, alias Viktor Runeberg, attacked with drawn automatic the bearer of the warrant for his arrest, Captain Richard Madden. The latter, in self-defense, inflicted the wound which brought about Runeberg's death. (Borges's note.)

England, a man accused of laxity and perhaps of treason, how could he fail to seize and be thankful for such a miraculous opportunity: the discovery, capture, maybe even the death of two agents of the German Reich? I went up to my room; absurdly I locked the door and threw myself on my back on the narrow iron cot. Through the window I saw the familiar roofs and the cloud-shaded six o'clock sun. It seemed incredible to me that that day without premonitions or symbols should be the one of my inexorable death. In spite of my dead father, in spite of having been a child in a symmetrical garden of Hai Feng,[5] was I—now—going to die? Then I reflected that everything happens to a man precisely, precisely *now*. Centuries of centuries and only in the present do things happen; countless men in the air, on the face of the earth and the sea, and all that really is happening is happening to me . . . The almost intolerable recollection of Madden's horselike face banished these wanderings. In the midst of my hatred and terror (it means nothing to me now to speak of terror, now that I have mocked Richard Madden, now that my throat yearns for the noose) it occurred to me that that tumultuous and doubtless happy warrior did not suspect that I possessed the Secret. The name of the exact location of the new British artillery park on the River Ancre.[6] A bird streaked across the gray sky and blindly I translated it into an airplane and that airplane into many (against the French sky) annihilating the artillery station with vertical bombs. If only my mouth, before a bullet shattered it, could cry out that secret name so it could be heard in Germany . . . My human voice was very weak. How might I make it carry to the ear of the Chief? To the ear of that sick and hateful man who knew nothing of Runeberg and me save that we were in Staffordshire[7] and who was waiting in vain for our report in his arid office in Berlin, endlessly examining newspapers . . . I said out loud: *I must flee*. I sat up noiselessly, in a useless perfection of silence, as if Madden were already lying in wait for me. Something—perhaps the mere vain ostentation of proving my resources were nil—made me look through my pockets. I found what I knew I would find. The American watch, the nickel chain and the square coin, the key ring with the incriminating useless keys to Runeberg's apartment, the notebook, a letter which I resolved to destroy immediately (and which I did not destroy), a crown, two shillings and a few pence, the red and blue pencil, the handkerchief, the revolver with one bullet. Absurdly, I took it in my hand and weighed it in order to inspire courage within myself. Vaguely I thought that a pistol report can be heard at a great distance. In ten minutes my plan was perfected. The telephone book listed the name of the only person capable of transmitting the message; he lived in a suburb of Fenton, less than a half hour's train ride away.

I am a cowardly man. I say it now, now that I have carried to its end a plan whose perilous nature no one can deny. I know its execution was terrible. I didn't do it for Germany, no. I care nothing for a barbarous country which imposed

5. Chinese gardens usually aim for the appearance of nature, so a symmetrical garden would be unusual. Hai Feng seems fictional, as many names here are, but Hai-fang is Chinese for the Vietnamese city of Haiphong and is near the Yunnan province mentioned later. 6. River in northeastern France. 7. County in West Central England.

upon me the abjection of being a spy. Besides, I know of a man from England—a modest man—who for me is no less great than Goethe. I talked with him for scarcely an hour, but during that hour he was Goethe . . . I did it because I sensed that the Chief somehow feared people of my race—for the innumerable ancestors who merge within me. I wanted to prove to him that a yellow man could save his armies. Besides, I had to flee from Captain Madden. His hands and his voice could call at my door at any moment. I dressed silently, bade farewell to myself in the mirror, went downstairs, scrutinized the peaceful street and went out. The station was not far from my home, but I judged it wise to take a cab. I argued that in this way I ran less risk of being recognized; the fact is that in the deserted street I felt myself visible and vulnerable, infinitely so. I remember that I told the cab driver to stop a short distance before the main entrance. I got out with voluntary, almost painful slowness; I was going to the village of Ashgrove but I bought a ticket for a more distant station. The train left within a very few minutes, at eight-fifty. I hurried; the next one would leave at nine-thirty. There was hardly a soul on the platform. I went through the coaches; I remember a few farmers, a woman dressed in mourning, a young boy who was reading with fervor the *Annals* of Tacitus,[8] a wounded and happy soldier. The coaches jerked forward at last. A man whom I recognized ran in vain to the end of the platform. It was Captain Richard Madden. Shattered, trembling, I shrank into the far corner of the seat, away from the dreaded window.

From this broken state I passed into an almost abject felicity. I told myself 5
that the duel had already begun and that I had won the first encounter by frustrating, even if for forty minutes, even if by a stroke of fate, the attack of my adversary. I argued that this slightest of victories foreshadowed a total victory. I argued (no less fallaciously) that my cowardly felicity proved that I was a man capable of carrying out the adventure successfully. From this weakness I took strength that did not abandon me. I foresee that man will resign himself each day to more atrocious undertakings; soon there will be no one but warriors and brigands; I give them this counsel: *The author of an atrocious undertaking ought to imagine that he has already accomplished it, ought to impose upon himself a future as irrevocable as the past.* Thus I proceeded as my eyes of a man already dead registered the elapsing of that day, which was perhaps the last, and the diffusion of the night. The train ran gently along, amid ash trees. It stopped, almost in the middle of the fields. No one announced the name of the station. "Ashgrove?" I asked a few lads on the platform. "Ashgrove," they replied. I got off.

A lamp enlightened the platform but the faces of the boys were in shadow. One questioned me, "Are you going to Dr. Stephen Albert's house?" Without waiting for my answer, another said, "The house is a long way from here, but you won't get lost if you take this road to the left and at every crossroads turn again to your left." I tossed them a coin (my last), descended a few stone steps

8. The annals of Cornelius Tacitus (55?–117?) treat the history of Rome from the death of Augustus in 14 to the end of Nero's reign in 68, and the military events of the period.

and started down the solitary road. It went downhill, slowly. It was of elemental earth; overhead the branches were tangled; the low, full moon seemed to accompany me.

For an instant, I thought that Richard Madden in some way had penetrated my desperate plan. Very quickly, I understood that that was impossible. The instructions to turn always to the left reminded me that such was the common procedure for discovering the central point of certain labyrinths. I have some understanding of labyrinths: not for nothing am I the great grandson of that Ts'ui Pên who was governor of Yunnan[9] and who renounced worldly power in order to write a novel that might be even more populous than the *Hung Lu Meng*[1] and to construct a labyrinth in which all men would become lost. Thirteen years he dedicated to these heterogeneous tasks, but the hand of a stranger murdered him—and his novel was incoherent and no one found the labyrinth. Beneath English trees I meditated on that lost maze: I imagined it inviolate and perfect at the secret crest of a mountain; I imagined it erased by rice fields or beneath the water; I imagined it infinite, no longer composed of octagonal kiosks and returning paths, but of rivers and provinces and kingdoms . . . I thought of a labyrinth of labyrinths, of one sinuous spreading labyrinth that would encompass the past and the future and in some way involve the stars. Absorbed in these illusory images, I forgot my destiny of one pursued. I felt myself to be, for an unknown period of time, an abstract perceiver of the world. The vague, living countryside, the moon, the remains of the day worked on me, as well as the slope of the road which eliminated any possibility of weariness. The afternoon was intimate, infinite. The road descended and forked among the now confused meadows. A high-pitched, almost syllabic music approached and receded in the shifting of the wind, dimmed by leaves and distance. I thought that a man can be an enemy of other men, of the moments of other men, but not of a country: not of fireflies, words, gardens, streams of water, sunsets. Thus I arrived before a tall, rusty gate. Between the iron bars I made out a poplar grove and a pavilion. I understood suddenly two things, the first trivial, the second almost unbelievable: the music came from the pavilion, and the music was Chinese. For precisely that reason I had openly accepted it without paying it any heed. I do not remember whether there was a bell or whether I knocked with my hand. The sparkling of the music continued.

From the rear of the house within a lantern approached: a lantern that the trees sometimes striped and sometimes eclipsed, a paper lantern that had the form of a drum and the color of the moon. A tall man bore it. I didn't see his face for the light blinded me. He opened the door and said slowly, in my own language: "I see that the pious Hsi P'êng persists in correcting my solitude. You no doubt wish to see the garden?"

I recognized the name of one of our consuls and I replied, disconcerted, "The garden?"

10 "The garden of forking paths."

9. Southwesternmost of China's eighteen traditional provinces; beautiful but sparsely populated, damp and malarial. 1. *Dream of the Red Chamber*, long semiautobiographical novel by Ts'ao Chan (1715–1763) with more than 430 characters.

Something stirred in my memory and I uttered with incomprehensible certainty, "The garden of my ancestor Ts'ui Pên."

"Your ancestor? Your illustrious ancestor? Come in."

The damp path zigzagged like those of my childhood. We came to a library of Eastern and Western books. I recognized bound in yellow silk several volumes of the Lost Encyclopedia, edited by the Third Emperor of the Luminous Dynasty[2] but never printed. The record on the phonograph revolved next to a bronze phoenix. I also recall a *famille rose*[3] vase and another, many centuries older, of that shade of blue which our craftsmen copied from the potters of Persia . . .

Stephen Albert observed me with a smile. He was, as I have said, very tall, sharp-featured, with gray eyes and a gray beard. He told me that he had been a missionary in Tientsin "before aspiring to become a Sinologist."

We sat down—I on a long, low divan, he with his back to the window and a tall circular clock. I calculated that my pursuer, Richard Madden, could not arrive for at least an hour. My irrevocable determination could wait.

"An astounding fate, that of Ts'ui Pên," Stephen Albert said. "Governor of his native province, learned in astronomy, in astrology and in the tireless interpretation of the canonical books,[4] chess player, famous poet and calligrapher—he abandoned all this in order to compose a book and a maze. He renounced the pleasures of both tyranny and justice, of his populous couch, of his banquets and even of erudition—all to close himself up for thirteen years in the Pavilion of the Limpid Solitude.[5] When he died, his heirs found nothing save chaotic manuscripts. His family, as you may be aware, wished to condemn them to the fire; but his executor—a Taoist or Buddhist monk—insisted on their publication."

"We descendants of Ts'ui Pên," I replied, "continue to curse that monk. Their publication was senseless. The book is an indeterminate heap of contradictory drafts. I examined it once: in the third chapter the hero dies, in the fourth he is alive. As for the other undertaking of Ts'ui Pên, his labyrinth . . ."

"Here is Ts'ui Pên's labyrinth," he said, indicating a tall lacquered desk.

"An ivory labyrinth!" I exclaimed. "A minimum labyrinth."

"A labyrinth of symbols," he corrected. "An invisible labyrinth of time. To me, a barbarous Englishman, has been entrusted the revelation of this diaphanous mystery. After more than a hundred years, the details are irretrievable; but it is not hard to conjecture what happened. Ts'ui Pên must have said once: *I am withdrawing to write a book*. And another time: *I am withdrawing to construct a labyrinth*. Every one imagined two works; to no one did it occur that the book and the maze were one and the same thing. The Pavilion of the Limpid Solitude stood in the center of a garden that was perhaps intricate; that circum-

2. The "Luminous" Dynasty is the Ming; its third emperor, Yung-lo, reigned 1402–1424. He commissioned a compilation of all significant work done on Chinese history, government, philosophy, geography, etc., which, though incomplete, ran to over 11,000 of the small Chinese volumes—too long to be printed. 3. "Rose family" Chinese porcelain, characterized by rose glaze over the decoration. 4. The Confucian classics which officials had to know thoroughly and apply to contemporary social and political issues. 5. The names of both Ts'ui Pên and the Pavilion seem fictitious.

stance could have suggested to the heirs a physical labyrinth. Ts'ui Pên died; no one in the vast territories that were his came upon the labyrinth; the confusion of the novel suggested to me that *it* was the maze. Two circumstances gave me the correct solution of the problem. One: the curious legend that Ts'ui Pên had planned to create a labyrinth which would be strictly infinite. The other: a fragment of a letter I discovered."

Albert rose. He turned his back on me for a moment; he opened a drawer of the black and gold desk. He faced me and in his hands he held a sheet of paper that had once been crimson, but was now pink and tenuous and cross-sectioned. The fame of Ts'ui Pên as a calligrapher had been justly won. I read, uncomprehendingly and with fervor, these words written with a minute brush by a man of my blood: *I leave to the various futures (not to all) my garden of forking paths.* Wordlessly, I returned the sheet. Albert continued:

"Before unearthing this letter, I had questioned myself about the ways in which a book can be infinite. I could think of nothing other than a cyclic volume, a circular one. A book whose last page was identical with the first, a book which had the possibility of continuing indefinitely. I remembered too that night which is at the middle of the Thousand and One Nights when Scheherazade (through a magical oversight of the copyist) begins to relate word for word the story of the Thousand and One Nights, establishing the risk of coming once again to the night when she must repeat it, and thus on to infinity. I imagined as well a Platonic, hereditary work, transmitted from father to son, in which each new individual adds a chapter or corrects with pious care the pages of his elders. These conjectures diverted me; but none seemed to correspond, not even remotely, to the contradictory chapters of Ts'ui Pên. In the midst of this perplexity, I received from Oxford the manuscript you have examined. I lingered, naturally, on the sentence: *I leave to the various futures (not to all) my garden of forking paths.* Almost instantly, I understood: 'The garden of forking paths' was the chaotic novel; the phrase 'the various futures (not to all)' suggested to me the forking in time, not in space. A broad rereading of the work confirmed the theory. In all fictional works, each time a man is confronted with several alternatives, he chooses one and eliminates the others; in the fiction of Ts'ui Pên, he chooses—simultaneously—all of them. *He creates,* in this way, diverse futures, diverse times which themselves also proliferate and fork. Here, then, is the explanation of the novel's contradictions. Fang, let us say, has a secret; a stranger calls at his door; Fang resolves to kill him. Naturally, there are several possible outcomes: Fang can kill the intruder, the intruder can kill Fang, they both can escape, they both can die, and so forth. In the work of Ts'ui Pên, all possible outcomes occur; each one is the point of departure for other forkings. Sometimes, the paths of this labyrinth converge: for example, you arrive at this house, but in one of the possible pasts you are my enemy, in another, my friend. If you will resign yourself to my incurable pronunciation, we shall read a few pages."

His face, within the vivid circle of the lamplight, was unquestionably that of an old man, but with something unalterable about it, even immortal. He read with slow precision two versions of the same epic chapter. In the first, an army marches to a battle across a lonely mountain; the horror of the rocks and shadows makes the men undervalue their lives and they gain an easy victory. In the second, the same army traverses a palace where a great festival is taking place; the resplendent battle seems to them a continuation of the celebration and they win the victory. I listened with proper veneration to these ancient narratives, perhaps less admirable in themselves than the fact that they had been created by my blood and were being restored to me by a man of a remote empire, in the course of a desperate adventure, on a Western isle. I remember the last words, repeated in each version like a secret commandment: *Thus fought the heroes, tranquil their admirable hearts, violent their swords, resigned to kill and to die.*

From that moment on, I felt about me and within my dark body an invisible, intangible swarming. Not the swarming of the divergent, parallel and finally coalescent armies, but a more inaccessible, more intimate agitation that they in some manner prefigured. Stephen Albert continued:

"I don't believe that your illustrious ancestor played idly with these variations. I don't consider it credible that he would sacrifice thirteen years to the infinite execution of a rhetorical experiment. In your country, the novel is a subsidiary form of literature; in Ts'ui Pên's time it was a despicable form. Ts'ui Pên was a brilliant novelist, but he was also a man of letters who doubtless did not consider himself a mere novelist. The testimony of his contemporaries proclaims—and his life fully confirms—his metaphysical and mystical interests. Philosophic controversy usurps a good part of the novel. I know that of all problems, none disturbed him so greatly nor worked upon him so much as the abysmal problem of time. Now then, the latter is the only problem that does not figure in the pages of the *Garden*. He does not even use the word that signifies *time*. How do you explain this voluntary omission?"

I proposed several solutions—all unsatisfactory. We discussed them. Finally, Stephen Albert said to me:

"In a riddle whose answer is chess, what is the only prohibited word?"

I thought a moment and replied, "The word *chess*."

"Precisely," said Albert. "*The Garden of Forking Paths* is an enormous riddle, or parable, whose theme is time; this recondite cause prohibits its mention. To omit a word always, to resort to inept metaphors and obvious periphrases, is perhaps the most emphatic way of stressing it. That is the tortuous method preferred, in each of the meanderings of his indefatigable novel, by the oblique Ts'ui Pên. I have compared hundreds of manuscripts, I have corrected the errors that the negligence of the copyists has introduced, I have guessed the plan of this chaos, I have re-established—I believe I have re-established—the primordial organization, I have translated the entire work: it is clear to me that not once does he employ the word 'time.' The explanation is obvious: *The Garden of Forking Paths* is an incomplete, but not false, image of the universe as Ts'ui Pên conceived it. In contrast to Newton and Schopenhauer, your ancestor did not believe in a uniform, absolute time. He believed in an infinite series of times, in a growing, dizzying net of divergent, convergent and parallel times. This network of times which approached one another, forked, broke off, or were unaware of one another for centuries, embraces *all* possibilities of time. We do not exist in the majority of these times; in some you exist, and not I; in others I, and not you; in others, both of us. In the present one, which a favorable fate has granted me, you have arrived at my house; in another, while crossing the garden, you found me dead; in still another, I utter these same words, but I am a mistake, a ghost."

30 "In every one," I pronounced, not without a tremble to my voice, "I am grateful to you and revere you for your re-creation of the garden of Ts'ui Pên."

"Not in all," he murmured with a smile. "Time forks perpetually toward innumerable futures. In one of them I am your enemy."

Once again I felt the swarming sensation of which I have spoken. It seemed to me that the humid garden that surrounded the house was infinitely saturated with invisible persons. Those persons were Albert and I, secret, busy and multiform in other dimensions of time. I raised my eyes and the tenuous nightmare dissolved. In the yellow and black garden there was only one man; but this man was as strong as a statue . . . this man was approaching along the path and he was Captain Richard Madden.

"The future already exists," I replied, "but I am your friend. Could I see the letter again?"

Albert rose. Standing tall, he opened the drawer of the tall desk; for the moment his back was to me. I had readied the revolver. I fired with extreme caution. Albert fell uncomplainingly, immediately. I swear his death was instantaneous—a lightning stroke.

35 The rest is unreal, insignificant. Madden broke in, arrested me. I have been condemned to the gallows. I have won out abominably; I have communicated to Berlin the secret name of the city they must attack. They bombed it yesterday; I read it in the same papers that offered to England the mystery of the learned Sinologist Stephen Albert who was murdered by a stranger, one Yu Tsun. The Chief had deciphered this mystery. He knew my problem was to indicate (through the uproar of the war) the city called Albert, and that I had found no other means to do so than to kill a man of that name. He does not know (no one can know) my innumerable contrition and weariness.

1962

QUESTIONS

1. Is the old man in the García Márquez story a symbol? If so, does he "stand for" something you can name or paraphrase? if he does, what is it? If not, how can he be a symbol? If we do not read this story symbolically, how can we deal with its fantastic elements? take the story as "serious literature"?

2. What humorous elements do you find in "A Very Old Man with Enormous Wings"? How do these function in the story?

3. What is the theme of "The Eye Altering"? How might it be related to all art? to racism? gender differences?

4. Explain in your own words Ts'ui Pên's theory of the universe in "The Garden of Forking Paths." Is this universe "fantasy"? In what ways may this story be considered science fiction?

5. Toward the end of Borges's story "the rest" is said to be "insignificant," though it includes what seem to be important matters like Yu's arrest and condemnation; explain. In what sense is the rest of the rest—the delivery of the message to The Chief—insignificant? Explain the final sentence of the story.

6. What is "the garden of forking paths"?

WRITING SUGGESTIONS

1. Compare the way people or "the public" view the unusual or extraordinary in "A Very Old Man with Enormous Wings" and "A Hunger Artist" and / or the way the stories view people or the public.

2. Compare the views of art and society or art and reality in "The Eye Altering" and one or more of the following: "The Zebra Storyteller," "The Real Thing," "A Hunger Artist."

3. "The garden of forking paths" is an image of the theme (as suggested in question 6 above) but it may also be an image of the path of your expectations as you read through the story. Retrace your anticipations of what would happen next or what things seem to mean when you first read at least the first eight paragraphs of the story.

Evaluating Fiction

To evaluate a work of literature—to determine its worth or quality—is one of the most fundamental, significant, and difficult activities in literary study. It is impossible to dodge such questions as "Is this story good?" "Is it great?" "Is it better than that one? . . . that other one?" "Is it worth reading? studying?" It is equally impossible to answer such questions definitively, for all time and for all readers.

It is, however, usually possible to answer the question, "Do you like this story?" and often possible to answer "Do you like this one more than or less than that other?" Whether you like a story or not when you first read it is therefore probably the proper place to *begin*. But it is a dangerous place to *stop* the process of evaluation. If our appreciation and understanding of literature is to grow, and if we are not content simply to accept without question the authority of "those who know best," we must learn to isolate, analyze, and articulate what it is *we* like about a story and to search out in our minds and experience the reasons *we* like it. We must listen to other readers' responses too, responses that may reinforce our own, may show us things to appreciate in the story that we missed, or may challenge the viability of our reasons, if not that of our responses.

Let us begin by reading a story together. Let's see how we like it, and what we can say about it.

RICHARD CONNELL

The Most Dangerous Game

"Off there to the right—somewhere—is a large island," said Whitney. "It's rather a mystery—"

"What island is it?" Rainsford asked.

The old charts call it 'Ship-Trap Island,' " Whitney replied. "A suggestive name, isn't it? Sailors have a curious dread of the place. I don't know why. Some superstition—"

"Can't see it," remarked Rainsford, trying to peer through the dank tropical night that was palpable as it pressed its thick warm blackness in upon the yacht.

"You've good eyes," said Whitney, with a laugh, "and I've seen you pick off a moose moving in the brown fall bush at four hundred yards, but even you can't see four miles or so through a moonless Caribbean night."

"Nor four yards," admitted Rainsford. "Ugh! It's like moist black velvet."

"It will be light in Rio," promised Whitney. "We should make it in a few days. I hope the jaguar guns have come from Purdey's. We should have some good hunting up the Amazon. Great sport, hunting."

"The best sport in the world," agreed Rainsford.

"For the hunter," amended Whitney. "Not for the jaguar."

"Don't talk rot, Whitney," said Rainsford. "You're a big-game hunter, not a philosopher. Who cares how a jaguar feels?"

"Perhaps the jaguar does," observed Whitney.

"Bah! They've no understanding."

"Even so, I rather think they understand one thing—fear. The fear of pain and the fear of death."

"Nonsense," laughed Rainsford. "This hot weather is making you soft, Whitney. Be a realist. The world is made up of two classes—the hunters and the huntees. Luckily, you and I are hunters. Do you think we've passed that island yet?"

"I can't tell in the dark. I hope so."

"Why? asked Rainsford.

"The place has a reputation—a bad one."

"Cannibals?" suggested Rainsford.

"Hardly. Even cannibals wouldn't live in such a God-forsaken place. But it's gotten into sailor lore, somehow. Didn't you notice that the crew's nerves seemed a bit jumpy today?"

"They were a bit strange, now you mention it. Even Captain Nielsen—"

"Yes, even that tough-minded old Swede, who'd go up to the devil himself and ask him for a light. Those fishy blue eyes held a look I never saw there before. All I could get out of him was: 'This place has an evil name among seafaring men, sir.' Then he said to me, very gravely: 'Don't you feel anything?'—as if the air about us was actually poisonous. Now, you mustn't laugh when I tell you this—I did feel something like a sudden chill.

"There was no breeze. The sea was as flat as a plate-glass window. We were drawing near the island then. What I felt was a—a mental chill; a sort of sudden dread."

"Pure imagination," said Rainsford. "One superstitious sailor can taint the whole ship's company with his fear."

"Maybe. But sometimes I think sailors have an extra sense that tells them when they are in danger. Sometimes I think evil is a tangible thing—with wave lengths, just as sound and light have. An evil place can, so to speak, broadcast vibrations of evil. Anyhow, I'm glad we're getting out of this zone. Well, I think I'll turn in now, Rainsford."

"I'm not sleepy," said Rainsford. "I'm going to smoke another pipe up on the after deck."

"Good night, then, Rainsford. See you at breakfast."

"Right. Good night, Whitney."

There was no sound in the night as Rainsford sat there, but the muffled throb of the engine that drove the yacht swiftly through the darkness, and the swish and ripple of the wash of the propeller.

Rainsford, reclining in a steamer chair, indolently puffed on his favorite brier. The sensuous drowsiness of the night was on him. "It's so dark," he thought, "that I could sleep without closing my eyes; the night would be my eyelids—"

An abrupt sound startled him. Off to the right he heard it, and his ears, expert in such matters, could not be mistaken. Again he heard the sound, and again. Somewhere, off in the blackness, some one had fired a gun three times.

Rainsford sprang up and moved quickly to the rail, mystified. He strained his eyes in the direction from which the reports had come, but it was like trying to see through a blanket. He leaped upon the rail and balanced himself there, to get greater elevation; his pipe, striking a rope, was knocked from his mouth. He lunged for it; a short, hoarse cry came from his lips as he realized he had reached too far and had lost his balance. The cry was pinched off short as the bloodwarm waters of the Caribbean Sea closed over his head.

He struggled up to the surface and tried to cry out, but the wash from the speeding yacht slapped him in the face and the salt water in his open mouth made him gag and strangle. Desperately he struck out with strong strokes after the receding lights of the yacht, but he stopped before he had swum fifty feet. A certain cool-headedness had come to him; it was not the first time he had been in a tight place. There was a chance that his cries could be heard by some one aboard the yacht, but that chance was slender, and grew more slender as the yacht raced on. He wrestled himself out of his clothes, and shouted with all his power. The lights of the yacht became faint and ever-vanishing fireflies; then they were blotted out entirely by the night.

Rainsford remembered the shots. They had come from the right, and doggedly he swam in that direction, swimming with slow, deliberate strokes, conserving his strength. For a seemingly endless time he fought the sea. He began to count his strokes; he could do possibly a hundred more and then—

Rainsford heard a sound. It came out of the darkness, a high screaming sound, the sound of an animal in an extremity of anguish and terror.

He did not recognize the animal that made the sound; he did not try to; with fresh vitality he swam toward the sound. He heard it again; then it was cut short by another noise, crisp, staccato.

"Pistol shot," muttered Rainsford, swimming on.

Ten minutes of determined effort brought another sound to his ears—the most welcome he had ever heard—the muttering and growling of the sea breaking on a rocky shore. He was almost on the rocks before he saw them; on a night less calm he would have been shattered against them. With his remaining strength he dragged himself from the swirling waters. Jagged crags appeared to jut into the opaqueness; he forced himself upward, hand over hand. Gasping, his hands raw, he reached a flat place at the top. Dense jungle came down to the very edge of the cliffs. What perils that tangle of trees and underbrush might hold for him did not concern Rainsford just them. All he knew was that he was safe from his enemy, the sea, and that utter weariness was on him. He flung himself down at the jungle edge and tumbled headlong into the deepest sleep of his life.

When he opened his eyes he knew from the position of the sun that it was late in the afternoon. Sleep had given him new vigor; a sharp hunger was picking at him. He looked about him, almost cheerfully.

"Where there are pistol shots, there are men. Where there are men, there is food," he thought. But what kind of men, he wondered, in so forbidding a place? An unbroken front of snarled and ragged jungle fringed the shore.

He saw no sign of a trail through the closely knit web of weeds and trees; it was easier to go along the shore, and Rainsford floundered along by the water. Not far from where he had landed, he stopped.

Some wounded thing, by the evidence a large animal, had thrashed about in the underbrush; the jungle weeds were crushed down and the moss was lacerated; one patch of weeds was stained crimson. A small, glittering object not far away caught Rainsford's eye and he picked it up. It was an empty cartridge.

"A twenty-two," he remarked. "That's odd. It must have been a fairly large animal too. The hunter had his nerve with him to tackle it with a light gun. It's clear that the brute put up a fight. I suppose the first three shots I heard was when the hunter flushed his quarry and wounded it. The last shot was when he trailed it here and finished it."

He examined the ground closely and found what he had hoped to find—the print of hunting boots. They pointed along the cliff in the direction he had been going. Eagerly, he hurried along, now slipping on a rotten log or a loose stone, but making headway; night was beginning to settle down on the island.

Bleak darkness was blacking out the sea and jungle when Rainsford sighted the lights. He came upon them as he turned a crook in the coast line, and his first thought was that he had come upon a village, for there were many lights. But as he forged along he saw to his great astonishment that all the lights were in one enormous building—a lofty structure with pointed towers plunging upward into the gloom. His eyes made out the shadowy outlines of a palatial château; it was set on a high bluff, and on three sides of it cliffs dived down to where the sea licked greedy lips in the shadows.

"Mirage," thought Rainsford. But it was no mirage, he found, when he opened the tall spiked iron gate. The stone steps were real enough; the massive door with a leering gargoyle for a knocker was real enough; yet about it all hung an air of unreality.

He lifted the knocker, and it creaked up stiffly, as if it had never before been used. He let it fall, and it startled him with its booming loudness. He thought he heard steps within; the door remained closed. Again Rainsford lifted the heavy knocker, and let it fall. The door opened then, opened as suddenly as if it were on a spring, and Rainsford stood blinking in the river of glaring gold light that poured out. The first thing Rainsford's eyes discerned was the largest man Rainsford had ever seen—a gigantic creature, solidly made and blackbearded to the waist. In his hand the man held a long-barreled revolver, and he was pointing it straight at Rainsford's heart.

Out of the snarl of beard two small eyes regarded Rainsford.

"Don't be alarmed," said Rainsford, with a smile which he hoped was disarming. "I'm no robber. I fell off a yacht. My name is Sanger Rainsford of New York City."

The menacing look in the eyes did not change. The revolver pointed as rigidly as if the giant were a statue. He gave no sign that he understood Rainsford's words, or that he had even heard them. He was dressed in uniform, a black uniform trimmed with gray astrakhan.

"I'm Sanger Rainsford of New York," Rainsford began again. "I fell off a yacht. I am hungry."

The man's only answer was to raise with his thumb the hammer of his revolver. Then Rainsford saw the man's free hand go to his forehead in a military salute, and he saw him click his heels together and stand at attention. Another man was coming down the broad marble steps, an erect, slender man in evening clothes. He advanced to Rainsford and held out his hand.

In a cultivated voice marked by a slight accent that gave it added precision and deliberateness, he said: "It is a very great pleasure and honor to welcome Mr. Sanger Rainsford, the celebrated hunter, to my home."

Automatically Rainsford shook the man's hand.

"I've read your book about hunting snow leopards in Tibet, you see" explained the man. "I am General Zaroff."

Rainsford's first impression was that the man was singularly handsome; his second was that there was an original, almost bizarre quality about the general's face. He was a tall man past middle age, for his hair was a vivid white; but his thick eyebrows and pointed military mustache were as black as the night from which Rainsford had come. His eyes, too, were black and very bright. He had high cheek bones, a sharp-cut nose, a spare, dark face, the face of a man used to giving orders, the face of an aristocrat. Turning to the giant in uniform, the general made a sign. The giant put away his pistol, saluted, withdrew.

"Ivan is an incredibly strong fellow," remarked the general, "but he has the misfortune to be deaf and dumb. A simple fellow, but, I'm afraid, like all his race, a bit of a savage."

"Is he Russian?"

"He is a Cossack," said the general, and his smile showed red lips and pointed teeth. "So am I."

"Come," he said, "we shouldn't be chatting here. We can talk later. Now you want clothes, food, rest. You shall have them. This is a most restful spot."

Ivan had reappeared, and the general spoke to him with lips that moved but gave forth no sound.

"Follow Ivan, if you please, Mr. Rainsford," said the general. "I was about to have my dinner when you came. I'll wait for you. You'll find that my clothes will fit you, I think."

It was to a huge, beam-ceilinged bedroom with a canopied bed big enough for six men that Rainsford followed the silent giant. Ivan laid out an evening suit, and Rainsford, as he put it on, noticed that it came from a London tailor who ordinarily cut and sewed for none below the rank of duke.

The dining room to which Ivan conducted him was in many ways remarkable. There was a medieval magnificence about it; it suggested a baronial hall of feudal times with its oaken panels, its high ceiling, its vast refectory table where twoscore men could sit down to eat. About the hall were the mounted heads of many animals—lions, tigers, elephants, moose, bears; larger or more perfect specimens Rainsford had never seen. At the great table the general was sitting, alone.

"You'll have a cocktail, Mr. Rainsford," he suggested. The cocktail was surpassingly good; and, Rainsford noted, the table appointments were of the finest—the linen, the crystal, the silver, the china.

They were eating *borsch*, the rich, red soup with whipped cream so dear to Russian palates. Half apologetically General Zaroff said: "We do our best to preserve the amenities of civilization here. Please forgive any lapses. We are well off the beaten track, you know. Do you think the champagne has suffered from its long ocean trip?"

"Not in the least," declared Rainsford. He was finding the general a most thoughtful and affable host, a true cosmopolite. But there was one small trait of the general's that made Rainsford uncomfortable. Whenever he looked up from his plate he found the general studying him, appraising him narrowly.

"Perhaps," said General Zaroff, "you were surprised that I recognized your name. You see, I read all books on hunting published in English, French, and Russian. I have but one passion in my life, Mr. Rainsford, and it is the hunt."

"You have some wonderful heads here," said Rainsford as he ate a particularly well cooked filet mignon. "That Cape buffalo is the largest I ever saw."

"Oh, that fellow. Yes, he was a monster."

"Did he charge you?"

"Hurled me against a tree," said the general. "Fractured my skull. But I got the brute."

"I've always thought," said Rainsford, "that the Cape buffalo is the most dangerous of all big game."

For a moment the general did not reply; he was smiling his curious red-lipped smile. Then he said slowly: "No. You are wrong, sir. The Cape buffalo is not the most dangerous big game." He sipped his wine. "Here in my preserve on this island," he said in the same slow tone, "I hunt more dangerous game."

Rainsford expressed his surprise. "Is there big game on this island?"

The general nodded. "The biggest."

"Really?"

"Oh, it isn't here naturally, of course. I have to stock the island."

"What have you imported, general?" Rainsford asked. "Tigers?"

The general smiled. "No," he said. "Hunting tigers ceased to interest me some years ago. I exhausted their possibilities, you see. No thrill left in tigers, no real danger. I live for danger, Mr. Rainsford."

The general took from his pocket a gold cigarette case and offered his guest a long black cigarette with a silver tip; it was perfumed and gave off a smell like incense.

"We will have some capital hunting, you and I," said the general. "I shall be most glad to have your society."

"But what game—" began Rainsford.

"I'll tell you," said the general. "You will be amused, I know. I think I may say, in all modesty, that I have done a rare thing. I have invented a new sensation. May I pour you another glass of port, Mr. Rainsford?"

"Thank you, general."

The general filled both glasses, and said: "God makes some men poets. Some He makes kings, some beggars. Me He made a hunter. My hand was made for the trigger, my father said. He was a very rich man with a quarter of a million acres in the Crimea, and he was an ardent sportsman. When I was only five years old he gave me a little gun, specially made in Moscow for me, to shoot sparrows with. When I shot some of his prize turkeys with it, he did not punish me; he complimented me on my marksmanship. I killed my first bear in the Caucasus when I was ten. My whole life has been one prolonged hunt. I went into the army—it was expected of noblemen's sons—and for a time commanded a division of Cossack cavalry, but my real interest was always the hunt. I have hunted every kind of game in every land. It would be impossible for me to tell you how many animals I have killed."

The general puffed at his cigarette.

"After the debacle in Russia[1] I left the country, for it was imprudent for an officer of the Czar to stay there. Many noble Russians lost everything. I, luckily, had invested heavily in American securities, so I shall never have to open a tea room in Monte Carlo or drive a taxi in Paris. Naturally, I continued to hunt—grizzlies in your Rockies, crocodiles in the Ganges, rhinoceroses in East Africa. It was in Africa that the Cape buffalo hit me and laid me up for six months. As soon as I recovered I started for the Amazon to hunt jaguars, for I had heard they were unusually cunning. They weren't." The Cossack sighed. "They were no match at all for a hunter with his wits about him, and a high-powered rifle. I was bitterly disappointed. I was lying in my tent with a splitting headache one night when a terrible thought pushed its way into my mind. Hunting was beginning to bore me! And hunting, remember, had been my life. I have heard that in America business men often go to pieces when they give up the business that has been their life."

"Yes, that's so," said Rainsford.

The general smiled. "I had no wish to go to pieces," he said. "I must do something. Now, mine is an analytical mind, Mr. Rainsford. Doubtless that is why I enjoy the problems of the chase."

1. The Revolution of 1917, which overthrew the Czar and prepared the way for Communist rule.

"No doubt, General Zaroff."

"So," continued the general, "I asked myself why the hunt no longer fascinated me. You are much younger than I am, Mr. Rainsford, and have not hunted as much, but you perhaps can guess the answer."

"What was it?"

"Simply this: hunting had ceased to be what you call 'a sporting proposition.' It had become too easy. I always got my quarry. Always. There is no greater bore than perfection."

The general lit a fresh cigarette.

"No animal had a chance with me any more. That is no boast; it is a mathematical certainty. The animal had nothing but his legs and his instinct. Instinct is no match for reason. When I thought of this it was a tragic moment for me, I can tell you."

Rainsford leaned across the table, absorbed in what his host was saying.

"It came to me as an inspiration what I must do," the general went on.

"And that was?"

The general smiled the quiet smile of one who had faced an obstacle and surmounted it with success. "I had to invent a new animal to hunt," he said.

"A new animal? You're joking."

"Not at all," said the general. "I never joke about hunting. I needed a new animal. I found one. So I bought this island, built this house, and here I do my hunting. The island is perfect for my purposes—there are jungles with a maze of trails in them, hills, swamps—"

"But the animal, General Zaroff?"

"Oh," said the general, "it supplies me with the most exciting hunting in the world. No other hunting compares with it for an instant. Every day I hunt, and I never grow bored now, for I have a quarry with which I can match my wits."

Rainsford's bewilderment showed in his face.

"I wanted the ideal animal to hunt," explained the general. "So I said: 'What are the attributes of an ideal quarry?' And the answer was, of course: 'It must have courage, cunning, and, above all, it must be able to reason.' "

"But no animal can reason," objected Rainsford.

"My dear fellow," said the general, "there is one that can."

"But you can't mean—" gasped Rainsford.

"And why not?"

"I can't believe you are serious, General Zaroff. This is a grisly joke."

"Why should I not be serious? I am speaking of hunting."

"Hunting? Good God, General Zaroff, what you speak of is murder."

The general laughed with entire good nature. He regarded Rainsford quizzically. "I refuse to believe that so modern and civilized a young man as you seem to be harbors romantic ideas about the value of human life. Surely your experiences in the war—"

"Did not make me condone cold-blooded murder," finished Rainsford stiffly.

Laughter shook the general. "How extraordinarily droll you are!" he said. "One does not expect nowadays to find a young man of the educated class, even in America, with such a naïve, and, if I may say so, mid-Victorian point of view.

It's like finding a snuff-box in a limousine. Ah, well, doubtless you had Puritan ancestors. So many Americans appear to have had. I'll wager you'll forget your notions when you go hunting with me. You've a genuine new thrill in store for you, Mr. Rainsford."

"Thank you, I'm a hunter, not a murderer."

"Dear me," said the general, quite unruffled, "again that unpleasant word. But I think I can show you that your scruples are quite ill founded."

"Yes?"

"Life is for the strong, to be lived by the strong, and, if need be, taken by the strong. The weak of the world were put here to give the strong pleasure. I am strong. Why should I not use my gift? If I wish to hunt, why should I not? I hunt the scum of the earth—sailors from tramp ships—lascars, blacks, Chinese, whites, mongrels—a thoroughbred horse or hound is worth more than a score of them."

"But they are men," said Rainsford hotly.

"Precisely," said the general. "That is why I use them. It gives me pleasure. They can reason, after a fashion. So they are dangerous."

"But where do you get them?"

The general's left eyelid fluttered down in a wink. "This island is called Ship-Trap," he answered. "Sometimes an angry god of the high seas sends them to me. Sometimes, when Providence is not so kind, I help Providence a bit. Come to the window with me."

Rainsford went to the window and looked out toward the sea.

"Watch! Out there!" exclaimed the general, pointing into the night. Rainsford's eyes saw only blackness, and then, as the general pressed a button, far out to sea Rainsford saw the flash of lights.

The general chuckled. "They indicate a channel," he said, "where there's none: giant rocks with razor edges crouch like a sea monster with wide-open jaws. They can crush a ship as easily as I crush this nut." He dropped a walnut on the hardwood floor and brought his heel grinding down on it. "Oh, yes," he said, casually, as if in answer to a question, "I have electricity. We try to be civilized here."

"Civilized? And you shoot down men?"

A trace of anger was in the general's black eyes, but it was there for but a second, and he said, in his most pleasant manner: "Dear me, what a righteous young man you are! I assure you I do not do the thing you suggest. That would be barbarous. I treat these visitors with every consideration. They get plenty of good food and exercise. They get into splendid physical condition. You shall see for yourself tomorrow."

"What do you mean?"

"We'll visit my training school," smiled the general. "It's in the cellar. I have about a dozen pupils down there now. They're from the Spanish bark San Lucar that had the bad luck to go on the rocks out there. A very inferior lot, I regret to say. Poor specimens and more accustomed to the deck than to the jungle."

He raised his hand, and Ivan, who served as waiter, brought thick Turkish coffee. Rainsford, with an effort, held his tongue in check.

"It's a game, you see," pursued the general blandly. "I suggest to one of them that we go hunting. I give him a supply of food and an excellent hunting knife. I give him three hours' start. I am to follow, armed only with a pistol of the smallest caliber and range. If my quarry eludes me for three whole days, he wins the game. If I find him"—the general smiled—"he loses."

"Suppose he refuses to be hunted?"

"Oh," said the general, "I give him his option, of course. He need not play that game if he doesn't wish to. If he does not wish to hunt, I turn him over to Ivan. Ivan once had the honor of serving as official knouter to the Great White Czar,[2] and he has his own ideas of sport. Invariably, Mr. Rainsford, invariably they choose the hunt."

"And if they win?"

The smile on the general's face widened. "To date I have not lost," he said.

Then he added, hastily: "I don't wish you to think me a braggart, Mr. Rainsford. Many of them afford only the most elementary sort of problem. Occasionally I strike a tartar. One almost did win. I eventually had to use the dogs."

"The dogs?"

"This way, please. I'll show you."

The general steered Rainsford to a window. The lights from the windows sent a flickering illumination that made grotesque patterns on the courtyard below, and Rainsford could see moving about there a dozen or so huge black shapes; as they turned toward him, their eyes glittered greenly.

"A rather good lot, I think," observed the general. "They are let out at seven every night. If anyone should try to get into my house—or out of it—something extremely regrettable would occur to him." He hummed a snatch of song from the Folies Bergère.[3]

"And now," said the general, "I want to show you my new collection of heads. Will you come with me to the library?"

"I hope," said Rainsford, "that you will excuse me tonight, General Zaroff. I'm really not feeling at all well."

"Ah, indeed?" the general inquired solicitously. "Well, I suppose that's only natural, after your long swim. You need a good, restful night's sleep. Tomorrow you'll feel like a new man, I'll wager. Then we'll hunt, eh? I've one rather promising prospect—"

Rainsford was hurrying from the room.

"Sorry you can't go with me tonight," called the general. "I expect rather fair sport—a big, strong black. He looks resourceful—Well, good night, Mr. Rainsford; I hope you have a good night's rest."

The bed was good, and the pajamas of the softest silk, and he was tired in every fiber of his being, but nevertheless Rainsford could not quiet his brain with the opiate of sleep. He lay, eyes wide open. Once he thought he heard stealthy steps in the corridor outside his room. He sought to throw open the door; it would not open. He went to the window and looked out. His room was high up in one of the towers. The lights of the château were out now; and it was dark

2. Probably Nicholas II (1868–1918) who was overthrown by the Revolution and executed; "White" designates those opposed to the Communists, or "Reds." 3. Paris theater and music hall.

and silent, but there was a fragment of sallow moon, and by its wan light he could see, dimly, the courtyard; there, weaving in and out in the pattern of shadow, were black, noiseless forms; the hounds heard him at the window and looked up, expectantly, with their green eyes. Rainsford went back to bed and lay down. By many methods he tried to put himself to sleep. He had achieved a doze when, just as morning began to come, he heard, far off in the jungle, the faint report of a pistol.

General Zaroff did not appear until luncheon. He was dressed faultlessly in the tweeds of a country squire. He was solicitous about the state of Rainsford's health.

"As for me," sighed the general, "I do not feel so well. I am worried, Mr. Rainsford. Last night I detected traces of my old complaint."

150 To Rainsford's questioning glance the general said: "Ennui. Boredom."

Then, taking a second helping of *crêpes suzette*, the general explained: "The hunting was not good last night. The fellow lost his head. He made a straight trail that offered no problems at all. That's the trouble with these sailors; they have dull brains to begin with, and they do not know how to get about in the woods. They do excessively stupid and obvious things. It's most annoying. Will you have another glass of Chablis, Mr. Rainsford?"

"General," said Rainsford firmly, "I wish to leave this island at once."

The general raised his thickets of eyebrows; he seemed hurt. "But, my dear fellow," the general protested, "you've only just come. You've had no hunting—"

"I wish to go today," said Rainsford. He saw the dead black eyes of the general on him, studying him. General Zaroff's face suddenly brightened.

155 He filled Rainsford's glass with venerable Chablis from a dusty bottle.

"Tonight," said the general," we will hunt—you and I."

Rainsford shook his head. "No, general," he said, "I will not hunt."

The general shrugged his shoulders and delicately ate a hothouse grape. "As you wish, my friend," he said. "The choice rests entirely with you. But may I not venture to suggest that you will find my idea of sport more diverting than Ivan's?"

He nodded toward the corner to where the giant stood, scowling, his thick arms crossed on his hogshead of a chest.

160 "You don't mean—" cried Rainsford.

"My dear fellow," said the general, "have I not told you I always mean what I say about hunting? This is really an inspiration. I drink to a foeman worthy of my steel—at last."

The general raised his glass, but Rainsford sat staring at him.

"You'll find this game worth playing," the general said enthusiastically. "Your brain against mine. Your woodcraft against mine. Your strength and stamina against mine. Outdoor chess! And the stake is not without value, eh?"

"And if I win—" began Rainsford huskily.

165 "I'll cheerfully acknowledge myself defeated if I do not find you by midnight of the third day," said General Zaroff. "My sloop will place you on the mainland near a town."

The general read what Rainsford was thinking.

"Oh, you can trust me," said the Cossack. "I will give you my word as a gentleman and a sportsman. Of course you, in turn, must agree to say nothing of your visit here."

"I'll agree to nothing of the kind," said Rainsford.

"Oh," said the general, "in that case—But why discuss that now? Three days hence we can discuss it over a bottle of Veuve Cliquot.[4] unless—"

The general sipped his wine.

Then a businesslike air animated him. "Ivan," he said to Rainsford, "will supply you with hunting clothes, food, a knife. I suggest you wear moccasins; they leave a poorer trail. I suggest too that you avoid the big swamp in the southeast corner of the island. We call it Death Swamp. There's quicksand there. One foolish fellow tried it. The deplorable part of it was that Lazarus followed him. You can imagine my feelings, Mr. Rainsford. I loved Lazarus; he was the finest hound in my pack. Well, I must beg you to excuse me now. I always take a siesta after lunch. You'll hardly have time for a nap, I fear. You'll want to start, no doubt. I shall not follow till dusk. Hunting at night is so much more exciting than by day, don't you think? Au revoir, Mr. Rainsford, au revoir."

General Zaroff, with a deep, courtly bow, strolled from the room.

From another door came Ivan. Under one arm he carried khaki hunting clothes, a haversack of food, a leather sheath containing a long-bladed hunting knife; his right hand rested on a cocked revolver thrust in the crimson sash about his waist. . . .

Rainsford had fought his way through the bush for two hours. "I must keep my nerve. I must keep my nerve," he said through tight teeth.

He had not been entirely clear-headed when the château gates snapped shut behind him. His whole idea at first was to put distance between himself and General Zaroff, and, to this end, he had plunged along, spurred on by the sharp rowels of something very like panic. Now he had got a grip on himself, had stopped, and was taking stock of himself and the situation.

He saw that straight flight was futile; inevitably it would bring him face to face with the sea. He was in a picture with a frame of water, and his operations, clearly, must take place within that frame.

"I'll give him a trail to follow," muttered Rainsford, and he struck off from the rude paths he had been following into the trackless wilderness. He executed a series of intricate loops; he doubled on his trail again and again, recalling all the lore of the fox hunt, and all the dodges of the fox. Night found him leg-weary, with hands and face lashed by the branches, on a thickly wooded ridge. He knew it would be insane to blunder on through the dark, even if he had the strength. His need for rest was imperative and he thought: "I have played the fox, now I must play the cat of the fable.[5] A big tree with a thick trunk and

4. A fine champagne; Chablis, above, is a very dry white Burgundy table wine. 5. The fox boasts of his many tricks to elude the hounds; the cat responds he knows only one—to climb the nearest tree—but that this is worth more than all the fox's tricks.

outspread branches was nearby, and, taking care to leave not the slightest mark, he climbed up into the crotch, and stretching out on one of the broad limbs, after a fashion, rested. Rest brought him new confidence and almost a feeling of security. Even so zealous a hunter as General Zaroff could not trace him there, he told himself; only the devil himself could follow that complicated trail through the jungle after dark. But, perhaps, the general was a devil—

An apprehensive night crawled slowly by like a wounded snake, and sleep did not visit Rainsford, although the silence of a dead world was on the jungle. Toward morning when a dingy gray was varnishing the sky, the cry of some startled bird focused Rainsford's attention in that direction. Something was coming through the bush, coming slowly, carefully, coming by the same winding way Rainsford had come. He flattened himself down on the limb, and through a screen of leaves almost as thick as tapestry, he watched. The thing that was approaching was a man.

It was General Zaroff. He made his way along with his eyes fixed in utmost concentration on the ground before him. He paused, almost beneath the tree, dropped to his knees and studied the ground. Rainsford's impulse was to hurl himself down like a panther, but he saw that the general's right hand held something metallic—a small automatic pistol.

The hunter shook his head several times, as if he were puzzled. Then he straightened up and took from his case one of his black cigarettes; its pungent incense-like smoke floated up to Rainsford's nostrils.

Rainsford held his breath. The general's eyes had left the ground and were traveling inch by inch up the tree. Rainsford froze there, every muscle tensed for a spring. But the sharp eyes of the hunter stopped before they reached the limb where Rainsford lay; a smile spread over his brown face. Very deliberately he blew a smoke ring into the air; then he turned his back on the tree and walked carelessly away, back along the trail he had come. The swish of the underbrush against his hunting boots grew fainter and fainter.

The pent-up air burst hotly from Rainsford's lungs. His first thought made him feel sick and numb. The general could follow a trail through the woods at night; he could follow an extremely difficult trail; he must have uncanny powers; only by the merest chance had the Cossack failed to see his quarry.

Rainsford's second thought was even more terrible. It sent a shudder of cold horror through his whole being. Why had the general smiled? Why had he turned back?

Rainsford did not want to believe what his reason told him was true, but the truth was as evident as the sun that had by now pushed through the morning mists. The general was playing with him! The general was saving him for another day's sport! The Cossack was the cat; he was the mouse.[6] Then it was that Rainsford knew the full meaning of terror.

"I will not lose my nerve. I will not."

He slid down the tree, and struck off again into the woods. His face was set and he forced the machinery of his mind to function. Three hundred yards from

6. A cat, sure of his prey, plays with a mouse before killing him.

his hiding place he stopped where a huge dead tree leaned precariously on a smaller, living one. Throwing off his sack of food, Rainsford took his knife from its sheath and began to work with all his energy.

The job was finished at last, and he threw himself down behind a fallen log a hundred feet away. He did not have to wait long. The cat was coming again to play with the mouse.

Following the trail with the sureness of a bloodhound, came General Zaroff. Nothing escaped those searching black eyes, no crushed blade of grass, no bent twig, no mark, no matter how faint, in the moss. So intent was the Cossack on his stalking that he was upon the thing Rainsford had made before he saw it. His foot touched the protruding bough that was the trigger. Even as he touched it, the general sensed his danger and leaped back with the agility of an ape. But he was not quite quick enough; the dead tree, delicately adjusted to rest on the cut living one, crashed down and struck the general a glancing blow on the shoulder as it fell; but for his alertness, he must have been smashed beneath it. He staggered, but he did not fall; nor did he drop his revolver. He stood there, rubbing his injured shoulder, and Rainsford, with fear again gripping his heart, heard the general's mocking laugh ring through the jungle.

"Rainsford," called the general, "if you are within sound of my voice, as I suppose you are, let me congratulate you. Not many men know how to make a Malay man-catcher. Luckily, for me, I too have hunted in Malacca. You are proving interesting, Mr. Rainsford. I am going now to have my wound dressed; it's only a slight one. But I shall be back. I shall be back."

When the general, nursing his bruised shoulder, had gone, Rainsford took up his flight again. It was flight now, a desperate, hopeless flight, that carried him on for some hours. Dusk came, then darkness, and still he pressed on. The ground grew softer under his moccasins; the vegetation grew ranker, denser; insects bit him savagely. Then, as he stepped forward, his foot sank into the ooze. He tried to wrench it back, but the muck sucked viciously at his foot as if it were a giant leech. With a violent effort, he tore his foot loose. He knew where he was now. Death Swamp and its quicksand.

His hands were tight closed as if his nerve were something tangible that someone in the darkness was trying to tear from his grip. The softness of the earth had given him an idea. He stepped back from the quicksand a dozen feet or so and, like some huge prehistoric beaver, he began to dig.

Rainsford had dug himself in in France[7] when a second's delay meant death. That had been a placid pastime compared to his digging now. The pit grew deeper; when it was above his shoulders, he climbed out and from some hard saplings cut stakes and sharpened them to a fine point. These stakes he planted in the bottom of the pit with the points sticking up. With flying fingers he wove a rough carpet of weeds and branches and with it he covered the mouth of the pit. Then, wet with sweat and aching with tiredness, he crouched behind the stump of a lightning-charred tree.

7. During World War I he had quickly dug a hole or trench to shelter himself from exploding shells, bullets, etc.

He knew his pursuer was coming; he heard the padding sound of feet on the soft earth, and the night breeze brought him the perfume of the general's cigarette. It seemed to Rainsford that the general was coming with unusual swiftness; he was not feeling his way along, foot by foot. Rainsford, crouching there, could not see the general, nor could he see the pit. He lived a year in a minute. Then he felt an impulse to cry aloud with joy, for he heard the sharp crackle of the breaking branches as the cover of the pit gave way; he heard the sharp scream of pain as the pointed stakes found their mark. He leaped up from his place of concealment. Then he cowered back. Three feet from the pit a man was standing, with an electric torch in his hand.

"You've done well, Rainsford," the voice of the general called. "Your Burmese tiger pit has claimed one of my best dogs. Again you score. I think, Mr. Rainsford, I'll see what you can do against my whole pack. I'm going home for a rest now. Thank you for a most amusing evening."

At daybreak Rainsford, lying near the swamp, was awakened by a sound that made him know that he had new things to learn about fear. It was a distant sound, faint and wavering, but he knew it. It was the baying of a pack of hounds.

Rainsford knew he could do one of two things. He could stay where he was and wait. That was suicide. He could flee. That was postponing the inevitable. For a moment he stood there, thinking. An idea that held a wild chance came to him, and, tightening his belt, he headed away from the swamp.

The baying of the hounds drew nearer, then still nearer, nearer, ever nearer. On a ridge Rainsford climbed a tree. Down a watercourse, not a quarter of a mile away, he could see the bush moving. Straining his eyes, he saw the lean figure of General Zaroff; just ahead of him Rainsford made out another figure whose wide shoulders surged through the tall jungle weeds; it was the giant Ivan, and he seemed pulled forward by some unseen force; Rainsford knew that Ivan must be holding the pack in leash.

They would be on him any minute now. His mind worked frantically. He thought of a native trick he had learned in Uganda. He slid down the tree. He caught hold of a springy young sapling and to it he fastened his hunting knife, with the blade pointing down the trail; with a bit of wild grapevine he tied back the sapling. Then he ran for his life. The hounds raised their voices as they hit the fresh scent. Rainsford knew now how an animal at bay feels.

He had to stop to get his breath. The baying of the hounds stopped abruptly, and Rainsford's heart stopped too. They must have reached the knife.

He shinnied excitedly up a tree and looked back. His pursuers had stopped. But the hope that was in Rainsford's brain when he climbed died, for he saw in the shallow valley that General Zaroff was still on his feet. But Ivan was not. The knife, driven by the recoil of the springing tree, had not wholly failed.

Rainsford had hardly tumbled to the ground when the pack took up the cry again.

"Nerve, nerve, nerve!" he panted, as he dashed along. A blue gap showed between the trees dead ahead. Ever nearer drew the hounds. Rainsford forced himself on toward that gap. He reached it. It was the shore of the sea. Across a cove he could see the gloomy gray stone of the château. Twenty feet below him the sea rumbled and hissed. Rainsford hesitated. He heard the hounds. Then he leaped far out into the sea. . . .

When the general and his pack reached the place by the sea, the Cossack stopped. For some minutes he stood regarding the blue-green expanse of water. He shrugged his shoulders. Then he sat down, took a drink of brandy from a silver flask, lit a perfumed cigarette, and hummed a bit from "Madame Butterfly."[8]

General Zaroff had an exceedingly good dinner in his great paneled dining hall that evening. With it he had a bottle of Pol Roger and half a bottle of Chambertin.[9] Two slight annoyances kept him from perfect enjoyment. One was the thought that it would be difficult to replace Ivan; the other was that his quarry had escaped him; of course the American hadn't played the game—so thought the general as he tasted his after-dinner liqueur. In his library he read, to soothe himself, from the works of Marcus Aurelius.[1] At ten he went up to his bedroom. He was deliciously tired, he said to himself, as he locked himself in. There was a little moonlight so, before turning on his light, he went to the window and looked down at the courtyard. He could see the great hounds, and he called: "Better luck another time," to them. Then he switched on the light.

A man, who had been hiding in the curtains of the bed, was standing there.

"Rainsford!" screamed the general. "How in God's name did you get here?"

"Swam," said Rainsford. "I found it quicker than walking through the jungle."

The general sucked in his breath and smiled. "I congratulate you," he said. "You have won the game."

Rainsford did not smile. "I am still a beast at bay," he said, in a low, hoarse voice. "Get ready, General Zaroff."

The general made one of his deepest bows. "I see," he said. "Splendid! One of us is to furnish a repast for the hounds. The other will sleep in this very excellent bed. On guard, Rainsford. . . ."

He had never slept in a better bed, Rainsford decided.

1924

A good many readers like "The Most Dangerous Game." In classes I teach it is often a favorite, or even *the* favorite. Yet other readers have urged me to drop this story from the anthology because it is "unworthy," not really Literature. Is this simply ignorance on the one hand or snobbery on the other?

8. Opera (1904) by Giacomo Puccini (1858–1924). 9. Pol Roger is champagne, Chambertin is a highly esteemed red Burgundy wine. 1. Roman emperor (A.D. 161–180), Stoic philosopher, writer, and humanitarian.

Here are two brief papers, somewhat like those a student might write in class, the first supporting "The Most Dangerous Game," the second responding to the first.

Why "The Most Dangerous Game" Is Good Literature

"The Most Dangerous Game" by Richard Connell is exciting. Things happen in it, and you want to read on because you want to find out what will happen next and how it will come out. Too often the things we need to read for class are boring, nothing happens, or, if something does happen, it happens inside somebody's head. But here things happen outside; I mean, there's real action.

Not only is there action, but that action is important, a real life-and-death struggle. This story is not just about whether somebody used the wrong fork or had a good time or didn't have a good time at a party.

The good guy wins, the story ends happily, and when you finish reading it, you feel good about things. Sometimes in class I think only real downers are supposed to be good stories, like life always has to be full of gloom and doom. Now all of us die sooner or later, of course, but that's only the end, a minute or a month or something, and there's all the rest of the time when we're not dead and not really in the process of dying. That's life, and that's what a good story should be about.

"The Most Dangerous Game" is fun to read. Sometimes I think that what are supposed to be the "good" stories are the ones I don't like. But popular stories can be good: there have been several movies made of "The Most Dangerous Game" and several stories adapted from it with just a few things changed. But, I'm told, the world of literature isn't a democracy--you don't vote for what's Literature. When I say I like Stephen King--and I'm sure not the only one, because he sells lots and lots of books--teachers or English majors say wait fifty years and see if his stuff is still around.

Well, "The Most Dangerous Game" is over sixty-five years old, older than at least three-quarters of the stories in this anthology, so it's stood the test of time, whatever that is.

Why "The Most Dangerous Game" Is Not Good Literature

Though "The Most Dangerous Game" may be "a good read," at least the first time through, and I have nothing against someone reading it or even liking it in its way, I don't think it ought to be in <u>The Norton Introduction to Literature.</u> Being in the anthology gives it a status it does not deserve. It makes it the subject of serious study by college students, and college students ought to be engaged in more challenging and thought-provoking reading material, even if outside of class they are reading Stephen King and the likes of "The Most Dangerous Game."

Though it's true that a life-and-death struggle is important--for the person involved--it has no relevance for us, no outreach: it does not relate to our experience nor does it really illuminate anything about our experience or the way we look at life. I don't mean that a worthy story must have a "message," necessarily, but it should have a "theme," something that explores a significant area of human experience and understanding.

I admit that there is something like suspense in Connell's story, but that is not enough. There's nothing wrong with suspense in itself--expectations of one sort or another are part of every good work--but here the suspense is manipulated at the price of consistency. Note how we're seeing things from Rainsford's perspective (not through his eyes and mind exactly, not in the first person, but over his shoulder) until near the end when he leaps into the sea. At that point, when we're supposed to want most to know what happens next, there's the more or less artificial suspense added by three dots and a break on the page, and then we're not with Rainsford but Zaroff, just to make us wonder if Rainsford did indeed die. It's a cheap trick. Besides, don't we know from the beginning that in this kind of story the hero never dies, so isn't the suspense really phony? What's wrong with stories like this is the unrealistic, wish-fulfilling way it looks at reality: it tells us that good guys always finish first; they win because they're good.

While good guys do sometimes finish first, and plenty of good stories end happily, more or less, like "My Man Bovanne," and "The Old People," life is not always like that, and this victory seems a little too easy.

Finally, Rainsford has no "character"; he's just a good guy because he's an American and his life is threatened by a bad guy who's a Russian; and the bad guy is just a bad guy, with no redeeming human qualities--it's all about guys in white hats versus guys in black hats.

These are not polished and conclusive arguments, of course. Had the writer of the first paper read the response, he might have had more to say. About the alleged absence of theme in "The Most Dangerous Game," for example:

There is a theme in Connell's story. It is a very important one, one that you have to think about, and that some people will agree with, though it is not a theme that you necessarily have to agree with in order to appreciate the story. Notice it is set just after the Russian Revolution, and Zaroff (the "son of the czar") is a cruel aristocrat from the czarist regime who believes in power, believes that might-makes-right, and believes some people are better than others and have a right to do what they will with their "inferiors," even kill them for pleasure. Rainsford at the beginning is a hunter/exploiter, never thinking what the "inferior" beast, the hunted, feels like. Having been put in the place of the hunted he will no doubt learn to have more reverence for life, more sympathy for the underdog.

The opponent, hearing this contention that there is a significant theme in the story, might well respond that the theme as described is too pat, and that it is presented through too convenient (as well as unbelievable) a situation, too much of a set-up.

This, then, is only one example of the kinds of arguments readers can use to support their judgments. We need to go on from there to consider what we read for ("a good read," "an illumination of human life and experience"), and what we mean by "the reader," the one judging the story to be "good".

Let us assume for the moment that "the readers" can be represented roughly by the people in this class—you, those who agree with you about stories, and those who, though they are more or less like you, do not always agree with you about which stories are good and what makes them good. We said earlier that if our appreciation and understanding of literature is to grow, and if we are not to merely accept what those considered "authorities" say is good or great, we must learn to isolate, analyze, and articulate what *we* like (or dislike) in a story. And, we said, we must listen to those with other responses as they articulate their reasons.

Now for the test. The next story is by a Nobel Laureate and much revered writer, William Faulkner, and this is one of his most admired stories. It has some of the same attractive qualities as "The Most Dangerous Game"—conflict, action, suspense—but there are those who find it critically flawed. Regardless of which side we are on, we must take seriously both those who have reservations and questions and the author's and the story's established reputation. But first, we must read it.

WILLIAM FAULKNER

Barn Burning

The store in which the Justice of the Peace's court was sitting smelled of cheese. The boy, crouched on his nail keg at the back of the crowded room, knew he smelled cheese, and more: from where he sat he could see the ranked shelves close-packed with the solid, squat, dynamic shapes of tin cans whose labels his stomach read, not from the lettering which meant nothing to his mind but from the scarlet devils and the silver curve of fish—this, the cheese which he knew he smelled and the hermetic meat which his intestines believed he smelled coming in intermittent gusts momentary and brief between the other constant one, the smell and sense just a little of fear because mostly of despair and grief, the old fierce pull of blood. He could not see the table where the Justice sat and before which his father and his father's enemy *(our enemy* he thought in that despair; *ourn! mine and hisn both! He's my father!)* stood, but he could hear them, the two of them that is, because his father had said no word yet:

"But what proof have you, Mr. Harris?"

"I told you. The hog got into my corn. I caught it up and sent it back to him. He had no fence that would hold it. I told him so, warned him. The next time I put the hog in my pen. When he came to get it I gave him enough wire to patch up his pen. The next time I put the hog up and kept it. I rode down to his house and saw the wire I gave him still rolled on to the spool in his yard. I told him he could have the hog when he paid me a dollar pound fee. That evening a nigger came with the dollar and got the hog. He was a strange nigger. He said, 'He say to tell you wood and hay kin burn.' I said, 'What?' 'That whut he say to tell you,' the nigger said. 'Wood and hay kin burn.' That night my barn burned. I got the stock out but I lost the barn."

"Where is the nigger? Have you got him?"

"He was a strange nigger, I tell you. I don't know what became of him." 5

"But that's not proof. Don't you see that's not proof?"

"Get that boy up here. He knows." For a moment the boy thought too that the man meant his older brother until Harris said, "Not him. The little one. The boy," and, crouching, small for his age, small and wiry like his father, in patched and faded jeans even too small for him, with straight, uncombed, brown hair and eyes gray and wild as storm scud, he saw the men between himself and the table part and become a lane of grim faces, at the end of which he saw the Justice, a shabby, collarless, graying man in spectacles, beckoning him. He felt no floor under his bare feet; he seemed to walk beneath the palpable weight of the grim turning faces. His father, stiff in his black Sunday coat donned not for the trial but for the moving, did not even look at him. *He aims for me to lie,* he thought, again with that frantic grief and despair. *And I will have to do hit.*

"What's your name, boy?" the Justice said.

"Colonel Sartoris Snopes," the boy whispered.

"Hey?" the Justice said. "Talk louder. Colonel Sartoris? I reckon anybody 10 named for Colonel Sartoris in this country can't help but tell the truth, can they?" The boy said nothing. *Enemy! Enemy!* he thought; for a moment he could not even see, could not see that the Justice's face was kindly nor discern that his voice was troubled when he spoke to the man named Harris: "Do you want me to question this boy?" But he could hear, and during those subsequent long seconds while there was absolutely no sound in the crowded little room save that of quiet and intent breathing it was as if he had swung outward at the end of a grape vine, over a ravine, and at the top of the swing had been caught in a prolonged instant of mesmerized gravity, weightless in time.

"No!" Harris said violently, explosively. "Damnation! Send him out of here!" Now time, the fluid world, rushed beneath him again, the voices coming to him again through the smell of cheese and sealed meat, the fear and despair and the old grief of blood:

"This case is closed. I can't find against you, Snopes, but I can give you advice. Leave this country and don't come back to it."

His father spoke for the first time, his voice cold and harsh, level, without emphasis: "I aim to. I don't figure to stay in a country among people who . . ." he said something unprintable and vile, addressed to no one.

"That'll do," the Justice said. "Take your wagon and get out of this country before dark. Case dismissed."

His father turned, and he followed the stiff black coat, the wiry figure walking a little stiffly from where a Confederate provost's man's[1] musket ball had taken him in the heel on a stolen horse thirty years ago, followed the two backs now, since his older brother had appeared from somewhere in the crowd, no taller than the father but thicker, chewing tobacco steadily, between the two lines of grim-faced men and out of the store and across the worn gallery and down the sagging steps and among the dogs and half-grown boys in the mild May dust, where as he passed a voice hissed:

"Barn burner!"

Again he could not see, whirling; there was a face in a red haze, moonlike, bigger than the full moon, the owner of it half again his size, he leaping in the red haze toward the face, feeling no blow, feeling no shock when his head struck the earth, scrabbling up and leaping again, feeling no blow this time either and tasting no blood, scrabbling up to see the other boy in full flight and himself already leaping into pursuit as his father's hand jerked him back, the harsh, cold voice speaking above him: "Go get in the wagon."

It stood in a grove of locusts and mulberries across the road. His two hulking sisters in their Sunday dresses and his mother and her sister in calico and sunbonnets were already in it, sitting on and among the sorry residue of the dozen and more movings which even the boy could remember—the battered stove, the broken beds and chairs, the clock inlaid with mother-of-pearl, which would not run, stopped at some fourteen minutes past two o'clock of a dead and forgotten day and time, which had been his mother's dowry. She was crying, though when

1. Military policeman.

she saw him she drew her sleeve across her face and began to descend from the wagon. "Get back," the father said.

"He's hurt. I got to get some water and wash his . . ."

"Get back in the wagon," his father said. He got in too, over the tail-gate. His father mounted to the seat where the older brother already sat and struck the gaunt mules two savage blows with the peeled willow, but without heat. It was not even sadistic; it was exactly that same quality which in later years would cause his descendants to overrun the engine before putting a motor car into motion, striking and reining back in the same movement. The wagon went on, the store with its quiet crowd of grimly watching men dropped behind; a curve in the road hid it. *Forever* he thought. *Maybe he's done satisfied now, now that he has* . . . stopping himself, not to say it aloud even to himself. His mother's hand touched his shoulder.

"Does hit hurt?" she said.

"Naw," he said. "Hit don't hurt. Lemme be."

"Can't you wipe some of the blood off before hit dries?"

"I'll wash to-night," he said. "Lemme be, I tell you."

The wagon went on. He did not know where they were going. None of them ever did or ever asked, because it was always somewhere, always a house of sorts waiting for them a day or two days or even three days away. Likely his father had already arranged to make a crop on another farm before he . . . Again he had to stop himself. He (the father) always did. There was something about his wolf-like independence and even courage when the advantage was at least neutral which impressed strangers, as if they got from his latent ravening ferocity not so much a sense of dependability as a feeling that his ferocious conviction in the rightness of his own actions would be of advantage to all whose interest lay with his.

That night they camped, in a grove of oaks and beeches where a spring ran. The nights were still cool and they had a fire against it, of a rail lifted from a nearby fence and cut into lengths—a small fire, neat, niggard almost, a shrewd fire; such fires were his father's habit and custom always, even in freezing weather. Older, the boy might have remarked this and wondered why not a big one; why should not a man who had not only seen the waste and extravagance of war, but who had in his blood an inherent voracious prodigality with material not his own, have burned everything in sight? Then he might have gone a step farther and thought that that was the reason: that niggard blaze was the living fruit of nights passed during those four years in the woods hiding from all men, blue or gray,[2] with his strings of horses (captured horses, he called them). And older still, he might have divined the true reason: that the element of fire spoke to some deep mainspring of his father's being, as the element of steel or of powder spoke to other men, as the one weapon for the preservation of integrity, else breath were not worth the breathing, and hence to be regarded with respect and used with discretion.

2. The color of Union and Confederate Civil War (1861–1865) uniforms, respectively.

But he did not think this now and he had seen those same niggard blazes all his life. He merely ate his supper beside it and was already half asleep over his iron plate when his father called him, and once more he followed the stiff back, the stiff and ruthless limp, up the slope and on to the starlit road where, turning, he could see his father against the stars but without face or depth—a shape black, flat, and bloodless as though cut from tin in the iron folds of the frockcoat which had not been made for him, the voice harsh like tin and without heat like tin:

"You were fixing to tell them. You would have told him." He didn't answer. His father struck him with the flat of his hand on the side of the head, hard but without heat, exactly as he had struck the two mules at the store, exactly as he would strike either of them with any stick in order to kill a horse fly, his voice still without heat or anger: "You're getting to be a man. You got to learn. You got to learn to stick to your own blood or you ain't going to have any blood to stick to you. Do you think either of them, any man there this morning, would? Don't you know all they wanted was a chance to get at me because they knew I had them beat? Eh?" Later, twenty years later, he was to tell himself, "If I had said they wanted only truth, justice, he would have hit me again." But now he said nothing. He was not crying. He just stood there. "Answer me," his father said.

"Yes," he whispered. His father turned.

"Get on to bed. We'll be there tomorrow."

Tomorrow they were there. In the early afternoon the wagon stopped before a paintless two-room house identical almost with the dozen others it had stopped before even in the boy's ten years, and again, as on the other dozen occasions, his mother and aunt got down and began to unload the wagon, although his two sisters and his father and brother had not moved.

"Likely hit ain't fitten for hawgs," one of the sisters said.

"Nevertheless, fit it will and you'll hog it and like it," his father said. "Get out of them chairs and help your Ma unload."

The two sisters got down, big, bovine, in a flutter of cheap ribbons; one of them drew from the jumbled wagon bed a battered lantern, the other a worn broom. His father handed the reins to the older son and began to climb stiffly over the wheel. "When they get unloaded, take the team to the barn and feed them." Then he said, and at first the boy thought he was still speaking to his brother: "Come with me."

"Me?" he said.

"Yes," his father said. "You."

"Abner," his mother said. His father paused and looked back—the harsh level stare beneath the shaggy, graying, irascible brows.

"I reckon I'll have a word with the man that aims to begin to-morrow owning me body and soul for the next eight months."

They went back up the road. A week ago—or before last night, that is—he would have asked where they were going, but not now. His father had struck him before last night but never before had he paused afterward to explain why; it was as if the blow and the following calm, outrageous voice still rang, repercussed, divulging nothing to him save the terrible handicap of being young, the light weight of his few years, just heavy enough to prevent his soaring free of the world as it seemed to be ordered but not heavy enough to keep him footed solid in it, to resist it and try to change the course of its events.

Presently he could see the grove of oaks and cedars and the other flowering 40
trees and shrubs, where the house would be, though not the house yet. They walked beside a fence massed with honeysuckle and Cherokee roses and came to a gate swinging open between two brick pillars, and now, beyond a sweep of drive, he saw the house for the first time and at that instant he forgot his father and the terror and despair both, and even when he remembered his father again (who had not stopped) the terror and despair did not return. Because, for all the twelve movings, they had sojourned until now in a poor country, a land of small farms and fields and houses, and he had never seen a house like this before. *Hit's big as a courthouse* he thought quietly, with a surge of peace and joy whose reason he could not have thought into words, being too young for that: *They are safe from him. People whose lives are a part of this peace and dignity are beyond his touch, he no more to them than a buzzing wasp: capable of stinging for a little moment but that's all; the spell of this peace and dignity rendering even the barns and stable and cribs which belong to it impervious to the puny flames he might contrive* . . . this, the peace and joy, ebbing for an instant as he looked again at the stiff black back, the stiff and implacable limp of the figure which was not dwarfed by the house, for the reason that it had never looked big anywhere and which now, against the serene columned backdrop, had more than ever that impervious quality of something cut ruthlessly from tin, depthless, as though, sidewise to the sun, it would cast no shadow. Watching him, the boy remarked the absolutely undeviating course which his father held and saw the stiff foot come squarely down in a pile of fresh droppings where a horse had stood in the drive and which his father could have avoided by a simple change of stride. But it ebbed only for a moment, though he could not have thought this into words either, walking on in the spell of the house, which he could even want but without envy, without sorrow, certainly never with that ravening and jealous rage which unknown to him walked in the ironlike black coat before him: *Maybe he will feel it too. Maybe it will even change him now from what maybe he couldn't help but be.*

They crossed the portico. Now he could hear his father's stiff foot as it came down on the boards with clocklike finality, a sound out of all proportion to the displacement of the body it bore and which was not dwarfed either by the white door before it, as though it had attained to a sort of vicious and ravening minimum not to be dwarfed by anything—the flat, wide, black hat, the formal coat of broadcloth which had once been black but which had now that friction-glazed greenish cast of the bodies of old house flies, the lifted sleeve which was too large, the lifted hand like a curled claw. The door opened so promptly that the boy knew the Negro must have been watching them all the time, an old man with neat grizzled hair, in a linen jacket, who stood barring the door with his body, saying, "Wipe yo foots, white man, fo you come in here. Major ain't home nohow."

"Get out of my way, nigger," his father said, without heat too, flinging the door back and the Negro also and entering, his hat still on his head. And now the boy saw the prints of the stiff foot on the doorjamb and saw them appear on the pale rug behind the machinelike deliberation of the foot which seemed to bear (or transmit) twice the weight which the body compassed. The Negro was shouting "Miss Lula! Miss Lula!" somewhere behind them, then the boy, deluged as though by a warm wave by a suave turn of carpeted stair and a pendant glitter of chandeliers and a mute gleam of gold frames, heard the swift feet and saw her too, a lady—perhaps he had never seen her like before either—in a gray, smooth gown with lace at the throat and an apron tied at the waist and the sleeves turned back, wiping cake or biscuit dough from her hands with a towel as she came up the hall, looking not at his father at all but at the tracks on the blond rug with an expression of incredulous amazement.

"I tried," the Negro cried. "I tole him to . . ."

"Will you please go away?" she said in a shaking voice. "Major de Spain is not at home. Will you please go away?"

His father had not spoken again. He did not speak again. He did not even look at her. He just stood stiff in the center of the rug, in his hat, the shaggy iron-gray brows twitching slightly above the pebble-colored eyes as he appeared to examine the house with brief deliberation. Then with the same deliberation he turned; the boy watched him pivot on the good leg and saw the stiff foot drag round the arc of the turning, leaving a final long and fading smear. His father never looked at it, he never once looked down at the rug. The Negro held the door. It closed behind them, upon the hysteric and indistinguishable womanwail. His father stopped at the top of the steps and scraped his boot clean on the edge of it. At the gate he stopped again. He stood for a moment, planted stiffly on the stiff foot, looking back at the house. "Pretty and white, ain't it?" he said. "That's sweat. Nigger sweat. Maybe it ain't white enough yet to suit him. Maybe he wants to mix some white sweat with it."

Two hours later the boy was chopping wood behind the house within which his mother and aunt and the two sisters (the mother and aunt, not the two girls, he knew that; even at this distance and muffled by walls the flat loud voices of the two girls emanated an incorrigible idle inertia) were setting up the stove to prepare a meal, when he heard the hooves and saw the linen-clad man on a fine sorrel mare, whom he recognized even before he saw the rolled rug in front of the Negro youth following on a fat bay carriage horse—a suffused, angry face vanishing, still at full gallop, beyond the corner of the house where his father and brother were sitting in the two tilted chairs; and a moment later, almost before he could have put the axe down, he heard the hooves again and watched the sorrel mare go back out of the yard, already galloping again. Then his father began to shout one of the sisters' names, who presently emerged backward from the kitchen door dragging the rolled rug along the ground by one end while the other sister walked behind it.

"If you ain't going to tote, go on and set up the wash pot," the first said.

"You, Sarty!" the second shouted. "Set up the wash pot!" His father appeared at the door, framed against that shabbiness, as he had been against that other bland perfection, impervious to either, the mother's anxious face at his shoulder.

"Go on," the father said. "Pick it up." The two sisters stooped, broad, lethargic; stooping, they presented an incredible expanse of pale cloth and a flutter of tawdry ribbons.

"If I thought enough of a rug to have to git hit all the way from France I wouldn't keep hit where folks coming in would have to tromp on hit," the first said. They raised the rug.

"Abner," the mother said. "Let me do it."

"You go back and git dinner," his father said. "I'll tend to this."

From the woodpile through the rest of the afternoon the boy watched them, the rug spread flat in the dust beside the bubbling wash-pot, the two sisters stooping over it with that profound and lethargic reluctance, while the father stood over them in turn, implacable and grim, driving them though never raising his voice again. He could smell the harsh homemade lye they were using; he saw his mother come to the door once and look toward them with an expression not anxious now but very like despair; he saw his father turn, and he fell to with the axe and saw from the corner of his eye his father raise from the ground a flattish fragment of field stone and examine it and return to the pot, and this time his mother actually spoke: "Abner. Abner. Please don't. Please, Abner."

Then he was done too. It was dusk; the whippoorwills had already begun. He could smell coffee from the room where they would presently eat the cold food remaining from the mid-afternoon meal, though when he entered the house he realized they were having coffee again probably because there was a fire on the hearth, before which the rug now lay spread over the backs of the two chairs. The tracks of his father's foot were gone. Where they had been were now long, water-cloudy scoriations resembling the sporadic course of a Lilliputian mowing machine.

It still hung there while they ate the cold food and then went to bed, scattered without order or claim up and down the two rooms, his mother in one bed, where his father would later lie, the older brother in the other, himself, the aunt, and the two sisters on pallets on the floor. But his father was not in bed yet. The last thing the boy remembered was the depthless, harsh silhouette of the hat and coat bending over the rug and it seemed to him that he had not even closed his eyes when the silhouette was standing over him, the fire almost dead behind it, the stiff foot prodding him awake. "Catch up the mule," his father said.

When he returned with the mule his father was standing in the black door, the rolled rug over his shoulder. "Ain't you going to ride?" he said.

"No. Give me your foot."

He bent his knee into his father's hand, the wiry, surprising power flowed smoothly, rising, he rising with it, on to the mule's bare back (they had owned a saddle once; the boy could remember it though not when or where) and with the same effortlessness his father swung the rug up in front of him. Now in the starlight they retraced the afternoon's path, up the dusty road rife with honeysuckle, through the gate and up the black tunnel of the drive to the lightless house, where he sat on the mule and felt the rough warp of the rug drag across his thighs and vanish.

"Don't you want me to help?" he whispered. His father did not answer and now he heard again that stiff foot striking the hollow portico with that wooden and clocklike deliberation, that outrageous overstatement of the weight it carried. The rug, hunched, not flung (the boy could tell that even in the darkness) from his father's shoulder struck the angle of wall and floor with a sound unbelievably loud, thunderous, then the foot again, unhurried and enormous; a light came on in the house and the boy sat, tense, breathing steadily and quietly and just a little fast, though the foot itself did not increase its beat at all, descending the steps now; now the boy could see him.

60 "Don't you want to ride now?" he whispered. "We kin both ride now," the light within the house altering now, flaring up and sinking. *He's coming down the stairs now,* he thought. He had already ridden the mule up beside the horse block; presently his father was up behind him and he doubled the reins over and slashed the mule across the neck, but before the animal could begin to trot the hard, thin arm came round him, the hard, knotted hand jerking the mule back to a walk.

In the first red rays of the sun they were in the lot, putting plow gear on the mules. This time the sorrel mare was in the lot before he heard it at all, the rider collarless and even bareheaded, trembling, speaking in a shaking voice as the woman in the house had done, his father merely looking up once before stooping again to the hame he was buckling, so that the man on the mare spoke to his stooping back:

"You must realize you have ruined that rug. Wasn't there anybody here, any of your women . . ." he ceased, shaking, the boy watching him, the older brother leaning now in the stable door, chewing, blinking slowly and steadily at nothing apparently. "It cost a hundred dollars. But you never had a hundred dollars. You never will. So I'm going to charge you twenty bushels of corn against your crop. I'll add it in your contract and when you come to the commissary you can sign it. That won't keep Mrs. de Spain quiet but maybe it will teach you to wipe your feet off before you enter her house again."

Then he was gone. The boy looked at his father, who still had not spoken or even looked up again, who was now adjusting the logger-head in the hame.

"Pap," he said. His father looked at him—the inscrutable face, the shaggy brows beneath which the gray eyes glinted coldly. Suddenly the boy went toward him, fast, stopping as suddenly. "You done the best you could!" he cried. "If he wanted hit done different why didn't he wait and tell you how? He won't git no twenty bushels! He won't git none! We'll gether hit and hide hit! I kin watch . . ."

65 "Did you put the cutter back in that straight stock like I told you?"

"No, sir," he said.

"Then go do it."

That was Wednesday. During the rest of that week he worked steadily, at what was within his scope and some which was beyond it, with an industry that did not need to be driven nor even commanded twice; he had this from his mother, with the difference that some at least of what he did he liked to do, such as splitting wood with the half-size axe which his mother and aunt had earned, or saved money somehow, to present him with at Christmas. In company with the two older women (and on one afternoon, even one of the sisters), he built pens for the shoat and the cow which were a part of his father's contract with the landlord, and one afternoon, his father being absent, gone somewhere on one of the mules, he went to the field.

They were running a middle buster[3] now, his brother holding the plow straight while he handled the reins, and walking beside the straining mule, the rich black soil shearing cool and damp against his bare ankles, he thought *Maybe this is the end of it. Maybe even that twenty bushels that seems hard to have to pay for just a rug will be a cheap price for him to stop forever and always from being what he used to be;* thinking, dreaming now, so that his brother had to speak sharply to him to mind the mule: *Maybe he even won't collect the twenty bushels. Maybe it will all add up and balance and vanish—corn, rug, fire; the terror and grief, the being pulled two ways like between two teams of horses—gone, done with for ever and ever.*

Then it was Saturday; he looked up from beneath the mule he was harnessing 70
and saw his father in the black coat and hat. "Not that," his father said. "The wagon gear." And then, two hours later, sitting in the wagon bed behind his father and brother on the seat, the wagon accomplished a final curve, and he saw the weathered paintless store with its tattered tobacco- and patent-medicine posters and the tethered wagons and saddle animals below the gallery. He mounted the gnawed steps behind his father and brother, and there again was the lane of quiet, watching faces for the three of them to walk through. He saw the man in spectacles sitting at the plank table and he did not need to be told this was a Justice of the Peace; he sent one glare of fierce, exultant, partisan defiance at the man in collar and cravat now, whom he had seen but twice before in his life, and that on a galloping horse, who now wore on his face an expression not of rage but of amazed unbelief which the boy could not have known was at the incredible circumstance of being sued by one of his own tenants, and came and stood against his father and cried at the Justice: "He ain't done it! He ain't burnt . . ."

"Go back to the wagon," his father said.

"Burnt?" the Justice said. "Do I understand this rug was burned too?"

"Does anybody here claim it was?" his father said. "Go back to the wagon." But he did not, he merely retreated to the rear of the room, crowded as that other had been, but not to sit down this time, instead, to stand pressing among the motionless bodies, listening to the voices:

"And you claim twenty bushels of corn is too high for the damage you did to the rug?"

"He brought the rug to me and said he wanted the tracks washed out of it. I 75
washed the tracks out and took the rug back to him."

"But you didn't carry the rug back to him in the same condition it was in before you made the tracks on it."

His father did not answer, and now for perhaps half a minute there was no sound at all save that of breathing, the faint, steady suspiration of complete and intent listening.

3. A double moldboard plow that throws a ridge of earth both ways.

"You decline to answer that, Mr. Snopes?" Again his father did not answer. "I'm going to find against you, Mr. Snopes. I'm going to find that you were responsible for the injury to Major de Spain's rug and hold you liable for it. But twenty bushels of corn seems a little high for a man in your circumstances to have to pay. Major de Spain claims it cost a hundred dollars. October corn will be worth about fifty cents. I figure that if Major de Spain can stand a ninety-five dollar loss on something he paid cash for, you can stand a five-dollar loss you haven't earned yet. I hold you in damages to Major de Spain to the amount of ten bushels of corn over and above your contract with him, to be paid to him out of your crop at gathering time. Court adjourned."

It had taken no time hardly, the morning was but half begun. He thought they would return home and perhaps back to the field, since they were late, far behind all other farmers. But instead his father passed on behind the wagon, merely indicating with his hand for the older brother to follow with it, and crossed the road toward the blacksmith shop opposite, pressing on after his father, overtaking him, speaking, whispering up at the harsh, calm face beneath the weathered hat: "He won't git no ten bushels neither. He won't git one. We'll . . ." until his father glanced for an instant down at him, the face absolutely calm, the grizzled eyebrows tangled above the cold eyes, the voice almost pleasant, almost gentle:

80 "You think so? Well, we'll wait till October anyway."

The matter of the wagon—the setting of a spoke or two and the tightening of the tires—did not take long either, the business of the tires accomplished by driving the wagon into the spring branch behind the shop and letting it stand there, the mules nuzzling into the water from time to time, and the boy on the seat with the idle reins, looking up the slope and through the sooty tunnel of the shed where the slow hammer rang and where his father sat on an upended cypress bolt, easily, either talking or listening, still sitting there when the boy brought the dripping wagon up out of the branch and halted it before the door.

"Take them on to the shade and hitch," his father said. He did so and returned. His father and the smith and a third man squatting on his heels inside the door were talking, about crops and animals; the boy, squatting too in the ammoniac dust and hoof-parings and scales of rust, heard his father tell a long and unhurried story out of the time before the birth of the older brother even when he had been a professional horsetrader. And then his father came up beside him where he stood before a tattered last year's circus poster on the other side of the store, gazing rapt and quiet at the scarlet horses, the incredible poisings and convolutions of tulle and tights and the painted leers of comedians, and said, "It's time to eat."

But not at home. Squatting beside his brother against the front wall, he watched his father emerge from the store and produce from a paper sack a segment of cheese and divide it carefully and deliberately into three with his pocket knife and produce crackers from the same sack. They all three squatted on the gallery and ate, slowly, without talking; then in the store again, they drank from a tin dipper tepid water smelling of the cedar bucket and of living beech trees. And still they did not go home. It was a horse lot this time, a tall rail fence upon and along which men stood and sat and out of which one by one horses were led, to be walked and trotted and then cantered back and forth along the road while the slow swapping and buying went on and the sun began to slant westward, they—the three of them—watching and listening, the older brother with his muddy eyes and his steady, inevitable tobacco, the father commenting now and then on certain of the animals, to no one in particular.

It was after sundown when they reached home. They ate supper by lamplight, then, sitting on the doorstep, the boy watched the night fully accomplish, listening to the whippoorwills and the frogs, when he heard his mother's voice: "Abner! No! No! Oh, God. Oh, God. Abner!" and he rose, whirled, and saw the altered light through the door where a candle stub now burned in a bottle neck on the table and his father, still in the hat and coat, at once formal and burlesque as though dressed carefully for some shabby and ceremonial violence, emptying the reservoir of the lamp back into the five-gallon kerosene can from which it had been filled, while the mother tugged at his arm until he shifted the lamp to the other hand and flung her back, not savagely or viciously, just hard, into the wall, her hands flung out against the wall for balance, her mouth open and in her face the same quality of hopeless despair as had been in her voice. Then his father saw him standing in the door.

"Go to the barn and get that can of oil we were oiling the wagon with," he 85
said. The boy did not move. Then he could speak.

"What . . ." he cried. "What are you . . ."

"Go get that oil," his father said. "Go."

Then he was moving, running, outside the house, toward the stable: this the old habit, the old blood which he had not been permitted to choose for himself, which had been bequeathed him willy nilly and which had run for so long (and who knew where, battening on what of outrage and savagery and lust) before it came to him. *I could keep on,* he thought. *I could run on and on and never look back, never need to see his face again. Only I can't. I can't,* the rusted can in his hand now, the liquid sploshing in it as he ran back to the house and into it, into the sound of his mother's weeping in the next room, and handed the can to his father.

"Ain't you going to even send a nigger?" he cried. "At least you sent a nigger before!"

This time his father didn't strike him. The hand came even faster than the blow had, the same hand which had set the can on the table with almost excruciating care flashing from the can toward him too quick for him to follow it, gripping him by the back of his shirt and on to tiptoe before he had seen it quit the can, the face stooping at him in breathless and frozen ferocity, the cold, dead voice speaking over him to the older brother, who leaned against the table, chewing with that steady, curious, sidewise motion of cows:

"Empty the can into the big one and go on. I'll catch up with you."

"Better tie him up to the bedpost," the brother said.

"Do like I told you," the father said. Then the boy was moving, his bunched shirt and the hard, bony hand between his shoulder-blades, his toes just touching the floor, across the room and into the other one, past the sisters sitting with spread heavy thighs in the two chairs over the cold hearth, and to where his mother and aunt sat side by side on the bed, the aunt's arms about his mother's shoulders.

"Hold him," the father said. The aunt made a startled movement. "Not you," the father said. "Lennie. Take hold of him. I want to see you do it." His mother took him by the wrist. "You'll hold him better than that. If he gets loose don't you know what he is going to do? He will go up yonder." He jerked his head toward the road. "Maybe I'd better tie him."

"I'll hold him," his mother whispered.

"See you do then." Then his father was gone, the stiff foot heavy and measured upon the boards, ceasing at last.

Then he began to struggle. His mother caught him in both arms, he jerking and wrenching at them. He would be stronger in the end, he knew that. But he had no time to wait for it. "Lemme go!" he cried. "I don't want to have to hit you!"

"Let him go!" the aunt said. "If he don't go, before God, I am going up there myself!"

"Don't you see I can't?" his mother cried. "Sarty! Sarty! No! No! Help me, Lizzie!"

Then he was free. His aunt grasped at him but it was too late. He whirled, running, his mother stumbled forward on to her knees behind him, crying to the nearer sister: "Catch him, Net! Catch him!" But that was too late too, the sister (the sisters were twins, born at the same time, yet either of them now gave the impression of being, encompassing as much living meat and volume and weight as any other two of the family) not yet having begun to rise from the chair, her head, face, alone merely turned, presenting to him in the flying instant an astonishing expanse of young female features untroubled by any surprise even, wearing only an expression of bovine interest. Then he was out of the room, out of the house, in the mild dust of the starlit road and the heavy rifeness of honeysuckle, the pale ribbon unspooling with terrific slowness under his running feet, reaching the gate at last and turning in, running, his heart and lungs drumming, on up the drive toward the lighted house, the lighted door. He did not knock, he burst in, sobbing for breath, incapable for the moment of speech; he saw the astonished face of the Negro in the linen jacket without knowing when the Negro had appeared.

"De Spain!" he cried, panted. "Where's . . ." then he saw the white man too emerging from a white door down the hall. "Barn!" he cried. "Barn!"

"What?" the white man said. "Barn?"

"Yes!" the boy cried. "Barn!"

"Catch him!" the white man shouted.

But it was too late this time too. The Negro grasped his shirt, but the entire sleeve, rotten with washing, carried away, and he was out that door too and in the drive again, and had actually never ceased to run even while he was screaming into the white man's face.

Behind him the white man was shouting, "My horse! Fetch my horse!" and he thought for an instant of cutting across the park and climbing the fence into the road, but he did not know the park nor how high the vine-massed fence might be and he dared not risk it. So he ran on down the drive, blood and breath roaring; presently he was in the road again though he could not see it. He could not hear either: the galloping mare was almost upon him before he heard her, and even then he held his course, as if the very urgency of his wild grief and need must in a moment more find his wings, waiting until the ultimate instant to hurl himself aside and into the weed-choked roadside ditch as the horse thundered past and on, for an instant in furious silhouette against the stars, the tranquil early summer night sky which, even before the shape of the horse and rider vanished, stained abruptly and violently upward: a long, swirling roar incredible and soundless, blotting the stars, and he springing up and into the road again, running again, knowing it was too late yet still running even after he heard the shot and, an instant later, two shots, pausing now without knowing he had ceased to run, crying "Pap! Pap!", running again before he knew he had begun to run, stumbling, tripping over something and scrabbling up again without ceasing to run, looking backward over his shoulder at the glare as he got up, running on among the invisible trees, panting, sobbing, "Father! Father!"

At midnight he was sitting on the crest of a hill. He did not know it was midnight and he did not know how far he had come. But there was no glare behind him now and he sat now, his back toward what he had called home for four days anyhow, his face toward the dark woods which he would enter when breath was strong again, small, shaking steadily in the chill darkness, hugging himself into the remainder of his thin, rotten shirt, the grief and despair now no longer terror and fear but just grief and despair. *Father. My father*, he thought. "He was brave!" he cried suddenly, aloud but not loud, no more than a whisper: "He was! He was in the war! He was in Colonel Sartoris' cav'ry!" not knowing that his father had gone to that war a private in the fine old European sense, wearing no uniform, admitting the authority of and giving fidelity to no man or army or flag, going to war as Malbrouck[4] himself did: for booty—it meant nothing and less than nothing to him if it were enemy booty or his own.

The slow constellations wheeled on. It would be dawn and then sun-up after a while and he would be hungry. But that would be to-morrow and now he was only cold, and walking would cure that. His breathing was easier now and he decided to get up and go on, and then he found that he had been asleep because he knew it was almost dawn, the night almost over. He could tell that from the whippoorwills. They were everywhere now among the dark trees below him, constant and inflectioned and ceaseless, so that, as the instant for giving over to the day birds drew nearer and nearer, there was no interval at all between them. He got up. He was a little stiff, but walking would cure that too as it would the cold, and soon there would be the sun. He went on down the hill, toward the dark woods within which the liquid silver voices of the birds called unceasing—the rapid and urgent beating of the urgent and quiring heart of the late spring night. He did not look back.

1939

4. The duke of Marlborough (1650–1722), an English general whose name became distorted as Malbrough and Malbrouch in English and French popular songs celebrating his exploits.

The reservations I hear most often can be summarized as three "charges":

1. Faulkner's style is bad. His sentences are often too long and complicated, vague, unnecessarily wordy and sometimes hard to read.

2. The structure of the story seems almost haphazard: it wanders off the subject or out of focus.

3. The reasons the story gives—and insists upon—for people acting the way they do are unrealistic and shallow.

Can a story with a dubious style, form, theme, and vision of human actions and motives be good, much less great? Should I, must I, like it, or at least recognize its "literary value"?

Let us see a few examples of what those who find the story flawed might isolate, analyze, and articulate. We can begin with Faulkner's awkward and obscure style and pick out an early sentence—the second sentence of the story—as evidence:

> The boy, crouched on his nail keg at the back of the crowded room, knew he smelled cheese, and more: from where he sat he could see the ranked shelves close-packed with the solid, squat, dynamic shapes of tin cans whose labels his stomach read, not from the lettering which meant nothing to his mind but from the scarlet devils and the silver curve of fish—this, the cheese which he knew he smelled and the hermetic meat which his intestines believed he smelled coming in intermittent gusts momentary and brief between the other constant one, the smell and sense just a little of fear because mostly of despair and grief, the old fierce pull of blood.

Even those who do not mind taking some pains in reading will probably acknowledge that this sentence is not immediately clear. The chief problem is how to relate the final phrase "the old fierce pull of blood" to the rest of the sentence, and so to discover what the sentence as a whole means. After a little work, you may decide that what the sentence says is that there is not only the smell of cheese and the imagined smell of canned meat but also the smell of despair and grief and even some smell of fear; and that despair, grief, and fear are in the boy's "blood," that is, inherited, in his genes. We still cannot be sure whether this implies that acquired traits or experiences are hereditary or whether "blood" means something else, and we still cannot be sure whether the smell of fear is imaginary—like the smell of the meat in the cans—or real—like the smell of the cheese (perhaps the smell of the sweat that comes with fear, or the odor some say fear gives off). But even if we have been successful in our unraveling of the meaning, what is the value of a sentence that has to be worked over so much and whose meaning even then is doubtful?

Now as to the matter of form. One reason "The Most Dangerous Game" is just a slick adventure story, some people say, is that everything in it is manipulated to heighten suspense. But if we criticize Connell for shifting focus for his own purposes, what can we say about the shifting of the focus in "Barn Burning"? One such shift occurs when the narrator is explaining why the man who burns other people's barns lights only a small neat fire when it is for his own use:

> Older, the boy might have remarked this and wondered why not a big one; why should not a man who had in his blood an inherent voracious prodigality with material not his own, have burned everything in sight? Then he might have gone a step farther and thought that that was the reason: that niggard blaze was the living fruit of nights passed during those four years in the woods hiding from all men, blue or gray, with his strings of horses (captured horses, he called them). And older still, he might have divined the true reason: that the element of fire spoke to some deep mainspring of his father's being, as the element of steel or of powder spoke to other men, as the one weapon for the preservation of integrity, else breath were not worth the breathing, and hence to be regarded with respect and used with discretion.

Is it okay to shift the focus temporally like this because the purpose of the shift is not "merely" to enhance the suspense but to clarify the meaning, to reveal "the true reason"?

Sometimes the focus shifts to a time outside the story's present, as it does here, but also away from the consciousness of the boy that, like Rainsford's in "The Most Dangerous Game," dominates the rest of the story. When the father climbs aboard the wagon and immediately starts hitting the mules with a willow switch, the narrator comments,

> It was not even sadistic; it was exactly the same quality which in later years would cause his descendants to over-run the engine before putting a motor car into motion, striking and reining back in the same movement.

The time moves backward as well as forward and it always seems to do so in order to clarify or emphasize the meaning or illustrate the concept of "blood"—inborn, inherited habits or feelings. So, when his father tells him to get a can of oil the boy knows will be used to burn still another barn, despite the boy's repugnance at the act, he does it:

> Then he was moving, running, outside the house, toward the stable: this the old habit, the old blood which he had not been permitted to choose for himself, which had been bequeathed him willy nilly and which had run for so long (and who knew where, battening on what of outrage and savagery and lust) before it came to him. *I could keep on*, he thought. *I could run on and on and never look back, never need to see his face again. Only I can't. I can't . . .*

This passage leads us directly into the third reservation or question, that having to do with the story's vision of the springs of human action. Can we accept that such habits, such capacities or incapacities, are bred into the "blood"? Can we even accept that this is a concept that can be taken seriously, even if we cannot accept it? And if a serious concept, where does it lead? to genetic determinism of one kind or another? to justify "class"? to racism?

And, to go back to the earlier passage about the fire: what does it mean that fire can be a "deep mainspring of his father's being, as the element of steel or powder spoke to other men"? And how is it that fire, swords, guns—violence—can be weapons "for the preservation of integrity" without which life is not worth living? What is the "integrity" that the father is so intent on preserving? And what kind of "discretion" does the father show in his use of fire? What makes our acceptance of what this passage seems to say crucial is that it is not embedded in the fiction, as part of the action and thoughts of the characters—the boy, let us say—but it is separated from them by the shift in focus and by the flat statement that we are being given the "true reason"; so it has the authority of the story / author and we either have to believe it or discount the whole vision of the story.

And if we look beneath the surface of these "true reasons" and the "pull of blood" and look at the events of the story itself, we begin to suspect a "hidden agenda," an ideology that determines what the characters are seen to do and why.

Why is it that the boy overcomes or betrays the "pull of blood" only when the "aristocratic" Major de Spain's barn is to be burned? Is the blood of the highborn somehow more valuable than that of the low? (Though a Snopes, the boy's first name is that of the aristocrat Colonel Sartoris.) Is some blood better than others? some loyalties better than others? Or is property a higher good than blood?

The selection of certain key passages or incidents, the analysis and interpretation of the text, can be used to directly confront these critical comments and questions, as well as to explore other, more positive areas of the story and its accomplishment. And the objections themselves can be examined in terms of what unspoken assumptions they make about what makes a story good, and what agendas they hide.

The long second sentence of "Barn Burning" does indeed put extraordinary emphasis on "blood." The concept here embodied in the word "blood" can stand such emphasis, even demands it, for "blood" is one of the forces that are in conflict within the boy. Therefore the sentence, though it may seem difficult, really gives ready access to the meaning of the story by calling attention to one of its key elements. Part of its length, too, consists in magnificent particularizing detail, the kind that convinces you that the author knows what he is talking about, and really "sees" the scene. (See the comments Ford Maddox Ford makes on the first sentence in "Odour of Chrysanthemums"; you can make the same kind of analysis of this sentence.) The density of detail is also necessary in realizing (making real) the boy's sensations. The detail and the focus of the sentence also indicate where the significant action of the story is to take place—that is, inside the boy—and so we are made to understand and perhaps feel with him. Finally, the move from the smell of cheese to the "smell" of canned meat, to that of fear, is crucial: the smell of cheese is real. The smell of meat is inside the can and though it cannot actually be smelled while the can is intact it is real and is there. So what this suggests is that the boy's sensory imagination does not falsify, it just penetrates into things beyond the immediate present sense perceptions. This gives reality to the smell of despair, grief, fear—not necessarily real to the senses, but really there beneath the surface, real to the imagination. What the sentence does, then, is open up our notions of reality to include not just what the senses tell us, but what the imagination can sense. And since it does so through sensory images that gradually shade off into the imaginative, we are not just told that the imaginative is valid but we are made to feel that this is so. Thus the sentence that seemed unnecessarily long, complex, and difficult turns out to be functional. It does what no short sentence or series of sentences would be likely to manage.

Complexity, even obscurity, is not in all cases "bad"—as the criticism of the sentence seemed to assume. The literary value of language and detail does not necessarily follow rules of usage but questions of function—whether they work to create, reveal, intensify, the meaning and effect of the story.

Before going on to address the issue of the structure or theme of "Barn Burning," it may be appropriate to suggest that it is precisely in this merging of the physical and the imaginative, moral or psychological, that one of the strengths of the story—and of Faulkner—lies. The force that opposes blood, we soon learn, is the boy's sense of right and wrong. His father is accused of maliciously burning down Mr. Harris's barn. The boy knows his father is guilty. But when Harris demands the boy be called before the judge, the boy knows that because his ties to his father are those of "blood," he must lie. When the judge asks if Harris really wants the boy questioned there is a pause. For a boy,

> . . . it was as if he had swung outward at the end of a grape vine, over a ravine, and at the top of the swing had been caught in a prolonged instant of mesmerized gravity, weightless in time.

Most readers would acknowledge the appropriateness of the image both to the feeling of suspense and to the experience of the boy, and the intervention of the image suspends the meaning and imitates the boy's suspense. When Harris says the boy does not have to testify, "the smell of cheese and sealed meat, the fear and despair and the old grief of blood" return to the boy's consciousness. The importance and meaning of fear, despair, and grief in the "blood" is now a little clearer.

Faulkner's complexity, "idiosyncrasies" (what some call "flaws"), and difficulty (sometimes called "obscurity") usually come from this interpenetration of imagination and sensory reality or other things that we usually keep separate, like past and present. Each episode, character, detail, is saturated with the full world of his fiction, and its function seems to be primarily to embody that world rather than to further the plot or make a statement. The present is informed by the past and informs the future. Characters (Major de Spain) and names (Colonel Sartoris) that are minor or casual here are central elsewhere in Faulkner's canon, like actors in a repertory theater. The fiction is all one seamless, interconnected, timeless world. The interpenetration of community and generations is essential to the vision.

This gives both a smaller and larger role to the concept of "blood." "Blood" alone—inherited traits, customs, motives—does not determine behavior, but it is one of the multitude of communal and traditional forces that condition behavior. Though "blood" can explain many acts and impulses, its force does not eliminate free will. The boy does, after all, choose to warn the Major of his father's intention, chooses morality over blood. To claim that it was only Major de Spain's class or property that moved the boy to consider betraying his father is to ignore the fact that the story opens with his being on the verge of doing so in the Harris case. The father's crimes went well beyond the destruction of property; indeed it was the primacy of property over principles in his scheme of values that led him to serve neither North nor South but Mammon (by being a non-partisan horse thief) during the Civil War.

Explaining the function of what may at first have seemed defects does not close the discussion about the merits of a work or the nature and function of literature. The discussion of the value of "Barn Burning" does not necessarily end here.

Until now, we have depersonalized the evaluations, assuming that the pros and cons are intellectual positions that have little or nothing to do with an individual reader, and that the "evidence" is always in the story. But already we have seen that some of the response to Faulkner is ideological, based on social or political values that have little to do with whether the focus shifts or the sentences are too long. We must admit that not all evidence of value is "on the page"; some beauty is in the eyes of the beholder. Let us keep this in mind—that is, be aware of our own responses and try at the same time to account for those responses both in terms of the narrative strategies and in terms of our own prejudices or predispositions.

BHARATI MUKHERJEE

The Management of Grief

A woman I don't know is boiling tea the Indian way in my kitchen. There are a lot of women I don't know in my kitchen, whispering, and moving tactfully. They open doors, rummage through the pantry, and try not to ask me where things are kept. They remind me of when my sons were small, on Mother's Day or when Vikram and I were tired, and they would make big, sloppy omelets. I would lie in bed pretending I didn't hear them.

Dr. Sharma, the treasurer of the Indo-Canada Society, pulls me into the hallway. He wants to know if I am worried about money. His wife, who has just come up from the basement with a tray of empty cups and glasses, scolds him. "Don't bother Mrs. Bhave with mundane details." She looks so monstrously pregnant her baby must be days overdue. I tell her she shouldn't be carrying heavy things. "Shaila," she says, smiling, "this is the fifth." Then she grabs a teenager by his shirttails. He slips his Walkman off his head. He has to be one of her four children, they have the same domed and dented foreheads. "What's the official word now?" she demands. The boy slips the headphones back on. "They're acting evasive, Ma. They're saying it could be an accident or a terrorist bomb."

All morning, the boys have been muttering, Sikh Bomb, Sikh Bomb. The men, not using the word, bow their heads in agreement. Mrs. Sharma touches her forehead at such a word. At least they've stopped talking about space debris and Russian lasers.

Two radios are going in the dining room. They are tuned to different stations. Someone must have brought the radios down from my boys' bedrooms. I haven't gone into their rooms since Kusum came running across the front lawn in her bathrobe. She looked so funny, I was laughing when I opened the door.

The big TV in the den is being whizzed through American networks and 5
cable channels.

"Damn!" some man swears bitterly. "How can these preachers carry on like nothing's happened?" I want to tell him we're not that important. You look at the audience, and at the preacher in his blue robe with his beautiful white hair, the potted palm trees under a blue sky, and you know they care about nothing.

The phone rings and rings. Dr. Sharma's taken charge. "We're with her," he keeps saying. "Yes, yes, the doctor has given calming pills. Yes, yes, pills are having necessary effect." I wonder if pills alone explain this calm. Not peace, just a deadening quiet. I was always controlled, but never repressed. Sound can reach me, but my body is tensed, ready to scream. I hear their voices all around me. I hear my boys and Vikram cry, "Mommy, Shaila!" and their screams insulate me, like headphones.

The woman boiling water tells her story again and again. "I got the news first. My cousin called from Halifax before six A.M., can you imagine? He'd gotten up for prayers and his son was studying for medical exams and he heard on a rock channel that something had happened to a plane. They said first it had disappeared from the radar, like a giant eraser just reached out. His father called me, so I said to him, what do you mean, 'something bad'? You mean a hijacking? And he said, *behn*[1], there is no confirmation of anything yet, but check with your neighbors because a lot of them must be on that plane. So I called poor Kusum straightaway. I knew Kusum's husband and daughter were booked to go yesterday."

Kusum lives across the street from me. She and Satish had moved in less than a month ago. They said they needed a bigger place. All these people, the Sharmas and friends from the Indo-Canada Society had been there for the housewarming. Satish and Kusum made homemade tandoori on their big gas grill and even the white neighbors piled their plates high with that luridly red, charred, juicy chicken. Their younger daughter had danced, and even our boys had broken away from the Stanley Cup telecast to put in a reluctant appearance. Everyone took pictures for their albums and for the community newspapers—another of our families had made it big in Toronto—and now I wonder how many of those happy faces are gone. "Why does God give us so much if all along He intends to take it away?" Kusum asks me.

I nod. We sit on carpeted stairs, holding hands like children. "I never once told him that I loved him," I say. I was too much the well brought up woman. I was so well brought up I never felt comfortable calling my husband by his first name.

"It's all right," Kusum says. "He knew. My husband knew. They felt it. Modern young girls have to say it because what they feel is fake."

Kusum's daughter, Pam, runs in with an overnight case. Pam's in her McDonald's uniform. "Mummy! You have to get dressed!" Panic makes her cranky. "A reporter's on his way here."

"Why?"

"You want to talk to him in your bathrobe?" She starts to brush her mother's long hair. She's the daughter who's always in trouble. She dates Canadian boys and hangs out in the mall, shopping for tight sweaters. The younger one, the goody-goody one according to Pam, the one with a voice so sweet that when she sang *bhajans*[2] for Ethiopian relief even a frugal man like my husband wrote out a hundred dollar check, *she* was on that plane. *She* was going to spend July and August with grandparents because Pam wouldn't go. Pam said she'd rather wait-

1. "No." 2. Hymns.

ress at McDonald's. "If it's a choice between Bombay and Wonderland, I'm picking Wonderland," she'd said.

"Leave me alone," Kusum yells. "You know what I want to do? If I didn't have to look after you now, I'd hang myself."

Pam's young face goes blotchy with pain. "Thanks," she says, "don't let me stop you."

"Hush," pregnant Mrs. Sharma scolds Pam. "Leave your mother alone. Mr. Sharma will tackle the reporters and fill out the forms. He'll say what has to be said."

Pam stands her ground. "You think I don't know what Mummy's thinking? *Why her?* that's what. That's sick! Mummy wishes my little sister were alive and I were dead."

Kusum's hand in mine is trembly hot. We continue to sit on the stairs.

She calls before she arrives, wondering if there's anything I need. Her name is Judith Templeton and she's an appointee of the provincial government. "Multiculturalism?" I ask, and she says, "partially," but that her mandate is bigger. "I've been told you knew many of the people on the flight," she says. "Perhaps if you'd agree to help us reach the others. . . ?"

She gives me time at least to put on tea water and pick up the mess in the front room. I have a few *samosas*[3] from Kusum's housewarming that I could fry up, but then I think, why prolong this visit?

Judith Templeton is much younger than she sounded. She wears a blue suit with a white blouse and a polka dot tie. Her blond hair is cut short, her only jewelry is pearl drop earrings. Her briefcase is new and expensive looking, a gleaming cordovan leather. She sits with it across her lap. When she looks out the front windows onto the street, her contact lenses seem to float in front of her light blue eyes.

"What sort of help do you want from me?" I ask. She has refused the tea, out of politeness, but I insist, along with some slightly stale biscuits.

"I have no experience," she admits. "That is, I have an MSW and I've worked in liaison with accident victims, but I mean I have no experience with a tragedy of this scale—"

"Who could?" I ask.

"—and with the complications of culture, language, and customs. Someone mentioned that Mrs. Bhave is a pillar—because you've taken it more calmly."

At this, perhaps, I frown, for she reaches forward, almost to take my hand. "I hope you understand my meaning, Mrs. Bhave. There are hundreds of people in Metro directly affected, like you, and some of them speak no English. There are some widows who've never handled money or gone on a bus, and there are old parents who still haven't eaten or gone outside their bedrooms. Some houses and apartments have been looted. Some wives are still hysterical. Some husbands are in shock and profound depression. We want to help, but our hands are tied in so many ways. We have to distribute money to some people, and

3. Fried turnovers filled with meat or vegetable mixtures.

there are legal documents—these things can be done. We have interpreters, but we don't always have the human touch, or maybe the right human touch. We don't want to make mistakes, Mrs. Bhave, and that's why we'd like to ask you to help us."

"More mistakes, you mean," I say.

"Police matters are not in my hands," she answers.

"Nothing I can do will make any difference," I say. "We must all grieve in our own way."

"But you are coping very well. All the people said, Mrs. Bhave is the strongest person of all. Perhaps if the others could see you, talk with you, it would help them."

"By the standards of the people you call hysterical, I am behaving very oddly and very badly, Miss Templeton." I want to say to her, *I wish I could scream, starve, walk into Lake Ontario, jump from a bridge.* "They would not see me as a model. I do not see myself as a model."

I am a freak. No one who has ever known me would think of me reacting this way. This terrible calm will not go away.

She asks me if she may call again, after I get back from a long trip that we all must make. "Of course," I say. "Feel free to call, anytime."

Four days later, I find Kusum squatting on a rock overlooking a bay in Ireland. It isn't a big rock, but it juts sharply out over water. This is as close as we'll ever get to them. June breezes balloon out her sari and unpin her knee-length hair. She has the bewildered look of a sea creature whom the tides have stranded.

It's been one hundred hours since Kusum came stumbling and screaming across my lawn. Waiting around the hospital, we've heard many stories. The police, the diplomats, they tell us things thinking that we're strong, that knowledge is helpful to the grieving, and maybe it is. Some, I know, prefer ignorance, or their own versions. The plane broke into two, they say. Unconsciousness was instantaneous. No one suffered. My boys must have just finished their breakfasts. They loved eating on planes, they loved the smallness of plates, knives, and forks. Last year they saved the airline salt and pepper shakers. Half an hour more and they would have made it to Heathrow.

Kusum says that we can't escape our fate. She says that all those people—our husbands, my boys, her girl with the nightingale voice, all those Hindus, Christians, Sikhs, Muslims, Parsis, and atheists on that plane—were fated to die together off this beautiful bay. She learned this from a swami in Toronto.

I have my Valium.

Six of us "relatives"—two widows and four widowers—choose to spend the day today by the waters instead of sitting in a hospital room and scanning photographs of the dead. That's what they call us now: relatives. I've looked through twenty-seven photos in two days. They're very kind to us, the Irish are very understanding. Sometimes understanding means freeing a tourist bus for this trip to the bay, so we can pretend to spy our loved ones through the glassiness of waves or in sunspeckled cloud shapes.

I could die here, too, and be content.

"What is that, out there?" She's standing and flapping her hands and for a moment I see a head shape bobbing in the waves. She's standing in the water, I, on the boulder. The tide is low, and a round, black, headsized rock has just risen from the waves. She returns, her sari end dripping and ruined and her face is a twisted remnant of hope, the way mine was a hundred hours ago, still laughing but inwardly knowing that nothing but the ultimate tragedy could bring two women together at six o'clock on a Sunday morning. I watch her face sag into blankness.

"That water felt warm, Shaila," she says at length.

"You can't," I say. "We have to wait for our turn to come."

I haven't eaten in four days, haven't brushed my teeth.

"I know," she says. "I tell myself I have no right to grieve. They are in a better place than we are. My swami says I should be thrilled for them. My swami says depression is a sign of our selfishness."

Maybe I'm selfish. Selfishly I break away from Kusum and run, sandals slapping against stones, to the water's edge. What if my boys aren't lying pinned under the debris? What if they aren't stuck a mile below that innocent blue chop? What if, given the strong currents. . . .

Now I've ruined my sari, one of my best. Kusum has joined me, knee-deep in water that feels to me like a swimming pool. I could settle in the water, and my husband would take my hand and the boys would slap water in my face just to see me scream.

"Do you remember what good swimmers my boys were, Kusum?"

"I saw the medals," she says.

One of the widowers, Dr. Ranganathan from Montreal, walks out to us, carrying his shoes in one hand. He's an electrical engineer. Someone at the hotel mentioned his work is famous around the world, something about the place where physics and electricity come together. He has lost a huge family, something indescribable. "With some luck," Dr. Ranganathan suggests to me, " a good swimmer could make it safely to some island. It is quite possible that there may be many, many microscopic islets scattered around."

"You're not just saying that?" I tell Dr. Ranganathan about Vinod, my elder son. Last year he took diving as well.

"It's a parent's duty to hope," he says. "It is foolish to rule out possibilities that have not been tested. I myself have not surrendered hope."

Kusum is sobbing once again. "Dear lady," he says, laying his free hand on her arm, and she calms down.

"Vinod is how old?" he asks me. He's very careful, as we all are. *Is*, not was.

"Fourteen. Yesterday he was fourteen. His father and uncle were going to take him down to the Taj and give him a big birthday party. I couldn't go with them because I couldn't get two weeks off from my stupid job in June." I process bills for a travel agent. June is a big travel month.

Dr. Ranganathan whips the pockets of his suit jacked inside out. Squashed roses, in darkening shades of pink, float on the water. He tore the roses off creepers in somebody's garden. He didn't ask anyone if he could pluck the roses, but now there's been an article about it in the local papers. When you see an Indian person, it says, please give him or her flowers.

"A strong youth of fourteen," he says, "can very likely pull to safety a younger one."

My sons, though four years apart, were very close. Vinod wouldn't let Mithun drown. *Electrical engineering*, I think, foolishly perhaps: this man knows important secrets of the universe, things closed to me. Relief spins me lightheaded. No wonder my boys' photographs haven't turned up in the gallery of photos of the recovered dead. "Such pretty roses," I say.

"My wife loved pink roses. Every Friday I had to bring a bunch home. I used to say, why? After twenty-odd years of marriage you're still needing proof positive of my love?" He has identified his wife and three of his children. Then others from Montreal, the lucky ones, intact families with no survivors. He chuckles as he wades back to shore. Then he swings around to ask me a question. "Mrs. Bhave, you are wanting to throw in some roses for your loved ones? I have two big ones left."

But I have other things to float: Vinod's pocket calculator; a half-painted model B-52 for my Mithun. They'd want them on their island. And for my husband? For him I let fall into the calm, glassy waters a poem I wrote in the hospital yesterday. Finally he'll know my feelings for him.

"Don't tumble, the rocks are slippery," Dr. Ranganathan cautions. He holds out a hand for me to grab.

Then it's time to get back on the bus, time to rush back to our waiting posts on hospital benches.

Kusum is one of the lucky ones. The lucky ones flew here, identified in multiplicate their loved ones, then will fly to India with the bodies for proper ceremonies. Satish is one of the few males who surfaced. The photos of faces we saw on the walls in an office at Heathrow and here in the hospital are mostly of women. Women have more body fat, a nun said to me matter-of-factly. They float better.

Today I was stopped by a young sailor on the street. He had loaded bodies, he'd gone into the water when—he checks my face for signs of strength—when the sharks were first spotted. I don't blush, and he breaks down. "It's all right," I say. "Thank you." I had heard about the sharks from Dr. Ranganathan. In his orderly mind, science brings understanding, it holds no terror. It is the shark's duty. For every deer there is a hunter, for every fish a fisherman.

The Irish are not shy; they rush to me and give me hugs and some are crying. I cannot imagine reactions like that on the streets of Toronto. Just strangers, and I am touched. Some carry flowers with them and give them to any Indian they see.

After lunch, a policeman I have gotten to know quite well catches hold of me. He says he thinks he has a match for Vinod. I explain what a good swimmer Vinod is.

"You want me with you when you look at photos?" Dr. Ranganathan walks ahead of me into the picture gallery. In these matters, he is a scientist, and I am grateful. It is a new perspective. "They have performed miracles," he says. "We are indebted to them."

The first day or two the policemen showed us relatives only one picture at a time; now they're in a hurry, they're eager to lay out the possibles, and even the probables.

The face on the photo is of a boy much like Vinod; the same intelligent eyes, the same thick brows dipping into a V. But this boy's features, even his cheeks, are puffier, wider, mushier.

"No." My gaze is pulled by other pictures. There are five other boys who look like Vinod.

The nun assigned to console me rubs the first picture with a fingertip. "When they've been in the water for a while, love, they look a little heavier." The bones under the skin are broken, they said on the first day—try to adjust your memories. It's important.

"It's not him. I'm his mother. I'd know."

"I know this one!" Dr. Ranganathan cries out suddenly from the back of the gallery. "And this one!" I think he senses that I don't want to find my boys. "They are the Kutty brothers. They were also from Montreal." I don't mean to be crying. On the contrary, I am ecstatic. My suitcase in the hotel is packed heavy with dry clothes for my boys.

The policeman starts to cry. "I am so sorry, I am so sorry, ma'am. I really thought we had a match."

With the nun ahead of us and the policeman behind, we, the unlucky ones without our children's bodies, file out of the makeshift gallery.

From Ireland most of us go on to India. Kusum and I take the same direct flight to Bombay, so I can help her clear customs quickly. But we have to argue with a man in uniform. He has large boils on his face. The boils swell and glow with sweat as we argue with him. He wants Kusum to wait in line and he refuses to take authority because his boss is on a tea break. But Kusum won't let her coffins out of sight, and I shan't desert her though I know that my parents, elderly and diabetic, must be waiting in a stuffy car in a scorching lot.

"You bastard!" I scream at the man with the popping boils. Other passengers press closer. "You think we're smuggling contraband in those coffins!"

Once upon a time we were well brought up women; we were dutiful wives who kept our heads veiled, our voices shy and sweet.

In India, I become, once again, an only child of rich, ailing parents. Old friends of the family come to pay their respects. Some are Sikh, and inwardly, involuntarily, I cringe. My parents are progressive people; they do not blame communities for a few individuals.

In Canada it is a different story now.

"Stay longer," my mother pleads. "Canada is a cold place. Why would you want to be all by yourself?" I stay.

Three months pass. Then another.

"Vikram wouldn't have wanted you to give up things!" they protest. They call my husband by the name he was born with. In Toronto he'd changed to Vik so the men he worked with at his office would find his name as easy as Rod or Chris. "You know, the dead aren't cut off from us!"

My grandmother, the spoiled daughter of a rich *zamindar*[4], shaved her head with rusty razor blades when she was widowed at sixteen. My grandfather died of childhood diabetes when he was nineteen, and she saw herself as the harbinger of bad luck. My mother grew up without parents, raised indifferently by an uncle, while her true mother slept in a hut behind the main estate house and took her food with the servants. She grew up a rationalist. My parents abhor mindless mortification.

The zamindar's daughter kept stubborn faith in Vedic rituals; my parents rebelled. I am trapped between two modes of knowledge. At thirty-six, I am too old to start over and too young to give up. Like my husband's spirit, I flutter between worlds.

Courting aphasia, we travel. We travel with our phalanx of servants and poor relatives. To hill stations and to beach resorts. We play contract bridge in dusty gymkhana clubs. We ride stubby ponies up crumbly mountain trails. At tea dances, we let ourselves be twirled twice round the ballroom. We hit the holy spots we hadn't made time for before. In Varanasi, Kalighat, Rishikesh, Hardwar, astrologers and palmists seek me out and for a fee offer me cosmic consolations.

Already the widowers among us are being shown new bride candidates. They cannot resist the call of custom, the authority of their parents and older brothers. They must marry; it is the duty of a man to look after a wife. The new wives will be young widows with children, destitute but of good family. They will make loving wives, but the men will shun them. I've had calls from the men over crackling Indian telephone lines. "Save me," they say, these substantial, educated, successful men of forty. "My parents are arranging a marriage for me." In a month they will have buried one family and returned to Canada with a new bride and partial family.

I am comparatively lucky. No one here thinks of arranging a husband for an unlucky widow.

Then, on the third day of the sixth month into this odyssey, in an abandoned temple in a tiny Himalayan village, as I make my offering of flowers and sweetmeats to the god of a tribe of animists, my husband descends to me. He is squatting next to a scrawny *sadhu* in moth-eaten robes. Vikram wears the vanilla suit he wore the last time I hugged him. The *sadhu* tosses petals on a butter-fed flame, reciting Sanskrit mantras and sweeps his face of flies. My husband takes my hands in his.

You're beautiful, he starts. Then, *What are you doing here?*

Shall I stay? I ask. He only smiles, but already the image is fading. *You must finish alone what we started together.* No seaweed wreathes his mouth. He speaks

4. Landowner.

too fast just as he used to when we were an envied family in our pink split-level. He is gone.

In the windowless altar room, smoky with joss sticks and clarified butter lamps, a sweaty hand gropes for my blouse. I do not shriek. The *sadhu* arranges his robe. The lamps hiss and sputter out.

When we come out of the temple, my mother says, "Did you feel something weird in there?"

My mother has no patience with ghosts, prophetic dreams, holy men, and cults.

"No," I lie. "Nothing."

But she knows that she's lost me. She knows that in days I shall be leaving.

Kusum's put her house up for sale. She wants to live in an ashram in Hardwar. Moving to Hardwar was her swami's idea. Her swami runs two ashrams, the one in Hardwar and another here in Toronto.

"Don't run away," I tell her.

"I'm not running away," she says. "I'm pursuing inner peace. You think you or that Ranganathan fellow are better off?"

Pam's left for California. She wants to do some modelling, she says. She says when she comes into her share of the insurance money she'll open a yoga-cum-aerobics studio in Hollywood. She sends me postcards so naughty I daren't leave them on the coffee table. Her mother has withdrawn from her and the world.

The rest of us don't lose touch, that's the point. Talk is all we have, says Dr. Ranganathan, who has also resisted his relatives and returned to Montreal and to his job, alone. He says, whom better to talk with than other relatives? We've been melted down and recast as a new tribe.

He calls me twice a week from Montreal. Every Wednesday night and every Saturday afternoon. He is changing jobs, going to Ottawa. But Ottawa is over a hundred miles away, and he is forced to drive two hundred and twenty miles a day. He can't bring himself to sell his house. The house is a temple, he says; the king-sized bed in the master bedroom is a shrine. He sleeps on a folding cot. A devotee.

There are still some hysterical relatives. Judith Templeton's list of those needing help and those who've "accepted" is in nearly perfect balance. Acceptance means you speak of your family in the past tense and you make active plans for moving ahead with your life. There are courses at Seneca and Ryerson[5] we could be taking. Her gleaming leather briefcase is full of college catalogues and lists of cultural societies that need our help. She has done impressive work, I tell her.

"In the textbooks on grief management," she replies—I am her confidante, I realize, one of the few whose grief has not sprung bizarre obsessions—"there are stages to pass through: rejection, depression, acceptance, reconstruction." She has compiled a chart and finds that six months after the tragedy, none of us

5. Seneca College of Applied Arts and Technology, in Willowdale; Ryerson Polytechnical Institute, Toronto.

still reject reality, but only a handful are reconstructing. "Depressed Acceptance" is the plateau we've reached. Remarriage is a major step in reconstruction (though she's a little surprised, even shocked, over *how* quickly some of the men have taken on new families). Selling one's house and changing jobs and cities is healthy.

105 How do I tell Judith Templeton that my family surrounds me, and that like creatures in epics, they've changed shapes? She sees me as calm and accepting but worries that I have no job, no career. My closest friends are worse off than I. I cannot tell her my days, even my nights, are thrilling.

She asks me to help with families she can't reach at all. An elderly couple in Agincourt whose sons were killed just weeks after they had brought their parents over from a village in Punjab. From their names, I know they are Sikh. Judith Templeton and a translator have visited them twice with offers of money for air fare to Ireland, with bank forms, power-of-attorney forms, but they have refused to sign, or to leave their tiny apartment. Their sons' money is frozen in the bank. Their sons' investment apartments have been trashed by tenants, the furnishings sold off. The parents fear that anything they sign or any money they receive will end the company's or the country's obligations to them. They fear they are selling their sons for two airline tickets to a place they've never seen.

The high-rise apartment is a tower of Indians and West Indians, with a sprinkling of Orientals. The nearest bus stop kiosk is lined with women in saris. Boys practice cricket in the parking lot. Inside the building, even I wince a bit from the ferocity of onion fumes, the distinctive and immediate Indianness of frying *ghee*, but Judith Templeton maintains a steady flow of information. These poor old people are in imminent danger of losing their place and all their services.

I say to her, "They are Sikh. They will not open up to a Hindu woman." And what I want to add is, as much as I try not to, I stiffen now at the sight of beards and turbans. I remember a time when we all trusted each other in this new country, it was only the new country we worried about.

The two rooms are dark and stuffy. The lights are off, and an oil lamp sputters on the coffee table. The bent old lady has let us in, and her husband is wrapping a white turban over his oiled, hip-length hair. She immediately goes to the kitchen, and I hear the most familiar sound of an Indian home, tap water hitting and filling a teapot.

110 They have not paid their utility bills, out of fear and the inability to write a check. The telephone is gone; electricity and gas and water are soon to follow. They have told Judith their sons will provide. They are good boys, and they have always earned and looked after their parents.

We converse a bit in Hindi. They do not ask about the crash and I wonder if I should bring it up. If they think I am here merely as a translator, then they may feel insulted. There are thousands of Punjabi-speakers, Sikhs, in Toronto to do a better job. And so I say to the old lady, "I too have lost my sons, and my husband, in the crash."

Her eyes immediately fill with tears. The man mutters a few words which sound like a blessing. "God provides and God takes away," he says.

I want to say, but only men destroy and give back nothing. "My boys and my husband are not coming back," I say. "We have to understand that."

Now the old woman responds. "But who is to say? Man alone does not decide these things." To this her husband adds his agreement.

Judith asks about the bank papers, the release forms. With a stroke of the 115
pen, they will have a provincial trustee to pay their bills, invest their money, send them a monthly pension.

"Do you know this woman?" I ask them.

The man raises his hand from the table, turns it over and seems to regard each finger separately before he answers. "This young lady is always coming here, we make tea for her and she leaves papers for us to sign." His eyes scan a pile of papers in the corner of the room. "Soon we will be out of tea, then will she go away?"

The old lady adds, "I have asked my neighbors and no one else gets *angrezi*[6] visitors. What have we done?"

"It's her job," I try to explain. "The government is worried. Soon you will have no place to stay, no lights, no gas, no water."

"Government will get its money. Tell her not to worry, we are honorable 120
people."

I try to explain the government wishes to give money, not take. He raises his hand. "Let them take," he says. "We are accustomed to that. That is no problem."

"We are strong people," says the wife. "Tell her that."

"Who needs all this machinery?" demands the husband. "It is unhealthy, the bright lights, the cold air on a hot day, the cold food, the four gas rings. God will provide, not government."

"When our boys return," the mother says. Her husband sucks his teeth. "Enough talk," he says.

Judith breaks in. "Have you convinced them?" The snaps on her cordovan 125
briefcase go off like firecrackers in that quiet apartment. She lays the sheaf of legal papers on the coffee table. "If they can't write their names, an X will do—I've told them that."

Now the old lady has shuffled to the kitchen and soon emerges with a pot of tea and two cups. "I think my bladder will go first on a job like this," Judith says to me, smiling. "If only there was some way of reaching them. Please thank her for the tea. Tell her she's very kind."

I nod in Judith's direction and tell them in Hindi, "She thanks you for the tea. She thinks you are being very hospitable but she doesn't have the slightest idea what it means."

I want to say, humor her. I want to say, my boys and my husband are with me too, more than ever. I look in the old man's eyes and I can read his stubborn, peasant's message: *I have protected this woman as best I can. She is the only person I have left. Give to me or take from me what you will, but I will not sign for it. I will not pretend that I accept.*

In the car, Judith says, "You see what I'm up against? I'm sure they're lovely

6. English, Anglo.

people, but their stubbornness and ignorance are driving me crazy. They think signing a paper is signing their sons' death warrants, don't they?"

I am looking out the window. I want to say, *In our culture, it is a parent's duty to hope.*

"Now Shaila, this next woman is a real mess. She cries day and night, and she refuses all medical help. We may have to—"

"—Let me out at the subway," I say.

"I beg your pardon?" I can feel those blue eyes staring at me.

It would not be like her to disobey. She merely disapproves, and slows at a corner to let me out. Her voice is plaintive. "Is there anything I said? Anything I did?"

I could answer her suddenly in a dozen ways, but I choose not to. "Shaila? Let's talk about it," I hear, then slam the door.

A wife and mother begins her new life in a new country, and that life is cut short. Yet her husband tells her: Complete what we have started. We, who stayed out of politics and came halfway around the world to avoid religious and political feuding have been the first in the New World to die from it. I no longer know what we started, nor how to complete it. I write letters to the editors of local papers and to members of Parliament. Now at least they admit it was a bomb. One MP answers back, with sympathy, but with a challenge. You want to make a difference? Work on a campaign. Work on mine. Politicize the Indian voter.

My husband's old lawyer helps me set up a trust. Vikram was a saver and a careful investor. He had saved the boys' boarding school and college fees. I sell the pink house at four times what we paid for it and take a small apartment downtown. I am looking for a charity to support.

We are deep in the Toronto winter, gray skies, icy pavements. I stay indoors, watching television. I have tried to assess my situation, how best to live my life, to complete what we began so many years ago. Kusum has written me from Hardwar that her life is now serene. She has seen Satish and has heard her daughter sing again. Kusum was on a pilgrimage, passing through a village when she heard a young girl's voice, singing one of her daughter's favorite *bhajans*. She followed the music through the squalor of a Himalayan village, to a hut where a young girl, an exact replica of her daughter, was fanning coals under the kitchen fire. When she appeared, the girl cried out, "Ma!" and ran away. What did I think of that?

I think I can only envy her.

Pam didn't make it to California, but writes me from Vancouver. She works in a department store, giving make-up hints to Indian and Oriental girls. Dr. Ranganathan has given up his commute, given up his house and job, and accepted an academic position in Texas where no one knows his story and he has vowed not to tell it. He calls me now once a week.

I wait, I listen, and I pray, but Vikram has not returned to me. The voices and the shapes and the nights filled with visions ended abruptly several weeks ago.

I take it as a sign.

One rare, beautiful, sunny day last week, returning from a small errand on Yonge Street, I was walking through the park from the subway to my apartment. I live equidistant from the Ontario Houses of Parliament and the University of Toronto. The day was not cold, but something in the bare trees caught my attention. I looked up from the gravel, into the branches and the clear blue sky beyond. I thought I heard the rustling of larger forms, and I waited a moment for voices. Nothing.

"What?" I asked.

Then as I stood in the path looking north to Queen's Park and west to the university, I heard the voices of my family one last time. *Your time has come*, they said. *Go, be brave*.

I do not know where this voyage I have begun will end. I do not know which direction I will take. I dropped the package on a park bench and started walking.

1988

Let us begin a reader-oriented discussion of this story, by thinking of ourselves first as a general reader reading the opening of this story for the first time:

> A woman I don't know is boiling tea the Indian way in my kitchen. There are a lot of women I don't know in my kitchen, whispering, and moving tactfully. They open doors, rummage through the pantry, and try not to ask me where things are kept. They remind me of when my sons were small, on Mother's Day or when Vikram and I were tired, and they would make big, sloppy omelets. I would lie in bed pretending I didn't hear them.

We are plunged immediately into the mind of an "I" whose identity we do not know, in a setting specified only as in or near a kitchen, and in a situation about which we know nothing. There is no exposition, no explanation. Even the use of the present tense, rather than the more familiar past tense of most stories, tends to thrust us into a narrative present without known precedent or purpose. The uncertainty makes us look at every word and detail for clues: "my kitchen" and "my sons . . . on Mother's Day" soon identifies the narrator as a mature female.

At this point, regardless of whether we find this indirection and uncertainty annoying or engaging (getting us into the story by making us figure out what is going on for ourselves), we may ask a question or two not about the story but about ourselves. The first two stories in this chapter were not only written by men but were almost entirely about men. (No women appear in "The Most Dangerous Game" and the mother, aunt, and daughter in "Barn Burning" are peripheral.) "The Management of Grief" is not only written by a woman but tells the story through the consciousness of a woman, a strong and intelligent woman. On the other hand, this woman is a mother, somewhat older than most college students. The boy in "Barn Burning," though younger than you, is living through a part of life you have already lived through and so know something about first-hand. How much does the age of the central character have to do not just with your understanding, but with your feelings, your affective response to what you are reading?

The name "Vikram" in the first paragraph for many of us suggests little except foreignness, but "Dr. Sharma, the treasurer of the Indo-Canada Society" (par. 2), tells us enough about the cultural setting for the moment. In the ensuing conversation we learn the name of the narrator—Shaila Bhave—and learn that there has been an accident, perhaps a terrorist bombing, which may explain what seems to be the confusion of the opening scene.

The bomb, the next sentence tells us, may have been a Sikh bomb, and in the eighth paragraph we learn that it was a passenger plane that was, or might have been, bombed. What is a Sikh? Why would a Sikh bomb a plane full of people? Does the average American read this story with the same attitudes and emotions as the average Canadian? Indian? Sikh?

This is not to say that an eighteen-year-old male of Polish descent living in Cleveland cannot read this story with strong emotions and with deep sympathy for and understanding of Shaila Bhave and her tragedy. But would his responses be the same in nature and intensity as those of a middle-aged Indian woman living in Toronto or Vancouver?

For Indians, Sikhs, and some Canadians, this incident (which seems to be based on an actual disaster) is also likely to be controversial, even though the story itself does not concentrate on assessing blame or on the political tensions or causes involved. Whether or not a story takes sides, touching on an issue that readers recognize as controversial inevitably affects how those readers evaluate the story. This does not necessarily mean that all Sikhs or all Indians hold one view. People often disagree with their own government's or community's actions—as many Americans did during the Vietnam war. And it is unlikely that most English readers would repudiate "Beyond the Pale" because of its implicit condemnation of certain English attitudes toward the Irish "troubles." The point is not that controversial stories are bad or that considering the politics or ideology of a work in evaluating it is bad. But we need to recognize the ideological or political factor in our assessment, to acknowledge who and where we are, where we are coming from, when we say, "This story is good" or "That story is lousy."

Evaluating a story, then, means reading carefully (and widely), learning as much as we can about the elements of fiction and of narrative strategies, and articulating our analyses; being honest about our own responses and feeling responsible for articulating them as clearly and convincingly as possible; taking our opinions seriously but listening with attention and an open mind to the judgments and reasoning of other readers. It requires as well some examination and knowledge of ourselves, of what in ourselves conditions our responses to fiction, and a willingness to look at what underlies our judgments and how we might learn and grow. Assessing the value of a story is difficult and a firm evaluation elusive in part because it means examining more than words on a page, it means examining so many ideas, beliefs, and feelings we take for granted. It means examining and, to a degree, evaluating our outer world and inner selves.

Reading More Fiction

LEO TOLSTOY

The Death of Iván Ilyich[1]

I

During an interval in the Melvínski trial in the large building of the Law Courts the members and public prosecutor met in Iván Egórovich Shébek's private room, where the conversation turned on the celebrated Krasóvski case. Fëdor Vasílievich warmly maintained that it was not subject to their jurisdiction, Iván Egórovich maintained the contrary, while Peter Ivánovich, not having entered into the discussion at the start, took no part in it but looked through the *Gazette* which had just been handed in.

"Gentlemen," he said, "Iván Ilyich has died!"

"You don't say!"

"Here read it yourself," replied Peter Ivánovich, handing Fëdor Vasílievich the paper still damp from the press. Surrounded by a black border were the words: "Praskóvya Fëdorovna Goloviná,[2] with profound sorrow, informs relatives and friends of the demise of her beloved husband Iván Ilyich Golovín, Member of the Court of Justice, which occurred on February the 4th of this year 1882. The funeral will take place on Friday at one o'clock in the afternoon."

5 Iván Ilyich had been a colleague of the gentlemen present and was liked by them all. He had been ill for some weeks with an illness said to be incurable. His post had been kept open for him, but there had been conjectures that in case of his death Alexéev might receive his appointment, and that either Vínnikov or Shtábel would succeed Alexéev. So on receiving the news of Iván Ilyich's death

1. Translated by Louise and Aylmer Maude. 2. Many Russian family names have masculine and feminine endings, so that Iván's name is *Golovín*, his wife's *Goloviná*. Russian "middle" names are patronymics—the father's name plus an ending that means "son of" or "daughter of": *Fëdorovna* = daughter of Fëdor; *Ilyich* = son of Ilya.

the first thought of each of the gentlemen in that private room was of the changes and promotions it might occasion among themselves or their acquaintances.

"I shall be sure to get Shtábel's place or Vínnikov's," thought Fëdor Vasílievich. "I was promised that long ago, and the promotion means an extra eight hundred rubles[3] a year for me besides the allowance."

"Now I must apply for my brother-in-law's transfer from Kalúga,"[4] thought Peter Ivánovich. "My wife will be very glad, and then she won't be able to say that I never do anything for her relations."

"I thought he would never leave his bed again," said Peter Ivánovich aloud. "It's very sad."

"But what really was the matter with him?"

"The doctors couldn't say—at least they could, but each of them said something different. When last I saw him I thought he was getting better."

"And I haven't been to see him since the holidays. I always meant to go."

"Had he any property?"

"I think his wife had a little—but something quite trifling."

"We shall have to go to see her, but they live so terribly far away."

"Far away from you, you mean. Everything's far away from your place."

"You see, he never can forgive my living on the other side of the river," said Peter Ivánovich, smiling at Shébek. Then, still talking of the distances between different parts of the city, they returned to the Court.

Besides considerations as to the possible transfers and promotions likely to result from Iván Ilyich's death, the mere fact of the death of a near acquaintance aroused, as usual, in all who heard of it the complacent feeling that, "it is he who is dead and not I."

Each one thought or felt, "Well, he's dead but I'm alive!" But the more intimate of Iván Ilyich's acquaintances, his so-called friends, could not help thinking also that they would now have to fulfil the very tiresome demands of propriety by attending the funeral service and paying a visit of condolence to the widow.

Fëdor Vasílievich and Peter Ivánovich had been his nearest acquaintances. Peter Ivánovich had studied law with Iván Ilyich and had considered himself to be under obligations to him.

Having told his wife at dinner-time of Iván Ilyich's death, and of his conjecture that it might be possible to get her brother transferred to their circuit, Peter Ivánovich sacrificed his usual nap, put on his evening clothes, and drove to Iván Ilyich's house.

At the entrance stood a carriage and two cabs. Leaning against the wall in the hall downstairs near the cloak-stand was a coffin-lid covered with cloth of gold, ornamented with gold cord and tassels, that had been polished up with metal powder. Two ladies in black were taking off their fur cloaks. Peter Ivánovich recognized one of them as Iván Ilyich's sister, but the other was a stranger to

3. A ruble was then roughly equivalent to a dollar, though its modern purchasing power is difficult to calculate: perhaps four or five dollars per ruble is close enough. 4. City about one hundred miles southwest of Moscow.

him. His colleague Schwartz was just coming downstairs, but on seeing Peter Ivánovich enter he stopped and winked at him, as if to say: "Iván Ilyich has made a mess of things—not like you and me."

Schwartz's face with his Piccadilly whiskers,[5] and his slim figure in evening dress, had as usual an air of elegant solemnity which contrasted with the playfulness of his character and had a special piquancy here, or so it seemed to Peter Ivánovich.

Peter Ivánovich allowed the ladies to precede him and slowly followed them upstairs. Schwartz did not come down but remained where he was, and Peter Ivánovich understood that he wanted to arrange where they should play bridge that evening. The ladies went upstairs to the widow's room, and Schwartz with seriously compressed lips but a playful look in his eyes, indicated by a twist of his eyebrows the room to the right where the body lay.

Peter Ivánovich, like everyone else on such occasions, entered feeling uncertain what he would have to do. All he knew was that at such times it is always safe to cross oneself. But he was not quite sure whether one should make obeisances while doing so. He therefore adopted a middle course. On entering the room he began crossing himself and made a slight movement resembling a bow. At the same time, as far as the motion of his head and arm allowed, he surveyed the room. Two young men—apparently nephews, one of whom was a high-school pupil—were leaving the room, crossing themselves as they did so. An old woman was standing motionless, and a lady with strangely arched eyebrows was saying something to her in a whisper. A vigorous, resolute Church Reader, in a frock-coat, was reading something in a loud voice with an expression that precluded any contradiction. The butler's assistant, Gerásim, stepping lightly in front of Peter Ivánovich, was strewing something on the floor. Noticing this, Peter Ivánovich was immediately aware of a faint odour of a decomposing body.

The last time he had called on Iván Ilyich, Peter Ivánovich had seen Gerásim in the study. Iván Ilyich had been particularly fond of him and he was performing the duty of a sick nurse.

Peter Ivánovich continued to make the sign of the cross slightly inclining his head in an intermediate direction between the coffin, the Reader, and the icons on the table in a corner of the room. Afterwards, when it seemed to him that this movement of his arm in crossing himself had gone on too long, he stopped and began to look at the corpse.

The dead man lay, as dead men always lie, in a specially heavy way, his rigid limbs sunk in the soft cushions of the coffin, with the head forever bowed on the pillow. His yellow waxen brow with bald patches over his sunken temples was thrust up in the way peculiar to the dead, the protruding nose seeming to press on the upper lip. He was much changed and had grown even thinner since Peter Ivánovich had last seen him, but, as is always the case with the dead, his face was handsomer and above all more dignified than when he was alive. The expression on the face said that what was necessary had been accomplished, and accomplished rightly. Besides this there was in that expression a reproach and a

5. Sideburns carefully combed out and worn as long as possible, a fashion that died out in the 1880s.

warning to the living. This warning seemed to Peter Ivánovich out of place, or at least not applicable to him. He felt a certain discomfort and so he hurriedly crossed himself once more and turned and went out of the door—too hurriedly and too regardless of propriety, as he himself was aware.

Schwartz was waiting for him in the adjoining room with legs spread wide apart and both hands toying with his top-hat behind his back. The mere sight of that playful, well-groomed, and elegant figure refreshed Peter Ivánovich. He felt that Schwartz was above all these happenings and could not surrender to any depressing influences. His very look said that this incident of a church service for Iván Ilyich could not be a sufficient reason for infringing the order of the session—in other words, that it would certainly not prevent his unwrapping a new pack of cards and shuffling them that evening while a footman placed four fresh candles on the table: in fact, that there was no reason for supposing that this incident would hinder their spending the evening agreeably. Indeed he said this in a whisper as Peter Ivánovich passed him, proposing that they should meet for a game at Fëdor Vasílievich's. But apparently Peter Ivánovich was not destined to play bridge that evening. Praskóvya Fëdorovna (a short, fat woman who despite all efforts to the contrary had continued to broaden steadily from her shoulders downwards and who had the same extraordinary arched eyebrows as the lady who had been standing by the coffin), dressed all in black, her head covered with lace, came out of her own room with some other ladies, conducted them to the room where the dead body lay, and said: "The service will begin immediately. Please go in."

Schwartz, making an indefinite bow, stood still, evidently neither accepting nor declining this invitation. Praskóvya Fëdorovna recognizing Peter Ivánovich, sighed, went close up to him, took his hand, and said: "I know you were a true friend to Iván Ilyich . . ." and looked at him awaiting some suitable response. And Peter Ivánovich knew that, just as it had been the right thing to cross himself in that room, so what he had to do here was to press her hand, sigh, and say, "Believe me . . ." So he did all this and as he did it felt that the desired result had been achieved: that both he and she were touched.

"Come with me. I want to speak to you before it begins," said the widow. "Give me your arm."

Peter Ivánovich gave her his arm and they went to the inner rooms, passing Schwartz who winked at Peter Ivánovich compassionately.

"That does for our bridge! Don't object if we find another player. Perhaps you can cut in when you do escape," said his playful look.

Peter Ivánovich sighed still more deeply and despondently, and Praskóvya Fëdorovna pressed his arm gratefully. When they reached the drawing-room, upholstered in pink cretonne and lighted by a dim lamp, they sat down at the table—she on a sofa and Peter Ivánovich on a low hassock, the springs of which yielded spasmodically under his weight. Praskóvya Fëdorovna had been on the point of warning him to take another seat, but felt that such a warning was out of keeping with her present condition and so changed her mind. As he sat down on the hassock Peter Ivánovich recalled how Iván Ilyich had arranged this room and had consulted him regarding this pink cretonne with green leaves. The whole room was full of furniture and knick-knacks, and on her way to the sofa the lace of the widow's black shawl caught on the carved edge of the table. Peter Ivánovich rose to detach it, and the springs of the hassock, relieved of his weight, rose also and gave him a push. The widow began detaching her shawl herself, and Peter Ivánovich again sat down, suppressing the rebellious springs of the hassock under him. But the widow had not quite freed herself and Peter Ivánovich got up again, and again the hassock rebelled and even creaked. When this was all over she took out a clean cambric handkerchief and began to weep. The episode with the shawl and the struggle with the hassock had cooled Peter Ivánovich's emotions and he sat there with a sullen look on his face. This awkward situation was interrupted by Sokolóv, Iván Ilyich's butler, who came to report that the plot in the cemetery that Praskóvya Fëdorovna had chosen would cost two hundred rubles. She stopped weeping and, looking at Peter Ivánovich with the air of a victim, remarked in French[6] that it was very hard for her. Peter Ivánovich made a silent gesture signifying his full conviction that it must indeed be so.

"Please smoke," she said in a magnanimous yet crushed voice, and turned to discuss with Sokolóv the price of the plot for the grave.

Peter Ivánovich while lighting his cigarette heard her inquiring very circumstantially into the prices of different plots in the cemetery and finally decide which she would take. When that was done she gave instructions about engaging the choir. Sokolóv then left the room.

"I look after everything myself," she told Peter Ivánovich, shifting the albums that lay on the table; and noticing that the table was endangered by his cigarette-ash, she immediately passed him an ashtray, saying as she did so: "I consider it an affectation to say that my grief prevents my attending to practical affairs. On the contrary, if anything can—I won't say console me, but—distract me, it is seeing to everything concerning him." She again took out her handkerchief as if preparing to cry, but suddenly, as if mastering her feeling, she shook herself and began to speak calmly. "But there is something I want to talk to you about."

Peter Ivánovich bowed, keeping control of the springs of the hassock, which immediately began quivering under him.

"He suffered terribly the last few days."

"Did he?" said Peter Ivánovich.

"Oh, terribly! He screamed unceasingly, not for minutes but for hours. For the last three days he screamed incessantly. It was unendurable. I cannot understand how I bore it; you could hear him three rooms off. Oh, what I have suffered!"

"Is it possible that he was conscious all that time?" asked Peter Ivánovich.

"Yes," she whispered. "To the last moment. He took leave of us a quarter of an hour before he died, and asked us to take Vásya[7] away."

The thought of the sufferings of this man he had known so intimately, first as a merry little boy, then as a school-mate, and later as a grown-up colleague, suddenly struck Peter Ivánovich with horror, despite an unpleasant conscious-

6. The Russian upper classes commonly spoke French. 7. Nickname for Vasílii, Iván Ilyich's son.

ness of his own and this woman's dissimulation. He again saw that brow, and that nose pressing down on the lip, and felt afraid for himself.

"Three days of frightful suffering and then death! Why, that might suddenly, at any time, happen to me," he thought, and for a moment felt terrified. But—he did not himself know how—the customary reflection at once occurred to him that this had happened to Iván Ilyich and not to him, and that it should not and could not happen to him, and that to think that it could would be yielding to depression which he ought not to do, as Schwartz's expression plainly showed. After which reflection Peter Ivánovich felt reassured, and began to ask with interest about the details of Iván Ilyich's death, as though death was an accident natural to Iván Ilyich but certainly not to himself.

After many details of the really dreadful physical sufferings Iván Ilyich had 45
endured (which details he learnt only from the effect those sufferings had produced on Praskóvya Fëdorovna's nerves) the widow apparently found it necessary to get to business.

"Oh, Peter Ivánovich, how hard it is! How terribly, terribly hard!" and she again began to weep.

Peter Ivánovich sighed and waited for her to finish blowing her nose. When she had done so he said, "Believe me . . ." and she again began talking and brought out what was evidently her chief concern with him—namely, to question him as to how she could obtain a grant of money from the government on the occasion of her husband's death. She made it appear that she was asking Peter Ivánovich's advice about her pension, but he soon saw that she already knew about that to the minutest detail, more even than he did himself. She knew how much could be got out of the government in consequence of her husband's death, but wanted to find out whether she could possibly extract something more. Peter Ivánovich tried to think of some means of doing so, but after reflecting for a while and, out of propriety, condemning the government for its niggardliness, he said he thought that nothing more could be got. Then she sighed and evidently began to devise means of getting rid of her visitor. Noticing this, he put out his cigarette, rose, pressed her hand, and went out into the anteroom.

In the dining-room where the clock stood that Iván Ilyich had liked so much and had bought at an antique shop, Peter Ivánovich met a priest and a few acquaintances who had come to attend the service, and he recognized Iván Ilyich's daughter, a handsome young woman. She was in black and her slim figure appeared slimmer than ever. She had a gloomy, determined, almost angry expression, and bowed to Peter Ivánovich as though he were in some way to blame. Behind her, with the same offended look, stood a wealthy young man, an examining magistrate, whom Peter Ivánovich also knew and who was her fiancé, as he had heard. He bowed mournfully to them and was about to pass into the death-chamber, when from under the stairs appeared the figure of Iván Ilyich's schoolboy son, who was extremely like this father. He seemed a little Iván Ilyich, such as Peter Ivánovich remembered when they studied law together. His tear-stained eyes had in them the look that is seen in the eyes of boys of thirteen or fourteen who are not pure-minded.

When he saw Peter Ivánovich he scowled morosely and shamefacedly. Peter Ivánovich nodded to him and entered the death-chamber. The service began: candles, groans, incense, tears, and sobs. Peter Ivánovich stood looking gloomily down at his feet. He did not look once at the dead man, did not yield to any depressing influence, and was one of the first to leave the room. There was no one in the anteroom, but Gerásim darted out of the dead man's room, rummaged with his strong hands among the fur coats to find Peter Ivánovich's and helped him on with it.

"Well, friend Gerásim," said Peter Ivánovich, so as to say something. "It's a sad affair, isn't it?"

"It's God's will. We shall all come to it some day," said Gerásim, displaying his teeth—the even, white teeth of a healthy peasant—and, like a man in the thick of urgent work, he briskly opened the front door, called the coachman, helped Peter Ivánovich into the sledge, and sprang back to the porch as if in readiness for what he had to do next.

Peter Ivánovich found the fresh air particularly pleasant after the smell of incense, the dead body, and carbolic acid.

"Where to, sir?" asked the coachman.

"It's not too late even now. . . . I'll call round on Fëdor Vasílievich."

He accordingly drove there and found them just finishing the first rubber, so that it was quite convenient for him to cut in.

II

Iván Ilyich's life had been most simple and most ordinary and therefore most terrible.

He had been a member of the Court of Justice, and died at the age of forty-five. His father had been an official who after serving in various ministries and departments in Petersburg[8] had made the sort of career which brings men to positions from which by reason of their long service they cannot be dismissed, though they are obviously unfit to hold any responsible position, and for whom therefore posts are specially created, which though fictitious, carry salaries of from six to ten thousand rubles that are not fictitious, and in receipt of which they live on to a great age.

Such was the Privy Councillor and superfluous member of various superfluous institutions, Ilya Efímovich Golovín.

He had three sons, of whom Iván Ilyich was the second. The eldest son was following in his father's footsteps only in another department, and was already approaching that stage in the service at which a similar sinecure would be reached. The third son was a failure. He had ruined his prospects in a number of positions and was now serving in the railway department. His father and brothers, and still more their wives, not merely disliked meeting him, but avoided remembering his existence unless compelled to do so. His sister had married Baron Greff, a Petersburg official of her father's type. Iván Ilyich was *le phénix de la famille*[9] as

8. St. Petersburg (now Leningrad), the capital of Russia (1712–1918) and its cultural and social center. 9. Prodigy of the family.

people said. He was neither as cold and formal as his elder brother nor as wild as the younger, but was a happy mean between them—an intelligent, polished, lively and agreeable man. He had studied with his younger brother at the School of Law, but the latter had failed to complete the course and was expelled when he was in the fifth class. Iván Ilyich finished the course well. Even when he was at the School of Law he was just what he remained for the rest of his life: a capable, cheerful, good-natured, and sociable man, though strict in the fulfilment of what he considered to be his duty: and he considered his duty to be what was so considered by those in authority. Neither as a boy nor as a man was he a toady, but from early youth was by nature attracted to people of high station as a fly is drawn to the light, assimilating their ways and views of life and establishing friendly relations with them. All the enthusiasms of childhood and youth passed without leaving much trace on him; he succumbed to sensuality, to vanity, and latterly among the highest classes to liberalism, but always within limits which his instinct unfailingly indicated to him as correct.

At school he had done things which had formerly seemed to him very horrid 60
and made him feel disgusted with himself when he did them; but when later on he saw that such actions were done by people of good position and that they did not regard them as wrong, he was able not exactly to regard them as right, but to forget about them entirely or not be at all troubled at remembering them.

Having graduated from the School of Law and qualified for the tenth rank of the civil service, and having received money from his father for his equipment, Iván Ilyich ordered himself clothes at Scharmer's, the fashionable tailor, hung a medallion inscribed *respice finem*[1] on his watch-chain, took leave of his professor and the prince who was patron of the school, had a farewell dinner with his comrades at Donon's first-class restaurant, and with his new and fashionable portmanteau, linen, clothes, shaving and other toilet appliances, and a travelling rug, all purchased at the best shops, he set off for one of the provinces where, through his father's influence, he had been attached to the governor as an official for special service.

In the province Iván Ilyich soon arranged as easy and agreeable a position for himself as he had at the School of Law. He performed his official tasks, made his career, and at the same time amused himself pleasantly and decorously. Occasionally he paid official visits to country districts, where he behaved with dignity both to his superiors and inferiors, and performed the duties entrusted to him, which related chiefly to the sectarians,[2] with an exactness and incorruptible honesty of which he could not but feel proud.

In official matters, despite his youth and taste for frivolous gaiety, he was exceedingly reserved, punctilious, and even severe; but in society he was often amusing and witty, and always good-natured, correct in his manner, and *bon enfant*,[3] as the governor and his wife—with whom he was like one of the family—used to say of him.

In the province he had an affair with a lady who made advances to the elegant young lawyer, and there was also a milliner; and there were carousals

1. Look to (or consider) the end. 2. A large sect (the "Old Believers") that had broken with the Orthodox church. 3. A good fellow.

with aides-de-camp who visited the district, and after-supper visits to a certain outlying street of doubtful reputation; and there was too some obsequiousness to his chief and even to his chief's wife, but all this was done with such a tone of good breeding that no hard names could be applied to it. It all came under the heading of the French saying: "*Il faut que jeunesse se passe.*"[4] It was all done with clean hands, in clean linen, with French phrases, and above all among people of the best society and consequently with the approval of people of rank.

65 So Iván Ilyich served for five years and then came a change in his official life. The new and reformed judicial institutions were introduced, and new men were needed. Iván Ilyich became such a new man. He was offered the post of Examining Magistrate, and he accepted it though the post was in another province and obliged him to give up the connexions he had formed and to make new ones. His friends met to give him a send-off; they had a group-photograph taken and presented him with a silver cigarette-case, and he set off to his new post.

As examining magistrate Iván Ilyich was just as *comme il faut* and decorous a man, inspiring general respect and capable of separating his official duties from his private life, as he had been when acting as an official on special service. His duties now as examining magistrate were far more interesting and attractive than before. In his former position it had been pleasant to wear an undress uniform made by Scharmer, and to pass through the crowd of petitioners and officials who were timorously awaiting an audience with the governor, and who envied him as with free and easy gait he went straight into his chief's private room to have a cup of tea and a cigarette with him. But not many people had then been directly dependent on him—only police officials and the sectarians when he went on special missions—and he liked to treat them politely, almost as comrades, as if he were letting them feel that he who had the power to crush them was treating them in this simple, friendly way. There were then but few such people. But now, as an examining magistrate, Iván Ilyich felt that everyone without exception, even the most important and self-satisfied, was in his power, and that he need only write a few words on a sheet of paper with a certain heading, and this or that important, self-satisfied person would be brought before him in the role of an accused person or a witness, and if he did not choose to allow him to sit down, would have to stand before him and answer his questions. Iván Ilyich never abused his power; he tried on the contrary to soften its expression, but the consciousness of it and of the possibility of softening its effect, supplied the chief interest and attraction of his office. In his work itself, especially in his examinations, he very soon acquired a method of eliminating all considerations irrelevant to the legal aspect of the case, and reducing even the most complicated case to a form in which it would be presented on paper only in its externals, completely excluding his personal opinion of the matter, while above all observing every prescribed formality. The work was new and Iván Ilyich was one of the first men to apply the new Code of 1864.[5]

On taking up the post of examining magistrate in a new town, he made new acquaintances and connexions, placed himself on a new footing, and assumed a

4. Youth must have its fling. (Translators' note) 5. The emancipation of the serfs in 1861 was followed by a thorough all-round reform of judicial proceedings. (Translators' note)

somewhat different tone. He took up an attitude of rather dignified aloofness towards the provincial authorities, but picked out the best circle of legal gentlemen and wealthy gentry living in the town and assumed a tone of slight dissatisfaction with the government, of moderate liberalism, and of enlightened citizenship. At the same time, without at all altering the elegance of his toilet, he ceased shaving his chin and allowed his beard to grow as it pleased.

Iván Ilyich settled down very pleasantly in this new town. The society there, which inclined towards opposition to the governor, was friendly, his salary was larger, and he began to play *vint* [a form of bridge], which he found added not a little to the pleasure of life, for he had a capacity for cards, played good-humouredly, and calculated rapidly and astutely, so that he usually won.

After living there for two years he met his future wife, Praskóvya Fëdorovna Míkhel, who was the most attractive, clever, and brilliant girl of the set in which he moved, and among other amusements and relaxations from his labours as examining magistrate, Iván Ilyich established light and playful relations with her.

While he had been an official on special service he had been accustomed to dance, but now as an examining magistrate it was exceptional for him to do so. If he danced now, he did it as if to show that though he served under the reformed order of things, and had reached the fifth official rank, yet when it came to dancing he could do it better than most people. So at the end of an evening he sometimes danced with Praskóvya Fëdorovna, and it was chiefly during these dances that he captivated her. She fell in love with him. Iván Ilyich had at first no definite intention of marrying, but when the girl fell in love with him he said to himself: "Really, why shouldn't I marry?"

Praskóvya Fëdorovna came of a good family, was not bad looking, and had some little property. Iván Ilyich might have aspired to a more brilliant match, but even this was good. He had his salary, and she, he hoped, would have an equal income. She was well connected, and was a sweet, pretty, and thoroughly correct young woman. To say that Iván Ilyich married because he fell in love with Praskóvya Fëdorovna and found that she sympathized with his views of life would be as incorrect as to say that he married because his social circle approved of the match. He was swayed by both these considerations: the marriage gave him personal satisfaction, and at the same time it was considered the right thing by the most highly placed of his associates.

So Iván Ilyich got married.

The preparations for marriage and the beginning of married life, with its conjugal caresses, the new furniture, new crockery, and new linen, were very pleasant until his wife became pregnant—so that Iván Ilyich had begun to think that marriage would not impair the easy, agreeable, gay, and always decorous character of his life, approved of by society and regarded by himself as natural, but would even improve it. But from the first months of his wife's pregnancy, something new, unpleasant, depressing, and unseemly, and from which there was no way of escape, unexpectedly showed itself.

His wife, without any reason—*de gaieté de coeur*[6] as Iván Ilyich expressed it

6. Wantonly.

to himself—began to disturb the pleasure and propriety of their life. She began to be jealous without any cause, expected him to devote his whole attention to her, found fault with everything, and made coarse and ill-mannered scenes.

At first Iván Ilyich hoped to escape from the unpleasantness of this state of affairs by the same easy and decorous relation to life that had served him heretofore: he tried to ignore his wife's disagreeable moods, continued to live in his usual easy and pleasant way, invited friends to his house for a game of cards, and also tried going out to his club or spending his evenings with friends. But one day his wife began upbraiding him so vigorously, using such coarse words, and continued to abuse him every time he did not fulfil her demands, so resolutely and with such evident determination not to give way till he submitted—that is, till he stayed at home and was bored just as she was—that he became alarmed. He now realized that matrimony—at any rate with Praskóvya Fëdorovna—was not always conducive to the pleasures and amenities of life, but on the contrary often infringed both comfort and propriety, and that he must therefore entrench himself against such infringement. And Iván Ilyich began to seek for means of doing so. His official duties were the one thing that imposed upon Praskóvya Fëdorovna, and by means of his official work and the duties attached to it he began struggling with his wife to secure his own independence.

With the birth of their child, the attempts to feed it and the various failures in doing so, and with the real and imaginary illnesses of mother and child, in which Iván Ilyich's sympathy was demanded but about which he understood nothing, the need of securing for himself an existence outside his family life became still more imperative.

As his wife grew more irritable and exacting and Iván Ilyich transferred the centre of gravity of his life more and more to his official work, so did he grow to like his work better and became more ambitious than before.

Very soon, within a year of his wedding, Iván Ilyich had realized that marriage, though it may add some comforts to life, is in fact a very intricate and difficult affair towards which in order to perform one's duty, that is, to lead a decorous life approved of by society, one must adopt a definite attitude just as towards one's official duties.

And Iván Ilyich evolved such an attitude towards married life. He only required of it those conveniences—dinner at home, housewife, and bed—which it could give him, and above all that propriety of external forms required by public opinion. For the rest he looked for light-hearted pleasure and propriety, and was very thankful when he found them, but if he met with antagonism and querulousness he at once retired into his separate fenced-off world of official duties, where he found satisfaction.

Iván Ilyich was esteemed a good official, and after three years was made Assistant Public Prosecutor. His new duties, their importance, the possibility of indicting and imprisoning anyone he chose, the publicity his speeches received, and the success he had in all these things, made his work still more attractive.

More children came. His wife became more and more querulous and ill-tempered, but the attitude Iván Ilyich had adopted towards his home life rendered him almost impervious to her grumbling.

After seven years' service in that town he was transferred to another province as Public Prosecutor. They moved, but were short of money and his wife did not like the place they moved to. Though the salary was higher the cost of living was greater, besides which two of their children died and family life became still more unpleasant for him.

Praskóvya Fëdorovna blamed her husband for every inconvenience they encountered in their new home. Most of the conversations between husband and wife, especially as to the children's education, led to topics which recalled former disputes, and those disputes were apt to flare up again at any moment. There remained only those rare periods of amorousness which still came to them at times but did not last long. These were islets at which they anchored for a while and then again set out upon that ocean of veiled hostility which showed itself in their aloofness from one another. This aloofness might have grieved Iván Ilyich had he considered that it ought not to exist, but he now regarded the position as normal, and even made it the goal at which he aimed in family life. His aim was to free himself more and more from those unpleasantnesses and to give them a semblance of harmlessness and propriety. He attained this by spending less and less time with his family, and when obliged to be at home he tried to safeguard his position by the presence of outsiders. The chief thing however was that he had his official duties. The whole interest of his life now centered in the official world and that interest absorbed him. The consciousness of his power, being able to ruin anybody he wished to ruin, the importance, even the external dignity of his entry into court, or meetings with his subordinates, his success with superiors and inferiors, and above all his masterly handling of cases, of which he was conscious—all this gave him pleasure and filled his life, together with chats with his colleagues, dinners, and bridge. So that on the whole Iván Ilyich's life continued to flow as he considered it should do—pleasantly and properly.

So things continued for another seven years. His eldest daughter was already sixteen, another child had died, and only one son was left, a schoolboy and a subject of dissensions. Iván Ilyich wanted to put him in the School of Law, but to spite him Praskóvya Fëdorovna entered him at the High School. The daughter had been educated at home and had turned out well: the boy did not learn badly either.

III

So Iván Ilyich lived for seventeen years after his marriage. He was already a 85
Public Prosecutor of long standing, and had declined several proposed transfers while awaiting a more desirable post, when an unanticipated and unpleasant occurrence quite upset the peaceful course of his life. He was expecting to be offered the post of presiding judge in a University town, but Hoppe somehow came to the front and obtained the appointment instead. Iván Ilyich became irritable, reproached Hoppe, and quarrelled both with him and with his immediate superiors—who became colder to him and again passed him over when other appointments were made.

This was in 1880, the hardest year of Iván Ilyich's life. It was then that it became evident on the one hand that his salary was insufficient for them to live on, and on the other that he had been forgotten, and not only this, but that what was for him the greatest and most cruel injustice appeared to others a quite ordinary occurrence. Even his father did not consider it his duty to help him. Iván Ilyich felt himself abandoned by everyone, and that they regarded his position with a salary of 3,500 rubles as quite normal and even fortunate. He alone knew that with the consciousness of the injustices done him, with his wife's incessant nagging, and with the debts he had contracted by living beyond his means his position was far from normal.

In order to save money that summer he obtained leave of absence and went with his wife to live in the country at her brother's place.

In the country, without his work, he experienced *ennui* for the first time in his life, and not only *ennui* but intolerable depression, and he decided that it was impossible to go on living like that, and that it was necessary to take energetic measures.

Having passed a sleepless night pacing up and down the veranda, he decided to go to Petersburg and bestir himself, in order to punish those who had failed to appreciate him and to get transferred to another ministry.

Next day, despite many protests from his wife and her brother, he started for Petersburg with the sole object of obtaining a post with a salary of five thousand rubles a year. He was no longer bent on any particular department, or tendency, or kind of activity. All he now wanted was an appointment to another post with a salary of five thousand rubles, either in the administration, in the banks, with the railways, in one of the Empress Márya's Institutions,[7] or even in the customs—but it had to carry with it a salary of five thousand rubles and be in a ministry other than that in which they had failed to appreciate him.

And this quest of Iván Ilyich's was crowned with remarkable and unexpected success. At Kursk an acquaintance of his, F. I. Ilyín, got into the first-class carriage, sat down beside Iván Ilyich, and told him of a telegram just received by the governor of Kursk announcing that a change was about to take place in the ministry: Peter Ivánovich was to be superseded by Iván Semënovich.

The proposed change, apart from its significance for Russia, had a special significance for Iván Ilyich, because by bringing forward a new man, Peter Petróvich, and consequently his friend Zachár Ivánovich, it was highly favourable for Iván Ilyich, since Zachár Ivánovich was a friend and colleague of his.

In Moscow his news was confirmed, and on reaching Petersburg Iván Ilyich found Zachár Ivánovich and received a definite promise of an appointment in his former department of Justice.

A week later he telegraphed to his wife: "Zachár in Miller's place. I shall receive appointment on presentation of report."

Thanks to this change of personnel, Iván Ilyich had unexpectedly obtained an appointment in his former ministry which placed him two stages above his former colleagues besides giving him five thousand rubles salary and three thou-

7. Charitable organization founded nearly a century earlier by the wife of Tsar Paul I.

sand five hundred rubles for expenses connected with his removal.[8] All his ill humour towards his former enemies and the whole department vanished, and Iván Ilyich was completely happy.

He returned to the country more cheerful and contented than he had been for a long time. Praskóvya Fëdorovna also cheered up and a truce was arranged between them. Iván Ilyich told of how he had been fêted by everybody in Petersburg, how all those who had been his enemies were put to shame and now fawned on him, how envious they were of his appointment, and how much everybody in Petersburg had liked him.

Praskóvya Fëdorovna listened to all this and appeared to believe it. She did not contradict anything, but only made plans for their life in the town to which they were going. Iván Ilyich saw with delight that these plans were his plans, that he and his wife agreed, and that, after a stumble, his life was regaining its due and natural character of pleasant lightheartedness and decorum.

Iván Ilyich had come back for a short time only, for he had to take up his new duties on the 10th of September. Moreover, he needed time to settle into the new place, to move all his belongings from the province, and to buy and order many additional things: in a word, to make such arrangements as he had resolved on, which were almost exactly what Praskóvya Fëdorovna too had decided on.

Now that everything had happened so fortunately, and that he and his wife were at one in their aims and moreover saw so little of one another they got on together better than they had done since the first years of marriage. Iván Ilyich had thought of taking his family away with him at once, but the insistence of his wife's brother and her sister-in-law, who had suddenly become particularly amiable and friendly to him and his family, induced him to depart alone.

So he departed, and the cheerful state of mind induced by his success and by the harmony between his wife and himself, the one intensifying the other, did not leave him. He found a delightful house, just the thing both he and his wife had dreamt of. Spacious, lofty reception rooms in the old style, a convenient and dignified study, rooms for his wife and daughter, a study for his son—it might have been specially built for them. Iván Ilyich himself superintended the arrangements, chose the wallpapers, supplemented the furniture (preferably with antiques which he considered particularly *comme il faut*), and supervised the upholstering. Everything progressed and progressed and approached the ideal he had set himself: even when things were only half completed they exceeded his expectations. He saw what a refined and elegant character, free from vulgarity, it would all have when it was ready. On falling asleep he pictured to himself how the reception-room would look. Looking at the yet unfinished drawing-room he could see the fireplace, the screen, the what-not, the little chairs dotted here and there, the dishes and plates on the walls, and the bronzes, as they would be when everything was in place. He was pleased by the thought of how his wife and daughter, who shared his taste in this matter, would be impressed by it. They were certainly not expecting as much. He had been particularly successful

8. Moving.

in finding, and buying cheaply, antiques which gave a particularly aristocratic character to the whole place. But in his letters he intentionally understated everything in order to be able to surprise them. All this so absorbed him that his new duties—though he liked his official work—interested him less than he had expected. Sometimes he even had moments of absent-mindedness during the Court Sessions, and would consider whether he should have straight or curved cornices for his curtains. He was so interested in it all that he often did things himself, rearranging the furniture, or rehanging the curtains. Once when mounting a step-ladder to show the upholsterer, who did not understand, how he wanted the hangings draped, he made a false step and slipped, but being a strong and agile man he clung on and only knocked his side against the knob of the window frame. The bruised place was painful but the pain soon passed, and he felt particularly bright and well just then. He wrote: "I feel fifteen years younger." He thought he would have everything ready by September, but it dragged on till mid-October. But the result was charming not only in his eyes but to everyone who saw it.

In reality it was just what is usually seen in the houses of people of moderate means who want to appear rich, and therefore succeed only in resembling others like themselves: there were damasks, dark wood, plants, rugs, and dull and polished bronzes—all the things people of a certain class have in order to resemble other people of that class. His house was so like the others that it would never have been noticed, but to him it all seemed to be quite exceptional. He was very happy when he met his family at the station and brought them to the newly furnished house all lit up, where a footman in a white tie opened the door into the hall decorated with plants, and when they went on into the drawing room and the study uttering exclamations of delight. He conducted them everywhere, drank in their praises eagerly, and beamed with pleasure. At tea that evening, when Praskóvya Fëdorovna among other things asked him about his fall, he laughed, and showed them how he had gone flying and had frightened the upholsterer.

"It's a good thing I'm a bit of an athlete. Another man might have been killed, but I merely knocked myself, just here; it hurts when it's touched, but it's passing off already—it's only a bruise."

So they began living in their new home—in which, as always happens, when they got thoroughly settled in they found they were just one room short—and with the increased income, which as always was just a little (some five hundred rubles) too little, but it was all very nice.

Things went particularly well at first, before everything was finally arranged and while something had still to be done: this thing bought, that thing ordered, another thing moved, and something else adjusted. Though there were some disputes between husband and wife, they were both so well satisfied and had so much to do that it all passed off without any serious quarrels. When nothing was left to arrange it became rather dull and something seemed to be lacking, but they were then making acquaintances, forming habits, and life was growing fuller.

Iván Ilyich spent his mornings at the law court and came home to dinner, and at first he was generally in a good humour, though he occasionally became irritable just on account of his house. (Every spot on the tablecloth or the upholstery, and every broken window-blind string, irritated him. He had devoted so much trouble to arranging it all that every disturbance of it distressed him.) But on the whole his life ran its course as he believed life should do: easily, pleasantly, and decorously.

He got up at nine, drank his coffee, read the paper, and then put on his undress uniform and went to the law courts. There the harness in which he worked had already been stretched to fit him and he donned it without a hitch: petitioners, inquiries at the chancery, the chancery itself, and the sittings public and administrative. In all this the thing was to exclude everything fresh and vital, which always disturbs the regular course of official business, and to admit only official relations with people, and then only on official grounds. A man would come, for instance, wanting some information. Iván Ilyich, as one in whose sphere the matter did not lie, would have nothing to do with him: but if the man had some business with him in his official capacity, something that could be expressed on officially stamped paper, he would do everything, positively everything he could within the limits of such relations, and in doing so would maintain the semblance of friendly human relations, that is, would observe the courtesies of life. As soon as the official relations ended, so did everything else. Iván Ilyich possessed this capacity to separate his real life from the official side of affairs and not mix the two, in the highest degree, and by long practice and natural aptitude had brought it to such a pitch that sometimes, in the manner of a virtuoso, he would even allow himself to let the human and official relations mingle. He let himself do this just because he felt that he could at any time he chose resume the strictly official attitude again and drop the human relation. And he did it all easily, pleasantly, correctly, and even artistically. In the intervals between the sessions he smoked, drank tea, chatted a little about politics, a little about general topics, a little about cards, but most of all about official appointments. Tired, but with the feelings of a virtuoso—one of the first violins who has played his part in an orchestra with precision—he would return home to find that his wife and daughter had been out paying calls, or had a visitor, and that his son had been to school, had done his homework with his tutor, and was duly learning what is taught at High Schools. Everything was as it should be. After dinner, if they had no visitors, Iván Ilyich sometimes read a book that was being much discussed at the time, and in the evening settled down to work, that is, read official papers, compared the depositions of witnesses, and noted paragraphs of the Code applying to them. This was neither dull nor amusing. It was dull when he might have been playing bridge, but if no bridge was available it was at any rate better than doing nothing or sitting with his wife. Iván Ilyich's chief pleasure was giving little dinners to which he invited men and women of good social position, and just as his drawing-room resembled all other drawing-rooms so did his enjoyable little parties resemble all other such parties.

Once they even gave a dance. Iván Ilyich enjoyed it and everything went off well, except that it led to a violent quarrel with his wife about the cakes and sweets. Praskóvya Fëdorovna had made her own plans, but Iván Ilyich insisted on getting everything from an expensive confectioner and ordered too many cakes, and the quarrel occurred because some of those cakes were left over and the confectioner's bill came to forty-five rubles. It was a great and disagreeable quarrel. Praskóvya Fëdorovna called him "a fool and an imbecile," and he clutched at his head and made angry allusions to divorce.

But the dance itself had been enjoyable. The best people were there, and Iván Ilyich had danced with Princess Trúfonova, a sister of the distinguished founder of the Society "Bear my Burden."

The pleasures connected with his work were pleasures of ambition; his social pleasures were those of vanity; but Iván Ilyich's greatest pleasure was playing bridge. He acknowledged that whatever disagreeable incident happened in his life, the pleasure that beamed like a ray of light above everything else was to sit down to bridge with good players, not noisy partners, and of course to four-handed bridge (with five players it was annoying to have to stand out, though one pretended not to mind), to play a clever and serious game (when the cards allowed it) and then to have supper and drink a glass of wine. After a game of bridge, especially if he had won a little (to win a large sum was unpleasant), Iván Ilyich went to bed in specially good humour.

110 So they lived. They formed a circle of acquaintances among the best people and were visited by people of importance and by young folk. In their views as to their acquaintances, husband, wife, and daughter were entirely agreed, and tacitly and unanimously kept at arm's length and shook off the various shabby friends and relations who, with much show of affection, gushed into the drawing-room with its Japanese plates on the walls. Soon these shabby friends ceased to obtrude themselves and only the best people remained in the Golovíns' set.

Young men made up to Lisa, and Petríshchev, an examining magistrate and Dmítri Ivánovich Petríschchev's son and sole heir, began to be so attentive to her that Iván Ilyich had already spoken to Praskóvya Fëdorovna about it, and considered whether they should not arrange a party for them, or get up some private theatricals.

So they lived, and all went well, without change, and life flowed pleasantly.

IV

They were all in good health. It could not be called ill health if Iván Ilyich sometimes said that he had a queer taste in his mouth and felt some discomfort in his left side.

But this discomfort increased and, though not exactly painful, grew into a sense of pressure in his side accompanied by ill humour. And his irritability became worse and worse and began to mar the agreeable, easy, and correct life that had established itself in the Golovín family. Quarrels between husband and wife became more and more frequent, and soon the ease and amenity disappeared and even the decorum was barely maintained. Scenes again became frequent, and very few of those islets remained on which husband and wife could meet without an explosion. Praskóvya Fëdorovna now had good reason to say that her husband's temper was trying. With characteristic exaggeration she said he had always had a dreadful temper, and that it had needed all her good nature to put up with it for twenty years. It was true that now the quarrels were started by him. His bursts of temper always came just before dinner, often just as he began to eat his soup. Sometimes he noticed that a plate or dish was chipped, or the food was not right, or his son put his elbow on the table, or his daughter's hair was not done as he liked it, and for all this he blamed Praskóvya Fëdorovna. At first she retorted and said disagreeable things to him, but once or twice he fell into such a rage at the beginning of dinner that she realized it was due to some physical derangement brought on by taking food, and so she restrained herself and did not answer, but only hurried to get the dinner over. She regarded this self-restraint as highly praiseworthy. Having come to the conclusion that her husband had a dreadful temper and made her life miserable, she began to feel sorry for herself, and the more she pitied herself the more she hated her husband. She began to wish he would die; yet she did not want him to die because then his salary would cease. And this irritated her against him still more. She considered herself dreadfully unhappy just because not even his death could save her, and though she concealed her exasperation, that hidden exasperation of hers increased his irritation also.

After one scene in which Iván Ilyich had been particularly unfair and after 115
which he had said in explanation that he certainly was irritable but that it was due to his not being well, she said that if he was ill it should be attended to, and insisted on his going to see a celebrated doctor.

He went. Everything took place as he had expected and as it always does. There was the usual waiting and the important air assumed by the doctor, with which he was so familiar (resembling that which he himself assumed in court), and the sounding and listening, and the questions which called for answers that were foregone conclusions and were evidently unnecessary, and the look of importance which implied that "if only you put yourself in our hands we will arrange everything—we know indubitably how it has to be done, always in the same way for everybody alike." It was all just as it was in the law courts. The doctor put on just the same air towards him as he himself put on towards an accused person.

The doctor said that so-and-so indicated that there was so-and-so inside the patient, but if the investigation of so-and-so did not confirm this, then he must assume that and that. If he assumed that and that, then . . . and so on. To Iván Ilyich only one question was important: was his case serious or not? But the doctor ignored that inappropriate question. From his point of view it was not the one under consideration, the real question was to decide between a floating kidney, chronic catarrh, or appendicitis. It was not a question of Iván Ilyich's life or death, but one between a floating kidney and appendicitis. And that question the doctor solved brilliantly, as it seemed to Iván Ilyich, in favour of the appendix, with the reservation that should an examination of the urine give fresh indications the matter would be reconsidered. All this was just what Iván Ilyich had himself brilliantly accomplished a thousand times in dealing with men on trial. The doctor summed up just as brilliantly, looking over his spectacles triumphantly and even gaily at the accused. From the doctor's summing up Iván Ilyich concluded that things were bad, but that for the doctor, and perhaps for everybody else, it was a matter of indifference, though for him it was bad. And this conclusion struck him painfully, arousing in him a great feeling of pity for himself and of bitterness towards the doctor's indifference to a matter of such importance.

He said nothing of this, but rose, placed the doctor's fee on the table, and remarked with a sigh: "We sick people probably often put inappropriate questions. But tell me, in general, is this complaint dangerous or not? . . ."

The doctor looked at him sternly over his spectacles with one eye, as if to say: "Prisoner, if you will not keep to the questions put to you, I shall be obliged to have you removed from the court."

"I have already told you what I consider necessary and proper. The analysis may show something more." And the doctor bowed.

Iván Ilyich went out slowly, seated himself disconsolately in his sledge, and drove home. All the way home he was going over what the doctor had said, trying to translate those complicated, obscure, scientific phrases into plain language and find in them an answer to the question: "Is my condition bad? Is it very bad? Or is there as yet nothing much wrong?" And it seemed to him that the meaning of what the doctor had said was it was very bad. Everything in the streets seemed depressing. The cabmen, the houses, the passers-by, and the shops, were dismal. His ache, this dull gnawing ache that never ceased for a moment, seemed to have acquired a new and more serious significance from the doctor's dubious remarks. Iván Ilyich now watched it with a new and oppressive feeling.

He reached home and began to tell his wife about it. She listened, but in the middle of his account his daughter came in with her hat on, ready to go out with her mother. She sat down reluctantly to listen to this tedious story, but could not stand it long, and her mother too did not hear him to the end.

"Well, I am very glad," she said. "Mind now to take your medicine regularly. Give me the prescription and I'll send Gerásim to the chemist's." And she went to get ready to go out.

While she was in the room Iván Ilyich had hardly taken time to breathe, but he sighed deeply when she left it.

"Well," he thought, "perhaps it isn't so bad after all."

He began taking his medicine and following the doctor's directions, which had been altered after the examination of the urine. But then it happened that there was a contradiction between the indications drawn from the examination of the urine and the symptoms that showed themselves. It turned out that what was happening differed from what the doctor had told him, and that he had either forgotten, or blundered, or hidden something from him. He could not, however, be blamed for that, and Iván Ilyich still obeyed his orders implicitly and at first derived some comfort from doing so.

From the time of his visit to the doctor, Iván Ilyich's chief occupation was the exact fulfilment of the doctor's instructions regarding hygiene and the taking of medicine, and the observation of his pain and his excretions. His chief interests came to be people's ailments and people's health. When sickness, deaths, or recoveries were mentioned in his presence, especially when the illness resembled his own, he listened with agitation which he tried to hide, asked questions, and applied what he heard to his own case.

The pain did not grow less, but Iván Ilyich made efforts to force himself to think that he was better. And he could do this so long as nothing agitated him. But as soon as he had any unpleasantness with his wife, any lack of success in his official work, or held bad cards at bridge, he was at once acutely sensible of his disease. He had formerly borne such mischances, hoping soon to adjust what was wrong, to master it and attain success, or make a grand slam. But now every mischance upset him and plunged him into despair. He would say to himself. "There now, just as I was beginning to get better and the medicine had begun to take effect, comes this accursed misfortune, or unpleasantness . . ." And he was furious with the mishap, or with the people who were causing the unpleasantness and killing him, for he felt that this fury was killing him but could not restrain it. One would have thought that it should have been clear to him that this exasperation with circumstances and people aggravated his illness, and that he ought therefore to ignore unpleasant occurrences. But he drew the very opposite conclusion: he said that he needed peace, and he watched for everything that might disturb it and became irritable at the slightest infringement of it. His condition was rendered worse by the fact that he read medical books and consulted doctors. The progress of his disease was so gradual that he could deceive himself when comparing one day with another—the difference was so slight. But when he consulted the doctors it seemed to him that he was getting worse, and even very rapidly. Yet despite this he was continually consulting them.

That month he went to see another celebrity, who told him almost the same as the first had done but put his questions rather differently, and the interview with this celebrity only increased Iván Ilyich's doubts and fears. A friend of a friend of his, a very good doctor, diagnosed his illness again quite differently from the others, and though he predicted recovery, his questions and suppositions bewildered Iván Ilyich still more and increased his doubts. A homeopathist diagnosed the disease in yet another way, and prescribed medicine which Iván Ilyich took secretly for a week. But after a week, not feeling any improvement and having lost confidence both in the former doctor's treatment and in this one's, he became still more despondent. One day a lady acquaintance mentioned a cure effected by a wonder-working icon. Iván Ilyich caught himself listening attentively and beginning to believe that it had occurred. This incident alarmed him. "Has my mind really weakened to such an extent?" he asked himself. "Nonsense! It's all rubbish. I mustn't give way to nervous fears but having chosen a doctor must keep strictly to his treatment. That is what I will do. Now it's all settled. I won't think about it, but will follow the treatment seriously till summer, and then we shall see. From now there must be no more of this wavering!" This was easy to say but impossible to carry out. The pain in his side oppressed him and seemed to grow worse and more incessant, while the taste in his mouth grew stranger and stranger. It seemed to him that his breath had a disgusting smell, and he was conscious of a loss of appetite and strength. There was no deceiving himself: something terrible, new, and more important than anything before in his life, was taking place within him of which he alone was aware. Those about him did not understand or would not understand it, but thought everything in the world was going on as usual. That tormented Iván Ilyich more than anything. He saw that his household, especially his wife and daughter who were in a perfect whirl of visiting, did not understand anything of it and were annoyed that he was so depressed and so exacting, as if he were to blame for it. Though they tried to disguise it he saw that he was an obstacle in their path, and that his wife had adopted a definite line in regard to his illness and kept to it regardless of anything he said or did. Her attitude was this: "You know," she would say to her friends, "Iván Ilyich can't do as other people do, and keep to the treatment prescribed for him. One day he'll take his drops and keep strictly to his diet and go to bed in good time, but the next day unless I watch him he'll suddenly forget his medicine, eat sturgeon—which is forbidden—and sit up playing cards till one o'clock in the morning."

"Oh, come, when was that?" Iván Ilyich would ask in vexation. "Only once at Peter Ivánovich's."

"And yesterday with Shébek."

"Well, even if I hadn't stayed up, this pain would have kept me awake."

"Be that as it may you'll never get well like that, but will always make us wretched."

Praskóvya Fédorovna's attitude to Iván Ilyich's illness, as she expressed it both to others and to him, was that it was his own fault and was another of the annoyances he caused her. Iván Ilyich felt that this opinion escaped her involuntarily—but that did not make it easier for him.

At the law courts too, Iván Ilyich noticed, or thought he noticed, a strange attitude towards himself. It sometimes seemed to him that people were watching him inquisitively as a man whose place might soon be vacant. Then again, his friends would suddenly begin to chaff him in a friendly way about his low spirits, as if the awful, horrible, and unheard-of thing that was going on within him, incessantly gnawing at him and irresistibly drawing him away, was a very agreeable subject for jests. Schwartz in particular irritated him by his jocularity, vivacity, and *savoir-faire*, which reminded him of what he himself had been ten years ago.

Friends came to make up a set and they sat down to cards. They dealt, bending the new cards to soften them, and he sorted the diamonds in his hand and found he had seven. His partner said "No trumps" and supported him with two diamonds. What more could be wished for? It ought to be jolly and lively. They would make a grand slam. But suddenly Iván Ilyich was conscious of that gnawing pain, that taste in his mouth, and it it seemed ridiculous that in such circumstances he should be pleased to make a grand slam.

He looked at his partner Mikháil Mikháylovich, who rapped the table with his strong hand and instead of snatching up the tricks pushed the cards courteously and indulgently towards Iván Ilyich that he might have the pleasure of gathering them up without the trouble of stretching out his hand for them. "Does he think I am too weak to stretch out my arm?" thought Iván Ilyich, and forgetting what he was doing he over-trumped his partner, missing the grand slam by three tricks. And what was most awful of all was that he saw how upset Mikháil Mikháylovich was about it but did not himself care. And it was dreadful to realize why he did not care.

They all saw that he was suffering, and said: "We can stop if you are tired. Take a rest." Lie down? No, he was not at all tired, and he finished the rubber. All were gloomy and silent. Iván Ilyich felt that he had diffused this gloom over them and could not dispel it. They had supper and went away, and Iván Ilyich was left alone with the consciousness that his life was poisoned and was poisoning the lives of others, and that this poison did not weaken but penetrated more and more deeply into his whole being.

With this consciousness, and with physical pain besides the terror, he must go to bed, often to lie awake the greater part of the night. Next morning he had to get up again, dress, go to the law courts, speak, and write; or if he did not go out, spend at home those twenty-four hours a day each of which was a torture. And he had to live thus all alone on the brink of an abyss, with no one who understood or pitied him.

V

So one month passed and then another. Just before the New Year his brother- 140
in-law came to town and stayed at their house. Iván Ilyich was at the law courts and Praskóvya Fëdorovna had gone shopping. When Iván Ilyich came home and entered his study he found his brother-in-law there—a healthy, florid man—unpacking his portmanteau himself. He raised his head on hearing Iván Ilyich's footsteps and looked up at him for a moment without a word. That stare told Iván everything. His brother-in-law opened his mouth to utter an exclamation of surprise but checked himself, and that action confirmed it all.

"I have changed, eh?"

"Yes, there is a change."

And after that, try as he would to get his brother-in-law to return to the subject of his looks, the latter would say nothing about it. Prakóvya Fëdorovna came home and her brother went out to her. Iván Ilyich locked the door and began to examine himself in the glass, first full face, then in profile. He took up a portrait of himself taken with his wife, and compared it with what he saw in the glass. The change in him was immense. Then he bared his arms to the elbow, looked at them, drew the sleeves down again, sat down on an ottoman, and grew blacker than night.

"No, no, this won't do!" he said to himself, and jumped up, went to the table, took up some law papers and began to read them, but could not continue. He unlocked the door and went into the reception-room. The door leading to the drawing-room was shut. He approached it on tiptoe and listened.

"No, you are exaggerating!" Praskóvya Fëdorovna was saying. 145

"Exaggerating! Don't you see it? Why, he's a dead man! Look at his eyes—there's no light in them. But what is it that is wrong with him?"

"No one knows. Nikoláevich [that was another doctor] said something, but I don't know what. And Leshchetítsky [this was the celebrated specialist] said quite the contrary. . ."

Iván Ilyich walked away, went to his own room, lay down and began musing: "The kidney, a floating kidney." He recalled all the doctors had told him of how it detached itself and swayed about. And by an effort of imagination he tried to catch that kidney and arrest it and support it. So little was needed for this, it seemed to him. "No, I'll go to see Peter Ivánovich again." [That was the friend whose friend was a doctor.] He rang, ordered the carriage, and got ready to go.

"Where are you going, *Jean?*"[9] asked his wife, with a specially sad and exceptionally kind look.

This exceptionally kind look irritated him. He looked morosely at her.

"I must go to see Peter Ivánovich."

He went to see Peter Ivánovich, and together they went to see his friend, the doctor. He was in, and Iván Ilyich had a long talk with him.

Reviewing the anatomical and physiological details of what in the doctor's opinion was going on inside him, he understood it all.

There was something, a small thing, in the vermiform appendix. It might all come right. Only stimulate the energy of one organ and check the activity of another, then absorption would take place and everything would come right. He got home rather late for dinner, ate his dinner, and conversed cheerfully, but could not for a long time bring himself to go back to work in his room. At last, however, he went to his study and did what was necessary, but the consciousness that he had put something aside—an important, intimate matter which he would revert to when his work was done—never left him. When he had finished his work he remembered that this intimate matter was the thought of his vermiform appendix. But he did not give himself up to it, and went to the drawing-room for tea. There were callers there, including the examining magistrate who was a desirable match for his daughter, and they were conversing, playing the piano, and singing. Iván Ilyich, as Praskóvya Fëdorovna remarked, spent that evening more cheerfully than usual, but he never for a moment forgot that he had postponed the important matter of the appendix. At eleven o'clock he said good-night and went to his bedroom. Since his illness he had slept alone in a small room next to his study. He undressed and took up a novel by Zola,[1] but instead of reading it he fell into thought, and in his imagination that desired improvement in the vermiform appendix occurred. There was the absorption and evacuation and the reestablishment of normal activity. "Yes, that's it!" he said to himself. "One need only assist nature, that's all." He remembered his medicine, rose, took it, and lay down on his back watching for the beneficent action of the medicine and for it to lessen the pain. "I need only take it regularly and avoid all injurious influences. I am already feeling better, much better." He began touching his side: it was not painful to the touch. "There, I really don't feel it. It's much better already." He put out the light and turned on his side. . . . "The

9. French for *Iván*. 1. The French naturalistic novelist Émile Zola (1840–1902) saw human life as merely a matter of biological and mechanistic functions.

appendix is getting better, absorption is occurring." Suddenly he felt the old, familiar, dull, gnawing pain, stubborn and serious. There was the same familiar loathsome taste in his mouth. His heart sank and he felt dazed. "My God! My God!" he muttered. "Again, again! And it will never cease." And suddenly the matter presented itself in a quite different aspect. "Vermiform appendix! Kidney!" he said to himself. "It's not a question of appendix or kidney, but of life and . . . death. Yes, life was there and now it is going, going and I cannot stop it. Yes. Why deceive myself? Isn't it obvious to everyone but me that I'm dying, and that it's only a question of weeks, days . . . it may happen this moment. There was light and now there is darkness. I was here and now I'm going there! Where?" A chill came over him, his breathing ceased, and he felt only the throbbing of his heart.

"When I am not, what will there be? There will be nothing. Then where 155
shall I be when I am no more? Can this be dying? No, I don't want to!" He jumped up and tried to light the candle, felt for it with trembling hands, dropped candle and candlestick on the floor, and fell back on his pillow.

"What's the use? It makes no difference," he said to himself, staring with wide-open eyes into the darkness. "Death. Yes, death. And none of them know or wish to know it, and they have no pity for me. Now they are playing." (He heard through the door the distant sound of a song and its accompaniment.) "It's all the same to them, but they will die too! Fools! I first, and they later, but it will be the same for them. And now they are merry . . . the beasts!"

Anger choked him and he was agonizingly, unbearably miserable. "It is impossible that all men have been doomed to suffer this awful horror!" He raised himself.

"Something must be wrong. I must calm myself—must think it all over from the beginning." And he again began thinking. "Yes, the beginning of my illness: I knocked my side, but I was still quite well that day and the next. It hurt a little, then rather more. I saw the doctors, then followed despondency and anguish, more doctors, and I drew nearer to the abyss. My strength grew less and I kept coming nearer and nearer, and now I have wasted away and there is no light in my eyes. I think of the appendix—but this is death! I think of mending the appendix, and all the while here is death! Can it really be death!" Again terror seized him and he gasped for breath. He leant down and began feeling for the matches, pressing with his elbow on the stand beside the bed. It was in his way and hurt him, he grew furious with it, pressed on it still harder, and upset it. Breathless and in despair he fell on his back, expecting death to come immediately.

Meanwhile the visitors were leaving. Praskóvya Fëdorovna was seeing them off. She heard something fall and came in.

"What has happened?" 160

"Nothing. I knocked it over accidentally."

She went out and returned with a candle. He lay there panting heavily, like a man who has run a thousand yards, and stared upwards at her with a fixed look.

"What is it, *Jean?*"

"No . . . o . . . thing. I upset it." ("Why speak of it? She won't understand," he thought.)

And in truth she did not understand. She picked up the stand, lit his candle, and hurried away to see another visitor off. When she came back he still lay on his back, looking upwards.

"What is it? Do you feel worse?"

"Yes."

She shook her head and sat down.

"Do you know, *Jean*, I think we must ask Leshchetítsky to come and see you here."

This meant calling in the famous specialist, regardless of expense. He smiled malignantly and said "No." She remained a little longer and then went up to him and kissed his forehead.

While she was kissing him he hated her from the bottom of his soul and with difficulty refrained from pushing her away.

"Good-night. Please God you'll sleep."

"Yes."

VI

Iván Ilyich saw that he was dying, and he was in continual despair.

In the depth of his heart he knew he was dying, but not only was he not accustomed to the thought, he simply did not and could not grasp it.

The syllogism he had learned from Kiesewetter's *Logic*:[2] "Caius is a man, men are mortal, therefore Caius is mortal," had always seemed to him correct as applied to Caius, but certainly not as applied to himself. That Caius—man in the abstract—was mortal, was perfectly correct, but he was not Caius, not an abstract man, but a creature quite, quite separate from all others. He had been little Ványa, with a mamma and a papa, with Mítya and Volódya, with the toys, a coachman and a nurse, afterwards with Kátenka and with all the joys, griefs, and delights of childhood, boyhood, and youth. What did Caius know of the smell of that striped leather ball Ványa had been so fond of? Had Caius kissed his mother's hand like that, and did the silk of her dress rustle so for Caius? Had he rioted like that at school when the pastry was bad? Had Caius been in love like that? Could Caius preside at a session as he did? "Caius really was mortal, and it was right for him to die; but for me, little Ványa, Iván Ilyich, with all my thoughts and emotions, it's altogether a different matter. It cannot be that I ought to die. That would be too terrible."

Such was his feeling.

"If I had to die like Caius I should have known it was so. An inner voice would have told me so, but there was nothing of the sort in me and I and all my friends felt that our case was quite different from that of Caius. And now here it is!" he said to himself. "It can't be. It's impossible! But here it is. How is this? How is one to understand it?"

2. Karl Kiesewetter (1766–1819), *Outline of Logic According to Kantian Principles* (1796), influential in Russia as basis for school textbooks.

He could not understand it, and tried to drive this false, incorrect, morbid thought away and to replace it by other proper and healthy thoughts. But that thought, and not the thought only but the reality itself, seemed to come and confront him.

And to replace that thought he called up a succession of others, hoping to find in them some support. He tried to get back into the former current of thoughts that had once screened the thought of death from him. But strange to say, all that had formerly shut off, hidden, and destroyed, his consciousness of death, no longer had that effect. Iván Ilyich now spent most of his time in attempting to re-establish that old current. He would say to himself: "I will take up my duties again—after all I used to live by them." And banishing all doubts he would go to the law courts, enter into conversation with his colleagues, and sit carelessly as was his wont, scanning the crowd with a thoughtful look and leaning both his emaciated arms on the arms of his oak chair; bending over as usual to a colleague and drawing his papers nearer he would interchange whispers with him, and then suddenly raising his eyes and sitting erect would pronounce certain words and open the proceedings. But suddenly in the midst of those proceedings the pain in his side, regardless of the stage the proceedings had reached, would begin its own gnawing work. Iván Ilyich would turn his attention to it and try to drive the thought of it away, but without success. *It* would come and stand before him and look at him, and he would be petrified and the light would die out of his eyes, and he would again begin asking himself whether *It* alone was true. And his colleagues and subordinates would see with surprise and distress that he, the brilliant and subtle judge, was becoming confused and making mistakes. He would shake himself, try to pull himself together, manage somehow to bring the sitting to a close, and return home with the sorrowful consciousness that his judicial labours could not as formerly hide from him what he wanted them to hide, and could not deliver him from *It*. And what was worst of all was that *It* drew his attention to itself not in order to make him take some action but only that he should look at *It*, look it straight in the face: look at it without doing anything, suffer inexpressibly.

And to save himself from this condition Iván Ilyich looked for consolations—new screens—and new screens were found and for a while seemed to save him, but then they immediately fell to pieces or rather became transparent, as *It* penetrated them and nothing could veil *It*.

In these latter days he would go into the drawing-room he had arranged—that drawing-room where he had fallen and for the sake of which (how bitterly ridiculous it seemed) he had sacrificed his life—for he knew that his illness originated with that knock. He would enter and see that something had scratched the polished table. He would look for the cause of this and find that it was the bronze ornamentation of an album, that had got bent. He would take up the expensive album which he had lovingly arranged, and feel vexed with his daughter and her friends for their untidiness—for the album was torn here and there and some of the photographs turned upside down. He would put it carefully in order and bend the ornamentation back into position. Then it would occur to him to place all those things in another corner of the room, near the plants. He would call the footman, but his daughter or wife would contradict him, and he would dispute and grow angry. But that was all right, for then he did not think about *It*. *It* was invisible.

But then, when he was moving something himself, his wife would say: "Let the servants do it. You will hurt yourself again." And suddenly *It* would flash through the screen and he would see it. It was just a flash, and he hoped it would disappear, but he would involuntarily pay attention to his side. "It sits there as before, gnawing just the same!" And he could no longer forget *It*, but could distinctly see it looking at him from behind the flowers. "What is it all for?"

"It really is so! I lost my life over that curtain as I might have done when storming a fort. Is that possible? How terrible and how stupid. It can't be true! It can't, but it is."

He would go to his study, lie down, and again be alone with *It*: face to face with *It*. And nothing could be done with *It* except to look at it and shudder.

VII

How it happened it is impossible to say because it came about step by step, unnoticed, but in the third month of Iván Ilyich's illness, his wife, his daughter, his son, his acquaintances, the doctors, the servants, and above all he himself, were aware that the whole interest he had for other people was whether he would soon vacate his place, and at last release the living from the discomfort caused by his presence and be himself released from his sufferings.

He slept less and less. He was given opium and hypodermic injections of morphine, but this did not relieve him. The dull depression he experienced in a somnolent condition at first gave him a little relief, but only as something new; afterwards it became as distressing as the pain itself or even more so.

Special foods were prepared for him by the doctors' orders, but all those foods became increasingly distasteful and disgusting to him.

For his excretions also special arrangements had to be made, and this was a torment to him every time—a torment from the uncleanliness, the unseemliness, and the smell, and from knowing that another person had to take part in it.

But just through this most unpleasant matter, Iván Ilyich obtained comfort. Gerásim, the butler's young assistant, always came in to carry the things out. Gerásim was a clean, fresh peasant lad, grown stout on town food and always cheerful and bright. At first the sight of him, in his clean Russian peasant costume, engaged on that disgusting task embarrassed Iván Ilyich.

Once when he got up from the commode too weak to draw up his trousers, he dropped into a soft armchair and looked with horror at his bare, enfeebled thighs with the muscles so sharply marked on them.

Gerásim with a firm light tread, his heavy boots emitting a pleasant smell of tar and fresh winter air, came in wearing a clean Hessian apron,[3] the sleeves of his print shirt tucked up over his strong bare young arms; and refraining from looking at his sick master out of consideration for his feelings, and restraining

3. Burlap apron.

the joy of life that beamed from his face, he went up to the commode.

"Gerásim!" said Iván Ilyich in a weak voice.

Gerásim started, evidently afraid he might have committed some blunder, and with a rapid movement turned his fresh, kind, simple young face which just showed the first downy sign of a beard.

"Yes, sir?"

"That must be very unpleasant for you. You must forgive me. I am helpless."

"Oh, why, sir," and Gerásim's eyes beamed and he showed his glistening white teeth, "what's a little trouble? It's a case of illness with you, sir."

And his deft strong hands did their accustomed task, and he went out of the room stepping lightly. Five minutes later he as lightly returned.

Iván Ilyich was still sitting in the same position in the armchair.

"Gerásim," he said when the latter had replaced the freshly-washed utensil. "Please come here and help me." Gerásim went up to him. "Lift me up. It is hard for me to get up, and I have sent Dmítri away."

Gerásim went up to him, grasped his master with his strong arms deftly but gently, in the same way that he stepped—lifted him, supported him with one hand, and with the other drew up his trousers and would have set him down again, but Iván Ilyich asked to be led to the sofa. Gerásim, without an effort and without apparent pressure, led him, almost lifting him, to the sofa and placed him on it.

"Thank you. How easily and well you do it all!"

Gerásim smiled again and turned to leave the room. But Iván Ilyich felt his presence such a comfort that he did not want to let him go.

"One thing more, please move up that chair. No, the other one—under my feet. It is easier for me when my feet are raised."

Gerásim brought the chair, set it down gently in place, and raised Iván Ilyich's legs on to it. It seemed to Iván Ilyich that he felt better while Gerásim was holding up his legs.

"It's better when my legs are higher," he said. "Place that cushion under them."

Gerásim did so. He again lifted the legs and placed them, and again Iván Ilyich felt better while Gerásim held his legs. When he set them down Iván Ilyich fancied he felt worse.

"Gerásim," he said. "Are you busy now?"

"Not at all, sir," said Gerásim, who had learnt from the townsfolk how to speak to gentlefolk.

"What have you still to do?"

"What have I to do? I've done everything except chopping the logs for to-morrow."

"Then hold my legs up a bit higher, can you?"

"Of course I can. Why not?" And Gerásim raised his master's legs higher and Iván Ilyich thought that in that position he did not feel any pain at all.

"And how about the logs?"

"Don't trouble about that, sir. There's plenty of time."

Iván Ilyich told Gerásim to sit down and hold his legs, and began to talk to him. And strange to say it seemed to him that he felt better while Gerásim held his legs up.

After that Iván Ilyich would sometimes call Gerásim and get him to hold his legs on his shoulders, and he liked talking to him. Gerásim did it all easily, willingly, simply, and with a good nature that touched Iván Ilyich. Health, strength, and vitality in other people were offensive to him, but Gerásim's strength and vitality did not mortify but soothed him.

What tormented Iván Ilyich most was the deception, the lie, which for some reason they all accepted, that he was not dying but was simply ill, and that he only need keep quiet and undergo a treatment and then something very good would result. He however knew that do what they would nothing would come of it, only still more agonizing suffering and death. This deception tortured him—their not wishing to admit what they all knew and what he knew, but wanting to lie to him concerning his terrible condition, and wishing and forcing him to participate in that lie. Those lies—lies enacted over him on the eve of his death and destined to degrade this awful, solemn act to the level of their visitings, their curtains, their sturgeon for dinner—were a terrible agony for Iván Ilyich. And strangely enough, many times when they were going through their antics over him he had been within a hairbreadth of calling out to them: "Stop lying! You know and I know that I am dying. Then at least stop lying about it!" But he had never had the spirit to do it. The awful, terrible act of his dying was, he could see, reduced by those about him to the level of a casual, unpleasant, and almost indecorous incident (as if someone entered a drawing-room diffusing an unpleasant odour) and this was done by that very decorum which he had served all his life long. He saw that no one felt for him, because no one even wished to grasp his position. Only Gerásim recognized and pitied him. And so Iván Ilyich felt at ease only with him. He felt comforted when Gerásim supported his legs (sometimes all night long) and refused to go to bed, saying: "Don't you worry, Iván Ilyich. I'll get sleep enough later on," or when he suddenly became familiar and exclaimed: "If you weren't sick it would be another matter, but as it is, why should I grudge a little trouble?" Gerásim alone did not lie; everything showed that he alone understood the facts of the case and did not consider it necessary to disguise them, but simply felt sorry for his emaciated and enfeebled master. Once when Iván Ilyich was sending him away he even said straight out: "We shall all of us die, so why should I grudge a little trouble?"—expressing the fact that he did not think his work burdensome, because he was doing it for a dying man and hoped someone would do the same for him when his time came.

Apart from this lying, or because of it, what most tormented Iván Ilyich was that no one pitied him as he wished to be pitied. At certain moments after prolonged suffering he wished most of all (though he would have been ashamed to confess it) for someone to pity him as a sick child is pitied. He longed to be petted and comforted. He knew he was an important functionary, that he had a beard turning grey, and that therefore what he longed for was impossible, but still he longed for it. And in Gerásim's attitude towards him there was something akin to what he wished for, and so that attitude comforted him. Iván Ilyich wanted to weep, wanted to be petted and cried over, and then his colleague

Shébek would come, and instead of weeping and being petted, Iván Ilyich would assume a serious, severe, and profound air, and by force of habit would express his opinion on a decision of the Court of Appeal and would stubbornly insist on that view. This falsity around him and within him did more than anything else to poison his last days.

VIII

It was morning. He knew it was morning because Gerásim had gone, and Peter the footman had come and put out the candles, drawn back one of the curtains, and begun quietly to tidy up. Whether it was morning or evening, Friday or Sunday, made no difference, it was all just the same: the gnawing, unmitigated, agonizing pain, never ceasing for an instant, the consciousness of life inexorably waning but not yet extinguished, the approach of that ever dreaded and hateful Death which was the only reality, and always the same falsity. What were days, weeks, hours, in such a case?

"Will you have some tea, sir?"

"He wants things to be regular, and wishes the gentlefolk to drink tea in the morning," thought Iván Ilyich, and only said "No."

"Wouldn't you like to move onto the sofa, sir?"

"He wants to tidy up the room, and I'm in the way. I am uncleanliness and disorder," he thought, and said only:

"No, leave me alone."

The man went on bustling about. Iván Ilyich stretched out his hand. Peter came up, ready to help.

"What is it, sir?"

"My watch."

Peter took the watch which was close at hand and gave it to his master.

"Half-past eight. Are they up?"

"No sir, except Vladímir Ivánich" (the son) "who has gone to school. Praskóvya Fëdorovna ordered me to wake her if you asked for her. Shall I do so?"

"No, there's no need to." "Perhaps I'd better have some tea," he thought, and added aloud: "Yes, bring me some tea."

Peter went to the door, but Iván Ilyich dreaded being left alone. "How can I keep him here? Oh yes, my medicine." "Peter, give me my medicine." "Why not? Perhaps it may still do me some good." He took a spoonful and swallowed it. "No, it won't help. It's all tomfoolery, all deception," he decided as soon as he became aware of the familiar, sickly, hopeless taste. "No, I can't believe in it any longer. But the pain, why this pain? If it would only cease just for a moment!" And he moaned. Peter turned towards him. "It's all right. Go and fetch me some tea."

Peter went out. Left alone Iván Ilyich groaned not so much with pain, terrible though that was, as from mental anguish. Always and forever the same, always these endless days and nights. If only it would come quicker! If only *what* would come quicker? Death, darkness? . . . No, no! Anything rather than death!

When Peter returned with the tea on a tray, Iván Ilyich stared at him for a time in perplexity, not realizing who and what he was. Peter was disconcerted by that look and his embarrassment brought Iván Ilyich to himself.

"Oh, tea! All right, put it down. Only help me to wash and put on a clean shirt."

And Iván Ilyich began to wash. With pauses for rest, he washed his hands and then his face, cleaned his teeth, brushed his hair, and looked in the glass. He was terrified by what he saw, especially by the limp way in which his hair clung to his pallid forehead.

While his shirt was being changed he knew that he would be still more frightened at the sight of his body, so he avoided looking at it. Finally he was ready. He drew on a dressing-gown, wrapped himself in a plaid, and sat down in the armchair to take his tea. For a moment he felt refreshed, but as soon as he began to drink the tea he was again aware of the same taste, and the pain also returned. He finished it with an effort, and then lay down stretching out his legs, and dismissed Peter.

Always the same. Now a spark of hope flashes up, then a sea of despair rages, and always pain; always pain, always despair, and always the same. When alone he had a dreadful and distressing desire to call someone, but he knew beforehand that with others present it would be still worse. "Another dose of morphine—to lose consciousness. I will tell him, the doctor, that he must think of something else. It's impossible, impossible, to go on like this."

An hour and another pass like that. But now there is a ring at the door bell. Perhaps it's the doctor? It is. He comes in fresh, hearty, plump, and cheerful, with that look on his face that seems to say: "There now, you're in a panic about something, but we'll arrange it all for you directly!" The doctor knows this expression is out of place here, but he has put it on once for all and can't take it off—like a man who has put on a frock-coat in the morning to pay a round of calls.

The doctor rubs his hands vigorously and reassuringly.

"Brr! How cold it is! There's such a sharp frost; just let me warm myself!" he says, as if it were only a matter of waiting till he was warm, and then he would put everything right.

"Well now, how are you?"

Iván Ilyich feels that the doctor would like to say: "Well, how are our affairs?" but that even he feels that this would not do, and says instead: "What sort of a night have you had?"

Iván Ilyich looks at him as much as to say: "Are you really never ashamed of lying?" But the doctor does not wish to understand this question, and Iván Ilyich says: "Just as terrible as ever. The pain never leaves me and never subsides. If only something . . ."

"Yes, you sick people are always like that. . . . There, now I think I'm warm enough. Even Praskóvya Fëdorovna, who is so particular, could find no fault with my temperature. Well, now I can say good-morning," and the doctor presses his patient's hand.

Then, dropping his former playfulness, he begins with a most serious face to examine the patient, feeling his pulse and taking his temperature, and then begins the sounding and auscultation.

Iván Ilyich knows quite well and definitely that all this is nonsense and pure deception, but when the doctor, getting down on his knee, leans over him, putting his ear first higher then lower, and performs various gymnastic movements over him with a significant expression on his face, Iván Ilyich submits to it all as he used to submit to the speeches of the lawyers, though he knew very well that they were all lying and why they were lying.

The doctor, kneeling on the sofa, is still sounding him when Praskóvya Fëdorovna's silk dress rustles at the door and she is heard scolding Peter for not having let her know of the doctor's arrival.

She comes in, kisses her husband, and at once proceeds to prove that she has been up a long time already, and only owing to a misunderstanding failed to be there when the doctor arrived.

Iván Ilyich looks at her, scans her all over, sets against her the whiteness and plumpness and cleanness of her hands and neck, the gloss of her hair, and the sparkle of her vivacious eyes. He hates her with his whole soul. And the thrill of hatred he feels for her makes him suffer from her touch.

Her attitude towards him and his disease is still the same. Just as the doctor had adopted a certain relation to his patient which he could not abandon, so had she formed one towards him—that he was not doing something he ought to do and was himself to blame, and that she reproached him lovingly for this—and she could not now change that attitude.

"You see he doesn't listen to me and doesn't take his medicine at the proper time. And above all he lies in a position that is no doubt bad for him—with his legs up."

She described how he made Gerásim hold his legs up.

The doctor smiled with a contemptuous affability that said: "What's to be done? These sick people do have foolish fancies of that kind, but we must forgive them."

When the examination was over the doctor looked at his watch, and then Praskóvya Fëdorovna announced to Iván Ilyich that it was of course as he pleased, but she had sent to-day for a celebrated specialist who would examine him and have a consultation with Michael Danílovich (their regular doctor).

"Please don't raise any objections. I am doing this for my own sake," she said ironically, letting it be felt that she was doing it all for his sake and only said this to leave him no right to refuse. He remained silent, knitting his brows. He felt that he was so surrounded and involved in a mesh of falsity that it was hard to unravel anything.

Everything she did for him was entirely for her own sake, and she told him she was doing for herself what she actually was doing for herself, as if that was so incredible that he must understand the opposite.

At half-past eleven the celebrated specialist arrived. Again the sounding began and the significant conversations in his presence and in other room, about the kidneys and the appendix, and the questions and answers, with such an air of importance that again, instead of the real question of life and death which now alone confronted him, the question arose of the kidney and the appendix which were not behaving as they ought to and would now be attacked by Michael Danílovich and the specialist and forced to amend their ways.

260 The celebrated specialist took leave of him with a serious though not hopeless look, and in reply to the timid question in Iván Ilyich, with eyes glistening with fear and hope, put to him as to whether there was a chance of recovery, said that he could not vouch for it but there was a possibility. The look of hope with which Iván Ilyich watched the doctor out was so pathetic that Praskóvya Fëdorovna, seeing it, even wept as she left the room to hand the doctor his fee.

The gleam of hope kindled by the doctor's encouragement did not last long. The same room, the same pictures, curtains, wallpaper, medicine bottles, were all there, and the same aching suffering body, and Iván Ilyich began to moan. They gave him a subcutaneous injection and he sank into oblivion.

It was twilight when he came to. They brought him his dinner and he swallowed some beef tea with difficulty, and then everything was the same again and night was coming on.

After dinner, at seven o'clock, Praskóvya Fëdorovna came into the room in evening dress, her full bosom pushed up by her corset, and with traces of powder on her face. She had reminded him in the morning that they were going to the theatre. Sarah Bernhardt was visiting the town and they had a box, which he had insisted on their taking. Now he had forgotten about it and her toilet offended him, but he concealed his vexation when he remembered that he had himself insisted on their securing a box and going because it would be an instructive and aesthetic pleasure for the children.

Praskóvya Fëdorovna came in, self-satisfied but yet with a rather guilty air. She sat down and asked how he was, but, as he saw, only for the sake of asking and not in order to learn about it, knowing that there was nothing to learn—and then went on to what she really wanted to say: that she would not on any account have gone but that the box had been taken and Helen and their daughter were going, as well as Petríshchev (the examining magistrate, their daughter's fiancé) and that it was out of the question to let them go alone; but that she would have much preferred to sit with him for a while; and he must be sure to follow the doctor's orders while she was away.

265 "Oh, and Fëdor Petróvich" (the fiancé) "would like to come in. May he? And Lisa?"

"All right."

Their daughter came in in full evening dress, her fresh young flesh exposed (making a show of that very flesh which in his own case caused so much suffering), strong, healthy, evidently in love, and impatient with illness, suffering, and death, because they interfered with her happiness.

Fëdor Petróvich came in too, in evening dress, his hair curled *à la Capoul*,[4] a tight stiff collar round his long sinewy neck, an enormous white shirt-front and narrow black trousers tightly stretched over his strong thighs. He had one white glove tightly drawn on, and was holding his opera hat in his hand.

Following him the schoolboy crept in unnoticed, in a new uniform, poor

4. With a part in the middle, hair brushed off the sides of the forehead but with two small curls over the middle of the forehead; after Joseph-Amédée-Victor Capoul (1839–1924), French singer and matinee idol.

little fellow, and wearing gloves. Terribly dark shadows showed under his eyes, the meaning of which Iván Ilyich knew well.

His son had always seemed pathetic to him, and now it was dreadful to see the boy's frightened look of pity. It seemed to Iván Ilyich that Vásya was the only one besides Gerásim who understood and pitied him.

They all sat down and again asked how he was. A silence followed. Lisa asked her mother about the opera-glasses, and there was an altercation between mother and daughter as to who had taken them and where they had been put. This occasioned some unpleasantness.

Fëdor Petróvich inquired of Iván Ilyich whether he had ever seen Sarah Bernhardt. Iván Ilyich did not at first catch the question, but then replied: "No, have you seen her before?"

"Yes, in *Adrienne Lecouvreur*."[5]

Praskóvya Fëdorovna mentioned some rôles in which Sarah Bernhardt was particularly good. Her daughter disagreed. Conversation sprang up as to the elegance and realism of her acting—the sort of conversation that is always repeated and is always the same.

In the midst of the conversation Fëdor Petróvich glanced at Iván Ilyich and became silent. The others also looked at him and grew silent. Iván Ilyich was staring with glittering eyes straight before him, evidently indignant with them. This had to be rectified, but it was impossible to do so. The silence had to be broken, but for a time no one dared to break it and they all became afraid that the conventional deception would suddenly become obvious and the truth become plain to all. Lisa was the first to pluck up courage and break that silence, but by trying to hide what everybody was feeling, she betrayed it.

"Well, if we are going it's time to start," she said, looking at her watch, a present from her father, and with a faint and significant smile at Fëdor Petróvich relating to something known only to them. She got up with a rustle of her dress.

They all rose, said good-night, and went away.

When they had gone it seemed to Iván Ilyich that he felt better; the falsity had gone with them. But the pain remained—that same pain and that same fear that made everything monotonously alike, nothing harder and nothing easier. Everything was worse.

Again minute followed minute and hour followed hour. Everything remained the same and there was no cessation. And the inevitable end of it all became more and more terrible.

"Yes, send Gerásim here," he replied to a question Peter asked.

IX

His wife returned late at night. She came in on tiptoe, but he heard her, opened his eyes, and made haste to close them again. She wished to send Gerásim away and to sit with him herself, but he opened his eyes and said: "No, go away."

5. An 1849 play by the prolific and popular French playwright Eugène Scribe (1791–1861), one of Bernhardt's most famous vehicles.

"Are you in great pain?"

"Always the same."

"Take some opium."

He agreed and took some. She went away.

Till about three in the morning he was in a state of stupefied misery. It seemed to him that he and his pain were being thrust into a narrow, deep black sack, but though they were pushed further and further in they could not be pushed to the bottom. And this, terrible enough in itself, was accompanied by suffering. He was frightened yet wanted to fall through the sack, he struggled but yet co-operated. And suddenly he broke through, fell, and regained consciousness. Gerásim was sitting at the foot of the bed dozing quietly and patiently, while he himself lay with his emaciated stockinged legs resting on Gerásim's shoulders; the same shaded candle was there and the same unceasing pain.

"Go away, Gerásim," he whispered.

"It's all right, sir. I'll stay a while."

"No. Go away."

He removed his legs from Gerásim's shoulders, turned sideways onto his arm, and felt sorry for himself. He only waited till Gerásim had gone into the next room and then restrained himself no longer but wept like a child. He wept on account of his helplessness, his terrible loneliness, the cruelty of man, the cruelty of God, and the absence of God.

"Why hast Thou done all this? Why hast Thou brought me here? Why, dost Thou torment me so terribly?"

He did not expect an answer and yet wept because there was no answer and could be none. The pain again grew more acute, but he did not stir and did not call. He said to himself: "Go on! Strike me! But what is it for? What have I done to Thee? What is it for?"

Then he grew quiet and not only ceased weeping but even held his breath and became all attention. It was as though he were listening not to an audible voice but to a voice of his soul, to the current of thoughts arising within him.

"What is it you want?" was the first clear conception capable of expression in words, that he heard.

"What do you want? What do you want?" he repeated to himself.

"What do I want? To live and not to suffer," he answered.

And again he listened with such concentrated attention that even his pain did not distract him.

"To live? How?" asked his inner voice.

"Why, to live as I used to—well and pleasantly."

"As you lived before, well and pleasantly?" the voice repeated.

And in imagination he began to recall the moments of his pleasant life. But strange to say none of those best moments of his pleasant life now seemed at all what they had then seemed—none of them except the first recollections of childhood. There, in childhood, there had been something really pleasant with which it would be possible to live if it could return. But the child who had experienced that happiness existed no longer, it was like a reminiscence of somebody else.

As soon as the period began which had produced the present Iván Ilyich, all that had then seemed joys now melted before his sight and turned into something trivial and often nasty.

And the further he departed from childhood and the nearer he came to the present the more worthless and doubtful were the joys. This began with the School of Law. A little that was really good was still found there—there was light-heartedness, friendship, and hope. But in the upper classes there had already been fewer of such good moments. Then during the first years of his official career, when he was in the service of the Governor, some pleasant moments again occurred: they were the memories of love for a woman. Then all became confused and there was still less of what was good; later on again there was still less that was good, and the further he went the less there was. His marriage, a mere accident, then the disenchantment that followed it, his wife's bad breath and the sensuality and hypocrisy: then that deadly official life and those preoccupations about money, a year of it, and two, and ten, and twenty, and always the same thing. And the longer it lasted the more deadly it became. "It is as if I had been going downhill while I imagined I was going up. And that is really what it was. I was going up in public opinion, but to the same extent life was ebbing away from me. And now it is all done and there is only death."

"Then what does it mean? Why? It can't be that life is so senseless and horrible. But if it really has been so horrible and senseless, why must I die and die in agony? There is something wrong!"

"Maybe I did not live as I ought to have done," it suddenly occurred to him. 305
"But how could that be, when I did everything properly?" he replied, and immediately dismissed from his mind this, the sole solution of all the riddles of life and death, as something quite impossible.

"Then what do you want now? To live? Live how? Live as you lived in the law courts when the usher proclaimed 'The judge is coming!' The judge is coming, the judge!" he repeated to himself. "Here he is, the judge. But I am not guilty!" he exclaimed angrily. "What is it for?" And he ceased crying, but turning his face to the wall continued to ponder on the same question: Why, and for what purpose, is there all this horror? But however much he pondered he found no answer. And whenever the thought occurred to him, as it often did, that it all resulted from his not having lived as he ought to have done, he at once recalled the correctness of his whole life, and dismissed so strange an idea.

X

Another fortnight passed. Iván Ilyich now no longer left his sofa. He would not lie in bed but lay on the sofa, facing the wall nearly all the time. He suffered ever the same unceasing agonies and in his loneliness pondered always on the same insoluble question: "What is this? Can it be that it is Death?" And the inner voice answered: "Yes, it is Death."

"Why these sufferings?" And the voice answered, "For no reason—they just are so." Beyond and besides this there was nothing.

From the very beginning of his illness, ever since he had first been to see the doctor, Iván Ilyich's life had been divided between two contrary and alternating moods: now it was despair and the expectation of this uncomprehended and terrible death, and now hope and an intently interested observation of the functioning of his organs. Now before his eyes there was only a kidney or an intestine that temporarily evaded its duty, and now only that incomprehensible and dreadful death from which it was impossible to escape.

These two states of mind had alternated from the very beginning of his illness, but the further it progressed the more doubtful and fantastic became the conception of the kidney, and the more real the sense of impending death.

He had but to call to mind what he had been three months before and what he was now, to call to mind with what regularity he had been going downhill, for every possibility of hope to be shattered.

Latterly during that loneliness in which he found himself as he lay facing the back of the sofa, a loneliness in the midst of a populous town and surrounded by numerous acquaintances and relations but that yet could not have been more complete anywhere—either at the bottom of the sea or under the earth—during that terrible loneliness Iván Ilyich had lived only in memories of the past. Pictures of his past rose before him one after another. They always began with what was nearest in time and then went back to what was most remote—to his childhood—and rested there. If he thought of the stewed prunes that had been offered him that day, his mind went back to the raw shrivelled French plums of his childhood, their peculiar flavour and the flow of saliva when he sucked their stones, and along with the memory of that taste came a whole series of memories of those days: his nurse, his brother, and their toys. "No, I mustn't think of that. . . . It is too painful," Iván Ilyich said to himself, and brought himself back to the present—to the button on the back of the sofa and the creases in its morocco. "Morocco is expensive, but it does not wear well: there had been a quarrel about it. It was a different kind of quarrel and a different kind of morocco that time when we tore father's portfolio and were punished, and mamma brought us some tarts. . . ." And again his thoughts dwelt on his childhood, and again it was painful and he tried to banish them and fix his mind on something else.

Then again together with that chain of memories another series passed through his mind—of how his illness had progressed and grown worse. There also the further back he looked the more life there had been. There had been more of what was good in life and more of life itself. The two merged together. "Just as the pain went on getting worse and worse, so my life grew worse and worse," he thought. "There is one bright spot there at the back, at the beginning of life, and afterwards all becomes blacker and blacker and proceeds more and more rapidly—in inverse ratio to the square of the distance from death," thought Iván Ilyich. And the example of a stone falling downwards with increasing velocity entered his mind. Life, a series of increasing sufferings, flies further and further towards its end—the most terrible suffering. "I am flying. . . ." He shuddered, shifted himself, and tried to resist, but was already aware that resistance was impossible, and again with eyes weary of gazing but unable to cease seeing what was before them, he stared at the back of the sofa and waited—awaiting that dreadful fall and shock and destruction.

"Resistance is impossible!" he said to himself. "If I could only understand what it is all for! But that too is impossible. An explanation would be possible if it could be said that I have not lived as I ought to. But it is impossible to say that," and he remembered all the legality, correctitude, and propriety of his life. "That at any rate can certainly not be admitted," he thought, and his lips smiled ironically as if someone could see that smile and be taken in by it. "There is no explanation! Agony, death. . . . What for?"

XI

Another two weeks went by in this way and during that fortnight an event occurred that Iván Ilyich and his wife had desired. Petríshchev formally proposed. It happened in the evening. The next day Praskóvya Fëdorovna came into her husband's room considering how best to inform him of it, but that very night there had been a fresh change for the worse in his condition. She found him still lying on the sofa but in a different position. He lay on his back, groaning and staring fixedly straight in front of him.

She began to remind him of his medicines, but he turned his eyes towards her with such a look that she did not finish what she was saying; so great an animosity, to her in particular, did that look express.

"For Christ's sake let me die in peace!" he said.

She would have gone away, but just then their daughter came in and went up to say good morning. He looked at her as he had done at his wife, and in reply to her inquiry about his health said dryly that he would soon free them all of himself. They were both silent and after sitting with him for a while went away.

"Is it our fault?" Lisa said to her mother. "It's as if we were to blame! I am sorry for papa, but why should we be tortured?"

The doctor came at his usual time. Iván Ilyich answered "Yes" and "No," never taking his angry eyes from him, and at last said: "You know you can do nothing for me, so leave me alone."

"We can ease your sufferings."

"You can't even do that. Let me be."

The doctor went into the drawing-room and told Praskóvya Fëdorovna that the case was very serious and that the only resource left was opium to allay her husband's sufferings, which must be terrible.

It was true, as the doctor said, that Iván Ilyich's physical sufferings were terrible, but worse than the physical sufferings were his mental sufferings which were his chief torture.

His mental sufferings were due to the fact that that night, as he looked at Gerásim's sleepy, good-natured face with its prominent cheek-bones, the question suddenly occurred to him: "What if my whole life has really been wrong?"

It occurred to him that what had appeared perfectly impossible before, namely that he had not spent his life as he should have done, might after all be true. It occurred to him that his scarcely perceptible attempts to struggle against what was considered good by the most highly placed people, those scarcely noticeable impulses which he had immediately suppressed, might have been the real thing, and all the rest false. And his professional duties and the whole arrangement of his life and of his family, and all his social and official interests, might all have been false. He tried to defend all those things to himself and suddenly felt the weakness of what he was defending. There was nothing to defend.

"But if that is so," he said to himself, "and I am leaving this life with the consciousness that I have lost all that was given me and it is impossible to rectify it—what then?"

He lay on his back and began to pass his life in review in quite a new way. In the morning when he saw first his footman, then his wife, then his daughter, and then the doctor, their every word and movement confirmed to him the awful truth that had been revealed to him during the night. In them he saw himself—all that for which he had lived—and saw clearly that it was not real at all, but a terrible and huge deception which had hidden both life and death. This consciousness intensified his physical suffering tenfold. He groaned and tossed about, and pulled at his clothing which choked and stifled him. And he hated them on that account.

He was given a large dose of opium and became unconscious, but at noon his sufferings began again. He drove everybody away and tossed from side to side.

His wife came to him and said:

"*Jean*, my dear, do this for me. It can't do any harm and often helps. Healthy people often do it."

He opened his eyes wide.

"What? Take communion? Why? It's unnecessary! However . . ."

She began to cry.

"Yes, do, my dear. I'll send for our priest. He is such a nice man."

"All right. Very well," he muttered.

When the priest came and heard his confession, Iván Ilyich was softened and seemed to feel a relief from his doubts and consequently from his sufferings, and for a moment there came a ray of hope. He again began to think of the vermiform appendix and the possibility of correcting it. He received the sacrament with tears in his eyes.

When they laid him down again afterwards he felt a moment's ease, and the hope that he might live awoke in him again. He began to think of the operation that had been suggested to him. "To live! I want to live!" he said to himself.

His wife came in to congratulate him after his communion, and when uttering the usual conventional words she added:

"You feel better, don't you?"

Without looking at her he said "Yes."

Her dress, her figure, the expression of her face, the tone of her voice, all revealed the same thing. "This is wrong, it is not as it should be. All you have lived for and still live for is falsehood and deception, hiding life and death from you." And as soon as he admitted that thought, his hatred and his agonizing physical suffering again sprang up, and with that suffering a consciousness of the unavoidable, approaching end. And to this was added a new sensation of grinding shooting pain and a feeling of suffocation.

The expression of his face when he uttered that "yes" was dreadful. Having uttered it, he looked her straight in the eyes, turned on his face with a rapidity extraordinary in his weak state and shouted:

"Go away! Go away and leave me alone!"

XII

From that moment the screaming began that continued for three days, and was 345
so terrible that one could not hear it through two closed doors without horror. At the moment he answered his wife he realized that he was lost, that there was no return, that the end had come, the very end, and his doubts were still unsolved and remained doubts.

"Oh! Oh! Oh!" he cried in various intonations. He had begun by screaming "I won't!" and continued screaming on the letter "o."

For three whole days, during which time did not exist for him, he struggled in that black sack into which he was being thrust by an invisible, resistless force. He struggled as a man condemned to death struggles in the hands of the executioner, knowing that he cannot save himself. And every moment he felt that despite all his efforts he was drawing nearer and nearer to what terrified him. He felt that his agony was due to his being thrust into that black hole and still more to his not being able to get right into it. He was hindered from getting into it by his conviction that his life had been a good one. That very justification of his life held him fast and prevented his moving forward, and it caused him most torment of all.

Suddenly some force struck him in the chest and side, making it still harder to breathe, and he fell through the hole and there at the bottom was a light. What had happened to him was like the sensation one sometimes experiences in a railway carriage when one thinks one is going backwards while one is really going forwards and suddenly becomes aware of the real direction.

"Yes, it was all not the right thing," he said to himself, "but that's no matter. It can be done. But what *is* the right thing?" he asked himself, and suddenly grew quiet.

This occurred at the end of the third day, two hours before his death. Just 350
then his schoolboy son had crept softly in and gone up to the bedside. The dying man was still screaming desperately and waving his arms. His hand fell on the boy's head, and the boy caught it, pressed it to his lips, and began to cry.

At that very moment Iván Ilyich fell through and caught sight of the light, and it was revealed to him that though his life had not been what it should have been, this could still be rectified. He asked himself, "What *is* the right thing?" and grew still, listening. Then he felt that someone was kissing his hand. He opened his eyes, looked at his son, and felt sorry for him. His wife came up to him and he glanced at her. She was gazing at him open-mouthed, with undried tears on her nose and cheek and a despairing look on her face. He felt sorry for her too.

"Yes, I am making them wretched," he thought. "They are sorry, but it will be better for them when I die." He wished to say this but had not the strength to utter it. "Besides, why speak? I must act," he thought. With a look at his wife he indicated his son and said: "Take him away . . . sorry for him . . . sorry for you too. . . ." He tried to add, "forgive me," but said "forego" and waved his hand, knowing that He whose understanding mattered would understand.

And suddenly it grew clear to him that what had been oppressing him and would not leave him was all dropping away at once from two sides, from ten sides, and from all sides. He was sorry for them, he must act so as not to hurt them: release them and free himself from these sufferings. "How good and how simple!" he thought. "And the pain?" he asked himself. "What has become of it? Where are you, pain?"

He turned his attention to it.

"Yes, here it is. Well, what of it? Let the pain be."

"And death . . . where is it?"

He sought his former accustomed fear of death and did not find it. "Where is it? What death?" There was no fear because there was no death.

In place of death there was light.

"So that's what it is!" he suddenly exclaimed aloud. "What joy!"

To him all this happened in a single instant, and the meaning of that instant did not change. For those present his agony continued for another two hours. Something rattled in his throat, his emaciated body twitched, then the gasping and rattle became less and less frequent.

"It is finished!" said someone near him.

He heard these words and repeated them in his soul.

"Death is finished," he said to himself. "It is no more!"

He drew in a breath, stopped in the midst of a sigh, stretched out, and died.

1886

KATE CHOPIN

Beyond the Bayou

The bayou curved like a crescent around the point of land on which La Folle's cabin stood. Between the stream and the hut lay a big abandoned field, where cattle were pastured when the bayou supplied them with enough water. Through the woods that spread back into unknown regions the woman had drawn an imaginary line, and past this circle she never stepped. This was the form of her only mania.

She was now a large, gaunt black woman, past thirty-five. Her real name was Jacqueline, but every one on the plantation called her La Folle,[1] because in childhood she had been frightened literally "out of her senses," and had never wholly regained them.

It was when there had been skirmishing and sharpshooting all day in the

1. The crazy woman.

woods. Evening was near when P'tit Maître,[2] black with powder and crimson with blood, had staggered into the cabin of Jacqueline's mother, his pursuers close at his heels. The sight had stunned her childish reason.

She dwelt alone in her solitary cabin, for the rest of the quarters had long since been removed beyond her sight and knowledge. She had more physical strength than most men, and made her patch of cotton and corn and tobacco like the best of them. But of the world beyond the bayou she had long known nothing, save what her morbid fancy conceived.

People at Bellissime had grown used to her and her way, and they thought 5
nothing of it. Even when "Old Mis' " died, they did not wonder that La Folle had not crossed the bayou, but had stood upon her side of it, wailing and lamenting.

P'tit Maître was now the owner of Bellissime. He was a middle-aged man, with a family of beautiful daughters about him, and a little son whom La Folle loved as if he had been her own. She called him Chéri,[3] and so did every one else because she did.

None of the girls had ever been to her what Chéri was. They had each and all loved to be with her, and to listen to her wondrous stories of things that always happened "yonda, beyon' de bayou."

But none of them had stroked her black hand quite as Chéri did, nor rested their heads against her knee so confidingly, nor fallen asleep in her arms as he used to do. For Chéri hardly did such things now, since he had become the proud possessor of a gun, and had had his black curls cut off.

That summer—the summer Chéri gave La Folle two black curls tied with a knot of red ribbon—the water ran so low in the bayou that even the little children at Bellissime were able to cross it on foot, and the cattle were sent to pasture down by the river. La Folle was sorry when they were gone, for she loved these dumb companions well, and liked to feel that they were there, and to hear them browsing by night up to her own inclosure.

It was Saturday afternoon, when the fields were deserted. The men had flocked 10
to a neighboring village to do their week's trading, and the women were occupied with household affairs,—La Folle as well as the others. It was then she mended and washed her handful of clothes, scoured her house, and did her baking.

In this last employment she never forgot Chéri. To-day she had fashioned croquignoles[4] of the most fantastic and alluring shapes for him. So when she saw the boy come trudging across the field with his gleaming little new rifle on his shoulder, she called out gayly to him, "Chéri! Chéri!"

But Chéri did not need the summons, for he was coming straight to her. His pockets all bulged out with almonds and raisins and an orange that he had secured for her from the very fine dinner which had been given that day up at his father's house.

He was a sunny-faced youngster of ten. When he had emptied his pockets, La Folle patted his round red cheek, wiped his soiled hands on her apron, and smoothed his hair. Then she watched him as, with his cakes in his hand, he

2. Little Master. 3. Darling. 4. Biscuits.

crossed her strip of cotton back of the cabin, and disappeared into the wood.

He had boasted of the things he was going to do with his gun out there.

"You think they got plenty deer in the wood, La Folle?" he had inquired, with the calculating air of an experienced hunter.

"*Non, non!*" the woman laughed. "Don't you look fo' no deer, Chéri. Dat's too big. But you bring La Folle one good fat squirrel fo' her dinner to-morrow, an' she goin' be satisfi'."

"One squirrel ain't a bite. I'll bring you mo' 'an one, La Folle," he had boasted pompously as he went away.

When the woman, an hour later, heard the report of the boy's rifle close to the wood's edge, she would have thought nothing of it if a sharp cry of distress had not followed the sound.

She withdrew her arms from the tub of suds in which they had been plunged, dried them upon her apron, and as quickly as her trembling limbs would bear her, hurried to the spot whence the ominous report had come.

It was as she feared. There she found Chéri stretched upon the ground, with his rifle beside him. He moaned piteously:—

"I'm dead, La Folle! I'm dead! I'm gone!"

"*Non, non!*" she exclaimed resolutely, as she knelt beside him. "Put you' arm 'roun' La Folle's nake, Chéri. Dat's nuttin'; dat goin' be nuttin'." She lifted him in her powerful arms.

Chéri had carried his gun muzzle-downward. He had stumbled,—he did not know how. He only knew that he had a ball lodged somewhere in his leg, and he thought that his end was at hand. Now, with his head upon the woman's shoulder, he moaned and wept with pain and fright.

"Oh, La Folle! La Folle! it hurt so bad! I can' stan' it, La Folle!"

"Don't cry, *mon bébé*[5] *mon bébé, mon Chéri!*" the woman spoke soothingly as she covered the ground with long strides. "La Folle goin' mine you; Doctor Bonfils goin' come make *mon Chéri* well agin."

She had reached the abandoned field. As she crossed it with her precious burden, she looked constantly and restlessly from side to side. A terrible fear was upon her,—the fear of the world beyond the bayou, the morbid and insane dread she had been under since childhood.

When she was at the bayou's edge she stood there, and shouted for help as if a life depended upon it:—

"Oh, P'tit Maître! P'tit Maître! Venez donc! Au secours! Au secours!"[6]

No voice responded. Chéri's hot tears were scalding her neck. She called for each and every one upon the place, and still no answer came.

She shouted, she wailed; but whether her voice remained unheard or unheeded, no reply came to her frenzied cries. And all the while Chéri moaned and wept and entreated to be taken home to his mother.

La Folle gave a last despairing look around her. Extreme terror was upon her. She clasped the child close against her breast, where he could feel her heart beat like a muffled hammer. Then shutting her eyes, she ran suddenly down the

5. My baby. 6. Come here! Help! Help!

shallow bank of the bayou, and never stopped till she had climbed the opposite shore.

She stood there quivering an instant as she opened her eyes. Then she plunged into the footpath through the trees.

She spoke no more to Chéri, but muttered constantly, "Bon Dieu, ayez pitié La Folle! Bon Dieu, ayez pitié moi!"[7]

Instinct seemed to guide her. When the pathway spread clear and smooth enough before her, she again closed her eyes tightly against the sight of that unknown and terrifying world.

A child, playing in some weeds, caught sight of her as she neared the quarters. The little one uttered a cry of dismay.

"La Folle!" she screamed, in her piercing treble. "La Folle done cross de bayer!"

Quickly the cry passed down the line of cabins.

"Yonda, La Folle done cross de bayou!"

Children, old men, old women, young ones with infants in their arms, flocked to doors and windows to see this awe-inspiring spectacle. Most of them shuddered with superstitious dread of what it might portend. "She totin' Chéri!" some of them shouted.

Some of the more daring gathered about her, and followed at her heels, only to fall back with new terror when she turned her distorted face upon them. Her eyes were bloodshot and the saliva had gathered in a white foam on her black lips.

Some one had run ahead of her to where P'tit Maître sat with his family and guests upon the gallery.

"P'tit Maître! La Folle done cross de bayou! Look her! Look her yonda totin' Chéri!" This startling intimation was the first which they had of the woman's approach.

She was now near at hand. She walked with long strides. Her eyes were fixed desperately before her, and she breathed heavily, as a tired ox.

At the foot of the stairway, which she could not have mounted, she laid the boy in his father's arms. Then the world that had looked red to La Folle suddenly turned black,—like that day she had seen powder and blood.

She reeled for an instant. Before a sustaining arm could reach her, she fell heavily to the ground.

When La Folle regained consciousness, she was at home again, in her own cabin and upon her own bed. The moon rays, streaming in through the open door and windows, gave what light was needed to the old black mammy who stood at the table concocting a tisane of fragrant herbs. It was very late.

Others who had come, and found that the stupor clung to her, had gone again. P'tit Maître had been there, and with him Doctor Bonfils, who said that La Folle might die.

But death had passed her by. The voice was very clear and steady with which she spoke to Tante[8] Lizette, brewing her tisane there in a corner.

7. Good Lord, have pity on La Folle! Good Lord, have pity on me! 8. Aunt.

"Ef you will give me one good drink tisane, Tante Lizette, I b'lieve I'm goin' sleep, me."

And she did sleep; so soundly, so healthfully, that old Lizette without compunction stole softly away, to creep back through the moonlit fields to her own cabin in the new quarters.

The first touch of the cool gray morning awoke La Folle. She arose, calmly, as if no tempest had shaken and threatened her existence but yesterday.

She donned her new blue cottonade[9] and white apron, for she remembered that this was Sunday. When she had made for herself a cup of strong black coffee, and drunk it with relish, she quitted the cabin and walked across the old familiar field to the bayou's edge again.

She did not stop there as she had always done before, but crossed with a long, steady stride as if she had done this all her life.

When she had made her way through the brush and scrub cottonwood-trees that lined the opposite bank, she found herself upon the border of a field where the white, bursting cotton, with the dew upon it, gleamed for acres and acres like frosted silver in the early dawn.

La Folle drew a long, deep breath as she gazed across the country. She walked slowly and uncertainly, like one who hardly knows how, looking about her as she went.

The cabins, that yesterday had sent a clamor of voices to pursue her, were quiet now. No one was yet astir at Bellissime. Only the birds that darted here and there from hedges were awake, and singing their matins.

When La Folle came to the broad stretch of velvety lawn that surrounded the house, she moved slowly and with delight over the springy turf, that was delicious beneath her tread.

She stopped to find whence came those perfumes that were assailing her senses with memories from a time far gone.

There they were, stealing up to her from the thousand blue violets that peeped out from green, luxuriant beds. There they were, showering down from the big waxen bells of the magnolias far above her head, and from the jessamine clumps around her.

There were roses, too, without number. To right and left palms spread in broad and graceful curves. It all looked like enchantment beneath the sparkling sheen of dew.

When La Folle had slowly and cautiously mounted the many steps that led up to the veranda, she turned to look back at the perilous ascent she had made. Then she caught sight of the river, bending like a silver bow at the foot of Bellissime. Exultation possessed her soul.

La Folle rapped softly upon a door near at hand. Chéri's mother soon cautiously opened it. Quickly and cleverly she dissembled the astonishment she felt at seeing La Folle.

"Ah, La Folle! Is it you, so early?"

"*Oui,*[1] madame. I come ax how my po' li'le Chéri to, 's mo'nin'. "

9. Cotton fabric made to resemble wool. 1. Yes.

"He is feeling easier, thank you, La Folle. Dr. Bonfils says it will be nothing serious. He's sleeping now. Will you come back when he awakes?"

"*Non*, madame. I'm goin' wait yair tell Chéri wake up." La Folle seated herself upon the topmost step of the veranda.

A look of wonder and deep content crept into her face as she watched for the first time the sun rise upon the new, the beautiful world beyond the bayou.

1894

ARLOTTE PERKINS GILMAN

It is very seldo … elf secure ancestral halls for the su …

A colonia … haunted house, and reach the hei … ng too much of fate!

Still I wil … about it.

Else, wh … stood so long untenanted?

John lau … marriage.

John is … with faith, an intense horror of su … hings not to be felt and seen and p …

John i … it to a living soul, of course, bu … mind—) *perhaps* that is one reaso …

You s …

And …

If a p … band, assures friends and relatives … ne but temporary nervous depressi … to do?

My … standing, and he says the same th …

So … t is, and tonics, and journeys, … dden to "work" until I am well a …

P …

P … xcitement and change, would do n …

… *loes* exhaust me a good deal—having to be so sly abou … vy opposition.

I sometimes fancy that in my condition … had less opposition and more society and stimulus—but John says the very worst thing I can do is to think about my condition, and I confess it always makes me feel bad.

So I will let it alone and talk about the house.

The most beautiful place! It is quite alone, standing well back from the road, quite three miles from the village. It makes me think of English places that you read about, for there are hedges and walls and gates that lock, and lots of separate little houses for the gardeners and people.

There is a *delicious* garden! I never saw such a garden—large and shady, full of box-bordered paths, and lined with long grape-covered arbors with seats under them.

There were greenhouses, too, but they are all broken now.

There was some legal trouble, I believe, something about the heirs and co-heirs; anyhow, the place has been empty for years.

That spoils my ghostliness, I am afraid, but I don't care—there is something strange about the house—I can feel it.

I even said so to John one moonlight evening, but he said what I felt was a *draught*, and shut the window.

I get unreasonably angry with John sometimes. I'm sure I never used to be so sensitive. I think it is due to this nervous condition.

But John says if I feel so, I shall neglect proper self-control; so I take pains to control myself—before him, at least, and that makes me very tired.

I don't like our room a bit. I wanted one downstairs that opened on the piazza and had roses all over the window, and such pretty old-fashioned chintz hangings! but John would not hear of it.

He said there was only one window and not room for two beds, and no near room for him if he took another.

He is very careful and loving, and hardly lets me stir without special direction.

I have a schedule prescription for each hour in the day; he takes all care from me, and so I feel basely ungrateful not to value it more.

He said we came here solely on my account, that I was to have perfect rest and all the air I could get. "Your exercise depends on your strength, my dear," said he, "and your food somewhat on your appetite; but air you can absorb all the time." So we took the nursery at the top of the house.

It is a big, airy room, the whole floor nearly, with windows that look all ways, and air and sunshine galore. It was nursery first and then playroom and gymnasium, I should judge; for the windows are barred for little children, and there are rings and things in the walls.

The paint and paper look as if a boys' school had used it. It is stripped off—the paper—in great patches all around the head of my bed, about as far as I can reach, and in a great place on the other side of the room low down. I never saw a worse paper in my life.

One of those sprawling flamboyant patterns committing every artistic sin.

It is dull enough to confuse the eye in following, pronounced enough to constantly irritate and provoke study, and when you follow the lame uncertain curves for a little distance they suddenly commit suicide—plunge off at outrageous angles, destroy themselves in unheard of contradictions.

The color is repellant, almost revolting; a smouldering unclean yellow, strangely faded by the slow-turning sunlight.

It is a dull yet lurid orange in some places, a sickly sulphur tint in others.

No wonder the children hated it! I should hate it myself if I had to live in this room long.

There comes John, and I must put this away,—he hates to have me write a word.

We have been here two weeks, and I haven't felt like writing before, since that first day.

I am sitting by the window now, up in this atrocious nursery, and there is nothing to hinder my writing as much as I please, save lack of strength.

John is away all day, and even some nights when his cases are serious.

I am glad my case is not serious!

But these nervous troubles are dreadfully depressing.

John does not know how much I really suffer. He knows there is no *reason* to suffer, and that satisfies him.

Of course it is only nervousness. It does weigh on me so not to do my duty in any way!

I mean to be such a help to John, such a real rest and comfort, and here I am a comparative burden already!

Nobody would believe what an effort it is to do what little I am able,—to dress and entertain, and order things.

It is fortunate Mary is so good with the baby. Such a dear baby!

And yet I *cannot* be with him, it makes me so nervous.

I suppose John never was nervous in his life. He laughs at me so about this wallpaper!

At first he meant to repaper the room, but afterwards he said that I was letting it get the better of me, and that nothing was worse for a nervous patient than to give way to such fancies.

He said that after the wallpaper was changed it would be the heavy bedstead, and then the barred windows, and then that gate at the head of the stairs, and so on.

"You know the place is doing you good," he said, "and really, dear, I don't care to renovate the house just for a three months' rental."

"Then do let us go downstairs," I said, "there are such pretty rooms there."

Then he took me in his arms and called me a blessed little goose, and said he would go down cellar, if I wished, and have it whitewashed into the bargain.

But he is right enough about the beds and windows and things.

It is an airy and comfortable room as any one need wish, and, of course, I would not be so silly as to make him uncomfortable just for a whim.

I'm really getting quite fond of the big room, all but that horrid paper.

Out of one window I can see the garden, those mysterious deep-shaded arbors, the riotous old-fashioned flowers, and bushes and gnarly trees.

Out of another I get a lovely view of the bay and a little private wharf belonging to the estate. There is a beautiful shaded lane that runs down there from the house. I always fancy I see people walking in these numerous paths and arbors, but John has cautioned me not to give way to fancy in the least. He says that with my imaginative power and habit of story-making, a nervous weakness like mine is sure to lead to all manner of excited fancies, and that I ought to use my will and good sense to check the tendency. So I try.

I think sometimes that if I were only well enough to write a little it would relieve the press of ideas and rest me.

But I find I get pretty tired when I try.

It is so discouraging not to have any advice and companionship about my work. When I get really well, John says we will ask Cousin Henry and Julia down for a long visit; but he says he would as soon put fireworks in my pillow-case as to let me have those stimulating people about now.

I wish I could get well faster.

But I must not think about that. This paper looks to me as if it *knew* what a vicious influence it had!

There is a recurrent spot where the pattern lolls like a broken neck and two bulbous eyes stare at you upside down.

I get positively angry with the impertinence of it and the everlastingness. Up and down and sideways they crawl, and those absurd, unblinking eyes are every-where. There is one place where two breadths didn't match, and the eyes go all up and down the line, one a little higher than the other.

I never saw so much expression in an inanimate thing before, and we all know how much expression they have! I used to lie awake as a child and get more entertainment and terror out of blank walls and plain furniture than most children could find in a toy-store.

I remember what a kindly wink the knobs of our big, old bureau used to have, and there was one chair that always seemed like a strong friend.

I used to feel that if any of the other things looked too fierce I could always hop into that chair and be safe.

The furniture in this room is no worse than inharmonious, however, for we had to bring it all from downstairs. I suppose when this was used as a playroom they had to take the nursery things out, and no wonder! I never saw such ravages as the children have made here.

The wallpaper, as I said before, is torn off in spots, and it sticketh closer than a brother—they must have had perseverance as well as hatred.

Then the floor is scratched and gouged and splintered, the plaster itself is dug out here and there, and this great heavy bed which is all we found in the room, looks as if it had been through the wars.

But I don't mind it a bit—only the paper.

There comes John's sister. Such a dear girl as she is, and so careful of me! I must not let her find me writing.

She is a perfect and enthusiastic housekeeper, and hopes for no better profes-sion. I verily believe she thinks it is the writing which made me sick!

But I can write when she is out, and see her a long way off from these windows.

There is one that commands the road, a lovely shaded winding road, and one that just looks off over the country. A lovely country, too, full of great elms and velvet meadows.

This wallpaper has a kind of sub-pattern in a different shade, a particularly irritating one, for you can only see it in certain lights, and not clearly then.

But in the places where it isn't faded and where the sun is just so—I can see a strange, provoking, formless sort of figure, that seems to skulk about behind that silly and conspicuous front design.

There's sister on the stairs!

Well, the Fourth of July is over! The people are all gone and I am tired out. John thought it might do me good to see a little company, so we just had mother and Nellie and the children down for a week.

Of course I didn't do a thing. Jennie sees to everything now.

But it tired me all the same.

John says if I don't pick up faster he shall send me to Weir Mitchell[1] in the fall.

But I don't want to go there at all. I had a friend who was in his hands once, and she says he is just like John and my brother, only more so!

Besides, it is such an undertaking to go so far.

I don't feel as if it was worth while to turn my hand over for anything, and I'm getting dreadfully fretful and querulous.

I cry at nothing, and cry most of the time.

Of course I don't when John is here, or anybody else, but when I am alone.

And I am alone a good deal just now. John is kept in town very often by serious cases, and Jennie is good and lets me alone when I want her to.

So I walk a little in the garden or down that lovely lane, sit on the porch under the roses, and lie down up here a good deal.

I'm getting really fond of the room in spite of the wallpaper. Perhaps *because* of the wallpaper.

It dwells in my mind so!

I lie here on this great immovable bed—it is nailed down, I believe—and follow that pattern about by the hour. It is as good as gymnastics, I assure you. I start, we'll say, at the bottom, down in the corner over there where it has not been touched, and I determine for the thousandth time that I *will* follow that pointless pattern to some sort of conclusion.

I know a little of the principle of design, and I know this thing was not arranged on any laws of radiation, or alternation, or repetition, or symmetry, or anything else that I ever heard of.

It is repeated, of course, by the breadths, but not otherwise.

Looked at in one way each breadth stands alone, the bloated curves and flourishes—a kind of "debased Romanesque" with *delirium tremens*—go waddling up and down in isolated columns of fatuity.

But, on the other hand, they connect diagonally, and the sprawling outlines

1. Silas Weir Mitchell (1829–1914), American physician, novelist, and specialist in nerve disorders, popularized the "rest cure."

run off in great slanting waves of optic horror, like a lot of wallowing seaweeds in full chase.

The whole thing goes horizontally, too, at least it seems so, and I exhaust myself in trying to distinguish the order of its going in that direction.

They have used a horizontal breadth for a frieze, and that adds wonderfully to the confusion.

There is one end of the room where it is almost intact, and there, when the crosslights fade and the low sun shines directly upon it, I can almost fancy radiation after all,—the interminable grotesque seem to form around a common center and rush off in headlong plunges of equal distraction.

It makes me tired to follow it. I will take a nap I guess.

I don't know why I should write this.

I don't want to.

I don't feel able.

And I know John would think it absurd. But I *must* say what I feel and think in some way—it is such a relief!

But the effort is getting to be greater than the relief.

Half the time now I am awfully lazy, and lie down ever so much.

John says I mustn't lose my strength, and has me take cod liver oil and lots of tonics and things, to say nothing of ale and wine and rare meat.

Dear John! He loves me very dearly, and hates to have me sick. I tried to have a real earnest reasonable talk with him the other day, and tell him how I wish he would let me go and make a visit to Cousin Henry and Julia.

But he said I wasn't able to go, nor able to stand it after I got there; and I did not make out a very good case for myself, for I was crying before I had finished.

It is getting to be a great effort for me to think straight. Just this nervous weakness I suppose.

And dear John gathered me up in his arms, and just carried me upstairs and laid me on the bed, and sat by me and read to me till it tired my head.

He said I was his darling and his comfort and all he had, and that I must take care of myself for his sake, and keep well.

He says no one but myself can help me out of it, that I must use my will and self-control and not let any silly fancies run away with me.

There's one comfort, the baby is well and happy, and does not have to occupy this nursery with the horrid wallpaper.

If we had not used it, that blessed child would have! What a fortunate escape! Why, I wouldn't have a child of mine, an impressionable little thing, live in such a room for worlds.

I never thought of it before, but it is lucky that John kept me here after all, I can stand it so much easier than a baby, you see.

Of course I never mention it to them any more—I am too wise,—but I keep watch of it all the same.

There are things in that paper that nobody knows but me, or ever will.

Behind that outside pattern the dim shapes get clearer every day.

It is always the same shape, only very numerous.

And it is like a woman stooping down and creeping about behind that pattern. I don't like it a bit. I wonder—I begin to think—I wish John would take me away from here!

It is so hard to talk with John about my case, because he is so wise, and because he loves me so.

But I tried it last night.

It was moonlight. The moon shines in all around just as the sun does.

I hate to see it sometimes, it creeps so slowly, and always comes in by one window or another.

John was asleep and I hated to waken him, so I kept still and watched the moonlight on that undulating wallpaper till I felt creepy.

The faint figure behind seemed to shake the pattern, just as if she wanted to get out.

I got up softly and went to feel and see if the paper *did* move, and when I came back John was awake.

"What is it, little girl?" he said. "Don't go walking about like that—you'll get cold."

I thought it was a good time to talk, so I told him that I really was not gaining here, and that I wished he would take me away.

"Why, darling!" said he, "our lease will be up in three weeks, and I can't see how to leave before.

"The repairs are not done at home, and I cannot possibly leave town just now. Of course if you were in any danger, I could and would, but you really are better, dear, whether you can see it or not. I am a doctor, dear, and I know. You are gaining flesh and color, your appetite is better, I feel really much easier about you."

"I don't weigh a bit more," said I, "nor as much; and my appetite may be better in the evening when you are here, but it is worse in the morning when you are away!"

"Bless her little heart!" said he with a big hug, "she shall be as sick as she pleases! But now let's improve the shining hours by going to sleep, and talk about it in the morning!"

"And you won't go away?" I asked gloomily.

"Why, how can I, dear? It is only three weeks more and then we will take a nice little trip of a few days while Jennie is getting the house ready. Really dear you are better!"

"Better in body perhaps—" I began, and stopped short, for he sat up straight and looked at me with such a stern, reproachful look that I could not say another word.

"My darling," said he, "I beg of you, for my sake and for our child's sake, as well as for your own, that you will never for one instant let that idea enter your mind! There is nothing so dangerous, so fascinating, to a temperament like yours. It is a false and foolish fancy. Can you not trust me as a physician when I tell you so?"

So of course I said no more on that score, and we went to sleep before long.

He thought I was asleep first, but I wasn't, and lay there for hours trying to decide whether that front pattern and the back pattern really did move together or separately.

On a pattern like this, by daylight, there is a lack of sequence, a defiance of law, that is a constant irritant to a normal mind.

The color is hideous enough, and unreliable enough, and infuriating enough, but the pattern is torturing.

You think you have mastered it, but just as you get well underway in following, it turns a back-somersault and there you are. It slaps you in the face, knocks you down, and tramples upon you. It is like a bad dream.

The outside pattern is a florid arabesque, reminding one of a fungus. If you can imagine a toadstool in joints, an interminable string of toadstools, budding and sprouting in endless convolutions—why, that is something like it.

That is, sometimes!

There is one marked peculiarity about this paper, a thing nobody seems to notice but myself, and that is that it changes as the light changes.

When the sun shoots in through the east window—I always watch for that first long, straight ray—it changes so quickly that I never can quite believe it.

That is why I watch it always.

By moonlight—the moon shines in all night when there is a moon—I wouldn't know it was the same paper.

At night in any kind of light, in twilight, candlelight, lamplight, and worst of all by moonlight, it becomes bars! The outside pattern I mean, and the woman behind it is as plain as can be.

I didn't realize for a long time what the thing was that showed behind, that dim sub-pattern, but now I am quite sure it is a woman.

By daylight she is subdued, quiet. I fancy it is the pattern that keeps her so still. It is so puzzling. It keeps me quiet by the hour.

I lie down ever so much now. John says it is good for me, and to sleep all I can.

Indeed he started the habit by making me lie down for an hour after each meal.

It is a very bad habit I am convinced, for you see I don't sleep.

And that cultivates deceit, for I don't tell them I'm awake—O no!

The fact is I am getting a little afraid of John.

He seems very queer sometimes, and even Jennie has an inexplicable look.

It strikes me occasionally, just as a scientific hypothesis,—that perhaps it is the paper!

I have watched John when he did not know I was looking, and come into the room suddenly on the most innocent excuses, and I've caught him several times *looking at the paper*! And Jennie too. I caught Jennie with her hand on it once.

She didn't know I was in the room, and when I asked her in a quiet, a very quiet voice, with the most restrained manner possible, what she was doing with the paper—she turned around as if she had been caught stealing, and looked quite angry—asked me why I should frighten her so!

Then she said that the paper stained everything it touched, that she had 165
found yellow smooches on all my clothes and John's, and she wished we would be more careful!

Did not that sound innocent? But I know she was studying that pattern, and I am determined that nobody shall find it out but myself!

Life is very much more exciting now than it used to be. You see I have something more to expect, to look forward to, to watch. I really do eat better, and am more quiet than I was.

John is so pleased to see me improve! He laughed a little the other day, and said I seemed to be flourishing in spite of my wallpaper.

I turned it off with a laugh. I had no intention of telling him it was *because* of the wallpaper—he would make fun of me. He might even want to take me away.

I don't want to leave now until I have found it out. There is a week more, 170
and I think that will be enough.

I'm feeling ever so much better! I don't sleep much at night, for it is so interesting to watch developments; but I sleep a good deal in the daytime.

In the daytime it is tiresome and perplexing.

There are always new shoots on the fungus, and new shades of yellow all over it. I cannot keep count of them, though I have tried conscientiously.

It is the strangest yellow, that wallpaper! It makes me think of all the yellow things I ever saw—not beautiful ones like buttercups, but old foul, bad yellow things.

But there is something else about that paper—the smell! I noticed it the 175
moment we came into the room, but with so much air and sun it was not bad. Now we have had a week of fog and rain, and whether the windows are open or not, the smell is here.

It creeps all over the house.

I find it hovering in the dining-room, skulking in the parlor, hiding in the hall, lying in wait for me on the stairs.

It gets into my hair.

Even when I go to ride, if I turn my head suddenly and surprise it—there is that smell!

Such a peculiar odor, too! I have spent hours in trying to analyze it, to find 180
what it smelled like.

It is not bad—at first, and very gentle, but quite the subtlest, most enduring odor I ever met.

In this damp weather it is awful, I wake up in the night and find it hanging over me.

It used to disturb me at first. I thought seriously of burning the house—to reach the smell.

But now I am used to it. The only thing I can think of that it is like is the *color* of the paper! A yellow smell.

There is a very funny mark on this wall, low down, near the mopboard. A streak that runs round the room. It goes behind every piece of furniture, except the bed, a long, straight, even *smooch*, as if it had been rubbed over and over.

I wonder how it was done and who did it, and what they did it for. Round and round and round—round and round and round—it makes me dizzy!

I really have discovered something at last.

Through watching so much at night, when it changes so, I have finally found out.

The front pattern *does* move—and no wonder! The woman behind shakes it!

Sometimes I think there are a great many women behind, and sometimes only one, and she crawls around fast, and her crawling shakes it all over.

Then in the very bright spots she keeps still, and in the very shady spots she just takes hold of the bars and shakes them hard.

And she is all the time trying to climb through. But nobody could climb through that pattern—it strangles so; I think that is why it has so many heads.

They get through, and then the pattern strangles them off and turns them upside down, and makes their eyes white!

If those heads were covered or taken off it would not be half so bad.

I think that woman gets out in the daytime!

And I'll tell you why—privately—I've seen her!

I can see her out of every one of my windows!

It is the same woman, I know, for she is always creeping, and most women do not creep by daylight.

I see her in that long shaded lane, creeping up and down. I see her in those dark grape arbors, creeping all around the garden.

I see her on that long road under the trees, creeping along, and when a carriage comes she hides under the blackberry vines.

I don't blame her a bit. It must be very humiliating to be caught creeping by daylight!

I always lock the door when I creep by daylight. I can't do it at night, for I know John would suspect something at once.

And John is so queer now, that I don't want to irritate him. I wish he would take another room! Besides, I don't want anybody to get that woman out at night but myself.

I often wonder if I could see her out of all the windows at once.

But, turn as fast as I can, I can only see out of one at one time.

And though I always see her, she *may* be able to creep faster than I can turn!

I have watched her sometimes away off in the open country, creeping as fast as a cloud shadow in a high wind.

If only that top pattern could be gotten off from the under one! I mean to try it, little by little.

I have found out another funny thing, but I shan't tell it this time! It does not do to trust people too much.

There are only two more days to get this paper off, and I believe John is beginning to notice. I don't like the look in his eyes.

And I heard him ask Jennie a lot of professional questions about me. She had a very good report to give.

She said I slept a good deal in the daytime.

John knows I don't sleep very well at night, for all I'm so quiet!

He asked me all sorts of questions, too, and pretended to be very loving and kind.

As if I couldn't see through him!

Still, I don't wonder he acts so, sleeping under this paper for three months.

It only interests me, but I feel sure John and Jennie are secretly affected by it.

Hurrah! This is the last day, but it is enough. John to stay in town over night, and won't be out until this evening.

Jennie wanted to sleep with me—the sly thing! but I told her I should undoubtedly rest better for a night all alone.

That was clever, for really I wasn't alone a bit! As soon as it was moonlight and that poor thing began to crawl and shake the pattern, I got up and ran to help her.

I pulled and she shook, I shook and she pulled, and before morning we had peeled off yards of that paper.

A strip about as high as my head and half around the room.

And then when the sun came and that awful pattern began to laugh at me, I declared I would finish it to-day!

We go away to-morrow, and they are moving all my furniture down again to leave things as they were before.

Jennie looked at the wall in amazement, but I told her merrily that I did it out of pure spite at the vicious thing.

She laughed and said she wouldn't mind doing it herself, but I must not get tired.

How she betrayed herself that time!

But I am here, and no person touches this paper but me,—not *alive!*

She tried to get me out of the room—it was too patent! But I said it was so quiet and empty and clean now that I believed I would lie down again and sleep all I could; and not to wake me even for dinner—I would call when I woke.

So now she is gone, and the servants are gone, and the things are gone, and there is nothing left but that great bedstead nailed down, with the canvas mattress we found on it.

We shall sleep downstairs to-night, and take the boat home to-morrow.

I quite enjoy the room, now it is bare again.

How those children did tear about here!

This bedstead is fairly gnawed!

But I must get to work.

I have locked the door and thrown the key down into the front path.

I don't want to go out, and I don't want to have anybody come in, till John comes.

I want to astonish him.

I've got a rope up here that even Jennie did not find. If that woman does get out, and tries to get away, I can tie her!

But I forgot I could not reach far without anything to stand on!

This bed will *not* move!

I tried to lift and push it until I was lame, and then I got so angry I bit off a little piece at one corner—but it hurt my teeth.

Then I peeled off all the paper I could reach standing on the floor. It sticks horribly and the pattern just enjoys it! All those strangled heads and bulbous eyes and waddling fungus growths just shriek with derision!

I am getting angry enough to do something desperate. To jump out of the window would be admirable exercise, but the bars are too strong even to try.

Besides I wouldn't do it. Of course not. I know well enough that a step like that is improper and might be misconstrued.

I don't like to *look* out of the windows even—there are so many of those creeping women, and they creep so fast.

I wonder if they all come out of that wallpaper as I did?

But I am securely fastened now by my well-hidden rope—you don't get *me* out in the road there!

I suppose I shall have to get back behind the pattern when it comes night, and that is hard!

It is so pleasant to be out in this great room and creep around as I please!

I don't want to go outside. I won't, even if Jennie asks me to.

For outside you have to creep on the ground, and everything is green instead of yellow.

But here I can creep smoothly on the floor, and my shoulder just fits in that long smooch around the wall, so I cannot lose my way.

Why there's John at the door!

It is no use, young man, you can't open it!

How he does call and pound!

Now he's crying for an axe.

It would be a shame to break down that beautiful door!

"John dear!" said I in the gentlest voice, "the key is down by the front steps, under a plantain leaf!"

That silenced him for a few moments.

Then he said—very quietly indeed, "Open the door, my darling!"

"I can't," said I. "The key is down by the front door under a plantain leaf!"

And then I said it again, several times, very gently and slowly, and said it so often that he had to go and see, and he got it of course, and came in. He stopped short by the door.

"What is the matter?" he cried. "For God's sake, what are you doing!"

I kept on creeping just the same, but I looked at him over my shoulder.

"I've got out at last," said I, "in spite of you and Jane? And I've pulled off most of the paper, so you can't put me back!"

Now why should that man have fainted? But he did, and right across my path by the wall, so that I had to creep over him every time!

1892

FRANZ KAFKA

A Hunger Artist[1]

During these last decades the interest in professional fasting has markedly diminished. It used to pay very well to stage such great performances under one's own management, but today that is quite impossible. We live in a different world now. At one time the whole town took a lively interest in the hunger artist; from day to day of his fast the excitement mounted; everybody wanted to see him at least once a day; there were people who bought season tickets for the last few days and sat from morning till night in front of his small barred cage; even in the nighttime there were visiting hours, when the whole effect was heightened by torch flares; on fine days the cage was set out in the open air, and then it was the children's special treat to see the hunger artist; for their elders he was often just a joke that happened to be in fashion, but the children stood open-mouthed, holding each other's hands for greater security, marveling at him as he sat there pallid in black tights, with his ribs sticking out so prominently, not even on a seat but down among straw on the ground, sometimes giving a courteous nod, answering questions with a constrained smile, or perhaps stretching an arm through the bars so that one might feel how thin it was, and then again withdrawing deep into himself, paying no attention to anyone or anything, not even to the all-important striking of the clock that was the only piece of furniture in his cage, but merely staring into vacancy with half shut eyes, now and then taking a sip from a tiny glass of water to moisten his lips.

Besides casual onlookers there were also relays of permanent watchers selected by the public, usually butchers, strangely enough, and it was their task to watch the hunger artist day and night, three of them at a time, in case he should have some secret recourse to nourishment. This was nothing but a formality, instituted to reassure the masses, for the initiates knew well enough that during his fast the artist would never in any circumstances, not even under forcible compulsion, swallow the smallest morsel of food: the honor of his profession forbade it. Not every watcher, of course, was capable of understanding this, there were often groups of night watchers who were very lax in carrying out their duties and deliberately huddled together in a retired corner to play cards with great absorption, obviously intending to give the hunger artist the chance of a little refresh-

1. Translated by Edwin and Willa Muir.

ment, which they supposed he could draw from some private hoard. Nothing annoyed the artist more than such watchers; they made him miserable; they made his fast seem unendurable; sometimes he mastered his feebleness sufficiently to sing during their watch for as long as he could keep going, to show them how unjust their suspicions were. But that was of little use; they only wondered at his cleverness in being able to fill his mouth even while singing. Much more to his taste were the watchers who sat close up to the bars, who were not content with the dim night lighting of the hall but focused him in the full glare of the electric pocket torch given them by the impresario. The harsh light did not trouble him at all, in any case he could never sleep properly, and he could always drowse a little, whatever the light, at any hour, even when the hall was thronged with noisy onlookers. He was quite happy at the prospect of spending a sleepless night with such watchers; he was ready to exchange jokes with them, to tell them stories out of his nomadic life, anything at all to keep them awake and demonstrate to them again that he had no eatables in his cage and that he was fasting as not one of them could fast. But his happiest moment was when the morning came and an enormous breakfast was brought them, at his expense, on which they flung themselves with the keen appetite of healthy men after a weary night of wakefulness. Of course there were people who argued that this breakfast was an unfair attempt to bribe the watchers, but that was going rather too far, and when they were invited to take on a night's vigil without a breakfast, merely for the sake of the cause, they made themselves scarce, although they stuck stubbornly to their suspicions.

Such suspicions, anyhow, were a necessary accompaniment to the profession of fasting. No one could possibly watch the hunger artist continuously, day and night, and so no one could produce first-hand evidence that the fast had really been rigorous and continuous; only the artist himself could know that, he was therefore bound to be the sole completely satisfied spectator of his own fast. Yet for other reasons he was never satisfied; it was not perhaps mere fasting that had brought him to such skeleton thinness that many people had regretfully to keep away from his exhibitions, because the sight of him was too much for them, perhaps it was dissatisfaction with himself that had worn him down. For he alone knew, what no other initiate knew, how easy it was to fast. It was the easiest thing in the world. He made no secret of this, yet people did not believe him, at the best they set him down as modest, most of them, however, thought he was out for publicity or else was some kind of cheat who found it easy to fast because he had discovered a way of making it easy, and then had the impudence to admit the fact, more or less. He had to put up with all that, and in the course of time had got used to it, but his inner dissatisfaction always rankled, and never yet, after any term of fasting—this must be granted to his credit—had he left the cage of his own free will. The longest period of fasting was fixed by his impresario at forty days, beyond that term he was not allowed to go, not even in great cities, and there was good reason for it, too. Experience had proved that for about forty days the interest of the public could be stimulated by a steadily increasing pressure of advertisement, but after that the town began to lose interest, sympathetic support began notably to fall off; there were of course local variations as between one town and another or one country and another, but as a general rule forty days marked the limit. So on the fortieth day the flower-bedecked cage was opened, enthusiastic spectators filled the hall, a military band played, two doctors entered the cage to measure the results of the fast, which were announced through a megaphone, and finally two young ladies appeared, blissful at having been selected for the honor, to help the hunger artist down the few steps leading to a small table on which was spread a carefully chosen invalid repast. And at this very moment the artist always turned stubborn. True, he would entrust his bony arms to the outstretched helping hands of the ladies bending over him, but stand up he would not. Why stop fasting at this particular moment, after forty days of it? He had held out for a long time, an illimitably long time; why stop now, when he was in his best fasting form, or rather, not yet quite in his best fasting form? Why should he be cheated of the fame he would get for fasting longer, for being not only the record hunger artist of all time, which presumably he was already, but for beating his own record by a performance beyond human imagination, since he felt that there were no limits to his capacity for fasting? His public pretended to admire him so much, why should it have so little patience with him; if he could endure fasting longer, why shouldn't the public endure it? Besides, he was tired, he was comfortable sitting in the straw, and now he was supposed to lift himself to his full height and go down to a meal the very thought of which gave him a nausea that only the presence of the ladies kept him from betraying, and even that with an effort. And he looked up into the eyes of the ladies who were apparently so friendly and in reality so cruel, and shook his head, which felt too heavy on its strengthless neck. But then there happened yet again what always happened. The impresario came forward, without a word—for the band made speech impossible—lifted his arms in the air above the artist, as if inviting Heaven to look down upon its creature here in the straw, this suffering martyr, which indeed he was, although in quite another sense; grasped him round the emaciated waist, with exaggerated caution, so that the frail condition he was in might be appreciated; and committed him to the care of the blenching ladies, not without secretly giving him a shaking so that his legs and body tottered and swayed. The artist now submitted completely; his head lolled on his breast as if it had landed there by chance; his body was hollowed out; his legs in a spasm of self-preservation clung close to each other at the knees, yet scraped on the ground as if it were not really solid ground, as if they were only trying to find solid ground; and the whole weight of his body, a feather-weight after all, relapsed onto one of the ladies, who, looking round for help and panting a little—this post of honor was not at all what she had expected it to be—first stretched her neck as far as she could to keep her face at least free from contact with the artist, when finding this impossible, and her more fortunate companion not coming to her aid but merely holding extended on her own trembling hand the little bunch of knucklebones that was the artist's, to the great delight of the spectators burst into tears and had to be replaced by an attendant who had long been stationed in readiness. Then came the food, a little of which the impresario managed to get between the artist's lips, while he sat in a kind of half-fainting trance, to the accompaniment of cheerful patter designed to distract the public's attention from the artist's condition; after that, a toast was drunk to the public, supposedly prompted by a whisper from the artist in the impresario's ear; the band confirmed it with a mighty flourish, the spectators melted away, and no one had any cause to be dissatisfied with the proceedings, no one except the hunger artist himself, he only, as always.

So he lived for many years, with small regular intervals of recuperation, in visible glory, honored by the world, yet in spite of that troubled in spirit, and all the more troubled because no one would take his trouble seriously. What comfort could he possibly need? What more could he possibly wish for? And if some good-natured person, feeling sorry for him, tried to console him by pointing out that his melancholy was probably caused by fasting, it could happen, especially when he had been fasting for some time, that he reacted with an outburst of fury and to the general alarm began to shake the bars of his cage like a wild animal. Yet the impresario had a way of punishing these outbreaks which he rather enjoyed putting into operation. He would apologize publicly for the artist's behavior, which was only to be excused, he admitted, because of the irritability caused by fasting; a condition hardly to be understood by well-fed people; then by natural transition he went on to mention the artist's equally incomprehensible boast that he could fast for much longer than he was doing; he praised the high ambition, the good will, the great self-denial undoubtedly implicit in such a statement; and then quite simply countered it by bringing out photographs, which were also on sale to the public, showing the artist on the fortieth day of a fast lying in bed almost dead from exhaustion. This perversion of the truth, familiar to the artist though it was, always unnerved him afresh and proved too much for him. What was a consequence of the premature ending of his fast was here presented as the cause of it! To fight against this lack of understanding, against a whole world of non-understanding, was impossible. Time and again in good faith he stood by the bars listening to the impresario, but as soon as the photographs appeared he always let go and sank with a groan back on to his straw, and the reassured public could once more come close and gaze at him.

A few years later when the witnesses of such scenes called them to mind, they often failed to understand themselves at all. For meanwhile the aforementioned change in public interest had set in; it seemed to happen almost overnight; there may have been profound causes for it, but who was going to bother about that; at any rate the pampered hunger artist suddenly found himself deserted one fine day by the amusement seekers, who went streaming past him to other more favored attractions. For the last time the impresario hurried him over half Europe to discover whether the old interest might still survive here and there; all in vain; everywhere, as if by secret agreement, a positive revulsion from professional fasting was in evidence. Of course it could not really have sprung up so suddenly as all that, and many premonitory symptoms which had not been sufficiently remarked or suppressed during the rush and glitter of success now came retrospectively to mind, but it was now too late to take any countermeasures. Fasting would surely come into fashion again at some future date, yet that was no comfort for those living in the present. What, then, was the hunger artist to do? He had been applauded by thousands in his time and could hardly come down to showing himself in a street booth at village fairs, and as for adopting another profession, he was not only too old for that but too fanatically devoted to fasting. So he took leave of the impresario, his partner in an unparalleled career, and hired himself to a large circus; in order to spare his own feelings he avoided reading the conditions of his contract.

A large circus with its enormous traffic in replacing and recruiting men, animals and apparatus can always find a use for people at any time, even for a hunger artist, provided of course that he does not ask too much, and in this particular case anyhow it was not only the artist who was taken on but his famous and long-known name as well, indeed considering the peculiar nature of his performance, which was not impaired by advancing age, it could not be objected that here was an artist past his prime, no longer at the height of his professional skill, seeking a refuge in some quiet corner of a circus; on the contrary, the hunger artist averred that he could fast as well as ever, which was entirely credible, he even alleged that if he were allowed to fast as he liked, and this was at once promised him without more ado, he could astound the world by establishing a record never yet achieved, a statement which certainly provoked a smile among the other professionals, since it left out of account the change in public opinion, which the hunger artist in his zeal conveniently forgot.

He had not, however, actually lost his sense of the real situation and took it as a matter of course that he and his cage should be stationed, not in the middle of the ring as a main attraction, but outside, near the animal cages, on a site that was after all easily accessible. Large and gaily painted placards made a frame for the cage and announced what was to be seen inside it. When the public came thronging out in the intervals to see the animals, they could hardly avoid passing the hunger artist's cage and stopping there for a moment, perhaps they might even have stayed longer had not those pressing behind them in the narrow gangway, who did not understand why they should be held up on their way toward the excitements of the menagerie, made it impossible for anyone to stand gazing quietly for any length of time. And that was the reason why the hunger artist, who had of course been looking forward to these visiting hours as the main achievement of his life, began instead to shrink from them. At first he could hardly wait for the intervals; it was exhilarating to watch the crowds come streaming his way, until only too soon—not even the most obstinate self-deception, clung to almost consciously, could hold out against the fact—the conviction was borne in upon him that these people, most of them, to judge from their actions, again and again, without exception, were all on their way to the menagerie. And the first sight of them from the distance remained the best. For when they reached his cage he was at once deafened by the storm of shouting and abuse that arose from the two contending factions, which renewed themselves continuously, of those who wanted to stop and stare at him—he soon began to dislike them more than the others—not out of real interest but only out of obstinate self-assertiveness, and those who wanted to go straight on to the animals. When the first great rush was past, the stragglers came along, and these, whom nothing could have prevented from stopping to look at him as long as they had breath, raced past with long strides, hardly even glancing at him, in their haste to get to the menagerie in time. And all too rarely did it happen that he had a stroke of luck, when some father of a family fetched up before him with his children, pointed a finger at the hunger artist and explained at length what the phenomenon meant, telling stories of earlier years when he himself had watched similar but much more thrilling performances, and the children, still rather uncomprehending, since neither inside nor outside school had they been sufficiently prepared for this lesson—what did they care about fasting?—yet showed by the brightness of their intent eyes that new and better times might be coming. Perhaps, said the hunger artist to himself many a time, things would be a little better if his cage were set not quite so near the menagerie. That made it too easy for people to make their choice, to say nothing of what he suffered from the stench of the menagerie, the animals' restlessness by night, the carrying past of raw lumps of flesh for the beasts of prey, the roaring at feeding times, which depressed him continually. But he did not dare to lodge a complaint with the management; after all, he had the animals to thank for the troops of people who passed his cage, among whom there might always be one here and there to take an interest in him, and who could tell where they might seclude him if he called attention to his existence and thereby to the fact that, strictly speaking, he was only an impediment on the way to the menagerie.

A small impediment, to be sure, one that grew steadily less. People grew familiar with the strange idea that they could be expected, in times like these, to take an interest in a hunger artist, and with this familiarity the verdict went out against him. He might fast as much as he could, and he did so; but nothing could save him now, people passed him by. Just try to explain to anyone the art of fasting! Anyone who has no feeling for it cannot be made to understand it. The fine placards grew dirty and illegible, they were torn down; the little notice board telling the number of fast days achieved, which at first was changed carefully every day, had long stayed at the same figure, for after the first few weeks even this small task seemed pointless to the staff; and so the artist simply fasted on and on, as he had once dreamed of doing, and it was no trouble to him, just as he had always foretold, but no one counted the days, no one, not even the artist himself, knew what records he was already breaking, and his heart grew heavy. And when once in a time some leisurely passer-by stopped, made merry over the old figure on the board and spoke of swindling, that was in its way the stupidest lie ever invented by indifference and inborn malice, since it was not the hunger artist who was cheating; he was working honestly, but the world was cheating him of his reward.

Many more days went by, however, and that too came to an end. An overseer's eye fell on the cage one day and he asked the attendants why this perfectly good cage should be left standing there unused with dirty straw inside it; nobody knew, until one man, helped out by the notice board, remembered about the hunger artist. They poked into the straw with sticks and found him in it. "Are you still fasting?" asked the overseer. "When on earth do you mean to stop?" "Forgive me, everybody," whispered the hunger artist; only the overseer, who had his ear to the bars, understood him. "Of course," said the overseer, and tapped his forehead with a finger to let the attendants know what state the man was in, "we forgive you." "I always wanted you to admire my fasting," said the hunger artist. "We do admire it," said the overseer, affably. "But you shouldn't admire it," said the hunger artist. "Well, then we don't admire it," said the overseer, "but why shouldn't we admire it?" "Because I have to fast, I can't help it," said the hunger artist. "What a fellow you are," said the overseer, "and why can't you help it?" "Because," said the hunger artist, lifting his head a little and speaking, with his lips pursed, as if for a kiss, right into the overseer's ear, so that no syllable might be lost, "because I couldn't find the food I liked. If I had found it, believe me, I should have made no fuss and stuffed myself like you or anyone else." These were his last words, but in his dimming eyes remained the firm though no longer proud persuasion that he was still continuing to fast.

"Well, clear this out now!" said the overseer, and they buried the hunger 10
artist, straw and all. Into the cage they put a young panther. Even the most insensitive felt it refreshing to see this wild creature leaping around the cage that had so long been dreary. The panther was all right. The food he liked was brought him without hesitation by the attendants; he seemed not even to miss his freedom; his noble body, furnished almost to the bursting point with all that it needed, seemed to carry freedom around with it too; somewhere in his jaws it seemed to lurk; and the joy of life streamed with such ardent passion from his throat that for the onlookers it was not easy to stand the shock of it. But they braced themselves, crowded round the cage, and did not want ever to move away.

1924

KATHERINE ANNE PORTER

The Fig Tree

Old Aunt Nannie had a habit of gripping with her knees to hold Miranda while she brushed her hair or buttoned her dress down the back. When Miranda wriggled, Aunt Nannie squeezed still harder, and Miranda wriggled more, but never enough to get away. Aunt Nannie gathered up Miranda's scalp lock firmly, snapped a rubber band around it, jammed a freshly starched white chambray bonnet over her ears and forehead, fastened the crown to the lock with a large safety pin, and said: "Got to hold you still someways. Here now, don't you take this off your head till the sun go down."

"I didn't want a bonnet, it's too hot, I wanted a hat," said Miranda.

"You not goin' to get a hat, you goin' to get just what you got," said Aunt Nannie in the bossy voice she used for washing and dressing time, "and mo'over some of these days I'm going' to *sew* this bonnet to your topknot. Your daddy says if you get freckles he blame me. Now, you're all ready to set out."

"Where are we going, Aunty?" Miranda could never find out about anything until the last minute. She was always being surprised. Once she went to sleep in her bed with her kitten curled on the pillow purring, and woke up in a stuffy tight bed in a train, hugging a hot-water bottle; and there was Grandmother stretched out beside her in her McLeod tartan dressing-gown, her eyes wide open. Miranda thought something wonderful had happened. "My goodness, Grandmother, where are we going?" And it was only for another trip to El Paso to see Uncle Bill.

Now Tom and Dick were hitched to the carry-all standing outside the gate with boxes and baskets tied on everywhere. Grandmother was walking alone through the house very slowly, taking a last look at everything. Now and then she put something else in the big leather portmoney on her arm until it was pretty bulgy. She carried a long black mohair skirt on her other arm, the one she put on over her other skirt when she rode horseback. Her son Harry, Miranda's father, followed her saying: "I can't see the sense in rushing off to Halifax on five minutes' notice."

Grandmother said, walking on: "It's five hours exactly." Halifax wasn't the name of Grandmother's farm at all, it was Cedar Grove, but Father always called it Halifax. "Hot as Halifax," he would say when he wanted to describe something very hot. Cedar Grove was very hot, but they went there every summer because Grandmother loved it. "I went to Cedar Grove for fifty summers before you were born," she told Miranda, who remembered last summer very well, and the summer before a little. Miranda liked it for watermelons and grasshoppers and the long rows of blooming chinaberry trees where the hounds flattened themselves out and slept. They whined and winked their eyelids and worked their feet and barked faintly in their sleep, and Uncle Jimbilly said it was because dogs always dreamed they were chasing something. In the middle of the day when Miranda looked down over the thick green fields towards the spring she could simply see it being hot: everything blue and sleepy and the mourning doves calling.

"Are we going to Halifax, Aunty?"

"Now just ask your dad if you wanta know so much."

"Are we going to Halifax, Dad?"

Her father twitched her bonnet straight and pulled her hair forward so it would show. "You mustn't get sunburned. No, let it alone. Show the pretty curls. You'll be wading in Whirlypool before supper this evening."

Grandmother said, "Don't say Halifax, child, say Cedar Grove. Call things by their right names."

"Yes, ma'am," said Miranda. Grandmother said again, to her son, "It's five hours, exactly, and your Aunt Eliza has had plenty of time to pack up her telescope, and take my saddle horse. She's been there three hours by now. I imagine she's got the telescope already set up on the hen-house roof. I hope nothing happens."

"You worry too much, Mammy," said her son, trying to conceal his impatience.

"I am not worrying," said Grandmother, shifting her riding skirt to the arm carrying the portmoney. "It will scarcely be any good taking this," she said; "I might in fact as well throw it away for this summer."

"Never mind, Mammy, we'll send to the Black Farm for Pompey, he's a good easy saddler."

"You may ride him yourself," said Grandmother. "I'll never mount Pompey while Fiddler is alive. Fiddler is my horse, and I hate having his mouth spoiled by a careless rider. Eliza never could ride, and she never will. . . ."

Miranda gave a little skip and ran away. So they were going to Cedar Grove. Miranda never got over being surprised at the way grown-up people simply did not seem able to give anyone a straight answer to any question, unless the answer was "No." Then it popped out with no trouble at all. At a little distance, she heard her grandmother say, "Harry, have you seen my riding crop lately?" and her father answered, at least maybe he thought it was an answer, "Now, Mammy, for God's sake let's get this thing over with." That was it, exactly.

Another strange way her father had of talking was calling Grandmother "Mammy." Aunt Jane was Mammy. Sometimes he called Grandmother "Mama," but she wasn't Mama either, she was really Grandmother. Mama was dead. Dead meant gone away forever. Dying was something that happened all the time, to people and everything else. Somebody died, and there was a long string of carriages going at a slow walk over the rocky ridge of the hill towards the river while the bell tolled and tolled, and that person was never seen again by anybody. Kittens and chickens and specially little turkeys died much oftener, and sometimes calves, but hardly ever cows or horses. Lizards on rocks turned into shells, with no lizard inside at all. If caterpillars all curled up and furry didn't move when you poked them with a stick, that meant they were dead—it was a sure sign.

When Miranda found any creature that didn't move or make a noise, or looked somehow different from the live ones, she always buried it in a little grave with flowers on top and a smooth stone at the head. Even grasshoppers. Everything dead had to be treated this way. "This way and no other!" Grandmother always said when she was laying down the law about all kinds of things. "It must be done *this* way, and no other!"

Miranda went down the crooked flat-stone walk hopping zigzag between the 20
grass tufts. First there were pomegranate and cape jessamine bushes mixed together; then it got very dark and shady and that was the fig grove. She went to her favorite fig tree where the deep branches bowed down level with her chin, and she could gather figs without having to climb and skin her knees. Grandmother hadn't remembered to take any figs to the country the last time, she said there were plenty of them at Cedar Grove. But the ones at Cedar Grove were big soft greenish white ones, and these at home were black and sugary. It was strange that Grandmother did not seem to notice the difference. The air was sweet among the fig trees, and chickens were always getting out of the run and rushing there to eat the figs off the ground. One mother hen was scurrying around scratching and clucking. She would scratch around a fig lying there in plain sight and cluck to her children as if it was a worm and she had dug it up for them.

"Old smarty," said Miranda, "you're just pretending."

When the little chickens all ran to their mother under Miranda's fig tree, one little chicken did not move. He was spread out on his side with his eyes shut and his mouth open. He was yellow fur in spots and pinfeathers in spots, and the rest of him was naked and sunburned. "Lazy," said Miranda, poking him with her toe. Then she saw that he was dead.

Oh, and in no time at all they'd be setting out for Halifax. Grandmother never went away, she always set out for somewhere. She'd have to hurry like anything to get him buried properly. Back into the house she went on tiptoe hoping not to be seen, for Grandmother always asked: "Where are you going, child? What are you doing? What is that you're carrying? Where did you get it? Who gave you permission?" and after Miranda had explained all that, even if there turned out not to be anything wrong in it, nothing ever seemed so nice any more. Besides it took forever to get away.

Miranda slid open her bureau drawer, third down, left-hand side where her new shoes were still wrapped in tissue paper in a nice white box the right size for a chicken with pinfeathers. She pushed the rustling white folded things and the lavender bags out of the way and trembled a little. Down in front the carry-all wheels screeched and crunched on the gravel, with Old Uncle Jimbilly yelling like a foghorn, "Hiyi, thar, back up, you steeds! Back up thar, you!" and of course, that meant he was turning Tom and Dick around so they would be pointing towards Halifax. They'd be after her, calling and hurrying her, and she wouldn't have time for anything and they wouldn't listen to a word.

It wasn't hard work digging a hole with her little spade in the loose dry soil. Miranda wrapped the slimpsy chicken in tissue paper, trying to make it look pretty, laid it in the box carefully, and covered it up with a nice mound, just like people's. She had hardly got it piled up grave shape, kneeling and leaning to smooth it over, when a strange sound came from somewhere, a very sad little crying sound. It said Weep, weep, weep, three times like that slowly, and it seemed to come from the mound of dirt. "My goodness," Miranda asked herself aloud, "what's that?" She pushed her bonnet off her ears and listened hard. "Weep, weep," said the tiny sad voice. And People began calling and urging her, their voices coming nearer. She began to clamor, too.

"Yes, Aunty, wait a minute, Aunty!"

"You come right on here this minute, we're goin'!"

"You *have* to wait, Aunty!"

Her father was coming along the edge of the fig trees. "Hurry up, Baby, you'll get left!"

Miranda felt she couldn't bear to be left. She ran all shaking with fright. Her father gave her the annoyed look he always gave her when he said something to upset her and then saw that she was upset. His words were kind but his voice scolded: "Stop getting so excited, Baby, you know we wouldn't leave you for anything." Miranda wanted to talk back: 'Then why did you say so?" but she was still listening for that tiny sound: "Weep, weep." She lagged and pulled backward, looking over her shoulder. but her father hurried her towards the carry-all. But things didn't make sounds if they were dead. They couldn't. That was one of the signs. Oh, but she had heard it.

Her father sat in front and drove, and old Uncle Jimbilly didn't do anything but get down and open gates. Grandmother and Aunt Nannie sat in the back seat, with Miranda between them. She loved setting out somewhere, with everybody smiling and settling down and looking up at the weather, with the horses bouncing and pulling on the reins, the springs jolting and swaying with a creaky noise that made you feel sure you were traveling. That evening she would go wading with Maria and Paul and Uncle Jimbilly, and that very night she would lie out on the grass in her nightgown to cool off, and they would all drink lemonade before going to bed. Sister Maria and Brother Paul would already be burned like muffins because they were sent on ahead the minute school was out. Sister Maria had got freckled and Father was furious. "Keep your bonnet on," he said to Miranda, sternly. "Now remember. I'm not going to have that face ruined, too." But oh, what had made that funny sound? Miranda's ears buzzed and she had a dull round pain in her just under her front ribs. She had to go back and let him out. He'd never get out by himself, all tangled up in tissue paper and that shoebox. He'd never get out without her.

"Grandmother, I've got to go back. Oh, I've *got* to go back!"

Grandmother turned Miranda's face around by the chin and looked at her closely, the way grown folks did. Grandmother's eyes were always the same. They never looked kind or sad or angry or tired or anything. They just looked, blue and still. "What is the matter with you, Miranda, what happened?"

"Oh, I've got to go back—I forg-got something important."

"Stop that silly crying and tell me what you want."

Miranda couldn't stop. Her father looked very anxious. "Mammy, maybe the Baby's sick." He reached out his handkerchief to her face. "What's the matter with my honey? Did you eat something?"

Miranda had to stand up to cry as hard as she wanted to. The wheels went grinding round in the road, the carry-all wobbled so that Grandmother had to take her by one arm, and her father by the other. They stared at each other over Miranda's head with a moveless gaze that Miranda had seen often, and their eyes looked exactly alike. Miranda blinked up at them, waiting to see who would win. Then Grandmother's hand fell away, and Miranda was handed over to her father. He gave the reins to Uncle Jimbilly, and lifted her over the top of the seat. She sprawled against his chest and knees as if he were an armchair and stopped crying at once. "We can't go back just for notions," he told her in the reasoning tone he always talked in when Grandmother scolded, and held the muffly handkerchief for her. "Now, blow hard. What did you forget, honey? We'll find another. Was it your doll?"

Miranda hated dolls. She never played with them. She always pulled the wigs off and tied them on the kittens, like hats. The kittens pulled them off instantly. It was fun. She put the doll clothes on the kittens and it took any one of them just half a minute to get them all off again. Kittens had sense. Miranda wailed suddenly, "Oh, I want my doll!" and cried again, trying to drown out the strange little sound, "Weep, weep"—

"Well now, if that's all," said her father comfortably, "there's a raft of dolls at Cedar Grove, and about forty fresh kittens. How'd you like that?"

"Forty?" asked Miranda.

"About," said Father.

Old Aunt Nannie leaned and held out her hand. "Look, honey, I toted you some nice black figs."

Her face was wrinkled and black and it looked like a fig upside down with a white ruffled cap. Miranda clenched her eyes tight and shook her head.

"Is that a pretty way to behave when Aunt Nannie offers you something nice?" asked Grandmother in her gentle reminding tone of voice.

"No, ma'am," said Miranda meekly. "Thank you, Aunt Nannie." But she did not accept the figs.

Great-Aunt Eliza, half way up a stepladder pitched against the flat-roofed chicken house, was telling Hinry just how to set up her telescope. "For a fellow who never saw or heard of a telescope," Great-Aunt Eliza said to Grandmother, who was really her sister Sophia Jane, "he doesn't do so badly so long as I tell him."

"I do wish you'd stop clambering up stepladders, Eliza," said Grandmother, "at your time of life."

"You're nothing but a nervous wreck, Sophia, I declare. When did you ever know me to get hurt?"

"Even so," said Grandmother tartly, "there is such a thing as appropriate behavior at our time of . . ."

Great-Aunt Eliza seized a fold of her heavy brown pleated skirt with one hand, with the other she grasped the ladder one rung higher and ascended another step. "Now Hinry," she called, "just swing it around facing west and leave it level. I'll fix it the way I want when I'm ready. You can come on down now." She came down then herself, and said to her sister: "So long as you can go bouncing off on that horse of yours, Sophia Jane, I s'pose I can climb ladders. I'm three years younger than you, and *at your time of life* that makes all the difference!"

Grandmother turned pink as the inside of a seashell, the one on her sewing table that had the sound of the sea in it; Miranda knew that she had always been the pretty one, and she was pretty still, but Great-Aunt Eliza was not pretty now and never had been. Miranda, watching and listening—for everything in the world was strange to her and something she had to know about—saw two old women, who were proud of being grandmothers, who spoke to children always as if they knew best about everything and children knew nothing, and they told children all day long to come here, go there, do this, do not do that, and they were always right and children never were except when they did anything they were told right away without a word. And here they were bickering like two little girls at school, or even the way Miranda and her sister Maria bickered and nagged and picked on each other and said things on purpose to hurt each other's feelings. Miranda felt sad and strange and a little frightened. She began edging away.

"Where are you going, Miranda?" asked Grandmother in her everyday voice.

"Just to the house," said Miranda, her heart sinking.

"Wait and walk with us," said Grandmother. She was very thin and pale and had white hair. Beside her, Great-Aunt Eliza loomed like a mountain with her grizzled iron-colored hair like a curly wig, her steel-rimmed spectacles over her snuff-colored eyes, and snuff-colored woollen skirts billowing about her, and her smell of snuff. When she came through the door she quite filled it up. When she sat down the chair disappeared under her, and she seemed to be sitting solidly on herself from her waistband to the floor.

Now with Grandmother sitting across the room rummaging in her work bas- 55
ket and pretending not to see anything, Great-Aunt Eliza took a small brown bottle out of her pocket, opened it, took a pinch of snuff in each nostril, sneezed loudly, wiped her nose with a big white starchy-looking handkerchief, pushed her spectacles up on her forehead, took a little twig chewed into a brush at one end, dipped and twisted it around in the little bottle, and placed it firmly between her teeth. Miranda had heard of this shameful habit in women of the lower classes, but no lady had been known to "dip snuff," and surely not in the family. Yet here was Great-Aunt Eliza, a lady even if not a very pretty one, dipping snuff. Miranda knew how her grandmother felt about it; she stared fascinated at Great-Aunt Eliza until her eyes watered. Great-Aunt Eliza stared back in turn.

"Look here, young one, d'ye s'pose if I gave you a gumdrop you'd get out from underfoot?"

She reached in the other pocket and took out a roundish, rather crushed-looking pink gumdrop with the sugar coating pretty badly crackled. "Now take this, and don't let me lay eyes on you any more today."

Miranda hurried away, clenching the gumdrop in her palm. When she reached the kitchen it was oozing through her fingers. She went to the tap and held her hand under the water and tried to wash off the snuffy smell. After this crime she did not really dare go near Great-Aunt Eliza again soon. "What did you do with that gumdrop so quickly, child?" she could almost hear her asking.

Yet Miranda almost forgot her usual interests, such as kittens and other little animals on the place, pigs, chickens, rabbits, anything at all so it was a baby and would let her pet and feed it, for Great-Aunt Eliza's ways and habits kept Miranda following her about, gazing, or sitting across the dining-table, gazing, for when Great-Aunt Eliza was not on the roof before her telescope, always just before daylight or just after dark, she was walking about with a microscope and a burning glass, peering closely at something she saw on a tree trunk, something she found in the grass; now and then she collected fragments that looked like dried leaves or bits of bark, brought them in the house, spread them out on a sheet of white paper, and sat there, poring, as still as if she were saying her prayers. At table she would dissect a scrap of potato peeling or anything else she might be eating, and sit there, bowed over, saying, "Hum," from time to time. Grandmother, who did not allow the children to bring anything to the table to play with and who forbade them to do anything but eat while they were there, ignored her sister's manners as long as she could, then remarked one day, when Great-Aunt Eliza was humming like a bee to herself over what her microscope had found in a raisin, "Eliza, if it is interesting save it for me to look at after dinner. Or tell me what it is."

"You wouldn't know if I told you," said Great-Aunt Eliza, coolly, putting 60
her microscope away and finishing off her pudding.

When at last, just before they were all going back to town again, Great-Aunt

Eliza invited the children to climb the ladder with her and see the stars through her telescope, they were so awed they looked at each other like strangers, and did not exchange a word. Miranda saw only a great pale flaring disk of cold light, but she knew it was the moon and called out in pure rapture, "Oh, it's like another world!"

"Why, of course, child," said Great-Aunt Eliza, in her growling voice, but kindly, "other worlds, a million other worlds."

"Like this one?" asked Miranda, timidly.

"Nobody knows, child. . . ."

"Nobody knows, nobody knows," Miranda sang to a tune in her head, and when the others walked on, she was so dazzled with joy she fell back by herself, walking a little distance behind Great-Aunt Eliza's swinging lantern and her wide-swinging skirts. They took the dewy path through the fig grove, much like the one in town, with the early dew bringing out the sweet smell of the milky leaves. They passed a fig tree with low hanging branches, and Miranda reached up by habit and touched it with her fingers for luck. From the earth beneath her feet came a terrible, faint troubled sound. "Weep weep, weep weep . . ." murmured a little crying voice from the smothering earth, the grave.

Miranda bounded like a startled pony against the back of Great-Aunt Eliza's knees, crying out, 'Oh, oh, oh, wait . . ."

"What on earth's the matter, child?"

Miranda seized the warm snuffly hand held out to her and hung on hard. "Oh, there's something saying 'weep weep' out of the ground!"

Great-Aunt Eliza stooped, put her arm around Miranda and listened carefully, for a moment. "Hear them?" she said. "They're not in the ground at all. They are the first tree frogs, means it's going to rain," she said, "weep weep—hear them?"

Miranda took a deep trembling breath and heard them. They were in the trees. They walked on again, Miranda holding Great-Aunt Eliza's hand.

"Just think," said Great-Aunt Eliza, in her most scientific voice, "when tree frogs shed their skins, they pull them off over their heads like little shirts, and they eat them. Can you imagine? They have the prettiest little shapes you ever saw—I'll show you one some time under the microscope."

"Thank you, ma'am," Miranda remembered finally to say through her fog of bliss at hearing the tree frogs sing, "Weep weep . . ."

1944

ERNEST HEMINGWAY

A Clean, Well-Lighted Place

It was late and every one had left the café except an old man who sat in the shadow the leaves of the tree made against the electric light. In the day time the street was dusty, but at night the dew settled the dust and the old man liked to sit late because he was deaf and now at night it was quiet and he felt the difference. The two waiters inside the café knew that the old man was a little drunk, and while he was a good client they knew that if he became too drunk he would leave without paying, so they kept watch on him.

"Last week he tried to commit suicide," one waiter said.

"Why?"

"He was in despair."

"What about?"

"Nothing."

"How do you know it was nothing?"

"He has plenty of money."

They sat together at a table that was close against the wall near the door of the café and looked at the terrace where the tables were all empty except where the old man sat in the shadow of the leaves of the tree that moved slightly in the wind. A girl and a soldier went by in the street. The street light shone on the brass number on his collar. The girl wore no head covering and hurried beside him.

"The guard will pick him up," one waiter said.

"What does it matter if he gets what he's after?"

"He had better get off the street now. The guard will get him. They went by five minutes ago."

The old man sitting in the shadow rapped on his saucer with his glass. The younger waiter went over to him.

"What do you want?"

The old man looked at him. "Another brandy," he said.

"You'll be drunk," the waiter said. The old man looked at him. The waiter went away.

"He'll stay all night," he said to his colleague. "I'm sleepy now. I never get into bed before three o'clock. He should have killed himself last week."

The waiter took the brandy bottle and another saucer from the counter inside the café and marched out to the old man's table. He put down the saucer and poured the glass full of brandy.

"You should have killed yourself last week," he said to the deaf man. The old man motioned with his finger. "A little more," he said. The waiter poured on into the glass so that the brandy slopped over and ran down the stem into the top saucer of the pile. "Thank you," the old man said. The waiter took the bottle back inside the café. He sat down at the table with his colleague again.

"He's drunk now," he said.

"He's drunk every night."

"What did he want to kill himself for?"

"How should I know."

"How did he do it?"

"He hung himself with a rope."

"Who cut him down?"

"His niece."

"Why did they do it?"

"Fear for his soul."

"How much money has he got?"

"He's got plenty."

"He must be eighty years old."

"Anyway I should say he was eighty."

"I wish he would go home. I never get to bed before three o'clock. What kind of hour is that to go to bed?"

"He stays up because he likes it."

"He's lonely. I'm not lonely. I have a wife waiting in bed for me."

"He had a wife once too."

"A wife would be no good to him now."

"You can't tell. He might be better with a wife."

"His niece looks after him. You said she cut him down."

"I know."

"I wouldn't want to be that old. An old man is a nasty thing."

"Not always. This old man is clean. He drinks without spilling. Even now, drunk. Look at him."

"I don't want to look at him. I wish he would go home. He has no regard for those who must work."

The old man looked from his glass across the square, then over at the waiters.

"Another brandy," he said, pointing to his glass. The waiter who was in a hurry came over.

"Finished," he said, speaking with that omission of syntax stupid people employ when talking to drunken people or foreigners. "No more tonight. Close now."

"Another," said the old man.

"No. Finished." The waiter wiped the edge of the table with a towel and shook his head.

The old man stood up, slowly counted the saucers, took a leather coin purse from his pocket and paid for the drinks, leaving half a peseta tip.

The waiter watched him go down the street, a very old man walking unsteadily but with dignity.

"Why didn't you let him stay and drink?" the unhurried waiter asked. They were putting up the shutters. "It is not half-past two."

"I want to go home to bed."

"What is an hour?"

"More to me than to him."

"An hour is the same."

"You talk like an old man yourself. He can buy a bottle and drink at home."

"It's not the same."

"No, it is not," agreed the waiter with a wife. He did not wish to be unjust. He was only in a hurry.

"And you? You have no fear of going home before your usual hour?"

"Are you trying to insult me?"

"No, hombre, only to make a joke."

"No," the waiter who was in a hurry said, rising from pulling down the metal shutters. "I have confidence. I am all confidence."

"You have youth, confidence, and a job," the older waiter said. "You have everything."

"And what do you lack?"

"Everything but work."

"You have everything I have."

"No. I have never had confidence and I am not young."

"Come on. Stop talking nonsense and lock up."

"I am of those who like to stay late at the café," the older waiter said. "With all those who do not want to go to bed. With all those who need a light for the night."

"I want to go home and into bed."

"We are of two different kinds," the older waiter said. He was now dressed to go home. "It is not only a question of youth and confidence although those things are very beautiful. Each night I am reluctant to close up because there may be some one who needs the café."

"Hombre, there are bodegas open all night long."

"You do not understand. This is a clean and pleasant café. It is well lighted. The light is very good and also, now, there are shadows of the leaves."

"Good night," said the younger waiter.

"Good night," the other said. Turning off the electric light he continued the conversation with himself. It is the light of course but it is necessary that the place be clean and pleasant. You do not want music. Certainly you do not want music. Nor can you stand before a bar with dignity although that is all that is provided for these hours. What did he fear? It was not fear or dread. It was a nothing that he knew too well. It was all a nothing and a man was nothing too. It was only that and light was all it needed and a certain cleanness and order. Some lived in it and never felt it but he knew it all was nada y pues nada[1] y nada y pues nada. Our nada who art in nada, nada be thy name thy kingdom nada thy will be nada in nada as it is in nada. Give us this nada our daily nada and nada us our nada as we nada our nadas and nada us not into nada but deliver us from nada; pues nada. Hail nothing full of nothing, nothing is with thee. He smiled and stood before a bar with a shining steam pressure coffee machine.

"What's yours?" asked the barman.

"Nada."

"Otro loco mas,"[2] said the barman and turned away.

"A little cup," said the waiter.

The barman poured it for him.

"The light is very bright and pleasant but the bar is unpolished," the waiter said.

The barman looked at him but did not answer. It was too late at night for conversation.

"You want another copita?" the barman asked.

"No, thank you," said the waiter and went out. He disliked bars and bodegas. A clean, well-lighted café was a very different thing. Now, without thinking

1. Nothing and then nothing. 2. One more nutcase.

further, he would go home to his room. He would lie in bed and finally, with daylight, he would go to sleep. After all, he said to himself, it is probably only insomnia. Many must have it.

1933

GRACE PALEY

A Conversation with My Father

My father is eighty-six years old and in bed. His heart, that bloody motor, is equally old and will not do certain jobs any more. It still floods his head with brainy light. But it won't let his legs carry the weight of his body around the house. Despite my metaphors, this muscle failure is not due to his old heart, he says, but to a potassium shortage. Sitting on one pillow, leaning on three, he offers last-minute advice and makes a request.

"I would like you to write a simple story just once more," he says, "the kind de Maupassant wrote, or Chekhov, the kind you used to write. Just recognizable people and then write down what happened to them next."

I say, "Yes, why not? That's possible." I want to please him, though I don't remember writing that way. I *would* like to try to tell such a story, if he means the kind that begins: "There was a woman . . ." followed by plot, the absolute line between two points which I've always despised. Not for literary reasons, but because it takes all hope away. Everyone, real or invented, deserves the open destiny of life.

Finally I thought of a story that had been happening for a couple of years right across the street. I wrote it down, then read it aloud. "Pa," I said, "how about this? Do you mean something like this?"

> 5 Once in my time there was a woman and she had a son. They lived nicely, in a small apartment in Manhattan. This boy at about fifteen became a junkie, which is not unusual in our neighborhood. In order to maintain her close friendship with him, she became a junkie too. She said it was part of the youth culture, with which she felt very much at home. After a while, for a number of reasons, the boy gave it all up and left the city and his mother in disgust. Hopeless and alone, she grieved. We all visit her.

"O.K., Pa, that's it," I said, "an unadorned and miserable tale."

"But that's not what I mean," my father said. "You misunderstood me on purpose. You know there's a lot more to it. You know that. You left everything out. Turgenev[1] wouldn't do that. Chekhov wouldn't do that. There are in fact Russian writers you never heard of, you don't have an inkling of, as good as anyone, who can write a plain ordinary story, who would not leave out what you

1. Ivan Sergevich Turgenev (1818–1883); his best-known novel, *Fathers and Sons*, deals with the conflict between generations.

have left out. I object not to facts but to people sitting in trees talking senselessly, voices from who knows where . . ."

"Forget that one, Pa, what have I left out now? In this one?"

"Her looks, for instance."

"Oh. Quite handsome, I think. Yes."

"Her hair?"

"Dark, with heavy braids, as though she were a girl or a foreigner."

"What were her parents like, her stock? That she became such a person. It's interesting, you know."

"From out of town. Professional people. The first to be divorced in their county. How's that? Enough?" I asked.

"With you, it's all a joke," he said. "What about the boy's father. Why didn't you mention him? Who was he? Or was the boy born out of wedlock?"

"Yes," I said. "He was born out of wedlock."

"For Godsakes, doesn't anyone in your stories get married? Doesn't anyone have the time to run down to City Hall before they jump into bed?"

"No," I said. "In real life, yes. But in my stories, no."

"Why do you answer me like that?"

"Oh, Pa, this is a simple story about a smart woman who came to N.Y.C. full of interest love trust excitement very up to date, and about her son, what a hard time she had in this world. Married or not, it's of small consequence."

"It is of great consequence," he said.

"O.K.," I said.

"O.K. O.K. yourself," he said, "but listen. I believe you that she's good-looking, but I don't think she was so smart."

"That's true," I said. "Actually that's the trouble with stories. People start out fantastic. You think they're extraordinary, but it turns out as the work goes along, they're just average with a good education. Sometimes the other way around, the person's a kind of dumb innocent, but he outwits you and you can't even think of an ending good enough."

"What do you do then?" he asked. He had been a doctor for a couple of decades and then an artist for a couple of decades and he's still interested in details, craft, technique.

"Well, you just have to let the story lie around till some agreement can be reached between you and the stubborn hero."

"Aren't you talking silly, now?" he asked. "Start again," he said. "It so happens I'm not going out this evening. Tell the story again. See what you can do this time."

"O.K.," I said. "But it's not a five-minute job." Second attempt:

Once, across the street from us, there was a fine handsome woman, our neighbor. She had a son whom she loved because she'd known him since birth (in helpless chubby infancy, and in the wrestling, hugging ages, seven to ten, as well as earlier and later). This boy, when he fell into the fist of adolescence, became a junkie. He was not a hopeless one. He was in fact hopeful, an ideologue and successful converter. With his busy brilliance, he wrote persuasive articles for his high-school newspaper. Seeking a wider audience, using important connections, he drummed into

Lower Manhattan newsstand distribution a periodical called *Oh! Golden Horse!*[2]

30 In order to keep him from feeling guilty (because guilt is the stony heart of nine tenths of all clinically diagnosed cancers in America today, she said), and because she had always believed in giving bad habits room at home where one could keep an eye on them, she too became a junkie. Her kitchen was famous for a while—a center for intellectual addicts who knew what they were doing. A few felt artistic like Coleridge and others were scientific and revolutionary like Leary.[3] Although she was often high herself, certain good mothering reflexes remained, and she saw to it that there was lots of orange juice around and honey and milk and vitamin pills. However, she never cooked anything but chili, and that no more than once a week. She explained, when we talked to her, seriously, with neighborly concern, that it was her part in the youth culture and she would rather be with the young, it was an honor, than with her own generation.

One week, while nodding[4] through an Antonioni[5] film, this boy was severely jabbed by the elbow of a stern and proselytizing girl, sitting beside him. She offered immediate apricots and nuts for his sugar level, spoke to him sharply, and took him home.

She had heard of him and his work and she herself published, edited, and wrote a competitive journal called *Man Does Live By Bread Alone*. In the organic heat of her continuous presence he could not help but become interested once more in his muscles, his arteries, and nerve connections. In fact he began to love them, treasure them, praise them with funny little songs in *Man Does Live* . . .

the fingers of my flesh transcend
my transcendental soul
the tightness in my shoulders end
my teeth have made me whole

To the mouth of his head (that glory of will and determination) he brought hard apples, nuts, wheat germ, and soybean oil. He said to his old friends, From now on, I guess I'll keep my wits about me. I'm going on the natch. He said he was about to begin a spiritual deep-breathing journey. How about you too, Mom? he asked kindly.

His conversion was so radiant, splendid, that neighborhood kids his age began to say that he had never been a real addict at all, only a journalist along for the smell of the story. The mother tried several times to give up what had become without her son and his friends a lonely habit. This effort only brought it to supportable levels. The boy and his girl took their electronic mimeograph and moved to the bushy edge of another borough. They were very strict. They said they would not see her again until she had been off drugs for sixty days.

35 At home alone in the evening, weeping, the mother read and reread the seven issues of *Oh! Golden Horse!* They seemed to her as truthful as ever. We often crossed the street to visit and console. But if we mentioned any of our children who were at college or in the hospital or dropouts at home, she would cry out, My baby! My baby! and burst into terrible, face-scarring, time-consuming tears. The End.

2. "Horse" is a slang term for heroin. **3.** Samuel Taylor Coleridge (1772–1834), English Romantic poet, wrote his allegedly unfinished poem *Kubla Khan* in an opium dream. Timothy Leary (b. 1920), American psychologist who promoted the use of psychedelic drugs. **4.** A slang term referring to the narcotic effect of heroin. **5.** Michelangelo Antonioni (b. 1912), Italian director (*Blow-Up, Zabriskie Point*).

First my father was silent, then he said, "Number One: You have a nice sense of humor. Number Two: I see you can't tell a plain story. So don't waste time." Then he said sadly, "Number Three: I suppose that means she was alone, she was left like that, his mother. Alone. Probably sick?"

I said, "Yes."

"Poor woman. Poor girl, to be born in a time of fools, to live among fools. The end. The end. You were right to put that down. The end."

I didn't want to argue, but I had to say, "Well, it is not necessarily the end, Pa."

"Yes," he said, "what a tragedy. The end of a person."

"No, Pa," I begged him. "It doesn't have to be. She's only about forty. She could be a hundred different things in this world as time goes on. A teacher or a social worker. An ex-junkie! Sometimes it's better than having a master's in education."

"Jokes," he said. "As a writer that's your main trouble. You don't want to recognize it. Tragedy! Plain tragedy! Historical tragedy! No hope. The end."

"Oh, Pa," I said. "She could change."

"In your own life, too, you have to look it in the face." He took a couple of nitroglycerin.[6] "Turn to five," he said, pointing to the dial on the oxygen tank. He inserted the tubes into his nostrils and breathed deep. He closed his eyes and said, "No."

I had promised the family to always let him have the last word when arguing, but in this case I had a different responsibility. That woman lives across the street. She's my knowledge and my invention. I'm sorry for her. I'm not going to leave her there in that house crying. (Actually neither would Life, which unlike me has no pity.)

Therefore: She did change. Of course her son never came home again. But right now, she's the receptionist in a storefront community clinic in the East Village. Most of the customers are young people, some old friends. The head doctor said to her, "If we only had three people in this clinic with your experiences . . ."

"The doctor said that?" My father took the oxygen tubes out of his nostrils and said, "Jokes. Jokes again."

"No, Pa, it could really happen that way, it's a funny world nowadays."

"No," he said. "Truth first. She will slide back. A person must have character. She does not."

"No, Pa," I said. "That's it. She's got a job. Forget it. She's in that storefront working."

"How long will it be?" he asked. "Tragedy! You too. When will you look it in the face?"

1974

6. Medicine for certain heart conditions.

WOODY ALLEN

The Kugelmass Episode

Kugelmass, a professor of humanities at City College, was unhappily married for the second time. Daphne Kugelmass was an oaf. He also had two dull sons by his first wife, Flo, and was up to his neck in alimony and child support.

"Did I know it would turn out so badly?" Kugelmass whined to his analyst one day. "Daphne had promise. Who suspected she'd let herself go and well up like a beach ball? Plus she had a few bucks, which is not in itself a healthy reason to marry a person, but it doesn't hurt, with the kind of operating nut[1] I have. You see my point?"

Kugelmass was bald and as hairy as a bear, but he had soul.

"I need to meet a new woman," he went on. "I need to have an affair. I may not look the part, but I'm a man who needs romance. I need softness, I need flirtation. I'm not getting younger, so before it's too late I want to make love in Venice, trade quips at '21,'[2] and exchange coy glances over red wine and candlelight. You see what I'm saying?"

Dr. Mandel shifted in his chair and said, "An affair will solve nothing. You're so unrealistic. Your problems run much deeper."

"And also this affair must be discreet," Kugelmass continued. "I can't afford a second divorce. Daphne would really sock it to me."

"Mr. Kugelmass—"

"But it can't be anyone at City College, because Daphne also works there. Not that anyone on the faculty at C.C.N.Y. is any great shakes, but some of those coeds . . ."

"Mr. Kugelmass—"

"Help me. I had a dream last night. I was skipping through a meadow holding a picnic basket and the basket was marked 'Options.' And then I saw there was a hole in the basket."

"Mr. Kugelmass, the worst thing you could do is act out. You must simply express your feelings here, and together we'll analyze them. You have been in treatment long enough to know there is no overnight cure. After all, I'm an analyst, not a magician."

"Then perhaps what I need is a magician," Kugelmass said, rising from his chair. And with that he terminated his therapy.

A couple of weeks later, while Kugelmass and Daphne were moping around in their apartment one night like two pieces of old furniture, the phone rang.

"I'll get it," Kugelmass said. "Hello."

"Kugelmass?" a voice said, "Kugelmass, this is Persky."

"Who?"

"Persky. Or should I say The Great Persky?"

"Pardon me?"

1. Budget, expenses 2. Celebrity nightclub and restaurant.

"I hear you're looking all over town for a magician to bring a little exotica into your life? Yes or no?"

"Sh-h-h," Kugelmass whispered. "Don't hang up. Where are you calling from, Persky?"

Early the following afternoon, Kugelmass climbed three flights of stairs in a broken-down apartment house in the Bushwick section of Brooklyn. Peering through the darkness of the hall, he found the door he was looking for and pressed the bell. I'm going to regret this, he thought to himself.

Seconds later, he was greeted by a short, thin, waxy-looking man.

"*You're* Persky the Great?" Kugelmass said.

"The Great Persky. You want a tea?"

"No, I want romance. I want music. I want love and beauty."

"But not tea, eh? Amazing. O.K., sit down."

Persky went to the back room, and Kugelmass heard the sounds of boxes and furniture being moved around. Persky reappeared, pushing before him a large object on squeaky roller-skate wheels. He removed some old silk handkerchiefs that were lying on its top and blew away a bit of dust. It was a cheap-looking Chinese cabinet, badly lacquered.

"Persky," Kugelmass said, "what's your scam?"[3]

"Pay attention," Persky said. "This is some beautiful effect. I developed it for a Knights of Pythias[4] date last year, but the booking fell through. Get into the cabinet."

"Why, so you can stick it full of swords or something?"

"You see any swords?"

Kugelmass made a face and, grunting, climbed into the cabinet. He couldn't help noticing a couple of ugly rhinestones glued onto the raw plywood just in front of his face. "If this is a joke" he said.

"Some joke. Now, here's the point. If I throw any novel into this cabinet with you, shut the doors, and tap it three times, you will find yourself projected into that book."

Kugelmass made a grimace of disbelief.

"It's the emess,"[5] Persky said. "My hand to God. Not just a novel, either. A short story, a play, a poem. You can meet any of the women created by the world's best writers. Whoever you dreamed of. You could carry on all you like with a real winner. Then when you've had enough you give a yell, and I'll see you're back here in a split second."

"Persky, are you some kind of outpatient?"

"I'm telling you it's on the level," Persky said.

Kugelmass remained skeptical. "What are you telling me—that this cheesy homemade box can take me on a ride like you're describing?"

"For a double sawbuck."[6]

Kugelmass reached for his wallet. "I'll believe this when I see it," he said.

Persky tucked the bills in his pants pocket and turned toward his bookcase.

3. Scheme, confidence trick. 4. Secret fraternal society. 5. Truth. 6. Twenty dollars.

"So who do you want to meet? Sister Carrie? Hester Prynne? Ophelia? Maybe someone by Saul Bellow? Hey, what about Temple Drake?[7] Although for a man your age she'd be a workout."

"French. I want to have an affair with a French lover."

"Nana?"[8]

"I don't want to have to pay for it."

"What about Natasha in 'War and Peace'?"[9]

"I said French. I know! What about Emma Bovary? That sounds to me perfect."

"You got it, Kugelmass. Give me a holler when you've had enough." Persky tossed in a paperback copy of Flaubert's novel.

"You sure this is safe?" Kugelmass asked as Persky began shutting the cabinet doors.

"Safe. Is anything safe in this crazy world?" Persky rapped three times on the cabinet and then flung open the doors.

Kugelmass was gone. At the same moment, he appeared in the bedroom of Charles and Emma Bovary's house at Yonville.[1] Before him was a beautiful woman, standing alone with her back turned to him as she folded some linen. I can't believe this, thought Kugelmass, staring at the doctor's ravishing wife. This is uncanny. I'm here. It's her.

Emma turned in surprise. "Goodness, you startled me," she said. "Who are you?" She spoke in the same fine English translation as the paperback.

It's simply devastating, he thought. Then, realizing that it was he whom she had addressed, he said, "Excuse me. I'm Sidney Kugelmass. I'm from City College. A professor of humanities. C.C.N.Y.? Uptown. I—oh, boy!"

Emma Bovary smiled flirtatiously and said, "Would you like a drink? A glass of wine, perhaps?"

She is beautiful, Kugelmass thought. What a contrast with the troglodyte who shared his bed! He felt a sudden impulse to take this vision into his arms and tell her she was the kind of woman he had dreamed of all his life.

"Yes, some wine" he said hoarsely. "White. No, red. No, white. Make it white."

"Charles is out for the day," Emma said, her voice full of playful implication.

After the wine, they went for a stroll in the lovely French countryside. "I've always dreamed that some mysterious stranger would appear and rescue me from the monotony of this crass rural existence," Emma said, clasping his hand. They passed a small church. "I love what you have on," she murmured. "I've never seen anything like it around here. It's so . . . so modern."

"It's called a leisure suit," he said romantically. 'It was marked down." Sud-

7. Respectively, the fallen heroine of Theodore Dreiser's *Sister Carrie* (1900); the adulterous heroine of Nathaniel Hawthorne's *The Scarlet Letter* (1850); Hamlet's fiancée, who drowns herself; Bellow's heroines are intensely neurotic, sexual, and vindictive; the victim of a bizarre rape in Faulkner's *Sanctuary* (1931), who is also the heroine of his *Requiem for a Nun* (1950).

8. Prostitute-heroine of Émile Zola's *Nana* (1880).

9. Saucy heroine of the novel (1865–1869) by Tolstoy.

1. Town in Normandy, France, where much of Flaubert's novel *Madame Bovary* (1857) is set.

denly he kissed her. For the next hour they reclined under a tree and whispered together and told each other deeply meaningful things with their eyes. Then Kugelmass sat up. He had just remembered he had to meet Daphne at Bloomingdale's.[2] "I must go," he told her. "But don't worry, I'll be back."

"I hope so," Emma said.

He embraced her passionately, and the two walked back to the house. He held Emma's face cupped in his palms, kissed her again, and yelled, "O.K., Persky! I got to be at Bloomingdale's by three-thirty."

There was an audible pop, and Kugelmass was back in Brooklyn.

"So? Did I lie?" Persky asked triumphantly.

"Look, Persky, I'm right now late to meet the ball and chain at Lexington Avenue, but when can I go again? Tomorrow?"

"My pleasure. Just bring a twenty. And don't mention this to anybody."

"Yeah. I'm going to call Rupert Murdoch."[3]

Kugelmass hailed a cab and sped off to the city. His heart danced on point. I am in love, he thought, I am the possessor of a wonderful secret. What he didn't realize was that at this very moment students in various classrooms across the country were saying to their teachers, "Who is this character on page 100? A bald Jew is kissing Madame Bovary?" A teacher in Sioux Falls, South Dakota, sighed and thought, Jesus, these kids, with their pot and acid. What goes through their minds!

Daphne Kugelmass was in the bathroom-accessories department at Bloomingdale's when Kugelmass arrived breathlessly. "Where've you been?" she snapped. "It's four-thirty."

"I got held up in traffic," Kugelmass said.

Kugelmass visited Persky the next day, and in a few minutes was again passed magically to Yonville. Emma couldn't hide her excitement at seeing him. The two spent hours together, laughing and talking about their different backgrounds. Before Kugelmass left, they made love. "My God, I'm doing it with Madame Bovary!" Kugelmass whispered to himself. "Me, who failed freshman English."

As the months passed, Kugelmass saw Persky many times and developed a close and passionate relationship with Emma Bovary. "Make sure and always get me into the book before page 120," Kugelmass said to the magician one day. "I always have to meet her before she hooks up with this Rodolphe character."[4]

"Why?" Persky asked. "You can't beat his time?"

"Beat his time. He's landed gentry. Those guys have nothing better to do than flirt and ride horses. To me, he's one of those faces you see in the pages of *Women's Wear Daily*.[5] With the Helmut Berger[6] hairdo. But to her he's hot stuff."

2. Chic New York department store. 3. Australian newspaper baron, who, in addition to several British papers, owns the New York *Post*, the *Village Voice*, and *New York* magazine. 4. The provincial aristocratic womanizer who seduces Emma, after she has a first romantic, idealistic flirtation with the mooning young Léon (who is mentioned below). The Abbé Bournisien and Binet, mentioned later, are minor characters in the novel. 5. Gossipy New York fashion newspaper. 6. Handsome German actor (b. 1942) who often plays decadent characters *(The Damned, Portrait of Dorian Gray)*.

"And her husband suspects nothing?"

"He's out of his depth. He's a lackluster little paramedic who's thrown in his lot with a jitterbug. He's ready to go to sleep by ten, and she's putting on her dancing shoes. Oh, well . . . See you later."

And once again Kugelmass entered the cabinet and passed instantly to the Bovary estate at Yonville. "How you doing, cupcake?" he said to Emma.

"Oh, Kugelmass," Emma sighed. "What I have to put up with. Last night at dinner, Mr. Personality dropped off to sleep in the middle of the dessert course. I'm pouring my heart out about Maxim's[7] and the ballet, and out of the blue I hear snoring."

"It's O.K., darling. I'm here now," Kugelmass said, embracing her. I've earned this, he thought, smelling Emma's French perfume and burying his nose in her hair. I've suffered enough. I've paid enough analysts. I've searched till I'm weary. She's young and nubile, and I'm here a few pages after Léon and just before Rodolphe. By showing up during the correct chapters, I've got the situation knocked.

Emma, to be sure, was just as happy as Kugelmass. She had been starved for excitement, and his tales of Broadway night life, of fast cars and Hollywood and TV stars, enthralled the young French beauty.

"Tell me again about O.J. Simpson," she implored that evening, as she and Kugelmass strolled past Abbé Bournisien's church.

"What can I say? The man is great. He sets all kinds of rushing records. Such moves. They can't touch him."

"And the Academy Awards?" Emma said wistfully. "I'd give anything to win one."

"First you've got to be nominated."

"I know. You explained it. But I'm convinced I can act. Of course, I'd want to take a class or two. With Strasberg[8] maybe. Then, if I had the right agent"—

"We'll see, we'll see. I'll speak to Persky."

That night, safely returned to Persky's flat, Kugelmass brought up the idea of having Emma visit him in the big city.

"Let me think about it," Persky said. "Maybe I could work it. Stranger things have happened." Of course, neither of them could think of one.

"Where the hell do you go all the time?" Daphne Kugelmass barked at her husband as he returned home late that evening. "You got a chippie stashed somewhere?"

"Yeah, sure, I'm just the type," Kugelmass said wearily. "I was with Leonard Popkin. We were discussing Socialist agriculture in Poland. You know Popkin. He's a freak on the subject."

"Well, you've been very odd lately," Daphne said. "Distant. Just don't forget about my father's birthday. On Saturday?"

"Oh, sure, sure," Kugelmass said, heading for the bathroom.

7. Fashionable Paris restaurant. 8. Lee Strasberg's acting school taught the natural acting style known as "The Method" to such stars as Marlon Brando.

"My whole family will be there. We can see the twins. And Cousin Hamish. You should be more polite to Cousin Hamish—he likes you."

"Right, the twins," Kugelmass said, closing the bathroom door and shutting out the sound of his wife's voice. He leaned against it and took a deep breath. In a few hours, he told himself, he would be back in Yonville again, back with his beloved. And this time, if all went well, he would bring Emma back with him.

At three-fifteen the following afternoon, Persky worked his wizardry again. Kugelmass appeared before Emma, smiling and eager. The two spent a few hours at Yonville with Binet and then remounted the Bovary carriage. Following Persky's instructions, they held each other tightly, closed their eyes, and counted to ten. When they opened them, the carriage was just drawing up at the side door of the Plaza Hotel, where Kugelmass had optimistically reserved a suite earlier in the day.

"I love it! It's everything I dreamed it would be," Emma said as she swirled joyously around the bedroom, surveying the city from their window. "There's F.A.O. Schwarz.[9] And there's Central Park, and the Sherry[1] is which one? Oh, there—I see. It's too divine."

On the bed there were boxes from Halston and Saint Laurent.[2] Emma 95
unwrapped a package and held up a pair of black velvet pants against her perfect body.

"The slacks suit is by Ralph Lauren," Kugelmass said. "You'll look like a million bucks in it. Come on, sugar, give us a kiss."

"I've never been so happy!" Emma squealed as she stood before the mirror. "Let's go out on the town. I want to see 'Chorus Line' and the Guggenheim and this Jack Nicholson character you always talk about. Are any of his flicks showing?"

"I cannot get my mind around this," a Stanford professor said. "First a strange character named Kugelmass, and now she's gone from the book. Well, I guess the mark of a classic is that you can reread it a thousand times and always find something new."

The lovers passed a blissful weekend. Kugelmass had told Daphne he would be away at a symposium in Boston and would return Monday. Savoring each moment, he and Emma went to the movies, had dinner in Chinatown, passed two hours at a discothèque, and went to bed with a TV movie. They slept till noon on Sunday, visited SoHo, and ogled celebrities at Elaine's.[3] They had caviar and champagne in their suite on Sunday night and talked until dawn. That morning, in the cab taking them to Persky's apartment, Kugelmass thought, It was hectic, but worth it. I can't bring her here too often, but now and then it will be a charming contrast with Yonville.

At Persky's, Emma climbed into the cabinet, arranged her new boxes of 100
clothes neatly around her, and kissed Kugelmass fondly. "My place next time,"

9. Well-known toy store. 1. Sherry-Netherland Hotel, also in Central Park area. 2. Famous and expensive fashion designers and couturiers, as is Ralph Lauren, below. 3. SoHo is the center of the contemporary art scene south of Greenwich Village. Elaine's restaurant is frequented by publishing and newspaper notables.

she said with a wink. Persky rapped three times on the cabinet. Nothing happened.

"Hmm," Persky said, scratching his head. He rapped again, but still no magic. "something must be wrong," he mumbled.

"Persky, you're joking!" Kugelmass cried. "How can it not work?"

"Relax, relax. Are you still in the box, Emma?"

"Yes."

Persky rapped again—harder this time.

"I'm still here, Persky."

"I know, darling. Sit tight."

"Persky, we *have* to get her back," Kugelmass whispered. "I'm a married man, and I have a class in three hours. I'm not prepared for anything more than a cautious affair at this point."

"I can't understand it," Persky muttered. "It's such a reliable little trick."

But he could do nothing. "It's going to take a little while," he said to Kugelmass. "I'm going to have to strip it down. I'll call you later."

Kugelmass bundled Emma into a cab and took her back to the Plaza. He barely made it to his class on time. He was on the phone all day, to Persky and to his mistress. The magician told him it might be several days before he got to the bottom of the trouble.

"How was the symposium?" Daphne asked him that night.

"Fine, fine," he said, lighting the filter end of a cigarette.

"What's wrong? You're as tense as a cat."

"Me? Ha, that's a laugh. I'm as calm as a summer night. I'm just going to take a walk." He eased out the door, hailed a cab, and flew to the Plaza.

"This is no good," Emma said. "Charles will miss me."

"Bear with me, sugar," Kugelmass said. He was pale and sweaty. He kissed her again, raced to the elevators, yelled at Persky over a pay phone in the Plaza lobby, and just made it home before midnight.

"According to Popkin, barley prices in Kraków have not been this stable since 1971," he said to Daphne, and smiled wanly as he climbed into bed.

The whole week went by like that. On Friday night, Kugelmass told Daphne there was another symposium he had to catch, this one in Syracuse. He hurried back to the Plaza, but the second weekend there was nothing like the first. "Get me back into the novel or marry me," Emma told Kugelmass. "Meanwhile, I want to get a job or go to class, because watching TV all day is the pits."

"Fine. We can use the money," Kugelmass said. "You consume twice your weight in room service."

"I met an Off Broadway producer in Central Park yesterday, and he said I might be right for a project he's doing," Emma said.

"Who is this clown?" Kugelmass asked.

"He's not a clown. He's sensitive and kind and cute. His name's Jeff Something-or-Other, and he's up for a Tony."[4]

4. A theater award, comparable to an Oscar.

Later that afternoon, Kugelmass showed up at Persky's drunk.

"Relax," Persky told him. "You'll get a coronary."

"Relax. The man says relax. I've got a fictional character stashed in a hotel room, and I think my wife is having me tailed by a private shamus."

"O.K., O.K. We know there's a problem." Persky crawled under the cabinet and started banging on something with a large wrench.

"I'm like a wild animal," Kugelmass went on. "I'm sneaking around town, and Emma and I have had it up to here with each other. Not to mention a hotel tab that reads like the defense budget."

"So what should I do? This is the world of magic," Persky said. "It's all nuance."

"Nuance, my foot. I'm pouring Dom Pérignon and black eggs[5] into this little mouse, plus her wardrobe, plus she's enrolled at the Neighborhood Playhouse and suddenly needs professional photos. Also, Persky, Professor Fivish Kopkind, who teaches Comp Lit and who has always been jealous of me, has identified me as the sporadically appearing character in the Flaubert book. He's threatened to go to Daphne. I see ruin and alimony jail. For adultery with Madame Bovary, my wife will reduce me to beggary."

"What do you want me to say? I'm working on it night and day. As far as your personal anxiety goes, that I can't help you with. I'm a magician, not an analyst."

By Sunday afternoon, Emma had locked herself in the bathroom and refused to respond to Kugelmass's entreaties. Kugelmass stared out the window at the Wollman Rink[6] and contemplated suicide. Too bad this is a low floor, he thought, or I'd do it right now. Maybe if I ran away to Europe and started life over . . . Maybe I could sell the *International Herald Tribune*, like those young girls used to.[7]

The phone rang. Kugelmass lifted it to his ear mechanically.

"Bring her over," Persky said. "I think I got the bugs out of it."

Kugelmass's heart leaped. "You're serious?" he said. "You got it licked?"

"It was something in the transmission. Go figure."

"Persky, you're a genius. We'll be there in a minute. Less than a minute."

Again the lovers hurried to the magician's apartment, and again Emma Bovary climbed into the cabinet with her boxes. This time there was no kiss. Persky shut the doors, took a deep breath, and tapped the box three times. There was the reassuring popping noise, and when Persky peered inside, the box was empty. Madame Bovary was back in her novel. Kugelmass heaved a great sigh of relief and pumped the magician's hand.

"It's over," he said. "I learned my lesson. I'll never cheat again, I swear it." He pumped Persky's hand again and made a mental note to sent him a necktie.

Three weeks later, at the end of a beautiful spring afternoon, Persky answered his doorbell. It was Kugelmass, with a sheepish expression on his face.

5. An especially fine champagne and caviar. 6. Skating rink in Central Park. 7. This was what some American dropouts of the 1950s did; Jean Seberg portrayed one in the 1959 film *Breathless*.

"O.K., Kugelmass," the magician said. "Where to this time?"

"It's just this once," Kugelmass said. "The weather is so lovely, and I'm not getting any younger. Listen, you've read 'Portnoy's Complaint'? Remember The Monkey?"[8]

"The price is now twenty-five dollars, because the cost of living is up, but I'll start you off with one freebie, due to all the trouble I caused you."

"You're good people," Kugelmass said, combing his few remaining hairs as he climbed into the cabinet again. "This'll work all right?"

"I hope. But I haven't tried it much since all that unpleasantness."

"Sex and romance," Kugelmass said from inside the box. "What we go through for a pretty face."

Persky tossed in a copy of "Portnoy's Complaint" and rapped three times on the box. This time, instead of a popping noise there was a dull explosion, followed by a series of crackling noises and a shower of sparks. Persky leaped back, was seized by a heart attack, and dropped dead. The cabinet burst into flames, and eventually the entire house burned down.

Kugelmass, unaware of this catastrophe, had his own problems. He had not been thrust into "Portnoy's Complaint," or into any other novel, for that matter. He had been projected into an old textbook, "Remedial Spanish" and was running for his life over a barren, rocky terrain as the word "*tener*" ("to have")—a large and hairy irregular verb—raced after him on its spindly legs.

p. 1977

LUISA VALENZUELA

The Redtown Chronicles[1]

I. Littleherb

He arrived in this no-man's town shouldering his bundle. He was tired of towns that belonged to someone, to the others.

The first thing he did was write his name on a rock: one way among many to assert himself and avenge himself on stones. They had made him suffer enough—stones, that is—especially when thrown in his face by unknown hands. The stones' fault? No, of course not. But stone he was familiar with and could avenge himself on confidently, whereas the hand that does the throwing is always anonymous. There are too many anonymous hands in the world, though few shameless enough to throw stones at him, who is usually so unobtrusive.

In this town, luckily, no hands, no feet, nothing human; only red sand, red stone; a town indistinguishable from the mountains and abandoned for years.

"Hello," was the first thing he said to the town in general, but most particu-

8. The leading character in Philip Roth's 1969 novel, The Monkey is less romantic than Flaubert's Emma Bovary and more sexually carefree and . . . experimental.

1. Translated by Christopher Leland

larly to one house there on the left, which appeared the coziest. Or at least, the most intact: walls of red stone, the color of the earth, and an absolute, spacious rooflessness that allowed him to see stars in a new, nonmetaphorical way. He dragged his bundle into that new home and settled in. He unrolled his sleeping bag and pulled out his little burner and pot, his gourd and his sipper.

Stingily preparing his maté, he said to himself: "Here I am." And he had never been so much there as in this town that belonged to no one, that was his alone.

The maté had a different flavor, though it was made with the herb from the towns where they had stoned him. He had little left. Littleherb, he called himself, which sounded much sweeter to him than his old name, now abandoned forever on that rock on the outskirts of town.

Stripped of his name, with only Littleherb to cover him, he felt much better—relieved, more in tune with the air of the town. He put more wood on the fire he had built, making a huge blaze inside the house, and he was glad there was neither roof nor door nor anything else combustible around.

Next morning he made a trip through the town, taking possession of places by putting up signs. With that in mind, he had not burned the wood that seemed most likely to be useful, planks on which he could write (for example) "Sheriff's Office" or "Hotel," "Church" or "Town Hall."

But the following day, the sun's first rays hadn't even waked him when the Indians, come down from the highlands, did. He saw them, a stain of color on the red town in their ponchos with geometric designs. To speak with him, they respectfully removed their hats.

"Pardon us, sir, but you can't build a fire here. There can be no life in this town."

"Why not?" he asked, astonished.

And they replied: "Because this is a dead town."

And he had to accept that, whether he liked it or not, because they refused to say anymore and, turning away, left him with that gentle advice that was almost a threat.

"Dead town, my ass," he said to himself. He mumbled a number of other things as he went from door to door nailing up his signs with growing enthusiasm, as if he were resuscitating the town. The noise of hammering made the adobe ring in a new way, and the old walls waggled like the tail of a grateful dog. Later, with the houses marked—posted—it was as if there were people around. "Bakery"—just imagine, there among the rocks—"General Store." "Saloon." "Jail" he never put up, it was too painful for him.

Littleherb went into each building—some almost completely in ruins—and went through a private ritual: "Do come in, ma'am," he would say to a passing breeze, "we have the best merchandise in these parts. What was it you were looking for?"

Dead town. Ha! He, Littleherb, knew it wasn't Deadtown. No! Redtown. Vital, radiant there in the sunshine. A little dry, true. Like the skin of a snake, which was the only animal he had seen during his long wanderings through the town. Not a bird. Not an ant. Nothing. So much the better, he said to himself, no need to worry about spiders crawling into his sleeping bag. But it wasn't very pleasant to find himself like that, with no company at all. A nothing town with nobody in it, only a tiny stream that ran some distance away, without even a fish in the water.

Littleherb was counting on the Indians to help him get a bit of food, but after that first day, they did not come down again. Occasionally, at night, Littleherb thought he heard their voices descending from on high: "Dead town! Dead town!" But they did not venture into the valley.

And Littleherb, involved in reviving the town, didn't notice how he was beginning to resemble it: red and dry. Red from the dust that settled into his pores; dry from that unforgiving sun. Poor Littleherb. He was Hardly-any-herb these days. Just stubble. Still and all, he continued drinking his maté, each time a little weaker, and thus passed days that seemed years to him, as he learned to be happy for long periods. He finally came to know how to lean quietly against an adobe wall and allow happiness slowly to infuse him. Happy while he contemplated the distinct tones of the red mountains or when he put up new and fantastic signs: "Dreameria," "Rainbow Shop," "Bordello de luxe," "Pink Corner." Happy as he wandered down those deserted desert streets. He didn't even hear the shouts of "dead town" that those up above cast down on him, or he thought they cast down. Shouts, after all, don't hurt, do they? Not like the stones he had been pelted with when he passed through living towns with his angelic, irritating air.

He wandered through the red town posting signs, and one night he slept in the town hall, and the next in the general store, the bordello, or the bakery. Happy each night, happy in his days of sign-posting, a happiness ever more solid, even if he was running out of paint.

Just as the last of his supplies were tap-dancing on the bottom of the basket he carried, he reached the far edge of town and found himself before a vast field sown with crosses. With all his accumulated happiness, he wrote "Cemetery" and sat down to wait. Peacefully.

II. Littleherb and the Infidels

Afterward came the time when the Indians tried to save Littleherb. They succeeded only in prolonging his life a bit, a few years at most, not much reckoned against the mountains.

Littleherb did not thank them, letting resignation lick the wounds of his soul. (Stupid Indians. Completely acculturated, having forgotten the secrets of their race, not knowing what constitutes the final self-realization, the ultimate, most profound surrender.)

They had been watching him from above, and only deigned to go down to him when they saw him fall after two days of standing guard at the old cemetery. Up to then, he had remained erect, casting shade like a tree. They went to rescue him even though they did not approve of his way of disturbing the peace of Deadtown—little signs all over the place! For what? Signs they couldn't read, but which nonetheless restored its proper name to each building, putting each in its place. Now nobody would forget. They, at least, would not forget, and to better remember—to better recount it all to coming generations—they descended a second time to Deadtown to bear the man to the heights, to those windy plateaus where their grandparents had settled.

The stranger was brought up unconscious, not much of a burden to carry up the craggy slope. It was like rescuing a stray sheep, a lost animal, and returning it to the heights.

When he first opened his eyes, Littleherb saw an eagle fly by and said to himself: "I'm dead. If there's something alive, it must mean I'm dead, because in this town there is absolutely nothing."

When he heard voices, he hadn't the slightest doubt, and when he was asked, "What is your name?" he replied, "Littleherb," since that was how he wanted to figure in the register of souls.

The name Littleherb sounded familiar to the Indians, and they decided this fellow with the kind eyes must be one of them, in spite of his beard. They gave him something to eat—an activity Littleherb had almost forgotten—and bathed him, more to get the stink of Deadtown off him than to clean him up.

After this, they took him to the shrine of Fewfleas, and Littleherb had no choice but to fall in love with the young shaman. She was like that: she had dazzling eyes. Dozens of lynx eyes, cleverly preserved, were arranged in an arc over her altar. The eyes formed a halo around Fewfleas, and Littleherb couldn't help but love her for her eyes.

When he was a bit fatter and somewhat recuperated, they were married most intimately, blessed by the winds.

The tenderness of Littleherb—who had achieved happiness and now needed nothing more—made Fewfleas forget some of her divinity and transformed her into the best of wives, two facts that cost her many subjects.

Within Littleherb, meanwhile, guilt began to blossom, growing and growing there high in the mountains till it reached the point that guilt almost sent him tumbling down the slope, back to Deadtown.

He took to spending long hours on the lip of the chasm, looking toward where Deadtown, Redtown, *His*town stood. But it was impossible, at that distance, to make it out. Because of its color and materials, it vanished into the landscape. Finally, as his own eyes were insufficient, he brought out to the cliff's edge the arc of lynx eyes from the altar of Fewfleas.

At night, the eyes served as tiny reflectors, and it was as if the invisible town was lit by thousands of fireflies. So Littleherb could locate exactly where he had christened every house.

Fewfleas, good wife to the end, came to fetch him when it got too late, and for a while would stand in wonder at the fireflies of the town. But only for a while. It seemed unwise to openly applaud other people's miracles.

Fewfleas wasn't the only one to wonder at the tiny, green lights that the lynx eyes seemed to project over Deadtown. Little by little, the whole tribe knew about the miracle and ended up clumped around Littleherb on the edge of the mountain.

Sometimes they had to forcefully restrain Littleherb, who wanted to launch himself head over heels to return to that peaceful felicity he had known in his adobe town. But more than the hands of the Indians, the voice of Fewfleas held him there, when she called him from their hut at that hour of a different joy, a moveable one.

While restraining Littleherb, the tribe embraced him, and finally came to worship him. That was the way Littleherb was: he awakened passions without wanting to, like the hatred of those people who had thrown stones at him.

Passions come and go. As it turned out, the Indians up above came to adore him as a god from the regions of light. And he himself began to believe that his ascension had not been in vain and that, in some yet unknowable way, he ought to return to the infidels what they had forgotten down in Redtown.

III. The Second Founding of Redtown

The Indians eventually took Littleherb for an oracle. Fewfleas dictated the words in his ear, and all he had to do was repeat them with great feeling, appending to each prophecy: "Happiness lies below in Redtown, Belletown, Towntown."

Fewfleas pinched him subtly to make him shut up, afraid the others might discover the subterfuge, now that the only thing her husband wanted, sickened by the highland winds, was to descend. But everyone looked upon him goggle-eyed, and thanks to the lights of Deadtown, they were even inclined to believe his words. He did work, it must be admitted, a certain number of miraculous cures by the laying on of hands, and he gave good counsel to the confused. In the end, one fine day, the Indians decided to undertake the journey down, bearing him along in a litter crowned with the halo of lynx eyes. First went the goats, as if opening up the road, then the pigs and the first men, single file, carrying cages of chickens. Admittedly, there was wisdom in all this: the animals knew how to choose the best path. It was not an easy descent. Surely not, hanging from the rocks! But still they went, singing and playing the flute from stone to stone, sometimes slipping right to the edge of the abyss.

They arrived at the end of an exhausting day's travel. After looking around a bit, they understood the mystery of the celebrated fireflies—nothing more than the sparkling, on moonlit nights, of the phosphorescent paint Littleherb had happened to use to make the signs. But the Indians chose not to investigate further, to leave things as they were.

They did, however, worship the rock on the outskirts of town. There, boldly writ, was what they intuited to be Littleherb's secret name. In a gesture of real affection, he took a piece of coal and added, "And Fewfleas," and drew a heart with an arrow, which the Indians interpreted as a sign of good omen. They entered the town singing so loudly that the adobe walls began to tremble. Finally, on one particularly high note, the walls tumbled down thunderously in an ugly cloud of dust.

At first panic reigned, but then the collapse gave rise to considerable mirth. Littleherb was the only one who failed to see much comedy in it: his poor town reduced to rubble. And when the children began to play war with shards of adobe, he feared getting a piece in the face as in other, unfortunate times. But no, there were no attacks here where everyone adored him, and after a while, he decided to see the positive side of the disaster: that no-place town had been his alone; the new town they would build would be of stone, more resilient.

They chose the most appropriate color of stone for each house—red for the distinguished, pinkest for those of pleasure. The house of Littleherb and Fewfleas was nearly crimson and Fewfleas began to recover her various dignities, even the arc of eyes. Littleherb ceded them to her with no regrets, as she had once ceded them to him. And he found much more to his liking the role of living god than that of miracle worker.

He took to sitting in the afternoons on the rock inscribed with his old name. Gazing west, he could recapture bits of that happiness he had known before.

He still played—perfectly, constantly—the part of a god, so deeply had he imbibed the idea. It wasn't for nothing that he had been born, suffered, and thought, and had come to the point of giving up there by the cemetery. He never returned there, and didn't much want to. His rock was enough. And he really did seem a god, sitting on that stone cross-legged, a soft wind or the cry of a bird rustling his beard. He had such wise eyes. He knew so many things, though he never spoke them.

A select member of the tribe had the honor of handing him his maté, made with aromatic herbs. Sometimes the sipper clogged, and as he sipped it made little noises that everyone marveled at. But the greatest marvel occurred the day he decided to teach them all to read, and at last they could decipher the meaning of those signs they revered as relics.

Veneration reached its peak when the entire tribe finally read effortlessly. That was indeed a glorious day for everyone, except for Littleherb. From then on, he had to write ever more complicated texts. The Indians loudly demanded new reading material, and complained bitterly when it wasn't to their liking. For more than a year, Littleherb wrote tirelessly while the others went about their simple labors—tilling the earth, tending the animals, or bartering with distant tribes.

Poor Littleherb! He didn't even have time to watch the rebirth of his old Deadtown, his beloved Redtown, so tightly did writing hem him in. Till the day arrived when he had written for the Indians their entire history and that of their town and, feeling himself fulfilled, he resigned from his task.

He forever renounced being a living god and lapsed into the comfortable role of priest-consort. It's the kind of life we all envy now, as we spend our days writing him stories. Like this one.

1987

BOBBIE ANN MASON

Shiloh

Leroy Moffitt's wife, Norma Jean, is working on her pectorals. She lifts three-pound dumbbells to warm up, then progresses to a twenty-pound barbell. Standing with her legs apart, she reminds Leroy of Wonder Woman.

"I'd give anything if I could just get these muscles to where they're real hard," says Norma Jean. "Feel this arm. It's not as hard as the other one."

"That's cause you're right-handed," says Leroy, dodging as she swings the barbell in an arc.

"Do you think so?"

5 "Sure."

Leroy is a truckdriver. He injured his leg in a highway accident four months ago, and his physical therapy, which involves weights and a pulley, prompted Norma Jean to try building herself up. Now she is attending a body-building class. Leroy has been collecting temporary disability since his tractor-trailer jackknifed in Missouri, badly twisting his left leg in its socket. He has a steel pin in his hip. He will probably not be able to drive his rig again. It sits in the backyard, like a gigantic bird that has flown home to roost. Leroy has been home in Kentucky for three months, and his leg is almost healed, but the accident frightened him and he does not want to drive any more long hauls. He is not sure what to do next. In the meantime, he makes things from craft kits. He started by building a miniature log cabin from notched Popsicle sticks. He varnished it and placed it on the TV set, where it remains. It reminds him of a rustic Nativity scene. Then he tried string art (sailing ships on black velvet), a macramé owl kit, a snap-together B-17 Flying Fortress,[1] and a lamp made out of a model truck, with a light fixture screwed in the top of the cab. At first the kits were diversions, something to kill time, but now he is thinking about building a full-scale log house from a kit. It would be considerably cheaper than building a regular house, and besides, Leroy has grown to appreciate how things are put together. He has begun to realize that in all the years he was on the road he never took time to examine anything. He was always flying past scenery.

"They won't let you build a log cabin in any of the new subdivisions," Norma Jean tells him.

"They will if I tell them it's for you," he says, teasing her. Ever since they were married, he has promised Norma Jean he would build her a new home one day. They have always rented, and the house they live in is small and nondescript. It does not even feel like a home, Leroy realizes now.

Norma Jean works at the Rexall drugstore, and she has acquired an amazing amount of information about cosmetics. When she explains to Leroy the three stages of complexion care, involving creams, toners, and moisturizers, he thinks happily of other petroleum products—axle grease, diesel fuel. This is a connec-

1. World War II bomber.

tion between him and Norma Jean. Since he has been home, he has felt unusually tender about his wife and guilty over his long absences. But he can't tell what she feels about him. Norma Jean has never complained about his traveling; she has never made hurt remarks, like calling his truck a "widow-maker." He is reasonably certain she has been faithful to him, but he wishes she would celebrate his permanent homecoming more happily. Norma Jean is often startled to find Leroy at home, and he thinks she seems a little disappointed about it. Perhaps he reminds her too much of the early days of their marriage, before he went on the road. They had a child who died as an infant, years ago. They never speak about their memories of Randy, which have almost faded, but now that Leroy is home all the time, they sometimes feel awkward around each other, and Leroy wonders if one of them should mention the child. He has the feeling that they are waking up out of a dream together—that they must create a new marriage, start afresh. They are lucky they are still married. Leroy has read that for most people losing a child destroys the marriage—or else he heard this on *Donahue*. He can't always remember where he learns things anymore.

At Christmas, Leroy bought an electric organ for Norma Jean. She used to 10
play the piano when she was in high school. "It don't leave you," she told him once. "It's like riding a bicycle."

The new instrument had so many keys and buttons that she was bewildered by it at first. She touched the keys tentatively, pushed some buttons, then pecked out "Chopsticks." It came out in an amplified fox-trot rhythm, with marimba sounds.

"It's an orchestra!" she cried.

The organ had a pecan-look finish and eighteen preset chords, with optional flute, violin, trumpet, clarinet, and banjo accompaniments. Norma Jean mastered the organ almost immediately. At first she played Christmas songs. Then she bought *The Sixties Songbook* and learned every tune in it, adding variations to each with the rows of brightly colored buttons.

"I didn't like these old songs back then," she said. "But I have this crazy feeling I missed something."

"You didn't miss a thing," said Leroy. 15

Leroy likes to lie on the couch and smoke a joint and listen to Norma Jean play "Can't Take My Eyes Off You" and "I'll Be Back."[2] He is back again. After fifteen years on the road, he is finally settling down with the woman he loves. She is still pretty. Her skin is flawless. Her frosted curls resemble pencil trimmings.

Now that Leroy has come home to stay, he notices how much the town has changed. Subdivisions are spreading across western Kentucky like an oil slick. The sign at the edge of town says "Pop: 11,500"—only seven hundred more than it said twenty years before. Leroy can't figure out who is living in all the new houses. The farmers who used to gather around the courthouse square on Saturday afternoons to play checkers and spit tobacco juice have gone. It has been

2. 1960s hit songs.

years since Leroy has thought about the farmers, and they have disappeared without his noticing.

Leroy meets a kid named Stevie Hamilton in the parking lot at the new shopping center. While they pretend to be strangers meeting over a stalled car, Stevie tosses an ounce of marijuana under the front seat of Leroy's car. Stevie is wearing orange jogging shoes and a T-shirt that says CHATTAHOOCHEE SUPER-RAT. His father is a prominent doctor who lives in one of the expensive subdivisons in a new white-columned brick house that looks like a funeral parlor. In the phone book under his name there is a separate number, with the listing "Teenagers."

"Where do you get this stuff?" asks Leroy. "From your pappy!"

"That's for me to know and you to find out," Stevie says. He is slit-eyed and skinny.

"What else you got?"

"What you interested in?'

"Nothing special. Just wondered."

Leroy used to take speed on the road. Now he has to go slowly. He needs to be mellow. He leans back against the car and says, "I'm aiming to build me a log house, soon as I get time. My wife, though, I don't think she likes the idea."

"Well, let me know when you want me again," Stevie says. He has a cigarette in his cupped palm, as though sheltering it from the wind. He takes a long drag, then stomps it on the asphalt and slouches away.

Stevie's father was two years ahead of Leroy in high school. Leroy is thirty-four. He married Norma Jean when they were both eighteen, and their child Randy was born a few months later, but he died at the age of four months and three days. He would be about Stevie's age now. Norma Jean and Leroy were at the drive-in, watching a double feature *(Dr. Strangelove* and *Lover Come Back)*,[3] and the baby was sleeping in the back seat. When the first movie ended, the baby was dead. It was the sudden infant death syndrome. Leroy remembers handing Randy to a nurse at the emergency room, as though he were offering her a large doll as a present. A dead baby feels like a sack of flour. "It just happens sometimes," said the doctor, in what Leroy always recalls as a nonchalant tone. Leroy can hardly remember the child anymore, but he still sees vividly a scene from *Dr. Strangelove* in which the President of the United States was talking in a folksy voice on the hot line to the Soviet premier about the bomber accidentally headed toward Russia. He was in the War Room, and the world map was lit up. Leroy remembers Norma Jean catatonically beside him in the hospital and himself thinking: Who is this strange girl? He had forgotten who she was. Now scientists are saying that crib death is caused by a virus. Nobody knows anything, Leroy thinks. The answers are always changing.

When Leroy gets home from the shopping center, Norma Jean's mother, Mabel Beasley, is there. Until this year, Leroy has not realized how much time she spends with Norma Jean. When she visits, she inspects the closets and then

3. A 1963 satire on nuclear war and a 1961 Rock Hudson–Doris Day romantic comedy satirizing the advertising business.

the plants, informing Norma Jean when a plant is droopy or yellow. Mabel calls the plants "flowers," although there are never any blooms. She always notices if Norma Jean's laundry is piling up. Mabel is a short, overweight woman whose tight, brown-dyed curls look more like a wig than the actual wig she sometimes wears. Today she has brought Norma Jean an off-white dust ruffle she made for the bed; Mabel works in a custom-upholstery shop.

"This is the tenth one I made this year," Mabel says. "I got started and couldn't stop."

"It's real pretty," says Norma Jean.

"Now we can hide things under the bed," says Leroy, who gets along with his mother-in-law primarily by joking with her. Mabel has never really forgiven him for disgracing her by getting Norma Jean pregnant. When the baby died, she said that fate was mocking her.

"What's that thing?" Mabel says to Leroy in a loud voice, pointing to a tangle of yarn on a piece of canvas.

Leroy holds it up for Mabel to see. "It's my needlepoint," he explains. "This is a *Star Trek* pillow cover."

"That's what a woman would do," says Mabel. "Great day in the morning!"

"All the big football players on TV do it," he says.

"Why, Leroy, you're always trying to fool me. I don't believe you for one minute. You don't know what to do with yourself—that's the whole trouble. Sewing!"

"I'm aiming to build us a log house," says Leroy. "Soon as my plans come."

"Like *heck* you are," says Norma Jean. She takes Leroy's needlepoint and shoves it into a drawer. "You have to find a job first. Nobody can afford to build now anyway."

Mabel straightens her girdle and says, "I still think before you get tied down y'all ought to take a little run to Shiloh."

"One of these days, Mama," Norma Jean says impatiently.

Mabel is talking about Shiloh, Tennessee. For the past few years, she has been urging Leroy and Norma Jean to visit the Civil War battleground there.[4] Mabel went there on her honeymoon—the only real trip she ever took. Her husband died of a perforated ulcer when Norma Jean was ten, but Mabel, who was accepted into the United Daughters of the Confederacy in 1975, is still preoccupied with going back to Shiloh.

"I've been to kingdom come and back in that truck out yonder," Leroy says to Mabel, "but we never yet set foot in that battleground. Ain't that something? How did I miss it?"

"It's not even that far," Mabel says.

After Mabel leaves, Norma Jean reads to Leroy from a list she has made. "Thing you could do," she announces. "You could get a job as a guard at Union Carbide, where they'd let you set on a stool. You could get on at the lumberyard.

4. Where, in April 1862, more than 23,000 troops of the North and South, one-quarter of those who fought there, died. This was the first real indication of how bitter and bloody the war was to be. General Ulysses S. Grant, when reinforcements arrived, drove the Confederate forces, which had gained an initial victory by a surprise attack, back to their base in Corinth, Mississippi.

You could do a little carpenter work, if you want to build so bad. You could—"

"I can't do something where I'd have to stand up all day."

"You ought to try standing up all day behind a cosmetics counter. It's amazing that I have strong feet, coming from two parents that never had strong feet at all." At the moment Norma Jean is holding on to the kitchen counter, raising her knees one at a time as she talks. She is wearing two-pound ankle weights.

"Don't worry," says Leroy. "I'll do something."

"You could truck calves to slaughter for somebody. You wouldn't have to drive any big old truck for that."

"I'm going to build you this house," says Leroy. "I want to make you a real home."

"I don't want to live in any log cabin."

"It's not a cabin. It's a house."

"I don't care. It looks like a cabin."

"You and me together could lift those logs. It's just like lifting weights."

Norma Jean doesn't answer. Under her breath, she is counting. Now she is marching through the kitchen. She is doing goose steps.

Before his accident, when Leroy came home he used to stay in the house with Norma Jean, watching TV in bed and playing cards. She would cook fried chicken, picnic ham, chocolate pie—all his favorites. Now he is home alone much of the time. In the mornings, Norma Jean disappears, leaving a cooling place in the bed. She eats a cereal called Body Buddies, and she leaves the bowl on the table, with soggy tan balls floating in a milk puddle. He sees things about Norma Jean that he never realized before. When she chops onions, she stares off into a corner, as if she can't bear to look. She puts on her house slippers almost precisely at nine o'clock every evening and nudges her jogging shoes under the couch. She saves bread heels for the birds. Leroy watches the birds at the feeder. He notices the peculiar way goldfinches fly past the window. They close their wings, then fall, then spread their wings to catch and lift themselves. He wonders if they close their eyes when they fall. Norma Jean closes her eyes when they are in bed. She wants the lights turned out. Even then, he is sure she closes her eyes.

He goes for long drives around town. He tends to drive a car rather carelessly. Power steering and an automatic shift make a car feel so small and inconsequential that his body is hardly involved in the driving process. His injured leg stretches out comfortably. Once or twice he has almost hit something, but even the prospect of an accident seems minor in a car. He cruises the new subdivisions, feeling like a criminal rehearsing for a robbery. Norma Jean is probably right about a log house being inappropriate here in the new subdivisions. All the houses look grand and complicated. They depress him.

One day when Leroy comes home from a drive he finds Norma Jean in tears. She is in the kitchen making a potato and mushroom-soup casserole, with grated-cheese topping. She is crying because her mother caught her smoking.

"I didn't hear her coming. I was standing here puffing away pretty as you please," Norma Jean says, wiping her eyes.

"I knew it would happen sooner or later," says Leroy, putting his arm around her.

"She don't know the meaning of the word 'knock,' " says Norma Jean. "It's a wonder she hadn't caught me years ago."

"Think of it this way," Leroy says. "What if she caught me with a joint?" 60

"You better not let her!" Norma Jean shrieks. "I'm warning you, Leroy Moffitt!"

"I'm just kidding. Here, play me a tune. That'll help you relax."

Norma Jean puts the casserole in the oven and sets the timer. Then she plays a ragtime tune, with horns and banjo, as Leroy lights up a joint and lies on the couch, laughing to himself about Mabel's catching him at it. He thinks of Stevie Hamilton—a doctor's son pushing grass. Everything is funny. The whole town seems crazy and small. He is reminded of Virgil Mathis, a boastful policeman Leroy used to shoot pool with. Virgil recently led a drug bust in a back room at a bowling alley, where he seized ten thousand dollars' worth of marijuana. The newspaper had a picture of him holding up the bags of grass and grinning widely. Right now, Leroy can imagine Virgil breaking down the door and arresting him with a lungful of smoke. Virgil would probably have been alerted to the scene because of all the racket Norma Jean is making. Now she sounds like a hard-rock band. Norma Jean is terrific. When she switches to a latin-rhythm version of "Sunshine Superman," Leroy hums along. Norma Jean's foot goes up and down, up and down.

"Well, what do you think?" Leroy says, when Norma Jean pauses to search through her music.

"What do I think about what?" 65

His mind has gone blank. Then he says, "I'll sell my rig and build us a house." That wasn't what he wanted to say. He wanted to know what she thought—what she *really* thought—about them.

"Don't start in on that again," says Norma Jean. She begins playing "Who'll Be the Next in Line?"

Leroy used to tell hitchhikers his whole life story—about his travels, his hometown, the baby. He would end with a question: "Well, what do you think?" It was just a rhetorical question. In time, he had the feeling that he'd been telling the same story over and over to the same hitchhikers. He quit talking to hitchhikers when he realized how his voice sounded—whining and self-pitying, like some teenage-tragedy song. Now Leroy has the sudden impulse to tell Norma Jean about himself, as if he had just met her. They have known each other so long they have forgotten a lot about each other. They could become reacquainted. But when the oven timer goes off and she runs to the kitchen, he forgets why he wants to do this.

The next day, Mabel drops by. It is Saturday and Norma Jean is cleaning. Leroy is studying the plans of his log house, which have finally come in the mail. He has them spread out on the table—big sheets of stiff blue paper, with diagrams and numbers printed in white. While Norma Jean runs the vacuum, Mabel drinks coffee. She sets her coffee cup on a blueprint.

"I'm just waiting for time to pass," she says to Leroy, drumming her fingers on the table.

As soon as Norma Jean switches off the vacuum, Mabel says in a loud voice, "Did you hear about the datsun dog that killed the baby?"

Norma Jean says, "The word is 'dachshund.' "

"They put the dog on trial. It chewed the baby's legs off. The mother was in the next room all the time." She raises her voice. "They thought it was neglect."

Norma Jean is holding her ears. Leroy manages to open the refrigerator and get some Diet Pepsi to offer Mabel. Mabel still has some coffee and she waves away the Pepsi.

"Datsuns are like that," Mabel says. "They're jealous dogs. They'll tear a place to pieces if you don't keep an eye on them."

"You better watch out what you're saying, Mabel," says Leroy.

"Well, facts is facts."

Leroy looks out the window at his rig. It is like a huge piece of furniture gathering dust in the backyard. Pretty soon it will be an antique. He hears the vacuum cleaner. Norma Jean seems to be cleaning the living room rug again.

Later, she says to Leroy, "She just said that about the baby because she caught me smoking. She's trying to pay me back."

"What are you talking about?" Leroy says, nervously shuffling blueprints.

"You know good and well," Norma Jean says. She is sitting in a kitchen chair with her feet up and her arms wrapped around her knees. She looks small and helpless. She says, "The very idea, her bringing up a subject like that! Saying it was neglect."

"She didn't mean that," Leroy says.

"She might not have *thought* she meant it. She always says things like that. You don't know how she goes on."

"But she didn't really mean it. She was just talking."

Leroy opens a king-sized bottle of beer and pours it into two glasses, dividing it carefully. He hands a glass to Norma Jean and she takes it from him mechanically. For a long time, they sit by the kitchen window watching the birds at the feeder.

Something is happening. Norma Jean is going to night school. She has graduated from her six-week body-building course and now she is taking an adult-education course in composition at Paducah Community College. She spends her evenings outlining paragraphs.

"First you have a topic sentence," she explains to Leroy. "Then you divide it up. Your secondary topic has to be connected to your primary topic."

To Leroy, this sounds intimidating. "I never was any good in English," he says.

"It makes a lot of sense."

"What are you doing this for, anyhow?"

She shrugs. "It's something to do." She stands up and lifts her dumbbells a few times.

"Driving a rig, nobody cared about my English."

"I'm not criticizing your English."

Norma Jean used to say, "If I lose ten minutes' sleep, I just drag all day." Now she stays up late, writing compositions. She got a B on her first paper—a how-to theme on soup-based casseroles. Recently Norma Jean has been cooking unusual foods—tacos, lasagna, Bombay chicken. She doesn't play the organ anymore, though her second paper was called "Why Music Is Important to Me." She sits at the kitchen table, concentrating on her outlines, while Leroy plays with his log house plans, practicing with a set of Lincoln Logs. The thought of getting a truckload of notched, numbered logs scares him, and he wants to be prepared. As he and Norma Jean work together at the kitchen table, Leroy has the hopeful thought that they are sharing something, but he knows he is a fool to think this. Norma Jean is miles away. He knows he is going to lose her. Like Mabel, he is just waiting for time to pass.

One day, Mabel is there before Norma Jean gets home from work, and Leroy 95
finds himself confiding in her. Mabel, he realizes, must know Norma Jean better than he does.

"I don't know what's got into that girl," Mabel says. "She used to go to bed with the chickens. Now you say she's up all hours. Plus her a-smoking. I like to died."

"I want to make her this beautiful home," Leroy says, indicating the Lincoln Logs. "I don't think she even wants it. Maybe she was happier with me gone."

"She don't know what to make of you, coming home like this."

"Is that it?"

Mabel takes the roof off his Lincoln Log cabin. "You couldn't get *me* in a 100
log cabin," she says. "I was raised in one. It's no picnic, let me tell you."

"They're different now," says Leroy.

"I tell you what," Mabel says, smiling oddly at Leroy.

"What?"

"Take her on down to Shiloh. Y'all need to get out together, stir a little. Her brain's all balled up over them books."

Leroy can see traces of Norma Jean's features in her mother's face. Mabel's 105
face has the texture of crinkled cotton, but suddenly she looks pretty. It occurs to Leroy that Mabel has been hinting all along that she wants them to take her with them to Shiloh.

"Let's all go to Shiloh," he says. "You and me and her. Come Sunday."

Mabel throws up her hands in protest. "Oh, no, not me. Young folks want to be by theirselves."

When Norma Jean comes in with groceries, Leroy says excitedly, "Your mama here's been dying to go to Shiloh for thirty-five years. It's about time we went, don't you think?"

"I'm not going to butt in on anybody's second honeymoon," Mabel says.

"Who's going on a honeymoon, for Christ's sake?" Norma Jean says loudly. 110

"I never raised no daughter of mine to talk that-a-way," Mabel says.

"You ain't seen nothing yet," says Norma Jean. She starts putting away boxes and cans, slamming cabinet doors.

"There's a log cabin at Shiloh." Mabel says, "It was there during the battle. There's bullet holes in it."

"When are you going to *shut up* about Shiloh, Mama?" asks Norma Jean.

"I always thought Shiloh was the prettiest place, so full of history," Mabel goes on. "I just hoped y'all could see it once before I die, so you could tell me about it." Later, she whispers to Leroy, "You do what I said. A little change is what she needs."

"Your name means 'the king,' " Norma Jean says to Leroy that evening. He is trying to get her to go to Shiloh, and she is reading a book about another century.

"Well, I reckon I ought to be right proud."

"I guess so."

"Am I still king around here?"

Norma Jean flexes her biceps and feels them for hardness. "I'm not fooling around with anybody, if that's what you mean," she says.

"Would you tell me if you were?"

"I don't know."

"What does *your* name mean?"

"It was Marilyn Monroe's real name."

"No kidding!"

"Norma comes from the Normans. They were invaders," she says. She closes her book and looks hard at Leroy. "I'll go to Shiloh with you if you'll stop staring at me."

On Sunday, Norma Jean packs a picnic and they go to Shiloh. To Leroy's relief, Mabel says she does not want to come with them. Norma Jean drives, and Leroy, sitting beside her, feels like some boring hitchhiker she has picked up. He tries some conversation, but she answers him in monosyllables. At Shiloh, she drives aimlessly through the park, past bluffs and trails and steep ravines. Shiloh is an immense place, and Leroy cannot see it as a battleground. It is not what he expected. He thought it would look like a golf course. Monuments are everywhere, showing through the thick clusters of trees. Norma Jean passes the log cabin Mabel mentioned. It is surrounded by tourists looking for bullet holes.

"That's not the kind of log house I've got in mind," says Leroy apologetically.

"I know *that*."

"This is a pretty place. Your mama was right."

"It's O.K.," says Norma Jean. "Well, we've seen it. I hope she's satisfied."

They burst out laughing together.

At the park museum, a movie on Shiloh is shown every half hour, but they decide that they don't want to see it. They buy a souvenir Confederate flag for Mabel, and then they find a picnic spot near the cemetery. Norma Jean has brought a picnic cooler, with pimiento sandwiches, soft drinks, and Yodels. Leroy eats a sandwich and then smokes a joint, hiding it behind the picnic cooler. Norma Jean has quit smoking altogether. She is picking cake crumbs from the cellophane wrapper, like a fussy bird.

Leroy says, "So the boys in gray ended up in Corinth. The Union soldiers zapped 'em finally. April 7, 1862."

They both know that he doesn't know any history. He is just talking about some of the historical plaques they have read. He feels awkward, like a boy on a date with an older girl. They are still just making conversation.

"Corinth is where Mama eloped to," says Norma Jean.

They sit in silence and stare at the cemetery for the Union dead and, beyond, at a tall cluster of trees. Campers are parked nearby, bumper to bumper, and small children in bright clothing are cavorting and squealing. Norma Jean wads up the cake wrapper and squeezes it tightly in her hand. Without looking at Leroy, she says, "I want to leave you."

Leroy takes a bottle of Coke out of the cooler and flips off the cap. He holds the bottle poised near his mouth but cannot remember to take a drink. Finally he says, "No, you don't."

"Yes, I do."

"I won't let you."

"You can't stop me."

"Don't do me that way."

Leroy knows Norma Jean will have her own way. "Didn't I promise to be home from now on?" he says.

"In some ways, a woman prefers a man who wanders," says Norma Jean. "That sounds crazy, I know."

"You're not crazy."

Leroy remembers to drink from his Coke. Then he says, "Yes, you *are* crazy. You and me could start all over again. Right back at the beginning."

"We *have* started all over again," says Norma Jean. "And this is how it turned out."

"What did I do wrong?"

"Nothing."

"Is this one of those women's lib things?" Leroy asks.

"Don't be funny."

The cemetery, a green slope dotted with white markers, looks like a subdivision site. Leroy is trying to comprehend that his marriage is breaking up, but for some reason he is wondering about white slabs in a graveyard.

"Everything was fine till Mama caught me smoking," says Norma Jean, standing up. "That set something off."

"What are you talking about?"

"She won't leave me alone—*you* won't leave me alone." Norma Jean seems to be crying, but she is looking away from him. "I feel eighteen again. I can't face that all over again." She starts walking away. "No, it *wasn't* fine. I don't know what I'm saying. Forget it."

Leroy takes a lungful of smoke and closes his eyes as Norma Jean's words sink in. He tries to focus on the fact that thirty-five hundred soldiers died on the grounds around him. He can only think of that war as a board game with plastic soldiers. Leroy almost smiles, as he compares the Confederates' daring attack on the Union camps and Virgil Mathis's raid on the bowling alley. General Grant, drunk and furious, shoved the Southerners back to Corinth, where Mabel and Jet Beasley were married years later, when Mabel was still thin and good-looking. The next day, Mabel and Jet visited the battleground, and then Norma Jean was born, and then she married Leroy and they had a baby, which they lost, and now Leroy and Norma Jean are here at the same battleground. Leroy knows he is leaving out a lot. He is leaving out the insides of history. History was always just names and dates to him. It occurs to him that building a house out of logs is similarly empty—too simple. And the real inner workings of a marriage, like most of history, have escaped him. Now he sees that building a log house is the dumbest idea he could have had. It was clumsy of him to think Norma Jean would want a log house. It was a crazy idea. He'll have to think of something else, quickly. He will wad the blueprints into tight balls and fling them into the lake. Then he'll get moving again. He opens his eyes. Norma Jean has moved away and is walking through the cemetery, following a serpentine brick path.

Leroy gets up to follow his wife, but his good leg is asleep and his bad leg still hurts him. Norma Jean is far away, walking rapidly toward the bluff by the river, and he tries to hobble toward her. Some children run past him, screaming noisily. Norma Jean has reached the bluff, and she is looking out over the Tennessee River. Now she turns toward Leroy and waves her arms. Is she beckoning to him? She seems to be doing an exercise for her chest muscles. The sky is unusually pale—the color of the dust ruffle Mabel made for their bed.

1982

RICHARD FORD

Great Falls

This is not a happy story. I warn you.

My father was a man named Jack Russell, and when I was a young boy in my early teens, we lived with my mother in a house to the east of Great Falls, Montana, near the small town of Highwood and the Highwood Mountains and the Missouri River. It is a flat, treeless benchland there, all of it used for wheat farming, though my father was never a farmer, but was brought up near Tacoma, Washington, in a family that worked for Boeing.

He—my father—had been an Air Force sergeant and had taken his discharge in Great Falls. And instead of going home to Tacoma, where my mother wanted to go, he had taken a civilian's job with the Air Force, working on planes, which was what he liked to do. And he had rented the house out of town from a farmer who did not want it left standing empty.

The house itself is gone now—I have been to the spot. But the double row of Russian olive trees and two of the outbuildings are still standing in the milkweeds. It was a plain, two-story house with a porch on the front and no place for the cars. At the time, I rode the school bus to Great Falls every morning, and my father drove in while my mother stayed home.

5 My mother was a tall pretty woman, thin, with black hair and slightly sharp features that made her seem to smile when she wasn't smiling. She had grown up in Wallace, Idaho, and gone to college a year in Spokane, then moved out

to the coast, which is where she met Jack Russell. She was two years older than he was, and married him, she said to me, because he was young and wonderful looking, and because she thought they could leave the sticks and see the world together—which I suppose they did for a while. That was the life she wanted, even before she knew much about wanting anything else or about the future.

When my father wasn't working on airplanes, he was going hunting or fishing, two things he could do as well as anyone. He had learned to fish, he said, in Iceland, and to hunt ducks up on the DEW line—stations he had visited in the Air Force. And during the time of this—it was 1960—he began to take me with him on what he called his "expeditions." I thought even then, with as little as I knew, that these were opportunities other boys would dream of having but probably never would. And I don't think that I was wrong in that.

It is a true thing that my father did not know limits. In the spring, when we would go east to the Judith River Basin and camp up on the banks, he would catch a hundred fish in a weekend, and sometimes more than that. It was all he did from morning until night, and it was never hard for him. He used yellow corn kernels stacked onto a #4 snelled hook, and he would rattle this rig-up along the bottom of a deep pool below a split-shot sinker, and catch fish. And most of the time, because he knew the Judith River and knew how to feel his bait down deep, he would catch fish of good size.

It was the same with ducks, the other thing he liked. When the northern birds were down, usually by mid-October, he would take me and we would build a cattail and wheatstraw blind on one of the tule ponds or sloughs he knew about down the Missouri, where the water was shallow enough to wade. We would set out his decoys to the leeward side of our blind, and he would sprinkle corn on a hunger-line from the decoys to where we were. In the evenings when he came home from the base, we would go and sit out in the blind until the roosting fights came and put down among the decoys—there was never calling involved. And after a while, sometimes it would be an hour and full dark, the ducks would find the corn, and the whole raft of them—sixty, sometimes—would swim in to us. At the moment he judged they were close enough, my father would say to me, "Shine, Jackie," and I would stand and shine a seal-beam car light out onto the pond, and he would stand up beside me and shoot all the ducks that were there, on the water if he could, but flying and getting up as well. He owned a Model 11 Remington with a long-tube magazine that would hold ten shells, and with that many, and shooting straight over the surface rather than down onto it, he could kill or wound thirty ducks in twenty seconds' time. I remember distinctly the report of that gun and the flash of it over the water into the dark air, one shot after another, not even so fast, but measured in a way to hit as many as he could.

What my father did with the ducks he killed, and the fish, too, was sell them. It was against the law then to sell wild game, and it is against the law now. And though he kept some for us, most he would take—his fish laid on ice, or his ducks still wet and bagged in the burlap corn sacks—down to the Great Northern Hotel, which was still open then on Second Street in Great Falls, and sell them to the Negro caterer who bought them for his wealthy customers and for the dining car passengers who came through. We would drive in my father's Plymouth to the back of the hotel—always this was after dark—to a concrete loading ramp and lighted door that were close enough to the yards that I could sometimes see passenger trains waiting at the station, their car lights yellow and warm inside, the passengers dressed in suits, all bound for someplace far away from Montana—Milwaukee or Chicago or New York City, unimaginable places to me, a boy fourteen years old, with my father in the cold dark selling illegal game.

The caterer was a tall, stooped-back man in a white jacket, who my father called "Professor Ducks" or "Professor Fish," and the Professor referred to my father as "Sarge." He paid a quarter per pound for trout, a dime for whitefish, a dollar for a mallard duck, two for a speckle or a blue goose, and four dollars for a Canada. I have been with my father when he took away a hundred dollars for fish he'd caught and, in the fall, more than that for ducks and geese. When he had sold game in that way, we would drive out 10th Avenue and stop at a bar called The Mermaid which was by the air base, and he would drink with some friends he knew there, and they would laugh about hunting and fishing while I played pinball and wasted money in the jukebox.

It was on such a night as this that the unhappy things came about. It was in late October. I remember the time because Halloween had not been yet, and in the windows of the houses that I passed every day on the bus to Great Falls, people had put pumpkin lanterns, and set scarecrows in their yards in chairs.

My father and I had been shooting ducks in a slough on the Smith River, upstream from where it enters on the Missouri. He had killed thirty ducks, and we'd driven them down to the Great Northern and sold them there, though my father had kept two back in his corn sack. And when we had driven away, he suddenly said, "Jackie, let's us go back home tonight. Who cares about those hard-dicks at The Mermaid. I'll cook these ducks on the grill. We'll do something different tonight." He smiled at me in an odd way. This was not a thing he usually said, or the way he usually talked. He liked The Mermaid, and my mother—as far as I knew—didn't mind it if he went there.

"That sounds good," I said.

"We'll surprise your mother," he said. "We'll make her happy."

We drove out past the air base on Highway 87, past where there were planes taking off into the night. The darkness was dotted by the green and red beacons, and the tower light swept the sky and trapped planes as they disappeared over the flat landscape toward Canada or Alaska and the Pacific.

"Boy-oh-boy," my father said—just out of the dark. I looked at him and his eyes were narrow, and he seemed to be thinking about something. "You know, Jackie" he said, "your mother said something to me once I've never forgotten. She said, 'Nobody dies of a broken heart.' This was somewhat before you were born. We were living down in Texas and we'd had some big blow-up, and that was the idea she had. I don't know why." He shook his head.

He ran his hand under the seat, found a half-pint bottle of whiskey, and held it up to the lights of the car behind us to see what there was left of it. He unscrewed the cap and took a drink, then held the bottle out to me. "Have a drink, son," he said. "Something oughta be good in life." And I felt that something was wrong. Not because of the whiskey, which I had drunk before and he had reason to know about, but because of some sound in his voice, something I didn't recognize and did not know the importance of, though I was certain it was important.

I took a drink and gave the bottle back to him, holding the whiskey in my mouth until it stopped burning and I could swallow it a little at a time. When we turned out the road to Highwood, the lights of Great Falls sank below the horizon, and I could see the small white lights of farms, burning at wide distances in the dark.

"What do you worry about, Jackie," my father said. "Do you worry about girls? Do you worry about your future sex life? Is that some of it?" He glanced at me, then back at the road.

"I don't worry about that," I said. 20

"Well, what then?" my father said. "What else is there?"

"I worry if you're going to die before I do," I said, though I hated saying that, "or if Mother is. That worries me."

"It'd be a miracle if we didn't," my father said, with the half-pint held in the same hand he held the steering wheel. I had seen him drive that way before. "Things pass too fast in your life, Jackie. Don't worry about that. If I were you, I'd worry we might not." He smiled at me, and it was not the worried, nervous smile from before, but a smile that meant he was pleased. And I don't remember him ever smiling at me that way again.

We drove on out behind the town of Highwood and onto the flat field roads toward our house. I could see, out on the prairie, a moving light where the farmer who rented our house to us was disking his field for winter wheat. "He's waited too late with that business," my father said and took a drink, then threw the bottle right out the window. "He'll lose that," he said, "the cold'll kill it." I did not answer him, but what I thought was that my father knew nothing about farming, and if he was right it would be an accident. He knew about planes and hunting game, and that seemed all to me.

"I want to respect your privacy," he said then, for no reason at all that I 25
understood. I am not even certain he said it, only that it is in my memory that way. I don't know what he was thinking of. Just words. But I said to him, I remember well, "It's all right. Thank you."

We did not go straight out the Geraldine Road to our house. Instead my father went down another mile and turned, went a mile and turned back again so that we came home from the other direction. "I want to stop and listen now," he said. "The geese should be in the stubble." We stopped and he cut the lights and engine, and we opened the car windows and listened. It was eight o'clock at night and it was getting colder, though it was dry. But I could hear nothing, just the sound of air moving lightly through the cut field, and not a goose sound. Though I could smell the whiskey on my father's breath and on mine, could hear the motor ticking, could hear him breathe, hear the sound we made sitting side by side on the car seat, our clothes, our feet, almost our hearts beating. And I could see out in the night the yellow lights of our house, shining through the olive trees south of us like a ship on the sea. "I hear them, by God," my father said, his head stuck out the window. "But they're high up. They won't stop here now, Jackie. They're high flyers, those boys. Long gone geese."

There was a car parked off the road, down the line of wind-break trees, beside a steel thresher the farmer had left there to rust. You could see moonlight off the taillight chrome. It was a Pontiac, a two-door hard-top. My father said nothing about it and I didn't either, though I think now for different reasons.

The floodlight was on over the side door of our house and lights were on inside, upstairs and down. My mother had a pumpkin on the front porch, and the wind chime she had hung by the door was tinkling. My dog, Major, came out of the quonset shed and stood in the car lights when we drove up.

"Let's see what's happening here," my father said, opening the door and stepping out quickly. He looked at me inside the car, and his eyes were wide and his mouth drawn tight.

We walked in the side door and up the basement steps into the kitchen, and a man was standing there—a man I had never seen before, a young man with blond hair, who might've been twenty or twenty-five. He was tall and was wearing a short-sleeved shirt and beige slacks with pleats. He was on the other side of the breakfast table, his fingertips just touching the wooden tabletop. His blue eyes were on my father, who was dressed in hunting clothes.

"Hello," my father said.

"Hello," the young man said, and nothing else. And for some reason I looked at his arms, which were long and pale. They looked like a young man's arms, like my arms. His short sleeves had each been neatly rolled up, and I could see the bottom of a small green tattoo edging out from underneath. There was a glass of whiskey on the table, but no bottle.

"What's your name?" my father said, standing in the kitchen under the bright ceiling light. He sounded like he might be going to laugh.

"Woody," the young man said and cleared his throat. He looked at me, then he touched the glass of whiskey, just the rim of the glass. He wasn't nervous, I could tell that. He did not seem to be afraid of anything.

"Woody," my father said and looked at the glass of whiskey. He looked at me, then sighed and shook his head. "Where's Mrs. Russell, Woody? I guess you aren't robbing my house, are you?"

Woody smiled. "No," he said. "Upstairs. I think she went upstairs."

"Good," my father said, "that's a good place." And he walked straight out of the room, but came back and stood in the doorway. "Jackie, you and Woody step outside and wait on me. Just stay there and I'll come out." He looked at Woody then in a way I would not have liked him to look at me, a look that meant he was studying Woody. "I guess that's your car," he said.

"That Pontiac." Woody nodded.

"Okay. Right," my father said. Then he went out again and up the stairs. At that moment the phone started to ring in the living room, and I heard my mother say, "Who's that?" And my father say, "It's me. It's Jack." And I decided I wouldn't go answer the phone. Woody looked at me, and I understood he wasn't sure what to do. Run, maybe. But he didn't have run in him. Though I thought he would probably do what I said if I would say it.

"Let's just go outside," I said.

And he said, "All right."

Woody and I walked outside and stood in the light of the floodlamp above the side door. I had on my wool jacket, but Woody was cold and stood with his hands in him pockets, and his arms bare, moving from foot to foot. Inside, the phone was ringing again. Once I looked up and saw my mother come to the window and look down at Woody and me. Woody didn't look up or see her, but I did. I waved at her, and she waved back at me and smiled. She was wearing a powder-blue dress. In another minute the phone stopped ringing.

Woody took a cigarette out of his shirt pocket and lit it. Smoke shot through his nose into the cold air, and he sniffed, looked around the ground and threw his match on the gravel. His blond hair was combed backwards and neat on the sides, and I could smell his aftershave on him, a sweet, lemon smell. And for the first time I noticed his shoes. They were twotones, black with white tops and black laces. They stuck out below his baggy pants and were long and polished and shiny, as if he had been planning on a big occasion. They looked like shoes some country singer would wear, or a salesman. He was handsome, but only like someone you would see beside you in a dime store and not notice again.

"I like it out here," Woody said, his head down, looking at his shoes. "Nothing to bother you. I bet you'd see Chicago if the world was flat. The Great Plains commence here."

"I don't know," I said.

Woody looked up at me, cupping his smoke with one hand. "Do you play football?"

"No," I said. I thought about asking him something about my mother. But I had no idea what it would be.

"I *have* been drinking," Woody said, "but I'm not drunk now."

The wind rose then, and from behind the house I could hear Major bark once from far away, and I could smell the irrigation ditch, hear it hiss in the field. It ran down from Highwood Creek to the Missouri, twenty miles away. It was nothing Woody knew about, nothing he could hear or smell. He knew nothing about anything that was here. I heard my father say the words, "That's a real joke," from inside the house, then the sound of a drawer being opened and shut, and a door closing. Then nothing else.

Woody turned and looked into the dark toward where the glow of Great Falls rose on the horizon, and we both could see the flashing lights of a plane lowering to land there. "I once passed my brother in the Los Angeles airport and didn't even recognize him," Woody said, staring into the night. "He recognized *me*, though. He said, 'Hey, bro, are you mad at me, or what?' I wasn't mad at him. We both had to laugh."

Woody turned and looked at the house. His hands were still in his pockets, his cigarette clenched between his teeth, his arms taut. They were, I saw, bigger, stronger arms than I had thought. A vein went down the front of each of them.

I wondered what Woody knew that I didn't. Not about my mother—I didn't know anything about that and didn't want to—but about a lot of things, about the life out in the dark, about coming out here, about airports, even about me. He and I were not so far apart in age, I knew that. But Woody was one thing, and I was another. And I wondered how I would ever get to be like him, since it didn't necessarily seem so bad a thing to be.

"Did you know your mother was married before?" Woody said.

"Yes," I said. "I knew that."

"It happens to all of them, now," he said. "They can't wait to get divorced."

Woody dropped his cigarette into the gravel and toed it out with his black-and-white shoe. He looked up at me and smiled the way he had inside the house, a smile that said he knew something he wouldn't tell, a smile to make you feel bad because you weren't Woody and never could be.

It was then that my father came out of the house. He still had on his plaid hunting coat and his wool cap, but his face was as white as snow, as white as I have ever seen a human being's face to be. It was odd. I had the feeling that he might've fallen inside, because he looked roughed up, as though he had hurt himself somehow.

My mother came out the door behind him and stood in the floodlight at the top of the steps. She was wearing the powder-blue dress I'd seen through the window, a dress I had never seen her wear before, though she was also wearing a car coat and carrying a suitcase. She looked at me and shook her head in a way that only I was supposed to notice, as if it was not a good idea to talk now.

My father had his hands in his pockets, and he walked right up to Woody. He did not even look at me. "What do you do for a living?" he said, and he was very close to Woody. His coat was close enough to touch Woody's shirt.

"I'm in the Air Force," Woody said. He looked at me and then at my father. He could tell my father was excited.

"Is this your day off, then?" my father said. He moved even closer to Woody, his hands still in his pockets. He pushed Woody with his chest, and Woody seemed willing to let my father push him.

"No," he said, shaking his head.

I looked at my mother. She was just standing, watching. It was as if someone had given her an order, and she was obeying it. She did not smile at me, though I thought she was thinking about me, which made me feel strange.

"What's the matter with you?" my father said into Woody's face, right into his face—his voice tight, as if it had gotten hard for him to talk. "Whatever in the world is the matter with you? Don't you understand something?" My father took a revolver pistol out of his coat and put it up under Woody's chin, into the soft pocket behind the bone, so that Woody's whole face rose, but his arms stayed at his sides, his hands open. "I don't know what to do with you," my father said. "I don't have any idea what to do with you. I just don't." Though I thought that what he wanted to do was hold Woody there just like that until something important took place, or until he could simply forget about all this.

My father pulled the hammer back on the pistol and raised it tighter under Woody's chin, breathing into Woody's face—my mother in the light with her suitcase, watching them, and me watching them. A half a minute must've gone by.

And then my mother said, "Jack, let's stop now. Let's just stop."

My father stared into Woody's face as if he wanted Woody to consider doing something—moving or turning around or anything on his own to stop this—that my father would then put a stop to. My father's eyes grew narrowed, and his teeth were gritted together, his lips snarling up to resemble a smile. "You're crazy, aren't you?" he said. "You're a goddamned crazy man. Are you in love with her, too? Are you, crazy man? Are you? Do you say you love her? Say you love her! Say you love her so I can blow your fucking brains in the sky."

"All right," Woody said. "No. It's all right."

"He doesn't love me, Jack. For God's sake," my mother said. She seemed so calm. She shook her head at me again. I do not think she thought my father would shoot Woody. And I don't think Woody thought so. Nobody did, I think, except my father himself. But I think he did, and was trying to find out how to.

My father turned suddenly and glared at my mother, his eyes shiny and moving, but with the gun still on Woody's skin. I think he was afraid, afraid he was doing this wrong and could mess all of it up and make matters worse without accomplishing anything.

"You're leaving," he yelled at her. "That's why you're packed. Get out. Go on."

"Jackie has to be at school in the morning," my mother said in just her normal voice. And without another word to any one of us, she walked out of the floodlamp light carrying her bag, turned the corner at the front porch steps and disappeared toward the olive trees that ran in rows back into the wheat.

My father looked back at me where I was standing in the gravel, as if he expected to see me go with my mother toward Woody's car. But I hadn't thought about that—though later I would. Later I would think I should have gone with her, and that things between them might've been different. But that isn't how it happened.

"You're sure you're going to get away now, aren't you, mister?" my father said into Woody's face. He was crazy himself, then. Anyone would've been. Everything must have seemed out of hand to him.

"I'd like to," Woody said. "I'd like to get away from here."

"And I'd like to think of some way to hurt you," my father said and blinked his eyes. "I feel helpless about it." We all heard the door to Woody's car close in the dark. "Do you think that I'm a fool?" my father said.

"No," Woody said. "I don't think that."

"Do you think you're important?"

"No," Woody said. "I'm not."

My father blinked again. He seemed to be becoming someone else at that moment, someone I didn't know. "Where are you from?"

And Woody closed his eyes. He breathed in, then out, a long sigh. I was as if this was somehow the hardest part, something he hadn't expected to be asked to say.

"Chicago," Woody said. "A suburb of there."

"Are your parents alive?" my father said, all the time with his blue magnum pistol pushed under Woody's chin.

"Yes," Woody said. "Yessir."

85 "That's too bad," my father said. "Too bad they have to know what you are. I'm sure you stopped meaning anything to them a long time ago. I'm sure they both wish you were dead. You didn't know that. But I know it. I can't help them out, though. Somebody else'll have to kill you. I don't want to have to think about you anymore. I guess that's it."

My father brought the gun down to his side and stood looking at Woody. He did not back away, just stood, waiting for what I don't know to happen. Woody stood a moment, then he cut his eyes at me uncomfortably. And I know that I looked down. That's all I could do. Though I remember wondering if Woody's heart was broken and what any of this meant to him. Not to me, or my mother, or my father. But to him, since he seemed to be the one left out somehow, the one who would be lonely soon, the one who had done something he would someday wish he hadn't and would have no one to tell him that it was all right, that they forgave him, that these things happen in the world.

Woody took a step back, looked at my father and at me again as if he intended to speak, then stepped aside and walked away toward the front of our house, where the wind chime made a noise in the new cold air.

My father looked at me, his big pistol in his hand. "Does this seem stupid to you?" he said. "All this? Yelling and threatening and going nuts? I wouldn't blame you if it did. You shouldn't even see this. I'm sorry. I don't know what to do now."

"It'll be all right," I said. And I walked out to the road. Woody's car started up behind the olive trees. I stood and watched it back out, its red taillights clouded by exhaust. I could see their two heads inside, with the headlights shining behind them. When they got into the road, Woody touched his brakes, and for a moment I could see that they were talking, their heads turned toward each other, nodding. Woody's head and my mother's. They sat that way for a few seconds, then drove slowly off. And I wondered what they had to say to each other, something important enough that they had to stop right at that moment and say it. Did she say, *I love you?* Did she say, *This is not what I expected to happen?* Did she say, *This is what I've wanted all along?* and did he say, *I'm sorry for all this,* or *I'm glad,* or *None of this matters to me?* These are not the kinds of things you can know if you were not there. And I was not there and did not want to be. It did not seem like I should be there. I heard the door slam when my father went inside, and I turned back from the road where I could still see their taillights disappearing, and went back into the house where I was to be alone with my father.

90 Things seldom end in one event. In the morning I went to school on the bus as usual, and my father drove in to the air base in his car. We had not said very much about all that had happened. Harsh words, in a sense, are all alike. You can make them up yourself and be right. I think we both believed that we were in a fog we couldn't see through yet, though in a while, maybe not even a long while, we would see lights and know something.

In my third-period class that day a messenger brought a note for me that said I was excused from school at noon, and I should meet my mother at a motel down 10th Avenue South—a place not so far from my school—and we would eat lunch together.

It was a gray day in Great Falls that day. The leaves were off the trees and the mountains to the east of town were obscured by a low sky. The night before had been cold and clear, but today it seemed as if it would rain. It was the beginning of winter in earnest. In a few days there would be snow everywhere.

The motel where my mother was staying was called the Tropicana, and was beside the city golf course. There was a neon parrot on the sign out front, and the cabins made a U shape behind a little white office building. Only a couple of cars were parked in front of cabins, and no car was in front of my mother's cabin. I wondered if Woody would be here, or if he was at the air base. I wondered if my father would see him there, and what they would say.

I walked back to cabin 9. The door was open, though a DO NOT DISTURB sign was hung on the knob outside. I looked through the screen and saw my mother sitting on the bed alone. The television was on, but she was looking at me. She was wearing the powder-blue dress she had had on the night before. She was smiling at me, and I liked the way she looked at that moment, through the screen, in shadows. Her features did not seem as sharp as they had before. She looked comfortable where she was, and I felt like we were going to get along, no matter what had happened, and that I wasn't mad at her—that I had never been mad at her. 95

She sat forward and turned the television off. "Come in, Jackie," she said, and I opened the screen door and came inside. "It's the height of grandeur in here, isn't it?" My mother looked around the room. Her suitcase was open on the floor by the bathroom door, which I could see through and out the window onto the golf course, where three men were playing under the milky sky. "Privacy can be a burden, sometimes," she said, and reached down and put on her highheeled shoes. "I didn't sleep very well last night, did you?"

"No," I said, though I had slept all night. I wanted to ask her where Woody was, but it occurred to me at that moment that he was gone now and wouldn't be back, that she wasn't thinking in terms of him and didn't care where he was or ever would be.

"I'd like a nice compliment from you," she said. "Do you have one of those to spend?"

"Yes," I said. "I'm glad to see you."

"That's a nice one," she said and nodded. She had both her shoes on now. "Would you like to go have lunch? We can walk across the street to the cafeteria. You can get hot food." 100

"No" I said. "I'm not really hungry now."

"That's okay," she said and smiled at me again. And, as I said before, I liked the way she looked. She looked pretty in a way I didn't remember seeing her, as if something that had had a hold on her had let her go, and she could be different about things. Even about me.

"Sometimes, you know," she said, "I'll think about something I did. Just anything. Years ago in Idaho, or last week, even. And it's as if I'd read it. Like a story. Isn't that strange?"

"Yes," I said. And it did seem strange to me because I was certain then what the difference was between what had happened and what hadn't, and knew I always would be.

"Sometimes," she said, and she folded her hands in her lap and stared out the little side window of her cabin at the parking lot and the curving row of other cabins. "Sometimes I even have a moment when I completely forget what life's like. Just altogether." She smiled. "That's not so bad, finally. Maybe it's a disease I have. Do you think I'm just sick and I'll get well?"

"No. I don't know," I said. "Maybe. I hope so." I looked out the bathroom window and saw the three men walking down the golf course fairway carrying golf clubs.

"I'm not very good at sharing things right now," my mother said. "I'm sorry." She cleared her throat, and then she didn't say anything for almost a minute while I stood there. "I *will* answer anything you'd like me to answer, though. Just ask me anything, and I'll answer it the truth, whether I want to or not. Okay? I will. You don't even have to trust me. That's not a big issue with us. We're both grown-ups now."

And I said, "Were you ever married before?"

My mother looked at me strangely. Her eyes got small, and for a moment she looked the way I was used to seeing her—sharp-faced, her mouth set and taut. "No," she said. "Who told you that? That isn't true. I never was. Did Jack say that to you? Did your father say that? That's an awful thing to say. I haven't been that bad."

"He didn't say that," I said.

"Oh, of course he did," my mother said. "He doesn't know just to let things go when they're bad enough."

"I wanted to know that," I said. "I just thought about it. It doesn't matter."

"No, it doesn't," my mother said. "I could've been married eight times. I'm just sorry he said that to you. He's not generous sometimes."

"He didn't say that," I said. But I'd said it enough, and I didn't care if she believed me or didn't. It was true that trust was not a big issue between us then. And in any event, I know now that the whole truth of anything is an idea that stops existing finally.

"Is that all you want to know, then?" my mother said. She seemed mad, but not at me, I didn't think. Just at things in general. And I sympathized with her. "Your life's your own business, Jackie," she said. "Sometimes it scares you to death it's so much your own business. You just want to run."

"I guess so," I said.

"I'd like a less domestic life, is all." She looked at me, but I didn't say anything. I didn't see what she meant by that, though I knew there was nothing I could say to change the way her life would be from then on. And I kept quiet.

In a while we walked across 10th Avenue and ate lunch in the cafeteria. When she paid for the meal I saw that she had my father's silver-dollar money clip in her purse and that there was money in it. And I understood that he had been to see her already that day, and no one cared if I knew it. We were all of us on our own in this.

When we walked out onto the street, it was colder and the wind was blowing. Car exhausts were invisible and some drivers had their lights on, though it was only two o'clock in the afternoon. My mother had called a taxi, and we stood and waited for it. I didn't know where she was going, but I wasn't going with her.

"Your father won't let me come back," she said, standing on the curb. It was just a fact to her, not that she hoped I would talk to him or stand up for her or take her part. But I did wish then that I had never let her go the night before. Things can be fixed by staying; but to go out into the night and not come back hazards life, and everything can get out of hand.

My mother's taxi came. She kissed me and hugged me very hard, then got inside the cab in her powder-blue dress and high heels and her car coat. I smelled her perfume on my cheeks as I stood watching her. "I used to be afraid of more things than I am now," she said, looking up at me, and smiled. "I've got a knot in my stomach, of all things." And she closed the cab door, waved at me, and rode away.

I walked back toward my school. I thought I could take the bus home if I got there by three. I walked a long way down 10th Avenue to Second Street, beside the Missouri River, then over to town. I walked by the Great Northern Hotel, where my father had sold ducks and geese and fish of all kinds. There were no passenger trains in the yard and the loading dock looked small. Garbage cans were lined along the edge of it, and the door was closed and locked.

As I walked toward school I thought to myself that my life had turned suddenly, and that I might not know exactly how or which way for possibly a long time. Maybe, in fact, I might never know. It was a thing that happened to you—I knew that—and it had happened to me in this way now. And as I walked on up the cold street that afternoon in Great Falls, the questions I asked myself were these: why wouldn't my father let my mother come back? Why would Woody stand in the cold with me outside my house and risk being killed? Why would he say my mother had been married before, if she hadn't been? And my mother herself—why would she do what she did? In five years my father had gone off to Ely, Nevada, to ride out the oil strike there, and been killed by accident. And in the years since then I have seen my mother from time to time—in one place or another, with one man or other—and I can say, at least, that we know each other. But I have never known the answer to these questions, have never asked anyone their answers. Though possibly it—the answer—is simple: it is just low-life, some coldness in us all, some helplessness that causes us to misunderstand life when it is pure and plain, makes our existence seem like a border between two nothings, and makes us no more or less than animals who meet on the road—watchful, unforgiving, without patience or desire.

1987

JAMAICA KINCAID

Girl

Wash the white clothes on Monday and put them on the stone heap; wash the color clothes on Tuesday and put them on the clothesline to dry; don't walk barehead in the hot sun; cook pumpkin fritters in very hot sweet oil; soak your little cloths right after you take them off; when buying cotton to make yourself a nice blouse, be sure that it doesn't have gum on it, because that way it won't hold up well after a wash; soak salt fish overnight before you cook it; is it true that you sing benna[1] in Sunday school?; always eat your food in such a way that it won't turn someone else's stomach; on Sundays try to walk like a lady and not like the slut you are so bent on becoming; don't sing benna in Sunday school; you mustn't speak to wharf-rat boys, not even to give directions; don't eat fruits on the street—flies will follow you; *but I don't sing benna on Sundays at all and never in Sunday school;* this is how to sew on a button; this is how to make a buttonhole for the button you have just sewed on; this is how to hem a dress when you see the hem coming down and so to prevent yourself from looking like the slut I know you are so bent on becoming; this is how you iron your father's khaki shirt so that it doesn't have a crease; this is how you iron your father's khaki pants so that they don't have a crease; this is how you grow okra—far from the house, because okra tree harbors red ants; when you are growing dasheen, make sure it gets plenty of water or else it makes your throat itch when you are eating it; this is how you sweep a corner; this is how you sweep a whole house; this is how you sweep a yard; this is how you smile to someone you don't like too much; this is how you smile to someone you don't like at all; this is how you smile to someone you like completely; this is how you set a table for tea; this is how you set a table for dinner; this is how you set a table for dinner with an important guest; this is how you set a table for lunch; this is how you set a table for breakfast; this is how to behave in the presence of men who don't know you very well, and this way they won't recognize immediately the slut I have warned you against becoming; be sure to wash every day, even if it is with your own spit; don't squat down to play marbles—you are not a boy, you know; don't pick people's flowers—you might catch something; don't throw stones at blackbirds, because it might not be a blackbird at all; this is how to make a bread pudding; this is how to make doukona;[2] this is how to make pepper pot; this is how to make a good medicine for a cold; this is how to make a good medicine to throw away a child before it even becomes a child; this is how to catch a fish; this is how to throw back a fish you don't like, and that way something bad won't fall on you; this is how to bully a man; this is how a man bullies you; this is how to love a man, and if this doesn't work there are other ways, and if they don't work don't feel too bad about giving up; this is how to spit up in the air if you feel like

1. Sing popular music, calypso.
2. A spicy pudding, often made from plantain and wrapped in a plantain or banana leaf.

it, and this is how to move quick so that it doesn't fall on you; this is how to make ends meet; always squeeze bread to make sure it's fresh; *but what if the baker won't let me feel the bread?*; you mean to say that after all you are really going to be the kind of woman who the baker won't let near the bread?

1983

POETRY

Reading Poetry

People seldom feel neutral about poetry. Those who love it sometimes give the impression that it is an adequate substitute for food, shelter, and love. It isn't. Words, no matter how satisfying, are never an equivalent for life itself and its human experiences. Those who dislike poetry on principle sometimes claim, on the other hand, that poetry is only words and good for nothing. That's not true either. It is easy to become frustrated by words—in poetry or in life—but when words represent and recreate genuine human feelings, as they often do in poetry, they can be crucially important. Poetry is, in fact, more than just words. It is an *experience* of words, and those who know how to read poetry can easily extend their experience of life, their sense of what other people are like, their awareness of themselves, and their range of human feelings.

One reason poetry can be so important is that it is so intimately concerned with feelings. Poetry is often full of ideas, too, and sometimes poems can be powerful experiences of the mind, but most poems are primarily about how people feel rather than how people think. Poems provide, in fact, a language for feeling, and one of poetry's most insistent virtues involves its attempt to express the inexpressible. How can anyone, for example, put into words what it means to be in love? or what it feels like to lose someone one cares about? Poetry tries, and it often captures exactly the shade of emotion that feels just right to a reader. No single poem can be said to express all the things that love or death feels like, or means, but one of the joys of experiencing poetry occurs when we read a poem and want to say, "Yes, that is just what it is like; I know exactly what that line means but I've never been able to express it so well." Poetry can be the voice of our feelings even when our minds are speechless with grief or joy. Reading is no substitute for living, but it can make living more abundant and more available.

Here are two poems that talk about the sincerity and depth of love between two people. Each is written as if it were spoken by one person to his or her lover, and each is definite and powerful about the intensity and quality of love; but the poems work in quite different ways—the first one asserting the strength and depth of love, the second implying intense feeling by reminiscing about events in the relationship between the two people.

ELIZABETH BARRETT BROWNING

How Do I Love Thee?

How do I love thee? Let me count the ways.
I love thee to the depth and breadth and height
My soul can reach, when feeling out of sight
For the ends of Being and ideal Grace.
I love thee to the level of every day's
Most quiet need, by sun and candlelight.
I love thee freely, as men strive for Right;
I love thee purely, as they turn from Praise;
I love thee with the passion put to use
In my old griefs, and with my childhood's faith.
I love thee with a love I seemed to lose
With my lost saints—I love thee with the breath,
Smiles, tears of all my life!—and, if God choose,
I shall but love thee better after death.

1850

JAROLD RAMSEY

The Tally Stick

Here from the start, from our first of days, look:
I have carved our lives in secret on this stick
of mountain mahogany the length of your arms
outstretched, the wood clear red, so hard and rare.
It is time to touch and handle what we know we share.

Near the butt, this intricate notch where the grains
converge and join: it is our wedding.
I can read it through with a thumb and tell you now
who danced, who made up the songs, who meant us joy.
These little arrowheads along the grain,
they are the births of our children. See,
they make a kind of design with these heavy crosses,
the deaths of our parents, the loss of friends.

Over it all as it goes, of course, I
have chiseled Events, History—random

hashmarks cut against the swirling grain.
See, here is the Year the World Went Wrong,
we thought, and here the days the Great Men fell.
The lengthening runes of our lives run through it all.
See, our tally stick is whittled nearly end to end;
delicate as scrimshaw, it would not bear you up.
Regrets have polished it, hand over hand.
Yet let us take it up, and as our fingers
like children leading on a trail cry back
our unforgotten wonders, sign after sign,
we will talk softly as of ordinary matters,
and in one another's blameless eyes go blind.

p. 1977

The first poem is direct, but fairly abstract. It lists several ways in which the poet feels love and connects them to some noble ideas of higher obligations—to justice (line 7), for example, and to spiritual aspiration (lines 2–4). It suggests a wide range of things that love can mean and notices a variety of emotions. It is an ardent statement of feeling and asserts a permanence that will extend even beyond death. It contains admirable thoughts and memorable phrases that many lovers would like to hear said to themselves. What it does not do is say very much about what the relationship between the two lovers is like on an everyday basis, what experiences they have had together, what distinguishes their relationship from that of other devoted or ideal lovers. Its appeal is to our general sense of what love is like and how intense feelings can be; it does not offer everyday details. Love may differ from person to person and even from moment to moment, and so can poems about love.

"The Tally Stick" is much more concrete. The whole poem concentrates on a single object that, like "How Do I Love Thee?", "counts" or "tallies" the ways in which this couple love one another. This stick stands for their love and becomes a kind of physical reminder of it: its natural features—the notches and arrowheads and cross marks (lines 6, 10, and 12) along with the marks carved on it (lines 15–16, 20–21)—indicate events in the story of the relationship. (We could say that the stick *symbolizes* their love; later on, we will look at a number of terms like this that can be used to make it easier to talk about some aspects of poems, but for now it is enough to notice that the stick serves the lovers as a reminder of some specific details of their love.) It is a special kind of reminder to them because its language is "secret" (line 2), something they can share privately (except that we as readers of the poem are sort of looking over their shoulders, not intruding but sharing their secret). The poet interprets the particular features of the stick as standing for particular events—their wedding and the births of their children, for example—and carves marks into it as reminders of other events (lines 15ff.). The stick itself becomes a very personal object, and in the last stanza of the poem it is as if we watch the lovers touching the stick together and reminiscing over it, gradually dissolving into their emotions and each other as they recall the "unforgotten wonders" (line 25) of their lives together.

Both poems are powerful statements of feelings, each in its own way. Some readers will prefer one and some the other. Personal preference does not mean that objective standards for poetry cannot be found (some poems are better than others, and later we will look in detail at features that help us to evaluate poems), but we need have no preconceived standard that all poetry must be one thing or another or work in one particular way. Some good poems are quite abstract, others quite specific. Any poem that helps us to articulate and clarify human feelings and ideas has a legitimate claim on us as readers.

Both "How Do I Love Thee?" and "The Tally Stick" are written as if they were addressed to the partner in the love relationship, and both talk directly about the intensity of the love. The poem below talks only indirectly about the quality and intensity of love. It is written as if it were a letter from a woman to her husband who has gone on a long journey on business. It directly expresses how much she misses him and indirectly suggests how much she cares about him.

EZRA POUND

The River-Merchant's Wife: A Letter

(after Rihaku[1])

While my hair was still cut straight across my forehead
I played about the front gate, pulling flowers.
You came by on bamboo stilts, playing horse,
You walked about my seat, playing with blue plums.
And we went on living in the village of Chokan:
Two small people, without dislike or suspicion.

At fourteen I married My Lord you.
I never laughed, being bashful.
Lowering my head, I looked at the wall.
Called to, a thousand times, I never looked back.

1. The Japanese name for Li Po, an 8th-century Chinese poet. Pound's poem is a loose paraphrase of Li Po's.

At fifteen I stopped scowling,
I desired my dust to be mingled with yours
For ever and for ever and for ever.
Why should I climb the look out?

At sixteen you departed,
You went into far Ku-to-yen, by river of swirling eddies,
And you have been gone five months.
The monkeys make sorrowful noise overhead.

You dragged your feet when you went out.
By the gate now, the moss is grown, the different mosses,
Too deep to clear them away!
The leaves fall early this autumn, in wind.
The paired butterflies are already yellow with August
Over the grass in the West garden;
They hurt me. I grow older,
If you are coming down through the narrows of the river Kiang,
Please let me know beforehand,
And I will come out to meet you
    As far as Cho-fu-Sa.

1915

The "letter" tells us only a few facts about the nameless merchant's wife: that she is about sixteen and a half years old, that she married at fourteen and fell in love with her husband a year later, that she is now very lonely. And about their relationship we know only that they were childhood playmates in a small Chinese village, that their marriage originally was not a matter of personal choice, and that the husband unwillingly went away on a long journey five months ago. But the words tell us a great deal about how the young wife feels, and the simplicity of her language suggests her sincere and deep longing. The daily noises she hears seem "sorrowful" (line 18), and she worries about the dangers of the far-away place where her husband is, thinking of it in terms of its perilous "river of swirling eddies" (line 16). She thinks of how moss has grown up over the unused gate, and more time seems to her to have passed than actually has (lines 22–25). Nostalgically she remembers their innocent childhood, when they played together without deeper love or commitment (lines 1–6), and contrasts that with her later satisfaction in their love (lines 11–14) and with her present anxiety, loneliness, and desire. We do not need to know the details of the geography of the river Kiang or how far Cho-fu-Sa is to sense that her wish to see him is very strong, that her desire is powerful enough to make her venture beyond the ordinary geographical bounds of her existence so that their reunion will come sooner. The closest she comes to a direct statement about her love is her statement that she desired that her dust be mingled with his "For ever and for ever and for ever" (lines 12–13). But her single-minded vision of the world, her perception of even the beauty of nature as only a record of her husband's absence and the passage of time, and her plain, apparently uncalculated language about her rejection of other suitors and her shutting out of the rest of the world all show her to be committed, desirous, nearly desperate for his presence. In a different sense, she has also counted the ways that she loves her man.

Here is another poem that reflects intense feelings a woman has for her lover, but here the emphasis is on the complexities of physical presence.

ADRIENNE RICH

Living in Sin

She had thought the studio would keep itself;
no dust upon the furniture of love.
Half heresy, to wish the taps less vocal,
the panes relieved of grime. A plate of pears,
a piano with a Persian shawl, a cat
stalking the picturesque amusing mouse
had risen at his urging.
Not that at five each separate stair would writhe
under the milkman's tramp; that morning light
so coldly would delineate the scraps
of last night's cheese and three sepulchral bottles;
that on the kitchen shelf among the saucers
a pair of beetle-eyes would fix her own—
envoy from some village in the moldings . . .
Meanwhile, he, with a yawn,
sounded a dozen notes upon the keyboard,
declared it out of tune, shrugged at the mirror,
rubbed at his beard, went out for cigarettes;
while she, jeered by the minor demons,
pulled back the sheets and made the bed and found
a towel to dust the table-top,
and let the coffee-pot boil over on the stove.
By evening she was back in love again,
though not so wholly but throughout the night
she woke sometimes to feel the daylight coming
like a relentless milkman up the stairs.

1955

Here the presence of the lover has just as insistent an effect as absence in "The River-Merchant's Wife." This poem contrasts the expectations of the central figure in the poem (a woman who is living "in sin" with her lover) with actual experience—what her days and nights now are actually like. The high expectations of romance and the old idealized fantasies about living together are set against grimy, cramped, and noisy realities: accumulating dust in the small apartment ("studio," line 1), noisy faucets (line 3), intrusive insects (lines 12–14), dirty windows (line 4), and the clutter of leftover food and empty bottles (lines 9–11). The earlier sense of her lover as a romantic figure in a painting (lines 4–7) disappears into his presence as an unshaven, yawning, impatient man who leaves an unmade bed to seek cigarettes, and the woman finds herself trying to recreate some sense of order, cleanliness, and alertness. Ultimately there is here too some small affirmation of the pleasures of affection and illusion, but the squeaking stairs of intrusion are as "relentless" as mornings and milkmen, and the poem insists on the everyday disillusionments of love and living.

Poems can be about the meaning of a relationship or about disappointment just as easily as about emotional fulfillment, and poets are often very good at suggesting the contradictions and uncertainties in relationships. Like other people, poets often find love and its complications quaint or downright funny, too, mainly because it involves human beings who, however serious their intentions and concerns, are often inept, uncertain, and self-contradictory—in short, human. Showing us ourselves as others see us is one of the more useful tasks that poems perform, but the poems that result can be just as entertaining and pleasurable as they are educational. Here is a poem that imagines a very strange scene, a kind of fantasy of what happens when we *think* too much about sex or love, and it is likely to leave us laughing, whether or not we take it seriously as a statement of human anxiety and of the tendency to intellectualize too much.

TOM WAYMAN

Wayman in Love

At last Wayman gets the girl into bed.
He is locked in one of those embraces
so passionate his left arm is asleep
when suddenly he is bumped in the back.
"Excuse me," a voice mutters, thick with German.
Wayman and the girl sit up astounded
as a furry gentleman in boots and a frock coat
climbs in under the covers.

"My name is Doktor Marx," the intruder announces
settling his neck comfortably on the pillow.

"I'm here to consider for you the cost of a kiss."
He pulls out a notepad. "Let's see now,
we have the price of the mattress, this room must be rented,
your time off work, groceries for two,
medical fees in case of accidents . . ."

"Look," Wayman says,
"couldn't we do this later?"
The philosopher sighs, and continues: "You are affected too, Miss.
If you are not working, you are going to resent
your dependent position. This will influence
I assure you, your most intimate moments . . ."

"Doctor, please," Wayman says. "All we want
is to be left alone."
But another beard, more nattily dressed,
is also getting into the bed.
There is a shifting and heaving of bodies
as everyone wriggles out room for themselves.
"I want you to meet a friend from Vienna,"
Marx says. "This is Doktor Freud."

The newcomer straightens his glasses,
peers at Wayman and the girl.
"I can see," he begins,
"that you two have problems . . ." 1973

▽ ▽ ▽

Another traditional subject of poetry is death, and on this subject, too, poets often describe frequent, recurrent human emotions in a variety of ways. In the following poem, a father struggles to understand and control his grief.

BEN JONSON

On My First Son

Farewell, thou child of my right hand,[2] and joy;
My sin was too much hope of thee, loved boy:
Seven years thou wert lent to me, and I thee pay,
Exacted by thy fate, on the just[3] day.
O could I lose all father now! for why
Will man lament the state he should envý,
To have so soon 'scaped world's and flesh's rage,
And, if no other misery, yet age?

2. A literal translation of the son's name, Benjamin. 3. Exact; the son died on his seventh birthday, in 1603.

Rest in soft peace, and asked, say, "Here doth lie
Ben Jonson his[4] best piece of poetry."
For whose sake henceforth all his vows be such
As what he loves may never like too much.

1616

This poem's attempts to rationalize the boy's death are quite conventional. Although the father tries to be comforted by pious thoughts, his feelings keep showing through. The poem's beginning—with its formal "farewell" and the rather distant-sounding address to the dead boy ("child of my right hand")—cannot be sustained for long: both of the first two lines end with bursts of emotion. It is as if the father is trying to explain the death to himself and to keep his emotions under control, but cannot quite manage it. Even the punctuation suggests the way his feelings compete with conventional attempts to put the death into some sort of perspective that will soften the grief, and the comma near the end of each of the first two lines marks a pause that cannot quite hold back the overflowing emotion. But finally the only "idea" that the poem supports is that the father wishes he did not feel so intensely; in the fifth line he fairly blurts that he wishes he could lose his fatherly emotions, and in the final lines he resolves never again to "like" so much that he can be this deeply hurt. Philosophy and religion offer their useful counsels in this poem, but they prove far less powerful than feeling. Rather than drawing some kind of moral about what death means, the poem presents the actuality of feeling as inevitable and nearly all-consuming.

The poem that follows similarly tries to suppress the rawness of feelings about the death of a loved one, but here the survivor is haunted by memories of his wife when he sees a physical object—a vacuum cleaner—that was important in her life.

HOWARD NEMEROV

The Vacuum

The house is so quiet now
The vacuum cleaner sulks in the corner closet,
Its bag limp as a stopped lung, its mouth
Grinning into the floor, maybe at my
Slovenly life, my dog-dead youth.

4. Ben Jonson's (a common Renaissance form of the possessive).

I've lived this way long enough,
But when my old woman died her soul
Went into that vacuum cleaner, and I can't bear
To see the bag swell like a belly, eating the dust
And the woolen mice, and begin to howl

Because there is old filth everywhere
She used to crawl, in the corner and under the stair.
I know now how life is cheap as dirt,
And still the hungry, angry heart
Hangs on and howls, biting at air. 1955

The poem is about a vacuum in the husband's life, but the title refers most obviously to the vacuum cleaner that, like the tally stick we looked at earlier, seems to stand for many of the things that were once important in their life together. The cleaner is a reminder of the dead wife ("my old woman," line 7) because of her devotion to cleanliness. But to the surviving husband buried in the filth of his life it seems as if the machine has become almost human, a kind of ghost of her: it "sulks" (line 2), it has lungs and a mouth (line 3), and it seems to grin, making fun of what has become of him. He "can't bear" (line 8) to see it in action because it then seems too much alive, too much a reminder of her life. The poem records his paralysis, his inability to do more than discover that life is "cheap as dirt" without her ordering and cleansing presence for him. At the end it is *his* angry heart that acts like the haunting machine, howling and biting at air as if he has merged with her spirit and the physical object that memorializes her. This poem puts a strong emphasis on the stillness of death and the way it makes things seem to stop; it captures in words the hurt, the anger, the inability to understand, the vacuum that remains when a loved one dies and leaves a vacant space. But here we do not see the body or hear a direct good-bye to the dead person; rather we encounter the feeling that lingers and won't go away, recalled through memory by an especially significant object, a mere thing but one that has been personalized to the point of becoming nearly human in itself. (The event described here is, by the way, fictional; the poet's wife did not in fact die. Like a dramatist or writer of fiction, the poet may simply *imagine* an event in order to analyze and articulate how such an event might feel in certain circumstances.)

Here is another poem about the death of a loved one:

SHARON OLDS

The Glass

I think of it with wonder now,
the glass of mucous that stood on the table
next to my father all weekend. The cancer
is growing fast in his throat now,
and as it grows it sends out pus like the
sun sending out flares, those pouring
tongues. So my father has to gargle, hack,
spit a mouth full of thick stuff
into the glass every ten minutes or so,
scraping the rim up his lower lip to
get the last bit off his skin, then he
sets the glass down on the table and it
sits there, like a glass of beer foam,
shiny and faintly golden, he gurgles and
coughs and reaches for it again and
gets the heavy sputum out,
full of bubbles and moving around like yeast—
he is like some god producing food from his own mouth.
He himself can eat nothing anymore,
just a swallow of milk sometimes,
cut with water, and even then it
can't always get past the tumor,
and the next time the saliva comes up it's
chalkish and ropey, he has to roll it in his
throat to form it and get it up and dis-
gorge the elliptical globule into the cup—
and the wonder to me is that it did not disgust me,
that glass of phlegm that stood there all day and
filled slowly with compound globes and I'd
empty it and it would fill again and
shimmer there on the table until the
room seemed to turn around it
in an orderly way, a model of the solar system
turning around the gold sun,
my father the dark earth that used to
lie at the center of the universe
now turning with the rest of us
around the bright glass of spit
on the table, these last mouthfuls.

1990

Like "The Vacuum," "The Glass" reflects on a loved one through unconventional images, material objects that suggest pain and unpleasantness rather than joy and love. The "glass" of the title is not a mirror that reflects a beautiful face, not a crafted objet d'art, but rather a simple tumbler, and it is full of mucus—not a very appealing object. The loved one, the father of the person who is speaking the poem, is dying of cancer, and the indicators of his condition are painfully detailed. The sights and sounds are disgusting rather than appealing; the body fluids are pus and spit, and the human sounds are gargling, gurgling, and hacking. It is almost as if the poem tries to create a picture as ugly as possible, for the father's physical struggle just to swallow and spit is chronicled moment by painful moment. "[T]he wonder to me," says the daughter who views the daily struggle and records it for us in the poem, "is that it did not disgust me" (line 27), and the poem transforms the central object of disgust ("that glass of phlegm," line 28) into something that stands for the daughter's love and the father's ability to accept it even in his deteriorating condition. The daughter's act of staying and emptying the glass represents not only fortitude and loyalty but the steadying influence of stability and predictability. She begins to see the glass itself—its regular filling and emptying of life and coming death—as a kind of center around which human activity revolves "in an orderly way" (line 33). The father, once the center of the family's universe, now seems to move with the others "around" (line 38) the act of death as represented by the glass. It is an awful picture—awful in its details, awful in its implications of loss—but it is also beautiful in its own way. The poem shows how even the most unattractive events, objects, and words can be used to suggest how life and love can be portrayed, explained, and imprinted on our memories.

Sometimes poems are a way of confronting feelings. Sometimes they explore feelings in detail and try to intellectualize or rationalize them. At other times, poems generate feelings by recalling an experience many years in the past. In the following two poems, for example, memories of childhood provide perspective on two very different kinds of events. In the first, written as if the person speaking the poem were in the fifth grade, a child's sense of death is portrayed through her exploration of a photograph that makes her grandfather's earlier presence vivid to her memory—a memory that lingers primarily through smell and touch. In the second poem, another childhood memory—this time of overshoes—takes an adult almost physically back into childhood.

RITA DOVE

Fifth Grade Autobiography

I was four in this photograph fishing
with my grandparents at a lake in Michigan.

My brother squats in poison ivy.
His Davy Crockett cap
sits squared on his head so the raccoon tail
flounces down the back of his sailor suit.

My grandfather sits to the far right
in a folding chair,
and I know his left hand is on
the tobacco in his pants pocket
because I used to wrap it for him
every Christmas. Grandmother's hips
bulge from the brush, she's leaning
into the ice chest, sun through the trees
printing her dress with soft
luminous paws.

I am staring jealously at my brother;
the day before he rode his first horse, alone.
I was strapped in a basket
behind my grandfather.
He smelled of lemons. He's died—

but I remember his hands.

1989

ANNE SEXTON

The Fury of Overshoes

They sit in a row
outside the kindergarten,
black, red, brown, all
with those brass buckles.
Remember when you couldn't
buckle your own
overshoe
or tie your own
shoe
or cut your own meat
and the tears
running down like mud
because you fell off your
tricycle?
Remember, big fish,
when you couldn't swim
and simply slipped under
like a stone frog?
The world wasn't
yours.

It belonged to
the big people.
Under your bed
sat the wolf
and he made a shadow
when cars passed by
at night.
They made you give up
your nightlight
and your teddy
and your thumb.
Oh overshoes,
don't you
remember me,
pushing you up and down
in the winter snow?
Oh thumb,
I want a drink,
it is dark,
where are the big people,
when will I get there,
taking giant steps
all day,
each day
and thinking
nothing of it?

1974

▽ ▽ ▽

There is much more going on in the poems that we have glanced at than we have taken time to consider, but even the quickest look at these poems suggests something of the range of feelings that poems can offer—the depth of feeling, the clarity, the experience that may be articulately and precisely shared. Not all poems are as accessible as those we've looked at so far, and even the ones that are accessible usually yield themselves to us more readily and more completely if we approach them systematically by developing specific reading habits and skills—just as someone learning to play tennis systematically learns the rules, the techniques, the things to watch out for that are distinctive to the pleasures and hazards of that skill or craft. It helps if you develop a sense of what to expect, and the chapters that follow will help you to an understanding of the things that poets can do—and thus of what poems can do for you.

But knowing what to expect isn't everything, and I have one bit of advice to offer every prospective reader of poetry before going any further: Be open. Be open to new experience, be open to new feelings, be open to new ideas. Every poem in the world is a potential new experience, and no matter how sophisticated you become, you can still be surprised (and delighted) by new poems—and by rereading old ones. Good poems bear many, many rereadings, and often one discovers something new with every new reading. Be willing to let poems surprise you when you come to them; let them come on their own terms, let them be themselves. If you are open to poetry, you are open to much that the world can offer you.

No one can give you a method that will offer you total experience of all poems. But because many characteristics of an individual poem are characteristics that one poem shares with other poems, there are guidelines that can prompt you to ask the right questions. The chapters that follow will help you in detail with a variety of problems, but meanwhile here is a checklist of some things to remember:

1. *Identify the poem's situation.* What is said is often conditioned by where it is said and by whom. Identifying the speaker and his or her place in the situation puts what he or she says in perspective.
2. *Read the syntax literally.* What the words say literally in normal sentences is only a starting point, but it is the place to start. Not all poems use normal prose syntax, but most of them do, and you can save yourself embarrassment by paraphrasing accurately (that is, rephrasing what the poem literally says, in plain prose) and not simply free-associating from an isolated word or phrase.
3. *Articulate for yourself what the title, subject, and situation make you expect.* Poets often use false leads and try to surprise you by doing shocking things, but defining expectation lets you be conscious of where you are when you begin.
4. *Be willing to be surprised.* Things often happen in poems that turn them around. A poem may seem to suggest one thing at first, then persuade you of its opposite, or at least of a significant qualification or variation.
5. *Find out what is implied by the traditions behind the poem.* Verse forms, poetic kinds, and metrical patterns all have a frame of reference, traditions of the way they are usually used and for what. For example, the anapest (two unstressed syllables followed by a stressed one, as in the word "Tennessee") is usually used for comic poems, and when poets use it "straight" they are aware of their "departure" and are probably making a point by doing it.
6. *Remember that poems exist in time, and times change.* Not only the meanings of words, but whole ways of looking at the universe vary in different ages. Consciousness of time works two ways: your knowledge

of history provides a context for reading the poem, and the poem's use of a word or idea may modify your notion of a particular age.

7. *Bother the reference librarian.* Look up anything you don't understand: an unfamiliar word (or an ordinary word used in an unfamiliar way), a place, a person, a myth, an idea—anything the poem uses. When you can't find what you need or don't know where to look, ask for help.
8. *Take a poem on its own terms.* Adjust to the poem; don't make the poem adjust to you. Be prepared to hear things you do not want to hear. Not all poems are about your ideas, nor will they always present emotions you want to feel. But be tolerant and listen to the poem's ideas, not only to your desire to revise them for yourself.
9. *Argue.* Discussion usually results in clarification and keeps you from being too dependent on personal biases and preoccupations that sometimes mislead even the best readers. Talking a poem over with someone else (especially someone very different) can expand your perspective.
10. *Assume there is a reason for everything.* Poets do make mistakes, but in poems that show some degree of verbal control it is usually safest to assume that the poet chose each word carefully; if the choice seems peculiar to us, it is often *we* who are missing something. Try to account for everything in a poem and see what kind of sense you can make of it. Poets make choices; try to figure out a coherent pattern that explains the text as it stands.

What *is* poetry? Let your definition be cumulative as you read more and more poems. No dictionary definition will cover all that you find, and it is better to discover for yourself poetry's many ingredients, its many effects, its many ways of acting. What can it do for you? Wait and see. Begin to add up its effects after you have read carefully—after you have studied and reread—a hundred or so poems; that will be a beginning, and you will be able to add to that total as long as you continue to read new poems or reread old ones.

▽ ▽ ▽

SIR THOMAS WYATT

They Flee from Me

They flee from me, that sometime did me seek,
With naked foot stalking in my chamber.
I have seen them, gentle, tame, and meek,

That now are wild, and do not remember
That sometime they put themselves in danger
To take bread at my hand; and now they range,
Busily seeking with a continual change.

Thankéd be Fortune it hath been otherwise,
Twenty times better; but once in special,
In thin array, after a pleasant guise,
When her loose gown from her shoulders did fall,
And she me caught in her arms long and small.[5]
And therewith all sweetly did me kiss
And softly said, "Dear heart, how like you this?"

It was no dream, I lay broad waking.
But all is turned, thorough[6] my gentleness,
Into a strange fashion of forsaking;
And I have leave to go, of her goodness,
And she also to use newfangleness.[7]
But since that I so kindely[8] am servéd,
I fain[9] would know what she hath deservéd.

1557

W. B. YEATS

A Last Confession

What lively lad most pleasured me
Of all that with me lay?
I answer that I gave my soul
And loved in misery,
But had great pleasure with a lad
That I loved bodily.

Flinging from his arms I laughed
To think his passion such
He fancied that I gave a soul
Did but our bodies touch,
And laughed upon his breast to think
Beast gave beast as much.

I gave what other women gave
That stepped out of their clothes,
But when this soul, its body off,
Naked to naked goes,
He it has found shall find therein
What none other knows,

5. Slender. 6. Through. 7. Fondness for novelty. 8. In a way natural to women.
9. Eagerly.

And give his own and take his own
And rule in his own right;
And though it loved in misery
Close and cling so tight,
There's not a bird of day that dare
Extinguish that delight.

1933

CAROL JANE BANGS

Touching Each Other's Surfaces

Skin meeting skin, we want to think
we know each other scientifically;
we want to believe
it is objective knowledge
gives this conviction of intimacy,
makes us say it feels so right.
That mole below your shoulder blade,
the soft hair over my thighs—
we examine our bodies with the precision
known only to lovers or surgeons,
all those whose profession is explication,
who have to believe their own words.
And yet, having memorized each turning,
each place where bone strains or bends,
each hollow, each hair, each failure of form,
we still encounter that stubborn wall,
that barrier which hides an infinite vastness
the most sincere gesture can't find.

Nor does emotion take us further
than the shared heat of bodies
aware of themselves,
the flattery of multiple desires.
We rest in each other's arms unexplained
by these currents of feeling rushing past
like ripples over a pool of water
whose substance never changes,
reflecting each wave, each ribboned crossing,
without being really moved.
We search each other's eyes so long
beyond our own reflections,
finding only the black centers,
the immeasurable interior we'll
never reach with candle,
never plumb with love.

Perhaps it is just this ignorance,
this absence of certainty, lack of clear view,
more than anything, brings us together,
draws us into and through each other
to the unknown inside us all,
that gray space from which
what we know of ourselves
emerges briefly, casts a transient
shadow across the earth
and learns to believe in itself just enough
to believe in some one else. 1983

EDNA ST. VINCENT MILLAY

[I, being born a woman and distressed]

I, being born a woman and distressed
By all the needs and notions of my kind,
Am urged by your propinquity to find
Your person fair, and feel a certain zest
To bear your body's weight upon my breast:
So subtly is the fume of life designed,
To clarify the pulse and cloud the mind,
And leave me once again undone, possessed.
Think not for this, however, the poor treason
Of my stout blood against my staggering brain,
I shall remember you with love, or season
My scorn with pity,—let me make it plain:
I find this frenzy insufficient reason
For conversation when we meet again. 1923

MARGE PIERCY

To Have Without Holding

Learning to love differently is hard,
love with the hands wide open, love
with the doors banging on their hinges,
the cupboard unlocked, the wind
roaring and whimpering in the rooms
rustling the sheets and snapping the blinds
that thwack like rubber bands
in an open palm.

It hurts to love wide open
stretching the muscles that feel

as if they are made of wet plaster,
then of blunt knives, then
of sharp knives.

It hurts to thwart the reflexes
of grab, of clutch; to love and let
go again and again. It pesters to remember
the lover who is not in the bed,
to hold back what is owed to the work
that gutters like a candle in a cave
without air, to love consciously,
conscientiously, concretely, constructively.

I can't do it, you say it's killing
me, but you thrive, you glow
on the street like a neon raspberry,
You float and sail, a helium balloon
bright bachelor's button blue and bobbing
on the cold and hot winds of our breath,
as we make and unmake in passionate
diastole and systole the rhythm
of our unbound bonding, to have
and not to hold, to love
with minimized malice, hunger
and anger moment by moment balanced. 1980

AUDRE LORDE

Recreation

Coming together
it is easier to work
after our bodies
meet
paper and pen
neither care nor profit
whether we write or not
but as your body moves
under my hands
charged and waiting
we cut the leash
you create me against your thighs
hilly with images
moving through our word countries
my body
writes into your flesh

the poem
you make of me

Touching you I catch midnight
as moon fires set in my throat
I love you flesh into blossom
I made you
and take you made
into me.

1978

WILLIAM SHAKESPEARE

[Let me not to the marriage of true minds]

Let me not to the marriage of true minds
Admit impediments.[1] Love is not love
Which alters when it alteration finds,
Or bends with the remover to remove:
Oh, no! it is an ever-fixéd mark,
That looks on tempests and is never shaken;
It is the star to every wandering bark,
Whose worth's unknown, although his height be taken.[2]
Love's not Time's fool, though rosy lips and cheeks
Within his bending sickle's compass come;
Love alters not with his brief hours and weeks,
But bears it out even to the edge of doom.
If this be error and upon me proved,
I never writ, nor no man ever loved.

1609

ANNE BRADSTREET

To My Dear and Loving Husband

If ever two were one, then surely we.
If ever man were loved by wife, then thee;
If ever wife was happy in a man,
Compare with me ye women if you can.
I prize thy love more than whole mines of gold,
Or all the riches that the East doth hold.

1. The Marriage Service contains this address to the witnesses: "If any of you know cause or just impediments why these persons should not be joined together. . . ." 2. I.e., measuring the altitude of stars (for purposes of navigation) is not a measurement of value.

My love is such that rivers cannot quench,
Nor ought but love from thee give recompense.
Thy love is such I can no way repay;
The heavens reward thee manifold, I pray.
Then while we live, in love let's so persever,
That when we live no more we may live ever. 1678

GALWAY KINNELL

After Making Love We Hear Footsteps

For I can snore like a bullhorn
or play loud music
or sit up talking with any reasonably sober Irishman
and Fergus will only sink deeper
into his dreamless sleep, which goes by all in one flash,
but let there be that heavy breathing
or a stifled come-cry anywhere in the house
and he will wrench himself awake
and make for it on the run—as now, we lie together,
after making love, quiet, touching along the length of our bodies,
familiar touch of the long-married,
and he appears—in his baseball pajamas, it happens,
the neck opening so small
he has to screw them on, which one day may make him wonder
about the mental capacity of baseball players—
and says, "Are you loving and snuggling? May I join?"
He flops down between us and hugs us and snuggles himself to sleep,
his face gleaming with satisfaction at being this very child.

In the half darkness we look at each other
and smile
and touch arms across his little, startlingly muscled body—
this one whom habit of memory propels to the ground of his making,
sleeper only the mortal sounds can sing awake,
this blessing love gives again into our arms. 1980

LI-YOUNG LEE

Persimmons

In sixth grade Mrs. Walker
slapped the back of my head
and made me stand in the corner
for not knowing the difference

between *persimmon* and *precision.*
How to choose

persimmons. This is precision.
Ripe ones are soft and brown-spotted.
Sniff the bottoms. The sweet one
will be fragrant. How to eat:
put the knife away, lay down newspaper.
Peel the skin tenderly, not to tear the meat.
Chew the skin, suck it,
and swallow. Now, eat
the meat of the fruit,
so sweet,
all of it, to the heart.

Donna undresses, her stomach is white.
In the yard, dewy and shivering
with crickets, we lie naked,
face-up, face-down.
I teach her Chinese.
Crickets: *chiu chiu.* Dew: I've forgotten.
Naked: I've forgotten.
Ni, wo: you and me.
I part her legs,
remember to tell her
she is beautiful as the moon.

Other words
that got me into trouble were
fight and *fright, wren* and *yarn.*
Fight was what I did when I was frightened,
fright was what I felt when I was fighting.
Wrens are small, plain birds,
yarn is what one knits with.
Wrens are soft as yarn.
My mother made birds out of yarn.
I loved to watch her tie the stuff;
a bird, a rabbit, a wee man.

Mrs. Walker brought a persimmon to class
and cut it up
so everyone could taste
a *Chinese apple.* Knowing
it wasn't ripe or sweet, I didn't eat
but watched the other faces.

My mother said every persimmon has a sun
inside, something golden, glowing,
warm as my face.

Once, in the cellar, I found two wrapped in newspaper,
forgotten and not yet ripe.
I took them and set both on my bedroom windowsill,
where each morning a cardinal
sang, *The sun, the sun.*

Finally understanding
he was going blind,
my father sat up all one night
waiting for a song, a ghost.
I gave him the persimmons,
swelled, heavy as sadness,
and sweet as love.

This year, in the muddy lighting
of my parents' cellar, I rummage, looking
for something I lost.
My father sits on the tired, wooden stairs,
black cane between his knees,
hand over hand, gripping the handle.

He's so happy that I've come home.
I ask how his eyes are, a stupid question.
All gone, he answers.

Under some blankets, I find a box.
Inside the box I find three scrolls.
I sit beside him and untie
three paintings by my father:
Hibiscus leaf and a white flower.
Two cats preening.
Two persimmons, so full they want to drop from the cloth.

He raises both hands to touch the cloth,
asks, *Which is this?*

This is persimmons, Father.

Oh, the feel of the wolftail on the silk,
the strength, the tense
precision in the wrist.
I painted them hundreds of times
eyes closed. These I painted blind.
Some things never leave a person:
scent of the hair of one you love,
the texture of persimmons,
in your palm, the ripe weight.

1986

ELLEN BRYANT VOIGT

For My Mother

When does the soul leave the body?
Since early morning you have not moved—
only your head moves, thrown back
with each deliberate breath,
the one sound that matters in the room.
My brother is here, my sister,
two of your sisters, ripples
widening from the bed.
The nurses check and measure,
keeping the many records.
Are you afraid?
Are you dreaming of what is past, lost,
or is this sleep some other preparation?
My sister has put your rings
on my finger; it seems like your hand
stroking the white brow,
unable to release you,
not even after you have asked for death—

And we know nothing about such pain,
except that it has weaned you from us,
and from the reedy, rusted
sunflowers outside the window,
drooping over the snow like tongueless bells.

1983

IRVING LAYTON

Keine Lazarovitch, 1870–1959

When I saw my mother's head on the cold pillow,
Her white waterfalling hair in the cheeks' hollows,
I thought, quietly circling my grief, of how
She had loved God but cursed extravagantly his creatures.

For her final mouth was not water but a curse,
A small black hole, a black rent in the universe,
Which damned the green earth, stars and trees in its stillness
And the inescapable lousiness of growing old.

And I record she was comfortless, vituperative,
Ignorant, glad, and much else besides; I believe
She endlessly praised her black eyebrows, their thick weave,
Till plagiarizing Death leaned down and took them for his mould.

And spoiled a dignity I shall not again find,
And the fury of her stubborn limited mind;
Now none will shake her amber beads and call God blind,
Or wear them upon a breast so radiantly.

O fierce she was, mean and unaccommodating;
But I think now of the toss of her gold earrings,
Their proud carnal assertion, and her youngest sings
While all the rivers of her red veins move into the sea.

DAVID WAGONER

My Father's Garden

On his way to the open hearth where white-hot steel
Boiled against furnace walls in wait for his lance
To pierce the fireclay and set loose demons
And dragons in molten tons, blazing
Down to the huge satanic caldrons,
Each day he would pass the scrapyard, his kind of garden.

In rusty rockeries of stoves and brake drums,
In grottoes of sewing machines and refrigerators,
He would pick flowers for us: small gears and cogwheels
With teeth like petals, with holes for anthers,
Long stalks of lead to be poured into toy soldiers,
Ball bearings as big as grapes to knock them down.

He was called a melter. He tried to keep his brain
From melting in those tyger-mouthed mills
Where the same steel reappeared over and over
To be reborn in the fire as something better
Or worse: cannons or cars, needles or girders,
Flagpoles, swords, or plowshares.

But it melted. His classical learning ran
Down and away from him, not burning bright.
His fingers culled a few cold scraps of Latin
And Greek, *magna sine laude*,[3] for crosswords
And brought home lumps of tin and sewer grills
As if they were his ripe prize vegetables.

1987

3. Without great distinction; a reversal of the usual *magna cum laude*.

DIANE WAKOSKI

The Photos

My sister in her well-tailored silk blouse hands me
the photo of my father
in naval uniform and white hat.
I say, "Oh, this is the one which Mama used to have on her dresser."

My sister controls her face and furtively looks at my mother,
a sad rag bag of a woman, lumpy and sagging everywhere,
like a mattress at the Salvation Army, though with no holes or tears,
and says, "No."

I look again,
and see that my father is wearing a wedding ring,
which he never did
when he lived with my mother. And that there is a legend on it,
"To my dearest wife,
        Love
        Chief"
And I realize the photo must have belonged to his second wife,
whom he left our mother to marry.

My mother says, with her face as still as the whole unpopulated part of the
state of North Dakota,
"May I see it too?"
She looks at it.

I look at my tailored sister
and my own blue-jeaned self. Have we wanted to hurt our mother,
sharing these pictures on this, one of the few days I ever visit or
spend with family? For her face is curiously haunted,
not now with her usual viperish bitterness,
but with something so deep it could not be spoken.

I turn away and say I must go on, as I have a dinner engagement with friends.
But I drive all the way to Pasadena from Whittier,
thinking of my mother's face; how I could never love her; how my father
could not love her either. Yet knowing I have inherited
the rag-bag body,
stony face with bulldog jaws.

I drive, thinking of that face.
Jeffers' California Medea[4] who inspired me to poetry.

4. Robinson Jeffers (1887–1962), American poet who migrated to California from the East, retold the Medea story in *Solstice* (1935). In Greek legend, Medea was a sorceress who killed her own children.

I killed my children,
but there as I am changing lanes on the freeway, necessarily glancing in the rearview mirror, I see the face,
not even a ghost, but always with me, like a photo in a beloved's wallet.

How I hate my destiny.

1978

Understanding the Text

1 TONE

Poetry is full of surprises. Poems express anger or outrage just as effectively as love or sadness, and good poems can be written about going to a rock concert or having lunch or cutting the lawn, as well as about making love or gazing at a cloudless sky or smelling flowers. Even poems on "predictable" subjects can surprise us with unpredicted attitudes, unusual events, or a sudden twist. Knowing that a poem is about some particular subject—love, for example, or death—may give us a general idea of what to expect, but it never tells us altogether what we will find in a particular poem. Experiencing a poem fully means being open to the poem and its surprises, being willing to let the poem guide us to its own attitudes, feelings, and ideas. Letting a poem speak to us means being willing to listen to *how* the poem says what it says—hearing the tone of voice implied in the way the words are spoken.

The following two poems—one about death and one about love—express rather different ideas and feelings from those we looked at in "Reading Poetry."

MARGE PIERCY

Barbie Doll

This girlchild was born as usual
and presented dolls that did pee-pee
and miniature GE stoves and irons

and wee lipsticks the color of cherry candy.
Then in the magic of puberty, a classmate said:
You have a great big nose and fat legs.

She was healthy, tested intelligent,
possessed strong arms and back,
abundant sexual drive and manual dexterity.
She went to and fro apologizing.
Everyone saw a fat nose on thick legs.

She was advised to play coy,
exhorted to come on hearty,
exercise, diet, smile and wheedle.
Her good nature wore out
like a fan belt.
So she cut off her nose and her legs
and offered them up.

In the casket displayed on satin she lay
with the undertaker's cosmetics painted on,
a turned-up putty nose,
dressed in a pink and white nightie.
Doesn't she look pretty? everyone said.
Consummation at last.
To every woman a happy ending.

1973

W. D. SNODGRASS

Leaving the Motel

Outside, the last kids holler
Near the pool: they'll stay the night.
Pick up the towels; fold your collar
Out of sight.

Check: is the second bed
Unrumpled, as agreed?
Landlords have to think ahead
In case of need,

Too. Keep things straight: don't take
The matches, the wrong keyrings—
We've nowhere we could keep a keepsake—
Ashtrays, combs, things

That sooner or later others
Would accidentally find.
Check: take nothing of one another's
And leave behind

Your license number only,
Which they won't care to trace;
We've paid. Still, should such things get lonely,
Leave in their vase

An aspirin to preserve
Our lilacs, the wayside flowers
We've gathered and must leave to serve
A few more hours;

That's all. We can't tell when
We'll come back, can't press claims,
We would no doubt have other rooms then,
Or other names.

1968

The first poem has the strong note of sadness that characterizes many death poems, but its emphasis is not on the response to the girl's death but on the disappointments in her life. The only "scene" in the poem (lines 19–23) portrays the unnamed girl at rest in her casket, but the still body in the casket contrasts not with vitality but with frustration and anxiety: her life since puberty (lines 5–6) had been full of apologies and attempts to change her physical appearance and emotional makeup. The rest she achieves in death is not, however, a triumph, despite what people say (line 23). Although the poem's last two words are "happy ending," this girl without a name has died in embarrassment and without fulfillment, and the final lines are ironic, meaning the opposite of what they say. The cheerful comments at the end lack force and truth because of what we already know; we understand them as ironic because they emphasize how unhappy the girl was and how false her cosmeticized corpse is to the sad truth of her life.

The poem's concern is to suggest the falsity and destructiveness of those standards of beauty that have led to the tragedy of the girl's life. In an important sense, the poem is not really *about* death at all in spite of the fact that the girl's death and her repaired corpse are central to it. As the title suggests, the poem dramatizes how standardized, commercialized notions of femininity and prettiness can be painful and destructive to those whose bodies do not precisely fit the conformist models, and the poem attacks vigorously those conventional standards and the widespread, unthinking acceptance of them.

"Leaving the Motel" similarly goes in quite a different direction from many poems on the subject of love. Instead of expressing assurance about how love lasts and endures, or about the sincerity and depth of affection, this poem dramatizes a brief sexual encounter. But it does not emphasize sexuality or eroticism in the meeting of the nameless lovers (we see them only as they prepare to leave), nor does it suggest why or how they have found each other, or what either of them is like as a person. Its emphasis is on how careful they must be not to get caught, how exact and calculating they must be in their planning, how finite and limited their encounter must be, how sealed off this encounter is from the rest of their lives. The poem stresses the tiny details the lovers must think of, the agreements they must observe, and the ritual checklist of their duties ("Check . . . Keep things straight . . . Check . . .", lines 5, 9, 15). Affection and sentiment have their small place in the poem (notice the care for the flowers, lines 19–24, and the thought of "pressing claims," line 26), but the emphasis is on temporariness, uncertainty, and limits. The poem is about an illicit, perhaps adulterous, sexual encounter, but there is no sex in the poem, only a kind of archeological record of lust.

Labeling a poem as a "love poem" or a "death poem" is primarily a matter of convenience, a grouping based on the **subject matter** in a poem or the event or **topic** it chooses to engage. But as the poems we have been looking at suggest, poems that may be loosely called love poems or death poems may differ widely from one another, express totally different attitudes or ideas, and concentrate on very different aspects of the subject. The main advantages of grouping poems in this way for study is that a reader can become conscious of individual differences: a reading of two poems side by side may suggest how each is distinctive in what it has to say and how it says it.

What a poem has to say is often called its **theme,** the kind of statement it makes about its subject. We could say, for example, that the theme of "Leaving the Motel" is that illicit love is secretive, careful, transitory, and short on emotion and sentiment, or that secret sexual encounters tend to be brief, calculated, and characterized by restrained and insecure feelings. The theme of a poem may be expressed in several different ways, and poems often have more than one theme. "Barbie Doll" suggests that commercialized standards destroy human values; that rigid and idealized notions of normality cripple people who are different; that false standards of appearance and behavior can destroy human beings and lead to personal tragedy; that people are easily and tragically led to accept evaluations thrust upon them by others; that American consumers tend to be conformists, easily influenced in their outlook by advertising and by commercial products; that children who do not conform to middle-class standards and notions don't have a chance. Each of these statements could be demonstrated to be said or implied in the poem and rather central to it. But none of these statements individually nor all of them together would be an adequate substitute for the poem itself. To state the theme in such a brief and abstract way—while it may be helpful in clarifying what the poem does and does not say—never does justice to the experience of the poem, the way it works on us as readers. Poems affect us in all sorts of ways—emotional and psychological as well as rational—and often a poem's dramatization of a story, an event, or a moment bypasses our rational responses and affects us far more deeply than a clear and logical argument would.

Sometimes poems express feelings directly and quite simply:

LINDA PASTAN

love poem

I want to write you
a love poem as headlong
as our creek
after thaw
when we stand
on its dangerous
banks and watch it carry
with it every twig
every dry leaf and branch
in its path
every scruple
when we see it
so swollen
with runoff
that even as we watch
we must grab
each other
and step back
we must grab each
other or
get our shoes
soaked we must
grab each other

1988

But even the simplicity and directness of this poem, though they express genuine and powerful feelings, suggest how the art and craft of poems work. The poem expresses the desire to write a love poem even as the love poem itself begins to proceed; the desire and the resultant poem exist side by side, and in reading the poem we seem to watch the poet's creative process at work in developing appropriate metaphors and means of expression. The poem must be "headlong" (line 2), expressing the power of a love that needs to be compared to the irresistible forces of nature. The poem should, like the love it expresses, sweep along everything just as does Spring itself, and it should represent (and reproduce) the sense of watching that the lovers have when they observe natural processes at work. The poem, like the action it represents, has to suggest to readers the kind of desire that grabbing each other means to the lovers.

The lovers in this poem seem, at least to themselves, to own the world they observe, but it has causal power over their relationship. The creek on whose banks they stand is "our creek" (line 3), and what they observe as they watch its rising currents requires them ("must," lines 16, 19, 22) to "grab each other" over and over again. It is as if their love is part of nature itself, and what they seem to own actually controls them by subjecting them to forces larger than themselves. Everything—twigs, leaves, branches, scruples—is carried along by the powerful currents after the "thaw" (line 4), and the poem replicates the repeated actions of the lovers as if to power along observant readers just as the lovers are powered along by what they see. But the poem (and their love) admits dangers too; in fact, it is the fact of danger that propels the lovers to each other. The poem suggests that love provides a kind of haven, but the haven hardly involves passivity or peace; instead, it requires the kind of grabbing that means activity and boldness and deep engagement. Love here is no quiet or simple matter even if the expression of it in poems can be direct and based on a simple observation of experience. The "love poem" itself—linked as it is with the headlong currents of the creek from which the lovers are protecting themselves—even represents that which is beyond love and that therefore both threatens it and at the same time makes it happen. The power of poetry is thus affirmed at the center of the poem, but what poetry is about (love and life) is suggested to be more important. Poetry makes things happen but is not itself a substitute for life, just a means to make it more energetic and meaningful.

Poems, then, differ widely from one another even when they share a common subject. And the subjects of poetry also vary widely. It isn't true that there are certain "poetic" subjects and that there are others that aren't appropriate to poetry. Any human activity, thought, or feeling can be the subject of poetry. Poetry often deals with beauty and the softer, more attractive human emotions, but it can deal with ugliness and less attractive human conduct as well, for poetry seeks to mirror human beings and human events, showing us ourselves not only as we would like to be but as we are. Good poetry gets written about all kinds of topics, in all kinds of forms, with all kinds of attitudes. Here, for example, is a poem about a prison inmate—and about the conflict between individual and societal values.

ETHERIDGE KNIGHT

Hard Rock Returns to Prison from the Hospital for the Criminal Insane

Hard Rock was "known not to take no shit
From nobody," and he had the scars to prove it:
Split purple lips, lumped ears, welts above
His yellow eyes, and one long scar that cut
Across his temple and plowed through a thick
Canopy of kinky hair.

The WORD was that Hard Rock wasn't a mean nigger
Anymore, that the doctors had bored a hole in his head,
Cut out part of his brain, and shot electricity
Through the rest. When they brought Hard Rock back,
Handcuffed and chained, he was turned loose,
Like a freshly gelded stallion, to try his new status.
And we all waited and watched, like indians at a corral,
To see if the WORD was true.

As we waited we wrapped ourselves in the cloak
Of his exploits: "Man, the last time, it took eight
Screws to put him in the Hole."[1] "Yeah, remember when he
Smacked the captain with his dinner tray?" "He set
The record for time in the Hole—67 straight days!"
"Ol Hard Rock! man, that's one crazy nigger."
And then the jewel of a myth that Hard Rock had once bit
A screw on the thumb and poisoned him with syphilitic spit.

The testing came, to see if Hard Rock was really tame.
A hillbilly called him a black son of a bitch
And didn't lose his teeth, a screw who knew Hard Rock
From before shook him down and barked in his face.
And Hard Rock did *nothing*. Just grinned and looked silly,
His eyes empty like knot holes in a fence.

And even after we discovered that it took Hard Rock
Exactly 3 minutes to tell you his first name,
We told ourselves that he had just wised up,
Was being cool; but we could not fool ourselves for long,
And we turned away, our eyes on the ground. Crushed.
He had been our Destroyer, the doer of things
We dreamed of doing but could not bring ourselves to do,
The fears of years, like a biting whip,
Had cut grooves too deeply across our backs.

1968

1. Solitary confinement. *Screws:* guards.

The picture of Hard Rock as a kind of hero to other prison inmates is established early in the poem through a retelling of the legends circulated about him; the straightforward chronology of the poem sets up the mystery of how he will react after his "treatment" in the hospital. The poem identifies with those who wait; they are hopeful that Hard Rock's spirit has not been broken by surgery or shock treatments, and the lines crawl almost to a stop with disappointment in stanza 4. The "*nothing*" (line 27) of Hard Rock's response to teasing and taunting and the emptiness of his eyes ("like knot holes in a fence," line 28) reduce the heroic hopes and illusions to despair. The final stanza recounts the observers' attempts to reinterpret, to hang onto hope that their symbol of heroism could stand up against the best efforts to tame him, but the spirit has gone out of the hero-worshipers too, and the poem records them as beaten, conformed, deprived of their spirit as Hard Rock has been of his. The poem records the despair of the hopeless and it protests against the exercise of power that can curb even as rebellious a figure as Hard Rock.

The following poem is equally full of anger and disappointment, but it expresses its attitudes in a very different way.

WILLIAM BLAKE

London

I wander through each chartered street,
Near where the chartered Thames does flow,
And mark in every face I meet
Marks of weakness, marks of woe.

In every cry of every man,
In every Infant's cry of fear,
In every voice, in every ban,
The mind-forged manacles I hear.

How the Chimney-sweeper's cry
Every black'ning Church appalls;
And the hapless Soldier's sigh
Runs in blood down Palace walls.

But most through midnight streets I hear
How the youthful Harlot's curse
Blasts the new-born Infant's tear,
And blights with plagues the Marriage hearse.

1794

The poem gives a strong sense of how London feels to this particular observer; it is cluttered, constricting, oppressive. The wordplay here articulates and connects the strong emotions he associates with London experiences. The repeated words—"every," for example, or "cry"—intensify the sense of total despair in the city and weld connections between things not necessarily related—the cries of street vendors, for example, with the cries for help. The word "chartered" implies strong feelings too, and the word gives a particularly rigid sense of streets. Instead of seeming alive with people or bustling with movement, they are rigidly, coldly determined, controlled, cramped. And the same word is used for the river, as if it too were planned, programmed, laid out by an oppressor. In fact, the course of the Thames had been altered (slightly) by the government before Blake's time, but most important is the word's emotional force, the sense it projects of constriction and artificiality: the person speaking experiences London as if human artifice had totally altered nature. According to the poem, people are victimized too, "marked" by their confrontations with urbanness and the power of institutions: the "soldier's sigh" that "runs in blood down Palace walls" vividly suggests, through a metaphor that visually dramatizes the speaker's feelings, both the powerlessness of the individual and the callousness of power. The "description" of the city has clearly become, by now, a subjective, highly emotional, and vivid expression of how the speaker feels about London and what it represents to him.

One more thing about "London": at first it looks like an account of a personal experience, as if the speaker is describing and interpreting as he goes along: "I wander through each chartered street." But soon it is clear that he is describing many wanderings, putting together impressions from many walks, recreating a generalized or typical walk—which shows him "every" person in the streets, allows him to generalize about the churches being "appalled" (literally, made white) by the cry of the representative Chimney-sweeper, and presents his conclusions about soldiers, prostitutes, and infants. What we are given is not a personal record of an event, but a re-presentation of it, as it seems in the mind in retrospect—not a story, not a narrative or chronological account of events, but a dramatization of self that compresses many experiences into one.

"London" is somber in spite of the poet's playfulness with words. Wordplay may be witty and funny if it calls attention to its own cleverness, but here it involves the discovery of unsuspected (but meaningful) connections between things. The term **tone** is used to describe the attitude a poem takes toward its subject and theme. If the theme of a poem is *what* the poem says, the tone involves *how* one says it. The tone of "London" is sad, despairing, and angry; reading "London" aloud, one would try to show in one's voice the strong feelings that the poem expresses, just as one would try to reproduce tenderness and caring and passion in reading aloud "The Tally Stick" or "How Do I Love Thee?"

The following two poems might be said to be about animals, although both of them place their final emphasis on what human beings are like: the animal in each case is only the means to the end of exploring human nature. The poems share a common assumption that animals reflect human habits and conduct and may reveal much about ourselves, and in each case the woman central to the poem is revealed to be surprisingly unlike the way she thinks of herself. But the poems are very different from one another. Read each poem aloud, and try to imagine what each main character is like. What tones of voice do you use to help express the character of the killer in the first poem? What demands on your voice does the second poem make?

MAXINE KUMIN

Woodchucks

Gassing the woodchucks didn't turn out right.
The knockout bomb from the Feed and Grain Exchange
was featured as merciful, quick at the bone
and the case we had against them was airtight,
both exits shoehorned shut with puddingstone,[2]
but they had a sub-sub-basement out of range.

Next morning they turned up again, no worse
for the cyanide than we for our cigarettes
and state-store Scotch, all of us up to scratch.
They brought down the marigolds as a matter of course
and then took over the vegetable patch
nipping the broccoli shoots, beheading the carrots.

The food from our mouths, I said, righteously thrilling
to the feel of the .22, the bullets' neat noses.
I, a lapsed pacifist fallen from grace
puffed with Darwinian pieties for killing,
now drew a bead on the littlest woodchuck's face.
He died down in the everbearing roses.

Ten minutes later I dropped the mother. She
flipflopped in the air and fell, her needle teeth
still hooked in a leaf of early Swiss chard.
Another baby next. O one-two-three
the murderer inside me rose up hard,
the hawkeye killer came on stage forthwith.

There's one chuck left. Old wily fellow, he keeps
me cocked and ready day after day after day.

2. A mixture of cement, pebbles, and gravel.

All night I hunt his humped-up form. I dream
I sight along the barrel in my sleep.
If only they'd all consented to die unseen
gassed underground the quiet Nazi way.
1972

ADRIENNE RICH

Aunt Jennifer's Tigers

Aunt Jennifer's tigers prance across a screen,
Bright topaz denizens of a world of green.
They do not fear the men beneath the tree;
They pace in sleek chivalric certainty.

Aunt Jennifer's fingers fluttering through her wool
Find even the ivory needle hard to pull.
The massive weight of Uncle's wedding band
Sits heavily upon Aunt Jennifer's hand.

When Aunt is dead, her terrified hands will lie
Still ringed with ordeals she was mastered by.
The tigers in the panel that she made
Will go on prancing, proud and unafraid.
1951

How would your tone of voice change if you read "Woodchucks" aloud from beginning to end? What tone would you use to read the ending? How does the hunter feel about her increasing attraction to violence? Why does the poem begin by calling the gassing of the woodchucks "merciful" and end by describing it as "the quiet Nazi way"? What names does the hunter call herself? How does the name-calling affect your feelings about her? Exactly when does the hunter begin to *enjoy* the feel of the gun and the idea of killing? How does the poet make that clear?

Why are tigers a particularly appropriate contrast to the quiet and subdued manner of Aunt Jennifer? What words used to describe the tigers seem particularly significant? In what ways is the tiger an opposite of Aunt Jennifer? In what ways does it externalize her secrets? Why are Aunt Jennifer's hands described as "terrified"? What clues does the poem give about why Aunt Jennifer is so afraid? How does the poem make you feel about Aunt Jennifer? about her tigers? about her life? How would you describe the tone of the poem? How does the poet feel about Aunt Jennifer?

Twenty years after writing "Aunt Jennifer's Tigers," Adrienne Rich said this about the poem:

> In writing this poem, composed and apparently cool as it is, I thought I was creating a portrait of an imaginary woman. But this woman suffers from the opposition of her imagination, worked out in tapestry, and her life style, "ringed with ordeals she was mastered by." It was important to me that Aunt Jennifer was a person as distinct from myself as possible—distanced by the formalism of the poem, by its objective, observant tone—even by putting the woman in a different generation. In those years formalism was part of the strategy—like asbestos gloves, it allowed me to handle materials I couldn't pick up bare-handed.[3]

Not often do we have such an explicit comment on a poem by its author, and we don't actually have to have it to understand and experience the force of the poem (although such a statement may clarify why the author chose particular modes of presentation and how the poem fits into the author's own patterns of thinking and growing). Most poems contain within them what we need to know in order to tap the human and artistic resources they offer us.

Subject, theme, and tone: each of these categories gives us a way to begin considering poems and showing how one poem differs from another. Comparing poems on the same subject, or with a similar theme or tone, can lead to a clearer understanding of each individual poem and can refine our responses to the subtleties of individual differences. The title of a poem ("Leaving the Motel," for example) or the way the poem first introduces its subject often can give us a sense of what to expect, but we need to be open to surprise too. No two poems are going to be exactly alike in their effect on us; the variety of possible poems multiplies when you think of all the possible themes and tones that can be explored within any single subject. Varieties of feeling often coincide with varieties of thinking, and readers open to the pleasures of the unexpected may find themselves learning, growing, becoming more sensitive to ideas and human issues as well as more articulate about feelings and thoughts they already have.

▽ ▽ ▽

TONE A Glossary

subject: the general or specific area of concern of a poem; also called topic
theme: the statement a poem makes about its subject
tone: the attitude a poem takes toward its subject and theme
topic: see subject

3. In "When We Dead Awaken: Writing as Re-Vision," a talk given in December 1971 at the Women's Forum of the Modern Language Association.

ROBERT HAYDEN

Those Winter Sundays

Sundays too my father got up early
and put his clothes on in the blueblack cold,
then with cracked hands that ached
from labor in the weekday weather made
banked fires blaze. No one ever thanked him.

I'd wake and hear the cold splintering, breaking.
When the rooms were warm, he'd call,
and slowly I would rise and dress,
fearing the chronic angers of that house,

Speaking indifferently to him,
who had driven out the cold
and polished my good shoes as well.
What did I know, what did I know
of love's austere and lonely offices?

1966

SYLVIA PLATH

Daddy

You do not do, you do not do
Any more, black shoe
In which I have lived like a foot
For thirty years, poor and white,
Barely daring to breathe or Achoo.

Daddy, I have had to kill you.
You died before I had time—
Marble-heavy, a bag full of God,
Ghastly statue with one gray toe
Big as a Frisco seal

And a head in the freakish Atlantic
Where it pours bean green over blue
In the waters off beautiful Nauset.[4]
I used to pray to recover you.
Ach, du.[5]

In the German tongue, in the Polish town
Scraped flat by the roller
Of wars, wars, wars.

4. An inlet on Cape Cod. 5. "Oh, you" in German. Plath often portrays herself as Jewish and her oppressors as German. *Ich* (below): German for "I."

But the name of the town is common.
My Polack friend

Says there are a dozen or two.
So I never could tell where you
Put your foot, your root,
I never could talk to you.
The tongue stuck in my jaw.

It stuck in a barb wire snare.
Ich, ich, ich, ich,
I could hardly speak.
I thought every German was you.
And the language obscene

An engine, an engine
Chuffing me off like a Jew.
A Jew to Dachau, Auschwitz, Belsen.[6]
I began to talk like a Jew.
I think I may well be a Jew.

The snows of the Tyrol,[7] the clear beer of Vienna
Are not very pure or true.
With my gypsy-ancestress and my weird luck
And my Taroc[8] pack and my Taroc pack
I may be a bit of a Jew.

I have always been scared of *you*,
With your Luftwaffe,[9] your gobbledygoo.
And your neat moustache
And your Aryan eye, bright blue.
Panzer-man, panzer-man, O You—

Not God but a swastika
So black no sky could squeak through.
Every woman adores a Fascist,
The boot in the face, the brute
Brute heart of a brute like you.

You stand at the blackboard, daddy,
In the picture I have of you,
A cleft in your chin instead of your foot
But no less a devil for that, no not
Any less the black man who

Bit my pretty red heart in two.
I was ten when they buried you.

6. Sites of World War II German death camps. 7. Alpine region in Austria and northern Italy. The snow there is, legendarily, as pure as the beer is clear in Vienna. 8. Tarot, playing cards used mainly for fortune-telling. 9. German air force.

At twenty I tried to die
And get back, back, back to you.
I thought even the bones would do

But they pulled me out of the sack,
And they stuck me together with glue.
And then I knew what to do.
I made a model of you,
A man in black with a Meinkampf[1] look

And a love of the rack and the screw.
And I said I do, I do.
So daddy, I'm finally through.
The black telephone's off at the root,
The voices just can't worm through.

If I've killed one man, I've killed two—
The vampire who said he was you
And drank my blood for a year,
Seven years, if you want to know.
Daddy, you can lie back now.

There's a stake in your fat black heart
And the villagers never liked you.
They are dancing and stamping on you.
They always *knew* it was you.
Daddy, daddy, you bastard, I'm through.

1966

ALAN DUGAN

Elegy

I know but will not tell
you, Aunt Irene, why there
are soap-subs in the whiskey:
Uncle Robert had to have
a drink while shaving. May
there be no bloodshed in your house
this morning of my father's death
and no unkept appearance
in the living, since he has
to wear the rouge and lipstick
of your ceremony, mother,
for the first and last time:
father, hello and goodbye.

1963

1. The title of Adolf Hitler's autobiography and manifesto (1925–27); German for "my struggle."

DOROTHY LIVESAY

Green Rain

I remember long veils of green rain
Feathered like the shawl of my grandmother—
Green from the half-green of the spring trees
Waving in the valley.

I remember the road
Like the one which leads to my grandmother's house,
A warm house, with green carpets,
Geraniums, a trilling canary
And shining horse-hair chairs;
And the silence, full of the rain's falling
Was like my grandmother's parlour
Alive with herself and her voice, rising and falling—
Rain and wind intermingled.

I remember on that day
I was thinking only of my love
And of my love's house.
But now I remember the day
As I remember my grandmother.
I remember the rain as the feathery fringe of her shawl.

p. 1929

ROBERT CREELEY

I Know a Man

As I sd to my
friend, because I am
always talking,—John, I

sd, which was not his
name, the darkness sur-
rounds us, what

can we do against
it, or else, shall we &
why not, buy a goddamn big car,

drive, he sd, for
christ's sake, look
out where yr going.

1962

TESS GALLAGHER

Unanswered Letter

Your silence is leaning toward judgment.
Yesterday I bragged, writing to calm
my paranoid friend, that I never assume
the worst when my pals don't write. Now
assuming the worst, I think what I must have
done, or not done. Surely some recognition
will brand the door of my house, or
rich attention flutter down.

How natural, in silence, to credit delay
with intention, like the word *oar*
insisting on water. The need also to
advise the self around exaggeration,
i.e., "nobody loves me," because nothing *is*
coming back, and, next to nothing, not
to act like a transistor radio left on into
the night, voices singing like an ear
baffled by the rain, or someone refused
because they think so.

Those others you loved elsewhere, you miss
what they haven't said. They belong
to some permission to go on as more
than yourself, a clarity that adds you back
to all you cast off, as when
you want to be the good light of a lamp
scanning the firmament, or rain—its pleasure
with an open boat.

So what is unanswered keeps you coming back
to yourself, telling you what you wanted
only when it didn't come, having now
to make up this difference.
Even moments you think empty, the world
doesn't stop speaking—the windshield
blurred suddenly by a sighting of gravestones,
before you are driven
                    through the underpass.

1984

EDWARD THOMAS

The Owl

Downhill I came, hungry, and yet not starved;
Cold, yet had heat within me that was proof
Against the North wind; tired, yet so that rest
Had seemed the sweetest thing under a roof.

Then at the inn I had food, fire, and rest,
Knowing how hungry, cold, and tired was I.
All of the night was quite barred out except
An owl's cry, a most melancholy cry

Shaken out long and clear upon the hill,
No merry note, nor cause of merriment,
But one telling me plain what I escaped
And others could not, that night, as in I went.

And salted was my food, and my repose,
Salted and sobered, too, by the bird's voice
Speaking for all who lay under the stars,
Soldiers and poor, unable to rejoice. 1917

EMILY DICKINSON

[A narrow Fellow in the Grass]

A narrow Fellow in the Grass
Occasionally rides—
You may have met Him—did you not
His notice sudden is—

The Grass divides as with a Comb—
A spotted shaft is seen—
And then it closes at your feet
And opens further on—

He likes a Boggy Acre
A Floor too cool for Corn—
Yet when a Boy, and Barefoot—
I more than once at Noon

Have passed, I thought, a Whip lash
Unbraiding in the Sun
When stooping to secure it
It wrinkled, and was gone—

Several of Nature's People
I know, and they know me—
I feel for them a transport
Of cordiality—

But never met this Fellow
Attended, or alone
Without a tighter breathing
And Zero at the Bone— 1866

W. S. MERWIN

Burning the Cat

In the spring, by the big shuck-pile
Between the bramble-choked brook where the copperheads
Curled in the first sun, and the mud road,
All at once it could no longer be ignored.
The season steamed with an odor for which
There has never been a name, but it shouted above all.
When I went near, the wood-lice were in its eyes
And a nest of beetles in the white fur of its armpit.
I built a fire there by the shuck-pile
But it did no more than pop the beetles
And singe the damp fur, raising a stench
Of burning hair that bit through the sweet day-smell.
Then thinking how time leches after indecency,
Since both grief is indecent and the lack of it,
I went away and fetched newspaper,
And wrapped it in dead events, days and days,
Soaked it in kerosene and put it in
With the garbage on a heaped nest of sticks:
It was harder to burn than the peels of oranges,
Bubbling and spitting, and the reek was like
Rank cooking that drifted with the smoke out
Through the budding woods and clouded the shining dogwood.
But I became stubborn: I would consume it
Though the pyre should take me a day to build
And the flames rise over the house. And hours I fed
That burning, till I was black and streaked with sweat;
And poked it out then, with charred meat still clustering
Thick around the bones. And buried it so
As I should have done in the first place, for
The earth is slow, but deep, and good for hiding;
I would have used it if I had understood
How nine lives can vanish in one flash of a dog's jaws,

A car or a copperhead, and yet how one small
Death, however reckoned, is hard to dispose of. 1955

QUESTIONS

1. Consider carefully how the tone of "Those Winter Sundays" is created. What activities of the father inspire the son's admiration? Which words of the son are especially effective in suggesting his attitude toward his father? Why is the phrase "what did I know" repeated in line 13? What are the connotations of the word "austere" in line 14? How old does the son seem to be at the time the poem is written? How can you tell?

2. What information presented in Sylvia Plath's "Daddy" explains the poem's attitude toward "Daddy"? What other charges are made or implied against "Daddy"? What tonal purpose is served by the portrayal of "Daddy" as a Nazi? What adjectives would you use to describe the basic tone of voice in which the poem is spoken?

3. What attitude does "Elegy" take toward Aunt Irene? toward Uncle Robert? toward the mother? toward the father? How can you tell about the attitudes toward each? What individual words or factual details help to suggest the attitudes? Is "Elegy" an appropriate title for the poem? Why?

4. How much information do we have about the "I" in "The Owl"? What kind of message does the owl's cry provide? What attitude does the "I" have toward the owl? toward the activities on the hill that he has left behind? Describe the tones of voice you would use in reading the poem aloud. At what points in the poem would you vary your voice? Exactly how?

5. Which words and phrases early in "[A narrow Fellow in the Grass]" are especially important in creating the poem's playful and cheerful tone in the beginning? How, and exactly where, is the transition made to suggest the scariness of the snake?

6. In "Burning the Cat," describe the poem's attitude toward the endurance of the dead cat. How does the person speaking the poem feel about himself? How can you tell?

WRITING SUGGESTIONS

1. Paraphrase—that is, put into different words line by line and stanza by stanza—Gallagher's "Unanswered Letter." Summarize the poem's basic state-

ment in one sentence. How accurately do your paraphrase and summary represent the tone of the poem?

2. Compare the tone of voice used in reading "Woodchucks" aloud to that in "Burning the Cat." Pick out three or four key words from each poem that seem to you to help to control the tone. Then, concentrating on the words you have isolated, write a short essay, of no more than 600 words, in which you compare the tones of the two poems.

2 SPEAKER

Poems are personal. The thoughts and feelings they express belong to a specific person, and however general or universal their sentiments seem to be, poems come to us as the expression of an individual human voice. That voice is often the voice of the poet. But not always. Poets sometimes create a "character" just as writers of fiction or drama do—people who speak for them only indirectly. A character may, in fact, be very different from the poet, just as a character in a play or story is different from the author, and that person, the **speaker** of the poem, may express ideas or feelings very different from the poet's own. In the following poem, *two* individual voices in fact speak, and it is clear that, rather than himself speaking directly to us, the poet has chosen to create two speakers, both female, each of whom has a distinctive voice, personality, and character.

THOMAS HARDY

The Ruined Maid

"O 'Melia,[1] my dear, this does everything crown!
Who could have supposed I should meet you in Town?
And whence such fair garments, such prosperi-ty?"—
"O didn't you know I'd been ruined?" said she.

—"You left us in tatters, without shoes or socks,
Tired of digging potatoes, and spudding up docks;[2]
And now you've gay bracelets and bright feathers three!"—
"Yes: that's how we dress when we're ruined," said she.

—"At home in the barton[3] you said 'thee' and 'thou,'
And 'thik oon,' and 'theäs oon,' and 't'other'; but now
Your talking quite fits 'ee for high compa-ny!"—
"Some polish is gained with one's ruin," said she.

—"Your hands were like paws then, your face blue and bleak
But now I'm bewitched by your delicate cheek,
And your little gloves fit as on any la-dy!"—
"We never do work when we're ruined," said she.

1. Short for Amelia. 2. Spading up weeds. 3. Farmyard.

—"You used to call home-life a hag-ridden dream,
And you'd sigh, and you'd sock;[4] but at present you seem
To know not of megrims[5] or melancho-ly!"—
"True. One's pretty lively when ruined," said she.

—"I wish I had feathers, a fine sweeping gown,
And a delicate face, and could strut about Town!"—
"My dear—a raw country girl, such as you be,
Cannot quite expect that. You ain't ruined," said she.

1866

The first voice, that of a young woman who has remained back on the farm, is designated typographically (that is, by the way the poem is printed): there are dashes at the beginning and end of each of her speeches. She speaks the first part of each stanza, usually the first three lines. The second young woman, a companion and co-worker on the farm in years gone by, regularly gets the last line in each stanza (and in the last stanza, two lines), so it is easy to tell who is talking at every point. Also, the two speakers are just as clearly distinguished by what they say, how they say it, and what sort of person each proves to be. The nameless stay-at-home shows little knowledge of the world, and everything surprises her: seeing her former companion at all, but especially seeing her well clothed, cheerful, and polished; and as the poem develops she shows increasing envy of her more worldly friend. She is the "raw country girl" (line 23) that the other speaker says she is, and she still speaks the country dialect ("fits 'ee," line 11, for example) that she notices her friend has lost (lines 9–11). The "ruined" young woman ('Melia), on the other hand, says little except to keep repeating the refrain about having been ruined, but even the slight variations she plays on that theme suggest her sophistication and amusement at her farm friend, although she still uses a rural "ain't" at the end. We are not told the full story of their lives (was the ruined young woman thrown out? did she run away from home or work?), but we know enough (that they've been separated for some time, that the stay-at-home did not know where the other had gone) to allow the dialogue to articulate the contrast between them. The style of speech of each speaker then does the rest.

It is equally clear that there is a speaker (or, in this case, actually a singer) in stanzas 2 through 9 of this poem:

4. Deliver angry blows. 5. Migraine headaches.

X. J. KENNEDY

In a Prominent Bar in Secaucus One Day

To the tune of "The Old Orange Flute" or the tune of "Sweet Betsy from Pike"

In a prominent bar in Secaucus[6] one day
Rose a lady in skunk with a topheavy sway,
Raised a knobby red finger—all turned from their beer—
While with eyes bright as snowcrust she sang high and clear:

"Now who of you'd think from an eyeload of me
That I once was a lady as proud as could be?
Oh I'd never sit down by a tumbledown drunk
If it wasn't, my dears, for the high cost of junk.

"All the gents used to swear that the white of my calf
Beat the down of a swan by a length and a half.
In the kerchief of linen I caught to my nose
Ah, there never fell snot, but a little gold rose.

"I had seven gold teeth and a toothpick of gold.
My Virginia cheroot was a leaf of it rolled
And I'd light it each time with a thousand in cash—
Why the bums used to fight if I flicked them an ash.

"Once the toast of the Biltmore,[7] the belle of the Taft,
I would drink bottle beer at the Drake, never draft,
And dine at the Astor on Salisbury steak
With a clean tablecloth for each bite I did take.

"In a car like the Roxy[8] I'd roll to the track,
A steel-guitar trio, a bar in the back,
And the wheels made no noise, they turned over so fast,
Still it took you ten minutes to see me go past.

"When the horses bowed down to me that I might choose,
I bet on them all, for I hated to lose.
Now I'm saddled each night for my butter and eggs
And the broken threads race down the backs of my legs.

"Let you hold in mind, girls, that your beauty must pass
Like a lovely white clover that rusts with its grass.
Keep your bottoms off barstools and marry you young
Or be left—an old barrel with many a bung.

6. A small town on the Hackensack River in New Jersey, a few miles west of Manhattan. 7. Like the Taft, Drake, and Astor, a once-fashionable New York hotel. 8. A luxurious old New York theater and movie house, the site of many "world premieres" in the heyday of Hollywood.

"For when time takes you out for a spin in his car
You'll be hard-pressed to stop him from going too far
And be left by the roadside, for all your good deeds,
Two toadstools for tits and a face full of weeds."

All the house raised a cheer, but the man at the bar
Made a phonecall and up pulled a red patrol car
And she blew us a kiss as they copped her away
From that prominent bar in Secaucus, N.J.

1961

Again, we learn about the character primarily through her own words, although we don't have to believe everything she tells us about her past. From her introduction in the first stanza we get some general notion of her appearance and condition, but it is she who tells us that she is a junkie (line 8), a prostitute (line 27), and that her face and figure are pretty well shot (lines 32, 36). That information could make her a sad case, and the poem might lament her state or allow her to lament it, but instead the poem presents her in a light and friendly way. She is anxious to give advice and sound moral (line 31, for example), but she's also enormously cheerful about herself, and her spirit repeatedly bursts through her song. Her performance gives her a lot of pleasure as she exaggerates outrageously about her former luxury and prominence, and even her departure in a patrol car she chooses to treat as a grand exit, throwing a kiss to her audience. The comedy is bittersweet, perhaps, but she is allowed to present herself, through her own words and attitudes, as a likable character. The glorious fiction of her life, narrated with energy and polish in the manner of a practiced and accomplished liar, betrays some rather naive notions of good taste and luxurious living (lines 18–26). But this "lady in skunk" has a picturesque and engaging style, a refreshing sense of humor about herself, and a flair for theatricality. Like the cheap fur she wears, her experiences in what she considers high life satisfy her sense of style and celebration. The self-portrait accumulates, almost completely through how she talks about herself, and the poet develops our attitude toward her by allowing her to recount her story herself, in her own words—or rather in words chosen for her by the author.

The following poem uses the idea of speaker in a very different way and for quite different tonal purposes.

ADRIENNE RICH

Letters in the Family

I: Catalonia, 1936

Dear Parents:
I'm the daughter
you didn't bless when she left,
an unmarried woman wearing a khaki knapsack
with a poor mark in Spanish.
I'm writing now
from a plaster-dusted desk in a town
pocked street by street with hand grenades,
some of them, dear ones, thrown by me.
This is a school: the children are at war.
You don't need honors in schoolroom Spanish here
to be of use and my right arm
's as strong as anyone's. I sometimes think
all languages are spoken here,
even mine, which you got zero in.
Don't worry. Don't try to write. I'm happy,
if you could know it.
Rochelle.

II: Yugoslavia, 1944[9]

Dear Chana,
where are you now?
Am sending this pocket-to-pocket
(though we both know pockets we'd hate to lie in).
They showed me that poem you gave Reuven,
about the match:
Chana, you know, I never was
for martyrdom. I thought we'd try our best,
ragtag mission that we were,
then clear out if the signals looked too bad.
Something in you drives things ahead for me
but if I can I mean to stay alive.
We're none of us giants, you know,
just small, frail, inexperienced romantic people.

9. See *Hannah Senesh: Her Life and Diary* (New York: Schocken, 1973). Born in Budapest, 1921, Hannah Senesh became a Zionist and emigrated to Palestine at the age of eighteen; her mother and brother remained in Europe. In 1943, she joined an expedition of Jews who trained under the British to parachute behind Nazi lines in Europe and connect with the partisan underground, to rescue Jews in Hungary, Romania, and Czechoslovakia. She was arrested by the Nazis, imprisoned, tortured, and executed in November 1944. Like the other letter-writers, "Esther" is an imagined person.

See also Ruth Whitman's long poem, *The Testing of Hannah Senesh* (Detroit: Wayne State University Press, 1986). [Author's note]

But there are things we learn.
You know the sudden suck of empty space
between the jump and the ripcord pull?
I hate it. I hate it so,
I've hated you for your dropping
ecstatically in free-fall, in the training,
your look, dragged on the ground, of knowing
precisely why you were there.
My mother's
still in Palestine. And yours
still there in Hungary. Well, there we are.
When this is over—
I'm
your earthbound friend to the end, still yours—
Esther.

III: Southern Africa, 1986

Dear children:
We've been walking nights
a long time over rough terrain,
sometimes through marshes. Days we hide
under what bushes we can find.
Our stars steer us. I write
on my knee by a river with a weary hand,
and the weariness will come through
this letter that should tell you
nothing but love. I can't say where we are,
what weeds are in bloom, what birds cry at dawn.
The less you know the safer.
But not to know how you are going on—
Matile's earache, Emma's lessons, those tell-tale
eyes and tongues, so quick—are you remembering
to be brave and wise and strong?
At the end of this hard road
we'll sit all together at one meal
and I'll tell you everything: the names
of our comrades, how the letters
were routed to you, why I left.
And I'll stop and say, "Now you,
grown so big, how was it for you, those times?
Look, I know you in detail, every inch of each
sweet body, haven't I washed and dried you
a thousand times?"
And we'll eat and tell our stories
together. That is my reason.
Ma.

1989

As in "The Ruined Maid," this poem uses different voices, and here they are clearly distinguished as different "historical" characters—Rochelle, Esther, and "Ma", women from three separate places and times who in letter form tell their own stories. In each case, the individual story is part of some larger historical moment, and although all three characters are (as the author's footnote points out) fictional, the three stories together present a kind of history of female heroism in difficult cultural moments.

Read the poem aloud and notice how different in tone the three voices sound; each woman has distinctive expressions and syntax of her own. All are in part defined by their relationships to families left behind, but all are defined even more fully by their own idealistic determination to resist the larger social and political forces in the cultures where they are at the time they write their letters. Telling stories, the pleasure identified by the third speaker as the ultimate purpose of her actions (lines 56–62), is important to all three speakers as a way of defining themselves in relation to their families; to the poem, the telling of separate stories by the different speakers becomes the collective means to exemplify the power of women in history in action.

Some speakers in poems are not, however, nearly so heroic or attractive, and some poems create a speaker who makes us dislike him or her, also because of what the poet makes him or her say, as the following poem does. Here the speaker, as the title implies, is a monk, but he shows himself to be most unmonklike: mean, self-righteous, and despicable.

ROBERT BROWNING

Soliloquy of the Spanish Cloister[1]

Gr-r-r—there go, my heart's abhorrence!
    Water your damned flower-pots, do!
If hate killed men, Brother Lawrence,
    God's blood, would not mine kill you!
What? your myrtle-bush wants trimming?
    Oh, that rose has prior claims—
Needs its leaden vase filled brimming?
    Hell dry you up with its flames!

At the meal we sit together:
    Salve tibi![2] I must hear
Wish talk of the kind of weather,
    Sort of season, time of year:

1. Monastery. 2. Hail to thee. Italics usually indicate the words of Brother Lawrence.

Not a plenteous cork-crop: scarcely
Dare we hope oak-galls,[3] *I doubt:*
What's the Latin name for "parsley"?
What's the Greek name for Swine's Snout?

Whew! We'll have our platter burnished,
Laid with care on our own shelf!
With a fire-new spoon we're furnished,
And a goblet for ourself,
Rinsed like something sacrificial
Ere 'tis fit to touch our chaps[4]—
Marked with L. for our initial!
(He-he! There his lily snaps!)

Saint, forsooth! While brown Dolores
Squats outside the Convent bank
With Sanchicha, telling stories,
Steeping tresses in the tank,
Blue-black, lustrous, thick like horsehairs,
—Can't I see his dead eye glow,
Bright as 'twere a Barbary corsair's?[5]
(That is, if he'd let it show!)

When he finishes refection,[6]
Knife and fork he never lays
Cross-wise, to my recollection,
As do I, in Jesu's praise.
I the Trinity illustrate,
Drinking watered orange-pulp—
In three sips the Arian[7] frustrate;
While he drains his at one gulp.

Oh, those melons? If he's able
We're to have a feast! so nice!
One goes to the Abbot's table,
All of us get each a slice.
How go on your flowers? None double?
Not one fruit-sort can you spy?
Strange!—And I, too, at such trouble,
Keep them close-nipped on the sly!

There's a great text in Galatians,
Once you trip on it, entails
Twenty-nine distinct damnations,[8]
One sure, if another fails:
If I trip him just a-dying,
Sure of heaven as sure can be,

3. Abnormal growth on oak trees, used for tanning. 4. Jaws. 5. African pirate's. 6. A meal. 7. A heretical sect that denied the Trinity. 8. Galatians 5:15–23 provides a long list of possible offenses, but they do not add up to 29.

Spin him round and send him flying
    Off to hell, a Manichee?[9]

Or, my scrofulous French novel
    On gray paper with blunt type!
Simply glance at it, you grovel
    Hand and foot in Belial's gripe:[1]
If I double down its pages
    At the woeful sixteenth print,
When he gathers his greengages,
    Ope a sieve and slip it in't?

Or, there's Satan!—one might venture
    Pledge one's soul to him, yet leave
Such a flaw in the indenture
    As he'd miss till, past retrieve,
Blasted lay that rose-acacia
    We're so proud of! *Hy, Zy, Hine* . . .[2]
'St, there's Vespers! *Plena gratiâ*
    Ave, Virgo.[3] Gr-r-r—you swine!

1842

Not many poems begin with a growl, and in this one it turns out to be fair warning that we are about to get to know a real beast, even though he is in the clothing of a religious man. In line 1, he has already shown himself to hold a most uncharitable attitude toward his fellow monk, Brother Lawrence, and by line 4 he has uttered two profanities and admitted his intense feelings of hatred and vengefulness. His ranting and roaring is full of exclamation points (four in the first stanza!), and he reveals his own personality and character when he imagines curses and unflattering nicknames for Brother Lawrence or plots malicious jokes on him. By the end, we have accumulated no knowledge of Brother Lawrence that makes him seem a fit target for such rage (except that he is pious, dutiful, and pleasant—perhaps enough to make this sort of speaker despise him), but we have discovered the speaker to be lecherous (stanza 4), full of false piety (stanza 5), malicious in trivial matters (stanza 6), ready to use his theological learning to sponsor damnation rather than salvation (stanza 7), a closet reader and viewer of pornography within the monastery (stanza 8)—even willing to risk his own soul in order to torment Brother Lawrence (last stanza).

The speaker is made to characterize himself; the details accrue and accumulate into a fairly full portrait, and here we do not have even an opening and

9. A heretic. According to the Manichean heresy, the world was divided into the forces of good and evil, equally powerful. 1. In the clutches of Satan. 2. Possibly the beginning of an incantation or curse. 3. The opening words of the *Ave Maria*, here reversed: "Full of grace, Hail, Virgin."

closing "objective" description (as in "In a Prominent Bar") or another speaker (as in "The Ruined Maid") to give us perspective. Except for the moments when the speaker mimics or parodies Brother Lawrence (usually in italic type), we have only the speaker's own words and thoughts. But that is enough; the poet has controlled them so carefully that we clearly know what he thinks of the speaker he has created—that he is a mean-spirited, vengeful hypocrite, a thoroughly disreputable and unlikable character. The whole poem has been about him and his attitudes; the point of the poem has been to characterize the speaker and develop in us a dislike of him and what he stands for—total hypocrisy.

In reading a poem like this aloud, we would want our voice to suggest all the unlikable features of a hypocrite. We would also need to suggest, through the tone of voice we used, the author's contemptuous mocking of the rage and hypocrisy, and we would want, like an actor, to create strong disapproval in the hearer. The poem's words (the ones the author has given to the speaker) clearly imply those attitudes, and we would want our voice to express them. Usually there is much more to a poem than the identification and characterization of the speaker, but in many cases it is necessary to identify the speaker and determine his or her character before we can appreciate what else goes on in the poem. And sometimes, as here, in looking for the speaker of the poem, we come near to the center of the poem itself.

Sometimes the effect of a poem depends on our recognizing the temporal position of the speaker as well as her or his identity. The following poem, for example, quickly makes plain that a childhood experience is at the center of the action and that the speaker is female:

TESS GALLAGHER

Sudden Journey

Maybe I'm seven in the open field—
the straw-grass so high
only the top of my head makes a curve
of brown in the yellow. Rain then.
First a little. A few drops on my
wrist, the right wrist. More rain.
My shoulders, my chin. Until I'm looking up
to let my eyes take the bliss.
I open my face. Let the teeth show. I
pull my shirt down past the collar-bones.
I'm still a boy under my breast spots.

I can drink anywhere. The rain. My
skin shattering. Up suddenly, needing
to gulp, turning with my tongue, my arms out
running, running in the hard, cold plenitude
of all those who reach earth by falling.

1984

The sense of adventure and wonder here has a lot to do with the childlike syntax and words at the beginning of the poem. Sentences are short, observations direct and simple. The rain becomes exciting and blissful and totally absorbing as the child's actions and reactions take over the poem in lines 2–13. But not all of the poem takes place in a child's mind in spite of the precise and impressive recreation of childish responses and feelings. The opening line makes clear that we are sliding into a supposition of the past; "maybe I'm seven" makes clear that we, as conspiring adults, are pretending ourselves into earlier time. And at the end the word "plenitude"—crucial to interpreting the poem's full effect and meaning—makes clear that we are finding an adult perspective on the incident. Elsewhere, too, the adult world gives the incident meaning. In line 12, for example, the joke about being able to drink anywhere depends on an adult sense of what being a boy might mean. The "journey" of the poem's title is not only the little girl's running in the rain but also the adult movement into a past recreated and newly understood.

The speaker in the following poem positions herself very differently, but we do not get a very full sense of her until the poem is well along. As you read, try to imitate the tone of voice you think this kind of person would use. Exactly when do you begin to feel that you know what she is like?

DOROTHY PARKER

A Certain Lady

Oh, I can smile for you, and tilt my head,
And drink your rushing words with eager lips,
And paint my mouth for you a fragrant red,
And trace your brows with tutored finger-tips.
When you rehearse your list of loves to me,
Oh, I can laugh and marvel, rapturous-eyed.
And you laugh back, nor can you ever see
The thousand little deaths my heart has died.
And you believe, so well I know my part,
That I am gay as morning, light as snow,
And all the straining things within my heart
You'll never know.

Oh, I can laugh and listen, when we meet,
  And you bring tales of fresh adventurings—
Of ladies delicately indiscreet,
  Of lingering hands, and gently whispered things.
And you are pleased with me, and strive anew
  To sing me sagas of your late delights.
Thus do you want me—marveling, gay, and true—
  Nor do you see my staring eyes of nights.
And when, in search of novelty, you stray,
  Oh, I can kiss you blithely as you go . . .
And what goes on, my love, while you're away,
  You'll never know.

1937

To whom does the speaker seem to be talking? What sort of person is he? How do you feel about him? Which habits and attitudes of his do you like least? How soon can you tell that the speaker is not altogether happy about his conversation and conduct? In what tone of voice would you read the first 22 lines aloud? What attitude would you try to express toward the person spoken to? What tone would you use for the last two lines? How would you describe the speaker's personality? What aspects of her behavior are most crucial to the poem's effect?

It is easy to assume that the speaker in a poem is an extension of the poet. Is the speaker in this poem Dorothy Parker? Maybe. A lot of Parker's poems present a similar world-weary posture and a kind of cynicism about romantic love (look, for example, at "Comment" in *Reading More Poetry*). But the poem is hardly an example of self-revelation, a giving away of personal secrets. If it were, it would be silly, not to say risky, to address her lover in a way that gives damaging facts about a pose she has been so careful to set up.

In poems such as "The Ruined Maid," "In a Prominent Bar," and "Soliloquy of the Spanish Cloister," we are in no danger of mistaking the speaker for the poet, once we have recognized that poets may create speakers who participate in specific situations much as in fiction or drama. When there is a pointed discrepancy between the speaker and what we know of the poet—when the speaker is a woman, for example, and the poet is a man—we know we have a created speaker to contend with and that the point (or at least *one* point) in the poem is to observe the characterization carefully. In "A Certain Lady" we may be less sure, and in other poems the discrepancy between speaker and poet may be even more uncertain. What are we to make, for example, of the speaker in "Woodchucks" in the previous chapter? Is that speaker the real Maxine Kumin? At best (without knowing something quite specific about the author) we can only say "maybe" to that question. What we can be sure of is the sort of person the speaker is portrayed to be—someone (man? or woman?) surprised to discover feelings and attitudes that contradict values apparently held confidently. And that is exactly what we need to know for the poem to have its effect.

A similar kind of self-mocking of the speaker is present in the following poem, but here the mockery is put to less revelatory, more comic ends.

A. R. AMMONS

Needs

I want something suited to my special needs
I want chrome hubcaps, pin-on attachments
and year round use year after year
I want a workhorse with smooth uniform cut,
dozer blade and snow blade & deluxe steering
wheel
I want something to mow, throw snow, tow
and sow with
I want precision reel blades
I want a console styled dashboard
I want an easy spintype recoil starter
I want combination bevel and spur gears, 14
gauge stamped steel housing and
washable foam element air cleaner
I want a pivoting front axle and extrawide
turf tires
I want an inch of foam rubber inside a vinyl
covering
and especially if it's not too much, if I
can deserve it, even if I can't pay for it
I want to mow while riding.

1970

The poet here may be teasing himself about his desire for comfort and ease—and showing how readily advertisements and catalog descriptions manipulate us. But the speaker doesn't have to be the author for the teasing to work. In fact, the effect is to tease those attitudes no matter who holds them by teasing a speaker who illustrates the attitudes. It doesn't matter to the poem whether the speaker is the poet himself or some totally invented character. If the speaker is a version of the poet himself—perhaps a *side* of his personality that he is exploring—the portrait is still fictional in an important sense. The poem presents not a whole human being (*no* poem could do that) but only a version of him—a mood perhaps, an aspect, an attitude, a part of that person. The poet presents someone with an obsession, in this case a small and not very damaging one, and allows him to spout phrases as if he were reciting from an ad. The "portrait" is made more comic by a clear sense the poem projects that what we have is only a part of the person, an interest grown too intense, gone askew, gotten out of proportion, something that happens to most of us from time to time. All we know about the speaker is that he has a one-track mind, that he is obsessed by his own luxurious comfort. He may not even be a "he": there is nothing in the poem that makes us certain that the speaker is male. It is customary to think of the speaker in a poem written by a man as "he" and in a poem written by a woman as "she" (as in Maxine Kumin's "Woodchucks") unless the poem presents contrary evidence, but it is merely a convenience, a habit, nothing more.

Even when poets present themselves as if they were speaking directly to us in their own voices, their poems present only a partial portrait, something considerably less than the full personality of the poet. Even when there is not an obviously created character—someone with distinct characteristics that are different from those of the poet—strategies of characterization are used to present the person speaking in one way and not another. Even in a poem like the following one, it is still a good idea to talk of the speaker instead of the poet, although here it is probable that the poet is writing about a personal, actual experience.

WILLIAM WORDSWORTH

She Dwelt among the Untrodden Ways

She dwelt among the untrodden ways
    Beside the springs of Dove,[4]
A Maid whom there were none to praise
    And very few to love:

A violet by a mossy stone
    Half hidden from the eye!
—Fair as a star, when only one
    Is shining in the sky.

She lived unknown, and few could know
    When Lucy ceased to be;
But she is in her grave, and, oh,
    The difference to me!

1800

It is hard to say whether this poem is more about Lucy or about how the speaker feels about her death. Her simple life, far removed from fame and

4. A small stream in the Lake District in northern England, near where Wordsworth lived in Dove Cottage at Grasmere.

known only to a few, is said nevertheless to have been beautiful. We know little else about her beyond her name and where she lived, in a beautiful but then-isolated section of northern England. We don't know if she was young or old, only that the speaker thinks of her as "fair" and compares her to a "violet by a mossy stone." What we do know is that the speaker feels her loss deeply, so deeply that he is almost inarticulate with grief, lapsing into simple exclamation ("oh," line 11) and unable to articulate the "difference" that her death makes.

Did Lucy actually live? Was she a friend of the poet? We don't know; the poem doesn't tell us, and even biographers of Wordsworth are unsure. What we do know is that Wordsworth was able to represent grief over the death very powerfully. Whether the speaker is the historical Wordsworth or not, that speaker is a major focus of the poem, and it is his feelings that the poem isolates and expresses. We need to recognize some characteristics of the speaker and be sensitive to his feelings for the poem to work.

The following poem similarly seems to draw upon an actual occurrence and present a speaker who is the poet herself.

SHARON OLDS

In the Hospital Near the End

Suddenly my father lifted up his nightie, I
turned my head away but he cried out
Share!, my nickname, so I turned and looked. He was
sitting in the cranked-up hospital bed with the
gown up around his neck
to show me what had happened. I looked where his
solid ruddy stomach had been and I
saw the skin fallen into loose
dark hairy rippled folds
lying in a pool of folds
down at the base of his abdomen,
the gaunt torso of a big man
who is dying soon. Right away
I saw how much his hips are like mine,
the long, white angles, and then how
much his pelvis is like my daughter's, a
chambered shell hollowed out,
I saw the sculptural folds of skin like
something poured, some rich thick matter, I
saw the rueful smile on his face,
the cast-up eyes, his innocence as he
shows me his old half-sloughed body
full of cancer, he knows I will be

interested, he knows I will find him
appealing. If you had ever told me I would
sit by him and he would pull up his nightie and I'd
look at him, at his naked body, if you'd
told me I would see the dark
thick bud of his penis in all that
dark hair and just look at him
in affection and uneasy wonder,
I would not have believed you. But now I can still
see the tiny snowflakes, white and
night-blue, on the cotton of the gown as it
rises the way we were promised at death it would rise,
the veils would fall from our eyes, we would know everything.

1990

Other poems by Olds written at about the same time also recount moments in the approaching death of a father—compare, for example, "The Glass" in *Reading Poetry*—and the similar situations may suggest that the poet was herself struggling with such an event. But even if we were to read enough about the poet's life to be sure that the poem was based on an actual event, we would still have to be careful about assuming that the speaker was, plainly and simply, the poet herself. It may well be that the "I" in this poem is very close to the historical Sharon Olds in 1990, but we are still well advised as readers to think of the speaker in the poem as the woman characterized specifically in the text and not necessarily as altogether identifiable with the poet.

The poems we have looked at in this chapter—and the group that follows at the end of the chapter—all suggest the value of beginning the reading of any poem with a simple question: Who is speaking and what do we know about him or her? Putting together the evidence that the poem presents in answer to this question can often take us a long way into the poem. For some poems, this question won't help a great deal because the speaking voice is too indistinct or the character behind the poem too scantily presented, but in many cases asking this question will lead you toward the central experience the poem offers.

▽ ▽ ▽

SPEAKER A Glossary

speaker: a person, not necessarily the author, who is the voice of the poem

HENRY REED

Lessons of the War

JUDGING DISTANCES

Not only how far away, but the way that you say it
Is very important. Perhaps you may never get
The knack of judging a distance, but at least you know
How to report on a landscape: the central sector,
The right of arc and that, which we had last Tuesday,
    And at least you know

That maps are of time, not place, so far as the army
Happens to be concerned—the reason being,
Is one which need not delay us. Again, you know
There are three kinds of tree, three only, the fir and the poplar,
And those which have bushy tops to; and lastly
    That things only seem to be things.

A barn is not called a barn, to put it more plainly,
Or a field in the distance, where sheep may be safely grazing.
You must never be over-sure. You must say, when reporting:
At five o'clock in the central sector is a dozen
Of what appear to be animals; whatever you do,
    Don't call the bleeders *sheep*.

I am sure that's quite clear; and suppose, for the sake of example,
The one at the end, asleep, endeavors to tell us
What he sees over there to the west, and how far away,
After first having come to attention. There to the west,
On the fields of summer the sun and the shadows bestow
    Vestments of purple and gold.

The still white dwellings are like a mirage in the heat,
And under the swaying elms a man and a woman
Lie gently together. Which is, perhaps, only to say
That there is a row of houses to the left of arc,
And that under some poplars a pair of what appear to be humans
    Appear to be loving.

Well that, for an answer, is what we might rightly call
Moderately satisfactory only, the reason being,
Is that two things have been omitted, and those are important.
The human beings, now: in what direction are they,
And how far away, would you say? And do not forget
    There may be dead ground in between.

There may be dead ground in between; and I may not have got
The knack of judging a distance; I will only venture

A guess that perhaps between me and the apparent lovers,
(Who, incidentally, appear by now to have finished,)
At seven o'clock from the houses, is roughly a distance
Of about one year and a half.

1946

AUDRE LORDE

Hanging Fire

I am fourteen
and my skin has betrayed me
the boy I cannot live without
still sucks his thumb
in secret
how come my knees are
always so ashy
what if I die
before morning
and momma's in the bedroom
with the door closed.

I have to learn how to dance
in time for the next party
my room is too small for me
suppose I die before graduation
they will sing sad melodies
but finally
tell the truth about me
There is nothing I want to do
and too much
that has to be done
and momma's in the bedroom
with the door closed.

Nobody even stops to think
about my side of it
I should have been on Math Team
my marks were better than his
why do I have to be
the one
wearing braces
I have nothing to wear tomorrow
will I live long enough
to grow up
and momma's in the bedroom
with the door closed.

1978

JOHN BETJEMAN

In Westminster Abbey[5]

Let me take this other glove off
As the *vox humana*[6] swells,
And the beauteous fields of Eden
Bask beneath the Abbey bells.
Here, where England's statesmen lie,
Listen to a lady's cry.

Gracious Lord, oh bomb the Germans.
Spare their women for Thy Sake,
And if that is not too easy
We will pardon Thy Mistake.
But, gracious Lord, whate'er shall be,
Don't let anyone bomb me.

Keep our Empire undismembered
Guide our Forces by Thy Hand,
Gallant blacks from far Jamaica,
Honduras and Togoland;
Protect them Lord in all their fights,
And, even more, protect the whites.

Think of what our Nation stands for,
Books from Boots[7] and country lanes,
Free speech, free passes, class distinction,
Democracy and proper drains.
Lord, put beneath Thy special care
One-eighty-nine Cadogan Square.[8]

Although dear Lord I am a sinner,
I have done no major crime;
Now I'll come to Evening Service
Whensoever I have the time.
So, Lord, reserve for me a crown,
And do not let my shares go down.

I will labor for Thy Kingdom,
Help our lads to win the war,
Send white feathers to the cowards[9]
Join the Women's Army Corps,[1]

5. Gothic church in London in which English monarchs are crowned and famous Englishmen are buried (see lines 5, 39–40). 6. Organ tones which resemble the human voice. 7. A chain of London pharmacies. 8. Presumably where the speaker lives, in a fairly fashionable area. 9. White feathers were sometimes given, or sent, to men not in uniform, to suggest that they were cowards and should join the armed forces. 1. The speaker uses the old World War I name (Women's Army Auxiliary Corps) of the Auxiliary Territorial Service, an organization that performed domestic (and some foreign) defense duties.

Then wash the Steps around Thy Throne
In the Eternal Safety Zone.

Now I feel a little better,
    What a treat to hear Thy Word
Where the bones of leading statesmen,
    Have so often been interred.
And now, dear Lord, I cannot wait
Because I have a luncheon date.

1940

MARGARET ATWOOD

Rat Song

When you hear me singing
you get the rifle down
and the flashlight, aiming for my brain,
but you always miss

and when you set out the poison
I piss on it
to warn the others.

You think: *That one's too clever,*
she's dangerous, because
I don't stick around to be slaughtered
and you think I'm ugly too
despite my fur and pretty teeth
and my six nipples and snake tail.
All I want is love, you stupid
humanist. See if you can.

Right, I'm a parasite, I live off your
leavings, gristle and rancid fat,
I take without asking
and make nests in your cupboards
out of your suits and underwear.
You'd do the same if you could,

if you could afford to share
my crystal hatreds.
It's your throat I want, my mate
trapped in your throat.
Though you try to drown him
with your greasy person voice,
he is hiding / between your syllables
I can hear him singing.

1974

SYLVIA PLATH

Mirror

I am silver and exact. I have no preconceptions.
Whatever I see I swallow immediately
Just as it is, unmisted by love or dislike.
I am not cruel, only truthful—
The eye of a little god, four-cornered.
Most of the time I meditate on the opposite wall.
It is pink, with speckles. I have looked at it so long
I think it is a part of my heart. But it flickers.
Faces and darkness separate us over and over.

Now I am a lake. A woman bends over me,
Searching my reaches for what she really is.
Then she turns to those liars, the candles or the moon.
I see her back, and reflect it faithfully.
She rewards me with tears and an agitation of hands.
I am important to her. She comes and goes.
Each morning it is her face that replaces the darkness.
In me she has drowned a young girl, and in me an old woman
Rises toward her day after day, like a terrible fish.

1961

TOM WAYMAN

Picketing Supermarkets

Because all this food is grown in the store
do not take the leaflet.
Cabbages, broccoli and tomatoes
are raised at night in the aisles.
Milk is brewed in the rear storage areas.
Beef produced in vats in the basement.
Do not take the leaflet.
Peanut butter and soft drinks
are made fresh each morning by store employees.
Our oranges and grapes
are so fine and round
that when held up to the lights they cast no shadow.
Do not take the leaflet.

And should you take one
do not believe it.
This chain of stores has no connection

with anyone growing food someplace else.
How could we have an effect on local farmers?
Do not believe it.

The sound here is Muzak, for your enjoyment.
It is not the sound of children crying.
There *is* a lady offering samples
to mark Canada Cheese Month.
There is no dark-skinned man with black hair beside her
wanting to show you the inside of a coffin.
You would not have to look if there was.
And there are no Nicaraguan heroes
in any way connected with the bananas.

Pay no attention to these people.
The manager is a citizen.
All this food is grown in the store.

1973

SEAMUS HEANEY

The Outlaw

Kelly's kept an unlicensed bull, well away
From the road: you risked fine but had to pay

The normal fee if cows were serviced there.
Once I dragged a nervous Friesian on a tether

Down a lane of alder, shaggy with catkin,
Down to the shed the bull was kept in.

I gave Old Kelly the clammy silver, though why
I could not guess. He grunted a curt 'Go by

Get up on that gate'. And from my lofty station
I watched the business-like conception.

The door, unbolted, whacked back against the wall.
The illegal sire fumbled from his stall

Unhurried as an old steam engine shunting,
He circled, snored and nosed. No hectic panting,

Just the unfussy ease of a good tradesman;
Then an awkward, unexpected jump, and

His knobbed forelegs straddling her flank,
He slammed life home, impassive as a tank,

Dropping off like a tipped-up load of sand.
'She'll do,' said Kelly and tapped his ash-plant

Across her hindquarters. 'If not, bring her back.'
I walked ahead of her, the rope now slack

While Kelly whooped and prodded his outlaw
Who, in his own time, resumed the dark, the straw. 1969

SUSAN MITCHELL

From the Journals of the Frog Prince[2]

In March I dreamed of mud,
sheets of mud over the ballroom chairs and table,
rainbow slicks of mud under the throne.
In April I saw mud of clouds and mud of sun.
Now in May I find excuses to linger in the kitchen
for wafts of silt and ale,
cinnamon and river bottom,
tender scallion and sour underlog.

At night I cannot sleep.
I am listening for the dribble of mud
climbing the stairs to our bedroom
as if a child in a wet bathing suit ran
up them in the dark.

Last night I said, "Face it, you're bored.
How many times can you live over
with the same excitement
that moment when the princess leans
into the well, her face a petal
falling to the surface of the water
as you rise like a bubble to her lips,
the golden ball bursting from your mouth?"
Remember how she hurled you against the wall,
your body cracking open,
skin shriveling to the bone,
the green pod of your heart splitting in two,
and her face imprinted with every moment
of your transformation?

I no longer tremble.

Night after night I lie beside her.
"Why is your forehead so cool and damp?" she asks.
Her breasts are soft and dry as flour.
The hand that brushes my head is feverish.

2. According to a popular fairy tale, a frog is transformed into a prince when a girl for whom he performs a favor kisses him and allows him to sleep in her bed.

At her touch I long for wet leaves,
the slap of water against rocks.

"What are you thinking of?" she asks.
How can I tell her
I am thinking of the green skin
shoved like wet pants behind the Directoire desk?
Or tell her I am mortgaged to the hilt
of my sword, to the leek-green tip of my soul?
Someday I will drag her by her hair
to the river—and what? Drown her?
Show her the green flame of my self rising at her feet?
But there's no more violence in her
than in a fence or a gate.

"What are you thinking of?" she whispers.
I am staring into the garden.
I am watching the moon
wind its trail of golden slime around the oak,
over the stone basin of the fountain.
How can I tell her
I am thinking that transformations are not forever?

1983

MARGARET ATWOOD

Death of a Young Son by Drowning

He, who navigated with success
the dangerous river of his own birth
once more set forth

on a voyage of discovery
into the land I floated on
but could not touch to claim.

His feet slid on the bank,
the currents took him;
he swirled with ice and trees in the swollen water

and plunged into distant regions,
his head a bathysphere;
through his eyes' thin glass bubbles

he looked out, reckless adventurer
on a landscape stranger than Uranus
we have all been to and some remember.

There was an accident; the air locked,
he was hung in the river like a heart.
They retrieved the swamped body,

cairn of my plans and future charts,
with poles and hooks
from among the nudging logs.

It was spring, the sun kept shining, the new grass
leapt to solidity;
my hands glistened with details.

After the long trip I was tired of waves.
My foot hit rock. The dreamed sails
collapsed, ragged.

I planted him in his country
like a flag.

1970

QUESTIONS

1. In "Lessons of the War: Judging Distances," what indicators are there that different voices speak within the poem? Where, exactly, do the changes of speaker take place? How would you characterize each speaker? What words or phrases are especially effective in establishing the different speakers' characters and values?

2. What, precisely, do we know about the speaker in "Hanging Fire"? How much self-confidence does she have? How can you tell? How does she feel about herself?

3. List all the facts we know about the speaker of "In Westminster Abbey." Which facts are especially important in our view of her? Explain the significance of the poem's setting.

4. Characterize the speaker in "The Outlaw." What in particular fascinates him about the breeding operation? What, exactly, does he see? How do the two participants respond to the central event? How do the observers respond? Why does the poem describe the path to Kelly's so fully? Why does the "nervous Friesian" have to be dragged? Why is the money paid to Kelly described as "clammy silver" (line 7)? Why does the speaker decide to employ an "unlicensed bull"? What or whom does the title of the poem refer to?

5. What kind of journey does the mother make in "Death of a Young Son by Drowning"? How are the son's and mother's journeys related? Explain the final image in lines 28–29.

WRITING SUGGESTIONS

1. Look up, in your college library, the fairy tale on which "From the Journal of the Frog Prince" is based. Read the tale carefully, and then record all the ways in which the poem departs from or adds to the tale. Try to account for all the revisions in terms of what the poem tries to do. What kind of character does it give to the frog prince? Write a three-page essay in which you analyze the ways the poem revises the tale, showing to what purposes the various revisions are put.

2. The speakers in "Needs" and "The Outlaw" both reveal themselves to have desires and needs that they are not themselves fully conscious of. Analyze carefully just what elements in the poem make clear to us the "secret" aspects of their character. Compare the character of the speaker (and the strategies used to characterize her) in Maxine Kumin's "Woodchucks" (chapter 1). Choose either "Needs" or "The Outlaw" to compare in detail with "Woodchucks," and write a short (600–700 word) essay in which you characterize the speakers in the two poems, making clear what kind of attitude each poem develops toward its speaker.

3. Analyze carefully the way "Rat Song" and "Mirror" are narrated. Evaluate the strategy in each of using a non-human speaker through which to present the words of the poem. Which poem seems to you more effective in its choice of speaker? Write a brief, two-paragraph account of each poem in which you explain the advantages and disadvantages of its choice of speaker.

3 SITUATION AND SETTING

Questions about speaker ("Who?" questions) in a poem almost always lead to questions of "Where?" "When?" and "Why?" Identifying the speaker usually is, in fact, part of a larger process of defining the entire imagined **situation** in a poem: What is happening? Where is it happening? Who is the speaker speaking to? Who else is present? Why is this event occurring? In order to understand the dialogue in "The Ruined Maid," for example, we need to become aware that the friends are meeting again after a period of absence and that they are meeting in a town large enough to seem substantially different in setting from the rural area in which they grew up together. And we infer (from the opening lines) that the meeting is accidental, and that no other friends are present for the conversation. The poem's whole "story" depends upon the fact of their situation: after leading separate lives for some time they have some catching up to do. We don't know what specific town is involved, or what year, season, or time of day because those details are not important to the poem's effect. But crucial to the poem are the where and when questions that define the situation and relationship of the two speakers, and the answer to the why question—that the meeting is by chance—is important too. In another poem we looked at in the previous chapter, "A Certain Lady," the specific moment and place are not important, but we do need to notice that the "lady" is talking to (or having an imaginary conversation with) her lover and that they are talking about a relationship of some duration.

Sometimes a *specific* time and place **(setting)** may be important. The "lady in skunk" sings her life story "in a prominent bar in Secaucus, N.J.," a smelly and unfashionable town, but on no particular occasion ("one day"). In "Soliloquy of the Spanish Cloister," the setting (a monastery) adds to the irony because of the gross inappropriateness of such sentiments and attitudes in such a supposedly holy place, and the setting of "In Westminster Abbey" similarly helps us to judge the speaker's ideas, attitudes, and self-conception.

The title of the following poem suggests that place may be important, and it is, although you may be surprised to discover exactly what exists at this address and what uses the speaker makes of it.

JAMES DICKEY

Cherrylog Road

Off Highway 106
At Cherrylog Road I entered
The '34 Ford without wheels,
Smothered in kudzu,[1]
With a seat pulled out to run
Corn whiskey down from the hills,

And then from the other side
Crept into an Essex
With a rumble seat of red leather
And then out again, aboard
A blue Chevrolet, releasing
The rust from its other color,

Reared up on three building blocks.
None had the same body heat;
I changed with them inward, toward
The weedy heart of the junkyard,
For I knew that Doris Holbrook
Would escape from her father at noon

And would come from the farm
To seek parts owned by the sun
Among the abandoned chassis,
Sitting in each in turn
As I did, leaning forward
As in a wild stock-car race

In the parking lot of the dead.
Time after time, I climbed in
And out the other side, like
An envoy or movie star
Met at the station by crickets.
A radiator cap raised its head,

Become a real toad or a kingsnake
As I neared the hub of the yard,
Passing through many states,
Many lives, to reach
Some grandmother's long Pierce-Arrow
Sending platters of blindness forth

1. A rapidly growing vine, introduced from Japan to combat erosion but now covering whole fields and groves of trees.

From its nickel hubcaps
And spilling its tender upholstery
On sleepy roaches,
The glass panel in between
Lady and colored driver
Not all the way broken out,

The back-seat phone
Still on its hook.
I got in as though to exclaim,
"Let us go to the orphan asylum,
John; I have some old toys
For children who say their prayers."

I popped with sweat as I thought
I heard Doris Holbrook scrape
Like a mouse in the southern-state sun
That was eating the paint in blisters
From a hundred car tops and hoods.
She was tapping like code,

Loosening the screws,
Carrying off headlights,
Sparkplugs, bumpers,
Cracked mirrors and gear-knobs,
Getting ready, already,
To go back with something to show

Other than her lips' new trembling
I would hold to me soon, soon,
Where I sat in the ripped back seat
Talking over the interphone,
Praying for Doris Holbrook
To come from her father's farm

And to get back there
With no trace of me on her face
To be seen by her red-haired father
Who would change, in the squalling barn,
Her back's pale skin with a strop,
Then lay for me

In a bootlegger's roasting car
With a string-triggered 12-gauge shotgun
To blast the breath from the air.
Not cut by the jagged windshields,
Through the acres of wrecks she came
With a wrench in her hand,

Through dust where the blacksnake dies
Of boredom, and the beetle knows

The compost has no more life.
Someone outside would have seen
The oldest car's door inexplicably
Close from within:
I held her and held her and held her,
Convoyed at terrific speed
By the stalled, dreaming traffic around us,
So the blacksnake, stiff
With inaction, curved back
Into life, and hunted the mouse

With deadly overexcitement,
The beetles reclaimed their field
As we clung, glued together,
With the hooks of the seat springs
Working through to catch us red-handed
Amidst the gray breathless batting

That burst from the seat at our backs.
We left by separate doors
Into the changed, other bodies
Of cars, she down Cherrylog Road
And I to my motorcycle
Parked like the soul of the junkyard

Restored, a bicycle fleshed
With power, and tore off
Up Highway 106, continually
Drunk on the wind in my mouth,
Wringing the handlebar for speed,
Wild to be wreckage forever.

1964

The *exact* location of the junkyard is not important (there is no Highway 106 near the real Cherrylog Road in North Georgia), but we do need to know that the setting is rural, that the time is summer and that the summer is hot, and that moonshine whiskey is native to the area. Following the story is no problem once we have sorted out these few facts, and we are prepared to meet the cast of characters: Doris Holbrook, her red-haired father, and the speaker. About each we learn just enough to appreciate the sense of vitality, adventure, and power that constitute the major effects of the poem.

The situation of lovemaking in another setting than the junkyard would not produce the same effects, and the exotic sense of a forbidden meeting in this unlikely place helps to recreate the speaker's sense of the episode. For him, it is memorable (notice all the tiny details he remembers), powerful (notice his reaction when he gets back on his motorcycle), dreamlike (notice the sense of time standing still, especially in lines 85–89), and important (notice how the speaker perceives his environment as changed by their lovemaking, lines 88–91 and 98–100). The wealth of details about setting also helps us to raise other, related questions. Why does the speaker fantasize about being shot by the father (lines 72–75)? Why, in a poem so full of details, do we find out so little about what Doris Holbrook looks like? What gives us the sense that this incident is a composite of episodes, an event that was repeated many times? What gives us the impression that the events occurred long ago? What makes the speaker feel so powerful at the end? What does he mean when he talks of himself as being "wild to be wreckage forever"? All of the poem's attention to the speaker's reactions, reflections, and memories is intricately tied up with the particulars of setting. Making love in a junkyard is crucial to the speaker's sense of both power and wreckage, and Doris is merely a matter of excitement, adventure, and pale skin, appreciated because she makes the world seem different and because she is willing to take risks and to suffer for meeting him like this. The more we probe the poem with questions about situation, the more likely we are to catch the poem's full effect.

"Cherrylog Road" is a fairly easy poem to read, but its effect is more complex than its simple story suggests. The next poem we will look at is, at first glance, much more difficult to follow. Part of the difficulty is that the poem is from an earlier age and its language is a little different, and part is because the action in the poem is so closely connected to what is being said. But its opening lines—addressed to someone who is resisting the speaker's suggestions—disclose the situation, and gradually we can figure out the scene: a man is trying to convince a woman that they should make love. When a flea happens by, the speaker uses it for an unlikely example; it becomes part of his argument. And once we recognize the situation, we can readily follow (and be amused by) the speaker's witty and intricate argument.

JOHN DONNE

The Flea

Mark but this flea, and mark in this[2]
How little that which thou deny'st me is;
It sucked me first, and now sucks thee,
And in this flea our two bloods mingled be;

2. Medieval preachers and rhetoricians asked their hearers to "mark" (look at) an object which illustrated a moral or philosophical lesson they wished to emphasize.

Thou know'st that this cannot be said
A sin, nor shame, nor loss of maidenhead.
Yet this enjoys before it woo,
And pampered[3] swells with one blood made of two,
And this, alas, is more than we would do.[4]

Oh stay, three lives in one flea spare,
Where we almost, yea more than, married are.
This flea is you and I, and this
Our marriage bed, and marriage temple is;
Though parents grudge, and you, we're met
And cloistered in these living walls of jet.
Though use[5] make you apt to kill me,
Let not to that, self-murder added be,
And sacrilege, three sins in killing three.

Cruel and sudden, hast thou since
Purpled thy nail in blood of innocence?
Wherein could this flea guilty be,
Except in that drop which it sucked from thee?
Yet thou triumph'st, and say'st that thou
Find'st not thyself, nor me, the weaker now;
'Tis true; then learn how false, fears be;
Just so much honor, when thou yield'st to me,
Will waste, as this flea's death took life from thee.

1633

The scene in "The Flea" develops almost as in a play. Action occurs even as the poem is being written. Between stanzas 1 and 2, the woman makes a move to kill the flea (as stanza 2 opens, the speaker is trying to stop her), and between stanzas 2 and 3 the woman has squished the flea with her fingernail. Once we try to make sense of what the speaker says, the action is just as clear from the words as if we had stage directions in the margin. All of the speaker's verbal cleverness and all of his specious arguments follow from the situation, and in this poem (as in "Soliloquy of the Spanish Cloister" or "In Westminster Abbey") we watch as if we were observing a scene on the stage. The speaker is, in effect, giving a dramatic monologue for our benefit.

Neither time nor place is important to "The Flea," except in the sense that the speaker and his friend have to be assumed to be in the same place and to have the leisure for some playfulness. The situation could occur in any place where a man, a woman, and a flea could be together. Indoors, outdoors, morning, evening, city, country—it is all one; the situation could occur in cot-

3. Fed luxuriously. 4. According to contemporary medical theory, conception involved the literal mingling of the lovers' blood. 5. Habit.

tage or palace, on a boat or in a bedroom. We do know, from the date of publication of the poem (1633), that the poet was writing about people of more than three centuries ago, but the conduct he describes might equally happen in later ages just as well. Only the habits of language (and perhaps the speaker's religious attitudes) date the poem; the situation could equally be set in any age or place.

The two poems that follow have simpler plots, but in each case the heart of the poem is in the basic situation:

RITA DOVE

Daystar

She wanted a little room for thinking:
but she saw diapers steaming on the line,
a doll slumped behind the door.

So she lugged a chair behind the garage
to sit out the children's naps.

Sometimes there were things to watch—
the pinched armor of a vanished cricket,
a floating maple leaf. Other days
she stared until she was assured
when she closed her eyes
she'd see only her own vivid blood.

She had an hour, at best, before Liza appeared
pouting from the top of the stairs.
And just *what* was mother doing
out back with the field mice? Why,

building a palace. Later
that night when Thomas rolled over and
lurched into her, she would open her eyes
and think of the place that was hers
for an hour—where
she was nothing,
pure nothing, in the middle of the day.

1986

LINDA PASTAN

To a Daughter Leaving Home

When I taught you
at eight to ride
a bicycle, loping along
beside you
as you wobbled away
on two round wheels,
my own mouth rounding
in surprise when you pulled
ahead down the curved
path of the park,
I kept waiting
for the thud
of your crash as I
sprinted to catch up,
while you grew
smaller, more breakable
with distance,
pumping, pumping
for your life, screaming
with laughter,
the hair flapping
behind you like a
handkerchief waving
goodbye.

1988

Both these poems involve motherhood, but they take entirely different stances about it and have very different tones. The mother in "Daystar" is overwhelmed by the demands of young children and needs a room of her own. All she can manage, however, is a brief hour in a chair behind the garage. The situation is virtually the whole story here. Nothing really happens except that daily events (washing diapers, picking up toys, looking at crickets and leaves, explaining the world to children, having sex) crowd her brief private hour and make it precious. Being "nothing" (lines 21 and 22) takes on great value in these circumstances, and the poem makes much of the setting: an isolated chair behind the garage. Setting in poems often means something much more specific, but here time and place are given value by the circumstances of the situation.

The particulars of time and place in "To a Daughter Leaving Home" are even less specific, but the incident the poem describes happened a long time ago, and it is important to notice that its vividness in the poem is a function of memory. The mother is the speaker here, and we are told very little about her, at least directly. But she is thinking back nostalgically to a moment long ago when her daughter made an earlier (but briefer) departure from home, and the poem implies the occasion for her doing so. The daughter now is old enough to "leave" home in a full sense; the poem does not tell us why or what the present circumstances are, but the title tells us the situation. We may infer quite a bit about the speaker here—her affection for the daughter, the kind of mother she has been, her anxiety at the new departure that seems to reflect the earlier wobbly ride into the distance—but as in "Daystar" the poem is all situation. There are almost no details of present action, and we have no specific information about place or time for either the remembered event or the present one.

Some poems, however, depend heavily on specifics of time and place, sometimes on a knowledge of actual places and events. The following short poem requires a reader's knowledge of historical information (it also assumes that we know the terminology of children's games).

ROBERT FROST

U. S. 1946 King's X

Having invented a new Holocaust,
And been the first with it to win a war,
How they make haste to cry with fingers crossed,
King's X—no fairs to use it any more!

p. 1946

Our knowledge of the relevant historical facts does not necessarily mean that we will agree with the poet's criticism of U.S. policy at the end of World War II, but we certainly can't understand or appreciate the poem's equation of nuclear policy with a child's fear of consequence unless we do know the facts. Shortly after exploding the two atomic bombs that ended the war, the United States proposed to share nuclear information with other countries in exchange for an agreement that the information would be used only for peaceful purposes. And in children's games, time out is sometimes signaled by crossing fingers and saying "King's X."

Often it is hard to place ourselves fully enough in another time or place to imagine sympathetically what a particular historical moment would have been like, and even the best poetic efforts do not necessarily transport us there. But poets sometimes record a particular moment or event in order to commemorate it or comment upon it. A poem written about a specific occasion is usually called an **occasional poem,** and such a poem is **referential;** that is, it refers to a specific historical moment or event. For such poems we need, at the least, specific historical information—plus a willingness on our part as readers to let the poem transport us imaginatively to that particular time, sometimes (as in "U. S. 1946 King's X") by mentioning explicitly a particular time, sometimes by recreating that moment in a dramatic situation.

Time or place may, of course, be used much less specifically and still be important to a poem, and the most common uses of setting involve drawing upon common notions of a particular time or place. Setting a poem in a garden, for example, or writing about apples almost inevitably reminds us of the Garden of Eden because it is part of our common heritage of belief or knowledge. Even people who don't read at all or who lack Judaeo-Christian religious commitments are likely to know about Eden, and a poet writing in our culture can count on that. An **allusion** is a reference to something outside the poem that carries a history of meaning and strong emotional associations. For example, gardens may carry suggestions of innocence and order, or temptation and the Fall, or both, depending on how the poem handles the allusion. Well-known places from history or myth may be popularly associated with particular ideas or values or ways of life.

The place involved in a poem is its **spatial setting,** and the time is its **temporal setting.** The temporal setting may involve a specific date or an era, a season of the year or a time of day. We tend, for example, to think of spring as a time of discovery and growth, and poems set in spring are likely to draw upon that association; morning usually suggests discovery as well—beginnings, vitality, the world fresh and new—even to those of us who in reality take our waking slow. Temporal or spatial setting is often used to influence our expectation of theme and tone in a specific way, although the poet may then go on to surprise us by making something very different of our expectation. Setting is often an important factor in creating the mood in poems just as in stories, plays, or films. Often the details of setting have a lot to do with the way we ultimately respond to the poem's subject or theme, as in this poem:

SYLVIA PLATH

Point Shirley

From Water-Tower Hill to the brick prison
The shingle booms, bickering under
The sea's collapse.
Snowcakes break and welter. This year
The gritted wave leaps
The seawall and drops onto a bier
Of quahog chips,[6]
Leaving a salty mash of ice to whiten

In my grandmother's sand yard. She is dead,
Whose laundry snapped and froze here, who
Kept house against
What the sluttish, rutted sea could do.
Squall waves once danced
Ship timbers in through the cellar window;
A thresh-tailed, lanced
Shark littered in the geranium bed—

Such collusion of mulish elements
She wore her broom straws to the nub.
Twenty years out
Of her hand; the house still hugs in each drab
Stucco socket
The purple egg-stones: from Great Head's knob
To the filled-in Gut
The sea in its cold gizzard ground those rounds.

Nobody wintering now behind
The planked-up windows where she set
Her wheat loaves
And apple cakes to cool. What is it
Survives, grieves
So, over this battered, obstinate spit
Of gravel? The waves'
Spewed relics clicker masses in the wind,

Gray waves the stub-necked eiders ride.
A labor of love, and that labor lost.
Steadily the sea
Eats at Point Shirley. She died blessed,
And I come by
Bones, bones only, pawed and tossed,
A dog-faced sea.
The sun sinks under Boston, bloody red.

6. Chips from quahog clam shells, common on the New England coast.

I would get from these dry-papped stones
The milk your love instilled in them.
The black ducks dive.
And though your graciousness might stream,
And I contrive,
Grandmother, stones are nothing of home
To that spumiest dove.
Against both bar and tower the black sea runs. 1960

One does not have to know the New England coast by personal experience to have it vividly recalled by Plath's poem. A reader who knows that coast or another like it may have an advantage in being able to respond more quickly to the poem's precision of description, but the poem does not depend on such knowledge from outside the poem. The precise location of Point Shirley, near Boston, is not especially important, but visualization of the setting is. Crucial to the poem's tone and mood is the sense of the sea as aggressor, a force powerful enough to change the contours of the coast and invade the privacy of yards and homes. The energy, relentlessness, and impersonality of the sea met their match, though a temporary one, in the speaker's grandmother who "Kept house against / What the sluttish, rutted sea could do" (lines 11–12). The grandmother *belonged* in this setting, and it seemed hers, but twenty years of her absence (since her death) now begin to show. Still, the marks of her obstinacy and love are there, although ultimately doomed by the sea's more enduring power.

Details—and how they are amassed—are important here rather than historic particulars of time and place. The grays and whites and drab colors of the sea and its leavings provide both a visual sense of the scene and the mood for the poem. The stubbornness that the speaker admired in the grandmother comes to seem a part of that tenacious grayness. Nothing happens rapidly here; things wear down. Even the "bloody red" (line 40) of the sun's setting—an ominous sign that adds a vivid fright to the dullness rather than brightening it—makes promises that seem slow and long-term. The toughness of the boarded-up house is a monument to the grandmother's loving care and becomes a way for the speaker to touch her human spirit, but the poem's final emphasis is on the relentless black sea, which continues to run against the landmarks and fortresses that had been identified with the setting in the very first line.

Questions about situation and setting begin as simple questions of identification but often become more complex when we sort out all the implications. Often it takes only a moment to determine a poem's situation, but it may take much longer to discover all of the things that time and place imply, for their meanings may depend upon visual details, or upon actual historical occurrences, or upon habitual ways of thinking about certain times and places—or all three at once. As you read the following poem, notice how the setting—another shore—prepares us for the speaker's moods and ideas, and then watch how the movement of his mind is affected by what he sees.

MATTHEW ARNOLD

Dover Beach[7]

The sea is calm tonight.
The tide is full, the moon lies fair
Upon the straits; on the French coast the light
Gleams and is gone; the cliffs of England stand,
Glimmering and vast, out in the tranquil bay.
Come to the window, sweet is the night-air!
Only, from the long line of spray
Where the sea meets the moon-blanched land,
Listen! you hear the grating roar
Of pebbles which the waves draw back, and fling,
At their return, up the high strand,
Begin, and cease, and then again begin,
With tremulous cadence slow, and bring
The eternal note of sadness in.

Sophocles long ago
Heard it on the Aegean, and it brought
Into his mind the turbid ebb and flow
Of human misery;[8] we
Find also in the sound a thought,
Hearing it by this distant northern sea.

The Sea of Faith
Was once, too, at the full, and round earth's shore
Lay like the folds of a bright girdle furled.
But now I only hear
Its melancholy, long, withdrawing roar,
Retreating, to the breath
Of the night-wind, down the vast edges drear
And naked shingles[9] of the world.

7. At the narrowest point on the English Channel. The lights on the French coast (lines 3–4) would be about 20 miles away. 8. In *Antigone*, lines 583–91, the chorus compares the fate of the house of Oedipus to the waves of the sea. 9. Pebble-strewn beaches.

Ah, love, let us be true
To one another! for the world, which seems
To lie before us like a land of dreams,
So various, so beautiful, so new,
Hath really neither joy, nor love, nor light,
Nor certitude, nor peace, nor help for pain;
And we are here as on a darkling plain
Swept with confused alarms of struggle and flight,
Where ignorant armies clash by night.

ca. 1851

Exactly what is the dramatic situation in "Dover Beach"? How soon are you aware that someone is being spoken to? How much are we told about the person spoken to? How would you describe the speaker's mood? What does the speaker's mood have to do with time and place? Do any details of present place and time help to account for his tendency to talk repeatedly of the past and the future? How important is it to the poem's total effect that the beach here involves an international border? What particulars of the Dover Beach seem especially important to the poem's themes? to its emotional effects?

Sometimes time and place may carry even greater resonance in a poem because pieces of history are recovered or rehearsed. In the following poem, for example, a whole history of Manifest Destiny ultimately is invoked in a situation that at first only seems to involve a quiet walk in a California small town. Here the "clear night in Live Oak" (line 1) quickly allows us to see large episodes in American and Mexican history.

ADRIENNE RICH

Walking down the Road

On a clear night in Live Oak you can see
the stars glittering low as from the deck
of a frigate.
In Live Oak without pavements you can walk
the fronts of old homesteads, past tattered palms,
original rosebushes, thick walnut trees
ghosts of the liveoak groves
the whitemen cleared. On a night like this
the old California thickens and bends
the Baja streams out like lava-melt
we are no longer the United States

we're a lost piece of Mexico
maybe dreaming the destruction
of the Indians, reading the headlines,
how the gringos marched into Mexico City
forcing California into the hand
of Manifest Destiny, law following greed.
And the pale lies trapped in the flickering boxes
here in Live Oak tonight, they too follow.
One thing follows on another, that is time:
Carmel in its death-infested prettiness,
thousands of skeletons stacked in the *campo santo:*[1]
the spring fouled by the pickaxe:
the flag dragged on to the moon:
the crystal goblet smashed: grains of the universe
flashing their angry tears, here in Live Oak.

1989

Not all poems have an identifiable situation or setting, just as not all poems have a speaker that is distinct from the author. Poems that simply present a series of thoughts and feelings directly, in a contemplative, meditative, or reflective way, may not set up any kind of action, plot, or situation at all, preferring to speak directly without the intermediary of a dramatic device. But most poems depend crucially upon a sense of place, a sense of time, and an understanding of human interaction in scenes that resemble the strategies of drama or film. And questions about these matters will often lead you to define not only the "facts" but also the feelings central to a poem's design upon us.

▽ ▽ ▽

SITUATION AND SETTING A Glossary

allusion: a reference to a text or myth, outside the poem itself, that carries its own history of meaning
occasional poem: a poem written about or for a specific occasion, public or private
referential: making use of a specific historical moment or event
setting: the time and place of the poem's action
situation: the context of the poem's action, what is happening when the poem begins
spatial setting: the place of a poem
temporal setting: the time of a poem

1. *Campo santo:* Sacred field, cemetary.

ROBERT BROWNING

My Last Duchess

FERRARA[2]

That's my last Duchess painted on the wall,
Looking as if she were alive. I call
That piece a wonder, now: Frà Pandolf's hands[3]
Worked busily a day, and there she stands.
Will't please you sit and look at her? I said
"Frà Pandolf" by design, for never read
Strangers like you that pictured countenance,
The depth and passion of its earnest glance,
But to myself they turned (since none puts by
The curtain I have drawn for you, but I)
And seemed as they would ask me, if they durst,
How such a glance came there; so, not the first
Are you to turn and ask thus. Sir, 'twas not
Her husband's presence only, called that spot
Of joy into the Duchess' cheek: perhaps
Frà Pandolf chanced to say "Her mantle laps
Over my lady's wrist too much," or "Paint
Must never hope to reproduce the faint
Half-flush that dies along her throat": such stuff
Was courtesy, she thought, and cause enough
For calling up that spot of joy. She had
A heart—how shall I say?—too soon made glad,
Too easily impressed; she liked whate'er
She looked on, and her looks went everywhere.
Sir, 'twas all one! My favor at her breast,
The dropping of the daylight in the West,
The bough of cherries some officious fool
Broke in the orchard for her, the white mule
She rode with round the terrace—all and each
Would draw from her alike the approving speech,
Or blush, at least. She thanked men,—good! but thanked
Somehow—I know not how—as if she ranked
My gift of a nine-hundred-years-old name
With anybody's gift. Who'd stoop to blame
This sort of trifling? Even had you skill
In speech—which I have not—to make your will
Quite clear to such an one, and say, "Just this

2. Alfonso II, Duke of Ferrara in Italy in the mid-16th century, is the presumed speaker of the poem, which is loosely based on historical events. The duke's first wife—whom he had married when she was 14—died under suspicious circumstances at 17, and he then negotiated through an agent (to whom the poem is spoken) for the hand of the niece of the Count of Tyrol in Austria. 3. Frà Pandolf is, like Claus (line 56), fictitious.

Or that in you disgusts me; here you miss,
Or there exceed the mark"—and if she let
Herself be lessoned so, nor plainly set
Her wits to yours, forsooth, and made excuse,
—E'en then would be some stooping; and I choose
Never to stoop. Oh sir, she smiled, no doubt,
Whene'er I passed her; but who passed without
Much the same smile? This grew; I gave commands;
Then all smiles stopped together. There she stands
As if alive. Will't please you rise? We'll meet
The company below, then. I repeat,
The Count your master's known munificence
Is ample warrant that no just pretense
Of mine for dowry will be disallowed;
Though his fair daughter's self, as I avowed
At starting, is my object. Nay, we'll go
Together down, sir. Notice Neptune, though,
Taming a sea-horse, thought a rarity,
Which Claus of Innsbruck cast in bronze for me!

1842

HEATHER McHUGH

20–200 on 737

Here and now is clear so we
can't see it (what we know too well
we notice least). In airplanes, chance
encounters want to know, so what
are your poems about? They're about

their business and their father's business
and their monkey's uncle, just about
undone, about themselves, and not about
being about, of of. This answer
drives them back to the snack tray every time.

One Phil Fenstermacher, for example, turns up
perfectly clear in my memory, perfectly attentive to
his Piedmont Vache Qui Rit[4] (that saddest cheese)—and let us now
commiserate with that engagement, for it takes what might
be years to open life's array

of incidental parcels—mysteries of red strips, tips and strings—
the tricks of tampons, band-aids, perforated notches on
detergent boxes, spatial reasoning milk carton quiz and subtle
eschatologies of toilet paper—O,
it's endless. Mister Fenstermacher is relieved

4. "Laughing Cow," a brand of processed cheese.

to fill his mind with the immediate
and masterable challenge of the cheese, after our brief
and chastening foray into the social arts. We part
before we part; indeed
we part before we meet. (I sense the French

philosophers nearby—I hope not in the cockpit—
furious about an act of metaphor, they rock
the plane and all the singers in it (contrary to popular
belief, the vehicle is one, the tenors many)—they intone

we're sunk, we're sunk, in our little container, our
story of starting and stopping.) Whose story
is it anyway? Out of my mouth
whose words emerge? Who's the self the self
surpasses? Look at your glasses, someone
whispers. Maybe the world is speckled

by your carelessness. Look at your glasses,
if you want to see. (Who says? It's night, we're not alone,
the town down there grows huge, one tiny runway will
engulf us. Is the whisperer Phil Fenstermacher, getting
a last word in before

the craft alights?) I look at my glasses.
I see what he means. They're a sight.

1988

DOUGLAS LOCHHEAD

Winter Landscape—Halifax

A bright hard day over harbour where sea
in chips of white and blue speaks and toys, while
flurries of gulls spinning in wide deploys swoon
in sleigh-rides giddy and cold off government wharf.

At Devil's[5] the sea spanks a winter's drum,
a hollow ballad and boom for sailors' throats
courting their winter mermaids battened down
somewhere off Scatari[6] and heading home.

Now in December the wind leans rude and hard,
snow heaps and hides in the cormorant rocks,
and at the Citadel[7] commissionaires
clap hands, stamp feet, turn backs against the cold.

1960

5. Island at the entrance to Halifax harbor. 6. Or Scatarie: an island, the easternmost part of Nova Scotia. 7. Stone fortress (1828) overlooking downtown Halifax.

LARRY RUBIN

The Houses of Emily Dickinson

It is, of course, the wrong house.
The one next door seems much more likely
To have sheltered an aging spinster
Rattling her chains in the garret
Or burning through beds with puritan heat.
Emily—and Charlotte—are names for the moors,[8]
For Victorian gables and turrets, gothic stairs;
But our Emily dwelt in a brick house
Suitable for a sorority in Charlottesville,[9]
Nor are there seven gables in this solid residence
Of the Amherst treasurer.[1]
Still, daughters with a literary bent
Can do funny things with their father's land.
They can take a tree, or a robin,
Or a garden,
And fiddle with it till its roots are screwed
Into the earth of words to such a depth
That dirt meets sky, and alabaster
Is the mode for every chamber—
Whether the structure be brick or frame.
She has pierced this heavy parasol with light;
All houses, for her, it seems, are right.

p. 1983

AGHA SHAHID ALI

Houses

FOR *Jon Anderson*

The man who buries his house in the sand
and digs it up again, each evening,
learns to put it together quickly

and just as quickly to take it apart.
My parents sleep like children in the dark.
I am too far to hear them breathe

8. Emily and Charlotte Brontë, the novelists, lived in the Yorkshire (England) moors. 9. Where the University of Virginia is located. 1. Emily Dickinson's father was treasurer of Amherst College. *The House of the Seven Gables* (1851) is a novel by Nathaniel Hawthorne (1804–64).

but I remember their house is safe
and I can sleep, the night's hair
black and thick in my hands.

My parents sleep in the dark.
When the moon rises, the night's hair
turns white in my arms.

I am thirteen thousand miles from home.
I comb the moon out of the night,
and my parents are sleeping like children.

"My father is dead," Vidur writes,
and a house in my neighborhood, next
to my parents', has burned down.

I keep reading the letter.
If I wake up,
my body will be water, reflecting the fire.

1987

TESS GALLAGHER

Not There

One whistle, a short husky breath—
like a child blowing into a metal pipe then
listening. The house shudders
as the train passes on the hillside.
Days, mornings—whatever I'm doing I stop
and rush to wave it by. But always
I'm too late for the engineer.
It's the man in the caboose
who's searched out my doorway.
His grave face and hand say *hello-goodbye*—

Other times the train is coming
and I don't go out. I go on
doing what I'm doing—reading, or staring
at the gulls rising and falling above
the waves. I don't
go out. A weight pulls
against the house. I think of his grave face
looking down at the house, of the woman
in the doorway. I don't go out and
I don't go out. These
are the moments when we meet.

1984

DIANE ACKERMAN

Driving through Farm Country at Sunset

As I drive through farm country,
a damp reek brewing by the roadway
hits me. Manure, cut grass, honeysuckle,
spearmint. The air feels light as rusk.
And I want to lie down in the newly turned
earth, amid the wheat-chaff and the chicory,
while sunlight creeps up a mountainside

off in the distant whelm of color.
Each cemetery, flanked by poplars, looks ready
to play as a chess set. A dozen washloads
blow on the line, sock lanterns ablaze,
towels bellied like a schooner's rigging.
In a dogwood's petaled salon, bees leave
their pollen footprints as calling cards.

The occasional samba of a dragonfly
tightens the puffy-lidded dusk.
Clouds begin to curdle overhead. And I want
to lie down with you in this boggy dirt,
our legs rubbing like locusts'.
I want you here with the scallions
sweet in the night air, to lie down with you
heavy in my arms, and take root. 1978

WILLIAM SHAKESPEARE

[Full many a glorious morning have I seen]

Full many a glorious morning have I seen
Flatter the mountain-tops with sovereign eye,
Kissing with golden face the meadows green,
Gilding pale streams with heavenly alchymy;
Anon permit the basest clouds to ride
With ugly rack[2] on his celestial face,
And from the forlorn world his visage hide,
Stealing unseen to west with this disgrace:
Even so my sun one early morn did shine,
With all-triumphant splendour on my brow;
But, out! alack! he was but one hour mine,
The region cloud hath mask'd him from me now.
  Yet him for this my love no whit disdaineth;
  Suns of the world may stain when heaven's sun staineth. 1609

2. Moss.

JOHN DONNE

The Good-Morrow

I wonder, by my troth, what thou and I
Did, till we loved? were we not weaned till then?
But sucked on country pleasures, childishly?
Or snorted we in the Seven Sleepers' den?[3]
'Twas so; but[4] this, all pleasures fancies be.
If ever any beauty I did see,
Which I desired, and got,[5] 'twas but a dream of thee.

And now good-morrow to our waking souls,
Which watch not one another out of fear;
For love, all love of other sights controls,
And makes one little room an everywhere.
Let sea-discoverers to new worlds have gone,
Let maps to other,[6] worlds on worlds have shown,
Let us possess one world, each hath one, and is one.

My face in thine eye, thine in mine appears,[7]
And true plain hearts do in the faces rest;
Where can we find two better hemispheres,
Without sharp north, without declining west?
Whatever dies was not mixed equally,[8]
If our two loves be one, or, thou and I
Love so alike that none do slacken, none can die.

1633

MARILYN CHIN

Aubade

The candle that would not burn
will never share its glory.

Waking is this easy:
Sunday; Haunauma Bay,[9] your birthday,
and we—too comfortable to notice
the sea forging inward,

that before the picture window
our special pine, dwarfed and hunched

3. According to tradition, seven Christian youths escaped Roman persecution by sleeping in a cave for 187 years. *Snorted:* snored. 4. Except for. 5. Sexually possessed. *Beauty:* Beautiful woman. 6. Other people. 7. I.e., each is reflected in the other's eyes. 8. Perfectly mixed elements, according to scholastic philosophy, were stable and immortal. 9. On Oahu, east of Honolulu.

through decades of seastorm and salty air,
has uprooted to die in the rain.

And in our sleep, the years have proceeded toward the horizon
like a school of uninteresting driftwood
or tortoises plodding disconsolately
to find what lurks at the edge.

What lurks there might be disaster:
the charred aftermath of Rome and Cathay, or
more deceptive, a sea of new aquatic flora
bathed in eternal dawn light.

But today as clouds give way to sunshine,
we wake as tourists of yet another decade.
Our tongues stale with last night's lovemaking,
our eyes bleared with tomorrow's dreams.

For now, let each candle gutter, as they do
and celebrate earth's mundane surprises:
family, lovers, friends,
clams in the mudflat for the taking. 1987

JONATHAN SWIFT

A Description of the Morning

Now hardly here and there a hackney-coach[1]
Appearing, showed the ruddy morn's approach.
Now Betty[2] from her master's bed had flown,
And softly stole to discompose her own.
The slip shod 'prentice from his master's door
Had pared the dirt, and sprinkled round the floor.
Now Moll had whirled her mop with dext'rous airs,
Prepared to scrub the entry and the stairs.
The youth with broomy stumps began to trace
The kennel-edge[3] where wheels had worn the place.
The small-coal man[4] was heard with cadence deep,
Till drowned in shriller notes of chimney-sweep:
Duns[5] at his lordship's gate began to meet;
And brick-dust Moll had screamed through half the street.[6]
The turnkey now his flock returning sees,

1. Hired coach. *Hardly*: Scarcely; i.e., they are just beginning to appear. 2. A stock name for a servant girl. Moll (lines 7, 14) is a frequent lower-class nickname. 3. Edge of the gutter that ran down the middle of the street. *Trace*: "To find old Nails." (Swift's note) 4. A seller of coal and charcoal. 5. Bill collectors. 6. Selling powdered brick that was used to clean knives.

Duly let out a-nights to steal for fees.[7]
The watchful bailiffs take their silent stands,[8]
And schoolboys lag with satchels in their hands. p. 1709

SYLVIA PLATH

Morning Song

Love set you going like a fat gold watch.
The midwife slapped your footsoles, and your bald cry
Took its place among the elements.

Our voices echo, magnifying your arrival. New statue.
In a drafty museum, your nakedness
Shadows our safety. We stand round blankly as walls.

I'm no more your mother
Than the cloud that distils a mirror to reflect its own slow
Effacement at the wind's hand.

All night your moth-breath
Flickers among the flat pink roses. I wake to listen:
A far sea moves in my ear.

One cry, and I stumble from bed, cow-heavy and floral
In my Victorian nightgown.
Your mouth opens clean as a cat's. The window square

Whitens and swallows its dull stars. And now you try
Your handful of notes;
The clear vowels rise like balloons. 1961

QUESTIONS

1. What facts do we actually have about the speaker of "My Last Duchess"? On what basis do we form our evaluation of him? How does the setting contribute to the characterization? At what point in reading the poem do you become aware of the precise situation?

2. Describe the "situation" in "20–200 on 737." What indications are there in the poem that a composite of several experiences is being represented here?

7. Jailers collected fees from prisoners for their keep and often let them out at night so they could steal to pay expenses. 8. Looking for those on their "wanted" lists.

Describe the poem's speaker. By what means is she characterized? What do you make of the wordplay in her description of her experiences? What attitude does the poem take toward the speaker? Explain the several meanings of the last sentence in the last line.

3. Paraphrase Rich's "Walking down the Road" by recasting it line by line into prose in different words. What kinds of distortions of meaning and tone do you perpetrate by recasting the poem in this way? Look back to "Living in Sin," an early poem by Rich in *Reading Poetry*, and look ahead to the collection of poems by Rich in chapter 11. What similarities do you see among the several Rich poems? What differences between the early poems and the later ones?

4. Compare "Not There" with the Gallagher poems in chapter 2 ("Sudden Journey") and chapter 1 ("Unanswered Letter"). In what ways are the situations in the three poems similar? Describe the use of speakers in the three poems.

5. What function does the sunset perform in "Driving through Farm Country at Sunset"? What other aspect of setting, either spatial or temporal, are important to the effects in the poem? Describe the tone of the poem.

WRITING SUGGESTIONS

1. Ask the reference librarian in your college library to help you find a reliable biography of Emily Dickinson, and find out about her way of life in Amherst, Massachusetts. What kind of house did she live in? What were the houses of her neighbors like? To what social and economic class did she belong?

Using the index to locate them, read all the Emily Dickinson poems in this book, taking notes on their subject matter and tone. Which poems are echoed or referred to directly in "The Houses of Emily Dickinson"? What does the last line of the poem mean? Write a short (2- or 3-page) account of Emily Dickinson's life in which you try to account for the range of her poems relative to the cultural background of her life.

2. Consult at least three handbooks of literary terms, and compare their definitions of *aubade* and *aube*. Consider the poems at the end of this chapter by Shakespeare, Donne, Chin, Swift, and Plath. Choose *one* of these poems and analyze how closely it relates to the tradition of morning poems described in the handbooks. Write a short essay (no more than two pages long) in which you explain how the poem achieves its effects by employing and modifying or rejecting the standard expectations of how mornings are to be described in poetry.

3. Consult a handbook of classical literature, and find out how Roman poets represented sunrises mythologically. (Hint: look up Phoebus, then—guided by the handbook or a reference librarian—look at several poems in which Phoebus or his fiery car is described in detail.) Consider carefully the opening lines of Swift's "A Description of the Morning." Write a short account (no more than three paragraphs) of how Swift's first two lines work: in what ways do they use and modify the standard mythological expectations? What do you make of the comparison of modern ordinary life to mythic patterns? What kind of evaluation of modern life (or of mythology) seems to be implied?

4 WORDS AND WORD ORDER

Fiction and drama depend upon language just as poetry does, but in a poem almost everything comes down to words. In stories and plays, we are likely to keep our attention primarily on character and plot—what is happening in front of us or in the action as we imagine it in our minds—and although words are crucial to how we imagine the characters and how we respond to what happens to them, we are not as likely to pause over any one word as we may need to in a poem. Besides, poems often are short and use only a few words, so a lot depends on every single one. Poetry sometimes feels like prose that is distilled: only the most essential words are there, just barely enough so that we communicate in the most basic way, using the most elemental signs of meaning and feeling—and each one chosen for exactly the right shade of meaning. But elemental does not necessarily mean simple, and these signs may be very rich in their meanings and complex in their effects.

Let's look first at two poems, each of which depends heavily upon a single key word.

RICHARD ARMOUR

Hiding Place

A speaker at a meeting of the New York State Frozen Food Locker Association declared that the best hiding place in event of an atomic explosion is a frozen-food locker, where "radiation will not penetrate."[1]

—News item

Move over, ham
    And quartered cow,
My Geiger says
    The time is now.

Yes, now I lay me
    Down to sleep,
And if I die,
    At least I'll keep.

1954

1. Before home freezers became popular, many Americans rented lockers in specially equipped commercial buildings.

YVOR WINTERS

At the San Francisco Airport

TO *my daughter*, 1954

This is the terminal: the light
Gives perfect vision, false and hard;
The metal glitters, deep and bright.
Great planes are waiting in the yard—
They are already in the night.

And you are here beside me, small,
Contained and fragile, and intent
On things that I but half recall—
Yet going whither you are bent.
I am the past, and that is all.

But you and I in part are one:
The frightened brain, the nervous will,
The knowledge of what must be done,
The passion to acquire the skill
To face that which you dare not shun.

The rain of matter upon sense
Destroys me momently. The score:
There comes what will come. The expense
Is what one thought, and something more—
One's being and intelligence.

This is the terminal, the break.
Beyond this point, on lines of air,
You take the way that you must take;
And I remain in light and stare—
In light, and nothing else, awake.

1954

In "Hiding Place," almost all the poem's comedy depends on the final word, "keep." In the child's prayer that the poem echoes, to "pray the Lord my soul to keep" does not exactly involve cold storage (though it implies, theologically, a distinct lack of afterlife heat), and so the poem depends upon an outrageous double meaning. The key word is chosen because it can mean more than one thing; in this case, the importance of the word involves its **ambiguity** (an ability to mean more than one thing) rather than its **precision** (exactness).

In the second poem, the several possible meanings of a single word are probed more soberly and thoughtfully. What does it *mean* to be in a place called a "terminal"? the poem asks. As the parting of father and daughter is explored, carefully, the place of parting and the means of transportation begin to take on meanings larger than their simple referential ones. The poem is full of contrasts—young and old, light and dark, past and present, security and adventure—as the parting of generations is pondered. The father ("I am the past," line 10) remains in the light, among known objects and experience familiar to his many years; the daughter is about to depart into the night, the unknown, the uncertain future. But they both share a sense of the necessity of the parting, of the need for the daughter to mature, gain knowledge, acquire experience. Is she going off to school? to college? to her first job? The specifics are not given, but her plane ride clearly means a new departure and a clean break with childhood, dependency, the past.

So much depends upon the meanings of "terminal." It is the airport building, of course, but it also implies a boundary, an extremity, an end, something that is limited, a place where a connection is broken. The clear, crisp meanings of other words are important too. The words "break," "point," "lines," "way," and "remain" all express literally and sharply what the event means. The final stanza of the poem is full of words that state flatly and **denote** exactly, as if the speaker has recovered completely from the momentary confusion of stanza 4, when "being and intelligence" are lost in the emotion of the parting itself. The crisp articulation of the last stanza puts an almost total emphasis on the precise meaning of each word, its **denotation,** what it precisely denotes or refers to. The words "break," "point," "way," and "remain" are almost completely unemotional and colorless; they do not make value judgments or offer personal views, but rather define and describe. It is as if the speaker is trying to disengage himself from the emotion of the situation and just give the facts.

Words, however, are more than hard blocks of meaning on whose sense everyone agrees. They also have a more personal side, and they carry emotional force and shades of suggestion. The words we use indicate not only what we mean but how we feel about it, and we choose words that we hope will carry a persuasive emotional engagement with others, in conversation and daily usage as well as in poems. A person who holds office is, quite literally (and unemotionally), an "officeholder," a word that clearly denotes what he or she does. But if we want to convince someone that an officeholder is wise, trustworthy, and deserving of political support we may call that person a "political leader" or perhaps a "statesman"; whereas if we want to promote distrust or contempt of officeholders we might call them "politicians" or "bureaucrats" or "political hacks." These latter words have clear **connotations**—suggestions of emotional coloration that imply our attitude and invite a similar one on the part of our hearers. What words **connote** can be just as important to a poem as what they denote, although some poems depend primarily on denotation and some more on connotation.

"At the San Francisco Airport" seems to depend primarily on denotation; the speaker tries to *specify* the meanings and implications of the parting with his daughter, and his tendency to split categories neatly for the two of them at first contributes to the sense of clarity and certainty which the speaker wants to project. He is the past (line 10) and what remains (line 24); he has age and experience, his life is the known quantity, he stands in the light. She, on the other hand, is committed to the adventure of going into the night; she seems small, fragile, and her identity exists in the uncertain future. Yet the connotations of some words carry strong emotional force as well as clear definition: that the daughter seems "small" and "fragile" to the speaker suggests his fear for her, something quite different from her sense of adventure. The neat, clean categories keep breaking down, and the speaker's feelings keep showing through. In stanza 1, the speaker tells us that the light in the terminal gives "perfect vision" but he also notices, indirectly, its artificial quality: it is "false" and "hard," suggesting the limits of the rationalism he tries to maintain. That artificial light shines over most of the poem and honors the speaker's effort, but the whole poem represents his struggle, and in stanza 4 the signals of disturbance are very strong as, despite an insistence on a vocabulary of calculation, his rational facade collapses completely. If we have observed his verbal strategies carefully, we should not be surprised to find him at the end just *staring* in the artificial light, merely awake, although the poem has shown him to be unconsciously awake to much more than he will candidly admit.

"At the San Francisco Airport" is an unusually intricate and complicated poem, and it offers us, if we are willing to examine very precisely its carefully crafted fabric, an unusually rich insight into how complex a thing it is to be human and have human feelings and foibles when we think we must be rational machines. Connotations often work more simply. The following poem, for example, even though it describes the mixed feelings one person has about another, depends heavily on the common connotations of fairly common words.

WALTER DE LA MARE

Slim Cunning Hands

Slim cunning hands at rest, and cozening eyes—
Under this stone one loved too wildly lies;
How false she was, no granite could declare;
    Nor all earth's flowers, how fair.

1950

What the speaker in "Slim Cunning Hands" remembers about the dead woman—her hands, her eyes—tells part of the story; her physical presence was clearly important to him, and the poem's other nouns—stone, granite, flowers—all remind us of her death and its finality. All these words denote objects having to do with rituals that memorialize a departed life. Granite and stone connote finality as well, and flowers connote fragility and suggest the shortness of life (which is why they have become the symbolic language of funerals). The way the speaker talks about the woman expresses, in just a few words, how complexly he feels about his love for her. She was loved, he says, too "wildly"—by him perhaps, and by others. The excitement she offered is suggested by the word, and also the lack of control. The words "cunning" and "cozening" help us interpret both her wildness and falsity; they suggest her calculation, cleverness, and untrustworthiness as well as her skill, persuasiveness, and ability to please. And the word "fair," a simple yet very inclusive word, suggests how totally attractive the speaker finds her: her beauty is just as incapable of being expressed by flowers as her fickleness is of being expressed in something as permanent as stone. Simple words here tell us perhaps all we need to know of a long story—or at least the speaker's version of it.

Words like "fair" and "cozening" are clearly loaded; they imply more emotionally than they literally mean. They have strong, clear connotations and tell us what to think, what evaluation to make, and they suggest the basis for the evaluation. Both words in the title of the following poem turn out to be key ones in its meaning and effect:

PAT MORA

Gentle Communion

Even the long-dead are willing to move.
Without a word, she came with me from the desert.
Mornings she wanders through my rooms
making beds, folding socks.

Since she can't hear me anymore,
Mamande[2] ignores the questions I never knew
to ask, about her younger days, her red
hair, the time she fell and broke her nose
in the snow. I will never know.

When I try to make her laugh,
to disprove her sad album face, she leaves

2. A child's conflation of *mama grande* ("grandmother").

the room, resists me as she resisted
grinning for cameras, make-up, English.

While I write, she sits and prays,
feet apart, legs never crossed,
the blue housecoat buttoned high
as her hair dries white, girlish
around her head and shoulders.

She closes her eyes, bows her head,
and like a child presses her hands together,
her patient flesh steeple, the skin
worn, like the pages of her prayer book.

Sometimes I sit in her wide-armed
chair as I once sat in her lap.
Alone, we played a quiet I Spy.
She peeled grapes I still taste.

She removes the thin skin, places
the luminous coolness on my tongue.
I know not to bite or chew. I wait
for the thick melt,
our private green honey.

1991

Neither of the words in the title appears in the text itself, but both resonate throughout the poem. "Communion" is the more powerful of the words; here, it comes to imply the close ritualized relationship between the speaker and "Mamande." Mamande has long been dead but now returns, recalling to the speaker a host of memories and providing a sense of history and family identity. To the speaker, the reunion has a powerful value, reminding her of rituals, habits, and beliefs that "place" her and affirm her heritage. The past is powerful in the speaker's mind and in the poem. Many details are recalled from album photographs—the blue housecoat (line 16), the sad face (line 11), the white hair that was once red (lines 7–8 and 17), the posture at prayer (lines 19–22), the big chair (lines 23–24), the plain old-fashioned style (line 13)—and the speaker's childhood memories fade into them as she recalls a specific intimate moment.

The full effect of the word "communion"—as an intimate moment of union and as ritual—comes only in the final lines when the speaker remembers the secret of the grapes and recalls their sensuous feel and taste. The moment brings together the experience of different generations and cultures and represents a sacred sharing: the Spanish grandmother had resisted English, modernity, and show (line 13), and the speaker is a poet, writing (and publishing) in

English, but the two have a common "private" (line 31) moment ritually shared and forever memorable. At the end, too, the full sense of "gentle" becomes evident—a word that sums up the softness, quietness, and understatedness of the experience, the personal qualities of "Mamande," and the unpretentious but dignified social level of the family heritage. Throughout the text, other words—ordinary, simple, and precise—are chosen with equal care to suggest the sense of personal dignity, revealed identity, and verbal power that the speaker comes to accept as her own. Look especially at the words "move" (line 1), "steeple" (line 21), and "luminous" (line 28).

In the two poems that follow we can readily see why the specific words are chosen because, although both poems express a male preference for the same sort of feminine appearance, the grounds of appeal are vastly different.

BEN JONSON

Still to Be Neat[3]

Still[4] to be neat, still to be dressed,
As you were going to a feast;
Still to be powdered, still perfumed;
Lady, it is to be presumed,
Though art's hid causes are not found,
All is not sweet, all is not sound.

Give me a look, give me a face
That makes simplicity a grace;
Robes loosely flowing, hair as free;
Such sweet neglect more taketh me
Than all th' adulteries of art.
They strike mine eyes, but not my heart.

1609

ROBERT HERRICK

Delight in Disorder

A sweet disorder in the dress
Kindles in clothes a wantonness.
A lawn[5] about the shoulders thrown
Into a fine distractiön;
An erring lace, which here and there

3. A song from Jonson's play *The Silent Woman* (1609–10). 4. Continually. 5. Scarf of fine linen.

Enthralls the crimson stomacher,[6]
A cuff neglectful, and thereby
Ribbands[7] to flow confusedly;
A winning wave, deserving note,
In the tempestuous petticoat;
A careless shoestring, in whose tie
I see a wild civility;
Do more bewitch me than when art
Is too precise[8] in every part.

1648

The poem "Still to Be Neat" begins by describing a woman who looks too neat and orderly; she seems too perfect to be believed, the speaker says, and he has to assume that there is a reason for such overly fastidious grooming, that she is covering up something. He worries that something is wrong underneath—that not all is "sweet" and "sound." "Sweet" could mean several possible things, and its meaning becomes clearer when it is repeated in the next stanza in a more specific context. But "sound" begins to suggest the speaker's moral earnestness: it is a strong word, implying a suspicion that something is deeply wrong.

When "sweet" is repeated in line 10, it has taken on specific attributes from what the speaker has said about things he likes in a less calculated physical appearance. Now it appears to mean easy, attractive, unpremeditated. And when the speaker springs "adulteries" on us in the next line as a description of the woman's cosmeticizing, it is clear what he fears—that the appearance of the too neat, too made-up woman covers serious flaws, things which try to make her appear someone she is not. "Adulteries" suggests the addition of something foreign, something unlike her own nature, and it is a strong, disapproving word. The "soundness" he had worried about involves her integrity; his objection is certainly moral, probably sexual. He wants a woman to be simple and chaste; he wants women to be just what they seem to be.

The speaker in "Delight in Disorder" wants his women easy and simple too, but for different reasons. He finds disorder "sweet" too (line 1), and seems almost to be answering the first speaker, providing a different rationale for artless appearance. His grounds of preference are clear early: his support of "wantonness" (line 2) is close to the opposite in its moral suppositions of the first speaker's disapproval of "adulteries." This speaker wants a careless look because

6. Ornamental covering for the breasts. 7. Ribbons. 8. In the 16th and 17th centuries Puritans were often called Precisians because of their fastidiousness.

he thinks it's sexy, and many of the words he chooses suggest sensuality and availability: "distraction" (line 4), "erring" (line 5), "tempestuous" (line 10), "wild" (line 12). The speakers in the two poems read informality of dress very differently and have very different expectations of the person who dresses in a particular way. We find out quite a lot about each speaker. Their common subject allows us to see clearly how different they are, and how what one sees is in the eye of the beholder, how values and assumptions are built into the words one chooses even for description. Jonson has created a speaker who wants an informally clad woman who has a natural grace and ease of manner because she is confident of herself, dependable, and chaste. Herrick has created a speaker who finds informality of dress fetching and sexy and indicative of sensuality and availability.

It would be hard to exaggerate how important words are to poems. Poets who know their craft pick each word with care, so that each word will express exactly what needs to be expressed and suggest every emotional shade that the poem is calculated to evoke in us. Often individual words qualify and amplify one another—suggestions clarify other suggestions, and meanings grow upon meanings—and thus the way the words are put together can be important too. Notice, for example, that in "Slim Cunning Hands" the final emphasis is on how *fair* in appearance the woman was; that is the speaker's last word, the thing he can't forget in spite of her lack of a different kind of fairness and his distrust of her, and that is where the poem chooses to leave the emphasis, on that one word which, even though it doesn't justify everything else, qualifies all the disappointment and hurt.

That word does not stand all by itself, however, any more than any other word in a poem can be considered all alone. Every word exists within larger units of meaning—sentences, patterns of comparisons and contrasts, the whole poem—and where the word is and how it is used are often important. The final word or words may be especially emphatic (as in "Slim Cunning Hands"), and words that are repeated take on a special intensity, as "terminal" does in "At the San Francisco Airport" or as "chartered" and "cry" do in "London," a poem we looked at in chapter 2. Certain words often stand out, because they are used in an unusual way (like "chartered" in "London" or "adulteries" in "Still to Be Neat") or because they are given an artificial prominence—through unusual sentence structure, for example, or because the title calls special attention to them.

Sometimes word choice in poems is less dramatic and less obviously "significant" but equally important. Simple appropriateness is often, in fact, what makes the words in a poem work, and when words do not call special attention to themselves they are sometimes the most effective. Precision of denotation may be just as impressive and productive of specific effects as the resonance or ambiguous suggestiveness of connotation. Often poems achieve their power by a combination of verbal effects, setting off elaborate figures of speech (which we will discuss in the next chapter) or other complicated strategies with simple words chosen to mark exact actions, moments, or states of mind. Notice, for example, how carefully the following poem produces its complex description of emotional patterns by delineating precise stages (which are then elaborated) of feeling.

EMILY DICKINSON

[After great pain, a formal feeling comes—]

After great pain, a formal feeling comes—
The Nerves sit ceremonious, like Tombs—
The stiff Heart questions was it He, that bore,
And Yesterday, or Centuries before?

The Feet, mechanical, go round—
Of Ground, or Air, or Ought—
A Wooden way
Regardless grown,
A Quartz contentment, like a stone—

This is the Hour of Lead—
Remembered, if outlived,
As Freezing Persons recollect the Snow—
First—Chill—then Stupor—then the letting go—

ca. 1862

In the following poem, notice how the title calls upon us to wonder, from the beginning, how playful and how patterned the boy's bedtime romp with his father is. As you read it, try to be conscious of the emotional effects created by the choice of words that seem to be key ones. Which words establish the bond between the two males?

THEODORE ROETHKE

My Papa's Waltz

The whiskey on your breath
Could make a small boy dizzy;
But I hung on like death:
Such waltzing was not easy.

We romped until the pans
Slid from the kitchen shelf;
My mother's countenance
Could not unfrown itself.

The hand that held my wrist
Was battered on one knuckle;
At every step you missed
My right ear scraped a buckle.

You beat time on my head
With a palm caked hard by dirt,
Then waltzed me off to bed
Still clinging to your shirt.

1948

Exactly what is the situation in "My Papa's Waltz"? What are the economic circumstances in the family? How can you tell? What indications are there of the family's social class? of the father's line of work? How would you characterize the speaker? How does the poem indicate his pleasure in the bedtime ritual? Which words suggest the boy's excitement? Which suggest his anxiety? How can you tell how the speaker feels about his father? What clues are there about what the mother is like? How can you tell that the experience is remembered at some years' distance? What clues are there in the word choice that an adult is remembering a childhood experience? In what sense is the poem a tribute to memories of the father? How would you describe the poem's tone?

The subtlety and force of word choice is sometimes very much affected by **word order,** the way the sentences are put together. Sometimes poems are driven to unusual word order because of the demands of rhyme and meter, but ordinarily poets use word order very much as prose writers do, to create a particular emphasis. When an unusual word order is used, you can be pretty sure that something worth noticing is going on. Notice, for example, the odd constructions in the second and third stanzas of "My Papa's Waltz." In the third stanza, the way the speaker talks about the abrasion of buckle on ear is very unusual. He does not say that the buckle scraped his ear, but rather puts it the other way round—a big difference in the kind of effect created, for it avoids placing blame and refuses to specify any unpleasant effect. Had he said that the buckle scraped his ear—the normal way of putting it—we would have to worry about the fragile ear. The **syntax** (sentence structure) of the poem channels our feeling and helps to control what we think of the waltz.

The most curious part of the poem is the second stanza, for it is there that the silent mother appears, and the syntax there is peculiar in two places. In lines 5–6, the connection between the romping and the pans falling is stated oddly: "We romped *until* the pans / Slid from the kitchen shelf." The speaker does not say that they knocked down the pans or imply that there was awkwardness, but he does suggest energetic activity and duration. He implies intensity, almost design—as though the romping were not complete until the pans fell. And the sentence about the mother—odd but effective—makes her position clear. She is a silent bystander in this male ritual, and her frown seems molded on her face. It is not as if she is frightened or angry but as if she too is performing a ritual, holding a frown on her face as if it is part of her role in the ritual, as well as perhaps a facet of her stern character. The syntax implies that she *has to* maintain the frown, and the falling of the pans almost seems to be for her benefit. She disapproves, but she is still their audience.

Word order is not always as complicated or crucial as it is in "My Papa's Waltz," but poets often manipulate the ordinary prose order of a sentence to make a specific point or create a specific emphasis or effect. In the passage below from *Paradise Lost*, for example, notice how the syntax first sets a formal tone for the passage, then calls attention to the complexities of theology that it expresses, and (in lines 44ff.) imitates, by holding back key elements of the grammar, the fall that is being described.

Sometimes poems create, as well, a powerful sense of the way minds and emotions work by varying normal syntactical order in special ways. Listen, for example, in the following poem to the speaker's sudden loss of vocal control in the midst of what seems to be a calm analysis of her feelings about sexual behavior.

SHARON OLDS

Sex Without Love

How do they do it, the ones who make love
without love? Beautiful as dancers,
gliding over each other like ice-skaters
over the ice, fingers hooked
inside each other's bodies, faces

red as steak, wine, wet as the
children at birth whose mothers are going to
give them away. How do they come to the
come to the   come to the   God   come to the
still waters, and not love
the one who came there with them, light
rising slowly as steam off their joined
skin? These are the true religious,
the purists, the pros, the ones who will not
accept a false Messiah, love the
priest instead of the God. They do not
mistake the lover for their own pleasure,
they are like great runners: they know they are alone
with the road surface, the cold, the wind,
the fit of their shoes, their over-all cardio-
vascular health—just factors, like the partner
in the bed, and not the truth, which is the
single body alone in the universe
against its own best time.   1984

The poem starts calmly enough, with a simple rhetorical question implying that the speaker just cannot understand sex without love. The second through fourth lines compare such sexual activity with some distant aesthetic, with two carefully delineated examples, and the speaker—although plainly disapproving—seems coolly, almost chillingly, in control of the analysis and evaluation. But by the end of the fourth line, something begins to seem odd: "hooked" seems too ugly and extreme a way to characterize the lovers' fingers, however much the speaker may disapprove, and by line 6, the syntax seems to break down. How does "wine" fit the syntax of the line? Is it parallel with "steak," another example of redness? or is it somehow related to the last part of the sentence, parallel with "faces"? But neither of these possibilities quite works. At best, the punctuation is faulty; at worst the speaker's mind is working too fast for the language it can generate and scrambling its images. We can't yet be quite sure what is going on, but by the ninth line the lack of control is manifest with the compulsive repeating (three times) of "come to the" and the interjected "God."

Such verbal behavior—here concretized by the way the poem orders its words—invites us to reevaluate the speaker's moralism relative to her emotional involvement with the issues and with her representation of sexuality itself. The speaker's values, as well as those who have sex without love, become a subject for evaluation.

Words are the basic building materials of poetry. They are of many kinds and are used in many different ways and in different—sometimes surprising—combinations. Words are seldom simple, even when we know their meanings and recognize their syntax as conventional and transparent. The careful examination of them individually and collectively is a crucial part of the process of reading poems, and learning exactly what kinds of questions to ask about the words that poems use and how poems use them is one of the most basic—and rewarding—skills a reader of poetry can develop.

▽ ▽ ▽

WORDS AND WORD ORDER A Glossary

ambiguity: the ability to mean more than one thing
connote: to suggest something in addition to explicit meaning
connotation: what is suggested by a word, apart from what it explicitly describes
denote: to mean or stand for
denotation: a direct and specific meaning (as distinct from implication)
precision: exactness, accuracy of language or description
syntax: the formal arrangement of words in a sentence
word order: the positioning of words in relation to one another

GERARD MANLEY HOPKINS

Pied Beauty[9]

Glory be to God for dappled things—
For skies of couple-color as a brinded[1] cow;
For rose-moles all in stipple[2] upon trout that swim;
Fresh-firecoal chestnut-falls;[3] finches' wings;
Landscape plotted and pieced—fold, fallow, and plow;
And all trades, their gear and tackle and trim.
All things counter, original, spare, strange;
Whatever is fickle, freckled (who knows how?)
With swift, slow; sweet, sour; adazzle, dim;
He fathers-forth whose beauty is past change:
Praise him.

1877

WILLIAM CARLOS WILLIAMS

The Red Wheelbarrow

so much depends
upon

a red wheel
barrow

glazed with rain
water

beside the white
chickens.

1923

SYLVIA PLATH

Black Rook in Rainy Weather

On the stiff twig up there
Hunches a wet black rook
Arranging and rearranging its feathers in the rain.
I do not expect a miracle
Or an accident

9. Particolored beauty: having patches or sections of more than one color. 1. Streaked or spotted. 2. Rose-colored dots or flecks. 3. Fallen chestnuts as red as burning coals.

To set the sight on fire
In my eye, nor seek
Any more in the desultory weather some design,
But let spotted leaves fall as they fall,
Without ceremony, or portent

Although, I admit, I desire,
Occasionally, some backtalk
From the mute sky, I can't honestly complain:
A certain minor light may still
Leap incandescent

Out of kitchen table or chair
As if a celestial burning took
Possession of the most obtuse objects now and then—
Thus hallowing an interval
Otherwise inconsequent

By bestowing largesse, honor,
One might say love. At any rate, I now walk
Wary (for it could happen
Even in this dull, ruinous landscape); skeptical,
Yet politic; ignorant

Of whatever angel may choose to flare
Suddenly at my elbow. I only know that a rook
Ordering its black feathers can so shine
As to seize my senses, haul
My eyelids up, and grant

A brief respite from fear
Of total neutrality. With luck,
Trekking stubborn through this season
Of fatigue, I shall
Patch together a content

Of sorts. Miracles occur,
If you care to call those spasmodic
Tricks of radiance miracles. The wait's begun again,
The long wait for the angel,
For that rare, random descent.[4]

1960

4. According to Acts 2, the Holy Ghost at Pentecost descended like a dove upon Jesus's disciples.

ERIC ORMSBY

My Mother in Old Age

As my mother ages and becomes
Ever more fragile and precarious,
Her hands dwindle under her rings
And the freckled skin at her throat
Gathers in tender pleats like some startled fabric.
The blue translucence of her veins gives
The texture of her skin an agate gleam
And the dark-blue, almost indigo
Capillaries of her cheeks and forehead
Resemble the gentle roots
Of cuttings of violets
In sheltered jars.

I love her now more urgently
Because there is an unfamiliar and relentless
Splendor in her face that terrifies me.
"Oh, don't prettify decrepitude,"
She demands. "Don't lie!
Don't make old age seem so *ornamental!*"

And yet she abets her metamorphosis,
Invests herself in voluminous costume
Jewels and shrill polyesters

—ambitious as a moth
To mime the dangerous leaf on which she rests.

p. 1989

X. J. KENNEDY

Nude Descending a Staircase[5]

Toe upon toe, a snowing flesh,
A gold of lemon, root and rind,
She sifts in sunlight down the stairs
With nothing on. Nor on her mind.

We spy beneath the banister
A constant thresh of thigh on thigh—
Her lips imprint the swinging air
That parts to let her parts go by.

5. A celebrated cubist-futurist painting (1913) by Marcel Duchamp (1887–1968).

One-woman waterfall, she wears
Her slow descent like a long cape
And pausing, on the final stair
Collects her motions into shape.

1961

JOHN MILTON

from Paradise Lost[6]

I

Of man's first disobedience, and the fruit[7]
Of that forbidden tree whose mortal taste
Brought death into the world, and all our woe,
With loss of Eden, till one greater Man
Restore us, and regain the blissful seat,
Sing, Heav'nly Muse,[8] that, on the secret top
Of Oreb, or Sinai, didst inspire
That shepherd who first taught the chosen seed
In the beginning how the Heav'ns and Earth
Rose out of Chaos: or, if Sion hill
Delight thee more, and Siloa's brook that flowed
Fast[9] by the oracle of God, I thence
Invoke thy aid to my adventurous song,
That with no middle flight intends to soar
Above th' Aonian mount,[1] while it pursues
Things unattempted yet in prose or rhyme.
And chiefly thou, O Spirit,[2] that dost prefer
Before all temples th' upright heart and pure,
Instruct me, for thou know'st; thou from the first
Wast present, and, with mighty wings outspread,
Dovelike sat'st brooding on the vast abyss,

6. The opening lines of Books I and II and a short passage from Book III. The first passage states the poem's subject, and the second describes Satan's beginning address to the council of fallen angels meeting to discuss strategy; in the third, God is looking down from Heaven at his new human creation and watching Satan approach the Earth. 7. The apple, but also the consequences. 8. Addressing one of the muses and asking for aid is a convention for the opening lines of an epic; Milton complicates the standard procedure here by describing sources and circumstances of Judeo-Christian revelation rather than specifically invoking one of the nine classical muses. Sinai is the spur of Mount Oreb, where Moses ("That shepherd," line 8, who was traditionally regarded as author of the first five books of the Bible) received the Law; Sion hill and Siloa (lines 10–11), near Jerusalem, correspond to the traditional mountain (Helicon) and springs of classical tradition. Later, in Book VII, Milton calls upon Urania, the muse of astronomy, but he does not mention by name the muse of epic poetry, Calliope. 9. Close. 1. Mt. Helicon, home of the classical muses. 2. The divine voice that inspired the Hebrew prophets. Genesis 1:2 says that "the Spirit of God moved upon the face of the waters" as part of the process of the original creation; Milton follows tradition in making the inspirational and communicative function of God present in creation itself. The passage echoes and merges many biblical references to divine creation and revelation.

And mad'st it pregnant: what in me is dark
Illumine; what is low, raise and support;
That, to the height of this great argument,[3]
I may assert Eternal Providence,
And justify the ways of God to men.
    Say first (for Heav'n hides nothing from thy view,
Nor the deep tract of Hell), say first what cause
Moved our grand parents, in that happy state,
Favored of Heav'n so highly, to fall off
From their Creator, and transgress his will
For one restraint, lords of the world besides?[4]
Who first seduced them to that foul revolt?
Th' infernal serpent; he it was, whose guile,
Stirred up with envy and revenge, deceived
The mother of mankind, what time[5] his pride
Had cast him out from Heav'n, with all his host
Of rebel angels, by whose aid, aspiring
To set himself in glory above his peers,
He trusted to have equaled the Most High,
If he opposed; and with ambitious aim
Against the throne and monarchy of God,
Raised impious war in Heav'n and battle proud,
With vain attempt. Him the Almighty Power
Hurled headlong flaming from th' ethereal sky,
With hideous ruin and combustion down
To bottomless perdition, there to dwell
In adamantine chains and penal fire,
Who durst defy th' Omnipotent to arms.[6]

* * *

II

High on a throne of royal state, which far
Outshone the wealth of Ormus and of Ind,[7]
Or where the gorgeous East with richest hand
Show'rs on her kings barbaric pearl and gold,
Satan exalted sat, by merit raised
To that bad eminence; and, from despair
Thus high uplifted beyond hope, aspires
Beyond thus high, insatiate to pursue
Vain war with Heav'n, and by success[8] untaught,
His proud imaginations thus displayed:
    "Powers and Dominions, Deities of Heav'n,
For since no deep within her gulf can hold
Immortal vigor, though oppressed and fall'n,

3. Subject. 4. In all other respects. *For:* because of. 5. When. 6. After invoking the muse and giving a brief summary of the poem's subject, an epic regularly begins *in medias res* (in the midst of things). 7. India. *Ormus:* Hormuz, an island in the Persian Gulf, famous for pearls. 8. Outcome, either good or bad.

I give not Heav'n for lost. From this descent
Celestial virtues rising will appear
More glorious and more dread than from no fall,
And trust themselves to fear no second fate.
Me though just right and the fixed laws of Heav'n
Did first create your leader, next, free choice,
With what besides, in council or in fight,
Hath been achieved of merit, yet this loss,
Thus far at least recovered, hath much more
Established in a safe unenvied throne
Yielded with full consent. The happier state
In Heav'n, which follows dignity, might draw
Envy from each inferior; but who here
Will envy whom the highest place exposes
Foremost to stand against the Thunderer's aim
Your bulwark, and condemns to greatest share
Of endless pain? Where there is then no good
For which to strive, no strife can grow up there
From faction; for none sure will claim in hell
Precédence, none, whose portion is so small
Of present pain, that with ambitious mind
Will covet more. With this advantage then
To union, and firm faith, and firm accord,
More than can be in Heav'n, we now return
To claim our just inheritance of old,
Surer to prosper than prosperity
Could have assured us; and by what best way,
Whether of open war or covert guile,
We now debate; who can advise, may speak."

* * *

III

* * *

Now had th' Almighty Father from above,
From the pure empyrean where he sits
High throned above all height, bent down his eye,
His own works and their works at once to view:
About him all the sanctities of Heav'n[9]
Stood thick as stars, and from his sight received
Beatitude past utterance; on his right
The radiant image of his glory sat,
His only Son. On earth he first beheld
Our two first parents, yet the only two
Of mankind, in the happy garden placed,
Reaping immortal fruits of joy and love,
Uninterrupted joy, unrivaled love,

9. The hierarchies of angels.

In blissful solitude. He then surveyed
Hell and the gulf between, and Satan there
Coasting the wall of Heav'n on this side Night
In the dun air sublime,[1] and ready now
To stoop[2] with wearied wings and willing feet
On the bare outside of this world, that seemed
Firm land embosomed without firmament,
Uncertain which, in ocean or in air.

1667

E. E. CUMMINGS

[anyone lived in a pretty how town]

anyone lived in a pretty how town
(with up so floating many bells down)
spring summer autumn winter
he sang his didn't he danced his did.

Women and men(both little and small)
cared for anyone not at all
they sowed their isn't they reaped their same
sun moon stars rain

children guessed(but only a few
and down they forgot as up they grew
autumn winter spring summer)
that noone loved him more by more

when by now and tree by leaf
she laughed his joy she cried his grief
bird by snow and stir by still
anyone's any was all to her

someones married their everyones
laughed their cryings and did their dance
(sleep wake hope and then)they
said their nevers they slept their dream

stars rain sun moon
(and only the snow can begin to explain
how children are apt to forget to remember
with up so floating many bells down)

one day anyone died i guess
(and noone stooped to kiss his face)

1. Aloft in the twilight atmosphere. 2. Swoop down, like a bird of prey.

busy folk buried them side by side
little by little and was by was

all by all and deep by deep
and more by more they dream their sleep
noone and anyone earth by april
wish by spirit and if by yes.

Women and men(both dong and ding)
summer autumn winter spring
reaped their sowing and went their came
sun moon stars rain

1940

EMILY DICKINSON

[I dwell in Possibility—]

I dwell in Possibility—
A fairer House than Prose—
More numerous of Windows—
Superior—for Doors—

Of Chambers as the Cedars—
Impregnable of Eye—
And for an Everlasting Roof
The Gambrels[3] of the Sky—

Of Visitors—the fairest—
For Occupation—This—
The spreading wide my narrow Hands
To gather Paradise—

ca. 1862

STEPHEN DUNN

Tenderness

Back then when so much was clear
    and I hadn't learned
young men learn from women

what it feels like to feel just right,
    I was twenty-three,
she thirty-four, two children, a husband

3. Roofs with double slopes.

in prison for breaking someone's head.
Yelled at, slapped
around, all she knew of tenderness

was how much she wanted it, and all
I knew
were back seats and a night or two

in a sleeping bag in the furtive dark.
We worked
in the same office, banter and loneliness

leading to the shared secret
that to help
National Biscuit sell biscuits

was wildly comic, which led to my body
existing with hers
like rain water that's found its way

underground to water it naturally joins.
I can't remember
ever saying the exact word, tenderness,

though she did. It's a word I see now
you must be older to use,
you must have experienced the absence of it

often enough to know what silk and deep balm
it is
when at last it comes. I think it was terror

at first that drove me to touch her
so softly,
then selfishness, the clear benefit

of doing something that would come back
to me twofold,
and finally, sometime later, it became

reflexive and motiveless in the high
ignorance of love.
Oh abstractions are just abstract

until they have an ache in them. I met
a woman never touched
gently, and when it ended between us,

I had new hands and new sorrow,
everything it meant
to be a man changed, unheroic, floating.

1988

HEATHER McHUGH

What Could Hold Us

Hats divide generally into three classes: offensive hats, defensive hats, and shrapnel.

—KATHERINE WHITEHORN

I

There are no accidents, or so
the lucky like to say.
In the department store she ran
smack into the clutches of
an unassuming man, and double-breasted them.
She drew away at once, but saw
he looked aghast at being
implicated so—with his offending
hands in air—they never meant
to take such liberties—and all around
stood mannequins, unmoved,
in shades of innocence,
in underwear.

II

In the togetherness department, stores
leave much to be desired. The couches seem malposed
beside the barbecues, the bicycles beside the bras,
the customers beside
themselves, or reasonable
facsimiles.

III

She hauled the bedroom suite to the public dump
where one man's paid to stay all day and oversee
the afterlife of wealth. She saw what trucks and trunks
delivered: headless dolls, dead televisions, tangles
of forgetful lamp, a signmaker's
unwanted ampersands. And over everything
the dump man passed, with mercy
and a yellow *machina* (it's he
who parts the earth, who heals the wound,
who tends the jilted and who calms the dead). She stood there
by the empty pickup while he dozed
the king-size thing and earth together,
burning and the bed.

IV

However big the pain, the earth can take it.
Habeas corpus, the raincoat wraps
the flasher's trouble up. Habits close about the nun's
uncustomary hurt. The earth's big headache (having so many
of us in mind) is soothed
by a pacifist sky, with a bright blue sash or a few white flags
or a green forgiving rain, whatever suits the hidden
haberdasher . . . 1987

ROO BORSON

Talk

The shops, the streets are full of old men
who can't think of a thing to say anymore.
Sometimes, looking at a girl, it
almost occurs to them, but they can't make it out,
they go pawing toward it through the fog.

The young men are still jostling shoulders
as they walk along, tussling at one another with words.
They're excited by talk, they can still see the danger.

The old women, thrifty with words,
haggling for oranges, their mouths
take bites out of the air. They know the value of oranges.
They had to learn everything
on their own.

The young women are the worst off, no one has bothered
to show them things.
You can see their minds on their faces,
they are like little lakes before a storm.
They don't know it's a confusion that makes them sad.
It's lucky in a way though, because the young men take
a look of confusion for inscrutability, and this
excites them and makes them want to own
this face they don't understand,
something to be tinkered with at their leisure.

1981

QUESTIONS

1. List all of the neologisms and other unusual words in "Pied Beauty." Find the most precise synonym you can for each. How can you tell exactly what these words contribute to the poem? Explain the effects of the repeated consonant sounds (alliteration) and repeated vowel sounds (assonance) in the poem. What are the advantages of making up original words to describe highly individualized effects? What are the disadvantages?

2. Look up in a dictionary the following words from "Black Rook in Rainy Weather": rook (title), hunches (line 2), desultory (line 8), design (line 8), portent (line 10), mute (line 13), incandescent (line 15), obtuse (line 18), hallowing (line 19), largesse (line 21), ruinous (line 24), ordering (line 28), trekking (line 33), spasmodic (line 37), descent (line 40). Consider carefully how and where each word is used in the poem, and try to sort out the most important *connotation* for each word as it appears in the poem. You may want to consult more than one dictionary to be sure you are considering the full range of meanings and connotations.

3. Explain the full effect of "snowing" (line 1) in "Nude Descending a Staircase," of "sifts" (line 3), of "thresh" (line 6), of "waterfall" (line 9), of "collects" (line 12). Beyond the literal meanings listed in the dictionary, what other implications of these words are suggested by their position and function in the poem?

4. Compare "[I dwell in Possibility—]" with the two Dickinson poems you read earlier ("[A narrow Fellow in the Grass]" and "[After great pain, a formal feeling comes—]"). What patterns of word use do you see in the three poems? What kinds of vocabulary do they have in common? what patterns of syntax? what strategies of organization?

5. Read aloud the passage from *Paradise Lost*. Then ask a friend to read the passage aloud as well. As the friend reads, note which words—and which choices of word order—provide especially useful guides for reading aloud. Make a list of all the lines in which the "normal" word order would be different if the poem were not written in a metrical form designed for reading aloud. In each case in which the poem uses unusual word order, try to figure out exactly what effect is produced by the variation.

WRITING SUGGESTIONS

1. In the arts section of your college library, find a copy of the Duchamp painting on which "Nude Descending a Staircase" is based. Write a short essay (of about 600 words) comparing the painting with Kennedy's interpretation of it. Which words in the poem seem especially appropriate for the visual strategies of Duchamp? In what ways is the structure of the poem a comment on Duchamp's style? Comment especially on the verbs ("sifts," line 3; "imprint," line 7; "parts," line 8; "wears," line 9; "collects," line 12) Kennedy chooses to try to capture the sense of motion in the painting.

2. Choose five words in "What Could Hold Us" that seem to you key ones in producing the poem's effects. Consider carefully exactly how those words are used in the poem, and organize a short (2-page) interpretive essay around your observations on the effects of those words. (Alternative: use "Tenderness" as the subject of your essay, and relate each of the words you choose to the governing title term in the poem.)

3. Read back through the poems you have read so far in the course, and pick out one in which a single word seems to you crucial to the poem's total effect. Write a short essay in which you work out carefully how the poem's meaning and tone depend upon that word.

5 FIGURATIVE LANGUAGE

Metaphor and Simile

The language of poetry is almost always visual and pictorial. Rather than depending primarily on abstract ideas and elaborate reasoning, poems depend mainly upon the creation of images in our minds, helping us to see things fresh and new, or to feel them suggestively through our other physical senses, such as hearing or touch. Poetry is most often visual in the sense that it helps us form, in our minds, visual impressions, images that communicate more directly than concepts. We "see" yellow leaves on a branch, a father and son waltzing precariously, or two lovers sitting together on the bank of a stream, so that our response begins from a vivid impression of exactly what is happening. Some people think that those media and arts that challenge the imagination of a hearer or reader—radio drama, for example, or poetry—allow us to respond more fully than those (such as television or theater) that actually show things more fully to our physical senses. Certainly they leave more to our imagination, to our mind's eye.

But being visual does not just mean describing, telling us facts, indicating shapes, colors, and specific details and giving us precise discriminations through exacting verbs, nouns, adverbs, and adjectives. Often the vividness of the picture in our minds depends upon comparisons. What we are trying to imagine is pictured in terms of something else familiar to us, and we are asked to think of one thing as if it were something else. Many such comparisons, or **figures of speech,** in which something is pictured or figured forth in terms of something already familiar to us, are taken for granted in daily life. Things we can't see or that aren't familiar to us are imaged as things we can; for example, God is said to be like a father, Italy is said to be shaped like a boot, life is compared to a forest, a journey, or a sea. Poems use **figurative language** much of the time. A poem may insist that death is like a sunset or sex like an earthquake or that the way to imagine how it feels to be spiritually secure is to think of the way a shepherd takes care of his sheep. The pictorialness of our imagination may *clarify* things for us—scenes, states of mind, ideas—but at the same time it stimulates us to think of how those pictures make us *feel*. Pictures, even when they are mental pictures or imagined visions, may be both denotative and connotative, just as individual words are: they may clarify and make precise, and they may channel our feelings.

In the poem that follows, the poet helps us to visualize the old age and approaching death of the speaker by making comparisons with familiar things—the coming of winter, the approach of sunset, and the dying embers of a fire.

WILLIAM SHAKESPEARE

[That time of year thou mayst in me behold]

That time of year thou mayst in me behold
When yellow leaves, or none, or few, do hang
Upon those boughs which shake against the cold,
Bare ruined choirs, where late the sweet birds sang.
In me thou see'st the twilight of such day
As after sunset fadeth in the west;
Which by and by[1] black night doth take away,
Death's second self,[2] that seals up all in rest.
In me thou see'st the glowing of such fire,
That on the ashes of his youth doth lie,
As the deathbed whereon it must expire,
Consumed with that which it was nourished by.
This thou perceiv'st, which makes thy love more strong,
To love that well which thou must leave ere long. 1609

The first four lines of "That time of year" make the comparison to seasonal change; but notice that the poet does not have the speaker say directly that his physical condition and age make him resemble autumn. He draws the comparison without stating that it is a comparison: you can see, he says, my own state in the coming of winter in late autumn when the leaves are almost all off the trees. The speaker portrays himself *indirectly* by talking about the passing of the year. The poem uses **metaphor**; that is, one thing is pictured *as if* it were something else. "That time of year" goes on to another metaphor in lines 5–8 and still another in lines 9–12, and each of the metaphors contributes to our understanding of the speaker's sense of his old age and approaching death. Even more important, however, is the way the metaphors give us feelings, an emotional sense of the speaker's age and of his own attitude toward aging. Through the metaphors we come to understand, appreciate, and to some extent share

1. Shortly. 2. Sleep.

the increasing sense of anxiety and urgency that the poem expresses. Our emotional sense of the poem is largely influenced by the way each metaphor is developed and by the way each metaphor leads, with its own kind of internal logic, to another.

The images of late autumn in the first four lines all suggest loneliness, loss, and nostalgia for earlier times. As in the rest of the poem, our eyes are imagined to be the main vehicle for noticing the speaker's age and condition; the phrase "thou mayst in me behold" (line 1) introduces what we are asked to see, and in both lines 5 and 9 we are similarly told "In me thou see'st. . . ." The picture of the trees shedding their leaves suggests that autumn is nearly over, and we can imagine trees either with yellow leaves, or without leaves, or with just a trace of foliage remaining—the latter perhaps most feelingly suggesting the bleakness and loneliness that characterize the change of seasons, the ending of the life cycle. But other senses are invoked too. The boughs shaking against the cold represent an appeal to our tactile sense, and the next line appeals to our sense of hearing, although only as a reminder that the birds no longer sing. (Notice how exact the visual representation is of the bare, or nearly bare, limbs, even as the cold and the lack of birds are noted; birds lined up like a choir on risers would have made a striking visual image on the barren limbs one above the other, but now there is only the *reminder* of what used to be. The present is quiet, bleak, trembly, and lonely.)

The next four lines are slightly different in tone, and the color changes. From a black-and-white landscape with a few yellow leaves, we come upon a rich and almost warm reminder of a faded sunset. But a somber note does enter the poem in these lines through another figure of speech, **personification,** which involves treating an abstraction, such as death or justice or beauty, as if it were a person. The poem is talking about the coming of night and of sleep, and Sleep is personified and identified as the "second self" of Death (that is, as a kind of "double" or reflection of death). The main emphasis is on how night and sleep close in on our sense of twilight, and only secondarily does a reminder of death enter the poem. But it does enter.

The third metaphor—that of the dying embers of a fire—begins in line 9 and continues to color and warm the bleak cold that the poem began with, but it also sharpens the reminder of death. The three main metaphors in the poem work in a way to make our sense of old age and approaching death more familiar, but also more immediate: moving from barren trees, to fading twilight, to dying embers suggests a sensuous increase of color and warmth, but also an increasing urgency. The first metaphor involves a whole season, or at least a segment of one, a matter of days or possibly weeks; the second involves the passing of a single day, reducing the time scale to a matter of minutes, and the third draws our attention to that split second when a glowing ember fades into a simple ash. The final part of the fire metaphor introduces the most explicit sense of death so far, as the metaphor of embers shifts into a direct reminder of death. Embers which had been a metaphor of the speaker's aging body now themselves become, metaphorically, a deathbed; the vitality that nourishes youth is used up just as a log in a fire is. The urgency of the reminder of coming death has now peaked. It is friendlier but now seems immediate and inevitable, a natural part of the life process, and the final two lines then make an explicit plea to make good and intense use of the remaining moments of human relationship.

"That time of year" represents an unusually intricate use of images to organize a poem and focus its emotional impact. Not all poems are so skillfully made, and not all depend on such a full and varied use of metaphor. But most poems use metaphors for at least part of their effect, and often a poem is based on a single metaphor that is fully developed as the major way of making the poem's statement and impact, as in the following poem about the role of a mother and wife.

LINDA PASTAN

Marks

My husband gives me an A
for last night's supper,
an incomplete for my ironing,
a B plus in bed.
My son says I am average,
an average mother, but if
I put my mind to it
I could improve.
My daughter believes
in Pass / Fail and tells me
I pass. Wait 'til they learn
I'm dropping out.

1978

The speaker in "Marks" is obviously not thrilled with the idea of continually being judged, and the metaphor of marks (or grades) as a way of talking about her performance of roles in the family suggests her irritation. The list of the roles implies the many things expected of her, and the three different systems of marking (letter grades, categories to be checked off on a chart, and pass / fail) detail the difficulties of multiple standards. The poem retains the language of schooldays all the way to the end ("learn," line 11; "dropping out," line 12), and the major effect of the poem depends on the irony of the speaker's surrendering to the metaphor the family has thrust upon her; if she is to be judged as if she were a student, she retains the right to drop out. Ironically, she joins the system (adopts the metaphor for herself) in order to defeat it.

Poets often are self-conscious and explicit about the ways they use language metaphorically, and sometimes (as in the following poem) they celebrate the richness of language that makes their art possible:

ROBERT FRANCIS

Hogwash

The tongue that mothered such a metaphor
Only the purest purist could despair of.

Nobody ever called swill sweet but isn't
Hogwash a daisy in a field of daisies?

What beside sports and flowers could you find
To praise better than the American language?

Bruised by American foreign policy
What shall I soothe me, what defend me with

But a handful of clean unmistakable words—
Daisies, daisies, in a field of daisies?

1965

The poet here claims little for his own invention and not much for the art of poetry, insisting that the American language itself is responsible for miraculous conceptions. The poet plays cheerfully here with what words offer—the pun on "purest" and "purist" (line 2), for example, and the taunting (but misleading) similarity of the beginnings of "swill" and "sweet" (line 3)—but insists that poems and poets only articulate things already realized in common speech, where metaphors are "mothered" (line 1). "Hogwash," although never explicitly glossed or discussed in the poem, is the primary example: What *does* "hogwash" mean? How do hogs wash themselves and in what? to what purpose and effect? How did the term get invented as a metaphor, and what are its visual implications? And what is it doing as an example of beauty in a poem about "clean unmistakable words" (line 9)? But then the poem plays even more fully with "daisy" (lines 4 and 10) as metaphor and idiomatic expression. A "daisy" is a great success, a breakthrough, a beaut, a perfect example, and the word "hogwash" is such a daisy, an instance of such a success: a "daisy in a field of daisies," a success of successes, a wonder in a language full of wonders.

Not everything American, according to this poem, is as praiseworthy as its language, and the word "hogwash" ultimately has its context established in the poem's fourth stanza when the speaker finally tells us why the word is so soothing and so pertinent. Poets, the poem says, need words and metaphors that are not always images of beauty because the world is full of things that are not altogether beautiful, and metaphors of ugliness can be "daisies" too.

Not all poets feel as positive as Robert Francis claims to be here about the raw materials they have to work with in language. Ultimately, of course, the modesty of the poet's claims about his own inventiveness becomes as comic as the metaphor of "hogwash" itself and the poem's characterization of foreign policy, for it is the poem that makes this particular use of the metaphor, no matter where or when it was invented: the wit belongs to the poem, not the language. Poets make use of whatever idioms, expressions, inherited metaphors, and traditions of language come their way, and they turn them to their own uses, sometimes quite surprisingly.

The difficulty of conveying what some experiences are like and how we feel about them sometimes leads poets to startling comparisons and figures of speech that may at first seem far-fetched but that, in one way or another, do in fact suggest the quality of the experience or the feelings associated with it. Sometimes it takes a series of metaphors, as if no single act of visualization will serve but several together may suggest the full complexity of the experience or cumulatively define the feeling precisely. Metaphors open up virtually endless possibilities of comparison, giving words a chance to be more than words, offering our mind's eye a challenge to keep up with the fertile and articulate imagination of writers who make it their business to see things that ordinary people miss, noticing the most surprising likenesses and conveying feelings more powerfully than politicians usually do.

Sometimes, in poetry as in prose, comparisons are made explicitly, as in the following poem.

ROBERT BURNS

A Red, Red Rose

O, my luve's like a red, red rose
That's newly sprung in June.

O, my luve is like the melodie
That's sweetly played in tune.

As fair art thou, my bonnie lass,
So deep in luve am I;
And I will luve thee still, my dear,
Till a' the seas gang[3] dry.

Till a' the seas gang dry, my dear,
And the rocks melt wi' the sun;
And I will luve thee still, my dear,
While the sands o' life shall run.

And fare thee weel, my only luve,
And fare thee weel a while!
And I will come again, my luve,
Though it were ten thousand mile.

1796

The first four lines make two explicit comparisons: the speaker says that his love is "like a rose" and "like a melodie." Such *explicit* comparison is called a **simile,** and usually (as here) the comparison involves the words "like" or "as." Similes work much as do metaphors, except that they usually are used more passingly, more incidentally; they make a quick comparison and usually do not elaborate, whereas metaphors often extend over a long section of a poem (in which case they are called **extended metaphors**) or even over the whole poem as in "Marks" (in which case they are called **controlling metaphors**).

The two similes in "A Red, Red Rose" assume that we already have a favorable opinion of roses and of melodies. Here the poet does not develop the comparison or even remind us of attractive details about roses or tunes. He pays the quick compliment and moves on. Similes sometimes develop more elaborate comparisons than this and occasionally even control long sections of a poem (in which case they are called **analogies**), but usually a simile is briefer and relies more fully on something we already know. The speaker in "My Papa's Waltz" says that he hung on "like death"; he doesn't have to explain or elaborate the comparison: we know the anxiety he refers to.

Like metaphors, similes may imply both meaning and feeling; they may both explain something and invoke feelings about it. All figurative language involves an attempt to clarify something *and* to help readers feel a certain way about it. Saying that one's love is like a rose implies a delicate and fragile

3. Go.

beauty and invites our senses into play so that we can share sensuously a response to fragrant appeal and soft touch, just as the shivering boughs and dying embers in "That time of year" explain separation and loss at the same time that they allow us to share the cold sense of loneliness and the warmth of old friendship.

Once you are alerted to look for them you will find figures of speech in poem after poem; they are among the most common devices through which poets share their vision with us.

The following poem uses a variety of metaphors to describe sexual experiences.

ADRIENNE RICH

Two Songs

1

Sex, as they harshly call it,
I fell into this morning
at ten o'clock, a drizzling hour
of traffic and wet newspapers.
I thought of him who yesterday
clearly didn't
turn me to a hot field
ready for plowing,
and longing for that young man
piercéd me to the roots
bathing every vein, etc.[4]
All day he appears to me
touchingly desirable,
a prize one could wreck one's peace for.
I'd call it love if love
didn't take so many years
but lust too is a jewel
a sweet flower and what
pure happiness to know
all our high-toned questions
breed in a lively animal.

2

That "old last act"!
And yet sometimes

4. See the opening lines of the Prologue to Chaucer's *Canterbury Tales*.

all seems post coitum triste[5]
and I a mere bystander.
Somebody else is going off,
getting shot to the moon.
Or, a moon-race!
my opposite number lands
Split seconds after
I make it—
we lie fainting together
at a crater-edge
heavy as mercury in our moonsuits
till he speaks
in a different language
yet one I've picked up
through cultural exchanges . . .
we murmur the first moonwords:
Spasibo.[6] *Thanks. O.K.*

1964

The first "song" begins straightforwardly as narration ("sex . . . I fell into this morning / at ten o'clock"), but the vividness of sex and desire is communicated mostly by figure. The narrator describes today's self (unlike yesterday's) as "a hot field / ready for plowing" (lines 7–8), and her longing is also described by metaphor, in this case an elaborate one borrowed from another poem. After so sensual and urgent a beginning, the song turns more thoughtful and philosophical, but even the intellectual sorting between love and lust comes to depend on figures: lust is a "jewel" (line 17) and a "flower" (line 18). After the opening pace and excitement those later metaphors seem calm and tame, moving the poem from the lust in action of its beginning to a contemplative reflection on the value and beauty of momentary physical pleasures.

The second song depends on two closely related metaphors, and here the metaphors for sex are highly self-conscious and a little comic. The song begins on a plaintive note, considering the classic melancholic feeling after sex; the speaker pictures herself as isolated, left out, "a bystander" (line 25), while someone else is having sexual pleasure. This pleasure of others is described through two colloquial expressions (both metaphors) for sexual climax: "going off" (line 26) and "getting shot to the moon" (line 27). Suddenly the narrator pretends to take sex as space travel seriously and creates a metaphor of her own: sexual partners running a "moon-race" (line 28). The rest of the poem enacts the metaphor in the context of the space race between the United States and Russia in the early 1960s. The race, not exactly even but close enough, is

5. Sadness after sexual union. 6. Russian for "thanks."

described in detail, and the speaker tells her story in a self-conscious comic way. These are international relations, foreign affairs, and the lovers appropriately say their thank-yous separately in Russian and English, then communicate an international *O.K.*

▽ ▽ ▽

METAPHOR AND SIMILE A Glossary

analogy: a comparison based on certain resemblances between things that are otherwise unlike one another

controlling metaphors: metaphors that dominate or organize an entire poem

extended metaphors: detailed and complex metaphors that extend over a long section of a poem

figurative language: language that uses figures of speech

figures of speech: comparisons in which something is pictured or figured forth in other, more familiar terms

metaphor: one thing pictured as if it were something else, suggesting a likeness or analogy between them

personification (or **prosopopeia**): treating an abstraction as if it were a person, endowing it with human-like qualities

simile: a direct, explicit comparison of one thing to another, and usually using the words "like" or "as" to draw the connection

RANDALL JARRELL

The Death of the Ball Turret Gunner[7]

From my mother's sleep I fell into the State,
And I hunched in its belly till my wet fur froze.
Six miles from earth, loosed from its dream of life,
I woke to black flak and the nightmare fighters.
When I died they washed me out of the turret with a hose.

1945

LINDA PASTAN

Erosion

We are slowly
undermined. Grain
by grain . . .
inch by inch . . .
slippage.
It happens as we watch.
The waves move their long row
of scythes over the beach.

It happens as we sleep,
the way the clock's hands
move continuously
just out of sight,
but more like an hourglass
than a clock,
for here sand
is running out.

We wake to water.
Implacably lovely
is this view
though it will swallow
us whole, soon
there will be
nothing left
but view.

7. "A ball turret was a plexiglass sphere set into the belly of a B-17 or B-24 and inhabited by two .50 caliber machine-guns and one man, a short, small man. When this gunner tracked with his machine-guns a fighter attacking his bomber from below, he revolved with the turret; hunched upside-down in his little sphere, he looked like the foetus in the womb. The fighters which attacked him were armed with cannon firing explosive shells. The hose was a steam hose." [Author's note]

We have tried a seawall.
We have tried prayer.
We have planted grasses
on the bank, small tentacles
hooks of green that catch
on nothing. For the wind
does its work, the water
does its sure work.

One day the sea will simply
take us. The children
press their faces to the glass
as if the windows were portholes,
and the house fills
with animals: two dogs,
a bird, cats—we are becoming
an ark already.

The gulls will follow
our wake.
We are made of water anyway,
I can feel it in the yielding
of your flesh, though sometimes
I think that you are sand,
moving slowly, slowly
from under me.

1988

JOHN DONNE

[Batter my heart, three-personed God . . .][8]

Batter my heart, three-personed God; for You
As yet but knock, breathe, shine, and seek to mend;
That I may rise and stand, o'erthrow me, and bend
Your force, to break, blow, burn, and make me new.
I, like an usurped town, to another due,
Labor to admit You, but Oh, to no end!
Reason, Your viceroy[9] in me, me should defend,
But is captived, and proves weak or untrue.
Yet dearly I love You, and would be loved fain.[1]
But am betrothed unto Your enemy:
Divorce me, untie or break that knot again,

8. *Holy Sonnets,* 14. 9. One who rules as the representative of a higher power. 1. Gladly.

Take me to You, imprison me, for I,
Except You enthrall me, never shall be free,
Nor ever chaste, except You ravish me.

1633

ANONYMOUS[2]

The Twenty-Third Psalm

The Lord is my shepherd; I shall not want.

He maketh me to lie down in green pastures: he leadeth me beside
the still waters.
He restoreth my soul: he leadeth me in the paths of righteousness
for his name's sake.
Yea, though I walk through the valley of the shadow of death,
I will fear no evil: for thou art with me;
thy rod and thy staff they comfort me.
Thou preparest a table before me in the presence of mine enemies:
thou anointest my head with oil; my cup runneth over.
Surely goodness and mercy shall follow me all the days of my life:
and I will dwell in the house of the Lord for ever.

JIM POWELL

It Was Fever that Made the World

It was fever that made the world
burn last summer, that afternoon
when I lay watching the sun pour
its incurable folly slantwise
into a plum tree's crest,

infusing it till the whole crown glowed
red as infected blood translucent
in a syringe. Sunlight was
the carnal fuel leaves burned for life—
obedient to hunger,

they turned their faces toward it
with such greed, in their recklessness
I could see fall's wreckage breeding:
motionless, each leaf swarmed
with an earthly fire

2. Traditionally attributed to King David.

commanding as the power I felt
churning inside me last night
listening to a guitar rant
dirty blues till the crowd eddied
open as everyone

started dancing: past will
or withstanding, in the hot dark
song after song grew stronger, thriving
like summer in our shaken limbs.
Outside, between sets,

after midnight in the sidewalk
company of strangers, all
the flushed faces reminded me:
sweat was a fever sign last June—now,
my drenched shirt cooling

felt like health, like strength, urgent as the sight
of taillights queuing at the tollbooths
Friday night, then streaming up the bridge
till all five lanes of their sharp reds merge
toward the city's bright towers.

1989

MARGE PIERCY

September Afternoon at Four O'Clock

Full in the hand, heavy
with ripeness, perfume spreading
its fan: moments now resemble
sweet russet pear glowing
on the bough, peaches warm
from the afternoon sun, amber
and juicy, flesh that can
make you drunk.

There is a turn in things
that makes the heart catch.
We are ripening, all the hard
green grasping, the stony will
swelling into sweetness, the acid
and sugar in balance, the sun
stored as energy that is pleasure
and pleasure that is energy.

Whatever happens, whatever,
we say, and hold hard and let

go and go on. In the perfect
moment the future coils,
a tree inside a pit. Take,
eat, we are each other's
perfection, the wine of our
mouths is sweet and heavy.

Soon enough comes the vinegar.
The fruit is ripe for the taking
and we take. There is
no other wisdom.

1980

ELI MANDEL

Houdini[3]

I suspect he knew that trunks are metaphors,
could distinguish between the finest rhythms
unrolled on rope or singing in a chain
and knew the metrics of the deepest pools

I think of him listening to the words
spoken by manacles, cells, handcuffs,
chests, hampers, roll-top desks, vaults,
especially the deep words spoken by coffins

escape, escape: quaint Harry in his suit
his chains, his desk, attached to all attachments
how he'd sweat in that precise struggle
with those binding words, wrapped around him
like that mannered style, his formal suit

and spoken when? by whom? What think first said
"there's no way out"?; so that he'd free himself,
leap, squirm, no matter how, to chain himself again,
once more jump out of the deep alive
with all his chains singing around his feet
like the bound crowds who sigh, who sigh.

1967

3. Harry Houdini (1874–1926), American magician and escape-artist; he was especially famous for spectacular "challenge" acts in which he allowed members of his audience to tie him up, handcuff him, and lock him in boxes, trunks, coffins, etc., and for an act in which he escaped from a Water Torture Cell while submerged upside down.

Symbol

The word "symbol" is often used sloppily and sometimes pretentiously, but properly used the term suggests one of the most basic things about poems—their ability to get beyond what words signify and make larger claims about meanings in the verbal world. All words go beyond themselves. They are not simply a collection of sounds: they signify something beyond their sounds, often things or actions or ideas. Words describe not only a verbal universe but a world in which actions occur, acts have implications, and events mean. Sometimes words not only signify something beyond themselves—a rock or a tree or a cloud—but symbolize something as well—solidity or life or dreams. Words can—when their implications are agreed on by tradition, convention, or habit—stand for things beyond their most immediate meanings or significations and become symbols, and even simple words that have accumulated no special power from previous use may be given special significance in special circumstances—either in poetry or in life itself.

A **symbol** is, put simply, something that stands for something else. The everyday world is full of common examples; a flag, a logo, a trademark, or a skull and crossbones all suggest things beyond themselves, and everyone is likely to understand what their display is meant to indicate, whether or not the viewer shares a commitment to what the object represents. In common usage a prison is a symbol of confinement, constriction, and loss of freedom, and in specialized traditional usage a cross may symbolize oppression, cruelty, suffering, death, resurrection, triumph, or the intersection of two separate things, traditions, or ideas (as in crossroads and crosscurrents, for example). The specific symbolic significance is controlled by the context; a reader may often decide what it is by looking at contiguous details in the poem and by examining the poem's attitude toward a particular tradition or body of beliefs. A star means one kind of thing to a Jewish poet and something else to a Christian poet, still something else to a sailor or actor. In a very literal sense, words themselves are all symbols (they stand for an object, action, or quality, not just for letters or sounds), but symbols in poetry are said to be those words and groups of words that have a range of reference beyond their literal signification or denotation.

Poems sometimes create a symbol out of a thing, action, or event that has no previously agreed upon symbolic significance. In the following poem, for example, a random gesture is given symbolic significance.

SHARON OLDS

Leningrad Cemetery, Winter of 1941[1]

That winter, the dead could not be buried.
The ground was frozen, the gravediggers weak from hunger,
the coffin wood used for fuel. So they were covered with something
and taken on a child's sled to the cemetery
in the sub-zero air. They lay on the soil,
some of them wrapped in dark cloth
bound with rope like the tree's ball of roots
when it waits to be planted; others wound in sheets,
their pale, gauze, tapered shapes
stiff as cocoons that will split down the center
when the new life inside is prepared;
but most lay like corpses, their coverings
coming undone, naked calves
hard as corded wood spilling
from under a cloak, a hand reaching out
with no sign of peace, wanting to come back
even to the bread made of glue and sawdust,
even to the icy winter, and the siege.

p. 1979

All of the corpses—frozen, neglected, beginning to be in disarray—vividly stamp upon our minds a sense of the horrors of war, and the detailed picture of the random, uncounted clutter of bodies is likely to stick in our minds long after we have finished reading the poem. Several of the details are striking, and the poem's language heightens our sense of them. The corpses wound in sheets, for example, are described in "their pale, gauze, tapered shapes," and they are compared to cocoons that one day will split and emit new life; and the limbs that dangle loose when the coverings come undone are said to be "hard as corded wood spilling." But clearly the most memorable sight is the hand dangling from one corpse that is coming unwrapped, for the poet invests that hand with special significance, giving its gesture *meaning*. The hand is described as "reaching out . . . wanting to come back": it is as if the dead can still gesture even if they cannot speak, and the gesture seems to signify the desire of the dead to come back at any price. They would be glad to be alive, even under the grim conditions that attend the living in Leningrad during this grim war. Suddenly the grimness that we—living—have been witnessing pales by comparison with what the dead have lost simply by being dead. The hand has been made to *symbolize* the desire of the dead to return, to be alive, to be

1. The 900-day siege of Leningrad during World War II began in September 1941.

still among us, anywhere. The hand reaches out in the poem as a gesture that means; the poet has made it a symbol of desire.

The whole array of dead bodies in the poem might be said to be symbolic as well. As a group, they stand for the human waste that the war has produced, and their dramatic visual presence on the scene provides the poem with a dramatic visualization of how war and its requirements have no time for decency, not even the decency of burial. The bodies are a symbol in the sense that they stand for what the poem as a whole asserts.

The poem that follows also arises out of a historical moment, but this time the event is a personal one that the poet gives a significance by the interpretation he puts upon it.

JAMES DICKEY

The Leap

The only thing I have of Jane MacNaughton
Is one instant of a dancing-class dance.
She was the fastest runner in the seventh grade,
My scrapbook says, even when boys were beginning
To be as big as the girls,
But I do not have her running in my mind,
Though Frances Lane is there, Agnes Fraser,
Fat Betty Lou Black in the boys-against-girls
Relays we ran at recess: she must have run

Like the other girls, with her skirts tucked up
So they would be like bloomers,
But I cannot tell; that part of her is gone.
What I do have is when she came,
With the hem of her skirt where it should be
For a young lady, into the annual dance
Of the dancing class we all hated, and with a light
Grave leap, jumped up and touched the end
Of one of the paper-ring decorations

To see if she could reach it. She could,
And reached me now as well, hanging in my mind
From a brown chain of brittle paper, thin
And muscular, wide-mouthed, eager to prove
Whatever it proves when you leap
In a new dress, a new womanhood, among the boys
Whom you easily left in the dust
Of the passionless playground. If I said I saw
In the paper where Jane MacNaughton Hill,

Mother of four, leapt to her death from a window
Of a downtown hotel, and that her body crushed-in
The top of a parked taxi, and that I held
Without trembling a picture of her lying cradled
In that papery steel as though lying in the grass,
One shoe idly off, arms folded across her breast,
I would not believe myself. I would say
The convenient thing, that it was a bad dream
Of maturity, to see that eternal process

Most obsessively wrong with the world
Come out of her light, earth-spurning feet
Grown heavy: would say that in the dusty heels
Of the playground some boy who did not depend
On speed of foot, caught and betrayed her.
Jane, stay where you are in my first mind:
It was odd in that school, at that dance.
I and the other slow-footed yokels sat in corners
Cutting rings out of drawing paper

Before you leapt in your new dress
And touched the end of something I began,
Above the couples struggling on the floor,
New men and women clutching at each other
And prancing foolishly as bears: hold on
To that ring I made for you, Jane—
My feet are nailed to the ground
By dust I swallowed thirty years ago—
While I examine my hands.

1967

Memory is crucial to "The Leap." The fact that Jane MacNaughton's graceful leap in dancing class has stuck in the speaker's mind for all these years means that this leap was important to him, meant something to him, stood for something in his mind. For the speaker, the leap is an "instant" and the "only thing" he has of Jane. Its grace and ease are what he remembers, and he struggles at several points to articulate its meaning (lines 15–26, 44–50), but even without articulation or explanation it is there in his head as a visual memory, a symbol for him of something beyond himself, something he cannot do, something he wanted to be. What that leap had stood for, or symbolized, was boldness, confidence, accomplishment, maturity, the ability to go beyond her fellow students in dancing class—the transcending of childhood by someone beginning to be a woman. Her feet now seem "earth-spurning" (line 38) in that original leap, and they separate her from everyone else. Jane MacNaughton was beyond the speaker's abilities and any attempt he could make to articulate his hopes, but not beyond his dreams. And even before articulation, she symbolized that dream.

The leap to her death seems cruelly ironic in the context of her earlier leap. In memory she is suspended in air, as if there were no gravity, no coming back to earth, as if life could exist as dream. And so the photograph, recreated in precise detail, is a cruel dashing of the speaker's dream—a detailed record of the ending of a leap, a denial of the suspension in which his memory had held her. His dream is grounded; her mortality is insistent. But what the speaker wants to hang on to (line 42) is still that symbolic moment which, although now confronted in more mature implications, will never be altogether replaced or surrendered.

The leap is ultimately symbolic in the *poem*, too, not just in the speaker's mind. In the poem (and for us as readers) the symbolism of the leap is double: the first leap is aspiration, and the second is frustration of high hopes; the two are complementary, one unable to be imagined without the other. The poem is horrifying in some ways, a dramatic reminder that human beings don't ultimately transcend their mortality, their limits, no matter how heroic or unencumbered by gravity they may seem to an observer. But it is not altogether sad and despairing either, partly because it notices and affirms the validity of the original leap and partly because another symbol is created and elaborated in the poem. That symbol is the paper chain.

The chain connects Jane to the speaker both literally and figuratively. It is, in part, *his* paper chain which she had leaped to touch in dancing class (lines 18–19), and he thinks of her first leap as "touch[ing] the end of something I began" (line 47). He and the other "slow footed," earthbound "yokels" (line 44) were the makers of the chain, and thus they are connected to her original leap, just as a photograph glimpsed in the paper connects the speaker to her second leap. The paper in the chain is "brittle" (line 21), and its creators seem dull artisans compared to the artistic performer that Jane was. They are heavy and left in the dust (lines 25, 52–53), and she is "light" (line 16) and able to transcend them but even in transcendence touching their lives and what they are able to do. And so the paper chain becomes the poem's symbol of linkage, connecting lower accomplishment to higher possibility, the artisan to the artist, material substance to the act of imagination. And the speaker at the end examines the hands that made the chain because those hands certify his connection to her and the imaginative leap she had made for him. The chain thus symbolizes not only the lower capabilities of those who cannot leap like the budding Jane could, but (later) the connection with her leap as both transcendence and mortality. Like the leap itself, the chain has been elevated to special meaning, given symbolic significance, by the poet's treatment of it. A leap and a chain have no necessary significance in themselves to most of us—at least no significance that we have all agreed upon together—but they may be given significance in specific circumstances or a specific text.

But some objects and acts do have a significance built in because of past usage. Over the years some things have acquired an agreed-upon significance, an accepted value in our minds. They already stand for something before the poet cites them; they are **traditional symbols.** Their uses in poetry have to do with the fact that poets can count on a recognition of their traditional suggestions and meanings outside the poem, and the poem does not have to propose or argue a particular symbolic value. Birds, for example, traditionally symbolize flight, freedom from confinement, detachment from earthbound limits, the ability to soar beyond rationality and transcend mortal limits. Traditionally, birds have also been linked with imagination, especially poetic imagination, and poets often identify with them as ideal singers of songs, as in Keats's "Ode to a Nightingale." One of the most traditional symbols is that of the rose. It may be a simple and fairly plentiful flower in its season, but it has been allowed to stand for particular qualities for so long that to name it raises predictable expectations. Its beauty, delicacy, fragility, shortness of life, and depth of color have made it a symbol of the transitoriness of beauty, and countless poets have counted on its accepted symbolism—sometimes to compliment a friend (as Burns does in "A Red, Red Rose") or sometimes to make a point about the nature of symbolism. The following poem draws on, in a quite traditional way, the traditional meanings.

JOHN CLARE

Love's Emblem

Go, rose, my Chloe's[2] bosom grace:
  How happy should I prove,
Could I supply that envied place
  With never-fading love.

Accept, dear maid, now summer glows,
  This pure, unsullied gem,
Love's emblem in a full-blown rose,
  Just broken from the stem.

2. A standard "poetic" name for a woman in traditional love poetry.

Accept it as a favorite flower
For thy soft breast to wear;
'Twill blossom there its transient hour,
A favorite of the fair.

Upon thy cheek its blossom glows,
As from a mirror clear,
Making thyself a living rose,
In blossom all the year.

It is a sweet and favorite flower
To grace a maiden's brow,
Emblem of love without its power—
A sweeter rose art thou.

The rose, like hues of insect wing,
May perish in an hour;
'Tis but at best a fading thing,
But thou'rt a living flower.

The roses steeped in morning dews
Would every eye enthrall,
But woman, she alone subdues;
Her beauty conquers all.

1873

The speaker in "Love's Emblem" sends the rose to Chloe to decorate her bosom (lines 1, 10) and reflect the blush of her cheek and brow (lines 13, 18), and he goes on to mention some of the standard meanings: the rose is pure (line 6), transitory (line 11), fragrant, beautiful, and always appreciated (line 17). The poet need not elaborate or argue these things; he can assume the reader's acquiescence. To say that the rose is an emblem of love is to say that it traditionally symbolizes love, and the speaker expects Chloe to accept his gift readily; she will understand it as a compliment, a pledge, and a bond. She will understand, too, that her admirer is being conventional and complimentary in going on to call her (and women in general) a rose (line 20), except that her qualities are said to be more lasting than those of a momentary flower.

Poems often use traditional symbols to invoke predictable responses—in effect using shortcuts to meaning and power by repeating acts of signification and symbolization sanctioned by time and habit. But often poets examine the tradition even as they employ it, and sometimes they revise or reverse meanings built into the tradition. Some of the poems at the end of this chapter question the usual meanings of roses in poetry and evaluate as they go. Symbols do not necessarily stay the same over time, and poets often turn even the most traditional of symbols to their own original uses. Knowing the traditions of poetry—

reading a lot of poems and observing how they tend to use certain words, metaphors, and symbols—can be very useful in reading new poems, but traditions modify and individual poems do highly individual things. Knowing the past never means being able to predict new texts with confidence. Symbolism makes things happen, but individual poets and texts determine what will happen and how.

Sometimes symbols—traditional or not—become so insistent in the world of a poem that the larger referential world is left almost totally behind. In such cases the symbol is everything, and the poem does not just *use* symbols but becomes a **symbolic poem,** usually a highly individualized one dependent on an internal system introduced by the individual poet.

Here is an example of such a poem:

WILLIAM BLAKE

The Sick Rose[3]

O rose, thou art sick.
The invisible worm
That flies in the night
In the howling storm

Has found out thy bed
Of crimson joy,
And his dark secret love
Does thy life destroy.

1794

The poem does not seem to be about a rose, but about what the rose represents—not in this case something altogether understandable through the traditional meanings of rose.

We know that the rose is usually associated with beauty and love, often with sex; and here several key terms have sexual connotations: "bed," "worm," and "crimson joy." The violation of the rose by the worm is the poem's main concern; the violation seems to have involved secrecy, deceit, and "dark" motives, and the result is sickness rather than the joy of love. The poem is sad; it involves a sense of hurt and tragedy, nearly of despair. The poem cries out against the misuse of the rose, against its desecration, implying that instead of a

3. In Renaissance emblem books, the scarab beetle, worm, and rose are closely associated: The beetle feeds on dung, and the smell of the rose is fatal to it.

healthy joy in sensuality and sexuality, in this case, there has been destruction and hurt because of misunderstanding and repression and lack of sensitivity.

But to say so much about this poem I have had to extrapolate from other poems by this poet, and have introduced information from outside the poem. Fully symbolic poems often require that, and thus they ask us to go beyond the normal procedures of reading that we have discussed so far. As presented in this poem, the rose is not part of the normal world that we ordinarily see, and it is symbolic in a special sense. The poet does not simply take an object from that everyday world and give it special significance, making it a symbol in the same sense that the leap is a symbol, or the corpse's hand. Here the rose seems to belong to its own world, a world made entirely inside the poem. The rose is not referential or not primarily so. The whole poem is symbolic; it is not paraphrasable; it lives in its own world. But what is the rose here a symbol of? In general terms, we can say from what the poem tells us; but we may not be as confident as we can be in the more nearly everyday world of "The Leap" or "Leningrad Cemetery, Winter of 1941," poems that contain actions we recognize from the world of probabilities in which we live. In "The Sick Rose," it seems inappropriate to ask the standard questions: What rose? Where? Which worm? What are the particulars here? In the world of this poem worms can fly and may be invisible. We are altogether in a world of meanings. We will only feel comfortable and confident in that world if we read many poems written by the poet (in this case William Blake) within the same symbolic system.

Negotiation of meanings in symbolic poems can be very difficult indeed. The skill of reading symbolic poems is an advanced skill that depends on special knowledge of authors and of the traditions they work from, but the symbols you will usually find in poems are referential, and these meanings are readily discoverable from the careful study of the poems themselves, as in poems like "The Leap" and "Love's Emblem."

▽ ▽ ▽

SYMBOL A Glossary

symbol: something that stands, or figures for, something else

symbolic poem: a poem in which the use of symbols is so pervasive and internally consistent that the larger referential world is distanced, if not forgotten

traditional symbols: symbols that, through years of usage, have acquired an agreed-on significance, an accepted meaning

EMILY DICKINSON

[Go not too near a House of Rose—]

Go not too near a House of Rose—
The depredation of a Breeze
Or inundation of a Dew
Alarms its walls away—

Nor try to tie the Butterfly,
Nor climb the Bars of Ecstasy,
In insecurity to lie.
Is Joy's insuring quality.

ca. 1878

WILLIAM CARLOS WILLIAMS

Poem

The rose fades
and is renewed again
by its seed, naturally
but where

save in the poem
shall it go
to suffer no diminution
of its splendor

1962

DOROTHY PARKER

One Perfect Rose

A single flow'r he sent me, since we met.
All tenderly his messenger he chose;
Deep-hearted, pure, with scented dew still wet—
One perfect rose.

I knew the language of the floweret;
"My fragile leaves," it said, "his heart enclose."
Love long has taken for his amulet
One perfect rose.

Why is it no one ever sent me yet
One perfect limousine, do you suppose?
Ah no, it's always just my luck to get
One perfect rose.

1937

DANNIE ABSE

Pathology of Colours

I know the colour rose, and it is lovely,
but not when it ripens in a tumour;
and healing greens, leaves and grass, so springlike,
in limbs that fester are not springlike.

I have seen red-blue tinged with hirsute mauve
in the plum-skin face of a suicide.
I have seen white, china white almost, stare
from behind the smashed windscreen of a car

And the criminal, multi-coloured flash
of an H-bomb is no more beautiful
than an autopsy when the belly's opened—
to show cathedral windows never opened.

So in the simple blessing of a rainbow,
in the bevelled edge of a sunlit mirror,
I have seen, visible, Death's artifact
like a soldier's ribbon on a tunic tacked.

1968

KATHA POLLITT

Two Fish

Those speckled trout we glimpsed in a pool last year
you'd take for an image of love: it too should be
graceful, elusive, tacit, moving surely
among half-lights of mingled dim and clear,
forced to no course, of no fixed residence,
its only end its own swift elegance.
What would you say
if you saw what I saw the other day:
that pool heat-choked and fevered where sick blue
bubbled green scum and blistered water lily?
A white like a rolled-back eye or fish's belly
I thought I saw far out—but doubtless you
prefer to think our trout had left together
to seek a place with less inclement weather.

1981

GEORGE PEELE

A Farewell to Arms[4]

His golden locks time hath to silver turned;
Oh, time too swift, oh, swiftness never ceasing!
His youth 'gainst time and age hath ever spurned,[5]
But spurned in vain; youth waneth by increasing.
Beauty, strength, youth, are flowers but fading seen;
Duty, faith, love, are roots, and ever green.

His helmet now shall make a hive for bees,
And lover's sonnets turned to holy psalms,
A man-at-arms must now serve on his knees,
And feed on prayers, which are age his[6] alms;
But though from court to cottage he depart,
His saint is sure of his unspotted heart.

And when he saddest sits in homely cell,
He'll teach his swains this carol for a song:
Blest be the hearts that wish my sovereign well,
Cursed be the souls that think her any wrong!
Goddess, allow this aged man his right,
To be your beadsman[7] now, that was your knight.

1590

WILLIAM MATTHEWS

The Psychopathology of Everyday Life[8]

Just as we were amazed to learn
that the skin itself is an organ—
I'd thought it a flexible sack,
always exact—we're stunned
to think the skimpiest mental
event, even forgetting, has meaning.
If one thinks of the sky as scenery,
like photographs of food, one stills it
with that wish and appetite,
but the placid expanse that results
is an illusion. The air is restless
everywhere inside our atmosphere

4. From *Polyhymnia*, a verse description of a 1590 jousting tournament on Queen Elizabeth's birthday. Sir Henry Lee, who had for years been the queen's champion in such contests, retired that year (at age 60) in favor of a younger man. 5. Kicked. 6. Age's (a common Elizabethan possessive form). 7. One who prays for the soul of another (OED). 8. Title of a book (1904) on psychoanalysis by Sigmund Freud (1856–1939).

but the higher and thinner it gets
the less it has to push around
(how else do we see air?) but itself.
It seems that the mind, too,
is like that sky, not shiftless;
and come to think of it, the body
is no slouch at constant commerce,
bicker and haggle, provide and deny.
When we tire of work we should think
how the mind and body relentlessly
work for our living, though since
their labors end in death we greet
their ceaseless fealty with mixed emotions.
Of course the mind must pay attention
to itself, vast sky in the small skull.
In this we like to think we are alone:
evolutionary pride: it's lonely
at the top, self-consciousness. We forget
that the trout isn't beautiful and stupid
but a system of urges that works
even when the trout's small brain is somewhere
else, watching its shadow on the streambed,
maybe, daydreaming of food.
Even when we think we're not,
we're paying attention to everything;
this may be the origin of prayer
(and if we listen to ourselves,
how much in our prayers is well-dressed
complaint, how much we are loneliest Sundays
though whatever we do, say, or forget
is prayer and daily bread):
Doesn't everything mean something?
O God who composed this dense
text, our only beloved planet
—at this point the supplicants look upward—
why have You larded it against our hope
with allusions to itself, and how
can it bear the weight of such
self-reference and such self-ignorance?

1984

QUESTIONS

1. How many different applications of the term "erosion" can you find in the poem of the same name? Look carefully at the words "undermined" (line 2) and "slippage" (line 5) and explain how they work in the poem. Which other words in the poem take part of their meaning from their relationship to the central metaphor of erosion?

2. Characterize as fully as you can the speaker in "Batter My Heart." Explain how the metaphor of invasion and resistance works in the poem. What effect does this central metaphor have on our conception of the speaker? Explain the terms "imprison" (line 12) and "enthrall" (line 13). Explain "chaste" and "ravish" (line 14). How do these two sets of terms relate to the poem's central metaphor?

3. List every term in "The Twenty-Third Psalm" that relates to the central metaphor of sheepherding. Explain the metaphors of anointing and the overfull cup in line 5. (If you have trouble with this metaphor and do not understand the historical/cultural reference, ask a reference librarian to guide you to biblical commentaries that explain the practices referred to here.) What is the "house of the Lord" (line 6), and how does it relate to the basic metaphor of the psalm? (Again, if you are not sure of the historical/cultural reference, consult biblical commentaries or other historical sources on social and economic structures of the ancient Middle East.)

4. Consider carefully the following words in "It Was Fever that Made the World": pour (line 3), infusing (line 6) carnal (line 9), wreckage (line 13), swarmed (line 14), eddied, (line 19), thriving (line 23), shaken (line 24). Explain the major metaphors in the poem, and relate as many of these terms as you can to those metaphors, showing one by one what they imply. What past events seem to be referred to in the poem? What do these events mean?

5. Is the central metaphor of "September Afternoon at Four O'Clock" fruit? sweetness? eating? drinking? ripening? How can you tell which metaphor subordinates the others?

6. Besides "rose," how many other words can you find in "Pathology of Colours" in which the traditional symbolic meaning is reversed or changed radically?

7. List all of the material objects and human activities in "A Farewell to Arms" that symbolize the active world of the knight? List all the objects and activities that symbolize the contemplative life of the beadsman. What, according to the poem, are the relative values of the "golden" and "silver" (line 1) worlds?

8. Compare the symbolism of the trout in "The Psychopathology of Everyday Life" with that of the two trout in "Two Fish."

WRITING SUGGESTIONS

1. With the help of a reference librarian, find several pictures of B-17 bombers, and study carefully the design and appearance of the ball turret. Try to find a picture of the gunner at work in the turret, and note carefully his body position. Explain, in a paragraph, how the poem uses the visual details of the ball turret to create the fetal and birth metaphors in the poem.

2. Consider carefully the symbolism of the trout in "Two Fish." Exactly how do the fish become symbolic to the lovers? How do they become invested with meaning? What do this year's trout look like? Is the difference between last year's trout and this year's in the fish themselves or in their settings? What power does the weather have over the fish? What is the implied moral for the lovers? What does each lover believe about what the trout represent? What are the temperamental differences between the two lovers? What does the poem conclude about the "meaning" of the fish? Write an essay of about three pages in which you show how the poem opens and develops the question of what "symbols" mean?

3. With the help of a reference librarian, find at least half a dozen more poems that are about roses. Read them all carefully, and make a list of all the things that the rose seems to stand for in the poems. Write a paragraph about each poem showing how a specific symbolism for rose is established.

6 STRUCTURE

Proper words in proper places": that is the way one great writer of English prose (Jonathan Swift) described good writing. Finding appropriate words is not the easiest of tasks for a poet, and in the last two chapters we have looked at some of the implications for readers of the choices a poet makes. But a poet's decision about where to put those words is also difficult, for individual words, metaphors, and symbols not only exist as part of a phrase or sentence or rhythmic pattern but also as part of the larger whole of the poem itself. How are the words to be ordered and the poem organized? What will come first and what last? What will be its "plot"? How will it be conceived as a whole? How is some sort of structure to be created? What principle will structure the poem? How are words, sentences, images, ideas, feelings to be put together into something that holds together, seems complete, and will have a certain effect upon us as readers?

Looking at these questions from the point of view of the maker of the poem (What shall I plan? Where shall I begin?) can have the advantage of helping us as readers to notice the effect of structural decisions. Every poem is different from every other one, and independent, individual decisions must therefore be made about how to organize. But there are also patterns of organization that poems fall into, sometimes because of the subject matter, sometimes because of the effect intended, sometimes for other reasons. Often poets consciously decide on a particular organizational strategy; sometimes they may reach instinctively for one or happen into a structure that suits the needs of the moment, one onto which a creater can hang the words one by one.

When there is a story to be told, the organization of a poem may be fairly simple, as in this popular ballad:

ANONYMOUS

Frankie and Johnny

Frankie and Johnny were lovers,
  Lordy, how they could love,
Swore to be true to each other,
  True as the stars up above,
    He was her man, but he done her wrong.

Frankie went down to the corner,
To buy her a bucket of beer,
Frankie says "Mister Bartender,
Has my lovin' Johnny been here?
He is my man, but he's doing me wrong."

"I don't want to cause you no trouble
Don't want to tell you no lie,
I saw your Johnny half-an-hour ago
Making love to Nelly Bly.
He is your man, but he's doing you wrong."

Frankie went down to the hotel
Looked over the transom so high,
There she saw her lovin Johnny
Making love to Nelly Bly.
He was her man; he was doing her wrong.

Frankie threw back her kimono,
Pulled out her big forty-four;
Rooty-toot-toot: three times she shot
Right through that hotel door,
She shot her man, who was doing her wrong.

"Roll me over gently,
Roll me over slow,
Roll me over on my right side,
'Cause these bullets hurt me so,
I was your man, but I done you wrong."

Bring all your rubber-tired hearses
Bring all your rubber-tired hacks,
They're carrying poor Johnny to the burying ground
And they ain't gonna bring him back,
He was her man, but he done her wrong.

Frankie says to the sheriff,
"What are they going to do?"
The sheriff he said to Frankie,
"It's the 'lectric chair for you.
He was your man, and he done you wrong."

"Put me in that dungeon,
Put me in that cell,
Put me where the northeast wind
Blows from the southeast corner of hell,
I shot my man, 'cause he done me wrong."

19th cent.

Even in a poem with as straightforward a **narrative structure** as that of "Frankie and Johnny," pure chronology is not the only consideration in finding places for the words. The first stanza of the poem provides an overview, some background, and even a hint of the catastrophe ("he done her wrong"). Stanza 2 and 3 move the story along swiftly, but not by the most economical narrative means possible; instead, the poem adds some color and flavor by including the dialogue between Frankie and the bartender. Except for the repeated refrain (which keeps the whole story continuously in view), the next three stanzas are straightforward, and efficient, up through the shooting and Johnny's confession of infidelity. The final three stanzas also proceed chronologically—through the funeral, the conversation between Frankie and the sheriff, and Frankie's final reflections. The poem does not ever violate chronology, strictly speaking, but one can readily imagine quite a different emphasis from the very same facts told in much the same order. Chronology has guided the construction of the poem, but the final effects depend just as much upon the decision of which details to include, on the decision to include so much dialogue, on the decision to follow Frankie's progress through the events rather than Johnny's, and on the decision to include a summary refrain in each stanza. The structure here is basically chronological, but there are several substructures.

Purely narrative poems are often very long, much longer than can be included in a book like this, and often there are many features that are not, strictly speaking, closely connected to the narrative or linked to a strict chronology. Very often a poem moves on from a narrative of an event to some sort of commentary or reflection upon it, as in "Auto Wreck" (at the end of this chapter). Reflection can be included along the way or may be implicit in the way the story is narrated, as in "Woodchucks" where our major attention is more on the narrator and her responses than on the events in the story as such.

Just as they sometimes take on a structure rather like that of a story, poems sometimes borrow the structures of plays. The following poem has a **dramatic structure**; it consists of a series of scenes, each of which is presented vividly and in detail:

HOWARD NEMEROV

The Goose Fish

On the long shore, lit by the moon
To show them properly alone,
Two lovers suddenly embraced
So that their shadows were as one.

The ordinary night was graced
For them by the swift tide of blood
That silently they took at flood.
And for a little time they prized
  Themselves emparadised.

Then, as if shaken by stage-fright
Beneath the hard moon's bony light,
They stood together on the sand
Embarrassed in each other's sight
But still conspiring hand in hand,
Until they saw, there underfoot,
As though the world had found them out,
The goose fish turning up, though dead,
  His hugely grinning head.

There in the china light he lay,
Most ancient and corrupt and gray
They hesitated at his smile,
Wondering what it seemed to say
To lovers who a little while
Before had thought to understand,
By violence upon the sand,
The only way that could be known
  To make a world their own.

It was a wide and moony grin
Together peaceful and obscene;
They knew not what he would express,
So finished a comedian
He might mean failure or success,
But took it for an emblem of
Their sudden, new and guilty love
To be observed by, when they kissed,
  That rigid optimist.

So he became their patriarch,
Dreadfully mild in the half-dark.
His throat that the sand seemed to choke,
His picket teeth, these left their mark
But never did explain the joke
That so amused him, lying there
While the moon went down to disappear
Along the still and tilted track
  That bears the zodiac.

1955

The first stanza sets the scene—a sandy shore in moonlight—and presents, in fact, the major action of the poem. The rest of the poem dramatizes the lovers' reactions: their initial embarrassment and feelings of guilt (stanza 2), their attempt to interpret the goose fish's smile (stanza 3), their decision to make him, whatever his meaning, the "emblem" of their love (stanza 4), and their acceptance of the fish's ambiguity and of their own relationship (stanza 5). The five stanzas do not exactly present five different scenes, but they do present separate dramatic moments, even if only a few minutes apart. Almost like a play of five very short acts, the poem traces the drama of the lovers' discovery of themselves, of their coming to terms with the meaning of their action. As in many plays, the central event (their love-making) is not the central focus of the drama, although the drama is based upon that event and could not take place without it. Here, that event is depicted only briefly but very vividly through figurative language: "they took at flood" the "swift tide of blood," and the immediate effect is to make them briefly feel "emparadised." But the poem concentrates on their later reactions, not on the act of love itself.

Their sudden discovery of the fish is a rude shock and injects a grotesque, almost macabre note into the poem. From a vision of paradise, the poem seems for a moment to turn toward a gothic horror story when the lovers discover that they have, after all, been seen—and by such a ghoulish spectator. The last three stanzas gradually recreate the intruder in their minds, as they are forced to admit that their act of love does not exist in isolation as they had at first hoped, and they begin to see it as part of a continuum, as part of their relationship to the larger world, even (at the end) putting it into the context of the rotating world and its seasons as the moon disappears into its zodiac. In retrospect, we can see that even at the moment of passion they were in touch with larger processes controlled by the presiding mood (the "swift tide of blood"), but neither the lovers nor we had understood their act as such then, and the poem is about their gradual recognition.

Stages of feeling and knowing rather than specific visual scenes are responsible for the poem's progress, and its dramatic structure depends upon internal perceptions and internal states of mind rather than dialogue and events. Visualization and images help to organize the poem too. Notice in particular how the two most striking visual features of the poem—the fish and the moon—are presented stanza by stanza. In stanza 1, the fish is not yet noticed, and the moon exists plain; it is only mentioned, not described, and its light serves as a stage spotlight to assure not center-stage attention, but rather total privacy: it is a kind of lookout for the lovers. The stage imagery, barely suggested by the light in stanza 1, is articulated in stanza 2, and there the moon is said to be "hard" and its light "bony"'; its features have characteristics that seem more appropriate to the fish which has now become visible. In stanza 3, the moon's light has come to seem fragile ("china") as it is said to expose the fish directly; the role of the moon as lookout and protector seems abandoned, or at least endangered. No moon appears in stanza 4, but the fish's grin is described as "wide and moony," almost as if the two onlookers, one earthly and dead, the other heavenly and eternal, had become merged in the poem, as they nearly had been by the imagery in stanza 2. And by stanza 5, the fish has become a friend—by now he is a comedian, optimist, emblem, and a patriarch of their love—and his new position in collaboration with the lovers is presided over by the moon going about its eternal business. The moon has provided the stage light for the poem and the means by which not only the fish but the meaning of the lovers' act has been discovered. The moon has also helped to organize the poem, partly as a dramatic accessory, partly as imagery.

The following poem is also dramatic, but it seems to represent a composite of several similar experiences rather than a single event—a fairly common pattern in dramatic poems:

PHILIP LARKIN

Church Going

Once I am sure there's nothing going on
I step inside, letting the door thud shut.
Another church: matting, seats, and stone,
And little books; sprawlings of flowers, cut
For Sunday, brownish now; some brass and stuff
Up at the holy end; the small neat organ;
And a tense, musty, unignorable silence,
Brewed God knows how long. Hatless, I take off
My cycle-clips in awkward reverence,

Move forward, run my hand around the font.
From where I stand, the roof looks almost new—
Cleaned, or restored? Someone would know: I don't.
Mounting the lectern, I peruse a few
Hectoring large-scale verses, and pronounce
"Here endeth" much more loudly than I'd meant.
The echoes snigger briefly. Back at the door
I sign the book, donate an Irish sixpence,
Reflect the place was not worth stopping for.

Yet stop I did: in fact I often do,
And always end much at a loss like this,
Wondering what to look for; wondering, too,
When churches fall completely out of use
What we shall turn them into, if we shall keep

A few cathedrals chronically on show,
Their parchment, plate and pyx in locked cases,
And let the rest rent-free to rain and sheep.
Shall we avoid them as unlucky places?

Or, after dark, will dubious women come
To make their children touch a particular stone;
Pick simples[1] for a cancer; or on some
Advised night see walking a dead one?
Power of some sort or other will go on
In games, in riddles, seemingly at random;
But superstition, like belief, must die,
And what remains when disbelief has gone?
Grass, weedy pavement, brambles, buttress, sky,

A shape less recognizable each week,
A purpose more obscure. I wonder who
Will be the last, the very last, to seek
This place for what it was; one of the crew
That tap and jot and know what rood-lofts[2] were?
Some ruin-bibber,[3] randy for antique,
Or Christmas-addict, counting on a whiff
Of gown-and-bands and organ-pipes and myrrh?
Or will he be my representative,

Bored, uninformed, knowing the ghostly silt
Dispersed, yet tending to this cross of ground
Through suburb scrub because it held unspilt
So long and equably what since is found
Only in separation—marriage, and birth,
And death, and thoughts of these—for whom was built
This special shell? For, though I've no idea
What this accoutered frowsty barn is worth,
It pleases me to stand in silence here;

A serious house on serious earth it is,
In whose blent air all our compulsions meet,
Are recognized, and robed as destinies.
And that much never can be obsolete,
Since someone will forever be surprising
A hunger in himself to be more serious,
And gravitating with it to this ground,
Which, he once heard, was proper to grow wise in,
If only that so many dead lie round.

1955

1. Medicinal herbs. 2. Galleries atop the screens (on which crosses are mounted) that divide the naves or main bodies of churches from the choirs or chancels. 3. Literally, ruin-drinker: someone extremely attracted to antiquarian objects.

Ultimately, the poem's emphasis is upon what it means to visit churches, what sort of phenomenon church buildings represent, and what one is to make of the fact that "church going" (in the usual sense of the word) has declined so much. The poem uses a *different* sort of church-going (visitation by tourists) to consider larger philosophical questions about the relationship of religion to culture and history. The poem is, finally, a rather philosophical one about the directions of English culture, and through an enumeration of religious objects and rituals it reviews the history of how we got to our present historical circumstance. It tells a kind of story first, through one lengthy dramatized scene, in order to comment later on what the place and the experience may mean, and the larger conclusion derives from the particulars of what the speaker does and touches. The action is really over by the end of stanza 2, and that action, we are told, stands for many such visits to similar churches; after that, all is reflection and discussion, five stanzas' worth.

"Church Going" is a curious poem in many ways. It goes to a lot of trouble to characterize its speaker, who seems a rather odd choice as a commentator on the state of religion. His informal attire (he takes off his cycle-clips at the end of stanza 1) and his not exactly worshipful behavior do not at first make us expect him to be a serious philosopher about what all this means. He is not disrespectful or sacrilegious, and before the end of stanza 1 he has tried to describe the "awkward reverence" he feels, but his overly somber imitation of part of the service stamps him as playful and as a tourist here, not someone who regularly drops in for prayer or meditation in the usual sense. And yet those early details do give him credentials, in a way; he clearly knows the names of religious objects and has some of the history of churches in his grasp. Clearly he does this sort of church-going often ("Yet stop I did; in fact I often do," line 19) because he wonders seriously what it all means—now—in comparison to what it meant to religious worshipers in times past. Ultimately, he takes the church itself seriously and its cultural meaning and function just as seriously (lines 55ff.), understanding its important place in the history of his culture. In this poem, the drama is, relatively speaking, brief, but it gives a context for the more digressive and rambling free-floating reflections that grow out of the dramatic experience.

Sometimes poems are organized by contrasts, setting one thing up conveniently against another that is quite different. Look, for example, at the two worlds in the following poem, and notice how carefully the contrasts between the two worlds are developed.

PAT MORA

Sonrisas

I live in a doorway
between two rooms, I hear
quiet clicks, cups of black
coffee, *click*, *click* like facts
    budgets, tenure, curriculum,
from careful women in crisp beige
suits, quick beige smiles
that seldom sneak into their eyes.

I peek
in the other room señoras
in faded dresses stir sweet
milk coffee, laughter whirls
with steam from fresh *tamales*
    sh, sh, mucho ruido,[4]
they scold one another,
press their lips, trap smiles
in their dark, Mexican eyes.

1986

Here different words, habits, and values characterize the different worlds of the two sets of characters, and the poem is largely organized on the basis of the contrasts between them. The meaning of the poem (the difference between the two worlds) is very nearly the same as the structure itself.

Poems often have **discursive structures** too; that is, they are sometimes organized like a treatise, an argument, or an essay. "First," they say, "and second . . . and third. . . ." This sort of 1–2–3 structure takes a variety of forms depending on what one is enumerating or arguing. Here, for example, is a poem that is about three people who have died. The poem honors all three, but makes clear and sharp distinctions between them. As you read the poem, try to articulate just what sort of person each of the three is represented to be.

4. A lot of noise.

JAMES WRIGHT

Arrangements with Earth for Three Dead Friends

Sweet earth, he ran and changed his shoes to go
Outside with other children through the fields.
He panted up the hills and swung from trees
Wild as a beast but for the human laughter
That tumbled like a cider down his cheeks.
Sweet earth, the summer has been gone for weeks,
And weary fish already sleeping under water
Below the banks where early acorns freeze.
Receive his flesh and keep it cured of colds.
Button his coat and scarf his throat from snow.

And now, bright earth, this other is out of place
In what, awake, we speak about as tombs.
He sang in houses when the birds were still
And friends of his were huddled round till dawn
After the many nights to hear him sing.
Bright earth, his friends remember how he sang
Voices of night away when wind was one.
Lonely the neighborhood beneath your hill
Where he is waved away through silent rooms.
Listen for music, earth, and human ways.

Dark earth, there is another gone away,
But she was not inclined to beg of you
Relief from water falling or the storm.
She was aware of scavengers in holes
Of stone, she knew the loosened stones that fell
Indifferently as pebbles plunging down a well
And broke for the sake of nothing human souls.
Earth, hide your face from her where dark is warm.
She does not beg for anything, who knew
The change of tone, the human hope gone gray.

1957

Why, in stanza 1, is the earth represented as a parent? What does addressing the earth here as "sweet" seem to mean? How does the address to earth as "bright" fit the dead person described in stanza 2? In what different senses is the person described in stanza 3 "dark"? Why is the earth asked to give attention secretly to this person? Exactly what kind of person was she? How does the poem make you feel about her? Is there any cumulative point in describing three such different people in the same poem? What is accomplished by having the poem's three stanzas addressed to various aspects of earth? Similar discursive structures help to organize poems such as Shelley's "Ode to the West Wind," where the wind is shown driving a leaf in Part I, a cloud in Part II, a wave in Part III, and then, after a summary and statement of the speaker's ambitious hope in Part IV, is asked to make the speaker a lyre in Part V.

Poems may borrow their organizational strategies from many places, imitating chronological, visual, or discursive shapes in reality or in other works of art. Sometimes poems strive to be almost purely descriptive of someone or something (using **descriptive structures**), in which case organizational decisions have to be made much as a painter or photographer would make them, deciding first how the whole scene should look, then putting the parts into proper place for the whole. But there are differences demanded by the poetic medium: a poem has to present the details sequentially, not all at once as an actual picture more or less can, so the poet must decide where the description starts (at the left? center? top?) and what sort of movement to use (linear across the scene? clockwise?). But if having words instead of paint or film has some disadvantages, it also has particular assets: figurative language can be a part of description, or an adjunct to it. A poet can insert a comparison at any point without necessarily disturbing the unity of what he or she describes.

Some poems use **imitative structures,** mirroring as exactly as possible the structure of something that already exists as an object and can be seen—another poem perhaps, as in Koch's "Variations on a Theme by William Carlos Williams" (p. 959) or a standard visual or vocal format, by asking and answering questions, as Levertov's "What Were They Like?" (p. 789) does. Or a poem may use **reflective** (or **meditative**) **structures,** pondering a subject, theme, or event, and letting the mind play with it, skipping (sometimes illogically but still usefully) from one sound to another, or to related thoughts or objects as the mind receives them.

Here is a poem that involves several different organizational principles but ultimately takes its structure from an important emotional shift in the speaker's attitude.

SHARON OLDS

The Victims

When Mother divorced you, we were glad. She took it and
took it, in silence, all those years and then
kicked you out, suddenly, and her
kids loved it. Then you were fired, and we

grinned inside, the way people grinned when
Nixon's helicopter lifted off the South
Lawn for the last time.[5] We were tickled
to think of your office taken away,
your secretaries taken away,
your lunches with three double bourbons,
your pencils, your reams of paper. Would they take your
suits back, too, those dark
carcasses hung in your closet, and the black
noses of your shoes with their large pores?
She had taught us to take it, to hate you and take it
until we pricked with her for your
annihilation, Father. Now I
pass the bums in doorways, the white
slugs of their bodies gleaming through slits in their
suits of compressed silt, the stained
flippers of their hands, the underwater
fire of their eyes, ships gone down with the
lanterns lit, and I wonder who took it and
took it from them in silence until they had
given it all away and had nothing
left but this. 1984

"The Victims" divides basically into two parts. In the first two-thirds of the poem (from line 1 to the middle of line 17), the speaker attacks the "you" of the poem (the speaker's father), remembering all his terrible habits and behavior when the speaker was young. Awful things happened to him in those years (he was kicked out suddenly and divorced by the speaker's mother [lines 1–3], fired from his job [line 4], and lost his whole way of life [lines 8–12]), and the speaker (taught by the mother, lines 15–17) celebrated every defeat and every loss ("we pricked with her for your annihilation," lines 16–17). All the sympathies in this part of the poem are with the mother; she seems the victim ("she took it and took it, in silence, all those years" [lines 1–2]), and the speaker forms an indivisible unit with her and the other children ("her kids," lines 3–4). They are the "we" of the first part of the poem. They are "glad" (line 1) at the divorce; they "loved it" (line 4) when the mother kicked out the father, they "grinned" (line 5) when the father was fired; they were "tickled" (line 7) when he lost his job, his secretaries, and his daily life. Only at the end of the first section does the speaker (now older but remembering what it was like to be a

5. When Richard Nixon resigned the U.S. presidency on August 8, 1974, his exit from the White House (by helicopter from the lawn) was televised live.

child) recognize that the mother was responsible for the easy childish vision of responsibility ("she had taught us to take it, to hate you and take it" [line 15]).

The imagery in this part of the poem is entirely unfavorable to the father. People react to him the way observers responded to the retreat in disgrace of Richard Nixon from the U.S. presidency. The father seems to lead a luxurious and insensitive life, with lots of support in his office (lines 8–11), fancy clothes (lines 12–14), and decadent lunches (line 10); his artificial identity seems haunting and daunting (lines 11–14) to the speaker as child. All the facts seem against the father, and the sympathies are entirely with the mother and children who seem bunched against him.

But in line 17, the poem shifts focus and shifts gears. The "you" in the poem is now, suddenly, "Father." A bit of sympathy begins to surface for "bums in doorways" (line 18) who suddenly begin to seem victims too; their bodies are "slugs" (line 19), their suits seem made of residual waste pressed into regimented usefulness (lines 19–20), and their hands are constricted into mechanical "flippers" (line 21). Their eyes contain fire (line 22), but it is as if they retain only a spark of life in their submerged and dying state. The speaker has not forgotten the cruelty and insensitivity remembered in the first part of the poem, but the blame seems to have shifted somewhat and the father is not the only villain, nor are the mother and children the only victims.

Imagery, words, attitudes, and narrative are different in the two parts of the poem, and the second half carefully qualifies the first, as if to illustrate the more mature and considered attitudes of the speaker in her older years—a qualification of the easy imitation of the earlier years when the mother's views were thoroughly dominant and seemed sensible and adequate. Change has governed the poem's structure here; differences in age, attitude, and tone are supported by entirely different sets of terms, attitudes, and versions of causality.

The paradigms (or models) for organizing poems are, finally, not all that different from those of prose. It may be easier to organize something short rather than something long, but the question of intensity becomes comparatively more important in shorter works. Basically, the problem of how to organize one's material is, for the writer, first of all a matter of deciding what kind of thing one wants to create, of having its purposes and effects clearly in mind. That means that every poem will differ somewhat from every other, but it also means that patterns of purpose—narrative, dramatic, discursive, descriptive, imitative, or reflective—may help writers organize and formulate their ideas. A consciousness of purpose and effect can help the reader see *how* a poem proceeds toward its goal. Seeing how a poem is organized is, in turn, often a good way of seeing where it is going and what its real concerns and purposes may be.

Often a poem's organization helps to make clear the particular effects that the poet wishes to generate. In a good poem, means and end are closely related, and a reader who is a good observer of one will be able to discover the other.

▽ ▽ ▽

STRUCTURE A Glossary

descriptive structure: determined by the requirements of describing someone or something

discursive structure: organized in the form of a treatise, argument, or essay

dramatic structure: consisting of a series of scenes, each of which is presented vividly and in detail

imitative structure: mirroring exactly, if possible, the structure of something that already exists as an object and can be seen

narrative structure: based on a straightforward chronological framework

reflective/meditative structure: pondering a subject, theme, or event, and letting the mind play with it, skipping from one sound to another, or to related thoughts or objects as the mind receives them

ANONYMOUS

Sir Patrick Spens

The king sits in Dumferling toune,[6]
Drinking the blude-reid[7] wine:
"O whar will I get guid sailor,
To sail this ship of mine?"

Up and spake an eldern knicht,
Sat at the king's richt knee:
"Sir Patrick Spens is the best sailor
That sails upon the sea."

The king has written a braid[8] letter
And signed it wi' his hand,
And sent it to Sir Patrick Spens,
Was walking on the sand.

The first line that Sir Patrick read,
A loud lauch[9] lauched he;
The next line that Sir Patrick read,
The tear blinded his ee.[1]

"O wha is this has done this deed,
This il deed done to me,
To send me out this time o' the year,
To sail upon the sea?

"Make haste, make haste, my merry men all,
Our guid ship sails the morn."
"O say na sae,[2] my master dear,
For I fear a deadly storm.

"Late, late yestre'en I saw the new moon
Wi' the auld moon in her arm,
And I fear, I fear, my dear mastér,
That we will come to harm."

O our Scots nobles were richt laith[3]
To weet their cork-heeled shoon,[4]
But lang owre a'[5] the play were played
Their hats they swam aboon.[6]

6. Town. 7. Blood-red. 8. Broad: explicit. 9. Laugh. 1. Eye. 2. Not so. 3. Right loath: very reluctant. 4. To wet their cork-heeled shoes. Cork was expensive, and therefore such shoes were a mark of wealth and status. 5. Before all. 6. They swam above their hats.

O lang, lang, may their ladies sit,
Wi' their fans into their hand,
Or ere they see Sir Patrick Spens
Come sailing to the land.

O lang, lang, may the ladies stand
Wi' their gold kems[7] in their hair,
Waiting for their ain[8] dear lords,
For they'll see them na mair.

Half o'er, half o'er to Aberdour
It's fifty fadom deep,
And there lies guid Sir Patrick Spens
Wi' the Scots lords at his feet.

Probably 13th cent.

T. S. ELIOT

Journey of the Magi[9]

"A cold coming we had of it,
Just the worst time of the year
For a journey, and such a long journey:
The ways deep and the weather sharp,
The very dead of winter."[1]
And the camels galled, sore-footed, refractory,
Lying down in the melting snow.
There were times we regretted
The summer palaces on slopes, the terraces,
And the silken girls bringing sherbet.
Then the camel men cursing and grumbling
And running away, and wanting their liquor and women,
And the night-fires going out, and the lack of shelters,
And the cities hostile and the towns unfriendly
And the villages dirty and charging high prices:
A hard time we had of it.
At the end we preferred to travel all night,
Sleeping in snatches,
With the voices singing in our ears, saying
That this was all folly.

Then at dawn we came down to a temperate valley,
Wet, below the snow line, smelling of vegetation;

7. Combs. 8. Own. 9. The wise men who followed the star of Bethlehem. See Matthew 2:1–12. 1. An adaptation of a passage from a 1622 sermon by Lancelot Andrewes.

With a running stream and a water-mill beating the darkness,
And three trees on the low sky,[2]
And an old white horse galloped away in the meadow.
Then we came to a tavern with vine-leaves over the lintel,
Six hands at an open door dicing for pieces of silver,
And feet kicking the empty wine-skins.
But there was no information, and so we continued
And arrived at evening, not a moment too soon
Finding the place; it was (you may say) satisfactory.

All this was a long time ago, I remember,
And I would do it again, but set down
This set down
This: were we led all that way for
Birth or Death? There was a Birth, certainly,
We had evidence and no doubt. I had seen birth and death,
But had thought they were different; this Birth was
Hard and bitter agony for us, like Death, our death.
We returned to our places, these Kingdoms,[3]
But no longer at ease here, in the old dispensation,
With an alien people clutching their gods.
I should be glad of another death.

1927

MARGARET ATWOOD

Landcrab I

A lie, that we come from water.
The truth is we were born
from stones, dragons, the sea's
teeth, as you testify,
with your crust and jagged scissors.

Hermit, hard socket
for a timid eye,
you're a soft gut scuttling
sideways, a blue skull,
round bone on the prowl.
Wolf of treeroots and gravelly holes,
a mouth on stilts,
the husk of a small demon.

2. Suggestive of the three crosses of the Crucifixion (Luke 23:32–33). The Magi see several objects that suggest later events in Christ's life: pieces of silver (see Matthew 26:14–16), the dicing (see Matthew 27:35), the white horse (see Revelation 6:2 and 19:11–16), and the empty wine-skins (see Matthew 9:14–17, possibly relevant also to lines 41–42). 3. The Bible only identifies the wise men as "from the East," and subsequent tradition has made them kings. In Persia, Magi were members of an ancient priestly caste.

Attack, voracious
eating, and flight:
it's a sound routine
for staying alive on edges.

Then there's the tide, and that dance
you do for the moon
on wet sand, claws raised
to fend off your mate,
your coupling a quick
dry clatter of rocks.
For mammals
with their lobes and tubers,
scruples and warm milk,
you've nothing but contempt.

Here you are, a frozen scowl
targeted in flashlight,
then gone: a piece of what
we are, not all,
my stunted child, my momentary
face in the mirror,
my tiny nightmare.

Landcrab II

The sea sucks at its own
edges, in and out with the moon.
Tattered brown fronds
(shredded nylon stockings,
feathers, the remnants of hands)
wash against my skin.

As for the crab, she's climbed
a tree and sticks herself
to the bark with her adroit
spikes; she jerks
her stalked eyes at me, seeing

a meat shadow,
food or a predator.
I smell the pulp
of her body, faint odour
of rotting salt,
as she smells mine,
working those martian palps:

seawater in leather.
I'm a category, a noun
in a language not human,
infra-red in moonlight,
a tidal wave in the air.

Old fingernail, old mother,
I'm up to scant harm
tonight; though you don't care,

you're no-one's metaphor,
you have your own paths
and rituals, frayed snails
and soaked nuts, waterlogged sacks
to pick over, soggy chips and crusts.

The beach is all yours, wordless
and ripe once I'm off it,
wading towards the moored boats
and blue lights of the dock. 1981

KARL SHAPIRO

Auto Wreck

Its quick soft silver bell beating, beating,
And down the dark one ruby flare
Pulsing out red light like an artery,
The ambulance at top speed floating down
Past beacons and illuminated clocks
Wings in a heavy curve, dips down,
And brakes speed, entering the crowd.
The doors leap open, emptying light;
Stretchers are laid out, the mangled lifted
And stowed into the little hospital.
Then the bell, breaking the hush, tolls once,
And the ambulance with its terrible cargo
Rocking, slightly rocking, moves away,
As the doors, an afterthought, are closed.

We are deranged, walking among the cops
Who sweep glass and are large and composed.
One is still making notes under the light.
One with a bucket douches ponds of blood
Into the street and gutter.
One hangs lanterns on the wrecks that cling,
Empty husks of locusts, to iron poles.

Our throats were tight as tourniquets,
Our feet were bound with splints, but now,
Like convalescents intimate and gauche,
We speak through sickly smiles and warn
With the stubborn saw of common sense,
The grim joke and the banal resolution.
The traffic moves around with care,
But we remain, touching a wound
That opens to our richest horror.
Already old, the question Who shall die?
Becomes unspoken Who is innocent?

For death in war is done by hands;
Suicide has cause and stillbirth, logic;
And cancer, simple as a flower, blooms.
But this invites the occult mind,
Cancels our physics with a sneer,
And spatters all we knew of denouement
Across the expedient and wicked stones. 1942

MIRIAM WADDINGTON

Advice to the Young

1

Keep bees and
grow asparagus,
watch the tides
and listen to the
wind instead of
the politicians
make up your own
stories and believe
them if you want to
live the good life.

2

All rituals
are instincts
never fully
trust them
study to im-
prove biology
with reason.

3

Digging trenches
for asparagus
is good for the
muscles and
waiting for the
plants to settle
teaches patience
to those who are
usually in too
much of a hurry.

4

There is mortality
in bee-keeping
it teaches how
not to be afraid
of the bee swarm
it teaches how
not to be afraid of
finding new places
and building them
all over again.

DENISE LEVERTOV

What Were They Like?

1) Did the people of Viet Nam
use lanterns of stone?
2) Did they hold ceremonies
to reverence the opening of buds?
3) Were they inclined to rippling laughter?
4) Did they use bone and ivory,
jade and silver, for ornament?
5) Had they an epic poem?
6) Did they distinguish between speech and singing?

1) Sir, their light hearts turned to stone.
It is not remembered whether in gardens
stone lanterns illumined pleasant ways.

2) Perhaps they gathered once to delight in blossom,
but after the children were killed
there were no more buds.
3) Sir, laughter is bitter to the burned mouth.
4) A dream ago, perhaps. Ornament is for joy.
All the bones were charred.
5) It is not remembered. Remember,
most were peasants; their life
was in rice and bamboo.
When peaceful clouds were reflected in the paddies
and the water buffalo stepped surely along terraces,
maybe fathers told their sons old tales.
When bombs smashed the mirrors
there was time only to scream.
6) There is an echo yet, it is said,
of their speech which was like a song.
It is reported their singing resembled
the flight of moths in moonlight.
Who can say? It is silent now. 1966

MARGARET ATWOOD

Siren Song

This is the one song everyone
would like to learn: the song
that is irresistible:

the song that forces men
to leap overboard in squadrons
even though they see the beached skulls

the song nobody knows
because anyone who has heard it
is dead, and the others can't remember.

Shall I tell you the secret
and if I do, will you get me
out of this bird suit?

I don't enjoy it here
squatting on this island
looking picturesque and mythical

with these two feathery maniacs,
I don't enjoy singing
this trio, fatal and valuable.

I will tell the secret to you,
to you, only to you.
Come closer. This song

is a cry for help: Help me!
Only you, only you can,
you are unique

at last. Alas
it is a boring song
but it works every time.

1974

WILLIAM CARLOS WILLIAMS

The Dance

In Brueghel's great picture, The Kermess,[4]
the dancers go round, they go round and
around, the squeal and the blare and the
tweedle of bagpipes, a bugle and fiddles
tipping their bellies (round as the thick-
sided glasses whose wash they impound)
their hips and their bellies off balance
to turn them. Kicking and rolling about
the Fair Grounds, swinging their butts, those
shanks must be sound to bear up under such
rollicking measures, prance as they dance
in Brueghel's great picture, The Kermess.

1944

LI-YOUNG LEE

Visions and Interpretations

Because this graveyard is a hill,
I must climb up to see my dead,
stopping once midway to rest
beside this tree.

It was here, between the anticipation
of exhaustion, and exhaustion,
between vale and peak,
my father came down to me

4. A drawing by Pieter Brueghel the elder (ca. 1525–1569).

and we climbed arm in arm to the top.
He cradled the bouquet I'd brought,
and I, a good son, never mentioned his grave,
erect like a door behind him.

And it was here, one summer day, I sat down
to read an old book. When I looked up
from the noon-lit page, I saw a vision
of a world about to come, and a world about to go.

Truth is, I've not seen my father
since he died, and, no, the dead
do not walk arm in arm with me.

If I carry flowers to them, I do so without their help,
the blossoms not always bright, torch-like,
but often heavy as sodden newspaper.

Truth is, I came here with my son one day,
and we rested against this tree,
and I fell asleep, and dreamed

a dream which, upon my boy waking me, I told.
Neither of us understood.
Then we went up.

Even this is not accurate.
Let me begin again:

Between two griefs, a tree.
Between my hands, white chrysanthemums, yellow chrysanthemums.

The old book I finished reading
I've since read again and again.

And what was far grows near,
and what is near grows more dear,

and all of my visions and interpretations
depend on what I see,

and between my eyes is always
the rain, the migrant rain. 1986

ALAN SHAPIRO

Familiar Story

Tonight they need to be both host and stranger,
talking together all evening after dinner;
the candle wavering down till they are half

in darkness as they lead each other back
through their accumulated separate lore,
telling the stories they have told before
to other lovers, who are stories now.
They give no truth here, but the practised glow
of truthfulness: even as they confess
wholeheartedly to niggling attentiveness
disguised as love, to no or too much care,
affection parceled out till it's not there—
the more one tells, the more the other sees
just how appealing is this honesty,
how generous they are to those who hurt them.
They think this kind shrewd vision won't desert them.
And tonight, at least, it won't as they forget
what all their lore will lead them to expect
of one another, what they'll later owe
day after each slow day when all they know
is the familiar story they are living,
restless, and remote, and unforgiving.
It's then, when they don't feel it, they will need
the love bad days require and impede.
But not tonight, the candle going, gone,
their eyes shut briefly as the light goes on.
Tonight desire is generosity,
desire in each other's all they see,
and all else now is no more than the light
hurting their eyes, too sudden and too bright.

1987

PERCY BYSSHE SHELLEY

Ode to the West Wind

I

O wild West Wind, thou breath of Autumn's being,
Thou, from whose unseen presence the leaves dead
Are driven, like ghosts from an enchanter fleeing,

Yellow, and black, and pale, and hectic red,
Pestilence-stricken multitudes: O thou,
Who chariotest to their dark wintry bed

The wingéd seeds, where they lie cold and low,
Each like a corpse within its grave, until
Thine azure sister of the Spring shall blow

Her clarion[5] o'er the dreaming earth, and fill
(Driving sweet buds like flocks to feed in air)
With living hues and odors plain and hill:

Wild Spirit, which art moving everywhere;
Destroyer and preserver; hear, oh, hear!

II

Thou on whose stream, mid the steep sky's commotion,
Loose clouds like earth's decaying leaves are shed,
Shook from the tangled boughs of Heaven and Ocean,

Angels[6] of rain and lightning: there are spread
On the blue surface of thine aëry surge,
Like the bright hair uplifted from the head

Of some fierce Maenad,[7] even from the dim verge
Of the horizon to the zenith's height,
The locks of the approaching storm. Thou dirge

Of the dying year, to which this closing night
Will be the dome of a vast sepulcher,
Vaulted with all thy congregated might

Of vapors, from whose solid atmosphere
Black rain, and fire, and hail will burst: oh, hear!

III

Thou who didst waken from his summer dreams
The blue Mediterranean, where he lay,
Lulled by the coil of his crystálline streams,

Beside a pumice isle in Baiae's bay,[8]
And saw in sleep old palaces and towers
Quivering within the wave's intenser day,

All overgrown with azure moss and flowers
So sweet, the sense faints picturing them! Thou
For whose path the Atlantic's level powers

Cleave themselves into chasms, while far below
The sea-blooms and the oozy woods which wear
The sapless foliage of the ocean, know

Thy voice, and suddenly grow gray with fear,
And tremble and despoil themselves:[9] oh, hear!

5. Trumpet-call. 6. Messengers. 7. A frenzied female votary of Dionysus, the Greek god of vegetation and fertility who was supposed to die in the Fall and rise again each Spring. 8. Where Roman emperors had erected villas, west of Naples. 9. "The vegetation at the bottom of the sea . . . sympathizes with that of the land in the change of seasons." [Author's note]

IV

If I were a dead leaf thou mightest bear;
If I were a swift cloud to fly with thee;
A wave to pant beneath thy power, and share

The impulse of thy strength, only less free
Than thou, O uncontrollable! If even
I were as in my boyhood, and could be

The comrade by thy wanderings over Heaven,
As then, when to outstrip thy skyey speed
Scarce seemed a vision; I would ne'er have striven

As thus with thee in prayer in my sore need.
Oh, lift me as a wave, a leaf, a cloud!
I fall upon the thorns of life! I bleed!

A heavy weight of hours has chained and bowed
One too like thee: tameless, and swift, and proud.

V

Make me thy lyre, even as the forest is:
What if my leaves are falling like its own!
The tumult of thy mighty harmonies

Will take from both a deep, autumnal tone,
Sweet though in sadness. Be thou, Spirit fierce,
My spirit! Be thou me, impetuous one!

Drive my dead thoughts over the universe
Like withered leaves to quicken a new birth!
And, by the incantation of this verse,

Scatter, as from an unextinguished hearth
Ashes and sparks, my words among mankind!
Be through my lips to unawakened earth

The trumpet of a prophecy! O Wind,
If Winter comes, can Spring be far behind? 1820

QUESTIONS

1. How many different "scenes" can you identify in "Sir Patrick Spens"? Where does each scene begin and end? How are the transitions made from scene to scene?

2. Compare the two Atwood poems entitled "Landcrab." How is each poem organized? Describe the structural differences between the two.

3. Look back over the poems you have read earlier in the course, and pick out one of them that seems to you particularly effective in the way it is put together. Read it over several times and consider carefully how it is organized. What does the choice of speaker, situation, and setting have to do with its structure? What other artistic decisions seem to you crucial in creating the poem's structure?

4. Read "Familiar Story" through quickly and notice the organizing role that time plays in the poem. What other structural principles are at work here? Within the temporal framework, which lines have nothing to do with the narrative sequence? What role does setting play in the transitions?

WRITING SUGGESTIONS

1. After doing the reading and analysis suggested in question 3 above, write a detailed essay in which you consider fully the structural principles at work in the poem. The length of your essay will depend on the length of the poem you choose—but also on the complexity of its structure.

2. Look back at "Cherrylog Road" (chapter 3) and re-read it carefully. Then look for another poem in which memory of a much earlier event plays an important structural function. Compare the poems in detail, noting how (in each case) memory influences the way the event is reconstructed. What details of the event are in each case omitted in the retelling? What parts are lengthened or dwelt upon? What, in each case, is the point of having the event recalled later rather than from an immediate recollection?

Write a 3- or 4-page essay comparing the structuring function of memory in the two poems, noting in each case exactly how the structural principles at work in the poem help to create the poem's final tone.

7 SOUND AND SIGHT

The Sounds of Poetry

A lot of what happens in a poem happens in your mind's eye, but some of it happens in your voice. Poems are full of sounds and silences as well as words and sentences that are meaningful. Besides choosing words for their meanings, poets sometimes choose words because they involve certain sounds, and poems use sound effects to create a mood or establish a tone, just as films do. Sometimes the sounds of words are crucial to what is happening in the text of the poem.

The following poem explores the sounds of a particular word, tries them on, and analyzes them in relation to the word itself.

HELEN CHASIN

The Word *Plum*

The word *plum* is delicious

pout and push, luxury of
self-love, and savoring murmur

full in the mouth and falling
like fruit

taut skin
pierced, bitten, provoked into
juice, and tart flesh

question
and reply, lip and tongue
of pleasure.

1968

The poem savors the sounds of the word as well as the taste and feel of the fruit itself. It is almost as if the poem is tasting the sounds and rolling them carefully on the tongue. The second and third lines even replicate the "p," "l," "uh," and "m" sounds of the word while at the same time imitating the squishy sounds of eating the fruit. Words like "delicious" and "luxury" sound juicy, and other words imitate sounds of satisfaction and pleasure—"murmur," for example. Even the process of eating is in part recreated aurally. The tight, clipped sounds of "taut skin / pierced" suggest the sharp breaking of the skin and solid flesh, and as the tartness is described, the words ("provoked," "question") force the lips to pucker and the tongue and palate to meet and hold, as if the mouth were savoring a tart fruit. The poet is having fun here recreating the various sense appeals of a plum, teasing the sounds and meanings out of available words. The words must mean something appropriate and describe something accurately first of all, of course, but when they can also imitate the sounds and feel of the process, they can do double duty. Not all poems manipulate sound as consciously or as fully as "The Word *Plum*," but many poems at least contain passages in which the sounds of life are reproduced by the human voice reading the poem. To get the full effect of this poem—and of many others—reading aloud is essential; that way, you can pay attention to the vocal rhythms and articulate the sounds as the poem calls for them to be reproduced by the human voice.

Almost always a poem's effect will be helped by reading it aloud, using your voice to pronounce the words so that the poem becomes a spoken communication. Historically, poetry began as an oral phenomenon, and often poems that seem very difficult when looked at silently come alive when they are turned into sound. Early bards chanted their verses, and the music of poetry—its cadences and rhythms—developed from this kind of performance. Often in primitive poetry (and sometimes in later ages) poetry performances have been accompanied by some kind of musical instrument. The rhythms of any poem become clearer when you say or hear them.

Poetry is, almost always, a vocal art, dependent on the human voice to become its full self (for some exceptions look at the shaped verse at the end of this chapter). In a sense, it begins to exist as a real phenomenon when a reader reads and actualizes it. Poems don't really achieve their full meaning when they merely exist on a page; a poem on a page is more a score or set of stage directions for a poem than a poem itself. Sometimes, in fact, it is hard to experience the poem at all unless you hear it. A good poetry reading might easily convince you of the importance of a good voice sensitive to the poem's requirements, but you can also persuade yourself by reading poems aloud in the privacy of your own room. An audience is even better, however, because then there is someone to share the pleasure in the sounds themselves and consider what they imply.

MONA VAN DUYN

What the Motorcycle Said

Br-r-r-am-m-m, rackety-am-m, OM, *Am:*
All—r-r-room, r-r-ram, ala-bas-ter—
Am, the world's my oyster.

I hate plastic, wear it black and slick,
hate hardhats, wear one on my head,
that's what the motorcycle said.

Passed phonies in Fords, knocked down billboards, landed
on the other side of The Gap, and Whee,
bypassed history.

When I was born (The Past), baby knew best.
They shook when I bawled, took Freud's path,
threw away their wrath.

R-r-rackety-am-m. *Am*. War, rhyme,
soap, meat, marriage, the Phantom Jet
are shit, and like that.

Hate pompousness, punishment, patience, am into Love,
hate middle-class moneymakers, live on Dad,
that's what the motorcycle said.

Br-r-r-am-m-m. It's Nowsville, man. Passed Oldies, Uglies,
Straighties, Honkies. I'll never be
mean, tired or unsexy.

Passed cigarette suckers, souses, mother-fuckers,
losers, went back to Nature and found
how to get VD, stoned.

Passed a cow, too fast to hear her moo, "*I* rolled
our leaves of grass into one ball.
I am the grassy All."

Br-r-r-am-m-m, rackety-am-m, OM, *Am:*
All—gr-r-rin, oooohgah, gl-l-utton—
Am, the world's my smilebutton.

1973

Saying this poem as if you were a motorcycle with the power of speech (sort of) is part of the poem's fun, and the rich, loud sounds of a motorcycle revving up concentrate and intensify the effect and enrich the pleasure. It's a shame not to hear a poem like this aloud; a lot of it is missed if you don't try to imitate the sounds or if you don't try to pick up the motor's rhythms in the poem. A performance here is clearly worth it: a human being as motorcycle, motorcycle as human being.

And it's a good poem, too. It does something interesting, important, and maybe a bit subversive. The speaking motorcycle seems to take on the values of some of its riders, the noisy and obtrusive ones that readers are most likely to associate with motorcycles. The riders made fun of here are themselves sort of mindless and mechanical; they are the sort who have cult feelings about their group, who travel in packs, and who live no life beyond their machines. The speaking motorcycle, like such riders, grooves on power and speed, lives for the moment, and has little respect for people, the past, for institutions, or for anything beyond its own small world. It is self-centered, modish, ignorant, and inarticulate; but proud, mighty proud, and feels important in its own sounds. That's what the motorcycle says.

The following poem uses sound effects efficiently, too.

KENNETH FEARING

Dirge

1-2-3 was the number he played but today the number came 3-2-1;
Bought his Carbide at 30, and it went to 29; had the favorite at Bowie[1] but the track was slow—

O executive type, would you like to drive a floating-power, knee-action, silk-upholstered six? Wed a Hollywood star? Shoot the course in 58? Draw to the ace, king, jack?
O fellow with a will who won't take no, watch out for three cigarettes on the same, single match; O democratic voter born in August under Mars, beware of liquidated rails—

Denouement to denouement, he took a personal pride in the certain, certain way he lived his own, private life,
But nevertheless, they shut off his gas; nevertheless, the bank foreclosed; nevertheless, the landlord called; nevertheless, the radio broke,

And twelve o'clock arrived just once too often,
Just the same he wore one gray tweed suit, bought one straw hat, drank one straight Scotch, walked one short step, took one long look, drew one deep breath,
Just one too many,

1. A racetrack in Maryland. *Carbide*: the Union Carbide Corporation.

And wow he died as wow he lived,
Going whop to the office and blooie home to sleep and biff got married and bam
had children and oof got fired,
Zowie did he live and zowie did he die,

With who the hell are you at the corner of his casket, and where the hell're we
going on the right-hand silver knob, and who the hell cares walking second
from the end with an American Beauty[2] wreath from why the hell not,

Very much missed by the circulation staff of the New York Evening Post; deeply,
deeply mourned by the B.M.T.[3]
Wham, Mr. Roosevelt; pow, Sears Roebuck; awk, big dipper; bop, summer rain;
Bong, Mr., bong, Mr., bong, Mr., bong.

1935

As the title implies, "Dirge" is a kind of musical lament, in this case for a certain sort of businessman who took a lot of chances and saw his investments and life go down the drain in the depression of the early thirties. Reading this poem aloud is a big help partly because it contains expressive words that echo the action, words like "oof" and "blooie" (which primarily carry their meaning in their sounds, for they have practically no literal or referential meaning). Reading aloud also helps us notice that the poem employs rhythms much as a song would and that it frequently shifts its pace and mood. Notice how carefully the first two lines are balanced, and then how quickly the rhythm shifts as the "executive type" begins to be addressed directly in line 3. (Line 2 is long and dribbles over in the narrow pages of a book like this; a lot of the lines here are especially long, and the irregularity of the line lengths is one aspect of the special sound effects the poem creates.) In the direct address, the poem first picks up a series of advertising features which it recites in rapid-fire order rather like the advertising phrases in "Needs" in Chapter 2. In stanza 3 here, the rhythm shifts again, but the poem gives us helpful clues about how to read. Line 5 sounds like prose and is long, drawn out, and rather dull (rather like its subject), but line 6 sets up a regular (and monotonous) rhythm with its repeated "nevertheless" which punctuates the rhythm like a drumbeat: "But nevertheless *tuh-tuh-tuh-tuh-tuh;* nevertheless *tuh-tuh-tuh-tuh;* nevertheless *tuh-tuh-tuh-tuh;* nevertheless *tuh-tuh-tuh-tuh-tuh.*" In the next stanza, the repetitive phrasing comes again, this time guided by the word "one" in cooperation with other words of one syllable: "wore *one* gray tweed suit, bought *one* straw hat, *tuh* one *tuh-tuh; tuh* one *tuh-tuh; tuh* one *tuh-tuh; tuh* one *tuh-tuh.*" And then a new rhythm and a new technique in stanza 5 as the language of comic books is

2. A variety of rose. 3. A New York subway line.

imitated to describe in violent, exaggerated terms the routine of his life. You have to say words like "whop" and "zowie" aloud and in the rhythm of the whole sentence to get the full effect of how boring his life is, no matter how he tries to jazz it up with exciting words. And so it goes—repeated words, shifting rhythms, emphasis on routine and averageness—until the final bell ("Bong . . . bong . . . bong . . . bong") tolls rhythmically for the dead man in the final clanging line.

Sometimes sounds in poems just provide special effects, rather like a musical score behind a film, setting mood and getting us into an appropriate frame of mind. But often sound and meaning go hand in hand, and the poet finds words that in their sounds echo the action. A word that captures or approximates the sound of what it describes, such as "splash" or "squish" or "murmur" is called an **onomatopoeic** word, and the device itself is called **onomatopoeia.** And similar things can be done poetically with pacing and rhythm, sounds and pauses. The punctuation, the length of vowels, and the combination of consonant sounds help to control the way we read so that we imitate what is being described. The poems at the end of this discussion (pp. 816–819) suggest several ways that such imitations of pace and pause may occur: by echoing the lapping of waves on a shore, for example ("Like as the Waves"), or mimicking the sounds of a train on a variable terrain ("The Express"), or reproducing the rhythms of a musical style ("Dear John, Dear Coltrane").

Here is a classic passage in which a skillful poet talks about the virtues of making the sound echo the sense—and shows at the same time how to do it:

ALEXANDER POPE

[Sound and Sense][4]

But most by numbers[5] judge a poet's song,
And smooth or rough, with them, is right or wrong;
In the bright muse though thousand charms conspire,[6]
Her voice is all these tuneful fools admire,
Who haunt Parnassus[7] but to please their ear,
Not mend their minds; as some to church repair,
Not for the doctrine, but the music there.

4. From *An Essay on Criticism,* Pope's poem on the art of poetry and the problems of literary criticism. The passage excerpted here follows a discussion of several common weaknesses of critics; failure to regard an author's intention, for example, or over-emphasis on clever metaphors and ornate style. 5. Meter, rhythm, sound. 6. Unite. 7. A mountain in Greece, traditionally associated with the muses and considered the seat of poetry and music.

These, equal syllables[8] alone require,
Though oft the ear the open vowels tire,
While expletives[9] their feeble aid do join,
And ten low words oft creep in one dull line,
While they ring round the same unvaried chimes,
With sure returns of still expected rhymes.
Where'er you find "the cooling western breeze,"
In the next line, it "whispers through the trees";
If crystal streams "with pleasing murmurs creep,"
The reader's threatened (not in vain) with "sleep."
Then, at the last and only couplet fraught
With some unmeaning thing they call a thought,
A needless Alexandrine[1] ends the song,
That, like a wounded snake, drags its slow length along.
Leave such to tune their own dull rhymes, and know
What's roundly smooth, or languishingly slow;
And praise the easy vigor of a line,
Where Denham's strength and Waller's[2] sweetness join.
True ease in writing comes from art, not chance,
As those move easiest who have learned to dance.
'Tis not enough no harshness gives offense,
The sound must seem an echo to the sense:
Soft is the strain when Zephyr[3] gently blows,
And the smooth stream in smoother numbers flows;
But when loud surges lash the sounding shore,
The hoarse, rough verse should like the torrent roar.
When Ajax[4] strives, some rock's vast weight to throw,
The line too labors, and the words move slow;
Not so, when swift Camilla[5] scours the plain,
Flies o'er th' unbending corn, and skims along the main.
Hear how Timotheus'[6] varied lays surprise,
And bid alternate passions fall and rise!
While, at each change, the son of Libyan Jove[7]
Now burns with glory, and then melts with love;
Now his fierce eyes with sparkling fury glow,
Now sighs steal out, and tears begin to flow:
Persians and Greeks like turns of nature[8] found,
And the world's victor stood subdued by sound!

8. Regular accents. 9. Filler words, such as "do." 1. A six-foot line, sometimes used in pentameter poems to vary the pace mechanically. Line 357 is an alexandrine. 2. Sir John Denham and Edmund Waller, 17th-century poets credited with perfecting the heroic couplet. 3. The west wind. 4. A Greek hero of the Trojan War, noted for his strength. 5. A woman warrior in *The Aeneid*. 6. The court-musician of Alexander the Great, celebrated in a famous poem by Dryden (see line 383) for the power of his music over Alexander's emotions. 7. In Greek tradition, the chief god of any people was often given the name Zeus (Jove), and the chief god of Libya (the Greek name for all of Africa) was called Zeus Ammon. Alexander visited his oracle and was proclaimed son of the god. 8. Similar alternations of emotion.

The pow'r of music all our hearts allow,
And what Timotheus was, is DRYDEN now.

1711

A lot of things go on here simultaneously. The poem uses a number of echoic or onomatopoeic words, and pleasant and unpleasant consonant sounds are used in some lines to underline a particular point or add some mood music. When the poet talks about a particular weakness in poetry, he illustrates it at the same time—by using open vowels (line 345), expletives (line 346), monosyllabic words (line 347), predictable rhymes (lines 350–353), or long, slow lines (line 357). And the good qualities of poetry he talks about and illustrates as well (line 360, for example). But the main effects of the passage come from an interaction of several strategies at once. The effects are fairly simple and easy to spot, but their causes involve a lot of poetic ingenuity. In line 340, for example, a careful cacophonous effect is achieved by the repetition of the o͞o vowel sound and the repetition of the L consonant sound together with the interruption (twice) of the rough F sound in the middle; no one wants to be caught admiring that music when the poet gets through with us, but the careful harmony of the preceding sounds has set us up beautifully. And in lines 347, 357, and 359, the pace of the lines is carefully controlled by consonant sounds as well as by the use of long vowels. Line 347 moves incredibly slowly and seems much longer than it is because almost all the one-syllable words end in a consonant that refuses to blend with the beginning of the next word, making the words hard to say without distinct, awkward pauses between them. And in lines 357 and 359, long vowels such as those in "wounded," "snake," "slow," "along," "roundly," and "smooth" help to slow down the pace, and the same trick of juxtaposing awkward, unpronounceable consonants is also employed. The commas also provide nearly a full stop in the midst of these lines to slow us down still more. Similarly, the harsh lashing of the shore in lines 368–69 is partly accomplished by onomatopoeia, partly by a shift in the pattern of stress, which creates irregular waves in line 368, and partly by the dominance of rough consonants in line 369. (In Pope's time, the English R was still trilled gruffly so that it could be made to sound extremely rrrough and harrrsh.) Almost every line in this passage could serve as a demonstration of how to make sound echo sense.

As the passage from Pope and the poem "Dirge" suggest, sound is most effectively manipulated in poetry when the rhythm of the voice is carefully controlled so that not only are the proper sounds heard, but they are heard at precisely the right moment. Pace and rhythm are nearly as important to a good poem as they are to a good piece of music. The human voice naturally develops certain rhythms in speech; some syllables and some words receive more stress than others, and a careful poet controls the flow of stresses so that, in many poems, a certain basic rhythm develops almost like a quiet percussion instrument in the background. Not all poems are metered, and not all metered poems follow a single dominant rhythm, but many poems are written in one pervasive pattern, and it is useful to look for patterns of stress.

Here is a poem that names and illustrates many of the meters. If you read it aloud and chart the unstressed (˘) and stressed (¯) syllables you should have a chart similar to that done by the poet himself in the text.

SAMUEL TAYLOR COLERIDGE

Metrical Feet

LESSON FOR A BOY

Trōchĕe trīps frŏm lōng tŏ shōrt;[9]
From long to long in solemn sort
Slōw Spōndēe stālks; strōng fo͞ot! yet ill able
Ēvĕr tŏ cōme ŭp wĭth Dācty̆l trĭsy̆llăblĕ.
Ĭāmbĭcs mārch frŏm shōrt tŏ lōng—
Wĭth ă le͞ap ănd ă bo͞und thĕ swĭft Ănāpĕsts thrōng;
One syllable long, with one short at each side,
Ămphĭbrăchy̆s hāstes wĭth ă stātely̆ stride—
Fīrst ănd lāst bēĭng lōng, mīddlĕ shōrt, Ămphĭmācer
Strīkes hĭs thūndĕrĭng ho͞ofs līke ă pro͞ud hīgh-brĕd Rācer.
If Derwent[1] be innocent, steady, and wise,
And delight in the things of earth, water, and skies;
Tender warmth at his heart, with these meters to show it,
With sound sense in his brains, may make Derwent a poet—
May crown him with fame, and must win him the love
Of his father on earth and his Father above.
My dear, dear child!
Could you stand upon Skiddaw,[2] you would not from its whole ridge
See a man who so loves you as your fond S. T. COLERIDGE.

1806

9. The long and short marks over syllables are Coleridge's. 1. Written originally for Coleridge's son Hartley, the poem was later adapted for his younger son, Derwent. 2. A mountain in the lake country of northern England (where Coleridge lived in his early years), near the town of Derwent.

The following poem exemplifies **dactylic rhythm (–⏑⏑, or a stressed syllable followed by two unstressed ones).**

ARTHUR W. MONKS

Twilight's Last Gleaming

Higgledy-piggledy
President Jefferson
Gave up the ghost on the
Fourth of July.

So did John Adams, which
Shows that such patriots
Propagandistically
Knew how to die.

1967

Limericks rely on **anapestic meter (⏑⏑–, or two unstressed syllables followed by a stressed one).**

ANONYMOUS

[A staid schizophrenic named Struther]

A staid schizophrenic named Struther,
When told of the death of his brother,
    Said: "Yes, I am sad;
    It makes me feel bad,
But then, I still have each other."

ANONYMOUS

[There once was a girl from St. Paul]

There once was a girl from St. Paul,
Wore a newspaper dress to a ball.
    The dress caught on fire
    And burned her entire
Front page, sporting section, and all.

ANONYMOUS

[There once was a spinster of Ealing]

There once was a spinster of Ealing,
Endowed with such delicate feeling,
    That she thought an armchair
    Should not have its legs bare—
So she kept her eyes trained on the ceiling.

The following poem is composed in the more common **trochaic** meter (–⌣, a stressed syllable followed by an unstressed one).

SIR JOHN SUCKLING

Song

Why so pale and wan, fond Lover?
    Prithee why so pale?
Will, when looking well can't move her,
    Looking ill prevail?
    Prithee why so pale?

Why so dull and mute, young Sinner?
    Prithee why so mute?
Will, when speaking well can't win her,
    Saying nothing do 't?
    Prithee why so mute?

Quit, quit, for shame, this will not move,
    This cannot take her;
If of her self she will not love,
    Nothing can make her,
    The Devil take her.

1646

The basic meter in the following poem is the most common one in English, **iambic** (⌣–, an unstressed syllable followed by a stressed one).

JOHN DRYDEN

To the Memory of Mr. Oldham[3]

Farewell, too little, and too lately known,
Whom I began to think and call my own;
For sure our souls were near allied, and thine
Cast in the same poetic mold with mine.
One common note on either lyre did strike,
And knaves and fools we both abhorred alike.
To the same goal did both our studies drive;
The last set out the soonest did arrive.
Thus Nisus fell upon the slippery place,
While his young friend performed and won the race.[4]
O early ripe! to thy abundant store
What could advancing age have added more?
It might (what nature never gives the young)
Have taught the numbers[5] of thy native tongue.
But satire needs not those, and wit will shine
Through the harsh cadence of a rugged line.[6]
A noble error, and but seldom made,
When poets are by too much force betrayed.
Thy generous fruits, though gathered ere their prime,
Still showed a quickness; and maturing time
But mellows what we write to the dull sweets of rhyme.
Once more, hail and farewell; farewell, thou young,
But ah too short, Marcellus[7] of our tongue;
Thy brows with ivy, and with laurels bound;
But fate and gloomy night encompass thee around. 1684

Once you have figured out the basic rhythm of a poem, you can often find some interesting things by looking carefully at the departures from the pattern. Departures from the basic iambic meter of "To the Memory of Mr. Oldham," for example, suggest some of the imaginative things that poets can do within the apparently very restrictive requirements of traditional meter. Try marking the stressed and unstressed syllables in "To the Memory of Mr. Oldham" and then look carefully at each of the places that vary from the basic iambic pattern. Which of these variations call special attention to a particular sound or

3. John Oldham (1653–83), who like Dryden (see lines 3–6) wrote satiric poetry. 4. In Vergil's *Aeneid* (Book V), Nisus (who is leading the race) falls and then trips the second runner so that his friend Euryalus can win. 5. Rhythms. 6. In Dryden's time, *r*'s were pronounced with a harsh, trilling sound. 7. The nephew of the Roman emperor Augustus; he died at 20, and Vergil celebrated him in the *Aeneid*, Book VI.

action being talked about in the poem? Which ones specifically mimic or echo the sense? Which variations seem to exist primarily for emphasis? Which ones seem primarily intended to mark structural breaks in the poem? (For a sample student paper analyzing the prosody of this poem, see p. 1977.)

▽ ▽ ▽

THE SOUNDS OF POETRY A Glossary

anapestic: two unstressed syllables followed by a stressed one
dactylic: a stressed syllable followed by two unstressed ones
iambic: an unstressed syllable followed by a stressed one
onamatopoeia: a word capturing or approximating the sound of what it describes
trochaic: a stressed syllable followed by an unstressed one

ALFRED, LORD TENNYSON

Break, Break, Break

Break, break, break,
    On thy cold gray stones, O Sea!
And I would that my tongue could utter
    The thoughts that arise in me.

O well for the fisherman's boy,
    That he shouts with his sister at play
O well for the sailor lad,
    That he sings in his boat on the bay!
And the stately ships go on
    To their haven under the hill;
But O for the touch of a vanished hand,
    And the sound of a voice that is still!

Break, break, break,
    At the foot of thy crags, O Sea!
But the tender grace of a day that is dead
    Will never come back to me.

ca. 1834

BEN JONSON

Slow, Slow, Fresh Fount[8]

Slow, slow, fresh fount, keep time with my salt tears;
Yet slower, yet, O faintly, gentle springs!
List to the heavy part the music bears,
Woe weeps out her division,[9] when she sings.
    Droop herbs and flowers;
    Fall grief in showers;
    Our beauties are not ours.
        O, I could still,
Like melting snow upon some craggy hill,
    Drop, drop, drop, drop,
Since nature's pride is now a withered daffodil.

1600

8. This lyric, from Jonson's play *Cynthia's Revels,* is a lament sung by Echo for Narcissus, who was entranced by his own reflection and ultimately transformed into a flower.
9. Grief at parting, but also a rapid melodic passage of music.

THOMAS NASHE

A Litany in Time of Plague

Adieu, farewell, earth's bliss;
This world uncertain is;
Fond[1] are life's lustful joys;
Death proves them all but toys;[2]
None from his darts can fly;
I am sick, I must die.
Lord, have mercy on us!

Rich men, trust not in wealth,
Gold cannot buy you health;
Physic himself must fade.
All things to end are made,
The plague full swift goes by;
I am sick, I must die.
Lord, have mercy on us!

Beauty is but a flower
Which wrinkles will devour;
Brightness falls from the air;
Queens have died young and fair;
Dust hath closed Helen's eye.
I am sick, I must die.
Lord, have mercy on us!

Strength stoops unto the grave,
Worms feed on Hector brave;
Swords may not fight with fate,
Earth still holds ope her gate.
"Come, come!" the bells do cry.
I am sick, I must die.
Lord, have mercy on us.

Wit with his wantonness
Tasteth death's bitterness;
Hell's executioner
Hath no ears for to hear
What vain art can reply.
I am sick, I must die.
Lord, have mercy on us.

Haste, therefore, each degree,
To welcome destiny;
Heaven is our heritage,

1. Foolish. 2. Trifles.

Earth but a player's stage;
Mount we unto the sky.
I am sick, I must die.
    Lord, have mercy on us.

1600

DONALD JUSTICE

Counting the Mad

This one was put in a jacket,
This one was sent home,
This one was given bread and meat
But would eat none,
And this one cried No No No No
All day long.

This one looked at the window
As though it were a wall,
This one saw things that were not there,
This one things that were,
And this one cried No No No No
All day long.

This one thought himself a bird,
This one a dog,
And this one thought himself a man,
An ordinary man,
And cried and cried No No No No
All day long.

1960

DIANE ACKERMAN

Beija-Flor[3]

(*Hummingbird*)

When you kiss me, moths flutter in my mouth;
when you kiss me, leaf-cutter ants lift up
their small burdens and carry them along
corridors of scent; when you kiss me,
caymans slither down wet banks in moonlight,
jaws yawning open, eyes bright red lasers;
when you kiss me, my tiny fist conceals
the bleached skull of a sloth; when you kiss me,
the waters wed in my ribs, dark and pale

3. Where the Sun Dines, Poems of Amazonia, IV.

rivers exchange their potions—she gives him
love's power, he gives her love's lure;
when you kiss me, my heart, surfacing, steals
a small breath like a pink river dolphin;
when you kiss me, the rain falls thick as rubber,
sunset pours molasses down my spine
and, in my hips, the green wings of the jungle flutter;
when you kiss me, blooms explode like land mines
in trees loud with monkey muttering
and the kazoo-istry of birds; when you kiss me,
a palm cradling the moon in its arms becomes
a pictograph for leisure; when you kiss me
my flesh sambas like an iguana; when you kiss me,
the river-mirror reflects an unknown land,
eyes glitter in the foliage, ships pass
like traveling miracle plays, and coca sets
brush fires in my veins; when you kiss me,
the river tilts its wet thighs around a bend;
when you kiss me, my tongue unfolds its wings
and flies through shadows as a leaf-nosed bat,
a ventriloquist of the twilight shore
which hurls its voice against the tender world
and aches to hear its echo rushing back;
when you kiss me, anthuria send up
small telescopes, the vine-clad trees wear
pantaloons, a reasonably evitable moon
rises among a signature of clouds,
the sky fills with the pandemonium
of swamp monkeys, the aerial slither
and looping confetti of butterflies;
when you kiss me, time's caravan pauses
to sip from the rich tropic of the heart,
find shade in the oasis of a touch,
bathe in Nature carnal, mute and radiant;
you find me there trembling and overawed;
for, when you kiss me, I become the all
you love: a peddler on your luminous river,
whose salted-fish are words, daughter
of a dolphin; when you kiss me, I smell
of night-blooming orchids; when you kiss me,
my mouth softens into scarlet feathers—
an ibis with curved bill and small dark smile;
when you kiss me, jaguars lope through my knees;
when you kiss me, my lips quiver like bronze
violets; oh, when you kiss me. . . .

1990

JAMES MERRILL

Watching the Dance

1. Balanchine's[4]

Poor savage, doubting that a river flows
But for the myriad eddies made
By unseen powers twirling on their toes,

Here in this darkness it would seem
You had already died, and were afraid.
Be still. Observe the powers. Infer the stream.

2. Discotheque.

Having survived entirely your own youth,
Last of your generation, purple gloom
Investing you, sit, Jonah,[5] beyond speech,

And let towards the brute volume VOOM whale mouth
VAM pounding viscera VAM VOOM
A teenage plankton luminously twitch.

1967

GERARD MANLEY HOPKINS

Spring and Fall:

TO *a Young Child*

Márgarét áre you gríeving
Over Goldengrove unleaving?
Leáves, like the things of man, you
With your fresh thoughts care for, can you?
Áh! ás the heart grows older
It will come to such sights colder
By and by, nor spare a sigh
Though worlds of wanwood leafmeal[6] lie;
And yet you wíll weep and know why.
Now no matter, child, the name:
Sórrow's spríngs áre the same.
Nor mouth had, no nor mind, expressed
What heart heard of, ghost[7] guessed:

4. George Balanchine (1904–1983), Russian-born ballet choreographer and teacher. 5. According to Jonah 4, Jonah sat in gloom near Nineveh after its residents repented and God decided to spare the city from destruction. 6. Broken up, leaf by leaf (analogous to "piecemeal"). *Wanwood:* pale, gloomy woods. 7. Soul.

It ís the blight man was born for,
1880 It is Margaret you mourn for.

P. K. PAGE

Photos of a Salt Mine

How innocent their lives look,
how like a child's
dream of caves and winter, both combined;
the steep descent to whiteness
and the stope
with its striated walls
their folds all leaning as if pointing to
the greater whiteness still,
that great white bank
with its decisive front,
that seam upon a slope,
salt's lovely ice.

And wonderful underfoot the snow of salt
the fine
particles a broom could sweep,
one thinks
muckers might make angels in its drifts
as children do in snow,
lovers in sheets,
lie down and leave imprinted where they lay
a feathered creature holier than they.

And in the outworked stopes
with lamps and ropes
up miniature matterhorns
the miners climb
probe with their lights
the ancient folds of rock—
syncline and anticline—
and scoop from darkness an Aladdin's cave:
rubies and opals glitter from its walls.

But hoses douse the brilliance of these jewels,
melt fire to brine.
Salt's bitter water trickles thin and forms,
slow fathoms down,
a lake within a cave,
lacquered with jet—
white's opposite.

There grey on black the boating miners float
to mend the stays and struts of that old stope
and deeply underground
their words resound,
are multiplied by echo, swell and grow
and make a climate of a miner's voice.

So all the photographs like children's wishes
are filled with caves or winter,
innocence
has acted as a filter,
selected only beauty from the mine.
Except in the last picture,
it is shot
from an acute high angle. In a pit
figures the size of pins are strangely lit
and might be dancing but you know they're not.
Like Dante's vision of the nether hell
men struggle with the bright cold fires of salt,
locked in the black inferno of the rock:
the filter here, not innocence but guilt.

1951

WILLIAM SHAKESPEARE

[Like as the waves make towards the pebbled shore]

Like as the waves make towards the pebbled shore,
So do our minutes hasten to their end,
Each changing place with that which goes before,
In sequent toil all forwards do contend.[8]
Nativity, once in the main[9] of light,
Crawls to maturity, wherewith being crowned,
Crooked[1] eclipses 'gainst his glory fight,
And Time that gave doth now his gift confound.[2]
Time doth transfix[3] the flourish set on youth
And delves the parallels[4] in beauty's brow,
Feeds on the rarities of nature's truth,
And nothing stands but for his scythe to mow.
And yet to times in hope[5] my verse shall stand,
Praising thy worth, despite his cruel hand.

1609

8. Struggle. *Sequent:* successive. 9. High seas. *Nativity:* newborn life. 1. Perverse. 2. Bring to nothing. 3. Pierce. 4. Lines, wrinkles. 5. In the future.

STEPHEN SPENDER

The Express

After the first powerful, plain manifesto
The black statement of pistons, without more fuss
But gliding like a queen, she leaves the station.
Without bowing and with restrained unconcern
She passes the houses which humbly crowd outside,
The gasworks, and at last the heavy page
Of death, printed by gravestones in the cemetery.
Beyond the town, there lies the open country
Where, gathering speed, she acquires mystery,
The luminous self-possession of ships on ocean.
It is now she begins to sing—at first quite low
Then loud, and at last with a jazzy madness—
The song of her whistle screaming at curves,
Of deafening tunnels, brakes, innumerable bolts.
And always light, aerial, underneath,
Retreats the elate meter of her wheels.
Steaming through metal landscape on her lines,
She plunges new eras of white happiness,
Where speed throws up strange shapes, broad curves
And parallels clean like trajectories from guns.
At last, further than Edinburgh or Rome,
Beyond the crest of the world, she reaches night
Where only a low stream-line brightness
Of phosphorus on the tossing hills is light.
Ah, like a comet through flame, she moves entranced,
Wrapt in her music no bird song, no, nor bough
Breaking with honey buds, shall ever equal.

1933

MICHAEL HARPER

Dear John, Dear Coltrane

a love supreme, a love supreme[6]
a love supreme, a love supreme

Sex fingers toes
in the marketplace
near your father's church

6. Coltrane's record of "A Love Supreme," released in 1965, represents his moment of greatest public acclaim.

in Hamlet, North Carolina—[7]
witness to this love
in this calm fallow
of these minds,
there is no substitute for pain:
genitals gone or going,
seed burned out,
you tuck the roots in the earth,
turn back, and move
by river through the swamps,
singing: *a love supreme, a love supreme;*
what does it all mean?
Loss, so great each black
woman expects your failure
in mute change, the seed gone.
You plod up into the electric city—
your song now crystal and
the blues. You pick up the horn
with some will and blow
into the freezing night:
a love supreme, a love supreme—

Dawn comes and you cook
up the thick sin 'tween
impotence and death, fuel
the tenor sax cannibal
heart, genitals and sweat
that makes you clean—
a love supreme, a love supreme—

Why you so black?
cause I am
why you so funky?
cause I am
why you so black
cause I am
why you so sweet?
cause I am
why you so black?
cause I am
a love supreme, a love supreme:

So sick
you couldn't play *Naima*,[8]
so flat we ached
for song you'd concealed

7. Coltrane's birthplace. His family shared a house with Coltrane's grandfather, who was the minister of St. Stephen's AME Zion Church there. 8. Another standard Coltrane song, recorded in 1966.

with your own blood,
your diseased liver gave
out its purity,
the inflated heart
pumps out, the tenor kiss,
tenor love:
a love supreme, a love supreme—
a love supreme, a love supreme—

1970

JUDITH WRIGHT

"Dove-Love"

The dove purrs—over and over the dove
purrs its declaration. The wind's tone
changes from tree to tree, the creek on stone
alters its sob and fall, but still the dove
goes insistently on, telling its love
    "I could eat you."

And in captivity, they say, doves do.
Gentle, methodical, starting with the feet
(the ham-pink succulent toes
on their thin stems of rose),
baring feather by feather the wincing meat:
    "I could eat you."

That neat suburban head, that suit of grey,
watchful conventional eye and manicured claw—
these also rhyme with us. The doves play
on one repetitive note that plucks the raw
helpless nerve, their soft "I do. I do.
    I could eat you."

1962

The Way a Poem Looks

The way a poem looks is not nearly so important as the way it sounds—usually. But there are exceptions. A few poems are written to be seen rather than heard, and their appearance on the page is crucial to their effect. The poem "[l(a]", for example, tries to visualize typographically what the poet asks you to see in your mind's eye. Occasionally, too, poems are composed in a specific shape so that the poem looks like a physical object. The poems that follow in this chapter—some old, some new—illustrate ways in which visual effects may be created. Even though poetry has traditionally been thought of as oral—words to be said, sung, or performed rather than looked at—the idea that poems can also be related to painting and the visual arts is also an old one. Theodoric in ancient Greece is credited with inventing **technopaegnia**—that is, the construction of poems with visual appeal. Once, the shaping of words to resemble an object was thought to have mystical power, but more recent attempts at **concrete poetry** or **shaped verse** are usually playful exercises (such as Robert Hollander's "You Too? Me Too—Why Not? Soda Pop" (p. 974) which is shaped like a Coke bottle), attempting to supplement (or replace) verbal meanings with devices from painting and sculpture.

Reading a poem like "Easter Wings" aloud wouldn't make much sense. Our eyes are everything for a poem like that. A more frequent poetic device is to ask us to use our eyes as a guide to sound. The following poem depends upon recognition of some standard typographical symbols and knowledge of their names. We have to say those names to read the poem.

FRANKLIN P. ADAMS

Composed in the Composing Room

At stated .ic times
I love to sit and—off rhymes
Till ,tose at last I fall
Exclaiming "I don't ∧ all."

Though I'm an * objection
By running this in this here §
This ☞ of the Fleeting Hour,
This lofty -ician Tower—

A ¶er's hope dispels
All fear of deadly ||.
You think these [ ] are a pipe?
Well, not on your †eotype.

1914

We create the right term here when we verbalize, putting the visual signs together with the words or letters printed in the poem, for example making the word "periodic" out of ".ic" or "high Phoenician" out of "-ician." This, too, involves an extreme instance and involves a game more than any serious emotional effect. More often poets give us—by the visual placement of sounds—a guide to reading, inviting us to regulate the pace of our reading, notice pauses or silences, pay attention both to the syntax of the poem and to the rhetoric of the voice, thus providing us a kind of musical score for reading.

E. E. CUMMINGS

[Buffalo Bill 's][1]

Buffalo Bill 's
defunct
            who used to
            ride a watersmooth-silver
                                                    stallion
and break onetwothreefourfive pigeonsjustlikethat
                                                                        Jesus
he was a handsome man
                                        and what i want to know is
how do you like your blueeyed boy
Mister Death

1923

The unusual spacing of words here, with some run together and others widely separated, provides a guide to reading, regulating both speed and sense, so that the poem can capture aloud some of the excitement and wonder of a boy's enthusiasm for a theatrical act as spectacular as that of Buffalo Bill. A good reader-aloud, with only this typographical guidance, can capture some of the wide-eyed boy's responses, remembered now in retrospect long after Buffalo Bill's act is out of business and the man himself is dead.

In prose, syntax and punctuation are the main guides to the voice of a reader, providing indicators of emphasis, pace, and speed, and in poetry they are also more conventional and more common guides than extreme forms of unusual typography as in "[Buffalo Bill 's]." Reading a poem sensitively is in some ways a lot like reading a piece of prose sensitively: one has to pay close attention to the way the sentences are put together and how they are punctuated. A good reader makes use of appropriate pauses as well as thundering emphasis; silence as well as sound is part of any poem, and reading punctuation is as important as knowing how to say the words.

Beyond punctuation, the placement and spacing of lines on the page may

1. Portraits XXI.

be helpful to a reader even when that placement is not as radical as in "[Buffalo Bill 's]." The fact that poetry looks different from prose is not an accident; decisions to make lines one length instead of another have as much to do with vocal breaks and phrasing as they have to do with functions of syntax or meaning. In a good poem, there are few accidents, not even in the way the poem meets the eye, for as readers our eyes are the most direct route to our voices; they are our scanner and director, our prompter and guide.

The eye also may help the ear in poetry in another way—guiding us to notice repeated sounds by repeated visual patterns in letters. The most common rhymes in poems occur at the ends of lines, and the arrangement of lines (the typography of the poem) often calls attention to the pattern of sounds because of the similar appearance of line-ending words. Not all words that rhyme have similar spellings, of course, but similarities of word appearance seem to imply a relationship of sound too, and many poems hint at their stanza patterns and verse forms (discussed in the next chapter) by their spatial arrangement and repeated patterns at ends of lines. The following poem takes advantage of such expectations and plays with them by forcing a letter into arbitrary line relationships, forcing words ("stew," line 2) in order to create rhymes, setting up rhyme patterns and then breaking them (lines 9–11), using false or near rhymes (lines 10–11), and creating long lines with multisyllabic rhymes that seem silly (the final two lines).

STEVIE SMITH

The Jungle Husband

Dearest Evelyn, I often think of you
Out with the guns in the jungle stew
Yesterday I hittapotamus
I put the measurements down for you but they got lost in the fuss
It's not a good thing to drink out here
You know, I've practically given it up dear.
Tomorrow I am going alone a long way
Into the jungle. It is all grey
But green on top
Only sometimes when a tree has fallen
The sun comes down plop, it is quite appalling.
You never want to go in a jungle pool
In the hot sun, it would be the act of a fool
Because it's always full of anacondas, Evelyn, not looking ill-fed
I'll say. So no more now, from your loving husband, Wilfred. 1957

Similar sight-to-sound expectations in the following two poems provide clues to the structure of the verse form. Note, for each poem, how the final words of each stanza are repeated (but in a different order) in subsequent stanzas, and see if you can predict the pattern of key words in the final stanza:

DAVID FERRY

The Guest Ellen at the Supper for Street People

The unclean spirits cry out in the body
Or mind of the guest Ellen in a loud voice,
Torment me not, and in the fury of her unclean
Hands beating the air in some kind of unending torment—
Nobody witnessing could possibly know the event
That cast upon her the spell of this enchantment.

Almost all the guests are under some kind of enchantment:
Of being poor day after day in the same body;
Of being witness still to some obscene event;
Of listening all the time to somebody's voice
Whispering in the ear things divine or unclean,
In the quotidian of unending torment.

One has to keep thinking there was some source of torment,
Something that happened someplace else, unclean.
One has to keep talking in a reasonable voice
About things done, say, by a father's body
To or upon the body of Ellen, in enchantment
Helpless, still by the old forgotten event

Enchanted, still in the unforgotten event
A prisoner of love, filthy Ellen in her torment,
Guest Ellen in the dining hall in her body,
Hands beating the air in her enchantment,
Sitting alone, gabbling in her garbled voice
The narrative of the spirits of the unclean.

She is wholly the possessed one of the unclean.
Maybe the spirits came from the river. The enchantment
Entered her, maybe, in the Northeast Kingdom. The torment,
A thing of the waters, gratuitous event,
Came up out of the waters and entered her body
And lived in her in torment and cried out in her voice.

It speaks itself over and over again in her voice,
Cursing maybe or not a familiar obscene event

Or only the pure event of original enchantment
From the birth of the river waters, the pure unclean
Rising from the source of things, in a figure of torment
Seeking out Ellen, finding its home in her poor body.

Her body witness is, so also is her voice,
Of torment coming from unknown event;
Unclean is the nature and name of the enchantment.

1988

HARRY MATHEWS

"Histoire"[2]

Tina and Seth met in the midst of an overcrowded militarism.
"Like a drink?" he asked her. "They make great Alexanders[3] over at the Marxism-Leninism."
She agreed. They shared cocktails. They behaved cautiously, as in a period of pre-fascism.
Afterwards he suggested dinner at a restaurant renowned for its Maoism.
"O.K.," she said, but first she had to phone a friend about her ailing Afghan, whose name was Racism.
Then she followed Seth across town past twilit alleys of sexism.

The waiter brought menus and announced the day's specials. He treated them with condescending sexism,
So they had another drink. Tina started her meal with a dish of militarism,
While Seth, who was hungrier, had a half portion of stuffed baked racism.
Their main dishes were roast duck for Seth, and for Tina broiled Marxism-Leninism.
Tina had pecan pie à la for dessert, Seth a compote of stewed Maoism.
They lingered. Seth proposed a liqueur. They rejected sambuca[4] and agreed on fascism.

During the meal, Seth took the initiative. He inquired into Tina's fascism,
About which she was reserved, not out of reticence but because Seth's sexism
Had aroused in her a desire she felt she should hide—as though her Maoism
Would willy-nilly betray her feelings for him. She was right. Even her deliberate militarism
Couldn't keep Seth from realizing that his attraction was reciprocated. His own Marxism-Leninism

2. French for "story." 3. Cocktail of brandy, cream, and crème de cacao. 4. Italian anise liqueur.

Became manifest, in a compulsive way that piled the Ossa of confusion on the Peleion[5] of racism.

Next, what? Food finished, drinks drunk, bills paid—what racism
Might not swamp their yearning in an even greater confusion of fascism?
But women are wiser than words. Tina rested her hand on his thigh and, a-twinkle with Marxism-Leninism,
Asked him, "My place?" Clarity at once abounded under the flood-lights of sexism,
They rose from the table, strode out, and he with the impetuousness of young militarism
Hailed a cab to transport them to her lair, heaven-haven of Maoism.

In the taxi he soon kissed her. She let him unbutton her Maoism
And stroke her resilient skin, which was quivering with shudders of racism.
When beneath her jeans he sensed the superior Lycra of her militarism,
His longing almost strangled him. Her little tongue was as potent as fascism
In its elusive certainty. He felt like then and there tearing off her sexism
But he reminded himself: "Pleasure lies in patience, not in the greedy violence of Marxism-Leninism."

Once home, she took over. She created a hungering aura of Marxism-Leninism
As she slowly undressed him where he sat on her overstuffed art-deco Maoism,
Making him keep still, so that she could indulge in caresses, in sexism,
In the pursuit of knowing him. He groaned under the exactness of her racism
—Fingertip sliding up his nape, nails incising his soles, teeth nibbling his fascism
At last she guided him to bed, and they lay down on a patchwork of Old American militarism.

Biting his lips, he plunged his militarism into the popular context of her Marxism-Leninism,
Easing one thumb into her fascism, with his free hand coddling the tip of her Maoism,
Until, gasping with appreciative racism, both together sink into the revealed glory of sexism.
1988

Both these poems are written in an intricate verse form called a sestina (see the next chapter) in which elaborate patterning and repetition is involved, and seeing the poem on the page helps the voice (and the mind) identify the pattern. Such elaborateness is very self-conscious, of course, and the second of the two poems here plays outrageously on the expectations of repetition.

5. To pile Ossa on Peleion (or vice versa) is to pile difficulty on difficulty. In Greek mythology, two giants attempted to reach heaven (to overthrow the gods) by piling Mt. Ossa on Mt. Olympus and Mt. Peleion on Mt. Ossa.

Stanzas—visual breaks in poems that indicate some kind of unit of meaning or measurement—ultimately are more than visual devices, for they point to structural questions and ultimately frame and formalize the content of poems. But they involve—as do the similar visual patterns of words that rhyme—part of the "score" of poems, and suggest one more way that sight becomes a guide to sound in many poems.

▽ ▽ ▽

THE WAY A POEM LOOKS A Glossary

concrete poetry/shaped verse: an attempt to supplement (or replace) verbal meaning with visual devices from painting and sculpture

technopaegnia: the construction of poems with visual appeal

GEORGE HERBERT

Easter Wings

Lord, who createdst man in wealth and store,[6]
Though foolishly he lost the same,
Decaying more and more,
Till he became
Most poor:
With thee
O let me rise
As larks,[7] harmoniously,
And sing this day thy victories:
Then shall the fall further the flight in me.

My tender age in sorrow did begin;
Andstillwithsicknessesandshame
Thou didst so punish sin,
That I became
Most thin.
With thee
Let me combine,
And feel this day thy victory;
For, if I imp[8] my wing on thine,
Affliction shall advance the flight in me.

1633

ROBERT HERRICK

The Pillar of Fame

Fame's pillar here, at last, we set,
Out-during *Marble*, *Brass*, or *Jet*,[9]
Charmed and enchanted so,
As to withstand the blow
Of overthrow:
Nor shall the seas,
Or OUTRAGES
Of storms o'erbear
What we up-rear,
Tho Kingdoms fall,
This pillar never shall
Decline or waste at all;
But stand for ever by his own
Firm and well fixed foundation.

1648

6. In plenty. 7. Which herald the morning. 8. Engraft. In falconry, to engraft feathers in a damaged wing, so as to restore the powers of flight (OED). 9. Black lignite or black marble. *Out-during*: out-lasting.

E. E. CUMMINGS

[l(a]

l(a

le
af
fa

ll

s)
one
l

iness

1958

NORA DAUENHAUER

Tlingit Concrete Poem

t’an
a i
a k
x’aax’x’aax’x’aax’x’aax’x’aax
aax’x’aax’x’aax’x’aax’x’aax’x’aax’x
’x’aax’x’aax’x’aax’x’aax’x’aax’x’aax’x’a
x’x’aax’x’aax’x’aax’x’aax’x’aax’x’aax’x’aax
aax’x’aax’x’aax’x’aax’x’aax’x’aax’x’aax’x’aax’
’aax’x’aax’x’aax’x’aax’x’aax’x’aax’x’aax’x’aax’x
x’aax’x’aax’x’aax’x’aax’x’aax’x’aax’x’aax’x’aax’x’
’x’aax’x’aax’x’aax’x’aax’x’aax’x’aax’x’aax’x’aax’x’
’x’aax’x’aax’x’aax’x’aax’x’aax’x’aax’x’aax’x’aax’x’a
’x’aax’x’aax’x’aax’x’aax’x’aax’x’aax’x’aax’x’aax’x’a
x’x’aax’x’aax’x’aax’x’aax’x’aax’x’aax’x’aax’x’aax’x’a
x’x’aax’x’aax’x’aax’x’aax’x’aax’x’aax’x’aax’x’aax’x’a
x’x’aax’x’aax’x’aax’x’aax’x’aax’x’aax’x’aax’x’aax’x’a
x’x’aax’x’aax’x’aax’x’aax’x’aax’x’aax’x’aax’x’aax’x’a
’x’aax’x’aax’x’aax’x’aax’x’aax’x’aax’x’aax’x’aax’x’a
’x’aax’x’aax’x’aax’x’aax’x’aax’x’aax’x’aax’x’aax’x’
x’aax’x’aax’x’aax’x’aax’x’aax’x’aax’x’aax’x’aax’x
x’aax’x’aax’x’aax’x’aax’x’aax’x’aax’x’aax’x’aax’x’
’aax’x’aax’x’aax’x’aax’x’aax’x’aax’x’aax’x’aax’x
’aax’x’aax’x’aax’x’aax’x’aax’x’aax’x’aax’x’aax’
aax’x’aax’x’aax’x’aax’x’aax’tl’ukwx’aax’x’aax’
ax’x’aax’x’aax’x’aax’x’aax’x’aax’x’aax’x’aax
x’x’aax x’aax’x’aax’x’aax’x’aax’x’aax’x’aa
’x’aax’x’aax’x’aax’x’aax’x’aax’x’aax’x’a
’aax’x’aax’x’aax’x’aax’x’aax’x’aax’x
ax’x’aax’x’aax’x’aax’x’aax’x’aax
’x’aax’x’aax’x’aax’x’aax’x’a
’aax’x’aax’x’aax’x’aax’x’
’x’aax’x’aax’x’aa
’x’aa

akat’ani = stem
x’aax’ = apple
tl’ukwx = worm

1984

QUESTIONS

1. Read “Persimmons” (*Reading Poetry*) and Galway Kinnell’s “Blackberry Eating” (*Reading More Poetry*), and compare the sound effects of each with those in “The Word *Plum*.” How visual an image does each poem create? To what purposes does Li-Young Lee put the visual qualities of the persimmon?

Which other of the five senses are evoked in each poem? to what specific purpose?

2. Read the following poems aloud: "Break, Break, Break," "Slow, Slow, Fresh Fount," and "Counting the Mad." As you read each, try to be especially conscious of the way punctuation guides your pauses and of the pace you develop as you become accustomed to the prevailing rhythms of the poem. At what points do you notice radical changes in rhythm or pace? (Pay special attention to the constantly changing patterns in "Slow, Slow, Fresh Fount," and notice at what points the "sense" of the poem guides its rhythms.) Compare the strategies of repetition in "Counting the Mad" with those in "A Litany in Time of Plague." (Read "Litany" aloud too, and then get someone else to read it aloud to you, comparing the way the two voices handle the insistently repeated refrain.)

3. Pick out all the onomatopoeic words in "Beija-Flor." What other strategies of sound help to recreate the sense of presence of the hummingbird? How, exactly, does the central analogy in the poem work?

4. Scan—that is, mark all of the stressed syllables and chart their pattern—"[Like as the waves make towards the pebbled shore]." What variations do you find on the basic iambic pentameter pattern? What functions do the variations perform in each case?

WRITING SUGGESTIONS

1. Read "[Sound and Sense]" over carefully twice—once silently and once aloud—and then mark the stressed and unstressed syllables. Draw up a chart indicating, line by line, exactly what the patterns of stress are, and then single out all the lines that have major variations from the basic iambic pentameter pattern. Pick out half a dozen lines with variations that seem to you worthy of comment, and write a paragraph on each in which you show how the metrical pattern contributes to the specific effects achieved in that line. (You will probably notice that in most of the lines other strategies also contribute to the sound effects, but confine your discussion to the achievement through metrical pattern.)

2. Try your hand at writing limericks in imitation of those in this chapter. Use "[There once was a spinster of Ealing]" as your model, and begin your limerick with "There once was a ——— of ———" (use a place name for

which you think you can find a comic rhyme). Study the rhythmic patterns and line lengths carefully, and imitate them exactly in your poem.

3. Scan line by line Suckling's "Song." In an essay of no more than 500 words, show in detail how the varied metrical pattern in the final stanza abruptly changes the tone of the poem and reverses the poem's direction.

4. Read "Beija-Flor" aloud. Then go through the poem line by line and pick out half a dozen words and patterns of sound that seem to you especially effective in creating vocal effects. Analyze carefully the effects created by each of these words or word groups, and try to account for exactly how the passage works. Then, using these examples as the primary (though not necessarily the exclusive) basis, write a three-page paper on the uses of sound in the poem.

8 STANZAS AND VERSE FORMS

Most poems of more than a few lines are divided into **stanzas,** groups of lines divided from other groups by white space on the page. Putting some space between the groupings of lines has the effect of sectioning off the poem, giving its physical appearance a series of divisions that often mark breaks in thought in the poem, changes of scenery or imagery, or other shifts in structure or direction. In "The Flea" (p. 690), for example, the stanza divisions mark distinctive stages in the action; between the first and second stanzas, the speaker stops his companion from killing the flea, and between the second and third stanzas, the companion follows through on her intention and kills the flea. And in "The Goose Fish" (p. 771), the stanzas mark stages in the self-perception of the lovers; each of the stanzas is a more or less distinct scene, and the stanzas unfold almost like a series of slides. Not all stanzas are quite so neatly patterned, but any poem divided into stanzas calls attention on the page to the fact of the divisions and invites some sort of response to what appear to be gaps or silences that may be structural indicators.

Historically, stanzas have most often been organized internally by patterns of rhyme, and thus stanza divisions have been a visual indicator of patterns in sound. In most traditional stanza forms, the pattern of rhyme is repeated in stanza after stanza throughout the poem, and the voice and ear become familiar with the pattern so that, in a sense, we come to depend on it. We can thus "hear" variations, just as we do in music. In a poem of more than a few stanzas, the accumulation of pattern may even mean that our ear comes to expect repetition and finds a kind of comfort in its increasing familiarity. The rhyme thus becomes an organizational device in the poem, and ordinarily the metrical patterns stay constant from stanza to stanza. In Shelley's "Ode to the West Wind," for example, the first and third lines in each stanza rhyme, and the middle line then rhymes with the first and third lines of the next stanza. (In indicating rhyme, a different letter of the alphabet is conventionally used to represent each sound; in the following example, if we begin with "being" as *a* and "dead" as *b*, then "fleeing" is also *a*, and "red" and "bed" are *b*.)

O wild West Wind, thou breath of Autumn's being, *a*
Thou, from whose unseen presence the leaves dead *b*
Are driven, like ghosts from an enchanter fleeing *a*

Yellow, and black, and pale, and hectic red, *b*
Pestilence-stricken multitudes: O thou, *c*
Who chariotest to their dark wintry bed *b*

The wingéd seeds, where they lie cold and low, *c*
Each like a corpse within its grave, until *d*
Thine azure sister of the Spring shall blow *c*

In this stanza form, known as **terza rima,** the stanzas are thus linked to each other by a common sound: one rhyme sound from each stanza is picked up in the next stanza, and so on to the end of the group of stanzas. This stanza form is the one used by the great Italian poet Dante in *The Divine Comedy,* written in the early 1300s. Its use is not all that common in English because it is a rhyme-rich stanza form—that is, it requires many rhymes—and English is, relatively speaking, a rhyme-poor language (not as rich in rhyme possibilities as are languages such as Italian or French). One reason for this is that English words derive from so many different language families that we have fewer similar word endings than languages that have remained more "pure," more dependent for vocabulary on roots and patterns in their own language system.

Contemporary poets seldom use rhyme, finding it neither necessary nor appealing, but until the twentieth century rhyme was central to most poems. Because poetry was originally an oral art (and its texts not always written down) various kinds of **memory devices** (sometimes called **mnemonic devices**) were built into poems to help reciters remember them. Rhyme was one such device, and most people still find it easier to memorize poetry that rhymes. The simple pleasure of hearing the repetition of familiar sounds may also help to account for the traditional popularity of rhyme, and perhaps plain habit (for both poets and hearers) had a lot to do with why rhyme flourished for so many centuries as a standard expectation. No doubt, too, rhyme helped to give poetry a special quality that distinguished it from prose, a significant advantage in ages that worried about decorum and propriety and that were anxious to preserve a strong sense of poetic tradition. Some ages have been very concerned that poetry should not in any way be mistaken for prose or made to serve prosaic functions, and the literary critics and theorists in those ages made extraordinary efforts to emphasize the distinctions between poetry, which was thought to be artistically superior, and prose, which was thought to be primarily utilitarian. A pride in elitism and a fear that an expanded reading public could ultimately mean a dilution of the possibilities of traditional art forms have been powerful cultural forces in Western civilization, and if such forces were not themselves responsible for creating rhyme in poetry, they at least helped to preserve a sense of its necessity.

But there are at least two other reasons for rhyme. One is complex and hard to state justly without long explanations. It involves traditional ideas of the symmetrical relationship of different aspects of the world and ideas about the function of poetry to reflect the universe as human learning understood it. Most poets in earlier centuries assumed that rhyme was proper to verse, perhaps even essential. They would have felt themselves eccentric to compose poems any other way. Some poets did experiment—very successfully—with **blank verse** (that is, verse that did not rhyme but that nevertheless had strict metrical requirements), but the cultural pressure for rhyme was almost constant. Why? Custom or habit may account for part of the assumption that rhyme was necessary, but probably not all of it. Rather, the poets' sense that poetry was an imitation of larger relationships in the universe made it seem natural to use rhyme to recreate a sense of harmony, correspondence, symmetry, and order. The sounds of poetry were thus faint reminders of the harmonious cosmos, of the music of the spheres that animated the planets, the processes of nature, the interrelationship of all created things and beings. Probably poets never said to themselves, "I shall now tunefully emulate the harmony of God's carefully ordered universe," but the tendency to use rhyme and other repetitions or reechoings of sound (such as **alliteration** or **assonance**) nevertheless stemmed ultimately from basic assumptions about how the universe worked. In a modern world increasingly perceived as fragmented, rambling, and unrelated, there is of course a much lessened tendency to testify to a sense of harmony and symmetry. It would be too easy and too mechanical to think that rhyme in a poem specifically means that the poet has a firm sense of cosmic order, and that an unrhymed poem testifies to chaos, but cultural assumptions do affect the expectations of both poets and readers, and cultural tendencies create a kind of pressure upon the individual creator.

One other reason for using rhyme is that it provides a kind of discipline for the poet, a way of harnessing poetic talents and keeping a rein on the imagination, so that the results are ordered, controlled, put into some kind of meaningful and recognizable form. Robert Frost used to be fond of saying that writing poems without rhyme was like playing tennis without a net. Writing good poetry does require a lot of discipline, and Frost speaks for many (perhaps most) traditional poets in suggesting that rhyme can be a major source of that discipline. But it is not the only possible source, and more recent poets have usually felt they would rather play by new rules or invent their own as they go along, and have therefore sought their sources of discipline elsewhere, preferring the more spare tones that unrhymed poetry provides. It is not that contemporary poets cannot think of rhyme words or that they do not care about the sounds of their poetry; rather, recent poets have consciously decided not to work with rhyme and to use instead other aural devices and other strategies for organizing stanzas, just as they have chosen to work with experimental and variable rhythms instead of writing primarily in the traditional English meters. Some few modern poets, though, have protested the abandonment of rhyme and have continued to write rhymed verse successfully in a more or less traditional way.

The amount and density of rhyme varies widely in stanza and verse forms, some requiring elaborate and intricate patterns of rhyme, others more casual or spare sound repetitions. The **Spenserian stanza,** for example, is even more rhyme rich than terza rima, using only three rhyme sounds in nine rhymed lines.

Her falt'ring hand upon the balustrade, *a*
Old Angela was feeling for the stair, *b*
When Madeline, St. Agnes' charméd maid, *a*
Rose, like a missioned spirit, unaware: *b*
With silver taper's light, and pious care, *b*
She turned, and down the agéd gossip led *c*
To a safe level matting. Now prepare, *b*
  Young Porphyro, for gazing on that bed; *c*
She comes, she comes again, like ring dove frayed and fled *c*

On the other hand, the **ballad stanza** has only one set of rhymes in four lines; lines 1 and 3 in each stanza do not rhyme at all.

The king sits in Dumferling toune *a*
  Drinking the blude-reid wine. *b*
"O whar will I get guid sailor, *c*
  To sail this ship of mine?" *b*

Most stanzas have a metrical pattern as well as a rhyme scheme. Terza rima, for example, involves iambic meter (unstressed and stressed syllables alternating regularly) and each line has five beats (pentameter). Most of the Spenserian stanza (the first 8 lines) is also in iambic pentameter, but the ninth line in each stanza has one extra foot (it is iambic hexameter). The ballad stanza, also iambic as are most English stanza and verse forms, alternates three-beat and four-beat lines; lines 1 and 3 are unrhymed iambic tetrameter, and lines 2 and 4 are rhymed iambic trimeter.

Several stanza forms are exemplified in this book, most of them based on rhyme schemes, but some (such as blank verse or syllabic verse) are based entirely on meter or other measures of sound, or on some more elaborate scheme such as the measured repetition of words, as in the **sestina,** or the repetition of whole lines, as in the **villanelle.** You can probably deduce the principles involved in each of the following stanza or verse forms by looking carefully at a poem which uses it; if you have trouble, look at the definitions in the glossary in this chapter.

heroic couplet	"[Sound and Sense]"	p. 802
tetrameter couplet	"To His Coy Mistress"	p. 954
limerick	"[There once was a spinster of Ealing]"	p. 807
free verse	"Dirge"	p. 800
blank verse	from *Paradise Lost*	p. 729

What are stanza forms good for? What use is it to recognize them? Why do poets bother? Matters discussed in this chapter so far have suggested two reasons: 1. Breaks between stanzas provide convenient pauses for reader and writer, something roughly equivalent to paragraphs in prose. The eye thus picks up the places where some kind of pause or break occurs. 2. Poets sometimes use stanza forms, as they do rhyme itself, as a discipline: writing in a certain kind of stanza form imposes a shape on their act of imagination.

To suggest some other uses, we will look in more detail at one particular verse form, the **sonnet.** A sonnet usually has only a single stanza and offers several related possibilities for its rhyme scheme, but it is always fourteen lines long and usually written in iambic pentameter. The sonnet has remained a popular verse form in English for more than four centuries, and even in an age that largely rejects rhyme it continues to attract a variety of poets, including (curiously) radical and even revolutionary poets who find its firm structure very useful. Its uses, although quite varied, can be illustrated fairly precisely. As a verse form, the sonnet is contained, compact, demanding; whatever it does, it must do concisely and quickly. To be effective, it must take advantage of the possibilities inherent in its shortness and its relative rigidity. It is best suited to intensity of feeling and concentration of expression. Not too surprisingly, one subject it frequently discusses is confinement itself.

WILLIAM WORDSWORTH

Nuns Fret Not

Nuns fret not at their convent's narrow room;
And hermits are contented with their cells;
And students with their pensive citadels;
Maids at the wheel, the weaver at his loom,
Sit blithe and happy; bees that soar for bloom,

High as the highest Peak of Furness-fells,[1]
Will murmur by the hour in foxglove bells:[2]
In truth the prison, unto which we doom
Ourselves, no prison is: and hence for me,
In sundry moods, 'twas pastime to be bound
Within the sonnet's scanty plot of ground;
Pleased if some souls (for such there needs must be)
Who have felt the weight of too much liberty,
Should find brief solace there, as I have found.
1807

Most sonnets are structured according to one of two principles of division. On one principle, the sonnet divides into three units of four lines each and a final unit of two lines. On the other, the fundamental break is between the first eight lines (called an octave) and the last six (called a sestet). The 4-4-4-2 sonnet is usually called the **English** or **Shakespearean sonnet,** and ordinarily its rhyme scheme reflects the structure: the scheme of *abab cdcd efef gg* is the classic one, but many variations from that pattern still reflect the basic 4-4-4-2 division. The 8-6 sonnet is usually called the **Italian** or **Petrarchan sonnet** (the Italian poet Petrarch was an early master of this structure), and its "typical" rhyme scheme is *abbaabba cdecde,* although it too produces many variations that still reflect the basic division into two parts.

The two kinds of sonnet structures are useful for two different sorts of argument. The 4-4-4-2 structure works very well for constructing a poem that wants to make a three-step argument (with a quick summary at the end), or for setting up brief, cumulative images. "[That time of year thou mayst in me behold]" (p. 740), for example, uses the 4-4-4-2 structure to mark the progressive steps toward death and the parting of friends by using three distinct images, then summarizing. "[Let me not to the marriage of true minds]" (p. 631) works very similarly, following the kind of organization that in chapter 6 I called the 1-2-3 structure—and doing it compactly and economically.

Here, on the other hand, is a poem that uses the 8-6 pattern:

1. Mountains in England's Lake District, where Wordsworth lived. 2. Flowers from which digitalis (a heart medicine) began to be made in 1799.

HENRY CONSTABLE

[My lady's presence makes the roses red]

My lady's presence makes the roses red,
Because to see her lips they blush for shame.
The lily's leaves, for envy, pale became,
And her white hands in them this envy bred.
The marigold the leaves abroad doth spread,
Because the sun's and her power is the same.
The violet of purple colour came.
Dyed in the blood she made my heart to shed.
In brief: all flowers from her their virtue take;
From her sweet breath their sweet smells do proceed;
The living heat which her eyebeams doth make
Warmeth the ground and quickeneth the seed.
The rain, wherewith she watereth the flowers,
Falls from mine eyes, which she dissolves in showers. 1594

The first eight lines argue that the lady's presence is responsible for the color of all of nature's flowers, and the final six lines summarize and extend that argument to smells and heat—and finally to the rain that the lady draws from the speaker's eyes. That kind of two-part structure, in which the octave states a proposition or generalization and the sestet provides a particularization or application of it, has a variety of uses. The final lines may, for example, reverse the first eight and achieve a paradox or irony in the poem, or the poem may nearly balance two comparable arguments. Basically, the 8-6 structure lends itself to poems with two points to make, or to those that wish to make one fairly brief point and illustrate it.

Sometimes the neat and precise structure I have described is altered—either slightly, as in "Nuns Fret Not" above (where the 8-6 structure is more of an 8½–5½ structure), or more radically as particular needs or effects may demand. And the two basic structures certainly do not define all the structural possibilities within a fourteen-line poem, even if they do suggest the most traditional ways of taking advantage of the sonnet's compact and well-kept container.

The sonnets here by Sidney, Shakespeare, and Constable survive from a golden age of sonnet writing in the late 16th century, an age that set the pattern for expectations of form, subject matter, and tone. The sonnet came to England from Italy via France, and imitations of Petrarch's famous sonnet sequence to Laura became the rage. Thousands upon thousands of sonnets were written in those years, often in sequences of a hundred or more sonnets each; the sequences explored the many moods of love and usually had a light thread of narrative that purported to recount a love affair between the male poet and a female lover who was almost always golden-haired, beautiful, disdainful, and inaccessible. Her beauty was described in a series of exaggerated comparisons: her eyes were like the sun ("[When Nature made her chief work, Stella's eyes]"), her teeth like pearls, her cheeks like roses, her skin like ivory, and so on, but the adherence to these conventions was always playful, and it became a game of wit to play variations upon expectations ("[My lady's presence makes the roses red]" and "[My mistress' eyes are nothing like the sun]"). Almost always teasing and witty, these poems were probably not as true to life as they pretended, but they provided historically an expectation of what sonnets were to be.

Many modern sonnets continue to be about love or private life, and many continue to use a personal, apparently open and sincere tone. But poets often find the sonnet's compact form and rigid demands equally useful for many varieties of subject, theme, and tone. Besides love, sonnets often treat other subjects: politics, philosophy, discovery of a new world. And tones vary widely too, from the anger and remorse of "[Th' expense of spirit in a waste of shame]" (p. 698) and righteous outrage of "On the Late Massacre in Piedmont" (p. 234) to the tender awe of "How Do I Love Thee?" (p. 4). Many poets seem to take the kind of comfort Wordsworth describes in the careful limits of the form, finding in its two basic variations (the English sonnet such as "My Mistress' Eyes" and the Italian sonnet such as "On First Looking") a sufficiency of convenient ways to organize their materials into coherent structures.

▽ ▽ ▽

STANZAS AND VERSE FORMS A Glossary

alliteration: the repetition of sounds in nearby words; alliteration usually involves the initial consonant sounds of words (and sometimes internal consonants in stressed syllables)

assonance: the repetition of vowel sounds in a line or series of lines; assonance often affects pace (by unbalancing short and long vowel patterns) and the way words included in the pattern tend to seem underscored

ballad stanza: a four-line stanza, the second and fourth of which are iambic trimeter and rhyme with each other; the first and third lines, in iambic tetrameter, do not rhyme

blank verse: unrhymed iambic pentameter

English or **Shakespearian sonnet**: three four-line stanzas and a couplet (two lines), rhymed *abab cdcd efef gg*

free verse: poetry that avoids regularized meter and has no significant recurrent stress rhythms, although it may use other repetitive patterns—of words, phrases, or structures

heroic couplet: a pair of rhymed lines of iambic pentameter

Italian or **Petrarchan sonnet**: an octave (eight lines) and a sestet (six lines); typically rhymed *abbaabba cdecde*, although it has many variations that still reflect the basic division into two parts

limerick: two lines of rhymed trimeter, two lines of rhymed dimeter, and an additional line of trimeter, the last word of which is the same as, or rhymes with, the last word of the first line

memory devices / mnemonic devices: forms, such as rhyme, built into poems to help reciters remember them

sestina: six six-line stanzas and a final three-line stanza, all unrhymed; but the final word in each line of the first stanza then becomes the final word in other stanzas (though in a different specific pattern); the final stanza uses these words again in a specified way, one in each half line

sonnet: a form, usually only a single stanza, that offers several related possibilities for its rhyme scheme, but is always fourteen lines long and usually written in iambic pentameter

Spenserian stanza: eight lines of iambic pentameter and a ninth line of iambic hexameter, called an alexandrine, rhymed *ababbcbcc*

stanzas: groups of lines with a specific cogency of their own and usually set off from one another by a space

terza rima: the three-line stanza in which Dante wrote *The Divine Comedy*; each iambic pentameter stanza *(aba)* interlocks with the next through rhyme (*bcb*, *cdc*, *ded*, etc.)

tetrameter couplet: a pair of rhymed, four-beat lines

villanelle: contains five three-line stanzas and a final four-line stanza; only two rhyme sounds are permitted in the entire poem, and the first and third lines of the first stanza are repeated, alternately, as the third line of subsequent stanzas until the last

JOHN KEATS

On the Sonnet

If by dull rhymes our English must be chained,
And like Andromeda,[3] the sonnet sweet
Fettered, in spite of painéd loveliness,
Let us find, if we must be constrained,
Sandals more interwoven and complete
To fit the naked foot of Poesy:[4]
Let us inspect the lyre, and weigh the stress
Of every chord,[5] and see what may be gained
By ear industrious, and attention meet;
Misers of sound and syllable, no less
Than Midas[6] of his coinage, let us be
Jealous of dead leaves in the bay-wreath crown;[7]
So, if we may not let the Muse be free,
1819 She will be bound with garlands of her own.

PERCY BYSSHE SHELLEY

Ozymandias[8]

I met a traveler from an antique land
Who said: Two vast and trunkless legs of stone
Stand in the desert. . . . Near them, on the sand,
Half sunk, a shattered visage lies, whose frown,
And wrinkled lip, and sneer of cold command,
Tell that its sculptor well those passions read
Which yet survive, stamped on these lifeless things,
The hand that mocked them, and the heart that fed:
And on the pedestal these words appear:
"My name is Ozymandias, King of Kings:
Look on my works, ye Mighty, and despair!"

3. Who, according to Greek myth, was chained to a rock so that she would be devoured by a sea monster. She was rescued by Perseus, who married her. When she died she was placed among the stars. 4. In a letter that contained this sonnet, Keats expressed impatience with the traditional Petrarchan and Shakespearean sonnet forms: "I have been endeavoring to discover a better sonnet stanza than we have." 5. Lyre-string. 6. The legendary king of Phrygia who asked, and got, the power to turn all he touched to gold. 7. The bay tree was sacred to Apollo, god of poetry, and bay wreaths came to symbolize true poetic achievement. The withering of the bay tree is sometimes considered an omen of death. *Jealous:* suspiciously watchful. 8. The Greek name for Rameses II, 13th-century B.C. pharaoh of Egypt. According to a first century B.C. Greek historian, Diodorus Siculus, the largest statue in Egypt was inscribed: "I am Ozymandias, king of kings; if anyone wishes to know what I am and where I lie, let him surpass me in some of my exploits."

Nothing beside remains. Round the decay
Of that colossal wreck, boundless and bare
The lone and level sands stretch far away.   1818

WILLIAM WORDSWORTH

London, 1802

Milton! thou should'st be living at this hour:
England hath need of thee: she is a fen
Of stagnant waters: altar, sword, and pen,
Fireside, the heroic wealth of hall and bower,
Have forfeited their ancient English dower
Of inward happiness. We are selfish men;
Oh! raise us up, return to us again;
And give us manners, virtue, freedom, power.
Thy soul was like a star, and dwelt apart:
Thou hadst a voice whose sound was like the sea:
Pure as the naked heavens, majestic, free,
So didst thou travel on life's common way,
In cheerful godliness; and yet thy heart
1802   The lowliest duties on herself did lay.

JOHN MILTON

On the Late Massacre in Piedmont[9]

Avenge, O Lord, thy slaughtered saints, whose bones
Lie scattered on the Alpine mountains cold;
Ev'n them who kept thy truth so pure of old,
When all our fathers worshiped stocks and stones,
Forget not: in thy book record their groans
Who were thy sheep, and in their ancient fold
Slain by the bloody Piedmontese, that rolled
Mother with infant down the rocks. Their moans
The vales redoubled to the hills, and they
To Heav'n. Their martyred blood and ashes sow
O'er all th' Italian fields, where still doth sway

9. On Easter Sunday, 1655, the Duke of Savoy's forces massacred 1700 members of the Waldensian sect in the Piedmont in northwestern Italy. The sect, founded in 1170, existed at first within the Roman Catholic Church, but its vigorous condemnation of church rites and policies (especially of the use of icons—see line 4) led to a total break. Until the year of the massacre the group had been allowed freedom of worship.

The triple Tyrant:[1] that from these may grow
A hundredfold who, having learnt thy way,
1655 Early may fly the Babylonian woe.[2]

GWENDOLYN BROOKS

First Fight. Then Fiddle.

First fight. Then fiddle. Ply the slipping string
With feathery sorcery; muzzle the note
With hurting love; the music that they wrote
Bewitch, bewilder. Qualify to sing
Threadwise. Devise no salt, no hempen thing
For the dear instrument to bear. Devote
The bow to silks and honey. Be remote
A while from malice and from murdering.
But first to arms, to armor. Carry hate
In front of you and harmony behind.
Be deaf to music and to beauty blind.
Win war. Rise bloody, maybe not too late
For having first to civilize a space
Wherein to play your violin with grace. 1949

LOUIS MacNEICE

Sunday Morning

Down the road someone is practicing scales,
The notes like little fishes vanish with a wink of tails,
Man's heart expands to tinker with his car
For this is Sunday morning, Fate's great bazaar;
Regard these means as ends, concentrate on this Now,
And you may grow to music or drive beyond Hindhead[3] anyhow,
Take corners on two wheels until you go so fast
That you can clutch a fringe or two of the windy past,
That you can abstract this day and make it to the week of time
A small eternity, a sonnet self-contained in rhyme.
But listen, up the road, something gulps, the church spire
Opens its eight bells out, skulls' mouths which will not tire
To tell how there is no music or movement which secures
Escape from the weekday time. Which deadens and endures. 1935

1. The Pope's tiara has three crowns. 2. Protestants in Milton's day associated Catholicism with Babylonian decadence, called the church "the whore of Babylon," and read the prophecy of Revelation 17 and 18 as an allegory of its coming destruction. 3. In Surrey; the direction of a typical Sunday outing from London.

E. E. CUMMINGS

[a salesman is an it that stinks Excuse]

a salesman is an it that stinks Excuse

Me whether it's president of the you were say
or a jennelman name misder finger isn't
important whether it's millions of other punks
or just a handful absolutely doesn't
matter and whether it's in lonjewray

or shrouds is immaterial it stinks

a salesman is an it that stinks to please

but whether to please itself or someone else
makes no more difference than if it sells
hate condoms education snakeoil vac
uumcleaners terror strawberries democ
ra (caveat emptor[4]) cy superfluous hair

or Think We've Met subhuman rights Before

1944

CLAUDE McKAY

The White House

Your door is shut against my tightened face,
And I am sharp as steel with discontent;
But I possess the courage and the grace
To bear my anger proudly and unbent.
The pavement slabs burn loose beneath my feet,
And passion rends my vitals as I pass,
A chafing savage, down the decent street,
Where boldly shines your shuttered door of glass.
Oh, I must search for wisdom every hour,
Deep in my wrathful bosom sore and raw,
And find in it the superhuman power
To hold me to the letter of your law!
Oh, I must keep my heart inviolate
Against the poison of your deadly hate.

1937

4. Literally, "let the buyer beware": the principle that the seller is not responsible for a product unless he provides a formal guarantee.

LINDA PASTAN

Turnabout

The old dog used to herd me through the street
As if the leash were for my benefit,
And when our walk was over he would sit
A friendly jailer, zealous, at my feet.
My children would pretend that they felt fine
When I was anxious at some hurt of theirs
As if they were the parents, for the tears
At their predicaments were often mine.

And now against the whiteness of the sheet
My mother, white faced, comforts with the story
of Brahms, the boy, who couldn't sleep for worry
Until a chord achieved its harmony,
So down the stairs he crept to play the C.
She means her death will make a circle complete.

1988

SIR PHILIP SIDNEY

[When Nature made her chief work, Stella's eyes][5]

When Nature made her chief work, Stella's eyes,
In color black[6] why wrapped she beams so bright?
Would she in beamy black, like painter wise,
Frame daintiest luster mixed of shades and light?
Or did she else that sober hue devise,
In object best to knit and strength our sight,
Lest if no veil those brave gleams did disguise.
They sunlike should more dazzle than delight?
Or would she her miraculous power show,
That, whereas black seems Beauty's contrary,
She even in black doth make all beauties flow?
Both so and thus: she, minding[7] Love should be
Placed ever there, gave him this mourning weed
To honor all their deaths who for her bleed.

1582

5. From Sidney's sonnet sequence *Astrophel and Stella*, usually credited with having started the vogue of sonnet sequences in Elizabethan England. 6. Black was frequently used in the Renaissance to mean absence of light, and ugly or foul (see line 10). 7. Remembering that.

WILLIAM SHAKESPEARE

[My mistress' eyes are nothing like the sun]

My mistress' eyes are nothing like the sun;
Coral is far more red than her lips' red;
If snow be white, why then her breasts are dun;[8]
If hairs be wires, black wires grow on her head.
I have seen roses damasked[9] red and white,
But no such roses see I in her cheeks;
And in some perfumes is there more delight
Than in the breath that from my mistress reeks.
I love to hear her speak, yet well I know
That music hath a far more pleasing sound;
I grant I never saw a goddess go;[1]
My mistress, when she walks, treads on the ground.
And yet, by heaven, I think my love as rare
As any she belied with false compare.

1609

DIANE ACKERMAN

Sweep Me Through Your Many-Chambered Heart

Sweep me through your many-chambered heart
if you like, or leave me here, flushed
amid the sap-ooze and blossom: one more dish
in the banquet called April, or think me hard-
won all your days full of women. Weeks
later, till I felt your arms around
me like a shackle, heard all the sundown
wizardries the fired body speaks.
Tell me why, if it was no more than this,
the unmuddled tumble, the renegade kiss,
today, rapt in a still life and unaware,
my paintbrush dropped like an amber hawk;
thinking I'd heard your footfall on the stair,
I listened, heartwise, for the knock.

1978

8. Mouse-colored. 9. Variegated. 1. Walk.

HELENE JOHNSON

Sonnet to a Negro in Harlem

You are disdainful and magnificent—
Your perfect body and your pompous gait,
Your dark eyes flashing solemnly with hate,
Small wonder that you are incompetent
To imitate those whom you so despise—
Your shoulders towering high above the throng,
Your head thrown back in rich, barbaric song,
Palm trees and mangoes stretched before your eyes.
Let others toil and sweat for labor's sake
And wring from grasping hands their meed of gold.
Why urge ahead your supercilious feet?
Scorn will efface each footprint that you make.
I love your laughter arrogant and bold.
You are too splendid for this city street.

p. 1927

CLAUDE McKAY

The Harlem Dancer

Applauding youths laughed with young prostitutes
And watched her perfect, half-clothed body sway;
Her voice was like the sound of blended flutes
Blown by black players upon a picnic day.
She sang and danced on gracefully and calm,
The light gauze hanging loose about her form;
To me she seemed a proudly-swaying palm
Grown lovelier for passing through a storm.
Upon her swarthy neck black shiny curls
Luxuriant fell; and tossing coins in praise,
The wine-flushed, bold-eyed boys, and even the girls,
Devoured her shape with eager, passionate gaze;
But looking at her falsely-smiling face,
I knew her self was not in that strange place.

1922

DICK ALLEN

Lost Love

You're in the city, somewhere. I suppose if I stood
On Times Square a year or two I'd find you,

Face pleasant and older, coming out of the subway crowd,
Or studying poinsettias in a florist's window.
A flicker—that would be all. Both of us
Looked so much like others, which of us could be sure
We were not others? Once, we met in a glance.
So, too, in a glance, should both of us disappear.

But I'm lying. Often, on West Coast or East,
I'll be at a movie before the lights go down
And Beauty flees through the meadows from the Beast
Or the boy steps out of a throng to claim his crown
When far down the aisles and rows I'll see you there,
Your body still young, your eyes, your taffeta hair!

p. 1987

QUESTIONS

1. Chart the rhyme scheme of Keats's "On the Sonnet," and then, after a careful reading of the poem aloud, mark the major structural breaks in the poem. At what points do the structural breaks and the breaks in rhyme pattern coincide? At what points do they conflict? Can you account for the variations in terms of the poem's meaning?

2. Study carefully the way "Sunday Morning" is put together structurally. How precisely does its structure conform to the patterns of structure characteristic of most sonnets? Are you comfortable thinking of this poem as a sonnet even though it is written in couplets?

3. Describe the structure of "Turnabout."

4. What conventions of description is "[My mistress' eyes are nothing like the sun]" working against? How can you tell? Describe the tone of the poem. What strategies, beyond the basic one of inverting conventions, help to create the poem's special tone?

5. Characterize the "you" in "Sonnet to a Negro in Harlem." Describe the speaker's tone toward him. Describe the function of setting in the poem.

WRITING SUGGESTIONS

1. Consider the structure of "The White House" and the poem's themes of confinement and exclusion. In what specific ways does the poem use the tight

restrictions of the sonnet form? Write an essay of about two pages on the merger of content and form in the poem.

2. Compare "The Harlem Dancer" (also by Claude McKay) with "The White House," considering the very different uses the sonnet form accommodates. Write a parallel essay to that above in which you show how "The Harlem Dancer" uses the sonnet form to further its themes and tones.

3. Consider carefully the structure and sequencing in "First Fight. Then Fiddle." Notice how various uses of sound in the poem (rhyme, onomatapoeia, and alliteration, for example) help to enforce its themes and tones. In an essay of about 600 words, show the relationship between "sound and sense" in the poem.

9 POETIC "KINDS"

There are all sorts of poems. By now you have experienced poems on a variety of subjects and with a variation of tones, short poems, long poems, poems that rhyme and poems that don't. And there are, of course, other sorts of poems that we haven't looked at. Some poems, for example, are thousands of lines long and differ rather substantially from the poems that can be included in a book like this.

Poems may be classified in a variety of ways, by subject, topic, or theme; by their length, appearance, and formal features; by the way they are organized; by the level of language they use; by the poet's intention and what kinds of effects the poem tries to generate.

Classification may be, of course, simply an intellectual exercise. Recognizing a poem that is an elegy, for example, or a satire, may be very much like the satisfaction involved in recognizing a scarlet tanager, a weeping willow, a French phrase, or a 1967 Ford Thunderbird. Just *knowing* what others don't know gives us a sense of importance, accomplishment, and power. But there are also *uses* for classification: we can experience a poem more fully if we understand early on exactly what kind of poem we are dealing with. A fuller response is possible because the poet has consciously chosen to play by certain defined rules, and the **conventions** he or she employs indicate that certain standard ways of saying things are being employed so as to achieve certain expected effects. The **tradition** that is involved in a particular poetic kind is thus employed by the poet in order to produce predictable standard responses.

A poem that calls itself an "elegy," for example, gives us fair warning of what to expect: its label tells that it will be a serious poem memorializing the death of someone, and we may reasonably expect that its tone will be sad or angry about the death, and reflective about the meaning and direction of the dead person's life, and perhaps ruminative about the implications of the death itself. For example, much of the humor and fun in the following poem is premised on the assumption that readers will recognize the kind of poem they are reading.

CHRISTOPHER MARLOWE

The Passionate Shepherd to His Love

Come live with me and be my love,
And we will all the pleasures prove[1]
That valleys, groves, hills, and fields,
Woods, or steepy mountain yields.

And we will sit upon the rocks,
Seeing the shepherds feed their flocks,
By shallow rivers to whose falls
Melodious birds sing madrigals.

And I will make thee beds of roses
And a thousand fragrant posies,
A cap of flowers, and a kirtle[2]
Embroidered all with leaves of myrtle;

A gown made of the finest wool
Which from our pretty lambs we pull;
Fair lined slippers for the cold,
With buckles of the purest gold;

A belt of straw and ivy buds,
With coral clasps and amber studs:
And if these pleasures may thee move,
Come live with me, and be my love.

The shepherd swains[3] shall dance and sing
For thy delight each May morning:
If these delights thy mind may move,
Then live with me and be my love.

1600

A naive reader might easily protest that a plea such as this one is unrealistic and fanciful and thus feel unsure of the poem's tone. What could such a reader think of a speaker who constructed his argument in such a dreamlike way? But the traditions behind the poem and the conventions of the poetic kind make its intention and effects quite clear. "The Passionate Shepherd" is a pastoral poem, a poetic kind that concerns itself with the simple life of country folk and describes that life in stylized, idealized terms. The people in a pastoral poem are usually (as here) shepherds, although they may be fishermen or other rustics who lead an outdoor life and are involved in tending basic human needs in a simplified society; the world of the poem is one of simplicity, beauty, music,

1. Try. 2. Gown. 3. Youths.

and love. The world always seems timeless in pastoral; people are eternally young, and the season is always spring, usually May. Nature seems endlessly green and the future entirely golden. Difficulty, frustration, disappointment, and obligation do not belong in this world at all; it is blissfully free of problems. Shepherds sing instead of tending sheep here, and they make love and play music instead of having to watch out for wolves in the night. If only the shepherd boy and shepherd girl can agree with each other to make love joyously and passionately, they will live happily ever after. The language of pastoral is informal and fairly simple, although always a bit more sophisticated than that of real shepherds with real problems and real sheep.

Unrealistic? Of course. No real shepherd gets to spend even a single whole day like that, and certainly the world of simple country folk has to cope with the ferocities of nature, human falsehood and knavery, disease, bad weather, old age, moments that are not all green and gold. And probably no poet ever thought that shepherds really live that way, but it is an attractive fantasy, and poets who write pastoral simply choose one formulaic way to isolate a series of idealized moments. Fantasies can be personal and private, of course, but there is also a certain pleasure in shared public fantasies, and one central moment is that moment in a love relationship when two people are contemplating the joys of ecstatic love.

Pastoral poems are not written by shepherds. No doubt shepherds have fantasies too, but theirs probably involve ways of life far removed from sheepfolds and nights outdoors. Pastoral poems are usually written, as here, by city poets who are consciously indulging their "isn't it pretty to think so" thoughts. Pastoral poems involve an urban fantasy of rural bliss. It can be lovely to contemplate a world in which the birds sing only for our delight and other shepherds take care of the sheep, a world in which there is no work that does not turn into magic and in which the lambs bring themselves to us so that we can transform their wool instantly into a beautiful gown. It is also fun to "answer" such a vision. A group of poems on pp. 957–959 provide responses to Marlowe's poem and thus offer a kind of critique of the pastoral vision. But in a sense none is necessary; the pastoral poet builds an awareness of artificiality into the whole idea of the poem. It is conceived in full consciousness that its fantasy avoids implication, and in filtering that implication carefully out of the poem, poets implicitly provide their own criticism of the fantasy world. Satire is, in a sense, the other side of the pastoral world—a city poet who fantasizes about being a shepherd usually knows all about dirt and grime and human failure and urban corruption—and satire and pastoral are often seen as complementary poetic kinds.

Several other poetic kinds are exemplified in this book; and each has its own characteristics and conventions that have become established by tradition, repetition, and habit.

epic	from *Paradise Lost*	p. 729
pastoral	"The Passionate Shepherd to His Love"	p. 851
elegy	"On My First Son"	p. 618
lyric	"The Lamb"	p. 992
ballad	"Frankie and Johnny"	p. 769
protest poem	"Hard Rock Returns . . ."	p. 645
aubade	"The Sun Rising"	p. 883
confessional poem	"Skunk Hour"	p. 1025
meditation	"Love Calls Us . . ."	p. 1072
dramatic monologue	"My Last Duchess"	p. 701
soliloquy	"Soliloquy of the Spanish Cloister"	p. 666

You will find definitions and brief descriptions of these poetic kinds in the glossary. Each of these established kinds is worthy of detailed discussion and study, and your teacher may want to examine in depth how the conventions of several different kinds work. But rather than go through kind after kind with you, I have chosen to include quite a few poems that typify one particular kind, the epigram, so that you can examine one kind in some depth.

The poems at the end of this chapter are all epigrams, and together they add up almost to a definition of that poetic kind. Like most poetic kinds, the epigram has a history that shaped its form and content. Originally, an **epigram** was an inscription upon some object such as a monument, triumphal arch, tombstone, or gate; hence it prized brevity and conciseness because they were absolutely necessary. But over a period of time, the term "epigram" came to mean a short poem that tried to attract attention in the same way that an inscription attracts the eyes of passersby.

As the poems here suggest, epigrams have been popular over a long period of time. The modern tradition of epigrams has two more or less separate ancient sources, one in Greece, one in Rome. In classical Greece, epigrams were composed over a period of 2,000 years; the earliest surviving ones date from the 8th century B.C. Apparently there were several anthologies of epigrams in early times, and fragments of these anthologies were later preserved, especially in large collections like the so-called *Greek Anthology*, which dates from the 10th century A.D. Largely short inscriptions, these epigrams also included some love poems (including many on homosexual love), comments on life and morality, riddles, etc. The father of the Roman tradition is generally agreed to be Martial (Marcus Valerius Martialis, A.D. 40–104 [?]), whose epigrams are witty and satirical. Modern epigrams have more frequently followed Martial's lead, but occasionally the distinctive influence of the older Greek tradition can be seen in the sadder poignancy of such poems as "Parting in Wartime."

Knowing what to do with a poem often is aided by knowing what it is, or what it means to be. Many modern poems are not consciously conceived in terms of a traditional kind, and not all older poems are either, but a knowledge of kind can often provide one more way of deciding what to look for in a poem, helping one to find the right questions to ask.

▽ ▽ ▽

POETIC "KINDS" A Glossary

aubade: a morning song in which the coming of dawn is either celebrated or denounced as a nuisance

ballad: a narrative poem which is, or originally was, meant to be sung; characterized by repetition and often by a repeated refrain (recurrent phrase or series of phrases), ballads were originally a folk creation, transmitted orally from person to person and age to age

confessional poem: a relatively new (or recently defined) kind in which the speaker describes a confused, chaotic state of mind, which becomes a metaphor for the larger world

conventions: standard ways of saying things in verse, employed so as to achieve certain expected effects

dramatic monologue: a monologue set in a specific situation and spoken to someone

elegy: in classical times, any poem on any subject written in "elegiac" meter, but since the Renaissance usually a formal lament for the death of a particular person

epic: a poem that celebrates, in a continuous narrative, the achievements of mighty heroes and heroines, usually in founding a nation or developing a culture, and uses elevated language and a grand, high style

epigram: originally any poem carved in stone (on tombstones, buildings, gates, etc.), but in modern usage a very short, usually witty verse with a quick turn at the end

lyric: originally designated poems meant to be sung to the accompaniment of a lyre; now a short poem in which the speaker expresses intense personal emotion rather than describing a narrative or dramatic situation

meditation: a contemplation of some physical object as a way of reflecting upon some larger truth, often (but not necessarily) a spiritual one

pastoral: a poem (also called an eclogue, a bucolic, or an idyll) that describes the simple life of country folk, usually shepherds who live a timeless, painless (and sheepless) life in a world that is full of beauty, music, and love, and that remains forever green

protest poem: an attack, sometimes indirect, on institutions or social injustices

soliloquy: a monoloque in which the character is alone and speaking only to him- or herself

tradition: an inherited, established, or customary practice

SAMUEL TAYLOR COLERIDGE

What Is an Epigram?

What is an epigram? a dwarfish whole,
Its body brevity, and wit its soul.

p. 1802

BEN JONSON

Epitaph on Elizabeth, L. H.

Wouldst thou hear what man can say
In a little? Reader, stay.
Underneath this stone doth lie
As much beauty as could die;
Which in life did harbor give
To more virtue than doth live.
If at all she had a fault,
Leave it buried in this vault.
One name was Elizabeth;
Th' other, let it sleep with death:
Fitter, where it died, to tell,
Than that it lived at all. Farewell.

1616

PALLADAS

[This life a theater we well may call][4]

This life a theater we well may call,
Where every actor must perform with art;
Or laugh it through and make a farce of all,
Or learn to bear with grace his tragic part.

ca. 400

MARTIAL

[You've told me, Maro, whilst you live][5]

You've told me, Maro, whilst you live
You'd not a single penny give,
But that whene'er you chanced to die,

4. From the *Greek Anthology*. Translated by Robert Bland.

5. Translated from the Latin by F. Lewis.

You'd leave a handsome legacy;
You must be mad beyond redress,
If my next wish you cannot guess.
ca. 100

MARTIAL

[Fair, rich, and young? How rare is her perfection][6]

Fair, rich, and young? How rare is her perfection,
Were it not mingled with one foul infection?
I mean, so proud a heart, so cursed a tongue,
As makes her seem, nor fair, nor rich, nor young.
ca. 80–85

TOM BROWN

[I do not love thee, Dr. Fell][7]

I do not love thee, Dr. Fell,
The reason why I cannot tell:
But this I know, and know full well,
I do not love thee, Dr. Fell.
ca. 1680

JOHN GAY

My Own Epitaph

Life is a jest; and all things show it.
I thought so once; but now I know it.
1720

J. V. CUNNINGHAM

Here Lies My Wife

Here lies my wife. Eternal peace
Be to us both with her decease.
1959

6. Translated from the Latin by Sir John Harington. 7. A version of Martial's "Non Amo Te." According to tradition, Brown while a student at Oxford got into trouble and was taken to the dean, Dr. John Fell; Brown was expelled, but Dr. Fell decided to waive the expulsion if he could translate, extempore, a Martial epigram: this was the result.

RICHARD CRASHAW

An Epitaph upon a Young Married Couple, Dead and Buried Together

To these, whom death again did wed,
This grave's their second marriage-bed.
For though the hand of fate could force
'Twixt soul and body a divorce,
It could not sunder man and wife
'Cause they both livéd but one life.
Peace, good reader. Do not weep.
Peace, the lovers are asleep.
They, sweet turtles,[8] folded lie
In the last knot love could tie.
And though they lie as they were dead,
Their pillow stone, their sheets of lead,
(Pillow hard, and sheets not warm)
Love made the bed; they'll take no harm;
Let them sleep, let them sleep on.
Till this stormy night be gone,
Till th' eternal morrow dawn;
Then the curtains will be drawn
And they wake into a light,
Whose day shall never die in night.

1646

ALEXANDER POPE

Three Epitaphs on John Hewet and Sarah Drew

I

EPITAPH ON JOHN HEWET AND SARAH DREW
IN THE CHURCHYARD AT STANTON HARCOURT

NEAR THIS PLACE LIE THE BODIES OF
JOHN HEWET AND SARAH DREW,
AN INDUSTRIOUS YOUNG MAN AND
VIRTUOUS MAIDEN OF THIS PARISH;
CONTRACTED IN MARRIAGE
WHO BEING WITH MANY OTHERS AT HARVEST
WORK, WHERE BOTH IN AN INSTANT KILLED
BY LIGHTNING ON THE LAST DAY OF JULY
1718

8. Turtledoves.

Think not by rigorous judgment seized,
  A pair so faithful could expire;
Victims so pure Heav'n saw well pleased
  And snatched them in celestial fire.

Live well and fear no sudden fate;
  When God calls virtue to the grave,
Alike 'tis justice, soon or late,
  Mercy alike to kill or save.

Virtue unmoved can hear the call,
And face the flash that melts the ball.

II

When Eastern lovers feed the fun'ral fire,
On the same pile the faithful fair expire;
Here pitying Heav'n that virtue mutual found,
And blasted both, that it might neither wound.
Hearts so sincere th' Almighty saw well pleased,
Sent his own lightning, and the victims seized.

III

Here lie two poor lovers, who had the mishap
1718 Though very chaste people, to die of a clap.

X. J. KENNEDY

Epitaph for a Postal Clerk

Here lies wrapped up tight in sod
Henry Harkins c/o God.
On the day of Resurrection
May be opened for inspection. 1961

DAVID McCORD

Epitaph on a Waiter

By and by
God caught his eye. 1935

COUNTEE CULLEN

For a Lady I Know

She even thinks that up in heaven
Her class lies late and snores,
While poor black cherubs rise at seven
To do celestial chores. 1925

J. V. CUNNINGHAM

All in Due Time

All in due time: love will emerge from hate,
And the due deference of truth from lies.
If not quite all things come to those who wait
They will not need them: in due time one dies. 1950

MATTHEW PRIOR

A True Maid

No, no; for my virginity,
  When I lose that, says Rose, I'll die:
Behind the elms, last night, cried Dick,
  Rose, were you not extremely sick? 1718

EZRA POUND

The Bathtub

As a bathtub lined with white porcelain,
When the hot water gives out or goes tepid,
So is the slow cooling of our chivalrous passion,
O my much praised but-not-altogether-satisfactory lady. p. 1913

FRANCIS QUARLES

[Be sad, my heart, deep dangers wait thy mirth]

Be sad, my heart, deep dangers wait thy mirth:
Thy soul's waylaid by sea, by hell, by earth:
Hell has her hounds; earth, snares; the sea, a shelf;
But, most of all, my heart, beware thyself. 1635

J. V. CUNNINGHAM

History of Ideas

God is love. Then by inversion
Love is God, and sex conversion. 1947

JOHN WILMOT, EARL OF ROCHESTER

Impromptu on Charles II

God bless our good and gracious king,
Whose promise none relies on,
Who never said a foolish thing,
ca. 1670–80 Nor ever did a wise one.

WALTER SAVAGE LANDOR

The Georges[9]

George the First was always reckoned
Vile, but viler George the Second;
And what mortal ever heard
Any good of George the Third?
When from earth the Fourth descended
(God be praised!) the Georges ended. p. 1855

9. British kings who ruled successively from 1714 to 1830.

PETER PINDAR

Epigram

Midas, they say, possessed the art of old
Of turning whatsoe'er he touched to gold;
This modern statesmen can reverse with ease—
Touch *them* with gold, *they'll turn to what you please.*

ca. 1780

HOWARD NEMEROV

Epigram: Political Reflexion

loquitur the sparrow in the zoo[1]

No bars are set too close, no mesh too fine
To keep me from the eagle and the lion,
Whom keepers feed that I may freely dine.
This goes to show that if you have the wit
To be small, common, cute, and live on shit,
Though the cage fret kings, you may make free with it.

1958

FRANCES CORNFORD

Parting in Wartime

How long ago Hector[2] took off his plume,
Not wanting that his little son should cry,
Then kissed his sad Andromache good-bye—
And now we three in Euston[3] waiting-room.

1948

QUESTIONS

1. List all the metaphors you can find in "An Epitaph upon a Young Married Couple, Dead and Buried Together." How closely are the metaphors related to each other? Which metaphors seem especially appropriate to an epitaph? to the epigram as a poetic kind?

1. I.e., the sparrow is the speaker. 2. The noblest chieftain in ancient Troy and husband to Andromache. 3. A London railway station.

2. Which epitaph in the chapter seems to you the most likely actually to end up on a tombstone? Why? What features would prevent most of the "epitaphs" here actually from being used? Which epitaph here seems to you the wittiest? In what, exactly, does the wit consist? Do you like the epigrams better or worse that have a "sting" at the end? Why?

3. Read through a number of the very short poems in this book and pick out one of no more than eight lines that does not seem to you to qualify as an epigram. What features of the poem make that label inappropriate? On the basis of what you know about poetic kinds, can you assign a label to it?

WRITING SUGGESTIONS

1. Using a poetry index (available in the reference section of your college library), find half a dozen poems that use the term "elegy" in their titles, and compare their tones and strategies. Try to decide what features and expectations seem to be central to the poetic kind. Then look back at "On My First Son," often said to be a typical elegy, and write a brief (two-page) analysis of the poem in which you show how it uses and transforms the expectations associated with the elegy as a poetic kind.

2. Choose randomly any six of the epigrams in this chapter, and try to decide on the basis of them what a good definition of the epigram might be. Write down your definition, mentioning any features of epigram that seem to you crucial to the kind. Then choose a seventh poem from the chapter, one that seems to you entirely typical of the epigram kind, and write a brief, three-paragraph analysis of it, showing exactly how it uses features mentioned in your definition.

3. Using one of the poems in this chapter as your model, try your hand at writing an epigram (of no more than four lines) of your own. When you have completed your poem, write a brief paragraph about it, describing how you have used features characteristic of the poetic kind.

10 THE WHOLE TEXT

In the previous nine chapters, we have been thinking about one thing at a time—symbolism, meter, stanza form, and so on—and each poem has been read and discussed primarily in terms of a single problem. Learning to deal with one problem at a time is good educational practice and in the long run will make you a more careful and more effective reader of poems. Still, the elements of poems do not work individually but in combination, and in considering even the simplest elements (speaker, for example, or setting) we have noticed how categories overlap—how, for example, the question of setting in "Cherrylog Road" quickly merges into questions about the speaker, his state of mind, his personality, his distance from the central events in the poem. Thinking about a single issue never fully does justice to an individual poem; no poem depends for all its effects on just one device or one element of craft. Poems are complex wholes that demand varieties of attention, and ultimately all the questions you have been learning to ask need to be applied to any poem you read. Reading any poem fully and well involves all the questions about craft, form, and tradition that you can think to ask. Not all questions are equally relevant to all poems, of course, but moving systematically through your whole list of questions will ultimately enable you to get beyond the fragmentation of particulars and approach the whole poem. It is now time to think about how the various elements of poems work together to create the effects of the whole poem.

Here is a short poem in which several of the issues we have considered come up almost simultaneously:

ELIZABETH JENNINGS

Delay

The radiance of that star that leans on me
Was shining years ago. The light that now
Glitters up there my eye may never see
And so the time lag teases me with how

Love that loves now may not reach me until
Its first desire is spent. The star's impulse
Must wait for eyes to claim it beautiful
And love arrived may find us somewhere else.

1953

In most poems, several issues come up more or less at once, and the separation of issues is a convenience rather than an assertion of priority or order. In "Delay," a lot of the basic questions (about speaker, situation, and setting, for example) seem to be put on hold in the beginning, but if we proceed systematically the poem begins to open itself to us. The first line identifies with "I" (or rather, in this case, "me") of the poem as an observer of the bright star that is the main object in the poem and the principal source of its imagery, its "plot," and its analogical argument. But we learn little detail about the speaker. She surfaces again in lines 4 and 5 and with someone else ("us") in line 8, but she is always in the objective case—acted on rather than acting—and the only "fact" we know about her is that she reasons deeply and at length about the meaning and effect of time lags. We have even less explicit detail about setting and situation; somewhere the speaker is watching a bright star and meditating on the knowledge that she is seeing it long, long after its actual light was sent forth. The time is probably night, but it could be any night, and the place is not specified. The speaker knows some basic facts about the speed of light and the distance of stars from Earth (and so we know that this observation must have taken place after some basic scientific discoveries and mathematical calculations were made), but the only other explicit clue we have about situation involves the "us" of the final line and the fact that the speaker's concern with time seems oddly personal, something that matters to her emotional life—not merely a matter of stellar knowledge.

The poem's language helps us understand much more about the speaker and her situation, as does the poem's structure and stanza form. The most crucial word in the first stanza is probably the verb "leans" (line 1); certainly it is the oddest and most surprising word. Because a star cannot literally *lean* on its observer, the word seems to suggest the speaker's perception of the relationship. Perhaps she feels that the star impinges on her, that she is somehow *subject* to its influence, though not in the popular astrological sense. Here the star influences the speaker because she understands something about the way the universe works and can apply her knowledge of light and light years in an analogical way to her own life: it "leans" because it tells her something about how observers are affected by their relationships to what they observe. And it is worth noticing how fully the speaker thinks of herself as object rather than actor. Here, as throughout the poem, she is acted upon; things happen *to* her—the star leans on her, the time lag teases her (line 4), love may not reach her (line 5), and she (along with someone else) is the object sought in the final line as well.

Other crucial words also help clarify the speaker and her situation. The words "radiance" (line 1) and "[g]litters" (line 3) are fairly standard ones to describe stars, but here their standard meanings are carefully qualified by their position in time. The radiance is from years ago and seems to be unavailable to the speaker, who now sees only glitter, something far less warm and resonant. And the word "impulse" in line 6 invokes technical knowledge about light. Here a star is not impulsive or quickly spent but must "wait" for its reception in the eye of the beholder where it becomes "beautiful"; in physics, an impulse combines force and duration. Hence, the receiver of light—the beholder, the acted upon—comes to be important, and we begin to see why the speaker always appears as object: she is the receiver and interpreter, and the light is not complete—its duration not established—until she receives and interprets it. The star does, after all, *lean* on (depend on) her in some objective sense as well as the subjective one in which she first seemed to report it.

The stanza form suggests that the poem may have stages and that its meaning may emerge in two parts, a suggestion that is in fact confirmed by the poem's structure. The first stanza is entirely about stars and star-gazing, but the second stanza establishes the analogy with love that becomes the poem's central metaphor. Now, too, more becomes clear about the speaker and her situation. Her concern is about delay, "time lag" (line 4), and the fact that "Love that loves now may not reach me until / Its first desire is spent" (lines 5–6), a strong indication that her initial observation of the star is driven by feeling and her emotional context. Her attempt to put the remoteness of feeling into a perspective that will enable understanding and patience becomes the "plot" of the poem, and her final calm recognition about "us"—that "love arrived may find us somewhere else"—is, if not comforting, nevertheless a recognition that patience is important and that some things do last. Even the sounds of the poem—in this case the way rhyme is used—help support the meaning of the poem and the tone it achieves. The rhymes in the first part of the poem are perfect rhymes reflecting the stable sense of ancient stars, while in the second stanza the sounds involve near-rhyme: there is harmony here, but in human life and emotion nothing is quite perfect.

Here is another short poem that deserves similar detailed attention to its several elements:

ANONYMOUS

Western Wind

Western wind, when wilt thou blow,
The small rain down can rain?
Christ, if my love were in my arms
And I in my bed again!

ca. 1300 15th century

Perhaps the most obvious thing to demand attention here is the poem's structure, for its first two lines seem to have little to do with the last two. How are we to account for these two distinct and apparently unrelated directions, the calm concern with natural processes in the first part and the emotional outburst about loneliness and lovelessness in the second? The best route to the whole poem is still to begin with the most simple of questions—who? when? where? what is happening?—and proceed to more difficult and complex ones.

As in "Delay," the speaker here offers little explicit autobiography. In the first two lines, there is no personal information. The question these lines ask could be delivered quite impersonally; they could be part of a philosophical meditation. The abbreviated syntax at the end of line 1 (the question of causality is not fully stated, and we have to supply the "so that" implied at the end of the line) may suggest strong feeling and emotional upset, but it tells us nothing intimate and offers little information except that the time is Spring (that is when the western wind blows). No place is indicated, no year, no particulars of situation. But the next two lines, while remaining inexplicit about exact details, make the speaker's situation clear enough: his love is no longer in his arms, and he wishes she were.

The poem's language is a study in contrast and guides us to see the two-part structure clearly. The question asked of the wind in the first two lines involves straightforward, steady language, but the third line bursts with agony and personal despair. The power of the first word of the third line—especially in an age of belief—suggests a speaker ready to state his loss in the strongest possible terms, and the parallel statements of loss in lines 3 and 4 suggest not only the speaker's physical relationship to his love but also his displacement from home: he is deprived of both place and love, human contact and contact with his past. His longing for a world ordered according to his past experience is structured to parallel his longing for the spring wind that brings the world back to life. The two parts of the poem both express a desire for return—to life, to order, to causal relationships within the world. Setting has in fact become a central theme in the poem, and what the poem expresses tonally involves a powerful desire for stability and belonging—an effect that grows out of our sense of the speaker's situation and character. Speaker, setting, language, and structure here intertwine to create the intense focus of the poem.

Here is another short poem in which the several elements noticeably interrelate:

ROBERT HERRICK

Upon Julia's Clothes

Whenas in silks my Julia goes
Then, then, methinks, how sweetly flows
That liquefaction of her clothes.

Next, when I cast mine eyes, and see
That brave[1] vibration, each way free,
O, how that glittering taketh me!

1648

The poem is unabashed in its admiration of the way Julia looks, and nearly everything in its six short lines contributes to its celebratory tone. Perhaps the most striking thing about the poem involves its unusual, highly suggestive use of words. "[G]oes" at the end of line 1 may be the first word to call special attention to itself, though we will return in a minute to the very first word of the poem. "Walks" or "moves" would seem to be more obvious choices; "goes" is more neutral and less specific and in most circumstances would seem an inferior choice, but here the point seems to be to describe Julia in a kind of seamless and unspecified motion, because the poem is anxious to record the effect on the speaker (already a second element becomes crucial) rather than the specifics of Julia. Another word that seems especially crucial is "liquefaction" (line 3), also an unusual and suggestive word about motion. Again it implies no specific kind of motion, just smoothness and seamlessness, and it is applied not to Julia but to her clothes—the kind of indirection that doesn't really fool anybody. Other words that might repay a close look include "vibration" in line 5 (the speaker is finally willing to be a little more direct), "brave" and "free" (also in line 5), and "glittering" and "taketh" in line 6.

Had we begun conventionally by thinking about speaker, situation, and setting, we would have quickly noticed the precise way that the speaker chose to

1. Handsome, showy.

clothe Julia: "in silks" in which her body and its clothing move almost as one. And we would have noticed that the speaker positions himself almost as voyeur (standing for us as observers, of course, but also himself the central figure in the poem). Not much detail about situation or setting is given (and the speaker is characterized only as a viewer and appreciator), but one thing about the scene is crucial. It takes us back to the first word of the poem, "whenas." The slightly quaint quality of the word may at first obscure, to a modern reader, just what it tells us about the situation, that it is a *kind* of scene rather than a single event. "Whenas" is very close to "whenever"; the speaker's claim seems to be that he responds this way *whenever* Julia dons her silks—apparently fairly often, at least in his memory or imagination.

Most of the speaker's language is sensual and rather provocative (he is anxious to share his responses with others so that *everyone* will know just how "taking" Julia is), but there is one rather elaborate (though somewhat disguised) metaphor that suggests his awareness of his own calculation and its consequences. In the beginning of the second stanza he describes how he "cast" his eyes: it is a metaphor from fishing, a frequent one in love poetry about luring, chasing, and catching. The metaphor continues two lines later, but the angler is himself caught: he is taken by the "glittering" lure. This turning of the tables, drawing as it does on a traditional, common image that is then modified to help characterize the speaker, gives a little depth to the show: whatever the slither and glitter, there is not just showing off and sensuality but a catch in this angling.

Many other elements in the poem are worth comment, especially because they quickly relate to each other. Look at the way the poem uses sounds, first of all picking words like "liquefaction" that are themselves virtually onomatopoeic, but then also using rhyme very cleverly. There are only two rhyme sounds in the poem, one in the first stanza, another in the second. The long *ee* of the second becomes almost an exclamation of its own, and the three words of the first set of rhymes seem to become linked in a kind of separate grammar of their own, as if goes, flows, and clothes are all part of a single action—pretty much what the poem claims on a thematic level. A lot is going on in this short and simple poem, and although a reader can get at it step by step by thinking about element after element, the interlocking of the elements is finally what is most impressive. We need to be flexible enough in our analysis and reading to consider not only all the analytical categories, but also the ways in which they work together.

Going back to poems read earlier in the course—with the methods and approaches you have learned since then—can be a useful exercise in seeing how different elements of poems interrelate. Look, for example, at the stanza divisions in "Cherrylog Road" and consider how the neatly spaced, apparently discrete units work against the sometimes frantic pacing of the poem. Or consider the character of the speaker, or the fundamental metaphor of "wreckage" that sponsors the poem, relative to the idea of speaker. Or go back and read "Woodchucks" while thinking about structural questions, or consider how the effaced speaker works in "Aunt Jennifer's Tigers," or think about metaphor in "The Vacuum."

Here are six new poems to analyze. As you read them, think about the elements discussed in the first nine chapters—but rather than thinking about a single element at a time, try to consider relationships, how the different elements combine to make a whole.

▽ ▽ ▽

W. H. AUDEN

Musée des Beaux Arts[2]

About suffering they were never wrong,
The Old Masters: how well they understood
Its human position; how it takes place
While someone else is eating or opening a window or just walking dully along;
How, when the aged are reverently, passionately waiting
For the miraculous birth, there always must be
Children who did not specially want it to happen, skating
On a pond at the edge of the wood:
They never forgot
That even the dreadful martyrdom must run its course
Anyhow in a corner, some untidy spot
Where the dogs go on with their doggy life and the torturer's horse
Scratches its innocent behind on a tree.

In Brueghel's *Icarus*,[3] for instance: how everything turns away
Quite leisurely from the disaster; the plowman may
Have heard the splash, the forsaken cry,
But for him it was not an important failure; the sun shone

2. The Museum of the Fine Arts, in Brussels. 3. "Landscape with the Fall of Icarus," by Pieter Brueghel the elder (1525?–1569), located in the Brussels Museum. According to Greek myth, Daedalus and his son Icarus escaped from imprisonment by using homemade wings of wax; but Icarus flew too near the sun, the wax melted, and he fell into the sea and drowned. In the Brueghel painting the central figure is a peasant plowing, and several other figures are more immediately noticeable than Icarus who, disappearing into the sea, is easy to miss in the lower right-hand corner. Equally ignored by the figures is a dead body in the woods.

As it had to on the white legs disappearing into the green
Water; and the expensive delicate ship that must have seen
Something amazing, a boy falling out of the sky,
Had somewhere to get to and sailed calmly on.

1938

GEORGE HERBERT

The Collar

I struck the board[4] and cried, "No more;
I will abroad!
What? shall I ever sigh and pine?
My lines[5] and life are free, free as the road,
Loose as the wind, as large as store.[6]
Shall I be still in suit?[7]
Have I no harvest but a thorn
To let me blood, and not restore
What I have lost with cordial[8] fruit?
Sure there was wine
Before my sighs did dry it; there was corn
Before my tears did drown it.
Is the year only lost to me?
Have I no bays[9] to crown it,
No flowers, no garlands gay? All blasted?
All wasted?
Not so, my heart; but there is fruit,
And thou hast hands.
Recover all thy sigh-blown age
On double pleasures: leave thy cold dispute
Of what is fit, and not. Forsake thy cage,
Thy rope of sands,[1]
Which petty thoughts have made, and made to thee
Good cable, to enforce and draw,
And be thy law,
While thou didst wink[2] and wouldst not see.
Away! take heed;
I will abroad.
Call in thy death's-head[3] there; tie up thy fears.
He that forbears
To suit and serve his need,
Deserves his load."

4. Table. 5. Lot. 6. A storehouse; i.e., in abundance. 7. In service to another. 8. Reviving, restorative. 9. Wreaths of triumph. 1. Moral restrictions. 2. I.e., close your eyes to the weaknesses of such restrictions. 3. *Memento mori*, a skull intended to remind people of their mortality.

But as I raved and grew more fierce and wild
At every word,
Methought I heard one calling, *Child!*
And I replied, *My Lord.* 1633

EMILY DICKINSON

[My Life had stood—a Loaded Gun]

My Life had stood—a Loaded Gun—
In Corners—till a Day
The Owner passed—identified—
And carried Me away—

And now We roam in Sovereign Woods—
And now We hunt the Doe—
And every time I speak for Him—
The Mountains straight reply—

And do I smile, such cordial light
Upon the Valley glow—
It is as a Vesuvian face
Had let its pleasure through—

And when at Night—Our good Day done—
I guard My Master's Head—
'Tis better than the Eider-Duck's
Deep Pillow—to have shared—

To foe of His—I'm deadly foe—
None stir the second time—
On whom I lay a Yellow Eye—
Or an emphatic Thumb—

Though I than He—may longer live
He longer must—than I—
For I have but the power to kill,
Without—the power to die—

ca. 1863

ROBERT FROST

Design

I found a dimpled spider, fat and white,
On a white heal-all,[4] holding up a moth

4. A plant, also called the "all-heal" and "self-heal," with tightly clustered violet-blue flowers.

Like a white piece of rigid satin cloth—
Assorted characters of death and blight
Mixed ready to begin the morning right,
Like the ingredients of a witches' broth—
A snow-drop spider, a flower like a froth,
And dead wings carried like a paper kite.

What had that flower to do with being white,
The wayside blue and innocent heal-all?
What brought the kindred spider to that height,
Then steered the white moth thither in the night?
What but design of darkness to appall?—
If design govern in a thing so small.

1936

WALLACE STEVENS

Anecdote of the Jar

I placed a jar in Tennessee,
And round it was, upon a hill.
It made the slovenly wilderness
Surround that hill.

The wilderness rose up to it,
And sprawled around, no longer wild.
The jar was round upon the ground
And tall and of a port in air.

It took dominion everywhere.
The jar was gray and bare.
It did not give of bird or bush,
Like nothing else in Tennessee.

1923

AMY CLAMPITT

Beethoven, Opus 111[5]

FOR *Norman Carey*

There are epochs . . . when mankind, not content with the present, longing for time's deeper layers, like the plowman, thirsts for the virgin soil of time.

—OSIP MANDELSTAM[6]

—Or, conversely, hungers
for the levitations of the concert hall:
the hands like rafts of *putti*[7]
out of a region where the dolorous stars
are fixed in glassy cerements of Art;
the *ancien régime*'s diaphanous plash
athwart the mounting throb of hobnails—
shod squadrons of vibration
mining the air, its struck ores hardening
into a plowshare,[8] a downward wandering
disrupting every formal symmetry:
from the supine harp-case, the strung-foot
tendons under the mahogany, the bulldozer
in the bass unearths a Piranesian[9]
catacomb: Beethoven ventilating,
with a sound he cannot hear,[1] the cave-in
of recurring rage.
                                In the tornado country
of mid-America, my father
might have been his twin—a farmer
hacking at sourdock, at the strangle-
roots of thistles and wild morning glories,
setting out rashly, one October,
to rid the fencerows of poison ivy:

5. "Beethoven's piano sonata No. 32, Opus 111 (the arabic numbers tend to be misread and even, unfortunately, misprinted as a Roman numeral III, which would make it an early rather than a late composition) is his last work in that form, dating to the early 1820s. It figures in Thomas Mann's *Dr. Faustus* (Knopf, 1948; Vintage Books edition pp. 53–56), in E. M. Forster's A *Room with a View* (Knopf, 1932, p. 54), and in Milan Kundera's *The Book of Laughter and Forgetting* (Knopf, 1981, p. 161). I was first exposed to it, so far as I know, at a recital by Norman Carey, to whom the poem is dedicated. The notes by Eric Blom to the recording by Artur Schnabel on the Seraphim label have added much to my own understanding of the music." (Author's note)

6. Russian poet (1891–1938).

7. "The stylized infant cherubs that appear to soar, plunge or hover in some Italian and Spanish paintings on Christian themes." (Author's note)

8. See Isaiah 2:4.

9. Giambattista Piranesi (1720–1778), Italian architect and artist.

1. Beethoven had lost his hearing by the time of this sonata's composition.

livid seed-globs turreted
in trinities of glitter, ripe
with the malefic glee no farmer doubts
lives deep down things. My father
was naïve enough—by nature
revolutionary, though he'd have
disowned the label—to suppose he might
in some way, minor but radical, disrupt
the givens of existence: set
his neighbors' thinking straight, undo
the stranglehold of reasons nations
send their boys off to war. That fall,
after the oily fireworks had cooled down
to trellises of hairy wicks,
he dug them up, rootstocks and all,
and burned them. Do-gooder!
The well-meant holocaust became
a mist of venom, sowing itself along
the sculptured hollows of his overalls,
braceleting wrists and collarbone—
a mesh of blisters spreading to a shirt
worn like a curse. For weeks
he writhed inside it. Awful.
                    High art
with a stiff neck: an upright Steinway[2]
bought in Chicago; a chromo of a Hobbema
tree-avenue, or of Millet's imagined peasant,
the lark she listens to invisible, perhaps
irrelevant: harpstrings and fripperies of air
congealed into an object nailed against the wall,
its sole ironic function (if it has any)
to demonstrate that one, though he may
grunt and sweat at work, is not a clod.
Beethoven might declare the air
his domicile, the winds kin,[3] the tornado
a kind of second cousin; here,
his labor merely shimmers—a deracinated
album leaf, a bagatelle, the "Moonlight"[4]
rendered with a dying fall[5] (the chords
subside, disintegrate, regroup

2. A famous make of piano, the one most often heard in concert halls. 3. "In a letter to Count Brunswick dated February 13, 1814, Beethoven wrote: 'As regards me, great heavens! my dominion is in the air; the tones whirl like the wind, and often there is a whirl in my soul.' Quoted in *Beethoven: The Man and the Artist, as Revealed in His Own Words,* edited by Frederick Kersh and H. E. Krehbiel (Dover, 1964)." (Author's note) 4. Beethoven's most famous piano sonata (Opus 27, No. 2, 1802). *Bagatelle:* a short, light piece for the piano. 5. Shakespeare, *Twelfth Night,* I.i.1: "If music be the food of love, play on; / Give me excess of it, that, surfeiting, / The appetite may sicken, and so die. / That strain again! it had a dying fall . . . ."

in climbing sequences *con brio*); there's
no dwelling on the sweet past here,
there being no past to speak of
other than the setbacks: typhoid
in the wells, half the first settlers
dead of it before a year was out;
diphtheria and scarlet fever
every winter; drought, the Depression,
a mortgage on the mortgage. High art
as a susurrus, the silk and perfume
of unsullied hands. Those hands!—
driving the impressionable wild with anguish
for another life entirely: the Lyceum circuit,
the doomed diving bell of Art.
Beethoven
in his workroom: ear trumpet,[6]
conversation book and pencil, candlestick,
broken crockery, the Graf piano[7]
wrecked by repeated efforts to hear himself—
out of a humdrum squalor the levitations,
the shakes and triplets, the *Adagio*
molto semplice e cantabile,[8] the Arietta
a disintegrating surf of blossom
opening along the keyboard, along the fencerows
the astonishment of sweetness. My father,
driving somewhere in Kansas or Colorado,
in dustbowl country, stopped the car
to dig up by the roots a flower
he'd never seen before—a kind
of prickly poppy most likely, its luminousness
wounding the blank plains like desire.
He mentioned in a letter the disappointment
of his having hoped it might transplant—
an episode that brings me near tears,
still, as even his dying does not—
that awful dying, months-long, hunkered,
irascible. From a clod no plowshare
could deliver, a groan for someone
(because he didn't want to look
at anything) to take away the flowers,
a bawling as of slaughterhouses, slogans
of a general uprising: *Freiheit!*[9]
Beethoven, shut up with the four walls
of his deafness, rehearsing the unhearable
semplice e cantabile, somehow reconstituting

6. A primitive hearing aid. 7. Beethoven played a piano made by Conrad Graf (1782–1851).
8. A slow tempo, "very simple and in a singing manner." 9. Freedom!

the blister shirt of the intolerable
into these shakes and triplets, a hurrying
into flowering along the fencerows: dying,
for my father, came to be like that
finally—in its messages the levitation
of serenity, as though the spirit might
aspire, in its last act,
to walk on air.

1983

QUESTIONS

1. Consider the setting of "Musée des Beaux Arts" both in the sense of the painting and of its location in the museum. In what different ways do the two settings become important? How does the use of setting relate to the way the speaker is conceived? Define the role played by all of the other characters in the poem, including the people on the ship. Whose attitudes (or perhaps words) are being echoed or parodied in line 20? Describe the poem's structure.

2. Consider the elements of speaker and situation simultaneously when you analyze "The Collar."

3. Consider the interrelation of the elements of speaker, words and word order, and stanza form in "[My Life had stood—a Loaded Gun]."

4. Consider the interrelationships among speaker, structure, stanza form, and tone in "Design."

5. Consider the interrelationships among structure, visual effect, stanza form, poetic kind, metaphor, and connotation in "Anecdote of the Jar."

6. Consider the relationship between characterization and structure in "Beethoven, Opus 111."

WRITING SUGGESTIONS

1. Find a reproduction of the Brueghel painting on which Auden's poem is based. "Read" the painting carefully, and notice which details Auden mentions and which he does not. What aspect(s) of the painting does he choose to emphasize? What does he ignore? Write a three-page essay in which you show exactly how Auden *uses* the Brueghel painting in his poem.

2. Consider "Design" as a sonnet. What features of the sonnet seem espe-

cially important to the effects Frost achieves here? Consider the structure, rhyme scheme, and imagery of the poem. Now look at another Frost poem, "Range-Finding" (p. 1006), and ask the same questions about this poem. Which poem seems to you to use the sonnet form more effectively?

Write a four- to five-page essay, comparing the two poems and evaluating their use of the sonnet form.

Exploring Contexts

11 THE AUTHOR'S WORK

Poems are not all written in the same style, as if they were produced by a corporation or put together in a committee. Even though all poets share the same medium (language) and usually have some common notions of their craft, they put the unique resources of their individual minds and consciousnesses into what they create. A poet may use the tradition extensively and share the crafts that others have developed without surrendering his or her own individuality, just as the integrity and uniqueness of an individual are not compromised by characteristics the individual may share with others—political affiliations, religious beliefs, tastes in clothes and music. Sometimes this uniqueness is hard to define—what exactly is it that defines the singular personality of an individual?—but it is always there, and we recognize and depend upon it in our relationships with other people. And so with poets: most don't make a conscious effort to put an individual stamp on their work; they don't have to. The stamp is there, just in the way they choose subjects, words, configurations. Every individual's consciousness uniquely marks what it records, imagines, and decides to print.

Experienced readers can often identify a poem as the distinctive work of an individual poet even though they may never have seen the poem before, much as experienced listeners can identify a particular singer or group after hearing only a few phrases of a new song. Such an ability depends upon a lot of reading of that author, or a lot of listening to music, but any reasonably sensitive reader can learn to do it with great accuracy. Developing such an ability, however, is not really an end in itself; rather, it is a by-product of learning to notice the particular, distinctive qualities in the workmanship of any poet. Once you've read several poems by the same person, you will usually begin to notice some features that they have in common, and gradually you may come to think of those features as characteristic. The poem that follows was written by Howard Nemerov, whose work you have read in some earlier chapters. Before you read it, you may want to look back at his poems printed earlier in this book and remind yourself of what those poems were like or to look ahead at two more of his poems later in the book. (The index will help you find them all.)

HOWARD NEMEROV

A Way of Life

It's been going on a long time.
For instance, these two guys, not saying much, who slog
Through sun and sand, fleeing the scene of their crime,
Till one turns, without a word, and smacks
His buddy flat with the flat of an axe,
Which cuts down on the dialogue
Some, but is viewed rather as normal than sad
By me, as I wait for the next ad.

It seems to me it's been quite a while
Since the last vision of blonde loveliness
Vanished, her shampoo and shower and general style
Replaced by this lean young lunk-
head parading along with a gun in his back to confess
How yestereve, being drunk
And in a state of existential despair,
He beat up his grandma and pawned her invalid chair.

But here at last is a pale beauty
Smoking a filter beside a mountain stream,
Brief interlude, before the conflict of love and duty
Gets moving again, as sheriff and posse expound,
Between jail and saloon, the American Dream
Where Justice, after considerable horsing around,
Turns out to be Mercy; when the villain is knocked off,
A kindly uncle offers syrup for my cough.

And now these clean-cut athletic types
In global hats are having a nervous debate
As they stand between their individual rocket ships
Which have landed, appropriately, on some rocks
Somewhere in Space, in an atmosphere of hate
Where one tells the other to pull up his socks

And get going, he doesn't say where; they fade,
And an angel food cake flutters in the void.

I used to leave now and again;
No more. A lot of violence in American life
These days, mobsters and cops all over the scene.
But there's a lot of love, too, mixed with the strife,
And kitchen-kindness, like a bedtime story
With rich food and a more kissable depilatory.
Still, I keep my weapons handy, sitting here
Smoking and shaving and drinking the dry beer. 1967

What does this poem have in common with Nemerov's other poems? The concern with contemporary life, the tendency to concentrate on modern conveniences and luxuries, and the interest in isolating and defining aspects of the distinctively modern sensibility are all characteristic of Nemerov, as is the tendency to create a short drama, with a speaker who is not altogether admirable. Several of Nemerov's other poems also share an attitude that seems deeply imbedded in this poem, a kind of anti-romanticism that emerges when someone tries to sound or feel *too* proud or cheerful and is shown, by events in the poem, to be part of a grimmer reality instead. The concentration upon one or more physical objects is also characteristic, and often (as in "The Vacuum") the main object is a mechanical one that symbolizes modernity and our modern dependency on things rather than our concern with human relationships. Americanness is made emphatic here too, as if the poem were concerned to help us define our culture and its habits and values. The mood of loneliness is also characteristic, and so is the poem's witty conversational style. The verbal wit here—although not as prominent as the puns and double-entendres of "Boom!"—is characteristically informal. Often it seems to derive from the language of commercials and street speech, and the undercutting of this language by the poet—having a paranoid and simple-minded speaker talk about a gangster in "a state of existential despair"—is similar to the strategy of "Boom!" or "The Vacuum." The regular stanzas, rhymed but not in a traditional or regular way and with a number of near-rhymes, are also typical. Nemerov's thematic interests and ideas, his verbal style, and his cast of mind are all plainly visible in "A Way of Life."

Noticing common features does not mean that every poem by a particular author will be predictable and contain all these features. Most poets like to experiment with new subjects, tones, forms, and various kinds of poetic strategies and devices. But a characteristic way of thinking—the distinct stamp imposed by a unique consciousness—is likely to be visible anyway. The work of any writer will have certain *tendencies* that are identifiable, although not all of them will show up in any one poem.

Of what practical use is it to notice the distinctive voice and mind of a particular poet? One use (not the most important one for the casual reader, but one that nonetheless gives pleasure) is the pleasant surprise that occurs when you recognize something familiar. Reading a new poem by a poet with whom you are already familiar is a bit like meeting an old friend whose face or conversation reminds you of experiences you have had together. Poetic friendships can be treasures just as personal friendships are, even though they are necessarily more distant and somewhat more abstract. Just as novelty—meeting something or someone altogether new to you—is one kind of pleasure, so revisiting or recalling the familiar is another, its equal and opposite. Just *knowing* and *recognizing* often feel good—in and for themselves.

But there are other reasons, also, to look at the various works of a single writer. Just as you learn from watching other people—seeing how they react and respond to people and events, observing how they cope with their lives—you also learn from watching poets at work, seeing how they learn and develop, how they change their minds, how they discover the reach and limits of their imaginations and talents, how they find their distinctive voices and come to terms with their own identities. Watching someone at work over a period of years (as you can Adrienne Rich in the selection at the end of this chapter) is a little like watching an autobiography unfold, except that the individual poems continue to exist separately and for themselves as well as provide a record of a distinctive but gradually changing and evolving consciousness.

A third reason to study in some detail the work of a single individual is a very practical one: the more you know about the poet, the better a reader you are likely to be of any individual poem by that poet. It is not so much that the external facts of a writer's life find their way into whatever he or she writes—be it poem, essay, letter, or autobiography—but that a reader gets used to habits and manners, of knowing what to expect. Coming to a new poem by a poet you already know is not completely an experience fresh and new. You adjust faster, know better what to look for, have some specific expectations (although they may be unconscious and unarticulated) of what the poem will be like. The more poems you read by any author, the better a reader you are likely to be of any one poem.

Before you read the following poem by John Donne, look at the poems by him that appear elsewhere in this book (check the index of authors). What features in these poems seem most striking and distinctive to you as you review them as a group?

JOHN DONNE

The Sun Rising

Busy old fool, unruly sun,
Why dost thou thus,
Through windows, and through curtains, call on us?
Must to thy motions lovers' seasons run?
Saucy pedantic wretch, go chide
Late schoolboys, and sour prentices,[1]
Go tell court-huntsmen that the king will ride,
Call country ants[2] to harvest offices;
Love, all alike, no season knows, nor clime,
Nor hours, days, months, which are the rags of time.

Thy beams, so reverend and strong
Why shouldst thou think?
I could eclipse and cloud them with a wink,
But that I would not lose her sight so long:
If her eyes have not blinded thine,
Look, and tomorrow late, tell me
Whether both the Indias[3] of spice and mine
Be where thou left'st them, or lie here with me.
Ask for those kings whom thou saw'st yesterday,
And thou shalt hear, all here in one bed lay.

She is all states, and all princes I,
Nothing else is.
Princes do but play us; compared to this,
All honor's mimic, all wealth alchemy.[4]
Thou, sun, art half as happy as we,
In that the world's contracted thus;
Thine age asks[5] ease, and since thy duties be
To warm the world, that's done in warming us.
Shine here to us, and thou art every where;
This bed thy center[6] is, these walls thy sphere. 1633

1. Apprentices. 2. Farmworkers. 3. The East and West Indies, commercial sources of spices and gold. 4. Imposture, like the "scientific" procedures for turning base metals into gold. *Mimic:* hypocritical. 5. Requires. 6. Of orbit.

Is "The Sun Rising" somewhat easier to read than the first Donne poem you read this term? What kind of expectations did you have of the poem, knowing it was by the same author as other poems you had read? How conscious were you of those expectations? Did they enable you to ask more intelligent questions of the poem as you read it? How conscious were you, as you read, of the subject matter of other Donne poems? of their themes? tone? style? form? sound effects? of other poetic devices? Did you consciously expect a speaker and a dramatic situation? How quickly did you decide what the situation was? How quickly did you identify the setting? Did you find that you had certain expectations of the speaker once you had sensed the poem's subject and situation? In retrospect, how similar to other Donne poems does this one seem? In what specific ways?

The skills involved here are progressive: they don't come all at once like a flash of lightning. Rather, they develop over time, as do most of the more sophisticated reading skills we will be considering in the final chapters of this book, and they develop in conjunction with skills you have already worked on in the previous chapters. Don't worry if you still have difficulty with a new Donne poem. You are in good company: Donne isn't easy. But the more you read, the better you will get. Reading ten or a dozen poems by a single author is better than reading three or four, not only because your generalizations and the expectations they create will be more reliable but also because you will feel increasingly comfortable. Spending some hours in the library reading several new poems by a poet you like and admire can be a very satisfying experience; work with any author long enough, and you will begin to feel positively at home. But even then, a good poet will still surprise you in every new poem, at least to some extent. Being reliable and distinctive is not the same as being totally predictable.

The two groups of poems that follow indicate both the distinctiveness of an individual poet's voice and the variety that often exists within that distinctiveness. The poems by John Keats suggest the pervasive sensuous and sensual quality of his work, his fascination with medieval times and gothic states of mind, his attraction both to nature and to highly ornate artifices, his distinctive patterns of phrasing and use of poetic devices, and the recurrent contrasts in his work between an external world of "objective" reality and internal states of "subjective" consciousness. Prose selections from a preface and from several of Keats's personal letters underscore some of his most persistent poetic and personal concerns. The poems are arranged chronologically, and a chronology of his life suggests the potential relevance of biographical information.

While Adrienne Rich's distinctive poetic voice emerges from the representative selection here, the corpus of her work also illustrates change and development. Rich herself describes these changes in the prose selections and in notes appended to "Snapshots of a Daughter-in-Law," "Orion," and "Planetarium." You may also want to look back at what Rich has said about "Aunt Jennifer's Tigers" (p. 000).

▽ ▽ ▽

JOHN KEATS

On First Looking into Chapman's Homer[7]

Much have I traveled in the realms of gold,
And many goodly states and kingdoms seen;
Round many western islands have I been
Which bards in fealty[8] to Apollo hold.
Oft of one wide expanse had I been told
That deep-browed Homer ruled as his demesne;
Yet did I never breathe its pure serene[9]
Till I heard Chapman speak out loud and bold:
Then felt I like some watcher of the skies
When a new planet swims into his ken;[1]
Or like stout Cortez[2] when with eagle eyes
He stared at the Pacific—and all his men
Looked at each other with a wild surmise—
Silent, upon a peak in Darien.

1816

On the Grasshopper and the Cricket

The poetry of earth is never dead:
When all the birds are faint with the hot sun,
And hide in cooling trees, a voice will run
From hedge to hedge about the new-mown mead;
That is the grasshopper's—he takes the lead
In summer luxury—he has never done
With his delights; for when tired out with fun

7. George Chapman's were among the most famous Renaissance translations; his *Iliad* was completed in 1611, *The Odyssey* in 1616. Keats wrote the sonnet after being led to Chapman by his former teacher and reading *The Iliad* all night long. 8. Literally, the loyalty owed by a vassal to his feudal lord. Apollo was the Greek god of poetry and music. 9. Atmosphere. 1. Range of vision. 2. Actually, Balboa; he first viewed the Pacific from Darien, in Panama.

He rests at ease beneath some pleasant weed.
The poetry of earth is ceasing never:
On a lone winter evening, when the frost
Has wrought a silence, from the stove there shrills
The cricket's song, in warmth increasing ever,
And seems to one in drowsiness half lost,
The grasshopper's among some grassy hills.

December 30, 1816

On Seeing the Elgin Marbles[3]

My spirit is too weak—mortality
Weighs heavily on me like unwilling sleep,
And each imagined pinnacle and steep
Of godlike hardship tells me I must die
Like a sick eagle looking at the sky.
Yet 'tis a gentle luxury to weep
That I have not the cloudy winds to keep
Fresh for the opening of the morning's eye.
Such dim-conceived glories of the brain
Bring round the heart an indescribable feud;
So do these wonders a most dizzy pain,
That mingles Grecian grandeur with the rude
Wasting of old Time—with a billowy main—
A sun—a shadow of a magnitude.

1817

from Endymion (Book I)[4]

A thing of beauty is a joy for ever:
Its loveliness increases; it will never
Pass into nothingness; but still will keep
A bower quiet for us, and a sleep
Full of sweet dreams, and health, and quiet breathing.
Therefore, on every morrow, are we wreathing
A flowery band to bind us to the earth,
Spite of despondence, of the inhuman dearth
Of noble natures, of the gloomy days,
Of all the unhealthy and o'er-darkened ways

3. Figures and friezes from the Athenian Parthenon. They were purchased from the Turks (who controlled Athens) by Lord Elgin, brought to England in 1806, and then sold to the British Museum, where Keats saw them.

4. Keats's long poem about the myth of a mortal (Endymion) loved by the goddess of the moon.

Made for our searching: yes, in spite of all,
Some shape of beauty moves away the pall
From our dark spirits. Such the sun, the moon,
Trees old, and young sprouting a shady boon
For simple sheep; and such are daffodils
With the green world they live in; and clear rills
That for themselves a cooling covert make
'Gainst the hot season; the mid forest brake,[5]
Rich with a sprinkling of fair musk-rose blooms:
And such too is the grandeur of the dooms[6]
We have imagined for the mighty dead;
All lovely tales that we have heard or read:
An endless fountain of immortal drink,
Pouring unto us from the heaven's brink.
Nor do we merely feel these essences
For one short hour; no, even as the trees
That whisper round a temple become soon
Dear as the temple's self, so does the moon,
The passion poesy, glories infinite,
Haunt us till they become a cheering light
Unto our souls, and bound to us so fast,
That, whether there be shine, or gloom o'ercast,
1817 They always must be with us, or we die.

When I Have Fears

When I have fears that I may cease to be
Before my pen has gleaned my teeming brain,
Before high-pilèd books, in charact'ry,
Hold like rich garners the full-ripened grain;
When I behold, upon the night's starred face,
Huge cloudy symbols of a high romance,
And think that I may never live to trace
Their shadows, with the magic hand of chance;
And when I feel, fair creature of an hour!
That I shall never look upon thee more,
Never have relish in the faery power
Of unreflecting love!—then on the shore
Of the wide world I stand alone, and think
1818 Till Love and Fame to nothingness do sink.

5. Thicket. 6. Judgments.

To Sleep

O soft embalmer of the still midnight,
Shutting, with careful fingers and benign,
Our gloom-pleased eyes, embowered from the light,
Enshaded in forgetfulness divine;
O soothest[7] Sleep! if so it please thee, close,
In midst of this thine hymn, my willing eyes,
Or wait the amen, ere thy poppy[8] throws
Around my bed its lulling charities;
Then save me, or the passéd day will shine
Upon my pillow, breeding many woes;
Save me from curious conscience, that still lords[9]
Its strength for darkness, burrowing like a mole;
Turn the key deftly in the oiléd wards,[1]
And seal the hushéd casket of my soul.

April 1819

Ode to a Nightingale

I

My heart aches, and a drowsy numbness pains
My sense, as though of hemlock I had drunk,
Or emptied some dull opiate to the drains
One minute past, and Lethe-wards[2] had sunk:
'Tis not through envy of thy happy lot,
But being too happy in thine happiness,
That thou, light-wingéd Dryad[3] of the trees,
In some melodious plot
Of beechen green, and shadows numberless,
Singest of summer in full-throated ease.

II

O, for a draught of vintage! that hath been
Cooled a long age in the deep-delvéd earth,
Tasting of Flora[4] and the country green,
Dance, and Provençal song,[5] and sunburnt mirth!
O for a beaker full of the warm South,

7. Softest. 8. Because opium derives from it, the poppy was associated with sleep. 9. Marshals. *Curious:* scrupulous. 1. Ridges in a lock that distinguish proper from improper keys. 2. Toward the river of forgetfulness (Lethe) in Hades. 3. Wood nymph. 4. Roman goddess of flowers. 5. The medieval troubadors of Provence were famous for their love songs.

Full of the true, the blushful Hippocrene,[6]
With beaded bubbles winking at the brim,
And purple-stainéd mouth;
That I might drink, and leave the world unseen,
And with thee fade away into the forest dim:

III

Fade far away, dissolve, and quite forget
What thou among the leaves hast never known,
The weariness, the fever, and the fret
Here, where men sit and hear each other groan;
Where palsy shakes a few, sad, last gray hairs,
Where youth grows pale, and specter-thin, and dies;
Where but to think is to be full of sorrow
And leaden-eyed despairs,
Where Beauty cannot keep her lustrous eyes,
Or new Love pine at them beyond tomorrow.

IV

Away! away! for I will fly to thee,
Not charioted by Bacchus and his pards,[7]
But on the viewless[8] wings of Poesy,
Though the dull brain perplexes and retards:
Already with thee! tender is the night,
And haply the Queen-Moon is on her throne,
Clustered around by all her starry Fays;[9]
But here there is no light,
Save what from heaven is with the breezes blown
Through verdurous glooms and winding mossy ways.

V

I cannot see what flowers are at my feet,
Nor what soft incense hangs upon the boughs,
But, in embalméd[1] darkness, guess each sweet
Wherewith the seasonable month endows
The grass, the thicket, and the fruit-tree wild;
White hawthorn, and the pastoral eglantine;[2]
Fast fading violets covered up in leaves;
And mid-May's eldest child,
The coming musk-rose, full of dewy wine,
The murmurous haunt of flies on summer eves.

6. The fountain of the Muses on Mt. Helicon, whose waters bring poetic inspiration. 7. The Roman god of wine was sometimes portrayed in a chariot drawn by leopards. 8. Invisible. 9. Fairies. 1. Fragrant, aromatic. 2. Sweetbriar or honeysuckle.

VI

Darkling[3] I listen; and, for many a time
I have been half in love with easeful Death,
Called him soft names in many a muséd rhyme,
To take into the air my quiet breath;
Now more than ever seems it rich to die,
To cease upon the midnight with no pain,
While thou art pouring forth thy soul abroad
In such an ecstasy!
Still wouldst thou sing, and I have ears in vain—
To thy high requiem become a sod.

VII

Thou wast not born for death, immortal Bird!
No hungry generations tread thee down;
The voice I hear this passing night was heard
In ancient days by emperor and clown:
Perhaps the selfsame song that found a path
Through the sad heart of Ruth,[4] when, sick for home,
She stood in tears amid the alien corn;
The same that ofttimes hath
Charmed magic casements, opening on the foam
Of perilous seas, in faery lands forlorn.

VIII

Forlorn! the very word is like a bell
To toll me back from thee to my sole self!
Adieu! the fancy cannot cheat so well
As she is famed to do, deceiving elf.
Adieu! adieu! thy plaintive anthem fades
Past the near meadows, over the still stream,
Up the hillside; and now 'tis buried deep
In the next valley-glades:
Was it a vision, or a waking dream?
Fled is that music:—Do I wake or sleep?

May 1819

3. In the dark. 4. A virtuous Moabite widow who, according to the Old Testament Book of Ruth, left her own country to accompany her mother-in-law Naomi back to Naomi's native land. She supported herself as a gleaner.

Ode on a Grecian Urn

I

Thou still unravished bride of quietness,
Thou foster-child of silence and slow time,
Sylvan[5] historian, who canst thus express
A flowery tale more sweetly than our rhyme:
What leaf-fringed legend haunts about thy shape
Of deities or mortals, or of both,
In Tempe or the dales of Arcady?[6]
What men or gods are these? What maidens loath?
What mad pursuit? What struggle to escape?
What pipes and timbrels? What wild ecstasy?

II

Heard melodies are sweet, but those unheard
Are sweeter; therefore, ye soft pipes, play on;
Not to the sensual[7] ear, but, more endeared,
Pipe to the spirit ditties of no tone:
Fair youth, beneath the trees, thou canst not leave
Thy song, nor ever can those trees be bare;
Bold Lover, never, never canst thou kiss,
Though winning near the goal—yet, do not grieve
She cannot fade, though thou hast not thy bliss,
For ever wilt thou love, and she be fair!

III

Ah, happy, happy boughs! that cannot shed
Your leaves, nor ever bid the Spring adieu;
And, happy melodist, unwearièd,
For ever piping songs for ever new;
More happy love! more happy, happy love!
For ever warm and still to be enjoyed,
For ever panting, and for ever young;
All breathing human passion far above,
That leaves a heart high-sorrowful and cloyed,
A burning forehead, and a parching tongue.

5. Rustic. The urn depicts a woodland scene. 6. Arcadia. Tempe is a beautiful valley near Mt. Olympus in Greece, and the valley ("dales") of Arcadia a picturesque section of the Peloponnesus; both came to be associated with the pastoral ideal. 7. Of the senses, as distinguished from the "ear" of the spirit or imagination.

IV

Who are these coming to the sacrifice?
To what green altar, O mysterious priest,
Lead'st thou that heifer lowing at the skies,
And all her silken flanks with garlands dressed?
What little town by river or sea shore,
Or mountain-built with peaceful citadel,
Is emptied of this folk, this pious morn?
And, little town, thy streets for evermore
Will silent be; and not a soul to tell
Why thou art desolate, can e'er return.

V

O Attic shape! Fair attitude! with brede[8]
Of marble men and maidens overwrought,[9]
With forest branches and the trodden weed;
Thou, silent form, dost tease us out of thought
As doth eternity: Cold Pastoral!
When old age shall this generation waste,
Thou shalt remain, in midst of other woe
Than ours, a friend to man, to whom thou say'st,
Beauty is truth, truth beauty[1]—that is all
Ye know on earth, and all ye need to know.

May 1819

Ode on Melancholy

I

No, no, go not to Lethe,[2] neither twist
Wolfsbane, tight-rooted, for its poisonous wine;[3]
Nor suffer thy pale forehead to be kissed
By nightshade, ruby grape of Proserpine;
Make not your rosary of yew-berries,[4]
Nor let the beetle, nor the death-moth be

8. Woven pattern. *Attic:* Attica was the district of ancient Greece surrounding Athens. 9. Ornamented all over. 1. In some texts of the poem "Beauty is truth, truth beauty" is in quotation marks and in some texts it is not, leading to critical disagreements about whether the last line and a half are also inscribed on the urn or spoken by the poet. 2. The river of forgetfulness in Hades. 3. Like nightshade (line 4), wolfsbane is a poisonous plant. "Proserpine": Queen of Hades. 4. Which often grow in cemeteries and which are traditionally associated with death.

Your mournful Psyche,[5] nor the downy owl
A partner in your sorrow's mysteries;
For shade to shade will come too drowsily,
And drown the wakeful anguish of the soul.

II

But when the melancholy fit shall fall
Sudden from heaven like a weeping cloud,
That fosters the droop-headed flowers all,
And hides the green hill in an April shroud;
Then glut thy sorrow on a morning rose,
Or on the rainbow of the salt sand-wave,
Or on the wealth of globéd peonies;
Or if thy mistress some rich anger shows,
Emprison her soft hand, and let her rave,
And feed deep, deep upon her peerless eyes.

III

She[6] dwells with Beauty—Beauty that must die;
And Joy, whose hand is ever at his lips
Bidding adieu; and aching Pleasure nigh,
Turning to poison while the bee-mouth sips:
Ay, in the very temple of Delight
Veiled Melancholy has her sov'reign shrine,
Though seen of none save him whose strenuous tongue
Can burst Joy's grape against his palate fine;[7]
His soul shall taste the sadness of her might,
And be among her cloudy trophies hung.[8]

May 1819

To Autumn

I

Season of mists and mellow fruitfulness,
Close bosom-friend of the maturing sun;
Conspiring with him how to load and bless
With fruit the vines that round the thatch-eves run;

5. *Psyche* means both "soul" and "breath," and sometimes it was anciently represented by a moth leaving the mouth at death. Owls and beetles were also traditionally associated with darkness and death. 6. The goddess Melancholy, whose chief place of worship ("shrine") is described in lines 25–26. 7. Sensitive, discriminating. 8. The ancient Greeks and Romans hung trophies in their gods' temples.

To bend with apples the mossed cottage-trees,
 And fill all fruit with ripeness to the core;
  To swell the gourd, and plump the hazel shells
With a sweet kernel; to set budding more,
 And still more, later flowers for the bees,
 Until they think warm days will never cease,
  For Summer has o'er-brimmed their clammy cells.

II

Who hath not seen thee oft amid thy store?
 Sometimes whoever seeks abroad may find
Thee sitting careless on a granary floor,
 Thy hair soft-lifted by the winnowing wind;[9]
Or on a half-reaped furrow sound asleep,
 Drowsed with the fume of poppies, while thy hook[1]
  Spares the next swath and all its twinéd flowers:
And sometimes like a gleaner thou dost keep
 Steady thy laden head across a brook;
 Or by a cider-press, with patient look,
  Thou watchest the last oozings hours by hours.

III

Where are the songs of Spring? Ay, where are they?
 Think not of them, thou hast thy music too—
While barréd clouds bloom the soft-dying day,
 And touch the stubble-plains with rosy hue;
Then in a wailful choir the small gnats mourn
 Among the river sallows,[2] borne aloft
  Or sinking as the light wind lives or dies;
And full-grown lambs loud bleat from hilly bourn;[3]
 Hedge-crickets sing; and now with treble soft
 The red-breast whistles from a garden-croft;[4]
  And gathering swallows twitter in the skies.

September 19, 1819

from Letter to Benjamin Bailey, November 22, 1817[5]

* * * I am certain of nothing but of the holiness of the Heart's affections and the truth of Imagination—What the imagination seizes as Beauty must be truth—whether it existed before or not—for I have the same Idea of all our Passions as

9. Which sifts the grain from the chaff. 1. Scythe or sickle. 2. Willows. 3. Domain.
4. An enclosed garden near a house. 5. Keats's private letters, often carelessly written, are reprinted uncorrected.

of Love they are all in their sublime, creative of essential Beauty * * The Imagination may be compared to Adam's dream[6]—he awoke and found it truth. I am the more zealous in this affair, because I have never yet been able to perceive how any thing can be known for truth by consequitive reasoning—and yet it must be—Can it be that even the greatest Philosopher ever ~~when~~ arrived at his goal without putting aside numerous objections—However it may be, O for a Life of Sensations rather than of Thoughts! It is "a Vision in the form of Youth" a Shadow of reality to come—and this consideration has further conv[i]nced me for it has come as auxiliary to another favorite Speculation of mine, that we shall enjoy ourselves here after by having what we called happiness on Earth repeated in a finer tone and so repeated—And yet such a fate can only befall those who delight in sensation rather than hunger as you do after Truth—Adam's dream will do here and seems to be a conviction that Imagination and its empyreal reflection is the same as human Life and its spiritual repetition. But as I was saying—the simple imaginative Mind may have its rewards in the repeti[ti]on of its own silent Working coming continually on the spirit with a fine suddenness—to compare great things with small—have you never by being surprised with an old Melody—in a delicious place—by a delicious voice, fe[l]t over again your very speculations and surmises at the time it first operated on your soul—do you not remember forming to yourself the singer's face more beautiful that [*for* than] it was possible and yet with the elevation of the Moment you did not think so—even then you were mounted on the Wings of Imagination so high—that the Prototype must be here after—that delicious face you will see—What a time! I am continually running away from the subject—sure this cannot be exactly the case with a complex Mind—one that is imaginative and at the same time careful of its fruits—who would exist partly on sensation partly on thought—to whom it is necessary that years should bring the philosophic Mind—such an one I consider your's and therefore it is necessary to your eternal Happiness that you not only ~~have~~ drink this old Wine of Heaven which I shall call the redigestion of our most ethereal Musings on Earth; but also increase in knowledge and know all things. * * *

from Letter to George and Thomas Keats, December 21, 1817

* * * I spent Friday evening with Wells[7] & went the next morning to see *Death on the Pale horse.*[8] It is a wonderful picture, when West's age is considered; But there is nothing to be intense upon; no women one feels mad to kiss, no face swelling into reality. the excellence of every Art is its intensity, capable of making all disagreeables evaporate, from their being in close relationship with Beauty & Truth—Examine King Lear & you will find this examplified throughout; but in

6. In *Paradise Lost*, VIII, 460–90. 7. Charles Wells (1800–1879), an author. 8. By Benjamin West (1738–1820), American painter and president of the Royal Academy; *Christ Rejected* (mentioned below) is also by West.

this picture we have unpleasantness without any momentous depth of speculation excited, in which to bury its repulsiveness—The picture is larger than Christ rejected—I dined with Haydon the sunday after you left, & had a very pleasant day, I dined too (for I have been out too much lately) with Horace Smith & met his two Brothers with Hill & Kingston & one Du Bois,[9] they only served to convince me, how superior humour is to wit in respect to enjoyment—These men say things which make one start, without making one feel, they are all alike; their manners are alike; they all know fashionables; they have a mannerism in their very eating & drinking, in their mere handling a Decanter—They talked of Kean[1] & his low company—Would I were with that company instead of yours said I to myself! I know such like acquaintance will never do for me & yet I am going to Reynolds, on wednesday—Brown & Dilke walked with me & back from the Christmas pantomime. I had not a dispute but a disquisition with Dilke, on various subjects; several things dovetailed in my mind, & at once it struck me, what quality went to form a Man of Achievement especially in Literature & which Shakespeare posessed so enormously—I mean *Negative Capability*, that is when man is capable of being in uncertainties, Mysteries, doubts, without any irritable reaching after fact & reason—Coleridge, for instance, would let go by a fine isolated verisimilitude caught from the Penetralium of mystery, from being incapable of remaining content with half knowledge. This pursued through Volumes would perhaps take us no further than this, that with a great poet the sense of Beauty overcomes every other consideration, or rather obliterates all consideration.

Letter to John Hamilton Reynolds, February 19, 1818

I have an idea that a Man might pass a very pleasant life in this manner—let him on any certain day read a certain Page of full Poesy or distilled Prose and let him wander with it, and muse upon it, and reflect from it, and bring home to it, and prophesy upon it, and dream upon it—untill it becomes stale—but when will it do so? Never—When Man has arrived at a certain ripeness in intellect any one grand and spiritual passage serves him as a starting post towards all "the two-and-thirty Pallaces"[2] How happy is such a "voyage of conception," what delicious diligent Indolence! A doze upon a Sofa does not hinder it, and a nap upon Clover engenders ethereal finger-pointings—the prattle of a child gives it wings, and the converse of middle age a strength to beat them—a strain of musick conducts to "an odd angle of the Isle",[3] and when the leaves whisper it puts a girdle round the earth",[4] Nor will this sparing touch of noble Books be any irreverance to their Writers—for perhaps the honors paid by Man to Man are

9. Thomas Hill (1760–1840), a book collector, and Edward duBois (1774–1850), a journalist.
1. Edmund Kean (1789–1833), a famous Shakespearean actor.
2. "Places of delight" in Buddhism.
3. *The Tempest*, Act I, scene ii, 223.
4. The phrase is from A *Midsummer Night's Dream*, Act II, scene i, 175.

trifles in comparison to the Benefit done by great Works to the "Spirit and pulse of good" by their mere passive existence. Memory should not be called knowledge—Many have original minds who do not think it—they are led away by Custom—Now it appears to me that almost any Man may like the Spider spin from his own inwards his own airy Citadel—the points of leaves and twigs on which the Spider begins her work are few and she fills the Air with a beautiful circuiting: man should be content with as few points to tip with the fine Webb of his Soul and weave a tapestry empyrean—full of Symbols for his spiritual eye, of softness for his spiritual touch, of space for his wandering of distinctness for his Luxury—But the Minds of Mortals are so different and bent on such diverse Journeys that it may at first appear impossible for any common taste and fellowship to exist ~~bettween~~ between two or three under these suppositions—It is however quite the contrary—Minds would leave each other in contrary directions, traverse each other in Numberless points, and all [*for* at] last greet each other at the Journeys end—An old Man and a child would talk together and the old Man be led on his Path, and the child left thinking—Man should not dispute or assert but whisper results to his neighbor, and thus by every germ of Spirit sucking the Sap from mould ethereal every human might become great, and Humanity instead of being a wide heath of Furse[5] and Briars with here and there a remote Oak or Pine, would become a grand democracy of Forest Trees. It has been an old Comparison for our urging on—the Bee hive—however it seems to me that we should rather be the flower than the Bee—for it is a false notion that more is gained by receiving than giving—no, the receiver and the giver are equal in their benefits—The f[l]ower I doubt not receives a fair guerdon from the Bee—its leaves blush deeper in the next spring—and who shall say between Man and Woman which is the most delighted? Now it is more noble to sit like Jove that [*for* than] to fly like Mercury—let us not therefore go hurrying about and collecting honey bee like, buzzing here and there impatiently from a knowledge of what is to be arrived at; but let us open our leaves like a flower and be passive and receptive—budding patiently under the eye of Apollo and taking hints from every noble insect that favors us with a visit—sap will be given us for Meat and dew for drink—I was led into these thoughts, my dear Reynolds, by the beauty of the morning operating on a sense of Idleness—I have not read any Books—the Morning said I was right—I had no Idea but of the Morning, and the Thrush said I was right—seeming to say—

> O thou whose face hath felt the Winter's wind,
> Whose eye has seen the snow-clouds hung in mist,
> And the black elm tops 'mong the freezing stars,
> To thee the spring will be a harvest-time.
> O thou, whose only book has been the light
> Of supreme darkness which thou feddest on
> Night after night when Phœbus was away,
> To thee the spring shall be a triple morn.
> O fret not after knowledge—I have none,

5. *The Tempest*, Act I, scene i, 68–69.

And yet my song comes native with the warmth.
O fret not after knowledge—I have none,
And yet the Evening listens. He who saddens
At thought of idleness cannot be idle,
And he's awake who thinks himself asleep.

Now I am sensible all this is a mere sophistication, however it may neighbor to any truths, to excuse my own indolence—so I will not deceive myself that Man should be equal with jove—but think himself very well off as a sort of scullion-Mercury, or even a humble Bee—It is not [*for* no] matter whether I am right or wrong either one way or another, if there is sufficient to lift a little time from your Shoulders.

from Letter to John Taylor, February 27, 1818

* * * It is a sorry thing for me that any one should have to overcome Prejudices in reading my Verses—that affects me more than any hyper-criticism on any particular Passage. In *Endymion* I have most likely but moved into the Go-cart from the leading strings. In Poetry I have a few Axioms, and you will see how far I am from their Centre. 1st I think Poetry should surprise by a fine excess and not by Singularity—it should strike the Reader as a wording of his own highest thoughts, and appear almost a Remembrance—2nd Its touches of Beauty should never be half way therby making the reader breathless instead of content: the rise, the progress, the setting of imagery should like the Sun come natural natural too him—shine over him and set soberly although in magnificence leaving him in the Luxury of twilight—but it is easier to think what Poetry should be than to write it—and this leads me on to another axiom. That if Poetry comes not as naturally as the Leaves to a tree it had better not come at all. However it may be with me I cannot help looking into new countries with "O for a Muse of fire to ascend!"[6]—If Endymion serves me as a Pioneer perhaps I ought to be content. I have great reason to be content, for thank God I can read and perhaps understand Shakspeare to his depths, and I have I am sure many friends, who, if I fail, will attribute any change in my Life and Temper to Humbleness rather than to Pride—to a cowering under the Wings of great Poets rather than to a Bitterness that I am not appreciated. I am anxious to get Endymion printed that I may forget it and proceed. * * *

6. Shakespeare, *Henry V*, Prologue, 1.

from the Preface to Endymion, dated April 10, 1818

The imagination of a boy is healthy, and the mature imagination of a man is healthy; but there is a space of life between, in which the soul is in a ferment, the character undecided, the way of life uncertain, the ambition thick-sighted: thence proceeds mawkishness, and all the thousand bitters which those men I speak of must necessarily taste in going over the following pages.

I hope I have not in too late a day touched the beautiful mythology of Greece, and dulled its brightness: for I wish to try once more, before I bid it farewell.

CHRONOLOGY

1795 John Keats born October 31 at Finsbury, just north of London, the eldest child of Thomas and Frances Jennings Keats. Thomas Keats was head ostler at a livery stable.

1797–1803 Birth of three younger brothers and sisters: George in 1797, Thomas in 1799, Frances Mary (Fanny) in 1803.

1803 With George, begins school in Enfield.

1804 Father killed by a fall from his horse, April 15. On June 27 his mother remarries, and the children go to live with their maternal grandparents at Enfield. The grandfather dies a year later, and the children move with their grandmother to Lower Edmonton.

1809 Begins a literary friendship with Charles Cowden Clarke, the son of the headmaster at the Enfield school, and develops a strong interest in reading.

1810 Mother dies of tuberculosis, after a long illness.

1811 Leaves school to become apprenticed to an apothecary-surgeon in Edmonton; completes a prose translation of the *Aeneid*, begun at school.

1814 Earliest known attempts at writing verse. In December his grandmother dies, and the family home is broken up.

1815 In October moves to next stage of his medical training at Guy's Hospital, south of the Thames in London.

1816 On May 5 his first published poem, *O Solitude*, appears in Leigh Hunt's *Examiner*. In October writes *On First Looking into Chapman's Homer*, published in December. Meets Hunt, Benjamin Haydon, John Hamilton Reynolds, and Shelley. By the spring of 1817, gives up the idea of medical practice.

1817 In March, moves with brothers to Hampstead, sees the Elgin Marbles with Haydon, and publishes his first collection of *Poems*. Composes *Endymion* between April and November. Reads Milton, Shakespeare, and Coleridge and rereads Wordsworth during the year.

1818 *Endymion* published in April, unfavorably reviewed in September, defended by Reynolds in October. During the summer goes on walking tour of the lake country and Scotland, but returns to London in mid-August with a sore throat and severe chills. His brother Tom also seriously ill by late summer, dying on December 1. In September, Keats first meets Fanny Brawne (18 years old), with whom he arrives at an "understanding" by Christmas.

1819 Writes *The Eve of St. Agnes* in January, revises it in September. Fanny Brawne and her mother move into the other half of the double house in which Keats lives in April. During April and May writes *La Belle Dame sans Merci* and all the major odes except *To Autumn*, written in September. Rental arrangements force separation from Fanny Brawne during the summer (Keats on Isle of Wight from June to August), and in the fall he tries to break his dependence on her, but they become engaged by Christmas. Earlier in December suffers a recurrence of his sore throat.

1820 In February has a severe hemorrhage and in June an attack of blood-spitting. In July his doctor orders him to Italy for the winter; he sails in September and finally arrives in Rome on November 15. In July a volume of poems published, *Lamia, Isabella, The Eve of St. Agnes and Other Poems*. Fanny Brawne nurses him through the late summer.

1821 Dies at 11 P.M., February 23. Buried in the English Cemetery at Rome.

ADRIENNE RICH

At a Bach Concert

Coming by evening through the wintry city
We said that art is out of love with life.
Here we approach a love that is not pity.

This antique discipline, tenderly severe,
Renews belief in love yet masters feeling,
Asking of us a grace in what we bear.

Form is the ultimate gift that love can offer—
The vital union of necessity
With all that we desire, all that we suffer.

A too-compassionate art is half an art.
Only such proud restraining purity
Restores the else-betrayed, too-human heart. 1951

Storm Warnings

The glass has been falling all the afternoon,
And knowing better than the instrument
What winds are walking overhead, what zone
Of gray unrest is moving across the land,

I leave the book upon a pillowed chair
And walk from window to closed window, watching
Boughs strain against the sky

And think again, as often when the air
Moves inward toward a silent core of waiting,
How with a single purpose time has traveled
By secret currents of the undiscerned
Into this polar realm. Weather abroad
And weather in the heart alike come on
Regardless of prediction.

Between foreseeing and averting change
Lies all the mastery of elements
Which clocks and weatherglasses cannot alter.
Time in the hand is not control of time,
Nor shattered fragments of an instrument
A proof against the wind; the wind will rise,
We can only close the shutters.

I draw the curtains as the sky goes black
And set a match to candles sheathed in glass
Against the keyhole draught, the insistent whine
Of weather through the unsealed aperture.
This is our sole defense against the season;
These are the things that we have learned to do
Who live in troubled regions.

1951

Snapshots of a Daughter-in-Law

1

You, once a belle in Shreveport,
with henna-colored hair, skin like a peachbud,
still have your dresses copied from that time,
and play a Chopin prelude
called by Cortot: "*Delicious recollections*
float like perfume through the memory."

Your mind now, mouldering like wedding-cake,
heavy with useless experience, rich
with suspicion, rumor, fantasy,
crumbling to pieces under the knife-edge
of mere fact. In the prime of your life.

Nervy, glowering, your daughter
wipes the teaspoons, grows another way.

2

Banging the coffee-pot into the sink
she hears the angels chiding, and looks out
past the raked gardens to the sloppy sky.
Only a week since They said: *Have no patience.*

The next time it was: *Be insatiable.*
Then: *Save yourself; others you cannot save.*[7]
Sometimes she's let the tapstream scald her arm,
a match burn to her thumbnail,

or held her hand above the kettle's snout
right in the woolly steam. They are probably angels,
since nothing hurts her any more, except
each morning's grit blowing into her eyes.

3

A thinking woman sleeps with monsters.
The beak that grips her, she becomes. And Nature,
that sprung-lidded, still commodious
steamer-trunk of *tempora* and *mores*[8]
gets stuffed with it all: the mildewed orange-flowers,
the female pills, the terrible breasts
of Boadicea[9] beneath flat foxes' heads and orchids.

Two handsome women, gripped in argument,
each proud, acute, subtle, I hear scream
across the cut glass and majolica
like Furies[1] cornered from their prey:
The argument *ad feminam,*[2] all the old knives
that have rusted in my back, I drive in yours,
ma semblable, ma soeur![3]

4

Knowing themselves too well in one another:
their gifts no pure fruition, but a thorn,

15
20
25
30
35
40

7. According the Matthew 27:42, the chief priests, scribes, and elders mocked the crucified Jesus by saying, "He saved others; himself he cannot save." 8. Times and customs. 9. Queen of the ancient Britons. When her husband died, the Romans seized the territory he ruled and scourged Boadicea; she then led a heroic but ultimately unsuccessful revolt. 1. In Roman mythology, the three sisters were the avenging spirits of retributive justice. 2. Argument to the woman. The *argumentum ad hominem* (literally, argument to the man) is (in logic) an argument aimed at a person's individual prejudices or special interests. 3. "My mirror-image (or 'double'), my sister." Baudelaire, in the prefatory poem to *Les Fleurs du Mal*, addresses (and attacks) his "hypocrite reader" as "mon semblable, mon frère" (my double, my brother).

the prick filed sharp against a hint of scorn . . .
Reading while waiting
for the iron to heat,
writing, *My Life had stood—a Loaded Gun—*[4]
in that Amherst pantry while the jellies boil and scum,
or, more often,
iron-eyed and beaked and purposed as a bird,
dusting everything on the whatnot every day of life.

5

Dulce ridens, dulce loquens,[5]
she shaves her legs until they gleam
like petrified mammoth-tusk.

6

When to her lute Corinna sings[6]
neither words nor music are her own;
only the long hair dipping
over her cheek, only the song
of silk against her knees
and these
adjusted in reflections of an eye.

Poised, trembling and unsatisfied, before
an unlocked door, that cage of cages,
tell us, you bird, you tragical machine—
is this *fertilisante douleur?*[7] Pinned down
by love, for you the only natural action,
are you edged more keen
to prise the secrets of the vault? has Nature shown
her household books to you, daughter-in-law,
that her sons never saw?

7

"To have in this uncertain world some stay
which cannot be undermined, is
of the utmost consequence."[8]

4. " 'My Life had stood—a Loaded Gun' [Poem No. 754], Emily Dickinson, *Complete Poems*, ed. T. H. Johnson, 1960, p. 369." (Rich's note) 5. "Sweet (or winsome) laughter, sweet chatter." The phrase (slightly modified here) concludes Horace's *Ode*, 1, 22, describing the appeal of a mistress. 6. The opening line of a famous Elizabethan lyric (by Thomas Campion) in which Corinna's music is said to control totally the poet's happiness or despair. 7. Enriching pain. 8. " '. . . is of the utmost consequence,' from Mary Wollstonecraft, *Thoughts on the Education of Daughters*, London, 1787." (Rich's note)

Thus wrote
a woman, partly brave and partly good,
who fought with what she partly understood.
Few men about her would or could do more,
hence she was labeled harpy, shrew and whore.

8

"You all die at fifteen," said Diderot,[9]
and turn part legend, part convention.
Still, eyes inaccurately dream
behind closed windows blankening with steam.
Deliciously, all that we might have been,
all that we were—fire, tears,
wit, taste, martyred ambition—
stirs like the memory of refused adultery
the drained and flagging bosom of our middle years.

9

Not that it is done well, but
that it is done at all?[1] Yes, think
of the odds! or shrug them off forever.
This luxury of the precocious child,
Time's precious chronic invalid,—
would we, darlings, resign it if we could?
Our blight has been our sinecure:
mere talent was enough for us—
glitter in fragments and rough drafts.

Sigh no more, ladies.
Time is male
and in his cups drinks to the fair.
Bemused by gallantry, we hear
our mediocrities over-praised,
indolence read as abnegation,
slattern thought styled intuition,
every lapse forgiven, our crime
only to cast too bold a shadow
or smash the mould straight off.

9. " 'Vous mourez toutes a quinze ans,' from the *Lettres à Sophie Volland*, quoted by Simone de Beauvoir in *Le Deuxième Sexe*, vol. II, pp. 123–4." (Rich's note) Editor of the *Encyclopédie* (the central document of the French Enlightenment), Diderot became disillusioned with the traditional education of women and undertook an experimental education for his own daughter. 1. Samuel Johnson's comment on women preachers: "Sir, a woman's preaching is like a dog's walking on his hinder legs. It is not done well, but you are surprised to find it done at all." (Boswell's *Life of Johnson*, ed. Birbeck-Hill, I, 463)

For that, solitary confinement,
tear gas, attrition shelling.
Few applicants for that honor.

10

Well,
she's long about her coming, who must be
more merciless to herself than history.[2]
Her mind full to the wind, I see her plunge
breasted and glancing through the currents,
taking the light upon her
at least as beautiful as any boy
or helicopter,
poised, still coming,
her fine blades making the air wince

but her cargo
no promise then:
delivered
palpable
ours.

1958–60

In *When We Dead Awaken,* Rich describes her consciousness during the time she was writing this poem:

> Over two years I wrote a 10-part poem called "Snapshots of a Daughter-in-Law," in a longer, looser mode than I've ever trusted myself with before. It was an extraordinary relief to write that poem. It strikes me now as too literary, too dependent on allusion; I hadn't found the courage yet to do without authorities, or even to use the pronoun "I"—the woman in the poem is always "she." One section of it, #2, concerns a woman who thinks she is going mad; she is haunted by voices telling her to resist and rebel, voices which she can hear but not obey.

Orion

Far back when I went zig-zagging
through tamarack pastures

2. "Cf. *Le Deuxième Sexe*, vol. II, p. 574: '. . . elle arrive du fond des ages, de Thèbes, de Minos, de Chichen Itza; et elle est aussi le totem planté au coeur de la brousse africaine; c'est un helicoptère et c'est un oiseau; et voilà la plus grande merveille: sous ses cheveux peints le bruissement des feuillages devient une pensée et des paroles s'échappent de ses seins.' " (Rich's note)

you were my genius, you
my cast-iron Viking, my helmed
lion-heart king in prison.
Years later now you're young

my fierce half-brother, staring
down from that simplified west
your breast open, your belt dragged down
by an oldfashioned thing, a sword
the last bravado you won't give over
though it weighs you down as you stride

and the stars in it are dim
and maybe have stopped burning
But you burn, and I know it;
as I throw back my head to take you in
an old transfusion happens again:
divine astronomy is nothing to it.

Indoors I bruise and blunder,
break faith, leave ill enough
alone, a dead child born in the dark.
Night cracks up over the chimney,
pieces of time, frozen geodes
come showering down in the grate.

A man reaches behind my eyes
and finds them empty
a woman's head turns away
from my head in the mirror
children are dying my death
and eating crumbs of my life.

Pity is not your forte.
Calmly you ache up there
pinned aloft in your crow's nest,
my speechless pirate!
You take it all for granted
and when I look you back

it's with a starlike eye
shooting its cold and egotistical spear
where it can do least damage.
Breathe deep! No hurt, no pardon
out here in the cold with you
you with your back to the wall.

1965

In *When We Dead Awaken*, Rich describes "Orion" as

> a poem of reconstruction with a part of myself I had felt I was losing—the active principle, the energetic imagination, the "half-brother" whom I projected, as I had for many years, into the constellation Orion. It's no accident that the words "cold and egotistical" appear in this poem, and are applied to myself. The choice still seemed to be between "love"—womanly, maternal love, altruistic love—a love defined and ruled by the weight of an entire culture—and egotism—a force directed by men into creation, achievement, ambition, often at the expense of others, but justifiably so. For weren't they men, and wasn't that their destiny as womanly love was ours? I know now that the alternatives are false ones—that the word "love" is itself in need of re-vision.

Planetarium

(Thinking of Caroline Herschel, 1750–1848,
astronomer, sister of William; and others)

A woman in the shape of a monster
a monster in the shape of a woman
the skies are full of them

a woman   "in the snow
among the Clocks and instruments
or measuring the ground with poles"

in her 98 years to discover
8 comets

she whom the moon ruled
like us
levitating into the night sky
riding the polished lenses

Galaxies of women, there
doing penance for impetuousness
ribs chilled
in those spaces   of the mind

An eye,
          "virile, precise and absolutely certain"
          from the mad webs of Uranisborg
                                        encountering the NOVA

every impulse of light exploding
from the core
as life flies out of us

Tycho[3] whispering at last
"Let me not seem to have lived in vain"

What we see, we see
and seeing is changing

the light that shrivels a mountain
and leaves a man alive

Heartbeat of the pulsar
heart sweating through my body

The radio impulse
pouring in from Taurus
I am bombarded yet I stand

I have been standing all my life in the
direct path of a battery of signals
the most accurately transmitted most
untranslatable language in the universe
I am a galactic cloud so deep so invo-
luted that a light wave could take 15
years to travel through me And has
taken I am an instrument in the shape
of a woman trying to translate pulsations
into images for the relief of the body
and the reconstruction of the mind.

1968

Rich describes this poem, in *When We Dead Awaken*, as a "companion poem to 'Orion,' " above:

> at last the woman in the poem and the woman writing the poem become the same person. . . . It was written after a visit to a real planetarium, where I read an account of the work of Caroline Herschel, the astronomer, who worked with her brother William, but whose name remained obscure, as his did not.

Diving into the Wreck

First having read the book of myths,
and loaded the camera,
and checked the edge of the knife-blade,
I put on

3. Tycho Brahe (1546–1601), Danish astronomer whose cosmology tried to fuse the Ptolemaic and Copernican systems. He discovered and described ("*De Nova Stella*, 1573) a new star in what had previously been considered a fixed star-system. Uranisborg (line 19) was Tycho's famous and elaborate palace-laboratory-observatory.

the body-armor of black rubber
the absurd flippers
the grave and awkward mask.
I am having to do this
not like Cousteau with his
assiduous team
aboard the sun-flooded schooner
but here alone.

There is a ladder.
The ladder is always there
hanging innocently
close to the side of the schooner.
We know what it is for,
we who have used it.
Otherwise
it's a piece of maritime floss
some sundry equipment.

I go down.
Rung after rung and still
the oxygen immerses me
the blue light
the clear atoms
of our human air.
I go down.
My flippers cripple me,
I crawl like an insect down the ladder
and there is no one
to tell me when the ocean
will begin.

First the air is blue and then
it is bluer and then green and then
black I am blacking out and yet
my mask is powerful
it pumps my blood with power
the sea is another story
the sea is not a question of power
I have to learn alone
to turn my body without force
in the deep element.

And now: it is easy to forget
what I came for
among so many who have always
lived here
swaying their crenellated fans
between the reefs

and besides
you breathe differently down here.

I came to explore the wreck.
The words are purposes.
The words are maps.
I came to see the damage that was done
and the treasures that prevail.
I stroke the beam of my lamp
slowly along the flank
of something more permanent
than fish or weed

the thing I came for:
the wreck and not the story of the wreck
the thing itself and not the myth
the drowned face always staring
toward the sun
the evidence of damage
worn by salt and sway into this threadbare beauty
the ribs of the disaster
curving their assertion
among the tentative haunters.

This is the place.
And I am here, the mermaid whose dark hair
streams black, the merman in his armored body
We circle silently
about the wreck
we dive into the hold.
I am she: I am he
whose drowned face sleeps with open eyes
whose breasts still bear the stress
whose silver, copper, vermeil cargo lies
obscurely inside barrels
half-wedged and left to rot
we are the half-destroyed instruments
that once held to a course
the water-eaten log
the fouled compass

We are, I am, you are
by cowardice or courage
the one who find our way
back to this scene
carrying a knife, a camera
a book of myths
in which
our names do not appear.

1972

Origins and History of Consciousness

I

Night-life. Letters, journals, bourbon
sloshed in the glass. Poems crucified on the wall,
dissected, their bird-wings severed
like trophies. No one lives in this room
without living through some kind of crisis.

No one lives in this room
without confronting the whiteness of the wall
behind the poems, planks of books,
photographs of dead heroines.
Without contemplating last and late
the true nature of poetry. The drive
to connect. The dream of a common language.

Thinking of lovers, their blind faith, their
experienced crucifixions,
my envy is not simple. I have dreamed of going to bed
as walking into clear water ringed by a snowy wood
white as cold sheets, thinking, *I'll freeze in there.*
My bare feet are numbed already by the snow
but the water
is mild, I sink and float
like a warm amphibious animal
that has broken the net, has run
through fields of snow leaving no print;
this water washes off the scent—
You are clear now
of the hunter, the trapper
the wardens of the mind—

yet the warm animal dreams on
of another animal
swimming under the snow-flecked surface of the pool,
and wakes, and sleeps again.

No one sleeps in this room without
the dream of a common language.

II

It was simple to meet you, simple to take your eyes
into mine, saying: these are eyes I have known
from the first. . . . It was simple to touch you
against the hacked background, the grain of what we
had been, the choices, years. . . . It was even simple
to take each other's lives in our hands, as bodies.

What is not simple: to wake from drowning
from where the ocean beat inside us like an afterbirth
into this common, acute particularity
these two selves who walked half a lifetime untouching—
to wake to something deceptively simple: a glass
sweated with dew, a ring of the telephone, a scream
of someone beaten up far down in the street
causing each of us to listen to her own inward scream

knowing the mind of the mugger and the mugged
as any woman must who stands to survive this city,
this century, this life . . .

each of us having loved the flesh in its clenched or loosened beauty
better than trees or music (yet loving those too
as if they were flesh—and they are—but the flesh
of beings unfathomed as yet in our roughly literal life).

III

It's simple to wake from sleep with a stranger,
dress, go out, drink coffee,
enter a life again. It isn't simple
to wake from sleep into the neighborhood
of one neither strange nor familiar
whom we have chosen to trust. Trusting, untrusting,
we lowered ourselves into this, let ourselves
downward hand over hand as on a rope that quivered
over the unsearched. . . . We did this. Conceived
of each other, conceived each other in a darkness
which I remember as drenched in light.
I want to call this, life.

But I can't call it life until we start to move
beyond this secret circle of fire
where our bodies are giant shadows flung on a wall
where the night becomes our inner darkness, and sleeps
like a dumb beast, head on her paws, in the corner.

1972–1974 1978

For the Record

The clouds and the stars didn't wage this war
the brooks gave no information
if the mountain spewed stones of fire into the river
it was not taking sides

the raindrop faintly swaying under the leaf
had no political opinions

and if here or there a house
filled with backed-up raw sewage
or poisoned those who lived there
with slow fumes, over years
the houses were not at war
nor did the tinned-up buildings

intend to refuse shelter
to homeless old women and roaming children
they had no policy to keep them roaming
or dying, no, the cities were not the problem
the bridges were non-partisan
the freeways burned, but not with hatred

Even the miles of barbed-wire
stretched around crouching temporary huts
designed to keep the unwanted
at a safe distance, out of sight
even the boards that had to absorb
year upon year, so many human sounds

so many depths of vomit, tears
slow-soaking blood
had not offered themselves for this
The trees didn't volunteer to be cut into boards
nor the thorns for tearing flesh
Look around at all of it

and ask whose signature
is stamped on the orders, traced
in the corner of the building plans
Ask where the illiterate, big-bellied
women were, the drunks and crazies,
the ones you fear most of all: ask where you were. 1983

from Talking with Adrienne Rich[4]

* * * I think of myself as using poetry as a chief means of self-exploration—one of several means, of which maybe another would be dreams, really thinking about, paying attention to dreams, but the poem, like the dream, does this through images and it is in the images of my poems that I feel I am finding out more about my own experience, my sense of things. But I don't think of myself as

4. A transcript of a conversation recorded March 9, 1971, and printed in the *Ohio Review*, Fall 1971.

having a position or a self-description which I'm then going to present in the poem.

When I started writing poetry I was tremendously conscious of, and very much in need of, a formal structure that could be obtained from outside, into which I could pour whatever I had, whatever I thought I had to express. But I think that was a part of a whole thing that I see, now as a teacher, very much with young writers, of using language more as a kind of façade than as either self-revelation or as a probe into one's own consciousness. I think I would attribute a lot of the change in my poetry simply to the fact of growing older, undergoing certain kinds of experiences, realizing that formal metrics were not going to suffice me in dealing with those experiences, realizing that experience itself is much more fragmentary, much more sort of battering, much ruder than these structures would allow, and it had to find its own form.

I have a very strong sense about the existence of poetry in daily life and poetry being part of the world as it is, and that the attempt to reduce poetry to what is indited on a page just limits you terribly. . . . The poem is the poetry of things lodged in the innate shape of the experience. My saying "The moment of change is the only poem" is the kind of extreme statement you feel the need to make at certain times if only to force someone to say, "But I always thought a poem is something written on a piece of paper," you know, and to say: "But look, how did those words get on that piece of paper." There had to be a mind; there had to be an experience; the mind had to go through certain shocks, certain stresses, certain strains, and if you're going to carry the poem back to its real beginnings it's that moment of change. I feel that we are always writing.

When I was in my twenties * * * I was going through a very sort of female thing—of trying to distinguish between the ego that is capable of writing poems, and then this other kind of being that you're asked to be if you're a woman, who is, in a sense, denying that ego. I had great feelings of split about that for many years actually, and there are a lot of poems I couldn't write even, because I didn't want to confess to having that much aggression, that much ego, that much sense of myself. I had always thought of my first book as being a book of very well-tooled poems of a sort of very bright student, which I was at that time, but poems in which the unconscious things never got to the surface. But there's a poem in that book about a woman who sews a tapestry and the tapestry has figures of tigers on it. But the woman is represented as being completely—her hand is burdened by the weight of the wedding band, and she's meek, and she's fearful, and the only way in which she can express any other side of her nature is in embroidering these tigers. Well, I thought of that as almost a formal exercise, but when I go back and look at that poem I really think it's saying something about what I was going through. And now that's lessened a great deal for all sorts of reasons—that split.

from An Interview with Adrienne Rich[5]

I would have said ten or fifteen years ago that I would not even want to identify myself as a woman poet. That term *has* been used pejoratively; I just don't think it can be at this point. You know, for a woman the act of creation is prototypically to produce children, while the act of creating with language—I'm not saying that women writers haven't been accepted; certainly, more have been accepted than women lawyers or doctors. Still, a woman writer feels, she is going against the grain—or there has been this sense until very recently (if there isn't still). Okay, it's all right to be a young thing and write verse. But a friend of mine was telling me about meeting a noted poet at a cocktail party. She'd sent him a manuscript for a contest he was judging. She went up to him and asked him about it, and he looked at her and said, "Young girls *are* poems; they shouldn't write them." This attitude toward women poets manifests itself so strongly that you are made to feel you are becoming the thing you are not.

If a man is writing, he's gone through all the nonsense and said "Okay, I am a poet and I'm still a man. They don't cancel each other out or, if they do, then I'll opt to be a poet." He's not writing for a hostile sex, a breed of critics who by virtue of their sex are going to look at his language and pass judgment on it. That does happen to a woman. I don't know why the woman poet has been slower than the woman novelist in taking risks though I'm very grateful that this is no longer so. I feel that I dare to think further than I would have dared to think ten years ago—and *that* certainly is going to affect my writing. And I now dare to entertain thoughts and speculations that then would have seemed unthinkable.

Many of the male writers whom I very much admire—Galway Kinnell, James Wright, W. S. Merwin—are writing poetry of such great desolation. They come from different backgrounds, write in different ways, and yet all seem to write out of a sense of doom, as if we were fated to carry on these terribly flawed relationships. I think it's expressive of a feeling that "we, the masters, have created a world that's impossible to live in and that probably may not be livable in, in a very literal sense. What we thought, what we'd been given to think is our privilege, our right, and our sexual prerogative has led to this, to our doom." I guess a lot of women—if not a lot of women poets—are feeling that there has to be some other way, that human life is messed-up but that it doesn't have to be *this* desolate.

Today, much poetry by women is charged with anger and uses voices of rage and anger that I don't think were ever used in poetry before. In poets like Sylvia Plath and Diane Wakoski, say, those voices are so convincing that it is impossible to describe them by using those favorite adjectives of phallic criticism—shrill and hysterical. Well, Sylvia Plath is dead. I always maintained from the first

5. By David Kalstone, in the *Saturday Review*, April 22, 1972.

time I read her last poems that her suicide was not necessary, that she could have gone on and written poems that would have given us even more insight into the states of anger and willfulness, even of self-destructiveness, that women experience. She didn't need literally to destroy herself in order to reflect and express those things. Diane Wakoski is a young woman. She's changing a lot and will continue to change. What I admire in her, besides her energy and dynamism and quite a beautiful gift for snatching the image that she wants out of the air, is her honesty. No woman has written before about her face and said she hated it, that it had served her ill, that she wished she could throw acid in it. That's very shocking. But I think all women, even the most beautiful women, at times have felt that in a kind of self-hatred. Because the *face* is supposed to be the *woman*.

A lot of poetry is becoming more oral. Certainly, it's true of women and black poets. Reading black poetry on the printed page gives no sense of the poem, if you're going to look at that poetry the way you look at poems by Richard Wilbur. Yet you can hear these poets read and realize it's the oldest kind of poetry.

I think the energy of language comes somewhat from the pressure and need and unbearableness of what's being done to you. It's not the same energy you find in the blues. The blues are a grief language, a lost language, and a cry of pain, usually in a woman's voice, which is interesting. For a long time you sing the blues, and then you begin to say, "I'm tired of singing the blues. I want something else." And that's what you're hearing now. There seems to be a connection between an oppressed condition and having access to certain kinds of energy, vitality, and subjectivity. For women as well as blacks. Though I don't feel there is a necessary cause-and-effect relationship; what seems to happen is that being on top, being in a powerful position leads to a divorce between one's unruly, chaotic, revolutionary sensitivity and one's reason, sense of order and of maintaining a hold. And, therefore, you have at the bottom of the pile, so to speak, a kind of churning energy that gets lost up there among the administrators.

I don't know how or whether poetry changes anything. But neither do I know how or whether bombing or even community organizing changes anything when we are pitted against a massive patriarchal system armed with supertechnology. I believe in subjectivity—that a lot of male Left leaders have turned into Omnipotent Administrators, because their "masculinity" forced them to deny their subjectivity. I believe in dreams and visions and "the madness of art." And at moments I can conceive of a women's movement that will show the way to humanizing technology and fusing dreams and skills and visions and reason to begin the healing of the human race. But I don't want women to take over the world and run it the way men have, or to take on—yet again!—the burden of carrying the subjectivity of the race. Women are a vanguard now, and I believe will increasingly become so, because we have—Western women, Third World women, all women—known and felt the pain of the human condition most consistently. But in the end it can't be women alone.

from When We Dead Awaken: Writing as Re-Vision

Most, if not all, human lives are full of fantasy—passive daydreaming which need not be acted on. But to write poetry or fiction, or even to think well, is not to fantasize or to put fantasies on paper. For a poem to coalesce, for a character or an action to take shape, there has to be an imaginative transformation of reality which is in no way passive. And a certain freedom of the mind is needed—freedom to press on, to enter the currents of your thought like a glider pilot, knowing that your motion can be sustained, that the buoyancy of your attention will not be suddenly snatched away. Moreover, if the imagination is to transcend and transform experience it has to question, to challenge, to conceive of alternatives, perhaps to the very life you are living at that moment. You have to be free to play around with the notion that day might be night, love might be hate, nothing can be too sacred for the imagination to turn into its opposite or to call experimentally by another name. For writing is re-naming.

Now, to be maternally with small children all day in the old way, to be with a man in the old way of marriage, requires a holding back, a putting aside of that imaginative activity, and seems to demand instead a kind of conservatism. I want to make it clear that I am *not* saying that in order to write well, or think well, it is necessary to become unavailable to others, or to become a devouring ego. This has been the myth of the masculine artist and thinker; and, I repeat, I do not accept it. But to be a female human being trying to fulfill traditional female functions in a traditional way *is* in direct conflict with the subversive function of the imagination. The word "traditional" is important here. There must be ways, and we will be finding out more and more about them, in which the energy of creation and the energy of relation can be united. But in those earlier years I always felt the conflict as a failure of love in myself. I had thought I was choosing a full life: the life available to most men, in which sexuality, work and parenthood could co-exist. But I felt, at 29, guilt toward the people closest to me, and guilty toward my own being.

I wanted, then, more than anything, the one thing of which there was never enough: time to think, time to write. The '50s and early '60s were years of rapid revelations: the sit-ins and marches in the South, the Bay of Pigs, the early antiwar movement, raised large questions—questions for which the masculine world of the academy around me seemed to have expert and fluent answers. But I needed desperately to think for myself—about pacifism and dissent and violence, about poetry and society, and about my own relationship to all these things. For about ten years I was reading in fierce snatches, scribbling in notebooks, writing poetry in fragments; I was looking desperately for clues, because if there were no clues then I thought I might be insane. I wrote in a notebook about this time:

> Paralyzed by the sense that there exists a mesh of relationships—e.g. between my anger at the children, my sensual life, pacifism, sex (I mean sex in its broadest significance, not merely sexual desire)—an interconnectedness which, if I could see it, make it valid, would give me back myself, make it possible to function lucidly and passionately. Yet I grope in and out among these dark webs.

I think I began at this point to feel that politics was not something "out there" but something "in here" and of the essence of my condition.

In the late '50s I was able to write, for the first time, directly about experiencing myself as a woman. The poem was jotted in fragments during children's naps, brief hours in a library, or at 3 A.M. after rising with a wakeful child. I despaired of doing any continuous work at this time. Yet I began to feel that my fragments and scraps had a common consciousness and a common theme, one which I would have been very unwilling to put on paper at an earlier time because I had been taught that poetry should be "universal," which meant, of course, non-female. Until then I had tried very much *not* to identify myself as a female poet.

CHRONOLOGY

1929 Born in Baltimore, Maryland, May 16. Began writing poetry as a child under the encouragement and supervision of her father, Dr. Arnold Rich, from whose "very Victorian, pre-Raphaelite" library, Rich later recalled, she read Tennyson, Keats, Arnold, Blake, Rossetti, Swinburne, Carlyle, and Pater.

1951 A.B., Radcliffe College. Phi Beta Kappa. *A Change of World* chosen by W. H. Auden for the Young Poets Award and published.

1952–53 Guggenheim Fellowship; travel in Europe and England. Marriage to Alfred H. Conrad, an economist who taught at Harvard. Residence in Cambridge, Massachusetts, 1953–66.

1955 Birth of David Conrad. Publication of *The Diamond Cutters and Other Poems*, which won the Ridgely Torrence Memorial Award of the Poetry Society of America.

1957 Birth of Paul Conrad.

1959 Birth of Jacob Conrad.

1960 National Institute of Arts and Letters Award for poetry. Phi Beta Kappa poet at William and Mary College.

1961–62 Guggenheim Fellowship; residence with family in the Netherlands.

1962 Bollingen Foundation grant for translation of Dutch poetry.

1962–63 Amy Lowell Travelling Fellowship.

1963 *Snapshots of a Daughter-in-Law* published. Bess Hokin Prize of *Poetry* magazine.

1965 Phi Beta Kappa poet at Swarthmore College.

1966 *Necessities of Life* published, nominated for the National Book Award. Phi

Beta Kappa poet at Harvard College. Move to New York City, where Alfred Conrad taught at City College of New York. Residence there from 1966 on. Increasingly active politically in protests against the Indochina war.

1966–68 Lecturer at Swarthmore College.

1967–69 Adjunct Professor of Writing in the Graduate School of the Arts, Columbia University.

1967 *Selected Poems* published in Britain. Litt.D., Wheaton College.

1968 Eunice Tietjens Memorial Prize of *Poetry* magazine. Began teaching in the SEEK and Open Admissions Programs at City College of New York.

1969 *Leaflets* published.

1970 Death of Alfred Conrad.

1971 *The Will to Change* published. Shelley Memorial Award of the Poetry Society of America. Increasingly identifies with the women's movement as a radical feminist.

1972–73 Fanny Hurst Visiting Professor of Creative Literature at Brandeis University.

1973 *Diving into the Wreck* published.

1973–74 Ingram Merrill Foundation research grant; began work on a book on the history and myths of motherhood.

1974 National Book Award for *Diving into the Wreck*. Rich rejected the award as an individual, but accepted it, in a statement written with Audre Lorde and Alice Walker, two other nominees, in the name of all women:

> We . . . together accept this award in the name of all the women whose voices have gone and still go unheard in a patriarchal world, and in the name of those who, like us, have been tolerated as token women in this culture, often at great cost and in great pain. . . . We symbolically join here in refusing the terms of patriarchal competition and declaring that we will share this prize among us, to be used as best we can for women. . . . We dedicate this occasion to the struggle for self-determination of all women, of every color, identification or derived class . . . the women who will not understand yet; the silent women whose voices have been denied us, the articulate women who have given us strength to do our work.

Professor of English, City College of New York.

1975 *Poems: Selected and New* published.

1976 Professor of English at Douglass College. *Of Woman Born: Motherhood as Experience and Institution* published. *Twenty-one Love Poems* published.

1978 *The Dream of a Common Language: Poems 1974–1977* published.

1979 *On Lies, Secrets, and Silence: Selected Prose 1966–1978* published. Leaves Douglass College and New York City; moves to Montague, Massachusetts; edits, with Michelle Cliff, the lesbian-feminist journal, *Sinister Wisdom*.

1981 *A Wild Patience Has Taken Me This Far: Poems 1978–1981* published.

1984 *The Fact of a Doorframe: Poems Selected and New 1950–1984* published. Moves to Santa Cruz, California.

1986 *Blood, Bread, and Poetry: Selected Prose 1979–1985* published. Professor of English at Stanford University.

1989 *Time's Power: Poems 1985–1988* published.

QUESTIONS

1. Once your have read at least half a dozen poems by Keats, make a list of the ideas that you have found repeated in more than one poem. Make a list as well of any distinctive stylistic features you have noticed. What kinds of experiences or events does he tend to write about? Do you notice any pattern in his use of speaker? Does he have favorite words that he uses in a particular way? What about metaphors? What are his habits in putting poems together? (You might want to look ahead to some examples of his revisions in chapter 14.) In which poems do you feel as if you want to know more about the author and his experiences before you can interpret them confidently?

2. Before you begin to read the poems in this chapter by Adrienne Rich, look back over the poems by her you have already read (there are some poems by her later on, too: the index can point you to all the Rich poems not in this chapter, including a number of very recent ones). What significant differences do you notice among the poems? Can you tell quickly an early Rich poem from a later one? What are the differences in subject matter? in style? in situation? in strategies of argument? Try to read all the Rich poems in the book at one sitting, working in poems to be found elsewhere in the text in their appropriate chronological place. In what ways does the voice in her poems seem to have changed. Characterize, as fully as you can, the voice of the poems written in the 50s; in the 60s; 70s; 80s. What, exactly, are the differences? What similarities do you see in her work from beginning to end?

WRITING SUGGESTION

For both Keats and Rich, try to pick out *one* poem that seems to you "typical" in the sense that it uses many of the strategies to be found in other poems and displays themes that seem central to the poet's work. Choose either Keats or Rich, and write a detailed paper (of 8–10 pages) in which you analyze the poem you have chosen, showing how it is typical of the poet's work.

12 HISTORICAL AND CULTURAL CONTEXTS

The more you know, the better a reader of poetry you are likely to be. Poems often draw upon a large fund of human knowledge, and sometimes they require a great deal from the reader. The earlier chapters in this book suggest some of the skills one needs to develop in order to cope with the demands poems make. In these final chapters we will look at the knowledge poets often expect. Very little that you know will ultimately go to waste in your reading of poetry. The best potential reader of a poem is someone who has already developed reading skills to perfection, read everything, thought deeply about all sorts of things, and who is wise beyond belief—but that is the ideal reader we all strive to be, not the one any of us actually is. Although no poet expects any reader to be all those things, good readers try.

The chapters that follow suggest some of the ways that poetry draws upon the traditional fund of human knowledge, how it uses the history of literature, science, philosophy, religion—the "wisdom of the ages" that is the cornerstone of a traditional humanistic education. This chapter considers some of the historical particulars, matters that relate specifically to the moment in time when a particular poem was written—for every poem is, in the beginning, a timely act of creation.

Things that happen every day frequently find their way into poetry in an easy and yet often forceful manner. Making love in a junkyard, as in "Cherrylog Road," is one kind of example; a reader doesn't need to know what particular junkyard was involved—or imaginatively involved—in order to understand the poem, but a reader does need to know what an auto junkyard was like in the middle of the 20th century, with more or less whole car bodies being scattered in various states of disarray over a large plot of ground. But what if, over the next generation or two, junkyards disappear as other ways are found to dispose of old cars? What if the metal is all melted down, or the junk is orbited into space? If something like that happens, readers will then need a footnote explaining what junkyards once were like. The history of junkyards will not be lost—there will be pictures, films, records, and someone will write definitive books about the forms and functions of junkyards, probably even including the fact that lovers occasionally visited them—but the public memory of junkyards will soon disappear. No social customs, no things that are made, no institutions or sites last forever.

Readers may still be able to experience "Cherrylog Road" when that happens, but they will need some help, and they may think its particulars a little quaint, much as we regard literature that involves horses and buggies—or even making love in the back seat of a parked car—as quaint now. Institutions change, habits change, times change, particulars change, even when people's wants, needs, and foibles pretty much go on in the same way. Footnotes never provide a precise or adequate substitute for the ease and pleasure that come from already knowing, but they can help us understand and pave the way for feeling and experience. A kind of imaginative historical sympathy can be simulated and in fact created, for poems from earlier times that refer to specific contemporary details (and that have now become to us, in our own time, *historical* details) often describe human nature and human experiences very much as we still know and experience them. Today's poem may need tomorrow's footnote, but the poem need not be tomorrow's puzzle or only a curiosity or fossil.

The following poem, not many years old, already requires some explanation, not only because the factual details of its occasion may not be known to every reader, but also because the whole spirit of the poem may be difficult to appreciate unless one knows its circumstances.

RAYMOND R. PATTERSON

You Are the Brave

You are the brave who do not break
In the grip of the mob when the blow comes straight
To the shattered bone; when the sockets shriek;
When your arms lie twisted under your back.

Good men holding their courage slack
In their frightened pockets see how weak
The work that is done; and feel the weight
Of your blood on the ground for their spirits' sake;

And build their anger, stone on stone;
Each silently, but not alone.

1962

I can remember teaching this poem in class during the Vietnam War and finding that a lot of students were hostile to it because they assumed it to be a poem in praise of patriotism and war. Sometimes the difficulty about factual information is that one doesn't know that one *needs* specific information. In a poem like "You Are the Brave," it is fairly easy to assume (incorrectly, but understandably) that the conflict involved is a war and that the speaker addresses, and honors, a group of soldiers. Actually, there are clues in the poem that this conflict is, if as bitter as war, one in which mob violence (line 2) and enforced restraint (line 4) are involved. The date of the poem is a clue too—1962, when the American civil rights struggle was at its height. Once that "fact" is noticed, the whole historical context of the poem, if not its *immediate* occasion in terms of one specific civil rights march in one place on one day, becomes clear. In fact, since the poem doesn't mention a particular time and place, we may assume that it is not about the particulars of one specific incident, but instead gathers the kind of details that characterized many moments of the early sixties. The poem's details (generalized details about mob resentments and brutalities in a situation of passive resistance), its metaphors in the second and third stanzas, and its dignified tone of praise for "the brave" all make sense readily when the right information is available. The poem does not mention specific time and place because its concern is not confined to one event, but its location in time is important to finding what it refers to. Poems may be referential to one single event or moment, or to some larger situation that may span weeks, months, or even years. The amount of particularity in the poem will tell you.

How do you know what you need to know? The easiest clue is your own puzzlement. When it seems that something is happening in a poem that you don't recognize—and yet the poem makes no apparent effort in itself to clarify it—you have a clue that readers at the time the poem was written must have recognized something that is not now such common knowledge. Once you know you don't know, it only takes a little work to find out: most college libraries contain far more information than you will ever need, and the trick is to learn to search efficiently. Your ability to find the information efficiently will depend upon how well you know the kinds of reference materials available to you. Practice helps. Knowledge accumulates. Most poems printed in textbooks like this one will be annotated for you with minimal facts, but often you may need additional information to interpret the poem's full meaning and resonance. An editor, trying to decide on the needs of a variety of readers, may not always have decided to write the footnote you yourself may need, so there may be digging to be done in the library for any poem you read, certainly for those you may come upon in magazines and books of poetry without footnotes. Few poets like to footnote their own work (they'd rather let you struggle a little to appreciate them), and besides, many things that now need footnotes didn't when they were first written, as in "You Are the Brave."

The two poems that follow both require from the reader some specific "referential" information, but they differ considerably in their emphasis on the particularities of time and place. The first poem, "Channel Firing," reflects and refers to a moment just before the outbreak of World War I when British naval forces were preparing for combat by taking gunnery practice in the English Channel. The second, "Sonnet: The Ladies' Home Journal," reflects a broader cultural moment in which attitudes and assumptions, rather than some specific event, are crucial to understanding what is happening in the poem.

THOMAS HARDY

Channel Firing

That night your great guns, unawares,
Shook all our coffins as we lay,
And broke the chancel window squares,[1]
We thought it was the Judgment-day

And sat upright. While drearisome
Arose the howl of wakened hounds:
The mouse let fall the altar-crumb,[2]
The worms drew back into the mounds,

The glebe cow[3] drooled. Till God called, "No;
It's gunnery practice out at sea
Just as before you went below;
The world is as it used to be:

"All nations striving strong to make
Red war yet redder. Mad as hatters
They do no more for Christés sake
Than you who are helpless in such matters.

"That this is not the judgment-hour
For some of them's a blessed thing,
For if it were they'd have to scour
Hell's floor for so much threatening . . .

"Ha, ha. It will be warmer when
I blow the trumpet (if indeed
I ever do; for you are men,
And rest eternal sorely need)."

So down we lay again. "I wonder,
Will the world ever saner be,"

1. The windows near the altar in a church. 2. Breadcrumbs from the sacrament. 3. Parish cow pastured on the meadow next to the churchyard.

Said one, "than when He sent us under
In our indifferent century!"

And many a skeleton shook his head.
"Instead of preaching forty year,"
My neighbor Parson Thirdly said,
"I wish I had stuck to pipes and beer."

Again the guns disturbed the hour,
Roaring their readiness to avenge.
As far inland as Stourton Tower,
And Camelot, and starlit Stonehenge.[4]

April, 1914

SANDRA GILBERT

Sonnet: The Ladies' Home Journal

The brilliant stills of food, the cozy
glossy, bygone life—mashed potatoes
posing as whipped cream, a neat mom
conjuring shapes from chaos, trimming the flame—
how we ached for all that,
that dance of love in the living room,
those paneled walls, that kitchen golden
as the inside of a seed: how we leaned
on those shiny columns of advice,
stroking the *thank yous*, the firm thighs, the wise
closets full of soap.

But even then
we knew it was the lies we loved, the lies
we wore like Dior coats,[5] the clean-cut airtight
lies that laid out our lives in black and white.

1984

"Channel Firing" is not ultimately *about* World War I, for its emphasis is finally on how human behavior stays the same from age to age, but it begins from a particular historical vantage point. It would be difficult to make much

4. Stourton Tower, built in the 18th century to commemorate King Alfred's ninth-century victory over the Danes, in Stourhead Park, Wiltshire. Camelot is the legendary site of King Arthur's court, said to have been in Cornwall or Somerset. Stonehenge, a circular formation of upright stones dating from about 1800 B.C., is on Salisbury Plain, Wiltshire; it is thought to have been a ceremonial site for political and religious occasions or an early scientific experiment in astronomy.

5. Designer coats by Christian Dior.

sense of the poem if the reader were not to recognize the importance of that specific reference, and the poem's situation (with a waking corpse as the main speaker) is difficult enough to sort out even with the clue of the careful dating at the end (the date here is actually a part of the poem, recorded on the manuscript by the author and always printed as part of the text). The firing of the guns has awakened the dead buried near the channel, and in their puzzlement they assume it is Judgment Day, time for them to arise, until God enters and tells them what is happening. Much of the poem's effect depends on character portrayal—a God who laughs and sounds cynical, a parson who regrets his selfless life and wishes he had indulged himself more—as well as the sense that nothing ever changes. But particularity of time and place are crucial to this sense of changelessness; even so important a contemporary moment as the beginning of a world war—a moment that seemed to most people at the time unique and world-changing—fades into a timeless parade of moments that stretches over centuries of history. The geographical particulars cited at the end—as the sound of the guns moves inland to be heard in place after place—make the same point. Great moments in history are all encompassed in the sound of the guns and its message about human behavior. Times, places, and events, however important they seem, all become part of some larger pattern that denies individuality or uniqueness.

The particulars in "Sonnet: The Ladies' Home Journal" work rather differently—to remind us not of a specific time that readers need to identify but to characterize a way of seeing and thinking. The referentiality here is more cultural than historical; it is based more on ideas and attitudes characteristic of a particular period of time than on a specific moment or location. The pictures in the magazine stand for a whole way of thinking about women—a way of thinking characteristic of the time when the *Ladies' Home Journal* flourished as a popular magazine. The poem implicitly contrasts the "lies" (line 12) of the magazine with the truth of the present—that women's lives and values are not to be seen as some fantasized sense of beautiful food, motherhood, social rituals, and commercial products. Two vastly different cultural attitudes—that of the poem's present, with its sceptical view of traditional women's roles, and that of a past that equated the superficiality of glossy photographs with gender identity—are at the heart of the poem. It is about cultural attitudes and their effects on actual human beings. Readers need to know what the *Ladies' Home Journal* was like in order to understand the poem; we do not need to know the date or contents of a specific issue, only that this popular magazine reflected the attitudes and values of a whole age and culture. The referentiality of this poem involves information about ideas and consciousness more than time and event.

To get at appropriate factual, cultural, and historical information, it is important to learn to ask three kinds of questions. One kind is obvious: it is the "Do I understand the reference to . . . ?" kind. When events, places, or people unfamiliar to you come up, you will need to find out what or who they are. The second kind of question is more difficult: How do you know, in a poem like "You Are the Brave," that you need to know more? When there are no specific references to look up, no people or events to identify, how do you know that there is a specific context? To get at this sort of question, you have to trust two people: the poet, and yourself. Learning to trust yourself, your own responses, is the more difficult—you can just decide to trust the poet. Usually, good poets know what they are doing. If they do, they will not want to puzzle you more than necessary, so that you can safely assume that something which is not self-explanatory will merit close attention and possibly some digging in the library. (Poets do make mistakes and miscalculations about their readers, but it is safest to assume they know what they are doing and why they are doing it.) References that are not in themselves clear (such as "the grip of the mob" or the "arms . . . twisted under your back" in "You Are the Brave") provide a strong clue that you need more information. And that is why you need to trust yourself: you need to be confident that when something doesn't click, when the information given you does not seem enough, you trust your puzzlement and try to find the missing facts that will allow the poem to make sense. But how? Often the date of the poem is a help, as in "You Are the Brave." Sometimes the title gives a clue or a point of departure. Sometimes you can discover, by reading about the author, some of the things he or she was interested in or concerned about. There is no single all-purpose way to discover what to look for, but that kind of research—looking for clues, adding up the evidence—can be interesting in itself and very rewarding when it is successful.

The third question is why? For every factual reference, one needs to ask why. Why does the poem refer to this particular person instead of some other? What function does the reference serve?

Beyond the level of simply understanding that a particular poem is about an event or place or movement is the matter of developing a full sense of historical context, a sense of the larger significance and resonance of the historical occurrence or attitude referred to. Often a poem expects you to bring with you some sense of that significance; equally often it works to continue your education, telling you more, wanting you to understand and appreciate on the level of feeling some further things about this occurrence.

What we need to bring to our reading varies from poem to poem. "Dulce et Decorum Est," for example, needs our knowledge that poison gas was used in

World War I; the green tint through which the speaker sees the world in lines 13–14 comes from green-lensed glass in the goggles of the gas mask he has just put on. But some broader matters are important as well. Harder to specify but probably even more important is the climate of opinion that surrounded the war. To idealists, it was "the war to end all wars," and many participants—as well as politicians and propagandists—considered it a sacred mission, regarding the threat of Germany's expansionist policy as the potential destruction of Western civilization. No doubt you will read the poem more intelligently—and with more feeling—if you know quite a bit about World War I, and the same is true of poems about any historical occurrence or of poems that refer to things that happen or situations that exist in a temporal or spatial context. But it is also true that your sense of these events will grow as a result of reading sensitively and thoughtfully the poems themselves. Facts are no substitute for skills. Once you have read individually the poems in this section, try taking a breather; and then at one sitting read them all again. Reading poetry can be a form of gaining knowledge as well as an aesthetic experience. One doesn't go to poetry to seek information as such, but poems often give us more than we came for. The ways to wisdom are paved with facts, and although poetry is not primarily a data-conscious art, it often requires us to be aware, sometimes in detail, of its referents in the real world.

Time and Event

CLAUDE McKAY

America

Although she feeds me bread of bitterness,
And sinks into my throat her tiger's tooth,
Stealing my breath of life, I will confess
I love this cultured hell that tests my youth!
Her vigor flows like tides into my blood,
Giving me strength erect against her hate.
Her bigness sweeps my being like a flood.
Yet as a rebel fronts a king in state,
I stand within her walls with not a shred
Of terror, malice, not a word of jeer.
Darkly I gaze into the days ahead,
And see her might and granite wonders there,
Beneath the touch of Time's unerring hand,
Like priceless treasures sinking in the sand.

1922

LANGSTON HUGHES

Harlem (A Dream Deferred)

What happens to a dream deferred?

Does it dry up
like a raisin in the sun?
Or fester like a sore—
And then run?
Does it stink like rotten meat?
Or crust and sugar over—
like a syrupy sweet?

Maybe it just sags
like a heavy load.

Or does it explode?

1951

JAMES A. EMANUEL

Emmett Till[6]

I hear a whistling
Through the water.
Little Emmett
Won't be still.
He keeps floating
Round the darkness,
Edging through
The silent chill.
Tell me, please,
That bedtime story
Of the fairy
River Boy
Who swims forever,
Deep in treasures,
Necklaced in
A coral toy.

1968

6. In 1955, Till, a fourteen-year-old from Chicago, was lynched in Mississippi for allegedly making sexual advances toward a white woman.

DUDLEY RANDALL

Ballad of Birmingham

(On the bombing of a church in Birmingham, Alabama, 1963)

"Mother dear, may I go downtown
Instead of out to play,
And march the streets of Birmingham
In a Freedom March today?"

"No, baby, no, you may not go,
For the dogs are fierce and wild,
And clubs and hoses, guns and jails
Aren't good for a little child."

"But, mother, I won't be alone.
Other children will go with me,
And march the streets of Birmingham
To make our country free."

"No, baby, no, you may not go,
For I fear those guns will fire.
But you may go to church instead
And sing in the children's choir."

She has combed and brushed her night-dark hair,
And bathed rose petal sweet,
And drawn white gloves on her small brown hands,
And white shoes on her feet.

The mother smiled to know her child
Was in the sacred place,
But that smile was the last smile
To come upon her face.

For when she heard the explosion,
Her eyes grew wet and wild.
She raced through the streets of Birmingham
Calling for her child.

She clawed through bits of glass and brick,
Then lifted out a shoe.
"Oh, here's the shoe my baby wore,
But, baby, where are you?"

1969

WILFRED OWEN

Dulce et Decorum Est[7]

Bent double, like old beggars under sacks,
Knock-kneed, coughing like hags, we cursed through sludge,
Till on the haunting flares we turned our backs
And towards our distant rest began to trudge.
Men marched asleep. Many had lost their boots
But limped on, blood-shod. All went lame; all blind;
Drunk with fatigue; deaf even to the hoots
Of disappointed shells that dropped behind.

Gas! Gas! Quick, boys!—An ecstasy of fumbling,
Fitting the clumsy helmets just in time;
But someone still was yelling out and stumbling
And floundering like a man in fire or lime.—
Dim, through the misty panes and thick green light
As under a green sea, I saw him drowning.

In all my dreams, before my helpless sight,
He plunges at me, guttering, choking, drowning.

If in some smothering dreams you too could pace
Behind the wagon that we flung him in,
And watch the white eyes writhing in his face,
His hanging face, like a devil's sick of sin;
If you could hear, at every jolt, the blood
Come gargling from the froth-corrupted lungs,
Obscene as cancer, bitter as the cud
Of vile, incurable sores on innocent tongues,—
My friend, you would not tell with such high zest
To children ardent for some desperate glory,
The old Lie: Dulce et decorum est
Pro patria mori.

1917

EZRA POUND

There Died a Myriad[8]

There died a myriad,
And of the best, among them,

7. Part of a phrase from Horace, quoted in full in the last lines: "It is sweet and proper to die for one's country." 8. Section V of "E. P. Ode pour L'Élection de Son Sépulcre."

For an old bitch gone in the teeth,
For a botched civilization,

Charm, smiling at the good mouth,
Quick eyes gone under earth's lid,

For two gross of broken statues,
For a few thousand battered books.

1920

W. B. YEATS

On Being Asked for a War Poem

I think it better that in times like these
A poet's mouth be silent, for in truth
We have no gift to set a statesman right;
He has had enough of meddling who can please
A young girl in the indolence of her youth,
Or an old man upon a winter's night.

p. 1915

ROBERT BRINGHURST

For the Bones of Josef Mengele, Disinterred June 1985

Master of Auschwitz, angel of death,
murderer, deep in Brazil they are breaking
your bones—or somebody's bones: my
bones, your bones, his bones, whose
bones does not matter. Deep in Brazil they are breaking
bones like loaves of old bread. The angel
of death is not drowning but eating.

Speak! they are saying. *Speak! speak!*
If you don't speak we will open and read you!
Something you too might have said in your time.
Are these bones guilty? they say. And the bones
are already talking. The bones, with guns
to their heads, are already saying, *Yes!*
Yes! It is true, we are guilty!

Butcher, baker, lampshade and candlestick
maker: yes, it is true. But the bones? The bones,
earth, metals, teeth, the body?

These are not guilty. The minds of the dead
are not to be found in the bones of the dead.
The minds of the dead are not anywhere to be found,
outside the minds of the living.

1986

MARY JO SALTER

Welcome to Hiroshima

is what you first see, stepping off the train:
a billboard brought to you in living English
by Toshiba Electric. While a channel
silent in the TV of the brain

projects those flickering re-runs of a cloud
that brims its risen columnful like beer
and, spilling over, hangs its foamy head,
you feel a thirst for history: what year

it started to be safe to breathe the air,
and when to drink the blood and scum afloat
on the Ohta River. But no, the water's clear,
they pour it for your morning cup of tea

in one of the countless sunny coffee shops
whose plastic dioramas advertise
mutations of cuisine behind the glass:
a pancake sandwich; a pizza someone tops

with a maraschino cherry. Passing by
the Peace Park's floral hypocenter (where
how bravely, or with what mistaken cheer,
humanity erased its own erasure),

you enter the memorial museum
and through more glass are served, as on a dish
of blistered grass, three mannequins. Like gloves
a mother clips to coatsleeves, strings of flesh

hang from their fingertips; or as if tied
to recall a duty for us, *Reverence*
the dead whose mourners too shall soon be dead,
but all commemoration's swallowed up

in questions of bad taste, how re-created
horror mocks the grim original,
and thinking at last *They should have left it all*
you stop. This is the wristwatch of a child.

Jammed on the moment's impact, resolute
to communicate some message, although mute,
it gestures with its hands at eight-fifteen
and eight-fifteen and eight-fifteen again

while tables of statistics on the wall
update the news by calling on a roll
of tape, death gummed on death, and in the case
adjacent, an exhibit under glass

is glass itself: a shard the bomb slammed in
a woman's arm at eight-fifteen, but some
three decades on—as if to make it plain
hope's only as renewable as pain,

and as if all the unsung
debasements of the past may one day come
rising to the surface once again—
worked its filthy way out like a tongue. 1984

WILLIAM STAFFORD

At the Bomb Testing Site

At noon in the desert a panting lizard
waited for history, its elbows tense,
watching the curve of a particular road
as if something might happen.

It was looking at something farther off
than people could see, an important scene
acted in stone for little selves
at the flute end of consequences.

There was just a continent without much on it
under a sky that never cared less.
Ready for a change, the elbows waited.
The hands gripped hard on the desert. 1966

SHARON OLDS

May, 1968

The Dean of the University said
the neighborhood people could not cross campus
until the students gave up the buildings
so we lay down in the street,

we said The cops will enter this gate
over our bodies. Spine-down on the cobbles—
hard bed, like a carton of eggs—
I saw the buildings of New York City
from dirt level, they soared up and stopped,
chopped off cleanly—beyond them the sky
black and neither sour nor sweet, the
night air over the island.
The mounted police moved near us
delicately. Flat out on our backs
we sang, and then I began to count,
12, 13, 14, 15, I
counted again, 15, 16, one
month since the day on that deserted beach when we
used nothing, 17, 18, my
mouth fell open, my hair in the soil,
if my period did not come tonight
I was pregnant. I looked up at the sole of the
cop's shoe, I looked up at the
horse's belly, its genitals—if they
took me to Women's Detention and did the
exam on me, jammed the unwashed
speculum high inside me, the guard's
three fingers—supine on Broadway, I looked
up into the horse's tail like a
dark filthed comet. All week, I had
wanted to get arrested, longed to
give myself away. I lay in the
tar, one brain in my head and another
tiny brain at the base of my tail and I
stared at the world, good-luck iron
arc of the gelding's shoe, the cop's
baton, the deep curve of the animal's
belly, the buildings streaming up
away from the earth. I knew I should get up and
leave, stand up to muzzle level, to the
height of the soft velvet nostrils and
walk away, turn my back on my
friends and danger, but I was a coward so I
lay there looking up at the sky,
black vault arched above us, I
lay there gazing up at God, at his
underbelly, till it turned deep blue and then
silvery, colorless, *Give me this one*
night, I said, *and I'll give this child*
the rest of my life, the horses' heads
drooping, dipping, until they slept in a
dark circle around my body and my daughter.

1988

Ideas and Consciousness

DIANE WAKOSKI

A Poet Recognizing the Echo of the Voice

I. Isolation of Beautiful Women

"How were you able to get ten of the world's
most beautiful women to marry you?"
"I just asked them. You know, men all over
the world dream about Lana Turner, desire
her want to be with her. But very very
few ever ask her to marry them."
—paraphrase of an interview with
Artie Shaw

We are burning
in our heads
at night,
bonfires of our own bodies.
Persia reduces our heads
to star sapphires and lapis lazuli.[9]
Silver threads itself
into the lines of our throats
and glitters every time we speak.

Old alchemical riddles[1]
are solved in the dreams of men
who marry other women and think of us.
Anyone who sees us
will hold our small hands,
like mirrors in which they see themselves,
and try to initial our arms
with desperation.
Everyone wants to come close to
the cinnamon of our ears.
Every man wants to explore our bodies
and fill up our minds.
Riding their motorcycles along collapsing grey highways,
they sequester their ambivalent hunting clothes
between our legs,

9. Blue gems. 1. Problems. Alchemy was devoted to finding an elixir which would turn baser metals to gold (line 31).

reminding themselves of their value
by quoting mining stock prices, and ours.
But men do not marry us,
do not ask us to share their lives,
do not survive the bonfires
hot enough to melt steel.
To alchemize rubies.

We live the loneliness
that men run after,
and we,
the precious rocks of the earth
are made harder,
more fiery
more beautiful,
more complex,
by all the pressing,
the burying,
the plundering;

even your desertions,
your betrayals,
your failure to understand and love us,
your unwillingness to face the world
as staunchly as we do;
these things
which ravage us,
cannot destroy our lives,
though they often take our bodies.
We are the earth.
We wake up
finding ourselves
glinting in the dark
after thousands of years
of pressing.

II. Movement to Establish My Identity

I know what wages beauty gives,
How hard a life her servant lives . . .
—"To A Young Beauty," W. B. YEATS

A woman wakes up
finds herself
glinting in the dark;
the earth holds her
as a precious rock
in a mine

her breath is a jumble
of sediments,
of mixed strata,
of the valuable,
beautiful,
of bulk.

All men are miners;
willing to work hard
and cover themselves with pit dirt;
to dig out;
to weigh;
to possess.

Mine is a place.
Mine is a designation.
A man says, "it is mine,"
but he hacks,
chops apart the mine
to discover,
to plunder,
what's in it / Plunder,
that is the word.
Plunder.

A woman wakes up
finds herself
scarred
but still glinting
in the dark.

III. Beauty

only God, my dear,
Could love you for yourself alone
And not your yellow hair.
—"For Anne Gregory," W. B. YEATS

and if I cut off my long hair,
if I stopped speaking,
if I stopped dreaming for other people about parts of the car,
stopped handing them tall creamy flowered silks
and loosing the magnificent hawks to fly in their direction,
stopped exciting them with the possibilities
of a thousand crystals under the fingernail
to look at while writing a letter,
if I stopped crying for the salvation of the tea ceremony,
stopped rushing in excitedly with a spikey bird-of-paradise,[2]

2. A bright, spectacular plant.

and never let them see how accurate my pistol shooting is,
who would I be?

Where is the real me
I want them all to love?

We are all the textures we wear.

We frighten men with our steel;
we fascinate them with our silk;
we seduce them with our cinnamon;
we rule them with our sensuous voices;
we confuse them with our submissions.
Is there anywhere
a man
who
will not punish us
for our beauty?

He is the one
we all search for,
chanting names for exotic oceans of the moon.

He is the one
we all anticipate,
pretending these small pedestrians
jaywalking into our lives
are he.
He is the one
we all anticipate;
beauty looks for its match,
confuses the issue
with a mystery that does not exist:
the rock
that cannot burn.

We are burning
in our heads at night
the incense of our histories, finding
you have used our skulls
for ashtrays.

1970

ADRIENNE RICH

Delta

If you have taken this rubble for my past
raking through it for fragments you could sell

know that I long ago moved on
deeper into the heart of the matter

If you think you can grasp me, think again:
my story flows in more than one direction
a delta springing from the riverbed
with its five fingers spread

1989

MARGE PIERCY

What's That Smell in the Kitchen?

All over America women are burning dinners.
It's lambchops in Peoria; it's haddock
in Providence; it's steak in Chicago;
tofu delight in Big Sur; red
rice and beans in Dallas.
All over America women are burning
food they're supposed to bring with calico
smile on platters glittering like wax.
Anger sputters in her brainpan, confined
but spewing out missiles of hot fat.
Carbonized despair presses like a clinker
from a barbecue against the back of her eyes.
If she wants to grill anything, it's
her husband spitted over a slow fire.
If she wants to serve him anything
it's a dead rat with a bomb in its belly
ticking like the heart of an insomniac.
Her life is cooked and digested,
nothing but leftovers in Tupperware.
Look, she says, once I was roast duck
on your platter with parsley but now I am Spam.
Burning dinner is not incompetence but war.

1983

LIZ ROSENBERG

Married Love

The trees are uncurling their first
green messages: Spring, and some man
lets his arm brush my arm in a darkened
theatre. Faint-headed, I fight the throb.
Later I dream
the gas attendant puts a cool hand

on my breast, asking a question.
Slowly I rise through the surface of the dream,
brushing his hand and my own heat away.

Young, I burned to marry. Married,
the smolder goes on underground,
clutching at weeds, writhing everywhere.
I'm trying to talk to a friend on burning
issues, flaming from the feet up,
drinking in his breath, touching his wrist.
I want to grab the pretty woman
on the street, seize the falcon
by its neck, beat my way into whistling steam.

I turn to you in the dark, oh husband,
watching your lit breath circle the pillow.
Then you turn to me, throwing first one limb
and then another over me, in the easy brotherly
lust of marriage. I cling to you
as if I were a burning ship and you
could save me, as if I won't go sliding down
beneath you soon; as if our lives are made of rise
and fall, and we could ride this out forever,
with longing's thunder rolling heavy in our arms.

1986

SHARON OLDS

The Elder Sister

When I look at my elder sister now
I think how she had to go first, down through the
birth canal, to force her way
head-first through the tiny channel,
the pressure of Mother's muscles on her brain,
the tight walls scraping her skin.
Her face is still narrow from it, the long
hollow cheeks of a Crusader on a tomb,
and her inky eyes have the look of someone who has
been in prison a long time and
knows they can send her back. I look at her
body and think how her breasts were the first to
rise, slowly, like swans on a pond.
By the time mine came along, they were just
two more birds in the flock, and when the hair
rose on the white mound of her flesh, like
threads of water out of the ground, it was the
first time, but when mine came

they knew about it. I used to think
only in terms of her harshness, sitting and
pissing on me in bed, but now I
see I had her before me always
like a shield. I look at her wrinkles, her clenched
jaws, her frown-lines—I see they are
the dents on my shield, the blows that did not reach me.
She protected me, not as a mother
protects a child, with love, but as a
hostage protects the one who makes her
escape as I made my escape, with my sister's
body held in front of me. 1984

DOROTHY PARKER

Indian Summer

In youth, it was a way I had
To do my best to please,
And change, with every passing lad,
To suit his theories.

But now I know the things I know,
And do the things I do;
And if you do not like me so,
To hell, my love, with you! 1937

WARING CUNEY

No Images

She does not know
Her beauty,
She thinks her brown body
Has no glory.

If she could dance
Naked,
Under palm trees
And see her image in the river
She would know.

But there are no palm trees
On the street,
And dish water gives back no images. p. 1926

RUTH STONE

Second-Hand Coat

I feel
in her pockets; she wore nice cotton gloves,
kept a handkerchief box, washed her undies,
ate at the Holiday Inn, had a basement freezer,
belonged to a bridge club.
I think when I wake in the morning
that I have turned into her.
She hangs in the hall downstairs,
a shadow with pulled threads.
I slip her over my arms, skin of a matron.
Where are you? I say to myself, to the orphaned body,
and her coat says,
Get your purse, have you got your keys?

1987

KAY SMITH

Annunciation

FOR *Kathy*

In all the old paintings
The Virgin is reading—
No one knows what,
When she is disturbed
By an angel with a higher mission,
Beyond books.

She looks up reluctantly,
Still marking the place with her finger.
The angel is impressive,
With red shoes and just
A hint of wing and shine everywhere.
Listening to the measured message
The Virgin bows her head,
Her eyes aslant
Between the angel and the book.

At the Uffizi[3]
We stood

3. The richest art gallery in Italy, located in Florence. Its collection includes a painting of the annunciation by the 14th-century Sienese painter Simone Martini.

Before a particularly beautiful angel
And a hesitant Sienese Virgin,
We two sometimes women.
Believing we could ignore
All messages,
Unobliged to wings or words,
We laughed in the vibrant space
Between the two,
Somewhere in the angled focus
Of the Virgin's eye.

Now, in the harder times,
I do not laugh so often;
Still the cheap postcard in my room
Glints with the angel's robe.
I look with envy
At the angel and the book,
Wishing I had chosen
One or the other,
Anything but the space between.

1986

PAULETTE JILES

Paper Matches

My aunts washed dishes while the uncles
squirted each other on the lawn with
garden hoses. Why are we in here,
I said, and they are out there.
That's the way it is,
said Aunt Hetty, the shrivelled-up one.
I have the rages that small animals have,
being small, being animal.
Written on me was a message,
"At Your Service" like a book of
paper matches. One by one we were
taken out and struck.
We come bearing supper.
our heads on fire.

1973

STEPHEN DUNN

The Man Who Closed Shop

To allow himself to be properly held
he had to let his body
soften, give it unguarded, willingly,

to her. It meant suspension
of achievement,
a celebration in a country

without government. Always he desired
the getting there,
loved, in fact, getting lost

on the way. But too often,
too soon,
he'd think of the office

or a program he was missing
on T.V.   He'd feel
his body pull back into itself

like a man closing his own shop
mid-day
for reasons he didn't understand.

He'd roll away, thinking to himself
"This is pleasure, too,"
knowing he'd need different words—

yet whatever his explanation
she knew it
beforehand, several touches ago.

1989

CYNTHIA MacDONALD

Two Brothers in a Field of Absence

Because as they cut it was that special green, they decided
To make a woman of the fresh hay. They wished to lie in green, to wrap
Themselves in it, light but not pale, silvered but not gray,
Green and ample, big enough so both of them could shelter together
In any of her crevices, the armpit, the join
Of hip and groin. They—who knew what there was to know about baling
The modern way with hay so you rolled it up like a carpet,

Rather than those loose stacks—they packed the green body tight
So she wouldn't fray. Each day they molted her to keep her
Green and soft. Only her hair was allowed to ripen into yellow tousle.

The next weeks whenever they stopped cutting they lay with her.
She was always there, waiting, reliable, their green woman.
She gathered them in, yes she did,
Into the folds of herself, like the mother they hadn't had.
Like the woman they had had, only more pliant, more graceful,
Welcoming in a way that you never just found.
They not only had the awe of taking her,
But the awe of having made her. They drank beer
Leaning against the pillow of her belly,
And one would tell the other, "Like two Adams creating."
And they marvelled as they placed
The cans at her ankles, at her neck, at her wrists so she
Glittered gold and silver. They adorned what they'd made.
After harrowing, they'd come to her, drawing
The fountains of the Plains, the long line
Of irrigating spray, and moisten her up.
And lean against her tight, green thighs to watch buzzards
Circle black against the pink stain of the sunset.
What time she began to smolder they never knew—
Sometime between night when they'd left her
And evening when they returned. Wet green hay
Can go a long time smoldering before you notice. It has a way
Of catching itself, of asserting that
There is no dominion over it but the air. And it flares suddenly,
Like a redhead losing its temper, and allows its long, bright hair
To tangle in the air, letting you know again
That what shelters you can turn incendiary in a flash.
And then there is only the space of what has been,
An absence in the field, memory in the shape of a woman. p. 1983

RICHARD HUGO

To Women

You start it all. You are lovely.
We look at you and we flow.
So a line begins, on the page, on air,
in the all of self. We have misused you,
invested you with primal sin. You bleed
for our regret we are not more.
The dragon wins. We come home and sob

and you hold us and say we are brave
and in the future will do better.
So far, so good.

Now some of you want out and I don't
blame you, not a tiny bit. You've caught on.
You have the right to veer off flaming
in a new direction, mud flat and diamond mine,
clavicord and dead drum. Whatever
Please know our need remains the same.
It's a new game every time, one on one.

In me today is less rage than ever, less hurt.
When I imagine some good woman young
I no longer imagine her cringing
in cornstalks, cruel father four rows away
beating corn leaves aside with a club.
That is release you never expected
from a past you never knew you had.
My horse is not sure he can make it
to the next star. You are free.

1980

QUESTIONS

1. What additional information would you like to have about the events referred to in "Emmett Till" and "Ballad of Birmingham"? What details in each poem seem to require additional information about the events on which it is based? On the basis of the poem's reference to the incident, how do you think Emmett Till died? What do you make of the mention of "dogs," "clubs," and "hoses" in "Ballad of Birmingham"? What did "Freedom March" mean in 1969? Given the poem's structure and its portrayal of children's voices and attitudes, what difference might it make to your reading of the poem if you had factual information about the actual casualties of the bombing? If you were editing this poem, what other footnotes would you provide?

2. What kinds of attitudes toward World War I might explain the stances taken by Pound and Yeats in "There Died a Myriad" and "On Being Asked for a War Poem"? Who is the "old bitch gone in the teeth" ("There Died a Myriad," line 3)? What, exactly, is meant by "times like these" ("On Being Asked for a War Poem," line 1)?

3. What details about the physical suffering from poison gas are specifically suggested in "Dulce et Decorum Est"? What details about the physical effects

of atomic explosions in "Welcome to Hiroshima"? How accurate are these representations? Using the reference resources in your college library, look up news accounts of gassings in World War I and the atomic bombing of Hiroshima, and compare the journalistic details with those given in the poems. How careful does each poet seem to have been in representing historical events? What evidence do you find of distortion or "poetic license"? Which details are specifically chosen for powerful rhetorical effects in each poem?

4. Compare the images of fire and burning in "A Poet Recognizing the Echo of the Voice," "What's That Smell in the Kitchen?," "Married Love," and "Paper Matches." To what different uses is the image put in each poem? What common thread of meaning informs the images in all the poems? On what kind of cultural assumptions about women and their roles does the image seem to be based? In what ways is this image like other images of passion in poems in this chapter or elsewhere in the book? In what ways is the image like other images of destruction?

5. What is the relationship between burning "to marry" (line 10), "burning issues" (lines 13–14), and the "burning ship" (line 24) in "Married Love"? What, exactly, is the dramatic situation in the poem? In what specific ways does the speaker's attitude change in the course of the poem? How do you interpret the poem's "as ifs" in final stanza? What is the poem's ultimate attitude toward "married love"? Explain the imagery of mines and mining in "A Poet Recognizing the Echo of the Voice." Explain the imagery of jewels. How does the poem's final image of skulls as ashtrays relate to the different patterns of imagery in the poem?

6. Which poems in the *Ideas and Consciousness* group are especially concerned to suggest the importance of physical space? In what ways do they portray its absence? In what ways do they represent the male sense of a woman's "place"? How does the image of "rubble" in "Delta" (line 1) relate to the images of place, material evidence, and destruction in other poems? Why does the speaker of "Delta" describe herself and her past as ungraspable (line 5)? In what sense has she "moved on" (line 3) beyond the "rubble"? Explain the ironies in the phrase "the heart of the matter" (line 4). Explain the poem's title.

7. What images of passivity, deferentiality, and compliance can you find in the poems in *Ideas and Consciousness?* How is each image treated in the individual poem? In what ways do images of assertion and resistance compete with these images?

WRITING SUGGESTIONS

1. Using reference materials available in your college's library, construct a short but detailed narrative (of about 500 to 700 words) of either the Emmett Till murder or the Birmingham bombing. Then "read" the poem in the context of the full story, showing how the poem uses specific details of the incident to create its effects.

2. In an essay of no more than 1,000 words, compare the structure of "Sonnet: The Ladies' Home Journal" with that of "Welcome to Hiroshima."

3. Compare the speaker of "May, 1968" with that of "The Elder Sister." In an essay of about 800 words, show how each speaker characterizes herself through attitudes toward other people.

13 LITERARY TRADITION

The more poetry you read, the better a reader of poetry you are likely to be. This is not just because your skills will improve and develop, but also because you will come to know more about the poetic tradition and can thus understand more fully how poets draw upon each other. Poets are conscious of other poets, and often they refer to each other's work or use it as a starting point for their own, in ways that may not be immediately obvious to an outsider. Poetry can be treated as a form of argument: poets agree or disagree over basic matters. Sometimes a quiet (or even noisy) competitiveness is at the bottom of their concern with what other poems have done or can do; at other times, playfulness and a sense of humor about poetic possibilities take over, and the competitiveness dwindles to fun and poetic games. And often poets want to tap the rich mine of artistic expression just to share in the bounty of our heritage. In any case, a poet's consciousness of what others have done leads to a sense of tradition that is often hard to articulate but nevertheless is very important to the effects of poetry—and this sense of tradition is something of a problem for a relatively new reader of poetry. How can I possibly read this poem intelligently, we are likely to ask sometimes in exasperation, until I've read all the other poems ever written? It's a real problem. Poets don't actually expect that all of their readers have Ph.D.s in literature, but sometimes it *seems* as if they do. For some poets—T. S. Eliot is one example—it does help if one has read practically everything imaginable.

Why are poets so dependent on each other? What is the point of their relentless consciousness of what has already been done by others? Why do they repeatedly answer, allude to, and echo other poems? Why is a sense of tradition so important to them?

A sense of common task, a kind of communality of purpose, accounts for some traditional poetic practice, and the desire of individual poets to achieve a place in the English and American poetic tradition accounts for more. Many poets are anxious to be counted among those who achieve, through their writing, a place in history; and a way of establishing that place is to define for oneself the relationship between one's own work and that of others whose place is already secure. There is, for many poets, a sense of a serious and abiding cultural tradition which they wish to share and pass on; but also important is a shared sense of playfulness, a kind of poetic gamesmanship. Making words dance on the page or in our heads provides in itself a satisfaction and delight for many writers—pride in craft that is rather like the pride of a painter or potter or tennis player. Often poets set themselves a particular task to see what they can do. One way of doing that is to introduce a standard traditional **motif** (a recurrent device, formula, or situation that deliberately connects a poem with common patterns of existing thought), and then to play variations on it much as a musician might do. Another way is to provide an alternative answer to a question that has repeatedly been asked and answered in a traditional way. Poetic playfulness by no means excludes serious intention—the poems in this chapter often make important statements about their subject, however humorous they may be in their method. Some teasing of the tradition and of other poets is pure fun, a kind of kidding among good friends; some is rather more harsh and represents an attempt to see the world very differently—to define and articulate a very different set of attitudes and values.

The English poetic tradition is a rich and varied heritage, and individual poets draw upon it in countless ways. You have probably noticed, in the poems you have read so far, a number of allusions, glances at the tradition or at individual expressions of it. The more poems you read, the more you will notice and the more you will yourself become a comfortable member of the audience poets write for. Poets do expect a lot—not always but often enough to make a new reader feel nervous and sometimes inadequate. The other side of that discomfort comes when you begin to notice things that other readers don't.

The three groups of poems in this chapter illustrate some of the ways that the tradition energizes individual poets and suggest some of the things poets like to do with their heritage. The poems in the first group specifically draw on a particular poem or a motif that runs through a series of traditional poems. "To His Coy Mistress," "[(ponder, darling, these busted statues]," and "To His Importunate Mistress . . ." share a common subject (love), theme (time is short), and urgency of tone (let's not wait; let's make love now). Often these poems seem rather self-conscious—as if each poet is aware of a common tradition and is trying to do something a little bit different. However "sincere" they are as seduction poems, their sense of play is equally important in its variation upon the standard *carpe diem* (seize the day: live for the moment) motif, which dates back at least to classical Roman times and is the source of countless poems. The next three poems pick on (playfully) Christopher Marlowe's "The Passionate Shepherd to His Love" (p. 851). In effect, all of them provide "answers" to that poem. It is as if "his love" were telling the shepherd what is the matter with his argument, and the poets are answering Marlowe, too. These poets know full well what Marlowe was doing in the fantasy of his original poem, and they clearly have a lot of fun telling him how people in various circumstances might feel about his fantasy. There is in the end a lot of joy in their "realistic" deflation of his magic, and not much hostility. The poems by Koch, Skirrow, and Hecht poke gentle fun at other famous works, offering a summary or another version of what might have happened in each. (See, respectively, "This Is Just to Say" [p. 1073], "Ode on a Grecian Urn" [p. 891], and "Dover Beach" [p. 698].) Strictly speaking, only one of these poems (the one by Koch) is a parody (that is, it pretends to write in the style of the original poem but comically exaggerates that style); the other two have a similar objective of answering an original, although they use very different styles to alter, totally, the poetic intention of that original. "Ode on a Grecian Urn Summarized" teases Keats as well as the whole notion of poetic summaries; the effects of the summary are not very much like those of the Keats poem. "Penelope" offers a different perspective—the woman's—on a famous episode in mythology and thus puts a wholly different interpretation on the event. "The Dover Bitch," on the other hand, is as its subtitle suggests much more than just a different perspective on the situation presented in "Dover Beach"; it uses the tradition to criticize art *and* life.

The poems in the *Mythology and Myth* group draw on a tradition that is larger than just "literary." Mythologies involve whole systems of belief, usually cultural in scope, and the familiar literary formulations of these mythologies are just the surface articulations of a larger explanation of why the world works the way it does.

Every culture develops stories to explain itself. These stories try to explain to us who we are and why we are the way we are. Taken together, they constitute what is often called a **myth.** Calling it a myth does not mean that it is false. In fact, it means nearly the opposite, for a culture takes its myths seriously as explanations of why things are the way they are, why the history of that culture has gone in a particular way. Myth, in the sense in which it is used here, involves the explanations that are more or less universally shared within a particular culture; it is a frame of reference that people within the culture understand and share. A sharing of this frame of reference does not mean that all people within a culture are carbon copies of each other or that popular stereotypes represent reality accurately, nor does it mean that every individual in the culture *knows* the perceived history and can articulate its events, ideas, and values. But it does mean that a shared history and a shared set of symbols lie behind any particular culture and that the culture is to some extent aware of its distinctiveness from other cultures.

A **culture** may be of many sizes and shapes. Often we think of a nation as a culture (and so speak of American culture, American history, the myth of

America, the American dream, the American frame of reference), and it is equally useful to make smaller and larger divisions—as long as there is some commonality of history and some cohesiveness of purpose within the group. One can speak of Southern culture, for example, or of urban culture, or of the drug culture, or of the various popular music cultures, or of a culture associated with a particular political belief, economic class, or social group. Most of us belong, willingly or not, to a number of such cultures at one time, and to some extent our identity and destiny are linked with the distinctive features of those cultures and with the ways each culture perceives its identity, values, and history. Some of these cultures we choose to join; some are thrust upon us by birth and circumstances. It is these larger and more persistent forms of culture that are illustrated in this chapter.

Poets, aware of their heritage, often like to probe its history and beliefs and plumb its depths, just as they like to articulate and play variations on the poetic tradition they feel a part of. For poetry written in the English language over the last 400 years or so, both the Judaeo-Christian frame of reference and the classical frame of reference (drawing on the civilizations of ancient Greece and Rome) have been quite important. Western culture, a broad culture that includes many nations and many religious and social groups, is largely defined within these two frames of reference—or it has been until quite recently. As religious belief has eroded over the past two or three centuries, and as classical civilization has been less emphasized and less studied, poets have felt increasingly less comfortable in assuming that their audiences share a knowledge of their systems, but they have often continued to use them to isolate and articulate human traits that have cultural continuity and importance. More recently, poets have drawn on other cultural myths—Native American, African, and Asian, for example—to expand our sense of common heritage and give new meaning to the "American" and "Western" experience.

The final group of poems in this chapter illustrate the familiar poetic strategy of echoing or alluding to other texts as a way of importing meaning into a particular poem. Strategies of echo and allusion can be very complicated, for the question of just how much of one text can carry over—or be forcibly brought over—into another one is not one that can be answered categorically.

Often poets quote—or echo with variations—a passage from another text in order to suggest some thematic, ideological, tonal, or other link. Sometimes the purpose is simply to invoke an idea or attitude from another text, another place, or another culture. Thus, in Adrienne Rich's "Two Songs" (p. 746) Chaucer's familiar formulation of the rites of Spring (with its description of all things coming to life, their vital juices flowing, as they follow the natural progress of the seasons) is introduced into the text to suggest the way the sap rises and bodies merge in ordinary lusty human beings. The speaker's attraction to a lover is thus put into a larger human perspective, and her sense of herself as a subject and object of lust comes to seem ordinary, part of the natural course of events.

The first poem in *Echo and Allusion* belongs, uncomfortably, in the *carpe diem* tradition with the first few poems in *Imitating and Answering*; but unlike ordinary *carpe diem* poems it is moralistic. It undercuts the speaker by having him allude to familiar biblical passages that imply a condemnation of live-for-today attitudes and ideas. By echoing Satan's tempting addresses to Eve in Genesis, the speaker in "Come, My Celia" condemns himself in the eyes of readers and becomes a seducer-tempter instead of a libertine-hero. The other three poems allude, respectively, to Ovid, Keats, and Auden, and the meaning of each poem derives primarily from a sorting through of the allusion. Poems do not necessarily need earlier texts to exist or mean, but prior texts may set up what happens in a particular poem or govern how it is to be construed. Allusion is the strategy of using one text to comment on—and influence the interpretation of—another. It is one of the most popular, familiar, and frequent strategies that poets use.

▽ ▽ ▽

Imitating and Answering

ANDREW MARVELL

To His Coy Mistress

Had we but world enough, and time,
This coyness,[1] lady, were no crime.
We would sit down, and think which way
To walk, and pass our long love's day.
Thou by the Indian Ganges' side
Shouldst rubies[2] find: I by the tide
Of Humber[3] would complain. I would
Love you ten years before the Flood,
And you should if you please refuse

1. Hesitancy, modesty (not necessarily suggesting calculation). 2. Talismans which are supposed to preserve virginity. 3. A small river which flows through Marvell's home town of Hull. *Complain:* write love complaints, conventional songs lamenting the cruelty of love.

Till the conversion of the Jews.[4]
My vegetable love[5] should grow
Vaster than empires, and more slow;
An hundred years should go to praise
Thine eyes, and on thy forehead gaze;
Two hundred to adore each breast,
But thirty thousand to the rest.
An age at least to every part,
And the last age should show your heart.
For, lady, you deserve this state;[6]
Nor would I love at lower rate.
    But at my back I always hear
Time's wingéd chariot hurrying near;
And yonder all before us lie
Deserts of vast eternity.
Thy beauty shall no more be found,
Nor, in thy marble vault, shall sound
My echoing song; then worms shall try
That long preserved virginity,
And your quaint honor turn to dust,
And into ashes all my lust:
The grave's a fine and private place,
But none, I think, do there embrace.
    Now therefore, while the youthful hue
Sits on thy skin like morning dew,[7]
And while thy willing soul transpires[8]
At every pore with instant fires,
Now let us sport us while we may,
And now, like am'rous birds of prey,
Rather at once our time devour
Than languish in his slow-chapped[9] pow'r.
Let us roll all our strength and all
Our sweetness up into one ball,
And tear our pleasures with rough strife
Thorough[1] the iron gates of life.
Thus, though we cannot make our sun
Stand still,[2] yet we will make him run.[3]

1681

4. Which, according to popular Christian belief, will occur just before the end of the world. 5. Which is capable only of passive growth, not of consciousness. The "Vegetable Soul" is lower than the other two divisions of the Soul, "Animal" and "Rational." 6. Dignity. 7. The text reads "glew." "Lew" (warmth) has also been suggested as an emendation. 8. Breathes forth. 9. Slow-jawed. Chronos (Time), ruler of the world in early Greek myth, devoured all of his children except Zeus, who was hidden. Later, Zeus seized power (see line 46 and note). 1. Through. 2. To lengthen his night of love with Alcmene, Zeus made the sun stand still. 3. Each sex act was believed to shorten life by one day.

E. E. CUMMINGS

[(ponder,darling,these busted statues]

(ponder,darling,these busted statues
of yon motheaten forum be aware
notice what hath remained
—the stone cringes
clinging to the stone,how obsolete

lips utter their extant smile . . .
remark

a few deleted of texture
or meaning monuments and dolls

resist Them Greediest Paws of careful
time all of which is extremely
unimportant) whereas Life

matters if or

when the your- and my-
idle vertical worthless
self unite in a peculiarly
momentary

partnership (to instigate
constructive
                    Horizontal
business . . . even so,let us make haste
—consider well this ruined aqueduct

lady,
which used to lead something into somewhere) 1926

PETER DE VRIES

To His Importunate Mistress

ANDREW MARVELL UPDATED

Had we but world enough, and time,
My coyness, lady, were a crime,
But at my back I always hear
Time's wingèd chariot, striking fear
The hour is nigh when creditors
Will prove to be my predators.
As wages of our picaresque,

Bag lunches bolted at my desk
Must stand as fealty to you
For each expensive rendezvous.
Obeisance at your marble feet
Deserves the best-appointed suite,
And would have, lacked I not the pelf
To pleasure also thus myself;
But aptly sumptuous amorous scenes
Rule out the rake of modest means.

Since mistress presupposes wife,
It means a doubly costly life;
For fools by second passion fired
A second income is required,
The earning which consumes the hours
They'd hoped to spend in rented bowers.
To hostelries the worst of fates
That weekly raise their daily rates!
I gather, lady, from your scoffing
A bloke more solvent in the offing.
So revels thus to rivals go
For want of monetary flow.
How vexing that inconstant cash
The constant suitor must abash,
Who with excuses vainly pled
Must rue the undishevelled bed,
And that for paltry reasons given
His conscience may remain unriven.

p. 1986

SIR WALTER RALEGH

The Nymph's Reply to the Shepherd

If all the world and love were young,
And truth in every shepherd's tongue,
These pretty pleasures might me move
To live with thee and be thy love.

Time drives the flocks from field to fold,
When rivers rage, and rocks grow cold,
And Philomel[4] becometh dumb;
The rest complain of cares to come.

The flowers do fade, and wanton fields
To wayward winter reckoning yields:

4. The nightingale.

A honey tongue, a heart of gall,
Is fancy's spring, but sorrow's fall.

Thy gowns, thy shoes, they beds of roses,
Thy cap, thy kirtle, and thy posies
Soon break, soon wither, soon forgotten;
In folly ripe, in reason rotten.

Thy belt of straw and ivy buds,
Thy coral clasps and amber studs,
All these in me no means can move
To come to thee and be thy love.

But could youth last, and love still breed,
Had joys no date,[5] nor age no need,
Then these delights my mind might move
To live with thee and be thy love.

1600

C. DAY LEWIS

Song

Come, live with me and be my love,
And we will all the pleasures prove
Of peace and plenty, bed and board,
That chance employment may afford.

I'll handle dainties on the docks
And thou shalt read of summer frocks:
At evening by the sour canals
We'll hope to hear some madrigals.

Care on thy maiden brow shall put
A wreath of wrinkles, and thy foot
Be shod with pain: not silken dress
But toil shall tire thy loveliness.

Hunger shall make thy modest zone
And cheat fond death of all but bone—
If these delights thy mind may move,
Then live with me and be my love.

1935

5. End.

WILLIAM CARLOS WILLIAMS

Raleigh Was Right

We cannot go to the country
for the country will bring us no peace
What can the small violets tell us
that grow on furry stems in
the long grass among lance shaped leaves?

Though you praise us
and call to mind the poets
who sung of our loveliness
it was long ago!
long ago! when country people
would plow and sow with
flowering minds and pockets at ease—
if ever this were true.

Not now. Love itself a flower
with roots in a parched ground.
Empty pockets make empty heads.
Cure it if you can but
do not believe that we can live
today in the country
for the country will bring us no peace.

1941

KENNETH KOCH

Variations on a Theme by William Carlos Williams

1

I chopped down the house that you had been saving to live in next
summer.
I am sorry, but it was morning, and I had nothing to do
and its wooden beams were so inviting.

2

We laughed at the hollyhocks together
and then I sprayed them with lye.
Forgive me. I simply do not know what I am doing.

3

I gave away the money that you had been saving to live on for the next ten years.
The man who asked for it was shabby
and the firm March wind on the porch was so juicy and cold.

4

Last evening we went dancing and I broke your leg.
Forgive me. I was clumsy, and
I wanted you here in the wards, where I am the doctor!

1962

DESMOND SKIRROW

Ode on a Grecian Urn Summarized

Gods chase
Round vase.
What say?
What play?
Don't know.
Nice, though.

p. 1960

ANTHONY HECHT

The Dover Bitch

A CRITICISM OF LIFE

FOR *Andrews Wanning*

So there stood Matthew Arnold and this girl
With the cliffs of England crumbling away behind them,
And he said to her, "Try to be true to me,
And I'll do the same for you, for things are bad
All over, etc., etc."
Well now, I knew this girl. It's true she had read
Sophocles in a fairly good translation
And caught that bitter allusion to the sea,[6]
But all the time he was talking she had in mind
The notion of what his whiskers would feel like

6. In Sophocles' *Antigone*, lines 583–91. See "Dover Beach," lines 9–18.

On the back of her neck. She told me later on
That after a while she got to looking out
At the lights across the channel, and really felt sad,
Thinking of all the wine and enormous beds
And blandishments in French and the perfumes.
And then she got really angry. To have been brought
All the way down from London, and then be addressed
As a sort of mournful cosmic last resort
Is really tough on a girl, and she was pretty.
Anyway, she watched him pace the room
And finger his watch-chain and seem to sweat a bit,
And then she said one or two unprintable things.
But you mustn't judge her by that. What I mean to say is,
She's really all right. I still see her once in a while
And she always treats me right. We have a drink
And I give her a good time, and perhaps it's a year
Before I see her again, but there she is,
Running to fat, but dependable as they come.
And sometimes I bring her a bottle of *Nuit d'Amour*.

1968

Mythology and Myth

A. D. HOPE

Imperial[7] Adam

Imperial Adam, naked in the dew,
Felt his brown flanks and found the rib was gone.
Puzzled he turned and saw where, two and two,
The mighty spoor of Jahweh marked the lawn.

Then he remembered through mysterious sleep
The surgeon fingers probing at the bone,
The voice so far away, so rich and deep:
"It is not good for him to live alone."

Turning once more he found Man's counterpart
In tender parody breathing at his side.
He knew her at first sight, he knew by heart
Her allegory of sense unsatisfied.

The pawpaw drooped its golden breasts above
Less generous than the honey of her flesh;

7. I.e., emperor.

The innocent sunlight showed the place of love;
The dew on its dark hairs winked crisp and fresh.

This plump gourd severed from his virile root,
She promised on the turf of Paradise
Delicious pulp of the forbidden fruit;
Sly as the snake she loosed her sinuous thighs,

And waking, smiled up at him from the grass;
Her breasts rose softly and he heard her sigh—
From all the beasts whose pleasant task it was
In Eden to increase and multiply

Adam had learned the jolly deed of kind:
He took her in his arms and there and then,
Like the clean beasts, embracing from behind,
Began in joy to found the breed of men.

Then from the spurt of seed within her broke
Her terrible and triumphant female cry,
Split upward by the sexual lightning stroke.
It was the beasts now who stood watching by:

The gravid elephant, the calving hind,
The breeding bitch, the she-ape big with young
Were the first gentle midwives of mankind;
The teeming lioness rasped her with her tongue;

The proud vicuña nuzzled her as she slept
Lax on the grass; and Adam watching too
Saw how her dumb breasts at their ripening wept,
The great pod of her belly swelled and grew,

And saw its water break, and saw, in fear,
Its quaking muscles in the act of birth,
Between her legs a pigmy face appear,
And the first murderer lay upon the earth.

1955

JOHN HOLLANDER

Adam's Task

And Adam gave names to all cattle, and to the fowl of the air, and to every beast of the field . . .

—Gen. 2:20

Thou, paw-paw-paw; thou, glurd; thou, spotted
    Glurd; thou, whitestap, lurching through
The high-grown brush; thou, pliant-footed,
    Implex; thou, awagabu.

Every burrower, each flier
  Came for the name he had to give:
Gay, first work, ever to be prior,
  Not yet sunk to primitive.

Thou, verdle; thou, McFleery's pomma;
  Thou; thou; thou—three types of grawl;
Thou, flisket; thou, kabasch; thou, comma-
  Eared mashawk; thou, all; thou, all.

Were, in a fire of becoming,
  Laboring to be burned away,
Then work, half-measuring, half-humming,
  Would be as serious as play.

Thou, pambler; thou, rivarn; thou, greater
  Wherret, and thou, lesser one;
Thou, sproal; thou, zant; thou, lily-eater.
  Naming's over. Day is done. 1971

CHRISTINA ROSSETTI

Eve

"While I sit at the door,
Sick to gaze within,
Mine eye weepeth sore
For sorrow and sin:
As a tree my sin stands
To darken all lands;
Death is the fruit it bore.

"How have Eden bowers grown
Without Adam to bend them!
How have Eden flowers blown,
Squandering their sweet breath,
Without me to tend them!
The Tree of Life was ours,
Tree twelvefold-fruited,[8]
Most lofty tree that flowers,
Most deeply rooted:
I chose the Tree of Death.[9]

8. The tree of life is so described in Revelation 22:2, 14, but the account there is of the New Jerusalem, not of Eden. 9. The Genesis account distinguishes between the tree of life and the tree of the knowledge of good and evil; the latter is forbidden, and eating of it brings labor, sickness, and death into the world. See Genesis 2:9, 3:1–24.

"Hadst thou but said me nay,
    Adam, my brother,
I might have pined away—
    I, but none other:
God might have let thee stay
Safe in our garden,
By putting me away
Beyond all pardon.

"I, Eve, sad mother
Of all who must live,
I, not another,
Plucked bitterest fruit to give
My friend, husband, lover.
O wanton eyes run over!
Who but I should grieve?—
Cain hath slain his brother:[1]
Of all who must die mother,
Miserable Eve!"
Thus she sat weeping,
Thus Eve our mother,
Where one lay sleeping
Slain by his brother.
Greatest and least
Each piteous beast
To hear her voice
Forgot his joys
And set aside his feast.

The mouse paused in his walk
And dropped his wheaten stalk;
Grave cattle wagged their heads
In rumination;
The eagle gave a cry
From his cloud station:
Larks on thyme beds
Forbore to mount or sing;
Bees dropped upon the wing;
The raven perched on high
Forgot his ration;
The conies[2] in their rock,
A feeble nation,
Quaked sympathetical;
The mocking-bird left off to mock;
Huge camels knelt as if
In deprecation;

1. Abel (see Genesis 4:1–15). 2. A common term for rabbits, but here probably the small pachyderms mentioned in Proverbs 30:26.

The kind hart's tears were falling;
Chattered the wistful stork;
Dove-voices with a dying fall
Cooed desolation
Answering grief by grief.

Only the serpent in the dust,
Wriggling and crawling,
Grinned an evil grin, and thrust
His tongue out with its fork.

1865

ROBERT FROST

Never Again Would Birds' Song Be the Same

He would declare and could himself believe
That the birds there in all the garden round
From having heard the daylong voice of Eve
Had added to their own an oversound,
Her tone of meaning but without the words.
Admittedly an eloquence so soft
Could only have had an influence on birds
When call or laughter carried it aloft.
Be that as may be, she was in their song.
Moreover her voice upon their voices crossed
Had now persisted in the woods so long
That probably it never would be lost.
Never again would birds' song be the same.
And to do that to birds was why she came.

1942

DAVID HELWIG

Lot[3]

should the pillar sing, should salt
talk aloud, it would be no wonder
in these days of miracles

in those cities
the frightened burghers gabbled

3. Nephew of Abraham who fled the destruction by fire of Sodom and Gomorrah (Genesis 19:1–25). Lot's wife looked behind her as she left the city and became a pillar of salt (Genesis 19:26).

as the fire came down
to punish their inventive appetites

oh who would not look back
to the familiar cities
the giddy degenerate afternoons
the daily chatter

should the pillar speak, what wonder

and I return now to listen
here in the desert

remember the hot afternoons
when I licked the sweat from her skin

by the light of the falling fire I wait
and my tongue, remembering, reaches,
touches salt and is stung

1969

ALFRED, LORD TENNYSON

Ulysses[4]

It little profits that an idle king,
By this still hearth, among these barren crags,
Matched with an agéd wife,[5] I mete and dole
Unequal laws unto a savage race,
That hoard, and sleep, and feed, and know not me.

I cannot rest from travel; I will drink
Life to the lees.[6] All times I have enjoyed
Greatly, have suffered greatly, both with those
That loved me, and alone; on shore, and when
Through scudding drifts the rainy Hyades[7]
Vexed the dim sea. I am become a name;
For always roaming with a hungry heart
Much have I seen and known—cities of men
And manners, climates, councils, governments,
Myself not least, but honored of them all—
And drunk delight of battle with my peers,
Far on the ringing plains of windy Troy.
I am a part of all that I have met;

4. After the end of the Trojan War, Ulysses (or Odysseus), King of Ithaca and one of the Greek heroes of the war, returned to his island home (line 34). Homer's account of the situation is in *The Odyssey*, Book XI, but Dante's account of Ulysses in *The Inferno*, XXVI, is the more immediate background of the poem. 5. Penelope. 6. All the way down to the bottom of the cup. 7. A group of stars which were supposed to predict rain when they rose at the same time as the sun.

Yet all experience is an arch wherethrough
Gleams that untraveled world, whose margin fades
For ever and for ever when I move.
How dull it is to pause, to make an end,
To rust unburnished, not to shine in use!
As though to breathe were life. Life piled on life
Were all too little, and of one to me
Little remains; but every hour is saved
From that eternal silence, something more,
A bringer of new things; and vile it were
For some three suns to store and hoard myself,
And this gray spirit yearning in desire
To follow knowledge like a sinking star,
Beyond the utmost bound of human thought.

This is my son, mine own Telemachus,
To whom I leave the scepter and the isle—
Well-loved of me, discerning to fulfill
This labor by slow prudence to make mild
A rugged people, and through soft degrees
Subdue them to the useful and the good.
Most blameless is he, centered in the sphere
Of common duties, decent not to fail
In offices of tenderness, and pay
Meet adoration to my household gods,
When I am gone. He works his work, I mine.

There lies the port; the vessel puffs her sail:
There gloom the dark, broad seas. My mariners,
Souls that have toiled, and wrought, and thought with me—
That ever with a frolic welcome took
The thunder and the sunshine, and opposed
Free hearts, free foreheads—you and I are old;
Old age hath yet his honor and his toil.
Death closes all; but something ere the end,
Some work of noble note, may yet be done,
Not unbecoming men that strove with Gods.
The lights begin to twinkle from the rocks;
The long day wanes; the slow moon climbs; the deep
Moans round with many voices. Come, my friends.
'Tis not too late to seek a newer world.
Push off, and sitting well in order smite
The sounding furrows; for my purpose holds
To sail beyond the sunset, and the baths
Of all the western stars, until I die.
It may be that the gulfs will wash us down;[8]

8. Beyond the Gulf of Gibraltar was supposed to be a chasm that led to Hades.

It may be we shall touch the Happy Isles,[9]
And see the great Achilles, whom we knew.
Though much is taken, much abides; and though
We are not now that strength which in old days
Moved earth and heaven, that which we are, we are:
One equal temper of heroic hearts,
Made weak by time and fate, but strong in will
To strive, to seek, to find, and not to yield.

1833

JAMES HARRISON

Penelope[1]

FOR *Ken*

Oh, I have no illusions as to what
he's been up to all these years—a sea
nymph here, a minor goddess there, and a free
for all with the odd monster to give the plot
the necessary epic tone. Not
that I'm saying he goes out of his way to be
led astray. It happens quite naturally,
I'm sure. But it happens.
So, since suitors squat
on my doorstep, why so squeamish? In the first
place because it's the property they're out
to get, with me as an afterthought perhaps.
Then they're so callow. But mostly, having nursed
forebearance for twenty years, I'm not about
to have him forgiving me my only lapse.

1983

LANGSTON HUGHES

The Negro Speaks of Rivers

I've known rivers:
I've known rivers ancient as the world and older than the flow of human blood
in human veins.

9. Elysium, the Islands of the Blessed, where heroes like Achilles (line 64) abide after death.
1. *Penelope*—wife of Ulysses, stuck at home the ten years he spent fighting Troy, and the further ten it took him to find his way back to Ithaca. (Author's note.)

My soul has grown deep like the rivers.

I bathed in the Euphrates when dawns were young.
I built my hut near the Congo and it lulled me to sleep.
I looked upon the Nile and raised the pyramids above it.
I heard the singing of the Mississippi when Abe Lincoln went down to New Orleans, and I've seen its muddy bosom turn all golden in the sunset.

I've known rivers:
Ancient, dusky rivers.

My soul has grown deep like the rivers.

1926

GABRIEL OKARA

Piano and Drums

When at break of day at a riverside
I hear jungle drums telegraphing
the mystic rhythm, urgent, raw
like bleeding flesh, speaking of
primal youth and the beginning,
I see the panther ready to pounce,
the leopard snarling about to leap
and the hunters crouch with spears poised;

And my blood ripples, turns torrent,
topples the years and at once I'm
in my mother's lap a suckling;
at once I'm walking simple
paths with no innovations,
rugged, fashioned with the naked
warmth of hurrying feet and groping hearts
in green leaves and wild flowers pulsing.

Then I hear a wailing piano
solo speaking of complex ways
in tear-furrowed concerto;
of far-away lands
and new horizons with
coaxing diminuendo, counterpoint,
crescendo. But lost in the labyrinth
of its complexities, it ends in the middle
of a phrase at a daggerpoint.

And I lost in the morning mist
of an age at a riverside keep
wandering in the mystic rhythm
of jungle drums and the concerto.

1963

MAYA ANGELOU

Africa

Thus she had lain
sugar cane sweet
deserts her hair
golden her feet
mountains her breasts
two Niles her tears
Thus she has lain
Black through the years.

Over the white seas
rime white and cold
brigands ungentled
icicle bold
took her young daughters
sold her strong sons
churched her with Jesus
bled her with guns.
Thus she has lain.

Now she is rising
remember her pain
remember the losses
her screams loud and vain
remember her riches
her history slain
now she is striding
although she had lain. 1975

ISHMAEL REED

I Am a Cowboy in the Boat of Ra

The devil must be forced to reveal any such physical evil (potions, charms, fetishes, etc.) still outside the body and these must be burned.

—*Rituale Romanum*, published 1947, endorsed by the coat of arms and introduction letter from Francis Cardinal Spellman

I am a cowboy in the boat of Ra,[2]
sidewinders in the saloons of fools
bit my forehead like O

2. Chief of the ancient Egyptian gods, creator and protector of humans and vanquisher of Evil.

the untrustworthiness of Egyptologists
Who do not know their trips. Who was that
dog-faced man?[3] they asked, the day I rode
from town.

School marms with halitosis cannot see
the Nefertiti[4] fake chipped on the run by slick
germans, the hawk behind Sonny Rollins' head or
the ritual beard of his axe,[5] a longhorn winding
its bells thru the Field of Reeds.

I am a cowboy in the boat of Ra. I bedded
down with Isis,[6] Lady of the Boogaloo, dove
down deep in her horny, stuck up her Wells-Far-ago
in daring midday get away. "Start grabbing the
blue," i said from top of my double crown.

I am a cowboy in the boat of Ra. Ezzard Charles[7]
of the Chisholm Trail. Took up the bass but they
blew off my thumb. Alchemist in ringmanship but a
sucker for the right cross.

I am a cowboy in the boat of Ra. Vamoosed from
the temple i bide my time. The price on the wanted
poster was a-going down, outlaw alias copped my stance
and moody greenhorns were making me dance; while my mouth's
shooting iron got its chambers jammed.

I am a cowboy in the boat of Ra. Boning-up in
the ol West i bide my time. You should see
me pick off these tin cans whippersnappers. I
write the motown long plays for the comeback of
Osiris.[8] Make them up when stars stare at sleeping
steer out here near the campfire. Women arrive
on the backs of goats and throw themselves on
my Bowie.[9]

I am a cowboy in the boat of Ra. Lord of the lash,
the Loup Garou[1] Kid. Half breed son of Pisces and
Aquarius. I hold the souls of men in my pot. I do
the dirty boogie with scorpions. I make the bulls
keep still and was the first swinger to grape the taste.

3. The Egyptian god of the dead Anubis was usually depicted as a man with the head of a dog or jackal. 4. Fourteenth-century B.C. Egyptian queen; elsewhere Reed says that German scholars are responsible for the notion that her dynasty was white. 5. Saxophone. *Sonny Rollins:* jazz great of the late 1950s and early 1960s. 6. Principal goddess of ancient Egypt. 7. World heavyweight boxing champion, 1949–51. 8. Husband of Isis and constant foe of his brother Set (line 48). Tricked by Set, he died violently but later rose from the dead. 9. Large hunting knife. 1. French for werewolf; in voodoo, a priest who has run amok or gone mad.

I am a cowboy in his boat. Pope Joan[2] of the
Ptah Ra. C / mere a minute willya doll?
Be a good girl and
Bring me my Buffalo horn of black powder
Bring me my headdress of black feathers
Bring me my bones of Ju-Ju snake
Go get my eyelids of red paint.
Hand me my shadow
I'm going into town after Set

I am a cowboy in the boat of Ra
look out Set   here i come Set
to get Set   to sunset Set
to unseat Set   to Set down Set
                    usurper of the Royal couch
                    imposter RAdio of Moses' bush[3]
                    party pooper O hater of dance
                    vampire outlaw of the milky way

1969

Echo and Allusion

BEN JONSON

Come, My Celia[4]

Come, my Celia, let us prove,[5]
While we can, the sports of love;
Time will not be ours forever:
He at length our good will sever.
Spend not, then, his gifts in vain;
Suns that set may rise again,
But if once we lose this light,
'Tis with us perpetual night.
Why should we defer our joys?
Fame and rumor are but toys.
Cannot we delude the eyes
Of a few poor household spies?
Or his easier ears beguile,
Thus removéd by our wile?
'Tis no sin love's fruits to steal,

2. Mythical female pope, supposed to have succeeded to the papacy in 855. *Ptah Ra:* chief god of Memphis, capital of ancient Egypt. **3.** Which, according to Exodus 3:2, burned but was not consumed and from which Moses heard the voice of God telling him to lead the Israelites out of Egypt. **4.** A song from *Volpone*, sung by the play's villain and would-be seducer. Part of the poem paraphrases Catullus, V. **5.** Try.

But the sweet thefts to reveal;
To be taken, to be seen,
These have crimes accounted been. 1606

D. G. JONES

Summer Is a Poem by Ovid[6]

FOR *Michael Ondaatje*

The fire falls, the night
Grows more profound.
The music is composed
Of clear chords
And silence. We become
Clear and simple as the forms
Of music; we are dumb
As water
Mirroring the stars.

Then summer is
Ovidian, and every sun
Is but a moth evolving
In the large gloom,
An excerpt from
Ars Amoris: flame
Is no more fleeting than the limbs
Of boy and girl: the conflagration
Is the same.

While the fire falls, and night
Grows more profound, the flesh,
The music and the flame
All undergo
Metamorphosis. The sounds
Of music make a close,
So with our several selv s,
Together, until silence shall compose
All but the ashes in the pale dawn
And even those. 1983

6. The most brilliant Roman poet of his generation, Ovid (43 B.C.–17 A.D.) was the author of *Ars Amoris (The Art of Love)*, a handbook of seduction, and of the *Metamorphoses*, his great work that brings together a treasure house of mythological stories with Pythagoras's philosophy of impermanence and unceasing change.

ROBERT HOLLANDER

You Too? Me Too—Why Not? Soda Pop

I am
look
ing at
the Co
caCola
bottle
which is
green wi
th ridges
just like
c c c
o o o
l l l
u u u
m m m
n n n
s s s
and on itself it says

COCA-COLA
reg. u.s. pat. off.

exactly like an art pop
statue of that kind of
bottle but not so green
that the juice inside
gives other than the co
lor it has when I pour
it out in a clear glass
glass on this table top
(It's making me thirsty
all this winking and
beading of Hippocrene
please let me pause
drinking the fluid in)
ah! it is enticing how
each color is the same
brown in green bottle
brown in uplifted glass
making each utensil on
the table laid a brown
fork in a brown shade
making me long to watch
them harvesting the crop
which makes the deep-aged
rich brown wine of America
that is to say which makes
soda pop

p. 1968

DANNIE ABSE

Brueghel in Naples

> About suffering they were never wrong,
> The Old Masters . . .
>
> —W. H. AUDEN

Ovid would never have guessed how far
and father's notion about wax melting, bah!
It's ice up there. Freezing.
Soaring and swooping over solitary altitudes
I was breezing along (a record I should think)
when my wings began to moult not melt.
These days, workmanship, I ask you.
Appalling.

There's a mountain down there on fire
and I'm falling, falling away from it.
Phew, the sun's on the horizon
or am I upside down?

Great Bacchus, the sea is rearing
up. Will I drown? My white legs
the last to disappear? (I have no trousers on)
A little to the left the ploughman,
a little to the right a galleon,
a sailor climbing the rigging,
a fisherman casting his line,
and now I hear a shepherd's dog barking.
I'm that near.

Lest I have no trace
but a few scattered feathers on the water
show me your face, sailor,
look up, fisherman,
look this way, shepherd,
turn around, ploughman.
Raise the alarm! Launch a boat!

My luck. I'm seen
only by a jackass of an artist
interested in composition, in the green
tinge of the sea, in the aesthetics
of disaster—not in me.

I drown, bubble by bubble,
(Help! Save me!)
while he stands ruthlessly
before the canvas, busy busy,
intent on becoming an Old Master.

1991

QUESTIONS

1. Read the Cummings poem, [(ponder,darling,these busted statues], closely in relation to Marvell's poem. In what specific ways does it echo "To His Coy Mistress"? Which images are specifically derived from Marvell? In what specific ways does the Cummings poem undercut the argument of the Marvell poem? In what ways does it undercut its own argument? To what purpose?

2. Indicate the specific ways in which Ralegh's poem "replies" to Marlowe's. In what points does Williams agree with Ralegh? How, exactly, does the C. Day Lewis poem "update" Marlowe? Describe its tone and attitude toward Marlowe. What, exactly, is "unfair" about Skirrow's summary of Keats? How do you think Keats would justify himself against Skirrow's summary?

3. What attitudes toward Adam and Eve are displayed in the Hope, Hollander, Rossetti, and Frost poems? Which poems develop the strongest negative attitudes toward their "heroes" or "heroines"? From what perspective does Helwig retell the story of Lot and his wife? How does Harrison's version of the Ulysses story differ from Tennyson's? What values are associated with Africa in the Okara, Angelou, and Reed poems? What is the "cowboy" doing in Reed's poem?

4. How, specifically, is the speaker undercut in Jonson's "Come, My Celia"? Explain how the strategy of allusion works in this poem. How seriously do you take Robert Hollander's allusion to Keats? Abse's allusion to Brueghel? to Auden? What effect does each allusion create?

WRITING SUGGESTIONS

1. In what specific ways is "To His Coy Mistress" anchored to its historical or cultural context? Can you tell that it is written by a 17th-century poet? How? What historical or cultural "allusions" anchor the poem to its specific moment in time? To its philosophical or thematic contexts? In what specific ways does the de Vries poem establish itself as contemporary? Write a short (500–700 word) essay in which you show how de Vries undercuts the assumptions of Marvell. (Alternative: write a short essay in which you show how Cummings undercuts the assumptions of Marvell.)

2. In an essay of about three pages, show how the primary effects of "I Am a Cowboy in the Boat of Ra" relate to its use of cultural myths. (Alternative: apply this same question to Rossetti's "Eve," Tennyson's "Ulysses," or Okara's "Piano and Drums.")

Evaluating Poetry

How do you know a good poem when you see one? It is not an easy question to answer—partly because deciding about the *value* of poems is a complex, difficult, and often lengthy process, and partly because there is no single and absolute criterion that will measure texts and neatly divide the good from the not so good. People who long for a nice infallible sorter—some test that will automatically pick out the best poems and distinguish variations of quality much as a litmus test separates acids from bases—often are frustrated at what they perceive to be the "relativity" of judgment in evaluating poems. But because an issue is complex does not mean it is impossible, and even if there is no easy and absolute standard to be discovered, there are nevertheless distinctions to be made. Some poems are better—that is, more consistently effective with talented and experienced readers—than others. Even if we cannot sensibly rate poems on a 1 to 10 scale or agree on the excellence of a single poem, it is possible to set out some criteria that are helpful to readers who may not yet have developed confidence in their own judgments. It isn't necessary, of course, to spend all of our time asking about quality and being judgmental about poetry (or anything else). But as life isn't long enough to read everything, it is often useful to sort among those things that are likely to be worth your time and those that aren't. Besides, the process of sorting—in which you begin to articulate your own judgments and poetic values—can be a very useful strategy in making yourself a better reader and a more informed, better-educated, and wiser person. Evaluating poems can be, among other things, a way to learn more about yourself, for what you like in poetry has a lot to say about where your own values really lie.

I like it. That simple, unreflective statement about a poem is often a way to begin the articulation of standards—as long as your next move is to ask yourself why. Answers to *why* questions are often, at first, quite simple, even for experienced and sophisticated readers. "I like the way it sounds" or "I like its rhythm and pace" might be good, if partial, reasons for liking a poem. The popularity of nursery rhymes and simple childish ditties, or even the haunting, predictable, and repeated sounds and phrases of a poem like "The Raven" owe a lot (if not necessarily everything) to the use of sound. Another frequent answer might be: "because it is TRUE" or "because I agree with what it says." All of us are apt to like sentiments or ideas that resemble our own more than those that challenge or disturb us, though bad formulations of some idea we treasure, like bad behavior in someone we love, can sometimes be more embarrassing than comforting. But the longer we struggle with our reasons for liking a poem, the more complex and revealing our answers are likely to be: "I like the *way* it expresses something I had thought but had never quite been able to articulate." "I like the way its sounds and rhythms imitate the sounds of what is being described." "I like the way it balances conflicting emotions, being fair to both negative and positive feelings that seem to exist at the same time in about equal intensity." "I like its precision in describing just how something like that affects a person." Such statements of "I like . . ." have quietly crossed the border into statements of "I admire," and they have begun to be statements of "because" that offer complex reasons for that admiration.

What kinds of reasons might we expect different readers to agree on? *Groups* of readers might well agree on certain ideas—questions of politics or economics or religion, for example—but not readers across the board. More likely to generate consensus are technical criteria, questions of craft. How precise are the word choices at crucial moments in the poem? How rich, suggestive, and resonant are the words that open up the poem to larger statements and claims? How appropriate are the metaphors and other figures of speech? How original and imaginative? How carefully is the poem's situation set up? How clearly? How full and appropriate is the characterization of the speaker? How well-matched are the speaker, situation, and setting with the poem's sentiments and ideas? How consistent is the poem's tone? How appropriate to its themes? How carefully worked out is the poem's structure? How appropriate to the desired effects are the line breaks, the stanza breaks, and the pattern of rhythms and sounds?

One way of seeing how good a poem is in its various aspects is to look at what it is not—to consider the choices *not* made by the poet. Often it is possible to consider what a poem would be like if a different artistic choice had been made, as a way of seeing the importance of the choice actually made. What if, for example, Sylvia Plath had described a black *crow* in rainy weather instead of a rook? What if William Carlos Williams had described a *white* wheelbarrow? Sometimes we have the benefit, if we have a working manuscript or an autobiographical account of composition, of actually watching the process of selection. Look, for example, at the several drafts of the first stanza of "Love Calls Us to the Things of This World":

(a) My eyes came open to the squeak of pulleys
My spirit, shocked from the brothel of itself

(b) My eyes came open to the shriek of pulleys,
And the soul, spirited from its proper wallow,
Hung in the air as bodiless and hollow

(c) My eyes came open to the pulleys' cry.
The soul, spirited from its proper wallow,
Hung, in the air as bodiless and hollow
As light that frothed upon the wall opposing;
But what most caught my eyes at their unclosing
Was two gray ropes that yanked across the sky.
One after one into the window frame
. . . the hosts of laundry came

(d) The eyes open to a dry of pulleys,
And the soul, so suddenly spirited from sleep,
As morning sunlight frothing on the floor,
While just outside the window
The air is solid with a dance of angels.

(e) The eyes open to a cry of pulleys,
And spirited from sleep, the astounded soul
Hangs for a moment bodiless and simple
As dawn light in the moment of its breaking:
Outside the open window
The air is crowded with a

(f) The eyes open to a cry of pulleys,
And spirited from sleep, the astounded soul
Hangs for a moment bodiless and simple
As false dawn
Outside the open window,
Their air is leaping with a rout of angels.
Some are in bedsheets, some are in dresses,
it does not seem to matter.

Notice how much more appropriate to the total poem is the choice of "cry" over "shriek" or "squeak" to describe the sound of pulleys or how much more effective than the metaphor of a spirit's "brothel" is the image of the soul hanging "bodiless." Notice the things Wilbur excised from the early drafts as well as the things he added when the poem became more clear and more of a piece in his mind. Read some of the other revised versions of poems or passages printed in that chapter. Do you think all the revisions improve on the originals? in what specific way? What are your criteria for deciding? Do any of the revisions seem pointless to you—or (worse) make the poem less than it was?

Let's look again at one of the first poems we discussed, Adrienne Rich's "Aunt Jennifer's Tigers" (p. 649). Some of the power of this poem comes from the poet's clear and sympathetic engagement with Aunt Jennifer's situation, but the effects are carefully generated through a series of specific technical choices. Rich herself may or may not have made all these choices consciously; her later comments on the poem suggest that her creative instincts, as well as her then-repressed sense of gender, may have governed some decisions more fully than her own deliberate calculations. But however conscious, the choices of speaker, situation, metaphor, and connotative words work brilliantly together to create a strong feminist statement, almost a manifesto on the subject of mastery and compliance.

In a sense there is no speaker in this poem, no specified personality—only a faceless niece who observes the central character—but the effacing of this speaker in the light of the vivid Jennifer amounts to a brilliant artistic decision. Jennifer, powerless to articulate and possibly even to understand her own plight, nevertheless is allowed through the poem almost to speak for herself, primarily through her hands. The refusal of the narrator to do more than simply describe Jennifer's hands and their product gives Jennifer the crucial central role; she is the center of attention throughout, and the poem emphasizes only what one sees, with little apparent "editorial" comment (though the speaker does make three evaluative statements, saying that Jennifer was "mastered" by her ordeals (line 10), and noting that her hands are "terrified" (line 9) and that the wedding band "sits heavily" (line 9) on one of them). But the tigers are ultimately more eloquent than the speaker seems to be: they "prance" (lines 1 and 12) and "pace" (line 4), and they are "proud" (line 12) and unafraid of men (lines 3 and 12), embodying the guarded message Jennifer sends to the world even though she herself is "mastered" and "ringed" (line 10). The brightly conceived colors in the tapestry, the expressive description of Jennifer's fingers and hands (note especially the excitement implied in "fluttering" [line 5]), and the action of the panel itself combine with the characterization of Jennifer to present a strong statement of generational repression—and boldness. Even the fact of the knitting as art, suggestive of the way the classical Fates determine the future and the nature of things, is conceived to suggest the implications of Jennifer's art—and Rich's. The quality of the poem lies in the care, precision, and imaginativeness of Rich's application of craft. In later years, Rich has become clearer and more vocal about her values, but here is a very early poem (from her very first book, published 40 years ago) that through its technical prowess makes clear the direction and intensity of her vision and creates in the process a first-rate poem.

Here is another celebrated poem that similarly accomplishes a great deal in a short space:

WILLIAM SHAKESPEARE

[Th' expense of spirit in a waste of shame]

Th' expense[1] of spirit in a waste[2] of shame
Is lust in action; and, till action, lust
Is perjured, murderous, bloody, full of blame,
Savage, extreme, rude, cruel, not to trust;
Enjoyed no sooner but despiséd straight:
Past reason hunted; and no sooner had,
Past reason hated, as a swallowed bait,
On purpose laid to make the taker mad:
Mad in pursuit, and in possession so;
Had, having, and in quest to have, extreme;
A bliss in proof;[3] and proved, a very woe;
Before, a joy proposed; behind, a dream.
All this the world well knows; yet none knows well
To shun the heaven that leads men to this hell.

1609

Here the speaker *is* fully characterized, and the economical skill with which the characterization takes place is one of the most striking accomplishments of the poem. The poem sets up its situation carefully and, at first, not altogether clearly. But the delay in clarity is functional: we do not know for a while just what disturbs the speaker so much, except that it has to do with "lust in action" (line 2). What we do know quickly is how powerful his feeling is. The two explosive p's in the first half of the first line get the poem off to a fast and powerful start, and by the fourth line the speaker has listed nine separate unpleasant human characteristics driven by lust. He virtually spits them out. Here is an angry speaker, and it swiftly becomes clear that he is speaking from (undescribed) personal experience.

But the poem is not only angry and negative about lust. It also admits that

1. Expending. 2. Using up; also, desert. 3. In the act.

there are definite, and powerful, pleasures in lust: it is "enjoyed" (line 5) at the time ("a bliss in proof," line 11), and anticipated with pleasure ("a joy proposed," line 12). Such inconsistencies (or at least complexities) in the speaker's opinion are characteristic of the poem. Everything about his views, and according to him about lust itself, is "extreme" (line 10). There are no easy conclusions about lust in the first 12 lines of the poem, just a confusing movement back and forth between positives and negatives. The powerful condemnation of lust in the beginning—detailed in terms of how it makes people feel about themselves and how it affects their actions—quickly shifts into admissions of pleasure and joy, but then shifts back again. No opinion sticks for long. The only consistent thing about the speaker's feelings involves his certainty of lust's power—to drive individuals to behavior that they may love or hate. Only at the end is there any kind of reasoned conclusion, and the "moral" is hardly comforting: everybody knows what I've been saying, the speaker says, and yet nobody knows how to avoid lust and its consequences ("the heaven that leads men to this hell").

The vacillation of the speaker's opinions and moods is not the only confusing thing about the poem's organization. His account of lust repeatedly skips around in time. Are we talking here about lust at the time it is being satisfied ("lust in action")? Or are we talking about desire and anticipation? Or are we talking about what happens afterward? The answer is all three, and the discussion is hardly systematic. The first line and a half describe the present, and the meter of the first line even imitates the rhythms and force of male ejaculation: note how the basic iambic pentameter strategy of the poem does not actually get going until near the end of the second line. But soon we are talking about what happens before lust in action ("till action," line 2), and by line 5, after. Lines 6 and 7 contrast before and after, and line 9 compares before and during. Line 10 describes all three positions in time ("Had, having, and in quest to have"). Line 11 compares during and after, line 12 before and after. The poem, or rather the speaker, does not seem able to make up his mind exactly what he wants to talk about and what he thinks of his subject.

All this shifting around in focus and in feelings could easily be regarded as a serious flaw. Don't we expect a short poem, and especially a sonnet, to be very carefully organized and carefully focussed toward a single end? Shouldn't the poet make up his mind about what he thinks and what the poem is about? It would be easy to construct an argument, on the basis of consistency or clarity of purpose, that this is not a very good poem, that perhaps the greatest poet in the English language was not, here, at the top of his form. But to do so would be to ignore the power of the poem's effects and to underrate another principle of consistency—that of character. If we regard the poem as representative of a mind wrestling with the complex feelings brought about by lust—someone out of control because of lust, conscious enough to see his plight but unable to do anything about it—we can see a higher consistency here that helps explain the poem's powerful effect on many readers. Here is an account of a human mind grappling with a universal human experience, the subject of many much longer works of literature. Lust is beautiful but terrifying, certainly to be avoided but impossible to avoid. Shakespeare has managed, in the unlikely space of 14 lines and in a form in which we expect tight organization and intense focus, to portray succinctly the human recognition of confusion and powerlessness in the face of a passion larger than our ability to control it.

Here is another poem that is something of a challenge to evaluate:

JOHN DONNE

Song

Go, and catch a falling star,
    Get with child a mandrake root,[4]
Tell me, where all past years are,
    Or who cleft the devil's foot,
Teach me to hear mermaids singing
Or to keep off envy's stinging,
        And find
        What wind
Serves to advance an honest mind.

If thou beest born to strange sights,[5]
    Things invisible to see,
Ride ten thousand days and nights,
    Till age snow white hairs on thee;
Thou, when thou return'st, wilt tell me
All strange wonders that befell thee,
        And swear
        No where
Lives a woman true, and fair.

If thou find'st one, let me know:
    Such a pilgrimage were sweet.
Yet do not, I would not go,
    Though at next door we might meet:

4. The forked mandrake root is said to look vaguely human. 5. I.e., if you have supernatural powers.

Though she were true when you met her,
And last till you write your letter,
Yet she
Will be
False, ere I come, to two, or three.

1633

One immediate problem to confront here is the irregular, jerky rhythm. In a poem called "Song," we are likely to expect music, harmony, something pleasant and (within limits) predictable in its rhythm and movement. But this "song" is nothing like that. At first its message sounds lyrical and romantic: to go and catch a falling star is, if impossible, a romantic thing to propose, a motif that often comes up (and has for centuries) in love poems and popular songs; and lines 3 and 5 propose similar traditional romantic activities that evoke wonder and pleasure in contemplation. But the activities suggested in the alternate lines (2, 4, and 6) are in sharp contrast; they are just as bold in their unromantic or anti-romantic sentiments. Making a mandrake root pregnant does not sound like an especially pleasant male activity, however much such a root may look like a female body, and knowledge of the devil's cleft foot or envy's stinging are not usually the stuff of romantic poems or songs. Besides, the strange interruptions of easy rhythm (indicated by commas) in otherwise pleasant lines like 1 and 3 suggest that something less than lyrical is going on there too.

By the time we get to the last stanza, what is going on is a lot clearer. We have here a portrait of an angry and disillusioned man who is obsessed with the infidelity of women. He is talking to another man, apparently someone who has far more positive, perhaps even romantic, notions of women, and the poem is a kind of argument, except that the disillusioned speaker does all the talking. He pretends to take into account some traditional romantic rhetoric but turns it all on its head, intermixing the traditional impossible quests of lovers with a quest of his own—to find a "woman true, and fair" (line 18). But he knows cynically—he would probably say from experience, though he offers no evidence of his experience and no account of why he feels the way he does—that all these quests are impossible. This is one bitter man, and the song he sings has nothing to do with love or romance.

If we were to evaluate this "song" on the basis of harmonic and romantic expectations, looking for evenness of rhythms, pleasant sounds, and an attractive series of images consonant with romantic attitudes, we would certainly find it wanting. But again (as with the Shakespeare poem above) a larger question of appropriateness begs to be applied. Is the musical, imagistic, and organizational strategy consonant with the poem's total focus and force? Do the sounds and tone of the poem "work" in terms of the speaker portrayed here and the kind of artistic project this poem represents? The displeasure we feel in the speaker's words, images, feelings, and attitudes ultimately needs to be directed toward the speaker; the poet has done a good job of portraying a character whose bitterness, however generated, is unpleasant and off-putting. The poem "works" in its own terms. We may or may not like to hear attitudes like this expressed in a poem; we may or may not approve of using a pretended "song" to mouth such sentiments. But whether we "like" the poem in terms of what it says, we can evaluate, through close analysis of its several different elements (much as we have been doing analytically in earlier chapters), how *well* it does what it does. There are, of course, still larger questions of whether what it tries to do is worth doing, and readers of different philosophical or political persuasions may differ widely in their opinions and evaluations of that matter.

Different people do admire different things, and when we talk about criteria for evaluating poetry, we are talking about, at best, elements that a fairly large number of people have, over a long period of time, agreed on as important. There may be substantial agreement about political or social values in a particular group, and a consensus may exist among, say, misogynists or feminists about the value of such a poem as Donne's "Song." But more general agreements that bridge social and ideological divisions are more likely to involve the kinds of matters that have come up for analysis in earlier chapters, matters involving how well a poem *works*, how well it uses the resources it has within its conceptual limits. For some readers, ideology is everything, and there is no such thing as quality beyond political "correctness." But for others, different, more pluralistic evaluations can be made about accomplishment and quality.

Consistency. Appropriateness. Coherence. Effectiveness. Such terms are likely to be key ones for most readers in making their evaluations—as they have been in this discussion. But individual critics or readers will often have their own emphases, their own axes to grind. For some critics in past generations, "organic unity" was the key to all evaluation, whether a poem achieved, like something grown in nature, a wholeness of conception and effect. For others, the key term may be "tension" or "ambiguity" or "complexity" or "simplicity" or "authenticity" or "representation" or "psychological accuracy." With experience, you will develop your own set of criteria that may or may not involve a single ruling concept or term. But wherever (and whenever) you come out, you will learn something about yourself and your values in the process of articulating exactly what you like and admire—and why.

WRITING SUGGESTIONS

1. Choose one poem that you especially admire and one that you do not. Write a two- or three-page essay about each in which you try to show what specific accomplishments (or lack of them) lead you to your evaluative conclusions. Treat each poem in detail, and suggest fully not only how but *why* things "work"—or don't work. Try to construct your argument as "objectively" as possible, so that you are not simply pitting your personal judgment against someone else's. (Alternative: find two poems that are very much alike in subject matter, theme, or situation, but that seem to you very different in their success. Write one *comparative* essay in which you account for the difference in quality by showing in detail the difference between what works and what does not.)

2. Discuss with classmates a variety of poems you have read this term, and choose one poem about which a number of you disagree. Discuss among yourselves the different perspectives you have on the poem, and try to sort out in the discussion exactly what issues are at stake. Take notes on the discussion, trying to be clear about how your position differs from that of other students. Once you believe that you have the issues sorted out and can be clear about your own position, write a two- or three-page personal letter to your instructor in which you outline a position contrary to your own and then answer it point by point. Be sure to make clear in your letter the *grounds* for your evaluative position, positive or negative—that is, the principles or values on which you base your evaluation. (Hint: in the conversation with classmates, try to steer the discussion to a clear disagreement on no more than two or three points, and in your letter focus carefully on these points. State the arguments of your classmates as effectively and forcefully as you can so that your own argument will be as probing and sophisticated as you can make it.)

3. Choose a poem you have read this term that you admire but really don't like very much. In thinking over the poem again, try to account for the conflict between your feelings and judgment: what questions of content or form, social or political assumption, personal style, or manner of argument in the poem seem to make it less attractive to you? In a personal letter to a friend who is not in the class and who thus has not heard the class discussions of the issues, describe your dilemma, being careful to first outline why you think the poem is admirable. Say frankly what your personal reservations about the poem are, and at the end use the discussion of the poem to talk about your own values, in poetry and in general.

Reading More Poetry

JOHN ASHBERY

City Afternoon

A veil of haze protects this
Long-ago afternoon forgotten by everybody
In this photograph, most of them now
Sucked screaming through old age and death.

If one could seize America
Or at least a fine forgetfulness
That seeps into our outline
Defining our volumes with a stain
That is fleeting too

But commemorates
Because it does define, after all:
Gray garlands, that threesome
Waiting for the light to change,
Air lifting the hair of one
Upside down in the reflecting pool.

1975

MARGARET ATWOOD

Tricks with Mirrors

I

It's no coincidence
this is a used
furniture warehouse.

I enter with you
and become a mirror.

Mirrors
are the perfect lovers,

that's it, carry me up the stairs
by the edges, don't drop me,

that would be bad luck,
throw me on the bed

reflecting side up,
fall into me,

it will be your own
mouth you hit, firm and glassy,

your own eyes you find you
are up against   closed   closed

II

There is more to a mirror
than you looking at

your full-length body
flawless but reversed,

there is more than this dead blue
oblong eye turned outwards to you.

Think about the frame.
The frame is carved, it is important,

it exists, it does not reflect you,
it does not recede and recede, it has limits

and reflections of its own.
There's a nail in the back

to hang it with; there are several nails,
think about the nails,

pay attention to the nail
marks in the wood,

they are important too.

III

Don't assume it is passive
or easy, this clarity

with which I give you yourself.
Consider what restraint it

takes: breath withheld, no anger
or joy disturbing the surface

of the ice.
You are suspended in me

beautiful and frozen, I
preserve you, in me you are safe.

It is not a trick either,
it is a craft:

mirrors are crafty.

IV

I wanted to stop this,
this life flattened against the wall,

mute and devoid of colour,
built of pure light,

this life of vision only, split
and remote, a lucid impasse.

I confess: this is not a mirror,
it is a door

I am trapped behind.
I wanted you to see me here,

say the releasing word, whatever
that may be, open the wall.

Instead you stand in front of me
combing your hair.

V

You don't like these metaphors.
All right:

Perhaps I am not a mirror.
Perhaps I am a pool.

Think about pools.

1974

W. H. AUDEN

In Memory of W. B. Yeats

(d. January, 1939)

I

He disappeared in the dead of winter:
The brooks were frozen, the airports almost deserted,
And snow disfigured the public statues;
The mercury sank in the mouth of the dying day.
What instruments we have agree
The day of his death was a dark cold day.

Far from his illness
The wolves ran on through the evergreen forests,
The peasant river was untempted by the fashionable quays;
By mourning tongues
The death of the poet was kept from his poems.

But for him it was his last afternoon as himself,
An afternoon of nurses and rumors;
The provinces of his body revolted,
The squares of his mind were empty,
Silence invaded the suburbs,
The current of his feeling failed; he became his admirers.

Now he is scattered among a hundred cities
And wholly given over to unfamiliar affections,
To find his happiness in another kind of wood
And be punished under a foreign code of conscience.
The words of a dead man
Are modified in the guts of the living.

But in the importance and noise of tomorrow
When the brokers are roaring like beasts on the floor of the Bourse,[1]
And the poor have the sufferings to which they are fairly accustomed,
And each in the cell of himself is almost convinced of his freedom,
A few thousand will think of this day
As one thinks of a day when one did something slightly unusual.
What instruments we have agree
The day of his death was a dark cold day.

II

You were silly like us; your gift survived it all:
The parish of rich women, physical decay,
Yourself. Mad Ireland hurt you into poetry.

1. The Paris stock exchange.

Now Ireland has her madness and her weather still,
For poetry makes nothing happen: it survives
In the valley of its making where executives
Would never want to tamper, flows on south
From ranches of isolation and the busy griefs,
Raw towns that we believe and die in; it survives,
A way of happening, a mouth.

III

Earth, receive an honored guest:
William Yeats is laid to rest.
Let the Irish vessel lie
Emptied of its poetry.

In the nightmare of the dark
All the dog of Europe bark,
And the living nations wait,
Each sequestered in its hate;

Intellectual disgrace
Stares from every human face,
And the seas of pity lie
Locked and frozen in each eye.

Follow, poet, follow right
To the bottom of the night,
With your unconstraining voice
Still persuade us to rejoice;

With the farming of a verse
Make a vineyard of the curse,
Sing of human unsuccess
In a rapture of distress;

In the deserts of the heart
Let the healing fountain start,
In the prison of his days
Teach the free man how to praise.

1939

APHRA BEHN

On Her Loving Two Equally

I

How strong does my passion flow,
Divided equally twixt[2] two?

2. Between.

Damon had ne'er subdued my heart
Had not Alexis took his part;
Nor could Alexis powerful prove,[3]
Without my Damon's aid, to gain my love.

II

When my Alexis present is,
Then I for Damon sigh and mourn;
But when Alexis I do miss,
Damon gains nothing but my scorn.
But if it chance they both are by,
For both alike I languish, sigh, and die.

III

Cure then, thou mighty wingéd god,[4]
This restless fever in my blood;
One golden-pointed dart take back:
But which, O Cupid, wilt thou take?
If Damon's, all my hopes are crossed;
Or that of my Alexis, I am lost. 1684

WILLIAM BLAKE

Ah Sunflower

Ah Sunflower! weary of time,
Who countest the steps of the Sun,
Seeking after that sweet golden clime
Where the traveler's journey is done,

Where the Youth pined away with desire,
And the pale Virgin shrouded in snow,
Arise from their graves and aspire,
Where my Sunflower wishes to go. 1794

The Lamb

Little Lamb, who made thee?
Dost thou know who made thee?

3. Show himself. 4. Cupid, who, according to myth, shot darts of lead and of gold at the hearts of lovers, corresponding to false and true love respectively.

Gave thee life, and bid thee feed
By the stream and o'er the mead;
Gave thee clothing of delight,
Softest clothing woolly bright;
Gave thee such a tender voice,
Making all the vales rejoice?
Little Lamb, who made thee?
Dost thou know who made thee?

Little Lamb, I'll tell thee!
Little Lamb, I'll tell thee:
He is calléd by thy name,
For he calls himself a Lamb,
He is meek and he is mild;
He became a little child.
I a child and thou a lamb,
We are calléd by his name.
Little Lamb, God bless thee!
Little Lamb, God bless thee!

1789

The Tiger

Tiger, Tiger, burning bright
In the forests of the night,
What immortal hand or eye
Could frame thy fearful symmetry?

In what distant deeps or skies
Burnt the fire of thine eyes?
On what wings dare he aspire?
What the hand dare seize the fire?

And what shoulder and what art,
Could twist the sinews of thy heart?
And when thy heart began to beat,
What dread hand, and what dread feet?

What the hammer? What the chain?
In what furnace was thy brain?
What the anvil? What dread grasp
Dare its deadly terrors clasp?

When the stars threw down their spears
And watered heaven with their tears,
Did he smile his work to see?
Did he who made the Lamb make thee?

Tiger, Tiger, burning bright
In the forests of the night,
What immortal hand or eye
Dare frame thy fearful symmetry? 1794

SAMUEL TAYLOR COLERIDGE

Kubla Khan: or, a Vision in a Dream[5]

In Xanadu did Kubla Khan
  A stately pleasure-dome decree:
Where Alph, the sacred river, ran
Through caverns measureless to man
  Down to a sunless sea.
So twice five miles of fertile ground
With walls and towers were girdled round:
And here were gardens bright with sinuous rills
Where blossomed many an incense-bearing tree;
And here were forests ancient as the hills,
Enfolding sunny spots of greenery.
But oh! that deep romantic chasm which slanted
Down the green hill athwart a cedarn cover![6]
A savage place! as holy and enchanted
As e'er beneath a waning moon was haunted
By woman wailing for her demon-lover![7]
And from this chasm, with ceaseless turmoil seething,
As if this earth in fast thick pants were breathing,
A mighty fountain momently was forced,
Amid whose swift half-intermitted burst
Huge fragments vaulted like rebounding hail,
Or chaffy grain beneath the thresher's flail:
And 'mid these dancing rocks at once and ever
It flung up momently the sacred river.
Five miles meandering with a mazy motion
Through wood and dale the sacred river ran,
Then reached the caverns measureless to man,
And sank in tumult to a lifeless ocean:
And 'mid this tumult Kubla heard from far
Ancestral voices prophesying war!

    The shadow of the dome of pleasure
    Floated midway on the waves;

5. Coleridge said he wrote this fragment immediately after waking from an opium dream and that after he was interrupted by a caller he was unable to finish the poem. 6. From side to side of a cover of cedar trees. 7. In a famous and often imitated German ballad, the lady Lenore is carried off on horseback by the specter of her lover and married to him at his grave.

Where was heard the mingled measure
From the fountain and the caves.
It was a miracle of rare device,
A sunny pleasure-dome with caves of ice!
A damsel with a dulcimer
In a vision once I saw:
It was an Abyssinian maid,
And on her dulcimer she played,
Singing of Mount Abora.
Could I revive within me
Her symphony and song,
To such a deep delight 'twould win me,
That with music loud and long,
I would build that dome in air,
That sunny dome! those caves of ice!
And all who heard should see them there,
And all should cry, Beware! Beware!
His flashing eyes, his floating hair!
Weave a circle round him thrice,
And close your eyes with holy dread,
For he on honey-dew hath fed,
And drunk the milk of Paradise.

1798

HART CRANE

To Emily Dickinson

You who desired so much—in vain to ask—
Yet fed your hunger like an endless task,
Dared dignify the labor, bless the quest—
Achieved that stillness ultimately best,

Being, of all, least sought for: Emily, hear!
O sweet, dead Silencer, most suddenly clear
When singing that Eternity possessed
And plundered momently in every breast;

—Truly no flower yet withers in your hand,
The harvest you descried and understand
Needs more than wit to gather, love to bind.
Some reconcilement of remotest mind—

Leaves Ormus rubyless, and Ophir[8] chill.
Else tears heap all within one clay-cold hill.

1933

8. An ancient country from which Solomon secured gold and precious stones. *Ormus:* Presumably Ormuz, an ancient city on the Persian gulf.

E. E. CUMMINGS

[in Just-][9]

in Just-
spring   when the world is mud-
luscious the little
lame balloonman

whistles   far   and wee

and eddieandbill come
running from marbles and
piracies and it's
spring

when the world is puddle-wonderful

the queer
old balloonman whistles
far   and   wee
and bettyandisbel come dancing

from hop-scotch and jump-rope and
it's
spring
and

          the

                    goat-footed

balloonMan   whistles
far
and
wee[1]

1923

EMILY DICKINSON

[Because I could not stop for Death—]

Because I could not stop for Death—
He kindly stopped for me—
The Carriage held but just Ourselves—
And Immortality.

We slowly drove—He knew no haste
And I had put away

9. *Chansons innocentes* I.   1. Pan, whose Greek name means "everything," is traditionally represented with a syrinx (or the pipes of Pan). The upper half of his body is human, the lower half goat, and as the father of Silenus he is associated with the spring rites of Dionysus.

My labor and my leisure too,
For His Civility—

We passed the School, where Children strove
At Recess—in the Ring—
We passed the Fields of Gazing Grain—
We passed the Setting Sun—

Or rather—He passed Us—
The Dews drew quivering and chill—
For only Gossamer,[2] my Gown—
My Tippet—only Tulle[3]—

We paused before a House that seemed
A Swelling of the Ground—
The Roof was scarcely visible—
The Cornice—in the Ground—

Since then—'tis Centuries—and yet
Feels shorter than the Day
I first surmised the Horses' Heads
Were toward Eternity—

ca. 1863

[The Brain—is wider than the Sky—]

The Brain—is wider than the Sky—
For—put them side by side—
The one the other will contain
With ease—and You—beside—

The Brain is deeper than the sea—
For—hold them—Blue to Blue—
The one the other will absorb—
As Sponges—Buckets—do—

The Brain is just the weight of God—
For—Heft them—Pound for Pound—
And they will differ—if they do—
As Syllable from Sound—

ca. 1862

[I reckon—when I count at all—]

I reckon—when I count at all—
First—Poets—Then the Sun—

2. A soft sheer fabric. 3. A fine net fabric. *Tippet:* scarf.

Then Summer—Then the Heaven of God—
And then—the List is done—

But, looking back—the First so seems
To Comprehend the Whole—
The Others look a needless Show—
So I write—Poets—All—

Their Summer—lasts a Solid Year—
They can afford a Sun
The East—would deem extravagant—
And if the Further Heaven—

Be Beautiful as they prepare
For Those who worship Them—
It is too difficult a Grace—
ca. 1862 To justify the Dream—

[My life closed twice before its close—]

My life closed twice before its close—
It yet remains to see
If Immortality unveil
A third event to me

So huge, so hopeless to conceive
As these that twice befell.
Parting is all we know of heaven,
And all we need of hell. 1896

[We do not play on Graves—]

We do not play on Graves—
Because there isn't Room—
Besides—it isn't even—it slants
And People come—

And put a Flower on it—
And hang their faces so—
We're fearing that their Hearts will drop—
And crush our pretty play—

And so we move as far
As Enemies—away—
Just looking round to see how far
ca. 1862 It is—Occasionally—

[Wild Nights—Wild Nights!]

Wild Nights—Wild Nights!
Were I with thee
Wild Nights should be
Our luxury!

Futile—the Winds—
To a Heart in port—
Done with the Compass—
Done with the Chart!

Rowing in Eden—
Ah, the Sea!
Might I but moor—Tonight—
In Thee!

ca. 1861

JOHN DONNE

The Canonization

For God's sake hold your tongue and let me love!
Or chide my palsy or my gout,
My five gray hairs or ruined fortune flout;
With wealth your state, your mind with arts improve,
Take you a course, get you a place,
Observe his Honor or his Grace,
Or the king's real or his stampéd face[4]
Contemplate; what you will, approve,
So you will let me love.

Alas, alas, who's injured by my love?
What merchant's ships have my sighs drowned?
Who says my tears have overflowed his ground?
When did my colds a forward spring remove?
When did the heats which my veins fill
Add one man to the plaguy bill?[5]
Soldiers find wars, and lawyers find out still
Litigious men which quarrels move,
Though she and I do love.

Call us what you will, we are made such by love.
Call her one, me another fly,
We're tapers[6] too, and at our own cost die;

4. On coins. 5. List of plague victims. 6. Which consume themselves. To "die" is Renaissance slang for consummating the sexual act, which was popularly believed to shorten life by one day. *Fly:* a traditional symbol of transitory life.

And we in us find th' eagle and the dove.[7]
The phoenix riddle[8] hath more wit[9]
By us; we two, being one, are it.
So to one neutral thing both sexes fit,
We die and rise the same, and prove
Mysterious by this love.

We can die by it, if not live by love;
And if unfit for tombs and hearse
Our legend be, it will be fit for verse;[1]
And if no piece of chronicle we prove,
We'll build in sonnets[2] pretty rooms
(As well a well-wrought urn becomes[3]
The greatest ashes, as half-acre tombs),
And by these hymns all shall approve
Us canonized for love.

And thus invoke us: "You whom reverent love
Made one another's hermitage,
You to whom love was peace, that now is rage,
Who did the whole world's soul extract, and drove[4]
Into the glasses of your eyes
(So made such mirrors and such spies
That they did all to you epitomize)
Countries, towns, courts; beg from above
A pattern of your love!" 1633

[Death be not proud, though some have calléd thee]

Death be not proud, though some have calléd thee
Mighty and dreadful, for thou art not so;
For those whom thou think'st thou dost overthrow
Die not, poor Death, nor yet canst thou kill me.
From rest and sleep, which but thy pictures[5] be,
Much pleasure; then from thee much more must flow,
And soonest[6] our best men with thee do go,
Rest of their bones, and soul's delivery.[7]
Thou art slave to Fate, Chance, kings, and desperate men,
And dost with Poison, War, and Sickness dwell;
And poppy or charms can make us sleep as well,
And better than thy stroke; why swell'st[8] thou then?

7. Traditional symbols of strength and purity. 8. According to tradition, only one phoenix existed at a time, dying in a funeral pyre of its own making and being reborn from its own ashes. The bird's existence was thus a riddle akin to a religious mystery (line 27), and a symbol sometimes fused with Christian representations of immortality. 9. Meaning. 1. I.e., if we don't turn out to be an authenticated piece of historical narrative. 2. Love poems. In Italian, *stanza* means room. 3. Befits. 4. Compressed. 5. Likenesses. 6. Most willingly. 7. Deliverance. 8. Puff with pride.

One short sleep past, we wake eternally
And death shall be no more; Death, thou shalt die. 1633

DAVID DONNELL

Potatoes

This poem is about the strength and sadness of potatoes.
Unknown in Portugal or China, England or France,
untasted by the legions of Hannibal or Caesar,
hardy, simple, variable tuber; plain dusty brown,
North Carolina, New Brunswick, Idaho,
of the new world, passed over by the Indians
who preferred the bright yellow of corn, its sweetness,
the liquor they made from it, pemmican and wild corn mush.
The potato was seized upon by the more spiritual Puritans
while their companions were enraptured
by the beauty of New World tobacco, cotton and squash.

The Puritans recognized something of themselves in the pale
potato. Its simple shape reminded them of the human soul;
the many eyes of the potato amazed them. They split it
in half and saw the indivisibility of man;
they looked at the many eyes of the potato
and saw God looking back at them.
Potatoes like many different kinds of soil, resist cold weather,
store well in cool cellars and are more nutritious than beets.
Potato dumplings became the pièce de résistance of eastern Europe.
They developed a considerable number of useful proverbs.
For example: "Love is not a potato, do not throw it out the window".
Or the famous Scottish lament—"What good is he to me?
For three days he has not even brought me a potato".

The potato is modest and develops its indivisible bounty
under the ground, taking from the ground some of its color
and just enough skin to resist an excess of moisture.
It can be harvested easily by young boys and girls working
in rows with bushel baskets and pausing at lunch
to lift up their skirts and make love under the fences.
Truckloads of potatoes can be sent to every part of the world.
The French make frites[9] with them. The Russians make vodka.
The Chinese have white and brown rice but all potatoes are the same.
Potato flour is not as sweet as corn but makes an excellent bread.
In the cellars of poor farmers all over America
the potatoes sit quietly on top of each other growing eyes. 1980

9. French fries.

JOHN DRYDEN

[Why should a foolish marriage vow][1]

Why should a foolish marriage vow,
  Which long ago was made,
Oblige us to each other now
  When passion is decayed?
We loved, and we loved, as long as we could,
  Till our love was loved out in us both;
But our marriage is dead when the pleasure is fled:
  'Twas pleasure first made it an oath.

If I have pleasures for a friend,
  And farther love in store,
What wrong has he whose joys did end,
  And who could give no more?
'Tis a madness that he should be jealous of me,
  Or that I should bar him of another:
For all we can gain is to give ourselves pain,
  When neither can hinder the other.

1671

PAUL LAWRENCE DUNBAR

We Wear the Mask

We wear the mask that grins and lies,
It hides our cheeks and shades our eyes,—
This debt we pay to human guile;
With torn and bleeding hearts we smile,
And mouth with myriad subtleties.

Why should the world be over-wise,
In counting all our tears and sighs?
Nay, let them only see us, while
    We wear the mask.

We smile, but, O great Christ, our cries
To thee from tortured souls arise.
We sing, but oh the clay is vile
Beneath our feet, and long the mile;
But let the world dream otherwise,
    We wear the mask!

1896

1. A song from Dryden's play, *Marriage à la Mode*.

STEPHEN DUNN

Dancing with God

At first the surprise
of being singled out,
the dance floor crowded
and me not looking my best,
a too-often-worn dress
and the man with me
a budding casualty
of one repetition too much.
God just touched his shoulder
and he left.
Then the confirmation of
an old guess:
God was a wild god,
into the most mindless rock,
but graceful,
looking—this excited me—
like no one I could love,
cruel mouth, eyes evocative
of promises unkept.
I never danced better, freer,
as if dancing were my way
of saying how easily
I could be with him, or apart.
When the music turned slow
God held me close
and I felt for a moment
I'd mistaken him,
that he was Death
and this the famous embrace
before the lights go out.
But God kept holding me
and I him
until the band stopped
and I stood looking at a figure
I wanted to slap
or forgive for something,
I couldn't decide which.
He left then, no thanks,
no sign
that he'd felt anything
more than an earthly moment
with someone who could've been
anyone on earth.

To this day I don't know why
I thought he was God,
though it was clear
there was no going back
to the man who brought me,
nice man
with whom I'd slept
and grown tired,
who danced wrong,
who never again
could do anything right.

1989

Men Talk

It was the winter I had to get away.
Though I didn't know it then,
I needed the kind of solace
you get at depressing movies
if they're good; all those others
just like you. In Orlando,
biding time, I watched peacocks
among people in a wooded preserve,
then drove further inland past cattle
to where my friend lived.

I was glad the peacocks made awful
sounds, and I was glad—
after we jogged his circular path
through the orange groves—
that our polite, complete sentences
broke down into talk
of his empty house, the woman who left,
and then my house far away.
I told him what staying meant, as if
I knew; the precipice in every room.
Friendship: someone leaning
to your side of the truth.

Next day was beautiful,
seventy-five degrees, and each of us
silent, back in control.
We walked into the countryside,
pointed away from ourselves
toward the landscape,
took possession of it for a while.

Kumquats were growing next to lemons
and white birds rode the backs of cows.
Though it wasn't, it seemed enough,
seemed we'd never have to speak again.
1989

RICHARD EBERHART

The Fury of Aerial Bombardment

You would think the fury of aerial bombardment
Would rouse God to relent; the infinite spaces
Are still silent. He looks on shock-pried faces.
History, even, does not know what is meant.

You would feel that after so many centuries
God would give man to repent; yet he can kill
As Cain could, but with multitudinous will,
No farther advanced than in his ancient furies.

Was man made stupid to see his own stupidity?
Is God by definition indifferent, beyond us all?
Is the eternal truth man's fighting soul
Wherein the Beast ravens in its own avidity?

Of Van Wettering I speak, and Averill,
Names on a list, whose faces I do not recall
But they are gone to early death, who late in school
Distinguished the belt feed lever from the belt holding pawl.[2]
1947

ELIZABETH

When I Was Fair and Young[3]

When I was fair and young, and favor graced me,
Of many was I sought, their mistress for to be;
But I did scorn them all, and answered them therefore,
"Go, go, go, seek some otherwhere,
Importune me no more!"

How many weeping eyes I made to pine with woe,
How many sighing hearts, I have no skill to show;
Yet I the prouder grew, and answered them therefore,

2. Machine-gun parts. 3. The attribution of this poem to Queen Elizabeth I of England (1533–1603) is by no means certain; but she was highly—and perhaps excessively—praised by her subjects for her poetic talents.

"Go, go, go, seek some otherwhere,
Importune me no more!"

Then spake fair Venus' son, that proud victorious boy,[4]
And said: "Fine dame, since that you be so coy,
I will so pluck your plumes that you shall say no more,
'Go, go, go, seek some otherwhere,
Importune me no more!' "

When he had spake these words, such change grew in my breast
That neither night nor day since that, I could take any rest.
Then lo! I did repent that I had said before,
"Go, go, go, seek some otherwhere,
Importune me no more!"

ca. 1585?

ROBERT FROST

Range-Finding

The battle rent a cobweb diamond-strung
And cut a flower beside a groundbird's nest
Before it stained a single human breast.
The stricken flower bent double and so hung.
And still the bird revisited her young.
A butterfly its fall had dispossessed,
A moment sought in air his flower of rest,
Then lightly stooped to it and fluttering clung.
On the bare upland pasture there had spread
O'ernight 'twixt mullein[5] stalks a wheel of thread
And straining cables wet with silver dew.
A sudden passing bullet shook it dry.
The indwelling spider ran to greet the fly,
But finding nothing, sullenly withdrew.

1916

The Road Not Taken

Two roads diverged in a yellow wood,
And sorry I could not travel both
And be one traveler, long I stood
And looked down one as far as I could
To where it bent in the undergrowth;

Then took the other, as just as fair,
And having perhaps the better claim,

4. Cupid. 5. Weed.

Because it was grassy and wanted wear;
Though as for that the passing there
Had worn them really about the same,

And both that morning equally lay
In leaves no step had trodden black.
Oh, I kept the first for another day!
Yet knowing how way leads on to way,
I doubted if I should ever come back.

I shall be telling this with a sigh
Somewhere ages and ages hence:
Two roads diverged in a wood, and I—
I took the one less traveled by,
And that has made all the difference.

1916

Stopping by Woods on a Snowy Evening

Whose woods these are I think I know.
His house is in the village, though;
He will not see me stopping here
To watch his woods fill up with snow.

My little horse must think it queer
To stop without a farmhouse near
Between the woods and frozen lake
The darkest evening of the year.

He gives his harness bells a shake
To ask if there is some mistake.
The only other sound's the sweep
Of easy wind and downy flake.

The woods are lovely, dark, and deep,
But I have promises to keep,
And miles to go before I sleep,
And miles to go before I sleep.

1923

ARTHUR GUITERMAN

On the Vanity of Earthly Greatness

The tusks that clashed in mighty brawls
Of mastodons, are billiard balls.

The sword of Charlemagne the Just
Is ferric oxide known as rust.

The grizzly bear whose potent hug
Was feared by all, is now a rug.

Great Caesar's bust is on the shelf,
And I don't feel so well myself! 1930

THOMAS HARDY

The Convergence of the Twain

LINES ON THE LOSS OF THE "TITANIC"[6]

I

In a solitude of the sea
Deep from human vanity,
And the Pride of Life that planned her, stilly couches she.

II

Steel chambers, late the pyres
Of her salamandrine[7] fires,
Cold currents thrid,[8] and turn to rhythmic tidal lyres.

III

Over the mirrors meant
To glass the opulent
The sea-worm crawls—grotesque, slimed, dumb, indifferent.

IV

Jewels in joy designed
To ravish the sensuous mind
Lie lightless, all their sparkles bleared and black and blind.

V

Dim moon-eyed fishes near
Gaze at the gilded gear
And query: "What does this vaingloriousness down here?" . . .

6. On the night of April 14, 1912, the *Titanic*, the largest ship afloat and on her maiden voyage to New York from Southampton, collided with an iceberg in the North Atlantic and sank in less than three hours; 1,500 of 2,206 passengers were lost. 7. Bright red; the salamander was supposed to be able to live in fire. 8. Thread.

VI

Well: while was fashioning
This creature of cleaving wing,
The Immanent Will that stirs and urges everything

VII

Prepared a sinister mate
For her—so gaily great—
A Shape of Ice, for the time far and dissociate.

VIII

And as the smart ship grew
In stature, grace, and hue,
In shadowy silent distance grew the Iceberg too.

IX

Alien they seemed to be:
No mortal eye could see
The intimate welding of their later history,

X

Or sign that they were bent
By paths coincident
On being anon twin halves of one august event,

XI

Till the Spinner of the Years
Said "Now!" And each one hears,
And consummation comes, and jars two hemispheres.

1914

The Darkling Thrush

I leant upon a coppice gate
When Frost was specter gray,
And Winter's dregs made desolate
The weakening eye of day.
The tangled bine-stems scored the sky
Like strings of broken lyres,
And all mankind that haunted nigh
Had sought their household fires.

The land's sharp features seemed to be
  The Century's corpse outleant,
His crypt the cloudy canopy,
  The wind his death-lament.
The ancient pulse of germ and birth
  Was shrunken hard and dry,
And every spirit upon earth
  Seemed fervorless as I.

At once a voice arose among
  The bleak twigs overhead
In a full-hearted evensong
  Of joy illimited;
An aged thrush, frail, gaunt, and small,
  In blast-beruffled plume,
Had chosen thus to fling his soul
  Upon the growing gloom.

So little cause for carolings
  Of such ecstatic sound
Was written on terrestrial things
  Afar or nigh around,
That I could think there trembled through
  His happy good-night air
Some blessed Hope, whereof he knew
  And I was unaware.

December 31, 1900

During Wind and Rain

They sing their dearest songs—
He, she, all of them—yea,
Treble and tenor and bass,
  And one to play;
With the candles mooning each face. . . .
  Ah, no; the years O!
How the sick leaves reel down in throngs!

They clear the creeping moss—
Elders and juniors—aye,
Making the pathway neat
  And the garden gay;
And they build a shady seat. . . .
  Ah, no; the years, the years;
See, the white stormbirds wing across!

They are blithely breakfasting all—
Men and maidens—yea,
Under the summer tree,
With a glimpse of the bay,
While pet fowl come to the knee. . . .
Ah, no; the years O!
And the rotten rose is ripped from the wall.

They change to a high new house,
He, she, all of them—aye,
Clocks and carpets, and chairs
On the lawn all day,
And brightest things that are theirs. . . .
Ah, no; the years, the years;
Down their carved names the rain drop ploughs.

1917

ROBERT HASS

Privilege of Being

Many are making love. Up above, the angels
in the unshaken ether and crystal of human longing
are braiding one another's hair, which is strawberry blond
and the texture of cold rivers. They glance
down from time to time at the awkward ecstasy—
it must look to them like featherless birds
splashing in the spring puddle of a bed—
and then one woman, she is about to come,
peels back the man's shut eyelids and says,
look at me, and he does. Or is it the man
tugging the curtain rope in that dark theater?
Anyway, they do, they look at each other;
two beings with evolved eyes, rapacious,
startled, connected at the belly in an unbelievably sweet
lubricious glue, stare at each other,
and the angels are desolate. They hate it. They shudder pathetically
like lithographs of Victorian beggars
with perfect features and alabaster skin hawking rags
in the lewd alleys of the novel.
All of creation is offended by this distress.
It is like the keening sound the moon makes sometimes,
rising. The lovers especially cannot bear it,
it fills them with unspeakable sadness, so that
they close their eyes again and hold each other, each
feeling the mortal singularity of the body
they have enchanted out of death for an hour or so,

and one day, running at sunset, the woman says to the man,
I woke up feeling so sad this morning because I realized
that you could not, as much as I love you,
dear heart, cure my loneliness,
wherewith she touched his cheek to reassure him
that she did not mean to hurt him with this truth.
And the man is not hurt exactly,
he understands that life has limits, that people
die young, fail at love,
fail of their ambitions. He runs beside her, he thinks
of the sadness they have gasped and crooned their way out of
coming, clutching each other with old, invented
forms of grace and clumsy gratitude, ready
to be alone again, or dissatisfied, or merely
companionable like the couples on the summer beach
reading magazine articles about intimacy between the sexes
to themselves, and to each other,
and to the immense, illiterate, consoling angels. 1989

ROBERT HAYDEN

Frederick Douglass[9]

When it is finally ours, this freedom, this liberty, this beautiful
and terrible thing, needful to man as air,
usable as earth; when it belongs at last to all,
when it is truly instinct, brain matter, diastole, systole,
reflex action; when it is finally won; when it is more
than the gaudy mumbo jumbo of politicians:
this man, this Douglass, this former slave, this Negro
beaten to his knees, exiled, visioning a world
where none is lonely, none hunted, alien,
this man, superb in love and logic, this man
shall be remembered. Oh, not with statues' rhetoric,
not with legends and poems and wreaths of bronze alone,
but with the lives grown out of his life, the lives
fleshing his dream of the beautiful, needful thing. 1966

9. Frederick Douglass (1817–1895), escaped slave. Douglass was involved in the Underground Railroad, and became the publisher of the famous abolitionist newspaper the *North Star,* in Rochester, N.Y.

ROBERT HERRICK

To the Virgins, to Make Much of Time

Gather ye rosebuds while ye may,
   Old time is still a-flying;
And this same flower that smiles today
   Tomorrow will be dying.

The glorious lamp of heaven, the sun,
   The higher he's a-getting,
The sooner will his race be run,
   And nearer he's to setting.

That age is best which is the first,
   When youth and blood are warmer;
But being spent, the worse, and worst
   Times still succeed the former.

Then be not coy, but use your time,
   And, while ye may, go marry;
For, having lost but once your prime,
   You may forever tarry.

1648

GERARD MANLEY HOPKINS

God's Grandeur

The world is charged with the grandeur of God.
   It will flame out, like shining from shook foil;[1]
   It gathers to a greatness, like the ooze of oil
Crushed. Why do men then now not reck his rod?[2]
Generations have trod, have trod, have trod;
   And all is seared with trade; bleared, smeared with toil;
   And wears man's smudge and shares man's smell: the soil
Is bare now, nor can foot feel, being shod.

And for all this, nature is never spent;
   There lives the dearest freshness deep down things;
And though the last lights off the black West went
   Oh, morning, at the brown brink eastward, springs—

1. "I mean foil in its sense of leaf or tinsel. . . . Shaken goldfoil gives off broad glares like sheet lightning and also, and this is true of nothing else, owing to its zig-zag dints and creasings and network of small many cornered facets, a sort of fork lightning too." *Letters of Gerard Manley Hopkins to Robert Bridges*, ed. C. C. Abbott, 1955, p. 169.

2. Heed his authority.

Because the Holy Ghost over the bent
World broods with warm breast and with ah! bright wings.

1918

The Windhover[3]

TO *Christ Our Lord*

I caught this morning morning's minion,[4] king-
dom of daylight's dauphin,[5] dapple-dawn-drawn Falcon, in his riding
Of the rolling level underneath him steady air, and striding
High there, how he rung upon the rein of a wimpling[6] wing
In his ecstasy! then off, off forth on swing,
As a skate's heel sweeps smooth on a bow-bend: the hurl and gliding
Rebuffed the big wind. My heart in hiding
Stirred for a bird,—the achieve of, the mastery of the thing!

Brute beauty and valor and act, oh, air, pride, plume, here
Buckle![7] AND the fire that breaks from thee then, a billion
Times told lovelier, more dangerous, O my chevalier![8]

No wonder of it: sheér plód makes plow down sillion[9]
Shine, and blue-bleak embers, ah my dear,
Fall, gall themselves, and gash gold-vermilion.

1877

A. E. HOUSMAN

To an Athlete Dying Young

The time you won your town the race
We chaired[1] you through the marketplace;
Man and boy stood cheering by,
And home we brought you shoulder-high.

Today, the road all runners come,
Shoulder-high we bring you home,
And set you at your threshold down,
Townsman of a stiller town.

3. A small hawk, the kestrel, which habitually hovers in the air, headed into the wind. 4. Favorite, beloved. 5. Heir to regal splendor. 6. Rippling. 7. Several meanings may apply: to join closely, to prepare for battle, to grapple with, to collapse. 8. Horseman, knight. 9. The narrow strip of land between furrows in an open field divided for separate cultivation. 1. Carried aloft in triumph.

Smart lad, to slip betimes away
From fields where glory does not stay,
And early though the laurel grows
It withers quicker than the rose.

Eyes the shady night has shut
Cannot see the record cut,
And silence sounds no worse than cheers
After earth has stopped the ears:

Now you will not swell the rout
Of lads that wore their honors out,
Runners whom renown outran
And the name died before the man.

So set, before its echoes fade,
The fleet foot on the sill of shade,
And hold to the low lintel up
The still-defended challenge-cup.

And round that early-laureled head
Will flock to gaze the strengthless dead,
And find unwithered on its curls
The garland briefer than a girl's.

1896

LANGSTON HUGHES

Theme for English B

The instructor said,

Go home and write
a page tonight.
And let that page come out of you—
Then, it will be true.

I wonder if it's that simple?
I am twenty-two, colored, born in Winston-Salem.
I went to school there, then Durham,[2] then here
to this college[3] on the hill above Harlem.
I am the only colored student in my class.
The steps from the hill lead down into Harlem,
through a park, then I cross St. Nicholas,[4]
Eighth Avenue, Seventh, and I come to the Y,
the Harlem Branch Y, where I take the elevator
up to my room, sit down, and write this page:

2. Cities in North Carolina. 3. Columbia University. 4. An avenue east of Columbia University.

It's not easy to know what is true for you or me
at twenty-two, my age. But I guess I'm what
I feel and see and hear, Harlem, I hear you:
hear you, hear me—we two—you, me, talk on this page.
(I hear New York, too.) Me—who?

Well, I like to eat, sleep, drink, and be in love.
I like to work, read, learn, and understand life.
I like a pipe for a Christmas present,
or records—Bessie,[5] bop, or Bach.
I guess being colored doesn't make me *not* like
the same things other folks like who are other races.
So will my page be colored that I write?

Being me, it will not be white.
But it will be
a part of you, instructor.
You are white—
yet a part of me, as I am a part of you.
That's American.
Sometimes perhaps you don't want to be a part of me.
Nor do I often want to be a part of you.
But we are, that's true!
As I learn from you,
I guess you learn from me—
although you're older—and white—
and somewhat more free.

This is my page for English B. 1959

RICHARD HUGO

Places and Ways to Live

Note the stump, a peach tree. We had to cut it down.
It banged the window every wind. Our garden
swayed with corn each summer. Our crops were legend
and our kindness. Whatever stranger came, we said,
'Come in.' We ran excited. 'Someone's come to see us.'
By night we were exhausted. The dark came early
in that home, came early for the last time soon.

Some nights in motels, I wake bewildered by the room.
Then I remember where I am. I turn the light on
and the girl's still there, smiling from the calendar
whatever the year. When I'm traveling, I'm hurt.

5. Bessie Smith (1898?–1937), famous blues singer.

I tune in certain radio stations by heart,
the ones that play old tunes like nothing worthwhile's
happened since that funeral in 1949.

When I'm in the house I've bought, I don't dwell on
the loss of trees, don't cry when neighbors move away
or dogs get killed by cars. I'm old enough to know
a small girl's tears are fated to return, years from now
in some Berlin hotel, though I seem to sit unfeeling
at the window watching it all like a patron.
I'm taking it in, deep where I hope it will bloom.

That is the crude self I've come to. The man who says
suffer, stay poor and I can create. Believe me, friends,
I offer you your homes and wish you well in them.
May kisses rain. May you find warm arms each morning.
May your favorite tree be blooming in December.
And may you never be dispossessed, forced to wander
a world the color of salt with no young music in it.

1975

BEN JONSON

To Penshurst[6]

Thou art not, Penshurst, built to envious show,
Of touch[7] or marble; nor canst boast a row
Of polished pillars, or a roof of gold;
Thou hast no lantern[8] whereof tales are told,
Or stair, or courts; but stand'st an ancient pile,
And, these grudged at,[9] art reverenced the while.
Thou joy'st in better marks, of soil, of air,
Of wood, of water; therein thou art fair.
Thou hast thy walks for health, as well as sport;
Thy mount, to which the dryads do resort,
Where Pan and Bacchus[1] their high feasts have made
Beneath the broad beech and the chestnut shade,
That taller tree, which of a nut was set
At his great birth[2] where all the Muses met.
There in the writhéd bark are cut the names

6. The country seat (in Kent) of the Sidney family, owned by Sir Robert, brother of the poet, Sir Philip. Jonson's celebration of the estate is one of the earliest "house" poems and a prominent example of topographical or didactic-descriptive poetry. 7. Touchstone: basanite, a smooth dark stone similar to black marble. 8. A glassed or open tower or dome atop the roof. 9. I.e., although these (more pretentious structures) are envied. *The while:* anyway. 1. Ancient gods of nature and wine, both associated with spectacular feasting and celebration. 2. Sir Philip Sidney's, on November 30, 1554; the tree stood for nearly 150 years.

Of many a sylvan, taken with his flames;[3]
And thence the ruddy satyrs oft provoke
The lighter fauns to reach thy Lady's Oak.[4]
Thy copse too, named of Gamage,[5] thou hast there,
That never fails to serve thee seasoned deer
When thou wouldst feast, or exercise, thy friends.
The lower land, that to the river bends,
Thy sheep, thy bullocks, kine, and calves do feed;
The middle grounds thy mares and horses breed.
Each bank doth yield thee conies;[6] and the tops,
Fertile of wood, Ashore and Sidney's copse,
To crown thy open table, doth provide
The purpled pheasant with the speckled side;
The painted partridge lies in every field,
And for thy mess is willing to be killed.
And if the high-swollen Medway[7] fail thy dish,
Thou hast thy ponds that pay thee tribute fish,
Fat agéd carps that run into thy net,
And pikes, now weary their own kind to eat,
As loath the second draught[8] or cast to stay,
Officiously[9] at first themselves betray;
Bright eels that emulate them, and leap on land
Before the fisher, or into his hand.
Then hath thy orchard fruit, thy garden flowers,
Fresh as the air, and new as are the hours.
The early cherry, with the later plum,
Fig, grape, and quince, each in his time doth come:
The blushing apricot and woolly peach
Hang on thy walls, that every child may reach.
And though thy walls be of the country stone,
They're reared with no man's ruin, no man's groan;
There's none that dwell about them wish them down,
But all come in, the farmer and the clown,[1]
And no one empty-handed, to salute
Thy lord and lady, though they have no suit.[2]
Some bring a capon, some a rural cake,
Some nuts, some apples; some that think they make
The better cheeses bring 'em, or else send
By their ripe daughters, whom they would commend
This way to husbands, and whose baskets bear
An emblem of themselves in plum or pear.
But what can this (more than express their love)
Add to thy free[3] provisions, far above
The need of such? whose liberal board doth flow

3. Inspired by Sidney's love poetry. 4. Where, according to legend, a former lady of the house (Lady Leicester) began labor pains. *Satyrs:* half-men, half-goats who participated in the rites of Bacchus. 5. The maiden name of the owner's wife. *Copse:* thicket. 6. Rabbits. 7. A river bordering the estate. 8. Of a net. *Stay:* await. 9. Obligingly. 1. Rustic, peasant. 2. Request for favors. 3. Generous.

With all that hospitality doth know;
Where comes no guest but is allowed to eat,
Without his fear, and of thy lord's own meat;
Where the same beer and bread, and selfsame wine,
That is his lordship's shall be also mine.
And I not fain[4] to sit (as some this day
At great men's tables), and yet dine away.[5]
Here no man tells[6] my cups; nor, standing by,
A waiter doth my gluttony envý,
But gives me what I call, and lets me eat;
He knows below he shall find plenty of meat.
Thy tables hoard not up for the next day;
Nor, when I take my lodging, need I pray
For fire, or lights, or livery;[7] all is there,
As if thou then wert mine, or I reigned here:
There's nothing I can wish, for which I stay.
That found King James when hunting late this way
With his brave son, the prince,[8] they saw thy fires
Shine bright on every hearth, as the desires
Of thy Penates had been set on flame
To entertain them; or the country came
With all their zeal to warm their welcome here.
What (great I will not say, but) sudden cheer
Didst thou then make 'em! and what praise was heaped
On thy good lady then! who therein reaped
The just reward of her high housewifery;[9]
To have her linen, plate, and all things nigh,
When she was far; and not a room but dressed
As if it had expected such a guest!
These, Penshurst, are thy praise, and yet not all.
Thy lady's noble, fruitful, chaste withal.
His children thy great lord may call his own,
A fortune in this age but rarely known.
They are, and have been, taught religion; thence
Their gentler spirits have sucked innocence.
Each morn and even they are taught to pray,
With the whole household, and may, every day,
Read in their virtuous parents' noble parts
The mysteries of manners, arms, and arts.
Now, Penshurst, they that will proportion[1] thee
With other edifices, when they see
Those proud, ambitious heaps, and nothing else,
May say, their lords have built, but thy lord dwells.

1616

4. Obliged. 5. Possibly, "elsewhere," because they do not get enough to eat; or "away" in the sense of far from the party of honor. 6. Counts. 7. Provisions (or, possibly, servants). 8. Prince Henry, who died in 1612. 9. Domestic economy. 1. Compare.

DONALD JUSTICE

Children Walking Home from School Through Good Neighborhood

They are like figures held in some glass ball,
One of those in which, when shaken, snowstorms occur;
But this one is not yet shaken.
        And they go unaccompanied still,
Out along this walkway between two worlds,
This almost swaying bridge.
        October sunlight checkers their path;
It frets their cheeks and bare arms now with shadow
Almost too pure to signify itself.
And they progress slowly, somewhat lingeringly,
Independent, yet moving all together,
Like polyphonic voices that crisscross
In short-lived harmonies.

        Today, a few stragglers.
One, a girl, stands there with hands spaced out, so—
A gesture in a story. Someone's school notebook spills,
And they bend down to gather up the loose pages.
(Bright sweaters knotted at the waist; solemn expressions.)
Not that they would shrink or hold back from what may come,
For now they all at once run to meet it, a little swirl of colors,
Like the leaves already blazing and falling farther north.

1987

GALWAY KINNELL

Blackberry Eating

I love to go out in late September
among the fat, overripe, icy, black blackberries
to eat blackberries for breakfast,
the stalks very prickly, a penalty
they earn for knowing the black art
of blackberry-making; and as I stand among them
lifting the stalks to my mouth, the ripest berries
fall almost unbidden to my tongue,
as words sometimes do, certain peculiar words
like *strengths* or *squinched*,
many-lettered, one-syllabled lumps,
which I squeeze, squinch open, and splurge well

in the silent, startled, icy, black language
of blackberry-eating in late September.

1980

A. M. KLEIN

Heirloom

My father bequeathed me no wide estates;
No keys and ledgers were my heritage;
Only some holy books with *yahrzeit*[2] dates
Writ mournfully upon a blank front page—

Books of the Baal Shem Tov,[3] and of his wonders;
Pamphlets upon the devil and his crew;
Prayers against road demons, witches, thunders;
And sundry other tomes for a good Jew.

Beautiful: though no pictures on them, save
The scorpion crawling on a printed track;
The Virgin floating on a scriptural wave,
Square letters twinkling in the Zodiac.

The snuff left on this page, now brown and old,
The tallow stains of midnight liturgy—
These are my coat of arms, and these unfold
My noble lineage, my proud ancestry!

And my tears, too, have stained this heirloomed ground,
When reading in these treatises some weird
Miracle, I turned a leaf and found
A white hair fallen from my father's beard.

1940

ETHERIDGE KNIGHT

The Idea of Ancestry

I

Taped to the wall of my cell[4] are 47 pictures: 47 black
faces: my father, mother, grandmothers (1 dead), grand

2. Anniversary of the death of a parent or near relative. 3. A title given to someone who possesses the secret knowledge of Jewish holy men and who therefore could work miracles. 4. This poem is from Knight's volume, *Poems from Prison;* Knight began to write poetry while serving a sentence for armed robbery in the Ohio State Penitentiary.

fathers (both dead), brothers, sisters, uncles, aunts,
cousins (1st & 2nd), nieces, and nephews. They stare
across the space at my sprawling on my bunk. I know
their dark eyes, they know mine. I know their style,
they know mine. I am all of them, they are all of me;
they are farmers, I am a thief, I am me, they are thee.

I have at one time or another been in love with my mother,
1 grandmother, 2 sisters, 2 aunts (1 went to the asylum),
and 5 cousins. I am now in love with a 7 yr old niece
(she sends me letters written in large block print, and
her picture is the only one that smiles at me).

I have the same name as 1 grandfather, 3 cousins, 3 nephews,
and 1 uncle. The uncle disappeared when he was 15, just took
off and caught a freight (they say). He's discussed each year
when the family has a reunion, he causes uneasiness in
the clan, he is an empty space. My father's mother, who is 93
and who keeps the Family Bible with everybody's birth dates
(and death dates) in it, always mentions him. There is no
place in her Bible for "whereabouts unknown."

II

Each Fall the graves of my grandfathers call me, the brown
hills and red gullies of mississippi send out their electric
messages, galvanizing my genes. Last yr / like a salmon quitting
the cold ocean—leaping and bucking up his birthstream / I
hitchhiked my way from L.A. with 16 caps[5] in my pocket and a
monkey on my back, and I almost kicked it with the kinfolks.
I walked barefooted in my grandmother's backyard / I smelled the old
land and the woods / I sipped cornwhiskey from fruit jars with the men /
I flirted with the women / I had a ball till the caps ran out
and my habit came down. That night I looked at my grandmother
and split / my guts were screaming for junk / but I was almost
contented / I had almost caught up with me.
The next day in Memphis I cracked a croaker's crib[6] / for a fix.

This yr there is a gray stone wall damming my stream, and when
the falling leaves stir my genes, I pace my cell or flop on my bunk
and stare at 47 black faces across the space. I am all of them,
they are all of me, I am me, they are thee, and I have no sons
to float in the space between.

1968

5. Doses of heroin (?); *Monkey on my back:* drug habit. 6. Burglarized a doctor's house (or a drugstore).

PHILIP LARKIN

Annus Mirabilis[7]

Sexual intercourse began
In nineteen sixty-three
(Which was rather late for me)
Between the end of the *Chatterley* ban[8]
And the Beatles' first LP.

Up till then there'd only been
A sort of bargaining,
A wrangle for a ring,
A shame that started at sixteen
And spread to everything.

Then all at once the quarrel sank:
Everyone felt the same,
And every life became
A brilliant breaking of the bank,
A quite unlosable game.

So life was never better than
In nineteen sixty three
(Though just too late for me)—
Between the end of the *Chatterley* ban
And the Beatles' first LP.

1974

IRVING LAYTON

Berry Picking

Silently my wife walks on the still wet furze
Now darkgreen the leaves are full of metaphors
Now lit up is each tiny lamp of blueberry.
The white nails of rain have dropped and the sun is free.

And whether she bends or straightens to each bush
To find the children's laughter among the leaves
Her quiet hands seem to make the quiet summer hush—
Berries or children, patient she is with these.

I only vex and perplex her; madness, rage
Are endearing perhaps put down upon the page;

7. Latin for "year of wonders." 8. D. H. Lawrence's novel *Lady Chatterley's Lover* had been banned in the U.S. as obscene until court rulings of the early sixties.

Even silence daylong and sullen can then
Enamour as restraint or classic discipline.

So I envy the berries she puts in her mouth,
The red and succulent juice that stains her lips;
I shall never taste that good to her, nor will they
Displease her with a thousand barbarous jests.

How they lie easily for her hand to take,
Part of the unoffending world that is hers;
Here beyond complexity she stands and stares
And leans her marvellous head as if for answers.

No more the easy soul my childish craft deceives
Nor the simpler one for whom yes is always yes;
No, now her voice comes to me from a far way off
Though her lips are redder than the raspberries. 1971

RICHARD LOVELACE

To Amarantha, that She Would Dishevel Her Hair

Amarantha sweet and fair,
Ah, braid no more that shining hair!
As my curious hand or eye
Hovering round thee, let it fly.

Let it fly as unconfined
As its calm ravisher, the wind,
Who hath left his darling, th' East,
To wanton o'er that spicy nest.

Every tress must be confessed
But neatly tangled at the best,
Like a clue[9] of golden thread,
Most excellently raveléd.

Do not then wind up that light
In ribands, and o'ercloud in night;
Like the sun in's early ray,
But shake your head and scatter day.

See, 'tis broke! Within this grove,
The bower and the walks of love,
Weary lie we down and rest
And fan each other's panting breast.

9. Ball.

Here we'll strip and cool our fire
In cream below, in milk-baths higher;
And when all wells are drawn dry,
I'll drink a tear out of thine eye.

Which our very joys shall leave,
That sorrows thus we can deceive;
Or our very sorrows weep,
That joys so ripe so little keep.
1649

ROBERT LOWELL

Skunk Hour

FOR *Elizabeth Bishop*

Nautilus Island's hermit
heiress still lives through winter in her Spartan cottage;
her sheep still graze above the sea.
Her son's a bishop. Her farmer
is first selectman[1] in our village,
she's in her dotage.

Thirsting for
the hierarchic privacy
of Queen Victoria's century,
she buys up all
the eyesores facing her shore,
and lets them fall.

The season's ill—
we've lost our summer millionaire,
who seemed to leap from an L. L. Bean[2]
catalogue. His nine-knot yawl
was auctioned off to lobstermen.
A red fox stain covers Blue Hill.

And now our fairy
decorator brightens his shop for fall,
his fishnet's filled with orange cork,
orange, his cobbler's bench and awl,
there is no money in his work,
he'd rather marry.

One dark night,
my Tudor Ford climbed the hill's skull,

1. An elected New England town official. 2. Famous old Maine sporting goods firm.

I watched for love-cars. Lights turned down,
they lay together, hull to hull,
where the graveyard shelves on the town. . . .
My mind's not right.

A car radio bleats,
"Love, O careless Love. . . ."[3] I hear
my ill-spirit sob in each blood cell,
as if my hand were at its throat. . . .
I myself am hell;
nobody's here—

only skunks, that search
in the moonlight for a bite to eat.
They march on their soles up Main Street:
white stripes, moonstruck eyes' red fire
under the chalk-dry and spar spire
of the Trinitarian Church.

I stand on top
of our back steps and breathe the rich air—
a mother skunk with her column of kittens swills the garbage pail.
She jabs her wedge head in a cup
of sour cream, drops her ostrich tail,
and will not scare.

1959

ARCHIBALD MacLEISH

Ars Poetica[4]

A poem should be palpable and mute
As a globed fruit,

Dumb
As old medallions to the thumb,

Silent as the sleeve-worn stone
Of casement ledges where the moss has grown—

A poem should be wordless
As the flight of birds.

A poem should be motionless in time
As the moon climbs.

Leaving, as the moon releases
Twig by twig the night-entangled trees,

3. A popular song. 4. "The Art of Poetry," title of a poetical treatise by the Roman poet Horace (65–8 B.C.).

Leaving, as the moon behind the winter leaves,
Memory by memory the mind—

A poem should be motionless in time
As the moon climbs.

A poem should be equal to:
Not true.

For all the history of grief
An empty doorway and a maple leaf.

For love
The leaning grasses and two lights above the sea—

A poem should not mean
But be.

1926

ANDREW MARVELL

The Garden

How vainly men themselves amaze[5]
To win the palm, the oak, or bays,[6]
And their incessant labors see
Crowned from some single herb, or tree,
Whose short and narrow-vergéd[7] shade
Does prudently their toils upbraid;
While all flowers and all trees do close[8]
To weave the garlands of repose!

Fair Quiet, have I found thee here,
And Innocence, thy sister dear?
Mistaken long, I sought you then
In busy companies of men.
Your sacred plants,[9] if here below,
Only among the plants will grow;
Society is all but rude[1]
To[2] this delicious solitude.

No white nor red was ever seen
So am'rous as this lovely green.
Fond lovers, cruel as their flame,
Cut in these trees their mistress' name:
Little, alas, they know, or heed
How far these beauties hers exceed!

5. Become frenzied. 6. Awards for athletic, civic, and literary achievements. 7. Narrowly cropped. 8. Unite. 9. Cuttings. 1. Barbarous. 2. Compared to.

Fair trees, wheresoe'er your barks I wound,
No name shall but your own be found.

When we have run our passion's heat,
Love hither makes his best retreat.
The gods, that mortal beauty chase,
Still in a tree did end their race:
Apollo hunted Daphne so,
Only that she might laurel grow;
And Pan did after Syrinx speed,
Not as a nymph, but for a reed.[3]

What wondrous life is this I lead!
Ripe apples drop about my head;
The luscious clusters of the vine
Upon my mouth do crush their wine;
The nectarine and curious[4] peach
Into my hands themselves do reach;
Stumbling on melons, as I pass,
Insnared with flowers, I fall on grass.

Meanwhile the mind, from pleasure less,
Withdraws into its happiness;[5]
The mind, that ocean where each kind
Does straight its own resemblance find;[6]
Yet it creates, transcending these,
Far other worlds and other seas,
Annihilating[7] all that's made
To a green thought in a green shade.

Here at the fountain's sliding foot,
Or at some fruit tree's mossy root,
Casting the body's vest[8] aside,
My soul into the boughs does glide:
There, like a bird, it sits and sings,
Then whets[9] and combs its silver wings,
And, till prepared for longer flight,
Waves in its plumes the various[1] light.

Such was that happy garden-state,
While man there walked without a mate:
After a place so pure, and sweet,
What other help could yet be meet![2]
But 'twas beyond a mortal's share

3. In Ovid's *Metamorphoses*, Daphne, pursued by Apollo, is turned into a laurel, and Syrinx, pursued by Pan, into a reed which Pan makes into a flute. 4. Exquisite. 5. I.e., the mind withdraws from lesser sense pleasure into contemplation. 6. All land creatures were supposed to have corresponding sea-creatures. 7. Reducing to nothing by comparison. 8. Vestment, clothing; the flesh is being considered as simply clothing for the soul. 9. Preens. 1. Many-colored. 2. Appropriate.

To wander solitary there:
Two paradises 'twere in one
To live in paradise alone.

How well the skillful gardener drew
Of flowers and herbs this dial[3] new,
Where, from above, the milder sun
Does through a fragrant zodiac run;
And as it works, th' industrious bee
Computes its time as well as we!
How could such sweet and wholesome hours
Be reckoned but with herbs and flowers?

1681

HEATHER McHUGH

A Physics

When you get down to it, Earth
has our own great ranges
of feeling—Rocky, Smoky, Blue—
and a heart that can melt stones.

The still pools fill with sky,
as if aloof, and we have eyes
for all of this and more, for Earth's
reminding moon. We too are ruled

by such attractions—spun and swaddled,
rocked and lent a light. We run
our clocks on wheels, our trains
on time. But all the while we want

to love each other endlessly—not only for
a hundred years, not only six feet up and down.
We want the suns and moons of silver
in ourselves, not only counted coins in a cup. The whole idea

of love was not to fall. And neither was
the whole idea of God. We put him well
above ourselves, because we meant,
in time, to measure up.

1987

3. A garden planted in the shape of a sundial, complete with zodiac.

JAMES MERRILL

Casual Wear

Your average tourist: Fifty. 2.3
Times married. Dressed, this year, in Ferdi Plinthbower
Originals. Odds 1 to 9^{10}
Against her strolling past the Embassy

Today at noon. Your average terrorist:
Twenty-five. Celibate. No use for trends,
At least in clothing. Mark, though, where it ends.
People have come forth made of colored mist

Unsmiling on one hundred million screens
To tell of his prompt phone call to the station,
"Claiming responsibility"—devastation
Signed with a flourish, like the dead wife's jeans. p. 1984

EDNA ST. VINCENT MILLAY

[What lips my lips have kissed, and where, and why]

What lips my lips have kissed, and where, and why,
I have forgotten, and what arms have lain
Under my head till morning; but the rain
Is full of ghosts tonight, that tap and sigh
Upon the glass and listen for reply,
And in my heart there stirs a quiet pain
For unremembered lads that not again
Will turn to me at midnight with a cry.
Thus in the winter stands the lonely tree,
Nor knows what birds have vanished one by one,
Yet knows its boughs more silent than before:
I cannot say what loves have come and gone;
I only know that summer sang in me
A little while, that in me sings no more.

1923

MARIANNE MOORE

Poetry

I, too, dislike it: there are things that are important beyond all this fiddle.
  Reading it, however, with a perfect contempt for it, one discovers in
  it after all, a place for the genuine.
    Hands that can grasp, eyes
    that can dilate, hair that can rise
      if it must, these things are important not because a

high-sounding interpretation can be put upon them but because they are
  useful. When they become so derivative as to become unintelligible,
  the same thing may be said for all of us, that we
    do not admire what
    we cannot understand: the bat
      holding on upside down or in quest of something to

eat, elephants pushing, a wild horse taking a roll, a tireless wolf under
  a tree, the immovable critic twitching his skin like a horse that feels a flea, the baseball fan, the statistician—
    nor is it valid
      to discriminate against "business documents and

school-books"[4]; all these phenomena are important. One must make a distinction
  however: when dragged into prominence by half poets, the result is not poetry,
  nor till the poets among us can be
    "literalists of
    the imagination"[5]—above
      insolence and triviality and can present

for inspection, "imaginary gardens with real toads in them," shall we have
  it. In the meantime, if you demand on the one hand,
  the raw material of poetry in
    all its rawness and
    that which is on the other hand
      genuine, you are interested in poetry.

1924

4. "*Diary of Tolstoy*, p. 84: 'Where the boundary between prose and poetry lies, I shall never be able to understand. The question is raised in manuals of style, yet the answer to it lies beyond me. Poetry is verse: prose is not verse. Or else poetry is everything with the exception of business documents and school books.' " (Moore's note)   5. " 'Literalists of the imagination.' Yeats, *Ideas of Good and Evil* (A. H. Bullen, 1903), p. 182. 'The limitation of his view was from the very intensity of his vision; he was a too literal realist of imagination, as others are of nature; and because he believed that the figures seen by the mind's eye, when exalted by inspiration, were "eternal existences," symbols of divine essences, he hated every grace of style that might obscure their lineaments.' " (Moore's note)

SUSAN MUSGRAVE

The Judas Goat

It was a bad sign I was born under,
half animal, half a cruel joke of nature.
The antlered ghosts of my ancestors were
vanishing; I envied them their shifty universe.

Fate made me plain and bitter,
my shape more symbol than pathfinder or
builder. I wandered from the herd to
escape humiliation—found more misery there
than mystery.

Where I grazed along the wayside
nothing would grow; when I lay down in the
garbage I gave no thought to the flowers.
Skirting the world's edge I thrived on spoils,
glutted my maw, grew reconciled to hunger.

Returning to the flock restored my
dignity. The fat ewes gathered to greet me;
I spoke to them in their own language
Where I led them to drink there was a warm trough and
plenty to eat. There was a dry place to
lie down; my ease did not betray cowardice.

Lord of everything pleasurable and defenceless,
I woke to their calling resurrected and holy.
There was no need for treachery in their
measure of life; too simple by origin they
followed me to the slaughterhouse.

My power was inimitable and blinding.
When they smelled their own blood they were
no longer afraid. They stumbled and fell
as if my will had supported them. I watched them
weakening, unashamed.

Even their whimpering made me feel ruthless,
the greatness of conquest far greater than
self-sacrifice. But when they lifted their
gentle heads to remind me all would be forgiven,
I turned and looked away.

There on the solitary block I sprawled
rootless and agonizing, Lord God of lolling tongues,
deliverer of carnage.

I prayed I had not become human.

1979

HOWARD NEMEROV

Boom!

SEES BOOM IN RELIGION, TOO

Atlantic City, June 23, 1957 (AP).—President Eisenhower's pastor said tonight that Americans are living in a period of "unprecedented religious activity" caused partially by paid vacations, the eight-hour day and modern conveniences.

"These fruits of material progress," said the Rev. Edward L. R. Elson of the National Presbyterian Church, Washington, "have provided the leisure, the energy, and the means for a level of human and spiritual values never before reached."

Here at the Vespasian-Carlton,[6] it's just one
religious activity after another; the sky
is constantly being crossed by cruciform
airplanes, in which nobody disbelieves
for a second and the tide, the tide
of spiritual progress and prosperity
miraculously keeps rising, to a level
never before attained. The churches are full,
the beaches are full, and the filling-stations
are full, God's great ocean is full
of paid vacationers praying an eight-hour day
to the human and spiritual values, the fruits,
the leisure, the energy, and the means, Lord,
the means for the level, the unprecedented level,
and the modern conveniences, which also are full.
Never before, O Lord, have the prayers and praises
from belfry and phonebooth, from ballpark and barbecue
the sacrifices, so endlessly ascended.

It was not thus when Job in Palestine
sat in the dust and cried, cried bitterly;[7]
when Damien kissed the lepers on their wounds
it was not thus;[8] it was not thus
when Francis worked a fourteen-hour day
strictly for the birds;[9] when Dante took

6. Vespasian was emperor of Rome 70–79, shortly after the reign of Nero. In French, *vespasienne* means public toilet. 7. According to the Book of Job, he was afflicted with the loss of prosperity, children, and health as a test of his faith. His name means, in Hebrew, "he cries"; see especially Job 2:7–13. 8. "Father Damien" (Joseph Damien de Veuster, 1840–1889), a Roman Catholic missionary from Belgium, was known for his work among lepers in Hawaii; he ultimately contracted leprosy himself and died there. 9. St. Francis of Assisi, 13th-century founder of the Franciscan order, was noted for his love of all living things, and one of the most famous stories about him tells of his preaching to the birds. "Strictly for the birds": a mid-20th-century expression for worthless or unfashionable activity.

a week's vacation without pay and it rained
part of the time,[1] O Lord, it was not thus.

But now the gears mesh and the tires burn
and the ice chatters in the shaker and the priest
in the pulpit and Thy Name, O Lord,
is kept before the public, while the fruits
ripen and religion booms and the level rises
and every modern convenience runneth over,
that it may never be with us as it hath been
with Athens and Karnak and Nagasaki,[2]
nor Thy sun for one instant refrain from shining
on the rainbow Buick by the breezeway
or the Chris Craft with the uplift life raft;
that we may continue to be the just folks we are,
plain people with ordinary superliners and
disposable diaperliners, people of the stop'n'shop
'n'pray as you go, of hotel, motel, boatel,
the humble pilgrims of no deposit no return
and please adjust thy clothing, who will give to Thee,
if Thee will keep us going, our annual
Miss Universe, for Thy Name's Sake, Amen. 1960

SHARON OLDS

Last Acts

I want to wash my father's face
to take cotton from the dirt of the earth
and run it over his face so the loops
press into his pores before he dies. I want
to be in him, the way I was once inside him,
riding in his balls the day before he cast me—
he carries me easily on his long legs up the
hills of San Francisco in war-time,
I am there between his legs where I belong,
I *am* his flesh, he can love me without
reserve. Soon I will be his pleasure.
Now I want him to feel me on his pitted
face, in the rowelling of the cloth, I want to
wash him the way I would wash my dolls,

1. Dante's journey through Hell, Purgatory, and Paradise (in *The Divine Comedy*) takes a week, beginning on Good Friday, 1300. It rains in the third chasm of Hell. 2. Athens, the cultural center of ancient Greek civilization; Karnak, a village on the Nile, built on the site of ancient Thebes; Nagasaki, a large Japanese port city, virtually destroyed by a U.S. atomic bomb in 1945.

scrub their faces expertly
before any great ceremony.

1990

The Moment of My Father's Death

When he breathed his last breath it was he,
my father, although he was so transformed
no one who had not been with him
for the last hours would know him, the skin
gold and physical as animal fat,
the eyes cast all way back into his head,
the whites gleaming like a white iris, the
nose growing steadily thinner,
the mouth open, racked open, and that
tongue so dried, scallopped, darkened and
material. We could see the fluid
risen like gorge into the back of his mouth
but it was he, the huge slack yellow arms,
the spots of blood under the skin
black and precise, we had come this far with him
step by step, it was he, his last
breath was his, not taken with desire but
his, light as the sphere of dandelion seeds
coming out of his mouth and floating across the room.
Then the nurse listened for his heart,
his stomach was silvery, it was his stomach,
she moved to the foot of the bed and stood there, she
did not shake her head she stood and
nodded at me. And for a minute it was fully
he, my father, dead but completely
himself, a man with an open mouth and
no breath, gold skin and
black spots on his arms. He looked like
someone killed in a bloodless struggle,
the strain in his neck, that look of pulling back,
the stillness he seemed to be holding at first
and then it was holding him, the skin
tightened slightly around his body
as if the purely physical were claiming him,
and then it was not my father,
it was not a man, it was not an animal, I
ran my hand through the silver hair,
slipped my fingers into it and
lifted them up slowly through the grey
waves of it, the unliving glistening
matter of this world.

1990

MICHAEL ONDAATJE

Light

FOR *Doris Gratiaen*

Midnight storm. Trees walking off across the fields in fury
naked in the spark of lightning.
I sit on the white porch on the brown hanging cane chair
coffee in my hand midnight storm midsummer night.
The past, friends and family, drift into the rain shower.
Those relatives in my favourite slides
re-shot from old minute photographs so they now stand
complex ambiguous grainy on my wall.

This is my Uncle who turned up to his marriage
on an elephant. He was a chaplain.
This shy looking man in the light jacket and tie was infamous,
when he went drinking he took the long blonde beautiful hair
of his wife and put one end in the cupboard and locked it
leaving her tethered in an armchair.
He was terrified of her possible adultery
and this way died peaceful happy to the end.
My Grandmother, who went to a dance in a muslin dress
with fireflies captured and embedded in the cloth, shining
and witty. This calm beautiful face
organized wild acts in the tropics.
She hid the mailman in her house
after he had committed murder and at the trial
was thrown out of the court for making jokes at the judge.
Her son became a Q.C.[3]
This is my brother at 6. With his cousin and his sister
and Pam de Voss who fell on a pen-knife and lost her eye.
My Aunt Christie. She knew Harold MacMillan[4] was a spy
communicating with her through pictures in the newspapers.
Every picture she believed asked her to forgive him,
his hound eyes pleading.
Her husband Uncle Fitzroy a doctor in Ceylon had a memory
sharp as scalpels into his 80's
though I never bothered to ask him about anything
—interested then more in the latest recordings of Bobby Darin.

And this is my Mother with her brother Noel in fancy dress.
They are 7 and 8 years old, a hand-coloured photograph,
it is the earliest picture I have. The one I love most.
A picture of my kids at Halloween

3. Queen's Counsel; a lawyer selected to serve the British crown. 4. British prime minister, 1957–1963.

has the same contact and laughter.
My Uncle dying at 68, and my Mother a year later dying at 68.
She told me about his death and the day he died
his eyes clearing out of illness as if seeing
right through the room the hospital and she said
he saw something so clear and good his whole body
for a moment became youthful and she remembered
when she sewed badges on his trackshirts.
Her voice joyous in telling me this, her face light and clear.
(My firefly Grandmother also dying at 68.)

These are the fragments I have of them, tonight
in this storm, the dogs restless on the porch.
They were all laughing, crazy, and vivid in their prime.
At a party my drunk Father
tried to explain a complex operation on chickens
and managed to kill them all in the process, the guests
having dinner an hour later while my Father slept
and the kids watched the servants clean up the litter
of beaks and feathers on the lawn.
These are their fragments, all I remember,
wanting more knowledge of them. In the mirror and in my kids
I see them in my flesh. Wherever we are
they parade in my brain and the expanding stories
connect to the grey grainy pictures on the wall,
as they hold their drinks or 20 years later
hold grandchildren, pose with favourite dogs,
coming through the light, the electricity, which the storm
destroyed an hour ago, a tree going down by the highway
so that now inside the kids play dominoes by candlelight
and out here the thick rain static the spark of my match
to a cigarette
and the trees across the fields leaving me, distinct
lonely in their own knife scars and cow-chewed bark
frozen in the jagged light as if snapped in their run
the branch arms waving to what was a second ago the dark sky
when in truth like me they haven't moved.
Haven't moved an inch from me.

1979

DOROTHY PARKER

Comment

Oh, life is a glorious cycle of song,
A medley of extemporanea;
And love is a thing that can never go wrong;
And I am Marie of Rumania.

1926

LINDA PASTAN

Ars Poetica

1. The Muse

You may catch
a butterfly
in a net
if you are swift enough

or if you keep
perfectly still
perhaps it will land
on your shoulder.

Often
it is just
a moth.

2. Writing

In the battle
between the typewriter
and the blank page
a certain rhythm evolves,
not unlike the hoofbeats
of a horse groomed for war
who would rather be
head down, grazing.

3. Rejection Slip

Darling, though you know
I admire your many
fine qualities
you don't fill all my needs
just now, and besides
there's a backlog
waiting to fit
in my bed.

4. Revision

The tree has been green
all summer, but now
it tries red . . . copper . . .
even gold. Soon
leaf after leaf

will be discarded,
there will be nothing
but bare tree, soon
it will be almost time
to start over again.

5. Ars poetica

Escape from the poem
by bus, by streetcar—
any way you can,
dragging a suitcase
tied together with twine
in which you've stuffed
all your singular belongings.

Leave behind
a room
washed by sun
or moonlight.
There should be a chair
on which you've draped a coat
that will fit anyone.

1988

SYLVIA PLATH

Lady Lazarus

I have done it again.
One year in every ten
I manage it——

A sort of walking miracle, my skin
Bright as a Nazi lampshade,
My right foot

A paperweight,
My face a featureless, fine
Jew linen.

Peel off the napkin
O my enemy.
Do I terrify?——

The nose, the eye pits, the full set of teeth?
The sour breath
Will vanish in a day.

Soon, soon the flesh
The grave cave ate will be
At home on me

And I a smiling woman.
I am only thirty.
And like the cat I have nine times to die.

This is Number Three.
What a trash
To annihilate each decade.

What a million filaments.
The peanut-crunching crowd
Shoves in to see

Them unwrap me hand and foot——
The big strip tease.
Gentlemen, ladies

These are my hands
My knees.
I may be skin and bone,

Nevertheless, I am the same, identical woman.
The first time it happened I was ten.
It was an accident.

The second time I meant
To last it out and not come back at all.
I rocked shut

As a seashell.
They had to call and call
And pick the worms off me like sticky pearls.

Dying
Is an art, like everything else.
I do it exceptionally well.

I do it so it fells like hell.
I do it so it feels real.
I guess you could say I've a call.

It's easy enough to do it in a cell.
It's easy enough to do it and stay put.
It's the theatrical

Comeback in broad day
To the same place, the same face, the same brute
Amused shout:

"A miracle!"
That knocks me out.
There is a charge

For the eyeing of my scars, there is a charge
For the hearing of my heart——
It really goes.

And there is a charge, a very large charge
For a word or a touch
Or a bit of blood

Or a piece of my hair or my clothes.
So, so Herr Doktor.
So, Herr Enemy.

I am your opus,
I am your valuable,
The pure gold baby

That melts to a shriek.
I turn and burn.
Do not think I underestimate your great concern

Ash, ash—
You poke and stir.
Flesh, bone, there is nothing there——

A cake of soap,
A wedding ring,
A gold filling.

Herr God, Herr Lucifer
Beware
Beware.

Out of the ash
I rise with my red hair
And I eat men like air.

1965

EDGAR ALLAN POE

The Raven

Once upon a midnight dreary, while I pondered, weak and weary,
Over many a quaint and curious volume of forgotten lore,
While I nodded, nearly napping, suddenly there came a tapping,
As of some one gently rapping, rapping at my chamber door.
" 'Tis some visitor," I muttered, "tapping at my chamber door—
Only this, and nothing more."

Ah, distinctly I remember it was in the bleak December,
And each separate dying ember wrought its ghost upon the floor.
Eagerly I wished the morrow;—vainly I had sought to borrow
From my books surcease of sorrow—sorrow for the lost Lenore—
For the rare and radiant maiden whom the angels name Lenore—
Nameless here for evermore.

And the silken sad uncertain rustling of each purple curtain
Thrilled me—filled me with fantastic terrors never felt before;
So that now, to still the beating of my heart, I stood repeating
" 'Tis some visitor entreating entrance at my chamber door;—
This it is, and nothing more."

Presently my soul grew stronger; hesitating then no longer,
"Sir," said I, "or Madam, truly your forgiveness I implore;
But the fact is I was napping, and so gently you came rapping,
And so faintly you came tapping, tapping at my chamber door,
That I scarce was sure I heard you"—here I opened wide the door;—
Darkness there, and nothing more.

Deep into that darkness peering, long I stood there wondering, fearing,
Doubting, dreaming dreams no mortal ever dared to dream before;
But the silence was unbroken, and the darkness gave no token,
And the only word there spoken was the whispered word, "Lenore!"
This I whispered, and an echo murmured back the word, "Lenore!"—
Merely this, and nothing more.

Back into the chamber turning, all my soul within me burning,
Soon I heard again a tapping somewhat louder than before.
"Surely," said I, "surely that is something at my window lattice;
Let me see, then, what thereat is, and this mystery explore—
Let my heart be still a moment and this mystery explore;—
'Tis the wind and nothing more!"

Open here I flung the shutter, when, with many a flirt and flutter,
In there stepped a stately raven of the saintly days of yore;
Not the least obeisance made he; not an instant stopped or stayed he;
But, with mien of lord or lady, perched above my chamber door—
Perched upon a bust of Pallas[5] just above my chamber door—
Perched, and sat, and nothing more.

Then this ebony bird beguiling my sad fancy into smiling,
By the grave and stern decorum of the countenance it wore,
"Though thy crest be shorn and shaven, thou," I said, "art sure no craven,
Ghastly grim and ancient raven wandering from the Nightly shore—
Tell me what thy lordly name is on the Night's Plutonian shore!"
Quoth the raven, "Nevermore."

5. Athena, the Greek goddess of wisdom.

Much I marvelled this ungainly fowl to hear discourse so plainly,
Though its answer little meaning—little relevancy bore,
For we cannot help agreeing that no living human being
Ever yet was blessed with seeing bird above his chamber door—
Bird or beast upon the sculptured bust above his chamber door,
With such name as "Nevermore."

But the raven, sitting lonely on the placid bust, spoke only
That one word, as if his soul in that one word he did outpour.
Nothing farther then he uttered—not a feather then he fluttered—
Till I scarcely more than muttered "Other friends have flown before—
On the morrow *he* will leave me, as my hopes have flown before."
Then the bird said "Nevermore."

Startled at the stillness broken by reply so aptly spoken,
"Doubtless," said I, "what it utters is its only stock and store
Caught from some unhappy master whom unmerciful Disaster
Followed fast and followed faster till his songs one burden bore—
Till the dirges of his Hope that melancholy burden bore
Of 'Never—nevermore.' "

But the raven still beguiling all my sad soul into smiling,
Straight I wheeled a cushioned seat in front of bird and bust and door;
Then, upon the velvet sinking, I betook myself to linking
Fancy unto fancy, thinking what this ominous bird of yore—
What this grim, ungainly, ghastly, gaunt, and ominous bird of yore
Meant in croaking "Nevermore."

This I sat engaged in guessing, but no syllable expressing
To the fowl whose fiery eyes now burned into my bosom's core;
This and more I sat divining, with my head at ease reclining
On the cushion's velvet lining that the lamplight gloated o'er,
But whose velvet violet lining with the lamplight gloating o'er,
She shall press, ah, nevermore!

Then, methought, the air grew denser, perfumed from an unseen censer
Swung by angels whose faint foot-falls tinkled on the tufted floor.
"Wretch," I cried, "thy God hath lent thee—by these angels he hath sent thee
Respite—respite and nepenthe[6] from thy memories of Lenore!
Quaff, oh quaff this kind nepenthe and forget this lost Lenore!"
Quoth the raven, "Nevermore."

"Prophet!" said I, "thing of evil!—prophet still, if bird or devil!—
Whether Tempter sent, or whether tempest tossed thee here ashore,
Desolate, yet all undaunted, on this desert land enchanted—
On this home by Horror haunted—tell me truly, I implore—
Is there—*is* there balm in Gilead?[7]—tell me—tell me, I implore!"
Quoth the raven, "Nevermore."

6. A drug reputed by the Greeks to cause forgetfulness of sorrow. 7. Cf. Jeremiah 8:22.

"Prophet!" said I, "thing of evil—prophet still, if bird or devil!
by that Heaven that bends above us—by that God we both adore—
Tell this soul with sorrow laden if, within the distant Aidenn,
It shall clasp a sainted maiden whom the angels name Lenore—
Clasp a rare and radiant maiden whom the angels name Lenore."
Quoth the raven, "Nevermore."

"Be that word our sign of parting, bird or fiend!" I shrieked upstarting—
"Get thee back into the tempest and the Night's Plutonian shore!
Leave no black plume as a token of that lie thy soul hath spoken!
Leave my loneliness unbroken!—quit the bust above my door!
Take thy beak from out my heart, and take thy form from off my door!"
Quoth the raven, "Nevermore."

And the raven, never flitting, still is sitting, still is sitting
On the pallid bust of Pallas just above my chamber door;
And his eyes have all the seeming of a demon's that is dreaming,
And the lamp-light o'er him streaming throws his shadow on the floor;
And my soul from out that shadow that lies floating on the floor
Shall be lifted—nevermore! 1844

EZRA POUND

The Garden

En robe de parade.
—SAMAIN[8]

Like a skein of loose silk blown against a wall
She walks by the railing of a path in Kensington Gardens,[9]
And she is dying piece-meal
of a sort of emotional anæmia.

And round about there is a rabble
Of the filthy, sturdy, unkillable infants of the very poor.
They shall inherit the earth.

In her is the end of breeding.
Her boredom is exquisite and excessive.
She would like some one to speak to her,
And is almost afraid that I
will commit that indiscretion. 1916

8. Albert Samain, late 19th-century French poet. The phrase is from the first line of the prefatory poem in his first book of poems, *Au Jardin de l'Infante*: "Mon âme est une infante en robe de parade" ("My soul is an Infanta in ceremonial dress"). An "Infanta" is a daughter of the Spanish royal family which, long inbred, had for many years been afflicted with a rare blood disease, hemophilia. 9. A fashionable park near the center of London.

In a Station of the Metro[1]

The apparition of these faces in the crowd;
Petals on a wet, black bough.

p. 1913

A Virginal

No, no! Go from me. I have left her lately.
I will not spoil my sheath with lesser brightness,
For my surrounding air hath a new lightness;
Slight are her arms, yet they have bound me straitly
And left me cloaked as with a gauze of æther;
As with sweet leaves; as with a subtle clearness.
Oh, I have picked up magic in her nearness
To sheathe me half in half the things that sheathe her.
No, no! Go from me, I have still the flavor,
Soft as spring wind that's come from birchen bowers.
Green come the shoots, aye April in the branches,
As winter's wound with her sleight hand she staunches,
Hath of the trees a likeness of the savor:
As white their bark, so white this lady's hours.

1912

JAROLD RAMSEY

Hand-Shadows

FOR *a daughter, eighteen*

Dear child, first-born, what I could give outright
I've given—now there is only a father's wishing.
What can I hang around your neck for magic,
or smuggle in your pocket? I would draw
you a contour map of the territory ahead
but in truth it could only show you X—*you are here.*
The rest would be your Terra Incognita.

Years ago, in the trees beside a mountain lake
after bedtime, your mother and I sat up
together, reading the fire. Each flame, leaping,
seemed a stroke of the future, a signal for us
for you asleep in your nest at the rim of firelight
where great jagged shadows danced like knives.
We faced our ignorance until the fire was ash.

1. The Paris subway.

Once, in the first transports of adolescence,
you wandered over the hills behind the Sky Ranch,
remember? Suddenly beyond your feet
the country plunged away to utter strangeness,
and you were lost. The south wind carried your cries
like birdsong. At last I found you quiet on a stone,
your eyes full of the world we do not own.

Now it is all before you—wonderful
beyond a father's bedtime reckoning,
beyond his fears. What is it love must say?
Go forth to the fullness of your being: may
a merry kindness look you in the face.
Where home was, may your travels bring
you to a fellowship of open hearts.

So love must change our parts, my child no longer
child. I stand rehearsing at the door,
and think how once at bedtime, a dozen years
ago, I taught you how to cross your wrists
in the bright lamp-light, and link your thumbs, *so*,
and there on the wall a great bird arose
and soared on shadow wings, to the wonderment of all. p. 1984

JOHN CROWE RANSOM

Bells for John Whiteside's Daughter

There was such speed in her little body,
And such lightness in her footfall,
It is no wonder her brown study[2]
Astonishes us all.

Her wars were bruited in our high window.
We looked among orchard trees and beyond
Where she took arms against her shadow,
Or harried unto the pond

The lazy geese, like a snow cloud
Dripping their snow on the green grass,
Tricking and stopping, sleepy and proud,
Who cried in goose, Alas,

For the tireless heart within the little
Lady with rod that made them rise
From their noon apple-dreams and scuttle
Goose-fashion under the skies!

2. Stillness, as if in meditation or deep thought.

But now go the bells, and we are ready,
In one house we are sternly stopped
To say we are vexed at her brown study,
Lying so primly propped. 1924

ISHMAEL REED

beware : do not read this poem

tonite , thriller was
abt an ol woman , so vain she
surrounded herself w /
  many mirrors

it got so bad that finally she
locked herself indoors & her
whole life became the
  mirrors

one day the villagers broke
into her house , but she was too
swift for them . she disappeared
  into a mirror

each tenant who bought the house
after that , lost a loved one to
  the ol woman in the mirror :
  first a little girl
  then a young woman
  then the young woman / s husband

the hunger of this poem is legendary
it has taken in many victims
back off from this poem
it has drawn in yr feet
back off from this poem
it has drawn in yr legs

back off from this poem
it is a greedy mirror
you are into this poem . from
  the waist down
nobody can hear you can they ?
this poem has had you up to here
  belch
this poem aint got no manners
you cant call out frm this poem
relax now & go w / this poem

move & roll on to this poem
do not resist this poem
this poem has yr eyes
this poem has his head
this poem has his arms
this poem has his fingers
this poem has his fingertips
this poem is the reader & the
reader this poem

statistic : the us bureau of missing persons reports
that in 1968 over 100,000 people disappeared
leaving no solid clues
nor trace only
a space in the lives of their friends

1970

ALBERTO RÍOS

Incident at Imuris

Mr. Aplinio Morales has reported this:
They were not after all
Watermelons, it was not the wild
Fruit patch they at first had thought;
In the manner of what moths do,
These were cocoons, as every child has
Picked up and squeezed,
But from in these came and they saw
Thousands of green-winged half moths,
Half moths and not exactly butterflies,
Not exactly puppies—
A name for them did not exist here.
Half this and some of that,
What was familiar and what might be European.
And when the fruit rotted, or seemed to rot—
Almost all of them on the same day—
From out of each husk the beasts flew
Fat, equipped, at ease
So that they were not so much
Hungry as curious.
The watermelons had been generous homes.
These were not begging animals,
Not raccoons, nor rats,
Not second or third class;
These were the kind that if human

They would have worn dinner jackets
And sniffed, not at anything in particular,
Just as general commentary.
Animals who had time for tea.
Easily distracted and obviously educated
In some inexplicable manner,
The beasts of the watermelons left
The same day, after putting their heads
In windows, bored already
From chasing the horses
And drinking too much from the town well.

1989

EDWIN ARLINGTON ROBINSON

Mr. Flood's Party

Old Eben Flood, climbing alone one night
Over the hill between the town below
And the forsaken upland hermitage
That held as much as he should ever know
On earth again of home, paused warily.
The road was his and not a native near;
And Eben, having leisure, said aloud,
For no man else in Tilbury Town to hear:

"Well, Mr. Flood, we have the harvest moon
Again, and we may not have many more;
The bird is on the wing, the poet says,[3]
And you and I have said it here before.
Drink to the bird." He raised up to the light
The jug that he had gone so far to fill,
And answered huskily: "Well, Mr. Flood,
Since you propose it, I believe I will."

Alone, as if enduring to the end
A valiant armor of scarred hopes outworn
He stood there in the middle of the road
Like Roland's ghost winding a silent horn.[4]
Below him, in the town among the trees,
Where friends of other days had honored him,
A phantom salutation of the dead
Rang thinly till old Eben's eyes were dim

Then, as a mother lays her sleeping child
Down tenderly, fearing it may awake

3. Edward Fitzgerald, in "The Rubáiyat of Omar Khayyám," so describes the "Bird of Time." 4. In French legend Roland's powerful ivory horn was used to warn his allies of impending attack.

He set the jug down slowly at his feet
With trembling care, knowing that most things break;
And only when assured that on firm earth
It stood, as the uncertain lives of men
Assuredly did not, he paced away,
And with his hand extended paused again:

"Well, Mr. Flood, we have not met like this
In a long time; and many a change has come
To both of us, I fear, since last it was
We had a drop together. Welcome home!"
Convivially returning with himself,
Again he raised the jug up to the light;
And with an acquiescent quaver said:
"Well, Mr. Flood, if you insist, I might.

"Only a very little, Mr. Flood—
For auld lang syne. No more, sir; that will do."
So, for the time, apparently it did,
And Eben evidently thought so too;
For soon amid the silver loneliness
Of night he lifted up his voice and sang,
Secure, with only two moons listening,
Until the whole harmonious landscape rang—

"For auld lang syne." The weary throat gave out,
The last word wavered, and the song was done.
He raised again the jug regretfully
And shook his head, and was again alone.
There was not much that was ahead of him,
And there was nothing in the town below—
Where strangers would have shut the many doors
That many friends had opened long ago.

1921

Uncle Ananias[5]

His words were magic and his heart was true,
 And everywhere he wandered he was blessed.
Out of all ancient men my childhood knew
 I choose him and I mark him for the best.
Of all authoritative liars, too,
 I crown him loveliest.

5. The biblical character of Ananias was famous because he lied to God. See Acts 5:1–10.

How fondly I remember the delight
That always glorified him in the spring;
The joyous courage and the benedight[6]
Profusion of his faith in everything!
He was a good old man, and it was right
That he should have his fling.

And often, underneath the apple-trees,
When we surprised him in the summer time,
With what superb magnificence and ease
He sinned enough to make the day sublime!
And if he liked us there about his knees,
Truly it was no crime.

All summer long we loved him for the same
Perennial inspiration of his lies;
And when the russet wealth of autumn came,
There flew but fairer visions to our eyes—
Multiple, tropical, winged with a feathery flame,
Like birds of paradise.

So to the sheltered end of many a year
He charmed the seasons out with pageantry
Wearing upon his forehead, with no fear,
The laurel of approved iniquity.
And every child who knew him, far or near,
Did love him faithfully.

1910

THEODORE ROETHKE

The Dream

1

I met her as a blossom on a stem
Before she ever breathed, and in that dream
The mind remembers from a deeper sleep:
Eye learned from eye, cold lip from sensual lip.
My dream divided on a point of fire;
Light hardened on the water where we were;
A bird sang low; the moonlight sifted in;
The water rippled, and she rippled on.

2

She came toward me in the flowing air,
A shape of change, encircled by its fire.

6. Blessed.

I watched her there, between me and the moon;
The bushes and the stones danced on and on;
I touched her shadow when the light delayed;
I turned my face away, and yet she stayed.
A bird sang from the center of a tree;
She loved the wind because the wind loved me.

3

Love is not love until love's vulnerable.
She slowed to sigh, in that long interval.
A small bird flew in circles where we stood;
The deer came down, out of the dappled wood.
All who remember, doubt. Who calls that strange?
I tossed a stone, and listened to its plunge.
She knew the grammar of least motion, she
Lent me one virtue, and I live thereby.

4

She held her body steady in the wind;
Our shadows met, and slowly swung around;
She turned the field into a glittering sea;
I played in flame and water like a boy
And I swayed out beyond the white seafoam;
Like a wet log, I sang within a flame.
In that last while, eternity's confine,
I came to love, I came into my own.

1958

The Waking

I wake to sleep, and take my waking slow.
I feel my fate in what I cannot fear.
I learn by going where I have to go.

We think by feeling. What is there to know?
I hear my being dance from ear to ear.
I wake to sleep, and take my waking slow.

Of those so close beside me, which are you?
God bless the Ground! I shall walk softly there,
And learn by going where I have to go.

Light takes the Tree; but who can tell us how?
The lowly worm climbs up a winding stair;
I wake to sleep, and take my waking slow.

Great Nature has another thing to do
To you and me; so take the lively air,
And, lovely, learn by going where to go.

This shaking keeps me steady. I should know.
What falls away is always. And is near.
I wake to sleep, and take my waking slow.
I learn by going where I have to go.

1953

PATTIANN ROGERS

The Family Is All There Is

Think of those old, enduring connections
found in all flesh—the channeling
wires and threads, vacuoles, granules,
plasma and pods, purple veins, ascending
boles and coral sapwood (sugar-
and light-filled), those common ligaments,
filaments, fibers and canals.

Seminal to all kin also is the open
mouth—in heart urchin and octopus belly,
in catfish, moonfish, forest lily,
and rugosa rose, in thirsty magpie,
wailing cat cub, barker, yodeler,
yawning coati.

And there is a pervasive clasping
common to the clan—the hard nails
of lichen and ivy sucker
on the church wall, the bean tendril
and the taproot, the bolted coupling
of crane flies, the hold of the shearwater
on its morning squid, guanine
to cytosine, adenine to thymine,
fingers around fingers, the grip
of the voice on presence, the grasp
of the self on place.

Remember the same hair on pygmy
dormouse and yellow-necked caterpillar,
covering red baboon, thistle seed
and willow herb? Remember the similar
snorts of warthog, walrus, male moose
and sumo wrestler? Remember the familiar
whinny and shimmer found in river birches,

bay mares and bullfrog tadpoles,
in children playing at shoulder tag
on a summer lawn?

The family—weavers, reachers, winders
and connivers, pumpers, runners, air
and bubble riders, rock-sitters, wave-gliders,
wire-wobblers, soothers, flagellators—all
brothers, sisters, all there is.

Name something else. 1989

WILLIAM SHAKESPEARE

[Hark, hark! the lark at heaven's gate sings][7]

Hark, hark! the lark at heaven's gate sings,
  And Phoebus'[8] gins arise,
His steeds to water at those springs
  On chaliced[9] flowers that lies;
And winking Mary-buds[1] begin
  To ope their golden eyes:
With every thing that pretty is,
  My lady sweet, arise!
ca. 1610 Arise, arise!

[Not marble, nor the gilded monuments]

Not marble, nor the gilded monuments
Of princes, shall outlive this powerful rhyme;
But you shall shine more bright in these conténts
Than unswept stone, besmeared with sluttish time.
When wasteful war shall statues overturn,
And broils root out the work of masonry,
Nor Mars his sword nor war's quick fire shall burn
The living record of your memory.
'Gainst death and all-oblivious enmity
Shall you pace forth; your praise shall still find room
Even in the eyes of all posterity

7. From *Cymbeline*, Act II, scene iii. 8. Apollo, the sun god. 9. Cup-shaped. 1. Buds of marigolds.

That wear this world out to the ending doom.[2]
So, till the judgment that yourself arise,
You live in this, and dwell in lovers' eyes.
1609

[Two loves I have of comfort and despair]

Two loves I have of comfort and despair,
Which like two spirits do suggest[3] me still:
The better angel is a man right fair,
The worser spirit a woman, color'd ill.[4]
To win me soon to hell, my female evil
Tempteth my better angel from my side,
And would corrupt my saint to be a devil,
Wooing his purity with her foul pride.
And whether that my angel be turn'd fiend
Suspect I may, but not directly tell
But being both from me,[5] both to each friend,
I guess one angel in another's hell:
  Yet this shall I ne'er know, but live in doubt,
  Till my bad angel fire[6] my good one out.
1609

Spring[7]

When daisies pied and violets blue
  And ladysmocks all silver-white
And cuckoobuds of yellow hue
  Do paint the meadows with delight,
The cuckoo then, on every tree,
Mocks married men;[8] for thus sings he,
    Cuckoo;
Cuckoo, cuckoo: Oh word of fear,
Unpleasing to a married ear!

When shepherds pipe on oaten straws,
  And merry larks are plowmen's clocks,
When turtles tread,[9] and rooks, and daws,
  And maidens bleach their summer smocks,

2. Judgment Day. 3. Tempt. "Still": constantly. 4. Badly. 5. Away from me, *Both to each friend*: friends to each other. 6. Drive out with fire ("fire" was Elizabethan slang for venereal disease). 7. Like "Winter" (below), a song from *Love's Labors Lost*, Act V, scene ii. 8. By the resemblance of its call to the word "cuckold." 9. Copulate. *Turtles*: turtledoves.

The cuckoo then, on every tree,
Mocks married men; for thus sings he,
Cuckoo;
Cuckoo, cuckoo: Oh word of fear,
Unpleasing to a married ear!
ca. 1595

Winter

When icicles hang by the wall
And Dick the shepherd blows[1] his nail,
And Tom bears logs into the hall,
And milk comes frozen home in pail.
When blood is nipped and ways be foul,
Then nightly sings the staring owl,
Tu-who;
Tu-whit, tu-who: a merry note,
While greasy Joan doth keel[2] the pot.

When all aloud the wind doth blow,
And coughing drowns the parson's saw,[3]
And birds sit brooding in the snow,
And Marian's nose looks red and raw,
When roasted crabs[4] hiss in the bowl,
Then nightly sings the staring owl,
Tu-who;
Tu-whit, tu-who: a merry note
While greasy Joan doth keel the pot.
ca. 1595

PERCY BYSSHE SHELLEY

Mont Blanc[5]

LINES WRITTEN IN THE VALE OF CHAMOUNI

I

The everlasting universe of things
Flows through the mind, and rolls its rapid waves,
Now dark—now glittering—now reflecting gloom—
Now lending splendor, where from secret springs
The source of human thought its tribute brings

1. Breathes on for warmth. *Nail*: fingernail; i.e., hands. 2. Cool: stir to keep it from boiling over. 3. Maxim, proverb. 4. Crabapples. 5. The highest peak in Europe. Its snows melt into the River Arve and the Chamonix valley in France, near the borders of Switzerland and Italy.

Of waters—with a sound but half its own,
Such as a feeble brook will oft assume
In the wild woods, among the mountains lone,
Where waterfalls around it leap forever,
Where woods and winds contend, and a vast river
Over its rocks ceaselessly bursts and raves.

II

Thus thou, Ravine of Arve—dark, deep Ravine—
Thou many-colored, many-voicéd vale,
Over whose pines, and crags, and caverns sail
Fast cloud-shadows and sunbeams: awful scene,
Where Power in likeness of the Arve comes down
From the ice-gulfs that gird his secret throne,
Bursting through these dark mountains like the flame
Of lightning through the tempest; thou dost lie,
Thy giant brood of pines around thee clinging,
Children of elder time, in whose devotion
The chainless winds still come and ever came
To drink their odors, and their mighty swinging
To hear—an old and solemn harmony;
Thine earthly rainbows stretched across the sweep
Of the ethereal waterfall, whose veil
Robes some unsculptured image; the strange sleep
Which when the voices of the desert fail
Wraps all in its own deep eternity;
Thy caverns echoing to the Arve's commotion,
A loud, lone sound no other sound can tame;
Thou art pervaded with that ceaseless motion,
Thou art the path of that unresting sound—
Dizzy Ravine! and when I gaze on thee
I seem as in a trance sublime and strange
To muse on my own separate fantasy,
My own, my human mind, which passively
Now renders and receives fast influencings,
Holding an unremitting interchange
With the clear universe of things around;
One legion of wild thoughts, whose wandering wings
Now float above thy darkness, and now rest
Where that or thou art no unbidden guest,
In the still cave of the witch Poesy,
Seeking among the shadows that pass by
Ghosts of all things that are, some shade of thee,
Some phantom, some faint image; till the breast
From which they fled recalls them, thou art there!

III

Some say that gleams of a remoter world
Visit the soul in sleep, that death is slumber,
And that its shapes the busy thoughts outnumber
Of those who wake and live. I look on high;
Has some unknown omnipotence unfurled
The veil of life and death? or do I lie
In dream, and does the mightier world of sleep
Spread far around and inaccessibly
Its circles? For the very spirit fails,
Driven like a homeless cloud from steep to steep
That vanishes among the viewless[6] gales!
Far, far above, piercing the infinite sky,
Mont Blanc appears—still, snowy, and serene—
Its subject mountains their unearthly forms
Pile around it, ice and rock; broad vales between
Of frozen floods, unfathomable deeps,
Blue as the overhanging heaven, that spread
And wind among the accumulated steeps;
A desert peopled by the storms alone,
Save when the eagle brings some hunter's bone,
And the wolf tracks her there—how hideously
Its shapes are heaped around! rude, bare, and high,
Ghastly, and scarred, and riven. Is this the scene
Where the old Earthquake-demon taught her young
Ruin? Were these their toys? or did a sea
Of fire envelop once this silent snow?[7]
None can reply—all seems eternal now.
The wilderness has a mysterious tongue
Which teaches awful doubt, or faith, so mild,
So solemn, so serene, that man may be,
But for such faith, with nature reconciled;
Thou hast a voice, great Mountain, to repeal
Large codes of fraud and woe; not understood
By all, but which the wise, and great, and good
Interpret, or make felt, or deeply feel.

IV

The fields, the lakes, the forests, and the streams,
Ocean, and all the living things that dwell
Within the daedal[8] earth; lightning, and rain,
Earthquake, and fiery flood, and hurricane,
The torpor of the year when feeble dreams

6. Invisible. 7. According to scientific theories of the time, the earth was originally round and smooth, and mountains resulted from floods, earthquakes, or fires bursting from the earth's center. 8. Varied.

Visit the hidden buds, or dreamless sleep
Holds every future leaf and flower; the bound
With which from that detested trance they leap;
The works and ways of man, their death and birth,
And that of him and all that his may be;
All things that move and breathe with toil and sound
Are born and die; revolve, subside, and swell.
Power dwells apart in its tranquillity,
Remote, serene, and inaccessible:
And *this*, the naked countenance of earth,
On which I gaze, even these primeval mountains
Teach the adverting mind. The glaciers creep
Like snakes that watch their prey, from their far fountains,
Slow rolling on; there, many a precipice,
Frost and the Sun in scorn of mortal power
Have piled: dome, pyramid, and pinnacle,
A city of death, distinct with many a tower
And wall impregnable of beaming ice.
Yet not a city, but a flood of ruin
Is there, that from the boundaries of the sky
Rolls its perpetual stream; vast pines are strewing
Its destined path, or in the mangled soil
Branchless and shattered stand; the rocks, drawn down
From yon remotest waste, have overthrown
The limits of the dead and living world,
Never to be reclaimed. The dwelling place
Of insects, beasts, and birds, becomes its spoil
Their food and their retreat for ever gone,
So much of life and joy is lost. The race
Of man flies far in dread; his work and dwelling
Vanish, like smoke before the tempest's stream,
And their place is not known. Below, vast caves
Shine in the rushing torrents' restless gleam,
Which from those secret chasms in tumult welling
Meet in the vale, and one majestic River,
The breath and blood of distant lands, forever
Rolls its loud waters to the ocean waves,
Breathes its swift vapors to the circling air.

V

Mont Blanc yet gleams on high—the power is there,
The still and solemn power of many sights,
And many sounds, and much of life and death.
In the calm darkness of the moonless nights,
In the lone glare of day, the snows descend
Upon that Mountain; none beholds them there,
Nor when the flakes burn in the sinking sun,

Or the star-beams dart through them—Winds contend
Silently there, and heap the snow with breath
Rapid and strong, but silently! Its home
The voiceless lightning in these solitudes
Keeps innocently, and like vapor broods
Over the snow. The secret Strength of things
Which governs thought, and to the infinite dome
Of Heaven is as a law, inhabits thee!
And what were thou, and earth, and stars, and sea,
If to the human mind's imaginings
Silence and solitude were vacancy? 1817

LOUIS SIMPSON

To the Western World

A siren sang, and Europe turned away
From the high castle and the shepherd's crook.
Three caravels went sailing to Cathay[9]
On the strange ocean, and the captains shook
Their banners out across the Mexique Bay.

And in our early days we did the same.
Remembering our fathers in their wreck
We crossed the sea from Palos[1] where they came
And saw, enormous to the little deck,
A shore in silence waiting for a name.

The treasures of Cathay were never found.
In this America, this wilderness
Where the axe echoes with a lonely sound,
The generations labor to possess
And grave by grave we civilize the ground. 1959

STEPHEN SPENDER

Judas Iscariot[2]

The eyes of twenty centuries
Pursue me along corridors to where
I am painted at their ends on many walls.

9. In medieval Europe, Northern China was referred to as Cathay. 1. The seaport in Spain from which Columbus set sail in 1492. 2. According to New Testament accounts, Judas, one of the twelve disciples, betrayed Jesus to his enemies for 30 pieces of silver. The betrayal occurred shortly after the Last Supper; Judas indicated to his confederates who Jesus was by kissing him.

Ever-revolving future recognize
This red hair and red beard, where I am seated
Within the dark cave of the feast of light.
Out of my heart-shaped shadow I stretch my hand
Across the white table into the dish
But not to dip the bread. It is as though
The cloth on each side of one dove-bright face
Spread dazzling wings on which the apostles ride
Uplifting them into the vision
Where their eyes watch themselves enthroned.
My russet hand across the dish
Plucks enviously against one feather
—But still the rushing wings spurn me below!

Saint Sebastian[3] of wickedness
I stand: all eyes legitimate arrows piercing through
The darkness of my wickedness. They recognize
My halo hammered from thirty silver pieces
And the hemp rope around my neck
Soft as that Spirit's hanging arms
When on my cheek he answered with the kiss
Which cuts for ever—
My strange stigmata,
All love and hate, all fire and ice!

But who betrayed whom? O you,
Whose light gaze forms the azure corridor
Through which those other pouring eyes
Arrow into me—answer! Who
Betrayed whom? Who read
In his mind's light from the first day
That the kingdom of heaven on earth must always
Reiterate the garden of Eden,
And each day's revolution be betrayed
Within man's heart, each day?
Who wrapped
The whispering serpent round the tree
And hung between the leaves the glittering purse
And trapped the fangs with God-appointed poison?
Who knew
I must betray the truth, and made the lie
Betray its truth in me?

Those hypocrite eyes which aimed at you
Now aim at me. And yet, beyond their world
Each turning on his pole of truth, your pole

3. Early Christian martyr who was a favorite subject of Renaissance painters. According to legend, St. Sebastian was sentenced to be shot with arrows, but his many wounds were miraculously healed.

Invisible light, and mine
Becoming what man is. We stare
Across two thousand years, and heaven, and hell,
Into each other's gaze. 1949

WALLACE STEVENS

The Emperor of Ice-Cream

Call the roller of big cigars,
The muscular one, and bid him whip
In kitchen cups concupiscent curds.[4]
Let the wenches dawdle in such dress
As they are used to wear, and let the boys
Bring flowers in last month's newspapers.
Let be be finale of seem.[5]
The only emperor is the emperor of ice-cream.

Take from the dresser of deal,
Lacking the three glass knobs, that sheet
On which she embroidered fantails[6] once
And spread it so as to cover her face.
If her horny feet protrude, they come
To show how cold she is, and dumb.
Let the lamp affix its beam.
The only emperor is the emperor of ice-cream. 1923

Sunday Morning

I

Complacencies of the peignoir, and late
Coffee and oranges in a sunny chair,
And the green freedom of a cockatoo
Upon a rug mingle to dissipate
The holy hush of ancient sacrifice.
She dreams a little, and she feels the dark

4. "The words 'concupiscent curds' have no genealogy; they are merely expressive: at least, I hope they are expressive. They express the concupiscence of life, but, by contrast with the things in relation in the poem, they express or accentuate life's destitution, and it is this that gives them something more than a cheap lustre" Wallace Stevens, *Letters* (New York: Knopf, 1966), p. 500. 5. ". . . the true sense of Let be be the finale of seem is let being become the conclusion or denouement of appearing to be: in short, ice cream is an absolute good. The poem is obviously not about ice cream, but about being as distinguished from seeming to be." *Letters*, p. 341. 6. Fantail pigeons.

Encroachment of that old catastrophe,[7]
As a calm darkens among water-lights.
The pungent oranges and bright, green wings
Seem things in some procession of the dead,
Winding across wide water, without sound,
The day is like wide water, without sound,
Stilled for the passing of her dreaming feet
Over the seas, to silent Palestine,
Dominion of the blood and sepulchre.

II

Why should she give her bounty to the dead?
What is divinity if it can come
Only in silent shadows and in dreams?
Shall she not find in comforts of the sun,
In pungent fruit and bright, green wings, or else
In any balm or beauty of the earth,
Things to be cherished like the thought of heaven.
Divinity must live within herself:
Passions of rain, or moods in falling snow;
Grievings in loneliness, or unsubdued
Elations when the forest blooms; gusty
Emotions on wet roads on autumn nights;
All pleasures and all pains, remembering
The bough of summer and the winter branch.
These are the measures destined for her soul.

III

Jove in the clouds has his inhuman birth.
No mother suckled him, no sweet land gave
Large-mannered motions to his mythy mind
He moved among us, as a muttering king,
Magnificent, would move among his hinds,[8]
Until our blood, commingling, virginal,
With heaven, brought such requital to desire
The very hinds discerned it, in a star.[9]
Shall our blood fail? Or shall it come to be
The blood of paradise? And shall the earth
Seem all of paradise that we shall know?
The sky will be much friendlier then than now,
A part of labor and a part of pain,
And next in glory to enduring love,
Not this dividing and indifferent blue.

7. The Crucifixion. 8. Lowliest rural subjects. 9. The star of Bethlehem.

IV

She says, "I am content when wakened birds,
Before they fly, test the reality
Of misty fields, by their sweet questionings;
But when the birds are gone, and their warm fields
Return no more, where, then, is paradise?"
There is not any haunt of prophecy,
Nor any old chimera of the grave,
Neither the golden underground, nor isle
Melodious, where spirits gat[1] them home,
Nor visionary south, nor cloudy palm
Remote on heaven's hill, that has endured
As April's green endures, or will endure
Like her remembrance of awakened birds,
Or her desire for June and evening, tipped
By the consummation of the swallow's wings.

V

She says, "But in contentment I still feel
The need of some imperishable bliss."
Death is the mother of beauty; hence from her,
Alone, shall come fulfillment to our dreams
And our desires. Although she strews the leaves
Of sure obliteration on our paths,
The path sick sorrow took, the many paths
Where triumph rang its brassy phrase, or love
Whispered a little out of tenderness,
She makes the willow shiver in the sun
For maidens who were wont to sit and gaze
Upon the grass, relinquished to their feet.
She causes boys to pile new plums and pears
On disregarded plate.[2] The maidens taste
And stray impassioned in the littering leaves.

VI

Is there no change of death in paradise?
Does ripe fruit never fall? Or do the boughs
Hang always heavy in that perfect sky,
Unchanging, yet so like our perishing earth,
With rivers like our own that seek for seas
They never find, the same receding shores

1. Got. 2. "Plate is used in the sense of so-called family plate. Disregarded refers to the disuse into which things fall that have been possessed for a long time. I mean, therefore, that death releases and renews. What the old have come to disregard, the young inherit and make use of." (*Letters*, pp. 183–184)

That never touch with inarticulate pang?
Why set the pear upon those river-banks
Or spice the shores with odors of the plum?
Alas, that they should wear our colors there,
The silken weavings of our afternoons,
And pick the strings of our insipid lutes!
Death is the mother of beauty, mystical,
Within whose burning bosom we devise
Our earthly mothers awaiting, sleeplessly.

VII

Supple and turbulent, a ring of men
Shall chant in orgy[3] on a summer morn
Their boisterous devotion to the sun,
Not as a god, but as a god might be,
Naked among them, like a savage source.
Their chant shall be a chant of paradise,
Out of their blood, returning to the sky;
And in their chant shall enter, voice by voice,
The windy lake wherein their lord delights,
The trees, like serafin,[4] and echoing hills,
That choir among themselves long afterward.
They shall know well the heavenly fellowship
Of men that perish and of summer morn.
And whence they came and whither they shall go
The dew upon their feet shall manifest.

VIII

She hears, upon that water without sound,
A voice that cries, "The tomb in Palestine
Is not the porch of spirits lingering.
It is the grave of Jesus, where he lay."
We live in an old chaos of the sun,
Or old dependency of day and night,
Or island solitude, unsponsored, free,
Of that wide water, inescapable.
Deer walk upon our mountains, and the quail
Whistle about us their spontaneous cries;
Sweet berries ripen in the wilderness;
And, in the isolation of the sky,
At evening, casual flocks of pigeons make
Ambiguous undulations as they sink,
Downward to darkness, on extended wings.

1915

3. Ceremonial revelry. 4. Seraphim, the highest of the nine orders of angels.

NANCY SULLIVAN

Burial in the Sand

The sand is a gritty flesh
mounding her aching mounds.
He piles her tight
                    up to her throat.
On her head a flare of cloth hat,
in her mouth the glare of gold teeth.
Pat, pat. The drooling sand dribbles
            over
her arthritis quiet under its warm compress.
He is Henry Moore[5] building his old woman.
            Then
from this burial in the sand his beach Venus[6]
rises out of the maw of Zeus,
            her jewelry toothy, her crown canvas.
He rises and she rises,
                    breaking the mold
the way it never happens out of
real statues, risky and rare,
although the same deep force
buried deep in the stone
is poised for the pounce.

1975

JONATHAN SWIFT

On Stella's Birthday, 1719

Stella this day is thirty-four,[7]
(We shan't dispute a year or more)
However Stella, be not troubled,
Although thy size and years are doubled,
Since first I saw thee at sixteen
The brightest virgin on the green,
So little is thy form declined
Made up so largely in thy mind.
Oh, would it please the gods to split
Thy beauty, size, and years, and wit,

5. English sculptor, b. 1898. 6. Roman goddess of love, usually said to have sprung from the foam of the sea or (alternatively) to have been the daughter of Dione and Jupiter (Greek name Zeus), the supreme deity. 7. Stella is Swift's pet name for Hester Johnson, a close friend for many years. She was actually 38.

No age could furnish out a pair
Of nymphs so graceful, wise and fair
With half the luster of your eyes,
With half your wit, your years and size:
And then before it grew too late,
How should I beg of gentle Fate,
(That either nymph might have her swain,[8])
To split my worship too in twain.

1719

ALFRED, LORD TENNYSON

Tears, Idle Tears[9]

Tears, idle tears, I know not what they mean,
Tears from the depth of some divine despair
Rise in the heart, and gather to the eyes,
In looking on the happy autumn-fields,
And thinking of the days that are no more.

Fresh as the first beam glittering on a sail,
That brings our friends up from the underworld,
Sad as the last which reddens over one
That sinks with all we love below the verge;
So sad, so fresh, the days that are no more.

Ah, sad and strange as in dark summer dawns
The earliest pipe of half-awakened birds
To dying ears, when unto dying eyes
The casement slowly grows a glimmering square;
So sad, so strange, the days that are no more.

Dear as remembered kisses after death,
And sweet as those by hopeless fancy feigned
On lips that are for others; deep as love,
Deep as first love, and wild with all regret;
O Death in Life, the days that are no more!

1847

8. Servant, admirer, lover.
9. A song from *The Princess,* a long narrative poem about what the mid-19th century called the "new woman."

DYLAN THOMAS

Do Not Go Gentle into That Good Night[1]

Do not go gentle into that good night,
Old age should burn and rave at close of day;
Rage, rage against the dying of the light.

Though wise men at their end know dark is right,
Because their words had forked no lightning they
Do not go gentle into that good night.

Good men, the last wave by, crying how bright
Their frail deeds might have danced in a green bay,
Rage, rage against the dying of the light.

Wild men who caught and sang the sun in flight,
And learn, too late, they grieved it on its way,
Do not go gentle into that good night.

Grave men, near death, who see with blinding sight
Blind eyes could blaze like meteors and be gay,
Rage, rage against the dying of the light.

And you, my father, there on the sad height,
Curse, bless, me now with your fierce tears, I pray.
Do not go gentle into that good night.
Rage, rage against the dying of the light. 1952

Fern Hill

Now as I was young and easy under the apple boughs
About the lilting house and happy as the grass was green,
    The night above the dingle starry,
        Time let me hail and climb
    Golden in the heydays of his eyes,
And honored among wagons I was prince of the apple towns
And once below a time I lordly had the trees and leaves
        Trail with daisies and barley
    Down the rivers of the windfall light.

And as I was green and carefree, famous among the barns
About the happy yard and singing as the farm was home,
    In the sun that is young once only,
        Time let me play and be
    Golden in the mercy of his means,

1. Written during the final illness of the poet's father.

And green and golden I was huntsman and herdsman, the calves
Sang to my horn, the foxes on the hills barked clear and cold,
And the sabbath rang slowly
In the pebbles of the holy streams.

All the sun long it was running, it was lovely, the hay
Fields high as the house, the tunes from the chimneys, it was air
And playing, lovely and watery
And fire green as grass.
And nightly under the simple stars
As I rode to sleep the owls were bearing the farm away,
All the moon long I heard, blessed among stables, the nightjars[2]
Flying with the ricks,[3] and the horses
Flashing into the dark.

And then to awake, and the farm, like a wanderer white
With the dew, come back, the cock on his shoulder: it was all
Shining, it was Adam and maiden,
The sky gathered again
And the sun grew round that very day.
So it must have been after the birth of the simple light
In the first, spinning place, the spellbound horses walking warm
Out of the whinnying green stable
On to the fields of praise.

And honored among foxes and pheasants by the gay house
Under the new made clouds and happy as the heart was long,
In the sun born over and over,
I ran my heedless ways,
My wishes raced through the house-high hay
And nothing I cared, at my sky-blue trades, that time allows
In all his tuneful turning so few and such morning songs
Before the children green and golden
Follow him out of grace,

Nothing I cared, in the lamb white days, that time would take me
Up to the swallow-thronged loft by the shadow of my hand,
In the moon that is always rising,
Nor that riding to sleep
I should hear him fly with the high fields
And wake to the farm forever fled from the childless land.
Oh as I was young and easy in the mercy of his means,
Time held me green and dying
Though I sang in my chains like the sea.

1946

2. Birds. 3. Haystacks.

In My Craft or Sullen Art

In my craft or sullen art
Exercised in the still night
When only the moon rages
And the lovers lie abed
With all their griefs in their arms,
I labor by singing light
Not for ambition or bread
Or the strut and trade of charms
On the ivory stages
But for the common wages
Of their most secret heart.

Not for the proud man apart
From the raging moon I write
On these spindrift[4] pages
Nor for the towering dead
With their nightingales and psalms
But for the lovers, their arms
Round the griefs of the ages,
Who pay no praise or wages
Nor heed my craft or art.

1946

JEAN TOOMER

Song of the Son[5]

Pour O pour that parting soul in song,
O pour it in the sawdust glow of night,
Into the velvet pine-smoke air tonight,
And let the valley carry it along.
And let the valley carry it along.

O land and soil, red soil and sweet-gum tree,
So scant of grass, so profligate of pines,
Now just before an epoch's sun declines
Thy son, in time, I have returned to thee,
Thy son, I have in time returned to thee.

In time, for though the sun is setting on
A song-lit race of slaves, it has not set;
Though late, O soil, it is not too late yet
To catch thy plaintive soul, leaving, soon gone,
Leaving, to catch thy plaintive soul soon gone.

4. Literally, wind-driven sea spray. 5. From the novel *Cane*.

O Negro slaves, dark purple ripened plums,
Squeezed, and bursting in the pine-wood air,
Passing, before they strip the old tree bare
One plum was saved for me, one seed becomes

An everlasting song, a singing tree,
Caroling softly souls of slavery,
What they were, and what they are to me,
Caroling softly souls of slavery.

1923

MIRIAM WADDINGTON

Old Women of Toronto

All old women sometimes come to this:
they go to live away, they cross ravines,
mornings they ride the subway, later look below
to read the red of dogwood and the print of snow.
They tread upon the contours of each month
with delicate feet that hardly sense its shape,
explore the mouth of March and with a hiss,
they spit at myth and swallow counter-bliss.

Their brows beetle, their plush hats tremble
they specially deplore without preamble
the palomino carpets on the lawns
steamy with manure in frosty air;
against all evidence and witnesses they'll swear
they never argued once or schemed to take
the room in front with the old Morris chair,
and partial view, at least, of the bright lake.

1972

WALT WHITMAN

I Saw in Louisiana a Live-Oak Growing

I saw in Louisiana a live-oak growing,
All alone stood it and the moss hung down from the branches,
Without any companion it grew there uttering joyous leaves of dark green,
And its look, rude, unbending, lusty, made me think of myself,
But I wonder'd how it could utter joyous leaves standing alone there without its
 friend near, for I knew I could not,

And I broke off a twig with a certain number of leaves upon it, and twined around it a little moss,
And brought it away, and I have placed it in sight in my room,
It is not needed to remind me as of my own dear friends,
(For I believe lately I think of little else than of them,)
Yet it remains to me a curious token, it makes me think of manly love;
For all that, and though the live-oak glistens there in Louisiana solitary in a wide flat space,
Uttering joyous leaves all its life without a friend a lover near,
I know very well I could not. 1860

RICHARD WILBUR

Love Calls Us to the Things of This World[6]

The eyes open to a cry of pulleys,[7]
And spirited from sleep, the astounded soul
Hangs for a moment bodiless and simple
As false dawn.
Outside the open window
The morning air is all awash with angels.

Some are in bed-sheets, some are in blouses,
Some are in smocks: but truly there they are.
Now they are rising together in calm swells
Of halcyon[8] feeling, filling whatever they wear
With the deep joy of their impersonal breathing;
Now they are flying in place,[9] conveying
The terrible speed of their omnipresence, moving
And staying like white water; and now of a sudden
They swoon down into so rapt a quiet
That nobody seems to be there.
The soul shrinks

From all that it is about to remember,
From the punctual rape of every blessèd day,
And cries,
"Oh, let there be nothing on earth but laundry,
Nothing but rosy hands in the rising steam
And clear dances done in the sight of heaven."

6. A phrase from St. Augustine's *Commentary on the Psalms.* 7. Laundry pulleys, designed so that clothes can be hung on the line inside and then sent outdoors to dry. 8. Serene. 9. Like planes in a formation.

Yet, as the sun acknowledges
With a warm look the world's hunks and colors,
The soul descends once more in bitter love
To accept the waking body, saying now
In a changed voice as the man yawns and rises,

"Bring them down from their ruddy gallows;
Let there be clean linen for the backs of thieves;
Let lovers go fresh and sweet to be undone,
And the heaviest nuns walk in a pure floating
Of dark habits,
keeping their difficult balance."

1956

WILLIAM CARLOS WILLIAMS

This Is Just to Say

I have eaten
the plums
that were in
the icebox

and which
you were probably
saving
for breakfast

Forgive me
they were delicious
so sweet
and so cold

1934

WILLIAM WORDSWORTH

Lines Composed a Few Miles above Tintern Abbey on Revisiting the Banks of the Wye During a Tour, July 13, 1798[1]

Five years have passed; five summers, with the length
Of five long winters! and again I hear
These waters, rolling from their mountain-springs
With a soft inland murmur. Once again

1. Wordsworth had first visited the Wye valley and the ruins of the medieval abbey there in 1793, while on a solitary walking tour. He was 23 then, 28 when he wrote this poem.

Do I behold these steep and lofty cliffs,
That on a wild secluded scene impress
Thoughts of more deep seclusion; and connect
The landscape with the quiet of the sky.
The day is come when I again repose
Here, under this dark sycamore, and view
These plots of cottage-ground, these orchard tufts,
Which at this season, with their unripe fruits,
Are clad in one green hue, and lose themselves
'Mid groves and copses.[2] Once again I see
These hedge-rows, hardly hedge-rows, little lines
Of sportive wood run wild: these pastoral farms,
Green to the very door; and wreaths of smoke
Sent up, in silence, from among the trees!
With some uncertain notice, as might seem
Of vagrant dwellers in the houseless woods,
Or of some hermit's cave, where by his fire
The hermit sits alone.
These beauteous forms,
Through a long absence, have not been to me
As is a landscape to a blind man's eye;
But oft, in lonely rooms, and 'mid the din
Of towns and cities, I have owed to them,
In hours of weariness, sensations sweet,
Felt in the blood, and felt along the heart;
And passing even into my purer mind,
With tranquil restoration—feelings too
Of unremembered pleasure: such, perhaps,
As have no slight or trivial influence
On that best portion of a good man's life,
His little, nameless, unremembered acts
Of kindness and of love. Nor less, I trust,
To them I may have owed another gift,
Of aspect more sublime; that blessèd mood,
In which the burthen[3] of the mystery,
In which the heavy and the weary weight
Of all this unintelligible world,
Is lightened—that serene and blessèd mood,
In which the affections gently lead us on—
Until, the breath of this corporeal frame
And even the motion of our human blood
Almost suspended, we are laid asleep
In body, and become a living soul;
While with an eye made quiet by the power
Of harmony, and the deep power of joy,
We see into the life of things.

2. Thickets. 3. Burden.

If this
Be but a vain belief, yet, oh! how oft—
In darkness and amid the many shapes
Of joyless daylight; when the fretful stir
Unprofitable, and the fever of the world,
Have hung upon the beatings of my heart—
How oft, in spirit, have I turned to thee,
O sylvan Wye! thou wanderer through the woods,
How often has my spirit turned to thee!

And now, with gleams of half-extinguished thought,
With many recognitions dim and faint,
And somewhat of a sad perplexity,
The picture of the mind revives again;
While here I stand, not only with the sense
Of present pleasure, but with pleasing thoughts
That in this moment there is life and food
For future years. And so I dare to hope,
Though changed, no doubt, from what I was when first
I came among these hills; when like a roe
I bounded o'er the mountains, by the sides
Of the deep rivers, and the lonely streams,
Wherever nature led: more like a man
Flying from something that he dreads than one
Who sought the thing he loved. For nature then
(The coarser[4] pleasures of my boyish days,
And their glad animal movements all gone by)
To me was all in all—I cannot paint
What then I was. The sounding cataract
Haunted me like a passion; the tall rock,
The mountain, and the deep and gloomy wood,
Their colors and their forms, were then to me
An appetite; a feeling and a love,
That had no need of a remoter charm.
By thought supplied, nor any interest
Unborrowed from the eye. That time is past,
And all its aching joys are now no more,
And all its dizzy raptures. Not for this
Faint I,[5] nor mourn nor murmur; other gifts
Have followed; for such loss, I would believe,
Abundant recompense. For I have learned
To look on nature, not as in the hour
Of thoughtless youth; but hearing oftentimes
The still, sad music of humanity,
Nor harsh nor grating, though of ample power
To chasten and subdue. And I have felt

4. Physical. 5. Am I discouraged.

A presence that disturbs me with the joy
Of elevated thoughts, a sense sublime
Of something far more deeply interfused,
Whose dwelling is the light of setting suns,
And the round ocean and the living air,
And the blue sky, and in the mind of man:
A motion and a spirit, that impels
All thinking things, all objects of all thought,
And rolls through all things. Therefore am I still
A lover of the meadows and the woods
And mountains; and of all that we behold
From this green earth; of all the mighty world
Of eye, and ear—both what they half create,
And what perceive; well pleased to recognize
In nature and the language of the sense
The anchor of my purest thoughts, the nurse,
The guide, the guardian of my heart, and soul
Of all my moral being.
Nor perchance,
If I were not thus taught, should I the more
Suffer my genial spirits[6] to decay:
For thou art with me here upon the banks
Of this fair river; thou my dearest Friend,[7]
My dear, dear Friend; and in thy voice I catch
The language of my former heart, and read
My former pleasures in the shooting lights
Of thy wild eyes. Oh! yet a little while
May I behold in thee what I was once,
My dear, dear Sister! and this prayer I make,
Knowing that Nature never did betray
The heart that loved her; 'tis her privilege,
Through all the years of this our life, to lead
From joy to joy: for she can so inform
The mind that is within us, so impress
With quietness and beauty, and so feed
With lofty thoughts, that neither evil tongues,
Rash judgments, nor the sneers of selfish men,
Nor greetings where no kindness is, nor all
The dreary intercourse of daily life,
Shall e'er prevail against us, or disturb
Our cheerful faith that all which we behold
Is full of blessings. Therefore let the moon
Shine on thee in thy solitary walk;
And let the misty mountain-winds be free
To blow against thee: and, in after years,
When these wild ecstasies shall be matured

6. Natural disposition; i.e., the spirits that are part of his individual genius.
7. His sister Dorothy.

Into a sober pleasure; when thy mind
Shall be a mansion for all lovely forms,
Thy memory be as a dwelling-place
For all sweet sounds and harmonies; oh! then,
If solitude, or fear, or pain, or grief,
Should be thy portion, with what healing thoughts
Of tender joy wilt thou remember me,
And these my exhortations! No, perchance—
If I should be where I no more can hear
Thy voice, nor catch from thy wild eyes these gleams
Of past existence—wilt thou then forget
That on the banks of this delightful stream
We stood together; and that I, so long
A worshiper of Nature, hither came
Unwearied in that service; rather say
With warmer love—oh! with far deeper zeal
Of holier love. Nor wilt thou then forget,
That after many wanderings, many years
Of absence, these steep woods and lofty cliffs,
And this green pastoral landscape, were to me
More dear, both for themselves and for thy sake!

1798

W. B. YEATS

Easter 1916[8]

I have met them at close of day
Coming with vivid faces
From counter or desk among gray
Eighteenth-century houses.
I have passed with a nod of the head
Or polite meaningless words,
Or have lingered awhile and said
Polite meaningless words,
And thought before I had done
Of a mocking tale or a gibe
To please a companion
Around the fire at the club,
Being certain that they and I
But lived where motley is worn:
All changed, changed utterly:
A terrible beauty is born.

8. On Easter Monday 1916, an Irish Republic was proclaimed by nationalist leaders, who launched an unsuccessful revolt against the British government. After a week of street fighting, the Easter Rebellion was put down. A number of prominent nationalists were executed, including the four leaders mentioned in lines 75–76, all of whom Yeats knew personally.

That woman's[9] days were spent
In ignorant good-will,
Her nights in argument
Until her voice grew shrill.
What voice more sweet than hers
When, young and beautiful,
She rode to harriers?
This man[1] had kept a school
And rode our wingéd horse;[2]
This other[3] his helper and friend
Was coming into his force;
He might have won fame in the end,
So sensitive his nature seemed,
So daring and sweet his thought.
This other man[4] I had dreamed
A drunken, vainglorious lout.
He had done most bitter wrong
To some who are near my heart,
Yet I number him in the song;
He, too, has resigned his part
In the casual comedy;
He, too, has been changed in his turn,
Transformed utterly:
A terrible beauty is born.

Hearts with one purpose alone
Through summer and winter seem
Enchanted to a stone
To trouble the living stream.
The horse that comes from the road,
The rider, the birds that range
From cloud to tumbling cloud,
Minute by minute they change;
A shadow of cloud on the stream
Changes minute by minute;
A horse-hoof slides on the brim,
And a horse plashes within it;
The long-legged moor-hens dive,
And hens to moor-cocks call;
Minute by minute they live:
The stone's in the midst of all.

9. Countess Constance Georgina Markiewicz, a beautiful and well-born young woman from County Sligo who became a vigorous and bitter nationalist. At first condemned to death, she later had her sentence commuted to life imprisonment, and she gained amnesty in 1917. 1. Patrick Pearse, who led the assault on the Dublin Post Office from which the proclamation of a republic was issued. A schoolmaster by profession, he had vigorously supported the restoration of the Gaelic language in Ireland and was an active political writer and poet. 2. Pegasus, a traditional symbol of poetic inspiration. 3. Thomas MacDonagh, also a writer and teacher. 4. Major John MacBride, who had married Yeats's beloved Maud Gonne in 1903 but separated from her two years later.

Too long a sacrifice
Can make a stone of the heart.
O when may it suffice?
That is Heaven's part, our part
To murmur name upon name,
As a mother names her child
When sleep at last has come
On limbs that had run wild.
What is it but nightfall?
No, no, not night but death;
Was it needless death after all?
For England may keep faith[5]
For all that is done and said.
We know their dream; enough
To know they dreamed and are dead;
And what if excess of love
Bewildered them till they died?
I write it out in a verse—
MacDonagh and MacBride
And Connolly[6] and Pearse
Now and in time to be,
Wherever green is worn,
Are changed, changed utterly;
A terrible beauty is born.

1916

The Second Coming[7]

Turning and turning in the widening gyre[8]
The falcon cannot hear the falconer;
Things fall apart; the center cannot hold;
Mere anarchy is loosed upon the world,
The blood-dimmed tide is loosed, and everywhere
The ceremony of innocence is drowned;
The best lack all conviction, while the worst
Are full of passionate intensity.
Surely some revelation is at hand;
Surely the Second Coming is at hand.

5. Before the uprising the English had promised eventual home rule to Ireland. 6. James Connolly, the leader of the Easter uprising. 7. The Second Coming of Christ, according to Matthew 24:29–44, will come after a time of "tribulation." Disillusioned by Ireland's continued civil strife, Yeats saw his time as the end of another historical cycle. In *A Vision* (1937) Yeats describes his view of history as dependent on cycles of about 2000 years: the birth of Christ had ended the cycle of Greco-Roman civilization, and now the Christian cycle seemed near an end, to be followed by an antithetical cycle, ominous in its portents. 8. Literally, the widening spiral of a falcon's flight. "Gyre" is Yeats's term for a cycle of history, which he diagramed in terms of a series of interpenetrating cones.

The Second Coming! Hardly are those words out
When a vast image out of *Spiritus Mundi*[9]
Troubles my sight: somewhere in sands of the desert
A shape with lion body and the head of a man,
A gaze blank and pitiless as the sun,
Is moving its slow thighs, while all about it
Reel shadows of the indignant desert birds.[1]
The darkness drops again; but now I know
That twenty centuries of stony sleep
Were vexed to nightmare by a rocking cradle,
And what rough beast, its hour come round at last,
Slouches towards Bethlehem to be born? p. 1920

Leda and the Swan[2]

A sudden blow: the great wings beating still
Above the staggering girl, her thighs caressed
By the dark webs, her nape caught in his bill,
He holds her helpless breast upon his breast.

How can those terrified vague fingers push
The feathered glory from her loosening thighs?
And how can body, laid in that white rush,
But feel the strange heart beating where it lies?

A shudder in the loins engenders there
The broken wall, the burning roof and tower
And Agamemnon dead.
Being so caught up,
So mastered by the brute blood of the air,
Did she put on his knowledge with his power
1923 Before the indifferent beak could let her drop?

9. Or *Anima Mundi*, the spirit or soul of the world. Yeats considered this universal consciousness or memory a fund from which poets drew their images and symbols. 1. Yeats later wrote of the "brazen winged beast . . . described in my poem *The Second Coming*" as "associated with laughing, ecstatic destruction." "Our civilization was about to reverse itself, or some new civilization about to be born from all that our age had rejected . . . ; because we had worshiped a single god it would worship many." 2. According to Greek myth, Zeus took the form of a swan to seduce Leda, who became the mother of Helen of Troy and also of Clytemnestra, Agamemnon's wife and murderer. Helen's abduction from her husband. Menelaus, brother of Agamemnon, began the Trojan War (line 10). Yeats described the visit of Zeus to Leda as an annunciation like that to Mary (see *Luke* 1:26–38): "I imagine the annunciation that founded Greece as made to Leda. . . ." (*A Vision*).

Sailing to Byzantium[3]

I

That[4] is no country for old men. The young
In one another's arms, birds in the trees
—Those dying generations—at their song,
The salmon-falls, the mackerel-crowded seas
Fish, flesh, or fowl, commend all summer long
Whatever is begotten, born, and dies.
Caught in that sensual music all neglect
Monuments of unaging intellect.

II

An aged man is but a paltry thing,
A tattered coat upon a stick, unless
Soul clap its hands and sing, and louder sing
For every tatter in its mortal dress,
Nor is there singing school but studying
Monuments of its own magnificence;
And therefore I have sailed the seas and come
To the holy city of Byzantium.

III

O sages standing in God's holy fire
As in the gold mosaic of a wall,
Come from the holy fire, perne in a gyre,[5]
And be the singing-masters of my soul.
Consume my heart away; sick with desire
And fastened to a dying animal
It knows not what it is; and gather me
Into the artifice of eternity.

IV

Once out of nature I shall never take
My bodily form from any natural thing,
But such a form as Grecian goldsmiths make
Of hammered gold and gold enameling

3. The ancient name of Istanbul, the capital and holy city of Eastern Christendom from the late fourth century until 1453. It was famous for its stylized and formal mosaics, its symbolic, nonnaturalistic art, and its highly developed intellectual life. Yeats repeatedly uses it to symbolize a world of artifice and timelessness, free from the decay and death of the natural and sensual world. 4. Ireland, as an instance of the natural, temporal world. 5. I.e., whirl in a coiling motion, so that his soul may merge with its motion as the timeless world invades the cycles of history and nature. "Perne" is Yeats's coinage (from the noun "pirn"): to spin around in the kind of spiral pattern that thread makes as it comes off a bobbin or spool.

To keep a drowsy Emperor awake;[6]
Or set upon a golden bough[7] to sing
To lords and ladies of Byzantium
Of what is past, or passing, or to come.

1927

Among School Children

I

I walk through the long schoolroom questioning;
A kind old nun in a white hood replies;
The children learn to cipher and to sing,
To study reading-books and history,
To cut and sew, be neat in everything
In the best modern way—the children's eyes
In momentary wonder stare upon
A sixty-year-old smiling public man.[8]

II

I dream of a Ledaean body,[9] bent
Above a sinking fire, a tale that she
Told of a harsh reproof, or trivial event
That changed some childish day to tragedy—
Told, and it seemed that our two natures blent
Into a sphere from youthful sympathy,
Or else, to alter Plato's parable,
Into the yolk and white of the one shell.[1]

III

And thinking of that fit of grief or rage
I look upon one child or t'other there
And wonder if she stood so at that age—
For even daughters of the swan can share

6. "I have read somewhere that in the Emperor's palace at Byzantium was a tree made of gold and silver, and artificial birds that sang." (Yeats's note) 7. In Book VI of *The Aeneid*, the sybil tells Aeneas that he must pluck a golden bough from a nearby tree in order to descend to Hades. There is only one such branch there, and when it is plucked an identical one takes its place. 8. At 60 (in 1925) Yeats had been a senator of the Irish Free State. 9. Like that of Helen of Troy, daughter of Leda. The memory dream is of Maud Gonne (see also lines 29–30), with whom Yeats had long been hopelessly in love. 1. In Plato's *Symposium*, the origin of human love is explained by parable: Human beings were once spheres, but Zeus was fearful of their power and cut them in half; now each half longs to be reunited with its missing half. Helen and Pollux were hatched from one of two eggs born to Leda after her union with Zeus in the form of a swan; the other contained Castor and Clytemnestra. According to Yeats in *A Vision*, "from one of [Leda's] eggs came Love and from the other War."

Something of every paddler's heritage—
And had that color upon cheek or hair,
And thereupon my heart is driven wild:
She stands before me as a living child.

IV

Her present image floats into the mind—
Did Quattrocento finger[2] fashion it
Hollow of cheek as though it drank the wind
And took a mess of shadows for its meat?
And I though never of Ledaean kind
Had pretty plumage once—enough of that,
Better to smile on all that smile, and show
There is a comfortable kind of old scarecrow.

V

What youthful mother, a shape upon her lap
Honey of generation[3] had betrayed,
And that must sleep, shriek, struggle to escape
As recollection or the drug decide,
Would think her son, did she but see that shape
With sixty or more winters on its head,
A compensation for the pang of his birth,
Or the uncertainty of his setting forth?

VI

Plato thought nature but a spume that plays
Upon a ghostly paradigm of things;[4]
Solider Aristotle played the taws
Upon the bottom of a king of kings;[5]
World-famous golden-thighed Pythagoras[6]
Fingered upon a fiddle-stick or strings
What a star sang and careless Muses heard:
Old clothes upon old sticks to scare a bird.

2. The hand of a fifteenth-century artist. Yeats especially admired Botticelli, and in *A Vision* praises his "deliberate strangeness everywhere [which] gives one an emotion of mystery which is new to painting." 3. Porphyry, a third-century Greek scholar and neoplatonic philosopher, says "honey of generation" means the "pleasure arising from copulation" which draws souls "downward" to generation. 4. Plato considered the world of nature an imperfect and illusory copy of the ideal world. 5. Aristotle, the teacher of Alexander the Great, disciplined him with a strap ("taw," line 43). His philosophy, insisting on the interdependence of form and matter, took the world of nature far more seriously than did Plato's. 6. Pythagoras (ca. 580–ca. 500 B.C.), the Greek mathematician and philosopher, was highly-revered, and one legend describes his godlike golden thighs.

VII

Both nuns and mothers worship images,
But those the candles light are not as those
That animate a mother's reveries
But keep a marble or a bronze repose.
And yet they too break hearts—O Presences
That passion, piety or affection knows,
And that all heavenly glory symbolize—
O self-born mockers of man's enterprise;

VIII

Labor is blossoming or dancing where
The body is not bruised to pleasure soul,
Nor beauty born out of its own despair,
Nor blear-eyed wisdom out of midnight oil.
O chestnut-tree, great-rooted blossomer,
Are you the leaf, the blossom or the bole?
O body swayed to music, O brightening glance,
How can we know the dancer from the dance?

1927

Byzantium

The unpurged images of day recede;
The Emperor's drunken soldiery are abed;
Night resonance recedes, night-walkers' song
After great cathedral gong;
A starlit or a moonlit dome[7] disdains
All that man is,
All mere complexities,
The fury and the mire of human veins.

Before me floats an image, man or shade,
Shade more than man, more image than a shade;
For Hades' bobbin bound in mummy-cloth
May unwind the winding path;
A mouth that has no moisture and no breath
Breatheless mouths may summon;
I hail the superhuman;
I call it death-in-life and life-in-death.

Miracle, bird or golden handiwork,
More miracle than bird or handiwork,

7. According to Yeats' philosophy, the full moon ("moonlit") represents the mind "completely absorbed in being."

Planted on the star-lit golden bough
Can like the cocks of Hades crow,[8]
Or, by the moon embittered, scorn aloud
In glory of changeless metal
Common bird or petal
And all complexities of mire or blood.

At midnight on the Emperor's pavement flit
Flames that no fagot feeds, nor steel has lit,
Nor storm disturbs, flames begotten of flame,
Where blood-begotten spirits come
And all complexities of fury leave,
Dying into a dance,
An agony of trance,
An agony of flame that cannot singe a sleeve.

Astraddle on the dolphin's mire and blood,[9]
Spirit after spirit! The smithies break the flood,
The golden smithies of the Emperor!
Marbles of the dancing floor
Break bitter furies of complexity,
Those images that yet
Fresh images beget,
That dolphin-torn, that gong-tormented sea. 1932

8. As the bird of dawn, the cock has from antiquity been a symbol of rebirth and resurrection.
9. In ancient art, dolphins symbolize the soul moving from one state to another, and sometimes they provide a vehicle for the dead. Palaemon, for example, in Greek tradition is often mounted on a dolphin.

DRAMA

Reading Drama

Plays are generally written to be performed—by actors, on a stage, for an audience. Playwrights create plays in full consciousness of the possibilities that go beyond words and texts and extend to physical actions, stage effects, and other bits of theatricality that can create special effects on an audience.

To see and hear a play—to be a part of an audience responding to it—represents a different kind of experience from the usually solitary act of reading. When plays are acted out on a stage you see actions and hear words spoken through your physical senses; real live human beings stand for imaginary characters and actually say speeches and perform actions that you can hear and watch. You sit with others who are also watching and responding to the play. You and the other members of the audience have, at a single instant, a common experience; you have assembled for the explicit purpose of seeing a play. Plays are performed before a live audience of real people who respond directly and immediately to it, unlike a text that may lie silent and undisturbed in a book for days or even years at a time.

But you are not directly experiencing the author's play. It has been mediated by the director and actors who have brought it to the stage and to your senses. These mediators are interpreters of the play, and they perform for viewers part of the act of imagination that readers must perform for themselves. In poems and stories, only the written text mediates between author and reader, but in plays all of the people involved in a particular production help to interpret the author's text for a specific audience. Consciously or not, every director puts an interpretation on every scene by the way he or she stages the action; timing, casting, set design, physical interaction, and the phrasing and tone of every speech affect how the play will play. Every syllable uttered by every actor in some sense affects the outcome; tone of voice and the slightest body gesture are, for an actor, equivalent to the choices of words and sentence rhythm for a writer.

Every performance is a unique expression of a collaborative effort. Actors must remember hundreds of lines and perform movements on stage at certain times; the stagehands must change sets and install props between scenes; light and sound effects must occur on certain visual and aural cues. In any of these areas a single change or error—a new inflection at the end of a line or a misplaced prop—guarantees that a given performance will be unique. Nor are any two audiences the same, and the character of an audience inevitably affects the performance. A warm, responsive audience will bring out the best in the performers, as any actor will tell you, while a crowd's cold indifference often results in a tepid or stiff production. For these reasons, no staged realization of a plan can ever duplicate another.

Yet it is common to speak of Olivier's Hamlet (meaning the performance of the title role by Sir Laurence Olivier), of Dame Maggie Smith's or Glenda Jackson's Hedda Gabler, or Zeffirelli's *Romeo and Juliet* (meaning the film directed by Franco Zeffirelli), because in each case the hand of the actor or director leads to a distinctive interpretation of the play. In the written text Hamlet may be regarded as indecisive, melancholy, conniving, mad, vindictive, ambitious, or some combination of these things; individual performances emphasize one attribute or another, always at some expense to other characteristics and interpretations. No play can be all things to an audience in any one performance.

It is this limitation of the performed play, its necessary restriction of the potential multiple meanings of the work to one interpretation, that led the nineteenth-century writer Charles Lamb to come home from the theater vowing never to go see another play of Shakespeare's on the stage. He found that no matter how good the performance, the enacted play restricted his imagination and robbed the play of some of the richness he found in reading it for himself.

It is not necessary to renounce the theater or deprive ourselves of the thrilling experience of a brilliantly directed and performed interpretation of a play, but it may be important in the 90s to reassert the quite different claims of reading drama as *literature*, as something written, the letters of the alphabet forming words on the page. It may be necessary to assert that reading drama (I am somewhat arbitrarily here using the term "drama" to mean the written and read play, as opposed to the performed one) is not a poor substitute for seeing a play; it is simply a different kind of experience, literary rather than theatrical.

In some ways reading a play is no different from reading a story or novel. In reading both we anticipate what is to happen next and what it all means. In reading both narrative and drama we imagine the characters, setting, action;

and in reading both we respond to the symbolic suggestiveness of images and we project configurations of thematic significance. The chief difference between narrative and drama is the absence, in drama, of a mediator, someone standing between the reader and the work and helping us relate to the characters, actions, and meanings. It is for this reason that reading drama is for many a greater strain on the imagination: the reader is his or her own mediator, narrator, interpreter.

Reading drama is not only a compelling literary experience in itself, but even the strain it puts upon our imagination is rewarding. For not only are we freer to incorporate the play into our own being, but in becoming our own mediator we see how our imagination or our response to story-telling language really works. It is customary to assume that we "cast characters" in our minds, paint in the scenic backdrops, place the furniture and props, and choreograph the action. While we do some of this, no doubt, it seems safe to say that most of our imaginations are not so fully furnished, and we certainly cannot claim to be able to recreate what the playwright had in her or his mind's eye. We can ask ourselves whom we might cast as Hamlet or Hedda Gabler, but, unless we are remembering a theatrical performance or movie, most of us do not have a full and fixed visual image of a character: we have a shape here, a profile there, adding a feature, mannerism, or gesture as we read on.

In reading drama where dialogue is more or less all we have, we reconstruct character and personality from what the character says; we do this by relating our own experiences to what we are reading. We've known someone who said things like this, or remember another play or story where such attitudes and statements suggested that. So what we imagine as we read depends greatly upon our repertoire of experiences of life and literature. A character, even at the end of a play, is less a solid reconstruction than a series of frames like those that go to make up a moving picture, each a little different. When we have seen an actress playing Blanche DuBois in *A Streetcar Named Desire* and see her as we read the play, we are no longer reading that play but watching it in our minds, more or less remembering a play we once saw.

This is not necessarily to agree with Charles Lamb—an actress can show us something in a part we might not have seen for ourselves. If we would go to the theater more often we would have a spectrum of performances to lend depth to our reading. But to read a play we have never seen is not to watch in the mind's eye a single, well-defined figure incorporating a character throughout the one, three, or five acts. We *watch* plays, but we *read* drama. Though we must take every opportunity to see a play performed to enrich our own repertoire of reading, and though we should take advantage of our silent reading to include all the alternatives we can, each time we read a play we do our own interpreting, make our own choices and omissions. Reading, we perform all the parts, and we may want to ask ourselves how we would act this or that role, read this or that line; what kind of person we should try to imagine ourselves being, what, if we were that person, our motivations might be, and so on. But most important, perhaps, we will want to be aware of what choices are available and what making one choice or another means.

Plays often reflect the drama of everyday life, but (like other forms of literature and art) they concentrate life and hold it up to examination. Many scenes in plays could be slices of actual conversations, and sometimes playwrights make a special effort to have their dialogue take on the informality—or even the sloppiness and banality—of ordinary talk. Sometimes, too, the actions portrayed are everyday actions—drinking a cup of coffee, watching a bus go by, working out the subtleties of a relationship with a friend. Not all plays are about grand machinations of state or great loves or noble deeds (although some are), and not all artistic shapings of actuality into drama are formalized into traditional structures (although many are). Plays may be short, have only two or three characters, portray the routine matters of everyday life, and present conflicts that are personal or even trivial as well as moments of national or cosmic significance. Sometimes it takes greater artistic control to make a very simple scene compelling than it does to portray grander actions that are more laden with deep conflict and greater in import. Here, for example, is a very brief contemporary piece of drama. Its author, Harold Pinter, does not call it a play but only a "sketch," a short piece suitable for staging and containing key elements of dramatic art.

HAROLD PINTER

The Black and White

The FIRST OLD WOMAN *is sitting at a milk bar table. Small.* A SECOND OLD WOMAN *approaches. Tall. She is carrying two bowls of soup, which are covered by two plates, on each of which is a slice of bread. She puts the bowls down on the table carefully.*

SECOND: You see that one come up and speak to me at the counter? [*She takes the bread plates off the bowls, takes two spoons from her pocket, and places the bowls, plates, and spoons.*]

FIRST: You got the bread, then?

SECOND: I didn't know how I was going to carry it. In the end I put the plates on top of the soup.

FIRST: I like a bit of bread with my soup. [*They begin the soup. Pause.*]

SECOND: Did you see that one come up and speak to me at the counter?

FIRST: Who?

SECOND: Comes up to me, he says, hullo, he says, what's the time by your clock? Bloody liberty. I was just standing there getting your soup.

FIRST: It's tomato soup.

SECOND: What's the time by your clock? he says.

FIRST: I bet you answered him back.

SECOND: I told him all right. Go on, I said, why don't you get back into your scraghole, I said, clear off out of it before I call a copper. [*Pause.*]

FIRST: I not long got here.

SECOND: Did you get the all-night bus?

FIRST: I got the all-night bus straight here.

SECOND: Where from?

FIRST: Marble Arch.

SECOND: Which one?

FIRST: The two-nine-four, that takes me all the way to Fleet Street.

SECOND: So does the two-nine-one. [*Pause.*] I see you talking to two strangers as I come in. You want to stop talking to strangers, old piece of boot like you, you mind who you talk to.

FIRST: I wasn't talking to any strangers. [*Pause. The* FIRST OLD WOMAN *follows the progress of a bus through the window.*] That's another all-night bus gone down. [*Pause.*] Going up the other way. Fulham way. [*Pause.*] That was a two-nine-seven. [*Pause.*] I've never been up that way. [*Pause.*] I've been down to Liverpool Street.

SECOND: That's up the other way.

FIRST: I don't fancy going down there, down Fulham way, and all up there.

SECOND: Uh-uh.

FIRST: I've never fancied that direction much. [*Pause.*]

SECOND: How's your bread? [*Pause.*]

FIRST: Eh?

SECOND: Your bread.

FIRST: All right. How's yours? [*Pause.*]

SECOND: They don't charge for the bread if you have soup.

FIRST: They do if you have tea.

SECOND: If you have tea they do. [*Pause.*] You talk to strangers they'll take you in. Mind my word. Coppers'll take you in.

FIRST: I don't talk to strangers.

SECOND: They took me away in the wagon once.

FIRST: They didn't keep you though.

SECOND: They didn't keep me, but that was only because they took a fancy to me. They took a fancy to me when they got me in the wagon.

FIRST: Do you think they'd take a fancy to me?

SECOND: I wouldn't back on it.

[*The* FIRST OLD WOMAN *gazes out of the window*.]

FIRST: You can see what goes on from this top table. [*Pause*.] It's better than going down to that place on the embankment, anyway.
SECOND: Yes, there's not too much noise.
FIRST: There's always a bit of noise.
SECOND: Yes, there's always a bit of life. [*Pause*.]
FIRST: They'll be closing down soon to give it a scrub-round.
SECOND: There's a wind out. [*Pause*.]
FIRST: I wouldn't mind staying.
SECOND: They won't let you.
FIRST: I know. [*Pause*.] Still, they only close hour and half, don't they? [*Pause*.] It's not long. [*Pause*.] You can go along, then come back.
SECOND: I'm going. I'm not coming back.
FIRST: When it's light I come back. Have my tea.
SECOND: I'm going. I'm going up to the Garden.
FIRST: I'm not going down there. [*Pause*.] I'm going up to Waterloo Bridge.
SECOND: You'll just about see the last two-nine-six come up over the river.
FIRST: I'll just catch a look of it. Time I get up there. [*Pause*.] It don't look like an all-night bus in daylight, do it?

1959

All the elements of drama are here in rather elementary form: there is a bit of story, mostly implied, about the lives of two women; action on a modest scale, with a lot of emphasis on timing and relatively insignificant movements and props in order to emphasize the women's dependence on the everyday; characterization sufficient to give a quite clear idea of what the two women's lives are like; dialogue enough to suggest the characters' thoughts and feelings and to show how their lives intersect. Even a small element of conflict is present, just enough to make the scene interesting and lively and to highlight the quiet desperation of the women's lives.

What is such a sketch about? Why is it interesting? What makes it worth seeing, worth reading, worth studying, worth writing? What makes it "drama"?

It's easy enough to say what it's "about"—the essentially eventless lives of two elderly, lonely women who create a simple kind of sociality between each other and in relation to their rather mechanized, anonymous, modern environment. The order of their lives is built on the predictable schedules of London's night buses and the odd opening and closing hours of an almost-all-night eatery. It reflects human routines in which not much—not even sleep—happens and in which little connection to other people exists. The women therefore create an artificial community with other riders and other patrons who are in fact unknown to them except by rituals, habits, and eccentricities.

And with each other they develop some elemental sense of human relationship—a sort of parody of a conventional domestic relationship. One might say (although it sounds almost too pretentious and formal to describe this piece) that the sketch is about loneliness and a quest for meaning. But the point is less to prove or assert something profound or thematic than to present, poignantly, a sense of what life—or a brief slice of life—is like for two isolated people who feel rather passed by.

The question of what makes the sketch interesting, memorable, and dramatic is more complicated. Once in a while we may witness, in life, a scene or vignette that seems to tell a story or offer a poignant sense of some aspect of human life. When we come upon such a moment, it is sort of art by accident, and in a way that is what Pinter manages to recreate here. We could just walk in on a scene like this, and the sketch goes out of its way to give that impression. The set is simple, the props are few and common, there is nothing especially complicated about the setting or about the way the action is set up. A production of the sketch is not likely to seem much like a production, and one can imagine the actors making it seem as little like a play—as untheatrical—as possible. They probably would not even seem to be actors. This is about as close to a segment of life as one can get, certainly far less portentous than a scene in *Oedipus* or *Hamlet*, far less organized and contrived than a carefully orchestrated confrontation in your favorite soap on television.

Yet the scene is very powerful. The action is efficient, there are no irrelevancies, except in the sense that the whole sketch depends on the conventional perceptions of two lives it presents as marginal. Its two main characters quickly reveal themselves. The setting gives them an opportunity to present, quickly and compactly, their situation and to imply their feelings. The action—almost a non-action—reflects that story of their lives and the theme of the sketch. And the setting and props—in their simplicity and spareness—not only set the stage for the dialogue but also reflect accurately the whole world of the women's lives. All things work together quickly and efficiently to create an impression, a vivid visual sense of the way some people (probably people most members of the audience wouldn't know much about) actually live, and a brief sense of both how those people feel about their lives and how we do.

The Brute, a short one-act play, like *The Black and White* isolates quite quickly the lives and feelings of two people. It is almost as limited in number of characters, set, and props as Pinter's sketch. It, too, has in its brief space all the elements of drama. Its effect, however, is very different from *The Black and White*. It has more of the kind of conflict that we are used to in drama and its subversion of stereotypes of men and women makes it seem to have a more traditional, social theme. It seems more theatrical, less realistic, less like something the author stumbled over or a scene you might run into tomorrow. And, rather than being touching and sad, it is very funny.

ANTON CHEKHOV

The Brute[1]

A JOKE IN ONE ACT

CHARACTERS

MRS. POPOV, *widow and landowner, small, with dimpled cheeks*

MR. GRIGORY S. SMIRNOV, *gentleman farmer, middle-aged*

LUKA, *Mrs. Popov's footman, an old man*

GARDENER, COACHMAN, HIRED MEN

The drawing room of a country house. MRS. POPOV, *in deep mourning, is staring hard at a photograph.* LUKA *is with her.*

LUKA: It's not right, ma'am, you're killing yourself. The cook has gone off with the maid to pick berries. The cat's having a high old time in the yard catching birds. Every living thing is happy. But you stay moping here in the house like it was a convent, taking no pleasure in nothing. I mean it, ma'am! It must be a full year since you set foot out of doors.

MRS. POPOV: I must never set foot out of doors again, Luka. Never! I have nothing to set foot out of doors *for.* My life is done. *He* is in his grave. I have buried myself alive in this house. We are *both* in our graves.

LUKA: You're off again, ma'am. I just won't listen to you no more. Mr. Popov is dead, but what we can we do about that? It's God's doing. God's will be done. You've cried over him, you've done your share of mourning, haven't you? There's a limit to everything. You can't go on weeping and wailing forever. My old lady died, for that matter, and I wept and wailed over her a whole month long. Well, that was it. I couldn't weep and wail all my life, she just wasn't worth it. [*He sighs.*] As for the neighbours, you've forgotten all about them, ma'am. You don't visit them and you don't let them visit you. You and I are like a pair of spiders—excuse the expression, ma'am—here we are in this house like a pair of spiders, we never see the light of day. And it isn't like there was no nice people around either. The whole country's swarming with 'em. There's a regiment quartered at Riblov, and the officers are so good-looking! The girls can't take their eyes off them—There's a ball at the camp every Friday—The military band plays most every day of the week—What do you say, ma'am? You're young, you're pretty, you could

1. Translated by Eric Bentley.

enjoy yourself! Ten years from now you may want to strut and show your feathers to the officers, and it'll be too late.

MRS. POPOV: [*Firmly.*] You must never bring this subject up again, Luka. Since Popov died, life has been an empty dream to me, you know that. *You* may think I am alive. Poor ignorant Luka! You are wrong. I am dead. I'm in my grave. Never more shall I see the light of day, never strip from my body this . . . raiment of death! Are you listening, Luka? Let his ghost learn how I love him! Yes, *I* know, and *you* know, he was often unfair to me, he was cruel to me, and he was unfaithful to me. What of it? *I* shall be faithful to *him*, that's all. I will show him how *I* can love. Hereafter, in a better world than this, he will welcome me back, the same loyal girl I always was—

LUKA: Instead of carrying on this way, ma'am, you should go out in the garden and take a bit of a walk, ma'am. Or why not harness Toby and take a drive? Call on a couple of the neighbours, ma'am?

MRS. POPOV: [*Breaking down.*] Oh, Luka!

LUKA: Yes, ma'am? What have I said, ma'am? Oh dear!

MRS. POPOV: Toby! You said Toby! He adored that horse. When he drove me out to the Korchagins and the Vlasovs, it was always with Toby! He was a wonderful driver, do you remember, Luka? So graceful! So strong! I can see him now, pulling at those reins with all his might and main! Toby! Luka, tell them to give Toby an extra portion of oats today.

LUKA: Yes, ma'am.

[*A bell rings.*]

MRS. POPOV: Who is that? Tell them I'm not at home.

LUKA: Very good, ma'am. [*Exit.*]

MRS. POPOV: [*Gazing again at the photograph.*] You shall see, my Popov, how a wife can love and forgive. Till death do us part. Longer than that. Till death re-unite us forever! [*Suddenly a titter breaks through her tears.*] Aren't you ashamed of yourself, Popov? Here's your little wife, being good, being faithful, so faithful she's locked up here waiting for her own funeral, while you—doesn't it make you ashamed, you naughty boy? You were terrible, you know. You were unfaithful, and you made those awful scenes about it, you stormed out and left me alone for weeks—

[*Enter* LUKA].

LUKA: [*Upset*] There's someone asking for you, ma'am. Says he must—

MRS. POPOV: I suppose you told him that since my husband's death I see no one?

LUKA: Yes, ma'am. I did, ma'am. But he wouldn't listen, ma'am. He says it's urgent.

MRS. POPOV: [*Shrilly.*] I see no one!!

LUKA: He won't take no for an answer, ma'am. He just curses and swears and comes in anyway. He's a perfect monster, ma'am. He's in the dining room right now.

MRS. POPOV: In the dining room, is he? I'll give him his come uppance. Bring him in here this minute. [*Exit* LUKA. *Suddenly sad again.*] Why do they do this to me? Why? Insulting my grief, intruding on my solitude? [*She sighs.*] I'm afraid I'll have to enter a convent. I will, I *must* enter a convent!

[*Enter* MR. SMIRNOV *and* LUKA]

SMIRNOV: [*To* LUKA] Dolt! Idiot! You talk too much! [*Seeing* MRS. POPOV. *With dignity.*] May I have the honour of introducing myself, madam? Grigory S. Smirnov, landowner and lieutenant of artillery, retired. Forgive me, madam, if I disturb your peace and quiet, but my business is both urgent and weighty.

MRS. POPOV: [*Declining to offer him her hand.*] What is it you wish, sir?

SMIRNOV: At the time of his death, your late husband—with whom I had the honour to be acquainted, ma'am—was in my debt to the tune of twelve hundred rubles. I have two notes to prove it. Tomorrow, ma'am, I must pay the interest on a bank loan. I have therefore no alternative, ma'am, but to ask you to pay me the money today.

MRS. POPOV: Twelve hundred rubles? But what did my husband owe it to you for?

SMIRNOV: He used to buy his oats from me, madam.

MRS. POPOV: [*To* LUKA, *with a sigh.*] Remember what I said, Luka: tell them to give Toby an extra portion of oats today! [*Exit* LUKA.] My dear Mr.—what was the name again?

SMIRNOV: Smirnov, ma'am.

MRS. POPOV: My dear Mr. Smirnov, if Mr. Popov owed you money, you shall be paid—to the last ruble, to the last kopeck. But today—you must excuse me, Mr.—what was it?

SMIRNOV: Smirnov, ma'am.

MRS. POPOV: Today, Mr. Smirnov, I have no ready cash in the house. [SMIRNOV *starts to speak.*] Tomorrow, Mr. Smirnov, no, the day after tomorrow, all will be well. My steward will be back from town. I shall see that he pays what is owing. Today, no. In any case, today is exactly seven months from Mr. Popov's death. On such a day you will understand that I am in no mood to think of money.

SMIRNOV: Madam, if you don't pay up now, you can carry me out feet foremost. They'll seize my estate.

MRS. POPOV: You can have your money. [*He starts to thank her.*] Tomorrow. [*He again starts to speak.*] That is: the day after tomorrow.

SMIRNOV: I don't need the money the day after tomorrow. I need it today.

MRS. POPOV: I'm sorry, Mr.—

SMIRNOV: [*Shouting.*] Smirnov!

MRS. POPOV: [*Sweetly.*] Yes, of course. But you can't have it today.

SMIRNOV: But I can't wait for it any longer!

MRS. POPOV: Be sensible, Mr. Smirnov. How can I pay you if I don't have it?

SMIRNOV: You don't have it?

MRS. POPOV: I don't have it.

SMIRNOV: Sure?

MRS. POPOV: Positive.

SMIRNOV: Very well. I'll make a note to that effect. [*Shrugging.*] And then they want me to keep cool. I meet the tax commissioner on the street, and he says, "Why are you always in such a bad humour, Smirnov?" Bad humour! How can I help it, in God's name? I need money, I need it desperately. Take yesterday: I leave home at the crack of dawn, I call on all my debtors. Not a one of them pays up. Footsore and weary, I creep at midnight into some little dive, and try to snatch a few winks of sleep on the floor by the vodka barrel. Then today, I come here, fifty miles from home, saying to myself, "At last, at last, I can be sure of something," and you're not in the mood! You give me a mood! Christ, how can I help getting all worked up?

MRS. POPOV: I thought I'd made it clear, Mr. Smirnov, that you'll get your money the minute my steward is back from town?

SMIRNOV: What the hell do I care about your steward? Pardon the expression, ma'am. But it was you I came to see.

MRS. POPOV: What language! What a tone to take to a lady! I refuse to hear another word. [*Quickly, exit.*]

SMIRNOV: Not in the mood, huh? "Exactly seven months since Popov's death," huh? How about me? [*Shouting after her.*] Is there this interest to pay, or isn't there? I'm asking you a question: is there this interest to pay, or isn't there? So your husband died, and you're not in the mood, and your steward's gone off some place, and so forth and so on, but what *I* can do about all that, huh? What do *you* think I should do? Take a running jump and shove my head through the wall? Take off in a balloon? You don't know my *other* debtors. I call on Gruzdeff. Not at home. I look for Yaroshevitch. He's hiding out. I find Kooritsin. He kicks up a row, and I have to throw him through the window. I work my way right down the list. Not a kopeck. Then I come to you, and God damn it to hell, if you'll pardon the expression, you're not in the mood! [*Quietly, as he realizes he's talking to air.*] I've spoiled them all, that's what, I've let them play me for a sucker. Well, I'll show them. I'll show this one. I'll stay right here till she pays up. Ugh! [*He shudders with rage.*] I'm in a rage! I'm in a positively towering rage! Every nerve in my body is trembling at forty to the dozen! I can't breathe, I feel ill, I think I'm going to faint, hey, you there!

[*Enter* LUKA.]

LUKA: Yes, sir? Is there anything you wish, sir?

SMIRNOV: Water! Water!! No, make it vodka. [*Exit* LUKA.] Consider the logic of it. A fellow creature is desperately in need of cash, so desperately in need that he has to seriously contemplate hanging himself, and this woman, this mere chit of a girl, won't pay up, and why not? Because, forsooth, she isn't in the mood! Oh, the logic of women! Come to that, I never have liked them, I could do without the whole sex. Talk to a woman? I'd rather sit on a barrel of dynamite, the very thought gives me gooseflesh. Women! Creatures of poetry and romance! Just to see one in the distance gets me mad. My legs start twitching with rage. I feel like yelling for help.

[*Enter* LUKA, *handing* SMIRNOV *a glass of water.*]

LUKA: Mrs. Popov is indisposed, sir. She is seeing no one.

SMIRNOV: Get out. [*Exit* LUKA.] Indisposed, is she? Seeing no one, huh? Well, she can see me or not, but I'll be here, I'll be right here till she pays up. If you're sick for a week, I'll be here for a week. If you're sick for a year, I'll be here for a year. You won't get around *me* with your widow's weeds and your schoolgirl dimples. I know all about dimples. [*Shouting through the window.*] Semyon, let the horses out of those shafts, we're not leaving, we're staying, and tell them to give the horses some oats, yes, oats, you fool, what do you think? [*Walking away from the window.*] What a mess, what an unholy mess! I didn't sleep last night, the heat is terrific today, not a damn one of 'em has paid up, and here's this—this skirt in mourning that's not in the mood! My head aches, where's that— [*He drinks from the glass.*] Water, ugh! You there!

[*Enter* LUKA.]

LUKA: Yes, sir. You wish for something, sir?

SMIRNOV: Where's that confounded vodka I asked for? [*Exit* LUKA.] [SMIRNOV *sits and looks himself over.*] Oof! A fine figure of a man *I* am! Unwashed, uncombed, unshaven straw on my vest, dust all over me. The little woman must've taken me for a highwayman. [*Yawns.*] I suppose it wouldn't be considered polite to barge into a drawing room in this state, but who cares? I'm not a visitor, I'm a creditor—most unwelcome of guests, second only to Death.

[*Enter* LUKA.]

LUKA: [*Handing him the vodka.*] If I may say so, sir, you take too many liberties, sir.

SMIRNOV: What?!

LUKA: Oh, nothing, sir, nothing.

SMIRNOV: Who in hell do you think you're talking to? Shut your mouth!

LUKA: [*Aside.*] There's an evil spirit abroad. The Devil must have sent him. Oh! [*Exit* LUKA.]

SMIRNOV: What a rage I'm in! I'll grind the whole world to powder. Oh, I feel ill again. You there!

[*Enter* MRS. POPOV.]

MRS. POPOV: [*Looking at the floor.*] In the solitude of my rural retreat, Mr. Smirnov, I've long since grown unaccustomed to the sound of the human voice. Above all, I cannot bear shouting. I must beg you not to break the silence.

SMIRNOV: Very well. Pay me my money and I'll go.

MRS. POPOV: I told you before, and I tell you again, Mr. Smirnov: I have no cash, you'll have to wait till the day after tomorrow. Can I express myself more plainly?

SMIRNOV: And *I* told *you* before, and *I* tell *you* again, that I need the money today, that the day after tomorrow is too late, and that if you don't pay, and pay now, I'll have to hang myself in the morning!

MRS. POPOV: But I have no cash. This is quite a puzzle.

SMIRNOV: You won't pay, huh?

MRS. POPOV: I *can't* pay, Mr. Smirnov.

SMIRNOV: In that case, I'm going to sit here and wait. [*Sits down.*] You'll pay up the day after tomorrow? Very good. Till the day after tomorrow, here I sit. [*Pause. He jumps up.*] Now look, do I have to pay that interest tomorrow, or don't I? Or do you think I'm joking?

MRS. POPOV: I must ask you not to raise your voice, Mr. Smirnov. This is not a stable.

SMIRNOV: Who said it was? Do I have to pay the interest tomorrow or not?

MRS. POPOV: Mr. Smirnov, do you know how to behave in the presence of a lady?

SMIRNOV: No, madam, I do not know how to behave in the presence of a lady.

MRS. POPOV: Just what I thought. I look at you, and I say: ugh! I hear you talk, and I say to myself: "That man doesn't know how to talk to a lady."

SMIRNOV: You'd like me to come simpering to you in French, I suppose. "*Enchanté, madame! Merci beaucoup* for not paying zee money, *madame! Pardonnez-moi* if I 'ave disturbed you, *madame!* How *charmante* you look in mourning, *madame!*"[2]

MRS. POPOV: Now you're being silly, Mr. Smirnov.

SMIRNOV: [*Mimicking.*] "Now you're being silly, Mr. Smirnov." "You don't know to talk to a lady, Mr. Smirnov." Look here, Mrs. Popov, I've known more women than you've known pussycats. I've fought three duels on their account. I've jilted twelve, and been jilted by nine others. Oh, yes, Mrs. Popov, I've played the fool in my time, whispered sweet nothings, bowed and scraped and endeavoured to please. Don't tell me I don't know what it is to love, to pine away with longing, to have the blues, to melt like butter, to be weak as water. I was full of tender emotion. I was carried away with passion. I squandered half my fortune on the sex. I chattered about women's emancipation. But there's an end to everything, dear madam. Burning eyes, dark eyelashes, ripe, red lips, dimpled cheeks, heaving bosoms, soft whisperings, the moon above, the lake below—I don't give a rap for that sort of nonsense any more, Mrs. Popov. I've found out about women. Present company excepted, they're liars. Their behaviour is mere play acting; their conversation is sheer gossip. Yes, dear lady, women, young or old, are false, petty, vain, cruel, malicious, unreasonable. As for intelligence, any sparrow could give them points. Appearances, I admit, can be deceptive. In appearance, a woman may be all poetry and romance, goddess and angel, muslin and fluff. To look at her exterior is to be transported to heaven. But I have looked at her interior, Mrs. Popov, and what did I find there—in her very soul? A crocodile. [*He has gripped the back of the chair so firmly that it snaps.*] And, what is more revolting, a crocodile with an illusion, a crocodile that imagines tender sentiments are its own special province, a crocodile that thinks itself queen of the realm of love! Whereas, in sober fact, dear madam, if a woman can love anything except a lapdog you can hang me by the feet on that nail. For a man, love is suffering, love is sacrifice. A woman just swishes her train around

2. Enchanted (to meet you), madame. Thank you very much . . . Pardon me . . . How charming . . .

and tightens her grip on your nose. Now, you're a woman, aren't you, Mrs. Popov? You must be an expert on some of this. Tell me, quite frankly, did you ever know a woman to be—faithful, for instance? Or even sincere? Only old hags, huh? Though some women are old hags from birth. But as for the others? You're right: a faithful woman is a freak of nature—like a cat with horns.

MRS. POPOV: Who *is* faithful, then? Who *have* you cast for the faithful lover? Not man?

SMIRNOV: Right first time, Mrs. Popov: man.

MRS. POPOV: [*Going off into a peal of bitter laughter.*] Man! Man is faithful! That's a new one! [*Fiercely.*] What right do you have to say, Mr. Smirnov? Men faithful? Let me tell you something. Of all the men I have ever known my late husband Popov was the best. I loved him, and there are women who know how to love, Mr. Smirnov. I gave him my youth, my happiness, my life, my fortune. I worshipped the ground he trod on—and what happened? The best of men was unfaithful to me, Mr. Smirnov. Not once in a while. All the time. After he died, I found his desk drawer full of love letters. While he was alive, he was always going away for the week-end. He squandered my money. He made love to other women before my very eyes. But, in spite of all, Mr. Smirnov, *I* was faithful. Unto death. And beyond. I am *still* faithful, Mr. Smirnov! Burlied alive in this house, I shall wear mourning till the day I, too, am called to my eternal rest.

SMIRNOV: [*Laughing scornfully.*] Expect me to believe that? As if I couldn't see through all this hocus-pocus. Buried alive! Till you're called to your eternal rest! Till when? Till some little poet—or some little subaltern with his first moustache—comes riding by and asks: "Can that be the house of the mysterious Tamara who for love of her late husband has buried herself alive, vowing to see no man?" Ha!

MRS. POPOV: [*Flaring up.*] How dare you? How dare you insinuate—?

SMIRNOV: You may have buried yourself alive, Mrs. Popov, but you haven't forgotten to powder your nose.

MRS. POPOV: [*Incoherent.*] How dare you? How—?

SMIRNOV: Who's raising his voice now? Just because I call a spade a spade. Because I shoot straight from the shoulder. Well, don't shout at me, I'm not your steward.

MRS. POPOV: I'm not shouting, you're shouting! Oh, leave me alone!

SMIRNOV: Pay me the money, and I will.

MRS. POPOV: You'll get no money out of me!

SMIRNOV: Oh, so that's it!

MRS. POPOV: Not a ruble, not a kopeck. Get out! Leave me alone!

SMIRNOV: Not being your husband, I must ask you not to make scenes with me. [*He sits.*] I don't like scenes.

MRS. POPOV: [*Choking with rage.*] You're sitting down?

SMIRNOV: Correct, I'm sitting down.

MRS. POPOV: I asked you to leave!

SMIRNOV: Then give me the money. [*Aside.*] Oh, what a rage I'm in, what a rage!

MRS. POPOV: The impudence of the man! I won't talk to you a moment longer. Get out. [*Pause.*] Are you going?

SMIRNOV: No.

MRS. POPOV: No?!

SMIRNOV: No.

MRS. POPOV: On your head be it. Luka! [*Enter* LUKA.] Show the gentleman out, Luka.

LUKA: [*Approaching.*] I'm afraid, sir, I'll have to ask you, um, to leave, sir, now, um—

SMIRNOV: [*Jumping up.*] Shut your mouth, you old idiot! Who do you think you're talking to? I'll make mincemeat of you.

LUKA: [*Clutching his heart.*] Mercy on us! Holy saints above! [*He falls into an armchair.*] I'm taken sick! I can't breathe!!

MRS. POPOV: Then where's Dasha? Dasha! Dasha! Come here at once! [*She rings.*]

LUKA: They gone picking berries, ma'am, I'm alone here—Water, water, I'm taken sick!

MRS. POPOV: [*To* SMIRNOV] Get out, you!

SMIRNOV: Can't you even be polite with me, Mrs. Popov?

MRS. POPOV: [*Clenching her fists and stamping her feet.*] With you? You're a wild animal, you were never housebroken!

SMIRNOV: What? What did you say?

MRS. POPOV: I said you were a wild animal, you were never housebroken.

SMIRNOV: [*Advancing upon her.*] And what right do you have to talk to me like that?

MRS. POPOV: Like what?

SMIRNOV: You have insulted me, madam.

MRS. POPOV: What of it? Do you think I'm scared of you?

SMIRNOV: So you think you can get away with it because you're a woman. A creature of poetry and romance, huh? Well, it doesn't go down with me. I hereby challenge you to a duel.

LUKA: Mercy on us! Holy saints alive! Water!

SMIRNOV: I propose we shoot it out.

MRS. POPOV: Trying to scare me again? Just because you have big fists and a voice like a bull? You're a brute.

SMIRNOV: No one insults Grigory S. Smirnov with impunity! And I don't care if you *are* a female.

MRS. POPOV: [*Trying to outshout him.*] Brute, brute, brute!

SMIRNOV: The sexes are equal, are they? Fine: then it's just prejudice to expect men alone to pay for insults. I hereby challenge—

MRS. POPOV: [*Screaming.*] All right! You want to shoot it out? All right! Let's shoot it out!

SMIRNOV: And let it be here and now!

MRS. POPOV: Here and now! All right! I'll have Popov's pistols here in one minute! [*Walks away, then turns.*] Putting one of Popov's bullets through your silly head will be a pleasure! *Au revoir.* [*Exit.*]

SMIRNOV: I'll bring her down like a duck, a sitting duck. I'm not one of your little poets, I'm no little subaltern with his first moustache. No, sir, there's no weaker sex where I'm concerned!

LUKA: Sir! Master! [*He goes down on his knees.*] Take pity on a poor old man, and do me a favour: go away. It was bad enough before, you nearly scared me to death. But a duel—!

SMIRNOV: [*Ignoring him.*] A duel! That's equality of the sexes for you! That's women's emancipation! Just as a matter of principle I'll bring her down like a duck. But what a woman! "Putting one of Popov's bullets through your silly head . . ." Her cheeks were flushed, her eyes were gleaming! And, by God, she's accepted the challenge! I never knew a woman like this before!

LUKA: Sir! Master! Please go away! I'll always pray for you!

SMIRNOV: [*Again ignoring him.*] What a woman! Phew!! *She's* no sourpuss, *she's* no crybaby. She's fire and brimstone. She's a human cannon ball. What a shame I have to kill her!

LUKA: [*Weeping.*] Please, kind sir, please, go away!

SMIRNOV: [*As before.*] I like her, isn't that funny? With those dimples and all? I like her. I'm even prepared to consider letting her off that debt. And where's my rage? It's gone. I never knew a woman like this before.

[*Enter* MRS. POPOV *with pistols.*]

MRS. POPOV: [*Boldly.*] Pistols, Mr. Smirnov! [*Matter of fact.*] But before we start, you'd better show me how it's done, I'm not too familiar with these things. In fact I never gave a pistol a second look.

LUKA: Lord, have mercy on us, I must go hunt up the gardener and the coachman. Why has this catastrophe fallen upon us, O Lord! [*Exit.*]

SMIRNOV: [*Examining the pistols.*] Well, it's like this. There are several makes: one is the Mortimer, with capsules, especially constructed for duelling. What you have here are Smith and Wesson triple-action revolvers, with extractor, first-rate job, worth ninety rubles at the very least. You hold it this way. [*Aside.*] My God, what eyes she has! They're setting me on fire.

MRS. POPOV: This way?

SMIRNOV: Yes, that's right. You cock the trigger, take aim like this, head up, arm out like this. Then you just press with this finger here, and it's all over. The main thing is, keep cool, take slow aim, and don't let your arm jump.

MRS. POPOV: I see. And if it's inconvenient to do the job here, we can go out in the garden.

SMIRNOV: Very good. Of course, I should warn you: I'll be firing in the air.

MRS. POPOV: What? This is the end. Why?

SMIRNOV: Oh, well—because—for private reasons.

MRS. POPOV: Scared, huh? [*She laughs heartily.*] Now don't you try to get out of it, Mr. Smirnov. My blood is up. I won't be happy till I've drilled a hole through that skull of yours. Follow me. What's the matter? Scared?

SMIRNOV: That's right. I'm scared.

MRS. POPOV: Oh, come on, what's the matter with you?

SMIRNOV: Well, um, Mrs. Popov, I, um, I like you.

MRS. POPOV: [*Laughing bitterly.*] Good God! He likes me, does he! The gall of the man. [*Showing him the door.*] You may leave, Mr. Smirnov.

SMIRNOV: [*Quietly puts the gun down, takes his hat, and walks to the door. Then he stops and the pair look at each other without a word. Then, approaching gingerly.*] Listen, Mrs. Popov. Are you still mad at me? I'm in the devil of a temper myself, of course. But then, you see—what I mean is—it's this way—the fact is—[*Roaring.*] Well, is it my fault, damn it, if I like you? [*Clutches the back of a chair. It breaks.*] Christ, what fragile furniture you have here. I like you. Know what I mean? I could fall in love with you.

MRS. POPOV: I hate you. Get out!

SMIRNOV: What a woman! I never saw anything like it. Oh, I'm lost, I'm done for, I'm a mouse in a trap.

MRS. POPOV: Leave this house, or I shoot!

SMIRNOV: Shoot away! What bliss to die of a shot that was fired by that little velvet hand! To die gazing into those enchanting eyes. I'm out of my mind. I know: you must decide at once. Think for one second, then decide. Because if I leave now, I'll never be back. Decide! I'm a pretty decent chap. Landed gentleman, I should say. Ten thousand a year. Good stable. Throw a kopeck up in the air, and I'll put a bullet through it. Will you marry me?

MRS. POPOV: [*Indignant, brandishing the gun.*] We'll shoot it out! Get going! Take your pistol!

SMIRNOV: I'm out of my mind. I don't understand any more. [*Shouting.*] You there! That vodka!

MRS. POPOV: No excuses! No delays! We'll shoot it out!

SMIRNOV: I'm out of my mind. I'm falling in love. I *have* fallen in love. [*He takes her hand vigorously; she squeals.*] I love you. [*He goes down on his knees.*] I love you as I've never loved before. I jilted twelve, and was jilted by nine others. But I didn't love a one of them as I love you. I'm full of tender emotion. I'm melting like butter. I'm weak as water. I'm on my knees like a fool, and I offer you my hand. It's a shame, it's a disgrace. I haven't been in love in five years. I took a vow against it. And now, all of a sudden, to be swept off my feet, it's a scandal. I offer you my hand, dear lady. Will you or won't you? You won't? Then don't! [*He rises and walks toward the door.*]

MRS. POPOV: I didn't say anything.

SMIRNOV: [*Stopping.*] What?

MRS. POPOV: Oh, nothing, you can go. Well, no, just a minute. No, you can go. Go! I detest you! But, just a moment. Oh, if you knew how furious I feel! [*Throws the gun on the table.*] My fingers have gone to sleep holding that horrid thing. [*She is tearing her handkerchief to shreds.*] And what are you standing around for? Get out of here!

SMIRNOV: Goodbye.

MRS. POPOV: Go, go, go! [*Shouting.*] Where are you going? Wait a minute! No, no, it's all right, just go. I'm fighting mad. Don't come near me, don't come near me!

SMIRNOV: [*Who is coming near her.*] I'm pretty disgusted with myself—falling in love like a kid, going down on my knees like some moongazing whippersnapper, the very thought gives me gooseflesh. [*Rudely.*] I love you. But it doesn't make sense. Tomorrow, I have to pay that interest, and we've already started mowing. [*He puts his arm about her waist.*] I shall never forgive myself for this.

MRS. POPOV: Take your hands off me, I hate you! Let's shoot it out!

[*A long kiss. Enter* LUKA *with an axe, the* GARDENER *with a rake, the* COACHMAN *with a pitchfork,* HIRE MEN *with sticks.*]

LUKA: [*Seeing the kiss.*] Mercy on us! Holy saints above!

MRS. POPOV: [*Dropping her eyes.*] Luka, tell them in the stable that Toby is *not* to have any oats today.

CURTAIN

1888

Understanding the Text

1 CHARACTERIZATION

People—their activities, habits, eccentricities, and personalities—are ultimately the center of almost all the stories that literature tells. Just as literature is written for human eyes and has no meaningful existence as text unless people read and respond, literature always has people at the center of attention within the text.

Someone who appears in a work is called a **character,** the same word we use to refer to those qualities of mind, spirit, and behavior that make one individual different from every other. The identity of terms is not mere coincidence, for the creation of an imaginary character by author and reader is almost always based on some conception of human character and of individual differences.

Plays have a special engagement with character because of the visual and concrete manner in which they portray people on the stage, and written drama must create its world only through stage directions and dialogue. Stories or poems may comment on a character or editorialize rather directly, but plays have to *reveal* character—that is, let characters dramatize the kind of people they are by their own words and actions. Other characters may, of course, express opinions about a particular character, and our feelings as readers or members of the audience may be influenced by such rumor and innuendo, but all characters who appear on the stage or on the drama's page ultimately have to be credible in their own terms.

It it thus the first task of a play to introduce the people with whose lives we are to be concerned and to establish the central facts of their characters. The first page of text of most plays contains a complete list of the persons whose lives are to be presented dramatically, the **dramatis personae.** Many play programs offer this list, the names of the actors playing the parts, and sometimes even a brief description of each of the characters and of the relationships among them. Some plays, older ones usually, have someone appear on stage and recite a prologue that explains directly what the audience needs to know about the plot and characters. Still, whatever textual aids may be provided for curious readers or introductory matter for the audience, the play on page or stage has to present characters as if from scratch.

In *The Brute*, for example, the opening conversation between Mrs. Popov and her servant Luka tells us essentially what we need to know about her and her situation—not only that her husband has recently died, but that she has decided that she will pine away in "grief" at his passing, and even that her grief is more anger at her dead husband than anything else: her notion of proper behavior is not based on personal feelings and desires but on some abstract romantic principle of what is likely to gain her the reputation of being a noble, self-sacrificing, and unappreciated widow. The attempts by Luka to talk her out of her silly resolution serve to get the play off the ground; within the first two or three minutes the dramatic situation is fully set up: romantic, unfulfilled, long-suffering, unhappy, self-deluded, lonely, adamant Mrs. Popov needs to be talked out of her pretensions and her underlying hopelessness. By the time the other main character, Smirnov, appears we need no further preparation or exposition. Just before he enters, Luka describes him as a perfect monster, cursing and swearing, and he reveals himself immediately by the way he speaks, rants, and storms about the stage or page in his desperation and rage. The characters "fit": though cleverly arranged and carefully drawn out to maximize the effect, the resolution is already almost inevitable.

In longer plays, it is often minor (or even inconsequential) characters who provide the initial information, sometimes hardly appearing again after performing their expository function. The main character seldom appears until he or she has been prepared for: Smirnov appears after eighty lines or so, Hedda after almost three times that number, her entrance anticipated and announced, as if with a flourish of trumpets.

Our first, indirect impressions of her are rather positive. We hear what a beauty she is, how sought-after she was, and how prominent her family is. She has just returned from her honeymoon, and it is from her new husband and his Aunt Juju that we hear about Hedda and learn how lucky they feel that she has—rather inexplicably—chosen to marry the unprepossessing Tesman. There are cautionary hints that Hedda is less than perfect, however. Tesman says she insisted on having all her baggage with her on the journey, which suggests self-indulgence or at least a certain amount of eccentricity that is hard to reconcile with her image as a cool and classy beauty. Aunt Juliana is a bit shocked by Hedda's having removed the chintz covers from the furniture and the pretension of using the drawing-room as a parlor. When Hedda enters, she is a bit snappy with both her husband and his aunt. It is quite possible, however, that the reader or audience shares Hedda's low opinion of her new groom and his family, and so we are on her side and are trying to figure out how she was trapped into marrying a rather unattractive, thick-skulled, bloodless oaf like Tesman. Her self-centeredness and cruelty are only very gradually revealed (and perhaps we, who have been on her side against the "inferior" Tesman, come to recognize that we too have been guilty of snobbishness, confusing class and worth).

The very titles of such plays as *Hamlet*, *Hedda Gabler*, and *Oedipus the King* imply that the play will center on a single character, and in most cases the expectations of titles are fulfilled in the play itself: the main character (or **protagonist**) is not only at the center of the action but is also the chief object of the playwright's (and the reader's or audience's) concern. Defining the character of that protagonist (sometimes by comparison with a competitor, or **antagonist**) often becomes the consuming interest of the play, and the action seems designed to illustrate, or clarify, or develop that character, or sometimes to make him or her a complex, unfathomable, mysterious being. Even titles that do not use proper names can indicate focus on a single character—*Death of a Salesman*, *The Doctor in Spite of Himself*—but already there is a suggestion that the emphasis is on a type rather than an individual. Occasionally, of course, a title may be a mere convenience (in which case it means nothing about the play's focus), or it may set up misleading or ambiguous expectations so that our attention can be aroused or diverted. Does the title of *The Brute* refer to Smirnov or to the absent Popov? Is either the real center of attention?

Not all plays center on characters, though all involve characters and characterization. The reader, without the image of a living actor in view, must imaginatively create or recreate that image. Or, to be more precise, the reader must be building, projecting, revising, compounding, and complicating the image of the character throughout the reading of the play.

This activity is necessary even when the play is not notably one of character. Such a play is Susan Glaspell's *Trifles*, which may be considered either as a mystery story or as a theme-centered, feminist play. The men in that play concentrate on "the big picture," the "important" things, and they are rather dismissive of women's petty concerns and their interest in "trifles." The "trifles" that concern the women, however, turn out to be more important than the larger, more worldly things with which the men are involved. Though the reader's sympathies are engaged primarily on the side of the women in a form of "sisterhood," there is differentiation of the two women characters and of the third woman who, though she never appears onstage, is in many ways at the center of the play. Indeed, there is something like conflict between the two women characters, the wife of the sheriff being more strongly influenced by "the law," which Mrs. Hale seems to consider only "*man's* law" and in general an instrument of the suppression of women. In reading the play we must distinguish the women, and we must distinguish between the young county attorney, the sheriff, farmer Hale, and the murder victim, John Wright.

Not all characters in a play are heroes or heroines or villains, protagonists or antagonists, and we must pay attention to them all if we are to people the play vividly and make sense of the action, structure, and themes of the work. There are, for example, supporting or minor characters. All these are categorized by their function within the play. But characters can also be categorized by the talents and strengths they require of those who are to act the part. There are demanding and challenging roles, juicy parts and dull or routine ones, roles for stars, character-actors, comedians, and novices. Characters can also be categorized by their cultural identities (Jewish mothers, Roumanian ravenhaired beauties, pious frauds, social climbers). These sometimes verge on (or are subsumed by) **stereotypes:** characters based on conscious or unconscious cultural assumptions that sex, age, ethnic or national identification, occupation, marital status, and so on are predictably accompanied by certain character traits, actions, even values. Stereotypes, especially disparaging ones, can be a weakness in a play if they involve important characters who do not develop or become individualized or explored in the course of the work. However, no matter how individualized characters ultimately turn out to be, they often begin as some identifiable "type" of person that the audience will recognize and have certain expectations about.

Usually these expectations are thereafter overturned or modified just as plot expectations often are, so the reader or audience is both surprised and, because the character began as a familiar type, convinced. Hedda Gabler, as we have seen, is at first a Great Beauty. She is also rich, spoiled, ambitious, used to having her own way. Less and less attractive as she reveals herself more and more, yet pitiable because she is beginning to age and panic, and more and more helpless in a trap only in part of her own making, she begins as a quite predictable stereotype but becomes more and more complex, as does our response to her.

Tesman similarly begins as a type, almost as a comic type—the otherworldly and somewhat absent-minded professor who does not really understand veiled allusions to pregnancy, who has little sense of money, who is affectionate without suspicion, who is generally unsophisticated about the ways of the world and very trusting of human nature. Although he is always more simple and straightforward than Hedda, and his annoying mannerisms (his habit of ending most of his sentences with "what," for example) continue to categorize him, he, too, as the play develops, becomes complicated, no longer simply a simple stereotype. His part, too, though not so challenging as that of Hedda, demands interpretation, nuance, and subtlety of an actor and understanding from the reader.

No matter how magnificent a performance may be, the actor or actress has to make choices—how to read a line, what body language to use, what gestures, if any, or stage "business" to bring to bear—and a choice means choosing not to perform some other way which may be equally true to the text and equally or similarly effective. A performance is an interpretation, a "reading" of the play one way rather than another—or any other.

How would you play Hedda Gabler? What are the possibilities reading the play reveals? You might play her as an aristocratic beauty trapped into a dull marriage in the ugly, tacky world of the bourgeoisie, driven by boredom, frustration, and abhorrence to acts of cruelty; or as a thoroughly spoiled brat, used to primacy and getting her own way, who lashes out at the weak and innocent and uses everyone to satisfy her need and greed; or as . . . Is her reverence for her dead father touching? admirable? unhealthy? To what degree is she more sinned against than sinning? Ibsen, in starkly realistic, hands-off fashion, does not mediate. Not one in the play seems to speak for him—or us. There may be clues in the context Ibsen sketches in, her social background and family upbringing, but the play does not seem to offer them either as "explanations" or justification of her nature and acts.

Suppose you wanted to show that she was some subtle mixture of both lady and brat. How would you read the lines early in the play where she seems more sympathetic in order to suggest the bitch beneath? And how would you read the later lines when her cruelty emerges so that we can see the pitiable lady beneath her selfishness and greed? How would you play off the emotions and sympathies of the "audience" yet play fair? For example, in a rather early episode Hedda mistakes Aunt Juliana's new hat for an old one that must belong to the maid. Still enthralled by her, we as readers or audience may have our own sense of social superiority tickled by her obvious superiority to the bumbling Tesmans. Later in the play, when Hedda's spoiled, unstable, cruel character has been more and more clearly revealed, we learn that this "mistake" was deliberate, that Hedda was deliberately trying to put down Tesman's doting, flighty, but well-meaning and vulnerable aunt. How do we reveal her cruelty for what it is, while still suggesting the lovely and suffering woman beneath? Do we simply play the early part for sympathy and the later portions of the play as a bitter exposé? That would have its own merit, engaging the reader/audience/ourselves in the romantic self-deception and then showing Hedda and ourselves up for what we are. But should we—and if so, how could we—suggest hypocrisy and selfishness from the beginning? No actress can completely embody all the suggestions and possibilities of the character as we imagine her in our reading, yet many great actresses have played the role, and when we have seen three or four portrayals, our image of the possibilities will surely be further enriched. No wonder actresses clamor for this role just as actors do for the part of Hamlet.

Every production of a play (and, in a sense, every performance) is an interpretation. Not just the "adaptations," setting a Greek or Elizabethan play in modern times and performing in modern dress, but even a production and performance that seeks to get at the "heart" or "essence" of the play is a "reading," a diagnosis or analysis of just what is vital and essential in the play. Interpretation does not necessarily mean getting the author's "intention," however. John Malkovich, in the 1983–84 production of *Death of a Salesman*, did not project Biff Loman as an outgoing, successful, hail-fellow-well-met jock, though that is what Arthur Miller intended and how he wanted the part played. Malkovich saw Biff as only pretending, playing the part of the jock. Big-time athletes, he insisted, don't glad-hand people; they wait for people to come to them. The actor did not change the author's words, but by body language, stage business, and carriage suggested his own view of the nature of the character.

Once the playwright sets down the words in the many-faceted language of the multiple communities of readers and audience, readers, directors, and actors are free to read those words as they will, within the limits of the language, the culture, and reason. The effect of Malkovich's interpretation and performance was revolutionary and convincing. Reading the play now, perhaps we will see Biff as more complex, more ambiguous—not the jock, for sure, but not a pretender for sure either.

Characterization on the stage involves four more or less separate processes. The first involves the **conception** of the character in the playwright's mind, at the moment when the play begins to be an idea, when the playwright first begins to construct—or even dream about—a plot, structure, or theme that will ultimately be an element of the drama. Characters may develop or change radically in the process of conception, and nothing in the process is really complete or final until the other three processes are also complete. The second process involves **presentation** of the character by the playwright through the words and actions specified in the text. The artistic decision about how much to present and when to present it (structural decisions, really) can have an important effect on how the audience responds to a character and what sort of character ultimately is realized in the play. But the full effect of characterization in a performed play is possible only when the play is fleshed out on the stage with a live actor playing the part and adding the final personal touches to the character, whether these are subtle shadings or bold new interpretations, with body gestures, facial expressions, and tones of voice. In **casting** a play—that is, in deciding what actors are to play the parts—a director takes a major step in determining how a character might seem to the audience, for the choice of actor determines not only the physical appearance, quality of voice, and degree of presence that a character will present on the stage, but also more subtle and more significant details of presentation. The **acting** itself is the last of the four steps in characterization. The embodying of a character onstage in a fully realized production is the ultimate creative act in an art that goes beyond words and stage directions and is ultimately an exercise in a complex form of impersonation. In this step one person becomes for a brief while someone different, first conceived in one form in the imagination of the playwright, developed in an inevitably somewhat different form in words by that playwright, partially interpreted by the director, and now embodied by the actor as someone other than him- or herself, but within his or her individual resources, experiences, abilities.

In a play performed on the stage we in the audience have a role, but a somewhat reduced role: the actor and director have made choices and limited our freedom to interpret—though, actors tell us, no two performances are exactly alike, in part due to the nature of the audience. In reading the play on the page, we are both director and actor—we are the richer for our freedom from the necessity of making choices and our opportunity to hold complex, even contradictory, possibilities in mind, to "change character" as the words shift, while retaining all the possibilities we have gone through. But we may be the poorer for lacking the inspired insights of a great director and the incorporation of the character by a great actor.

▽ ▽ ▽

CHARACTERIZATION A Glossary

acting: the last of the four steps in characterization in a performed play, for in the actual production the actor makes something distinctive of her or his talents in relation to the author's original conception and to the author's presentation.

antagonist: the opponent of the protagonist or main character; the villain

casting: the third step in the creation of a character on the stage; deciding what actors are to play the parts

character: someone who acts, appears, or is referred to in a work

conception: the first step in the creation of a dramatic character, whether for written text or performed play; the original idea, when the playwright first begins to construct—or even dream about—a plot, or the characters, structure, or theme that will be an element of the play

dramatis personae: a list of the persons either in the play program or at the top of the first page of the written play whose lives are to be presented dramatically

hero/heroine: the leading male/female character, usually larger than life. See **protagonist.**

presentation: the second step in the creation of a character for the written text and the performed play; the representation of the character by the playwright in the words and actions specified in the text

protagonist: the main character of a play

stereotype: characters based on conscious or unconscious cultural assumptions that sex, age, ethnic or national identification, occupation, marital status, and so on are predictably accompanied by certain character traits, actions, even values

SUSAN GLASPELL

Trifles

CHARACTERS

SHERIFF	MRS. PETERS, *Sheriff's wife*
COUNTY ATTORNEY	MRS. HALE
HALE	

SCENE: *The kitchen is the now abandoned farmhouse of* JOHN WRIGHT, *a gloomy kitchen, and left without having been put in order—unwashed pans under the sink, a loaf of bread outside the bread-box, a dish-towel on the table—other signs of incompleted work. At the rear the outer door opens and the* SHERIFF *comes in followed by the* COUNTY ATTORNEY *and* HALE. *The* SHERIFF *and* HALE *are men in middle life, the* COUNTY ATTORNEY *is a young man; all are much bundled up and go at once to the stove. They are followed by the two women—the* SHERIFF's *wife first; she is a slight wiry woman, a thin nervous face.* MRS. HALE *is larger and would ordinarily be called more comfortable looking, but she is disturbed now and looks fearfully about as she enters. The women have come in slowly, and stand close together near the door.*

COUNTY ATTORNEY: [*Rubbing his hands.*] This feels good. Come up to the fire, ladies.

MRS. PETERS: [*After taking a step forward.*] I'm not—cold.

SHERIFF: [*Unbuttoning his overcoat and stepping away from the stove as if to mark the beginning of official business.*] Now, Mr. Hale, before we move things about, you explain to Mr. Henderson just what you saw when you came here yesterday morning.

COUNTY ATTORNEY: By the way, has anything been moved? Are things just as you left them yesterday?

SHERIFF: [*Looking about.*] It's just the same. When it dropped below zero last night I thought I'd better send Frank out this morning to make a fire for us—no use getting pneumonia with a big case on, but I told him not to touch anything except the stove—and you know Frank.

COUNTY ATTORNEY: Somebody should have been left here yesterday.

SHERIFF: Oh—yesterday. When I had to send Frank to Morris Center for that man who went crazy—I want you to know I had my hands full yesterday. I knew you could get back from Omaha by today and as long as I went over everything here myself—

COUNTY ATTORNEY: Well, Mr. Hale, tell just what happened when you came here yesterday morning.

HALE: Harry and I had started to town with a load of potatoes. We came along the road from my place and as I got here I said, "I'm going to see if I can't get John Wright to go in with me on a party telephone." I spoke to Wright about it once before and he put me off, saying folks talked too much anyway, and all he asked was peace and quiet—I guess you know about how much he talked himself; but I thought maybe if I went to the house and talked about it before his wife, though I said to Harry that I didn't know as what his wife wanted made much difference to John—

COUNTY ATTORNEY: Let's talk about that later, Mr. Hale. I do want to talk about that, but tell now just what happened when you got to the house.

HALE: I didn't hear or see anything; I knocked at the door, and still it was all quiet inside. I knew they must be up, it was past eight o'clock. So I knocked again, and I thought I heard somebody say, "Come in." I wasn't sure, I'm not sure yet, but I opened the door—this door [*Indicating the door by which the two women are still standing.*] and there in that rocker—[*Pointing to it.*] sat Mrs. Wright.

[*They all look at the rocker.*]

COUNTY ATTORNEY: What—was she doing?

HALE: She was rockin' back and forth. She had her apron in her hand and was kind of—pleating it.

COUNTY ATTORNEY: And how did she—look?

HALE: Well, she looked queer.

COUNTY ATTORNEY: How do you mean—queer?

HALE: Well, as if she didn't know what she was going to do next. And kind of done up.

COUNTY ATTORNEY: How did she seem to feel about your coming?

HALE: Why, I don't think she minded—one way or other. She didn't pay much attention. I said, "How do, Mrs. Wright, it's cold, ain't it?" And she said, "Is it?"—and went on kind of pleating at her apron. Well, I was surprised; she didn't ask me to come up to the stove, or to set down, but just sat there, not even looking at me, so I said, "I want to see John." And then she—laughed. I guess you would call it a laugh. I thought of Harry and the team outside, so I said a little sharp: "Can't I see John?" "No," she says, kind o' dull like. "Ain't he home?" says I. "Yes," says she, "he's home." "Then why can't I see him?" I asked her, out of patience. " 'Cause he's dead," says she. "*Dead?*" says I. She just nodded her head, not getting a bit excited, but rockin' back and forth. "Why—where is he?" says I, not knowing what to say. She just pointed upstairs—like that [*Himself pointing to the room above.*] I got up, with the idea of going up there. I walked from there to here—then I says, "Why, what did he die of?" "He died of a rope round his neck," says she, and just went on pleatin' at her apron. Well, I went out and called Harry. I thought I might—need help. We went upstairs and there he was lyin'—

COUNTY ATTORNEY: I think I'd rather have you go into that upstairs, where you can point it all out. Just go on now with the rest of the story.

HALE: Well, my first thought was to get that rope off. It looked . . . [*Stops, his face twitches.*] . . . but Harry, he went up to him, and he said, "No, he's dead all right, and we'd better not touch anything." So we went back down stairs. She was still sitting that same way. "Has anybody been notified?" I asked. "No," says she unconcerned. "Who did this, Mrs. Wright?" said Harry.

He said it business-like—and she stopped pleatin' of her apron. "I don't know," she says. "You don't *know?*" says Harry. "No," says she. "Weren't you sleepin' in the bed with him?" says Harry. "Yes," says she, "but I was on the inside." "Somebody slipped a rope round his neck and strangled him and you didn't wake up?" says Harry. "I didn't wake up," she said after him. We must 'a looked as if we didn't see how that could be, for after a minute she said, "I sleep sound." Harry was going to ask her more questions but I said maybe we ought to let her tell her story first to the coroner, or the sheriff, so Harry went fast as he could to Rivers' place, where there's a telephone.

COUNTY ATTORNEY: And what did Mrs. Wright do when she knew that you had gone for the coroner?

HALE: She moved from that chair to this one over here [*Pointing to a small chair in the corner.*] and just sat there with her hands held together and looking down. I got a feeling that I ought to make some conversation, so I said I had come in to see if John wanted to put in a telephone, and at that she started to laugh, and then she stopped and looked at me—scared. [*The* COUNTY ATTORNEY, *who has had his notebook out, makes a note.*] I dunno, maybe it wasn't scared. I wouldn't like to say it was. Soon Harry got back, and then Dr. Lloyd came, and you, Mr. Peters, and so I guess that's all I know that you don't.

COUNTY ATTORNEY: [*Looking around.*] I guess we'll go upstairs first—and then out to the barn and around there. [*To the* SHERIFF.] You're convinced that there was nothing important here—nothing that would point to any motive.

SHERIFF: Nothing here but kitchen things.

[*The* COUNTY ATTORNEY, *after again looking around the kitchen, opens the door of a cupboard closet. He gets up on a chair and looks on a shelf. Pulls his hand away, sticky.*]

COUNTY ATTORNEY: Here's a nice mess.

[*The women draw nearer.*]

MRS. PETERS: [*To the other woman.*] Oh, her fruit; it did freeze. [*To the* LAWYER.] She worried about that when it turned so cold. She said the fire'd go out and her jars would break.

SHERIFF: Well, can you beat the women! Held for murder and worryin' about her preserves.

COUNTY ATTORNEY: I guess before we're through she may have something more serious than preserves to worry about.

HALE: Well, women are used to worrying over trifles.

[*The two women move a little closer together.*]

COUNTY ATTORNEY: [*With the gallantry of a young politician.*] And yet, for all their worries, what would we do without the ladies? [*The women do not unbend. He goes to the sink, takes a dipperful of water from the pail and pouring it into a basin, washes his hands. Starts to wipe them on the roller-towel, turns it for a cleaner place.*] Dirty towels! [*Kicks his foot against the pans under the sink.*] Not much of a housekeeper, would you say, ladies?

MRS. HALE: [*Stiffly.*] There's a great deal of work to be done on a farm.

COUNTY ATTORNEY: To be sure. And yet [*With a little bow to her.*] I know there are some Dickson county farmhouses which do not have such roller towels.

[*He gives it a pull to expose its length again.*]

MRS. HALE: Those towels get dirty awful quick. Men's hands aren't always as clean as they might be.

COUNTY ATTORNEY: Ah, loyal to your sex, I see. But you and Mrs. Wright were neighbors. I suppose you were friends, too.

MRS. HALE: [*Shaking her head.*] I've not seen much of her of late years. I've not been in this house—it's more than a year.

COUNTY ATTORNEY: And why was that? You didn't like her?

MRS. HALE: I liked her all well enough. Farmers' wives have their hands full, Mr. Henderson. And then—

COUNTY ATTORNEY: YES—?

MRS. HALE: [*Looking about.*] It never seemed a very cheerful place.

COUNTY ATTORNEY: No—it's not cheerful. I shouldn't say she had the homemaking instinct.

MRS. HALE: Well, I don't know as Wright had, either.

COUNTY ATTORNEY: You mean that they didn't get on very well?

MRS. HALE: No, I don't mean anything. But I don't think a place'd be any cheerfuller for John Wright's being in it.

COUNTY ATTORNEY: I'd like to talk more of that a little later. I want to get the lay of things upstairs now.

[*He goes to the left, where three steps lead to a stair door.*]

SHERIFF: I suppose anything Mrs. Peters does'll be all right. She was to take in some clothes for her, you know, and a few little things. We left in such a hurry yesterday.

COUNTY ATTORNEY: Yes, but I would like to see what you take, Mrs. Peters, and keep an eye out for anything that might be of use to us.

MRS. PETERS: Yes, Mr. Henderson.

[*The women listen to the men's steps on the stairs, then look about the kitchen.*]

MRS. HALE: I'd hate to have men coming into my kitchen, snooping around and criticizing.

[*She arranges the pans under sink which the* LAWYER *had shoved out of place.*]

MRS. PETERS: Of course it's no more than their duty.

MRS. HALE: Duty's all right, but I guess that deputy sheriff that came out to make the fire might have got a little of this on. [*Gives the roller towel a pull.*] Wish I'd thought of that sooner. Seems mean to talk about her for not having things slicked up when she had to come away in such a hurry.

MRS. PETERS: [*Who has gone to a small table in the left rear corner of the room, and lifted one end of a towel that covers a pan.*] She had bread set. [*Stands still.*]

MRS. HALE: [*Eyes fixed on a loaf of bread beside the bread-box, which is on a low shelf at the other side of the room. Moves slowly toward it.*] She was going to put this in there. [*Picks up loaf, then abruptly drops it. In a manner of returning to familiar things.*] It's a shame about her fruit. I wonder if it's all gone. [*Gets up on the chair and looks.*] I think there's some here that's all right, Mrs. Peters. Yes—here; [*Holding it toward the window.*] this is cherries, too. [*Looking again.*] I declare I believe that's the only one. [*Gets down, bottle in her hand. Goes to the sink and wipes it off on the outside.*] She'll feel awful bad after all her hard work in the hot weather. I remember the afternoon I put up my cherries last summer.

[*She puts the bottle on the big kitchen table, center of the room. With a sigh, is about to sit down in the rocking-chair. Before she is seated realizes what chair it is; with a slow look at it, steps back. The chair which she has touched rocks back and forth.*]

MRS. PETERS: Well, I must get those things from the front room closet. [*She goes to the door at the right, but after looking into the other room, steps back.*] You coming with me, Mrs. Hale? You could help me carry them.

[*They go in the other room; reappear,* MRS. PETERS *carrying a dress and skirt,* MRS. HALE *following with a pair of shoes.*]

MRS. PETERS: My, it's cold in there.

[*She puts the clothes on the big table, and hurries to the stove.*]

MRS. HALE: [*Examing the skirt.*] Wright was close. I think maybe that's why she kept so much to herself. She didn't even belong to the Ladies Aid. I suppose she felt she couldn't do her part, and then you don't enjoy things when you feel shabby. She used to wear pretty clothes and be lively, when she was Minnie Foster, one of the town girls singing in the choir. But that—oh, that was thirty years ago. This all you was to take in?

MRS. PETERS: She said she wanted an apron. Funny thing to want, for there isn't much to get you dirty in jail, goodness knows. But I suppose just to make her feel more natural. She said they was in the top drawer in this cupboard. Yes, here. And then her little shawl that always hung behind the door. [*Opens stair door and looks.*] Yes, here it is. [*Quickly shuts door leading upstairs.*]

MRS. HALE: [*Abruptly moving toward her.*] Mrs. Peters?

MRS. PETERS: Yes, Mrs. Hale?

MRS. HALE: Do you think she did it?

MRS. PETERS: [*In a frightened voice.*] Oh, I don't know.

MRS. HALE: Well, I don't think she did. Asking for an apron and her little shawl. Worrying about her fruit.

MRS. PETERS: [*Starts to speak, glances up, where footsteps are heard in the room above. In a low voice.*] Mr. Peters says it looks bad for her. Mr. Henderson is awful sarcastic in a speech and he'll make fun of her sayin' she didn't wake up.

MRS. HALE: Well, I guess John Wright didn't wake when they was slipping that rope under his neck.

MRS. PETERS: No, it's strange. It must have been done awful crafty and still. They say it was such a—funny way to kill a man, rigging it all up like that.

MRS. HALE: That's just what Mr. Hale said. There was a gun in the house. He says that's what he can't understand.

MRS. PETERS: Mr. Henderson said coming out that what was needed for the case was a motive; something to show anger, or—sudden feeling.

MRS. HALE: [*Who is standing by the table.*] Well, I don't see any signs of anger around here. [*She puts her hand on the dish towel which lies on the table, stands looking down at table, one half of which is clean, the other half messy.*] It's wiped to here. [*Makes a move as if to finish work, then turns and looks at loaf of bread outside the breadbox. Drops towel. In that voice of coming back to familiar things.*] Wonder how they are finding things upstairs. I hope she had it a little more red-up[1] up there. You know, it seems kind of *sneaking*. Locking her up in town and then coming out here and trying to get her own house to turn against her!

MRS. PETERS: But Mrs. Hale, the law is the law.

MRS. HALE: I s'pose 'tis. [*Unbuttoning her coat.*] Better loosen up your things, Mrs. Peters. You won't feel them when you go out.

[MRS. PETERS *takes off her fur tippet, goes to hang it on hook at back of room, stands looking at the under part of the small corner table.*]

MRS. PETERS: She was piecing a quilt.

[*She brings the large sewing basket and they look at the bright pieces.*]

MRS. HALE: It's log cabin pattern. Pretty, isn't it? I wonder if she was goin' to quilt it or just knot it?

[*Footsteps have been heard coming down the stairs. The* SHERIFF *enters followed by* HALE *and the* COUNTY ATTORNEY.]

SHERIFF: They wonder if she was going to quilt it or just knot it!

[*The men laugh, the women look abashed.*]

COUNTY ATTORNEY: [*Rubbing his hands over the stove.*] Frank's fire didn't do much up there, did it? Well, let's go out to the barn and get that cleared up.

[*The men go outside.*]

MRS. HALE: [*Resentfully.*] I don't know as there's anything so strange, our takin' up our time with little things while we're waiting for them to get the evidence. [*She sits down at the big table smoothing out a block with decision.*] I don't see as it's anything to laugh about.

MRS. PETERS: [*Apologetically.*] Of course they've got awful important things on their minds.

[*Pulls up a chair and joins* MRS. HALE *at the table.*]

1. Tidied up.

MRS. HALE: [*Examining another block.*] Mrs. Peters, look at this one. Here, this is the one she was working on, and look at the sewing! All the rest of it has been so nice and even. And look at this! It's all over the place! Why, it looks as if she didn't know what she was about!

[*After she has said this they look at each other, then start to glance back at the door. After an instant* MRS. HALE *has pulled at a knot and ripped the sewing.*]

MRS. PETERS: Oh, what are you doing, Mrs. Hale?

MRS. HALE: [*Mildly.*] Just pulling out a stitch or two that's not sewed very good. [*Threading the needle.*] Bad sewing always made me fidgety.

MRS. PETERS: [*Nervously.*] I don't think we ought to touch things.

MRS. HALE: I'll just finish up this end. [*Suddenly stopping and leaning forward.*] Mrs. Peters?

MRS. PETERS: Yes, Mrs. Hale?

MRS. HALE: What do you suppose she was so nervous about?

MRS. PETERS: Oh—I don't know. I don't know as she was nervous. I sometimes sew awful queer when I'm just tired. [MRS. HALE *starts to say something, looks at* MRS. PETERS, *then goes on sewing.*] Well I must get these things wrapped up. They may be through sooner than we think. [*Putting apron and other things together.*] I wonder where I can find a piece of paper, and string.

MRS. HALE: In that cupboard, maybe.

MRS. PETERS: [*Looking in cupboard.*] Why, here's a bird-cage. [*Holds it up.*] Did she have a bird, Mrs. Hale?

MRS. HALE: Why, I don't know whether she did or not—I've not been here for so long. There was a man around last year selling canaries cheap, but I don't know as she took one; maybe she did. She used to sing real pretty herself.

MRS. PETERS: [*Glancing around.*] Seems funny to think of a bird here. But she must have had one, or why would she have a cage? I wonder what happened to it.

MRS. HALE: I s'pose maybe the cat got it.

MRS. PETERS: No, she didn't have a cat. She's got that feeling some people have about cats—being afraid of them. My cat got in her room and she was real upset and asked me to take it out.

MRS. HALE: My sister Bessie was like that. Queer, ain't it?

MRS. PETERS: [*Examing the cage.*] Why, look at this door. It's broke. One hinge is pulled apart.

MRS. HALE: [*Looking too.*] Looks as if someone must have been rough with it.

MRS. PETERS: Why, yes.

[*She brings the cage forward and puts it on the table.*]

MRS. HALE: I wish if they're going to find any evidence they'd be about it. I don't like this place.

MRS. PETERS: But I'm awful glad you came with me, Mrs. Hale. It would be lonesome for me sitting here alone.

MRS. HALE: It would, wouldn't it? [*Dropping her sewing.*] But I tell you what I do wish, Mrs. Peters. I wish I had come over sometimes when *she* was here. I—[*Looking around the room.*]—wish I had.

MRS. PETERS: But of course you were awful busy, Mrs. Hale—your house and your children.

MRS. HALE: I could've come. I stayed away because it weren't cheerful—and that's why I ought to have come. I—I've never liked this place. Maybe because it's down in a hollow and you don't see the road. I dunno what it is, but it's a lonesome place and always was. I wish I had come over to see Minnie Foster sometimes. I can see now—[*Shakes her head.*]

MRS. PETERS: Well, you mustn't reproach yourself, Mrs. Hale. Somehow we just don't see how it is with other folks until—something comes up.

MRS. HALE: Not having children makes less work—but it makes a quiet house, and Wright out to work all day, and no company when he did come in. Did you know John Wright, Mrs. Peters?

MRS. PETERS: Not to know him; I've seen him in town. They say he was a good man.

MRS. HALE: Yes—good; he didn't drink, and kept his word as well as most, I guess, and paid his debts. But he was a hard man, Mrs. Peters. Just to pass the time of day with him—[*Shivers.*] Like a raw wind that gets to the bone. [*Pauses, her eye falling on the cage.*] I should think she would 'a wanted a bird. But what do you suppose went with it?

MRS. PETERS: I don't know, unless it got sick and died.

[*She reaches over and swings the broken door, swings it again, both women watch it.*]

MRS. HALE: You weren't raised round here, were you? [MRS. PETERS *shakes her head.*] You didn't know—her?

MRS. PETERS: Not till they brought her yesterday.

MRS. HALE: She—come to think of it, she was kind of like a bird herself—real sweet and pretty, but kind of timid and—fluttery. How—she—did—change. [*Silence; then as if struck by a happy thought and relieved to get back to everyday things.*] Tell you what, Mrs. Peters, why don't you take the quilt in with you? It might take up her mind.

MRS. PETERS: Why, I think that's a real nice idea, Mrs. Hale. There couldn't possibly be any objection to it, could there? Now, just what would I take? I wonder if her patches are in here—and her things.

[*They look in the sewing basket.*]

MRS. HALE: Here's some red. I expect this has got sewing things in it. [*Brings out a fancy box.*] What a pretty box. Looks like something somebody would give you. Maybe her scissors are in here. [*Opens box. Suddenly puts her hand to her nose.*] Why— [MRS. PETERS *bends nearer, then turns her face away.*] There's something wrapped up in this piece of silk.

MRS. PETERS: Why, this isn't her scissors.

MRS. HALE: [*Lifting the silk.*] Oh, Mrs. Peters—it's—

[MRS. PETERS *bends closer.*]

MRS. PETERS: It's the bird.

MRS. HALE: [*Jumping up.*] But, Mrs. Peters—look at it! It's neck! Look at its neck! It's all—other side *to*.

MRS. PETERS: Somebody—wrung—its—neck.

[*Their eyes meet. A look of growing comprehension, of horror. Steps are heard outside.* MRS. HALE *slips box under quilt pieces, and sinks into her chair. Enter* SHERIFF *and* COUNTY ATTORNEY. MRS. PETERS *rises.*]

COUNTY ATTORNEY: [*As one turning from serious things to little pleasantries.*] Well ladies, have you decided whether she was going to quilt it or knot it?

MRS. PETERS: We think she was going to—knot it.

COUNTY ATTORNEY: Well, that's interesting, I'm sure. [*Seeing the birdcage.*] Has the bird flown?

MRS. HALE: [*Putting more quilt pieces over the box.*] We think the—cat got it.

COUNTY ATTORNEY: [*Preoccupied.*] Is there a cat?

[MRS. HALE *glances in a quick covert way at* MRS. PETERS.]

MRS. PETERS: Well, not *now*. They're superstitious, you know. They leave.

COUNTY ATTORNEY: [*To* SHERIFF PETERS, *continuing an interrupted conversation.*] No sign at all of anyone having come from the outside. Their own rope. Now let's go up again and go over it piece by piece. [*They start upstairs.*] It would have to have been someone who knew just the—

[MRS. PETERS *sits down. The two women sit there not looking at one another, but as if peering into something and at the same time holding back. When they talk now it is in the manner of feeling their way over strange ground, as if afraid of what they are saying, but as if they cannot help saying it.*]

MRS. HALE: She liked the bird. She was going to bury it in that pretty box.

MRS. PETERS: [*In a whisper.*] When I was a girl—my kitten—there was a boy took a hatchet, and before my eyes—and before I could get there—[*Covers her face an instant.*] If they hadn't held me back I would have—[*Catches herself, looks upstairs where steps are heard, falters weakly.*]—hurt him.

MRS. HALE: [*With a slow look around her.*] I wonder how it would seem never to have had any children around. [*Pause.*] No, Wright wouldn't like the bird—a thing that sang. She used to sing. He killed that, too.

MRS. PETERS: [*Moving uneasily.*] We don't know who killed the bird.

MRS. HALE: I knew John Wright.

MRS. PETERS: It was an awful thing was done in this house that night, Mrs. Hale. Killing a man while he slept, slipping a rope around his neck that choked the life out of him.

MRS. HALE: His neck. Choked the life out of him.

[*Her hand goes out and rests on the bird-cage.*]

MRS. PETERS: [*With rising voice.*] We don't know who killed him. We don't *know*.

MRS. HALE: [*Her own feeling not interrupted.*] If there's been years and years of nothing, then a bird to sing to you, it would be awful—still, after the bird was still.

MRS. PETERS: [*Something within her speaking.*] I know what stillness is. When we homesteaded in Dakota, and my first baby died—after he was two years old, and me with no other then—

MRS. HALE: [*Moving.*] How soon do you suppose they'll be through, looking for the evidence?

MRS. PETERS: I know what stillness is. [*Pulling herself back.*] The law has got to punish crime, Mrs. Hale.

MRS. HALE: [*Not as if answering that.*] I wish you'd seen Minnie Foster when she wore a white dress with blue ribbons and stood up there in the choir and sang. [*A look around the room.*] Oh, I *wish* I'd come over here once in a while! That was a crime! That was a crime! Who's going to punish that?

MRS. PETERS: [*Looking upstairs.*] We mustn't—take on.

MRS. HALE: I might have known she needed help! I know how things can be—for women. I tell you, it's queer, Mrs. Peters. We live close together and we live far apart. We all go through the same things—it's all just a different kind of the same thing. [*Brushes her eyes, noticing the bottle of fruit, reaches out for it.*] If I was you, I wouldn't tell her her fruit was gone. Tell her it *ain't*. Tell her it's all right. Take this in to prove it to her. She—she may never know whether it was broke or not.

MRS. PETERS: [*Takes the bottle, looks about for something to wrap it in; takes petticoat from the clothes brought from the other room, very nervously begins winding this around the bottle. In a false voice.*] My, it's a good thing the men couldn't hear us. Wouldn't they just laugh! Getting all stirred up over a little thing like a—dead canary. As if that could have anything to do with—with—wouldn't they *laugh!*

[*The men are heard coming down stairs.*]

MRS. HALE: [*Under her breath.*] Maybe they would—maybe they wouldn't.

COUNTY ATTORNEY: No, Peters, it's all perfectly clear except a reason for doing it. But you know juries when it comes to women. If there was some definite thing. Something to show—something to make a story about—a thing that would connect up with this strange way of doing it—

[*The women's eyes meet for an instant. Enter* HALE *from outer door.*]

HALE: Well, I've got the team around. Pretty cold out there.

COUNTY ATTORNEY: I'm going to stay here a while by myself. [*To the* SHERIFF.] You can send Frank out for me, can't you? I want to go over everything. I'm not satisfied that we can't do better.

SHERIFF: Do you want to see what Mrs. Peters is going to take in?

[*The* LAWYER *goes to the table, picks up the apron, laughs.*]

COUNTY ATTORNEY: Oh, I guess they're not very dangerous things the ladies have picked out. [*Moves a few things about, disturbing the quilt pieces which cover the box. Steps back.*] No, Mrs. Peters doesn't need supervising. For that matter, a sheriff's wife is married to the law. Ever think of it that way, Mrs. Peters?

MRS. PETERS: Not—just that way.

SHERIFF: [*Chuckling.*] Married to the law. [*Moves toward the other room.*] I just want you to come in here a minute, George. We ought to take a look at these windows.

COUNTY ATTORNEY: [*Scoffingly.*] Oh, windows!

SHERIFF: We'll be right out, Mr. Hale.

[HALE *goes outside. The* SHERIFF *follows the* COUNTY ATTORNEY *into the other room. Then* MRS. HALE *rises, hands tight together, looking intensely at* MRS. PETERS, *whose eyes make a slow turn, finally meeting* MRS. HALE'*s. A moment* MRS. HALE *holds her, then her own eyes point the way to where the box is concealed. Suddenly* MRS. PETERS *throws back quilt pieces and tries to put the box in the bag she is wearing. It is too big. She opens box, starts to take bird out, cannot touch it, goes to pieces, stands there helpless. Sound of a knob turning in the other room.* MRS. HALE *snatches the box and puts it in the pocket of her big coat. Enter* COUNTY ATTORNEY *and* SHERIFF.]

COUNTY ATTORNEY: [*Facetiously.*] Well, Henry, at least we found out that she was not going to quilt it. She was going to—what is it you call it, ladies?

MRS. HALE: [*Her hand against her pocket.*] We call it—knot it, Mr. Henderson.

CURTAIN

1920

HENRIK IBSEN

Hedda Gabler[1]

CHARACTERS

GEORGE TESMAN, *research graduate in cultural history*
HEDDA, *his wife*
MISS JULIANA TESMAN, *his aunt*
MRS. ELVSTED
JUDGE BRACK
EILERT LOEVBORG
BERTHA, *a maid*

The action takes place in TESMAN'S *villa in the fashionable quarter of town.*

ACT I

SCENE: A *large drawing room, handsomely and tastefully furnished; decorated in dark colors. In the rear wall is a broad open doorway, with curtains drawn back to either side. It leads to a smaller room, decorated in the same style as the*

1. Translated by Michael Meyer.

drawing room. In the right-hand wall of the drawing room, a folding door leads out to the hall. The opposite wall, on the left, contains french windows, also with curtains drawn back on either side. Through the glass we can see part of a verandah, and trees in autumn colors. Downstage stands an oval table, covered by a cloth and surrounded by chairs. Downstage right, against the wall, is a broad stove tiled with dark porcelain; in front of it stand a high-backed armchair, a cushioned footrest, and two footstools. Upstage right, in an alcove, is a corner sofa, with a small, round table. Downstage left, a little away from the wall, is another sofa. Upstage of the french windows, a piano. On either side of the open doorway in the rear wall stand what-nots holding ornaments of terra cotta and majolica. Against the rear wall of the smaller room can be seen a sofa, a table, and a couple of chairs. Above this sofa hangs the portrait of a handsome old man in general's uniform. Above the table a lamp hangs from the ceiling, with a shade of opalescent, milky glass. All round the drawing room bunches of flowers stand in vases and glasses. More bunches lie on the tables. The floors of both rooms are covered with thick carpets. Morning light. The sun shines in through the french windows.

MISS JULIANA TESMAN, *wearing a hat and carrying a parasol, enters from the hall, followed by* BERTHA, *who is carrying a bunch of flowers wrapped in paper.* MISS TESMAN *is about sixty-five, of pleasant and kindly appearance. She is neatly but simply dressed in grey outdoor clothes.* BERTHA, *the maid, is rather simple and rustic-looking. She is getting on in years.*

MISS TESMAN: [*Stops just inside the door, listens, and says in a hushed voice.*] No, bless my soul! They're not up yet.

BERTHA: [*Also in hushed tones.*] What did I tell you, miss? The boat didn't get in till midnight. And when they did turn up—Jesus, miss, you should have seen all the things Madam made me unpack before she'd go to bed!

MISS TESMAN: Ah, well. Let them have a good lie in. But let's have some nice fresh air waiting for them when they do come down. [*Goes to the french windows and throws them wide open.*]

BERTHA: [*Bewildered at the table, the bunch of flowers in her hand.*] I'm blessed if there's a square inch left to put anything. I'll have to let it lie here, miss. [*Puts it on the piano.*]

MISS TESMAN: Well, Bertha dear, so now you have a new mistress. Heaven knows it nearly broke my heart to have to part with you.

BERTHA: [*Snivels.*] What about me, Miss Juju? How do you suppose I felt? After all the happy years I've spent with you and Miss Rena?

MISS TESMAN: We must accept it bravely, Bertha. It was the only way. George needs you to take care of him. He could never manage without you. You've looked after him ever since he was a tiny boy.

BERTHA: Oh, but Miss Juju, I can't help thinking about Miss Rena, lying there all helpless, poor dear. And that new girl! She'll never learn the proper way to handle an invalid.

MISS TESMAN: Oh, I'll manage to train her. I'll do most of the work myself, you know. You needn't worry about my poor sister, Bertha dear.

BERTHA: But Miss Juju, there's another thing. I'm frightened Madam may not find me suitable.

MISS TESMAN: Oh, nonsense, Bertha. There may be one or two little things to begin with——

BERTHA: She's a real lady. Wants everything just so.

MISS TESMAN: But of course she does! General Gabler's daughter! Think of what she was accustomed to when the General was alive. You remember how we used to see her out riding with her father? In that long black skirt? With the feather in her hat?

BERTHA: Oh, yes, miss. As if I could forget! But, Lord! I never dreamed I'd live to see a match between her and Master Georgie.

MISS TESMAN: Neither did I. By the way, Bertha, from now on you must stop calling him Master Georgie. You must say: Dr. Tesman.

BERTHA: Yes, Madam said something about that too. Last night—the moment they'd set foot inside the door. Is it true, then, miss?

MISS TESMAN: Indeed it is. Just imagine, Bertha, some foreigners have made him a doctor.[2] It happened while they were away. I had no idea till he told me when they got off the boat.

BERTHA: Well, I suppose there's no limit to what he won't become. He's that clever. I never thought he'd go in for hospital work, though.

MISS TESMAN: No, he's not that kind of doctor. [*Nods impressively.*] In any case, you may soon have to address him by an even grander title.

BERTHA: You don't say! What might that be, miss?

MISS TESMAN: [*Smiles.*] Ah! If you only knew! [*Moved.*] Dear God, if only poor dear Joachim could rise out of his grave and see what his little son has grown into! [*Looks round.*] But Bertha, why have you done this? Taken the chintz covers off all the furniture!

BERTHA: Madam said I was to. Can't stand chintz covers on chairs, she said.

MISS TESMAN: But surely they're not going to use this room as a parlor?

BERTHA: So I gathered, miss. From what Madam said. He didn't say anything. The Doctor.

[GEORGE TESMAN *comes into the rear room, from the right, humming, with an open, empty traveling bag in his hand. He is about thirty-three, of medium height and youthful appearance, rather plump, with an open, round, contented face, and fair hair and beard. He wears spectacles, and is dressed in comfortable, indoor clothes.*]

MISS TESMAN: Good morning! Good morning, George!

TESMAN: [*In open doorway.*] Auntie Juju! Dear Auntie Juju! [*Comes forward and shakes her hand.*] You've come all the way out here! And so early! What?

MISS TESMAN: Well, I had to make sure you'd settled in comfortably.

TESMAN: But you can't have had a proper night's sleep.

MISS TESMAN: Oh, never mind that.

TESMAN: We were so sorry we couldn't give you a lift. But you saw how it was—

2. Awarded him a doctoral degree.

Hedda had so much luggage—and she insisted on having it all with her.

MISS TESMAN: Yes, I've never seen so much luggage.

BERTHA: [*To* TESMAN.] Shall I go and ask Madam if there's anything I can lend her a hand with?

TESMAN: Er—thank you, Bertha; no, you needn't bother. She says if she wants you for anything she'll ring.

BERTHA: [*Over to right.*] Oh. Very good.

TESMAN: Oh, Bertha—take this bag, will you?

BERTHA: [*Takes it.*] I'll put it in the attic. [*Goes out into the hall.*]

TESMAN: Just fancy, Auntie Juju, I filled that whole bag with notes for my book. You know, it's really incredible what I've managed to find rooting through those archives. By Jove! Wonderful old things no one even knew existed——

MISS TESMAN: I'm sure you didn't waste a single moment of your honeymoon, George dear.

TESMAN: No, I think I can truthfully claim that. But, Auntie Juju, do take your hat off. Here. Let me untie it for you. What?

MISS TESMAN: [*As he does so.*] Oh dear, oh dear! It's just as if you were still living at home with us.

TESMAN: [*Turns the hat in his hand and looks at it.*] I say! What a splendid new hat!

MISS TESMAN: I bought it for Hedda's sake.

TESMAN: For Hedda's sake? What?

MISS TESMAN: So that Hedda needn't be ashamed of me, in case we ever go for a walk together.

TESMAN: [*Pats her cheek.*] You still think of everything, don't you, Auntie Juju? [*Puts the hat down on a chair by the table.*] Come on, let's sit down here on the sofa. And have a little chat while we wait for Hedda.

[*They sit. She puts her parasol in the corner of the sofa.*]

MISS TESMAN: [*Clasps both his hands and looks at him.*] Oh, George, it's so wonderful to have you back, and be able to see you with my own eyes again! Poor dear Joachim's own son!

TESMAN: What about me! It's wonderful for me to see you again, Auntie Juju. You've been a mother to me. And a father, too.

MISS TESMAN: You'll always keep a soft spot in your heart for your old aunties, won't you, George dear?

TESMAN: I suppose Auntie Rena's no better? What?

MISS TESMAN: Alas, no. I'm afraid she'll never get better, poor dear. She's lying there just as she has for all these years. Please God I may be allowed to keep her for a little longer. If I lost her I don't know what I'd do. Especially now I haven't you to look after.

TESMAN: [*Pats her on the back.*] There, there, there!

MISS TESMAN: [*With a sudden change of mood.*] Oh but George, fancy you being a married man! And to think it's you who've won Hedda Gabler! The beautiful Hedda Gabler! Fancy! She was always so surrounded by admirers.

TESMAN: [*Hums a little and smiles contentedly.*] Yes, I suppose there are quite a few people in this town who wouldn't mind being in my shoes. What?

MISS TESMAN: And what a honeymoon! Five months! Nearly six.

TESMAN: Well, I've done a lot of work, you know. All those archives to go through. And I've had to read lots of books.

MISS TESMAN: Yes, dear, of course. [*Lowers her voice confidentially.*] But tell me, George—haven't you any—any extra little piece of news to give me?

TESMAN: You mean, arising out of the honeymoon?

MISS TESMAN: Yes.

TESMAN: No, I don't think there's anything I didn't tell you in my letters. My doctorate, of course—but I told you about that last night, didn't I?

MISS TESMAN: Yes, yes, I didn't mean that kind of thing. I was just wondering—are you—are you expecting——?

TESMAN: Expecting what?

MISS TESMAN: Oh, come on George, I'm your old aunt!

TESMAN: Well actually—yes, I am expecting something.

MISS TESMAN: I knew it!

TESMAN: You'll be happy to hear that before very long I expect to become a professor.

MISS TESMAN: Professor?

TESMAN: I think I may say that the matter has been decided. But, Auntie Juju, you know about this.

MISS TESMAN: [*Gives a little laugh.*] Yes, of course. I'd forgotten. [*Changes her tone.*] But we were talking about your honeymoon. It must have cost a dreadful amount of money, George?

TESMAN: Oh well, you know, that big research grant I got helped a good deal.

MISS TESMAN: But how on earth did you manage to make it do for two?

TESMAN: Well, to tell the truth it was a bit tricky. What?

MISS TESMAN: Especially when one's traveling with a lady. A little bird tells me that makes things very much more expensive.

TESMAN: Well, yes, of course it does make things a little more expensive. But Hedda has to do things in style, Auntie Juju. I mean, she has to. Anything less grand wouldn't have suited her.

MISS TESMAN: No, no, I suppose not. A honeymoon abroad seems to be the vogue nowadays. But tell me, have you had time to look round the house?

TESMAN: You bet. I've been up since the crack of dawn.

MISS TESMAN: Well, what do you think of it?

TESMAN: Splendid. Absolutely splendid. I'm only wondering what we're going to do with those two empty rooms between that little one and Hedda's bedroom.

MISS TESMAN: [*Laughs slyly.*] Ah, George dear, I'm sure you'll manage to find some use for them—in time.

TESMAN: Yes, of course, Auntie Juju, how stupid of me. You're thinking of my books. What?

MISS TESMAN: Yes, yes, dear boy. I was thinking of your books.

TESMAN: You know, I'm so happy for Hedda's sake that we've managed to get this house. Before we became engaged she often used to say this was the only house in town she felt she could really bear to live in. It used to belong to Mrs. Falk—you know, the Prime Minister's widow.

MISS TESMAN: Fancy that! And what a stroke of luck it happened to come into the market. Just as you'd left on your honeymoon.

TESMAN: Yes, Auntie Juju, we've certainly had all the luck with us. What?

MISS TESMAN: But, George dear, the expense! It's going to make a dreadful hole in your pocket, all this.

TESMAN: [*A little downcast.*] Yes, I—I suppose it will, won't it?

MISS TESMAN: Oh, George, really!

TESMAN: How much do you think it'll cost? Roughly, I mean? What?

MISS TESMAN: I can't possibly say till I see the bills.

TESMAN: Well, luckily Judge Brack's managed to get it on very favorable terms. He wrote and told Hedda so.

MISS TESMAN: Don't you worry, George dear. Anyway I've stood security for all the furniture and carpets.

TESMAN: Security? But dear, sweet Auntie Juju, how could you possibly stand security?

MISS TESMAN: I've arranged a mortgage on our annuity.

TESMAN: [*Jumps up.*] What? On your annuity? And—Auntie Rena's?

MISS TESMAN: Yes. Well, I couldn't think of any other way.

TESMAN: [*Stands in front of her.*] Auntie Juju, have you gone completely out of your mind? That annuity's all you and Auntie Rena have.

MISS TESMAN: All right, there's no need to get so excited about it. It's a pure formality, you know. Judge Brack told me so. He was so kind as to arrange it all for me. A pure formality; those were his very words.

TESMAN: I dare say. All the same——

MISS TESMAN: Anyway, you'll have a salary of your own now. And, good heavens, even if we did have to fork out a little—tighten our belts for a week or two—why, we'd be happy to do so for your sake.

TESMAN: Oh, Auntie Juju! Will you never stop sacrificing yourself for me?

MISS TESMAN: [*Gets up and puts her hands on his shoulders.*] What else have I to live for but to smooth your road a little, my dear boy? You've never had any mother or father to turn to. And now at last we've achieved our goal. I won't deny we've had our little difficulties now and then. But now, thank the good Lord, George dear, all your worries are past.

TESMAN: Yes, it's wonderful really how everything's gone just right for me.

MISS TESMAN: Yes! And the enemies who tried to bar your way have been struck down. They have been made to bite the dust. The man who was your most dangerous rival has had the mightiest fall. And now he's lying there in the pit he dug for himself, poor misguided creature.

TESMAN: Have you heard any news of Eilert? Since I went away?

MISS TESMAN: Only that he's said to have published a new book.

TESMAN: What! Eilert Loevborg? You mean—just recently? What?

MISS TESMAN: So they say. I don't imagine it can be of any value, do you? When your new book comes out, that'll be another story. What's it going to be about?

TESMAN: The domestic industries of Brabant[3] in the Middle Ages.

MISS TESMAN: Oh, George! The things you know about!

TESMAN: Mind you, it may be some time before I actually get down to writing it. I've made these very extensive notes, and I've got to file and index them first.

MISS TESMAN: Ah, yes! Making notes; filing and indexing; you've always been wonderful at that. Poor dear Joachim was just the same.

TESMAN: I'm looking forward so much to getting down to that. Especially now I've a home of my own to work in.

MISS TESMAN: And above all, now that you have the girl you set your heart on, George dear.

TESMAN: [*Embraces her.*] Oh, yes, Auntie Juju, yes! Hedda's the loveliest thing of all! [*Looks towards the doorway.*] I think I hear her coming. What?

[HEDDA *enters the rear room from the left, and comes into the drawing room. She is a woman of twenty-nine. Distinguished, aristocratic face and figure. Her complexion is pale and opalescent. Her eyes are steel-grey, with an expression of cold, calm serenity. Her hair is of a handsome auburn color, but is not especially abundant. She is dressed in an elegant, somewhat loose-fitting morning gown.*]

MISS TESMAN: [*Goes to greet her.*] Good morning, Hedda dear! Good morning!

HEDDA: [*Holds out her hand.*] Good morning, dear Miss Tesman. What an early hour to call. So kind of you.

MISS TESMAN. [*Seems somewhat embarrassed.*] And has the young bride slept well in her new home?

HEDDA: Oh—thank you, yes. Passably well.

TESMAN: [*Laughs.*] Passably. I say, Hedda, that's good! When I jumped out of bed, you were sleeping like a top.

HEDDA: Yes. Fortunately. One has to accustom oneself to anything new, Miss Tesman. It takes time. [*Looks left.*] Oh, that maid's left the french windows open. This room's flooded with sun.

MISS TESMAN. [*Goes towards the windows.*] Oh—let me close them.

HEDDA: No, no, don't do that. Tesman dear, draw the curtains. This light's blinding me.

TESMAN: [*At the windows.*] Yes, yes, dear. There, Hedda, now you've got shade and fresh air.

HEDDA: This room needs fresh air. All these flowers—But my dear Miss Tesman, won't you take a seat?

MISS TESMAN: No, really not, thank you. I just wanted to make sure you have everything you need. I must see about getting back home. My poor dear sister will be waiting for me.

3. Prosperous duchy (1190–1477), now divided between Belgium and the Netherlands.

TESMAN: Be sure to give her my love, won't you? Tell her I'll run over and see her later today.

MISS TESMAN: Oh yes, I'll tell her that. Oh, George——[*Fumbles in the pocket of her skirt.*] I almost forgot. I've brought something for you.

TESMAN. What's that, Auntie Juju? What?

MISS TESMAN: [*Pulls out a flat package wrapped in newspaper and gives it to him.*] Open and see, dear boy.

TESMAN: [*Opens the package.*] Good heavens! Auntie Juju, you've kept them! Hedda, this is really very touching. What?

HEDDA: [*By the what-nots, on the right.*] What is it, Tesman?

TESMAN: My old shoes! My slippers, Hedda!

HEDDA: Oh, them. I remember you kept talking about them on our honeymoon.

TESMAN: Yes, I missed them dreadfully. [*Goes over to her.*] Here, Hedda, take a look.

HEDDA: [*Goes away towards the stove.*] Thanks, I won't bother.

TESMAN: [*Follows her.*] Fancy, Hedda, Auntie Rena's embroidered them for me. Despite her being so ill. Oh, you can't imagine what memories they have for me.

HEDDA: [*By the table.*] Not for me.

MISS TESMAN: No, Hedda's right there, George.

TESMAN: Yes, but I thought since she's one of the family now——

HEDDA: [*Interrupts.*] Tesman, we really can't go on keeping this maid.

MISS TESMAN: Not keep Bertha?

TESMAN: What makes you say that, dear? What?

HEDDA: [*Points.*] Look at that! She's left her old hat lying on the chair.

TESMAN: [*Appalled, drops his slippers on the floor.*] But, Hedda——!

HEDDA: Suppose someone came in and saw it?

TESMAN: But Hedda—that's Auntie Juju's hat.

HEDDA: Oh?

MISS TESMAN: [*Picks up the hat.*] Indeed it's mine. And it doesn't happen to be old, Hedda dear.

HEDDA: I didn't look at it very closely, Miss Tesman.

MISS TESMAN: [*Tying on the hat.*] As a matter of fact, it's the first time I've worn it. As the good Lord is my witness.

TESMAN: It's very pretty, too. Really smart.

MISS TESMAN: Oh, I'm afraid it's nothing much really. [*Looks round.*] My parasol? Ah, here it is. [*Takes it.*] This is mine, too. [*Murmurs.*] Not Bertha's.

TESMAN: A new hat and a new parasol! I say, Hedda, fancy that!

HEDDA: Very pretty and charming.

TESMAN: Yes, isn't it? What? But Auntie Juju, take a good look at Hedda before you go. Isn't she pretty and charming?

MISS TESMAN: Dear boy, there's nothing new in that. Hedda's been a beauty ever since the day she was born. [*Nods and goes right.*]

TESMAN: [*Follows her.*] Yes, but have you noticed how strong and healthy she's looking? And how she's filled out since we went away?

MISS TESMAN: [*Stops and turns.*] Filled out?

HEDDA: [*Walks across the room.*] Oh, can't we forget it?

TESMAN: Yes, Auntie Juju—you can't see it so clearly with that dress on. But I've good reason to know——

HEDDA: [*By the french windows, impatiently.*] You haven't good reason to know anything.

TESMAN: It must have been the mountain air up there in the Tyrol——

HEDDA: [*Curtly, interrupts him.*] I'm exactly the same as when I went away.

TESMAN: You keep on saying so. But you're not. I'm right, aren't I, Auntie Juju?

MISS TESMAN: [*Has folded her hands and is gazing at her.*] She's beautiful—beautiful. Hedda is beautiful. [*Goes over to* HEDDA, *takes her head between her hands, draws it down and kisses her hair.*] God bless and keep you, Hedda Tesman. For George's sake.

HEDDA: [*Frees herself politely.*] Oh—let me go, please.

MISS TESMAN: [*Quietly, emotionally.*] I shall come see you both every day.

TESMAN: Yes, Auntie Juju, please do. What?

MISS TESMAN: Good-bye! Good-bye!

[*She goes out into the hall.* TESMAN *follows her. The door remains open.* TESMAN *is heard sending his love to* AUNT RENA *and thanking* MISS TESMAN *for his slippers. Meanwhile* HEDDA *walks up and down the room raising her arms and clenching her fists as though in desperation. Then she throws aside the curtains from the french windows and stands there, looking out. A few moments later,* TESMAN *returns and closes the door behind him.*]

TESMAN: [*Picks up his slippers from the floor.*] What are you looking at, Hedda?

HEDDA: [*Calm and controlled again.*] Only the leaves. They're so golden. And withered.

TESMAN: [*Wraps up the slippers and lays them on the table.*] Well, we're in September now.

HEDDA: [*Restless again.*] Yes. We're already into September.

TESMAN: Auntie Juju was behaving rather oddly, I thought, didn't you? Almost as though she was in church or something. I wonder what came over her. Any idea?

HEDDA: I hardly know her. Does she often act like that?

TESMAN: Not to the extent she did today.

HEDDA: [*Goes away from the french windows.*] Do you think she was hurt by what I said about the hat?

TESMAN: Oh, I don't think so. A little at first, perhaps——

HEDDA: But what a thing to do, throw her hat down in someone's drawing room. People don't do such things.

TESMAN: I'm sure Auntie Juju doesn't do it very often.

HEDDA: Oh well, I'll make it up with her.

TESMAN: Oh Hedda, would you?

HEDDA: When you see them this afternoon invite her to come out here this evening.

TESMAN: You bet I will! I say, there's another thing which would please her enormously.

HEDDA: Oh?

TESMAN: If you could bring yourself to call her Auntie Juju. For my sake, Hedda? What?

HEDDA: Oh no, really Tesman, you mustn't ask me to do that. I've told you so once before. I'll try to call her Aunt Juliana. That's as far as I'll go.

TESMAN: [*After a moment.*] I say, Hedda, is anything wrong? What?

HEDDA: I'm just looking at my old piano. It doesn't really go with all this.

TESMAN: As soon as I start getting my salary we'll see about changing it.

HEDDA: No, no, don't let's change it. I don't want to part with it. We can move it into that little room and get another one to put in here.

TESMAN: [*A little downcast.*] Yes, we—might do that.

HEDDA: [*Picks up the bunch of flowers from the piano.*] These flowers weren't here when we arrived last night.

TESMAN: I expect Auntie Juju brought them.

HEDDA: Here's a card. [*Takes it out and reads.*] "Will come back later today." Guess who it's from?

TESMAN: No idea. Who? What?

HEDDA: It says: "Mrs. Elvsted."

TESMAN: No, really? Mrs. Elvsted! She used to be Miss Rysing, didn't she?

HEDDA: Yes. She was the one with that irritating hair she was always showing off. I hear she used to be an old flame of yours.

TESMAN: [*Laughs.*] That didn't last long. Anyway, that was before I got to know you, Hedda. By Jove, fancy her being in town!

HEDDA: Strange she should call. I only knew her at school.

TESMAN: Yes, I haven't seen her for—oh, heaven knows how long. I don't know how she manages to stick it out up there in the north. What?

HEDDA: [*Thinks for a moment, then says suddenly.*] Tell me, Tesman, doesn't he live somewhere up in those parts? You know—Eilert Loevborg?

TESMAN: Yes, that's right. So he does. [BERTHA *enters from the hall.*]

BERTHA. She's here again, madam. The lady who came and left the flowers. [*Points.*] The ones you're holding.

HEDDA: Oh, is she? Well, show her in.

[BERTHA *opens the door for* MRS. ELVSTED *and goes out.* MRS. ELVSTED *is a delicately built woman with gentle, attractive features. Her eyes are light blue, large, and somewhat prominent, with a frightened, questioning expression. Her hair is extremely fair, almost flaxen, and is exceptionally wavy and abundant. She is two or three years younger than* HEDDA. *She is wearing a dark visiting dress, in good taste but not quite in the latest fashion.*]

HEDDA: [*Goes cordially to greet her.*] Dear Mrs. Elvsted, good morning. How delightful to see you again after all this time.

MRS. ELVSTED: [*Nervously, trying to control herself.*] Yes, it's many years since we met.

TESMAN: And since *we* met. What?

HEDDA: Thank you for your lovely flowers.

MRS. ELVSTED: Oh, please—I wanted to come yesterday afternoon. But they told me you were away——

TESMAN: You've only just arrived in town, then? What?

MRS. ELVSTED: I got here yesterday, around midday. Oh, I became almost desperate when I heard you weren't here.

HEDDA: Desperate? Why?

TESMAN: My dear Mrs. Rysing—Elvsted——

HEDDA: There's nothing wrong, I hope?

MRS. ELVSTED: Yes, there is. And I don't know anyone else here whom I can turn to.

HEDDA: [*Puts the flowers down on the table.*] Come and sit with me on the sofa——

MRS. ELVSTED: Oh, I feel too restless to sit down.

HEDDA: You must. Come along, now. [*She pulls* MRS. ELVSTED *down on to the sofa and sits beside her.*]

TESMAN: Well? Tell us, Mrs.—er——

HEDDA: Has something happened at home?

MRS. ELVSTED: Yes—that is, yes and no. Oh, I do hope you won't misunderstand me——

HEDDA: Then you'd better tell us the whole story, Mrs. Elvsted.

TESMAN: That's why you've come. What?

MRS. ELVSTED: Yes—yes, it is. Well, then—in case you don't already know—Eilert Loevborg is in town.

HEDDA: Loevborg here?

TESMAN: Eilert back in town? By Jove, Hedda, did you hear that?

HEDDA: Yes, of course I heard.

MRS. ELVSTED: He's been here a week. A whole week! In this city. Alone. With all those dreadful people——

HEDDA: But my dear Mrs. Elvsted, what concern is he of yours?

MRS. ELVSTED: [*Gives her a frightened look and says quickly.*] He's been tutoring the children.

HEDDA: Your children?

MRS. ELVSTED: My husband's. I have none.

HEDDA: Oh, you mean your stepchildren.

MRS. ELVSTED: Yes.

TESMAN: [*Gropingly.*] But was he sufficiently—I don't know how to put it—sufficiently regular in his habits to be suited to such a post? What?

MRS. ELVSTED: For the past two to three years he has been living irreproachably.

TESMAN: You don't say! By Jove, Hedda, hear that?

HEDDA: I hear.

MRS. ELVSTED: Quite irreproachably, I assure you. In every respect. All the same—in this big city—with money in his pockets—I'm so dreadfully frightened something may happen to him.

TESMAN: But why didn't he stay up there with you and your husband?

MRS. ELVSTED: Once his book had come out, he became restless.

TESMAN: Oh, yes—Auntie Juju said he's brought out a new book.

MRS. ELVSTED: Yes, a big new book about the history of civilization. A kind of general survey. It came out a fortnight ago. Everyone's been buying it and reading it—it's created a tremendous stir——

TESMAN: Has it really? It must be something he's dug up, then.

MRS. ELVSTED: You mean from the old days?

TESMAN: Yes.

MRS. ELVSTED: No, he's written it all since he came to live with us.

TESMAN: Well, that's splendid news, Hedda. Fancy that!

MRS. ELVSTED: Oh, yes! If only he can go on like this!

HEDDA: Have you met him since you came here?

MRS. ELVSTED: No, not yet, I had such dreadful difficulty finding his address. But this morning I managed to track him down at last.

HEDDA: [*Looks searchingly at her.*] I must say I find it a little strange that your husband—hm——

MRS. ELVSTED: [*Starts nervously.*] My husband! What do you mean?

HEDDA: That he should send you all the way here on an errand of this kind. I'm surprised he didn't come himself to keep an eye on his friend.

MRS. ELVSTED: Oh, no, no—my husband hasn't the time. Besides, I—er—wanted to do some shopping here.

HEDDA: [*With a slight smile.*] Ah. Well, that's different.

MRS. ELVSTED: [*Gets up quickly, restlessly.*] Please, Mr. Tesman, I beg you—be kind to Eilert Loevborg if he comes here. I'm sure he will. I mean, you used to be such good friends in the old days. And you're both studying the same subject, as far as I can understand. You're in the same field, aren't you?

TESMAN: Well, we used to be, anyway.

MRS. ELVSTED: Yes—so I beg you earnestly, do please, please, keep an eye on him. Oh, Mr. Tesman, do promise me you will.

TESMAN: I shall be only too happy to do so, Mrs. Rysing.

HEDDA: Elvsted.

TESMAN: I'll do everything for Eilert that lies in my power. You can rely on that.

MRS. ELVSTED: Oh, how good and kind you are! [*Presses his hands.*] Thank you, thank you, thank you. [*Frightened.*] My husband's so fond of him, you see.

HEDDA: [*Gets up.*] You'd better send him a note, Tesman. He may not come to you of his own accord.

TESMAN: Yes, that'd probably be the best plan, Hedda. What?

HEDDA: The sooner the better. Why not do it now?

MRS. ELVSTED: [*Pleadingly.*] Oh yes, if only you would!

TESMAN: I'll do it this very moment. Do you have his address, Mrs.—er—Elvsted?

MRS. ELVSTED: Yes. [*Takes a small piece of paper from her pocket and gives it to him.*]

TESMAN: Good, good. Right, well I'll go inside and——[*Looks round.*] Where are my slippers? Oh yes, here. [*Picks up the package and is about to go.*]

HEDDA: Try to sound friendly. Make it a nice long letter.

TESMAN: Right, I will.

MRS. ELVSTED: Please don't say anything about my having seen you.

TESMAN: Good heavens no, of course not. What? [*Goes out through the rear room to the right.*]

HEDDA: [*Goes over to* MRS. ELVSTED, *smiles, and says softly.*] Well! Now we've killed two birds with one stone.

MRS. ELVSTED: What do you mean?
HEDDA: Didn't you realize I wanted to get him out of the room?
MRS. ELVSTED: So that he could write the letter?
HEDDA: And so that I could talk to you alone.
MRS. ELVSTED: [*Confused*.] About this?
HEDDA: Yes, about this.
MRS. ELVSTED: [*In alarm*.] But there's nothing more to tell, Mrs. Tesman. Really there isn't.
HEDDA: Oh, yes there is. There's a lot more. I can see that. Come along, let's sit down and have a little chat.

[*She pushes* MRS. ELVSTED *down into the armchair by the stove and seats herself on one of the footstools*.]

MRS. ELVSTED: [*Looks anxiously at her watch*] Really, Mrs. Tesman, I think I ought to be going now.
HEDDA: There's no hurry. Well? How are things at home?
MRS. ELVSTED: I'd rather not speak about that.
HEDDA: But my dear, you can tell me. Good heavens, we were at school together.
MRS. ELVSTED: Yes, but you were a year senior to me. Oh, I used to be terribly frightened of you in those days.
HEDDA: Frightened of me?
MRS. ELVSTED: Yes, terribly frightened. Whenever you met me on the staircase you used to pull my hair.
HEDDA: No, did I?
MRS. ELVSTED: Yes. And once you said you'd burn it all off.
HEDDA: Oh, that was only in fun.
MRS. ELVSTED: Yes, but I was so silly in those days. And then afterwards—I mean, we've drifted so far apart. Our backgrounds were so different.
HEDDA: Well, now we must try to drift together again. Now listen. When we were at school we used to call each other by our Christian names——
MRS. ELVSTED: No, I'm sure you're mistaken.
HEDDA: I'm sure I'm not. I remember it quite clearly. Let's tell each other our secrets, as we used to in the old days. [*Moves closer on her footstool*.] There, now. [*Kisses her on the cheek*.] You must call me Hedda.
MRS. ELVSTED: [*Squeezes her hands and pats them*.] Oh, you're so kind. I'm not used to people being so nice to me.
HEDDA: Now, now, now. And I shall call you Tora, the way I used to.
MRS. ELVSTED: My name is Thea.
HEDDA: Yes, of course. Of course. I meant Thea. [*Looks at her sympathetically*.] So you're not used to kindness, Thea? In your own home?
MRS. ELVSTED: Oh, if only I had a home! But I haven't. I've never had one.
HEDDA: [*Looks at her for a moment*.] I thought that was it.
MRS. ELVSTED: [*Stares blankly and helplessly*.] Yes—yes—yes.
HEDDA: I can't remember exactly now, but didn't you first go to Mr. Elvsted as a housekeeper?
MRS. ELVSTED: Governess, actually. But his wife—at the time, I mean—she was

an invalid, and had to spend most of her time in bed. So I had to look after the house too.

HEDDA: But in the end, you became mistress of the house.

MRS. ELVSTED: [*Sadly.*] Yes, I did.

HEDDA: Let me see. Roughly how long ago was that?

MRS. ELVSTED: When I got married, you mean?

HEDDA: Yes.

MRS. ELVSTED: About five years.

HEDDA: Yes; it must be about that.

MRS. ELVSTED: Oh, those five years! Especially that last two or three. Oh, Mrs. Tesman, if you only knew——

HEDDA: [*Slaps her hand gently.*] Mrs. Tesman? Oh, Thea!

MRS. ELVSTED: I'm sorry, I'll try to remember. Yes—if you had any idea——

HEDDA: [*Casually.*] Eilert Loevborg's been up here too, for about three years, hasn't he?

MRS. ELVSTED: [*Looks at her uncertainly.*] Eilert Loevborg? Yes, he has.

HEDDA: Did you know him before? When you were here?

MRS. ELVSTED: No, not really. That is—I knew him by name, of course.

HEDDA: But up there, he used to visit you?

MRS. ELVSTED: Yes, he used to come and see us every day. To give the children lessons. I found I couldn't do that as well as manage the house.

HEDDA: I'm sure you couldn't. And your husband——? I suppose being a magistrate he has to be away from home a good deal?

MRS. ELVSTED: Yes. You see, Mrs.—— you see, Hedda, he has to cover the whole district.

HEDDA: [*Leans against the arm of* MRS. ELVSTED'S *chair.*] Poor, pretty little Thea! Now you must tell me the whole story. From beginning to end.

MRS. ELVSTED: Well—what do you want to know?

HEDDA: What kind of a man is your husband, Thea? I mean, as a person. Is he kind to you?

MRS. ELVSTED: [*Evasively.*] I'm sure he does his best to be.

HEDDA: I only wonder if he isn't too old for you. There's more than twenty years between you, isn't there?

MRS. ELVSTED: [*Irritably.*] Yes, there's that too. Oh, there are so many things. We're different in every way. We've nothing in common. Nothing whatever.

HEDDA: But he loves you, surely? In his own way?

MRS. ELVSTED: Oh, I don't know. I think he just finds me useful. And then I don't cost much to keep. I'm cheap.

HEDDA: Now you're being stupid.

MRS. ELVSTED: [*Shakes her head.*] It can't be any different. With him. He doesn't love anyone except himself. And perhaps the children—a little.

HEDDA: He must be fond of Eilert Loevborg, Thea.

MRS. ELVSTED: [*Looks at her.*] Eilert Loevborg? What makes you think that?

HEDDA: Well, if he sends you all the way down here to look for him——[*Smiles almost imperceptibly.*] Besides, you said so yourself to Tesman.

MRS. ELVSTED: [*With a nervous twitch.*] Did I? Oh yes, I suppose I did. [*Impulsively, but keeping her voice low.*] Well, I might as well tell you the whole story. It's bound to come out sooner or later.

HEDDA: But my dear Thea——?

MRS. ELVSTED: My husband had no idea I was coming here.

HEDDA: What? Your husband didn't know?

MRS. ELVSTED: No, of course not. As a matter of fact, he wasn't even there. He was away at the assizes. Oh, I couldn't stand it any longer, Hedda! I just couldn't. I'd be so dreadfully lonely up there now.

HEDDA: Go on.

MRS. ELVSTED: So I packed a few things. Secretly. And went.

HEDDA: Without telling anyone?

MRS. ELVSTED: Yes. I caught the train and came straight here.

HEDDA: But my dear Thea! How brave of you!

MRS. ELVSTED: [*Gets up and walks across the room.*] Well, what else could I do?

HEDDA: But what do you suppose your husband will say when you get back?

MRS. ELVSTED: [*By the table, looks at her.*] Back there? To him?

HEDDA: Yes. Surely——?

MRS. ELVSTED: I shall never go back to him.

HEDDA: [*Gets up and goes closer.*] You mean you've left your home for good?

MRS. ELVSTED: Yes. I didn't see what else I could do.

HEDDA: But to do it so openly!

MRS. ELVSTED: Oh, it's no use trying to keep a thing like that secret.

HEDDA: But what do you suppose people will say?

MRS. ELVSTED: They can say what they like. [*Sits sadly, wearily on the sofa.*] I had to do it.

HEDDA: [*After a short silence.*] What do you intend to do now? How are you going to live?

MRS. ELVSTED: I don't know. I only know that I must live wherever Eilert Loevborg is. If I am to go on living.

HEDDA: [*Moves a chair from the table, sits on it near* MRS. ELVSTED *and strokes her hands.*] Tell me, Thea, how did this—friendship between you and Eilert Loevborg begin?

MRS. ELVSTED: Oh, it came about gradually. I developed a kind of—power over him.

HEDDA: Oh?

MRS. ELVSTED: He gave up his old habits. Not because I asked him to. I'd never have dared to do that. I suppose he just noticed I didn't like that kind of thing. So he gave it up.

HEDDA: [*Hides a smile.*] So you've made a new man of him. Clever little Thea!

MRS. ELVSTED: Yes—anyway, he says I have. And he's made a —sort of—real person of me. Taught me to think—and to understand all kinds of things.

HEDDA: Did he give you lessons too?

MRS. ELVSTED: Not exactly lessons. But he talked to me. About—oh, you've no idea—so many things! And then he let me work with him. Oh, it was wonderful. I was so happy to be allowed to help him.

HEDDA: Did he allow you to help him!

MRS. ELVSTED: Yes. Whenever he wrote anything we always—did it together.

HEDDA: Like good pals?

MRS. ELVSTED: [*Eagerly.*] Pals! Yes—why, Hedda, that's exactly the word he used! Oh, I ought to feel so happy. But I can't. I don't know if it will last.

HEDDA: You don't seem very sure of him.

MRS. ELVSTED: [*Sadly.*] Something stands between Eilert Loevberg and me. The shadow of another woman.

HEDDA: Who can that be?

MRS. ELVSTED: I don't know. Someone he used to be friendly with in—in the old days. Someone he's never been able to forget.

HEDDA: What has he told you about her?

MRS. ELVSTED: Oh, he only mentioned her once, casually.

HEDDA: Well! What did he say?

MRS. ELVSTED: He said when he left her she tried to shoot him with a pistol.

HEDDA: [*Cold, controlled.*] What nonsense. People don't do such things. The kind of people we know.

MRS. ELVSTED: No, I think it must have been that red-haired singer he used to—

HEDDA: Ah yes, very probably.

MRS. ELVSTED: I remember they used to say she always carried a loaded pistol.

HEDDA: Well then, it must be her.

MRS. ELVSTED: But Hedda, I hear she's come back, and is living here. Oh, I'm so desperate——!

HEDDA: [*Glances toward the rear room.*] Ssh! Tesman's coming. [*Gets up and whispers.*] Thea, we mustn't breathe a word about this to anyone.

MRS. ELVSTED: [*Jumps up.*] Oh, no, no! Please don't!

[GEORGE TESMAN *appears from the right in the rear room with a letter in his hand, and comes into the drawing room.*]

TESMAN: Well, here's my little epistle all signed and sealed.

HEDDA: Good. I think Mrs. Elvsted wants to go now. Wait a moment—I'll see you as far as the garden gate.

TESMAN: Er—Hedda, do you think Bertha could deal with this?

HEDDA: [*Takes the letter.*] I'll give her instructions.

[BERTHA *enters from the hall.*]

BERTHA: Judge Brack is here and asks if he may pay his respects to Madam and the Doctor.

HEDDA: Yes, ask him to be so good as to come in. And—wait a moment—drop this letter in the post box.

BERTHA: [*Takes the letter.*] Very good, madam.

[*She opens the door for* JUDGE BRACK, *and goes out.* JUDGE BRACK *is forty-five; rather short, but well-built, and elastic in his movements. He has a roundish face with an aristocratic profile. His hair, cut short, is still almost black, and is carefully barbered. Eyes lively and humorous. Thick eyebrows. His moustache is also thick, and is trimmed square at the ends. He is wearing outdoor clothes which are elegant but a little too youthful for him. He has a monocle in one eye; now and then he lets it drop.*]

BRACK: [*Hat in hand, bows.*] May one presume to call so early?

HEDDA: One may presume.

TESMAN: [*Shakes his hand.*] You're welcome here any time. Judge Brack—Mrs. Rysing.

[HEDDA *sighs.*]

BRACK: [*Bows.*] Ah—charmed——

HEDDA: [*Looks at him and laughs.*] What fun to be able to see you by daylight for once, Judge.

BRACK: Do I look—different?

HEDDA: Yes. A little younger, I think.

BRACK: Obliged.

TESMAN: Well, what do you think of Hedda? What? Doesn't she look well? Hasn't she filled out——?

HEDDA: Oh, do stop it. You ought to be thanking Judge Brack for all the inconvenience he's put himself to——

BRACK: Nonsense, it was a pleasure——

HEDDA: You're a loyal friend. But my other friend is pining to get away. Au revoir, Judge. I won't be a minute.

[*Mutual salutations.* MRS. ELVSTED *and* HEDDA *go out through the hall.*]

BRACK: Well, is your wife satisfied with everything?

TESMAN: Yes, we can't thank you enough. That is—we may have to shift one or two things around, she tells me. And we're short of one or two little items we'll have to purchase.

BRACK: Oh? Really?

TESMAN: But you musn't worry your head about that. Hedda says she'll get what's needed. I say, why don't we sit down? What?

BRACK: Thanks, just for a moment. [*Sits at the table.*] There's something I'd like to talk to you about, my dear Tesman.

TESMAN: Oh? Ah yes, of course. [*Sits.*] After the feast comes the reckoning. What?

BRACK: Oh, never mind about the financial side—there's no hurry about that. Though I could wish we'd arranged things a little less palatially.

TESMAN: Good heavens, that'd never have done. Think of Hedda, my dear chap. You know her. I couldn't possibly ask her to live like a suburban housewife.

BRACK: No, no—that's just the problem.

TESMAN: Anyway, it can't be long now before my nomination[4] comes through.

BRACK: Well, you know, these things often take time.

TESMAN: Have you heard any more news? What?

BRACK: Nothing definite. [*Changing the subject.*] Oh, by the way, I have one piece of news for you.

4. To a professorship at the university.

TESMAN: What?

BRACK: Your old friend Eilert Loevborg is back in town.

TESMAN: I know that already.

BRACK: Oh? How did you hear that?

TESMAN: She told me. That lady who went out with Hedda.

BRACK: I see. What was her name? I didn't catch it.

TESMAN: Mrs. Elvsted.

BRACK: Oh, the magistrate's wife. Yes, Loevborg's been living up near them, hasn't he?

TESMAN: I'm delighted to hear he's become a decent human being again.

BRACK: Yes, so they say.

TESMAN: I gather he's published a new book, too. What?

BRACK: Indeed he has.

TESMAN: I hear it's created rather a stir.

BRACK: Quite an unusual stir.

TESMAN: I say, isn't that splendid news! He's such a gifted chap—and I was afraid he'd gone to the dogs for good.

BRACK: Most people thought he had.

TESMAN: But I can't think what he'll do now. How on earth will he manage to make ends meet? What?

[*As he speaks his last words,* HEDDA *enters from the hall.*]

HEDDA: [*To* BRACK, *laughs slightly scornfully.*] Tesman is always worrying about making ends meet.

TESMAN: We were talking about poor Eilert Loevborg, Hedda dear.

HEDDA: [*Gives him a quick look.*] Oh, were you? [*Sits in the armchair by the stove and asks casually.*] Is he in trouble?

TESMAN: Well, he must have run through his inheritance long ago by now. And he can't write a new book every year. What? So I'm wondering what's going to become of him.

BRACK: I may be able to enlighten you there.

TESMAN: Oh?

BRACK: You mustn't forget he has relatives who wield a good deal of influence.

TESMAN: Relatives? Oh, they've quite washed their hands of him, I'm afraid.

BRACK: They used to regard him as the hope of the family.

TESMAN: Used to, yes. But he's put an end to that.

HEDDA: Who knows? [*With a little smile.*] I hear the Elvsteds have made a new man of him.

BRACK: And then this book he's just published——

TESMAN: Well, let's hope they find something for him. I've just written him a note. Oh, by the way, Hedda, I asked him to come over and see us this evening.

BRACK: But my dear chap, you're coming to me this evening. My bachelor party. You promised me last night when I met you at the boat.

HEDDA: Had you forgotten, Tesman?

TESMAN: Good heavens, yes, I'd quite forgotten.

BRACK: Anyway, you can be quite sure he won't turn up here.

TESMAN: Why do you think that? What?

BRACK: [*A little unwillingly, gets up and rests his hands on the back of his chair.*] My dear Tesman—and you, too, Mrs. Tesman—there's something I feel you ought to know.

TESMAN: Concerning Eilert?

BRACK: Concerning him and you.

TESMAN: Well, my dear Judge, tell us, please!

BRACK: You must be prepared for your nomination not to come through quite as quickly as you hope and expect.

TESMAN: [*Jumps up uneasily.*] Is anything wrong? What?

BRACK: There's a possibility that the appointment may be decided by competition——

TESMAN: Competition! By Jove, Hedda, fancy that!

HEDDA: [*Leans further back in her chair.*] Ah! How interesting!

TESMAN: But who else——? I say, you don't mean——?

BRACK: Exactly. By competition with Eilert Loevborg.

TESMAN: [*Clasps his hands in alarm.*] No, no, but this is inconceivable! It's absolutely impossible! What?

BRACK: Hm. We may find it'll happen, all the same.

TESMAN: No, but—Judge Brack, they couldn't be so inconsiderate toward me! [*Waves his arms.*] I mean, by Jove, I—I'm a married man! It was on the strength of this that Hedda and I *got* married! We ran up some pretty hefty debts. And borrowed money from Auntie Juju! I mean, good heavens, they practically promised me the appointment. What?

BRACK: Well, well, I'm sure you'll get it. But you'll have to go through a competition.

HEDDA: [*Motionless in her armchair.*] How exciting, Tesman. It'll be a kind of duel, by Jove.

TESMAN: My dear Hedda, how can you take it so lightly?

HEDDA: [*As before.*] I'm not. I can't wait to see who's going to win.

BRACK: In any case, Mrs. Tesman, it's best you should know how things stand. I mean before you commit yourself to these little items I hear you're threatening to purchase.

HEDDA: I can't allow this to alter my plans.

BRACK: Indeed? Well, that's your business. Good-bye. [*To* TESMAN.] I'll come and collect you on the way home from my afternoon walk.

TESMAN: Oh, yes, yes. I'm sorry, I'm all upside down just now.

HEDDA: [*Lying in her chair, holds out her hand.*] Good-bye, Judge. See you this afternoon.

BRACK: Thank you. Good-bye, good-bye.

TESMAN: [*Sees him to the door.*] Good-bye, my dear Judge. You will excuse me, won't you?

[JUDGE BRACK *goes out through the hall.*]

TESMAN: [*Pacing up and down.*] Oh, Hedda! One oughtn't to go plunging off on wild adventures. What?

HEDDA: [*Looks at him and smiles.*] Like you're doing?

TESMAN: Yes. I mean, there's no denying it, it was a pretty big adventure to go off and get married and set up house merely on expectation.

HEDDA: Perhaps you're right.

TESMAN: Well, anyway, we have our home, Hedda. By Jove, yes. The home we dreamed of. And set our hearts on. What?

HEDDA: [*Gets up slowly, wearily.*] You agreed that we should enter society. And keep open house. That was the bargain.

TESMAN: Yes. Good heavens, I was looking forward to it all so much. To seeing you play hostess to a select circle! By Jove! What? Ah, well, for the time being we shall have to make do with each other's company, Hedda. Perhaps have Auntie Juju in now and then. Oh dear, this wasn't all what you had in mind——

HEDDA: I won't be able to have a liveried footman. For a start.

TESMAN: Oh no, we couldn't possibly afford a footman.

HEDDA: And that thoroughbred horse you promised me——

TESMAN: [*Fearfully.*] Thoroughbred horse!

HEDDA: I mustn't even think of that now.

TESMAN: Heaven forbid!

HEDDA: [*Walks across the room.*] Ah, well. I still have one thing left to amuse myself with.

TESMAN: [*Joyfully.*] Thank goodness for that. What's that, Hedda? What?

HEDDA: [*In the open doorway, looks at him with concealed scorn.*] My pistols, George darling.

TESMAN: [*Alarmed.*] Pistols!

HEDDA: [*Her eyes cold.*] General Gabler's pistols. [*She goes into the rear room and disappears.*]

TESMAN: [*Runs to the doorway and calls after her.*] For heaven's sake, Hedda dear, don't touch those things. They're dangerous. Hedda—please—for my sake! What?

ACT II

SCENE—*The same as in Act I except that the piano has been removed and an elegant little writing table, with a bookcase, stands in its place. By the sofa on the left a smaller table has been placed. Most of the flowers have been removed.* MRS. ELVSTED's *bouquet stands on the larger table, downstage. It is afternoon.*

HEDDA, *dressed to receive callers, is alone in the room. She is standing by the open french windows, loading a revolver. The pair to it is lying in an open pistol case on the writing table.*

HEDDA: [*Looks down into the garden and calls.*] Good afternoon, Judge.

BRACK: [*In the distance, below.*] Afternoon, Mrs. Tesman.

HEDDA: [*Raises the pistol and takes aim.*] I'm going to shoot you, Judge Brack.

BRACK: [*Shouts from below.*] No no, no! Don't aim that thing at me!

HEDDA: This'll teach you to enter houses by the back door. [*Fires.*]

BRACK: [*Below.*] Have you gone completely out of your mind?

HEDDA: Oh dear! Did I hit you?

BRACK: [*Still outside.*] Stop playing these silly tricks.
HEDDA: All right, Judge. Come along in.

[JUDGE BRACK, *dressed for a bachelor party, enters through the french windows. He has a light overcoat on his arm.*]

BRACK: For God's sake! Haven't you stopped fooling around with those things yet? What are you trying to hit?
HEDDA: Oh, I was just shooting at the sky.
BRACK: [*Takes the pistol gently from her hand.*] By your leave, ma'am. [*Looks at it.*] Ah, yes—I know this old friend well. [*Looks around.*] Where's the case? Oh, yes. [*Puts the pistol in the case and closes it.*] That's enough of that little game for today.
HEDDA: Well, what on earth *am* I to do?
BRACK: You haven't had any visitors?
HEDDA: [*Closes the french windows.*] Not one. I suppose the best people are all still in the country.
BRACK: Your husband isn't home yet?
HEDDA: [*Locks the pistol case away in a drawer of the writing table.*] No. The moment he'd finished eating he ran off to his aunties. He wasn't expecting you so early.
BRACK: Ah, why didn't I think of that? How stupid of me.
HEDDA: [*Turns her head and looks at him.*] Why stupid?
BRACK: I'd have come a little sooner.
HEDDA: [*Walks across the room.*] There'd have been no one to receive you. I've been in my room since lunch, dressing.
BRACK: You haven't a tiny crack in the door through which we might have negotiated?
HEDDA: You forgot to arrange one.
BRACK: Another stupidity.
HEDDA: Well, we'll have to sit down here. And wait. Tesman won't be back for some time.
BRACK: Sad. Well, I'll be patient.

[HEDDA *sits on the corner of the sofa.* BRACK *puts his coat over the back of the nearest chair and seats himself, keeping his hat in his hand. Short pause. They look at each other.*]

HEDDA: Well?
BRACK: [*In the same tone of voice.*] Well?
HEDDA: I asked first.
BRACK: [*Leans forward slightly.*] Yes, well, now we can enjoy a nice, cosy little chat—Mrs. Hedda.
HEDDA: [*Leans further back in her chair.*] It seems such ages since we had a talk. I don't count last night or this morning.
BRACK: You mean: *à deux?*
HEDDA: Mm—yes. That's roughly what I meant.

BRACK: I've been longing so much for you to come home.

HEDDA: So have I.

BRACK: You? Really, Mrs. Hedda? And I thought you were having such a wonderful honeymoon.

HEDDA: Oh, yes. Wonderful!

BRACK: But your husband wrote such ecstatic letters.

HEDDA: He! Oh, yes! He thinks life has nothing better to offer than rooting around in libraries and copying old pieces of parchment, or whatever it is he does.

BRACK: [*A little maliciously.*] Well, that *is* his life. Most of it, anyway.

HEDDA: Yes, I know. Well, it's all right for him. But for me! Oh no, my dear Judge. I've been bored to death.

BRACK: [*Sympathetically.*] Do you mean that? Seriously?

HEDDA: Yes. Can you imagine? Six whole months without ever meeting a single person who was one of us, and to whom I could talk about the kind of things we talk about.

BRACK: Yes, I can understand. I'd miss that, too.

HEDDA: That wasn't the worst, though.

BRACK: What was?

HEDDA: Having to spend every minute of one's life with—with the same person.

BRACK: [*Nods.*] Yes. What a thought! Morning; noon; and——

HEDDA: [*Coldly.*] As I said: every minute of one's life.

BRACK: I stand corrected. But dear Tesman is such a clever fellow, I should have thought one ought to be able——

HEDDA: Tesman is only interested in one thing, my dear Judge. His special subject.

BRACK: True.

HEDDA: And people who are only interested in one thing don't make the most amusing company. Not for long, anyway.

BRACK: Not even when they happen to be the person one loves?

HEDDA: Oh, don't use that sickly, stupid word.

BRACK: [*Starts.*] But, Mrs. Hedda——!

HEDDA: [*Half laughing, half annoyed.*] You just try it, Judge. Listening to the history of civilization morning, noon and——

BRACK: [*Corrects her.*] Every minute of one's life.

HEDDA: All right. Oh, and those domestic industries of Brabant in the Middle Ages! That really is beyond the limit.

BRACK: [*Looks at her searchingly.*] But, tell me—if you feel like this why on earth did you—? Ha——

HEDDA: Why on earth did I marry George Tesman?

BRACK: If you like to put it that way.

HEDDA: Do you think it so very strange?

BRACK: Yes—and no, Mrs. Hedda.

HEDDA: I'd danced myself tired, Judge. I felt my time was up——[*Gives a slight shudder.*] No, I mustn't say that. Or even think it.

BRACK: You've no rational cause to think it.

HEDDA: Oh—cause, cause——[*Looks searchingly at him.*] After all, George Tesman—well, I mean, he's a very respectable man.

BRACK: Very respectable, sound as a rock. No denying that.

HEDDA: And there's nothing exactly ridiculous about him. Is there?

BRACK: Ridiculous? No-no, I wouldn't say that.

HEDDA: Mm. He's very clever at collecting material and all that, isn't he? I mean, he may go quite far in time.

BRACK: [*Looks at her a little uncertainly.*] I thought you believed, like everyone else, that he would become a very prominent man.

HEDDA: [*Looks tired.*] Yes, I did. And when he came and begged me on his bended knees to be allowed to love and to cherish me, I didn't see why I shouldn't let him.

BRACK: No, well—if one looks at it like that——

HEDDA: It was more than my other admirers were prepared to do, Judge dear.

BRACK: [*Laughs.*] Well, I can't answer for the others. As far as I myself am concerned, you know I've always had a considerable respect for the institution of marriage. As an institution.

HEDDA: [*Lightly.*] Oh, I've never entertained any hopes of you.

BRACK: All I want is to have a circle of friends whom I can trust, whom I can help with advice or—or by any other means, and into whose houses I may come and go as a—trusted friend.

HEDDA: Of the husband?

BRACK: [*Bows.*] Preferably, to be frank, of the wife. And of the husband too, of course. Yes, you know, this kind of—triangle is a delightful arrangement for all parties concerned.

HEDDA: Yes, I often longed for a third person while I was away. Oh, those hours we spent alone in railway compartments——

BRACK: Fortunately your honeymoon is now over.

HEDDA: [*Shakes her head.*] There's a long way still to go. I've only reached a stop on the line.

BRACK: Why not jump out and stretch your legs a little, Mrs. Hedda?

HEDDA: I'm not the jumping sort.

BRACK: Aren't you?

HEDDA: No. There's always someone around who——

BRACK: [*Laughs.*] Who looks at one's legs?

HEDDA: Yes. Exactly.

BRACK: Well, but surely——

HEDDA: [*With a gesture of rejection.*] I don't like it. I'd rather stay where I am. Sitting in the compartment. *À deux.*

BRACK: But suppose a third person were to step into the compartment?

HEDDA: That would be different.

BRACK: A trusted friend—someone who understood——

HEDDA: And was lively and amusing——

BRACK: And interested in—more subjects than one——

HEDDA: [*Sighs audibly.*] Yes, that'd be a relief.

BRACK: [*Hears the front door open and shut.*] The triangle is completed.
HEDDA: [*Half under breath.*] And the train goes on.

[GEORGE TESMAN, *in grey walking dress with a soft felt hat, enters from the hall. He has a number of paper-covered books under his arm and in his pockets.*]

TESMAN: [*Goes over to the table by the corner sofa.*] Phew! It's too hot to be lugging all this around. [*Puts the books down.*] I'm positively sweating, Hedda. Why, hullo, hullo! You here already, Judge? What? Bertha didn't tell me.
BRACK: [*Gets up.*] I came in through the garden.
HEDDA: What are all those books you've got there?
TESMAN: [*Stands glancing through them.*] Oh, some new publications dealing with my special subject. I had to buy them.
HEDDA. Your special subject?
BRACK: His special subject, Mrs. Tesman.

[BRACK *and* HEDDA *exchange a smile.*]

HEDDA: Haven't you collected enough material on your special subject?
TESMAN: My dear Hedda, one can never have too much. One must keep abreast of what other people are writing.
HEDDA: Yes. Of course.
TESMAN: [*Rooting among the books.*] Look—I bought a copy of Eilert Loevborg's new book, too. [*Holds it out to her.*] Perhaps you'd like to have a look at it, Hedda? What?
HEDDA. No, thank you. Er—yes, perhaps I will, later.
TESMAN: I glanced through it on my way home.
BRACK: What's your opinion—as a specialist on the subject?
TESMAN: I'm amazed how sound and balanced it is. He never used to write like that. [*Gathers his books together.*] Well, I must get down to these at once. I can hardly wait to cut the pages.[5] Oh, I've got to change, too. [*To* BRACK.] We don't have to be off just yet, do we? What?
BRACK: Heavens, no. We've plenty of time yet.
TESMAN: Good, I needn't hurry, then. [*Goes with his books, but stops and turns in the doorway.*] Oh, by the way, Hedda, Auntie Juju won't be coming to see you this evening.
HEDDA: Won't she? Oh—the hat, I suppose.
TESMAN: Good heavens, no. How could you think such a thing of Auntie Juju? Fancy——! No, Auntie Rena's very ill.
HEDDA: She always is.
TESMAN: Yes, but today she's been taken really bad.
HEDDA: Oh, then it's quite understandable that the other one should want to stay with her. Well, I shall have to swallow my disappointment.

5. Books used to be sold with the pages folded but uncut as they came from the printing press; the owner had to cut the pages in order to read the book.

TESMAN: You can't imagine how happy Auntie Juju was in spite of everything. At your looking so well after the honeymoon!

HEDDA: [*Half beneath her breath, as she rises.*] Oh, these everlasting aunts!

TESMAN: What?

HEDDA: [*Goes over to the french windows.*] Nothing.

TESMAN: Oh. All right. [*Goes into the rear room and out of sight.*]

BRACK: What was that about the hat?

HEDDA: Oh, something that happened with Miss Tesman this morning. She'd put her hat down on a chair. [*Looks at him and smiles.*] And I pretended to think it was the servant's.

BRACK: [*Shakes his head.*] But my dear Mrs. Hedda, how could you do such a thing? To that poor old lady?

HEDDA: [*Nervously, walking across the room.*] Sometimes a mood like that hits me. And I can't stop myself. [*Throws herself down in the armchair by the stove.*] Oh, I don't know how to explain it.

BRACK: [*Behind her chair.*] You're not really happy. That's the answer.

HEDDA: [*Stares ahead of her.*] Why on earth should I be happy? Can you give me a reason?

BRACK: Yes. For one thing you've got the home you always wanted.

HEDDA: [*Looks at him.*] You really believe that story?

BRACK: You mean it isn't true?

HEDDA: Oh, yes, it's partly true.

BRACK: Well?

HEDDA: It's true I got Tesman to see me home from parties last summer——

BRACK: It was a pity my home lay in another direction.

HEDDA: Yes. Your interests lay in another direction, too.

BRACK: [*Laughs.*] That's naughty of you, Mrs. Hedda. But to return to you and Tesman——

HEDDA: Well, we walked past this house one evening. And poor Tesman was fidgeting in his boots trying to find something to talk about. I felt sorry for the great scholar——

BRACK: [*Smiles incredulously.*] Did you? Hm.

HEDDA: Yes, honestly I did. Well, to help him out of his misery, I happened to say quite frivolously how much I'd love to live in this house.

BRACK: Was that all?

HEDDA: That evening, yes.

BRACK: But—afterwards?

HEDDA: Yes. My little frivolity had its consequences, my dear Judge.

BRACK: Our little frivolities do. Much too often, unfortunately.

HEDDA: Thank you. Well, it was our mutual admiration for the late Prime Minister's house that brought George Tesman and me together on common ground. So we got engaged, and we got married, and we went on our honeymoon, and—Ah well, Judge, I've—made my bed and I must lie in it, I was about to say.

BRACK: How utterly fantastic! And you didn't really care in the least about the house?

HEDDA: God knows I didn't.

BRACK: Yes, but now that we've furnished it so beautifully for you?

HEDDA: Ugh—all the rooms smell of lavender and dried roses. But perhaps Auntie Juju brought that in.

BRACK: [*Laughs.*] More likely the Prime Minister's widow, rest her soul.

HEDDA: Yes, it's got the odor of death about it. It reminds me of the flowers one has worn at a ball—the morning after. [*Clasps her hands behind her neck, leans back in the chair and looks up at him.*] Oh, my dear Judge, you've no idea how hideously bored I'm going to be out here.

BRACK: Couldn't you find some kind of occupation, Mrs. Hedda? Like your husband?

HEDDA: Occupation? That'd interest me?

BRACK: Well—preferably.

HEDDA: God knows what. I've often thought——[*Breaks off.*] No, that wouldn't work either.

BRACK: Who knows? Tell me about it.

HEDDA: I was thinking—if I could persuade Tesman to go into politics, for example.

BRACK: [*Laughs.*] Tesman! No, honestly, I don't think he's quite cut out to be a politician.

HEDDA: Perhaps not. But if I could persuade him to have a go at it?

BRACK: What satisfaction would that give you? If he turned out to be no good? Why do you want to make him do that?

HEDDA: Because I'm bored. [*After a moment.*] You feel there's absolutely no possibility of Tesman becoming Prime Minister, then?

BRACK: Well, you know, Mrs. Hedda, for one thing he'd have to be pretty well off before he could become that.

HEDDA: [*Gets up impatiently.*] There you are! [*Walks across the room.*] It's this wretched poverty that makes life so hateful. And ludicrous. Well, it is!

BRACK: I don't think that's the real cause.

HEDDA: What is, then?

BRACK: Nothing really exciting has ever happened to you.

HEDDA: Nothing serious, you mean?

BRACK: Call it that if you like. But now perhaps it may.

HEDDA: [*Tosses her head.*] Oh, you're thinking of this competition for that wretched professorship? That's Tesman's affair. I'm not going to waste my time worrying about that.

BRACK: Very well, let's forget about that then. But suppose you were to find yourself faced with what people call—to use the conventional phrase—the most solemn of human responsibilities? [*Smiles.*] A new responsibility, little Mrs. Hedda.

HEDDA: [*Angrily.*] Be quiet! Nothing like that's going to happen.

BRACK: [*Warily.*] We'll talk about it again in a year's time. If not earlier.

HEDDA: [*Curtly.*] I've no leanings in that direction, Judge. I don't want any—responsibilities.

BRACK: But surely you must feel some inclination to make use of that—natural talent which every woman—

HEDDA: [*Over by the french windows.*] Oh, be quiet, I say! I often think there's only one thing for which I have any natural talent.

BRACK: [*Goes closer.*] And what is that, if I may be so bold as to ask?

HEDDA: [*Stands looking out.*] For boring myself to death. Now you know. [*Turns, looks toward the rear room and laughs.*] Talking of boring, here comes the Professor.

BRACK: [*Quietly, warningly.*] Now, now, now, Mrs. Hedda!

[GEORGE TESMAN, *in evening dress, with gloves and hat in his hand, enters through the rear room from the right.*]

TESMAN: Hedda, hasn't any message come from Eilert? What?

HEDDA: No.

TESMAN: Ah, then we'll have him here presently. You wait and see.

BRACK: You really think he'll come?

TESMAN: Yes, I'm almost sure he will. What you were saying about him this morning is just gossip.

BRACK: Oh?

TESMAN: Yes. Auntie Juju said she didn't believe he'd ever dare to stand in my way again. Fancy that!

BRACK: Then everything in the garden's lovely.

TESMAN: [*Puts his hat, with his gloves in it, on a chair, right.*] Yes, but you really must let me wait for him as long as possible.

BRACK: We've plenty of time. No one'll be turning up at my place before seven or half past.

TESMAN: Ah, then we can keep Hedda company a little longer. And see if he turns up. What?

HEDDA: [*Picks up* BRACK's *coat and hat and carries them over to the corner sofa.*] And if the worst comes to the worst, Mr. Loevborg can sit here and talk to me.

BRACK: [*Offering to take his things from her.*] No, please. What do you mean by "if the worst comes to the worst"?

HEDDA: If he doesn't want to go with you and Tesman.

TESMAN: [*Looks doubtfully at her.*] I say, Hedda, do you think it'll be all right for him to stay here with you? What? Remember Auntie Juju isn't coming.

HEDDA: Yes, but Mrs. Elvsted is. The three of us can have a cup of tea together.

TESMAN: Ah, that'll be all right then.

BRACK: [*Smiles.*] It's probably the safest solution as far as he's concerned.

HEDDA: Why?

BRACK: My dear Mrs. Tesman, you always say of my little bachelor parties that they should be attended only by men of the strongest principles.

HEDDA: But Mr. Loevborg is a man of principle now. You know what they say about a reformed sinner——

[BERTHA *enters from the hall.*]

BERTHA: Madam, there's a gentleman here who wants to see you——

HEDDA: Ask him to come in.

TESMAN: [*Quietly.*] I'm sure it's him. By Jove. Fancy that!

[EILERT LOEVBORG *enters from the hall. He is slim and lean, of the same age as* TESMAN, *but looks older and somewhat haggard. His hair and beard are of a blackish-brown; his face is long and pale, but with a couple of reddish patches on his cheekbones. He is dressed in an elegant and fairly new black suit, and carries black gloves and a top hat in his hand. He stops just inside the door and bows abruptly. He seems somewhat embarrassed.*]

TESMAN: [*Goes over and shakes his hand.*] My dear Eilert! How grand to see you again after all these years!

EILERT LOEVBORG: [*Speaks softly.*] It was good of you to write, George. [*Goes nearer to* HEDDA.] May I shake hands with you, too, Mrs. Tesman?

HEDDA: [*Accepts his hand.*] Delighted to see you, Mr. Loevborg. [*With a gesture.*] I don't know if you two gentlemen——

LOEVBORG: [*Bows slightly.*] Judge Brack, I believe.

BRACK: [*Also with a slight bow.*] Correct. We—met some years ago——

TESMAN: [*Puts his hands on* LOEVBORG'S *shoulders.*] Now you're to treat this house just as though it were your own home, Eilert. Isn't that right, Hedda? I hear you've decided to settle here again? What?

LOEVBORG: Yes, I have.

TESMAN: Quite understandable. Oh, by the bye—I've just bought your new book. Though to tell the truth I haven't found time to read it yet.

LOEVBORG: You needn't bother.

TESMAN: Oh? Why?

LOEVBORG: There's nothing much in it.

TESMAN: By Jove, fancy hearing that from you!

BRACK: But everyone's praising it.

LOEVBORG: That was exactly what I wanted to happen. So I only wrote what I knew everyone would agree with.

BRACK: Very sensible.

TESMAN: Yes, but my dear Eilert——

LOEVBORG: I want to try to re-establish myself. To begin again—from the beginning.

TESMAN: [*A little embarrassed.*] Yes, I—er—suppose you do. What?

LOEVBORG: [*Smiles, puts down his hat and takes a package wrapped in paper from his coat pocket.*] But when this gets published—George Tesman—read it. This is my real book. The one in which I have spoken with my own voice.

TESMAN: Oh, really? What's it about?

LOEVBORG: It's the sequel.

TESMAN: Sequel? To what?

LOEVBORG: To the other book.

TESMAN: The one that's just come out?

LOEVBORG: Yes.

TESMAN: But my dear Eilert, that covers the subject right up to the present day.

LOEVBORG: It does. But this is about the future.

TESMAN: The future! But, I say, we don't know anything about that.

LOEVBORG: No. But there are one or two things that need to be said about it. [*Opens the package.*] Here, have a look.

TESMAN: Surely that's not your handwriting?

LOEVBORG: I dictated it. [*Turns the pages.*] It's in two parts. The first deals with the forces that will shape our civilization. [*Turns further on towards the end.*] And the second indicates the direction in which that civilization may develop.

TESMAN: Amazing! I'd never think of writing about anything like that.

HEDDA: [*By the french windows, drumming on the pane.*] No. You wouldn't.

LOEVBORG: [*Puts the pages back into their cover and lays the package on the table.*] I brought it because I thought I might possibly read you a few pages this evening.

TESMAN: I say, what a kind idea! Oh, but this evening——? [*Glances at* BRACK] I'm not quite sure whether——

LOEVBORG: Well, some other time, then. There's no hurry.

BRACK: The truth is, Mr. Loevborg, I'm giving a little dinner this evening. In Tesman's honor, you know.

LOEVBORG: [*Looks round for his hat.*] Oh—then I mustn't——

BRACK: No, wait a minute. Won't you do me the honor of joining us?

LOEVBORG: [*Curtly, with decision.*] No I can't. Thank you so much.

BRACK: Oh, nonsense. Do—please. There'll only be a few of us. And I can promise you we shall have some good sport, as Mrs. Hed—as Mrs. Tesman puts it.

LOEVBORG: I've no doubt. Nevertheless——

BRACK: You could bring your manuscript along and read it to Tesman at my place. I could lend you a room.

TESMAN: By Jove, Eilert, that's an idea. What?

HEDDA: [*Interposes.*] But Tesman, Mr. Loevborg doesn't want to go. I'm sure Mr. Loevborg would much rather sit here and have supper with me.

LOEVBORG: [*Looks at her.*] With you, Mrs. Tesman?

HEDDA: And Mrs. Elvsted.

LOEVBORG: Oh. [*Casually.*] I ran into her this afternoon.

HEDDA: Did you? Well, she's coming here this evening. So you really must stay, Mr. Loevborg. Otherwise she'll have no one to see her home.

LOEVBORG: That's true. Well—thank you, Mrs. Tesman, I'll stay then.

HEDDA: I'll just tell the servant.

[*She goes to the door which leads into the hall, and rings.* BERTHA *enters.* HEDDA *talks softly to her and points towards the rear room.* BERTHA *nods and goes out.*]

TESMAN: [*To* LOEVBORG, *as* HEDDA *does this.*] I say, Eilert. This new subject of yours—the—er—future—is that the one you're going to lecture about?

LOEVBORG: Yes.

TESMAN: They told me down at the bookshop that you're going to hold a series of lectures here during the autumn.

LOEVBORG: Yes, I am, I—hope you don't mind, Tesman.

TESMAN: Good heavens, no! But——?

LOEVBORG: I can quite understand it might queer your pitch a little.

TESMAN: [*Dejectedly.*] Oh well, I can't expect you to put them off for my sake.

LOEVBORG: I'll wait till your appointment's been announced.

TESMAN: You'll wait! But—but—aren't you going to compete with me for the post? What?

LOEVBORG: No. I only want to defeat you in the eyes of the world.

TESMAN: Good heavens! Then Auntie Juju was right after all! Oh, I knew it, I knew it! Hear that, Hedda? Fancy! Eilert *doesn't* want to stand in our way.

HEDDA: [*Curtly.*] Our? Leave me out of it, please.

[*She goes towards the rear room, where* BERTHA *is setting a tray with decanters and glasses on the table.* HEDDA *nods approval, and comes back into the drawing room.* BERTHA *goes out.*]

TESMAN: [*While this is happening.*] Judge Brack, what do you think about all this? What?

BRACK: Oh, I think honor and victory can be very splendid things——

TESMAN: Of course they can. Still——

HEDDA: [*Looks at* TESMAN *with a cold smile.*] You look as if you'd been hit by a thunderbolt.

TESMAN: Yes, I feel rather like it.

BRACK: There was a black cloud looming up, Mrs. Tesman. But it seems to have passed over.

HEDDA: [*Points toward the rear room.*] Well, gentlemen, won't you go in and take a glass of cold punch?

BRACK: [*Glances at his watch.*] A stirrup cup? Yes, why not?

TESMAN: An admirable suggestion, Hedda. Admirable! Oh, I feel so relieved!

HEDDA: Won't you have one, too, Mr. Loevborg?

LOEVBORG: No, thank you. I'd rather not.

BRACK: Great heavens, man, cold punch isn't poison. Take my word for it.

LOEVBORG: Not for everyone, perhaps.

HEDDA: I'll keep Mr. Loevborg company while you drink.

TESMAN: Yes, Hedda dear, would you?

[*He and* BRACK *go into the rear room, sit down, drink punch, smoke cigarettes and talk cheerfully during the following scene.* EILERT LOEVBORG *remains standing by the stove.* HEDDA *goes to the writing table.*]

HEDDA: [*Raising her voice slightly.*] I've some photographs I'd like to show you, if you'd care to see them. Tesman and I visited the Tyrol[6] on our way home.

[*She comes back with an album, places it on the table by the sofa and sits in the upstage corner of the sofa.* EILERT LOEVBORG *comes toward her, stops and looks at her. Then he takes a chair and sits down on her left, with his back toward the rear room.*]

6. Region in the Alps, now primarily in Austria, near the Italian border.

HEDDA: [*Opens the album.*] You see these mountains, Mr. Loevborg? That's the Ortler group. Tesman has written the name underneath. You see: "The Ortler Group near Meran."

LOEVBORG: [*Has not taken his eyes from her; says softly, slowly.*] Hedda—Gabler!

HEDDA: [*Gives him a quick glance.*] Ssh!

LOEVBORG: [*Repeats softly.*] Hedda Gabler!

HEDDA: [*Looks at the album.*] Yes, that used to be my name. When we first knew each other.

LOEVBORG: And from now on—for the rest of my life—I must teach myself never to say: Hedda Gabler.

HEDDA: [*Still turning the pages.*] Yes, you must. You'd better start getting into practice. The sooner the better.

LOEVBORG: [*Bitterly.*] Hedda Gabler married? And to George Tesman?

HEDDA: Yes. Well—that's life.

LOEVBORG: Oh, Hedda, Hedda! How could you throw yourself away like that?

HEDDA: [*Looks sharply at him.*] Stop it.

LOEVBORG: What do you mean?

[TESMAN *comes in and goes toward the sofa.*]

HEDDA: [*Hears him coming and says casually.*] And this, Mr. Loevborg, is the view from the Ampezzo valley. Look at those mountains. [*Glances affectionately up at* TESMAN.] What did you say those curious mountains were called, dear?

TESMAN: Let me have a look. Oh, those are the Dolomites.

HEDDA: Of course. Those are the Dolomites, Mr. Loevborg.

TESMAN: Hedda, I just wanted to ask you, can't we bring some punch in here? A glass for you, anyway. What?

HEDDA: Thank you, yes. And a biscuit or two, perhaps.

TESMAN: You wouldn't like a cigarette?

HEDDA: No.

TESMAN: Right.

[*He goes into the rear room and over to the right.* BRACK *is sitting there, glancing occasionally at* HEDDA *and* LOEVBORG.]

LOEVBORG: [*Softly, as before.*] Answer me, Hedda. How could you do it?

HEDDA: [*Apparently absorbed in the album.*] If you go on calling me Hedda I won't talk to you any more.

LOEVBORG: Mayn't I even when we're alone?

HEDDA: No. You can think it. But you mustn't say it.

LOEVBORG: Oh, I see. Because you love George Tesman.

HEDDA: [*Glances at him and smiles.*] Love? Don't be funny.

LOEVBORG: You don't love him?

HEDDA: I don't intend to be unfaithful to him. That's not what I want.

LOEVBORG: Hedda—just tell me one thing——

HEDDA: Ssh!

[TESMAN *enters from the rear room, carrying a tray.*]

TESMAN: Here we are! Here come the goodies! [*Puts the tray down on the table.*]

HEDDA: Why didn't you ask the servant to bring it in?

TESMAN: [*Fills the glasses.*] I like waiting on you, Hedda.

HEDDA: But you've filled both glasses. Mr. Loevborg doesn't want to drink.

TESMAN: Yes, but Mrs. Elvsted'll be here soon.

HEDDA: Oh yes, that's true. Mrs. Elvsted——

TESMAN: Had you forgotten her? What?

HEDDA: We're so absorbed with these photographs. [*Shows him one.*] You remember this little village?

TESMAN: Oh, that one down by the Brenner Pass. We spent a night there——

HEDDA: Yes, and met all those amusing people.

TESMAN: Oh yes, it was there, wasn't it? By Jove, if only we could have had you with us, Eilert! Ah, well. [*Goes back into the other room and sits down with* BRACK.]

LOEVBORG: Tell me one thing, Hedda.

HEDDA: Yes?

LOEVBORG: Didn't you love me either? Not—just a little?

HEDDA: Well now, I wonder? No, I think we were just good pals—Really good pals who could tell each other anything. [*Smiles.*] You certainly poured your heart out to me.

LOEVBORG: You begged me to.

HEDDA: Looking back on it, there was something beautiful and fascinating—and brave—about the way we told each other everything. That secret friendship no one else knew about.

LOEVBORG: Yes, Hedda, yes! Do you remember? How I used to come up to your father's house in the afternoon—and the General sat by the window and read his newspapers—with his back toward us——

HEDDA: And we sat on the sofa in the corner——

LOEVBORG: Always reading the same illustrated magazine——

HEDDA: We hadn't any photograph album.

LOEVBORG: Yes, Hedda. I regarded you as a kind of confessor. Told you things about myself which no one else knew about—then. Those days and nights of drinking and— Oh, Hedda, what power did you have to make me confess such things?

HEDDA: Power? You think I had some power over you?

LOEVBORG: Yes—I don't know how else to explain it. And all those—oblique questions you asked me——

HEDDA: You knew what they meant.

LOEVBORG: But that you could sit there and ask me such questions! So unashamedly——

HEDDA: I thought you said they were oblique.

LOEVBORG: Yes, but you asked them so unashamedly. That you could question me about—about that kind of thing!

HEDDA: You answered willingly enough.

LOEVBORG: Yes—that's what I can't understand—looking back on it. But tell me,

Hedda—what you felt for me—wasn't that—love? When you asked me those questions and made me confess my sins to you, wasn't it because you wanted to wash me clean?

HEDDA: No, not exactly.

LOEVBORG: Why did you do it, then?

HEDDA: Do you find it so incredible that a young girl, given the chance to do so without anyone knowing, should want to be allowed a glimpse into a forbidden world of whose existence she is supposed to be ignorant?

LOEVBORG: So that was it?

HEDDA: One reason. One reason—I think.

LOEVBORG: You didn't love me, then. You just wanted—knowledge. But if that was so, why did you break it off?

HEDDA: That was your fault.

LOEVBORG: It was you who put an end to it.

HEDDA: Yes, when I realized that our friendship was threatening to develop into something—something else. Shame on you, Eilert Loevborg! How could you abuse the trust of your dearest friend?

LOEVBORG: [*Clenches his fists.*] Oh, why didn't you do it? Why didn't you shoot me dead? As you threatened to?

HEDDA: I was afraid. Of the scandal.

LOEVBORG: Yes, Hedda. You're a coward at heart.

HEDDA: A dreadful coward. [*Changes her tone.*] Luckily for you. Well, now you've found consolation with the Elvsteds.

LOEVBORG: I know what Thea's been telling you.

HEDDA: I dare say you told her about us.

LOEVBORG: Not a word. She's too silly to understand that kind of thing.

HEDDA: Silly?

LOEVBORG: She's silly about that kind of thing.

HEDDA: And I am a coward. [*Leans closer to him, without looking him in the eyes, and says quietly.*] But let me tell you something. Something you don't know.

LOEVBORG: [*Tensely.*] Yes?

HEDDA: My failure to shoot you wasn't my worst act of cowardice that evening.

LOEVBORG: [*Looks at her for a moment, realizes her meaning and whispers passionately.*] Oh, Hedda! Hedda Gabler! Now I see what was behind those questions. Yes! It wasn't knowledge you wanted! It was life!

HEDDA: [*Flashes a look at him and says quietly.*] Take care! Don't you delude yourself!

[*It has begun to grow dark.* BERTHA, *from outside, opens the door leading into the hall.*]

HEDDA: [*Closes the album with a snap and cries, smiling.*] Ah, at last! Come in, Thea dear!

[MRS. ELVSTED *enters from the hall, in evening dress. The door is closed behind her.*]

HEDDA: [*On the sofa, stretches out her arms toward her.*] Thea darling, I thought you were never coming!

[MRS. ELVSTED *makes a slight bow to the gentlemen in the rear room as she passes the open doorway, and they to her. Then she goes to the table and holds out her hand to* HEDDA. EILERT LOEVBORG *has risen from his chair. He and* MRS. ELVSTED *nod silently to each other.*]

MRS. ELVSTED: Perhaps I ought to go in and say a few words to your husband?

HEDDA: Oh, there's no need. They're happy by themselves. They'll be going soon.

MRS. ELVSTED: Going?

HEDDA. Yes, they're off on a spree this evening.

MRS. ELVSTED: [*Quickly, to* LOEVBORG.] You're not going with them?

LOEVBORG: No.

HEDDA: Mr. Loevborg is staying here with us.

MRS. ELVSTED: [*Takes a chair and is about to sit down beside him.*] Oh, how nice it is to be here!

HEDDA: No, Thea darling, not there. Come over here and sit beside me. I want to be in the middle.

MRS. ELVSTED: Yes, just as you wish.

[*She goes right the table and sits on the sofa, on* HEDDA'S *right.* LOEVBORG *sits down again in his chair.*]

LOEVBORG: [*After a short pause, to* HEDDA.] Isn't she lovely to look at?

HEDDA: [*Strokes her hair gently.*] Only to look at?

LOEVBORG: Yes. We're just good pals. We trust each other implicitly. We can talk to each other quite unashamedly.

HEDDA: No need to be oblique?

MRS. ELVSTED: [*Nestles close to* HEDDA *and says quietly.*] Oh, Hedda, I'm so happy. Imagine—he says I've inspired him!

HEDDA: [*Looks at her with a smile.*] Dear Thea! Does he really?

LOEVBORG: She has the courage of her convictions, Mrs. Tesman.

MRS. ELVSTED: I? Courage?

LOEVBORG: Absolute courage. Where friendship is concerned.

HEDDA: Yes. Courage. Yes. If only one had that——

LOEVBORG: Yes?

HEDDA. One might be able to live. In spite of everything. [*Changes her tone suddenly.*] Well, Thea darling, now you're going to drink a nice glass of cold punch.

MRS. ELVSTED: No, thank you. I never drink anything like that.

HEDDA: Oh. You, Mr. Loevborg?

LOEVBORG: Thank you, I don't either.

MRS. ELVSTED: No, he doesn't, either.

HEDDA: [*Looks into his eyes.*] But if I want you to?

LOEVBORG: That doesn't make any difference.

HEDDA: [*Laughs.*] Have I no power over you at all? Poor me!

LOEVBORG: Not where this is concerned.

HEDDA: Seriously, I think you should. For your own sake.

MRS. ELVSTED: Hedda!

LOEVBORG: Why?

HEDDA: Or perhaps I should say for other people's sake.

LOEVBORG: What do you mean?

HEDDA: People might think you didn't feel absolutely and unashamedly sure of yourself. In your heart of hearts.

MRS. ELVSTED: [*Quietly.*] Oh, Hedda, no!

LOEVBORG: People can think what they like. For the present.

MRS. ELVSTED: [*Happily.*] Yes, that's true.

HEDDA: I saw it so clearly in Judge Brack a few minutes ago.

LOEVBORG: Oh. What did you see?

HEDDA: He smiled so scornfully when he saw you were afraid to go in there and drink with them.

LOEVBORG: Afraid! I wanted to stay here and talk to you.

MRS. ELVSTED: That was only natural, Hedda.

HEDDA: But the Judge wasn't to know that. I saw him wink at Tesman when you showed you didn't dare to join their wretched little party.

LOEVBORG: Didn't dare! Are you saying I didn't dare?

HEDDA: I'm not saying so. But that was what Judge Brack thought.

LOEVBORG: Well, let him.

HEDDA: You're not going, then?

LOEVBORG: I'm staying here with you and Thea.

MRS. ELVSTED: Yes, Hedda, of course he is.

HEDDA: [*Smiles, and nods approvingly to* LOEVBORG.] Firm as a rock! A man of principle! That's how a man should be! [*Turns to* MRS. ELVSTED *and strokes her cheek.*] Didn't I tell you so this morning when you came here in such a panic——

LOEVBORG: [*Starts.*] Panic?

MRS. ELVSTED: [*Frightened.*] Hedda! But—Hedda!

HEDDA: Well, now you can see for yourself. There's no earthly need for you to get scared to death just because——[*Stops.*] Well! Let's all three cheer up and enjoy ourselves.

LOEVBORG: Mrs. Tesman, would you mind explaining to me what this is all about?

MRS. ELVSTED: Oh, my God, my God, Hedda, what are you saying? What are you doing?

HEDDA: Keep calm. That horrid Judge has his eye on you.

LOEVBORG: Scared to death, were you? For my sake?

MRS. ELVSTED: [*Quietly, trembling.*] Oh, Hedda! You've made me so unhappy!

LOEVBORG: [*Looks coldly at her for a moment. His face is distorted.*] So that was how much you trusted me.

MRS. ELVSTED: Eilert dear, please listen to me——

LOEVBORG: [*Takes one of the glasses of punch, raises it and says quietly, hoarsely.*] Skoal, Thea! [*Empties the glass, puts it down and picks up one of the others.*]

MRS. ELVSTED: [*Quietly.*] Hedda, Hedda! Why did you want this to happen?
HEDDA: I—want it? Are you mad?
LOEVBORG: Skoal to you too, Mrs. Tesman. Thanks for telling me the truth. Here's to the truth! [*Empties his glass and refills it.*]
HEDDA: [*Puts her hand on his arm.*] Steady. That's enough for now. Don't forget the party.
MRS. ELVSTED: No, no, no!
HEDDA: Ssh! They're looking at you.
LOEVBORG: [*Puts down his glass.*] Thea, tell me the truth——
MRS. ELVSTED: Yes!
LOEVBORG: Did your husband know you were following me?
MRS. ELVSTED: Oh, Hedda!
LOEVBORG: Did you and he have an agreement that you should come here and keep an eye on me? Perhaps he gave you the idea? After all, he's a magistrate. I suppose he needed me back in his office. Or did he miss my companionship at the card table?
MRS. ELVSTED: [*Quietly, sobbing.*] Eilert, Eilert!
LOEVBORG: [*Seizes a glass and is about to fill it.*] Let's drink to him, too.
HEDDA: No more now. Remember you're going to read your book to Tesman.
LOEVBORG: [*Calm again, puts down his glass.*] That was silly of me, Thea. To take it like that, I mean. Don't be angry with me, my dear. You'll see—yes, and they'll see, too—that though I fell, I—I have raised myself up again. With your help, Thea.
MRS. ELVSTED: [*Happily.*] Oh, thank God!

[BRACK *has meanwhile glanced at his watch. He and* TESMAN *get up and come into the drawing room.*]

BRACK: [*Takes his hat and overcoat.*] Well, Mrs. Tesman. It's time for us to go.
HEDDA: Yes, I suppose it must be.
LOEVBORG: [*Gets up.*] Time for me too, Judge.
MRS. ELVSTED: [*Quietly, pleadingly.*] Eilert, please don't!
HEDDA: [*Pinches her arm.*] They can hear you.
MRS. ELVSTED: [*Gives a little cry.*] Oh!
LOEVBORG: [*To* BRACK.] You were kind enough to ask me to join you.
BRACK: Are you coming?
LOEVBORG: If I may.
BRACK: Delighted.
LOEVBORG: [*Puts the paper package in his pocket and says to* TESMAN.] I'd like to show you one or two things before I send it off to the printer.
TESMAN: I say, that'll be fun. Fancy——! Oh, but Hedda, how'll Mrs. Elvsted get home? What?
HEDDA: Oh, we'll manage somehow.
LOEVBORG: [*Glances over toward the ladies.*] Mrs. Elvsted? I shall come back and collect her, naturally. [*Goes closer.*] About ten o'clock, Mrs. Tesman? Will that suit you?
HEDDA: Yes. That'll suit me admirably.
TESMAN: Good, that's settled. But you mustn't expect me back so early, Hedda.

HEDDA: Stay as long as you c—as long as you like, dear.

MRS. ELVSTED: [*Trying to hide her anxiety.*] Well then, Mr. Loevborg, I'll wait here till you come.

LOEVBORG: [*His hat in his hand.*] Pray do, Mrs. Elvsted.

BRACK: Well, gentlemen, now the party begins. I trust that, in the words of a certain fair lady, we shall enjoy good sport.

HEDDA: What a pity the fair lady can't be there, invisible.

BRACK: Why invisible?

HEDDA: So as to be able to hear some of your uncensored witticisms, your honor.

BRACK: [*Laughs.*] Oh, I shouldn't advise the fair lady to do that.

TESMAN: [*Laughs too.*] I say, Hedda, that's good. By Jove! Fancy that!

BRACK: Well, good night, ladies, good night!

LOEVBORG: [*Bows farewell.*] About ten o'clock, then.

[BRACK, LOEVBORG *and* TESMAN *go out through the hall. As they do so* BERTHA *enters from the rear room with a lighted lamp. She puts it on the drawing-room table, then goes out the way she came.*]

MRS. ELVSTED: [*Has got up and is walking uneasily to and fro.*] Oh Hedda, Hedda! How is all this going to end?

HEDDA: At ten o'clock, then. He'll be here. I can see him. With a crown of vine-leaves in his hair. Burning and unashamed!

MRS. ELVSTED: Oh, I do hope so!

HEDDA: Can't you see? Then he'll be himself again! He'll be a free man for the rest of his days!

MRS. ELVSTED: Please God you're right.

HEDDA: That's how he'll come! [*Gets up and goes closer.*] You can doubt him as much as you like. I believe in him! Now we'll see which of us——

MRS. ELVSTED: You're after something, Hedda.

HEDDA: Yes, I am. For once in my life I want to have the power to shape a man's destiny.

MRS. ELVSTED: Haven't you that power already?

HEDDA: No, I haven't. I've never had it.

MRS. ELVSTED: What about your husband?

HEDDA: Him! Oh, if you could only understand how poor I am. And you're allowed to be so rich, so rich! [*Clasps her passionately.*] I think I'll burn your hair off after all!

MRS. ELVSTED: Let me go! Let me go! You frighten me, Hedda!

BERTHA: [*In the open doorway.*] I've laid tea in the dining room, madam.

HEDDA: Good, we're coming.

MRS. ELVSTED: No, no, no! I'd rather go home alone! Now—at once!

HEDDA: Rubbish! First you're going to have some tea, you little idiot. And then—at ten o'clock—Eilert Loevborg will come. With a crown of vine-leaves in his hair![7] [*She drags* MRS. ELVSTED *almost forcibly toward the open doorway.*]

7. Worshippers of Dionysus, Greek god of wine, wore garlands of vine leaves as a sign of divine intoxication.

ACT III

SCENE: *The same. The curtains are drawn across the open doorway, and also across the french windows. The lamp, half turned down, with a shade over it, is burning on the table. In the stove, the door of which is open, a fire has been burning, but it is now almost out.*

MRS. ELVSTED, *wrapped in a large shawl and with her feet resting on a footstool, is sitting near the stove, huddled in the armchair.* HEDDA *is lying asleep on this sofa, fully dressed, with a blanket over her.*

MRS. ELVSTED: [*After a pause, suddenly sits up in her chair and listens tensely. Then she sinks wearily back again and sighs.*] Not back yet! Oh, God! Oh, God! Not back yet!

[BERTHA *tiptoes cautiously in from the hall. She has a letter in her hand.*]

MRS. ELVSTED: [*Turns and whispers.*] What is it? Has someone come?
BERTHA: [*Quietly.*] Yes, a servant's just called with this letter.
MRS. ELVSTED: [*Quickly, holding out her hand.*] A letter! Give it to me!
BERTHA: But it's for the Doctor, madam.
MRS. ELVSTED: Oh. I see.
BERTHA: Miss Tesman's maid brought it. I'll leave it here on the table.
MRS. ELVSTED: Yes, do.
BERTHA: [*Puts down the letter.*] I'd better put the lamp out. It's starting to smoke.
MRS. ELVSTED: Yes, put it out. It'll soon be daylight.
BERTHA: [*Puts out the lamp.*] It's daylight already, madam.
MRS. ELVSTED: Yes. Broad day. And not home yet.
BERTHA: Oh dear, I was afraid this would happen.
MRS. ELVSTED: Were you?
BERTHA: Yes. When I heard that a certain gentleman had returned to town, and saw him go off with them. I've heard all about him.
MRS. ELVSTED: Don't talk so loud. You'll wake your mistress.
BERTHA: [*Looks at the sofa and sighs.*] Yes. Let her go on sleeping, poor dear. Shall I put some more wood on the fire?
MRS. ELVSTED: Thank you, don't bother on my account.
BERTHA: Very good. [*Goes quietly out through the hall.*]
HEDDA: [*Wakes as the door closes and looks up.*] What's that?
MRS. ELVSTED: It was only the maid.
HEDDA: [*Looks round.*] What am I doing here? Oh, now I remember. [*Sits up on the sofa, stretches herself and rubs her eyes.*] What time is it, Thea?
MRS. ELVSTED: It's gone seven.
HEDDA: When did Tesman get back?
MRS. ELVSTED: He's not back yet.
HEDDA: Not home yet?
MRS. ELVSTED: [*Gets up.*] No one's come.
HEDDA: And we sat up waiting for them till four o'clock.
MRS. ELVSTED: God! How I waited for him!

HEDDA: [*Yawns and says with her hand in front of her mouth.*] Oh, dear. We might have saved ourselves the trouble.

MRS. ELVSTED: Did you manage to sleep?

HEDDA: Oh, yes. Quite well, I think. Didn't you get any?

MRS. ELVSTED: Not a wink. I couldn't, Hedda. I just couldn't.

HEDDA: [*Gets up and comes over to her.*] Now, now, now. There's nothing to worry about. I know what's happened.

MRS. ELVSTED: What? Please tell me.

HEDDA: Well, obviously the party went on very late——

MRS. ELVSTED: Oh dear, I suppose it must have. But——

HEDDA: And Tesman didn't want to come home and wake us all up in the middle of the night. [*Laughs.*] Probably wasn't too keen to show his face either, after a spree like that.

MRS. ELVSTED: But where could he have gone?

HEDDA: I should think he's probably slept at his aunts'. They keep his old room for him.

MRS. ELVSTED: No, he can't be with them. A letter came for him just now from Miss Tesman. It's over there.

HEDDA: Oh? [*Looks at the envelope.*] Yes, it's Auntie Juju's handwriting. Well, he must still be at Judge Brack's, then. And Eilert Loevborg is sitting there, reading to him. With a crown of vine-leaves in his hair.

MRS. ELVSTED: Hedda, you're only saying that. You don't believe it.

HEDDA: Thea, you really are a little fool.

MRS. ELVSTED: Perhaps I am.

HEDDA: You look tired to death.

MRS. ELVSTED: Yes. I am tired to death.

HEDDA: Go to my room and lie down for a little. Do as I say, now; don't argue.

MRS. ELVSTED: No, no. I couldn't possibly sleep.

HEDDA: Of course you can.

MRS. ELVSTED: But your husband'll be home soon. And I must know at once——

HEDDA: I'll tell you when he comes.

MRS. ELVSTED: Promise me, Hedda?

HEDDA: Yes, don't worry. Go and get some sleep.

MRS. ELVSTED: Thank you. All right, I'll try.

[*She goes out through the rear room.* HEDDA *goes to the french windows and draws the curtains. Broad daylight floods into the room. She goes to the writing table, takes a small hand mirror from it and arranges her hair. Then she goes to the door leading into the hall and presses the bell. After a few moments,* BERTHA *enters.*]

BERTHA: Did you want anything, madam?

HEDDA: Yes, put some more wood on the fire. I'm freezing.

BERTHA: Bless you, I'll soon have this room warmed up. [*She rakes the embers together and puts a fresh piece of wood on them. Suddenly she stops and listens.*] There's someone at the front door, madam.

HEDDA: Well, go and open it. I'll see to the fire.

BERTHA: It'll burn up in a moment.

[*She goes out through the hall.* HEDDA *kneels on the footstool and puts more wood in the stove. After a few seconds,* GEORGE TESMAN *enters from the hall. He looks tired, and rather worried. He tiptoes toward the open doorway and is about to slip through the curtains.*]

HEDDA: [*At the stove, without looking up.*] Good morning.

TESMAN: [*Turns.*] Hedda! [*Comes nearer.*] Good heavens, are you up already? What?

HEDDA: Yes, I got up very early this morning.

TESMAN: I was sure you'd still be sleeping. Fancy that!

HEDDA: Don't talk so loud. Mrs. Elvsted's asleep in my room.

TESMAN: Mrs. Elvsted? Has she stayed the night here?

HEDDA: Yes. No one came to escort her home.

TESMAN: Oh. No, I suppose not.

HEDDA: [*Closes the door of the stove and gets up.*] Well. Was it fun?

TESMAN: Have you been anxious about me? What?

HEDDA: Not in the least. I asked if you'd had fun.

TESMAN: Oh yes, rather! Well, I thought, for once in a while—The first part was the best; when Eilert read his book to me. We arrived over an hour too early—what about that, eh? By Jove! Brack had a lot of things to see to, so Eilert read to me.

HEDDA: [*Sits at the right-hand side of the table.*] Well? Tell me about it.

TESMAN: [*Sits on a footstool by the stove.*] Honestly, Hedda, you've no idea what a book that's going to be. It's really one of the most remarkable things that's ever been written. By Jove!

HEDDA: Oh, never mind about the book—

TESMAN: I'm going to make a confession to you, Hedda. When he'd finished reading a sort of beastly feeling came over me.

HEDDA: Beastly feeling?

TESMAN: I found myself envying Eilert for being able to write like that. Imagine that, Hedda!

HEDDA: Yes. I can imagine.

TESMAN: What a tragedy that with all those gifts he should be so incorrigible.

HEDDA: You mean he's less afraid of life than most men?

TESMAN: Good heavens, no. He just doesn't know the meaning of the word moderation.

HEDDA: What happened afterwards?

TESMAN: Well, looking back on it I suppose you might almost call it an orgy, Hedda.

HEDDA: Had he vine-leaves in his hair?

TESMAN: Vine-leaves? No, I didn't see any of them. He made a long, rambling oration in honor of the woman who'd inspired him to write this book. Yes, those were the words he used.

HEDDA: Did he name her?

TESMAN: No. But I suppose it must be Mrs. Elvsted. You wait and see!

HEDDA: Where did you leave him?

TESMAN: On the way home. We left in a bunch—the last of us, that is—and Brack came with us to get a little fresh air. Well, then, you see, we agreed we ought to see Eilert home. He'd had a drop too much.

HEDDA: You don't say?

TESMAN: But now comes the funny part, Hedda. Or I should really say the tragic part. Oh, I'm almost ashamed to tell you. For Eilert's sake, I mean——

HEDDA: Why, what happened?

TESMAN: Well, you see, as we were walking toward town I happened to drop behind for a minute. Only for a minute—er—you understand——

HEDDA: Yes, yes——?

TESMAN: Well then, when I ran on to catch them up, what do you think I found by the roadside. What?

HEDDA: How on earth should I know?

TESMAN: You mustn't tell anyone, Hedda. What? Promise me that—for Eilert's sake. [*Takes a package wrapped in paper from his coat pocket.*] Just fancy! I found this.

HEDDA: Isn't this the one he brought here yesterday?

TESMAN: Yes! The whole of that precious, irreplaceable manuscript! And he went and lost it! Didn't even notice! What about that? By Jove! Tragic.

HEDDA: But why didn't you give it back to him?

TESMAN: I didn't dare to, in the state he was in.

HEDDA: Didn't you tell any of the others?

TESMAN: Good heavens, no. I didn't want to do that. For Eilert's sake, you understand.

HEDDA: Then no one else knows you have his manuscript?

TESMAN: No. And no one must be allowed to know.

HEDDA: Didn't it come up in the conversation later?

TESMAN: I didn't get a chance to talk to him any more. As soon as we got into the outskirts of town, he and one or two of the others gave us the slip. Disappeared, by Jove!

HEDDA: Oh? I suppose they took him home.

TESMAN: Yes, I imagine that was the idea. Brack left us, too.

HEDDA: And what have you been up to since then?

TESMAN: Well, I and one or two of the others—awfully jolly chaps, they were—went back to where one of them lived, and had a cup of morning coffee. Morning-after coffee—what? Ah, well. I'll just lie down for a bit and give Eilert time to sleep it off, poor chap, then I'll run over and give this back to him.

HEDDA: [*Holds out her hand for the package.*] No, don't do that. Not just yet. Let me read it first.

TESMAN: Oh no, really, Hedda dear, honestly, I daren't do that.

HEDDA: Daren't?

TESMAN: No—imagine how desperate he'll be when he wakes up and finds his manuscript's missing. He hasn't any copy, you see. He told me so himself.

HEDDA: Can't a thing like that be rewritten?

TESMAN: Oh no, not possibly, I shouldn't think. I mean, the inspiration, you know——

HEDDA: Oh, yes. I'd forgotten that. [*Casually.*] By the way, there's a letter for you.

TESMAN: Is there? Fancy that!

HEDDA: [*Holds it out to him.*] It came early this morning.

TESMAN: I say, it's from Auntie Juju! What on earth can it be? [*Puts the package on the other footstool, opens the letter, reads it and jumps up.*] Oh, Hedda! She says poor Auntie Rena's dying.

HEDDA: Well, we've been expecting that.

TESMAN: She says if I want to see her I must go quickly. I'll run over at once.

HEDDA: [*Hides a smile.*] Run?

TESMAN: Hedda dear, I suppose you wouldn't like to come with me? What about that, eh?

HEDDA: [*Gets up and says wearily and with repulsion.*] No, no, don't ask me to do anything like that. I can't bear illness or death. I loathe anything ugly.

TESMAN: Yes, yes. Of course. [*In a dither.*] My hat? My overcoat? Oh yes, in the hall. I do hope I won't get there too late, Hedda? What?

HEDDA: You'll be all right if you run.

[BERTHA *enters from the hall.*]

BERTHA: Judge Brack's outside and wants to know if he can come in.

TESMAN: At this hour? No, I can't possibly receive him now.

HEDDA: I can. [*To* BERTHA.] Ask his honor to come in.

[BERTHA *goes.*]

HEDDA: [*Whispers quickly.*] The manuscript, Tesman. [*She snatches it from the footstool.*]

TESMAN: Yes, give it to me.

HEDDA: No, I'll look after it for now.

[*She goes over to the writing table and puts it in the bookcase.* TESMAN *stands dithering, unable to get his gloves on.* JUDGE BRACK enters from the hall.]

HEDDA: [*Nods to him*] Well, you're an early bird.

BRACK: Yes, aren't I? [*To* TESMAN.] Are you up and about, too?

TESMAN: Yes, I've got to go and see my aunts. Poor Auntie Rena's dying.

BRACK: Oh dear, is she? Then you mustn't let me detain you. At so tragic a——

TESMAN: Yes, I really must run. Good-bye! Good-bye! [*Runs out through the hall.*]

HEDDA: [*Goes nearer.*] You seem to have had excellent sport last night—Judge.

BRACK: Indeed yes, Mrs. Hedda. I haven't even had time to take my clothes off.

HEDDA: *You* haven't either?

BRACK: As you see. What's Tesman told you about last night's escapades?

HEDDA: Oh, only some boring story about having gone and drunk coffee somewhere.

BRACK: Yes, I've heard about that coffee party. Eilert Loevborg wasn't with them, I gather?
HEDDA: No, they took him home first.
BRACK: Did Tesman go with him?
HEDDA: No, one or two of the others, he said.
BRACK: [*Smiles.*] George Tesman is a credulous man, Mrs. Hedda.
HEDDA: God knows. But—has something happened?
BRACK: Well, yes, I'm afraid it has.
HEDDA: I see. Sit down and tell me. [*She sits on the left of the table,* BRACK *at the long side of it, near her.*] Well?
BRACK: I had a special reason for keeping track of my guests last night. Or perhaps I should say some of my guests.
HEDDA: Including Eilert Loevborg?
BRACK: I must confess—yes.
HEDDA: You're beginning to make me curious.
BRACK: Do you know where he and some of my other guests spent the latter half of last night, Mrs. Hedda?
HEDDA: Tell me. If it won't shock me.
BRACK: Oh, I don't think it'll shock you. They found themselves participating in an exceedingly animated *soirée*.
HEDDA: Of a sporting character?
BRACK: Of a highly sporting character.
HEDDA: Tell me more.
BRACK: Loevborg had received an invitation in advance—as had the others. I knew all about that. But he had refused. As you know, he's become a new man.
HEDDA: Up at the Elvsteds', yes. But he went?
BRACK: Well, you see, Mrs. Hedda, last night at my house, unhappily, the spirit moved him.
HEDDA: Yes, I hear he became inspired.
BRACK: Somewhat violently inspired. And as a result, I suppose, his thoughts strayed. We men, alas, don't always stick to our principles as firmly as we should.
HEDDA: I'm sure you're an exception, Judge Brack. But go on about Loevborg.
BRACK: Well, to cut a long story short, he ended up in the establishment of a certain Mademoiselle Danielle.
HEDDA: Mademoiselle Danielle?
BRACK: She was holding the *soirée*. For a selected circle of friends and admirers.
HEDDA: Has she got red hair?
BRACK: She has.
HEDDA: A singer of some kind?
BRACK: Yes—among other accomplishments. She's also a celebrated huntress—of men, Mrs. Hedda. I'm sure you've heard about her. Eilert Loevborg used to be one of her most ardent patrons. In his salad days.
HEDDA: And how did all this end?
BRACK: Not entirely amicably, from all accounts. Mademoiselle Danielle began

by receiving him with the utmost tenderness and ended by resorting to her fists.

HEDDA: Against Loevborg?

BRACK: Yes. He accused her, or her friends, of having robbed him. He claimed his pocketbook had been stolen. Among other things. In short, he seems to have made a bloodthirsty scene.

HEDDA: And what did this lead to?

BRACK: It led to a general free-for-all, in which both sexes participated. Fortunately, in the end the police arrived.

HEDDA: The police too?

BRACK: Yes. I'm afraid it may turn out to be rather an expensive joke for Master Eilert. Crazy fool!

HEDDA: Oh?

BRACK: Apparently he put up a very violent resistance. Hit one of the constables on the ear and tore his uniform. He had to accompany them to the police station.

HEDDA: Where did you learn all this?

BRACK: From the police.

HEDDA: [*To herself.*] So that's what happened. He didn't have a crown of vine-leaves in his hair.

BRACK: Vine-leaves, Mrs. Hedda?

HEDDA: [*In her normal voice again.*] But, tell me, Judge, why do you take such a close interest in Eilert Loevborg?

BRACK: For one thing it'll hardly be a matter of complete indifference to me if it's revealed in court that he came there straight from my house.

HEDDA: Will it come to court?

BRACK: Of course. Well, I don't regard that as particularly serious. Still, I thought it my duty, as a friend of the family, to give you and your husband a full account of his nocturnal adventures.

HEDDA: Why?

BRACK: Because I've a shrewd suspicion that he's hoping to use you as a kind of screen.

HEDDA: What makes you think that?

BRACK: Oh, for heaven's sake, Mrs. Hedda, we're not blind. You wait and see. This Mrs. Elvsted won't be going back to her husband just yet.

HEDDA: Well, if there were anything between those two there are plenty of other places where they could meet.

BRACK: Not in anyone's home. From now on every respectable house will once again be closed to Eilert Loevborg.

HEDDA: And mine should be too, you mean?

BRACK: Yes. I confess I should find it more than irksome if this gentleman were to be granted unrestricted access to this house. If he were superfluously to intrude into——

HEDDA: The triangle?

BRACK: Precisely. For me it would be like losing a home.

HEDDA: [*Looks at him and smiles.*] I see. You want to be the cock of the walk.

BRACK: [*Nods slowly and lowers his voice.*] Yes, that is my aim. And I shall fight for it with—every weapon at my disposal.

HEDDA: [*As her smile fades.*] You're a dangerous man, aren't you? When you really want something.

BRACK: You think so?

HEDDA: Yes. I'm beginning to think so. I'm deeply thankful you haven't any kind of hold over me.

BRACK: [*Laughs equivocally.*] Well, well, Mrs. Hedda—perhaps you're right. If I had, who knows what I might not think up?

HEDDA: Come, Judge Brack. That sounds almost like a threat.

BRACK: [*Gets up.*] Heaven forbid! In the creation of a triangle—and its continuance—the question of compulsion should never arise.

HEDDA: Exactly what I was thinking.

BRACK: Well, I've said what I came to say. I must be getting back. Good-bye, Mrs. Hedda. [*Goes toward the french windows.*]

HEDDA: [*Gets up.*] Are you going out through the garden?

BRACK: Yes, it's shorter.

HEDDA: Yes. And it's the back door, isn't it?

BRACK: I've nothing against back doors. They can be quite intriguing—sometimes.

HEDDA: When people fire pistols out of them, for example?

BRACK: [*In the doorway, laughs.*] Oh, people don't shoot tame cocks.

HEDDA: [*Laughs too.*] I suppose not. When they've only got one.

[*They nod good-bye, laughing. He goes. She closes the french windows behind him, and stands for a moment, looking out pensively. Then she walks across the room and glances through the curtains in the open doorway. Goes to the writing table, takes* LOEVBORG'*s package from the bookcase and is about to leaf through the pages when* BERTHA *is heard remonstrating loudly in the hall.* HEDDA *turns and listens. She hastily puts the package back in the drawer, locks it and puts the key on the inkstand.* EILERT LOEVBORG, *with his overcoat on and his hat in his hand, throws the door open. He looks somewhat confused and excited.*]

LOEVBORG: [*Shouts as he enters.*] I must come in, I tell you! Let me pass! [*He closes the door, turns, sees* HEDDA, *controls himself immediately and bows.*]

HEDDA: [*At the writing table.*] Well, Mr. Loevborg, this is rather a late hour to be collecting Thea.

LOEVBORG: And an early hour to call on you. Please forgive me.

HEDDA: How do you know she's still here?

LOEVBORG: They told me at her lodgings that she has been out all night.

HEDDA: [*Goes to the table.*] Did you notice anything about their behavior when they told you?

LOEVBORG: [*Looks at her, puzzled.*] Notice anything?

HEDDA: Did they sound as if they thought it—strange?

LOEVBORG: [*Suddenly understands.*] Oh, I see what you mean. I'm dragging her down with me. No, as a matter of fact I didn't notice anything. I suppose Tesman isn't up yet?

HEDDA: No, I don't think so.

LOEVBORG: When did he get home?

HEDDA: Very late.

LOEVBORG: Did he tell you anything?

HEDDA: Yes. I gather you had a merry party at Judge Brack's last night.

LOEVBORG: He didn't tell you anything else?

HEDDA. I don't think so. I was so terribly sleepy——

[MRS. ELVSTED *comes through the curtains in the open doorway.*]

MRS. ELVSTED: [*Runs toward him.*] Oh, Eilert! At last!

LOEVBORG: Yes—at last. And too late.

MRS. ELVSTED: What is too late?

LOEVBORG: Everything—now. I'm finished, Thea.

MRS. ELVSTED: Oh, no, no! Don't say that!

LOEVBORG: You'll say it yourself, when you've heard what I——

MRS. ELVSTED: I don't want to hear anything!

HEDDA: Perhaps you'd rather speak to her alone? I'd better go.

LOEVBORG: No, stay.

MRS. ELVSTED: But I don't want to hear anything, I tell you!

LOEVBORG: It's not about last night.

MRS. ELVSTED: Then what——?

LOEVBORG: I want to tell you that from now on we must stop seeing each other.

MRS. ELVSTED: Stop seeing each other!

HEDDA: [*Involuntarily.*] I knew it!

LOEVBORG: I have no further use for you, Thea.

MRS. ELVSTED: You can stand there and say that! No further use for me! Surely I can go on helping you? We'll go on working together, won't we?

LOEVBORG: I don't intend to do any more work from now on.

MRS. ELVSTED: [*Desperately.*] Then what use have I for my life?

LOEVBORG: You must try to live as if you had never known me.

MRS. ELVSTED: But I can't!

LOEVBORG: Try to, Thea. Go back home——

MRS. ELVSTED: Never! I want to be wherever you are! I won't let myself be driven away like this! I want to stay here—and be with you when the book comes out.

HEDDA: [*Whispers.*] Ah, yes! The book!

LOEVBORG: [*Looks at her.*] Our book; Thea's and mine. It belongs to both of us.

MRS. ELVSTED: Oh, yes! I feel that, too! And I've a right to be with you when it comes into the world. I want to see people respect and honor you again. And the joy! The joy! I want to share it with you!

LOEVBORG: Thea—our book will never come into the world.

HEDDA: Ah!

MRS. ELVSTED: Not——?

LOEVBORG: It cannot. Ever.

MRS. ELVSTED: Eilert—what have you done with the manuscript? Where is it?

LOEVBORG: Oh Thea, please don't ask me that!

MRS. ELVSTED: Yes, yes—I must know. I've a right to know. Now!

LOEVBORG: The manuscript. I've torn it up.

MRS. ELVSTED: [*Screams.*] No, no!

HEDDA: [*Involuntarily.*] But that's not——!

LOEVBORG: [*Looks at her.*] Not true, you think?

HEDDA: [*Controls herself.*] Why—yes, of course it is, if you say so. It just sounded so incredible——

LOEVBORG: It's true, nevertheless.

MRS. ELVSTED: Oh, my God, my God, Hedda—he's destroyed his own book!

LOEVBORG: I have destroyed my life. Why not my life's work, too?

MRS. ELVSTED: And you—did this last night?

LOEVBORG: Yes, Thea. I tore it into a thousand pieces. And scattered them out across the fjord. It's good, clean, salt water. Let it carry them away; let them drift in the current and the wind. And in a little while, they will sink. Deeper and deeper. As I shall, Thea.

MRS. ELVSTED: Do you know, Eilert—this book—all my life I shall feel as though you'd killed a little child?

LOEVBORG: You're right. It is like killing a child.

MRS. ELVSTED: But how could you? It was my child, too!

HEDDA. [*Almost inaudibly.*] Oh—the child——!

MRS. ELVSTED: [*Breathes heavily.*] It's all over, then. Well—I'll go now, Hedda.

HEDDA: You're not leaving town?

MRS. ELVSTED: I don't know what I'm going to do. I can't see anything except—darkness. [*She goes out through the hall.*]

HEDDA: [*Waits a moment.*] Aren't you going to escort her home, Mr. Loevborg?

LOEVBORG: I? Through the streets? Do you want me to let people see her with me?

HEDDA: Of course I don't know what else may have happened last night. But is it so utterly beyond redress?

LOEVBORG: It isn't just last night. It'll go on happening. I know it. But the curse of it is, I don't want to live that kind of life. I don't want to start all that again. She's broken my courage. I can't spit in the eyes of the world any longer.

HEDDA: [*As though to herself.*] That pretty little fool's been trying to shape a man's destiny. [*Looks at him.*] But how could you be so heartless toward her?

LOEVBORG: Don't call me heartless!

HEDDA: To go and destroy the one thing that's made her life worth living? You don't call that heartless?

LOEVBORG: Do you want to know the truth, Hedda?

HEDDA: The truth?

LOEVBORG: Promise me first—give me your word—that you'll never let Thea know about this.

HEDDA: I give you my word.

LOEVBORG: Good. Well; what I told her just now was a lie.

HEDDA: About the manuscript?

LOEVBORG: Yes. I didn't tear it up. Or throw it in the fjord.

HEDDA: You didn't? But where is it, then?

LOEVBORG: I destroyed it, all the same. I destroyed it, Hedda!

HEDDA: I don't understand.

LOEVBORG: Thea said that what I had done was like killing a child.

HEDDA: Yes. That's what she said.

LOEVBORG: But to kill a child isn't the worst thing a father can do to it.

HEDDA: What could be worse than that?

LOEVBORG: Hedda—suppose a man came home one morning, after a night of debauchery, and said to the mother of his child: "Look here. I've been wandering round all night. I've been to—such-and-such a place and such-and-such a place. And I had our child with me. I took him to—these places. And I've lost him. Just—lost him. God knows where he is or whose hands he's fallen into."

HEDDA: I see. But when all's said and done, this was only a book——

LOEVBORG: Thea's heart and soul were in that book. It was her whole life.

HEDDA: Yes. I understand.

LOEVBORG: Well, then you must also understand that she and I cannot possibly ever see each other again.

HEDDA: Where will you go?

LOEVBORG: Nowhere. I just want to put an end to it all. As soon as possible.

HEDDA: [*Takes a step toward him.*] Eilert Loevborg, listen to me. Do it—beautifully!

LOEVBORG: Beautifully? [*Smiles.*] With a crown of vine-leaves in my hair? The way you used to dream of me—in the old days?

HEDDA: No. I don't believe in that crown any longer. But—do it beautifully, all the same. Just this once. Good-bye. You must go now. And don't come back.

LOEVBORG: Adieu, madam. Give my love to George Tesman. [*Turns to go.*]

HEDDA: Wait. I want to give you a souvenir to take with you.

[*She goes over to the writing table, opens the drawer and the pistol-case, and comes back to* LOEVBORG *with one of the pistols.*]

LOEVBORG: [*Looks at her.*] This? Is this the souvenir?

HEDDA: [*Nods slowly.*] You recognize it? You looked down its barrel once.

LOEVBORG: You should have used it then.

HEDDA: Here! Use it now!

LOEVBORG: [*Puts the pistol in his breast pocket.*] Thank you.

HEDDA: Do it beautifully, Eilert Loevborg. Only promise me that!

LOEVBORG: Good-bye, Hedda Gabler.

[*He goes out through the hall.* HEDDA *stands by the door for a moment, listening. Then she goes over to the writing table, takes out the package containing the manuscript, glances inside it, pulls some of the pages half out and looks at them. Then she takes it to the armchair by the stove and sits down with the package in her lap. After a moment, she opens the door of the stove; then she opens the packet.*]

HEDDA: [*Throws one of the pages into the stove and whispers to herself.*] I'm burning your child, Thea! You with your beautiful wavy hair! [*She throws a few more pages into the stove.*] The child Eilert Loevborg gave you. [*Throws the rest of the manuscript in.*] I'm burning it! I'm burning your child!

ACT IV

SCENE: *The same. It is evening. The drawing room is in darkness. The small room is illuminated by the hanging lamp over the table. The curtains are drawn across the french windows.* HEDDA, *dressed in black, is walking up and down in the darkened room. Then she goes into the small room and crosses to the left. A few chords are heard from the piano. She comes back into the drawing room.*

BERTHA *comes through the small room from the right with a lighted lamp, which she places on the table in front of the corner sofa in the drawing room. Her eyes are red with crying, and she has black ribbons on her cap. She goes quietly out, right.* HEDDA *goes over to the french windows, draws the curtains slightly to one side and looks out into the darkness.*

A few moments later, MISS TESMAN *enters from the hall. She is dressed in mourning, with a black hat and veil.* HEDDA *goes to meet her and holds out her hand.*

MISS TESMAN: Well, Hedda, here I am in the weeds of sorrow. My poor sister has ended her struggles at last.

HEDDA: I've already heard. Tesman sent me a card.

MISS TESMAN: Yes, he promised me he would. But I thought, no, I must go and break the news of death to Hedda myself—here, in the house of life.

HEDDA: It's very kind of you.

MISS TESMAN: Ah, Rena shouldn't have chosen a time like this to pass away. This is no moment for Hedda's house to be a place of mourning.

HEDDA: [*Changing the subject.*] She died peacefully, Miss Tesman?

MISS TESMAN: Oh, it was quite beautiful! The end came so calmly. And she was so happy at being able to see George once again. And say good-bye to him. Hasn't he come home yet?

HEDDA: No. He wrote that I mustn't expect him too soon. But please sit down.

MISS TESMAN: No, thank you, Hedda dear—bless you. I'd like to. But I've so little time. I must dress her and lay her out as well as I can. She shall go to her grave looking really beautiful.

HEDDA: Can't I help with anything?

MISS TESMAN: Why, you mustn't think of such a thing! Hedda Tesman mustn't let her hands be soiled by contact with death. Or her thoughts. Not at this time.

HEDDA: One can't always control one's thoughts.

MISS TESMAN: [*Continues.*] Ah, well, that's life. Now we must start to sew poor

Rena's shroud. There'll be sewing to be done in this house too before long, I shouldn't wonder. But not for a shroud, praise God.

[GEORGE TESMAN *enters from the hall.*]

HEDDA: You've come at last! Thank heavens!

TESMAN: Are you here, Auntie Juju? With Hedda? Fancy that!

MISS TESMAN: I was just on the point of leaving, dear boy. Well, have you done everything you promised me?

TESMAN: No, I'm afraid I forgot half of it. I'll have to run over again tomorrow. My head's in a complete whirl today. I can't collect my thoughts.

MISS TESMAN: But George dear, you mustn't take it like this.

TESMAN: Oh? Well—er—how should I?

MISS TESMAN: You must be happy in your grief. Happy for what's happened. As I am.

TESMAN: Oh, yes, yes. You're thinking of Aunt Rena.

HEDDA: It'll be lonely for you now, Miss Tesman.

MISS TESMAN: For the first few days, yes. But it won't last long, I hope. Poor dear Rena's little room isn't going to stay empty.

TESMAN: Oh? Whom are you going to move in there? What?

MISS TESMAN: Oh, there's always some poor invalid who needs care and attention.

HEDDA: Do you really want another cross like that to bear?

MISS TESMAN: Cross! God forgive you, child. It's been no cross for me.

HEDDA: But now—if a complete stranger comes to live with you——?

MISS TESMAN: Oh, one soon makes friends with invalids. And I need so much to have someone to live for. Like you, my dear. Well, I expect there'll soon be work in this house too for an old aunt, praise God!

HEDDA: Oh—please!

TESMAN: By Jove, yes! What a splendid time the three of us could have together if——

HEDDA: If?

TESMAN: [*Uneasily.*] Oh, never mind. It'll all work out. Let's hope so—what?

MISS TESMAN: Yes, yes. Well, I'm sure you two would like to be alone. [*Smiles.*] Perhaps Hedda may have something to tell you, George. Good-bye. I must go home to Rena. [*Turns to the door.*] Dear God, how strange! Now Rena is with me and with poor dear Joachim.

TESMAN: Fancy that. Yes, Auntie Juju! What?

[MISS TESMAN *goes out through the hall.*]

HEDDA: [*Follows* TESMAN *coldly and searchingly with her eyes.*] I really believe this death distresses you more than it does her.

TESMAN: Oh, it isn't just Auntie Rena. It's Eilert I'm so worried about.

HEDDA: [*Quickly.*] Is there any news of him?

TESMAN: I ran over to see him this afternoon. I wanted to tell him his manuscript was in safe hands.

HEDDA: Oh? You didn't find him?

TESMAN: No. He wasn't at home. But later I met Mrs. Elvsted and she told me he'd been here early this morning.
HEDDA: Yes, just after you'd left.
TESMAN: It seems he said he'd torn the manuscript up. What?
HEDDA: Yes, he claimed to have done so.
TESMAN: You told him we had it, of course?
HEDDA: No. [*Quickly.*] Did you tell Mrs. Elvsted?
TESMAN: No, I didn't like to. But you ought to have told him. Think if he should go home and do something desperate! Give me the manuscript, Hedda. I'll run over to him with it right away. Where did you put it?
HEDDA: [*Cold and motionless, leaning against the armchair.*] I haven't got it any longer.
TESMAN: Haven't got it? What on earth do you mean?
HEDDA: I've burned it.
TESMAN: [*Starts, terrified.*] Burned it! Burned Eilert's manuscript!
HEDDA: Don't shout. The servant will hear you.
TESMAN: Burned it! But in heaven's name——! Oh, no, no, no! This is impossible!
HEDDA: Well, it's true.
TESMAN: But Hedda, do you realize what you've done? That's appropriating lost property! It's against the law! By Jove! You ask Judge Brack and see if I'm not right.
HEDDA: You'd be well advised not to talk about it to Judge Brack or anyone else.
TESMAN: But how could you go and do such a dreadful thing? What on earth put the idea into your head? What came over you? Answer me! What?
HEDDA: [*Represses an almost imperceptible smile.*] I did it for your sake, George.
TESMAN: For my sake?
HEDDA: When you came home this morning and described how he'd read his book to you——
TESMAN: Yes, yes?
HEDDA: You admitted you were jealous of him.
TESMAN: But, good heavens, I didn't mean it literally!
HEDDA: No matter. I couldn't bear the thought that anyone else should push you into the background.
TESMAN: [*Torn between doubt and joy.*] Hedda—is this true? But—but—but I never realized you loved me like that! Fancy——
HEDDA: Well, I suppose you'd better know. I'm going to have—— [*Breaks off and says violently.*] No, no—you'd better ask your Auntie Juju. She'll tell you.
TESMAN: Hedda! I think I understand what you mean. [*Clasps his hands.*] Good heavens, can it really be true! What?
HEDDA: Don't shout. The servant will hear you.
TESMAN: [*Laughing with joy.*] The servant! I say, that's good! The servant! Why, that's Bertha! I'll run out and tell her at once!
HEDDA: [*Clenches her hands in despair.*] Oh, it's destroying me, all this—it's destroying me!

TESMAN: I say, Hedda, what's up? What?

HEDDA: [*Cold, controlled.*] Oh, it's all so—absurd—George.

TESMAN: Absurd? That I'm so happy? But surely——? Ah, well—perhaps I won't say anything to Bertha.

HEDDA: No, do. She might as well know too.

TESMAN: No, no, I won't tell her yet. But Auntie Juju—I must let her know! And you—you called me George! For the first time! Fancy that! Oh, it'll make Auntie Juju so happy, all this! So very happy!

HEDDA: Will she be happy when she hears I've burned Eilert Loevborg's manuscript—for your sake?

TESMAN: No, I'd forgotten about that. Of course no one must be allowed to know about the manuscript. But that you're burning with love for me, Hedda, I must certainly let Auntie Juju know that. I say, I wonder if young wives often feel like that toward their husbands? What?

HEDDA: You might ask Auntie Juju about that too.

TESMAN: I will, as soon as I get the chance. [*Looks uneasy and thoughtful again.*] But I say, you know, that manuscript. Dreadful business. Poor Eilert!

[MRS. ELVSTED, *dressed as on her first visit, with hat and overcoat, enters from the hall.*]

MRS. ELVSTED: [*Greets them hastily and tremulously.*] Oh, Hedda dear, do please forgive me for coming here again.

HEDDA: Why, Thea, what's happened?

TESMAN: Is it anything to do with Eilert Loevborg? What?

MRS. ELVSTED: Yes—I'm so dreadfully afraid he may have met with an accident.

HEDDA: [*Grips her arm.*] You think so?

TESMAN: But, good heavens, Mrs. Elvsted, what makes you think that?

MRS. ELVSTED: I heard them talking about him at the boarding-house, as I went in. Oh, there are the most terrible rumors being spread about him in town today.

TESMAN: Fancy. Yes, I heard about them too. But I can testify that he went straight home to bed. Fancy that!

HEDDA: Well—what did they say in the boarding-house?

MRS. ELVSTED: Oh, I couldn't find out anything. Either they didn't know, or else—— They stopped talking when they saw me. And I didn't dare to ask.

TESMAN: [*Fidgets uneasily.*] We must hope—we must hope you misheard them, Mrs. Elvsted.

MRS. ELVSTED: No, no, I'm sure it was he they were talking about. I heard them say something about a hospital——

TESMAN: Hospital!

HEDDA: Oh no, surely that's impossible!

MRS. ELVSTED: Oh, I became so afraid. So I went up to his rooms and asked to see him.

HEDDA: Do you think that was wise, Thea?

MRS. ELVSTED: Well, what else could I do? I couldn't bear the uncertainty any longer.

TESMAN: But you didn't manage to find him either? What?

MRS. ELVSTED: No. And they had no idea where he was. They said he hadn't been home since yesterday afternoon.

TESMAN: Since yesterday? Fancy that!

MRS. ELVSTED: I'm sure he must have met with an accident.

TESMAN: Hedda, I wonder if I ought to go into town and make one or two enquiries?

HEDDA: No, no, don't you get mixed up in this.

[JUDGE BRACK *enters from the hall, hat in hand.* BERTHA, *who has opened the door for him, closes it. He looks serious and greets them silently.*]

TESMAN: Hullo, my dear Judge. Fancy seeing you!

BRACK: I had to come and talk to you.

TESMAN: I can see Auntie Juju's told you the news.

BRACK: Yes, I've heard about that too.

TESMAN: Tragic, isn't it?

BRACK: Well, my dear chap, that depends how you look at it.

TESMAN: [*Looks uncertainly at him.*] Has something else happened?

BRACK: Yes.

HEDDA: Another tragedy?

BRACK: That also depends on how you look at it, Mrs. Tesman.

MRS. ELVSTED: Oh, it's something to do with Eilert Loevborg!

BRACK: [*Looks at her for a moment.*] How did you guess? Perhaps you've heard already——?

MRS. ELVSTED: [*Confused.*] No, no, not at all—I——

TESMAN: For heaven's sake, tell us!

BRACK: [*Shrugs his shoulders.*] Well, I'm afraid they've taken him to the hospital. He's dying.

MRS. ELVSTED: [*Screams.*] Oh God, God!

TESMAN: The hospital! Dying!

HEDDA: [*Involuntarily.*] So quickly!

MRS. ELVSTED: [*Weeping.*] Oh, Hedda! And we parted enemies!

HEDDA: [*Whispers.*] Thea—Thea!

MRS. ELVSTED: [*Ignoring her.*] I must see him! I must see him before he dies!

BRACK: It's no use, Mrs. Elvsted. No one's allowed to see him now.

MRS. ELVSTED: But what's happened to him? You must tell me!

TESMAN: He hasn't tried to do anything to himself? What?

HEDDA: Yes, he has. I'm sure of it.

TESMAN: Hedda, how can you——?

BRACK: [*Who has not taken his eyes from her.*] I'm afraid you've guessed correctly, Mrs. Tesman.

MRS. ELVSTED: How dreadful!

TESMAN: Attempted suicide! Fancy that!

HEDDA: Shot himself!

BRACK: Right again, Mrs. Tesman.

MRS. ELVSTED: [*Tries to compose herself.*] When did this happen, Judge Brack?

BRACK: This afternoon. Between three and four.

TESMAN: But, good heavens—where? What?

BRACK: [*A little hesitantly.*] Where? Why, my dear chap, in his rooms of course.

MRS. ELVSTED: No, that's impossible. I was there soon after six.

BRACK: Well, it must have been somewhere else, then. I don't know exactly. I only know that they found him. He'd shot himself—through the breast.

MRS. ELVSTED: Oh, how horrible! That he should end like that!

HEDDA: [*To* BRACK.] Through the breast, you said?

BRACK: That is what I said.

HEDDA: Not through the head?

BRACK: Through the breast, Mrs. Tesman.

HEDDA: The breast. Yes; yes. That's good, too.

BRACK: Why, Mrs. Tesman?

HEDDA: Oh—no, I didn't mean anything.

TESMAN: And the wound's dangerous you say? What?

BRACK: Mortal. He's probably already dead.

MRS. ELVSTED: Yes, yes—I feel it! It's all over. All over. Oh Hedda——!

TESMAN: But, tell me, how did you manage to learn all this?

BRACK: [*Curtly.*] From the police. I spoke to one of them.

HEDDA: [*Loudly, clearly.*] At last! Oh, thank God!

TESMAN: [*Appalled.*] For God's sake, Hedda, what are you saying?

HEDDA: I am saying there's beauty in what he has done.

BRACK: Mm—Mrs. Tesman——

TESMAN: Beauty! Oh, but I say!

MRS. ELVSTED: Hedda, how can you talk of beauty in connection with a thing like this?

HEDDA: Eilert Loevborg has settled his account with life. He's had the courage to do what—what he had to do.

MRS. ELVSTED: No, that's not why it happened. He did it because he was mad.

TESMAN: He did it because he was desperate.

HEDDA: You're wrong! I know!

MRS. ELVSTED: He must have been mad. The same as when he tore up the manuscript.

BRACK: [*Starts.*] Manuscript? Did he tear it up?

MRS. ELVSTED: Yes. Last night.

TESMAN: [*Whispers.*] Oh, Hedda, we shall never be able to escape from this.

BRACK: Hm. Strange.

TESMAN: [*Wanders round the room.*] To think of Eilert dying like that. And not leaving behind him the thing that would have made his name endure.

MRS. ELVSTED: If only it could be pieced together again!

TESMAN: Yes, fancy! If only it could! I'd give anything——

MRS. ELVSTED: Perhaps it can, Mr. Tesman.

TESMAN: What do you mean?

MRS. ELVSTED: [*Searches in the pocket of her dress.*] Look! I kept the notes he dictated it from.

HEDDA: [*Takes a step nearer.*] Ah!

TESMAN: You kept them, Mrs. Elvsted! What?

MRS. ELVSTED: Yes, here they are. I brought them with me when I left home. They've been in my pocket ever since.

TESMAN: Let me have a look.

MRS. ELVSTED: [*Hands him a wad of small sheets of paper.*] They're in a terrible muddle. All mixed up.

TESMAN: I say, just fancy if we can sort them out! Perhaps if we work on them together——?

MRS. ELVSTED: Oh, yes! Let's try, anyway!

TESMAN: We'll manage it. We must! I shall dedicate my life to this.

HEDDA: *You*, George? Your life?

TESMAN: Yes—well, all the time I can spare. My book'll have to wait. Hedda, you do understand? What? I owe it to Eilert's memory.

HEDDA: Perhaps.

TESMAN: Well, my dear Mrs. Elvsted, you and I'll have to pool our brains. No use crying over spilt milk, what? We must try to approach this matter calmly.

MRS. ELVSTED: Yes, yes, Mr. Tesman. I'll do my best.

TESMAN: Well, come over here and let's start looking at these notes right away. Where shall we sit? Here? No, the other room. You'll excuse us, won't you, Judge? Come along with me, Mrs. Elvsted.

MRS. ELVSTED: Oh, God! If only we can manage to do it!

[TESMAN *and* MRS. ELVSTED *go into the rear room. He takes off his hat and overcoat. They sit at the table beneath the hanging lamp and absorb themselves in the notes.* HEDDA *walks across to the stove and sits in the armchair. After a moment,* BRACK *goes over to her.*]

HEDDA: [*Half aloud.*] Oh, Judge! This act of Eilert Loevborg's—doesn't it give one a sense of release!

BRACK: Release, Mrs. Hedda? Well, it's a release for him, of course——

HEDDA: Oh, I don't mean him—I mean me! The release of knowing that someone can do something really brave! Something beautiful!

BRACK: [*Smiles.*] Hm—my dear Mrs. Hedda——

HEDDA: Oh, I know what you're going to say. You're a bourgeois at heart too, just like—ah, well!

BRACK: [*Looks at her.*] Eilert Loevborg has meant more to you than you're willing to admit to yourself. Or am I wrong?

HEDDA: I'm not answering questions like that from you. I only know that Eilert Loevborg has had the courage to live according to his own principles. And now, at last, he's done something big! Something beautiful! To have the courage and the will to rise from the feast of life so early!

BRACK: It distresses me deeply, Mrs. Hedda, but I'm afraid I must rob you of that charming illusion.

HEDDA: Illusion?

BRACK: You wouldn't have been allowed to keep it for long, anyway.

HEDDA: What do you mean?

BRACK: He didn't shoot himself on purpose.

HEDDA: Not on purpose?

BRACK: No. It didn't happen quite the way I told you.

HEDDA: Have you been hiding something? What is it?

BRACK: In order to spare poor Mrs. Elvsted's feelings, I permitted myself one or two small—equivocations.

HEDDA: What?

BRACK: To begin with, he is already dead.

HEDDA: He died at the hospital?

BRACK: Yes. Without regaining consciousness.

HEDDA: What else haven't you told us?

BRACK: The incident didn't take place at his lodgings.

HEDDA: Well, that's utterly unimportant.

BRACK: Not utterly. The fact is, you see, that Eilert Loevborg was found shot in Mademoiselle Danielle's boudoir.

HEDDA: [*Almost jumps up, but instead sinks back in her chair.*] That's impossible. He can't have been there today.

BRACK: He was there this afternoon. He went to ask for something he claimed they'd taken from him. Talked some crazy nonsense about a child which had got lost——

HEDDA: Oh! So that was the reason!

BRACK: I thought at first he might have been referring to his manuscript. But I hear he destroyed that himself. So he must have meant his pocketbook—I suppose.

HEDDA: Yes, I suppose so. So they found him there?

BRACK: Yes; there. With a discharged pistol in his breast pocket. The shot had wounded him mortally.

HEDDA: Yes. In the breast.

BRACK: No. In the—hm—stomach. The—lower part——

HEDDA: [*Looks at him with an expression of repulsion.*] That too! Oh, why does everything I touch become mean and ludicrous? It's like a curse!

BRACK: There's something else, Mrs. Hedda. It's rather disagreeable, too.

HEDDA: What?

BRACK: The pistol he had on him——

HEDDA: Yes? What about it?

BRACK: He must have stolen it.

HEDDA: [*Jumps up.*] Stolen it! That isn't true! He didn't!

BRACK: It's the only explanation. He must have stolen it. Ssh!

[TESMAN *and* MRS. ELVSTED *have got up from the table in the rear room and come into the drawing room.*]

TESMAN. [*His hands full of papers.*] Hedda, I can't see properly under that lamp. Think!

HEDDA: I am thinking.

TESMAN: Do you think we could possibly use your writing table for a little? What?

HEDDA: Yes, of course. [*Quickly.*] No, wait! Let me tidy it up first.

TESMAN: Oh, don't you trouble about that. There's plenty of room.

HEDDA: No, no, let me tidy it up first, I say. I'll take this in and put them on the piano. Here.

[*She pulls an object, covered with sheets of music, out from under the bookcase, puts some more sheets on top and carries it all into the rear room and away to the left.* TESMAN *puts his papers on the writing table and moves the lamp over from the corner table. He and* MRS. ELVSTED *sit down and begin working again.* HEDDA *comes back.*]

HEDDA: [*Behind* MRS. ELVSTED*'s chair, ruffles her hair gently.*] Well, my pretty Thea! And how is work progressing on Eilert Loevborg's memorial?

MRS. ELVSTED: [*Looks up at her, dejectedly.*] Oh, it's going to be terribly difficult to get these into any order.

TESMAN: We've got to do it. We must! After all, putting other people's papers into order is rather my specialty, what?

[HEDDA *goes over to the stove and sits on one of the footstools.* BRACK *stands over her, leaning against the armchair.*]

HEDDA: [*Whispers.*] What was that you were saying about the pistol?

BRACK: [*Softly.*] I said he must have stolen it.

HEDDA: Why do you think that?

BRACK: Because any other explanation is unthinkable, Mrs. Hedda, or ought to be.

HEDDA: I see.

BRACK: [*Looks at her for a moment.*] Eilert Loevborg was here this morning. Wasn't he?

HEDDA: Yes.

BRACK: Were you alone with him?

HEDDA: For a few moments.

BRACK: You didn't leave the room while he was here?

HEDDA: No.

BRACK: Think again. Are you sure you didn't go out for a moment?

HEDDA: Oh—yes, I might have gone into the hall. Just for a few seconds.

BRACK: And where was your pistol-case during this time?

HEDDA: I'd locked it in that——

BRACK: Er—Mrs. Hedda?

HEDDA: It was lying over there on my writing table.

BRACK: Have you looked to see if both the pistols are still there?

HEDDA: No.

BRACK: You needn't bother. I saw the pistol Loevborg had when they found him. I recognized it at once. From yesterday. And other occasions.

HEDDA: Have you got it?

BRACK: No. The police have it.

HEDDA: What will the police do with this pistol?

BRACK: Try to trace the owner.

HEDDA: Do you think they'll succeed?

BRACK: [*Leans down and whispers.*] No, Hedda Gabler. Not as long as I hold my tongue.

HEDDA: [*Looks nervously at him.*] And if you don't?

BRACK: [*Shrugs his shoulders.*] You could always say he'd stolen it.

HEDDA: I'd rather die!

BRACK: [*Smiles.*] People say that. They never do it.

HEDDA: [*Not replying.*] And suppose the pistol wasn't stolen? And they trace the owner? What then?

BRACK: There'll be a scandal, Hedda.

HEDDA: A scandal!

BRACK: Yes, a scandal. The thing you're so frightened of. You'll have to appear in court. Together with Mademoiselle Danielle. She'll have to explain how it all happened. Was it an accident, or was it—homicide? Was he about to take the pistol from his pocket to threaten her? And did it go off? Or did she snatch the pistol from his hand, shoot him and then put it back in his pocket? She might quite easily have done it. She's a resourceful lady, is Mademoiselle Danielle.

HEDDA: But I had nothing to do with this repulsive business.

BRACK: No. But you'll have to answer one question. Why did you give Eilert Loevborg this pistol? And what conclusions will people draw when it is proved you did give it to him?

HEDDA: [*Bows her head.*] That's true. I hadn't thought of that.

BRACK: Well, luckily there's no danger as long as I hold my tongue.

HEDDA: [*Looks up at him.*] In other words, I'm in your power, Judge. From now on, you've got your hold over me.

BRACK: [*Whispers, more slowly.*] Hedda, my dearest—believe me—I will not abuse my position.

HEDDA: Nevertheless, I'm in your power. Dependent on your will, and your demands. Not free. Still not free! [*Rises passionately.*] No. I couldn't bear that. No.

BRACK: [*Looks half-derisively at her.*] Most people resign themselves to the inevitable, sooner or later.

HEDDA: [*Returns his gaze.*] Possibly they do. [*She goes across to the writing table.*]

HEDDA: [*Represses an involuntary smile and says in* TESMAN'*s voice.*] Well, George. Think you'll be able to manage? What?

TESMAN: Heaven knows, dear. This is going to take months and months.

HEDDA: [*In the same tone as before.*] Fancy that, by Jove! [*Runs her hands gently through* MRS. ELVSTED'*s hair.*] Doesn't it feel strange, Thea? Here you are working away with Tesman just the way you used to work with Eilert Loevborg.

MRS. ELVSTED: Oh—if only I can inspire your husband too!

HEDDA: Oh, it'll come. In time.

TESMAN: Yes—do you know, Hedda, I really think I'm beginning to feel a bit—well—that way. But you go back and talk to Judge Brack.

HEDDA: Can't I be of use to you two in any way?

TESMAN: No, none at all. [*Turns his head.*] You'll have to keep Hedda company from now on, Judge, and see she doesn't get bored. If you don't mind.

BRACK: [*Glances at* HEDDA.] It'll be a pleasure.

HEDDA: Thank you. But I'm tired this evening. I think I'll lie down on the sofa in there for a little while.

TESMAN: Yes, dear—do. What?

[HEDDA *goes into the rear room and draws the curtain behind her. Short pause. Suddenly she begins to play a frenzied dance melody on the piano.*]

MRS. ELVSTED: [*Starts up from her chair.*] Oh, what's that?

TESMAN: [*Runs to the doorway.*] Hedda dear, please! Don't play dance music tonight! Think of Auntie Rena. And Eilert.

HEDDA: [*Puts her head out through the curtains.*] And Auntie Juju. And all the rest of them. From now on I'll be quiet. [*Closes the curtains behind her.*]

TESMAN: [*At the writing table.*] It distresses her to watch us doing this. I say, Mrs. Elvsted, I've an idea. Why don't you move in with Auntie Juju? I'll run over each evening, and we can sit and work there. What?

MRS. ELVSTED: Yes, that might be the best plan.

HEDDA: [*From the rear room.*] I can hear what you're saying, Tesman. But how shall I spend the evenings out here?

TESMAN: [*Looking through his papers.*] Oh, I'm sure Judge Brack'll be kind enough to come over and keep you company. You won't mind my not being here, Judge?

BRACK: [*In the armchair, calls gaily.*] I'll be delighted, Mrs. Tesman. I'll be here every evening. We'll have great fun together, you and I.

HEDDA: [*Loud and clear.*] Yes, that'll suit you, won't it, Judge? The only cock on the dunghill——!

[*A shot is heard from the rear room.* TESMAN, MRS. ELVSTED *and* JUDGE BRACK *start from their chairs.*]

TESMAN: Oh, she's playing with those pistols again.

[*He pulls the curtains aside and runs in.* MRS. ELVSTED *follow him.* HEDDA *is lying dead on the sofa. Confusion and shouting.* BERTHA *enters in alarm from the right.*]

TESMAN: [*Screams to* BRACK.] She's shot herself! Shot herself in the head! By Jove! Fancy that!

BRACK: [*Half paralyzed in the armchair.*] But, good God! People don't do such things!

1890

QUESTIONS

Trifles

1. How do each of these "trifles" function in the play, what does each tell you, and what is your emotional response to each at the time it is introduced?

- the loaf of bread?
- the burst jar of preserves?
- the botched quilt square?
- the bird cage?
- the bird?

Hedda Gabler

1. How much do you learn of Hedda's life, of Tesman, of the situation, in the brief conversation between Miss Tesman and Bertha that opens the play? What indications are there of differences in class (or "life-style") between the Tesmans and Gablers in that conversation?

2. In what way did Tesman not "waste time" on his honeymoon? What does this suggest about him? his marriage? the future? What other details in the first five or six pages reinforce your understanding of his character, his professional accomplishments, and your expectations of what will happen later in the play? How is Tesman distinguished from the stereotypical absent-minded professor?

3. What is the important element in Hedda's attire when she first enters?

4. What expectations are aroused by the first part of the scene in act 1 in which Mrs. Elvsted pays a call (before Tesman leaves the room)? What does Hedda get out of Mrs. Elvsted after Tesman leaves? How does she do it? Why? What new expectations are aroused by the Hedda–Thea conversation? Hedda is amazed by Mrs. Elvsted's open break with social conformity in deserting her husband; what are Hedda's attitudes toward society and the appearance that she makes in that society?

5. Why is Hedda so intrigued by the "competition" between George Tesman and Loevborg? Why does Judge Brack find the competition suited to his purposes?

6. How does the first act end? What is the effect of that ending? What does it fill in about the past and what expectations does it arouse about what is to happen later?

7. What are Loevborg's strengths? weaknesses? How are they related?

8. Why is George so shocked at the subject of Loevborg's new book? How are their approaches to their professions and to life different?

9. When Hedda suggests to George that Loevborg is "less afraid of life than most men," George responds, "Good heavens, no. He just doesn't know the meaning of the word moderation." Whose assessment is more accurate?

10. Does Mrs. Elvsted's inspiration of George and her plans to move in with Miss Tesman complete a new triangle excluding Hedda? What does Hedda's imitation of George in the last scene ("Fancy that, by Jove!") indicate regarding this turn of events?

WRITING SUGGESTIONS

1. Note the similarities in the stage directions describing the sets (and, indeed, in the rooms themselves) in *Hedda Gabler* and *The Little Foxes*. Beginning with setting, write a comparative analysis of the two plays as examples of realism.

2. Write on the relation of social class to character and events in *Hedda Gabler*, in the course of your essay suggesting what segments of society Hedda, George, Loevborg, and Judge Brack represent.

3. Write on the themes of courage and cowardice in *Hedda Gabler*. You will probably want to treat the scenes between Hedda and Loevborg, and between Hedda, Mrs. Elvsted, and Loevborg in act 2, and, of course, Hedda's suicide.

4. Write a "response" to *Trifles* in which the county attorney, having found the dead bird in Mrs. Hale's coat pocket, cites her for obstructing justice, concealing evidence, and accessory after the fact to murder.

5. Compare the exploration of gender stereotypes in *Trifles* and *The Brute*.

2 STRUCTURE

An important part of the task of any storyteller, whether the story is to be narrative or dramatic, is the invention, selection, and arrangement of the action. What is going to happen—the characters to be introduced, the events that will unfold, the themes to be introduced, and the situational problems to be solved—cannot properly be said to exist as a full-scale **plot** until some principles of order and organization are introduced and questions of character, plot, and idea are somehow brought together.

Plot in plays usually involves a conflict, and dramatic structure centrally concerns the presentation—quite literally the embodiment or fleshing out—of that conflict. A conflict whose outcome is never in doubt may have other kinds of interest, but it is not truly dramatic. In a dramatic conflict each of the opposing forces—whether one character versus another, one group of characters versus another group, the values of an individual versus those of a group or society or nature, or one idea or ideology versus another one—at some point or other seems to have a chance to triumph.

In *Hamlet*, for example, our interest in the struggle between Hamlet and Claudius depends on their being evenly matched. Claudius has possession of the throne and the queen, but Hamlet has his relation to the late king and his popularity with the people to balance his opponent's strengths. Early in the play Claudius has the upper hand, but he realizes that he has underestimated Hamlet, and he overreacts. Until he stops the play-within-the-play, the king seems firmly in command; the odds seem to favor him. The play, however, does not end with Claudius's triumph.

The king's outburst in *Hamlet* is an example of the kind of event around which dramatic structure is built. A typical dramatic structure involves five distinguishable parts that mark different stages in the progression of the conflict. The first of these, the **exposition**, presents the situation as it exists at the opening of the play, introducing the characters and defining the relationships among them. In *The Brute* most of the exposition is presented before Luka goes to answer the bell, and the rest of it—the introduction of Smirnov and his information about Popov's debt—is given immediately thereafter. The second part of dramatic structure, the **rising action**, consists in a series of events that complicate the original situation and create conflicts among characters or values. It often begins before the exposition is complete because some action needs to be taking place even while we are learning about the situation and the characters involved. During the rising action, the flow of the action is in a single direction, but at some crucial moment an event occurs that changes the direction of that flow, sometimes just by a sudden revelation. In *The Brute*, for example, the hostile Smirnov suddenly realizes he is falling in love with Mrs. Popov. This is the third part of dramatic structure, the **climax** or **turning point.** The fourth part is the **falling action,** the changes that characterize the unwinding or unknotting of the complication, and often this unwinding happens much more quickly than the rising action. The final part of dramatic structure is its **conclusion,** sometimes called the **catastrophe** (from a Greek word meaning "to overturn"). The central conflict is resolved, a stable situation is re-established, and the drama is done.

Structure does not work in exactly the same way in every play, but the basic pattern in most plays is quite similar. In *Hamlet*, the exposition—the situation at the beginning of the play—is mostly set forth in the first act. What do we need to know to understand the major conflicts in the play? We must know about the death of the old king, the accession of Claudius rather than young Hamlet, the marriage of Claudius and Gertrude, Hamlet's return from Wittenberg, and the threat of invasion from Fortinbras. We also need to know something about the nature of the characters involved in the situation. Shakespeare uses two major devices to present this information: the recent return of Horatio from Wittenberg (and his need to be brought up to date) and Claudius's speech at the beginning of act 1, scene 2. In these and other ways we learn where things stand. But even as these basic facts are unfolding, things begin to happen. The rising action begins, the introduction of new elements that are to affect the action of the play: the appearance of the ghost, Claudius's refusal to allow Hamlet to return to Wittenberg, Hamlet's growing involvement with Ophelia, the return of Rosencrantz and Guildenstern, and so forth. These and other complications affect the action without changing its basic direction. They also set up or prepare us for events that are to happen later in the play: for example, Laertes' departure for Paris sets up his return in act 4. The climax, or turning point, occurs when the king loses control of himself at the play-within-the-play. He loses his advantage over Hamlet, who from then on is more or less in control of the situation. During the falling action the various strands of the plot begin to work themselves out. What happens to Ophelia? What is the result of Rosencrantz and Guildenstern's return? When such questions have been settled, we move to the conclusion of the play, the re-establishment of a new stable situation. The conclusion takes place in the final scene, where order is finally restored by the promise of Fortinbras as king.

Similarly in *The Little Foxes*, the opening scenes establish the characters and outline the various kinds of emotional and thematic conflict. There is regional conflict between the values of the South, as represented by the Hubbard and Giddens families, and the North, as represented by the Chicago interests of William Marshall. There is class conflict between the old landed South of Birdie and the new commercialization represented by Oscar and Ben—the paternalistic values represented by Lionnet versus those of stores and factories. There are racial conflicts, generational conflicts, conflicts among siblings and between husbands and wives.

And most immediately and powerfully, there are struggles of will among strong individuals, most notably involving Regina and her several antagonists—both her brothers, her daughter, her husband.

But even before all the givens of character and situation are clear to us, the tension (rising action) begins to develop over details of the family's deal with Mr. Marshall, a deal that is designed to ease some of the major ideological conflicts (North and South, land and commerce) but that heightens other conflicts instead (between generations, between siblings, marriage partners, and other individuals). The climax comes near the end of act 2 when Ben and Oscar decide to steal the bonds and leave Regina out of the deal. The falling action sorts out the implications for the several characters and families and leads to the final struggle between Regina and Horace and the related struggles between Regina and Zan and Regina and her brothers, and the conclusion involves baring the loneliness and fears of Regina and a recognition on all sides of the way their continued existence depends on silence and lies.

Even a sketch like *The Black and White* or a short play like *The Brute* contains all five of the parts, although some are in abbreviated or truncated form. In *Black and White,* for example, the exposition is barely completed when the play ends. The action is minimal and so is the conflict. What little disagreement there is between the two characters—the rising action—quickly climaxes through their discussion of how to handle strangers as their joint worry about uselessness and pointlessness surfaces, and together they face the fact that they both have no place to go when the milk bar closes (the falling action). The brief conclusion shows them planning how to cope individually with the alien world (by mentioning familiar sights and going to familiar places) as the night ends and dawn comes on. This is not high drama with fireworks and physical conflict, but even in their shortened and subdued form a basic dramatic structure shapes the single scene.

There are other structural devices by which a play can be organized and made meaningful and effective. Thematic concerns, for example, often hold together varieties of characters and winding plots. In *The Little Foxes*, the concern to define southern culture and values brings together the various kinds of conflict—between races, classes, generations, families, individuals, and ways of life. Careful and intricate plot calculations, in which difficult situations are created to keep in tension the precise strengths and weaknesses of crucial characters, also structure plays in subtle but analyzable ways. In *The Little Foxes*, the negotiable bonds in Leo's possession make possible not only the theft of Regina's share in the family investment but also set up the final isolation of Regina from both her husband and daughter. Making Leo an assistant at the bank, creating him as a weak, immature, opportunistic, and gossipy character, and having his private knowledge of the bonds in the safe deposit box surface at precisely the right moment, allow developments in the plot to come into conflict with aspects of Regina's character—her greed and ambition, her romanticism, her lack of human loyalty and inability to love—in ways that make event after event seem nearly inevitable.

Another structural device involves **dramatic irony**, the fulfillment of a plan, action, or expectation in a surprising way, often the opposite of what was intended. One example occurs in *Trifles* when the women keep noticing all the everyday things—"trifles"—in the house while the official investigators—the men—keep looking for large and unusual things. When the men find "nothing . . . but kitchen things," they think they have no clues at all and condescend to what women are concerned about. "Women are used to worrying about trifles," they observe ironically, but the irony is on them. Here the play's title sets up the dramatic irony of moment after moment and observation after observation, for two wholly different ways of observing and reasoning are explored from beginning to end, and the action continually comments on the dominant male assumptions.

Another example involves the way, at the end of *The Little Foxes*, Regina's clever manipulativeness first seems to be rewarded and then is thwarted. Her insistence that Horace return home from Baltimore so that she can persuade him to join in the family's get-rich-quick scheme becomes a nighmare for her when he proves to have become, during his absence, both stronger and smarter, and when Horace reveals the terms of his will she recognizes that her own "will"—to be rich and have a new life in Chicago—is going to be defeated. But there are yet more turns of dramatic irony. When Horace's sudden attack again gives Regina control over his medicine, his life, and his ability to make the will, she again seems not only to have triumphed over her husband but over her brothers as well—only to find again that her shrewdest and most cruel plans fail to get her what she wants.

Such paralleled ironies are only one way of achieving thematic resonance through plotting. In *Death of a Salesman*, the unfolding story of Willy's life moves backward and forward through time so that Willy experiences the past as if it were the present, and we hear almost simultaneously conversations between friends inhabiting his grim present and those from an idealized past. These concurrent "plots"—the stories of Willy before and after the Depression—proceed chronologically as revealed to the reader and viewer through Willy's consciousness.

Besides structures like dramatic irony or thematic coherence that pull parts of the play together, and the five dramatic structural divisions that shape the action, most plays also have formal divisions, such as acts and scenes. In the Greek theater scenes were separated by choral odes. In many French plays, a new scene begins with any significant entrance or exit. Many "classic" plays have five acts (because the poet Horace suggested that number), but modern plays tend to have two or three acts. Formal divisions are the result of the content of the individual play—where sharp breaks can be emotionally effective by creating suspense or giving readers a relief from tension—or the conventions of the period: the expectation in the modern theater, for example, that audiences will have one or two intermissions in a public performance. Divisions may vary from the one-act, one-scene play—such as *The Brute*—to such long multi-act plays as Eugene O'Neill's *Mourning Becomes Electra*.

The ways that interest is sustained, that the rise and fall of emotion are controlled, and that character and plot are revealed depend heavily on length and the mode of presentation conceived for the drama. Closet dramas written primarily for private reading are likely to have a different pace from that of musicals or farces that depend heavily on physical movement or pratfalls, and soap operas or serials broken into many episodes are likely to use all kinds of subplots and subconflicts to create smaller structural units within some larger shape. Dramas that are written as performance texts but read as literary texts retain in their printed state features that may have been dictated by conventions, circumstances, or accidents of performance.

Dramatic structures, dramatic irony, and even the formal divisions of a play are present to the reader as well as the viewer of the performance of a play, but of course in performance a play takes definite form on a stage or acting area rather than in the less defined theater of the reader's mind. The design and significance of the acting area vary in different times and places, and it is often useful for readers to know something about stage history so as to appreciate how features of the text came to be and how the action might be imagined. In the Greek theater, the audience was seated on a raised semicircle of seats (**amphitheater**) halfway around a circular area (**orchestra**) used primarily for dancing by the chorus. At the back of the orchestra was the **skene** or stage house, which represented the palace or temple before which the action took place. Shakespeare's stage, in contrast, basically involved a rectangular area built inside one end of a generally round enclosure, so that the audience was on three sides of the principal acting area. There were additional acting areas on either side of this stage, as well as a recessed area at the back of the stage, which could represent Gertrude's chamber in *Hamlet*, for example, and an upper acting area, which could serve as Juliet's balcony, for example.

Modern stages are of three basic types. The **proscenium** stage evolved during the nineteenth century and is still the most common. For such a stage, the proscenium or proscenium arch is an architectural element that separates the auditorium from the stage and makes the action seem more real because the audience is viewing it through an invisible fourth wall. The proscenium stage lends itself to the use of a curtain, which can be lowered and raised—or closed and parted—between acts or scenes. Sometimes a part of the acting area is on the auditorium side of the proscenium. Such an area is an **apron** or forestage. The second type of modern stage is the **thrust stage,** in which the audience is seated around three-fourths of the major acting area. All of the action may take place on this projecting area, or some may occur in the extended area of the fourth side. In an **arena stage,** the third type, the audience is seated around the acting area. Entrances and exits are made through the auditorium, and restrictions on the sets are required to insure visibility. At any given time and place the idea of what a stage is like is generally shared by audience and stage personnel, and most authors work with this generally understood notion of the kind of stage involved when they write a play. Of course, authors will sometimes innovate and they, the director, or set designer will work out new ways of using the stage, as in the flashbacks of *Death of a Salesman.* But even then Miller and his associates were working with the general understanding of the nature of one stage. Even greater differences are involved when we examine plays of different periods that have radically different conventions.

One such convention involves the notion of place. The audience knows that the stage is a stage, but they accept it for a public square or a room in a castle or an empty road. In *The Brute* we accept the stage as a drawing room in a Russian country house. There must be at least one door, leading to the entrance of the house, and the rest of the house and window. There must be at least two (fragile) straight chairs and an armchair. The play is written for a proscenium stage. If the play is to work, the designer must make the audience aware of the objects, doors, windows, chairs, and so on, required by the action. Many medieval plays were, by contrast, written to be performed on small wagons that could be moved from town to town, and although the action could spill into the street or the audience, no elaborate stage settings or entrances or exits could be physically represented: much more of the "place" had to be left to the audience's imagination, as in radio plays or plays written primarily for readers.

Films, on the other hand, can change location quickly and without asking for acts of spatial imagination on the part of viewers (though they may require another kind of imagination because of the temporal jumps involved in changing scenes). But films may also choose to create a sense of place that is more dreamy, or symbolic, or suggestive, since the mode has no scenes to change or physical stage to be limited by. The film script of *Hiroshima, Mon Amour,* for example, uses a different kind of film resource, the ability to create mood through juxtaposed images that may operate irrespective of time and place, instead of exploiting its photographic ability to reproduce an exact sense of particulars.

The convention of place also involves how place is changed in a stage production. In a modern play like *The Little Foxes,* such a change would involve lowering a curtain or darkening the stage while the sets and props were changed to produce the new place. In Greek drama, generally there was no change of place and the action was set up to involve only one place. If the presence of Tiresias was required, someone would be sent to bring him.

In Shakespeare's theater the conventions of place are quite different: the acting area does not represent a specific place, but assumes a temporary identity from the characters who inhabit it, their costumes, and their speeches. At the opening of the play we know we are at a sentry station because a man dressed as a soldier challenges two others. By line 15, we know what that we are in Denmark because the actors profess to be "liegemen to the Dane." At the end of the scene the actors leave the stage and in a sense take the sentry station with them. Shortly a group of people dressed in court costumes and a man and a woman wearing crowns appear. A theater audience must surmise, from costumes and dialogue, that the acting area has now become a "chamber of state"; as readers of the text, we could also infer the change of place from the identity of the characters and their words, but our text provides more information than a performance can, identifying the changed place in a stage direction. Often, in fact, readers of plays have more—and more accurate—guidance than viewers of plays, for they have the clues beyond dialogue from which actors and directors make decisions about tone or staging.

Readers of plays usually have the convenience of stage directions to indicate exactly where they are, but readers have greater demands placed on them as well, for they are allowed to keep open matters of interpretation that viewers of a play will have had decided by the director. Readers, for example, can put to work their own strategies of textual interpretation to decide how "real" the ghost is, and they can juggle more than one possibility at a time, while a viewer of a performance will have "seen" either an apparent illusion or a realistic presence. The mists can only cover so much in a production, but for a reader the mist can linger much longer, until an entire coherent interpretation of events merges. Thus, in one sense, a reader's text of a play is richer and more uncertain, more open to individual interpretation, than a production mediated by a director and acting company.

Production conventions also govern the treatment of time on stage, and such conventions have an impact on readers as well as viewers of plays because the conventions often have an influence on the way the text is written. Renaissance commentators on classical drama argued that in order to insure maximum dramatic impact the action of a play should be restricted to a very short time—sometimes as short as the actual performance (two or three hours), and certainly no longer than a single day. It is this concentration or **unity of time** that impels a dramatist to select the moment when a stable situation is on the verge of change and to fill in the necessary prior details by exposition or even by some more elaborate device, such as the enacted dreams and memories in *Death of a Salesman.* The action from the beginning to the end of the play thus can be concentrated in a very short period of represented time, rather than spread over fifteen years, moving toward the present crisis scene by scene, act by act. You might look back over the plays you have read so far and note how much time elapses from beginning to end and what devices, if any, preserve the restriction of represented time so as to concentrate the action and thus heighten the impact.

Even within the classical drama with its restricted time span, there are conventions to mark the passing of represented time when it is supposed to pass at a greater rate than that of viewing or reading time. The choral odes in *Oedipus the King* are an example of one convention for representing the passage of time. The elapsed time between scenes may be that necessary to send for the shepherd from Mount Cithaeron and allow for his return or the much shorter time needed for Oedipus to enter his palace, discover Jocasta's suicide, blind himself, and return.

The time covered by the ode is shorter or longer as necessary, without real reference to the length of the ode. In the Elizabethan theater the break between scenes covered whatever time was necessary without a formal device like the choral odes. Sometimes the time was short, like the break between Hamlet's departure to see his mother at the end of act 3, scene 2, and the opening of the king's prayer at the beginning of the next scene; at other times the elapsed time between might be as long as that between scenes 4 and 5 of act 4, in which the news of Polonius's death reached Paris and Laertes returned to Denmark and there rallied his friends. In *Hamlet* we cannot tell exactly what the time span is, but in a time of relatively primitive transportation Laertes goes to Paris, remains there for a time, and returns to Denmark; Fortinbras goes from Norway to Poland, fights a war, and returns to Denmark; and news of the deaths of Rosencrantz and Guildenstern, who left England between acts 3 and 4, is brought back. The point is not that Shakespeare was sloppy about time; he worked, as did other playwrights of his time, within conventions that audiences and readers understood, and modern readers of his text have to adjust to these assumptions or they will spend a lot of energy worrying about "inconsistencies" or "inaccuracies" that are readily explained by historical habits of performance, reading, and interpretation.

In reading fiction we recognize that what is going on in represented time is often supposed to be taking much longer than it takes us to read the words describing it. The time that is supposed to pass within one sentence can vary greatly from that which passes in another. In reading fiction, we are used to making such adjustments. In plays, however, modern readers or audiences expect the passage of time to be more clearly marked—by stage directions, or scene or act endings.

Not so, necessarily, in Shakespeare. The first scene of *Hamlet*, for example, opens just on the stroke of midnight, yet in less than forty lines—with no obvious warning to the reader that so much time is passing—we learn it is one o'clock. And a hundred lines later the cock crows, and soon Horatio says that it is dawn. In reading this scene, we have little difficulty in adjusting represented time to reading time, but if we enact plays within our imagination while we read them we need to become very aware of this "undramatic" handling of time. In performance, some sort of stage business must suggest the passing of represented time: those watching for the ghost may sit still for what seems to an audience a long time—a couple of minutes—or get up and stretch and walk about the stage, or lie down, toss and turn, perhaps sleep.

Drama is both a literary and performed art, and a play exists separately on page and stage. In reading plays, we use our imagination much as we do in stories to portray to ourselves the way the action is unfolding, but there is a difference. When we read stories we have a mediator, a narrator to guide us. When we read plays, we know that in another manifestation they are staged, produced, performed, and that another set of consciousnesses would mediate how we are led to imagine if we were viewing the plays in performance. As readers, we take all the roles ourselves and do not portion them out to actors; we set our own stage in our own minds. We become, in effect, our own producers, directors, and actors, but with the reader's latitude to keep multiple possibilities in mind. We become not just viewers of a staged production created by an intermediary, but imagining readers of a play—staging and re-staging it in the mind's eye, mediated by our producer-selves.

▽ ▽ ▽

STRUCTURE A Glossary

amphitheater: the raised semicircle of seats on which the audience sat in ancient Greek theater

apron: a forestage, an area of the stage in proscenium theater that extends outward from the curtain, toward the audience

arena stage: a stage in which the action takes place in the midst of the audience, that is, with the audience seated all around the stage action. Also called theater-in-a-circle.

catastrophe: the conclusion, the fifth part of dramatic structure

climax: the turning point between rising and falling action, the third part of dramatic structure

conclusion: the final part of dramatic structure, the catastrophe

conflict: the central tension in drama. Conflict may be between individuals or groups, between an individual and some particular group, between ideas or values, or various combinations of the above.

exposition: the situation of events and the givens of character at the beginning of a play; the first part of dramatic structure

falling action: the unwinding of the plot toward a conclusion, the fourth part of dramatic structure

orchestra: the circular area in ancient Greek theater, which was used primarily for dancing by the chorus

plot: the entire conception of action and character in a play, including its structure

proscenium: the kind of stage in which the action takes place in a designated area isolated from the audience. A proscenium arch, often with a pull or drop curtain, normally divides the stage cleanly from the audience, and the illusion created is of an audience seeing through one wall of a room or from one side of an outdoor scene.

rising action: the tangling of the plot, the setting up of conflict; the second part of dramatic structure

skene: in ancient Greek theater, the stage house representing the palace or temple in front of which the action takes place

thrust stage: a stage surrounded on three sides by the audience

turning point: the climax, the third part of dramatic structure: the point at which rising action ends and falling action begins

unity of time: the critical doctrine that the represented action in a play should not exceed the performance time on the stage. Literally understood, unity of time would mean that a play that takes two hours to perform represents fictional time of two hours, but in practice even the most rigid proponents of unity of time allow a play to represent fictional time up to [not to exceed] a single twenty-four-hour day.

WILLIAM SHAKESPEARE

Hamlet

CHARACTERS

CLAUDIUS, *King of Denmark*
HAMLET, *son of the former and nephew to the present King*
POLONIUS, *Lord Chamberlain*
HORATIO, *friend of Hamlet*
LAERTES, *son of Polonius*
VOLTEMAND, CORNELIUS, ROSENCRANTZ, GUILDENSTERN, OSRIC, A GENTLEMAN } *courtiers*
A PRIEST
MARCELLUS, BERNARDO } *officers*
FRANCISCO, *a soldier*
REYNALDO, *servant to Polonius*
PLAYERS
TWO CLOWNS, *gravediggers*
FORTINBRAS, *Prince of Norway*
A NORWEGIAN CAPTAIN
ENGLISH AMBASSADORS
GERTRUDE, *Queen of Denmark, and mother of Hamlet*
OPHELIA, *daughter of Polonius*
GHOST OF HAMLET'S FATHER
LORDS, LADIES, OFFICERS, SOLDIERS, SAILORS, MESSENGERS, AND ATTENDANTS

SCENE: *The action takes place in or near the royal castle of Denmark at Elsinore.*

ACT I

SCENE 1

A guard station atop the castle. Enter BERNARDO *and* FRANCISCO, *two sentinels.*

BERNARDO: Who's there?
FRANCISCO: Nay, answer me. Stand and unfold yourself.
BERNARDO: Long live the king!
FRANCISCO: Bernardo?
BERNARDO: He.
FRANCISCO: You come most carefully upon your hour.
BERNARDO: 'Tis now struck twelve. Get thee to bed, Francisco.
FRANCISCO: For this relief much thanks. 'Tis bitter cold,
And I am sick at heart.
BERNARDO: Have you had quiet guard?
FRANCISCO: Not a mouse stirring.
BERNARDO: Well, good night.
If you do meet Horatio and Marcellus,
The rivals[1] of my watch, bid them make haste.

[*Enter* HORATIO *and* MARCELLUS.]

1. Companions.

FRANCISCO: I think I hear them. Stand, ho! Who is there?
HORATIO: Friends to this ground.
MARCELLUS: And liegemen to the Dane.[2]
FRANCISCO: Give you good night.
MARCELLUS: O, farewell, honest soldier!
Who hath relieved you?
FRANCISCO: Bernardo hath my place.
Give you good night. [*Exit* FRANCISCO.]
MARCELLUS: Holla, Bernardo!
BERNARDO: Say—
What, is Horatio there?
HORATIO: A piece of him.
BERNARDO: Welcome, Horatio. Welcome, good Marcellus.
HORATIO: What, has this thing appeared again tonight?
BERNARDO: I have seen nothing.
MARCELLUS: Horatio says 'tis but our fantasy,
And will not let belief take hold of him
Touching this dreaded sight twice seen of us.
Therefore I have entreated him along
With us to watch the minutes of this night,
That if again this apparition come,
He may approve[3] our eyes and speak to it.
HORATIO: Tush, tush, 'twill not appear.
BERNARDO: Sit down awhile,
And let us once again assail your ears,
That are so fortified against our story,
What we have two nights seen.
HORATIO: Well, sit we down.
And let us hear Bernardo speak of this.
BERNARDO: Last night of all,
When yond same star that's westward from the pole[4]
Had made his course t' illume that part of heaven
Where now it burns, Marcellus and myself,
The bell then beating one—

[*Enter* GHOST.]

MARCELLUS: Peace, break thee off. Look where it comes again.
BERNARDO: In the same figure like the king that's dead.
MARCELLUS: Thou art a scholar; speak to it, Horatio.
BERNARDO: Looks 'a[5] not like the king? Mark it, Horatio.
HORATIO: Most like. It harrows me with fear and wonder.
BERNARDO: It would be spoke to.

2. The "Dane" is the King of Denmark, who is also called "Denmark," as in line 48 of this scene. In line 61 the same figure is used for the King of Norway. 3. Confirm the testimony of. 4. Polestar. 5. He.

MARCELLUS: Speak to it, Horatio.
HORATIO: What art thou that usurp'st this time of night
Together with that fair and warlike form
In which the majesty of buried Denmark
Did sometimes march? By heaven I charge thee, speak.
MARCELLUS: It is offended.
BERNARDO: See, it stalks away.
HORATIO: Stay. Speak, speak. I charge thee, speak. [*Exit* GHOST.]
MARCELLUS: 'Tis gone and will not answer.
BERNARDO: How now, Horatio! You tremble and look pale.
Is not this something more than fantasy?
What think you on't?
HORATIO: Before my God, I might not this believe
Without the sensible[6] and true avouch
Of mine own eyes.
MARCELLUS: Is it not like the king?
HORATIO: As thou art to thyself.
Such was the very armor he had on
When he the ambitious Norway combated.
So frowned he once when, in an angry parle,[7]
He smote the sledded Polacks on the ice.
'Tis strange.
MARCELLUS: Thus twice before, and jump[8] at this dead hour,
With martial stalk hath he gone by our watch.
HORATIO: In what particular thought to work I know not,
But in the gross and scope of mine opinion,
This bodes some strange eruption to our state.
MARCELLUS: Good now, sit down, and tell me he that knows,
Why this same strict and most observant watch
So nightly toils the subject[9] of the land,
And why such daily cast of brazen cannon
And foreign mart for implements of war;
Why such impress of shipwrights, whose sore task
Does not divide the Sunday from the week.
What might be toward that this sweaty haste
Doth make the night joint-laborer with the day?
Who is't that can inform me?
HORATIO: That can I.
At last, the whisper goes so. Our last king,
Whose image even but now appeared to us,
Was as you know by Fortinbras of Norway,
Thereto pricked on by a most emulate pride,
Dared to the combat; in which our valiant Hamlet
(For so this side of our known world esteemed him)

6. Of the senses. 7. Parley. 8. Precisely. 9. People.

Did slay this Fortinbras; who by a sealed compact
Well ratified by law and heraldry,
Did forfeit, with his life, all those his lands
Which he stood seized of,[1] to the conqueror;
Against the which a moiety competent[2]
Was gagéd[3] by our king; which had returned
To the inheritance of Fortinbras,
Had he been vanquisher; as, by the same covenant
And carriage of the article designed,
His fell to Hamlet. Now, sir, young Fortinbras,
Of unimprovéd mettle hot and full,
Hath in the skirts of Norway here and there
Sharked up a list of lawless resolutes
For food and diet to some enterprise
That hath a stomach in't; which is no other,
As it doth well appear unto our state,
But to recover of us by strong hand
And terms compulsatory, those foresaid lands
So by his father lost; and this, I take it,
Is the main motive of our preparations,
The source of this our watch, and the chief head
Of this post-haste and romage[4] in the land.

BERNARDO: I think it be no other but e'en so.
Well may it sort[5] that this portentous figure
Comes armed through our watch so like the king
That was and is the question of these wars.

HORATIO: A mote[6] it is to trouble the mind's eye.
In the most high and palmy state of Rome,
A little ere the mightiest Julius fell,
The graves stood tenantless, and the sheeted dead
Did squeak and gibber in the Roman streets;
As stars with trains of fire, and dews of blood,
Disasters in the sun; and the moist star,
Upon whose influence Neptune's empire stands,[7]
Was sick almost to doomsday with eclipse.
And even the like precurse[8] of feared events,
As harbingers preceding still the fates
And prologue to the omen coming on,
Have heaven and earth together demonstrated
Unto our climatures[9] and countrymen.

[*Enter* GHOST.]

1. Possessed. 2. Portion of similar value. 3. Pledged. 4. Stir. 5. Chance. 6. Speck of dust. 7. Neptune was the Roman sea god; the "moist star" is the moon. 8. Precursor. 9. Regions.

But soft, behold, lo where it comes again!
I'll cross it[1] though it blast me.—Stay, illusion.

[*It spreads (its) arms.*]

If thou hast any sound or use of voice,
Speak to me.
If there be any good thing to be done,
That may to thee do ease, and grace to me,
Speak to me.
If thou art privy to thy country's fate,
Which happily foreknowing may avoid,
O, speak!
Or if thou hast uphoarded in thy life
Extorted treasure in the womb of earth,
For which, they say, you spirits oft walk in death,

[*The cock crows.*]

Speak of it. Stay, and speak. Stop it, Marcellus.
MARCELLUS: Shall I strike at it with my partisan[2]?
HORATIO: Do, if it will not stand.
BERNARDO: 'Tis here.
HORATIO: 'Tis here.
MARCELLUS: 'Tis gone. [*Exit* GHOST.]
We do it wrong, being so majestical,
To offer it the show of violence;
For it is as the air, invulnerable,
And our vain blows malicious mockery.
BERNARDO: It was about to speak when the cock crew.
HORATIO: And then it started like a guilty thing
Upon a fearful summons. I have heard
The cock, that is the trumpet to the morn,
Doth with his lofty and shrill-sounding throat
Awake the god of day, and at his warning,
Whether in sea or fire, in earth or air,
Th' extravagant and erring[3] spirit hies
To his confine; and of the truth herein
This present object made probation.[4]
MARCELLUS: It faded on the crowing of the cock.
Some say that ever 'gainst that season comes
Wherein our Savior's birth is celebrated,
This bird of dawning singeth all night long,
And then, they say, no spirit dare stir abroad,

1. Horatio means either that he will move across the Ghost's path in order to stop him or that he will make the sign of the cross to gain power over him. The stage direction which follows is somewhat ambiguous. "It" seems to refer to the Ghost, but the movement would be appropriate to Horatio.
2. Halberd. 3. Wandering out of bounds. 4. Proof.

The nights are wholesome, then no planets strike,
No fairy takes,[5] nor witch hath power to charm,
So hallowed and so gracious is that time.
HORATIO: So have I heard and do in part believe it.
But look, the morn in russet mantle clad
Walks o'er the dew of yon high eastward hill.
Break we our watch up, and by my advice
Let us impart what we have seen tonight
Unto young Hamlet, for upon my life
This spirit, dumb to us, will speak to him.
Do you consent we shall acquaint him with it,
As needful in our loves, fitting our duty?
MARCELLUS: Let's do't, I pray, and I this morning know
Where we shall find him most convenient. [*Exeunt.*]

SCENE 2

A *chamber of state. Enter* KING CLAUDIUS, QUEEN GERTRUDE, HAMLET, POLONIUS, LAERTES, OPHELIA, VOLTEMAND, CORNELIUS *and other members of the court.*

KING: Though yet of Hamlet our dear brother's death
The memory be green, and that it us befitted
To bear our hearts in grief, and our whole kingdom
To be contracted in one brow of woe,
Yet so far hath discretion fought with nature
That we with wisest sorrow think on him,
Together with remembrance of ourselves.
Therefore our sometime sister, now our queen,
Th' imperial jointress[6] to this warlike state,
Have we, as 'twere with a defeated joy,
With an auspicious and a dropping eye,
With mirth in funeral, and with dirge in marriage,
In equal scale weighing delight and dole,
Taken to wife; nor have we herein barred
Your better wisdoms, which have freely gone
With this affair along. For all, our thanks.
Now follows that you know young Fortinbras,
Holding a weak supposal of our worth,
Or thinking by our late dear brother's death
Our state to be disjoint and out of frame,
Colleaguéd with this dream of his advantage,
He hath not failed to pester us with message
Importing the surrender of those lands

5. Enchants. 6. A "jointress" is a widow who holds a *jointure* or life interest in the estate of her deceased husband.

Lost by his father, with all bands of law,
To our most valiant brother. So much for him.
Now for ourself, and for this time of meeting,
Thus much the business is: we have here writ
To Norway, uncle of young Fortinbras—
Who, impotent and bedrid, scarcely hears
Of this his nephew's purpose—to suppress
His further gait[7] herein, in that the levies,
The lists, and full proportions are all made
Out of his subject; and we here dispatch
You, good Cornelius, and you, Voltemand,
For bearers of this greeting to old Norway,
Giving to you no further personal power
To business with the king, more than the scope
Of these dilated[8] articles allow.
Farewell, and let your haste commend your duty.

CORNELIUS: } In that, and all things will we show our duty.
VOLTEMAND: }

KING: We doubt it nothing, heartily farewell.

[*Exeunt* VOLTEMAND *and* CORNELIUS.]

And now, Laertes, what's the news with you?
You told us of some suit. What is't, Laertes?
You cannot speak of reason to the Dane
And lose your voice. What wouldst thou beg, Laertes,
That shall not be my offer, not thy asking?
The head is not more native to the heart,
The hand more instrumental[9] to the mouth,
Than is the throne of Denmark to thy father.
What wouldst thou have, Laertes?

LAERTES: My dread lord,
Your leave and favor to return to France,
From whence, though willingly, I came to Denmark
To show my duty in your coronation,
Yet now I must confess, that duty done,
My thoughts and wishes bend again toward France,
And bow them to your gracious leave and pardon.

KING: Have you your father's leave? What says Polonius?

POLONIUS: He hath, my lord, wrung from me my slow leave
By laborsome petition, and at last
Upon his will I sealed my hard consent.
I do beseech you give him leave to go.

KING: Take thy fair hour, Laertes. Time be thine,
And thy best graces spend it at thy will.

7. Progress. 8. Fully expressed. 9. Serviceable.

But now, my cousin[1] Hamlet, and my son—
HAMLET: [*Aside.*] A little more than kin, and less than kind.
KING: How is it that the clouds still hang on you?
HAMLET: Not so, my lord. I am too much in the sun.
QUEEN: Good Hamlet, cast thy nighted color off,
And let thine eye look like a friend on Denmark.
Do not for ever with thy vailéd lids[2]
Seek for thy noble father in the dust.
Thou know'st 'tis common—all that lives must die,
Passing through nature to eternity.
HAMLET: Ay, madam, it is common.
QUEEN: If it be,
Why seems it so particular with thee?
HAMLET: Seems, madam? Nay, it is. I know not "seems."
'Tis not alone my inky cloak, good mother,
Nor customary suits of solemn black,
Nor windy suspiration of forced breath,
No, nor the fruitful river in the eye,
Nor the dejected havior[3] of the visage,
Together with all forms, moods, shapes of grief,
That can denote me truly. These indeed seem,
For they are actions that a man might play,
But I have that within which passes show—
These but the trappings and the suits of woe.
KING: 'Tis sweet and commendable in your nature, Hamlet,
To give these mourning duties to your father,
But you must know your father lost a father,
That father lost, lost his, and the survivor bound
In filial obligation for some term
To do obsequious[4] sorrow. But to persever
In obstinate condolement is a course
Of impious stubbornness. 'Tis unmanly grief.
It shows a will most incorrect to[5] heaven,
A heart unfortified, a mind impatient,
An understanding simple and unschooled.
For what we know must be, and is as common
As any the most vulgar thing to sense,
Why should we in our peevish opposition
Take it to heart? Fie, 'tis a fault to heaven,
A fault against the dead, a fault to nature,
To reason most absurd, whose common theme
Is death of fathers, and who still hath cried,
From the first corse[6] till he that died today,

1. "Cousin" is used here as a general term of kinship. 2. Lowered eyes. 3. Appearance.
4. Suited for funeral obsequies. 5. Uncorrected toward. 6. Corpse.

"This must be so." We pray you throw to earth
This unprevailing woe, and think of us
As of a father, for let the world take note
You are the most immediate[7] to our throne,
And with no less nobility of love
Than that which dearest father bears his son
Do I impart toward you. For your intent
In going back to school in Wittenberg,
It is most retrograde[8] to our desire,
And we beseech you, bend you to remain
Here in the cheer and comfort of our eye,
Our chiefest courtier, cousin, and our son.

QUEEN: Let not thy mother lose her prayers, Hamlet.
I pray thee stay with us, go not to Wittenberg.

HAMLET: I shall in all my best obey you, madam.

KING: Why, 'tis a loving and a fair reply.
Be as ourself in Denmark. Madam, come.
This gentle and unforced accord of Hamlet
Sits smiling to my heart, in grace whereof,
No jocund health that Denmark drinks today
But the great cannon to the clouds shall tell,
And the king's rouse the heaven shall bruit[9] again,
Respeaking earthly thunder. Come away.

[*Flourish. Exeunt all but* HAMLET.]

HAMLET: O, that this too too solid flesh would melt,
Thaw, and resolve itself into a dew,
Or that the Everlasting had not fixed
His canon[1] 'gainst self-slaughter. O God, God,
How weary, stale, flat, and unprofitable
Seem to me all the uses of this world!
Fie on't, ah, fie, 'tis an unweeded garden
That grows to seed. Things rank and gross in nature
Possess it merely.[2] That it should come to this,
But two months dead, nay, not so much, not two.
So excellent a king, that was to this
Hyperion to a satyr,[3] so loving to my mother,
That he might not beteem[4] the winds of heaven
Visit her face too roughly. Heaven and earth,
Must I remember? Why, she would hang on him
As if increase of appetite had grown
By what it fed on, and yet, within a month—
Let me not think on't. Frailty, thy name is woman—
A little month, or ere those shoes were old

7. Next in line. 8. Contrary. 9. Echo. *Rouse:* carousal. 1. Law. 2. Entirely.
3. Hyperion, a Greek god, stands here for beauty in contrast to the monstrous satyr, a lecherous creature, half man and half goat. 4. Permit.

With which she followed my poor father's body
Like Niobe,[5] all tears, why she, even she—
O God, a beast that wants discourse of reason
Would have mourned longer—married with my uncle,
My father's brother, but no more like my father
Than I to Hercules.[6] Within a month,
Ere yet the salt of most unrighteous tears
Had left the flushing in her galléd eyes,
She married. O, most wicked speed, to post
With such dexterity to incestuous sheets!
It is not, nor it cannot come to good.
But break my heart, for I must hold my tongue.

[*Enter* HORATIO, MARCELLUS, *and* BERNARDO.]

HORATIO: Hail to your lordship!
HAMLET: I am glad to see you well.
Horatio—or I do forget myself.
HORATIO: The same, my lord, and your poor servant ever.
HAMLET: Sir, my good friend, I'll change[7] that name with you.
And what make you from Wittenberg, Horatio?
Marcellus?
MARCELLUS: My good lord!
HAMLET: I am very glad to see you. [*To* BERNARDO.] Good even, sir.—
But what, in faith, make you from Wittenberg?
HORATIO: A truant disposition, good my lord.
HAMLET: I would not hear your enemy say so,
Nor shall you do my ear that violence
To make it truster of your own report
Against yourself. I know you are no truant.
But what is your affair in Elsinore?
We'll teach you to drink deep ere you depart.
HORATIO: My lord, I came to see your father's funeral.
HAMLET: I prithee do not mock me, fellow-student,
I think it was to see my mother's wedding.
HORATIO: Indeed, my lord, it followed hard upon.
HAMLET: Thrift, thrift, Horatio. The funeral-baked meats
Did coldly furnish forth the marriage tables.
Would I had met my dearest[8] foe in heaven
Or ever I had seen that day, Horatio!
My father—methinks I see my father.
HORATIO: Where, my lord?
HAMLET: In my mind's eye, Horatio.

5. In Greek mythology Niobe was turned to stone after a tremendous fit of weeping over the death of her fourteen children, a misfortune brought about by her boasting over her fertility. 6. The demigod Hercules was noted for his strength and the series of spectacular labors which it allowed him to accomplish. 7. Exchange. 8. Bitterest.

HORATIO: I saw him once, 'a was a goodly king.
HAMLET: 'A was a man, take him for all in all,
I shall not look upon his like again.
HORATIO: My lord, I think I saw him yesternight.
HAMLET: Saw who?
HORATIO: My lord, the king your father.
HAMLET: The king my father?
HORATIO: Season your admiration[9] for a while
With an attent ear till I may deliver[1]
Upon the witness of these gentlemen
This marvel to you.
HAMLET: For God's love, let me hear!
HORATIO: Two nights together had these gentlemen,
Marcellus and Bernardo, on their watch
In the dead waste and middle of the night
Been thus encountered. A figure like your father,
Armed at point exactly, cap-a-pe,[2]
Appears before them, and with solemn march
Goes slow and stately by them. Thrice he walked
By their oppressed and fear-surprisèd eyes
Within his truncheon's[3] length, whilst they, distilled
Almost to jelly with the act of fear,
Stand dumb and speak not to him. This to me
In dreadful secrecy impart they did,
And I with them the third night kept the watch,
Where, as they had delivered, both in time,
Form of the thing, each word made true and good,
The apparition comes. I knew your father.
These hands are not more like.
HAMLET: But where was this?
MARCELLUS: My lord, upon the platform where we watch.
HAMLET: Did you not speak to it?
HORATIO: My lord, I did,
But answer made it none. Yet once methought
It lifted up it head and did address
Itself to motion, like as it would speak;
But even then the morning cock crew loud,
And at the sound it shrunk in haste away
And vanished from our sight.
HAMLET: 'Tis very strange.
HORATIO: As I do live, my honored lord, 'tis true,
And we did think it writ down in our duty
To let you know of it.

9. Moderate your wonder. 1. Relate. *Attent:* attentive. 2. From head to toe. *Exactly:* completely. 3. Baton of office.

HAMLET: Indeed, sirs, but
This troubles me. Hold you the watch tonight?
ALL: We do, my lord.
HAMLET: Armed, say you?
ALL: Armed, my lord.
HAMLET: From top to toe?
ALL: My lord, from head to foot.
HAMLET: Then saw you not his face.
HORATIO: O yes, my lord, he wore his beaver[4] up.
HAMLET: What, looked he frowningly?
HORATIO: A countenance more in sorrow than in anger.
HAMLET: Pale or red?
HORATIO: Nay, very pale.
HAMLET: And fixed his eyes upon you?
HORATIO: Most constantly.
HAMLET: I would I had been there.
HORATIO: It would have much amazed you.
HAMLET: Very like.
Stayed it long?
HORATIO: While one with moderate haste might tell a hundred.
BOTH: Longer, longer.
HORATIO: Not when I saw't.
HAMLET: His beard was grizzled, no?
HORATIO: It was as I have seen it in his life,
A sable silvered.
HAMLET: I will watch tonight.
Perchance 'twill walk again.
HORATIO: I warr'nt it will.
HAMLET: If it assume my noble father's person,
I'll speak to it though hell itself should gape[5]
And bid me hold my peace. I pray you all,
If you have hitherto concealed this sight,
Let it be tenable[6] in your silence still,
And whatsomever else shall hap tonight,
Give it an understanding but no tongue.
I will requite your loves. So fare you well.
Upon the platform 'twixt eleven and twelve
I'll visit you.
ALL: Our duty to your honor.
HAMLET: Your loves, as mine to you. Farewell. [*Exeunt all but* HAMLET.]
My father's spirit in arms? All is not well.
I doubt[7] some foul play. Would the night were come!
Till then sit still, my soul. Foul deeds will rise,
Though all the earth o'erwhelm them, to men's eyes. [*Exit.*]

4. Movable face protector. 5. Open (its mouth) wide. 6. Held. 7. Suspect.

Scene 3

The dwelling of POLONIUS. *Enter* LAERTES *and* OPHELIA.

LAERTES: My necessaries are embarked. Farewell.
And, sister, as the winds give benefit
And convoy is assistant,[8] do not sleep,
But let me hear from you.
OPHELIA: Do you doubt that?
LAERTES: For Hamlet, and the trifling of his favor,
Hold it a fashion and a toy in blood,
A violet in the youth of primy[9] nature,
Forward, not permanent, sweet, not lasting,
The perfume and suppliance of a minute,
No more.
OPHELIA: No more but so?
LAERTES: Think it no more.
For nature crescent[1] does not grow alone
In thews and bulk, but as this temple[2] waxes
The inward service of the mind and soul
Grows wide withal. Perhaps he loves you now,
And now no soil nor cautel[3] doth besmirch
The virtue of his will, but you must fear,
His greatness weighted,[4] his will is not his own,
For he himself is subject to his birth.
He may not, as unvalued persons do,
Carve for himself, for on his choice depends
The safety and health of this whole state,
And therefore must his choice be circumscribed
Unto the voice[5] and yielding of that body
Whereof he is the head. Then if he says he loves you,
It fits your wisdom so far to believe it
As he in his particular act and place
May give his saying deed, which is no further
Than the main voice of Denmark goes withal.
Then weigh what loss your honor may sustain
If with too credent ear you list[6] his songs,
Or lose your heart, or your chaste treasure open
To his unmastered importunity.
Fear it, Ophelia, fear it, my dear sister,
And keep you in the rear of your affection,
Out of the shot and danger of desire.
The chariest[7] maid is prodigal enough

8. Means of transport is available. 9. Of the spring. 1. Growing. 2. Body. 3. Deceit. 4. Rank considered. 5. Assent. 6. Too credulous ear you listen to. 7. Most circumspect.

If she unmask her beauty to the moon.
Virtue itself scapes not calumnious strokes.
The canker[8] galls the infants of the spring
Too oft before their buttons[9] be disclosed,
And in the morn and liquid dew of youth
Contagious blastments[1] are most imminent.
Be wary then; best safety lies in fear.
Youth to itself rebels, though none else near.

OPHELIA: I shall the effect of this good lesson keep
As watchman to my heart. But, good my brother,
Do not as some ungracious pastors do,
Show me the steep and thorny way to heaven,
Whiles like a puffed and reckless libertine
Himself the primrose path of dalliance treads
And recks not his own rede.[2]

LAERTES: O, fear me not.

[*Enter* POLONIUS.]

I stay too long. But here my father comes.
A double blessing is a double grace;
Occasion smiles upon a second leave.

POLONIUS: Yet here, Laertes? Aboard, aboard, for shame!
The wind sits in the shoulder of your sail,
And you are stayed for. There—my blessing with thee,
And these few precepts in thy memory
Look thou character.[3] Give thy thoughts no tongue,
Nor any unproportioned thought his act.
Be thou familiar, but by no means vulgar.
Those friends thou hast, and their adoption tried,
Grapple them unto thy soul with hoops of steel;
But do not dull[4] thy palm with entertainment
Of each new-hatched, unfledged comrade. Beware
Of entrance to a quarrel, but being in,
Bear't that th' opposéd[5] may beware of thee.
Give every man thy ear, but few thy voice;[6]
Take each man's censure, but reserve thy judgment.
Costly thy habit as thy purse can buy,
But not expressed in fancy; rich not gaudy,
For the apparel oft proclaims the man,
And they in France of the best rank and station
Are of a most select and generous chief[7] in that.
Neither a borrower nor a lender be,
For loan oft loses both itself and friend,

8. Rose caterpillar. 9. Buds. 1. Blights. 2. Heeds not his own advice. 3. Write. 4. Make callous. 5. Conduct it so that the opponent. 6. Approval. 7. Eminence.

And borrowing dulls th' edge of husbandry.
This above all, to thine own self be true,
And it must follow as the night the day
Thou canst not then be false to any man.
Farewell. My blessing season this in thee!
LAERTES: Most humbly do I take my leave, my lord.
POLONIUS: The time invites you. Go, your servants tend.[8]
LAERTES: Farewell, Ophelia, and remember well
What I have said to you.
OPHELIA: 'Tis in my memory locked,
And you yourself shall keep the key of it.
LAERTES: Farewell. [*Exit.*]
POLONIUS: What is't, Ophelia, he hath said to you?
OPHELIA: So please you, something touching the Lord Hamlet.
POLONIUS: Marry, well bethought.
'Tis told me he hath very oft of late
Given private time to you, and you yourself
Have of your audience been most free and bounteous.
If it be so—as so 'tis put on me,
And that in way of caution—I must tell you,
You do not understand yourself so clearly
As it behooves my daughter and your honor.
What is between you? Give me up the truth.
OPHELIA: He hath, my lord, of late made many tenders
Of his affection to me.
POLONIUS: Affection? Pooh! You speak like a green girl,
Unsifted in such perilous circumstance.
Do you believe his tenders, as you call them?
OPHELIA: I do not know, my lord, what I should think.
POLONIUS: Marry, I will teach you. Think yourself a baby
That you have ta'en these tenders for true pay
Which are not sterling. Tender yourself more dearly,
Or (not to crack the wind of the poor phrase,
Running it thus) you'll tender me a fool.
OPHELIA: My lord, he hath importuned me with love
In honorable fashion.
POLONIUS: Ay, fashion you may call it. Go to, go to.
OPHELIA: And hath given countenance[9] to his speech, my lord,
With almost all the holy vows of heaven.
POLONIUS: Ay, springes[1] to catch woodcocks. I do know,
When the blood burns, how prodigal the soul
Lends the tongue vows. These blazes, daughter,
Giving more light than heat, extinct in both
Even in their promise, as it is a-making,

8. Await. 9. Confirmation. 1. Snares.

You must not take for fire. From this time
Be something scanter of your maiden presence.
Set your entreatments[2] at a higher rate
Than a command to parle. For Lord Hamlet,
Believe so much in him that he is young,
And with a larger tether may he walk
Than may be given you. In few, Ophelia,
Do not believe his vows, for they are brokers,[3]
Not of that dye which their investments[4] show,
But mere implorators[5] of unholy suits,
Breathing like sanctified and pious bawds,
The better to beguile. This is for all:
I would not, in plain terms, from this time forth
Have you so slander any moment leisure
As to give words or talk with the Lord Hamlet.
Look to't, I charge you. Come your ways.

OPHELIA: I shall obey, my lord. [*Exeunt.*]

SCENE 4

The guard station. Enter HAMLET, HORATIO *and* MARCELLUS.

HAMLET: The air bites shrewdly[6]; it is very cold.
HORATIO: It is a nipping and an eager[7] air.
HAMLET: What hour now?
HORATIO: I think it lacks of twelve.
MARCELLUS: No, it is struck.
HORATIO: Indeed? I heard it not. It then draws near the season
Wherein the spirit held his wont to walk.

[*A flourish of trumpets, and two pieces go off.*]

What does this mean, my lord?
HAMLET: The king doth wake tonight and takes his rouse.
Keeps wassail, and the swagg'ring up-spring[8] reels,
And as he drains his draughts of Rhenish down,
The kettledrum and trumpet thus bray out
The triumph of his pledge.
HORATIO: Is it a custom?
HAMLET: Ay, marry, is't,
But to my mind, though I am native here
And to the manner born, it is a custom
More honored in the breach than the observance.
This heavy headed revel east and west
Makes us traduced and taxed of other nations.

2. Negotiations before a surrender. 3. Panders. 4. Garments. 5. Solicitors.
6. Sharply. 7. Keen. 8. A German dance.

They clepe[9] us drunkards, and with swinish phrase
Soil our addition,[1] and indeed it takes
From our achievements, though performed at height,
The pith and marrow of our attribute.[2]
So oft it chances in particular men,
That for some vicious mole of nature in them,
As in their birth, wherein they are not guilty
(Since nature cannot choose his origin),
By the o'ergrowth of some complexion,
Oft breaking down the pales[3] and forts of reason,
Or by some habit that too much o'er-leavens
The form of plausive[4] manners—that these men,
Carrying, I say, the stamp of one defect,
Being nature's livery or fortune's star,
His virtues else, be they as pure as grace,
As infinite as man may undergo,
Shall in the general censure take corruption
From that particular fault. The dram of evil
Doth all the noble substance often doubt[5]
To his own scandal.

[*Enter* GHOST.]

HORATIO: Look, my lord, it comes.
HAMLET: Angels and ministers of grace defend us!
Be thou a spirit of health or goblin damned,
Bring with thee airs from heaven or blasts from hell,
Be thy intents wicked or charitable,
Thou com'st in such a questionable[6] shape
That I will speak to thee. I'll call thee Hamlet,
King, father, royal Dane. O, answer me!
Let me not burst in ignorance, but tell
Why thy canonized[7] bones, hearsèd in death,
Have burst their cerements[8]; why the sepulchre
Wherein we saw thee quietly interred
Hath oped his ponderous and marble jaws
To cast thee up again. What may this mean
That thou, dead corse, again in complete steel[9]
Revisits thus the glimpses of the moon,
Making night hideous, and we fools of nature
So horridly to shake our disposition
With thoughts beyond the reaches of our souls?
Say, why is this? wherefore? What should we do?

9. Call. 1. Reputation. 2. Honor. 3. Barriers. 4. Pleasing. 5. Put out.
6. Prompting question. 7. Buried in accordance with church canons. 8. Gravecloths.
9. Armor.

[GHOST *beckons.*]

HORATIO: It beckons you to go away it,
As if it some impartment[1] did desire
To you alone.
MARCELLUS: Look with what courteous action
It waves you to a more removéd[2] ground.
But do not go with it.
HORATIO: No, by no means.
HAMLET: It will not speak; then I will follow it.
HORATIO: Do not, my lord.
HAMLET: Why, what should be the fear?
I do not set my life at a pin's fee,[3]
And for my soul, what can it do to that,
Being a thing immortal as itself?
It waves me forth again. I'll follow it
HORATIO: What if it tempt you toward the flood, my lord,
Or to the deathful summit of the cliff
That beetles[4] o'er his base into the sea,
And there assume some other horrible form,
Which might deprive your sovereignty of reason[5]
And draw you into madness? Think of it.
The very place puts toys of desperation,[6]
Without more motive, into every brain
That looks so many fathoms to the sea
And hears it roar beneath.
HAMLET: It waves me still.
Go on. I'll follow thee.
MARCELLUS: You shall not go, my lord.
HAMLET: Hold off your hands.
HORATIO: Be ruled, You shall not go.
HAMLET: My fate cries out
And makes each petty artere in this body
As hardy as the Nemean lion's nerve.[7]
Still am I called. Unhand me, gentlemen.
By heaven, I'll make a ghost of him that lets[8] me.
I say, away! Go on. I'll follow thee. [*Exeunt* GHOST *and* HAMLET.]
HORATIO: He waxes desperate with imagination.
MARCELLUS: Let's follow. 'Tis not fit thus to obey him.
HORATIO: Have after. To what issue will this come?
MARCELLUS: Something is rotten in the state of Denmark.

1. Communication. 2. Beckons you to a more distant. 3. Price. 4. Juts out. 5. Rational power. *Deprive:* take away. 6. Desperate fancies. 7. The Nemean lion was a mythological monster slain by Hercules as one of his twelve labors. 8. Hinders.

HORATIO: Heaven will direct it.
MARCELLUS: Nay, let's follow him. [*Exeunt.*]

Scene 5

Near the guard station. Enter GHOST *and* HAMLET.

HAMLET: Whither wilt thou lead me? Speak. I'll go no further.
GHOST: Mark me.
HAMLET: I will.
GHOST: My hour is almost come,
When I to sulph'rous and tormenting flames
Must render up myself.
HAMLET: Alas, poor ghost!
GHOST: Pity me not, but lend thy serious hearing
To what I shall unfold.
HAMLET: Speak. I am bound to hear.
GHOST: So art thou to revenge, when thou shalt hear.
HAMLET: What?
GHOST: I am thy father's spirit,
Doomed for a certain term to walk the night,
And for the day confined to fast in fires,
Till the foul crimes done in my days of nature[9]
Are burnt and purged away. But that I am forbid
To tell the secrets of my prison house,
I could a tale unfold whose lightest word
Would harrow up thy soul, freeze thy young blood,
Make thy two eyes like stars start from their spheres,
Thy knotted and combinéd[1] locks to part,
And each particular hair to stand an end,
Like quills upon the fretful porpentine.[2]
But this eternal blazon[3] must not be
To ears of flesh and blood. List, list, O, list!
If thou didst every thy dear father love—
HAMLET: O God!
GHOST: Revenge his foul and most unnatural murder.
HAMLET: Murder!
GHOST: Murder most foul, as in the best it is,
But this most foul, strange, and unnatural.
HAMLET: Haste me to know't, that I, with wings as swift
As meditation or the thoughts of love,
May sweep to my revenge.
GHOST: I find thee apt.
And duller shouldst thou be than the fat weed

9. I.e., while I was alive. 1. Tangled. 2. Porcupine. 3. Description of eternity.

That rots itself in ease on Lethe[4] wharf,—
Wouldst thou not stir in this. Now, Hamlet, hear.
'Tis given out that, sleeping in my orchard,
A serpent stung me. So the whole ear of Denmark
Is by a forgéd process[5] of my death
Rankly abused. But know, thou noble youth,
The serpent that did sting thy father's life
Now wears his crown.

HAMLET: O my prophetic soul!
My uncle!

GHOST: Ay, that incestuous, that adulterate beast,
With witchcraft of his wits, with traitorous gifts—
O wicked wit and gifts that have the power
So to seduce!—won to his shameful lust
The will of my most seeming virtuous queen.
O Hamlet, what a falling off was there,
From me, whose love was of that dignity
That it went hand in hand even with the vow
I made to her in marriage, and to decline[6]
Upon a wretch whose natural gifts were poor
To those of mine!
But virtue, as it never will be moved,
Though lewdness court it in a shape of heaven,
So lust, though to a radiant angel linked,
Will sate itself in a celestial bed
And prey on garbage.
But soft, methinks I scent the morning air.
Brief let me be. Sleeping within my orchard,
My custom always of the afternoon,
Upon my secure hour thy uncle stole,
With juice of cursed hebona[7] in a vial,
And in the porches of my ears did pour
The leperous distilment, whose effect
Holds such an enmity with blood of man
That swift as quicksilver it courses through
The natural gates and alleys of the body,
And with a sudden vigor it doth posset[8]
And curd, like eager[9] droppings into milk,
The thin and wholesome blood. So did it mine,
And a most instant tetter barked about[1]
Most lazar-like[2] with vile and loathsome crust
All my smooth body.

4. The Lethe was one of the rivers of the classical underworld. Its specific importance was that its waters when drunk induced forgetfulness. The "fat weed" is the asphodel which grew there.
5. False report. 6. Sink. 7. A poison. 8. Coagulate. 9. Acid. *Curd:* curdle.
1. Covered like bark. *Tetter:* a skin disease. 2. Leper-like.

Thus was I sleeping by a brother's hand
Of life, of crown, of queen at once dispatched,
Cut off even in the blossoms of my sin,
Unhouseled, disappointed, unaneled,[3]
No reck'ning made, but sent to my account
With all my imperfections on my head.
O, horrible! O, horrible! most horrible!
If thou hast nature in thee, bear it not.
Let not the royal bed of Denmark be
A couch of luxury[4] and damnéd incest.
But howsomever thou pursues this act,
Taint not thy mind, nor let thy soul contrive
Against thy mother aught. Leave her to heaven,
And to those thorns that in her bosom lodge
To prick and sting her. Fare thee well at once.
The glowworm shows the matin[5] to be near,
And gins to pale his uneffectual fire.
Adieu, adieu, adieu. Remember me. [*Exit.*]

HAMLET: O all you host of heaven! O earth! What else?
And shall I couple hell? O, fie! Hold, hold, my heart,
And you, my sinews, grow not instant old,
But bear me stiffly up. Remember thee?
Ay, thou poor ghost, whiles memory holds a seat
In this distracted globe.[6] Remember thee?
Yea, from the table[7] of my memory
I'll wipe away all trivial fond[8] records,
All saws of books, all forms, all pressures past
That youth and observation copied there,
And thy commandment all alone shall live
Within the book and volume of my brain,
Unmixed with baser matter. Yes, by heaven!
O most pernicious woman!
O villain, villain, smiling, damnéd villian!
My tables—meet it is I set it down
That one may smile, and smile, and be a villain.
At least I am sure it may be so in Denmark.
So, uncle, there you are. Now to my word[9]:
It is "Adieu, adieu. Remember me."
I have sworn't.

[*Enter* HORATIO *and* MARCELLUS.]

HORATIO: My lord, my lord!

3. The Ghost means that he died without the customary rites of the church, that is, without receiving the sacrament, without confession, and without extreme unction. 4. Lust. 5. Morning. 6. Skull. 7. Writing tablet. 8. Foolish. 9. For my motto.

MARCELLUS: Lord Hamlet!
HORATIO: Heavens secure him!
HAMLET: So be it!
MARCELLUS: Illo, ho, ho, my lord!
HAMLET: Hillo, ho, ho, boy![1] Come, bird, come.
MARCELLUS: How is't, my noble lord?
HORATIO: What news, my lord?
HAMLET: O, wonderful!
HORATIO: Good my lord, tell it.
HAMLET: No, you will reveal it.
HORATIO: Not I, my lord, by heaven.
MARCELLUS: Nor I, my lord.
HAMLET: How say you then, would heart of man once think it?
But you'll be secret?
BOTH: Ay, by heaven, my lord.
HAMLET: There's never a villain dwelling in all Denmark
But he's an arrant knave.
HORATIO: There needs no ghost, my lord, come from the grave
To tell us this.
HAMLET: Why, right, you are in the right,
And so without more circumstance at all
I hold it fit that we shake hands and part,
You, as your business and desire shall point you,
For every man hath business and desire
Such as it is, and for my own poor part,
I will go pray.
HORATIO: These are but wild and whirling words, my lord.
HAMLET: I am sorry they offend you, heartily;
Yes, faith, heartily.
HORATIO: There's no offence, my lord.
HAMLET: Yes, by Saint Patrick, but there is, Horatio,
And much offence too. Touching this vision here,
It is an honest ghost, that let me tell you.
For your desire to know what is between us,
O'ermaster't as you may. And now, good friends,
As you are friends, scholars, and soldiers,
Give me one poor request.
HORATIO: What is't, my lord? We will.
HAMLET: Never make known what you have seen tonight.
BOTH: My lord, we will not.
HAMLET: Nay, but swear't.
HORATIO: In faith,
My lord, not I.
MARCELLUS: Nor I, my lord, in faith.

1. A falconer's cry.

HAMLET: Upon my sword.
MARCELLUS: We have sworn, my lord, already.
HAMLET: Indeed, upon my sword, indeed.

[GHOST *cries under the stage.*]

GHOST: Swear.
HAMLET: Ha, ha, boy, say'st thou so? Art thou there, truepenny[2]?
Come on. You hear this fellow in the cellarage.[3]
Consent to swear.
HORATIO: Propose the oath, my lord.
HAMLET: Never to speak of this that you have seen,
Swear by my sword.
GHOST: [*Beneath.*] Swear.
HAMLET: Hic et ubique?[4] Then we'll shift our ground.
Come hither, gentlemen,
And lay your hands again upon my sword.
Swear by my sword
Never to speak of this that you have heard.
GHOST: [*Beneath.*] Swear by his sword.
HAMLET: Well said, old mole! Canst work i' th' earth so fast?
A worthy pioneer![5] Once more remove, good friends.
HORATIO: O day and night, but this is wondrous strange!
HAMLET: And therefore as a stranger give it welcome.
There are more things in heaven and earth, Horatio,
Than are dreamt of in your philosophy.
But come.
Here as before, never, so help you mercy,
How strange or odd some'er I bear myself
(As I perchance hereafter shall think meet
To put an antic[6] disposition on),
That you, at such times, seeing me, never shall,
With arms encumbered[7] thus, or this head-shake,
Or by pronouncing of some doubtful phrase,
As "Well, well, we know," or "We could, and if we would"
Or "If we list to speak," or "There be, and if they might"
Or such ambiguous giving out, to note
That you know aught of me—this do swear,
So grace and mercy at your most needed help you.
GHOST: [*Beneath.*] Swear. [*They swear.*]
HAMLET: Rest, rest, perturbéd spirit! So, gentlemen,
With all my love I do commend me to you,
And what so poor a man as Hamlet is
May do t'express his love and friending[8] to you,

2. Old fellow. 3. Below. 4. Here and everywhere. 5. Soldier who digs trenches. 6. Mad. 7. Folded. 8. Friendship.

God willing, shall not lack. Let us go in together,
And still your fingers on your lips, I pray.
The time is out of joint. O curséd spite
That ever I was born to set it right!
Nay, come, let's go together. [*Exeunt.*]

ACT II

SCENE 1

The dwelling of POLONIUS. *Enter* POLONIUS *and* REYNALDO.

POLONIUS: Give him this money and these notes, Reynaldo.
REYNALDO: I will, my lord.
POLONIUS: You shall do marvellous wisely, good Reynaldo,
Before you visit him, to make inquire[9]
Of his behavior.
REYNALDO: My lord, I did intend it.
POLONIUS: Marry, well said, very well said. Look you, sir.
Enquire me first what Danskers[1] are in Paris,
And how, and who, what means, and where they keep,[2]
What company, at what expense; and finding
By this encompassment[3] and drift of question
That they do know my son, come you more nearer
Than your particular demands[4] will touch it.
Take you as 'twere some distant knowledge of him,
As thus, "I know his father and his friends,
And in part him." Do you mark this, Reynaldo?
REYNALDO: Ay, very well, my lord.
POLONIUS: "And in part him, but," you may say, "not well,
But if't be he I mean, he's very wild,
Addicted so and so." And there put on him
What forgeries you please; marry, none so rank[5]
As may dishonor him. Take heed of that.
But, sir, such wanton, wild, and usual slips
As are companions noted and most known
To youth and liberty.
REYNALDO: As gaming, my lord.
POLONIUS: Ay, or drinking, fencing, swearing, quarrelling,
Drabbing[6]—you may go so far.
REYNALDO: My lord, that would dishonor him.
POLONIUS: Faith, no, as you may season it in the charge.[7]
You must not put another scandal on him,
That he is open to incontinency.[8]

9. Inquiry. 1. Danes. 2. Live. 3. Indirect means. 4. Direct questions. 5. Foul. *Forgeries:* lies. 6. Whoring. 7. Soften the accusation. 8. Sexual excess.

That's not my meaning. But breathe his faults so quaintly[9]
That they may seem the taints of liberty,[1]
The flash and outbreak of a fiery mind,
A savageness in unreclaiméd[2] blood,
Of general assault.[3]
REYNALDO: But, my good lord—
POLONIUS: Wherefore should you do this?
REYNALDO: Ay, my lord,
I would know that.
POLONIUS: Marry, sir, here's my drift,
And I believe it is a fetch of warrant.[4]
You laying these slight sullies on my son,
As 'twere a thing a little soiled i' th' working,
Mark you,
Your party in converse,[5] him you would sound,
Having ever seen in the prenominate[6] crimes
The youth you breathe[7] of guilty, be assured
He closes with you in this consequence,
"Good sir," or so, or "friend," or "gentleman,"
According to the phrase or the addition
Of man and country.
REYNALDO: Very good, my lord.
POLONIUS: And then, sir, does 'a this—'a does—What was I about to say?
By the mass, I was about to say something.
Where did I leave?
REYNALDO: At "closes in the consequence."
POLONIUS: At "closes in the consequence"—ay, marry,
He closes thus: "I know the gentleman.
I saw him yesterday, or th' other day,
Or then, or then, with such, or such, and as you say,
There was 'a gaming, there o'ertook in's rouse,
There falling out at tennis," or perchance
"I saw him enter such a house of sale,"
Videlicet,[8] a brothel, or so forth.
See you, now—
Your bait of falsehood takes this carp of truth,
And thus do we of wisdom and of reach,[9]
With windlasses and with assays of bias,[1]
By indirections find directions out;
So by my former lecture and advice
Shall you my son. You have me, have you not?
REYNALDO: My lord, I have.

9. With delicacy. 1. Faults of freedom. 2. Untamed. 3. Touching everyone. 4. Permissible trick. 5. Conversation. 6. Already named. 7. Speak. 8. Namely. 9. Ability. 1. Indirect tests.

POLONIUS: God b'wi' ye; fare ye well.
REYNALDO: Good my lord.
POLONIUS: Observe his inclination in yourself.
REYNALDO: I shall, my lord.
POLONIUS: And let him ply[2] his music.
REYNALDO: Well, my lord.
POLONIUS: Farewell. [*Exit* REYNALDO.]

[*Enter* OPHELIA.]

How now, Ophelia, what's the matter?
OPHELIA: O my lord, my lord, I have been so affrighted!
POLONIUS: With what, i' th' name of God?
OPHELIA: My lord, as I was sewing in my closet,[3]
Lord Hamlet with his doublet all unbraced,[4]
No hat upon his head, his stockings fouled,
Ungartered and down-gyvéd[5] to his ankle,
Pale as his shirt, his knees knocking each other,
And with a look so piteous in purport
As if he had been looséd out of hell
To speak of horrors—he comes before me.
POLONIUS: Mad for thy love?
OPHELIA: My lord, I do not know,
But truly I do fear it.
POLONIUS: What said he?
OPHELIA: He took me by the wrist, and held me hard,
Then goes he to the length of all his arm,
And with his other hand thus o'er his brow,
He falls to such perusal of my face
As 'a would draw it. Long stayed he so.
At last, a little shaking of mine arm,
And thrice his head thus waving up and down,
He raised a sigh so piteous and profound
As it did seem to shatter all his bulk,[6]
And end his being. That done, he lets me go,
And with his head over his shoulder turned
He seemed to find his way without his eyes,
For out adoors he went without their helps,
And to the last bended[7] their light on me.
POLONIUS: Come, go with me. I will go seek the king.
This is the very ecstasy of love,
Whose violent property fordoes[8] itself,
And leads the will to desperate undertakings
As oft as any passion under heaven

2. Practice. 3. Chamber. 4. Unlaced. *Doublet*: jacket. 5. Fallen down like fetters. 6. Body. 7. Directed. 8. Destroys. *Property*: character.

That does afflict our natures. I am sorry.
What, have you given him any hard words of late?
OPHELIA: No, my good lord, but as you did command
I did repel[9] his letters, and denied
His access to me.
POLONIUS: That hath made him mad.
I am sorry that with better heed and judgment
I had not quoted[1] him. I feared he did but trifle,
And meant to wrack[2] thee; but beshrew my jealousy.
By heaven, it is as proper to our age
To cast beyond ourselves in our opinions
As it is common for the younger sort
To lack discretion. Come, go we to the king.
This must be known, which being kept close, might move
More grief to hide than hate to utter love.
Come. [*Exeunt.*]

SCENE 2

A *public room. Enter* KING, QUEEN, ROSENCRANTZ *and* GUILDENSTERN.

KING: Welcome, dear Rosencrantz and Guildenstern.
Moreover that[3] we much did long to see you,
The need we have to use you did provoke
Our hasty sending. Something have you heard
Of Hamlet's transformation—so call it,
Sith[4] nor th' exterior nor the inward man
Resembles that it was. What it should be,
More than his father's death, that thus hath put him
So much from th' understanding of himself,
I cannot deem of. I entreat you both
That, being of so young days[5] brought up with him,
And sith so neighbored[6] to his youth and havior,
That you vouchsafe your rest here in our court
Some little time, so by your companies
To draw him on to pleasures, and to gather
So much as from occasion you may glean,
Whether aught to us unknown afflicts him thus,
That opened lies within our remedy.
QUEEN: Good gentlemen, he hath much talked of you,
And sure I am two men there are not living
To whom he more adheres. If it will please you
To show us so much gentry[7] and good will
As to expend your time with us awhile

9. Refuse. 1. Observed. 2. Harm. 3. In addition to the fact that. 4. Since.
5. From childhood. 6. Closely allied. 7. Courtesy.

For the supply and profit of our hope,
Your visitation shall receive such thanks
As fits a king's remembrance.
ROSENCRANTZ: Both your majesties
Might, by the sovereign power you have of us,
Put your dread pleasures more into command
Than to entreaty.
GUILDENSTERN: But we both obey,
And here give up ourselves in the full bent[8]
To lay our service freely at your feet,
To be commanded.
KING: Thanks, Rosencrantz and gentle Guildenstern.
QUEEN: Thanks, Guildenstern and gentle Rosencrantz.
And I beseech you instantly to visit
My too much changed son. Go, some of you,
And bring these gentlemen where Hamlet is.
GUILDENSTERN: Heavens make our presence and our practices
Pleasant and helpful to him!
QUEEN: Ay, amen!

[*Exeunt* ROSENCRANTZ *and* GUILDENSTERN.]

[*Enter* POLONIUS.]

POLONIUS: Th' ambassadors from Norway, my good lord,
Are joyfully returned.
KING: Thou still[9] hast been the father of good news.
POLONIUS: Have I, my lord? I assure you, my good liege,
I hold my duty as I hold my soul,
Both to my God and to my gracious king;
And I do think—or else this brain of mine
Hunts not the trial of policy[1] so sure
As it hath used to do—that I have found
The very cause of Hamlet's lunacy.
KING: O, speak of that, that do I long to hear.
POLONIUS: Give first admittance to th' ambassadors.
My news shall be the fruit[2] to that great feast.
KING: Thyself do grace to them, and bring them in. [*Exit* POLONIUS.]
He tells me, my dear Gertrude, he hath found
The head and source of all your son's distemper.
QUEEN: I doubt it is no other but the main,
His father's death and our o'erhasty marriage.
KING: Well, we shall sift[3] him.

[*Enter Ambassadors* (VOLTEMAND *and* CORNELIUS) *with* POLONIUS.]

Welcome, my good friends,
Say, Voltemand, what from our brother Norway?

8. Completely. 9. Ever. 1. Statecraft. 2. Dessert. 3. Examine.

VOLTEMAND: Most fair return of greetings and desires.
Upon our first,[4] he sent out to suppress
His nephew's levies, which to him appeared
To be a preparation 'gainst the Polack,
But better looked into, he truly found
It was against your highness, whereat grieved,
That so his sickness, age, and impotence
Was falsely borne in hand, sends out arrests[5]
On Fortinbras, which he in brief obeys,
Receives rebuke from Norway, and in fine,
Makes vow before his uncle never more
To give th' assay[6] of arms against your majesty.
Whereon old Norway, overcome with joy,
Gives him threescore thousand crowns in annual fee,
And his commission to employ those soldiers,
So levied as before, against the Polack,
With an entreaty, herein further shown, [*Gives* CLAUDIUS *a paper.*]
That it might please you to give quiet pass[7]
Through your dominions for this enterprise,
On such regards of safety and allowance
As therein are set down.

KING: It likes[8] us well,
And at our more considered time[9] we'll read,
Answer, and think upon this business.
Meantime we thank you for your well-took[1] labor.
Go to your rest; at night we'll feast together.
Most welcome home! [*Exeunt* AMBASSADORS.]

POLONIUS: This business is well ended.
My liege and madam, to expostulate[2]
What majesty should be, what duty is,
Why day is day, night night, and time is time,
Were nothing but to waste night, day, and time.
Therefore, since brevity is the soul of wit,
And tediousness the limbs and outward flourishes,[3]
I will be brief. Your noble son is mad.
Mad call I it, for to define true madness,
What is't but to be nothing else but mad?
But let that go.

QUEEN: More matter with less art.

POLONIUS: Madam, I swear I use no art at all.
That he is mad, 'tis true: 'tis true 'tis pity,
And pity 'tis 'tis true. A foolish figure,
But farewell it, for I will use no art.
Mad let us grant him, then, and now remains

4. I.e., first appearance. 5. Orders to stop. *Falsely borne in hand:* deceived. 6. Trial. 7. Safe conduct. 8. Pleases. 9. Time for more consideration. 1. Successful. 2. Discuss. 3. Adornments.

That we find out the cause of this effect,
Or rather say the cause of this defect,
For this effect defective comes by cause.
Thus it remains, and the remainder thus.
Perpend.[4]
I have a daughter—have while she is mine—
Who in her duty and obedience, mark,
Hath given me this. Now gather, and surmise.
"To the celestial, and my soul's idol, the most beautified Ophelia."—That's an ill phrase, a vile phrase, "beautified" is a vile phrase. But you shall hear. Thus:
"In her excellent white bosom, these, etc."

QUEEN: Came this from Hamlet to her?

POLONIUS: Good madam, stay awhile. I will be faithful.
"Doubt thou the stars are fire,
Doubt that the sun doth move;
Doubt truth to be a liar;
But never doubt I love.

O dear Ophelia, I am ill at these numbers.[5] I have not art to reckon my groans, but that I love thee best, O most best, believe it. Adieu.

Thine evermore, most dear lady, whilst this machine[6] is to him, Hamlet."

This in obedience hath my daughter shown me,
And more above, hath his solicitings,
As they fell out by time, by means, and place,
All given to mine ear.

KING: But how hath she
Received his love?

POLONIUS: What do you think of me?

KING: As of a man faithful and honorable.

POLONIUS: I would fain prove so. But what might you think,
When I had seen this hot love on the wing.
(As I perceived it, I must tell you that,
Before my daughter told me), what might you,
Or my dear majesty your queen here, think,
If I had played the desk or table-book,
Or given my heart a winking, mute and dumb,
Or looked upon this love with idle sight,[7]
What might you think? No, I went round[8] to work,
And my young mistress thus I did bespeak:

4. Consider. 5. Verses. 6. Body. 7. Polonius means that he would have been at fault if, having seen Hamlet's attention to Ophelia, he had winked at it or not paid attention, an "idle sight," and if he had remained silent and kept the information to himself, as if it were written in a "desk" or "table-book." 8. Directly.

"Lord Hamlet is a prince out of thy star.[9]
This must not be." And then I prescripts[1] gave her,
That she should lock herself from his resort,
Admit no messengers, receive no tokens.
Which done, she took[2] the fruits of my advice;
And he repelled, a short tale to make,
Fell into a sadness, then into a fast,
Thence to a watch, thence into a weakness,
Thence to a lightness, and by this declension,
Into the madness wherein now he raves,
And all we mourn for.

KING: Do you think 'tis this?

QUEEN: It may be, very like.

POLONIUS: Hath there been such a time—I would fain know that—
That I have positively said "Tis so,"
When it proved otherwsie?

KING: Not that I know.

POLONIUS: [*Pointing to his head and shoulder.*] Take this from this, if this be otherwise.
If circumstances lead me, I will find
Where truth is hid, though it were hid indeed
Within the centre.[3]

KING: How may we try it further?

POLONIUS: You know sometimes he walks four hours together
Here in the lobby.

QUEEN: So he does, indeed.

POLONIUS: At such a time I'll loose[4] my daughter to him.
Be you and I behind an arras[5] then.
Mark the encounter. If he love her not,
And be not from his reason fall'n thereon,
Let me be no assistant for a state,
But keep a farm and carters.

KING: We will try it.

[*Enter* HAMLET *reading a book.*]

QUEEN: But look where sadly the poor wretch comes reading.

POLONIUS: Away, I do beseech you both away,
I'll board[6] him presently. [*Exeunt* KING *and* QUEEN.]
O, give me leave.
How does my good Lord Hamlet?

HAMLET: Well, God-a-mercy.

POLONIUS: Do you know me, my lord?

HAMLET: Excellent well, you are a fishmonger.

9. Beyond your sphere. 1. Orders. 2. Followed. 3. Of the earth. 4. Let loose.
5. Tapestry. 6. Accost.

POLONIUS: Not I, my lord.

HAMLET: Then I would you were so honest a man.

POLONIUS: Honest, my lord?

HAMLET: Ay, sir, to be honest as this world goes, is to be one man picked out of ten thousand.

POLONIUS: That's very true, my lord.

HAMLET: For if the sun breed maggots in a dead dog, being a god kissing carrion[7]—Have you a daughter?

POLONIUS: I have, my lord.

HAMLET: Let her not walk i' th' sun. Conception is a blessing, but as your daughter may conceive—friend, look to't.

POLONIUS: How say you by that? [*Aside.*] Still harping on my daughter. Yet he knew me not at first. 'A said I was a fishmonger. 'A is far gone. And truly in my youth I suffered much extremity for love. Very near this. I'll speak to him again.—What do you read, my lord?

HAMLET: Words, words, words.

POLONIUS: What is the matter, my lord?

HAMLET: Between who?

POLONIUS: I mean the matter that you read, my lord.

HAMLET: Slanders, sir; for the satirical rogue says here that old men have grey beards, that their faces are wrinkled, their eyes purging thick amber and plum-tree gum, and that they have a plentiful lack of wit, together with most weak hams[8]—all which, sir, though I have it thus set down, for yourself, sir, shall grow old as I am, if like a crab you could go backward.

POLONIUS: [*Aside.*] Though this be madness, yet there is method in't.—Will you walk out of the air, my lord?

HAMLET: Into my grave?

POLONIUS: [*Aside.*] Indeed, that's out of the air. How pregnant sometime his replies are! a happiness that often madness hits on, which reason and sanity could not so prosperously be delivered of. I will leave him, and suddenly contrive the means of meeting between him and my daughter.—My lord. I will take my leave of you.

HAMLET: You cannot take from me anything that I will more willingly part withal—except my life, except my life, except my life.

[*Enter* GUILDENSTERN *and* ROSENCRANTZ.]

POLONIUS: Fare you well, my lord.

HAMLET: These tedious old fools!

POLONIUS: You go to seek the Lord Hamlet. There he is.

ROSENCRANTZ: [*To* POLONIUS.] God save you, sir! [*Exit* POLONIUS.]

GUILDENSTERN: My honored lord!

ROSENCRANTZ: My most dear lord!

HAMLET: My excellent good friends! How dost thou, Guildenstern?
Ah, Rosencrantz! Good lads, how do you both?

7. A reference to the belief of the period that maggots were produced spontaneously by the action of sunshine on carrion. 8. Limbs.

ROSENCRANTZ: As the indifferent[9] children of the earth.
GUILDENSTERN: Happy in that we are not over-happy;
On Fortune's cap we are not the very button.[1]
HAMLET: Nor the soles of her shoe?
ROSENCRANTZ: Neither, my lord.
HAMLET: Then you live about her waist, or in the middle of her favors.
GUILDENSTERN: Faith, her privates we.
HAMLET: In the secret parts of Fortune? O, most true, she is a strumpet.[2] What news?
ROSENCRANTZ: None, my lord, but that the world's grown honest.
HAMLET: Then is doomsday near. But your news is not true. Let me question more in particular. What have you, my good friends, deserved at the hands of Fortune, that she sends you to prison hither?
GUILDENSTERN: Prison, my lord?
HAMLET: Denmark's a prison.
ROSENCRANTZ: Then is the world one.
HAMLET: A goodly one, in which there are many confines, wards[3] and dungeons. Denmark being one o' th' worst.
ROSENCRANTZ: We think not so, my lord.
HAMLET: Why then 'tis none to you; for there is nothing either good or bad, but thinking makes it so. To me it is a prison.
ROSENCRANTZ: Why then your ambition makes it one. 'Tis too narrow for your mind.
HAMLET: O God, I could be bounded in a nutshell and count myself a king of infinite space, where it not that I have bad dreams.
GUILDENSTERN: Which dreams indeed are ambition; for the very substance of the ambitious is merely the shadow of a dream.
HAMLET: A dream itself is but a shadow.
ROSENCRANTZ: Truly, and I hold ambition of so airy and light a quality that it is but a shadow's shadow.
HAMLET: Then are our beggars bodies, and our monarchs and outstretched heroes the beggars' shadows. Shall we to th' court? for, by my fay,[4] I cannot reason.
BOTH: We'll wait upon you.
HAMLET: No such matter. I will not sort[5] you with the rest of my servants; for to speak to you like an honest man, I am most dreadfully attended. But in the beaten way of friendship, what make you at Elsinore?
ROSENCRANTZ: To visit you, my lord; no other occasion.
HAMLET: Beggar that I am, I am even poor in thanks, but I thank you; and sure, dear friends, my thanks are too dear a halfpenny.[6] Were you not sent for? Is it your own inclining? Is it a free visitation? Come, come, deal justly with me. Come, come, nay speak.
GUILDENSTERN: What should we say, my lord?
HAMLET: Why anything but to th' purpose. You were sent for, and there is a kind

9. Ordinary. 1. I.e., on top. 2. Prostitute. Hamlet is indulging in characteristic ribaldry. Guildenstern means that they are "privates" = ordinary citizens, but Hamlet takes him to mean "privates" = sexual organs and "middle of her favors" = waist = sexual organs. 3. Cells. 4. Faith. 5. Include. 6. Not worth a halfpenny.

of confession in your looks, which your modesties have not craft enough to color. I know the good king and queen have sent for you.

ROSENCRANTZ: To what end, my lord?

HAMLET: That you must teach me. But let me conjure you by the rights of our fellowship, by the consonancy of our youth, by the obligation of our ever-preserved love, and by what more dear a better proposer can charge you withal, be even and direct[7] with me whether you were sent for or no.

ROSENCRANTZ: [*Aside to* GUILDENSTERN.] What say you?

HAMLET: [*Aside.*] Nay, then, I have an eye of you.—If you love me, hold not off.

GUILDENSTERN: My lord, we were sent for.

HAMLET: I will tell you why; so shall my anticipation prevent your discovery,[8] and your secrecy to the king and queen moult no feather. I have of late—but wherefore I know not—lost all my mirth, forgone all custom of exercises; and indeed it goes so heavily with my disposition, that this goodly frame the earth seems to me a sterile promontory, this most excellent canopy the air, look you, this brave o'er-hanging firmament, this majestical roof fretted[9] with golden fire, why it appeareth nothing to me but a foul and pestilent congregation of vapors. What a piece of work is a man, how noble in reason, how infinite in faculties, in form and moving, how express[1] and admirable in action, how like an angel in apprehension, how like a god: the beauty of the world, the paragon of animals. And yet to me, what is this quintessence of dust? Man delights not me, nor woman neither, though by your smiling you seem to say so.

ROSENCRANTZ: My lord, there was no such stuff in my thoughts.

HAMLET: Why did ye laugh, then, when I said "Man delights not me"?

ROSENCRANTZ: To think, my lord, if you delight not in man, what lenten entertainment the players shall receive from you. We coted[2] them on the way, and hither are they coming to offer you service.

HAMLET: He that plays the king shall be welcome—his majesty shall have tribute on me; the adventurous knight shall use his foil and target; the lover shall not sigh gratis; the humorous[3] man shall end his part in peace; the clown shall make those laugh whose lungs are tickle o' th' sere[4]; and the lady shall say her mind freely, or the blank verse shall halt for't. What players are they?

ROSENCRANTZ: Even those you were wont to take such delight in, the tragedians of the city.

HAMLET: How chances it they travel? Their residence, both in reputation and profit, was better both ways.

ROSENCRANTZ: I think their inhibition comes by the means of the late innovation.

HAMLET: Do they hold the same estimation they did when I was in the city? Are they so followed?

ROSENCRANTZ: No, indeed, are they not.

HAMLET: How comes it? Do they grow rusty?

7. Straightforward. 8. Disclosure. 9. Ornamented with fretwork. 1. Well built. 2. Passed. *Lenten:* scanty. 3. Eccentric. *Foil and target:* sword and shield. 4. Easily set off.

ROSENCRANTZ: Nay, their endeavor keeps in the wonted pace; but there is, sir, an eyrie of children, little eyases,[5] that cry out on the top of question,[6] and are most tyrannically clapped for't. These are now the fashion, and so berattle the common stages (so they call them) that many wearing rapiers are afraid of goose quills[7] and dare scarce come thither.[8]

HAMLET: What, are they children? Who maintains 'em? How are they escoted[9]? Will they pursue the quality no longer than they can sing? Will they not say afterwards, if they should grow themselves to common players (as it is most like, if their means are no better), their writers do them wrong to make them exclaim against their own succession[1]?

ROSENCRANTZ: Faith, there has been much to do on both sides; and the nation holds it no sin to tarre[2] them to controversy. There was for a while no money bid for argument,[3] unless the poet and the player went to cuffs[4] in the question.

HAMLET: Is't possible?

GUILDENSTERN: O, there has been much throwing about of brains.

HAMLET: Do the boys carry it away?

ROSENCRANTZ: Ay, that they do, my lord. Hercules and his load too.[5]

HAMLET: It is not very strange, for my uncle is King of Denmark, and those that would make mouths[6] at him while my father lived give twenty, forty, fifty, a hundred ducats apiece for his picture in little.[7] 'Sblood, there is something in this more than natural, if philosophy could find it out.

[A flourish.]

GUILDENSTERN: There are the players.

HAMLET: Gentlemen, you are welcome to Elsinore. Your hands. Come then, th' appurtenance of welcome is fashion and ceremony. Let me comply with you in this garb, lest my extent[8] to the players, which I tell you must show fairly outwards should more appear like entertainment[9] than yours. You are welcome. But my uncle-father and aunt-mother are deceived.

GUILDENSTERN: In what, my dear lord?

HAMLET: I am but mad north-north-west; when the wind is southerly
I know a hawk from a handsaw.[1]

[Enter POLONIUS.]

POLONIUS: Well be with you, gentlemen.

305

310

315

320

325

330

5. Little hawks. 6. With a loud, high delivery. 7. Pens of satirical writers. 8. The passage refers to the emergence at the time of the play of theatrical companies made up of children from London choir schools. Their performances became fashionable and hurt the business of the established companies. Hamlet says that if they continue to act, "pursue the quality," when they are grown, they will find that they have been damaging their own future careers. 9. Supported.
1. Future careers. 2. Urge. 3. Paid for a play plot. 4. Blows. 5. During one of his labors Hercules assumed for a time the burden of the Titan Atlas, who supported the heavens on his shoulder. Also a reference to the effect on business at Shakespeare's theater, the Globe.
6. Sneer. 7. Miniature. 8. Fashion. Comply with: welcome. 9. Cordiality. 1. A "hawk" is a plasterer's tool; Hamlet may also be using "handsaw" = hernshaw = heron.

HAMLET: Hark you, Guildenstern—and you too—at each ear a hearer.
That great baby you see there is not yet out of his swaddling clouts.[2]

ROSENCRANTZ: Happily he is the second time come to them, for they say an old man is twice a child.

HAMLET: I will prophesy he comes to tell me of the players. Mark it.
—You say right, sir, a Monday morning, 'twas then indeed.

POLONIUS: My lord, I have news to tell you.

HAMLET: My lord, I have news to tell you.
When Roscius was an actor in Rome—[3]

POLONIUS: The actors are come hither, my lord.

HAMLET: Buzz, buzz.

POLONIUS: Upon my honor—

HAMLET: Then came each actor on his ass—

POLONIUS: The best actors in the world, either for tragedy, comedy, history, pastoral, pastoral-comical, historical-pastoral, tragical-historical, tragical-comical-historical-pastoral, scene individable, or poem unlimited. Seneca cannot be too heavy nor Plautus too light. For the law of writ and the liberty, these are the only men.[4]

HAMLET: O Jephtha, judge of Israel, what a treasure hadst thou![5]

POLONIUS: What a treasure had he, my lord?

HAMLET: Why—

"One fair daughter, and no more,
The which he loved passing well."

POLONIUS: [*Aside.*] Still on my daughter.

HAMLET: Am I not i' th' right, old Jephtha?

POLONIUS: If you call me Jephtha, my lord, I have a daughter that I love passing well.

HAMLET: Nay, that follows not.

POLONIUS: What follows then, my lord?

HAMLET: Why—

"As by lot, God wot"

and then, you know,

"It came to pass, as most like it was."

The first row of the pious chanson[6] will show you more, for look where my abridgement[7] comes.

2. Wrappings for an infant. 3. Roscius was the most famous actor of classical Rome. 4. Seneca and Plautus were Roman writers of tragedy and comedy, respectively. The "law of writ" refers to plays written according to such rules as the three unities; the "liberty" to those written otherwise. 5. To insure victory, Jephtha promised to sacrifice the first creature to meet him on his return. Unfortunately, his only daughter outstripped his dog and was the victim of his vow. The biblical story is told in Judges 11. 6. Song. *Row:* stanza. 7. That which cuts short by interrupting.

[*Enter the* PLAYERS.]

You are welcome, masters; welcome, all.—I am glad to see thee well.—Welcome, good friends.—O, old friend! Why thy face is valanced[8] since I saw thee last. Com'st thou to beard me in Denmark?—What, my young lady and mistress? By'r lady, your ladyship is nearer to heaven than when I saw you last by the altitude of a chopine.[9] Pray God your voice, like a piece of uncurrent gold, be not cracked within the ring.—Masters, you are all welcome. We'll e'en to't like French falconers, fly at anything we see. We'll have a speech straight. Come give us a taste of your quality,[1] come a passionate speech.

FIRST PLAYER: What speech, my good lord?

HAMLET: I heard thee speak me a speech once, but it was never acted, or if it was, not above once, for the play, I remember, pleased not the million; 'twas caviary to the general.[2] But it was—as I received it, and others whose judgments in such matters cried in the top of[3] mine—an excellent play, well digested[4] in the scenes, set down with as much modesty as cunning. I remember one said there were no sallets[5] in the lines to make the matter savory, nor no matter in the phrase that might indict the author of affectation, but called it an honest method, as wholesome as sweet, and by very much more handsome than fine. One speech in't I chiefly loved. 'Twas Æneas' tale to Dido, and thereabout of it especially where he speaks of Priam's slaughter.[6] If it live in your memory, begin at this line—let me see, let me see:

"The rugged Pyrrhus, like th' Hyrcanian beast"[7]—

'tis not so; it begins with Pyrrhus—

"The rugged Pyrrhus, he whose sable arms,
Black as his purpose, did the night resemble
When he lay couchéd in th' ominous horse,[8]
Hath now this dread and black complexion smeared
With heraldry more dismal; head to foot
Now is he total gules, horridly tricked[9]
With blood of fathers, mothers, daughters, sons,
Baked and impasted with the parching[1] streets,

8. Fringed (with a beard) 9. A reference to the contemporary theatrical practice of using boys to play women's parts. The company's "lady" has grown in height by the size of a woman's thick-soled shoe, "chopine," since Hamlet saw him last. The next sentence refers to the possibility, suggested by his growth, that the young actor's voice may soon begin to change. 1. Trade. 2. Masses. *Caviary*: caviar. 3. Were weightier than. 4. Arranged. 5. Spicy passages. 6. Aeneas, fleeing with his band from fallen Troy (Ilium), arrives in Carthage, where he tells Dido, the Queen of Carthage, of the fall of Troy. Here he is describing the death of Priam, the aged king of Troy, at the hands of Pyrrhus, the son of the slain Achilles. 7. Tiger. 8. I.e., the Trojan horse. 9. Adorned. *Total gules*: completely red. 1. Burning. *Impasted*: crusted.

That lend a tyrannous and a damnéd light
To their lord's murder. Roasted in wrath and fire,
And thus o'er-sizéd with coagulate[2] gore,
With eyes like carbuncles, the hellish Pyrrhus
Old grandsire Priam seeks."

So proceed you.

POLONIUS: Fore God, my lord, well spoken, with good accent and good discretion.

FIRST PLAYER: "Anon he finds him[3]
Striking too short at Greeks. His antique[4] sword,
Rebellious[5] to his arm, lies where it falls,
Repugnant to command. Unequal matched,
Pyrrhus at Priam drives, in rage strikes wide.
But with the whiff and wind of his fell sword
Th' unnervéd father falls. Then senseless[6] Ilium,
Seeming to feel this blow, with flaming top
Stoops[7] to his base, and with a hideous crash
Takes prisoner Pyrrhus' ear. For, lo! his sword,
Which was declining[8] on the milky head
Of reverend Priam, seemed i' th' air to stick.
So as a painted tyrant Pyrrhus stood,
And like a neutral to his will and matter,[9]
Did nothing.
But as we often see, against some storm,
A silence in the heavens, the rack[1] stand still,
The bold winds speechless, and the orb below
As hush as death, anon the dreadful thunder
Doth rend the region; so, after Pyrrhus' pause,
A rouséd vengeance sets him new awork,[2]
And never did the Cyclops' hammers fall
On Mars's armor, forged for proof eterne,[3]
With less remorse than Pyrrhus' bleeding sword
Now falls on Priam.
Out, out, thou strumpet, Fortune! All you gods,
In general synod take away her power,
Break all the spokes and fellies[4] from her wheel,
And bowl the round nave[5] down the hill of heaven
As low as to the fiends."

2. Clotted. *O'er-sized:* glued over. 3. I.e., Pyrrhus finds Priam. 4. Which he used when young. 5. Refractory. 6. Without feeling. 7. Falls. 8. About to fall. 9. Between his will and the fulfillment of it. 1. Clouds. 2. To work. 3. Mars, as befits a Roman war god, had armor made for him by the blacksmith god Vulcan and his assistants, the Cyclops. It was suitably impenetrable, of "proof eterne." 4. Parts of the rim. 5. Hub. *Bowl:* roll.

POLONIUS: This is too long.

HAMLET: It shall to the barber's with your beard.—Prithee say on. He's for a jig,[6] or a tale of bawdry, or he sleeps. Say on; come to Hecuba.[7]

FIRST PLAYER: "But who, ah woe! had seen the mobled[8] queen—"

HAMLET: "The mobled queen"?

POLONIUS: That's good. "Mobled queen" is good.

FIRST PLAYER: "Run barefoot up and down, threat'ning the flames
With bisson rheum, a clout[9] upon that head
Where late the diadem stood, and for a robe,
About her lank and all o'er-teeméd loins,
A blanket, in the alarm of fear caught up—
Who this had seen, with tongue in venom steeped,
'Gainst Fortune's state[1] would treason have pronounced.
But if the gods themselves did see her then,
When she saw Pyrrhus make malicious sport
In mincing[2] with his sword her husband's limbs,
The instant burst of clamor that she made,
Unless things mortal move them not at all,
Would have made milch[3] the burning eyes of heaven,
And passion in the gods."

POLONIUS: Look whe'r[4] he has not turned his color, and has tears in's eyes. Prithee no more.

HAMLET: 'Tis well. I'll have thee speak out the rest of this soon.—Good my lord, will you see the players well bestowed?[5] Do you hear, let them be well used, for they are the abstract[6] and brief chronicles of the time; after your death you were better have a bad epitaph than their ill report while you live.

POLONIUS: My lord, I will use them according to their desert.

HAMLET: God's bodkin, man, much better. Use every man after his desert, and who shall 'scape whipping? Use them after your own honor and dignity. The less they deserve, the more merit is in your bounty. Take them in.

POLONIUS: Come, sirs.

HAMLET: Follow him, friends. We'll hear a play tomorrow. [*Aside to* FIRST PLAYER.] Dost thou hear me, old friend, can you play "The Murder of Gonzago"?

FIRST PLAYER: Ay, my lord.

HAMLET: We'll ha't tomorrow night. You could for a need study a speech of some dozen or sixteen lines which I would set down and insert in't, could you not?

FIRST PLAYER: Ay, my lord.

HAMLET: Very well. Follow that lord, and look you mock him not.

[*Exeunt* POLONIUS *and* PLAYERS.]

440

445

450

455

460

465

470

475

6. A comic act. 7. Hecuba was the wife of Priam and Queen of Troy. Her "loins" are described below as "o'erteemed" because of her unusual fertility. The number of her children varies in different accounts, but twenty is a safe minimum. 8. Muffled (in a hood). 9. Cloth. *Bisson rheum*: blinding tears. 1. Government. 2. Cutting up. 3. Tearful (*lit.* milk-giving). 4. Whether. 5. Provided for. 6. Summary.

My good friends, I'll leave you till night. You are welcome to Elsinore.

ROSENCRANTZ: Good my lord.

[*Exeunt* ROSENCRANTZ *and* GUILDENSTERN.]

HAMLET: Ay, so God b'wi'ye. Now I am alone.
O, what a rogue and peasant slave am I!
Is it not monstrous that this player here,
But in a fiction, in a dream of passion,
Could force his soul so to his own conceit[7]
That from her working all his visage wanned;[8]
Tears in his eyes, distraction in his aspect[9]
A broken voice, and his whole function suiting
With forms to his conceit? And all for nothing,
For Hecuba!
What's Hecuba to him or he to Hecuba,
That he should weep for her? What would he do
Had he the motive and the cue for passion
That I have? He would drown the stage with tears,
And cleave the general ear with horrid speech,
Make mad the guilty, and appal the free,
Confound the ignorant, and amaze indeed
The very faculties of eyes and ears.
Yet I,
A dull and muddy-mettled rascal, peak[1]
Like John-a-dreams, unpregnant[2] of my cause,
And can say nothing; no, not for a king
Upon whose property and most dear life
A damned defeat was made. Am I a coward?
Who calls me villain, breaks my pate across,
Plucks off my beard and blows it in my face,
Tweaks me by the nose, gives me the lie i' th' throat
As deep as to the lungs? Who does me this?
Ha, 'swounds, I should take it; for it cannot be
But I am pigeon-livered and lack gall[3]
To make oppression bitter, or ere this
I should 'a fatted all the region kites[4]
With this slave's offal. Bloody, bawdy villain!
Remorseless, treacherous, lecherous, kindless[5] villain!
Why, what an ass am I! This is most brave,
That I, the son of a dear father murdered,
Prompted to my revenge by heaven and hell,
Must like a whore unpack[6] my heart with words,
And fall a-cursing like a very drab,

7. Imagination. 8. Grew pale. 9. Face. 1. Mope. *Muddy-mettled:* dull-spirited. 2. Not quickened by. *John-a-dreams:* a man dreaming. 3. Bitterness. 4. Birds of prey of the area. 5. Unnatural. 6. Relieve.

A scullion![7] Fie upon't! foh!
About, my brains. Hum—I have heard
That guilty creatures sitting at a play,
Have by the very cunning of the scene
Been struck so to the soul that presently
They have proclaimed[8] their malefactions;
For murder, though it have no tongue, will speak
With most miraculous organ. I'll have these players
Play something like the murder of my father
Before mine uncle. I'll observe his looks.
I'll tent him to the quick. If 'a do blench,[9]
I know my course. The spirit that I have seen
May be a devil, and the devil hath power
T' assume a pleasing shape, yea, and perhaps
Out of my weakness and my melancholy,
As he is very potent with such spirits,
Abuses me to damn me. I'll have grounds
More relative[1] than this. The play's the thing
Wherein I'll catch the conscience of the king. [*Exit.*]

ACT III

Scene 1

A room in the castle. Enter KING, QUEEN, POLONIUS, OPHELIA, ROSENCRANTZ *and* GUILDENSTERN.

KING: And can you by no drift of conference[2]
Get from him why he puts on this confusion,
Grating so harshly all his days of quiet
With turbulent[3] and dangerous lunacy?
ROSENCRANTZ: He does confess he feels himself distracted,
But from what cause 'a will by no means speak.
GUILDENSTERN: Nor do we find him forward to be sounded,[4]
But with a crafty madness keeps aloof
When we would bring him on to some confession
Of his true state.
QUEEN: Did he receive you well?
ROSENCRANTZ: Most like a gentleman.
GUILDENSTERN: But with much forcing of his disposition.[5]
ROSENCRANTZ: Niggard of question, but of our demands[6]
Most free in his reply.

7. In some versions of the play, the word "stallion," a slang term for a prostitute, appears in place of "scullion." 8. Admitted. 9. Turn pale. *Tent:* try. 1. Conclusive. 2. Line of conversation. 3. Disturbing. 4. Questioned. *Forward:* eager. 5. Conversation. 6. To our questions.

QUEEN: Did you assay[7] him
To any pastime?
ROSENCRANTZ: Madam, it so fell out that certain players
We o'er-raught[8] on the way. Of these we told him,
And there did seem in him a kind of joy
To hear of it. They are here about the court,
And as I think, they have already order
This night to play before him.
POLONIUS: 'Tis most true,
And he beseeched me to entreat your majesties
To hear and see the matter.[9]
KING: With all my heart, and it doth much content me
To hear him so inclined.
Good gentlemen, give him a further edge,
And drive his purpose[1] into these delights.
ROSENCRANTZ: We shall, my lord. [*Exeunt* ROSENCRANTZ *and* GUILDENSTERN.]
KING: Sweet Gertrude, leave us too,
For we have closely sent for Hamlet hither,
That he, as 'twere by accident, may here
Affront[2] Ophelia.
Her father and myself (lawful espials[3])
Will so bestow ourselves that, seeing unseen,
We may of their encounter frankly judge,
And gather by him, as he is behaved,
If't be th' affiction of his love or no
That thus he suffers for.
QUEEN: I shall obey you.—
And for your part, Ophelia, I do wish
That your good beauties be the happy cause
Of Hamlet's wildness. So shall I hope your virtues
Will bring him to his wonted[4] way again,
To both your honors.
OPHELIA: Madam, I wish it may. [*Exit* QUEEN]
POLONIUS: Ophelia, walk you here.—Gracious,[5] so please you,
We will bestow ourselves.—[*To* OPHELIA.] Read on this book,
That show of such an exercise may color[6]
Your loneliness.—We are oft to blame in this,
'Tis too much proved, that with devotion's visage
And pious action we do sugar o'er
The devil himself.
KING: [*Aside.*] O, 'tis too true.
How smart a lash that speech doth give my conscience!
The harlot's cheek, beautied with plast'ring[7] art,

7. Tempt. 8. Passed. 9. Performance. 1. Sharpen his intention. 2. Confront. 3. Justified spies. 4. Usual. 5. Majesty. 6. Explain. *Exercise:* act of devotion. 7. Thickly painted.

Is not more ugly to the thing that helps it
Than is my deed to my most painted word.
O heavy burden!

POLONIUS: I hear him coming. Let's withdraw, my lord.

[*Exeunt* KING *and* POLONIUS.]

[*Enter* HAMLET.]

HAMLET: To be, or not to be, that is the question:
Whether 'tis nobler in the mind to suffer
The slings and arrows of outrageous fortune,
Or to take arms against a sea of troubles,
And by opposing end them. To die, to sleep—
No more; and by a sleep to say we end
The heartache, and the thousand natural shocks
That flesh is heir to. 'Tis a consummation
Devoutly to be wished—to die, to sleep—
To sleep, perchance to dream, ay there's the rub;
For in that sleep of death what dreams may come
When we have shuffled off this mortal coil[8]
Must give us pause—there's the respect[9]
That makes calamity of so long life.
For who would bear the whips and scorns of time,
Th' oppressor's wrong, the proud man's contumely,[1]
The pangs of despised love, the law's delay,
The insolence of office, and the spurns[2]
That patient merit of th' unworthy takes,
When he himself might his quietus[3] make
With a bare bodkin? Who would fardels[4] bear,
To grunt and sweat under a weary life,
But that the dread of something after death,
The undiscovered country, from whose bourn[5]
No traveller returns, puzzles the will,
And makes us rather bear those ills we have
Than fly to others that we know not of?
Thus conscience does make cowards of us all;
And thus the native[6] hue of resolution
Is sicklied o'er with the pale cast of thought,
And enterprises of great pitch[7] and moment
With this regard their currents turn awry
And lose the name of action.—Soft you now,
The fair Ophelia.—Nymph, in thy orisons[8]
Be all my sins remembered.

8. Turmoil. 9. Consideration. 1. Insulting behavior. 2. Rejections. 3. Settlement. 4. Burdens. *Bodkin:* dagger. 5. Boundary. 6. Natural. 7. Importance. *Pitch:* height. 8. Prayers.

OPHELIA: Good my lord,
How does your honor for this many a day?
HAMLET: I humbly thank you, well, well, well.
OPHELIA: My lord, I have remembrances of yours
That I have longed long to re-deliver.
I pray you now receive them.
HAMLET: No, not I,
I never gave you aught.
OPHELIA: My honored lord, you know right well you did,
And with them words of so sweet breath composed
As made the things more rich. Their perfume lost,
Take these again, for to the noble mind
Rich gifts wax[9] poor when givers prove unkind.
There, my lord.
HAMLET: Ha, ha! are you honest?[1]
OPHELIA: My lord?
HAMLET: Are you fair?
OPHELIA: What means your lordship?
HAMLET: That if you be honest and fair, your honesty should admit no discourse to your beauty.
OPHELIA: Could beauty, my lord, have better commerce[2] than with honesty?
HAMLET: Ay, truly, for the power of beauty will sooner transform honesty from what it is to a bawd than the force of honesty can translate beauty into his likeness. This was sometimes a paradox, but now the time gives it proof. I did love you once.
OPHELIA: Indeed, my lord, you made me believe so.
HAMLET: You should not have believed me, for virtue cannot so inoculate[3] our old stock but we shall relish of it. I loved you not.
OPHELIA: I was the more deceived.
HAMLET: Get thee to a nunnery.[4] Why wouldst thou be a breeder of sinners? I am myself indifferent[5] honest, but yet I could accuse me of such things that it were better my mother had not borne me: I am very proud, revengeful, ambitious, with more offences at my beck[6] than I have thoughts to put them in, imagination to give them shape, or time to act them in. What should such fellows as I do crawling between earth and heaven? We are arrant[7] knaves all; believe none of us. Go thy ways to a nunnery. Where's your father?
OPHELIA: At home, my lord.
HAMLET: Let the doors be shut upon him, that he may play the fool nowhere but in's own house. Farewell.
OPHELIA: O, help him, you sweet heavens!
HAMLET: If thou dost marry, I'll give thee this plague for thy dowry: be thou as

9. Become. 1. Chaste. 2. Intercourse. 3. Change by grafting. 4. With typical ribaldry Hamlet uses "nunnery" in two senses, the second as a slang term for brothel. 5. Moderately. 6. Command. 7. Thorough.

chaste as ice, as pure as snow, thou shalt not escape calumny. Get thee to a nunnery, farewell. Or if thou wilt needs marry, marry a fool, for wise men know well enough what monsters[8] you make of them. To a nunnery, go, and quickly too. Farewell.

OPHELIA: Heavenly powers, restore him!

HAMLET: I have heard of your paintings well enough. God hath given you one face, and you make yourselves another. You jig, you amble, and you lisp;[9] you nickname God's creatures, and make your wantonness your ignorance.[1] Go to, I'll no more on't, it hath made me mad. I say we will have no more marriage. Those that are married already, all but one, shall live. The rest shall keep as they are. To a nunnery, go. [*Exit.*]

OPHELIA: O, what a noble mind is here o'erthrown!
The courtier's, soldier's, scholar's, eye, tongue, sword,
Th' expectancy and rose[2] of the fair state,
The glass of fashion and the mould[3] of form,
Th' observed of all observers, quite quite down!
And I of ladies most deject and wretched,
That sucked the honey of his music[4] vows,
Now see that noble and most sovereign reason
Like sweet bells jangled, out of time and harsh;
That unmatched form and feature of blown[5] youth
Blasted with ecstasy. O, woe is me
T' have seen what I have seen, see what I see!

[*Enter* KING *and* POLONIUS.]

KING: Love! His affections do not that way tend,
Nor what he spake, though it lacked form a little,
Was not like madness. There's something in his soul
O'er which his melancholy sits on brood,[6]
And I do doubt the hatch and the disclose[7]
Will be some danger; which to prevent,
I have in quick determination
Thus set it down: he shall with speed to England
For the demand of our neglected tribute.
Haply the seas and countries different,
With variable objects, shall expel
This something-settled matter in his heart
Whereon his brains still beating puts him thus
From fashion of himself. What think you on't?

POLONIUS: It shall do well. But yet do I believe
The origin and commencement of his grief
Sprung from neglected love.—How now, Ophelia?

8. Horned because cuckolded. 9. Walk and talk affectedly. 1. Hamlet means that women call things by pet names and then blame the affectation on ignorance. 2. Ornament. *Expectancy:* hope. 3. Model. *Glass:* mirror. 4. Musical. 5. Full-blown. 6. I.e., like a hen. 7. Result. *Doubt:* fear.

You need not tell us what Lord Hamlet said,
We heard it all.—My lord, do as you please,
But if you hold it fit, after the play
Let his queen-mother all alone entreat him
To show his grief. Let her be round[8] with him,
And I'll be placed, so please you, in the ear[9]
Of all their conference. If she find him not,[1]
To England send him; or confine him where
Your wisdom best shall think.

KING: It shall be so.
Madness in great ones must not unwatched go. [*Exeunt*.]

SCENE 2

A *public room in the castle. Enter* HAMLET *and three of the* PLAYERS.

HAMLET: Speak the speech, I pray you, as I pronounced it to you, trippingly on the tongue; but if you mouth it as many of our players do, I had as lief the town-crier spoke my lines. Nor do not saw the air too much with your hand thus, but use all gently, for in the very torrent, tempest, and as I may say, whirlwind of your passion, you must acquire and beget a temperance that may give it smoothness. O, it offends me to the soul to hear a robustious periwig-pated[2] fellow tear a passion to tatters, to very rags, to split the ears of the groundlings, who for the most part are capable of[3] nothing but inexplicable dumb shows and noise. I would have such a fellow whipped for o'erdoing Termagant. It out-herods Herod.[4] Pray you avoid it.

FIRST PLAYER: I warrant your honor.

HAMLET: Be not too tame neither, but let your own discretion be your tutor. Suit the action to the word, the word to the action, with this special observance, that you o'erstep not the modesty of nature; for anything so o'erdone is from[5] the purpose of playing, whose end both at the first, and now, was and is, to hold as 'twere the mirror up to nature, to show virtue her own feature, scorn her own image, and the very age and body of the time his form and pressure.[6] Now this overdone, or come tardy off, though it makes the unskilful[7] laugh, cannot but make the judicious grieve, the censure[8] of the which one must in your allowance o'erweigh a whole theatre of others. O, there be players that I have seen play—and heard others praise, and that highly—not to speak it profanely, that neither having th' accent of Christians, nor the gait of Christian, pagan, nor man, have so strutted and bellowed that I have thought some of nature's journeymen[9] had made men, and not made them well, they imitated humanity so abominably.

8. Direct. 9. Hearing. 1. Discover his problem. 2. Bewigged. *Robustius:* noisy. 3. I.e., capable of understanding. *Groundlings:* the spectators who paid least. 4. Termagant, a "Saracen" deity, and the biblical Herod were stock characters in popular drama noted for the excesses of sound and fury used by their interpreters. 5. Contrary to. 6. Shape. 7. Ignorant. 8. Judgment. 9. Inferior craftsmen.

FIRST PLAYER: I hope we have reformed that indifferently[1] with us.

HAMLET: O, reform it altogether. And let those that play your clowns speak no more than is set down for them, for there be of them that will themselves laugh, to set on some quantity of barren[2] spectators to laugh too, though in the meantime some necessary question of the play be then to be considered. That's villainous, and shows a most pitiful ambition in the fool that uses it. Go, make you ready. [*Exeunt* PLAYERS.]

[*Enter* POLONIUS, GUILDENSTERN, *and* ROSENCRANTZ.]

How now, my lord? Will the king hear this piece of work?

POLONIUS: And the queen too, and that presently.

HAMLET: Bid the players make haste. [*Exit* POLONIUS.]
Will you two help to hasten them?

ROSENCRANTZ: Ay, my lord. [*Exeunt they two.*]

HAMLET: What, ho, Horatio!

[*Enter* HORATIO.]

HORATIO: Here, sweet lord, at your service.

HAMLET: Horatio, thou art e'en as just a man
As e'er my conversation coped[3] withal.

HORATIO: O my dear lord!

HAMLET: Nay, do not think I flatter,
For what advancement may I hope from thee,
That no revenue hast but thy good spirits
To feed and clothe thee? Why should the poor be flattered?
No, let the candied tongue lick absurd pomp,
And crook the pregnant[4] hinges of the knee
Where thrift[5] may follow fawning. Dost thou hear?
Since my dear soul was mistress of her choice
And could of men distinguish her election,
S'hath sealed thee for herself, for thou hast been
As one in suff'ring all that suffers nothing,
A man that Fortune's buffets and rewards
Hast ta'en with equal thanks; and blest are those
Whose blood and judgment are so well commingled
That they are not a pipe[6] for Fortune's finger
To sound what stop[7] she please. Give me that man
That is not passion's slave, and I will wear him
In my heart's core, ay, in my heart of heart,
As I do thee. Something too much of this.
There is a play tonight before the king.
One scene of it comes near the circumstance
Which I have told thee of my father's death.

1. Somewhat. 2. Dull-witted. 3. Encountered. 4. Quick to bend. 5. Profit. 6. Musical instrument. 7. Note. *Sound:* play.

I prithee, when thou seest that act afoot,
Even with the very comment[8] of thy soul
Observe my uncle. If his occulted[9] guilt
Do not itself unkennel[1] in one speech,
It is a damnéd ghost that we have seen,
And my imaginations are as foul
As Vulcan's stithy. Give him heedful note,[2]
For I mine eyes will rivet to his face,
And after we will both our judgments join
In censure of his seeming.[3]

HORATIO: Well, my lord.
If 'a steal aught the whilst this play in playing,
And 'scape detecting, I will pay[4] the theft.

[*Enter Trumpets and Kettledrums,* KING, QUEEN, POLONIUS, OPHELIA, ROSENCRANTZ, GUILDENSTERN, *and other* LORDS *attendant.*]

HAMLET: They are coming to the play. I must be idle.
Get you a place.

KING: How fares our cousin Hamlet?

HAMLET: Excellent, i' faith, of the chameleon's dish.[5] I eat the air, promise-crammed. You cannot feed capons so.

KING: I have nothing with this answer, Hamlet. These words are not mine.

HAMLET: No, nor mine now. [*To* POLONIUS] My lord, you played once i' th' university, you say?

POLONIUS: That did I, my lord, and was accounted a good actor.

HAMLET: What did you enact?

POLONIUS: I did enact Julius Cæsar. I was killed i' th' Capitol; Brutus killed me.[6]

HAMLET: It was a brute part of him to kill so capital a calf there. Be the players ready?

ROSENCRANTZ: Ay, my lord, they stay upon your patience.[7]

QUEEN: Come hither, my dear Hamlet, sit by me.

HAMLET: No, good mother, here's metal more attractive.

POLONIUS: [*To the* KING.] O, ho! do you mark that?

HAMLET: Lady, shall I lie in your lap?

[*Lying down at* OPHELIA'S *feet.*]

OPHELIA: No, my lord.

HAMLET: I mean, my head upon your lap?

OPHELIA: Ay, my lord.

HAMLET: Do you think I meant country matters?[8]

8. Keenest observation. 9. Hidden. 1. Break loose. 2. Careful attention. *Stithy:* smithy. 3. Manner. 4. Repay. 5. A reference to a popular belief that the chameleon subsisted on a diet of air. Hamlet has deliberately misunderstood the king's question. 6. The assassination of Julius Caesar by Brutus and others is the subject of another play by Shakespeare. 7. Leisure. *Stay:* wait. 8. Presumably, rustic misbehavior, but here and elsewhere in this exchange Hamlet treats Ophelia to some ribald double meanings.

OPHELIA: I think nothing, my lord.

HAMLET: That's a fair thought to lie between maids' legs.

OPHELIA: What is, my lord?

HAMLET: Nothing.

OPHELIA: You are merry, my lord.

HAMLET: Who, I?

OPHELIA: Ay, my lord.

HAMLET: O God, your only jig-maker![9] What should a man do but be merry? For look you how cheerfully my mother looks, and my father died within's two hours.

OPHELIA: Nay, 'tis twice two months, my lord.

HAMLET: So long? Nay then, let the devil wear black, for I'll have a suit of sables. O heavens! die two months ago, and not forgotten yet? Then there's hope a great man's memory may outlive his life half a year, but by'r lady 'a must build churches then, or else shall 'a suffer not thinking on, with the hobby-horse, whose epitaph is "For O, for O, the hobby-horse is forgot!"[1]

The trumpets sound. Dumb Show follows. Enter a KING *and a* QUEEN *very lovingly; the* QUEEN *embracing him and he her. She kneels, and makes show of protestation unto him. He takes her up, and declines*[2] *his head upon her neck. He lies him down upon a bank of flowers; she, seeing him asleep, leaves him. Anon come in another man, takes off his crown, kisses it, pours poison in the sleeper's ears, and leaves him. The* QUEEN *returns, finds the* KING *dead, makes passionate action. The* POISONER *with some three or four come in again, seem to condole with her. The dead body is carried away. The* POISONER *woos the* QUEEN *with gifts; she seems harsh awhile, but in the end accepts love.*

[*Exeunt.*]

OPHELIA: What means this, my lord?

HAMLET: Marry, this is miching mallecho;[3] it means mischief.

OPHELIA: Belike this show imports the argument[4] of the play.

[*Enter* PROLOGUE.]

HAMLET: We shall know by this fellow. The players cannot keep counsel; they'll tell all.

OPHELIA: Will 'a tell us what this show meant?

HAMLET: Ay, or any show that you will show him. Be not you ashamed to show, he'll not shame to tell you what it means.

OPHELIA: You are naught, you are naught. I'll mark[5] the play.

PROLOGUE: *For us, and for our tragedy,*
Here stooping to your clemency,
We beg your hearing patiently. [*Exit.*]

HAMLET: Is this a prologue, or the posy[6] of a ring?

9. Writer of comic scenes. 1. In traditional games and dances one of the characters was a man respresented as riding a horse. The horse was made of something like cardboard and was worn about the "rider's" waist. 2. Lays. 3. Sneaking crime. 4. Plot. *Imports:* explains. 5. Attend to. *Naught:* obscene. 6. Motto engraved inside.

OPHELIA: 'Tis brief, my lord.
HAMLET: As woman's love.

[*Enter the* PLAYER KING *and* QUEEN.]

PLAYER KING: *Full thirty times hath Phœbus' cart gone round*
Neptune's salt wash and Tellus' orbéd ground,
And thirty dozen moons with borrowed sheen[7]
About the world have times twelve thirties been,
Since love our hearts and Hymen did our hands
Unite comutual in most sacred bands.[8]
PLAYER QUEEN: *So many journeys may the sun and moon*
Make us again count o'er ere love be done!
But woe is me, you are so sick of late,
So far from cheer and from your former state,
That I distrust[9] *you. Yet though I distrust,*
Discomfort you, my lord, it nothing must.
For women's fear and love hold quantity,[1]
In neither aught, or in extremity.[2]
Now what my love is proof hath made you know,
And as my love is sized,[3] *my fear is so.*
Where love is great, the littlest doubts are fear;
Where little fears grow great, great love grows there.
PLAYER KING: *Faith, I must leave thee, love, and shortly too;*
My operant powers their functions leave[4] *to do.*
And thou shalt live in this fair world behind,
Honored, beloved, and haply one as kind
For husband shalt thou—
PLAYER QUEEN: *O, confound the rest!*
Such love must needs be treason in my breast.
In second husband let me be accurst!
None wed the second but who killed the first.[5]
HAMLET: That's wormwood.
PLAYER QUEEN: *The instances*[6] *that second marriage move*
Are base respects[7] *of thrift, but none of love.*
A second time I kill my husband dead,
When second husband kisses me in bed.
PLAYER KING: *I do believe you think what now you speak,*
But what we do determine oft we break.
Purpose is but the slave to memory,
Of violent birth, but poor validity;

7. Light. 8. The speech contains several references to Greek mythology. "Phoebus" was the sun god, and his chariot or "cart" the sun. The "salt wash" of Neptune is the ocean; "Tellus" was an earth goddess, and her "orbed ground" is the earth, or globe. Hymen was the god of marriage. *Comutual:* Mutually. 9. Fear for. 1. Agree in weight. 2. The lady means without regard to too much or too little. 3. In size. 4. Cease. *Operant powers:* active forces. 5. Though there is some ambiguity, she seems to mean that the only kind of woman who would remarry is one who has killed or would kill her first husband. 6. Causes. 7. Concerns.

Which now, like fruit unripe, sticks on the tree,
But fall unshaken when they mellow be.
Most necessary 'tis that we forget
To pay ourselves what to ourselves is debt.
What to ourselves in passion we propose,
The passion ending, doth the purpose lose.
The violence of either grief or joy
Their own enactures[8] *with themselves destroy.*
Where joy most revels, grief doth most lament;
Grief joys, joy grieves, on slender accident.
This world is not for aye,[9] *nor 'tis not strange*
That even our loves should with our fortunes change;
For 'tis a question left us yet to prove,
Whether love lead fortune, or else fortune love.
The great man down, you mark his favorite flies;
The poor advanced makes friends of enemies;
And hitherto doth love on fortune tend,
For who not needs shall never lack a friend,
And who in want a hollow[1] *friend doth try,*
Directly seasons him[2] *his enemy.*
But orderly to end where I begun,
Our wills and fates do so contrary run
That our devices[3] *still are overthrown;*
Our thoughts are ours, their ends none of our own.
So think thou wilt no second husband wed,
But die thy thoughts when thy first lord is dead.

PLAYER QUEEN: *Nor earth to me give food, nor heaven light,*
Sport and repose lock from me day and night,
To desperation turn my trust and hope,
An anchor's cheer[4] *in prison be my scope,*
Each opposite that blanks[5] *the face of joy*
Meet what I would have well, and it destroy,
Both here and hence[6] *pursue me lasting strife,*
If once a widow, ever I be wife!

HAMLET: If she should break it now!

PLAYER KING: *'Tis deeply sworn. Sweet, leave me here awhile.*
My spirits grow dull, and fain I would beguile
The tedious day with sleep. [*Sleeps.*]

PLAYER QUEEN: *Sleep rock thy brain,*
And never come mischance between us twain! [*Exit.*]

HAMLET: Madam, how like you this play?

QUEEN: The lady doth protest too much, methinks.

HAMLET: O, but she'll keep her word.

KING: Have you heard the argument? Is there no offence in't?

8. Actions. 9. Eternal. 1. False. 2. Ripens him into. 3. Plans. 4. Anchorite's food. 5. Blanches. 6. In the next world.

HAMLET: No, no, they do but jest, poison in jest; no offence i' th' world.

KING: What do you call the play?

HAMLET: "The Mouse-trap." Marry, how? Tropically.[7] This play is the image of a murder done in Vienna. Gonzago is the duke's name; his wife, Baptista. You shall see anon. 'Tis a knavish piece of work, but what of that? Your majesty, and we that have free souls, it touches us not. Let the galled jade wince, our withers are unwrung.[8]

[*Enter* LUCIANUS.]

This is one Lucianus, nephew to the king.

OPHELIA: You are as good as a chorus, my lord.

HAMLET: I could interpret between you and your love, if I could see the puppets dallying.

OPHELIA: You are keen, my lord, you are keen.

HAMLET: It would cost you a groaning to take off mine edge.

OPHELIA: Still better, and worse.

HAMLET: So you mis-take your husbands.—Begin, murderer. Leave thy damnable faces and begin. Come, the croaking raven doth bellow for revenge.

LUCIANUS: *Thoughts black, hands apt, drugs fit, and time agreeing,*
Confederate season,[9] *else no creature seeing,*
Thou mixture rank, of midnight weeds collected,
With Hecate's ban thrice blasted, thrice infected,[1]
Thy natural magic[2] *and dire property*
On wholesome life usurps immediately. [*Pours the poison in his ears.*]

HAMLET: 'A poisons him i' th' garden for his estate. His name's Gonzago. The story is extant, and written in very choice Italian. You shall see anon how the murderer gets the love of Gonzago's wife.

OPHELIA: The king rises.

HAMLET: What, frighted with false fire?

QUEEN: How fares my lord?

POLONIUS: Give o'er the play.

KING: Give me some light. Away!

POLONIUS: Lights, lights, lights! [*Exeunt all but* HAMLET *and* HORATIO.]

HAMLET:

Why, let the strucken deer go weep,
    The hart ungallèd[3] play.
For some must watch while some must sleep;
    Thus runs the world away.

Would not this, sir, and a forest of feathers[4]—if the rest of my fortunes turn Turk with me—with two Provincial roses on my razed shoes, get me a fellowship in a cry of players?[5]

7. Figuratively. 8. A "galled jade" is a horse, particularly one of poor quality, with a sore back. The "withers" are the ridge between a horse's shoulders; "unwrung withers" are not chafed by the harness. 9. A helpful time for the crime. 1. Hecate was a classical goddess of witchcraft. 2. Native power. 3. Uninjured. 4. Plumes. 5. Hamlet asks Horatio if "this" recitation, accompanied with a player's costume, including plumes and rosettes on shoes which have been

HORATIO: Half a share.
HAMLET: A whole one, I.

> For thou dost know, O Damon dear,[6]
> This realm dismantled was
> Of Jove himself, and now reigns here
> A very, very—peacock.

HORATIO: You might have rhymed.
HAMLET: O good Horatio, I'll take the ghost's word for a thousand pound. Didst perceive?
HORATIO: Very well, my lord.
HAMLET: Upon the talk of the poisoning.
HORATIO: I did very well note[7] him.
HAMLET: Ah, ha! Come, some music. Come, the recorders.[8]

> For if the king like not the comedy,
> Why then, belike he likes it not, perdy.[9]

Come, some music.

[*Enter* ROSENCRANTZ *and* GUILDENSTERN.]

GUILDENSTERN: Good my lord, vouchsafe me a word with you.
HAMLET: Sir, a whole history.
GUILDENSTERN: The king, sir—
HAMLET: Ay, sir, what of him?
GUILDENSTERN: Is in his retirement marvellous distempered.[1]
HAMLET: With drink, sir?
GUILDENSTERN: No, my lord, with choler.[2]
HAMLET: Your wisdom should show itself more richer to signify this to the doctor, for for me to put him to his purgation[3] would perhaps plunge him into more choler.
GUILDENSTERN: Good my lord, put your discourse into some frame,[4] and start not so wildly from my affair.
HAMLET: I am tame, sir. Pronounce.
GUILDENSTERN: The queen your mother, in most great affliction of spirit, hath sent me to you.
HAMLET: You are welcome.
GUILDENSTERN: Nay, good my lord, this courtesy is not of the right breed. If it shall please you to make me a wholesome[5] answer, I will do your mother's

---

slashed for decorative effect, might not entitle him to become a shareholder in a theatrical company in the event that Fortune goes against him, "turn Turk." *Cry:* company. 6. Damon was a common name for a young man or a shepherd in lyric, especially pastoral poetry. Jove was the chief god of the Romans. The reader may supply for himself the rhyme referred to by Horatio. 7. Observe. 8. Wooden end-blown flutes. 9. *Par Dieu* (by God). 1. Vexed. *Retirement:* place to which he has retired. 2. Bile. 3. Treatment with a laxative. 4. Order. *Discurse:* speech. 5. Reasonable.

commandment. If not, your pardon and my return[6] shall be the end of my business.

HAMLET: Sir, I cannot.

ROSENCRANTZ: What, my lord?

HAMLET: Make you a wholesome answer; my wit's diseased. But, sir, such answer as I can make, you shall command, or rather, as you say, my mother. Therefore no more, but to the matter. My mother, you say—

ROSENCRANTZ: Then thus she says: your behavior hath struck her into amazement and admiration.[7]

HAMLET: O wonderful son, that can so stonish a mother! But is there no sequel at the heels of his mother's admiration? Impart.[8]

ROSENCRANTZ: She desires to speak with you in her closet[9] ere you go to bed.

HAMLET: We shall obey, were she ten times our mother. Have you any further trade[1] with us?

ROSENCRANTZ: My lord, you once did love me.

HAMLET: And do still, by these pickers and stealers.[2]

ROSENCRANTZ: Good my lord, what is your cause of distemper? You do surely bar the door upon your own liberty, if you deny your griefs to your friend.

HAMLET: Sir, I lack advancement.

ROSENCRANTZ: How can that be, when you have the voice of the king himself for your succession in Denmark?

HAMLET: Ay, sir, but "while the grass grows"—the proverb[3] is something musty.

[*Enter the* PLAYERS *with recorders.*]

O, the recorders! Let me see one. To withdraw with you[4]—why do you go about to recover the wind of me, as if you would drive me into a toil?[5]

GUILDENSTERN: O my lord, if my duty be too bold, my love is too unmannerly.

HAMLET: I do not well understand that. Will you play upon this pipe?[6]

GUILDENSTERN: My lord, I cannot.

HAMLET: I pray you.

GUILDENSTERN: Believe me, I cannot.

HAMLET: I do beseech you.

GUILDENSTERN: I know no touch of it,[7] my lord.

HAMLET: It is as easy as lying. Govern these ventages[8] with your fingers and thumb, give it breath with your mouth, and it will discourse most eloquent music. Look you, these are the stops.[9]

GUILDENSTERN: But these cannot I command to any utt'rance of harmony. I have not the skill.

HAMLET: Why, look you now, how unworthy a thing you make of me! You would play upon me, you would seem to know my stops, you would pluck out the heart of my mystery, you would sound[1] me from my lowest note to

6. I.e., to the queen. 7. Wonder. 8. Tell me. 9. Bedroom. 1. Business. 2. Hands. 3. The proverb ends "the horse starves." 4. Let me step aside. 5. The figure is from hunting. "You will approach me with the wind blowing from me toward you in order to drive me into the net." 6. Recorder. 7. Have no ability. 8. Holes. *Govern:* cover and uncover. 9. Wind-holes. 1. Play.

the top of my compass[2]; and there is much music, excellent voice, in this little organ, yet cannot you make it speak. 'Sblood, do you think I am easier to be played on than a pipe? Call me what instrument you will, though you can fret[3] me, you cannot play upon me.

[*Enter* POLONIUS.]

God bless you, sir!

POLONIUS: My lord, the queen would speak with you, and presently.[4]

HAMLET: Do you see yonder cloud that's almost in shape of a camel?

POLONIUS: By th' mass, and 'tis like a camel indeed.

HAMLET: Methinks it is like a weasel.

POLONIUS: It is backed like a weasel.

HAMLET: Or like a whale.

POLONIUS: Very like a whale.

HAMLET: Then I will come to my mother by and by. [*Aside.*] They fool me to the top of my bent.[5]—I will come by and by.

POLONIUS: I will say so. [*Exit.*]

HAMLET: "By and by" is easily said. Leave me, friends. [*Exeunt all but* HAMLET.]

'Tis now the very witching time of night,
When churchyards yawn, and hell itself breathes out
Contagion to this world. Now could I drink hot blood,
And do such bitter business as the day
Would quake to look on. Soft, now to my mother.
O heart, lose not thy nature; let not ever
The soul of Nero[6] enter this firm bosom.
Let me be cruel, not unnatural;
I will speak daggers to her, but use none.
My tongue and soul in this be hypocrites—
How in my words somever she be shent,[7]
To give them seals[8] never, my soul, consent! [*Exit.*]

Scene 3

A *room in the castle. Enter* KING, ROSENCRANTZ *and* GUILDENSTERN.

KING: I like him not,[9] nor stands it safe with us
To let his madness range.[1] Therefore prepare you.
I your commission will forthwith dispatch,
And he to England shall along with you.
The terms of our estate[2] may not endure
Hazard so near's as doth hourly grow
Out of his brows.

2. Range. 3. "Fret" is used in a double sense, to annoy and to play a guitar or similar instrument using the "frets" or small bars on the neck. 4. At once. 5. Treat me as an utter fool. 6. The Roman emperor Nero, known for his excesses, was believed to have been responsible for the death of his mother. 7. Shamed. 8. Fulfillment in action. 9. Distrust him.
1. Roam freely. 2. Condition of the state.

GUILDENSTERN: We will ourselves provide,[3]
Most holy and religious fear it is
To keep those many many bodies safe
That live and feed upon your majesty.
ROSENCRANTZ: The single and peculiar[4] life is bound
With all the strength and armor of the mind
To keep itself from noyance,[5] but much more
That spirit upon whose weal[6] depends and rests
The lives of many. The cess[7] of majesty
Dies not alone, but like a gulf[8] doth draw
What's near it with it. It is a massy[9] wheel
Fixed on the summit of the highest mount,
To whose huge spokes ten thousand lesser things
Are mortised and adjoined,[1] which when it falls,
Each small annexment, petty consequence,
Attends[2] the boist'rous ruin. Never alone
Did the king sigh, but with a general groan.
KING: Arm you, I pray you, to this speedy voyage,
For we will fetters put about this fear,
Which now goes too free-footed.
ROSENCRANTZ: We will haste us.
[*Exeunt* ROSENCRANTZ *and* GUILDENSTERN.]

[*Enter* POLONIUS.]

POLONIUS: My lord, he's going to his mother's closet.
Behind the arras I'll convey[3] myself
To hear the process. I'll warrant she'll tax him home,[4]
And as you said, and wisely was it said,
'Tis meet that some more audience than a mother,
Since nature makes them partial, should o'erhear
The speech, of vantage.[5] Fare you well, my liege.
I'll call upon you ere you go to bed,
And tell you what I know.
KING: Thanks, dear my lord. [*Exit* POLONIUS.]
O, my offence is rank, it smells to heaven;
It hath the primal eldest curse[6] upon't,
A brother's murder. Pray can I not,
Though inclination be as sharp as will.
My stronger guilt defeats my strong intent,
And like a man to double business[7] bound,
I stand in pause where I shall first begin,
And both neglect. What if this curséd hand

3. Equip (for the journey). 4. Individual. 5. Harm. 6. Welfare. 7. Cessation. 8. Whirlpool. 9. Massive. 1. Attached. 2. Joins in. 3. Station. 4. Sharply. *Process:* proceedings. 5. From a position of vantage. 6. I.e., of Cain. 7. Two mutually opposed interests.

Were thicker than itself with brothers' blood,
Is there not rain enough in the sweet heavens
To wash it white as snow? Whereto serves mercy
But to confront the visage of offence?
And what's in prayer but this twofold force,
To be forestalléd[8] ere we come to fall,
Or pardoned being down.[9]? Then I'll look up.
My fault is past, But, O, what form of prayer
Can serve my turn? "Forgive me my foul murder"?
That cannot be, since I am still possessed
Of those effects[1] for which I did the murder—
My crown, mine own ambition, and my queen.
May one be pardoned and retain th' offence[2]?
In the corrupted currents of this world
Offence's gilded[3] hand may shove by justice,
And oft 'tis seen the wicked prize itself
Buys out the law. But 'tis not so above.
There is no shuffling; there the action[4] lies
In his true nature, and we ourselves compelled,
Even to the teeth and forehead of[5] our faults,
To give in evidence. What then? What rests[6]?
Try what repentance can. What can it not?
Yet what can it when one can not repent?
O wretched state? O bosom black as death!
O liméd[7] soul, that struggling to be free
Art more engaged! Help, angels! Make assay.
Bow, stubborn knees, and heart with strings of steel,
Be soft as sinews of the new-born babe.
All may be well. [*He kneels.*]

[*Enter* HAMLET.]

HAMLET: Now might I do it pat,[8] now 'a is a-praying,
And now I'll do't—and so 'a goes to heaven,
And so am I revenged. That would be scanned.[9]
A villain kills my father, and for that,
I, his sole son, do this same villain send
To heaven.
Why, this is hire and salary, not revenge.
'A took my father grossly, full of bread,[1]
With all his crimes broad blown, as flush[2] as May;
And how his audit stands who knows save heaven?
But in our circumstance and course of thought

8. Prevented (from sin). 9. Having sinned. 1. Gains. 2. I.e., benefits of the offence. 3. Bearing gold as a bribe. 4. Case at law. 5. Face-to-face with. 6. Remains. 7. Caught as with bird-lime. 8. Easily. 9. Deserves consideration. 1. In a state of sin and without fasting. 2. Vigorous. *Blown:* full-blown.

'Tis heavy with him; and am I then revenged
To take him in the purging of his soul,
When he is fit and seasoned[3] for his passage?
No.
Up, sword, and know thou a more horrid hent.[4]
When he is drunk, asleep, or in his rage,
Or in th' incestuous pleasure of his bed,
At game a-swearing, or about some act
That has no relish[5] of salvation in't—
Then trip him, that his heels may kick at heaven,
And that his soul may be as damned and black
As hell, whereto it goes. My mother stays.
This physic[6] but prolongs thy sickly days. [*Exit.*]

KING: [*Rising.*] My words fly up, my thoughts remain below.
Words without thoughts never to heaven go. [*Exit.*]

Scene 4

The Queen's chamber. Enter QUEEN *and* POLONIUS.

POLONIUS: 'A will come straight. Look you lay home to[7] him.
Tell him his pranks have been too broad[8] to bear with,
And that your grace hath screen'd[9] and stood between
Much heat and him. I'll silence me even here.
Pray you be round.

QUEEN: I'll warrant you. Fear[1] me not.
Withdraw, I hear him coming.

[POLONIUS *goes behind the arras. Enter* HAMLET.]

HAMLET: Now, mother, what's the matter?

QUEEN: Hamlet, thou hast thy father much offended.

HAMLET: Mother, you have my father much offended.

HAMLET: Come, come, you answer with an idle tongue.

HAMLET: Go, go, you question with a wicked tongue.

QUEEN: Why, how now, Hamlet?

HAMLET: What's the matter now?

QUEEN: Have you forgot me?

HAMLET: No, by the rood,[2] not so.
You are the queen, your husband's brother's wife,
And would it were not so, you are my mother.

QUEEN: Nay, then I'll set those to you that can speak.

HAMLET: Come, come, and sit you down. You shall not budge.
You go not till I set you up a glass[3]

3. Ready. 4. Opportunity. 5. Flavor. 6. Medicine. 7. Be sharp with. 8. Outrageous. 9. Acted as a fire screen. 1. Doubt. 2. Cross. 3. Mirror.

Where you may see the inmost part of you.
QUEEN: What wilt thou do? Thou wilt not murder me?
Help, ho!
POLONIUS: [*Behind.*] What, ho! help!
HAMLET: [*Draws.*] How now, a rat?
Dead for a ducat, dead!

[*Kills* POLONIUS *with a pass through the arras.*]

POLONIUS: [*Behind.*] O, I am slain!
QUEEN: O me, what hast thou done?
HAMLET: Nay, I know not.
Is it the king?
QUEEN: O, what a rash and bloody deed is this!
HAMLET: A bloody deed!—almost as bad, good mother,
As kill a king and marry with his brother.
QUEEN: As kill a king?
HAMLET: Ay, lady, it was my word. [*Parting the arras.*]
Thou wretched, rash, intruding fool, farewell!
I took thee for thy better. Take thy fortune.
Thou find'st to be too busy[4] is some danger.—
Leave wringing of your hands. Peace, sit you down
And let me wring your heart, for so I shall
If it be made of penetrable stuff,
If damnéd custom have not brazed it[5] so
That it be proof and bulwark against sense.[6]
QUEEN: What have I done that thou dar'st wag thy tongue
In noise so rude against me?
HAMLET: Such an act
That blurs the grace and blush of modesty,
Calls virtue hypocrite, takes off the rose
From the fair forehead of an innocent love.
And sets a blister[7] there, makes marriage-vows
As false as dicers' oaths. O, such a deed
As from the body of contraction[8] plucks
The very soul, and sweet religion makes
A rhapsody of words. Heaven's face does glow
And this solidity and compound mass[9]
With heated visage, as against the doom[1]—
Is though-sick at the act.
QUEEN: Ay me, what act
That roars so loud and thunders in the index[2]?
HAMLET: Look here upon this picture[3] and on this,
The counterfeit presentment of two brothers.

4. Officious. 5. Plated it with brass 6. Feeling. *Proof*: armor. 7. Brand. 8. The marriage contract. 9. Meaningless mass (Earth). 1. Judgment Day. 2. Table of contents. 3. Portrait.

See what a grace was seated on this brow:
Hyperion's curls, the front[4] of Jove himself,
An eye like Mars, to threaten and command,
A station like the herald Mercury[5]
New lighted[6] on a heaven-kissing hill—
A combination and a form indeed
Where every god did seem to set his seal,[7]
To give the world assurance of a man.
This was your husband. Look you now what follows.
Here is your husband, like a mildewed ear
Blasting his wholesome brother. Have you eyes?
Could you on this fair mountain leave to feed,
And batten[8] on this moor? Ha! have you eyes?
You cannot call it love, for at your age
The heyday in the blood is tame, it's humble,
And waits upon the judgment, and what judgment
Would step from this to this? Sense sure you have
Else could you not have motion, but sure that sense
Is apoplexed[9] for madness would not err,
Nor sense to ecstasy was ne'er so thralled
But it reserved some quantity[1] of choice
To serve in such a difference. What devil was't
That thus hath cozened you at hoodman-blind[2]?
Eyes without feeling, feeling without sight,
Ears without hands or eyes, smelling sans[3] all,
Or but a sickly part of one true sense
Could not so mope.[4] O shame! where is thy blush?
Rebellious hell,
If thou canst mutine[5] in a matron's bones,
To flaming youth let virtue be as wax
And melt in her own fire. Proclaim no shame
When the compulsive ardor gives the charge,[6]
Since frost itself as actively doth burn,
And reason panders[7] will.

QUEEN: O Hamlet, speak no more!
Thou turn'st my eyes into my very soul;
And there I see such black and grainéd[8] spots
As will not leave their tinct.[9]

HAMLET: Nay, but to live
In the rank sweat of an enseamèd[1] bed,
Stewed in curruption, honeying and making love

4. Forehead. 5. In Roman mythology, Mercury served as the messenger of the gods. *Station:* bearing. 6. Newly alighted. 7. Mark of approval. 8. Feed greedily. 9. Paralyzed. 1. Power. 2. Blindman's buff. *Cozened:* cheated. 3. Without. 4. Be stupid. 5. Commit mutiny. 6. Attacks. 7. Pimps for. 8. Ingrained. 9. Lose their color. 1. Greasy.

Over the nasty sty—
QUEEN: O, speak to me no more!
These words like daggers enter in my ears;
No more, sweet Hamlet.
HAMLET: A murderer and a villain,
A slave that is not twentieth part the tithe[2]
Of your precedent lord, a vice of kings,[3]
A cutpurse[4] of the empire and the rule,
That from a shelf the precious diadem stole
And put it in his pocket—
QUEEN: No more.

[*Enter* GHOST.]

HAMLET: A king of shreds and patches—
Save me and hover o'er me with your wings,
You heavenly guards! What would your gracious figure?
QUEEN: Alas, he's mad.
HAMLET: Do you not come your tardy[5] son to chide,
That lapsed in time and passion lets go by
Th' important acting of your dread command?
O, say!
GHOST: Do not forget. This visitation
Is but to whet thy almost blunted purpose.
But look, amazement on thy mother sits.
O, step between her and her fighting soul!
Conceit[6] in weakest bodies strongest works.
Speak to her, Hamlet.
HAMLET: How is it with you, lady?
QUEEN: Alas, how is't with you,
That you do bend[7] your eye on vacancy,
And with th' incorporal air do hold discourse?
Forth at your eyes your spirits wildly peep,
And as the sleeping soldiers in th' alarm,
Your bedded hairs like life in excrements[8]
Start up and stand an end. O gentle son,
Upon the heat and flame of thy distemper
Sprinkle cool patience. Whereon do you look?
HAMLET: On him, on him! Look you how pale he glares.
His form and cause conjoined,[9] preaching to stones,
Would make them capable.[1]—Do not look upon me,
Lest with piteous action you convert
My stern effects.[2] Then what I have to do

2. One-tenth. 3. The "Vice," a common figure in the popular drama, was a clown or buffoon. *Precedent lord:* first husband. 4. Pickpocket. 5. Slow to act. 6. Imagination. 7. Turn. 8. Nails and hair. 9. Working together. 1. Of responding. 2. Deeds.

Will want true color—tears perchance for blood.
QUEEN: To whom do you speak this?
HAMLET: Do you see nothing there?
QUEEN: Nothing at all, yet all that is I see.
HAMLET: Nor did you nothing hear?
QUEEN: No, nothing but ourselves.
HAMLET: Why, look you there. Look how it steals away.
My father, in his habit[3] as he lived!
Look where he goes even now out at the portal. [*Exit* GHOST.]
QUEEN: This is the very coinage[4] of your brain.
Ths bodiless creation ecstasy[5]
Is very cunning[6] in.
HAMLET: My pulse as yours doth temperately keep time,
And makes as healthful music. It is not madness
That I have uttered. Bring me to the test,
And I the matter will re-word, which madness
Would gambol[7] from. Mother, for love of grace,
Lay not that flattering unction[8] to your soul,
That not your trespass but my madness speaks.
It will but skin and film the ulcerous place
Whiles rank corruption, mining[9] all within,
Infects unseen. Confess yourself to heaven,
Repent what's past, avoid what is to come.
And do not spread the compost on the weeds,
To make them ranker. Forgive me this my virtue,
For in the fatness of these pursy[1] times
Virtue itself of vice must pardon beg,
Yea, curb[2] and woo for leave to do him good.
QUEEN: O Hamlet, thou hast cleft my heart in twain.
HAMLET: O, throw away the worser part of it,
And live the purer with the other half.
Good night—but go not to my uncle's bed.
Assume a virtue, if you have it not.
That monster custom[3] who all sense doth eat
Of habits evil, is angel yet in this,
That to the use of actions fair and good
He likewise gives a frock or livery
That aptly[4] is put on. Refrain tonight,
And that shall lend a kind of easiness
To the next abstinence; the next more easy;
For use almost can change the stamp of nature,
And either curb the devil, or throw him out
With wondrous potency. Once more, good night,

3. Costume. 4. Invention. 5. Madness. 6. Skilled. 7. Shy away. 8. Ointment.
9. Undermining. 1. Bloated. 2. Bow. 3. Habit. 4. Easily.

And when you are desirous to be blest,
I'll blessing beg of you. For this same lord
I do repent; but heaven hath pleased it so,
To punish me with this, and this with me,
That I must be their scourge and minister.
I will bestow[5] him and will answer well
The death I gave him. So, again, good night.
I must be cruel only to be kind.
Thus bad begins and worse remains behind.
One word more, good lady.

QUEEN: What shall I do?

HAMLET: Not this, by no means, that I bid you do:
Let the bloat[6] king tempt you again to bed,
Pinch wanton[7] on your cheek, call you his mouse,
And let him, for a pair of reechy[8] kisses,
Or paddling in your neck with his damned fingers,
Make you to ravel[9] all this matter out,
That I essentially am not in madness,
But mad in craft. 'Twere good you let him know,
For who that's but a queen, fair, sober, wise,
Would from a paddock, from a bat, a gib,[1]
Such dear concernings hide? Who would so do?
No, in despite of sense and secrecy,
Unpeg the basket on the house's top,
Let the birds fly, and like the famous ape,
To try conclusions, in the basket creep
And break your own neck down.[2]

QUEEN: Be thou assured, if words be made of breath
And breath of life, I have no life to breathe
What thou hast said to me.

HAMLET: I must to England; you know that?

QUEEN: Alack,
I had forgot. 'Tis so concluded on.

HAMLET: There's letters sealed, and my two school-fellows,
Whom I will trust as I will adders fanged,
They bear the mandate; they must sweep[3] my way
And marshal me to knavery. Let it work,
For 'tis the sport to have the enginer
Hoist with his own petar; and't shall go hard
But I will delve[4] one yard below their mines
And blow them at the moon. O, 'tis most sweet

5. Dispose of. 6. Bloated. 7. Lewdly. 8. Foul. 9. Reveal. 1. Tomcat. *Paddock:* toad. 2. Apparently a reference to a now-lost fable in which an ape, finding a basket containing a cage of birds on a housetop, opens the cage. The birds fly away. The ape, thinking that if he were in the basket he too could fly, enters, jumps out, and breaks his neck. 3. Prepare. *Mandate:* command. 4. Dig.

When in one line two crafts directly meet.[5]
This man shall set me packing.
I'll lug the guts into the neighbor room.
Mother, good night. Indeed, this counsellor
Is now most still, most secret, and most grave,
Who was in life a foolish prating knave.
Come sir, to draw toward an end with you.
Good night, mother.

[*Exit the* QUEEN. *Then exit* HAMLET *tugging* POLONIUS.]

ACT IV

Scene 1

A room in the castle. Enter KING, QUEEN, ROSENCRANTZ *and* GUILDENSTERN.

KING: There's matter in these sighs, these profound heaves,
You must translate[6]; 'tis fit we understand them.
Where is your son?
QUEEN: Bestow this place on us a little while.

[*Exeunt* ROSENCRANTZ *and* GUILDENSTERN.]

Ah, mine own lord, what have I seen tonight!
KING: What, Gertrude? How does Hamlet?
QUEEN: Mad as the sea and wind when both contend
Which is the mightier. In his lawless fit,
Behind the arras hearing something stir,
Whips out his rapier, cries "A rat, a rat!"
And in this brainish apprehension[7] kills
The unseen good old man.
KING: O heavy deed!
It had been so with us had we been there.
His liberty is full of threats to all—
To your yourself, to us, to every one.
Alas, how shall this bloody deed be answered?
It will be laid to us, whose providence[8]
Should have kept short, restrained, and out of haunt,[9]
This mad young man. But so much was our love,
We would not understand what was most fit;
But, like the owner of a foul disease,
To keep it from divulging, let it feed
Even on the pith of life. Where is he gone?

5. The "enginer" or engineer is a military man who is here described as being blown up by a bomb of his own construction, "hoist with his own petar." The military figure continues in the succeeding lines where Hamlet describes himself as digging a countermine or tunnel beneath the one Claudius is digging to defeat Hamlet. In line 214 the two tunnels unexpectedly meet. 6. Explain. 7. Insane notion. 8. Prudence. 9. Away from court.

QUEEN: To draw apart the body he hath killed,
O'er whom his very madness, like some ore
Among a mineral of metals base,
Shows itself pure: 'a weeps for what is done.
KING: O Gertrude, come away!
The sun no sooner shall the mountains touch
But we will ship him hence, and this vile deed
We must with all our majesty and skill
Both countenance and excuse. Ho, Guildenstern!

[*Enter* ROSENCRANTZ *and* GUILDENSTERN.]

Friends both, go join you with some further aid.
Hamlet in madness hath Polonius slain,
And from his mother's closet hath he dragged him.
Go seek him out; speak fair, and bring the body
Into the chapel. I pray you haste in this.
[*Exeunt* ROSENCRANTZ *and* GUILDENSTERN.]
Come, Gertrude, we'll call up our wisest friends
And let them know both what we mean to do
And what's untimely done;
Whose whisper o'er the world's diameter,
As level as the cannon to his blank,[1]
Transports his poisoned shot—may miss our name,
And hit the woundless air. O, come away!
My soul is full of discord and dismay. [*Exeunt.*]

Scene 2

A *passageway. Enter* HAMLET.

HAMLET: Safely stowed.—But soft, what noise? Who calls on Hamlet?
O, here they come.

[*Enter* ROSENCRANTZ, GUILDENSTERN, *and* OTHERS.]

ROSENCRANTZ: What have you done, my lord, with the dead body?
HAMLET: Compounded it with dust, whereto 'tis kin.
ROSENCRANTZ: Tell us where 'tis, that we may take it thence
And bear it to the chapel.
HAMLET: Do not believe it.
ROSENCRANTZ: Believe what?
HAMLET: That I can keep your counsel and not mine own. Besides, to be demanded of a sponge—what replication[2] should be made by the son of a king?
ROSENCRANTZ: Take you me for a sponge, my lord?
HAMLET: Ay, sir, that soaks up the king's countenance,[3] his rewards, his author-

1. Mark. *Level*: direct. 2. Answer. *Demanded of*: questioned by. 3. Favor.

ities. But such officers do the king best service in the end. He keeps them like an apple in the corner of his jaw, first mouthed to be last swallowed. When he needs what you have gleaned, it is but squeezing you and, sponge, you shall be dry again.

ROSENCRANTZ: I understand you not, my lord.

HAMLET: I am glad of it. A knavish speech sleeps in a foolish ear.

ROSENCRANTZ: My lord, you must tell us where the body is, and go with us to the king.

HAMLET: The body is with the king, but the king is not with the body.
The king is a thing—

GUILDENSTERN: A thing, my lord!

HAMLET: Of nothing. Bring me to him. Hide fox, and all after.[4] [*Exeunt*.]

Scene 3

A room in the castle. Enter KING.

KING: I have sent to seek him, and to find the body.
How dangerous is it that this man goes loose!
Yet must not we put the strong law on him.
He's loved of the distracted[5] multitude,
Who like not in their judgment but their eyes,
And where 'tis so, th' offender's scourge[6] is weighed,
But never the offence. To bear all smooth and even,
This sudden sending him away must seem
Deliberate pause.[7] Diseases desperate grown
By desperate appliance are relieved,
Or not at all.

[*Enter* ROSENCRANTZ, GUILDENSTERN, *and all the rest*.]

How now! what hath befall'n?

ROSENCRANTZ: Where the dead body is bestowed, my lord,
We cannot get from him.

KING: But where is he?

ROSENCRANTZ: Without, my lord; guarded, to know[8] your pleasure.

KING: Bring him before us.

ROSENCRANTZ: Ho! bring in the lord.

[*They enter with* HAMLET.]

KING: Now, Hamlet, where's Polonius?

HAMLET: At supper.

KING: At supper? Where?

HAMLET: Not where he eats, but where 'a is eaten. A certain convocation of politic[9] worms are e'en at him. Your worm is your only emperor for diet.

4. Apparently a reference to a children's game like hide-and-seek. 5. Confused. 6. Punishment. 7. I.e., not an impulse. 8. Await. 9. Statemanlike. *Convocation:* gathering.

We fat all creatures else to fat us, and we fat ourselves for maggots. Your fat king and your lean beggar is but variable service—two dishes, but to one table. That's the end.

KING: Alas, alas!

HAMLET: A man may fish with the worm that hath eat of a king, and eat of the fish that hath fed of that worm.

KING: What dost thou mean by this?

HAMLET: Nothing but to show you how a king may go a progress through the guts of a beggar.

KING: Where is Polonius?

HAMLET: In heaven. Send thither to see. If your messenger find him not there, seek him i' th' other place yourself. But if, indeed, you find him not within this month, you shall nose[1] him as you go up the stairs into the lobby.

KING: [*To* ATTENDANTS.] Go seek him there.

HAMLET: 'A will stay till you come. [*Exeunt* ATTENDANTS.]

KING: Hamlet, this deed, for thine especial safety—
Which we do tender, as we dearly[2] grieve
For that which thou hast done—must send thee hence
With fiery quickness. Therefore prepare thyself.
The bark is ready, and the wind at help,
Th' associates tend, and everything is bent
For England.

HAMLET: For England?

KING: Ay, Hamlet.

HAMLET: Good.

KING: So it is, if thou knew'st our purposes.

HAMLET: I see a cherub that sees them. But come, for England!
Farewell, dear mother.

KING: Thy loving father, Hamlet.

HAMLET: My mother. Father and mother is man and wife, man and wife is one flesh. So, my mother. Come, for England. [*Exit.*]

KING: Follow him at foot[3]; tempt him with speed aboard.
Delay it not; I'll have him hence tonight.
Away! for everything is sealed and done
That else leans on th' affair. Pray you make haste. [*Exeunt all but the* KING.]
And, England, if my love thou hold'st at aught—
As my great power thereof may give thee sense,[4]
Since yet thy cicatrice[5] looks raw and red
After the Danish sword, and thy free awe
Pays homage to us—thou mayst not coldly set[6]
Our sovereign process,[7] which imports at full
By letters congruing[8] to that effect
The present death of Hamlet. Do it, England,

1. Smell. 2. Deeply. *Tender:* consider. 3. Closely. 4. Of its value. 5. Wound scar. 6. Set aside. 7. Mandate. 8. Agreeing.

For like the hectic[9] in my blood he rages,
And thou must cure me. Till I know 'tis done,
Howe'er my haps, my joys were ne'er begun. [*Exit.*]

SCENE 4

Near Elsinore. Enter FORTINBRAS *with his army.*

FORTINBRAS: Go, captain, from me greet the Danish king.
Tell him that by his license Fortinbras
Craves the conveyance[1] of a promised march
Over his kingdom. You know the rendezvous.
If that his majesty would aught with us,
We shall express our duty in his eye,[2]
And let him know so.
CAPTAIN: I will do't, my lord.
FORTINBRAS: Go softly on. [*Exeunt all but the* CAPTAIN.]

[*Enter* HAMLET, ROSENCRANTZ, GUILDENSTERN, *and* OTHERS.]

HAMLET: Good sir, whose powers are these?
CAPTAIN: They are of Norway, sir.
HAMLET: How purposed, sir, I pray you?
CAPTAIN: Against some part of Poland.
HAMLET: Who commands them, sir?
CAPTAIN: The nephew to old Norway, Fortinbras.
HAMLET: Goes it against the main[3] of Poland, sir,
Or for some frontier?
CAPTAIN: Truly to speak, and with no addition,[4]
We go to gain a little patch of ground
That hath in it no profit but the name.
To pay five ducats,[5] five, I would not farm it;
Nor will it yield to Norway or the Pole
A ranker rate should it be sold in fee.[6]
HAMLET: Why, then the Polack never will defend it.
CAPTAIN: Yes, it is already garrisoned.
HAMLET: Two thousand souls and twenty thousand ducats
Will not debate the question of this straw.
This is th' imposthume[7] of much wealth and peace,
That inward breaks, and shows no cause without
Why the man dies. I humbly thank you, sir.
CAPTAIN: God b'wi'ye, sir. [*Exit.*]
ROSENCRANTZ: Will't please you go, my lord?
HAMLET: I'll be with you straight. Go a little before. [*Exeunt all but* HAMLET.]
How all occasions do inform against me,

9. Chronic fever. 1. Escort. 2. Presence. 3. Central part. 4. Exaggeration. 5. I.e., in rent. 6. Outright. *Ranker:* higher. 7. Abscess.

And spur my dull revenge! What is a man,
If his chief good and market[8] of his time
Be but to sleep and feed? A beast, no more.
Sure he that made us with such large discourse,[9]
Looking before and after, gave us not
That capability and godlike reason
To fust[1] in us unused. Now, whether it be
Bestial oblivion, or some craven scruple
Of thinking too precisely on th' event[2]—
A thought which, quartered, hath but one part wisdom
And ever three parts coward—I do not know
Why yet I live to say "This thing's to do,"
Sith[3] I have cause, and will, and strength, and means,
To do't. Examples gross as earth exhort me.
Witness this army of such mass and charge,[4]
Led by a delicate and tender prince,
Whose spirit, with divine ambition puffed,
Makes mouths at[5] the invisible event,
Exposing what is mortal and unsure
To all that fortune, death, and danger dare,
Even for an eggshell. Rightly to be great
Is not to stir without great argument,
But greatly to find quarrel in a straw
When honor's at the stake. How stand I then,
That have a father killed, a mother stained,
Excitements of my reason and my blood,
And let all sleep, while to my shame I see
The imminent death of twenty thousand men
That for a fantasy and trick of fame
Go to their graves like beds, fight for a plot
Whereon the numbers cannot try the cause,
Which is not tomb enough and continent
To hide the slain?[6] O, from this time forth,
My thoughts be bloody, or be nothing worth! [*Exit.*]

Scene 5

A room in the castle. Enter QUEEN, HORATIO *and a* GENTLEMAN.

QUEEN: I will not speak with her.
GENTLEMAN: She is importunate, indeed distract.
Her mood will needs to be pitied.

8. Occupation. 9. Ample reasoning power. 1. Grow musty. 2. Outcome. 3. Since. 4. Expense. 5. Scorns. 6. The plot of ground involved is so small that it cannot contain the number of men involved in fighting nor furnish burial space for the number of those who will die.

QUEEN: What would she have?
GENTLEMAN: She speaks much of her father, says she hears
There's tricks i' th' world, and hems, and beats her heart,
Spurns enviously at straws,[7] speaks things in doubt
That carry but half sense. Her speech is nothing,
Yet the unshaped use of it doth move
The hearers to collection[8]; they yawn at it,
And botch the words up fit to their own thoughts,
Which, as her winks and nods and gestures yield them,
Indeed would make one think there might be thought,
Though nothing sure, yet much unhappily.
HORATIO: 'Twere good she were spoken with, for she may strew
Dangerous conjectures in ill-breeding minds.
QUEEN: Let her come in. [*Exit* GENTLEMAN.]
[*Aside.*] To my sick soul, as sin's true nature is,
Each toy seems prologue to some great amiss.[9]
So full of artless jealousy is guilt,
It spills itself in fearing to be spilt.

[*Enter* OPHELIA *distracted.*]

OPHELIA: Where is the beauteous majesty of Denmark?
QUEEN: How now, Ophelia!

[OPHELIA *sings.*]

How should I your true love know
From another one?
By his cockle hat and staff,[1]
And his sandal shoon.[2]

QUEEN: Alas, sweet lady, what imports this song?
OPHELIA: Say you? Nay, pray you mark.

[*Sings.*]

He is dead and gone, lady,
He is dead and gone;
At his head a grass-green turf,
At his heels a stone.

O, ho!
QUEEN: Nay, but Ophelia—
OPHELIA: Pray you mark.

[*Sings.*]

White his shroud as the mountain snow—

7. Takes offense at trifles. 8. An attempt to order. 9. Catastrophe. *Toy:* trifle. 1. A "cockle hat," one decorated with a shell, indicated that the wearer had made a pilgrimage to the shrine of St. James at Compostela in Spain. The staff also marked the carrier as a pilgrim. 2. Shoes.

[*Enter* KING.]

QUEEN: Alas, look here, my lord.

[OPHELIA:]

Larded all with sweet flowers;
Which bewept to the grave did not go
With true-love showers.

KING: How do you, pretty lady?

OPHELIA: Well, God dild[3] you! They say the owl was a baker's daughter. Lord, we know what we are, but know not what we may be. God be at your table!

KING: Conceit[4] upon her father.

OPHELIA: Pray let's have no words of this, but when they ask you what it means, say you this:

[*Sings.*]

Tomorrow is Saint Valentine's day,
All in the morning betime,
And I a maid at your window,
To be your Valentine.

Then up he rose, and donn'd his clo'es,
And dupped[5] the chamber-door,
Let in the maid, that out a maid
Never departed more.

KING: Pretty Ophelia!

OPHELIA: Indeed, without an oath, I'll make an end on't.

[*Sings.*]

By Gis[6] and by Saint Charity,
Alack, and fie for shame!
Young men will do't, if they come to't;
By Cock,[7] they are to blame.

Quoth she "before you tumbled me,
You promised me to wed."

He answers:

"So would I'a done, by yonder sun,
An thou hadst not come to my bed."

KING: How long hath she been thus?

OPHELIA: I hope all will be well. We must be patient, but I cannot choose but weep to think they would lay him i' th' cold ground. My brother shall know of it, and so I thank you for your good counsel. Come, my coach! Good

3. Yield. 4. Thought. 5. Opened. 6. Jesus. 7. God.

night, ladies, good night. Sweet ladies, good night, good night. [*Exit.*]

KING: Follow her close; give her good watch, I pray you.
[*Exeunt* HORATIO *and* GENTLEMAN.]
O, this is the poison of deep grief; it springs
All from her father's death, and now behold!
O Gertrude, Gertrude!
When sorrows come, they come not single spies,
But in battalions: first, her father slain;
Next, your son gone, and he most violent author
Of his own just remove; the people muddied,[8]
Thick and unwholesome in their thoughts and whispers
For good Polonius' death; and we have done but greenly[9]
In hugger-mugger[1] to inter him; poor Ophelia
Divided from herself and her fair judgment,
Without the which we are pictures, or mere beasts;
Last, and as much containing as all these,
Her brother is in secret come from France,
Feeds on his wonder, keeps himself in clouds,
And wants not buzzers to infect his ear
With pestilent speeches of his father's death,
Wherein necessity, of matter beggared,[2]
Will nothing stick our person to arraign[3]
In ear and ear.[4] O my dear Gertrude, this,
Like to a murd'ring piece,[5] in many places
Gives me superfluous death. Attend,

[*A noise within. Enter a* MESSENGER.]

Where are my Switzers[6]? Let them guard the door.
What is the matter?

MESSENGER: Save yourself, my lord.
The ocean, overpeering of his list,[7]
Eats not the flats with more impiteous[8] haste
Then young Laertes, in a riotous head,[9]
O'erbears your officers. The rabble call him lord,
And as the world were now but to begin,
Antiquity forgot, custom not known,
The ratifiers and props of every word,
They cry "Choose we, Laertes shall be king."
Caps, hands, and tongues, applaud it to the clouds,
"Laertes shall be king, Laertes king."

QUEEN: How cheerfully on the false trail they cry[1]!

8. Disturbed. 9. Without judgment. 1. Haste. 2. Short on facts. 3. Accuse. *Stick:* hesitate. 4. From both sides. 5. A weapon designed to scatter its shot. 6. Swiss guards. 7. Towering above its limits. 8. Pitiless. 9. With an armed band. 1. As if following the scent.

[*A noise within.*]

O, this is counter,[2] you false Danish dogs!
KING: The doors are broke.

[*Enter* LAERTES, *with* OTHERS.]

LAERTES: Where is this king?—Sirs, stand you all without.
ALL: No, let's come in.
LAERTES: I pray you give me leave.
ALL: We will, we will. [*Exeunt his followers.*]
LAERTES: I thank you. Keep[3] the door.—O thou vile king,
Give me my father!
QUEEN: Calmly, good Laertes.
LAERTES: That drop of blood that's calm proclaims me bastard,
Cries cuckold to my father, brands the harlot
Even here between the chaste unsmirchéd brow
Of my true mother.
KING: What is the cause, Laertes,
That thy rebellion looks so giant-like?
Let him go, Gertrude. Do not fear[4] our person.
There's such divinity doth hedge a king
That treason can but peep to[5] what it would,
Acts little of his will. Tell me, Laertes.
Why thou art thus incensed. Let him go, Gertrude.
Speak, man.
LAERTES: Where is my father?
KING: Dead.
QUEEN: But not by him.
KING: Let him demand[6] his fill.
LAERTES: How came he dead? I'll not be juggled with.
To hell allegiance, vows to the blackest devil,
Conscience and grace to the profoundest pit!
I dare damnation. To this point I stand,
That both the worlds I give to negligence,[7]
Let come what comes, only I'll be revenged
Most throughly for my father.
KING: Who shall stay you?
LAERTES: My will, not all the world's.
And for my means, I'll husband[8] them so well
They shall go far with little.
KING: Good Laertes,
If you desire to know the certainty
Of your dear father, is't writ in your revenge

2. Backward. 3. Guard. 4. Fear for. 5. Look at over or through a barrier. 6. Question. 7. Disregard. *Both the worlds:* i.e., this and the next. 8. Manage.

That, swoopstake,[9] you will draw both friend and foe,
Winner and loser?

KING: None but his enemies.

KING: Will you know them, then?

LAERTES: To his good friends thus wide I'll ope my arms,
And like the kind life-rend'ring pelican,[1]
Repast them with my blood.

KING: Why, now you speak
Like a good child and a true gentleman.
That I am guiltless of your father's death,
And am most sensibly in grief for it,
It shall as level[2] to your judgment 'pear
As day does to your eye.

[*A noise within*: "Let her come in."]

LAERTES: How now? What noise is that?

[*Enter* OPHELIA.]

O, heat dry up my brains! tears seven times salt
Burn out the sense and virtue[3] of mine eye!
By heaven, thy madness shall be paid with weight
Till our scale turn the beam. O rose of May,
Dear maid, kind sister, sweet Ophelia!
O heavens! is't possible a young maid's wits
Should be as mortal as an old man's life?
Nature is fine[4] in love, and where 'tis fine
It sends some precious instances of itself
After the thing it loves.[5]

[OPHELIA *sings*.]

They bore him barefac'd on the bier;
Hey non nonny, nonny, hey nonny;
And in his grave rain'd many a tear—

Fare you well, my dove!

LAERTES: Hadst thou thy wits, and didst persuade revenge,
It could not move thus.

OPHELIA: You must sing "A-down, a-down, and you call him a-down-a." O, how the wheel becomes it! It is the false steward, that stole his master's daughter.[6]

9. Sweeping the board. 1. The pelican was believed to feed her young with her own blood. 2. Plain. 3. Function. *Sense*: feeling. 4. Refined. 5. Laertes means that Ophelia, because of her love for her father, gave up her sanity as a token of grief at his death. 6. The "wheel" refers to the "burden" or refrain of a song, in this case "A-down, a-down, and you call him a-down-a." The ballad to which she refers was about a false steward. Others have suggested that the "wheel" is the Wheel of Fortune, a spinning wheel to whose rhythm such a song might have been sung or a kind of dance movement performed by Ophelia as she sings.

LAERTES: This nothing's more than matter.
OPHELIA: There's a rosemary, that's for remembrance. Pray you, love, remember. And there is pansies, that's for thoughts.
LAERTES: A document[7] in madness, thoughts and remembrance fitted.
OPHELIA: There's fennel for you, and columbines. There's rue for you, and here's some for me. We may call it herb of grace a Sundays. O, you must wear your rue with a difference. There's a daisy. I would give you some violets, but they withered all when my father died. They say 'a made a good end.

[*Sings.*]

For bonny sweet Robin is all my joy.

LAERTES: Thought and affliction, passion, hell itself,
She turns to favor[8] and to prettiness.

[OPHELIA *sings.*]

And will 'a not come again?
And will 'a not come again?
No, no, he is dead,
Go to thy death-bed,
He never will come again.

His beard was as white as snow,
All flaxen was his poll[9];
He is gone, he is gone,
And we cast away moan:
God-a-mercy on his soul!

And of all Christian souls, I pray God. God b'wi'you. [*Exit.*]
LAERTES: Do you see this, O God?
KING: Laertes, I must commune with your grief,
Or you deny me right. Go but apart,
Make choice of whom your wisest friends you will,
And they shall hear and judge 'twixt you and me.
If by direct or by collateral[1] hand
They find us touched,[2] we will our kingdom give,
Our crown, our life, and all that we call ours,
To you in satisfaction; but if not,
Be you content to lend your patience to us,
And we shall jointly labor with your soul
To give it due content.
LAERTES: Let this be so.
His means of death, his obscure funeral—
No trophy, sword, nor hatchment,[3] o'er his bones,
No noble rite nor formal ostentation[4]—

7. Lesson. 8. Beauty. 9. Head. 1. Indirect. 2. By guilt. 3. Coat of arms. 4. Pomp.

Cry to be heard, as 'twere from heaven to earth,
That I must call't in question.

KING: So you shall;
And where th' offence is, let the great axe fall.
I pray you go with me. [*Exeunt.*]

SCENE 6

Another room in the castle. Enter HORATIO *and a* GENTLEMAN.

HORATIO: What are they that would speak with me?

GENTLEMAN: Sea-faring men, sir. They say they have letters for you.

HORATIO: Let them come in. [*Exit* GENTLEMAN.]
I do not know from what part of the world
I should be greeted, if not from Lord Hamlet.

[*Enter* SAILORS.]

SAILOR: God bless you, sir.

HORATIO: Let him bless thee too.

SAILOR: 'A shall, sir, an't please him. There's a letter for you, sir—it came from th' ambassador that was bound for England—if your name be Horatio, as I am let to know[5] it is.

HORATIO: [*Reads*]. "Horatio, when thou shalt have overlooked[6] this, give these fellows some means[7] to the king. They have letters for him. Ere we were two days old at sea, a pirate of very warlike appointment[8] gave us chase. Finding ourselves too slow of sail, we put on a compelled valor, and in the grapple I boarded them. On the instant they got clear of our ship, so I alone became their prisoner. They have dealt with me like thieves of mercy, but they knew what they did; I am to do a good turn for them. Let the king have the letters I have sent, and repair thou to me with as much speed as thou wouldest fly death. I have words to speak in thine ear will make thee dumb; yet are they much too light for the bore of the matter.[9] These good fellows will bring thee where I am. Rosencrantz and Guildenstern hold their course for England. Of them I have much to tell thee. Farewell.
He that thou knowest thine, HAMLET."

Come, I will give you way[1] for these your letters,
And do't the speedier that you may direct me
To him from whom you brought them. [*Exeunt.*]

5. Informed. 6. Read through. 7. Access. 8. Equipment. 9. A figure from gunnery, referring to shot which is too small for the size of the weapons to be fired. 1. Means of delivery.

Scene 7

Another room in the castle. Enter KING *and* LAERTES.

KING: Now must your conscience my acquittance seal,[2]
And you must put me in your heart for friend,
Sith you have heard, and with a knowing ear,
That he which hath your noble father slain
Pursued my life.
LAERTES: It well appears. But tell me
Why you proceeded not against these feats,
So criminal and so capital in nature,
As by your safety, greatness, wisdom, all things else,
You mainly were stirred up.
KING: O, for two special reasons,
Which may to you, perhaps, seem much unsinewed,[3]
But yet to me th' are strong. The queen his mother
Lives almost by his looks, and for myself—
My virtue or my plague, be it either which—
She is so conjunctive[4] to my life and soul
That, as the star moves not but in his sphere,[5]
I could not but by her. The other motive,
Why to a public count[6] I might not go,
Is the great love the general gender[7] bear him,
Who, dipping all his faults in their affection,
Work like the spring that turneth wood to stone,[8]
Convert his gyves[9] to graces; so that my arrows,
Too slightly timbered[1] for so loud a wind,
Would have reverted to my bow again,
But not where I have aimed them.
LAERTES: And so have I a noble father lost,
A sister driven into desp'rate terms,
Whose worth, if praises may go back again,
Stood challenger on mount of all the age
For her perfections. But my revenge will come.
KING: Break not your sleeps for that. You must not think
That we are made of stuff so flat and dull
That we can let our beard be shook with danger,
And think it pastime. You shortly shall hear more.
I loved you father, and we love our self,
And that, I hope, will teach you to imagine—

2. Grant me innocent. 3. Weak. 4. Closely joined. 5. A reference to the Ptolemaic cosmology in which planets and stars were believed to revolve about the earth in crystalline spheres concentric with the earth. 6. Reckoning. 7. Common people. 8. Certain English springs contain so much lime in the water than a lime covering will be deposited on a log placed in one of them for a length of time. 9. Fetters. 1. Shafted.

[*Enter a* MESSENGER *with letters.*]

MESSENGER: These to your majesty; this to the queen.
KING: From Hamlet! Who brought them?
MESSENGER: Sailors, my lord, they say. I saw them not.
They were given me by Claudio; he received them
Of him that brought them.
KING: Laertes, you shall hear them.—
Leave us. [*Exit* MESSENGER.]
[*Reads.*] "High and mighty, you shall know I am set naked on your kingdom. Tomorrow shall I beg leave to see your kingly eyes; when I shall, first asking your pardon thereunto, recount the occasion of my sudden and more strange return.
Hamlet."
What should this mean? Are all the rest come back?
Or is it some abuse,[2] and no such thing?
LAERTES: Know you the hand?
KING: 'Tis Hamlet's character.[3] "Naked"!
And in a postscript here, he says "alone."
Can you devise[4] me?
LAERTES: I am lost in it, my lord. But let him come.
It warms the very sickness in my heart
That I shall live and tell him to his teeth
"Thus didest thou."
KING: If it be so, Laertes—
As how should it be so, how otherwise?—
Will you be ruled by me?
LAERTES: Ay, my lord,
So you will not o'errule me to a peace.
KING: To thine own peace. If he be now returned,
As checking at[5] his voyage, and that he means
No more to undertake it, I will work him
To an exploit now ripe in my device,
Under the which he shall not choose but fall;
And for his death no wind of blame shall breathe
But even his mother shall uncharge[6] the practice
And call it accident.
LAERTES: My lord, I will be ruled;
The rather if you could devise it so
That I might be the organ.[7]
KING: It falls right.
You have been talked of since your travel much,
And that in Hamlet's hearing, for a quality

2. Trick. 3. Handwriting. 4. Explain it to. 5. Turning aside from. 6. Not accuse.
7. Instrument.

Wherein they say you shine. Your sum of parts
Did not together pluck such envy from him
As did that one, and that, in my regard,
Of the unworthiest siege.[8]

LAERTES: What part is that, my lord?

KING: A very riband in the cap of youth,
Yet needful too, for youth no less becomes
The light and careless livery that it wears
Than settled age his sables and his weeds,[9]
Importing health and graveness. Two months since
Here was a gentleman of Normandy.
I have seen myself, and served against, the French,
And they can[1] well on horseback, but this gallant
Had witchcraft in't. He grew unto his seat,
And to such wondrous doing brought his horse,
As had he been incorpsed and demi-natured
With the brave beast. So far he topped my thought
That I, in forgery[2] of shapes and tricks,
Come short of what he did.[3]

LAERTES: A Norman was't?

KING: A Norman.

LAERTES: Upon my life, Lamord.

KING: The very same.

LAERTES: I know him well. He is the brooch indeed
And gem of all the nation.

KING: He made confession[4] of you,
And gave you such a masterly report
For art and exercise in your defence,[5]
And for your rapier most especial,
That he cried out 'twould be a sight indeed
If one could match you. The scrimers[6] of their nation
He swore had neither motion, guard, nor eye,
If you opposed them. Sir, this report of his
Did Hamlet so envenom with his envy
That he could nothing do but wish and beg
Your sudden coming o'er, to play with you.
Now out of this—

LAERTES: What out of this, my lord?

KING: Laertes, was your father dear to you?

8. Rank. 9. Dignified clothing. 1. Perform. 2. Imagination. 3. The gentleman referred to was so skilled in horsemanship that he seemed to share one body with the horse, "incorpsed." The king further extends the compliment by saying that he appeared like the mythical centaur, a creature who was man from the waist up and horse from the waist down, therefore "demi-natured." 4. Gave a report. 5. Skill in fencing. 6. Fencers.

Or are you like the painting of a sorrow,
A face without a heart?

LAERTES: Why ask you this?

KING: Not that I think you did not love your father,
But that I know love is begun by time,
And that I see in passages of proof,[7]
Time qualifies the spark and fire of it.
There lives within the very flame of love
A kind of wick or snuff that will abate it,
And nothing is at a like goodness still,
For goodness, growing to a plurisy,[8]
Dies in his own too much.[9] That we would do,
We should do when we would; for this "would" changes,
And hath abatements and delays as many
As there are tongues, are hands, are accidents,
And then this "should" is like a spendthrift's sigh
That hurts by easing. But to the quick of th' ulcer—
Hamlet comes back; what would you undertake
To show yourself in deed your father's son
More than in words?

LAERTES: To cut his throat i' th' church.

KING: No place indeed should murder sanctuarize[1];
Revenge should have no bounds. But, good Laertes,
Will you do this? Keep close within your chamber.
Hamlet returned shall know you are come home.
We'll put on those shall praise your excellence,
And set a double varnish[2] on the fame
The Frenchman gave you, bring you in fine[3] together,
And wager on your heads. He, being remiss,[4]
Most generous, and free from all contriving,
Will not peruse[5] the foils, so that with ease,
Or with a little shuffling, you may choose
A sword unbated,[6] and in a pass of practice
Requite him for your father.

LAERTES: I will do't,
And for that purpose I'll anoint my sword.
I bought an unction of a mountebank
So mortal that but dip a knife in it,
Where it draws blood no cataplasm[7] so rare,
Collected from all simples[8] that have virtue
Under the moon, can save the thing from death
That is but scratched withal. I'll touch my point

7. Tests of experience. 8. Fullness. 9. Excess. 1. Provide sanctuary for murder. 2. Gloss. 3. In short. 4. Careless. 5. Examine. 6. Not blunted. 7. Poultice. 8. Herbs.

With this contagion, that if I gall[9] him slightly,
It may be death.

KING: Let's further think of this,
Weigh what convenience both of time and means
May fit us to our shape. If this should fail,
And that our drift look[1] through our bad performance,
'Twere better not assayed. Therefore this project
Should have a back or second that might hold
If this did blast in proof.[2] Soft, let me see.
We'll make a solemn wager on your cunnings—
I ha't.
When in your motion you are hot and dry—
As make your bouts more violent to that end—
And that he calls for drink, I'll have preferred him
A chalice for the nonce, whereon but sipping,
If he by chance escape your venomed stuck,[3]
Our purpose may hold there.—But stay, what noise?

[*Enter* QUEEN.]

QUEEN: One woe doth tread upon another's heel,
So fast they follow. Your sister's drowned, Laertes.

LAERTES: Drowned? O, where?

QUEEN: There is a willow grows aslant the brook
That shows his hoar leaves in the glassy stream.
Therewith fantastic garlands did she make
Of crowflowers, nettles, daisies, and long purples
That liberal shepherds give a grosser[4] name,
But our cold[5] maids do dead men's fingers call them.
There on the pendent boughs her coronet weeds
Clamb'ring to hang, an envious[6] sliver broke,
When down her weedy trophies and herself
Fell in the weeping brook. Her clothes spread wide,
And mermaid-like awhile they bore her up,
Which time she chanted snatches of old tunes,
As one incapable[7] of her own distress,
Or like a creature native and indued[8]
Unto that element. But long it could not be
Till that her garments, heavy with their drink,
Pulled the poor wretch from her melodious lay
To muddy death.

LAERTES: Alas, then she is drowned?

QUEEN: Drowned, drowned.

LAERTES: Too much of water hast thou, poor Ophelia,

9. Scratch. 1. Intent become obvious. 2. Fail when tried. 3. Thrust. 4. Coarser. *Liberal*: vulgar. 5. Chaste. 6. Malicious. 7. Unaware. 8. Habituated.

And therefore I forbid my tears; but yet
It is our trick; nature her custom holds,
Let shame say what it will. When these are gone,
The woman will be out. Adieu, my lord.
I have a speech o' fire that fain would blaze
But that this folly drowns it. [*Exit.*]

KING: Let's follow, Gertrude.
How much I had to do to calm his rage!
Now fear I this will give it start again;
Therefore let's follow. [*Exeunt.*]

ACT V

SCENE 1

A churchyard. Enter two CLOWNS.[9]

CLOWN: Is she to be buried in Christian burial when she wilfully seeks her own salvation?

OTHER: I tell thee she is. Therefore make her grave straight. The crowner hath sat on her,[1] and finds it Christian burial.

CLOWN: How can that be, unless she drowned herself in her own defence?

OTHER: Why, 'tis found so.

CLOWN: It must be "se offendendo";[2] it cannot be else. For here lies the point: if I drown myself wittingly, it argues an act, and an act hath three branches—it is to act, to do, to perform; argal,[3] she drowned herself wittingly.

OTHER: Nay, but hear you, Goodman Delver.

CLOWN: Give me leave. Here lies the water; good. Here stands the man; good. If the man go to this water and drown himself, it is, will he, nill he, he goes—mark you that. But if the water come to him and drown him, he drowns not himself. Argal, he that is not guilty of his own death shortens not his own life.

OTHER: But is this law?

CLOWN: Ay, marry, is't; crowner's quest[4] law.

OTHER: Will you ha' the truth on't? If this had not been a gentle woman, she should have been buried out o' Christian burial.

CLOWN: Why, there thou say'st. And the more pity that great folk should have count'nance[5] in this world to drown or hang themselves more than their even-Christen.[6] Come, my spade. There is no ancient gentlemen but gard'ners, ditchers, and grave-makers. They hold up Adam's profession.

OTHER: Was he a gentleman?

CLOWN: 'A was the first that ever bore arms.

OTHER: Why, he had none.

9. Rustics. 1. Held an inquest. *Crowner: coroner.* 2. An error for *se defendendo,* in self-defense. 3. Therefore. 4. Inquest. 5. Approval. 6. Fellow Christians.

CLOWN: What, art a heathen? How dost thou understand the Scripture? The Scripture says Adam digged. Could he dig without arms? I'll put another question to thee. If thou answerest me not to the purpose, confess thyself—

OTHER: Go to.

CLOWN: What is he that builds stronger than either the mason, the shipwright, or the carpenter?

OTHER: The gallows-maker, for that frame outlives a thousand tenants.

CLOWN: I like thy wit well, in good faith. The gallows does well. But how does it well? It does well to those that do ill. Now thou dost ill to say the gallows is built stronger than the church. Argal, the gallows may do well to thee. To't again,[7] come.

OTHER: Who builds stronger than a mason, a shipwright, or a carpenter?

CLOWN: Ay tell me that, and unyoke.[8]

OTHER: Marry, now I can tell.

CLOWN: To't.

OTHER: Mass, I cannot tell.

CLOWN: Cudgel thy brains no more about it, for your dull ass will not mend his pace with beating. And when you are asked this question next, say "a grave-maker." The houses he makes lasts till doomsday. Go, get thee in, and fetch me a stoup[9] of liquor. [*Exit* OTHER CLOWN.]

[*Enter* HAMLET *and* HORATIO *as* CLOWN *digs and sings.*]

In youth, when I did love, did love,
Methought it was very sweet,
To contract the time for-a my behove,[1]
O, methought there-a was nothing-a meet.[2]

HAMLET: Has this fellow no feeling of his business, that 'a sings in grave-making?

HORATIO: Custom hath made it in him a property of easiness.

HAMLET: 'Tis e'en so. The hand of little employment hath the daintier sense.

[CLOWN *sings.*]

But age, with his stealing steps,
Hath clawed me in his clutch,
And hath shipped me into the land,
As if I had never been such.

[*Throws up a skull.*]

HAMLET: That skull had a tongue in it, and could sing once. How the knave jowls[3] it to the ground, as if 'twere Cain's jawbone, that did the first murder! This might be the pate of a politician, which this ass now o'erreaches[4]; one that would circumvent God, might it not?

7. Guess again. 8. Finish the matter. 9. Mug. 1. Advantage. *Contract:* shorten. 2. The gravedigger's song is a free version of "The aged lover renounceth love" by Thomas, Lord Vaux, published in *Tottel's Miscellany*, 1557. 3. Hurls. 4. Gets the better of.

HORATIO: It might, my lord.

HAMLET: Or of a courtier, which could say, "Good morrow, sweet lord! How does thou, sweet lord?" This might be my Lord Such-a-one, that praised my Lord Such-a-one's horse, when 'a meant to beg it, might it not?

HORATIO: Ay, my lord.

HAMLET: Why, e'en so, and now my Lady Worm's, chapless,[5] and knock'd abut the mazzard[6] with a sexton's spade. Here's fine revolution,[7] an we had the trick to see't. Did these bones cost no more the breeding but to play at loggets with them?[8] Mine ache to think on't.

[CLOWN *sings.*]

A pick-axe and a spade, a spade,
For and a shrouding sheet:
O, a pit of clay for to be made
For such a guest is meet.

[*Throws up another skull.*]

HAMLET: There's another. Why may not that be the skull of a lawyer? Where be his quiddities now, his quillets, his cases, his tenures, and his tricks? Why does he suffer this mad knave now to knock him about the sconce[9] with a dirty shovel, and will not tell him of his action of battery? Hum! This fellow might be in's time a great buyer of land, with his statutes, his recognizances, his fines, his double vouchers, his recoveries. Is this the fine[1] of his fines, and the recovery of his recoveries, to have his fine pate full of fine dirt? Will his vouchers vouch him no more of his purchases, and double ones too, than the length and breadth of a pair of indentures[2]? The very conveyances of his lands will scarcely lie in this box, and must th' inheritor himself have no more, ha?[3]

HORATIO: Not a jot more, my lord.

HAMLET: Is not parchment made of sheepskins?

HORATIO: Ay, my lord, and of calves' skins too.

HAMLET: They are sheep and calves which seek out assurance in that. I will speak to this fellow. Whose grave's this, sirrah?

CLOWN: Mine, sir.

[*Sings.*]

O, a pit of clay for to be made—

HAMLET: I think it be thine indeed, for thou liest in't.

CLOWN: You lie out on't, sir, and therefore 'tis not yours. For my part, I do not lie in't, yet it is mine.

HAMLET: Thou dost lie in't, to be in't and say it is thine. 'Tis for the dead, not for the quick[4]; therefore thou liest.

5. Lacking a lower jaw. 6. Head. 7. Skill. 8. "Loggets" were small pieces of wood thrown as part of a game. 9. Head. 1. End. 2. Contracts. 3. In this speech Hamlet reels off a list of legal terms relating to property transactions. 4. Living.

CLOWN: 'Tis a quick lie, sir; 'twill away again from me to you.
HAMLET: What man dost thou dig it for?
CLOWN: For no man, sir.
HAMLET: What woman, then?
CLOWN: For none neither.
HAMLET: Who is to be buried in't?
CLOWN: One that was a woman, sir; but, rest her soul, she's dead.
HAMLET: How absolute the knave is! We must speak by the card,[5] or equivocation will undo us. By the Lord, Horatio, this three years I have took note of it, the age is grown so picked[6] that the toe of the peasant comes so near the heel of the courtier, he galls his kibe.[7] How long hast thou been a grave-maker?
CLOWN: Of all the days i' th' year, I came to't that day that our last King Hamlet overcame Fortinbras.
HAMLET: How long is that since?
CLOWN: Cannot you tell that? Every fool can tell that. It was that very day that young Hamlet was born—he that is mad, and sent into England.
HAMLET: Ay, marry, why was he sent into England?
CLOWN: Why, because 'a was mad. 'A shall recover his wits there; or, if 'a do not, 'tis no great matter there.
HAMLET: Why?
CLOWN: 'Twill not be seen in him there. There the men are as mad as he.
HAMLET: How came he mad?
CLOWN: Very strangely, they say.
HAMLET: How strangely?
CLOWN: Faith, e'en with losing his wits.
HAMLET: Upon what ground?
CLOWN: Why, here in Denmark. I have been sexton here, man and boy, thirty years.
HAMLET: How long will a man lie i' th' earth ere he rot?
CLOWN: Faith, if 'a be not rotten before 'a die—as we have many pocky[8] corses now-a-days that will scarce hold the laying in—'a will last you some eight year or nine year. A tanner will last you nine year.
HAMLET: Why he more than another?
CLOWN: Why, sir, his hide is so tanned with his trade that 'a will keep out water a great while; and your water is a sore decayer of your whoreson dead body. Here's a skull now hath lien[9] you i' th' earth three and twenty years.
HAMLET: Whose was it?
CLOWN: A whoreson mad fellow's it was. Whose do you think it was?
HAMLET: Nay, I know not.
CLOWN: A pestilence on him for a mad rogue! 'A poured a flagon of Rhenish on my head once. This same skull, sir, was, sir, Yorick's skull, the king's jester.
HAMLET: [*Takes the skull.*] This?
CLOWN: E'en that.

5. Exactly. *Absolute:* precise. 6. Refined. 7. Rubs a blister on his heel. 8. Corrupted by syphilis 9. Lain. *Whoreson:* bastard (not literally).

HAMLET: Alas, poor Yorick! I knew him, Horatio—a fellow of infinite jest, of most excellent fancy. He hath bore me on his back a thousand times, and now how abhorred in my imagination it is! My gorge[1] rises at it. Here hung those lips that I have kissed I know not how oft. Where be your gibes now, your gambols, your songs, your flashes of merriment that were wont to set the table on a roar? Not one now to mock your own grinning? Quite chap-fall'n[2]? Now get you to my lady's chamber, and tell her, let her paint an inch thick, to this favor[3] she must come. Make her laugh at that. Prithee, Horatio, tell me one thing.

HORATIO: What's that, my lord?

HAMLET: Dost thou think Alexander looked o' this fashion i' th' earth?

HORATIO: E'en so.

HAMLET: And smelt so? Pah! [*Throws down the skull.*]

HORATIO: E'en so, my lord.

HAMLET: To what base uses we may return, Horatio! Why may not imagination trace the noble dust of Alexander till 'a find it stopping a bung-hole?

HORATIO: 'Twere to consider too curiously[4] to consider so.

HAMLET: No, faith, not a jot, but to follow him thither with modesty[5] enough, and likelihood to lead it. Alexander died, Alexander was buried, Alexander returneth to dust; the dust is earth; of earth we make loam; and why of that loam whereto he was converted might they not stop a beerbarrel?

Imperious Cæsar, dead and turned to clay,
Might stop a hole to keep the wind away.
O, that that earth which kept the world in awe
Should patch a wall t'expel the winter's flaw![6]

But soft, but soft awhile! Here comes the king,
The queen, the courtiers.

[*Enter* KING, QUEEN, LAERTES, *and the Corse with a* PRIEST *and* LORDS *attendant.*]

Who is this they follow?
And with such maiméd[7] rites? This doth betoken
The corse they follow did with desperate hand
Fordo it own life. 'Twas of some estate.[8]
Couch[9] we awhile and mark. [*Retires with* HORATIO.]

LAERTES: What ceremony else[1]?

HAMLET: That is Laertes, a very noble youth. Mark.

LAERTES: What ceremony else?

PRIEST: Here obsequies have been as far enlarged[2]
As we have warranty. Her death was doubtful,

1. Throat. 2. Lacking a lower jaw. 3. Appearance. 4. Precisely. 5. Moderation. 6. Gusty wind. 7. Cut short. 8. Rank. *Fordo:* destroy. 9. Conceal ourselves.
1. More. 2. Extended.

And but that great command o'ersways the order,[3]
She should in ground unsanctified been lodged
Till the last trumpet. For charitable prayers,
Shards, flints, and pebbles, should be thrown on her.
Yet here she is allowed her virgin crants,[4]
Her maiden strewments,[5] and the bringing home
Of bell and burial.

LAERTES: Must there no more be done?

PRIEST: No more be done.
We should profane the service of the dead
To sing a requiem and such rest to her
As to peace-parted souls.

LAERTES: Lay her i' th' earth,
And from her fair and unpolluted flesh
May violets spring! I tell thee, churlish priest,
A minist'ring angel shall my sister be
When thou liest howling.[6]

HAMLET: What, the fair Ophelia!

QUEEN: Sweets to the sweet. Farewell! [*Scatters flowers.*]
I hoped thou shouldst have been my Hamlet's wife.
I thought thy bride-bed to have decked, sweet maid,
And not have strewed thy grave.

LAERTES: O, treble woe
Fall ten times treble on that curséd head
Whose wicked deed thy most ingenious sense[7]
Deprived thee of! Hold off the earth awhile,
Till I have caught her once more in mine arms. [*Leaps into the grave.*]
Now pile your dust upon the quick and dead,
Till of this flat a mountain you have made
T' o'er-top old Pelion or the skyish head
Of blue Olympus.[8]

HAMLET: [*Coming forward.*] What is he whose grief
Bears such an emphasis, whose phrase of sorrow
Conjures[9] the wand'ring stars, and makes them stand
Like wonder-wounded hearers? This is I,
Hamlet the Dane.

[HAMLET *leaps into the grave and they grapple.*]

LAERTES: The devil take thy soul!

HAMLET: Thou pray'st not well.

3. Usual rules. 4. Wreaths. 5. Flowers strewn on the grave. 6. In Hell. 7. Lively mind. 8. The rivalry between Laertes and Hamlet in this scene extends even to their rhetoric. Pelion and Olympus, mentioned here by Laertes, and Ossa, mentioned below by Hamlet, were Greek mountains noted in mythology for their height. Olympus was the reputed home of the gods, and the other two were piled one on top of the other by the Giants in an attempt to reach the top of Olympus and overthrow the gods. 9. Casts a spell on.

I prithee take thy fingers from my throat,
For though I am not splenitive[1] and rash,
Yet have I in me something dangerous,
Which let thy wisdom fear. Hold off thy hand.

KING: Pluck them asunder.

QUEEN: Hamlet! Hamlet!

ALL: Gentlemen!

HORATIO: Good my lord, be quiet.

[*The* ATTENDANTS *part them, and they come out of the grave.*]

HAMLET: Why, I will fight with him upon this theme
Until my eyelids will no longer wag.[2]

QUEEN: O my son, what theme?

HAMLET: I loved Ophelia. Forty thousand brothers
Could not with all their quantity of love
Make up my sum. What wilt thou do for her?

KING: O, he is mad, Laertes.

QUEEN: For love of God, forbear[3] him.

HAMLET: 'Swounds, show me what th'owt do.
Woo't[4] weep, woo't fight, woo't fast, woo't tear thyself,
Woo't drink up eisel,[5] eat a crocodile?
I'll do't. Dost come here to whine?
To outface[6] me with leaping in her grave?
Be buried quick with her, and so will I.
And if thou prate of mountains, let them throw
Millions of acres on us, till our ground,
Singeing his pate against the burning zone,[7]
Make Ossa like a wart! Nay, an thou'lt mouth,
I'll rant as well as thou.

QUEEN: This is mere madness;
And thus awhile the fit will work on him.
Anon, as patient as the female dove
When that her golden couplets[8] are disclosed,
His silence will sit drooping.

HAMLET: Hear you, sir.
What is the reason that you use me thus?
I loved you ever. But it is no matter.
Let Hercules himself do what he may,
The cat will mew, and dog will have his day.

KING: I pray thee, good Horatio, wait upon[9] him.

[*Exeunt* HAMLET *and* HORATIO.]

1. Hot-tempered. 2. Move. 3. Bear with. 4. Will you. 5. Vinegar. 6. Get the best of. 7. Sky in the torrid zone. 8. Pair of eggs. 9. Attend.

[*To* LAERTES.] Strengthen your patience in our last night's speech.
We'll put the matter to the present push.[1]—
Good Gertrude, set some watch over your son.—
This grave shall have a living monument.
An hour of quiet shortly shall we see;
Till then in patience our proceeding be. [*Exeunt.*]

SCENE 2

A hall or public room. Enter HAMLET *and* HORATIO.

HAMLET: So much for this, sir; now shall you see the other.
You do remember all the circumstance?
HORATIO: Remember it, my lord!
HAMLET: Sir, in my heart there was a kind of fighting
That would not let me sleep. Methought I lay
Worse than the mutines in the bilboes.[2] Rashly,
And praised be rashness for it—let us know,
Our indiscretion sometime serves us well,
When our deep plots do pall; and that should learn[3] us
There's a divinity that shapes our ends,
Rough-hew them how we will—
HORATIO: That is most certain.
HAMLET: Up from my cabin,
My sea-gown scarfed[4] about me, in the dark
Groped I to find out them, had my desire,
Fingered their packet, and in fine[5] withdrew
To mine own room again, making so bold,
My fears forgetting manners, to unseal
Their grand commission; where I found, Horatio—
Ah, royal knavery!—an exact[6] command,
Larded[7] with many several sorts of reasons,
Importing Denmark's health, and England's too,
With, ho! such bugs and goblins in my life,[8]
That on the supervise,[9] no leisure bated,
No, not to stay the grinding of the axe,
My head should be struck off.
HORATIO: Is't possible?
HAMLET: Here's the commission; read it at more leisure.
But wilt thou hear now how I did proceed?
HORATIO: I beseech you.
HAMLET: Being thus benetted[1] round with villainies,

1. Immediate trial. 2. Stocks. *Mutines:* mutineers. 3. Teach. 4. Wrapped. 5. Quickly. *Fingered:* stole. 6. Precisely stated. 7. Garnished. 8. Such dangers if I remained alive. 9. As soon as the commission was read. 1. Caught in a net.

Or I could make a prologue to my brains,
They had begun the play. I sat me down,
Devised a new commission, wrote it fair.[2]
I once did hold it, as our statists[3] do,
A baseness to write fair, and labored much
How to forget that learning; but sir, now
It did me yeoman's service. Wilt thou know
Th' effect[4] of what I wrote?

HORATIO: Ay, good my lord.

HAMLET: An earnest conjuration from the king,
As England was his faithful tributary,[5]
As love between them like the palm might flourish,
As peace should still her wheaten garland wear
And stand a comma 'tween their amities[6]
And many such like as's of great charge,[7]
That on the view and knowing of these contents,
Without debatement[8] further more or less,
He should those bearers put to sudden death,
Not shriving-time allowed.[9]

HORATIO: How was this sealed?

HAMLET: Why, even in that was heaven ordinant,[1]
I had my father's signet in my purse,
Which was the model of that Danish seal,
Folded the writ up in the form of th' other,
Subscribed it, gave't th' impression,[2] placed it safely,
The changeling[3] never known. Now, the next day
Was our sea-fight, and what to this was sequent[4]
Thou knowest already.

HORATIO: So Guildenstern and Rosencrantz go to't.

HAMLET: Why, man, they did make love to this employment.
They are not near my conscience; their defeat[5]
Does by their own insinuation grow.
'Tis dangerous when the baser nature comes
Between the pass and fell[6] incensèd points
Of mighty opposites.

HORATIO: Why, what a king is this!

HAMLET: Does it not, think thee, stand me now upon—
He that hath killed my king and whored my mother,
Popped in between th' election and my hopes,
Thrown out his angle[7] for my proper life,
And with such coz'nage[8]—is't not perfect conscience
To quit[9] him with this arm? And is't not be be damned

2. Legibly. *Devised:* made. 3. Politicians. 4. Contents. 5. Vassal. 6. Link friendships. 7. Import. 8. Consideration. 9. Without time for confession. 1. Operative. 2. Of the seal. 3. Alteration. 4. Followed. 5. Death. *Are not near:* do not touch. 6. Cruel. *Pass:* thrust. 7. Fishhook. 8. Trickery. 9. Repay.

To let this canker of our nature come
In further evil?

HORATIO: It must be shortly known to him from England
What is the issue[1] of the business there.

HAMLET: It will be short[2]; the interim is mine.
And a man's life's no more than to say "one."
But I am very sorry, good Horatio,
That to Laertes I forgot myself;
For by the image of my cause I see
The portraiture of his. I'll court his favors.
But sure the bravery[3] of his grief did put me
Into a tow'ring passion.

HORATIO: Peace; who comes here?

[*Enter* OSRIC.]

OSRIC: Your lordship is right welcome back to Denmark.

HAMLET: I humbly thank you, sir. [*Aside to* HORATIO.] Dost know this water-fly?

HORATIO: [*Aside to* HAMLET.] No, my good lord.

HAMLET: [*Aside to* HORATIO.] Thy state is the more gracious, for 'tis a vice to know him. He hath much land, and fertile. Let a beast be lord of beasts, and his crib shall stand at the king's mess. 'Tis a chough,[4] but as I say, spacious in the possession of dirt.

OSRIC: Sweet lord, if your lordship were at leisure, I should impart a thing to you from his majesty.

HAMLET: I will receive it, sir, with all diligence of spirit. Put your bonnet to his right use. 'Tis for the head.

OSRIC: I thank your lordship, it is very hot.

HAMLET: No, believe me, 'tis very cold; the wind is northerly.

OSRIC: It is indifferent[5] cold, my lord, indeed.

HAMLET: But yet methinks it is very sultry and hot for my complexion.[6]

OSRIC: Exceedingly, my lord; it is very sultry, as 'twere—I cannot tell how. My lord, his majesty bade me signify to you that 'a has laid a great wager on your head. Sir, this is the matter—

HAMLET: I beseech you, remember. [*moves him to put on his hat.*]

OSRIC: Nay, good my lord; for my ease, in good faith. Sir, here is newly come to court Laertes; believe me, an absolute[7] gentleman, full of most excellent differences,[8] of very soft society and great showing.[9] Indeed, to speak feelingly of him, he is the card or calendar of gentry, for you shall find in him the continent[1] of what part a gentleman would see.

HAMLET: Sir, his definement[2] suffers no perdition in you, though I know to divide him inventorially would dozy[3] th' arithmetic of memory, and yet but yaw[4] neither in respect of his quick sail. But in the verity of extolment, I take

1. Outcome. 2. Soon. 3. Exaggerated display. 4. Jackdaw. 5. Moderately. 6. Temperament. 7. Perfect. 8. Qualities. 9. Good manners. 1. Sum total. *Calendar:* measure. 2. Description. 3. Daze. *Divide him inventorially:* examine bit by bit. 4. Steer wildly.

him to be a soul of great article,[5] and his infusion[6] of such dearth and rareness as, to make true diction of him, his semblage[7] is his mirror, and who else would trace him, his umbrage,[8] nothing more.

OSRIC: Your lordship speaks most infallibly of him.

HAMLET: The concernancy,[9] sir? Why do we wrap the gentleman in our more rawer breath?[1]

OSRIC: Sir?

HORATIO: Is't not possible to understand in another tongue? You will to't, sir, really.

HAMLET: What imports the nomination[2] of this gentleman?

OSRIC: Of Laertes?

HORATIO: [*Aside.*] His purse is empty already. All's golden words are spent.

HAMLET: Of him, sir.

OSRIC: I know you are not ignorant—

HAMLET: I would you did, sir; yet, in faith, if you did, it would not much approve me. Well, sir.

OSRIC: You are not ignorant of what excellence Laertes is—

HAMLET: I dare not confess that, lest I should compare[3] with him in excellence; but to know a man well were to know himself.

OSRIC: I mean, sir, for his weapon; but in the imputation[4] laid on him by them, in his meed he's unfellowed.[5]

HAMLET: What's his weapon?

OSRIC: Rapier and dagger.

HAMLET: That's two of his weapons—but well.

OSRIC: The king, sir, hath wagered with him six Barbary horses, against the which he has impawned,[6] as I take it, six French rapiers and poniards, with their assigns,[7] as girdle, hangers, and so. Three of the carriages, in faith, are very dear to fancy,[8] very responsive to the hilts, most delicate carriages, and of very liberal conceit.[9]

HAMLET: What call you the carriages?

HORATIO: [*Aside to* HAMLET.] I knew you must be edified by the margent[1] ere you had done.

OSRIC: The carriages, sir, are the hangers.

HAMLET: The phrase would be more germane to the matter if we could carry a cannon by our sides. I would it might be hangers till then. But on! Six Barbary horses against six French swords, their assigns, and three liberal conceited carriages; that's the French bet against the Danish. Why is this all impawned, as you call it?

OSRIC: The king, sir, hath laid, sir, that in a dozen passes between yourself and him he shall not exceed you three hits; he hath laid on twelve for nine, and

5. Scope. 6. Nature. 7. Rival. *Diction:* telling. 8. Shadow. *Trace:* keep pace with. 9. Meaning. 1. Cruder words. 2. Naming. 3. I.e., compare myself. 4. Reputation. 5. Unequaled in his excellence. 6. Staked. 7. Appurtenances. 8. Finely designed. 9. Elegant design. *Delicate:* well adjusted. 1. Marginal gloss.

it would come to immediate trial if your lordship would vouchsafe the answer.

HAMLET: How if I answer no?

OSRIC: I mean, my lord, the opposition of your person in trial.

HAMLET: Sir, I will walk here in the hall. If it please his majesty, it is the breathing time[2] of day with me. Let the foils be brought, the gentleman willing, and the king hold his purpose; I will win for him an I can. If not, I will gain nothing but my shame and the odd hits.

OSRIC: Shall I deliver you so?

HAMLET: To this effect, sir, after what flourish your nature will.

OSRIC: I commend my duty to your lordship.

HAMLET: Yours, yours. [*Exit* OSRIC.] He does well to commend it himself; there are no tongues else for's turn.

HORATIO: This lapwing runs away with the shell on his head.[3]

HAMLET: 'A did comply, sir, with his dug[4] before 'a sucked it. Thus has he, and many more of the same bevy that I know the drossy age dotes on, only got the tune of the time; and out of an habit of encounter, a king of yesty[5] collection which carries them through and through the most fanned and winnowed opinions; and do but blow them to their trial, the bubbles are out.

[*Enter a* LORD.]

LORD: My lord, his majesty commended him to you by young Osric, who brings back to him that you attend[6] him in the hall. He sends to know if your pleasure hold to play with Laertes, or that you will take longer time.

HAMLET: I am constant to my purposes; they follow the king's pleasure. If his fitness speaks, mine is ready; now or whensoever, provided I be so able as now.

LORD: The king and queen and all are coming down.

HAMLET: In happy time.

LORD: The queen desires you to use some gentle entertainment[7] to Laertes before you fall to play.

HAMLET: She well instructs me. [*Exit* LORD.]

HORATIO: You will lose this wager, my lord.

HAMLET: I do not think so. Since he went into France I have been in continual practice. I shall win at the odds. But thou wouldst not think how ill[8] all's here about my heart. But it's no matter.

HORATIO: Nay, good my lord—

HAMLET: It is but foolery, but it is such a kind of gaingiving[9] as would perhaps trouble a woman.

HORATIO: If your mind dislike anything, obey it. I will forestall their repair[1] hither, and say you are not fit.

2. Time for exercise. 3. The lapwing was thought to be so precocious that it could run immediately after being hatched, even as here with bits of the shell still on its head. 4. Mother's breast. *Comply:* deal formally. 5. Yeasty. 6. Await. 7. Cordiality. 8. Uneasy. 9. Misgiving. 1. Coming.

HAMLET: Not a whit, we defy augury. There is special providence in the fall of a sparrow. If it be now, 'tis not to come; if it be not to come, it will be now; if it be not now, yet it will come. The readiness is all. Since no man of aught he leaves knows, what is't to leave betimes? Let be.

[*A table prepared. Enter* TRUMPETS, DRUMS, *and* OFFICERS *with cushions;* KING, QUEEN, OSRIC *and* ATTENDANTS *with foils, daggers, and* LAERTES.]

KING: Come, Hamlet, come and take this hand from me.

[*The* KING *puts* LAERTES' *hand into* HAMLET'*s.*]

HAMLET: Give me your pardon, sir. I have done you wrong,
But pardon 't as you are a gentleman.
This presence[2] knows, and you must needs have heard,
How I am punished with a sore distraction.
What I have done
That might your nature, honor, and exception,[3]
Roughly awake, I here proclaim was madness.
Was 't Hamlet wronged Laertes? Never Hamlet.
If Hamlet from himself be ta'en away,
And when he's not himself does wrong Laertes,
Then Hamlet does it not, Hamlet denies it.
Who does it then? His madness. If't be so,
Hamlet is of the faction that is wronged;
His madness is poor Hamlet's enemy.
Sir, in this audience,
Let my disclaiming from[4] a purposed evil
Free[5] me so far in your most generous thoughts
That I have shot my arrow o'er the house
And hurt my brother.

LAERTES: I am satisfied in nature,
Whose motive in this case should stir me most
To my revenge. But in my terms of honor
I stand aloof, and will no reconcilement
Till by some elder masters of known honor
I have a voice[6] and precedent of peace
To keep my name ungored.[7] But till that time
I do receive your offered love like love,
And will not wrong it.

HAMLET: I embrace it freely,
And will this brother's wager frankly[8] play.
Give us the foils.

LAERTES: Come, one for me.

HAMLET: I'll be your foil, Laertes. In mine ignorance

2. Company. 3. Resentment. 4. Denying of. 5. Absolve. 6. Authority. 7. Unshamed. 8. Without rancor.

Your skill shall, like a star i' th' darkest night,
Stick fiery off[9] indeed.

LAERTES: You mock me, sir.

HAMLET: No, by this hand.

KING: Give them the foils, young Osric. Cousin Hamlet,
You know the wager?

HAMLET: Very well, my lord;
Your Grace has laid the odds o' th' weaker side.

KING: I do not fear it, I have seen you both;
But since he is bettered[1] we have therefore odds.

LAERTES: This is too heavy; let me see another.

HAMLET: This likes me well. These foils have all a[2] length?

[*They prepare to play.*]

OSRIC: Ay, my good lord.

KING: Set me the stoups of wine upon that table.
If Hamlet give the first or second hit,
Or quit in answer of[3] the third exchange,
Let all the battlements their ordnance fire.
The king shall drink to Hamlet's better breath,
And in the cup an union[4] shall he throw,
Richer than that which four successive kings
In Denmark's crown have worn. Give me the cups,
And let the kettle[5] to the trumpet speak,
The trumpet to the cannoneer without,
The cannons to the heavens, the heaven to earth,
"Now the king drinks to Hamlet." Come, begin—

[*Trumpets the while.*]

And you, the judges, bear a wary eye.

HAMLET: Come on, sir.

LAERTES: Come, my lord.

[*They play.*]

HAMLET: One.

LAERTES: No.

HAMLET: Judgment?

OSRIC: A hit, a very palpable hit.

[*Drums, trumpets, and shot. Flourish; a piece goes off.*]

LAERTES: Well, again.

KING: Stay, give me drink. Hamlet, this pearl is thine.
Here's to thy health. Give him the cup.

9. Shine brightly. 1. Reported better. 2. The same. *Likes:* suits. 3. Repay. 4. Pearl.
5. Kettledrum.

HAMLET: I'll play this bout first; set it by awhile.
Come.

[*They play.*]

Another hit; what say you?
LAERTES: I do confess't.
KING: Our son shall win.
QUEEN: He's fat,[6] and scant of breath.
Here, Hamlet, take my napkin, rub thy brows.
The queen carouses to thy fortune, Hamlet.
HAMLET: Good madam!
KING: Gertrude, do not drink.
QUEEN: I will, my lord; I pray you pardon me.
KING: [*Aside.*] It is the poisoned cup; it is too late.
HAMLET: I dare not drink yet, madam; by and by.
QUEEN: Come, let me wipe thy face.
LAERTES: My lord, I'll hit him now.
KING: I do not think't.
LAERTES: [*Aside.*] And yet it is almost against my conscience.
HAMLET: Come, for the third, Laertes. You do but dally.
I pray you pass[7] with your best violence;
I am afeard you make a wanton of me.[8]
LAERTES: Say you so? Come on.

[*They play.*]

OSRIC: Nothing, neither way.
LAERTES: Have at you now!

[LAERTES *wounds* HAMLET: *then, in scuffling, they change rapiers, and* HAMLET *wounds* LAERTES.]

KING: Part them. They are incensed.
HAMLET: Nay, come again.

[*The* QUEEN *falls.*]

OSRIC: Look to the queen there, ho!
HORATIO: They bleed on both sides. How is it, my lord?
OSRIC: How is't, Laertes?
LAERTES: Why, as a woodcock to mine own springe,[9] Osric.
I am justly killed with mine own treachery.
HAMLET: How does the queen?
KING: She swoons to see them bleed.
QUEEN: No, no, the drink, the drink! O my dear Hamlet!
The drink, the drink! I am poisoned. [*Dies.*]

6. Out of shape. 7. Attack. 8. Trifle with me. 9. Snare.

HAMLET: O, villainy! Ho! let the door be locked.
Treachery! seek it out.
LAERTES: It is here, Hamlet. Hamlet, thou art slain;
No med'cine in the world can do thee good.
In thee there is not half an hour's life.
The treacherous instrument is in thy hand,
Unbated[1] and envenomed. The foul practice
Hath turned itself on me. Lo, here I lie,
Never to rise again. Thy mother's poisoned.
I can no more. The king, the king's to blame.
HAMLET: The point envenomed too?
Then, venom, to thy work. [*Hurts the* KING.]
ALL: Treason! treason!
KING: O, yet defend me, friends. I am but hurt.[2]
HAMLET: Here, thou incestuous, murd'rous, damnéd Dane,
Drink off this potion. Is thy union here?
Follow my mother.

[*The* KING *dies.*]

LAERTES: He is justly served.
It is a poison tempered[3] by himself.
Exchange forgiveness with me, noble Hamlet.
Mine and my father's death come not upon thee,
Nor thine on me! [*Dies.*]
HAMLET: Heaven make thee free of[4] it! I follow thee.
I am dead, Horatio. Wretched queen, adieu!
You that look pale and tremble at this chance,[5]
That are but mutes or audience to this act,
Had I but time, as this fell sergeant Death
Is strict in his arrest,[6] O, I could tell you—
But let it be. Horatio, I am dead:
Thou livest; report me and my cause aright
To the unsatisfied.[7]
HORATIO: Never believe it.
I am more an antique Roman than a Dane.
Here's yet some liquor left.
HAMLET: As th'art a man,
Give me the cup. Let go. By heaven, I'll ha't.
O God, Horatio, what a wounded name,
Things standing thus unknown, shall live behind me!
If thou didst ever hold me in thy heart,
Absent thee from felicity awhile,

1. Unblunted. 2. Wounded. 3. Mixed. 4. Forgive. 5. Circumstance. 6. Summons to court. 7. Uninformed.

And in this harsh world draw thy breath in pain,
To tell my story.

[*A march afar off.*]

What warlike noise is this?

OSRIC: Young Fortinbras, with conquest come from Poland,
To th' ambassadors of England gives
This warlike volley.[8]

HAMLET: O, I die, Horatio!
The potent poison quite o'er-crows[9] my spirit.
I cannot live to hear the news from England,
But I do prophesy th' election lights
On Fortinbras. He has my dying voice.[1]
So tell him, with th' occurrents,[2] more and less,
Which have solicited[3]—the rest is silence. [*Dies.*]

HORATIO: Now cracks a noble heart. Good night, sweet prince,
And flights of angels sing thee to thy rest!

[*March within.*]

Why does the drum come hither?

[*Enter* FORTINBRAS, *with the* AMBASSADORS *and with drum, colors, and* ATTENDANTS.]

FORTINBRAS: Where is this sight?

HORATIO: What is it you would see?
If aught of woe or wonder, cease your search.

FORTINBRAS: This quarry cries on havoc.[4] O proud death,
What feast is toward[5] in thine eternal cell
That thou so many princes at a shot
So bloodily hast struck?

AMBASSADORS: The sight is dismal;
And our affairs from England come too late.
The ears are senseless[6] that should give us hearing
To tell him his commandment is fulfilled,
That Rosencrantz and Guildenstern are dead.
Where should we have our thanks?

HORATIO: Not from his mouth,
Had it th' ability of life to thank you.
He never gave commandment for their death.
But since, so jump[7] upon this bloody question,

8. The staging presents some difficulties here. If Osric is not clairvoyant, he must have left the stage at some point and returned. One possibility is that he might have left to carry out Hamlet's order to lock the door (line 291) and returned when the sound of the distant march is heard. 9. Overcomes. 1. Support. 2. Circumstances. 3. Brought about this scene. 4. The game killed in the hunt proclaims a slaughter. 5. In preparation. 6. Without sense of hearing. 7. Exactly.

You from the Polack wars, and you from England,
Are here arrived, give orders that these bodies
High on a stage be placed to the view,
And let me speak to th' yet unknowing world
How these things came about. So shall you hear
Of carnal, bloody, and unnatural acts;
Of accidental judgments, casual[8] slaughters;
Of deaths put on by cunning and forced cause;
And, in this upshot,[9] purposes mistook
Fall'n on th' inventors' heads. All this can I
Truly deliver.

FORTINBRAS: Let us haste to hear it,
And call the noblest to the audience.[1]
For me, with sorrow I embrace my fortune.
I have some rights of memory[2] in this kingdom,
Which now to claim my vantage[3] doth invite me.

HORATIO: Of that I shall have also cause to speak,
And from his mouth whose voice will draw on more.
But let this same be presently performed,
Even while men's minds are wild, lest more mischance
On plots and errors happen.

FORTINBRAS: Let four captains
Bear Hamlet like a soldier to the stage,
For he was likely, had he been put on,[4]
To have proved most royal; and for his passage
The soldier's music and the rite of war
Speak loudly for him.
Take up the bodies. Such a sight as this
Becomes the field, but here shows much amiss.
Go, bid the soldiers shoot.

[*Exeunt marching. A peal of ordnance shot off.*]

ca. 1600

8. Brought about by apparent accident. 9. Result. 1. Hearing. 2. Succession. 3. Position. 4. Elected king.

LILLIAN HELLMAN

The Little Foxes

Take us the foxes, the little foxes,
that spoil the vines:
for our vines have tender grapes.[1]

CHARACTERS

ADDIE
CAL
OSCAR HUBBARD
BIRDIE HUBBARD, *his wife*
LEO HUBBARD, *Oscar and Birdie's son*
HORACE GIDDENS
REGINA GIDDENS, *Horace's wife*
ALEXANDRA GIDDENS, *Horace and Regina's daughter*
BENJAMIN HUBBARD
WILLIAM MARSHALL

The scene of the play is the living room of the Giddens house, in a small town in the South.

Act I: The Spring of 1900, evening.

Act II: A week later, early morning.

Act III: Two weeks later, late afternoon.

There has been no attempt to write Southern dialect. It is to be understood that the accents are Southern.

ACT I

SCENE: *The living room of the Giddens house, in a small town in the deep South, the Spring of 1900. Upstage is a staircase leading to the second story. Upstage, right, are double doors to the dining room. When these doors are open we see a section of the dining room and the furniture. Upstage, left, is an entrance hall with a coat-rack and umbrella stand. There are large lace-curtained windows on the left wall. The room is lit by a center gas chandelier and painted china oil lamps on the tables. Against the wall is a large piano. Downstage, right, are a high couch, a large table, several chairs. Against the left back wall are a table and several chairs. Near the window there are a smaller couch and tables. The room is good-looking, the furniture expensive; but it reflects no particular taste. Everything is of the best and that is all.*

AT RISE: ADDIE, *a tall, nice-looking Negro woman of about fifty-five, is closing the windows. From behind the closed dining-room doors there is the sound of voices. After a second,* CAL, *a middle-aged Negro, comes in from the entrance hall carrying a tray with glasses and a bottle of port.* ADDIE *crosses, takes the tray from him, puts it on table, begins to arrange it.*

ADDIE: [*Pointing to the bottle.*] You gone stark out of your head?
CAL: No, smart lady, I ain't. Miss Regina told me to get out that bottle. [*Points*

1. Song of Solomon 2:15.

to bottle.] That very bottle for the mighty honored guest. When Miss Regina changes orders like that you can bet your dime she got her reason.

ADDIE: [*Points to dining room.*] Go on. You'll be needed.

CAL: Miss Zan she had two helpings frozen fruit cream and she tell that honored guest, she tell him that you make the best frozen fruit cream in all the South.

ADDIE: [*Smiles, pleased.*] Did she? Well, see that Belle saves a little for her. She like it right before she go to bed. Save a few little cakes, too, she like—

[*The dining-room doors are opened and quickly closed again by* BIRDIE HUBBARD. BIRDIE *is a woman of about forty, with a pretty, well-bred, faded face. Her movements are usually nervous and timid, but now, as she comes running into the room, she is gay and excited.* CAL *turns to* BIRDIE.]

BIRDIE: Oh, Cal. [*Closes door.*] I want you to get one of the kitchen boys to run home for me. He's to look in my desk drawer and—[*To* ADDIE.] My, Addie. What a good supper! Just as good as good can be.

ADDIE: You look pretty this evening, Miss Birdie, and young.

BIRDIE: [*Laughing.*] Me, young? [*Turns back to* CAL.] Maybe you better find Simon and tell him to do it himself. He's too look in my desk, the left drawer, and bring my music album right away. Mr. Marshall is very anxious to see it because of his father and the opera in Chicago. [*To* ADDIE.] Mr. Marshall is such a polite man with his manners and very educated and cultured and I've told him all about how my mama and papa used to go to Europe for the music—[*Laughs. To* ADDIE.] Imagine going all the way to Europe just to listen to music. Wouldn't that be nice, Addie? Just to sit there and listen and—[*Turns and steps to* CAL.] *Left* drawer, Cal. Tell him that twice because he forgets. And tell him not to let any of the things drop out of the album and to bring it right in here when he comes back.

[*The dining-room doors are opened and quickly closed by* OSCAR HUBBARD. *He is a man in his late forties.*]

CAL: Yes'm. But Simon he won't get it right. But I'll tell him.

BIRDIE: Left drawer, Cal, and tell him to bring the blue book and—

OSCAR: [*Sharply.*] Birdie.

BIRDIE: [*Turning nervously.*] Oh, Oscar. I was just sending Simon for my music album.

OSCAR: [*To* CAL.] Never mind about the album. Miss Birdie has changed her mind.

BIRDIE: But, really, Oscar. Really I promised Mr. Marshall. I—

[CAL *looks at them, exits.*]

OSCAR: Why do you leave the dinner table and go running about like a child?

BIRDIE: [*Trying to be gay.*] But, Oscar, Mr. Marshall said most specially he *wanted* to see my album. I told him about the time Mama met Wagner,[2] and Mrs. Wagner gave her the signed program and the big picture. Mr. Marshall wants to see that. Very, very much. We had such a nice talk and—

2. Richard Wagner (1813–1883), German composer.

OSCAR: [*Taking a step to her.*] You have been chattering to him like a magpie. You haven't let him be for a second. I can't think he came South to be bored with you.

BIRDIE: [*Quickly, hurt.*] He wasn't bored. I don't believe he was bored. He's a very educated, cultured gentleman. [*Her voice rises.*] I just don't believe it. You always talk like that when I'm having a nice time.

OSCAR: [*Turning to her, sharply.*] You have had too much wine. Get yourself in hand now.

BIRDIE: [*Drawing back, about to cry, shrilly.*] What am I doing? I am not doing anything. What am I doing?

OSCAR: [*Taking a step to her, tensely.*] I said get yourself in hand. Stop acting like a fool.

BIRDIE: [*Turns to him, quietly.*] I don't believe he was bored. I just don't believe it. Some people like music and like to talk about it. That's all I was doing.

[LEO HUBBARD *comes hurrying through the dining-room door. He is a young man of twenty, with a weak kind of good looks.*]

LEO: Mama! Papa! They are coming in now.

OSCAR: [*Softly.*] Sit down, Birdie. Sit down now.

[BIRDIE *sits down, bows her head as if to hide her face. The dining-room doors are opened by* CAL. *We see people beginning to rise from the table.* REGINA GIDDENS *comes in with* WILLIAM MARSHALL. REGINA *is a handsome woman of forty.* MARSHALL *is forty-five, pleasant-looking, self-possessed. Behind them comes* ALEXANDRIA GIDDENS, *a very pretty, rather delicate-looking girl of seventeen. She is followed by* BENJAMIN HUBBARD, *fifty-five, with a large jovial face and the light graceful movements that one often finds in large men.*]

REGINA: Mr. Marshall, I think you're trying to console me. Chicago may be the noisiest, dirtiest city in the world but I should still prefer it to the sound of our horses and the smell of our azaleas. I should like crowds of people, and theatres, and lovely women—*Very* lovely women, Mr. Marshall?

MARSHALL: [*Crossing to sofa.*] In Chicago? Oh, I suppose so. But I can tell you this: I've never dined there with three *such* lovely ladies.

[ADDIE *begins to pass the port.*]

BEN: Our Southern women are well favored.

LEO: [*Laughs.*] But one must go to Mobile for the ladies, sir. Very elegant worldly ladies, too.

BEN: [*Looks at him very deliberately.*] Worldly, eh? *Worldly,* did you say?

OSCAR: [*Hastily, to* LEO.] Your Uncle Ben means that worldliness is not a mark of beauty in any woman.

LEO: [*Quickly.*] Of course, Uncle Ben. I didn't mean—

MARSHALL: Your port is excellent, Mrs. Giddens.

REGINA: Thank you, Mr. Marshall. We had been saving that bottle, hoping we could open it just for you.

ALEXANDRA: [*As* ADDIE *comes to her with the tray.*] Oh. May I *really,* Addie?

ADDIE: Better ask Mama.

ALEXANDRA: May I, Mama?

REGINA: [*Nods, smiles.*] In Mr. Marshall's honor.

ALEXANDRA: [*Smiles.*] Mr. Marshall, this will be the first taste of port I've ever had.

[ADDIE *serves* LEO.]

MARSHALL: No one ever had their first taste of a better port. [*He lifts his glass in a toast; she lifts hers; they both drink.*] Well, I suppose it is all true, Mrs. Giddens.

REGINA: What is true?

MARSHALL: That you Southerners occupy a unique position in America. You live better than the rest of us, you eat better, you drink better. I wonder you find time, or want to find time, to do business.

BEN: A great many Southerners don't.

MARSHALL: Do all of you live here together?

REGINA: Here with me? [*Laughs.*] Oh, no. My brother Ben lives next door. My brother Oscar and his family live in the next square.

BEN: But we are a very close family. We've always *wanted* it that way.

MARSHALL: That is very pleasant. Keeping your family together to share each other's lives. My family moves around too much. My children seem never to come home. Away at school in the winter; in the summer, Europe with their mother—

REGINA: [*Eagerly.*] Oh, yes. Even down here we read about Mrs. Marshall in the society pages.

MARSHALL: I dare say. She moves about a great deal. And all of you are part of the same business? Hubbard Sons?

BEN: [*Motions to* OSCAR.] Oscar and me. [*Motions to* REGINA.] My sister's good husband is a banker.

MARSHALL: [*Looks at* REGINA, *surprised.*] Oh.

REGINA: I am so sorry that my husband isn't here to meet you. He's been very ill. He is at Johns Hopkins.[3] But he will be home soon. We think he is getting better now.

LEO: I work for Uncle Horace. [REGINA *looks at him.*] I mean I work for Uncle Horace at his bank. I keep an eye on things while he's away.

REGINA: [*Smiles.*] Really, Leo?

BEN: [*Looks at* LEO, *then to* MARSHALL.] Modesty in the young is as excellent as it is rare. [*Looks at* LEO *again.*]

OSCAR: [*To* LEO.] Your uncle means that a young man should speak more modestly.

LEO: [*Hastily, taking a step to* BEN.] Oh, I didn't mean, sir—

MARSHALL: Oh, Mrs. Hubbard. Where's that Wagner autograph you promised to let me see? My train will be leaving soon and—

BIRDIE: The autograph? Oh. Well. Really, Mr. Marshall, I didn't mean to chat-

3. A well-respected hospital in Baltimore.

ter so about it. Really I—[*Nervously, looking at* OSCAR.] You must excuse me. I didn't get it because, well, because I had—I—I had a little headache and—

OSCAR: My wife is a miserable victim of headaches.

REGINA: [*Quickly.*] Mr. Marshall said at supper that he would like you to play for him, Alexandra.

ALEXANDRA: [*Who has been looking at* BIRDIE.] It's not I who play well, sir. It's my aunt. She plays just wonderfully. She's my teacher. [*Rises. Eagerly.*] May we play a duet? May we, Mama?

BIRDIE: [*Taking* ALEXANDRA*'s hand.*] Thank you, dear. But I have my headache now. I—

OSCAR: [*Sharply.*] Don't be stubborn, Birdie. Mr. Marshall wants you to play.

MARSHALL: Indeed I do. If your headache isn't—

BIRDIE: [*Hesitates, then gets up, pleased.*] But I'd like to, sir. Very much. [*She and* ALEXANDRA *go to the piano.*]

MARSHALL: It's very remarkable how you Southern aristocrats have kept together. Kept together and kept what belonged to you.

BEN: You misunderstand, sir. Southern aristocrats have *not* kept together and have *not* kept what belonged to them.

MARSHALL: [*Laughs, indicates room.*] You don't call this keeping what belongs to you?

BEN: But we are not aristocrats. [*Points to* BIRDIE *at the piano.*] Our brother's wife is the only one of us who belongs to the Southern aristocracy.

[BIRDIE *looks towards* BEN.]

MARSHALL: [*Smiles.*] My information is that you people have been here, and solidly here, for a long time.

OSCAR: And so we have. Since our great-grandfather.

BEN: [*Smiles.*] Who was *not* an aristocrat, like Birdie's.

MARSHALL: [*A little sharply.*] You make great distinctions.

BEN: Oh, they have been made for us. And maybe they are important distinctions. [*Leans forward, intimately.*] Now you take Birdie's family. When my great-grandfather came here they were the highest-tone plantation owners in this state.

LEO: [*Steps to* MARSHALL. *Proudly.*] My mother's grandfather was *governor* of the state before the war.

OSCAR: They owned the plantation, Lionnet. You may have heard of it, sir?

MARSHALL: [*Laughs.*] No, I've never heard of anything but brick houses on a lake, and cotton mills.

BEN: Lionnet in its day was the best cotton land in the South. It still brings us in a fair crop. [*Sits back.*] Ah, they were great days for those people—even when I can remember. They had the best of everything. [BIRDIE *turns to them.*] Cloth from Paris, trips to Europe, horses you can't raise any more, niggers to lift their fingers—

BIRDIE: [*Suddenly.*] We were good to our people. Everybody knew that. We were better to them than—

[MARSHALL *looks up at* BIRDIE.]

REGINA: Why, Birdie. You aren't playing.

BEN: But when the war comes these fine gentlemen ride off and leave the cotton, *and* the women, to rot.

BIRDIE: My father was killed in the war. He was a fine soldier, Mr. Marshall. A fine man.

REGINA: Oh, certainly, Birdie. A famous soldier.

BEN: [*To* BIRDIE.] But that isn't the tale I am telling Mr. Marshall. [*To* MARSHALL.] Well, sir, the war ends. [BIRDIE *goes back to piano.*] Lionnet is almost ruined, and the sons finish ruining it. And there were thousands like them. Why? [*Leans forward.*] Because the Southern aristocrat can adapt himself to nothing. Too high-tone to try.

MARSHALL: Sometimes it is difficult to learn new ways.

[BIRDIE *and* ALEXANDRA *begin to play.* MARSHALL *leans forward, listening.*]

BEN: Perhaps, perhaps. [*He sees that* MARSHALL *is listening to the music. Irritated, he turns to* BIRDIE *and* ALEXANDRA *at the piano, then back to* MARSHALL.] You're right, Mr. Marshall. It is difficult to learn new ways. But maybe that's why it's profitable. *Our* grandfather and *our* father learned the new ways and learned how to make them pay. They work. [*Smiles nastily.*] *They* are in trade. Hubbard Sons, Merchandise. Others, Birdie's family, for example, look down on them. [*Settles back in chair.*] To make a long story short, Lionnet now belongs to *us.* [BIRDIE *stops playing.*] Twenty years ago we took over their land, their cotton, and their daughter.

[BIRDIE *rises and stands stiffly by the piano.* MARSHALL, *who has been watching her, rises.*]

MARSHALL: May I bring you a glass of port, Mrs. Hubbard?

BIRDIE: [*Softly.*] No, thank you, sir. You are most polite.

REGINA: [*Sharply, to* BEN.] You are boring Mr. Marshall with these ancient family tales.

BEN: I hope not. I hope not. I am trying to make an important point—[*Bows to* MARSHALL.] for our future business partner.

OSCAR: [*To* MARSHALL.] My brother always says that it's folks like us who have struggled and fought to bring to our land some of the posperity of your land.

BEN: Some people call that patriotism.

REGINA: [*Laughs gaily.*] I hope you don't find my brothers too obvious, Mr. Marshall. I'm afraid they mean that this is the time for the ladies to leave the gentlemen to talk business.

MARSHALL: [*Hastily.*] Not at all. We settled everything this afternoon. [MARSHALL *looks at his watch.*] I have only a few minutes before I must leave for the train. [*Smiles at her.*] And I insist they be spent with you.

REGINA: *And* with another glass of port.

MARSHALL: Thank you.

BEN: [*To* REGINA.] My sister is right. [*To* MARSHALL.] I am a plain man and I am trying to say a plain thing. A man ain't only in business for what he can get out of it. It's got to give him something here. [*Puts hand to his breast.*] That's every bit as true for the nigger picking cotton for a silver quarter, as it is for you and me. [REGINA *gives* MARSHALL *a glass of port.*] If it don't give him something here, then he don't pick the cotton right. Money isn't all. Not by three shots.

MARSHALL: Really? Well, I always thought it was a great deal.

REGINA: And so did I, Mr. Marshall.

MARSHALL: [*Leans forward. Pleasantly, but with meaning.*] Now you don't have to convince me that you are the right people for the deal. I wouldn't be here if you hadn't convinced me six months ago. You want the mill here, and I want it here. It isn't my business to find out *why* you want it.

BEN: To bring the machine to the cotton, and not the cotton to the machine.

MARSHALL: [*Amused.*] You have a turn for neat phrases, Hubbard. Well, however grand your reasons are, mine are simple: I want to make money and I believe I'll make it on you. [*As* BEN *starts to speak, he smiles.*] Mind you, I have no objections to more high-minded reasons. They are mighty valuable in business. It's fine to have partners who so closely follow the teachings of Christ. [*Gets up.*] And now I must leave for my train.

REGINA: I'm sorry you won't stay over with us, Mr. Marshall, but you'll come again. Any time you like.

BEN: [*Motions to* LEO, *indicating the bottle.*] Fill them up, boy, fill them up. [LEO *moves around filling the glasses as* BEN *speaks.*] Down here, sir, we have a strange custom. We drink the *last* drink for a toast. That's to prove that the Southerner is always still on his feet for the last drink. [*Picks up his glass.*] It was Henry Frick, your Mr. Henry Frick,[4] who said, "Railroads are the Rembrandts of investments." Well, *I* say, "Southern cotton mills *will be* the Rembrandts of investment." So I give you the firm of Hubbard Sons and Marshall, Cotton Mills, and to it a long and prosperous life.

[*They all pick up their glasses.* MARSHALL *looks at them, amused. Then he, too, lifts his glass, smiles.*]

OSCAR: The children will drive you to the depot. Leo! Alexandra! You will drive Mr. Marshall down.

LEO: [*Eagerly, looks at* BEN *who nods.*] Yes, sir. [*To* MARSHALL.] Not often Uncle Ben lets *me* drive the horses. And a beautiful pair they are. [*Starts for hall.*] Come on, Zan.

ALEXANDRA: May I drive tonight, Uncle Ben, please? I'd like to and—

BEN: [*Shakes his head, laughs.*] In your evening clothes? Oh, no, my dear.

ALEXANDRA: But Leo always—[*Stops, exits quickly.*]

REGINA: I don't like to say good-bye to you, Mr. Marshall.

MARSHALL: Then we won't say good-bye. You have promised that you would come and let me show you Chicago. Do I have to make you promise again?

4. (1849–1919), American industrialist; "your" because he was a Northerner. *Rembrandts*: valuable paintings by the great Dutch artist (1606–1669), here representing the highest quality.

REGINA: [*Looks at him as he presses her hand.*] I promise again.

MARSHALL: [*Touches her hand again, then moves to* BIRDIE.] Good-bye, Mrs. Hubbard.

BIRDIE: [*Shyly, with sweetness and dignity.*] Good-bye, sir.

MARSHALL: [*As he passes* REGINA.] Remember.

REGINA: I will.

OSCAR: We'll see you to the carriage.

[MARSHALL *exits, followed by* BEN *and* OSCAR. *For a second* REGINA *and* BIRDIE *stand looking after them. Then* REGINA *throws up her arms, laughs happily.*]

REGINA: And there, Birdie, goes the man who has opened the door to our future.

BIRDIE: [*Surprised to the unaccustomed friendliness.*] What?

REGINA: [*Turning to her.*] *Our future.* Yours and mine, Ben's and Oscar's, the children—[*Looks at* BIRDIE*'s puzzled face, laughs.*] Our future! [*Gaily.*] You were charming at supper, Birdie. Mr. Marshall certainly thought so.

BIRDIE: [*Pleased.*] Why, Regina! Do you think he did?

REGINA: Can't you tell when you're being admired?

BIRDIE: Oscar said I bored Mr. Marshall. [*Then quietly.*] But he admired *you*. He told me so.

REGINA: What did he say?

BIRDIE: He said to me, "I hope your sister-in-law will come to Chicago. Chicago will be at her feet." He said the ladies would bow to your manners and the gentlemen to your looks.

REGINA: Did he? He seems a lonely man. Imagine being lonely with all that money. I don't think he likes his wife.

BIRDIE: Not like his wife? What a thing to say.

REGINA: She's away a great deal. He said that several times. And once he made fun of her being so social and high-tone. But that fits in all right. [*Sits back, arms on back of sofa, stretches.*] Her being social, I mean. She can introduce me. It won't take long with an introduction from her.

BIRDIE: [*Bewildered.*] Introduce you? In Chicago? You mean you really might go? Oh, Regina, you can't leave here. What about Horace?

REGINA: Don't look so scared about everything, Birdie. I'm going to live in Chicago. I've always wanted to. And now there'll be plenty of money to go with.

BIRDIE: But Horace won't be able to move around. You know what the doctor wrote.

REGINA: There'll be millions, Birdie, millions. You know what I've always said when people told me we were rich? I said I think you should either be a nigger or a millionaire. In between, like us, what for? [*Laughs. Looks at* BIRDIE.] But I'm not going away tomorrow, Birdie. There's plenty of time to worry about Horace when he comes home. If he ever decides to come home.

BIRDIE: Will we be going to Chicago? I mean, Oscar and Leo and me?

REGINA: You? I shouldn't think so. [*Laughs.*] Well, we must remember tonight. It's a very important night and we mustn't forget it. We shall plan all the things we'd like to have and then we'll really have them. Make a wish, Birdie, any wish. It's bound to come true now.

[BEN *and* OSCAR *enter.*]

BIRDIE: [*Laughs.*] Well. Well, I don't know. Maybe. [REGINA *turns to look at* BEN.] Well, I guess I'd know right off what I wanted.

[OSCAR *stands by the upper window, waves to the departing carriage.*]

REGINA [*Looks up at* BEN, *smiles. He smiles back at her.*] Well, you did it.
BEN: Looks like it might be we did.
REGINA: [*Springs up, laughs.*] Looks like it! Don't pretend. You're like a cat who's been licking the cream. [*Crosses to wine bottle.*] Now we must all have a drink to celebrate.
OSCAR: The children, Alexandra and Leo, make a very handsome couple, Regina. Marshall remarked himself what fine young folks they were. How well they looked together!
REGINA: [*Sharply.*] Yes. You said that before, Oscar.
BEN: Yes, sir. It's beginning to look as if the deal's all set. I may not be a subtle man—but—[*Turns to them. After a second.*] Now somebody ask me how I know the deal is set.
OSCAR: What do you mean, Ben?
BEN: You remember I told him that down here we drink the *last* drink for a toast?
OSCAR: [*Thoughtfully.*] Yes. I never heard that before.
BEN: Nobody's ever heard it before. God forgives those who invent what they need. I already had his signature. But we've all done business with men whose word over a glass is better than a bond. Anyway it don't hurt to have both.
OSCAR: [*Turns to* REGINA.] You understand what Ben means?
REGINA: [*Smiles.*] Yes, Oscar. I understand. I understood immediately.
BEN: [*Looks at her admiringly.*] Did you, Regina? Well, when he lifted his glass to drink, I closed my eyes and saw the bricks going into place.
REGINA: And *I* saw a lot more than that.
BEN: Slowly, slowly. As yet we have only our hopes.
REGINA: Birdie and I have just been planning what we want. I know what I want. What will you want, Ben?
BEN: Caution. Don't count the chickens. [*Leans back, laughs.*] Well, God would allow us a little daydreaming. Good for the soul when you've worked hard enough to deserve it. [*Pauses.*] I think I'll have a stable. For a long time I've had my good eyes on Carter's in Savannah. A rich man's pleasure, the sport of kings, why not the sport of Hubbards? Why not?
REGINA: [*Smiles.*] Why not? What will you have, Oscar?
OSCAR: I don't know. [*Thoughtfully.*] The pleasure of seeing the bricks grow will be enough for me.
BEN: Oh, of course. Our *greatest* pleasure will be to see the bricks grow. But we are all entitled to a little side indulgence.
OSCAR: Yes, I suppose so. Well, then, I think we might take a few trips here and there, eh, Birdie?
BIRDIE: [*Surprised at being consulted.*] Yes, Oscar. I'd like that.

OSCAR: We might even make a regular trip to Jekyll Island.[5] I've heard the Cornelly place is for sale. We might think about buying it. Make a nice change. Do you good, Birdie, a change of climate. Fine shooting on Jekyll, the best.

BIRDIE: I'd like—

OSCAR: [*Indulgently.*] What would you like?

BIRDIE: *Two* things. Two things I'd like most.

REGINA: Two! I should like a thousand. You are modest, Birdie.

BIRDIE: [*Warmly, delighted with the unexpected interest.*] I should like to have Lionnet back. I know you own it now, but I'd like to see it fixed up again, the way Mama and Papa had it. Every year it used to get a nice coat of paint—Papa was very particular about the paint—and the lawn was so smooth all the way down to the river, with the trims of zinnias and red-feather plush. And the figs and blue little plums and the scuppernongs—[*Smiles. Turns to* REGINA.] The organ is still there and it wouldn't cost much to fix. We could have parties for Zan, the way Mama used to have for me.

BEN: That's a pretty picture, Birdie. Might be a most pleasant way to live. [*Dismissing* BIRDIE.] What do you want, Regina?

BIRDIE: [*Very happily, not noticing that they are no longer listening to her.*] I could have a cutting garden. Just where Mama's used to be. Oh, I do think we could be happier there. Papa used to say that *nobody* had ever lost their temper at Lionnet, and *nobody* ever would. Papa would never let anybody be nasty-spoken or mean. No, sir. He just didn't like it.

BEN: What do you want, Regina?

REGINA: I'm going to Chicago. And when I'm settled there and know the right people and the right things to buy—because I certainly don't now—I shall go to Paris and buy them. [*Laughs.*] I'm going to leave you and Oscar to count the bricks.

BIRDIE: Oscar. Please let me have Lionnet back.

OSCAR: [*To* REGINA.] You are serious about moving to Chicago?

BEN: She is going to see the great world and leave us in the little one. Well, we'll come and visit you and meet all the great and be proud to think you are our sister.

REGINA: [*Gaily.*] Certainly. And you won't even have to learn to be subtle, Ben. Stay as you are. You will be rich and the rich don't have to be subtle.

OSCAR: But what about Alexandra? She's seventeen. Old enough to be thinking about marrying.

BIRDIE: And, Oscar, I have one more wish. Just one more wish.

OSCAR: [*Turns.*] What is it, Birdie? What are you saying?

BIRDIE: I want you to stop shooting. I mean, so much. I don't like to see animals and birds killed just for the killing. You only throw them away—

BEN: [*To* REGINA.] It'll take a great deal of money to live as you're planning, Regina.

REGINA: Certainly. But there'll be plenty of money. You have estimated the profits very high.

5. In Georgia, on the Atlantic coast.

BEN: I have—

BIRDIE: [OSCAR *is looking at her furiously*.] And you never let anybody else shoot, and the niggers need it so much to keep from starving. It's wicked to shoot food just because you like to shoot, when poor people need it so—

BEN: [*Laughs*.] I have estimated the profits very high—for myself.

REGINA: What did you say?

BIRDIE: I've always wanted to speak about it, Oscar.

OSCAR: [*Slowly, carefully*.] What are you chattering about?

BIRDIE: [*Nervously*.] I was talking about Lionnet and—and about your shooting—

OSCAR: You are exciting yourself.

REGINA: [*To* BEN.] I didn't hear you. There was so much talking.

OSCAR: [*To* BIRDIE.] You have been acting very childish, very excited, all evening.

BIRDIE: Regina asked me what I'd like.

REGINA: What did you say, Ben?

BIRDIE: Now that we'll be so rich everybody was saying what they would like, so *I* said what *I* would like, too.

BEN: I said—[*He is interrupted by* OSCAR.]

OSCAR: [*To* BIRDIE.] Very well, We've all heard you. That's enough now.

BEN: I am waiting. [*They stop*.] I am waiting for you to finish. You and Birdie. Four conversations are three too many. [BIRDIE *slowly sits down*. BEN *smiles, to* REGINA.] I said that I had, and I do, estimate the profits very high—for myself, and Oscar, of course.

REGINA: [*Slowly*.] And what does that mean?

[BEN *shrugs, looks towards* OSCAR.]

OSCAR: [*Looks at* BEN, *clears throat*.] Well, Regina, it's like this. For forty-nine per cent Marshall will put up four hundred thousand dollars. For forty-one per cent—[*Smiles archly*.] a controlling interest, mind you, we will put up two hundred and twenty-five thousand dollars besides offering him certain benefits that our [*Looks at* BEN.] local position allows us to manage. Ben means that two hundred and twenty-five thousand dollars is a lot of money.

REGINA: I know the terms and I know it's a lot of money.

BEN: [*Nodding*.] It is.

OSCAR: Ben means that we are ready with our two-thirds of the money. Your third, Horace's I mean, doesn't seem to be ready. [*Raises his hand as* REGINA *starts to speak*.] Ben has written to Horace, I have written, and you have written. He answers. But he never mentions this business. Yet we have explained it to him in great detail, and told him the urgency. Still he never mentions it. Ben has been very patient, Regina. Naturally, you are our sister and we want you to benefit from anything we do.

REGINA: And in addition to your concern for me, you do not want control to go out of the family. [*To* BEN.] That right, Ben?

BEN: That's cynical. [*Smiles*.] Cynicism is an unpleasant way of saying the truth.

OSCAR: No need to be cynical. We'd have no trouble raising the third share, the share that you want to take.

REGINA: I am sure you could get the third share, the share you were saving for me. But that would give you a strange partner. And strange partners sometimes want a great deal. [*Smiles unpleasantly.*] But perhaps it would be wise for you to find him.

OSCAR: Now, now. Nobody says we *want* to do that. We would like to have you in and you would like to come in.

REGINA: Yes. I certainly would.

BEN: [*Laughs, puts up his hand.*] But we haven't heard from Horace.

REGINA: I've given my word that Horace will put up the money. That should be enough.

BEN: Oh, it was enough. I took your word. But I've got to have more than your word now. The contracts will be signed this week, and Marshall will want to see our money soon after. Regina, Horace has been in Baltimore for five months. I know that you've written him to come home, and that he hasn't come.

OSCAR: It's beginning to look as if he doesn't want to come home.

REGINA: Of course he wants to come home. You can't move around with heart trouble at any moment you choose. You know what doctors are like once they get their hands on a case like this—

OSCAR: They can't very well keep him from answering letters, can they? [REGINA *turns to* BEN.] They couldn't keep him from arranging for the money if he wanted to—

REGINA: Has it occurred to you that Horace is also a good business man?

BEN: Certainly. He is a shrewd trader. Always has been. The bank is proof of that.

REGINA: Then, possibly, he may be keeping silent because he doesn't think he is getting enough for his money. [*Looks at* OSCAR.] Seventy-five thousand he has to put up. That's a lot of money, too.

OSCAR: Nonsense. He knows a good thing when he hears it. He knows that we can make *twice* the profit on cotton goods manufactured *here* than can be made in the North.

BEN: That isn't what Regina means. [*Smiles.*] May I interpret you, Regina? [*To* OSCAR.] Regina is saying that Horace wants *more* than a third of our share.

OSCAR: But he's only putting up a third of the money. You put up a third and you get a third. What else *could* he expect?

REGINA: Well, *I* don't know. I don't know about these things. It would seem that if you put up a third you should only get a third. But then again, there's no law about it, is there? I should think that if you knew your money was very badly needed, well, you just might say, I want more, I want a bigger share. You boys have done that. I've heard you say so.

BEN: [*After a pause, laughs.*] So you believe he has deliberately held out? For a larger share? [*Leaning forward.*] Well, I *don't* believe it. But I *do* believe that's what *you* want. Am I right, Regina?

REGINA: Oh, I shouldn't like to be too definite. But I *could* say that I wouldn't like to persuade Horace unless he did get a larger share. I must look after his interests. It seems only natural—

OSCAR: And where would the larger share come from?

REGINA: I don't know. That's not my business. [*Giggles.*] But perhaps it could come off your share, Oscar.

[REGINA *and* BEN *laugh.*]

OSCAR: [*Rises and wheels furiously on both of them as they laugh.*] What kind of talk is this?

BEN: I haven't said a thing.

OSCAR: [*To* REGINA.] *You* are talking very big tonight.

REGINA: [*Stops laughing.*] Am I? Well, you should know me well enough to know that I wouldn't be asking for things I didn't think I could get.

OSCAR: Listen. I don't believe you can even get Horace to come home, much less get money from him or talk quite so big about what you want.

REGINA: Oh, I can get him home.

OSCAR: Then why haven't you?

REGINA: I thought I should fight his battles for him, before he came home. Horace is a very sick man. And even if *you* don't care how sick he is, I do.

BEN: Stop this foolish squabbling. How can you get him home?

REGINA: I will send Alexandra to Baltimore. She will ask him to come home. She will say that she *wants* him to come home, and that *I* want him to come home.

BIRDIE: [*Suddenly.*] Well, of course she wants him here, but he's sick and maybe he's happy where he is.

REGINA: [*Ignores* BIRDIE, *to* BEN.] You agree that he will come home if she asks him to, if she says that I miss him and want him—

BEN: [*Looks at her, smiles.*] I admire you, Regina. And I agree. That's settled now and—[*Starts to rise.*]

REGINA: [*Quickly.*] But before she brings him home, I want to know what he's going to get.

BEN: What do you want?

REGINA: Twice what you offered.

BEN: Well, you won't get it.

OSCAR: [*To* REGINA.] I think you've gone crazy.

REGINA: I don't want to fight, Ben—

BEN: I don't either. You won't get it. There isn't any chance of that. [*Roguishly.*] You're holding us up, and that's not pretty, Regina, not pretty. [*Holds up his hand as he sees she is about to speak.*] But we need you, and I don't want to fight. Here's what I'll do: I'll give Horace forty percent, instead of the thirty-three and a third he really should get. I'll do that, provided he is home and his money is up within two weeks. How's that?

REGINA: All right.

OSCAR: I've asked before: where is this extra share coming from?

BEN: [*Pleasantly.*] From you. From your share.

OSCAR: [*Furiously.*] From me, is it? That's just fine and dandy. That's my reward. For thirty-five years I've worked my hands to the bone for you. For thirty-five years I've done all the things you didn't want to do. And this is what I—

BEN: [*Turns slowly to look at* OSCAR. OSCAR *breaks off.*] My, my. I am being attacked tonight on all sides. First by my sister, then by my brother. And I ain't a man who likes being attacked. I can't believe that God wants the strong to parade their strength, but I don't mind doing it if it's got to be done. [*Leans back in his chair.*] You ought to take these things better, Oscar. I've made you money in the past. I'm going to make you more money now. You'll be a very rich man. What's the difference to any of us if a little more goes here, a little less goes there—it's all in the family. And it will stay in the family. I'll never marry. [ADDIE *enters, begins to gather the glasses from the table.* OSCAR *turns to* BEN.] So my money will go to Alexandra and Leo. They may even marry some day and—

[ADDIE *looks at* BEN.]

BIRDIE: [*Rising.*] Marry—Zan and Leo—

OSCAR: [*Carefully.*] That would make a great difference in my feelings. If they married.

BEN: Yes, that's what I mean. Of course it would make a difference.

OSCAR: [*Carefully.*] Is that what *you* mean, Regina?

REGINA: Oh, it's too far away. We'll talk about it in a few years.

OSCAR: I want to talk about it now.

BEN: [*Nods.*] Naturally.

REGINA: There's a lot of things to consider. They are first cousins, and—

OSCAR: That isn't unusual. Our grandmother and grandfather were first cousins.

REGINA: [*Giggles.*] And look at us.

[BEN *giggles.*]

OSCAR: [*Angrily.*] You're both being very gay with my money.

BEN: [*Sighs.*] These quarrels. I dislike them so. [*Leans forward to* REGINA.] A marriage might be a very wise arrangement, for several reasons. And then, Oscar has given up something for you. You should try to manage something for him.

REGINA: I haven't said I was opposed to it. But Leo is a wild boy. There were those times when he took a little money from the bank and—

OSCAR: That's all past history—

REGINA: Oh, I know. And I know all young men are wild. I'm only mentioning it to show you that there are considerations—

BEN: [*Irritated because she does not understand that he is trying to keep* OSCAR *quiet.*] All right, so there are. But please assure Oscar that you will think about it very seriously.

REGINA: [*Smiles, nods.*] Very well. I assure Oscar that I will think about it seriously.

OSCAR: [*Sharply.*] That is not an answer.

REGINA: [*Rises.*] My, you're in a bad humor and you shall put me in one. I have said all that I am willing to say now. After all, Horace has to give his consent too.

OSCAR: Horace will do what you tell him to.

REGINA: Yes, I think he will.
OSCAR: And I have your word that you will try to—
REGINA: [*Patiently.*] Yes, Oscar. You have my word that I will think about it. Now do leave me alone.

[*There is the sound of the front door being closed.*]

BIRDIE: I—Alexandra is only seventeen. She—
REGINA: [*Calling.*] Alexandra? Are you back?
ALEXANDRA: Yes, Mama.
LEO: [*Comes into the room.*] Mr. Marshall got off safe and sound. Weren't those fine clothes he had? You can always spot clothes made in a good place. Looks like maybe they were done in England. Lots of men in the North send all the way to England for their stuff.
BEN: [*To* LEO.] Were you careful driving the horses?
LEO: Oh, yes, sir. I was.

[ALEXANDRA *has come in on* BEN's *question, hears the answer, looks angrily at* LEO.]

ALEXANDRA: It's a lovely night. You should have come, Aunt Birdie.
REGINA: Were you gracious to Mr. Marshall?
ALEXANDRA: I think so, Mama. I liked him.
REGINA: Good. And now I have great news for you. You are going to Baltimore in the morning to bring your father home.
ALEXANDRA: [*Gasps, then delighted.*] Me? Papa said I should come? That must mean—[*Turns to* ADDIE.] Addie, he must be well. Think of it, he'll be back home again. We'll bring him home.
REGINA: You are going alone, Alexandra.
ADDIE: [ALEXANDRA *has turned in surprise.*] Going alone? Going by herself? A child that age! Mr. Horace ain't going to like Zan traipsing up there by herself.
REGINA: [*Sharply.*] Go upstairs and lay out Alexandra's things.
ADDIE: He'd expect me to be along—
REGINA: I'll be up in a few minutes to tell you what to pack. [ADDIE *slowly begins to climb the steps. To* ALEXANDRA.] I should think you'd like going alone. At your age it certainly would have delighted me. You're a strange girl, Alexandra. Addie has babied you so much.
ALEXANDRA: I only thought it would be more fun if Addie and I went together.
BIRDIE: [*Timidly.*] Maybe I could go with her, Regina. I'd really like to.
REGINA: She is going alone. She is getting old enough to take some responsibilities.
OSCAR: She'd better learn now. She's almost old enough to get married. [*Jovially, to* LEO, *slapping him on shoulder.*] Eh, son?
LEO: Huh?
OSCAR: [*Annoyed with* LEO *for not understanding.*] Old enough to get married, you're thinking, eh?

LEO: Oh, yes, sir. [*Feebly.*] Lots of girls get married at Zan's age. Look at Mary Prester and Johanna and—

REGINA: Well, she's not getting married tomorrow. But she is going to Baltimore tomorrow, so let's talk about that. [*To* ALEXANDRA.] You'll be glad to have Papa home again.

ALEXANDRA: I wanted to go before, Mama. You remember that. But you said *you* couldn't go, and that *I* couldn't go alone.

REGINA: I've changed my mind. [*Too casually.*] You're to tell Papa how much you missed him, and that he must come home now—for your sake. Tell him that you *need* him home.

ALEXANDRA: Need him home? I don't understand.

REGINA: There is nothing for you to understand. You are simply to say what I have told you.

BIRDIE: [*Rises.*] He may be too sick. She couldn't do that—

ALEXANDRA: Yes. He may be too sick to travel. I couldn't make him think he had to come home for me, if he is too sick to—

REGINA: [*Looks at her, sharply, challengingly.*] You *couldn't* do what I tell you to do, Alexandra?

ALEXANDRA: [*Quietly.*] No. I couldn't. If I thought it would hurt him.

REGINA: [*After a second's silence, smiles pleasantly.*] But you are doing this for Papa's own good. [*Takes* ALEXANDRA'*s hand.*] You must let me be the judge of his condition. It's the best possible cure for him to come home and be taken care of here. He mustn't stay there any longer and listen to those alarmist doctors. You are doing this entirely for his sake. Tell your papa that I want him to come home, that I miss him very much.

ALEXANDRA: [*Slowly.*] Yes, Mama.

REGINA: [*To the others. Rises.*] I must go and start getting Alexandra ready now. Why don't you all go home?

BEN: [*Rises.*] I'll attend to the railroad ticket. One of the boys will bring it over. Good night, everybody. Have a nice trip, Alexandra. The food on the train is very good. The celery is so crisp. Have a good time and act like a little lady. [*Exits.*]

REGINA: Good night, Ben. Good night, Oscar—[*Playfully.*] Don't be so glum, Oscar. It makes you look as if you had chronic indigestion.

BIRDIE: Good night, Regina.

REGINA: Good night, Birdie. [*Exits upstairs.*]

OSCAR: [*Starts for hall.*] Come along.

LEO: [*To* ALEXANDRA.] Imagine your not wanting to go! What a little fool you are. Wish it were me. What I could do in a place like Baltimore!

ALEXANDRA: [*Angrily, looking away from him.*] Mind your business. I can guess the kind of things *you* could do.

LEO: [*Laughs.*] Oh, no, you couldn't. [*He exits.*]

REGINA: [*Calling from the top of the stairs.*] Come on, Alexandra.

BIRDIE: [*Quickly, softly.*] Zan.

ALEXANDRA: I don't understand about my going, Aunt Birdie. [*Shrugs.*] But anyway, Papa will be home again. [*Pats* BIRDIE's *arm.*] Don't worry about me. I can take care of myself. Really I can.

BIRDIE: [*Shakes her head, softly.*] That's not what I'm worried about. Zan—

ALEXANDRA: [*Comes close to her.*] What's the matter?

BIRDIE: It's about Leo—

ALEXANDRA: [*Whispering.*] He beat the horses. That's why we were late getting back. We had to wait until they cooled off. He always beats the horses as if—

BIRDIE: [*Whispering frantically, holding* ALEXANDRA's *hands.*] He's my son. My own son. But you are more to me—more to me than my own child. I love you more than anybody else—

ALEXANDRA: Don't worry about the horses. I'm sorry I told you.

BIRDIE: [*Her voice rising.*] I am not worrying about the horses. I am worrying about *you*. You are *not* going to marry Leo. I am not going to let them do that to you—

ALEXANDRA: Marry? To Leo? [*Laughs.*] I wouldn't marry, Aunt Birdie. I've never even thought about it—

BIRDIE: But they have thought about it. [*Wildly.*] Zan, I couldn't stand to think about such a thing. You and—

[OSCAR *has come into the doorway on* ALEXANDRA's *speech. He is standing quietly, listening.*]

ALEXANDRA: [*Laughs.*] But I'm not going to marry. And I'm certainly not going to marry Leo.

BIRDIE: Don't you understand? They'll make you. They'll make you—

ALEXANDRA: [*Takes* BIRDIE's *hands, quietly, firmly.*] That's foolish, Aunt Birdie. I'm grown now. Nobody can make me do anything.

BIRDIE: I just couldn't stand—

OSCAR: [*Sharply.*] Birdie. [BIRDIE *looks up, draws quickly away from* ALEXANDRA. *She stands rigid, frightened. Quietly.*] Birdie, get your hat and coat.

ADDIE: [*Calls from upstairs.*] Come on, baby. Your mama's waiting for you, and she ain't nobody to keep waiting.

ALEXANDRA: All right. [*Then softly, embracing* BIRDIE.] Good night, Aunt Birdie. [*As she passes* OSCAR.] Good night, Uncle Oscar. [BIRDIE *begins to move slowly towards the door as* ALEXANDRA *climbs the stairs.* ALEXANDRA *is almost out of view when* BIRDIE *reaches* OSCAR *in the doorway. As* BIRDIE *quietly attempts to pass him, he slaps her hard, across the face.* BIRDIE *cries out, puts her hand to her face. On the cry,* ALEXANDRA *turns, begins to run down the stairs.*] Aunt Birdie! What happened? What happened? I—

BIRDIE: [*Softly, without turning.*] Nothing, darling. Nothing happened. [*Quickly, as if anxious to keep* ALEXANDRA *from coming close.*] Now go to bed. [OSCAR *exits.*] Nothing happened. [*Turns to* ALEXANDRA *who is holding her hand.*] I only—I only twisted my ankle. [*She goes out.* ALEXANDRA *stands on the stairs looking after her as if she were puzzled and frightened.*]

CURTAIN

ACT II

SCENE: *Same as Act I. A week later, morning.*

AT RISE: *The light comes from the open shutter of the right window; the other shutters are tightly closed.* ADDIE *is standing at the window, looking out. Near the dining-room doors are brooms, mops, rags, etc. After a second,* OSCAR *comes into the entrance hall, looks in the room, shivers, decides not to take his hat and coat off, comes into the room. At the sound of the door,* ADDIE *turns to see who has come in.*

ADDIE: [*Without interest.*] Oh, it's you, Mr. Oscar.

OSCAR: What is this? It's not night. What's the matter here? [*Shivers.*] Fine thing at this time of the morning. Blinds all closed. [ADDIE *begins to open shutters.*] Where's Miss Regina? It's cold in here.

ADDIE: Miss Regina ain't down yet.

OSCAR: She had any word?

ADDIE: [*Wearily.*] No, sir.

OSCAR: Wouldn't you think a girl that age could get on a train at one place and have sense enough to get off at another?

ADDIE: Something must have happened. If Zan say she was coming last night, she's coming last night. Unless something happened. Sure fire disgrace to let a baby like that go all that way alone to bring home a sick man without—

OSCAR: You do a lot of judging around here, Addie, eh? Judging of your white folks, I mean.

ADDIE: [*Looks at him, sighs.*] I'm tired. I been up all night watching for them.

REGINA: [*Speaking from the upstairs hall.*] Who's downstairs, Addie? [*She appears in a dressing gown, peers down from the landing.* ADDIE *picks up broom, dustpan and brush and exits.*] Oh, it's you, Oscar. What are you doing here so early? I haven't been down yet. I'm not finished dressing.

OSCAR: [*Speaking up to her.*] You had any word from them?

REGINA: No.

OSCAR: Then something certainly has happened. People don't just say they are arriving on Thursday night, and they haven't come by Friday morning.

REGINA: Oh, nothing has happened. Alexandra just hasn't got sense enough to send a message.

OSCAR: If nothing's happened, then why aren't they here?

REGINA: You asked me that ten times last night. My, you do fret so, Oscar. Anything might have happened. They may have missed connections in Atlanta, the train may have been delayed—oh, a hundred things could have kept them.

OSCAR: Where's Ben?

REGINA: [*As she disappears upstairs.*] Where should he be? At home, probably. Really, Oscar, I don't tuck him in his bed and I don't take him out of it. Have some coffee and don't worry so much.

OSCAR: Have some coffee? There isn't any coffee. [*Looks at his watch, shakes his head. After a second* CAL *enters with a large silver tray, coffee urn, small cups, newspaper.*] Oh, there you are. Is everything in this fancy house always late?

CAL: [*Looks at him surprised.*] You ain't out shooting this morning, Mr. Oscar?

OSCAR: First day I missed since I had my head cold. First day I missed in eight years.

CAL: Yes, sir. I bet you. Simon he say you had a mighty good day yesterday morning. That's what Simon say. [*Brings* OSCAR *coffee and newspaper.*]

OSCAR: Pretty good, pretty good.

CAL: [*Laughs slyly.*] Bet you got enough bobwhite and squirrel to give every nigger in town a Jesus-party. Most of 'em ain't had no meat since the cotton picking was over. Bet they'd give anything for a little piece of that meat—

OSCAR: [*Turns his head to look at* CAL.] Cal, if I catch a nigger in this town going shooting, you know what's going to happen.

[LEO *enters.*]

CAL: [*Hastily.*] Yes, sir, Mr. Oscar. I didn't say nothing about nothing. It was Simon who told me and— Morning, Mr. Leo. You gentlemen having your breakfast with us here?

LEO: The boys in the bank don't know a thing. They haven't had any message.

[CAL *waits for an answer, gets none, shrugs, moves to door, exits.*]

OSCAR: [*Peers at* LEO.] What you doing here, son?

LEO: You told me to find out if the boys at the bank had any message from Uncle Horace or Zan—

OSCAR: I told you if they had a message to bring it here. I told you that if they didn't have a message to stay at the bank and do your work.

LEO: Oh, I guess I misunderstood.

OSCAR: You didn't misunderstand. You just were looking for any excuse to take an hour off. [LEO *pours a cup of coffee.*] You got to stop that kind of thing. You got to start settling down. You going to be a married man one of these days.

LEO: Yes, sir.

OSCAR: You also got to stop with that woman in Mobile. [*As* LEO *is about to speak.*] You're young and I haven't got no objections to outside women. That is, I haven't got no objections so long as they don't interfere with serious things. Outside women are all right in their place, but *now* isn't their place. You got to realize that.

LEO: [*Nods.*] Yes, sir. I'll tell her. She'll act all right about it.

OSCAR: Also, you got to start working harder at the bank. You got to convince your Uncle Horace you going to make a fit husband for Alexandra.

LEO: What do you think has happened to them? Supposed to be here last night— [*Laughs.*] Bet you Uncle Ben's mighty worried. Seventy-five thousand dollars worried.

OSCAR: [*Smiles happily.*] Ought to be worried. Damn well ought to be. First he don't answer the letters, then he don't come home— [*Giggles.*]

LEO: What will happen if Uncle Horace don't come home or don't—

OSCAR: Or don't put up the money? Oh, we'll get it from outside. Easy enough.

LEO: [*Surprised.*] But *you* don't want outsiders.

OSCAR: What do I care who gets my share? I been shaved already. Serve Ben right if he had to give away some of his.

LEO: Damn shame what they did to you.

OSCAR: [*Looking up the stairs.*] Don't talk so loud. Don't you worry. When I die, you'll have as much as the rest. You might have yours *and* Alexandra's. I'm not so easily licked.

LEO: I wasn't thinking of myself, Papa—

OSCAR: Well, you should be, you should be. It's every man's duty to think of himself.

LEO: You think Uncle Horace don't want to go in on this?

OSCAR: [*Giggles.*] That's my hunch. He hasn't showed any signs of loving it yet.

LEO: [*Laughs.*] But he hasn't listened to Aunt Regina yet, either. Oh, he'll go along. It's too good a thing. Why wouldn't he want to? He's got plenty and plenty to invest with. He don't even have to sell anything. Eighty-eight thousand worth of Union Pacific bonds sitting right in his safe deposit box. All he's got to do is open the box.

OSCAR: [*After a pause. Looks at his watch.*] Mighty late breakfast in this fancy house. Yes, he's had those bonds for fifteen years. Bought them when they were low and just locked them up.

LEO: Yeah. Just has to open the box and take them out. That's all. Easy as easy can be. [*Laughs.*] The things in that box! There's all those bonds, looking mighty fine. [OSCAR *slowly puts down his newspaper and turns to* LEO.] Then right next to them is a baby shoe of Zan's and a cheap old cameo on a string, and, *and*—nobody'd believe this—a piece of an old violin. Not even a whole violin. Just a piece of an old thing, a piece of a violin.

OSCAR: [*Very softly, as if he were trying to control his voice.*] A piece of a violin! What do you think of that!

LEO: Yes, sirree. A lot of other crazy things, too. A poem, I guess it is, signed with his mother's name, and two old schoolbooks with notes and—[LEO *catches* OSCAR's *look. His voice trails off. He turns his head away.*]

OSCAR: [*Very softly.*] How do you know what's in the box, son?

LEO: [*Stops, draws back, frightened, realizing what he has said.*] Oh, well. Well, er. Well, one of the boys, sir. It was one of the boys at the bank. He took old Manders' keys. It was Joe Horns. He just up and took Manders' keys and, and—well, took the box out. [*Quickly.*] Then they all asked me if I wanted to see, too. So I looked a little, I guess, but then I made them close up the box quick and I told them never—

OSCAR: [*Looks at him.*] Joe Horns, you say? He opened it?

LEO: Yes, sir, yes, he did. My word of honor. [*Very nervously looking away.*] I suppose that don't excuse *me* for looking—[*Looking at* OSCAR.] but I did make him close it up and put the keys back in Manders' drawer—

OSCAR: [*Leans forward, very softly.*] Tell me the truth, Leo. I am not going to be angry with you. Did you open the box yourself?

LEO: No, sir, I didn't. I told you I didn't. No, I—

OSCAR: [*Irritated, patient.*] I am *not* going to be angry with you. [*Watching* LEO *carefully.*] Sometimes a young fellow deserves credit for looking round him to see what's going on. Sometimes that's a good sign in a fellow your age. [OSCAR *rises.*] Many great men have made their fortune with their eyes. Did you open the box?

LEO: [*Very puzzled.*] No. I—

OSCAR: [*Moves to* LEO.] Did you open the box? It may have been—well, it may have been a good thing if you had.

LEO: [*After a long pause.*] I opened it.

OSCAR: [*Quickly.*] Is that the truth? [LEO *nods.*] Does anybody else know that you opened it? Come, Leo, don't be afraid of speaking the truth to me.

LEO: No. Nobody knew. Nobody was in the bank when I did it. But—

OSCAR: Did your Uncle Horace ever know you opened it?

LEO: [*Shakes his head.*] He only looks in it once every six months when he cuts the coupons,[6] and sometimes Manders even does that for him. Uncle Horace don't even have the keys. Manders keeps them for him. Imagine not looking at all that. You can bet if I had the bonds, I'd watch 'em like—

OSCAR: If you had them. [LEO *watches him.*] *If* you had them. Then you could have a share in the mill, you and me. A fine, big share, too. [*Pauses, shrugs.*] Well, a man can't be shot for wanting to see his son get on in the world, can he, boy?

LEO: [*Looks up, begins to understand.*] No, he can't. Natural enough. [*Laughs.*] But I haven't got the bonds and Uncle Horace has. And now he can just sit back and wait to be a millionaire.

OSCAR: [*Innocently.*] You think your Uncle Horace likes you well enough to lend you the bonds if he decides not to use them himself?

LEO: Papa, it must be that you haven't had your breakfast! [*Laughs loudly.*] Lend me the bonds! My God—

OSCAR: [*Disappointed.*] No, I suppose not. Just a fancy of mine. A loan for three months, maybe four, easy enough for us to pay it back then. Anyway, this is only April—[*Slowly counting the months on his fingers.*] and if he doesn't look at them until Fall, he wouldn't even miss them out of the box.

LEO: That's it. He wouldn't even miss them. Ah, well—

OSCAR: No, sir. Wouldn't even miss them. How could he miss them if he never looks at them? [*Sighs as* LEO *stares at him.*] Well, here we are sitting around waiting for him to come home and invest his money in something he hasn't lifted his hand to get. But I can't help thinking he's acting strange. You laugh when I say he could lend you the bonds if he's not going to use them himself. But would it hurt him?

LEO: [*Slowly looking at* OSCAR.] No. No, it wouldn't.

OSCAR: People ought to help other people. But that's not always the way it happens. [BEN *enters, hangs his coat and hat in hall. Very carefully.*] And so sometimes you got to think of yourself. [*As* LEO *stares at him,* BEN *appears in the doorway.*] Morning, Ben.

6. In order to receive his interest payments.

BEN: [*Coming in, carrying his newspaper.*] Fine sunny morning. Any news from the runaways?

REGINA: [*On the staircase.*] There's no news or you would have heard it. Quite a convention so early in the morning, aren't you all? [*Goes to coffee urn.*]

OSCAR: You rising mighty late these days. Is that the way they do things in Chicago society?

BEN: [*Looking at his paper.*] Old Carter died up in Senateville. Eighty-one is a good time for us all, eh? What do you think has really happened to Horace, Regina?

REGINA: Nothing.

BEN: [*Too casually.*] You don't think maybe he never started from Baltimore and never intends to start?

REGINA: [*Irritated.*] Of course they've started. Didn't I have a letter from Alexandra? What is so strange about people arriving late? He has that cousin in Savannah he's so fond of. He may have stopped to see him. They'll be along today some time, very flattered that you and Oscar are so worried about them.

BEN: I'm a natural worrier. Especially when I am getting ready to close a business deal and one of my partners remains silent *and* invisible.

REGINA: [*Laughs.*] Oh, is that it? I thought you were worried about Horace's health.

OSCAR: Oh, that too. Who could help but worry? I'm worried. This is the first day I haven't shot since my head cold.

REGINA: [*Starts towards dining room.*] Then you haven't had your breakfast. Come along.

[OSCAR *and* LEO *follow her.*]

BEN: Regina. [*She turns at dining-room door.*] That cousin of Horace's has been dead for years and, in any case, the train does not go through Savannah.

REGINA: [*Laughs, continues into dining room, seats herself.*] Did he die? You're always remembering about people dying. [BEN *rises.*] Now I intend to eat my breakfast in peace, and read my newspaper.

BEN: [*Goes towards dining room as he talks.*] This is second breakfast for me. My first was bad. Celia ain't the cook she used to be. Too old to have taste any more. If she hadn't belonged to Mama, I'd send her off to the country.

[OSCAR *and* LEO *start to eat.* BEN *seats himself.*]

LEO: Uncle Horace will have some tales to tell, I bet. Baltimore is a lively town.

REGINA: [*To* CAL.] The grits isn't hot enough. Take it back.

CAL: Oh, yes'm. [*Calling into kitchen as he exits.*] Grits didn't hold the heat. Grits didn't hold the heat.

LEO: When I was at school three of the boys and myself took a train once and went over to Baltimore. It was so big we thought we were in Europe. I was just a kid then—

REGINA: I find it very pleasant [ADDIE *enters.*] to have breakfast alone. I hate chattering before I've had something hot. [CAL *closes the dining-room doors.*] Do be still, Leo.

[ADDIE *comes into the room, begins gathering up the cups, carries them to the large tray. Outside there are the sounds of voices. Quickly* ADDIE *runs into the hall. A few seconds later she appears again in the doorway, her arm around the shoulders of* HORACE GIDDENS, *supporting him.* HORACE *is a tall man of about forty-five. He has been good looking, but now his face is tired and ill. He walks stiffly, as if it were an enormous effort, and carefully, as if he were unsure of his balance.* ADDIE *takes off his overcoat and hangs it on the hall tree. She then helps him to a chair.*]

HORACE: How are you, Addie? How have you been?

ADDIE: I'm all right, Mr. Horace. I've just been worried about you.

[ALEXANDRA *enters. She is flushed and excited, her hat awry, her face dirty. Her arms are full of packages, but she comes quickly to* ADDIE.]

ALEXANDRA: Now don't tell me how worried you were. We couldn't help it and there was no way to send a message.

ADDIE: [*Begins to take packages from* ALEXANDRA.] Yes, sir, I was mighty worried.

ALEXANDRA: We had to stop in Mobile over night. Papa— [*Looks at him.*] Papa didn't feel well. The trip was too much for him, and I made him stop and rest— [*As* ADDIE *takes the last package.*] No, don't take that. That's father's medicine. I'll hold it. It mustn't break. Now, about the stuff outside. Papa must have his wheel chair. I'll get that and the valises—

ADDIE: [*Very happy, holding* ALEXANDRA'*s arms.*] Since when you got to carry your own valises? Since when I ain't old enough to hold a bottle of medicine? [HORACE *coughs.*] You feel all right, Mr. Horace?

HORACE: [*Nods.*] Glad to be sitting down.

ALEXANDRA: [*Opening package of medicine.*] He doesn't feel all right. [ADDIE *looks at her, then at* HORACE.] He just says that. The trip was very hard on him, and now he must go right to bed.

ADDIE: [*Looking at him carefully.*] Them fancy doctors, they give you help?

HORACE: They did their best.

ALEXANDRA: [*Has become conscious of the voices in the dining room.*] I bet Mama was worried. I better tell her we're here now. [*She starts for door.*]

HORACE: Zan. [*She stops.*] Not for a minute, dear.

ALEXANDRA: Oh, Papa, you feel bad again. I knew you did. Do you want your medicine?

HORACE: No, I don't feel that way. I'm just tired, darling. Let me rest a little.

ALEXANDRA: Yes, but Mama will be mad if I don't tell her we're here.

ADDIE: They're all in there eating breakfast.

ALEXANDRA: Oh, are they all here? Why do they *always* have to be here? I was hoping Papa wouldn't have to see anybody, that it would be nice for him and quiet.

ADDIE: Then let your papa rest for a minute.

HORACE: Addie, I bet your coffee's as good as ever. They don't have such good coffee up North. [*Looks at the urn.*] Is it as good, Addie? [ADDIE *starts for coffee urn.*]

ALEXANDRA: No. Dr. Reeves said not much coffee. Just now and then. I'm the nurse now, Addie.

ADDIE: You'd be a better one if you didn't look so dirty. Now go and take a bath, Miss Grown-up. Change your linens, get out a fresh dress and give your hair a good brushing—go on—

ALEXANDRA: Will you be all right, Papa?

ADDIE: Go on.

ALEXANDRA: [*On stairs, talks as she goes up.*] The pills Papa must take once every four hours. And the bottle only when—only if he feels very bad. Now don't move until I come back and don't talk much and remember about his medicine, Addie—

ADDIE: Ring for Belle and have her help you and then I'll make you a fresh breakfast.

ALEXANDRA: [*As she disappears.*] How's Aunt Birdie? Is she here?

ADDIE: It ain't right for you to have coffee? It will hurt you?

HORACE: [*Slowly.*] Nothing can make much difference now. Get me a cup, Addie. [*She looks at him, crosses to urn, pours a cup.*] Funny. They can't make coffee up North. [ADDIE *brings him a cup.*] They don't like red pepper, either. [*He takes the cup and gulps it greedily.*] God, that's good. You remember how I used to drink it? Ten, twelve cups a day. So strong it had to stain the cup. [*Then slowly.*] Addie, before I see anybody else, I want to know why Zan came to fetch me home. She's tried to tell me, but she doesn't seem to know herself.

ADDIE: [*Turns away.*] I don't know. All I know is big things are going on. Everybody going to be high-tone rich. Big rich. You too. All because smoke's going to start out of a building that ain't even up yet.

HORACE: I've heard about it.

ADDIE: And, er— [*Hesitates—steps to him.*] And—well, Zan, she going to marry Mr. Leo in a little while.

HORACE: [*Looks at her, then very slowly.*] What are you talking about?

ADDIE: That's right. That's the talk. God help us.

HORACE: [*Angrily.*] *What's* the talk?

ADDIE: I'm telling you. There's going to be a wedding— [*Angrily turns away.*] Over my dead body there is.

HORACE: [*After a second, quietly.*] Go and tell them I'm home.

ADDIE: [*Hesitates.*] Now you ain't to get excited. You're to be in your bed—

HORACE: Go on, Addie. Go and say I'm back. [ADDIE *opens dining-room doors. He rises with difficulty, stands stiff, as if he were in pain, facing the dining room.*]

ADDIE: Miss Regina. They're home. They got here—

REGINA: Horace! [REGINA *quickly rises, runs into the room. Warmly.*] Horace! You've finally arrived. [*As she kisses him, the others come forward, all talking together.*]

BEN: [*In doorway, carrying a napkin.*] Well, sir, you had us all mighty worried.

[*He steps forward. They shake hands.* ADDIE *exits.*]

OSCAR: You're a sight for sore eyes.

HORACE: Hello, Ben.

[LEO *enters, eating a biscuit.*]

OSCAR: And what is that costume you have on?

BIRDIE: [*Looking at* HORACE.] Now that you're home, you'll feel better. Plenty of good rest and we'll take such fine care of you. [*Stops.*] But where is Zan? I missed her so much.

OSCAR: I asked you what is that strange costume you're parading around in?

BIRDIE: [*Nervously, backing towards stairs.*] Me? Oh! It's my wrapper. I was so excited about Horace I just rushed out of the house—

OSCAR: Did you come across the square dressed that way? My dear Birdie, I—

HORACE: [*To* REGINA, *wearily.*] Yes, it's just like old times.

REGINA: [*Quickly to* OSCAR.] Now, no fights. This is a holiday.

BIRDIE: [*Runs quickly up the stairs.*] Zan! Zannie!

OSCAR: Birdie! [*She stops.*]

BIRDIE: Oh. Tell Zan I'll be back in a little while. [*Whispers.*] Sorry, Oscar. [*Exits.*]

REGINA: [*To* OSCAR *and* BEN.] Why don't you go finish your breakfast and let Horace rest for a minute?

BEN: [*Crossing to dining room with* OSCAR.] Never leave a meal unfinished. There are too many poor people who need the food. Mighty glad to see you home, Horace. Fine to have you back. Fine to have you back.

OSCAR: [*To* LEO *as* BEN *closes dining-room doors.*] Your mother has gone crazy. Running around the streets like a woman—

[*The moment* REGINA *and* HORACE *are alone, they become awkward and self-conscious.*]

REGINA: [*Laughs awkwardly.*] Well. Here we are. It's been a long time. [HORACE *smiles.*] Five months. You know, Horace, I wanted to come and be with you in the hospital, but I didn't know where my duty was. Here, or with you. But you know how much I *wanted* to come.

HORACE: That's kind of you, Regina. There was no need to come.

REGINA: Oh, but there was. Five months lying there all by yourself, no kinfolks, no friends. Don't try to tell me you didn't have a bad time of it.

HORACE: I didn't have a bad time. [*As she shakes her head, he becomes insistent.*] No, I didn't, Regina. Oh, at first when I—when I heard the news about myself—but after I got used to that, I liked it there.

REGINA: You *liked* it? [*Coldly.*] Isn't that strange. You liked it so well you didn't want to come home?

HORACE: That's not the way to put it. [*Then, kindly, as he sees her turn her head away.*] But there I was and I got kind of used to it, kind of to like lying there and thinking. [*Smiles.*] I never had much time to think before. And time's become valuable to me.

REGINA: It sounds almost like a holiday.

HORACE: [*Laughs.*] It was, sort of. The first holiday I've had since I was a little kid.

REGINA: And here I was thinking you were in pain and—

HORACE: [*Quietly.*] I was in pain.

REGINA: And instead you were having a holiday! A holiday of thinking. Couldn't you have done that here?

HORACE: I wanted to do it before I came here. I was thinking about us.

REGINA: About us? About you and me? Thinking about you and me after all these years. [*Unpleasantly.*] You shall tell me everything you thought—some day.

HORACE: [*There is silence for a minute.*] Regina. [*She turns to him.*] Why did you send Zan to Baltimore?

REGINA: Why? Because I wanted you home. You can't make anything suspicious out of that, can you?

HORACE: I didn't mean to make anything suspicious about it. [*Hesitantly, taking her hand.*] Zan said you wanted me to come home. I was so pleased at that and touched, it made me feel good.

REGINA: [*Taking away her hand, turns.*] Touched that I should want you home?

HORACE: [*Sighs.*] I'm saying all the wrong things as usual. Let's try to get along better. There isn't so much more time. Regina, what's all this crazy talk I've been hearing about Zan and Leo? Zan and Leo marrying?

REGINA: [*Turning to him, sharply.*] Who gossips so much around here?

HORACE: [*Shocked.*] Regina!

REGINA: [*Annoyed, anxious to quiet him.*] It's some foolishness that Oscar thought up. I'll explain later. I have no intention of allowing any such arrangement. It was simply a way of keeping Oscar quiet in all this business I've been writing you about—

HORACE: [*Carefully.*] What has Zan to do with any business of Oscar's? Whatever it is, you had better put it out of Oscar's head immediately. You know what I think of Leo.

REGINA: But there's no need to talk about it now.

HORACE: There is no need to talk about it ever. Not as long as I live. [HORACE *stops, slowly turns to look at her.*] As long as I live. I've been in a hospital for five months. Yet since I've been here you have not once asked me about—about my health. [*Then gently.*] Well, I suppose they've written you. I can't live very long.

REGINA: [*Coldly.*] I've never understood why people have to talk about this kind of thing.

HORACE: [*There is a silence. Then he looks up at her, his face cold.*] You misunderstand. I don't intend to gossip about my sickness. I thought it was only fair to tell you. I was not asking for your sympathy.

REGINA: [*Sharply, turns to him.*] What do the doctors think caused your bad heart?

HORACE: What do you mean?

REGINA: They didn't think it possible, did they, that your fancy women may have—

HORACE: [*Smiles unpleasantly.*] Caused my heart to be bad? I don't think that's the best scientific theory. You don't catch heart trouble in bed.

REGINA: [*Angrily.*] I didn't think you did. I only thought you might catch a bad conscience—in bed, as you say.

HORACE: I didn't tell them about my bad conscience. Or about my fancy women. Nor did I tell them that my wife has not wanted me in bed with her for—[*Sharply.*] How long is it, Regina? [REGINA *turns to him.*] Ten years? Did you bring me home for this, to make me feel guilty again? That means you want something. But you'll not make me feel guilty any more. My "thinking" has made a difference.

REGINA: I see that it has. [*She looks towards dining-room door. Then comes to him, her manner warm and friendly.*] It's foolish for us to fight this way. I didn't mean to be unpleasant. I was stupid.

HORACE: [*Wearily.*] God knows I didn't either. I came home wanting so much not to fight, and then all of a sudden there we were. I got hurt and—

REGINA: [*Hastily.*] It's all my fault. I didn't ask about—about your illness because I didn't want to remind you of it. Anyway I never believe doctors when they talk about—[*Brightly.*] when they talk like that.

HORACE: [*Not looking at her.*] Well, we'll try our best with each other. [*He rises.*]

REGINA: [*Quickly.*] I'll try. Honestly, I will. Horace, Horace, I know you're tired but, but—couldn't you stay down here a few minutes longer? I want Ben to tell you something.

HORACE: Tomorrow.

REGINA: I'd like to now. It's very important to me. It's very important to all of us. [*Gaily, as she moves toward dining room.*] Important to your beloved daughter. She'll be a very great heiress—

HORACE: Will she? That's nice.

REGINA: [*Opens doors.*] Ben, are you finished breakfast?

HORACE: Is this the mill business I've had so many letters about?

REGINA: [*To* BEN.] Horace would like to talk to you now.

HORACE: Horace would not like to talk to you now. I am very tired, Regina—

REGINA: [*Comes to him.*] Please. You've said we'll try our best with each other. I'll try. Really, I will. Please do this for me now. You will see what I've done while you've been away. How I watched your interests. [*Laughs gaily.*] And I've done very well too. But things can't be delayed any longer. Everything must be settled this week— [HORACE *sits down.* BEN *enters.* OSCAR *has stayed in the dining room, his head turned to watch them.* LEO *is pretending to read the newspaper.*] Now you must tell Horace all about it. Only be quick because he is very tired and must go to bed. [HORACE *is looking up at her. His face hardens as she speaks.*] But I think your news will be better for him than all the medicine in the world.

BEN: [*Looking at* HORACE.] It could wait. Horace may not feel like talking today.

REGINA: What an old faker you are! You know it can't wait. You know it must be finished this week. You've been just as anxious for Horace to get here as I've been.

BEN: [*Very jovial.*] I suppose I have been. And why not? Horace has done Hubbard Sons many a good turn. Why shouldn't I be anxious to help him now?

REGINA: [*Laughs.*] Help him! Help him when you need him, that's what you mean.

BEN: What a woman you married, Horace. [*Laughs awkwardly when* HORACE *does not answer.*] Well, then I'll make it quick. You know what I've been telling you for years. How I've always said that every one of us little Southern business men had great things—[*Extends his arms.*]—right beyond our finger tips. It's been my dream: my dream to make those fingers grow longer. I'm a lucky man, Horace, a lucky man. To dream and to live to get what you've dreamed of. That's *my* idea of a lucky man. [*Looks at his fingers as his arm drops slowly.*] For thirty years I've cried bring the cotton mills to the cotton. [HORACE *opens medicine bottle.*] Well, finally I got up nerve to go to Marshall Company in Chicago.

HORACE: I know all this. [*He takes the medicine.* REGINA *rises, steps to him.*]

BEN: Can I get you something?

HORACE: Some water, please.

REGINA: [*Turns quickly.*] Oh, I'm sorry. Let me. [*Brings him a glass of water. He drinks as they wait in silence.*] You fell all right now?

HORACE: Yes. You wrote me. I know all that.

[OSCAR *enters from dining room.*]

REGINA: [*Triumphantly.*] But you don't know that in the last few days Ben has agreed to give us—you, I mean—a much larger share.

HORACE: Really? That's very generous of him.

BEN: [*Laughs.*] It wasn't so generous of me. It was smart of Regina.

REGINA: [*As if she were signaling* HORACE.] I explained to Ben that perhaps you hadn't answered his letters because you didn't think he was offering you enough, and that the time was getting short and you could guess how much he needed you—

HORACE: [*Smiles at her, nods.*] And I could guess that he wants to keep control in the family?

REGINA: [*To* BEN, *triumphantly.*] Exactly. [*To* HORACE.] So I did a little bargaining for you and convinced my brothers they weren't the only Hubbards who had a business sense.

HORACE: Did you have to convince them of that? How little people know about each other! [*Laughs.*] But you'll know better about Regina next time, eh, Ben? [BEN, REGINA, HORACE *laugh together.* OSCAR'*s face is angry.*] Now let's see. We're getting a bigger share. [*Looking at* OSCAR.] Who's getting less?

BEN: Oscar.

HORACE: Well, Oscar, you've grown very unselfish. What's happened to you?

[LEO *enters from dining room.*]

BEN: [*Quickly, before* OSCAR *can answer.*] Oscar doesn't mind. Not worth fighting about now, eh, Oscar?

OSCAR: [*Angrily.*] I'll get mine in the end. You can be sure of that. I've got my son's future to think about.

HORACE: [*Sharply.*] Leo? Oh, I see. [*Puts his head back, laughs.* REGINA *looks at him nervously.*] I am beginning to see. Everybody will get theirs.

BEN: I knew you'd see it. Seventy-five thousand, and that seventy-five thousand will make you a million.

OSCAR: And how you feel? Tip-top, I bet, because that's the way you're looking.

HORACE: [*Coldly, irritated with* OSCAR'*s lie.*] Hello, Oscar. Hello, Leo, how are you?

LEO: [*Shaking hands.*] I'm fine, sir. But a lot better now that you're back.

REGINA: Now sit down. What did happen to you and where's Alexandra? I am so excited about seeing you that I almost forgot about her.

HORACE: I didn't feel good, a little weak, I guess, and we stopped over night to rest. Zan's upstairs washing off the train dirt.

REGINA: Oh, I am so sorry the trip was hard on you. I didn't think that—

HORACE: Well, it's just as if I had never been away. All of you here—

BEN: Waiting to welcome you home.

[BIRDIE *bursts in. She is wearing a flannel kimono and her face is flushed and excited.*]

BIRDIE: [*Runs to him, kisses him.*] Horace!

HORACE: [*Warmly pressing her arm.*] I was just wondering where you were, Birdie.

BIRDIE: [*Excited.*] Oh, I would have been here. I didn't know you were back until Simon said he saw the buggy. [*She draws back to look at him. Her face sobers.*] Oh, you don't look well, Horace. No, you don't.

REGINA: [*Laughs.*] Birdie, what a thing to say—

HORACE: [*Looking at* OSCAR.] Oscar thinks I look very well.

OSCAR: [*Annoyed. Turns on* LEO.] Don't stand there holding that biscuit in your hand.

LEO: Oh, well. I'll just finish my breakfast, Uncle Horace, and then I'll give you all the news about the bank— [*He exits into the dining room.*]

REGINA: [*Steps to table, leaning forward.*] It will, Horace, it will.

HORACE: I believe you. [*After a second.*] Now I can understand Oscar's self-sacrifice, but what did you have to promise Marshall Company besides the money you're putting up?

BEN: They wouldn't take promises. They wanted guarantees.

HORACE: Of what?

BEN: [*Nods.*] Water power. Free and plenty of it.

HORACE: You got them that, of course.

BEN: Cheap. You'd think the Governor of a great state would make his price a little higher. From pride, you know. [HORACE *smiles.* BEN *smiles.*] Cheap wages. "What do you mean by cheap wages?" I say to Marshall. "Less than Massachusetts," he says to me, "and that averages eight a week." "Eight a week! By God," I tell him, "*I'd* work for eight a week myself." Why, there ain't a mountain white or a town nigger but wouldn't give his right arm for three silver dollars every week, eh, Horace?

HORACE: Sure. And they'll take less than that when you get around to playing them off against each other. You can save a little money that way, Ben.

[*Angrily.*] And make them hate each other just a little more than they do now.

REGINA: What's all this about?

BEN: [*Laughs.*] There'll be no trouble from anybody, white or black. Marshall said that to me. "What about strikes? That's all we've had in Massachusetts for the last three years." I say to him, "What's a strike? I never heard of one. Come South, Marshall. We got good folks and we don't stand for any fancy fooling."

HORACE: You're right. [*Slowly.*] Well, it looks like you made a good deal for yourselves, and for Marshall, too. [*To* BEN.] Your father used to say he made the thousands and you boys would make the millions. I think he was right. [*Rises.*]

REGINA: [*They are all looking at* HORACE. *She laughs nervously.*] Millions for *us*, too.

HORACE: Us? You and me? I don't think so. We've got enough money, Regina. We'll just sit by and watch the boys grow rich. [*They watch* HORACE *tensely as he begins to move towards the staircase. He passes* LEO, *looks at him for a second.*] How's everything at the bank, Leo?

LEO: Fine, sir. Everything is fine.

HORACE: How are all the ladies in Mobile? [HORACE *turns to* REGINA, *sharply.*] Whatever made you think I'd let Zan marry—

REGINA: Do you mean that you are turning this down? Is it possible that's what you mean?

BEN: No, that's not what he means. Turning down a fortune. Horace is tired. He'd rather talk about it tomorrow—

REGINA: We can't keep putting it off this way. Oscar must be in Chicago by the end of the week with the money and contracts.

OSCAR: [*Giggles, pleased.*] Yes, sir. Got to be there end of the week. No sense going without the money.

REGINA: [*Tensely.*] I've waited long enough for your answer. I'm not going to wait any longer.

HORACE: [*Very deliberately.*] I'm very tired now, Regina.

BEN: [*Hastily.*] Now, Horace probably has his reasons. Things he'd like explained. Tomorrow will do. I can—

REGINA: [*Turns to* BEN, *sharply.*] I want to know his reasons now! [*Turns back to* HORACE.]

HORACE: [*As he climbs the steps.*] I don't know them all myself. Let's leave it at that.

REGINA: We shall not leave it at that! We have waited for you here like children. Waited for you to come home.

HORACE: So that you could invest my money. So this is why you wanted me home? Well, I had hoped— [*Quietly.*] If you are disappointed, Regina, I'm sorry. But I must do what I think best. We'll talk about it another day.

REGINA: We'll talk about it now. Just you and me.

HORACE: [*Looks down at her. His voice is tense.*] Please, Regina. It's been a hard trip. I don't feel well. Please leave me alone now.

REGINA: [*Quietly.*] I want to talk to you, Horace. I'm coming up. [*He looks at her for a minute, then moves on again out of sight. She begins to climb the stairs.*]

BEN: [*Softly.* REGINA *turns to him as he speaks.*] Sometimes it is better to wait for the sun to rise again. [*She does not answer.*] And sometimes, as our mother used to tell you, [REGINA *starts up stairs.*] it's unwise for a good-looking woman to frown. [BEN *rises, moves towards stairs.*] Softness and a smile do more to the heart of men—

[*She disappears.* BEN *stands looking up the stairs. There is a long silence. Then, suddenly,* OSCAR *giggles.*]

OSCAR: Let us hope she'll change his mind. Let us hope.

[*After a second* BEN *crosses to table, picks up his newspaper.* OSCAR *looks at* BEN. *The silence makes* LEO *uncomfortable.*]

LEO: The paper says twenty-seven cases of yellow fever in New Orleans. Guess the flood-waters caused it. [*Nobody pays attention.*] Thought they were building the levees high enough. Like the niggers always say: a man born of woman can't build nothing high enough for the Mississippi. [*Gets no answer. Gives an embarrassed laugh.*]

[*Upstairs there is the sound of voices. The voices are not loud, but* BEN, OSCAR, LEO *become conscious of them.* LEO *crosses to landing, looks up, listens.*]

OSCAR: [*Pointing up.*] Now just suppose she don't change his mind? Just suppose he keeps on refusing?

BEN: [*Without conviction.*] He's tired. It was a mistake to talk to him today. He's a sick man, but he isn't a crazy one.

OSCAR: [*Giggles.*] But just suppose he is crazy. What then?

BEN: [*Puts down his paper, peers at* OSCAR.] Then we'll go outside for the money. There's plenty who would give it.

OSCAR: And plenty who will want a lot for what they give. The ones who are rich enough to give will be smart enough to want. That means we'd be working for them, don't it, Ben?

BEN: You don't have to tell me the things I told you six months ago.

OSCAR: Oh, you're right not to worry. She'll change his mind. She always has. [*There is a silence. Suddenly* REGINA's *voice becomes louder and sharper. All of them begin to listen now. Slowly* BEN *rises, goes to listen by the staircase.* OSCAR, *watching him, smiles. As they listen* REGINA's *voice becomes very loud.* HORACE's *voice is no longer heard.*] Maybe. But I don't believe it. I never did believe he was going in with us.

BEN: [*Turning on him.*] What the hell do you expect me to do?

OSCAR: [*Mildly.*] Nothing. You done your almighty best. Nobody could blame you if the whole thing just dripped away right through our fingers. You can't do a thing. But there may be something I could do for us. [OSCAR *rises.*] Or, I might better say, Leo could do for us. [BEN *stops, turns, looks at* OSCAR.

LEO *is staring at* OSCAR.] Ain't that true, son? Ain't it true you might be able to help your own kinfolks?

LEO: [*Nervously taking a step to him.*] Papa, I—

BEN: [*Slowly.*] How would he help us, Oscar?

OSCAR: Leo's got a friend. Leo's friend owns eighty-eight thousand dollars in Union Pacific bonds. [BEN *turns to look at* LEO.] Leo's friend don't look at the bonds much—not for five or six months at a time.

BEN: [*After a pause.*] Union Pacific. Uh, huh. Let me understand. Leo's friend would—would lend him these bonds and he—

OSCAR: [*Nods.*] Would be kind enough to lend them to us.

BEN: Leo.

LEO: [*Excited, comes to him.*] Yes, sir?

BEN: When would your friend be wanting the bonds back?

LEO: [*Very nervous.*] I don't know. I—well, I—

OSCAR: [*Sharply. Steps to him.*] You told me he won't look at them until Fall—

LEO: Oh, that's right. But I—not till Fall. Uncle Horace never—

BEN: [*Sharply.*] Be still.

OSCAR: [*Smiles at* LEO.] Your uncle doesn't wish to know your friend's name.

LEO: [*Starts to laugh.*] That's a good one. Not know his name—

OSCAR: Shut up, Leo! [LEO *turns away slowly, moves to table.* BEN *turns to* OSCAR.] He won't look at them again until September. That gives us five months. Leo will return the bonds in three months. And we'll have no trouble raising the money once the mills are going up. Will Marshall accept bonds?

[BEN *stops to listen to sudden sharp voices from above. The voices are now very angry and very loud.*]

BEN: [*Smiling.*] Why not? Why not? [*Laughs.*] Good. We are lucky. We'll take the loan from Leo's friend—I think he will make a safer partner than our sister. [*Nods towards stairs. Turns to* LEO.] How soon can you get them?

LEO: Today. Right now. They're in the safe-deposit box and—

BEN: [*Sharply.*] I don't want to know where they are.

OSCAR: [*Laughs.*] We will keep it secret from you. [*Pats* BEN'*s arm.*]

BEN: [*Smiles.*] Good. Draw a check for our part. You can take the night train for Chicago. Well, Oscar [*holds out his hand*], good luck to us.

OSCAR: Leo will be taken care of?

LEO: I'm entitled to Uncle Horace's share. I'd enjoy being a partner—

BEN: [*Turns to stare at him.*] You would? You can go to hell, you little—[*Starts towards* LEO.]

OSCAR: [*Nervously.*] Now, now. He didn't mean that. I only want to be sure he'll get something out of all this.

BEN: Of course. We'll take care of him. We won't have any trouble about that. I'll see you at the store.

OSCAR: [*Nods.*] That's settled then. Come on, son. [*Starts for door.*]

LEO: [*Puts out his hand.*] I didn't mean just that. I was only going to say what a great day this was for me and—

[BEN *ignores his hand.*]

BEN: Go on.

[LEO *looks at him, turns, follows* OSCAR *out.* BEN *stands where he is, thinking. Again the voices upstairs can be heard.* REGINA'S *voice is high and furious.* BEN *looks up, smiles, winces at the noise.*]

ALEXANDRA: [*Upstairs.*] Mama—Mama—don't . . . [*The noise of running footsteps is heard and* ALEXANDRA *comes running down the steps, speaking as she comes.*] Uncle Ben! Uncle Ben! Please go up. Please make Mama stop. Uncle Ben, he's sick, he's so sick. How can Mama talk to him like that—please, make her stop. She'll—

BEN: Alexandra, you have a tender heart.

ALEXANDRA: [*Crying.*] Go on up, Uncle Ben, please—

[*Suddenly the voices stop. A second later there is the sound of a door being slammed.*]

BEN: Now you see. Everything is over. Don't worry. [*He starts for the door.*] Alexandra, I want you to tell your mother how sorry I am that I had to leave. And don't worry so, my dear. Married folk frequently raise their voices, unfortunately. [*He starts to put on his hat and coat as* REGINA *appears on the stairs.*]

ALEXANDRA: [*Furiously.*] How can you treat Papa like this? He's sick. He's very sick. Don't you know that? I won't let you.

REGINA: Mind your business, Alexandra. [*To* BEN. *Her voice is cold and calm.*] How much longer can you wait for the money?

BEN: [*Putting on his coat.*] He has refused? My, that's too bad.

REGINA: He will change his mind. I'll find a way to make him. What's the longest you can wait now?

BEN: I could wait until next week. But I can't wait until next week. [*He giggles, pleased at the joke.*] I could but I can't. Could and can't. Well, I must go now. I'm very late—

REGINA: [*Coming downstairs towards him.*] You're not going. I want to talk to you.

BEN: I was about to give Alexandra a message for you. I wanted to tell you that Oscar is going to Chicago tonight, so we can't be here for our usual Friday supper.

REGINA: [*Tensely.*] Oscar is going to Chi— [*Softly.*] What do you mean?

BEN: Just that. Everything is settled. He's going on to deliver to Marshall—

REGINA: [*Taking a step to him.*] I demand to know what— You are lying. You are trying to scare me. *You haven't got the money.* How could you have it? You can't have— [BEN *laughs.*] You will wait until I—

[HORACE *comes into view on the landing.*]

BEN: You are getting out of hand. Since when do I take orders from you?

REGINA: Wait, you—[BEN *stops.*] How *can* he go to Chicago? Did a ghost arrive with the money? [BEN *starts for the hall.*] I don't believe you. Come back here. [REGINA *starts after him.*] Come back here, you— [*The door slams. She stops in the doorway, staring, her fists clenched. After a pause she turns slowly.*]

HORACE: [*Very quietly.*] It's a great day when you and Ben cross swords. I've been waiting for it for years.

ALEXANDRA: Papa, Papa, please go back! You will—

HORACE: And so they don't need you, and so you will not have your millions, after all.

REGINA: [*Turns slowly.*] You hate to see anybody live now, don't you? You hate to think that I'm going to be alive and have what I want.

HORACE: I should have known you'd think that was the reason.

REGINA: Because you're going to die and you know you're going to die.

ALEXANDRA: [*Shrilly.*] Mama! Don't— Don't listen, Papa. Just don't listen. Go away—

HORACE: Not to keep you from getting what you want. Not even partly that. [*Holding to the rail.*] I'm sick of you, sick of this house, sick of my life here. I'm sick of your brothers and their dirty tricks to make a dime. There must be better ways of getting rich than cheating niggers on a pound of bacon. Why should I give you the money? [*Very angrily.*] To pound the bones of this town to make dividends for you to spend? You wreck the town, you and your brothers, *you* wreck the town and live on it. Not me. Maybe it's easy for the dying to be honest. But it's not my fault I'm dying. [ADDIE *enters, stands at door quietly.*] I'll do no more harm now. I've done enough. I'll die my own way. And I'll do it without making the world any worse. I leave that to you.

REGINA: [*Looks up at him slowly, calmly.*] I hope you die. I hope you die soon. [*Smiles.*] I'll be waiting for you to die.

ALEXANDRA: [*Shrieking.*] Papa! Don't—Don't listen—Don't—

ADDIE: Come here, Zan. Come out of this room.

[ALEXANDRA *runs quickly to* ADDIE, *who holds her.* HORACE *turns slowly and starts upstairs.*]

CURTAIN

ACT III

SCENE: *Same as Act I. Two weeks later. It is late afternoon and it is raining.*

AT RISE: HORACE *is sitting near the window in a wheel chair. On the table next to him is a safe-deposit box, and a small bottle of medicine.* BIRDIE *and* ALEXANDRA *are playing the piano. On a chair is a large sewing basket.*

BIRDIE: [*Counting for* ALEXANDRA.] One and two and three and four. One and two and three and four. [*Nods—turns to* HORACE.] We once played together, Horace. Remember?

HORACE: [*Has been looking out of the window.*] What, Birdie?

BIRDIE: We played together. You and me.

ALEXANDRA: *Papa* used to play?

BIRDIE: Indeed he did. [ADDIE *appears at the door in a large kitchen apron. She is wiping her hands on a towel.*] He played the fiddle and very well, too.

ALEXANDRA: [*Turns to smile at* HORACE.] I never knew—

ADDIE: Where's your mama?

ALEXANDRA: Gone to Miss Safronia's to fit her dresses.

[ADDIE *nods, starts to exit.*]

HORACE: Addie.

ADDIE: Yes, Mr. Horace.

HORACE: [*Speaks as if he had made a sudden decision.*] Tell Cal to get on his things. I want him to go an errand.

[ADDIE *nods, exits.* HORACE *moves nervously in his chair, looks out of the window.*]

ALEXANDRA: [*Who has been watching him.*] It's too bad it's been raining all day, Papa. But you can go out in the yard tomorrow. Don't be restless.

HORACE: I'm not restless, darling.

BIRDIE: I remember so well the time we played together, your papa and me. It was the first time Oscar brought me here to supper. I had never seen all the Hubbards together before, and you know what a ninny I am and how shy. [*Turns to look at* HORACE.] You said you could play the fiddle and you'd be much obliged if I'd play with you. *I* was obliged to *you*, all right, all right. [*Laughs when he does not answer her.*] Horace, you haven't heard a word I've said.

HORACE: Birdie, when did Oscar get back from Chicago?

BIRDIE: Yesterday. Hasn't he been here yet?

ALEXANDRA: [*Stops playing.*] No. Neither has Uncle Ben since—since that day.

BIRDIE: Oh, I didn't know it was *that* bad. Oscar never tells me anything—

HORACE: [*Smiles, nods.*] The Hubbards have had their great quarrel. I knew it would come some day. [*Laughs.*] It came.

ALEXANDRA: It came. It certainly came all right.

BIRDIE: [*Amazed.*] But Oscar was in such a good humor when he got home, I didn't—

HORACE: Yes, I can understand that.

[ADDIE *enters carrying a large tray with glasses, a carafe of elderberry wine and a plate of cookies, which she puts on the table.*]

ALEXANDRA: Addie! A party! What for?

ADDIE: Nothing for. I had the fresh butter, so I made the cakes, and a little elderberry does the stomach good in the rain.

BIRDIE: Isn't this nice! A party just for us. Let's play party music, Zan. [ALEXANDRA *begins to play a gay piece.*]

ADDIE: [*To* HORACE, *wheeling his chair to center.*] Come over here, Mr. Horace, and don't be thinking so much. A glass of elderberry will do more good.

[ALEXANDRA *reaches for a cake.* BIRDIE *pours herself a glass of wine.*]

ALEXANDRA: Good cakes, Addie. It's nice here. Just us. Be nice if it could always be this way.

BIRDIE: [*Nods happily.*] Quiet and restful.

ADDIE: Well, it won't be that way long. Little while now, even sitting here, you'll hear the red bricks going into place. The next day the smoke'll be pushing out the chimneys and by church time that Sunday every human born of woman will be living on chicken. That's how Mr. Ben's been telling the story.

HORACE: [*Looks at her.*] They believe it that way?

ADDIE: Believe it? They use to believing what Mr. Ben orders. There ain't been so much talk around here since Sherman's army didn't come near.[7]

HORACE: [*Softly.*] They are fools.

ADDIE: [*Nods, sits down with the sewing basket.*] You ain't born in the South unless you're a fool.

BIRDIE: [*Has drunk another glass of wine.*] But we didn't play together after that night. Oscar said he didn't like me to play on the piano. [*Turns to* ALEXANDRA.] You know what he said that night?

ALEXANDRA: Who?

BIRDIE: Oscar. He said that music made him nervous. He said he just sat and waited for the next note. [ALEXANDRA *laughs.*] He wasn't poking fun. He meant it. Ah, well—[*She finishes her glass, shakes her head.* HORACE *looks at her, smiles.*] Your papa don't like to admit it, but he's been mighty kind to me all these years. [*Running the back of her hand along his sleeve.*] Often he'd step in when somebody said something and once—[*She stops, turns away, her face still.*] Once he stopped Oscar from—[*She stops, turns. Quickly.*] I'm sorry I said that. Why, here I am so happy and yet I think about bad things. [*Laughs nervously.*] That's not right, now, is it?

[*She pours a drink.* CAL *appears in the door. He has on an old coat and is carrying a torn umbrella.*]

ALEXANDRA: Have a cake, Cal.

CAL: [*Comes in, takes a cake.*] Yes'm. You want me, Mr. Horace?

HORACE: What time is it, Cal?

CAL: 'Bout ten minutes before it's five.

HORACE: All right. Now you walk yourself down to the bank.

CAL: It'll be closed. Nobody'll be there but Mr. Manders, Mr. Joe Horns, Mr. Leo—

HORACE: Go in the back way. They'll be at the table, going over the day's business. [*Points to the deposit box.*] See that box?

CAL: [*Nods.*] Yes, sir.

7. Union general William Tecumseh Sherman (1820–1891) fought vigorously in the Deep South in the Civil War, most notably in his famous and destructive march from Atlanta to Savannah, November–December 1864.

HORACE: You tell Mr. Manders that Mr. Horace says he's much obliged to him for bringing the box, it arrived all right.

CAL: [*Bewildered.*] He know you got the box. He bring it himself Wednesday. I opened the door to him and he say, "Hello, Cal, coming on to summer weather."

HORACE: You say just what I tell you. Understand?

[BIRDIE *pours another drink, stands at table.*]

CAL: No, sir. I ain't going to say I understand. I'm going down and tell a man he give you something he already know he give you, and you say "understand."

HORACE: Now, Cal.

CAL: Yes, sir. I just going to say you obliged for the box coming all right. I ain't going to understand it, but I'm going to say it.

HORACE: And tell him I want him to come over here after supper, and to bring Mr. Sol Fowler with him.

CAL: [*Nods.*] He's to come after supper and bring Mr. Sol Fowler, your attorney-*at*-law, with him.

HORACE: [*Smiles.*] That's right. Just walk right in the back room and say your piece. [*Slowly.*] In front of everybody.

CAL: Yes, sir. [*Mumbles to himself as he exits.*]

ALEXANDRA: [*Who has been watching* HORACE.] Is anything the matter, Papa?

HORACE: Oh, no. Nothing.

ADDIE: Miss Birdie, that elderberry going to give you a headache spell.

BIRDIE: [*Beginning to be drunk. Gaily.*] Oh, I don't think so. I don't think it will.

ALEXANDRA: [*As* HORACE *puts his hand to this throat.*] Do you want your medicine, Papa?

HORACE: No, no. I'm all right, darling.

BIRDIE: Mama used to give me elderberry wine when I was a little girl. For hiccoughs. [*Laughs.*] You know, I don't think people get hiccoughs any more. Isn't that funny? [BIRDIE *laughs.* HORACE *and* ALEXANDRA *laugh.*] I used to get hiccoughs just when I shouldn't have.

ADDIE: [*Nods.*] And nobody gets growing pains no more. That is funny. Just as if there was some style in what you get. One year an ailment's stylish and the next year it ain't.

BIRDIE: [*Turns.*] I remember. It was my first big party, at Lionnet I mean, and I was so excited, and there I was with hiccoughs and Mama laughing. [*Softly. Looking at carafe.*] Mama always laughed. [*Picks up carafe.*] A big party, a lovely dress from Mr. Worth[8] in Paris, France, and hiccoughs. [*Pours drink.*] My brother pounding me on the back and Mama with the elderberry bottle, laughing at me. Everybody was on their way to come, and I was such a ninny, hiccoughing away. [*Drinks.*] You know, that was the first day I ever saw Oscar Hubbard. The Ballongs were selling their horses and he was going there to buy. He passed and lifted his hat—we could see him from the window—and my brother, to tease Mama, said maybe we should have invited

8. Charles Frederick Worth (1825–1895), founder of the influential fashion house Maison Worth.

the Hubbards to the party. He said Mama didn't like them because they kept a store, and he said that was old-fashioned of her. [*Her face lights up.*] And then, and *then*, I saw Mama angry for the first time in my life. She said that wasn't the reason. She said she was old-fashioned, but not that way. She said she was old-fashioned enough not to like people who killed animals they couldn't use, and who made their money charging awful interest to poor, ignorant niggers and cheating them on what they bought. She was very angry, Mama was. I had never seen her face like that. And then suddenly she laughed and said, "Look, I've frightened Birdie out of the hiccoughs." [*Her head drops. Then softly.*] And so she had. They were all gone. [*Moves to sofa, sits.*]

ADDIE: Yeah, they got mighty well off cheating niggers. Well, there are people who eat the earth and eat all the people on it like in the Bible with the locusts.[9] Then there are people who stand around and watch them eat it. [*Softly.*] Sometimes I think it ain't right to stand and watch them do it.

BIRDIE: [*Thoughtfully.*] Like I say, if we could only go back to Lionnet. Everybody'd be better there. They'd be good and kind. I like people to be kind. [*Pours drink.*] Don't you, Horace; don't you like people to be kind?

HORACE: Yes, Birdie.

BIRDIE: [*Very drunk now.*] Yes, that was the first day I ever saw Oscar. Who would have thought— [*Quickly.*] You all want to know something? Well, I don't like Leo. My very own son, and I don't like him. [*Laughs, gaily.*] My, I guess I even like Oscar more.

ALEXANDRA: Why did you marry Uncle Oscar?

ADDIE: [*Sharply.*] That's no question for you to be asking.

HORACE: [*Sharply.*] Why not? She's heard enough around here to ask anything.

ALEXANDRA: Aunt Birdie, why did you marry Uncle Oscar?

BIRDIE: I don't know. I thought I liked him. He was kind to me and I thought it was because he liked me too. But that wasn't the reason— [*Wheels on* ALEXANDRA.] Ask why *he* married *me*. I can tell you that: He's told it to me often enough.

ADDIE: [*Leaning forward.*] Miss Birdie, don't—

BIRDIE: [*Speaking very rapidly, tensely.*] My family was good and the cotton on Lionnet's fields was better. Ben Hubbard wanted the cotton and [*Rises.*] Oscar Hubbard married it for him. He was kind to me, then. He used to smile at me. He hasn't smiled at me since. Everybody knew that's what he married me for. [ADDIE *rises.*] Everybody but me. Stupid, stupid me.

ALEXANDRA: [*To* HORACE, *holding his hand, softly.*] I see. [*Hesitates.*] Papa, I mean—when you feel better couldn't we go away? I mean, by ourselves. Couldn't we find a way to go—

HORACE: Yes, I know what you mean. We'll try to find a way. I promise you, darling.

ADDIE: [*Moves to* BIRDIE.] Rest a bit, Miss Birdie. You get talking like this you'll get a headache and—

BIRDIE: [*Sharply, turning to her.*] I've never had a headache in my life. [*Begins*

9. Exodus 10: 12–16.

to cry hysterically.] You know it as well as I do. [*Turns to* ALEXANDRA.] I never had a headache, Zan. That's a lie they tell for me. I drink. All by myself, in my own room, by myself, I drink. Then, when they want to hide it, they say, "Birdie's got a headache again"—

ALEXANDRA: [*Comes to her quickly.*] Aunt Birdie.

BIRDIE: [*Turning away.*] Even you won't like me now. You won't like me any more.

ALEXANDRA: I love you. I'll always love you.

BIRDIE: [*Furiously.*] Well, don't Don't love me. Because in twenty years you'll just be like me. They'll do all the same things to you. [*Begins to laugh hysterically.*] You know what? In twenty-two years I haven't had a whole day of happiness. Oh, a little, like today with you all. But never a single, whole day. I say to myself, if only I had one more *whole* day, then— [*The laugh stops.*] And that's the way you'll be. And you'll trail after them, just like me, hoping they won't be so mean that day or say something to make you feel so bad—only you'll be worse off because you haven't got my Mama to remember— [*Turns away, her head drops. She stands quietly, swaying a little, holding onto the sofa.* ALEXANDRA *leans down, puts her cheek on* BIRDIE'S *arm.*]

ALEXANDRA: [*To* BIRDIE.] I guess we were all trying to make a happy day. You know, we sit around and try to pretend nothing's happened. We try to pretend we are not here. We make believe we are just by ourselves, some place else, and it doesn't seem to work. [*Kisses* BIRDIE'S *hand.*] Come now, Aunt Birdie, I'll walk you home. You and me. [*She takes* BIRDIE'S *arm. They move slowly out.*]

BIRDIE: [*Softly as they exit.*] You and me.

ADDIE: [*After a minute.*] Well. First time I ever heard Miss Birdie say a word. [HORACE *looks at her.*] Maybe it's good for her. I'm just sorry Zan had to hear it. [HORACE *moves his head as if he were uncomfortable.*] You feel bad, don't you? [*He shrugs.*]

HORACE: So you didn't want Zan to hear? It would be nice to let her stay innocent, like Birdie at her age. Let her listen now. Let her see everything. How else is she going to know that she's got to get away? I'm trying to show her that. I'm trying, but I've only got a little time left. She can even hate me when I'm dead, if she'll only learn to hate and fear this.

ADDIE: Mr. Horace—

HORACE: Pretty soon there'll be nobody to help her but you.

ADDIE: [*Crossing to him.*] What can I do?

HORACE: Take her away.

ADDIE: How can I do that? Do you think they'd let me just go away with her?

HORACE: I'll fix it so they can't stop you when you're ready to go. You'll go, Addie?

ADDIE: [*After a second, softly.*] Yes, sir. I promise.

[*He touches her arm, nods.*]

HORACE: [*Quietly.*] I'm going to have Sol Fowler make me a new will. They'll make trouble, but you make Zan stand firm and Fowler'll do the rest. Addie,

I'd like to leave you something for yourself. I always wanted to.

ADDIE: [*Laughs.*] Don't you do that, Mr. Horace. A nigger woman in a white man's will! I'd never get it nohow.

HORACE: I know. But upstairs in the armoire drawer there's seventeen hundred dollar bills. It's money left from my trip. It's in an envelope with your name. It's for you.

ADDIE: Seventeen hundred dollar bills! My God, Mr. Horace, I won't know how to count up that high. [*Shyly.*] It's mighty kind and good of you. I don't know what to say for thanks—

CAL: [*Appears in doorway.*] I'm back. [*No answer.*] I'm back.

ADDIE: So we see.

HORACE: Well?

CAL: Nothing. I just went down and spoke my piece. Just like you told me. I say, "Mr. Horace he thank you mightily for the safe box arriving in good shape and he say you come right after supper to his house and bring Mr. Attorney-at-law Sol Fowler with you." Then I wipe my hands on my coat. Every time I ever told a lie in my whole life, I wipe my hands right after. Can't help doing it. Well, while I'm wiping my hands, Mr. Leo jump up and say to me, "What box? What you talking about?"

HORACE: [*Smiles.*] Did he?

CAL: And Mr. Leo say he got to leave a little early cause he got something to do. And then Mr. Manders say Mr. Leo should sit right down and finish up his work and stop acting like somebody made him Mr. President. So he sit down. Now, just like I told you, Mr. Manders was mighty surprised with the message because he knows right well he brought the box—[*Points to box, sighs.*] But he took it all right. Some men take everything easy and some do not.

HORACE: [*Puts his head back, laughs.*] Mr. Leo was telling the truth; he *has* got something to do. I hope Manders don't keep him too long. [*Outside there is the sound of voices.* CAL *exits.* ADDIE *crosses quickly to* HORACE, *puts basket on table, begins to wheel his chair towards the stairs. Sharply.*] No. Leave me where I am.

ADDIE: But that's Miss Regina coming back.

HORACE: [*Nods, looking at door.*] Go away, Addie.

ADDIE: [*Hesitates.*] Mr. Horace. Don't talk no more today. You don't feel well and it won't do no good—

HORACE: [*As he hears footsteps in the hall.*] Go on.

[*She looks at him for a second, then picks up her sewing from table and exits as* REGINA *comes in from hall.* HORACE'S *chair is now so placed that he is in front of the table with the medicine.* REGINA *stands in the hall, shakes umbrella, stands it in the corner, takes off her cloak and throws it over the banister. She stares at* HORACE.]

REGINA: [*As she takes off her gloves.*] We had agreed that you were to stay in your part of this house and I in mine. This room is *my* part of the house. Please don't come down here again.

HORACE: I won't.

REGINA: [*Crosses towards bell-cord.*] I'll get Cal to take you upstairs.

HORACE: [*Smiles.*] Before you do I want to tell you that after all, we have invested our money in Hubbard Sons and Marshall, Cotton Manufacturers.

REGINA: [*Stops, turns, stares at him.*] What are you talking about? You haven't seen Ben— When did you change your mind?

HORACE: I didn't change my mind. *I* didn't invest the money. [*Smiles.*] It was invested for me.

REGINA: [*Angrily.*] What—?

HORACE: I had eighty-eight thousand dollars' worth of Union Pacific bonds in that safe-deposit box. They are not there now. Go and look. [*As she stares at him, he points to the box.*] Go and look, Regina. [*She crosses quickly to the box, opens it.*] Those bonds are as negotiable as money.

REGINA: [*Turns back to him.*] What kind of joke are you playing now? Is this for my benefit?

HORACE: I don't look in that box very often, but three days ago, on Wednesday it was, because I had made a decision—

REGINA: I want to know what you are talking about.

HORACE: [*Sharply.*] Don't interrupt me again. Because I had made a decision, I sent for the box. The bonds were gone. Eighty-eight thousand dollars gone. [*He smiles at her.*]

REGINA: [*After a moment's silence, quietly.*] Do you think I'm crazy enough to believe what you're saying?

HORACE: [*Shrugs.*] Believe anything you like.

REGINA: [*Stares at him, slowly.*] Where did they go to?

HORACE: They are in Chicago. With Mr. Marshall, I should guess.

REGINA: What did they do? Walk to Chicago? Have you really gone crazy?

HORACE: Leo took the bonds.

REGINA: [*Turns sharply then speaks softly, without conviction.*] I don't believe it.

HORACE: [*Leans forward.*] I wasn't there but I can guess what happened. This fine gentleman, to whom you were willing to marry your daughter, took the keys and opened the box. You remember that the day of the fight Oscar went to Chicago? Well, he went with my bonds that his son Leo had stolen for him. [*Pleasantly.*] And for Ben, of course, too.

REGINA: [*Slowly, nods.*] When did you find out the bonds were gone?

HORACE: Wednesday night.

REGINA: I thought that's what you said. Why have you waited three days to do anything? [*Suddenly laughs.*] This *will* make a fine story.

HORACE: [*Nods.*] Couldn't it?

REGINA: [*Still laughing.*] A fine story to hold over their heads. How could they be such fools? [*Turns to him.*]

HORACE: But I'm not going to hold it over their heads.

REGINA: [*The laugh stops.*] What?

HORACE: [*Turns his chair to face her*] I'm going to let them keep the bonds—as a loan from you. An eighty-eight-thousand-dollar loan; they should be grateful to you. They will be, I think.

REGINA: [*Slowly, smiles.*] I see. You are punishing me. But I won't let you punish me. If you won't do anything, I will. Now. [*She starts for door.*]

HORACE: You won't do anything. Because you can't. [REGINA *stops.*] It won't do you any good to make trouble because I shall simply say that I lent them the bonds.

REGINA: [*Slowly.*] You would do that?

HORACE: Yes. For once in your life I am tying your hands. There is nothing for you to do.

[*There is silence. Then she sits down.*]

REGINA: I see. You are going to lend them the bonds and let them keep all the profit they make on them, and there is nothing I can do about it. Is that right?

HORACE: Yes.

REGINA: [*Softly.*] Why did you say that I was making this gift?

HORACE: I was coming to that. I am going to make a new will, Regina, leaving you eighty-eight thousand dollars in Union Pacific bonds. The rest will go to Zan. It's true that your brothers have borrowed your share for a little while. After my death I advise you to talk to Ben and Oscar. They won't admit anything and Ben, I think, will be smart enough to see that he's safe. Because I knew about the theft and said nothing. Nor will I say anything as long as I live. Is that clear to you?

REGINA: [*Nods, softly, without looking at him.*] You will not say anything as long as you live.

HORACE: That's right. And by that time they will probably have replaced your bonds, and then they'll belong to you and nobody but us will ever know what happened. [*Stops, smiles.*] They'll be around any minute to see what I am going to do. I took good care to see that word reached Leo. They'll be mighty relieved to know I'm going to do nothing and Ben will think it all a capital joke on you. And that will be the end of that. There's nothing you can do to them, nothing you can do to me.

REGINA: You hate me very much.

HORACE: No.

REGINA: Oh, I think you do. [*Puts her head back, sighs.*] Well, we haven't been very good together. Anyway, I don't hate you either. I have only contempt for you. I've always had.

HORACE: From the very first?

REGINA: I think so.

HORACE: I was in love with *you*. But why did *you* marry *me?*

REGINA: I was lonely when I was young.

HORACE: *You* were lonely?

REGINA: Not the way people usually mean. Lonely for all the things I wasn't going to get. Everybody in this house was so busy and there was so little place for what I wanted. I wanted the world. Then, and then— [*Smiles.*] Papa died and left the money to Ben and Oscar.

HORACE: And you married me?

REGINA: Yes, I thought—But I was wrong. You were a small-town clerk then. You haven't changed.

HORACE: [*Nods, smiles.*] And that wasn't what you wanted.

REGINA: No. No, it wasn't what I wanted. [*Pauses, leans back, pleasantly.*] It took me a little while to find out I had made a mistake. As for you—I don't know. It was almost as if I couldn't stand the kind of man you were— [*Smiles, softly.*] I used to lie there at night, praying you wouldn't come near—

HORACE: Really? It was as bad as that?

REGINA: [*Nods.*] Remember when I went to Doctor Sloan and I told you he said there was something the matter with me and that you shouldn't touch me any more?

HORACE: I remember.

REGINA: But you believed it. I couldn't understand that. I couldn't understand that anybody could be such a soft fool. That was when I began to despise you.

HORACE: [*Puts his hand to his throat, looks at the bottle of medicine on table.*] Why didn't you leave me?

REGINA: I told you I married you for something. It turned out it was only for this. [*Carefully.*] This wasn't what I wanted, but it was something. I never thought about it much but if I had [HORACE *puts his hand to his throat.*] I'd have known that you would die before I would. But I couldn't have known that you would get heart trouble so early and so bad. I'm lucky, Horace. I've always been lucky. [HORACE *turns slowly to the medicine.*] I'll be lucky again.

[HORACE *looks at her. The he puts his hand to his throat. Because he cannot reach the bottle he moves the chair closer. He reaches for the medicine, takes out the cork, picks up the spoon. The bottle slips and smashes on the table. He draws in his breath, gasps.*]

HORACE: Please. Tell Addie— The other bottle is upstairs. [REGINA *has not moved. She does not move now. He stares at her. Then, suddenly as if he understood, he raises his voice. It is a panic-stricken whisper, too small to be heard outside the room.*] Addie! Addie! Come—

[*Stops as he hears the softness of his voice. He makes a sudden, furious spring from the chair to the stairs, taking the first few steps as if he were a desperate runner. On the fourth step he slips, gasps, grasps the rail, makes a great effort to reach the landing. When he reaches the landing, he is on his knees. His knees give way, he falls on the landing, out of view.* REGINA *has not turned during his climb up the stairs. Now she waits a second. Then she goes below the landing, speaks up.*]

REGINA: Horace. Horace. [*When there is no answer, she turns, calls.*] Addie! Cal! Come in here. [*She starts up the steps.* ADDIE *and* CAL *appear. Both run towards the stairs.*] He's had an attack. Come up here. [*They run up the steps quickly.*]

CAL: My God. Mr. Horace—

[*They cannot be seen now.*]

REGINA: [*Her voice comes from the head of the stairs.*] Be still, Cal. Bring him in here.

[*Before the footsteps and the voices have completely died away,* ALEXANDRA *appears in the hall door, in her raincloak and hood. She comes into the room, begins to unfasten the cloak, suddenly looks around, sees the empty wheel chair, begins to move swiftly as if to look in the dining room. At the same moment* ADDIE *runs down the stairs.* ALEXANDRA *turns and stares up at* ADDIE.]

ALEXANDRA: Addie! What?

ADDIE: [*Takes* ALEXANDRA *by the shoulders.*] I'm going for the doctor. Go upstairs.

[ALEXANDRA *looks at her, then quickly breaks away and runs up the steps.* ADDIE *exits. The stage is empty for a minute. Then the front door bell begins to ring. When there is no answer, it rings again. A second later* LEO *appears in the hall, talking as he comes in.*]

LEO: [*Very nervous.*] Hello. [*Irritably.*] Never saw any use ringing a bell when a door was open. If you are going to ring a bell, then somebody should answer it. [*Gets in the room, looks around, puzzled, listens, hears no sound.*] Aunt Regina. [*He moves around restlessly.*] Addie. [*Waits.*] Where the hell— [*Crosses to the bell cord, rings it impatiently, waits, gets no answer, calls.*] Cal! Cal!

[CAL *appears on the stair landing.*]

CAL: [*His voice is soft, shaken.*] Mr. Leo. Miss Regina says you stop that screaming noise.

LEO: [*Angrily.*] Where is everybody?

CAL: Mr. Horace he got an attack. He's bad. Miss Regina says you stop that noise.

LEO: Uncle Horace—What—What happened? [CAL *starts down the stairs, shakes his head, begins to move swiftly off.* LEO *looks around wildly.*] But when— You seen Mr. Oscar or Mr. Ben? [CAL *shakes his head. Moves on.* LEO *grabs him by the arm.*] Answer me, will you?

CAL: No, I ain't seen 'em. I ain't got time to answer you. I got to get things. [CAL *runs off.*]

LEO: But what's the matter with him? When did this happen—[*Calling after* CAL.] You'd think Papa'd be some place where you could find him. I been chasing him all afternoon.

[OSCAR *and* BEN *come into the room, talking excitedly.*]

OSCAR: I hope it's not a bad attack.

BEN: It's the first one he's had since he came home.

LEO: Papa, I've been looking all over town for you and Uncle Ben—

BEN: Where is he?

OSCAR: Addie said it was sudden.

BEN: [*To* LEO.] Where is he? When did it happen?

LEO: Upstairs. Will you listen to me, please? I been looking for you for—

OSCAR: [*To* BEN.] You think we should go up?

[BEN, *looking up the steps, shakes his head.*]

BEN: I don't know. I don't know.

OSCAR: [*Shakes his head.*] But he was all right—

LEO: [*Yelling.*] *Will you listen to me?*

OSCAR: [*Sharply.*] What is the matter with you?

LEO: I been trying to tell you. I been trying to find you for an hour—

OSCAR: Tell me what?

LEO: Uncle Horace knows about the bonds. He knows about them. He's had the box since Wednesday—

BEN: [*Sharply.*] Stop shouting! What the hell are you talking about?

LEO: [*Furiously.*] I'm telling you he knows about the bonds. Ain't that clear enough—

OSCAR: [*Grabbing* LEO'S *arm.*] You God-damn fool! Stop screaming!

BEN: Now what happened? Talk quietly.

LEO: You heard me. Uncle Horace knows about the bonds. He's known since Wednesday.

BEN: [*After a second.*] How do you known that?

LEO: Because Cal comes down to Manders and says the box came O.K. and—

OSCAR: [*Trembling.*] That might not mean a thing—

LEO: [*Angrily.*] No? It might not, huh? Then he says Manders should come here tonight and bring Sol Fowler with him. I guess that don't mean a thing either.

OSCAR: [*To* BEN.] Ben— What— Do you think he's seen the—

BEN: [*Motions to the box.*] There's the box. [*Both* OSCAR *and* LEO *turn sharply.* LEO *makes a leap to the box.*] You ass. Put it down. What are you going to do with it, eat it?

LEO: I'm going to— [*Starts.*]

BEN: [*Furiously.*] Put it down. Don't touch it again. Now sit down and shut up for a minute.

OSCAR: Since Wednesday. [*To* LEO.] You said he had it since Wednesday. Why didn't he say something— [*To* BEN.] I don't understand—

LEO: [*Taking a step.*] I can put it back. I can put it back before anybody knows.

BEN: [*Who is standing at the table, softly.*] He's had it since Wednesday. Yet he hasn't said a word to us.

OSCAR: *Why? Why?*

LEO: What's the difference why? He was getting ready to say plenty. He was going to say it to Fowler tonight—

OSCAR: [*Angrily.*] Be still. [*Turns to* BEN, *looks at him, waits.*]

BEN: [*After a minute.*] I don't believe that.

LEO: [*Wildly.*] *You* don't believe it? What do I care what *you* believe? I do the dirty work and then—

BEN: [*Turning his head sharply to* LEO.] I'm remembering that. I'm remembering that, Leo.

OSCAR: What do you mean?

LEO: You—

BEN: [*To* OSCAR.] If you don't shut that little fool up, I'll show you what I mean. For some reason he knows, but he don't say a word.

OSCAR: Maybe he didn't know that *we*—

BEN: [*Quickly.*] That *Leo*— He's no fool. Does Manders know the bonds are missing?

LEO: How could I tell? I was half crazy. I don't think so. Because Manders seemed kind of puzzled and—

OSCAR: But we got to find out—[*He breaks off as* CAL *comes into the room carrying a kettle of hot water.*]

BEN: How is he, Cal?

CAL: I don't know, Mr. Ben. He was bad. [*Going towards stairs.*]

OSCAR: But when did it happen?

CAL: [*Shrugs.*] He wasn't feeling bad early. [ADDIE *comes in quickly from the hall.*] Then there he is next thing on the landing, fallen over, his eyes tight—

ADDIE: [*To* CAL.] Dr. Sloan's over at the Ballongs. Hitch the buggy and go get him. [*She takes the kettle and cloths from him, pushes him, runs up the stair.*] Go on.

[*She disappears.* CAL *exits.*]

BEN: Never seen Sloan anywhere when you need him.

OSCAR: [*Softly.*] Sounds bad.

LEO: He would have told *her* about it. Aunt Regina. He would have told his own wife—

BEN: [*Turning to* LEO.] Yes, he might have told her. But they weren't on such pretty terms and maybe he didn't. Maybe he didn't. [*Goes quickly to* LEO.] Now, listen to me. If she doesn't know, it may work out all right. If she does know, you're to say he lent you the bonds.

LEO: Lent them to me! Who's going to believe that?

BEN: Nobody.

OSCAR: [*To* LEO.] Don't you understand? It can't do no harm to say it—

LEO: Why should I say he lent them to me? Why not to you? [*Carefully.*] Why not to Uncle Ben?

BEN: [*Smiles.*] Just because he didn't lend them to me. Remember that.

LEO: But all he has to do is say he didn't lend them to me—

BEN: [*Furiously.*] But for some reason, he doesn't seem to be talking, does he?

[*There are footsteps above. They all stand looking at the stairs.* REGINA *begins to come slowly down.*]

BEN: What happened?

REGINA: He's had a bad attack.

OSCAR: Too bad. I'm so sorry we weren't here when—when Horace needed us.

BEN: When *you* needed us.

REGINA: [*Looks at him.*] Yes.

BEN: How is he? Can we—can we go up?

REGINA: [*Shakes her head.*] He's not conscious.

OSCAR: [*Pacing around.*] It's that—it's that bad? Wouldn't you think Sloan could be found quickly, just once, just once?

REGINA: I don't think there is much for him to do.

BEN: Oh, don't talk like that. He's come through attacks before. He will now.

[REGINA *sits down. After a second she speaks softly.*]

REGINA: Well. We haven't seen each other since the day of our fight.

BEN: [*Tenderly.*] That was nothing. Why, you and Oscar and I used to fight when we were kids.

OSCAR: [*Hurriedly.*] Don't you think we should go up? Is there anything we can do for Horace—

BEN: You don't feel well. Ah—

REGINA: [*Without looking at them.*] No, I don't. [*Slight pause.*] Horace told me about the bonds this afternoon.

[*There is an immediate shocked silence.*]

LEO: The bonds. What do you mean? What bonds? What—

BEN: [*Looks at him furiously. Then to* REGINA.] The Union Pacific bonds? *Horace's* Union Pacific bonds?

REGINA: Yes.

OSCAR: [*Steps to her, very nervously.*] Well. Well what—what about them? What—what could he say?

REGINA: He said that Leo had stolen the bonds and given them to you.

OSCAR: [*Aghast, very loudly.*] That's ridiculous, Regina, absolutely—

LEO: I don't know what you're talking about. What would I— Why—

REGINA: [*Wearily to* BEN.] Isn't it enough that he stole them from me? Do I have to listen to this in the bargain?

OSCAR: You are talking—

LEO: I didn't steal anything. I don't know why—

REGINA: [*To* BEN.] Would you ask them to stop that, please?

[*There is silence for a minute.* BEN *glowers at* OSCAR *and* LEO.]

BEN: Aren't we starting at the wrong end, Regina? What did Horace tell you?

REGINA: [*Smiles at him.*] He told me that Leo had stolen the bonds.

LEO: I didn't steal—

REGINA: Please. Let me finish. Then he told me that he was going to pretend that he had lent them to you [LEO *turns sharply to* REGINA, *then looks at* OSCAR, *then looks back at* REGINA.] as a present from me—to my brothers. He said there was nothing I could do about it. He said the rest of his money would go to Alexandra. That is all.

[*There is a silence.* OSCAR *coughs,* LEO *smiles slyly.*]

LEO: [*Taking a step to her.*] I told you he had lent them—I could have told you—

REGINA: [*Ignores him, smiles sadly at* BEN.] So I'm very badly off, you see. [*Carefully.*] But Horace said there was nothing I could do about it as long as he was alive to say he had lent you the bonds.

BEN: You shouldn't feel that way. It can all be explained, all be adjusted. It isn't as bad—

REGINA: So you, at least, are willing to admit that the bonds were stolen?

[OSCAR *laughs nervously.*]

BEN: I admit no such thing. It's possible that Horace made up that part of the story to tease you—[*Looks at her.*] Or perhaps to punish you. Punish you.

REGINA: [*Sadly.*] It's not a pleasant story. I feel bad, Ben, naturally. I hadn't thought—

BEN: Now you shall have the bonds safely back. That was the understanding, wasn't it, Oscar?

OSCAR: Yes.

REGINA: I'm glad to know that. [*Smiles.*] Ah, I had greater hopes—

BEN: Don't talk that way. That's foolish. [*Looks at his watch.*] I think we ought to drive out for Sloan ourselves. If we can't find him we'll go over to Senateville for Doctor Morris. And don't think I'm dismissing this other business. I'm not. We'll have it all out on a more appropriate day.

REGINA: [*Looks up, quietly.*] I don't think you had better go yet. I think you had better stay and sit down.

BEN: We'll be back with Sloan.

REGINA: Cal has gone for him. I don't want you to go.

BEN: Now don't worry and—

REGINA: You will come back in this room and sit down. I have something more to say.

BEN: [*Turns, comes towards her.*] Since when do I take orders from you?

REGINA: [*Smiles.*] You don't—yet. [*Sharply.*] Come back, Oscar. You too, Leo.

OSCAR: [*Sure of himself, laughs.*] My dear Regina—

BEN: [*Softly, pats her hand.*] Horace has already clipped your wings and very wittily. Do I have to clip them, too? [*Smiles at her.*] You'd get farther with a smile, Regina. I'm a soft man for a woman's smile.

REGINA: I'm smiling, Ben. I'm smiling because you are quite safe while Horace lives. But I don't think Horace will live. And if he doesn't live I shall want seventy-five per cent in exchange for the bonds.

BEN: [*Steps back, whistles, laughs.*] Greedy! What a greedy girl you are! You want so much of everything.

REGINA: Yes. And if I don't get what I want I am going to put all three of you in jail.

OSCAR: [*Furiously.*] You're mighty crazy. Having just admitted—

BEN: And on what evidence would you put Oscar and Leo in jail?

REGINA: [*Laughs, gaily.*] Oscar, listen to him. He's getting ready to swear that it was you and Leo! What do you say to that? [OSCAR *turns furiously towards* BEN.] Oh, don't be angry, Oscar. I'm going to see that he goes in with you.

BEN: Try anything you like, Regina. [*Sharply.*] And now we can stop all this and say good-bye to you. [ALEXANDRA *comes slowly down the steps.*] It's his money and he's obviously willing to let us borrow it. [*More pleasantly.*] Learn to make threats when you can carry them through. For how many years have I told you a good-looking woman gets more by being soft and appealing? Mama used to tell you that. [*Looks at his watch.*] Where the hell is Sloan? [*To* OSCAR.] Take the buggy and—

[*As* BEN *turns to* OSCAR, *he sees* ALEXANDRA. *She walks stiffly. She goes slowly to the lower window, her head bent. They all turn to look at her.*]

OSCAR: [*After a second, moving toward her.*] What? Alexandra—

[*She does not answer. After a second,* ADDIE *comes slowly down the stairs, moving as if she were very tired. At the foot of steps, she looks at* ALEXANDRA, *then turns and slowly crosses to door and exits.* REGINA *rises.* BEN *looks nervously at* ALEXANDRA, *at* REGINA.]

OSCAR: [*As* ADDIE *passes him, irritably to* ALEXANDRA.] Well, what is— [*Turns into room—sees* ADDIE *at foot of steps.*] —what's? [BEN *puts up a hand, shakes his head.*] My God, I didn't know—who *could* have known—I didn't know he was that sick. Well, well—I—

[REGINA *stands quietly, her back to them.*]

BEN: [*Softly, sincerely.*] Seems like yesterday when he first came here.

OSCAR: [*Sincerely, nervously.*] Yes, that's true. [*Turns to* BEN.] The whole town loved him and respected him.

ALEXANDRA: [*Turns.*] Did you love him, Uncle Oscar?

OSCAR: Certainly, I— What a strange thing to ask! I—

ALEXANDRA: Did you love him, Uncle Ben?

BEN: [*Simply.*] He had—

ALEXANDRA: [*Suddenly starts to laugh very loudly.*] And you, Mama, did you love him, too?

REGINA: I know what you feel, Alexandra, but please try to control yourself.

ALEXANDRA: [*Still laughing.*] I'm trying, Mama. I'm trying very hard.

BEN: Grief makes some people laugh and some people cry. It's better to cry, Alexandra.

ALEXANDRA: [*The laugh has stopped. Tensely moves toward* REGINA.] What was Papa doing on the staircase?

[BEN *turns to look at* ALEXANDRA.]

REGINA: Please go and lie down, my dear. We all need time to get over shocks like this. [ALEXANDRA *does not move.* REGINA'S *voice becomes softer, more insistent.*] Please go, Alexandra.

ALEXANDRA: No, Mama. I'll wait. I've got to talk to you.

REGINA: Later. Go and rest now.

ALEXANDRA: [*Quietly.*] I'll wait, Mama. I've plenty of time.

REGINA: [*Hesitates, stares, makes a half shrug, turns back to* BEN.] As I was saying. Tomorrow morning I am going up to Judge Simmes. I shall tell him about Leo.

BEN: [*Motioning toward* ALEXANDRA.] Not in front of the child, Regina. I—

REGINA: [*Turns to him. Sharply.*] I didn't ask her to stay. Tomorrow morning I go to Judge Simmes—

OSCAR: And what proof? What proof of all this—

REGINA: [*Turns sharply.*] None. I won't need any. The bonds are missing and they are with Marshall. That will be enough. If it isn't, I'll add what's necessary.

BEN: I'm sure of that.

REGINA: [*Turns to* BEN.] You can be quite sure.

OSCAR: We'll deny—

REGINA: Deny your heads off. You couldn't find a jury that wouldn't weep for a woman whose brothers steal from her. And you couldn't find twelve men in this state you haven't cheated and hate you for it.

OSCAR: What kind of talk is this? You couldn't do anything like that! We're your own brothers. [*Points upstairs.*] How can you talk that way when upstairs not five minutes ago—

REGINA: [*Slowly.*] There are people who can never go back, who must finish what they start. I am one of those people, Oscar. [*After a slight pause.*] Where was I? [*Smiles at* BEN.] Well, they'll convict you. But I won't care much if they don't. [*Leans forward, pleasantly.*] Because by that time you'll be ruined. I shall also tell my story to Mr. Marshall, who likes me, I think, and who will not want to be involved in your scandal. A respectable firm like Marshall and Company. The deal would be off in an hour. [*Turns to them angrily.*] And you know it. Now I don't want to hear any more from any of you. *You'll do no more bargaining in this house.* I'll take my seventy-five per cent and we'll forget the story forever. That's one way of doing it, and the way I prefer. You know me well enough to know that I don't mind taking the other way.

BEN: [*After a second, slowly.*] None of us have ever known you well enough, Regina.

REGINA: You're getting old, Ben. Your tricks aren't as smart as they used to be. [*There is no answer. She waits, then smiles.*] All right. I take it that's settled and I get what I asked for.

OSCAR: [*Furiously to* BEN.] Are you going to let her do this—

BEN: [*Turns to look at him, slowly.*] You have a suggestion?

REGINA: [*Puts her arms above her head, stretches, laughs.*] No, he hasn't. All right. Now, Leo, I have forgotten that you ever saw the bonds. [*Archly, to* BEN *and* OSCAR.] And as long as you boys both behave yourselves, I've forgotten that we ever talked about them. You can draw up the necessary papers tomorrow.

[BEN *laughs,* LEO *stares at him, starts for door. Exits.* OSCAR *moves towards door angrily.* REGINA *looks at* BEN, *nods, laughs with him. For a second,* OSCAR *stands in the door, looking back at them. Then he exits.*]

REGINA: You're a good loser, Ben. I like that.

BEN: [*He picks up his coat, then turns to her.*] Well, I say to myself, what's the good? You and I aren't like Oscar. We're not sour people. I think that comes from a good digestion. Then, too, one loses today and wins tomorrow. I say to myself, years of planning and I get what I want. Then I don't get it. But I'm not discouraged. The century's turning, the world is open. Open for people like you and me. Ready for us, waiting for us. After all this is just the beginning. There are hundreds of Hubbards sitting in rooms like this throughout the country. All their names aren't Hubbard, but they are all Hubbards and they will own this country some day. We'll get along.

REGINA: [*Smiles.*] I think so.

BEN: Then, too, I say to myself, things may change. [*Looks at* ALEXANDRA.] I agree with Alexandra. What is a man in a wheel chair doing on a staircase? I ask myself that.

REGINA: [*Looks up at him.*] And what do you answer?

BEN: I have no answer. But maybe some day I will. Maybe never, but maybe some day. [*Smiles. Pats her arm.*] When I do, I'll let you know. [*Goes towards hall.*]

REGINA: When you do, write me. I will be in Chicago. [*Gaily.*] Ah, Ben, if Papa had only left me his money.

BEN: I'll see you tomorrow.

REGINA: Oh, yes. Certainly. You'll be sort of working for me now.

BEN: [*As he passes* ALEXANDRA, *smiles.*] Alexandra, you're turning out to be a right interesting girl. [*Looks at* REGINA.] Well, good night all. [*He exits.*]

REGINA: [*Sits quietly for a second, stretches, turns to look at* ALEXANDRA.] What do you want to talk to me about, Alexandra?

ALEXANDRA: [*Slowly.*] I've changed my mind. I don't want to talk. There's nothing to talk about now.

REGINA: You're acting very strange. Not like yourself. You've had a bad shock today. I know that. And you loved Papa, but you must have expected this to come some day. You know how sick he was.

ALEXANDRA: I knew. We all knew.

REGINA: It will be good for you to get away from here. Good for me, too. Time heals most wounds, Alexandra. You're young, you shall have all the things I wanted. I'll make the world for you the way I wanted it to be for me. [*Uncomfortably.*] Don't sit there staring. You've been around Birdie so much you're getting just like her.

ALEXANDRA: [*Nods.*] Funny. That's what Aunt Birdie said today.

REGINA: [*Nods.*] Be good for you to get away from all this.

[ADDIE *enters.*]

ADDIE: Cal is back, Miss Regina. He says Dr. Sloan will be coming in a few minutes.

REGINA: We'll go in a few weeks. A few weeks! That means two or three Saturdays, two or three Sundays. [*Sighs.*] Well, I'm very tired. I shall go to bed. I don't want any supper. Put the lights out and lock up. [ADDIE *moves to the piano lamp, turns it out.*] You go to your room, Alexandra. Addie will bring you something hot. You look very tired. [*Rises. To* ADDIE.] Call me when

Dr. Sloan gets here. I don't want to see anybody else. I don't want any condolence calls tonight. The whole town will be over.

ALEXANDRA: Mama, I'm not coming with you. I'm not going to Chicago.

REGINA: [*Turns to her.*] You're very upset, Alexandra.

ALEXANDRA: [*Quietly.*] I mean what I say. With all my heart.

REGINA: We'll talk about it tomorrow. The morning will make a difference.

ALEXANDRA: It won't make any difference. And there isn't anything to talk about. I am going away from you. Because I want to. Because I know Papa would want me to.

REGINA: [*Puzzled, careful, polite.*] You *know* your papa wanted you to go away from me?

ALEXANDRA: Yes.

REGINA: [*Softly.*] And if I say no?

ALEXANDRA: [*Looks at her.*] Say it, Mama, say it. And see what happens.

REGINA: [*Softly, after a pause.*] And if I make you stay?

ALEXANDRA: That would be foolish. It wouldn't work in the end.

REGINA: You're very serious about it, aren't you? [*Crosses to stairs.*] Well, you'll change your mind in a few days.

ALEXANDRA: You only change your mind when you want to. And I won't want to.

REGINA: [*Going up the steps.*] Alexandra, I've come to the end of my rope. Somewhere there has to be what I want, too. Life goes too fast. Do what you want; think what you want; go where you want. I'd like to keep you with me, but I won't make you stay. Too many people used to make me do too many things. No, I won't make you stay.

ALEXANDRA: You couldn't, Mama, because I want to leave here. As I've never wanted anything in my life before. Because now I understand what Papa was trying to tell me. [*Pause.*] All in one day: Addie said there were people who ate the earth and other people who stood around and watched them do it. And just now Uncle Ben said the same thing. Really, he said the same thing. [*Tensely.*] Well, tell him for me, Mama, I'm not going to stand around and watch you do it. Tell him I'll be fighting as hard as he'll be fighting [*Rises.*] some place where people don't just stand around and watch.

REGINA: Well, you have spirit, after all. I used to think you were all sugar water. We don't have to be bad friends. I don't want us to be bad friends, Alexandra. [*Starts, stops, turns to* ALEXANDRA.] Would you like to come and talk to me, Alexandra? Would you—would you like to sleep in my room tonight?

ALEXANDRA: [*Takes a step towards her.*] Are you afraid, Mama?

[REGINA *does not answer. She moves slowly out of sight.* ADDIE *comes to* ALEXANDRA, *presses her arm.*]

CURTAIN

1939

QUESTIONS

Hamlet

1. Read over the first act of the play carefully, and make a list of all the exposition we are given here—relationships between characters, events that have taken place before the play begins, conflicts of various kinds and issues at stake. What *else* happens in Act I? What kinds of emotions are aroused? With what issues do we become concerned? With whose problems do we care about? In what specific ways is the action moved forward?

2. Review carefully all the action in Act III, Scene 2. Summarize exactly what happens in the scene, and specify exactly what we learn. Do we learn the same thing that Hamlet does? What structural functions does the scene perform? If you were producing the play, how would you have Claudius act at the end of the scene when he calls for more light? What facial expressions would you give him? What hand gestures?

3. How are Rosencrantz and Guildenstern characterized in the play? In what ways are they alike? In what ways different? What suggestions do you find in the text as to why their fate is paired so closely? What other "pairs" of characters are in the play? Which characters are specifically compared to each other in terms of temperament or habit? How does the device of pairing have to do with the play's structure?

4. What different strategies are used to characterize Laertes? Describe his relationship to his sister; to his father; to Hamlet. Describe his "role" in the plot. What if he were to be eliminated from the play? What specific things that seem to you crucial to the play's structure and effects would be missing? Can you conceive of another character or group of characters that could be introduced into the play to perform those structural functions? Make a list of all the things that such a character or group would have to be or do.

5. Study the character of Polonius carefully and review all of his lines and actions. What other characters is he paired with, by relationship or parallel function? How do those pairings help us to evaluate Polonius and draw conclusions about him? What structural role does he perform in the play?

The Little Foxes

1. How much of Act I seems to you to be exposition? Exactly what are we told and by whom? At what point in Act I do you begin to have a sense of what individual characters are like and how they are related to each other? Where does the rising action begin?

2. Exactly what part of Act II constitutes the play's turning point? Where does the falling action begin? In what does the play's final stability consist?

3. What different parts haunt the different characters in the play? In what specific ways do memories of the past, or nostalgia for it, affect the motivations of individual characters? How much of the plot is driven by a sense of the past? Which characters are motivated by the future? In what ways are economic status and social class related to a sense of the past?

4. In what specific ways is the setting of the play important? Does it make any difference that the action occurs in the spring? In what ways are the material objects mentioned in the stage directions important to characterization? to the play's themes?

5. Who is the most important character in the play? On what basis did you decide: centrality to the plot? attractiveness? psychological complexity? obsession to manipulate others? power?

6. What does the play's title mean?

WRITING SUGGESTIONS

Hamlet

1. Paraphrase, as exactly as you can, Hamlet's "To be or not to be" soliloquy. Summarize it in no more than two sentences. In your summary, what distortions are you particularly concerned about? In what ways did you find it difficult to communicate tone in your paraphrase?

2. Pretend that you have been given the job of reading the play in order to prepare actors for their performance in it. Choose five characters from the play, and write (as if for the actor about to play the part) a full description of each of them (about 300 words each) Describe physical appearance, voice, gestures, personality, temperament, conflicts, character flaws, everything you think the actor needs to know to play the part according to your interpretation of the play.

3. In an essay of about 4 pages, analyze the characterization of Ophelia and assess her structural function in the play.

The Little Foxes

1. Write a brief character sketch of Leo, outlining his most obvious characteristics. Then read back through the play carefully and notice at what points his various stereotypical characteristics reveal themselves. How important to the

play are other people's opinions of Leo? When do you become aware that you have formed a strong opinion about him? Exactly what function does he perform in the plot? Which of his distinctive characteristics are crucial to the plot? In an essay of about the pages, analyze Leo's role in the plot and show exactly how structure of the play depends on the gradual revelation of his character.

2. Write a short (600-word) essay describing Birdie's role in the plot.

3. "Chicago" has a specific symbolic value for several of the play's characters, a symbolism that does not necessarily correspond to the "real" Chicago Mr. Marshall is from. Which characters, develop a particular "image" of Chicago—either from the past or because of what it might hold in the future? Make a list of the qualities Chicago represents to individual characters. Note especially what kinds of notions Regina has about Chicago. In an essay about Regina's character (an essay of about 1,000 words), show the importance of "Chicago" to her consciousness, and note how other people's visions of the city help to clarify Regina's character and values.

3 THE WHOLE TEXT

Though plot, dramatic structure, characterization, and other elements such as symbol and theme are useful concepts, they do not really exist as discrete, separable parts of a finished work. In analyzing a play—in breaking it down into pieces you can handle—you may find it necessary to talk or write about it in terms of its "elements." But as you read (especially when you are reading for pleasure) you do not say to yourself, "ah, a bit of characterization," or "yes, here ends the exposition." These distinctions are useful but they are arbitrary, for the words and details of a play have multiple functions, and the play as a whole is a sum of inter-working parts. The opening passages of *Trifles* illustrate how some of the elements interact, suggest some of the differences between the act of reading a play and viewing it on the stage, and demonstrate the holistic nature of reading.

Reading *Trifles*, we have an advantage over those who take their seats in the theater and watch a young man enter, rubbing his hands and saying, "This feels good. Come up to the fire, ladies." If those in the theater audience have had a chance to look at their programs, they know that the young man is the county attorney. Depending on the director, set designer, and prop manager, the theater audience may see the unwashed pans under the sink or the loaf outside the bread-box, but they will not know for sure whether these are "signs of incompleted work." Indeed, if they are males like those in the play, they might not even notice that the kitchen is messed up. The director may have cast a "slight wiry woman" as Mrs. Peters, but the acting company may have had no such actress, or there may be an actress in the company who, although not slight or wiry, fits other aspects of the part. Her "nervous" face may be acted out in a number of ways, ways that not every member of the audience will identify as "nervous," and the actress playing Mrs. Hale might not be thought of by every member of the theater audience as "more *comfortable* looking." The director, then, may ignore or modify the stage directions, but you as reader must embody them or keep them as signs within your imagination. Since you know Mrs. Peters has a nervous face, you may likely read the dash in her first spoken line, "I'm not—cold," as a sign of nervousness. (It would be easy, seeing the play on the stage, to think that the pause was not the result of nervousness but of the cold weather.) Mr. Hale, at the invitation of the sheriff, tells the county attorney and us that he had stopped by the Wrights the day before and found Mrs. Wright "kind of done up" in the rocking chair and Mr. Wright upstairs, dead, and with a rope around his neck. Virtually all the exposition we will need has been supplied by his story.

But more than exposition has been going on. Mr. Hale's testimony is at first delayed by the county attorney's asking if anything has been moved, the sheriff's detailed explanation of what has been done, the other's admonition that "Somebody should have been left here yesterday." We have the image of the young official's officiousness, his going "by the book," and the more realistic practicality of the middle-aged sheriff. We also notice the county attorney's interrupting Mr. Hale when he starts talking about John Wright's character or behavior toward his wife. He wants only the "facts," indeed only the "important facts," about what happened yesterday. We already have a sense, if a somewhat stereotypical one, of this character.

By the time Mr. Hale finishes his story, we know who the murderer is, and so do all the characters in the play. There's not much mystery, so we are quite sure we do not have a mystery story before us. Just what kind of play is this, then? If it's not going to be about "who done it?" what *is* it going to be about?

Immediately after Mr. Hale's story, the attorney decides they will first look upstairs and then in the barn for clues. There's nothing important here, the sheriff says, for there is "nothing here but kitchen things." Among the "kitchen things," the attorney finds a burst jar of preserved fruit. Mrs. Peters says Mrs. Wright was worried that the frost might get to her preserves, and the attorney, always the cocksure official, says ominously that she'll have more to worry about than that. "Well," Mr. Hale says, "women are used to worrying over trifles."

The word alerts us, for the author has singled it out as the title of the play. We ourselves now worry over trifles—kitchen things, burst jars, unwashed pans, misplaced loaves and towels. And the speaker's tone, dismissive of the concerns of "women," characterizes the speaker and his male companions and raises the "kitchen things" to almost symbolic value. The ironic yoking together of trifles and women also hints that the plot may well overturn conventional values: women and trifles may turn out to be more important than men and other "important things."

From this point on, the ingredients in the mix—the symbolic trifles and the theme of gender difference, for example—are so blended that it is difficult to separate character from theme or plot, symbol from clue, character, plot, or theme. The words, actions, and details all function together.

There are remarkable similarities in the subject matter of the serious one-act play *Trifles* and *The Doctor in Spite of Himself*, the comic full-length play by Molière that follows: both plots involve a husband's abuse of his wife and her revenge.

MOLIÈRE

The Doctor in Spite of Himself[1]

CHARACTERS

SGANARELLE, *husband of Martine*
MARTINE, *wife of Sganarelle*
MONSIEUR ROBERT, *neighbor of Sganarelle*
VALÈRE, *servant of Géronte*
LUCAS, *husband of Jacqueline*
GÉRONTE, *father of Lucinde*
JACQUELINE, *wet-nurse at Géronte's and wife of Lucas*
LUCINDE, *daughter of Géronte*
LÉANDRE, *in love with Lucinde*
THIBAUT, *a peasant, father of Perrin*
PERRIN, *a peasant, son of Thibaut*

ACT I

A *clearing. The houses of* SGANARELLE *and* MONSIEUR ROBERT *may be seen through the trees.*

SCENE 1

SGANARELLE, MARTINE, *who enter quarreling.*

SGANARELLE: No, I tell you I won't do anything of the sort, and I'm the one to say and be the master.

MARTINE: And *I* tell *you* that I want you to live to suit me, and I didn't marry you to put up with your carryings-on.

SGANARELLE: Oh, what a weary business it is to have a wife, and how right Aristotle is when he says a wife is worse than a demon!

MARTINE: Just listen to that smart fellow with his half-wit Aristotle!

SGANARELLE: Yes, a smart fellow. Just find me a woodcutter who knows how to reason about things, like me, who served a famous doctor for six years, and who as a youngster knew his elementary Latin book by heart.

MARTINE: A plague on the crazy fool!

SGANARELLE: A plague on the slut!

MARTINE: Cursed by the day when I went and said yes!

SGANARELLE: Cursed by the hornified[2] notary who had me sign my own ruin!

MARTINE: Really, it's a fine thing for you to complain of that affair! Should you

1. Translated by Donald M. Frame. 2. Cuckolded.

let a single moment go by without thanking Heaven for having me for your wife? And did you deserve to marry a person like me?

SGANARELLE: Oh, yes, you did me too much honor, and I had reason to congratulate myself on our wedding night! Oh, my Lord! Don't get me started on that! I'd have a few things to say . . .

MARTINE: What? What would you say?

SGANARELLE: Let it go at that; let's drop that subject. Enough that we know what we know, and that you were very lucky to find me.

MARTINE: What do you mean, lucky to find you? A man who drags me down to the poorhouse, a debauchee, a traitor, who eats up everything I own?

SGANARELLE: That's a lie. I drink part of it.

MARTINE: Who sells, piece by piece, everything in the house.

SGANARELLE: That's living on our means.

MARTINE: Who's taken even my bed from under me.

SGANARELLE: You'll get up all the earlier in the morning.

MARTINE: In short, who doesn't leave a stick of furniture in the whole house.

SGANARELLE: All the easier to move out.

MARTINE: And who does nothing but gamble and drink from morning to night.

SGANARELLE: That's so I won't get bored.

MARTINE: And what do you expect me to do with my family in the meantime?

SGANARELLE: Whatever you like.

MARTINE: I have four poor little children on my hands.

SGANARELLE: Set them on the floor.

MARTINE: Who are constantly asking me for bread.

SGANARELLE: Give them the whip. When I've had plenty to eat and drink, I want everyone in my house to have his fill.

MARTINE: And you, you drunkard, do you expect things to go on forever like this?

SGANARELLE: My good wife, let's go easy, if you please.

MARTINE: And me to endure your insolence and debauchery to all eternity?

SGANARELLE: Let's not get excited, my good wife.

MARTINE: And that I can't find a way to make you do your duty?

SGANARELLE: My good wife, you know that my soul isn't very patient and my arm is pretty good.

MARTINE: You make me laugh with your threats.

SGANARELLE: My good little wife, my love, you're itching for trouble, as usual.

MARTINE: I'll show you I'm not afraid of you.

SGANARELLE: My dear better half, you're asking for something.

MARTINE: Do you think your words frighten me?

SGANARELLE: Sweet object of my eternal vows, I'll box your ears.

MARTINE: Drunkard that you are!

SGANARELLE: I'll beat you.

MARTINE: Wine-sack!

SGANARELLE: I'll wallop you.

MARTINE: Wretch!

SGANARELLE: I'll tan your hide.

MARTINE: Traitor, wiseacre, deceiver, coward, scoundrel, gallowsbird, beggar, good-for-nothing, rascal, villain, thief . . .

SGANARELLE: [*Takes a stick and beats her.*] Ah! So you want it, eh?

MARTINE: Oh, oh, oh, oh!

SGANARELLE: That's the right way to pacify you.

Scene 2

MONSIEUR ROBERT, SGANARELLE, MARTINE.

MONSIEUR ROBERT: Hey there, hey there, hey there! Fie! What's this? What infamy! Confound the rascal for beating his wife that way!

MARTINE: [*Arms akimbo, forces* MONSIEUR ROBERT *back as she talks, and finally gives him a slap.*] And as for me, I want him to beat me.

MONSIEUR ROBERT: Oh! Then with all my heart, I consent.

MARTINE: What are you meddling for?

MONSIEUR ROBERT: I'm wrong.

MARTINE: Is it any business of yours?

MONSIEUR ROBERT: You're right.

MARTINE: Just look at this meddler, trying to keep husbands from beating their wives.

MONSIEUR ROBERT: I take it all back.

MARTINE: What have you got to do with it?

MONSIEUR ROBERT: Nothing.

MARTINE: Have you any right to poke your nose in?

MONSIEUR ROBERT: No.

MARTINE: Mind your own business.

MONSIEUR ROBERT: I won't say another word.

MARTINE: I like to be beaten.

MONSIEUR ROBERT: All right.

MARTINE: It's no skin off your nose.

MONSIEUR ROBERT: That's true.

MARTINE: And you're a fool to come butting in where it's none of your business.

[*Slaps* MONSIEUR ROBERT. *He turns toward* SGANARELLE, *who likewise forces him back as he talks, threatening him with the same stick and finally beating and routing him with it.*]

MONSIEUR ROBERT: Neighbor, I beg your pardon with all my heart. Go on, beat your wife and thrash her to your heart's content; I'll help you if you want.

SGANARELLE: Me, I don't want to.

MONSIEUR ROBERT: Oh well, that's another matter.

SGANARELLE: I want to beat her if I want to; and I don't want to beat her if I don't want to.

MONSIEUR ROBERT: Very well.

SGANARELLE: She's my wife, not yours.

MONSIEUR ROBERT: Undoubtedly.

SGANARELLE: I don't take orders from you.

MONSIEUR ROBERT: Agreed.

SGANARELLE: I don't need any help from you.

MONSIEUR ROBERT: That's fine with me.

SGANARELLE: And you're a meddler to interfere in other people's affairs. Learn that Cicero says that you mustn't put the bark between the tree and your finger. [*Beats* MONSIEUR ROBERT *and drives him offstage, then returns to his wife and clasps her hand.*] Well now, let's us two make peace. Shake on it.

MARTINE: Oh yes! After beating me that way!

SGANARELLE: That's nothing. Shake.

MARTINE: I will not.

SGANARELLE: Eh?

MARTINE: No.

SGANARELLE: My little wife!

MARTINE: No sir.

SGANARELLE: Come on, I say.

MARTINE: I won't do anything of the kind.

SGANARELLE: Come, come, come.

MARTINE: No, I want to be angry.

SGANARELLE: Fie! It's nothing. Come on, come on.

MARTINE: Let me be.

SGANARELLE: Shake, I say.

MARTINE: You've treated me too badly.

SGANARELLE: All right then, I ask your pardon: give me your hand.

MARTINE: I forgive you; [*Aside.*] but you'll pay for it.

SGANARELLE: You're crazy to pay any attention to that: those little things are necessary from time to time for a good friendship; and five or six cudgel-blows between people in love only whet their affection. There now, I'm off to the woods, and I promise you more than a hundred bundles of kindling wood today.

SCENE 3

MARTINE *(alone)*.

MARTINE: All right, whatever face I put on, I'm not forgetting my resentment; and I'm burning inside to find ways to punish you for the beatings you give me. I know very well that a wife always has in hand means of taking revenge on a husband; but that's too delicate a punishment for my gallowsbird. I want a vengeance that he'll feel a bit more; and that would be no satisfaction for the offense I've received.

SCENE 4

VALÈRE, LUCAS, MARTINE.

LUCAS: Doggone it! We sure both tooken on one heck of a job; and me, I don't know what I'm gonna come up with.

VALÈRE: Well, what do you expect as the wet-nurse's husband? We have to obey our master; and then we both have an interest in the health of the mistress, his daughter; and no doubt her marriage, put off by her illness, would be worth some kind of present to us. Horace, who is generous, has the best chances of anyone to win her hand; and although she has shown a fondness for a certain Léandre, you know very well that her father has never consented to accept him as a son-in-law.

MARTINE: [*Musing, aside.*] Can't I think up some scheme to get revenge?

LUCAS: But what kind of wild idea has the master tooken into his head, now that the doctors have used up all their Latin?

VALÈRE: You sometimes find, by looking hard, what you don't find at first; and often in simple places . . .

MARTINE: Yes, I must get revenge, whatever the price; that beating sticks in my crop, I can't swallow it, and . . . [*She says all this still musing, not noticing the two men, so that when she turns around she bumps into them.*] Oh! Gentlemen, I beg your pardon; I didn't see you, and I was trying to think of something that's bothering me.

VALÈRE: Everyone has his problems in this world, and we too are looking for something we would very much like to find.

MARTINE: Would it be anything I might help you with?

VALÈRE: It just might. We're trying to find some able man, some special doctor, who might give some relief to our master's daughter, ill with a disease that has suddenly taken away the use of her tongue. Several doctors have already exhausted all their learning on her; but you sometimes find people with wonderful secrets, with certain special remedies, who can very often do what the others couldn't; and that's what we're looking for.

MARTINE: [*Aside.*] Oh! What a wonderful scheme Heaven inspires me with to get revenge on my gallowsbird! [*Aloud.*] You couldn't have come to a better place to find what you're looking for; and we have a man here, the most marvelous man in the world for hopeless illnesses.

VALÈRE: And, pray, where can we find him?

MARTINE: You'll find him right now in that little clearing over there, spending his time cutting wood.

LUCAS: A doctor cutting wood?

VALÈRE: Spending his time gathering herbs, do you mean?

MARTINE: No, he's an extraordinary man who enjoys that—strange, fantastic, crotchety—you'd never take him for what he is. He goes around dressed in an eccentric way, sometimes affects ignorance, keeps his knowledge hidden, and every day avoids nothing so much as exercising the marvelous talents Heaven has given him for medicine.

VALÈRE: It's an amazing thing that all great men always have some caprice, some little grain of folly mingled with their learning.

MARTINE: This one's mania is beyond all belief, for it sometimes goes to the point of his wanting to be beaten before he'll acknowledge his capacity; and I'm telling you you'll never get the better of him, he'll never admit he's a doctor, if he's in that mood, unless you each take a stick and beat him into confessing in the end what he'll hide from you at first. That's what *we* do when we need him.

VALÈRE: That's a strange mania!

MARTINE: That's true; but afterward, you'll see he does wonders.

VALÈRE: What's his name?

MARTINE: His name is Sganarelle, but he's easy to recognize. He's a man with a big black beard, wearing a ruff and a green and yellow coat.

LUCAS: A green and yaller coat? So he's a parrot doctor?[3]

VALÈRE: But is it really true that he's as skillful as you say?

MARTINE: What? He's a man who works miracles. Six months ago a woman was abandoned by all the other doctors. They thought she'd been dead for a good six hours, and were getting ready to bury her, when they forced the man we're talking about to come. After he'd looked her over, he put a little drop of something or other in her mouth, and that very moment she got up out of bed and right away started walking around her room as if nothing had happened.

LUCAS: Ah!

VALÈRE: It must have been a drop of elixir of gold.

MARTINE: That might well be. Then again, not three weeks ago a youngster twelve years old fell down from the top of the steeple and broke his head, arms, and legs on the pavement. They had no sooner brought our man in than he rubbed the boy's whole body with a certain ointment he knows how to make; and right away the boy got up on his feet and ran off to play marbles.

LUCAS: Ah!

VALÈRE: That man must have a universal cure.

MARTINE: Who doubts it?

LUCAS: By jingo, that's sure the man we need. Let's go get him quick.

VALÈRE: We thank you for the favor you're doing us.

MARTINE: But anyway, be sure to remember what I warned you about.

LUCAS: Tarnation! Leave it to us. If a beating is all it takes, she's our cow.

VALÈRE: That certainly was a lucky encounter for us; and for my part, I'm very hopeful about it.

SCENE 5

SGANARELLE, VALÈRE, LUCAS.

SGANARELLE: [*Enters singing, bottle in hand.*] La, la, la!

VALÈRE: I hear someone singing and cutting wood.

SGANARELLE: La, la, la . . . ! My word, that's enough work for a while. Let's take a little breather. [*Drinks.*] That wood is salty as the devil.

[*Sings.*]

Sweet glug-glug,
How I love thee!

3. In Molière's time, doctors always wore black robes. [Translator's note]

Sweet glug-glug
Of my little jug!
But everybody would think me too smug
If you were as full as you can be.
Just never be empty, that's my plea.
Come, sweet, let me give you a hug.

[*Speaks again.*] Come on, good Lord, we mustn't breed melancholy.

VALÈRE: There's the man himself.

LUCAS: I think you're right, and we done stumbled right onto him.

VALÈRE: Let's get a closer look.

SGANARELLE: [*Seeing them, looks at them, turning first toward one then toward the other, and lowers his voice.*] Ah! my little hussy! How I love you, my little jug!

But everybody . . . would think . . . me . . . too smug,
If . . .

What the devil! What do these people want?

VALÈRE: That's the one, no doubt about it.

LUCAS: That's him, his spit an' image, just like they prescribed him to us.

SGANARELLE: [*Aside.*] They're looking at me and consulting. What can they have in mind?

[*He puts his bottle on the ground. As* VALÈRE *bows to greet him,* SGANARELLE *thinks he is reaching down to take his bottle away, and so puts it on the other side of him. When* LUCAS *bows in turn, he picks it up again and clutches it to his belly, with much other byplay.*]

VALÈRE: Sir, isn't your name Sganarelle?

SGANARELLE: How's that?

VALÈRE: I'm asking you if you're not the man named Sganarelle?

SGANARELLE: [*Turning toward* VALÈRE, *then toward* LUCAS.] Yes and no, depending on what you want with him.

VALÈRE: All we want is to pay him all the civilities we can.

SGANARELLE: In that case, my name *is* Sganarelle.

VALÈRE: Sir, we are delighted to see you. We have been addressed to you for something we're looking for; and we come to implore your aid, which we need.

SGANARELLE: If it's something, sirs, connected with my little line of business, I am all ready to serve you.

VALÈRE: Sir, you are too kind. But sir, put on your hat, please; the sun might give you trouble.

LUCAS: Slap it on, sir.

SGANARELLE: [*Aside.*] These are very ceremonious people.

VALÈRE: Sir, you must not find it strange that we should come to you. Able men are always sought out, and we are well informed about your capability.

SGANARELLE: It is true, gentlemen, that I'm the best man in the world for cutting kindling wood.

VALÈRE: Ah, sir . . . !

SGANARELLE: I spare no pains, and cut it in such a way that it's above criticism.

VALÈRE: Sir, that's not the point.

SGANARELLE: But also I sell it at a hundred and ten sous for a hundred bundles.

VALÈRE: Let's not talk about that, if you please.

SGANARELLE: I promise you I can't let it go for less.

VALÈRE: Sir, we know how things stand.

SGANARELLE: If you know how things stand, you know that that's what I sell them for.

VALÈRE: Sir, you're joking when . . .

SGANARELLE: I'm not joking, I can't take anything off for it.

VALÈRE: Let's talk in other terms, please.

SGANARELLE: You can find it for less elsewhere: there's kindling and kindling; but as for what I cut . . .

VALÈRE: What? Sir, let's drop this subject.

SGANARELLE: I swear you couldn't get it for a penny less.

VALÈRE: Fie now!

SGANARELLE: No, on my conscience, that's what you'll pay. I'm speaking sincerely, and I'm not the man to overcharge.

VALÈRE: Sir, must a person like you waste his time on these crude pretenses and stoop to speaking like this? Must such a learned man, a famous doctor like yourself, try to disguise himself in the eyes of the world and keep his fine talents buried?

SGANARELLE: [*Aside.*] He's crazy.

VALÈRE: Please, sir, don't dissimulate with us.

SGANARELLE: What?

LUCAS: All this here fiddle-faddle don't do no good; we knows what we knows.

SGANARELLE: What about it? What are you trying to tell me? Whom do you take me for?

VALÈRE: For what you are: for a great doctor.

SGANARELLE: Doctor yourself: I'm not one and I've never been one.

VALÈRE: [*Aside.*] That's his madness gripping him [*Aloud.*] Sir, please don't deny things any longer; and pray let's not come to regrettable extremes.

SGANARELLE: To what?

VALÈRE: To certain things that we would be sorry for.

SGANARELLE: Good Lord! Come to whatever you like. I'm no doctor, and I don't know what you're trying to tell me.

VALÈRE: [*Aside.*] I can certainly see we'll have to use the remedy. [*Aloud.*] Once more, sir, I beg you to admit what you are.

LUCAS: Dad bust it! No more messin' around; confess frank-like that you're a doctor.

SGANARELLE: I'm getting mad.

VALÈRE: Why deny what everybody knows?

LUCAS: Why all this fuss and feathers? And what good does that done you?

SGANARELLE: Gentlemen, I tell you in one word as well as in two thousand: *I'm not a doctor.*

VALÈRE: You're not a doctor?

SGANARELLE: No.

LUCAS: You ain't no doc?

SGANARELLE: No, I tell you.

VALÈRE: Since you insist, we'll have to go ahead.

[*They each take a stick and beat him.*]

SGANARELLE: Oh, oh, oh! Gentlemen, I'm whatever you like.

VALÈRE: Why, sir, do you force us to this violence?

LUCAS: Why do you give us the botherment of beating you?

VALÈRE: I assure you that I could not regret it more.

LUCAS: By jeepers, I'm sorry about it, honest.

SGANARELLE: What the devil is this, gentlemen? I ask you, is it a joke, or are you both crazy, to insist I'm a doctor?

VALÈRE: What? You still won't give in, and you deny you're a doctor?

SGANARELLE: Devil take me if I am!

LUCAS: It ain't true that you're a doc?

SGANARELLE: No, plague take me!

[*They start beating him again.*]

Oh, oh! Well, gentlemen, since you insist, I'm a doctor, I'm a doctor; an apothecary too, if you see fit. I'd rather consent to anything than get myself beaten to death.

VALÈRE: Ah! That's fine, sir; I'm delighted to find you in a reasonable mood.

LUCAS: You fair cram my heart with joy when I see you talk thataway.

VALÈRE: I beg your pardon with all my heart.

LUCAS: I begs your excuse for the liberty I done tooken.

SGANARELLE: [*Aside.*] Well now! Suppose I'm the one that's mistaken? Could I have become a doctor without noticing it?

VALÈRE: Sir, you won't regret showing us what you are; and you'll certainly be satisfied with your treatment.

SGANARELLE: But, gentlemen, aren't you making a mistake yourselves? Is it quite certain that I'm a doctor?

LUCAS: Yup, by jiminy!

SGANARELLE: Honestly?

VALÈRE: Beyond a doubt.

SGANARELLE: Devil take me if I knew it!

VALÈRE: What? You're the ablest doctor in the world.

SGANARELLE: Aha!

LUCAS: A doc which has cureded I don't know how many maladies.

SGANARELLE: My Lord!

VALÈRE: A woman had been taken for dead six hours before; she was ready to be buried, when, with a drop of something or other, you brought her back to life and set her walking around the room right away.

SGANARELLE: I'll be darned!

LUCAS: A little boy twelve years old left himself fall from the top of a steeple, from which he got his head, legs, and arms busted; and you, with some kind of ointment or other, you fixed him so he gets right up on his feet and goes off to play marbles.

SGANARELLE: The devil you say!

VALÈRE: In short, sir, you will have every satisfaction with us; and you'll earn whatever you like if you'll let us take you where we mean to.

SGANARELLE: I'll earn whatever I like?

VALÈRE: Yes.

SGANARELLE: Oh! I'm a doctor, there's no denying it. I'd forgotten, but now I remember. What's the problem? Where do we have to go?

VALÈRE: We'll take you. The problem is to go see a girl who's lost her speech.

SGANARELLE: My word! I haven't found it.

VALÈRE: He likes his little joke. Let's go, sir.

SGANARELLE: Without a doctor's gown?

VALÈRE: We'll get one.

SGANARELLE: [*Presenting his bottle to* VALÈRE.] Hold that, you: that's where I put my potions. [*Turning toward* LUCAS *and spitting on the ground.*] You, step on that; doctor's orders.

LUCAS: Land's sakes! That's a doctor I like. I reckon he'll do all right, 'cause he's a real comic.

ACT II

A room in GÉRONTE's house.

SCENE 1

GÉRONTE, VALÈRE, LUCAS, JACQUELINE.

VALÈRE: Yes, sir, I think you'll be satisfied; and we've brought you the greatest doctor in the world.

LUCAS: Oh, gee whillikins! You gotta pull up the ladder after that one, and all the rest ain't good enough to take off his shoon.

VALÈRE: He's a man who has performed wonderful cures.

LUCAS: As has cureded some folk as were dead.

VALÈRE: He's a bit capricious, as I've told you; and sometimes he has moments when his mind wanders and he doesn't seem what he really is.

LUCAS: Yup, he likes to clown; and sometimes you'd say, with no offense, that he'd been hit on the head with an axe.

VALÈRE: But underneath it, he's all learning, and very often he says quite lofty things.

LUCAS: When he gets to it, he talks right straight out just like he was reading out of a book.

VALÈRE: His reputation has already spread hereabouts, and everybody is coming to see him.

GÉRONTE: I'm dying to meet him. Bring him to me quick.

VALÈRE: I'll go and get him.

JACQUELINE: Land's sakes, sir, this'un'll do just what the others done. I reckon it'll be just the same old stuff; and the bestest med'cine anyone could slip your daughter, if you're asking me, would be a good handsome husband she had a hankering for.

GÉRONTE: Well now! My good wet-nurse, you certainly meddle in lots of things.

LUCAS: Be quiet, Jacqueline, keep to your housework: you ain't the one to stick your nose in there.

JACQUELINE: I told you before and I'll tell you some more that all these here doctors won't do nothing more for her than plain branch water, that your daughter needs something mighty different from rhubarb and senna, and that a husband is the kind of poultice that'll cure all a girl's troubles.

GÉRONTE: Is she in condition now for anyone to want to take her on, with the infirmity she has? And when I was minded to have her married, didn't she oppose my will?

JACQUELINE: I should think she did: you was wanting to pass her a man she don't love. Why didn't you take that Monsieur Léandre that she had a soft spot for? She would've been real obedient; and I'm gonna bet you he'd take her just like she is, if you'd give her to him.

GÉRONTE: That Léandre is not what she needs; he's not well off like the other.

JACQUELINE: He's got such a rich uncle, and he's his hair.

GÉRONTE: All this property to come is just so much nonsense to me. There's nothing like what you've got; and you run a big risk of fooling yourself when you count on what someone else is keeping for you. Death doesn't always keep her ears open to the wishes and prayers of their honors the heirs; and you can grow a long set of teeth when you're waiting for someone's death so as to have a livelihood.

JACQUELINE: Anyway I've always heard that in marriage, as elsewhere, happiness counts more than riches. The pas and mas, they have that goldarned custom of always asking "How much has he got?" and "How much has she got?" and neighbor Peter married off his daughter Simonette to fat Thomas 'cause he had a quarter vineyard more than young Robin, which she'd set her heart on; and now, poor critter, it's turned her yellow as a quince, and she hasn't got her property in all the time since. That's a fine example for *you*, sir. All we got in this world is our pleasure; and I'd rather give my daughter a good husband which she liked than all the revenues in Beauce.

GÉRONTE: Plague take it, Madame Nurse, how you do spit it out! Be quiet, please; you're getting too involved and you're heating up your milk.

LUCAS: [*By mistake, tapping* GÉRONTE *on the chest instead of* JACQUELINE.] Gosh darn it! Shut up, you're just a meddler. The master don't have no use for your speeches, and he knows what he's got to do. You see to nursing the child you're nurse to, and don't give us none of your big ideas. The master is his daughter's father, and he's good enough and wise enough to see what she needs.

GÉRONTE: Easy! Oh! Easy!

LUCAS: Sir, I want to mortify her a bit, and teach her the *re*spect she owes you.
GÉRONTE: Yes, but those gestures aren't necessary.

Scene 2

VALÈRE, SGANARELLE, GÉRONTE, LUCAS, JACQUELINE.

VALÈRE: Sir, prepare yourself. Here comes our doctor.
GÉRONTE: Sir, I'm delighted to have you in my house, and we need you badly.
SGANARELLE: [*In a doctor's gown, with a sharply pointed hat.*] Hippocrates[4] says . . . that we should both put our hats on.
GÉRONTE: Hippocrates says that?
SGANARELLE: Yes.
GÉRONTE: In what chapter, if you please?
SGANARELLE: In his chapter on hats.
GÉRONTE: Since Hippocrates says it, we must do it.
SGANARELLE: Sir Doctor, since I have heard the wonderful things . . .
GÉRONTE: Whom are you speaking to, pray?
SGANARELLE: You.
GÉRONTE: I'm not a doctor.
SGANARELLE: You're not a doctor?
GÉRONTE: No, really.
SGANARELLE: [*Takes a stick and beats him just as he himself was beaten.*] You really mean it?
GÉRONTE: I really mean it. Oh, oh, oh!
SGANARELLE: You're a doctor now. I never got any other license.
GÉRONTE: What the devil kind of a man have you brought me?
VALÈRE: I told you he was a joker of a doctor.
GÉRONTE: Yes, but I'd send him packing with his jokes.
LUCAS: Don't pay no attention to that, sir: that's just for a laugh.
GÉRONTE: I don't like that kind of a laugh.
SGANARELLE: Sir, I ask your pardon for the liberty I took.
GÉRONTE: Your servant, sir.
SGANARELLE: I'm sorry . . .
GÉRONTE: That's nothing.
SGANARELLE: For the cudgeling . . .
GÉRONTE: No harm done.
SGANARELLE: That I had the honor of giving you.
GÉRONTE: Let's say no more about it. Sir, I have a daughter who has caught a strange disease.
SGANARELLE: Sir, I'm delighted that your daughter needs me; and I wish with all my heart that you and your whole family needed me too, just to show you how much I want to serve you.
GÉRONTE: I am obliged to you for those sentiments.
SGANARELLE: I assure you that I'm speaking straight from the heart.

4. (ca. 460–ca. 370 B.C.), Greek physician and "father of medicine."

GÉRONTE: You do me too much honor.
SGANARELLE: What's your daughter's name?
GÉRONTE: Lucinde.
SGANARELLE: Lucinde! Oh, what a fine name to prescribe for! Lucinde!
GÉRONTE: I'll just go and have a look to see what she's doing.
SGANARELLE: Who's that big buxom woman?
GÉRONTE: She's the wet-nurse of a little baby of mine.
SGANARELLE: Plague take it! That's a pretty piece of goods! Ah, nurse, charming nurse, my medicine is the very humble slave of your nurseship, and I'd certainly like to be the lucky little doll who sucked the milk [*Puts his hand on her breast.*] of your good graces. All my remedies, all my learning, all my capacity is at your service, and . . .
LUCAS: With your pummission, Mister Doctor, leave my wife be, I beg you.
SGANARELLE: What? Is she your wife?
LUCAS: Yes.
SGANARELLE: [*Makes as if to embrace* LUCAS, *then, turning toward the nurse, embraces her.*] Oh! really! I didn't know that, and I'm delighted for the sake of you both.
LUCAS: [*Pulling him away.*] Easy now, please.
SGANARELLE: I assure you I'm delighted that you're united. I congratulate her [*He again makes as if to embrace* LUCAS, *and, passing under his arms, throws himself on* JACQUELINE'*s neck.*] on having a husband like you; and you, I congratulate you on having a wife as beautiful, modest, and well-built as she is.
LUCAS: [*Pulling him away again.*] Hey! Goldarn it! Not so much compliment, I ask you now.
SGANARELLE: Don't you want me to rejoice with you at such a fine assembly?
LUCAS: With me, all you like; but with my wife, let's skip these kind of formalities.
SGANARELLE: I take part in the happiness of you both alike; and [*Same business as before.*] if I embrace you to attest my joy to you, I embrace her as well to attest my joy to her too.
LUCAS: [*Pulling him away once more.*] Oh! Dad blast it, Mister Doctor, what a lot of fiddle-faddle!

Scene 3

SGANARELLE, GÉRONTE, LUCAS, JACQUELINE.

GÉRONTE: Sir, they're going to bring my daughter to you. She'll be here right away.
SGANARELLE: I await her sir, and all medicine with me.
GÉRONTE: Where is it?
SGANARELLE: [*Tapping his forehead.*] In there.
GÉRONTE: Very good.
SGANARELLE: [*Trying to touch the nurse's breasts.*] But since I am interested in

your whole family, I must take a small sample of your nurse's milk, and inspect her bosom.

LUCAS: [*Pulling him away and spinning him around.*] Nah, nah, I don't want no truck with that.

SGANARELLE: It's the doctor's job to examine nurses' breasts.

LUCAS: Job nor no job, I'm your servant.

SGANARELLE: Do you really have the audacity to set yourself up against the doctor? Begone!

LUCAS: The heck with that!

SGANARELLE: [*Looking at him askance.*] I'll give you the fever.

JACQUELINE: [*Taking* LUCAS *by the arm and spinning him around.*] That's right, get out of there. Ain't I big enough to defend myself if he does something to me as a person hadn't ought?

LUCAS: Well, me, I don't want him a-feeling you.

SGANARELLE: Fie! The peasant! He's jealous of his wife!

GÉRONTE: Here is my daughter.

SCENE 4

LUCINDE, VALÈRE, GÉRONTE, LUCAS, SGANARELLE, JACQUELINE.

SGANARELLE: Is this the patient?

GÉRONTE: Yes, she's the only daughter I have, and I'd be heart-broken if she were to die.

SGANARELLE: She'd better not! She mustn't die except on doctor's orders.

GÉRONTE: Come, come, a chair![5]

SGANARELLE: That's not such a bad-looking patient, and I maintain that a really healthy man would make out all right with her.

GÉRONTE: You've made her laugh, sir.

SGANARELLE: That's fine. When the doctor makes the patient laugh, that's the best possible sign. Well! What's the problem? What's wrong with you? Where does it hurt?

LUCINDE: [*Answers in sign language, putting her hand to her mouth, her head, and under her chin.*] Hah, heeh, hoh, hah.

SGANARELLE: Eh? What's that you say?

LUCINDE: [*Same gestures as before.*] Hah, heeh, hoh, hah, hah, heeh, hoh.

SGANARELLE: What?

LUCINDE: Hah, heeh, hoh.

SGANARELLE: [*Imitating her.*] Hah, heeh, hoh, hah, hah: I don't understand you. What the devil kind of language is that?

GÉRONTE: Sir, that's her illness. She's been struck dumb, and up to now no one has been able to learn the reason why; and it's an accident that has put off her marriage.

SGANARELLE: And why so?

5. Chairs were relatively rare luxuries in Molière's France. By ordering a regular chair, not a folding stool, Géronte shows his respect for the learned doctor. [Translator's note]

GÉRONTE: The man she is to marry wants to wait until she's cured to make things final.

SGANARELLE: And who is the fool that doesn't want his wife to be dumb? Would God mine had that disease! I'd be the last one to want to cure her.

GÉRONTE: Anyway, sir, we beg you to make every effort to relieve her of her trouble.

SGANARELLE: Oh! Don't worry. Tell me now, does this trouble bother her a lot?

GÉRONTE: Yes, sir.

SGANARELLE: Very good. Does she feel great pains?

GÉRONTE: Very great.

SGANARELLE: That's just fine. Does she go—you know where?

GÉRONTE: Yes.

SGANARELLE: Copiously?

GÉRONTE: I don't know anything about that.

SGANARELLE: Does she achieve laudable results?

GÉRONTE: I'm no expert in those matters.

SGANARELLE: [*Turning to the patient.*] Give me your arm. That pulse shows your daughter is dumb.

GÉRONTE: Why yes, sir, that's her trouble! You found it the very first thing.

SGANARELLE: Aha!

JACQUELINE: Just lookit how he guessed her illness!

SGANARELLE: We great doctors, we know things right away. An ignorant one would have been embarrassed and would have gone and told you "It's this" or "It's that"; but *I* hit the mark on the first shot, and I inform you that your daughter is dumb.

GÉRONTE: Yes; but I wish you could tell me what it comes from.

SGANARELLE: Nothing easier: it comes from the fact that she has lost her speech.

GÉRONTE: Very good; but the reason, please, why she has lost her speech?

SGANARELLE: All our best authors will tell you that it's the stoppage of the action of her tongue.

GÉRONTE: But still, what are your views about this stoppage of the action of her tongue?

SGANARELLE: Aristotle, on that subject, says . . . some very fine things.

GÉRONTE: I believe it.

SGANARELLE: Oh! He was a great man!

GÉRONTE: No doubt.

SGANARELLE: [*Raising his forearm.*] An utterly great man: a man who was greater than I by all of that! So, to get back to our reasoning, I hold that this stoppage of the action of her tongue is caused by certain humors, which among us scholars we call peccant humors: peccant, that is to say . . . peccant humors; because the vapors formed by the exhalations of the influences arising in the region where the maladies lie, when they come . . . so to speak . . . to . . . Do you understand Latin?

GÉRONTE: Not in the least.

SGANARELLE: [*Getting up in astonishment.*] You don't understand Latin?

GÉRONTE: No.

SGANARELLE: [*Assuming various comical poses.*] *Cabricias arci thuram, catalamus, singulariter, nominativo haec Musa,* "the Muse," *bonus, bona, bonum, Deus sanctus, estne oratio latinas? Etiam,* "yes." *Quare,* "why?" *Quia substantivo et adjectivum concordat in generi, numerum, et casus.*

GÉRONTE: Oh! Why did I never study?

JACQUELINE: Land! That's an able man!

LUCAS: Yup, that's so purty I can't make out a word of it.

SGANARELLE: Now when these vapors I'm speaking of come to pass from the left side, where the liver is, to the right side, where the heart is, it happens that the lungs, which in Latin we call *armyan,* having communication with the brain, which in Greek we call *nasmus,* by means of the vena cava, which in Hebrew we call *cubile,*[6] on its way encounters the said vapors, which fill the ventricles of the omoplate; and because the said vapors—follow this reasoning closely, I beg you—and because the said vapors have a certain malignity . . . Listen to this carefully, I conjure you.

GÉRONTE: Yes.

SGANARELLE: Have a certain malignity, which is caused . . . Be attentive, please.

GÉRONTE: I am.

SGANARELLE: Which is caused by acridity of the humors engendered in the concavity of the diaphragm, it happens that these vapors . . . *Ossabandus, nequeys, nequer, potarinum, quipsa milus.* That's exactly what is making your daughter dumb.

JACQUELINE: Oh! That man of ourn! Ain't that well said?

LUCAS: Why ain't *my* tongue that slick?

GÉRONTE: No one could reason any better, no doubt about it. There's just one thing that surprised me: the location of the liver and the heart. It seems to me that you place them otherwise than they are; that the heart is on the left side and the liver on the right side.

SGANARELLE: Yes, it used to be that way; but we have changed all that, and now we practice medicine in a completely new way.

GÉRONTE: That's something I didn't know, and I beg your pardon for my ignorance.

SGANARELLE: No harm done, and you're not obliged to be as able as we are.

GÉRONTE: To be sure. But, sir, what do you think needs to be done for this illness?

SGANARELLE: What I think needs to be done?

GÉRONTE: Yes.

SGANARELLE: My advice is to put her back in bed and have her take, as a remedy, a lot of bread steeped in wine.

GÉRONTE: And why that, sir?

SGANARELLE: Because in bread and wine mixed together there is a sympathetic virtue that makes people speak. Haven't you noticed that they don't give anything else to parrots, and that they learn to speak by eating that?

GÉRONTE: That's true. Oh, what a great man! Quick, lots of bread and wine!

6. These are all invented names, except that *cubile* is Latin for *bed.* [Translator's note]

SGANARELLE: I'll come back toward evening and see how she is. [*To the nurse.*] Hold on, you. Sir, here is a nurse to whom I must administer a few little remedies.

JACQUELINE: Who? Me? I couldn't be in better health.

SGANARELLE: Too bad, nurse, too bad. Such good health is alarming, and it won't be a bad thing to give you a friendly little bloodletting, a little dulcifying enema.

GÉRONTE: But, sir, that's a fashion I don't understand. Why should we go and be bled when we haven't any illness?

SGANARELLE: No matter, it's a salutary fashion; and just as we drink on account of the thirst to come, so we must have ourselves bled on account of the illness to come.

JACQUELINE: [*Starting to go off.*] My Lord! The heck with that, and I don't want to make my body into a drugstore.

SGANARELLE: You are resistant to remedies, but we'll manage to bring you to reason. [*Exit* JACQUELINE. *To* GÉRONTE.] I bid you good day.

GÉRONTE: Wait a bit, please.

SGANARELLE: What do you want to do?

GÉRONTE: Give you some money, sir.

SGANARELLE: [*Holding out his hand behind, beneath his gown, while* GÉRONTE *opens his purse.*] I won't take any, sir.

GÉRONTE: Sir . . .

SGANARELLE: Not at all.

GÉRONTE: Just a moment.

SGANARELLE: By no means.

GÉRONTE: Please!

SGANARELLE: You're joking.

GÉRONTE: That's that.

SGANARELLE: I'll do nothing of the sort.

GÉRONTE: Eh?

SGANARELLE: Money is no motive to me.

GÉRONTE: I believe it.

SGANARELLE: [*After taking the money.*] Is this good weight?

GÉRONTE: Yes, sir.

SGANARELLE: I'm not a mercenary doctor.

GÉRONTE: I'm well aware of it.

SGANARELLE: I'm not ruled by self-interest.

GÉRONTE: I have no such idea.

SCENE 5

SGANARELLE, LÉANDRE.

SGANARELLE: [*Looking at his money.*] My word! That's not too bad; and if only . . .

LÉANDRE: Sir, I've been waiting for you a long time, and I come to implore your assistance.

SGANARELLE: [*Taking his wrist.*] That's a very bad pulse.

LÉANDRE: I'm not sick, sir, and that's not why I've come to see you.

SGANARELLE: If you're not sick, why the devil don't you say so?

LÉANDRE: No. To put the whole thing in a word, my name is Léandre, and I'm in love with Lucinde, whom you've just examined; and since, because of her father's bad disposition, I'm denied all access to her, I'm venturing to beg you to serve my love, and give me a chance to carry out a scheme I've thought up to say a word or two to her on which my happiness and my life depend absolutely.

SGANARELLE: [*Feigning anger.*] Whom do you take me for? How can you dare come up and ask me to serve you in your love, and try to degrade the dignity of a doctor to this type of employment?

LÉANDRE: Sir, don't make so much noise.

SGANARELLE: *I* want to make noise. You're an impertinent young man.

LÉANDRE: Ah! Gently, sir.

SGANARELLE: A dunderhead.

LÉANDRE: Please!

SGANARELLE: I'll teach you that I'm not the kind of man for that, and that it's the height of insolence . . .

LÉANDRE: [*Pulling out a purse and giving it to him.*] Sir . . .

SGANARELLE: To want to use me . . . I'm speaking about you, for you're a gentleman, and I would be delighted to do you a service; but there are some impertinent people in the world who come and take people for what they're not; and I admit that makes me angry.

LÉANDRE: I ask your pardon, sir, for the liberty that . . .

SGANARELLE: Don't be silly. What's the problem?

LÉANDRE: You shall know, then, sir, that this illness that you want to cure is make-believe. The doctors have reasoned in due form about it, and have not failed to say that it came, some say from the brain, some from the intestines, some from the spleen, some from the liver; but it is certain that love is the real cause of it, and that Lucinde hit upon this illness only to deliver herself from a threatened marriage. But, for fear we may be seen together, let's get out of here, and as we walk I'll tell you what I would like from you.

SGANARELLE: Let's go, sir: you've given me an inconceivable fondness for your love; and unless I'm no doctor, either the patient will die or else she'll be yours.

ACT III

GÉRONTE'*s garden.*

SCENE 1

SGANARELLE, LÉANDRE.

LÉANDRE: It seems to me I don't look bad this way as an apothecary; and since the father has scarcely ever seen me, this change of costume and wig may well succeed, I think, in disguising me to his eyes.

SGANARELLE: No doubt about it.

LÉANDRE: All I could wish would be to know five or six big medical terms to adorn my speech and make me seem like a learned man.

SGANARELLE: Come, come, all that is unnecessary: the costume is enough, and I know no more about it than you.

LÉANDRE: What?

SGANARELLE: Devil take me if I know anything about medicine! You're a good sort, and I'm willing to confide in you, just as you are confiding in me.

LÉANDRE: What? You're not really . . . ?

SGANARELLE: No, I tell you: they made me a doctor in spite of me. I had never bothered my head about being that learned; and all my studies went only up to seventh grade. I don't know what put this idea into their heads; but when I saw that they absolutely insisted on my being a doctor, I decided to be one, at the expense of whom it may concern. However, you'd never believe how the mistaken idea has gotten around, and how everybody is hell-bent on thinking me a learned man. They come looking for me from all directions; and if things keep on this way, I believe I'll stick to medicine all my life. I think it's the best trade of all; for whether you do well or badly, you're always paid just the same. Bad work never comes back onto our backs, and we cut the material we work on as we please. A cobbler making shoes could never botch a piece of leather without paying for the broken crockery; but in this work we can botch a man without its costing us anything. The blunders are never ours, and it's always the fault of the person who dies. In short, the best part of this profession is that there's a decency, an unparalleled discretion, among the dead; and you never see one of them complaining of the doctor who killed him.

LÉANDRE: It's true that dead men are very decent folk on that score.

SGANARELLE: [*Seeing some men coming toward him.*] There are some people who look as though they were coming to consult me. Go ahead and wait for me near your sweetheart's house.

Scene 2

THIBAUT, PERRIN, SGANARELLE.

THIBAUT: Sir, we done come to see you, my son Perrin and me.

SGANARELLE: What's the matter?

THIBAUT: His poor mother, her name is Perrette, is sick in bed these six months now.

SGANARELLE: [*Holding out his hand to receive money.*] And what do you expect me to do about it?

THIBAUT: We'd like, sir, for you to slip us some kind of funny business for to cure her.

SGANARELLE: I'll have to see what she's sick of.

THIBAUT: She's sick of a proxy, sir.

SGANARELLE: Of a proxy?

THIBAUT: Yes, that is to say she's all swelled up all over; and they say it's a whole lot of seriosities she's got inside her, and that her liver, her belly, or her spleen, whatever you want to call it, 'stead of making blood don't make nothing but water. Every other day she has a quotigian fever, with pains and lassitules in the muskles of her legs. You can hear in her throat phleg-ums like to choke her; and sometimes she gets tooken with syncopations and compulsions till I think she done passed away. In our village we got a 'pothecary, all respect to him, who's given her I don't know how many kinds of stuff; and it costs me more'n a dozen good crowns in enemas, no offense, and beverages he had her take, in jacinth confusions and cordial portions. But all that stuff, like the feller said, was just a kind of salve that didn't make her no better nor no worse. He wanted to slip her one certain drug that they call hermetic wine; but me, frankly, I got scared that would send her to join her ancestors; and they do say those big doctors are killing off I don't know how many people with that there invention.[7]

SGANARELLE: [*Still holding out his hand and signaling with it for money.*] Let's get to the point, my friend, let's get to the point.

THIBAUT: The fact is, sir, that we done come to ask you to tell us what we should do.

SGANARELLE: I don't understand you at all.

PERRIN: Sir, my mother is sick; and here be two crowns that we've brung you so you'll give us some cure.

SGANARELLE: Oh! Now *you*, I understand you. Here's a lad who speaks clearly and explains himself properly. You say that your mother is ill with dropsy, that her whole body is swollen, that she has a fever and pains in her legs, and that she is sometimes seized with syncopes and convulsions, that is to say, fainting spells?

PERRIN: Oh, yes, sir, that's exactly it.

SGANARELLE: I understood you right away. You have a father who doesn't know what he's talking about. Now you're asking me for a remedy?

PERRIN: Yes, sir.

SGANARELLE: A remedy to cure her?

PERRIN: That's what we got in mind.

SGANARELLE: Look, here's a piece of cheese that you must have her take

PERRIN: Cheese, sir?

SGANARELLE: Yes, it's a specially prepared cheese containing gold, coral, pearls, and lots of other precious things.

PERRIN: Sir, we be much obliged to you; and we'll have her take this right away.

SGANARELLE: Go ahead. If she dies, don't fail to give her the best burial you can.

Scene 3

JACQUELINE, SGANARELLE, LUCAS [*backstage*].

SGANARELLE: Here's that beautiful nurse. Ah, nurse of my heart, I'm delighted that we meet again, and the sight of you is the rhubarb, cassia, and senna that purge my soul of all its melancholy!

7. A big medical controversy of the time concerned the value of emetic wine, which contained antimony. [Translator's note]

JACQUELINE: Well I swan, Mister Doctor, you say that too purty for me, and I don't understand none of your Latin.

SGANARELLE: Fall ill, nurse, I beg you; fall ill for my sake: it would give me all the pleasure in the world to cure you.

JACQUELINE: I'm your servant, sir: I'd much rather not have no one cure me.

SGANARELLE: How sorry I am for you, fair nurse, for having a jealous, troublesome husband like the one you have!

JACQUELINE: What would you have me do, sir? It's a penance for my sins. Where the goat is tied, that's where she's got to graze.

SGANARELLE: What? A clod like that! A man who's always watching you, and won't let anyone talk to you!

JACQUELINE: Mercy me, you ain't seen nothin' yet, and that's only a little sample of his bad humor.

SGANARELLE: Is it possible? And can a man have a soul so base as to mistreat a person like you? Ah, lovely nurse, I know people, and not far from here either, who would think themselves happy just to kiss the little tips of your footsies! Why must so lovely a person have fallen into such hands, and must a mere animal, a brute, a lout, a fool . . . ? Pardon me, nurse, if I speak in this way of your husband.

JACQUELINE: Oh, sir, I know good and well he deserves all them names.

SGANARELLE: Yes, nurse, he certainly does deserve them; and he would also deserve to have you plant a certain decoration on his head,[8] to punish him for his suspicions.

JACQUELINE: It's quite true that if I was only thinking about him, he might drive me to some strange carryings-on.

SGANARELLE: My word! It wouldn't be a bad idea for you to take vengeance on him with someone else. He's a man, I tell you, who really deserves that; and if I were fortunate enough, beautiful nurse, to be chosen to . . .

[*At this point they both notice* LUCAS, *who was in back of them all the time listening to their talk. They go off in opposite directions, the doctor with comical byplay.*]

SCENE 4

GÉRONTE, LUCAS.

GÉRONTE: Hey there, Lucas! Haven't you seen our doctor around?

LUCAS: Yup, tarnation take it! I seen him, and my wife too.

GÉRONTE: Then where can he be?

LUCAS: I dunno, but I wish he'd go to the devil in hell.

GÉRONTE: Go take a look and see what my daughter is doing.

8. Horns, the traditional sign of the cuckold.

Scene 5

SGANARELLE, LÉANDRE, GÉRONTE.

GÉRONTE: Ah, sir! I was just asking where you were.

SGANARELLE: I was busy in your courtyard—expelling the superfluity of my potations. How is the patient?

GÉRONTE: A little worse since taking your prescription.

SGANARELLE: Very good: that's a sign that it's working.

GÉRONTE: Yes, but as it works, I'm afraid it will choke her.

SGANARELLE: Don't worry; I have remedies that make light of everything, and I'll wait for her in her death agony.

GÉRONTE: Who's this man you're bringing with you?

SGANARELLE: [*Gesturing like an apothecary giving an enema.*] He's . . .

GÉRONTE: What?

SGANARELLE: The one . . .

GÉRONTE: Eh?

SGANARELLE: Who . . .

GÉRONTE: I understand.

SGANARELLE: Your daughter will need him.

Scene 6

JACQUELINE, LUCINDE, GÉRONTE, LÉANDRE, SGANARELLE.

JACQUELINE: Sir, here's your daughter as wants to take a little walk.

SGANARELLE: That will do her good. Mister Apothecary, go along and take her pulse a bit so that I can discuss her illness with you presently. [*At this point he draws* GÉRONTE *to one side of the stage, and, passing one arm over his shoulders, puts his hand under his chin and turns him back toward himself whenever* GÉRONTE *tries to watch what his daughter and the apothecary are doing together.*] Sir, it's a great and subtle question among the learned whether women are easier to cure than men. I beg you to listen to this, if you please. Some say no, others say yes; and *I* say yes and no: inasmuch as the incongruity of the opaque humors that are found in the natural temperament of women, is the reason why the brutish part always tries to gain power over the sensitive part, we see that the inequality of their opinions depends on the oblique movement of the moon's circle; and since the sun, which darts its rays over the concavity of the earth, finds . . .

LUCINDE: No, I'm utterly incapable of changing my feelings.

GÉRONTE: That's my daughter speaking! Oh, what wonderful virtue in that remedy! Oh, what an admirable doctor! How obliged I am to you for this marvelous cure! And what can I do for you after such a service?

SGANARELLE: [*Walking around the stage and wiping his brow.*] That's an illness that gave me a lot of trouble!

LUCINDE: Yes, father, I've recovered my speech; but I've recovered it to tell you that I shall never have any other husband than Léandre, and that there's no use your trying to give me Horace.
GÉRONTE: But . . .
LUCINDE: Nothing can shake my resolution.
GÉRONTE: What . . . ?
LUCINDE: All your fine objections will be in vain.
GÉRONTE: If . . .
LUCINDE: All your arguments will be no use.
GÉRONTE: I . . .
LUCINDE: It's a thing I'm determined on.
GÉRONTE: But . . .
LUCINDE: There is no paternal authority that can force me to marry in spite of myself.
GÉRONTE: I've . . .
LUCINDE: All your efforts will not avail.
GÉRONTE: He . . .
LUCINDE: My heart could never submit to this tyranny.
GÉRONTE: There . . .
LUCINDE: And I'll cast myself into a convent rather than marry a man I don't love.
GÉRONTE: But . . .
LUCINDE: [*In a deafening voice.*] No. By no means. Nothing doing. You're wasting your time. I won't do anything of the sort. That's settled.
GÉRONTE: Oh! What a rush of words! There's no way to resist it. Sir, I beg you to make her dumb again.
SGANARELLE: That's impossible for me. All I can do for your service is to make you deaf, if you want.
GÉRONTE: Many thanks! [*To* LUCINDE.] Then do you think . . . ?
LUCINDE: No. All your reasons will make no impression on my soul.
GÉRONTE: You shall marry Horace this very evening.
LUCINDE: I'll sooner marry death.
SGANARELLE: Good Lord! Stop, let me medicate this affair. Her illness still grips her, and I know the remedy we must apply.
GÉRONTE: Is it possible, sir that you can also cure this illness of the mind?
SGANARELLE: Yes. Leave it to me, I have remedies for everything, and our apothecary will serve us for this cure. [*Calls the apothecary.*] One word. You see that the ardor she has for this Léandre is completely contrary to her father's will, that there is no time to lose, that the humors are very inflamed, and that it is necessary to find a remedy promptly for this ailment, which could get worse with delay. For my part, I see only one, which is a dose of purgative flight, which you will combine properly with two drams of matrimonium in pill form. She may make some difficulty about taking this remedy; but since you are an able man at your trade, it's up to you to persuade her and make her swallow the dose as best you can. Go along and get her to take a little turn around the garden, so as to prepare the humors, while I talk to her

father here; but above all don't waste time. The remedy, quickly, the one specific remedy!

Scene 7

GÉRONTE, SGANARELLE.

GÉRONTE: What are those drugs, sir, that you just mentioned? It seems to me I've never heard of them.

SGANARELLE: They are drugs used in great emergencies.

GÉRONTE: Did you ever see such insolence as hers?

SGANARELLE: Daughters are sometimes a little headstrong.

GÉRONTE: You wouldn't believe how crazy she is about this Léandre.

SGANARELLE: The heat of the blood does this to young minds.

GÉRONTE: For my part, ever since I discovered the violence of this love, I've managed to keep my daughter always locked up.

SGANARELLE: You've done wisely.

GÉRONTE: And I've kept them from having any communication together.

SGANARELLE: Very good.

GÉRONTE: Some folly would have resulted if I'd allowed them to see each other.

SGANARELLE: No doubt.

GÉRONTE: And I think she'd have been just the girl to run off with him.

SGANARELLE: That's prudent reasoning.

GÉRONTE: I've been warned that he's making every effort to speak to her.

SGANARELLE: What a clown!

GÉRONTE: But he'll be wasting his time.

SGANARELLE: Ha, ha!

GÉRONTE: And I'll keep him from seeing her, all right.

SGANARELLE: He's not dealing with a dolt, and you know tricks of the game that he doesn't. Smarter than you is no fool.

Scene 8

LUCAS, GÉRONTE, SGANARELLE.

LUCAS: Dad blast it, sir, here's a lot of ruckus: your daughter's done run off with her Léandre. The 'pothecary, that was him; and Mister Doctor here's the one as pufformed that fine operation.

GÉRONTE: What? Assassinate me in that way! Here, get a policeman! Don't let him get out. Ah, traitor! I'll have the law on you.

LUCAS: Hah! By jingo, Mister Doctor, you'll be hung: just don't move outa there.

Scene 9

MARTINE, SGANARELLE, LUCAS.

MARTINE: Oh, Good Lord! What a time I've had finding this house! Tell me, what's the news of the doctor I provided for you?

LUCAS: Here he be. Gonna be hung.

MARTINE: What? My husband hanged? Alas! What's he done?

LUCAS: He fixed it for our master's daughter to get run away with.

MARTINE: Alas! My dear husband, is it really true they're going to hang you?

SGANARELLE: As you see. Oh!

MARTINE: Must you let yourself die in the presence of all these people?

SGANARELLE: What do you expect me to do about it?

MARTINE: At least if you'd finished cutting our wood, I'd have some consolation.

SGANARELLE: Get out of here, you're breaking my heart.

MARTINE: No, I mean to stay to give you courage in the face of death, and I won't leave you until I see you hanged.

SGANARELLE: Oh!

SCENE 10

GÉRONTE, SGANARELLE, MARTINE, LUCAS.

GÉRONTE: The constable will be here soon, and they'll put you in a place where they'll be answerable for you to me.

SGANARELLE: [*Hat in hand.*] Alas! Can't this be changed to a modest cudgeling?

GÉRONTE: No, no, justice will take its course . . . But what's this I see?

SCENE 11

LÉANDRE, LUCINDE, JACQUELINE, LUCAS, GÉRONTE, SGANARELLE, MARTINE.

LÉANDRE: Sir, I come to reveal Léandre to you and restore Lucinde to your power. We both intended to run away and get married; but this plan has given way to a more honorable procedure. I do not aim to steal your daughter from you, and it is only from your hands that I wish to receive her. I will tell you this, sir: I have just received letters informing me that my uncle has died and that I am heir to all his property.

GÉRONTE: Sir, I have highest consideration for your virtues, and I give you my daughter with the greatest pleasure in the world.

SGANARELLE: That was a close shave for medicine!

MARTINE: Since you're not going to be hanged, you can thank me for being a doctor; for I'm the one who procured you that honor.

SGANARELLE: Yes, you're the one who procured me quite a beating.

LÉANDRE: The result is too fine for you to harbor resentment.

SGANARELLE: All right: I forgive you for the beatings in consideration of the dignity you've raised me to; but prepare henceforth to live in the greatest respect with a man of my consequence, and bear in mind that the wrath of a doctor is more to be feared than anyone can ever believe.

The exposition in the first scene of Molière's play is presented through action: Sganarelle's beating his wife both takes place on stage as present action and suggests the relationship between husband and wife that has roots in the past. The dialogue and the action define the characters, though in somewhat stereotypical fashion—the aggressive male, the shrewish female. The dialogue, especially Sganarelle's—"You did me too much honor, and I had reason to congratulate myself on our wedding night!"; "My good little wife, my love . . . My dear better half . . . Sweet object of my eternal vows"—also relates to the hostility between husband and wife, and in its sarcasm (hostile, sneering irony) prepares the way for the overall irony of the plot that Martine has set in motion by seeking revenge. This irony is heightened in the second scene (scenes in French Renaissance drama do not necessarily involve change of place or time but of the entrances and exits of characters) when Martine turns on Monsieur Robert who is trying to protect her. We are momentarily puzzled by her character; she seemed in the first fighting scene to be an independent, self-respecting woman, while here she seems to be defending her husband's right to abuse her. But the brief third scene contributes to her characterization, the plot, the comic, ironic tone, and the theme of gender conflict in the play: Martine is revealed as slyly plotting revenge under the cover of proper womanly submissiveness.

The conventional Renaissance subplot, with its "low" comic characters and young lovers whose situation both parallels and contrasts with the main couple, is introduced in the fourth scene of *The Doctor in Spite of Himself.* When Valère, the servant of Lucinde's father, and Lucas, husband of the wet-nurse at Lucinde's family's home, tell Martine, who literally bumps into them, of Lucinde's need for a doctor with miraculous cures, she invents her means of revenge. The plot and subplot are fused and the meaning of the title, *The Doctor in Spite of Himself,* emerges: Sganarelle will be beaten until, in spite of himself, he will act the part of a doctor. Martine will have her revenge and Lucinde her cure. Plot, subplot, theme, and character, dialogue, comedy, and the irony that pervades all the elements work together.

QUESTIONS

1. What does Martine mean, when she says in I. 3, "A wife always has in hand means of taking revenge on a husband"? Why does she reject that means?

In what way is her eventual scheme foolproof? How do her comment and choice relate to her character? to the action? to the plot? to the gender theme?

2. What are Sganarelle's reasons (note: there are at least two) for accepting his identity as a doctor? How do these relate to character? plot? theme?

3. By the end of the first act the "single action" of the play—Sganarelle beats Martine, she swears revenge, plots it, achieves it—is complete. How are the second and third acts related to that action? What difference do the later acts make in the characterization, structure, theme, of the play?

4. What is the function of Jacqueline in the subplot? love theme? characterization of Sganarelle? What is gained by having her identified specifically as a wet-nurse rather than as a general servant?

5. How is Lucinde cured? Why does her father agree to her marrying Léandre, whose suit he previously opposed?

WRITING SUGGESTIONS

1. Using the discussion in this chapter of the interaction of the elements of drama in *Trifles* as a model, write an essay showing how characterization, structure, theme, language and, where relevant, symbol interact in either *The Brute* or *The Black and White.* (For a longer paper, write on *Hamlet* or *The Little Foxes.*)

2. Deduce from the text of *The Doctor in Spite of Himself* Molière's view of doctors, using specific lines and incidents from the play to support your analysis.

3. The structure of comedy often involves at the beginning the disruption of a situation and at the end the restoration of the situation to some kind of stability. Describe Molière's play in these terms.

Exploring Contexts

4 THE AUTHOR'S WORK

Making comparisons is an inevitable activity of the mind, and as we read drama we can enlarge our understanding of a work by making comparisons—between this play and our own experience, between this play and other plays of the season, between this play and others by the same dramatist. No doubt you have already been making such comparisons as you've been reading the plays in this book.

Take *Hamlet* as an example: if you have read other tragedies or histories by Shakespeare, you may already be aware that the question of royal succession was of paramount importance to Shakespeare and his audience and may thus understand the emphasis laid upon it in this play. Moreover, whatever Shakespeare plays you have read or will go on to read, comparisons will show you how Shakespeare continually made his verse line more fluid and dramatic. Thus every new Shakespeare play you encounter will increase your knowledge of Shakespeare's "world." The present chapter provides some materials for the entry into another major playwright's world—that of Tennessee Williams.

The basic text is *A Streetcar Named Desire* (1947), Williams's second major success and considered by many his finest play. In order to amplify Williams's world for you beyond that play, we also include passages from his essays and memoirs.

Before we look at Williams's work, however, we might take a brief look at his life. If he called *The Glass Menagerie* (1945) a "memory play," to what extent does it mirror the playwright's own memories? And does his biography infuse the characters or moods of later plays?

Williams's mother, "Miss Edwina," the daughter of an Episcopalian minister, was repressed and genteel, very much the Southern belle in her youth; his father, Cornelius, was a traveling salesman, often away from his family and often violent and drunken when at home. The young Williams was a sickly child, overly protected by his mother, who fussed at him throughout her life; he was closely attached to his sister Rose, repelled by the roughhouse world of boys, and alienated from his father. The family's move from Mississippi to St. Louis, where Cornelius became a sales manager of the shoe company he had traveled for, was a shock to both Mrs. Williams and her young children, used to living in small southern towns where a minister's daughter was an important person. The change must also have made the strange city even more forbidding and hostile than it was. Yet Mrs. Williams was a woman who could take care of herself, a "survivor." The young Williams went to the University of Missouri, but left after two years: his father then found him a job in the shoe-factory warehouse. He worked there for ten months, writing at night, before succumbing to a heart attack. (Traumatized by this experience, which he called a "living death," he would later say that he had worked there for three years.) After recovering at his grandparents' home, he went on to further studies, finally graduating at the age of twenty-seven. Meanwhile Rose, who had been suffering from increasing mental imbalance, was allowed by her parents to be "tragically becalmed" by a prefrontal lobotomy; she has since spent the rest of her life in institutions. The next year Williams left for New Orleans, determined to become a writer.

"These are the cards life dealt Williams," the novelist Gore Vidal has cynically remarked, "and he played them for the rest of his life." But in comparing his life with the plays, we can see how art transmutes the autobiographical. In *The Glass Menagerie*, for example, the father has deserted his family years before; while Cornelius never deserted completely, his frequent absences must have made him shadowy indeed, and his presence must have been even harder to bear. Similarly, Edwina's ability to survive, her underlying strength of character, appears in the figure of Amanda Wingfield in the play. Yet, as our first passage from the *Memoirs* shows, Amanda is not Williams's mother: the character has been transformed into somebody unique and different. Finally, Laura both is and is not Rose. Laura's physical handicap is a transmutation of Rose's emotional one, and the sexuality implicit in Laura's relationship to the glass unicorn with his single phallic horn is based on Williams's intuition of Rose's mental illness—a plight that possessed him throughout his life, as is evinced by the appearance of a Rose-like character or rose imagery in many later plays.

There are no indictments in Williams's early life remotely like those that take place in *Streetcar*, despite some similarities between Williams's warehouse friend Kowalski, a lover of Williams's named Pancho, and the Stanley of the play. Williams's biographer Donald Spoto tells us that the first image of the earliest drafts of *Streetcar* was "simply that of a woman, sitting with folded hands near a window, while moonlight streamed in and she awaited in vain the arrival of her boy friend"; she was intended first as a younger Amanda. Even though Elia Kazan, who directed *Streetcar,* said that he "saw Blanche as Williams, an ambivalent figure who is attracted to the harshness and vulgarity around him at the same time that he fears it, because it threatens his life," in this play again art is the transmuting force.

Blanche speaks a heightened, rhythmic, southern language that may remind us of Flannery O'Connor—a language that differentiates her from the other characters whom she confronts and that she tries to use to distance herself from her confusion and her doom. It is worth comparing Stanley's speech rhythms as his attacks mount, and the breathlessness of his cornered victim.

You may also notice that Williams had an almost painterly vision of his settings: he wants scene 3 of *Streetcar* to look like a Van Gogh painting (elsewhere, he asks for a lightning like that of El Greco in *Menagerie* and he suggests that the bedroom in *Cat on a Hot Tin Roof* (1955) look like an old photograph of Robert Louis Stevenson's home in the South Seas). More importantly, we see that not only in scene 3 of *Streetcar* but throughout the play the action does not remain enclosed within the walls of the Kowalskis' apartment, but moves freely from the interior to the exterior street, with other buildings looming over the protagonists' dwelling.

In realizing this movement on the stage—a theatrical innovation at the time—Williams was happily served by his scenic designer Jo Mielziner, who also, as a matter of fact, designed the settings for *Cat* and for Arthur Miller's *Death of a Salesman.* Mielziner was developing special translucent scenery that, with the proper lighting, could be either opaque or transparent, but he gave some credit to Williams, saying later that "even as an inexperienced young writer, Tennessee Williams revealed a strong instinct for the visual qualities of the theatre. If he had written plays before the technical development of translucent and transparent scenery, I believe he would have invented it."

Mielziner went on to say of *Streetcar* that "throughout the play the brooding atmosphere is like an impressionistic X-ray. We are always conscious of the skeleton of this house of terror, even though we have peripheral impressions, like the chant of the Mexican woman which forms a background to a solo scene of Stella in her bedroom downstage." This is enhanced by full orchestration of other theatrical effects: special lighting within the settings, such as Blanche's paper lantern—lighting perhaps symbolic of the character herself;

music, such as the "Blue Piano" and the "Varsouviana," each of which introduces a mood within the play; and sounds, as in the "inhuman noises like cries in a jungle" in scene 10. All these, with language and setting, constitute what Williams liked to call "poetic realism" and which is uniquely his.

In reading *Streetcar*, we may also begin to see some characteristic themes that preoccupied Williams's writing throughout his life. One of these is a deep concern, an obsession, with sexuality. For Williams, as for D. H. Lawrence—in whose writings he was, especially in his early career, passionately interested—sexuality was a powerful and intense force: for Williams, however, the physical aspects of sex are a more dangerous, if not malevolent, force. There is no doubt that the ever-increasing intensity of Blanche and Stanley's effect on each other, with its consummation in scene 10, is what drives her into madness. That their confrontation came out of Williams's self has been noted by his director, Elia Kazan, and by his biographer, Donald Spoto, who writes that "in his creative struggles with himself and in his domestic struggles with Pancho [his lover at the time] . . . he met both the protective and destructive Stanley, and the gentle, needy, spiritual but manipulative sensualist Blanche."

The theme of the outsider is also central for Williams; he once said that he "existed outside of conventional society, while contriving somewhat precariously to remain in contact with it. For me this was not only precarious but a matter of dark unconscious disturbances." Tom Wingfield in *Menagerie* is only beginning the quest to become the outsider that, for Williams, it was necessary to become when he left home for New Orleans to be a writer. Blanche also may be seen as an outsider: in entering Stella's and Stanley's marriage, not only does her hold on her own life diminish increasingly, but at the same time she increasingly disturbs the life the Kowalskis have found. For to be an outsider can be, as well, to disrupt the "conventions" of the society one enters into, as the gentleman caller disrupts life in the Wingfield family.

In his *Memoirs* (1975), Williams wrote that "there is more sensibility—which is equivalent to more talent—among the 'gays' of both sexes than among the 'norms' . . . (Why? They must compensate for so much.)." In so saying, he links the life of the loner, the outsider, with the idea that art may arise out of suffering and deprivation—a compensation for pain or loss. In *Menagerie,* the unhappiness, the sense of lost or unexperienced adventure, the routine of life, make Tom into a poet. This is expressed most poignantly in his description of the young couples coming out of the dance hall across the alley and embracing among the garbage cans. The pleasure of those stolen embraces is denied him, but the deprivation provides him with the artistic impulse to describe them. He cannot take on the role of the gentleman caller, the young man who sets about making himself ready to be a good husband and father. He cannot take a girl out into the alley and embrace her because that would constitute a promise, a disposition to become something he is not: an ordinary person. Nor is Blanche an ordinary person; yet in celebrating her loneliness, Williams makes her speak for his tormented dramatic vision.

TENNESSEE WILLIAMS

A Streetcar Named Desire

And so it was I entered the broken world
To trace the visionary company of love, its voice
An instant in the wind (I know not whither hurled)
But not for long to hold each desperate choice.
—"The Broken Tower" by HART CRANE[1]

CHARACTERS

BLANCHE	PABLO
STELLA	A NEGRO WOMAN
STANLEY	A DOCTOR
MITCH	A NURSE (MATRON)
EUNICE	A YOUNG COLLECTOR
STEVE	A MEXICAN WOMAN

SCENE 1

The exterior of a two-story corner building on a street in New Orleans which is named Elysian Fields and runs between the L & N tracks and the river.[2] *The section is poor but, unlike corresponding sections in other American cities, it has a raffish charm. The houses are mostly white frame, weathered grey, with rickety outside stairs and galleries and quaintly ornamented gables. This building contains two flats, upstairs and down. Faded white stairs ascend to the entrances of both.*

It is first dark of an evening early in May. The sky that shows around the dim white building is a peculiarly tender blue, almost a turquoise, which invests the scene with a kind of lyricism and gracefully attenuates the atmosphere of decay. You can almost feel the warm breath of the brown river beyond the river warehouses with their faint redolences of bananas and coffee. A corresponding air is evoked by the music of Negro entertainers at a barroom around the corner. In this

1. Americn poet (1899–1932). 2. Elysian Fields is in fact a New Orleans street at the northern tip of the French Quarter, between the Louisville & Nashville railroad tracks and the Mississippi River. In Greek mythology, the Elysian Fields are the abode of the blessed in the afterlife; in Paris, the Champs Elysées is a grand boulevard.

part of New Orleans you are practically always just around the corner, or a few doors down the street, from a tinny piano being played with the infatuated fluency of brown fingers. This "Blue Piano" expresses the spirit of the life which goes on here.

Two women, one white and one colored, are taking the air on the steps of the building. The white woman is EUNICE, *who occupies the upstairs flat; the colored woman a neighbor, for New Orleans is a cosmopolitan city where there is a relatively warm and easy intermingling of races in the old part of town.*

Above the music of the "Blue Piano" the voices of people on the street can be heard overlapping.

[*Two men come around the corner,* STANLEY KOWALSKI *and* MITCH. *They are about twenty-eight, or thirty years old, roughly dressed in blue denim work clothes.* STANLEY *carries his bowling jacket and a red-stained package from a butcher's. They stop at the foot of the steps.*]

STANLEY: [*Bellowing.*] Hey there! Stella, baby!

[STELLA *comes out on the first floor landing, a gentle young woman, about twenty-five, and of a background obviously quite different from her husband's.*]

STELLA: [*Mildly.*] Don't holler at me like that. Hi, Mitch.
STANLEY: Catch!
STELLA: What?
STANLEY: Meat!

[*He heaves the package at her. She cries out in protest but manages to catch it: then she laughs breathlessly. Her husband and his companion have already started back around the corner.*]

STELLA: [*Calling after him.*] Stanley! Where are you going?
STANLEY: Bowling!
STELLA: Can I come watch?
STANLEY: Come on. [*He goes out.*]
STELLA: Be over soon. [*To the white woman.*] Hello, Eunice. How are you?
EUNICE: I'm all right. Tell Steve to get him a poor boy's sandwich[3] 'cause nothing's left here.

[*They all laugh; the colored woman does not stop.* STELLA *goes out.*]

COLORED WOMAN: What was that package he th'ew at 'er? [*She rises from steps, laughing louder.*]
EUNICE: You hush, now!
NEGRO WOMAN: Catch *what!*

[*She continues to laugh.* BLANCHE *comes around the corner, carrying a valise. She looks at a slip of paper, then at the building, then again at the slip and*

3. Usually called just "poor boy" or "po' boy." Similar to a hero or submarine sandwich.

again at the building. Her expression is one of shocked disbelief. Her appearance is incongruous to this setting. She is daintily dressed in a white suit with a fluffy bodice, necklace and earrings of pearl, white gloves and hat, looking as if she were arriving at a summer tea or cocktail party in the garden district. She is about five years older than STELLA. *Her delicate beauty must avoid a strong light. There is something about her uncertain manner, as well as her white clothes, that suggests a moth.*]

EUNICE: [*Finally.*] What's the matter, honey? Are you lost?

BLANCHE: [*With faintly hysterical humor.*] They told me to take a street-car named Desire, and then transfer to one called Cemeteries[4] and ride six blocks and get off at—Elysian Fields!

EUNICE: That's where you are now.

BLANCHE: At Elysian Fields?

EUNICE: This here is Elysian Fields.

BLANCHE: They mustn't have—understood—what number I wanted . . .

EUNICE: What number you lookin' for?

[BLANCHE *wearily refers to the slip of paper.*]

BLANCHE: Six thirty-two.

EUNICE: You don't have to look no further.

BLANCHE: [*Uncomprehendingly.*] I'm looking for my sister, Stella DuBois, I mean—Mrs. Stanley Kowalski.

EUNICE: That's the party.—You just did miss her, though.

BLANCHE: This—can this be—her home?

EUNICE: She's got the downstairs here and I got the up.

BLANCHE: Oh. She's—out?

EUNICE: You noticed that bowling alley around the corner?

BLANCHE: I'm—not sure I did.

EUNICE: Well, that's where she's at, watchin' her husband bowl. [*There is a pause.*] You want to leave your suitcase here an' go find her?

BLANCHE: No.

NEGRO WOMAN: I'll go tell her you come.

BLANCHE: Thanks.

NEGRO WOMAN: You welcome. [*She goes out.*]

EUNICE: She wasn't expecting you?

BLANCHE: No. No, not tonight.

EUNICE: Well, why don't you just go in and make yourself at home till they get back.

BLANCHE: How could I—do that?

EUNICE: We own this place so I can let you in.

[*She gets up and opens the downstairs door. A light goes on behind the blind, turning it light blue.* BLANCHE *slowly follows her into the downstairs flat. The surrounding areas dim out as the interior is lighted. Two rooms can be seen,*

4. Desire is a street in New Orleans, Cemeteries the end of a streetcar line that stopped at a cemetery.

not too clearly defined. The one first entered is primarily a kitchen but contains a folding bed to be used by BLANCHE. *The room beyond this is a bedroom. Off this room is a narrow door to a bathroom.*]

EUNICE: [*Defensively, noticing* BLANCHE'*s look.*] It's sort of messed up right now but when it's clean it's real sweet.

BLANCHE: Is it?

EUNICE: Uh-huh, I think so. So you're Stella's sister?

BLANCHE: Yes. [*Wanting to get rid of her.*] Thanks for letting me in.

EUNICE: *Por nada*, as the Mexicans say, *por nada!*[5] Stella spoke of you.

BLANCHE: Yes?

EUNICE: I think she said you taught school.

BLANCHE: Yes.

EUNICE: And you're from Mississippi, huh?

BLANCHE: Yes.

EUNICE: She showed me a picture of your home-place, the plantation.

BLANCHE: Belle Reve?[6]

EUNICE: A great big place with white columns.

BLANCHE: Yes . . .

EUNICE: A place like that must be awful hard to keep up.

BLANCHE: If you will excuse me, I'm just about to drop.

EUNICE: Sure, honey. Why don't you set down?

BLANCHE: What I meant was I'd like to be left alone.

EUNICE: [*Offended.*] Aw. I'll make myself scarce, in that case.

BLANCHE: I didn't meant to be rude, but—

EUNICE: I'll drop by the bowling alley an' hustle her up. [*She goes out the door.*]

[BLANCHE *sits in a chair very stiffly with her shoulders slightly hunched and her legs pressed close together and her hands tightly clutching her purse as if she were quite cold. After a while the blind look goes out of her eyes and she begins to look slowly around. A cat screeches. She catches her breath with a startled gesture. Suddenly she notices something in a half opened closet. She springs up and crosses to it, and removes a whiskey bottle. She pours a half tumbler of whiskey and tosses it down. She carefully replaces the bottle and washes out the tumbler at the sink. Then she resumes her seat in front of the table.*]

BLANCHE: [*Faintly to herself.*] I've got to keep hold of myself!

[*Stella comes quickly around the corner of the building and runs to the door of the downstairs flat.*]

STELLA: [*Calling out joyfully.*] *Blanche!*

[*For a moment they stare at each other. Then* BLANCHE *springs up and runs to her with a wild cry.*]

BLANCHE: Stella, oh, Stella, Stella! Stella for Star!

5. "It's nothing." 6. "Beautiful Dream."

[*She begins to speak with feverish vivacity as if she feared for either of them to stop and think. They catch each other in a spasmodic embrace.*]

BLANCHE: Now, then, let me look at you. But don't you look at me, Stella, no, no, no, not till later, not till I've bathed and rested! And turn that over-light off! Turn that off! I won't be looked at in this merciless glare! [STELLA *laughs and complies.*] Come back here now! Oh, my baby! Stella! Stella for Star! [*She embraces her again.*] I thought you would never come back to this horrible place! What am I saying? I didn't mean to say that. I meant to be nice about it and say—Oh, what a convenient location and such—Ha-a-ha! Precious lamb! You haven't said a *word* to me.

STELLA: You haven't given me a chance to, honey! [*She laughs, but her glance at* BLANCHE *is a little anxious.*]

BLANCHE: Well, now you talk. Open your pretty mouth and talk while I look around for some liquor! I know you must have some liquor on the place! Where could it be, I wonder? Oh, I spy, I spy! [*She rushes to the closet and removes the bottle; she is shaking all over and panting for breath as she tries to laugh. The bottle nearly slips from her grasp.*]

STELLA: [*Noticing.*] Blanche, you sit down and let me pour the drinks. I don't know what we've got to mix with. Maybe a coke in the icebox. Look'n see, honey, while I'm—

BLANCHE: No coke, honey, not with my nerves tonight! Where—where—where is—?

STELLA: Stanley? Bowling! He loves it. They're having a—found some soda!—tournament . . .

BLANCHE: Just water, baby, to chase it! Now don't get worried, your sister hasn't turned into a drunkard, she's just all shaken up and hot and tired and dirty! You sit down, now, and explain this place to me! What are you doing in a place like this?

STELLA: Now, Blanche—

BLANCHE: Oh, I'm not going to be hypocritical, I'm going to be honestly critical about it! Never, never, never in my worst dreams could I picture— Only Poe! Only Mr. Edgar Allan Poe!—could do it justice! Out there I suppose is the ghoul-haunted woodland of Weir![7] [*She laughs.*]

STELLA: No, honey, those are the L & N tracks.

BLANCHE: No, now seriously, putting joking aside. Why didn't you tell me, why didn't you write me, honey, why didn't you let me know?

STELLA: [*Carefully, pouring herself a drink.*] Tell you what, Blanche?

BLANCHE: Why, that you had to live in these conditions!

STELLA: Aren't you being a little intense about it? It's not that bad at all! New Orleans isn't like other cities.

BLANCHE: This has got nothing to do with New Orleans. You might as well say—forgive me, blessed baby! [*She suddenly stops short.*] The subject is closed!

STELLA: [*A little drily.*] Thanks.

7. From the refrain of Poe's gothic ballad *Ulalume* (1847).

[*During the pause,* BLANCHE *stares at her. She smiles at* BLANCHE.]

BLANCHE: [*Looking down at her glass, which shakes in her hand.*] You're all I've got in the world, and you're not glad to see me!

STELLA: [*Sincerely.*] Why, Blanche, you know that's not true.

BLANCHE: No?—I'd forgotten how quiet you were.

STELLA: You never did give me a chance to say much, Blanche. So I just got in the habit of being quiet around you.

BLANCHE: [*Vaguely.*] A good habit to get into . . . [*Then, abruptly.*] You haven't asked me how I happened to get away from the school before the spring term ended.

STELLA: Well, I thought you'd volunteer that information—if you wanted to tell me.

BLANCHE: You thought I'd been fired?

STELLA: No, I—thought you might have—resigned . . .

BLANCHE: I was so exhausted by all I'd been through my—nerves broke. [*Nervously tamping cigarette.*] I was on the verge of—lunacy, almost! So Mr. Graves—Mr. Graves is the high school superintendent—he suggested I take a leave of absence. I couldn't put all of those details into the wire . . . [*She drinks quickly.*] Oh, this buzzes right through me and feels so *good!*

STELLA: Won't you have another?

BLANCHE: No, one's my limit.

STELLA: Sure?

BLANCHE: You haven't said a word about my appearance.

STELLA: You look just fine.

BLANCHE: God love you for a liar! Daylight never exposed so total a ruin! But you—you've put on some weight, yes, you're just as plump as a little partridge! And it's so becoming to you!

STELLA: Now, Blanche—

BLANCHE: Yes, it is, it is or I wouldn't say it! You just have to watch around the hips a little. Stand up.

STELLA: Not now.

BLANCHE: You hear me? I said stand up! [STELLA *complies reluctantly.*] You messy child, you, you've spilt something on that pretty white lace collar! About your hair—you ought to have it cut in a feather bob with your dainty features. Stella, you have a maid, don't you?

STELLA: No. With only two rooms it's—

BLANCHE: What? *Two* rooms, did you say?

STELLA: This one and—[*She is embarrassed.*]

BLANCHE: The other one? [*She laughs sharply. There is an embarrassed silence.*]

BLANCHE: I am going to take just one little tiny nip more, sort of to put the stopper on, so to speak. . . . Then put the bottle away so I won't be tempted. [*She rises.*] I want you to look at *my* figure! [*She turns around.*] You know I haven't put on one ounce in ten years, Stella? I weigh what I weighed the summer you left Belle Reve. The summer Dad died and you left us . . .

STELLA: [*A little wearily.*] It's just incredible, Blanche, how well you're looking.

BLANCHE: [*They both laugh uncomfortably.*] But, Stella, there's only two rooms, I don't see where you're going to put me!

STELLA: We're going to put you in here.

BLANCHE: What kind of bed's this—one of those collapsible things? [*She sits on it.*]

STELLA: Does it feel all right?

BLANCHE: [*Dubiously.*] Wonderful, honey. I don't like a bed that gives much. But there's no door between the two rooms, and Stanley—will it be decent?

STELLA: Stanley is Polish, you know.

BLANCHE: Oh, yes. They're something like Irish, aren't they?

STELLA: Well—

BLANCHE: Only not so—highbrow? [*They both laugh again in the same way.*] I brought some nice clothes to meet all your lovely friends in.

STELLA: I'm afraid you won't think they are lovely.

BLANCHE: What are they like?

STELLA: They're Stanley's friends.

BLANCHE: Polacks?

STELLA: They're a mixed lot, Blanche.

BLANCHE: Heterogeneous—types?

STELLA: Oh, yes. Yes, types is right!

BLANCHE: Well—anyhow—I brought nice clothes and I'll wear them. I guess you're hoping I'll say I'll put up at a hotel, but I'm not going to put up at a hotel. I want to be *near* you, got to be *with* somebody, I *can't* be *alone!* Because—as you must have noticed—I'm—*not* very *well*. . . . [*Her voice drops and her look is frightened.*]

STELLA: You seem a little bit nervous or overwrought or something.

BLANCHE: Will Stanley like me, or will I be just a visiting in-law, Stella? I couldn't stand that.

STELLA: You'll get along fine together, if you'll just try not to—well—compare him with men that we went out with at home.

BLANCHE: Is he so—different?

STELLA: Yes. A different species.

BLANCHE: In what way; what's he like?

STELLA: Oh, you can't describe someone you're in love with! Here's a picture of him! [*She hands a photograph to* BLANCHE.]

BLANCHE: An officer?

STELLA: A Master Sergeant in the Engineers' Corps. Those are decorations!

BLANCHE: He had those on when you met him?

STELLA: I assure you I wasn't just blinded by all the brass.

BLANCHE: That's not what I—

STELLA: But of course there were things to adjust myself to later on.

BLANCHE: Such as his civilian background! [STELLA *laughs uncertainly.*] How did he take it when you said I was coming?

STELLA: Oh, Stanley doesn't know yet.

BLANCHE: [*Frightened.*] You—haven't told him?

STELLA: He's on the road a good deal.

BLANCHE: Oh. Travels?
STELLA: Yes.
BLANCHE: Good. I mean—isn't it?
STELLA: [*Half to herself.*] I can hardly stand it when he is away for a night . . .
BLANCHE: Why, Stella!
STELLA: When he's away for a week I nearly go wild!
BLANCHE: Gracious!
STELLA: And when he comes back I cry on his lap like a baby . . . [*She smiles to herself.*]
BLANCHE: I guess that is what is meant by being in love . . . [STELLA *looks up with a radiant smile.*] Stella—
STELLA: What?
BLANCHE: [*In an uneasy rush.*] I haven't asked you the things you probably thought I was going to ask. And so I'll expect you to be understanding about what *I* have to tell *you*.
STELLA: What, Blanche? [*Her face turns anxious.*]
BLANCHE: Well, Stella—you're going to reproach me, I know that you're bound to reproach me—but before you do—take into consideration—you left! I stayed and struggled! You came to New Orleans and looked out for yourself! *I* stayed at Belle Reve and tried to hold it together! I'm not meaning this in any reproachful way, but *all* the burden descended on *my* shoulders.
STELLA: The best I could do was make my own living, Blanche.

[BLANCHE *begins to shake again with intensity.*]

BLANCHE: I know, I know. But you are the one that abandoned Belle Reve, not I! I stayed and fought for it, bled for it, almost died for it!
STELLA: Stop this hysterical outburst and tell me what's happened? What do you mean fought and bled? What kind of—
BLANCHE: I knew you would, Stella. I knew you would take this attitude about it!
STELLA: About—what?—please!
BLANCHE: [*Slowly.*] The loss—the loss . . .
STELLA: Belle Reve? Lost, is it? No!
BLANCHE: Yes, Stella.

[*They stare at each other across the yellow-checked linoleum of the table.* BLANCHE *slowly nods her head and* STELLA *looks slowly down at her hands folded on the table. The music of the "Blue Piano" grows louder.* BLANCHE *touches her handkerchief to her forehead.*]

STELLA: But how did it go? What happened?
BLANCHE: [*Springing up.*] You're a fine one to ask me how it went!
STELLA: Blanche!
BLANCHE: You're a fine one to sit there *accusing me* of it!
STELLA: *Blanche!*
BLANCHE: I, I, *I* took the blows in my face and my body! All of those deaths! The long parade to the graveyard! Father, mother! Margaret, that dreadful way! So big with it, it couldn't be put in a coffin! But had to be burned like

rubbish! You just came home in time for the funerals, Stella. And funerals are pretty compared to deaths. Funerals are quiet, but deaths—not always. Sometimes their breathing is hoarse, and sometimes it rattles, and sometimes they even cry out to you, "Don't let me go!" Even the old, sometimes, say, "Don't let me go." As if you were able to stop them! But funerals are quiet, with pretty flowers. And, oh, what gorgeous boxes they pack them away in! Unless you were there at the bed when they cried out, "Hold me!" you'd never suspect there was the struggle for breath and bleeding. You didn't dream, but I saw! *Saw! Saw!* And now you sit there telling me with your eyes that I let the place go! How in hell do you think all that sickness and dying was paid for? Death is expensive, Miss Stella! And old Cousin Jessie's right after Margaret's, hers! Why, the Grim Reaper had put up his tent on our doorstep! . . . Stella. Belle Reve was his headquarters! Honey—that's how it slipped through my fingers! Which of them left us a fortune? Which of them left a cent of insurance even? Only poor Jessie—one hundred to pay for her coffin. That was all, Stella! And I with my pitiful salary at the school. Yes, accuse me! Sit there and stare at me, thinking I let the place go! *I* let the place go? Where were *you!* In bed with your—Polack!

STELLA: [*Springing.*] Blanche! You be still! That's enough! [*She starts out.*]
BLANCHE: Where are you going?
STELLA: I'm going into the bathroom to wash my face.
BLANCHE: Oh, Stella, Stella, you're crying!
STELLA: Does that surprise you?
BLANCHE: Forgive me—I didn't mean to—

[*The sound of men's voices is heard.* STELLA *goes into the bathroom, closing the door behind her. When the men appear, and* BLANCHE *realizes it must be* STANLEY *returning, she moves uncertainly from the bathroom door to the dressing table, looking apprehensively toward the front door.* STANLEY *enters, followed by* STEVE *and* MITCH. STANLEY *pauses near his door,* STEVE *by the foot of the spiral stair, and* MITCH *is slightly above and to the right of them, about to go out. As the men enter, we hear some of the following dialogue.*]

STANLEY: Is that how he got it?
STEVEN: Sure that's how he got it. He hit the old weather-bird for 300 bucks on a six-number-ticket.
MITCH: Don't tell him those things; he'll believe it. [*Mitch starts out.*]
STANLEY: [*Restraining Mitch.*] Hey, Mitch—come back here.

[BLANCHE, *at the sound of voices, retires in the bedroom. She picks up* STANLEY*'s photo from dressing table, looks at it, puts it down. When* STANLEY *enters the apartment, she darts and hides behind the screen at the head of bed.*]

STEVE: [*To* STANLEY *and* MITCH.] Hey, are we playin' poker tomorrow?
STANLEY: Sure—at Mitch's.
MITCH: [*Hearing this, returns quickly to the stair rail.*] No—not at my place. My mother's still sick!

STANLEY: Okay, at my place . . . [MITCH *starts out again.*] But you bring the beer!

[MITCH *pretends not to hear—calls out "Good night, all," and goes out, singing.* EUNICE'*s voice is heard, above.*]

EUNICE: Break it up down there! I made the spaghetti dish and ate it myself.
STEVE: [*Going upstairs.*] I told you and phoned you we was playing. [*To the men.*] Jax[8] beer!
EUNICE: You never phoned me once.
STEVE: I told you at breakfast—and phoned you at lunch . . .
EUNICE: Well, never mind about that. You just get yourself home here once in a while.
STEVE: You want it in the papers?

[*More laughter and shouts of parting come from the men.* STANLEY *throws the screen door of the kitchen open and comes in. He is of medium height, about five feet eight or nine, and strongly, compactly built. Animal joy in his being is implicit in all his movements and attitudes. Since earliest manhood the center of his life has been pleasure with women, the giving and taking of it, not with weak indulgence, dependently, but with the power and pride of a richly feathered male bird among hens. Branching out from this complete and satisfying center are all the auxiliary channels of his life, such as his heartiness with men, his appreciation of rough humor, his love of good drink and food and games, his car, his radio, everything that is his, that bears his emblem of the gaudy seed-bearer. He sizes women up at a glance, with sexual classifications, crude images flashing into his mind and determining the way he smiles at them.*]

BLANCHE: [*Drawing involuntarily back from his stare.*] You must be Stanley. I'm Blanche.
STANLEY: Stella's sister?
BLANCHE: Yes.
STANLEY: H'lo. Where's the little woman?
BLANCHE: In the bathroom.
STANLEY: Oh. Didn't know you were coming in town.
BLANCHE: I—uh—
STANLEY: Where you from, Blanche?
BLANCHE: Why, I—live in Laurel.

[*He has crossed to the closet and removed the whiskey bottle.*]

STANLEY: In Laurel, huh? Oh, yeah. Yeah, in Laurel, that's right. Not in my territory. Liquor goes fast in hot weather. [*He holds the bottle to the light to observe its depletion.*] Have a shot?
BLANCHE: No, I—rarely touch it.
STANLEY: Some people rarely touch it, but it touches them often.

8. A local brand.

BLANCHE: [*Faintly.*] Ha-ha.

STANLEY: My clothes're stickin' to me. Do you mind if I make myself comfortable? [*He starts to remove his shirt.*]

BLANCHE: Please, please do.

STANLEY: Be comfortable is my motto.

BLANCHE: It's mine, too. It's hard to stay looking fresh. I haven't washed or even powdered my face and—here you are!

STANLEY: You know you can catch cold sitting around in damp things, especially when you been exercising hard like bowling is. You're a teacher, aren't you?

BLANCHE: Yes.

STANLEY: What do you teach, Blanche?

BLANCHE: English.

STANLEY: I never was a very good English student. How long you here for, Blanche?

BLANCHE: I—don't know yet.

STANLEY: You going to shack up here?

BLANCHE: I thought I would if it's not inconvenient for you all.

STANLEY: Good.

BLANCHE: Traveling wears me out.

STANLEY: Well, take it easy.

[*A cat screeches near the window.* BLANCHE *springs up.*]

BLANCHE: What's that?

STANLEY: Cats . . . Hey, Stella!

STELLA: [*Faintly, from the bathroom.*] Yes, Stanley.

STANLEY: Haven't fallen in, have you? [*He grins at* BLANCHE. *She tries unsuccessfully to smile back. There is a silence.*] I'm afraid I'll strike you as being the unrefined type. Stella's spoke of you a good deal. You were married once, weren't you?

[*The music of the polka rises up, faint in the distance.*]

BLANCHE: Yes. When I was quite young.

STANLEY: What happened?

BLANCHE: The boy—the boy died. [*She sinks back down.*] I'm afraid I'm—going to be sick! [*Her head falls on her arms.*]

SCENE 2

It is six o'clock the following evening. BLANCHE *is bathing.* STELLA *is completing her toilette.* BLANCHE*'s dress, a flowered print, is laid out on* STELLA*'s bed.*

STANLEY *enters the kitchen from outside, leaving the door open on the perpetual "Blue Piano" around the corner.*

STANLEY: What's all this monkey doings?

STELLA: Oh, Stan! [*She jumps up and kisses him, which he accepts with lordly composure.*] I'm taking Blanche to Galatoire's for supper and then to a show, because it's your poker night.

STANLEY: How about my supper, huh? I'm not going to no Galatoire's[9] for supper!

STELLA: I put you a cold plate on ice.

STANLEY: Well, isn't that just dandy!

STELLA: I'm going to try to keep Blanche out till the party breaks up because I don't know how she would take it. So we'll go to one of the little places in the Quarter afterward and you'd better give me some money.

STANLEY: Where is she?

STELLA: She's soaking in a hot tub to quiet her nerves. She's terribly upset.

STANLEY: Over what?

STELLA: She's been through such an ordeal.

STANLEY: Yeah?

STELLA: Stan, we've—lost Belle Reve!

STANLEY: The place in the country?

STELLA: Yes.

STANLEY: How?

STELLA: [*Vaguely.*] Oh, it had to be—sacrificed or something. [*There is a pause while* STANLEY *considers.* STELLA *is changing into her dress.*] When she comes in be sure to say something nice about her appearance. And, oh! Don't mention the baby. I haven't said anything yet, I'm waiting until she gets in a quieter condition.

STANLEY: [*Ominously.*] So?

STELLA: And try to understand her and be nice to her, Stan.

BLANCHE: [*Singing in the bathroom.*] "From the land of the sky blue water, They brought a captive maid!"

STELLA: She wasn't expecting to find us in such a small place. You see I'd tried to gloss things over a little in my letters.

STANLEY: So?

STELLA: And admire her dress and tell her she's looking wonderful. That's important with Blanche. Her little weakness!

STANLEY: Yeah. I get the idea. Now let's skip back a little to where you said the country place was disposed of.

STELLA: Oh!—yes . . .

STANLEY: How about that? Let's have a few more details on that subjeck.

STELLA: It's best not to talk much about it until she's calmed down.

STANLEY: So that's the deal, huh? Sister Blanche cannot be annoyed with business details right now!

STELLA: You saw how she was last night.

STANLEY: Uh-hum, I saw how she was. Now let's have a gander at the bill of sale.

STELLA: I haven't seen any.

STANLEY: She didn't show you no papers, no deed of sale or nothing like that, huh?

STELLA: It seems like it wasn't sold.

9. A famous old restaurant on Bourbon Street in the French Quarter.

STANLEY: Well, what in hell was it then, give away? To charity?

STELLA: Shhh! She'll hear you.

STANLEY: I don't care if she hears me. Let's see the papers!

STELLA: There weren't any papers, she didn't show any papers, I don't care about papers.

STANLEY: Have you ever heard of the Napoleonic code?[1]

STELLA: No, Stanley, I haven't heard of the Napoleonic code and if I have, I don't see what it—

STANLEY: Let me enlighten you on a point or two, baby.

STELLA: Yes?

STANLEY: In the state of Louisiana we have the Napoleonic code according to which what belongs to the wife belongs to the husband and vice versa. For instance if I had a piece of property, or you had a piece of property—

STELLA: My head is swimming!

STANLEY: All right. I'll wait till she gets through soaking in a hot tub and then I'll inquire if *she* is acquainted with the Napoleonic code. It looks to me like you have been swindled, baby, and when you're swindled under the Napoleonic code I'm swindled *too*. And I don't like to be *swindled*.

STELLA: There's plenty of time to ask her questions later but if you do now she'll go to pieces again. I don't undertand what happened to Belle Reve but you don't know how ridiculous you are being when you suggest that my sister or I or anyone of our family could have perpetrated a swindle on anyone else.

STANLEY: Then where's the money if the place was sold?

STELLA: Not sold—*lost, lost!* [*He stalks into bedroom, and she follows him.*] *Stanley!*

[*He pulls open the wardrobe trunk standing in middle of room and jerks out an armful of dresses.*]

STANLEY: Open your eyes to this stuff! You think she got them out of a teacher's pay?

STELLA: Hush!

STANLEY: Look at these feathers and furs that she come here to preen herself in! What's this here? A solid-gold dress, I believe! And this one! What is these here? Fox-pieces! [*He blows on them.*] Genuine fox fur-pieces, a half a mile long! Where are your fox-pieces, Stella? Bushy snowwhite ones, no less! Where are your white fox-pieces?

STELLA: Those are inexpensive summer furs that Blanche has had a long time.

STANLEY: I got an acquaintance who deals in this sort of merchandise. I'll have him in here to appraise it. I'm willing to bet you there's thousands of dollars invested in this stuff here!

STELLA: Don't be such an idiot, Stanley!

[*He hurls the furs to the day bed. Then he jerks open small drawer in the trunk and pulls up a fistful of costume jewelry.*]

1. This codification of French law (1802), made by Napoleon as emperor, is the basis for Louisiana's civil law.

STANLEY: And what have we here? The treasure chest of a pirate!

STELLA: Oh, Stanley!

STANLEY: Pearls! Ropes of them! What is this sister of yours, a deep-sea diver? Bracelets of solid gold, too! Where are your pearls and gold bracelets?

STELLA: Shhh! Be still, Stanley!

STANLEY: And diamonds! A crown for an empress!

STELLA: A rhinestone tiara she wore to a costume ball.

STANLEY: What's rhinestone?

STELLA: Next door to glass.

STANLEY: Are you kidding? I have an acquaintance that works in a jewelry store. I'll have him in here to make an appraisal of this. Here's your plantation, or what was left of it, here!

STELLA: You have no idea how stupid and horrid you're being! Now close that trunk before she comes out of the bathroom!

[*He kicks the trunk partly closed and sits on the kitchen table.*]

STANLEY: The Kowalskis and the DuBoises have different notions.

STELLA: [*Angrily.*] Indeed they have, thank heavens!—*I'm* going outside. [*She snatches up her white hat and gloves and crosses to the outside door.*] You come out with me while Blanche is getting dressed.

STANLEY: Since when do you give me orders?

STELLA: Are you going to stay here and insult her?

STANLEY: You're damn tootin' I'm going to stay here.

[STELLA *goes out to the porch.* BLANCHE *comes out of the bathroom in a red satin robe.*]

BLANCHE: [*Airily.*] Hello, Stanley! Here I am, all freshly bathed and scented, and feeling like a brand new human being!

[*He lights a cigarette.*]

STANLEY: That's good.

BLANCHE: [*Drawing the curtains at the windows.*] Excuse me while I slip on my pretty new dress!

STANLEY: Go right ahead, Blanche.

[*She closes the drapes between the rooms.*]

BLANCHE: I undertsand there's to be a little card party to which we ladies are cordially *not* invited!

STANLEY: [*ominously*] Yeah?

[BLANCHE *throws off her robe and slips into a flowered print dress.*]

BLANCHE: Where's Stella?

STANLEY: Out on the porch.

BLANCHE: I'm going to ask a favor of you in a moment.

STANLEY: What could that be, I wonder?

BLANCHE: Some buttons in back! You may enter! [*He crosses through drapes with a smoldering look.*] How do I look?
STANLEY: You look all right.
BLANCHE: Many thanks! Now the buttons!
STANLEY: I can't do nothing with them.
BLANCHE: You men with your big clumsy fingers. May I have a drag on your cig?
STANLEY: Have one for yourself.
BLANCHE: Why, thanks! . . . It looks like my trunk has exploded.
STANLEY: Me an' Stella were helping you unpack.
BLANCHE: Well, you certainly did a fast and thorough job of it!
STANLEY: It looks like you raided some stylish shops in Paris.
BLANCHE: Ha-ha! Yes—clothes are my passion!
STANLEY: What does it cost for a string of fur-pieces like that?
BLANCHE: Why, those were a tribute from an admirer of mine!
STANLEY: He must have had a lot of—admiration!
BLANCHE: Oh, in my youth I excited some admiration. But look at me now! [*She smiles at him radiantly.*] Would you think it possible that I was once considered to be—attractive?
STANLEY: Your looks are okay.
BLANCHE: I was fishing for a compliment, Stanley.
STANLEY: I don't go in for that stuff.
BLANCHE: What—stuff?
STANLEY: Compliments to women about their looks. I never met a woman that didn't know if she was good-looking or not without being told, and some of them give themselves credit for more than they've got. I once went out with a doll who said to me, "I am the glamorous type, I am the glamorous type!" I said, "So what?
BLANCHE: And what did she say then?
STANLEY: She didn't say nothing. That shut her up like a clam.
BLANCHE: Did it end the romance?
STANLEY: It ended the conversation—that was all. Some men are took in by this Hollywood glamor stuff and some men are not.
BLANCHE: I'm sure you belong in the second category.
STANLEY: That's right.
BLANCHE: I cannot imagine any witch of a woman casting a spell over you.
STANLEY: That's—right.
BLANCHE: You're simple, straightforward and honest, a little bit on the primitive side I should think. To interest you a woman would have to—[*She pauses with an indefinite gesture.*]
STANLEY: [*Slowly.*] Lay . . . her cards on the table.
BLANCHE: [*Smiling.*] Well, I never cared for wishy-washy people. That was why, when you walked in here last night, I said to myself—"My sister has married a man!"—Of course that was all that I could tell about you.
STANLEY: [*Booming.*] Now let's cut the re-bop![2]

2. Nonsense syllables (from "bop," a form of jazz).

BLANCHE: [*Pressing hands to her ears.*] Ouuuuu!

STELLA: [*Calling from the steps.*] Stanley! You come out here and let Blanche finish dressing!

BLANCHE: I'm through dressing, honey.

STELLA: Well, you come out, then.

STANLEY: Your sister and I are having a little talk.

BLANCHE: [*Lightly.*] Honey, do me a favor. Run to the drugstore and get me a lemon Coke with plenty of chipped ice in it!—Will you do that for me, sweetie?

STELLA: [*Uncertainly.*] Yes. [*She goes around the corner of the building.*]

BLANCHE: The poor little thing was out there listening to us, and I have an idea she doesn't understand you as well as I do. . . . All right; now, Mr. Kowalski, let us proceed without any more double-talk. I'm ready to answer all questions. I've nothing to hide. What is it?

STANLEY: There is such a thing in this state of Louisiana as the Napoleonic code, according to which whatever belongs to my wife is also mine—and vice versa.

BLANCHE: My, but you have an impressive judicial air!

[*She sprays herself with her atomizer; then playfully sprays him with it. He seizes the atomizer and slams it down on the dresser. She throws back her head and laughs.*]

STANLEY: If I didn't know that you was my wife's sister I'd get ideas about you!

BLANCHE: Such as what!

STANLEY: Don't play so dumb. You know what!

BLANCHE: [*She puts the atomizer on the table.*] All right. Cards on the table. That suits me. [*She turns to* STANLEY.] I know I fib a good deal. After all, a woman's charm is fifty per cent illusion, but when a thing is important I tell the truth, and this is the truth: I haven't cheated my sister or you or anyone else as long as I have lived.

STANLEY: Where's the papers? In the trunk?

BLANCHE: Everything that I own is in that trunk.

[STANLEY *crosses to the trunk, shoves it roughly open and begins to open compartments.*]

BLANCHE: What in the name of heaven are you thinking of! What's in the back of that little boy's mind of yours? That I am absconding with something, attempting some kind of treachery on my sister?—Let me do that! It will be faster and simpler . . . [*She crosses to the trunk and takes out a box.*] I keep my papers mostly in this tin box. [*She opens it.*]

STANLEY: What's them underneath? [*He indicates another sheaf of paper.*]

BLANCHE: These are love-letters, yellowing with antiquity, all from one boy. [*He snatches them up. She speaks fiercely.*] Give those back to me!

STANLEY: I'll have a look at them first!

BLANCHE: The touch of your hands insults them!

STANLEY: Don't pull that stuff!

[*He rips off the ribbon and starts to examine them.* BLANCHE *snatches them from him, and they cascade to the floor.*]

BLANCHE: Now that you've touched them I'll burn them!

STANLEY: [*Staring, baffled.*] What in hell are they?

BLANCHE: [*On the floor gathering them up.*] Poems a dead boy wrote. I hurt him the way that you would like to hurt me, but you can't! I'm not young and vulnerable any more. But my young husband was and I—never mind about that! Just give them back to me!

STANLEY: What do you mean by saying you'll have to burn them?

BLANCHE: I'm sorry, I must have lost my head for a moment. Everyone has something he won't let others touch because of their—intimate nature . . . [*She now seems faint with exhaustion and she sits down with the strong box and puts on a pair of glasses and goes methodically through a large stack of papers.*] Ambler & Ambler. Hmmmmm. . . . Crabtree. . . . More Ambler & Ambler.

STANLEY: What is Ambler & Ambler?

BLANCHE: A firm that made loans on the place.

STANLEY: Then it *was* lost on a mortgage?

BLANCHE: [*Touching her forehead.*] That must've been what happened.

STANLEY: I don't want no ifs, ands or buts! What's all the rest of them papers?

[*She hands him the entire box. He carries it to the table and starts to examine the papers.*]

BLANCHE: [*Picking up a large envelope containing more papers.*] There are thousands of papers, stretching back over hundreds of years, affecting Belle Reve as, piece by piece, our improvident grandfathers and father and uncles and brothers exchanged the land for their epic fornications—to put it plainly! [*She removes her glasses with an exhausted laugh.*] The four-letter word deprived us of our plantation, till finally all that was left—and Stella can verify that!—was the house itself and about twenty acres of ground, including a graveyard, to which now all but Stella and I have retreated. [*She pours the contents of the envelope on the table.*] Here all of them are, all papers! I hereby endow you with them! Take them, peruse them—commit them to memory, even! I think it's wonderfully fitting that Belle Reve should finally be this bunch of old papers in your big, capable hands! . . . I wonder if Stella's come back with my lemon Coke . . . [*She leans back and closes her eyes.*]

STANLEY: I have a lawyer acquaintance who will study these out.

BLANCHE: Present them to him with a box of aspirin tablets.

STANLEY: [*becoming somewhat sheepish*] You see, under the Napoleonic code—a man has to take an interest in his wife's affairs—especially now that she's going to have a baby.

[BLANCHE *opens her eyes. The "Blue Piano" sounds louder.*]

BLANCHE: Stella? Stella going to have a baby? [*Dreamily.*] I didn't know she was going to have a baby!

[*She gets up and crosses to the outside door.* STELLA *appears around the corner with a carton from the drugstore.* STANLEY *goes into the bedroom with the envelope and the box. The inner rooms fade to darkness and the outside wall of the house is visible.* BLANCHE *meets* STELLA *at the foot of the steps to the sidewalk.*]

BLANCHE: Stella, Stella for star! How lovely to have a baby! It's all right. Everything's all right.

STELLA: I'm sorry he did that to you.

BLANCHE: Oh, I guess he's just not the type that goes for jasmine perfume, but maybe he's what we need to mix with our blood now that we've lost Belle Reve. We thrashed it out. I feel a bit shaky, but I think I handled it nicely, I laughed and treated it all as a joke. [STEVE *and* PABLO *appear, carrying a case of beer.*] I called him a little boy and laughed and flirted. Yes, I was flirting with your husband! [*As the men approach.*] The guests are gathering for the poker party. [*The two men pass between them, and enter the house.*] Which way do we go now, Stella—this way?

STELLA: No, this way. [*She leads* BLANCHE *away.*]

BLANCHE: [*Laughing.*] The blind are leading the blind!

[A *tamale* VENDOR *is heard calling.*]

VENDOR'S VOICE: Red-hot!

Scene 3. The Poker Night

There is a picture of Van Gogh's of a billiard-parlor at night.[3] *The kitchen now suggests that sort of lurid nocturnal brilliance, the raw colors of childhood's spectrum. Over the yellow linoleum of the kitchen table hangs an electric bulb with a vivid green glass shade. The poker players—*STANLEY, STEVE, MITCH *and* PABLO*—wear colored shirts, solid blues, a purple, a red-and-white check, a light green, and they are men at the peak of their physical manhood, as coarse and direct and powerful as the primary colors. There are vivid slices of watermelon on the table, whiskey bottles and glasses. The bedroom is relatively dim with only the light that spills between the portieres and through the wide window on the street.*

For a moment, there is absorbed silence as a hand is dealt.

STEVE: Anything wild this deal?

PABLO: One-eyed jacks are wild.

STEVE: Give me two cards.

PABLO: You, Mitch?

MITCH: I'm out.

PABLO: One.

MITCH: Anyone want a shot?

STANLEY: Yeah. Me.

3. *The Night Café*, by Vincent Van Gogh, Dutch post-impressionist painter (1853–1890). *The Poker Night* was Williams's first title for *A Streetcar Named Desire*.

PABLO: Why don't somebody go to the Chinaman's and bring back a load of chop suey?

STANLEY: When I'm losing you want to eat! Ante up! Openers? Openers! Get y'r ass off the table, Mitch. Nothing belongs on a poker table but cards, chips and whiskey. [*He lurches up and tosses some watermelon rinds to the floor.*]

MITCH: Kind of on your high horse, ain't you?

STANLEY: How many?

STEVE: Give me three.

STANLEY: One.

MITCH: I'm out again. I oughta go home pretty soon.

STANLEY: Shut up.

MITCH: I gotta sick mother. She don't go to sleep until I come in at night.

STANLEY: Then why don't you stay home with her?

MITCH: She says to go out, so I go, but I don't enjoy it. All the while I keep wondering how she is.

STANLEY: Aw, for the sake of Jesus, go home, then!

PABLO: What've you got?

STEVE: Spade flush.

MITCH: You all are married. But I'll be alone when she goes.—I'm going to the bathroom.

STANLEY: Hurry back and we'll fix you a sugar-tit.

MITCH: Aw, go rut. [*He crosses through the bedroom into the bathroom.*]

STEVE: [*Dealing a hand.*] Seven card stud. [*Telling his joke as he deals.*] This ole farmer is out in back of his house sittin' down th'owing corn to the chickens when all at once he hears a loud cackle and this young hen comes lickety split around the side of the house with the rooster right behind her and gaining on her fast.

STANLEY: [*Impatient with the story.*] Deal!

STEVE: But when the rooster catches sight of the farmer th'owing the corn he puts on the brakes and lets the hen get away and starts pecking corn. And the old farmer says, "Lord God, I hopes I never gits *that* hongry!"

[STEVE *and* PABLO *laugh. The sisters appear around the corner of the building.*]

STELLA: The game is still going on.

BLANCHE: How do I look?

STELLA: Lovely, Blanche.

BLANCHE: I feel so hot and frazzled. Wait till I powder before you open the door. Do I look done in?

STELLA: Why no. You are as fresh as a daisy.

BLANCHE: One that's been picked a few days.

[STELLA *opens the door and they enter.*]

STELLA: Well, well, well. I see you boys are still at it?

STANLEY: Where you been?

STELLA: Blanche and I took in a show. Blanche, this is Mr. Gonzales and Mr. Hubbell.

BLANCHE: Please don't get up.

STANLEY: Nobody's going to get up, so don't be worried.

STELLA: How much longer is this game going to continue?

STANLEY: Till we get ready to quit.

BLANCHE: Poker is so fascinating. Could I kibitz?

STANLEY: You could not. Why don't you women go up and sit with Eunice?

STELLA: Because it is nearly two-thirty. [*Blanche crosses into the bedroom and partially closes the portieres.*] Couldn't you call it quits after one more hand?

[*A chair scrapes.* STANLEY *gives a loud whack of his hand on her thigh.*]

STELLA: [*Sharply.*] That's not fun, Stanley.

[*The men laugh.* STELLA *goes into the bedroom.*]

STELLA: It makes me so mad when he does that in front of people.

BLANCHE: I think I will bathe.

STELLA: Again?

BLANCHE: My nerves are in knots. Is the bathroom occupied?

STELLA: I don't know.

[BLANCHE *knocks.* MITCH *opens the door and comes out, still wiping his hands on a towel.*]

BLANCHE: Oh!—good evening.

MITCH: Hello. [*He stares at her.*]

STELLA: Blanche, this is Harold Mitchell. My sister, Blanche DuBois.

MITCH: [*With awkward courtesy.*] How do you do, Miss DuBois.

STELLA: How is your mother now, Mitch?

MITCH: About the same, thanks. She appreciated your sending over that custard.—Excuse me, please.

[*He crosses slowly back into the kitchen, glancing back at* BLANCHE *and coughing a little shyly. He realizes he still has the towel in his hands and with an embarrassed laugh hands it to* STELLA. BLANCHE *looks after him with a certain interest.*]

BLANCHE: That one seems—superior to the others.

STELLA: Yes, he is.

BLANCHE: I thought he had a sort of sensitive look.

STELLA: His mother is sick.

BLANCHE: Is he married?

STELLA: No.

BLANCHE: Is he a wolf?

STELLA: Why, Blanche! [BLANCHE *laughs.*] I don't think he would be.

BLANCHE: What does—what does he do? [*She is unbuttoning her blouse.*]

STELLA: He's on the precision bench in the spare parts department. At the plant Stanley travels for.

BLANCHE: Is that something much?

STELLA: No. Stanley's the only one of his crowd that's likely to get anywhere.

BLANCHE: What makes you think Stanley will?

STELLA: Look at him.

BLANCHE: I've looked at him.

STELLA: Then you should know.

BLANCHE: I'm sorry, but I haven't noticed the stamp of genius even on Stanley's forehead.

[*She takes off the blouse and stands in her pink silk brassiere and white skirt in the light through the portieres. The game has continued in undertones.*]

STELLA: It isn't on his forehead and it isn't genius.

BLANCHE: Oh. Well, what is it, and where? I would like to know.

STELLA: It's a drive that he has. You're standing in the light, Blanche!

BLANCHE: Oh, am I!

[*She moves out of the yellow streak of light.* STELLA *has removed her dress and put on a light blue satin kimona.*]

STELLA: [*With girlish laughter.*] You ought to see their wives.

BLANCHE: [*Laughingly.*] I can imagine. Big, beefy things, I suppose.

STELLA: You know that one upstairs? [*More laughter.*] One time [*Laughing.*] the plaster—[*Laughing.*] cracked—

STANLEY: You hens cut out that conversation in there!

STELLA: You can't hear us.

STANLEY: Well, you can hear me and I said to hush up!

STELLA: This is my house and I'll talk as much as I want to!

BLANCHE: Stella, don't start a row.

STELLA: He's half drunk!—I'll be out in a minute.

[*She goes into the bathroom.* BLANCHE *rises and crosses leisurely to a small white radio and turns it on.*]

STANLEY: Awright, Mitch, you in?

MITCH: What? Oh!—No, I'm out!

[BLANCHE *moves back into the streak of light. She raises her arms and stretches, as she moves indolently back to the chair. Rhumba music comes over the radio.* MITCH *rises at the table.*]

STANLEY: Who turned that on in there?

BLANCHE: I did. Do you mind?

STANLEY: Turn it off!

STEVE: Aw, let the girls have their music.

PABLO: Sure, that's good, leave it on!

STEVE: Sounds like Xavier Cugat![4] [STANLEY *jumps up and, crossing to the radio, turns it off. He stops short at the sight of* BLANCHE *in the chair. She returns*

4. Cuban band leader, well known for composing and playing rhumbas.

his look without flinching. Then he sits again at the poker table. Two of the men have started arguing hotly.] I didn't hear you name it.

PABLO: Didn't I name it, Mitch?

MITCH: I wasn't listenin'.

PABLO: What were you doing, then?

STANLEY: He was looking through them drapes. [*He jumps up and jerks roughly at curtains to close them.*] Now deal the hand over again and let's play cards or quit. Some people get ants when they win.

[MITCH *rises as* STANLEY *returns to his seat.*]

STANLEY: [*Yelling.*] Sit down!

MITCH: I'm going to the "head." Deal me out.

PABLO: Sure he's got ants now. Seven five-dollar bills in his pants pocket folded up tight as spitballs.

STEVE: Tomorrow you'll see him at the cashier's window getting them changed into quarters.

STANLEY: And when he goes home he'll deposit them one by one in a piggy bank his mother give him for Christmas. [*Dealing.*] This game is Spit in the Ocean.

[MITCH *laughs uncomfortably and continues through the portieres. He stops just inside.*]

BLANCHE: [*Softly.*] Hello! The Little Boys' Room is busy right now.

MITCH: We've—been drinking beer.

BLANCHE: I hate beer.

MITCH: It's—a hot weather drink.

BLANCHE: Oh, I don't think so; it always makes me warmer. Have you got any cigs? [*She has slipped on the dark red satin wrapper.*]

MITCH: Sure.

BLANCHE: What kind are they?

MITCH: Luckies.

BLANCHE: Oh, good. What a pretty case. Silver?

MITCH: Yes. Yes; read the inscription.

BLANCHE: Oh, is there an inscription? I can't make it out. [*He strikes a match and moves closer.*] Oh! [*Reading with feigned difficulty.*] "And if God choose, / I shall but love thee better—after—death!" Why, that's from my favorite sonnet by Mrs. Browning![5]

MITCH: You know it?

BLANCHE: Certainly I do!

MITCH: There's a story connected with that inscription.

BLANCHE: It sounds like a romance.

MITCH: A pretty sad one.

BLANCHE: Oh?

MITCH: The girl's dead now.

5. Elizabeth Barrett Browning, 19th-century British poet, was most famous for her sequence of love poems, *Sonnets from the Portuguese*.

BLANCHE: [*In a tone of deep sympathy.*] Oh!

MITCH: She knew she was dying when she give me this. A very strange girl, very sweet—very!

BLANCHE: She must have been fond of you. Sick people have such deep, sincere attachments.

MITCH: That's right, they certainly do.

BLANCHE: Sorrow makes for sincerity, I think.

MITCH: It sure brings it out in people.

BLANCHE: The little there is belongs to people who have experienced some sorrow.

MITCH: I believe you are right about that.

BLANCHE: I'm positive that I am. Show me a person who hasn't known any sorrow and I'll show you a shuperficial—Listen to me! My tongue is a little—thick! You boys are responsible for it. The show let out at eleven and we couldn't come home on account of the poker game so we had to go somewhere and drink. I'm not accustomed to having more than one drink. Two is the limit—and *three!* [*She laughs.*] Tonight I had three.

STANLEY: Mitch!

MITCH: Deal me out. I'm talking to Miss—

BLANCHE: DuBois.

MITCH: Miss DuBois?

BLANCHE: It's a French name. It means woods and Blanche means white, so the two together mean white woods. Like an orchard in spring! You can remember it by that.

MITCH: You're French?

BLANCHE: We are French by extraction. Our first American ancestors were French Huguenots.

MITCH: You are Stella's sister, are you not?

BLANCHE: Yes, Stella is my precious little sister. I call her little in spite of the fact she's somewhat older than I. Just slightly. Less than a year. Will you do something for me?

MITCH: Sure. What?

BLANCHE: I bought this adorable little colored paper lantern at a Chinese shop on Bourbon. Put it over the light bulb! Will you, please?

MITCH: Be glad to.

BLANCHE: I can't stand a naked light bulb, any more than I can a rude remark or a vulgar action.

MITCH: [*Adjusting the lantern.*] I guess we strike you as being a pretty rough bunch.

BLANCHE: I'm very adaptable—to circumstances.

MITCH: Well, that's a good thing to be. You are visiting Stanley and Stella?

BLANCHE: Stella hasn't been so well lately, and I came down to help her for a while. She's very run down.

MITCH: You're not—?

BLANCHE: Married? No, no. I'm an old maid schoolteacher!

MITCH: You may teach school but you're certainly not an old maid.

BLANCHE: Thank you, sir! I appreciate your gallantry!
MITCH: So you are in the teaching profession?
BLANCHE: Yes. Ah, yes . . .
MITCH: Grade school or high school or—
STANLEY: [*Bellowing.*] Mitch!
MITCH: Coming!
BLANCHE: Gracious, what lung-power! . . . I teach high school. In Laurel.
MITCH: What do you teach? What subject?
BLANCHE: Guess!
MITCH: I bet you teach art or music? [BLANCHE *laughs delicately.*] Of course I could be wrong. You might teach arithmetic.
BLANCHE: Never arithmetic, sir; never arithmetic! [*With a laugh.*] I don't even know my multiplication tables! No, I have the misfortune of being an English instructor. I attempt to instill a bunch of bobby-soxers and drugstore Romeos with reverence for Hawthorne and Whitman and Poe!
MITCH: I guess that some of them are more interested in other things.
BLANCHE: How very right you are! Their literary heritage is not what most of them treasure above all else! But they're sweet things! And in the spring, it's touching to notice them making their first discovery of love! As if nobody had ever known it before! [*The bathroom door opens and* STELLA *comes out.* BLANCHE *continues talking to* MITCH.] Oh! Have you finished? Wait—I'll turn on the radio.

[*She turns the knobs on the radio and it begins to play "Wien, Wien, nur du allein."*[6] BLANCHE *waltzes to the music with romantic gestures.* MITCH *is delightd and moves in awkward imitation like a dancing bear.* STANLEY *stalks fiercely through the portieres into the bedroom. He crosses to the small white radio and snatches it off the table. With a shouted oath, he tosses the instrument out the window.*]

STELLA: *Drunk—drunk—animal thing, you!* [*She rushes through to the poker table.*] All of you—please go home! If any of you have one spark of decency in you—
BLANCHE: [*Wildly.*] Stella, watch out, he's—

[STANLEY *charges after* STELLA.]

MEN: [*Feebly.*] Take it easy, Stanley. Easy, fellow.—Let's all—
STELLA: You lay your hands on me and I'll—

[*She backs out of sight. He advances and disappears. There is the sound of a blow,* STELLA *cries out.* BLANCHE *screams and runs into the kitchen. The men rush forward and there is grappling and cursing. Something is overturned with a crash.*]

BLANCHE: [*Shrilly.*] My sister is going to have a baby!
MITCH: This is terrible.

6. "Vienna, Vienna, you are my only," a waltz from an operetta by Franz Lehár (1870–1948).

BLANCHE: Lunacy, absolute lunacy!

MITCH: Get him in here, men.

[STANLEY *is forced, pinioned by the two men, into the bedroom. He nearly throws them off. Then all at once he subsides and is limp in their grasp. They speak quietly and lovingly to him and he leans his face on one of their shoulders.*]

STELLA: [*In a high, unnatural voice, out of sight.*] I want to go away, I want to go away!

MITCH: Poker shouldn't be played in a house with women.

[BLANCHE *rushes into the bedroom.*]

BLANCHE: I want my sister's clothes! We'll go to that woman's upstairs!

MITCH: Where is the clothes?

BLANCHE: [*Opening the closet.*] I've got them! [*She rushes through to* STELLA.] Stella, Stella, precious! Dear, dear little sister, don't be afraid!

[*With her arm around* STELLA, BLANCHE *guides her to the outside door and upstairs.*]

STANLEY: [*Dully.*] What's the matter; what's happened?

MITCH: You just blew your top, Stan.

PABLO: He's okay, now.

STEVE: Sure, my boy's okay!

MITCH: Put him on the bed and get a wet towel.

PABLO: I think coffee would do him a world of good, now.

STANLEY: [*Thickly.*] I want water.

MITCH: Put him under the shower!

[*The men talk quietly as they lead him to the bathroom.*]

STANLEY: Let the rut go of me, you sons of bitches!

[*Sounds of blows are heard. The water goes on full tilt.*]

STEVE: Let's get quick out of here!

[*They rush to the poker table and sweep up their winnings on their way out.*]

MITCH: [*Sadly but firmly.*] Poker should not be played in a house with women.

[*The door closes on them and the place is still. The Negro entertainers in the bar around the corner play "Paper Doll"*[7] *slow and blue. After a moment* STANLEY *comes out of the bathroom dripping water and still in his clinging wet polka dot drawers.*]

STANLEY: Stella! [*There is a pause.*] My baby doll's left me! [*He breaks into sobs. Then he goes to the phone and dials, still shuddering with sobs.*] Eunice? I want my baby! [*He waits a moment; then he hangs up and dials again.*]

7. Popular song of the early 1940s.

Eunice! I'll keep on ringin' until I talk with my *baby!* [*An indistinguishable shrill voice is heard. He hurls phone to floor. Dissonant brass and piano sounds as the rooms dim out to darkness and the outer walls appear in the night light. The "Blue Piano" plays for a brief interval. Finally,* STANLEY *stumbles half-dressed out to the porch and down the wooden steps to the pavement before the building. There he throws back his head like a baying hound and bellows his wife's name:* "STELLA! STELLA, *sweetheart!* STELLA!"] Stell-*lahhhhh!*

EUNICE: [*Calling down from the door of her upper apartment.*] Quit that howling out there an' go back to bed!

STANLEY: I want my baby down here. Stella, Stella!

EUNICE: She ain't comin' down so you quit! Or you'll git th' law on you!

STANLEY: Stella!

EUNICE: You can't beat on a woman an' then call 'er back! She won't come! And her goin' t' have a baby! . . . You stinker! You whelp of a Polack, you! I hope they do haul you in and turn the fire hose on you, same as the last time!

STANLEY: [*Humbly.*] Eunice, I want my girl to come down with me!

EUNICE: Hah! [*She slams her door.*]

STANLEY: [*With heaven-splitting violence.*] *STELL-LAHHHHH!*

[*The low-tone clarinet moans. The door upstairs opens again.* STELLA *slips down the rickety stairs in her robe. Her eyes are glistening with tears and her hair loose about her throat and shoulders. They stare at each other. Then they come together with low, animal moans. He falls to his knees on the steps and presses his face to her belly, curving a little with maternity. Her eyes go blind with tenderness as she catches his head and raises him level with her. He snatches the screen door open and lifts her off her feet and bears her into the dark flat.* BLANCHE *comes out the upper landing in her robe and slips fearfully down the steps.*]

BLANCHE: Where is my little sister? Stella? Stella?

[*She stops before the dark entrance of her sister's flat. Then catches her breath as if struck. She rushes down to the walk before the house. She looks right and left as if for a sanctuary. The music fades away.* MITCH *appears from around the corner.*]

MITCH: Miss DuBois?

BLANCHE: Oh!

MITCH: All quiet on the Potomac now?

BLANCHE: She ran downstairs and went back in there with him.

MITCH: Sure she did.

BLANCHE: I'm terrified!

MITCH: Ho-ho! There's nothing to be scared of. They're crazy about each other.

BLANCHE: I'm not used to such—

MITCH: Naw, it's a shame this had to happen when you just got here. But don't take it serious.

BLANCHE: Violence! Is so—

MITCH: Set down on the steps and have a cigarette with me.
BLANCHE: I'm not properly dressed.
MITCH: That don't make no difference in the Quarter.
BLANCHE: Such a pretty silver case.
MITCH: I showed you the inscription, didn't I?
BLANCHE: Yes. [*During the pause, she looks up at the sky.*] There's so much—so much confusion in the world . . . [*He coughs diffidently.*] Thank you for being so kind! I need kindness now.

Scene 4

It is early the following morning. There is a confusion of street cries like a choral chant.

STELLA *is lying down in the bedroom. Her face is serene in the early morning sunlight. One hand rests on her belly, rounding slightly with new maternity. From the other dangles a book of colored comics. Her eyes and lips have that almost narcotized tranquility that is in the faces of Eastern idols.*

The table is sloppy with remains of breakfast and the debris of the preceding night, and STANLEY'*s gaudy pyjamas lie across the threshold of the bathroom. The outside door is slightly ajar on a sky of summer brilliance.*

BLANCHE *appears at this door. She has spent a sleepless night and her appearance entirely contrasts with* STELLA'*s. She presses her knuckles nervously to her lips as she looks through the door, before entering.*

BLANCHE: Stella?
STELLA: [*Stirring lazily.*] Hmmh?

[BLANCHE *utters a moaning cry and runs into the bedroom, throwing herself down beside* STELLA *in a rush of hysterical tenderness.*]

BLANCHE: Baby, my baby sister!
STELLA: [*Drawing away from her.*] Blanche, what is the matter with you?

[BLANCHE *straightens up slowly and stands beside the bed looking down at her sister with knuckles pressed to her lips.*]

BLANCHE: He's left?
STELLA: Stan? Yes.
BLANCHE: Will he be back?
STELLA: He's gone to get the car greased. Why?
BLANCHE: Why! I've been half crazy, Stella! When I found out you'd been insane enough to come back in here after what happened—I started to rush in after you!
STELLA: I'm glad you didn't.
BLANCHE: What were you thinking of? [STELLA *makes an indefinite gesture.*] Answer me! What? What?
STELLA: Please, Blanche! Sit down and stop yelling.

BLANCHE: All right, Stella. I will repeat the question quietly now. How could you come back in this place last night? Why, you must have slept with him!

[STELLA *gets up in a calm and leisurely way.*]

STELLA: Blanche, I'd forgotten how excitable you are. You're making much too much fuss about this.

BLANCHE: Am I?

STELLA: Yes, you are, Blanche. I know how it must have seemed to you and I'm awful sorry it had to happen, but it wasn't anything as serious as you seem to take it. In the first place, when men are drinking and playing poker anything can happen. It's always a powder-keg. He didn't know what he was doing. . . . He was as good as a lamb when I came back and he's really very, very ashamed of himself.

BLANCHE: And that—that makes it all right?

STELLA: No, it isn't all right for anybody to make such a terrible row, but—people do sometimes. Stanley's always smashed things. Why, on our wedding night—soon as we came in here—he snatched off one of my slippers and rushed about the place smashing light bulbs with it.

BLANCHE: He did—*what?*

STELLA: He smashed all the lightbulbs with the heel of my slipper! [*She laughs.*]

BLANCHE: And you—you *let* him? Didn't *run,* didn't *scream?*

STELLA: I was—sort of—thrilled by it. [*She waits for a moment.*] Eunice and you had breakfast?

BLANCHE: Do you suppose I wanted any breakfast?

STELLA: There's some coffee left on the stove.

BLANCHE: You're so—matter-of-fact about it, Stella.

STELLA: What other can I be? He's taken the radio to get it fixed. It didn't land on the pavement so only one tube was smashed.

BLANCHE: And you are standing there smiling!

STELLA: What do you want me to do?

BLANCHE: Pull yourself together and face the facts.

STELLA: What are they, in your opinion?

BLANCHE: In my opinion? You're married to a madman!

STELLA: No!

BLANCHE: Yes, you are, your fix is worse than mine is! Only you're not being sensible about it. I'm going to *do* something. Get hold of myself and make myself a new life!

STELLA: Yes?

BLANCHE: But you've given in. And that isn't right, you're not old! You can get out.

STELLA: [*Slowly and emphatically.*] I'm not in anything I want to get out of.

BLANCHE: [*Incredulously.*] What—Stella?

STELLA: I said I am not in anything that I have a desire to get out of. Look at the mess in this room! And those empty bottles! They went through two cases last night! He promised this morning that he was going to quit having these poker parties, but you know how long such a promise is going to keep. Oh, well, it's his pleasure, like mine is movies and bridge. People have got to tolerate each other's habits, I guess.

BLANCHE: I don't understand you. [*Stella turns toward her.*] I don't understand your indifference. Is this a Chinese philosophy you've—cultivated?

STELLA: Is what—what?

BLANCHE: This—shuffling about and mumbling—"One tube smashed—beer bottles—mess in the kitchen!"—as if nothing out of the ordinary has happened! [STELLA *laughs uncertainly and picking up the broom, twirls it in her hands.*] Are you deliberately shaking that thing in my face?

STELLA: No.

BLANCHE: Stop it. Let go of that broom. I won't have you cleaning up for him!

STELLA: Then who's going to do it? Are you?

BLANCHE: I? I!

STELLA: No, I didn't think so.

BLANCHE: Oh, let me think, if only my mind would function! We've got to get hold of some money, that's the way out!

STELLA: I guess that money is always nice to get hold of.

BLANCHE: Listen to me. I have an idea of some kind. [*Shakily she twists a cigarette into her holder.*] Do you remember Shep Huntleigh? [STELLA *shakes her head.*] Of course you remember Shep Huntleigh. I went out with him at college and wore his pin for a while. Well—

STELLA: Well?

BLANCHE: I ran into him last winter. You know I went to Miami during the Christmas holidays?

STELLA: No.

BLANCHE: Well, I did. I took the trip as an investment, thinking I'd meet someone with a million dollars.

STELLA: Did you?

BLANCHE: Yes. I ran into Shep Huntleigh—I ran into him on Biscayne Boulevard, on Christmas Eve, about dusk . . . getting into his car—Cadillac convertible; must have been a block long!

STELLA: I should think it would have been—inconvenient in traffic!

BLANCHE: You've heard of oil wells?

STELLA: Yes—remotely.

BLANCHE: He has them, all over Texas. Texas is literally spouting gold in his pockets.

STELLA: My, my.

BLANCHE: Y'know how indifferent I am to money. I think of money in terms of what it does for you. But he could do it, he could certainly do it!

STELLA: Do what, Blanche?

BLANCHE: Why—set us up in a—shop!

STELLA: What kind of shop?

BLANCHE: Oh, a—shop of some kind! He could do it with half what his wife throws away at the races.

STELLA: He's married?

BLANCHE: Honey, would I be here if the man weren't married? [STELLA *laughs a little.* BLANCHE *suddenly springs up and crosses to phone. She speaks shrilly.*] How do I get Western Union?—Operator! Western Union!

STELLA: That's a dial phone, honey.

BLANCHE: I can't dial, I'm too—

STELLA: Just dial O.

BLANCHE: O?

STELLA: Yes, "O" for Operator!

[BLANCHE *considers a moment; then she puts the phone down.*]

BLANCHE: Give me a pencil. Where is a slip of paper? I've got to write it down first—the message, I mean . . . [*She goes to the dressing table, and grabs up a sheet of Kleenex and an eyebrow pencil for writing equipment.*] Let me see now . . . [*She bites the pencil.*] "Darling Shep. Sister and I in desperate situation."

STELLA: I beg your pardon!

BLANCHE: "Sister and I in desperate situation. Will explain details later. Would you be interested in—?" [*She bites the pencil again.*] "Would you be—interested—in . . ." [*She smashes the pencil on the table and springs up.*] You never get anywhere with direct appeals!

STELLA: [*With a laugh.*] Don't be so ridiculous, darling!

BLANCHE: But I'll think of something, I've *got* to think of—*some*thing! Don't laugh at me, Stella! Please, please don't—I—I want you to look at the contents of my purse! Here's what's in it! [*She snatches her purse open.*] Sixty-five measly cents in coin of the realm!

STELLA: [*Crossing to bureau.*] Stanley doesn't give me a regular allowance, he likes to pay bills himself, but—this morning he gave me ten dollars to smooth things over. You take five of it, Blanche, and I'll keep the rest.

BLANCHE: Oh, no. No, Stella.

STELLA: [*Insisting.*] I know how it helps your morale just having a little pocket-money on you.

BLANCHE: No, thank you—I'll take to the streets!

STELLA: Talk sense! How did you happen to get so low on funds?

BLANCHE: Money just goes—it goes places. [*She rubs her forehead.*] Sometime today I've got to get hold of a Bromo![8]

STELLA: I'll fix you one now.

BLANCHE: Not yet—I've got to keep thinking!

STELLA: I wish you'd just let things go, at least for a—while.

BLANCHE: Stella, I can't live with him! You can, he's your husband. But how could I stay here with him, after last night, with just those curtains between us?

STELLA: Blanche, you saw him at his worst last night.

BLANCHE: On the contrary, I saw him at his best! What such a man has to offer is animal force and he gave a wonderful exhibition of that! But the only way

8. Short for "Bromo Seltzer," a headache remedy.

to live with such a man is to—go to bed with him! And that's your job—not mine!

STELLA: After you've rested a little, you'll see it's going to work out. You don't have to worry about anything while you're here. I mean—expenses . . .

BLANCHE: I have to plan for us both, to get us both—out!

STELLA: You take it for granted that I am in something that I want to get out of.

BLANCHE: I take it for granted that you still have sufficient memory of Belle Reve to find this place and these poker players impossible to live with.

STELLA: Well, you're taking entirely too much for granted.

BLANCHE: I can't believe you're in earnest.

STELLA: No?

BLANCHE: I understand how it happened—a little. You saw him in uniform, an officer, not here but—

STELLA: I'm not sure it would have made any difference where I saw him.

BLANCHE: Now don't say it was one of those mysterious electric things between people! If you do I'll laugh in your face.

STELLA: I am not going to say anything more at all about it!

BLANCHE: All right, then, don't!

STELLA: But there are things that happen between a man and a woman in the dark—that sort of make everything else seem—unimportant. [*Pause.*]

BLANCHE: What you are talking about is brutal desire—just—Desire!—the name of that rattle-trap streetcar that bangs through the Quarter, up one old narrow street and down another . . .

STELLA: Haven't you ever ridden on that streetcar?

BLANCHE: It brought me here.—Where I'm not wanted and where I'm ashamed to be . . .

STELLA: Then don't you think your superior attitude is a bit out of place?

BLANCHE: I am not being or feeling at all superior, Stella. Believe me I'm not! It's just this. This is how I look at it. A man like that is someone to go out with—once—twice—three times when the devil is in you. But live with? Have a child by?

STELLA: I have told you I love him.

BLANCHE: Then I *tremble* for you! I just—*tremble* for you. . . .

STELLA: I can't help your trembling if you insist on trembling!

[*There is a pause.*]

BLANCHE: May I—speak—*plainly?*

STELLA: Yes, do. Go ahead. As plainly as you want to.

[*Outside, a train approaches. They are silent till the noise subsides. They are both in the bedroom. Under cover of the train's noise* STANLEY *enters from outside. He stands unseen by the women, holding some packages in his arms, and overhears their following conversation. He wears an undershirt and grease-stained seersucker pants.*]

BLANCHE: Well—if you'll forgive me—he's *common!*

STELLA: Why, yes, I suppose he is.

BLANCHE: Suppose! You can't have forgotten that much of our bringing up, Stella, that you just *suppose* that any part of a gentleman's in his nature! *Not one particle, no!* Oh, if he was just—*ordinary!* Just *plain*—but good and wholesome, but—*no.* There's something downright—*bestial*—about him! You're hating me saying this, aren't you?

STELLA: [*Coldly.*] Go on and say it all, Blanche.

BLANCHE: He acts like an animal, has an animal's habits! Eats like one, moves like one, talks like one! There's even something—sub-human—something not quite to the stage of humanity yet! Yes, something—ape-like about him, like one of those pictures I've seen in—anthropological studies! Thousands and thousands of years have passed him right by, and there he is—Stanley Kowalski—survivor of the Stone Age! Bearing the raw meat home from the kill in the jungle! And you—*you* here—*waiting* for him! Maybe he'll strike you or maybe grunt and kiss you! That is, if kisses have been discovered yet! Night falls and the other apes gather! There in the front of the cave, all grunting like him, and swilling and gnawing and hulking! His poker night! you call it—this party of apes! Somebody growls—some creature snatches at something—the fight is on! *God!* Maybe we are a long way from being made in God's image, but Stella—my sister—there has been *some* progress since then! Such things as art—as poetry and music—such kinds of new light have come into the world since then! In some kinds of people some tenderer feelings have had some little beginning! That we have got to make *grow!* And *cling* to, and hold as our flag! In this dark march toward whatever it is we're approaching. . . . *Don't—don't hang back with the brutes!*

[*Another train passes outside.* STANLEY *hesitates, licking his lips. Then suddenly he turns stealthily about and withdraws through front door. The women are still unaware of his presence. When the train has passed he calls through the closed front door.*]

STANLEY: Hey! Hey, Stella!

STELLA: [*who has listened gravely to Blanche.*] Stanley!

BLANCHE: Stell, I—

[*But* STELLA *has gone to the front door.* STANLEY *enters casually with his packages.*]

STANLEY: Hiyuh, Stella. Blanche back?

STELLA: Yes, she's back.

STANLEY: Hiyuh, Blanche. [*He grins at her.*]

STELLA: You must've got under the car.

STANLEY: Them darn mechanics at Fritz's don't know their ass fr'm—*Hey!*

[STELLA *has embraced him with both arms, fiercely, and full in the view of* BLANCHE. *He laughs and clasps her head to him. Over her head he grins through the curtains at* BLANCHE. *As the lights fade away, with a lingering brightness on their embrace, the music of the "Blue Piano" and trumpet and drums is heard.*]

SCENE 5

BLANCHE *is seated in the bedroom fanning herself with a palm leaf as she reads over a just-completed letter. Suddenly she bursts into a peal of laughter.* STELLA *is dressing in the bedroom.*

STELLA: What are you laughing at, honey?

BLANCHE: Myself, myself, for being such a liar! I'm writing a letter to Shep. [*She picks up the letter.*] "Darling Shep. I am spending the summer on the wing, making flying visits here and there. And who knows, perhaps I shall take a sudden notion to *swoop* down on *Dallas!* How would you feel about that? Ha-ha! [*She laughs nervously and brightly, touching her throat as if actually talking to Shep.*] Forewarned is forearmed, as they say!"—How does that sound?

STELLA: Uh-huh . . .

BLANCHE: [*Going on nervously.*] "Most of my sister's friends go north in the summer but some have homes on the Gulf and there has been a continued round of entertainments, teas, cocktails, and luncheons—"

[*A disturbance is heard upstairs at the Hubbells' apartment.*]

STELLA: Eunice seems to be having some trouble with Steve. [EUNICE*'s voice shouts in terrible wrath.*]

EUNICE: I heard about you and that blonde!

STEVE: That's a damn lie!

EUNICE: You ain't pulling the wool over my eyes! I wouldn't mind if you'd stay down at the Four Deuces, but you always going up.

STEVE: Who ever seen me up?

EUNICE: I seen you chasing her 'round the balcony—I'm gonna call the vice squad!

STEVE: Don't you throw that at me!

EUNICE: [*Shrieking.*] You hit me! I'm gonna call the police!

[*A clatter of aluminum striking a wall is heard, followed by a man's angry roar, shouts and overturned furniture. There is a crash; then a relative hush.*]

BLANCHE: [*Brightly.*] Did he *kill* her?

[EUNICE *appears on the steps in daemonic disorder.*]

STELLA: No! She's coming downstairs.

EUNICE: Call the police, I'm going to call the police! [*She rushes around the corner.*]

[*They laugh lightly.* STANLEY *comes around the corner in his green and scarlet silk bowling shirt. He trots up the steps and bangs into the kitchen.* BLANCHE *registers his entrance with nervous gestures.*]

STANLEY: What's a matter with Eun-uss?

STELLA: She and Steve had a row. Has she got the police?

STANLEY: Naw. She's gettin' a drink.
STELLA: That's much more practical!

[*Steve comes down nursing a bruise on his forehead and looks in the door.*]

STEVE: *She here?*
STANLEY: Naw, naw. At the Four Deuces.
STEVE: That rutting hunk! [*He looks around the corner a bit timidly, then turns with affected boldness and runs after her.*]
BLANCHE: I must jot that down in my notebook. Ha-ha! I'm compiling a notebook of quaint little words and phrases I've picked up here.
STANLEY: You won't pick up nothing here you ain't heard before.
BLANCHE: Can I count on that?
STANLEY: You can count on it up to five hundred.
BLANCHE: That's a mighty high number. [*He jerks open the bureau drawer, slams it shut and throws shoes in a corner. At each noise* BLANCHE *winces slightly. Finally she speaks.*] What sign were you born under?
STANLEY: [*While he is dressing.*] Sign?
BLANCHE: Astrological sign. I bet you were born under Aries. Aries people are forceful and dynamic. They dote on noise! They love to bang things around! You must have had lots of banging around in the army and now that you're out, you make up for it by treating inanimate objects with such a fury!

[STELLA *has been going in and out of closet during this scene. Now she pops her head out of the closet.*]

STELLA: Stanley was born just five minutes after Christmas.
BLANCHE: Capricorn—the Goat!
STANLEY: What sign were *you* born under?
BLANCHE: Oh, my birthday's next month, the fifteenth of September; that's under Virgo.
STANLEY: What's Virgo?
BLANCHE: Virgo is the Virgin.
STANLEY: [*Contemptuously.*] *Hah!* [*He advances a little as he knots his tie.*] Say, do you happen to know somebody named Shaw?

[*Her face expresses a faint shock. She reaches for the cologne bottle and dampens her handkerchief as she answers carefully.*]

BLANCHE: Why, everybody knows somebody named Shaw!
STANLEY: Well, this somebody named Shaw is under the impression he met you in Laurel, but I figure he must have got you mixed up with some other party because this other party is someone he met at a hotel called the Flamingo.

[BLANCHE *laughs breathlessly as she touches the cologne-dampened handkerchief to her temples.*]

BLANCHE: I'm afraid he does have me mixed up with this "other party." The Hotel Flamingo is not the sort of establishment I would dare to be seen in!
STANLEY: You know of it?

BLANCHE: Yes, I've seen it and smelled it.
STANLEY: You must've got pretty close if you could smell it.
BLANCHE: The odor of cheap perfume is penetrating.
STANLEY: That stuff you use is expensive?
BLANCHE: Twenty-five dollars an ounce! I'm nearly out. That's just a hint if you want to remember my birthday! [*She speaks lightly but her voice has a note of fear.*]
STANLEY: Shaw must've got you mixed up. He goes in and out of Laurel all the time so he can check on it and clear up any mistake.

[*He turns away and crosses to the portieres.* BLANCHE *closes her eyes as if faint. Her hand trembles as she lifts the handkerchief again to her forehead.* STEVE *and* EUNICE *come around corner.* STEVE*'s arm is around* EUNICE*'s shoulder and she is sobbing luxuriously and he is cooing love-words. There is a murmur of thunder as they go slowly upstairs in a tight embrace.*]

STANLEY: [*To* STELLA.] I'll wait for you at the Four Deuces!
STELLA: Hey! Don't I rate one kiss?
STANLEY: Not in front of your sister.

[*He goes out.* BLANCHE *rises from her chair. She seems faint; looks about her with an expression of almost panic.*]

BLANCHE: Stella! What have you heard about me?
STELLA: Huh?
BLANCHE: What have people been telling you about me?
STELLA: Telling?
BLANCHE: You haven't heard any—unkind—gossip about me?
STELLA: Why, no, Blanche, of course not!
BLANCHE: Honey, there was—a good deal of talk in Laurel.
STELLA: About *you*, Blanche?
BLANCHE: I wasn't so good the last two years or so, after Belle Reve had started to slip through my fingers.
STELLA: All of us do things we—
BLANCHE: I never was hard or self-sufficient enough. When people are soft—soft people have got to shimmer and glow—they've got to put on soft colors, the colors of butterfly wings, and put a—paper lantern over the light. . . . It isn't enough to be soft *and attractive*. And I—I'm fading now! I don't know how much longer I can turn the trick. [*The afternoon has faded to dusk.* STELLA *goes into the bedroom and turns on the light under the paper lantern. She holds a bottled soft drink in her hand.*] Have you been listening to me?
STELLA: I don't listen to you when you are being morbid! [*She advances with the bottled Coke.*]
BLANCHE: [*With abrupt change to gaiety.*] Is that Coke for me?
STELLA: Not for anyone else!
BLANCHE: Why, you precious thing, you! Is it just Coke?
STELLA: [*Turning.*] You mean you want a shot in it!

BLANCHE: Well, honey, a shot never does a Coke any harm! Let me! You mustn't wait on me!

STELLA: I like to wait on you, Blanche. It makes it seem more like home. [*She goes into the kitchen, finds a glass and pours a shot of whiskey into it.*]

BLANCHE: I have to admit I love to be waited on . . . [*She rushes into the bedroom.* STELLA *goes to her with the glass.* BLANCHE *suddenly clutches* STELLA'*s free hand with a moaning sound and presses the hand to her lips.* STELLA *is embarrassed by her show of emotion.* BLANCHE *speaks in a choked voice.*] You're—you're—so *good* to me! And I—

STELLA: Blanche.

BLANCHE: I know, I won't! You hate me to talk sentimental! But honey, *believe* I feel things more than I *tell* you! I *won't* stay long! I won't, I *promise* I—

STELLA: Blanche!

BLANCHE: [*hysterically.*] I won't, I promise, *I'll* go! Go *soon!* I will *really!* I *won't* hang around until he—throws me out . . .

STELLA: Now will you stop talking foolish?

BLANCHE: Yes, honey. Watch how you pour—that fizzy stuff foams over!

[BLANCHE *laughs shrilly and grabs the glass, but her hand shakes so it almost slips from her grasp.* STELLA *pours the Coke into the glass. It foams over and spills.* BLANCHE *gives a piercing cry.*]

STELLA: [*Shocked by the cry.*] Heavens!

BLANCHE: Right on my pretty white skirt!

STELLA: Oh . . . Use my hanky. Blot gently.

BLANCHE: [*Slowly recovering.*] I know—gently—gently . . .

STELLA: Did it stain?

BLANCHE: Not a bit. Ha-ha! Isn't that lucky? [*She sits down shakily, taking a grateful drink. She holds the glass in both hands and continues to laugh a little.*]

STELLA: Why did you scream like that?

BLANCHE: I don't know why I screamed! [*Continuing nervously.*] Mitch—Mitch is coming at seven. I guess I am just feeling nervous about our relations. [*She begins to talk rapidly and breathlessly.*] He hasn't gotten a thing but a good-night kiss, that's all I have given him, Stella. I want his respect. And men don't want anything they get too easy. But on the other hand men lose interest quickly. Especially when the girl is over—thirty. They think a girl over thirty ought to—the vulgar term is—"put out." . . . And I—I'm not "putting out." Of course he—he doesn't know—I mean I haven't informed him—of my real age!

STELLA: Why are you sensitive about your age?

BLANCHE: Because of hard knocks my vanity's been given. What I mean is—he thinks I'm sort of—prim and proper, you know! [*She laughs out sharply.*] I want to *deceive* him enough to make him—want me . . .

STELLA: Blanche, do you want *him?*

BLANCHE: I want to *rest!* I want to breathe quietly again! Yes—I *want* Mitch . . .

very badly! Just think! If it happens! I can leave here and not be anyone's problem . . .

[STANLEY *comes around the corner with a drink under his belt.*]

STANLEY: [*Bawling.*] Hey, Steve! Hey, Eunice! Hey, Stella!

[*There are joyous calls from above. Trumpet and drums are heard from around the corner.*]

STELLA: [*Kissing* BLANCHE *impulsively.*] It *will* happen!

BLANCHE: [*Doubtfully.*] It will?

STELLA: It *will!* [*She goes across into the kitchen, looking back at* BLANCHE.] It will, honey, *it will*. . . . But don't take another drink! [*Her voice catches as she goes out the door to meet her husband.*]

[BLANCHE *sinks faintly back in her chair with her drink.* EUNICE *shrieks with laughter and runs down the steps.* STEVE *bounds after her with goat-like screeches and chases her around corner.* STANLEY *and* STELLA *twine arms as they follow, laughing. Dusk settles deeper. The music from the Four Deuces is slow and blue.*]

BLANCHE: Ah, me, ah, me, ah, me . . . [*Her eyes fall shut and the palm leaf fan drops from her fingers. She slaps her hand on the chair arm a couple of times. There is a little glimmer of lightning about the building.* A YOUNG MAN *comes along the street and rings the bell.*] Come in.

[*The* YOUNG MAN *appears through the portieres. She regards him with interest.*]

BLANCHE: Well, well! What can I do for *you?*

YOUNG MAN: I'm collecting for *The Evening Star.*

BLANCHE: I didn't know that stars took up collections.

YOUNG MAN: It's the paper.

BLANCHE: I know, I was joking—feebly! Will you—have a drink?

YOUNG MAN: No, ma'am. No, thank you. I can't drink on the job.

BLANCHE: Oh, well, now, let's see. . . . No, I don't have a dime! I'm not the lady of the house. I'm her sister from Mississippi. I'm one of those poor relations you've heard about.

YOUNG MAN: That's all right. I'll drop by later. [*He starts to go out. She approaches a little.*]

BLANCHE: Hey! [*He turns back shyly. She puts a cigarette in a long holder.*] Could you give me a light? [*She crosses toward him. They meet at the door between the two rooms.*]

YOUNG MAN: Sure. [*He takes out a lighter.*] This doesn't always work.

BLANCHE: It's temperamental? [*It flares.*] Ah!—thank you. [*He starts away again.*] Hey! [*He turns again, still more uncertainly. She goes close to him.*] Uh—what time is it?

YOUNG MAN: Fifteen of seven, ma'am.

BLANCHE: So late? Don't you just love these long rainy afternoons in New Orleans when an hour isn't just an hour—but a little piece of eternity dropped into your hands—and who knows what to do with it? [*She touches his shoulders.*] You—uh—didn't get wet in the rain?

YOUNG MAN: No, ma'am. I stepped inside.

BLANCHE: In a drugstore? And had a soda?

YOUNG MAN: Uh-huh.

BLANCHE: Chocolate?

YOUNG MAN: No, ma'am. Cherry.

BLANCHE: [*Laughing.*] Cherry!

YOUNG MAN: A cherry soda.

BLANCHE: You make my mouth water. [*She touches his cheek lightly, and smiles. Then she goes to the trunk.*]

YOUNG MAN: Well, I'd better be going—

BLANCHE: [*Stopping him.*] Young man! [*He turns. She takes a large, gossamer scarf from the trunk and drapes it about her shoulders. In the ensuing pause, the "Blue Piano" is heard. It continues through the rest of this scene and the opening of the next. The young man clears his throat and looks yearningly at the door.*] Young man! Young, young, young man! Has anyone ever told you that you look like a young Prince out of the Arabian Nights? [*The* YOUNG MAN *laughs uncomfortably and stands like a bashful kid.* BLANCHE *speaks softly to him.*] Well, you do, honey lamb! Come here. I want to kiss you, just once, softly and sweetly on your mouth! [*Without waiting for him to accept, she crosses quickly to him and presses her lips to his.*] Now run along, now, quickly! It would be nice to keep you, but I've got to be good—and keep my hands off children.

[*He stares at her a moment. She opens the door for him and blows a kiss at him as he goes down the steps with a dazed look. She stands there a little dreamily after he has disappeared. Then* MITCH *appears around the corner with a bunch of roses.*]

BLANCHE: [*gaily.*] Look who's coming! My Rosenkavalier![9] Bow to me first . . . now present them! *Ahhhh—Merciiii!*

[*She looks at him over them, coquettishly pressing them to her lips. He beams at her self-consciously.*]

Scene 6

It is about two AM *on the same evening. The outer wall of the building is visible.* BLANCHE *and* MITCH *come in. The utter exhaustion which only a neurasthenic personality can know is evident in* BLANCHE'*s voice and manner.* MITCH *is stolid but depressed. They have probably been out to the amusement park on Lake Pontchartrain, for* MITCH *is bearing, upside down, a plaster statuette of Mae West, the sort of prize won at shooting galleries and carnival games of chance.*

9. *Knight of the Rose,* title of a romantic opera (1911) by Richard Strauss (1864–1949). *"Merci"*: thank you.

BLANCHE: [*Stopping lifelessly at the steps.*] Well—[MITCH *laughs uneasily.*] Well . . .

MITCH: I guess it must be pretty late—and you're tired.

BLANCHE: Even the hot tamale man has deserted the street, and he hangs on till the end. [MITCH *laughs uneasily again.*] How will you get home?

MITCH: I'll walk over to Bourbon and catch an owl-car.

BLANCHE: [*Laughing grimly.*] Is that street-car named Desire still grinding along the tracks at this hour?

MITCH: [*Heavily.*] I'm afraid you haven't gotten much fun out of this evening, Blanche.

BLANCHE: I spoiled it for *you*.

MITCH: No, you didn't, but I felt all the time that I wasn't giving you much—entertainment.

BLANCHE: I simply couldn't rise to the occasion. That was all. I don't think I've ever tried so hard to be gay and made such a dismal mess of it. I get ten points for trying!—I *did* try.

MITCH: Why did you try if you didn't feel like it, Blanche?

BLANCHE: I was just obeying the law of nature.

MITCH: Which law is that?

BLANCHE: The one that says the lady must entertain the gentleman—or no dice! See if you can locate my door key in this purse. When I'm so tired my fingers are all thumbs!

MITCH: [*Rooting in her purse.*] This it?

BLANCHE: No, honey, that's the key to my trunk which I must soon be packing.

MITCH: You mean you are leaving here soon?

BLANCHE: I've outstayed my welcome.

MITCH: This it?

[*The music fades away.*]

BLANCHE: Eureka! Honey, you open the door while I take a last look at the sky. [*She leans on the porch rail. He opens the door and stands awkwardly behind her.*] I'm looking for the Pleiades,[1] the Seven Sisters, but these girls are not out tonight. Oh, yes they are, there they are! God bless them! All in a bunch going home from their little bridge party. . . . Y' get the door open? Good boy! I guess you—want to go now . . .

[*He shuffles and coughs a little.*]

MITCH: Can I—uh—kiss you—good night?

BLANCHE: Why do you always ask me if you may?

MITCH: I don't know whether you want me to or not.

BLANCHE: Why should you be so doubtful?

MITCH: That night when we parked by the lake and I kissed you, you—

BLANCHE: Honey, it wasn't the kiss I objected to. I liked the kiss very much. It was the other little—familiarity—that I—felt obliged to—discourage. . . . I didn't resent it! Not a bit in the world! In fact, I was somewhat flattered that

1. The seven daughters of Atlas who were metemorphosed into stars.

you—desired me! But, honey, you know as well as I do that a single girl, a girl alone in the world, has got to keep a firm hold on her emotions or she'll be lost!

MITCH: [*Solemnly.*] Lost?

BLANCHE: I guess you are used to girls that like to be lost. The kind that get lost immediately, on the first date!

MITCH: I like you to be exactly the way that you are, because in all my—experience—I have never known anyone like you. [BLANCHE *looks at him gravely; then she bursts into laughter and then claps a hand to her mouth.*] Are you laughing at me?

BLANCHE: No, honey. The lord and lady of the house have not yet returned, so come in. We'll have a nightcap. Let's leave the lights off. Shall we?

MITCH: You just—do what you want to.

[BLANCHE *precedes him into the kitchen. The outer wall of the building disappears and the interiors of the two rooms can be dimly seen.*]

BLANCHE: [*Remaining in the first room.*] The other room's more comfortable—go on in. This crashing around in the dark is my search for some liquor.

MITCH: You want a drink?

BLANCHE: I want *you* to have a drink! You have been so anxious and solemn all evening, and so have I; we have both been anxious and solemn and now for these few last remaining moments of our lives together—I want to create—*joie de vivre!* I'm lighting a candle.

MITCH: That's good.

BLANCHE: We are going to be very Bohemian. We are going to pretend that we are sitting in a little artists' cafe on the Left Bank in Paris! [*She lights a candle stub and puts it in a bottle.*] *Je suis la Dame aux Camellias! Vous êtes—Armand!*[2] Understand French?

MITCH: [*Heavily.*] Naw. Naw, I—

BLANCHE: *Voulez-vous couchez avec moi ce soir? Vous ne comprenez pas? Ah, quelle dommage!*[3]—I mean it's a damned good thing. . . . I've found some liquor! Just enough for two shots without any dividends, honey . . .

MITCH: [*Heavily.*] That's—good.

[*She enters the bedroom with the drinks and the candle.*]

BLANCHE: Sit down! Why don't you take off your coat and loosen your collar?

MITCH: I better leave it on.

BLANCHE: No. I want you to be comfortable.

MITCH: I am ashamed of the way I perspire. My shirt is sticking to me.

BLANCHE: Perspiration is healthy. If people didn't perspire they would die in five minutes. [*She takes his coat from him.*] This is a nice coat. What kind of material is it?

2. "I am the Lady of the Camellias! You are—Armand!" Both are characters in the popular romantic play *La Dame aux Camélias* (1852) by the French author Alexandre Dumas (1824–1895); she is a courtesan who gives up her true love, Armand.

3. "Would you like to sleep with me this evening? You don't understand? Ah, what a pity!"

MITCH: They call that stuff alpaca.

BLANCHE: Oh. Alpaca.

MITCH: It's very light-weight alpaca.

BLANCHE: Oh. Light-weight alpaca.

MITCH: I don't like to wear a wash-coat even in summer because I sweat through it.

BLANCHE: Oh.

MITCH: And it don't look neat on me. A man with a heavy build has got to be careful of what he puts on him so he don't look too clumsy.

BLANCHE: You are not too heavy.

MITCH: You don't think I am?

BLANCHE: You are not the delicate type. You have a massive bone-structure and a very imposing physique.

MITCH: Thank you. Last Christmas I was given a membership to the New Orleans Athletic Club.

BLANCHE: Oh, good.

MITCH: It was the finest present I ever was given. I work out there with the weights and I swim and I keep myself fit. When I started there, I was getting soft in the belly but now my belly is hard. It is so hard now that a man can punch me in the belly and it don't hurt me. Punch me! Go on! See? [*She pokes lightly at him.*]

BLANCHE: Gracious. [*Her hand touches her chest.*]

MITCH: Guess how much I weigh, Blanche?

BLANCHE: Oh, I'd say in the vicinity of—one hundred and eighty?

MITCH: Guess again.

BLANCHE: Not that much?

MITCH: No. More.

BLANCHE: Well, you're a tall man and you can carry a good deal of weight without looking awkward.

MITCH: I weigh two hundred and seven pounds and I'm six feet one and one half inches tall in my bare feet—without shoes on. And that is what I weigh stripped.

BLANCHE: Oh, my goodness, me! It's awe-inspiring.

MITCH: [*Embarrassed.*] My weight is not a very interesting subject to talk about. [*He hesitates for a moment.*] What's yours?

BLANCHE: My weight?

MITCH: Yes.

BLANCHE: Guess!

MITCH: Let me lift you.

BLANCHE: Samson![4] Go on, lift me. [*He comes behind her and puts his hands on her waist and raises her lightly off the ground.*] Well?

MITCH: You are light as a feather.

BLANCHE: Ha-ha! [*He lowers her but keeps his hands on her waist.* BLANCHE *speaks with an affectation of demureness.*] You may release me now.

4. Legendary strong man, in the Old Testament.

MITCH: Huh?

BLANCHE: [*Gaily.*] I said unhand me, sir. [*He fumblingly embraces her. Her voice sounds gently reproving.*] Now, Mitch. Just because Stanley and Stella aren't at home is no reason why you shouldn't behave like a gentleman.

MITCH: Just give me a slap whenever I step out of bounds.

BLANCHE: That won't be necessary. You're a natural gentleman, one of the very few that are left in the world. I don't want you to think that I am severe and old maid school-teacherish or anything like that. It's just—well—

MITCH: Huh?

BLANCHE: I guess it is just that I have—old-fashioned ideals! [*She rolls her eyes, knowing he cannot see her face.* MITCH *goes to the front door. There is a considerable silence between them.* BLANCHE *sighs and* MITCH *coughs self-consciously.*]

MITCH: [*Finally.*] Where's Stanley and Stella tonight?

BLANCHE: They have gone out. With Mr. and Mrs. Hubbell upstairs.

MITCH: Where did they go?

BLANCHE: I think they were planning to go to a midnight prevue at Loew's State.

MITCH: We should all go out together some night.

BLANCHE: No. That wouldn't be a good plan.

MITCH: Why not?

BLANCHE: You are an old friend of Stanley's?

MITCH: We was together in the Two-forty-first.[5]

BLANCHE: I guess he talks to you frankly?

MITCH: Sure.

BLANCHE: Has he talked to you about me?

BLANCHE: Oh—not very much.

BLANCHE: The way you say that, I suspect that he has.

MITCH: No, he hasn't said much.

BLANCHE: But what he *has* said. What would you say his attitude toward me was?

MITCH: Why do you want to ask that?

BLANCHE: Well—

MITCH: Don't you get along with him?

BLANCHE: What do you think?

MITCH: I don't think he understands you.

BLANCHE: That is putting it mildly. If it weren't for Stella about to have a baby, I wouldn't be able to endure things here.

MITCH: He isn't—nice to you?

BLANCHE: He is insufferably rude. Goes out of his way to offend me.

MITCH: In what way, Blanche?

BLANCHE: Why, in every conceivable way.

MITCH: I'm surprised to hear that.

BLANCHE: Are you?

MITCH: Well, I—don't see how anybody could be rude to you.

BLANCHE: It's really a pretty frightful situation. You see, there's no privacy here.

5. Battalion of Engineers, in World War II.

There's just these portieres between the two rooms at night. He stalks through the rooms in his underwear at night. And I have to ask him to close the bathroom door. That sort of commonness isn't necessary. You probably wonder why I don't move out. Well, I'll tell you frankly. A teacher's salary is barely sufficient for her living expenses. I didn't save a penny last year and so I had to come here for the summer. That's why I have to put up with my sister's husband. And he has to put up with me, apparently so much against his wishes. . . . Surely he must have told you how much he hates he!

MITCH: I don't think he hates you.

BLANCHE: He hates me. Or why would he insult me? The first time I laid eyes on him I thought to myself, that man is my executioner! That man will destroy me, unless——

MITCH: Blanche—

BLANCHE: Yes, honey?

MITCH: Can I ask you a question?

BLANCHE: Yes. What?

MITCH: How old are you?

[*She makes a nervous gesture.*]

BLANCHE: Why do you want to know?

MITCH: I talked to my mother about you and she said, "How old is Blanche?" And I wasn't able to tell her. [*There is another pause.*]

BLANCHE: You talked to your mother about me?

MITCH: Yes.

BLANCHE: Why?

MITCH: I told my mother how nice you were, and I liked you.

BLANCHE: Were you sincere about that?

MITCH: You know I was.

BLANCHE: Why did your mother want to know my age?

MITCH: Mother is sick.

BLANCHE: I'm sorry to hear it. Badly?

MITCH: She won't live long. Maybe just a few months.

BLANCHE: Oh.

MITCH: She worries because I'm not settled.

BLANCHE: Oh.

MITCH: She wants me to be settled down before she—[*His voice is hoarse and he clears his throat twice, shuffling nervously around with his hands in and out of his pockets.*]

BLANCHE: You love her very much, don't you?

MITCH: Yes.

BLANCHE: I think you have a great capacity for devotion. You will be lonely when she passes on, won't you? [MITCH *clears his throat and nods.*] I understand what that is.

MITCH: To be lonely?

BLANCHE: I loved someone, too, and the person I loved I lost.

MITCH: Dead? [*She crosses to the window and sits on the sill, looking out. She pours herself another drink.*] A man?

BLANCHE: He was a boy, just a boy, when I was a very young girl. When I was sixteen, I made the discovery—love. All at once and much, much too completely. It was like you suddenly turned a blinding light on something that had always been half in shadow, that's how it struck the world for me. But I was unlucky. Deluded. There was something different about the boy, a nervousness, a softness and tenderness which wasn't like a man's, although he wasn't the least bit effeminate looking—still—that thing was there. . . . He came to me for help. I didn't know that. I didn't find out anything till after our marriage when we'd run away and come back and all I knew was I'd failed him in some mysterious way and wasn't able to give the help he needed but couldn't speak of! He was in the quicksands and clutching at me—but I wasn't holding him out, I was slipping in with him! I didn't know that. I didn't know anything except I loved him unendurably but without being able to help him or help myself. Then I found out. In the worst of all possible ways. By coming suddenly into a room that I thought was empty—which wasn't empty, but had two people in it . . . the boy I had married and an older man who had been his friend for years . . . [*A locomotive is heard approaching outside. She claps her hands to her ears and crouches over. The headlight of the locomotive glares into the room as it thunders past. As the noise recedes she straightens slowly and continues speaking.*] Afterward we pretended that nothing had been discovered. Yes, the three of us drove out to Moon Lake Casino, very drunk and laughing all the way. [*Polka music sounds, in a minor key faint with distance.*] We danced the Varsouviana![6] Suddenly in the middle of the dance the boy I had married broke away from me and ran out of the casino. A few moments later—a shot! [*The polka stops abruptly.* BLANCHE *rises stiffly. Then, the polka resumes in a major key.*] I ran out—all did!—all ran and gathered about the terrible thing at the edge of the lake! I couldn't get near for the crowding. Then somebody caught my arm. "Don't go any closer! Come back! You don't want to see!" See? See what! Then I heard voices say—Allan! Allan! The Grey boy! He'd stuck the revolver into his mouth, and fired—so that the back of his head had been—blown away! [*She sways and covers her face.*] It was because—on the dance floor—unable to stop myself—I'd suddenly said—"I saw! I know! You disgust me . . ." And then the searchlight which had been turned on the world was turned off again and never for one moment since has there been any light that's stronger than this—kitchen—candle . . .

[MITCH *gets up awkwardly and moves toward her a little. The polka music increases.* MITCH *stands beside her.*]

MITCH: [*Drawing her slowly into his arms.*] You need somebody. And I need somebody, too. Could it be—you and me, Blanche?

6. Fast Polish dance, similar to the polka.

[*She stares at him vacantly for a moment. Then with a soft cry huddles in his embrace. She makes a sobbing effort to speak but the words won't come. He kisses her forehead and her eyes and finally her lips. The Polka tune fades out. Her breath is drawn and released in long, grateful sobs.*]

BLANCHE: Sometimes—there's God—so quickly!

SCENE 7

It is late afternoon in mid-September.

The portieres are open and a table is set for a birthday supper, with cake and flowers.

STELLA *is completing the decorations as* STANLEY *comes in.*

STANLEY: What's all this stuff for?
STELLA: Honey, it's Blanche's birthday.
STANLEY: She here?
STELLA: In the bathroom.
STANLEY: [*Mimicking.*] "Washing out some things"?
STELLA: I reckon so.
STANLEY: How long she been in there?
STELLA: All afternoon.
STANLEY: [*Mimicking.*] "Soaking in a hot tub"?
STELLA: Yes.
STANLEY: Temperature 100 on the nose, and she soaks herself in a hot tub.
STELLA: She says it cools her off for the evening.
STANLEY: And you run out an' get her cokes, I suppose? And serve 'em to Her Majesty in the tub? [STELLA *shrugs.*] Set down here a minute.
STELLA: Stanley, I've got things to do.
STANLEY: Set down! I've got th' dope on your big sister, Stella.
STELLA: Stanley, stop picking on Blanche.
STANLEY: That girl calls *me* common!
STELLA: Lately you been doing all you can think of to rub her the wrong way, Stanley, and Blanche is sensitive and you've got to realize that Blanche and I grew up under very different circumstances than you did.
STANLEY: So I been told. And told and told and told! You know she's been feeding us a pack of lies here?
STELLA: No, I don't and—
STANLEY: Well, she has, however. But now the cat's out of the bag! I found out some things!
STELLA: What—things?
STANLEY: Things I already suspected. But now I got proof from the most reliable sources—which I have checked on!

[BLANCHE *is singing in the bathroom a saccharine popular ballad which is used contrapuntally with* STANLEY*'s speech.*]

STELLA: [*To* STANLEY.] Lower your voice!

STANLEY: Some canary bird, huh!

STELLA: Now please tell me quietly what you think you've found out about my sister.

STANLEY: Lie Number One: All this squeamishness she puts on! You should just know the line she's been feeding to Mitch. He thought she had never been more than kissed by a fellow! But Sister Blanche is no lily! Ha-ha! Some lily she is!

STELLA: What have you heard and who from?

STANLEY: Our supply-man down at the plant has been going through Laurel for years and he knows all about her and everybody else in the town of Laurel knows all about her. She is as famous in Laurel as if she was the President of the United States, only she is not respected by any party! This supply-man stops at a hotel called the Flamingo.

BLANCHE: [*Singing blithely.*] "Say, it's only a paper moon, Sailing over a cardboard sea—But it wouldn't be make-believe If you believed in me!"[7]

STELLA: What about the—Flamingo?

STANLEY: She stayed there, too.

STELLA: My sister lived at Belle Reve.

STANLEY: This is after the home-place had slipped through her lily-white fingers! She moved to the Flamingo! A second-class hotel which has the advantage of not interfering in the private social life of the personalities there! The Flamingo is used to all kinds of goings-on. But even the management of the Flamingo was impressed by Dame Blanche! In fact they was so impressed by Dame Blanche that they requested her to turn in her room key—for permanently! This happened a couple of weeks before she showed here.

BLANCHE: [*Singing.*] "It's a Barnum and Bailey world, Just as phony as it can be—But it wouldn't be make-believe If you believed in me!"

STELLA: What—contemptible—lies!

STANLEY: Sure, I can see how you would be upset by this. She pulled the wool over your eyes as much as Mitch's!

STELLA: It's pure invention! There's not a word of truth in it and if I were a man and this creature had dared to invent such things in my presence—

BLANCHE: [*Singing.*] "Without your love, it's a honky-tonk parade! Without your love, It's a melody played In a penny arcade . . ."

STANLEY: Honey, I told you I thoroughly checked on these stories! Now wait till I finish. The trouble with Dame Blanche was that she couldn't put on her act any more in Laurel! They got wised up after two or three dates with her and then they quit, and she goes on to another, the same old line, same old act, same old hooey! But the town was too small for this to go on forever! And as time went by she became a town character. Regarded as not just different but downright loco—nuts. [STELLA *draws back.*] And for the last year or two she has been washed up like poison. That's why she's here this

7. From "It's Only a Paper Moon" (1933), a popular song by Harold Arlen.

summer, visiting royalty, putting on all this act—because she's practically told by the mayor to get out of town! Yes, did you know there was an army camp near Laurel and your sister's was one of the places called "Out-of-Bounds"?

BLANCHE: "It's only a paper moon, Just as phony as it can be—But it wouldn't be make-believe If you believed in me!"

STANLEY: Well, so much for her being such a refined and particular type of girl. Which brings us to Lie Number Two.

BLANCHE: I don't want to hear any more!

STANLEY: She's not going back to teach school! In fact I am willing to bet you that she never had no idea of returning to Laurel! She didn't resign temporarily from the high school because of her nerves! No, siree, Bob! She didn't. They kicked her out of that high school before the spring term ended—and I hate to tell you the reason that step was taken! A seventeen-year-old boy—she'd gotten mixed up with!

BLANCHE: "It's a Barnum and Bailey world, Just as phony as it can be—"

[*In the bathroom the water goes on loud; little breathless cries and peals of laughter are heard as if a child were frolicking in the tub.*]

STELLA: This is making me—sick!

STANLEY: The boy's dad learned about it and got in touch with the high school superintendent. Boy, oh, boy, I'd like to have been in that office when Dame Blanche was called on the carpet! I'd like to have seen her trying to squirm out of that one! But they had her on the hook good and proper that time and she knew that the jig was all up! They told her she better move on to some fresh territory. Yep, it was practickly a town ordinance passed against her!

[*The bathroom door is opened and* BLANCHE *thrusts her head out, holding a towel about her hair.*]

BLANCHE: Stella!

STELLA: [*Faintly.*] Yes, Blanche?

BLANCHE: Give me another bath-towel to dry my hair with. I've just washed it.

STELLA: Yes, Blanche. [*She crosses in a dazed way from the kitchen to the bathroom door with a towel.*]

BLANCHE: What's the matter, honey?

STELLA: Matter? Why?

BLANCHE: You have such a strange expression on your face!

STELLA: Oh—[*She tries to laugh.*] I guess I'm a little tired!

BLANCHE: Why don't you bathe, too, soon as I get out?

STANLEY: [*Calling from the kitchen.*] How soon is that going to be?

BLANCHE: Not so terribly long! Possess your soul in patience!

STANLEY: It's not my soul, it's my kidneys I'm worried about! [BLANCHE *slams the door.* STANLEY *laughs harshly.* STELLA *comes slowly back into the kitchen.*] Well, what do you think of it?

STELLA: I don't believe all of those stories and I think your supply-man was mean and rotten to tell them. It's possible that some of the things he said are partly true. There are things about my sister I don't approve of—things that caused sorrow at home. She was always—flighty!

STANLEY: Flighty!

STELLA: But when she was young, very young, she married a boy who wrote poetry. . . . He was extremely good-looking. I think Blanche didn't just love him but worshipped the ground he walked on! Adored him and thought him almost too fine to be human! But then she found out—

STANLEY: What?

STELLA: This beautiful and talented young man was a degenerate. Didn't your supply-man give you that information?

STANLEY: All we discussed was recent history. That must have been a pretty long time ago.

STELLA: Yes, it was—a pretty long time ago . . .

[STANLEY *comes up and takes her by the shoulders rather gently. She gently withdraws from him. Automatically she starts sticking little pink candles in the birthday cake.*]

STANLEY: How many candles you putting in that cake?

STELLA: I'll stop at twenty-five.

STANLEY: Is company expected?

STELLA: We asked Mitch to come over for cake and ice-cream.

[STANLEY *looks a little uncomfortable. He lights a cigarette from the one he has just finished.*]

STANLEY: I wouldn't be expecting Mitch over tonight.

[STELLA *pauses in her occupation with candles and looks slowly around at* STANLEY.]

STELLA: *Why?*

STANLEY: Mitch is a buddy of mine. We were in the same outfit together—Two-forty-first Engineers. We work in the same plant and now on the same bowling team. You think I could face him if—

STELLA: Stanley Kowalski, did you—did you repeat what that—?

STANLEY: You're goddam right I told him! I'd have that on my conscience the rest of my life if I knew all that stuff and let my best friend get caught!

STELLA: Is Mitch through with her?

STANLEY: Wouldn't you be if—?

STELLA: I said, *Is Mitch through with her?*

[BLANCHE'*s voice is lifted again, serenely as a bell. She sings "But it wouldn't be make-believe If you believed in me."*]

STANLEY: No, I don't think he's necessarily through with her—just wised up!

STELLA: Stanley, she thought Mitch was—going to—going to marry her. I was hoping so, too.

STANLEY: Well, he's not going to marry her. Maybe he *was*, but he's not going to jump in a tank with a school of sharks—now! [*He rises.*] Blanche! Oh,

Blanche! Can I please get in my bathroom? [*There is a pause.*]

BLANCHE: Yes, indeed, sir! Can you wait one second while I dry?

STANLEY: Having waited one hour I guess one second ought to pass in a hurry.

STELLA: And she hasn't got her job? Well, what will she do!

STANLEY: She's not stayin' here after Tuesday. You know that, don't you? Just to make sure I bought her ticket myself. A bus ticket.

STELLA: In the first place, Blanche wouldn't go on a bus.

STANLEY: She'll go on a bus and like it.

STELLA: No, she won't, no, she won't, Stanley!

STANLEY: *She'll go!* Period. P.S. She'll go *Tuesday!*

STELLA: [*slowly*] What'll—she—do? What on earth will she—*do!*

STANLEY: Her future is mapped out for her.

STELLA: What do you mean?

[BLANCHE *sings.*]

STANLEY: Hey, canary bird! Toots! Get *OUT* of the *BATHROOM!*

[*The bathroom door flies open and* BLANCHE *emerges with a gay peal of laughter, but as* STANLEY *crosses past her, a frightened look appears in her face, almost a look of panic. He doesn't look at her but slams the bathroom door shut as he goes in.*

BLANCHE: [*Snatching up a hair-brush.*] Oh, I feel so good after my long, hot bath, I feel so good and cool and—rested!

STELLA: [*Sadly and doubtfully from the kitchen.*] Do you, Blanche?

BLANCHE: [*Snatching up a hairbrush.*] Yes, I do, so refreshed! [*She tinkles her highball glass.*] A hot bath and a long, cold drink always give me a brand new outlook on life! [*She looks through the portieres at* STELLA, *standing between them, and slowly stops brushing.*] Something has happened!—What is it?

STELLA: [*Turning away quickly.*] Why, nothing has happened, Blanche.

BLANCHE: You're lying! Something has!

[*She stares fearfully at* STELLA, *who pretends to be busy at the table. The distant piano goes into a hectic breakdown.*]

SCENE 8

Three quarters of an hour later.

The view through the big windows is fading gradually into a still-golden dusk. A torch of sunlight blazes on the side of a big water-tank or oil-drum across the empty lot toward the business district which is now pierced by pinpoints of lighted windows or windows reflecting the sunset.

The three people are completing a dismal birthday supper. STANLEY *looks sullen. Stella is embarrassed and sad.*

BLANCHE *has a tight, artificial smile on her drawn face. There is a fourth place at the table which is left vacant.*

BLANCHE: [*Suddenly.*] Stanley, tell us a joke, tell us a funny story to make us all laugh. I don't know what's the matter, we're all so solemn. Is it because I've been stood up by my beau? [STELLA *laughs feebly.*] It's the first time in my entire experience with men, and I've had a good deal of all sorts, that I've actually been stood up by anybody! Ha-ha! I don't know how to take it. . . . Tell us a funny little story, Stanley! Something to help us out.

STANLEY: I didn't think you liked my stories, Blanche.

BLANCHE: I like them when they're amusing but not indecent.

STANLEY: I don't know any refined enough for your taste.

BLANCHE: Then let me tell one.

STELLA: Yes, you tell one, Blanche. You used to know lots of good stories.

[*The music fades.*]

BLANCHE: Let me see, now. . . . I must run through my repertoire! Oh, yes—I love parrot stories! Do you all like parrot stories? Well, this one's about the old maid and the parrot. This old maid, she had a parrot that cursed a blue streak and knew more vulgar expressions than Mr. Kowalski!

STANLEY: Huh.

BLANCHE: And the only way to hush the parrot up was to put the cover back on its cage so it would think it was night and go back to sleep. Well, one morning the old maid had just uncovered the parrot for the day—when who should she see coming up the front walk but the preacher! Well, she rushed back to the parrot and slipped the cover back on the cage and then she let in the preacher. And the parrot was perfectly still, just as quiet as a mouse, but just as she was asking the preacher how much sugar he wanted in his coffee—the parrot broke the silence with a loud—[*She whistles.*]—and said—"God *damn*, but that was a short day!"

[*She throws back her head and laughs.* STELLA *also makes an ineffectual effort to seem amused.* STANLEY *pays no attention to the story but reaches way over the table to spear his fork into the remaining chop which he eats with his fingers.*]

BLANCHE: Apparently Mr. Kowalski was not amused.

STELLA: Mr. Kowalski is too busy making a pig of himself to think of anything else!

STANLEY: That's right, baby.

STELLA: Your face and your fingers are disgustingly greasy. Go and wash up and then help me clear the table.

[*He hurls a plate to the floor.*]

STANLEY: That's how I'll clear the table! [*He seizes her arm.*] Don't ever talk that way to me! "Pig—Polack—disgusting—vulgar—greasy!"—them kind of words have been on your tongue and your sister's too much around here! What do you two think you are? A pair of queens? Remember what Huey Long[8] said—

8. Demagogic Louisiana political leader, governor, and senator (1893–1935).

"Every Man is a King!" And I am the king around here, so don't forget it! [*He hurls a cup and saucer to the floor.*] My place is cleared! You want me to clear your places?

[STELLA *begins to cry weakly.* STANLEY *stalks out on the porch and lights a cigarette. The Negro entertainers around the corner are heard.*]

BLANCHE: What happened while I was bathing? What did he tell you, Stella?
STELLA: Nothing, nothing, nothing!
BLANCHE: I think he told you something about Mitch and me! You know why Mitch didn't come but you won't tell me! [STELLA *shakes her head helplessly.*] I'm going to call him!
STELLA: I wouldn't call him, Blanche.
BLANCHE: I am, I'm going to call him on the phone.
STELLA: [*Miserably.*] I wish you wouldn't.
BLANCHE: I intend to be given some explanation from someone!

[*She rushes to the phone in the bedroom.* STELLA *goes out on the porch and stares reproachfully at her husband. He grunts and turns away from her.*]

STELLA: I hope you're pleased with your doings. I never had so much trouble swallowing food in my life, looking at that girl's face and the empty chair! [*She cries quietly.*]
BLANCHE: [*At the phone.*] Hello. Mr. Mitchell, please. . . . Oh. . . . I would like to leave a number if I may. Magnolia 9047. And say it's important to call. . . . Yes, very important. . . . Thank you. [*She remains by the phone with a lost, frightened look.*]

[STANLEY *turns slowly back toward his wife and takes her clumsily in his arms.*]

STANLEY: Stell, it's gonna be all right after she goes and after you've had the baby. It's gonna be all right again between you and me the way that it was. You remember the way that it was? Them nights we had together? God, honey, it's gonna be sweet when we can make noise in the night the way that we used to and get the colored lights going with nobody's sister behind the curtains to hear us! [*Their upstairs neighbors are heard in bellowing laughter at something.* STANLEY *chuckles.*] Steve an' Eunice . . .
STELLA: Come on back in. [*She returns to the kitchen and starts lighting the candles on the white cake.*] Blanche?
BLANCHE: Yes. [*She returns from the bedroom to the table in the kitchen.*] Oh, those pretty, pretty little candles! Oh, don't burn them, Stella.
STELLA: I certainly will.

[STANLEY *comes back in.*]

BLANCHE: You ought to save them for baby's birthdays. Oh, I hope candles are going to glow in his life and I hope that his eyes are going to be like candles, like two blue candles lighted in a white cake!
STANLEY: [*Sitting down.*] What poetry!

BLANCHE: [*She pauses reflectively for a moment.*] I shouldn't have called him.

STELLA: There's lots of things could have happened.

BLANCHE: There's no excuse for it, Stella. I don't have to put up with insults. I won't be taken for granted.

STANLEY: Goddamn, it's hot in here with the steam from the bathroom.

BLANCHE: I've said I was sorry three times. [*The piano fades out.*] I take hot baths for my nerves. Hydrotherapy, they call it. You healthy Polack, without a nerve in your body, of course you don't know what anxiety feels like!

STANLEY: I am not a Polack. People from Poland are Poles, not Polacks. But what I am is a one-hundred-per-cent American, born and raised in the greatest country on earth and proud as hell of it, so don't ever call me a Polack.

[*The phone rings.* BLANCHE *rises expectantly.*]

BLANCHE: Oh, that's for me, I'm sure.

STANLEY: *I'm* not sure. Keep your seat. [*He crosses leisurely to phone.*] H'lo. Aw, yeh, hello, Mac.

[*He leans against wall, staring insultingly in at* BLANCHE. *She sinks back in her chair with a frightened look.* STELLA *leans over and touches her shoulder.*]

BLANCHE: Oh, keep your hands off me, Stella. What is the matter with you? Why do you look at me with that pitying look?

STANLEY: [*Bawling.*] QUIET IN THERE!—We've got a noisy woman on the place.—Go on, Mac. At Riley's? No, I don't wanta bowl at Riley's. I had a little trouble with Riley last week. I'm the team captain, ain't I? All right, then, we're not gonna bowl at Riley's, we're gonna bowl at the West Side or the Gala! All right, Mac. See you! [*He hangs up and returns to the table.* BLANCHE *fiercely controls herself, drinking quickly from her tumbler of water. He doesn't look at her but reaches in a pocket. Then he speaks slowly and with false amiability.*] Sister Blanche, I've got a little birthday remembrance for you.

BLANCHE: Oh, have you, Stanley? I wasn't expecting any, I—I don't know why Stella wants to observe my birthday! I'd much rather forget it—when you—reach twenty-seven! Well—age is a subject that you'd prefer to—ignore!

STANLEY: Twenty-seven?

BLANCHE: [*Quickly.*] What is it? Is it for *me?*

[*He is holding a little envelope toward her.*]

STANLEY: Yes, I hope you like it!

BLANCHE: Why, why—Why, it's a—

STANLEY: Ticket! Back to Laurel! On the Greyhound! Tuesday! [*The Varsouviana music steals in softly and continues playing.* STELLA *rises abruptly and turns her back.* BLANCHE *tries to smile. Then she tries to laugh. Then she gives both up and springs from the table and runs into the next room. She clutches her throat and then runs into the bathroom. Coughing, gagging sounds are heard.*] Well!

STELLA: You didn't need to do that.

STANLEY: Don't forget all that I took off her.

STELLA: You needn't have been so cruel to someone alone as she is.

STANLEY: Delicate piece she is.

STELLA: She is. She was. You didn't know Blanche as a girl. Nobody, nobody, was tender and trusting as she was. But people like you abused her, and forced her to change. [*He crosses into the bedroom, ripping off his shirt, and changes into a brilliant silk bowling shirt. She follows him.*] Do you think you're going bowling now?

STANLEY: Sure.

STELLA: You're not going bowling. [*She catches hold of his shirt.*] Why did you do this to her?

STANLEY: I done nothing to no one. Let go of my shirt. You've torn it.

STELLA: I want to know why. Tell me why.

STANLEY: When we first met, me and you, you thought I was common. How right you was, baby. I was common as dirt. You showed me the snapshot of the place with the columns. I pulled you down off them columns and how you loved it, having them colored lights going! And wasn't we happy together, wasn't it all okay till she showed here? [STELLA *makes a slight movement. Her look goes suddenly inward as if some interior voice had called her name. She begins a slow, shuffling progress from the bedroom to the kitchen, leaning and resting on the back of the chair and then on the edge of a table with a blind look and listening expression.* STANLEY, *finishing with his shirt, is unaware of her reaction.*] And wasn't we happy together? Wasn't it all okay? Till she showed here. Hoity-Toity, describing me as an ape. [*He suddenly notices the change in* STELLA.] Hey, what is it, Stell? [*He crosses to her.*]

STELLA: [*Quietly.*] Take me to the hospital.

[*He is with her now, supporting her with his arm, murmuring indistinguishably as they go outside.*]

Scene 9

A *while later that evening.* BLANCHE *is seated in a tense hunched position in a bedroom chair that she has recovered with diagonal green and white stripes. She has on her scarlet satin robe. On the table beside chair is a bottle of liquor and a glass. The rapid, feverish polka tune, the "Varsouviana," is heard. The music is in her mind; she is drinking to escape it and the sense of disaster closing in on her, and she seems to whisper the words of the song. An electric fan is turning back and forth across her.*

MITCH *comes around the corner in work clothes: blue denim shirt and pants. He is unshaven. He climbs the steps to the door and rings.* BLANCHE *is startled.*

BLANCHE: Who is it, please?

MITCH: [*Hoarsely.*]: Me. Mitch.

[*The polka tune stops.*]

BLANCHE: Mitch!—Just a minute. [*She rushes about frantically, hiding the bottle in a closet, crouching at the mirror and dabbing her face with cologne and powder. She is so excited that her breath is audible as she dashes about. At last she rushes to the door in the kitchen and lets him in.*] Mitch!—Y'know, I really shouldn't let you in after the treatment I have received from you this evening! So utterly uncavalier! But hello, beautiful! [*She offers him her lips. He ignores it and pushes past her into the flat. She looks fearfully after him as he stalks into the bedroom.*] My, my, what a cold shoulder! And such uncouth apparel! Why, you haven't even shaved! The unforgivable insult to a lady! But I forgive you. I forgive you because it's such a relief to see you. You've stopped that polka tune that I had caught in my head. Have you ever had anything caught in your head? No, of course you haven't, you dumb angel-puss, you'd never get anything awful caught in your head!

[*He stares at her while she follows him while she talks. It is obvious that he has had a few drinks on the way over.*]

MITCH: Do we have to have that fan on?

BLANCHE: No!

MITCH: I don't like fans.

BLANCHE: Then let's turn it off, honey. I'm not partial to them! [*She presses the switch and the fan nods slowly off. She clears her throat uneasily as* MITCH *plumps himself down on the bed in the bedroom and lights a cigarette.*] I don't know what there is to drink. I—haven't investigated.

MITCH: I don't want Stan's liquor.

BLANCHE: It isn't Stan's. Everything here isn't Stan's. Some things on the premises are actually mine! How is your mother? Isn't your mother well?

MITCH: Why?

BLANCHE: Something's the matter tonight, but never mind. I won't cross-examine the witness. I'll just— [*She touches her forehead vaguely. The polka tune starts up again.*]—pretend I don't notice anything different about you! That—music again . . .

MITCH: What music?

BLANCHE: The "Varsouviana"! The polka tune they were playing when Allan—Wait! [*A distant revolver shot is heard.* BLANCHE *seems relieved.*] There now, the shot! It always stops after that. [*The polka music dies out again.*] Yes, now it's stopped.

MITCH: Are you boxed out of your mind?

BLANCHE: I'll go and see what I can find in the way of— [*She crosses into the closet, pretending to search for the bottle.*] Oh, by the way, excuse me for not being dressed. But I'd practically given you up! Had you forgotten your invitation to supper?

MITCH: I wasn't going to see you any more.

BLANCHE: Wait a minute. I can't hear what you're saying and you talk so little that when you do say something, I don't want to miss a single syllable of it. . . . What am I looking around here for? Oh, yes—liquor! We've had so much excitement around here this evening that I *am* boxed out of my mind! [*She pretends suddenly to find the bottle. He draws his foot up on the bed and stares at her contemptuously.*] Here's something. Southern Comfort! What is that, I wonder?

MITCH: If you don't know, it must belong to Stan.

BLANCHE: Take your foot off the bed. It has a light cover on it. Of course you boys don't notice things like that. I've done so much with this place since I've been here.

MITCH: I bet you have.

BLANCHE: You saw it before I came. Well, look at it now! This room is almost—dainty! I want to keep it that way. I wonder if this stuff ought to be mixed with something? Ummm, it's sweet! It's terribly, terribly sweet! Why, it's a *liqueur*, I believe! Yes, that's what it *is*, a liqueur! [MITCH *grunts.*] I'm afraid you won't like it, but try it, and maybe you will.

MITCH: I told you already I don't want none of his liquor and I mean it. You ought to lay off his liquor. He says you been lapping it up all summer like a wild-cat!

BLANCHE: What a fantastic statement! Fantastic of him to say it, fantastic of you to repeat it! I won't descend to the level of such cheap accusations to answer them, even!

MITCH: Huh.

BLANCHE: What's in your mind? I see something in your eyes!

MITCH: [*Getting up.*]: It's dark in here.

BLANCHE: I like it dark. The dark is comforting to me.

MITCH: I don't think I ever seen you in the light. [BLANCHE *laughs breathlessly.*] That's a fact!

BLANCHE: Is it?

MITCH: I've never seen you in the afternoon.

BLANCHE: Whose fault is that?

MITCH: You never want to go out in the afternoon.

BLANCHE: Why, Mitch, you're at the plant in the afternoon!

MITCH: Not Sunday afternoon. I've asked you to go out with me sometimes on Sundays but you always make an excuse. You never want to go out till after six and then it's always some place that's not lighted much.

BLANCHE: There is some obscure meaning in this but I fail to catch it.

MITCH: What it means is I've never had a real good look at you, Blanche. Let's turn the light on here.

BLANCHE: [*Fearfully.*]: Light? Which light? What for?

MITCH: This one with the paper thing on it.

[*He tears the paper lantern off the light bulb. She utters a frightened gasp.*]

BLANCHE: What did you do that for?

MITCH: So I can take a look at you good and plain!

BLANCHE: Of course you don't really mean to be insulting!

MITCH: No, just realistic.

BLANCHE: I don't want realism. I want magic! [MITCH *laughs.*] Yes, yes, magic! I try to give that to people. I misrepresent things to them. I don't tell truth, I tell what *ought* to be truth. And if that is sinful, then let me be damned for it!—*Don't turn the light on!*

[MITCH *crosses to the switch. He turns the light on and stares at her. She cries out and covers her face. He turns the lights off again.*]

MITCH: [*Slowly and bitterly.*] I don't mind you being older than what I thought. But all the rest of it—Christ! That pitch about your ideals being so old-fashioned and all the malarkey that you've dished out all summer. Oh, I knew you weren't sixteen any more. But I was a fool enough to believe you was straight.

BLANCHE: Who told you I wasn't—"straight"? My loving brother-in-law. And you believed him.

MITCH: I called him a liar at first. And then I checked on the story. First I asked our supply-man who travels through Laurel. And then I talked directly over long-distance to this merchant.

BLANCHE: Who is this merchant?

MITCH: Kiefaber.

BLANCHE: The merchant Kiefaber of Laurel! I know the man. He whistled at me. I put him in his place. So now for revenge he makes up stories about me.

MITCH: Three people, Kiefaber, Stanley and Shaw, swore to them!

BLANCHE: Rub-a-dub-dub, three men in a tub! And such a filthy tub!

MITCH: Didn't you stay at a hotel called The Flamingo?

BLANCHE: Flamingo? No! Tarantula was the name of it! I stayed at a hotel called The Tarantula Arms!

MITCH: [*Stupidly*] Tarantula?

BLANCHE: Yes, a big spider! That's where I brought my victims. [*She pours herself another drink.*] Yes, I had many intimacies with strangers. After the death of Allan—intimacies with strangers was all I seemed able to fill my empty heart with. . . . I think it was panic, just panic, that drove me from one to another, hunting for some protection—here and there, in the most—unlikely places—even, at last, in a seventeen-year-old boy but—somebody wrote the superintendent about it—"This woman is morally unfit for her position!" [*She throws back her head with convulsive, sobbing laughter. Then she repeats the statement, gasps, and drinks.*] True? Yes, I suppose—unfit somehow—anyway. . . . So I came here. There was nowhere else I could go. I was played out. You know what played out is? My youth was suddenly gone up the water-spout, and—I met you. You said you needed somebody. Well, I needed somebody, too. I thanked God for you, because you seemed to be gentle—a cleft in the rock of the world that I could hide in! But I guess I was asking, hoping—too much! Kiefaber, Stanley and Shaw have tied an old tin can to the tail of the kite.

[*There is a pause.* MITCH *stares at her dumbly.*]

MITCH: You lied to me, Blanche.

BLANCHE: Don't say I lied to you.

MITCH: Lies, lies, inside and out, all lies.

BLANCHE: Never inside, I didn't lie in my heart . . .

[*A Vendor comes around the corner. She is a blind Mexican woman in a dark shawl, carrying bunches of those gaudy tin flowers that lower-class Mexicans display at funerals and other festive occasions. She is calling barely audibly. Her figure is only faintly visible outside the building.*]

MEXICAN WOMAN: Flores. Flores, Flores para los muertos.[9] Flores. Flores.

BLANCHE: What? Oh! Somebody outside . . . [*She goes to the door, opens it and stares at the* MEXICAN WOMAN.]

MEXICAN WOMAN: [*She is at the door and offers* BLANCHE *some of her flowers.*] Flores? Flores para los muertos?

BLANCHE: [*Frightened.*] No, no! Not now! Not now! [*She darts back into the apartment, slamming the door.*]

MEXICAN WOMAN: [*She turns away and starts to move down the street.*] Flores para los muertos.

[*The polka tune fades in.*]

BLANCHE: [*As if to herself.*] Crumble and fade and—regrets—recriminations . . . "If you'd done this, it wouldn't've cost me that!"

MEXICAN WOMAN: Corones[1] para los muertos. Corones . . .

BLANCHE: Legacies! Huh. . . . And other things such as bloodstained pillow-slips—"Her linen needs changing"—"Yes, Mother. But couldn't we get a colored girl to do it?" No, we couldn't of course. Everything gone but the—

MEXICAN WOMAN: Flores.

BLANCHE: Death—I used to sit here and she used to sit over there and death was as close as you are. . . . We didn't dare even admit we had ever heard of it!

MEXICAN WOMAN: Flores para los muertos, flores—flores . . .

BLANCHE: The opposite is desire. So do you wonder? How could you possibly wonder! Not far from Belle Reve, before we had lost Belle Reve, was a camp where they trained young soldiers. On Sunday nights they would go in town to get drunk—

MEXICAN WOMAN: [*Softly.*] Corones . . .

BLANCHE: —and on the way back they would stagger onto my lawn and call—"Blanche! Blanche!"—the deaf old lady remaining suspected nothing. But sometimes I slipped outside to answer their calls. . . . Later the paddy-wagon would gather them up like daisies . . . the long way home . . . [*The* MEXICAN WOMAN *turns slowly and drifts back off with her soft mournful cries.* BLANCHE *goes to the dresser and leans forward on it. After a moment,* MITCH *rises and follows her purposefully. The polka music fades away. He places his hands on her waist and tries to turn her about.*] What do you want?

MITCH: [*Fumbling to embrace her.*] What I been missing all summer.

BLANCHE: Then marry me, Mitch!

MITCH: I don't think I want to marry you any more.

BLANCHE: No?

MITCH: [*Dropping his hands from her waist.*] You're not clean enough to bring in the house with my mother.

9. "Flowers for the dead." 1. "Wreaths."

BLANCHE: Go away, then. [*He stares at her.*] Get out of here quick before I start screaming fire! [*Her throat is tightening with hysteria.*] Get out of here quick before I start screaming fire. [*He still remains staring. She suddenly rushes to the big window with its pale blue square of the soft summer light and cries wildly.*] Fire! Fire! Fire!

[*With a startled gasp,* MITCH *turns and goes out the outer door, clatters awkwardly down the steps and around the corner of the building.* BLANCHE *staggers back from the window and falls to her knees. The distant piano is slow and blue.*]

SCENE 10

It is a few hours later that night.

BLANCHE *has been drinking fairly steadily since* MITCH *left. She has dragged her wardrobe trunk into the center of the bedroom. It hangs open with flowery dresses thrown across it. As the drinking and packing went on, a mood of hysterical exhilaration came into her and she has decked herself out in a somewhat soiled and crumpled white satin evening gown and a pair of scuffed silver slippers with brilliants set in their heels.*

Now she is placing the rhinestone tiara on her head before the mirror of the dressing-table and murmuring excitedly as if to a group of spectral admirers.

BLANCHE: How about taking a swim, a moonlight swim at the old rock-quarry? If anyone's sober enough to drive a car! Ha-ha! Best way in the world to stop your head buzzing! Only you've got to be careful to dive where the deep pool is—if you hit a rock you don't come up till tomorrow . . . [*Tremblingly she lifts the hand mirror for a closer inspection. She catches her breath and slams the mirror face down with such violence that the glass cracks. She moans a little and attempts to rise.* STANLEY *appears around the corner of the building. He still has on the vivid green silk bowling shirt. As he rounds the corner the honky-tonk music is heard. It continues softly throughout the scene. He enters the kitchen, slamming the door. As he peers in at* BLANCHE, *he gives a low whistle. He has had a few drinks on the way and has brought some quart beer bottles home with him.*] How is my sister?

STANLEY: She is doing okay.

BLANCHE: And how is the baby?

STANLEY: [*Grinning amiably.*] The baby won't come before morning so they told me to go home and get a little shut-eye.

BLANCHE: Does that mean we are to be alone in here?

STANLEY: Yep. Just me and you, Blanche. Unless you got somebody hid under the bed. What've you got on those fine feathers for?

BLANCHE: Oh, that's right. You left before my wire came.

STANLEY: You got a wire?

BLANCHE: I received a telegram from an old admirer of mine.

STANLEY: Anything good?

BLANCHE: I think so. An invitation.

STANLEY: What to? A fireman's ball?

BLANCHE: [*Throwing back her head.*] A cruise of the Caribbean on a yacht!

STANLEY: Well, well. What do you know?

BLANCHE: I have never been so surprised in my life.

STANLEY: I guess not.

BLANCHE: It came like a bolt from the blue!

STANLEY: Who did you say it was from?

BLANCHE: An old beau of mine.

STANLEY: The one that give you the white fox-pieces?

BLANCHE: Mr. Shep Huntleigh. I wore his ATO pin my last year at college. I hadn't seen him again until last Christmas. I ran in to him on Biscayne Boulevard. Then—just now—this wire—inviting me on a cruise of the Caribbean! The problem is clothes. I tore into my trunk to see what I have that's suitable for the tropics!

STANLEY: And come up with that—gorgeous—diamond—tiara?

BLANCHE: This old relic? Ha-ha! It's only rhinestones.

STANLEY: Gosh. I thought it was Tiffany diamonds. [*He unbuttons his shirt.*]

BLANCHE: Well, anyhow, I shall be entertained in style.

STANLEY: Uh-huh. It goes to show, you never know what is coming.

BLANCHE: Just when I thought my luck had begun to fail me—

STANLEY: Into the picture pops this Miami millionaire.

BLANCHE: This man is not from Miami. This man is from Dallas.

STANLEY: This man is from Dallas?

BLANCHE: Yes, this man is from Dallas where gold spouts out of the ground!

STANLEY: Well, just so he's from somewhere! [*He starts removing his shirt.*]

BLANCHE: Close the curtains before you undress any further.

STANLEY: [*Amiably.*] This is all I'm going to undress right now. [*He rips the sack off a quart beer bottle.*] Seen a bottle-opener? [*She moves slowly toward the dresser, where she stands with her hands knotted together.*] I used to have a cousin who could open a beer bottle with his teeth. [*Pounding the bottle cap on the corner of table.*] That was his only accomplishment, all he could do—he was just a human bottle-opener. And then one time, at a wedding party, he broke his front teeth off! After that he was so ashamed of himself he used t' sneak out of the house when company came . . . [*The bottle cap pops off and a geyser of foam shoots up.* STANLEY *laughs happily, holding up the bottle over his head.*] Ha-ha! Rain from heaven! [*He extends the bottle toward her.*] Shall we bury the hatchet and make it a loving-cup? Huh?

BLANCHE: No, thank you.

STANLEY: Well, it's a red-letter night for us both. You having an oil millionaire and me having a baby. [*He goes to the bureau in the bedroom and crouches to remove something from the bottom drawer.*]

BLANCHE: [*Drawing back.*] What are you doing in here?

STANLEY: Here's something I always break out on special occasions like this. The silk pyjamas I wore on my wedding night!

BLANCHE: Oh.

STANLEY: When the telephone rings and they say, "You've got a son!" I'll tear this off and wave it like a flag! [*He shakes out a brilliant pyjama coat.*] I guess we are both entitled to put on the dog. [*He goes back to the kitchen with the coat over his arm.*]

BLANCHE: When I think of how divine it is going to be to have such a thing as privacy once more—I could weep with joy!

STANLEY: This millionaire from Dallas is not going to interfere with your privacy any?

BLANCHE: It won't be the sort of thing you have in mind. This man is a gentleman and he respects me. [*Improvising feverishly.*] What he wants is my companionship. Having great wealth sometimes makes people lonely! A cultivated woman, a woman of intelligence and breeding, can enrich a man's life—immeasurably! I have those things to offer, and this doesn't take them away. Physical beauty is passing. A transitory possession. But beauty of the mind and richness of the spirit and tenderness of the heart—and I have all of those things—aren't taken away, but grow! Increase with the years! How strange that I should be called a destitute woman! When I have all of these treasures locked in my heart. [*A choked sob comes from her.*] I think of myself as a very, very rich woman! But I have been foolish—casting my pearls before swine!

STANLEY: Swine, huh?

BLANCHE: Yes, swine! Swine! And I'm thinking not only of you but of your friend, Mr. Mitchell. He came to see me tonight. He dared to come here in his work clothes! And to repeat slander to me, vicious stories that he had gotten from you! I gave him his walking papers . . .

STANLEY: You did, huh?

BLANCHE: But then he came back. He returned with a box of roses to beg my forgiveness! He implored my forgiveness. But some things are not forgivable. Deliberate cruelty is not forgivable. It is the one unforgivable thing in my opinion and it is the one thing of which I have never, ever been guilty. And so I told him, I said to him, "Thank you," but it was foolish of me to think that we could ever adapt ourselves to each other. Our ways of life are too different. Our attitudes and our backgrounds are incompatible. We have to be realistic about such things. So farewell, my friend! And let there be no hard feelings . . .

STANLEY: Was this before or after the telegram came from the Texas oil millionaire?

BLANCHE: What telegram? No! No, after! As a matter of fact, the wire came just as—

STANLEY: As a matter of fact there wasn't no wire at all!

BLANCHE: Oh, oh!

STANLEY: There isn't no millionaire! And Mitch didn't come back with roses 'cause I know where he is—

BLANCHE: Oh!

STANLEY: There isn't a goddam thing but imagination!

BLANCHE: Oh!

STANLEY: And lies and conceit and tricks!

BLANCHE: Oh!

STANLEY: And look at yourself! Take a look at yourself in that worn-out Mardi Gras outfit, rented for fifty cents from some ragpicker! And with the crazy crown on! What queen do you think you are?

BLANCHE: Oh—God . . .

STANLEY: I've been on to you from the start! Not once did you pull any wool over this boy's eyes! You come in here and sprinkle the place with powder and spray perfume and cover the light-bulb with a paper lantern, and lo and behold the place has turned into Egypt and you are the Queen of the Nile! Sitting on your throne and swilling down my liquor! I say—*Ha!—Ha!* Do you hear me? *Ha—ha—ha!* [*He walks into the bedroom.*]

BLANCHE: Don't come in here! [*Lurid reflections appear on the walls around* BLANCHE. *The shadows are of a grotesque and menacing form. She catches her breath, crosses to the phone and jiggles the hook.* STANLEY *goes into the bathroom and closes the door.*] Operator, operator! Give me long-distance, please. . . . I want to get in touch with Mr. Shep Huntleigh of Dallas. He's so well known he doesn't require any address. Just ask anybody who—Wait!!—No, I couldn't find it right now. . . . Please understand, I—No! No, wait! . . . One moment! Someone is—Nothing! Hold on, please! [*She sets the phone down and crosses warily into the kitchen. The night is filled with inhuman voices like cries in a jungle. The shadows and lurid reflections move sinuously as flames along the wall spaces. Through the back wall of the rooms, which have become transparent, can be seen the sidewalk. A prostitute has rolled a drunkard. He pursues her along the walk, overtakes her and there is a struggle. A policeman's whistle breaks it up. The figures disappear. Some moments later the* NEGRO WOMAN *appears around the corner with a sequined bag which the prostitute had dropped on the walk. She is rooting excitedly through it.* BLANCHE *presses her knuckles to her lips and returns slowly to the phone. She speaks in a hoarse whisper.*] Operator! Operator! Never mind long-distance. Get Western Union. There isn't time to be—Western—Western Union! [*She waits anxiously.*] Western Union? Yes! I—want to—Take down this message! "In desperate, desperate circumstances! Help me! Caught in a trap. Caught in—" *Oh!*

[*The bathroom door is thrown open and* STANLEY *comes out in the brilliant silk pyjamas. He grins at her as he knots the tassled sash about his waist. She gasps and backs away from the phone. He stares at her for a count of ten. Then a clicking becomes audible from the telephone, steady and rasping.*]

STANLEY: You left th' phone off th' hook.

[*He crosses to it deliberately and sets it back on the hook. After he has replaced it, he stares at her again, his mouth slowly curving into a grin, as he weaves between* BLANCHE *and the outer door. The barely audible "Blue Piano" begins to drum up louder. The sound of it turns into the roar of an approaching locomotive.* BLANCHE *crouches, pressing her fists to her ears until it has gone by.*]

BLANCHE: [*Finally straightening.*] Let me—let me get by you!
STANLEY: Get by me? Sure. Go ahead. [*He moves back a pace in the doorway.*]
BLANCHE: You—you stand over there! [*She indicates a further position.*]
STANLEY: You got plenty of room to walk by me now.
BLANCHE: Not with you there! But I've got to get out somehow!
STANLEY: You think I'll interfere with you? Ha-ha! [*The "Blue Piano" goes softy. She turns confusedly and makes a faint gesture. The inhuman jungle voices rise up. He takes a step toward her, biting his tongue which protrudes between his lips. Softly.*] Come to think of it—maybe you wouldn't be bad to—interfere with . . .

[BLANCHE *moves backward through the door into the bedroom.*]

BLANCHE: Stay back! Don't you come toward me another step or I'll—
STANLEY: What?
BLANCHE: Some awful thing will happen! It will!
STANLEY: What are you putting on now?

[*They are now both inside the bedroom.*]

BLANCHE: I warn you, don't, I'm in danger!

[*He takes another step. She smashs a bottle on the table and faces him, clutching the broken top.*]

STANLEY: What did you do that for?
BLANCHE: So I could twist the broken end in your face!
STANLEY: I bet you would do that!
BLANCHE: I would! I will if you—
STANLEY: Oh! So you want some roughhouse! All right, let's have some roughhouse! [*He springs toward her, overturning the table. She cries out and strikes at him with the bottle top but he catches her wrist.*] Tiger—tiger! Drop the bottle-top! Drop it! We've had this date with each other from the beginning!

[*She moans. The bottle-top falls. She sinks to her knees: He picks up her inert figure and carries her to the bed. The hot trumpet and drums from the Four Deuces sound loudly.*]

Scene 11

It is some weeks later. STELLA *is packing* BLANCHE'*s things. Sounds of water can be heard running in the bathroom.*

The portieres are partly open on the poker players—STANLEY, STEVE, MITCH *and* PABLO—*who sit around the table in the kitchen. The atmosphere of the kitchen is now the same raw, lurid one of the disastrous poker night.*

The building is framed by the sky of turquoise. STELLA *has been crying as she arranges the flowery dresses in the open trunk.*

EUNICE *comes down the steps from her flat above and enters the kitchen. There is an outburst from the poker table.*

STANLEY: Drew to an inside straight and made it, by God.
PABLO: *Maldita sea tu suerto!*
STANLEY: Put it in English, greaseball.
PABLO: I am cursing your rutting luck.
STANLEY: [*Prodigiously elated.*] You know what luck is? Luck is believing you're lucky. Take at Salerno.[2] I believed I was lucky. I figured that 4 out of 5 would not come through but I would . . . and I did. I put that down as a rule. To hold front position in this rat-race you've got to believe you are lucky.
MITCH: You . . . you . . . you . . . Brag . . . brag . . . bull . . . bull.

[STELLA *goes into the bedroom and starts folding a dress.*]

STANLEY: What's the matter with him?
EUNICE: [*Walking past the table.*] I always did say that men are callous things with no feelings but this does beat anything. Making pigs of yourselves. [*She comes through the portieres into the bedroom.*]
STANLEY: What's the matter with her?
STELLA: How is my baby?
EUNICE: Sleeping like a little angel. Brought you some grapes. [*She puts them on a stool and lowers her voice.*] Blanche?
STELLA: Bathing.
EUNICE: How is she?
STELLA: She wouldn't eat anything but asked for a drink.
EUNICE: What did you tell her?
STELLA: I—just told her that—we'd made arrangements for her to rest in the country. She's got it mixed in her mind with Shep Huntleigh.

[BLANCHE *opens the bathroom door slightly.*]

BLANCHE: Stella.
STELLA: Yes.
BLANCHE: That cool yellow silk—the bouclé. See if it's crushed. If it's not too crushed I'll wear it and on the lapel that silver and turquoise pin in the shape of a seahorse. You will find them in the heart-shaped box I keep my accessories in. And Stella . . . Try and locate a bunch of artificial violets in that box, too, to pin with the seahorse on the lapel of the jacket.

[*She closes the door.* STELLA *turns to* EUNICE.]

STELLA: I don't know if I did the right thing.
EUNICE: What else could you do?
STELLA: I couldn't believe her story and go on living with Stanley.
EUNICE: Don't ever believe it. Life has got to go on. No matter what happens, you've got to keep on going.

2. Important beachhead in the Allied invasion of Italy in World War II.

[*The bathroom door opens a little.*]

BLANCHE: [*Looking out.*] Is the coast clear?
STELLA: Yes, Blanche. [*To* EUNICE.] Tell her how well she's looking.
BLANCHE: Please close the curtains before I come out.
STELLA: They're closed.
STANLEY: —How many for you?
PABLO: Two.
STEVE: Three.

[BLANCHE *appears in the amber light of the door. She has a tragic radiance in her red satin robe following the sculptural lines of her body. The "Varsouviana" rises audibly as* BLANCHE *enters the bedroom.*]

BLANCHE: [*With faintly hysterical vivacity.*] I have just washed my hair.
STELLA: Did you?
BLANCHE: I'm not sure I got the soap out.
EUNICE: Such fine hair!
BLANCHE: [*Accepting the compliment.*] It's a problem. Didn't I get a call?
STELLA: Who from, Blanche?
BLANCHE: Shep Huntleigh . . .
STELLA: Why, not yet, honey!
BLANCHE: How strange! I—

[*At the sound of* BLANCHE*'s voice* MITCH*'s arm supporting his cards has sagged and his gaze is dissolved into space.* STANLEY *slaps him on the shoulder.*]

STANLEY: Hey, Mitch, come to!

[*The sound of this new voice shocks* BLANCHE. *She makes a shocked gesture, forming his name with her lips.* STELLA *nods and looks quickly away.* BLANCHE *stands quite still for some moments—the silver-backed mirror in her hand and a look of sorrowful perplexity as though all human experience shows on her face.* BLANCHE *finally speaks but with sudden hysteria.*]

BLANCHE: What's going on here? [*She turns from* STELLA *to* EUNICE *and back to* STELLA. *Her rising voice penetrates the concentration of the game.* MITCH *ducks his head lower but* STANLEY *shoves back his chair as if about to rise.* STEVE *places a restraining hand on his arm. Continuing.*] What's happened here? I want an explanation of what's happened here.
STELLA: [*Agonizingly.*] Hush! Hush!
EUNICE: Hush! Hush! Honey.
STELLA: Please, Blanche.
BLANCHE: Why are you looking at me like that? Is something wrong with me?
EUNICE: You look wonderful, Blanche. Don't she look wonderful?
STELLA: Yes.
EUNICE: I understand you are going on a trip.
STELLA: Yes, Blanche *is.* She's going on a vacation.
EUNICE: I'm green with envy.

BLANCHE: Help me, help me get dressed!
STELLA: [*Handing her dress.*] Is this what you—
BLANCHE: Yes, it will do! I'm anxious to get out of here—this place is a trap!
EUNICE: What a pretty blue jacket.
STELLA: It's lilac colored.
BLANCHE: You're both mistaken. It's Della Robbia blue.[3] The blue of the robe in the old Madonna pictures. Are these grapes washed? [*She fingers the bunch of grapes which* EUNICE *had brought in.*]
EUNICE: Huh?
BLANCHE: Washed, I said. Are they washed?
EUNICE: They're from the French Market.
BLANCHE: That doesn't mean they've been washed. [*The cathedral bells chime.*] Those cathedral bells—they're the only clean thing in the Quarter. Well, I'm going now. I'm ready to go.
EUNICE: [*Whispering.*] She's going to walk out before they get here.
STELLA: Wait, Blanche.
BLANCHE: I don't want to pass in front of those men.
EUNICE: Then wait'll the game breaks up.
STELLA: Sit down and . . .

[BLANCHE *turns weakly, hesitantly about. She lets them push her into a chair.*]

BLANCHE: I can smell the sea air. The rest of my time I'm going to spend on the sea. And when I die, I'm going to die on the sea. You know what I shall die of? [*She plucks a grape.*] I shall die of eating an unwashed grape one day out on the ocean. I will die—with my hand in the hand of some nice-looking ship's doctor, a very young one with a small blond mustache and a big silver watch. "Poor lady," they'll say, "the quinine did her no good. That unwashed grape has transported her soul to heaven." [*The cathedral chimes are heard.*] And I'll be buried at sea sewn up in a clean white sack and dropped overboard—at noon—in the blaze of summer—and into an ocean as blue as [*Chimes again.*] my first lover's eyes!

[A DOCTOR *and a* MATRON *have appeared around the corner of the building and climbed the steps to the porch. The gravity of their profession is exaggerated—the unmistakable aura of the state institution with its cynical detachment. The* DOCTOR *rings the doorbell. The murmur of the game is interrupted.*]

EUNICE: [*Whispering to* STELLA.] That must be them.

[STELLA *presses her fists to her lips.*]

BLANCHE: [*Rising slowly.*] What is it?
EUNICE: [*Affectedly casual.*] Excuse me while I see who's at the door.
STELLA: Yes.

[EUNICE *goes into the kitchen.*]

3. A shade of light blue seen in terra cottas made by the Della Robbia family in the Italian Renaissance.

BLANCHE: [*Tensely.*] I wonder if it's for me.

[*A whispered colloquy takes place at the door.*]

EUNICE: [*Returning, brightly.*] Someone is calling for Blanche.

BLANCHE: It *is* for me, then! [*She looks fearfully from one to the other and then to the portieres. The "Varsouviana" faintly plays.*] Is it the gentleman I was expecting from Dallas?

EUNICE: I think it is, Blanche.

BLANCHE: I'm not quite ready.

STELLA: Ask him to wait outside.

BLANCHE: I . . .

[EUNICE *goes back to the portieres. Drums sound very softly.*]

STELLA: Everything packed?

BLANCHE: My silver toilet articles are still out.

STELLA: Ah!

EUNICE: [*Returning.*] They're waiting in front of the house.

BLANCHE: They! Who's "they"?

EUNICE: There's a lady with him.

BLANCHE: I cannot imagine who this "lady" could be! How is she dressed?

EUNICE: Just—just a sort of a—plain-tailored outfit.

BLANCHE: Possibly she's—[*Her voice dies out nervously.*]

STELLA: Shall we go, Blanche?

BLANCHE: Must we go through that room?

STELLA: I will go with you.

BLANCHE: How do I look?

STELLA: Lovely.

EUNICE: [*Echoing.*] Lovely.

[BLANCHE *moves fearfully to the portieres.* EUNICE *draws them open for her.* BLANCHE *goes into the kitchen.*]

BLANCHE: [*To the men.*] Please don't get up. I'm only passing through.

[*She crosses quickly to outside door.* STELLA *and* EUNICE *follow. The poker players stand awkwardly at the table—all except* MITCH, *who remains seated, looking down at the table.* BLANCHE *steps out on a small porch at the side of the door. She stops short and catches her breath.*]

DOCTOR: How do you do?

BLANCHE: You are not the gentleman I was expecting. [*She suddenly gasps and starts back up the steps. She stops by* STELLA, *who stands just outside the door, and speaks in a frightening whisper.*] That man isn't Shep Huntleigh.

[*The "Varsouviana" is playing distantly.* STELLA *stares back at* BLANCHE. EUNICE *is holding* STELLA's *arm. There is a moment of silence—no sound but that of* STANLEY *steadily shuffling the cards.* BLANCHE *catches her breath again and slips back into the flat. She enters the flat with a peculiar smile, her eyes wide and brilliant. As soon as her sister goes past her,* STELLA *closes her eyes and clenches her hands.* EUNICE *throws her arms comfortingly about her. Then she starts up to her flat.* BLANCHE *stops just inside the door.* MITCH *keeps staring down at his hands on the table, but the other men look at her curiously. At last she starts around the table toward the bedroom. As she does,* STANLEY *suddenly pushes back his chair and rises as if to block her way. The* MATRON *follows her into the flat.*]

STANLEY: Did you forget something?
BLANCHE: [*Shrilly.*] Yes! Yes, I forgot something!

[*She rushes past him into the bedroom. Lurid reflections appear on the walls in odd, sinuous shapes. The "Varsouviana" is filtered into a weird distortion, accompanied by the cries and noises of the jungle.* BLANCHE *seizes the back of a chair as if to defend herself.*]

STANLEY: [*Sotto voce.*] Doc, you better go in.
DOCTOR: [*Sotto voce, motioning to the* MATRON.] Nurse, bring her out.

[*The* MATRON *advances on one side,* STANLEY *on the other. Divested of all the softer properties of womanhood, the* MATRON *is a peculiarly sinister figure in her severe dress. Her voice is bold and toneless as a firebell.*]

MATRON: Hello, Blanche.

[*The greeting is echoed and re-echoed by other mysterious voices behind the walls, as if reverberated through a canyon of rock.*]

STANLEY: She says that she forgot something.

[*The echo sounds in threatening whispers.*]

MATRON: That's all right.
STANLEY: What did you forget, Blanche?
BLANCHE: I—I—
MATRON: It don't matter. We can pick it up later.
STANLEY: Sure. We can send it along with the trunk.
BLANCHE: [*Retreating in panic.*] I don't know you—I don't know you. I want to be—left alone—please!
MATRON: Now, Blanche!
ECHOES: [*Rising and falling.*] Now, Blanche—now, Blanche—now, Blanche!
STANLEY: You left nothing here but spilt talcum and old empty perfume bottles—unless it's the paper lantern you want to take with you. You want the lantern?

[*He crosses to dressing table and seizes the paper lantern, tearing it off the light bulb, and extends it toward her. She cries out as if the lantern was herself. The* MATRON *steps boldly toward her. She screams and tries to break past the* MATRON. *All the men spring to their feet.* STELLA *runs out to the porch, with* EUNICE *following to comfort her, simultaneously with the confused voices of the men in the kitchen.* STELLA *rushes into* EUNICE*'s embrace on the porch.*]

STELLA: Oh, my God, Eunice help me! Don't let them do that to her, don't let them hurt her! Oh, God, oh, please God, don't hurt her! What are they doing to her? What are they doing? [*She tries to break from* EUNICE'*s arms.*]

EUNICE: No, honey, no, no, honey. Stay here. Don't go back in there. Stay with me and don't look.

STELLA: What have I done to my sister? Oh, God, what have I done to my sister?

EUNICE: You done the right thing, the only thing you could do. She couldn't stay here; there wasn't no other place for her to go.

[*While* STELLA *and* EUNICE *are speaking on the porch the voices of the men in the kitchen overlap them.* MITCH *has started toward the bedroom.* STANLEY *crosses to block him.* STANLEY *pushes him aside.* MITCH *lunges and strikes at* STANLEY. STANLEY *pushes* MITCH *back.* MITCH *collapses at the table, sobbing. During the preceding scenes, the* MATRON *catches hold of* BLANCHE'*s arm and prevents her flight.* BLANCHE *turns wildly and scratches at the* MATRON. *The heavy woman pinions her arms.* BLANCHE *cries out hoarsely and slips to her knees.*]

MATRON: These fingernails have to be trimmed. [*The* DOCTOR *comes into the room and she looks at him.*] Jacket, Doctor?

DOCTOR: Not unless necessary.

[*He takes off his hat and now he becomes personalized. The unhuman quality goes. His voice is gentle and reassuring as he crosses to* BLANCHE *and crouches in front of her. As he speaks her name, her terror subsides a little. The lurid reflections fade from the walls, the inhuman cries and noises die out and her own hoarse crying is calmed.*]

DOCTOR: Miss DuBois. [*She turns her face to him and stares at him with desperate pleading. He smiles; then he speaks to the* MATRON.] It won't be necessary.

BLANCHE: [*Faintly.*] Ask her to let go of me.

DOCTOR: [*To the* MATRON.] Let go.

[*The* MATRON *releases her.* BLANCHE *extends her hands toward the* DOCTOR. *He draws her up gently and supports her with his arm and leads her through the portieres.*]

BLANCHE: [*Holding tight to his arm.*] Whoever you are—I have always depended on the kindness of strangers.

[*The poker players stand back as* BLANCHE *and the* DOCTOR *cross the kitchen to the front door. She allows him to lead her as if she were blind. As they go out on the porch,* STELLA *cries out her sister's name from where she is crouched a few steps up on the stairs.*]

STELLA: Blanche! Blanche, Blanche!

[BLANCHE *walks on without turning, followed by the* DOCTOR *and the* MATRON. *They go around the corner of the building.* EUNICE *descends to* STELLA *and places the child in her arms. It is wrapped in a pale blue blanket.* STELLA *accepts the child, sobbingly.* EUNICE *continues downstairs and enters the kitchen where the men, except for* STANLEY, *are returning silently to their places about the table.* STANLEY *has gone out on the porch and stands at the foot of the steps looking at* STELLA.]

STANLEY: [*A bit uncertainly.*] Stella? [*She sobs with inhuman abandon. There is something luxurious in her complete surrender to crying now that her sister is gone. Voluptuously, soothingly.*] Now, honey. Now, love. Now, now, love. [*He kneels beside her and his fingers find the opening of her blouse.*] Now, now, love, Now, love. . . .

[*The luxurious sobbing, the sensual murmur fade away under the swelling music of the "Blue Piano" and the muted trumpet.*]

STEVE: This game is seven-card stud.

CURTAIN

1947

TENNESSEE WILLIAMS

Passages from Essays and Memoirs

from "On a Streetcar Named Success"[1]

AN ARTIST'S WORK

It is only in his work that an artist can find reality and satisfaction, for the actual world is less intense than the world of his invention, and consequently his life, without recourse to violent disorder, does not seem very substantial. The right condition for him is that in which his work is not only convenient but unavoidable.

from "The Timeless World of a Play"[2]

Carson McCullers[3] concludes one of her lyric poems with the line: "Time, the endless idiot, runs screaming 'round the world." It is this continual rush of time, so violent that it appears to be screaming, that deprives our actual lives of so much dignity and meaning, and it is, perhaps more than anything else, the *arrest of time* which has taken place in a completed work of art that gives to certain plays their feeling of depth and significance. In the London notices of *Death of*

1. First published in the *New York Times* (Nov. 30, 1947), a few days before the opening of *Streetcar*; later collected in *Where I Live* (1978). 2. First published in the *New York Times* (Jan. 14, 1951), and later collected in *Where I Live* (1978). 3. American writer (1917–1967), a close friend of Williams's for a time.

a Salesman a certain notoriously skeptical critic made the remark that Willy Loman was the sort of man that almost any member of the audience would have kicked out of an office had he applied for a job or detained one for conversation about his troubles. The remark itself possibly holds some truth. But the implication that Willy Loman is consequently a character with whom we have no reason to concern ourselves in drama, reveals a strikingly false conception of what plays are. Contemplation is something that exists outside of time, and so is the tragic sense. Even in the actual world of commerce, there exists in some persons a sensibility to the unfortunate situations of others, a capacity for concern and compassion, surviving from a more tender period of life outside the present whirling wire-cage of business activity. Facing Willy Loman across an office desk, meeting his nervous glance and hearing his querulous voice, we would be very likely to glance at our wrist watch and our schedule of other appointments. We would not kick him out of the office, no, but we would certainly *ease* him out with more expedition than Willy had feebly hoped for. But suppose there had been no wrist watch or office clock and suppose there had *not* been the schedule of pressing appointments, and suppose that we were not actually facing Willy across a desk—and facing a person is *not* the best way to *see* him!—suppose, in other words, that the meeting with Willy Loman had somehow occurred in a world *outside* of time. Then I think we would receive him with concern and kindness and even with respect. If the world of a play did not offer us this occasion to view its characters under that special condition of a *world without time*, then, indeed, the characters and occurrences of drama would become equally pointless, equally trivial, as corresponding meetings and happenings in life.

The classic tragedies of Greece had tremendous nobility. The actors wore great masks, movements were formal, dance-like, and the speeches had an epic quality which doubtless was as removed from the normal conversation of their contemporary society as they seem today. Yet they did not seem false to the Greek audiences: the magnitude of the events and the passions aroused by them did not seem ridiculously out of proportion to common experience. And I wonder if this was not because the Greek audiences knew, instinctively or by training, that the created world of a play is removed from that element which makes people *little* and their emotions fairly inconsequential.

Great sculpture often follows the lines of the human body: yet the repose of great sculpture suddenly transmutes those human lines to something that has an absoluteness, a purity, a beauty, which would not be possible in a living mobile form.

A play may be violent, full of motion: yet it has that special kind of repose which allows contemplation and produces the climate in which tragic importance is a possible thing, provided that certain modern conditions are met.

In actual existence the moments of love are succeeded by the moments of satiety and sleep. The sincere remark is followed by a cynical distrust. Truth is fragmentary, at best: we love and betray each other in not quite the same breath but in two breaths that occur in fairly close sequence. But the fact that passion occurred in *passing*, that it then declined into a more familiar sense of indifference, should not be regarded as proof of its inconsequence. And this is the very truth that drama wished to bring us. . . .

Whether or not we admit it to ourselves, we are all haunted by a truly awful sense of impermanence. . . .

About their lives, people ought to remember that when they are finished, everything in them will be contained in a marvelous state of repose which is the same as that which they unconsciously admired in drama. The rush is temporary. The great and only possible dignity of man lies in his power deliberately to choose certain moral values by which to live as steadfastly as if he, too, like a character in a play, were immured against the corrupting rush of time. Snatching the eternal out of the desperately fleeting is the great magic trick of human existence. . . .

from "Person—to—Person"[4]

Of course it is a pity that so much of all creative work is so closely related to the personality of the one who does it.

It is sad and embarrassing and unattractive that those emotions that stir him deeply enough to demand expression, and to charge their expression with some measure of light and power, are nearly all rooted, however changed in their surface, in the particular and sometimes peculiar concerns of the artist himself, that special world, the passions and images of it that each of us weaves about him from birth to death, a web of monstrous complexity, spun forth at a speed that is incalculable to a length beyond measure, from the spider mouth of his own singular perceptions.

It is a lonely idea, a lonely condition, so terrifying to think of that we usually don't. And so we talk to each other, write and wire each other, call each other, call each other short and long distance across land and sea, clasp hands with each other at meeting and at parting, fight each other and even destroy each other because of this always somewhat thwarted effort to break through walls to each other. As a character in a play once said, "We're all of us sentenced to solitary confinement inside our own skins."

Personal lyricism is the outcry of prisoner to prisoner from the cell in solitary where each is confined for the duration of his life.

I once saw a group of little girls on a Mississippi sidewalk, all dolled up in their mothers' and sisters' cast-off finery, old raggedy ball gowns and plumed hats and high-heeled slippers, enacting a meeting of ladies in a parlor with a perfect mimicry of polite Southern gush and simper. But one child was not satisfied with the attention paid her enraptured performance by the others, they were too involved in their own performances to suit her, so she stretched out her skinny arms and threw back her skinny neck and shrieked to the deaf heavens and her equally oblivious playmates, "Look at me, look at me, look at me!"

And then her mother's high-heeled slippers threw her off balance and she

4. First published in the *New York Times* Sunday drama section in 1955; later published as the introduction to *Cat on a Hot Tin Roof* (1955) and collected in *Where I Live* (1978).

fell to the sidewalk in a great howling tangle of soiled white satin and torn pink net, and still nobody looked at her.

I wonder if she is not, now, a Southern writer.

Of course it is not only Southern writers, of lyrical bent, who engage in such histrionics and shout, "Look at me!" Perhaps it is a parable of all artists. And not always do we topple over and land in a tangle of trappings that don't fit us. However, it is well to be aware of that peril, and not to content yourself with a demand for attention, to know that out of your personal lyricism, your sidewalk histrionics, something has to be created that will not only attract observers but participants in the performance.

I try very hard to do that.

The fact that I want you to observe what I do for your possible pleasure and to give you knowledge of things that I feel I may know better than you, because my world is different from yours, as different as every man's world is from the world of others, is not enough excuse for a personal lyricism that has not yet mastered its necessary trick of rising above the singular to the plural concern, from personal to general import. But for years and years now, which may have passed like a dream because of this obsession, I have been trying to learn how to perform this trick and make it truthful, and sometimes I feel that I am able to do it. Sometimes, when the enraptured street-corner performer in me cries out "Look at me!" I feel that my hazardous footwear and fantastic regalia may not quite throw me off balance. Then, suddenly, you fellow performers in the sidewalk show may turn to give me your attention and allow me to hold it, at least for the interval between 8:40 and 11 something P.M.

from Memoirs[1]

THE GLASS MENAGERIE, HIS MOTHER, AND LAURETTE TAYLOR

On the Broadway opening night of *Menagerie,* the performers took bow after bow, and finally they tried to get me up on the stage. I was sitting in the fourth row, and somebody extended a hand to me and I went up on the stage. And I felt embarrassed; I don't think I felt any great sense of triumph. I think writing is continually a pursuit of a very evasive quarry, and you never quite catch it.

In the essay that accompanies one of the printed editions of *Cat on a Hot Tin Roof,* I talk very honestly about my goal in writing, what I want to do.[2] That goal is just somehow to capture the constantly evanescent quality of existence. When I do that, then I have accomplished something, but I have done it, I think, relatively few times compared to the times I have attempted it. I don't have any sense of being a fulfilled artist. And when I was writing *Menagerie,* I did not know that I was capturing it, and I agree with Brooks Atkinson[3] that the narrations are not up to the play. I didn't feel they were at the time, either. Thank God, in the 1973 television version of it, they cut the narrations down.

1. Williams published *Memoirs* in 1975, when both his critical reputation and his self-esteem were at a low ebb. As strict autobiography it is not reliable, but it contains extraordinary insights into his life and work. 2. See "Person-to-Person," above. 3. Then drama critic for the *New York Times.*

There was too much of them. And the play itself holds without much narration.

Maybe I am a machine, a typist. A compulsive typist and a compulsive writer. But that's my life, and what is in these memoirs is mostly the barest periphery of that which is my intense life, for my intense life is my work.

Mother came up to Chicago for the opening there of *Menagerie* in the late December of 1944. I don't recall her precise reaction to the play but it was probably favorable, for Mother was very concerned with my long-delayed success. I do recall her coming backstage after the performance which she attended and paying her respects to Laurette.[4]

"Well, Mrs. Williams," said Laurette, briefly scrutinizing Edwina Williams in her dressing-room mirror, "how did you like yourself?"

"Myself?" said Mother innocently.

Laurette was as kind a person as I have known in a theatre mostly inhabited by jungle beasts, but even she, being Irish, was not one to pass by an opportunity to be mischievous.

"You notice these bangs I wear? I have to wear them playing this part because it's the part of a fool and I have a high, intellectual forehead."

Miss Edwina did not pick up on this either. She let it go by her without a sign of offense. She was probably bedazzled by Laurette's somewhat supernatural quality on a stage.

CRAFT AND CAT ON A HOT TIN ROOF

Well, now, about plays, what about them? Plays are written and then, if they are lucky, they are performed, and if their luck still holds, which is not too frequently the case, their performance is so successful that both audience and critics at the first night are aware that they are being offered a dramatic work which is both honest and entertaining and also somehow capable of engaging their aesthetic appreciation.

I have never liked to talk about the professional side of my life. Am I afraid that it is a bird that will be startled away by discussion, as by a hawk's shadow? Something like that, I suppose.

People are always asking me, at those symposia to which I've been subjected in recent years, which is my favorite among the plays I have written, the number of which eludes my recollection, and I either say to them, "Always the latest" or I succumb to my instinct for the truth and say, "I suppose it must be the published version of *Cat on a Hot Tin Roof*."[5]

That play comes closest to being both a work of art and a work of craft. It is really very well put together, in my opinion, and all its characters are amusing and credible and touching. Also it adheres to the valuable edict of Aristotle that a tragedy must have unity of time and place and magnitude of theme.

4. The role of Amanda Wingfield was created by Laurette Taylor (1884–1946). Her first great success had been in 1912 (*Peg o' My Heart*), and she had been in virtual retirement for a number of years until her performance in this play.

5. The published version includes Williams's original version of Act III, which he preferred to the Broadway version.

The set in *Cat* never changes and its running time is exactly the time of its action, meaning that one act, timewise, follows directly upon the other, and I know of no other modern American play in which this is accomplished.

However my reasons for liking *Cat* best are deeper than that. I believe that in *Cat* I reached beyond myself, in the second act, to a kind of crude eloquence of expression in Big Daddy that I have managed to give no other character of my creation.

DRAMATIC FORM AND "LITTLE PEOPLE"

I realize how very old-fashioned I am as a dramatist to be so concerned with classic form but this does not embarrass me, since I feel that the absence of form is nearly always, if not always, as dissatisfying to an audience as it is to me. I persist in considering *Cat* my best work of the long plays because of its classic unities of time and place and the kingly magnitude of Big Daddy. Yet I seem to contradict myself. I write so often of people with no magnitude, at least on the surface. I write of "little people." But are there "little people"? I sometimes think there are only little conceptions of people. Whatever is living and feeling with intensity is not little and, examined in depth, it would seem to me that most "little people" are living with that intensity that I can use as a writer.

Was Blanche a "little person"? Certainly not. She was a demonic creature, the size of her feeling was too great for her to contain without the escape of madness. . . .

"SENSATIONS OF BEING"

The work of a fine painter, committed only to vision, abstract and allusive as he pleases, is better able to create for you his moments of intensely perceptive being. Jackson Pollock could paint ecstasy as it could not be written. Van Gogh could capture for you moments of beauty, indescribable as descent into madness.[6]

And those who painted and sculpted the sensuous and the sensual of naked life in its moments of glory made them palpable to you as we can never feel with our fingertips and the erogenous parts of our flesh.

A poet such as the young Rimbaud[7] is the only writer of whom I can think, at this moment, who could escape from words into the sensations of being, through his youth, turbulent with revolution, permitted articulation by nights of absinthe. And of course there is Hart Crane.[8] Both of these poets touched fire that burned them alive. And perhaps it is only through self-immolation of such a nature that we living beings can offer to you the entire truth of ourselves within the reasonable boundaries of a book.

6. Jackson Pollock (1912–1956), American abstract expressionist painter; Vincent Van Gogh (1853–90), Dutch post-impressionist painter. 7. Arthur Rimbaud (1854–91), French poet who deeply influenced the Symbolists. 8. American poet (1899–1932), much admired by Williams. All four of the artists Williams cites combined tempestuous lives with their art.

5 TRAGEDY AND COMEDY

Classifying literary texts serves a variety of purposes for historians and literary critics who may need to "place" a literary work in history, suggest its relationship to other texts, or make a value judgment about its literary quality or cultural value. But classification is not just an activity for "professionals," and a knowledge of literary categories and definitions is not merely useful for those who enjoy sorting and labeling. Classification can also be important to students and ordinary readers, for a knowledge of categories and what they stand for can aid in the interpretation and enjoyment of individual texts. Just as the generic divisions of poetry, fiction, and drama tell you something about what to expect when you pick up a text, so particular kinds of dramas—tragedies, for example, or comedies—provide certain expectations of what will go on and how. Knowing something about the nature of tragedy can make you a better, more attentive reader of *Oedipus the King*, and understanding the nature of literary categories can help you to a more satisfying relationship with literary texts more generally.

Authors sometimes label their texts specifically to help readers know what to expect, thereby entering into a kind of contract of expectation with readers. Fiction writers who call their books "romances," for example, immediately tell their readers just what kind of story—romantic, idealistic, improbable, full of fantasy, and characterized by love and emotional fulfillment—to expect. Playwrights similarly have historically labeled their texts to lure or warn readers. **Pastoral plays** promise to be about shepherds living in an idealized world that will remind us of the idealistic values of some primitive golden age. **Farces** promise broad humor and wild antics, perhaps slapstick or pratfalls or other physical humor or perhaps easy puns and verbal highjinks, but certainly something entertaining, not too taxing, and not too serious. **Satires** promise critical commentary on some person or situation or event, often political or involving some specific cultural or social situation of contemporary relevance. Not all pastoral plays, farces, and satires do exactly what they promise, but if they label themselves as such they are setting up readers to expect a certain kind of text—a text that will treat predictable subject matter and behave in predictable fashion. Often these labels imply a certain kind of structure, a certain kind of language, and a value structure that they invite readers to share. When Shakespeare calls a play *The Tragedy of Hamlet, Prince of Denmark*, we have some idea from the moment of reading the title of what to expect—not just a plot, ending, and tone of a particular kind but an imagined world that operates according to habits and laws.

Not all plays (or texts of any other kind) are given labels by their authors, but many unlabeled texts are nevertheless conceived along lines that have to do with previous practice and traditional classifications, and many texts are therefore classified by critics or by their earliest views and readers as belonging to traditional groups. We might, for example, describe a film we saw last night as a whodunit or a spaghetti Western, or we might call a TV program a sitcom or a soap, and have a reasonable expectation that others would know, at least roughly speaking, what kind of thing we had been watching.

Tragedy and **comedy** are two of the oldest and most enduring dramatic forms, and many contemporary plays are still called, by their authors or by critics, by these names. Many people believe that tragedy and comedy still provide convenient ways to organize and present experience because they testify to, and reflect, basic ways of viewing human history. You can sometimes get into a pretty lively argument about whether a particular play should properly be called a tragedy; when *Death of a Salesman* first appeared, all kinds of critics, students, theatergoers, and readers argued with its author and with each other about whether the play was truly tragic. Individuals often have very different opinions about the propriety of labels for particular texts, and often they have somewhat different notions of the idea of tragedy itself, but they share a common belief that classification is a proper way to define and characterize and they at least believe that some common agreement about definition is possible.

But beginning with Aristotle, who first tried to define tragedy by describing contemporary examples in the fourth century B.C., there has been (in spite of many disagreements about details) some general agreement about the nature of tragedy and comedy. The most fundamental aspects of definition may be summarized as depending upon three categories of assumption—the order of values implicit in the play, the nature of character in the play, and the nature of the conclusion.

In a tragedy like *Oedipus the King*, values are universal and beyond the control of mankind. Right and wrong are determined not by any agreement between humans, but by the will of the gods, or some other preterhuman force. When the oracle tells Oedipus that his fate is to kill his father and marry his mother, Oedipus is revolted by the prospect. In human terms such a fate is unthinkable, and Oedipus is certainly right to try to avoid such a fate—but in terms of the value system that rules the play, his attempt to circumvent the will of the gods is what destroys him.

In a comedy like *The Importance of Being Earnest*, on the other hand, values are social and determined by the general opinion of society. In moral terms there is no reason why Jack and Gwendolen should not marry and get about the business of establishing a family. They are healthy unmarried people; the only problems about their intention to marry are social ones. Gwendolen's children cannot achieve their "proper" place in society unless her husband is a suitable choice, a man of good family, some social position, and suitable means to provide an appropriate education for them. Implicit in this consideration is the fact that comedy tends to endorse the values of the society, sometimes at the expense of individual needs or values. Lady Bracknell may be amusing, but she is also right, because she understands how her society works, what is acceptable and what is not.

A second characteristic feature of a dramatic genre is its treatment of character. Tragedy, for example, tends to focus on a single individual, a person of high rank who confronts the universe and his fate as an individual, a hero. He is ultimately doomed to defeat because, although a good and noble person, the tragic figure has a flaw of character or a limitation of knowledge—some mark of humanity—that offsets all his goodness. Oedipus wishes to know and to control his own destiny, but he learns too much and is destroyed. Had Oedipus been the son of a shepherd rather than of a king, perhaps the gods would not have taken such an unfortunate interest in his fate.

Comic figures are quite different. Since the plays are concerned with society and social roles, comic characters are often defined in those terms. In *The Importance of Being Earnest* both Jack and Algernon are, for plot purposes, unmarried young men who are not eminently eligible husbands-to-be, Jack because of his uncertain parentage and Algernon because of his lack of money. They have individual traits—Algernon eats too much and enjoys pretense, Jack is more straightforward, or wishes to be—but their individuality is not so important as their definition by the common social standard. Many comic characters go even further and become stereotypes. Lady Bracknell, for example, is a middle-aged meddling matron, ideally placed by age and position to exert tremendous social influence. However ridiculous Lady Bracknell appears, she understands her society and its rules thoroughly. Other stereotypes in the same play are Miss Prism, the desperate spinster, and Dr. Chasuble, the slightly dim clergyman.

A third feature of the dramatic genres can be found in their endings. In most tragedies, the hero is enlightened; he or she comes to understand the meaning of his or her deeds and to accept an appropriate punishment. At the end of *Oedipus the King* the blind hero sees and understands. He accepts his ostracism, and when he leaves Thebes he is a chastened but wiser man. Many tragic heroes die, as Hamlet does, but it is not death that ends the tragedy, it is understanding. Hamlet understands what has happened and in his last moments tries to restore order to the kingdom, asking for himself only that people may know the truth about what he has done. In comedy, on the other hand, the resolution occurs when one or more characters take a proper social role. This is most frequently defined in terms of the marriage of an eligible young woman and an equally eligible young man. The society of *Earnest* believes that young men like Jack and Algernon and young women like Gwendolen and Cecily should marry and get about the business of having children and raising them to provide for the continuation of the society. Even the marriage of Miss Prism and Dr. Chasuble serves social purposes. The society of the play prefers married clergymen to celibates and has no really useful function for a middle-aged spinster.

The two plays that follow represent tragedy and comedy in something close to pure form, and in each the assumptions as well as the features of their genre are manifest. Many good plays are examples far less clear, and over the years many plays have consciously mixed the conventions and assumptions of these two lasting kinds. Many other categories have been used over the centuries to describe the shape and assumptions of groups of dramatic texts. Modern and post-modern plays most often mix genres in a conscious way, and they tend to emphasize their desire to reflect and depict ordinary reality as their authors perceive it to be (that is, they aim to be *mimetic*) rather than following some predetermined shape or set of assumptions about some universal tone and standard kind of ending.

SOPHOCLES

Oedipus the King[1]

CHARACTERS

OEDIPUS, *king of Thebes*
A PRIEST *of Zeus*
CREON, *brother of Jocasta*
A CHORUS *of Theban citizens and their* LEADER
TIRESIAS, *a blind prophet*
JOCASTA, *the queen, wife of Oedipus*
A MESSENGER *from Corinth*
A SHEPHERD
A MESSENGER *from inside the palace*
ANTIGONE, ISMENE, *daughters of Oedipus and Jocasta*
GUARDS *and attendants*
PRIESTS *of Thebes*

TIME AND SCENE: *The royal house of Thebes. Double doors dominate the façade; a stone altar stands at the center of the stage.*

1. Translated by Robert Fagles. Annotated by Bernard Knox.

Many years have passed since OEDIPUS *solved the riddle of the Sphinx and ascended the throne of Thebes, and now a plague has struck the city. A procession of priests enters; suppliants, broken and despondent, they carry branches wound in wool and lay them on the altar.*

The doors open. GUARDS *assemble.* OEDIPUS *comes forward, majestic but for a telltale limp, and slowly views the condition of his people.*

OEDIPUS: Oh my children, the new blood of ancient Thebes,
why are you here? Huddling at my altar,
praying before me, your branches wound in wool.[2]
Our city reeks with the smoke of burning incense,
rings with cries for the Healer[3] and wailing for the dead.
I thought it wrong, my children, to hear the truth
from others, messengers. Here I am myself—
you all know me, the world knows my fame:
I am Oedipus.

[*Helping a* PRIEST *to his feet.*]

Speak up, old man. Your years,
your dignity—you should speak for the others.
Why here and kneeling, what preys upon you so?
Some sudden fear? some strong desire?
You can trust me. I am ready to help,
I'll do anything. I would be blind to misery
not to pity my people kneeling at my feet.

PRIEST: Oh Oedipus, king of the land, our greatest power!
You see us before you now, men of all ages
clinging to your altars. Here are boys,
still too weak to fly from the nest,
and here the old, bowed down with the years,
the holy ones—a priest of Zeus myself—and here
the picked, unmarried men, the young hope of Thebes.
And all the rest, your great family gathers now,
branches wreathed, massing in the squares,
kneeling before the two temples of queen Athena
or the river-shrine where the embers glow and die
and Apollo sees the future in the ashes.[4]

Our city—
look around you, see with your own eyes—
our ship pitches wildly, cannot lift her head
from the depths, the red waves of death . . .
Thebes is dying. A blight on the fresh crops

2. The insignia of suppliants, laid on the altar and left there until the suppliant's request was granted. At the end of the scene, when Oedipus promises action, he will tell them to take the branches away.
3. A title of Apollo.
4. At a temple of Apollo in Thebes the priests foretold the future according to patterns they saw in the ashes of the burned flesh of sacrificial victims.

and the rich pastures, cattle sicken and die,
and the women die in labor, children stillborn,
and the plague, the fiery god of fever hurls down
on the city, his lightning slashing through us—
raging plague in all its vengeance, devastating
the house of Cadmus![5] And black Death luxuriates
in the raw, wailing miseries of Thebes.
Now we pray to you. You cannot equal the gods,
your children know that, bending at your altar.
But we do rate you first of men,
both in the common crises of our lives
and face-to-face encounters with the gods.
You freed us from the Sphinx,[6] you came to Thebes
and cut us loose from the bloody tribute[7] we had paid
that harsh, brutal singer. We taught you nothing,
no skill, no extra knowledge, still you triumphed.
A god was with you, so they say, and we believe it—
you lifted up our lives.
So now again,
Oedipus, king, we bend to you, your power—
we implore you, all of us on our knees:
find us strength, rescue! Perhaps you've heard
the voice of a god or something from other men,
Oedipus . . . what do you know?
The man of experience—you see it every day—
his plans will work in a crisis, his first of all.

Act now—we beg you, best of men, raise up our city!
Act, defend yourself, your former glory!
Your country calls you savior now
for your zeal, your action years ago.
Never let us remember of your reign:
you helped us stand, only to fall once more.
Oh raise up our city, set us on our feet.
The omens were good that day you brought us joy—
be the same man today!
Rule our land, you know you have the power,
but rule a land of the living, not a wasteland.
Ship and towered city are nothing, stripped of men
alive within it, living all as one.

OEDIPUS: My children,

5. Mythical founder of Thebes and its first king. 6. The winged female monster which terrorized the city of Thebes until her riddle was finally answered by Oedipus. The riddle was: "What is it that walks on four feet and two feet and three feet and has only one voice; when it walks on most feet, it is weakest?" Oedipus' answer was Man. (He has four feet as a child crawling on "all fours," and three feet in old age when he walks with the aid of a stick.) 7. Many young men of Thebes had tried to answer the riddle, failed, and been killed.

I pity you. I see—how could I fail to see
what longings bring you here? Well I know
you are sick to death, all of you,
but sick as you are, not one is sick as I.
Your pain strikes each of you alone, each
in the confines of himself, no other. But my spirit
grieves for the city, for myself and all of you.
I wasn't asleep, dreaming. You haven't wakened me—
I've wept through the nights, you must know that,
groping, laboring over many paths of thought.
After a painful search I found one cure:
I acted at once. I sent Creon,
my wife's own brother, to Delphi[8]—
Apollo the Prophet's oracle—to learn
what I might do or say to save our city.
Today's the day. When I count the days gone by
it torments me . . . what is he doing?
Strange, he's late, he's gone too long.
But once he returns, then, then I'll be a traitor
if I do not do all the god makes clear.

PRIEST: Timely words. The men over there
are signaling—Creon's just arriving.

OEDIPUS: [*Sighting* CREON, *then turning to the altar.*]
Lord Apollo,
let him come with a lucky word of rescue,
shining like his eyes!

PRIEST: Welcome news, I think—he's crowned, look,
and the laurel wreath is bright with berries.[9]

OEDIPUS: We'll soon see. He's close enough to hear—

[*Enter* CREON *from the side; his face is shaded with a wreath.*]

Creon, prince, my kinsman, what do you bring us?
What message from the god?

CREON: Good news.
I tell you even the hardest things to bear,
if they should turn out well, all would be well.

OEDIPUS: Of course, but what were the god's *words?* There's no hope
and nothing to fear in what you've said so far.

CREON: If you want my report in the presence of these people,

[*Pointing to the* PRIESTS *while drawing* OEDIPUS *toward the palace.*]

I'm ready now, or we might go inside.

OEDIPUS: Speak out,

8. The oracular shrine of Apollo at Delphi, below Mount Parnassus in central Greece. 9. Creon is wearing a crown of laurel as a sign that he brings good news.

speak to us all. I grieve for these, my people,
far more than I fear for my own life.
CREON: Very well,
I will tell you what I heard from the god.
Apollo commands us—he was quite clear—
"Drive the corruption from the land,
don't harbor it any longer, past all cure,
don't nurse it in your soil—root it out!"
OEDIPUS: How can we cleanse ourselves—what rites?
What's the source of the trouble?
CREON: Banish the man, or pay back blood with blood.
Murder sets the plague-storm on the city.
OEDIPUS: Whose murder?
Whose fate does Apollo bring to light?
CREON: Our leader,
my lord, was once a man named Laius,
before you came and put us straight on course.
OEDIPUS: I know—
or so I've heard. I never saw the man myself.
CREON: Well, he was killed, and Apollo commands us now—
he could not be more clear,
"Pay the killers back—whoever is responsible."
OEDIPUS: Where on earth are they? Where to find it now,
the trail of the ancient guilt so hard to trace?
CREON: "Here in Thebes," he said.
Whatever is sought for can be caught, you know,
whatever is neglected slips away.
OEDIPUS: But where,
in the palace, the fields or foreign soil,
where did Laius meet his bloody death?
CREON: He went to consult an oracle, Apollo said,
and he set out and never came home again.
OEDIPUS: No messenger, no fellow-traveler saw what happened?
Someone to cross-examine?
CREON: No,
they were all killed but one. He escaped,
terrified, he could tell us nothing clearly,
nothing of what he saw—just one thing.
OEDIPUS: What's that?
one thing could hold the key to it all,
a small beginning give us grounds for hope.
CREON: He said thieves attacked them—a whole band,
not single-handed, cut King Laius down.
OEDIPUS: A thief,
so daring, so wild, he'd kill a king? Impossible,
unless conspirators paid him off in Thebes.

CREON: We suspected as much. But with Laius dead
no leader appeared to help us in our troubles.
OEDIPUS: Trouble? Your *king* was murdered—royal blood!
What stopped you from tracking down the killer
then and there?
CREON: The singing, riddling Sphinx.
She . . . persuaded us to let the mystery go
and concentrate on what lay at our feet.
OEDIPUS: No,
I'll start again—I'll bring it all to light myself!
Apollo is right, and so are you, Creon,
to turn our attention back to the murdered man.
Now you have *me* to fight for you, you'll see:
I am the land's avenger by all rights,
and Apollo's champion too.
But not to assist some distant kinsman, no,
for my own sake I'll rid us of this corruption.
Whoever killed the king may decide to kill me too,
with the same violent hand—by avenging Laius
I defend myself.

[*To the* PRIESTS.]

Quickly, my children.
Up from the steps, take up your branches now.

[*To the* GUARDS.]

One of you summon the city[1] here before us,
tell them I'll do everything. God help us,
we will see our triumph—or our fall.

[OEDIPUS *and* CREON *enter the palace, followed by the guards.*]

PRIEST: Rise, my sons. The kindness we came for
Oedipus volunteers himself.
Apollo has sent his word, his oracle—
Come down, Apollo, save us, stop the plague.

[*The* PRIESTS *rise, remove their branches and exit to the side.*]
[*Enter a* CHORUS, *the citizens of Thebes, who have not heard the news that* CREON *brings. They march around the altar, chanting.*]

CHORUS: Zeus!
Great welcome voice of Zeus,[2] what do you bring?
What word from the gold vaults of Delphi
comes to brilliant Thebes? Racked with terror—
terror shakes my heart

1. Represented by the chorus which comes on to the circular dancing floor immediately after this scene. 2. Apollo was his son, and spoke for him.

and I cry your wild cries, Apollo, Healer of Delos[3]
I worship you in dread . . . what now, what is your price?
some new sacrifice? some ancient rite from the past
come round again each spring?—
    what will you bring to birth?
Tell me, child of golden Hope
    warm voice that never dies!

You are the first I call, daughter of Zeus
deathless Athena—I call your sister Artemis,[4]
heart of the market place enthroned in glory,
    guardian of our earth—
I call Apollo, Archer astride the thunderheads of heaven—
O triple shield against death, shine before me now!
If ever, once in the past, you stopped some ruin
launched against our walls
    you hurled the flame of pain
far, far from Thebes—you gods
    come now, come down once more!
                No, no
the miseries numberless, grief on grief, no end—
too much to bear, we are all dying
O my people . . .
    Thebes like a great army dying
and there is no sword of thought to save us, no
and the fruits of our famous earth, they will not ripen
no and the women cannot scream their pangs to birth—
screams for the Healer, children dead in the womb
    and life on life goes down
        you can watch them go
    like seabirds winging west, outracing the day's fire
down the horizon, irresistibly
    streaking on to the shores of Evening
                Death
so many deaths, numberless deaths on deaths, no end—
Thebes is dying, look, her children
stripped of pity . . .
    generations strewn on the ground
unburied, unwept, the dead spreading death
and the young wives and gray-haired mothers with them
cling to the altars, trailing in from all over the city—
Thebes, city of death, one long cortege
    and the suffering rises
        wails for mercy rise
    and the wild hymn for the Healer blazes out

3. Apollo was born on the sacred island of Delos. 4. Sister of Apollo: a goddess associated with hunting, and also a protector of women in childbirth.

clashing with our sobs our cries of mourning—
O golden daughter of god,[5] send rescue
radiant as the kindness in your eyes!
Drive him back!—the fever, the god of death
that raging god of war[6]
not armored in bronze, not shielded now, he burns me,
battle cries in the onslaught burning on—
O rout him from our borders!
Sail him, blast him out to the Sea-queen's chamber
the black Atlantic gulfs
or the northern harbor, death to all
where the Thracian surf[7] comes crashing.
Now what the night spares he comes by day and kills—
the god of death.
O lord of the stormcloud,
you who twirl the lightning, Zeus, Father,
thunder Death to nothing!

Apollo, lord of the light, I beg you—
whip your longbow's golden cord
showering arrows on our enemies—shafts of power
champions strong before us rushing on!

Artemis, Huntress,
torches flaring over the eastern ridges—
ride Death down in pain!

God of the headdress gleaming gold, I cry to you—
your name and ours are one, Dionysus—
come with your face a flame with wine
your raving women's[8] cries
your army on the march! Come with the lightning
come with torches blazing, eyes ablaze with glory!
Burn that god of death that all gods hate!

[OEDIPUS *enters from the palace to address the* CHORUS, *as if addressing the entire city of Thebes*.]

OEDIPUS: You pray to the gods? Let me grant your prayers.
Come, listen to me—do what the plague demands:
you'll find relief and lift your head from the depths.

I will speak out now as a stranger to the story,
a stranger to the crime. If I'd been present then,

5. Athena, daughter of Zeus. 6. The plague is identified with Ares, the war-god, though he comes now without armor and shield. Ares is not elsewhere connected with plague; this passage may be an allusion to the early years of the Peloponnesian War, when Spartan troops threatened the city from outside and the plague raged inside the walls. 7. Ares was thought to be at home among the savages of Thrace, to the northeast of Greece proper. 8. The Bacchanals, nymphs or human female votaries of the god Dionysus (Bacchus) who celebrated him with wild dancing rites.

there would have been no mystery, no long hunt
without a clue in hand. So now, counted
a native Theban years after the murder,
to all of Thebes I make this proclamation:
if any one of you knows who murdered Laius,
the son of Labdacus, I order him to reveal
the whole truth to me. Nothing to fear,
even if he must denounce himself,
let him speak up
and so escape the brunt of the charge—
he will suffer no unbearable punishment,
nothing worse than exile, totally unharmed.

[*Pauses, waiting for a reply.*]

Next,
if anyone knows the murderer is a stranger,
a man from alien soil, come, speak up.
I will give him a handsome reward, and lay up
gratitude in my heart for him besides.

[*Silence again, no reply.*]

But if you keep silent, if anyone panicking,
trying to shield himself or friend or kin,
rejects my offer, then hear what I will do.
I order you, every citizen of the state
where I hold throne and power: banish this man—
whoever he may be—never shelter him, never
speak a word to him, never make him partner
to your prayers, your victims burned to the gods.
Never let the holy water touch his hands
Drive him out, each of you, from every home.
He is the plague, the heart of our corruption,
as Apollo's oracle has just revealed to me.
So I honor my obligations:
I fight for the god and for the murdered man.

Now my curse on the murderer. Whoever he is,
a lone man unknown in his crime
or one among many, let that man drag out
his life in agony, step by painful step—
I curse myself as well . . . if by any chance
he proves to be an intimate of our house,
here at my hearth, with my full knowledge,
may the curse I just called down on him strike me!
These are your orders: perform them to the last.
I command you, for my sake, for Apollo's, for this country
blasted root and branch by the angry heavens.

Even if god had never urged you on to act,
how could you leave the crime uncleansed so long?
A man so noble—your king, brought down in blood—
you should have searched. But I am the king now,
I hold the throne that he held then, possess his bed
and a wife who shares our seed . . . why, our seed
might be the same, children born of the same mother
might have created blood-bonds between us
if his hope of offspring hadn't met disaster—
but fate swooped at his head and cut him short.
So I will fight for him as if he were my father,
stop at nothing, search the world
to lay my hands on the man who shed his blood,
the son of Labdacus descended of Polydorus,
Cadmus of old and Agenor, founder of the line:
their power and mine are one.
Oh dear gods,
my curse on those who disobey these orders!
Let no crops grow out of the earth for them—
shrivel their women, kill their sons,
burn them to nothing in this plague
that hits us now, or something even worse.
But you, loyal men of Thebes who approve my actions,
may our champion, Justice, may all the gods
be with us, fight beside us to the end!

LEADER: In the grip of your curse, my king, I swear
I'm not the murderer, I cannot point him out.
As for the search, Apollo pressed it on us—
he should name the killer.

OEDIPUS: Quite right,
but to force the gods to act against their will—
no man has the power.

LEADER: Then if I might mention
the next best thing . . .

OEDIPUS: The third best too—
don't hold back, say it.

LEADER: I still believe . . .
Lord Tiresias[9] sees with the eyes of Lord Apollo.
Anyone searching for the truth, my king,
might learn it from the prophet, clear as day.

OEDIPUS: I've not been slow with that. On Creon's cue
I sent the escorts, twice, within the hour.
I'm surprised he isn't here.

LEADER: We need him—

9. The blind prophet of Thebes (whose ghost Odysseus goes to consult in Hades in *Odyssey* XI).

without him we have nothing but old, useless rumors.
OEDIPUS: Which rumors? I'll search out every word.
LEADER: Laius was killed, they say, by certain travelers.
OEDIPUS: I know—but no one can find the murderer.
LEADER: If the man has a trace of fear in him
he won't stay silent long,
not with your curses ringing in his ears.
OEDIPUS: He didn't flinch at murder,
he'll never flinch at words.

[*Enter* TIRESIAS, *the blind prophet, led by a boy with escorts in attendance. He remains at a distance.*]

LEADER: Here is the one who will convict him, look,
they bring him on at last, the seer, the man of god.
The truth lives inside him, him alone.
OEDIPUS: O Tiresias,
master of all the mysteries of our life,
all you teach and all you dare not tell,
signs in the heavens, signs that walk the earth!
Blind as you are, you can feel all the more
what sickness haunts our city. You, my lord,
are the one shield, the one savior we can find.

We asked Apollo—perhaps the messengers
haven't told you—he sent his answer back:
"Relief from the plague can only come one way.
Uncover the murderers of Laius,
put them to death or drive them into exile."
So I beg you, grudge us nothing now, no voice,
no message plucked from the birds, the embers
or the other mantic ways within your grasp.
Rescue yourself, your city, rescue me—
rescue everything infected by the dead.
We are in your hands. For a man to help others
with all his gifts and native strength:
that is the noblest work.
TIRESIAS: How terrible—to see the truth
when the truth is only pain to him who sees!
I knew it well, but I put it from my mind,
else I never would have come.
OEDIPUS: What's this? Why so grim, so dire?
TIRESIAS: Just send me home. You bear your burdens,
I'll bear mine. It's better that way,
please believe me.
OEDIPUS: Strange response . . . unlawful,
unfriendly too to the state that bred and reared you—
you withhold the word of god.

TIRESIAS: I fail to see
that your own words are so well-timed.
I'd rather not have the same thing said of me . . .
OEDIPUS: For the love of god, don't turn away,
not if you know something. We beg you,
all of us on our knees.
TIRESIAS: None of you knows—
and I will never reveal my dreadful secrets,
not to say your own.
OEDIPUS: What? You know and you won't tell?
You're bent on betraying us, destroying Thebes?
TIRESIAS: I'd rather not cause pain for you or me.
So why this . . . useless interrogation?
You'll get nothing from me.
OEDIPUS: Nothing! You,
you scum of the earth, you'd enrage a heart of stone!
You won't talk? Nothing moves you?
Out with it, once and for all!
TIRESIAS: You criticize my temper . . . unaware
of the one[1] *you* live with, you revile me.
OEDIPUS: Who could restrain his anger hearing you?
What outrage—you spurn the city!
TIRESIAS: What will come will come.
Even if I shroud it all in silence.
OEDIPUS: What will come? You're bound to *tell* me that.
TIRESIAS: I'll say no more. Do as you like, build your anger
to whatever pitch you please, rage your worst—
OEDIPUS: Oh I'll let loose, I have such fury in me—
now I see it all. You helped hatch the plot,
you did the work, yes, short of killing him
with your own hands—and given eyes I'd say
you did the killing single-handed!
TIRESIAS: Is that so!
I charge you, then, submit to that decree
you just laid down: from this day onward
speak to no one, not these citizens, not myself.
You are the curse, the corruption of the land!
OEDIPUS: You, shameless—
aren't you appalled to start up such a story?
You think you can get away with this?
TIRESIAS: I have already.
The truth with all its power lives inside me.
OEDIPUS: Who primed you for this? Not your prophet's trade.

1. In the Greek the veiled reference to Jocasta is more forceful, since the word translated "the one" has a feminine ending (agreeing with the feminine noun *orgê*—"temper").

TIRESIAS: You did, you forced me, twisted it out of me.
OEDIPUS: What? Say it again—I'll understand it better.
TIRESIAS: Didn't you understand, just now?
Or are you tempting me to talk?
OEDIPUS: No, I can't say I grasped your meaning.
Out with it, again!
TIRESIAS: I say you are the murderer you hunt.
OEDIPUS: That obscenity, twice—by god, you'll pay.
TIRESIAS: Shall I say more, so you can really rage?
OEDIPUS: Much as you want. Your words are nothing—
futile.
TIRESIAS: You cannot imagine . . . I tell you,
you and your loved ones live together in infamy,
you cannot see how far you've gone in guilt.
OEDIPUS: You think you can keep this up and never suffer?
TIRESIAS: Indeed, if the truth has any power.
OEDIPUS: It does
but not for you, old man. You've lost your power,
stone-blind, stone-deaf—senses, eyes blind as stone!
TIRESIAS: I pity you, flinging at me the very insults
each man here will fling at you so soon.
OEDIPUS: Blind,
lost in the night, endless night that cursed you!
You can't hurt me or anyone else who sees the light—
you can never touch me.
TIRESIAS: True, it is not your fate
to fall at my hands. Apollo is quite enough,
and he will take some pains to work this out.
OEDIPUS: Creon! Is this conspiracy his or yours?
TIRESIAS: Creon is not your downfall, no, you are your own.
OEDIPUS: O power—
wealth and empire, skill outstripping skill
in the heady rivalries of life,
what envy lurks inside you! Just for this,
the crown the city gave me—I never sought it,
they laid it in my hands—for this alone, Creon,
the soul of trust, my loyal friend from the start
steals against me . . . so hungry to overthrow me
he sets this wizard on me, this scheming quack,
this fortune-teller peddling lies, eyes peeled
for his own profit—seer blind in his craft!

Come here, you pious fraud. Tell me,
when did you ever prove yourself a prophet?
When the Sphinx, that chanting Fury kept her deathwatch here,
why silent then, not a word to set our people free?

There was a riddle, not for some passer-by to solve—
it cried out for a prophet. Where were you?
Did you rise to the crisis? Not a word,
you and your birds, your gods—nothing.
No, but I came by, Oedipus the ignorant,
I stopped the Sphinx! With no help from the birds,
the flight of my own intelligence hit the mark.

And this is the man you'd try to overthrow?
You think you'll stand by Creon when he's king?
You and the great mastermind—
you'll pay in tears, I promise you, for this,
this witch-hunt. If you didn't look so senile
the lash would teach you what your scheming means!

LEADER: I would suggest his words were spoken in anger,
Oedipus . . . yours too, and it isn't what we need.
The best solution to the oracle, the riddle
posed by god—we should look for that.

TIRESIAS: You are the king no doubt, but in one respect,
at least, I am your equal: the right to reply.
I claim that privilege too.
I am not your slave. I serve Apollo.
I don't need Creon to speak for me in public.
So,
you mock my blindness? Let me tell you this.
You with your precious eyes,
you're blind to the corruption of your life,
to the house you live in, those you live with—
who *are* your parents? Do you know? All unknowing
you are the scourge of your own flesh and blood,
the dead below the earth and the living here above,
and the double lash of your mother and your father's curse
will whip you from this land one day, their footfall
treading you down in terror, darkness shrouding
your eyes that now can see the light!
Soon, soon
you'll scream aloud—what haven won't reverberate?
What rock of Cithaeron[2] won't scream back in echo?
That day you learn the truth about your marriage,
the wedding-march that sang you into your halls,
the lusty voyage home to the fatal harbor!
And a crowd of other horrors you'd never dream
will level you with yourself and all your children.

There. Now smear us with insults—Creon, myself,
and every word I've said. No man will ever

2. The mountain range near Thebes, on which Oedipus was left to die when an infant.

be rooted from the earth as brutally as you.
OEDIPUS: Enough! Such filth from him? Insufferable—
what, still alive? Get out—
faster, back where you came from—vanish!
TIRESIAS: I would never have come if you hadn't called me here.
OEDIPUS: If I thought you would blurt out such absurdities,
you'd have died waiting before I'd had you summoned.
TIRESIAS: Absurd, am I! To you, not to your parents:
the ones who bore you found me sane enough.
OEDIPUS: Parents—who? Wait . . . who is my father?
TIRESIAS: This day will bring your birth and your destruction.
OEDIPUS: Riddles—all you can say are riddles, murk and
darkness.
TIRESIAS: Ah, but aren't you the best man alive at solving riddles?
OEDIPUS: Mock me for that, go on, and you'll reveal my greatness.
TIRESIAS: Your great good fortune, true, it was your ruin.
OEDIPUS: Not if I saved the city—what do I care?
TIRESIAS: Well then, I'll be going.

[*To his attendant.*]

Take me home, boy.
OEDIPUS: Yes, take him away. You're a nuisance here.
Out of the way, the irritation's gone.

[*Turning his back on* TIRESIAS, *moving toward the palace.*[3]]

TIREIAS: I will go,
once I have said what I came here to say.
I'll never shrink from the anger in your eyes—
you can't destroy me. Listen to me closely:
the man you've sought so long, proclaiming,
cursing up and down, the murderer of Laius—
he is here. A stranger,
you may think, who lives among you,
he soon will be revealed a native Theban
but he will take no joy in the revelation.
Blind who now has eyes, beggar who now is rich,
he will grope his way toward a foreign soil,
a stick tapping before him step by step.

[OEDIPUS *enters the palace.*]

Revealed at last, brother and father both
to the children he embraces, to his mother

3. There are no stage directions in our texts. It is suggested here that Oedipus moves off stage and does not hear the critical section of Tiresias' speech (520 ff) which he could hardly fail to connect with the prophecy made to him by Apollo many years ago.

son and husband both—he sowed the loins
his father sowed, he spilled his father's blood!

Go in and reflect on that, solve that.
And if you find I've lied
from this day onward call the prophet blind.

[TIRESIAS *and the boy exit to the side.*]

CHORUS: Who—
who is the man the voice of god denounces
resounding out of the rocky gorge of Delphi?
The horror too dark to tell,
whose ruthless bloody hands have done the work?
His time has come to fly
to outrace the stallions of the storm
his feet a streak of speed—
Cased in armor, Apollo son of the Father
lunges on him, lightning-bolts afire!
And the grim unerring Furies[4]
closing for the kill.
Look,
the word of god has just come blazing
flashing off Parnassus'[5] snowy heights!
That man who left no trace—
after him, hunt him down with all our strength!
Now under bristling timber
up through rocks and caves he stalks
like the wild mountain bull—
cut off from men, each step an agony, frenzied, racing blind
but he cannot outrace the dread voices of Delphi
ringing out of the heart of Earth,
the dark wings beating around him shrieking doom
the doom that never dies, the terror—
The skilled prophet scans the birds and shatters me with terror!
I can't accept him, can't deny him, don't know what to say,
I'm lost, and the wings of dark foreboding beating—
I cannot see what's come, what's still to come . . .
and what could breed a blood feud between
Laius' house and the son of Polybus?[6]
I know of nothing, not in the past and not now,
no charge to bring against our king, no cause
to attack his fame that rings throughout Thebes—

4. Avenging spirits who pursued a murderer when no earthly avenger was at hand. 5. A mountain range in central Greece. The great oracular shrine of Apollo at Delphi was on its lower slopes. 6. King of Corinth and, so far as anyone except Tiresias knows, the father of Oedipus.

not without proof—not for the ghost of Laius,
not to avenge a murder gone without a trace.
Zeus and Apollo know, they know, the great masters
of all the dark and depth of human life.
But whether a mere man can know the truth,
whether a seer can fathom more than I—
there is no test, no certain proof
though matching skill for skill
a man can outstrip a rival. No, not till I see
these charges proved will I side with his accusers.
We saw him then, when the she-hawk[7] swept against him,
saw with our own eyes his skill, his brilliant triumph—
there was the test—he was the joy of Thebes!
Never will I convict my king, never in my heart.

[*Enter* CREON *from the side.*]

CREON: My fellow-citizens, I hear King Oedipus
levels terrible charges at me. I had to come.
I resent it deeply. If, in the present crisis
he thinks he suffers any abuse from me,
anything I've done or said that offers him
the slightest injury, why, I've no desire
to linger out this life, my reputation in ruins.
The damage I'd face from such an accusation
is nothing simple. No, there's nothing worse:
branded a traitor in the city, a traitor
to all of you and my good friends.

LEADER: True,
but a slur might have been forced out of him,
by anger perhaps, not any firm conviction.

CREON: The charge was made in public, wasn't it?
I put the prophet up to spreading lies?

LEADER: Such things were said . . .
I don't know with what intent, if any.

CREON: Was his glance steady, his mind right
when the charge was brought against me?

LEADER: I really couldn't say. I never look
to judge the ones in power.

[*The doors open.* OEDIPUS *enters.*]

Wait,
here's Oedipus now.

OEDIPUS: You—here? You have the gall
to show your face before the palace gates?

7. The Sphinx.

You, plotting to kill me, kill the king—
I see it all, the marauding thief himself
scheming to steal my crown and power!
Tell me,
in god's name, what did you take me for,
coward or fool, when you spun out your plot?
Your treachery—you think I'd never detect it
creeping against me in the dark? Or sensing it,
not defend myself? Aren't you the fool,
you and your high adventure. Lacking numbers,
powerful friends, out for the big game of empire—
you need riches, armies to bring that quarry down!
CREON: Are you quite finished? It's your turn to listen
for just as long as you've . . . instructed me.
Hear me out, then judge me on the facts.
OEDIPUS: You've a wicked way with words, Creon,
but I'll be slow to learn—from you.
I find you a menace, a great burden to me.
CREON: Just one thing, hear me out in this.
OEDIPUS: Just one thing,
don't tell *me* you're not the enemy, the traitor.
CREON: Look, if you think crude, mindless stubbornness
such a gift, you've lost your sense of balance.
OEDIPUS: If you think you can abuse a kinsman,
then escape the penalty, you're insane.
CREON: Fair enough, I grant you. But this injury
you say I've done you, what is it?
OEDIPUS: Did you induce me, yes or no,
to send for that sanctimonious prophet?
CREON: I did. And I'd do the same again.
OEDIPUS: All right then, tell me, how long is it now
since Laius . . .
CREON: Laius—what did *he* do?
OEDIPUS: Vanished,
swept from sight, murdered in his tracks.
CREON: The count of the years would run you far back. . .
OEDIPUS: And that far back, was the prophet at his trade?
CREON: Skilled as he is today, and just as honored.
OEDIPUS: Did he ever refer to me then, at that time?
CREON: No,
never, at least, when I was in his presence.
OEDIPUS: But you did investigate the murder, didn't you?
CREON: We did our best, of course, discovered nothing.
OEDIPUS: But the great seer never accused me then—why not?
CREON: I don't know. And when I don't, *I* keep quiet.

OEDIPUS: You do know this, you'd tell it too—
if you had a shred of decency.
CREON: What?
If I know, I won't hold back.
OEDIPUS: Simply this:
if the two of you had never put heads together,
we would never have heard about *my* killing Laius.
CREON: If that's what he says . . . well, you know best.
But now I have a right to learn from you
as you just learned from me.
OEDIPUS: Learn your fill,
you never will convict me of the murder.
CREON: Tell me, you're married to my sister, aren't you?
OEDIPUS: A genuine discovery—there's no denying that.
CREON: And you rule the land with her, with equal power?
OEDIPUS: She receives from me whatever she desires.
CREON: And I am the third, all of us are equals?
OEDIPUS: Yes, and it's there you show your stripes—
you betray a kinsman.
CREON: Not at all.
Not if you see things calmly, rationally,
as I do. Look at it this way first:
who in his right mind would rather rule
and live in anxiety than sleep in peace?
Particularly if he enjoys the same authority.
Not I, I'm not the man to yearn for kingship,
not with a king's power in my hands. Who would?
No one with any sense of self-control.
Now, as it is, you offer me all I need,
not a fear in the world. But if I wore the crown . . .
there'd be many painful duties to perform,
hardly to my taste.
How could kingship
please me more than influence, power
without a qualm? I'm not that deluded yet,
to reach for anything but privilege outright,
profit free and clear.
Now all men sing my praises, all salute me,
now all who request your favors curry mine.
I am their best hope: success rests in me.
Why give up that, I ask you, and borrow trouble?
A man of sense, someone who sees things clearly
would never resort to treason.
No, I've no lust for conspiracy in me,
nor could I ever suffer one who does.

Do you want proof? Go to Delphi yourself,
examine the oracle and see if I've reported
the message word-for-word. This too:
if you detect that I and the clairvoyant
have plotted anything in common, arrest me,
execute me. Not on the strength of one vote,
two in this case, mine as well as yours.
But don't convict me on sheer unverified surmise.
How wrong it is to take the good for bad,
purely at random, or take the bad for good.
But reject a friend, a kinsman? I would as soon
tear out the life within us, priceless life itself.
You'll learn this well, without fail, in time.
Time alone can bring the just man to light—
the criminal you can spot in one short day.

LEADER: Good advice,
my lord, for anyone who wants to avoid disaster.
Those who jump to conclusions may go wrong.

OEDIPUS: When my enemy moves against me quickly
plots in secret, I move quickly too, I must,
I plot and pay him back. Relax my guard a moment,
waiting his next move—he wins his objective,
I lose mine.

CREON: What do you want?
You want me banished?

OEDIPUS: No, I want you dead.

CREON: Just to show how ugly a grudge can . . .

OEDIPUS: So,
still stubborn? you don't think I'm serious?

CREON: I think you're insane.

OEDIPUS: Quite sane—in my behalf.

CREON: Not just as much in mine?

OEDIPUS: You—my mortal enemy?

CREON: What if you're wholly wrong?

OEDIPUS: No matter—I must rule.

CREON: Not if you rule unjustly.

OEDIPUS: Hear him, Thebes, my city!

CREON: My city too, not yours alone!

LEADER: Please, my lords.

[*Enter* JOCASTA *from the palace*.]

Look, Jocasta's coming,
and just in time too. With her help
you must put this fighting of yours to rest.

JOCASTA: Have you no sense? Poor misguided men,
such shouting—why this public outburst?

Aren't you ashamed, with the land so sick,
to stir up private quarrels?

[*To* OEDIPUS.]

Into the palace now. And Creon, you go home.
Why make such a furor over nothing?
CREON: My sister, it's dreadful . . . Oedipus, your husband,
he's bent on choice of punishments for me,
banishment from the fatherland or death.
OEDIPUS: Precisely. I caught him in the act, Jocasta,
plotting, about to stab me in the back.
CREON: Never—curse me, let me die and be damned
if I've done you any wrong you charge me with.
JOCASTA: Oh god, believe it, Oedipus,
honor the solemn oath he swears to heaven.
Do it for me, for the sake of all your people.

[*The* CHORUS *begins to chant.*]

CHORUS: Believe it, be sensible
give way, my king, I beg you!
OEDIPUS: What do you want from me, concessions?
CHORUS: Respect him—he's been no fool in the past
and now he's strong with the oath he swears to god.
OEDIPUS: You know what you're asking?
CHORUS: I do.
OEDIPUS: Then out with it!
CHORUS: The man's your friend, your kin, he's under oath—
don't cast him out, disgraced
branded with guilt on the strength of hearsay only.
OEDIPUS: Know full well, if that is what you want
you want me dead or banished from the land.
CHORUS: Never—
no, by the blazing Sun, first god of the heavens!
Stripped of the gods, stripped of loved ones,
let me die by inches if that ever crossed my mind.
But the heart inside me sickens, dies as the land dies
and now on top of the old griefs you pile this,
your fury—both of you!
OEDIPUS: Then let him go,
even if it does lead to my ruin, my death
or my disgrace, driven from Thebes for life.
It's you, not him I pity—your words move me.
He, wherever he goes, my hate goes with him.
CREON: Look at you, sullen in yielding, brutal in your rage—
you'll go too far. It's perfect justice:
natures like yours are hardest on themselves.

OEDIPUS: Then leave me alone—get out!

CREON: I'm going.
You're wrong, so wrong. These men know I'm right.

[*Exit to the side. The* CHORUS *turns to* JOCASTA.]

CHORUS: Why do you hesitate, my lady
why not help him in?

JOCASTA: Tell me what's happened first.

CHORUS: Loose, ignorant talk started dark suspicions
and a sense of injustice cut deeply too.

JOCASTA: On both sides?

CHORUS: Oh yes.

JOCASTA: What did they say?

CHORUS: Enough, please, enough! The land's so racked already
or so it seems to me . . .
End the trouble here, just where they left it.

OEDIPUS: You see what comes of your good intentions now?
And all because you tried to blunt my anger.

CHORUS: My king,
I've said it once, I'll say it time and again—
I'd be insane, you know it,
senseless, ever to turn my back on you.
You who set our beloved land—storm-tossed, shattered—
straight on course. Now again, good helmsman,
steer us through the storm!

[*The* CHORUS *draws away, leaving* OEDIPUS *and* JOCASTA *side by side.*]

JOCASTA: For the love of god,
Oedipus, tell me too, what is it?
Why this rage? You're so unbending.

OEDIPUS: I will tell you. I respect you, Jocasta,
much more than these men here . . .

[*Glancing at the* CHORUS.]

Creon's to blame, Creon schemes against me.

JOCASTA: Tell me clearly, how did the quarrel start?

OEDIPUS: He says *I* murdered Laius—I am guilty.

JOCASTA: How does he know? Some secret knowledge
or simple hearsay?

OEDIPUS: Oh, he sent his prophet in
to do his dirty work. You know Creon,
Creon keeps his own lips clean.

JOCASTA: A prophet?
Well then, free yourself of every charge!
Listen to me and learn some peace of mind:
no skill in the world,

nothing human can penetrate the future.
Here is proof, quick and to the point.
An oracle came to Laius one fine day
(I won't say from Apollo himself
but his underlings, his priests) and it declared
that doom would strike him down at the hands of a son,
our son, to be born of our own flesh and blood. But Laius,
so the report goes at least, was killed by strangers,
thieves, at a place where three roads meet . . . my son—
he wasn't three days old and the boy's father
fastened his ankles, had a henchman fling him away
on a barren, trackless mountain.
There, you see?
Apollo brought neither thing to pass. My baby
no more murdered his father than Laius suffered—
his wildest fear—death at his own son's hands.
That's how the seers and all their revelations
mapped out the future. Brush them from your mind.
Whatever the god needs and seeks
he'll bring to light himself, with ease.

OEDIPUS: Strange,
hearing you just now . . . my mind wandered,
my thoughts racing back and forth.

JOCASTA: What do you mean? Why so anxious, startled?

OEDIPUS: I thought I heard you say that Laius
was cut down at a place where three roads meet.

JOCASTA: That was the story. It hasn't died out yet.

OEDIPUS: Where did this thing happen? Be precise.

JOCASTA: A place called Phocis, where two branching roads,
one from Daulia, one from Delphi,
come together—a crossroads.

OEDIPUS: When? How long ago?

JOCASTA: The heralds no sooner reported Laius dead
than you appeared and they hailed you king of Thebes.

OEDIPUS: My god, my god—what have you planned to do to me?

JOCASTA: What, Oedipus? What haunts you so?

OEDIPUS: Not yet.
Laius—how did he look? Describe him.
Had he reached his prime?

JOCASTA: He was swarthy,
and the gray had just begun to streak his temples,
and his build . . . wasn't far from yours.

OEDIPUS: Oh no no,
I think I've just called down a dreadful curse
upon myself—I simply didn't know!

JOCASTA: What are you saying? I shudder to look at you.
OEDIPUS: I have a terrible fear the blind seer can see.
I'll know in a moment. One thing more—
JOCASTA: Anything,
afraid as I am—ask, I'll answer, all I can.
OEDIPUS: Did he go with a light or heavy escort,
several men-at-arms, like a lord, a king?
JOCASTA: There were five in the party, a herald among them,
and a single wagon carrying Laius.
OEDIPUS: Ai—
now I can see it all, clear as day.
Who told you all this at the time, Jocasta?
JOCASTA: A servant who reached home, the lone survivor.
OEDIPUS: So, could he still be in the palace—even now?
JOCASTA: No indeed. Soon as he returned from the scene
and saw you on the throne with Laius dead and gone,
he knelt and clutched my hand, pleading with me
to send him into the hinterlands, to pasture,
far as possible, out of sight of Thebes.
I sent him away. Slave though he was,
he'd earned that favor—and much more.
OEDIPUS: Can we bring him back, quickly?
JOCASTA: Easily. Why do you want him so?
OEDIPUS: I'm afraid,
Jocasta, I have said too much already.
That man—I've got to see him.
JOCASTA: Then he'll come.
But even I have a right, I'd like to think,
to know what's torturing you, my lord.
OEDIPUS: And so you shall—I can hold nothing back from you,
now I've reached this pitch of dark foreboding.
Who means more to me than you? Tell me,
whom would I turn toward but you
as I go through all this?
My father was Polybus, king of Corinth.
My mother, a Dorian, Merope. And I was held
the prince of the realm among the people there,
till something struck me out of nowhere,
something strange . . . worth remarking perhaps,
hardly worth the anxiety I gave it.
Some man at a banquet who had drunk too much
shouted out—he was far gone, mind you—
that I am not my father's son. Fighting words!
I barely restrained myself that day
but early the next I went to mother and father,

questioned them closely, and they were enraged
at the accusation and the fool who let it fly.
So as for my parents I was satisfied,
but still this thing kept gnawing at me,
the slander spread—I had to make my move.
And so,
unknown to mother and father I set out for Delphi,
and the god Apollo spurned me, sent me away
denied the facts I came for,
but first he flashed before my eyes a future
great with pain, terror, disaster—I can hear him cry,
"You are fated to couple with your mother, you will bring
a breed of children into the light no man can bear to see—
you will kill your father, the one who gave you life!"
I heard all that and ran. I abandoned Corinth,
from that day on I gauged its landfall only
by the stars, running, always running
toward some place where I would never see
the shame of all those oracles come true.
And as I fled I reached that very spot
where the great king, you say, met his death.
Now, Jocasta, I will tell you all.
Making my way toward this triple crossroad
I began to see a herald, then a brace of colts
drawing a wagon, and mounted on the bench . . . a man,
just as you've described him, coming face-to-face,
and the one in the lead and the old man himself
were about to thrust me off the road—brute force—
and the one shouldering me aside, the driver,
I strike him in anger!—and the old man, watching me
coming up along his wheels—he brings down
his prod, two prongs straight at my head!
I paid him back with interest!
Short work, my god—with one blow of the staff
in this right hand I knock him out of his high seat,
roll him out of the wagon, sprawling headlong—
I killed them all—every mother's son!

Oh, but if there is any blood-tie
between Laius and this stranger . . .
what man alive more miserable than I?
More hated by the gods? *I* am the man
no alien, no citizen welcomes to his house,
law forbids it—not a word to me in public,
driven out of every hearth and home.
And all these curses I—no one but I

brought down these piling curses on myself!
And you, his wife, I've touched your body with these,
the hands that killed your husband cover you with blood.

Wasn't I born for torment? Look me in the eyes!
I am abomination—heart and soul!
I must be exiled, and even in exile
never see my parents, never set foot
on native ground again. Else I am doomed
to couple with my mother and cut my father down . . .
Polybus who reared me, gave me life.
But why, why?
Wouldn't a man of judgment say—and wouldn't he be right—
some savage power has brought this down upon my head?

Oh no, not that, you pure and awesome gods,
never let me see that day! Let me slip
from the world of man, vanish without a trace
before I see myself stained with such corruption,
stained to the heart.

LEADER: My lord, you fill our hearts with fear.
But at least until you question the witness,
do take hope.

OEDIPUS: Exactly. He is my last hope—
I am waiting for the shepherd. He is crucial.

JOCASTA: And once he appears, what then? Why so urgent?

OEDIPUS: I will tell you. If it turns out that his story
matches yours, I've escaped the worst.

JOCASTA: What did I say? What struck you so?

OEDIPUS: You said *thieves*—
he told you a whole band of them murdered Laius.
So, if he still holds to the same number,
I cannot be the killer. One can't equal many.
But if he refers to one man, one alone,
clearly the scales come down on me:
I am guilty.

JOCASTA: Impossible. Trust me,
I told you precisely what he said,
and he can't retract it now;
the whole city heard it, not just I.
And even if he should vary his first report
by one man more or less, still, my lord,
he could never make the murder of Laius
truly fit the prophecy. Apollo was explicit:
my son was doomed to kill my husband . . . my son,
poor defenseless thing, he never had a chance

to kill his father. They destroyed him first.

So much for prophecy. It's neither here nor there.
From this day on, I wouldn't look right or left.

OEDIPUS: True, true. Still, that shepherd,
someone fetch him—now!

JOCASTA: I'll send at once. But do let's go inside.
I'd never displease you, least of all in this.

[OEDIPUS *and* JOCASTA *enter the palace*.]

CHORUS: Destiny guide me always
Destiny find me filled with reverence
pure in word and deed.
Great laws tower above us, reared on high
born for the brilliant vault of heaven—
Olympian Sky their only father,
nothing mortal, no man gave them birth,
their memory deathless, never lost in sleep:
within them lives a mighty god, the god does not
grow old.

Pride breeds the tyrant
violent pride, gorging, crammed to bursting
with all that is overripe and rich with ruin—
clawing up to the heights, headlong pride
crashes down the abyss—sheer doom!
No footing helps, all foothold lost and gone.
But the healthy strife that makes the city strong—
I pray that god will never end that wrestling:
god, my champion, I will never let you go.
But if any man comes striding, high and mighty
in all he says and does,
no fear of justice, no reverence
for the temples of the gods—
let a rough doom tear him down,
repay his pride, breakneck, ruinous pride!
If he cannot reap his profits fairly
cannot restrain himself from outrage—
mad, laying hands on the holy things untouchable!

Can such a man, so desperate, still boast
he can save his life from the flashing bolts of god?
If all such violence goes with honor now
why join the sacred dance?

Never again will I go reverent to Delphi,
the inviolate heart of Earth
or Apollo's ancient oracle at Abae

or Olympia[8] of the fires—
unless these prophecies all come true
for all mankind to point toward in wonder.
King of kings, if you deserve your titles
Zeus, remember, never forget!
You and your deathless, everlasting reign.

They are dying, the old oracles sent to Laius,
now our masters strike them off the rolls.
Nowhere Apollo's golden glory now—
the gods, the gods go down.

[*Enter* JOCASTA *from the palace, carrying a suppliant's branch wound in wool.*]

JOCASTA: Lords of the realm,[9] it occurred to me,
just now, to visit the temples of the gods,
so I have my branch in hand and incense too.
Oedipus is beside himself. Racked with anguish,
no longer a man of sense, he won't admit
the latest prophecies are hollow as the old—
he's at the mercy of every passing voice
if the voice tells of terror.
I urge him gently, nothing seems to help,
so I turn to you, Apollo, you are nearest.

[*Placing her branch on the altar, while an old herdsman enters from the side, not the one just summoned by the King but an unexpected* MESSENGER *from Corinth.*]

I come with prayers and offerings . . . I beg you,
cleanse us, set us free of defilement!
Look at us, passengers in the grip of fear,
watching the pilot of the vessel go to pieces.

MESSENGER: [*Approaching* JOCASTA *and the* CHORUS.]
Strangers, please, I wonder if you could lead us
to the palace of the king . . . I think it's Oedipus.
Better, the man himself—you know where he is?

LEADER: This is his palace, stranger. He's inside.
But here is his queen, his wife and mother
of his children.

MESSENGER: Blessings on you, noble queen,
queen of Oedipus crowned with all your family—
blessings on you always!

JOCASTA: And the same to you, stranger, you deserve it . . .
such a greeting. But what have you come for?
Have you brought us news?

8. Abae was a city in central Greece, and Olympia a site in the western Peloponnese, where there were important oracles of Apollo and Zeus, respectively. 9. She is addressing the chorus.

MESSENGER: Wonderful news—
for the house, my lady, for your husband too.
JOCASTA: Really, what? Who sent you?
MESSENGER: Corinth.
I'll give you the message in a moment.
You'll be glad of it—how could you help it?—
though it costs a little sorrow in the bargain.
JOCASTA: What can it be, with such a double edge?
MESSENGER: The people there, they want to make your Oedipus
king of Corinth, so they're saying now.
JOCASTA: Why? Isn't old Polybus still in power?
MESSENGER: No more. Death has got him in the tomb.
JOCASTA: What are you saying? Polybus, dead?—dead?
MESSENGER: If not,
if I'm not telling the truth, strike me dead too.

[*To a servant.*]

JOCASTA: Quickly, go to your master, tell him this!
You prophecies of the gods, where are you now?
This is the man that Oedipus feared for years,
he fled him, not to kill him—and now he's dead,
quite by chance, a normal, natural death,
not murdered by his son.

[*Emerging from the palace.*]

OEDIPUS: Dearest,
what now? Why call me from the palace?
JOCASTA: [*Bringing the* MESSENGER *closer.*]
Listen to *him*, see for yourself what all
those awful prophecies of god have come to.
OEDIPUS: And who is he? What can he have for me?
JOCASTA: He's from Corinth, he's come to tell you
your father is no more—Polybus—he's dead!
OEDIPUS: [*Wheeling on the* MESSENGER.]
What? Let me have it from your lips.
MESSENGER: Well,
if that's what you want first, then here it is:
make no mistake, Polybus is dead and gone.
OEDIPUS: How—murder? sickness?—what? what killed him?
MESSENGER: A light tip of the scales can put old bones to rest.
OEDIPUS: Sickness then—poor man, it wore him down.
MESSENGER: That,
and the long count of years he's measured out.
OEDIPUS: So!
Jocasta, why, why look to the Prophet's hearth,
the fires of the future? Why scan the birds

that scream above our heads? They winged me on
to the murder of my father, did they? That was my doom?
Well look, he's dead and buried, hidden under the earth,
and here I am in Thebes, I never put hand to sword—
unless some longing for me wasted him away,
then in a sense you'd say I caused his death.
But now, all those prophecies I feared—Polybus
packs them off to sleep with him in hell!
They're nothing, worthless.

JOCASTA: There.
Didn't I tell you from the start?

OEDIPUS: So you did. I was lost in fear.

JOCASTA: No more, sweep it from your mind forever.

OEDIPUS: But my mother's bed, surely I must fear—

JOCASTA: Fear?
What should a man fear? It's all chance,
chance rules our lives. Not a man on earth
can see a day ahead, groping through the dark.
Better to live at random, best we can.
And as for this marriage with your mother—
have no fear. Many a man before you,
in his dreams, has shared his mother's bed.
Take such things for shadows, nothing at all—
Live, Oedipus,
as if there's no tomorrow!

OEDIPUS: Brave words,
and you'd persuade me if mother weren't alive.
But mother lives, so for all your reassurances
I live in fear, I must.

JOCASTA: But your father's death,
that, at least, is a great blessing, joy to the eyes!

OEDIPUS: Great, I know . . . but I fear *her*—she's still alive.

MESSENGER: Wait, who is this woman, makes you so afraid?

OEDIPUS: Merope, old man. The wife of Polybus.

MESSENGER: The queen? What's there to fear in her?

OEDIPUS: A dreadful prophecy, stranger, sent by the gods.

MESSENGER: Tell me, could you? Unless it's forbidden
other ears to hear.

OEDIPUS: Not at all.
Apollo told me once—it is my fate—
I must make love with my own mother,
shed my father's blood with my own hands.
So for years I've given Corinth a wide berth,
and it's been my good fortune too. But still,
to see one's parents and look into their eyes
is the greatest joy I know.

MESSENGER: You're afraid of that?
That kept you out of Corinth?
OEDIPUS: My *father*, old man—
so I wouldn't kill my father.
MESSENGER: So that's it.
Well then, seeing I came with such good will, my king,
why don't I rid you of that old worry now?
OEDIPUS: What a rich reward you'd have for that!
MESSENGER: What do you think I came for, majesty?
So you'd come home and I'd be better off.
OEDIPUS: Never, I will never go near my parents.
MESSENGER: My boy, it's clear, you don't know what you're doing.
OEDIPUS: What do you mean, old man? For god's sake, explain.
MESSENGER: If you ran from *them*, always dodging home . . .
OEDIPUS: Always, terrified Apollo's oracle might come true—
MESSENGER: And you'd be covered with guilt, from both your parents.
OEDIPUS: That's right, old man, that fear is always with me.
MESSENGER: Don't you know? You've really nothing to fear.
OEDIPUS: But why? If I'm their son—Merope, Polybus?
MESSENGER: Polybus was nothing to you, that's why, not in blood.
OEDIPUS: What are you saying—Polybus was not my father?
MESSENGER: No more than I am. He and I are equals.
OEDIPUS: My father—
how can my father equal nothing? You're nothing to me!
MESSENGER: Neither was he, no more your father than I am.
OEDIPUS: Then why did he call me his son?
MESSENGER: You were a gift,
years ago—know for a fact he took you
from my hands.
OEDIPUS: No, from another's hands?
Then how could he love me so? He loved me, deeply . . .
MESSENGER: True, and his early years without a child
made him love you all the more.
OEDIPUS: And you, did you . . .
buy me? find me by accident?
MESSENGER: I stumbled on you,
down the woody flanks of Mount Cithaeron.
OEDIPUS: So close,
what were you doing here, just passing through?
MESSENGER: Watching over my flocks, grazing them on the slopes.
OEDIPUS: A herdsman, were you? A vagabond, scraping for wages?
MESSENGER: Your savior too, my son, in your worst hour.
OEDIPUS: Oh—
when you picked me up, was I in pain? What exactly?
MESSENGER: Your ankles . . . they tell the story. Look at them.
OEDIPUS: Why remind me of that, that old affliction?

MESSENGER: Your ankles were pinned together. I set you free.
OEDIPUS: That dreadful mark—I've had it from the cradle.
MESSENGER: And you got your name[1] from that misfortune too,
the name's still with you.
OEDIPUS: Dear god, who did it?—
mother? father? Tell me.
MESSENGER: I don't know.
The one who gave you to me, he'd know more.
OEDIPUS: What? You took me from someone else?
You didn't find me yourself?
MESSENGER: No sir,
another shepherd passed you on to me.
OEDIPUS: Who? Do you know? Describe him.
MESSENGER: He called himself a servant of . . .
if I remember rightly—Laius.

[JOCASTA *turns sharply*.]

OEDIPUS: The king of the land who ruled here long ago?
MESSENGER: That's the one. That herdsman was *his* man.
OEDIPUS: Is he still alive? Can I see him?
MESSENGER: They'd know best, the people of these parts.

[OEDIPUS *and the* MESSENGER *turn to the* CHORUS.]

OEDIPUS: Does anyone know that herdsman,
the one he mentioned? Anyone seen him
in the fields, here in the city? Out with it!
The time has come to reveal this once for all.
LEADER: I think he's the very shepherd you wanted to see,
a moment ago. But the queen, Jocasta,
she's the one to say.
OEDIPUS: Jocasta,
you remember the man we just sent for?
Is *that* the one he means?
JOCASTA: That man . . .
why ask? Old shepherd, talk, empty nonsense,
don't give it another thought, don't even think—
OEDIPUS: What—give up now, with a clue like this?
Fail to solve the mystery of my birth?
Not for all the world!
JOCASTA: Stop—in the name of god,
if you love your own life, call off this search!
My suffering is enough.
OEDIPUS: Courage!

1. In Greek the name *Oidipous* suggests "swollen foot."

Even if my mother turns out to be a slave,
and I a slave, three generations back,
you would not seem common.

JOCASTA: Oh no,
listen to me, I beg you, don't do this.

OEDIPUS: Listen to you? No more. I must know it all,
must see the truth at last.

JOCASTA: No, please—
for your sake—I want the best for you!

OEDIPUS: Your best is more than I can bear.

JOCASTA: You're doomed—
may you never fathom who you are!

OEDIPUS: [*To a servant.*] Hurry, fetch me the herdsman, now!
Leave her to glory in her royal birth.

JOCASTA: Aieeeeee—
man of agony—
that is the only name I have for you,
that, no other—ever, ever, ever!

[*Flinging through the palace doors. A long, tense silence follows.*]

LEADER: Where's she gone, Oedipus?
Rushing off, such wild grief . . .
I'm afraid that from this silence
something monstrous may come bursting forth.

OEDIPUS: Let it burst! Whatever will, whatever must!
I must know my birth, no matter how common
it may be—I must see my origins face-to-face.
She perhaps, she with her woman's pride
may well be mortified by my birth,
but I, I count myself the son of Chance,
the great goddess, giver of all good things—
I'll never see myself disgraced. She is my mother!
And the moons have marked me out, my blood-brothers,
one moon on the wane, the next moon great with power.
That is my blood, my nature—I will never betray it,
never fail to search and learn my birth!

CHORUS: Yes—if I am a true prophet
if I can grasp the truth,
by the boundless skies of Olympus,
at the full moon of tomorrow, Mount Cithaeron
you will know how Oedipus glories in you—
you, his birthplace, nurse, his mountain-mother!
And we will sing you, dancing out your praise—
you lift our monarch's heart!
Apollo, Apollo, god of the wild cry
may our dancing please you!

Oedipus—
son, dear child, who bore you?
Who of the nymphs who seem to live forever[2]
mated with Pan,[3] the mountain-striding Father?
Who was your mother? who, some bride of Apollo
the god who loves the pastures spreading toward the sun?
Or was it Hermes, king of the lightning ridges?
Or Dionysus,[4] lord of frenzy, lord of the barren peaks—
did he seize you in his hands, dearest of all his lucky finds?—
found by the nymphs, their warm eyes dancing, gift
to the lord who loves them dancing out his joy!

[OEDIPUS *strains to see a figure coming from the distance. Attended by palace guards, an old* SHEPHERD *enters slowly, reluctant to approach the king.*]

OEDIPUS: I never met the man, my friends . . . still,
if I had to guess, I'd say that's the shepherd,
the very one we've looked for all along.
Brothers in old age, two of a kind,
he and our guest here. At any rate
the ones who bring him in are my own men,
I recognize them.

[*Turning to the* LEADER.]

But you know more than I,
you should, you've seen the man before.
LEADER: I know him, definitely. One of Laius' men,
a trusty shepherd, if there ever was one.
OEDIPUS: You, I ask you first, stranger,
you from Corinth—is this the one you mean?
MESSENGER: You're looking at him. He's your man.
OEDIPUS: [*To the* SHEPHERD.] You, old man, come over here—
look at me. Answer all my questions.
Did you ever serve King Laius?
SHEPHERD: So I did . . .
a slave, not bought on the block though,
born and reared in the palace.
OEDIPUS: Your duties, your kind of work?
SHEPHERD: Herding the flocks, the better part of my life.
OEDIPUS: Where, mostly? Where did you do your grazing?
SHEPHERD: Well,
Cithaeron sometimes, or the foothills round about.
OEDIPUS: This man—you know him? ever see him there?

2. Nymphs were not immortal, like gods, but lived much longer than mortals. 3. A woodland god; patron of shepherds and flocks. 4. Dionysus like Pan and Hermes haunted the wild country, woods and mountains. Hermes was born on Mount Kyllene in Arcadia.

SHEPHERD: [*Confused, glancing from the* MESSENGER *to the King.*]
Doing what?—what man do you mean?
OEDIPUS: [*Pointing to the* MESSENGER.]
This one here—ever have dealings with him?
SHEPHERD: Not so I could say, but give me a chance,
my memory's bad . . .
MESSENGER: No wonder he doesn't know me, master.
But let me refresh his memory for him.
I'm sure he recalls old times we had
on the slopes of Mount Cithaeron;
he and I, grazing our flocks, he with two
and I with one—we both struck up together,
three whole seasons, six months at a stretch
from spring to the rising of Arcturus in the fall,[5]
then with winter coming on I'd drive my herds
to my own pens, and back he'd go with his
to Laius' folds.

[*To the* SHEPHERD.]

Now that's how it was,
wasn't it—yes or no?
SHEPHERD: Yes, I suppose . . .
it's all so long ago.
MESSENGER: Come, tell me,
you gave me a child back then, a boy, remember?
A little fellow to rear, my very own.
SHEPHERD: What? Why rake up that again?
MESSENGER: Look, here he is, my fine old friend—
the same man who was just a baby then.
SHEPHERD: Damn you, shut your mouth—quiet!
OEDIPUS: Don't lash out at him, old man—
you need lashing more than he does.
SHEPHERD: Why,
master, majesty—what have I done wrong?
OEDIPUS: You won't answer his question about the boy.
SHEPHERD: He's talking nonsense, wasting his breath.
OEDIPUS: So, you won't talk willingly—
then you'll talk with pain.

[*The guards seize the* SHEPHERD.]

SHEPHERD: No, dear god, don't torture an old man!
OEDIPUS: Twist his arms back, quickly!

5. Arcturus is the principal star in the constellation Boötes. Its "rising" (i.e., its reappearance in the night sky just before dawn in September) signaled the end of summer.

SHEPHERD: God help us, why?—
what more do you need to know?
OEDIPUS: Did you give him that child? He's asking.
SHEPHERD: I did . . . I wish to god I'd died that day.
OEDIPUS: You've got your wish if you don't tell the truth.
SHEPHERD: The more I tell, the worse the death I'll die.
OEDIPUS: Our friend here wants to stretch things out, does he?

[*Motions to his men for torture.*]

SHEPHERD: No, no, I gave it to him—I just said so.
OEDIPUS: Where did you get it? Your house? Someone else's?
SHEPHERD: It wasn't mine, no, I got it from . . . someone.
OEDIPUS: Which one of them?

[*Looking at the citizens.*]

Whose house?
SHEPHERD: No—
god's sake, master, no more questions!
OEDIPUS: You're a dead man if I have to ask again.
SHEPHERD: Then—the child came from the house . . .
of Laius.
OEDIPUS: A slave? or born of his own blood?
SHEPHERD: Oh no,
I'm right at the edge, the horrible truth—I've got to say it!
OEDIPUS: And I'm at the edge of hearing horrors, yes, but I must hear!
SHEPHERD: All right! His son, they said it was—his son!
But the one inside, your wife,
she'd tell it best.
OEDIPUS: My wife—
she gave it to you?
SHEPHERD: Yes, yes, my king.
OEDIPUS: Why, what for?
SHEPHERD: To kill it.
OEDIPUS: Her own child,
how could she?
SHEPHERD: She was afraid—
frightening prophecies.
OEDIPUS: What?
SHEPHERD: They said—
he'd kill his parents.
OEDIPUS: But you gave him to this old man—why?
SHEPHERD: I pitied the little baby, master,
hoped he'd take off to his own country,
far away, but he saved him for this, this fate.
If you are the man he says you are, believe me,
you were born for pain.

OEDIPUS: O god—
all come true, all burst to light!
O light—now let me look my last on you!
I stand revealed at last—
cursed in my birth, cursed in marriage,
cursed in the lives I cut down with these hands!

[*Rushing through the doors with a great cry. The Corinthian* MESSENGER, *the* SHEPHERD *and attendants exit slowly to the side.*]

CHORUS: O the generations of men
the dying generations—adding the total
of all your lives I find they come to nothing . . .
does there exist, is there a man on earth
who seizes more joy than just a dream, a vision?
And the vision no sooner dawns than dies
blazing into oblivion.

You are my great example, you, your life
your destiny, Oedipus, man of misery—
I count no man blest.
You outranged all men!
Bending your bow to the breaking-point
you captured priceless glory, O dear god,
and the Sphinx came crashing down,
the virgin, claws hooked
like a bird of omen singing, shrieking death—
like a fortress reared in the face of death
you rose and saved our land.

From that day on we called you king
we crowned you with honors, Oedipus, towering over all—
mighty king of the seven gates of Thebes.
But now to hear your story—is there a man more agonized?
More wed to pain and frenzy? Not a man on earth,
the joy of your life ground down to nothing
O Oedipus, name for the ages—
one and the same wide harbor served you
son and father both
son and father came to rest in the same bridal chamber.
How, how could the furrows your father plowed
bear you, your agony, harrowing on
in silence O so long?

But now for all your power
Time, all-seeing Time has dragged you to the light,
judged your marriage monstrous from the start—
the son and the father tangling, both one—
O child of Laius, would to god

I'd never seen you, never never!
        Now I weep like a man who wails the dead
and the dirge comes pouring forth with all my heart!
I tell you the truth, you gave me life
my breath leapt up in you
and now you bring down night upon my eyes.

[*Enter a* MESSENGER *from the palace.*]

MESSENGER: Men of Thebes, always first in honor,
what horrors you will hear, what you will see,
what a heavy weight of sorrow you will shoulder . . .
if you are true to your birth, if you still have
some feeling for the royal house of Thebes.
I tell you neither the waters of the Danube
nor the Nile[6] can wash this palace clean.
Such things it hides, it soon will bring to light—
terrible things, and none done blindly now,
all done with a will. The pains
we inflict upon ourselves hurt most of all.

LEADER: God knows we have pains enough already.
What can you add to them?

MESSENGER: The queen is dead.

LEADER: Poor lady—how?

MESSENGER: By her own hand. But you are spared the worst,
you never had to watch . . . I saw it all,
and with all the memory that's in me
you will learn what that poor woman suffered.

Once she'd broken in through the gates,
dashing past us, frantic, whipped to fury,
ripping her hair out with both hands—
straight to her rooms she rushed, flinging herself
across the bridal-bed, doors slamming behind her—
once inside, she wailed for Laius, dead so long,
remembering how she bore his child long ago
the life that rose up to destroy him, leaving
its mother to mother living creatures
with the very son she'd borne.
Oh how she wept, mourning the marriage-bed
where she let loose that double brood—monsters—
husband by her husband, children by her child.
                                        And then—
but how she died is more than I can say. Suddenly
Oedipus burst in, screaming, he stunned us so

6. The Greek says Phasis—a river in Asia Minor. The translator has substituted a big river more familiar to modern readers.

we couldn't watch her agony to the end,
our eyes were fixed on him. Circling
like a maddened beast, stalking, here, there,
crying out to us—
Give him a sword![7] His wife,
no wife, his mother, where can he find the mother earth
that cropped two crops at once, himself and all his children?
He was raging—one of the dark powers pointing the way,
none of us mortals crowding around him, no,
with a great shattering cry—someone, something leading him on—
he hurled at the twin doors and bending the bolts back
out of their sockets, crashed through the chamber.
And there we saw the woman hanging by the neck,
cradled high in a woven noose, spinning,
swinging back and forth. And when he saw her,
giving a low, wrenching sob that broke our hearts,
slipping the halter from her throat, he eased her down,
in a slow embrace he laid her down, poor thing . . .
then, what came next, what horror we beheld!
He rips off her brooches, the long gold pins
holding her robes—and lifting them high,
looking straight up into the points,
he digs them down the sockets of his eyes, crying, "You,
you'll see no more the pain I suffered, all the pain I caused!
Too long you looked on the ones you never should have seen,
blind to the ones you longed to see, to know! Blind
from this hour on! Blind in the darkness—blind!"
His voice like a dirge, rising, over and over
raising the pins, raking them down his eyes.
And at each stroke blood spurts from the roots,
splashing his beard, a swirl of it, nerves and clots—
black hail of blood pulsing, gushing down.

These are the griefs that burst upon them both,
coupling man and woman. The joy they had so lately,
the fortune of their old ancestral house
was deep joy indeed. Now, in this one day,
wailing, madness and doom, death, disgrace,
all the griefs in the world that you can name,
all are theirs forever.

LEADER: Oh poor man, the misery—
has he any rest from pain now?

[*A voice within, in torment.*]

7. Presumably so that he could kill himself.

MESSENGER: He's shouting,
"Loose the bolts, someone, show me to all of Thebes!
My father's murderer, my mother's—"
No, I can't repeat it, it's unholy.
Now he'll tear himself from his native earth,
not linger, curse the house with his own curse.
But he needs strength, and a guide to lead him on.
This is sickness more than he can bear.

[*The palace doors open.*]

Look,
he'll show you himself. The great doors are opening—
you are about to see a sight, a horror
even his mortal enemy would pity.

[*Enter* OEDIPUS, *blinded, led by a boy. He stands at the palace steps, as if surveying his people once again.*]

CHORUS: O the terror—
the suffering, for all the world to see,
the worst terror that ever met my eyes.
What madness swept over you? What god,
what dark power leapt beyond all bounds,
beyond belief, to crush your wretched life?—
godforsaken, cursed by the gods!
I pity you but I can't bear to look.
I've much to ask, so much to learn,
so much fascinates my eyes,
but you . . . I shudder at the sight.

OEDIPUS: Oh, Ohh—
the agony! I am agony—
where am I going? where on earth?
where does all this agony hurl me?
where's my voice?—
winging, swept away on a dark tide—
My destiny, my dark power, what a leap you made!

CHORUS: To the depths of terror, too dark to hear, to see.

OEDIPUS: Dark, horror of darkness
my darkness, drowning, swirling around me
Crashing wave on wave—unspeakable, irresistible
headwind, fatal harbor! Oh again,
the misery, all at once, over and over
the stabbing daggers, stab of memory
raking me insane.

CHORUS: No wonder you suffer
twice over, the pain of your wounds,
the lasting grief of pain.

OEDIPUS: Dear friend, still here?
Standing by me, still with a care for me,
the blind man? Such compassion,
loyal to the last. Oh it's you,
I know you're here, dark as it is
I'd know you anywhere, your voice—
it's yours, clearly yours.
CHORUS: Dreadful, what you've done . . .
how could you bear it, gouging out your eyes?
What superhuman power drove you on?
OEDIPUS: Apollo, friends, Apollo—
he ordained my agonies—these, my pains on pains!
But the hand that struck my eyes was mine,
mine alone—no one else—
I did it all myself!
What good were eyes to me?
Nothing I could see could bring me joy.
CHORUS: No, no, exactly as you say.
OEDIPUS: What can I ever see?
What love, what call of the heart
can touch my ears with joy? Nothing, friends.
Take me away, far, far from Thebes,
quickly, cast me away, my friends—
this great murderous ruin, this man cursed to heaven,
the man the deathless gods hate most of all!
CHORUS: Pitiful, you suffer so, you understand so much . . .
I wish you'd never known.
OEDIPUS: Die, die—
whoever he was that day in the wilds
who cut my ankles free of the ruthless pins,
he pulled me clear of death, he saved my life
for this, this kindness—
Curse him, kill him!
If I'd died then, I'd never have dragged myself,
my loved ones through such hell.
CHORUS: Oh if only . . . would to god.
OEDIPUS: I'd never have come to this,
my father's murderer—never been branded
mother's husband, all men see me now! Now,
loathed by the gods, son of the mother I defiled
coupling in my father's bed, spawning lives in the loins
that spawned my wretched life. What grief can crown this grief?
It's mine alone, my destiny—I am Oedipus!
CHORUS: How can I say you've chosen for the best?
Better to die than be alive and blind.
OEDIPUS: What I did was best—don't lecture me,

no more advice. I, with *my* eyes,
how could I look my father in the eyes
when I go down to death? Or mother, so abused . . .
I have done such things to the two of them,
crimes too huge for hanging.
Worse yet,
the sight of my children, born as they were born,
how could I long to look into their eyes?
No, not with these eyes of mine, never.
Not this city either, her high towers,
the sacred glittering images of her gods—
I am misery! I, her best son, reared
as no other son of Thebes was ever reared,
I've stripped myself I gave the command myself.
All men must cast away the great blasphemer,
the curse now brought to light by the gods,
the son of Laius—I, my father's son!

Now I've exposed my guilt, horrendous guilt,
could I train a level glance on you, my countrymen?
Impossible! No, if I could just block off my ears,
the springs of hearing, I would stop at nothing—
I'd wall up my loathsome body like a prison,
blind to the sound of life, not just the sight.
Oblivion—what a blessing . . .
for the mind to dwell a world away from pain.

O Cithaeron, why did you give me shelter?
Why didn't you take me, crush my life out on the spot?
I'd never have revealed my birth to all mankind.

O Polybus, Corinth, the old house of my fathers,
so I believed—what a handsome prince you raised
under the skin, what sickness to the core.
Look at me! Born of outrage, outrage to the core.
O triple roads—it all comes back, the secret,
dark ravine, and the oaks closing in
where the three roads join . . .
You drank my father's blood, my own blood
spilled by my own hands—you still remember me?
What things you saw me do? Then I came here
and did them all once more!
Marriages! O marriage,
you gave me birth, and once you brought me into the world
you brought my sperm rising back, springing to light
fathers, brothers, sons—one murderous breed—
brides, wives, mothers. The blackest things
a man can do, I have done them all!

No more—
it's wrong to name what's wrong to do. Quickly,
for the love of god, hide me somewhere,
kill me, hurl me into the sea
where you can never look on me again.

[*Beckoning to the* CHORUS *as they shrink away.*]

Closer,
it's all right. Touch the man of grief.
Do. Don't be afraid. My troubles are mine
and I am the only man alive who can sustain them.

[*Enter* CREON *from the palace, attended by palace guards.*]

LEADER: Put your requests to Creon. Here he is,
just when we need him. He'll have a plan, he'll act.
Now that he's the sole defense of the country
in your place.
OEDIPUS: Oh no, what can I say to him?
How can I ever hope to win his trust?
I wronged him so, just now, in every way.
You must see that—I was so wrong, so wrong.
CREON: I haven't come to mock you, Oedipus,
or to criticize your former failings.

[*Turning to the guards.*]

You there,
have you lost all respect for human feelings?
At least revere the Sun, the holy fire
that keeps us all alive. Never expose a thing
of guilt and holy dread so great it appalls
the earth, the rain from heaven, the light of day!
Get him into the halls—quickly as you can.
Piety demands no less. Kindred alone
should see a kinsman's shame. This is obscene.
OEDIPUS: Please, in god's name . . . you wipe my fears away,
coming so generously to me, the worst of men.
Do one thing more, for your sake, not mine.
CREON: What do you want? Why so insistent?
OEDIPUS: Drive me out of the land at once, far from sight,
where I can never hear a human voice.
CREON: I'd have done that already, I promise you.
First I wanted the god to clarify my duties.
OEDIPUS: The god? His command was clear, every word:
death for the father-killer, the curse—
he said destroy me!

CREON: So he did. Still, in such a crisis
it's better to ask precisely what to do.
OEDIPUS: So miserable—
you'd consult the god about a man like me?
CREON: By all means. And this time, I assume,
even you will obey the god's decrees.
OEDIPUS: I will,
I will. And you, I command you—I beg you . . .
the woman inside, bury her as you see fit.
It's the only decent thing,
to give your own the last rites. As for me,
never condemn the city of my fathers
to house my body, not while I'm alive, no,
let me live on the mountains, on Cithaeron,
my favorite haunt, I have made it famous.
Mother and father marked out that rock
to be my everlasting tomb—buried alive.
Let me die there, where they tried to kill me.

Oh but this I know: no sickness can destroy me,
nothing can. I would never have been saved
from death—I have been saved
for something great and terrible, something strange.
Well let my destiny come and take me on its way!
About my children, Creon, the boys at least,
don't burden yourself. They're men,
wherever they go, they'll find the means to live.
But my two daughters, my poor helpless girls,
clustering at our table, never without me
hovering near them . . . whatever I touched,
they always had their share. Take care of them,
I beg you. Wait, better—permit me, would you?
Just to touch them with my hands and take
our fill of tears. Please . . . my king.
Grant it, with all your noble heart.
If I could hold them, just once, I'd think
I had them with me, like the early days
when I could see their eyes.

[ANTIGONE *and* ISMENE, *two small childen, are led in from the palace by a nurse.*]

What's that
O god! Do I really hear you sobbing?—
my two children. Creon, you've pitied me?
Sent me my darling girls, my own flesh and blood!
Am I right?

CREON: Yes, it's my doing.
I know the joy they gave you all these years,
the joy you must feel now.

OEDIPUS: Bless you, Creon!
May god watch over you for this kindness,
better than he ever guarded me.
Children, where are you?
Here, come quickly—

[*Groping for* ANTIGONE *and* ISMENE, *who approach their father cautiously, then embrace him.*]

Come to these hands of mine,
your brother's hands, your own father's hands
that served his once bright eyes so well—
that made them blind. Seeing nothing, children,
knowing nothing, I became your father,
I fathered you in the soil that gave me life.

How I weep for you—I cannot see you now . . .
just thinking of all your days to come, the bitterness,
the life that rough mankind will thrust upon you.
Where are the public gatherings you can join,
the banquets of the clans? Home you'll come,
in tears, cut off from the sight of it all,
the brilliant rites unfinished.
And when you reach perfection, ripe for marriage,
who will he be, my dear ones? Risking all
to shoulder the curse that weighs down my parents,
yes and you too—that wounds us all together.
What more misery could you want?
Your father killed his father, sowed his mother,
one, one and the selfsame womb sprang you—
he cropped the very roots of his existence.

Such disgrace, and you must bear it all!
Who will marry you then? Not a man on earth.
Your doom is clear: you'll wither away to nothing,
single, without a child.

[*Turning to* CREON.]

Oh Creon,
you are the only father they have now . . .
we who brought them into the world
are gone, both gone at a stroke—
Don't let them go begging, abandoned,
women without men. Your own flesh and blood!

Never bring them down to the level of my pains.
Pity them. Look at them, so young, so vulnerable,
shorn of everything—you're their only hope.
Promise me, noble Creon, touch my hand!

[*Reaching toward* CREON, *who draws back.*]

You, little ones, if you were old enough
to understand, there is much I'd tell you.
Now, as it is, I'd have you say a prayer.
Pray for life, my children,
live where you are free to grow and season.
Pray god you find a better life than mine,
the father who begot you.

CREON: Enough.
You've wept enough. Into the palace now.
OEDIPUS: I must, but I find it very hard.
CREON: Time is the great healer, you will see.
OEDIPUS: I am going—you know on what condition?
CREON: Tell me. I'm listening.
OEDIPUS: Drive me out of Thebes, in exile.
CREON: Not I. Only the gods can give you that.
OEDIPUS: Surely the gods hate me so much—
CREON: You'll get your wish at once.
OEDIPUS: You consent?
CREON: I try to say what I mean; it's my habit.
OEDIPUS: Then take me away. It's time.
CREON: Come along, let go of the children.
OEDIPUS: No—
don't take them away from me, not now! No no no!

[*Clutching his daughters as the guards wrench them loose and take them through the palace doors.*]

CREON: Still the king, the master of all things?
No more: here your power ends.
None of your power follows you through life.

[*Exit* OEDIPUS *and* CREON *to the palace. The* CHORUS *comes forward to address the audience directly.*]

CHORUS: People of Thebes, my countrymen, look on Oedipus.
He solved the famous riddle with his brilliance,
he rose to power, a man beyond all power.
Who could behold his greatness without envy?

Now what a black sea of terror has overwhelmed him.
Now as we keep our watch and wait the final day,
count no man happy till he dies, free of pain at last.

[*Exit in procession.*]

ca. 429 B.C.

OSCAR WILDE

The Importance of Being Earnest

CHARACTERS

ALGERNON MONCRIEFF	MISS PRISM
LANE	CECILY CARDEW
ERNEST WORTHING	CANON CHASUBLE
LADY AUGUSTA BRACKNELL	MERRIMAN
GWENDOLEN FAIRFAX	

ACT I

SCENE: *Morning room in* ALGERNON*'s flat in Half-Moon Street.*[1]

The room is luxuriously and artistically furnished. The sound of a piano is heard in the adjoining room.

[LANE *is arranging afternoon tea on the table, and after the music has ceased,* ALGERNON *enters.*]

ALGERNON: Did you hear what I was playing, Lane?

LANE: I didn't think it polite to listen, sir.

ALGERNON: I'm sorry for that, for your sake. I don't play accurately—anyone can play accurately—but I play with wonderful expression. As far as the piano is concerned, sentiment is my forte. I keep science for Life.

LANE: Yes, sir.

ALGERNON: And, speaking of the science of Life, have you got the cucumber sandwiches cut for Lady Bracknell?

LANE: Yes, sir. [*Hands them on a salver.*]

ALGERNON: [*Inspects them, takes two, and sits down on the sofa.*] Oh! . . . by the way, Lane, I see from your book that on Thursday night, when Lord Shoreham and Mr. Worthing were dining with me, eight bottles of champagne are entered as having been consumed.

LANE: Yes, sir; eight bottles and a pint.

1. Half-Moon Street runs north from Piccadilly near Hyde Park. Like many of the addresses in the play, it is in Mayfair, a very fashionable section of London.

ALGERNON: Why is it that at a bachelor's establishment the servants invariably drink the champagne? I ask merely for information.

LANE: I attribute it to the superior quality of the wine, sir. I have often observed that in married households the champagne is rarely of a first-rate brand.

ALGERNON: Good Heavens! Is marriage so demoralizing as that?

LANE: I believe it *is* a very pleasant state, sir. I have had very little experience of it myself up to the present. I have only been married once. That was in consequence of a misunderstanding between myself and a young person.

ALGERNON: [*Languidly.*] I don't know that I am much interested in your family life, Lane.

LANE: No, sir; it is not a very interesting subject. I never think of it myself.

ALGERNON: Very natural, I am sure. That will do, Lane, thank you.

LANE: Thank you, sir. [LANE *goes out.*]

ALGERNON: Lane's views on marriage seem somewhat lax. Really, if the lower orders don't set us a good example, what on earth is the use of them? They seem, as a class, to have absolutely no sense of moral responsibility.

[*Enter* LANE.]

LANE: Mr. Ernest Worthing.

[*Enter* JACK. LANE *goes out.*]

ALGERNON: How are you, my dear Ernest? What brings you up to town?

JACK: Oh, pleasure, pleasure! What else should bring one anywhere? Eating as usual, I see, Algy!

ALGERNON: [*Stiffly.*] I believe it is customary in good society to take some slight refreshment at five o'clock. Where have you been since last Thursday?

JACK: [*Sitting down on the sofa.*] In the country.

ALGERNON: What on earth do you do there?

JACK: [*Pulling off his gloves.*] When one is in town one amuses oneself. When one is in the country one amuses other people. It is excessively boring.

ALGERNON: And who are the people you amuse?

JACK: [*Airily.*] Oh, neighbors, neighbors.

ALGERNON: Got nice neighbors in your part of Shropshire?

JACK: Perfectly horrid! Never speak to one of them.

ALGERNON: How immensely you must amuse them! [*Goes over and takes sandwich.*] By the way, Shropshire is your county, is it not?

JACK: Eh? Shropshire? Yes, of course.[2] Hallo! Why all these cups? Why cucumber sandwiches? Why such reckless extravagance in one so young? Who is coming to tea?

ALGERNON: Oh! merely Aunt Augusta and Gwendolen.

JACK: How perfectly delightful!

ALGERNON: Yes, that is all very well; but I am afraid Aunt Augusta won't quite approve of your being here.

2. As we learn later, Jack's country place is in Hertfordshire, to the north of London. He is attempting to deceive Algernon by giving a false location to the west, on the Welsh border.

JACK: May I ask why?

ALGERNON: My dear fellow, the way you flirt with Gwendolen is perfectly disgraceful. It is almost as bad as the way Gwendolen flirts with you.

JACK: I am in love with Gwendolen. I have come up to town expressly to propose to her.

ALGERNON: I thought you had come up for pleasure? . . . I call that business.

JACK: How utterly unromantic you are!

ALGERNON: I really don't see anything romantic in proposing. It is very romantic to be in love. But there is nothing romantic about a definite proposal. Why, one may be accepted. One usually is, I believe. Then the excitement is all over. The very essence of romance is uncertainty. If ever I get married, I'll certainly try to forget the fact.

JACK: I have no doubt about that, dear Algy. The Divorce Court was specially invented for people whose memories are so curiously constituted.

ALGERNON: Oh! there is no use speculating on that subject. Divorces are made in Heaven—[JACK *puts out his hand to take a sandwich.* ALGERNON *at once interferes.*] Please don't touch the cucumber sandwiches. They are ordered specially for Aunt Augusta. [*Takes one and eats it.*]

JACK: Well, you have been eating them all the time.

ALGERNON: That is quite a different matter. She is my aunt. [*Takes plate from below.*] Have some bread and butter. The bread and butter is for Gwendolen. Gwendolen is devoted to bread and butter.

JACK: [*Advancing to table and helping himself.*] And very good bread and butter it is too.

ALGERNON: Well, my dear fellow, you need not eat as if you were going to eat it all. You behave as if you were married to her already. You are not married to her already, and I don't think you ever will be.

JACK: Why on earth do you say that?

ALGERNON: Well, in the first place, girls never marry the men they flirt with. Girls don't think it right.

JACK: Oh, that is nonsense!

ALGERNON: It isn't. It is a great truth. It accounts for the extraordinary number of bachelors that one sees all over the place. In the second place, I don't give my consent.

JACK: Your consent!

ALGERNON: My dear fellow, Gwendolen is my first cousin. And before I allow you to marry her, you will have to clear up the whole question of Cecily. [*Rings bell.*]

JACK: Cecily! What on earth do you mean? What do you mean, Algy, by Cecily? I don't know anyone of the name of Cecily.

[*Enter* LANE.]

ALGERNON: Bring me that cigarette case Mr. Worthing left in the smoking-room the last time he dined here.

LANE: Yes, sir. [LANE *goes out.*]

JACK: Do you mean to say you have had my cigarette case all this time? I wish to goodness you had let me know. I have been writing frantic letters to Scotland Yard about it. I was very nearly offering a large reward.

ALGERNON: Well, I wish you would offer one. I happen to be more than usually hard up.

JACK: There is no good offering a large reward now that the thing is found.

[*Enter* LANE *with the cigarette case on a salver.* ALGERNON *takes it at once.* LANE *goes out.*]

ALGERNON: I think that is rather mean of you, Ernest, I must say. [*Opens case and examines it.*] However, it makes no matter, for, now that I look at the inscription inside, I find that the thing isn't yours after all.

JACK: Of course it's mine. [*Moving to him.*] You have seen me with it a hundred times, and you have no right whatsoever to read what is written inside. It is a very ungentlemanly thing to read a private cigarette case.

ALGERNON: Oh! it is absurd to have a hard-and-fast rule about what one should read and what one shouldn't. More than half of modern culture depends on what one shouldn't read.

JACK: I am quite aware of the fact, and I don't propose to discuss modern culture. It isn't the sort of thing one should talk of in private. I simply want my cigarette case back.

ALGERNON: Yes; but this isn't your cigarette case. This cigarette case is a present from someone of the name of Cecily, and you said you didn't know anyone of that name.

JACK: Well, if you want to know, Cecily happens to be my aunt.

ALGERNON: Your aunt!

JACK: Yes. Charming old lady she is, too. Lives at Tunbridge Wells.[3] Just give it back to me, Algy.

ALGERNON: [*Retreating to back of sofa.*] But why does she call herself Cecily if she is your aunt and lives at Tunbridge Wells? [*Reading.*] "From little Cecily with her fondest love."

JACK: [*Moving to sofa and kneeling upon it.*] My dear fellow, what on earth is there in that? Some aunts are tall, some aunts are not tall. That is a matter that surely an aunt may be allowed to decide for herself. You seem to think that every aunt should be exactly like your aunt! That is absurd! For Heaven's sake give me back my cigarette case. [*Follows* ALGY *round the room.*]

ALGERNON: Yes. But why does your aunt call you her uncle? "From little Cecily, with her fondest love to her dear Uncle Jack." There is no objection, I admit, to an aunt being a small aunt, but why an aunt, no matter what her size may be, should call her own nephew her uncle, I can't quite make out. Besides, your name isn't Jack at all; it is Ernest.

JACK: It isn't Ernest; it's Jack.

ALGERNON: You have always told me it was Ernest. I have introduced you to everyone as Ernest. You answer to the name of Ernest. You look as if your name was Ernest. You are the most earnest looking person I ever saw in my

3. Tunbridge Wells is a resort town in Kent, to the southeast of London.

life. It is perfectly absurd your saying that your name isn't Ernest. It's on your cards. Here is one of them. [*Taking it from case.*] "Mr. Ernest Worthing, B. 4, The Albany."[4] I'll keep this as a proof that your name is Ernest if ever you attempt to deny it to me, or to Gwendolen, or to anyone else. [*Puts the card in his pocket.*]

JACK: Well, my name is Ernest in town and Jack in the country, and the cigarette case was given to me in the country.

ALGERNON: Yes, but that does not account for the fact that your small Aunt Cecily, who lives at Tunbridge Wells, calls you her dear uncle. Come, old boy, you had much better have the thing out at once.

JACK: My dear Algy, you talk exactly as if you were a dentist. It is very vulgar to talk like a dentist when one isn't a dentist. It produces a false impression.

ALGERNON: Well, that is exactly what dentists always do. Now, go on! Tell me the whole thing. I may mention that I have always suspected you of being a confirmed and secret Bunburyist; and I am quite sure of it now.

JACK: Bunburyist? What on earth do you mean by a Bunburyist?

ALGERNON: I'll reveal to you the meaning of that incomparable expression as soon as you are kind enough to inform me why you are Ernest in town and Jack in the country.

JACK: Well, produce my cigarette case first.

ALGERNON: Here it is. [*Hands cigarette case.*] Now produce your explanation, and pray make it improbable. [*Sits on sofa.*]

JACK: My dear fellow, there is nothing improbable about my explanation at all. In fact it's perfectly ordinary. Old Mr. Thomas Cardew, who adopted me when I was a little boy, made me in his will guardian to his granddaughter, Miss Cecily Cardew. Cecily, who addresses me as her uncle from motives of respect that you could not possibly appreciate, lives at my place in the country under the charge of her admirable governess, Miss Prism.

ALGERNON: Where is that place in the country, by the way?

JACK: That is nothing to you, dear boy. You are not going to be invited. . . . I may tell you candidly that the place is not in Shropshire.

ALGERNON: I suspected that, my dear fellow! I have Bunburyed all over Shropshire on two separate occasions. Now, go on. Why are you Ernest in town and Jack in the country?

JACK: My dear Algy, I don't know whether you will be able to understand my real motives. You are hardly serious enough. When one is placed in the position of guardian, one has to adopt a very high moral tone on all subjects. It's one's duty to do so. And as a high moral tone can hardly be said to conduce very much to either one's health or one's happiness, in order to get up to town I have always pretended to have a younger brother of the name of Ernest, who lives in the Albany, and gets into the most dreadful scrapes. That, my dear Algy, is the whole truth pure and simple.

ALGERNON: The truth is rarely pure and never simple. Modern life would be very tedious if it were either, and modern literature a complete impossibility!

4. An apartment building for single gentlemen on Piccadilly, to the east of Algernon's flat.

JACK: That wouldn't be at all a bad thing.

ALGERNON: Literary criticism is not your forte, my dear fellow. Don't try it. You should leave that to people who haven't been at a University. They do it so well in the daily papers. What you really are is a Bunburyist. I was quite right in saying you were a Bunburyist. You are one of the most advanced Bunburyists I know.

JACK: What on earth do you mean?

ALGERNON: You have invented a very useful young brother called Ernest, in order that you may be able to come up to town as often as you like. I have invented an invaluable permanent invalid called Bunbury, in order that I may be able to go down into the country whenever I choose. Bunbury is perfectly invaluable. If it wasn't for Bunbury's extraordinary bad health, for instance, I wouldn't be able to dine with you at Willis's[5] tonight, for I have been really engaged to Aunt Augusta for more than a week.

JACK: I haven't asked you to dine with me anywhere tonight.

ALGERNON: I know. You are absurdly careless about sending out invitations. It is very foolish of you. Nothing annoys people so much as not receiving invitations.

JACK: You had much better dine with your Aunt Augusta.

ALGERNON: I haven't the smallest intention of doing anything of the kind. To begin with, I dined there on Monday, and once a week is quite enough to dine with one's own relations. In the second place, whenever I do dine there I am always treated as a member of the family, and sent down with either no woman at all, or two. In the third place, I know perfectly well whom she will place me next to, tonight. She will place me next Mary Farquhar, who always flirts with her own husband across the dinner table. That is not very pleasant. Indeed, it is not even decent . . . and that sort of thing is enormously on the increase. The amount of women in London who flirt with their own husbands is perfectly scandalous. It looks so bad. It is simply washing one's clean linen in public. Besides, now that I know you to be a confirmed Bunburyist, I naturally want to talk to you about Bunburying. I want to tell you the rules.

JACK: I'm not a Bunburyist at all. If Gwendolen accepts me, I am going to kill my brother, indeed I think I'll kill him in any case. Cecily is a little too much interested in him. It is rather a bore. So I am going to get rid of Ernest. And I strongly advise you to do the same with Mr. . . . with your invalid friend who has the absurd name.

ALGERNON: Nothing will induce me to part with Bunbury, and if you ever get married, which seems to me extremely problematic, you will be very glad to know Bunbury. A man who marries without knowing Bunbury has a very tedious time of it.

JACK: That is nonsense. If I marry a charming girl like Gwendolen, and she is the only girl I ever saw in my life that I would marry, I certainly won't want to know Bunbury.

5. A well-known establishment for dining on King Street, off St. James's Street and quite near Picadilly.

ALGERNON: Then your wife will. You don't seem to realize, that in married life three is company and two is none.

JACK: [*Sententiously.*] That, my dear young friend, is the theory that the corrupt French Drama has been propounding for the last fifty years.[6]

ALGERNON: Yes; and that the happy English home has proved in half the time.

JACK: For heaven's sake, don't try to be cynical. It's perfectly easy to be cynical.

ALGERNON: My dear fellow, it isn't easy to be anything nowadays. There's such a lot of beastly competition about. [*The sound of an electric bell is heard.*] Ah! that must be Aunt Augusta. Only relatives, or creditors, ever ring in that Wagnerian manner.[7] Now, if I get her out of the way for ten minutes, so that you can have an opportunity for proposing to Gwendolen, may I dine with you tonight at Willis's?

JACK: I suppose so, if you want to.

ALGERNON: Yes, but you must be serious about it. I hate people who are not serious about meals. It is so shallow of them.

[*Enter* LANE.]

LANE: Lady Bracknell and Miss Fairfax.

[ALGERNON *goes forward to meet them. Enter* LADY BRACKNELL *and* GWENDOLEN.]

LADY BRACKNELL: Good afternoon, dear Algernon, I hope you are behaving very well.

ALGERNON: I'm feeling very well, Aunt Augusta.

LADY BRACKNELL: That's not quite the same thing. In fact the two things rarely go together. [*Sees* JACK *and bows to him with icy coldness.*]

ALGERNON: [*To* GWENDOLEN.] Dear me, you are smart!

GWENDOLEN: I am always smart! Aren't I, Mr. Worthing?

JACK: You're quite perfect, Miss Fairfax.

GWENDOLEN: Oh! I hope I am not that. It would leave no room for developments, and I intend to develop in many directions. [GWENDOLEN *and* JACK *sit down together in the corner.*]

LADY BRACKNELL: I'm sorry if we are a little late, Algernon, but I was obliged to call on dear Lady Harbury. I hadn't been there since her poor husband's death. I never saw a woman so altered; she looks quite twenty years younger. And now I'll have a cup of tea, and one of those nice cucumber sandwiches you promised me.

ALGERNON: Certainly, Aunt Augusta. [*Goes over to teatable.*]

LADY BRACKNELL: Won't you come and sit here, Gwendolen?

GWENDOLEN: Thanks, mamma, I'm quite comfortable where I am.

ALGERNON: [*Picking up empty plate in horror.*] Good heavens! Lane! Why are

6. Beginning in the middle of the 19th century, French drama produced plays dealing with subjects such as adultery, prostitution, and illegitimacy. The heavily censored English theater either avoided such subjects or dealt with them more circumspectly.

7. Many earlier listeners to the music of Richard Wagner found it extremely loud and, consequently, peremptory in demanding attention.

there no cucumber sandwiches? I ordered them specially.

LANE: [*Gravely.*] There were no cucumbers in the market this morning, sir. I went down twice.

ALGERNON: No cucumbers!

LANE: No, sir. Not even for ready money.

ALGERNON: That will do, Lane, thank you.

LANE: Thank you, sir.

ALGERNON: I am greatly distressed, Aunt Augusta, about there being no cucumbers, not even for ready money.

LADY BRACKNELL: It really makes no matter, Algernon. I had some crumpets with Lady Harbury, who seems to me to be living entirely for pleasure now.

ALGERNON: I hear her hair has turned quite gold from grief.

LADY BRACKNELL: It certainly has changed its color. From what cause I, of course, cannot say. [ALGERNON *crosses and hands tea.*] Thank you. I've quite a treat for you tonight, Algernon. I am going to send you down with Mary Farquhar. She is such a nice woman, and so attentive to her husband. It's delightful to watch them.

ALGERNON: I am afraid, Aunt Augusta, I shall have to give up the pleasure of dining with you tonight after all.

LADY BRACKNELL: [*Frowning.*] I hope not, Algernon. It would put my table completely out. Your uncle would have to dine upstairs. Fortunately he is accustomed to that.

ALGERNON: It is a great bore, and, I need hardly say, a terrible disappointment to me, but the fact is I have just had a telegram to say that my poor friend Bunbury is very ill again. [*Exchanges glances with* JACK.] They seem to think I should be with him.

LADY BRACKNELL: It is very strange. This Mr. Bunbury seems to suffer from curiously bad health.

ALGERNON: Yes; poor Bunbury is a dreadful invalid.

LADY BRACKNELL: Well, I must say, Algernon, that I think it is high time that Mr. Bunbury made up his mind whether he was going to live or to die. This shilly-shallying with the question is absurd. Nor do I in any way approve of the modern sympathy with invalids. I consider it morbid. Illness of any kind is hardly a thing to be encouraged in others. Health is the primary duty of life. I am always telling that to your poor uncle, but he never seems to take much notice . . . as far as any improvement in his ailments goes. I should be obliged if you would ask Mr. Bunbury, from me, to be kind enough not to have a relapse on Saturday, for I rely on you to arrange my music for me. It is my last reception, and one wants something that will encourage conversation, particularly at the end of the season when everyone has practically said whatever they had to say, which, in most cases, was probably not much.

ALGERNON: I'll speak to Bunbury, Aunt Augusta, if he is still conscious, and I think I can promise you he'll be all right by Saturday. Of course the music is a great difficulty. You see, if one plays good music, people don't listen, and if one plays bad music, people don't talk. But I'll run over the program I've drawn out, if you will kindly come into the next room for a moment.

LADY BRACKNELL: Thank you, Algernon. It is very thoughtful of you. [*Rising, and following* ALGERNON.] I'm sure the program will be delightful, after a few expurgations. French songs I cannot possibly allow. People always seem to think that they are improper, and either look shocked, which is vulgar, or laugh, which is worse. But German sounds a thoroughly respectable language, and indeed, I believe is so. Gwendolen, you will accompany me.

GWENDOLEN: Certainly, mamma.

[LADY BRACKNELL *and* ALGERNON *go into the music room,* GWENDOLEN *remains behind.*]

JACK: Charming day it has been, Miss Fairfax.

GWENDOLEN: Pray don't talk to me about the weather, Mr. Worthing. Whenever people talk to me about the weather, I always feel quite certain that they mean something else. And that makes me so nervous.

JACK: I do mean something else.

GWENDOLWN: I thought so. In fact, I am never wrong.

JACK: And I would like to be allowed to take advantage of Lady Bracknell's temporary absence . . .

GWENDOLEN. I would certainly advise you to do so. Mamma has a way of coming back suddenly into a room that I have often had to speak to her about.

JACK: [*Nervously.*] Miss Fairfax, ever since I met you I have admired you more than any girl . . . I have ever met since . . . I met you.

GWENDOLEN: Yes, I am quite aware of the fact. And I often wish that in public, at any rate, you had been more demonstrative. For me you have always had an irresistible fascination. Even before I met you I was far from indifferent to you. [JACK *looks at her in amazement.*] We live, as I hope you know, Mr. Worthing, in an age of ideals. The fact is constantly mentioned in the more expensive monthly magazines, and has reached the provincial pulpits, I am told: and my ideal has always been to love someone of the name of Ernest. There is something in that name that inspires absolute confidence. The moment Algernon first mentioned to me that he had a friend called Ernest, I knew I was destined to love you.

JACK: You really love me, Gwendolen?

GWENDOLEN: Passionately!

JACK: Darling! You don't know how happy you've made me.

GWENDOLEN: My own Ernest!

JACK: But you don't really mean to say that you couldn't love me if my name wasn't Ernest?

GWENDOLEN: But your name is Ernest.

JACK: Yes, I know it is. But supposing it was something else? Do you mean to say you couldn't love me then?

GWENDOLEN: [*Glibly.*] Ah! that is clearly a metaphysical speculation, and like most metaphysical speculations has very little reference at all to the actual facts of real life, as we know them.

JACK: Personally, darling, to speak quite candidly, I don't much care about the name of Ernest . . . I don't think the name suits me at all.

GWENDOLEN: It suits you perfectly. It is a divine name. It has a music of its own. It produces vibrations.

JACK: Well, really, Gwendolen, I must say that I think there are lots of other much nicer names. I think Jack, for instance, a charming name.

GWENDOLEN: Jack? . . . No, there is very little music in the name Jack, if any at all, indeed. It does not thrill. It produces absolutely no vibrations. . . . I have known several Jacks, and they all, without exception, were more than usually plain. Besides, Jack is a notorious domesticity for John! And I pity any woman who is married to a man called John. She would probably never be allowed to know the entrancing pleasure of a single moment's solitude. The only really safe name is Ernest.

JACK: Gwendolen, I must get christened at once—I mean we must get married at once. There is no time to be lost.

GWENDOLWN: Married, Mr. Worthing?

JACK: [*Astounded.*] Well . . . surely. You know that I love you, and you led me to believe, Miss Fairfax, that you were not absolutely indifferent to me.

GWENDOLEN: I adore you. But you haven't proposed to me yet. Nothing has been said at all about marriage. The subject has not even been touched on.

JACK: Well . . . may I propose to you now?

GWENDOLEN: I think it would be an admirable opportunity. And to spare you any possible disappointment, Mr. Worthing, I think it only fair to tell you quite frankly beforehand that I am fully determined to accept you.

JACK: Gwendolen!

GWENDOLEN: Yes, Mr. Worthing, what have you got to say to me?

JACK: You know what I have got to say to you.

GWENDOLEN: Yes, but you don't say it.

JACK: Gwendolen, will you marry me? [*Goes on his knees.*]

GWENDOLEN: Of course I will, darling. How long you have been about it! I am afraid you have had very little experience in how to propose.

JACK: My own one, I have never loved anyone in the world but you.

GWENDOLEN: Yes, but men often propose for practice. I know my brother Gerald does. All my girlfriends tell me so. What wonderfully blue eyes you have, Ernest! They are quite, quite blue. I hope you will always look at me just like that, especially when there are other people present.

[*Enter* LADY BRACKNELL.]

LADY BRACKNELL: Mr. Worthing! Rise, sir, from this semi-recumbent posture. It is most indecorous.

GWENDOLEN: Mamma! [*He tries to rise; she restrains him.*] I must beg you to retire. This is no place for you. Besides, Mr. Worthing has not quite finished yet.

LADY BRACKNELL: Finished what, may I ask?

GWENDOLEN: I am engaged to Mr. Worthing, mamma.

[*They rise together.*]

LADY BRACKNELL: Pardon me, you are not engaged to anyone. When you do become engaged to someone, I, or you father, should his health permit him, will inform you of the fact. An engagement should come on a young girl as a surprise, pleasant or unpleasant, as the case may be. It is hardly a matter that she could be allowed to arrange for herself. . . . And now I have a few questions to put to you, Mr. Worthing. While I am making these inquiries, you, Gwendolen, will wait for me below in the carriage.

GWENDOLEN: [*Reproachfully.*] Mamma!

LADY BRACKNELL: In the carriage, Gwendolen! [GWENDOLEN *goes to the door. She and* JACK *blow kisses to each other behind* LADY BRACKNELL*'s back.* LADY BRACKNELL *looks vaguely about as if she could not understand what the noise was. Finally turns round.*] Gwendolen, the carriage!

GWENDOLEN: Yes, mamma. [*Goes out, looking back at* JACK.]

LADY BRACKNELL: [*Sitting down.*] You can take a seat, Mr. Worthing.

[*Looks in her pocket for notebook and pencil.*]

JACK: Thank you, Lady Bracknell, I prefer standing.

LADY BRACKNELL: [*Pencil and notebook in hand.*] I feel bound to tell you that you are not down on my list of eligible young men, although I have the same list as the dear Duchess of Bolton has. We work together, in fact. However, I am quite ready to enter your name, should your answers be what a really affectionate mother requires. Do you smoke?

JACK: Well, yes, I must admit I smoke.

LADY BRACKNELL: I am glad to hear it. A man should always have an occupation of some kind. There are far too many idle men in London as it is. How old are you?

JACK: Twenty-nine.

LADY BRACKNELL: A very good age to be married at. I have always been of opinion that a man who desires to get married should know either everything or nothing. Which do you know?

JACK: [*After some hesitation.*] I know nothing, Lady Bracknell.

LADY BRACKNELL: I am pleased to hear it. I do not approve of anything that tampers with natural ignorance. Ignorance is like a delicate exotic fruit; touch it and the bloom is gone. The whole theory of modern education is radically unsound. Fortunately in England, at any rate, education produces no effect whatsoever. If it did, it would prove a serious danger to the upper classes, and probably lead to acts of violence in Grosvenor Square.[8] What is your income?

JACK: Between seven and eight thousand a year.[9]

LADY BRACKNELL: [*Makes a note in her book.*] In land, or in investments?

JACK: In investments, chiefly.

LADY BRACKNELL: That is satisfactory. What between the duties expected of one during one's lifetime, and the duties exacted from one after one's death, land has ceased to be either a profit or a pleasure. It gives one position, and prevents one from keeping it up. That's all that can be said about land.

JACK: I have a country house with some land, of course, attached to it, about

8. A fashionable location in Mayfair. 9. A considerable income for the time.

fifteen hundred acres, I believe; but I don't depend on that for my real income. In fact, as far as I can make out, the poachers are the only people who make anything out of it.

LADY BRACKNELL: A country house! How many bedrooms? Well, that point can be cleared up afterwards. You have a town house, I hope? A girl with a simple, unspoiled nature, like Gwendolen, could hardly be expected to reside in the country.

JACK: Well, I own a house in Belgrave Square,[1] but it is let by the year to Lady Bloxham. Of course, I can get it back whenever I like, at six months' notice.

LADY BRACKNELL: Lady Bloxham? I don't know her.

JACK: Oh, she goes about very little. She is a lady considerably advanced in years.

LADY BRACKNELL: Ah, nowadays that is no guarantee of respectability of character. What number in Belgrave Square?

JACK: 149.

LADY BRACKNELL: [*Shaking her head.*] The unfashionable side. I thought there was something. However, that could easily be altered.

JACK: Do you mean the fashion, or the side?

LADY BRACKNELL: [*Sternly.*] Both, if necessary, I presume. What are your politics?

JACK: Well, I am afraid I really have none. I am a Liberal Unionist.

LADY BRACKNELL: Oh, they count as Tories.[2] They dine with us. Or come in the evening, at any rate. Now to minor matters. Are your parents living?

JACK: I have lost both my parents.

LADY BRACKNELL: Both? To lose one parent may be regarded as a misfortune—to lose *both* seems like carelessness. Who was your father? He was evidently a man of some wealth. Was he born in what the Radical papers call the purple of commerce, or did he rise from the ranks of aristocracy?

JACK: I am afraid I really don't know. The fact is, Lady Bracknell, I said I had lost my parents. It would be nearer the truth to say that my parents seem to have lost me. . . . I don't actually know who I am by birth. I was . . . well, I was found.

LADY BRACKNELL: Found!

JACK: The late Mr. Thomas Cardew, an old gentleman of a very charitable and kindly disposition, found me, and gave me the name of Worthing, because he happened to have a first-class ticket for Worthing in his pocket at the time. Worthing is a place in Sussex. It is a seaside resort.

LADY BRACKNELL: Where did the charitable gentleman who had a first-class ticket for this seaside resort find you?

JACK: [*Gravely.*] In a handbag.

LADY BRACKNELL: A handbag?

JACK: [*Very seriously.*] Yes, Lady Bracknell. I was in a handbag—a somewhat

1. Belgrave Square is near the southeast corner of Hyde Park in Belgravia, another fashionable section of London. 2. Members of the Conservative Party. Opposed to home rule for Ireland, they joined forces with the Liberal Unionists, who had split from the Liberal Party over the issue.

large, black leather handbag, with handles to it—an ordinary handbag, in fact.

LADY BRACKNELL: In what locality did this Mr. James, or Thomas, Cardew come across this ordinary handbag?

JACK: In the cloak room at Victoria Station.[3] It was given to him in mistake for his own.

LADY BRACKNELL: The cloak room at Victoria Station?

JACK: Yes. The Brighton line.

LADY BRACKNELL: The line is immaterial. Mr. Worthing, I confess I feel somewhat bewildered by what you have just told me. To be born, or at any rate, bred in a handbag, whether it had handles or not, seems to me to display a contempt for the ordinary decencies of family life that reminds one of the worst excesses of the French Revolution. And I presume you know what that unfortunate movement led to? As for the particular locality in which the handbag was found, a cloak room at a railway station might serve to conceal a social indiscretion—has probably, indeed, been used for that purpose before now—but it could hardly be regarded as an assured basis for a recognized position in good society.

JACK: May I ask you then what you would advise me to do? I need hardly say I would do anything in the world to ensure Gwendolen's happiness.

LADY BRACKNELL: I would strongly advise you, Mr. Worthing, to try and acquire some relations as soon as possible, and to make a definite effort to produce at any rate one parent, of either sex, before the season is quite over.

JACK: Well, I don't see how I could possibly manage to do that. I can produce the handbag at any moment, it is in my dressing room at home. I really think that should satisfy you, Lady Bracknell.

LADY BRACKNELL: Me, sir! What has it to do with me? You can hardly imagine that I and Lord Bracknell would dream of allowing our only daughter—a girl brought up with the utmost care—to marry into a cloak room, and form an alliance with a parcel? Good morning, Mr. Worthing!

[LADY BRACKNELL *sweeps out in majestic indignation.*]

JACK: Good morning! [ALGERNON, *from the other room, strikes up the Wedding March.* JACK *looks perfectly furious, and goes to the door.*] For goodness' sake don't play that ghastly tune, Algy! How idiotic you are!

[*The music stops, and* ALGERNON *enters cheerily.*]

ALGERNON: Didn't it go off all right, old boy? You don't mean to say Gwendolen refused you? I know it is a way she has. She is always refusing people. I think it is most ill-natured of her.

JACK: Oh, Gwendolen is as right as a trivet.[4] As far as she is concerned, we are engaged. Her mother is perfectly unbearable. Never met such a Gorgon[5]

3. Major railroad terminus in London. 4. A proverbial expression, referring to the solidity of a tripod on its three legs. 5. A mythological creature of horrible aspect, the Gorgon had snakes in place of hair. According to myth, those who looked on a Gorgon were turned to stone by the experience.

. . . I don't really know what a Gorgon is like, but I am quite sure that Lady Bracknell is one. In any case, she is a monster, without being a myth, which is rather unfair . . . I beg your pardon, Algy, I suppose I shouldn't talk about your own aunt in that way before you.

ALGERNON: My dear boy, I love hearing my relations abused. It is the only thing that makes me put up with them at all. Relations are simply a tedious pack of people who haven't got the remotest knowledge of how to live, nor the smallest instinct about when to die.

JACK: Oh, that is nonsense!

ALGERNON: It isn't!

JACK: Well, I won't argue about the matter. You always want to argue about things.

ALGERNON: That is exactly what things were originally made for.

JACK: Upon my word, if I thought that, I'd shoot myself . . . [*A pause.*] You don't think there is any chance of Gwendolen becoming like her mother in about a hundred and fifty years, do you, Algy?

ALGERNON: All women become like their mothers. That is their tragedy. No man does. That's his.

JACK: Is that clever?

ALGERNON: It is perfectly phrased! and quite as true as any observation in civilized life should be.

JACK: I am sick to death of cleverness. Everybody is clever nowadays. You can't go anywhere without meeting clever people. The thing has become an absolute public nuisance. I wish to goodness we had a few fools left.

ALGERNON: We have.

JACK: I should extremely like to meet them. What do they talk about?

ALGERNON: The fools? Oh! about the clever people, of course.

JACK: What fools!

ALGERNON: By the way, did you tell Gwendolen the truth about your being Ernest in town, and Jack in the country?

JACK: [*In a very patronizing manner.*] My dear fellow, the truth isn't quite the sort of thing one tells to a nice sweet refined girl. What extraordinary ideas you have about the way to behave to a woman!

ALGERNON: The only way to behave to a woman is to make love to her, if she is pretty, and to someone else if she is plain.

JACK: Oh, that is nonsense.

ALGERNON: What about your brother? What about the profligate Ernest?

JACK: Oh, before the end of the week I shall have got rid of him. I'll say he died in Paris of apoplexy. Lots of people die of apoplexy, quite suddenly, don't they?

ALGERNON: Yes, but it's hereditary, my dear fellow. It's a sort of thing that runs in families. You had much better say a severe chill.

JACK: You are sure a severe chill isn't hereditary, or anything of that kind?

ALGERNON: Of course it isn't!

JACK: Very well, then. My poor brother Ernest is carried off suddenly in Paris, by a severe chill. That gets rid of him.

ALGERNON: But I thought you said that . . . Miss Cardew was a little too much interested in your poor brother Ernest? Won't she feel his loss a good deal?

JACK: Oh, that is all right. Cecily is not a silly romantic girl, I am glad to say. She has got a capital appetite, goes on long walks, and pays no attention at all to her lessons.

ALGERNON: I would rather like to see Cecily.

JACK: I will take very good care you never do. She is excessively pretty, and she is only just eighteen.

ALGERNON: Have you told Gwendolen yet that you have an excessively pretty ward who is only just eighteen?

JACK: Oh! one doesn't blurt these things out to people. Cecily and Gwendolen are perfectly certain to be extremely great friends. I'll bet you anything you like that half an hour after they have met, they will be calling each other sister.

ALGERNON: Women only do that when they have called each other a lot of other things first. Now, my dear boy, if we want to get a good table at Willis's, we really must go and dress. Do you know it is nearly seven?

JACK: [*Irritably.*] Oh! it always is nearly seven.

ALGERNON: Well, I'm hungry.

JACK: I never knew you when you weren't. . . .

ALGERNON: What shall we do after dinner? Go to the theater?

JACK: Oh no! I loathe listening.

ALGERNON: Well, let us go to the club?

JACK: Oh, no! I hate talking.

ALGERNON: Well, we might trot around to the Empire[6] at ten?

JACK: Oh no! I can't bear looking at things. It is so silly.

ALGERNON: Well, what shall we do?

JACK: Nothing!

ALGERNON: It is awfully hard work doing nothing. However, I don't mind hard work where there is no definite object of any kind.

[*Enter* LANE.]

LANE: Miss Fairfax.

[*Enter* GWENDOLEN. LANE *goes out.*]

ALGERNON: Gwendolen, upon my word!

GWENDOLEN: Algy, kindly turn your back. I have something very particular to say to Mr. Worthing.

ALGERNON: Really, Gwendolen, I don't think I can allow this at all.

GWENDOLEN: Algy, you always adopt a strictly immoral attitude towards life. You are not quite old enough to do that.

[ALGERNON *retires to the fireplace.*]

JACK: My own darling!

GWENDOLEN: Ernest, we may never be married. From the expression on mam-

6. The Empire Theatre of Varieties, a music hall on Leicester Square.

ma's face I fear we never shall. Few parents nowadays pay any regard to what their children say to them. The old-fashioned respect for the young is fast dying out. Whatever influence I ever had over mamma, I lost at the age of three. But although she may prevent us from becoming man and wife, and I may marry someone else, and marry often, nothing that she can possibly do can alter my eternal devotion to you.

JACK: Dear Gwendolen!

GWENDOLEN: The story of your romantic origin, as related to me by mamma, with unpleasing comments, has naturally stirred the deeper fibers of my nature. Your Christian name has an irresistible fascination. The simplicity of your character makes you exquisitely incomprehensible to me. Your town address at the Albany I have. What is your address in the country?

JACK: The Manor House, Woolton, Hertfordshire.

[ALGERNON, *who has been carefully listening, smiles to himself, and writes the address on his shirt-cuff. Then picks up the Railway Guide.*]

GWENDOLEN: There is a good postal service, I suppose? It may be necessary to do something desperate. That of course will require serious consideration. I will communicate with you daily.

JACK: My own one!

GWENDOLEN: How long do you remain in town?

JACK: Till Monday.

GWENDOLEN: Good! Algy, you may turn round now.

ALGERNON: Thanks, I've turned round already.

GWENDOLEN: You may also ring the bell.

JACK: You will let me see you to your carriage, my own darling?

GWENDOLEN: Certainly.

JACK: [*To* LANE, *who now enters.*] I will see Miss Fairfax out.

LANE: Yes, sir.

[JACK *and* GWENDOLEN *go off.* LANE *presents several letters on a salver to* ALGERNON. *It is to be surmised that they are bills, as* ALGERNON *after looking at the envelopes, tears them up.*]

ALGERNON: A glass of sherry, Lane.

LANE: Yes, sir.

ALGERNON: Tomorrow, Lane, I'm going Bunburying.

LANE: Yes, sir.

ALGERNON: I shall probably not be back till Monday. You can put up my dress clothes, my smoking jacket, and all the Bunbury suits . . .

LANE: Yes, sir. [*Handing sherry.*]

ALGERNON: I hope tomorrow will be a fine day, Lane.

LANE: It never is, sir.

ALGERNON: Lane, you're a perfect pessimist.

LANE: I do my best to give satisfaction, sir.

[*Enter* JACK. LANE *goes off.*]

JACK: There's a sensible, intellectual girl! the only girl I ever cared for in my life. [ALGERNON *is laughing immoderately.*] What on earth are you so amused at?

ALGERNON: Oh, I'm a little anxious about poor Bunbury, that is all.

JACK: If you don't take care, your friend Bunbury will get you into a serious scrape some day.

ALGERNON: I love scrapes. They are the only things that are never serious.

JACK: Oh, that's nonsense, Algy. You never talk anything but nonsense.

ALGERNON: Nobody ever does.

[JACK *looks indignantly at him, and leaves the room.* ALGERNON *lights a cigarette, reads his shirt-cuff, and smiles.*]

ACT-DROP

ACT II

SCENE: *Garden at the Manor House. A flight of gray stone steps leads up to the house. The garden, an old-fashioned one, full of roses. Time of year, July. Basket chairs, and a table covered with books, are set under a large yew tree.*

[MISS PRISM *discovered seated at the table.* CECILY *is at the back watering flowers.*]

MISS PRISM: [*Calling.*] Cecily, Cecily! Surely such a utilitarian occupation as the watering of flowers is rather Moulton's duty than yours? Especially at a moment when intellectual pleasures await you. Your German grammar is on the table. Pray open it at page fifteen. We will repeat yesterday's lesson.

CECILY: [*Coming over very slowly.*] But I don't like German. It isn't at all a becoming language. I know perfectly well that I look quite plain after my German lesson.

MISS PRISM: Child, you know how anxious your guardian is that you should improve yourself in every way. He laid particular stress on your German, as he was leaving for town yesterday. Indeed, he always lays stress on your German when he is leaving for town.

CECILY: Dear Uncle Jack is so very serious! Sometime he is so serious that I think he cannot be quite well.

MISS PRISM: [*Drawing herself up.*] Your guardian enjoys the best of health, and his gravity of demeanor is especially to be commended in one so comparatively young as he is. I know no one who has a higher sense of duty and responsibility.

CECILY: I suppose that is why he often looks a little bored when we three are together.

MISS PRISM: Cecily! I am surprised at you. Mr. Worthing has many troubles in his life. Idle merriment and triviality would be out of place in his conversation. You must remember his constant anxiety about that unfortunate young man his brother.

CECILY: I wish Uncle Jack would allow that unfortunate young man, his brother, to come down here sometimes. We might have a good influence over him,

Miss Prism. I am sure you certainly would. You know German, and geology, and things of that kind influence a man very much. [CECILY *begins to write in her diary.*]

MISS PRISM: [*Shaking her head.*] I do not think that even I could produce any effect on a character that according to his own brother's admission is irretrievably weak and vacillating. Indeed I am not sure that I would desire to reclaim him. I am not in favor of this modern mania for turning bad people into good people at a moment's notice. As a man sows so let him reap. You must put away your diary, Cecily. I really don't see why you should keep a diary at all.

CECILY: I keep a diary in order to enter the wonderful secrets of my life. If I didn't write them down I should probably forget all about them.

MISS PRISM: Memory, my dear Cecily, is the diary that we all carry about with us.

CECILY: Yes, but it usually chronicles the things that have never happened, and couldn't possibly have happened. I believe that Memory is responsible for nearly all the three-volume novels that Mudie sends us.[7]

MISS PRISM: Do not speak slightingly of the three-volume novel, Cecily. I wrote one myself in earlier days.

CECILY: Did you really, Miss Prism? How wonderfully clever you are! I hope it did not end happily? I don't like novels that end happily. They depress me so much.

MISS PRISM: The good ended happily, and the bad unhappily. That is what Fiction means.

CECILY: I suppose so. But it seems very unfair. And was your novel ever published?

MISS PRISM: Alas! no. The manuscript unfortunately was abandoned. I use the word in the sense of lost or mislaid. To your work, child, these speculations are profitless.

CECILY: [*Smiling.*] But I see dear Dr. Chasuble coming up through the garden.

MISS PRISM: [*Rising and advancing.*] Dr. Chasuble! This is indeed a pleasure.

[*Enter* CANON CHASUBLE.]

CHASUBLE: And how are we this morning? Miss Prism, you are, I trust, well?

CECILY: Miss Prism has just been complaining of a slight headache. I think it would do her so much good to have a short stroll with you in the Park, Dr. Chasuble.

MISS PRISM: Cecily, I have not mentioned anything about a headache.

CECILY: No, dear Miss Prism, I know that, but I felt instinctively that you had a headache. Indeed I was thinking about that, and not about my German lesson, when the Rector came in.

CHASUBLE: I hope, Cecily, you are not inattentive.

CECILY: Oh, I am afraid I am.

7. From the 1860s to the 1880s most novels were published in three volumes. Because of the resultant price, most readers could not afford to buy copies and obtained them by subscription from lending libraries, of which Mudie's in London was by far the largest.

CHASUBLE: That is strange. Were I fortunate enough to be Miss Prism's pupil, I would hang upon her lips. [MISS PRISM *glares.*] I spoke metaphorically.—My metaphor was drawn from bees. Ahem! Mr. Worthing, I suppose, has not returned from town yet?

MISS PRISM: We do not expect him till Monday afternoon.

CHASUBLE: Ah yes, he usually likes to spend his Sunday in London. He is not one of those whose sole aim is enjoyment, as, by all accounts, that unfortunate young man his brother seems to be. But I must not disturb Egeria[8] and her pupil any longer.

MISS PRISM: Egeria? My name is Laetitia, Doctor.

CHASUBLE: [*Bowing.*] A classical allusion merely, drawn from the Pagan authors. I shall see you both no doubt at Evensong?[9]

MISS PRISM: I think, dear Doctor, I will have a stroll with you. I find I have a headache after all, and a walk might do it good.

CHASUBLE: With pleasure, Miss Prism, with pleasure. We might go as far as the schools and back.

MISS PRISM: That would be delightful. Cecily, you will read your Political Economy[1] in my absence. The chapter on the Fall of the Rupee you may omit. It is somewhat too sensational. Even these metallic problems have their melodramatic side. [*Goes down the garden with* CANON CHASUBLE.]

CECILY: [*Picks up books and throws them back on table.*] Horrid Political Economy! Horrid Geography! Horrid, horrid German!

[*Enter* MERRIMAN *with a card on a salver.*]

MERRIMAN: Mr. Ernest Worthing has just driven over from the station. He has brought his luggage with him.

CECILY: [*Takes the card and reads it.*] "Mr. Ernest Worthing, B. 4, The Albany, W." Uncle Jack's brother! Did you tell him Mr. Worthing was in town?

MERRIMAN: Yes, Miss. He seemed very much disappointed. I mentioned that you and Miss Prism were in the garden. He said he was anxious to speak to you privately for a moment.

CECILY. Ask Mr. Ernest Worthing to come here. I suppose you had better talk to the housekeeper about a room for him.

MERRIMAN: Yes, Miss. [MERRIMAN *goes off.*]

CECILY: I have never met any really wicked person before. I feel rather frightened. I am so afraid he will look just like everyone else. [*Enter* ALGERNON, *very gay and debonair.*] He does!

ALGERNON: [*Raising his hat.*] You are my little cousin Cecily, I'm sure.

CECILY: You are under some strange mistake. I am not little. In fact, I believe I am more than usually tall for my age. [ALGERNON *is rather taken aback.*] But I am your cousin Cecily. You, I see from your card, are Uncle Jack's brother, my cousin Ernest, my wicked cousin Ernest.

8. A nymph in classical mythology, famous as the wise counselor of Numa Pompilius, the second of the legendary kings of Rome. 9. Evening church services. 1. I.e., book about economies. The rupee is the currency unit of India.

ALGERNON: Oh! I am not really wicked at all, cousin Cecily. You mustn't think that I am wicked.

CECILY: If you are not, then you have certainly been deceiving us all in a very inexcusable manner. I hope you have not been leading a double life, pretending to be wicked and being really good all the time. That would be hypocrisy.

ALGERNON: [*Looks at her in amazement.*] Oh! Of course I have been rather reckless.

CECILY: I am glad to hear it.

ALGERNON: In fact, now you mention the subject, I have been very bad in my own small way.

CECILY: I don't think you should be so proud of that, though I am sure it must have been very pleasant.

ALGERNON: It is much pleasanter being here with you.

CECILY: I can't understand how you are here at all. Uncle Jack won't be back till Monday afternoon.

ALGERNON: That is a great disappointment. I am obliged to go up by the first train on Monday morning. I have a business appointment that I am anxious . . . to miss.

CECILY: Couldn't you miss it anywhere but in London?

ALGERNON: No: the appointment is in London.

CECILY: Well, I know, of course, how important it is not to keep a business engagement, if one wants to retain any sense of the beauty of life, but still I think you had better wait till Uncle Jack arrives. I know he wants to speak to you about your emigrating.

ALGERNON: About my what?

CECILY: Your emigrating. He has gone up to buy your outfit.

ALGERNON: I certainly wouldn't let Jack buy my outfit. He has no taste in neckties at all.

CECILY: I don't think you will require neckties. Uncle Jack is sending you to Australia.

ALGERNON: Australia? I'd sooner die.

CECILY: Well, he said at dinner on Wednesday night, that you would have to choose between this world, the next world, and Australia.

ALGERNON: Oh, well! The accounts I have received of Australia and the next world are not particularly encouraging. This world is good enough for me, cousin Cecily.

CECILY: Yes, but are you good enough for it?

ALGERNON: I'm afraid I'm not that. That is why I want you to reform me. You might make that your mission, if you don't mind, cousin Cecily.

CECILY: I'm afraid I've no time, this afternoon.

ALGERNON: Well, would you mind my reforming myself this afternoon?

CECILY: It is rather Quixotic of you. But I think you should try.

ALGERNON: I will. I feel better already.

CECILY: You are looking a little worse.

ALGERNON: That is because I am hungry.

CECILY: How thoughtless of me. I should have remembered that when one is going to lead an entirely new life, one requires regular and wholesome meals. Won't you come in?

ALGERNON: Thank you. Might I have a buttonhole[2] first? I never have any appetite unless I have a buttonhole first.

CECILY: A Maréchal Niel? [*Picks up scissors.*]

ALGERNON: No, I'd sooner have a pink rose.

CECILY: Why? [*Cuts a flower.*]

ALGERNON: Because you are like a pink rose, cousin Cecily.

CECILY: I don't think it can be right for you to talk to me like that. Miss Prism never says such things to me.

ALGERNON: Then Miss Prism is a shortsighted old lady. [CECILY *puts the rose in his buttonhole.*] You are the prettiest girl I ever saw.

CECILY: Miss Prism says that all good looks are a snare.

ALGERNON: They are a snare that every sensible man would like to be caught in.

CECILY: Oh! I don't think I would care to catch a sensible man. I shouldn't know what to talk to him about.

[*They pass into the house.* MISS PRISM *and* DR. CHASUBLE *return.*]

MISS PRISM: You are too much alone, dear Dr. Chasuble. You should get married. A misanthrope I can understand—a womanthrope, never!

CHASUBLE: [*With a scholar's shudder.*] Believe me, I do not deserve so neologistic a phrase. The precept as well as the practice of the Primitive Church was distinctly against matrimony.

MISS PRISM: [*Sententiously.*] That is obviously the reason why the Primitive Church has not lasted up to the present day. And you do not seem to realize, dear Doctor, that by persistently remaining single, a man converts himself into a permanent public temptation. Men should be more careful; this very celibacy leads weaker vessels astray.

CHASUBLE: But is a man not equally attractive when married?

MISS PRISM: No married man is ever attractive except to his wife.

CHASUBLE: And often, I've been told, not even to her.

MISS PRISM: That depends on the intellectual sympathies of the woman. Maturity can always be depended on. Ripeness can be trusted. Young women are green. [DR. CHASUBLE *starts.*] I spoke horticulturally. My metaphor was drawn from fruits. But where is Cecily?

CHASUBLE: Perhaps she followed us to the schools.

[*Enter* JACK *slowly from the back of the garden. He is dressed in the deepest mourning, with crape hat-band and black gloves.*]

MISS PRISM: Mr. Worthing!

CHASUBLE: Mr. Worthing?

2. A "buttonhole" is a flower to be worn on the lapel of a man's coat, in this case the Maréchal Niel, a popular yellow rose of the period.

MISS PRISM: This is indeed a surprise. We did not look for you till Monday afternoon.

JACK: [*Shakes* MISS PRISM*'s hand in a tragic manner.*] I have returned sooner than I expected. Dr. Chasuble, I hope you are well?

CHASUBLE: Dear Mr. Worthing, I trust this garb of woe does not betoken some terrible calamity?

JACK: My brother.

MISS PRISM: More shameful debts and extravagance?

CHASUBLE: Still leading his life of pleasure?

JACK: [*Shaking his head.*] Dead!

CHASUBLE: Your brother Ernest dead?

JACK: Quite dead.

MISS PRISM: What a lesson for him! I trust he will profit by it.

CHASUBLE: Mr. Worthing, I offer you my sincere condolence. You have at least the consolation of knowing that you were always the most generous and forgiving of brothers.

JACK: Poor Ernest! He had many faults, but it is a sad, sad blow.

CHASUBLE: Very sad indeed. Were you with him at the end?

JACK: No. He died abroad; in Paris, in fact. I had a telegram last night from the manager of the Grand Hotel.

CHASUBLE: Was the cause of death mentioned?

JACK: A severe chill, it seems.

MISS PRISM: As a man sows, so shall he reap.

CHASUBLE: [*Raising his hand.*] Charity, dear Miss Prism, charity! None of us are perfect. I myself am peculiarly susceptible to drafts. Will the interment take place here?

JACK: No. He seemed to have expressed a desire to be buried in Paris.

CHASUBLE: In Paris! [*Shakes his head.*] I fear that hardly points to any very serious state of mind at the last. You would no doubt wish me to make some slight allusion to this tragic domestic affliction next Sunday. [JACK *presses his hand convulsively.*] My sermon on the meaning of the manna in the wilderness can be adapted to almost any occasion, joyful, or, as in the present case, distressing. [*All sigh.*] I have preached it at harvest celebrations, christenings, confirmations, on days of humiliation and festal days. The last time I delivered it was in the Cathedral, as a charity sermon on behalf of the Society for the Prevention of Discontent among the Upper Orders. The Bishop, who was present, was much struck by some of the analogies I drew.

JACK: Ah! That reminds me, you mentioned christenings, I think, Dr. Chasuble? I suppose you know how to christen all right? [DR. CHASUBLE *looks astounded.*] I mean, of course, you are continually christening, aren't you?

MISS PRISM: It is, I regret to say, one of the Rector's most constant duties in this parish. I have often spoken to the poorer classes on the subject. But they don't seem to know what thrift is.

CHASUBLE: But is there any particular infant in whom you are interested, Mr. Worthing? Your brother was, I believe, unmarried, was he not?

JACK: Oh yes.

MISS PRISM: [*Bitterly.*] People who live entirely for pleasure usually are.

JACK: But it is not for any child, dear Doctor. I am very fond of children. No! the fact is, I would like to be christened myself, this afternoon, if you have nothing better to do.

CHASUBLE: But surely, Mr. Worthing, you have been christened already?

JACK: I don't remember anything about it.

CHASUBLE: But have you any grave doubts on the subject?

JACK: I certainly intend to have. Of course I don't know if the thing would bother you in any way, or if you think I am a little too old now.

CHASUBLE: Not at all. The sprinkling, and, indeed, the immersion of adults is a perfectly canonical practice.

JACK: Immersion!

CHASUBLE: You need have no apprehensions. Sprinkling is all that is necessary, or indeed I think advisable. Our weather is so changeable. At what hour would you wish the ceremony performed?

JACK: Oh, I might trot round about five if that would suit you.

CHASUBLE: Perfectly, perfectly! In fact I have two similar ceremonies to perform at that time. A case of twins that occurred recently in one of the outlying cottages on your own estate. Poor Jenkins the carter, a most hard-working man.

JACK: Oh! I don't see much fun in being christened along with other babies. It would be childish. Would half-past five do?

CHASUBLE: Admirably! Admirably! [*Takes out watch.*] And now, dear Mr. Worthing, I will not intrude any longer into a house of sorrow. I would merely beg you not to be too much bowed down by grief. What seem to us bitter trials are often blessings in disguise.

MISS PRISM: This seems to me a blessing of an extremely obvious kind.

[*Enter* CECILY *from the house.*]

CECILY: Uncle Jack! Oh, I am pleased to see you back. But what horrid clothes you have got on! Do go and change them.

MISS PRISM: Cecily!

CHASUBLE: My child! my child!

[CECILY *goes towards* JACK; *he kisses her brow in a melancholy manner.*]

CECILY: What is the matter, Uncle Jack? Do look happy! You look as if you had toothache, and I have got such a surprise for you. Who do you think is in the dining room? Your brother!

JACK: Who?

CECILY: Your brother Ernest. He arrived about half an hour ago.

JACK: What nonsense! I haven't got a brother!

CECILY: Oh, don't say that. However badly he may have behaved to you in the past he is still your brother. You couldn't be so heartless as to disown him. I'll tell him to come out. And you will shake hands with him, won't you, Uncle Jack? [*Runs back into the house.*]

CHASUBLE: These are very joyful tidings.

MISS PRISM: After we had all been resigned to his loss, his sudden return seems to me peculiarly distressing.

JACK: My brother is in the dining room? I don't know what it all means. I think it is perfectly absurd. [*Enter* ALGERNON *and* CECILY *hand in hand. They come slowly up to* JACK.] Good heavens! [*Motions* ALGERNON *away.*]

ALGERNON: Brother John, I have come down from town to tell you that I am very sorry for all the trouble I have given you, and that I intend to lead a better life in the future. [JACK *glares at him and does not take his hand.*]

CECILY: Uncle Jack, you are not going to refuse your own brother's hand?

JACK: Nothing will induce me to take his hand. I think his coming down here disgraceful. He knows perfectly well why.

CECILY: Uncle Jack, do be nice. There is some good in everyone. Ernest has just been telling me about his poor invalid friend Mr. Bunbury whom he goes to visit so often. And surely there must be much good in one who is kind to an invalid, and leaves the pleasures of London to sit by a bed of pain.

JACK: Oh! he has been talking about Bunbury, has he?

CECILY: Yes, he has told me all about poor Mr. Bunbury, and his terrible state of health.

JACK: Bunbury! Well, I won't have him talk to you about Bunbury or about anything else. It is enough to drive one perfectly frantic.

ALGERNON: Of course I admit that the faults were all on my side. But I must say that I think that Brother John's coldness to me is peculiarly painful. I expected a more enthusiastic welcome, especially considering it is the first time I have come here.

CECILY: Uncle Jack, if you don't shake hands with Ernest, I will never forgive you.

JACK: Never forgive me?

CECILY: Never, never, never!

JACK: Well, this is the last time I shall ever do it. [*Shakes hands with* ALGERNON *and glares.*]

CHASUBLE: It's pleasant, is it not, to see so perfect a reconciliation? I think we might leave the two brothers together.

MISS PRISM: Cecily, you will come with us.

CECILY: Certainly, Miss Prism. My little task of reconciliation is over.

CHASUBLE: You have done a beautiful action today, dear child.

MISS PRISM: We must not be premature in our judgments.

CECILY: I feel very happy.

[*They all go off.*]

JACK: You young scoundrel, Algy, you must get out of this place as soon as possible. I don't allow any Bunburying here.

[*Enter* MERRIMAN.]

MERRIMAN: I have put Mr. Ernest's things in the room next to yours, sir. I suppose that is all right?

JACK: What?

MERRIMAN: Mr. Ernest's luggage, sir. I have unpacked it and put it in the room next to your own.

JACK: His luggage?

MERRIMAN: Yes, sir. Three portmanteaus, a dressing case, two hat-boxes, and a large luncheon basket.

ALGERNON: I am afraid I can't stay more than a week this time.

JACK: Merriman, order the dogcart[3] at once. Mr. Ernest has been suddenly called back to town.

MERRIMAN: Yes, sir. [*Goes back into the house.*]

ALGERNON: What a fearful liar you are, Jack. I have not been called back to town at all.

JACK: Yes, you have.

ALGERNON: I haven't heard anyone call me.

JACK: Your duty as a gentleman calls you back.

ALGERNON: My duty as a gentleman has never interfered with my pleasures in the smallest degree.

JACK: I can quite understand that.

ALGERNON: Well, Cecily is a darling.

JACK: You are not to talk of Miss Cardew like that. I don't like it.

ALGERNON: Well, I don't like your clothes. You look perfectly ridiculous in them. Why on earth don't you go up and change? It is perfectly childish to be in deep mourning for a man who is actually staying for a whole week with you in your house as a guest. I call it grotesque.

JACK: You are certainly not staying with me for a whole week as a guest or anything else. You have got to leave . . . by the four-five train.

ALGERNON: I certainly won't leave you so long as you are in mourning. It would be most unfriendly. If I were in mourning you would stay with me, I suppose. I should think it very unkind if you didn't.

JACK: Well, will you go if I change my clothes?

ALGERNON: Yes, if you are not too long. I never saw anybody take so long to dress, and with such little result.

JACK: Well, at any rate, that is better than being always overdressed as you are.

ALGERNON: If I am occasionally a little overdressed, I make up for it by being always immensely overeducated.

JACK: Your vanity is ridiculous, your conduct an outrage, and your presence in my garden utterly absurd. However, you have got to catch the four-five, and I hope you will have a pleasant journey back to town. This Bunburying, as you call it, has not been a great success for you. [*Goes into the house.*]

ALGERNON: I think it has been a great success. I'm in love with Cecily, and that is everything. [*Enter* CECILY *at the back of the garden. She picks up the can and begins to water the flowers.*] But I must see her before I go, and make arrangements for another Bunbury. Ah, there she is.

3. A light, two-wheeled carriage, usually drawn by one horse; it has two transverse seats positioned back to back.

CECILY: Oh, I merely came back to water the roses. I thought you were with Uncle Jack.

ALGERNON: He's gone to order the dogcart for me.

CECILY: Oh, is he going to take you for a nice drive?

ALGERNON: He's going to send me away.

CECILY: Then have we got to part?

ALGERNON: I am afraid so. It's very painful parting.

CECILY: It is always painful to part from people whom one has known for a very brief space of time. The absence of old friends one can endure with equanimity. But even a momentary separation from anyone to whom one has just been introduced is almost unbearable.

ALGERNON: Thank you.

[*Enter* MERRIMAN.]

MERRIMAN: The dogcart is at the door, sir. [ALGERNON *looks appealingly at* CECILY.]

CECILY: It can wait, Merriman . . . for . . . five minutes.

MERRIMAN: Yes, Miss. [*Exit* MERRIMAN.]

ALGERNON: I hope, Cecily, I shall not offend you if I state quite frankly and openly that you seem to me to be in every way the visible personification of absolute perfection.

CECILY: I think your frankness does you great credit, Ernest. If you will allow me I will copy your remarks into my diary. [*Goes over to table and begins writing in diary.*]

ALGERNON: Do you really keep a diary? I'd give anything to look at it. May I?

CECILY: Oh no. [*Puts her hand over it.*] You see, it is simply a very young girl's record of her own thoughts and impressions, and consequently meant for publication. When it appears in volume form I hope you will order a copy. But pray, Ernest, don't stop. I delight in taking down from dictation. I have reached "absolute perfection." You can go on. I am quite ready for more.

ALGERNON: [*Somewhat taken aback.*] Ahem! Ahem!

CECILY: Oh, don't cough, Ernest. When one is dictating one should speak fluently and not cough. Besides, I don't know how to spell a cough. [*Writes as* ALGERNON *speaks.*]

ALGERNON: [*Speaking very rapidly.*] Cecily, ever since I first looked upon your wonderful and incomparable beauty, I have dared to love you wildly, passionately, devotedly, hopelessly.

CECILY: I don't think that you should tell me that you love me wildly, passionately, devotedly, hopelessly. Hopelessly doesn't seem to make much sense, does it?

ALGERNON: Cecily!

[*Enter* MERRIMAN.]

MERRIMAN: The dogcart is waiting, sir.

ALGERNON: Tell it to come round next week, at the same hour.

MERRIMAN: [*Looks at* CECILY, *who makes no sign.*] Yes, sir. [MERRIMAN *retires.*]

CECILY: Uncle Jack would be very much annoyed if he knew you were staying on till next week, at the same hour.

ALGERNON: Oh, I don't care about Jack. I don't care for anybody in the whole world but you. I love you, Cecily. You will marry me, won't you?

CECILY: You silly boy! Of course. Why, we have been engaged for the last three months.

ALGERNON: For the last three months?

CECILY: Yes, it will be exactly three months on Thursday.

ALGERNON: But how did we become engaged?

CECILY: Well, ever since dear Uncle Jack first confessed to us that he had a younger brother who was very wicked and bad, you of course have formed the chief topic of conversation between myself and Miss Prism. And of course a man who is much talked about is always very attractive. One feels there must be something in him after all. I daresay it was foolish of me, but I fell in love with you, Ernest.

ALGERNON: Darling! And when was the engagement actually settled?

CECILY: On the 14th of February last. Worn out by your entire ignorance of my existence, I determined to end the matter one way or the other, and after a long struggle with myself I accepted you under this dear old tree here. The next day I bought this little ring in your name, and this is the little bangle with the true lovers' knot I promised you always to wear.

ALGERNON: Did I give you this? It's very pretty, isn't it?

CECILY: Yes, you've wonderfully good taste, Ernest. It's the excuse I've always given for your leading such a bad life. And this is the box in which I keep all your dear letters. [*Kneels at table, opens box, and produces letters tied up with blue ribbon.*]

ALGERNON: My letters! But my own sweet Cecily, I have never written you any letters.

CECILY: You need hardly remind me of that, Ernest. I remember only too well that I was forced to write your letters for you. I always wrote three times a week, and sometimes oftener.

ALGERNON: Oh, do let me read them, Cecily?

CECILY: Oh, I couldn't possibly. They would make you far too conceited. [*Replaces box.*] The three you wrote me after I had broken off the engagement are so beautiful, and so badly spelled, that even now I can hardly read them without crying a little.

ALGERNON: But was our engagement ever broken off?

CECILY: Of course it was. On the 22nd of last March. You can see the entry if you like [*Shows diary.*] "Today I broke off my engagement with Ernest. I feel it is better to do so. The weather still continues charming."

ALGERNON: But why on earth did you break if off? What had I done? I had done nothing at all. Cecily, I am very much hurt indeed to hear you broke it off. Particularly when the weather was so charming.

CECILY: It would hardly have been a really serious engagement if it hadn't been broken off at least once. But I forgave you before the week was out.

ALGERNON: [*Crossing to her, and kneeling.*] What a perfect angel you are, Cecily.

CECILY: You dear romantic boy. [*He kisses her, she puts her fingers through his hair.*] I hope your hair curls naturally, does it?

ALGERNON: Yes, darling, with a little help from others.

CECILY: I am so glad.

ALGERNON: You'll never break off our engagement again, Cecily?

CECILY: I don't think I could break it off now that I have actually met you. Besides, of course, there is the question of your name.

ALGERNON: Yes, of course. [*Nervously.*]

CECILY: You must not laugh at me, darling, but it had always been a girlish dream of mine to love someone whose name was Ernest. [ALGERNON *rises,* CECILY *also.*] There is something in that name that seems to inspire absolute confidence. I pity any poor married woman whose husband is not called Ernest.

ALGERNON: But, my dear child, do you mean to say you could not love me if I had some other name?

CECILY: But what name?

ALGERNON: Oh, any name you like—Algernon—for instance . . .

CECILY: But I don't like the name of Algernon.

ALGERNON: Well, my own dear, sweet, loving little darling, I really can't see why you should object to the name of Algernon. It is not at all a bad name. In fact, it is rather an aristocratic name. Half of the chaps who get into the Bankruptcy Court are called Algernon. But seriously, Cecily . . . [*Moving to her.*] . . . if my name was Algy, couldn't you love me?

CECILY: [*Rising.*] I might respect you, Ernest, I might admire your character, but I fear that I should not be able to give you my undivided attention.

ALGERNON: Ahem! Cecily! [*Picking up hat.*] Your Rector here is, I suppose, thoroughly experienced in the practice of all the rites and ceremonials of the Church?

CECILY: Oh, yes. Dr. Chasuble is a most learned man. He has never written a single book, so you can imagine how much he knows.

ALGERNON: I must see him at once on a most important christening—I mean on most important business.

CECILY: Oh!

ALGERNON: I shan't be away more than half an hour.

CECILY: Considering that we have been engaged since February the 14th, and that I only met you today for the first time, I think it is rather hard that you should leave me for so long a period as half an hour. Couldn't you make it twenty minutes?

ALGERNON: I'll be back in no time. [*Kisses her and rushes down the garden.*]

CECILY: What an impetuous boy he is! I like his hair so much. I must enter his proposal in my diary.

[*Enter* MERRIMAN.]

MERRIMAN: A Miss Fairfax has just called to see Mr. Worthing. On very important business, Miss Fairfax states.

CECILY: Isn't Mr. Worthing in his library?

MERRIMAN: Mr. Worthing went over in the direction of the Rectory some time ago.

CECILY: Pray ask the lady to come out here; Mr. Worthing is sure to be back soon. And you can bring tea.

MERRIMAN: Yes, Miss. [*Goes out.*]

CECILY: Miss Fairfax! I suppose one of the many good elderly women who are associated with Uncle Jack in some of his philanthropic work in London. I don't quite like women who are interested in philanthropic work. I think it is so forward of them.

[*Enter* MERRIMAN.]

MERRIMAN: Miss Fairfax.

[*Enter* GWENDOLEN. *Exit* MERRIMAN.]

CECILY: [*Advancing to meet her.*] Pray let me introduce myself to you. My name is Cecily Cardew.

GWENDOLEN: Cecily Cardew? [*Moving to her and shaking hands.*] What a very sweet name! Something tells me that we are going to be great friends. I like you already more than I can say. My first impressions of people are never wrong.

CECILY: How nice of you to like me so much after we have known each other such a comparatively short time. Pray sit down.

GWENDOLEN: [*Still standing up.*] I may call you Cecily, may I not?

CECILY: With pleasure!

GWENDOLEN: And you will always call me Gwendolen, won't you?

CECILY: If you wish.

GWENDOLEN: Then that is all quite settled, is it not?

CECILY: I hope so. [*A pause. They both sit down together.*]

GWENDOLEN: Perhaps this might be a favorable opportunity for my mentioning who I am. My father is Lord Bracknell. You have never heard of papa, I suppose?

CECILY: I don't think so.

GWENDOLEN: Outside the family circle, papa, I am glad to say, is entirely unknown. I think that is quite as it should be. The home seems to me to be the proper sphere for the man. And certainly once a man begins to neglect his domestic duties he becomes painfully effeminate, does he not? And I don't like that. It makes men so very attractive. Cecily, mamma, whose views on education are remarkably strict, has brought me up to be extremely shortsighted; it is part of her system; so do you mind my looking at you through my glasses?

CECILY: Oh! not at all, Gwendolen. I am very fond of being looked at.

GWENDOLEN: [*After examining* CECILY *carefully through a lorgnette.*] You are here on a short visit, I suppose.

CECILY: Oh no! I live here.

GWENDOLEN: [*Severely.*] Really? Your mother, no doubt, or some female relative of advanced years, resides here also?

CECILY: Oh no! I have no mother, nor, in fact, any relations.

GWENDOLEN: Indeed?

CECILY: My dear guardian, with the assistance of Miss Prism, has the arduous task of looking after me.

GWENDOLEN: Your guardian?

CECILY: Yes, I am Mr. Worthing's ward.

GWENDOLEN: Oh! It is strange he never mentioned to me that he had a ward. How secretive of him! He grows more interesting hourly. I am not sure, however, that the news inspires me with feelings of unmixed delight. [*Rising and going to her.*] I am very fond of you, Cecily; I have liked you ever since I met you! But I am bound to state that now that I know that you are Mr. Worthing's ward, I cannot help expressing a wish you were—well just a little older than you seem to be—and not quite so very alluring in appearance. In fact, if I may speak candidly——

CECILY: Pray do! I think that whenever one has anything unpleasant to say, one should always be quite candid.

GWENDOLEN: Well, to speak with perfect candor, Cecily, I wish that you were fully forty-two, and more than usually plain for your age. Ernest has a strong upright nature. He is the very soul of truth and honor. Disloyalty would be as impossible to him as deception. But even men of the noblest possible moral character are extremely susceptible to the influence of the physical charms of others. Modern, no less than Ancient History, supplies us with many most painful examples of what I refer to. If it were not so, indeed, History would be quite unreadable.

CECILY: I beg your pardon, Gwendolen, did you say Ernest?

GWENDOLEN: Yes.

CECILY: Oh, but it is not Mr. Ernest Worthing who is my guardian. It is his brother—his elder brother.

GWENDOLEN: [*Sitting down again.*] Ernest never mentioned to me that he had a brother.

CECILY: I am sorry to say they have not been on good terms for a long time.

GWENDOLEN: Ah! that accounts for it. And now that I think of it I have never heard any man mention his brother. The subject seems distasteful to most men. Cecily, you have lifted a load from my mind. I was growing almost anxious. It would have been terrible if any cloud had come across a friendship like ours, would it not? Of course you are quite, quite sure that it is not Mr. Ernest Worthing who is your guardian?

CECILY: Quite sure. [*A pause.*] In fact, I am going to be his.

GWENDOLEN: [*Inquiringly.*] I beg your pardon?

CECILY: [*Rather shy and confidingly.*] Dearest Gwendolen, there is no reason why I should make a secret of it to you. Our little county newspaper is sure to chronicle the fact next week. Mr. Ernest Worthing and I are engaged to be married.

GWENDOLEN: [*Quite politely, rising.*] My darling Cecily, I think there must be some slight error. Mr. Ernest Worthing is engaged to me. The announcement will appear in the *Morning Post* on Saturday at the latest.

CECILY: [*Very politely, rising.*] I am afraid you must be under some misconception. Ernest proposed to me exactly ten minutes ago. [*Shows diary.*]

GWENDOLEN: [*Examines diary through her lorgnette carefully.*] It is certainly very curious, for he asked me to be his wife yesterday afternoon at 5:30. If you would care to verify the incident, pray do so. [*Produces diary of her own.*] I never travel without my diary. One should always have something sensational to read in the train. I am so sorry, dear Cecily, if it is any disappointment to you, but I am afraid *I* have the prior claim.

CECILY: It would distress me more than I can tell you, dear Gwendolen, if it caused you any mental or physical anguish, but I feel bound to point out that since Ernest proposed to you he clearly has changed his mind.

GWENDOLEN: [*Meditatively.*] If the poor fellow has been entrapped into any foolish promise I shall consider it my duty to rescue him at once, and with a firm hand.

CECILY: [*Thoughtfully and sadly.*] Whatever unfortunate entanglement my dear boy may have got into, I will never reproach him with it after we are married.

GWENDOLEN: Do you allude to me, Miss Cardew, as an entanglement? You are presumptuous. On an occasion of this kind it becomes more than a moral duty to speak one's mind. It becomes a pleasure.

CECILY: Do you suggest, Miss Fairfax, that I entrapped Ernest into an engagement? How dare you? This is no time for wearing the shallow mask of manners. When I see a spade I call it a spade.

GWENDOLEN: [*Satirically.*] I am glad to say that I have never seen a spade. It is obvious that our social spheres have been widely different.

[*Enter* MERRIMAN, *followed by the footman. He carries a salver, tablecloth, and plate stand.* CECILY *is about to retort. The presence of the servants exercises a restraining influence, under which both girls chafe.*]

MERRIMAN: Shall I lay tea here as usual, Miss?

CECILY: [*Sternly, in a calm voice.*] Yes, as usual.

[MERRIMAN *begins to clear table and lay cloth. A long pause.* CECILY *and* GWENDOLEN *glare at each other.*]

GWENDOLEN: Are there many interesting walks in the vicinity, Miss Cardew?

CECILY: Oh! yes! a great many. From the top of one of the hills quite close one can see five counties.

GWENDOLEN: Five counties! I don't think I should like that. I hate crowds.

CECILY: [*Sweetly.*] I suppose that is why you live in town?

[GWENDOLEN *bites her lip, and beats her foot nervously with her parasol.*]

GWENDOLEN: [*Looking round.*] Quite a well-kept garden this is, Miss Cardew.

CECILY: So glad you like it, Miss Fairfax.

GWENDOLEN: I had no idea there were any flowers in the country.

CECILY: Oh, flowers are as common here, Miss Fairfax, as people are in London.

GWENDOLEN: Personally I cannot understand how anybody manages to exist in the country, if anybody who is anybody does. The country always bores me to death.

CECILY: Ah! This is what the newspapers call agricultural depression, is it not? I believe the aristocracy are suffering very much from it just at present. It is almost an epidemic amongst them, I have been told. May I offer you some tea, Miss Fairfax?

GWENDOLEN: [*With elaborate politeness.*] Thank you. [*Aside.*] Detestable girl! But I require tea!

CECILY: [*Sweetly.*] Sugar?

GWENDOLEN: [*Superciliously.*] No, thank you. Sugar is not fashionable any more.

[CECILY *looks angrily at her, takes up the tongs and puts four lumps of sugar into the cup.*]

CECILY: [*Severely.*] Cake or bread and butter?

GWENDOLEN: [*In a bored manner.*] Bread and butter, please. Cake is rarely seen at the best houses nowadays.

CECILY. [*Cuts a very large slice of cake, and puts it on the tray.*] Hand that to Miss Fairfax.

[MERRIMAN *does so, and goes out with footman.* GWENDOLEN *drinks the tea and makes a grimace. Puts down cup at once, reaches out her hand to the bread and butter, looks at it, and finds it is cake. Rises in indignation.*]

GWENDOLEN: You have filled my tea with lumps of sugar, and though I asked most distinctly for bread and butter, you have given me cake. I am known for the gentleness of my disposition, and the extraordinary sweetness of my nature, but I warn you, Miss Cardew, you may go too far.

CECILY: [*Rising.*] To save my poor, innocent, trusting boy from the machinations of any other girl there are no lengths to which I would not go.

GWENDOLEN: From the moment I saw you I distrusted you. I felt that you were false and deceitful. I am never deceived in such matters. My first impressions of people are invariably right.

CECILY: It seems to me, Miss Fairfax, that I am trespassing on your valuable time. No doubt you have many other calls of a similar character to make in the neighborhood.

[*Enter* JACK.]

GWENDOLEN: [*Catching sight of him.*] Ernest! My own Ernest!

JACK: Gwendolen! Darling! [*Offers to kiss her.*]

GWENDOLEN: [*Drawing back.*] A moment! May I ask if you are engaged to be married to this young lady? [*Points to* CECILY.]

JACK: [*Laughing.*] To dear little Cecily! Of course not! What could have put such an idea into your pretty little head?

GWENDOLEN: Thank you. You may! [*Offers her cheek.*]

CECILY: [*Very sweetly.*] I knew there must be some misunderstanding, Miss Fairfax. The gentleman whose arm is at present round your waist is my dear guardian, Mr. John Worthing.

GWENDOLEN: I beg your pardon?

CECILY: This is Uncle Jack.

GWENDOLEN: [*Receding.*] Jack! Oh!

[*Enter* ALGERNON.]

CECILY: Here is Ernest.

ALGERNON: [*Goes straight over to* CECILY *without noticing anyone else.*] My own love! [*Offers to kiss her.*]

CECILY: [*Drawing back.*] A moment, Ernest! May I ask you—are you engaged to be married to this young lady?

ALGERNON: [*Looking round.*] To what young lady? Good heavens! Gwendolen!

CECILY: Yes! to good heavens, Gwendolen, I mean to Gwendolen.

ALGERNON: [*Laughing.*] Of course not! What could have put such an idea into your pretty little head?

CECILY: Thank you. [*Presenting her cheek to be kissed.*] You may. [ALGERNON *kisses her.*]

GWENDOLEN: I felt there was some slight error, Miss Cardew. The gentleman who is now embracing you is my cousin, Mr. Algernon Moncrieff.

CECILY. [*Breaking away from* ALGERNON.] Algernon Moncrieff! Oh! [*The two girls move towards each other and put their arms round each other's waists as if for protection.*] Are you called Algernon?

ALGERNON: I cannot deny it.

CECILY: Oh!

GWENDOLEN: Is your name really John?

JACK: [*Standing rather proudly.*] I could deny it if I liked, I could deny anything if I liked. But my name certainly is John. It has been John for years.

CECILY: [*To* GWENDOLEN.] A gross deception has been practiced on both of us.

GWENDOLEN: My poor wounded Cecily!

CECILY: My sweet wronged Gwendolen!

GWENDOLEN: [*Slowly and seriously.*] You will call me sister, will you not?

[*They embrace.* JACK *and* ALGERNON *groan and walk up and down.*]

CECILY: [*Rather brightly.*] There is just one question I would like to be allowed to ask my guardian.

GWENDOLEN: An admirable idea! Mr. Worthing, there is just one question I would like to be permitted to put to you. Where is your brother Ernest? We are both engaged to be married to your brother Ernest, so it is a matter of some importance to us to know where your brother Ernest is at present.

JACK: [*Slowly and hesitatingly.*] Gwendolen—Cecily—it is very painful for me to be forced to speak the truth. It is the first time in my life that I have ever been reduced to such a painful position, and I am really quite inexperienced in doing anything of the kind. However I will tell you quite frankly that I have no brother Ernest. I have no brother at all. I never had a brother in my life, and I certainly have not the smallest intention of ever having one in the future.

CECILY: [*Surprised.*] No brother at all?

JACK: [*Cheerily.*] None!

GWENDOLEN: [*Severely.*] Had you never a brother of any kind?

JACK: [*Pleasantly.*] Never. Not even of any kind.

GWENDOLEN: I am afraid it is quite clear, Cecily, that neither of us is engaged to be married to anyone.

CECILY: It is not a very pleasant position for a young girl suddenly to find herself in. Is it?

GWENDOLEN: Let us go into the house. They will hardly venture to come after us there.

CECILY: No, men are so cowardly, aren't they?

[*They retire into the house with scornful looks.*]

JACK: This ghastly state of things is what you call Bunburying, I suppose?

ALGERNON: Yes, and a perfectly wonderful Bunbury it is. The most wonderful Bunbury I have ever had in my life.

JACK: Well, you've no right whatsoever to Bunbury here.

ALGERNON: That is absurd. One has a right to Bunbury anywhere one chooses. Every serious Bunburyist knows that.

JACK: Serious Bunburyist! Good heavens!

ALGERNON: Well, one must be serious about something, if one wants to have any amusement in life. I happen to be serious about Bunburying. What on earth you are serious about I haven't got the remotest idea. About everything, I should fancy. You have such an absolutely trivial nature.

JACK: Well, the only small satisfaction I have in the whole of this wretched business is that your friend Bunbury is quite exploded. You won't be able to run down to the country quite so often as you used to do, dear Algy. And a very good thing too.

ALGERNON: Your brother is a little off-color, isn't he, dear Jack? You won't be able to disappear to London quite so frequently as your wicked custom was. And not a bad thing either.

JACK: As for your conduct towards Miss Cardew, I must say that your taking in a sweet, simple, innocent girl like that is quite inexcusable. To say nothing of the fact that she is my ward.

ALGERNON: I can see no possible defense at all for your deceiving a brilliant, clever, thoroughly experienced young lady like Miss Fairfax. To say nothing of the fact that she is my cousin.

JACK: I wanted to be engaged to Gwendolen, that is all. I love her.

ALGERNON: Well, I simply wanted to be engaged to Cecily. I adore her.

JACK: There is certainly no chance of your marrying Miss Cardew.

ALGERNON: I don't think there is much likelihood, Jack, of you and Miss Fairfax being united.

JACK: Well, that is no business of yours.

ALGERNON: If it was my business, I wouldn't talk about it. [*Begins to eat muffins.*] It is very vulgar to talk about one's business. Only people like stockbrokers do that, and then merely at dinner parties.

JACK: How can you sit there, calmly eating muffins when we are in this horrible trouble, I can't make out. You seem to me to be perfectly heartless.

ALGERNON: Well, I can't eat muffins in an agitated manner. The butter would probably get on my cuffs. One should always eat muffins quite calmly. It is the only way to eat them.

JACK: I say it's perfectly heartless your eating muffins at all, under the circumstances.

ALGERNON: When I am in trouble, eating is the only thing that consoles me. Indeed, when I am in really great trouble, as anyone who knows me intimately will tell you, I refuse everything except food and drink. At the present moment I am eating muffins because I am unhappy. Besides, I am particularly fond of muffins. [*Rising.*]

JACK: [*Rising.*] Well, that is no reason why you should eat them all in that greedy way. [*Takes muffins from* ALGERNON.]

ALGERNON: [*Offering tea cake.*] I wish you would have tea cake instead. I don't like tea cake.

JACK: Good heavens! I suppose a man may eat his own muffins in his own garden.

ALGERNON: But you have just said it was perfectly heartless to eat muffins.

JACK: I said it was perfectly heartless of you, under the circumstances. That is a very different thing.

ALGERNON: That may be. But the muffins are the same. [*He seizes the muffin dish from* JACK.]

JACK: Algy, I wish to goodness you would go.

ALGERNON: You can't possibly ask me to go without having some dinner. It's absurd. I never go without my dinner. No one ever does, except vegetarians and people like that. Besides I have just made arrangements with Dr. Chasuble to be christened at a quarter to six under the name of Ernest.

JACK: My dear fellow, the sooner you give up that nonsense the better. I made arrangements this morning with Dr. Chasuble to be christened myself at 5:30, and I naturally will take the name of Ernest. Gwendolen would wish it. We can't both be christened Ernest. It's absurd. Besides, I have a perfect right to be christened if I like. There is no evidence at all that I ever have been christened by anybody. I should think it extremely probable I never was, and so does Dr. Chasuble. It is entirely different in your case. You have been christened already.

ALGERNON: Yes, but I have not been christened for years.

JACK: Yes, but you have been christened. That is the important thing.

ALGERNON: Quite so. So I know my constitution can stand it. If you are not quite sure about your ever having been christened, I must say I think it rather dangerous your venturing on it now. It might make you very unwell. You can hardly have forgotten that someone very closely connected with you was very nearly carried off this week in Paris by a severe chill.

JACK: Yes, but you said yourself that a severe chill was not hereditary.

ALGERNON: It usen't to be, I know—but I daresay it is now. Science is always making wonderful improvements in things.

JACK: [*Picking up the muffin dish.*] Oh, that is nonsense; you are always talking nonsense.

ALGERNON: Jack, you are at the muffins again! I wish you wouldn't. There are only two left. [*Takes them.*] I told you I was particularly fond of muffins.

JACK: But I hate tea cake.

ALGERNON: Why on earth then do you allow tea cake to be served up for your guests? What ideas you have of hospitality!

JACK: Algernon! I have already told you to go. I don't want you here. Why don't you go!

ALGERNON: I haven't quite finished my tea yet! and there is still one muffin left.

[JACK *groans, and sinks into a chair.* ALGERNON *still continues eating.*]

ACT-DROP

ACT III

SCENE: *Morning room at the Manor House.*

[GWENDOLEN *and* CECILY *are at the window, looking out into the garden.*]

GWENDOLEN: The fact that they did not follow us at once into the house, as anyone else would have done, seems to me to show that they have some sense of shame left.

CECILY: They have been eating muffins. That looks like repentance.

GWENDOLEN: [*After a pause.*] They don't seem to notice us at all. Couldn't you cough?

CECILY: But I haven't got a cough.

GWENDOLEN: They're looking at us. What effrontery!

CECILY: They're approaching. That's very forward of them.

GWENDOLEN: Let us preserve a dignified silence.

CECILY: Certainly. It's the only thing to do now.

[*Enter* JACK *followed by* ALGERNON. *They whistle some dreadful popular air from a British Opera.*]

GWENDOLEN: This dignified silence seems to produce an unpleasant effect.

CECILY: A most distasteful one.

GWENDOLEN: But we will not be the first to speak.

CECILY: Certainly not.

GWENDOLEN: Mr. Worthing, I have something very particular to ask you. Much depends on your reply.

CECILY: Gwendolen, your common sense is invaluable. Mr. Moncrieff, kindly answer me the following question. Why did you pretend to be my guardian's brother?

ALGERNON: In order that I might have an opportunity of meeting you.

CECILY: [*To* GWENDOLEN.] That certainly seems a satisfactory explanation, does it not?

GWENDOLEN: Yes, dear, if you can believe him.

CECILY: I don't. But that does not affect the wonderful beauty of his answer.

GWENDOLEN: True. In matters of grave importance, style, not sincerity is the vital thing. Mr. Worthing, what explanation can you offer to me for pretending to have a brother? Was it in order that you might have an opportunity of coming up to town to see me as often as possible?

JACK: Can you doubt it, Miss Fairfax?

GWENDOLEN: I have the gravest doubts upon the subject. But I intend to crush them. This is not the moment for German skepticism.[4] [*Moving to* CECILY.] Their explanations appear to be quite satisfactory, especially Mr. Worthing's. That seems to me to have the stamp of truth upon it.

CECILY: I am more than content with what Mr. Moncrieff said. His voice alone inspires one with absolute credulity.

GWENDOLEN: Then you think we should forgive them?

CECILY: Yes. I mean no.

GWENDOLEN: True! I had forgotten. There are principles at stake that one cannot surrender. Which of us should tell them? The task is not a pleasant one.

CECILY: Could we not both speak at the same time?

GWENDOLEN: An excellent idea! I nearly always speak at the same time as other people. Will you take the time from me?

CECILY: Certainly [GWENDOLEN *beats time with uplifted finger.*]

GWENDOLEN AND CECILY: [*Speaking together.*] Your Christian names are still an insuperable barrier. That is all!

JACK AND ALGERNON: [*Speaking together.*] Our Christian names! Is that all? But we are going to be christened this afternoon.

GWENDOLEN: [*To* JACK.] For my sake you are prepared to do this terrible thing?

JACK: I am.

CECILY: [*To* ALGERNON.] To please me you are ready to face this fearful ordeal?

ALGERNON: I am!

GWENDOLEN: How absurd to talk of the equality of the sexes! Where questions of self-sacrifice are concerned, men are infinitely beyond us.

JACK: We are. [*Clasps hands with* ALGERNON.]

CECILY: They have moments of physical courage of which we women know absolutely nothing.

GWENDOLEN: [*To* JACK.] Darling!

ALGERNON: [*To* CECILY.] Darling. [*They fall into each other's arms.*]

[*Enter* MERRIMAN. *When he enters he coughs loudly, seeing the situation.*]

MERRIMAN: Ahem! Ahem! Lady Bracknell!

JACK: Good heavens!

[*Enter* LADY BRACKNELL. *The couples separate in alarm. Exit* MERRIMAN.]

LADY BRACKNELL: Gwendolen! What does this mean?

GWENDOLEN: Merely that I am engaged to be married to Mr. Worthing, mamma.

LADY BRACKNELL: Come here. Sit down. Sit down immediately. Hesitation of any kind is a sign of mental decay in the young, of physical weakness in the

4. A reference to such philosophical movements as the Materialism of Ludwig Feuerbach (1804–1872) and such theological movements as the "Higher Criticism," a movement which subjected the Bible to the same kind of study as that accorded other books.

old. [*Turns to* JACK.] Apprised, sir, of my daughter's sudden flight by her trusty maid, whose confidence I purchased by means of a small coin, I followed her at once by a luggage train. Her unhappy father is, I am glad to say, under the impression that she is attending a more than usually lengthy lecture by the University Extension Scheme on the Influence of a permanent income on Thought. I do not propose to undeceive him. Indeed I have never undeceived him on any question. I would consider it wrong. But of course, you will clearly understand that all communication between yourself and my daughter must cease immediately from this moment. On this point, as indeed on all points, I am firm.

JACK: I am engaged to be married to Gwendolen, Lady Bracknell!

LADY BRACKNELL: You are nothing of the kind, sir. And now, as regards Algernon! . . . Algernon!

ALGERNON: Yes, Aunt Augusta.

LADY BRACKNELL: May I ask if it is in this house that your invalid friend Mr. Bunbury resides?

ALGERNON: [*Stammering.*] Oh! No! Bunbury doesn't live here. Bunbury is somewhere else at present. In fact, Bunbury is dead.

LADY BRACKNELL: Dead! When did Mr. Bunbury die? His death must have been extremely sudden.

ALGERNON: [*Airily.*] Oh! I killed Bunbury this afternoon. I mean poor Bunbury died this afternoon.

LADY BRACKNELL: What did he die of?

ALGERNON: Bunbury? Oh, he was quite exploded.

LADY BRACKNELL: Exploded! Was he the victim of a revolutionary outrage? I was not aware that Mr. Bunbury was interested in social legislation. If so, he is well punished for his morbidity.

ALGERNON: My dear Aunt Augusta, I mean he was found out! The doctors found out that Bunbury could not live, that is what I mean—so Bunbury died.

LADY BRACKNELL: He seems to have had great confidence in the opinion of his physicians. I am glad, however, that he made up his mind at the last to some definite course of action, and acted under proper medical advice. And now that we have finally got rid of this Mr. Bunbury, may I ask, Mr. Worthing, who is that young person whose hand my nephew Algernon is now holding in what seems to me a peculiarly unnecessary manner?

JACK: That lady is Miss Cecily Cardew, my ward.

[LADY BRACKNELL *bows coldly to* CECILY.]

ALGERNON: I am engaged to be married to Cecily, Aunt Augusta.

LADY BRACKNELL: I beg your pardon?

CECILY: Mr. Moncrieff and I are engaged to be married, Lady Bracknell.

LADY BRACKNELL: [*With a shiver, crossing to the sofa and sitting down.*] I do not know whether there is anything peculiarly exciting in the air of this particular part of Hertfordshire, but the number of engagements that go on seems to me considerably above the proper average that statistics have laid down for our guidance. I think some preliminary inquiry on my part would not be out of place. Mr. Worthing, is Miss Cardew at all connected with any of the larger railway stations in London? I merely desire information. Until yesterday I had no idea that there were any families or persons whose origin was a Terminus.

[JACK *looks perfectly furious, but restrains himself.*]

JACK: [*In a clear, cold voice.*] Miss Cardew is the granddaughter of the late Mr. Thomas Cardew of 149, Belgrave Square, S.W.; Gervase Park, Dorking, Surrey; and the Sporran, Fifeshire, N.B.[5]

LADY BRACKNELL: That sounds not unsatisfactory. Three addresses always inspire confidence, even in tradesmen. But what proof have I of their authenticity?

JACK: I have carefully preserved the Court Guides of the period. They are open to your inspection, Lady Bracknell.

LADY BRACKNELL: [*Grimly.*] I have known strange errors in that publication.

JACK: Miss Cardew's family solicitors are Messrs. Markby, Markby, and Markby.

LADY BRACKNELL: Markby, Markby, and Markby? A firm of the very highest position in their profession. Indeed I am told that one of the Mr. Markbys is occasionally to be seen at dinner parties. So far I am satisfied.

JACK: [*Very irritably.*] How extremely kind of you, Lady Bracknell! I have also in my possession, you will be pleased to hear, certificates of Miss Cardew's birth, baptism, whooping cough, registration, vaccination, confirmation, and the measles; both the German and the English variety.

LADY BRACKNELL: Ah! A life crowded with incident, I see; though perhaps somewhat too exciting for a young girl. I am not myself in favor of premature experiences. [*Rises, looks at her watch.*] Gwendolen! the time approaches for our departure. We have not a moment to lose. As a matter of form, Mr. Worthing, I had better ask you if Miss Cardew has any little fortune?

JACK: Oh! about a hundred and thirty thousand pounds in the Funds.[6] That is all. Good-bye, Lady Bracknell. So pleased to have seen you.

LADY BRACKNELL: [*Sitting down again.*] A moment, Mr. Worthing. A hundred and thirty thousand pounds! And in the Funds! Miss Cardew seems to me a most attractive young lady, now that I look at her. Few girls of the present day have any really solid qualities, any of the qualities that last, and improve with time. We live, I regret to say, in an age of surfaces. [*To* CECILY.] Come over here, dear. [CECILY *goes across.*] Pretty child! your dress is sadly simple, and your hair seems almost as Nature might have left it. But we can soon alter all that. A thoroughly experienced French maid produces a really marvelous result in a very brief space of time. I remember recommending one to young Lady Lancing, and after three months her own husband did not know her.

JACK: [*Aside.*] And after six months nobody knew her.

LADY BRACKNELL: [*Glares at* JACK *for a few moments. Then bends, with a practiced smile, to* CECILY.] Kindly turn round, sweet child. [CECILY *turns completely*

5. In addition to his London residence in Belgrave Square (already referred to in Act 1), Mr. Cardew maintained establishments inthe south of England (Dorking, Surrey) and in Scotland (Fifeshire).
6. Stock of the British National Debt.

round.] No, the side view is what I want. [CECILY *presents her profile.*] Yes, quite as I expected. There are distinct social possibilities in your profile. The two weak points in our age are its want of principle and its want of profile. The chin a little higher, dear. Style largely depends on the way the chin is worn. They are worn very high, just at present. Algernon!

ALGERNON: Yes, Aunt Augusta!

LADY BRACKNELL: There are distinct social possibilities in Miss Cardew's profile.

ALGERNON: Cecily is the sweetest, dearest, prettiest girl in the whole world. And I don't care twopence about social possibilities.

LADY BRACKNELL: Never speak disrespectfully of Society, Algernon. Only people who can't get into it do that. [*To* CECILY.] Dear child, of course you know that Algernon has nothing but his debts to depend upon. But I do not approve of mercenary marriages. When I married Lord Bracknell I had no fortune of any kind. But I never dreamed for a moment of allowing that to stand in my way. Well, I suppose I must give my consent.

ALGERNON: Thank you, Aunt Augusta.

LADY BRACKNELL: Cecily, you may kiss me!

CECILY: [*Kisses her.*] Thank you, Lady Bracknell.

LADY BRACKNELL: You may also address me as Aunt Augusta for the future.

CECILY: Thank you, Aunt Augusta.

LADY BRACKNELL: The marriage, I think, had better take place quite soon.

ALGERNON: Thank you, Aunt Augusta.

CECILY: Thank you, Aunt Augusta.

LADY BRACKNELL: To speak frankly, I am not in favor of long engagements. They give people the opportunity of finding out each other's character before marriage, which I think is never advisable.

JACK: I beg your pardon for interrupting you, Lady Bracknell, but this engagement is quite out of the question. I am Miss Cardew's guardian, and she cannot marry without my consent until she comes of age. That consent I absolutely decline to give.

LADY BRACKNELL: Upon what grounds may I ask? Algernon is an extremely, I may almost say an ostentatiously, eligible young man. He has nothing, but he looks everything. What more can one desire?

JACK: It pains me very much to have to speak frankly to you, Lady Bracknell, about your nephew, but the fact is that I do not approve at all of his moral character. I suspect him of being untruthful.

[ALGERNON *and* CECILY *look at him in indignant amazement.*]

LADY BRACKNELL: Untruthful! My nephew Algernon? Impossible! He is an Oxonian.[7]

JACK: I fear there can be no possible doubt about the matter. This afternoon, during my temporary absence in London on an important question of romance, he obtained admission to my house by means of the false pretense of being my brother. Under an assumed name he drank, I've just been informed by

7. A graduate of Oxford University.

my butler, an entire pint bottle of my Perrier-Jouet, Brut, '89;[8] a wine I was specially reserving for myself. Continuing his disgraceful deception, he succeeded in the course of the afternoon in alienating the affections of my only ward. He subsequently stayed to tea, and devoured every single muffin. And what makes his conduct all the more heartless is, that he was perfectly well aware from the first that I have no brother, that I never had a brother, and that I don't intend to have a brother, not even of any kind. I distinctly told him so myself yesterday afternoon.

LADY BRACKNELL: Ahem! Mr. Worthing, after careful consideration I have decided entirely to overlook my nephew's conduct to you.

JACK: That is very generous of you, Lady Bracknell. My own decision, however, is unalterable. I decline to give my consent.

LADY BRACKNELL: [*To* CECILY.] Come here, sweet child. [CECILY *goes over.*] How old are you, dear?

CECILY: Well, I am really only eighteen, but I always admit to twenty when I go to evening parties.

LADY BRACKNELL: You are perfectly right in making some slight alteration. Indeed, no woman should ever be quite accurate about her age. It looks so calculating. . . . [*In a meditative manner.*] Eighteen, but admitting to twenty at evening parties. Well, it will not be very long before you are of age and free from the restraints of tutelage. So I don't think your guardian's consent is, after all, a matter of any importance.

JACK: Pray excuse me, Lady Bracknell, for interrupting you again, but it is only fair to tell you that according to the terms of her grandfather's will Miss Cardew does not come legally of age till she is thirty-five.

LADY BRACKNELL: That does not seem to me to be a grave objection. Thirty-five is a very attractive age. London society is full of women of the very highest birth who have, of their own free choice, remained thirty-five for years. Lady Dumbleton is an instance in point. To my own knowledge she has been thirty-five ever since she arrived at the age of forty, which was many years ago now. I see no reason why our dear Cecily should not be even still more attractive at the age you mention than she is at present. There will be a large accumulation of property.

CECILY: Algy, could you wait for me till I was thirty-five?

ALGERNON: Of course I could, Cecily. You know I could.

CECILY: Yes, I felt it instinctively, but I couldn't wait all that time. I hate waiting even five minutes for anybody. It always makes me rather cross. I am not punctual myself, I know, but I do like punctuality in others, and waiting, even to be married, is quite out of the question.

ALGERNON: Then what is to be done, Cecily?

CECILY: I don't know, Mr. Moncrieff.

LADY BRACKNELL: My dear Mr. Worthing, as Miss Cardew states positively that she cannot wait till she is thirty-five—a remark which I am bound to say

8. A very fine champagne.

seems to me to show a somewhat impatient nature—I would beg of you to reconsider your decision.

JACK: But my dear Lady Bracknell, the matter is entirely in your own hands. The moment you consent to my marriage with Gwendolen, I will most gladly allow your nephew to form an alliance with my ward.

LADY BRACKNELL: [*Rising and drawing herself up.*] You must be quite aware that what you propose is out of the question.

JACK: Then a passionate celibacy is all that any of us can look forward to.

LADY BRACKNELL: This is not the destiny I propose for Gwendolen. Algernon, of course, can choose for himself. [*Pulls out her watch.*] Come, dear; [GWENDOLEN *rises.*] we have already missed five, if not six, trains. To miss any more might expose us to comment on the platform.

[*Enter* CANON CHASUBLE.]

CHASUBLE: Everything is quite ready for the christenings.

LADY BRACKNELL: The christenings, sir! Is not that somewhat premature!

CHASUBLE: [*Looking rather puzzled, and pointing to* JACK *and* ALGERNON.] Both these gentlemen have expressed a desire for immediate baptism.

LADY BRACKNELL: At their age? The idea is grotesque and irreligious! Algernon, I forbid you to be baptized. I will not hear of such excesses. Lord Bracknell would be highly displeased if he learned that that was the way in which you wasted your time and money.

CHASUBLE: Am I to understand then that there are to be no christenings at all this afternoon?

JACK: I don't think that, as things are now, it would be of much practical value to either of us, Dr. Chasuble.

CHASUBLE: I am grieved to hear such sentiments from you, Mr. Worthing. They savor of the heretical views of the Anabaptists,[9] views that I have completely refuted in four of my unpublished sermons. However, as your present mood seems to be one peculiarly secular, I will return to the church at once. Indeed, I have just been informed by the pew-opener[1] that for the last hour and a half Miss Prism has been waiting for me in the vestry.

LADY BRACKNELL: [*Starting.*] Miss Prism! Did I hear you mention a Miss Prism?

CHASUBLE: Yes, Lady Bracknell. I am on my way to join her.

LADY BRACKNELL: Pray allow me to detain you for a moment. This matter may prove to be one of vital importance to Lord Bracknell and myself. Is this Miss Prism a female of repellent aspect, remotely connected with education?

CHASUBLE: [*Somewhat indignantly.*] She is the most cultivated of ladies, and the very picture of respectability.

9. A 16th-century religious group, most nearly like contemporary Mennonites. Dr. Chasuble, however, is probably using the term loosely to apply to a group more like contemporary Baptists.

1. An usher. Since most pews were completely enclosed, his duties would have included opening the gate that provided entrance for the worshipers. In addition, since most pews were rented for the use of specific persons, he would have been responsible for seeing that worshipers were seated in the correct pews.

LADY BRACKNELL: It is obviously the same person. May I ask what position she holds in your household?

CHASUBLE: [*Severely.*] I am a celibate, madam.

JACK: [*Interposing.*] Miss Prism, Lady Bracknell, has been for the last three years Miss Cardew's esteemed governess and valued companion.

LADY BRACKNELL: In spite of what I hear of her, I must see her at once. Let her be sent for.

CHASUBLE: [*Looking off.*] She approaches; she is nigh.

[*Enter* MISS PRISM *hurriedly.*]

MISS PRISM: I was told you expected me in the vestry, dear Canon. I have been waiting for you there for an hour and three quarters. [*Catches sight of* LADY BRACKNELL *who has fixed her with a stony glare.* MISS PRISM *grows pale and quails. She looks anxiously round as if desirous to escape.*]

LADY BRACKNELL: [*In a severe, judicial voice.*] Prism! [MISS PRISM *bows her head in shame.*] Come here, Prism! [MISS PRISM *approaches in a humble manner.*] Prism! Where is that baby? [*General consternation.* THE CANON *starts back in horror.* ALGERNON *and* JACK *pretend to be anxious to shield* CECILY *and* GWENDOLEN *from hearing the details of a terrible public scandal.*] Twenty-eight years ago, Prism, you left Lord Bracknell's house, Number 104, Upper Grosvenor Street, in charge of a perambulator that contained a baby, of the male sex. You never returned. A few weeks later, through the elaborate investigations of the Metropolitan police, the perambulator was discovered at midnight, standing by itself in a remote corner of Bayswater.[2] It contained the manuscript of a three-volume novel of more than usually revolting sentimentality. [MISS PRISM *starts in involuntary indignation.*] But the baby was not there! [*Everyone looks at* MISS PRISM.] Prism! Where is that baby? [*A pause.*]

MISS PRISM: Lady Bracknell, I admit with shame that I do not know. I only wish I did. The plain facts of the case are these. On the morning of the day you mention, a day that is forever branded on my memory, I prepared as usual to take the baby out in its perambulator. I had also with me a somewhat old, but capacious handbag, in which I had intended to place the manuscript of a work of fiction that I had written during my few unoccupied hours. In a moment of mental abstraction, for which I never can forgive myself, I deposited the manuscript in the bassinette, and placed the baby in the handbag.

JACK: [*Who has been listening attentively.*] But where did you deposit the handbag?

MISS PRISM: Do not ask me, Mr. Worthing.

JACK: Miss Prism, this is a matter of no small importance to me. I insist on knowing where you deposited the handbag that contained that infant.

MISS PRISM: I left it in the cloak room of one of the larger railway stations in London.

JACK: What railway station?

2. A fashionable residential section to the north of Hyde Park and Kensington Gardens.

MISS PRISM: [*Quite crushed.*] Victoria. The Brighton line. [*Sinks into a chair.*]
JACK: I must retire to my room for a moment. Gwendolen, wait here for me.
GWENDOLEN: If you are not too long, I will wait here for you all my life.

[*Exit* JACK *in great excitement.*]

CHASUBLE: What do you think this means, Lady Bracknell?
LADY BRACKNELL: I dare not even suspect, Dr. Chasuble. I need hardly tell you that in families of high position strange coincidences are not supposed to occur. They are hardly considered the thing.

[*Noises heard overhead as if someone was throwing trunks about. Everyone looks up.*]

CECILY: Uncle Jack seems strangely agitated.
CHASUBLE: Your guardian has a very emotional nature.
LADY BRACKNELL: This noise is extremely unpleasant. It sounds as if he was having an argument. I dislike arguments of any kind. They are always vulgar, and often convincing.
CHASUBLE: [*Looking up.*] It has stopped now. [*The noise is redoubled.*]
LADY BRACKNELL: I wish he would arrive at some conclusion.
GWENDOLEN: This suspense is terrible. I hope it will last.

[*Enter* JACK *with a handbag of black leather in his hand.*]

JACK: [*Rushing over to* MISS PRISM.] Is this the handbag, Miss Prism? Examine it carefully before you speak. The happiness of more than one life depends on your answer.
MISS PRISM: [*Calmly.*] It seems to be mine. Yes, here is the injury it received through the upsetting of a Gower Street omnibus in younger and happier days. Here is the stain on the lining caused by the explosion of a temperance beverage, an incident that occurred at Leamington. And here, on the lock, are my initials. I had forgotten that in an extravagant mood I had had them placed there. The bag is undoubtedly mine. I am delighted to have it so unexpectedly restored to me. It has been a great inconvenience being without it all these years.
JACK: [*In a pathetic voice.*] Miss Prism, more is restored to you than this handbag. I was the baby you placed in it.
MISS PRISM: [*Amazed.*] You!
JACK: [*Embracing her.*] Yes . . . mother!
MISS PRISM: [*Recoiling in indignant astonishment.*] Mr. Worthing! I am unmarried!
JACK: Unmarried! I do not deny that is a serious blow. But after all, who has the right to cast a stone against one who has suffered? Cannot repentance wipe out an act of folly? Why should there be one law for men, and another for women? Mother, I forgive you. [*Tries to embrace her again.*]
MISS PRISM: [*Still more indignant.*] Mr. Worthing, there is some error. [*Pointing to* LADY BRACKNELL.] There is the lady who can tell you who you really are.

JACK: [*After a pause.*] Lady Bracknell, I hate to seem inquisitive, but would you kindly inform me who I am?

LADY BRACKNELL: I am afraid that the news I have to give you will not altogether please you. You are the son of my poor sister, Mrs. Moncrieff, and consequently Algernon's elder brother.

JACK: Algy's elder brother! Then I have a brother after all. I knew I had a brother! I always said I had a brother! Cecily—how could you have ever doubted that I had a brother? [*Seizes hold of* ALGERNON.] Dr. Chasuble, my unfortunate brother. Miss Prism, my unfortunate brother. Gwendolen, my unfortunate brother. Algy, you young scoundrel, you will have to treat me with more respect in the future. You have never behaved to me like a brother in all your life.

ALGERNON: Well, not till today, old boy, I admit. I did my best, however, though I was out of practice. [*Shakes hands.*]

GWENDOLEN: [*To* JACK.] My own! But what own are you? What is your Christian name, now that you have become someone else?

JACK: Good heavens! . . . I had quite forgotten that point. Your decision on the subject of my name is irrevocable, I suppose?

GWENDOLEN: I never change, except in my affections.

CECILY: What a noble nature you have, Gwendolen!

JACK: Then the question had better be cleared up at once. Aunt Augusta, a moment. At the time when Miss Prism left me in the handbag, had I been christened already?

LADY BRACKNELL: Every luxury that money could buy, including christening, had been lavished on you by your fond and doting parents.

JACK: Then I was christened! That is settled. Now, what name was I given? Let me know the worst.

LADY BRACKNELL: Being the eldest son you were naturally christened after your father.

JACK: [*Irritably.*] Yes, but what was my father's Christian name?

LADY BRACKNELL: [*Meditatively.*] I cannot at the present moment recall what the General's Christian name was. But I have no doubt he had one. He was eccentric, I admit. But only in later years. And that was the result of the Indian climate, and marriage, and indigestion, and other things of that kind.

JACK: Algy! Can't you recollect what our father's Christian name was?

ALGERNON: My dear boy, we were never even on speaking terms. He died before I was a year old.

JACK: His name would appear in the Army Lists of the period, I suppose, Aunt Augusta?

LADY BRACKNELL: The General was essentially a man of peace, except in his domestic life. But I have no doubt his name would appear in any military directory.

JACK: The Army Lists of the last forty years are here. These delightful records should have been my constant study. [*Rushes to bookcase and tears the books out.*] M. Generals . . . Mallam, Maxbohm, Magley, what ghastly names they have—Markby, Migsby, Mobbs, Moncrieff! Lieutenant 1840, Captain,

Lieutenant Colonel, Colonel, General 1869, Christian names, Ernest John. [*Puts book very quietly down and speaks quite calmly.*] I always told you, Gwendolen, my name was Ernest, didn't I? Well it is Ernest after all. I mean it naturally is Ernest.

LADY BRACKNELL: Yes, I remember now that the General was called Ernest. I knew I had some particular reason for disliking the name.

GWENDOLEN: Ernest! My own Ernest! I felt from the first that you could have no other name!

JACK: Gwendolen, it is a terrible thing for a man to find out suddenly that all his life he has been speaking nothing but the truth. Can you forgive me?

GWENDOLEN: I can. For I feel that you are sure to change.

JACK: My own one!

CHASUBLE: [*To* MISS PRISM.] Laetitia! [*Embraces her.*]

MISS PRISM: [*Enthusiastically.*] Frederick! At last!

ALGERNON: Cecily! [*Embraces her.*] At last!

JACK: Gwendolen! [*Embraces her.*] At last!

LADY BRACKNELL: My nephew, you seem to be displaying signs of triviality.

JACK: On the contrary, Aunt Augusta, I've now realized for the first time in my life the vital Importance of Being Earnest.

CURTAIN

1899

QUESTIONS

Oedipus the King

1. Summarize the story before the play opens. What actually happens in the play itself? What period of time is covered? How important is setting to this play? In what specific ways?

2. How, exactly, does the chorus function in this play? What is the significance of the chorus being made up of Theban citizens? Which opinions of the chorus are most important to the effects of the play?

3. Characterize Tiresias. How much does the play itself actually tell us about Tiresias? What function does he perform in the plot? in the play's structure?

4. In what specific ways is the plot *Oedipus* tragic?

The Importance of Being Earnest

1. What initial obstacles are there to a comic resolution of the romantic plot? How are they resolved? Trace the structure of the resolution, and show

where the various structural parts of the play (exposition, rising action, climax, falling action, and conclusion) occur in the text.

2. Characterize Lady Bracknell. Trace the different ways that the character and her role are made clear. What is her structural role in the play?

3. What characters in the play seem to you simple stereotypes? Exactly how are attitudes toward these characters developed? Which characters rise "above" or go "beyond" stereotypes? What kinds of qualities separate stereotypes from the more complex characters? Which names are especially significant in suggesting the nature of character? Which names are non-characterizing or neutral?

4. Wilde is often praised for his wit and the skill with which he develops conversational repartee. Choose three speeches that seem to you especially witty, and explain in detail exactly how they work, in what their wit consists. What patterns of verbal wit do you notice in the play? How dependent is the tone on language? What human values does the play seem to support/What has the preoccupation of the play with language to do with these values?

WRITING SUGGESTIONS

1. In an essay of about three pages, compare Oedipus at the beginning of the play with Oedipus at the end. Explain the differences in terms of tragic form.

2. Try to recount the events of the play from the point of view of Jocasta. In what sense is the play a tragedy for her? Write a persuasive essay in which you argue that the play is Jocasta's story.

3. What are the more significant and distinctive elements in the character of Oedipus? In what sense is he responsible for his fate? In what sense is he a victim? How heroic is he? Write an essay appraising Oedipus's character and assessing his responsibility for the things that befall him.

The Importance of Being Earnest

1. Recount in as few words as possible the plot of the play. Then retell the story structurally as a "typical" comic plot. On the basis our this retelling, write a short (2-page) essay in which you show how Wilde structures his play along classical comic lines.

2. Choose one character in the play who seems to you not as fully developed as he or she might be. Construct a new scene for the play in which this

character is allowed, through dialogue and action, to reveal him or herself more fully.

3. Defend the use of comic stereotypes in the play in an essay that suggested how the various stereotypical characters help to create the basic comic plot.

6 HISTORICAL SETTING

Time conditions all texts, but a sense of time is particularly important for readers of drama. Events in drama often seem more immediate than in poems or stories, and the demands of time seem more pressing. Immediacy is an important feature of drama, and not only in performance. Reading drama involves a strong sense of presentness as well, for all the action takes place in the present tense regardless of what time period is being represented. Nothing in drama is narrated or recounted: action is all in words and gestures happening right now. And all the action takes place rather fast; novels often take many hours to read, but most plays can easily be read in the time it would take to perform them on stage, two or three hours, even when the action they represent covers several years in time.

But whatever the illusion of presentness, plays often deal with extensive and complicated dislocations in time, and readers of drama are often asked to make sophisticated moves that involve an adjustment to more than the illusion of immediacy. Even though action seems to be taking place as we read, the plot may be set far in the past, and we are often asked as readers to bring to bear specific historical information on the times being represented. Sensitive reading of a play may depend on making some fairly complicated distinctions between different time frames.

Three different levels of time operate in most plays. First, play texts represent some particular time—the temporal setting—in which the action takes place. We can call this **plot time.** Second, texts reflect the time when the author was writing, and the conditions and assumptions of that time find their way into the conception and style of the text. This feature of textual time we may call **authorial time.** Third, readers read a text in a particular time frame of their own, and sometimes conditions and assumptions then are very different from those that obtain in either the text's present or the author's present. We may call this time **reader time.**

These three levels of time often interact importantly in the way we interpret a text. When, for example, we read—as American readers in the 1990s—a play written by Shakespeare in the early seventeenth century about the Danish court of many centuries earlier, we have three time schemes operating at once as we read. We are reading about a time (and place) centuries remote from us, and the text in which these events are represented reflects values, writing conditions, habits of language, and dramatic conventions of a second time—centuries later than the action but still almost four centuries earlier than the time in which we read. Values in these three times are not going to be identical, and how we interpret the actions and thoughts of Hamlet in part depends not only on our own assumptions about what he ought to do or might do, but on what we know about the expectations of human events in two earlier ages. Suspending these three "settings" in our minds as we read—and consciously making comparisons when we perceive conflicts of values—is an important part of interpretation and response. We perceive at one and the same time three different Hamlets—ours (the reader's), Shakespeare's (the text's), and the "historical" Hamlet known to his contemporaries in medieval Denmark. In this particular case, the play does not ask us to know anything very specific about the historical Hamlet; we do not need to know, for example, the history of ancient Elsinore. All we really need to know is that the Danish monarchy passes within families but not necessarily to the eldest son.

Many plays explicitly invoke a particular era as the time of action, and often they specify (in stage directions or interjected comments) information about the era that is relevant to the interpretation of specific episodes. But sometimes we have to supply historical or cultural facts from outside the text, and often we have to adjust our expectations because the "world" of the play—its "present" time in some past age in some specific place—is very different from our own time. People may share some characteristics across ages and cultures, but behavior and motivation are often conditioned by cultural habits and situations, and often we are asked to think carefully about the particulars of a time and place very different from our own. Identifying the setting of a play—in both time and place—and considering carefully its historical situation are often crucial to understanding what happens and why.

The 1957 setting of *Fences*, for example, is very important to the interpretation of Troy Maxon's resistance to his son's participation in sports. Troy is fifty-three at the time the play begins; he had himself been a talented athlete and had played in the Negro League against players like Satchel Paige who had gone on to become well-known stars after major-league baseball finally admitted black players in 1947. Troy often reminisces about his youthful athletic exploits (hitting homers off Paige, for example), and he is clearly proud of his accomplishments, but his athletic success has brought him nothing in later life except memories. He had been well past his peak when blacks were first allowed in the major leagues (and thus when significant salaries and public fame became available to black players). He doesn't say so but it is clear that, at forty-three, he never got the chance that the younger Jackie Robinson did.

In 1946, just after the end of World War II, Robinson became the first black to be signed in what was then called "organized baseball"—that is, the elaborate system of major and minor professional leagues for white players. The Negro League, in which the quality of play was thought by many to be as high as in the majors, was not part of "organized baseball," and salaries there were very much lower, and most of white America knew nothing of the players. After a year in the minors (at Montreal, which was then the top farm team of the Brooklyn Dodgers), Robinson—at age twenty-eight—was promoted to the "parent" Dodgers and immediately became a star, thus opening careers for scores of young black athletes. Robinson went on to bat over .300 for six consecutive years in the late '40s and early '50s, and he compiled a lifetime average of .311, even though he was over thirty years old for most of his major-league career. He retired at the end of the 1956 season, just a year before the action of *Fences* begins.

Troy's slighting references to Robinson and other black players younger than himself who had major-league careers reflect his frustration and bitterness at having been left out of the reform, and he still finds it impossible to believe that sports can be the road to success for blacks, even though by 1957 a great many professional black athletes had achieved national fame and commanded large salaries. By 1981, when the play was written, sports had come to be considered one of the most direct routes from the ghetto to public success, and Troy's combination of self-pity and blindness to his son's opportunities makes him a figure both pathetic and repressive. His refusal to encourage his son's potential to advance beyond the status of Troy's own generation becomes one of the play's "fences"—one of the text's reminders that some barriers are sustained by human failings within the black culture as well as by white systems. Troy's attitudes about the relationship between athletic prowess and later success in life would be a good bit more understandable in 1957 than 1981. The irony of Troy's insistence that his son quit football to work at the A & P and that he refuse athletic scholarship opportunities depends heavily on what happened between 1957 and 1981. Readers or viewers in 1981—or in the '90s—are likely to regard this aspect of Troy's fathering more critically then the historically based text implies; the text does not ask us to like Troy for these attitudes, only to understand what his world looked like, to him, at a time when history had not yet taken some of the turns we take for granted.

The fact of World War II is also important to the play. Gabriel is a casualty of the war and receives a small pension as a result of the disabling head wound that has altered his mind. Like Troy, he is a victim of white society and public policy, and he bears his wound publicly (though he is himself unaware of his condition) as a reminder of the sacrifice he has made. Unlike Troy, he bears no bitterness; he simply does not understand what has happened to him, and he sees his inheritance beyond racial terms. He is able to imagine himself as Heaven's trumpeter, right there with St. Peter, largely because he does not understand the fences that govern expectations. (Lyons, by contrast, is painfully aware of the limits imposed on him by his color, his background, and his education, and the most he can imagine for his musicianship is a marginal living.)

In 1957, the present of the play. World War II was still a vivid memory, and daily life was still conditioned by its aftermath. The relative plenty and peace that seemed impressive when compared to the scarcities and dangers of the war were frequently celebrated, and if we remember the complacent and self-satisfied attitudes generally attributed now to the '50s, we will understand better the weekly struggle Troy faces. He has a menial job and little chance for promotion, though he is affected enough by the general optimism about success and fairness that he protests the discrimination that divides black and white expectations on his job. And then he is unable to take advantage of the opportunity when fairness unexpectedly triumphs, because he has never learned to drive and doesn't understand the "rules" about "qualification."

The war shadows the action of the play well beyond the specific wound to Gabriel; 1957 takes us back in time to a world related to our own but quite different in both the events of daily life and the expectations created by them. But the play invites us to make connections between that world and ours, causal connections. We are conscious of looking back to an earlier time because the text emphasizes the distance.

Authorial time here is 1981, a quarter century later. The play's events are self-consciously distanced in time; the twenty-four intervening years provide some perspective. In 1981, World War II seemed distant, well over, and any portrayal of postwar optimism was far removed from the moment—the Iranian hostage crisis, runaway inflation, a new administration elected under the banner of returning to old-fashioned values, a tough stance on national defense and the shadow of the debacle in Vietnam, the public display of patriotism and a chauvinistic championing of American frontier values, a retreat from affirmative action and a reliance on competitive, appetitive instincts. *Fences* recalls a world that in 1981 was a generation old; when Troy describes the habits he has fallen into and is made to seem the cause that some problems have been passed along to a new generation, he seems to represent old attitudes and old solutions that are up against the values of a rising generation that will be in some ways different, in some ways more like, the values blackness embodied in 1981.

The author of *Fences*, August Wilson, has continued to write plays about the past of black families, self-consciously going back to different decades in different plays to suggest not only different stages in growing black consciousness but the kinds of attitudes and responses to crises that obtained within black families set apart from, but always circumscribed by, the larger white world of America. Wilson's interest is very much in suggesting what present-day life is like, especially for black people, and his play of 1990, *The Piano Lesson,* is self-consciously a play of the '90s even though its action takes place a generation before *Fences* and involves the history of an old material object, a piano, that has been passed down through several generations. For Wilson (and for most playwrights who set their plays in earlier times), the past leads to the present and helps the present learn how it got here. It not only represents events (World War II, or the integration of major-league baseball) that helped to cause change; it also represents attitudes and individual acts of behavior that lead to new conditions and an evolved set of issues and problems. The kind of fencing that this play is about suggests both the power of family and generational influence (a theme that is universal) and the kinds of particulars associated with one family's story conditioned by specific patterns of social and cultural history. *Fences* is about America in the 1950s in much the same way that *Death of a Salesman* is about the American '50s—the values, the consciousness, the habits, the immediate outcomes—except that *Fences* emphatically distances itself in time and makes the audience conscious of the difference as a way of articulating the power of a past on the present, whereas *Death of a Salesman*—written in 1949 about present events—is itself implicated in those values and assumptions.

Recreating a sense of a historical past is, we have been noticing, important to the act of reading when a text is set in an earlier time. But we have also been noticing difference—the implied contrast between the world represented in a play (plot time) and the world at the time the play is written (authorial time). But we are not reading *Fences* in 1981 or *Death of a Salesman* in 1949. Often the perspective from which we read, especially when we are reading relatively recent plays, is quite similar to that in authorial time, for often it is simply pastness that is at stake, but in older plays—*Oedipus the King,* for example, or *Hamlet*—we are often conscious of being far removed from the text's assumptions and values. We do not share the sense of urgency about Greek history and myth, and we are, as late-twentieth-century American readers, not so anxious about how power and control are passed along in monarchies (though there are plenty of other urgencies that translate readily—anxieties about whether our actions are somehow predetermined, for example, or about what we should do with our knowledge of evil). And sometimes, too, even more recent plays already are distanced from us by events that have intervened between authorial time and reader time.

Readers of the 1990s are not all that far removed in years from the time in which Wilson wrote *Fences*, but some things have changed that well may influence how we respond. Some readers of this book will hardly be able to remember what life was like for themselves in 1981, let alone what the world was doing in larger terms. In the '90s, we are much more removed now from World War II, the shifts in Eastern Europe and in China having made us think in quite different international terms. The self-conscious removal from the '50s that we described as having been built into the play is now even more striking to readers. Reader time has begun to be quite distinct from authorial time, and we may have to reach back further to retrieve the relevant facts about baseball, or the war, or daily life in Pittsburgh to understand the issues in the play. And we also read with a somewhat different perspective. In 1981 the integration of baseball seemed a powerful symbol of progress and disappearing distinctions between black and white opportunity. In the '90s the symbol has become more mixed. Statistical studies have emphasized the difference between the opportunities available to blacks and to whites as "fringe" players, the lack of blacks in managerial and management positions in baseball has drawn a lot of attention, and the exploitation of football players, especially black players, by colleges has gotten a lot of press. We therefore read Troy's skepticism about the sports opportunities for his son rather differently than we would have in 1981; Troy sounds like some of the spokespeople for black capitalism in the Reagan administration. Generally speaking, the longer the time between the writing of a text and the reading of it, the more differences of attitude and assumption will have appeared. Often readers must adjust their sights somewhat to understand the perspective that went into the positioning of the action that the act of writing represents, as well as adjusting to the historical present of the play.

Plays that represent a specific historical event—the Lizzie Borden case in *Blood Relations*, for example—make the act of reading at once easier and more difficult. The easy part is that we are alerted to the fact that we have to know something about that historical moment. We may well have heard the familiar rhyme:

> Lizzie Borden took an ax
> And gave her mother forty whacks;
> When she saw what she had done
> She gave her father forty-one!

And we may well know that the murder of Lizzie's parents (actually it was her father and stepmother) occurred in 1892 and that Lizzie was ultimately acquitted. We might even have heard something, rumors at least, of Lizzie's character and behavior and be aware of her reputation for oddness. If we don't know these things we can readily find them out, and texts that consciously represent public historical events usually count on this knowledge. But there are more subtle aspects of historical consciousness that do not come from going to the library to research an event, and Pollock's play is very much about these subtleties.

What was life like in Fall River, Massachusetts, in the late nineteenth century? What was it like to be a spinster in such a time and such a community? What kinds of expectations of behavior and value were imposed then on a woman like Lizzie? How free were individuals in this "Victorian" age to behave eccentrically, and what sorts of conclusions were drawn about "odd" behavior? Such information is not readily found in encyclopedia articles about an event or even in "factual" books on the subject. Often, as in *Blood Relations,* the text will reconstruct ordinary life so as to make us aware of the subtle particularities of the historical moment, but we have to be open to that re-creation and not assume we have mastered the "history" when we disinter "facts" about the event. It is often easy to mislead ourselves, in any text that renders a historical event, into thinking that factual research prepares us with the "right" knowledge. The "right" knowledge may in fact be far more complex, and it is important to allow the text to lead us to the "right" history rather than imposing the standard public version of history. Writers are often attracted to historical events and historical moments because they want to reinterpret history or to examine some kind of motivation or behavior within a definable cultural context. Fact and legend interact in *Blood Relations* with a highly subjective interpretation of history, culture, and the psychological analysis of human behavior, and readers of the '90s may want to know just as much about authorial time here as about historical time—just as much about the playwright of 1981 and her Canadian context as about the Lizzie Borden of a century earlier and her New England context.

SHARON POLLOCK

Blood Relations

CHARACTERS

MISS LIZZIE, *who will play* BRIDGET, *the Irish maid.*
THE ACTRESS, *who will play* LIZZIE BORDEN.
HARRY, *Mrs. Borden's brother.*
EMMA, *Lizzie's older sister.*
ANDREW [MR. BORDEN], *Lizzie's father.*
ABIGAIL [MRS. BORDEN], *Lizzie's stepmother.*
DR. PATRICK, *the Irish doctor, sometimes* THE DEFENSE.

SETTING

The time proper is late Sunday afternoon and evening, late fall, in Fall River,[1] *1902; the year of the "dream thesis," if one might call it that, is 1892.*

The playing areas include (a) within the Borden house: the dining room from which there is an exit to the kitchen; the parlour; a flight of stairs leading to the second floor; and (b) in the Borden yard: the walk outside the house; the area in which the birds are kept.

PRODUCTION NOTE: *Action must be free-flowing. There can be no division of the script into scenes by blackout, movement of furniture, or sets. There may be freezes of some characters while other scenes are being played. There is no necessity to "get people off" and "on" again for, with the exception of* THE ACTRESS *and* MISS LIZZIE *(and* EMMA *in the final scene), all characters are imaginary, and all action in reality would be taking place between* MISS LIZZIE *and* THE ACTRESS *in the dining room and parlour of her home.*

THE DEFENSE *may actually be seen, may be a shadow, or a figure behind a scrim.*

While MISS LIZZIE *exits and enters with her* BRIDGET *business, she is a presence, often observing unobtrusively when as* BRIDGET *she takes no part in the action.*

ACT I

Lights up on the figure of a woman standing centre stage. It is a somewhat formal pose. A pause. She speaks.

[THE ACTRESS:]

"Since what I am about to say must be but that
Which contradicts my accusation, and
The testimony on my part no other
But what comes from myself, it shall scare boot[2] me
To say "Not Guilty."
But, if Powers Divine
Behold our human action as they do,
I doubt not than but innocence shall make
False accusation blush and tyranny
Tremble at . . . at . . ."

[*She wriggles the fingers of an outstretched hand searching for the word.*]

"Aaaat" . . . Bollocks!![3]

[*She raises her script, takes a bite of chocolate.*]

"Tremble at Patience," patience patience! . . .

[MISS LIZZIE *enters from the kitchen with tea service.* THE ACTRESS*'s attention drifts to* MISS LIZZIE. THE ACTRESS *watches* MISS LIZZIE *sit in the parlour and*

1. Town in southeastern Massachusetts. 2. Profit. 3. Balls!

proceed to pour two cups of tea. THE ACTRESS *sucks her teeth a bit to clear the chocolate as she speaks.*]

THE ACTRESS: Which . . . is proper, Lizzie?

MISS LIZZIE: Proper?

THE ACTRESS: To pour first the cream, and add the tea—or first tea and add cream. One is proper. Is the way you do the proper way, the way it's done in circles where it counts?

MISS LIZZIE: Sugar?

THE ACTRESS: Well, is it?

MISS LIZZIE: I don't know, sugar?

THE ACTRESS: Mmmn. [MISS LIZZIE *adds sugar.*] I suppose if we had Mrs. Beeton's *Book of Etiquette,* we could look it up.

MISS LIZZIE: I do have it, shall I get it?

THE ACTRESS: No. . . . You could ask your sister, she might know.

MISS LIZZIE: Do you want this tea or not?

THE ACTRESS: I hate tea.

MISS LIZZIE: You drink it every Sunday.

THE ACTRESS: I drink it because you like to serve it.

MISS LIZZIE: Pppu.

THE ACTRESS: It's true. You've no idea how I suffer from this toast and tea ritual. I really do. The tea upsets my stomach and the toast makes me fat because I eat so much of it.

MISS LIZZIE: Practice some restraint then.

THE ACTRESS: Mmmmm. . . . Why don't we ask your sister which is proper?

MISS LIZZIE: You ask her.

THE ACTRESS: How can I? She doesn't speak to me. I don't think she even sees me. She gives no indication of it. [*She looks up the stairs.*] What do you suppose she does up there every Sunday afternoon?

MISS LIZZIE: She sulks.

THE ACTRESS: And reads the Bible I suppose, and Mrs. Beeton's *Book of Etiquette.* Oh Lizzie. . . . What a long day. The absolutely longest day. . . . When does that come anyway, the longest day?

MISS LIZZIE: June.

THE ACTRESS: Ah yes, June. [*She looks at* MISS LIZZIE.] June?

MISS LIZZIE: June.

THE ACTRESS: Mmmmmm. . . .

MISS LIZZIE: I know what you're thinking.

THE ACTRESS: Of course you do. . . . I'm thinking . . . shall I pour the sherry—or will you.

MISS LIZZIE: No.

THE ACTRESS: I'm thinking . . . June . . . in Fall River.

MISS LIZZIE: No.

THE ACTRESS: August in Fall River? [*She smiles. Pause.*]

MISS LIZZIE: We could have met in Boston.

THE ACTRESS: I prefer it here.

MISS LIZZIE: You don't find it . . . a trifle boring?

THE ACTRESS: Au contraire. [MISS LIZZIE *gives a small laugh at the affectation.*] What?

MISS LIZZIE: I find it a trifle boring . . . I know what you're doing. You're soaking up the ambience.

THE ACTRESS: Nonsense, Lizzie. I come to see you.

MISS LIZZIE: Why?

THE ACTRESS: Because . . . of us. [*Pause.*]

MISS LIZZIE: You were a late arrival last night. Later than usual.

THE ACTRESS: Don't be silly.

MISS LIZZIE: I wonder why.

THE ACTRESS: The show was late, late starting, late coming down.

MISS LIZZIE: And?

THE ACTRESS: And—then we all went out for drinks.

MISS LIZZIE: We?

THE ACTRESS: The other members of the cast.

MISS LIZZIE: Oh yes.

THE ACTRESS: And then I caught a cab . . . all the way from Boston. . . . Do you know what it cost?

MISS LIZZIE: I should. I paid the bill, remember?

THE ACTRESS: [*Laughs.*] Of course. What a jumble all my thoughts are. There're too many words running round inside my head today. It's terrible.

MISS LIZZIE: It sounds it.

[*Pause.*]

THE ACTRESS: . . . You know . . . you do this thing . . . you stare at me . . . You look directly at my eyes. I think . . . you think . . . that if I'm lying . . . it will come up, like lemons on a slot machine. [*She makes a gesture at her eyes.*] Tick. Tick . . . [*Pause.*] In the alley, behind the theater the other day, there were some kids. You know what they were doing?

MISS LIZZIE: How could I?

THE ACTRESS: They were playing skip rope, and you know what they were singing?

[*She sings, and claps her hands arhythmically to:*]

"Lizzie Borden took an ax
Gave her mother forty whacks,
When the job was nicely done,
She gave her father forty-one."

MISS LIZZIE: Did you stop them?

THE ACTRESS: No.

MISS LIZZIE: Did you tell them I was acquitted?

THE ACTRESS: No.

MISS LIZZIE: What did you do?

THE ACTRESS: I shut the window.

MISS LIZZIE: A noble gesture on my behalf.

THE ACTRESS: We were doing lines—the noise they make is dreadful. Sometimes they play ball, ka-thunk, ka-thunk, ka-thunk against the wall. Once I saw them with a cat and—

MISS LIZZIE: And you didn't stop them?

THE ACTRESS: That time I stopped them. [THE ACTRESS *crosses to table where there is a gramophone. She prepares to play a record. She stops.*] Should I?

MISS LIZZIE: Why not?

THE ACTRESS: Your sister, the noise upsets her.

MISS LIZZIE: And she upsets me. On numerous occasions.

THE ACTRESS: You're incorrigible, Lizzie. [THE ACTRESS *holds out her arms to* MISS LIZZIE. *They dance the latest "in" dance, a Scott Joplin composition. It requires some concentration, but they chat while dancing rather formally in contrast to the music.*] . . . Do you think your jawline's heavy?

MISS LIZZIE: Why do you ask?

THE ACTRESS: They said you had jowls.

MISS LIZZIE: Did they.

THE ACTRESS: The reports of the day said you were definitely jowly.

MISS LIZZIE: That was ten years ago.

THE ACTRESS: Imagine. You were only thirty-four.

MISS LIZZIE: Yes.

THE ACTRESS: It happened here, this house.

MISS LIZZIE: You're leading.

THE ACTRESS: I know.

MISS LIZZIE: . . . I don't think I'm jowly. Then or now. Do you?

THE ACTRESS: Lizzie? Lizzie.

MISS LIZZIE: What?

THE ACTRESS: . . . did you?

MISS LIZZIE: Did I what?

[*Pause.*]

THE ACTRESS: You never tell *me* anything. [*She turns off the music.*]

MISS LIZZIE: I tell you everything.

THE ACTRESS: No you don't!

MISS LIZZIE: Oh yes, I tell you the most personal things about myself, my thoughts, my dreams, my—

THE ACTRESS: But never that one thing. . . . [*She lights a cigarette.*]

MISS LIZZIE: And don't smoke those—they stink. [THE ACTRESS *ignores her, inhales, exhales a volume of smoke in* MISS LIZZIE*'s direction.*] Do you suppose . . . people buy you drinks . . . or cast you even . . . because you have a "liaison" with Lizzie Borden? Do you suppose they do that?

THE ACTRESS: They cast me because I'm good at what I do.

MISS LIZZIE: They never pry? They never ask? What's she really like? Is she really jowly? Did she? Didn't she?

THE ACTRESS: What could I tell them? You never tell me anything.

MISS LIZZIE: I tell you everything.

THE ACTRESS: But that! [*Pause.*] You think everybody talks about you—they don't.
MISS LIZZIE: Here they do.
THE ACTRESS: You think they talk about you.
MISS LIZZIE: But never to me.
THE ACTRESS: Well . . . you give them lots to talk about.
MISS LIZZIE: You know you're right, your mind is a jumble.
THE ACTRESS: I told you so.

[*Pause.*]

MISS LIZZIE: You remind me of my sister.
THE ACTRESS: Oh God, in what way?
MISS LIZZIE: Day in, day out, ten years now, sometimes at breakfast as she rolls little crumbs of bread in little balls, sometimes at noon, or late at night . . . "Did you, Lizzie?" "Lizzie, did you?"
THE ACTRESS: Ten years, day in, day out?
MISS LIZZIE: Oh yes. She sits there where Papa used to sit and I sit there, where I have always sat. She looks at me and at her plate, then at me, and at her plate, then at me and then she says "Did you Lizzie?" "Lizzie, did you?"
THE ACTRESS: [*A nasal imitation of Emma's voice.*] "Did-you-Lizzie—Lizzie-did-you." [*Laughs.*]
MISS LIZZIE: Did I what?
THE ACTRESS: [*Continues her imitation of Emma.*] "You know."
MISS LIZZIE: Well, what do you think?
THE ACTRESS: "Oh, I believe you didn't, in fact I know you didn't, what a thought! After all, you were acquitted."
MISS LIZZIE: Yes, I was.
THE ACTRESS: "But sometimes when I'm on the street . . . or shopping . . . or at the church even, I catch somebody's eye, they look away . . . and I think to myself "Did-you-Lizzie—Lizzie-did-you."
MISS LIZZIE: [*Laughs.*] Ah, poor Emma.
THE ACTRESS: [*Dropping her Emma immitation.*] Well, did you?
MISS LIZZIE: Is it important?
THE ACTRESS: Yes.
MISS LIZZIE: Why?
THE ACTRESS: I have . . . a compulsion to know the truth.
MISS LIZZIE: The truth?
THE ACTRESS: Yes.
MISS LIZZIE: . . . Sometimes I think you look like me, and you're not jowly.
THE ACTRESS: No.
MISS LIZZIE: You look like me, or how I think I look, or how I ought to look . . . sometimes you think like me . . . do you feel that?
THE ACTRESS: Sometimes.
MISS LIZZIE: [*Triumphant.*] You shouldn't have to ask then. You should know. "Did I, didn't I." You tell me.
THE ACTRESS: I'll tell you what I think . . . I think . . . that you're aware there is a certain fascination in the ambiguity. . . . You always paint the background

but leave the rest to my imagination. Did Lizzie Borden take an axe? . . . If you didn't I should be disappointed . . . and if you did I should be horrified.

MISS LIZZIE: And which is worse?

THE ACTRESS: To have murdered one's parents, or to be a pretentious small-town spinster? I don't know.

MISS LIZZIE: Why're you so cruel to me?

THE ACTRESS: I'm teasing, Lizzie. I'm only teasing. Come on, paint the background again.

MISS LIZZIE: Why?

THE ACTRESS: Perhaps you'll give something away.

MISS LIZZIE: Which you'll dine out on.

THE ACTRESS: Of course. [*Laughs.*] Come on, Lizzie. Come on.

MISS LIZZIE: A game.

THE ACTRESS: What?

MISS LIZZIE: A game? . . . And you'll play me.

THE ACTRESS: Oh—

MISS LIZZIE: It's your stock in trade, my love.

THE ACTRESS: All right. . . . A game!

MISS LIZZIE: Let me think . . . Bridget . . . Brrridget. We had a maid then. And her name was Bridget. Oh, she was a great one for stories, stood like this, very straight back, and her hair . . . and there she was in the courtroom in her new dress on the stand. "Do you swear to tell the truth, the whole truth, and nothing but the truth, so help you God?" [*Imitates Irish accent.*]
"I do sir," she said.
"Would you give the court your name."
"Bridget O'Sullivan, sir."

[*Very faint echo of the voice of* THE DEFENSE *under* MISS LIZZIE*'s next line.*]

"And occupation."
"I'm like what you'd call a maid, sir. I do a bit of everything, cleanin' and cookin'."

[*The actual voice of* THE DEFENSE *is heard alone; he may also be seen.*]

THE DEFENSE: You've been in Fall River how long?

MISS LIZZIE: [*Who continues as* BRIDGET, *while* THE ACTRESS (*who will play* LIZZIE) *observes.*] Well now, about five years sir, ever since I came over. I worked up on the hill for a while but it didn't—well, you could say, suit me, too lah-de-dah—so I—

THE DEFENSE: Your employer in June of 1892 was?

BRIDGET: Yes sir. Mr. Borden, sir. Well, more rightly, Mrs. Borden for she was the one who—

THE DEFENSE: Your impression of the household?

BRIDGET: Well . . . the man of the house, Mr. Borden, was a bit of a . . . tightwad, and Mrs. B. could nag you into the grave, still she helped with the dishes and things which not everyone does when they hire a maid. [*Harry appears on the stairs; approaches* BRIDGET *stealthily. She is unaware of him.*]

Then there was the daughters, Miss Emma and Lizzie, and that day, Mr. Wingate, Mrs. B's brother who'd stayed for the night and was—[*He grabs her ass with both hands. She screams.*] Get off with you!

HARRY: Come on, Bridget, give me a kiss!

BRIDGET: I'll give you a good poke in the nose if you don't keep your hands to yourself.

HARRY: Ohhh-hh-hh Bridget!

BRIDGET: Get away you old sod!

HARRY: Haven't you missed me?

BRIDGET: I have not! I was pinched black and blue last time—and I'll be sufferin' the same before I see the end of you this time.

HARRY: [*Tilts his ass at her.*] You want to see my end?

BRIDGET: You're a dirty old man.

HARRY: If Mr. Borden hears that, you'll be out on the street. [*Grabs her.*] Where's my kiss!

BRIDGET: [*Dumps glass of water on his head.*] There! [HARRY *splutters.*] Would you like another? You silly thing you—and leave me towels alone!

HARRY: You've soaked my shirt.

BRIDGET: Shut up and pour yourself a cup of coffee.

HARRY: You got no sense of fun, Bridget.

BRIDGET: Well now, if you tried actin' like the gentleman farmer you're supposed to be, Mr. Wingate—

HARRY: I'm tellin' you you can't take a joke.

BRIDGET: If Mr. Borden sees you jokin', it's not his maid he'll be throwin' out on the street, but his brother-in-law, and that's the truth.

HARRY: What's between you and me's between you and me, eh?

BRIDGET: There ain't nothin' between you and me.

HARRY: . . . Finest cup of coffee in Fall River.

BRIDGET: There's no gettin' on the good side of me now, it's too late for that.

HARRY: . . . Bridget? . . . You know what tickles my fancy?

BRIDGET: No and I don't want to hear.

HARRY: It's your Irish temper.

BRIDGET: It is, is it? . . . Can I ask you something?

HARRY: Ooohhh—anything.

BRIDGET: [*Innocently.*] Does Miss Lizzie know you're here? . . . I say does Miss Lizzie—

HARRY: Why do you bring her up.

BRIDGET: She don't then, eh? [*Teasing.*] It's a surprise visit?

HARRY: No surprise to her father.

BRIDGET: Oh?

HARRY: We got business.

BRIDGET: I'd of thought the last bit of business was enough.

HARRY: It's not for— [you to say]

BRIDGET: You don't learn a thing, from me or Lizzie, do you?

HARRY: Listen here—

BRIDGET: You mean you've forgotten how mad she was when you got her father to sign the rent from the mill house over to your sister? Oh my.

HARRY: She's his wife, isn't she?

BRIDGET: [*Lightly.*] Second wife.

HARRY: She's still got her rights.

BRIDGET: Who am I to say who's got a right? But I can tell you this—Miss Lizzie don't see it that way.

HARRY: It don't matter how Miss Lizzie sees it.

BRIDGET: Oh it matters enough—she had you thrown out last time, didn't she? By jasus that was a laugh!

HARRY: You mind your tongue.

BRIDGET: And after you left, you know what happened?

HARRY: Get away.

BRIDGET: She and sister Emma got her father's rent money from the other mill house to make it all even-steven—and now, here you are back again? What kind of business you up to this time? [*Whispers in his ear.*] Mind Lizzie doesn't catch you.

HARRY: Get away!

BRIDGET: [*Laughs.*] Ohhhh—would you like some more coffee, sir? It's the finest coffee in all Fall River! [*She pours it.*] Thank you sir. You're welcome, sir. [*She exits to the kitchen.*]

HARRY: There'll be no trouble this time! Do you hear me!

BRIDGET: [*Off.*] Yes sir.

HARRY: There'll be no trouble. [*Sees a basket of crusts.*] What the hell's this? I said is this for breakfast!

BRIDGET: [*Entering.*] Is what for—oh no—Mr. Borden's not economizin' to that degree yet, it's the crusts for Miss Lizzie's birds.

HARRY: What birds?

BRIDGET: Some kind of pet pigeons she's raisin' out in the shed. Miss Lizzie loves her pigeons.

HARRY: Miss Lizzie loves kittens and cats and horses and dogs. What Miss Lizzie doesn't love is people.

BRIDGET: *Some* people. [*She looks past* HARRY *to* THE ACTRESS / LIZZIE. HARRY *turns to follow* BRIDGET'*s gaze. Bridget speaks, encouraging an invitation for* THE ACTRESS *to join her.*] Good mornin' Lizzie.

THE ACTRESS: [*She is a trifle tentative in the role of* LIZZIE.] Is the coffee on?

BRIDGET: Yes ma'am.

LIZZIE: I'll have some then.

BRIDGET: Yes ma'am.

[*She makes no move to get it, but watches as* LIZZIE *stares at Harry.*]

HARRY: Well . . . I think . . . maybe I'll . . . just split a bit of that kindling out back.

[*He exits.* LIZZIE *turns to* BRIDGET.]

LIZZIE: Silly ass.

BRIDGET: Oh Lizzie.

[*She laughs. She enjoys* THE ACTRESS / LIZZIE*'s comments as she guides her into her role by "painting the background."*]

LIZZIE: Well, he is. He's a silly ass.

BRIDGET: Can you remember him last time with your Papa? Oh, I can still hear him. "Now Andrew, I've spent my life raisin' horses and I'm gonna tell you somethin'—a *woman* is just like a *horse!* You keep her on a tight rein, or she'll take the bit in her teeth and next thing you know, road, destination, and purpose is all behind you, and you'll be damn lucky if she don't pitch you right in a sewer ditch!"

LIZZIE: Stupid bugger.

BRIDGET: Oh Lizzie, what language! What would your father say if he heard you?

LIZZIE: Well . . . I've never used a word I didn't hear from him first.

BRIDGET: Do you think he'd be congratulatin' you?

LIZZIE: Possibly. [BRIDGET *gives a subtle shake of her head.*] Not.

BRIDGET: Possibly not is right. . . . And what if *Mrs.* B. should hear you?

LIZZIE: I hope and pray that she does. . . . Do you know what I think, Bridget? I think there's nothing wrong with Mrs. B. . . . that losing eighty pounds and tripling her intellect wouldn't cure.

BRIDGET: [*Loving it.*] You ought to be ashamed.

LIZZIE: It's the truth, isn't it?

BRIDGET: Still, what a way to talk of your mother.

LIZZIE: Step-mother.

BRIDGET: Still you don't mean it, do you?

LIZZIE: Don't I? [*Louder.*] She's a *silly ass* too!

BRIDGET: Shhhh.

LIZZIE: It's all right, she's deaf as a picket fence when she wants to be. . . . What's he here for?

BRIDGET: Never said.

LIZZIE: He's come to worm more money out of Papa I bet.

BRIDGET: Lizzie.

LIZZIE: What.

BRIDGET: Your sister, Lizzie.

[BRIDGET *indicates* EMMA, LIZZIE *turns to see her on the stairs.*]

EMMA: You want to be quiet, Lizzie, a body can't sleep for the racket upstairs.

LIZZIE: Oh?

EMMA: You've been makin' too much noise.

LIZZIE: It must have been Bridget, she dropped a pot, didn't you, Bridget.

EMMA: A number of pots from the sound of it.

BRIDGET: I'm all thumbs this mornin', ma'am.

EMMA: You know it didn't sound like pots.

LIZZIE: Oh.

EMMA: Sounded more like voices.

LIZZIE: Oh?

EMMA: Sounded like your voice, Lizzie.

LIZZIE: Maybe you dreamt it.
EMMA: I wish I had, for someone was using words no lady would use.
LIZZIE: When Bridget dropped the pot, she did say "pshaw!" didn't you, Bridget.
BRIDGET: Pshaw! That's what I said.
EMMA: That's not what I heard.

[BRIDGET *will withdraw.*]

LIZZIE: Pshaw?
EMMA: If mother heard you, you know what she's say.
LIZZIE: She's not my mother or yours.
EMMA: Well she married our father twenty-seven years ago, if that doesn't make her our mother—
LIZZIE: It doesn't.
EMMA: Don't talk like that.
LIZZIE: I'll talk as I like.
EMMA: We're not going to fight, Lizzie. We're going to be quiet and have our breakfast!
LIZZIE: Is that what we're going to do?
EMMA: Yes.
LIZZIE: Oh.
EMMA: At least—that's what I'm going to do.
LIZZIE: Bridget, Emma wants her breakfast!
EMMA: I could have yelled myself.
LIZZIE: You could, but you never do.

[BRIDGET *serves* EMMA, EMMA *is reluctant to argue in front of* BRIDGET.]

EMMA: Thank you, Bridget.
LIZZIE: Did you know Harry Wingate's back for a visit? . . . He must have snuck in late last night so I wouldn't hear him. Did you? [*Emma shakes her head. Lizzie studies her.*] Did you know he was coming?
EMMA: No.
LIZZIE: No?
EMMA: But I do know he wouldn't be here unless Papa asked him.
LIZZIE: That's not the point. You know what happened last time he was here. Papa was signing property over to her.
EMMA: Oh Lizzie.
LIZZIE: Oh Lizzie nothing. It's bad enough Papa's worth thousands of dollars, and here we are, stuck in this tiny bit of a house on Second Street, when we should be up on the hill—and that's her doing. Or hers and Harry's.
EMMA: Shush.
LIZZIE: I won't shush. They cater to Papa's worst instincts.
EMMA: They'll hear you.
LIZZIE: I don't care if they do. It's true, isn't it? Papa tends to be miserly, he probably has the first penny he ever earned—or more likely *she* has it.
EMMA: You talk rubbish.
LIZZIE: Papa *can* be very warm-hearted and generous *but he needs encouragement.*

EMMA: If Papa didn't save his money, Papa wouldn't have any money.

LIZZIE: And neither will we if he keeps signing things over to her.

EMMA: I'm not going to listen.

LIZZIE: Well try thinking.

EMMA: Stop it.

LIZZIE: [*Not a threat, a simple statement of fact.*] Someday Papa will die—

EMMA: Don't say that.

LIZZIE: Some day Papa will die. And I don't intend to spend the rest of my life licking Harry Wingate's boots, or toadying to his sister.

MRS. BORDEN: [*From the stairs.*] What's that?

LIZZIE: Nothing.

MRS. BORDEN: [*Making her way downstairs.*] Eh?

LIZZIE: I said, nothing!

BRIDGET: [*Holds out basket of crusts.* LIZZIE *looks at it.*] For your birds, Miss Lizzie.

LIZZIE: [*She takes the basket.*] You want to know what I think? I think she's a fat cow and I hate her. [*She exits.*]

EMMA: Morning, Mother.

MRS. BORDEN: Morning Emma.

EMMA: . . . Did you have a good sleep.

[BRIDGET *will serve breakfast.*]

MRS. BORDEN: So so. . . . It's the heat you know. It never cools off proper at night. It's too hot for a good sleep.

EMMA: . . . Is Papa up?

MRS. BORDEN: He'll be down in a minute . . . sooo. . . . What's wrong with Lizzie this morning?

EMMA: Nothing.

MRS. BORDEN: . . . Has Harry come down?

EMMA: I'm not sure.

MRS. BORDEN: Bridget. Has Harry come down?

BRIDGET: Yes ma'am.

MRS. BORDEN: And?

BRIDGET: And he's gone out back for a bit.

MRS. BORDEN: Lizzie see him?

BRIDGET: Yes ma'am. [*Beats it back to the kitchen.*]

[EMMA *concentrates on her plate.*]

MRS. BORDEN: . . . You should have said so. . . . She have words with him?

EMMA: Lizzie has more manners than that.

MRS. BORDEN: She's incapable of disciplining herself like a lady and we all know it.

EMMA: Well she doesn't make a habit of picking fights with people.

MRS. BORDEN: That's just it. She does.

EMMA: Well—she may—

MRS. BORDEN: And you can't deny that.

EMMA: [*Louder.*] Well this morning she may have been a bit upset because no one told her he was coming and when she came down he was here. But that's all there was to it.

MRS. BORDEN: If your father wants my brother in for a stay, he's to ask Lizzie's permission I suppose.

EMMA: No.

MRS. BORDEN: You know, Emma—

EMMA: She didn't argue with him or anything like that.

MRS. BORDEN: You spoiled her. You may have had the best of intentions, but you spoiled her.

[MISS LIZZIE / BRIDGET *is speaking to* ACTRESS / LIZZIE.]

MISS LIZZIE / BRIDGET: I was thirty-four years old, and I still daydreamed. . . . I did . . . I daydreamed . . . I dreamt that my name was Lisbeth . . . and I lived up on the hill in a corner house . . . and my hair wasn't red. I hate red hair. When I was little, everyone teased me. . . . When I was little, we never stayed in this house for the summer, we'd go to the farm. . . . I remember . . . my knees were always covered with scabs, god knows how I got them, but you know what I'd do? I'd sit in the field, and haul up my skirts, and my petticoat and my bloomers and roll down my stockings and I'd *pick* the scabs on my knees! And Emma would catch me! You know what she'd say? "Nice little girls don't have scabs on their knees!"

[*They laugh.*]

LIZZIE: Poor Emma.

MISS LIZZIE / BRIDGET: I dreamt . . . someday I'm going to live . . . in a corner house on the hill. . . . I'll have parties, grand parties. I'll be . . . witty, not biting, but witty. Everyone will be witty. Everyone who is *any*one will want to come to my parties . . . and if . . . I can't . . . live in a corner house on the hill . . . I'll live on the farm, all by myself on the farm! There was a barn there, with barn cats and barn kittens and two horses and barn swallows that lived in the eaves. . . . The birds I kept here were pigeons, not swallows. . . . They were grey, a dull grey . . . but . . . when the sun struck their feathers, I'd see blue, a steel blue with a sheen, and when they'd move in the sun they were bright blue and maroon and over it all, an odd sparkle as if you'd . . . grated a new silver dollar and the gratings caught in their feathers. . . . Most of the time they were dull . . . and stupid perhaps . . . but they weren't really. They were . . . hiding I think. . . . They knew me. . . . They liked me. . . . The truth . . . is . . .

ACTRESS / LIZZIE: The truth is . . . thirty-four is too old to daydream. . . .

MRS. BORDEN: The truth is she's spoilt rotten. [MR. BORDEN *will come downstairs and take his place at the table.* MRS. BORDEN *continues for his benefit.* MR. BORDEN *ignores her. He has learned the fine art of tuning her out. He is not intimidated or hen-pecked.*] And we're paying the piper for that. In most of the places I've been the people who pay the piper call the tune. Of course I haven't had the advantage of a trip to Europe with a bunch of lady friends like our Lizzie had three years ago, all expenses paid by her father.

EMMA: Morning Papa.
MR. BORDEN: Mornin'.
MRS. BORDEN: I haven't had the benefit of that experience. . . . Did you know Lizzie's seen Harry?
MR. BORDEN: Has she.
MRS. BORDEN: You should have met him down town. You should never have asked him to stay over.
MR. BORDEN: Why not?
MRS. BORDEN: You know as well as I do why not. I don't want a repeat of last time. She didn't speak civil for months.
MR. BORDEN: There's no reason for Harry to pay for a room when we've got a spare one. . . . Where's Lizzie?
EMMA: Out back feeding the birds.
MR. BORDEN: She's always out at those birds.
EMMA: Yes Papa.
MR. BORDEN: And tell her to get a new lock for the shed. There's been someone in it again.
EMMA: All right.
MR. BORDEN: It's those little hellions from next door. We had no trouble with them playin' in that shed before, they always played in their own yard before.
EMMA: . . . Papa?
MR. BORDEN: It's those damn birds, that's what brings them into the yard.
EMMA: . . . About Harry . . .
MR. BORDEN: What about Harry?
EMMA: Well . . . I was just wondering why . . . [he's here]
MR. BORDEN: You never mind Harry—did you speak to Lizzie about Johnny MacLeod?
EMMA: I ah—
MR. BORDEN: Eh?
EMMA: I said I tried to—
MR. BORDEN: What do you mean, you tried to.
EMMA: Well, I was working my way round to it but—
MR. BORDEN: What's so difficult about telling Lizzie Johnny MacLeod wants to call?
EMMA: Then why don't you tell her? I'm always the one that has to go running to Lizzie telling her this and telling her that, and taking the abuse for it!
MRS. BORDEN: We all know why that is, she can wrap her father round her little finger, always has, always could. If everything else fails, she throws a tantrum and her father buys her off, trip to Europe, rent to the mill house, it's all the same.
EMMA: Papa, what's Harry here for?
MR. BORDEN: None of your business.
MRS. BORDEN: And don't you go runnin' to Lizzie stirring things up.
EMMA: You know I've never done that!
MR. BORDEN: What she means—
EMMA: [*With anger but little fatigue.*] I'm tired, do you hear? Tired!

[*She gets up from the table and leaves for upstairs.*]

MR. BORDEN: Emma!

EMMA: You ask Harry here, you know there'll be trouble, and when I try to find out what's going on, so once again good old Emma can stand between you and Lizzie, all you've got to say is "none of your business!" Well then, it's *your* business, you look after it, because I'm not! [*She exits.*]

MRS. BORDEN: . . . She's right.

MR. BORDEN: That's enough. I've had enough. I don't want to hear from you too.

MRS. BORDEN: I'm only saying she's right. You have to talk straight and plain to Lizzie and tell her things she don't want to hear.

MR. BORDEN: About the farm?

MRS. BORDEN: About Johnny MacLeod! Keep your mouth shut about the farm and she won't know the difference.

MR. BORDEN: All right.

MRS. BORDEN: Speak to her about Johnny MacLeod.

MR. BORDEN: All right!

MRS. BORDEN: You know what they're sayin' in town. About her and that doctor.

[MISS LIZZIE / BRIDGET *is speaking to* THE ACTRESS / LIZZIE.]

MISS LIZZIE / BRIDGET: They're saying if you live on Second Street and you need a housecall, and you don't mind the Irish, call Dr. Patrick. Dr. Patrick is very prompt with his Second Street house calls.

ACTRESS / LIZZIE: Do they really say that?

MISS LIZZIE / BRIDGET: No they don't. I'm telling a lie. But he is very prompt with a Second Street call, do you know why that is?

ACTRESS / LIZZIE: Why?

MISS LIZZIE / BRIDGET: Well—he's hoping to see someone who lives on Second Street—someone who's yanking up her skirt and showing her ankle—so she can take a decent-sized step—and forgetting everything she was ever taught in Miss Cornelia's School for Girls, and talking to the Irish as if she never heard of the Pope! Oh yes, he's very prompt getting to Second Street . . . getting away is something else. . . .

DR. PATRICK: Good morning, Miss Borden!

LIZZIE: I haven't decided . . . if it is . . . or it isn't. . . .

DR. PATRICK: No, you've got it all wrong. The proper phrase is "good morning, Dr. Patrick," and then you smile, discreetly of course, and lower the eyes just a titch, twirl the parasol—

LIZZIE: The parasol?

DR. PATRICK: The parasol, but not too fast; and then you murmur in a voice that was ever sweet and low, "And how are you doin' this morning, Dr. Patrick?" Your education's been sadly neglected, Miss Borden.

LIZZIE: You're forgetting something. You're married—and Irish besides—I'm supposed to ignore you.

DR. PATRICK: No.

LIZZIE: Yes. Don't you realize Papa and Emma have fits everytime we engage in "illicit conversation." They're having fits right now.

DR. PATRICK: Well, does Mrs. Borden approve?

LIZZIE: Ahhh. She's the real reason I keep stopping and talking. Mrs. Borden is easily shocked. I'm hoping she dies from the shock.

DR. PATRICK: [*Laughs.*] Why don't you . . . run away from home, Lizzie?

LIZZIE: Why don't you "run away" with me?

DR. PATRICK: Where'll we go?

LIZZIE: Boston.

DR. PATRICK: Boston?

LIZZIE: For a start.

DR. PATRICK: And when will we go?

LIZZIE: Tonight.

DR. PATRICK: But you don't really mean it, you're havin' me on.

LIZZIE: I do mean it.

DR. PATRICK: How can you joke—and look so serious?

LIZZIE: It's a gift.

DR. PATRICK: [*Laughs.*] Oh Lizzie—

LIZZIE: Look!

DR. PATRICK: What is it?

LIZZIE: It's those little beggars next door. Hey! Hey get away! Get away there! . . . They break into the shed to get at my birds and Papa gets angry.

DR. PATRICK: It's a natural thing.

LIZZIE: Well Papa doesn't like it.

DR. PATRICK: They just want to look at them.

LIZZIE: Papa says what's his is his own—you need a formal invitation to get into our yard. . . . [*Pause.*] How's your wife?

DR. PATRICK: My wife.

LIZZIE: Shouldn't I ask that? I thought nice polite ladies always inquired after the wives of their friends or acquaintances or . . . whatever.

[HARRY *observes them.*]

DR. PATRICK: You've met my wife, my wife is always the same.

LIZZIE: How boring for you.

DR. PATRICK: Uh-huh.

LIZZIE: And for her—

DR. PATRICK: Yes indeed.

LIZZIE: And for me.

DR. PATRICK: Do you know what they say, Lizzie? They say if you live on Second Street, and you need a house call, and you don't mind the Irish, call Dr. Patrick. Dr. Patrick is very prompt with his Second Street house calls.

LIZZIE: I'll tell you what I've heard them say—Second Street is a nice place to visit, but you wouldn't want to live there. I certainly don't.

HARRY: Lizzie.

LIZZIE: Well, look who's here. Have you had the pleasure of meeting my uncle, Mr. Wingate.

DR. PATRICK: No Miss Borden, that pleasure has never been mine.

LIZZIE: That's exactly how I feel.

DR. PATRICK: Mr. Wingate, sir.

HARRY: Dr. . . . Patrick is it?

DR. PATRICK: Yes it is, sir.

HARRY: Who's sick? [In other words, "What the hell are you doing here?"]

LIZZIE: No one. He just dropped by for a visit; you see Dr. Patrick and I are very old, very dear friends, isn't that so?

[HARRY *stares at* DR. PATRICK.]

DR. PATRICK: Well . . . [LIZZIE *jabs him in the ribs.*] Ouch! . . . It's her sense of humor, sir . . . a rare trait in a woman. . .

HARRY: You best get in, Lizzie, it's gettin' on for lunch.

LIZZIE: Don't be silly, we just had breakfast.

HARRY: You best get in!

LIZZIE: . . . Would you give me your arm, Dr. Patrick?

[*She moves away with* DR. PATRICK, *ignoring* HARRY.]

DR. PATRICK: Now see what you've done?

LIZZIE: What?

DR. PATRICK: You've broken two of my ribs and ruined my reputation all in one blow.

LIZZIE: It's impossible to ruin an Irishman's reputation.

DR. PATRICK: [*Smiles.*] . . . I'll be seeing you, Lizzie . . .

MISS LIZZIE / BRIDGET: They're sayin' it's time you were married.

LIZZIE: What time is that?

MISS LIZZIE / BRIDGET: You need a place of your own.

LIZZIE: How would getting married get me that?

MISS LIZZIE / BRIDGET: Though I don't know what man would put up with your moods!

LIZZIE: What about me putting up with his!

MISS LIZZIE / BRIDGET: Oh Lizzie!

LIZZIE: What's the matter, don't men have moods?

HARRY: I'm tellin' you, as God is my witness, she's out in the walk talkin' to that Irish doctor, and he's fallin' all over her.

MRS. BORDEN: What's the matter with you. For her own sake you should speak to her.

MR. BORDEN: I will.

HARRY: The talk around town can't be doin' you any good.

MRS. BORDEN: Harry's right.

HARRY: Yes sir.

MRS. BORDEN: He's tellin' you what you should know.

HARRY: If a man can't manage his own daughter, how the hell can he manage a business—that's what people say, and it don't matter a damn whether there's any sense in it or not.

MR. BORDEN: I know that.

MRS. BORDEN: Knowin' is one thing, doin' something about it is another. What're you goin' to do about it?

MR. BORDEN: God damn it! I said I was goin' to speak to her and I am!

MRS. BORDEN: Well speak good and plain this time!
MR. BORDEN: Jesus Christ woman!
MRS. BORDEN: Your "speakin' to Lizzie" is a ritual around here.
MR. BORDEN: Abbie—
MRS. BORDEN: She talks, you listen, and nothin' changes!
MR. BORDEN: That's enough!
MRS. BORDEN: Emma isn't the only one that's fed to the teeth!
MR. BORDEN: Shut up!
MRS. BORDEN: You're gettin' old, Andrew! You're gettin' old! [*She exits.*]

[*An air of embarrassment from* MR. BORDEN *at having words in front of* HARRY. MR. BORDEN *fumbles with his pipe.*]

HARRY: [*Offers his pouch of tobacco.*] Here . . . have some of mine.
MR. BORDEN: Don't mind if I do. . . . Nice mix.
HARRY: It is.
MR. BORDEN: . . . I used to think . . . by my seventies . . . I'd be bouncin' a grandson on my knee. . . .
HARRY: Not too late for that.
MR. BORDEN: Nope . . . never had any boys . . . and girls . . . don't seem to have the same sense of family. . . . You know it's all well and good to talk about speakin' plain to Lizzie, but the truth of the matter is, if Lizzie puts her mind to a thing, she does it, and if she don't, she don't.
HARRY: It's up to you to see she does.
MR. BORDEN: It's like Abigail says, knowin' is one thing, doin' is another. . . . You're lucky you never brought any children into the world, Harry, you don't have to deal with them.
HARRY: Now that's no way to be talkin'.
MR. BORDEN: There's Emma . . . Emma's a good girl . . . when Abbie and I get on, there'll always be Emma. . . . Well! You're not sittin' here to listen to me and my girls, are you, you didn't come here for that. Business, eh Harry?

[HARRY *whips out a sheet of figures.*]

MISS LIZZIE / BRIDGET: I can remember distinctly . . . that moment I was undressing for bed, and I looked at my knees—and there were no scabs! At last! I thought I'm the nice little girl Emma wants me to be! . . . But it wasn't that at all. I was just growing up. I didn't fall down so often. . . . [*She smiles.*] Do you suppose . . . do you suppose there's a formula, a magic formula for being "a woman"? Do you suppose every girl baby receives it at birth, it's the last thing that happens just before birth, the magic formula is stamped indelibly on the brain—Ka Thud!! [*Her mood of amusement changes.*] . . . and . . . through some terrible oversight . . . perhaps the death of my mother . . . I didn't get that Ka Thud!! I was born . . . defective. . . . [*She looks at* THE ACTRESS.]
LIZZIE: [*Low.*] No.
MISS LIZZIE / BRIDGET: Not defective?
LIZZIE: Just . . . born.

THE DEFENSE: Gentlemen of the Jury! I ask you to look at the defendant, Miss Lizzie Borden. I ask you to recall the nature of the crime of which she is accused. I ask you—do you believe Miss Lizzie Borden, the youngest daughter of a scion of our community, a recipient of the fullest amenities our society can bestow upon its most fortunate members, do you believe Miss Lizzie Borden capable of wielding the murder weapon—thirty-two blows, gentlemen, thirty-two blows—fracturing Abigail Borden's skull, leaving her bloody and broken body in an upstairs bedroom, then, Miss Borden, with no hint of frenzy, hysteria, or trace of blood upon her person, engages in casual conversation with the maid, Bridget O'Sullivan, while awaiting her father's return home, upon which, after sending Bridget to her attic room, Miss Borden deals thirteen blows to the head of her father, and minutes later—in a state utterly comparable with that of a loving daughter upon discovery of murder most foul—Miss Borden calls for aid! Is this the aid we give her? Accusation of the most heinous and infamous of crimes? Do you believe Miss Lizzie Borden capable of these acts? I can tell you I do not!! I can tell you these acts of violence are acts of madness!! Gentlemen! If this gentlewoman is capable of such an act—I say to you—look to your daughters—if this gentlewoman is capable of such an act, which of us can lie abed at night, hear a step upon the stairs, a rustle in the hall, a creak outside the door. . . . Which of you can plump your pillow, nudge your wife, close your eyes, and sleep? Gentlemen, Lizzie Borden is not mad. Gentlemen, Lizzie Borden is not guilty.

MR. BORDEN: Lizzie?
LIZZIE: Papa . . . have you and Harry got business?
HARRY: 'lo Lizzie. I'll ah . . . finish up later.

[*He exits with the figures.* LIZZIE *watches him go.*].

MR. BORDEN: Lizzie?
LIZZIE: What?
MR. BORDEN: Could you sit down a minute?
LIZZIE: If it's about Dr. Patrick again, I—
MR. BORDEN: It isn't.
LIZZIE: Good.
MR. BORDEN: But we could start there.
LIZZIE: Oh Papa.
MR. BORDEN: Sit down Lizzie.
LIZZIE: But I've heard it all before, another chat for a wayward girl.
MR. BORDEN: [*Gently.*] Bite your tongue, Lizzie.

[*She smiles at him, there is affection between them. She has the qualities he would like in a son but deplores in a daughter.*]

MR. BORDEN: Now . . . first off . . . I want you to know that I . . . understand about you and the doctor.
LIZZIE: What do you understand?
MR. BORDEN: I understand . . . that it's a natural thing.

LIZZIE: What is?

MR. BORDEN: I'm saying there's nothing unnatural about an attraction between a man and a woman. That's a natural thing.

LIZZIE: I find Dr. Patrick . . . amusing and entertaining . . . if that's what you mean . . . is that what you mean?

MR. BORDEN: This attraction . . . points something up—you're a woman of thirty-four years—

LIZZIE: I know that.

MR. BORDEN: Just listen to me, Lizzie. . . . I'm choosing my words, and I want you to listen. Now . . . in most circumstances . . . a woman of your age would be married, eh? have children, be running her own house, that's the natural thing, eh? [*Pause.*] Eh, Lizzie?

LIZZIE: I don't know.

MR. BORDEN: Of course you know.

LIZZIE: You're saying I'm unnatural . . . am I supposed to agree, is that what you want?

MR. BORDEN: No, I'm not saying that! I'm saying the opposite to that! . . . I'm saying the feelings you have towards Dr. Patrick—

LIZZIE: What feelings?

MR. BORDEN: What's . . . what's happening here, I can understand, but what you have to understand is that he's a married man, and there's nothing for you there.

LIZZIE: If he weren't married, Papa, I wouldn't be bothered talking to him! . . . It's just a game, Papa, it's a game.

MR. BORDEN: A game.

LIZZIE: You have no idea how boring it is looking eligible, interested, and alluring, when I feel none of the three. So I play games. And it's a blessed relief to talk to a married man.

MR. BORDEN: What're his feelings for you?

LIZZIE: I don't know, I don't care. Can I go now?

MR. BORDEN: I'm not finished yet! . . . You know Mr. MacLeod, Johnny MacLeod?

LIZZIE: I know his three little monsters.

MR. BORDEN: He's trying to raise three boys with no mother!

LIZZIE: That's not my problem! I'm going.

MR. BORDEN: Lizzie!

LIZZIE: What!

MR. BORDEN: Mr. MacLeod's asked to come over next Tuesday.

LIZZIE: I'll be out that night.

MR. BORDEN: No you won't!

LIZZIE: Yes I will! . . . Whose idea was this?

MR. BORDEN: No one's.

LIZZIE: That's a lie. She wants to get rid of me.

MR. BORDEN: I want what's best for you!

LIZZIE: No you don't! 'Cause you don't care what I want!

MR. BORDEN: You don't know what you want!

LIZZIE: But I know what you want! You want me living my life by the Farmer's

Almanac; having everyone over for Christmas dinner, waiting up for my husband; and *serving at socials!*

MR. BORDEN: It's good enough for your mother!

LIZZIE: She is *not* my *mother!*

MR. BORDEN: . . . John MacLeod is looking for a wife.

LIZZIE: No, god damn it, he isn't!

MR. BORDEN: Lizzie!

LIZZIE: He's looking for a housekeeper and it isn't going to be me!

MR. BORDEN: You've a filthy mouth!

LIZZIE: Is that why you hate me?

MR. BORDEN: You don't make sense.

LIZZIE: Why is it when I pretend things I don't feel, that's when you like me?

MR. BORDEN: You talk foolish.

LIZZIE: I'm supposed to be a mirror. I'm supposed to reflect what you want to see, but everyone wants something different. If no one looks in the mirror, I'm not even there, I don't exist!

MR. BORDEN: Lizzie, you talk foolish!

LIZZIE: No, I don't, that isn't true.

MR. BORDEN: About Mr. MacLeod—

LIZZIE: You can't make me get married!

MR. BORDEN: Lizzie, do you want to spend the rest of your life in this house?

LIZZIE: No . . . No . . . I want out of it, but I won't get married to do it.

MRS. BORDEN: [*On her way through to the kitchen.*] You've never been asked.

LIZZIE: Oh listen to her! I must be some sort of failure, then, eh? You had no son and a daughter that failed? What does that make you, Papa?!

MR. BORDEN: I want you to think about Johnny MacLeod!

LIZZIE: To hell with him!!! [MR. BORDEN *appears defeated. After a moment,* LIZZIE *goes to him, she holds his hand, strokes his hair.*] Papa? . . . Papa, I love you, I try to be what you want, really I do try, I try . . . but . . . I don't want to get married. I wouldn't be a good mother, I—

MR. BORDEN: How do you know—

LIZZIE: I know it! . . . I want out of all this . . . I hate this house, I hate . . . I want out. Try to understand how I feel. . . . Why can't I do something? . . . Eh? I mean . . . I could . . . I could go into your office. . . . I could . . . learn how to keep books?

MR. BORDEN: Lizzie.

LIZZIE: Why can't I do something like that?

MR. BORDEN: For god's sake, talk sensible.

LIZZIE: All right then! Why can't we move up on the hill to a house where we aren't in each other's laps!

MRS. BORDEN: [*Returning from kitchen.*] Why don't you move out!

LIZZIE: Give me the money and I'll go!

MRS. BORDEN: Money.

LIZZIE: And give me enough that I won't ever have to come back!

MRS. BORDEN: She always gets round to money!

LIZZIE: You drive me to it!

MRS. BORDEN: She's crazy!

LIZZIE: You drive me to it!

MRS. BORDEN: She should be locked up!

LIZZIE: [*Begins to smash the plates in the dining-room*] There!! There!!

MR. BORDEN: Lizzie!

MRS. BORDEN: Stop her!

LIZZIE: There!

[MR. BORDEN *attempts to restrain her.*]

MRS. BORDEN: For god's sake, Andrew!

LIZZIE: Lock me up! Lock me up!

MR. BORDEN: Stop it! Lizzie!

[*She collapses against him, crying.*]

LIZZIE: Oh, Papa, I can't stand it.

MR. BORDEN: There, there, come on now, it's all right, listen to me, Lizzie, it's all right.

MRS. BORDEN: You may as well get down on your knees.

LIZZIE: Look at her. She's jealous of me. She can't stand it whenever you're nice to me.

MR. BORDEN: There now.

MRS. BORDEN: Ask her about Dr. Patrick.

MR. BORDEN: I'll handle this my way.

LIZZIE: He's an entertaining person, there're very few around!

MRS. BORDEN: Fall River ain't Paris and ain't that a shame for our Lizzie!

LIZZIE: One trip three years ago and you're still harping on it; it's true, Papa, an elephant never forgets!

MR. BORDEN: Show some respect!

LIZZIE: She's a fat cow and I hate her!

[MR. BORDEN *slaps* LIZZIE. *There is a pause as he regains control of himself.*]

MR. BORDEN: Now . . . now . . . you'll see Mr. MacLeod Tuesday night.

LIZZIE: No.

MR. BORDEN: God damn it!! I said you'll see Johnny MacLeod Tuesday night!!

LIZZIE: No.

MR. BORDEN: Get the hell upstairs to your room!

LIZZIE: No.

MR. BORDEN: I'm telling you to go upstairs to your room!!

LIZZIE: I'll go when I'm ready.

MR. BORDEN: I said, Go!

[*He grabs her arm to move her forcibly, she hits his arm away.*]

LIZZIE: No! . . . There's something you don't understand, Papa. You can't make me do one thing that I don't want to do. I'm going to keep on doing just what I want just when I want—like always!

MR. BORDEN: [*Shoves her to the floor to gain a clear exit from the room. He stops on the stairs, looks back to her on the floor.*] . . . I'm . . . [*He continues off.*]

MRS. BORDEN: [*Without animosity.*] You know, Lizzie, your father keeps you. You know you got nothing but what he gives you. And that's a fact of life. You got to come to deal with facts. I did.

LIZZIE: And married Papa.

MRS. BORDEN: And married your father. You never made it easy for me. I took on a man with two little ones, and Emma was your mother.

LIZZIE: You got stuck so I should too, is that it?

MRS. BORDEN: What?

LIZZIE: The reason I should marry Johnny MacLeod.

MRS. BORDEN: I just know, this time, in the end, you'll do what your Papa says, you'll see.

LIZZIE: No, I won't. I have a right. A right that frees me from all that.

MRS. BORDEN: No, Lizzie, you got no rights.

LIZZIE: I've a legal right to one-third because I am his flesh and blood.

MRS. BORDEN: What you don't understand is your father's not dead yet, your father's got many good years ahead of him, and when his time comes, well, we'll see what his will says then. . . . Your father's no fool, Lizzie. . . . Only a fool would leave money to you. [*She exits.*]

[*After a moment,* BRIDGET *enters from the kitchen.*]

BRIDGET: Ah Lizzie . . . you outdid yourself that time. [*She is comforting* LIZZIE.] . . . Yes you did . . . an elephant never forgets!

LIZZIE: Oh Bridget.

BRIDGET: Come on now.

LIZZIE: I can't help it.

BRIDGET: Sure you can . . . sure you can . . . stop your cryin' and come and sit down . . . you want me to tell you a story?

LIZZIE: No.

BRIDGET: Sure, a story. I'll tell you a story. Come on now . . . now . . . before I worked here I worked up on the hill and the lady of the house . . . are you listenin'? Well, she swore by her cook, finest cook in creation, yes, always bowin' and scrapin' and smilin' and givin' up her day off if company arrived. Oh the lady of the house she loved that cook—and I'll tell you her name! It was Mary! Now listen! Do you know what Mary was doin'? [LIZZIE *shakes her head.*] Before eatin' the master'd serve drinks in the parlour—and out in the kitchen, Mary'd be spittin' in the soup!

LIZZIE: What?

BRIDGET: She'd spit in the soup! And she'd smile when they served it!

LIZZIE: No.

BRIDGET: Yes. I've seen her cut up hair for an omelette.

LIZZIE: You're lying.

BRIDGET: Cross me heart. . . . They thought it was pepper!

LIZZIE: Oh, Bridget!

BRIDGET: These two eyes have seen her season up mutton stew when it's off and gone bad.

LIZZIE: Gone bad?

BRIDGET: Oh and they et it, every bit, and the next day they was hit with . . . *stomach flu*! so cook called it. By jasus, Lizzie, I daren't tell you what she served up in their food, for fear you'd be sick!!

LIZZIE: That's funny. . . . [*A fact*—LIZZIE *does not appear amused.*]

BRIDGET: [*Starts to clear up the dishes.*] Yes, well, I'm tellin' you I kept on the good side of cook.

[LIZZIE *watches her for a moment.*]

LIZZIE: . . . Do you . . . like me?

BRIDGET: Sure I do. . . . You should try bein' more like cook, Lizzie. Smile and get round them. You can do it.

LIZZIE: It's not . . . *fair* that I have to.

BRIDGET: There ain't nothin' fair in this world.

LIZZIE: Well then . . . well then, I don't want to!

BRIDGET: You dream, Lizzie . . . you dream dreams . . . Work. Be sensible. What could you do?

LIZZIE: I could

MISS LIZZIE / BRIDGET: No.

LIZZIE: I could

MISS LIZZIE / BRIDGET: No.

LIZZIE: I could

MISS LIZZIE / BRIDGET: No!

LIZZIE: I . . . dream.

MISS LIZZIE / BRIDGET: You dream . . . of a carousel . . . you see a carousel . . . you see lights that go on and go off . . . you see yourself on a carousel horse, a red-painted horse with its head in the air, and green staring eyes, and a white flowing mane, it looks wild! . . . It goes up and comes down, and the carousel whirls round with music and lights, on and off . . . and you watch . . . watch yourself on the horse. You're wearing a mask, a white mask like the mane of the horse, it looks like your face except that it's rigid and white . . . and it changes! With each flick of the lights, the expression, it changes, but always so rigid and hard, like the flesh of the horse that is red that you ride. You ride with no hands! No hands on this petrified horse, its head flung in the air, its wide staring eyes like those of a doe run down by the dogs! . . . And each time you go round, your hands rise a fraction nearer the mask . . . and the music and the carousel and the horse . . . they all three slow down, and they stop. . . . You can reach out and touch . . . you . . . you on the horse . . . with your hands so at the eyes. . . . You look into the eyes! [*A sound from* LIZZIE, *she is horrified and frightened. She covers her eyes.*] There are none! None! Just black holes in a white mask. . . . [*Pause.*] Only a dream. . . . The eyes of your birds . . . are round . . . and bright . . . a light shines from inside . . . they . . . can see into your heart . . . they're pretty . . . they love you. . . .

MR. BORDEN: I want this settled, Harry, I want it settled while Lizzie's out back.

[MISS LIZZIE / BRIDGET *draws* LIZZIE'S *attention to the* MR. BORDEN / HARRY *scene.* LIZZIE *listens, will move closer.*]

HARRY: You know I'm for that.
MR. BORDEN: I want it all done but the signin' of the papers tomorrow, that's if I decide to—
HARRY: You can't lose, Andrew. The farm's just lyin' fallow.
MR. BORDEN: Well, let's see what you got.
HARRY: [*Gets out his papers.*] Look at this . . . I'll run horse auctions and a buggy rental—now I'll pay no rent for the house or pasturage but you get twenty percent, eh? That figure there—
MR. BORDEN: Mmmn.
HARRY: From my horse auctions last year, it'll go up on the farm and you'll get twenty percent off the top. . . . My buggy rental won't do so well . . . that's that figure there, approximate . . . but it all adds up, eh? Adds up for you.
MR. BORDEN: It's a good deal, Harry, but . . .
HARRY: Now I know why you're worried—but the farm will still be in the family, 'cause aren't I family? and whenever you or the girls want to come over for a visit, why I'll send a buggy from the rental, no need for you to have the expense of a horse, eh?
MR. BORDEN: It looks good on paper.
HARRY: There's . . . ah . . . something else, it's a bit awkward but I got to mention it; I'll be severin' a lot of my present connections, and what I figure I've a right to, is some kind of guarantee. . . .
MR. BORDEN: You mean a renewable lease for the farm?
HARRY: Well—what I'm wondering is . . . No offense, but you're an older man, Andrew . . . now if something should happen to you, where would the farm stand in regards to your will? That's what I'm wondering.
MR. BORDEN: I've not made a will.
HARRY: You know best—but I wouldn't want to be in a position where Lizzie would be havin' anything to do with that farm. The less she knows now the better, but she's bound to find out—I don't feel I'm steppin' out of line by bringin' this up.

[LIZZIE *is within earshot. She is staring at* HARRY *and* MR. BORDEN. *They do not see her.*]

MR. BORDEN: No.
HARRY: If you mind you come right out and say so.
MR. BORDEN: That's all right.
HARRY: Now . . . if you . . . put the farm—in Abbie's name, what do you think?
MR. BORDEN: I don't know, Harry.
HARRY: I don't want to push.
MR. BORDEN: . . . I should make a will . . . I want the girls looked after, it don't seem like they'll marry . . . and Abbie, she's younger than me, I know Emma will see to her, still . . .money-wise I got to consider these things . . . it makes a difference no men in the family.

HARRY: You know you can count on me for whatever.

MR. BORDEN: If . . . *If* I changed title to the farm, Abbie'd have to come down to the bank, I wouldn't want Lizzie to know.

HARRY: You can send a note for her when you get to the bank; she can say it's a note from a friend, and come down and meet you. Simple as that.

MR. BORDEN: I'll give it some thought.

HARRY: You see, Abbie owns the farm, it's no difference to you, but it gives me protection.

MR. BORDEN: Who's there?

HARRY: It's Lizzie.

MR. BORDEN: What do you want? . . . Did you lock the shed? . . . Is the shed locked! [LIZZIE *makes a slow motion which* MR. BORDEN *takes for assent*.] Well you make sure it stays locked! I don't want anymore of those god damned. . . . I . . . ah . . . I think we about covered everything, Harry, we'll . . . ah . . . we'll let it go till tomorrow.

HARRY: Good enough . . . well . . . I'll just finish choppin' that kindlin', give a shout when it's lunchtime. [*He exits.*]

[LIZZIE *and* MR. BORDEN *stare at each other for a moment.*]

LIZZIE: [*Very low.*] What are you doing with the farm? [MR. BORDEN *slowly picks up the papers, places them in his pocket.*] Papa! . . . Papa. I want you to show me what you put in your pocket.

MR. BORDEN: It's none of your business.

LIZZIE: The farm is my business.

MR. BORDEN: It's nothing.

LIZZIE: Show me!

MR. BORDEN: I said it's nothing!

[LIZZIE *makes a quick move towards her father to seize the paper from his pocket. Even more quickly and smartly he slaps her face. It is all very quick and clean. A pause as they stand frozen.*]

HARRY: [*Off.*] Andrew, there's a bunch of kids broken into the shed!

MR. BORDEN: Jesus Christ.

LIZZIE: [*Whispers.*] What about the farm.

MR. BORDEN: You! You and those god damn birds! I've told you! I've told you time and again!

LIZZIE: What about the farm!

MR. BORDEN: Jesus Christ . . . You never listen! Never!

HARRY: [*Enters carrying the hand hatchet.*] Andrew!!

MR. BORDEN: [*Grabs the hand hatchet from* HARRY, *turns to* LIZZIE.] There'll be no more of your god damn birds in this yard!!

LIZZIE: No! [MR. BORDEN *raises the hatchet and smashes it into the table as* LIZZIE *screams.*] No Papa!! Nooo!!

[*The hatchet is embedded in the table.* MR. BORDEN *and* HARRY *assume a soft freeze as* ACTRESS / LIZZIE *whirls to see* MISS LIZZIE / BRIDGET *observing the scene.*]

LIZZIE: Nooo!
MISS LIZZIE: I loved them.

BLACKOUT

ACT II

Lights come up on THE ACTRESS / LIZZIE *sitting at the dining room table. She is very still, her hands clasped in her lap.* MISS LIZZIE / BRIDGET *is near her. She too is very still. A pause.*

ACTRESS / LIZZIE: [*Very low.*] Talk to me.
MISS LIZZIE / BRIDGET: I remember . . .
ACTRESS / LIZZIE: [*Very low.*] No.
MISS LIZZIE / BRIDGET: On the farm, Papa's farm, Harry's farm, when I was little and thought it was my farm and I loved it, we had some puppies, the farm dog had puppies, brown soft little puppies with brown ey . . . [*She does not complete the word "eyes."*] And one of the puppies got sick. I didn't know it was sick, it seemed like the others, but the mother, she knew. It would lie at the back of the box, she would lie in front of it while she nursed all the others. They ignored it, that puppy didn't exist for the others. . . . I think inside it was different, and the mother thought the difference she sensed was a sickness . . . and after a while . . . anyone could tell it was sick. It had nothing to eat! . . . And papa took it and drowned it. That's what you do on a farm with things that are different.
ACTRESS / LIZZIE: Am I different?
MISS LIZZIE / BRIDGET: You kill them.

[ACTRESS / LIZZIE *looks at* MISS LIZZIE / BRIDGET. MISS LIZZIE / BRIDGET *looks towards the top of the stairs.* BRIDGET *gets up and exits to the kitchen.* EMMA *appears at the top of the stairs. She is dressed for travel and carries a small suitcase and her gloves. She stares down at* LIZZIE *still sitting at the table. After several moments* LIZZIE *becomes aware of that gaze and turns to look at* EMMA. EMMA *then descends the stairs. She puts down her suitcase. She is not overjoyed at seeing* LIZZIE, *having hoped to get away before* LIZZIE *arose, nevertheless she begins with an excess of enthusiasm to cover the implications of her departure.*]

EMMA: Well! You're up early . . . Bridget down? . . . did you put the coffee on? [*She puts her gloves on the table.*] My goodness, Lizzie, cat got your tongue?

[*She exits to the kitchen.* LIZZIE *picks up the gloves.* EMMA *returns.*]

Bridget's down, she's in the kitchen. . . . Well . . . looks like a real scorcher today, doesn't it? . . .
LIZZIE: What's the bag for?
EMMA: I . . . decided I might go for a little trip, a day or two, get away from the heat. . . . The girls've rented a place out beach way and I thought . . . with the weather and all . . .

LIZZIE: How can you do that?
EMMA: Do What? . . . Anyway I thought I might stay with them a few days. . . . Why don't you come with me?
LIZZIE: No.
EMMA: Just for a few days, come with me.
LIZZIE: No.
EMMA: You know you like the water.
LIZZIE: I said no!
EMMA: Oh, Lizzie.

[*Pause.*]

LIZZIE: I don't see how you can leave me like this.
EMMA: I asked you to come with me.
LIZZIE: You know I can't do that.
EMMA: Why not?
LIZZIE: Someone has to *do* something, you just run away from things.

[*Pause.*]

EMMA: . . . Lizzie . . . I'm sorry about the—[birds]
LIZZIE: No!
EMMA: Papa was angry.
LIZZIE: I don't want to talk about it.
EMMA: He's sorry now.
LIZZIE: Nobody *listens* to me, can't you hear me? I said *don't* talk about it. I don't want to talk about it. Stop talking about it!!

[BRIDGET *enters with the coffee.*]

EMMA: Thank you, Bridget. [BRIDGET *withdraws.*] Well! . . . I certainly can use this this morning. . . . Your coffee's there.
LIZZIE: I don't want it.
EMMA: You're going to ruin those gloves.
LIZZIE: I don't care.
EMMA: Since they're not yours.

[LIZZIE *bangs the gloves down on the table. A pause. Then* EMMA *picks them up and smooths them out.*]

LIZZIE: Why are you leaving me?
EMMA: I feel like a visit with the girls. Is there something wrong with that?
LIZZIE: How can you go now?
EMMA: I don't know what you're getting at.
LIZZIE: I heard them. I heard them talking yesterday. Do you know what they're saying?
EMMA: How could I
LIZZIE: "How could I?" What do you mean "How could I?" Did you know?
EMMA: No, Lizzie, I did not.
LIZZIE: *Did-not-what.*

EMMA: Know.
LIZZIE: But you know now. How do you know now?
EMMA: I've put two and two together and I'm going over to the girls for a visit!
LIZZIE: Please Emma!
EMMA: It's too hot.
LIZZIE: I need you, don't go.
EMMA: I've been talking about this trip.
LIZZIE: That's a lie.
EMMA: They're expecting me.
LIZZIE: You're lying to me!
EMMA: I'm going to the girls' place. You can come if you want, you can stay if you want. I planned this trip and I'm taking it!
LIZZIE: Stop lying!
EMMA: If I want to tell a little white lie to avoid an altercation in this house, I'll do so. Other people have been doing it for years!
LIZZIE: You don't understand, you don't understand anything.
EMMA: Oh, I understand enough.
LIZZIE: You don't! Let me explain it to you. You listen carefully, you listen. . . . Harry's getting the farm, can you understand that? Harry is here and he's moving on the farm and he's going to be there, on the farm, living on the farm. *Our farm*. Do you understand that? . . . Do you understand that!
EMMA: Yes.
LIZZIE: Harry's going to be on the farm. That's the first thing. . . . No . . . no it isn't. . . . The first thing . . . was the mill house, that was the first thing! And *now* the farm. You see there's a pattern, Emma, you can see that, can't you?
EMMA: I don't—
LIZZIE: You can see it! The mill house, then the farm, and the next thing is the papers for the farm—do you know what he's doing, Papa's doing? He's signing the farm over to her. It will never be ours, we will never have it, not ever. It's ours by rights, don't you feel that?
EMMA: The farm—has always meant a great deal to me, yes.
LIZZIE: Then what are you doing about it! You can't leave me now . . . but that's not all. Papa's going to make a will, and you can see the pattern, can't you, and if the pattern keeps on, what do you suppose his will will say. What do you suppose, answer me!
EMMA: I don't know.
LIZZIE: Say it!
EMMA: He'll see we're looked after.
LIZZIE: I don't want to be looked after! What's the matter with you? Do you really want to spend the rest of your life with that cow, listening to her drone on and on for years! That's just what they think you'll do. Papa'll leave you a monthly allowance, just like he'll leave me, just enough to keep us all living together. We'll be worth millions on paper, and be stuck in this house and by and by Papa will die and Harry will move in and you will wait on that cow while she gets fatter and fatter and I—will—sit in my room.

EMMA: Lizzie.

LIZZIE: We have to do something, you can see that. We have to do something!

EMMA: There nothing we can do.

LIZZIE: Don't say that.

EMMA: All right, then, what can we do?

LIZZIE: I . . . I . . . don't know. But we have to do something, you have to help me, you can't go away and leave me alone, you can't do that.

EMMA: Then—

LIZZIE: You know what I thought? I thought you could talk to him, really talk to him, make him understand that we're people. *Individual people*, and we have to live separate lives, and his will should make it possible for us to do that. And the farm can't go to Harry.

EMMA: You know it's no use.

LIZZIE: I can't talk to him anymore. Everytime I talk to him I make everything worse. I hate him, no. No I don't. I hate her. [EMMA *looks at her broach watch.*] Don't look at the time.

EMMA: I'll miss my connections.

LIZZIE: No!

EMMA: [*Puts on her gloves.*] Lizzie. There's certain things we have to face. One of them is, we can't change a thing.

LIZZIE: I won't let you go!

EMMA: I'll be back on the week-end.

LIZZIE: He killed my birds! He took the ax and he killed them! Emma, I ran out and held them in my hands, I felt their hearts throbbing and pumping and the blood gushed out of their necks, it was all over my hands, don't you care about that?

EMMA: I . . . I . . . have a train to catch.

LIZZIE: He didn't care how much he hurt me and you don't care either. Nobody cares.

EMMA: I . . . have to go now.

LIZZIE: That's right. Go away. I don't even like you, Emma. Go away! [EMMA *leaves,* LIZZIE *runs after her calling.*] I'm sorry for all the things I told you! Things I really felt! You pretended to me, and I don't like you!! Go away!! [LIZZIE *runs to the window and looks out after* EMMA'S *departing figure. After a moment she slowly turns back into the room.* MISS LIZZIE / BRIDGET *is there.*] I want to die . . . I want to die, but something inside won't let me . . . inside something says *no.* [*She shuts her eyes.*] I can do anything.

DEFENSE: Miss Borden. [*Both* LIZZIES *turn.*] Could you describe the sequence of events upon your father's arrival home?

LIZZIE: [*With no animation.*] Papa came in . . . we exchanged a few words . . . Bridget and I spoke of the yard goods sale down town, whether she would buy some. She went up to her room . . .

DEFENSE: And then?

LIZZIE: I went out back . . . through the yard . . . I picked up several pears from the ground beneath the trees . . . I went into the shed . . . I stood looking out the window and ate the pears . . .

DEFENSE: How many?
LIZZIE: Four.
DEFENSE: It wasn't warm, stifling in the shed?
LIZZIE: No, it was cool.
DEFENSE: What were you doing, apart from eating the pears?
LIZZIE: I suppose I was thinking. I just stood there, looking out the window, thinking, and eating the pears I'd picked up.
DEFENSE: You're fond of pears?
LIZZIE: Otherwise, I wouldn't eat them.
DEFENSE: Go on.
LIZZIE: I returned to the house. I found—Papa. I called for Bridget.

[MRS. BORDEN *descends the stairs.* LIZZIE *and* BRIDGET *turn to look at her.* MRS. BORDEN *is only aware of* LIZZIE'S *stare. Pause.*]

MRS. BORDEN: . . . What're you staring at? I said what're you staring at?
LIZZIE: [*Continuing to stare at* MRS. BORDEN.] Bridget.
BRIDGET: Yes ma'am.

[*Pause.*]

MRS. BORDEN: Just coffee and a biscuit this morning, Bridget, it's too hot for a decent breakfast.
BRIDGET: Yes ma'am.

[*She exits for the biscuit and coffee.* LIZZIE *continues to stare at* MRS. BORDEN.]

MRS. BORDEN: . . . Tell Bridget I'll have it in the parlour.

[LIZZIE *is making an effort to be pleasant, to be "good."* MRS. BORDEN *is more aware of this as unusual behavior from* LIZZIE *than were she to be rude, biting, or threatening.* LIZZIE, *at the same time, feels caught in a dimension other than the one in which the people around her are operating.* For LIZZIE, *a bell-jar effect. Simple acts seem filled with significance.* LIZZIE *is trying to fulfill other people's expectations of "normal."*]

LIZZIE: It's not me, is it?
MRS. BORDEN: What?
LIZZIE: You're not moving into the parlor because of me, are you?
MRS. BORDEN: What?
LIZZIE: I'd hate to think I'd driven you out of your own dining-room.
MRS. BORDEN: No.
LIZZIE: Oh good, because I'd hate to think that was so.
MRS. BORDEN: It's cooler in the parlor.
LIZZIE: You know, you're right.
MRS. BORDEN: Eh?
LIZZIE: It is cooler. . . . [BRIDGET *enters with the coffee and biscuit.*] I will, Bridget.
[*She takes the coffee and biscuit, gives it to* MRS. BORDEN. LIZZIE *watches her*

eat and drink. MRS. BORDEN *eats the biscuit delicately.* LIZZIE'S *attention is caught by it.*] Do you like that biscuit?

MRS. BORDEN: It could be lighter.

LIZZIE: You're right. [MR. BORDEN *enters, makes his way into the kitchen,* LIZZIE *watches him pass.*] You know, Papa doesn't look well, Papa doesn't look well at all. Papa looks sick.

MRS. BORDEN: He had a bad night.

LIZZIE: Oh?

MRS. BORDEN: Too hot.

LIZZIE: But it's cooler in here, isn't it . . . [*Not trusting her own evaluation of the degree of heat.*] Isn't it?

MRS. BORDEN: Yes, yes, it's cooler in here.

[MR. BORDEN *enters with his coffee.* LIZZIE *goes to him.*]

LIZZIE: Papa? You should go in the parlor. It's much cooler in there, really it is.

[*He goes into the parlor.* LIZZIE *remains in the dining-room She sits at the table, folds her hands in her lap.* MR. BORDEN *begins to read the paper.*]

MRS. BORDEN: . . . I think I'll have Bridget do the windows today . . . they need doing . . . get them out of the way first thing. . . . Anything in the paper, Andrew?

MR. BORDEN: [*As he continues to read.*] Nope.

MRS. BORDEN: There never is . . . I don't know why we buy it.

MR. BORDEN: [*Reading.*] Yup.

MRS. BORDEN: You going out this morning?

MR. BORDEN: Business.

MRS. BORDEN: . . . Harry must be having a bit of a sleep-in.

MR. BORDEN: Yup.

MRS. BORDEN: He's always up by—[HARRY *starts down the stairs.*] Well, speak of the devil—coffee and biscuits?

HARRY: Sounds good to me.

[MRS. BORDEN *starts off to get it.* LIZZIE *looks at her, catching her eye.* MRS. BORDEN *stops abruptly.*]

LIZZIE: [*Her voice seems too loud.*] Emma's gone over to visit at the girls' place. [MR. BORDEN *lowers his paper to look at her.* HARRY *looks at her. Suddenly aware of the loudness of her voice, she continues softly, too softly.*] . . . Till the week-end.

MR. BORDEN: She didn't say she was going, when'd she decide that?

[LIZZIE *looks down at her hands, doesn't answer. A pause. Then* MRS. BORDEN *continues out to the kitchen.*]

HARRY: Will you be ah . . . going down today?

MR. BORDEN: This mornin'. I got . . . business at the bank.

[*A look between them. They are very aware of* LIZZIE'S *presence in the dining-room.*]

HARRY: This mornin' eh? Well now . . . that works out just fine for me. I can . . . I got a bill to settle in town myself.

[LIZZIE *turns her head to look at them.*]

HARRY: I'll be on my way after that.
MR. BORDEN: Abbie'll be disappointed you're not stayin' for lunch.
HARRY: 'Nother time.
MR. BORDEN: [*Aware of* LIZZIE'S *gaze.*] I . . . I don't know where she is with that coffee. I'll—
HARRY: Never you mind, you sit right there, I'll get it.

[*He exits.* LIZZIE *and* MR. BORDEN *look at each other. The bell-jar effect is lessened.*]

LIZZIE: [*Softly.*] Good mornin' Papa.
MR. BORDEN: Mornin' Lizzie.
LIZZIE: Did you have a good sleep?
MR. BORDEN: Not bad.
LIZZIE: Papa?
MR. BORDEN: Yes Lizzie.
LIZZIE: You're a very strong-minded person, Papa, do you think I'm like you?
MR. BORDEN: In some ways . . . perhaps.
LIZZIE: I must be like someone.
MR. BORDEN: You resemble your mother.
LIZZIE: I look like my mother?
MR. BORDEN: A bit like your mother.
LIZZIE: But my mother's dead.
MR. BORDEN: Lizzie—
LIZZIE: I remember you told me she died because she was sick . . . I was born and she died . . . Did you love her?
MR. BORDEN: I married her.
LIZZIE: Can't you say if you loved her.
MR. BORDEN: Of course I did, Lizzie.
LIZZIE: Did you hate me for killing her?
MR. BORDEN: You don't think of it that way, it was just something that happened.
LIZZIE: Perhaps she just got tired and died. She didn't want to go on, and the chance came up and she took it. I could understand that. . . . Perhaps she was like a bird, she could see all the blue sky and she wanted to fly away but she couldn't. She was caught, Papa, she was caught in a horrible snare, and she saw a way out and she took it. . . . Perhaps it was a very brave thing to do, Papa, perhaps it was the only way, and she hated to leave because she loved us so much, but she couldn't breathe all caught in the snare. . . . [*Long pause.*] Some people have very small wrists, have you noticed. Mine aren't . . . [*There is a murmur from the kitchen, then muted laughter.* MR. BORDEN *looks towards it.*] Papa! . . . I'm a very strong person.
MRS. BORDEN: [*Off, laughing.*] You're tellin' tales out of school, Harry!
HARRY: [*Off.*] God's truth. You should have seen the buggy when they brought it back.

MRS. BORDEN: [*Off.*] You've got to tell Andrew. [*Pokes her head in.*] Andrew, come on out here, Harry's got a story. [*Off.*] Now you'll have to start at the beginning again, oh my goodness.

[MRS. BORDEN *starts for the kitchen. He stops, and looks back at* LIZZIE.]

LIZZIE: Is there anything you want to tell me, Papa?
MRS. BORDEN: [*Off.*] Andrew!
LIZZIE: [*Softly, an echo.*] Andrew.
MR. BORDEN: What is it, Lizzie?
LIZZIE: If I promised to be a good girl forever and ever, would anything change?
MR. BORDEN: I don't know what you're talkin' about.
LIZZIE: I would be lying . . . Papa! . . . Don't do any business today. Don't go out. Stay home.
MR. BORDEN: What for?
LIZZIE: Everyone's leaving. Going away. Everyone's left.
MRS. BORDEN: [*Off.*] Andrew!
LIZZIE: [*Softly, an echo.*] Andrew.
MR. BORDEN: What is it?
LIZZIE: I'm calling you. [MR. BORDEN *looks at her for a moment, then leaves for the kitchen.* DR. PATRICK *is heard whistling very softly.* LIZZIE *listens.*] Listen . . . can you hear it . . . can you?
MISS LIZZIE / BRIDGET: I can hear it. . . . It's stopped.

[DR. PATRICK *can't be seen. Only his voice is heard.*]

DR. PATRICK: [*Very low.*] Lizzie?
LIZZIE: [*Realization.*] I could hear it before [you]. [*Pause.*] It sounded so sad I wanted to cry.
MISS LIZZIE / BRIDGET: You mustn't cry.
LIZZIE: I mustn't cry.
DR. PATRICK: I bet you know this one. [*He whistles an Irish jig.*]
LIZZIE: I know that! [*She begins to dance.*]

[DR. PATRICK *enters. He claps in time to the dance.* LIZZIE *finishes the jig.* DR. PATRICK *applauds.*]

DR. PATRICK: Bravo! Bravo!!
LIZZIE: You didn't know I could do that, did you?
DR. PATRICK: You're a woman of many talents, Miss Borden.
LIZZIE: You're not making fun of me?
DR. PATRICK: I would never do that.
LIZZIE: I can do anything I want.
DR. PATRICK: I'm sure you can.
LIZZIE: If I wanted to die—I could even do that, couldn't I.
DR. PATRICK: Well now, I don't think so.
LIZZIE: Yes, I could!
DR. PATRICK: Lizzie—
LIZZIE: You wouldn't know—you can't see into my heart.

DR. PATRICK: I think I can.
LIZZIE: Well you can't!
DR. PATRICK: . . . It's only a game.
LIZZIE: I never play games.
DR. PATRICK: Sure you do.
LIZZIE: I hate games.
DR. PATRICK: You're playin' one now.
LIZZIE: You don't even know me!
DR. PATRICK: Come on Lizzie, we don't want to fight. I know what we'll do . . . we'll start over. . . . Shut your eyes, Lizzie. [*She does so.*] Good mornin' Miss Borden. . . . Good mornin' Miss Borden. . . .
LIZZIE: . . . I haven't decided. . . . [*She slowly opens her eyes.*] . . . if it is or it isn't.
DR. PATRICK: Much better . . . and now . . . would you take my arm, Miss Borden? How about a wee promenade?
LIZZIE: There's nowhere to go.
DR. PATRICK: That isn't so. . . . What about Boston? . . . Do you think it's too far for a stroll? . . . I know what we'll do, we'll walk 'round to the side and you'll show me your birds. [*They walk.*] . . . I waited last night but you never showed up . . . there I was, travellin' bag and all, and you never appeared . . . I know what went wrong! We forgot to agree on an hour! Next time, Lizzie, you must set the hour. . . . Is this where they're kept? [LIZZIE *nods, she opens the cage and looks in it.*] It's empty. [*He laughs.*] And you say you never play games?
LIZZIE: They're gone.
DR. PATRICK: You've been havin' me on again, yes you have.
LIZZIE: They've run away.
DR. PATRICK: Did they really exist?
LIZZIE: I had blood on my hands.
DR. PATRICK: What do you say?
LIZZIE: You can't see it now, I washed it off, see?
DR. PATRICK: [*Takes her hands.*] Ah Lizzie. . . .
LIZZIE: Would you . . . help someone die?
DR. PATRICK: Why do you ask that?
LIZZIE: Some people are better off dead. I might be better off dead.
DR. PATRICK: You're a precious and unique person, Lizzie, and you shouldn't think things like that.
LIZZIE: Precious and unique?
DR. PATRICK: All life is precious and unique.
LIZZIE: I am precious and unique? . . . I *am* precious and unique. You said that.
DR. PATRICK: Oh, I believe it.
LIZZIE: And I am. I know it. People mix things up on you, you have to be careful. I am a person of worth.
DR. PATRICK: Sure you are.
LIZZIE: Not like that fat cow in there.
DR. PATRICK: Her life too is—

LIZZIE: No!
DR. PATRICK: Liz—
LIZZIE: Do you know her?
DR. PATRICK: That doesn't matter.
LIZZIE: Yes it does, it does matter.
DR. PATRICK: You can't be—
LIZZIE: You're a doctor, isn't that right?
DR. PATRICK: Right enough there.
LIZZIE: So, tell me, tell me, if a dreadful accident occurred . . . and two people were dying . . . but you could only save one. . . . Which would you save?
DR. PATRICK: You can't ask questions like that.
LIZZIE: Yes I can, come on, it's a game. How does a doctor determine? If one were old and the other were young—would you save the younger one first?
DR. PATRICK: Lizzie.
LIZZIE: You said you liked games! If one were a bad person and the other was good, was trying to be good, would you save the one who was good and let the bad person die?
DR. PATRICK: I don't know.
LIZZIE: Listen! If you could go back in time . . . what would you do if you met a person who was evil and wicked?
DR. PATRICK: Who?
LIZZIE: I don't know, Attila the Hun!
DR. PATRICK: [*Laughs.*] Oh my.
LIZZIE: Listen, if you met Attila the Hun, and you were in a position to kill him, would you do it?
DR. PATRICK: I don't know.
LIZZIE: Think of the suffering he caused, the unhappiness.
DR. PATRICK: Yes, but I'm a doctor, not an assassin.
LIZZIE: I think you're a coward.

[*Pause.*]

DR. PATRICK: What I do is try to save lives . . .
LIZZIE: But you put poison out for the slugs in your garden.
DR. PATRICK: You got something mixed up.
LIZZIE: I've never been clearer. Everything's clear. I've lived all of my life for this one moment of absolute charity! If war were declared, would you serve?
DR. PATRICK: I would fight in a war.
LIZZIE: You wouldn't fight, you would kill—you'd take a gun and shoot people, people who'd done nothing to you, people who were trying to be good, you'd kill them! And you say you wouldn't kill Attila the Hun, or that that stupid cow's life is precious—*My life is precious!!*
DR. PATRICK: To you.
LIZZIE: Yes to me, are you stupid!?
DR. PATRICK: And hers is to her.
LIZZIE: I don't care about her! [*Pause.*] I'm glad you're not my doctor, you can't

make decisions, can you? You are a coward. [DR. PATRICK *starts off.*] You're afraid of your wife . . . you can *only* play games. . . . If I really wanted to go to Boston, you wouldn't come with me because you're a coward! *I'm not a coward!!* [LIZZIE *turns to watch* MRS. BORDEN *sit with needle work. After a moment* MRS. BORDEN *looks at* LIZZIE, *aware of her scrutiny.*] . . . Where's Papa?

MRS. BORDEN: Out.

LIZZIE: And Mr. Wingate?

MRS. BORDEN: He's out too.

LIZZIE: So what are you going to do . . . Mrs. Borden?

MRS. BORDEN: I'm going to finish this up.

LIZZIE: You do that. . . . [*Pause.*] Where's Bridget?

MRS. BORDEN: Out back washing windows. . . . You got clean clothes to go upstairs, they're in the kitchen.

[*Pause.*]

LIZZIE: Did you know Papa killed my birds with the ax? He chopped off their heads. [*Mrs. Borden is uneasy.*] . . . It's all right. At first I felt bad, but I feel better now. I feel much better now. . . . I am a woman of decision, Mrs. Borden. When I decide to do things, I do them, yes, I do. [*Smiles.*] How many times has Papa said—when Lizzie puts her mind to a thing, she does it—and I do. . . . It's always me who puts the slug poison out because they eat all the flowers and you don't like that, do you? They're bad things, they must die. You see, not all life is precious, is it? [MRS. BORDEN *after a moment makes an attempt casually to gather together her things, to go upstairs. She does not want to be in the room with* LIZZIE.] Where're you going?

MRS. BORDEN: Upstairs. . . . [*An excuse.*] The spare room needs changing.

[*A knock at the back door. . . . A second knock.*]

LIZZIE: Someone's at the door. . . . [*A third knock.*] I'll get it. [*She exits to the kitchen.* MRS. BORDEN *waits.* LIZZIE *returns. She's a bit out of breath. She carries a pile of clean clothes which she puts on the table. She looks at* MRS. BORDEN.] Did you want something?

MRS. BORDEN: Who was it?—the door?

LIZZIE: Oh yes. I forgot. I had to step out back for a moment and—it's a note. A message for you.

MRS. BORDEN: Oh.

LIZZIE: Shall I open it?

MRS. BORDEN: That's all right. [*She holds out her hand.*]

LIZZIE: Looks like Papa's handwriting. . . . [*She passes over the note.*] Aren't you going to open it?

MRS. BORDEN: I'll read it upstairs.

LIZZIE: Mrs. Borden! . . . Would you mind . . . putting my clothes in my room? [*She gets some clothes from the table, Mrs. Borden takes them, something she would never normally do. Before she can move away, Lizzie grabs her arm.*]

Just a minute . . . I would like you to look into my eyes. What's the matter? Nothing's wrong. It's an experiment. . . . Look right into them. Tell me . . . what do you see . . . can you see anything?

MRS. BORDEN: . . . Myself.

LIZZIE: Yes. When a person dies, retained on her eye is the image of the last thing she saw. Isn't that interesting? [*Pause.* MRS. BORDEN *slowly starts upstairs.* LIZZIE *picks up remaining clothes on table. The hand hatchet is concealed beneath them. She follows* MRS. BORDEN *up the stairs.*] Do you know something? If I were to kill someone, I would come up behind them very slowly and quietly. They would never even hear me, they would never turn around. [MRS. BORDEN *stops on the stairs. She turns around to look at* LIZZIE *who is behind her.*] They would be too frightened to turn around even if they heard me. They would be so afraid they'd see what they feared. [MRS. BORDEN *makes a move which might be an effort to go past* LIZZIE *back down the stairs.* LIZZIE *stops her.*] Careful. Don't fall. [MRS. BORDEN *turns and slowly continues up the stairs with* LIZZIE *behind her.*] And then, I would strike them down. With them not turning around, they would retain no image of me on their eye. It would be better that way. [LIZZIE *and* MRS. BORDEN *disappear at the top of the stairs. The stage is empty for a moment.* BRIDGET *enters. She carries the pail for washing the windows. She sets the pail down, wipes her forehead. She stands for a moment looking towards the stairs as if she might have heard a sound. She picks up the pail and exits to the kitchen.* LIZZIE *appears on the stairs. She is carrying the pile of clothes she carried upstairs. The hand hatchet is concealed under the clothes.* LIZZIE *descends the stairs, she seems calm, self-possessed. She places the clothes on the table. She pauses, then she slowly turns to look at* MRS. BORDEN'S *chair at the table. After a moment she moves to it, pauses a moment, then sits down in it. She sits there at ease, relaxed, thinking.* BRIDGET *enters from the kitchen, she sees* LIZZIE, *she stops, she takes in* LIZZIE *sitting in* MRS. BORDEN'S *chair.* BRIDGET *glances towards the stairs, back to* LIZZIE. LIZZIE *looks, for the first time, at* BRIDGET.] We must hurry before Papa gets home.

BRIDGET: Lizzie?

LIZZIE: I have it all figured out, but you have to help me, Bridget, you have to help me.

BRIDGET: What have you done?

LIZZIE: He would never leave me the farm, not with her on his back, but now [*She gets up from the chair.*] I will have the farm, and I will have the money, yes, to do what I please! And you too Bridget, I'll give you some of my money but you've got to help me. [*She moves towards Bridget who backs away a step.*] Don't be afraid, it's me, it's Lizzie, you like me!

BRIDGET: What have you done? [*Pause. She moves towards the stairs.*]

LIZZIE: Don't go up there!

BRIDGET: You killed her!

LIZZIE: Someone broke in and they killed her.

BRIDGET: They'll know!

LIZZIE: Not if you help me.

BRIDGET: I can't, Miss Lizzie, I can't!

LIZZIE: [*Grabs Bridget's arm.*] Do you want them to hang me? Is that what you want? Oh Bridget, look! Look! [*She falls to her knees.*] I'm begging for my life, I'm begging. Deny me, and they will kill me. Help me, Bridget, please help me.

BRIDGET: But . . . what . . . could we do?

LIZZIE: [*Up off her knees.*] Oh I have it all figured out. I'll go down town as quick as I can and you leave the doors open and go back outside and work on the windows.

BRIDGET: I've finished them, Lizzie.

LIZZIE: Then do them again! Remember last year when the burglar broke in? Today someone broke in and she caught them.

BRIDGET: They'll never believe us.

LIZZIE: Have coffee with Lucy next door, stay with her till Papa gets home and he'll find her, and then each of us swears she was fine when we left, she was all right when we left!—it's going to work, Bridget, I know it!

BRIDGET: Your papa will guess.

LIZZIE: [*Getting ready to leave for downtown.*] If he found me here he might guess, but he won't.

BRIDGET: Your papa will know!

LIZZIE: Papa loves me, if he has another story to believe, he'll believe it. He'd want to believe it, he'd have to believe it.

BRIDGET: Your papa will know.

LIZZIE: Why aren't you happy? I'm happy. We both should be happy! [LIZZIE *embraces* BRIDGET. LIZZIE *steps back a pace.*] Now—how do I look? [MR. BORDEN *enters.* BRIDGET *sees him.* LIZZIE *slowly turns to see what* BRIDGET *is looking at.*] Papa?

MR. BORDEN: What is it? Where's Mrs. Borden?

BRIDGET: I . . . don't know . . . sir . . . I . . . just came in, sir.

MR. BORDEN: Did she leave the house?

BRIDGET: Well, sir . . .

LIZZIE: She went out. Someone delivered a message and she left. [LIZZIE *takes off her hat and looks at her father.*] . . . You're home early, Papa.

MR. BORDEN: I wanted to see Abbie. She's gone out, has she? Which way did she go? [LIZZIE *shrugs, he continues, more thinking aloud.*] Well . . . I . . . I . . . best wait for her here. I don't want to miss her again.

LIZZIE: Help Papa off with his coat, Bridget. . . . I hear there's a sale of dress goods on downtown. Why don't you go buy yourself a yard?

BRIDGET: Oh . . . I don't know, ma'am.

LIZZIE: You don't want any?

BRIDGET: I don't know.

LIZZIE: Then . . . why don't you go upstairs and lie down. Have a rest before lunch.

BRIDGET: I don't think I should.

LIZZIE: Nonsense.

BRIDGET: Lizzie, I—

LIZZIE: You go up and lie down. I'll look after things here. [LIZZIE *smiles at* BRIDGET. BRIDGET *starts up the stairs, suddenly stops. She looks back at* LIZZIE.] It's all right go on . . . it's all right. [BRIDGET *continues up the stairs. For the last bit of interchange,* MR. BORDEN *has lowered the paper he's reading.* LIZZIE *looks at him.*] Hello papa. You look so tired. . . . I make you unhappy. . . . I don't like to make you unhappy. I love you.

MR. BORDEN: [*Smiles and takes her hand.*] I'm just getting old, Lizzie.

LIZZIE: You've got on my ring. Do you remember when I gave you that? . . . When I left Miss Cornelia's—it was in a little blue velvet box, you hid it behind your back, and you said, "Guess which hand, Lizzie!" And I guessed. And you gave it to me and you said, "It's real gold, Lizzie, it's for you because you are very precious to me." Do you remember, Papa? [MR. BORDEN *nods.*] And I took it out of the little blue velvet box, and I took your hand, and I put my ring on your finger and I said "thank you, Papa, I love you." . . . You've never taken it off . . . see how it bites into the flesh of your finger. [*She presses his hand to her face.*] I forgive you, Papa, I forgive you for killing my birds. . . . You look so tired, why don't you lie down and rest, put your feet up, I'll undo your shoes for you. [*She kneels and undoes his shoes.*]

MR. BORDEN: You're a good girl.

LIZZIE: I could never stand to have you hate me, Papa. Never. I would do anything rather than have you hate me.

MR. BORDEN: I don't hate you, Lizzie.

LIZZIE: I would not want you to find out anything that would make you hate me. Because I love you.

MR. BORDEN: And I love you, Lizzie, you'll always be precious to me.

LIZZIE: [*Looks at him, and then smiles.*] Was I—when I had scabs on my knees?

MR. BORDEN: [*Laughs.*] Oh yes. Even then.

LIZZIE: [*Laughs.*] Oh Papa! . . . Kiss me! [*He kisses her on the forehead.*] Thank you, Papa.

MR. BORDEN: Why're you crying?

LIZZIE: Because I'm so happy. Now . . . put your feet up and get to sleep . . . that's right . . . shut your eyes . . . go to sleep . . . go to sleep . . .

[*She starts to hum, continues humming as* MR. BORDEN *falls asleep.* MISS LIZZIE / BRIDGET *appears on the stairs unobstrusively.* LIZZIE *still humming, moves to the table, slips her hand under the clothes, withdraws the hatchet. She approaches her father with the hatchet behind her back. She stops humming. A pause, then she slowly raises the hatchet very high to strike him. Just as the hatchet is about to start its descent, there is a black out. Children's voices are heard singing:*

"Lizzie Borden took an ax,
Gave her mother forty whacks,
When the job was nicely done,
She gave her father forty-one!

Forty-one!
Forty-one!"

The singing increases in volume and in distortion as it nears the end of the verse till the last words are very loud but discernible, just. Silence. Then the sound of slow measured heavy breathing which is growing into a wordless sound of hysteria. Light returns to the stage, dim light from late in the day. THE ACTRESS *stands with the hatchet raised in the same position in which we saw her before the blackout, but the couch is empty. Her eyes are shut. The sound comes from her.* MISS LIZZIE is at the foot of the stairs. She moves to THE ACTRESS, *reaches up to take the hatchet from her. When* MISS LIZZIE'S *hand touches* THE ACTRESS'S, THE ACTRESS *releases the hatchet and whirls around to face* MISS LIZZIE *who is left holding the hatchet.* THE ACTRESS *backs away from* MISS LIZZIE. *There is a flickering of light at the top of the stairs.*]

EMMA: [*From upstairs.*] Lizzie! Lizzie! You're making too much noise! [EMMA *descends the stairs carrying an oil lamp.* THE ACTRESS *backs away from* LIZZIE, *turns and runs into the kitchen.* MISS LIZZIE *turns to see* EMMA. *The hand hatchet is behind* MISS LIZZIE'S *back concealed from* EMMA. EMMA *pauses for a moment.*] Where is she?

MISS LIZZIE: Who?

[*A pause, then* EMMA *moves to the window and glances out.*]

EMMA: It's raining.
MISS LIZZIE: I know.
EMMA: [*Puts the lamp down, sits, lowers her voice.*] Lizzie.
MISS LIZZIE: Yes?
EMMA: I want to speak to you, Lizzie.
MISS LIZZIE: Yes Emma.
EMMA: That . . . actress who's come up from Boston.
MISS LIZZIE: What about her?
EMMA: People talk.
MISS LIZZIE: You needn't listen.
EMMA: In your position you should do nothing to *inspire talk*.
MISS LIZZIE: People need so little in the way of inspiration. And Miss Cornelia's classes didn't cover "Etiquette for Acquitted Persons."
EMMA: Common sense should tell you what you ought or ought not do.
MISS LIZZIE: Common sense is repugnant to me. I prefer uncommon sense.
EMMA: I forbid her in this house, Lizzie!

[*Pause.*]

MISS LIZZIE: Do you?
EMMA: [*Backing down, softly.*] It's . . . disgraceful.
MISS LIZZIE: I see. [*She turns away from* EMMA *a few steps.*]
EMMA: I simply cannot—
MISS LIZZIE: You could always leave.
EMMA: Leave?

MISS LIZZIE: Move. Away. Why don't you?

EMMA: I—

MISS LIZZIE: You could never, could you?

EMMA: If I only—

MISS LIZZIE: Knew.

EMMA: Lizzie, did you?

MISS LIZZIE: Oh Emma, do you intend asking me that question from now till death us do part?

EMMA: It's just—

MISS LIZZIE: For if you do, I may well take something sharp to you.

EMMA: Why do you joke like that!

MISS LIZZIE: [*Turning back to* EMMA *who sees the hatchet for the first time.* EMMA'S *reaction is not any verbal or untoward movement. She freezes as* MISS LIZZIE *advances on her.*] Did you never stop and think that if I did, then you were guilty too?

EMMA: What?

[THE ACTRESS *will enter unobtrusively on the periphery. We are virtually unaware of her entrance until she speaks and moves forward.*]

MISS LIZZIE: It was you who brought me up, like a mother to me. Almost like a mother. Did you ever stop and think that I was like a puppet, your puppet. My head your hand, yes, your hand working my mouth, me saying all the things you felt like saying, me doing all the things you felt like doing, me spewing forth, me hitting out, and you, you—!

THE ACTRESS: [*Quietly.*] Lizzie.

[MISS LIZZIE *is immediately in control of herself.*]

EMMA: [*Whispers.*] I wasn't even here that day.

MISS LIZZIE: I can swear to that.

EMMA: Do you want to drive me mad?

MISS LIZZIE: Oh yes.

EMMA: You didn't . . . did you?

MISS LIZZIE: Poor . . . Emma.

THE ACTRESS: Lizzie. [*She takes the hatchet from* MISS LIZZIE.] Lizzie, you did.

MISS LIZZIE: I didn't. [THE ACTRESS *looks to the hatchet—then to the audience.*] You did.

BLACKOUT

1981

AUGUST WILSON

Fences

CHARACTERS

TROY MAXON
JIM BONO, *Troy's friend*
ROSE, *Troy's wife*
LYONS, *Troy's oldest son by previous marriage*
GABRIEL, *Troy's brother*
CORY, *Troy and Rose's son*
RAYNELL, *Troy's daughter*

SETTING

The setting is the yard that fronts the only entrance to the MAXON *household, an ancient two-story brick house set back off a small alley in a big-city neighborhood. The entrance to the house is gained by two or three steps leading to a wooden porch badly in need of paint.*

A relatively recent addition to the house and running its full width, the porch lacks congruence. It is a sturdy porch with a flat roof. One or two chairs of dubious value sit at one end where the kitchen window opens onto the porch. An old-fashioned icebox stands silent guard at the opposite end.

The yard is a small dirt yard, partially fenced, except for the last scene, with a wooden sawhorse, a pile of lumber, and other fence-building equipment set off to the side. Opposite is a tree from which hangs a ball made of rags. A baseball bat leans against the tree. Two oil drums serve as garbage receptacles and sit near the house at right.

THE PLAY

Near the turn of the century, the destitute of Europe sprang on the city with tenacious claws and an honest and solid dream. The city devoured them. They swelled its belly until it burst into a thousand furnaces and sewing machines, a thousand butcher shops and bakers' ovens, a thousand churches and banks and hospitals and funeral parlors. The city grew. It nourished itself and offered each man a partnership limited only by his talent, his guile, and his willingness and capacity for hard work. For the immigrants of Europe, a dream dared and won true.

The descendants of African slaves were offered no such welcome or participation. They came from places called the Carolinas and the Virginias, Georgia, Alabama, Mississippi, and Tennessee. They came strong, eager, searching. The city rejected them and they fled and settled along the riverbanks and under bridges in shallow, ramshackle houses made of sticks and tar paper. They collected rags and wood. They sold the use of their muscles and their bodies. They cleaned houses and washed clothes, they shined shoes, and in quiet desperation and vengeful pride, they stole, and lived in pursuit of their own dream: that they could breathe free, finally, and stand to meet life with the force of dignity and whatever eloquence the heart could call upon.

By 1957, the hard-won victories of the European immigrants had solidified the industrial might of America. War had been confronted and won with new energies that used loyalty and patriotism as its fuel. Life was rich, full, and flourishing. The Milwaukee Braves won the World Series, and the hot winds of change that would make the sixties a turbulent, racing, dangerous, and provocative decade had not yet begun to blow full.

ACT I

Scene 1

It is 1957. TROY *and* BONO *enter the yard engaged in conversation.* TROY *is fifty-three years old, a large man with thick heavy hands; it is this largeness that he strives to fill out and make an accommodation with. Together with his blackness, his largeness informs his sensibilities and the choices he has made in his life. Of the two men,* BONO *is obviously the follower. His commitment to their friendship of thirty-odd years is rooted in his admiration of* TROY*'s honesty, capacity for hard work, and his strength, which* BONO *seeks to emulate.*

It is Friday night, payday, and the one night of the week the two men engage in a ritual of talk and drink. TROY *is usually the most talkative and at times he can be crude and almost vulgar, though he is capable of rising to profound heights of expression. The men carry lunch buckets and wear or carry burlap aprons and are dressed in clothes suitable to their jobs as garbage collectors.*

BONO: Troy, you ought to stop that lying!

TROY: I ain't lying! The nigger had a watermelon this big. [TROY *indicates with his hands.*] Talking about . . . "What watermelon, Mr. Rand?" I liked to fell out! "What watermelon, Mr. Rand?" . . . And it sitting there big as life.

BONO: What did Mr. Rand say?

TROY: Ain't said nothing. Figure if the nigger too dumb to know he carrying a watermelon, he wasn't gonna get much sense out of him. Trying to hide that great big old watermelon under his coat. Afraid to let the white man see him carry it home.

BONO: I'm like you . . . I ain't got no time for them kind of people.

TROY: Now what he look like getting mad 'cause he see the man from the union talking to Mr. Rand?

BONO: Well, as long as you got your complaint filed, they can't fire you. That's what one of them white fellows tell me.

TROY: I ain't worried about them firing me. They gonna fire me 'cause I asked a question? That's all I did. I went to Mr. Rand and asked him why. "Why you got the white mens driving and the colored lifting?" Told him, "What's the matter, don't I count? You think only white fellows got sense enough to drive a truck. That ain't no paper job! Hell, anybody can drive a truck. How come you got all whites driving and the colored lifting?" He told me take it to the union. Well, hell, that's what I done! Now they wanna come up with this pack of lies.

BONO: I told Brownie if the man come and ask him any questions . . . just tell the truth! It ain't nothing but something they done trumped up on you 'cause you filed a complaint on them.

TROY: Brownie don't understand nothing. All I want them to do is change the job description. Give everybody a chance to drive the truck. Brownie can't see that. He ain't got that much sense.

BONO: How you figure he making out with that gal be up at Taylor's all the time . . . that Alberta gal?

TROY: Same as you and me. Getting just as much as we is. Which is to say nothing.

BONO: It is, huh? I figure you doing a little better than me . . . and I ain't saying what I'm doing.

TROY: Aw, nigger, look here . . . I know you. If you had got anywhere near that gal, twenty minutes later you gonna be looking to tell somebody. And the first one you gonna tell . . . that you gonna want to brag to . . . is gonna be me.

BONO: I ain't saying that. I see where you be eyeing her.

TROY: I eye all the women. I don't miss nothing. Don't never let nobody tell you Troy Maxson don't eye the women.

BONO: You been doing more than eyeing her. You done bought her a drink or two.

TROY: Hell yeah, I bought her a drink! What that mean? I bought you one, too. What that mean 'cause I buy her a drink? I'm just being polite.

BONO: It's all right to buy her one drink. That's what you call being polite. But when you wanna be buying two or three . . . that's what you call eyeing her.

TROY: Look here, as long as you known me . . . you ever known me to chase after women?

BONO: Hell yeah! Long as I done known you. You forgetting I knew you when.

TROY: Naw, I'm talking about since I been married to Rose?

BONO: Not since you been married to Rose. That's the truth. I can say that.

TROY: All right then! Case closed.

BONO: I see you be walking up around Alberta's house.

TROY: What you watching where I'm walking for? I ain't watching after you.

BONO: I seen you walking around there more than once.

TROY: Hell, you liable to see me walking anywhere! That don't mean nothing 'cause you see me walking around there.

BONO: Where she come from anyway? She just kinda showed up one day.

TROY: Tallahassee. You can look at her and tell she one of them Florida gals. They got some big healthy women down there. Grow them right up out the ground. Got a little bit of Indian in her. Most of them niggers down in Florida got some Indian in them.

BONO: I don't know about that Indian part. But she damn sure big and healthy. Woman wear some big stockings. Got them great big old legs and hips as wide as the Mississippi River.

TROY: Legs don't mean nothing. You don't do nothing but push them out of the way. But them hips cushion the ride.

BONO: Troy, you ain't got no sense.

TROY: It's the truth! Like you riding on Goodyears!

[ROSE *enters from the house. She is ten years younger than* TROY, *and her devotion to him stems from her recognition of the possibilities of her life without him: a succession of abusive men and their babies, a life of partying and running the streets, the church, or aloneness with its attendant pain and frustration. She recognizes* TROY'*s spirit as a fine and illuminating one and she either ignores or forgives his faults, only some of which she recognizes. Though she doesn't drink, her presence is an integral part of the Friday-night rituals. She alternates between the porch and the kitchen, where supper preparations are under way.*]

ROSE: What you all out here getting into?

TROY: What you worried about what we getting into for? This is men talk, woman.

ROSE: What I care what you are talking about? Bono, you gonna stay for supper?

BONO: I thank you, Rose. But Lucille say she cooking up a pot of pig feet.

TROY: Pig feet! Hell, I'm going home with you! Might even stay the night if you got some pig feet. You got something in there to top them pig feet, Rose?

ROSE: I'm cooking up some chicken. I got some chicken and collard greens.

TROY: Well, go on back in the house and let me and Bono finish what we was talking about. This is men talk. I got some talk for you later. You know what kind of talk I mean. You go on and powder it up.

ROSE: Troy Maxson, don't you start that now!

TROY: [*Puts his arm around* ROSE.] Aw, woman . . . come here. Look here, Bono . . . when I met this woman . . . I got out that place, say, "Hitch up my pony, saddle up my mare . . . there's a woman out there for me somewhere." I looked here. Looked there. Saw Rose and latched on to her. I latched on to her and told her—I'm gonna tell you the truth—I told her, "Baby, I don't wanna marry, I just wanna be your man." Rose told me . . . Tell him what you told me, Rose.

ROSE: I told him if he wasn't the marrying kind, then move out the way so the marrying kind could find me.

TROY: That's what she told me. "Nigger, you in my way. You blocking the view! Move out the way so I can find me a husband." I thought it over two or three days. Come back—

ROSE: [*Interrupting.*] Ain't no two or three days nothing. You was back the same night.

TROY: Come back, told her, "Okay, baby . . . but I'm gonna buy me a banty rooster and put him out there in the backyard, and when he see a stranger come, he'll flap his wings and crow . . ." Look here, Bono, I could watch the front door by myself; it was that backdoor I was worried about.

ROSE: Troy, you ought not talk like that. Troy ain't doing nothing but telling a lie.

TROY: Only thing is, when we first got married—forget the rooster—we ain't had no yard!

BONO: I hear you tell it. Me and Lucille was staying down there on Logan Street.

Had two rooms with the outhouse in the back. I ain't mind the outhouse none. But when that goddamn wind blow through there in the winter, that's what I'm talking about! To this day I wonder why in the hell I ever stayed down there for six long years. But see, I didn't know I could do better. I thought only white folks had inside toilets and things.

ROSE: There's a lot of people don't know they can do better than they doing now. That's just something you got to learn. A lot of folks still shop at Bella's.

TROY: Ain't nothing wrong with shopping at Bella's. She got fresh food.

ROSE: I ain't said nothing about if she got fresh food. I'm talking about what she charge. She charge ten cents more than the A&P.

TROY: The A&P ain't never done nothing for me. I spends my money where I'm treated right. I go down to Bella, say, "I need a loaf of bread, I'll pay you on Friday," she give it to me. What sense that make when I got money to go and spend it somewhere else and ignore the person who done right by me? That ain't in the Bible.

ROSE: We ain't talking about what's in the Bible. What sense it make to shop there when she overcharge?

TROY: You shop where you want to. I'll do my shopping where the people been good to me.

ROSE: Well, I don't think it's right for her to overcharge. That's all I was saying.

BONO: Look here . . . I got to get on. Lucille going be raising all kind of hell.

TROY: Where you going, nigger? We ain't finished this pint. Come on, finish this pint.

BONO: Well, hell, I am . . . if you ever turn the bottle loose.

TROY: [*Hands him the bottle.*] The only thing I say about the A&P is I'm glad Cory got that job down there. Help him take care of his school clothes and things. Gabe done moved out and things getting tight around here. He got that job. He can start to look out for himself.

ROSE: Cory done went and got recruited by a college football team.

TROY: I told that boy about that football stuff. The white man ain't gonna let him get nowhere with that football. I told him when he first come to me with it. Now you come telling me he done went and got more tied up in it. He need to go and get recruited in how to fix cars or something where he can make a living.

ROSE: He ain't talking about making no living playing football. It's just something the boys in school do. They gonna send a recruiter by to talk to you. He'll tell you he ain't talking about making no living playing football. It's a honor to be recruited.

TROY: It ain't gonna get him nowhere. Bono'll tell you that.

BONO: If he be like you in the sports, he's gonna be all right. Ain't but two men ever played baseball as good as you. That's Babe Ruth and Josh Gibson. Thems the only two men hit a baseball farther than you.

TROY: What it ever get me? Ain't got a pot to piss in or a window to throw it out of.

ROSE: Times have changed since you was playing baseball, Troy. That was before the war. Times have changed a lot since then.

TROY: It's the same now as it was then. The white man ain't gonna let him get nowhere with that football.

ROSE: They got lots of colored boys playing ball now. Baseball and football.

BONO: You right about that, Rose. Times have changed. Troy just come along too early.

TROY: There ought not never have been no time called too early! Now you take that fellow . . . What's that fellow they had playing left field for the Yankees back then? You know who I'm talking about, Bono. Used to play left field for the Yankees?

ROSE: Selkirk?

TROY: Selkirk! That's it! Man batting .269, understand? .269. What kind of sense that make? I was hitting .432 with thirty-seven home runs! Man batting .269 and playing left field for the Yankees! I saw Josh Gibson's daughter yesterday. She walking around with raggedy shoes on her feet. Now I bet you Selkirk's daughter ain't walking around with raggedy shoes. I bet you that!

ROSE: They got a lot of colored baseball players now. Jackie Robinson was the first. Folks had to wait for Jackie Robinson.

TROY: I done seen a hundred niggers play baseball better than Jackie Robinson. Hell, I know some teams Jackie Robinson couldn't even make! What you talking about Jackie Robinson. Jackie Robinson wasn't nobody. I'm talking about if you could play ball, then they ought to have let you play. Don't care what color you were. Come telling me I come along too early. If you could play, then they ought to have let you play. [TROY *takes a long drink from the bottle.*]

ROSE: You gonna drink yourself to death. You don't need to be drinking like that.

TROY: Death ain't nothing. I done seen him, done wrestled with him. You can't tell me nothing about death. Death ain't nothing but a fastball on the outside corner. And you know what I'll do to that! Look here, Bono . . . am I lying? You get one of them fastballs about waist high over the outside corner of the plate where you can get the meat of the bat on it . . . and good God! You can kiss it good-bye. Now, am I lying?

BONO: Naw, you telling the truth there. I seen you do it.

TROY: If I'm lying, that's 450 feet worth of lying! [*Pause.*] That's all death is to me. A fastball on the outside corner.

ROSE: I don't know why you want to get on talking about Death.

TROY: Ain't nothing wrong with talking about Death. That's part of life. Everybody gonna die. You gonna die, I'm gonna die, Bono's gonna die. Hell, we all gonna die.

ROSE: But you ain't got to talk about it. I don't like to talk about it.

TROY: You the one brought it up. Me and Bono was talking about baseball . . . you tell me I'm gonna drink myself to Death. Ain't that right, Bono? You know I don't drink this but one night out of the week. That's Friday night. I'm gonna drink just enough to where I can handle it. Then I cuts it loose. I leave it alone. So don't you worry about me drinking myself to death. 'Cause I ain't worried about Death. I done seen him. I done wrestled with him.

Look here, Bono . . . I looked up one day and Death was marching straight at me. Like Soldiers on Parade! The Army of Death marching straight at me. The middle of July, 1941. It got real cold just like to be winter. It seem like Death himself reached out and touched me on the shoulder. He touch me just like I touch you. I got cold as ice and Death standing there grinning at me.

ROSE: Troy, why don't you hush that talk.

TROY: I say, "What you want, Mr. Death? You be wanting me? You done brought your army to be getting me?" I looked him dead in the eye. I wasn't fearing nothing. I was ready to tangle. Just like I'm ready to tangle now. The Bible say be ever vigilant. That's why I don't get but so drunk. I got to keep watch.

ROSE: Troy was right down there in Mercy Hospital. You remember he had pneumonia? Laying there with a fever talking plumb out of his head.

TROY: Death, he ain't said nothing. He just stared at me. He had a thousand men to do his bidding and he wasn't going to get a thousand and one. Not then! Hell, I wasn't but thirty-seven years old. [*Pause.*] Death standing there staring at me . . . carrying that sickle in his hand. Finally he say, "You want bound over for another year?" See, just like that . . . "You want bound over for another year?" I told him, "Bound over hell! Let's settle this now!" It seem like he kinda fell back when I said that, and all the cold went out of me. I reached out and grabbed that sickle and threw it just as far as I could throw it . . . and me and him commenced to wrestling. We wrestled for three days and three nights. I can't say where I found the strength from. Every time it seemed like he was gonna get the best of me, I'd reach way down deep inside myself and find the strength to do him one better.

ROSE: Every time Troy tell that story he find different ways to tell it. Different things to make up about it.

TROY: I ain't making up nothing. I'm telling you the facts of what happened. I wrestled with Death for three days and three nights and I'm standing here to tell you about it. [*Pause.*] All right. At the end of the third night we done weakened each other to where both of us could hardly move. Death stood up, throwed on his robe . . . had him a white robe with a hood on it. He throwed on that robe and went off to look for his sickle. Say, "I'll be back." Just like that, "I'll be back." I told him, say, "You gonna have to find me!" I wasn't no fool. I wasn't going looking for him. Death ain't nothing to play with. And I know he's gonna get me. I know I got to join his army. . . . his camp followers. But as long as I keep my strength and see him coming, as long as I keep up my vigilance, he's gonna have to fight to get me. I ain't going easy.

BONO: Well, look here, since you got to keep up your vigilance . . . let me have the bottle.

TROY: Aw hell, I shouldn't have told you that part. I should have left out that part. That vigilance part.

ROSE: Troy be talking that stuff and half the time don't even know what he be talking about.

TROY: Bono know me better than that. He know I don't talk nothing lessen I got a good handle on it as the truth. Ain't that right, Bono?

BONO: That's right. I know you. I know you got some Uncle Remus in your blood. You got more stories than the devil got sinners.

TROY: Aw hell, I done seen him too! Done talked with the devil.

ROSE: Troy, don't nobody wanna be hearing all that stuff.

[LYONS *enters the yard from the street. Thirty-four years old,* TROY'S *son by a previous marriage, he sports a neatly trimmed goatee, sport coat, white shirt, tieless and buttoned at the collar. Though he fancies himself a musician, he is more caught up in the rituals and "idea" of being a musician than in the actual practice of the music. The music offers him a "life-style and stance from which he can ignore the sociological context of his existence and celebrate the music's ability to provide a maintenance of equilibrium despite the precarious circumstances of day-to-day living." He has come to borrow money from* TROY, *and while he knows he will be successful, he is uncertain as to what extent his life-style will be held up to scrutiny and ridicule.*]

LYONS: Hey, Pop.

TROY: What you come Hey, Popping me for?

LYONS: How you doing, Rose? [*He kisses her.*] Mr. Bono, how you doing?

BONO: Hey, Lyons, how you been?

TROY: He must have been doing all right. I ain't seen him around here last week.

ROSE: Troy, leave the boy alone. He come by to see you and you wanna start all that nonsense.

TROY: I ain't bothering Lyons. [*Offers him the bottle.*] Here . . . get you a drink. We got an understanding. I know why he come by to see me and he know I know.

LYONS: Come on, Pop . . . I just stopped by to say hi, see how you was doing.

TROY: You ain't stopped by yesterday.

ROSE: You gonna stay for supper, Lyons? I got some chicken cooking in the oven.

LYONS: No, Rose . . . thanks. I was just in the neighborhood and thought I'd stop by for a minute.

TROY: You was in the neighborhood all right, nigger. You telling the truth there. You was in the neighborhood 'cause it's my payday.

LYONS: Well, hell, since you mentioned it, let me have ten dollars.

TROY: I'll be damned! I'll die and go to hell and play blackjack with the devil before I give you ten dollars.

BONO: That's what I wanna know about . . . this devil you done seen.

LYONS: What? Pop done seen the devil? You too much, Pops.

TROY: Yeah, I done seen him. Talked to him too!

ROSE: You ain't seen no devil. I done told you that man ain't had nothing to do with the devil. Anything you can't understand, you want to call it the devil.

TROY: Look here, Bono . . . I went down to see Hertzberger about some furniture. Got three rooms for two-ninety-eight. That what it say on the radio. Three rooms . . . two-ninety-eight. Even made up a little song about it. Go down there . . . man tell me I can't get no credit. I'm working every day and can't get no credit. What to do? I got an empty house with some raggedy furniture in it. Cory ain't got no bed. He's sleeping on a pile of rags on the floor. Working every day and can't get no credit. Come back home—Rose'll tell you—madder than hell. Sit down, try to figure what I'm gonna do. Come a knock on the door. Ain't been living here but three days. Who know I'm here? Open the door . . . devil standing there bigger than life. White fellow . . . got on good clothes and everything. Standing there with a clipboard in his hand. I ain't had to say nothing. First words come out of his mouth was "I understand you need some furniture and can't get no credit." I liked to fell over. He say I'll give you all the credit you want, but you got to pay the interest on it. I told him give me three rooms worth and charge whatever you want. Next day a truck pulled up here and two men unloaded them three rooms. Man what drove the truck give me a book. Say send ten dollars a month to the address in the book and everything will be all right. Say if I miss a payment the devil was coming back and it'll be hell to pay. That was fifteen years ago. To this day, the first of the month I send my ten dollars, Rose'll tell you.

ROSE: Troy lying.

TROY: I ain't never seen that man since. Now, you tell me who else that could have been but the devil? I ain't sold my soul or nothing, you understand. I wouldn't have truck with the devil about nothing like that. He ain't mentioned nothing like that. I just got my furniture and pays my ten dollars the first of the month just like clockwork.

BONO: How long you say you been paying this ten dollars a month?

TROY: Fifteen years!

BONO: Hell, ain't you finished paying for it yet? How much the man done charged you.

TROY: Aw hell, I done paid for it. I done paid for it ten times over! The fact is I'm scared to stop paying it.

ROSE: Troy lying. We got that furniture from Mr. Glickman. He ain't paying no ten dollars a month to nobody.

TROY: Aw hell, woman. Bono know I ain't that big a fool.

LYONS: I was just getting ready to say . . . I know where there's a bridge for sale.

TROY: Look here, I'll tell you this . . . it don't matter to me if he was the devil. It don't matter if the devil give credit. Somebody has got to give it.

ROSE: It ought to matter. You going around talking about having truck with the devil . . . God's the one you gonna have to answer to. He's the one gonna be at the judgment.

LYONS: Yeah, well, look here, Pop . . . let me have that ten dollars. I'll give it back to you. Bonnie got a job working at the hospital.

TROY: What I tell you, Bono? The only time I see this nigger is when he wants something. That's the only time I see him.

LYONS: Come on, Pop, Mr. Bono don't want to hear all that. Let me have the ten dollars. I told you Bonnie working.

TROY: What that mean to me? "Bonnie working." I don't care if she working. Go ask her for the ten dollars if she working. Talking about Bonnie working . . . why ain't you working?

LYONS: Aw, Pop, you know I can't find no decent job. Where am I gonna get a job at? You know I can't get no job.

TROY: I told you I know some people down there. I can get you on the rubbish if you want to work. I told you that the last time you came by here asking me for something.

LYONS: Naw, Pop . . . thanks. That ain't for me. I don't wanna be carrying nobody's rubbish. I don't wanna be punching nobody's time clock.

TROY: What's the matter? You too good to carry rubbish? Where you think that ten dollars you talking about come from? I'm just supposed to haul people's rubbish and give my money to you 'cause you too lazy to work. You too lazy to work and wanna know why you ain't got what I got.

ROSE: What hospital Bonnie working at? Mercy?

LYONS: She's down at Passavant working in the laundry.

TROY: Ain't got nothing as it is. I give you that ten dollars and I got to eat beans the rest of the week. Naw, you ain't getting no ten dollars here.

LYONS: You ain't got to be eating no beans. I don't know why you wanna say that.

TROY: I ain't got no extra money. Gabe done moved over to Miss Pearl's paying her the rent and things done got tight around here. I can't afford to be giving you every payday.

LYONS: I ain't asked you to give me nothing. I asked you to loan me ten dollars. I know you got ten dollars.

TROY: Yeah, I got it. Why you think I got it? 'Cause I don't throw my money away out there in the streets. You living the fast life, wanna be a musician, running around in them clubs and things . . . then you learn to take care of yourself. You ain't gonna find me going and asking nobody for nothing. I done spent too many years without.

LYONS: You and me is two different people, Pop.

TROY: I done learned my mistake and learned to do what's right by it. You still trying to get something for nothing. Life don't owe you nothing. You owe it to yourself. Ask Bono. He'll tell you I'm right.

LYONS: You got your way of dealing with the world . . . I got mine. The only thing that matters to me is the music.

TROY: Hell, I can see that! It don't matter how you gonna eat, where your next dollar is coming from. You telling the truth there.

LYONS: I know I got to eat. But I got to live too. I need something that gonna help me to get out of the bed in the morning. Make me feel like I belong in the world. I don't bother nobody. I just stay with my music 'cause that's the only way I can find to live in the world. Otherwise there ain't no telling what I might do. Now I don't come by here criticizing you and the way you live. I just come by to ask you for ten dollars. I don't wanna hear all that about how I live.

TROY: Boy, your mama did a hell of a job raising you.

LYONS: You can't change me, Pop. I'm thirty-four years old.

ROSE: Let the boy have ten dollars, Troy.

TROY: [*To* LYONS.] What the hell you looking at me for? I ain't got no ten dollars.

You know what I do with my money. [*To* ROSE.] Give him ten dollars if you want him to have it.

ROSE: I will. Just as soon as you turn it loose.

TROY: [*Handing* ROSE *the money.*] There it is. Seventy-six dollars and forty-two cents. You see this, Bono? Now, I ain't gonna get but six of that back.

ROSE: You ought to stop telling that lie. Here, Lyons. [*She hands him the money.*]

LYONS: Thanks, Rose. Look . . . I got to run. I'll see you later.

TROY: Wait a minute. You gonna say, "Thanks, Rose," and ain't gonna look to see where she got that ten dollars from?

LYONS: I know she got it from you, Pop. Thanks. I'll give it back to you.

TROY: There he go telling another lie. Time I see that ten dollars he'll be owed me thirty more.

LYONS: See you, Mr. Bono. Thanks, Pop. I'll see you again. [LYONS *exits the yard.*]

TROY: I don't know why he don't go and get him a decent job and take care of that woman he got.

BONO: He'll be all right, Troy. The boy's still young.

TROY: The boy is thirty-four years old.

ROSE: Let's not get off into all that.

BONO: Look here . . I got to be going. I got to be getting on. Lucille gonna be waiting.

TROY: [*Puts his arm around* ROSE.] See this woman, Bono? I love this woman. I love this woman so much it hurts. I love her so much . . . I done run out of ways to love her. So I got to go back to basics. Don't you come by my house Monday morning talking about time to go to work . . . 'cause I'm still gonna be stroking!

ROSE: Troy! Stop it now!

BONO: I ain't paying him no mind, Rose. That ain't nothing but gin-talk. Go on, Troy. I'll see you Monday.

TROY: Don't you come by my house, nigger! I done told you what I'm gonna be doing.

[*The lights go down to black.*]

Scene 2

The lights come up on ROSE *hanging up clothes. She hums and sings softly to herself.* TROY *enters from the house. It is the following morning.*

ROSE: 'Morning. You ready for breakfast? I can fix it soon as I finish hanging up these clothes?

TROY: I got the coffee on. That'll be all right. I'll just drink some of that this morning.

ROSE: That 642 hit yesterday. That's the second time this month. Miss Pearl hit for a dollar . . . seem like those that need the least always get lucky. Poor folks can't get nothing.

TROY: Them numbers don't know nobody. I don't know why you fool with them. You and Lyons both.

ROSE: It's something to do.

TROY: You ain't doing nothing but throwing your money away.

ROSE: Troy, you know I don't play foolishly. I just play a nickel here and a nickel there.

TROY: That's two nickels you done thrown away.

ROSE: Now I hit sometimes . . . that makes up for it. It always comes in handy when I do hit. I don't hear you complaining then.

TROY: I ain't complaining. I just say it's foolish. Trying to guess out of six hundred ways which way the number gonna come. If I had all the money niggers throw away on numbers for one week—just one week—I'd be a rich man.

ROSE: Well, you wishing and calling it foolish ain't gonna stop folks from playing numbers. That's one thing for sure. Besides, some good things come from playing numbers. Look where Pope done bought him that restaurant off of numbers.

TROY: I can't stand niggers like that. Man ain't had two dimes to rub together. He walking around with his shoes all run over bumming money for cigarettes. All right. Got lucky there and hit the numbers—

ROSE: Troy, I know all about it.

TROY: Had good sense, I'll say that for him. He ain't throwed his money away. I seen niggers hit the numbers and go through two thousand dollars in four days. Man bought him that restaurant down there, fixed it up real nice, and then didn't want nobody to come in it! A Negro go in there and can't get no kind of service. I seen a white fellow come in there and order a bowl of stew. Pope picked all the meat out the pot for him. Man ain't had nothing but a bowl of meat! Negro come behind him and ain't got nothing but the potatoes and carrots. Talking about what numbers do for people you picked a wrong example. Ain't done nothing but make him a worse fool than he was before. [*Pause.*] Where's Cory? Cory in the house? [*Calls.*] Cory?

ROSE: He gone out.

TROY: Out, huh? He gone out 'cause he know I want him to help me with this fence. I know how he is. That boy afraid of work. He ain't done a lick of work in his life.

ROSE: He had to go to football practice. Coach wanted them to get in a little extra practice before the season start.

TROY: I got his practice . . . running out of here before he get his chores done.

ROSE: Troy, what is wrong with you this morning? Don't nothing set right with you. Go on back in there and go to bed . . . get up on the other side.

TROY: Why something got to be wrong with me? I ain't said nothing wrong with me.

ROSE: You got something to say about everything. First it's the numbers, then it's the way the man runs his restaurant, then you done got on Cory. What's it gonna be next? Take a look up there and see if the weather suits you . . . or is it gonna be how you gonna put up the fence with the clothes hanging in the yard.

TROY: You hit the nail on the head there! Damn if that wasn't what I was thinking.

ROSE: I know you like I know the back of my hand. Go on in there and get you some coffee . . . see if that straighten you up. 'Cause you ain't right this morning.

[GABRIEL *is heard singing off stage.* TROY'S *brother, he is seven years younger than* TROY. *Injured in World War II, he has a metal plate in his head. He carries an old trumpet tied around his waist and believes with every fiber of his being that he is the Archangel Gabriel. He carries a chip basket with an assortment of discarded fruits and vegetables he has picked up in the strip district and which he attempts to sell.*]

[GABRIEL *singing.*]

Yes mam I got plums
You ask me how I sell them.

TROY: [*Hearing* GABRIEL.] Just what I need this morning.

[GABRIEL *singing.*]

Oh ten cents apiece
Three for a quarter
Come and buy now
'Cause I'm here today
And tomorrow I'll be gone

[GABRIEL *enters.*]

GABRIEL: Hey, Rose!

ROSE: How you doing, Gabe?

GABRIEL: There's Troy. Hey, Troy!

TROY: Hey, Gabe.

ROSE: [*To* GABRIEL.] What you got there?

GABRIEL: You know what I got, Rose. I got fruits and vegetables.

ROSE: [*Looking in basket.*] Where's all these plums you talking about?

GABRIEL: I ain't got no plums today, Rose. I was just singing that. Have some tomorrow. Put me in a big order for plums. Have enough plums tomorrow for St. Peter and everybody. [*To* ROSE.] Troy's mad at me.

TROY: I ain't mad at you. What I got to be mad at you about? You ain't done nothing to me.

GABRIEL: I just moved over to Miss Pearl's to keep out from in your way. I ain't mean no harm by it.

TROY: Who said anything about that? I ain't said nothing about that.

GABRIEL: You ain't mad at me, is you?

TROY: Naw, I ain't mad at you Gabe. If I was mad at you I'd tell you about it.

GABRIEL: Got me two rooms. In the basement. Got my own door too. Wanna see my key? [*He holds up a key.*] That's my own key! Ain't nobody else got a key like that. That's my key! My two rooms!

TROY: Well, that's good, Gabe. You got your own key . . . that's good.

ROSE: You hungry, Gabe? I was just fixing to cook Troy his breakfast.

GABRIEL: You got some biscuits? I'll take some biscuits. Did you know when I was in heaven, every morning me and St. Peter would sit down by the gate and eat some big fat biscuits? Oh, yeah! We had us a good time. We'd eat us them biscuits and then St. Peter would go off to sleep and tell me to wake him up when it's time to open the gates for the judgment.

ROSE: Well, come on . . . I'll make up a batch of biscuits. [ROSE *exits into the house.*]

GABRIEL: Troy, St. Peter got your name in the book. I seen it. It say, "Troy Maxson." I say, "I know him! He got the same name like what I got. That's my brother!"

TROY: How many times you gonna tell me that, Gabe? He got your name in there too?

GABRIEL: Ain't got my name in the book. Don't have to have my name. I done died and went to heaven. He got your name, though. One morning St. Peter was looking at his book, marking it up for the judgment, and he let me see your name. Got it in there under M. Got Rose's name too. I ain't seen it like I seen yours, but I know it's in there. Great big book. Got everybody's name what was ever been born. That's what he told me. But I seen your name. Seen it with my own eyes.

TROY: Go on in the house there. Rose going to fix you something to eat.

GABRIEL: Oh, I ain't hungry. I done had breakfast with Aunt Jemima. She come by and cooked me up a whole mess of flapjacks. Remember how we used to eat them flapjacks?

TROY: Yeah, I remember. Go on in the house and get you something to eat now.

GABRIEL: I got to go sell my plums. I done sold some tomatoes. Got me two quarters. Wanna see? [*He shows* TROY *his quarters.*] I'm gonna save them and buy me a new horn so St. Peter can hear me when it's time to open the gates. [GABRIEL *stops suddenly. Listens.*] Hear that? That's the hellhounds. I got to chase them out of here. Go on get out of here! Get out!

[GABRIEL *exits singing.*]

Better get ready for the judgment
Better get ready for the judgment
My lord is coming down
Better get ready for the judgment
Better get ready for the judgment morning
Better get ready for the judgment
My god is coming down

[ROSE *enters from the house.*]

TROY: He gone off somewhere.

ROSE: He ain't eating right. Miss Pearl say she can't get him to eat nothing.

TROY: What you want me to do about it, Rose? I done did everything I can for the man. I can't make him get well. Man got half his head blown away . . . what you expect?

ROSE: Seem like something ought to be done to help him.

TROY: Man don't bother nobody. He just mixed up from that metal plate he got in his head. Ain't no sense for him to go back into the hospital.

ROSE: Least he be eating right. They can help him take care of himself.

TROY: Don't nobody wanna be locked up, Rose. What you wanna lock him up for? Man go over there and fight the war, get half his head blown off, and they give him a lousy three thousand dollars. And I had to swoop down on that.

ROSE: Is you fixing to go into that again?

TROY: That's the only way I got a roof over my head . . . 'cause of that metal plate.

ROSE: Ain't no sense you blaming yourself for nothing. You done what was right by him. Can't nobody say you ain't done what was right by him. Look how long you took care of him . . . till he wanted to have his own place and moved over there with Miss Pearl.

TROY: That ain't what I'm saying, woman! I'm just stating the facts. If my brother didn't have that metal plate in his head, I wouldn't have a pot to piss in or a window to throw it out of. And I'm fifty-three years old. Now you try and understand that! [TROY *gets up from the porch and starts to exit the yard.*]

ROSE: Where you going off to? You been running out of here every Saturday for weeks. I thought you was gonna work on this fence?

TROY: I'm gonna walk down to Taylor's. Listen to the ballgame. I'll be back in a bit. I'll work on it when I get back.

[TROY *exits the yard. The lights go to black.*]

SCENE 3

The lights come up on the yard. It is four hours later. ROSE *is taking down the clothes from the line.* CORY *enters carrying his football equipment.*

ROSE: Your daddy liked to had a fit with you running out of here this morning without doing your chores.

CORY: I told you I had to go to practice.

ROSE: He say you were supposed to help him with this fence.

CORY: He always say that every Saturday and then he don't never do nothing. Did you tell him about the recruiter?

ROSE: Yeah, I told him.

CORY: What he say?

ROSE: He ain't said nothing too much. You go in there and get started on your chores before he gets back. Go on and scrub down them steps before he gets back here hollering and carrying on.

CORY: I'm hungry. What you got to eat, Mama?

ROSE: Go on and get started on your chores. I got some meat loaf in there. Go on and make you a sandwich . . . and don't leave no mess in there. [CORY *exits into the house.* ROSE *continues to take down the clothes.* TROY *enters the yard and sneaks up and grabs her from behind.*] Troy! Go on, now. You liked to scared me to death. What was the score of the game? Lucille had me on the phone and I couldn't keep up with it.

TROY: What I care about the game? Come here, woman. [*He tries to kiss her.*]

ROSE: I thought you went down Taylor's to listen to the game. Go on, Troy! You supposed to be putting up this fence.

TROY: [*Attempting to kiss her again.*] I'll put it up when I finish with what is at hand.

ROSE: Go on, Troy. I ain't studying you.

TROY: [*Chasing after her.*] I'm studying you . . . fixing to do my homework!

ROSE: Troy, you better leave me alone.

TROY: Where's Cory? That boy brought his butt home yet?

ROSE: He's in the house doing his chores.

TROY: [*Calling.*] Cory! Get your butt out here, boy! [ROSE *exits into the house with the laundry.* TROY *goes over to the pile of wood, picks up a board, and starts sawing.* CORY *enters from the house.*] You just now coming in here from leaving this morning?

CORY: Yeah, I had to go to football practice.

TROY: Yeah, what? What kind of talk is that?

CORY: Yessir.

TROY: I ain't but two seconds off you noway. The garbage sitting in there overflowing . . . you ain't done none of your chores . . . and you come in here talking about, "Yeah."

CORY: I was just getting ready to do my chores now.

TROY: Your first chore is to help me with this fence on Saturday. Everything else come after that. Now get that saw and cut them boards.

[CORY *takes the saw and begins cutting the boards.* TROY *continues working. There is a long pause.*]

CORY: The Pirates done won five in a row.

TROY: I ain't thinking about the Pirates. Got an all-white team. Got that boy . . . that Puerto Rican boy . . . Clemente. Don't even half-play him. That boy could be something if they give him a chance. Play him one day and sit him on the bench the next.

CORY: He gets a lot of chances to play.

TROY: I'm talking about playing regular. Playing every day so you can get your timing. That's what I'm talking about.

CORY: They got some white guys on the team that don't play every day. You can't play everybody at the same time.

TROY: If they got a white fellow sitting on the bench, you can bet your last dollar he can't play! The colored guy got to be twice as good before he get on the team. That's why I don't want you to get all tied up in them sports. Man on the team and what it get him? They got colored on the team and don't play them. Same as not having them. All them teams the same.

CORY: The Braves got Hank Aaron and Wes Covington. Hank Aaron hit two home runs today. That makes forty-three.

TROY: Hank Aaron ain't nobody. That's the way you supposed to do. That's how you supposed to play the game. Ain't nothing to it. It's just a matter of timing . . . getting the right follow-through. Hell, I can hit forty-three home runs right now!

CORY: Not off no major-league pitching you couldn't.

TROY: We had better pitching in the Negro League. I hit seven home runs off of Satchel Paige. You can't get no better than that!

CORY: Sandy Koufax. He's leading the league in strikeouts.

TROY: I ain't thinking of no Sandy Koufax nothing.

CORY: You got Warren Spahn and Lew Burdette. I bet you couldn't hit no home runs off of Warren Spahn.

TROY: I'm through with it now. You go on and get them boards cut. [*Pause.*] Your mama tells me you got recruited by a college football team? Is that right?

CORY: Yeah. Coach Zellman say the recruiter gonna be coming by to talk to you. Get you to sign the permission papers.

TROY: I thought you supposed to be working down there at the A&P. Ain't you supposed to be working down there after school?

CORY: Mr. Stawicki say he gonna hold my job for me until after the football season. Say starting next week I can work weekends.

TROY: I thought we had an understanding about this football stuff? You suppose to keep up with your chores and hold that job down at the A&P. Ain't been around here all day on a Saturday. Ain't none of your chores done . . . and now you telling me you done quit your job.

CORY: I'm gonna be working weekends.

TROY: You damn right you are! And ain't no need for nobody coming around here to talk to me about signing nothing.

CORY: Hey, Pop, you can't do that. He's coming all the way from North Carolina.

TROY: I don't care where he coming from. The white man ain't gonna let you get nowhere with that football no way. You go and get your book-learning where you can learn to do something besides carrying people's garbage.

CORY: I get good grades, Pop. That's why the recruiter wants to talk with you. You got to keep up your grades to get recruited. This way I'll be going to college. I'll get a chance—

TROY: You gonna get your butt down there to the A&P and get your job back.

CORY: Mr. Stawicki done already hired somebody else 'cause I told him I was playing football.

TROY: You a bigger fool than I thought . . . to let somebody take away your job so you can play some football. That's downright foolishness. Where you gonna get your money to take out your girlfriend and whatnot? What kind of foolishness is that to let somebody take away your job?

CORY: I'm still gonna be working weekends.

TROY: Naw . . . naw. You getting your butt out of here and finding you another job.

CORY: Come on, Pop! I got to practice. I can't work after school and play football too. Coach Zellman say the team needs me—say—

TROY: I don't care what nobody else say. I'm the boss . . . you understand? I'm the boss around here. I do the only saying what counts.

CORY: Come on, Pop!

TROY: I asked you. Did you understand?

CORY: Yeah . . . Yessir.

TROY: You go down there to that A&P and see if you can get your job back. If you can't do both, then you quit the football team. You've got to take the crooked with the straights.

CORY: Yessir. [*Pause.*] Can I ask you a question?

TROY: What the hell you wanna ask me? Mr. Stawicki the one you got the questions for.

CORY: How come you ain't never liked me?

TROY: Liked you? Who the hell say I got to like you? What law is there say I got to like you? Wanna stand up in my face and ask a damn fool-ass question like that. Talking about liking somebody. Come here, boy, when I talk to you. [CORY *comes over to where* TROY *is working. He stands slouched over and* TROY *shoves him on his shoulder.*] Straighten up, goddammit! I asked you a question. What law is there say I got to like you?

CORY: None.

TROY: Well, all right then! Don't you eat every day? [*Pause.*] Answer me when I talk to you! Don't you eat every day?

CORY: Yeah.

TROY: Nigger, as long as you in my house you put that sir on the end of it when you talk to me!

CORY: Yes . . . sir.

TROY: You eat every day. Got a roof over your head. Got clothes on your back.

CORY: Yessir.

TROY: Why you think that is?

CORY: 'Cause of you.

TROY: Aw, hell I know it's 'cause of me . . . but why do you think that is?

CORY: [*Hesitant.*] 'Cause you like me.

TROY: Like you? I go out of here every morning, bust my butt, putting up with them crackers every day . . . 'cause I like you? You about the biggest fool I ever saw. [*Pause.*] It's my job. It's my responsibility! You understand that? A man got to take care of his family. You live in my house, sleep you behind on my bedclothes, fill you belly up with my food . . . 'cause you my son. You my flesh and blood. Not 'cause I like you! 'Cause I owe a responsibility to you! 'Cause it's my duty to take care of you. Let's get this straight right here—before it go along any further—I ain't got to like you. Mr. Rand don't give me my money come payday 'cause he likes me. He gives me 'cause he owe me. I done give you everything I had to give you. I gave you your life! Me and your mama worked that out between us. And liking your black ass wasn't part of the bargain. Don't you try and go through life worrying about if somebody like you or not. You best be making sure they doing right by you. You understand what I'm saying, boy?

CORY: Yessir.

TROY: Then get the hell out of my face, and get on down to that A&P.

[ROSE *has been standing behind the screen door for much of the scene. She enters as* CORY *exits.*]

ROSE: Why don't you let the boy go ahead and play football, Troy? Ain't no harm in that. He's just trying to be like you with the sports.

TROY: I don't want him to be like me! I want him to move as far away from my life as he can get. You the only decent thing that ever happened to me. I wish him that. But I don't wish him a thing else from my life. I decided seventeen years ago that boy wasn't getting involved in no sports. Not after what they did to me in the sports.

ROSE: Troy, why don't you admit you was too old to play in the major leagues? For once . . . why don't you admit that?

TROY: What do you mean too old? Don't come telling me I was too old. I just wasn't the right color. Hell, I'm fifty-three years old and I can do better than Selkirk's .269 right now!

ROSE: How was you gonna play ball when you was over forty? Sometimes I can't get no sense out of you.

TROY: I got good sense, woman. I got sense enough not to let my boy get hurt over playing no sports. You been mothering that boy too much. Worried about if people like him.

ROSE: Everything that boy do he do for you. He wants you to say "Good job, son." That's all.

TROY: Rose, I ain't got time for that. He's alive. He's healthy. He's got to make his own way. I made mine. Ain't nobody gonna hold his hand when he get out there in that world.

ROSE: Times have changed from when you was young, Troy. People change. The world's changing around you and you can't even see it.

TROY: [*Slow, methodical.*] Woman . . . I do the best I can do. I come in here every Friday. I carry a sack of potatoes and a bucket of lard. You all line up at the door with your hands out. I give you the lint from my pockets. I give you my sweat and my blood. I ain't got no tears. I done spent them. We go upstairs in that room at night and I fall down on you and try to blast a hole into forever. I get up Monday morning . . . find my lunch on the table. I go out. Make my way. Find my strength to carry me through to the next Friday. [*Pause.*] That's all I got, Rose. That's all I got to give. I can't give nothing else.

[TROY *exits into the house. The lights go down to black.*]

SCENE 4

It is Friday, two weeks later. CORY *enters from the house carrying his football equipment. The phone rings.*

CORY: [*Calling.*] I got it! [*He answers the phone and stands in the screendoor talking.*] Hello? Hey, Jesse. Naw . . . I was just leaving now.

ROSE: [*Calling from inside the house.*] Cory!

CORY: I told you man, them spikes is all tore up. You can use them if you want but they ain't no good. Earl got some spikes.

ROSE: [*Calling.*] Cory!

CORY: Size nine, I think. [*Calling to* ROSE.] Mam? I'm talking to Jesse. [*Into phone.*] When she say that? Aw, you lying, man. I'm gonna tell her you said that.

ROSE: [*Calling.*] Cory, don't you go nowhere!

CORY: I got to go to the game, Ma! [*Into the phone.*] Yeah, hey look, I'll talk to you later. Yeah, I'll meet you over Earl's house. [*He hangs up the phone and calls to* ROSE.] Bye, Ma!

[ROSE *enters from the house.*]

ROSE: Cory, where you going off to? You got all that stuff pulled out and thrown all over your room.

CORY: I was looking for my spikes. Jesse wanted to borrow my spikes.

ROSE: Get up there and get that cleaned up before your daddy gets back in here.

CORY: I got to go. I'll clean it up when I get back. [CORY *exits.*]

ROSE: That's all he need to do is see that room all messed up.

[ROSE *exits into the house as* TROY *and* BONO *enter the yard.* TROY *is dressed in clothes other than his work clothes.*]

BONO: He told him the same thing he told you. Take it to the union.

TROY: Brownie ain't got that much sense. Man wasn't thinking about nothing. He wait until I confront them on it, then he wanna come crying seniority. [*Calls.*] Hey, Rose!

BONO: I wish I could have seen Mr. Rand's face when he told you.

TROY: He couldn't get it out of his mouth! Liked to bit his tongue! When they called me down there to the commissioner's office, he thought they was gonna fire me . . . like everybody else.

BONO: I didn't think they was gonna fire you . . . I thought they was gonna put you on the warning paper.

TROY: Hey, Rose! [*To* BONO.] Yeah . . . Mr. Rand like to bit his tongue. [TROY *breaks the seal on the bottle, takes a drink, and hands it to* BONO.] Hey, Rose!

ROSE: [*Entering from the house.*] Hush all that hollering man! I know you out here. What they say down there at the commissioner's office?

TROY: You supposed to come when I call you, woman. Bono'll tell you that. [*To* BONO.] Don't Lucille come when you call her?

ROSE: Man, hush your mouth. I ain't no dog . . . talk about come when you call me.

TROY: [*Puts his arm around* ROSE.] You hear this, Bono? I had me an old dog used to get uppity like that. You say, comere, Blue . . . and he just lay there and look at you. End up getting a stick and chasing him away trying to make him come.

ROSE: I ain't studying you and your dog. I remember you used to sing that old song.

[TROY *sings:*]

I had a dog his name was Blue
You know Blue was mighty true
You know Blue was a good old dog
Blue treed a possum in a hollow log.

ROSE: Don't nobody wanna hear you sing that old song. Used to have Cory running around here singing that song.

BONO: Hell, I remember that myself.

TROY: That was my daddy's song. My daddy made up that song.

ROSE: I don't care who made it up. Don't nobody wanna hear you sing it.

TROY: [*Makes a song like calling a dog.*] Come here, woman.

ROSE: You come in here carrying on, I reckon they ain't fired you. What they say down there at the commissioner's office?

TROY: Look here, Rose . . . Mr. Rand called me into his office today when I got back from talking to them people down there. It come from up top . . . he called me in and told me they was making me a driver.

ROSE: Troy, you kidding!

TROY: No I ain't. Ask Bono.

ROSE: Well, that's great, Troy. Now you don't have to hassle them people no more.

TROY: Brownie got mad when he heard about . . . run to Mr. Rand talking about he got seniority. Tell her what Mr. Rand told him, Bono.

BONO: Told him take it to the union . . . same as he told Troy.

[LYONS *enters from the street.*]

TROY: Aw hell, I wasn't looking to see you today. I thought you was in jail. Got it all over the front page of the *Courier* about them raiding Sefus' place . . . where you be hanging out with all them thugs.

LYONS: Hey, Pop . . . that ain't got nothing to do with me. I don't go down there gambling. I go down there to sit in with the band. I ain't got nothing to do with the gambling part. They got some good music down there.

TROY: They got some rogues . . . is what they got.

LYONS: How you been, Mr. Bono? Hi, Rose.

BONO: I see where you playing down at the Crawford Grill tonight.

ROSE: How come you ain't brought Bonnie like I told you. You should have brought Bonnie with you, she ain't been over in a month of Sundays.

LYONS: I was just in the neighborhood . . . thought I'd stop by.

TROY: Here he come with that I-was-in-the-neighborhood stuff.

BONO: Your daddy got a promotion on the rubbish. He's gonna be the first colored driver. Ain't got to do nothing but sit up there and read the paper like them white fellows.

LYONS: Hey, Pop . . . if you knew how to read you'd be all right.

TROY: What you care if I can read or not? I read about all them thugs you be hanging out with. I read about them going to jail. I read that.

BONO: Naw . . . naw . . . you mean if the nigger knew how to *drive* he'd be all right. Been fighting with them people about driving and ain't even got a license. Mr. Rand know you ain't got no driver's license?

TROY: Driving ain't nothing. All you do is point the truck where you want it to go and keep from hitting the rest of them cars and things out there. Driving ain't nothing.

BONO: Do Mr. Rand know you ain't got no driver's license? That's what I'm talking about. I ain't asked if driving was easy. I asked if Mr. Rand know you ain't got no driver's license.

TROY: He ain't got to know. The man ain't got to know my business.

LYONS: [*Going into his pocket.*] Say, look here, Pop . . .

TROY: I knew it was coming. Didn't I tell you, Bono? I know what kind of "Look here, Pop" that was. The nigger fixing to ask me for some money. It's Friday night. It's my payday. All them rogues down there on the avenue—the ones that ain't in jail—and Lyons is hopping in his shoes to get down there with them.

LYONS: See, Pop . . . if you give somebody else a chance to talk sometime, you'd see that I was fixing to pay you back your ten dollars like I told you. Here . . . told you I'd pay you when Bonnie got paid.

TROY: Naw . . . you go ahead and keep that ten dollars. Put it in the bank. The next time you feel like you wanna come by here and ask me for something, you go on down there and get that.

LYONS: Here's your ten dollars, Pop. I told you I don't want you to give me nothing. I just wanted to borrow ten dollars.

TROY: Naw . . . you go on and keep that for the next time you want to ask me.

LYONS: Come on, Pop . . . here go your ten dollars.

ROSE: Why don't you go on and let the boy pay you back, Troy?

LYONS: Here you go, Rose. If you don't take it I'm gonna have to hear about it for the next six months. [*He hands her the money.*]

ROSE: You can hand yours over here too, Troy.

TROY: You see this, Bono. You see how they do me.

BONO: Yeah, Lucille do me the same way.

[GABRIEL *is heard singing off stage. He enters.*]

GABRIEL: Hey! Hey! There's Troy's boy!

LYONS: How you doing, Uncle Gabe?

GABRIEL: Lyons . . . the King of the Jungle! Rose . . . hey, Rose. Got a flower for you. [*He takes a rose from his pocket.*] Picked it myself. That's the same rose like what you is!

ROSE: That's right nice of you, Gabe.

LYONS: What you been doing, Uncle Gabe?

GABRIEL: Oh, I been chasing hellhounds and waiting on the time to tell St. Peter to open the gates.

LYONS: You been chasing hellhounds, huh? Well, you doing the right thing, Uncle Gabe. Somebody got to chase them.

GABRIEL: Oh, yeah . . . I know it. The devil's strong. The devil ain't no push-over. Hellhounds snipping at everybody's heels. But I got my trumpet waiting on the judgment time.

LYONS: Waiting on the battle of Armageddon, huh?

GABRIEL: Ain't gonna be too much of a battle when God get to waving that judgment sword. But the peoples gonna have a hell of a time trying to get into heaven if them gates ain't open.

LYONS: [*Putting his arm around* GABRIEL.] You hear this, Pop. Uncle Gabe, you all right!

GABRIEL: [*Laughing with* LYONS.] Lyons! King of the Jungle.

ROSE: You gonna stay for supper, Gabe. Want me to fix you a plate?

GABRIEL: I'll take a sandwich, Rose. Don't want no plate. Just wanna eat with my hands. I'll take a sandwich.

ROSE: How about you, Lyons? You staying? Got some short ribs cooking.

LYONS: Naw, I won't eat nothing till after we finished playing. [*Pause.*] You ought to come down and listen to me play, Pop.

TROY: I don't like that Chinese music. All that noise.

ROSE: Go on in the house and wash up, Gabe . . . I'll fix you a sandwich.

GABRIEL: [*To* LYONS *as he exits.*] Troy's mad at me.

LYONS: What you mad at Uncle Gabe for, Pop.

ROSE: He thinks Troy's mad at him 'cause he moved over to Miss Pearl's.

TROY: I ain't mad at the man. He can live where he want to live at.

LYONS: What he move over there for? Miss Pearl don't like nobody.

ROSE: She don't mind him none. She treats him real nice. She just don't allow all that singing.

TROY: She don't mind that rent he be paying . . . that's what she don't mind.

ROSE: Troy, I ain't going through that with you no more. He's over there 'cause he want to have his own place. He can come and go as he please.

TROY: Hell, he could come and go as he please here. I wasn't stopping him. I ain't put no rules on him.

ROSE: It ain't the same thing, Troy. And you know it. [GABRIEL *comes to the door.*] Now, that's the last I wanna hear about that. I don't wanna hear nothing else about Gabe and Miss Pearl. And next week . . .

GABRIEL: I'm ready for my sandwich, Rose.

ROSE: . . . when that recruiter come from that school, I want you to sign that paper and go on and let Cory play football. Then that'll be the last I have to hear about that.

TROY: [*To* ROSE *as she exits into the house.*] I ain't thinking about Cory nothing.

LYONS: What? Cory got recruited? What school he going to?

TROY: That boy walking around here smelling his piss, thinking he's grown. Thinking he's gonna do what he want irrespective of what I say. Look here, Bono . . . I left the commissioner's office and went down to the A&P—that boy ain't working down there. He lying to me all the time. Telling me he got his job back, telling me he working weekends, telling me he working after school. Mr. Stawicki tell me he ain't working down there at all!

LYONS: Cory just growing up. He's just busting at the seams trying to fill out your shoes.

TROY: I don't care what he's doing. When he get to the point where he wanna disobey me . . . then it's time for him to move on. Bono'll tell you that. I bet he ain't never disobeyed his daddy without paying the consequences.

BONO: I ain't never had a chance. My daddy came on through, but I ain't never knew him to see him . . . or what he had on his mind or where he went. Just moving on through. Searching for the New Land. That's what the old folks used to call it. See a fellow moving around from place to place, woman to woman, called it searching for the New Land. I can't say if he ever found it. I come along, didn't want no kids. Didn't know if I was gonna be in one place long enough to fix on them right as their daddy. I figured I was going searching too. As it turned out, I been hooked up with Lucille near about as long as your daddy been with Rose. Going on sixteen years.

TROY: Sometimes I wish I hadn't known my daddy. My daddy ain't cared nothing about no kids. A kid to him wasn't nothing. All he wanted was for you to learn how to walk so he could start you to working. When it come time for eating, he ate first. If there was anything left over, that's what you got. Man would sit down and eat two chickens and give you the wing.

LYONS: You ought to stop that, Pop. Everybody feed their kids. No matter how hard times is, everybody care about their kids. Make sure they have something to eat.

TROY: The only thing my daddy cared about was getting them bales of cotton in to Mr. Lubin. That's the only thing that mattered to him. Sometimes I used to wonder why he was living. Wonder why the devil hadn't come and got him. Get them bales in to Mr. Lubin and find out he owe him money . . . and don't do nothing but walk around cussing for the next two months. That was the worse time to cross his path. Seem like he was mad at the world and would strike out at anything underfoot.

LYONS: He should have just went on and left when he saw he couldn't get nowhere. That's what I would have done.

TROY: How he gonna leave with eleven kids? And where he gonna go? He ain't knew how to do nothing but farm. No, he was trapped, and I think he knew it. But I'll say this for him: he felt a responsibility toward us. Maybe he ain't treated us the way I felt he should have, but without that responsibility he could have walked off and left us, made his own way.

BONO: A lot of them did. Back in those days what you talking about, niggers used to travel all over. They get up one day and see where the day ain't sitting right with them and they walk out their front door and just take on down one road or another and keep on walking.

LYONS: There you go! That's what I'm talking about.

BONO: Ain't owned nothing but what was on their back, so you didn't have to worry about leaving nothing behind or carrying nothing with you for that matter. Just walk on till you come to something else. Ain't you never heard of nobody having the walking blues? Well, that's what you call it when you just take off like that.

TROY: My daddy ain't had them walking blues what you talking about. He stayed right there with his family. But he was just as evil as he could be. My mama couldn't stand him . . . couldn't stand that evilness. She run off when I was about eight. She sneaked off one night after he had gone to sleep. Told me she was coming back for me. I ain't never seen her no more. All his women run off and left him. He wasn't good for nobody. When my turn come to head out, I was fourteen and got to sniffing around Joe Canewell's daughter. Had us an old mule we called Greyboy. My daddy sent me out to do some plowing and I tied up Greyboy and went to fooling around with Joe Canewell's daughter. We done found us a nice little spot, got real cozy with each other. She about thirteen and we done figured we was grown anyway, so we down there enjoying ourselves . . . ain't thinking about nothing. We didn't know Greyboy had got loose and wandered back to the house and my daddy was looking for me. We down there by the creek enjoying ourselves when my daddy come up on us, surprised us. He had them leather straps off the mule and commenced to whupping me like there was no tomorrow. I jumped up, mad and embarrassed. I was scared of my daddy. When he commenced to whupping on me, quite naturally I run to get out of the way. [*Pause.*] Now I thought he was mad 'cause I ain't done my work. But I see where he was chasing me off so he could have the gal for himself. When I see what the matter of it was, I lost all fear of my daddy. Right there is where I become a man . . . at fourteen years of age. [*Pause.*] Now it was my turn to run him off. I picked up the same reins that he had used on me. I picked up them reins and commenced to whupping on him. The gal jumped up and run off, and when my daddy turned to face me, I could see why the devil had never come to get him: 'cause he was the devil himself. I don't know what happened. When I woke up I was laying right there by the creek and Blue—this old dog we had—was licking my face. I thought I was blind. I couldn't see nothing. Both my eyes were swollen shut. I layed there and cried. I didn't know what I was gonna do. The only thing I knew was the time had come for me to leave my daddy's house. And right there the world suddenly got big. And it was a long time before I could cut it down to where I could handle it. Part of that cutting down was when I got to the place where I could feel him kicking in my blood and knew that the only thing that separated us was the matter of a few years.

[GABRIEL *enters from the house with a sandwich.*]

LYONS: What you got there, Uncle Gabe?

GABRIEL: Got me a ham sandwich. Rose gave me a ham sandwich.

TROY: I don't know what happened to him. I done lost touch with everybody except Gabriel. But I hope he's dead. I hope he found some peace.

LYONS: That's a heavy story, Pop. I didn't know you left home when you was fourteen?

[*The telephone rings.*]

TROY: And didn't know nothing. The only part of the world I knew was the forty-two acres of Mr. Lubin's land. That's all I knew about life.

LYONS: Fourteen's kinda young to be out on your own. I don't even think I was ready to be out on my own at fourteen. I don't know what I would have done.

TROY: I got up from the creek and walked on down to Mobile. I was through with farming. Figured I could do better in the city. So I walked the two hundred miles to Mobile.

LYONS: Wait a minute . . . you ain't walked no two hundred miles, Pop. Ain't nobody gonna walk no two hundred miles. You talking about some walking there.

BONO: That's the only way you got anywhere back in them days.

LYONS: Shhh. Damn if I wouldn't have hitched a ride with somebody.

TROY: Who you gonna hitch it with? They ain't had no cars and things like they got now. We talking about 1918.

ROSE: [*Entering.*] What you all out here getting into?

TROY: [*To* ROSE.] I'm telling Lyons how good he got it. He don't know nothing about this I'm talking.

ROSE: Lyons, that was Bonnie on the phone. She say you supposed to pick her up.

LYONS: Yeah, okay, Rose.

TROY: I walked on down to Mobile and hitched up with some of them fellows that was heading this way. Got up here and found out not only couldn't you get a job, you couldn't find no place to live. I thought I was in freedom. Shhh. Colored folks living down there on the riverbanks in whatever kind of shelter they could make for themselves. Right down there under the Brady Street Bridge. Living in shacks made of sticks an' tar paper. Messed around there and went from bad to worse. Started stealing. First it was food. Then I figured, hell, if I steal money I can buy me some food. Buy me some shoes, too. One thing led to another. Met your mama—I was young and anxious to be a man—met your mama and had you. What I do that for? Now I got to worry about feeding you and her. Got to steal three times as much. Went out one day looking for somebody to rob . . . That's what I was, a robber. I'll tell you the truth. I'm ashamed of it today. But it's the truth. Went to rob this fellow—pulled out my knife, and he pulled out a gun. Shot me in the chest. It felt just like somebody had taken a hot branding iron and laid it on me. When he shot me, I jumped at him with my knife. They tell me I killed him. They put me in the penitentiary and locked me up for fifteen years. That's where I met Bono. That's where I learned how to play baseball. Got out that place and your mama had taken you and went on to make life without me. Fifteen years was a long time for her to wait. But that fifteen years cured me of that robbing stuff. Rose'll tell you. She asked me when I met her if I had gotten all that foolishness out of my system. And I told her, "Baby, it's you and baseball all what count with me." You hear me, Bono? I meant it too. She say, "Which one comes first?" I told her, "Baby, there ain't no doubt it's baseball, but you stick and get old with me and we'll both outlive this baseball." Am I right, Rose? And it's true.

ROSE: Man, hush your mouth. You ain't said no such thing. Talking about, "Baby, you know you'll always be number one with me." That's what you was talking.

TROY: You hear that, Bono? That's why I love her.

BONO: Rose'll keep you straight. You get off the track, she'll straighten you up.

ROSE: Lyons, you better get on home and get Bonnie. She waiting on you.

LYONS: [*Getting up to go.*] Hey, Pop, why don't you come down to the Grill and hear me play?

TROY: I ain't' going down there. I got to get up in the morning. I'm too old to be sitting around in them clubs.

LYONS: You ain't got to stay long.

TROY: Naw, I'm gonna get my supper and go on to bed.

LYONS: Well, I got to go. I'll see you again.

TROY: Don't you come around here on my payday!

ROSE: Pick up the phone and let somebody know you coming. And bring Bonnie with you. You know I'm always glad to see her.

LYONS: Yeah, I'll do that, Rose. You take care now. See you, Pop. See you, Mr. Bono. See you, Uncle Gabe.

GABRIEL: Lyons! King of the Jungle!

[LYONS *exits.*]

TROY: Is supper ready, woman? Me and you got some business to take care of. I'm gonna tear it up too!

ROSE: Troy, I done told you now!

TROY: [*Puts his arm around* BONO.] Aw hell, woman . . . this is Bono. Bono like family. I done known this nigger since . . . How long I done know you?

BONO: It's been a long time.

TROY: I done known this nigger since Skippy was a pup. Me and him done been through some times.

BONO: You sure right about that.

TROY: Hell, I done know him longer than I known you. And we still standing shoulder to shoulder. Hey, look here, Bono . . . a man can't ask for no more than that. [*Drinks to him.*] I love you, nigger.

BONO: Hell, I love you too, but I got to get home to see my woman. You got yours. I got to go get mine.

[BONO *starts to exit as* CORY *enters the yard dressed in his football uniform. He gives* TROY *a hard, uncompromising look.*]

CORY: What you do that for, Pop? [*He throws his helmet down in the direction of* TROY.]

ROSE: What's the matter? Cory, what's the matter?

CORY: Papa done went up to the school and told Coach Zellman I can't play football no more. Wouldn't even let me play the game. Told him to tell the recruiter not to come.

ROSE: Troy—

TROY: What you Troying me for. Yeah, I did it. And the boy know why I did it.

CORY: Why you wanna do that to me? This the one chance I had.

ROSE: Ain't nothing wrong with Cory playing football, Troy.

TROY: The boy lied to me, Rose. I told the nigger if he wanna play football to keep up his chores and hold down that job at the A&P. That was the conditions. Stopped down there to see Mr. Stawicki—

CORY: I can't work after school during football season, Pop! I tried to tell you that Mr. Stawicki's holding my job for me. You don't ever want to listen to nobody. And then you wanna go and do this to me!

TROY: I ain't done nothing to you. You done it to yourself.

CORY: Just 'cause you didn't have a chance! You just scared I'm gonna be better than you, that's all.

TROY: Come here.

ROSE: Troy—

[CORY *reluctantly crosses over to* TROY.]

TROY: All right! See. You done made a mistake.

CORY: I didn't even do nothing!

TROY: I'm gonna tell you what your mistake was. See . . . you swung at the ball and didn't hit it. That's strike one. See, you in the batter's box now. You swung and you missed. That's strike one. Don't you strike out!

[*Lights fade to black.*]

ACT II

Scene 1

The following morning. CORY *is at the tree hitting the ball with the bat. He tries to mimic* TROY, *but his swing is awkward, less sure.* ROSE *enters from the house.*

ROSE: Cory, I want you to help me with this cupboard.

CORY: I ain't quitting the team. I don't care what Poppa say.

ROSE: I'll talk to him when he gets back. He had to go see about your Uncle Gabe. The police done arrested him. Say he was disturbing the peace. He'll be back directly. Come on in here and help me clean out the top of this cupboard. [CORY *exits into the house.* ROSE *sees* TROY *and* BONO *coming down the alley.*] Troy, what they say down there?

TROY: Ain't said nothing. I give them fifty dollars and they let him go. I'll talk to you about it. Where's Cory?

ROSE: He's in there helping me clean out these cupboards.

TROY: Tell him to get his butt out here. [ROSE *exits into the house.* TROY *and* BONO *go over to the pile of wood.* BONO *picks up the saw and begins sawing.*] All they want is the money. That makes six or seven times I done went down there and got him out. See me coming they stick out their hands.

BONO: Yeah, I know what you mean. That's all they care about is that money. They don't care about what's right. [*Pause.*] Nigger, why you got to go and get some hard wood? You ain't doing nothing but building a little old fence. Get you some soft pine wood. That's all you need.

TROY: I know what I'm doing. This is outside wood. You put pine wood inside the house. Pine wood is inside wood. This here is outside wood. Now you tell me where the fence is gonna be?

BONO: You don't need this wood. You can put it up with pine wood and it'll stand as long as you gonna be here looking at it.

TROY: How you know how long I'm gonna be here, nigger? Hell, I might just live forever. Live longer than old man Horsely.

BONO: That's what Magee used to say.

TROY: Magee was a damn fool. Now you tell me who you ever heard of gonna pull their own teeth with a pair of rusty pliers?

BONO: The old folks . . . my granddaddy used to pull his teeth with pliers. They ain't had no dentists for the colored folks back then.

TROY: Get clean pliers! You understand? Clean pliers! Sterilize them! Besides we ain't living back then. All Magee had to do was walk over to Doc Goldblums.

BONO: I see you and that Tallahassee gal—that Alberta—I see you all done got tight.

TROY: What you mean "got tight"?

BONO: I see where you be laughing and joking with her all the time.

TROY: I laughs and jokes with all of them, Bono. You know me.

BONO: That ain't the kind of laughing and joking I'm talking about.

[CORY *enters from the house.*]

CORY: How you doing, Mr. Bono?

BONO: How you doing, Cory?

TROY: Get that saw from Bono and cut some wood. He talking about the wood's too hard to cut. Stand back there, Jim, and let that young boy show you how it's done.

BONO: He's sure welcome to it. [CORY *takes the saw and begins to cut the wood.*] Look at that. Big old strong boy. Look like Joe Louis. Hell, I must be getting old the way I'm watching that boy whip through that wood.

CORY: I don't see why Mama want a fence around the yard noways.

TROY: Damn if I know either. What the hell she keeping out with it? She ain't got nothing nobody want.

BONO: Some people build fences to keep people out . . . and some people build fences to keep people in. Rose wants to hold on to you all. She loves you.

TROY: Hell, nigger, I don't need nobody to tell me my wife loves me. Cory, go on in the house and see if you can find that other saw.

CORY: Where's it at?

TROY: I said find it! Look for it till you find it. [CORY *exits into the house.*] What's that supposed to mean? Wanna keep us in?

BONO: Troy, I done known you seem like damn near all my life. You and Rose both. I done known both of you all for a long time. I remember when you met Rose. When you was hitting them baseballs out the park. A lot of them old gals was after you then, You had the pick of the litter. When you picked Rose, I was happy for you. That was the first time I knew you had any sense. I said, "My man Troy knows what he's doing; I'm gonna follow this nigger, he might take me somewhere." I been following you too. I done learned a whole heap of things about life watching you. I done learned how to tell where the shit lies, how to tell it from the alfalfa. You done learned me a lot of things. You showed me how to not make the same mistakes, to take life as it comes along and keep putting one foot in front of the other. [*Pause.*] Rose a good woman, Troy.

TROY: Hell, nigger, I know she a good woman. I been married to her for eighteen years. What you got on your mind, Bono?

BONO: I just say she a good woman. Just like I say anything. I ain't got to have nothing on my mind.

TROY: You just gonna say she a good woman and leave it hanging out there like that? Why, you telling me she a good woman?

BONO: She loves you, Troy. Rose loves you.

TROY: You saying I don't measure up. That's what you trying to say. I don't measure up 'cause I'm seeing this other gal. I know what you trying to say.

BONO: I know what Rose means to you, Troy. I'm just trying to say I don't want to see you mess up.

TROY: Yeah, I appreciate that, Bono. If you was messing around on Lucille, I'd be telling you the same thing.

BONO: Well, that's all I got to say. I just say that because I love you both.

TROY: Hell, you know me . . . I wasn't out there looking for nothing. You can't find a better woman than Rose. I know that. But seems like this woman just stuck on to me where I can't shake her loose. I done wrestled with it, tried to throw her off me, but she just stuck tighter. Now she's stuck on for good.

BONO: You's in control . . . that's what you tell me all the time. You responsible for what you do.

TROY: I ain't ducking the responsibility of it. As long as it sets right in my heart, then I'm okay. 'Cause that's all I listen to. It'll tell me right from wrong every time. And I ain't talking about doing Rose no bad turn. I love Rose. She done carried me a long ways and I love and respect her for that.

BONO: I know you do. That's why I don't want to see you hurt her. But what you gonna do when she find out? What you got then? If you try and juggle both of them, sooner or later you gonna drop one of them. That's common sense.

TROY: Yeah, I hear what you saying, Bono. I been trying to figure a way to work it out.

BONO: Work it out right, Troy. I don't want to be getting all up between you and Rose's business, but work it so it come out right.

TROY: Aw hell, I get all up between you and Lucille's business. When you gonna get that woman that refrigerator she been wanting? Don't tell me you ain't got no money now. I know who your banker is. Mellon don't need that money bad as Lucille want that refrigerator. I'll tell you that.

BONO: Tell you what I'll do. When you finish building this fence for Rose, I'll buy Lucille that refrigerator.

TROY: You done stuck your foot in your mouth now! [TROY *grabs up a board and begins to saw.* BONO *starts to walk out the yard.*] Hey, nigger . . . where you going?

BONO: I'm going home. I know you don't expect me to help you now. I'm protecting my money. I wanna see you put that fence up by yourself. That's what I want to see. You'll be here another six months without me.

TROY: Nigger, you ain't right.
BONO: When it comes to my money, I'm right as fireworks on the Fourth of July.
TROY: All right, we gonna see now. You better get out your bank book.

[BONO *exits, and* TROY *continues to work.* ROSE *enters from the house.*]

ROSE: What they say down there? What's happening with Gabe?
TROY: I went down there and got him out. Cost me fifty dollars. Say he was disturbing the peace. Judge set up a hearing for him in three weeks. Say to show cause why he shouldn't be recommitted.
ROSE: What was he doing that cause them to arrest him?
TROY: Some kids was teasing him and he run them off home. Say he was howling and carrying on. Some folks seen him and called the police. That's all it was.
ROSE: Well, what'd you say? What'd you tell the judge?
TROY: Told him I'd look after him. It didn't make no sense to recommit the man. He stuck out his big greasy palm and told me to give him fifty dollars and take him on home.
ROSE: Where's he at now? Where'd he go off to?
TROY: I ain't the man's keeper. He's gone on about his business. He don't need nobody to hold his hand.
ROSE: Well, I don't know. Seem like that would be the best place for him if they did put him into the hospital. I know what you're gonna say. But that's what I think would be best.
TROY: I'm gonna go down there and show cause all right. The man done had his life ruined fighting for what? And they wanna take and lock him up. Let him be free. He don't bother nobody.
ROSE: Well, everybody got their own way of looking at it, I guess. Come on and get your lunch. I got a bowl of lima beans and some cornbread in the oven. Come on get something to eat. Ain't no sense you fretting over Gabe. [ROSE *turns to go into the house.*]
TROY: Rose, I got something to tell you.
ROSE: Well, come on, wait till I get this food on the table.
TROY: Rose! [*She stops and turns around.*] I don't know how to say this. [*Pause.*] I can't explain it none. It just sort of grows on you till it gets out of hand. It starts out like a little bush . . . and the next thing you know it's a whole forest.
ROSE: Troy . . . what are you talking about?
TROY: I'm talking, woman, let me talk. I'm trying to find a way to tell you . . . I'm gonna be a daddy. I'm gonna be somebody's daddy.
ROSE: Troy . . you're not telling me this? You're gonna be . . . what?
TROY: Rose . . . now . . . see . . .
ROSE: You telling me you gonna be somebody's daddy? You telling your *wife* this?

[GABRIEL *enters from the street. He carries a rose in his hand.*]

GABRIEL: Hey, Troy! Hey, Rose!
ROSE: I have to wait eighteen years to hear something like this.

GABRIEL: Hey, Rose . . . got a flower for you. [*He hands it to her.*] That's a rose. Same rose like what you is.

ROSE: Thanks, Gabe.

GABRIEL: Troy, you ain't mad at me, is you? Them bad mens come and put me away. You ain't mad at me, is you?

TROY: Naw, Gabe, I ain't mad at you.

ROSE: Eighteen years and you wanna come with this.

GABRIEL: [*Takes a quarter out of his pocket.*] See what I got? Got a brand-new quarter.

TROY: Rose, it's just—

ROSE: Ain't nothing you can say, Troy. Ain't no way of explaining that.

GABRIEL: Fellow that give me this quarter had a whole mess of them. I'm gonna keep this quarter till it stops shining.

ROSE: Gabe, go on in the house there. I got some watermelon in the frigidaire. Go on and get you a piece.

GABRIEL: Say, Rose . . . you know I was chasing hellhounds and them bad mens come and get me and take me away. Troy helped me. He come down there and told them they better let me go before he beat them up. Yeah, he did!

ROSE: You go on and get you a piece of watermelon, Gabe. Them bad mens is gone now.

GABRIEL: Okay, Rose . . . gonna get me some watermelon. The kind with the stripes on it. [GABRIEL *exits into the house.*]

ROSE: Why, Troy? Why? After all these years to come dragging this in to me now. It don't make no sense at your age. I could have expected this ten or fifteen years ago, but not now.

TROY: Age ain't got nothing to do with it, Rose.

ROSE: I done tried to be everything a wife should be. Everything a wife could be. Been married eighteen years and I got to live to see the day you tell me you been seeing another woman and done fathered a child by her. And you know I ain't never wanted no half-nothing in my family. My whole family is half. Everybody got different fathers and mothers . . . my two sisters and my brother. Can't hardly tell who's who. Can't never sit down and talk about Papa and Mama. It's your papa and your mama and my papa and my mama—

TROY: Rose, stop it now.

ROSE: I ain't never wanted that for none of my children. And now you wanna drag your behind in here and tell me something like this.

TROY: You ought to know. It's time for you to know.

ROSE: Well, I don't want to know, goddamn it!

TROY: I can't just make it go away. It's done now. I can't wish the circumstances of the thing away.

ROSE: And you don't want to either. Maybe you want to wish me and my boy away. Maybe that's what you want? Well, you can't wish us away. I've got eighteen years of my life invested in you. You ought to have stayed upstairs in my bed, where you belong.

TROY: Rose, now listen to me, we can get a handle on this thing. We can talk this out, come to an understanding.

ROSE: All of a sudden it's "we." Where was "we" at when you was down there rolling around with some Godforsaken woman? "We" should have come to an understanding before you started making a damn fool of yourself. You're a day late and a dollar short when it comes to an understanding with me.

TROY: It's just . . . She gives me a different idea, a different understanding about myself. I can step out of this house and get away from the pressures and problems . . . be a different man. I ain't got to wonder how I'm gonna pay the bills or get the roof fixed. I can just be a part of myself that I ain't never been.

ROSE: What I want to know is, do you plan to continue seeing her? That's all you can say to me.

TROY: I can sit up in her house and laugh. Do you understand what I'm saying. I can laugh out loud . . . and it feels good. It reaches all the way down to the bottom of my shoes. [*Pause.*] Rose, I can't give that up.

ROSE: Maybe you ought to go on and stay down there with her . . . if she a better woman than me.

TROY: It ain't about nobody being a better woman or nothing. You ain't the blame, Rose. A man couldn't ask for no woman to be a better wife than you've been. I'm responsible for it. I done locked myself into a pattern trying to take care of you all that I forgot about myself.

ROSE: What the hell was I there for? That was my job, not somebody else's.

TROY: Rose, I done tried all my life to live decent . . . to live a clean, hard, useful life. I tried to be a good husband to you. In every way I knew. Maybe I come into the world backwards, I don't know. But you born with two strikes on you before you come to the plate. You got to guard it closely . . . looking for the curveball on the inside corner. You can't afford to let none get past you. You can't afford a call strike. If you going down, you going down swinging. Everything lined up against you. What you gonna do? I fooled them, Rose. I bunted. When I found you and Cory and a halfway decent job, I was safe. Couldn't nothing touch me. I wasn't gonna strike out no more. I wasn't going back to the penitentiary. I wasn't gonna lay in the streets with a bottle of wine. I was safe. I had me a family. A job. I wasn't gonna get that last strike. I was on first looking for one of them boys to knock me in. To get me home.

ROSE: You should have stayed in my bed, Troy.

TROY: Then, when I saw that gal, she firmed up my backbone. And I got to thinking that if I tried, I just might be able to steal second. Do you understand . . . after eighteen years I wanted to steal second.

ROSE: You should have held me tight. You should have grabbed me and held on.

TROY: I stood on first base for eighteen years and I thought . . . Well, goddamn it, go on for it!

ROSE: We're not talking about baseball! We're talking about you going off to lay in bed with another woman . . . and then bring it home to me. That's what we're talking about. We ain't talking about baseball.

TROY: Rose, you're not listening to me. I'm trying the best I can to explain it to you. It's not easy for me to admit that I been standing in the same place for eighteen years.

ROSE: I been standing with you! I been right here with you, Troy. I got a life too. I gave eighteen years of my life to stand in the same spot with you. Don't you think I ever wanted other things? Don't you think I had dreams and hopes? What about my life? What about me? Don't you think it ever crossed my mind to want to know other men? That I wanted to lay up somewhere and forget about my responsibilities? That I wanted someone to make me laugh so I could feel good? You not the only one who's got wants and needs. But I held on to you, Troy. I took all my feelings, my wants and needs, my dreams, and I buried them inside you. I planted a seed and watched and prayed over it. I planted myself inside you and waited to bloom. And it didn't take me no eighteen years to find out the soil was hard and rocky and it wasn't never gonna bloom. But I held on to you, Troy. I held you tighter. You was my husband. I owed you everything I had. Every part of me I could find to give you. And upstairs in that room, with the darkness falling in on me, I gave everything I had to try and erase the doubt that you wasn't the finest man in the world. And wherever you was going I wanted to be there with you. 'Cause you was my husband, 'cause that's the only way I was gonna survive as your wife. You always talking about what you give and what you don't have to give. But you take too. You take and don't even know nobody's giving!

[ROSE *turns to exit into the house;* TROY *grabs her arm.*]

TROY: You're gonna listen to me. It ain't like what you saying!
ROSE: Troy, let go of my arm. You're hurting me.
TROY: You say I take and don't give.
ROSE: Troy, you're hurting my arm. Let go.
TROY: I done give you everything I got. Don't you tell me about not taking and giving. Don't you tell that lie on me.
ROSE: Troy!
TROY: Don't you tell that lie on me!

[CORY *enters from the house.*]

CORY: Mama!
ROSE: Troy, you're hurting me.
TROY: Don't you tell me about no taking and giving.

[CORY *comes up behind* TROY *and grabs him.* TROY, *surprised, is thrown off balance just as* CORY *throws a glancing blow that catches him on the chest and knocks him down.* TROY *is stunned, as is* CORY.]

ROSE: Troy. Troy. NO! [TROY *gets to his feet and starts at* CORY.] Troy . . . no. Please! Troy!

[ROSE *pulls on* TROY *to hold him back.* TROY *stops himself.*]

TROY: [*To* CORY.] All right. That's strike two. You stay away from around me, boy. Don't you strike out. You living with a full count. Don't you strike out.

[TROY *exits out the yard as the lights go down.*]

Scene 2

It is six months later, early afternoon. TROY *enters from the house and starts to exit the yard.* ROSE *enters from the house.*

ROSE: Troy, I want to talk to you.

TROY: All of a sudden, after all this time, you want to talk to me, huh? You ain't wanted to talk to me for months. You ain't wanted to talk to me last night. You ain't wanted no part of me then. What you wanna talk to me about now?

ROSE: Tomorrow's Friday.

TROY: I know what day tomorrow is. You think I don't know tomorrow's Friday? My whole life I ain't done nothing but look to see Friday coming, and you got to tell me it's Friday.

ROSE: I want to know if you're coming home.

TROY: I always come home, Rose. You know that. There ain't never been a night I ain't come home.

ROSE: That ain't what I mean, Troy, and you know it. I want to know if you're coming straight home after work.

TROY: I figure I'd cash my check, hang out at Taylor's with the fellows . . . maybe play a game of checkers.

ROSE: Troy, I can't live like this. I won't live like this. It's been going on six months now you ain't been coming home.

TROY: I be here every night. Every night of the year. That's 365 days.

ROSE: I want you to come home tomorrow after work.

TROY: Rose, I don't mess up my pay. You know that now. I take my pay and I give it to you. I don't have no money but what you give me back. I just want to have a little time to myself . . . a little time to enjoy life.

ROSE: What about me? When's my time to enjoy life?

TROY: I don't know what to tell you, Rose. I'm doing the best I can do.

ROSE: You ain't been home from work but time enough to change your clothes and run out . . . and you wanna call that the best you can do?

TROY: I'm going over to the hospital to see Alberta. She went into the hospital this afternoon. Look like she might have the baby early. I won't be gone long.

ROSE: Well, you ought to know. . . . They went over to Miss Pearl's and got Gabe today. She said you told them to go ahead and lock him up.

TROY: I ain't said no such thing. Whoever told you that is a liar. Miss Pearl ain't doing nothing but telling a big fat lie.

ROSE: She ain't had to tell me. I read it on the papers.

TROY: I ain't told them nothing of the kind.

ROSE: I saw it right there on the papers.

TROY: What it say, huh? What it say?

ROSE: It said you told them to take him.

TROY: They got that all screwed up. The way they screw up everything. I ain't worried about what they got on the paper.

ROSE: Say the government send part of his check to the hospital and the other part to you.

TROY: I ain't got nothing to do with that if that's the way it works. I ain't made up the rules about how it work.

ROSE: You did Gabe just like you did Cory. You wouldn't sign the paper for Cory, but you signed for Gabe. You signed that paper.

[*The telephone is heard ringing inside the house.*]

TROY: I told you I ain't signed nothing, woman. The only thing I signed was the release form. I ain't signed nothing about sending Gabe away.

ROSE: I said send him to the hospital—you said let him be free—now you done went down there and signed him to the hospital for half his money. You went back on yourself, Troy. You gonna have to answer for that. [ROSE *exits into the house to answer the phone.*]

TROY: [*Calling after her.*] See now . . . you been over there talking to Miss Pearl. She done got mad 'cause she ain't getting Gabe's rent money. That's all it is. She's liable to say anything.

ROSE: [*From inside the house.*] Troy, I seen where you signed the paper.

TROY: What she doing got papers on my brother anyway? Miss Pearl telling a big fat lie. And I'm gonna tell her about it too! [TROY *paces about the yard. Presently* ROSE *enters.*] You ain't seen nothing I signed.

ROSE: Troy, that was the hospital. Alberta had the baby.

TROY: What she have? What is it?

ROSE: It's a girl.

TROY: I better get on down to the hospital to see her.

ROSE: Troy . . .

TROY: Rose, I got to go see her now. That's only right. What's the matter? The baby's all right, ain't it?

ROSE: Alberta died having the baby.

TROY: Died? You say she's dead? Alberta's dead?

ROSE: They said they done all they could. They couldn't do nothing for her.

TROY: The baby? How's the baby?

ROSE: They say it's healthy.

TROY: [*More to himself than* ROSE.] I had that sickle in my hand. I just didn't throw it far enough.

ROSE: I wonder who's gonna bury her?

TROY: She had family, Rose. She wasn't living in the world by herself.

ROSE: I know she wasn't living in the world by herself.

TROY: Next thing you gonna want to know if she had any insurance.

ROSE: Troy, you ain't got to talk like that.

TROY: That's the first thing that jumped out your mouth. "Who's gonna bury her?" Like I'm fixing to take on that task for myself.

ROSE: I am your wife. Don't push me away.

TROY: I ain't pushing nobody away. Just give me some space. That's all. Just give me some room to breathe.

[ROSE *exits into the house.* TROY *walks about the yard.*]

TROY: [*With a quiet rage that threatens to consume him.*] All right, Mr. Death. See now . . . I'm gonna tell you what I'm gonna do. I'm gonna take and build me a fence around this yard. See? I'm gonna build me a fence around what belongs to me. And then I want you to stay on the other side. See? You stay over there until you're ready for me. Then you come on. Bring your army. Bring your sickle. Bring your wrestling clothes. I ain't gonna fall down on my vigilance this time. You ain't gonna sneak up on me no more. When you ready for me, when the top of your list say Troy Maxson, that's when you come around here. You come up and knock on the front door and ask for me. Then we gonna find out what manner of man you are. Ain't nobody else got nothing to do with this. This is between you and me. Man to man. You stay on the other side of that fence until you ready for me. Then you come up and knock on the front door. Anytime you want. I'll be ready for you.

[*The lights go down to black.*]

SCENE 3

The lights come up on the porch. It is late evening three days later. ROSE *sits listening to the ball game waiting for* TROY. *The final out of the game is made and* ROSE *switches off the radio and enters the house. Presently* TROY *enters the yard carrying an infant wrapped in blankets. He stands back from the house and calls.*

TROY: Rose . . . Rose! [ROSE *enters and stands on the porch. There is a long, awkward silence, the weight of which grows heavier with each passing second.*] Rose . . . I'm standing here with my daughter in my arms. She ain't but a wee bitty little old thing. She don't know nothing about grown-ups' business. She innocent . . . and she ain't got no mamma.

ROSE: What you telling me for, Troy? [*She turns and exits into the house.*]

TROY: Well . . . I guess we'll just sit out here on the porch. [*He sits down on the porch. There is an awkward indelicateness about the way he handles the baby. His largeness engulfs and seems to swallow it. He speaks loud enough for* ROSE *to hear.*] A man's got to do what's right for him. I ain't sorry for nothing I done. It felt right in my heart, and if it set right there, a man can't be blamed. [*To the baby.*] Ain't that right? What you smiling at? You smiling 'cause your daddy's telling the truth? Your daddy's a big man. Got these great big old hands. But sometimes he's scared. And right now your daddy's scared 'cause we sitting out here and ain't got no home. Oh, I been homeless before. I ain't had no little baby with me. But I been homeless. You just be out on the road by your lonesome and you see one of them trains coming and you just kinda go like this.

[*He sings as a lullaby.*]

Please, Mr. Engineer, let a man ride the line
Please, Mr. Engineer, let a man ride the line
I ain't got no ticket, please let me ride the blinds

[ROSE *enters from the house.* TROY, *hearing her steps behind him, stands and faces her.*]

She's my daughter, Rose. My own flesh and blood. I can't deny her no more than I can deny them boys. We's the same. They my children. [*Pause.*] You and them boys is my family. You and them and this child is all I got in the world. World get so big sometimes a man can't hardly wrestle with it none. He need some help. This here little bitty thing is my daughter. I don't know too much about babies. So I guess what I'm saying is, I'd appreciate it if you'd help me take care of her.

ROSE: Okay, Troy. You're right. I'll take care of your baby for you 'cause, like you say, she's innocent and you can't visit the sins of the father upon the child. A motherless child has got a hard time. [*She takes the baby from him.*] From right now . . . this child got a mother. But you a womanless man.

[ROSE *turns and exits into the house with the baby. Lights go down to black.*]

Scene 4

It is two months later. LYONS *enters from the street. He knocks on the door and calls.*

LYONS: Hey, Rose! [*Pause.*] Rose!

ROSE: [*From inside the house.*] Stop all that hollering. You gonna wake up Raynell. I just got her to sleep.

LYONS: I just stopped by to pay Papa this twenty dollars I owe him. Where's everybody at?

ROSE: He should be here in a minute. I'm getting ready to go down to the church. Sit down and wait on him.

LYONS: I got to go pick up Bonnie over her mother's house.

ROSE: Well, sit it down there on the table. He'll get it.

LYONS: [*Enters the house and sets the money on the table.*] Tell Papa I said thanks. I'll see you again.

ROSE: All right, Lyons. We'll see you.

[LYONS *starts to exit as* CORY *enters.*]

CORY: Hey, Lyons.

LYONS: What's happening, Cory. Say man, I'm sorry I missed your graduation. You know I had a gig and couldn't get away. Otherwise you know I would have been there. So what you doing?

CORY: I'm trying to find a job.
LYONS: I know how that go. It's rough out here. Jobs are scarce.
CORY: Yeah, I know. I been looking all over.
LYONS: Look here, I got to run. Talk to Papa . . . he know some people. He'll be able to help get you a job. Talk to him . . . see what he say.
CORY: Yeah, okay, Lyons.
LYONS: You take care. I'll talk to you soon. We'll find some time to talk.

[LYONS *exits the yard.* CORY *wanders over to the tree, picks up the bat and assumes a batting stance. He studies an imaginary pitcher and swings. Dissatisfied with the result, he tries again.* TROY *enters. They eye each other for a beat.* CORY *puts the bat down and exits the yard.* TROY *starts into the house as* ROSE *exits with* RAYNELL. *She is carrying a cake.*]

TROY: I'm coming in and everybody's going out.
ROSE: I'm taking this cake down to the church for the bake sale. Lyons was by to see you. He stopped by to pay you your twenty dollars. It's laying in there on the table.
TROY: [*Going into his pocket.*] Well, here go this money.
ROSE: Put it there on the table, Troy. I'll get it.
TROY: What time you coming back?
ROSE: Ain't no use in you studying me. It don't matter what time I come back.
TROY: I just asked you a question, woman. What's the matter . . . can't I ask you a question?
ROSE: Troy, I don't want to go into it. Your dinner's in there on the stove. All you got to do is heat it up. And don't you be eating the rest of them cakes in there. I'm coming back for them. We having a bake sale at the church tomorrow.

[ROSE *exits the yard.* TROY *sits down on the steps, takes a pint bottle from his pocket, opens it, and drinks. He begins to sing.*]

[TROY:]

Had an old dog his name was Blue
You know Blue was a good old dog
Blue treed a possum in a hollow log
You know from that he was a good old dog.

[BONO *enters the yard.*]

BONO: Hey, Troy.
TROY: Hey, what's happening, Bono?
BONO: I just thought I'd stop by to see you.
TROY: What you stop by and see me for? You ain't stopped by in a month of Sundays. Hell, I must owe you money or something.
BONO: Since you got your promotion I can't keep up with you. Used to see you every day. Now I don't even know what route you working.

TROY: They keep switching me around. Got me out in Greentree now . . . hauling white folks' garbage.

BONO: Greentree, huh? Well, at least you ain't got to be lifting them barrels. Damn if they ain't getting heavier. I'm gonna put in my two years and call it quits.

TROY: I'm thinking about retiring myself. How's Lucille?

BONO: She all right. Her arthritis get to acting up on her sometime. Saw Rose on my way in. She going down to the church, huh?

TROY: Yeah, she took up going down there. All them preachers looking for somebody to fatten their pockets. [*Pause.*] Got some gin here.

BONO: Naw, thanks. I just stopped by to say hello.

TROY: Hell, nigger, you can take a drink. I ain't never known you to say no to a drink. You ain't got to work tomorrow.

BONO: I just stopped by. I'm fixing to go over to Skinner's. We got us a domino game going over his house every Friday.

TROY: Nigger, you can't play no dominoes. I used to whup you four games out of five.

BONO: Well, that learned me. I'm getting better.

TROY: Yeah? Well, that's all right. You sure had a good teacher.

BONO: Look here . . . I got to be getting on. Stop by sometime, huh?

TROY: Yeah, I'll do that, Bono. Lucille told Rose you bought her a new refrigerator.

BONO: Yeah, I finally broke down on that score.

TROY: I knew you would. I knew she'd get you.

BONO: Yeah . . . okay. I'll be talking to you.

TROY: Yeah, take care, Bono. Good to see you. I'm gonna stop over.

BONO: Yeah, okay, Troy. [BONO *exits.*]

[TROY *drinks from the bottle and sings:*]

Old Blue's feets was big and round
Never 'llowed a possum to touch the ground
Old Blue died and I dig his grave
Let him down with a golden chain
Every night when I hear old Blue bark
I know Blue treed a possum in Noah's Ark.

[CORY *enters the yard. They eye each other for a beat.* TROY *is sitting in the middle of the steps.* CORY *walks over.*]

CORY: I got to get by.

TROY: Say what? What's you say?

CORY: You in my way. I got to get by.

TROY: You got to get by where? This is my house. Bought and paid for. In full. Took me fifteen years. And if you wanna go in my house and I'm sitting on the steps you say excuse me. Like your mama taught you.

CORY: Come on, Pop . . . I got to get by.

[CORY *starts to maneuver his way past* TROY. TROY *grabs his leg and shoves him back.*]

TROY: You just gonna walk over top of me?

CORY: I live here too!

TROY: [*Advancing toward him.*] You just gonna walk over top of me in my own house?

CORY: I ain't scared of you.

TROY: I ain't asked if you was scared of me. I asked you if you was fixing to walk over top of me in my own house? That's the question. You ain't gonna say excuse me? You just gonna walk over top of me?

CORY: If you wanna put it like that.

TROY: How else am I gonna put it?

CORY: I was walking by you to go into the house 'cause you sitting on the steps drunk, singing to yourself. You can put it like that.

TROY: Without saying excuse me? [CORY *doesn't respond.*] I asked you a question. Without saying excuse me?

CORY: I ain't got to say excuse me to you. You don't count around here no more.

TROY: Oh, I see . . . I don't count around here no more. You ain't got to say excuse me to your daddy. All of a sudden you done got so grown that your daddy don't count around here no more. Around here in his own house and yard that he done paid for with the sweat of his brow. You done got so grown to where you gonna take over. You gonna take over my house. Is that right? You gonna wear my pants. You gonna go in there and stretch out on my bed. You ain't got to say excuse me 'cause I don't count around here no more. Is that right?

CORY: That's right. You always talking this dumb stuff. Now, why don't you just get out my way.

TROY: I guess you got someplace to sleep and something to put in your belly. You got that, huh? You got that? That's what you need. You got that, huh?

CORY: You don't know what I got. You ain't got to worry about what I got.

TROY: You right! You one hundred percent right! I done spent the last seventeen years worrying about what you got. Now it's your turn, see? I'll tell you what you do. You grown . . . we done established that. You a man. Now, let's see you act like one. Turn your behind around and walk out this yard. And when you get out there in the alley, you can forget about this house. See? 'Cause this is my house. You go on and be a man and get your own house. You can forget about this. 'Cause this is mine. You go on and get yours 'cause I'm through with doing for you.

CORY: You talking about what you did for me . . . What'd you ever give me?

TROY: Them feet and bones! That pumping heart! I give you more than anybody else is ever gonna give you.

CORY: You ain't never gave me nothing. You ain't never done nothing but hold me back. Afraid I was gonna be better than you. All you ever did was try and make me scared of you. I used to tremble every time you called my name. Every time I heard your footsteps in the house. Wondering all the time,

What's Papa gonna say if I do this? What's he gonna say if I do that? What's Papa gonna say if I turn on the radio? And Mama, too—she tries, but she's scared of you.

TROY: You leave your mama out of this. She ain't got nothing to do with this.

CORY: I don't know how she stands you . . . after what you did to her.

TROY: I told you to leave your mama out of this! [*He advances toward* CORY.]

CORY: What you gonna do . . . give me a whupping? You can't whup me no more. You're too old. You just an old man.

TROY: [*Shoves him on his shoulder.*] Nigger! That's what you are. You just another nigger on the street to me!

CORY: You crazy! You know that?

TROY: Go on now! You got the devil in you. Get on away from me!

CORY: You just a crazy old man . . . talking about I got the devil in me.

TROY: Yeah, I'm crazy! If you don't get on the other side of that yard, I'm gonna show you how crazy I am! Go on . . . get out my yard.

CORY: It ain't your yard. You took Uncle Gabe's money he got from the army to buy the house . . . and then you put him out.

TROY: [*Advances to him.*] You get your black ass out my yard!

[TROY'*s advance backs* CORY *up against the tree.* CORY *grabs up the bat.*]

CORY: I ain't going nowhere! Come on . . . put me out! I ain't scared of you.

TROY: That's my bat! Put my bat down!

CORY: Come on! Put me out.

[TROY *stops his advance.*]

CORY: What's the matter? You so bad . . . put me out!

TROY: That's strike three. You done struck out now. All right! Let's see what you gonna do now!

CORY: [*Backing up.*] Come on! Come on!

TROY: You gonna have to use it. You want to draw back that bat on me . . . you gonna have to use it.

[CORY *has retreated to the alley as* ROSE *enters carrying the baby.*]

ROSE: Cory! What you doing with that bat?

TROY: [*To* CORY.] Go on . . . don't you come around here no more.

ROSE: Troy, what's going on?

TROY: Rose, this boy don't live here no more. If he want to come back in here, he's gonna have to use that bat. [*To* CORY.] Go on! Get on away from around my house.

CORY: [*Throws the bat down in* TROY'*s direction.*] I'll be back for my things, Mama.

TROY: They better be out there on the other side of that yard.

[CORY *exits down the alley.* TROY *watches after him.*]

ROSE: Cory! Troy, you just can't put the boy out like that.

TROY: I don't want to hear it, Rose, I promised myself when the day come that boy want to get up in my face and challenge me, he going on away from here. So I don't want to hear nothing you got to say. [ROSE *turns and exits into the house.*] 'Cause it don't matter no more. I can't taste nothing. Hallelujah! I can't taste nothing no more!

[*The lights fade to black.*]

SCENE 5

The time is 1965. An unpainted, weather-beaten fence surrounds the house. RAYNELL, *a rather tall, gangly girl of seven, barefoot and wearing a flannel nightgown, enters the yard and crosses over to a small plot of ground off to the side. The screen door bangs shut.* ROSE *calls from the house.*

ROSE: Raynell!
RAYNELL: Mam?
ROSE: What you doing out there?
RAYNELL: Nothing.
ROSE: [*Coming to the door.*] Girl, get in here and get your shoes on. What you doing?
RAYNELL: Seeing if my garden growed.
ROSE: I told you it ain't gonna grow overnight. You got to wait.
RAYNELL: It don't look like it never gonna grow, dag!
ROSE: I told you a watched pot never boils. Get in here and get your shoes on.
RAYNELL: This ain't even no pot, Mama!
ROSE: You got to give it a chance. It'll grow. Now you come on and do what I told you. We got to be getting ready. This ain't no morning to be playing around. Hear me?
RAYNELL: Yes, mam.

[ROSE *turns and goes into the house.* RAYNELL *pokes at her garden with a stick.* CORY *enters. He is dressed in a Marine sergeant's uniform and carries a duffel bag. His posture is that of a military man and his speech has a clipped sternness.*]

CORY: Hi. [*Pause.*] I bet your name is Raynell.
RAYNELL: Uh huh.
CORY: Is your mama home?

[RAYNELL *runs up on the porch to the screen door.*]

RAYNELL: Mama . . . there's some man out here. Mama?

[ROSE *comes to the door.*]

ROSE: Cory? Lord have mercy! [ROSE *and* CORY *embrace in a tearful reunion.*] Look at you. My goodness . . . just look at you.
CORY: How have you been, Mama? It's good to see you.
ROSE: If you ain't a sight for sore eyes! Done got all grown up.
CORY: Don't cry, Mama. What you crying about?

ROSE: I'm just so glad to see you. I didn't know if you was gonna make it or not. What took you so long?

CORY: You know how the Marines are, Mama. They have to have all their paperwork straight before they let you do anything.

ROSE: You seen Raynell? Isn't she grown? Raynell?

RAYNELL: Mam?

ROSE: Come here and say hello to your brother. Come on . . . this is your brother, Cory. You remember Cory?

RAYNELL: No, mam.

CORY: She don't remember me, Mama.

ROSE: Well, we talk about you. She heard us talk about you. [*To* RAYNELL.] This is your brother, Cory. Come on and say hello.

RAYNELL: Hi.

CORY: Hi. So you're Raynell. Mama told me a lot about you.

ROSE: Now, you go on in there and put your shoes on and lay out that dress like I told you.

RAYNELL: Mama, it's too big. Can't I wear the other one with the bow?

ROSE: Don't you give me no sass now. You go on and do what I told you.

RAYNELL: [*As she exits.*] Yes, mam.

ROSE: She's a good girl. She give me a little back talk every now and then. But she's a good child. [*Pause.*] I was hoping you'd bring your girlfriend so I could get a chance to meet her.

CORY: She had to work. She told me to tell you hello and she'd meet you some other time.

ROSE: Well, I'm sure glad you made it. I done called up there about Lyons. They say they gonna let him come. Gabriel's still in the hospital. I don't know if they gonna let him come or not. If it wasn't for Jim Bono and Miss Pearl I don't know how I would have made it these past few days. Ain't had nobody but me. And Raynell . . . she too young to understand. I try to get down to see Lyons every chance I get. But with working and taking care of Raynell and going to church and whatnot . . . there just ain't that many hours in the day.

CORY: I didn't know you was working, Mama.

ROSE: Ain't been but about a year or so. Your daddy retired and I got tired of sitting in the house doing nothing. The ward chairman got me on down there cleaning up at the courthouse. I could have got Miss Pearl to write and tell you, but her arthritis got so bad I hate to ask her anymore.

CORY: I see you got your fence built.

ROSE: Oh, that's been up there ever since Raynell wasn't but a wee little bitty old thing. Your daddy finally got around to putting that up to keep her in the yard. The thing's near about fallen down now. Ain't too much else changed. He still got that old piece of rag tied to that tree. He was out here swinging that bat. I was just ready to go back in the house. He swung that bat and then he just fell over. Seem like he swung it and stood there with this grin on his face . . . and then he just fell over. They carried him on down to the hospital, but I knew there wasn't no need.

CORY: Mama . . . I don't know how to tell you this, but I've got to tell you. I'm not going to Papa's funeral.

ROSE: Boy, hush your mouth. That's your daddy you're talking about. I don't wanna hear that kind of talk this morning. I done raised you to come to this? You standing there all healthy and grown talking about you ain't going to your daddy's funeral?

CORY: Mama, listen . . .

ROSE: I don't want to hear it, Cory. You just get that thought out your head.

CORY: I can't drag Papa with me everywhere I go. I've got to say no to him. One time in my life I've got to say no.

ROSE: Don't nobody have to listen to nothing like that. I know you and your daddy ain't seen eye to eye, but I ain't got to listen to that kind of talk this morning. Whatever was between you and your daddy . . . the time has come to put it aside. Just take it and set it over there on the shelf and forget about it. Disrespecting your daddy ain't gonna make you a man, Cory. You got to find a way to come to that on your own. Not going to your daddy's funeral ain't gonna make you a man.

CORY: The whole time I was growing up, living in his house, Papa was like a shadow that followed you everywhere. It weighed on you and sunk in your flesh. It would wrap around you and lay there until you couldn't tell which one was you anymore. That shadow digging in your flesh. Trying to crawl in. Trying to live through you. Everywhere I looked Troy Maxson was staring back at me: hiding under the bed, in the closet. I'm just saying I've got to find a way to get rid of that shadow, Mama.

ROSE: You just like him. You got him in you good.

CORY: Don't tell me that, Mama.

TROY: You Troy Maxson all over again.

CORY: I don't want to be Troy Maxson. I want to be me.

ROSE: You can't be nobody but who you are, Cory. That shadow wasn't nothing but you growing into yourself. You either got to grow into it or cut it down to fit you. But that's all you got to make life with. That's all you got to measure yourself against that world out there. Your daddy wanted you to be everything he wasn't . . . and at the same time he tried to make you into everything he was. I don't know if he was right or wrong, but I know he meant to do more good than he meant to do harm. He wasn't always right. Sometimes when he touched, he bruised. And sometimes when he took me in his arms, he cut. When I first met your daddy I thought, Here is a man I can lay down with and make a baby. That's the first thing I thought when I seen him. I was thirty years old and had done seen my share of men. But when he walked up to me and said, "I can dance a waltz that'll make you dizzy," I thought, Rose Lee, here is a man that you can open yourself up to and be filled to bursting. Here is a man that can fill all them empty spaces you been tipping around the edges of. One of them empty spaces was being somebody's mother. I married your daddy and settled down to cooking his supper and keeping clean sheets on the bed. When your daddy walked through the house, he was so big he filled it up. That was my first mistake. Not to make him leave some room for me, for my part in the matter. But at that time I wanted that. I wanted a house that I could sing in. And that's what your daddy gave me. I didn't know to keep up his strength I had to give up little pieces of mine. I did that. I took on his life as mine and mixed up the pieces so that you couldn't hardly tell which was which anymore. It was my choice. It was my life and I didn't have to live it like that. But that's what life offered me in the way of being a woman, and I took it. I grabbed hold of it with both hands. After a while he didn't seem so big no more. Sometimes I'd catch him just sitting and staring at his hands, just sitting there staring like he was watching the silence eat away at them. By the time Raynell came into the house, me and your daddy had done lost touch with each other. I didn't want to make my blessing off of nobody's misfortune, but I took on to Raynell like she was all them babies I had wanted and never had. Like I'd been blessed to relive a part of my life. And if the Lord see fit to keep up my strength, I'm gonna do her just like your daddy did you . . . I'm gonna give her the best of what's in me.

[RAYNELL *enters from the house.*]

RAYNELL: Mama, can I wear my white shoes? This here hurt my feet.

ROSE: Well, they just gonna have to hurt your feet for a while. You ain't said they hurt your feet when you went down there to the store and got them.

RAYNELL: They ain't hurt then. My feet done got bigger.

ROSE: You leave them shoes on your feet and go back in there and get that black belt like I told you.

RAYNELL: I can't find it. These here look all right to me.

ROSE: Girl, go on back in that house and get that belt like I told you!

RAYNELL: [*As she exits.*] Dag! I told you I don't know where to find it.

ROSE: Don't you give me no back talk. You look around and find that belt. Look in that drawer upstairs.

[LYONS *enters from the street.*]

LYONS: Hey . . . hey, look here . . . is that Cory?

CORY: Hey, Lyons.

ROSE: [*Embracing* LYONS.] Lord have mercy.

LYONS: It'll be all right, Rose. Everything's gonna be all right. Looking at Cory standing there. He done come home. Standing there all big and grown. It's gonna be all right now. [LYONS *and* CORY *embrace awkwardly.*] Look at you, man. Look at you. A sergeant in the United States Marines! How you been, man?

CORY: I been all right.

LYONS: You look good. Don't he look good, Rose.

ROSE: Yeah . . . He come in a little while ago. A sight for sore eyes.

LYONS: Where's Uncle Gabe? He in the house?

ROSE: They don't know if they gonna let him come or not. I just talked to them a little while ago.

LYONS: Where's Raynell? Cory, you seen Raynell?

CORY: Yeah, she was in the yard when I came in.

LYONS: Ain't she precious? She gonna break a whole lot of hearts.

ROSE: You all come on in the house and let me fix you some breakfast . . . keep your strength up.

CORY: I ain't hungry, Mama.

LYONS: You can fix me something, Rose. I'll be in there in a minute. I'm gonna stay out here and talk to Cory a minute.

ROSE: Cory, you sure you don't want nothing? I know they ain't feeding you right.

CORY: No, Mama . . . thanks. I don't feel like eating. I'll get something later.

[ROSE *exits into the house.*]

LYONS: So how you been?

CORY: I been doing okay.

LYONS: Yeah. So when you get in?

CORY: A little while ago. This morning.

LYONS: Look at you . . . Got them sergeant stripes! [*Pause.*] I heard you thinking about getting married?

CORY: Yeah, I am. I figure it's about time.

LYONS: Me and Bonnie been split up about four years now. I guess she just got tired of all the changes I was putting her through. [*Pause.*] The Marines, huh? Sergeant. I knew you was gonna make something of yourself. Your head always was in the right direction. You gonna stay in. You gonna make it a career? Put in your twenty years?

CORY: I don't know. I got six in already. I think that's enough.

LYONS: Stick with Uncle Sam and retire early. There ain't nothing out here. I guess Rose told you what happened to me. They got me down the workhouse.

CORY: Yeah, she told me.

LYONS: You got to take the crooked with the straight. That's what Papa used to say. I thought I was being slick cashing other people's checks.

CORY: How much time you doing?

LYONS: They gave me three years. I got that beat now. I ain't got but nine months. It ain't so bad. You just learn to deal with it like anything else.

CORY: You still playing?

LYONS: Hey, you know I'm gonna do that. There's some fellows down there . . . we got us a band. We gonna stay together when we get out and see if we can make something out of it. But, yeah, I'm still playing. It still help me to get out of the bed in the morning. As long as it do that, I'm gonna be right there playing to make some sense out of it.

ROSE: [*At the screen door.*] Lyons, I got these eggs in the pan.

LYONS: Let me go get these eggs, man. Go eat and get ready to bury Papa. [LYONS *starts toward the house. He stops at the door and salutes.*] Sergeant! [*To* RAYNELL.] Hey, precious!

[LYONS *exits into the house.* CORY *walks about the yard. He goes over to the tree and picks up* TROY*'s bat.* RAYNELL *enters from the house.*]

RAYNELL: You in the Army or the Marines?
CORY: The Marines.
RAYNELL: Papa said it was the Army. [*Pause.*] Did you know Blue?
CORY: Blue? Who's Blue?
RAYNELL: Papa's dog what he sing about all the time.

[*After a long pause,* CORY *begins singing.*]

[CORY:]

I had a dog his name was Blue
You know how Blue was mighty true
You know Blue was a good old dog
Blue treed a possum in a hollow log
You know from that he was a good old dog.

[RAYNELL *joining the singing.*]

[CORY *and* RAYNELL:]

Blue treed a possum out on a limb
Blue looked at me and I looked at him
Grabbed that possum and put him in a sack
Blue stayed there till I came back
Old Blue's feets was big and round
Never allowed a possum to touch the ground.

Old Blue died and I dug his grave
I dug his grave with a silver spade
Let him down with a golden chain
And every night I call his name
Go on, Blue, you good dog, you!
Go on, Blue, you good dog, you!

Old Blue laid down and died like a man
Now he's treeing possums in the Promised Land.
I'm gonna tell you this to let you know:
Blue's gone where the good dogs go.
When I hear old Blue bark
When I hear old Blue bark

Blue treed a possum in Noah's Ark
Blue treed a possum in Noah's Ark.

ROSE: [*Comes to the door and calls.*] Raynell. Get in here and get them other shoes like I told you.
RAYNELL: I'll be back.

[RAYNELL *exits into the house.* ROSE *comes out into the yard.*]

ROSE: Cory, we gonna be ready to go in a few minutes.

[GABRIEL *enters waving his trumpet. He is dressed in a crumpled suit, shirt and tie, and a battered hat.*]

GABRIEL: Hey, Rose! I'm here, Rose. Hey, Rose. I'm here!
ROSE: Gabe? Lord . . . look here Lyons!

[LYONS *enters from the house, followed by* RAYNELL.]

GABRIEL: Hey, Rose. It's time. It's time to tell St. Peter to open the gates. Troy, you ready? You ready, Troy? I'm gonna tell St. Peter to open the gates. You get ready now. [*With great fanfare, he braces himself to blow. The trumpet is without a mouthpiece. He puts the end of it into his mouth and blows with great force, like a man who has been waiting some twenty-odd years for this single moment. No sound comes out of the trumpet. He braces himself and blows again with the same result. A third time he blows. There is a weight of impossible description that falls away and leaves him bare and exposed to a frightful realization. It is a trauma that a sane and normal mind would be unable to withstand. He begins to dance. A slow, strange dance, eerie and life-giving. A dance of atavistic signature and ritual. He begins to howl in what is an attempt at song, or perhaps a song turning back into itself in an attempt at speech. He finishes his dance and the gates of heaven stand open as wide as God's closet.*] That's the way that go!

1986

QUESTIONS

Blood Relations

1. What does the stage direction mean in asserting, at the beginning, that ". . . with the exception of THE ACTRESS and MISS LIZZIE (and EMMA in the final scene, all characters are imaginary . . ."?

2. Explain the relationship between the time frames of 1892 and 1902. In what ways does the play show its consciousness of having been written almost 90 years after the deaths took place? What effects in the play depend on the reader's (or audience's) distance from the historical events?

3. Given the uncertainties of time and identity in *Blood Relations*, it is not always easy to know exactly what the "facts" are. How do you get your bearings in the play? How do you *know* what really happened? What authority do you trust here?

Fences

1. How many meanings does the title take on in the course of the play? If you were staging the play, what strategies of staging and lighting would you use

to highlight the visual suggestions of the title? How finished or permanent would you make the fence seem? What other aspects of setting help to set up the major themes of the play?

2. Which characters in the play seem to you the most sympathetic? What devices of characterization make their distinctive individualities clear? What strategies are used to make them sympathetic? How sympathetic is Troy?

3. Examine carefully the play's attitudes toward the male characters as a group and toward the female characters. Does the play take a stand on gendered behaviors? Does more blame seem to be placed on one gender or the other?

4. in what specific ways do the values and habits of the white world impinge on the characters? What attitude does the play take toward white behavior and white institutions?

WRITING SUGGESTIONS

Blood Relations

1. With the help of a reference librarian, discover as many facts as you can about the actual episode involving Lizzie Borden, her trial, and daily life in the town in which Lizzie lived. Which events in the play are based on accepted historical "facts"? What things in the play seem invented purposely to distort or contradict "historical facts"? For what purpose?

2. How does the play reveal the character of Lizzie Borden—her values, desires, motivations? Write an essay on the characterization of Lizzie in *Blood Relations* in which you show what is revealed when and make clear what aspects of her life and character are left ambiguous.

Fences

1. Like the other plays of August Wilson, *Fences* seems to be very much about conflicts and continuities between generations. Write a four- or five-page essay on the theme of generations in *Fences*, showing the various manifestations of generational influence that the play fetures. How powerful, according to the play, is tradition from generation to generation? How powerful is generational rebellion?

2. In the reference department of your college library, look up Satchell Paige, and find out as much as you can about his career in the Negro League before he moved to "organized baseball." How long did he pitch in the majors? How old was he on his last appearance in the majors? Look up the roster for

the world-champion Milwaukee Braves in 1957, and check the record of black plays on that team. What additional ironies does Troy's attitude bear in the light of that particular baseball year?

3. According to this play, how do people free themselves from the power of the past? Write a three- or four-page interpretive essay in which you show how the play resolves the question of the tyranny of the past.

4. According to the play, who is responsible for the kinds of difficulties faced by Troy and his family? Write an interpretive essay in which you show how the play investigates themes of responsibility and causality.

Evaluating Drama

How can you tell if a play is good? Why are some plays said to be "great"? On what grounds are plays like *Hamlet* or *Oedipus the King* agreed to be so important that they are performed, season after season, in place after place, for hundreds or thousands of years? Why do actors try to build reputations on playing classic parts—like Ophelia or Hamlet, Hedda Gabler or Willy Loman—rather than staking their careers on new plays or less famous roles? Who decides that a particular play is that important? Why do people continue to buy and read some plays over and over while others die on the shelf or never get printed at all? Is there a qualitative difference between "great" and "good," or between "good" and "satisfactory," or are such distinctions subjective, arbitrary, or accidental? What criteria are useful in trying to assess the literary or dramatic quality of a play? What other kinds of values—political, cultural, social, moral, or ideological—are relevant in judging plays?

These questions are important ones, but the answers are not always easy. Even intelligent, knowledgeable, and well-meaning people do not always agree about matter of pleasure, importance, or quality. Besides, judgments vary from age to age and culture to culture, and plays judged highly in one time and place do not necessarily hold their reputation later and elsewhere. Some plays are better when read and some better when performed. Some are effective in some ways, ineffective in others. It is not easy to develop a logical, consistent, and useful set of criteria that will automatically sort plays into the great, the good, the indifferent, and the bad, and it is not clear that such a system would be a good idea even if it were workable. Systems that try to be "timeless" quickly discover that times do change and that both cultural and historical considerations do influence "objective" judgments in ways that cannot always be understood, let alone predicted.

Still, quality is not an irrelevant consideration, and if judgments are sometimes difficult and frustrating, they are also inevitable. We all judge all the time, and the question is whether we try to judge on some reasonable basis that we can communicate to others or whether we settle for gut feelings and first impressions. Evaluating is not, of course, something that only critics or experts do. We all do it all the time, often from the moment a curtain goes up or we read the opening words of a text. Timing can, in fact, be a major issue, for sometimes we are tempted to evaluate too fast, before we have appropriate grounds for deciding. We may be confident in our likes and dislikes and feel that we are entitled to make a judgment right away, but haste can be a problem if we go on inadequate or inaccurate information. We might, for example, decide from the moment that Willy Loman makes his first speech in *Death of a Salesman* that we just don't like him. We might decide quickly that he is too pathetic, self-pitying, whiny, inconsistent, and confused for our taste. And that could turn out to be a good judgment. But some crucial questions need to be confronted before a final judgment is made. Is his first appearance misleading, and will we like him better later if we stay tuned? Are his unattractive qualities part of the point? Are his weaknesses a crucial part of the plot, a way of suggesting complexity of character, or developing the play's structural conflicts, or setting up its themes? Seeing the implications of the way we respond to Willy, and relating them to the total play, add up to an evaluation, but the initial feelings might not, in themselves, represent the total evaluation.

Still, most evaluation does begin with feelings, and first impressions are not to be ignored. At the very least, our feelings and impressions—even when they are not fully thought through or rationalized—are guides to responses. And, finally, our own feelings are all—or nearly all—we have, at least to begin with. But feelings and impressions may be modified by clear thinking about various issues, and feelings can sometimes be educated to become more sensitive. Besides, whether it is feelings or thoughts that lead us to like or admire (or despise or distrust) a particular work, sorting out the reasons is a useful part of learning to read effectively and resonantly.

Before we cast our first impressions in cement we need to finish reading the play and think back on its parts—character, structure, theme—to see how they relate, to see the play as a whole. Discovering a play's wholeness—its fundamental direction and thrust—is not of course an easy matter. In fact, it is impossible to do all at once. But you have been learning, in this course, how to think carefully about wholeness by looking systematically at parts, and in fact you can readily apply the kinds of issues brought up chapter by chapter in this book to get at some sense of the whole as chapter 3 attempts to do. Ask yourself about the play's themes; the way it conceives character and how it defines, reveals, and values individual characters; the kinds of conflicts that are developed and resolved; the responses the play achieves. How well are the parts or elements put together? Your considered evaluation—the one you are willing to stand behind, at least for the moment—involves first of all close reading and a careful analysis of the relationship of parts to the whole.

Let's go back to the issue of first impressions and the character of Willy Loman in *Death of a Salesman*. Willy is plainly the central figure in the play. The title suggests that it is his death—and the kind of life that leads to it—that the play is about. Willy's inability to cope with his problems, from the very first moment of the play when he returns home from a disastrous sales trip, is the focus of almost all the action. We learn quickly that his mental and emotional health is in jeopardy, that he is failing as a salesman, that he likes to think that he is successful and very well liked but that he is increasingly aware that his notions of himself do not match well with reality. His image of himself as a father and husband is similarly fraught with contradiction: his "boys"—now grown men—have no jobs, no directions for their lives, no prospects of success, and no clear values. What they really believe in is pleasure to be achieved without personal effort or developed skills, and their disappointment promises to become as disastrous as Willy's. And Willy's marriage, haunted by trivial on-the-road episodes that sound like dramatizations of conventional jokes about traveling salesmen, is characterized by pain and disillusionment too. Willy, for all his bluff and hot air, is a disappointment to himself in all parts of his life, and the text leads us to be judgmental about a number of aspects of Willy's behavior—his bad fathering, his self-delusion, his philandering, his nostalgia for the past which repeatedly keeps him from facing problems in the present. It is his character which seems central to the play's focus and effect—do we despise him or pity him for his flaws?—and the themes of dream and disillusion play themselves out in relation to his career and his life.

Structurally, the play reveals Willy's character through a combination of present incident and flashbacks to the past. We actually "see" much of Willy's failure, and "watch" the various dramatic ironies that underscore the loss of the dream—for example, the flashback to the woman in Hartford to whom Willy gives nylon stockings (rare and expensive in the years just after World War II), framed by two scenes in which Linda is mending old hosiery. And the repeated juxtaposition of scenes involving Willy's dreams and ambitions with those involving his compromises and failures dramatizes over and over both his fallings short and the reasons behind them.

The theme of responsibility or blame seems closely related to questions of character that the play highlights from the first scene onward, so that, in one sense, the play seems to be, like *Hedda Gabler*, primarily an examination of character. But the play also articulates some larger questions of responsibility, asking whether Willy is fully responsible for himself and implying (also as in

Hedda Gabler) that societal values may have in part made Willy who he is. "Nobody dast blame this man," Linda insists after his death. Is she just being sentimental at such a moment? Is she unwilling to accept Willy's flaws for what they are? Is she as a character unable to understand the implications of individual behavior, or is her understanding superior to that of others (including us as readers) who find Willy culpable for his own misery? Are people like Uncle Ben—more consistent, more focussed in their goals, more ruthless—to be preferred to the impressionable and trusting Willy who seems to believe what he has been told about how life works, about dreams of success, about the values that are appreciated in American society? What are we ultimately to make of unquestioned conventional values and the way society tells us that ordinary people should live? How does what we believe about individual responsibility and social forces influence our judgment of the play? How do the questions raised by the play influence our beliefs?

Questions about how to read Linda's eulogy come close to the center of the play's meaning, and we will return in a moment to the implications of such questions for an evaluation of the total play. But first let's review the issues of evaluation growing out of the analysis of character that we have been discussing. We might expect a character to be consistent, but Willy is not. (There are several striking passages early on that you might cite as evidence—when, for example, Willy accuses Biff of being "a lazy bum" and only two lines later says, "There's one thing about Biff—he's not lazy"; or when, a little later in act 1, he calls Chevrolet "the greatest car ever built" and a few moments later rails against "that goddam Chevrolet, they ought to prohibit the manufacture of the car!") Yet Willy is convincing, for, if we think about it, most people we know are *not* consistent. In that respect, Willy is more realistic than mere consistency would make him. In the case of Willy, then, if we do not leap too immediately to a first impression, we evaluate not the consistency of character, but the consistency of characterization—how fully and how well does the play portray Willy's inconsistency? And we might wish to ask quite a variety of questions about Willy's characterization. How clear is the presentation of inconsistency? How well does what Willy says establish his character? Are they things someone like him might really say and not just words put in his mouth to illustrate a point? What other facets of Willy's character are related to his inconsistency, and are they all fully integrated into some total portrait of a person who then seems both whole (a fully portrayed or "three-dimensional" character) and representative (someone we recognize as like actual human beings we have seen or know about?) Does the sequence of events in the presentation of character make sense? Do the scenes illustrate the character and persuade us that Willy is actually like that? Do they succeed in developing a certain attitude—hatred, sympathy, contempt—toward him? Do we care about his existence and have an interest in his fate? Are we clearer, for reading the play, about what makes human beings act in the way they do?

Evaluative questions almost tumble over one another once you begin to raise them in a particular category. You could ask similar questions about other characters in the play—about consistency and effectiveness, about meaning, about relationship to other characters, to the play's total effect and theme—and you could ask related questions about structure and the way the play works out, and presents, the plot and stage action in order to render theme and idea into feeling and effect. How carefully is Willy's character differentiated from that of other characters? And you could raise questions of functionality about minor characters and small incidents: What does Uncle Ben do for the play? How does the character of Bernard work to clarify other characters and further the play's theme? Why is the woman from Boston introduced into the play?

Careful evaluation always takes us back to the text to look for evidence and to an examination of our own values and beliefs. It is important to accumulate that evidence to answer individual questions you might raise and to examine the evidence thoughtfully. One important reason for such care is that it helps us mediate between rational considerations and emotional ones. Both are important, for plays are neither logical syllogisms nor structures of pure feeling, and we respond to them not as robots or pure bundles of passion, but as human beings who both feel and think. Let us return to Linda's eulogy for Willy to see if we can sort out what the issues are in how we read—and evaluate—her statement of non-blame.

Death of a Salesman has now held the stage for more than forty years, and both audiences and readers have come to regard it as a "classic" American play. Hundreds of thousands of people seem to have been moved by it, moved enough to pay money to see or read it and to tell others to do so as well. What do they see in it? We cannot know the answer for every single viewer or reader. We can, however, get some idea of the issues that repeatedly are said to be at stake by listening to what issues they argue about. One that has surfaced most frequently has to do with Linda's evaluation of Willy. Do we agree with her? Should we? Does Arthur Miller agree? Does the text of the play offer a clear answer, or is the indeterminacy of the text crucial to the play's continued popularity and success?

Again, the issue of evaluation comes down to questions of consistency and inconsistency, though this time of a different kind. Is the statement that Willy cannot be blamed for his fate consistent with the play's portrayal of him and its presentation of questions of cause and effect? We have looked enough at the characterization here to say with certainty that Willy is presented as having made important mistakes: he has not always been a good role model for his sons, he has been an unfaithful husband, he deludes himself about his likability and his ambition, he vacillates in what he thinks about important issues, he sometimes seems to hold strong traditional values (about the wrongness of stealing, for example) and sometimes he seems to wink at violations of these values. But how fully is he responsible? How much of his attitude derives from a shared sense of how life works, of what is rewarded in an economy of salesmanship and being well liked, of what American culture is about? To discuss the issue intelligently, we have to consider not only the question of why Linda lets Willy off the hook but whether the whole play does. Is the play about personal responsibility or about societal influence? How well and how clearly does the play makes its point? Does the play divide the responsibility between individual and society? How effective is it in making us face questions of value and questions of responsibility? Answering such questions takes us back once again deep into the language of the play and forces us to examine not only what Willy says but how he says it, how often he seems to be echoing some master language of the culture. And relevant too are the languages of other characters in the play—Linda, Biff, Hap, Bernard, Uncle Ben, Howard. Do they all speak the language of value? Are they all subject to some larger system of determined values to which they can only respond with some limited individuality? How does the question of individuality and characterization relate to Linda's assertion about blame and to the larger cause-effect themes of the play?

Evaluation may be closely related to interpretation: if you believe the play says that society is to blame but you yourself believe this is a dodge of personal responsibility, of morality, you may not like the play. If you agree about what the play says and agree *with* what it says you may like the play. There is even another possibility. You may believe in either society's or the individual's responsibility but recognize that there are those who believe otherwise, that the issue is complex, that the best presentation of the issue is such that it can be read either way.

Even though evaluation may ultimately depend on highly subjective judgments and good readers may reasonably differ from each other, questions of evaluation are very close to analytical questions, and determining meaning and effect takes you very quickly to questions of value. And vice versa. Often asking questions about how good a play is will get you closer to questions of what it is about and of what you value than you may at first be aware. Questions of value are not, finally, of a different order from other questions that help us read more carefully and enjoyably, and evaluation is not only an understandable outcome of reading texts but an integral part of the process of reading itself.

Samuel Johnson, the most respected arbiter of taste in England in the late eighteenth century, said that "nothing can please many and please long but just representations of general nature." Johnson was trying to explain why Shakespeare had continued to charm readers and playgoers for a century and a half, and what he says is both a common-sense argument about actual responses to texts (based on consensus and durability) and a proposition about what literature has to say about reality. Good literature, says Johnson, accurately reflects patterns that exist across culture and time; to last, literature must have something important ("just") to say about what does not change from time to time or place to place ("general nature"). Plays last, says Johnson, when they accurately portray what human nature is like, the way things are, the universals that transcend the interests of individuals and local times and places.

Not everyone in Johnson's own time agreed that such a universal standard could be found, and in the enlarged and varied world of cultural relativity of the late twentieth century, fewer still believe that any universals exist. Still, his point is an interesting one even for relativists. We still want to believe that literature can teach us something, that it has a vision of reality from which we can learn, and even if we do not expect universal plots and characters that assure us that life and times are ever the same, we continue to expect representations of reality that we can recognize as related to our own. The accuracy of that representation (its "just"-ness, in Johnson's terms) is likely to remain important; we want our playwrights to know the world and be able to represent it faithfully, and we are apt to want the representation to seem enough like our own world for it to seem in some sense applicable. We are interested in people in other times and other cultures primarily because their experiences, even in other circumstances, have some potential analogy to us. We want a playwright's sense of reality—of what the world is like, and how people will behave—to be similar enough to our own that our own world will seem clearer after reading about the one represented in the play.

A play like *A Midsummer Night's Dream* may not at first seem to be of a kind that can be evaluated according to Johnson's test, for the characters, the plot, and the language of the play all are fairly strange by "normal," "realistic" standards. Johnson himself, in fact, wrote some fairly critical things about the play, objecting especially to the way Shakespeare combines the fairy mythology of one historical period with the court world of an entirely different age, though he did finally approve—and enjoy—the "wild, Fantastical . . ." Certainly, there is plenty in the play to like—the hijinks of Puck, the romantic plot at court with its solvable complications, the lunkish physical comedy of the mechanic players, the verbal wit in line after line, the memorable (and by now famous and familiar) lines about the "course of true love" that plainly state the play's theme, the careful and lively presentation of a wide variety of characters, the ingenious plotting, the engaging resolution of human conflicts. It is easy to find good, solid textual evidence that would enable us to analyze, and praise, the conception and presentation of characters, the effective and appropriate uses of language to delineate characters and further plot and theme, and the careful interlocking of the several plots and the three entirely different sets of characters. But what about the question of whether the play represents some recognizable reality that we can relate to in a sympathetic way? What are we to think of a world that presents royal lovers alongside simple laborers trying to mount a theatrical production and that then mixes in a magical group of fairies? Is this a mix from which we are likely to garner useful knowledge about what life is like?

Whether a text accurately represents human life, behavior, and conversation as we know it is often very important to readers. We want to think about the probable, if not necessarily the real, and often we want to feel that we are learning about the way the world works, what people are like, what kinds of stories other people are involved in. We do not necessarily expect to find ourselves in other people's stories, but we expact to find recognizable people. They do not have to be "universal" in the way that Johnson seems to imly—we have to believe that all times, places, and people are pretty much alike to regard literature as representational—but they need to represent people we can understand in predicaments we can sympathize with.

But how can we "understand" or "sympathize with" a group of characters like this one: a duke and a queen impatient to marry each other, a set of clumsy would-be actors who are really a carpenter, a weaver, a bellows-mender, a tinker, a joiner, and a tailor, and then another group characters of another order altogether—fairies, no less, with their king and queen? If the first set of characters is a little hard to relate to because of their high position, the next group (at least as Shakespeare presents them) seems difficult because too low. Even in our most awkward and most unself-possessed moments we are not likely to "identify" with figures like these. And watching fairies at work and play around their court does not seem a very promising way to find human "representation."

In this play, however, representation comes to mean something else: the play openly operates as fantasy, and the three different worlds that seem impossible to conceive on the same stage all ultimately become so tangled up with each other—and in such creative and entertaining ways—that we have the illusion of complicated conflicts and relationships being worked out across whole orders of being. To ask whether we have ever seen anyone in the real world who resembles Puck would be to ask, for this play, the wrong question. A key to seeing what is going on in this play is flexibility in applying standards and terms—even so basic a term and standard as representation. Ultimately, many readers feel that they *are* represented by the characters in A *Midsummer Night's Dream*, not because they resemble some one character in the play but because the play gives us insights into human aspiration and the pleasures and perils of romantic love in a social class or order of beings. Not all discovery in literature is solemn and high-minded; some is odd and unpredictable and full of belly laughs.

Questions about evaluation are ultimately questions about what values we share and with whom. Some readers will find it easier to appreciate—and like—a world like that of A *Midsummer Night's Dream* than will others. Sometimes, values shared throughout a whole culture or an entire age determine how a text will be received and evaluated; sometimes the sharing involves smaller, more local or more select groups—people of a particular political persuasion, or of a certain social class, or of a certain age or ethnic group, or those with common religious or philosophical beliefs. To some extent your values are determined by your community, but if you are strong enough you can choose your group by choosing your values, in your readings as in your social and political life.

Evaluations of some features of plays—of whether language is used precisely or effectively, for example, or whether characters are presented consistently and winningly—may sometimes seem almost value-free. Can't we decide such issues without regard to our social, economic, religious, or political biases and presuppositions? The answer seems to be that what we bring to a text, and where we bring it from, is likely to influence our judgment at every point. But the fact that our judgments are both highly subjective—subject to our individual biases and preferences—and influenced by the ideologies and cultural identities we participate in does not mean that evaluation is predetermined and beyond discussion or change. The more we read, the more conscious we are of how literary meaning and effect are conditioned by the text, the more aware we are of what we believe and why, of what we bring to a text. We are therefore more open to other influences. The better we can articulate our values and adduce evidence from the text, the more we will be able to learn, to grow, and to teach. For we may have to bring our values into discussion in class and papers to try to convince—and be convinced.

Agreeing about the quality of a play is not ultimately the point. You may never convince someone else that a particular play is as good (or bad) as you think it to be. And you may never be convinced by the arguments of someone else. But having discussions of quality has virtues of its own. The grounds of judgment are ultimately more important than the judgment of any single play, and argument helps clarify the grounds of judgment. Knowing your own grounds of judgment may make a play more enjoyable and meaningful to you; certainly it will make you more aware of who you are as a reader and as a person, and allow you to grow.

ARTHUR MILLER

Death of a Salesman

CERTAIN PRIVATE CONVERSATIONS IN

TWO ACTS AND A REQUIEM

CHARACTERS

WILLY LOMAN	UNCLE BEN
LINDA	HOWARD WAGNER
BIFF	JENNY
HAPPY	STANLEY
BERNARD	MISS FORSYTHE
THE WOMAN	LETTA
CHARLEY	

The action takes place in WILLY LOMAN*'s house and yard and in various places he visits in the New York and Boston of today.*

ACT I

A melody is heard, playing upon a flute. It is small and fine, telling of grass and trees and the horizon. The curtain rises.

Before us is the Salesman's house. We are aware of towering, angular shapes behind it, surrounding it on all sides. Only the blue light of the sky falls upon the house and forestage; the surrounding area shows an angry flow of orange. As more light appears, we see a solid vault of apartment houses around the small, fragile-seeming home. An air of the dream clings to the place, a dream rising out of reality. The kitchen at center seems actual enough, for there is a kitchen table with three chairs, and a refrigerator. But no other fixtures are seen. At the back of the kitchen there is a draped entrance, which leads to the living-room. To the right of the kitchen, on a level raised two feet, is a bedroom furnished only with a brass bedstead and a straight chair. On a shelf over the bed a silver athletic trophy stands. A window opens onto the apartment house at the side.

Behind the kitchen, on a level raised six and a half feet, is the boys' bedroom, at present barely visible. Two beds are dimly seen, and at the back of the room a dormer window. (This bedroom is above the unseen living-room.) At the left a stairway curves up to it from the kitchen.

The entire setting is wholly or, in some places, partially transparent. The roof-line of the house is one-dimensional; under and over it we see the apartment buildings. Before the house lies an apron, curving beyond the forestage into the orchestra. This forward area serves as the back yard as well as the locale of all WILLY'S *imaginings and of his city scenes. Whenever the action is in the present the actors observe the imaginary wall-lines, entering the house only through its door at the left. But in the scenes of the past these boundaries are broken, and characters enter or leave a room by stepping "through" a wall onto the forestage.*

From the right, WILLY LOMAN, *the Salesman, enters, carrying two large sample cases. The flute plays on. He hears but is not aware of it. He is past sixty years of age, dressed quietly. Even as he crosses the stage to the doorway of the house, his exhaustion is apparent. He unlocks the door, comes into the kitchen, and thankfully lets his burden down, feeling the soreness of his palms. A word-sigh escapes his lips—it might be "Oh, boy, oh, boy." He closes the door, then carries his cases out into the living-room, through the draped kitchen doorway.*

LINDA, *his wife, has stirred in her bed at the right. She gets out and puts on a robe, listening. Most often jovial, she has developed an iron repression of her exceptions to* WILLY'S *behavior—she more than loves him, she admires him, as though his mercurial nature, his temper, his massive dreams and little cruelties, served her only as sharp reminders of the turbulent longings within him, longings which she shares but lacks the temperament to utter and follow to their end.*

LINDA: [*Hearing* WILLY *outside the bedroom, calls with some trepidation.*] Willy!

WILLY: It's all right. I came back.

LINDA: Why? What happened? [*Slight pause.*] Did something happen, Willy?

WILLY: No, nothing happened.

LINDA: You didn't smash the car, did you?

WILLY: [*With casual irritation.*] I said nothing happened. Didn't you hear me?

LINDA: Don't you feel well?

WILLY: I'm tired to the death. [*The flute has faded away. He sits on the bed beside her, a little numb.*] I couldn't make it. I just couldn't make it, Linda.

LINDA: [*Very carefully, delicately.*] Where were you all day? You look terrible.

WILLY: I got as far as a little above Yonkers. I stopped for a cup of coffee. Maybe it was the coffee.

LINDA: What?

WILLY: [*After a pause.*] I suddenly couldn't drive any more. The car kept going off onto the shoulder, y'know?

LINDA: [*Helpfully.*] Oh. Maybe it was the steering again. I don't think Angelo knows the Studebaker.

WILLY: No, it's me, it's me. Suddenly I realize I'm goin' sixty miles an hour and I don't remember the last five minutes. I'm—I can't seem to—keep my mind to it.

LINDA: Maybe it's your glasses. You never went for your new glasses.

WILLY: No, I see everything. I came back ten miles an hour. It took me nearly four hours from Yonkers.

LINDA: [*Resigned.*] Well, you'll just have to take a rest, Willy, you can't continue this way.

WILLY: I just got back from Florida.

LINDA: But you didn't rest your mind. Your mind is overactive, and the mind is what counts, dear.

WILLY: I'll start out in the morning. Maybe I'll feel better in the morning. [*She is taking off his shoes.*] These goddam arch supports are killing me.

LINDA: Take an aspirin. Should I get you an aspirin? It'll soothe you.

WILLY: [*With wonder.*] I was driving along, you understand? And I was fine. I was even observing the scenery. You can imagine, me looking at scenery, on the road every week of my life. But it's so beautiful up there, Linda, the trees are so thick, and the sun is warm. I opened the windshield and just let the warm air bathe over me. And then all of a sudden I'm goin' off the road! I'm tellin' ya, I absolutely forgot I was driving. If I'd've gone the other way over the white line I might've killed somebody. So I went on again—and five minutes later I'm dreamin' again, and I nearly—[*He presses two fingers against his eyes.*] I have such thoughts, I have such strange thoughts.

LINDA: Willy, dear. Talk to them again. There's no reason why you can't work in New York.

WILLY: They don't need me in New York. I'm the New England man. I'm vital in New England.

LINDA: But you're sixty years old. They can't expect you to keep traveling every week.

WILLY: I'll have to send a wire to Portland. I'm supposed to see Brown and Morrison tomorrow morning at ten o'clock to show the line. Goddammit, I could sell them! [*He starts putting on his jacket.*]

LINDA: [*Taking the jacket from him.*] Why don't you go down to the place tomorrow and tell Howard you've simply got to work in New York? You're too accommodating, dear.

WILLY: If old man Wagner was alive I'd a been in charge of New York now! That man was a prince, he was a masterful man. But that boy of his, that Howard, he don't appreciate. When I went north the first time, the Wagner Company didn't know where New England was!

LINDA: Why don't you tell those things to Howard, dear?

WILLY: [*Encouraged.*] I will, I definitely will. Is there any cheese?

LINDA: I'll make you a sandwich.

WILLY: No, go to sleep. I'll take some milk. I'll be up right away. The boys in?

LINDA: They're sleeping. Happy took Biff on a date tonight.

WILLY: [*Interested.*] That so?

LINDA: It was so nice to see them shaving together, one behind the other, in the bathroom. And going out together. You notice? The whole house smells of shaving lotion.

WILLY: Figure it out. Work a lifetime to pay off a house. You finally own it, and there's nobody to live in it.

LINDA: Well, dear, life is a casting off. It's always that way.

WILLY: No, no, some people—some people accomplish something. Did Biff say anything after I went this morning?

LINDA: You shouldn't have criticized him, Willy, especially after he just got off the train. You mustn't lose your temper with him.

WILLY: When the hell did I lose my temper? I simply asked him if he was making any money. Is that a criticism?

LINDA: But, dear, how could he make any money?

WILLY: [*Worried and angered.*] There's such an undercurrent in him. He became a moody man. Did he apologize when I left this morning?

LINDA: He was crestfallen, Willy. You know how he admires you. I think if he finds himself, then you'll both be happier and not fight any more.

WILLY: How can he find himself on a farm? Is that a life? A farmhand? In the beginning, when he was young, I thought, well, a young man, it's good for him to tramp around, take a lot of different jobs. But it's more than ten years now and he has yet to make thirty-five dollars a week?

LINDA: He's finding himself, Willy.

WILLY: Not finding yourself at the age of thirty-four is a disgrace!

LINDA: Shh!

WILLY: The trouble is he's lazy, goddammit!

LINDA: Willy, please!

WILLY: Biff is a lazy bum!

LINDA: They're sleeping. Get something to eat. Go on down.

WILLY: Why did he come home? I would like to know what brought him home.

LINDA: I don't know. I think he's still lost, Willy. I think he's very lost.

WILLY: Biff Loman is lost. In the greatest country in the world a young man with such—personal attractiveness, gets lost. And such a hard worker. There's one thing about Biff—he's not lazy.

LINDA: Never.

WILLY: [*With pity and resolve.*] I'll see him in the morning; I'll have a nice talk with him. I'll get him a job selling. He could be big in no time. My God! Remember how they used to follow him around in high school? When he smiled at one of them their faces lit up. When he walked down the street . . . [*He loses himself in reminiscences.*]

LINDA: [*Trying to bring him out of it.*] Willy, dear, I got a new kind of American-type cheese today. It's whipped.

WILLY: Why do you get American when I like Swiss?

LINDA: I just thought you'd like a change—

WILLY: I don't want a change! I want Swiss cheese. Why am I always being contradicted?

LINDA: [*With a covering laugh.*] I thought it would be a surprise.

WILLY: Why don't you open a window in here, for God's sake?

LINDA: [*With infinite patience.*] They're all open, dear.

WILLY: The way they boxed us in here. Bricks and windows, windows and bricks.

LINDA: We should've bought the land next door.

WILLY: The street is lined with cars. There's not a breath of fresh air in the neighborhood. The grass don't grow any more, you can't raise a carrot in the back yard. They should've had a law against apartment houses. Remember those two beautiful elm trees out there? When I and Biff hung the swing between them?

LINDA: Yeah, like being a million miles from the city.

WILLY: They should've arrested the builder for cutting those down. They massacred the neighborhood. [*Lost.*] More and more I think of those days, Linda. This time of year it was lilac and wisteria. And then the peonies would come out, and the daffodils. What fragrance in this room!

LINDA: Well, after all, people had to move somewhere.

WILLY: No, there's more people now.

LINDA: I don't think there's more people. I think—

WILLY: There's more people! That's what ruining this country! Population is getting out of control. The competition is maddening! Smell the stink from that apartment house! And another one on the other side . . . How can they whip cheese?

[*On* WILLY*'s last line,* BIFF *and* HAPPY *raise themselves up in their beds, listening.*]

LINDA: Go down, try it. And be quiet.

WILLY: [*Turning to* LINDA*, guiltily.*] You're not worried about me, are you, sweetheart?

BIFF: What's the matter?

HAPPY: Listen!

LINDA: You've got too much on the ball to worry about.

WILLY: You're my foundation and my support, Linda.

LINDA: Just try to relax, dear. You make mountains out of mole-hills.

WILLY: I won't fight with him any more. If he wants to go back to Texas, let him go.

LINDA: He'll find his way.

WILLY: Sure. Certain men just don't get started till later in life. Like Thomas Edison, I think. Or B. F. Goodrich. One of them was deaf. [*He starts for the bedroom doorway.*] I'll put my money on Biff.

LINDA: And Willy—if it's warm Sunday we'll drive in the country. And we'll open the windshield, and take lunch.

WILLY: No, the windshields don't open on the new cars.

LINDA: But you opened it today.

WILLY: Me? I didn't. [*He stops.*] Now isn't that peculiar! Isn't that a remarkable— [*He breaks off in amazement and fright as the flute is heard distantly.*]

LINDA: What, darling?

WILLY: That is the most remarkable thing.

LINDA: What, dear?

WILLY: I was thinking of the Chevvy. [*Slight pause.*] Nineteen twenty-eight . . .

when I had that red Chevvy— [*Breaks off.*] That funny? I couda sworn I was driving that Chevvy today.

LINDA: Well, that's nothing. Something must've reminded you.

WILLY: Remarkable. *Ts.* Remember those days? The way Biff used to simonize that car? The dealer refused to believe there was eighty thousand miles on it. [*He shakes his head.*] Heh! [*To* LINDA.] Close your eyes, I'll be right up. [*He walks out of the bedroom.*]

HAPPY: [*To* BIFF.] Jesus, maybe he smashed up the car again!

LINDA: [*Calling after* WILLY.] Be careful on the stairs, dear! The cheese is on the middle shelf! [*She turns, goes over to the bed, takes his jacket, and goes out of the bedroom.*]

[*Light has risen on the boys' room. Unseen,* WILLY *is heard talking to himself, "Eighty thousand miles," and a little laugh.* BIFF *gets out of bed, comes downstage a bit, and stands attentively.* BIFF *is two years older than his brother* HAPPY, *well built, but in these days bears a worn air and seems less self-assured. He has succeeded less, and his dreams are stronger and less acceptable than* HAPPY'S. HAPPY *is tall, powerfully made. Sexuality is like a visible color on him, or a scent that many women have discovered. He, like his brother, is lost, but in a different way, for he has never allowed himself to turn his face toward defeat and is thus more confused and hard-skinned, although seemingly more content.*]

HAPPY: [*Getting out of bed.*] He's going to get his license taken away if he keeps that up. I'm getting nervous about him, y'know, Biff?

BIFF: His eyes are going.

HAPPY: No, I've driven with him. He sees all right. He just doesn't keep his mind on it. I drove into the city with him last week. He stops at a green light and then it turns red and he goes. [*He laughs.*]

BIFF: Maybe he's color-blind.

HAPPY: Pop? Why he's got the finest eye for color in the business. You know that.

BIFF: [*Sitting down on his bed.*] I'm going to sleep.

HAPPY: You're not still sour on Dad, are you Biff?

BIFF: He's all right, I guess.

WILLY: [*Underneath them, in the living-room.*] Yes, sir, eighty thousand miles—eighty-two thousand!

BIFF: You smoking?

HAPPY: [*Holding out a pack of cigarettes.*] Want one?

BIFF: [*Taking a cigarette.*] I can never sleep when I smell it.

WILLY: What a simonizing job, heh!

HAPPY: [*With deep sentiment.*] Funny, Biff, y'know? Us sleeping in here again? The old beds. [*He pats his bed affectionately.*] All the talk that went across those two beds, huh? Our whole lives.

BIFF: Yeah. Lotta dreams and plans.

HAPPY: [*With a deep and masculine laugh.*] About five hundred women would like to know what was said in this room.

[*They share a soft laugh.*]

BIFF: Remember that big Betsy something—what the hell was her name—over on Bushwick Avenue?

HAPPY: [*Combing his hair.*] With the collie dog!

BIFF: That's the one. I got you in there, remember?

HAPPY: Yeah, that was my first time—I think. Boy, there was a pig! [*They laugh, almost crudely.*] You taught me everything I know about women. Don't forget that.

BIFF: I bet you forgot how bashful you used to be. Especially with girls.

HAPPY: Oh, I still am, Biff.

BIFF: Oh, go on.

HAPPY: I just control it, that's all. I think I got less bashful and you got more so. What happened, Biff? Where's the old humor, the old confidence? [*He shakes* BIFF*'s knee.* BIFF *gets up and moves restlessly about the room.*] What's the matter?

BIFF: Why does Dad mock me all the time?

HAPPY: He's not mocking you, he—

BIFF: Everything I say there's a twist of mockery on his face. I can't get near him.

HAPPY: He just wants you to make good, that's all. I wanted to talk to you about Dad for a long time, Biff. Something's—happening to him. He—talks to himself.

BIFF: I noticed that this morning. But he always mumbled.

HAPPY: But not so noticeable. It got so embarrassing I sent him to Florida. And you know something? Most of the time he's talking to you.

BIFF: What's he say about me?

HAPPY: I can't make it out.

BIFF: What's he say about me?

HAPPY: I think the fact that you're not settled, that you're still kind of up in the air. . . .

BIFF: There's one or two things depressing him, Happy.

HAPPY: What do you mean?

BIFF: Never mind. Just don't lay it all to me.

HAPPY: But I think if you just got started—I mean—is there any future for you out there?

BIFF: I tell ya, Hap, I don't know what the future is. I don't know—what I'm supposed to want.

HAPPY: What do you mean?

BIFF: Well, I spent six or seven years after high school trying to work myself up. Shipping clerk, salesman, business of one kind or another. And it's a measly manner of existence. To get on that subway on the hot mornings in summer. To devote your whole life to keeping stock, or making phone calls, or selling or buying. To suffer fifty weeks of the year for the sake of a two-week vacation, when all you really desire is to be outdoors, with your shirt off. And always to have to get ahead of the next fella. And still—that's how you build a future.

HAPPY: Well, you really enjoy it on a farm? Are you content out there?

BIFF: [*With rising agitation.*] Hap, I've had twenty or thirty different kinds of jobs since I left home before the war, and it always turns out the same. I just realized it lately. In Nebraska when I herded cattle, and the Dakotas, and Arizona, and now in Texas. It's why I came home now, I guess, because I realized it. This farm I work on, it's spring there now, see? And they've got about fifteen new colts. There's nothing more inspiring or—beautiful than the sight of a mare and a new colt. And it's cool there now, see? Texas is cool now, and it's spring. And whenever spring comes to where I am, I suddenly get the feeling, my God, I'm not gettin' anywhere! What the hell am I doing, playing around with horses, twenty-eight dollars a week! I'm thirty-four years old. I oughta be makin' my future. That's when I come running home. And now, I get there, and I don't know what to do with myself. [*After a pause.*] I've always made a point of not wasting my life, and everytime I come back here I know that all I've done is to waste my life.

HAPPY: You're a poet, you know that, Biff? You're a—you're an idealist!

BIFF: No, I'm mixed up very bad. Maybe I oughta get married. Maybe I oughta get stuck into something. Maybe that's my trouble. I'm like a boy. I'm not married. I'm not in business, I just—I'm like a boy. Are you content, Hap? You're a success, aren't you? Are you content?

HAPPY: Hell, no!

BIFF: Why? You're making money, aren't you?

HAPPY: [*Moving about with energy, expressiveness.*] All I can do now is wait for the merchandise manager to die. And suppose I get to be merchandise manager? He's a good friend of mine, and he just built a terrific estate on Long Island. And he lived there about two months and sold it, and now he's building another one. He can't enjoy it once it's finished. And I know that's just what I would do. I don't know what the hell I'm workin' for. Sometimes I sit in my apartment—all alone. And I think of the rent I'm paying. And it's crazy. But then, it's what I always wanted. My own apartment, a car, and plenty of women. And still, goddammit, I'm lonely.

BIFF: [*With enthusiasm.*] Listen, why don't you come out West with me?

HAPPY: You and I, heh?

BIFF: Sure, maybe we could buy a ranch. Raise cattle, use our muscles. Men built like we are should be working out in the open.

HAPPY: [*Avidly.*] The Loman Brothers, heh?

BIFF: [*With vast affection.*] Sure, we'd be known all over the counties!

HAPPY: [*Enthralled.*] That's what I dream about, Biff. Sometimes I want to just rip my clothes off in the middle of the store and outbox that goddam merchandise manager. I mean I can outbox, outrun, and outlift anybody in that store, and I have to take orders from those common, petty sons-of-bitches till I can't stand it any more.

BIFF: I'm tellin' you, kid, if you were with me I'd be happy out there.

HAPPY: [*Enthused.*] See, Biff, everybody around me is so false that I'm constantly lowering my ideals . . .

BIFF: Baby, together we'd stand up for one another, we'd have someone to trust.

HAPPY: If I were around you—

BIFF: Hap, the trouble is we weren't brought up to grub for money. I don't know how to do it.

HAPPY: Neither can I!

BIFF: Then let's go!

HAPPY: The only thing is—what can you make out there?

BIFF: But look at your friend. Builds an estate and then hasn't the peace of mind to live in it.

HAPPY: Yeah, but when he walks into the store the waves part in front of him. That's fifty-two thousand dollars a year coming through the revolving door, and I got more in my pinky finger than he's got in his head.

BIFF: Yeah, but you just said—

HAPPY: I gotta show some of those pompous, self-important executives over there that Hap Loman can make the grade. I want to walk into the store the way he walks in. Then I'll go with you, Biff. We'll be together yet, I swear. But take those two we had tonight. Now weren't they gorgeous creatures?

BIFF: Yeah, yeah, most gorgeous I've had in years.

HAPPY: I get that any time I want, Biff. Whenever I feel disgusted. The only trouble is, it gets like bowling or something. I just keep knockin' them over and it doesn't mean anything. You still run around a lot?

BIFF: Naa. I'd like to find a girl—steady, somebody with substance.

HAPPY: That's what I long for.

BIFF: Go on! You'd never come home.

HAPPY: I would! Somebody with character, with resistance! Like Mom, y'know? You're gonna call me a bastard when I tell you this. That girl Charlotte I was with tonight is engaged to be married in five weeks. [*He tries on his new hat.*]

BIFF: No kiddin'!

HAPPY: Sure, the guy's in line for the vice-presidency of the store. I don't know what gets into me, maybe I just have an overdeveloped sense of competition or something, but I went and ruined her, and furthermore I can't get rid of her. And he's the third executive I've done that to. Isn't that a crummy characteristic? And to top it all, I go to their weddings! [*Indignantly, but laughing.*] Like I'm not supposed to take bribes. Manufacturers offer me a hundred-dollar bill now and then to throw an order their way. You know how honest I am, but it's like this girl, see. I hate myself for it. Because I don't want the girl, and, still, I take it and—I love it!

BIFF: Let's go to sleep.

HAPPY: I guess we didn't settle anything, heh?

BIFF: I just got one idea that I'm going to try.

HAPPY: What's that?

BIFF: Remember Bill Oliver?

HAPPY: Sure, Oliver is very big now. You want to work for him again?

BIFF: No, but when I quit he said something to me. He put his arm on my shoulder, and he said, "Biff, if you ever need anything, come to me."

HAPPY: I remember that. That sounds good.

BIFF: I think I'll go to see him. If I could get ten thousand or even seven or eight thousand dollars I could buy a beautiful ranch.

HAPPY: I bet he'd back you. 'Cause he thought highly of you, Biff. I mean, they all do. You're well liked, Biff. That's why I say to come back here, and we both have the apartment. And I'm tellin' you, Biff, any babe you want . . .

BIFF: No, with a ranch I could do the work I like and still be something. I just wonder though. I wonder if Oliver still thinks I stole that carton of basketballs.

HAPPY: Oh, he probably forgot that long ago. It's almost ten years. You're too sensitive. Anyway, he didn't really fire you.

BIFF: Well, I think he was going to. I think that's why I quit. I was never sure whether he knew or not. I know he thought the world of me, though. I was the only one he'd let lock up the place.

WILLY: [*Below.*] You gonna wash the engine, Biff?

HAPPY: Shh! [BIFF *looks at* HAPPY, *who is gazing down, listening.* WILLY *is mumbling in the parlor.*] You hear that?

[*They listen.* WILLY *laughs warmly.*]

BIFF: [*Growing angry.*] Doesn't he know Mom can hear that?

WILLY: Don't get your sweater dirty, Biff!

[*A look of pain crosses* BIFF*'s face.*]

HAPPY: Isn't that terrible? Don't leave again, will you? You'll find a job here. You gotta stick around. I don't know what to do about him, it's getting embarrassing.

WILLY: What a simonizing job!

BIFF: Mom's hearing that!

WILLY: No kiddin', Biff, you got a date? Wonderful!

HAPPY: Go on to sleep. But talk to him in the morning, will you?

BIFF: [*Reluctantly getting into bed.*] With her in the house. Brother!

HAPPY: [*Getting into bed.*] I wish you'd have a good talk with him.

[*The light on their room begins to fade.*]

BIFF: [*To himself in bed.*] That selfish, stupid . . .

HAPPY: Sh . . . Sleep, Biff.

[*Their light is out. Well before they have finished speaking,* WILLY*'s form is dimly seen below in the darkened kitchen. He opens the refrigerator, searches in there, and takes out a bottle of milk. The apartment houses are fading out, and the entire house and surroundings become covered with leaves. Music insinuates itself as the leaves appear.*]

WILLY: Just wanna be careful with those girls, Biff, that's all. Don't make any promises. No promises of any kind. Because a girl, y'know, they always believe what you tell 'em, and you're very young, Biff, you're too young to be talking serously to girls.

[*Light rises on the kitchen.* WILLY, *talking, shuts the refrigerator door and comes downstage to the kitchen table. He pours milk into a glass. He is totally immersed in himself, smiling faintly.*]

WILLY: Too young entirely, Biff. You want to watch your schooling first. Then when you're all set, there'll be plenty of girls for a boy like you. [*He smiles broadly at a kitchen chair.*] That so? The girls pay for you? [*He laughs.*] Boy, you must really be makin' a hit.

[WILLY *is gradually addressing—physically—a point offstage, speaking through the wall of the kitchen, and his voice has been rising in volume to that of a normal conversation.*]

WILLY: I been wondering why you polish the car so careful. Ha! Don't leave the hubcaps, boys. Get the chamois to the hubcaps. Happy, use newspaper on the windows, it's the easiest thing. Show him how to do it, Biff! You see, Happy? Pad it up, use it like a pad. That's it, that's it, good work. You're doin' all right, Hap. [*He pauses, then nods in approbation for a few seconds, then looks upward.*] Biff, first thing we gotta do when we get time is clip that big branch over the house. Afraid it's gonna fall in a storm and hit the roof. Tell you what. We get a rope and sling her around, and then we climb up there with a couple of saws and take her down. Soon as you finish the car, boys, I wanna see ya. I got a surprise for you, boys.

BIFF: [*Offstage.*] Whatta ya got, Dad?

WILLY: No, you finish first. Never leave a job till you're finished—remember that. [*Looking toward the "big trees."*] Biff, up in Albany I saw a beautiful hammock. I think I'll buy it next trip, and we'll hang it right between those two elms. Wouldn't that be something? Just swingin' there under those branches. Boy, that would be . . .

[YOUNG BIFF *and* YOUNG HAPPY *appear from the direction* WILLY *was addressing.* HAPPY *carries rags and a pail of water.* BIFF, *wearing a sweater with a block "S," carries a football.*]

BIFF: [*Pointing in the direction of the car offstage.*] How's that, Pop, professional?

WILLY: Terrific. Terrific job, boys. Good work, Biff.

HAPPY: Where's the surprise, Pop?

WILLY: In the back seat of the car.

HAPPY: Boy! [*He runs off.*]

BIFF: What is it, Dad? Tell me, what'd you buy?

WILLY: [*Laughing, cuffs him.*] Never mind, something I want you to have.

BIFF: [*Turns and starts off.*] What is it, Hap?

HAPPY: [*Offstage.*] It's a punching bag!

BIFF: Oh, Pop!

WILLY: It's got Gene Tunney's[1] signature on it!

1. Tunney (1897–1978) was world heavyweight boxing champion from 1926 to 1928 and retired undefeated.

[HAPPY *runs onstage with a punching bag.*]

BIFF: Gee, how'd you know we wanted a punching bag?

WILLY: Well, it's the finest thing for the timing.

HAPPY: [*Lies down on his back and pedals with his feet.*] I'm losing weight, you notice, Pop?

WILLY: [*To* HAPPY.] Jumping rope is good too.

BIFF: Did you see the new football I got?

WILLY: [*Examining the ball.*] Where'd you get a new ball?

BIFF: The coach told me to practice my passing.

WILLY: That so? And he gave you the ball, heh?

BIFF: Well, I borrowed it from the locker room. [*He laughs confidentially.*]

WILLY: [*Laughing with him at the theft.*] I want you to return that.

HAPPY: I told you he wouldn't like it!

BIFF: [*Angrily.*] Well, I'm bringing it back!

WILLY: [*Stopping the incipient argument, to* HAPPY.] Sure, he's gotta practice with a regulation ball, doesn't he? [*To* BIFF.] Coach'll probably congratulate you on your initiative!

BIFF: Oh, he keeps congratulating my initiative all the time, Pop.

WILLY: That's because he likes you. If somebody else took that ball there'd be an uproar. So what's the report, boys, what's the report?

BIFF: Where'd you go this time, Dad? Gee we were lonesome for you.

WILLY: [*Pleased, puts an arm around each boy and they come down to the apron.*] Lonesome, heh?

BIFF: Missed you every minute.

WILLY: Don't say? Tell you a secret, boys. Don't breathe it to a soul. Someday I'll have my own business, and I'll never have to leave home any more.

HAPPY: Like Uncle Charley, heh?

WILLY: Bigger than Uncle Charley! Because Charley is not—liked. He's liked, but he's not—well liked.

BIFF: Where'd you go this time, Dad?

WILLY: Well, I got on the road, and I went north to Providence. Met the Mayor.

BIFF: The Mayor of Providence!

WILLY: He was sitting in the hotel lobby.

BIFF: What'd he say?

WILLY: He said, "Morning!" And I said, "You got a fine city here, Mayor." And then he had coffee with me. And then I went to Waterbury. Waterbury is a fine city. Big clock city, the famous Waterbury clock. Sold a nice bill there. And then Boston—Boston is the cradle of the Revolution. A fine city. And a couple of other towns in Mass., and on to Portland and Bangor and straight home!

BIFF: Gee, I'd love to go with you sometime, Dad.

WILLY: Soon as summer comes.

HAPPY: Promise?

WILLY: You and Hap and I, and I'll show you all the towns. America is full of beautiful towns and fine, upstanding people. And they know me, boys, they know me up and down New England. The finest people. And when I bring you fellas up, there'll be open sesame for all of us, 'cause one thing, boys: I have friends. I can park my car in any street in New England, and the cops protect it like their own. This summer, heh?

BIFF and HAPPY: [*Together.*] Yeah! You bet!

WILLY: We'll take our bathing suits.

HAPPY: We'll carry your bags, Pop!

WILLY: Oh, won't that be something! Me comin' into the Boston stores with you boys carryin' my bags. What a sensation! [BIFF *is prancing around, practicing passing the ball.*] You nervous, Biff, about the game?

BIFF: Not if you're gonna be there.

WILLY: What do they say about you in school, now that they made you captain?

HAPPY: There's a crowd of girls behind him everytime the classes change.

BIFF: [*Taking* WILLY*'s hand.*] This Saturday, Pop, this Saturday—just for you, I'm going to break through for a touchdown.

HAPPY: You're supposed to pass.

BIFF: I'm takin' one play for Pop. You watch me, Pop, and when I take off my helmet, that means I'm breakin' out. Then you watch me crash through that line!

WILLY: [*Kisses* BIFF.] Oh, wait'll I tell this in Boston!

[BERNARD *enters in knickers. He is younger than* BIFF, *earnest and loyal, a worried boy.*]

BERNARD: Biff, where are you? You're supposed to study with me today.

WILLY: Hey, looka Bernard. What're you lookin' so anemic about, Bernard?

BERNARD: He's gotta study, Uncle Willy. He's got Regents[2] next week.

HAPPY: [*Tauntingly, spinning* BERNARD *around.*] Let's box, Bernard!

BERNARD: Biff! [*He gets away from* HAPPY.] Listen, Biff, I heard Mr. Birnbaum say that if you don't start studyin' math he's gonna flunk you, and you won't graduate. I heard him!

WILLY: You better study with him, Biff. Go ahead now.

BERNARD: I heard him!

BIFF: Oh, Pop, you didn't see my sneakers! [*He holds up a foot for* WILLY *to look at.*]

WILLY: Hey, that's a beautiful job of printing!

BERNARD: [*Wiping his glasses.*] Just because he printed University of Virginia on his sneakers doesn't mean they've got to graduate him, Uncle Willy!

WILLY: [*Angrily.*] What're you talking about? With scholarships to three universities they're gonna flunk him?

BERNARD: But I heard Mr. Birnbaum say—

WILLY: Don't be a pest, Bernard! [*To his boys.*] What an anemic!

BERNARD: Okay, I'm waiting for you in my house, Biff.

[BERNARD *goes off. The Lomans laugh.*]

2. A statewide examination administered to New York high school students.

WILLY: Bernard is not well liked, is he?
BIFF: He's liked, but he's not well liked.
HAPPY: That's right, Pop.
WILLY: That's just what I mean. Bernard can get the best marks in school, y'understand, but when he gets out in the business world, y'understand, you are going to be five times ahead of him. That's why I thank Almighty God you're both built like Adonises. Because the man who makes an appearance in the business world, the man who creates personal interest, is the man who gets ahead. Be liked and you will never want. You take me, for instance. I never have to wait in line to see a buyer. "Willy Loman is here!" That's all they have to know, and I go right through.
BIFF: Did you knock them dead, Pop?
WILLY: Knocked 'em cold in Providence, slaughtered 'em in Boston.
HAPPY: [*On his back, pedaling again.*] I'm losing weight, you notice, Pop?

[LINDA *enters, as of old, a ribbon in her hair, carrying a basket of washing.*]

LINDA: [*With youthful energy.*] Hello, dear!
WILLY: Sweetheart!
LINDA: How'd the Chevvy run?
WILLY: Chevrolet, Linda, is the greatest car ever built. [*To the boys.*] Since when do you let your mother carry wash up the stairs?
BIFF: Grab hold there, boy!
HAPPY: Where to, Mom?
LINDA: Hang them up on the line. And you better go down to your friends, Biff. The cellar is full of boys. They don't know what to do with themselves.
BIFF: Ah, when Pop comes home they can wait!
WILLY: [*Laughs appreciatively.*] You better go down and tell them what to do, Biff.
BIFF: I think I'll have them sweep out the furnace room.
WILLY: Good work, Biff.
BIFF: [*Goes through wall-line of kitchen to doorway at back and calls down.*] Fellas! Everybody sweep out the furnace room! I'll be right down!
VOICES: All right! Okay, Biff.
BIFF: George and Sam and Frank, come out back! We're hangin' up the wash! Come on, Hap, on the double!

[*He and* HAPPY *carry out the basket.*]

LINDA: The way they obey him!
WILLY: Well, that training, the training. I'm tellin' you, I was sellin' thousands and thousands, but I had to come home.
LINDA: Oh, the whole block'll be at that game. Did you sell anything?
WILLY: I did five hundred gross in Providence and seven hundred gross in Boston.
LINDA: No! Wait a minute, I've got a pencil. [*She pulls pencil and paper out of her apron pocket.*] That makes your commission . . . Two hundred—my God! Two hundred and twelve dollars!
WILLY: Well, I didn't figure it yet, but . . .

LINDA: How much did you do?

WILLY: Well, I—I did—about a hundred and eighty gross in Providence. Well, no—it came to—roughly two hundred gross on the whole trip.

LINDA: [*Without hesitation.*] Two hundred gross. That's . . . [*She figures.*]

WILLY: The trouble was that three of the stores were half closed for inventory in Boston. Otherwise I woulda broke records.

LINDA: Well, it makes seventy dollars and some pennies. That's very good.

WILLY: What do we owe?

LINDA: Well, on the first there's sixteen dollars on the refrigerator—

WILLY: Why sixteen?

LINDA: Well, the fan belt broke, so it was a dollar eighty.

WILLY: But it's brand new.

LINDA: Well, the man said that's the way it is. Till they work themselves in, y'know.

[*They move through the wall-line into the kitchen.*]

WILLY: I hope we didn't get stuck on that machine.

LINDA: They got the biggest ads of any of them!

WILLY: I know, it's a fine machine. What else?

LINDA: Well, there's nine-sixty for the washing machine. And for the vacuum cleaner there's three and a half due on the fifteenth. Then the roof, you got twenty-one dollars remaining.

WILLY: It don't leak, does it?

LINDA: No, they did a wonderful job. Then you owe Frank for the carburetor.

WILLY: I'm not going to pay that man! That goddam Chevrolet, they ought to prohibit the manufacture of that car!

LINDA: Well, you owe him three and a half. And odds and ends, comes to around a hundred and twenty dollars by the fifteenth.

WILLY: A hundred and twenty dollars! My God, if business don't pick up I don't know what I'm gonna do!

LINDA: Well, next week you'll do better.

WILLY: Oh, I'll knock 'em dead next week. I'll go to Hartford. I'm very well liked in Hartford. You know, the trouble is, Linda, people don't seem to take to me.

[*They move onto the forestage.*]

LINDA: Oh, don't be foolish.

WILLY: I know it when I walk in. They seem to laugh at me.

LINDA: Why? Why would they laugh at you? Don't talk that way, Willy.

[WILLY *moves to the edge of the stage.* LINDA *goes into the kitchen and starts to darn stockings.*]

WILLY: I don't know the reason for it, but they just pass me by. I'm not noticed.

LINDA: But you're doing wonderful, dear. You're making seventy to a hundred dollars a week.

WILLY: But I gotta be at it ten, twelve hours a day. Other men—I don't know—

they do it easier. I don't know why—I can't stop myself—I talk too much. A man oughta come in with a few words. One thing about Charley. He's a man of few words, and they respect him.

LINDA: You don't talk too much, you're just lively.

WILLY: [*Smiling.*] Well, I figure, what the hell, life is short, a couple of jokes. [*To himself.*] I joke too much! [*The smile goes.*]

LINDA: Why? You're—

WILLY: I'm fat. I'm very—foolish to look at, Linda. I didn't tell you, but Christmas time I happened to be calling on F. H. Stewarts, and a salesman I know, as I was going in to see the buyer I heard him say something about—walrus. And I—I cracked him right across the face. I won't take that. I simply will not take that. But they do laugh at me. I know that.

LINDA: Darling . . .

WILLY: I gotta overcome it. I know I gotta overcome it. I'm not dressing to advantage, maybe.

LINDA: Willy, darling, you're the handsomest man in the world—

WILLY: Oh, no, Linda.

LINDA: To me you are. [*Slight pause.*] The handsomest. [*From the darkness is heard the laughter of a woman.* WILLY *doesn't turn to it, but it continues through* LINDA*'s lines.*] And the boys, Willy. Few men are idolized by their children the way you are.

[*Music is heard as behind a scrim, to the left of the house,* THE WOMAN, *dimly seen, is dressing.*]

WILLY: [*With great feeling.*] You're the best there is, Linda, you're a pal, you know that? On the road—on the road I want to grab you sometimes and just kiss the life outa you. [*The laughter is loud now, and he moves into a brightening area at the left, where* THE WOMAN *has come from behind the scrim and is standing, putting on her hat, looking into a "mirror" and laughing.*] 'Cause I get so lonely—especially when business is bad and there's nobody to talk to. I get the feeling that I'll never sell anything again, that I won't make a living for you, or a business, a business for the boys. [*He talks through* THE WOMAN*'s subsiding laughter!* THE WOMAN *primps at the "mirror."*] There's so much I want to make for—

THE WOMAN: Me? You didn't make me, Willy. I picked you.

WILLY: [*Pleased.*] You picked me?

THE WOMAN: [*Who is quite proper-looking, Willy's age.*] I did. I've been sitting at that desk watching all the salesmen go by, day in, day out. But you've got such a sense of humor, and we do have such a good time together, don't we?

WILLY: Sure, sure. [*He takes her in his arms.*] Why do you have to go now?

THE WOMAN: It's two o'clock . . .

WILLY: No, come on in! [*He pulls her.*]

THE WOMAN: . . . my sisters'll be scandalized. When'll you be back?

WILLY: Oh, two weeks about. Will you come up again?

THE WOMAN: Sure thing. You do make me laugh. It's good for me. [*She squeezes his arm, kisses him.*] And I think you're a wonderful man.

WILLY: You picked me, heh?

THE WOMAN: Sure. Because you're so sweet. And such a kidder.

WILLY: Well, I'll see you next time I'm in Boston.

THE WOMAN: I'll put you right through to the buyers.

WILLY: [*Slapping her bottom.*] Right. Well, bottoms up!

THE WOMAN: [*Slaps him gently and laughs.*] You just kill me, Willy. [*He suddenly grabs her and kisses her roughly.*] You kill me. And thanks for the stockings. I love a lot of stockings. Well, good night.

WILLY: Good night. And keep your pores open!

THE WOMAN: Oh, Willy!

[THE WOMAN *bursts out laughing, and* LINDA*'s laughter blends in.* THE WOMAN *disappears into the dark. Now the area at the kitchen table brightens.* LINDA *is sitting where she was at the kitchen table, but now is mending a pair of her silk stockings.*]

LINDA: You are, Willy. The handsomest man. You've got no reason to feel that—

WILLY: [*Coming out of* THE WOMAN*'s dimming area and going over to* LINDA.] I'll make it all up to you, Linda. I'll—

LINDA: There's nothing to make up, dear. You're doing fine, better than—

WILLY: [*Noticing her mending.*] What's that?

LINDA: Just mending my stockings. They're so expensive—

WILLY: [*Angrily, taking them from her.*] I won't have you mending stockings in this house! Now throw them out!

[LINDA *puts the stockings in her pocket.*]

BERNARD: [*Entering on the run.*] Where is he? If he doesn't study!

WILLY: [*Moving to the forestage, with great agitation.*] You'll give him the answers!

BERNARD: I do, but I can't on a Regents! That's a state exam! They're liable to arrest me!

WILLY: Where is he? I'll whip him, I'll whip him!

LINDA: And he'd better give back that football, Willy, it's not nice.

WILLY: Biff! Where is he? Why is he taking everything?

LINDA: He's too rough with the girls, Willy. All the mothers are afraid of him!

WILLY: I'll whip him!

BERNARD: He's driving the car without a license!

[THE WOMAN*'s laugh is heard.*]

WILLY: Shut up!

LINDA: All the mothers—

WILLY: Shut up!

BERNARD: [*Backing quietly away and out.*] Mr. Birnbaum says he's stuck up.

WILLY: Get outa here!

BERNARD: If he doesn't buckle down he'll flunk math! [*He goes off.*]

LINDA: He's right, Willy, you've gotta—

WILLY: [*Exploding at her.*] There's nothing the matter with him! You want him to be a worm like Bernard? He's got spirit, personality . . . [*As he speaks,*

LINDA, *almost in tears, exits into the living room.* WILLY *is alone in the kitchen, wilting and staring. The leaves are gone. It is night again, and the apartment houses look down from behind.*] Loaded with it. Loaded! What is he stealing? He's giving it back, isn't he? Why is he stealing? What did I tell him? I never in my life told him anything but decent things.

[HAPPY *in pajamas has come down the stairs;* WILLY *suddenly becomes aware of* HAPPY*'s presence.*]

HAPPY: Let's go now, come on.
WILLY: [*Sitting down at the kitchen table.*] Huh! Why did she have to wax the floors herself? Everytime she waxes the floors she keels over. She knows that!
HAPPY: Shh! Take it easy. What brought you back tonight?
WILLY: I got an awful scare. Nearly hit a kid in Yonkers. God! Why didn't I go to Alaska with my brother Ben that time! Ben! That man was a genius, that man was success incarnate! What a mistake! He begged me to go.
HAPPY: Well, there's no use in—
WILLY: You guys! There was a man started with the clothes on his back and ended up with diamond mines!
HAPPY: Boy, someday I'd like to know how he did it.
WILLY: What's the mystery? The man knew what he wanted and went out and got it! Walked into a jungle, and comes out, the age of twenty-one, and he's rich! The world is an oyster, but you don't crack it open on a mattress!
HAPPY: Pop, I told you I'm gonna retire you for life.
WILLY: You'll retire me for life on seventy goddam dollars a week? And your women and your car and your apartment, and you'll retire me for life! Christ's sake, I couldn't get past Yonkers today! Where are you guys, where are you? The woods are burning! I can't drive a car!

[CHARLEY *has appeared in the doorway. He is a large man, slow of speech, laconic, immovable. In all he says, despite what he says, there is pity, and now, trepidation. He has a robe over pajamas, slippers on his feet. He enters the kitchen.*]

CHARLEY: Everything all right?
HAPPY: Yeah, Charley, everything's . . .
WILLY: What's the matter?
CHARLEY: I heard some noise. I thought something happened. Can't we do something about the walls? You sneeze in here, and in my house hats blow off.
HAPPY: Let's go to bed, Dad. Come on.

[CHARLEY *signals to* HAPPY *to go.*]

WILLY: You go ahead, I'm not tired at the moment.
HAPPY: [*To* WILLY.] Take it easy, huh? [*He exits.*]
WILLY: What're you doin' up?
CHARLEY: [*Sitting down at the kitchen table opposite* WILLY.] Couldn't sleep good. I had a heartburn.
WILLY: Well, you don't know how to eat.

CHARLEY: I eat with my mouth.
WILLY: No, you're ignorant. You gotta know about vitamins and things like that.
CHARLEY: Come on, let's shoot. Tire you out a little.
WILLY: [*Hesitantly.*] All right. You got cards?
CHARLEY: [*Taking a deck from his pocket.*] Yeah, I got them. Someplace. What is it with those vitamins?
WILLY: [*Dealing.*] They build up your bones. Chemistry.
CHARLEY: Yeah, but there's no bones in a heartburn.
WILLY: What are you talkin' about? Do you know the first thing about it?
CHARLEY: Don't get insulted.
WILLY: Don't talk about something you don't know anything about.

[*They are playing. Pause.*]

CHARLEY: What're you doin' home?
WILLY: A little trouble with the car.
CHARLEY: Oh. [*Pause.*] I'd like to take a trip to California.
WILLY: Don't say.
CHARLEY: You want a job?
WILLY: I got a job, I told you that. [*After a slight pause.*] What the hell are you offering me a job for?
CHARLEY: Don't get insulted.
WILLY: Don't insult me.
CHARLEY: I don't see no sense in it. You don't have to go on this way.
WILLY: I got a good job. [*Slight pause.*] What do you keep comin' in here for?
CHARLEY: You want me to go?
WILLY: [*After a pause, withering.*] I can't understand it. He's going back to Texas again. What the hell is that?
CHARLEY: Let him go.
WILLY: I got nothin' to give him, Charley, I'm clean, I'm clean.
CHARLEY: He won't starve. None a them starve. Forget about him.
WILLY: Then what have I got to remember?
CHARLEY: You take it too hard. To hell with it. When a deposit bottle is broken you don't get your nickel back.
WILLY: That's easy enough for you to say.
CHARLEY: That ain't easy for me to say.
WILLY: Did you see the ceiling I put up in the living-room?
CHARLEY: Yeah, that's a piece of work. To put up a ceiling is a mystery to me. How do you do it?
WILLY: What's the difference?
CHARLEY: Well, talk about it.
WILLY: You gonna put up a ceiling?
CHARLEY: How could I put up a ceiling?
WILLY: Then what the hell are you bothering me for?
CHARLEY: You're insulted again.
WILLY: A man who can't handle tools is not a man. You're disgusting.
CHARLEY: Don't call me disgusting, Willy.

[UNCLE BEN, *carrying a valise and an umbrella, enters the forestage from around the right corner of the house. He is a stolid man, in his sixties, with a mustache and an authoritative air. He is utterly certain of his destiny, and there is an aura of far places about him. He enters exactly as* WILLY *speaks.*]

WILLY: I'm getting awfully tired, Ben.

[BEN*'s music is heard.* BEN *looks around at everything.*]

CHARLEY: Good, keep playing; you'll sleep better. Did you call me Ben?

[BEN *looks at his watch.*]

WILLY: That's funny. For a second there you reminded me of my brother Ben.

BEN: I only have a few minutes. [*He strolls, inspecting the place.* WILLY *and* CHARLEY *continue playing.*]

CHARLEY: You never heard from him again, heh? Since that time?

WILLY: Didn't Linda tell you? Couple of weeks ago we got a letter from his wife in Africa. He died.

CHARLEY: That so.

BEN: [*Chuckling.*] So this is Brooklyn, eh?

CHARLEY: Maybe you're in for some of his money.

WILLY: Naa, he had seven sons. There's just one opportunity I had with that man . . .

BEN: I must make a train, William. There are several properties I'm looking at in Alaska.

WILLY: Sure, sure! If I'd gone with him to Alaska that time, everything would've been totally different.

CHARLEY: Go on, you'd froze to death up there.

WILLY: What're you talking about?

BEN: Opportunity is tremendous in Alaska, William. Surprised you're not up there.

WILLY: Sure, tremendous.

CHARLEY: Heh?

WILLY: There was the only man I ever met who knew the answers.

CHARLEY: Who?

BEN: How are you all?

WILLY: [*Taking a pot, smiling.*] Fine, fine.

CHARLEY: Pretty sharp tonight.

BEN: Is Mother living with you?

WILLY: No, she died a long time ago.

CHARLEY: Who?

BEN: That's too bad. Fine specimen of a lady, Mother.

WILLY: [*To* CHARLEY.] Heh?

BEN: I'd hoped to see the old girl.

CHARLEY: Who died?

BEN: Heard anything from Father, have you?

WILLY: [*Unnerved.*] What do you mean, who died?

CHARLEY: [*Taking a pot.*] What're you talkin' about?
BEN: [*Looking at his watch.*] William, it's half-past eight!
WILLY: [*As though to dispel his confusion he angrily stops* CHARLEY*'s hand.*] That's my build!
CHARLEY: I put the ace—
WILLY: If you don't know how to play the game I'm not gonna throw my money away on you!
CHARLEY: [*Rising.*] It was my ace, for God's sake!
WILLY: I'm through, I'm through!
BEN: When did Mother die?
WILLY: Long ago. Since the beginning you never knew how to play cards.
CHARLEY: [*Picks up the cards and goes to the door.*] All right! Next time I'll bring a deck with five aces.
WILLY: I don't play that kind of game!
CHARLEY: [*Turning to him.*] You ought to be ashamed of yourself!
WILLY: Yeah?
CHARLEY: Yeah! [*He goes out.*]
WILLY: [*Slamming the door after him.*] Ignoramus!
BEN: [*As* WILLY *comes toward him through the wall-line of the kitchen.*] So you're William.
WILLY: [*Shaking* BEN*'s hand.*] Ben! I've been waiting for you so long! What's the answer? How did you do it?
BEN: Oh, there's a story in that.

[LINDA *enters the forestage, as of old, carrying the wash basket.*]

LINDA: Is this Ben?
BEN: [*Gallantly.*] How do you do, my dear.
LINDA: Where've you been all these years? Willy's always wondered why you—
WILLY: [*Pulling* BEN *away from her impatiently.*] Where is Dad? Didn't you follow him? How did you get started?
BEN: Well, I don't know how much you remember.
WILLY: Well, I was just a baby, of course, only three or four years old—
BEN: Three years and eleven months.
WILLY: What a memory, Ben!
BEN: I have many enterprises, William, and I have never kept books.
WILLY: I remember I was sitting under the wagon in—was it Nebraska?
BEN: It was South Dakota, and I gave you a bunch of wild flowers.
WILLY: I remember you walking away down some open road.
BEN: [*Laughing.*] I was going to find Father in Alaska.
WILLY: Where is he?
BEN: At that age I had a very faulty view of geography, William. I discovered after a few days that I was heading due south, so instead of Alaska, I ended up in Africa.
LINDA: Africa!
WILLY: The Gold Coast!
BEN: Principally diamond mines.

LINDA: Diamond mines!

BEN: Yes, my dear. But I've only a few minutes—

WILLY: No! Boys! Boys! [*Young* BIFF *and* HAPPY *appear.*] Listen to this. This is your Uncle Ben, a great man! Tell my boys, Ben!

BEN: Why, boys, when I was seventeen I walked into the jungle, and when I was twenty-one I walked out. [*He laughs.*] And by God I was rich.

WILLY: [*To the boys.*] You see what I been talking about? The greatest things can happen!

BEN: [*Glancing at his watch.*] I have an appointment in Ketchikan Tuesday week.

WILLY: No, Ben! Please tell about Dad. I want my boys to hear. I want them to know the kind of stock they spring from. All I remember is a man with a big beard, and I was in Mamma's lap, sitting around a fire, and some kind of high music.

BEN: His flute. He played the flute.

WILLY: Sure, the flute, that's right!

[*New music is heard, a high, rollicking tune.*]

BEN: Father was a very great and a very wild-hearted man. We would start in Boston, and he'd toss the whole family into the wagon, and then he'd drive the team right across the country; through Ohio, and Indiana, Michigan, Illinois, and all the Western states. And we'd stop in the towns and sell the flutes that he'd made on the way. Great inventor, Father. With one gadget he made more in a week than a man like you could make in a lifetime.

WILLY: That's just the way I'm bringing them up, Ben—rugged, well liked, all-around.

BEN: Yeah? [*To* BIFF.] Hit that, boy—hard as you can. [*He pounds his stomach.*]

BIFF: Oh, no, sir!

BEN: [*Taking boxing stance.*] Come on, get to me! [*He laughs.*]

WILLY: Go to it, Biff! Go ahead, show him!

BIFF: Okay! [*He cocks his fist and starts in.*]

LINDA: [*To* WILLY.] Why must he fight, dear?

BEN: [*Sparring with* BIFF.] Good boy! Good boy!

WILLY: How's that, Ben, heh?

HAPPY: Give him the left, Biff!

LINDA: Why are you fighting?

BEN: Good boy! [*Suddenly comes in, trips* BIFF, *and stands over him, the point of his umbrella poised over* BIFF*'s eye.*]

LINDA: Look out, Biff!

BIFF: Gee!

BEN: [*Patting* BIFF*'s knee.*] Never fight fair with a stranger, boy. You'll never get out of the jungle that way. [*Taking* LINDA*'s hand and bowing.*] It was an honor and a pleasure to meet you, Linda.

LINDA: [*Withdrawing her hand coldly, frightened.*] Have a nice—trip.

BEN: [*To* WILLY.] And good luck with your—what do you do?

WILLY: Selling.

BEN: Yes. Well . . . [*He raises his hand in farewell to all.*]

WILLY: No, Ben, I don't want you to think . . . [*He takes* BEN*'s arm to show him.*] It's Brooklyn, I know, but we hunt too.

BEN: Really, now.

WILLY: Oh, sure, there's snakes and rabbits and—that's why I moved out here. Why, Biff can fell any one of these trees in no time! Boys! Go right over to where they're building the apartment house and get some sand. We're gonna rebuild the entire front stoop right now! Watch this, Ben!

BIFF: Yes, sir! On the double, Hap!

HAPPY: [*As he and* BIFF *run off.*] I lost weight, Pop, you notice?

[CHARLEY *enters in knickers, even before the boys are gone.*]

CHARLEY: Listen, if they steal any more from that building the watchman'll put the cops on them!

LINDA: [*To* WILLY.] Don't let Biff . . .

[BEN *laughs lustily.*]

WILLY: You shoulda seen the lumber they brought home last week. At least a dozen six-by-tens worth all kinds a money.

CHARLEY: Listen, if that watchman—

WILLY: I gave them hell, understand. But I got a couple of fearless characters there.

CHARLEY: Willy, the jails are full of fearless characters.

BEN: [*Clapping* WILLY *on the back, with a laugh at* CHARLEY.] And the stock exchange, friend!

WILLY: [*Joining in* BEN*'s laughter.*] Where are the rest of your pants?

CHARLEY: My wife bought them.

WILLY: Now all you need is a golf club and you can go upstairs and go to sleep. [*To* BEN.] Great athlete! Between him and his son Bernard they can't hammer a nail!

BERNARD: [*Rushing in.*] The watchman's chasing Biff!

WILLY: [*Angrily.*] Shut up! He's not stealing anything!

LINDA: [*Alarmed, hurrying off left.*] Where is he? Biff, dear! [*She exits.*]

WILLY: [*Moving toward the left, away from* BEN.] There's nothing wrong. What's the matter with you?

BEN: Nervy boy. Good!

WILLY: [*Laughing.*] Oh, nerves of iron, that Biff!

CHARLEY: Don't know what it is. My New England man comes back and he's bleedin', they murdered him up there.

WILLY: It's contacts, Charley, I got important contacts!

CHARLEY: [*Sarcastically.*] Glad to hear it, Willy. Come in later, we'll shoot a little casino. I'll take some of your Portland money. [*He laughs at* WILLY *and exits.*]

WILLY: [*Turning to* BEN.] Business is bad, it's murderous. But not for me, of course.

BEN: I'll stop by on my way back to Africa.

WILLY: [*Longingly.*] Can't you stay a few days? You're just what I need, Ben, because I—I have a fine position here, but I—well, Dad left when I was such a baby and I never had a chance to talk to him and I still feel—kind of temporary about myself.

BEN: I'll be late for my train.

[*They are at opposite ends of the stage.*]

WILLY: Ben, my boys—can't we talk? They'd go into the jaws of hell for me, see, but I—

BEN: William, you're being first-rate with your boys. Outstanding, manly chaps!

WILLY: [*Hanging on to his words.*] Oh, Ben, that's good to hear! Because sometimes I'm afraid that I'm not teaching them the right kind of— Ben, how should I teach them?

BEN: [*Giving great weight to each word, and with a certain vicious audacity.*] William, when I walked into the jungle, I was seventeen. When I walked out I was twenty-one. And, by God, I was rich! [*He goes off into darkness around the right corner of the house.*]

WILLY: . . . was rich! That's just the spirit I want to imbue them with! To walk into a jungle! I was right! I was right! I was right!

[BEN *is gone, but* WILLY *is still speaking to him as* LINDA, *in nightgown and robe, enters the kitchen, glances around for* WILLY, *then goes to the door of the house, looks out and sees him. Comes down to his left. He looks at her.*]

LINDA: Willy, dear? Willy?

WILLY: I was right!

LINDA: Did you have some cheese? [*He can't answer.*] It's very late, darling. Come to bed, heh?

WILLY: [*Looking straight up.*] Gotta break your neck to see a star in this yard.

LINDA: You coming in?

WILLY: Whatever happened to that diamond watch fob? Remember? When Ben came from Africa that time? Didn't he give me a watch fob with a diamond in it?

LINDA: You pawned it, dear. Twelve, thirteen years ago. For Biff's radio correspondence course.

WILLY: Gee, that was a beautiful thing. I'll take a walk.

LINDA: But you're in your slippers.

WILLY: [*Starting to go around the house at the left.*] I was right! I was! [*Half to* LINDA, *as he goes, shaking his head.*] What a man! There was a man worth talking to. I was right!

LINDA: [*Calling after* WILLY.] But in your slippers, Willy!

[WILLY *is almost gone when* BIFF, *in his pajamas, comes down the stairs and enters the kitchen.*]

BIFF: What is he doing out there?

LINDA: Sh!

BIFF: God Almighty, Mom, how long has he been doing this?

LINDA: Don't, he'll hear you.

BIFF: What the hell is the matter with him?
LINDA: It'll pass by morning.
BIFF: Shouldn't we do anything?
LINDA: Oh, my dear, you should do a lot of things, but there's nothing to do, so go to sleep.

[HAPPY *comes down the stair and sits on the steps.*]

HAPPY: I never heard him so loud, Mom.
LINDA: Well, come around more often; you'll hear him. [*She sits down at the table and mends the lining of* WILLY's *jacket.*]
BIFF: Why didn't you ever write me about this, Mom?
LINDA: How would I write to you? For over three months you had no address.
BIFF: I was on the move. But you know I thought of you all the time. You know that, don't you, pal?
LINDA: I know, dear, I know. But he likes to have a letter. Just to know that there's still a possibility for better things.
BIFF: He's not like this all the time, is he?
LINDA: It's when you come home he's always the worst.
BIFF: When I come home?
LINDA: When you write you're coming, he's all smiles, and talks about the future, and—he's just wonderful. And then the closer you seem to come, the more shaky he gets, and then, by the time you get here, he's arguing, and he seems angry at you. I think it's just that maybe he can't bring himself to—to open up to you. Why are you so hateful to each other? Why is that?
BIFF: [*Evasively.*] I'm not hateful, Mom.
LINDA: But you no sooner come in the door than you're fighting!
BIFF: I don't know why. I mean to change. I'm tryin', Mom, you understand?
LINDA: Are you home to stay now?
BIFF: I don't know. I want to look around, see what's doin'.
LINDA: Biff, you can't look around all your life, can you?
BIFF: I just can't take hold, Mom. I can't take hold of some kind of a life.
LINDA: Biff, a man is not a bird, to come and go with the springtime.
BIFF: Your hair . . . [*He touches her hair.*] Your hair got so gray.
LINDA: Oh, it's been gray since you were in high school. I just stopped dyeing it, that's all.
BIFF: Dye it again, will ya? I don't want my pal looking old. [*He smiles.*]
LINDA: You're such a boy! You think you can go away for a year and . . . You've got to get it into your head now that one day you'll knock on this door and there'll be strange people here—
BIFF: What are you talking about? You're not even sixty, Mom.
LINDA: But what about your father?
BIFF: [*Lamely.*] Well, I meant him too.
HAPPY: He admires Pop.
LINDA: Biff, dear, if you don't have any feeling for him, then you can't have any feeling for me.
BIFF: Sure I can, Mom.

LINDA: No. You can't just come to see me, because I love him. [*With a threat, but only a threat, of tears.*] He's the dearest man in the world to me, and I won't have anyone making him feel unwanted and low and blue. You've got to make up your mind now, darling, there's no leeway any more. Either he's your father and you pay him that respect, or else you're not to come here. I know he's not easy to get along with—nobody knows that better than me—but . . .

WILLY: [*From the left, with a laugh.*] Hey, hey, Biffo!

BIFF: [*Starting to go out after* WILLY.] What the hell is the matter with him? [HAPPY *stops him.*]

LINDA: Don't—don't go near him!

BIFF: Stop making excuses for him! He always, always wiped the floor with you. Never had an ounce of respect for you.

HAPPY: He's always had respect for—

BIFF: What the hell do you know about it?

HAPPY: [*Surlily.*] Just don't call him crazy!

BIFF: He's got no character—Charley wouldn't do this. Not in his own house—spewing out that vomit from his mind.

HAPPY: Charley never had to cope with what he's got to.

BIFF: People are worse off than Willy Loman. Believe me, I've seen them!

LINDA: Then make Charley your father, Biff. You can't do that, can you? I don't say he's a great man. Willy Loman never made a lot of money. His name was never in the paper. He's not the finest character that ever lived. But he's a human being, and a terrible thing is happening to him. So attention must be paid. He's not to be allowed to fall into his grave like an old dog. Attention, attention must be finally paid to such a person. You called him crazy—

BIFF: I didn't mean—

LINDA: No, a lot of people think he's lost his—balance. But you don't have to be very smart to know what his trouble is. The man is exhausted.

HAPPY: Sure!

LINDA: A small man can be just as exhausted as a great man. He works for a company thirty-six years this March, opens up unheard-of territories to their trademark, and now in his old age they take his salary away.

HAPPY: [*Indignantly.*] I didn't know that, Mom.

LINDA: You never asked, my dear! Now that you get your spending money someplace else you don't trouble your mind with him.

HAPPY: But I gave you money last—

LINDA: Christmas time, fifty dollars! To fix the hot water it cost ninety-seven fifty! For five weeks he's been on straight commission, like a beginner, an unknown!

BIFF: Those ungrateful bastards!

LINDA: Are they any worse than his sons? When he brought them business, when he was young, they were glad to see him. But now his old friends, the old buyers that loved him so and always found some order to hand him in a pinch—they're all dead, retired. He used to be able to make six, seven calls a day in Boston. Now he takes his valises out of the car and puts them back and takes them out again and he's exhausted. Instead of walking he talks now. He drives seven hundred miles, and when he gets there no one knows him any more, no one welcomes him. And what goes through a man's mind, driving seven hundred miles home without having earned a cent? Why shouldn't he talk to himself? Why? When he has to go to Charley and borrow fifty dollars a week and pretend to me that it's his pay? How long can that go on? How long? You see what I'm sitting here and waiting for? And you tell me he has no character? The man who never worked a day but for your benefit? When does he get the medal for that? Is this his reward—to turn around at the age of sixty-three and find his sons, who he loved better than his life, one a philandering bum—

HAPPY: Mom!

LINDA: That's all you are, my baby! [*To* BIFF.] And you! What happened to the love you had for him? You were such pals! How you used to talk to him on the phone every night! How lonely he was till he could come home to you!

BIFF: All right, Mom. I'll live here in my room, and I'll get a job. I'll keep away from him, that's all.

LINDA: No, Biff. You can't stay here and fight all the time.

BIFF: He threw me out of this house, remember that.

LINDA: Why did he do that? I never knew why.

BIFF: Because I know he's a fake and he doesn't like anybody around who knows!

LINDA: Why a fake? In what way? What do you mean?

BIFF: Just don't lay it all at my feet. It's between me and him—that's all I have to say. I'll chip in from now on. He'll settle for half my pay check. He'll be all right. I'm going to bed. [*He starts for the stairs.*]

LINDA: He won't be all right.

BIFF: [*Turning on the stairs, furiously.*] I hate this city and I'll stay here. Now what do you want?

LINDA: He's dying, Biff.

[HAPPY *turns quickly to her, shocked.*]

BIFF: [*After a pause.*] Why is he dying?

LINDA: He's been trying to kill himself.

BIFF: [*With great horror.*] How?

LINDA: I live from day to day.

BIFF: What're you talking about?

LINDA: Remember I wrote you that he smashed up the car again? In February?

LINDA: The insurance inspector came. He said that they have evidence. That all these accidents in the last year—weren't—weren't—accidents.

HAPPY: How can they tell that? That's a lie.

LINDA: It seems there's a woman . . . [*She takes a breath as.*]

{ BIFF: [*Sharply but contained.*] What woman?
{ LINDA: [*Simultaneously.*] . . . and this woman . . .

LINDA: What?

BIFF: Nothing. Go ahead.

LINDA: What did you say?

BIFF: Nothing. I just said what woman?

HAPPY: What about her?

LINDA: Well, it seems she was walking down the road and saw his car. She says that he wasn't driving fast at all, and that he didn't skid. She says he came to that little bridge, and then deliberately smashed into the railing, and it was only the shallowness of the water that saved him.

BIFF: Oh, no, he probably just fell asleep again.

LINDA: I don't think he fell asleep.

BIFF: Why not?

LINDA: Last month . . . [*With great difficulty.*] Oh, boys, it's so hard to say a thing like this! He's just a big stupid man to you, but I tell you there's more good in him than in many other people. [*She chokes, wipes her eyes.*] I was looking for a fuse. The lights blew out, and I went down the cellar. And behind the fuse box—it happened to fall out—was a length of rubber pipe—just short.

HAPPY: No kidding?

LINDA: There's a little attachment on the end of it. I knew right away. And sure enough, on the bottom of the water heater there's a new little nipple on the gas pipe.

HAPPY: [*Angrily.*] That—jerk.

BIFF: Did you have it taken off?

LINDA: I'm—I'm ashamed to. How can I mention it to him? Every day I go down and take away that little rubber pipe. But, when he comes home, I put it back where it was. How can I insult him that way? I don't know what to do. I live from day to day, boys. I tell you, I know every thought in his mind. It sounds so old-fashioned and silly, but I tell you he put his whole life into you and you've turned your backs on him. [*She is bent over in the chair, weeping, her face in her hands.*] Biff, I swear to God! Biff, his life is in your hands!

HAPPY: [*To* BIFF.] How do you like that damned fool!

BIFF: [*Kissing her.*] All right, pal, all right. It's all settled now. I've been remiss. I know that, Mom. But now I'll stay, and I swear to you, I'll apply myself. [*Kneeling in front of her, in a fever of self-reproach.*] It's just—you see, Mom, I don't fit in business. Not that I won't try. I'll try, and I'll make good.

HAPPY: Sure you will. The trouble with you in business was you never tried to please people.

BIFF: I know, I—

HAPPY: Like when you worked for Harrison's. Bob Harrison said you were tops, and then you go and do some damn fool thing like whistling whole songs in the elevator like a comedian.

BIFF: [*Against* HAPPY.] So what? I like to whistle sometimes.

HAPPY: You don't raise a guy to a responsible job who whistles in the elevator!

LINDA: Well, don't argue about it now.

HAPPY: Like when you'd go off and swim in the middle of the day instead of taking the line around.

BIFF: [*His resentment rising.*] Well, don't you run off? You take off sometimes, don't you? On a nice summer day?

HAPPY: Yeah, but I cover myself!

LINDA: Boys!

HAPPY: If I'm going to take a fade the boss can call any number where I'm supposed to be and they'll swear to him that I just left. I'll tell you something that I hate to say, Biff, but in the business world some of them think you're crazy.

BIFF: [*Angered.*] Screw the business world!

HAPPY: All right, screw it! Great, but cover yourself!

LINDA: Hap, Hap!

BIFF: I don't care what they think! They've laughed at Dad for years, and you know why? Because we don't belong in this nuthouse of a city! We should be mixing cement on some open plain, or—or carpenters. A carpenter is allowed to whistle!

[WILLY *walks in from the entrance of the house, at left.*]

WILLY: Even your grandfather was better than a carpenter. [*Pause. They watch him.*] You never grew up. Bernard does not whistle in the elevator, I assure you.

BIFF: [*As though to laugh* WILLY *out of it.*] Yeah, but you do, Pop.

WILLY: I never in my life whistled in an elevator! And who in the business world thinks I'm crazy?

BIFF: I didn't mean it like that, Pop. Now don't make a whole thing out of it, will ya?

WILLY: Go back to the West! Be a carpenter, a cowboy, enjoy yourself!

LINDA: Willy, he was just saying—

WILLY: I heard what he said!

HAPPY: [*Trying to quiet* WILLY.] Hey, Pop, come on now . . .

WILLY: [*Continuing over* HAPPY'*s line.*] They laugh at me, heh? Go to Filene's, go to the Hub, go to Slattery's Boston. Call out the name Willy Loman and see what happens! Big Shot!

BIFF: All right, Pop.

WILLY: Big!

BIFF: All right!

WILLY: Why do you always insult me?

BIFF: I didn't say a word. [*To* LINDA.] Did I say a word?

LINDA: He didn't say anything, Willy.

WILLY: [*Going to the doorway of the living-room.*] All right, good night, good night.

LINDA: Willy, dear, he just decided . . .

WILLY: [*To* BIFF.] If you get tired hanging around tomorrow, paint the ceiling I put up in the living-room.

BIFF: I'm leaving early tomorrow.

HAPPY: He's going to see Bill Oliver, Pop.

WILLY: [*Interestedly.*] Oliver? For what?

BIFF: [*With reserve, but trying, trying.*] He always said he'd stake me. I'd like to go into business, so maybe I can take him up on it.

LINDA: Isn't that wonderful?

WILLY: Don't interrupt. What's wonderful about it? There's fifty men in the City of New York who'd stake him. [*To* BIFF.] Sporting goods?

BIFF: I guess so. I know something about it and—

WILLY: He knows something about it! You know sporting goods better than Spalding, for God's sake! How much is he giving you?

BIFF: I don't know, I didn't even see him yet, but—

WILLY: Then what're you talkin' about?

BIFF: [*Getting angry.*] Well, all I said was I'm gonna see him, that's all!

WILLY: [*Turning away.*] Ah, you're counting your chickens again.

BIFF: [*Starting left for the stairs.*] Oh, Jesus, I'm going to sleep!

WILLY: [*Calling after him.*] Don't curse in this house!

BIFF: [*Turning.*] Since when did you get so clean?

HAPPY: [*Trying to stop them.*] Wait a . . .

WILLY: Don't use that language to me! I won't have it!

HAPPY: [*Grabbing* BIFF, *shouts.*] Wait a minute! I got an idea. I got a feasible idea. Come here, Biff, let's talk this over now, let's talk some sense here. When I was down in Florida last time, I thought of a great idea to sell sporting goods. It just came back to me. You and I, Biff—we have a line, the Loman Line. We train a couple of weeks, and put on a couple of exhibitions, see?

WILLY: That's an idea!

HAPPY: Wait! We form two basketball teams, see? Two water-polo teams. We play each other. It's a million dollars' worth of publicity. Two brothers, see? The Loman Brothers. Displays in the Royal Palms—all the hotels. And banners over the ring and the basketball court: "Loman Brothers." Baby, we could sell sporting goods!

WILLY: That is a one-million-dollar idea!

LINDA: Marvelous!

BIFF: I'm in great shape as far as that's concerned.

HAPPY: And the beauty of it is, Biff, it wouldn't be like a business. We'd be out playin' ball again . . .

BIFF: [*Enthused.*] Yeah, that's . . .

WILLY: Million-dollar . . .

HAPPY: And you wouldn't get fed up with it, Biff. It'd be the family again. There'd be the old honor, and comradeship, and if you wanted to go off for a swim or somethin'—well, you'd do it! Without some smart cooky gettin' up ahead of you!

WILLY: Lick the world! You guys together could absolutely lick the civilized world.

BIFF: I'll see Oliver tomorrow. Hap, if we could work that out . . .

LINDA: Maybe things are beginning to—

WILLY: [*Wildly enthused, to* LINDA.] Stop interrupting! [*To* BIFF.] But don't wear sport jacket and slacks when you see Oliver.

BIFF: No, I'll—

WILLY: A business suit, and talk as little as possible, and don't crack any jokes.

BIFF: He did like me. Always liked me.

LINDA: He loved you!

WILLY: [*To* LINDA.] Will you stop! [*To* BIFF.] Walk in very serious. You are not applying for a boy's job. Money is to pass. Be quiet, fine, and serious. Everybody likes a kidder, but nobody lends him money.

HAPPY: I'll try to get some myself, Biff. I'm sure I can.

WILLY: I see great things for you kids, I think your troubles are over. But remember, start big and you'll end big. Ask for fifteen. How much you gonna ask for?

BIFF: Gee, I don't know—

WILLY: And don't say "Gee." "Gee" is a boy's word. A man walking in for fifteen thousand dollars does not say "Gee!"

BIFF: Ten, I think, would be top though.

WILLY: Don't be so modest. You always started too low. Walk in with a big laugh. Don't look worried. Start off with a couple of your good stories to lighten things up. It's not what you say, it's how you say it—because personality always wins the day.

LINDA: Oliver always thought the highest of him—

WILLY: Will you let me talk?

BIFF: Don't yell at her, Pop, will ya?

WILLY: [*Angrily*.] I was talking, wasn't I?

BIFF: I don't like you yelling at her all the time, and I'm tellin' you, that's all.

WILLY: What're you, takin' over this house?

LINDA: Willy—

WILLY: [*Turning on her*.] Don't take his side all the time, goddammit!

BIFF: [*Furiously*.] Stop yelling at her!

WILLY: [*Suddenly pulling on his cheek, beaten down, guilt ridden*.] Give my best to Bill Oliver—he may remember me. [*He exits through the living-room doorway*.]

LINDA: [*Her voice subdued*.] What'd you have to start that for? [BIFF *turns away*.] You see how sweet he was as soon as you talked hopefully? [*She goes over to* BIFF.] Come up and say good night to him. Don't let him go to bed that way.

HAPPY: Come on, Biff, let's buck him up.

LINDA: Please, dear. Just say good night. It takes so little to make him happy. Come. [*She goes through the living-room doorway, calling upstairs from within the living-room*.] Your pajamas are hanging in the bathroom, Willy!

HAPPY: [*Looking toward where* LINDA *went out*.] What a woman! They broke the mold when they made her. You know that, Biff?

BIFF: He's off salary. My God, working on commission!

HAPPY: Well, let's face it: he's no hot-shot selling man. Except that sometimes, you have to admit, he's a sweet personality.

BIFF: [*Deciding*.] Lend me ten bucks, will ya? I want to buy some new ties.

HAPPY: I'll take you to a place I know. Beautiful stuff. Wear one of my striped shirts tomorrow.

BIFF: She got gray. Mom got awful old. Gee, I'm gonna go in to Oliver tomorrow and knock him for a—

HAPPY: Come on up. Tell that to Dad. Let's give him a whirl. Come on.

BIFF: [*Steamed up.*] You know, with ten thousand bucks, boy!

HAPPY: [*As they go into the living-room.*] That's the talk, Biff, that's the first time I've heard the old confidence out of you! [*From within the living-room, fading off.*] You're gonna live with me, kid, and any babe you want just say the word . . .

[*The last lines are hardly heard. They are mounting the stairs to their parents' bedroom.*]

LINDA: [*Entering her bedroom and addressing* WILLY *who is in the bathroom. She is straightening the bed for him.*] Can you do anything about the shower? It drips.

WILLY: [*From the bathroom.*] All of a sudden everything falls to pieces! Goddam plumbing, oughta be sued, those people. I hardly finished putting it in and the thing . . . [*His words rumble off.*]

LINDA: I'm just wondering if Oliver will remember him. You think he might?

WILLY: [*Coming out of the bathroom in his pajamas.*] Remember him? What's the matter with you, you crazy? If he'd've stayed with Oliver he'd be on top by now! Wait'll Oliver gets a look at him. You don't know the average caliber any more. The average young man today—[*He is getting into bed.*]—is got a caliber of zero. Greatest thing in the world for him was to bum around. [BIFF *and* HAPPY *enter the bedroom. Slight pause.* WILLY *stops short, looking at* BIFF.] Glad to hear it, boy.

HAPPY: He wanted to say good night to you, sport.

WILLY: [*To* BIFF.] Yeah. Knock him dead, boy. What'd you want to tell me?

BIFF: Just take it easy, Pop. Good night. [*He turns to go.*]

WILLY: [*Unable to resist.*] And if anything falls off the desk while you're talking to him—like a package or something—don't you pick it up. They have office boys for that.

LINDA: I'll make a big breakfast—

WILLY: Will you let me finish? [*To* BIFF.] Tell him you were in the business in the West. Not farm work.

BIFF: All right, Dad.

LINDA: I think everything—

WILLY: [*Going right through her speech.*] And don't undersell yourself. No less than fifteen thousand dollars.

BIFF: [*Unable to bear him.*] Okay. Good night, Mom. [*He starts moving.*]

WILLY: Because you got a greatness in you, Biff, remember that. You got all kinds of greatness . . . [*He lies back, exhausted.* BIFF *walks out.*]

LINDA: [*Calling after* BIFF.] Sleep well, darling!

HAPPY: I'm gonna get married, Mom. I wanted to tell you.

LINDA: Go to sleep, dear.

HAPPY: [*Going.*] I just wanted to tell you.

WILLY: Keep up the good work. [HAPPY *exits.*] God . . . remember that Ebbets Field[3] game? The championship of the city?

3. A Brooklyn sports stadium named after Charles H. Ebbets (1859–1925) and torn down in 1960.

LINDA: Just rest. Should I sing to you?

WILLY: Yeah. Sing to me. [LINDA *hums a soft lullaby.*] When that team came out—he was the tallest, remember?

LINDA: Oh, yes. And in gold.

[BIFF *enters the darkened kitchen, takes a cigarette, and leaves the house. He comes downstage into a golden pool of light. He smokes, staring at the night.*]

WILLY: Like a young god. Hercules—something like that. And the sun, the sun all around him. Remember how he waved to me? Right up from the field, with the representatives of three colleges standing by? And the buyers I brought, and the cheers when he came out—Loman, Loman, Loman! God Almighty, he'll be great yet. A star like that, magnificent, can never really fade away!

[*The light on* WILLY *is fading. The gas heater begins to glow through the kitchen wall, near the stairs, a blue flame beneath red coils.*]

LINDA: [*Timidly.*] Willy dear, what has he got against you?

WILLY: I'm so tired. Don't talk any more.

[BIFF *slowly returns to the kitchen. He stops, stares toward the heater.*]

LINDA: Will you ask Howard to let you work in New York?

WILLY: First thing in the morning. Everything'll be all right.

[BIFF *reaches behind the heater and draws out a length of rubber tubing. He is horrified and turns his head toward* WILLY'*s room, still dimly lit, from which the strains of* LINDA'*s desperate but monotonous humming rise.*]

WILLY: [*Staring through the window into the moonlight.*] Gee, look at the moon moving between the buildings!

[BIFF *wraps the tubing around his hand and quickly goes up the stairs.*]

CURTAIN

ACT II

Music is heard, gay and bright. The curtain rises as the music fades away. WILLY, *in shirt sleeves, is sitting at the kitchen table, sipping coffee, his hat in his lap.* LINDA *is filling his cup when she can.*

WILLY: Wonderful coffee. Meal in itself.

LINDA: Can I make you some eggs?

WILLY: No. Take a breath.

LINDA: You look so rested, dear.

WILLY: I slept like a dead one. First time in months. Imagine, sleeping till ten on a Tuesday morning. Boys left nice and early, heh?

LINDA: They were out of here by eight o'clock.

WILLY: Good work!

LINDA: It was so thrilling to see them leaving together. I can't get over the shaving lotion in this house!

WILLY: [*Smiling.*] Mmm—

LINDA: Biff was very changed this morning. His whole attitude seemed to be hopeful. He couldn't wait to get downtown to see Oliver.

WILLY: He's heading for a change. There's no question, there simply are certain men that take longer to get—solidified. How did he dress?

LINDA: His blue suit. He's so handsome in that suit. He could be a—anything in that suit!

[WILLY *gets up from the table.* LINDA *holds his jacket for him.*]

WILLY: There's no question, no question at all. Gee, on the way home tonight I'd like to buy some seeds.

LINDA: [*Laughing.*] That'd be wonderful. But not enough sun gets back there. Nothing'll grow any more.

WILLY: You wait, kid, before it's all over we're gonna get a little place out in the country, and I'll raise some vegetables, a couple of chickens . . .

LINDA: You'll do it yet, dear.

[WILLY *walks out of his jacket.* LINDA *follows him.*]

WILLY: And they'll get married, and come for a weekend. I'd build a little guest house. 'Cause I got so many fine tools, all I'd need would be a little lumber and some peace of mind.

LINDA: [*Joyfully.*] I sewed the lining . . .

WILLY: I could build two guest houses, so they'd both come. Did he decide how much he's going to ask Oliver for?

LINDA: [*Getting him into the jacket.*] He didn't mention it, but I imagine ten or fifteen thousand. You going to talk to Howard today?

WILLY: Yeah. I'll put it to him straight and simple. He'll just have to take me off the road.

LINDA: And Willy, don't forget to ask for a little advance, because we've got the insurance premium. It's the grace period now.

WILLY: That's a hundred . . . ?

LINDA: A hundred and eight, sixty-eight. Because we're a little short again.

WILLY: Why are we short?

LINDA: Well, you had the motor job on the car . . .

WILLY: That goddam Studebaker!

LINDA: And you got one more payment on the refrigerator . . .

WILLY: But it just broke again!

LINDA: Well, it's old, dear.

WILLY: I told you we should've bought a well-advertised machine. Charley bought a General Electric and it's twenty years old and it's still good, that son-of-a-bitch.

LINDA: But, Willy—

WILLY: Whoever heard of a Hastings refrigerator? Once in my life I would like to own something outright before it's broken! I'm always in a race with the junkyard! I just finished paying for the car and it's on its last legs. The refrigerator consumes belts like a goddam maniac. They time those things. They time them so when you finally paid for them, they're used up.

LINDA: [*Buttoning up his jacket as he unbuttons it.*] All told, about two hundred dollars would carry us, dear. But that includes the last payment on the mortgage. After this payment, Willy, the house belongs to us.

WILLY: It's twenty-five years!

LINDA: Biff was nine years old when we bought it.

WILLY: Well, that's a great thing. To weather a twenty-five year mortgage is—

LINDA: It's an accomplishment.

WILLY: All the cement, the lumber, the reconstruction I put in this house! There ain't a crack to be found in it any more.

LINDA: Well, it served its purpose.

WILLY: What purpose? Some stranger'll come along, move in, and that's that. If only Biff would take this house, and raise a family . . . [*He starts to go.*] Good-by, I'm late.

LINDA: [*Suddenly remembering.*] Oh, I forgot! You're supposed to meet them for dinner.

WILLY: Me?

LINDA: At Frank's Chop House on Forty-eighth near Sixth Avenue.

WILLY: Is that so! How about you?

LINDA: No, just the three of you. They're gonna blow you to a big meal!

WILLY: Don't say! Who thought of that?

LINDA: Biff came to me this morning, Willy, and he said, "Tell Dad, we want to blow him to a big meal." Be there six o'clock. You and your two boys are going to have dinner.

WILLY: Gee whiz! That's really somethin'. I'm gonna knock Howard for a loop, kid. I'll get an advance, and I'll come home with a New York job. Goddammit, now I'm gonna do it!

LINDA: Oh, that's the spirit, Willy!

WILLY: I will never get behind a wheel the rest of my life!

LINDA: It's changing, Willy, I can feel it changing!

WILLY: Beyond a question. G'by, I'm late. [*He starts to go again.*]

LINDA: [*Calling after him as she runs to the kitchen table for a handkerchief.*] You got your glasses?

WILLY: [*Feels for them, then comes back in.*] Yeah, yeah, got my glasses.

LINDA: [*Giving him the handkerchief.*] And a handkerchief.

WILLY: Yeah, handkerchief.

LINDA: And your saccharine?

WILLY: Yeah, my saccharine.

LINDA: Be careful on the subway stairs.

[*She kisses him, and a silk stocking is seen hanging from her hand.* WILLY *notices it.*]

WILLY: Will you stop mending stockings? At least while I'm in the house. It gets me nervous. I can't tell you. Please.

[LINDA *hides the stocking in her hand as she follows* WILLY *across the forestage in front of the house.*]

LINDA: Remember, Frank's Chop House.

WILLY: [*Passing the apron.*] Maybe beets would grow out there.

LINDA: [*Laughing.*] But you tried so many times.

WILLY: Yeah. Well, don't work hard today. [*He disappears around the right corner of the house.*]

LINDA: Be careful! [*As* WILLY *vanishes,* LINDA *waves to him. Suddenly the phone rings. She runs across the stage and into the kitchen and lifts it.*] Hello? Oh, Biff! I'm so glad you called, I just . . . Yes, sure, I just told him. Yes, he'll be there for dinner at six o'clock, I didn't forget. Listen, I was just dying to tell you. You know that little rubber pipe I told you about? That he connected to the gas heater? I finally decided to go down the cellar this morning and take it away and destroy it. But it's gone! Imagine? He took it away himself, it isn't there! [*She listens.*] When? Oh, then you took it. Oh—nothing, it's just that I'd hoped he'd taken it away himself. Oh, I'm not worried, darling, because this morning he left in such high spirits, it was like the old days! I'm not afraid any more. Did Mr. Oliver see you? . . . Well, you wait there then. And make a nice impression on him, darling. Just don't perspire too much before you see him. And have a nice time with Dad. He may have big news too! . . . That's right, a New York job. And be sweet to him tonight, dear. Be loving to him. Because he's only a little boat looking for a harbor. [*She is trembling with sorrow and joy.*] Oh, that's wonderful, Biff, you'll save his life. Thanks, darling. Just put your arm around him when he comes into the restaurant. Give him a smile. That's the boy . . . Good-by, dear. . . . You got your comb? . . . That's fine. Good-by, Biff dear.

[*In the middle of her speech,* HOWARD WAGNER, *thirty-six, wheels on a small typewriter table on which is a wire-recording machine and proceeds to plug it in. This is on the left forestage. Light slowly fades on* LINDA *as it rises on* HOWARD. HOWARD *is intent on threading the machine and only glances over his shoulder as* WILLY *appears.*]

WILLY: Pst! Pst!

HOWARD: Hello, Willy, come in.

WILLY: Like to have a little talk with you, Howard.

HOWARD: Sorry to keep you waiting. I'll be with you in a minute.

WILLY: What's that, Howard?

HOWARD: Didn't you ever see one of these? Wire recorder.

WILLY: Oh. Can we talk a minute?

HOWARD: Records things. Just got delivery yesterday. Been driving me crazy, the most terrific machine I ever saw in my life. I was up all night with it.

WILLY: What do you do with it?

HOWARD: I bought it for dictation, but you can do anything with it. Listen to this. I had it home last night. Listen to what I picked up. The first one is my daughter. Get this. [*He flicks the switch and "Roll out the Barrel" is heard being whistled.*] Listen to that kid whistle.

WILLY: That is lifelike, isn't it?

HOWARD: Seven years old. Get that tone.
WILLY: Ts, ts. Like to ask a little favor if you . . .

[*The whistling breaks off, and the voice of* HOWARD*'s daughter is heard.*]

HIS DAUGHTER: "Now you, Daddy."
HOWARD: She's crazy for me! [*Again the same song is whistled.*] That's me! Ha! [*He winks.*]
WILLY: You're very good!

[*The whistling breaks off again. The machine runs silent for a moment.*]

HOWARD: Sh! Get this now, this is my son.
HIS SON: "The capital of Alabama is Montgomery; the capital of Arizona is Phoenix; the capital of Arkansas is Little Rock; the capital of California is Sacramento . . ." [*And on, and on.*]
HOWARD: [*Holding up five fingers.*] Five years old, Willy!
WILLY: He'll make an announcer some day!
HIS SON: [*Continuing.*] "The capital. . ."
HOWARD: Get that—alphabetical order! [*The machine breaks off suddenly.*] Wait a minute. The maid kicked the plug out.
WILLY: It certainly is a—
HOWARD: Sh, for God's sake!
HIS SON: "It's nine o'clock, Bulova watch time. So I have to go to sleep."
WILLY: That really is—
HOWARD: Wait a minute! The next is my wife.

[*They wait.*]

HOWARD'S VOICE: "Go on, say something." [*Pause.*] "Well, you gonna talk?"
HIS WIFE: "I can't think of anything."
HOWARD'S VOICE: "Well, talk—it's turning."
HIS WIFE: [*Shyly, beaten.*] "Hello." [*Silence.*] "Oh, Howard, I can't talk into this . . ."
HOWARD: [*Snapping the machine off.*] That was my wife.
WILLY: That is a wonderful machine. Can we—
HOWARD: I tell you, Willy, I'm gonna take my camera, and my bandsaw, and all my hobbies, and out they go. This is the most fascinating relaxation I ever found.
WILLY: I think I'll get one myself.
HOWARD: Sure, they're only a hundred and a half. You can't do without it. Supposing you wanna hear Jack Benny,[4] see? But you can't be at home at that hour. So you tell the maid to turn the radio on when Jack Benny comes on, and this automatically goes on with the radio . . .
WILLY: And when you come home you . . .
HOWARD: You can come home twelve o'clock, one o'clock, any time you like,

4. Jack Benny (1894–1974), a vaudeville, radio, television, and motion picture star, hosted America's most popular radio show form 1932 to 1955.

and you get yourself a Coke and sit yourself down, throw the switch, and there's Jack Benny's program in the middle of the night!

WILLY: I'm definitely going to get one. Because lots of time I'm on the road, and I think to myself, what I must be missing on the radio!

HOWARD: Don't you have a radio in the car?

WILLY: Well, yeah, but who ever thinks of turning it on?

HOWARD: Say, aren't you supposed to be in Boston?

WILLY: That's what I want to talk to you about, Howard. You got a minute? [*He draws a chair in from the wing.*]

HOWARD: What happened? What're you doing here?

WILLY: Well . . .

HOWARD: You didn't crack up again, did you?

WILLY: Oh, no. No . . .

HOWARD: Geez, you had me worried there for a minute. What's the trouble?

WILLY: Well, tell you the truth, Howard. I've come to the decision that I'd rather not travel any more.

HOWARD: Not travel! Well, what'll you do?

WILLY: Remember, Christmas time, when you had the party here? You said you'd try to think of some spot for me here in town.

HOWARD: With us?

WILLY: Well, sure.

HOWARD: Oh, yeah, yeah. I remember. Well, I couldn't think of anything for you, Willy.

WILLY: I tell ya, Howard. The kids are all grown up, y'know. I don't need much any more. If I could take home—well, sixty-five dollars a week, I could swing it.

HOWARD: Yeah, but Willy, see I—

WILLY: I tell ya why, Howard. Speaking frankly and between the two of us, y'know—I'm just a little tired.

HOWARD: Oh, I could understand that, Willy. But you're a road man, Willy, and we do a road business. We've only got a half-dozen salesmen on the floor here.

WILLY: God knows, Howard, I never asked a favor of any man. But I was with the firm when your father used to carry you in here in his arms.

HOWARD: I know that, Willy, but—

WILLY: Your father came to me the day you were born and asked me what I thought of the name of Howard, may he rest in peace.

HOWARD: I appreciate that, Willy, but there just is no spot here for you. If I had a spot I'd slam you right in, but I just don't have a single solitary spot.

[*He looks for his lighter.* WILLY *has picked it up and gives it to him. Pause.*]

WILLY: [*With increasing anger.*] Howard, all I need to set my table is fifty dollars a week.

HOWARD: But where am I going to put you, kid?

WILLY: Look, it isn't a question of whether I can sell merchandise, is it?

HOWARD: No, but it's a business, kid, and everybody's gotta pull his own weight.

WILLY: [*Desperately*.] Just let me tell you a story, Howard—

HOWARD: 'Cause you gotta admit, business is business.

WILLY: [*Angrily*.] Business is definitely business, but just listen for a minute. You don't understand this. When I was a boy—eighteen, nineteen—I was already on the road. And there was a question in my mind as to whether selling had a future for me. Because in those days I had a yearning to go to Alaska. See, there were three gold strikes in one month in Alaska, and I felt like going out. Just for the ride, you might say.

HOWARD: [*Barely interested*.] Don't say.

WILLY: Oh, yeah, my father lived many years in Alaska. He was an adventurous man. We've got quite a little streak of self-reliance in our family. I thought I'd go out with my older brother and try to locate him, and maybe settle in the North with the old man. And I was almost decided to go, when I met a salesman in the Parker House. His name was Dave Singleman. And he was eighty-four years old, and he'd drummed merchandise in thirty-one states. And old Dave, he'd go up to his room, y'understand, put on his green velvet slippers—I'll never forget—and pick up his phone and call the buyers, and without ever leaving his room, at the age of eighty-four, he made a living. And when I saw that, I realized that selling was the greatest career a man could want. 'Cause what could be more satisfying than to be able to go, at the age of eighty-four, into twenty or thirty different cities, and pick up his phone and be remembered and loved and helped by so many different people? Do you know? when he died—and by the way he died the death of a salesman, in his green velvet slippers in the smoker of the New York, New Haven and Hartford, going into Boston—when he died, hundreds of salesmen and buyers were at his funeral. Things were sad on a lotta trains for months after that. [*He stands up.* HOWARD *has not looked at him*.] In those days there was personality in it, Howard. There was respect, and comradeship, and gratitude in it. Today, it's all cut and dried, and there's no chance for bringing friendship to bear—or personality. You see what I mean? They don't know me any more.

HOWARD: [*Moving away, toward the right*.] That's just the thing, Willy.

WILLY: If I had forty dollars a week—that's all I'd need. Forty dollars, Howard.

HOWARD: Kid, I can't take blood from a stone, I—

WILLY: [*Desperation is on him now*.] Howard, the year Al Smith[5] was nominated, your father came to me and—

HOWARD: [*Starting to go off*.] I've got to see some people, kid.

WILLY: [*Stopping him*.] I'm talking about your father! There were promises made across this desk! You mustn't tell me you've got people to see—I put thirty-four years into this firm, Howard, and now I can't pay my insurance! You can't eat the orange and throw the peel away—a man is not a piece of fruit! [*After a pause*.] Now pay attention. Your father—in 1928 I had a big year. I averaged a hundred and seventy dollars a week in commissions.

5. Alfred E. Smith (1873–1944) was the Democratic presidential nominee who lost to Herbert Hoover in 1928.

HOWARD: [*Impatiently.*] Now, Willy, you never averaged—

WILLY: [*Banging his hand on the desk.*] I averaged a hundred and seventy dollars a week in the year of 1928! And your father came to me—or rather, I was in the office here—it was right over this desk—and he put his hand on my shoulder—

HOWARD: [*Getting up.*] You'll have to excuse me, Willy, I gotta see some people. Pull yourself together. [*Going out.*] I'll be back in a little while.

[*On* HOWARD*'s exit, the light on his chair grows very bright and strange.*]

WILLY: Pull myself together! What the hell did I say to him? My God, I was yelling at him! How could I! [WILLY *breaks off, staring at the light, which occupies the chair, animating it. He approaches this chair, standing across the desk from it.*] Frank, Frank, don't you remember what you told me that time? How you put your hand on my shoulder, and Frank . . . [*He leans on the desk and as he speaks the dead man's name he accidentally switches on the recorder, and instantly.*]

HOWARD'S SON: ". . . of New York is Albany. The capital of Ohio is Cincinnati, the capital of Rhode Island is . . ." [*The recitation continues.*]

WILLY: [*Leaping away with fright, shouting.*] Ha! Howard! Howard! Howard!

HOWARD: [*Rushing in.*] What happened?

WILLY: [*Pointing at the machine, which continues nasally, childishly, with the capital cities.*] Shut it off! Shut it off!

HOWARD: [*Pulling the plug out.*] Look, Willy . . .

WILLY: [*Pressing his hands to his eyes.*] I gotta get myself some coffee. I'll get some coffee . . .

[WILLY *starts to walk out.* HOWARD *stops him.*]

HOWARD: [*Rolling up the cord.*] Willy, look . . .

WILLY: I'll go to Boston.

HOWARD: Willy, you can't go to Boston for us.

WILLY: Why can't I go?

HOWARD: I don't want you to represent us. I've been meaning to tell you for a long time now.

WILLY: Howard, are you firing me?

HOWARD: I think you need a good long rest, Willy.

WILLY: Howard—

HOWARD: And when you feel better, come back, and we'll see if we can work something out.

WILLY: But I gotta earn money, Howard. I'm in no position to—

HOWARD: Where are your sons? Why don't your sons give you a hand?

WILLY: They're working on a very big deal.

HOWARD: This is no time for false pride, Willy. You go to your sons and you tell them that you're tired. You've got two great boys, haven't you?

WILLY: Oh, no question, no question, but in the meantime . . .

HOWARD: Then that's that, heh?

WILLY: All right, I'll go to Boston tomorrow.

HOWARD: No, no.
WILLY: I can't throw myself on my sons. I'm not a cripple!
HOWARD: Look, kid, I'm busy, I'm busy this morning.
WILLY: [*Grasping* HOWARD's *arm*.] Howard, you've got to let me go to Boston!
HOWARD: [*Hard, keeping himself under control*.] I've got a line of people to see this morning. Sit down, take five minutes, and pull yourself together, and then go home, will ya? I need the office, Willy. [*He starts to go turns, remembering the recorder, starts to push off the table holding the recorder*.] Oh, yeah. Whenever you can this week, stop by and drop off the samples. You'll feel better, Willy, and then come back and we'll talk. Pull yourself together, kid, there's people outside.

[HOWARD *exits, pushing the table off left*. WILLY *stares into space, exhausted. Now the music is heard—*BEN*'s music—first distantly, then closer, closer. As* WILLY *speaks,* BEN *enters from the right. He carries valise and umbrella*.]

WILLY: Oh, Ben, how did you do it? What is the answer? Did you wind up the Alaska deal already?
BEN: Doesn't take much time if you know what you're doing. Just a short business trip. Boarding ship in an hour. Wanted to say good-by.
WILLY: Ben, I've got to talk to you.
BEN: [*Glancing at his watch*.] Haven't the time, William.
WILLY: [*Crossing the apron to* BEN.] Ben, nothing's working out. I don't know what to do.
BEN: Now, look here, William. I've bought timberland in Alaska and I need a man to look after things for me.
WILLY: God, timberland! Me and my boys in those grand outdoors!
BEN: You've a new continent at your doorstep, William. Get out of these cities, they're full of talk and time payments and courts of law. Screw on your fists and you can fight for a fortune up there.
WILLY: Yes, yes! Linda, Linda!

[LINDA *enters as of old, with the wash*.]

LINDA: Oh, you're back?
BEN: I haven't much time.
WILLY: No, wait! Linda, he's got a proposition for me in Alaska.
LINDA: But you've got—[*To* BEN.] He's got a beautiful job here.
WILLY: But in Alaska, kid, I could—
LINDA: You're doing well enough, Willy!
BEN: [*To* LINDA.] Enough for what, my dear?
LINDA: [*Frightened of* BEN *and angry at him*.] Don't say those things to him! Enough to be happy right here, right now. [*To* WILLY, *while* BEN *laughs*.] Why must everybody conquer the world? You're well liked, and the boys love you, and someday—[*To* BEN.]—why, old man Wagner told him just the other day that if he keeps it up he'll be a member of the firm, didn't he, Willy?
WILLY: Sure, sure. I am building something with this firm, Ben, and if a man is

building something he must be on the right track, mustn't he?

BEN: What are you building? Lay your hand on it. Where is it?

WILLY: [*Hesitantly.*] That's true, Linda, there's nothing.

LINDA: Why? [*To* BEN.] There's a man eighty-four years old—

WILLY: That's right, Ben, that's right. When I look at that man I say, what is there to worry about?

BEN: Bah!

WILLY: It's true, Ben. All he has to do is go into any city, pick up the phone, and he's making his living and you know why?

BEN: [*Picking up his valise.*] I've got to go.

WILLY: [*Holding* BEN *back.*] Look at this boy! [BIFF, *in his high school sweater, enters carrying suitcase.* HAPPY *carries* BIFF'*s shoulder guards, gold helmet, and football pants.*] Without a penny to his name, three great universities are begging for him, and from there the sky's the limit, because it's not what you do, Ben. It's who you know and the smile on your face! It's contacts, Ben, contacts! The whole wealth of Alaska passes over the lunch table at the Commodore Hotel, and that's the wonder, the wonder of this country, that a man can end with diamonds here on the basis of being liked! [*He turns to* BIFF.] And that's why when you get out on that field today it's important. Because thousands of people will be rooting for you and loving you. [*To* BEN, *who has again begun to leave.*] And Ben! when he walks into a business office his name will sound out like a bell and all the doors will open to him! I've seen it, Ben, I've seen it a thousand times! You can't feel it with your hand like timber, but it's there!

BEN: Good-by, William.

WILLY: Ben, am I right? Don't you think I'm right? I value your advice.

BEN: There's a new continent at your doorstep, William. You could walk out rich. Rich! [*He is gone.*]

WILLY: We'll do it here, Ben! You hear me? We're gonna do it here!

[*Young* BERNARD *rushes in. The gay music of the Boys is heard.*]

BERNARD: Oh, gee, I was afraid you left already!

WILLY: Why? What time is it?

BERNARD: It's half-past one!

WILLY: Well, come on, everybody! Ebbets Field next stop! Where's the pennants? [*He rushes through the wall-line of the kitchen and out into the living room.*]

LINDA: [*To* BIFF.] Did you pack fresh underwear?

BIFF: [*Who has been limbering up.*] I want to go!

BERNARD: Biff, I'm carrying your helmet, ain't I?

HAPPY: No, I'm carrying the helmet.

BERNARD: Oh, Biff, you promised me.

HAPPY: I'm carrying the helmet.

BERNARD: How am I going to get in the locker room?

LINDA: Let him carry the shoulder guards. [*She puts her coat and hat on in the kitchen.*]

BERNARD: Can I, Biff? 'Cause I told everybody I'm going to be in the locker room.

HAPPY: In Ebbets Field its the clubhouse.

BERNARD: I meant the clubhouse, Biff!

HAPPY: Biff!

BIFF: [*Grandly, after a slight pause.*] Let him carry the shoulder guards.

HAPPY: [*As he gives* BERNARD *the shoulder guards.*] Stay close to us now.

[WILLY *rushes in with the pennants.*]

WILLY: [*Handing them out.*] Everybody wave when Biff comes out on the field. [HAPPY *and* BERNARD *run off.*] You set now, boy?

[*The music has died away.*]

BIFF: Ready to go, Pop. Every muscle is ready.

WILLY: [*At the edge of the apron.*] You realize what this means?

BIFF: That's right, Pop.

WILLY: [*Feeling* BIFF*'s muscles.*] You're comin' home this afternoon captain of the All-Scholastic Championship Team of the City of New York.

BIFF: I got it, Pop. And remember, pal, when I take off my helmet, that touchdown is for you.

WILLY: Let's go! [*He is starting out, with his arm around* BIFF, *when* CHARLEY *enters, as of old, in knickers.*] I got no room for you, Charley.

CHARLEY: Room? For what?

WILLY: In the car.

CHARLEY: You goin' for a ride? I wanted to shoot some casino.

WILLY: [*Furiously.*] Casino! [*Incredulously.*] Don't you realize what today is?

LINDA: Oh, he knows, Willy. He's just kidding you.

WILLY: That's nothing to kid about!

CHARLEY: No, Linda, what's goin' on?

LINDA: He's playing in Ebbets Field.

CHARLEY: Baseball in this weather?

WILLY: Don't talk to him. Come on, come on! [*He is pushing them out.*]

CHARLEY: Wait a minute, didn't you hear the news?

WILLY: What?

CHARLEY: Don't you listen to the radio? Ebbets Field just blew up.

WILLY: You go to hell! [CHARLEY *laughs. Pushing them out.*] Come on, come on! We're late.

CHARLEY: [*As they go.*] Knock a homer, Biff, knock a homer!

WILLY: [*The last to leave, turning to* CHARLEY.] I don't think that was funny, Charley. This is the greatest day of my life.

CHARLEY: Willy, when are you going to grow up?

WILLY: Yeah, heh? When this game is over, Charley, you'll be laughing out of the other side of your face. They'll be calling him another Red Grange.[6] Twenty-five thousand a year.

6. Harold Edward Grange, All-American halfback at the University of Illinois (1923–1925), who played professionally for the Chicago Bears.

CHARLEY: [*Kidding.*] Is that so?
WILLY: Yeah, that's so.
CHARLEY: Well, then, I'm sorry, Willy. But tell me something.
WILLY: What?
CHARLEY: Who is Red Grange?
WILLY: Put up your hands. Goddam you, put up your hands! [CHARLEY, *chuckling, shakes his head and walks away, around the left corner of the stage.* WILLY *follows him. The music rises to a mocking frenzy.*] Who the hell do you think you are, better than everybody else? You don't know everything, you big, ignorant, stupid . . . Put up your hands! [*Light rises, on the right side of the forestage, on a small table in the reception room of* CHARLEY'*s office. Traffic sounds are heard.* BERNARD, *now mature, sits whistling to himself. A pair of tennis rackets and an overnight bag are on the floor beside him.*] [*Offstage.*] What are you walking away for? Don't walk away! If you're going to say something say it to my face! I know you laugh at me behind my back. You'll laugh out of the other side of your goddam face after this game. Touchdown! Touchdown! Eighty thousand people! Touchdown! Right between the goal posts.

[BERNARD *is a quiet, earnest, but self-assured young man.* WILLY'*s voice is coming from right upstage now.* BERNARD *lowers his feet off the table and listens.* JENNY, *his father's secretary, enters.*]

JENNY: [*Distressed.*] Say, Bernard, will you go out in the hall?
BERNARD: What is that noise? Who is it?
JENNY: Mr. Loman. He just got off the elevator.
BERNARD: [*Getting up.*] Who's he arguing with?
JENNY: Nobody. There's nobody with him. I can't deal with him any more, and your father gets all upset everytime he comes. I've got a lot of typing to do, and your father's waiting to sign it. Will you see him?
WILLY: [*Entering.*] Touchdown! Touch—[*He sees* JENNY.] Jenny, Jenny, good to see you. How're ya? Workin'? Or still honest?
JENNY: Fine. How've you been feeling?
WILLY: Not much any more, Jenny. Ha, ha! [*He is surprised to see the rackets.*]
BERNARD: Hello, Uncle Willy.
WILLY: [*Almost shocked.*] Bernard! Well, look who's here! [*He comes quickly, guiltily to* BERNARD *and warmly shakes his hand.*]
BERNARD: How are you? Good to see you.
WILLY: What are you doing here?
BERNARD: Oh, just stopped by to see Pop. Get off my feet till my train leaves. I'm going to Washington in a few minutes.
WILLY: Is he in?
BERNARD: Yes, he's in his office with the accountant. Sit down.
WILLY: [*Sitting down.*] What're you going to do in Washington?
BERNARD: Oh, just a case I've got there, Willy.
WILLY: That so? [*Indicating the rackets.*] You going to play tennis there?
BERNARD: I'm staying with a friend who's got a court.
WILLY: Don't say. His own tennis court. Must be fine people, I bet.

BERNARD: They are, very nice. Dad tells me Biff's in town.

WILLY: [*With a big smile.*] Yeah, Biff's in. Working on a very big deal, Bernard.

BERNARD: What's Biff doing?

WILLY: Well, he's been doing very big things in the West. But he decided to establish himself here. Very big. We're having dinner. Did I hear your wife had a boy?

BERNARD: That's right. Our second.

WILLY: Two boys! What do you know!

BERNARD: What kind of a deal has Biff got?

WILLY: Well, Bill Oliver—very big sporting-goods man—he wants Biff very badly. Called him in from the West. Long distance, carte blanche, special deliveries. Your friends have their own private tennis court?

BERNARD: You still with the old firm, Willy?

WILLY: [*After a pause.*] I'm—I'm overjoyed to see how you made the grade, Bernard, overjoyed. It's an encouraging thing to see a young man really—really— Looks very good for Biff—very—[*He breaks off, then.*] Bernard—[*He is so full of emotion, he breaks off again.*]

BERNARD: What is it, Willy?

WILLY: [*Small and alone.*] What—what's the secret?

BERNARD: What secret?

WILLY: How—how did you? Why didn't he ever catch on?

BERNARD: I wouldn't know that, Willy.

WILLY: [*Confidentially, desperately.*] You were his friend, his boyhood friend. There's something I don't understand about it. His life ended after that Ebbets Field game. From the age of seventeen nothing good ever happened to him.

BERNARD: He never trained himself for anything.

WILLY: But he did, he did. After high school he took so many correspondence courses. Radio mechanics; television; God knows what, and never made the slightest mark.

BERNARD: [*Taking off his glasses.*] Willy, do you want to talk candidly?

WILLY: [*Rising, faces* BERNARD.] I regard you as a very brilliant man, Bernard. I value your advice.

BERNARD: Oh, the hell with the advice, Willy. I couldn't advise you. There's just one thing I've always wanted to ask you. When he was supposed to graduate, and the math teacher flunked him—

WILLY: Oh, that son-of-a-bitch ruined his life.

BERNARD: Yeah, but, Willy, all he had to do was go to summer school and make up that subject.

WILLY: That's right, that's right.

BERNARD: Did you tell him not to go to summer school?

WILLY: Me? I begged him to go. I ordered him to go!

BERNARD: Then why wouldn't he go?

WILLY: Why? Why! Bernard, that question has been trailing me like a ghost for the last fifteen years. He flunked the subject, and laid down and died like a hammer hit him!

BERNARD: Take it easy, kid.

WILLY: Let me talk to you—I got nobody to talk to. Bernard, Bernard, was it my fault? Y'see? It keeps going around in my mind, maybe I did something to him. I got nothing to give him.

BERNARD: Don't take it so hard.

WILLY: Why did he lay down? What is the story there? You were his friend!

BERNARD: Willy, I remember, it was June, and our grades came out. And he'd flunked math.

WILLY: That son-of-a-bitch!

BERNARD: No, it wasn't right then. Biff just got very angry, I remember, and he was ready to enroll in summer school.

WILLY: [*Surprised.*] He was?

BERNARD: He wasn't beaten by it at all. But then, Willy, he disappeared from the block for almost a month. And I got the idea that he'd gone up to New England to see you. Did he have a talk with you then? [WILLY *stares in silence.*] Willy?

WILLY: [*With a strong edge of resentment in his voice.*] Yeah, he came to Boston. What about it?

BERNARD: Well, just that when he came back—I'll never forget this, it always mystifies me. Because I'd thought so well of Biff, even though he'd always taken advantage of me. I loved him, Willy, y'know? And he came back after that month and took his sneakers—remember those sneakers with "University of Virginia" printed on them? He was so proud of those, wore them every day. And he took them down in the cellar, and burned them up in the furnace. We had a fist fight. It lasted at least half an hour. Just the two of us, punching each other down the cellar, and crying right through it. I've often thought of how strange it was that I knew he'd given up his life. What happened in Boston, Willy? [WILLY *looks at him as at an intruder.*] I just bring it up because you asked me.

WILLY: [*Angrily.*] Nothing. What do you mean, "What happened?" What's that got to do with anything?

BERNARD: Well, don't get sore.

WILLY: What are you trying to do, blame it on me? If a boy lays down is that my fault?

BERNARD: Now, Willy, don't get—

WILLY: Well, don't—don't talk to me that way! What does that mean, "What happened?"

[CHARLEY *enters. He is in his vest, and he carries a bottle of bourbon.*]

CHARLEY: Hey, you're going to miss that train. [*He waves the bottle.*]

BERNARD: Yeah, I'm going. [*He takes the bottle.*] Thanks, Pop. [*He picks up his rackets and bag.*] Good-by, Willy, and don't worry about it. You know, "If at first you don't succeed . . ."

WILLY: Yes, I believe in that.

BERNARD: But sometimes, Willy, it's better for a man just to walk away.

WILLY: Walk away?

BERNARD: That's right.

WILLY: But if you can't walk away?

BERNARD: [*After a slight pause.*] I guess that's when it's tough. [*Extending his hand.*] Good-by, Willy.

WILLY: [*Shaking* BERNARD'*s hand.*] Good-by, boy.

CHARLEY: [*An arm on* BERNARD'*s shoulder.*] How do you like this kid? Gonna argue a case in front of the Supreme Court.

BERNARD: [*Protesting.*] Pop!

WILLY: [*Genuinely shocked, pained, and happy.*] No! The Supreme Court!

BERNARD: I gotta run. 'By, Dad!

CHARLEY: Knock 'em dead, Bernard!

[BERNARD *goes off.*]

WILLY: [*As* CHARLEY *takes out his wallet.*] The Supreme Court! And he didn't even mention it!

CHARLEY: [*Counting out money on the desk.*] He don't have to—he's gonna do it.

WILLY: And you never told him what to do, did you? You never took any interest in him.

CHARLEY: My salvation is that I never took any interest in anything. There's some money—fifty dollars. I got an accountant inside.

WILLY: Charley, look . . . [*With difficulty.*] I got my insurance to pay. If you can manage it—I need a hundred and ten dollars. [CHARLEY *doesn't reply for a moment; merely stops moving.*] I'd draw it from my bank but Linda would know, and I . . .

CHARLEY: Sit down, Willy.

WILLY: [*Moving toward the chair.*] I'm keeping an account of everything, remember. I'll pay every penny back. [*He sits.*]

CHARLEY: Now listen to me, Willy.

WILLY: I want you to know I appreciate . . .

CHARLEY: [*Sitting down on the table.*] Willy, what're you doin'? What the hell is goin' on in your head?

WILLY: Why? I'm simply . . .

CHARLEY: I offered you a job. You can make fifty dollars a week. And I won't send you on the road.

WILLY: I've got a job.

CHARLEY: Without pay? What kind of job is a job without pay? [*He rises.*] Now, look kid, enough is enough. I'm no genius but I know when I'm being insulted.

WILLY: Insulted!

CHARLEY: Why don't you want to work for me?

WILLY: What's the matter with you? I've got a job.

BERNARD: Then what're you walkin' in here every week for?

WILLY: [*Getting up.*] Well, if you don't want me to walk in here—

CHARLEY: I am offering you a job!

WILLY: I don't want your goddam job!

CHARLEY: When the hell are you going to grow up?

WILLY: [*Furiously.*] You big ignoramus, if you say that to me again I'll rap you one! I don't care how big you are! [*He's ready to fight. Pause.*]

CHARLEY: [*Kindly, going to him.*] How much do you need, Willy?

WILLY: Charley, I'm strapped, I'm strapped. I don't know what to do. I was just fired.

CHARLEY: Howard fired you?

WILLY: That snotnose. Imagine that? I named him. I named him Howard.

CHARLEY: Willy, when're you gonna realize that them things don't mean anything? You named him Howard, but you can't sell that. The only thing you got in this world is what you can sell. And the funny thing is that you're a salesman, and you don't know that.

WILLY: I've always tried to think otherwise. I guess. I always felt that if a man was impressive, and well liked, that nothing—

CHARLEY: Why must everybody like you? Who liked J. P. Morgan? Was he impressive? In a Turkish bath he'd look like a butcher. But with his pockets on he was very well liked. Now listen, Willy, I know you don't like me, and nobody can say I'm in love with you, but I'll give you a job because—just for the hell of it, put it that way. Now what do you say?

WILLY: I—I just can't work for you, Charley.

CHARLEY: What're you, jealous of me?

WILLY: I can't work for you, that's all, don't ask me why.

CHARLEY: [*Angered, takes out more bills.*] You been jealous of me all your life, you damned fool! Here, pay your insurance. [*He puts the money in* WILLY's *hand.*]

WILLY: I'm keeping strict accounts.

CHARLEY: I've got some work to do. Take care of yourself. And pay your insurance.

WILLY: [*Moving to the right.*] Funny, y'know? After all the highways and the trains, and the appointments, and the years, you end up worth more dead than alive.

CHARLEY: Willy, nobody's worth nothin' dead. [*After a slight pause.*] Did you hear what I said? [WILLY *stands still, dreaming.*] Willy!

WILLY: Apologize to Bernard for me when you see him. I didn't mean to argue with him. He's a fine boy. They're all fine boys, and they'll end up big—all of them. Someday they'll all play tennis together. Wish me luck, Charley. He saw Bill Oliver today.

CHARLEY: Good luck.

WILLY: [*On the verge of tears.*] Charley, you're the only friend I got. Isn't that a remarkable thing? [*He goes out.*]

CHARLEY: Jesus!

[CHARLEY *stares after him a moment and follows. All light blacks out. Suddenly raucous music is heard, and a red glow rises behind the screen at right.* STANLEY, *a young waiter, appears, carrying a table, followed by* HAPPY, *who is carrying two chairs.*]

STANLEY: [*Putting the table down.*] That's all right, Mr. Loman, I can handle it myself. [*He turns and takes the chairs from* HAPPY *and places them at the table.*]

HAPPY: [*Glancing around.*] Oh, this is better.

STANLEY: Sure, in the front there you're in the middle of all kinds a noise. Whenever you got a party. Mr. Loman, you just tell me and I'll put you back here. Y'know, there's a lotta people they don't like it private, because when they go out they like to see a lotta action around them because they're sick and tired to stay in the house by theirself. But I know you, you ain't from Hackensack. You know what I mean?

HAPPY: [*Sitting down.*] So how's it coming, Stanley?

STANLEY: Ah, it's a dog life. I only wish during the war they'd a took me in the Army. I couda been dead by now.

HAPPY: My brother's back, Stanley.

STANLEY: Oh, he come back, heh? From the Far West.

HAPPY: Yeah, big cattle man, my brother, so treat him right. And my father's coming too.

STANLEY: Oh, your father too!

HAPPY: You got a couple of nice lobsters?

STANLEY: Hundred per cent, big.

HAPPY: I want them with the claws.

STANLEY: Don't worry, I don't give you no mice. [HAPPY *laughs.*] How about some wine? It'll put a head on the meal.

HAPPY: No. You remember, Stanley, that recipe I brought you from overseas? With the champagne in it?

STANLEY: Oh, yeah, sure. I still got it tacked up yet in the kitchen. But that'll have to cost a buck apiece anyways.

HAPPY: That's all right.

STANLEY: What'd you, hit a number or somethin'?

HAPPY: No, it's a little celebration. My brother is—I think he pulled off a big deal today. I think we're going into business together.

STANLEY: Great! That's the best for you. Because a family business, you know what I mean?—that's the best.

HAPPY: That's what I think.

STANLEY: 'Cause what's the difference? Somebody steals? It's in the family. Know what I mean? [*Sotto voce.*] Like this bartender here. The boss is goin' crazy what kinda leak he's got in the cash register. You put it in but it don't come out.

HAPPY: [*Raising his head.*] Sh!

STANLEY: What?

HAPPY: You notice I wasn't lookin' right or left, was I?

STANLEY: No.

HAPPY: And my eyes are closed.

STANLEY: So what's the—?

HAPPY: Strudel's comin'.

STANLEY: [*Catching on, looks around.*] Ah, no there's no—[*He breaks off as a furred, lavishly dressed girl enters and sits at the next table. Both follow her with their eyes.*] Geez, how'd ya know?

HAPPY: I got radar or something. [*Staring directly at her profile.*] Oooooooo . . . Stanley.

STANLEY: I think, that's for you, Mr. Loman.

HAPPY: Look at that mouth. Oh, God. And the binoculars.
STANLEY: Geez, you got a life, Mr. Loman.
HAPPY: Wait on her.
STANLEY: [*Going to the girl's table.*] Would you like a menu, ma'am?
GIRL: I'm expecting someone, but I'd like a—
HAPPY: Why don't you bring her—excuse me, miss, do you mind? I sell champagne, and I'd like you to try my brand. Bring her a champagne, Stanley.
GIRL: That's awfully nice of you.
HAPPY: Don't mention it. It's all company money. [*He laughs*].
GIRL: That's a charming product to be selling, isn't it?
HAPPY: Oh, gets to be like everything else. Selling is selling, y'know.
GIRL: I suppose.
HAPPY: You don't happen to sell, do you?
GIRL: No, I don't sell.
HAPPY: Would you object to a compliment from a stranger? You ought to be on a magazine cover.
GIRL: [*Looking at him a little archly.*] I have been.

[STANLEY *comes in with a glass of champagne.*]

HAPPY: What'd I say before, Stanley? You see? She's a cover girl.
STANLEY: Oh, I could see, I could see.
HAPPY: [*To the* GIRL.] What magazine?
GIRL: Oh, a lot of them. [*She takes the drink.*] Thank you.
HAPPY: You know what they say in France, don't you? "Champagne is the drink of the complexion"—Hya, Biff!

[BIFF *has entered and sits with* HAPPY.]

BIFF: Hello, kid. Sorry I'm late.
HAPPY: I just got here. Uh, Miss—?
GIRL: Forsythe.
HAPPY: Miss Forsythe, this is my brother.
BIFF: Is Dad here?
HAPPY: His name is Biff. You might've heard of him. Great football player.
GIRL: Really? What team?
HAPPY: Are you familiar with football?
GIRL: No, I'm afraid I'm not.
HAPPY: Biff is quarterback with the New York Giants.
GIRL: Well, that's nice, isn't it? [*She drinks.*]
HAPPY: Good health.
GIRL: I'm happy to meet you.
HAPPY: That's my name, Hap. It's really Harold, but at West Point they called me Happy.
GIRL: [*Now really impressed.*] Oh, I see. How do you do? [*She turns her profile.*]
BIFF: Isn't Dad coming?
HAPPY: You want her?

BIFF: Oh, I could never make that.

HAPPY: I remember the time that idea would never come into your head. Where's the old confidence, Biff?

BIFF: I just saw Oliver—

HAPPY: Wait a minute. I've got to see that old confidence again. Do you want her? She's on call.

BIFF: Oh, no. [*He turns to look at the* GIRL.]

HAPPY: I'm telling you. Watch this. [*Turning to see the* GIRL.] Honey? [*She turns to him.*] Are you busy?

GIRL: Well, I am . . . but I could make a phone call.

HAPPY: Do that, will you, honey? And see if you can get a friend. We'll be here for a while. Biff is one of the greatest football players in the country.

GIRL: [*Standing up.*] Well, I'm certainly happy to meet you.

HAPPY: Come back soon.

GIRL: I'll try.

HAPPY: Don't try, honey, try hard. [*The* GIRL *exits.* STANLEY *follows, shaking his head in bewildered admiration.*] Isn't that a shame now? A beautiful girl like that? That's why I can't get married. There's not a good woman in a thousand. New York is loaded with them, kid!

BIFF: Hap, look—

HAPPY: I told you she was on call!

BIFF: [*Strangely unnerved.*] Cut it out, will ya? I want to say something to you.

HAPPY: Did you see Oliver?

BIFF: I saw him all right. Now look, I want to tell Dad a couple of things and I want you to help me.

HAPPY: What? Is he going to back you?

BIFF: Are you crazy? You're out of your goddam head, you know that?

HAPPY: Why? What happened?

BIFF: [*Breathlessly.*] I did a terrible thing today, Hap. It's been the strangest day I ever went through. I'm all numb, I swear.

HAPPY: You mean he wouldn't see you?

BIFF: Well, I waited six hours for him, see? All day. Kept sending my name in. Even tried to date his secretary so she'd get me to him, but no soap.

HAPPY: Because you're not showin' the old confidence, Biff. He remembered you, didn't he?

BIFF: [*Stopping* HAPPY *with a gesture.*] Finally, about five o'clock, he comes out. Didn't remember who I was or anything. I felt like such an idiot, Hap.

HAPPY: Did you tell him my Florida idea?

BIFF: He walked away. I saw him for one minute. I got so mad I could've torn the walls down! How the hell did I ever get the idea I was a salesman there? I even believed myself that I'd been a salesman for him! And then he gave me one look and—I realized what a ridiculous lie my whole life has been! We've been talking in a dream for fifteen years. I was a shipping clerk.

HAPPY: What'd you do?

BIFF: [*With great tension and wonder.*] Well, he left, see. And the secretary went out. I was all alone in the waiting-room. I don't know what came over me,

Hap. The next thing I know I'm in his office—paneled walls, everything. I can't explain it. I—Hap, I took his fountain pen.

HAPPY: Geez, did he catch you?

BIFF: I ran out. I ran down all eleven flights. I ran and ran and ran.

HAPPY: That was an awful dumb—what'd you do that for?

BIFF: [*Agonized.*] I don't know, I just—wanted to take something, I don't know. You gotta help me, Hap, I'm gonna tell Pop.

HAPPY: You crazy? What for?

BIFF: Hap, he's got to understand that I'm not the man somebody lends that kind of money to. He thinks I've been spiting him all these years and it's eating him up.

HAPPY: That's just it. You tell him something nice.

BIFF: I can't.

HAPPY: Say you got a lunch date with Oliver tomorrow.

BIFF: So what do I do tomorrow?

HAPPY: You leave the house tomorrow and come back at night and say Oliver is thinking it over. And he thinks it over for a couple of weeks, and gradually it fades away and nobody's the worse.

BIFF: But it'll go on forever!

HAPPY: Dad is never so happy as when he's looking forward to something! [WILLY *enters.*] Hello, scout!

WILLY: Gee, I haven't been here in years!

[STANLEY *has followed* WILLY *in and sets a chair for him.* STANLEY *starts off but* HAPPY *stops him.*]

HAPPY: Stanley!

[STANLEY *stands by, waiting for an order.*]

BIFF: [*Going to* WILLY *with guilt, as to an invalid.*] Sit down, Pop. You want a drink?

WILLY: Sure, I don't mind.

BIFF: Let's get a load on.

WILLY: You look worried.

BIFF: N-no. [*To* STANLEY.] Scotch all around. Make it doubles.

STANLEY: Doubles, right. [*He goes.*]

WILLY: You had a couple already, didn't you?

BIFF: Just a couple, yeah.

WILLY: Well, what happened, boy? [*Nodding affirmatively, with a smile.*] Everything go all right?

BIFF: [*Takes a breath, then reaches out and grasps* WILLY*'s hand.*] Pal . . . [*He is smiling bravely, and* WILLY *is smiling too.*] I had an experience today.

HAPPY: Terrific, Pop.

WILLY: That so? What happened?

BIFF: [*High, slightly alcoholic, above the earth.*] I'm going to tell you everything from first to last. It's been a strange day. [*Silence. He looks around, composes himself as best he can, but his breath keeps breaking the rhythm of his voice.*] I had to wait quite a while for him, and—

WILLY: Oliver?

BIFF: Yeah, Oliver. All day, as a matter of cold fact. And a lot of—instances—facts, Pop, facts about my life came back to me. Who was it, Pop? Who ever said I was a salesman with Oliver?

WILLY: Well, you were.

BIFF: No, Dad, I was shipping clerk.

WILLY: But you were practically—

BIFF: [*With determination.*] Dad, I don't know who said it first, but I was never a salesman for Bill Oliver.

WILLY: What're you talking about?

BIFF: Let's hold on to the facts tonight, Pop. We're not going to get anywhere bullin' around. I was a shipping clerk.

WILLY: [*Angrily.*] All right, now listen to me—

BIFF: Why don't you let me finish?

WILLY: I'm not interested in stories about the past or any crap of that kind because the woods are burning, boys, you understand? There's a big blaze going on all around. I was fired today.

BIFF: [*Shocked.*] How could you be?

WILLY: I was fired, and I'm looking for a little good news to tell your mother, because the woman has waited and the woman has suffered. The gist of it is that I haven't got a story left in my head, Biff. So don't give me a lecture about facts and aspects. I am not interested. Now what've you got to say to me? [STANLEY *enters with three drinks. They wait until he leaves.*] Did you see Oliver?

BIFF: Jesus, Dad!

WILLY: You mean you didn't go up there?

HAPPY: Sure he went up there.

BIFF: I did. I—saw him. How could they fire you?

WILLY: [*On the edge of his chair.*] What kind of a welcome did he give you?

BIFF: He won't even let you work on commission?

WILLY: I'm out. [*Driving.*] So tell me, he gave you a warm welcome?

HAPPY: Sure, Pop, sure!

BIFF: [*Driven.*] Well, it was kind of—

WILLY: I was wondering if he'd remember you. [*To* HAPPY.] Imagine, man doesn't see him for ten, twelve years and gives him that kind of a welcome!

HAPPY: Damn right!

BIFF: [*Trying to return to the offensive.*] Pop, look—

WILLY: You know why he remembered you, don't you? Because you impressed him in those days.

BIFF: Let's talk quietly and get this down to the facts, huh?

WILLY: [*As though* BIFF *had been interrupting.*] Well, what happened? It's great news, Biff. Did he take you into his office or'd you talk in the waiting-room?

BIFF: Well, he came in, see and—

WILLY: [*With a big smile.*] What'd he say? Betcha he threw his arm around you.
BIFF: Well, he kinda—
WILLY: He's a fine man. [*To* HAPPY.] Very hard man to see, y'know.
HAPPY: [*Agreeing.*] Oh, I know.
WILLY: [*To* BIFF.] Is that where you had the drinks?
BIFF: Yeah, he gave me a couple of—no, no!
HAPPY: [*Cutting in.*] He told him my Florida idea.
WILLY: Don't interrupt. [*To* BIFF.] How'd he react to the Florida idea?
BIFF: Dad, will you give me a minute to explain?
WILLY: I've been waiting for you to explain since I sat down here! What happened? He took you into his office and what?
BIFF: Well—I talked. And—he listened, see.
WILLY: Famous for the way he listens, y'know. What was his answer?
BIFF: His answer was—[*He breaks off, suddenly angry.*] Dad, you're not letting me tell you what I want to tell you!
WILLY: [*Accusing, angered.*] You didn't see him, did you?
BIFF: I did see him!
WILLY: What'd you insult him or something? You insulted him, didn't you?
BIFF: Listen, will you let me out of it, will you just let me out of it!
HAPPY: What the hell!
WILLY: Tell me what happened!
BIFF: [*To* HAPPY.] I can't talk to him!

[*A single trumpet note jars the ear. The light of green leaves stains the house, which holds the air of night and a dream.* YOUNG BERNARD *enters and knocks on the door of the house.*]

YOUNG BERNARD: [*Frantically.*] Mrs. Loman, Mrs. Loman!
HAPPY: Tell him what happened!
BIFF: [*To* HAPPY.] Shut up and leave me alone!
WILLY: No, no. You had to go and flunk math!
BIFF: What math? What're you talking about?
YOUNG BERNARD: Mrs. Loman, Mrs. Loman!

[LINDA *appears in the house, as of old.*]

WILLY: [*Wildly.*] Math, math, math!
BIFF: Take it easy, Pop!
YOUNG BERNARD: Mrs. Loman!
WILLY: [*Furiously.*] If you hadn't flunked you'd've been set by now!
BIFF: Now, look, I'm gonna tell you what happened, and you're going to listen to me.
YOUNG BERNARD: Mrs. Loman!
BIFF: I waited six hours—
HAPPY: What the hell are you saying?
BIFF: I kept sending in my name but he wouldn't see me. So finally he . . . [*He continues unheard as light fades low on the restaurant.*]
YOUNG BERNARD: Biff flunked math!

LINDA: No!

YOUNG BERNARD: Birnbaum flunked him! They won't graduate him!

LINDA: But they have to. He's gotta go to the university. Where is he? Biff! Biff!

YOUNG BERNARD: No, he left. He went to Grand Central.

LINDA: Grand— You mean he went to Boston!

YOUNG BERNARD: Is Uncle Willy in Boston?

LINDA: Oh, maybe Willy can talk to the teacher. Oh, the poor, poor boy!

[*Light on house area snaps out.*]

BIFF: [*At the table, now audible, holding up a gold fountain pen.*] . . . so I'm washed up with Oliver, you understand? Are you listening to me?

WILLY: [*At a loss.*] Yeah, sure. If you hadn't flunked—

BIFF: Flunked what? What're you talking about?

WILLY: Don't blame everything on me! I didn't flunk math—you did! What pen?

HAPPY: That was awful dumb, Biff, a pen like that is worth—

WILLY: [*Seeing the pen for the first time.*] You took Oliver's pen?

BIFF: [*Weakening.*] Dad, I just explained it to you.

WILLY: You stole Bill Oliver's fountain pen!

BIFF: I didn't exactly steal it! That's just what I've been explaining to you!

HAPPY: He had it in his hand and just then Oliver walked in, so he got nervous and stuck it in his pocket!

WILLY: My God, Biff!

BIFF: I never intended to do it, Dad!

OPERATOR'S VOICE: Standish Arms, good evening!

WILLY: [*Shouting.*] I'm not in my room!

BIFF: [*Frightened.*] Dad, what's the matter? [*He and* HAPPY *stand up.*]

OPERATOR: Ringing Mr. Loman for you!

BIFF: [*Horrified, gets down on one knee before* WILLY.] Dad, I'll make good, I'll make good. [WILLY *tries to get to his feet.* BIFF *holds him down.*] Sit down now.

WILLY: No, you're no good, you're no good for anything.

BIFF: I am, Dad, I'll find something else, you understand? Now don't worry about anything. [*He holds up* WILLY'*s face.*] Talk to me, Dad.

OPERATOR: Mr. Loman does not answer. Shall I page him?

WILLY: [*Attempting to stand, as though to rush and silence the* OPERATOR.] No, no, no!

HAPPY: He'll strike something, Pop.

WILLY: No, no . . .

BIFF: [*Desperately, standing over* WILLY.] Pop, listen! Listen to me! I'm telling you something good. Oliver talked to his partner about the Florida idea. You listening? He—he talked to his partner, and he came to me . . . I'm going to be all right, you hear? Dad, listen to me, he said it was just a question of the amount!

WILLY: Then you . . . got it?

HAPPY: He's gonna be terrific, Pop!

WILLY: [*Trying to stand.*] Then you got it, haven't you? You got it! You got it!

BIFF: [*Agonized, holds* WILLY *down.*] No, no. Look, Pop. I'm supposed to have lunch with them tomorrow. I'm just telling you this so you'll know that I can still make an impression, Pop. And I'll make good somewhere, but I can't go tomorrow, see?

WILLY: Why not? You simply—

BIFF: But the pen, Pop!

WILLY: You give it to him and tell him it was an oversight!

HAPPY: Sure, have lunch tomorrow!

BIFF: I can't say that—

WILLY: You were doing a crossword puzzle and accidentally used his pen!

BIFF: Listen, kid, I took those balls years ago, now I walk in with his fountain pen? That clinches it, don't you see? I can't face him like that! I'll try elsewhere.

PAGE'S VOICE: Paging Mr. Loman!

WILLY: Don't you want to be anything?

BIFF: Pop, how can I go back?

WILLY: You don't want to be anything, is that what's behind it?

BIFF: [*Now angry at* WILLY *for not crediting his sympathy.*] Don't take it that way! You think it was easy walking into that office after what I'd done to him? A team of horses couldn't have dragged me back to Bill Oliver!

WILLY: Then why'd you go?

BIFF: Why did I go? Why did I go! Look at you! Look at what's become of you!

[*Off left,* THE WOMAN *laughs.*]

WILLY: Biff, you're going to go to that lunch tomorrow, or—

BIFF: I can't go. I've got an appointment!

HAPPY: Biff for . . . !

WILLY: Are you spiting me?

BIFF: Don't take it that way! Goddammit!

WILLY: [*Strikes* BIFF *and falters away from the table.*] You rotten little louse! Are you spiting me?

THE WOMAN: Someone's at the door, Willy!

BIFF: I'm no good, can't you see what I am?

HAPPY: [*Separating them.*] Hey, you're in a restaurant! Now cut it out, both of you? [*The girls enter.*] Hello, girls, sit down.

[THE WOMAN *laughs, off left.*]

MISS FORSYTHE: I guess we might as well. This is Letta.

THE WOMAN: Willy, are you going to wake up?

BIFF: [*Ignoring* WILLY.] How're ya, miss, sit down. What do you drink?

MISS FORSYTHE: Letta might not be able to stay long.

LETTA: I gotta get up early tomorrow. I got jury duty. I'm so excited! Were you fellows ever on a jury?

BIFF: No, but I been in front of them! [*The girls laugh.*] This is my father.

LETTA: Isn't he cute? Sit down with us, Pop.

HAPPY: Sit him down, Biff!

BIFF: [*Going to him.*] Come on, slugger, drink us under the table. To hell with it! Come on, sit down, pal.

[*On* BIFF'S *last insistence,* WILLY *is about to sit.*]

THE WOMAN: [*Now urgently.*] Willy, are you going to answer the door!

[THE WOMAN'S *call pulls* WILLY *back. He starts right, befuddled.*]

BIFF: Hey, where are you going?
WILLY: Open the door.
BIFF: The door?
WILLY: The washroom . . . the door . . . where's the door?
BIFF: [*Leading* WILLY *to the left.*] Just go straight down.

[WILLY *moves left.*]

THE WOMAN: Willy, Willy, are you going to get up, get up, get up, get up?

[WILLY *exits left.*]

LETTA: I think it's sweet you bring your daddy along.
MISS FORSYTHE: Oh, he isn't really your father!
BIFF: [*At left, turning to her resentfully.*] Miss Forsythe, you've just seen a prince walk by. A fine, troubled prince. A hardworking, unappreciated prince. A pal, you understand? A good companion. Always for his boys.
LETTA: That's so sweet.
HAPPY: Well, girls, what's the program? We're wasting time. Come on, Biff. Gather round. Where would you like to go?
BIFF: Why don't you do something for him?
HAPPY: Me!
BIFF: Don't you give a damn for him, Hap?
HAPPY: What're you talking about? I'm the one who—
BIFF: I sense it, you don't give a good goddam about him. [*He takes the rolled-up hose from his pocket and puts it on the table in front of* HAPPY.] Look what I found in the cellar, for Christ's sake. How can you bear to let it go on?
HAPPY: Me? Who goes away? Who runs off and—
BIFF: Yeah, but he doesn't mean anything to you. You could help him—I can't! Don't you understand what I'm talking about? He's going to kill himself, don't you know that?
HAPPY: Don't I know it! Me!
BIFF: Hap, help him! Jesus . . . help him . . . Help me, help me, I can't bear to look at his face! [*Ready to weep, he hurries out, up right.*]
HAPPY: [*Starting after him.*] Where are you going?
MISS FORSYTHE: What's he so mad about?
HAPPY: Come on, girls, we'll catch up with him.
MISS FORSYTHE: [*As* HAPPY *pushes her out.*] Say, I don't like that temper of his!
HAPPY: He's just a little overstrung, he'll be all right!
WILLY: [*Off left, as* THE WOMAN *laughs.*] Don't answer! Don't answer!
LETTA: Don't you want to tell your father—

HAPPY: No, that's not my father. He's just a guy. Come on, we'll catch Biff, and, honey, we're going to paint this town! Stanley, where's the check! Hey, Stanley!

[*They exit.* STANLEY *looks toward left.*]

STANLEY: [*Calling to* HAPPY *indignantly.*] Mr. Loman! Mr. Loman!

[STANLEY *picks up a chair and follows them off. Knocking is heard off left.* THE WOMAN *enters, laughing.* WILLY *follows her. She is in a black slip; he is buttoning his shirt. Raw, sensuous music accompanies their speech.*]

WILLY: Will you stop laughing? Will you stop?

THE WOMAN: Aren't you going to answer the door? He'll wake the whole hotel.

WILLY: I'm not expecting anybody.

THE WOMAN: Whyn't you have another drink, honey, and stop being so damn self-centered?

WILLY: I'm so lonely.

THE WOMAN: You know you ruined me, Willy? From now on, whenever you come to the office, I'll see that you go right through to the buyers. No waiting at my desk any more, Willy. You ruined me.

WILLY: That's nice of you to say that.

THE WOMAN: Gee, you are self-centered! Why so sad? You are the saddest, self-centerdest soul I ever did see-saw. [*She laughs. He kisses her.*] Come on inside, drummer boy. It's silly to be dressing in the middle of the night. [*As knocking is heard.*] Aren't you going to answer the door?

WILLY: They're knocking on the wrong door.

THE WOMAN: But I felt the knocking. And he heard us talking in here. Maybe the hotel's on fire!

WILLY: [*His terror rising.*] It's a mistake.

THE WOMAN: Then tell them to go away!

WILLY: There's nobody there.

THE WOMAN: It's getting on my nerves, Willy. There's somebody standing out there and it's getting on my nerves!

WILLY: [*Pushing her away from him.*] All right, stay in the bathroom here, and don't come out. I think there's a law in Massachusetts about it, so don't come out. It may be that new room clerk. He looked very mean. So don't come out. It's a mistake, there's no fire.

[*The knocking is heard again. He takes a few steps away from her, and she vanishes into the wing. The light follows him, and now he is facing* YOUNG BIFF, *who carries a suitcase.* BIFF *steps toward him. The music is gone.*]

BIFF: Why didn't you answer?

WILLY: Biff! What are you doing in Boston?

BIFF: Why didn't you answer? I've been knocking for five minutes, I called you on the phone—

WILLY: I just heard you. I was in the bathroom and had the door shut. Did anything happen home?

BIFF: Dad—I let you down.
WILLY: What do you mean?
BIFF: Dad . . .
WILLY: Biffo, what's this about? [*Putting his arm around* BIFF.] Come on, let's go downstairs and get you a malted.
BIFF: Dad, I flunked math.
WILLY: Not for the term?
BIFF: The term. I haven't got enough credits to graduate.
WILLY: You mean to say Bernard wouldn't give you the answers?
BIFF: He did, he tried, but I only got a sixty-one.
WILLY: And they wouldn't give you four points?
BIFF: Birnbaum refused absolutely. I begged him, Pop, but he won't give me those points. You gotta talk to him before they close the school. Because if he saw the kind of man you are, and you just talked to him in your way, I'm sure he'd come through for me. The class came right before practice, see, and I didn't go enough. Would you talk to him? He'd like you, Pop. You know the way you could talk.
WILLY: You're on. We'll drive right back.
BIFF: Oh, Dad, good work! I'm sure he'll change for you!
WILLY: Go downstairs and tell the clerk I'm checkin' out. Go right down.
BIFF: Yes, sir! See, the reason he hates me, Pop—one day he was late for class so I got up at the blackboard and imitated him. I crossed my eyes and talked with a lithp.
WILLY: [*Laughing.*] You did? The kids like it?
BIFF: They nearly died laughing!
WILLY: Yeah? What'd you do?
BIFF: The thquare root of thixthy twee is . . . [WILLY *bursts out laughing;* BIFF *joins him.*] And in the middle of it he walked in!

[WILLY *laughs and* THE WOMAN *joins in offstage.*]

WILLY: [*Without hesitation.*] Hurry downstairs and—
BIFF: Somebody in there?
WILLY: No, that was next door.

[THE WOMAN *laughs offstage.*]

BIFF: Somebody got in your bathroom!
WILLY: No, it's the next room, there's a party—
THE WOMAN: [*Enters laughing. She lisps this.*] Can I come in? There's something in the bathtub, Willy, and it's moving!

[WILLY *looks at* BIFF, *who is staring open-mouthed and horrified at* THE WOMAN.]

WILLY: Ah—you better go back to your room. They must be finished painting by now. They're painting her room so I let her take a shower here. Go back, go back . . . [*He pushes her.*]
THE WOMAN: [*Resisting.*] But I've got to get dressed, Willy, I can't—
WILLY: Get out of here! Go back, go back . . . [*Suddenly striving for the ordi-*

nary.] This is Miss Francis, Biff, she's a buyer. They're painting her room. Go back, Miss Francis, go back . . .

THE WOMAN: But my clothes, I can't go out naked in the hall!

WILLY: [*Pushing her offstage.*] Get outa here! Go back, go back!

[BIFF *slowly sits down on his suitcase as the argument continues offstage.*]

THE WOMAN: Where's my stockings? You promised me stockings, Willy!

WILLY: I have no stockings here!

THE WOMAN: You had two boxes of size nine sheers for me, and I want them!

WILLY: Here, for God's sake, will you get outa here!

THE WOMAN: [*Enters holding a box of stockings.*] I just hope there's nobody in the hall. That's all I hope. [*To* BIFF.] Are you football or baseball?

BIFF: Football.

THE WOMAN: [*Angry, humiliated.*] That's me too. G'night. [*She snatches her clothes from* WILLY, *and walks out.*]

WILLY: [*After a pause.*] Well, better get going. I want to get to the school first thing in the morning. Get my suits out of the closet. I'll get my valise. [BIFF *doesn't move.*] What's the matter? [BIFF *remains motionless, tears falling.*] She's a buyer. Buys for J. H. Simmons. She lives down the hall—they're painting. You don't imagine—[*He breaks off. After a pause.*] Now listen, pal, she's just a buyer. She sees merchandise in her room and they have to keep it looking just so . . . [*Pause. Assuming command.*] All right, get my suits. [BIFF *doesn't move.*] Now stop crying and do as I say. I gave you an order. Biff, I gave you an order! Is that what you do when I give you an order? How dare you cry! [*Putting his arm around* BIFF.] Now look, Biff, when you grow up you'll understand about these things. You mustn't—you mustn't overemphasize a thing like this. I'll see Birnbaum first thing in the morning.

BIFF: Never mind.

WILLY: [*Getting down beside* BIFF.] Never mind! He's going to give you those points. I'll see to it.

BIFF: He wouldn't listen to you.

WILLY: He certainly will listen to me. You need those points for the U. of Virginia.

BIFF: I'm not going there.

WILLY: Heh? If I can't get him to change that mark you'll make it up in summer school. You've got all summer to—

BIFF: [*His weeping breaking from him.*] Dad . . .

WILLY: [*Infected by it.*] Oh, my boy . . .

BIFF: Dad . . .

WILLY: She's nothing to me, Biff. I was lonely, I was terribly lonely.

BIFF: You—you gave her Mama's stockings! [*His tears break through and he rises to go.*]

WILLY: [*Grabbing for* BIFF.] I gave you an order!

BIFF: Don't touch me, you—liar!

WILLY: Apologize for that!

BIFF: You fake! You phony little fake! You fake!

[*Overcome, he turns quickly and weeping fully goes out with his suitcase.* WILLY *is left on the floor on his knees.*]

WILLY: I gave you an order! Biff, come back here or I'll beat you! Come back here! I'll whip you! [STANLEY *comes quickly in from the right and stands in front of* WILLY. WILLY *Shouts at* STANLEY.] I gave you an order . . .

STANLEY: Hey, let's pick it up, pick it up, Mr. Loman. [*He helps* WILLY *to his feet.*] Your boys left with the chippies. They said they'll see you home.

[*A second waiter watches some distance away.*]

WILLY: But we were supposed to have dinner together.

[*Music is heard,* WILLY'S *theme.*]

STANLEY: Can you make it?

WILLY: I'll—sure, I can make it. [*Suddenly concerned about his clothes.*] Do I—I look all right?

STANLEY: Sure, you look all right. [*He flicks a speck off* WILLY'S *lapel.*]

WILLY: Here—here's a dollar.

STANLEY: Oh, your son paid me. It's all right.

WILLY: [*Putting it in* STANLEY'S *hand.*] No, take it. You're a good boy.

STANLEY: Oh, no, you don't have to . . .

WILLY: Here—here's some more, I don't need it any more. [*After a slight pause.*] Tell me—is there a seed store in the neighborhood?

STANLEY: Seeds? You mean like to plant?

[*As* WILLY *turns,* STANLEY *slips the money back into his jacket pocket.*]

WILLY: Yes. Carrots, peas . . .

STANLEY: Well, there's hardware stores on Sixth Avenue, but it may be too late now.

WILLY: [*Anxiously.*] Oh, I'd better hurry. I've got to get some seeds. [*He starts off to the right.*] I've got to get some seeds, right away. Nothing's planted. I don't have a thing in the ground.

[WILLY *hurries out as the light goes down.* STANLEY *moves over to the right after him, watches him off. The other waiter has been staring at* WILLY.]

STANLEY: [*To the waiter.*] Well, whatta you looking at?

[*The waiter picks up the chairs and moves off right.* STANLEY *takes the table and follows him. The light fades on this area. There is a long pause, the sound of the flute coming over. The light gradually rises on the kitchen, which is empty.* HAPPY *appears at the door of the house, followed by* BIFF. HAPPY *is carrying a large bunch of long-stemmed roses. He enters the kitchen, looks around for* LINDA. *Not seeing her, he turns to* BIFF, *who is just outside the house door, and makes a gesture with his hands, indicating "Not here, I guess." He looks into the living-room and freezes. Inside,* LINDA, *unseen, is seated,*

WILLY's *coat on her lap. She rises ominously and quietly and moves toward* HAPPY, *who backs up into the kitchen, afraid.*]

HAPPY: Hey, what're you doing up? [LINDA *says nothing but moves toward him implacably.*] Where's Pop? [*He keeps backing to the right, and now* LINDA *is in full view in the doorway to the living room.*] Is he sleeping?

LINDA: Where were you?

HAPPY: [*Trying to laugh it off.*] We met two girls, Mom, very fine types. Here, we brought you some flowers. [*Offering them to her.*] Put them in your room, Ma. [*She knocks them to the floor at* BIFF's *feet. He has now come inside and closed the door behind him. She stares at* BIFF, *silent.*] Now what'd you do that for? Mom, I want you to have some flowers—

LINDA: [*Cutting* HAPPY *off, violently to* BIFF.] Don't you care whether he lives or dies?

HAPPY: [*Going to the stairs.*] Come upstairs, Biff.

BIFF: [*With a flare of disgust, to* HAPPY.] Go away from me! [*To* LINDA.] What do you mean, lives or dies? Nobody's dying around here, pal.

LINDA: Get out of my sight! Get out of here!

BIFF: I wanna see the boss.

LINDA: You're not going near him!

BIFF: Where is he? [*He moves into the living-room and* LINDA *follows.*]

LINDA: [*Shouting after* BIFF.] You invite him for dinner. He looks forward to it all day—[BIFF *appears in his parents' bedroom, looks around and exits.*]—and then you desert him there. There's no stranger you'd do that to!

HAPPY: Why? He had a swell time with us. Listen, when I— [LINDA *comes back into the kitchen.*]—desert him I hope I don't outlive the day!

LINDA: Get out of here!

HAPPY: Now look, Mom . . .

LINDA: Did you have to go to women tonight? You and your lousy rotten whores!

[BIFF *re-enters the kitchen.*]

HAPPY: Mom, all we did was follow Biff around trying to cheer him up! [*To* BIFF.] Boy, what a night you gave me!

LINDA: Get out of here, both of you, and don't come back! I don't want you tormenting him any more. Go on now, get your things together! [*To* BIFF.] You can sleep in his apartment. [*She starts to pick up the flowers and stops herself.*] Pick up this stuff, I'm not your maid any more. Pick it up, you bum, you! [HAPPY *turns his back to her in refusal.* BIFF *slowly moves over and gets down on his knees, picking up the flowers.*] You're a pair of animals! Not one, not another living soul would have had the cruelty to walk out on that man in a restaurant!

BIFF: [*Not looking at her.*] Is that what he said?

LINDA: He didn't have to say anything. He was so humiliated he nearly limped when he came in.

HAPPY: But, Mom, he had a great time with us—

BIFF: [*Cutting him off violently.*] Shut up!

[*Without another word,* HAPPY *goes upstairs.*]

LINDA: You! You didn't even go in to see if he was all right!

BIFF: [*Still on the floor in front of* LINDA, *the flowers in his hand; with self-loathing.*] No. Didn't. Didn't do a damned thing. How do you like that, heh? Left him babbling in a toilet.

LINDA: You louse. You . . .

BIFF: Now you hit it on the nose! [*He gets up, throws the flowers in the wastebasket.*] The scum of the earth, and you're looking at him!

LINDA: Get out of here!

BIFF: I gotta talk to the boss, Mom. Where is he?

LINDA: You're not going near him. Get out of this house!

BIFF: [*With absolute assurance, determination.*] No. We're gonna have an abrupt conversation, him and me.

LINDA: You're not talking to him! [*Hammering is heard from outside the house, off right.* BIFF *turns toward the noise. Suddenly pleading.*] Will you please leave him alone?

BIFF: What's he doing out there?

LINDA: He's planting the garden!

BIFF: [*Quietly.*] Now? Oh, my God!

[BIFF *moves outside,* LINDA *following. The light dies down on them and comes up on the center of the apron as* WILLY *walks into it. He is carrying a flashlight, a hoe, and a handful of seed packets. He raps the top of the hoe sharply to fix it firmly, and then moves to the left, measuring off the distance with his foot. He holds the flashlight to look at the seed packets, reading off the instructions. He is in the blue of night.*]

WILLY: Carrots . . . quarter-inch apart. Rows . . . one-foot rows. [*He measures it off.*] One foot. [*He puts down a package and measures off.*] Beets. [*He puts down another package and measures again.*] Lettuce. [*He reads the package, puts it down.*] One foot—[*He breaks off as* BEN *appears at the right and moves slowly down to him.*] What a proposition, ts, ts. Terrific, terrific. 'Cause she's suffered, Ben, the woman has suffered. You understand me? A man can't go out the way he came in, Ben, a man has got to add up to something. You can't, you can't—[BEN *moves toward him as though to interrupt.*] You gotta consider, now. Don't answer so quick. Remember, it's a guaranteed twenty-thousand-dollar proposition. Now look, Ben, I want you to go through the ins and outs of this thing with me. I've got nobody to talk to, Ben, and the woman has suffered, you hear me?

BEN: [*Standing still, considering.*] What's the proposition?

WILLY: It's twenty thousand dollars on the barrelhead. Guaranteed, gilt-edged, you understand?

BEN: You don't want to make a fool of yourself. They might not honor the policy.

WILLY: How can they dare refuse? Didn't I work like a coolie to meet every premium on the nose? And now they don't pay off! Impossible!

BEN: It's called a cowardly thing, William.

WILLY: Why? Does it take more guts to stand here the rest of my life ringing up a zero?

BEN: [*Yielding.*] That's a point, William. [*He moves, thinking, turns.*] And twenty thousand—that *is* something one can feel with the hand, it is there.

WILLY: [*Now assured, with rising power.*] Oh, Ben, that's the whole beauty of it! I see it like a diamond, shining in the dark, hard and rough, that I can pick up and touch in my hand. Not like—like an appointment! This would not be another damned-fool appointment, Ben, and it changes all the aspects. Because he thinks I'm nothing, see, and so he spites me. But the funeral—[*Straightening up.*] Ben, that funeral will be massive! They'll come from Maine, Massachusetts, Vermont, New Hampshire! All the old-timers with the strange license plates—that boy will be thunder-struck, Ben, because he never realized—I am known! Rhode Island, New York, New Jersey—I am known, Ben, and he'll see it with his eyes once and for all. He'll see what I am, Ben! He's in for a shock, that boy!

BEN: [*Coming down to the edge of the garden.*] He'll call you a coward.

WILLY: [*Suddenly fearful.*] No, that would be terrible.

BEN: Yes. And a damned fool.

WILLY: No, no, he mustn't, I won't have that! [*He is broken and desperate.*]

BEN: He'll hate you, William.

[*The gay music of the Boys is heard.*]

WILLY: Oh, Ben, how do we get back to all the great times? Used to be so full of light, and comradeship, the sleigh-riding in winter, and the ruddiness on his cheeks. And always some kind of good news coming up, always something nice coming up ahead. And never even let me carry the valises in the house, and simonizing, simonizing that little red car! Why, why can't I give him something and not have him hate me?

BEN: Let me think about it. [*He glances at his watch.*] I still have a little time. Remarkable proposition, but you've got to be sure you're not making a fool of yourself.

[BEN *drifts off upstage and goes out of sight.* BIFF *comes down from the left.*]

WILLY: [*Suddenly conscious of* BIFF, *turns and looks up at him, then begins picking up the packages of seeds in confusion.*] Where the hell is that seed? [*Indignantly.*] You can't see nothing out here! They boxed in the whole goddam neighborhood!

BIFF: There are people all around here. Don't you realize that?

WILLY: I'm busy. Don't bother me.

BIFF: [*Taking the hoe from* WILLY.] I'm saying good-by to you, Pop. [WILLY *looks at him, silent, unable to move.*] I'm not coming back any more.

WILLY: You're not going to see Oliver tomorrow?

BIFF: I've got no appointment, Dad.

WILLY: He put his arm around you, and you've got no appointment?

BIFF: Pop, get this now, will you? Everytime I've left it's been a fight that sent me out of here. Today I realized something about myself and I tried to explain it to you and I—I think I'm just not smart enough to make any sense out of it for you. To hell with whose fault it is or anything like that. [*He takes* WILLY*'s arm.*] Let's just wrap it up, heh? Come on in, we'll tell Mom. [*He gently tries to pull* WILLY *to left.*]

WILLY: [*Frozen, immobile, with guilt in his voice.*] No, I don't want to see her.

BIFF: Come on! [*He pulls again, and* WILLY *tries to pull away.*]

WILLY: [*Highly nervous.*] No, no, I don't want to see her.

BIFF: [*Tries to look into* WILLY*'s face, as if to find the answer there.*] Why don't you want to see her?

WILLY: [*More harshly now.*] Don't bother me, will you?

BIFF: What do you mean, you don't want to see her? You don't want them calling you yellow, do you? This isn't your fault; it's me, I'm a bum. Now come inside! [WILLY *strains to get away.*] Did you hear what I said to you?

[WILLY *pulls away and quickly goes by himself into the house.* BIFF *follows.*]

LINDA: [*To* WILLY.] Did you plant, dear?

BIFF: [*At the door, to* LINDA.] All right, we had it out. I'm going and I'm not writing any more.

LINDA: [*Going to* WILLY *in the kitchen.*] I think that's the best way, dear. 'Cause there's no use drawing it out, you'll just never get along.

[WILLY *doesn't respond.*]

BIFF: People ask where I am and what I'm doing, you don't know, and you don't care. That way it'll be off your mind and you can start brightening up again. All right? That clears it, doesn't it? [WILLY *is silent, and* BIFF *goes to him.*] You gonna wish me luck, scout? [*He extends his hand.*] What do you say?

LINDA: Shake his hand, Willy.

WILLY: [*Turning to her, seething with hurt.*] There's no necessity to mention the pen at all, y'know.

BIFF: [*Gently.*] I've got no appointment, Dad.

WILLY: [*Erupting fiercely.*] He put his arm around . . . ?

BIFF: Dad, you're never going to see what I am, so what's the use of arguing? If I strike oil I'll send you a check. Meantime forget I'm alive.

WILLY: [*To* LINDA.] Spite, see?

BIFF: Shake hands, Dad.

WILLY: Not my hand.

BIFF: I was hoping not to go this way.

WILLY: Well, this is the way you're going. Good-by. [BIFF *looks at him a moment, then turns sharply and goes to the stairs.* WILLY *stops him with*—] May you rot in hell if you leave this house!

BIFF: [*Turning.*] Exactly what is it that you want from me?

WILLY: I want you to know, on the train, in the mountains, in the valleys, wherever you go, that you cut down your life for spite!

BIFF: No, no.

WILLY: Spite, spite, is the word of your undoing! And when you're down and out, remember what did it. When you're rotting somewhere beside the railroad tracks, remember, and don't you dare blame it on me!

BIFF: I'm not blaming it on you!

WILLY: I won't take the rap for this, you hear?

[HAPPY *comes down the stairs and stands on the bottom step, watching.*]

BIFF: That's just what I'm telling you!

WILLY: [*Sinking into a chair at the table, with full accusation.*] You're trying to put a knife in me—don't think I don't know what you're doing!

BIFF: All right, phony! Then let's lay it on the line. [*He whips the rubber tube out of his pocket and puts it on the table.*]

HAPPY: You crazy—

LINDA: Biff!

[*She moves to grab the hose, but* BIFF *holds it down with his hand.*]

BIFF: Leave it there! Don't move it!

WILLY: [*Not looking at it.*] What is that?

BIFF: You know goddam well what that is.

WILLY: [*Caged, wanting to escape.*] I never saw that.

BIFF: You saw it. The mice didn't bring it into the cellar! What is this supposed to do, make a hero out of you? This supposed to make me sorry for you?

WILLY: Never heard of it.

BIFF: There'll be no pity for you, you hear it? No pity!

WILLY: [*To* LINDA.] You hear the spite!

BIFF: No, you're going to hear the truth—what you are and what I am!

LINDA: Stop it!

WILLY: Spite!

HAPPY: [*Coming down toward* BIFF.] You cut it now!

BIFF: [*To* HAPPY.] The man don't know who we are! The man is gonna know! [*To* WILLY.] We never told the truth for ten minutes in this house!

HAPPY: We always told the truth!

BIFF: [*Turning on him.*] You big blow, are you the assistant buyer? You're one of the two assistants to the assistant, aren't you?

HAPPY: Well, I'm practically—

BIFF: You're practically full of it! We all are! And I'm through with it. [*To* WILLY.] Now hear this, Willy, this is me.

WILLY: I know you!

BIFF: You know why I had no address for three months? I stole a suit in Kansas City and I was in jail. [*To* LINDA, *who is sobbing.*] Stop crying. I'm through with it.

[LINDA *turns away from them, her hands covering her face.*]

WILLY: I suppose that's my fault!

BIFF: I stole myself out of every good job since high school!

WILLY: And whose fault is that?

BIFF: And I never got anywhere because you blew me so full of hot air I could never stand taking orders from anybody! That's whose fault it is!

WILLY: I hear that!

LINDA: Don't, Biff!

BIFF: It's goddam time you heard that! I had to be boss big shot in two weeks, and I'm through with it!

WILLY: Then hang yourself! For spite, hang yourself!

BIFF: No! Nobody's hanging himself, Willy! I ran down eleven flights with a pen in my hand today. And suddenly I stopped, you hear me? And in the middle of that office building, do you hear this? I stopped in the middle of that building and I saw—the sky. I saw the things that I love in this world. The work and the food and time to sit and smoke. And I looked at the pen and said to myself, what the hell am I grabbing this for? Why am I trying to become what I don't want to be? What am I doing in an office, making a contemptuous, begging fool of myself, when all I want is out there, waiting for me the minute I say I know who I am! Why can't I say that, Willy? [*He tries to make* WILLY *face him, but* WILLY *pulls away and moves to the left*.]

WILLY: [*With hatred, threateningly*.] The door of your life is wide open!

BIFF: Pop! I'm a dime a dozen, and so are you!

WILLY: [*Turning on him now in an uncontrolled outburst*.] I am not a dime a dozen! I am Willy Loman, and you are Biff Loman!

[BIFF *starts for* WILLY, *but is blocked by* HAPPY. *In his fury*, BIFF *seems on the verge of attacking his father*.]

BIFF: I am not a leader of men, Willy, and neither are you. You were never anything but a hard-working drummer who landed in the ash can like all the rest of them! I'm one dollar an hour, Willy! I tried seven states and couldn't raise it. A buck an hour! Do you gather my meaning? I'm not bringing home any prizes any more, and you're going to stop waiting for me to bring them home!

WILLY: [*Directly to* BIFF.] You vengeful, spiteful mut!

[BIFF *breaks from* HAPPY. WILLY, *in fright, starts up the stairs*. BIFF grabs him.]

BIFF: [*At the peak of his fury*.] Pop, I'm nothing! I'm nothing, Pop. Can't you understand that? There's no spite in it any more. I'm just what I am, that's all.

[BIFF's *fury has spent itself, and he breaks down, sobbing, holding on to* WILLY, *who dumbly fumbles for* BIFF's *face*.]

WILLY: [*Astonished*.] What're you doing? What're you doing? [*To* LINDA.] Why is he crying?

BIFF: [*Crying, broken*.] Will you let me go, for Christ's sake? Will you take that phony dream and burn it before something happens? [*Struggling to contain himself, he pulls away and moves to the stairs*.] I'll go in the morning. Put him—put him to bed. [*Exhausted*, BIFF *moves up the stairs to his room*.]

WILLY: [*After a long pause, astonished, elevated.*] Isn't that—isn't that remarkable? Biff—he likes me!

LINDA: He loves you, Willy!

HAPPY: [*Deeply moved.*] Always did, Pop.

WILLY: Oh, Biff! [*Staring wildly.*] He cried! Cried to me. [*He is choking with his love, and now cries out his promise.*] That boy—that boy is going to be magnificent!

[BEN *appears in the light just outside the kitchen.*]

BEN: Yes, outstanding, with twenty thousand behind him.

LINDA: [*Sensing the racing of his mind, fearfully, carefully.*] Now come to bed, Willy. It's all settled now.

WILLY: [*Finding it difficult not to rush out of the house.*] Yes, we'll sleep. Come on. Go to sleep, Hap.

BEN: And it does take a great kind of man to crack the jungle.

[*In accents of dread,* BEN's *idyllic music starts up.*]

HAPPY: [*His arm around* LINDA.] I'm getting married, Pop, don't forget it. I'm changing everything. I'm gonna run that department before the year is up. You'll see, Mom. [*He kisses her.*]

BEN: The jungle is dark but full of diamonds, Willy.

[WILLY *turns, moves, listening to* BEN.]

LINDA: Be good. You're both good boys, just act that way, that's all.

HAPPY: 'Night, Pop. [*He goes upstairs.*]

LINDA: [*To* WILLY.] Come, dear.

BEN: [*With greater force.*] One must go in to fetch a diamond out.

WILLY: [*To* LINDA, *as he moves slowly along the edge of the kitchen, toward the door.*] I just want to get settled down, Linda. Let me sit alone for a little.

LINDA: [*Almost uttering her fear.*] I want you upstairs.

WILLY: [*Taking her in his arms.*] In a few minutes, Linda. I couldn't sleep right now. Go on, you look awful tired. [*He kisses her.*]

BEN: Not like an appointment at all. A diamond is rough and hard to the touch.

WILLY: Go on now. I'll be right up.

LINDA: I think this is the only way, Willy.

WILLY: Sure, it's the best thing.

BEN: Best thing!

WILLY: The only way. Everything is gonna be—go on, kid, get to bed. You look so tired.

LINDA: Come right up.

WILLY: Two minutes. [LINDA *goes into the living-room, then reappears in her bedroom.* WILLY *moves just outside the kitchen door.*] Loves me. [*Wonderingly.*] Always loved me. Isn't that a remarkable thing? Ben, he'll worship me for it!

BEN: [*With promise.*] It's dark there, but full of diamonds.

WILLY: Can you imagine that magnificence with twenty thousand dollars in his pocket?

LINDA: [*Calling from her room.*] Willy! Come up!

WILLY: [*Calling into the kitchen.*] Yes! Yes. Coming! It's very smart, you realize that, don't you, sweetheart? Even Ben sees it. I gotta go, baby. 'By! 'By! [*Going over to* BEN, *almost dancing.*] Imagine? When the mail comes he'll be ahead of Bernard again!

BEN: A perfect proposition all around.

WILLY: Did you see how he cried to me? Oh, if I could kiss him, Ben!

BEN: Time, William, time!

WILLY: Oh, Ben, I always knew one way or another we were gonna make it, Biff and I!

BEN: [*Looking at his watch.*] The boat. We'll be late. [*He moves slowly off into the darkness.*]

WILLY: [*Elegiacally, turning to the house.*] Now when you kick off, boy, I want a seventy-yard boot, and get right down the field under the ball, and when you hit, hit low and hit hard, because it's important, boy. [*He swings around and faces the audience.*] There's all kinds of important people in the stands, and the first thing you know . . . [*Suddenly realizing he is alone.*] Ben! Ben, where do I . . . ? [*He makes a sudden movement of search.*] Ben, how do I . . . ?

LINDA: [*Calling.*] Willy, you coming up?

WILLY: [*Uttering a gasp of fear, whirling about as if to quiet her.*] Sh! [*He turns around as if to find his way; sounds, faces, voices, seem to be swarming in upon him and he flicks at them, crying.*] Sh! Sh! [*Suddenly music, faint and high, stops him. It rises in intensity, almost to an unbearable scream. He goes up and down on his toes, and rushes off around the house.*] Shhh!

LINDA: Willy? [*There is no answer.* LINDA *waits.* BIFF *gets up off his bed. He is still in his clothes.* HAPPY *sits up.* BIFF *stands listening.*] [*With real fear.*] Willy, answer me! Willy! [*There is the sound of a car starting and moving away at full speed.*] No!

BIFF: [*Rushing down the stairs.*] Pop!

[*As the car speeds off, the music crashes down in a frenzy of sound, which becomes the soft pulsation of a single cello string.* BIFF *slowly returns to his bedroom. He and* HAPPY *gravely don their jackets.* LINDA *slowly walks out of her room. The music has developed into a dead march. The leaves of day are appearing over everything.* CHARLEY *and* BERNARD, *somberly dressed, appear and knock on the kitchen door.* BIFF *and* HAPPY *slowly descend the stairs to the kitchen as* CHARLEY *and* BERNARD *enter. All stop a moment when* LINDA, *in clothes of mourning, bearing a little bunch of roses, comes through the draped doorway into the kitchen. She goes to* CHARLEY *and takes his arm. Now all move toward the audience, through the wall-line of the kitchen. At the limit of the apron,* LINDA *lays down the flowers, kneels, and sits back on her heels. All stare down at the grave.*]

REQUIEM

CHARLEY: It's getting dark, Linda.

[LINDA *doesn't react. She stares at the grave.*]

BIFF: How about it, Mom? Better get some rest, heh? They'll be closing the gate soon.

[LINDA *makes no move. Pause.*]

HAPPY: [*Deeply angered.*] He had no right to do that. There was no necessity for it. We would've helped him.

CHARLEY [*Grunting.*] Hmmm.

BIFF: Come along, Mom.

LINDA: Why didn't anybody come?

CHARLEY: It was a very nice funeral.

LINDA: But where are all the people he knew? Maybe they blame him.

CHARLEY: Naa. It's a rough world, Linda. They wouldn't blame him.

LINDA: I can't understand it. At this time especially. First time in thirty-five years we were just about free and clear. He only needed a little salary. He was even finished with the dentist.

CHARLEY: No man only needs a little salary.

LINDA: I can't understand it.

BIFF: There were a lot of nice days. When he'd come home from a trip; or on Sundays, making the stoop; finishing the cellar; putting on the new porch; when he built the extra bathroom; and put up the garage. You know something, Charley, there's more of him in that front stoop than in all the sales he ever made.

CHARLEY: Yeah. He was a happy man with a batch of cement.

LINDA: He was so wonderful with his hands.

BIFF: He had the wrong dreams. All, all, wrong.

HAPPY: [*Almost ready to fight* BIFF.] Don't say that!

BIFF: He never knew who he was.

CHARLEY: [*Stopping* HAPPY*'s movement and reply. To* BIFF.] Nobody dast blame this man. You don't understand: Willy was a salesman. And for a salesman, there is no rock bottom to the life. He don't put a bolt to a nut, he don't tell you the law or give you medicine. He's a man way out there in the blue, riding on a smile and a shoeshine. And when they start not smiling back—that's an earthquake. And then you get yourself a couple of spots on your hat, and you're finished. Nobody dast blame this man. A salesman is got to dream, boy. It comes with the territory.

BIFF: Charley, the man didn't know who he was.

HAPPY: [*Infuriated.*] Don't say that!

BIFF: Why don't you come with me, Happy?

HAPPY: I'm not licked that easily. I'm staying right in this city, and I'm gonna beat this racket! [*He looks at* BIFF, *his chin set.*] The Loman Brothers!

BIFF: I know who I am, kid.

HAPPY: All right, boy. I'm gonna show you and everybody else that Willy Loman did not die in vain. He had a good dream. It's the only dream you can have—to come out number-one-man. He fought it out here, and this is where I'm gonna win it for him.

BIFF: [*With a hopeless glance at* HAPPY, *bends toward his mother.*] Let's go, Mom.

LINDA: I'll be with you in a minute. Go on, Charley. [*He hesitates.*] I want to, just for a minute. I never had a chance to say good-by. [CHARLEY *moves away, followed by* HAPPY. BIFF *remains a slight distance up and left of* LINDA. *She sits there, summoning herself. The flute begins, not far away, playing behind her speech.*] Forgive me, dear. I can't cry. I don't know what it is, but I can't cry. I don't understand it. Why did you ever do that? Help me, Willy, I can't cry. It seems to me that you're just on another trip. I keep expecting you. Willy, dear, I can't cry. Why did you do it? I search and search and I search, and I can't understand it, Willy. I made the last payment on the house today. Today, dear. And there'll be nobody home. [*A sob rises in her throat.*] We're free and clear. [*Sobbing more fully, released.*] We're free. [BIFF *comes slowly toward her.*] We're free . . . We're free . . .

[BIFF *lifts her to her feet and moves out up right with her in his arms.* LINDA *sobs quietly.* BERNARD *and* CHARLEY *come together and follow them, followed by* HAPPY. *Only the music of the flute is left on the darkening stage as over the house the hard towers of the apartment buildings rise into sharp focus.*]

CURTAIN

1949

WILLIAM SHAKESPEARE

A Midsummer Night's Dream[1]

CHARACTERS

THESEUS, *Duke of Athens*
EGEUS, *father to Hermia*
LYSANDER, DEMETRIUS, *in love with Hermia*
PHILOSTRATE, *Master of the Revels to Theseus*
QUINCE, *a carpenter*
SNUG, *a joiner*
BOTTOM, *a weaver*
FLUTE, *a bellows-maker*
SNOUT, *a tinker*
STARVELING, *a tailor*
HIPPOLYTA, *Queen of the Amazons, betrothed to Theseus*
HERMIA, *daughter to Egeus, in love with Lysander*
HELENA, *in love with Demetrius*
OBERON, *King of the Fairies*
TITANIA, *Queen of the Fairies*
PUCK, *or Robin Goodfellow*
PEASEBLOSSOM, COBWEB, MOTH, MUSTARDSEED, *fairies.*
Other FAIRIES *attending their king and queen*
ATTENDANTS *on Theseus and Hippolyta*

SCENE: *Athens, and a wood near it*

ACT I

Scene 1[2]

Enter THESEUS, HIPPOLYTA, PHILOSTRATE, *with others.*

THESEUS: Now, fair Hippolyta, our nuptial hour
Draws on apace. Four happy days bring in
Another moon; but, O, methinks, how slow
This old moon wanes! She lingers[3] my desires,
Like to a step-dame or a dowager[4]
Long withering out a young man's revenue.
HIPPOLYTA: Four days will quickly steep themselves in night,
Four nights will quickly dream away the time;
And then the moon, like to a silver bow
New-bent in heaven, shall behold the night
Of our solemnities.
THESEUS: Go, Philostrate,
Stir up the Athenian youth to merriments,
Awake the pert and nimble spirit of mirth,
Turn melancholy forth to funerals;

1. Edited and annotated by David Bevington. 2. Location: Athens. The palace of Theseus. 3. Lengthens, protracts. 4. Widow with a jointure or dower. *Step-dame:* stepmother.

The pale companion is not for our pomp.[5] [*Exit* PHILOSTRATE.]
Hippolyta, I woo'd thee with my sword,[6]
And won thy love doing thee injuries;
But I will wed thee in another key,
With pomp, with triumph,[7] and with reveling.

[*Enter* EGEUS *and his daughter* HERMIA, *and* LYSANDER, *and* DEMETRIUS.]

EGEUS: Happy be Theseus, our renowned Duke!
THESEUS: Thanks, good Egeus. What's the news with thee?
EGEUS: Full of vexation come I, with complaint
Against my child, my daughter Hermia.
Stand forth, Demetrius. My noble lord,
This man hath my consent to marry her.
Stand forth, Lysander. And, my gracious Duke,
This man hath bewitch'd the bosom of my child.
Thou, thou, Lysander, thou hast given her rhymes
And interchang'd love-tokens with my child.
Thou hast by moonlight at her window sung
With feigning[8] voice verses of feigning love,
And stol'n the impression of her fantasy[9]
With bracelets of thy hair, rings, gauds, conceits,[1]
Knacks,[2] trifles, nosegays, sweetmeats—messengers
Of strong prevailment in unhardened youth.
With cunning hast thou filch'd my daughter's heart,
Turn'd her obedience, which is due to me,
To stubborn harshness. And, my gracious Duke,
Be it so she will not here before your Grace
Consent to marry with Demetrius,
I beg the ancient privilege of Athens:
As she is mine, I may dispose of her,
Which shall be either to this gentleman
Or to her death, according to our law
Immediately[3] provided in that case.
THESEUS: What say you, Hermia? Be advis'd, fair maid.
To you your father should be as a god—
One that compos'd your beauties, yea, and one
To whom you are but as a form in wax
By him imprinted and within his power
To leave the figure or disfigure[4] it.
Demetrius is a worthy gentleman.

5. Ceremonial magnificence. *Companion:* fellow. 6. I.e., in a military engagement against the Amazons, when Hippolyta was taken captive. 7. Public festivity. 8. (1) counterfeiting; (2) faining, desirous. 9. Made her fall in love with you (imprinting your image on her imagination) by stealthy and dishonest means. 1. Fanciful trifles. *Gauds:* playthings. 2. Knickknacks. 3. Expressly. 4. Obliterate. *Leave:* i.e., leave unaltered.

HERMIA: So is Lysander.
THESEUS: In himself he is;
But in this kind, wanting your father's voice,[5]
The other must be held the worthier.
HERMIA: I would my father look'd but with my eyes.
THESEUS: Rather your eyes must with his judgment look.
HERMIA: I do entreat your Grace to pardon me.
I know not by what power I am made bold,
Nor how it may concern[6] my modesty,
In such a presence here to plead my thoughts;
But I beseech your Grace that I may know
The worst that may befall me in this case,
If I refuse to wed Demetrius.
THESEUS: Either to die the death, or to abjure
Forever the society of men.
Therefore, fair Hermia, question your desires,
Know of your youth, examine well your blood,[7]
Whether, if you yield not to your father's choice,
You can endure the livery[8] of a nun,
For aye to be in shady cloister mew'd,[9]
To live a barren sister all your life,
Chanting faint hymns to the cold fruitless moon.
Thrice blessed they that master so their blood
To undergo such maiden pilgrimage;
But earthlier happy[1] is the rose distill'd,
Than that which withering on the virgin thorn
Grows, lives, and dies in single blessedness.
HERMIA: So will I grow, so live, so die, my lord,
Ere I will yield my virgin patent[2] up
Unto his lordship, whose unwished yoke
My soul consents not to give sovereignty.
THESEUS: Take time to pause; and, by the next new moon—
The sealing-day betwixt my love and me,
For everlasting bond of fellowship—
Upon that day either prepare to die
For disobedience to your father's will,
Or[3] else to wed Demetrius, as he would,
Or on Diana's altar to protest[4]
For aye austerity and single life.
DEMETRIUS: Relent, sweet Hermia, and, Lysander, yield
Thy crazed[5] title to my certain right.
LYSANDER: You have her father's love, Demetrius;

5. Approval. *Kind:* respect. *Wanting:* lacking. 6. Befit. 7. Passions. 8. Habit. 9. Shut in (said of a hawk, poultry, and so on). *Aye:* ever. 1. Happier as respects this world. 2. Privilege. 3. Either. 4. Vow. 5. Cracked, unsound.

Let me have Hermia's. Do you marry him.
EGEUS: Scornful Lysander! True, he hath my love,
And what is mine my love shall render him.
And she is mine, and all my right of her
I do estate unto[6] Demetrius.
LYSANDER: I am, my lord, as well deriv'd[7] as he,
As well possess'd;[8] my love is more than his;
My fortunes every way as fairly[9] rank'd,
If not with vantage,[1] as Demetrius';
And, which is more than all these boasts can be,
I am belov'd of beauteous Hermia.
Why should not I then prosecute my right?
Demetrius, I'll avouch it to his head,[2]
Made love to Nedar's daughter, Helena,
And won her soul; and she, sweet lady, dotes,
Devoutly dotes, dotes in idolatry,
Upon this spotted[3] and inconstant man.
THESEUS: I must confess that I have heard so much,
And with Demetrius thought to have spoke thereof;
But, being over-full of self-affairs,
My mind did lose it. But, Demetrius, come,
And come, Egeus, you shall go with me;
I have some private schooling for you both.
For you, fair Hermia, look you arm[4] yourself
To fit your fancies[5] to your father's will;
Or else the law of Athens yields you up—
Which by no means we may extenuate[6]—
To death, or to a vow of single life.
Come, my Hippolyta. What cheer, my love?
Demetrius and Egeus, go[7] along.
I must employ you in some business
Against[8] our nuptial, and confer with you
Of something nearly that[9] concerns yourselves.
EGEUS: With duty and desire we follow you.
[*Exeunt* (*all but* LYSANDER *and* HERMIA).]
LYSANDER: How now, my love, why is your cheek so pale?
How chance the roses there do fade so fast?
HERMIA: Belike[1] for want of rain, which I could well
Beteem[2] them from the tempest of my eyes.
LYSANDER: Ay me! For aught that I could ever read,
Could ever hear by tale or history,

6. Settle or bestow upon. 7. Descended; i.e., as well born. 8. Endowed with wealth. 9. Handsomely. 1. Superiority. 2. I.e., face. 3. I.e., morally stained. 4. Take care you prepare. 5. Likings, thought of love. 6. Mitigate. 7. I.e., come. 8. In preparation for. 9. That closely. 1. Very likely. 2. Grant, afford.

The course of true love never did run smooth;
But either it was different in blood[3]—
HERMIA: O cross,[4] too high to be enthrall'd to low!
LYSANDER: Or else misgraffed[5] in respect of years—
HERMIA: O spite, too old to be engag'd to young!
LYSANDER: Or else it stood upon the choice of friends[6]—
HERMIA: O hell, to choose love by another's eyes!
LYSANDER: Or, if there were a sympathy in choice,
War, death, or sickness did lay siege to it,
Making it momentany[7] as a sound,
Swift as a shadow, short as any dream,
Brief as the lightning in the collied[8] night,
That, in a spleen, unfolds[9] both heaven and earth,
And ere a man hath power to say "Behold!"
The jaws of darkness do devour it up.
So quick bright things come to confusion.[1]
HERMIA: If then true lovers have been ever cross'd,[2]
It stands as an edict in destiny.
Then let us teach our trial patience,[3]
Because it is a customary cross,
As due to love as thoughts and dreams and sighs,
Wishes and tears, poor fancy's[4] followers.
LYSANDER: A good persuasion. Therefore, hear me, Hermia.
I have a widow aunt, a dowager
Of great revenue, and she hath no child.
From Athens is her house remote seven leagues;
And she respects[5] me as her only son.
There, gentle Hermia, may I marry thee,
And to that place the sharp Athenian law
Cannot pursue us. If thou lovest me, then,
Steal forth thy father's house tomorrow night;
And in the wood, a league without the town,
Where I did meet thee once with Helena
To do observance to a morn of May,[6]
There will I stay for thee.
HERMIA: My good Lysander!
I swear to thee, by Cupid's strongest bow,
By his best arrow[7] with the golden head,
By the simplicity of Venus' doves,[8]

3. Hereditary station. 4. Vexation. 5. Ill grafted, badly matched. 6. Relatives. 7. Lasting but a moment. 8. Blackened (as with coal-dust), darkened. 9. Discloses. *In a spleen:* in a swift impulse, in a violent flash. 1. Ruin. *Quick:* quickly; or, perhaps, living, alive. 2. Always thwarted. 3. I.e., teach ourselves patience in this trial. 4. Amorous passion's. 5. Regards. 6. Perform the ceremonies of May Day. 7. (Cupid's best gold-pointed arrows were supposed to induce love, his blunt leaden arrows aversion.) 8. I.e., those that drew Venus's chariot. *Simplicity:* innocence.

By that which knitteth souls and prospers loves,
And by that fire which burn'd the Carthage queen,
When the false Troyan[9] under sail was seen,
By all the vows that ever men have broke,
In number more than ever women spoke,
In that same place thou hast appointed me
Tomorrow truly will I meet with thee.

LYSANDER: Keep promise, love. Look, here comes Helena.

[*Enter* HELENA.]

HERMIA: God speed fair[1] Helena, whither away?

HELENA: Call you me fair? That fair again unsay.
Demetrius loves your fair. O happy fair![2]
Your eyes are lodestars, and your tongue's sweet air[3]
More tuneable[4] than lark to shepherd's ear
When wheat is green, when hawthorn buds appear.
Sickness is catching. O, were favor[5] so,
Yours would I catch, fair Hermia, ere I go;
My ear should catch your voice, my eye your eye,
My tongue should catch your tongue's sweet melody.
Were the world mine, Demetrius being bated,[6]
The rest I'd give to be to you translated.[7]
O, teach me how you look, and with what art
You sway the motion[8] of Demetrius' heart.

HERMIA: I frown upon him, yet he loves me still.

HELENA: O that your frowns would teach my smiles such skill!

HERMIA: I give him curses, yet he gives me love.

HELENA: O that my prayers could such affection move![9]

HERMIA: The more I hate, the more he follows me.

HELENA: The more I love, the more he hateth me.

HERMIA: His folly, Helena, is no fault of mine.

HELENA: None, but your beauty. Would that fault were mine!

HERMIA: Take comfort. He no more shall see my face.
Lysander and myself will fly this place.
Before the time I did Lysander see,
Seem'd Athens as a paradise to me.
O, then, what graces in my love do dwell,
That he hath turn'd a heaven unto a hell!

LYSANDER: Helen, to you our minds we will unfold.
Tomorrow night, when Phoebe[1] doth behold
Her silver visage in the wat'ry glass,[2]

9. (Dido, Queen of Carthage, immolated herself on a funeral pyre after having been deserted by the Trojan hero Aeneas.) 1. Fair-complexioned (generally regarded by the Elizabethans as more beautiful than dark complexion). 2. Lucky fair one. *Fair:* beauty (even though Hermia is dark-complexioned). 3. Music. *Lodestars:* guiding stars. 4. Tuneful, melodious. 5. Appearance, looks. 6. Excepted. 7. Transformed. 8. Impulse. 9. Arouse. *Affection:* passion. 1. Diana, the moon. 2. Mirror.

Decking with liquid pearl the bladed grass,
A time that lovers' flights doth still[3] conceal,
Through Athens' gates have we devis'd to steal.
HERMIA: And in the wood, where often you and I
Upon faint[4] primrose beds were wont to lie,
Emptying our bosoms of their counsel[5] sweet,
There my Lysander and myself shall meet;
And thence from Athens turn away our eyes,
To seek new friends and stranger companies.
Farewell, sweet playfellow. Pray thou for us,
And good luck grant thee thy Demetrius!
Keep word, Lysander. We must starve our sight
From lovers' food till morrow deep midnight. [*Exit.*]
LYSANDER: I will, my Hermia.
Helena, adieu.
As you on him, Demetrius dote on you! [*Exit.*]
HELENA: How happy some o'er other some can be![6]
Through Athens I am thought as fair as she.
But what of that? Demetrius thinks not so;
He will not know what all but he do know.
And as he errs, doting on Hermia's eyes,
So I, admiring[7] of his qualities.
Things base and vile, holding no quantity,[8]
Love can transpose to form and dignity.
Love looks not with the eyes, but with the mind,
And therefore is wing'd Cupid painted blind.
Nor hath Love's mind of any judgment taste;[9]
Wings, and no eyes, figure[1] unheedy haste.
And therefore is Love said to be a child,
Because in choice he is so oft beguil'd.
As waggish boys in game[2] themselves forswear,
So the boy Love is perjur'd everywhere.
For ere Demetrius look'd on Hermia's eyne,[3]
He hail'd down oaths that he was only mine;
And when this hail some heat from Hermia felt,
So he dissolv'd, and show'rs of oaths did melt.
I will go tell him of fair Hermia's flight.
Then to the wood will he tomorrow night
Pursue her; and for this intelligence[4]
If I have thanks, it is a dear expense.[5]
But herein mean I to enrich my pain,
To have his sight thither and back again. [*Exit.*]

3. Always. 4. Pale. 5. Secret thought. 6. Can be in comparison to some others. 7. Wondering at. 8. I.e., unsubstantial, unshapely. 9. I.e., nor has Love, which dwells in the fancy or imagination, any taste or least bit of judgment or reason. 1. Are a symbol of. 2. Sport, jest. 3. Eyes (old form of plural). 4. Information. 5. I.e., a trouble worth taking. *Dear:* costly.

SCENE 2[6]

Enter QUINCE *the Carpenter, and* SNUG *the Joiner, and* BOTTOM *the Weaver, and* FLUTE *the Bellows Mender, and* SNOUT *the Tinker, and* STARVELING *the Tailor.*

QUINCE: Is all our company here?

BOTTOM: You were best to call them generally,[7] man by man, according to the scrip.[8]

QUINCE: Here is the scroll of every man's name which is thought fit, through all Athens, to play in our interlude before the Duke and the Duchess on his wedding-day at night.

BOTTOM: First, good Peter Quince, say what the play treats on, then read the names of the actors, and so grow to[9] a point.

QUINCE: Marry,[1] our play is "The most lamentable comedy and most cruel death of Pyramus and Thisby."

BOTTOM: A very good piece of work, I assure you, and a merry. Now, good Peter Quince, call forth your actors by the scroll. Masters, spread yourselves.

QUINCE: Answer as I call you. Nick Bottom, the weaver.

BOTTOM: Ready. Name what part I am for, and proceed.

QUINCE: You, Nick Bottom, are set down for Pyramus.

BOTTOM: What is Pyramus? A lover, or a tyrant?

QUINCE: A lover, that kills himself most gallant for love.

BOTTOM: That will ask some tears in the true performing of it. If I do it, let the audience look to their eyes. I will move storms; I will condole[2] in some measure. To the rest—yet my chief humor[3] is for a tyrant. I could play Ercles rarely, or a part to tear a cat in, to make all split.[4]

> "The raging rocks
> And shivering shocks
> Shall break the locks
> Of prison gates;
> And Phibbus' car[5]
> Shall shine from far
> And make and mar
> The foolish Fates."

This was lofty! Now name the rest of the players. This is Ercles' vein, a tyrant's vein. A lover is more condoling.

QUINCE: Francis Flute, the bellows-mender.

FLUTE: Here, Peter Quince.

QUINCE: Flute, you must take Thisby on you.

FLUTE: What is Thisby? A wand'ring knight?

5

10

15

20

25

30

35

6. Location: Athens. Quince's house (?) 7. (Bottom's blunder for *individually*.) 8. Script, written list. 9. Come to. 1. (A mild oath, originally the name of the Virgin Mary.) 2. Lament, arouse pity. 3. Inclination, whim. 4. I.e., cause a stir, bring the house down. *Ercles*: Hercules (the tradition of ranting came from Seneca's *Hercules Furens*). *Tear a cat*: i.e., rant. 5. Phoebus', the sun-god's, chariot.

QUINCE: It is the lady that Pyramus must love.

FLUTE: Nay, faith, let not me play a woman. I have a beard coming.

QUINCE: That's all one.[6] You shall play it in a mask, and you may speak as small[7] as you will.

BOTTOM: An[8] I may hide my face, let me play Thisby too. I'll speak in a monstrous little voice, "Thisne, Thisne!" "Ah, Pyramus, my lover dear! Thy Thisby dear, and lady dear!"

QUINCE: No, no; you must play Pyramus; and, Flute, you Thisby.

BOTTOM: Well, proceed.

QUINCE: Robin Starveling, the tailor.

STARVELING: Here, Peter Quince.

QUINCE: Robin Starveling, you must play Thisby's mother. Tom Snout, the tinker.

SNOUT: Here, Peter Quince.

QUINCE: You, Pyramus' father; myself, Thisby's father; Snug, the joiner, you, the lion's part; and I hope here is a play fitted.

SNUG: Have you the lion's part written? Pray you, if it be, give it me, for I am slow of study.

QUINCE: You may do it extempore, for it is nothing but roaring.

BOTTOM: Let me play the lion too. I will roar that I will do any man's heart good to hear me. I will roar that I will make the Duke say, "Let him roar again, let him roar again."

QUINCE: An you should do it too terribly, you would fright the Duchess and the ladies, that they would shriek; and that were enough to hang us all.

ALL: That would hang us, every mother's son.

BOTTOM: I grant you, friends, if you should fright the ladies out of their wits, they would have no more discretion but to hang us; but I will aggravate[9] my voice so that I will roar[1] you as gently as any sucking dove; I will roar you an 'twere any nightingale.

QUINCE: You can play no part but Pyramus; for Pyramus is a sweet-fac'd man, a proper[2] man as one shall see in a summer's day, a most lovely gentleman-like man. Therefore you must needs play Pyramus.

BOTTOM: Well, I will undertake it. What beard were I best to play it in?

QUINCE: Why, what you will.

BOTTOM: I will discharge it in either your[3] straw-color beard, your orange-tawny beard, your purple-in-grain beard, or your French-crown-color[4] beard, your perfect yellow.

QUINCE: Some of your French crowns[5] have no hair at all, and then you will play barefac'd. But, masters, here are your parts. [*He distributes parts.*] And I am to entreat you, request you, and desire you, to con[6] them by tomorrow night; and meet me in the palace wood, a mile without the town, by moonlight. There will we rehearse; for if we meet in the city, we shall be dogg'd

6. It makes no difference. 7. High-pitched. 8. If. 9. (Bottom's blunder for *diminish.*)
1. I.e., roar for you. 2. Handsome. 3. I.e., you know the kind I mean. *Discharge:* perform. 4. I.e., color of a French crown, a gold coin. *Purple-in-grain:* dyed a very deep red (from *grain*, the name applied to the dried insect used to make the dye). 5. Heads bald from syphilis, the "French disease." 6. Learn by heart.

with company, and our devices[7] known. In the meantime I will draw a bill[8] of properties, such as our play wants. I pray you, fail me not.

BOTTOM: We will meet, and there we may rehearse most obscenely[9] and courageously. Take pains, be perfect;[1] adieu.

QUINCE: At the Duke's oak we meet.

BOTTOM: Enough. Hold, or cut bow-strings.[2] [*Exeunt.*]

ACT II

SCENE 1[3]

Enter a FAIRY *at one door, and Robin Goodfellow* (PUCK) *at another.*

PUCK: How now, spirit! Whither wander you?

FAIRY: Over hill, over dale,
Thorough bush, thorough[4] brier,
Over park, over pale,[5]
Thorough flood, thorough fire,
I do wander every where,
Swifter than the moon's sphere;
And I serve the Fairy Queen,
To dew her orbs[6] upon the green.
The cowslips tall her pensioners[7] be.
In their gold coats spots you see;
Those be rubies, fairy favors,[8]
In those freckles live their savors.[9]
I must go seek some dewdrops here
And hang a pearl in every cowslip's ear.
Farewell, thou lob[1] of spirits; I'll be gone.
Our Queen and all her elves come here anon.[2]

PUCK: The King doth keep his revels here tonight.
Take heed the Queen come not within his sight.
For Oberon is passing fell and wrath,[3]
Because that she as her attendant hath
A lovely boy, stolen from an Indian king;
She never had so sweet a changeling.[4]
And jealous Oberon would have the child
Knight of his train, to trace[5] the forests wild.
But she perforce[6] withholds the loved boy,

7. Plans. 8. List. 9. (An unintentionally funny blunder, whatever Bottom meant to say.) 1. I.e., letter-perfect in memorizing your parts. 2. (An archer's expression not definitely explained, but probably meaning here "keep your promises, or give up the play.") 3. Location: A wood near Athens. 4. Through. 5. Enclosure. 6. Circles; i.e., fairy rings. 7. Retainers, members of the royal bodyguard. 8. Love tokens. 9. Sweet smells. 1. Country bumpkin. 2. At once. 3. Wrathful. *Fell:* exceedingly angry. 4. Child exchanged for another by the fairies. 5. Range through. 6. Forcibly.

Crowns him with flowers and makes him all her joy.
And now they never meet in grove or green,
By fountain[7] clear, or spangled starlight sheen,
But they do square,[8] that all their elves for fear
Creep into acorn-cups and hide them there.

FAIRY: Either I mistake your shape and making quite,
Or else you are that shrewd and knavish sprite[9]
Call'd Robin Goodfellow. Are not you he
That frights the maidens of the villagery,
Skim milk, and sometimes labor in the quern,[1]
And bootless[2] make the breathless huswife churn,
And sometime make the drink to bear no barm,[3]
Mislead night-wanderers, laughing at their harm?
Those that Hobgoblin call you and sweet Puck,
You do their work, and they shall have good luck.
Are you not he?

PUCK: Thou speakest aright;
I am that merry wanderer of the night.
I jest to Oberon and make him smile
When I a fat and bean-fed horse beguile,
Neighing in likeness of a filly foal;
And sometime lurk I in a gossip's[4] bowl,
In very likeness of a roasted crab,[5]
And when she drinks, against her lips I bob
And on her withered dewlap[6] pour the ale.
The wisest aunt,[7] telling the saddest[7] tale,
Sometime for three-foot stool mistaketh me;
Then slip I from her bum, down topples she,
And "tailor"[8] cries, and falls into a cough;
And then the whole quire[9] hold their hips and laugh,
And waxen in their mirth and neeze[1] and swear
A merrier hour was never wasted there.
But, room, fairy! Here comes Oberon.

FAIRY: And here my mistress. Would that he were gone!

[*Enter* OBERON *the King of Fairies at one door, with his train; and* TITANIA *the Queen at another, with hers.*]

OBERON: Ill met by moonlight, proud Titania.

TITANIA: What, jealous Oberon? Fairies, skip hence.
I have forsworn his bed and company.

OBERON: Tarry, rash wanton.[2] Am not I thy lord?

7. Spring. 8. Quarrel 9. Spirit. *Shrewd:* mischievous. 1. Handmill. 2. In vain. 3. Yeast, head on the ale. 4. Old woman's. 5. Crab apple. 6. Loose skin on neck. 7. Most serious. *Aunt:* old woman. 8. (Possibly because she ends up sitting cross-legged on the floor, looking like a tailor.) 9. Company. 1. Sneeze. *Waxen:* increase. 2. Head-strong creature.

TITANIA: Then I must be thy lady; but I know
When thou hast stolen away from fairy land,
And in the shape of Corin[3] sat all day,
Playing on pipes of corn[4] and versing love
To amorous Phillida. Why art thou here,
Come from the farthest steep[5] of India,
But that, forsooth, the bouncing Amazon,
Your buskin'd[6] mistress and your warrior love,
To Theseus must be wedded, and you come
To give their bed joy and prosperity.
OBERON: How canst thou thus for shame, Titania,
Glance at my credit with Hippolyta,[7]
Knowing I know thy love to Theseus?
Didst not thou lead him through the glimmering night
From Perigenia,[8] whom he ravished?
And make him with fair Aegles[9] break his faith,
With Ariadne and Antiopa?[1]
TITANIA: These are the forgeries of jealousy;
And never, since the middle summer's spring,[2]
Met we on hill, in dale, forest, or mead,
By paved[3] fountain or by rushy[3] brook,
Or in the beached margent[4] of the sea,
To dance our ringlets[5] to the whistling wind,
But with thy brawls thou hast disturb'd our sport.
Therefore the winds, piping to us in vain,
As in revenge, have suck'd up from the sea
Contagious[6] fogs; which falling in the land
Hath every pelting[7] river made so proud
That they have overborne their continents.[8]
The ox hath therefore stretch'd his yoke in vain,
The ploughman lost his sweat, and the green corn[9]
Hath rotted ere his youth attain'd a beard;
The fold[1] stands empty in the drowned field,
And crows are fatted with the murrion[2] flock;

3. Corin and Phillida are conventional names of pastoral lovers. 4. (Here, oat stalks.) 5. Mountain range. 6. Wearing half-boots called buskins. 7. Make insinuations about my favored relationship with Hippolyta. 8. I.e., Perigouna, one of Theseus' conquests. (This and the following women are named in Thomas North's translation of Plutarch's *Life of Theseus*.) 9. I.e., Aegle, for whom Theseus deserted Ariadne according to some accounts. 1. Queen of the Amazons and wife of Theseus; elsewhere identified with Hippolyta, but here thought of as a separate woman. *Ariadne:* the daughter of Minos, King of Crete, who helped Theseus to escape the labyrinth after killing the Minotaur; later she was abandoned by Theseus. 2. Beginning of midsummer. 3. Bordered with rushes. *Paved:* with pebbled bottom. 4. Edge, border. *In:* on. 5. Dances in a ring. (See *orbs* in I.9.) 6. Noxious. 7. Paltry; or, striking, moving forcefully. 8. Banks that contain them. 9. Grain of any kind. 1. Pen for sheep or cattle. 2. Having died of the murrain, plague.

The nine men's morris[3] is fill'd up with mud,
And the quaint mazes in the wanton[4] green
For lack of tread are undistinguishable.
The human mortals want their winter[5] here;
No night is now with hymn or carol bless'd.
Therefore[6] the moon, the governess of floods,
Pale in her anger, washes all the air,
That rheumatic[7] diseases do abound.
And thorough this distemperature[8] we see
The seasons alter: hoary-headed frosts
Fall in the fresh lap of the crimson rose,
And on old Hiems'[9] thin and icy crown
An odorous chaplet of sweet summer buds
Is, as in mockery, set. The spring, the summer,
The childing[1] autumn, angry winter, change
Their wonted liveries, and the mazed[2] world,
By their increase,[3] now knows not which is which.
And this same progeny of evils comes
From our debate,[4] from our dissension;
We are their parents and original.[5]

OBERON: Do you amend it then; it lies in you.
Why should Titania cross her Oberon?
I do but beg a little changeling boy,
To be my henchman.[6]

TITANIA: Set your heart at rest.
The fairy land buys not the child of me.
His mother was a vot'ress of my order,
And, in the spiced Indian air, by night,
Full often hath she gossip'd by my side,
And sat with me on Neptune's yellow sands,
Marking th' embarked traders on the flood,[7]
When we have laugh'd to see the sails conceive
And grow big-bellied with the wanton[8] wind;
Which she, with pretty and with swimming gait,
Following—her womb then rich with my young squire—
Would imitate, and sail upon the land
To fetch me trifles, and return again,
As from a voyage, rich with merchandise.

3. I.e., portion of the village green marked out in a square for a game played with nine pebbles or pegs. 4. Luxuriant. *Mazes:* i.e., intricate paths marked out on the village green to be followed rapidly on foot as a kind of contest. 5. I.e., regular winter season; or, proper observances of winter, such as the *hymn* or *carol* in the next line. *Want:* lack. 6. I.e., as a result of our quarrel. 7. Colds, flu, and other respiratory infections. 8. Disturbance in nature. 9. The winter god's. 1. Fruitful, pregnant. 2. Bewildered. *Liveries:* usual apparel. 3. Their yield, what they produce. 4. Quarrel. 5. Origin. 6. Attendant, page. 7. Flood tide. *Traders:* trading vessels. 8. Sportive.

But she, being mortal, of that boy did die;
And for her sake do I rear up her boy,
And for her sake I will not part with him.
OBERON: How long within this wood intend you stay?
TITANIA: Perchance till after Theseus' wedding-day.
If you will patiently dance in our round[9]
And see our moonlight revels, go with us;
If not, shun me, and I will spare[1] your haunts.
OBERON: Give me that boy, and I will go with thee.
TITANIA: Not for thy fairy kingdom. Fairies, away!
We shall chide downright, if I longer stay. [*Exeunt* TITANIA *with her train*.]
OBERON: Well, go thy way. Thou shalt not from[2] this grove
Till I torment thee for this injury.
My gentle Puck, come hither. Thou rememb'rest
Since[3] once I sat upon a promontory,
And heard a mermaid on a dolphin's back
Uttering such dulcet and harmonious breath[4]
That the rude sea grew civil at her song
And certain stars shot madly from their spheres,
To hear the sea-maid's music.
PUCK: I remember.
OBERON: That very time I saw, but thou couldst not,
Flying between the cold moon and the earth,
Cupid all[5] arm'd. A certain aim he took
At a fair vestal[6] throned by the west,
And loos'd his love-shaft smartly from his bow,
As[7] it should pierce a hundred thousand hearts;
But I might[8] see young Cupid's fiery shaft
Quench'd in the chaste beams of the wat'ry moon,
And the imperial vot'ress passed on,
In maiden meditation, fancy-free.[9]
Yet mark'd I where the bolt of Cupid fell:
It fell upon a little western flower,
Before milk-white, now purple with love's wound,
And maidens call it love-in-idleness.[1]
Fetch me that flow'r; the herb I showed thee once.
The juice of it on sleeping eyelids laid
Will make or man or[2] woman madly dote
Upon the next live creature that it sees.
Fetch me this herb, and be thou here again
Ere the leviathan[3] can swim a league.

9. Circular dance. 1. Shun. 2. Go from. 3. When. 4. Voice, song. 5. Fully. 6. Vestal virgin (contains a complimentary allusion to Queen Elizabeth as a votaress of Diana and probably refers to an actual entertainment in her honor at Elvetham in 1591). 7. As if. 8. Could. 9. Free of love's spell. 1. Pansy, heartsease. 2. Either . . . or. 3. Sea-monster, whale.

PUCK: I'll put a girdle round about the earth
In forty[4] minutes. [*Exit.*]
OBERON: Having once this juice,
I'll watch Titania when she is asleep,
And drop the liquor of it in her eyes.
The next thing then she waking looks upon,
Be it on lion, bear, or wolf, or bull,
On meddling monkey, or on busy ape,
She shall pursue it with the soul of love.
And ere I take this charm from off her sight,
As I can take it with another herb,
I'll make her render up her page to me.
But who comes here? I am invisible,
And I will overhear their conference.

[*Enter* DEMETRIUS, HELENA *following him.*]

DEMETRIUS: I love thee not, therefore pursue me not.
Where is Lysander and fair Hermia?
The one I'll slay, the other slayeth me.
Thou told'st me they were stol'n unto this wood;
And here am I, and wode[5] within this wood,
Because I cannot meet my Hermia.
Hence, get thee gone, and follow me no more.
HELENA: You draw me, you hard-hearted adamant;[6]
But yet you draw not iron, for my heart
Is true as steel. Leave[7] you your power to draw,
And I shall have no power to follow you.
DEMETRIUS: Do I entice you? Do I speak you fair?[8]
Or, rather, do I not in plainest truth
Tell you I do not nor I cannot love you?
HELENA: And even for that do I love you the more.
I am your spaniel; and, Demetrius,
The more you beat me, I will fawn on you.
Use me but as your spaniel, spurn me, strike me,
Neglect me, lose me; only give me leave,
Unworthy as I am, to follow you.
What worser place can I beg in your love—
And yet a place of high respect with me—
Than to be used as you use your dog?
DEMETRIUS: Tempt not too much the hatred of my spirit,
For I am sick when I do look on thee.
HELENA: And I am sick when I look not on you.

4. (Used indefinitely.) 5. Mad (pronounced *wood* and often spelled so). 6. Lodestone, magnet (with pun on *hard-hearted*, since adamant was also thought to be the hardest of all stones and was confused with the diamond). 7. Give up. 8. Courteously.

DEMETRIUS: You do impeach[9] your modesty too much
To leave the city and commit yourself
Into the hands of one that loves you not,
To trust the opportunity of night
And the ill counsel of a desert[1] place
With the rich worth of your virginity.
HELENA: Your virtue is my privilege. For that[2]
It is not night when I do see your face,
Therefore I think I am not in the night;
Nor doth this wood lack worlds of company,
For you in my respect[3] are all the world.
Then how can it be said I am alone,
When all the world is here to look on me?
DEMETRIUS: I'll run from thee and hide me in the brakes,[4]
And leave thee to the mercy of wild beasts.
HELENA: The wildest hath not such a heart as you.
Run when you will, the story shall be chang'd:
Apollo flies and Daphne holds the chase,[5]
The dove pursues the griffin, the mild hind[6]
Makes speed to catch the tiger—bootless[7] speed,
When cowardice pursues and valor flies.
DEMETRIUS: I will not stay thy questions.[8] Let me go!
Or if thou follow me, do not believe
But I shall do thee mischief in the wood.
HELENA: Ay, in the temple, in the town, the field,
You do me mischief. Fie, Demetrius!
Your wrongs do set a scandal on my sex.
We cannot fight for love, as men may do;
We should be woo'd and were not made to woo. [*Exit* DEMETRIUS.]
I'll follow thee and make a heaven of hell,
To die upon[9] the hand I love so well. [*Exit*.]
OBERON: Fare thee well, nymph. Ere he do leave this grove,
Thou shalt fly him and he shall seek thy love.

[*Enter* PUCK.]

Hast thou the flower there? Welcome, wanderer.
PUCK: Ay, there it is. [*Offers the flower*.]
OBERON: I pray thee, give it me.
I know a bank where the wild thyme blows,[1]
Where oxlips[2] and the nodding violet grows,

9. Call into question. 1. Deserted. 2. Because. *Virtue:* goodness or power to attract. *Privilege:* safeguard, warrant. 3. As far as I am concerned. 4. Thickets. 5. (In the ancient myth, Daphne fled from Apollo and was saved from rape by being transformed into a laurel tree; here it is the female who *holds the chase,* or pursues, instead of the male.) 6. Female deer. *Griffin:* a fabulous monster with the head of an eagle and the body of a lion. 7. Fruitless. 8. Talk or argument. *Stay:* wait for. 9. By. 1. Blooms. 2. Flowers resembling cowslip and primrose.

Quite over-canopied with luscious woodbine,[3]
With sweet musk-roses and with eglantine.[4]
There sleeps Titania sometime of the night,
Lull'd in these flowers with dances and delight;
And there the snake throws[5] her enamel'd skin,
Weed[6] wide enough to wrap a fairy in.
And with the juice of this I'll streak[7] her eyes,
And make her full of hateful fantasies.
Take thou some of it, and seek through this grove. [*Gives some love-juice.*]
A sweet Athenian lady is in love
With a disdainful youth. Anoint his eyes,
But do it when the next thing he espies
May be the lady. Thou shalt know the man
By the Athenian garments he hath on.
Effect it with some care, that he may prove
More fond on[8] her than she upon her love;
And look thou meet me ere the first cock crow.

PUCK: Fear not, my lord, your servant shall do so. [*Exeunt.*]

SCENE 2[9]

Enter TITANIA, *Queen of Fairies, with her train.*

TITANIA: Come, now a roundel[1] and a fairy song;
Then, for the third part of a minute, hence—
Some to kill cankers[2] in the musk-rose buds,
Some war with rere-mice[3] for their leathern wings,
To make my small elves coats, and some keep back
The clamorous owl, that nightly hoots and wonders
At our quaint[4] spirits. Sing me now asleep.
Then to your offices and let me rest.

[FAIRIES *sing.*]

[FIRST FAIRY:]

You spotted snakes with double[5] tongue,
Thorny hedgehogs, be not seen;
Newts[6] and blindworms, do no wrong,
Come not near our fairy queen.
[*Chorus.*] Philomel,[7] with melody
Sing in our sweet lullaby;

3. Honeysuckle. 4. Sweetbriar, a kind of rose. *Musk-rose:* a kind of large, sweet-scented rose. 5. Sloughs off, sheds. 6. Garment. 7. Anoint, touch gently. 8. Doting on. 9. Location: The wood. 1. Dance in a ring. 2. Cankerworms. 3. Bats. 4. Dainty. 5. Forked. 6. Water lizards (considered poisonous, as were *blindworms*—small snakes with tiny eyes—and spiders). 7. The nightingale (Philomela, daughter of King Pandion, was transformed into a nightingale, according to Ovid's *Metamorphoses* VI, after she had been raped by her sister

Lulla, lulla, lullaby, lulla, lulla, lullaby.
Never harm,
Nor spell nor charm,
Come our lovely lady nigh.
So, good night, with lullaby.

[FIRST FAIRY:]

Weaving spiders, come not here;
Hence, you long-legg'd spinners, hence!
Beetles black, approach not near;
Worm nor snail, do no offense.
[*Chorus.*] Philomel, with melody, etc.

[SECOND FAIRY:]

Hence, away! Now all is well.
One aloof stand sentinel.
[*Exeunt* FAIRIES. TITANIA *sleeps.*]

[*Enter* OBERON *and squeezes the flower on* TITANIA'*s eyelids.*]

OBERON: What thou seest when thou dost wake,
Do it for thy true-love take;
Love and languish for his sake.
Be it ounce,[8] or cat, or bear,
Pard,[9] or boar with bristled hair,
In thy eye that shall appear
When thou wak'st, it is thy dear.
Wake when some vile thing is near. [*Exit.*]

[*Enter* LYSANDER *and* HERMIA.]

LYSANDER: Fair love, you faint with wand'ring in the wood;
And to speak troth,[1] I have forgot our way.
We'll rest us, Hermia, if you think it good,
And tarry for the comfort of the day.
HERMIA: Be 't so, Lysander. Find you out a bed,
For I upon this bank will rest my head.
LYSANDER: One turf shall serve as pillow for us both,
One heart, one bed, two bosoms, and one troth.[2]
HERMIA: Nay, good Lysander; for my sake, my dear,
Lie further off yet, do not lie so near.
LYSANDER: O, take the sense, sweet, of my innocence![3]
Love takes the meaning in love's conference.[4]

Procne's husband, Tereus). 8. Lynx. 9. Leopard. 1. Truth. 2. Faith, troth-plight. 3. I.e., interpret my intention as innocent. 4. I.e., when lovers confer, love teaches each lover to interpret the others' meaning lovingly.

I mean, that my heart unto yours is knit
So that but one heart we can make of it;
Two bosoms interchained with an oath—
So then two bosoms and a single troth.
Then by your side no bed-room me deny,
For lying so, Hermia, I do not lie.[5]

HERMIA: Lysander riddles very prettily.
Now much beshrew[6] my manners and my pride
If Hermia meant to say Lysander lied.
But, gentle friend, for love and courtesy
Lie further off, in human[7] modesty;
Such separation as may well be said
Becomes a virtuous bachelor and a maid,
So far be distant; and, good night, sweet friend.
Thy love ne'er alter till thy sweet life end!

LYSANDER: Amen, amen, to that fair prayer, say I,
And then end life when I end loyalty!
Here is my bed. Sleep give thee all his rest!

HERMIA: With half that wish the wisher's eyes be press'd![8]

[*They sleep, separated by a short distance. Enter* PUCK.]

PUCK: Through the forest have I gone,
But Athenian found I none
On whose eyes I might approve[9]
This flower's force in stirring love.
Night and silence.—Who is here?
Weeds of Athens he doth wear.
This is he, my master said,
Despised the Athenian maid;
And here the maiden, sleeping sound,
On the dank and dirty ground.
Pretty soul! She durst not lie
Near this lack-love, this kill-courtesy.
Churl, upon thy eyes I throw
All the power this charm doth owe.[1] [*Applies the love-juice.*]
When thou wak'st, let love forbid
Sleep his seat on thy eyelid.
So awake when I am gone,
For I must now to Oberon. [*Exit.*]

[*Enter* DEMETRIUS *and* HELENA, *running.*]

HELENA: Stay, though thou kill me, sweet Demetrius.

DEMETRIUS: I charge thee, hence, and do not haunt me thus.

5. Tell a falsehood (with a riddling pun on *lie*, recline). 6. Curse (but mildly meant).
7. Courteous. 8. I.e., may we share your wish, so that your eyes too are *press'd*, closed, in sleep.
9. Test. 1. Own.

HELENA: O, wilt thou darkling[2] leave me? Do not so.
DEMETRIUS: Stay, on thy peril![3] I alone will go. [*Exit.*]
HELENA: O, I am out of breath in this fond[4] chase!
The more my prayer, the lesser is my grace.[5]
Happy is Hermia, wheresoe'er she lies,[6]
For she hath blessed and attractive eyes.
How came her eyes so bright? Not with salt tears;
If so, my eyes are oft'ner wash'd than hers.
No, no, I am as ugly as a bear;
For beasts that meet me run away for fear.
Therefore no marvel though Demetrius
Do, as a monster, fly my presence thus.
What wicked and dissembling glass of mine
Made me compare with Hermia's sphery eyne?[7]
But who is here? Lysander, on the ground?
Dead, or asleep? I see no blood, no wound.
Lysander, if you live, good sir, awake.
LYSANDER: [*Awaking.*] And run through fire I will for thy sweet sake.
Transparent[8] Helena! Nature shows art,
That through thy bosom makes me see thy heart.
Where is Demetrius? O, how fit a word
Is that vile name to perish on my sword!
HELENA: Do not say so, Lysander, say not so.
What though he love your Hermia? Lord, what though?
Yet Hermia still loves you. Then be content.
LYSANDER: Content with Hermia? No! I do repent
The tedious minutes I with her have spent.
Not Hermia but Helena I love.
Who will not change a raven for a dove?
The will of man is by his reason sway'd,
And reason says you are the worthier maid.
Things growing are not ripe until their season;
So I, being young, till now ripe[9] not to reason.
And touching now the point of human skill,[1]
Reason becomes the marshal to my will
And leads me to your eyes, where I o'erlook[2]
Love's stories written in love's richest book.
HELENA: Wherefore was I to this keen mockery born?
When at your hands did I deserve this scorn?
Is 't not enough, is 't not enough, young man,
That I did never, no, nor never can,
Deserve a sweet look from Demetrius' eye,

2. In the dark. 3. I.e., on pain of danger to you if you don't obey me and stay. 4. Doting. 5. The favor I obtain. 6. Dwells. 7. Eyes as bright as stars in their spheres. 8. (1) radiant; (2) able to be seen through. 9. (Am) not ripened. 1. Judgment. *Touching:* reaching. *Point:* summit. 2. Read.

But you must flout my insufficiency?
Good troth, you do me wrong, good sooth,[3] you do,
In such disdainful manner me to woo.
But fare you well. Perforce I must confess
I thought you lord of more true gentleness.[4]
O, that a lady, of[5] one man refus'd,
Should of another therefore be abus'd![6] [*Exit.*]

LYSANDER: She sees not Hermia. Hermia, sleep thou there,
And never mayst thou come Lysander near!
For as a surfeit of the sweetest things
The deepest loathing to the stomach brings,
Or as the heresies that men do leave
Are hated most of those they did deceive,
So thou, my surfeit and my heresy,
Of all be hated, but the most of me!
And, all my powers, address your love and might
To honor Helen and to be her knight! [*Exit.*]

HERMIA: [*Awaking.*] Help me, Lysander, help me! Do thy best
To pluck this crawling serpent from my breast!
Ay me, for pity! What a dream was here!
Lysander, look how I do quake with fear.
Methought a serpent eat[7] my heart away,
And you sat smiling at his cruel prey.[8]
Lysander! What, remov'd? Lysander! Lord!
What, out of hearing? Gone? No sound, no word?
Alack, where are you? Speak, an if you hear.
Speak, of all loves![9] I swoon almost with fear.
No? Then I well perceive you are not nigh.
Either death, or you, I'll find immediately.

[*Exit. Manet* TITANIA *lying asleep.*]

ACT III

SCENE 1[1]

Enter the Clowns (QUINCE, SNUG, BOTTOM, FLUTE, SNOUT, *and* STARVELING.)

BOTTOM: Are we all met?

QUINCE: Pat, pat; and here's a marvailes convenient place for our rehearsal. This green plot shall be our stage, this hawthorn brake our tiring-house,[2] and we will do it in action as we will do it before the Duke.

BOTTOM: Peter Quince?

3. I.e., indeed, truly. 4. Courtesy. *Lord of:* i.e., possessor of. 5. By. 6. Ill treated. 7. Ate (pronounced *et*). 8. Act of preying. 9. For all love's sake. 1. Location: Scene continues. 2. Attiring area, hence back stage. *Brake:* thicket.

QUINCE: What sayest thou, bully[3] Bottom?

BOTTOM: There are things in this comedy of Pyramus and Thisby that will never please. First, Pyramus must draw a sword to kill himself, which the ladies cannot abide. How answer you that?

SNOUT: By 'r lakin, a parlous[4] fear.

STARVELING: I believe we must leave the killing out, when all is done.[5]

BOTTOM: Not a whit. I have a device to make all well. Write me[6] a prologue; and let the prologue seem to say, we will do no harm with our swords and that Pyramus is not kill'd indeed; and, for the more better assurance, tell them that I Pyramus am not Pyramus, but Bottom the weaver. This will put them out of fear.

QUINCE: Well, we will have such a prologue, and it shall be written in eight and six.[7]

BOTTOM: No, make it two more; let it be written in eight and eight.

SNOUT: Will not the ladies be afeard of the lion?

STARVELING: I fear it, I promise you.

BOTTOM: Masters, you ought to consider with yourselves, to bring in—God shield us!—a lion among ladies,[8] is a most dreadful thing. For there is not a more fearful[9] wild-fowl than your lion living; and we ought to look to 't.

SNOUT: Therefore another prologue must tell he is not a lion.

BOTTOM: Nay, you must name his name, and half his face must be seen through the lion's neck, and he himself must speak through, saying thus, or to the same defect:[1] "Ladies"—or "Fair ladies—I would wish you"—or "I would request you"—or "I would entreat you—not to fear, not to tremble; my life for yours.[2] If you think I come hither as a lion, it were pity of my life.[3] No, I am no such thing; I am a man as other men are." And there indeed let him name his name, and tell them plainly he is Snug the joiner.

QUINCE: Well, it shall be so. But there is two hard things: that is, to bring the moonlight into a chamber; for, you know, Pyramus and Thisby meet by moonlight.

SNOUT: Doth the moon shine that night we play our play?

BOTTOM: A calendar, a calendar! Look in the almanac. Find out moonshine, find out moonshine. [*They consult an almanac.*]

QUINCE: Yes, it doth shine that night.

BOTTOM: Why then may you leave a casement of the great chamber window, where we play, open, and the moon may shine in at the casement.

QUINCE: Ay; or else one must come in with a bush of thorns and a lantern, and

3. I.e., worthy, jolly, fine fellow. 4. Perilous. *By 'r lakin:* by our ladykin; i.e., the Virgin Mary. 5. I.e., when all is said and done. 6. I.e., write at my suggestion. (*Me* is the ethical dative.) 7. Alternate lines of eight and six syllables, a common ballad measure. 8. (A contemporary pamphlet tells how at the christening in 1594 of Prince Henry, eldest son of King James VI of Scotland, later James I of England, a "blackmoor" instead of a lion drew the triumphal chariot since the lion's presence might have "brought some fear to the nearest.") 9. Fear-inspiring. 1. (Bottom's blunder for *effect*.) 2. I.e., I pledge my life to make your lives safe. 3. My life would be endangered.

say he comes to disfigure,[4] or to present,[5] the person of Moonshine. Then there is another thing: we must have a wall in the great chamber; for Pyramus and Thisby, says the story, did talk through the chink of a wall.

SNOUT: You can never bring in a wall. What say you, Bottom?

BOTTOM: Some man or other must present Wall. And let him have some plaster, or some loam, or some roughcast[6] about him, to signify wall; and let him hold his fingers thus, and through that cranny shall Pyramus and Thisby whisper.

QUINCE: If that may be, then all is well. Come, sit down, every mother's son, and rehearse your parts. Pyramus, you begin. When you have spoken your speech, enter into that brake, and so every one according to his cue.

[*Enter Robin* (PUCK).]

PUCK: What hempen home-spuns have we swagg'ring here,
So near the cradle of the Fairy Queen?
What, a play toward?[7] I'll be an auditor;
An actor too perhaps, if I see cause.

QUINCE: Speak, Pyramus. Thisby, stand forth.

BOTTOM: "Thisby, the flowers of odious savors sweet,"—

QUINCE: Odors, odors.

BOTTOM: —"Odors savors sweet;
So hath thy breath, my dearest Thisby dear.
But hark, a voice! Stay thou but here awhile,
And by and by I will to thee appear." [*Exit.*]

PUCK: A stranger Pyramus than e'er played here.[8] [*Exit.*]

FLUTE: Must I speak now?

QUINCE: Ay, marry, must you; for you must understand he goes but to see a noise that he heard, and is to come again.

FLUTE: "Most radiant Pyramus, most lily-white of hue,
Of color like the red rose on triumphant brier,
Most brisky juvenal and eke most lovely Jew,[9]
As true as truest horse that yet would never tire.
I'll meet thee, Pyramus, at Ninny's tomb."

QUINCE: "Ninus'[1] tomb," man. Why, you must not speak that yet. That you answer to Pyramus. You speak all your part at once, cues and all. Pyramus enter. Your cue is past; it is, "never tire."

FLUTE: O—"As true as truest horse, that yet would never tire."

4. (Quince's blunder for *prefigure.*) *Bush of thorns:* bundle of thornbush faggots (part of the accoutrements of the man in the moon, according to the popular notions of the time, along with his lantern and his dog). 5. Represent 6. A mixture of lime and gravel used to plaster the outside of buildings. 7. About to take place. 8. I.e., in this theatre (?). 9. (Probably an absurd repetition of the first syllable of *juvenal.*) *Briskly juvenal:* brisk youth. *Eke:* also. 1. Mythical founder of Nineveh (whose wife, Semiramis, was supposed to have built the walls of Babylon where the story of Pyramis and Thisbe (Thisby) takes place).

[*Enter* PUCK, *and* BOTTOM *as Pyramus with the ass head.*][2]

BOTTOM: "If I were fair,[3] Thisby, I were only thine."

QUINCE: O monstrous! O strange! We are haunted. Pray, masters! Fly, masters! Help! [*Exeunt* QUINCE, SNUG, FLUTE, SNOUT, *and* STARVELING.]

PUCK: I'll follow you, I'll lead you about a round,[4]
Through bog, through bush, through brake, through brier.
Sometime a horse I'll be, sometime a hound,
A hog, a headless bear, sometime a fire;[5]
And neigh, and bark, and grunt, and roar, and burn,
Like horse, hound, hog, bear, fire, at every turn. [*Exit.*]

BOTTOM: Why do they run away? This is a knavery of them to make me afeard.

[*Enter* SNOUT.]

SNOUT: O Bottom, thou art chang'd! what do I see on thee?

BOTTOM: What do you see? You see an ass-head of your own, do you? [*Exit* SNOUT.]

[*Enter* QUINCE.]

QUINCE: Bless thee, Bottom, bless thee! Thou art translated.[6] [*Exit.*]

BOTTOM: I see their knavery. This is to make an ass of me, to fright me, if they could. But I will not stir from this place, do what they can. I will walk up and down here, and I will sing, that they shall hear I am not afraid.

[*Sings.*]

The woosel cock[7] so black of hue,
With orange-tawny bill,
The throstle[8] with his note so true,
The wren with little quill[9]—

TITANIA: [*Awakening.*] What angel wakes me from my flow'ry bed?

[BOTTOM *Sings.*]

The finch, the sparrow, and the lark,
The plain-song[1] cuckoo grey,
Whose note full many a man doth mark,
And dares not answer nay[2]—

For, indeed, who would set his wit to so foolish a bird? Who would give a bird the lie,[3] though he cry "cuckoo" never so?[4]

TITANIA: I pray thee, gentle mortal, sing again.

2. (This stage direction, taken from the Folio, presumably refers to a standard stage property.) 3. Handsome. 4. Roundabout. 5. Will-o'-the-wisp. 6. Transformed. 7. Male ousel or ouzel, blackbird. 8. Song thrush. 9. (Literally, a reed pipe; hence, the bird's piping song.) 1. Singing a melody without variations. 2. I.e., cannot deny that he is a cuckold. 3. Call the bird a liar. 4. Ever so much.

Mine ear is much enamored of thy note;
So is mine eye enthralled to thy shape;
And thy fair virtue's force[5] perforce doth move me
On the first view to say, to swear, I love thee.

BOTTOM: Methinks, mistress, you should have little reason for that. And yet, to say the truth, reason and love keep little company together nowadays. The more the pity that some honest neighbors will not make them friends. Nay, I can gleek[6] upon occasion.

TITANIA: Thou art as wise as thou art beautiful.

BOTTOM: Not so, neither. But if I had wit enough to get out of this wood, I have enough to serve mine own turn.[7]

TITANIA: Out of this wood do not desire to go.
Thou shalt remain here, whether thou wilt or no.
I am a spirit of no common rate.[8]
The summer still doth tend upon my state;[9]
And I do love thee. Therefore, go with me.
I'll give thee fairies to attend on thee,
And they shall fetch thee jewels from the deep,
And sing while thou on pressed flowers dost sleep.
And I will purge thy mortal grossness so
That thou shalt like an airy spirit go.
Peaseblossom, Cobweb, Moth,[1] and Mustardseed!

[*Enter four Fairies* (PEASEBLOSSOM, COBWEB, MOTH, and MUSTARDSEED).]

PEASEBLOSSOM: Ready.
COBWEB: And I.
MOTH: And I.
MUSTARDSEED: And I.
ALL: Where shall we go?

TITANIA: Be kind and courteous to this gentleman.
Hop in his walks and gambol in his eyes;
Feed him with apricocks and dewberries,
With purple grapes, green figs, and mulberries;
The honey-bags steal from the humble-bees,
And for the night-tapers crop their waxen thighs
And light them at the fiery glow-worm's eyes,
To have my love to bed and to arise;
And pluck the wings from painted butterflies
To fan the moonbeams from his sleeping eyes.
Nod to him, elves, and do him courtesies.

5. The power of your beauty. 6. Scoff, jest. 7. Answer my purpose. 8. Rank, value. 9. Waits upon me as a part of my royal retinue. *Still:* ever, always. 1. I.e., mote, speck. (The two words *moth* and *mote* were pronounced alike.)

PEASEBLOSSOM: Hail, mortal!
COBWEB: Hail!
MOTH: Hail!
MUSTARDSEED: Hail!
BOTTOM: I cry your worships mercy, heartily. I beseech your worship's name.
COBWEB: Cobweb.
BOTTOM: I shall desire you of more acquaintance, good Master Cobweb. If I cut my finger, I shall make bold with you.[2] Your name, honest gentleman?
PEASEBLOSSOM: Peaseblossom.
BOTTOM: I pray you, commend me to Mistress Squash,[3] your mother, and to Master Peascod,[4] your father. Good Master Peaseblossom, I shall desire you of more acquaintance too. Your name, I beseech you, sir?
MUSTARDSEED: Mustardseed.
BOTTOM: Good Master Mustardseed, I know your patience well.[5] That same cowardly, giant-like ox-beef hath devour'd many a gentleman of your house. I promise you your kindred hath made my eyes water ere now. I desire you of more acquaintance, good Master Mustardseed.
TITANIA: Come wait upon him; lead him to my bower.
The moon methinks looks with a wat'ry eye;
And when she weeps,[6] weeps every little flower,
Lamenting some enforced[7] chastity.
Tie up my lover's tongue, bring him silently. [*Exeunt.*]

SCENE 2[8]

Enter OBERON, *King of Fairies.*

OBERON: I wonder if Titania be awak'd;
Then, what it was that next came in her eye,
Which she must dote on in extremity.

[*Enter Robin Goodfellow* (PUCK).]

Here comes my messenger. How now, mad spirit?
What night-rule now about this haunted[9] grove?
PUCK: My mistress with a monster is in love.
Near to her close[1] and consecrated bower,
While she was in her dull[2] and sleeping hour,
A crew of patches, rude mechanicals,[3]

2. (Cobwebs were used to stanch bleeding.) 3. Unripe pea pod. 4. Ripe pea pod. 5. What you have endured. 6. I.e., she causes dew. 7. Forced, violated; or, possibly, constrained (since Titania at this moment is hardly concerned about chastity). 8. Location: The wood. 9. Much frequented. *Night-rule:* diversion for the night. 1. Secret, private. 2. Drowsy. 3. Ignorant artisans. *Patches:* clowns, fools.

That work for bread upon Athenian stalls,
Were met together to rehearse a play
Intended for great Theseus' nuptial day.
The shallowest thick-skin of that barren sort,[4]
Who Pyramus presented,[5] in their sport
Forsook his scene[6] and ent'red in a brake.
When I did him at this advantage take,
An ass's nole[7] I fixed on his head.
Anon his Thisby must be answered,
And forth my mimic[8] comes. When they him spy,
As wild geese that the creeping fowler eye,
Or russet-pated choughs, many in sort,[9]
Rising and cawing at the gun's report,
Sever[1] themselves and madly sweep the sky,
So, at his sight, away his fellows fly;
And, at our stamp, here o'er and o'er one falls;
He murder cries and help from Athens calls.
Their sense thus weak, lost with their fears thus strong,
Made senseless things begin to do them wrong,
For briers and thorns at their apparel snatch;
Some, sleeves—some, hats; from yielders all things catch.
I led them on in this distracted fear
And left sweet Pyramus translated there,
When in that moment, so it came to pass,
Titania wak'd and straightway lov'd an ass.

OBERON: This falls out better than I could devise.
But hast thou yet latch'd[2] the Athenian's eyes
With the love-juice, as I did bid thee do?

PUCK: I took him sleeping—that is finish'd too—
And the Athenian woman by his side,
That, when he wak'd, of force[3] she must be ey'd.

[*Enter* DEMETRIUS *and* HERMIA.]

OBERON: Stand close. This is the same Athenian.

PUCK: This is the woman, but not this the man. [*They stand aside.*]

DEMETRIUS: O, why rebuke you him that loves you so?
Lay breath so bitter on your bitter foe.

HERMIA: Now I but chide; but I should use thee worse,
For thou, I fear, hast given me cause to curse.
If thou hast slain Lysander in his sleep,
Being o'er shoes in blood, plunge in the deep,

4. Stupid company or crew. 5. Acted. 6. Playing area. 7. Noddle, head. 8. Burlesque actor. 9. In a flock. *Russet-pated choughs:* grey-headed jackdaws. 1. I.e., scatter. 2. Moistened, anointed. 3. Perforce.

And kill me too.
The sun was not so true unto the day
As he to me. Would he have stolen away
From sleeping Hermia? I'll believe as soon
This whole[4] earth may be bor'd and that the moon
May through the center creep and so displease
Her brother's noontide with th' Antipodes.[5]
It cannot be but thou hast murd'red him;
So should a murderer look, so dead,[6] so grim.

DEMETRIUS: So should the murdered look, and so should I,
Pierc'd through the heart with your stern cruelty.
Yet you, the murderer, look as bright, as clear,
As yonder Venus in her glimmering sphere.

HERMIA: What's this to my Lysander? Where is he?
Ah, good Demetrius, wilt thou give him me?

DEMETRIUS: I had rather give his carcass to my hounds.

HERMIA: Out, dog! Out, cur! Thou driv'st me past the bounds
Of maiden's patience. Hast thou slain him, then?
Henceforth be never numb'red among men!
O, once tell true, tell true, even for my sake!
Durst thou have look'd upon him being awake,
And hast thou kill'd him sleeping? O brave touch![7]
Could not a worm,[8] an adder, do so much?
An adder did it; for with doubler tongue
Than thine, thou serpent, never adder stung.

DEMETRIUS: You spend your passion on a mispris'd mood.[9]
I am not guilty of Lysander's blood,
Nor is he dead, for aught that I can tell.

HERMIA: I pray thee, tell me then that he is well.

DEMETRIUS: An if I could, what should I get therefore?

HERMIA: A privilege never to see me more.
And from thy hated presence part I so.
See me no more, whether he be dead or no. [*Exit.*]

DEMETRIUS: There is no following her in this fierce vein.
Here therefore for a while I will remain.
So sorrow's heaviness doth heavier[1] grow
For debt that bankrupt[2] sleep doth sorrow owe;
Which now in some slight measure it will pay,
If for his tender here I make some stay.[3] [*They lie down and sleep.*]

4. Solid. 5. The people on the opposite side of the earth. *Her brother's:* i.e., the sun's. 6. Deadly, or deathly pale. 7. Noble exploit (said ironically). 8. Serpent. 9. Anger based on misconception. *Passion:* violent feelings. 1. (1) harder to bear; (2) more drowsy. 2. (Demetrius is saying that his sleepiness adds to the weariness caused by sorrow.) 3. I.e., to a small extent I will be able to "pay back" and hence find some relief from sorrow, if I pause here a while *(make some stay)* while sleep "tenders" or offers itself by way of paying the debt owed to sorrow.

OBERON: What hast thou done? Thou hast mistaken quite
And laid the love-juice on some true-love's sight.
Of thy misprision[4] must perforce ensue
Some true love turn'd and not a false turn'd true.
PUCK: Then fate o'er-rules, that, one man holding troth,[5]
A million fail, confounding[6] oath on oath.
OBERON: About the wood go swifter than the wind,
And Helena of Athens look thou find.
All fancy-sick she is and pale of cheer[7]
With sighs of love, that cost the fresh blood[8] dear.
By some illusion see thou bring her here.
I'll charm his eyes against she do appear.[9]
PUCK: I go, I go; look how I go,
Swifter than arrow from the Tartar's bow.[1] [*Exit.*]
OBERON: Flower of this purple dye,
Hit with Cupid's archery.
Sink in apple of his eye. [*Applies love-juice to* DEMETRIUS'*s eyes.*]
When his love he doth espy,
Let her shine as gloriously
As the Venus of the sky.
When thou wak'st, if she be by,
Beg of her for remedy.

[*Enter* PUCK.]

PUCK: Captain of our fairy band,
Helena is here at hand,
And the youth, mistook by me,
Pleading for a lover's fee.[2]
Shall we their fond pageant[3] see?
Lord, what fools these mortals be!
OBERON: Stand aside. The noise they make
Will cause Demetrius to awake.
PUCK: Then will two at once woo one;
That must needs be sport alone;[4]
And those things do best please me
That befall prepost'rously.[5] [*They stand aside.*]

[*Enter* LYSANDER *and* HELENA.]

4. Mistake. 5. Faith. 6. I.e., invalidating one oath with another. 7. Face. *Fancy-sick:* lovesick. 8. (An allusion to the physiological theory that each sigh costs the heart a drop of blood.) 9. In anticipation of her coming. 1. (Tartars were famed for their skill with the bow.) 2. Privilege, reward. 3. Foolish exhibition. 4. Unequaled. 5. Out of the natural order.

LYSANDER: Why should you think that I should woo in scorn?
Scorn and derision never come in tears.
Look when[6] I vow, I weep; and vows so born,
In their nativity all truth appears.[7]
How can these things in me seem scorn to you,
Bearing the badge[8] of faith, to prove them true?
HELENA: You do advance[9] your cunning more and more.
When truth kills truth,[1] O devilish-holy fray!
These vows are Hermia's. Will you give her o'er?
Weigh oath with oath, and you will nothing weigh.
Your vows to her and me, put in two scales,
Will even weigh, and both as light as tales.[2]
LYSANDER: I had no judgment when to her I swore.
HELENA: Nor none, in my mind, now you give her o'er.
LYSANDER: Demetrius loves her, and he loves not you.
DEMETRIUS: [*Awaking.*] O Helen, goddess, nymph, perfect, divine!
To what, my love, shall I compare thine eyne?
Crystal is muddy. O, how ripe in show[3]
Thy lips, those kissing cherries, tempting grow!
That pure congealed white, high Taurus'[4] snow,
Fann'd with the eastern wind, turns to a crow[5]
When thou hold'st up thy hand. O, let me kiss
This princess of pure white, this seal[6] of bliss!
HELENA: O spite! O hell! I see you all are bent
To set against me for your merriment.
If you were civil and knew courtesy,
You would not do me thus much injury.
Can you not hate me, as I know you do,
But you must join in souls to mock me too?
If you were men, as men you are in show,
You would not use a gentle lady so—
To vow, and swear, and superpraise my parts,[7]
When I am sure you hate me with your hearts.
You both are rivals, and love Hermia;
And now both rivals, to mock Helena.
A trim[8] exploit, a manly enterprise,
To conjure tears up in a poor maid's eyes
With your derision! None of noble sort

6. Whenever. 7. I.e., vows made by one who is weeping give evidence thereby of their sincerity. 8. Identifying device such as that worn on servants' livery. 9. Carry forward, display. 1. I.e., one of Lysander's vows must invalidate the other. 2. Lies. 3. Appearance. 4. A lofty mountain range in Asia Minor. 5. I.e., seems black by contrast. 6. Pledge. 7. Qualities. *Superpraise:* overpraise. 8. Pretty, fine (said ironically).

Would so offend a virgin and extort[9]
A poor soul's patience, all to make you sport.
LYSANDER: You are unkind, Demetrius. Be not so;
For you love Hermia; this you know I know.
And here, with all good will, with all my heart,
In Hermia's love I yield you up my part;
And yours of Helena to me bequeath,
Whom I do love and will do till my death.
HELENA: Never did mockers waste more idle breath.
DEMETRIUS: Lysander, keep thy Hermia; I will none.[1]
If e'er I lov'd her, all that love is gone.
My heart to her but as guest-wise sojourn'd,
And now to Helen is it home return'd,
There to remain.
LYSANDER: Helen, it is not so.
DEMETRIUS: Disparage not the faith thou dost not know,
Lest, to thy peril, thou aby[2] it dear.
Look, where thy love comes; yonder is thy dear.

[*Enter* HERMIA.]

HERMIA: Dark night, that from the eye his[3] function takes,
The ear more quick of apprehension makes;
Wherein it doth impair the seeing sense,
It pays the hearing double recompense.
Thou art not by mine eye, Lysander, found;
Mine ear, I thank it, brought me to thy sound.
But why unkindly didst thou leave me so?
LYSANDER: Why should he stay, whom love doth press to go?
HERMIA: What love could press Lysander from my side?
LYSANDER: Lysander's love, that would not let him bide,
Fair Helena, who more engilds the night
Than all yon fiery oes[4] and eyes of light.
Why seek'st thou me? Could not this make thee know,
The hate I bear thee made me leave thee so?
HERMIA: You speak not as you think. It cannot be.
HELENA: Lo, she is one of this confederacy!
Now I perceive they have conjoin'd all three
To fashion this false sport, in spite of me.[5]
Injurious Hermia, most ungrateful maid!
Have you conspir'd, have you with these contriv'd[6]
To bait[7] me with this foul derision?

9. Twist, torture. 1. I.e., wish none of her. 2. Pay for. 3. Its. 4. I.e., circles, orbs, stars. 5. To vex me. 6. Plotted. 7. Torment, as one sets on dogs to bait a bear.

Is all the counsel[8] that we two have shar'd,
The sisters' vows, the hours that we have spent,
When we have chid the hasty-footed time
For parting us—O, is all forgot?
All school-days friendship, childhood innocence?
We, Hermia, like two artificial[9] gods,
Have with our needles created both one flower,
Both on one sampler, sitting on one cushion,
Both warbling of one song, both in one key,
As if our hands, our sides, voices, and minds
Had been incorporate. So we grew together,
Like to a double cherry, seeming parted,
But yet an union in partition;
Two lovely[1] berries molded on one stem;
So, with two seeming bodies, but one heart;
Two of the first, like coats in heraldry,
Due but to one and crowned with one crest.[2]
And will you rent[3] our ancient love asunder,
To join with men in scorning your poor friend?
It is not friendly, 'tis not maidenly.
Our sex, as well as I, may chide you for it,
Though I alone do feel the injury.

HERMIA: I am amazed at your passionate words.
I scorn you not. It seems that you scorn me.

HELENA: Have you not set Lysander, as in scorn,
To follow me and praise my eyes and face?
And made your other love, Demetrius,
Who even but now did spurn me with his foot,
To call me goddess, nymph, divine and rare,
Precious, celestial? Wherefore speaks he this
To her he hates? And wherefore doth Lysander
Deny your love, so rich within his soul,
And tender[4] me, forsooth, affection,
But by your setting on, by your consent?
What though I be not so in grace[5] as you,
So hung upon with love, so fortunate,
But miserable most, to love unlov'd?
This you should pity rather than despise.

HERMIA: I understand not what you mean by this.

HELENA: Ay, do! Persever, counterfeit sad[6] looks,
Make mouths upon[7] me when I turn my back,

8. Confidential talk. 9. Skilled in art or creation. 1. Loving. 2. I.e., we have two separate bodies, just as a coat of arms in heraldry can be represented twice on a shield but surmounted by a single crest. 3. Rend. 4. Offer. 5. Favor. 6. Grave, serious. 7. I.e., makes mows, faces, grimaces at.

Wink each at other, hold the sweet jest up.
This sport, well carried,[8] shall be chronicled.
If you have any pity, grace, or manners,
You would not make me such an argument.[9]
But fare ye well. 'Tis partly my own fault,
Which death, or absence, soon shall remedy.

LYSANDER: Stay, gentle Helena; hear my excuse,
My love, my life, my soul, fair Helena!

HELENA: O excellent!

HERMIA: Sweet, do not scorn her so.

DEMETRIUS: If she cannot entreat,[1] I can compel.

LYSANDER: Thou canst compel no more than she entreat.
Thy threats have no more strength than her weak prayers.
Helen, I love thee, by my life, I do!
I swear by that which I will lose for thee,
To prove him false that says I love thee not.

DEMETRIUS: I say I love thee more than he can do.

LYSANDER: If thou say so, withdraw, and prove it too.

DEMETRIUS: Quick, come!

HERMIA: Lysander, whereto tends all this?

LYSANDER: Away, you Ethiope![2] [*He tries to break away from* HERMIA.]

DEMETRIUS: No, no; he'll
Seem to break loose; take on as you would follow,
But yet come not. You are a tame man, go!

LYSANDER: Hang off,[3] thou cat, thou burr! Vile thing, let loose,
Or I will shake thee from me like a serpent!

HERMIA: Why are you grown so rude? What change is this,
Sweet love?

LYSANDER: Thy love? Out, tawny Tartar, out!
Out, loathed med'cine![4] O hated potion, hence!

HERMIA: Do you not jest?

HELENA: Yes, sooth,[5] and so do you.

LYSANDER: Demetrius, I will keep my word with thee.

DEMETRIUS: I would I had your bond, for I perceive
A weak bond[6] holds you. I'll not trust your word.

LYSANDER: What, should I hurt her, strike her, kill her dead?
Although I hate her, I'll not harm her so.

HERMIA: What, can you do me greater harm than hate?
Hate me? Wherefore? O me, what news,[7] my love?
Am not I Hermia? Are not you Lysander?
I am as fair now as I was erewhile.[8]

8. Managed. 9. Subject for a jest. 1. I.e., succeed by entreaty. 2. (Referring to Hermia's relatively dark hair and complexion; see also *tawny Tartar* six lines later.) 3. Let go. 4. I.e., poison. 5. Truly. 6. I.e., Hermia's arm (with a pun on *bond*, oath, in the previous line). 7. What is the matter. 8. Just now.

Since night you lov'd me; yet since night you left me.
Why, then you left me—O, the gods forbid!—
In earnest, shall I say?

LYSANDER: Ay, by my life!
And never did desire to see thee more.
Therefore be out of hope, of question, of doubt;
Be certain, nothing truer. 'Tis no jest
That I do hate thee and love Helena.

HERMIA: O me! You juggler! You cankerblossom![9]
You thief of love! What, have you come by night
And stol'n my love's heart from him?

HELENA: Fine, i' faith!
Have you no modesty, no maiden shame,
No touch of bashfulness? What, will you tear
Impatient answers from my gentle tongue?
Fie, fie! You counterfeit, you puppet,[1] you!

HERMIA: Puppet? Why so? Ay, that way goes the game.
Now I perceive that she hath made compare
Between our statures; she hath urg'd her height,
And with her personage, her tall personage,
Her height, forsooth, she hath prevail'd with him.
And are you grown so high in his esteem,
Because I am so dwarfish and so low?
How low am I, thou painted maypole? Speak!
How low am I? I am not yet so low
But that my nails can reach unto thine eyes.

[*She flails at* HELENA, *but is restrained.*]

HELENA: I pray you, though you mock me, gentlemen,
Let her not hurt me. I was never curst;[2]
I have no gift at all in shrewishness;
I am a right[3] maid for my cowardice.
Let her not strike me. You perhaps may think,
Because she is something[4] lower than myself,
That I can match her.

HERMIA: Lower! Hark, again!

HELENA: Good Hermia, do not be so bitter with me.
I evermore did love you, Hermia,
Did ever keep your counsels, never wrong'd you;
Save that, in love unto Demetrius,
I told him of your stealth[5] unto this wood.
He followed you; for love I followed him.
But he hath chid me hence and threat'ned me

9. Worm that destroys the flower bud (?). 1. (1) counterfeit; (2) dwarfish woman (in reference to Hermia's smaller stature). 2. Shrewish. 3. True. 4. Somewhat. 5. Stealing away.

To strike me, spurn me, nay, to kill me too.
And now, so[6] you will let me quiet go,
To Athens will I bear my folly back
And follow you no further. Let me go.
You see how simple and how fond[7] I am.

HERMIA: Why, get you gone, Who is 't that hinders you?
HELENA: A foolish heart, that I leave here behind.
HERMIA: What, with Lysander?
HELENA: With Demetrius.
LYSANDER: Be not afraid; she shall not harm thee, Helena.
DEMETRIUS: No, sir, she shall not, though you take her part.
HELENA: O, when she is angry, she is keen and shrewd![8]
She was a vixen when she went to school;
And though she be but little, she is fierce.
HERMIA: "Little" again! Nothing but "low" and "little"!
Why will you suffer her to flout me thus?
Let me come to her.
LYSANDER: Get you gone, you dwarf!
You minimus, of hind'ring knot-grass[9] made!
You bead, you acorn!
DEMETRIUS: You are too officious
In her behalf that scorns your services.
Let her alone. Speak not of Helena;
Take not her part. For, if thou dost intend[1]
Never so little show of love to her,
Thou shalt aby[2] it.
LYSANDER: Now she holds me not;
Now follow, if thou dar'st, to try whose right,
Of thine or mine, is most in Helena. [*Exit.*]
DEMETRIUS: Follow? Nay, I'll go with thee, cheek by jowl.[3]
[*Exit, following* LYSANDER.]
HERMIA: You, mistress, all this coil is 'long of[4] you.
Nay, go not back.[5]
HELENA: I will not trust you, I,
Nor longer stay in your curst company.
Your hands than mine are quicker for a fray;
My legs are longer, though, to run away. [*Exit.*]
HERMIA: I am amaz'd, and know not what to say. [*Exit.*]
OBERON: This is thy negligence. Still thou mistak'st,
Or else committ'st thy knaveries willfully.
PUCK: Believe me, king of shadows, I mistook.

6. If only. 7. Foolish. 8. Shrewish. 9. A weed, an infusion of which was thought to stunt the growth. *Minimus:* diminutive creature. 1. Give sign of. 2. Pay for. 3. I.e., side by side. 4. On account of. *Coil:* turmoil, dissension. 5. I.e., don't retreat (Hermia is again proposing a fight).

Did not you tell me I should know the man
By the Athenian garments he had on?
And so far blameless proves my enterprise
That I have 'nointed an Athenian's eyes;
And so far am I glad it so did sort[6]
As this their jangling I esteem a sport.
OBERON: Thou see'st these lovers seek a place to fight.
Hie therefore, Robin, overcast the night;
The starry welkin[7] cover thou anon
With drooping fog as black as Acheron,[8]
And lead these testy rivals so astray
As[9] one come not within another's way.
Like to Lysander sometime frame thy tongue,
Then stir Demetrius up with bitter wrong;[1]
And sometime rail thou like Demetrius.
And from each other look thou lead them thus,
Till o'er their brows death-counterfeiting sleep
With leaden legs and batty[2] wings doth creep.
Then crush this herb[3] into Lysander's eye, [*Gives herb.*]
Whose liquor hath this virtuous[4] property,
To take from thence all error with his[5] might
And make his eyeballs roll with wonted[6] sight.
When they next wake, all this derision[7]
Shall seem a dream and fruitless vision,
And back to Athens shall the lovers wend
With league whose date[8] till death shall never end.
Whiles I in this affair do thee employ,
I'll to my queen and beg her Indian boy;
And then I will her charmed eye release
From monster's view, and all things shall be peace.
PUCK: My fairy lord, this must be done with haste,
For night's swift dragons[9] cut the clouds full fast,
And yonder shines Aurora's harbinger,[1]
At whose approach, ghosts, wand'ring here and there,
Troop home to churchyards. Damned spirits all,
That in crossways and floods have burial,[2]
Already to their wormy beds are gone.
For fear lest day should look their shames upon,

6. Turn out. 7. Sky. 8. River of Hades (here representing Hades itself). 9. That.
1. Insults. 2. Batlike. 3. I.e., the antidote (mentioned in II.i.184) to love-in-idleness.
4. Efficacious. 5. Its. 6. Accustomed. 7. Laughable business. 8. Term of existence.
9. (Supposed by Shakespeare to be yoked to the car of the goddess of night.) 1. The morning star, precursor of dawn. 2. (Those who had committed suicide were buried at crossways, with a stake driven through them; those drowned, i.e., buried in floods or great waters, would be condemned to wander disconsolate for want of burial rites.)

They willfully themselves exile from light
And must for aye[3] consort with black-brow'd night.

OBERON: But we are spirits of another sort.
I with the Morning's love[4] have oft made sport,
And, like a forester,[5] the groves may tread
Even till the eastern gate, all fiery-red,
Opening on Neptune with fair blessed beams,
Turns into yellow gold his salt green streams.
But, notwithstanding, haste; make no delay.
We may effect this business yet ere day. [*Exit.*]

PUCK: Up and down, up and down,
I will lead them up and down.
I am fear'd in field and town.
Goblin, lead them up and down.
Here comes one.

[*Enter* LYSANDER.]

LYSANDER: Where art thou, proud Demetrius? Speak thou now.

PUCK: [*Mimicking* DEMETRIUS.] Here, villain, drawn[6] and ready. Where art thou?

LYSANDER: I will be with thee straight.[7]

PUCK: Follow me, then,
To plainer[8] ground.

[LYSANDER *wanders about,*[9] *following the voice. Enter* DEMETRIUS.]

DEMETRIUS: Lysander! Speak again!
Thou runaway, thou coward, art thou fled?
Speak! In some bush? Where dost thou hide thy head?

PUCK: [*Mimicking* LYSANDER.] Thou coward, art thou bragging to the stars,
Telling the bushes that thou look'st for wars,
And wilt not come? Come, recreant;[1] come, thou child,
I'll whip thee with a rod. He is defil'd
That draws a sword on thee.

DEMETRIUS: Yea, art thou there?

PUCK: Follow my voice. We'll try[2] no manhood here. [*Exeunt.*]

[LYSANDER *returns.*]

LYSANDER: He goes before me and still dares me on.
When I come where he calls, then he is gone.
The villain is much lighter-heel'd than I.
I followed fast, but faster he did fly,
That fallen am I in dark uneven way,

3. Forever. 4. Cephalus, a beautiful youth beloved by Aurora; or perhaps the goddess of the dawn herself. 5. Keeper of a royal forest. 6. With drawn sword. 7. Immediately. 8. Smoother. 9. (It is not clearly necessary that Lysander exit at this point; neither exit nor reentrance is indicated in the early texts.) 1. Cowardly wretch. 2. Test.

And here will rest me. [*Lies down.*] Come, thou gentle day!
For if but once thou show me thy grey light,
I'll find Demetrius and revenge this spite. [*Sleeps.*]

[*Enter Robin* (PUCK) *and* DEMETRIUS.]

PUCK: Ho, ho, ho! Coward, why com'st thou not?
DEMETRIUS: Abide me, if thou dar'st; for well I wot[3]
Thou runn'st before me, shifting every place,
And dar'st not stand nor look me in the face.
Where art thou now?
PUCK: Come hither. I am here.
DEMETRIUS: Nay, then, thou mock'st me. Thou shalt buy this dear,[4]
If ever I thy face by daylight see.
Now, go thy way. Faintness constraineth me
To measure out my length on this cold bed.
By day's approach look to be visited. [*Lies down and sleeps.*]

[*Enter* HELENA.]

HELENA: O weary night, O long and tedious night,
Abate[5] thy hours! Shine, comforts, from the east,
That I may back to Athens by daylight,
From these that my poor company detest;
And sleep, that sometimes shuts up sorrow's eye,
Steal me awhile from mine own company. [*Lies down and sleeps.*]
PUCK: Yet but three? Come one more;
Two of both kinds makes up four.
Here she comes, curst and sad.
Cupid is a knavish lad,
Thus to make poor females mad.

[*Enter* HERMIA.]

HERMIA: Never so weary, never so in woe,
Bedabbled with the dew and torn with briers,
I can no further crawl, no further go;
My legs can keep no pace with my desires.
Here will I rest me till the break of day.
Heavens shield Lysander, if they mean a fray! [*Lies down and sleeps.*]
PUCK:
On the ground
Sleep sound.
I'll apply
To your eye,
Gentle lover, remedy. [*Squeezing the juice on* LYSANDER'*s eyes.*]
When thou wak'st,

3. Know. 4. Pay dearly for this. 5. Lessen, shorten.

Thou tak'st
True delight
In the sight
Of thy former lady's eye;
And the country proverb known,
That every man should take his own,
In your waking shall be shown:
Jack shall have Jill;
Nought shall go ill;
The man shall have his mare again, and all
shall be well. [*Exit. Manent the four lovers.*]

ACT IV

SCENE 1[6]

Enter TITANIA, *Queen of Fairies, and* BOTTOM *the Clown, and* FAIRIES: *and* OBERON, *the King, behind them.*

TITANIA: Come, sit thee down upon this flow'ry bed,
While I thy amiable cheeks do coy,[7]
And stick musk-roses in thy sleek smooth head,
And kiss thy fair large ears, my gentle joy.

[*They recline.*]

BOTTOM: Where's Peaseblossom?

PEASEBLOSSOM: Ready.

BOTTOM: Scratch my head, Peaseblossom. Where's Mounsieur Cobweb?

COBWEB: Ready.

BOTTOM: Mounsieur Cobweb, good mounsieur, get you your weapons in your hand, and kill me a red-hipp'd humble-bee on the top of a thistle; and, good mounsieur, bring me the honey-bag. Do not fret yourself too much in the action, mounsieur; and, good mounsieur, have a care the honey-bag break not; I would be loath to have you overflown with a honey-bag, signior. Where's Mounsieur Mustardseed?

MUSTARDSEED: Ready.

BOTTOM: Give me your neaf,[8] Mounsieur Mustardseed. Pray you, leave your curtsy,[9] good mounsieur.

MUSTARDSEED: What's your will?

BOTTOM: Nothing, good mounsieur, but to help Cavalery Cobweb[1] to scratch. I must to the barber's, mounsieur; for methinks I am marvailes hairy about the face; and I am such a tender ass, if my hair do but tickle me, I must scratch.

6. Location: Scene continues. The four lovers are still asleep on stage. 7. Caress. *Amiable:* lovely. 8. Fist. 9. I.e., put on your hat. 1. (Seemingly an error, since Cobweb has been sent to bring honey while Peaseblossom has been asked to scratch.) *Cavalier:* (Form of address for a gentleman.)

TITANIA: What, wilt thou hear some music, my sweet love?
BOTTOM: I have a reasonable good ear in music. Let's have the tongs and the bones.[2]

[*Music: tongs, rural music.*][3]

TITANIA: Or say, sweet love, what thou desirest to eat.
BOTTOM: Truly, a peck of provender. I could munch your good dry oats. Methinks I have a great desire to a bottle of hay. Good hay, sweet hay, hath no fellow.[4]
TITANIA: I have a venturous fairy that shall seek
The squirrel's hoard, and fetch thee new nuts.
BOTTOM: I had rather have a handful or two of dried peas. But, I pray you, let none of your people stir me. I have an exposition[5] of sleep come upon me.
TITANIA: Sleep thou, and I will wind thee in my arms.
Fairies, be gone, and be all ways[6] away. [*Exeunt* FAIRIES.]
So doth the woodbine the sweet honeysuckle
Gently entwist; the female ivy so
Enrings the barky fingers of the elm.
Oh, how I love thee! How I dote on thee! [*They sleep.*]

[*Enter Robin Goodfellow* (PUCK).]

OBERON: [*Advancing.*] Welcome, good Robin. See'st thou this sweet sight?
Her dotage now I do begin to pity.
For, meeting her of late behind the wood,
Seeking sweet favors[7] for this hateful fool,
I did upbraid her and fall out with her.
For she his hairy temples then had rounded
With coronet of fresh and fragrant flowers;
And that same dew, which sometime[8] on the buds
Was wont to swell like round and orient pearls,[9]
Stood now within the pretty flouriets'[1] eyes
Like tears that did their own disgrace bewail.
When I had at my pleasure taunted her,
And she in mild terms begg'd my patience,
I then did ask of her her changeling child;
Which straight she gave me, and her fairy sent
To bear him to my bower in fairy land.
And, now I have the boy, I will undo
This hateful imperfection of her eyes.
And, gentle Puck, take this transformed scalp
From off the head of this Athenian swain,
That, he awaking when the other[2] do,

2. Instruments for rustic music. (The tongs were played like a triangle, whereas the bones were held between the fingers and used as clappers.) 3. (This stage direction is added from the Folio.) 4. Equal. *Bottle:* bundle. 5. (Bottom's word for *disposition.*) 6. In all directions. 7. I.e., gifts of flowers. 8. Formerly. 9. I.e., the most beautiful of all pearls, those coming from the Orient. 1. Flowerets'. 2. Others.

May all to Athens back again repair,
And think no more of this night's accidents
But as the fierce vexation of a dream.
But first I will release the Fairy Queen. [*Squeezes juice in her eyes.*]
Be as thou wast wont to be;
See as thou wast wont to see.
Dian's bud[3] o'er Cupid's flower
Hath such force and blessed power.
Now, my Titania, wake you, my sweet queen.

TITANIA: [*Waking.*] My Oberon! What visions have I seen!
Methought I was enamor'd of an ass.

OBERON: There lies your love.

TITANIA: How came these things to pass?
O, how mine eyes do loathe his visage now!

OBERON: Silence awhile. Robin, take off this head.
Titania, music call, and strike more dead
Than common sleep of all these five[4] the sense.

TITANIA: Music, ho! Music, such as charmeth sleep!

[*Music.*]

PUCK: [*Removing the ass's head.*] Now, when thou wak'st, with thine own fool's eyes peep.

OBERON: Sound, music! Come, my queen, take hands with me,
And rock the ground whereon these sleepers be.

[*Dance.*]

Now thou and I are new in amity,
And will tomorrow midnight solemnly[5]
Dance in Duke Theseus' house triumphantly
And bless it to all fair prosperity.
There shall the pairs of faithful lovers be
Wedded, with Theseus, all in jollity.

PUCK: Fairy King, attend, and mark:
I do hear the morning lark.

OBERON: Then, my queen, in silence sad,[6]
Trip we after night's shade.
We the globe can compass soon,
Swifter than the wand'ring moon.

TITANIA: Come, my lord, and in our flight
Tell me how it came this night
That I sleeping here was found
With these mortals on the ground. [*Exeunt.*]

3. (Perhaps the flower of the *agnus castus* or chaste-tree, supposed to preserve chastity; or perhaps referring simply to Oberon's herb by which he can undo the effects of "Cupid's flower," the love-in-idleness of II.i.166 f.). 4. I.e., the four lovers and Bottom. 5. Ceremoniously. 6. Sober.

[*Wind horn within. Enter* THESEUS *and all his train;* HIPPOLYTA, EGEUS.]

THESEUS: Go, one of you, find out the forester,
For now our observation[7] is perform'd;
And since we have the vaward[8] of the day,
My love shall hear the music of my hounds.
Uncouple in the western valley; let them go.
Dispatch, I say, and find the forester. [*Exit an Attendant.*]
We will, fair queen, up to the mountain's top
And mark the musical confusion
Of hounds and echo in conjunction.
HIPPOLYTA: I was with Hercules and Cadmus[9] once,
When in a wood of Crete they bay'd[1] the bear
With hounds of Sparta.[2] Never did I hear
Such gallant chiding; for, besides the groves,
The skies, the fountains, every region near
Seem'd all one mutual cry. I never heard
So musical a discord, such sweet thunder.
THESEUS: My hounds are bred out of the Spartan kind,
So flew'd, so sanded;[3] and their heads are hung
With ears that sweep away the morning dew;
Crook-knee'd, and dewlapp'd[4] like Thessalian bulls;
Slow in pursuit, but match'd in mouth like bells,
Each under each. A cry more tuneable[5]
Was never holla'd to, nor cheer'd with horn,
In Crete, in Sparta, nor in Thessaly.
Judge when you hear. [*Sees the sleepers.*] But, soft! What nymphs are these?
EGEUS: My lord, this' my daughter here asleep;
And this, Lysander; this Demetrius is;
This Helena, old Nedar's Helena.
I wonder of their being here together.
THESEUS: No doubt they rose up early to observe
The rite of May, and, hearing our intent,
Came here in grace of our solemnity.[6]
But speak, Egeus. Is not this the day
That Hermia should give answer of her choice?
EGEUS: It is, my lord.
THESEUS: Go, bid the huntsmen wake them with their horns.
[*Exit an Attendant.*]

7. I.e., observance to a morn of May (I.i.167). 8. Vanguard, i.e., earliest part. 9. Mythical founder of Thebes. (This story about him is unknown.) 1. Brought to bay. 2. (A breed famous in antiquity for their hunting skill.) 3. Of sandy color. *So flew'd:* similarly having large hanging chaps or fleshy covering of the jaw. 4. Having pendulous folds of skin under the neck. 5. Well tuned, melodious. *Match'd . . . each:* i.e., harmoniously matched in their various cries like a set of bells, from treble down to bass. *Cry:* pack of hounds. 6. I.e., observance of these same rites of May.

[*Shout within. Wind horns. They all start up.*]

Good morrow, friends. Saint Valentine[7] is past.
Begin these wood-birds but to couple now?

LYSANDER: Pardon, my lord. [*They kneel.*]

THESEUS: I pray you all, stand up.
I know you two are rival enemies;
How comes this gentle concord in the world,
That hatred is so far from jealousy
To sleep by hate and fear no enmity?

LYSANDER: My lord, I shall reply amazedly,
Half sleep, half waking; but as yet, I swear,
I cannot truly say how I came here.
But, as I think—for truly would I speak,
And now I do bethink me, so it is—
I came with Hermia hither. Our intent
Was to be gone from Athens, where[8] we might,
Without[9] the peril of the Athenian law—

EGEUS: Enough, enough, my lord; you have enough.
I beg the law, the law, upon his head.
They would have stol'n away; they would, Demetrius,
Thereby to have defeated you and me,
You of your wife and me of my consent,
Of my consent that she should be your wife.

DEMETRIUS: My lord, fair Helen told me of their stealth,
Of this their purpose hither to this wood,
And I in fury hither followed them,
Fair Helena in fancy following me.
But, my good lord, I wot not by what power—
But by some power it is—my love to Hermia,
Melted as the snow, seems to me now
As the remembrance of an idle gaud[1]
Which in my childhood I did dote upon;
And all the faith, the virtue of my heart,
The object and the pleasure of mine eye,
Is only Helena. To her, my lord,
Was I betroth'd ere I saw Hermia,
But like a sickness did I loathe this food;
But, as in health, come to my natural taste,
Now I do wish it, love it, long for it,
And will for evermore be true to it.

7. (Birds were supposed to choose their mates on St. Valentine's Day.)
8. Wherever; or, to where.
9. Outside of, beyond.
1. Worthless trinket.

THESEUS: Fair lovers, you are fortunately met.
Of this discourse we more will hear anon.
Egeus, I will overbear your will;
For in the temple, by and by, with us
These couples shall eternally be knit.
And, for the morning now is something[2] worn,
Our purpos'd hunting shall be set aside.
Away with us to Athens. Three and three,
We'll hold a feast in great solemnity.
Come, Hippolyta. [*Exeunt* THESEUS, HIPPOLYTA, EGEUS, and train.]
DEMETRIUS: These things seem small and undistinguishable,
Like far-off mountains turned into clouds.
HERMIA: Methinks I see these things with parted[3] eye,
When every thing seems double.
HELENA: So methinks;
And I have found Demetrius like a jewel,
Mine own, and not mine own.[4]
DEMETRIUS: Are you sure
That we are awake? It seems to me
That yet we sleep, we dream. Do not you think
The Duke was here, and bid us follow him?
HERMIA: Yea, and my father.
HELENA: And Hippolyta.
LYSANDER: And he did bid us follow to the temple.
DEMETRIUS: Why, then, we are awake. Let's follow him,
And by the way let us recount our dreams. [*Exeunt.*]

BOTTOM: [*Awaking.*] When my cue comes, call me, and I will answer. My next is, "Most fair Pyramus." Heigh-ho! Peter Quince! Flute, the bellows-mender! Snout, the tinker! Starveling! God's my life, stol'n hence, and left me asleep! I have had a most rare vision. I have had a dream, past the wit of man to say what dream it was. Man is but an ass, if he go about[5] to expound this dream. Methought I was—there is no man can tell what. Methought I was—and methought I had—but man is but a patch'd fool, if he will offer[6] to say what methought I had. The eye of man hath not heard, the ear of man hath not seen, man's hand is not able to taste, his tongue to conceive, nor his heart to report, what my dream was. I will get Peter Quince to write a ballad of this dream. It shall be called "Bottom's Dream," because it hath no bottom; and I will sing it in the latter end of a play, before the Duke. Peradventure, to make it the more gracious, I shall sing it at her[7] death.
[*Exit.*]

2. Somewhat. *For:* since. 3. Improperly focused. 4. I.e., like a jewel that one finds by chance and therefore possesses but cannot certainly consider one's own property. 5. Attempt. 6. Venture. *Patch'd:* wearing motley, i.e., a dress of various colors. 7. Thisby's (?)

SCENE 2[8]

Enter QUINCE, FLUTE, SNOUT, *and* STARVELING.

QUINCE: Have you sent to Bottom's house? Is he come home yet?

STARVELING: He cannot be heard of. Out of doubt he is transported.[9]

FLUTE: If he come not, then the play is marr'd. It goes not forward, doth it?

QUINCE: It is not possible. You have not a man in all Athens able to discharge[1] Pyramus but he.

FLUTE: No, he hath simply the best wit of any handicraft man in Athens.

QUINCE: Yea, and the best person too; and he is a very paramour for a sweet voice.

FLUTE: You must say "paragon." A paramour is, God bless us, a thing of naught.

[*Enter* SNUG *the Joiner.*]

SNUG: Masters, the Duke is coming from the temple, and there is two or three lords and ladies more married. If our sport had gone forward, we had all been made men.

FLUTE: O sweet bully Bottom! Thus hath he lost sixpence a day[2] during his life; he could not have scap'd sixpence a day. An the Duke had not given him sixpence a day for playing Pyramus, I'll be hang'd. He would have deserv'd it. Sixpence a day in Pyramus, or nothing.

[*Enter* BOTTOM.]

BOTTOM: Where are these lads? Where are these hearts?[3]

QUINCE: Bottom! O most courageous day! O most happy hour!

BOTTOM: Masters, I am to discourse wonders.[4] But ask me not what; for if I tell you, I am no true Athenian. I will tell you everything, right as it fell out.

QUINCE: Let us hear, sweet Bottom.

BOTTOM: Not a word of[5] me. All that I will tell you is, that the Duke hath din'd. Get your apparel together, good strings to your beards, new ribands[6] to your pumps; meet presently[7] at the palace; every man look o'er his part; for the short and the long is, our play is preferr'd.[8] In any case, let Thisby have clean linen; and let not him that plays the lion pare his nails, for they shall hang out for the lion's claws. And, most dear actors, eat no onions nor garlic, for we are to utter sweet breath; and I do not doubt but to hear them say, it is a sweet comedy. No more words. Away! Go away! [*Exeunt.*]

8. Location: Athens. Quince's house (?) 9. Carried off by fairies; or, possibly, transformed. 1. Per- form. 2. I.e., as a royal pension. 3. Good fellows. 4. Have wonders to relate. 5. Out of. 6. Ribbons. *Strings*: (to attach the beards). 7. Immediately. 8. Selected for consideration.

ACT V

Scene 1[9]

Enter THESEUS, HIPPOLYTA, *and* PHILOSTRATE, *Lords, and Attendants.*

HIPPOLYTA: 'Tis strange, my Theseus, that[1] these lovers speak of.
THESEUS: More strange than true. I never may[2] believe
These antic fables, nor these fairy toys.[3]
Lovers and madmen have such seething brains,
Such shaping fantasies,[4] that apprehend
More than cool reason ever comprehends.
The lunatic, the lover, and the poet
Are of imagination all compact.[5]
One sees more devils than vast hell can hold;
That is the madman. The lover, all as frantic,
Sees Helen's beauty in a brow of Egypt.[6]
The poet's eye, in a fine frenzy rolling,
Doth glance from heaven to earth, from earth to heaven;
And as imagination bodies forth
The forms of things unknown, the poet's pen
Turns them to shapes and gives to airy nothing
A local habitation and a name.
Such tricks hath strong imagination
That, if it would but apprehend some joy,
It comprehends some bringer[7] of that joy;
Or in the night, imagining some fear,[8]
How easy is a bush suppos'd a bear!
HIPPOLYTA: But all the story of the night told over,
And all their minds transfigur'd so together,
More witnesseth than fancy's images[9]
And grows to something of great constancy;[1]
But, howsoever, strange and admirable.[2]

[*Enter lovers:* LYSANDER, DEMETRIUS, HERMIA, *and* HELENA.]

THESEUS: Here come the lovers, full of joy and mirth.
Joy, gentle friends! Joy and fresh days of love
Accompany your hearts!
LYSANDER: More than to us
Wait in your royal walks, your board, your bed!
THESEUS: Come now, what masques, what dances shall we have,

9. V.i. Location: Athens. The palace of Theseus. 1. That which. 2. Can. 3. Trifling stories about fairies. *Antic:* strange, grotesque (with additional punning sense of *antique*, ancient. 4. Imaginations. 5. Formed, composed. 6. I.e., face of a gypsy. *Helen's:* i.e., of Helen of Troy, pattern of beauty. 7. I.e., source. 8. Object of fear. 9. Testifies to something more substantial than mere imaginings. 1. Certainty. 2. Source of wonder. *Howsoever:* in any case.

To wear away this long age of three hours
Between our after-supper and bed-time?
Where is our usual manager of mirth?
What revels are in hand? Is there no play,
To ease the anguish of a torturing hour?
Call Philostrate.

PHILOSTRATE: Here, mighty Theseus.

THESEUS: Say, what abridgement[3] have you for this evening?
What masque? What music? How shall we beguile
The lazy time, if not with some delight?

PHILOSTRATE: There is a brief[4] how many sports are ripe.
Make choice of which your Highness will see first. [*Giving a paper.*]

THESEUS: [*Reads.*] "The battle with the Centaurs,[5] to be sung
By an Athenian eunuch to the harp."
We'll none of that. That have I told my love,
In glory of my kinsman[6] Hercules.
[*Reads.*] "The riot of the tipsy Bacchanals,
Tearing the Thracian singer in their rage."[7]
That is an old device; and it was play'd
When I from Thebes came last a conqueror.
[*Reads.*] "The thrice three Muses mourning for the death
Of Learning, late deceas'd in beggary."[8]
That is some satire, keen and critical,
Not sorting with[9] a nuptial ceremony.
[*Reads.*] "A tedious brief scene of young Pyramus
And his love Thisby; very tragical mirth."
Merry and tragical? Tedious and brief?
That is, hot ice and wondrous strange[1] snow.
How shall we find the concord of this discord?

PHILOSTRATE: A play there is, my lord, some ten words long,
Which is as brief as I have known a play;
But by ten words, my lord, it is too long,
Which makes it tedious. For in all the play
There is not one word apt, one player fitted.
And tragical, my noble lord, it is,
For Pyramus therein doth kill himself.
Which, when I saw rehears'd, I must confess,

3. Pastime (to abridge or shorten the evening). 4. Short written statement, list. 5. (Probably refers to the battle of the Centaurs and the Lapithae, when the Centaurs attempted to carry off Hippodamia, bride of Theseus' friend Pirothous.) 6. (Plutarch's *Life of Theseus* states that Hercules and Theseus were near kinsmen. Theseus is referring to a version of the battle of the Centaurs in which Hercules was said to be present.) 7. (This was the story of the death of Orpheus, as told in *Metamorphoses*, XI.) 8. (Possibly an allusion to Spenser's *Teares of the Muses*, 1591, though "satires" deploring the neglect of learning and the creative arts were commonplace.) 9. Befitting. 1. (Seemingly an error for some adjective that would contrast with *snow*, just as *hot* contrasts with *ice*.)

Made mine eyes water; but more merry tears
The passion of loud laughter never shed.
THESEUS: What are they that do play it?
PHILOSTRATE: Hard-handed men that work in Athens here,
Which never labor'd in their minds till now,
And now have toil'd their unbreathed[2] memories
With this same play, against[3] your nuptial.
THESEUS: And we will hear it.
PHILOSTRATE: No, my noble lord,
It is not for you. I have heard it over,
And it is nothing, nothing in the world;
Unless you can find sport in their intents,
Extremely stretch'd and conn'd[4] with cruel pain,
To do you service.
THESEUS: I will hear that play;
For never anything can be amiss
When simplenss and duty tender it.
Go, bring them in; and take your places, ladies.

[PHILOSTRATE *goes to summon the players.*]

HIPPOLYTA: I love not to see wretchedness o'ercharg'd[5]
And duty in his service[6] perishing.
THESEUS: Why, gentle sweet, you shall see no such thing.
HIPPOLYTA: He says they can do nothing in this kind.[7]
THESEUS: The kinder we, to give them thanks for nothing.
Our sport shall be to take what they mistake;
And what poor duty cannot do, noble respect
Takes it in might, not merit.[8]
Where I have come, great clerks[9] have purposed
To greet me with premeditated welcomes;
Where I have seen them shiver and look pale,
Make periods in the midst of sentences,
Throttle their practic'd accent[1] in their fears,
And in conclusion dumbly have broke off,
Not paying me a welcome. Trust me, sweet,
Out of this silence yet I pick'd a welcome;
And in the modesty of fearful duty
I read as much as from the rattling tongue
Of saucy and audacious eloquence.
Love, therefore, and tongue-tied simplicity
In least speak most, to my capacity.[2]

2. Unexercised. *Toll'd:* taxed. 3. In preparation for. 4. Memorized. *Stretch'd:* strained. 5. Incompetence overburdened. 6. Its attempt to serve. 7. Kind of thing. 8. Values it for the effort made rather than for the excellence achieved. 9. Learned men. 1. I.e., rehearsed speech; or, usual way of speaking. 2. In my judgment and understanding. *Least:* i.e., saying least.

[PHILOSTRATE *returns.*]

PHILOSTRATE: So please your Grace, the Prologue is address'd.[3]

THESEUS: Let him approach.

[*Flourish of trumpets. Enter the Prologue* (QUINCE).]

PROLOGUE: If we offend, it is with our good will.
That you should think, we come not to offend,
But with good will. To show our simple skill,
That is the true beginning of our end.
Consider, then, we come but in despite.
We do not come, as minding[4] to content you,
Our true intent is. All for your delight
We are not here. That you should here repent you,
The actors are at hand; and, by their show,
You shall know all that you are like to know.

THESEUS: This fellow doth not stand upon points.[5]

LYSANDER: He hath rid his prologue like a rough[6] colt; he knows not the stop.[7] A good moral, my lord: it is not enough to speak, but to speak true.

HIPPOLYTA: Indeed he hath play'd on his prologue like a child on a recorder; a sound, but not in government.[8]

THESEUS: His speech was like a tangled chain, nothing[9] impair'd, but all disorder'd. Who is next?

[*Enter* PYRAMUS *and* THISBY, *and* WALL, *and* MOONSHINE, *and* LION.]

PROLOGUE: Gentles, perchance you wonder at this show;
But wonder on, till truth make all things plain.
This man is Pyramus, if you would know;
This beauteous lady Thisby is certain.
This man, with lime and rough-cast, doth present
Wall, that vile Wall which did these lovers sunder;
And through Wall's chink, poor souls, they are content
To whisper. At the which let no man wonder.
This man, with lantern, dog, and bush of thorn,
Presenteth Moonshine; for, if you will know,
By moonshine did these lovers think no scorn[1]
To meet at Ninus' tomb, there, there to woo.
This grisly beast, which Lion hight[2] by name,
The trusty Thisby, coming first by night,
Did scare away, or rather did affright;
And, as she fled, her mantle she did fall,[3]

3. Ready. *Prologue:* speaker of the prologue. 4. Intending 5. (1) heed niceties or small points; (2) pay attention to punctuation in his reading. (The humor of Quince's speech is in the blunders of its punctuation.) 6. Unbroken. 7. (1) the stopping of a colt by reining it in; (2) punctuation mark. 8. Control. *Recorder:* a wind instrument like a flute or flageolet. 9. Not at all. 1. Think it no disgraceful matter. 2. Is called. 3. Let fall.

Which Lion vile with bloody mouth did stain.
Anon comes Pyramus, sweet youth and tall,[4]
And finds his trusty Thisby's mantle slain;
Whereat, with blade, with bloody blameful blade,
He bravely broach'd[5] his boiling bloody breast.
And Thisby, tarrying in mulberry shade,
His dagger drew, and died. For all the rest,
Let Lion, Moonshine, Wall, and lovers twain
At large[6] discourse, while here they do remain.

[*Exeunt* LION, THISBY, *and* MOONSHINE.]

THESEUS: I wonder if the lion be to speak.

DEMETRIUS: No wonder, my lord. One lion may, when many asses do.

WALL: In this same interlude it doth befall
That I, one Snout by name, present a wall;
And such a wall, as I would have you think,
That had in it a crannied hole or chink,
Through which the lovers, Pyramus and Thisby,
Did whisper often very secretly.
This loam, this rough-cast, and this stone doth show
That I am that same wall; the truth is so.
And this the cranny is, right and sinister,[7]
Through which the fearful lovers are to whisper.

THESEUS: Would you desire lime and hair to speak better?

DEMETRIUS: It is the wittiest partition[8] that ever I heard discourse, my lord.

[PYRAMUS *comes forward.*]

THESEUS: Pyramus draws near the wall. Silence!

PYRAMUS: O grim-look'd[9] night! O night with hue so black!
O night, which ever art when day is not!
O night, O night! Alack, alack, alack,
I fear my Thisby's promise is forgot.
And thou, O wall, O sweet, O lovely wall,
That stand'st between her father's ground and mine,
Thou wall, O wall, O sweet and lovely wall,
Show me thy chink, to blink through with mine eyne!

[WALL *holds up his fingers.*]

Thanks, courteous Wall. Jove shield thee well for this!
But what see I? No Thisby do I see.
O wicked wall, through whom I see no bliss!
Curs'd be thy stones for thus deceiving me!

THESEUS: The wall, methinks, being sensible,[1] should curse again.

4. Courageous. 5. Stabbed. 6. In full, at length. 7. I.e., the right side of it and the left; or, running from right to left, horizontally. 8. (1) wall; (2) section of a learned treatise or oration. 9. Grim-looking. 1. Capable of feeling.

PYRAMUS: No, in truth, sir, he should not. "Deceiving me" is Thisby's cue: she is to enter now, and I am to spy her through the wall. You shall see, it will fall pat as I told you. Yonder she comes.

[*Enter* THISBY.]

THISBY: O wall, full often hast thou heard my moans,
For parting my fair Pyramus and me.
My cherry lips have often kiss'd thy stones,
Thy stones with lime and hair knit up in thee.
PYRAMUS: I see a voice. Now will I to the chink,
To spy an[2] I can hear my Thisby's face.
Thisby!
THISBY: My love! Thou art my love, I think.
PYRAMUS: Think what thou wilt, I am thy lover's grace;[3]
And, like Limander, am I trusty still.
THISBY: And I like Helen,[4] till the Fates me kill.
PYRAMUS: Not Shafalus[5] to Procrus was so true.
THISBY: As Shafalus to Procrus, I to you.
PYRAMUS: O, kiss me through the hole of this vile wall!
THISBY: I kiss the wall's hole, not your lips at all.
PYRAMUS: Wilt thou at Ninny's tomb meet me straightway?
THISBY: 'Tide life, 'tide[6] death, I come without delay.

[*Exeunt* PYRAMUS *and* THISBY.]

WALL: Thus have I, Wall, my part discharged so;
And, being done, thus Wall away doth go. [*Exit.*]

THESEUS: Now is the mural down between the two neighbors.

DEMETRIUS: No remedy, my lord, when walls are so willful to hear without warning.[7]

HIPPOLYTA: This is the silliest stuff that ever I heard.

THESEUS: The best in this kind are but shadows;[8] and the worst are no worse, if imagination amend them.

HIPPOLYTA: It must be your imagination then, and not theirs.

THESEUS: If we imagine no worse of them than they of themselves, they may pass for excellent men. Here come two noble beasts in, a man and a lion.

[*Enter* LION *and* MOONSHINE.]

LION: You, ladies, you, whose gentle hearts do fear
The smallest monstrous mouse that creeps on floor,
May now perchance both quake and tremble here,
When lion rough in widest rage doth roar.
Then know that I, as Snug the joiner, am
A lion fell,[9] nor else no lion's dam;

2. If. 3. I.e., gracious lover. 4. (Blunders for "Leander" and "Hero.") 5. (Blunders for "Cephalus" and "Procris," also famous lovers.) 6. Betide, come. 7. I.e., without warning the parents. *To hear:* as to hear. 8. Likenesses, representations. *In this kind:* of this sort. 9. Fierce lion (with a play on the idea of *lion skin*).

For, if I should as lion come in strife
Into this place, 'twere pity on my life.

THESEUS: A very gentle beast, and of a good conscience.

DEMETRIUS: The very best at a beast, my lord, that e'er I saw.

LYSANDER: This lion is a very fox for his valor.[1]

THESEUS: True; and a goose for his discretion.[2]

DEMETRIUS: Not so, my lord; for his valor cannot carry his discretion; and the fox carries the gooe.

THESEUS: His discretion, I am sure, cannot carry his valor; for the goose carries not the fox. It is well. Leave it to his discretion, and let us listen to the moon.

MOON: This lanthorn[3] doth the horned moon present—

DEMETRIUS: He should have worn the horns on his head.[4]

THESEUS: He is no crescent, and his horns are invisible within the circumference.

MOON: This lanthorn doth the horned moon present;
Myself the man i' th' moon do seem to be.

THESEUS: This is the greatest error of all the rest. The man should be put into the lanthorn. How is it else the man i' th' moon?

DEMETRIUS: He dares not come there for the[5] candle; for, you see, it is already in snuff.[6]

HIPPOLYTA: I am aweary of this moon. Would he would change!

THESEUS: It appears, by his small light of discretion, that he is in the wane; but yet, in courtesy, in all reason, we must stay the time.

LYSANDER: Proceed, Moon.

MOON: All that I have to say is to tell you that the lanthorn is the moon, I, the man in the moon, this thorn-bush my thorn-bush, and this dog my dog.

DEMETRIUS: Why, all these should be in the lanthorn; for all these are in the moon. But silence! Here comes Thisby.

[*Enter* THISBY.]

THISBY: This is old Ninny's tomb. Where is my love?

LION: [*Roaring.*] Oh— [THISBY *runs off.*]

DEMETRIUS: Well roar'd, Lion.

THESEUS: Well run, Thisby.

HIPPOLYTA: Well shone, Moon. Truly, the moon shines with a good grace.

[*The* LION *shakes* THISBY'*s mantle, and exit.*]

THESEUS: Well mous'd,[7] Lion.

DEMETRIUS: And then came Pyramus.

LYSANDER: And so the lion vanish'd.

1. I.e., his valor consists of craftiness and discretion. 2. I.e., as discreet as a goose, that is, more foolish than discreet. 3. (This original spelling, *lanthorn*, may suggest a play on the *horn* of which lanterns were made, and also on a cuckold's horns; but the spelling *lanthorn* is not used consistently for comic effect in this play or elsewhere. At V.i.134, for example, the word is *lantern* in the original.) 4. (As a sign of cuckoldry.) 5. Because of the. 6. (1) offended; (2) in need of snuffing. 7. Shaken.

[*Enter* PYRAMUS.]

PYRAMUS: Sweet Moon, I thank thee for thy sunny beams;
I thank thee, Moon, for shining now so bright;
For, by thy gracious, golden, glittering gleams,
I trust to take of truest Thisby sight.
But stay, O spite!
But mark, poor knight,
What dreadful dole[8] is here!
Eyes, do you see?
How can it be?
O dainty duck! O dear!
Thy mantle good,
What, stain'd with blood!
Approach, ye Furies fell![9]
O Fates, come, come,
Cut thread and thrum;[1]
Quail, crush, conclude, and quell![2]

THESEUS: This passion, and the death of a dear friend, would go near to make a man look sad.[3]

HIPPOLYTA: Beshrew my heart, but I pity the man.

PYRAMUS: O wherefore, Nature, didst thou lions frame?
Since lion vile hath here deflow'r'd my dear,
Which is—no, no—which was the fairest dame
That liv'd, that lov'd, that lik'd, that look'd with cheer.[4]
Come, tears, confound,
Out, sword, and wound
The pap of Pyramus;
Ay, that left pap,
Where heart doth hop. [*Stabs himself.*]
Thus die I, thus, thus, thus.
Now am I dead,
Now am I fled;
My soul is in the sky.
Tongue, lose thy light;
Moon, take thy flight. [*Exit* MOONSHINE.]
Now die, die, die, die, die. [*Dies.*]

DEMETRIUS: No die, but an ace,[5] for him; for he is but one.[6]

LYSANDER: Less than an ace, man; for he is dead, he is nothing.

THESEUS: With the help of a surgeon he might yet recover, and yet prove an ass.[7]

8. Grievous event. 9. Fierce. 1. The warp in weaving and the loose end of the warp. 2. Kill, destroy. *Quail:* overpower. 3. I.e., if one had other reason to grieve, one might be sad, but not from this absurd portrayal of passion. 4. Countenance. 5. The side of the die featuring the single pip, or spot. (The pun is on *die* as a singular of *dice*; Bottom's performance is not worth a whole *die* but rather one single face of it, one small portion.) 6. (1) an individual person; (2) unique. 7. (With a pun on *ace*.)

HIPPOLYTA: How chance Moonshine is gone before Thisby comes back and finds her lover?

THESEUS: She will find him by starlight. Here she comes; and her passion ends the play.

[*Enter* THISBY.]

HIPPOLYTA: Methinks she should not use a long one for such a Pyramus. I hope she will be brief.

DEMETRIUS: A mote will turn the balance, which Pyramus, which[8] Thisby, is the better: he for a man, God warr'nt us; she for a woman, God bless us.

LYSANDER: She hath spied him already with those sweet eyes.

DEMETRIUS: And thus she means, videlicet:[9]

THISBY: Asleep, my love?
What, dead, my dove?
O Pyramus, arise!
Speak, speak. Quite dumb?
Dead, dead? A tomb
Must cover thy sweet eyes.
These lily lips,
This cherry nose,
These yellow cowslip cheeks,
Are gone, are gone!
Lovers, make moan.
His eyes were green as leeks.
O Sisters Three,[1]
Come, come to me,
With hands as pale as milk;
Lay them in gore,
Since you have shore[2]
With shears his thread of silk.
Tongue, not a word.
Come, trusty sword,
Come, blade, my breast imbrue![3] [*Stabs herself.*]
And farewell, friends.
Thus Thisby ends.
Adieu, adieu, adieu. [*Dies.*]

THESEUS: Moonshine and Lion are left to bury the dead.

DEMETRIUS: Ay, and Wall too.

BOTTOM: [*Starting up.*] No, I assure you; the wall is down that parted their fathers. Will it please you to see the epilogue, or to hear a Bergomask dance[4] between two of our company?

THESEUS: No epilogue, I pray you; for your play needs no excuse. Never excuse; for when the players are all dead, there need none to be blam'd. Marry, if

8. Whether . . . or. 9. To wit. *Means:* moans, laments. 1. The Fates. 2. Shorn. 3. Stain with blood. 4. A rustic dance named from Bergamo, a province in the state of Venice.

he that writ it had play'd Pyramus and hang'd himself in Thisby's garter, it would have been a fine tragedy; and so it is, truly, and very notably discharg'd. But, come, your Bergomask. Let your epilogue alone. [*A dance.*]
The iron tongue of midnight hath told[5] twelve.
Lovers, to bed; 'tis almost fairy time.
I fear we shall outsleep the coming morn
As much as we this night have overwatch'd.[6]
This palpable-gross[7] play hath well beguil'd
The heavy[8] gait of night. Sweet friends, to bed.
A fortnight hold we this solemnity,
In nightly revels and new jollity. [*Exeunt.*]

[*Enter* PUCK.]

PUCK: Now the hungry lion roars,
And the wolf behowls the moon;
Whilst the heavy ploughman snores,
All with weary task fordone.[9]
Now the wasted brands[1] do glow,
Whilst the screech-owl, screeching loud,
Puts the wretch that lies in woe
In remembrance of a shroud.
Now it is the time of night
That the graves, all gaping wide,
Every one lets forth his sprite,[2]
In the churchway paths to glide.
And we fairies, that do run
By the triple Hecate's[3] team
From the presence of the sun,
Following darkness like a dream,
Now are frolic.[4] Not a mouse
Shall disturb this hallowed house.
I am sent with broom before,
To sweep the dust behind[5] the door.

[*Enter* OBERON *and* TITANIA, *King and Queen of Fairies, with all their train.*]

OBERON: Through the house give glimmering light,
By the dead and drowsy fire;
Every elf and fairy sprite
Hop as light as bird from brier;
And this ditty, after me,
Sing, and dance it trippingly.

5. Counted, struck ("tolled"). 6. Stayed up too late. 7. Palpably gross, obviously crude. 8. Drowsy, dull. 9. Exhausted. 1. Burned-out logs. 2. Every grave lets forth its ghost. 3. (Hecate ruled in three capacities: as Luna or Cynthia in heaven, as Diana on earth, and as Proserpina in hell.) 4. Merry. 5. From behind. (Robin Goodfellow was a household spirit who helped good housemaids and punished lazy ones.)

TITANIA: First, rehearse your song by rote,
To each word a warbling note.
Hand in hand, with fairy grace,
Will we sing, and bless this place.

[*Song and dance.*]

OBERON: Now, until the break of day,
Through this house each fairy stray.
To the best bride-bed will we,
Which by us shall blessed be;
And the issue there create[6]
Ever shall be fortunate.
So shall all the couples three
Ever true in loving be;
And the blots of Nature's hand
Shall not in their issue stand;
Never mole, hare lip, nor scar,
Nor mark prodigious,[7] such as are
Despised in nativity,
Shall upon their children be.
With this field-dew consecrate,[8]
Every fairy take his gait,[9]
And each several[1] chamber bless,
Through this palace, with sweet peace;
And the owner of it blest
Ever shall in safety rest.
Trip away; make no stay;
Meet me all by break of day. [*Exeunt* OBERON, TITANIA, *and train.*]

PUCK: If we shadows have offended,
Think but this, and all is mended,
That you have but slumb'red here[2]
While these visions did appear.
And this weak and idle theme,
No more yielding but[3] a dream,
Gentles, do not reprehend.
If you pardon, we will mend.
And, as I am an honest Puck,
If we have unearned luck
Now to scape the serpent's tongue,[4]
We will make amends ere long;
Else the Puck a liar call.

6. Created. 7. Monstrous, unnatural. 8. Consecrated. 9. Go his way. 1. Separate.
2. I.e., that it is a "midsummer night's dream." 3. Yielding no more than. 4. I.e., hissing.

So, good night unto you all.
Give me your hands,[5] if we be friends,
And Robin shall restore amends. [*Exit.*]

ca. 1594–1595

5. Applaud.

Reading More Drama

ARISTOPHANES

Lysistrata[1]

CHARACTERS[2]

LYSISTRATA, CALONICE, MYRRHINE — *Athenian women*
LAMPITO, *a Spartan woman*
LEADER OF THE CHORUS OF OLD MEN
CHORUS OF OLD MEN
LEADER OF THE CHORUS OF OLD WOMEN
CHORUS OF OLD WOMEN
ATHENIAN MAGISTRATE
THREE ATHENIAN WOMEN
CINESIAS, *an Athenian, husband of Myrrhine*
SPARTAN HERALD
SPARTAN AMBASSADORS
ATHENIAN AMBASSADORS
TWO ATHENIAN CITIZENS
CHORUS OF ATHENIANS
CHORUS OF SPARTANS

SCENE: *In Athens, beneath the Acropolis. In the center of the stage is the Propylaea, or gate-way to the Acropolis; to one side is a small grotto, sacred to Pan. The Orchestra represents a slope leading up to the gate-way.*

It is early in the morning. LYSISTRATA *is pacing impatiently up and down.*

LYSISTRATA: If they'd been summoned to worship the God of Wine, or Pan, or to visit the Queen of Love, why, you couldn't have pushed your way through the streets for all the timbrels.[3] But now there's not a single woman here—except my neighbor; here she comes.

[*Enter* CALONICE.]

1. Translated by Charles T. Murphy. Annotated by Bernard Knox. 2. As is usual in ancient comedy, the leading characters have significant names. *Lysistrata* is "She who disbands the armies"; Lampito is a celebrated Spartan name; *Cinesias*, although a real name in Athens, is chosen to suggerst a Greek verb *kinein*, *to move*, then *to make love, to have intercourse*, and the name of his deme, *Paionidai*, suggests the verb *paiein*, which has about the same significance. 3. These instruments were used in most orgiastic cults, especially in the worship of Dionysus, the "God of Wine."

Good day to you, Calonice.

CALONICE: And to you, Lysistrata. [*Noticing* LYSISTRATA'S *impatient air.*] But what ails you? Don't scowl, my dear; it's not becoming to you to knit your brows like that.

LYSISTRATA: [*Sadly.*] Ah, Calonice, my heart aches; I'm so annoyed at us women. For among men we have a reputation for sly trickery—

CALONICE: And rightly too, on my word!

LYSISTRATA: —but when they were told to meet here to consider a matter of no small importance, they lie abed and don't come.

CALONICE: Oh, they'll come all right, my dear. It's not easy for a woman to get out, you know. One is working on her husband, another is getting up the maid, another has to put the baby to bed, or wash and feed it.

LYSISTRATA: But after all, there are other matters more important than all that.

CALONICE: My dear Lysistrata, just what is this matter you've summoned us women to consider? What's up? Something big?

LYSISTRATA: Very big.

CALONICE: [*Interested.*] Is it stout, too?

LYSISTRATA: [*Smiling.*] Yes indeed—both big and stout.

CALONICE: What? And the women still haven't come?

LYSISTRATA: It's not what you suppose; they'd have come soon enough for *that*. But I've worked up something, and for many a sleepless night I've turned it this way and that.

CALONICE: [*In mock disappointment.*] Oh, I guess it's pretty fine and slender, if you've turned it this way and that.

LYSISTRATA: So fine that the safety of the whole of Greece lies in us women.

CALONICE: In us women? It depends on a very slender reed then.

LYSISTRATA: Our country's fortunes are in our hands; and whether the Spartans shall perish—

CALONICE: Good! Let them perish, by all means.

LYSISTRATA: —and the Boeotians shall be completely annihilated.

CALONICE: Not completely! Please spare the eels.[4]

LYSISTRATA: As for Athens, I won't use any such unpleasant words. But you understand what I mean. But if the women will meet here—the Spartans, the Boeotians, and we Athenians—then all together we will save Greece.

CALONICE: But what could women do that's clever or distinguished? We just sit around all dolled up in silk robes, looking pretty in our sheer gowns and evening slippers.

LYSISTRATA: These are just the things I hope will save us: these silk robes, perfumes, evening slippers, rouge, and our chiffon blouses.

CALONICE: How so?

LYSISTRATA: So never a man alive will lift a spear against the foe—

CALONICE: I'll get a silk gown at once.

LYSISTRATA: —or take up his shield—

4. A favorite Athenian delicacy from the Boeotian lakes, eels were then very rare in Athens because of the war.

CALONICE: I'll put on my sheerest gown!

LYSISTRATA: —or sword.

CALONICE: I'll buy a pair of evening slippers.

LYSISTRATA: Well then, shouldn't the women have come?

CALONICE: Come? Why, they should have *flown* here.

LYSISTRATA: Well, my dear, just watch: they'll act in true Athenian fashion—everything too late! And now there's not a woman here from the shore or from Salamis.[5]

CALONICE: They're coming. I'm sure; at daybreak they were laying—to their oars to cross the straits.

LYSISTRATA: And those I expected would be the first to come—the women of Acharnae[6]—they haven't arrived.

CALONICE: Yet the wife of Theagenes[7] means to come: she consulted Hecate about it. [*Seeing a group of women approaching.*] But look! Here come a few. And there are some more over here. Hurrah! Where do they come from?

LYSISTRATA: From Anagyra.[8]

CALONICE: Yes indeed! We've raised up quite a stink from Anagyra anyway.

[*Enter* MYRRHINE *in haste, followed by several other women.*]

MYRRHINE: [*Breathlessly.*] Have we come in time, Lysistrata? What do you say? Why so quiet?

LYSISTRATA: I can't say much for you, Myrrhine, coming at this hour on such important business.

MYRRHINE: Why, I had trouble finding my girdle in the dark. But if it's so important, we're here now; tell us.

LYSISTRATA: No. Let's wait a little for the women from Boeotia and the Peloponnesus.

MYRRHINE: That's a much better suggestion. Look! Here comes Lampito now.

[*Enter* LAMPITO *with two other women.*]

LYSISTRATA. Greetings, my dear Spartan friend. How pretty you look, my dear. What a smooth complexion and well-developed figure! You could throttle an ox.

LAMPITO: Faith, yes, I think I could. I take exercises and kick my heels against my bum. [*She demonstrates with a few steps of the Spartan "bottom-kicking" dance.*]

LYSISTRATA: And what splendid breasts you have.

LAMPITO: La! You handle me like a prize steer.

LYSISTRATA: And who is this young lady with you?

LAMPITO: Faith, she's an Ambassadress from Boeotia.

LYSISTRATA: Oh yes, a Boeotian, and blooming like a garden too.

5. Just across the bay from Piraeus, the port of Athens. 6. A large village a few miles northwest of Athens. 7. A very superstitious Athenian (perhaps he was sitting in the audience) who never went out without consulting the shrine of Hecate at his doorstep. 8. A district south of Athens. It was also the name of a bad-smelling shrub and the phrase "to stir up the anagyra" was poverbially used to describe people who brought trouble on themselves by interfering.

CALONICE: [*Lifting up her skirt.*] My word! How neatly her garden's weeded!

LYSISTRATA: And who is the other girl?

LAMPITO: Oh, she's a Corinthian swell.

MYRRHINE: [*After a rapid examination.*] Yes indeed. She swells very nicely [*Pointing.*] here and here.

LAMPITO: Who has gathered together this company of women?

LYSISTRATA: I have.

LAMPITO: Speak up, then. What do you want?

MYRRHINE: Yes, my dear, tell us what this important matter is.

LYSISTRATA: Very well, I'll tell you. But before I speak, let me ask you a little question.

MYRRHINE: Anything you like.

LYSISTRATA: [*Earnestly.*] Tell me: don't you yearn for the fathers of your children, who are away at the wars? I know you all have husbands abroad.

CALONICE: Why, yes; mercy me! My husband's been away for five months in Thrace keeping guard on—Eucrates.[9]

MYRRHINE: And mine for seven whole months in Pylus.[1]

LAMPITO: And mine, as soon as ever he returns from the fray, readjusts his shield and flies out of the house again.

LYSISTRATA: And as for lovers, there's not even a ghost of one left. Since the Milesians revolted from us,[2] I've not even seen an eight-inch dingus to be a leather consolation for us widows. Are you willing, if I can find a way, to help me end the war?

MYRRHINE: Goodness, yes! I'd do it, even if I had to pawn my dress and—get drunk on the spot!

CALONICE: And I, even if I had to let myself be split in two like a flounder.

LAMPITO: I'd climb up Mt. Taygetus[3] if I could catch a glimpse of peace.

LYSISTRATA: I'll tell you, then, in plain and simple words. My friends, if we are going to force our men to make peace, we must do without—

MYRRHINE: Without what? Tell us.

LYSISTRATA: Will you do it?

MYRRHINE: We'll do it, if it kills us.

LYSISTRATA: Well, then we must do without sex altogether.

[*General consternation.*]

Why do you turn away? Where go you? Why turn so pale? Why those tears? Will you do it or not? What means this hestitation?

MYRRHINE: I won't do it! Let the war go on.

CALONICE: Nor I! Let the war go on.

LYSISTRATA: So, my little flounder? Didn't you say just now you'd split yourself in half?

9. We have no details on this campign in Thrace. 1. A point on the west coast of the Peloponnese held by an Athenian garrison. 2. The city of Miletus, an Athenian ally ever since the Persian war, had deserted the Athenian cause in the previous year. The objects Lysistrata speaks of were supposed to be manufactured there. 3. The mountain which towers over Sparta.

CALONICE: Anything else you like. I'm willing, even if I have to walk through fire. Anything rather than sex. There's nothing like it, my dear.

LYSISTRATA: [*To* MYRRHINE.] What about you?

MYRRHINE: [*Sullenly.*] I'm willing to walk through fire, too.

LYSISTRATA: Oh vile and cursed breed! No wonder they make tragedies about us: we're naught but "love-affairs and bassinets."[4] But you, my dear Spartan friend, if you alone are with me, our enterprise might yet succeed. Will you vote with me?

LAMPITO: 'Tis cruel hard, by my faith, for a woman to sleep alone without her nooky; but for all that, we certainly do need peace.

LYSISTRATA: O my dearest friend! You're the only real woman here.

CALONICE: [*Wavering.*] Well, if we do refrain from—[*Shuddering.*] what you say (God forbid!), would that bring peace?

LYSISTRATA: My goodness, yes! If we sit at home all rouged and powdered, dressed in our sheerest gowns, and neatly depilated, our men will get excited and want to take us; but if you don't come to them and keep away, they'll soon make a truce.

LAMPITO: Aye; Menelaus caught sight of Helen's naked breast and dropped his sword, they say.

CALONICE: What if the men give us up?

LYSISTRATA: "Flay a skinned dog,"[5] as Pherecrates says.

CALONICE: Rubbish! These make-shifts are no good. But suppose they grab us and drag us into the bedroom?

LYSISTRATA: Hold on to the door.

CALONICE: And if they beat us?

LYSISTRATA: Give in with a bad grace. There's no pleasure in it for them when they have to use violence. And you must torment them in every possible way. They'll give up soon enough; a man gets no joy if he doesn't get along with his wife.

MYRRHINE: If this is your opinion, we agree.

LAMPITO: As for our own men, we can persuade them to make a just and fair peace; but what about the Athenian rabble? Who will persuade them not to start any more monkey-shines?

LYSISTRATA: Don't worry. We guarantee to convince them.

LAMPITO: Not while their ships are rigged so well and they have that mighty treasure in the temple of Athene.

LYSISTRATA: We've taken good care for that too: we shall seize the Acropolis today. The older women have orders to do this, and while we are making our arrangements, they are to pretend to make a sacrifice and occupy the Acropolis.

LAMPITO: All will be well then. That's a very fine idea.

LYSISTRATA: Let's ratify this, Lampito, with the most solemn oath.

4. In the *Tyro* of Sophocles, which had recently been produced, the heroine, who had borne twin sons to the god Poseidon, left them exposed in a bassinet. 5. A proverb for useless activity. *Pherecrates:* a fifth-century comic poet.

LAMPITO: Tell us what oath we shall swear.

LYSISTRATA: Well said. Where's our Policewoman? [*To a Scythian slave.*] What are you gaping at? Set a shield upside-down here in front of me, and give me the sacred meats.

CALONICE: Lysistrata, what sort of an oath are we to take?

LYSISTRATA: What oath? I'm going to slaughter a sheep over the shield, as they do in Aeschylus.[6]

CALONICE: Don't, Lysistrata! No oaths about peace over a shield.

LYSISTRATA: What shall the oath be, then?

CALONICE: How about getting a white horse somewhere and cutting out its entrails for the sacrifice?

LYSISTRATA: White horse indeed!

CALONICE: Well then, how shall we swear?

MYRRHINE: I'll tell you: let's place a large black bowl upside-down and then slaughter—a flask of Thasian wine.[7] And then let's swear—not to pour in a single drop of water.

LAMPITO: Lord! How I like that oath!

LYSISTRATA: Someone bring out a bowl and a flask.

[*A slave brings the utensils for the sacrifice.*]

CALONICE: Look, my friends! What a big jar! Here's a cup that 'twould give me joy to handle. [*She picks up the bowl.*]

LYSISTRATA: Set it down and put your hands on our victim. [*As* CALONICE *places her hands on the flask.*] O Lady of Persuasion and dear Loving Cup, graciously vouchsafe to receive this sacrifice from us women. [*She pours the wine into the bowl.*]

CALONICE: The blood has a good colour and spurts out nicely.

LAMPITO: Faith, it has a pleasant smell, too.

MYRRHINE: Oh, let me be the first to swear, ladies!

CALONICE: No, by our Lady! Not unless you're allotted the first turn.

LYSISTRATA: Place all your hands on the cup, and one of you repeat on behalf of all what I say. Then all will swear and ratify the oath. *I will suffer no man, be he husband or lover,*

CALONICE: *I will suffer no man, be he husband or lover,*

LYSISTRATA: *To approach me all hot and horny.* [*As* CALONICE *hesitates.*] Say it!

CALONICE: [*Slowly and painfully.*] *To approach me all hot and horny.* O Lysistrata, I feel so weak in the knees!

LYSISTRATA: *I will remain at home unmated,*

CALONICE: *I will remain at home unmated,*

LYSISTRATA: *Wearing my sheerest gown and carefully adorned,*

CALONICE: *Wearing my sheerest gown and carefully adorned,*

6. In Aeschylus' *Seven Against Thebes*, the enemy champions are described as swearing loyalty to each other and slaughtering a bull so that the blood flowed into the hollow of a shield. 7. Strong wine from the island of Thasos in the northern Aegean. In Athens the wife was in charge of the household supplies and it is a frequent Aristophanic joke to present her as addicted to the bottle.

LYSISTRATA: *That my husband may burn with desire for me.*
CALONICE: *That my husband may burn with desire for me.*
LYSISTRATA: *And if he takes me by force against my will,*
CALONICE: *And if he takes me by force against my will,*
LYSISTRATA: *I shall do it badly and keep from moving.*
CALONICE: *I shall do it badly and keep from moving.*
LYSISTRATA: *I will not stretch my slippers toward the ceiling,*
CALONICE: *I will not stretch my slippers toward the ceiling,*
LYSISTRATA: *Nor will I take the posture of the lioness on the knife-handle.*
CALONICE: *Nor will I take the posture of the lioness on the knife-handle.*
LYSISTRATA: *If I keep this oath, may I be permitted to drink from this cup,*
CALONICE: *If I keep this oath, may I be permitted to drink from this cup,*
LYSISTRATA: *But if I break it, may the cup be filled with water.*
CALONICE: *But if I break it, may the cup be filled with water.*
LYSISTRATA: Do you all swear to this?
ALL: I do, so help me!
LYSISTRATA: Come then, I'll just consummate this offering.

[*She takes a long drink from the cup.*]

CALONICE: [*Snatching the cup away.*] Shares, my dear! Let's drink to our continued friendship.

[*A shout is heard from off-stage.*]

LAMPITO: What's that shouting?
LYSISTRATA: That's what I was telling you: the women have just seized the Acropolis. Now, Lampito, go home and arrange matters in Sparta; and leave these two ladies here as hostages. We'll enter the Acropolis to join our friends and help them lock the gates.
CALONICE: Don't you suppose the men will come to attack us?
LYSISTRATA: Don't worry about them. Neither threats nor fire will suffice to open the gates, except on the terms we've stated.
CALONICE: I should say not! Else we'd belie our reputation as unmanageable pests.

[LAMPITO *leaves the stage. The other women retire and enter the Acropolis through the Propylaea. Enter the* CHORUS OF OLD MEN, *carrying fire-pots and a load of heavy sticks.*]

LEADER OF MEN: Onward, Draces, step by step, though your shoulder's aching.
Cursèd logs of olive-wood, what a load you're making!

FIRST SEMI-CHORUS OF OLD MEN: [*Singing.*]

Aye, many surprises await a man who lives to a ripe old age;
For who could suppose, Strymodorus my lad, that the women
we've nourished (alas!),
Who sat at home to vex our days,
Would seize the holy image here

And occupy this sacred shrine,
With bolts and bars, with fell design,
To lock the Propylaea?

LEADER OF MEN: Come with speed, Philourgus, come! to the temple hast'ning.
There we'll heap these logs about in a circle round them,
And whoever has conspired, raising this rebellion,
Shall be roasted, scorched, and burnt, all without exception,
Doomed by one unanimous vote—but first the wife of Lycon.[8]

SECOND SEMI-CHORUS: [*Singing.*]

No, no! by Demeter, while I'm alive, no woman shall mock at me.
Not even the Spartan Cleomenes,[9] our citadel first to seize,
Got off unscathed; for all his pride
And haughty Spartan arrogance,
He left his arms and sneaked away,
Stripped to his shirt, unkempt, unshav'd,
With six years' filth still on him.

LEADER OF MEN: I besieged that hero bold, sleeping at my station,
Marshalled at these holy gates sixteen deep against him.
Shall I not these cursèd pests punish for their daring,
Burning these Euripides-and-God-detested women?[1]
Aye! or else may Marathon overturn my trophy.[2]

FIRST SEMI-CHORUS: [*Singing.*]

There remains of my road
Just this brow of the hill;
There I speed on my way.
Drag the logs up the hill, though we've got no ass to help.
(God! my shoulder's bruised and sore!)
Onward still must we go
Blow the fire! Don't let it go out
Now we're near the end of our road.

ALL: [*Blowing on the fire-pots.*] Whew! Whew! Drat the smoke!

8. The ancient commentaries tell us that she was called Rhodia and was not too careful about her reputation. 9. In 508 B.C., the Athenians expelled the tyrant Hippias and were about to install a democratic regime under the leadership of Cleisthenes when the oligarchic party appealed to Sparta for help. The Spartan king Cleomenes invaded Attica, seized the city, and began a purge of the democrats. A popular uprising, however, forced him into the Acropolis, where he was besieged; after two days he was allowed to withdraw with his troops and Cleisthenes began the reforms which established the democracy. 1. Euripides is always presented in Aristophanic comedy as a misogynist and hence hated by women in return. There does not seem to be any foundation for Aristophanes' view, though Euripides' realistic (if sympathetic) presentation of women may possibly have enraged Athenian society ladies. 2. If the chorus really fought at Marathon, they are very old men. The trophy was on a high mound which covered the Athenian dead and is still in place.

SECOND SEMI-CHORUS: [*Singing.*]

Lord, what smoke rushing forth
From the pot, like a dog
Running mad, bites my eyes!
This must be Lemnos-fire.[3] What a sharp and stinging smoke!
Rushing onward to the shrine
Aid the gods. Once for all
Show your mettle, Laches my boy!
To the rescue hastening all!

ALL: [*Blowing on the fire-pots.*] Whew! Whew! Drat the smoke!

[*The chorus has now reached the edge of the Orchestra nearest the stage, in front of the Propylaea. They begin laying their logs and fire-pots on the ground.*]

LEADER OF MEN: Thank heaven, this fire is still alive. Now let's first put down these logs here and place our torches in the pots to catch; then let's make a rush for the gates with a battering-ram. If the women don't unbar the gate at our summons, we'll have to smoke them out.

Let me put down my load. Ouch! That hurts! [*To the audience.*] Would any of the generals in Samos[4] like to lend a hand with this log? [*Throwing down a log.*] Well, *that* won't break my back any more, at any rate. [*Turning to his fire-pot.*] Your job, my little pot, is to keep those coals alive and furnish me shortly with a red-hot torch.

O mistress Victory, be my ally and grant me to rout these audacious women in the Acropolis.

[*While the men are busy with their logs and fires, the* CHORUS OF OLD WOMEN *enters, carrying pitchers of water.*]

LEADER OF WOMEN: What's this I see? Smoke and flames? Is that a fire ablazing? Let's rush upon them. Hurry up! They'll find us women ready.

FIRST SEMI-CHORUS OF OLD WOMEN: [*Singing.*]

With wingèd foot onward I fly,
Ere the flames consume Neodice;
Lest Critylla be overwhelmed
By a lawless, accurst herd of old men.
I shudder with fear. Am I too late to aid them?
At break of the day filled we our jars with water
Fresh from the spring, pushing our way straight through the crowds.
Oh, what a din!
Mid crockery crashing, jostled by slave-girls,
Sped we to save them, aiding our neighbors,
Bearing this water to put out the flames.

3. Lemnos is a volcanic island in the Aegean.
4. At this time, the headquarters of the Athenian fleet.

SECOND SEMI-CHORUS OF OLD WOMEN: [*Singing.*]

Such news I've heard: doddering fools
Come with logs, like furnace-attendants,
Loaded down with three hundred pounds,
Breathing many a vain, blustering threat,
That all these abhorred sluts will be burnt to charcoal.
O goddess, I pray never may they be kindled;
Grant them to save Greece and our men; madness and war help them to end.
With this as our purpose, golden-plumed Maiden,
Guardian of Athens, seized we thy precinct.
Be my ally, Warrior-maiden,
'Gainst these old men, bearing water with me.

[*The women have now reached their position in the Orchestra, and their* LEADER *advances toward the* LEADER OF THE MEN.]

LEADER OF WOMEN: Hold on there! What's this, you utter scoundrels? No decent, God-fearing citizens would act like this.

LEADER OF MEN: Oho! Here's something unexpected: a swarm of women have come out to attack us.

LEADER OF WOMEN: What, do we frighten you? Surely you don't think we're too many for you. And yet there are ten thousand times more of us whom you haven't even seen.

LEADER OF MEN: What say, Phaedria?[5] Shall we let these women wag their tongues? Shan't we take our sticks and break them over their backs?

LEADER OF WOMEN: Let's set our pitchers on the ground; then if anyone lays a hand on us, they won't get in our way.

LEADER OF MEN: By God! If someone gave them two or three smacks on the jaw, like Bupalus,[6] they wouldn't talk so much!

LEADER OF WOMEN: Go on, hit me, somebody! Here's my jaw! But no other bitch will bite a piece out of you before me.

LEADER OF MEN: Silence! or I'll knock out your—senility!

LEADER OF WOMEN: Just lay one finger on Stratyllis, I dare you!

LEADER OF MEN: Suppose I dust you off with this fist? What will you do?

LEADER OF WOMEN: I'll tear the living guts out of you with my teeth.

LEADER OF MEN: No poet is more clever than Euripides: "There is no beast so shameless as a woman."

LEADER OF WOMEN: Let's pick up our jars of water, Rhodippe.

LEADER OF MEN: Why have you come here with water, you detestable slut?

LEADER OF WOMEN: And why have you come with fire, you funeral vault? To cremate yourself?

LEADER OF MEN: To light a fire and singe your friends.

LEADER OF WOMEN: And I've brought water to put out your fire.

5. A man's name; the remark is addressed to another member of the male chorus. 6. A sixth-century sculptor, the target of the poet Hipponax's satirical attacks.

LEADER OF MEN: What? You'll put out my fire?
LEADER OF WOMEN: Just try and see!
LEADER OF MEN: I wonder: shall I scorch you with this torch of mine?
LEADER OF WOMEN: If you've got any soap, I'll give you a bath.
LEADER OF MEN: Give *me* a bath, you stinking hag?
LEADER OF WOMEN: Yes—a bridal bath!
LEADER OF MEN: Just listen to her! What crust!
LEADER OF WOMEN: Well, I'm a free citizen.
LEADER OF MEN: I'll put an end to your bawling.

[*The men pick up their torches.*]

LEADER OF WOMEN: You'll never do jury-duty[7] again.

[*The women pick up their pitchers.*]

LEADER OF MEN: Singe her hair for her!
LEADER OF WOMEN: Do your duty, water!

[*The women empty their pitchers on the men.*]

LEADER OF MEN: Ow! Ow! For heaven's sake!
LEADER OF WOMEN: Is it too hot?
LEADER OF MEN: What do you mean "hot"? Stop! What are you doing?
LEADER OF WOMEN: I'm watering you, so you'll be fresh and green.
LEADER OF MEN: But I'm all withered up with shaking.
LEADER OF WOMEN: Well, you've got a fire; why don't you dry yourself?

[*Enter an* ATHENIAN MAGISTRATE, *accompanied by four Scythian policemen.*[8]]

MAGISTRATE: Have these wanton women flared up again with their timbrels and their continual worship of Sabazius?[9] Is this another Adonis-dirge[1] upon the roof-tops—which we heard not long ago in the Assembly? That confounded Demostratus was urging us to sail to Sicily, and the whirling women shouted, "Woe for Adonis!" And then Demostratus said we'd best enroll the infantry from Zacynthus, and a tipsy woman on the roof shrieked, "Beat your breasts for Adonis!" And that vile and filthy lunatic forced his measure through. Such license do our women take.

LEADER OF MEN: What if you heard of the insolence of these women here? Besides their other violent acts, they threw water all over us, and we have to shake out our clothes just as if we'd leaked in them.

MAGISTRATE: And rightly, too, by God! For we ourselves lead the women astray

7. Paid attendance of the courts, the usual source of income for older Athenians. 8. The regular police of Athens. They carried bows and arrows. 9. The cult of the oriental deity Sabazius had been recently introduced in Athens. It was considered somewhat disorderly and immoral by religious conservatives. 1. The lament of the women of Adonis (Tammuz), another oriental cult. When the great expedition to Sicily set sail, the women were mourning the death of Adonis—a bad omen which proved all too true. Demostratus was one of the supporters of the expedition (the most prominent was Alcibiades) and he proposed to enroll heavy armed infantry from the island of Zacynthus, off the west coast of Greece, on the way to Sicily.

and teach them to play the wanton; from these roots such notions blossom forth. A man goes into the jeweler's shop and says, "About that necklace you made for my wife, goldsmith: last night, while she was dancing, the fastening-bolt slipped out of the hole. I have to sail over to Salamis today; if you're free, do come around tonight and fit in a new bolt for her." Another goes to the shoe-maker, a strapping young fellow with manly parts, and says, "See here, cobbler, the sandal-strap chafes my wife's little—toe; it's so tender. Come around during the siesta and stretch it a little, so she'll be more comfortable." Now we see the results of such treatment: here I'm a special Councillor and need money to procure oars for the galleys; and I'm locked out of the Treasury by these women.

But this is no time to stand around. Bring up crow-bars there! I'll put an end to their insolence. [*To one of the policemen.*] What are you gaping at, you wretch? What are you staring at? Got an eye out for a tavern, eh? Set your crow-bars here to the gates and force them open. [*Retiring to safe distance.*] I'll help from over here.

[*The gates are thrown open and* LYSISTRATA *comes out followed by several other women.*]

LYSISTRATA: Don't force the gates; I'm coming out of my own accord. We don't need crow-bars here; what we need is good sound common-sense.

MAGISTRATE: Is that so, you strumpet? Where's my policeman? Officer, arrest her and tie her arms behind her back.

LYSISTRATA: By Artemis, if he lays a finger on me, he'll pay for it, even if he is a public servant.

[*The policeman retires in terror.*]

MAGISTRATE: You there, are you afraid? Seize her round the waist—and you, too. Tie her up, both of you!

FIRST WOMAN: [*As the second policeman approaches* LYSISTRATA.] By Pandrosus,[2] if you but touch her with your hand, I'll kick the stuffings out of you.

[*The second policeman retires in terror.*]

MAGISTRATE: Just listen to that: "kick the stuffings out." Where's another policeman? Tie *her* up first, for her chatter.

SECOND WOMAN: By the Goddess of the Light, if you lay the tip of your finger on her, you'll soon need a doctor.

[*The third policeman retires in terror.*]

MAGISTRATE: What's this? Where's my policeman? Seize *her* too. I'll soon stop your sallies.

THIRD WOMAN: By the Goddess to Tauros,[3] if you go near her, I'll tear out your hair until it shrieks with pain.

[*The fourth policeman retires in terror.*]

2. A mythical Athenian princess. 3. Artemis.

MAGISTRATE: Oh, damn it all! I've run out of policemen. But women must never defeat us. Officers, let's charge them all together. Close up your ranks!

[*The policemen rally for a mass attack.*]

LYSISTRATA: By heaven, you'll soon find out that we have four companies of warrior-women, all fully equipped within!
MAGISTRATE: [*Advancing.*] Twist their arms off, men!
LYSISTRATA: [*Shouting.*] To the rescue, my valiant women!
O sellers-of-barley-green-stuffs-and-eggs,
O sellers-of-garlic, ye keepers-of-taverns, and vendors-of-bread,
Grapple! Smite! Smash!
Won't you heap filth on them? Give them a tongue-lashing!

[*The women beat off the policemen.*]

Halt! Withdraw! No looting on the field.

MAGISTRATE: Damn it! My police-force has put up a very poor show.
LYSISTRATA: What did you expect? Did you think you were attacking slaves? Didn't you know that women are filled with passion?
MAGISTRATE: Aye, passion enough—for a good strong drink!
LEADER OF MEN: O chief and leader of this land, why spend your words in vain?
Don't argue with these shameless beasts. You know not how we've fared:
A soapless bath they've given us; our clothes are soundly soaked.
LEADER OF WOMEN: Poor fool! You never should attack or strike a peaceful girl.
But if you do, your eyes must swell. For I am quite content
To sit unmoved, like modest maids, in peace and cause no pain;
But let a man stir up my hive, he'll find me like a wasp.

CHORUS OF MEN: [*Singing.*]

O God, whatever shall we do with creatures like Womankind?
This can't be endured by any man alive. Question them!
Let us try to find out what this means.
To what end have they seized on this shrine,
This steep and rugged, high and holy,
Undefiled Acropolis?

LEADER OF MEN: Come, put your questions; don't give in, and probe her every statement.
For base and shameful it would be to leave this plot untested.
MAGISTRATE: Well then, first of all I wish to ask her this: for what purpose have you barred us from the Acropolis?
LYSISTRATA: To keep the treasure safe, so you won't make war on account of it.
MAGISTRATE: What? Do we make war on account of the treasure?
LYSISTRATA: Yes, and you cause all our other troubles for it, too. Peisander[4] and

4. A leader of the war party.

those greedy office-seekers keep things stirred up so they can find occasions to steal. Now let them do what they like: they'll never again make off with any of this money.

MAGISTRATE: What will you do?

LYSISTRATA: What a question! We'll administer it ourselves.

MAGISTRATE: *You* will administer the treasure?

LYSISTRATA: What's so strange in that? Don't we administer the household money for you?

MAGISTRATE: That's different.

LYSISTRATA: How is it different?

MAGISTRATE: We've got to make war with this money.

LYSISTRATA: But that's the very first thing: you mustn't make war.

MAGISTRATE: How else can we be saved?

LYSISTRATA: We'll save you.

MAGISTRATE: *You?*

LYSISTRATA: Yes, we!

MAGISTRATE: God forbid!

LYSISTRATA: We'll save you, whether you want it or not.

MAGISTRATE: Oh! This is terrible!

LYSISTRATA: You don't like it, but we're going to do it none the less.

MAGISTRATE: Good God! it's illegal!

LYSISTRATA: We *will* save you, my little man!

MAGISTRATE: Suppose I don't want you to?

LYSISTRATA: That's all the more reason.

MAGISTRATE: What business have you with war and peace?

LYSISTRATA: I'll explain.

MAGISTRATE: [*Shaking his fist.*] Speak up, or you'll smart for it.

LYSISTRATA: Just listen, and try to keep your hands still.

MAGISTRATE: I can't. I'm so mad I can't stop them.

FIRST WOMAN: Then you'll be the one to smart for it.

MAGISTRATE: Croak to yourself, old hag! [*To* LYSISTRATA.] Now then, speak up.

LYSISTRATA: Very well. Formerly we endured the war for a good long time with our usual restraint, no matter what you men did. You wouldn't let us say "boo," although nothing you did suited us. But we watched you well, and though we stayed at home we'd often hear of some terribly stupid measure you'd proposed. Then, though grieving at heart, we'd smile sweetly and say, "What was passed in the Assembly today about writing on the treaty-stone?"[5] "What's that to you?" my husband would say. "Hold your tongue!" And I held my tongue.

FIRST WOMAN: But I wouldn't have—not I!

MAGISTRATE: You'd have been soundly smacked, if you hadn't kept still.

LYSISTRATA: So I kept still at home. Then we'd hear of some plan still worse than the first; we'd say, "Husband, how could you pass such a stupid proposal?"

5. The text of a treaty was inscribed on a stone which was set up in a public place.

He'd scowl at me and say, "If you don't mind your spinning, your head will be sore for weeks. *War shall be the concern of Men.*"[6]

MAGISTRATE: And he was right, upon my word!

LYSISTRATA: Why right, you confounded fool, when your proposals were so stupid and we weren't allowed to make suggestions?

"There's not a *man* left in the country," says one. "No, not one," says another. Therefore all we women have decided in council to make a common effort to save Greece. How long should we have waited? Now, if you're willing to listen to our excellent proposals and keep silence for us in your turn, we still may save you.

MAGISTRATE: We men keep silence for you? That's terrible; I won't endure it!

LYSISTRATA: Silence!

MAGISTRATE: Silence for *you*, you wench, when you're wearing a snood? I'd rather die!

LYSISTRATA: Well, if that's all that bothers you—here! take my snood and tie it round your head. [*During the following words the women dress up the* MAGISTRATE *in women's garments.*] And *now* keep quiet! Here, take this spinning-basket, too, and card your wool with robes tucked up, munching on beans. *War shall be the concern of Women!*

LEADER OF WOMEN: Arise and leave your pitchers, girls; no time is this to falter. We too must aid our loyal friends; our turn has come for action.

CHORUS OF WOMEN: [*Singing.*]

I'll never tire of aiding them with song and dance; never may
Faintness keep my legs from moving to and fro endlessly.
For I yearn to do all for my friends;
They have charm, they have wit, they have grace,
With courage, brains, and best of virtues—
Patriotic sapience.

LEADER OF WOMEN: Come, child of manliest ancient dames, offspring of stinging nettles,
Advance with rage unsoftened; for fair breezes speed you onward.

LYSISTRATA: If only sweet Eros and the Cyprian Queen of Love shed charm over our breasts and limbs and inspire our men with amorous longing and priapic spasms, I think we may soon be called Peacemakers among the Greeks.

MAGISTRATE: What will you do?

LYSISTRATA: First of all, we'll stop those fellows who run madly about the Marketplace in arms.

FIRST WOMAN: Indeed we shall, by the Queen of Paphos.[7]

LYSISTRATA: For now they roam about the market, amid the pots and greenstuffs, armed to the teeth like Corybantes.[8]

MAGISTRATE: That's what manly fellows ought to do!

6. Hector to Andromache, *Iliad* VI, 492. 7. Aphrodite. 8. The armed priests of the goddess Cybele.

LYSISTRATA: But it's so silly: a chap with a Gorgon-emblazoned shield buying pickled herring.

FIRST WOMAN: Why, just the other day I saw one of those long-haired dandies who command our cavalry ride up on horseback and pour into his bronze helmet the egg-broth he'd bought from an old dame. And there was a Thracian slinger too, shaking his lance like Tereus;[9] he'd scared the life out of the poor fig-peddler and was gulping down all her ripest fruit.

MAGISTRATE: How can you stop all the confusion in the various states and bring them together?

LYSISTRATA: Very easily.

MAGISTRATE: Tell me how.

LYSISTRATA: Just like a ball of wool, when it's confused and snarled: we take it thus, and draw out a thread here and a thread there with our spindles; thus we'll unsnarl this war, if no one prevents us, and draw together the various states with embassies here and embassies there.

MAGISTRATE: Do you suppose you can stop this dreadful business with balls of wool and spindles, you nit-wits?

LYSISTRATA: Why, if *you* had any wits, you'd manage all affairs of state like our wool-working.

MAGISTRATE: How so?

LYSISTRATA: First you ought to treat the city as we do when we wash the dirt out of a fleece: stretch it out and pluck and thrash out of the city all those prickly scoundrels; aye, and card out those who conspire and stick together to gain office, pulling off their heads. Then card the wool, all of it, into one fair basket of goodwill, mingling in the aliens residing here, any loyal foreigners, and anyone who's in debt to the Treasury; and consider that all our colonies lie scattered round about like remnants; from all of these collect the wool and gather it together here, wind up a great ball, and then weave a good stout cloak for the democracy.

MAGISTRATE: Dreadful! Talking about thrashing and winding balls of wool, when you haven't the slightest share in the war!

LYSISTRATA: Why, you dirty scoundrel, we bear more than twice as much as you. First, we bear children and send off our sons as soldiers.

MAGISTRATE: Hush! Let bygones be bygones!

LYSISTRATA: Then, when we ought to be happy and enjoy our youth, we sleep alone because of your expeditions abroad. But never mind us married women: I grieve most for the maids who grow old at home unwed.

MAGISTRATE: Don't men grow old, too?

LYSISTRATA: For heaven's sake! That's not the same thing. When a man comes home, no matter how grey he is, he soon finds a girl to marry. But woman's bloom is short and fleeting; if she doesn't grasp her chance, no man is willing to marry her and she sits at home a prey to every fortune-teller.

MAGISTRATE: [*Coarsely.*] But if a man can still get it up—

9. A mythical kind of Thrace. Thracian mercenaries had served in the Athenian ranks during the war.

LYSISTRATA: See here, you: what's the matter? Aren't you dead yet? There's plenty of room for you. Buy yourself a shroud and I'll bake you a honey-cake.[1] [*Handing him a copper coin for his passage across the Styx.*] Here's your fare! Now get yourself a wreath.

[*During the following dialogue the women dress up the* MAGISTRATE *as a corpse.*]

FIRST WOMAN: Here, take these fillets.
SECOND WOMAN: Here, take this wreath.
LYSISTRATA: What do you want? What's lacking? Get moving; off to the ferry! Charon is calling you; don't keep him from sailing.
MAGISTRATE: Am I to endure these insults? By God! I'm going straight to the magistrates to show them how I've been treated.
LYSISTRATA: Are you grumbling that you haven't been properly laid out? Well, the day after tomorrow we'll send around all the usual offerings early in the morning.

[*The* MAGISTRATE *goes out still wearing his funeral decorations.* LYSISTRATA *and the women retire into the Acropolis.*]

LEADER OF MEN: Wake, ye sons of freedom, wake! 'Tis no time for sleeping. Up and at them, like a man! Let us strip for action.

[*The* CHORUS OF MEN *remove their outer cloaks.*]

CHORUS OF MEN: [*Singing.*]

Surely there is something here greater than meets the eye;
For without a doubt I smell Hippias' tyranny.[2]
Dreadful fear assails me lest certain bands of Spartan men,
Meeting here with Cleisthenes,[3] have inspired through treachery
All these god-detested women secretly to seize
Athens' treasure in the temple, and to stop that pay
  Whence I live at my ease.

LEADER OF MEN: Now isn't it terrible for them to advise the state and chatter about shields, being mere women?

And they think to reconcile us with the Spartans—men who hold nothing sacred any more than hungry wolves. Surely this is a web of deceit, my friends, to conceal an attempt at tyranny. But they'll never lord it over me; I'll be on my guard and from now on,

"The blade I bear   A myrtle spray shall wear."

I'll occupy the market under arms and stand next to Aristogeiton.[4]

1. The dead were provided with a honey cake to throw to Cerberus, the three-headed dog which guarded the entry to the underworld. The copper coin was to pay the fare required by Charon, the ferryman over the river Styx. 2. The last tyrant of Athens, driven out in 510 B.C. 3. Not the great reformer who set up the democracy, but a contemporary of Aristophanes, notorious for his effeminacy (and therefore suspect as a fellow-conspirator of the women). 4. One of the two heroes of the democracy who assassinated Hipparchus, the brother of the tyrant Hippias. A drinking song which was frequently heard at Athenian banquets ran: "In a branch of myrtle, I'll hide my

Thus I'll stand beside him. [*He strikes the pose of the famous statue of the tyrannicides, with one arm raised.*] And here's my chance to take this accurst old hag and—[*Striking the* LEADER OF WOMEN.] smack her on the jaw!

LEADER OF WOMEN: You'll go home in such a state your Ma won't recognize you! Ladies all, upon the ground let us place these garments.

[*The* CHORUS OF WOMEN *remove their outer garments.*]

CHORUS OF WOMEN: [*Singing.*]

Citizens of Athens, hear useful words for the state.
Rightly; for it nurtured me in my youth royally.
As a child of seven years carried I the sacred box;[5]
Then I was a Miller-maid, grinding at Athene's shrine;
Next I wore the saffron robe and played Brauronia's Bear;
And I walked as Basket-bearer, wearing chains of figs,
As a sweet maiden fair.

LEADER OF WOMEN: Therefore, am I not bound to give good advice to the city?

Don't take it ill that I was born a woman, if I contribute something better than our present troubles. I pay my share; for I contribute men. But you miserable old fools contribute nothing, and after squandering our ancestral treasure, the fruit of the Persian Wars, you make no contribution in return. And now, all on account of you, we're facing ruin.

What, muttering, are you? If you annoy me, I'll take this hard, rough slipper and—[*Striking the* LEADER OF MEN.] smack you on the jaw!

CHORUS OF MEN: [*Singing.*]

This is outright insolence! Things go from bad to worse.
If you're men with any guts, prepare to meet the foe.
Let us strip our tunics off! We need the smell of male
Vigor. And we cannot fight all swaddled up in clothes.

[*They strip off their tunics.*]

Come then, my comrades, on to the battle, ye who once to Leipsydrion[6] came;
Then ye were MEN. Now call back your youthful vigor.
With light, wingèd footstep advance,
Shaking old age from your frame.

---

sword, like Harmodius and Aristogeiton, who killed the tyrant, and made Athens free." 5. This and the next four lines describe the religious duties of a well-born Athenian girl. The sacred box contained religious objects connected with the worship of Athena in the Erechtheum. The miller-maids ground flour for sacred cakes. At Brauron in Attica, young girls who represented themselves as bears (the saffron robe was a substitute for a more primitive bearskin) worshipped Artemis. In the Panathenaic procession certain selected girls carried baskets on their heads. 6. The base of the aristocratic family of the Almaeonidae (the family of Perides) in their first attempt to overthrow Hippias.

LEADER OF MEN: If any of us give these wenches the slightest hold, they'll stop at nothing: such is their cunning.

They will even build ships and sail against us, like Artemisia.[7] Or if they turn to mounting, I count our Knights as done for: a woman's such a tricky jockey when she gets astraddle, with a good firm seat for trotting. Just look at those Amazons that Micon[8] painted, fighting on horseback against men!

But we must throw them all in the pillory—[*Seizing and choking the* LEADER OF WOMEN.] grabbing hold of yonder neck!

CHORUS OF WOMEN: [*Singing.*]

'Ware my anger! Like a boar 'twill rush upon you men.
Soon you'll bawl aloud for help, you'll be so soundly trimmed!
Come, my friends, let's strip with speed, and lay aside these robes;
Catch the scent of women's rage. Attack with tooth and nail!

[*They strip off their tunics.*]

Now then, come near me, you miserable man! you'll never eat garlic or black beans again.
And if you utter a single hard word, in rage I will "nurse" you as once
The beetle[9] requited her foe.

LEADER OF WOMEN: For you don't worry me; no, not so long as my Lampito lives and our Theban friend, the noble Ismenia.

You can't do anything, not even if you pass a dozen—decrees! You miserable fool, all our neighbours hate you. Why, just the other day when I was holding a festival for Hecate, I invited as playmate from our neighbours the Boeotians a charming, well-bred Copaic—eel. But they refused to send me one on account of your decrees.

And you'll never stop passing decrees until I grab your foot and—[*Tripping up the* LEADER OF MEN.] toss you down and break your neck!

[*Here an interval of five days is supposed to elapse.* LYSISTRATA *comes out from the Acropolis.*]

LEADER OF WOMEN: [*Dramatically.*] Empress[1] of this great emprise and undertaking,
Why come you forth, I pray, with frowning brow?

LYSISTRATA: Ah, these cursèd women! Their deeds and female notions make me pace up and down in utter despair.

LEADER OF WOMEN: Ah, what sayest thou?

LYSISTRATA: The truth, alas! the truth.

7. Queen of Halicarnassus in Asia Minor. She played a prominent part in Xerxes' invasion of Greece and her ships fought at Salamis. 8. A painter who had lately decorated several public buildings with frescos. The battles of the Greeks and Amazons were favorite subjects of sculptors and painters all through the fifth century. 9. In a fable of Aesop the beetle revenges itself on the eagle by breaking its eggs. 1. The tone of the following passage is mock-tragic.

LEADER OF WOMEN: What dreadful tale hast thou to tell thy friends?
LYSISTRATA: 'Tis shame to speak, and not to speak is hard.
LEADER OF WOMEN: Hide not from me whatever woes we suffer.
LYSISTRATA: Well then, to put it briefly, we want—laying!
LEADER OF WOMEN: O Zeus, Zeus!
LYSISTRATA: Why call on Zeus? That's the way things are. I can no longer keep them away from the men, and they're all deserting. I caught one wriggling through a hole near the grotto of Pan, another sliding down a rope, another deserting her post; and yesterday I found one getting on a sparrow's back to fly off to Orsilochus,[2] and had to pull her back by the hair. They're digging up all sorts of excuses to get home. Look, here comes one of them now. [*A woman comes hastily out of the Acropolis.*] Here you! Where are you off to in such a hurry?
FIRST WOMAN: I want to go home. My very best wool is being devoured by moths.
LYSISTRATA: Moths? Nonsense! Go back inside.
FIRST WOMAN: I'll come right back; I swear it. I just want to lay it out on the bed.
LYSISTRATA: Well, you won't lay it out, and you won't go home, either.
FIRST WOMAN: Shall I let my wool be ruined?
LYSISTRATA: If necessary, yes.

[*Another woman comes out.*]

SECOND WOMAN: Oh dear! Oh dear! My precious flax! I left it at home all unpeeled.
LYSISTRATA: Here's another one, going home for her "flax." Come back here!
SECOND WOMAN: But I just want to work it up a little and then I'll be right back.
LYSISTRATA: No indeed! If you start this, all the other women will want to do the same.

[A *third woman comes out.*]

THIRD WOMAN: O Eilithyia, goddess of travail, stop my labor till I come to a lawful spot![3]
LYSISTRATA: What's this nonsense?
THIRD WOMAN: I'm going to have a baby—right now!
LYSISTRATA: But you weren't even pregnant yesterday.
THIRD WOMAN: Well, I am today. O Lysistrata, do send me home to see a midwife, right away.
LYSISTRATA: What are you talking about? [*Putting her hand on her stomach.*] What's this hard lump here?
THIRD WOMAN: A little boy.
LYSISTRATA: My goodness, what have you got there? It seems hollow; I'll just find out. [*Pulling aside her robe.*] Why, you silly goose, you've got Athene's sacred helmet there. And you said you were having a baby!
THIRD WOMAN: Well, I *am* having one, I swear!
LYSISTRATA: Then what's this helmet for?
THIRD WOMAN: If the baby starts coming while I'm still in the Acropolis, I'll creep

2. The sparrow, Aphrodite's bird, pulled her chariot. *Orsilochus* ran a house of ill-fame. 3. The Acropolis was holy ground, and would be polluted by either birth or death.

into this like a pigeon and give birth to it there.

LYSISTRATA: Stuff and nonsense! It's plain enough what you're up to. You just wait here for the christening of this—helmet.

THIRD WOMAN: But I can't sleep in the Acropolis since I saw the sacred snake.[4]

FIRST WOMAN: And I'm dying for lack of sleep: the hooting of the owls[5] keeps me awake.

LYSISTRATA: Enough of these shams, you wretched creatures. You want your husbands, I suppose. Well, don't you think they want us? I'm sure they're spending miserable nights. Hold out, my friends, and endure for just a little while. There's an oracle that we shall conquer, if we don't split up. [*Producing a roll of paper.*] Here it is.

FIRST WOMAN: Tell us what it says.

LYSISTRATA: Listen.

"When in the length of time the Swallows shall gather together,
Fleeing the Hoopoe's amorous flight and the Cockatoo shunning,
Then shall your woes be ended and Zeus who thunders in heaven
Set what's below on top—"

FIRST WOMAN: What? Are we going to be on top?

LYSISTRATA: "But if the Swallows rebel and flutter away from the temple,
Never a bird in the world shall seem more wanton and worthless."

FIRST WOMAN: That's clear enough, upon my word!

LYSISTRATA: By all that's holy, let's not give up the struggle now. Let's go back inside. It would be a shame, my dear friends, to disobey the oracle.

[*The women all retire to the Acropolis again.*]

CHORUS OF MEN: [*Singing.*]

I have a tale to tell,
Which I know full well.
It was told me
In the nursery.

Once there was a likely lad,
Melanion they name him;
The thought of marriage made him mad,
For which I cannot blame him.[6]

So off he went to mountains fair;
(No women to unbraid him!)
A mighty hunter of the hare,
He had a dog to aid him.

He never came back home to see
Detested women's faces.

4. A snake was kept in the Erechtheum. 5. The sacred bird of Athene. 6. The chorus of men here recasts a well-known myth for its own purposes. In the myth it was Atalanta who avoided marriage, challenging her suitors to a foot race which she always won; Melanion threw a golden apple in front of her; when she stopped to pick it up, she lost the race to him.

He showed a shrewd mentality.
With him I'd fain change places!

ONE OF THE MEN: [*To one of the women.*] Come here, old dame, give me a kiss.
WOMAN: You'll ne'er eat garlic, if you dare!
MAN: I want to kick you—just like this!
WOMAN: Oh, there's a leg with bushy hair!
MAN: Myronides and Phormio[7]
Were hairy—and they thrashed the foe.

CHORUS OF WOMEN: [*Singing.*]

I have another tale,
With which to assail
Your contention
'Bout Melanion.
Once upon a time a man
Named Timon[8] left our city,
To live in some deserted land.
(We thought him rather witty.)

He dwelt alone amidst the thorn;
In solitude he brooded.
From some grim Fury he was born:
Such hatred he exuded.

He cursed you men, as scoundrels through
And through, till life he ended.
He couldn't stand the sight of YOU!
But women he befriended.

WOMAN: [*To one of the men.*] I'll smash your face in, if you like.
MAN: Oh no, please don't! You frighten me.
WOMAN: I'll lift my foot—and thus I'll strike.
MAN: Aha! Look there! What's that I see?
WOMAN: Whate'er you see, you cannot say
That I'm not neatly trimmed today.

[LYSISTRATA *appears on the wall of the Acropolis.*]

LYSISTRATA: Hello! Hello! Girls, come here quick!

[*Several women appear beside her.*]

WOMAN: What is it? Why are you calling?
LYSISTRATA: I see a man coming: he's in a dreadful state. He's mad with passion.
O Queen of Cyprus, Cythera, and Paphos, just keep on this way!
WOMAN: Where is the fellow?

7. Successful Athenian generals. 8. The famous misanthrope, the subject of Shakespeare's play. There is no evidence that he "befriended" women; his hatred seems to have been directed at the whole human race.

LYSISTRATA: There, beside the shrine of Demeter.
WOMAN: Oh yes, so he is. Who is he?
LYSISTRATA: Let's see. Do any of you know him?
MYRRHINE: Yes indeed. That's my husband, Cinesias.
LYSISTRATA: It's up to you, now: roast him, rack him, fool him, love him—and leave him! Do everything, except what our oath forbids.
MYRRHINE: Don't worry; I'll do it.
LYSISTRATA: I'll stay here to tease him and warm him up a bit. Off with you.

[*The other women retire from the wall. Enter* CINESIAS *followed by a slave carrying a baby.* CINESIAS *is obviously in great pain and distress.*]

CINESIAS: [*Groaning.*] Oh-h! Oh-h-h! This is killing me! O God, what tortures I'm suffering!
LYSISTRATA: [*From the wall.*] Who's that within our lines?
CINESIAS: Me.
LYSISTRATA: A *man?*
CINESIAS: [*Pointing.*] A *man,* indeed!
LYSISTRATA: Well, go away!
CINESIAS: Who are you to send me away?
LYSISTRATA: The captain of the guard.
CINESIAS: Oh, for heaven's sake, call out Myrrhine for me.
LYSISTRATA: Call Myrrhine? Nonsense! Who are you?
CINESIAS: Her husband, Cinesias of Paionidai.
LYSISTRATA: [*Appearing much impressed.*] Oh, greetings, friend. Your name is not without honor here among us. Your wife is always talking about you, and whenever she takes an egg or an apple, she says, "Here's to my dear Cinesias!"
CINESIAS: [*Quivering with excitement.*] Oh, ye gods in heaven!
LYSISTRATA: Indeed she does! And whenever our conversations turn to men, your wife immediately says, "All others are mere rubbish compared with Cinesias."
CINESIAS: [*Groaning.*] Oh! Do call her for me.
LYSISTRATA: Why should I? What will you give me?
CINESIAS: Whatever you want. All I have is yours—and you see what I've got.
LYSISTRATA: Well then, I'll go down and call her. [*She descends.*]
CINESIAS: And hurry up! I've had no joy of life ever since she left home. When I go in the house, I feel awful: everything seems so empty and I can't enjoy my dinner. I'm in such a state all the time!
MYRRHINE: [*From behind the wall.*] I *do* love him so. But he won't let me love him. No, no! Don't ask me to see him!
CINESIAS: O my darling, O Myrrhine honey, why do you do this to me? [MYRRHINE *appears on the wall.*] Come down here!
MYRRHINE: No, I won't come down.
CINESIAS: *Don't want you?* I'm in agony!
MYRRHINE: No; you don't want me.
CINESIAS: *Don't want you?* I'm in agony!

MYRRHINE: I'm going now.

CINESIAS: Please don't! At least, listen to your baby. [*To the baby.*] Here you, call your mamma! [*Pinching the baby.*]

BABY: Ma-ma! Ma-ma! Ma-ma!

CINESIAS: [*To* MYRRHINE.] What's the matter with you? Have you no pity for your child, who hasn't been washed or fed for five whole days?

MYRRHINE: Oh, poor child; your father pays no attention to you.

CINESIAS: Come down then, you heartless wretch, for the baby's sake.

MYRRHINE: Oh, what it is to be a mother! I've got to come down, I suppose. [*She leaves the wall and shortly reappears at the gate.*]

CINESIAS: [*To himself.*] She seems much younger, and she has such a sweet look about her. Oh, the way she teases me! And her pretty, provoking ways make me burn with longing

MYRRHINE: [*Coming out of the gate and taking the baby.*] O my sweet little angel. Naughty papa! Here, let Mummy kiss you, Mamma's little sweetheart! [*She fondles the baby lovingly.*]

CINESIAS: [*In despair.*] You heartless creature, why do you do this? Why follow these other women and make both of us suffer so? [*He tries to embrace her.*]

MYRRHINE: Don't touch me!

CINESIAS: You're letting all our things at home go to wrack and ruin.

MYRRHINE: I don't care.

CINESIAS: You don't care that your wool is being plucked to pieces by the chickens?

MYRRHINE: Not in the least.

CINESIAS: And you haven't celebrated the rites of Aphrodite for ever so long. Won't you come home?

MYRRHINE: Not on your life, unless you men make a truce and stop the war.

CINESIAS: Well then, if that pleases you, we'll do it.

MYRRHINE: Well then, if that pleases *you*, I'll come home—afterwards! Right now I'm on oath not to.

CINESIAS: Then just lie down here with me for a moment.

MYRRHINE: No—[*In a teasing voice.*] and yet, I won't say I don't love you.

CINESIAS: You love me? Oh, do lie down here, Myrrhine dear!

MYRRHINE: What, you silly fool! in front of the baby?

CINESIAS: [*Hastily thrusting the baby at the slave.*] Of course not. Here—home! Take him, Manes! [*The slave goes off with the baby.*] See, the baby's out of the way. Now won't you lie down?

MYRRHINE: But where, my dear?

CINESIAS: Where? The grotto of Pan's a lovely spot.

MYRRHINE: How could I purify myself before returning to the shrine?

CINESIAS: Easily: just wash here in the Clepsydra.[9]

MYRRHINE: And then, shall I go back on my oath?

CINESIAS: On my head be it! Don't worry about the oath.

MYRRHINE: All right, then. Just let me bring out a bed.

9. A spring on the Acropolis.

CINESIAS: No, don't. The ground's all right.

MYRRHINE: Heavens, no! Bad as you are, I won't let you lie on the bare ground. [*She goes into the Acropolis.*]

CINESIAS: Why, she really loves me; it's plain to see.

MYRRHINE: [*Returning with a bed.*] There! Now hurry up and lie down. I'll just slip off this dress. But—let's see: oh yes, I must fetch a mattress.

CINESIAS: Nonsense! No mattress for me.

MYRRHINE: Yes indeed! It's not nice on the bare springs.

CINESIAS: Give me a kiss.

MYRRHINE: [*Giving him a hasty kiss.*] There! [*She goes.*]

CINESIAS: [*In mingled distress and delight.*] Oh-h! Hurry back!

MYRRHINE: [*Returning with a mattress.*] Here's the mattress; lie down on it. I'm taking my things off now—but—let's see: you have no pillow.

CINESIAS: I don't *want* a pillow!

MYRRHINE: But I do. [*She goes.*]

CINESIAS: Cheated again, just like Heracles and his dinner![1]

MYRRHINE: [*Returning with a pillow.*] Here, lift your head. [*To herself, wondering how else to tease him.*] Is that all?

CINESIAS: Surely that's all! Do come here, precious!

MYRRHINE: I'm taking off my girdle. But remember: don't go back on your promise about the truce.

CINESIAS: Hope to die, if I do.

MYRRHINE: You don't have a blanket.

CINESIAS: [*Shouting in exasperation.*] *I don't want one!* I want to—

MYRRHINE: Sh-h! There, there, I'll be back in a minute. [*She goes.*]

CINESIAS: She'll be the death of me with these bed-clothes.

MYRRHINE: [*Returning with a blanket.*] Here, get up.

CINESIAS: I've got *this* up!

MYRRHINE: Would you like some perfume?

CINESIAS: Good heavens, no! I won't have it!

MYRRHINE: Yes, you shall, whether you want it or not. [*She goes.*]

CINESIAS: O lord! Confound all perfumes anyway!

MYRRHINE: [*Returning with a flask.*] Stretch out your hand and put some on.

CINESIAS: [*Suspiciously.*] By God, I don't much like this perfume. It smells of shilly-shallying, and has no scent of the marriage-bed.

MYRRHINE: Oh dear! This is Rhodian perfume I've brought.

CINESIAS: It's quite all right dear. Never mind.

MYRRHINE: Don't be silly! [*She goes out with the flask.*]

CINESIAS: Damn the man who first concocted perfumes!

MYRRHINE: [*Returning with another flask.*] Here, try this flask.

CINESIAS: I've got another one all ready for you. Come, you wretch, lie down and stop bringing me things.

1. The point of this proberb seems to be that the hero is such a glutton that his hosts are never quick enough with their entertainment.

MYRRHINE: All right; I'm taking off my shoes. But, my dear, see that you vote for peace.

CINESIAS: [*Absently.*] I'll consider it. [MYRRHINE *runs away to the Acropolis.*] I'm ruined! The wretch has skinned me and run away! [*Chanting, in tragic style.*] Alas! Alas! Deceived, deserted by this fairest of women, whom shall I—lay? Ah, my poor little child, how shall I nurture thee? Where's Cynalopex?[2] I needs must hire a nurse!

LEADER OF MEN: [*Chanting.*] Ah, wretched man, in dreadful wise beguiled, bewrayed, thy soul is sore distressed. I pity thee, alas! alas! What soul, what loins, what liver could stand this strain? How firm and unyielding he stands, with naught to aid him of a morning.

CINESIAS: O lord! O Zeus! What tortures I endure!

LEADER OF MEN: This is the way she's treated you, that vile and cursèd wanton.

LEADER OF WOMEN: Nay, not vile and cursèd, but sweet and dear.

LEADER OF MEN: Sweet, you say? Nay, hateful, hateful!

CINESIAS: Hateful indeed! O Zeus, Zeus!
Seize her and snatch her away,
Like a handful of dust, in a mighty,
Fiery tempest! Whirl her aloft, then let her drop
Down to the earth, with a crash, as she falls—
On the point of this waiting
Thingummybob! [*He goes out.*]

[*Enter a* SPARTAN HERALD, *in an obvious state of excitement, which he is doing his best to conceal.*]

HERALD: Where can I find the Senate or the Prytanes?[3] I've got an important message.

[*The* ATHENIAN MAGISTRATE *enters.*]

MAGISTRATE: Say there, are you a man or Priapus?[4]

HERALD: [*In annoyance.*] I'm a herald, you lout! I've come from Sparta about the truce.

MAGISTRATE: Is that a spear you've got under your cloak?

HERALD: No, of course not!

MAGISTRATE: Why do you twist and turn so? Why hold your cloak in front of you? Did you rupture yourself on the trip?

HERALD: By gum, the fellow's an old fool.

MAGISTRATE: [*Pointing.*] Why, you dirty rascal, you're all excited.

HERALD: Not at all. Stop this tom-foolery.

MAGISTRATE: Well, what's that I see?

HERALD: A Spartan message-staff.[5]

2. A local brothel-keeper. 3. The permanent committee of the Council (Senate). 4. A god whose grossly phallic statue was set to guard orchards and gardens. 5. An encoding device. The papyrus was wrapped round the staff on a spiral and the message could be read only when the papyrus was wound round an exactly similar staff.

MAGISTRATE: Oh, certainly! That's just the kind of message-staff I've got. But tell me the honest truth: How are things going in Sparta?

HERALD: All the land of Sparta is up in arms—and our allies are up, too. We need Pellene.[6]

MAGISTRATE: What brought this trouble on you? A sudden Panic?

HERALD: No, Lampito started it and then all the other women in Sparta with one account chased their husbands out of their beds.

MAGISTRATE: How do you feel?

HERALD: Terrible. We walk around the city bent over like men lighting matches in a wind. For our women won't let us touch them until we all agree and make peace throughout Greece.

MAGISTRATE: This is a general conspiracy of the women; I see it now. Well, hurry back and tell the Spartans to send ambassadors here with full powers to arrange a truce. And I'll go tell the Council to choose ambassadors from here; I've got a little something here that will soon persuade them!

HERALD: I'll fly there; for you've made an excellent suggestion.

[*The* HERALD *and the* MAGISTRATE *depart on opposite sides of the stage.*]

LEADER OF MEN: No beast or fire is harder than womankind to tame.
Nor is the spotted leopard so devoid of shame.

LEADER OF WOMEN: Knowing this, you dare provoke us to attack?
I'd be your steady friend, if you'd but take us back.

LEADER OF MEN: I'll never cease my hatred keen of womankind.

LEADER OF WOMEN: Just as you will. But now just let me help you find
That cloak you threw aside. You look so silly there
Without your clothes. Here, put it on and don't go bare.

LEADER OF MEN: That's very kind, and shows you're not entirely bad.
But I threw off my things when I was good and mad.

LEADER OF WOMEN: At last you seem a man, and won't be mocked, my lad.
If you'd been nice to me, I'd take this little gnat
That's in your eye and pluck it out for you, like that.

LEADER OF MEN: So that's what's bothered me and bit my eye so long!
Please dig it out for me. I own that I've been wrong.

LEADER OF WOMEN: I'll do so, though you've been a most ill-natured brat.
Ye gods! See here! A huge and monstrous little gnat!

LEADER OF MEN: Oh, how that helps! For it was digging wells in me.
And now it's out, my tears can roll down hard and free.

LEADER OF WOMEN: Here, let me wipe them off, although you're such a knave
And kiss me.

LEADER OF MEN: No!

LEADER OF WOMEN: Whate'er you say, a kiss I'll have. [*She kisses him.*]

LEADER OF MEN: Oh, confound these women! They've a coaxing way about them.
He was wise and never spoke a truer word, who said,

6. A city held by the Athenians and claimed by the Spartans; also the name of a famous Athenian prostitute.

"We can't live with women, but we cannot live without them."
Now I'll make a truce with you. We'll fight no more: instead, I will not injure you if you do me no wrong.
And now let's join our ranks and then begin a song.

COMBINED CHORUS: [*Singing.*]

Athenians, we're not prepared,
To say a single ugly word
About our fellow-citizens.
Quite the contrary: we desire but to say and to do
Naught but good. Quite enough are the ills now on hand.
Men and women, be advised:
If anyone requires
Money—minae two or three—
We've got what he desires.

My purse is yours, on easy terms:
When Peace shall reappear,
Whate'er you've borrowed will be due.
So speak up without fear.

You needn't pay me back, you see,
If you can get a cent from me!

We're about to entertain
Some foreign gentlemen;
We've soup and tender, fresh-killed pork.
Come round to dine at ten.
Come early; wash and dress with care,
And bring the children, too.
Then step right in, no "by your leave."
We'll be expecting you.

Walk in as if you owned the place.
You'll find the door—shut in your face!

[*Enter a group of* SPARTAN AMBASSADORS; *they are in the same desperate condition as the* HERALD *in the previous scene.*]

LEADER OF CHORUS: Here come the envoys from Sparta, sprouting long beards and looking for all the world as if they were carrying pig-pens in front of them.

Greetings, gentlemen of Sparta. Tell me, in what state have you come?

SPARTAN: Why waste words? You can plainly see what state we're come in!

LEADER OF CHORUS: Wow! You're in a pretty high-strung condition, and it seems to be getting worse.

SPARTAN: It's indescribable. Won't someone please arrange a peace for us—in any way you like.

LEADER OF CHORUS: Here come our own, native ambassadors, crouching like wrestlers and holding their clothes in front of them; this seems an athletic kind of malady.

[*Enter several* ATHENIAN AMBASSADORS.]

ATHENIAN: Can anyone tell us where Lysistrata is? You see our condition.

LEADER OF CHORUS: Here's another case of the same complaint. Tell me, are the attacks worse in the morning?

ATHENIAN: No, we're always afflicted this way. If someone doesn't soon arrange this truce, you'd better not let me get my hands on—Cleisthenes!

LEADER OF CHORUS: If you're smart, you'll arrange your cloaks so none of the fellows who smashed the Hermae[7] can see you.

SPARTAN: Right you are; a very good suggestion.

ATHENIAN: Greetings, Spartan. We've suffered dreadful things.

SPARTAN: My dear fellow, we'd have suffered still worse if one of those fellows had seen us in this condition.

ATHENIAN: Well, gentlemen, we must get down to business. What's your errand here?

SPARTAN: We're ambassadors about peace.

ATHENIAN: Excellent; so are we. Only Lysistrata can arrange things for us; shall we summon her?

SPARTAN: Aye, and Lysistratus too, if you like.

LEADER OF CHORUS: No need to summon her, it seems. She's coming out of her own accord.

[*Enter* LYSISTRATA *accompanied by a statue of a nude female figure, which represents Reconciliation.*]

Hail, noblest of women; now must thou be
A judge shrewd and subtle, mild and severe,
Be sweet yet majestic: all manners employ.
The leaders of Hellas, caught by thy love-charms
Have come to thy judgment, their charges submitting.

LYSISTRATA: This is no difficult task, if one catch them still in amorous passion, before they've resorted to each other. But I'll soon find out. Where's Reconciliation? Go, first bring the Spartans here, and don't seize them rudely and violently, as our tactless husbands used to do, but as befits a woman, like an old, familiar friend; if they won't give you their hands, take them however you can. Then go fetch these Athenians here, taking hold of whatever they offer you. Now then, men of Sparta, stand here beside me, and you Athenians on the other side, and listen to my words.

I am a woman, it is true, but I have a mind; I'm not badly off in native wit, and by listening to my father and my elders, I've had a decent schooling.

Now I intend to give you a scolding which you both deserve. With one

7. Small statues of the god Hermes equipped with phalluses, which stood at the door of most Athenian houses. Just before the great expedition left for Sicily, rioters (probably oligarchic conspirators opposed to the expedition) smashed many of these statues.

common font you worship at the same altars, just like brothers, at Olympia, at Thermopylae, at Delphi—how many more might I name, if time permitted;—and the Barbarians stand by waiting with their armies; yet you are destroying the men and towns of Greece.

ATHENIAN: Oh, this tension is killing me!

LYSISTRATA: And now, men of Sparta,—to turn to you—don't you remember how the Spartan Pericleidas came here once as a suppliant, and sitting at our altar, all pale with fear in his crimson cloak, begged us for an army?[8] For all Messene had attacked you and the god sent an earthquake too? Then Cimon went forth with four thousand hoplites and saved all Lacedaemon. Such was the aid you received from Athens, and now you lay waste the country which once treated you so well.

ATHENIAN: [*Hotly.*] They're in the wrong, Lysistrata, upon my word, they are!

SPARTAN: [*Absently, looking at the statue of Reconciliation.*] We're in the wrong. What hips! How lovely they are!

LYSISTRATA: Don't think I'm going to let you Athenians off. Don't you remember how the Spartans came in arms when you were wearing the rough, sheepskin cloak of slaves and slew the host of Thessalians, the comrades and allies of Hippias?[9] Fighting with you on that day, alone of all the Greeks, they set you free and instead of a sheepskin gave your folk a handsome robe to wear.

SPARTAN: [*Looking at* LYSISTRATA.] I've never seen a more distinguished woman.

ATHENIAN: [*Looking at Reconciliation.*] I've never seen a more voluptuous body!

LYSISTRATA: Why then, with these many noble deeds to think of, do you fight each other? Why don't you stop this villainy? Why not make peace? Tell me, what prevents it?

SPARTAN: [*Waving vaguely at Reconciliation.*] We're willing, if you're willing to give up your position on yonder flank.

LYSISTRATA: What position, my good man?

SPARTAN: Pylus; we've been panting for it for ever so long.

ATHENIAN: No, by God! You shan't have it!

LYSISTRATA: Let them have it, my friend.

ATHENIAN: Then, what shall we have to rouse things up?

LYSISTRATA: Ask for another place in exchange.

ATHENIAN: Well, let's see: first of all [*Pointing to various parts of Reconciliation's anatomy.*] give us Echinus[1] here, this Maliac Inlet in back there, and these two Megarian legs.

SPARTAN: No, by heavens! You can't have *everything*, you crazy fool!

LYSISTRATA: Let it go. Don't fight over a pair of legs.

ATHENIAN: [*Taking off his cloak.*] I think I'll strip and do a little planting now.

8. After a disastrous earthquake the Spartans were in great danger as a result of a rebellion of their serfs, the Helots. The Athenians under Cimon sent a large force of soldiers to help them (464 B.C.).
9. Hippias the tyrant had allowed exiled democrats to return to Attica but they had to stay outside the city and wear sheepskins so that they could readily be identified. With the help of Spartan soldiers the exiles and the people of Attica finally defeated the Thessalian troops of Hippias.
1. Like Pylus (on the "flank" of the Peloponnese), these names are all double-barrelled references to territories in dispute in the war and salient portions of the anatomy of Reconciliation.

SPARTAN: [*Following suit.*] And I'll just do a little fertilizing, by gosh!

LYSISTRATA: Wait until the truce is concluded. Now if you've decided on this course, hold a conference and discuss the matter with your allies.

ATHENIAN: Allies? Don't be ridiculous! They're in the same state we are. Won't all our allies want the same thing we do—to jump in bed with their women?

SPARTAN: Ours will, I know.

ATHENIAN: Especially the Carystians,[2] by God!

LYSISTRATA: Very well. Now purify yourselves, that your wives may feast and entertain you in the Acropolis; we've provisions by the basketful. Exchange your oaths and pledges there, and then each of you may take his wife and go home.

ATHENIAN: Let's go at once.

SPARTAN: Come on, where you will.

ATHENIAN: For God's sake, let's hurry!

[*They all go into the Acropolis.*]

CHORUS: [*Singing.*]

Whate'er I have of coverlets
  And robes of varied hue
And golden trinkets,—without stint
  I offer them to you.

Take what you will and bear it home,
  Your children to delight,
Or if your girl's a Basket-maid;
  Just choose whate'er's in sight.

There's naught within so well secured
  You cannot break the seal
And bear it off; just help yourselves;
  No hesitation feel.
But you'll see nothing, though you try,
Unless you've sharper eyes than I!

If anyone needs bread to feed
  A growing family,
I've lots of wheat and full-grown loaves;
  So just apply to me.

Let every poor man who desires
  Come round and bring a sack
To fetch the grain; my slave is there
  To load it on his back.

But don't come near my door, I say.
Beware the dog, and stay away!

2. The people of Carystus on the island of Euboea were supposed to be of pre-Hellenic stock and therefore primitive and savage.

[*An* ATHENIAN *enters carrying a torch; he knocks at the gate.*]

ATHENIAN: Open the door! [*To the* CHORUS, *which is clustered around the gate.*] Make way, won't you! What are you hanging around for? Want me to singe you with this torch? [*To himself.*] No; it's a stale trick, I won't do it! [*To the audience.*] Still, if I've got to do it to please *you,* I suppose I'll have to take the trouble.

[A SECOND ATHENIAN *comes out of the gate.*]

SECOND ATHENIAN: And I'll help you.

FIRST ATHENIAN: [*Waving his torch at the* CHORUS.] Get out! Go bawl your heads off! Move on there, so the Spartans can leave in peace when the banquet's over.

[*They brandish their torches until the* CHORUS *leaves the Orchestra.*]

SECOND ATHENIAN: I've never seen such a pleasant banquet: the Spartans are charming fellows, indeed they are! And we Athenians are very witty in our cups.

FIRST ATHENIAN: Naturally: for when we're sober we're never at our best. If the Athenians would listen to me, we'd always get a little tipsy on our embassies. As things are now, we go to Sparta when we're sober and look around to stir up trouble. And then we don't hear what they say—and as for what they *don't* say, we have all sorts of suspicions. And then we bring back varying reports about the mission. But this time everything is pleasant; even if a man should sing the Telamon-song when he ought to sing "Cleitagoras,"[3] we'd praise him and swear it was excellent.

[*The two* CHORUSES *return, as a* CHORUS OF ATHENIANS *and a* CHORUS OF SPARTANS.]

Here they come back again. Go to the devil, you scoundrels!

SECOND ATHENIAN: Get out, I say! They're coming out from the feast.

[*Enter the* SPARTAN AND ATHENIAN AMBASSADORS, *followed by* LYSISTRATA *and all the women.*]

SPARTAN: [*To one of his fellow-envoys.*] My good fellow, take up your pipes; I want to do a fancy two-step and sing a jolly song for the Athenians.

ATHENIAN: Yes, do take your pipes, by all means. I'd love to see you dance.

SPARTAN: [*Singing and dancing with the* CHORUS OF SPARTANS.]

These youths inspire
To song and dance, O Memory;
Stir up my Muse, to tell how we
And Athens' men, in our galleys clashing

3. At an Athenian banquet each guest in turn, when the time came to sing, was supposed to cap the singer before him by choosing an appropriate drinking song.

At Artemisium,[4] 'gainst foemen dashing
  In godlike ire,
Conquered the Persian and set Greece free.

  Leonidas
Led on his valiant warriors
Whetting their teeth like angry boars.
Abundant foam on their lips was flow'ring,
A stream of sweat from their limbs was show'ring.
  The Persian was
Numberless as the sand on the shores.

O Huntress[5] who slayest the beasts in the glade,
O Virgin divine, hither come to our truce,
Unite us in bonds which all time will not loose.
Grant us to find in this treaty, we pray,
An unfailing source of true friendship today,
And all of our days, helping us to refrain
From weaseling tricks which bring war in their train.
  Then hither, come hither! O huntress maid.

LYSISTRATA: Come then, since all is fairly done, men of Sparta, lead away your wives, and you, Athenians, take yours. Let every man stand beside his wife, and every wife beside her man, and then, to celebrate our fortune, let's dance. And in the future, let's take care to avoid these misunderstandings.

CHORUS OF ATHENIANS: [*Singing and dancing.*]

Lead on the dances, your graces revealing.
Call Artemis hither, call Artemis' twin,
Leader of dances, Apollo the Healing,
Kindly God—hither! let's summon him in!
  Nysian Bacchus call,
Who with his Maenads, his eyes flashing fire,
  Dances, and last of all
Zeus of the thunderbolt flaming, the Sire.
  And Hera in majesty,
  Queen of prosperity.

  Come, ye Powers who dwell above
  Unforgetting, our witnesses be
Of Peace with bonds of harmonious love—
The Peace which Cypris has wrought for me.
  Alleluia! Io Paean!
  Leap in joy—hurrah! hurrah!
  'Tis victory—hurrah! hurrah!
  Euoi! Euoi! Euai! Euai!

4. The indecisive naval battle which took place off the coast while Leonidas held the pass at Thermopylae. 5. Artemis.

LYSISTRATA: [*To the* SPARTANS.] Come now, sing a new song to cap ours.

CHORUS OF SPARTANS: [*Singing and dancing.*]

Leaving Taygetus fair and renown'd,
Muse of Laconia,[6] hither come:
Amyclae's god in hymns resound,
Athene of the Brazen Home,[7]
And Castor and Pollux, Tyndareus' sons,
Who sport where Eurotas[8] murmuring runs.

On with the dance! Heia! Ho!
All leaping along,
Mantles a-swinging as we go!
Of Sparta our song.
There the holy chorus ever gladdens,
There the beat of stamping feet,
As our winsome fillies, lovely maidens,
Dance, beside Eurotas' banks a-skipping,—
Nimbly go to and fro
Hast'ning, leaping feet in measures tripping,
Like the Bacchae's revels, hair a-streaming.
Leda's child, divine and mild,
Leads the holy dance, her fair face beaming.
On with the dance! as your hand
Presses the hair
Streaming away unconfined.
Leap in the air
Light as the deer; footsteps resound
Aiding our dance, beating the ground.
Praise Athene, Maid divine, unrivalled in her might,
Dweller in the Brazen Home, unconquered in the fight.

[*All go out singing and dancing.*]

411 B.C.

6. The Spartan region. *Amyclae:* Part of Sparta. 7. The bronze-plated temple of Athena in Sparta. 8. The river of Sparta.

SAMUEL BECKETT

Krapp's Last Tape

A PLAY IN ONE ACT

A late evening in the future.

Krapp's den.

Front centre a small table, the two drawers of which open towards audience.

Sitting at the table, facing front, i.e. across from the drawers, a wearish old man: Krapp.

Rusty black narrow trousers too short for him. Rusty black sleeveless waistcoat, four capacious pockets. Heavy silver watch and chain. Grimy white shirt open at neck, no collar. Surprising pair of dirty white boots, size ten at least, very narrow and pointed.

White face. Purple nose. Disordered grey hair. Unshaven.

Very nearsighted (but unspectacled). Hard of hearing.

Cracked voice. Distinctive intonation.

Laborious walk.

On the table a tape-recorder with microphone and a number of cardboard boxes containing reels of recorded tapes.

Table and immediately adjacent area in strong white light. Rest of stage in darkness.

Krapp remains a moment motionless, heaves a great sigh, looks at his watch, fumbles in his pockets, takes out an envelope, puts it back, fumbles, takes out a small bunch of keys, raises it to his eyes, chooses a key, gets up and moves to front of table. He stoops, unlocks first drawer, peers into it, feels about inside it, takes out a reel of tape, peers at it, puts it back, locks drawer, unlocks second drawer, peers into it, feels about inside it, takes out a large banana, peers at it, locks drawer, puts keys back in his pocket. He turns, advances to edge of stage, halts, strokes banana, peels it, drops skin at his feet, puts end of banana in his mouth and remains motionless, staring vacuously before him. Finally he bites off the end, turns aside and begins pacing to and fro at edge of stage, in the light, i.e. not more than four or five paces either way, meditatively eating banana. He treads on skin, slips, nearly falls, recovers himself, stoops and peers at skin and finally pushes it, still stooping, with his foot over the edge of stage into pit. He resumes his pacing, finishes banana, returns to table, sits down, remains a moment motionless, heaves a great sigh, takes keys from his pocket, raises them to his eyes, chooses key, gets up and moves to front of table, unlocks second drawer, takes out a second large banana, peers at it, locks drawer, puts back keys in his pocket, turns, advances to edge of stage, halts, strokes banana, peels it, tosses skin into pit, puts end of banana in his mouth and remains motionless, staring vacuously before him. Finally he has an idea, puts banana in his waistcoat pocket, the end emerging, and goes with all the speed he can muster backstage into darkness. Ten seconds. Loud pop of cork. Fifteen seconds. He comes back into light carrying an old ledger and sits down at table. He lays ledger on table, wipes his mouth, wipes his hands on the front of his waistcoat, brings them smartly together and rubs them.

KRAPP: [*Briskly.*] Ah! [*He bends over ledger, turns the pages, finds the entry he wants, reads.*] Box . . . thrree . . . spool . . . five. [*He raises his head and stares front. With relish.*] Spool! [*Pause.*] Spooool! [*Happy smile. Pause. He bends over table, starts peering and poking at the boxes.*] Box . . . thrree . . . thrree . . . four . . . two . . . [*With surprise.*] nine! good God! . . . seven . . . ah! the little rascal! [*He takes up box, peers at it.*] Box thrree. [*He lays it on table, opens it and peers at spools inside.*] Spool . . . [*He peers at ledger*] . . . five . . . [*He peers at spools.*] . . . five . . . five . . . ah! the little scoundrel! [*He takes out a spool, peers at it.*] Spool five. [*He lays it on table, closes box three, puts it back with the others, takes up the spool.*] Box thrree, spool five. [*He bends over the machine, looks up. With relish.*] Spooool! [*Happy smile. He bends, loads spool on machine, rubs his hands.*] Ah! [*He peers at ledger, reads entry at foot of page.*] Mother at rest at last . . . Hm . . . The black ball . . . [*He raises his head, stares blankly front. Puzzled.*] Black ball? . . . [*He peers again at ledger, reads.*] The dark nurse . . . [*He raises his head, broods, peers again at ledger, reads.*] Slight improvement in bowel condition . . . Hm . . . Memorable . . . what? [*He peers closer.*] Equinox, memorable equinox. [*He raises his head, stares blankly front. Puzzled.*] Memorable equinox? . . . [*Pause. He shrugs his shoulders, peers again at ledger, reads.*] Farewell to—[*He turns the page*]—love.

[*He raises his head, broods, bends over machine, switches on and assumes listening posture, i.e. leaning forward, elbows on table, hand cupping ear towards machine, face front.*]

TAPE: [*Strong voice, rather pompous, clearly Krapp's at a much earlier time.*] Thirty-nine today, sound as a—[*Settling himself more comfortably he knocks one of the boxes off the table, curses, switches off, sweeps boxes and ledger violently to the ground, winds tape back to beginning, switches on, resumes posture.*] Thirty-nine today, sound as a bell, apart from my old weakness, and intellectually I have now every reason to suspect at the . . . [*Hesitates.*] . . . crest of the wave—or thereabouts. Celebrated the awful occasion, as in recent years, quietly at the Winehouse. Not a soul. Sat before the fire with closed eyes, separating the grain from the husks. Jotted down a few notes, on the back of an envelope. Good to be back in my den, in my old rags. Have just eaten I regret to say three bananas and only with difficulty refrained from a fourth. Fatal things for a man with my condition. [*Vehemently.*] Cut 'em out! [*Pause.*] The new light above my table is a great improvement. With all this darkness round me I feel less alone. [*Pause.*] In a way. [*Pause.*] I love to get up and move about in it, then back here to . . . [*Hesitates.*] . . . me. [*Pause.*] Krapp.

[*Pause.*]

The grain, now what I wonder do I mean by that, I mean . . . [*Hesitates.*] . . . I suppose I mean those things worth having when all the dust has—when all *my* dust has settled. I close my eyes and try and imagine them.

[*Pause. Krapp closes his eyes briefly.*]

Extraordinary silence this evening, I strain my ears and do not hear a sound. Old Miss McGlome always sings at this hour. But not tonight. Songs of her girlhood, she says. Hard to think of her as a girl. Wonderful woman though. Connaught, I fancy. [*Pause.*] Shall I sing when I am her age, if I ever am? No. [*Pause.*]. Did I sing as a boy? No. [*Pause.*] Did I ever sing? No.

[*Pause.*]

Just been listening to an old year, passages at random. I did not check in the book, but it must be at least ten or twelve years ago. At that time I think I was still living on and off with Bianca in Kedar Street. Well out of that; Jesus yes! Hopeless business. [*Pause.*] Not much about her, apart from a tribute to her eyes. Very warm. I suddenly saw them again. [*Pause.*] Incomparable! [*Pause.*] Ah well . . . [*Pause.*] These old P.M.s are gruesome, but I often find them—[*Krapp switches off, broods, switches on.*]—a help before embarking on a new . . . [*Hesitates.*] . . . retrospect. Hard to believe I was ever that young whelp. The voice! Jesus! And the aspirations! [*Brief laugh in which Krapp joins.*] And the resolutions! [*Brief laugh in which Krapp joins.*] To drink less, in particular. [*Brief laugh of Krapp alone.*] Statistics. Seventeen hundred hours, out of the preceding eight thousand odd, consumed on licensed premises alone. More than 20 percent, say 40 percent of his waking life. [*Pause.*] Plans for a less . . . [*Hesitates.*] . . . engrossing sexual life. Last illness of his father. Flagging pursuit of happiness. Unattainable laxation. Sneers at what he calls his youth and thanks to God that it's over. [*Pause.*] False ring there. [*Pause.*] Shadows of the opus . . . magnum. Closing with a—[*Brief laugh.*]—yelp to Providence. [*Prolonged laugh in which Krapp joins.*] What remains of all that misery? A girl in a shabby green coat, on a railway-station platform? No?

[*Pause.*]

When I look—

[*Krapp switches off, broods, looks at his watch, gets up, goes backstage into darkness. Ten seconds. Pop of cork. Ten seconds. Second cork. Ten seconds. Third cork. Ten seconds. Brief burst of quavering song.*

[*Sings.*]

Now the day is over,
Night is drawing nigh-igh,
Shadows—

[*Fit of coughing. He comes back into light, sits down, wipes his mouth, switches on, resumes his listening posture.*]

TAPE: —back on the year that is gone, with what I hope is perhaps a glint of the old eye to come, there is of course the house on the canal where mother lay a-dying, in the late autumn, after her long viduity [*Krapp gives a start*], and the—[*Krapp switches off, winds back tape a little, bends his ear closer to machine, switches on*]—a-dying, after her long viduity, and the—

[*Krapp switches off, raises his head, stares blankly before him. His lips move in the syllables of "viduity." No sound. He gets up, goes backstage into darkness, comes back with an enormous dictionary, lays it on table, sits down and looks up the word.*]

KRAPP: [*Reading from dictionary.*] State—or condition of being—or remaining—a widow—or widower. [*Looks up. Puzzled.*] Being—or remaining? . . . [*Pause. He peers again at dictionary. Reading.*] "Deep weeds of viduity" . . . Also of an animal, especially a bird . . . the vidua or weaver-bird . . . Black plumage of male . . . [*He looks up. With relish.*] The vidua-bird!

[*Pause. He closes dictionary, switches on, resumes listening posture.*]

TAPE: —bench by the weir from where I could see her window. There I sat, in the biting wind, wishing she were gone. [*Pause.*] Hardly a soul, just a few regulars, nursemaids, infants, old men, dogs. I got to know them quite well—oh by appearance of course I mean! One dark young beauty I recollect particularly, all white and starch, incomparable bosom, with a big black hooded perambulator, most funereal thing. Whenever I looked in her direction she had her eyes on me. And yet when I was bold enough to speak to her—not having been introduced—she threatened to call a policeman. As if I had designs on her virtue! [*Laugh. Pause.*] The face she had! The eyes! Like . . . [*Hesitates.*] . . . chrysolite! [*Pause.*] Ah well . . . [*Pause.*] I was there when—[*Krapp switches off, broods, switches on again.*]—the blind went down, one of those dirty brown roller affairs, throwing a ball for a little white dog, as chance would have it. I happened to look up and there it was. All over and done with, at last. I sat on for a few moments with the ball in my hand and the dog yelping and pawing at me. [*Pause.*] Moments. Her moments, my moments. [*Pause.*] The dog's moments. [*Pause.*] In the end I held it out to him and he took it in his mouth, gently, gently. A small, old, black, hard, solid rubber ball. [*Pause.*] I shall feel it, in my hand, until my dying day. [*Pause.*] I might have kept it. [*Pause.*] But I gave it to the dog.

[*Pause.*]

Ah well . . .

[*Pause.*]

Spiritually a year of profound gloom and indigence until that memorable night in March, at the end of the jetty, in the howling wind, never to be forgotten, when suddenly I saw the whole thing. The vision, at last. This I fancy is what I have chiefly to record this evening, against the day when my work will be done and perhaps no place left in my memory, warm or cold, for the miracle that . . . [*Hesitates.*] . . . for the fire that set it alight. What I suddenly saw then was this, that the belief I had been going on all my life, namely—[*Krapp switches off impatiently, winds tape forward, switches on again.*]—great granite rocks the foam flying up in the light of the lighthouse and the wind-gauge spinning like a propellor, clear to me at last that the dark I have always struggled to keep under is in reality my most—[*Krapp curses, switches off, winds tape forward, switches on again.*]—unshatterable association until my dissolution of storm and night with the light of the understanding and the fire—[*Krapp curses louder, switches off, winds tape forward, switches on again.*]—my face in her breasts and my hand on her. We lay there without moving. But under us all moved, and moved us, gently, up and down, and from side to side.

[*Pause.*]

Past midnight. Never knew such silence. The earth might be uninhabited.

[*Pause.*]

Here I end—

[*Krapp switches off, winds tape back, switches on again.*]

—upper lake, with the punt, bathed off the bank, then pushed out into the stream and drifted. She lay stretched out on the floorboards with her hands under her head and her eyes closed. Sun blazing down, bit of a breeze, water nice and lively. I noticed a scratch on her thigh and asked her how she came by it. Picking gooseberries, she said. I said again I thought it was hopeless and no good going on, and she agreed, without opening her eyes. [*Pause.*] I asked her to look at me and after a few moments—[*Pause.*]—after a few moments she did, but the eyes just slits, because of the glare. I bent over her to get them in the shadow and they opened. [*Pause. Low.*] Let me in. [*Pause.*] We drifted in among the flags and stuck. The way they went down, sighing, before the stem! [*Pause.*] I lay down across her with my face in her breasts and my hand on her. We lay there without moving. But under us all moved, and moved us, gently, up and down, and from side to side.

[*Pause.*]

Past midnight. Never knew—

[*Krapp switches off, broods. Finally he fumbles in his pockets, encounters the banana, takes it out, peers at it, puts it back, fumbles, brings out the envelope, fumbles, puts back envelope, looks at his watch, gets up and goes backstage into darkness. Ten seconds. Sound of bottle against glass, then brief siphon. Ten seconds. Bottle against glass alone. Ten seconds. He comes back a little unsteadily into light, goes to front of table, takes out keys, raises them to his eyes, chooses key, unlocks first drawer, peers into it, feels about inside, takes out reel, peers at it, locks drawer, puts keys back in his pocket, goes and sits down, takes reel off machine, lays it on dictionary, loads virgin reel on machine, takes envelope from his pocket, consults back of it, lays it on table, switches on, clears his throat and begins to record.*]

KRAPP: Just been listening to that stupid bastard I took myself for thirty years ago, hard to believe I was ever as bad as that. Thank God that's all done with anyway. [*Pause.*] The eyes she had!! [*Broods, realizes he is recording silence, switches off, broods. Finally.*] Everything there, everything, all the—[*Realizes this is not being recorded, switches on.*] Everything there, everything on this old muckball, all the light and dark and famine and feasting of . . . [*Hesitates.*] . . . the ages! [*In a shout.*] Yes! [*Pause.*] Let that go! Jesus! Take his mind off his homework! Jesus! [*Pause. Weary.*] Ah well, maybe he was right. [*Pause.*] Maybe he was right. [*Broods. Realizes. Switches off. Consults envelope.*] Pah! [*Crumples it and throws it away. Broods. Switches on.*] Nothing to say, not a squeak. What's a year now? The sour cud and the iron stool. [*Pause.*] Reveled in the word spool. [*With relish.*] Spooool! Happiest moment of the past half million. [*Pause.*] Seventeen copies sold, of which eleven at trade price to free circulating libraries beyond the seas. Getting known. [*Pause.*] One pound six and something, eight I have little doubt. [*Pause.*] Crawled out once or twice before the summer was cold. Sat shivering in the park, drowned in dreams and burning to be gone. Not a soul. [*Pause.*] Last fancies. [*Vehemently.*] Keep 'em under! [*Pause.*] Scalded the eyes out of me reading *Effie* again, a page a day, with tears again. Effie . . . [*Pause.*] Could have been happy with her, up there on the Baltic, and the pines, and the dunes. [*Pause.*] Could I? [*Pause.*] And she? [*Pause.*] Pah! [*Pause.*] Fanny came in a couple of times. Bony old ghost of a whore. Couldn't do much, but I suppose better than a kick in the crutch. The last time wasn't so bad. How do you manage it, she said, at your age? I told her I'd been saving up for her all my life. [*Pause.*] Went to Vespers once, like when I was in short trousers.

[*Pause. Sings.*]

Now the day is over,
Night is drawing nigh-igh,
Shadows—[*Coughing, then almost inaudible.*]—of the evening
Steal across the sky.

[*Gasping.*] Went to sleep and fell off the pew. [*Pause.*] Sometimes wondered in the night if a last effort mightn't—[*Pause.*] Ah finish your booze now and get to your bed. Go on with this drivel in the morning. Or leave it at that. [*Pause.*] Leave it at that. [*Pause.*] Lie propped up in the dark—and wander. Be again in the dingle on a Christmas Eve, gathering holly, the red-berried. [*Pause.*] Be again on Croghan[1] on a Sunday morning, in the haze, with the bitch, stop and listen to the bells. [*Pause.*] And so on. [*Pause.*] Be again, be again. [*Pause.*] All that old misery. [*Pause.*] Once wasn't enough for you. [*Pause.*] Lie down across her.

1. Mountain in southeastern Ireland.

[*Long pause. He suddenly bends over machine, switches off, wrenches off tape, throws it away, puts on the other, winds it forward to the passage he wants, switches on, listens staring front.*]

TAPE: —gooseberries, she said. I said again I thought it was hopeless and no good going on, and she agreed, without opening her eyes. [*Pause.*] I asked her to look at me and after a few moments—[*Pause.*]—after a few moments she did, but the eyes just slits, because of the glare. I bent over her to get them in the shadow and they opened. [*Pause. Low.*] Let me in. [*Pause.*] We drifted in among the flags and stuck. The way they went down, sighing, before the stem! [*Pause.*] I lay down across her with my face in her breasts and my hand on her. We lay there without moving. But under us all moved, and moved us, gently, up and down, and from side to side.

[*Pause. Krapp's lips move. No sound.*]

Past midnight. Never knew such silence. The earth might be uninhabited.

[*Pause.*]

Here I end this reel. Box—[*Pause.*]—three, spool—[*Pause.*]—five. [*Pause.*] Perhaps my best years are gone. When there was a chance of happiness. But I wouldn't want them back. Not with the fire in me now. No, I wouldn't want them back.

[*Krapp motionless staring before him. The tape runs on in silence.*]

CURTAIN

1958

MARGUERITE DURAS

Hiroshima Mon Amour[1]

PART I

As the film opens, two pair of bare shoulders appear, little by little. All we see are these shoulders—cut off from the body at the height of the head and hips—in an embrace, and as if drenched with ashes, rain, dew, or sweat, whichever is preferred. The main thing is that we get the feeling that this dew, this perspiration, has been deposited by the atomic "mushroom"[2] *as it moves away and evaporates. It should produce a violent, conflicting feeling of freshness and desire. The shoulders are of different colors, one dark, one light. Fusco's music*[3] *accompanies this almost shocking embrace. The difference between the hands is also very marked.*

1. Translated by Richard Seaver. Annotated by Sarah Lawall. 2. The immense, mushroom-shaped cloud of radioactive hot vapor that follows a nuclear explosion. 3. Giovanni Fusco, who with George Delerue composed the music for the film.

The woman's hand lies on the darker shoulder: "lies" is perhaps not the word; "grips" would be closer to it. A man's voice, flat and calm, as if reciting, says:

HE: You saw nothing in Hiroshima. Nothing.

[*To be used as often as desired. A woman's voice, also flat, muffled, monotonous, the voice of someone reciting, replies.*]

SHE: I saw *everything. Everything.*

[*Fusco's music, which has faded before this initial exchange, resumes just long enough to accompany the woman's hand tightening on the shoulder again, then letting go, then caressing it. The mark of fingernails on the darker flesh. As if this scratch could give the illusion of being a punishment for:* "No. You saw nothing in Hiroshima." *Then the woman's voice begins again, still calm, colorless, incantatory.*]

The hospital, for instance, I saw it. I'm sure I did. There is a hospital in Hiroshima. How could I help seeing it?

[*The hospital, hallways, stairs, patients, the camera coldly objective.*[4] (*We never see her seeing.*) *Then we come back to the hand gripping—and not letting go of—the darker shoulder.*]

HE: You did not see the hospital in Hiroshima. You saw nothing in Hiroshima.

[*Then the woman's voice becomes more . . . more impersonal. Shots of the museum.*[5] *The same blinding light, the same ugly light here as at the hospital. Explanatory signs, pieces of evidence from the bombardment, scale models, mutilated iron, skin, burned hair, wax models, etc.*]

SHE: Four times at the museum. . . .
HE: What museum in Hiroshima?
SHE: Four times at the museum in Hiroshima. I saw the people walking around, the people walk around, lost in thought, among the photographs, the reconstructions, for want of something else, among the photographs, the photographs, the reconstructions, for want of something else, the explanations, for want of something else.[6]

Four times at the museum in Hiroshima.

I looked at the people I myself looked thoughtfully at the iron. The burned iron. The broken iron, the iron made vulnerable as flesh. I saw the bouquet of bottle caps: who would have suspected that? Human skin floating, surviving, still in the bloom of its agony. Stones. Burned stones. Shattered stones. Anonymous heads of hair that the women of Hiroshima, when they awoke in the morning, discovered had fallen out.

4. With only a schematic initial text to go on, Resnais brought back a great number of documents from Japan. Thus the initial text was modified and considerably enlarged during the cutting of the film. [Author's note] 5. With a return, at regular intervals, to the bodies. [Author's note] 6. She describes actual exhibits in the Hiroshima Peace Memorial Museum, established in 1949.

I was hot at Peace Square. Ten thousand degrees at Peace Square[7] I know it. The temperature of the sun at Peace Square. How can you not know it? . . . The grass, it's quite simple . . .

HE: You saw nothing in Hiroshima. Nothing.

[*More shots of the museum. Then a shot of Peace Square taken with a burned skull in the foreground. Glass display cases with burned models inside. Newsreel shots of Hiroshima.*]

SHE: The reconstructions have been made as authentically as possible.

The films have been made as authentically as possible.

The illusion, it's quite simple, the illusion is so perfect that the tourists cry.

One can always scoff, but what else can a tourist do, really, but cry?

I've always wept over the fate of Hiroshima. Always.

[*A panorama of photographs taken of Hiroshima after the bomb, a "new desert" without reference to the other deserts of the world.*]

HE: No. What would you have cried about?

[*Peace Square, empty under a blinding sun that recalls the blinding light of the bomb. Newsreels taken after August 6, 1945.*[8] *Ants, worms, emerge from the ground. Interspersed with shots of the shoulders. The woman's voice begins again, gone mad, as the sequence of pictures has also gone mad.*]

SHE: I saw the newsreels.

On the second day, History tells, I'm not making it up, on the second day certain species of animals rose again from the depths of the earth and from the ashes.

Dogs were photographed.

For all eternity.

I saw them.

I *saw* the newsreels.

I *saw* them.

On the first day.

On the second day.

On the third day.

HE: [Interrupting her.] You saw nothing. Nothing.

[*A dog with a leg amputated. People, children. Wounds. Burned children screaming.*]

SHE: . . . on the fifteenth day too.

Hiroshima was blanketed with flowers. There were cornflowers and gla-

7. The museum, the Hiroshima Peace Memorial Hall, and the Hiroshima City Auditorium are located in Hiroshima Peace Memorial Park. The heat generated by the exploding bomb reached several million degrees centigrade (roughly 5.5 million degrees Fahrenheit); the temperature on the ground was 3,000–4,000°C (5,400–7,200°F).

8. The day the bomb was dropped.

diolas everywhere, and morning glories and day lilies that rose again from the ashes with an extraordinary vigor, quite unheard of for flowers till then.[9]

I didn't make anything up.

HE: You made it *all* up.

SHE: *Nothing.*

Just as in love this illusion exists, this illusion of being able never to forget, so I was under the illusion that I would never forget Hiroshima.

Just as in love.

[*Surgical forceps approach an eye to extract it. More newsreel shots.*]

I also saw the survivors and those who were in the wombs of the women of Hiroshima.

[*Shots of various survivors: a beautiful child who, upon turning around, is blind in one eye; a girl looking at her burned face in the mirror; a blind girl with twisted hands playing the zither; a woman praying near her dying children; a man, who has not slept for several years, dying.* (*Once a week they bring his children to see him.*)]

I saw the patience, the innocence, the apparent meekness with which the temporary survivors of Hiroshima adapted themselves to the fate so unjust that the imagination, normally so fertile, cannot conceive it.

[*And again a return to the perfect embrace of the bodies.*]

Listen . . .
I know . . .
I know *everything.*
It went on.

HE: *Nothing.* You know *nothing.*

[*A spiraling atomic cloud. People marching in the streets in the rain. Fishermen tainted with radioactivity. Unedible fish. Thousands of unedible fish buried.*]

SHE: Women risk giving birth to malformed children, to monsters, but it goes on.

Men risk becoming sterile, but it goes on.
People are afraid of the rain.
The rain of ashes on the waters of the Pacific.
The waters of the Pacific kill.
Fishermen of the Pacific are dead.
People are afraid of the food.
The food of an entire city is thrown away.
The food of entire cities is buried.
An entire city rises up in anger.
Entire cities rise up in anger.

9. This sentence is taken almost verbatim from John Hersey's admirable report on Hiroshima. All I did was apply it to the martyred children. [Author's note]

[*Newsreels: demonstrations.*]

Against whom, the anger of entire cities?

The anger of entire cities, whether they like it or not, against the inequality set forth as a principle by certain people against other people, against the inequality set forth as a principle by certain races against other races, against the inequality set forth as a principle by certain classes against other classes.

[*Processions of demonstrators. "Mute" speeches from loudspeakers.*]

SHE: [*Softly.*] . . . Listen to me.
Like you, I know what it is to forget.

HE: No, you don't know what it is to forget.

SHE: Like you, I have a memory. I know what it is to forget.

HE: No, you don't have a memory.

SHE: Like you, I too have tried with all my might not to forget. Like you, I forgot. Like you, I wanted to have an inconsolable memory, a memory of shadows and stone.

[*The shot of a shadow, "photographed" on stone, of someone killed at Hiroshima.*]

For my part, I struggled with all my might, every day, against the horror of no longer understanding at all the reason for remembering. Like you, I forgot. . . .

[*Shops with hundreds of scale models of the Palace of Industry, the only monument whose twisted skeleton remained standing after the bomb—and was afterward preserved. An empty shop. A busload of Japanese tourists. Tourists on Peace Square. A cat crossing Peace Square.*]

Why deny the obvious necessity for memory? . . .

[*A second punctuated by shots of the framework of the Palace of Industry.*]

. . . Listen to me. I know something else. It will begin all over again.
Two hundred thousand dead.
Eighty thousand wounded.
In nine seconds. These figures are official. It will begin all over again.

[*Trees. Church. Merry-go-round. Hiroshima rebuilt. Banality.*]

There will be ten thousand degrees on the earth. Ten thousand suns, they will say. The asphalt will burn.

[*Church. Japanese advertising poster.*]

Chaos will prevail. A whole city will be raised from the earth and fall back in ashes. . . .

[*Sand. A package of "Peace" cigarettes. A fat plant spread out like a spider on the sand.*]

New vegetation will rise from the sands. . . .

[*Four "dead" students chat beside the river. The river. The tides. The daily piers of Hiroshima rebuilt.*]

Four students await together a fraternal and legendary death.

The seven branches of the delta estuary in the Ota River[1] drain and fill at the usual hour, exactly at the usual hours, with water that is fresh and rich with fish, gray or blue depending on the hour or the season. Along the muddy banks people no longer watch the tide rising slowly in the seven branches of the delta estuary of the river Ota.

[*The incantatory tone ceases. The streets of Hiroshima, more streets. Bridges. Covered lanes. Streets. Suburbs. Railroad tracks. Suburbs. Universal banality.*]

. . . I meet you.
I remember you.
Who are you?
You destroy me.[2]
You're so good for me.
How could I have known that this city was made to the size of love?
How could I have known that you were made to the size of my body?
You're great. How wonderful. You're great.
How slow all of a sudden.
And how sweet.
More than you can know.
You destroy me.
You're so good for me.
You destroy me.
You're so good for me.
Plenty of time.
Please.
Take me.
Deform me, make me ugly.
Why not you?
Why not you in this city and in this night so like the others you can't tell the difference?
Please. . .

[*With exaggerated suddenness the woman's face appears, filled with tenderness, turned toward the man's.*]

It's extraordinary how beautiful your skin is.

1. The city of Hiroshima is built on a delta where the Ota River flows into the sea; the seven branches of the delta split the city into six small islands which are connected by bridges. 2. The lyrical effect of this famous monologue is heightened in French by the identical sound of "you" (intimate form) and "destroy": "*tu* me *tues*."

[*He sighs.*]

You. . .

[*His face appears. He laughs ecstatically, which has nothing to do with their words. He turns.*]

HE: Yes, me. You will have seen me.

[*The two naked bodies reappear. Same voice of the woman, muted, but this time not declamatory.*]

SHE: Are you completely Japanese or aren't you completely Japanese?
HE: Completely. I am Japanese.
Your eyes are green. Correct?
SHE: I think so . . . yes . . . I think they're green.
HE: [*Softly, looking at her.*] You are like a thousand women in one. . . .
SHE: It's because you don't know me. That's why.
HE: Perhaps that's not the only reason.
SHE: It's a rather nice idea, being a thousand women in one for you.

[*She kisses his shoulder and snuggles into the hollow of that shoulder. Her head is facing the open window, facing Hiroshima, the night. A man passes in the street and coughs. (We don't see him, only hear him.) She raises herself.*]

Listen. . . . It's four o'clock. . . .
HE: Why?
SHE: I don't know who it is. Every day he passes at four o'clock. And he coughs.

[*Silence. They look at each other.*]

You were here, at Hiroshima. . . .
HE: [*Laughing, as he might at a childish question.*] No . . . Of course I wasn't.
SHE: [*Caressing his naked shoulder again.*] That's true. . . . How stupid of me. [*Almost smiling.*]
HE: [*Serious, hesitant.*] But my family was at Hiroshima. I was off fighting the war.
SHE: [*Timidly, smiling now.*] A stroke of luck, eh?
HE: [*Not looking at her, weighing the pro and con.*] Yes.
SHE: Lucky for me too.

[*Pause.*]

HE: What are you doing at Hiroshima?
SHE: A film.
HE: What, a film?
SHE: I'm playing in a film.
HE: And before coming to Hiroshima, where were you?
SHE: In Paris.

[*A longer pause.*]

HE: And before Paris? . . .
SHE: Before Paris? . . . I was at Nevers.[3] *Ne-vers.*
HE: Nevers?
SHE: It's in the province of Nièvre. You don't know it.

[*Pause. Then he asks, as though he had just discovered a link between Hiroshima and Nevers:*]

HE: And why did you want to see everything at Hiroshima?
SHE: [*Trying to be sincere.*] Because it interested me. I have my own ideas about it. For instance, I think looking closely at things is something that has to be learned.

PART II

A swarm of bicycles passes in the street, the noise growing louder, then fading. She is on the balcony of the hotel, in a dressing gown. She is looking at him. She holds a cup of coffee in her hand. He is still asleep, lying on his stomach, his arms crossed, bare to the waist. She looks very intently at his hands, which tremble slightly, as children's hands do sometimes when they are asleep. He has very beautiful, very virile hands.

While she is looking at them, there suddenly appears, in place of the Japanese, the body of a young man, lying in the same position, but in a posture of death, on the bank of a river, in full daylight. (The room is in semi-darkness.) The young man is near death. He too has beautiful hands, strikingly like those of the Japanese. The approach of death makes them jerk violently.

The shot is an extremely brief one.

She remains frozen, leaning against the window. He awakes and smiles at her. She doesn't return his smile immediately. She continues to look at him attentively, without moving. Then she takes the coffee over to him.

SHE: Do you want some coffee?

[*He assents, takes the cup. Pause.*]

What were you dreaming about?
HE: I don't remember. . . . Why?

[*She has become herself again, extremely nice.*]

SHE: I was looking at your hands. They move when you're asleep.
HE: [*Examining his hands, perhaps moving his fingers.*] Maybe it's when you dream without knowing it.
SHE: [*Calmly, pleasantly, but seeming to doubt his words.*] Hmm, hmm.

[*They're together in the shower of the hotel room. In a gay mood. He puts his hand on her forehead and arches her head back.*]

3. The capital city of the Nièvre, south of Paris in the middle of France; an industrial city that was heavily bombed in the war.

HE: You're a beautiful woman, do you know that?
SHE: Do you think so?
HE: I think so.
SHE: A trifle worn out, no?
HE: [*Laughingly.*] A trifle ugly.
SHE: [*Smiling at his caress.*] Don't you mind?
HE: That's what I noticed last night in that café. The way you're ugly. And also . . .
SHE: [*Very relaxed.*] And also? . . .
HE: And also how bored you were.
SHE: [*Her curiosity aroused.*] Tell me more. . . .
HE: You were bored in a way that makes men want to know a woman.
SHE: [*Smiling, lowering her eyes.*] You speak French very well.
HE: [*Gaily.*] Don't I though! I'm glad you finally noticed how well I speak French. [Pause.] I hadn't noticed that you didn't speak Japanese. . . . have you ever noticed that it's always in the same sense[4] that people notice things?
SHE: No. I noticed you, that's all.

[*Laughter.*]

[*After the bath. Her hair is wet. She is munching slowly on an apple. She is on the balcony, dressed in a bathrobe; she looks at him, stretches, and as if to "pinpoint" their situation, says slowly, as though savoring the words:*]

To-meet-in-Hiroshima. It doesn't happen every day.

[*Already dressed—his shirt collar open—he joins her on the balcony and sits down opposite her. After a moment's hesitation, he asks:*]

HE: What did Hiroshima mean for you, in France?
SHE: The end of the war, I mean, really the end. Amazement . . . at the idea that they had dared . . . amazement at the idea that they had succeeded. And then too, for us, the beginning of an unknown fear. And then, indifference. And also the fear of indifference. . . .
HE: Where were you?
SHE: I had left Nevers. I was in Paris. In the street.
HE: That's a pretty French word, Nevers.
SHE: [*After a pause.*] It's a word like any other. Like the city.

[*She moves away. They begin to talk, about ordinary things.*]

[*He's seated on the bed; he lights a cigarette, looks at her intently, then asks:*]

HE: Have you met many Japanese at Hiroshima?
SHE: I've met some, yes . . . but no one like you. . . .
HE: [*Smiling, gay.*] I'm the first Japanese in your life?
SHE: Yes.

4. That is, people always see things from their own perspective.

[*Her laughter off-camera. She reappears while she is getting dressed.*]

Hi-ro-shi-ma.

HE: [*Lowering his eyes, calmly.*] The whole world was happy. You were happy with the whole world. [*Continuing, in the same tone.*] I heard it was a beautiful summer day in Paris that day, is that right?
SHE: Yes, it was a beautiful day.
HE: How old were you?
SHE: Twenty. And you?
HE: Twenty-two.
SHE: The same age, really.
HE: Yes, practically.

[*She appears completely dressed, just as she is putting on her Red Cross nurse's kerchief. She bends down beside him with a sudden gesture, or lies down beside him. She plays with his hand, kisses his bare arm. They talk about ordinary things.*]

SHE: What do you do in life?
HE: Architecture. And politics too.
SHE: Oh, so that's why you speak such good French.
HE: That's why. To read about the French Revolution.

[*They laugh. Any precise indications about his politics would be absolutely impossible, since he would be immediately tagged. And besides, it would be naive. Nor should it be forgotten that only a man of liberal opinions would have made the preceding remark.*]

What's the film you're playing in?

SHE: A film about Peace. What else do you expect them to make in Hiroshima except a picture about Peace?

[*A noisy swarm of bicycles passes.*]

HE: I'd like to see you again.
SHE: [*Gesturing negatively.*] At this time tomorrow I'll be on my way back to France.
HE: Is that true? You didn't tell me.
SHE: It's true. [*Pause.*] There was no point in telling you.
HE: [*Serious, taken aback.*] Is that why you let me come up to your room last night? . . . Because it was your last day at Hiroshima?
SHE: Not at all. The thought never even crossed my mind.
HE: When you talk, I wonder whether you lie or tell the truth.
SHE: I lie. And I tell the truth. But I don't have any reason to lie to you. Why? . . .
HE: Tell me . . . do things like . . . this happen to you often?
SHE: Not very often. But it happens. I have a weakness for men. [*Pause.*] I have doubtful morals, you know. [*She laughs.*]
HE: What do you call having doubtful morals?
SHE: Being doubtful about the morals of other people.

[*He laughs heartily.*]

HE: I'd like to see you again. Even if the plane is leaving tomorrow. Even if you do have doubtful morals.

[*Pause. A feeling of love returning.*]

SHE: No.
HE: Why?
SHE: [*With irritation.*] Because. [*He doesn't pursue the conversation.*] Don't you want to talk to me any more?
HE: [*After a pause.*] I'd like to see you again. [*They are in the hotel corridor.*] Where are you going in France? To Nevers?
SHE: No. To Paris. [*A pause.*] I don't ever go to Nevers any more.
HE: Not ever?
SHE: [*Grimacing as she says it.*] Not ever. [*Then, caught in her own trap, she adds.*] In Nevers I was younger than I've ever been. . . .
HE: Young-in-Nevers.
SHE: Yes. Young in Nevers. And then too, once, mad in Nevers.

[*They are pacing back and forth in front of the hotel. She is waiting for the car that is supposed to come and pick her up to take her to Peace Square. Few people, but lots of cars passing. It's a boulevard. The dialogue is almost shouted because of the noise of the cars.*]

You see, Nevers is the city in the world, and even the thing in the world, I dream about most often at the night. And at the same time it's the thing I think about the least.
HE: What was your madness like at Nevers?
SHE: Madness is like intelligence, you know. You can't explain it. Just like intelligence. It comes on you, it fills you, and then you understand it. But when it goes away you can't understand it at all any longer.
HE: Were you full of hate?
SHE: That was what my madness was. I was mad with hate. I had the impression it would be possible to make a real career of hate. All I cared about was hate. Do you understand?
HE: Yes.
SHE: It's true. I suppose you must understand that too.
HE: Did it ever happen to you again?
SHE: No. [*In a near whisper.*] It's all over.
HE: During the war?
SHE: Right after it.

[*Pause.*]

HE: Was that part of the difficulties of life in France after the war?
SHE: Yes, that's one way of putting it.
HE: When did you get over your madness?

SHE: [*In a low voice, as she would talk in normal circumstances.*] It went away little by little. And then of course when I had children.

[*The noise of the cars grows and fades in inverse proportion to the seriousness of their remarks.*]

HE: What did you say?

SHE: I said it went away little by little. And then of course when I had children. . . .

HE: I'd really like to spend a few days with you somewhere, sometime.

SHE: I would too.

HE: Seeing you again today wouldn't really be seeing you again. You can't see people again in such a short time. I really would.

SHE: No.

[*She stops in front of him, obstinate, motionless, silent. He almost accepts.*]

HE: All right.

[*She laughs, but it's a little forced. She seems slightly, but actually, spiteful. The taxi arrives.*]

SHE: It's because you know I'm leaving tomorrow.

[*They laugh, but his is less hearty than hers.* A *pause.*]

HE: It's possible that's part of it. But that's as good a reason as any, no? The thought of not seeing you again . . . ever . . . in a few hours.

[*The taxi has arrived and stopped at the intersection. She signals to it that she's coming. She takes her time, looks at the Japanese, and says:*]

SHE: No.

[*His eyes follow her. Perhaps he smiles.*]

PART III

It's four P.M. *at Peace Square in Hiroshima. In the distance a group of film technicians is moving away carrying a camera, lights, and reflectors. Japanese workers are dismantling the official grandstand that has just been used in the last scene of the film.*

An important note: we will always see the technicians in the distance and will never know what film it is they're shooting at Hiroshima. All we'll ever see is the scenery being taken down.

*Stagehands are carrying posters in various languages—Japanese, French, German, etc.—*NEVER ANOTHER HIROSHIMA. *The workmen are thus busy dismantling the official grandstands and removing the bunting. On the set we see the French woman. She is asleep. Her nurse's kerchief has slipped partly off her head. She is lying in the shadow of one of the stands.*

We gather that they have just finished shooting an enlightening film on Peace at Hiroshima. It's not necessarily a ridiculous film, merely an enlightening one. A crowd passes along the square where they have just been shooting the film. The crowd is indifferent. Except for a few children, no one looks, they are used to seeing films being shot at Hiroshima.

But one man passes, stops, and looks, the man we had seen previously in her hotel room. He approaches the nurse, and watches her sleeping. His gaze is what finally wakes her up, but only after he has been looking at her for a good while.

During the scene perhaps we see a few details in the distance, such as a scale model of the Palace of Industry, a guide surrounded by tourists, a couple of war invalids in white, begging, a family chatting on a street corner. She awakes. Her fatigue vanishes. They suddenly find themselves involved again with their own story. This personal story always dominates the necessarily demonstrative Hiroshima story.

She gets up and goes toward him. He laughs, a bit stiffly. Then they become serious again.

HE: It was easy to find you in Hiroshima.

[*She laughs happily. A pause. He looks at her again. Two workers—carrying an enlarged photograph from the picture* The Children of Hiroshima[5] *showing a dead mother and a child crying in the smoking ruins of Hiroshima—pass between them. They don't look at the photograph. Another photograph, of Einstein,*[6] *follows immediately after the one of the mother and child.*]

Is it a French film?

SHE: No. International. On Peace.

HE: Is it finished?

SHE: Yes, for me it's finished. They still have some crowd scenes to shoot. . . . We have lots of filmed commercials to sell soap. So . . . by stressing it . . . perhaps.

HE: [*With very clear ideas on the subject.*] Yes, by stressing it. Here, at Hiroshima, we don't joke about films on Peace.

[*He turns back toward her. The photographs have gone completely by. Instinctively they move closer together. She readjusts her kerchief, which has slipped partly off while she was sleeping.*]

Are you tired?

SHE: [*Looking at him in a way that is both provocative and gentle. Then, with an almost sad smile, she says.*] No more than you are.

HE: [*Meaningfully.*] I thought of Nevers in France.

5. A semidocumentary film produced in 1952 by the Japanese director Kaneto Shindo, echoing Arata Osada's 1951 *Children of the Atomic Bomb*, a compilation of 105 memoirs written by children who had lost parents or relatives to the bomb. 6. The picture of Albert Einstein (1879–1955), whose theoretical work led to the discovery of nuclear fission and the creation of the bomb, shows him sticking out his tongue (specifically mentioned in the French text).

[*She smiles.*]

I've been thinking of you. Is your plane still leaving tomorrow?

SHE: Still tomorrow.

HE: Irrevocably tomorrow?

SHE: Yes. The picture is behind schedule. I'm a month overdue returning to Paris.

[*She looks squarely at him. Slowly he takes her kerchief off. Either she is very heavily made up, in which case her lips are so dark they seem black, or else she is hardly made up at all and seems pale under the sun.*

The man's gesture is extremely free, composed, producing much the same erotic shock as in the opening scenes. Her hair is as mussed as it was in bed the night before. She lets him take off her kerchief, she lets him have his way as she must have let him have his way in love the night before. (Here, give him an erotically functional role.)

She lowers her eyes. An incomprehensible pout. She toys with something on the ground, then raises her eyes again.]

HE: You give me a great desire to love.

[*She doesn't answer right away. His words upset her, and she lowers her eyes again. The cat of Peace Square rubbing against her foot?*]

SHE: [*Slowly.*] Always . . . chance love affairs. . . . Me too.

[*Some extraordinary object, not clearly defined, passes between them. I see a square frame, some (atomic?) very precise form, but without the least idea what it's used for. They pay no attention to it.*]

HE: No. Not always like this. You know it.

[*Shouts in the distance. Then children singing. But it doesn't distract them. She makes an incomprehensible face (licentious would be the word). She raises her eyes again, but this time to the sky, and says, again incomprehensibly, as she wipes the sweat from her forehead:*]

SHE: They say there'll be a thunderstorm before nightfall.

[*A shot of the sky she sees. Clouds scudding . . . The singing becomes more distinct. Then (the end of) the parade begins. They back away. She clings to him (like the postures in women's magazines), her hand on his shoulder. His face against her hair. When she raises her eyes she sees him. He'll try and lead her away from the parade. She'll resist. But she'll go anyway, without realizing she's leaving.*

Children parading carrying posters.]

FIRST SERIES OF POSTERS

1st Poster

If 14 A-bombs equal 100 million ordinary bombs.

2nd Poster

And if the H-bomb equals 1500 A-bombs.

3rd Poster

How much do the 40,000 A- and H-bombs actually manufactured in the world equal?

4th Poster

10 H-bombs dropped on the world mean prehistory again.

5th Poster

What do 40,000 H- and A-bombs mean?

SECOND SERIES OF POSTERS

I

This extraordinary achievement bears witness to man's scientific inteligence.[7]

II

But it's regrettable that man's political intelligence is 100 times less developed than his scientific intelligence.

III

Which keeps us from really admiring man.

[*Men, women, follow the singing children. Dogs follow the children. Cats at the windows. (The Peace Square cat is used to it, and is asleep.)*

Posters. More posters. Everyone very hot. The sky, above the parade, is threatening. Clouds cover the sun. There are lots of children, beautiful children. They are hot, and sing heartily as children will. Irresistibly, and almost without realizing it, the Japanese pushes the French woman in the same—or in the opposite—direction the parade is moving. She closes her eyes and sighs, and while she is sighing:]

HE: I hate to think about your leaving. Tomorrow. I think I love you.

[*He buries his lips in her hair. Her hand tight on his shoulder. Slowly her eyes open. The parade goes on. The children's faces are made up white. Dots of sweat stand out on the white powder. Two of them argue over an orange, angrily. A man, made up as if burned in the bombing, passes. He probably had played in the film. The wax on his neck melts and falls off. Perhaps disgusting, terrifying. They look at each other.*]

You're coming with me, once more.

[*She doesn't answer. A beautiful Japanese woman, sitting on a float, passes. She looses a flock of pigeons (or maybe some other allegorical float—an atomic ballet, for instance).*]

Answer me.

[*She doesn't answer. He bends and whispers in her ear.*]

7. Resnais decided to leave in the error in spelling. [Author's note]

Are you afraid?

SHE: [*Smiling, shaking her head.*] No.

[*The formless songs of the children continue, but fading away. A monitor scolds the two children arguing over the orange. The big one takes the orange. The big one begins to eat the orange. All this lasts longer than it should. Behind the crying child, the five hundred Japanese students arrive. It's a little terrifying, and he pulls her against him. They look upset. He looking at her, she looking at the parade. One should have the feeling that this parade is depriving them of the short time they have left. They are silent. He leads her by the hand. She lets him. They exit, moving against the current of the parade. We lose sight of them.*[8]

We see them next in the middle of a large room in a Japanese house. Soft light. A feeling of freshness after the heat of the parade. A modern house, with chairs, etc. She stands there, like a guest. Almost intimidated. He approaches her from the far side of the room (as if he had just closed the door, or come from the garage, etc.).]

HE: Sit down.

[*She doesn't sit down. Both remain standing. We feel that eroticism is held in check between them by love, at least for the moment. He is facing her. And in the same state, almost awkward. The opposite of what a man would do if this were an* aubaine.[9]]

SHE: [*Making conversation.*] You're alone at Hiroshima? . . . Where's your wife?

HE: She's at Unzen,[1] in the mountains. I'm alone.

SHE: When is she coming back?

HE: In a few days.

SHE: [*Softly, as if in an aside.*] What is your wife like?

HE: [*Purposefully.*] Beautiful. I'm a man who's happy with his wife.

[*Pause.*]

SHE: So am I. I'm a woman who's happy with her husband.

[*This exchange charged with real emotion, which the ensuing moment covers.*]

SHE: Don't you work in the afternoon?

HE: Yes. A lot. Mainly in the afternoon.

SHE: The whole thing is stupid. . . .

[*As she would say "I love you." They kiss as the telephone rings. He doesn't answer.*]

Is it because of me you're wasting your afternoon?

[*He still doesn't answer the phone.*]

8. Resnais has them get lost in the crowd. [Author's note] 9. French for windfall, sudden stroke of luck. 1. A hot springs resort on the island of Kyushu.

Tell me. What difference does it make?

[*At Hiroshima. The light is already different. Later. After they have made love.*]

HE: Was he French, the man you loved during the war?

[*At Nevers. A German crosses a square at dusk.*]

SHE: No . . . he wasn't French.

[*At Hiroshima. She is lying on the bed, pleasantly tired. Darker now.*]

Yes. It was at Nevers.

[*Nevers. A shot of love at Nevers. Bicycles racing. The forest, etc.*]

At first we met in barns. Then among the ruins. And then in rooms. Like anywhere else.

[*Hiroshima. In the room, the light faded even more. Their bodies in a peaceful embrace.*]

And then he was dead.

[*Nevers. Shot of Nevers. Rivers. Quays. Poplar trees in the wind, etc. The quay deserted. The garden. Then at Hiroshima again.*]

I was eighteen and he was twenty-three.

[*Nevers. In a "hut" at night. The "marriage" at Nevers. During the shots of Nevers she answers the questions that he is presumed to have asked, but doesn't out loud. The sequence of shots of Nevers continues. Then:*]

SHE: [*Calmly.*] Why talk of him rather than the others?
HE: Why not?
SHE: No. Why?
HE: Because of Nevers. I can only begin to know you, and among the many thousands of things in your life, I'm choosing Nevers.
SHE: Like you'd choose anything else?
HE: Yes.

[*Do we know he's lying? We suspect it. She becomes almost violent, searching for something to say.*]

SHE: No, it's not by chance. [*Pause.*] You have to tell me why.

[*He can reply—a very important point for the film—either:*]

HE: It was there, I seem to have understood, that you were so young . . . so young you still don't belong to anyone in particular. I like that.

[*or:*]

SHE: No, that's not it.

HE: It was there, I seem to have understood, that I almost . . . lost you . . . and that I risked never knowing you.

[*or else:*]

It was there, I seem to have understood, that you must have begun to be what you are today.

[*Choose from among the three possibilities, or use all three, either one after the other, or separately, at random with the movements of love in the bed. The last is the solution I would prefer, if it doesn't make the scene too long.*[2]

One last time we come back to them.]

SHE: [*Shouting.*] I want to leave here. [*She clings to him almost savagely.*]

[*They are dressed and in the same room where they were earlier. The lights are on now. They are both standing.*]

HE: [*Very calmly.*] All we can do now is kill the time left before your departure. Still sixteen hours before your plane leaves.

SHE: [*Terribly upset, distressed.*] That's a terribly long time. . . .

HE: [*Gently.*] No. You mustn't be afraid.

PART IV

Night falls over Hiroshima, leaving long trails of light. The river drains and fills with the hours, the tides. Sometimes people along the muddy banks watch the tide rising slowly.

Opposite this river is a café. A modern café, Americanized, with a wide bay window. Those seated at the back of the café don't see the banks of the river, but only the river itself. The mouth of the river is only vaguely outlined. There Hiroshima ends and the Pacific begins. The place is half empty. They are seated at a table in the back of the room, facing each other, either cheek-to-cheek, or forehead against forehead. In the previous scene they had been overwhelmed by the thought that their final separation was only sixteen hours away. When we see them now they are almost happy. They don't notice the time passing. A miracle has occurred. What miracle? The resurrection of Nevers. And in this posture of hopelessly happy love, he says.

HE: Aside from that, Nevers doesn't mean anything else in French?

SHE: No. Nothing.

HE: Would you have been cold in that cellar at Nevers, if we had loved each other there?

SHE: I would have been cold. In Nevers the cellars are cold, both summer and winter. The city is built along a river called the Loire.

HE: I can't picture Nevers.

[*Shots of Nevers. The Loire.*]

2. Instead of using only one, Resnais decided to use all three. [Author's note]

SHE: Nevers. Forty thousand inhabitants. Built like a capital—(but). A child can walk around it. [*She moves away from him.*] I was born in Nevers [*She drinks.*], I grew up in Nevers. I learned how to read in Nevers. And it was there I became twenty.

HE: And the Loire?

[*He takes her head in his hands. Nevers.*]

SHE: It's a completely unnavigable river, always empty, because of its irregular course and its sand bars. In France, the Loire is considered a very beautiful river, especially because of its light . . . so soft, if you only knew.

[*Ecstatic tone. He frees her head and listens closely.*]

HE: When you are in the cellar, am I dead?

SHE: You are dead . . . and . . .

[*Nevers: the German is dying very slowly on the quay.*]

. . . how is it possible to bear such pain?
The cellar is small.

[*To show with her hands how small it is, she withdraws her cheek from his. Then she goes on, still very close to him, but no longer touching him. No incantation. She speaks to him with passionate enthusiasm.*]

. . . very small. The *Marseillaise* passes above my head. It's . . . deafening. . . .

[*She blocks her ears, in this café (at Hiroshima). The café is suddenly very quiet. Shots of Nevers' cellars. Riva's bloody hands.*]

Hands become useless in cellars. They scrape. They rub the skin off . . . against the walls . . .

[*Somewhere at Nevers, bleeding hands. Hers, on the table, are intact. Riva licks her own blood.*]

. . . that's all you can find to do, to make you feel better . . . and also to remember . . . I loved blood since I had tasted yours.

[*They scarcely look at each other as she talks. They look at Nevers. Both of them act as if they were somehow possessed by Nevers. There are two glasses on the table. She drinks avidly. He more slowly. Their hands are flat on the table.*]
[*Nevers.*]

The world moves along over my head. Instead of the sky . . . of course . . . I see the world walking. Quickly during the week. Slowly on Sunday. It doesn't know I'm in the cellar. They pretend I'm dead, dead a long way from Nevers. That's what my father wants. Because I'm disgraced, that's what my father wants.

[*Nevers: a father, a Nevers druggist, behind the window of his drug store.*]

HE: Do you scream?

[*The room at Nevers.*]

SHE: Not in the beginning; no, I don't scream: I call you softly.
HE: But I'm dead.
SHE: Nevertheless I call you. Even though you're dead. Then one day, I scream, I scream as loud as I can, like a deaf person would. That's when they put me in the cellar. To punish me.
HE: What do you scream?
SHE: Your German name. Only your name. I only have one memory left, your name.

[*Room at Nevers, mute screams.*]

I promise not to scream any more. Then they take me back to my room.

[*Room at Nevers. Lying down, one leg raised, filled with desire.*]

SHE: I want you so badly I can't bear it any more.
HE: Are you afraid?
SHE: I'm afraid. Everywhere. In the cellar. In my room.
HE: Of what?

[*Spots on the ceiling of the room at Nevers, terrifying objects at Nevers.*]

SHE: Of not ever seeing you again. Ever, ever.

[*They move closer together again, as at the beginning of the scene.*]

One day, I'm twenty years old. It's in the cellar. My mother comes and tells me I'm twenty. [*A pause, as if remembering.*] My mother's crying.
HE: You spit in your mother's face?
SHE: Yes.

[*As if they were aware of these things together. He moves away from her.*]

HE: Drink something.
SHE: Yes.

[*He holds the glass for her to drink. She is worn out from remembering.*]

SHE: [*Suddenly.*] Afterward, I don't remember any more. I don't remember any more . . .
HE: [*Trying to encourage her.*] These cellars are very old, and very damp, these Nevers cellars. . . . You were saying . . .
SHE: Yes. Full of saltpeter.

[*Her mouth against the walls of the Nevers cellar, biting.*]

SHE: Sometimes a cat comes in and looks. It's not a mean cat. I don't remember any more.

[*A cat comes in the Nevers cellar and looks at this woman.*]

Afterward, I don't remember any more.

HE: How long?

SHE: [*Still in a trancelike state.*] Eternity.

[*Someone, a solitary man, puts a record of French bal-musette*[3] *music on the juke box. To make the miracle of the lost memories of Nevers last, to keep anything from "moving," the Japanese pours the contents of his glass into hers.*

In the Nevers cellar the cat's eyes and Riva's eyes glow.

When she hears the music of the record she (drunk or mad) smiles and screams:]

Oh, how young I was, once!

[*She comes back to Nevers, having hardly left it. She is* haunted *(the choice of adjectives is voluntarily varied).*]

At night . . . my mother takes me down into the garden. She looks at my head. Every night she looks carefully at my head. She still doesn't dare come near me. . . . It's at night that I can look at the square, so I look at it. It's enormous [*Gesturing.*]! It curves in the middle.

[*The air shaft at the Nevers cellar. Through it, the rainbowlike wheels of bicycles passing at dawn at Nevers.*]

Sleep comes at dawn.

HE: Does it rain sometimes?

SHE: . . . along the walls.

[*She searches, searches, searches.*]

SHE: [*Almost evil.*] I think of you, but I don't think about it any more.

[*They move closer together again.*]

HE: Mad.

SHE: Madly in love with you. [*Pause.*] My hair is growing back. I can feel it every day, with my hand. I don't care. But nevertheless my hair is growing back. . . .

[*Riva in her bed at Nevers, her hand in her hair. She runs her hands through her hair.*]

HE: Do you scream, before the cellar?

SHE: No. I'm numb.

[*They are cheek-to-cheek, their eyes half-closed, at Hiroshima.*]

They shave my head carefully till they're finished. They think it's their duty to do a good job shaving the women's heads.

HE: [*Very clearly.*] Are you ashamed for them, my love?

3. Popular dancing music, often played on an accordion, for dances such as the waltz or fox trot.

[*The hair-cutting.*]

SHE: No. You're dead. I'm much too busy suffering. [*Dusk deepens. The following said with complete immobility.*] All I hear is the sound of the scissors on my head. It makes me feel a little bit better about . . . your death . . . like . . . like, oh! I can't give you a better example, like my nails, the walls . . . for my anger.

[*She goes on, desperately against him at Hiroshima.*]

Oh! What pain. What pain in my heart. It's unbelievable. Everywhere in the city they're singing the *Marseillaise.* Night falls. My dead love is an enemy of France. Someone says she should be made to walk through the city. My father's drug store is closed because of the disgrace. I'm alone. Some of them laugh. At night I return home.

[*Scene of the square at Nevers. She screams, not words, but a formless scream understandable in any language as the cry of a child for its mother. He is still against her, holding her hands.*]

HE: And then, one day, my love, you come out of eternity.

[*The room at Nevers. Riva paces the floor. Overturns objects. Savage, conscious animality.*]

SHE: Yes, it takes a long time.

They told me it had taken a very long time.

At six in the evening, the bells of the St. Etienne Cathedral[4] ring, winter and summer. One day, it is true, I hear them. I remember having heard them before—before—when we were in love, when we were happy.

I'm beginning to see.

I remember having already seen before—before—when we were in love, when we were happy.

I remember.

I see the ink.

I see the daylight.

I see my life. Your death.

My life that goes on. Your death that goes on

[*Room and cellar Nevers.*]

and that it took the shadows longer now to reach the corners of the room. And that it took the shadows longer now to reach the corners of the cellar walls. About half past six.

Winter is over.

[*A pause. Hiroshima. She is trembling. She moves away from his face.*]

Oh! It's horrible. I'm beginning to remember you less clearly.

4. A church in Nevers: "St. Stephen's."

[*He holds the glass and makes her drink. She's horrified by herself.*]

. . . I'm beginning to forget you. I tremble at the thought of having forgotten so much love . . .

. . . More. [*He makes her drink again.*]

[*She wanders. This time. Alone. He loses her.*]

We were supposed to meet you at noon on the quays of the Loire. I was going to leave with him. When I arrived at noon on the quay of the Loire, he wasn't quite dead yet. Someone had fired on him from a garden.

[*The garden above the quay of the Loire. She becomes delirious, no longer looking at him.*]

I stay near his body all that day and then all the next night. The next morning they came to pick him up and they put him in a truck. It was that night Nevers was liberated. The bells of St. Etienne were ringing, ringing . . . Little by little he grew cold beneath me. Oh! how long it took him to die! When? I'm not quite sure. I was lying on top of him . . . yes . . . the moment of his death actually escaped me, because . . . even at that very moment, and even afterward, yes, even afterward, I can say that I couldn't feel the slightest difference between this dead body and mine. All I could find between this body and mine were obvious similarities, do you understand? [*Shouting.*] He was my first love. . . .

[*The Japanese slaps her. (Or, if you prefer, crushes her hands in his.) She acts as though she didn't know where it had come from. But she snaps out of it, and acts as though she realized it had been necessary.*]

And then one day . . . I had screamed again. So they put me back in the cellar.

[*Her voice resumes its normal rhythm. Here the entire scene of the marble that enters the cellar, the marble she picks up, the warm marble she encloses in her hand, etc., and that she gives back to the children outside, etc.*]

. . . it was warm. . . .

[*He lets her talk, without understanding. She goes on.*]

SHE: [*After a pause.*] I think then is when I got over my hate. [*Pause.*] I don't scream any more. [*Pause.*] I'm becoming reasonable. They say: "She's becoming reasonable." [*Pause.*] One night, a holiday, they let me go out.

[*Dawn, at Nevers, beside a river.*]

The banks of the Loire. Dawn. People are crossing the bridge, sometimes many, sometimes few, depending on the hour. From afar, it's no one.

[*Republic Square, at Nevers, at night.*]

Not long after that my mother tells me I have to leave for Paris, by night. She give me some money. I leave for Paris, on a bicycle, at night. It's summery. The nights are warm. When I reach Paris two days later the name of Hiroshima is in all the newspapers. My hair is now a decent length. I'm in the street with the people.

[*Someone puts another bal-musette record on the juke box.*]

SHE: [*As if she were waking up.*] Fourteen years have passed.

[*He gives her something to drink. She drinks. She apparently becomes quite calm. They are emerging from the Nevers tunnel.*]

I don't even remember his hands very well. . . . The pain, I still remember the pain a little.

HE: Tonight?

SHE: Yes, tonight, I remember. But one day I won't remember it any more. Not at all. Nothing.

SHE: [*Raising her head to look at him.*] Tomorrow at this time I'll be thousands of miles away from you.

HE: Does your husband know about this?

SHE: [*Hesitating.*] No.

HE: Then I'm the only one who does?

SHE: Yes.

[*He gets up, takes her in his arms, forcing her to get up too, and holds her very tightly, shockingly. People look at them. They don't understand. He is overwhelmingly happy. He laughs.*]

HE: I'm the only one who knows. No one else?

SHE: [*Closing her eyes.*] Don't say any more.

[*She moves even closer to him. She raises her hand, and caresses his lips very lightly. Then, as if she were suddenly very happy:*]

Oh, how good it is to be with someone, sometimes.

[*They separate, very slowly, he sits back down again.*]

HE: Yes.

[*Somewhere a lamp goes out, either on the river bank or in the bar. She jumps. She withdraws her hand, which she had placed again on his lips. He hasn't forgotten the passing time.*]

Tell me more.

SHE: All right.

[*Searches, can't find anything.*]

HE: Tell me more.

SHE: I want to have lived through that moment. That incomparable moment.

[*She drinks. He speaks, as though divorced from the present.*]

HE: In a few years, when I'll have forgotten you, and when other such adventures, from sheer habit, will happen to me, I'll remember you as the symbol of love's forgetfulness. I'll think of this adventure as of the horror of oblivion. I already know it.

[*People enter the café. She looks at them.*]

SHE: [*Hopefully.*] Doesn't anything ever stop at night, in Hiroshima?

[*They begin a final game of mutual deception.*]

HE: Never, it never stops in Hiroshima.

[*She puts down her glass, smiles, her smiling concealing a feeling of distress.*]

SHE: I love that . . . cities where there are always people awake, day or night . . .

[*The proprietress of the bar turns out a light. The record stops playing. They're in semi-darkness. The late but ineluctable hour when the cafés close is fast approaching. They both close their eyes, as if seized by a feeling of modesty. The well-ordered world has thrown them out, for their adventure has no place in it. No use fighting. She suddenly understands this. When they raise their eyes again, they literally smile "in order not to cry." She gets up. He does nothing to restrain her. They are outside, in the night, in front of the café. She stands facing him.*]

It's sometimes necessary to keep from thinking about these difficulties the world makes. If we didn't we'd suffocate.

[*A last light goes out in the café. Both their eyes are lowered.*]

Go away, leave me.

[*He starts to leave, looks up at the sky.*]

HE: It isn't daylight yet. . . .
SHE: No. [*Pause.*] Probably we'll die without ever seeing each other again.
HE: Yes, probably. [*Pause.*] Unless, perhaps, someday, a war. . . .

[*Pause.*]

SHE: [*Ironically.*] Yes, a war. . . .

PART V

After a further time lapse. We see her in the street, walking quickly. Then we see her in the lobby of the hotel. She takes her key. Then we see her on the stairway. Then we see her open the door to her room. Enter the room and stop short as before an abyss, or as if she had discovered someone already in the room. Then she backs out and closes the door softly.

Climbing the stairs, descending, going back up, etc. Retracing her steps. Coming and going in the hallway. Wringing her hands, searching for a solution, not finding it, returning to her room all of a sudden. And this time coming to terms with the room.

She goes to the basin, splashes water on her face. And we hear the first sentence of her interior dialogue:

SHE: You think you know. And then, no. You don't.
In Nevers she had a German love when she was young. . . .
We'll go to Bavaria, my love, and there we'll marry.
She never went to Bavaria. [*Looking at herself in the mirror.*]
I dare those who have never gone to Bavaria to speak to her of love.
You were not yet quite dead.
I told our story.
I was unfaithful to you tonight with this stranger.
I told our story.
It was, you see, a story that could be told.
For fourteen years I hadn't found . . . the taste of an impossible love again.
Since Nevers.
Look how I'm forgetting you . . .
Look how I've forgotten you.
Look at me.

[*Through the open window we see the new Hiroshima, peacefully asleep. She suddenly raises her head, sees her wet face in the mirror—like tears—grown old, haggard. And this time, disgusted, she closes her eyes. She dries her face and quickly leaves, crossing the lobby.*]

[*When we see her again she is sitting on a bench, or on a pile of gravel, about fifty feet from the same bar where they had spent the evening together. The restaurant's light is in her eyes. Banal, almost empty: he is no longer there. She (lies down, sits down) on the gravel and continues to look at the café. (Now only one light is left on in the bar. The room where they had been a short while before is closed. The door into that room is slightly ajar, and by the dim light it is just possible to make out the arrangement of chairs and tables, which are no more than vague, vain shadows.)*]

[*She closes her eyes. Then opens them again. She seems to be asleep. But she is not. When she opens her eyes, she opens them suddenly. Like a cat. Then we hear her voice, an interior monologue:*]

SHE: I'm going to stay in Hiroshima. With him, every night. In Hiroshima. [*Opening her eyes.*] I'm going to stay here. Here.

[*She looks away from the café and gazes around her. Then suddenly she curls up as tightly as she can, a childlike movement, her head cuddled in her arms, her feet pulled up under her. The Japanese approaches her. She sees him, doesn't move, doesn't react. Their absence "from each other" has begun. No astonishment. He is smoking a cigarette.*]

HE: Stay in Hiroshima.

SHE: [*Glancing at him.*] Of course I'm going to stay in Hiroshima, with you. [*She buries her head again and says, in a childish tone:*] Oh, how miserable I am. . . .

[*He moves nearer to her.*]

I never expected this would happen, really. . . . Go away.

HE: [*Moving away.*] Impossible to leave you.

[*We see them now on a boulevard. In the background, the lighted signs of nightclubs. The boulevard is perfectly straight. She is walking, he following. We see first one, then the other. Distress on both their faces. He catches up with her.*]

HE: [*Softly.*] Stay in Hiroshima with me.

[*She doesn't reply. Then we hear her voice in an interior monologue, loud and uncontrolled:*]

SHE: He's going to come toward me, he's going to take me by the shoulders, he's-going-to-kiss-me. . . .

He'll kiss me . . . and I'll be lost. [*The word "lost" is said almost ecstatically.*]

[*A shot of him. And we notice he's walking more slowly to let the distance between them grow. That instead of coming toward her he's moving farther away. She doesn't turn back.*]

[*A succession of streets in Hiroshima and Nevers. Riva's interior monologue.*]

SHE: I meet you.

I remember you.
This city was made to the size of love.
You were made to the size of my body.
Who are you?
You destroy me.
I was hungry. Hungry for infidelity, for adultery, for lies, hungry to die.
I have always been.
I always expected that one day you would descend on me.
I waited for you calmly, with infinite patience.

Take me. Deform me to your likeness so that no one, after you, can understand the reason for so much desire.

We're going to remain alone, my love.
The night will never end.
The sun will never rise again on anyone.
Never. Never more. At last.
You destroy me.

You're so good for me.
In good conscience, with good will, we'll mourn the departed day.
We'll have nothing else to do, nothing but to mourn the departed day.
And a time is going to come.
A time will come. When we'll no more know what thing it is that binds us. By slow degrees the word will fade from our memory.
Then it will disappear altogether.

[*This time he accosts her face to face—for the last time—but from a distance. Henceforth she is inviolable. It is raining. They are under a store awning.*]

HE: Maybe it's possible for you to stay.
SHE: You know it's not. Still more impossible than to leave.
HE: A week.
SHE: No.
HE: Three days.
SHE: Time enough for what? To live from it? To die from it?
HE: Time enough to know which.
SHE: That doesn't exist. Neither time enough to live from it. Nor time enough to die from it. So I don't give a damn.
HE: I would have preferred that you had died at Nevers.
SHE: So would I. But I didn't die at Nevers.

[*She is seated on a bench in the waiting room of the Hiroshima railroad station. Still more time has elapsed. An elderly Japanese woman is seated beside her. Another interior monologue.*]

Nevers, that I'd forgotten, I'd like to see you again tonight. Every night for months on end I set you on fire, while my body was aflame with his memory.

[*Like a shadow the Japanese enters and sits on the same bench, on the opposite side of the old woman. He doesn't look at the French woman. His face is soaked from the rain. His lips are trembling slightly.*]

While my body is still on fire with your memory, I would like to see Nevers again . . . the Loire.

[*Shot of Nevers.*]

Lovely poplar trees of Nièvre, I offer you to oblivion. [*The word "lovely" should be spoken like a word of love.*]
Three-penny story, I bequeath you to oblivion.

[*The ruins at Nevers.*]

One night without you and I waited for daylight to free me.

[*The "marriage" at Nevers.*]

One day without his eyes was enough to kill her.
Little girl of Nevers.

Shameless child of Nevers.
One day without his hands and she thinks how sad it is to love.
Silly little girl.
Who dies of love at Nevers.
Little girl with shaven head, I bequeath you to oblivion.
Three-penny story.
As it was for him, oblivion will begin with your eyes.
Just the same.
Then, as it was for him, it will encompass your voice.
Just the same.
Then, as it was for him, it will encompass you completely, little by little.
You will become a song.

[*They are separated by the old Japanese woman. He takes a cigarette, rises slightly, and offers the French woman the package. "That's all I can do for you, offer you a cigarette, as I would offer one to anybody, to this old woman." She doesn't smoke. He offers the package to the old woman, lights her cigarette.*

The Nevers forest moves past in the twilight. And Nevers. While the loudspeaker at the Hiroshima station blares: "Hiroshima, Hiroshima!" during the shots of Nevers.

The French woman seems to be asleep. The two Japanese beside her speak softly to keep from waking her up.]

THE OLD WOMAN: Who is she?
HE: A French woman.
THE OLD WOMAN: What's the matter?
HE: She's leaving Japan in a little while. We're sad at having to leave each other.[5]

[*She is gone. We see her again just outside the station. She gets into a taxi. Stops before a night club. "The Casablanca." Then he arrives after her.*

She is alone at a table. He sits down at another table facing hers. It's the end. The end of the night which marks the beginning of their eternal separation. A Japanese who was in the room goes over to her and engages her in conversation.]

THE JAPANESE: Are you alone?[6]

[*She replies only by signs.*]

Do you mind talking with me a little?

[*The place is almost empty. People are bored.*]

It is very late to be lonely.

5. This exchange takes place in Japanese. Not translated in the film. [Author's note] 6. This passage in English in the film. [Author's note]

[*She lets herself be accosted by another man in order to "lose" the one we know. But not only is that not possible, it's useless. For the other one is already lost.*]

May I sit down? Are you just visiting Hiroshima?
Do you like Japan?
Do you live in Paris?

[*We can see day beginning to break (through the windows). The interior monologue has stopped. This unknown Japanese is talking to her. She looks at the other. The unknown Japanese stops talking to her. And then, terrifying, "the dawn of the damned" can be seen breaking through the windows of the night club.*]

[*She is next seen leaning against the door inside her hotel room. Her hand is on her heart. A knock. She opens*]

HE: Impossible not to come.

[*They are standing in the room, facing each other, their arms at their sides, their bodies not touching. The room is in order. The ashtrays are empty. It is now full daylight. The sun is up. They don't even smoke. The bed is still made. They say nothing. They look at each other. The silence of dawn weighs on the whole city. He enters her room. In the distance, Hiroshima is still sleeping. All of a sudden, she sits down. She buries her head in her hands, clenches her fist, closes her eyes, and moans. A moan of utter sadness. The light of the city in her eyes.*]

SHE: I'll forget you! I'm forgetting you already! Look how I'm forgetting you! Look at me!

[*He takes her arms (wrists), she faces him, her head thrown back. She suddenly breaks away from him. He helps her by an effort of self-abstraction. As if she were in danger. He looks at her, she at him, as she would look at the city, and suddenly, very softly, she calls him. She calls him from afar, lost in wonder. She has succeeded in drowning him in universal oblivion. And it is a source of amazement to her.*]

Hi-ro-shi-ma.
Hi-ro-shi-ma. That's your name.

[*They look at each other without seeing each other. Forever.*]

HE: That's my name. Yes. Your name is Nevers. Ne-vers-in-France.

1960

DAVID HENRY HWANG

M. Butterfly

PLAYWRIGHT'S NOTES

> A former French diplomat and a Chinese opera singer have been sentenced to six years in jail for spying for China after a two-day trial that traced a story of clandestine love and mistaken sexual identity. . . . Mr. Bouriscot was accused of passing information to China after he fell in love with Mr. Shi, whom he believed for twenty years to be a woman.
>
> —*The New York Times*, May 11, 1986

This play was suggested by international newspaper accounts of a recent espionage trial. For purposes of dramatization, names have been changed, characters created, and incidents devised or altered, and this play does not purport to be a factual record of real events or real people.

> I could escape this feeling
> With my China girl . . .
>
> —DAVID BOWIE & IGGY POP

CHARACTERS

RENE GALLIMARD / PINKERTON
SONG LILING / BUTTERFLY
MARC / SHARPLESS
COMRADE CHIN / SUZUKI
HELGA
AMBASSADOR MANUEL TOULON
RENEE
JUDGE

SETTING: *The action of the play takes place in a Paris prison in the present, and in recall, during the decade 1960 to 1970 in Beijing, and from 1966 to the present in Paris.*

ACT I

SCENE 1

M. GALLIMARD'S *prison cell. Paris. Present.*

Lights fade up to reveal RENE GALLIMARD, *65, in a prison cell. He wears a comfortable bathrobe, and looks old and tired. The sparsely furnished cell contains a wooden crate upon which sits a hot plate with a kettle, and a portable tape recorder.* GALLIMARD *sits on the crate staring at the recorder, a sad smile on his face.*

Upstage SONG, *who appears as a beautiful woman in traditional Chinese garb, dances a traditional piece from the Peking Opera, surrounded by the percussive clatter of Chinese music.*

Then, slowly, lights and sound cross-fade; the Chinese opera music dissolves into a Western opera, the "Love Duet" from Puccini's Madame Butterfly. SONG *continues dancing, now to the Western accompaniment. Though her movements are the same, the difference in music now gives them a balletic quality.*

GALLIMARD *rises, and turns upstage towards the figure of* SONG, *who dances without acknowledging him.*

GALLIMARD: Butterfly, Butterfly . . . [*He forces himself to turn away, as the image of* SONG *fade outs, and talks to us.*] The limits of my cell are as such: four-and-a-half meters by five. There's one window against the far wall; a door, very strong, to protect me from autograph hounds. I'm responsible for the tape recorder, the hot plate, and this charming coffee table.

When I want to eat, I'm marched off to the dining room—hot, steaming slop appears on my plate. When I want to sleep, the light bulb turns itself off—the work of fairies. It's an enchanted space I occupy. The French—we know how to run a prison.

But, to be honest, I'm not treated like an ordinary prisoner. Why? Because I'm a celebrity. You see, I make people laugh.

I never dreamed this day would arrive. I've never been considered witty or clever. In fact, as a young boy, in an informal poll among my grammar school classmates, I was voted "least likely to be invited to a party." It's a title I managed to hold onto for many years. Despite some stiff competition.

But now, how the tables turn! Look at me: the life of every social function in Paris. Paris? Why be modest? My fame has spread to Amsterdam, London, New York. Listen to them! In the world's smartest parlors. I'm the one who lifts their spirits!

[*With a flourish,* GALLIMARD *directs our attention to another part of the stage.*]

SCENE 2

A party. Present.

Lights go up on a chic-looking parlor, where a well-dressed trio, two men and one woman, make conversation. GALLIMARD *also remains lit; he observes them from his cell.*

WOMAN: And what of Gallimard?
MAN 1: Gallimard?
MAN 2: Gallimard!
GALLIMARD: [*To us.*] You see? They're all determined to say my name, as if it were some new dance.
WOMAN: He still claims not to believe the truth.
MAN 1: What? Still? Even since the trial?
WOMAN: Yes. Isn't it mad?
MAN 2: [*Laughing.*] He says . . . it was dark . . . and she was very modest!

[*The trio break into laughter.*]

MAN 1: So—what? He never touched her with his hands?

MAN 2: Perhaps he did, and simply misidentified the equipment. A compelling case for sex education in the schools.

WOMAN: To protect the National Security—the Church can't argue with that.

MAN 1: That's impossible! How could he not know?

MAN 2: Simple ignorance.

MAN 1: For twenty years?

MAN 2: Time flies when you're being stupid.

WOMAN: Well, I thought the French were ladies' men.

MAN 2: It seems Monsieur Gallimard was overly anxious to live up to his national reputation.

WOMAN: Well, he's not very good-looking.

MAN 1: No, he's not.

MAN 2: Certainly not.

WOMAN: Actually, I feel sorry for him.

MAN 2: A toast! To Monsieur Gallimard!

WOMAN: Yes! To Gallimard!

MAN 1: To Gallimard!

MAN 2: Vive la différence!

[*They toast, laughing. Lights down on them.*]

Scene 3

M. GALLIMARD'S *cell.*

GALLIMARD: [*Smiling.*] You see? They toast me. I've become patron saint of the socially inept. Can they really be so foolish? Men like that—they should be scratching at my door, begging to learn my secrets! For I, Rene Gallimard, you see, I have known, and been loved by . . . the Perfect Woman.

Alone in this cell, I sit night after night, watching our story play through my head, always searching for a new ending, one which redeems my honor, where she returns at last to my arms. And I imagine you—my ideal audience—who come to understand and even, perhaps just a little, to envy me. [*He turns on his tape recorder. Over the house speakers, we hear the opening phrases of* Madame Butterfly.] In order for you to understand what I did and why, I must introduce you to my favorite opera: *Madame Butterfly*. By Giacomo Puccini.[1] First produced at La Scala, Milan, in 1904, it is now beloved throughout the Western world. [*As* GALLIMARD *describes the opera, the tape segues in and out to sections he may be describing.*] And why not? Its heroine, Cio-Cio-San, also known as Butterfly, is a feminine ideal, beautiful and brave. And its hero, the man for whom she gives up everything, is—[*He pulls out a naval officer's cap from under his crate, pops it on his head, and struts about.*]—not very good-looking, not too bright, and pretty much a

1. (1858–1924), Italian composer.

wimp: Benjamin Franklin Pinkerton of the U.S. Navy. As the curtain rises, he's just closed on two great bargains: one on a house, the other on a woman—call it a package deal.

Pinkerton purchased the rights to Butterfly for one hundred yen—in modern currency, equivalent to about . . . sixty-six cents. So, he's feeling pretty pleased with himself as Sharpless, the American consul, arrives to witness the marriage.

[MARC, *wearing an official cap to designate* SHARPLESS, *enters and plays the character.*]

SHARPLESS / MARC: Pinkerton!

PINKERTON / GALLIMARD: Sharpless! How's it hangin'? It's a great day, just great. Between my house, my wife, and the rickshaw ride in from town, I've saved nineteen cents just this morning.

SHARPLESS: Wonderful. I can see the inscription on your tombstone already: "I saved a dollar, here I lie." [*He looks around.*] Nice house.

PINKERTON: It's artistic. Artistic, don't you think? Like the way the shoji screens slide open to reveal the wet bar and disco mirror ball? Classy, huh? Great for impressing the chicks.

SHARPLESS: "Chicks"? Pinkerton, you're going to be a married man!

PINKERTON: Well, sort of.

SHARPLESS: What do you mean?

PINKERTON: This country—Sharpless, it is okay. You got all these geisha girls running around—

SHARPLESS: I know! I live here!

PINKERTON: Then, you know the marriage laws, right? I split for one month, it's annulled!

SHARPLESS: Leave it to you to read the fine print. Who's the lucky girl?

PINKERTON: Cio-Cio-San. Her friends call her Butterfly. Sharpless, she eats out of my hand!

SHARPLESS: She's probably very hungry.

PINKERTON: Not like American girls. It's true what they say about Oriental girls. They want to be treated bad!

SHARPLESS: Oh, please!

PINKERTON: It's true!

SHARPLESS: Are you serious about this girl?

PINKERTON: I'm marrying her, aren't I?

SHARPLESS: Yes—with generous trade-in terms.

PINKERTON: When I leave, she'll know what it's like to have loved a real man. And I'll even buy her a few nylons.

SHARPLESS: You aren't planning to take her with you?

PINKERTON: Huh? Where?

SHARPLESS: Home!

PINKERTON: You mean, America? Are you crazy? Can you see her trying to buy rice in St. Louis?

SHARPLESS: So, you're not serious.

[*Pause.*]

PINKERTON / GALLIMARD: [*As* PINKERTON.] Consul, I am a sailor in port. [*As* GALLIMARD.] They then proceed to sing the famous duet, "The Whole World Over."

[*The duet plays on the speakers.* GALLIMARD, *as* PINKERTON, *lip-syncs his lines from the opera.*]

GALLIMARD: To give a rough translations: "The whole world over, the Yankee travels, casting his anchor wherever he wants. Life's not worth living unless he can win the hearts of the fairest maidens, then hotfoot it off the premises ASAP." [*He turns towards* MARC.] In the preceding scene, I played Pinkerton, the womanizing cad, and my friend Marc from school . . . [MARC *bows grandly for our benefit.*] played Sharpless, the sensitive soul of reason. In life, however, our positions were usually—no, always—reversed.

SCENE 4

Ecole Nationale. Aix-en-Provence. 1947.

GALLIMARD: No, Marc, I think I'd rather stay home.

MARC: Are you crazy?! We are going to Dad's condo in Marseille! You know what happened last time?

GALLIMARD: Of course I do.

MARC: Of course you don't! You never know. . . . They stripped, Rene!

GALLIMARD: Who stripped?

MARC: The girls!

GALLIMARD: Girls? Who said anything about girls?

MARC: Rene, we're a buncha university guys goin' up to the woods. What are we gonna do—talk philosophy?

GALLIMARD: What girls? Where do you get them?

MARC: Who cares? The point is, they come. On trucks. Packed in like sardines. The back flips open, babes hop out, we're ready to roll.

GALLIMARD: You mean, they just—?

MARC: Before you know it, every last one of them—they're stripped and splashing around my pool. There's no moon out, they can't see what's going on, their boobs are flapping, right? You close your eyes, reach out—it's grab bag, get it? Doesn't matter whose ass is between whose legs, whose teeth are sinking into who. You're just in there, going at it, eyes closed, on and on for as long as you can stand. [*Pause.*] Some fun, huh?

GALLIMARD: What happens in the morning?

MARC: In the morning, you're ready to talk some philosophy. [*Beat.*[2]] So how 'bout it?

GALLIMARD: Marc, I can't . . . I'm afraid they'll say no—the girls. So I never ask.

MARC: You don't have to ask! That's the beauty—don't you see? They don't have

2. That is, he pauses for one beat.

to say yes. It's perfect for a guy like you, really.

GALLIMARD: You go ahead . . . I may come later.

MARC: Hey, Rene—it doesn't matter that you're clumsy and got zits—they're not looking!

GALLIMARD: Thank you very much.

MARC: Wimp. [MARC *walks over to the other side of the stage, and starts waving and smiling at women in the audience.*]

GALLIMARD: [*To us.*] We now return to my version of *Madame Butterfly* and the events leading to my recent conviction for treason. [GALLIMARD *notices* MARC *making lewd gestures.*]

MARC: Huh? [*Sotto voce.*] Rene, there're a lotta great babes out there. They're probably lookin' at me and thinking, "What a dangerous guy."

GALLIMARD: Yes—how could they help but be impressed by your cool sophistication?

[GALLIMARD *pops the Sharpless cap on* MARC'S *head, and points him offstage.* MARC *exits, leering.*]

SCENE 5

M. GALLIMARD'*s cell.*

GALLIMARD: Next, Butterfly makes her entrance. We learn her age—fifteen . . . but very mature for her years. [*Lights come up on the area where we saw* SONG *dancing at the top of the play. She appears there again, now dressed as Madame Butterfly, moving to the "Love Duet."* GALLIMARD *turns upstage slightly to watch, transfixed.*] But as she slides past him, beautiful, laughing softly behind her fan, don't we who are men sigh with hope? We, who are not handsome, nor brave, nor powerful, yet somehow believe, like Pinkerton, that we deserve a Butterfly. She arrives with all her possessions in the folds of her sleeves, lays them all out, for her man to do with as he pleases. Even her life itself—she bows her head as she whispers that she's not even worth the hundred yen he paid for her. He's already given too much, when we know he's really had to give nothing at all. [*Music and lights on* SONG *out.* GALLIMARD *sits at his crate.*] In real life, women who put their total worth at less than sixty-six cents are quite hard to find. The closest we come is in the pages of these magazines. [*He reaches into his crate, pulls out a stack of girlie magazines, and begins flipping through them.*] Quite a necessity in prison. For three or four dollars, you get seven or eight women.

I first discovered these magazines at my uncle's house. One day, as a boy of twelve. The first time I saw them in his closet . . . all lined up—my body shook. Not with lust—no, with power. Here were women—a shelfful—who would do exactly as I wanted.

[*The "Love Duet" creeps in over the speakers. Special comes up,*[3] *revealing, not* SONG *this time, but a pinup girl in a sexy negligee, her back to us.* GALLIMARD *turns upstage and looks at her.*]

3. That is, light comes up on the upstage special area.

GIRL: I know you're watching me.
GALLIMARD: My throat . . . it's dry.
GIRL: I leave my blinds open every night before I go to bed.
GALLIMARD: I can't move.
GIRL: I leave my blinds open and the lights on.
GALLIMARD: I'm shaking. My skin is hot, but my penis is soft. Why?
GIRL: I stand in front of the window.
GALLIMARD: What is she going to do?
GIRL: I toss my hair, and I let my lips part . . . barely.
GALLIMARD: I shouldn't be seeing this. It's so dirty. I'm so bad.
GIRL: Then, slowly, I lift off my nightdress.
GALLIMARD: Oh, god. I can't believe it. I can't—
GIRL: I toss it to the ground.
GALLIMARD: Now, she's going to walk away. She's going to—
GIRL: I stand there, in the light, displaying myself.
GALLIMARD: No. She's—why is she naked?
GIRL: To you.
GALLIMARD: In front of a window? This is wrong. No—
GIRL: Without shame.
GALLIMARD: No, she must . . . like it.
GIRL: I like it.
GALLIMARD: She . . . she wants me to see.
GIRL: I want you to see.
GALLIMARD: I can't believe it! She's getting excited!
GIRL: I can't see you. You can do whatever you want.
GALLIMARD: I can't do a thing. Why?
GIRL: What would you like me to do . . . next?

[*Lights go down on her. Music off. Silence, as* GALLIMARD *puts away his magazines. Then he resumes talking to us.*]

GALLIMARD: Act Two begins with Butterfly staring at the ocean. Pinkerton's been called back to the U.S., and he's given his wife a detailed schedule of his plans. In the column marked "return date," he's written "when the robins nest." This failed to ignite her suspicions. Now, three years have passed without a peep from him. Which brings a response from her faithful servant, Suzuki.

[COMRADE CHIN *enters, playing* SUZUKI.]

SUZUKI: Girl, he's a loser. What'd he ever give you? Nineteen cents and those ugly Day-Glo stockings? Look, it's finished! Kaput! Done! And you should be glad! I mean, the guy was a woofer! He tried before, you know—before he met you, he went down to geisha central and plunked down his spare change in front of the usual candidates—everyone else gagged! These are hungry prostitutes, and they were not interested, get the picture? Now, stop slathering when an American ship sails in, and let's make some bucks—I mean, yen! We are broke!

Now, what about Yamadori? Hey, hey—don't look away—the man is a prince—figuratively, and, what's even better, literally. He's rich, he's handsome, he says he'll die if you don't marry him—and he's even willing to overlook the little fact that you've been deflowered all over the place by a foreign devil. What do you mean, "But he's Japanese?" You're Japanese! You think you've been touched by the whitey god? He was a sailor with dirty hands! [SUZUKI *stalks offstage*.]

GALLIMARD: She's also visited by Consul Sharpless, sent by Pinkerton on a minor errand.

[MARC *enters, as* SHARPLESS.]

SHARPLESS: I hate this job.

GALLIMARD: This Pinkerton—he doesn't show up personally to tell his wife he's abandoning her. No, he sends a government diplomat . . . at taxpayer's expense.

SHARPLESS: Butterfly? Butterfly? I have some bad—I'm going to be ill. Butterfly, I came to tell you—

GALLIMARD: Butterfly says she knows he'll return and if he doesn't she'll kill herself rather than go back to her own people. [*Beat*.] This causes a lull in the conversation.

SHARPLESS: Let's put it this way . . .

GALLIMARD: Butterfly runs into the next room, and returns holding—

[*Sound cue: a baby crying*. SHARPLESS, *"seeing" this, backs away*.]

SHARPLESS: Well, good. Happy to see things going so well. I suppose I'll be going now. Ta ta. Ciao. [*He turns away. Sound cue out*.] I hate this job. [*He exits*.]

GALLIMARD: At that moment, Butterfly spots in the harbor an American ship—the *Abramo Lincoln*![4] [*Music cue: "The Flower Duet."* SONG, *still dressed as* BUTTERFLY, *changes into a wedding kimono, moving to the music*.] This is the moment that redeems her years of waiting. With Suzuki's help, they cover the room with flowers—[CHIN, *as* SUZUKI, *trudges onstage and drops a lone flower without much enthusiasm*.]—and she changes into her wedding dress to prepare for Pinkerton's arrival. [SUZUKI *helps* BUTTERFLY *change*. HELGA *enters, and helps* GALLIMARD *change into a tuxedo*.] I married a woman older than myself—Helga.

HELGA: My father was ambassador to Australia. I grew up among criminals and kangaroos.

GALLIMARD: Hearing that brought me to the altar—[HELGA *exits*.]—where I took a vow renouncing love. No fantasy woman would ever want me, so, yes, I would settle for a quick leap up the career ladder. Passion, I banish, and in its place—practicality!

But my vows had long since lost their charm by the time we arrived in China. The sad truth is that all men want a beautiful woman, and the uglier the man, the greater the want. [SUZUKI *makes final adjustments of* BUTTERFLY*'s costume, as does* GALLIMARD *of his tuxedo*.] I married late, at age thirty-

4. "Abramo" because it's an Italian opera.

one. I was faithful to my marriage for eight years. Until the day when, as a junior-level diplomat in puritanical Peking, in a parlor at the German ambassador's house, during the "Reign of a Hundred Flowers," I first saw her . . . singing the death scene from *Madame Butterfly*.

[SUZUKI *runs offstage.*]

SCENE 6

German ambassador's house. Beijing. 1960.

The upstage special area now becomes a stage. Several chairs face upstage, representing seating for some twenty guests in the parlor. A few "diplomats"— RENEE, MARC, TOULON*—in formal dress enter and take seats.*

GALLIMARD *also sits down, but turns towards us and continues to talk. Orchestral accompaniment on the tape is now replaced by a simple piano.* SONG *picks up the death scene from the point where* BUTTERFLY *uncovers the hara-kiri knife.*

GALLIMARD: The ending is pitiful. Pinkerton, in an act of great courage, stays home and sends his American wife to pick up Butterfly's child. The truth, long deferred, has come up to her door.

[SONG, *playing* BUTTERFLY, *sings the lines from the opera in her own voice—which, though not classical, should be decent.*]

SONG: "Con onor muore/ chi non puo serbar/ vita con onore."

GALLIMARD: [*Simultaneously.*] "Death with honor/ Is better than life/ Life with dishonor." [*The stage is illuminated; we are now completely within an elegant diplomat's residence.* SONG *proceeds to play out an abbreviated death scene. Everyone in the room applauds.* SONG, *shyly, takes her bows. Others in the room rush to congratulate her.* GALLIMARD *remains with us.*] They say in opera the voice is everything. That's probably why I'd never before enjoyed opera. Here . . . here was a Butterfly with little or no voice—but she had the grace, the delicacy . . . I believed this girl. I believed her suffering. I wanted to take her in my arms—so delicate, even I could protect her, take her home, pamper her until she smiled.

[*Over the course of the preceeding speech,* SONG *has broken from the upstage crowd and moved directly upstage of* GALLIMARD.]

SONG: Excuse me. Monsieur . . . ?

[GALLIMARD *turns upstage, shocked.*]

GALLIMARD: Oh! Gallimard. Mademoiselle . . . ? A beautiful . . .

SONG: Song Liling.

GALLIMARD: A beautiful performance.

SONG: Oh, please.

GALLIMARD: I usually—

SONG: You make me blush. I'm no opera singer at all.

GALLIMARD: I usually don't like *Butterfly*.
SONG: I can't blame you in the least.
GALLIMARD: I mean, the story—
SONG: Ridiculous.
GALLIMARD: I like the story, but . . . what?
SONG: Oh, you like it?
GALLIMARD: I . . . what I mean is, I've always seen it played by huge women in so much bad makeup.
SONG: Bad makeup is not unique to the West.
GALLIMARD: But, who can believe them?
SONG: And you believe me?
GALLIMARD: Absolutely. You were utterly convincing. It's the first time—
SONG: Convincing? As a Japanese woman? The Japanese used hundreds of our people for medical experiments during the war, you know. But I gather such an irony is lost on you.
GALLIMARD: No! I was about to say, it's the first time I've seen the beauty of the story.
SONG: Really?
GALLIMARD: Of her death. It's a . . . a pure sacrifice. He's unworthy, but what can she do? She loves him . . . so much. It's a very beautiful story.
SONG: Well, yes, to a Westerner.
GALLIMARD: Excuse me?
SONG: It's one of your favorite fantasies, isn't it? The submissive Oriental woman and the cruel white man.
GALLIMARD: Well, I didn't quite mean . . .
SONG: Consider it this way: what would you say if a blonde homecoming queen fell in love with a short Japanese businessman? He treats her cruelly, then goes home for three years, during which time she prays to his picture and turns down marriage from a young Kennedy. Then, when she learns he has remarried, she kills herself. Now, I believe you would consider this girl to be a deranged idiot, correct? But because it's an Oriental who kills herself for a Westerner—ah!—you find it beautiful.

[*Silence.*]

GALLIMARD: Yes . . . well . . . I see your point . . .
SONG: I will never do Butterfly again, Monsieur Gallimard. If you wish to see some real theater, come to the Peking Opera sometime. Expand your mind.

[SONG *walks offstage.*]

GALLIMARD: [*To us.*] So much for protecting her in my big Western arms.

SCENE 7

M. GALLIMARD'*s apartment. Beijing. 1960.*
GALLIMARD *changes from his tux into a casual suit.* HELGA *enters.*

GALLIMARD: The Chinese are an incredibly arrogant people.
HELGA: They warned us about that in Paris, remember?

GALLIMARD: Even Parisians consider them arrogant. That's a switch.

HELGA: What is it that Madame Su says? "We are a very old civilization." I never know if she's talking about her country or herself.

GALLIMARD: I walk around here, all I hear every day, everywhere is how *old* this culture is. The fact that "old" may be synonymous with "senile" doesn't occur to them.

HELGA: You're not going to change them. "East is east, west is west, and . . ." whatever that guy said.

GALLIMARD: It's just that—silly. I met . . . at Ambassador Koening's tonight—you should've been there.

HELGA: Koening? Oh god, no. Did he enchant you all again with the history of Bavaria?

GALLIMARD: No. I met, I suppose, the Chinese equivalent of a diva. She's a singer in the Chinese opera.

HELGA: They have an opera, too? Do they sing in Chinese? Or maybe—in Italian?

GALLIMARD: Tonight, she did sing in Italian.

HELGA: How'd she manage that?

GALLIMARD: She must've been educated in the West before the Revolution. Her French is very good also. Anyway, she sang the death scene from *Madame Butterfly*.

HELGA: *Madame Butterfly!* Then I should have come. [*She begins humming, floating around the room as if dragging long kimono sleeves.*] Did she have a nice costume? I think it's a classic piece of music.

GALLIMARD: That's what *I* thought, too. Don't let her hear you say that.

HELGA: What's wrong?

GALLIMARD: Evidently the Chinese hate it.

HELGA: She hated it, but she performed it anyway? Is she perverse?

GALLIMARD: They hate it because the white man gets the girl. Sour grapes if you ask me.

HELGA: Politics again? Why can't they just hear it as a piece of beautiful music? So, what's in their opera?

GALLIMARD: I don't know. But, whatever it is, I'm sure it must be *old*.

[HELGA *exits.*]

SCENE 8

Chinese opera house and the streets of Beijing. 1960.
The sound of gongs clanging fills the stage.

GALLIMARD: My wife's innocent question kept ringing in my ears. I asked around, but no one knew anything about the Chinese opera. It took four weeks, but my curiosity overcame my cowardice. This Chinese diva—this unwilling Butterfly—what did she do to make her so proud?

The room was hot, and full of smoke. Wrinkled faces, old women, teeth missing—a man with a growth on his neck, like a human toad. All smiling, pipes falling from their mouths, cracking nuts between their teeth, a live chicken pecking at my foot—all looking, screaming, gawking . . . at her.

[*The upstage area is suddenly hit with a harsh white light. It has become the stage for the Chinese opera performance. Two dancers enter, along with* SONG. GALLIMARD *stands apart, watching.* SONG *glides gracefully amidst the two dancers. Drums suddenly slam to a halt.* SONG *strikes a pose, looking straight at* GALLIMARD. *Dancers exit. Light change. Pause, then* SONG *walks right off the stage and straight up to* GALLIMARD.]

SONG: Yes. You. White man. I'm looking straight at you.

GALLIMARD: Me?

SONG: You see any other white men? It was too easy to spot you. How often does a man in my audience come in a tie? [SONG *starts to remove her costume. Underneath, she wears simple baggy clothes. They are now backstage. The show is over.*] So, you are an adventurous imperialist?

GALLIMARD: I . . . thought it would further my education.

SONG: It took you four weeks. Why?

GALLIMARD: I've been busy.

SONG: Well, education has always been undervalued in the West, hasn't it?

GALLIMARD: [*Laughing.*] I don't think it's true.

SONG: No, you wouldn't. You're a Westerner. How can you objectively judge your own values?

GALLIMARD: I think it's possible to achieve some distance.

SONG: Do you? [*Pause.*] It stinks in here. Let's go.

GALLIMARD: These are the smells of your loyal fans.

SONG: I love them for being my fans, I hate the smell they leave behind. I too can distance myself from my people. [*She looks around, then whispers in his ear.*] "Art for the masses" is a shitty excuse to keep artists poor. [*She pops a cigarette in her mouth.*] Be a gentleman, will you? And light my cigarette.

[GALLIMARD *fumbles for a match.*]

GALLIMARD: I don't . . . smoke.

SONG: [*Lighting her own.*] Your loss. Had you lit my cigarette, I might have blown a puff of smoke right between your eyes. Come. [*They start to walk about the stage. It is a summer night on the Beijing streets. Sounds of the city play on the house speakers.*] How I wish there were even a tiny cafe to sit in. With capuccinos, and men in tuxedos and bad expatriate jazz.

GALLIMARD: If my history serves me correctly, you weren't even allowed into the clubs in Shanghai before the Revolution.

SONG: Your history serves you poorly, Monsieur Gallimard. True, there were signs reading "No dogs and Chinamen." But a woman, especially a delicate Oriental woman—we always go where we please. Could you imagine it otherwise? Clubs in China filled with pasty, big-thighed white women, while thousands of slender lotus blossoms wait just outside the door? Never. The clubs would be empty. [*Beat.*] We have always held a certain fascination for you Caucasian men, have we not?

GALLIMARD: But . . . that fascination is imperialist, or so you tell me.

SONG: Do you believe everything I tell you? Yes. It is always imperialist. But sometimes . . . sometimes, it is also mutual. Oh—this is my flat.

GALLIMARD: I didn't even—

SONG: Thank you. Come another time and we will further expand your mind.

[SONG *exits.* GALLIMARD *continues roaming the streets as he speaks to us.*]

GALLIMARD: What was that? What did she mean, "Sometimes . . . it is mutual?" Women do not flirt with me. And I normally can't talk to them. But tonight, I held up my end of the conversation.

SCENE 9

GALLIMARD*'s bedroom. Beijing. 1960.*
HELGA *enters.*

HELGA: You didn't tell me you'd be home late.

GALLIMARD: I didn't intend to. Something came up.

HELGA: Oh? Like what?

GALLIMARD: I went to the . . . to the Dutch ambassador's home.

HELGA: Again?

GALLIMARD: There was a reception for a visiting scholar. He's writing a six-volume treatise on the Chinese revolution. We all gathered that meant he'd have to live here long enough to actually write six volumes, and we all expressed our deepest sympathies.

HELGA: Well, I had a good night too. I went with the ladies to a martial arts demonstration. Some of those men—when they break those thick boards—[*She mimes fanning herself.*] whoo-whoo!

[HELGA *exits. Lights dim.*]

GALLIMARD: I lied to my wife. Why? I've never had any reason to lie before. But what reason did I have tonight? I didn't do anything wrong. That night, I had a dream. Other people, I've been told, have dreams where angels appear. Or dragons, or Sophia Loren in a towel. In my dream, Marc from school appeared.

[MARC *enters, in a nightshirt and cap.*]

MARC: Rene! You met a girl!

[GALLIMARD *and* MARC *stumble down the Beijing streets. Night sounds over the speakers.*]

GALLIMARD: It's not that amazing, thank you.

MARC: No! It's so monumental, I heard about it halfway around the world in my sleep!

GALLIMARD: I've met girls before, you know.

MARC: Name one. I've come across time and space to congratulate you. [*He hands* GALLIMARD *a bottle of wine.*]

GALLIMARD: Marc, this is expensive.

MARC: On those rare occasions when you become a formless spirit, why not steal the best? [MARC *pops open the bottle, begins to share it with* GALLIMARD.]

GALLIMARD: You embarrass me. She . . . there's no reason to think she likes me.

MARC: "Sometimes, it is mutual"?

GALLIMARD: Oh.

MARC: "Mutual"? "Mutual"? What does that mean?

GALLIMARD: You heard!

MARC: It means the money is in the bank, you only have to write the check!

GALLIMARD: I am a married man!

MARC: And an excellent one too. I cheated after . . . six months. Then again and again, until now—three hundred girls in twelve years.

GALLIMARD: I don't think we should hold that up as a model.

MARC: Of course not! My life—it is disgusting! Phooey! Phooey! But, you—you are the model husband.

GALLIMARD: Anyway, it's impossible. I'm a foreigner.

MARC: Ah, yes. She cannot love you, it is taboo, but something deep inside her heart . . . she cannot help herself . . . she must surrender to you. It is her destiny.

GALLIMARD: How do you imagine all this?

MARC: The same way you do. It's an old story. It's in our blood. They fear us, Rene. Their women fear us. And their men—their men hate us. And, you know something? They are all correct.

[*They spot a light in a window.*]

MARC: There! There, Rene!

GALLIMARD: It's her window.

MARC: Late at night—it burns. The light—it burns for you.

GALLIMARD: I won't look. It's not respectful.

MARC: We don't have to be respectful. We're foreign devils.

[*Enter* SONG, *in a sheer robe. The "One Fine Day" aria creeps in over the speakers. With her back to us,* SONG *mimes attending to her toilette. Her robe comes loose, revealing her white shoulders.*]

MARC: All your life you've waited for a beautiful girl who would lay down for you. All your life you've smiled like a saint when it's happened to every other man you know. And you see them in magazines and you see them in movies. And you wonder, what's wrong with me? Will anyone beautiful ever want me? As the years pass, your hair thins and you struggle to hold onto even your hopes. Stop struggling, Rene. The wait is over. [*He exits.*]

GALLIMARD: Marc? Marc? [*At that moment* SONG, *her back still towards us, drops her robe. A second of her naked back, then a sound cue: a phone ringing, very loud. Blackout, followed in the next beat by a special up on the bedroom area, where a phone now sits.* GALLIMARD *stumbles across the stage and picks up the phone. Sound cue out. Over the course of his conversation, area lights fill in the vicinity of his bed. It is the following morning.*] Yes? Hello?

SONG: [*Offstage.*] Is it very early?
GALLIMARD: Why, yes.
SONG: [*Offstage.*] How early?
GALLIMARD: It's . . . it's 5:30. Why are you—?
SONG: [*Offstage.*] But it's light outside. Already.
GALLIMARD: It is. The sun must be in confusion today.

[*Over the course of* SONG*'s next speech, her upstage special comes up again. She sits in a chair, legs crossed, in a robe, telephone to her ear.*]

SONG: I waited until I saw the sun. That was as much discipline as I could manage for one night. Do you forgive me?
GALLIMARD: Of course . . . for what?
SONG: Then I'll ask you quickly. Are you really interested in the opera?
GALLIMARD: Why, yes. Yes I am.
SONG: Then come again next Thursday. I am playing *The Drunken Beauty*. May I count on you?
GALLIMARD: Yes. You may.
SONG: Perfect. Well, I must be getting to bed. I'm exhausted. It's been a very long night for me.

[SONG *hangs up; special on her goes off.* GALLIMARD *begins to dress for work.*]

Scene 10

SONG LILING*'s apartment. Beijing. 1960.*

GALLIMARD: I returned to the opera that next week, and the week after that . . . she keeps our meetings so short—perhaps fifteen, twenty minutes at most. So I am left each week with a thirst which is intensified. In this way, fifteen weeks have gone by. I am starting to doubt the words of my friend Marc. But no, not really. In my heart, I know she has . . . an interest in me. I suspect this is her way. She is outwardly bold and outspoken, yet her heart is shy and afraid. It is the Oriental in her at war with her Western education.
SONG: [*Offstage.*] I will be out in an instant. Ask the servant for anything you want.
GALLIMARD: Tonight, I have finally been invited to enter her apartment. Though the idea is almost beyond belief, I believe she is afraid of me.

[GALLIMARD *looks around the room. He picks up a picture in a frame, studies it. Without his noticing,* SONG *enters, dressed elegantly in a black gown from the twenties. She stands in the doorway looking like Anna May Wong.*[5]]

SONG: That is my father.
GALLIMARD: [*Surprised.*] Mademoiselle Song . . .

[*She glides up to him, snatches away the picture.*]

5. Chinese-American actress (1907–1961) who played sultry roles.

SONG: It is very good that he did not live to see the Revolution. They would, no doubt, have made him kneel on broken glass. Not that he didn't deserve such a punishment. But he is my father. I would've hated to see it happen.
GALLIMARD: I'm very honored that you've allowed me to visit your home.

[SONG *curtsies.*]

SONG: Thank you. Oh! Haven't you been poured any tea?
GALLIMARD: I'm really not—
SONG: [*To her offstage servant.*] Shu-Fang! Cha! Kwai-lah![6] [*To* GALLIMARD.] I'm sorry. You want everything to be perfect—
GALLIMARD: Please.
SONG:—and before the evening even begins—
GALLIMARD: I'm really not thirsty.
SONG: —it's ruined.
GALLIMARD: [*Sharply.*] Mademoiselle Song! [SONG *sits down.*]
SONG: I'm sorry.
GALLIMARD: What are you apologizing for now?

[*Pause;* SONG *starts to giggle.*]

SONG: I don't know!

[GALLIMARD *laughs.*]

GALLIMARD: Exactly my point.
SONG: Oh, I am silly. Lightheaded. I promise not to apologize for anything else tonight, do you hear me?
GALLIMARD: That's a good girl.

[SHU-FANG, *a servant girl, comes out with a tea tray and starts to pour.*]

SONG: [*To* SHU-FANG.] No! I'll pour myself for the gentleman! [SHU-FANG, *staring at* GALLIMARD, *exits.*] No, I . . . I don't even know why I invited you up.
GALLIMARD: Well, I'm glad you did.

[SONG *looks around the room.*]

SONG: There is an element of danger to your presence.
GALLIMARD: Oh?
SONG: You must know.
GALLIMARD: It doesn't concern me. We both know why I'm here.
SONG: It doesn't concern me either. No . . . well perhaps . . .
GALLIMARD: What?
SONG: Perhaps I am slightly afraid of scandal.
GALLIMARD: What are we doing?
SONG: I'm entertaining you. In my parlor.
GALLIMARD: In France, that would hardly—
SONG: France. France is a country living in the modern era. Perhaps even ahead

6. "Shu-Fang [the servant's name]! Tea! Quickly!"

of it. China is a nation whose soul is firmly rooted two thousand years in the past. What I do, even pouring the tea for you now . . . it has . . . implications. The walls and windows say so. Even my own heart, strapped inside this Western dress . . . even it says things—things I don't care to hear.

[SONG *hands* GALLIMARD *a cup of tea.* GALLIMARD *puts his hand over both the teacup and* SONG*'s hand.*]

GALLIMARD: This is a beautiful dress.

SONG: Don't.

GALLIMARD: What?

SONG: I don't even know if it looks right on me.

GALLIMARD: Believe me—

SONG: You are from France. You see so many beautiful women.

GALLIMARD: France? Since when are the European women—?

SONG: Oh! What am I trying to do, anyway?! [SONG *runs to the door, composes herself, then turns towards* GALLIMARD.] Monsieur Gallimard, perhaps you should go.

GALLIMARD: But . . . why?

SONG: There's something wrong about this.

GALLIMARD: I don't see what.

SONG: I feel . . . I am not myself.

GALLIMARD: No. You're nervous.

SONG: Please. Hard as I try to be modern, to speak like a man, to hold a Western woman's strong face up to my own . . . in the end, I fail. A small, frightened heart beats too quickly and gives me away. Monsieur Gallimard, I'm a Chinese girl. I've never . . . never invited a man up to my flat before. The forwardness of my actions makes my skin burn.

GALLIMARD: What are you afraid of? Certainly not me, I hope.

SONG: I'm a modest girl.

GALLIMARD: I know. And very beautiful. [*He touches her hair.*]

SONG: Please—go now. The next time you see me, I shall again be myself.

GALLIMARD: I like you the way you are right now.

SONG: You are a cad.

GALLIMARD: What do you expect? I'm a foreign devil.

[GALLIMARD *walks downstage.* SONG *exits.*]

GALLIMARD: [*To us.*] Did you hear the way she talked about Western women? Much differently than the first night. She does—she feels inferior to them—and to me.

SCENE 11

The French embassy. Beijing. 1960.
GALLIMARD *moves towards a desk.*

GALLIMARD: I determined to try an experiment. In *Madame Butterfly*, Cio-Cio-San fears that the Western man who catches a butterfly will pierce its heart with a needle, then leave it to perish. I began to wonder: had I, too, caught a butterfly who would writhe on a needle?

[MARC *enters, dressed as a bureaucrat, holding a stack of papers.* As GALLIMARD *speaks,* MARC *hands papers to him. He peruses, then signs, stamps or rejects them.*]

GALLIMARD: Over the next five weeks, I worked like a dynamo. I stopped going to the opera, I didn't phone or write her. I knew this little flower was waiting for me to call, and, as I wickedly refused to do so, I felt for the first time that rush of power—the absolute power of a man.

[MARC *continues acting as the bureaucrat, but he now speaks as himself.*]

MARC: Rene! It's me!

GALLIMARD: Marc—I hear your voice everywhere now. Even in the midst of work.

MARC: That's because I'm watching you—all the time.

GALLIMARD: You were always the most popular guy in school.

MARC: Well, there's no guarantee of failure in life like happiness in high school. Somehow I knew I'd end up in the suburbs working for Renault and you'd be in the Orient picking exotic women off the trees. And they say there's no justice.

GALLIMARD: That's why you were my friend?

MARC: I gave you a little of my life, so that now you can give me some of yours [*Pause.*] Remember Isabelle?

GALLIMARD: Of course I remember! She was my first experience.

MARC: We all wanted to ball her. But she only wanted me.

GALLIMARD: I had her.

MARC: Right. You balled her.

GALLIMARD: You were the only one who ever believed me.

MARC: Well, there's a good reason for that. [*Beat.*] C'mon. You must've guessed.

GALLIMARD: You told me to wait in the bushes by the cafeteria that night. The next thing I knew, she was on me. Dress up in the air.

MARC: She never wore underwear.

GALLIMARD: My arms were pinned to the dirt.

MARC: She loved the superior position. A girl ahead of her time.

GALLIMARD: I looked up, and there was this woman . . . bouncing up and down on my loins.

MARC: Screaming, right?

GALLIMARD: Screaming, and breaking off the branches all around me, and pounding my butt up and down into the dirt.

MARC: Huffing and puffing like a locomotive.

GALLIMARD; And in the middle of all this, the leaves were getting into my mouth, my legs were losing circulation, I thought, "God. So this is *it*?"

MARC: You thought that?

GALLIMARD: Well, I was worried about my legs falling off.

MARC: You didn't have a good time?

GALLIMARD: No, that's not what I—I had a great time!
MARC: You're sure?
GALLIMARD: Yeah. Really.
MARC: 'Cuz I wanted you to have a good time.
GALLIMARD: I did.

[*Pause.*]

MARC: Shit. [*Pause.*] When all is said and done, she was kind of a lousy lay, wasn't she? I mean, there was a lot of energy there, but you never knew what she was doing with it. Like when she yelled "I'm coming!"—hell, it was so loud, you wanted to go "Look, it's not that big a deal."
GALLIMARD: I got scared. I thought she meant someone was actually coming. [*Pause.*] But, Marc?
MARC: What?
GALLIMARD: Thanks.
MARC: Oh, don't mention it.
GALLIMARD: It was my first experience.
MARC: Yeah. You got her.
GALLIMARD: I got her.
MARC: Wait! Look at that letter again!

[GALLIMARD *picks up one of the papers he's been stamping, and rereads it.*]

GALLIMARD: [*To us.*] After six weeks, they began to arrive. The letters.

[*Upstage special on* SONG, *as Madame Butterfly. The scene is underscored by the* "*Love Duet.*"]

SONG: Did we fight? I do not know. Is the opera no longer of interest to you? Please come—my audiences miss the white devil in their midst.

[GALLIMARD *looks up from the letter, towards us.*]

GALLIMARD: [*To us.*] A concession, but much too dignified. [*Beat; he discards the letter.*] I skipped the opera again that week to complete a position paper on trade.

[*The bureaucrat hands him another letter.*]

SONG: Six weeks have passed since last we met. Is this your practice—to leave friends in the lurch? Sometimes I hate you, sometimes I hate myself, but always I miss you.
GALLIMARD: [*To us.*] Better, but I don't like the way she calls me "friend." When a woman calls a man her "friend," she's calling him a eunuch or a homosexual. [*Beat; he discards the letter.*] I was absent from the opera for the seventh week, feeling a sudden urge to clean out my files.

[*Bureaucrat hands him another letter.*]

SONG: Your rudeness is beyond belief. I don't deserve this cruelty. Don't bother to call. I'll have you turned away at the door.

GALLIMARD: [*To us.*] I didn't. [*He discards the letter; bureaucrat hands him another.*] And then finally, the letter that concluded my experiment.

SONG: I am out of words. I can hide behind dignity no longer. What do you want? I have already given you my shame.

[GALLIMARD *gives the letter back to* MARC, *slowly. Special on* SONG *fades out.*]

GALLIMARD: [*To us.*] Reading it, I became suddenly ashamed. Yes, my experiment had been a success. She was turning on my needle. But the victory seemed hollow.

MARC: Hollow?! Are you crazy?

GALLIMARD: Nothing, Marc. Please go away.

MARC: [*Exiting, with papers.*] Haven't I taught you anything?

GALLIMARD: "I have already given you my shame." I had to attend a reception that evening. On the way, I felt sick. If there is a God, surely he would punish me now. I had finally gained power over a beautiful woman, only to abuse it cruelly. There must be justice in the world. I had the strange feeling that the ax would fall this very evening.

SCENE 12

AMBASSADOR TOULON'S *residence. Beijing. 1960.*

Sound cue: party noises. Light change. We are now in a spacious residence. TOULON, *the French ambassador, enters and taps* GALLIMARD *on the shoulder.*

TOULON: Gallimard? Can I have a word? Over here.

GALLIMARD: [*To us.*] Manuel Toulon. French ambassador to China. He likes to think of us all as his children. Rather like God.

TOULON: Look, Gallimard, there's not much to say. I've liked you. From the day you walked in. You were no leader, but you were tidy and efficient.

GALLIMARD: Thank you, sir.

TOULON: Don't jump the gun. Okay, our needs in China are changing. It's embarrassing that we lost Indochina. Someone just wasn't on the ball there. I don't mean you personally, of course.

GALLIMARD: Thank you, sir.

TOULON: We're going to be doing a lot more information-gathering in the future. The nature of our work here is changing. Some people are just going to have to go. It's nothing personal.

GALLIMARD: Oh.

TOULON: Want to know a secret? Vice-Consul LeBon is being transferred.

GALLIMARD: [*To us.*] My immediate superior!

TOULON: And most of his department.

GALLIMARD: [*To us.*] Just as I feared! God has seen my evil heart—

TOULON: But not you.

GALLIMARD: [*To us.*]—and he's taking her away just as . . . [*To* TOULON.] Excuse me, sir?

TOULON: Scare you? I think I did. Cheer up, Gallimard. I want you to replace LeBon as vice-consul.

GALLIMARD: You—? Yes, well, thank you, sir.

TOULON: Anytime.

GALLIMARD: I . . . accept with great humility.

TOULON: Humility won't be part of the job. You're going to coordinate the revamped intelligence division. Want to know a secret? A year ago, you would've been out. But the past few months, I don't know how it happened, you've become this new aggressive confident . . . thing. And they also tell me you get along with the Chinese. So I think you're a lucky man, Gallimard. Congratulations.

[*They shake hands.* TOULON *exits.* Party noises out. GALLIMARD stumbles across a darkened stage.]

GALLIMARD: Vice-consul? Impossible! As I stumbled out of the party, I saw it written across the sky: There is no God. Or, no—say that there is a God. But that God . . . understands. Of course! God who creates Eve to serve Adam, who blesses Solomon with his harem but ties Jezebel to a burning bed[7]—that God is a man. And he understands! At age thirty-nine, I was suddenly initiated into the way of the world.

SCENE 13

SONG LILING'*s apartment. Beijing. 1960.*
SONG *enters, in a sheer dressing gown.*

SONG: Are you crazy?

GALLIMARD: Mademoiselle Song—

SONG: To come here—at this hour? After . . . after eight weeks?

GALLIMARD: It's the most amazing—

SONG: You bang on my door? Scare my servants, scandalize the neighbors?

GALLIMARD: I've been promoted. To vice-consul.

[*Pause.*]

SONG: And what is that supposed to mean to me?

GALLIMARD: Are you my Butterfly?

SONG: What are you saying?

GALLIMARD: I've come tonight for an answer: are you my Butterfly?

SONG: Don't you know already?

GALLIMARD: I want you to say it.

SONG: I don't want to say it.

GALLIMARD: So, that is your answer?

SONG: You know how I feel about—

7. For the last, see Revelation 2:22.

GALLIMARD: I do remember one thing.

SONG: What?

GALLIMARD: In the letter I received today.

SONG: Don't.

GALLIMARD: "I have already given you my shame."

SONG: It's enough that I even wrote it.

GALLIMARD: Well, then—

SONG: I shouldn't have it splashed across my face.

GALLIMARD:—if that's all true—

SONG: Stop!

GALLIMARD: Then what is one more short answer?

SONG: I don't want to!

GALLIMARD: Are you my Butterfly? [*Silence; he crosses the room and begins to touch her hair.*] I want from you honesty. There should be nothing false between us. No false pride.

[*Pause.*]

SONG: Yes, I am. I am your Butterfly.

GALLIMARD: Then let me be honest with you. It is because of you that I was promoted tonight. You have changed my life forever. My little Butterfly, there should be no more secrets: I love you.

[*He starts to kiss her roughly. She resists slightly.*]

SONG: No . . . no . . . gently . . . please, I've never . . .

GALLIMARD: No?

SONG: I've tried to appear experienced, but . . . the truth is . . . no.

GALLIMARD: Are you cold?

SONG: Yes. Cold.

GALLIMARD: Then we will go very, very slowly. [*He starts to caress her; her gown begins to open.*]

SONG: No . . . let me . . . keep my clothes . . .

GALLIMARD: But . . .

SONG: Please . . . it all frightens me. I'm a modest Chinese girl.

GALLIMARD: My poor little treasure.

SONG: I am your treasure. Though inexperienced, I am not . . . ignorant. They teach us things, our mothers, about pleasing a man.

GALLIMARD: Yes?

SONG: I'll do my best to make you happy. Turn off the lights.

[GALLIMARD *gets up and heads for a lamp.* SONG, *propped up on one elbow, tosses her hair back and smiles.*]

Monsieur Gallimard?

GALLIMARD: Yes, Butterfly?

SONG: "Vieni, vieni!"

GALLIMARD: "Come, darling."

SONG: "Ah! Dolce notte!"

GALLIMARD: "Beautiful night."
SONG: "Tutto estatico d'amor ride il ciel!"
GALLIMARD: "All ecstatic with love, the heavens are filled with laughter."

[*He turns off the lamp. Blackout.*]

ACT II

SCENE 1

M. GALLIMARD'*s cell. Paris. Present.*
Lights up on GALLIMARD. *He sits in his cell, reading from a leaflet.*

GALLIMARD: This, from a contemporary critic's commentary on *Madame Butterfly*: "Pinkerton suffers from . . . being an obnoxious bounder whom every man in the audience itches to kick." Bully for us men in the audience! Then, in the same note: "Butterfly is the most irresistibly appealing of Puccini's 'Little Women.' Watching the succession of her humiliations is like watching a child under torture." [*He tosses the pamphlet over his shoulder.*] I suggest that, while we men may all want to kick Pinkerton, very few of us would pass up the opportunity to *be* Pinkerton.

[GALLIMARD *moves out of his cell.*]

SCENE 2

GALLIMARD *and* BUTTERFLY'*s flat. Beijing. 1960.*
We are in a simple but well-decorated parlor. GALLIMARD *moves to sit on a sofa, while* SONG, *dressed in a chong sam, enters and curls up at his feet.*

GALLIMARD: [*To us.*] We secured a flat on the outskirts of Peking. Butterfly, as I was calling her now, decorated our "home" with Western furniture and Chinese antiques. And there, on a few stolen afternoons or evenings each week, Butterfly commenced her education.
SONG: The Chinese men—they keep us down.
GALLIMARD: Even in the "New Society"?
SONG: In the "New Society," we are all kept ignorant equally. That's one of the exciting things about loving a Western man. I know you are not threatened by a woman's education.
GALLIMARD: I'm no saint, Butterfly.
SONG: But you come from a progressive society.
GALLIMARD: We're not always reminding each other how "old" we are, if that's what you mean.
SONG: Exactly. We Chinese—once, I suppose, it is true, we ruled the world. But so what? How much more exciting to be part of the society ruling the world today. Tell me—what's happening in Vietnam?

GALLIMARD: Oh, Butterfly—you want me to bring my work home?

SONG: I want to know what you know. To be impressed by my man. It's not the particulars so much as the fact that you're making decisions which change the shape of the world.

GALLIMARD: Not the world. At best, a small corner.

[TOULON *enters, and sits at a desk upstage.*]

SCENE 3

French embassy. Beijing. 1961.

GALLIMARD *moves downstage, to* TOULON*'s desk.* SONG *remains upstage, watching.*

TOULON: And a more troublesome corner is hard to imagine.

GALLIMARD: So, the Americans plan to begin bombing?

TOULON: This is very secret, Gallimard: yes. The Americans don't have an embassy here. They're asking us to be their eyes and ears. Say Jack Kennedy signed an order to bomb North Vietnam, Laos. How would the Chinese react?

GALLIMARD: I think the Chinese will squawk—

TOULON: Uh-huh.

GALLIMARD:—but, in their hearts, they don't even like Ho Chi Minh.[8]

[*Pause.*]

TOULON: What a bunch of jerks. Vietnam was *our* colony. Not only didn't the Americans help us fight to keep them, but now, seven years later, they've come back to grab the territory for themselves. It's very irritating.

GALLIMARD: With all due respect, sir, why should the Americans have won our war for us back in '54 if we didn't have the will to win it ourselves?

TOULON: You're kidding, aren't you?

[*Pause.*]

GALLIMARD: The Orientals simply want to be associated with whoever shows the most strength and power. You live with the Chinese, sir. Do you think they like Communism?

TOULON: I live in China. Not with the Chinese.

GALLIMARD: Well, I—

TOULON: *You* live with the Chinese.

GALLIMARD: Excuse me?

TOULON: I can't keep a secret.

GALLIMARD: What are you saying?

TOULON: Only that I'm not immune to gossip. So, you're keeping a native mistress. Don't answer. It's none of my business. [*Pause.*] I'm sure she must be gorgeous.

GALLIMARD: Well . . .

TOULON: I'm impressed. You have the stamina to go out into the streets and hunt

8. (1890–1969), Communist leader of the North Vietnamese.

one down. Some of us have to be content with the wives of the expatriate community.

GALLIMARD: I do feel . . . fortunate.

TOULON: So, Gallimard, you've got the inside knowledge—what *do* the Chinese think?

GALLIMARD: Deep down, they miss the old days. You know, cappuccinos, men in tuxedos—

TOULON: So what do we tell the Americans about Vietnam?

GALLIMARD: Tell them there's a natural affinity between the West and the Orient.

TOULON; And that you speak from experience?

GALLIMARD: The Orientals are people too. They want the good things we can give them. If the Americans demonstrate the will to win, the Vietnamese will welcome them into a mutually beneficial union.

TOULON: I don't see how the Vietnamese can stand up to American firepower.

GALLIMARD: Orientals will always submit to a greater force.

TOULON: I'll note your opinions in my report. The Americans always love to hear how "welcome" they'll be. [*He starts to exit.*]

GALLIMARD: Sir?

TOULON: Mmmm?

GALLIMARD: This . . . rumor you've heard.

TOULON: Uh-huh?

GALLIMARD: How . . . widespread do you think it is?

TOULON: It's only widespread within this embassy. Where nobody talks because everybody is guilty. We were worried about you, Gallimard. We thought you were the only one here without a secret. Now you go and find a lotus blossom . . . and top us all. [*He exits.*]

GALLIMARD: [*To us.*] Toulon knows! And he approves! I was learning the benefits of being a man. We form our own clubs, sit behind thick doors, smoke—and celebrate the fact that we're still boys. [*He starts to move downstage, towards* SONG.] So, over the—

[*Suddenly* COMRADE CHIN *enters.* GALLIMARD *backs away.*]

GALLIMARD: [*To* SONG.] No! Why does she have to come in?

SONG: Rene, be sensible. How can they understand the story without her? Now, don't embarrass yourself.

[GALLIMARD *moves down center.*]

GALLIMARD: [*To us.*] Now, you will see why my story is so amusing to so many people. Why they snicker at parties in disbelief. Please—try to understand it from my point of view. We are all prisoners of our time and place. [*He exits.*]

SCENE 4

GALLIMARD *and* BUTTERFLY'S *flat. Beijing. 1961.*

SONG: [*To us.*] 1961. The flat Monsieur Gallimard rented for us. An evening after he has gone.

CHIN: Okay, see if you can find out when the Americans plan to start bombing Vietnam. If you can find out what cities, even better.
SONG: I'll do my best, but I don't want to arouse his suspicions.
CHIN: Yeah, sure, of course. So, what else?
SONG: The Americans will increase troops in Vietnam to 170,000 soldiers with 120,000 militia and 11,000 American advisors.
CHIN: [*Writing.*] Wait, wait. 120,000 militia and—
SONG: —11,000 American—
CHIN: —American advisors. [*Beat.*] How do you remember so much?
SONG: I'm an actor.
CHIN: Yeah. [*Beat.*] Is that how come you dress like that?
SONG: Like what, Miss Chin?
CHIN: Like that dress! You're wearing a dress. And every time I come here, you're wearing a dress. Is that because you're an actor? Or what?
SONG: It's a . . . disguise, Miss Chin.
CHIN: Actors, I think they're all weirdos. My mother tells me actors are like gamblers or prostitutes or—
SONG: It helps me in my assignment.

[*Pause.*]

CHIN: You're not gathering information in any way that violates Communist Party principles, are you?
SONG: Why would I do that?
CHIN: Just checking. Remember: when working for the Great Proletarian State, you represent our Chairman Mao in every position you take.
SONG: I'll try to imagine the Chairman taking my positions.
CHIN: We all think of him this way. Good-bye, comrade. [*She starts to exit.*] Comrade?
SONG: Yes?
CHIN: Don't forget: there is no homosexuality in China!
SONG: Yes, I've heard.
CHIN: Just checking. [*She exits.*]
SONG: [*To us.*] What passes for a woman in modern China.

[GALLIMARD *sticks his head out from the wings.*]

GALLIMARD: Is she gone?
SONG: Yes, Rene. Please continue in your own fashion.

SCENE 5

Beijing. 1961–63.

GALLIMARD *moves to the couch where* SONG *still sits. He lies down in her lap, and she strokes his forehead.*

GALLIMARD: [*To us.*] And so, over the years 1961, '62, '63, we settled into our routine, Butterfly and I. She would always have prepared a light snack and then, ever so delicately, and only if I agreed, she would start to pleasure me. With her hands, her mouth . . . too many ways to explain, and too sad, given my present situation. But mostly we would talk. About my life. Perhaps there is nothing more rare than to find a woman who passionately listens.

[SONG *remains upstage, listening, as* HELGA *enters and plays a scene downstage with* GALLIMARD.]

HELGA: Rene, I visited Dr. Bolleart this morning.

GALLIMARD: Why? Are you ill?

HELGA: No, no. You see, I wanted to ask him . . . that question we've been discussing.

GALLIMARD: And I told you, it's only a matter of time. Why did you bring a doctor into this? We just have to keep trying—like a crapshoot, actually.

HELGA: I went, I'm sorry. But listen: he says there's nothing wrong with me.

GALLIMARD: You see? Now, will you stop—?

HELGA: Rene, he says he'd like you to go in and take some tests.

GALLIMARD: Why? So he can find there's nothing wrong with both of us?

HELGA: Rene, I don't ask for much. One trip! One visit! And then, whatever you want to do about it—you decide.

GALLIMARD: You're assuming he'll find something defective!

HELGA: No! Of course not! Whatever he finds—if he finds nothing, we decide what to do about nothing! But go!

GALLIMARD: If he finds nothing, we keep trying. Just like we do now.

HELGA: But at least we'll know! [*Pause.*] I'm sorry. [*She starts to exit.*]

GALLIMARD: Do you really want me to see Dr. Bolleart?

HELGA: Only if you want a child, Rene. We have to face the fact that time is running out. Only if you want a child. [*She exits.*]

GALLIMARD: [*To* SONG.] I'm a modern man, Butterfly. And yet, I don't want to go. It's the same old voodoo. I feel like God himself is laughing at me if I can't produce a child.

SONG: You men of the West—you're obsessed by your odd desire for equality. Your wife can't give you a child, and *you're* going to the doctor?

GALLIMARD: Well, you see, she's already gone.

SONG: And because this incompetent can't find the defect, you now have to subject yourself to him? It's unnatural.

GALLIMARD: Well, what is the "natural" solution?

SONG: In Imperial China, when a man found that one wife was inadequate, he turned to another—to give him his son.

GALLIMARD: What do you—? I can't . . . marry you, yet.

SONG: Please. I'm not asking you to be my husband. But I am already your wife.

GALLIMARD: Do you want to . . . have my child?

SONG: I thought you'd never ask.

GALLIMARD: But, your career . . . your—

SONG: Phooey on my career! That's your Western mind, twisting itself into strange shapes again. Of course I love my career. But what would I love most of all? To feel something inside me—day and night—something I know is yours.

[*Pause.*] Promise me . . . you won't go to this doctor. Who is this Western quack to set himself as judge over the man I love? I know who is a man, and who is not. [*She exits.*]

GALLIMARD: [*To us.*] Dr. Bolleart? Of course I didn't go. What man would?

Scene 6

Beijing. 1963

Party noises over the house speakers. RENEE *enters, wearing a revealing gown.*

GALLIMARD: 1963. A party at the Austrian embassy. None of us could remember the Austrian ambassador's name, which seemed somehow appropriate. [*To* RENEE.] So, I tell the Americans, Diem[9] must go. The U.S. wants to be respected by the Vietnamese, and yet they're propping up this nobody seminarian as her president. A man whose claim to fame is his sister-in-law imposing fanatic "moral order" campaigns? Oriental women—when they're good, they're very good, but when they're bad, they're Christians.

RENEE: Yeah.

GALLIMARD: And what do you do?

RENEE: I'm a student. My father exports a lot of useless stuff to the Third World.

GALLIMARD: How useless?

RENEE: You know. Squirt guns, confectioner's sugar, hula hoops . . .

GALLIMARD: I'm sure they appreciate the sugar.

RENEE: I'm here for two years to study Chinese.

GALLIMARD: Two years?

RENEE: That's what everybody says.

GALLIMARD: When did you arrive?

RENEE: Three weeks ago.

GALLIMARD: And?

RENEE: I like it. It's primitive, but . . . well, this is the place to learn Chinese, so here I am.

GALLIMARD: Why Chinese?

RENEE: I think it'll be important someday.

GALLIMARD: You do?

RENEE: Don't ask me when, but . . . that's what I think.

GALLIMARD: Well, I agree with you. One hundred percent. That's very far-sighted.

RENEE: Yeah. Well of course, my father thinks I'm a complete weirdo.

GALLIMARD: He'll thank you someday.

RENEE: Like when the Chinese start buying hula hoops?

GALLIMARD: There're a billion bellies out there.

RENEE: And if they end up taking over the world—well, then I'll be lucky to know Chinese too, right?

[*Pause.*]

9. Ngo Dinh Diem (1901–1963), prime minister of South Vietnam.

GALLIMARD: At this point, I don't see how the Chinese can possible take—
RENEE: You know what I *don't* like about China?
GALLIMARD: Excuse me? No—what?
RENEE: Nothing to do at night.
GALLIMARD: You come to parties at embassies like everyone else.
RENEE: Yeah, but they get out at ten. And then what?
GALLIMARD: I'm afraid the Chinese idea of a dance hall is a dirt floor and a man with a flute.
RENEE: Are you married?
GALLIMARD: Yes. Why?
RENEE: You wanna . . . fool around?

[*Pause.*]

GALLIMARD: Sure.
RENEE: I'll wait for you outside. What's your name?
GALLIMARD: Gallimard. Rene.
RENEE: Weird. I'm Renee too. [*She exits.*]
GALLIMARD: [*To us.*] And so, I embarked on my first extra-extramarital affair. Renee was picture perfect. With a body like those girls in the magazines. If I put a tissue paper over my eyes, I wouldn't have been able to tell the difference. And it was exciting to be with someone who wasn't afraid to be seen completely naked. But is it possible for a woman to be *too* uninhibited, *too* willing, so as to seem almost too . . . masculine?

[*Chuck Berry*[1] *blares from the house speakers, then comes down in volume as* RENEE *enters, toweling her hair.*]

RENEE: You have a nice weenie.
GALLIMARD: What?
RENEE: Penis. You have a nice penis.
GALLIMARD: Oh. Well, thank you. That's very . . .
RENEE: What—can't take a compliment?
GALLIMARD: No, it's very . . . reassuring.
RENEE: But most girls don't come out and say it, huh?
GALLIMARD: And also . . . what did you call it?
RENEE: Oh. Most girls don't call it a "weenie," huh?
GALLIMARD: It sounds very—
RENEE: Small, I know.
GALLIMARD: I was going to say, "young."
RENEE: Yeah. Young, small, same thing. Most guys are pretty, uh, sensitive about that. Like, you know, I had a boyfriend back home in Denmark. I got mad at him once and called him a little weeniehead. He got so mad! He said at least I should call him a great big weeniehead.
GALLIMARD: I suppose I just say "penis."
RENEE: Yeah. That's pretty clinical. There's "cock," but that sounds like a chicken.

1. (b. 1900), early rock-and-roll singer.

And "prick" is painful, and "dick" is like you're talking about someone who's not in the room.

GALLIMARD: Yes. It's a . . . bigger problem than I imagined.

RENEE: I—I think maybe it's because I really don't know what to do with them—that's why I call then "weenies."

GALLIMARD: Well, you did quite well with . . . mine.

RENEE: Thanks, but I mean, really *do* with them. Like, okay, have you ever looked at one? I mean, really?

GALLIMARD: No, I suppose when it's part of you, you sort of take it for granted.

RENEE: I guess. But, like, it just hangs there. This little . . . flap of flesh. And there's so much fuss that we make about it. Like, I think the reason we fight wars is because we wear clothes. Because no one knows—between the men, I mean—who has the bigger . . . weenie. So, if I'm a guy with a small one, I'm going to build a really big building or take over a really big piece of land or write a really long book so the other men don't know, right? But, see, it never really works, that's the problem. I mean, you conquer the country, or whatever, but you're still wearing clothes, so there's no way to prove absolutely whose is bigger or smaller. And that's what we call a civilized society. The whole world run by a bunch of men with pricks the size of pins. [*She exits.*]

GALLIMARD: [*To us.*] This was simply not acceptable. [*A high-pitched chime rings through the air.* SONG, *dressed as* BUTTERFLY, *appears in the upstage special. She is obviously distressed. Her body swoons as she attempts to clip the stems of flowers she's arranging in a vase.*] But I kept up our affair, wildly, for several months. Why? I believe because of Butterfly. She knew the secret I was trying to hide. But, unlike a Western woman, she didn't confront me, threaten, even pout. I remembered the words of Puccini's *Butterfly:*

SONG: "Noi siamo gente avvezza/ alle piccole cose/ umili e silenziose."

GALLIMARD: I come from a people/ Who are accustomed to little/ Humble and silent." I saw Pinkerton and Butterfly, and what she would say if he were unfaithful . . . nothing. She would cry, alone, into those wildly soft sleeves, once full of possessions, now empty to collect her tears. It was her tears and her silence that excited me, every time I visited Renee.

TOULON: [*Offstage.*] Gallimard! [TOULON *enters.* GALLIMARD *turns towards him. During the next section,* SONG, *up center, begins to dance with the flowers. It is a drunken dance, where she breaks small pieces off the stems.*] They're killing him.

GALLIMARD: Who? I'm sorry? What?

TOULON: Bother you to come over at this late hour?

GALLIMARD: No . . . of course not.

TOULON: Not after you hear my secret. Champagne?

GALLIMARD: Um . . . thank you.

TOULON: You're surprised. There's something that you've wanted, Gallimard. No, not a promotion. Next time. Something in the world. You're not aware of this, but there's an informal gossip circle among intelligence agents. And some of ours heard from some of the Americans—

GALLIMARD: Yes?

TOULON: That the U.S. will allow the Vietnamese generals to stage a coup . . . and assassinate President Diem.

[*The chime rings again.* TOULON *freezes.* GALLIMARD *turns upstage and looks at* BUTTERFLY, *who slowly and deliberately clips a flower off its stem.* GALLIMARD *turns back towards* TOULON.]

GALLIMARD: I think . . . that's a very wise move!

[TOULON *unfreezes.*]

TOULON: It's what you've been advocating. A toast?

GALLIMARD: Sure. I consider this a vindication.

TOULON: Not exactly. "To the test. Let's hope you pass."

[*They drink. The chime rings again.* TOULON *freezes.* GALLIMARD *turns upstage, and* SONG *clips another flower.*]

GALLIMARD: [*To* TOULON.] The test?

TOULON: [*Unfreezing.*] It's a test of everything you've been saying. I personally think the generals probably will stop the Communists. And you'll be a hero. But if anything goes wrong, then your opinions won't be worth a pig's ear. I'm sure that won't happen. But sometimes it's easier when they don't listen to you.

GALLIMARD: They're your opinions too, aren't they?

TOULON: Personally, yes.

GALLIMARD: So we agree.

TOULON: But my opinions aren't on that report. Yours are. Cheers.

[TOULON *turns away from* GALLIMARD *and raises his glass. At that instant* SONG *picks up the vase and hurls it to the ground. It shatters.* SONG *sinks down amidst the shards of the vase, in a calm, childlike trance. She sings softly, as if reciting a child's nursery rhyme.*]

SONG: [*Repeat as necessary.*] "The whole world over, the white man travels, setting anchor, wherever he likes. Life's not worth living, unless he finds, the finest maidens, of every land . . ."[2]

[GALLIMARD *turns downstage towards us.* SONG *continues singing.*]

GALLIMARD: I shook as I left his house. That coward! That worm! To put the burden for his decisions on my shoulders!

I started for Renee's. But no, that was all I needed. A schoolgirl who would question the role of the penis in modern society. What I wanted was revenge. A vessel to contain my humiliation. Though I hadn't seen her in several weeks, I headed for Butterfly's.

[GALLIMARD *enters* SONG*'s apartment.*]

2. From "The Whole World Over," sung by Pinkerton and Sharpless.

SONG: Oh! Rene . . . I was dreaming!

GALLIMARD: You've been drinking?

SONG: If I can't sleep, then yes, I drink. But then, it gives me these dreams which—Rene, it's been almost three weeks since you visited me last.

GALLIMARD: I know. There's been a lot going on in the world.

SONG: Fortunately I am drunk. So I can speak freely. It's not the world, it's you and me. And an old problem. Even the softest skin becomes like leather to a man who's touched it too often. I confess I don't know how to stop it. I don't know how to become another woman.

GALLIMARD: I have a request.

SONG: Is this a solution? Or are you ready to give up the flat?

GALLIMARD: It may be a solution. But I'm sure you won't like it.

SONG: Oh well, that's very important. "Like it?" Do you think I "like" lying here alone, waiting, always waiting for your return? Please—don't worry about what I may not "like."

GALLIMARD: I want to see you . . . naked.

[*Silence.*]

SONG: I thought you understood my modesty. So you want me to—what—strip? Like a big cowboy girl? Shiny pasties on my breasts? Shall I fling my kimono over my head and yell "ya-hoo" in the process? I thought you respected my shame!

GALLIMARD: I believe you gave me your shame many years ago.

SONG: Yes—and it is just like a white devil to use it against me. I can't believe it. I thought myself so repulsed by the passive Oriental and the cruel white man. Now I see—we are always most revolted by the things hidden within us.

GALLIMARD: I just mean—

SONG: Yes?

GALLIMARD: —that it will remove the only barrier left between us.

SONG: No, Rene. Don't couch your request in sweet words. Be yourself—a cad—and know that my love is enough, that I submit—submit to the worst you can give me. [*Pause.*] Well, come. Strip me. Whatever happens, know that you have willed it. Our love, in your hands. I'm helpless before my man.

[GALLIMARD *starts to cross the room.*]

GALLIMARD: Did I not undress her because I knew, somewhere deep down, what I would find? Perhaps. Happiness is so rare that our mind can turn somersaults to protect it.

At the time, I only knew that I was seeing Pinkerton stalking towards his Butterfly, ready to reward her love with his lecherous hands. The image sickened me, pulled me to my knees, so I was crawling towards her like a worm. By the time I reached her, Pinkerton . . . had vanished from my heart. To be replaced by something new, something unnatural, that flew in the face of all I'd learned in the world—something very close to love. [*He grabs her around the waist; she strokes his hair.*] Butterfly, forgive me.

SONG: Rene . . .

GALLIMARD: For everything. From the start.
SONG: I'm . . .
GALLIMARD: I want to—
SONG: I'm pregnant. [*Beat.*] I'm pregnant. [*Beat.*] I'm pregnant. [*Beat.*]
GALLIMARD: I want to marry you!

SCENE 7

GALLIMARD *and* BUTTERFLY'*s flat. Beijing. 1963.*

Downstage, SONG *paces as* COMRADE CHIN *reads from her notepad. Upstage,* GALLIMARD *is still kneeling. He remains on his knees throughout the scene, watching it.*

SONG: I need a baby.
CHIN: [*From pad.*] He's been spotted going to a dorm.
SONG: I need a baby.
CHIN: At the Foreign Language Institute.
SONG: I need a baby.
CHIN: The room of a Danish girl . . . What do you mean, you need a baby?!
SONG: Tell Comrade Kang—last night, the entire mission, it could've ended.
CHIN: What do you mean?
SONG: Tell Kang—he told me to strip.
CHIN: *Strip?!*
SONG: Write!
CHIN: I tell you, I don't understand nothing about this case anymore. Nothing.
SONG: He told me to strip, and I took a chance. Oh, we Chinese, we know how to gamble.
CHIN: [*Writing.*] ". . . told him to strip."
SONG: My palms were wet, I had to make a split-second decision.
CHIN: Hey! Can you slow down?!

[*Pause.*]

SONG: You write faster, I'm the artist here. Suddenly, it hit me—"All he wants is for her to submit. Once a woman submits, a man is always ready to become 'generous.' "
CHIN: You're just gonna end up with rough notes.
SONG: And it worked! He gave in! Now, if I can just present him with a baby. A Chinese baby with blond hair—he'll be mine for life!
CHIN: Kang will never agree! The trading of babies has to be a counterrevolutionary act!
SONG: Sometimes, a counterrevolutionary act is necessary to counter a counterrevolutionary act.

[*Pause.*]

CHIN: Wait.
SONG: I need one . . . in seven months. Make sure it's a boy.

CHIN: This doesn't sound like something the Chairman would do. Maybe you'd better talk to Comrade Kang yourself.

SONG: Good. I will. [CHIN *gets up to leave.*] Miss Chin? Why, in the Peking Opera, are women's roles played by men?

CHIN: I don't know. Maybe, a reactionary remnant of male—

SONG: No. [*Beat.*] Because only a man knows how a woman is supposed to act.

[CHIN *exits.* SONG *turns upstage, towards* GALLIMARD.]

GALLIMARD: [*Calling after* CHIN.] Good riddance! [*To* SONG.] I could forget all that betrayal in an instant, you know. If you'd just come back and become Butterfly again.

SONG: Fat chance. You're here in prison, rotting in a cell. And I'm on a plane, winging my way back to China. Your President pardoned me of our treason, you know.

GALLIMARD: Yes, I read about that.

SONG: Must make you feel . . . lower than shit.

GALLIMARD: But don't you, even a little bit, wish you were here with me?

SONG: I'm an artist, Rene. You were my greatest . . . acting challenge. [*She laughs.*] It doesn't matter how rotten I answer, does it? You still adore me. That's why I love you, Rene. [*She points to us.*] So—you were telling your audience about the night I announced I was pregnant.

[GALLIMARD *puts his arms around* SONG*'s waist. He and* SONG *are in the positions they were in at the end of Scene 6.*]

Scene 8

Same.

GALLIMARD: I'll divorce my wife. We'll live together here, and then later in France.

SONG: I feel so . . . ashamed.

GALLIMARD: Why?

SONG: I had begun to lose faith. And now, you shame me with your generosity.

GALLIMARD: Generosity? No, I'm proposing for very selfish reasons.

SONG: Your apologies only make me feel more ashamed. My outburst a moment ago!

GALLIMARD: Your outburst? What about my request?!

SONG: You've been very patient dealing with my . . . eccentricities. A Western man, used to women freer with their bodies—

GALLIMARD: It was sick! Don't make excuses for me.

SONG: I have to. You don't seem willing to make them for yourself.

[*Pause.*]

GALLIMARD: You're crazy.

SONG: I'm happy. Which often looks like crazy.

GALLIMARD: Then make me crazy. Marry me.

[*Pause.*]

SONG: No.

GALLIMARD: What?

SONG: Do I sound silly, a slave, if I say I'm not worthy?

GALLIMARD: Yes. In fact you do. No one has loved me like you.

SONG: Thank you. And no one ever will. I'll see to that.

GALLIMARD: So what is the problem?

SONG: Rene, we Chinese are realists. We understand rice, gold, and guns. You are a diplomat. Your career is skyrocketing. Now, what would happen if you divorced your wife to marry a Communist Chinese actress?

GALLIMARD: That's not being realistic. That's defeating yourself before you begin.

SONG: We must conserve our strength for the battles we can win.

GALLIMARD: That sounds like a fortune cookie!

SONG: Where do you think fortune cookies come from?

GALLIMARD: I don't care.

SONG: You do. So do I. And we should. That is why I say I'm not worthy. I'm worthy to love and even to be loved by you. But I am not worthy to end the career of one of the West's most promising diplomats.

GALLIMARD: It's not that great a career! I made it sound like more than it is!

SONG: Modesty will get you nowhere. Flatter yourself, and you flatter me. I'm flattered to decline your offer. [*She exits.*]

GALLIMARD: [*To us.*] Butterfly and I argued all night. And, in the end, I left, knowing I would never be her husband. She went away for several months—to the countryside, like a small animal. Until the night I received her call.

[*A baby's cry from offstage.* SONG *enters, carrying a child.*]

SONG: He looks like you.

GALLIMARD: Oh! [*Beat; he approaches the baby.*] Well, babies are never very attractive at birth.

SONG: Stop!

GALLIMARD: I'm sure he'll grow more beautiful with age. More like his mother.

SONG: "Chi vide mai/ a bimbo del Giappon . . ."

GALLIMARD: "What baby, I wonder, was ever born in Japan"—or China, for that matter—

SONG: ". . . occhi azzurrini?"

GALLIMARD: "With azure eyes"—they're actually sort of brown, wouldn't you say?

SONG: "E il labbro."

GALLIMARD: "And such lips!" [*He kisses* SONG.] And such lips.

SONG: "E i ricciolini d'oro schietto?"

GALLIMARD: "And such a head of golden"—if slightly patchy—"curls?"

SONG: I'm going to call him "Peepee."

GALLIMARD: Darling, could you repeat that because I'm sure a rickshaw just flew by overhead.

SONG: You heard me.

GALLIMARD: "Song Peepee"? May I suggest Michael, or Stephan, or Adolph?

SONG: You may, but I won't listen.

GALLIMARD: You can't be serious. Can you imagine the time this child will have in school?

SONG: In the West, yes.

GALLIMARD: It's worse than naming him Ping Pong or Long Dong or—

SONG: But he's never going to live in the West, is he?

[*Pause.*]

GALLIMARD: That wasn't my choice.

SONG: It is mine. And this is my promise to you: I will raise him, he will be our child, but he will never burden you outside of China.

GALLIMARD: Why do you make these promises? I want to be burdened! I want a scandal to cover the papers!

SONG: [*To us.*] Prophetic.

GALLIMARD: I'm serious.

SONG: So am I. His name is as I registered it. And he will never live in the West. [SONG *exits with the child.*]

GALLIMARD: [*To us.*] It is possible that her stubbornness only made me want her more. That drawing back at the moment of my capitulation was the most brilliant strategy she could have chosen. It is possible. But it is also possible that by this point she could have said, could have done . . . anything, and I would have adored her still.

Scene 9

Beijing. 1966.

A driving rhythm of Chinese percussion fills the stage.

GALLIMARD: And then, China began to change. Mao became very old, and his cult became very strong. And, like many old men, he entered his second childhood. So he handed over the reins of state to those with minds like his own. And children ruled the Middle Kingdom[3] with complete caprice. The doctrine of the Cultural Revolution implied continuous anarchy. Contact between Chinese and foreigners became impossible. Our flat was confiscated. Her fame and my money now counted against us. [*Two dancers in Mao suits and red-starred caps enter, and begin crudely mimicking revolutionary violence, in an agitprop fashion.*] And somehow the American war went wrong too. Four hundred thousand dollars were being spent for every Viet Cong[4] killed; so General Westmoreland's remark that the Oriental does not value life the way Americans do was oddly accurate. Why weren't the Vietnamese people giving in? Why were they content instead to die and die and die again?

3. Chung Kuo or Zhonghua, the Chinese name for China. 4. Communist insurgent in South Vietnam. William C. Westmoreland (b. 1914) commanded U.S. forces in Vietnam.

[TOULON *enters.*]

TOULON: Congratulations, Gallimard.

GALLIMARD: Excuse me, sir?

TOULON: Not a promotion. That was last time. You're going home.

GALLIMARD: What?

TOULON: Don't say I didn't warn you.

GALLIMARD: I'm being transferred . . . because I was wrong about the American war?

TOULON: Of course not. We don't care about the Americans. We care about your mind. The quality of your analysis. In general, everything you've predicted here in the Orient . . . just hasn't happened.

GALLIMARD: I think that's premature.

TOULON: Don't force me to be blunt. Okay, you said China was ready to open to Western trade. The only thing they're trading out there are Western heads. And, yes, you said the Americans would succeed in Indochina. You were kidding, right?

GALLIMARD: I think the end is in sight.

TOULON: Don't be pathetic. And don't take this personally. You were wrong. It's not your fault.

GALLIMARD: But I'm going home.

TOULON: Right. Could I have the number of your mistress? [*Beat.*] Joke! Joke! Eat a croissant for me.

[TOULON *exits.* SONG, *wearing a Mao suit, is dragged in from the wings as part of the upstage dance. They "beat" her, then lampoon the acrobatics of the Chinese opera, as she is made to kneel onstage.*]

GALLIMARD: [*Simultaneously.*] I don't care to recall how Butterfly and I said our hurried farewell. Perhaps it was better to end our affair before it killed her.

[GALLIMARD *exits.* COMRADE CHIN *walks across the stage with a banner reading: "The Actor Renounces His Decadent Profession!" She reaches the kneeling* SONG. *Percussion stops with a thud. Dancers strike poses.*]

CHIN: Actor-oppressor, for years you have lived above the common people and looked down on their labor. While the farmer ate millet—

SONG: I ate pastries from France and sweetmeats from silver trays.

CHIN: And how did you come to live in such an exalted position?

SONG: I was a plaything for the imperialists!

CHIN: What did you do?

SONG: I shamed China by allowing myself to be corrupted by a foreigner . . .

CHIN: What does this mean? The People demand a full confession!

SONG: I engaged in the lowest perversions with China's enemies!

CHIN: What perversions? Be more clear!

SONG: I let him put it up my ass!

[*Dancers look over, disgusted.*]

CHIN: Aaaa-ya! How can you use such sickening language?!
SONG: My language . . . is only as foul and the crimes I committed . . .
CHIN: Yeah. That's better. So—what do you want to do now?
SONG: I want to serve the people.

[*Percussion starts up, with Chinese strings.*]

CHIN: What?
SONG: I want to serve the people!

[*Dancers regain their revolutionary smiles, and begin a dance of victory.*]

CHIN: What?!
SONG: I want to serve the people!!

[*Dancers unveil a banner: "The Actor Is Rehabilitated!"* SONG *remains kneeling before* CHIN, *as the dancers bounce around them, then exit. Music out.*]

SCENE 10

A commune. Hunan Province. 1970.

CHIN: How you planning to do that?
SONG: I've already worked four years in the fields of Hunan, Comrade Chin.
CHIN: So? Farmers work all their lives. Let me see your hands. [SONG *holds them out for her inspection.*] Goddamn! Still so smooth! How long does it take to turn you actors into good anythings? Hunh. You've just spent too many years in luxury to be any good to the Revolution.
SONG: I served the Revolution.
CHIN: Serve the Revolution? Bullshit! You wore dresses! Don't tell me—I was there. I saw you! You and your white vice-consul! Stuck up there in your flat, living off the People's Treasury! Yeah, I knew what was going on! You two . . . homos! Homos! Homos! [*Pause; she composes herself.*] Ah! Well . . . you will serve the people, all right. But not with the Revolution's money. This time, you use your own money.
SONG: I have no money.
CHIN: Shut up! And you won't stink up China anymore with your pervert stuff. You'll pollute the place where pollution begins—the West.
SONG: What do you mean?
CHIN: Shut up! You're going to France. Without a cent in your pocket. You find your consul's house, you make him pay your expenses—
SONG: No.
CHIN: And you give us weekly reports! Useful information!
SONG: That's crazy. It's been four years.
CHIN: Either that, or back to rehabilitation center!
SONG: Comrade Chin, he's not going to support me! Not in France! He's a white man! I was just his plaything—
CHIN: Oh yuck! Again with the sickening language? Where's my stick?
SONG: You don't understand the mind of a man.

[*Pause.*]

CHIN: Oh no? No I don't? Then how come I'm married, huh? How come I got a man? Five, six years ago, you always tell me those kind of things, I felt very bad. But not now! Because what does the Chairman say? He tells us *I'm* now the smart one, you're now the nincompoop! *You're* the blockhead, the hare-brain, the nitwit! You think you're so smart? You understand "The Mind of a Man"? Good! Then *you* go to France and be a pervert for Chairman Mao!

[CHIN *and* SONG *exit in opposite directions.*]

SCENE 11

Paris. 1968–70.
GALLIMARD *enters.*

GALLIMARD: And what was waiting for me back in Paris? Well, better Chinese food than I'd eaten in China. Friends and relatives. A little accounting, regular schedule, keeping track of traffic violations in the suburbs . . . And the indignity of students shouting the slogans of Chairman Mao at me—in French.

HELGA: Rene? Rene? [*She enters, soaking wet.*] I've had a . . . a problem. [*She sneezes.*]

GALLIMARD: You're wet.

HELGA: Yes, I . . . coming back from the grocer's. A group of students, waving red flags, they—[GALLIMARD *fetches a towel.*]—they ran by, I was caught up along with them. Before I knew what was happening—[GALLIMARD *gives her the towel.*] Thank you. The police started firing water cannons at us. I tried to shout, to tell them I was the wife of a diplomat, but—you know how it is . . . [*Pause.*] Needless to say, I lost the groceries. Rene, what's happening to France?

GALLIMARD: What's—? Well, nothing, really.

HELGA: Nothing?! The storefronts are in flames, there's glass in the streets, buildings are toppling—and I'm wet!

GALLIMARD: Nothing! . . . that I care to think about.

HELGA: And is that why you stay in this room?

GALLIMARD: Yes, in fact.

HELGA: With the incense burning? You know something? I hate incense. It smells so sickly sweet.

GALLIMARD: Well, I hate the French. Who just smell—period!

HELGA: And the Chinese were better?

GALLIMARD: Please—don't start.

HELGA: When we left, this exact same thing, the riots—

GALLIMARD: No, no . . .

HELGA: Students screaming slogans, smashing down doors—

GALLIMARD: Helga—

HELGA: It was all going on in China, too. Don't you remember?!

GALLIMARD: Helga! Please! [*Pause.*] You have never understood China, have you? You walk in here with these ridiculous ideas, that the West is falling apart, that China was spitting in our faces. You come in, dripping of the streets, and you leave water all over my floor. [*He grabs* HELGA*'s towel, begins mopping up the floor.*]

HELGA: But it's the truth!

GALLIMARD: Helga, I want a divorce.

[*Pause;* GALLIMARD *continues mopping the floor.*]

HELGA: I take it back. China is . . . beautiful. Incense, I like incense.

GALLIMARD: I've had a mistress.

HELGA: So?

GALLIMARD: For eight years.

HELGA: I knew you would. I knew you would the day I married you. And now what? You want to marry her?

GALLIMARD: I can't. She's in China.

HELGA: I see. You want to leave. For someone who's not here, is that right?

GALLIMARD: That's right.

HELGA: You can't live with her, but still you don't want to live with me.

GALLIMARD: That's right.

[*Pause.*]

HELGA: Shit. How terrible that I can figure that out. [*Pause.*] I never thought I'd say it. But, in China, I was happy. I knew, in my own way, I knew that you were not everything you pretended to be. But the pretense—going on your arm to the embassy ball, visiting your office and the guards saying, "Good morning, good morning, Madame Gallimard"—the pretense . . . was very good indeed. [*Pause.*] I hope everyone is mean to you for the rest of your life. [*She exits.*]

GALLIMARD: [*To us.*] Prophetic. [MARC *enters with two drinks.*] [*To* MARC.] In China, I was different from all other men.

MARC: Sure. You were white. Here's your drink.

GALLIMARD: I felt . . . touched.

MARC: In the head? Rene, I don't want to hear about the Oriental love goddess. Okay? One night—can we just drink and throw up without a lot of conversation?

GALLIMARD: You still don't believe me, do you?

MARC: Sure I do. She was the most beautiful, et cetera, et cetera, blasé blasé.

[*Pause.*]

GALLIMARD: My life in the West has been such a disappointment.

MARC: Life in the West is like that. You'll get used to it. Look, you're driving me away. I'm leaving. Happy, now? [*He exits, then returns.*] Look, I have a date tomorrow night. You wanna come? I can fix you up with—

GALLIMARD: Of course. I would love to come.

[*Pause.*]

MARC: Uh—on second thought, no. You'd better get ahold of yourself first.

[*He exits;* GALLIMARD *nurses his drink.*]

GALLIMARD: [*To us.*] This is the ultimate cruelty, isn't it? That I can talk and talk and to anyone listening, it's only air—too rich a diet to be swallowed by a mundane world. Why can't anyone understand? That in China, I once loved, and was loved by, very simply, the Perfect Woman. [SONG *enters, dressed as* BUTTERFLY *in wedding dress. To* SONG.] Not again. My imagination is hell. Am I asleep this time? Or did I drink too much?

SONG: Rene?

GALLIMARD: God, it's too painful! That you speak?

SONG: What are you talking about? Rene—touch me.

GALLIMARD: Why?

SONG: I'm real. Take my hand.

GALLIMARD: Why? So you can disappear again and leave me clutching at the air? For the entertainment of my neighbors who—?

[SONG *touches* GALLIMARD.]

SONG: Rene?

[GALLIMARD *takes* SONG*'s hand. Silence.*]

GALLIMARD: Butterfly? I never doubted you'd return.

SONG: You hadn't . . . forgotten—?

GALLIMARD: Yes, actually, I've forgotten everything. My mind, you see—there wasn't enough room in this hard head—not for the world *and* for you. No, there was only room for one. [*Beat.*] Come, look. See? Your bed has been waiting, with the Klimt[5] poster you like, and—see? The xiang lu[6] you gave me?

SONG: I . . . I don't know what to say.

GALLIMARD: There's nothing to say. Not at the end of a long trip. Can I make you some tea?

SONG: But where's your wife?

GALLIMARD: She's by my side. She's by my side at last. [GALLIMARD *reaches to embrace* SONG. SONG *sidesteps, dodging him.*] Why?!

SONG: [*To us.*] So I did return to Rene in Paris. Where I found—

GALLIMARD: Why do you run away? Can't we show them how we embraced that evening?

SONG: Please. I'm talking.

GALLIMARD: You have to do what I say! I'm conjuring you up in *my* mind!

SONG: Rene, I've never done what you've said. Why should it be any different in your mind? Now split—the story moves on, and I must change.

5. Gustav Klimt (1862–1918), Austrian painter.   6. Incense burner. [Author's note]

GALLIMARD: I welcomed you into my home! I didn't have to, you know! I could've left you penniless on the streets of Paris! But I took you in!

SONG: Thank you.

GALLIMARD: So . . . please . . . don't change.

SONG: You know I have to. You know I will. And anyway, what difference does it make? No matter what your eyes tell you, you can't ignore the truth. You already know too much. [GALLIMARD *exits.* SONG *turns to us.*] The change I'm going to make requires about five minutes. So I thought you might want to take this opportunity to stretch your legs, enjoy a drink, or listen to the musicians. I'll be here, when you return, right where you left me.

[SONG *goes to a mirror in front of which is a wash basin of water. She starts to remove her makeup as stagelights go to half and houselights come up.*]

ACT III

Scene 1

A courthouse in Paris. 1986.

As he promised, SONG *has completed the bulk of his transformation, onstage by the time the houselights go down and the stagelights come up full. He removes his wig and kimono, leaving them on the floor. Underneath, he wears a well-cut suit.*

SONG: So I'd done my job better than I had a right to expect. Well, give him some credit, too. He's right—I was in a fix when I arrived in Paris. I walked from the airport into town, then I located, by blind groping, the Chinatown district. Let me make one thing clear: whatever else may be said about the Chinese, they are stingy! I slept in doorways three days until I could find a tailor who would make me this kimono on credit. As it turns out, maybe I didn't even need it. Maybe he would've been happy to see me in a simple shift and mascara. But . . . better safe than sorry.

That was 1970, when I arrived in Paris. For the next fifteen years, yes, I lived a very comfy life. Some relief, believe me, after four years on a fucking commune in Nowheresville, China. Rene supported the boy and me, and I did some demonstrations around the country as part of my "cultural exchange" cover. And then there was the spying. [SONG *moves upstage, to a chair.* TOULON *enters as a judge, wearing the appropriate wig and robes. He sits near* SONG. *It's 1986, and* SONG *is testifying in a courtroom.*] Not much at first. Rene had lost all his high-level contacts. Comrade Chin wasn't very interested in parking-ticket statistics. But finally, at my urging, Rene got a job as a courier, handling sensitive documents. He'd photograph them for me, and I'd pass them on to the Chinese embassy.

JUDGE: Did he understand the extent of his activity?

SONG: He didn't ask. He knew that I needed those documents, and that was enough.

JUDGE: But he must've known he was passing classified information.

SONG: I can't say.
JUDGE: He never asked what you were going to do with them?
SONG: Nope.

[*Pause.*]

JUDGE: There is one thing that the court—indeed, that all of France—would like to know.
SONG: Fire away.
JUDGE: Did Monsieur Gallimard know you were a man?
SONG: Well, he never saw me completely naked. Ever.
JUDGE: But surely, he must've . . . how can I put this?
SONG: Put it however you like. I'm not shy. He must've felt around?
JUDGE: Mmmmm.
SONG: Not really. I did all the work. He just laid back. Of course we did enjoy more . . . complete union, and I suppose he *might* have wondered why I was always on my stomach, but . . . But what you're thinking is, "Of course a wrist must've brushed . . . a hand hit . . . over twenty years!" Yeah. Well, Your Honor, it was my job to make him think I was a woman. And chew on this: it wasn't all that hard. See, my mother was a prostitute along the Bundt[7] before the Revolution. And, uh, I think it's fair to say she learned a few things about Western men. So I borrowed her knowledge. In service to my country.
JUDGE: Would you care to enlighten the court with this secret knowledge? I'm sure we're all very curious.
SONG: I'm sure you are. [*Pause.*] Okay, Rule One is: Men always believe what they want to hear. So a girl can tell the most obnoxious lies and the guys will believe them every time—"This is my first time"—"That's the biggest I've ever seen"—or *both*, which, if you really think about it, is not possible in a single lifetime. You've maybe heard those phrases a few times in your own life, yes, Your Honor?
JUDGE: It's not my life, Monsieur Song, which is on trial today.
SONG: Okay, okay, just trying to lighten up the proceedings. Tough room.
JUDGE: Go on.
SONG: Rule Two: As soon as a Western man comes into contact with the East—he's already confused. The West has sort of an international rape mentality towards the East. Do you know rape mentality?
JUDGE: Give us your definition, please.
SONG: Basically, "Her mouth says no, but her eyes say yes."

The West thinks of itself as masculine—big guns, big industry, big money—so the East is feminine—weak, delicate, poor . . . but good at art, and full of inscrutable wisdom—the feminine mystique.

Her mouth says no, but her eyes say yes. The West believes the East, deep down, *wants* to be dominated—because a woman can't think for herself.

7. Waterfront boulevard in Shanghai.

JUDGE: What does this have to do with my question?

SONG: You expect Oriental countries to submit to your guns, and you expect Oriental women to be submissive to your men. That's why you say they make the best wives.

JUDGE: But why would that make it possible for you to fool Monsieur Gallimard? Please—get to the point.

SONG: One, because when he finally met his fantasy woman, he wanted more than anything to believe that she was, in fact, a woman. And second, I am an Oriental. And being an Oriental, I could never be completely a man.

[*Pause.*]

JUDGE: Your armchair political theory is tenuous, Monsieur Song.

SONG: You think so? That's why you'll lose in all your dealings with the East.

JUDGE: Just answer my question: did he know you were a man?

[*Pause.*]

SONG: You know, Your Honor, I never asked.

SCENE 2

Same.

Music from the "Death Scene" from Butterfly *blares over the house speakers. It is the loudest thing we've heard in this play.*

GALLIMARD *enters, crawling towards* SONG*'s wig and kimono.*

GALLIMARD: Butterfly? Butterfly?

[SONG *remains a man, in the witness box, delivering a testimony we do not hear.*]

GALLIMARD: [*To us.*] In my moment of greatest shame, here, in this courtroom—with that . . . person up there, telling the world. . . . What strikes me especially is how shallow he is, how glib and obsequious . . . completely . . . without substance! The type that prowls around discos with a gold medallion stinking of garlic. So little like my Butterfly.

Yet even in this moment my mind remains agile, flip-flopping like a man on a trampoline. Even now, my picture dissolves, and I see that . . . witness . . . talking to me.

[SONG *suddenly stands straight up in his witness box, and looks at* GALLIMARD.]

SONG: Yes. You. White man.

[SONG *steps out of the witness box, and moves downstage towards* GALLIMARD. *Light change.*]

GALLIMARD: [*To* SONG.] Who? Me?

SONG: Do you see any other white men?

GALLIMARD: Yes. There're white men all around. This is a French courtroom.
SONG: So you are an adventurous imperialist. Tell me, why did it take you so long? To come back to this place?
GALLIMARD: What place?
SONG: This theater in China. Where we met many years ago.
GALLIMARD: [*To us.*] And once again, against my will, I am transported.

[*Chinese opera music comes up on the speakers.* SONG *begins to do opera moves, as he did the night they met.*]

SONG: Do you remember? The night you gave your heart?
GALLIMARD: It was a long time ago.
SONG: Not long enough. A night that turned your world upside down.
GALLIMARD: Perhaps.
SONG: Oh, be honest with me. What's another bit of flattery when you've already given me twenty years' worth? It's a wonder my head hasn't swollen to the size of China.
GALLIMARD: Who's to say it hasn't?
SONG: Who's to say? And what's the shame? In pride? You think I could've pulled this off if I wasn't already full of pride when we met? No, not just pride. Arrogance. It takes arrogance, really—to believe you can will, with your eyes and your lips, the destiny of another. [*He dances.*] C'mon. Admit it. You still want me. Even in slacks and a button-down collar.
GALLIMARD: I don't see what the point of—
SONG: You don't? Well maybe, Rene, just maybe—I want you.
GALLIMARD: You do?
SONG: Then again, maybe I'm just playing with you. How can you tell? [*Reprising his feminine character, he sidles up to* GALLIMARD.] "How I wish there were even a small cafe to sit in. With men in tuxedos, and cappuccinos, and bad expatriate jazz." Now you want to kiss me, don't you?
GALLIMARD: [*Pulling away.*] What makes you—?
SONG: —so sure? See? I take the words from your mouth. Then I wait for you to come and retrieve them. [*He reclines on the floor.*]
GALLIMARD: Why?! Why do you treat me so cruelly?
SONG: Perhaps I *was* treating you cruelly. But now—I'm being nice. Come here, my little one.
GALLIMARD: I'm not your little one!
SONG: My mistake. It's I who am *your* little one, right?
GALLIMARD: Yes, I—
SONG: So come get your little one. If you like. I may even let you strip me.
GALLIMARD: I mean, you were! Before . . . but not like this!
SONG: I was? Then perhaps I still am. If you look hard enough. [*He starts to remove his clothes.*]
GALLIMARD: What—what are you doing?
SONG: Helping you to see through my act.
GALLIMARD: Stop that! I don't want to! I don't—
SONG: Oh, but you asked me to strip, remember?

GALLIMARD: What? That was years ago! And I took it back!

SONG: No. You postponed it. Postponed the inevitable. Today, the inevitable has come calling.

[*From the speakers, cacophony: Butterfly mixed in with Chinese gongs.*]

GALLIMARD: No! Stop! I don't want to see!

SONG: Then look away.

GALLIMARD: You're only in my mind! All this is in my mind! I order you! To stop!

SONG: To what? To strip? That's just what I'm—

GALLIMARD: No! Stop! I want you—!

SONG: You want me?

GALLIMARD: To stop!

SONG: You know something, Rene? Your mouth says no, but your eyes say yes. Turn them away. I dare you.

GALLIMARD: I don't have to! Every night, you say you're going to strip, but then I beg you and you stop!

SONG: I guess tonight is different.

GALLIMARD: Why? Why should that be?

SONG: Maybe I've become frustrated. Maybe I'm saying "Look at me, you fool!" Or maybe I'm just feeling . . . sexy. [*He is down to his briefs.*]

GALLIMARD: Please. This is unnecessary. I know what you are.

SONG: Do you? What am I?

GALLIMARD: A—a man.

SONG: You don't really believe that.

GALLIMARD: Yes I do! I knew all the time somewhere that my happiness was temporary, my love a deception. But my mind kept the knowledge at bay. To make the wait bearable.

SONG: Monsieur Gallimard—the wait is over.

[SONG *drops his briefs. He is naked. Sound cue out. Slowly, we and* SONG *come to the realization that what we had thought to be* GALLIMARD*'s sobbing is actually his laughter.*]

GALLIMARD: Oh god! What an idiot! Of course!

SONG: Rene—what?

GALLIMARD: Look at you! You're a man! [*He bursts into laughter again.*]

SONG: I fail to see what's so funny!

GALLIMARD: "You fail to see—!" I mean, you never did have much of a sense of humor, did you? I just think it's ridiculously funny that I've wasted so much time on just a man!

SONG: Wait. I'm not "just a man."

GALLIMARD: No? Isn't that what you've been trying to convince me of?

SONG: Yes, but what I mean—

GALLIMARD: And now, I finally believe you, and you tell me it's not true? I think you must have some kind of identity problem.

SONG: Will you listen to me?

GALLIMARD: Why?! I've been listening to you for twenty years. Don't I deserve a vacation?
SONG: I'm not just any man!
GALLIMARD: Then, what exactly are you?
SONG: Rene, how can you ask—? Okay, what about this?

[*He picks up* BUTTERFLY'*s robes, starts to dance around. No music.*]

GALLIMARD: Yes, that's very nice. I have to admit.

[SONG *holds out his arm to* GALLIMARD.]

SONG: It's the same skin you've worshiped for years. Touch it.
GALLIMARD: Yes, it does feel the same.
SONG: Now—close your eyes.

[SONG *covers* GALLIMARD'*s eyes with one hand. With the other,* SONG *draws* GALLIMARD'*s hand up to his face.* GALLIMARD, *like a blind man, lets his hands run over* SONG'*s face.*]

GALLIMARD: This skin, I remember. The curve of her face, the softness of her cheek, her hair against the back of my hand . . .
SONG: I'm your Butterfly. Under the robes, beneath everything, it was always me. Now, open your eyes and admit it—you adore me. [*He removes his hand from* GALLIMARD'*s eyes.*]
GALLIMARD: You, who knew every inch of my desires—how could you, of all people, have made such a mistake?
SONG: What?
GALLIMARD: You showed me your true self. When all I loved was the lie. A perfect lie, which you let fall to the ground—and now, it's old and soiled.
SONG: So—you never really loved me? Only when I was playing a part?
GALLIMARD: I'm a man who loved a woman created by a man. Everything else—simply falls short.

[*Pause.*]

SONG: What am I supposed to do now?
GALLIMARD: You were a fine spy, Monsieur Song, with an even finer accomplice. But now I believe you should go. Get out of my life!
SONG: Go where? Rene, you can't live without me. Not after twenty years.
GALLIMARD: I certainly can't live with you—not after twenty years of betrayal.
SONG: Don't be so stubborn! Where will you go?
GALLIMARD: I have a date . . . with my Butterfly.
SONG: So, throw away your pride. And come . . .
GALLIMARD: Get away from me! Tonight, I've finally learned to tell fantasy from reality. And, knowing the difference, I choose fantasy.
SONG: *I'm* your fantasy!
GALLIMARD: You? You're as real as hamburger. Now get out! I have a date with my Butterfly and I don't want your body polluting the room! [*He tosses* SONG'*s suit at him.*] Look at these—you dress like a pimp.

SONG: Hey! These are Armani slacks and—! [*He puts on his briefs and slacks.*] Let's just say . . . I'm disappointed in you, Rene. In the crush of your adoration, I thought you'd become something more. More like . . . a woman.

But no. Men. You're like the rest of them. It's all in the way we dress, and make up our faces, and bat our eyelashes. You really have so little imagination!

GALLIMARD: You, Monsieur Song? Accuse me of too little imagination? You, if anyone, should know—I am pure imagination. And in imagination I will remain. Now get out! [GALLIMARD *bodily removes* SONG *from the stage, taking his kimono.*]

SONG: Rene! I'll never put on those robes again! You'll be sorry!

GALLIMARD: [*To* SONG.] I'm already sorry! [*Looking at the kimono in his hands.*] Exactly as sorry . . . as a Butterfly.

Scene 3

M. GALLIMARD'*s prison cell. Paris. Present.*

GALLIMARD: I've played out the events of my life night after night, always searching for a new ending to my story, one where I leave this cell and return forever to my Butterfly's arms.

Tonight I realize my search is over. That I've looked all along in the wrong place. And now, to you, I will prove that my love was not in vain—by returning to the world of fantasy where I first met her. [*He picks up the kimono; dancers enter.*] There is a vision of the Orient that I have. Of slender women in chong sams and kimonos who die for the love of unworthy foreign devils. Who are born and raised to be the perfect women. Who take whatever punishment we give them, and bounce back, strengthened by love, unconditionally. It is a vision that has become my life. [*Dancers bring the wash basin to him and help him make up his face.*] In public, I have continued to deny that Song Liling is a man. This brings me headlines, and is a source of great embarrassment to my French colleagues, who can now be sent into a coughing fit by the mere mention of Chinese food. But alone, in my cell, I have long since faced the truth.

And the truth demands a sacrifice. For mistakes made over the course of a lifetime. My mistakes were simple and absolute—the man I loved was a cad, a bounder. He deserved nothing but a kick in the behind, and instead I gave him . . . all my love.

Yes—love. Why not admit it all? That was my undoing, wasn't it? Love warped my judgment, blinded my eyes, rearranged the very lines on my face . . . until I could look in the mirror and see nothing but . . . a woman. [*Dancers help him put on the Butterfly wig.*] I have a vision. Of the Orient. That, deep within its almond eyes, there are still women. Women willing to sacrifice themselves for the love of a man. Even a man whose love is completely without worth. [*Dancers assist* GALLIMARD *in donning the kimono. They hand him a knife.*] Death with honor is better than life . . . life with dishonor. [*He sets himself center stage, in a seppuku position.*] The love of a Butterfly can withstand many things—unfaithfulness, loss, even abandonment. But how can it face the one sin that implies all others? The devastating knowledge that, underneath it all, the object of her love was nothing more, nothing less than . . . a man. [*He sets the tip of the knife against his body.*] It is 19——. And I have found her at last. In a prison on the outskirts of Paris. My name is Rene Gallimard—also known as Madame Butterfly.

[GALLIMARD *turns upstage and plunges the knife into his body, as music from the "Love Duet" blares over the speakers. He collapses into the arms of the dancers, who lay him reverently on the floor. The image holds for several beats. Then a tight special up on* SONG, *who stands as a man, staring at the dead* GALLIMARD. *He smokes a cigarette; the smoke filters up through the lights. Two words leave his lips.*[8]]

SONG: Butterfly? Butterfly?

[*Smoke rises as lights fade slowly to black.*]

END OF PLAY

1986

8. They are also the last words in *Madame Butterfly,* in which they are sung by Pinkerton.

WRITING ABOUT LITERATURE

INTRODUCTION

Writing about literature ought to be easier than writing about anything else. When you write about painting, for example, you have to translate shapes and colors and textures into words. When you write about music, you have to translate various aspects and combinations of sounds into words. When you write about that complex, mysterious, fleeting thing called "reality" or "life," you have an even more difficult task. Worst of all, perhaps, is trying to put into words all that is going on at any given moment inside your particular and unique self. So you ought to be relieved to know that you are going to write—that is, use words—about literature—again, words.

But writing about literature will not be easy if you haven't learned to *read* literature, for in order to write about anything you have to know that something rather well. Helping you to learn to read literature is what the rest of this book is about; this chapter is about the writing. (But, as you will see, you cannot fully separate the writing from the reading.)

Another thing keeps writing about literature from being easy: writing itself is not easy. Writing well requires a variety of language skills—a good working vocabulary, for example—and a sense of ordering your ideas, of how to link one idea or statement to another, of what to put in and what to leave out. Worse, writing is not a finite or definite skill or art; you never really "know how to write," you just learn how to write a little better about a little more. These very words you are reading have been written and revised several times, even though your editors have had a good many years in which to practice.

REPRESENTING THE LITERARY TEXT

Copying

If writing about literature is using words about words, what words should you use? Since most writers work very hard to get each word exactly right and in exactly the right order, there are no better words to use in discussing what the literature is about than those of the literary work itself. Faced with writing about a story, then, you could just write the story over again, word for word:

> Once upon a time there was a Siamese cat who pretended to be a lion and spoke inappropriate Zebraic . . .

and so on until the end. Copying texts was useful in medieval monasteries, but nowadays, what with printing, word processors, and Fax machines, it would not seem to be very useful. Besides, if you try to copy a text, you will probably find that spelling or punctuation errors, reversed word order, missing or added or just different words seem mysteriously to appear. Still, it's a good exercise for teaching yourself accuracy and attention to detail, and you will probably discover things about the text you are copying that you would be unlikely to notice otherwise. Early in a literature course, particularly, copying can serve as a useful step in the direction of learning how to read and write about fiction, poetry, or drama; later, being able to copy a passage accurately will help when you want to quote a passage to illustrate or prove a point you are making. But copying is not, in itself, writing *about* literature.

Reading aloud, a variation of copying, may be a more original and interpretive exercise than copying itself, since by tone, emphasis, and pace you are clarifying the text or indicating the way you understand the text. But it, too, is not *writing* about literature, and you will not long be satisfied with merely repeating someone else's words. You will have perceptions, responses, and ideas that you will want to express for yourself about what you are reading. And having something to say and wanting to say or write it is the first and most significant step in learning to write about literature.

Paraphrase

If you look away from the text for a while and then write the same material but in your own words, you are writing a **paraphrase**.

For example, let's try to paraphrase the first sentence of Jane Austen's *Pride and Prejudice:* "It is a truth universally acknowledged that a single man in possession of a good fortune, must be in want of a wife." We can start by making "It is a truth" a little less formal: *It's true that,* perhaps. Now "universally acknowledged": *everybody acknowledges,* or, a little more loosely, *everybody agrees.* Now we may choose to drop the whole first clause and begin, *Everybody agrees that* "a single man"—*a bachelor*—"in possession of a good fortune"—*rich*—"must be in want of a wife"—*wants a wife.* Or is it *needs a wife?* Okay, *Everybody agrees that a rich bachelor needs* (or *wants*) *a wife.* You can see that the process of paraphrase is something like that of translation. We are translating Austen's nineteenth-century formal English prose into twentieth-century informal American prose.

But what good is that? First of all, it enables us to test whether we really understand what we are reading. Second, certain elements of the text become clearer: we may see now that Austen's sentence is meant to be ironic or humorous, and we now understand the two possible meanings of "in want of." Third, we can check our paraphrase with those of others, our classmates' versions, for example, to compare our understanding of the passage with theirs. Finally, we have learned how dependent literature is upon words. A paraphrase, no matter how precise, can render only an approximate equivalent of the meaning of a text—how *good* Austen's sentence is, how *flat* our paraphrase.

Paraphrasing, like copying, is not in itself an entirely satisfactory way of writing about literature, but, like copying, it can be a useful tool when you write about literature in other ways. In trying to explain or clarify a literary text for someone, to illustrate a point you are making about that text, or to remind your readers of or to acquaint them with a text or passage, you will at times want to paraphrase. Unlike an exact copy, a paraphrase, being in your own words, adds something of yours to the text or passage—your emphasis, your perspective, your understanding.

Summary

Paraphrase follows faithfully the outlines of the text. But if you stand back far enough from the text so as not to see its specific words or smaller details and put down briefly in your own words what you believe the work is about, you will have a **summary.** How briefly? Well, you could summarize the 108 lines of Poe's "The Raven" in about 180 words or so, like this, for example:

> The speaker of Poe's "The Raven" is sitting in his room late at night reading in order to forget the death of his beloved Lenore. There's a tap at the door; after some hesitation he opens it and calls Lenore's name, but there is only an echo. When he goes back into his room he hears the rapping again, this time at his window, and when he opens it a raven enters. He asks the raven its name, and it answers very clearly, "Nevermore." When the speaker says that the bird, like his friends, will leave, the raven again says, "Nevermore." As the speaker's thoughts run back to Lenore, he realizes the aptness of the raven's word: she shall sit there nevermore. But, he says, sooner or later he will forget her and the grief will lessen. "Nevermore," the raven says again, too aptly. Now the speaker wants the bird to leave, but "Nevermore," the raven says once again. At the end, the speaker knows he'll never escape the raven or his dark message.

Or you could summarize the story of the whole long play *Hamlet* in a single sentence: "A young man, seeking to avenge the murder of his father by his uncle, kills his uncle, but he himself and others die in the process." Has *too* much been left out? What do you feel it essential to add? Let's try again: "In Denmark, many centuries ago, a young prince avenged the murder of his father, the king, by his uncle, who had usurped the throne, but the prince himself was killed as were others, and a well-led foreign army had no trouble successfully invading the decayed and troubled state." A classmate may have written this summary: "From the ghost of his murdered father a young prince learns that his uncle, who has married the prince's mother, much to the young man's shame and disgust, is the father's murderer, and he plots revenge, feigning madness, acting erratically—even to insulting the woman he loves—and, though gaining his revenge, causes the suicide of his beloved and the deaths of others and, finally, of himself."

The last two, though accurate enough, sound like two different plays, don't they? To summarize means to select and emphasize and so to interpret: that is, not to replicate the text in miniature, as a reduced photograph might replicate the original, but while reducing it to change the angle of vision and even the filter, to represent the essentials as the reader or summarizer sees them. When you write a summary you should try to be as objective as possible; nevertheless, your summary will reflect not only the literary text but also your own understanding and attitudes. There's nothing wrong with your fingerprints or "mindprints" appearing on the summary, so long as you recognize that in summarizing you are doing more than copying, paraphrasing, or merely reflecting the literary text. You might learn something about both literature and yourself by comparing your summaries of, say, three or four short poems, a couple of short stories, or a play with summaries of the same works by several of your classmates. Try to measure the refraction of the text as it passes through the lens of each student's mind. You might then write a composite summary that would include all that any one reader felt important. You might try the same exercise again on different texts. Has the practice made you more careful? More inclusive? Is there a greater degree of uniformity or inclusiveness in your summaries?

A good summary can be a form of literary criticism. Though you will seldom be called upon merely to summarize a work, a good deal of writing about literature requires that at some point or other you do summarize—a whole work, a particular incident or aspect, a stanza, chapter, or scene. But beware: a mere summary, no matter how accurate, will seldom satisfy the demand for a critical essay.

REPLYING TO THE TEXT

Imitation and Parody

While paraphrase is something like translation—a faithful following of the original text but in different words—and summary is the faithful, but inevitably interpretive, reduction of the matter, there is another kind of writing about literature that faithfully follows the manner or matter or both of a literary text, but that does so for different ends. It's called **imitation.**

Art students learn to paint by copying the Old Masters; "writing from models," was for many generations the way students were taught to write. Many serious works are, in one way or another, imitations: *The Aeneid,* for example, may be said to be an imitation of *The Odyssey,* and, in a very different way, so might James Joyce's *Ulysses.* You too may be able to learn a good deal about writing—and reading—by trying your hand at an imitation.

But how would *you* go about writing an imitation? You first analyze the original—that is, break it down into its characteristics or qualities—and decide just what you want to preserve in your version. Sometimes you can poke fun at a work by imitating it but at the same time exaggerating its style or prominent characteristics, or placing it in an inappropriate context; that kind of imitation, a kind that is still popular, is called a **parody.** The list of qualities and the model might be much the same for a serious imitation and for a parody, only in a parody you can exaggerate a little—or a lot.

To parody Poe's "The Raven," we may decide to stick closely to Poe's rhythms, his use of repetitive mood words or of several words that mean almost the same thing, and his frequent use of alliteration (words that begin with the same sound). We might want to exaggerate the characteristic stylistic devices as C. L. Edson does in his parody; it begins,

> Once upon a midnight dreary, eerie, scary,
> I was wary, I was weary, full of worry, thinking of my lost Lenore,
> Of my cheery, airy, faerie, fierie Dearie—(Nothing more).

We may choose another kind of parody, keeping the form as close as possible to the original but applying it to a ludicrously unsuitable subject, as Pope does in his mock epic "The Rape of the Lock," where he uses all the grand epic machinery in a poem about cutting off a lock of a lady's hair. In writing such a parody of "The Raven," we will keep the rhythm closer to Poe's and the subject matter less close. How about this?

> Once upon a midday murky, crunching on a Christmas turkey,
> And guzzling giant Jereboams of gin . . .

And maybe we could use the "Nevermore" refrain as if it were an antacid commercial.

You will have noticed that in order to write a good imitation or parody you must read and re-read the original very carefully, examine it, and identify just those elements and qualities that go to make it up and be itself. Since you admire works you wish to imitate, such close study should be a pleasure. You may or may not greatly admire a work you wish to parody, but parody itself is fun to do and fun to read. In either case, you are having fun while gaining a deeper, more intimate knowledge of the nature and details of a work of literature. Moreover, such close attention to how a professional piece of writing is put together and how its parts function together to do what it does along with your effort to reproduce the effects in your own imitation or parody are sure to help you understand the process of writing and so help you improve your own ability to write about literature knowledgeably.

Re-creation and Reply

Sometimes a story, poem, or play will seem so partial, biased, or unrealistic that it will stimulate a response that is neither an imitation or a parody but a retort. While Christopher Marlowe's "shepherd" in "The Passionate Shepherd to His Love" paints an idyllic scene of love in the country for his beloved and pleads, "Come live with me and be my love," Sir Walter Ralegh apparently feels obliged to reply in the name of the beloved "nymph": it won't always be spring, she says in "The Nymph's Reply to the Shepherd"; we won't always be young, and, besides, I can scarcely trust myself to someone who offers me such a phony view of reality.

Ralegh's nymph confronts the invitation and the words of Marlowe's shepherd directly and almost detail for detail. In fiction the reply is less likely to be so directly verbal a retort and is more likely to involve a shift in perspective. It may tell the same story as the original but from a different angle, not only giving a different view of the same events and people but also adding details that the original focus ignored or could not perceive. In *Jane Eyre,* for example, Bertha Mason Rochester is the hero's bestial, mad wife, whom he has locked away upstairs and whose existence, when it comes to light, prevents for a time our heroine, our Jane, from marrying her heart's desire; Bertha is, in effect, the villainess. In *Wide Sargasso Sea*, Jean Rhys not only gives Bertha's side of Charlotte Brontë's story but tells us more details about Bertha's earlier life: poor Bertha was more sinned against than sinning, it turns out.

We may respond to a work whose view seems partial or distorted by shifting the perspective in time as well as in space. Are Francis Weed's marital and other problems solved by his recognition, at the end of "The Country Husband," that life in the suburbs can be, in its own way, as adventurous as more romantic kinds of existence? What will happen to him next spring? On his fortieth birthday? As he lies dying? What will the speaker of "My Papa's Waltz" be thinking about as he plays or dances with *his* daughter?

You may have noticed that while retorts can often be witty, they are also serious. Usually they say not merely, "That's not how the story went," but "That's not what life is really like." We must always read literature initially with the aim of understanding it and taking it at its highest value (rather than reducing it and quibbling). We must try to "hear" what it is saying and not impose our own notions of reality prematurely upon a work but if possible learn from it and broaden our own views. We must finally, however, read it critically as well, asking, "Is this the way things *really* are?" or, more generously, "If I were standing over there, where the story (author, character) is, would things really look that way?"

Perhaps the most familiar kind of literary re-creation or reply is the **adaptation,** especially that of fiction into film. (Among the stories in this anthology that have been made into feature-length films are "The Most Dangerous Game," "An Occurrence at Owl Creek Bridge," "The Lady with the Dog," and "The Rocking-Horse Winner.") In adaptation, the rather contradictory demands of faithfulness to the original and appropriateness to the new medium can teach us a great deal about both the content and the medium of the original. It is unlikely you will have the opportunity in this course to make a film based on a story but you can still try your hand at adapting a work or piece of a work to a new medium. You might want to turn "The Cask of Amontillado" into verse (probably as a dramatic monologue) or write a short story called *Hamlet* or a one-act play called "Young Goodman Brown." It is quite likely that you will learn not only about the nature of the original work but also something of the nature of the medium in which you are trying to work.

EXPLAINING THE TEXT

Description

To give an account of the form of a work or passage rather than merely a brief version of its content or plot (and a plot summary, even of a poem, is usually what we mean by "summary") you may wish to write a **description.** We have given a summary of Poe's "The Raven" earlier, concentrating there, as summaries tend to do, on subject and plot. A description, on the other hand, may concentrate on the form of the stanzas, the lines, the rhyme scheme, perhaps like this:

> Poe's "The Raven" is a poem of 108 lines divided into eighteen 6-line stanzas. If in describing the rhyme scheme you were to look just at the ends of the lines, you would notice only one or two unusual features: not only is there only one rhyme sound per stanza, lines 2, 4, 5, and 6 rhyming, but that one rhyme sound is the same in all eighteen stanzas, so that there are 72 lines ending with the sound "ore"; in addition, the fourth and fifth lines of each stanza end with the identical word, and in six of the stanzas that word is "door" and in four others "Lenore." There is even more repetition: the last line of six of the first seven stanzas ends with the words "nothing more," and the last eleven stanzas end with the word "Nevermore." The rhyming lines—other than the last, which is very short—in each stanza are fifteen syllables long, the unrhymed lines sixteen. The longer lines give the effect of shorter ones, however, and add still further to the frequency of repeated sounds, for the first half of each opening line rhymes with the second half of the line, and so do the halves of line three. There is still more: the first half of line 4 rhymes with the halves of line 3 (in the first stanza the rhymes are "dreary" /"weary" and "napping" / "tapping" /"rapping"). So at least nine words in each eight-line stanza are involved in the regular rhyme scheme, and in many stanzas there are added instances of rhyme or repetition. As if this were not enough, all the half-line rhymes are rich feminine rhymes, where both the accented and the following unaccented syllables rhyme—"drēary̆" /"wēary̆."

This is a detailed and complicated description of a complex and unusual pattern of rhymes. Though there are many other elements of the poem we could describe—images and symbols, for example—the unusual and dominant element in this poem is clearly the intricate and insistent pattern of rhyme and repetition. Moreover, this paragraph shows how you can describe at length, in depth, and with considerable complexity, certain aspects of a work without mentioning the content at all. You can describe a play in comparable terms—acts, scenes, settings, time lapses perhaps—and you might describe a novel in terms of chapters, books, summary narration, dramatized scenes. In addition to describing the narrative structure or focus and voice of a short story, you might also describe the diction (word choice), the sentence structure, the amount of description of the characters or landscape, and so on.

Analysis

Like copying, paraphrase, and summary, a description of a work or passage rarely stands alone as a piece of writing about literature. It is, instead, a tool, a means of supporting a point or opinion. Even the description we have given above borders on **analysis.** To analyze is to break something down into its parts to discover what they are, and, usually, how they function in and relate to the whole. The description of the rhyme scheme of "The Raven" tells you what that scheme or pattern is but says nothing about how it functions in the poem. If you were to add such an account to the description, then, you would have analyzed one aspect of the poem. In order to do so, however, you would first have to decide what, in a general way, the poem is about: what its *theme* is. If you defined the theme of "The Raven" as "inconsolable grief," you could then write an analytical paper suggesting how the rhyme scheme reinforces that theme. You might begin something like this:

> Obsessive Rhyme in "The Raven"
>
> We all know that gloomy poem with that gloomy bird, Edgar Allan Poe's "The Raven." The time is midnight, the room is dark, the bird is black, and the poem is full of words like "dreary," "sad," "mystery," and "ghastly." We all know too it has a rather sing-song rhythm and repeated rhymes, but we do not often stop to think how the rhymes contribute to the mood or meaning. Before we do so here, perhaps it would be a good idea to describe in detail just what that rhyme scheme is.

—Then follow with the description of the rhyme scheme, and go on like this:

> Of course the most obvious way in which the rhyme scheme reinforces the theme of inconsolable loss is through the emphatic repetition of "Nevermore." Since this refrain comes at the very end of each of the last stanzas it is even more powerful in its effect.
>
> What is not so obvious as the effect of repeating "Nevermore" is the purpose of the over-all abundance and richness of rhyme. Some might say it is not abundant

and rich but excessive and cloying. These harsh critics cynically add that in a way the rhymes and repetitions are appropriate to this poem because the whole poem is excessive and cloying: grief over loss, even intense grief, does, human experience tells us, pass away. This criticism is just, however, only if we have accurately defined the theme of the poem as "inconsolable sorrow." The very insistence of the rhyme and repetition, however, suggests we may need to adjust slightly our definition of that theme. Perhaps the poem is not about "inconsolable sorrow" in so neutral a way; maybe it would be better to say it is about obsessive grief. Then the insistent, pounding rhyme and repetition make sense (just as the closed-in dark chamber does). Obsessive repetition of words and sounds thus helps to create the meaning of the poem almost as much as the words themselves do.

Interpretation

Principles and Procedures

If you have been reading carefully, you may have noticed what looks like a catch: to turn description into analysis, you must relate what you are describing to the theme, the overall effect and meaning of the work of literature. But how do you know what the theme is? If analysis relates the part to the whole, how can you know the "whole" before you have analyzed each part? But then, how can you analyze each part—relating it to the whole—if you don't know what that whole is?

Interpretation, or the expression of your understanding of a literary work and its meaning, involves an initial general impression that is then supported and, often, modified by analysis of the particulars. It involves looking at the whole, the part, the whole, the part, the whole, the part, in a series of approximations and adjustments. (Note, in particular, that you must keep your mind open for modifications or changes rather than forcing your analysis to confirm your first impressions.)

This procedure should in turn suggest something of the nature and even the form of the critical essay, or essay of interpretation. The essay should present the overall theme and support that generalization with close analyses of the major elements of the text (or, in some essays, an analysis of one significant element)—showing how one or more of such elements as rhyme or speaker, plot or setting reinforce, define, or modify the theme of the story. Often the conclusion of such an essay will be a fuller, more refined statement of the theme.

Both the definition of and the procedures for interpreting a work suggest that a literary text is unified, probably around a theme, a meaning and effect. In interpreting, you therefore keep asking of each element or detail, "How does it fit? How does it contribute to *the* theme or whole?" In most instances, especially when you are writing on shorter works, if you dig hard and deep enough, you will find a satisfactory interpretation or central theme. Even after you have done your best, however, you must hold your "reading" or interpretation as a hypothesis rather than a final truth. Your experience of reading criticism has probably already shown you that more than one reading of a literary work is possible and that no reading exhausts the meaning and totality of a work. Nonetheless, you must begin reading a literary text as if it were going to make a central statement and create a single effect, no matter how complex. You must try as conscientiously as you can to "make sense" of the work, to analyze it, show how its elements work together. In analyzing elements, you kept your initial sense of the whole as hypothesis and did not try to force evidence to fit your first impression. So, too, you must hold your interpretation as a hypothesis even in its final stages, even at the end. It is, you must be sure, the fullest and best "reading" of the text you are capable of at this time, with the evidence and knowledge you have at this moment; but only that. In other words, an interpretation is "only an opinion." But just as your political and other opinions are not lightly held but are what you really feel and believe based on all you know and have experienced and all you have thought and felt, so your opinion or interpretation of a literary work should be as responsible as you can make it. Your opinions are a measure of your knowledge, intelligence, and sensibility. They should not be lightly changed but neither should they be obstinately and inflexibly held.

Reading and Theme Making

Because you need a sense of the whole text before you can analyze it, analysis and interpretation would seem to be possible only after repeated readings. Though obvious, logical, and partially true, this may not be *entirely* true. In reading, we actually anticipate theme or meaning much as we anticipate what will happen next. Often this anticipation or expectation of theme or effect begins with our first opening a book—or even before, in reading the title. If you were to read *Hamlet* in an edition that gives its full title—*The Tragedy of Hamlet, Prince of Denmark*—even if, as unlikely as it may seem, you had never heard of the play or its author before—you would have some idea or hypothesis about who the protagonist is, where the action will more than likely be set, how the play will end, and even some of the feelings it will arouse.

Such anticipation of theme and effect, projecting and modifying understanding and response, continues as you read. When you read the first four words of "The Zebra Storyteller"—"Once upon a time . . ."—the strange title is to some extent explained and the kind of story you are about to read and its relation to everyday reality has been established. The title and the first short section of "The Most Dangerous Game" arouse expectations of the supernatural, the frightening, the adventurous, creating suspense: "What will happen next?" we ask as we read the first few paragraphs. The brief conversation about hunting, toward the end of that section, not only educates our expectations but also generates a moral and thematic question: "Are there really two animal classes—the hunters and the hunted—and does being lucky enough to be among the hunters justify insensitivity toward the feelings of the hunted?" While the question may recede from the foreground of our attention for a while, it has nonetheless been raised. It is, in addition, reinforced by the break on the page, which forces us to pause and, even if but momentarily, reflect. It comes forward again when General Zaroff introduces the subject of hunting. At these two points, at least, a thematic hypothesis based on hunters and hunted begins forming, however faintly, in our minds. That is enough to give us grounds—even as we read the story for the first time—for an analysis of elements and their relationship to our very tentatively formulated theme, and perhaps for beginning to modify or modulate our articulation of that theme. Many details in the story indicate that there is a political coloring to the theme: Zaroff is a Cossack—a people noted for fierceness—and is, or was, a Czarist general; he keeps a giant Cossack servant who was an official flogger under the Czar; he refers to the Revolution of 1917 in Russia as a "debacle"; he is clearly a racist. We may want to alter "hunter" and "hunted" in our first version of the anticipated theme to something broader—"strong" and "weak," perhaps, or "privileged" and "underprivileged," or we may need fuller definitions of the implications of the terms "hunter" and "hunted."

Just as we have more than one expectation of what may happen next as we read a story, poem, or play, so we may have more than one expectation of what it is going to be "about" in the more general sense: as we read along we have expectations or hypotheses of meaning, and so we consciously or unconsciously try to fit together the pieces of elements of what we are reading into a pattern of significance. By the end of our first reading we should have a fairly well-defined sense of what the work is "about," what it means, even how some of the elements have worked together to produce that meaning and effect. Indeed, isn't this the way we read when we are not reading for a class or performance?

Don't most people read most stories, poems, plays only once? And don't we usually think we have understood what we have read? Shouldn't we be able to read a very short story in class just once and immediately write an interpretive paper based on that first reading?

This is not to say that we cannot understand more about a work by repeated re-readings, or that there is some virtue or purity of response in the naive first reading that is lost in closer study. Our first "reading"—"reading" in the sense of both "casting our eye over" and "interpretation"—is almost certain to be modified or refined by re-reading: if nothing else, we know from the beginning what the most dangerous game is, and that the behavior of the English couples from "beyond the pale" is crass, insensitive, unacceptable. The theme or meaning is likely to be modulated by later readings, the way the elements function in defining or embodying meaning is likely to be clearer; the effect of the second reading is certain to be different from that of the first. It may be instructive to re-read several times the short work we interpreted in class after a single reading, write a new interpretive essay, and see how our understanding has been changed and enriched by subsequent readings.

Opinions, Right and Wrong

Just as each of our separate readings is different, so naturally one reader's fullest and "final" reading, interpretation, or opinion will differ somewhat from another's. Seldom will readers agree entirely with any full statement of the theme of a literary text. Nor is one of these interpretations entirely "right" and all the others necessarily "wrong." For no thematic summary, no analysis or interpretation, no matter how full, can exhaust the affective or intellectual significance of a major literary text. There are various approximate readings of varying degrees of acceptability, various competent or "good" readings, not just one single "right" reading.

Anyone who has heard two accomplished musicians faithfully perform the same work, playing all the "same" notes; or anyone who has seen two performances of *Hamlet*, will recognize how "interpretations" can be both correct and different. You might try to get hold of several recordings of one or more of Hamlet's soliloquies—by John Barrymore, Sir John Gielgud, Richard Burton, Sir Lawrence Olivier, for example—and notice how each of these actors lends to identical passages his own emphasis, pacing, tone, color, his own effect, and so, ultimately, his own meaning. These actors reading the identical words are, in effect, "copying," not paraphrasing or putting Shakespeare's Elizabethan poetry into modern American prose, not "interpreting" as we have defined it, or putting his play into their own words. If merely performing or reading the words aloud generates significant differences in interpretation, it is no wonder that when you write an interpretive essay about literature, when you give your conception of the meaning and effect of the literary text in your own words, your interpretation will differ from other interpretations, even when each of the different interpretations is competent and "correct."

Any communication, even a work of literature, is refracted by the recipient, and, in one sense, it is not complete until it is received, just as, in a sense, a musical score is not "music" until it is played. Philip Roth reported, not too long ago, how perturbed he was by what the critics and other readers said of his first novel—that was not at all what he intended, what the novel really was, he thought at first. But then he realized that once he had had his say in the novel, it was "out there," and each reader had to understand it within the limits and range of his or her own perspectives and literary and life experiences. His novel, once in print, was no longer merely "his," and rightly so.

That quite different interpretations may be "correct" is not to say, with Alice's Humpty-Dumpty, that a word or a work "means just what I choose it to mean." Though there may not be one "right" reading, some readings are more appropriate and convincing than others and some readings are demonstrably wrong.

What would you say about this reading of *Hamlet?*

> The play is about the hero's sexual love for his mother. He sees his father's "ghost" because he feels guilty, somehow responsible for his father's death, more than likely because he had often wished his father dead. To free himself from this feeling of guilt, he imagines that he sees his father's ghost and that the ghost tells him that his uncle murdered his father. He focuses upon his uncle because he is fiercely jealous that it is his uncle not himself who has replaced his father in his mother's bed. He so resents his mother's choice of so unworthy a mate, he attributes it not to love but to mere lust, clearly a projection of his own lust for his mother, which he calls love. His mother's lust so disgusts him that he hates all women now, even Ophelia. When his father was alive he could be fond of Ophelia, for his sexual feeling for his mother was deflected by his father-the-king's powerful presence. Now, however, he must alienate Ophelia not only because of his new hatred of women but because he has a chance of winning his mother, especially if he can get rid of Claudius, his uncle.

Such a reading explains more or less convincingly certain details in the play, but it wrenches some out of context and it leaves a good deal out and a good deal unexplained: why, for example, do others see the ghost of Hamlet's father if it is just a figment of his imagination? What are Horatio and Fortinbras and the political elements doing in the play? *If* you accept certain Freudian premises about human psychology and see life in Freudian terms; *if* you see literary texts as the *author's* psychic fantasy stimulating your own psychic fantasies and believe that interpretation of *Hamlet* is not merely a reading of the play itself but an analysis of Shakespeare's psyche, you will find this reading convincing. You will perhaps explain away some of the details of the play that do not seem to fit your Freudian reading as a cover-up, an attempt by Shakespeare to disguise the true but hidden meaning of his dramatic fantasy from others—and from himself. Such a reading is probably neither right nor wrong but only a way of interpreting *Hamlet* based on certain assumptions about psychology and about the way literature *means* and so it would be "right" or acceptable to those who share those assumptions.

Suppose one of your ingenious classmates were to argue that the real subject of *Hamlet* is that the hero has tuberculosis. This would explain, your classmate would say, the hero's moodiness, his pretended madness that sometimes seems real, his rejection of Ophelia (he wouldn't want their children to suffer from the disease), his father's ghost (he, too, died of consumption), his anger at his uncle (who carries the disease, of course) for marrying Hamlet's mother, and so on. Your classmate might even argue that the text of the play is flawed, that it was just copied down during a performance by someone in the audience or was printed from an actor's imperfect copy. Therefore, "O that this too too *solid flesh*" should read "*sullied flesh*," as many scholars have argued (and might not "sullied flesh" suggest tuberculosis?). And, therefore, isn't it quite possible that the most famous soliloquy in the play really began or was meant to begin, "TB or not TB"? "No way!" we'd say. We would be reasonably sure that this is not just "not proved" but just plain *wrong*. It might be interesting and illuminating to rebut that reading in a paper of your own and to notice what kinds of evidence you bring to bear on an interpretive argument.

Reader and Text

If it is difficult to say exactly what a piece of literature *says*, it is usually not because it is vague or meaning*less* but because it is too specific and meaning*ful* to paraphrase satisfactorily in any language other than its own. Since no two human beings are identical and no two people can inhabit the same space at the same time, no two people can see exactly the same reality from the same angle and vantage point. Most of us get around this awkward truth by saying that we see—or by only actually seeing—what we are "supposed" to see, a generalized, common-sense approximation of reality. We are all, in effect, like

Polonius in the third act of *Hamlet*, who sees in a cloud a camel, a weasel, a whale—whatever Hamlet tells him he sees.

Some individuals struggle to see things as fully and clearly as possible from their own unique vantage point and to communicate to others their particular—even peculiar—vision. But here too we are individuated, for though we speak of our "common language," we each speak a unique language, made up of "dialects" that are not only regional and ethnic but also conditioned by our age group, our profession, our education, travel, reading—all our experiences. Yet if we want to express our unique vision to others who have different visions and different "languages" we must find some medium that is both true to ourselves and understandable to others.

There is for these individuals—these writers of literature—a constant tug-of-war between the uniqueness of their individual visions and the generalizing nature of language. The battle does not always result in sheer loss, however. Often, in the very struggle to get their own perceptions into language, writers sharpen those perceptions or discover what they themselves did not know when they began to write. You have probably made similar discoveries some time or other in the process of writing a letter or an assigned paper. But writers also find that what they have written does not perfectly embody what they meant it to, just as you perhaps have found that your finished papers have been not quite so brilliant as your original idea.

"Understanding" is not a passive reception of a text but an active reaching out from our own experiences toward the text. At least at first we need to do so by meeting the author on the ground of a common or general language and set of conventions—things that everybody "knows." The first task of the reader, therefore, is to get not to the author's intention, but to the general statement that the work itself makes—that is, its theme or thesis. After a few readings we can usually make a stab at articulating the theme of most works. What a work says in the way of a general theme, however, is not necessarily its full or ultimate meaning; otherwise we would read theme summaries and not stories. The theme is the meaning accessible to all through close reading of the text and common to all, but a literary text is not all statement. There are often cloudy areas in the text where we cannot be sure what is **implication,** the suggestion of the text, and what is our **inference,** or interpretation, of the text. Why does Doris Lessing's Judith prefer having a tomcat put to death to having him neutered but does not suggest that the female kitten who has been ruined for procreation be put death? Does this suggest that males, including human males, exist only to fertilize eggs, but that females have other functions as well? Or, at least, that this is what Judith believes? Does this give us more insight into

Judith's life, her singleness, her refusal to marry the Greek professor, her ultimate flight from Luigi? The story does not *say* this, but many readers will find this inference convincing. If accepted, this changes the meaning of the story to some degree. Still, it need not be accepted; the story does not, will never say. The meaning of the story for the reader who is convinced will differ from the meaning for the reader who is not convinced.

The full meaning of a work for you is not only in its stated theme, one that everyone can agree on, but in the meaning you derive by bringing together that generalized theme, the precise language of the text, and your own applicable experiences—including reading experience—and imagination. That "meaning" is not the total meaning of the work, not what the author originally perceived and "meant to say"; it is the vision of the author as embodied in the work *and re-viewed from your own angle of vision.*

Your role in producing a meaning from the text does not free you, please note, from paying very close attention to the precise language of the text, the words and their meanings, their order, the syntax of the sentences, and even such mundane details as punctuation. You cannot impose a meaning on the text, no matter how sincerely and intensely you feel it, in defiance of the rules of grammar and the nature of the language.

Still, the reader must be an artist too, trying to experience the reality of the work as the author experienced reality, and with the same reverence and sense of responsibility for the original. To write about literature you must try to embody your reading experience—or interpretation—of the work in language. Alas, writing about literature, using words about words, is not as easy as it sounded at first. But it is more exciting, giving you a chance to see with another's eyes, to explore another's perceptions or experiences, and to explore and more fully understand your own in the process, thus expanding the horizon of your experience, perception, consciousness.

When some rich works of literature, like *Hamlet,* seem to have more than one meaning or no entirely satisfactory meaning or universally agreed upon single theme, it is not that they are not saying something, and saying something very specific, but that what they are saying is too specific, and complex, and profound, and true, perhaps, to be generalized or paraphrased in a few dozen words. The literary work is meaning*ful*—that is, full of meaning or meanings; but it is the reader who produces each particular meaning from the work, using the work itself, the language of the community and of the work, and his or her own language, experience, and imagination.

As readers trying to understand the unique perception and language of the author, we must translate the text as best we can into terms we can understand for ourselves. We try not to reduce the text to our own earlier, limited understanding but to stretch our minds and feelings toward its vision.

An interpretation, then, is not a clarification of what the writer "was trying to say"; it is a process that itself says, in effect, "The way I am trying to understand this work is . . . ."

CRITICAL APPROACHES

The way you read and talk about a literary text depends on your assumptions, usually unconscious or unarticulated, about what a work of literature is, what is it supposed to do, and what makes it good. Literary critics, however, often define their assumptions about literature and the proper way to go about reading it and writing about it. The results are critical theories or critical approaches. Looking at a few of these, you may recognize some of your own assumptions, see new and exciting ways of looking at literature, or, at the very least, become aware of your own critical premises and prejudices.

Objectivism

We might begin by asking just what, quite literally, a work of literature *is.* There are critics who think of it as a fixed and freestanding object made up of words on a page. It is "freestanding" in that it has no connection on the one hand with the author or his or her intention or life, nor, on the other hand, with the historical or cultural context of the author or the reader. These we might call **objectivist** critics; they believe that a text is an independent object, free from the subjectivity of author and reader.

Formalism

Among the objectivist critics are the **formalists.** One common formalist conception is that a work is **autotelic,** that is, complete in itself, written for its own sake, and unified by its form—that which makes it a work of art. Content is less important than form. Literature involves a special kind of language that sets it apart from merely utilitarian writing; the formal strategies that organize and animate that language valorize literature and give it a special, almost religious character.

NEW CRITICISM One group of formalists, the **New Critics,** dominated literary criticism in the middle of the 20th century, and New Criticism remains an important influence today. Their critical practice is to demonstrate formal unity by showing how every part of a work—every word, every image, every element—contributes to a central unifying theme. Because the details of the work relate to a theme or idea, they are generally treated as *symbolic*, as figurative or allegorical, representations of that central, unifying idea. The kind of unity thus demonstrated, in which every part is related to the whole and the whole is reflected in each part, is called **organic unity.** The New Critics differentiate organic unity from (and much prefer it to) **mechanical unity,** the external, preconceived structure or rules that do not arise from the individuality of the work but from the type or genre. New Critical analysis, or **explication of the text,** is especially effective in the critical reading of lyric poetry. It has become so universally accepted as *at least the first step* in the understanding of literature that it is almost everywhere the critical approach taught in introductory literature courses. It is, indeed, the basic approach of the "Understanding the Text" sections in *The Norton Introduction to Literature.*

The New Critics' focus on theme or meaning as well as form means that for them literature is **referential:** it points to something outside itself, things in the real, external world or in human experience—a tree, a sound wave, love. The New Critics, in general, do not question the reality of the phenomenal world or the ability of language to represent it.

Structuralism

For many formalists, however, literature is not referential. The words in a story, poem, or play no longer point outward to the things, people, or world they are supposed to denote, as they might do in ordinary, "nonliterary" discourse, but point inward to each other and to the formal system they create. The critic still focuses on interrelatedness but is less concerned with "meaning"; words are treated not as symbols with meaning but like numbers; poetry is likened to mathematics or music.

Structuralism focuses on the text as an independent aesthetic object and also tends to detach literature from history and social and political implications, but much more than New Criticism, structuralism emphasizes systematic analysis, aspiring to make literary criticism a branch of scientific inquiry. It sees every literary work as a separate "system" and seeks to discover the principles or general laws that govern the interaction of parts within the system. Structuralism has its roots in modern linguistic theory; it looks especially to the work of Ferdinand de Saussure (1857–1913), the founder of structural linguistics early in the 20th century. Structuralism in criticism did not, however, flourish internationally until the early 1960s when a combination of space-age preoccupation with science and cold-war fear of implication led to a view of literature as intellectually challenging yet socially and politically noncontroversial.

Although based on linguistic theory, structuralism tries to extend newly discovered principles about language to other aspects of literature. Drawing on the **semiotic** principle that a vast and intricate system of signs enables human beings to communicate through language, structuralism asks readers to consider the way that other kinds of sign systems within a work—structures all—combine to produce meaning. Language and its characteristic habits are important to structuralists, but it is not enough to consider any single part of a work or any single kind of sign—linguistic or otherwise—within it. Structuralism aspires to elucidate the meaning of a work of literature by seeing the way all of its parts work relationally toward some wholeness of structure and meaning. Like formalism, it shows little interest in the creative process as such and has virtually no interest in authors, their intentions, or the circumstances or contexts of creation. It takes texts to represent interactions of words and ideas apart from individual human identities or socio-political commitments, and concentrates its analytical attention on what can be said about how different elements or processes in a text operate in relation to one another. Structuralists are less likely than formalists to concentrate their attention on some single all-explaining characteristic of literature (such as Cleanth Brooks's "tension" or William Empson's "ambiguity") and its practitioners are less likely to privilege a particular text for its revelation or authority. Structuralism may be seen as a sort of secular equivalent of formalism; it is less mysterious and authoritarian, and it has both the advantage and disadvantage of seeming to be less arbitrary and more "objectively" reliable. But in some ways it seems to promise too much for method and "objectivity," and by the 1970s its insights into the ways of language were already beginning to be used against it to attack the certitudes it appeared to promise and to emphasize instead the uncertainties and indeterminateness of texts.

Post-structuralism

Post-structuralism is the broad term used to designate the several directions of literary criticism that, while depending crucially on the insights of science-based theory, attack the very idea that any kind of certitude can exist about the meaning, understandability, or sharability of texts. Post-structuralists, disturbed at the optimism of positivist philosophy in suggesting that the world is knowable and explainable, ultimately doubt the possibility of certainties of any kind, and they see language as especially elusive and unfaithful. Much of post-structuralism involves undoing; the best-known variety of post-structuralism, **deconstruction,** suggests as much in its very name.

DECONSTRUCTION Deconstruction takes the observations of structuralism to their logical conclusion, arguing that the elaborate web of semiotic differentiations created by the principle of difference in language means that no text can ultimately have any stable, definite, or discoverable meaning.

For the deconstructionist, language consists just in black marks on a page that repeat or differ from each other and the reader is the only author, one who can find whatever can be found in, or be made to appear in, those detached, isolated marks. The deconstructionist conception of literature is thus very broad—almost any writing will do. While this may seem "subjective," in that the critical reader has great freedom, it is the object—the black marks on the blank page—that is the sole subject/object of intention/attention.

As practiced by its most famous proponent, the French philosopher Jacques Derrida (b. 1930), deconstruction endeavors to trace the way texts challenge or cancel their explicit meanings and wrestle themselves into stasis or neutrality. Many deconstructionists have strong radical political commitments (it is possible to argue that the radical counterculture of the 1960s and especially the political events in Paris of 1968 are the crucial context for understanding the origins of deconstructionism), but the retreat from meaning and denial of clear signification that characterizes deconstruction also has affinities with formalism and structuralism, particularly as deconstruction is practiced by American critics. Rather than emphasizing form over content, however, deconstruction tries to deny the possibility of content and places value instead on verbal play as a characteristic outlet of a fertile, adroit, and supple human mind. Like structuralism, it lives almost completely in a self-referential verbal world rather than a world in which texts represent some larger or other reality, but unlike structuralism it denies that the verbal world adds up to anything coherent, consistent, or meaningful in itself. Deconstruction also influences other varieties of post-structuralism with different kinds of interests in history and ideology. Michel Foucault (1926–1984), Julia Kristeva (b. 1941), and Jacques Lacan (1901–1981)—though their disciplinary interests are in social history, feminist philosophy, and psychoanalysis, respectively, all come out of deconstructionist assumptions and carry the indeterminacies of post-structuralism (and of post-modernism more generally) into kinds of literary criticism with interests fundamentally different from those of structuralism.

Subjectivism

Opposed to objectivism is what might be called **subjectivism.** This loose term can be used to embrace many forms of psychological and self-, subject-, or reader-centered criticism.

Psychological Criticism

The assumption is that literature is the expression of the author's psyche, often his or her unconscious, and, like dreams, needs to be interpreted.

FREUDIAN CRITICISM The dominant school is the **Freudian,** based on the work of Sigmund Freud (1856–1939). Many of its practitioners assert that the meaning of a literary work does not lie on its surface but in the psyche (some would even claim, in the neuroses) of the author. The value of the work, then, lies in how powerfully and convincingly it expresses the author's unconscious and how universal the psychological elements are. A well-known Freudian reading of *Hamlet*, for example, insists that Hamlet is upset because he is jealous of his uncle, for he, *like all male children*, unconsciously wants to go to bed with his mother. The ghost, in such a reading, is a figment of Hamlet's unconscious desire; his madness is not just acting but is the result of this frustrated desire; his cruelly gross mistreatment of Ophelia is a deflection of his disgust at his mother's being "lecherous," "unfaithful" in her love for him. A Freudian critic may assume then that Hamlet is suffering from an Oedipus complex, a Freudian term for the desire of the son for his mother, its name derived from the Greek myth that is the basis of Sophocles' play *Oedipus the King*.

Some Freudian critics stress the author's psyche and find *Hamlet* the expression of Shakespeare's own Oedipus complex. Others stress the effect on the reader, the work having a purgative or cleansing effect by expressing in socially and morally acceptable ways unconscious desires that would be unacceptable if expressed directly.

LACANIAN CRITICISM As it absorbs the indeterminacies of post-structuralism under the influence of thinkers such as Jacques Lacan, psychological criticism has become increasingly complex. Accepting the Oedipal paradigm and the unconscious as the realm of repressed desire, Lacanian psychology (and the critical theory that depends from that psychology) conflates these concepts with the deconstructionist emphasis on language as expressing absence—you use a word to represent an absent object but you cannot make it present. The word, then, like the unconscious desire, is something that cannot be fulfilled. Language, reaching out with one word after the other, striving for but never reaching its object, is the arena of desire.

JUNGIAN CRITICISM Just as a Freudian assumes that human psyches have similar histories and structures, the **Jungian** critic assumes that we all share a universal or **collective unconscious** (as well as having a racial and individual unconscious). According to Carl Gustav Jung (1875–1961) and his followers, in the collective and in our individual unconscious are universal images, patterns, and forms of human experiences or **archetypes.** These archetypes can never be known directly, but they surface in art in an imperfect, shadowy way, taking the form of **archetypal images**—the snake with its tail in its mouth, rebirth, mother, the double, the descent into Hell. To get a sense of the archetype beneath the archetypal images or shadows in the characters, plot, language, and images of a work, to bring these together in an archetypal interpretation, is the function of the Jungian critic. He is guided by his belief that there is a central myth common to all literature. Just as, for the Freudian literary critic, the "family romance," out of which the Oedipus story comes, is central, so the Jungian assumes there is a **monomyth** that underlies the archetypal images and gives a clue as to how they can be related to suggest the archetypes themselves. The myth is that of the quest. In that all-encompassing myth the hero struggles to free himself (the gender of the pronoun is specific and significant) from the Great Mother, to become a separate, self-sufficient being who is then rewarded by union with his ideal other, the feminine *anima*.

Phenomenological Criticism

Another kind of subjectivist criticism is **phenomenology,** especially as it is practiced by **critics of consciousness.** They consider all the writings of an author—laundry lists and letters as well as lyrics—as the expression of his or her mind-set or way of looking at reality. Such a critic looks for repeated or obsessive use of certain key words, incidents, patterns, and angles of vision, and maps out thereby the inner world of the writer.

Reader-response Criticism

The formalists focus on the text. Though the psychological critics focus most frequently on the author, their assumptions about the similarity or universality of the human mind make them consider as well the role of the reader. There is another approach that, though not psychological in the usual sense of the word, also focuses on the reception of the text, on **reader response.** The conventional notion of reading is that a writer or speaker has an "idea," **encodes** it—that is, turns it into words—and the reader or listener decodes it, deriving, when successful, the writer/speaker's "idea." What the reader-response critic assumes, however, is that such equivalency between sender and receiver is impossible. The literary **work** therefore does *not* exist on the page; that is only the **text.** The text becomes a work only when it is read, just as a score becomes music only when it is played. And just as every musical performance, even of exactly the same notes, is somewhat different, a different "interpretation," so no two readers read or perform exactly the same work from identical texts. Besides the individual differences of readers, space is made for different readings or interpretations by **gaps** in a text itself. Some of these are temporary—such as the withholding of the name of the murderer until the end—and are closed by the text sooner or later, though each reader will in the meantime fill them differently. But others are permanent, and can never be filled with certainty; the result is a degree of uncertainty or **indeterminacy** in the text.

The reader-response critic's focus on the reading process is especially useful in the study of long works such as novels. The critic follows the text sequentially, observing what **expectations** are being aroused, how they are being satisfied or modified, how the reader recapitulates "evidence" from the portion of the text he has read to project forward a **configuration,** a tentative assumption of what the work as a whole will be and mean once it is done. The expectations are in part built by the text and in part by the repertoire of the reader, the reader's reading experience and social and cultural knowledge.

Historical Criticism

Dialogism

Another critical approach that gives a significant role to the reader and is particularly useful for long fiction is **dialogism,** largely identified with the work of Mikhail Bakhtin (1895–1975). The dialogic critic bases the study of language and literature on the individual utterance, taking into account the specific time, the place, the speaker, and the listener or reader. Such critics thus see language as a continuous dialogue, each utterance being a reply to what has gone before. Even thought, which they define as inner speech, is a dialogue between utterances that you have taken in. Even your own language (and thus thought) is itself dialogic, for it is made up of the dialogue in which you are engaged, that which you have heard from parents and peers, teachers and television, all kinds of social and professional discourse and reading. Indeed, you speak many "languages"—those of your ethnic, social, economic, national, professional, gender, and other identities. Your individual language consists in the combination of those languages. The literary form in which the dialogic is most interesting, complex, and significant is the novel, for there you have the languages not only of the characters (as you do in drama), but also that of a mediator or narrator and passages of description or analysis or information that seem to come from other voices—newspapers, whaling manuals, legal cases, and so on. Because the world is growing more interrelated and we have multiple voices rather than one dominant voice or language, the novel has become the most appropriate form for the representation of that world.

Because the dialogic sees utterances, including literary utterances or works, as specific to a time and place, one of its dimensions, unlike formalist, structuralist, or psychological criticism, is *historical*. Nineteenth-century **historical criticism** took the obvious fact that a work is created in a specific historical and cultural context and that the author is a member of that context and treated literature as a product of the culture. Formalists and others emphasizing the **aesthetic** value of literature saw this as reducing the literary work to the status of a mere historical document and the abandonment of literary study to history. The dialogic critic sees the work in relation to its host context, a part of the dialogue of the culture. The work in turn helps to create the context for other utterances, literary and otherwise. Some even consider dialogic criticism a form of sociological criticism.

SOCIOLOGICAL CRITICISM More recently, as the scientists from psychology to physics recognized the role of the perceiver in perception, historians realized that they were not only discovering and looking at facts but were finding what they were looking for, selecting facts to fit preconceived views or interpretations. Literary historians or historical critics began to see literature not as a mere passive product of "history" but a contributor and even creator of history. An early form of this kind of historicism was **sociological criticism,** in which literature is seen as one aspect of the larger processes of history, especially those processes involving people acting in social groups or as members of social institutions or movements. Much sociological criticism uses literary texts to illustrate social attitudes and tendencies—and therefore has been strongly resisted by formalists, structuralists, and other "objectivist" critics as not being properly literary—but sociological criticism also attempts to relate what happens in texts to social events and patterns and is as concerned about the effects of texts on human events as about the effects of historical events on texts. Sociological criticism assumes that the most significant aspects of human beings are social and that the most important functions of literature thus involve the way that literature both portrays and influences human interactions. Much sociological criticism centers its attention on contemporary life and texts, seeking to affect both societal directions and literary ones in the present, but some sociological criticism is historical, concerned with differences in different times and places and anxious to interpret directions of literature in terms of historical emphases and patterns.

MARXIST CRITICISM The most insistent and vigorous historicism through most of the 20th century has been **Marxism**, based on the work of Karl Marx (1818–1883). Marxist criticism, like other historical critical methods in the 19th century, treated literature as a passive product of the culture, specifically of the economic aspect, and therefore of class warfare. Economics, the underlying cause of history, was thus the *base*, and culture, including literature and the other arts, the *superstructure*. The literary works of a period would, then, properly viewed from the Marxist perspective, reveal the state of the struggle between classes in the historical place and moment.

Marxist critics, however, early on recognized the role of perception. They insisted that all use of language, including literary and critical language, is **ideological**, that is, that it derives from and expresses preconceived ideas, particularly economic or class values. Criticism is thus not just the product of the culture but part of the discourse or "conversation" that is what we call history. Formalism and even the extreme apolitical position of **aestheticism**, "art for art's sake," by placing art in a realm above the grubbiness of everyday life—above such mundane things as politics and money—removes art from having any importance in that life. This "bourgeois mystification of art" tends to support the class in power. Marxism has traditionally been sensitive to and articulate about power politics in both life and literature, and both its social and literary analysis has often been based on an explicit or implicit political agenda, though many Marxist critics are motivated more by theoretical than practical aims. In recent years, especially in the wake of post-structuralism and the psychoanalytical criticism of the 70s and 80s, Marxist criticism has become increasingly theoretical and less doctrinaire politically. Critics such as Raymond Williams, Fredric Jameson, Terry Eagleton, Pierre Macherey, Walter

Benjamin, and Louis Althusser have gained wide audiences among readers with a variety of political and literary commitments. Over the course of the century, it has been Marxism that has most often and most consistently raised referential and historical issues about literature, and those readers who have been interested in the interactive relationship between literature and life have most often turned for their guidance on such issues to Marxist analysts, whether or not they share their philosophical or political assumptions. In the past decade, however, two other critical schools with strong commitments to historical and cultural issues have become very powerful intellectually and have attracted many practitioners and adherents. These two, feminism and new historicism, have (along with Marxism and, in its way, dialogism) turned critical attention powerfully toward historical and representational issues, and since the mid-1980s they have set the dominant directions in literary criticism.

FEMINIST CRITICISM Like Marxist criticism, feminist criticism derives from firm political and ideological commitments and insists that literature both reflects and influences human behavior in the larger world. Feminist criticism often, too, has practical and political aims. Strongly conscious that most of recorded history has given grossly disproportionate attention to the interests, thoughts, and actions of men, feminist thought endeavors both to extend contemporary attention to distinctively female concerns, ideas, and accomplishments and to recover the largely unrecorded and unknown history of women in earlier times. Not all directions of feminist criticism are historical; feminism has, in fact, taken many different directions and forms in recent years, and it has many different concerns. French feminist criticism, for example, has been deeply influenced by psychoanalysis, especially Lacanian psychoanalysis, and by French post-structuralist emphasis on language. Beyond their common aim of explicating and furthering specifically female interests, feminist critics may differ substantially in their assumptions and emphases. Like Marxism, feminism draws creatively on various other approaches and theories for its several methodologies. The most common historical directions of American feminism in particular involve the recovery of neglected or forgotten texts written by women in earlier times, the redrawing of literary values to include forms of writing (letters and autobiography, for example) that women were able to create when more public and accepted forms were denied to them, the discovery of the roles (positive and negative) that reading played in the lives and consciousnesses of women when they were unable to pursue more "active" and "public" courses, and the sorting out of cultural values implicit in the way women are represented in the texts of particular times and places.

New Historicism

New historicism has less obvious ideological commitments than Marxism or feminism, but it shares their interest in the investigation of how power is distributed and used in different cultures. Drawing on the insights of modern anthropology (and especially on the work of Clifford Geertz), new historicism wishes to isolate the fundamental values in texts and cultures, and it regards texts both as evidence of basic cultural patterns and as forces in cultural and social change. Many of the most influential practitioners of the new historicism come out of the ranks of Marxism and feminism, and new historicists are usually knowledgeable about most varieties of literary theory. Like Marxists and feminists, they are anxious to uncover the ideological commitments in texts, and they care deeply about historical and cultural difference and the way texts represent it. But personal commitments and specific political agendas usually are less important—at least explicitly—to new historicists, and one of the main contentions between feminists and new historicists—or between Marxists and new historicists—involves disagreement about the role that one's own politics should play in the practice of criticism. Many observers regard new historicism as politically to the left in its analysis of traditional cultural values, but critics on the left are suspicious of new historicism, especially of its reluctance to state its premises openly, and they generally regard its assumptions as conservative. Whatever its fundamental political commitments, however (or whether its commitments can be fairly described as having a consistent and specifiable bias), new historicism is far more interested than any other literary approach in social groups generally ignored by literary historians, and it refuses to privilege "literature" over other printed, oral, or material texts. "Popular literature" often gets major attention in the work of new historicists, who see all texts in a culture as somehow expressive of its values and directions and thus as equally useful in determining the larger intellectual, epistemological, and ethical system of which any text is a part. Texts here are thus seen as less specifically individual and distinctive than in most objectivist criticisms, and although new historicists are sometimes interested in the psychology of authors or readers their main concern is with the prevailing tendencies shared across a culture and thus shared across all kinds of texts, whatever their class status, literary value, or political aim.

Pluralism

These classifications are not pigeonholes, and you will notice that many of the approaches overlap: many feminists, especially French feminist critics, are Lacanian or post-structuralist as well, while British feminists often lean toward sociological, especially Marxist, criticism; dialogic critics accept many of the starting points and methods of reader-response and sociological critics, and so on. These crossovers or combinations are generally enriching; they cause problems only when the critic seems to be operating out of contradictory assumptions.

There is a lively debate among critics and theorists at present involving the question of whether readers should bring together the insights and methods of different schools (practitioners of the mixing of methods are usually called **pluralists**) or whether they should commit themselves wholeheartedly to a single system. Pluralists contend that they make use of promising insights or methods wherever they find them and argue that putting together the values of different approaches leads to a more fair and balanced view of texts and their uses. Opponents—those who insist on a consistency of ideological commitment—argue that pluralists are simply unwilling to state or admit their real commitments, and that any mixing of methods leads to confusion, uncertainty, and inconsistency rather than fairness. Readers, conscious or not of their assumptions and their methods, make this basic choice—to follow one lead or many—and the kind of reading they do and the conclusions they come to depend not only on this basic choice but many others suggested by the dominant strands of recent criticism that have been described here. Not all critics are aware of their assumptions, methodologies, or values, and some would even deny that they begin with any particular assumptions or biases, but is is often useful, especially to readers newly learning to practice literary criticism, to sort out their own beliefs carefully and see exactly what kind of difference it makes in the way they read literature and ask questions of it.

Further Reading on Critical Approaches

For good introductions to the issues discussed here, see the following books from which we have drawn in our discussion and definitions:

Robert Alter, *The Pleasures of Reading in an Ideological Age*, New York, 1989
Jonathan Culler, *The Pursuit of Signs*, London, 1981

Jonathan Culler, *On Deconstruction*, London, 1983
Robert Con Davis and Ronald Schleifer, *Contemporary Literary Criticism*, 2d ed., New York, 1989
Mary Eagleton (ed.), *Feminist Literary Theory: A Reader*, Oxford, 1986
Terry Eagleton, *Literary Theory: An Introduction*, Minneapolis, 1983
Nannerl Keohane, Michelle Z. Rosaldo, and Barbara C. Gelpi (eds.), *Feminist Theory: A Critique of Ideology*, Chicago, 1982
Dominick LaCapra, *History and Criticism*, Ithaca, N.Y., 1985
Frank Lentricchia, *After the New Criticism*, Chicago, 1980
Frank Lentricchia and Thomas Mclaughlin (eds.), *Critical Terms for Literary Study*, Chicago, 1990
Richard Macksey and Eugenio Donato (eds.), *The Structuralist Controversy: The Languages of Criticism and the Sciences of Man*, Baltimore, 1972
Toril Moi, *Sexual-Textual Politics*, New York, 1985
Jean Piaget (translated by Chanihan Maschler), *Structuralism*, New York, 1970
Tzvetan Todorov, *Mikhail Bakhtin: The Dialogic Principle*, Minneapolis, 1984

WRITING ABOUT FICTION, POETRY, DRAMA

So far we have been discussing writing about literature in general, rather than writing about a story, a poem, or a play in particular, though we have used specific works as examples. There are topics, such as a study of imagery, symbol, or theme, that are equally applicable to all three genres: you can write a paper on the images or symbols in or the theme of a story, a poem, or a play. Indeed, you can write an essay comparing imagery, say, in a story, poem, and play—comparing the water imagery in James Baldwin's story "Sonny's Blues," for example, with the air or wind imagery in Shelley's "Ode to the West Wind," and the fire or burning imagery in Ibsen's *Hedda Gabler*. Fiction and drama also have action and character in common, so that you can not only choose to write on the plot of a story or play or on characters or characterization in a particular story or play, but you can compare, for example, a character in a story with a character in a play—Atwood's Emma with Ibsen's Hedda perhaps.

Narrative

A story has not only elements common to all three genres, such as plot and character, however; it also has something special—a narrator, someone who tells the story. Everything in fiction—action, character, theme, structure, even the language—is mediated: everything comes to us through an intervening mind or voice; we often see the story from a particular vantage point or several vantage points (*focus*) and always are told the story by someone, whether that someone is identified or is merely a disembodied *voice*. We must be aware of the narration, the means by which the story comes to us. We must be aware that the action, characters, all the elements in a story, are always mediated (there is someone between us and the story), and that the mediation contributes greatly to the meaning, structure, and effect of the story. Who is telling us the story of "The Lame Shall Enter First"? What is the physical and emotional relationship of the narrator of that story to its characters? How would you describe the language or voice of the narration? These are essential questions to ask about Flannery O'Connor's superb story, and in answering them you may want to write a paper called "The Narrator in 'The Lame Shall Enter First' " (or, if you want to be more dramatic, "The Ghostly Reporter of 'The Lame Shall Enter First' ". A story is told *to* someone as well as by someone, and you might want to ask yourself what the relationship is supposed to be between us—the audience—and the narrator. To what kind of audience is the narrator of "Our Friend Judith" telling her story? How do we, as readers, differ from that audience? What impression of the narrator do we form that she does not intend? Such questions might lead to an analysis of the tone of that story—and a paper we might sardonically call "With Friends Like Judith's . . ." These are the kinds of questions raised by the simple but central fact that stories do not come to us directly but are narrated; these are therefore the kinds of questions of special importance to readers of fiction and the kinds of questions writing about fiction frequently centers upon.

Even the conventional past tense in fiction that we take for granted implies a narrator. Since the story is not happening "now," in the present, is not being enacted before us but is over with, having already happened in the past, it is being recalled, and someone must be recalling it, someone who knows what happened and how it all came out. That someone is the narrator. Knowing the end, the narrator has been able to select and shape the events and details. For that reason everything in a well-constructed story is relevant and significant.

Even narrative time is purposefully structured. Stories, unlike actual time as we know it, have beginnings and endings, but they do not have to begin at the beginning and proceed in a uniform direction at a uniform pace toward the end. They can be told from end to beginning, or even from middle to beginning to end, as in "Sonny's Blues." In a story an hour, day, or decade can be skipped or condensed into a narrative moment (a phrase or sentence), or a moment can be expanded to fill pages. Since this manipulation of time affects the meaning and effect of the story, we must pay close attention to it and question its significance. For example, the beginning of the third chapter of "An Occurrence at Owl Creek Bridge" follows immediately from the end of the first chapter, so why is the second chapter there at all? Why does the first chapter cover only a few minutes of action but the third chapter, only a little longer, cover what seems to be a whole day? Can you explain why—in terms of meaning and effect—each of the lengthy scenes in "The Lady with the Dog" is dwelled upon? Why other, longer periods are briefly summarized or skipped? Why do some stories, such as "Her First Ball," cover only a very short period of time, while other, such as "A Rose for Emily" cover years and years? Why are stories such as "Her First Ball" presented largely through dialogue, while others, such as "A Rose for Emily," are "told" rather than presented, with few dramatized scenes and little dialogue?

Dramatization

Scenes presented more or less immediately (that is, without mediation) through dialogue and action, taking place over a short period of time, are said to be *dramatized*. Though there may be gaps of time *between* the senes or acts of a play, once the action begins it takes exactly as much time on the stage as it would in actuality: the actors speak and move in "real" time. Though there is, of course, a playwright who knew how it would all come out and has shaped the play accordingly, the language of the play that we respond to is in the present tense, the dialogue and action are happening in the present, right before our eyes. And though the playwright has written all the lines, his or her voice is not directly heard: only the characters speak. Neither the playwright nor a surrogate in the form of a narrator stands at your elbow to tell you who are the good guys and who the bad, what each character is like or whether what is being said is true, distorted, false. Only very rarely—as in the Shakespearean soliloquy or aside—do we know what a character is thinking. In plays such as *Oedipus the King* and even *Hamlet*, there are only very brief indications of setting, costume, movement of characters, tone of voice, if they are present at Such stage directions—which may be as elaborate as the detailed description of setting and costumes and the instructions for action and tone in *Hedda Gabler*—are not, in a sense, purely dramatic. Watching a play being performed on a stage, we do not see or hear these words at all. On the page, they are usually distinguished from the text of the play by italics or some other typographical device, so as we read we register—or are supposed to register—them as separate from "the play itself." They seen to belong to some other dimension and clearly belong to a voice other than that of any character.

When we read a play we tend to imagine it—in the literal sense of putting it into images—in our minds as if it were being performed on a stage. We act, as it were, as our own directors; if we were to put into words all that would be necessary to stage the play as we see it in our minds, we would be writing the stage directions, or narrative, of the play. The relative absence of such narrative in drama makes our part in the imaging or staging of a play as we read more crucial than it is in reading fiction. How you would stage a play or a scene in order to bring out its full meaning and effect as you imagined it can serve as a significant topic for writing about drama. You might ask yourself such questions as, What instructions would I give the actors for speaking the apparently banal lines of "The Black and White" and what effect would I strive for? What scene or passage would I use as the best example of how the play should be read? How would I costume Oedipus in the first and last scenes in order to bring out the main movement and theme of the play? How can I, in the early scenes, subtly reveal that Oedipus has an injured ankle without detracting from the power and majesty of his presence at that time? . . . In the middle of his stage directions describing the set for *Hedda Gabler*, Ibsen specifies that on the rear wall of the smaller room there "hangs the portrait of a handsome old man in general's uniform." What, precisely, should this portrait look like? What expression should be on the general's face? How prominent should the picture be in the set as a whole?

Though you may wish to write on the theme, characters, action, imagery, or language of a play from time to time, one central element you will certainly want to write about sooner or later is the staging, or dramatization—the set, costumes, acting, moving of characters about on the stage, even lighting—and how this can enhance the effect and meaning of the play on the page.

Words

Some plays, like *Hamlet*, are written partly or entirely in verse. Though we may be able to make a distinction between poetry and verse, it is reasonable to say that as the term is generally used, poetry itself is not so much a literary genre as it is a medium. It might be more logical to break literature down into "prose" and "poetry" rather than into "fiction," "drama," and "poetry." For besides poetic dramas like *Hamlet*, there are also dramatic poems, such as Browning's "My Last Duchess" and John Donne's "The Flea," poems in which a distinguishable character speaks in a definable, almost "stageable" situation. There are also narrative poems, those that tell a story through a narrator, such as "Sir Patrick Spens" or *Paradise Lost*. What these and other poems—lyrics, for example—have in common is rhythmical language (and, some people would add, highly figurative language).

All literature is embodied in words, of course, but poetry uses words most intensely, most fully. It uses not only the statements words make, what they signify or *denote*, using them with great precision; not only what words suggest or *connote*, usually with wide-ranging sensitivity and inclusiveness; but the very sounds of the words themselves. Not all poems have highly patterned or very regular meter, but almost all poetry is more highly patterned than almost any prose. Not all poems rhyme, but it seems safe to say that all extensively rhymed works are poems. So much writing about poetry concentrates on the words themselves: some treats the patterns of sounds, the rhythms or rhymes, some the precision or suggestiveness of the language, and some the relation of sounds to shades of meaning. This is not to say that excellent papers may not be written on the themes, characters, settings of poems. There are many excellent topics as well for comparative papers; the themes of a poem and a story may be compared—"Dover Beach" and "The Lady with the Dog," for example—or of a poem and a play—"[a salesman is an it that stinks Excuse]" and *Death of a Salesman*, perhaps. But in writing about poetry, even when discussing theme or other elements, at some point one usually comes to concentrate on the medium itself, the sound, precision, suggestiveness of the language. The sample paper on Dryden's "To the Memory of Mr. Oldham" (p. 1977) is an example of how one writes about this central element of poetry, words.

Sample Topics and Titles

We have been stressing, on the one hand, writing about the most characteristic elements of stories, plays, and poems—narration, dramatization, and words—and on the other hand, writing about the elements common to all three genres, like theme or symbols. For further hints about likely topics you might look at the chapter headings in the table of contents of this volume and read the introductory material to the chapter, or chapters, that looks most interesting or most promising for your immediate purpose. You might look, too, at the list of sample topics that follows, not so much for the topic that you will actually come to write on but as a trigger for your own imagination and ideas.

Fiction

1. A Plotless Story about Plot: Grace Paley's "A Conversation with My Father"
2. The Selection and Ordering of the Scenes in "The Country Husband"
3. What does the voice in "Love Medicine" contribute to the story's structure, tone, and effect?
4. Who Am I? The Nature of the Narrator in "Our Friend Judith"

5. The Self-Characterization of Montresor in "The Cask of Amontillado"
6. Sonny's Brother's Character
7. Beyond the Literal: Symbolism in "Beyond the Pale"
8. The Image and Import of the Sea in "The Lady with the Dog"
9. "Only a Girl": The Theme of "Boys and Girls"
10. What is the theme of "The Rocking-Horse Winner," and how does it relate to the title of the story?

Poetry

1. Attitudes toward Authority in "Sir Patrick Spens"
2. Scene, Sequence, and Time in "Sir Patrick Spens"
3. Sir Patrick Spens as a Tragic Hero
4. Why "Facts" Are Missing in "Western Wind"
5. Birth and Death Imagery in "The Death of the Ball Turret Gunner"
6. Varieties of Violence in Frost's "Range-Finding"
7. The Characterization of God in "Channel Firing"
8. The Idea of Flight in "Ode to a Nightingale"
9. Attitudes toward the Past in "Mr. Flood's Party" and "They Flee from Me"
10. Satire of Distinctive American Traits in "Boom," "Dirge" and "What the Motorcycle Said"

Drama

1. What is the conflict and what is the reversal (peripety) in *The Brute?*
2. What is the effect on the reader or audience of having so much of the major actions of *Hedda Gabler* (or *Oedipus*) happen offstage?
3. Rosencrantz and Guildenstern as Half-Men in *Hamlet*
4. The Past Recaptured: What We Know (or can Infer) about Blanche's Life in A *Streetcar Named Desire*
5. Varieties of Verbal Wit as a Device of Characterization in *The Importance of Being Earnest*
6. Realistic Drama versus Comedy: Love and Marriage in *Hedda Gabler* and *The Importance of Being Earnest*
7. Staging Polonius: Language and Cliché as Guides to Gestures, Facial Expression, and Character in *Hamlet*
8. How important is the visual impression that Hedda makes in *Hedda Gabler?* How would you stage her appearance? How would you clothe

her? What gestures would you give her? How would you instruct the actress playing her to speak? What textual clues lead you to your decisions?

Intergeneric Topics

1. Motivation in *Hedda Gabler* and "Aunt Jennifer's Tigers"
2. The Functions of Spare Language in "A Clean, Well-Lighted Place" and "On My First Son"
3. The Uses of Fantasy in "Araby" and "[Wild Nights—Wild Nights!]"
4. The Disillusioned Lovers in Joyce's "Araby" and Wyatt's "They Flee from Me"
5. The Loyalty of the Survivor: de Maupassant's "The Jewelry" and Chekhov's "The Brute"
6. Francis Weed and Troy Maxon: A Comparison
7. The Murderer Confesses: Browning's Duke of Ferrara and Poe's Montresor
8. Remembering Grandma: Dorothy Livesay's "Green Rain" and Mordecai Richler's "The Summer My Grandmother Was Supposed to Die"

Creative Topics

1. The speaker in "My Last Duchess" has been charged with the murder of his last duchess. On the basis on his words in the poem, prepare a case for the prosecution.
2. Write a "reply" to the speaker of "To His Coy Mistress," declining his invitation and picking out the flaws in his argument.
3. Write a soliloquy for Gertrude *(Hamlet)* in which she defends herself against the most serious charges made against her motives and conduct.
4. Reconstruct the events and sentiments in "Dover Beach" as a short mood play by writing dialogue and stage directions for a scene between the speaker and the woman.
5. Retell (in poetry or prose) the story in "Cherrylog Road" from the point of view of the woman who is looking back on the experience twenty years later.
6. Using "Fern Hill" as a model, write the kind of imaginary reverie Hedda Gabler might have written about her childhood.
7. What would happen in your neighborhood (town) if one morning there appeared a very old man with enormous wings?

8. Elo's (Joe Lee's) Version of the Dance in "My Man Bovanne"
9. Select three scenes for a one-act play called "The Rocking-Horse Winner"
10. Choose a story from *Reading More Fiction* that you have not read before (perhaps "The Yellow Wallpaper"), read to a crucial point or a pause marked by the author, and describe your expectations of how the story will develop and conclude.

DECIDING WHAT TO WRITE ABOUT

Having Something to Say

Deciding what to write about—what approach to use, which questions to ask—seems like the first step in the process of writing a paper about a work of literature. It isn't. Before that, you have to have confidence that you have something to say. If you are a beginner at this kind of writing, you are likely to have deep doubts about that. Developing confidence is not, at the beginning, easy. You may feel as if you can *never* begin and want to put off the paper forever, or you may want to plunge in fast and get it over with. Either of these approaches, though common and tempting, is a mistake: the best way is to begin preparing for the paper as soon as possible—the moment you know you have one to write—but not to hurry into the writing itself.

The first step is to get close enough to the work to feel comfortable with it. Before you can tell anyone else about what you have read—and writing about literature is just another form of talking about literature, although a more formal and organized one—you need to "know" the work, to have a sure sense of what the work itself is like, how its parts function, what ideas it expresses, how it creates particular effects, how it makes you feel. And the only way you will get to know the work is to spend time with it, reading it carefully and thoughtfully and turning it over in your mind. There is no substitute for reading, several times and with care, the work you are going to write about *before* you pick up a pen and prepare to write. And let your reading be the *work itself,* not something *about* that work, at least at first; later, your instructor may steer you to background materials or to critical readings about the work, but at first you should encounter the work alone and become aware of your own private responses to the work.

Begin, then, by reading, several times, the work you are going to write about. The first time, read it straight through at one sitting: read slowly, pausing at its natural divisions—between paragraphs or stanzas, or at the ends of scenes—to consider how you are responding to the work. Later, when your knowledge of the work is more nearly complete and when you have the "feel" of the whole, you can compare your early responses with your more considered thoughts about the work, in effect "correcting" your first impressions in whatever way seems necessary on the basis of new and better knowledge. But if you are non-committal at first, refusing to notice what you think and feel, you will have nothing to correct, and you may cut yourself off from the most direct routes of response. Feelings are not always reliable—about literature any more than about people—but they are always the first point of contact with a literary work: you feel before you think. Try to start with your mind open, as if it were a blank sheet of paper ready to receive an impression from what you read.

When you have finished a first reading, think about your first impressions. Think about how the work began, how it gained your interest, how its conflicts and issues were resolved, how it ended, how it made you feel from beginning to end. Write down any phrases or events that you remember especially vividly, anything you are afraid you might forget. Look back at any parts that puzzled you at first. Write down in one sentence what you think the story, poem, or play is about. Then read it again, this time much more slowly, making notes as you go on any passages that seem especially significant and pausing over any features or passages that puzzle you. Then write a longer statement—three or four sentences—summarizing the work and suggesting more fully what it seems to be about. Try to write the kind of summary described above on pages 1377–79.

Stop. Do something else for a while, something as different as possible—see a movie, do math problems, ride a bicycle, listen to music, have a meal, take a nap, mow the lawn, build a loft. Do NOT do some other reading you have been meaning to do. When you go back to the work and finish reading it for the third time—rapidly and straight through—write down in a sentence the most important thing you would want to tell someone else who was about to read it for the first time: not just whether you liked it or not, but what exactly you liked, how the whole story seems to have worked.

Now you are ready to choose a topic.

Choosing a Topic

Once you are ready to choose a topic, the chances are that you have already—quietly and unconsciously—chosen one. The clue is in the last statement you wrote. The desire to tell someone about a work of literature is a wonderful place to begin. Good papers almost always grow out of a desire to communicate. Desire is not enough, of course—the substance (and most of the work, sentence by sentence) is still ahead of you; but desire will get you started. Chances are that what you wrote down as the one thing you most wanted to say is close to the heart of the central issue in the work you are going to write about. Your statement will become, perhaps, in somewhat revised form, your thesis.

The next step is to convert your personal feelings and desire to communicate into something communicable—into an "objective" statement about the work, a statement that will mean something to someone else. Again, you may already be further along than you realize. Look at the "summary" you wrote after your second reading. The summary will probably sound factual, objective, and general about the work; the personal statement you wrote after the third reading will be more emotional, subjective, and particular about some aspect of the work. In combining the two successfully lies the key to a good paper: what you need to do is to write persuasively an elaboration and explanation of the last statement so that your reader comes to share the "objective" view of the whole work that your summary expresses. The summary you have written will, in short, be implicit in the whole essay; your total essay will suggest to your reader the wholeness of the work you are writing about, but it will do so by focusing its attention on some particular aspect of the work—on a part that leads to, or suggests, or represents the whole. What you want to do is build an essay on the basis of your first statement, taking a firm hold on the handle you have found. The summary is your limit and guide: it reminds you of where you will come out. Any good topic ultimately leads back to the crucial perceptions involved in a summary. Ultimately, any good writing about literature leads to a full and resonant sense of the central thrust of the work, but the most effective way to find that center is by discovering a pathway that particularly interests you. The best writing about literature presents a clear—and well-argued—thesis about a work or works and presents it from the perspective of personal, individual perception. But the thesis should clarify the central thrust of the work, helping it to open itself up to readers more completely and more satisfyingly.

Topics often suggest themselves after a second or third reading, simply because one feature or problem stands out so prominently that it almost demands to be talked about. What is real in "The Real Thing"? Will the love between Gurov and the lady with the dog last? Sometimes you may be lucky: your instructor may *assign* a topic instead of asking you to choose your own. At first glance, that may not seem like a good break: it often feels confining to follow specific directions or to have to operate within limits and rules prescribed by someone else. The advantage is that it may save a lot of time and prevent floundering around. If your instructor assigns a topic, it is almost certain to be one that will work, one that has a payoff if you approach it creatively and without too much resentment at being directed so closely and precisely. It is time-consuming, even when you have tentatively picked a topic, to think through its implications and be sure it works. And an instructor's directions, especially if they are detailed and call attention to particular questions or passages, may aid greatly in helping you focus on particular issues or in leading you to evidence crucial to the topic.

If your instructor does *not* give you a topic and if no topic suggests itself to you after you have read a particular work three or four times, you may sometimes have to settle for the kind of topic that will—more or less—be safe for any literary work. Some topics are almost all-purpose. You can always analyze devices of characterization in a story, showing how descriptive detail, dialogue, and the reactions of other people in the story combine to present a particular character and evoke the reader's response to him or her; with a poem you can almost always write an adequate paper analyzing rhythm, or verse form, or imagery, or the connotations of key words. Such "fall-back" topics are, however, best used only as last resorts, when your instincts have failed you in a particular instance. When choice is free, a more lively and committed paper is likely to begin from a particular insight or question, something that grabs you and makes you want to say something, or solve a problem, or formulate a thesis. The best papers are usually very personal in origin; even when a topic is set by the assignment, the best papers come from a sense of having personally found an answer to a significant question. To turn a promising idea into a good paper, however, personal responses usually need to be supported by a considerable mass of evidence; the process often resembles the testing of "evidence" in a laboratory or the formulation of hypotheses and arguments in a law case—and they will usually need to go through repeated written revisions that will sharpen and refine them.

Considering Your Audience

Thinking of your paper as an argument or an explanation will also help with one of the most sensitive issues in writing about literature. The issue: To whom are you writing? Who is your audience? The obvious answer is, your instructor, but in an important sense, that is the wrong answer. It is wrong because, although it could literally be true that your instructor will be the only person (besides you) who will ever read your paper, your object in writing about literature is to learn to write for an audience of peers, people a lot like yourself who are sensible, pretty well educated, and need to have something (in this case a literary work) explained to them so that they will be able to understand it more fully. Picture your ideal reader as someone about your own age and with about the same educational background. Assume that the person is intelligent and has some idea of what literature is like and how it works, but that he or she has just read this particular literary work for the first time and has not yet had a chance to think about it carefully. Don't be insulting and explain the obvious, but don't assume either that your reader has noticed and considered every detail. The object is to inform and convince your reader, not to try to impress.

Should you, then, altogether ignore the obvious fact that it is an instructor—probably with a master's degree or Ph.D. in literature—who is your actual reader? Not altogether: you don't want to get so carried away with speaking to people of your own age and interests that you slip into slang, or feel the need to explain what a stanza is, or leave an allusion to a rock star unexplained, and you do want to learn from the kind of advice your instructor has given in class or from comments he or she may have made on other papers you have written. But don't become preoccupied with the idea that you are writing for someone in "authority" or someone you need to please. Most of all, don't think of yourself as writing for a captive audience, for a reader who *has* to read what you write. It is not always easy to know exactly who your audience is or how interested your readers may be, so you have to make the most of every single word. It is your job to get the reader's attention. And you will have to do it subtly, making conscious assumptions about what your reader already knows and what he or she can readily understand. You cannot, as in a conversation, watch the facial expressions, the eyes, the gestures of your audience and improvise. The tone of your paper should be serious and straightforward and its attitude respectful toward the reader, as well as toward the literary work. But its approach and vocabulary, while formal enough for academic writing, should be readily understandable by someone with your own background and reading experience. And it should be lively enough to interest someone like you. Try to imagine, as your ideal reader, the person in your class whom you most respect. Write to get, and hold, that person's serious attention. Try to communicate, try to teach.

FROM TOPIC TO ROUGH DRAFT

Writing about literature is very much like talking about literature. But there is one important difference. When we talk, we organize as we go—trying to get a handle, experimenting, working toward an understanding. And the early stages of preparing a paper—the notetaking, the outlining, the rough drafts—are much like that. A "finished" paper, however, has the uncertainties and tentativeness worked out and presents an argument that moves carefully and compellingly toward a conclusion. How does one get from here to there?

Once you have decided on a topic, the process of planning is fairly straightforward, but it can be time consuming and (often) frustrating. There are three basic steps in the planning process: first you gather the evidence, then you sort it into order, and (finally) you develop it into a convincing argument. The easiest way is to take these steps one by one.

Gathering Evidence

The first step involves accumulating evidence that supports the statement you have decided to make about your topic (that is, your thesis), and that takes you back (yet once more) to the text. But before you read the text again, look over the notes you have already made in the margin of that text or on separate pieces of paper. Which of them have something to do with the topic you have now defined? Which of them will be useful to you in making your main point? Which ones can you now set aside as irrelevant to the topic you have decided on?

Reading over the notes you have already made is a good preparation for rereading the work again, for this time as you read it (at least the fourth time you will have read it) you will be looking at it in a new and quite specific way, looking for all the things in it that relate to the topic you have decided on. This time you will, in effect, be flagging everything—words, phrases, structural devices, changes of tone, anything—that bears upon your topic. As you read—very slowly and single-mindedly, with your topic always in mind—keep your pen constantly poised to mark useful points. Be ready to say something about the points as you come upon them; it's a good idea to write down, immediately, any sentences that occur to you as you re-read this time. Some of these sentences will turn out to be useful when you actually begin to write your paper. Some will be incorporated in your paper; but some will not: you will find that a lot of the notes you take, like a lot of the footage shot in making a film, will end up on the cutting room floor.

No one can tell you exactly how to take notes. Good notetaking is a highly individualized skill; precisely what notes you will need to take and how will depend on the particulars of the paper you are about to write. Ultimately, you will develop a style that is right for you, but some general guidelines may be useful. Here are five hints toward successful notetaking.

1. Keep your topic and your thesis about your topic constantly in mind as you re-read and take notes. Mark all passages in the work that bear on your topic, and for each one write on a note card a single sentence that describes how the passage relates to your topic and thesis. Indicate, for each passage, the specific location in the text—by page or paragraph number if you are working on a story; by line number if you are writing about a poem; by act, scene, and line number if you are writing about a play.

2. Keep re-reading and taking notes until one of five things happens:
   a. You get too tired and lose your concentration. (If that happens, stop and then start again when you are rested, preferably the next day.)
   b. You stop finding relevant passages or perceive a noticeable drying up of your ideas. (Again, time to pause; give the work at least one more reading later when your mind is fresh and see whether the juices start anew. If they don't, you may be ready to outline and write.)
   c. You begin to find yourself annotating every single sentence or line, and the evidence all begins to run together into a single blob. (Stop and sort out your thesis again, simplifying and narrowing it so that you don't try to include everything. Then go back to your notetaking and discriminate more carefully between what actually is important to your thesis and what only relates at some distance.)
   d. You become impatient with your notetaking and can't wait to get started writing. (Start writing. Use scrap paper, and be prepared to go back to systematic notetaking if your ideas or your energy fade. The chances are that the prose passages you write this way will find a place in your paper, but they may not belong exactly where you think they do when you first write them down.)
   e. You find that there is insufficient evidence for your thesis, that the evidence points in another direction, or that the evidence contradicts

your thesis. (Revise your topic to reflect the evidence, and begin re-reading once more.)

3. When you think you have finished your notetaking, read all your note cards over slowly, one by one, and jot down any further ideas as they occur to you, each one on a separate note card. (Sometimes it will seem as if note cards beget note cards. Too much is better than too little at the notetaking stage: you can always discard them before the final draft. Don't worry if you seem to have too many notes and too much material. But later, when you boil down to essentials, you will have to be ruthless with yourself and omit some of your favorite ideas.)

4. Transfer all of your notes to pieces of paper—or note cards—that are all the same size, one note on each. It is easier to sort them this way when you get ready to organize and outline. If you like to write notes in the margin of your text (or on the backs of envelopes, or on dinner napkins, or shirtsleeves), systematically transfer every note to uniform sheets of paper or cards before you begin to outline. Having everything easily recorded on sortable cards that can be moved from one pile to another makes organizing easier later, especially when you change your mind (as you will) and decide to move a point from one part of your paper to another. Index cards—either 3 × 5, if you write small and make economical notes, or 4 × 6, if you need more space—are ideal for notetaking and sorting.

5. When you think you are done taking notes (because you are out of ideas, or out of time, or getting beyond a manageable number of pieces of evidence), read through the whole pile one more time, again letting any new ideas—or ideas that take on a fresh look because you combine them in a new way—spawn new sentences for new note cards.

How many times should you read a story, poem, or play before you stop taking notes? There is no right answer. If you have read the work three times before settling on a topic, two more readings may do. But it could take several more. Common sense, endurance, and deadlines will all have an effect on how many re-readings you do. Let your conscience, your judgment, and your clock be your guides.

Organizing Your Notes

The notes you have taken will become, in the next few hours, almost the whole content of your paper. The task remaining is to give that content the form and shape that will make it appealing and persuasive. But it is not an easy task: the best content in the world isn't worth much if it isn't effectively presented. The key to the task is getting all your ideas into the right order, that is, into a sequence that will allow them to argue your thesis most persuasively.

In order to put your notes into a proper order, you will need (ironically) to get a little distance from your notes. (The key to good planning and writing—and to many other pursuits—is in knowing when to back away and get some perspective.) Set your notes aside, but not too far away. On a fresh sheet of paper, write down all the major points you want to be sure to make. Write them down randomly, as they occur to you. Now read quickly through your pack of note cards and add to your list any important points you have left out. Then decide which ideas should go first, which should go second, and so on.

Putting your points in order is something of a guess at this point. You may well want to re-order them before you begin to write—or later when you are writing a first (or even later) draft. But make your best guess. The easiest way to try out an order is to take your random list and put a 1 in front of the point you will probably begin with, a 2 before the probable second point, and so on. Then copy the list, in numerical order, onto a clean sheet of paper, revising (if you need to) as you go. Do not be surprised if later you have to revise your list further. Your next task is to match up your note cards (and the examples they contain) with the points on your outline.

Putting things in a particular order is a spatial problem, and by having your notes on cards or pieces of paper of a uniform size you can do much of your organizing physically. Do your sorting on a large table or sit in the middle of the floor. Prepare a title card for each point in your outline, writing on it the point and its probable place in your paper, then line them up on the table or floor in order before you begin writing.

Two-thirds of this exercise is quite easy: most examples and ideas you have written down will match quite easily with a particular point. But some cards will resist classification. Some cards will seem to belong in two or more places; others will not seem to belong at all. If a card seems to belong to more than one point, put it in the pile with the lowest number (but write on it the number or numbers of other possible locations). If, for example, a card might belong in point 2 but could also belong in point 6 or 9, put it in the pile of 2's and write "maybe 6 or 9" on the card; if you don't use it in writing about point 2 move it to pile 6; if you don't use it in 6, move it to 9. Remember that you will work your way through the piles in numerical order, so that you have a safety system for notes that don't seem to belong where you first thought but that still belong somewhere in your paper. Move them to a possible later point, or put them in a special pile (marked "?" or "use in revised draft") and, once you have completed a first draft on your paper, go through this pile, carefully looking for places in your paper where these ideas may belong. Almost never will everything fit neatly into your first draft. If everything does seem to fit exactly as you had originally planned, you have either done an incredible job of planning and guessing about the organization of your paper, or you are forcing things into inappropriate places.

Don't be surprised if you have a large number of leftover note cards, that is, cards whose ideas you haven't yet used, after you have written your first draft. You will probably find places for many of these ideas later, but some just won't fit and won't be needed for the paper you ultimately write, no matter how good the ideas are. No paper will do everything it could do. Writing a paper is a *human* project; it has limits.

Before you actually start writing, you may want to develop a more elaborate outline, incorporating your examples and including topic sentences for each paragraph, or you may wish to work from your sketchy outline and the accompanying packs of cards. Do the more detailed outline if it seems right to you, but don't delay the writing too long. You are probably ready right now, and any exercises you invent to delay writing are probably just excuses.

Developing an Argument

Once you have decided on your major points and assembled your evidence, you have to decide how you are going to present your argument and how you are going to present *yourself*. What you say is, of course, more important than how you say it, but your manner of presentation can make a world of difference. Putting your evidence together effectively—in a coherent and logical order so that your readers' curiosities and questions are answered systematically and fully—is half the task in developing a persuasive argument. The other half involves your choice of a voice and tone that will make readers want to read on—and make them favorably disposed toward what you say.

The tone of your paper is the basis of your relationship with your reader. "I will be just *me*," you may say, "and write naturally." But writing is not a "natural" act, any more than swinging a tennis racket, carrying a football, or dancing a pirouette. The "me" you choose to present is only one of several possible me's; you will project a certain mood, a certain attitude toward your subject, a certain confidence. How do you want your readers to feel about you and your argument? Being too positive can make your readers fell stupid and inadequate and can turn them into defensive, resistant readers who will rebel at your every point. Friendship with your reader is better than an adversary relationship. Sounding like a nice person who is talking reasonably and sensibly is not enough if in fact you don't make sense or have nothing to say, but the purpose of the tone you choose is to make your reader receptive to your content, not hostile. The rest of the job depends on the argument itself.

It has been said that all good papers should be organized in the same way:

1. Tell 'em what you're going to tell 'em.
2. Tell 'em.
3. Tell 'em what you told 'em.

That description fits—in pretty general terms—the most common kind of organization, which includes an introduction, a body of argument, and a conclusion, but if it is followed too simplistically it can lead to a paper that sounds simple-minded. The beginning does need to introduce the subject, sort out the essential issues, and suggest what your perspective will be, and the conclusion does need to sum up what you have said in the main part of your paper, but the first paragraph shouldn't give *everything* away, nor should the final one simply repeat what is already clear. Lead into your subject clearly but with a little subtlety; arrange your main points in the most effective manner you can think of, building a logical argument and supporting your general points with clear textual evidence, concisely phrased and presented, and at the end show *how* your argument has added up—don't just *say* that it did.

There are, of course, other ways to organize than the basic Tell-3 method, but the imagination and originality that can be exercised in a straightforward Tell-3 paper are practically unlimited.

Writing the First Draft

It is now time to set pen to paper. No one can help you much now for a while. The main thing is to get started right with a clear first sentence that expresses your sense of direction and arrests the attention of your readers. (If you can't think of a good first sentence, don't pause over it too long. Write down a paraphrase of what you want it to say—something like the statement you wrote down after your third reading—and go on to start writing about your main points. Your "first" sentence may sometimes be the last one you will write.)

And then you inch along, word by word and sentence by sentence, as you follow your outline from one paragraph to another. Keep at it. Struggle. Stare into space. Bite your pen when you feel like it. Get up and stride about the room. Scratch your head. Sharpen a pencil. Run your fingers through your hair. Groan. Snap your fingers. Pray. But keep writing.

It is often frustrating as you search for the right word or struggle to decide how the next sentence begins, but it is satisfying when you get it right. Stay with it until you complete a draft you think you can live with. Write "The End" at the bottom and set it aside. Breathe a sigh of relief.

And try not to think about the revisions you will do tomorrow.

FROM ROUGH DRAFT TO COMPLETED PAPER

Revising

This final stage of the process is the most important of all, and it is the easiest one to mismanage. There is a world of difference between a bunch of ideas that present a decent interpretation of a work of literature and a cogent, coherent, persuasive essay that will stir your readers to a nod of agreement and shared pleasure in a moment of insight. If you haven't done good literary analysis and sorted out your insights earlier, nothing you do at this stage will help much, but if what you have done so far is satisfactory, this is the stage that can turn your paper into something special.

The important thing is not to allow yourself to be too easily satisfied. If you have struggled with earlier stages, it may be tempting to think you are finished when you have put a period to the last sentence in your first draft. It will often feel as if you are done: you may feel drained, tired of the subject, anxious to get on to other things, such as sleep or food or friends or another project. And it *is* a good idea to take a break once you've finished a draft and let what you have done settle for a few hours, preferably overnight. (The Roman poet and critic Horace suggested putting a draft aside for nine years, but most instructors won't wait that long.) Re-reading it "cold" may be discouraging, though: all those sentences that felt so good when you wrote them often seem flat and stale, or even worthless, when a little time has elapsed. The biggest struggle in moving from a first draft to a second one is to keep from throwing what you have written into a wastebasket—or to keep from throwing up on top of it. Resist. It will get better, but not without your help.

It may take *several* more drafts to produce your best work. Often it is tempting to cut corners—to smooth out a troublesome paragraph by obscuring the issue or by omitting the difficult point altogether instead of confronting it, or to ask a roommate or friend for help in figuring out what is wrong with a particular passage. But you will learn more in the long run—and probably do better in the short run as well—if you make yourself struggle a bit. When a particular word or phrase you have used turns out to be imprecise, or misleading, or ambiguous, search until you find the *right* word or phrase. (At the least put a big X in the margin so that you will come back and fix it later.) If a paragraph is incomplete or poorly organized, fill it out or reorganize it. If a transition from one point to another does not work, look again at your outline and see if another way of ordering your points would help. *Never* decide that the problem can best be solved by hoping that your reader will not notice. The satisfaction of finally solving the problem will build your confidence and sooner or later make your writing easier and better.

Reviewing Your Work and Revising Again

Precisely how you move from one draft to another is up to you and will properly depend on the ways you work best; the key is to find all the things that bother you (and that *should* bother you) and then gradually correct them, moving toward a better paper with each succeeding draft. Here are some things to watch for.

Thesis and central thrust: Is it clear what your main point is? Do you state it clearly, effectively, and early? Do you make clear what the work is about? Are you fair to the spirit and emphasis of the work? Do you make clear the relationship between your thesis and the central thrust of the work? Do you explain *how* the work creates its effect rather than just asserting it?

Organization: Does your paper move logically from beginning to end? Does your first paragraph set up the main issue you are going to discuss and suggest the direction of your discussion? Do your paragraphs follow each other in a coherent and logical order? Does the first sentence of each paragraph accurately suggest what that paragraph will contain? Does your final paragraph draw a conclusion that follows from the body of your paper? Do you resolve the issues you say you resolve?

Use of evidence: Do you use enough examples? Too many? Does each example prove what you say it does? Do you explain each example fully enough? Are the examples sufficiently varied? Are any of them labored, or over-explained, or made to bear more weight than they can stand? Have you left out any examples useful to your thesis? Do you include any gratuitous ones just because you like them? Have you achieved a good balance between examples and generalizations?

Tone: How does your voice sound in the paper? Confident? Arrogant?

Boastful? Does it show off too much? Is it too timid or self-effacing? Do you ever sound smug? Too tentative? Too dogmatic? Would a neutral reader be put off by any of your assertions? By your way of arguing? By your choice of examples? By the language you use?

Sentences: Does each sentence read clearly and crisply? Have you rethought and rewritten any sentences you can't explain? Is the first sentence of your paper a strong, clear one likely to gain the interest of a neutral reader? Is the first sentence of each paragraph an especially vigorous one? Are your sentences varied enough? Do you avoid the passive voice and "there is/there are" sentences?

Word Choice: Have you used any words whose meaning you are not sure of? In any cases in which you were not sure of what word to use, did you stay with the problem until you found the exact word? Do your metaphors and figures of speech make literal sense? Are all the idioms used correctly? Is your terminology correct? Are your key words always used to mean *exactly* the same thing? Have you avoided sounding repetitive by varying your sentences rather than using several different terms to mean precisely the same thing?

Conciseness: Have you eliminated all the padding you put in when you didn't think your paper would be long enough? Have you gone through your paper, sentence by sentence, to eliminate all the unnecessary words and phrases? Have you looked for sentences (or even paragraphs) that essentially repeat what you have already said—and eliminated all repetition? Have you checked for multiple examples and pared down to the best and most vivid ones? Have you got rid of all inflated phrasing calculated to impress readers? Have you eliminated all roundabout phrases and rewritten long, complicated, or confusing sentences into shorter, clearer ones? Are you convinced that you have trimmed every possible bit of excess and that you cannot say what you have to say any more economically?

Mechanics: Have you checked the syntax in each *separate* sentence? Have you checked the spelling of any words that you are not sure of or that look funny? Have you examined each sentence separately for punctuation? Have you checked every quotation word by word against the original? Have you given proper credit for all material—written or oral—that you have borrowed from others? Have you followed the directions your instructor gave you for citations, footnotes, and form?

The most effective way to revise in the final stages is to read through your paper looking for one problem at a time, that is, to go through it once looking at paragraphing, another time looking at individual sentences, still another for word choice or problems of grammar. It is almost impossible to check too many things too often—although you can get so absorbed with little things that you overlook larger matters. With practice, you will learn to watch carefully for the kinds of mistakes you are most prone to. Everyone has individual weaknesses and flaws. Here are some of the most common temptations that beginning writers fall for:

1. Haste. (Don't start too late, or finish too soon after you begin.)
2. Pretentiousness. (Don't use words you don't understand, tackle problems that are too big for you, or write sentences you can't explain; it is more important to make sense than to make a big, empty impression.)
3. Boredom. (The quickest way to bore others is to be bored yourself. If you think your paper will be a drag, you are probably right. It is hard to fake interest in something you can't get excited about; keep at it until you find a spark.)
4. Randomness. (Don't try to string together half a dozen unrelated ideas or insights and con yourself into thinking that you have written a paper.)
5. Imprecision. (Don't settle for approximation, either in words or ideas; something that is 50 percent right is also 50 percent wrong.)
6. Universalism. (Don't try to be a philosopher and make grand statements about life; stick to what is in the work you are writing about.)
7. Vagueness. (Don't settle for a general "sense" of the work you are talking about; get it detailed, get it right.)
8. Wandering. (Don't lose track of your subject or the work that you are talking about.)
9. Sloppiness. (Don't sabotage all your hard work on analysis and writing by failing to notice misspelled words, grammatical mistakes, misquotations, incorrect citations or references, or typographical errors. Little oversights make readers suspicious.)
10. Impatience. (Don't be too anxious to get done. Enjoy the experience; savor the process. Have fun watching yourself learn.)

Being flexible—being willing to rethink your ideas and reorder your argument as you go—is crucial to success in writing, especially in writing about literature. You will find different (and better) ways to express your ideas and feelings as you struggle with revisions, and you will also find that—in the course of analyzing the work, preparing to write, writing, and rewriting—your response to the work itself will have grown and shifted somewhat. Part of the reason is that you will have become more knowledgeable as a result of the time and effort you have spent, and you will have a more subtle understanding of the work. But part of the reason will also be that the work itself will not be exactly the same. Just as a work is a little different for every reader, it is also a little different with every successive reading by the *same* reader, and what you will be capturing in your words is some of the subtlety of the work, its capacity to produce effects that are alive and that are therefore always changing just slightly. You need not, therefore, feel that you must say the final word about the work you are writing about—but you do want to say whatever word you have to say in the best possible way.

You can turn all this into a full-time job, of course, but you needn't. It is hard work, and at first the learning seems slow and the payoff questionable. A basketball novice watching the magic of Magic Johnson may find it hard to see the point of practicing lay-ups, but even creative geniuses have to go through those awful moments of sitting down and putting pen to paper (and then crossing out and rewriting again and again). But that's the way you learn to make it seem easy. Art is mostly craft, and craft means methodical work.

It *will* come more easily with practice. But you needn't aspire to professional writing to take pleasure in what you accomplish. Learning to write well about literature will help you with all sorts of tasks, some of them having little to do with writing. Writing trains the mind, creates habits, teaches you procedures that will have all kinds of long-range effects that you may not immediately recognize or be able to predict. And ultimately it is very satisfying, even if it is not easy, to be able to stand back and say, "That is mine. Those are my words. I know what I'm talking about. I understand, and I can make someone else understand."

One final bit of advice: do not follow, too rigidly or too closely, anyone's advice, including ours. We have suggested some general strategies and listed some common pitfalls. But writing is a very personal experience, and you will have talents (and faults) that are a little different from anyone else's. Learn to play to your own strengths and avoid the weaknesses that you are especially prone to. Pay attention to your instructor's comments; learn from your own mistakes.

A SUMMARY OF THE PROCESS

Here, briefly, is a summary, step by step, of the stages we have suggested you move through in preparing a paper about literature.

Stage One: Deciding what to write about

- Read the work straight through, thoughtfully. Make notes at the end on any points that caught your special attention.
- Read the work again more slowly, pausing to think through all the parts you don't understand. When you finish, write a three- or four-sentence summary.
- Read the work again, carefully but quite quickly. Decide what you feel most strongly about in the work, and write down the one thing you would most want to explain to a friend about how the story, poem, or play works, or (if the work still puzzles you) the one question you would most like to be able to answer.
- Decide how the statement you made at the end of your third reading relates to the summary you wrote down after the second reading.
- Write a one-paragraph "promise" of what your paper is going to argue.

Stage Two: Planning your paper

- Read the work at least twice more and make notes on anything that relates to your thesis.
- Read through all your notes so far, and for each write a sentence articulating how it relates to your thesis.
- Transfer all your notes to note cards of uniform size.
- Read through all your notes again and record any new observations or ideas on additional note cards.
- Set aside your note cards for the moment, and make a brief outline of the major points you intend to make.
- Sort the note cards into piles corresponding to the major points in your outline. Sort the cards in each separate pile into the most likely order of their use in the paper.
- Make a more detailed outline (including the most significant examples) from your pile of note cards on each point.

- Reconsider your order of presentation and make any necessary adjustments.
- Begin writing.

Stage Three: Rewriting

- Go over your writing, word by word, sentence by sentence, and paragraph by paragraph, in draft after draft until your writing is worthy of the ideas you want to express.

Stage Four: Final preparation

- Type or word-process. Chances are that your instructor does not have a degree in hieroglyphics.
- Proofread. Who wants to read a paper you did not care enough about to read yourself?
- Proofread again. Find your mistakes before someone else does.
- Read it one more time.
- Keep your fingers crossed.

THREE SAMPLE PAPERS

The essays that follow were written by Geoffrey Clement and Christine Woodside in their first year at Emory University and by Jeanette Sperhac in her first year at the University of Chicago. We are grateful to them for their kind permission to reprint their papers here.

The Struggle to Surface in the Water of "Sonny's Blues"

Geoffrey Clement

In "Sonny's Blues," James Baldwin employs water as a symbol that enables him to concentrate more clearly on the lack of and the crucial need for a real sense of communication among members of society. As Baldwin captures the intensity of Sonny's and his brother's struggles to understand their situation, he vividly depicts a society that seeks to swallow up the souls of its inhabitants and gradually to drown them spiritually. Thus, Baldwin illustrates quite clearly his sense of the hopelessness in man's plight. In portraying the struggle of street life in Harlem, he uses water in its opposite forms—frozen water and boiling water—and toward the end of the story, as Sonny's and his brother's revelations help to resolve the conflict, the water becomes calm.

Initially, and as a result of Sonny's arrest, Sonny's brother gradually realizes that he has not fulfilled his promise and that his feelings of love for his brother have certainly gone unexpressed, if indeed they exist. As a result, he feels physically the coldness that has permeated his emotional life: "It was a special kind of ice. It kept melting, sending trickles of ice water all up and down my veins, but it never got less. Sometimes it hardened and seemed to expand . . ." (par. 2). So the ice represents his guilt and his fears, both of which will lessen little. Although he learns to adapt to these feelings, they occasionally resurface. Upon Sonny's return from prison, for example, his brother thinks, "and thank God she [his wife] was there, for I was filled with that icy dread again. Everything I did seemed awkward to me, and everything I said sounded freighted with hidden meaning. . . . I was dying to hear him tell me he was safe" (par. 76). In addition to this guilt, Sonny's brother experiences much of the same emotional turmoil that Sonny has endured. In this passage in particular, he is seeking reassurance that there is a way to survive their imprisonment without having to feel the pain Sonny felt. Baldwin not only uses ice to show the brother's disappointment in his failures as a brother but also to point to the brother's own struggle for security, identity, and communication.

As Sonny's brother begins to realize that within him there has grown a heart hardened and haunted by the cold darkness of Harlem's streets, he also begins to recognize many of the realities that his brother has faced and that he too must eventually face. Sonny's brother is spiritually walking through "the vivid, killing streets of our childhood. These streets hadn't changed, though housing projects jutted up out of them now like rocks in the middle of a boiling sea" (par. 73). Here, Baldwin paints an almost hellish picture of pain and suffering, of emotional torment and fears, and of spiritual drowning and isolation, all of which slowly become real in the mind of Sonny's brother. He begins to feel for the first time in his life the depth of his denial of his brother. Tragically, he finds that when he is ready to reach out to help Sonny, he cannot, for he is even more lost and confused than Sonny himself. Sonny's brother wants desperately to save Sonny from the inevitable struggle, yet he learns from Sonny that "the storm inside" (par. 217) will pass over only with the constant expression of love. Clearly, the process of revelation is a very dramatic one, since Sonny's brother comes to understand Sonny's need for a giving, communicating, responsible relationship, a commitment filled with careful listening, compassion, and understanding. Sonny does not believe he can make his brother understand his experiences with drugs: "I can never tell you. I was all by myself at the bottom of something, and I thought

I'd die if I couldn't get away from it and yet, all the same, I knew that everything I was doing was just locking me in with it" (par. 220). Once his brother grasps the importance of listening with love and understanding, however, Sonny is finally able to reach out.

Toward the end of the story, the ice and the boiling sea come together, and there is peace; Sonny is able to reach out, and he starts to swim in the calmer water. Now, he finds freedom in expressing his struggles through his music, while at the same time alerting his audience to the lessons he has learned. Creole "wanted Sonny to leave the shoreline and strike out for the deep water. He was Sonny's witness that deep water and drowning were not the same thing" (par. 234). As Sonny ventures further and further into his own understanding of life's struggles, he tries, his brother tells us, "to find new ways to make us listen. For, while the tale of how we suffer, and how we are delighted, and how we may triumph is never new, it always must be heard. . . . it's the only light we've got in all this darkness" (par. 238). In a powerful way, Sonny taught the audience to listen: "Freedom lurked around us and I understood, at last, that he could help us be free if we would listen, that we would never be free until we did" (par. 240). The boiling rage of the streets and the coldness within his heart are reconciled as the brother finally witnesses "Sonny's world" (par. 231). Finally, he recognizes that Sonny has found the strength of knowing that he has discovered in music the outlet through which he can express himself and warn others of his mistakes. He sends up to the bandstand not water, not ice, but Scotch and milk. Sonny sips it in a sort of communion and puts it back on top of the piano, where "it glowed and shook about . . . [his] head like the very cup of trembling" (par. 241).

Thoughout his story, Baldwin stresses the lack of companionship to try to manipulate the reader's emotions. Playing on the contrasts between forms of water, he draws parallels to the theme of emotional conflict within the minds of Sonny and his brother. While the sea is calmer toward the end, there is still a sense of rage, because only in the expression of his struggle is Sonny able to find meaning, satisfaction, and forgiveness for his brother. The streets, society's common ground, still try to isolate its members as each person individually struggles to reach the surface. But if the struggler can find a listening helper, which Sonny finds in his brother, then he will reach the surface and breathe the fulfilling breath of love. The cup of trembling will be taken out of the struggler's hands, the Bible tells us, and will be put "into the hands of them that afflict thee" (p. 300n.). Light gracefully touches and penetrates the surface of the water, and the cup of trembling is still.

Metrical Variation and Meaning in "To the Memory of Mr. Oldham"

Christine Woodside

In his poem "To the Memory of Mr. Oldham," John Dryden rationalizes the death of a fellow satirist by comparing himself to the dead man. He begins by saying they were "cast in the same poetic mold," then considers the fact that Oldham's youth did not prevent him from reaching the "same goal" before the older speaker. Dryden also notes that while age—and thus experience—would have given Oldham a smoother command of the English language, satire and wit do not need such polishing and will "shine" through a less-experienced poet's "rugged line." He points out the possible stagnant quality that experience can nurture and seems to imply both that experience is unnecessary to produce good satire and that Oldham's death was timely, since he had already succeeded. Still, the poem ends in a tired, labored farewell, suggesting that Oldham's death was <u>not</u> timely, and that "fate and gloomy night" surround him. Since this poem is a single stanza, the shifts in thought and tone are subtle. The occasional exceptions to the iambic pentameter emphasize the different themes Dryden addresses. Although the variations in meter do not drastically alter the poem's significance, they do clarify some of the main <u>ideas</u> in the poem.

The first notable idea is the alliance Dryden

feels with Oldham, which is emphasized by four separate metrical variations. The word "allied" in the third line is accented on the first syllable, which disturbs the metrical flow that requires a stress on the second. In the next line, "cast in the same" throws off the iambic rhythm with an unexpected stress on the word "cast." (This also highlights the word "same," since two small words are unaccented between the two.) A third metrical surprise is in the fifth line, where the first three words, "One common note," receive accents. These accents not only emphasize the words, but actually slow down the reader. Another emphasis on unity is in the seventh line, where the first two words yield to stresses on the third and fourth in "To the same goal." All of these unsettling accent changes illustrate Dryden's conviction that both he and Oldham had the same goals in their poetry.

There are two variances in meter that emphasize youth. The first of these occurs when Dryden mentions that Oldham has surpassed his older and more experienced ally in a short amount of time: "While his young friend performed and won the race." Here the word "young" receives the unexpected accent. Not surprisingly, Dryden goes on to discuss Oldham's youth and youth's lack of control over the language. The second metrical variation deals with this inexperience with language, saying that a young poet's work must show "Through the harsh cadence of a rugged line." By position, neither "harsh" nor "cadence" would normally receive the accent, but both stand out noticeably. Interestingly, Dryden chooses to emphasize, metrically, youthful inexperience while at the same time saying that satire does not need an experienced control of the language. By doing this, he is contending that youth is not a handicap, at least not in satire. Still, he does choose to emphasize the "harsh cadence" (the consonants are hard to pronounce) of inexperienced work.

The next three metrical variations shift the attention to experience, which, he says, only "mellows what we write to the dull sweets of rhyme." The word "dull" receives an unexpected accent and, together with "sweets," gives the line a tired, heavy quality. This mirrors Dryden's thought that "maturing time" will only make his work "dull." (Also, as he mentions that rhyme can become stagnant, he has just completed three consecutive rhyming lines; the pattern calls for two.) The second "dull" metrical difference appears in line 22. "Once more, hail" is also slow and heavy because all three words need an accent. Finally, the last line contains six iambic feet instead of five, and the last word is redundant: "But fate and gloomy night encompass thee around." To say "encompass thee" would imply the word "around"; the last word does not change or clarify anything. It merely shows that Dryden allows the "dull sweets of rhyme" to control his choice of words! In the three metrical variations above, Dryden generates the very dullness he criticizes as characteristic of an older, experienced poet such as himself.

This poem discusses the "one common note" Dryden shares with Oldham; it then considers Oldham's youth; then deals with Dryden's age and experience in relation to the dead man's youth. All three of these ideas are reflected in the variations of the iambic pentameter, and the variations strengthen their impact.

The Play's the Thing: Deception in Hamlet

Jeanette Sperhac

Early in Act 1 we are introduced to the young Prince Hamlet who, distraught over his father's death, is defending the utter sincerity of his grief. Alongside the wily banter of the court and the murky circumstances of his mother's marriage, Hamlet's distress is astonishingly genuine and true. But Hamlet's honesty does not appear to last; his hopelessness leads him to don an "antic disposition" and reciprocate the deceit of those around him. He is driven to feign madness, to toy with the sensibilities of courtiers, friends, and even his mother, and to plot the exposure of the king's monstrous crime; these acts seem to be breaches of his honesty, yet all actually uphold a higher end, avenging King Hamlet's murder. Hamlet's seeming descent from sincerity to deceit, and the nested plots and false appearances that ensnare him, can be traced to his first speech, that of an "honest" man.

Hamlet's opening speech resounds with his ideals. "I know not 'seems,'" he claims (I, 2, 81), seeking to dispel his mother's misgivings about his mourning. Not merely claiming sincerity, Hamlet is making a statement fundamental to his character; all that he knows, all that he recognizes, is what is. Appearances are transitory and fleeting; in his distracted state, Hamlet knows and acknowledges only that his father is dead, that his mother's remarriage is suspect, that his grief is warranted. When Hamlet learns later that his father's ghost desires revenge, that fact becomes Hamlet's warrant to do whatever he must to frame Claudius. Further insight into Hamlet's character can be ascertained from "I have that within which passeth show" (I, 2, 90), which, on the surface, articulates the all-encompassing nature of his grief. Once again, there are strong undercurrents; Hamlet knows that he is able to project a false appearance, to act a part that still "passes show" and seems true. Hamlet's first speech makes evident two seemingly contradictory qualities, his conviction and honesty opposite his ability to lie and deceive.

It can hardly be surprising that Hamlet plunges into the rampant currents of deception, feigning madness and playing parts for those around him. The "actions that a man might play" to which Hamlet alluded in his opening speech (I, 2, 89) begin to unfold. Of Polonius he makes a "tedious old fool" (II, 2, 236) by bantering endlessly with the man until he is certain that the prince is mad with unrequited love; Hamlet is harsher with Polonius' daughter, berating Ophelia and mocking his own fond letters to her: "I did love you once . . . [but] you should not have believed me . . . I loved you not" (III, i,

125, 127, 129). Hamlet is torn upon the subject of his mother; though he is tempted to reproach her, though she is playing along with Claudius, his father's ghost has warned him to leave her alone. With his mother, as throughout, Hamlet's justification for his actions and his play-acting lies in the genuine motive that lies paradoxically behind his antic disposition. The ghost of King Hamlet has given irrevocable orders; Hamlet, in his distress, is compelled to obey them, and is drawn deeper into his playing.

Most fundamental of all Hamlet's play-acting is that which involves Claudius, for revenge upon Claudius is Hamlet's true objective. Directly connected to the king is Hamlet's playing and counterplaying with Rosencrantz and Guildenstern, who, at Claudius' request, assume the guises of concerned friends. The perceptive prince cuts instantly through what "seems"; he knows that they are informers. His uncanny sense for what "is" identifies their true intent. In the course of their three-way playing, Hamlet taunts Rosencrantz and Guildenstern with his knowledge, continually mocks them, and even forces them to admit to their doings. "Though you can fret me, you cannot play upon me," Hamlet laughs (III, 2, 379); though Rosencrantz and Guildenstern are hired to spy on him, though it is purportedly their game, Hamlet is the one in control; it is he who plays upon them.

Of the final and most shattering instances of

"playing", the framing of Claudius belongs completely to Hamlet; the exposure of the king's monstrous crime is Hamlet's great scheme. The prince's interest in the travelling players is misinterpreted by Claudius as a healthy diversion; the king never suspects that the crux of Hamlet's revenge lies in the players' art. Claudius' forced admission of the King's murder happens bizarrely, paradoxically, not acknowledged under confrontation, but whimpered in the dark in the response to posed figures on a stage. Hamlet has surpassed his own play-acting and the guile and tact of the court; he turns the false projection of an actor into a vehicle of justice. In his finest moment, Hamlet harnesses the actor's art to accuse Claudius; it is as if the prince is gone so far into playing that he must use puppets for his true intent.

The final scene could be viewed as Claudius' reply to the "Mousetrap." Challenged to an apparently harmless fencing match, Hamlet is doomed to lose his life, either to the tainted foil of Laeertes, his "sporting" opponent, or to the poisoned goblet held by Claudius. The prince is hopelessly trapped; no guise can transport him now, no perception foresee the consequences of the scene. Deception heaped upon deception has caught up with Hamlet at last, and upstaged by Claudius' guile, the prince drags Denmark down with him.

Central to Hamlet are currents of deception:

apparent truths, apparent sentiments, apparent relationships and the submerged realities which they misrepresent. Though the prince's opening speech shows a veneer of sincerity, it foreshadows the trickery that Hamlet is capable of, the playing and seeming that he will undertake to serve an ironically pure end. To obey his murdered father, a loyal son plays at deception, aiming to achieve justice; labyrinths of deceit produce a kind of final truth, once appearances are shed and the actual emerges. These entangled plots and jumbled motives within Hamlet are all evident from the prince's opening speech.

BIOGRAPHICAL SKETCHES

DIANE ACKERMAN (b. 1948)

"Poetry," says Ackerman, "is my form of celebration and prayer, but it is also the way in which I enquire about the world." In her verse can be seen a rich mixture of passionate intensity and cool, almost scientific detachment. Born in Waukegan, Illinois, Ackerman attended Boston, Pennsylvania State, and Cornell universities. Driven perhaps by what she calls "an intense, nomadic curiosity," she has held a variety of jobs, including social worker, government researcher, and editorial assistant, before settling on teaching. In addition to her poetry collections, which include *Wife of Light* (1978), *Lady Faustus* (1983), and *Jaguar of Sweet Laughter* (1990), Ackerman has written plays and books of nonfiction.

WOODY ALLEN (b. 1935)

A native of Brooklyn, Allen Stewart Konigsberg is a comedian, actor, playwright, screenwriter, writer, and director. He began his career in 1952, when he joined the National Broadcasting Corporation as a staff writer. His screenplays began with *What's New Pussycat?* (1965) and include a number of critically acclaimed films in which he was also actor and director, his latest being *Crimes and Misdemeanors* (1989). He has also written several Broadway plays. His books *Getting Even* (1971), *Without Feathers* (1975), and *Side Effects* (1980), primarily composed of essays and sketches previously published in *The New Yorker*, take a humorous look at the modern American city dweller and at such concerns as death, God, and sex. Allen has won several Academy Awards for his films; "The Kugelmass Episode" won the annual O. Henry Award as the best story of 1978.

ARISTOPHANES (450–385? B.C.)

We know little about the life of Aristophanes, the only Greek comic poet of the fifth century whose work survives today. The earliest of his known plays, *The Acharnians* (425 B.C.) takes the Peloponnesian War (431–404 B.C.) as its comic target, and most of his extant work dates from the war years. War was by no means his only subject, however; he attacked politicians in *The Knights* (424 B.C.), philosophers in *The Clouds* (423 B.C.), and even poets in *The Frogs* (405 B.C.). The range of Aristophanes' satire, its brilliant fusion of poetry and ribald humor, has no parallel in Western literature; it can be described only in its own terms, as "Aristophanic."

MARGARET ATWOOD (b. 1939)

Atwood spent her first eleven years in sparsely populated areas of northern Ontario and Quebec, where her father worked as an entomologist. After her education at the University of Toronto and Harvard, she held various jobs in Canada, America, England, and Italy. Atwood published her first poem when she was just nineteen, and she has won numerous prizes for her poetry as well as her fiction, which has become increasingly political over the years. Her novels include *The Edible Woman* (1969), *Surfacing* (1972),

Lady Oracle (1976), *Life Before Man* (1979), *Bodily Harm* (1982), *The Handmaid's Tale* (1985), and *Cat's Eye* (1988). Many of her stories have been collected in *Dancing Girls and Other Stories* (1978), *Murder in the Dark* (1983), and *Bluebeard's Egg* (1983).

JAMES BALDWIN (1924–1987)

Baldwin was for some time perhaps the leading literary spokesman for black Americans. Born in Harlem, long a resident of France, he first attracted critical attention with two extraordinary novels, *Go Tell It on the Mountain* (1953) and *Giovanni's Room* (1956), which dealt, somewhat autobiographically, with religious awakening (Baldwin was a minister at fourteen but later left his church) and the anguish of being black and homosexual in a white and heterosexual society. Baldwin was also a dramatist and an outstanding essayist, his best-known nonfiction prose being *Notes of a Native Son* (1955), *Nobody Knows My Name* (1961), and *The Fire Next Time* (1963), aimed at unraveling the repressive myths of white society and at healing the disastrous estrangement he found in the lives of black people in America. His stories are collected in *Going to Meet the Man* (1965), from which "Sonny's Blues" is taken.

TONI CADE BAMBARA (b. 1939)

Born in New York City, Bambara grew up in Harlem and Bedford-Stuyvesant, two of its poorest neighborhoods. She began writing while still a child. After graduating from Queens College, she worked at various jobs while studying for her M.A. at the City College of New York, writing fiction all the while in "the predawn in-betweens." Bambara began to publish her stories in 1962. She has also been a dancer, teacher, editor, and critic, and has worked in psychiatric and drug therapy, youth organizing, and settlement houses. Her work includes two anthologies, *The Black Woman* (1970) and *Stories for Black Folks* (1971), and two collections of stories, *Gorilla My Love* (1972) and *The Sea Birds Are Still Alive* (1977). She has also written a novel, *The Salt Eaters* (1980).

ANN BEATTIE (b. 1947)

Beattie grew up in the Washington suburb of Chevy Chase, Maryland. She received a B.A. from American University and went on to the University of Connecticut as a graduate student in English literature. Beattie's first published story, "A Rose for Judy Garland's Casket," appeared in 1972, and after many rejections she began publishing in *The New Yorker* shortly thereafter. Beattie's stories have made her a spokesperson for a generation that came of age in the sixties as they adapt to or are baffled and worn out by the oncoming years. Many of them have been collected in *Distortions* (1976), *Secrets and Surprises* (1979), *Jacklighting* (1981), *The Burning House* (1982), and *Where You'll Find Me* (1986). Her novels are *Chilly Scenes of Winter* (1976), *Falling in Place* (1980), *Love Always* (1985), and *Picturing Will* (1990).

SAMUEL BECKETT (1906–1990)

Beckett's world—presented most memorably in his great trilogy of novels, *Molloy* (1951), *Malone Dies* (1951), and *The Unnamable* (1953), and in works that have profoundly altered the course of modern drama, including *Waiting for Godot* (1952) and *Endgame* (1957)—is haunted by an absence of meaning at its core. Born in Ireland, Beckett, like James Joyce, chose to live abroad for most of his life, making Paris his permanent home in 1937. After World War II, he turned almost exclusively to French as his preferred language for original composition, often translating the texts afterwards into English; in

French, he explained, it was easier for him to strip his language bare, to write "without style." Beckett sought to fashion from his art "the expression that there is nothing to express, nothing with which to express, nothing from which to express, no power to express, no desire to express, together with the obligation to express."

AMBROSE BIERCE (1842–1914?)

The tenth child of a poor Ohio family, Bierce rose during the Civil War to the rank of major, was twice wounded and cited fifteen times for bravery. He stayed in the army for a time after the war, then was a journalist in California and London, where his boisterous Western mannerisms and savage wit made him a celebrity and earned him the name "Bitter Bierce." He published *Tales of Soldiers and Civilians* (later called *In the Midst of Life*) (1891) and another volume of short stories, *Can Such Things Be?* (1893). The death of his two sons in 1889 and 1901, along with his divorce in 1891, might well have led him to Mexico, where he reportedly rode with Pancho Villa's revolutionaries. He disappeared and is presumed to have died there. Bierce is well known as the author of *The Cynic's Wordbook* (later called *The Devil's Dictionary*) (1906), but his short stories are his finest achievement.

WILLIAM BLAKE (1757–1828)

In defense of his unorthodox and original work, Blake once said: "That which can be made Explicit to the Idiot . . . is not worth my care." The son of a London haberdasher, he studied drawing at ten and at fourteen was apprenticed to an engraver for seven years. After a first book of poems, *Poetical Sketches* (1783), he began experimenting with what he called "illuminated printing"—the words and pictures of each page were engraved in relief on copper and the printed sheets partly colored by hand—a laborious and time-consuming process which resulted in books of singular beauty, no two of which were exactly alike. His great *Songs of Innocence* (1789) and *Songs of Experience* (1794) were printed in this manner, as were his increasingly mythic and prophetic books, which include *The Marriage of Heaven and Hell* (1793), *The Four Zoas* (1803), *Milton* (1804), and *Jerusalem* (1809). Blake devoted his later life to pictorial art, illustrating *The Canterbury Tales*, the Book of Job, and *The Divine Comedy*, on which he was hard at work when he died.

JORGE LUIS BORGES (1899–1986)

A fifth-generation Argentinian, Borges moved with his family to Europe in 1914 and remained there until 1921, associating himself with avant-garde literary groups. Until the 1930s he was primarily a poet and a leader in *Ultraismo*, a literary movement based on Imagism and Surrealism, but he turned to prose—both fiction and essays—as his varied intellectual interests came together to suggest new forms. A vastly erudite man who directed the Biblioteca Nacional until the dictator Juan Peron for political reasons demoted him to the rank of chicken inspector, Borges created a "literature about literature"; his brief narratives and essays are often miniature encyclopedias of literary history and theory. His works available in English include *Labyrinths* (1962), *Ficciones* (1962), *Dreamtigers* (1964), *The Book of Imaginary Beings* (1969), *The Aleph and Other Stories* (1970), *Dr. Brodie's Report* (1972), and *The Book of Sand* (1979). He lost his sight in 1955.

JOHN CHEEVER (1912–1982)

Cheever was born in Quincy, Massachusetts. His formal education ended when he was expelled from Thayer Academy at the age of seventeen; thereafter he devoted himself completely to fiction writing, except for brief interludes of teaching at Barnard College and the University of Iowa, and script-writing for television. Cheever published his first story when he was sixteen, and until his first novel, *The Wapshot Chronicle*, won the National Book Award in 1958, he was known primarily as a superb and prolific writer of short stories. Built around a strong moral core and tinged with melancholy nostalgia for the past, they form a running commentary on the tensions, manners, and crippled aspirations of urban and suburban life. Many have won awards, including the O. Henry Award in 1956 for "The Country Husband." *The Stories of John Cheever* (1978) won the Pulitzer Prize.

ANTON CHEKHOV (1860–1904)

Son of a serf, Chekhov became a physician and author of a handful of classic plays and of hundreds of stories which changed the course of both genres. His first published work (1880) was written, it was said, to earn enough money to buy his mother a pie for her birthday. His first story collection, *The Tales of Melpomene*, was published in 1884, the year he completed his medical studies and went into practice in Moscow; the lung disease from which he was increasingly to suffer had already appeared the year before. The newly founded Moscow Art Company assured his success as a dramatist when it performed *The Sea Gull* in 1898 (a play that had failed two years earlier), *Uncle Vanya* the next year, *Three Sisters* in 1901, and *The Cherry Orchard* in 1904, the year of his death at a German health resort. Around the turn of the century his collected works appeared in ten volumes. He was diffident about the immense success of his works, thinking they would scarcely outlive him, and despite that success he never forgot his own early poverty and struggle for education—and the plight of those who had not been able to escape such conditions.

KATE CHOPIN (1851–1904)

The St. Louis–born Kate O'Flaherty married Oscar Chopin in 1879 and moved first to New Orleans, then to a Louisiana plantation, then, after her husband's death from swamp fever, back to St. Louis, where she began to fashion a literary career out of her experience of Louisiana life. When she was nearly forty years old she published her first novel, *At Fault* (1890). Her two volumes of short stories, *Bayou Folk* (1894) and *A Night in Acadie* (1897), were for a long time dismissed as mere tales of "local color." Recent attention to her last work, a short novel *The Awakening* (1899), which treats sex and marriage from a woman's point of view, has sparked renewed interest in and reassessment of her works.

SAMUEL TAYLOR COLERIDGE (1772–1834)

Born in the small town of Ottery St. Mary, in rural Devonshire, England, Coleridge was one of the greatest and most original of the 19th-century Romantic poets. He wrote three of the most haunting poems in the English tradition—*The Rime of the Ancient Mariner* (1798), *Christabel* (1816), and *Kubla Khan* (1816)—as well as immensely influential literary criticism and a revolutionary treatise on biology, *Hints Towards the Formation of a More Comprehensive Theory of Life*. In 1795, in the midst of a failed experiment to establish a "Pantisocracy" (his form of ideal community), he met William Wordsworth, and in 1798 they published together their *Lyrical Ballads*, which was to influence the course of English Romanticism for decades to come. Coleridge's physical ailments, addiction to opium, and profound sense of despair have to this day shaped our sense of the poet suffering for the sake of art.

RICHARD CONNELL (1893–1949)

Connell, like Ernest Hemingway, began his writing career as a journalist. At the age of sixteen, he was city editor of his native *Poughkeepsie News-Press;* later he was editor of both the *Crimson* and the *Lampoon* at Harvard, from which he graduated in 1915. After World War I, he left his New York job as an advertising editor to become a freelance writer, traveling to Paris and London and finally settling in Beverly Hills, California. His works include volumes of short stories—*Apes and Angels* (1924), *The Sin of Monsieur Pettipon* (1925), *Variety* (1925), and *Ironies* (1930)—and novels: *Mad Lover* (1927), *Murder at Sea* (1929), *Playboy* (1936), and *What Ho!* (1937).

JOSEPH CONRAD (1857–1924)

Jozeph Teodor Konrad Nalecz Korzeniowski was born in Berdyczew, Polish Ukraine. At five he accompanied his parents into exile in northern Russia and later near Kiev; he was left an orphan at eleven. Before he was seventeen he was off to Marseille, making several trips to the West Indies as an apprentice seaman. After some veiled troubles in France, involving gambling debts and an apparent suicide attempt, he sailed on a British ship, landed in England in 1878, and spent the next sixteen years in the British merchant service, rising to master in 1886, the year he became a British subject. In 1890, he worked on a boat that sailed up the Congo, the inspiration for *Heart of Darkness* (1899). He began writing in 1889 but did not publish his first novel, *Almayer's Folly*, until 1896. Though a successful writer, he was not truly popular or financially independent until the publication of *Chance* in 1912–13. Among his major novels are *The Nigger of the "Narcissus"* (1897), *Lord Jim* (1900), *Nostromo* (1904), *Under Western Eyes* (1910), and *Victory* (1915). His short-story collections include *Tales of Unrest* (1898), *Typhoon and Other Stories* (1903), *'Twixt Land and Sea* (1912), from which "The Secret Sharer" is taken, and *Within the Tides: Tales* (1915).

E. E. CUMMINGS (1894–1962)

Cummings' variety of modernism was distinguished by its playful sense of humor, its formal experimentation, its lyrical directness, and above all by its celebration of the individual against mass society. Born in Cambridge, Massachusetts, the son of a Congregationalist minister, Edward Estlin Cummings attended Harvard University where he wrote poetry in the Pre-Raphaelite and Metaphysical traditions. He joined the ambulance corps in France the day after the United States entered World War I and was imprisoned by his own side for his outspoken letters and disdain for bureaucracy; he transmuted the experience into his first literary success, *The Enormous Room* (1922). After the war, Cummings established himself as a poet and artist in Greenwich Village, made frequent trips to France and New Hampshire, and showed little interest in wealth or his growing celebrity.

EMILY DICKINSON (1830–1886)

From childhood on, Dickinson's life was sequestered and obscure. Yet her verse had a power and influence which has traveled far beyond the cultured yet relatively circumscribed environment in which she lived her life: her room, her father's house, her family, a few close friends, and the small town of Amherst, Massachusetts. Indeed, along with Walt Whitman, her far more public contemporary, she all but invented American poetry. Born in Amherst, the daughter of a respected lawyer and revered father ("His heart was pure and terrible," she once wrote), Dickinson studied for less than a year at the Mount Holyoke Female Seminary, returning permanently to Amherst. In later life she became more and more of a recluse, dressing in white, seeing no visitors, yet working without stint at her poems—nearly 1800 in all, only a few of which were published during her lifetime.

JOHN DONNE (1572–1631)

The first and greatest of what came to be known as the "Metaphysical school" of poets, Donne wrote in a style, revolutionary at the time, that combined highly intellectual conceits with complex, compressed phrasing. Born into an old Roman Catholic family at a time when Catholics were subject to constant harassment, Donne quietly abandoned his religion and had a brilliant early career until a politically disastrous marriage ruined his worldly hopes and forced him to struggle for years to support a large and growing family; impoverished and despairing, he even wrote a treatise (*Biathanatos*) on the lawfulness of suicide. King James (who had ambitions for him as a preacher) eventually forced Donne to take Anglican orders in 1615, and indeed he became one of the great sermonizers of his day, rising to dean of St. Paul's Cathedral in 1621. Donne's private devotions were published in 1624, and he continued to write sacred poetry until a few years before his death.

RITA DOVE (b. 1952)

When Rita Dove won the 1987 Pulitzer Prize in Poetry for *Thomas and Beulah* (1986), she was, surprisingly, only the second black poet (after Gwendolyn Brooks in 1950) to receive such high recognition. A native of Akron, Ohio, Dove attended Miami University in Ohio, studied for a year in West Germany as a Fulbright scholar, and received an M.F.A. in creative writing from the University of Iowa. She taught creative writing at Arizona State University and is now professor of English at the University of Virginia as well as an associate editor of *Callaloo*, the journal of African-American and African arts and letters. Dove's books include *The Yellow House on the Corner* (1980), *Museum* (1983), and *Grace Notes* (1989).

STEPHEN DUNN (b. 1939)

According to Dunn, the poet's task is the discovery and communication of *strangeness:* "A poem that speaks convincingly to strangeness, to otherness, brings us and others into the common fold, even if that common fold is a place that may not hold for us safety or certainty." Born in Forest Hills, New York, Dunn attended Hofstra and Syracuse Universities—and traveled widely—before publishing his first book of poetry, *Looking for Holes in the Ceiling*, in 1974. He is currently professor of creative writing at Stockton State College in New Jersey. Dunn's poems have been published in a number of journals; his seven collections include *Full of Lust and Good Usage* (1976), *A Circus of Needs* (1978), *Not Dancing* (1984), *Local Time* (1986), and *Between Angels* (1989).

MARGUERITE DURAS (b. 1914)

Born Marguerite Donnadieu in Indochina (now Vietnam), Duras spent most of her childhood on the banks of the Mekong River, before moving to Paris in 1932 to study mathematics, law, and political science. She was working as a secretary in the civil service when her first novel, *The Impudent Ones*, was published in 1943. A politically committed writer, Duras worked with the French Resistance during World War II, joined the Communist Party after the war (she was expelled in 1955), and attacked French colonial rule during the Algerian War (1954–62). During the course of her long career, she has moved away from more traditional narrative forms to increasingly experimental pieces, which include plays, films, and film scenarios. Her works, many of which draw from her experience in Asia, include *The Sea Wall* (1950), *Moderato Cantabile* (1958), *The Vice-Consul* (1965), *India Song* (1973), and *The Lover* (1984).

T. S. ELIOT (1888–1965)

Thomas Stearns Eliot—from his formally experimental and oblique writings to his brilliant arguments in defense of "orthodoxy" and "tradition"—dominated the world of English poetry between the world wars. Born in St. Louis, Missouri of New England stock, Eliot studied literature and philosophy at Harvard, and later in France and Germany. He came to England in 1914, read Greek philosophy at Oxford, and published his first major poem, "The Love Song of J. Alfred Prufrock," the next year. In 1922, with the help of his great supporter and adviser, Ezra Pound, Eliot published his long poem, *The Waste Land* (1922), which would profoundly influence a whole generation of poets. In his later work, particularly the *Four Quartets* (completed in 1945), Eliot explored religious questions in a quieter, more controlled idiom. He was awarded the Nobel Prize for Literature in 1948.

LOUISE ERDRICH (b. 1954)

Born in Little Falls, Minnesota, of German-American and Chippewa descent, Erdrich grew up in Wahpeton, North Dakota, as a member of the Turtle Mountain Band of Chippewa, and attended Dartmouth College. After graduation, she returned to teach in North Dakota's Poetry in the Schools Program. She received an M.A. in creative writing from Johns Hopkins University in 1979. In the same year, *Jacklight*, a collection of poetry, was published. Her novels are *Love Medicine* (1984), *The Beet Queen* (1986), and *Tracks* (1988). *Love Medicine*, which has been praised as a landmark work in its depiction of the lives of contemporary Native Americans, was the winner of the National Book Critics' Circle Award for fiction.

WILLIAM FAULKNER (1897–1962)

Faulkner spent almost his entire life in his native state of Mississippi. He left high school without graduating, joined the Royal Canadian Air Force in 1918, and in the mid-1920s lived briefly in New Orleans, where he was encouraged by Sherwood Anderson. He then spent a few miserable months as a clerk in a New York bookstore, published a collection of poems, *The Marble Faun*, in 1924, and took a long walking tour of Europe in 1925. In later years he made several visits to Hollywood, writing a screenplay for *The Big Sleep*, among others, and spent his last years in Charlottesville, Virginia. With the publication of *Sartoris* in 1929, Faulkner began a cycle of works interrelated by his fictional Yoknapatawpha County and the reappearance of characters or families from work to work. These include *As I Lay Dying* (1930), *Light in August* (1932), *Absalom, Absalom!* (1936), *The Unvanquished* (1939), *The Hamlet* (1940), and *Go Down, Moses* (1942), in which "The Old People" appears. His short fiction can be found in *The Collected Stories of William Faulkner* (1950). He received the Nobel Prize for Literature in 1950.

RICHARD FORD (b. 1944)

Ford was born in Jackson, Mississippi, attended Michigan State University, and received an M.F.A. in creative writing from the University of California. Since that time he has been awarded a Guggenheim Foundation fellowship and lived in western Montana, New York, Mississippi, and currently New Orleans. His first novel, *A Piece of My Heart*, was published in 1976. He has published three more novels, *The Ultimate Good Luck* (1981),

The Sportswriter (1986), and *Wildlife* (1990), and a volume of short stories, *Rock Springs* (1987).

ROBERT FROST (1874–1963)

Though his poetry forever identified Frost with rural New England, he was born and lived to the age of eleven in San Francisco. Coming to New England after his father's death, Frost studied classics in high school, entered and dropped out of both Dartmouth and Harvard, and spent difficult years as an unrecognized poet before his first book, *A Boy's Will* (1913), was accepted and published in England. Frost's character was full of contradiction—he held "that we get forward as much by hating as by loving"—yet by the end of his long life he was one of the most honored poets of his time. In 1961, two years before his death, he was invited to read a poem at John F. Kennedy's presidential inauguration ceremony.

TESS GALLAGHER (b. 1943)

Gallagher likens writing poetry to fishing—in which the people and circumstances of her life are bait. She recalls salmon fishing with her father: "I used to lean out over the water and try to look past my own face, past the reflection of the boat, past the sun and the darkness, down to where the fish were surely swimming. I made up charm songs and word-hopes to tempt the fish." Born in Port Angeles, Washington, Gallagher studied at the University of Washington and the University of Iowa before publishing her first book, *Stepping Outside* (1974). Since then she has taught at a number of colleges and universities. Gallagher's books include *Instructions to the Double* (1976), *Under Stars* (1978), and *Willingly* (1984).

GABRIEL GARCÍA MÁRQUEZ (b. 1928)

Born in Aracataca, a remote town in Magdalena province near the Caribbean coast of Colombia, García Márquez studied law at the University of Bogotá and then worked as a journalist in Latin America, Europe, and the United States. In 1967 he took up permanent residence in Barcelona, Spain. His first published book, *Leaf Storm* (1955, translated 1972), in which "A Very Old Man with Enormous Wings" appears, is set in the fictional small town of Macondo, based on the myths and legends of his childhood home. His most famous novel, *One Hundred Years of Solitude* (1967, translated 1970) presents six generations of one family in Macondo, fusing magic, reality, fable, and fantasy in a way which also allows the town to serve as a microcosm of many of the social, political, and economic problems of Latin America. Among his works are *The Autumn of the Patriarch* (1975, translated 1976), *Innocent Eréndira and Other Stories* (1972, translated 1978), *Chronicle of a Death Foretold* (1981, translated 1982), and *Love in the Time of Cholera* (1987, translated 1988). Garcia Márquez won the Nobel Prize for Literature in 1982.

CHARLOTTE PERKINS GILMAN (1860–1935)

Charlotte Anna Perkins was born in Hartford, Connecticut. After a painful, lonely childhood and several years supporting herself as a governess, art teacher, and designer of greeting cards, Charlotte Perkins married the artist Charles Stetson. Following several extended periods of depression, she was put by her husband into the hands of Dr. S. Weir Mitchell, who "sent me home with the solemn advice to 'live as domestic a life as . . . possible,' to 'have but two hours' intellectual life a day,' and 'never to touch pen, brush, or pencil again' as long as I lived." Three months of this, ending "near the borderline of utter mortal ruin," became the inspiration for "The Yellow Wallpaper." In 1900 she married George Houghton Gilman, having divorced Stetson in 1892. Her nonfiction works, which placed her at the center of the early women's movement, include *Women and Economics* (1898) and *Man-Made World* (1911). She also wrote several utopian novels, including *Moving the Mountain* (1911) and *Herland* (1915).

SUSAN GLASPELL (1882–1948)

Born and raised in Davenport, Iowa, Glaspell graduated from Drake University and worked on the staff of the *Des Moines Daily News* until her stories began appearing in magazines such as *Harper's* and the *Ladies' Home Journal*. In 1922, Glaspell moved to New York City where she married George Cram Cook, a talented director. In 1915 they founded the Provincetown Playhouse on Cape Cod, an extraordinary gathering of actors, directors, and playwrights, including Eugene O'Neill, Edna St. Vincent Millay, and John Reed. She spent the last part of her life in Provincetown, devoting herself to writing novels. Glaspell's plays include *The Verge* (1921) and *Alison's House* (1930). Among her novels are *The Visionary* (1911), *Fidelity* (1915), and *The Morning Is Near Us* (1939).

NADINE GORDIMER (b. 1923)

Gordimer was born in a gold-mining town in South Africa and has lived all her life in that country, exploring, through her writing, the effects of apartheid in all its forms with intelligence and acute sensitivity. Her novels include *The Lying Days* (1953), *A World of Strangers* (1958), *A Guest of Honor* (1970), *The Conservationist* (1975), *Burger's Daughter* (1979), and *A Sport of Nature* (1987). Among her short-story collections are *Six Feet of the Country* (1956), *Friday's Footprint and Other Stories* (1960), and *A Soldier's Embrace*. (1980). Her *Selected Stories* were published in 1976. For Gordimer, "a short story *occurs*, in the most imaginative sense. To write one is to express from a situation in the exterior or interior world the life-giving drop . . . that will spread an intensity on the page; burn a hole in it."

THOMAS HARDY (1840–1928)

In a preface dated 1901, Hardy called his poems "unadjusted impressions," which nevertheless might, by "humbly recording diverse readings of phenomena as they are forced upon us by chance and change," lead to a philosophy. Indeed, though he was essentially retrospective in his outlook, Hardy anticipated the concerns of modern poetry by treating the craft as an awkward, often skeptical means of penetrating the facade of language. Born at Upper Bockhampton in Dorset, England, the son of a master mason, Hardy began to write while in the midst of an architectural career. After a long and successful career as a novelist, he turned exclusively to poetry; he died in the midst of preparing his last book, *Winter Words* (1929), for publication.

NATHANIEL HAWTHORNE (1804–1864)

Hawthorne was born in Salem, Massachusetts, a descendent of Puritan immigrants; one ancestor had been a judge in the Salem witchcraft trials. Educated at Bowdoin College, he was agonizingly slow in winning acclaim for his work, and supported himself from time to time in government service—working in the custom houses of Boston and Salem and serving as the United States consul in Liverpool. His early collections of stories, *Twice-Told Tales* (1837) and *Mosses from an Old Manse* (1846), in which "Young Goodman Brown" appears, did not sell well, and it was not until the publication in 1850 of his most famous novel, *The Scarlet Letter*, that his fame spread beyond a discerning few.

His other novels include *The House of the Seven Gables* (1851) and *The Blithedale Romance* (1852).

SEAMUS HEANEY (b. 1939)

Heaney, like many of his contemporaries in the rich Northern Irish tradition, has sought in his poetry to clear some sort of imaginative ground, somewhere beyond his region's seemingly insoluble dilemmas. In early collections—*Death of a Naturalist* (1966) and *Door into the Dark* (1969)—he did so by sticking close to the land, the sounds and sights of a superbly evoked local world. With *Wintering Out* (1973) and *North* (1975) Heaney dug deeply into the "antediluvean" myths of his Irish ancestors. More recently, he has taken Dante's *Inferno* as his example—in *Field Work* (1979) and *Station Island* (1984)—and even created myths of his own in *The Haw Lantern* (1987). Far from his roots in rural County Derry, Heaney is now a professor at Harvard University and at Oxford.

LILLIAN HELLMAN (1907–1984)

Hellman's toughness and pragmatism allowed her to stretch the rigid conventions of the Broadway stage to explore unconventional subjects and to stand up to Senator Joseph McCarthy during a period when most writers were terrified to speak out. Born into a Jewish family in New Orleans, Hellman moved to New York where she attended New York and Columbia Universities and worked briefly in publishing. Her first successful play, *The Children's Hour* (1934), explored the pain of two women accused of lesbianism at a rigidly conventional private school. During the McCarthy period, Hellman was blacklisted for her "left-wing" politics. Nevertheless she refused to inform on other writers, explaining that "to hurt innocent people whom I knew many years ago in order to save myself is, to me, inhuman and indecent and dishonorable." After the death of the writer Dashiell Hammett, her companion for many years, Hellman began work on her memoirs, which were published in three volumes, *An Unfinished Woman* (1969), *Pentimento*, and *Scoundrel Time* (1976).

ERNEST HEMINGWAY (1899–1961)

Born in Oak Park, Illinois, Hemingway was first a reporter, then an ambulance-service volunteer in France and infantryman in Italy in 1918, when he was wounded and decorated for valor. After the war and more reporting, he settled for a time in Paris, where he knew Gertrude Stein and Ezra Pound, among others. From 1925 to 1935 he published two volumes of stories, *In Our Time* (1925) and *Death in the Afternoon* (1932), and two major novels, *The Sun Also Rises* (1926) and *A Farewell to Arms* (1929), which established his international reputation. Hemingway helped the Loyalists in the Spanish Civil War, the subject of *For Whom the Bell Tolls* (1940), served as a war correspondent in the Second World War, and from 1950 to 1962 lived in Cuba. *The Old Man and the Sea* was published in 1952, winning a Pulitzer Prize. Hemingway was awarded the Nobel Prize for Literature in 1954. He committed suicide in 1961.

ROBERT HERRICK (1591–1674)

The son of a London goldsmith, Herrick would have liked nothing better than to live a life of leisured study, discussing literature and drinking sack with his hero, Ben Jonson. For a number of reasons, though, he decided to take religious orders and moved to a parish in Devonshire. Herrick eventually made himself at home there, inventing dozens of imaginary mistresses with exotic names (his housekeeper was prosaically named Prudence) and practicing, half-seriously, his own peculiar form of paganism. When the

Puritans came to power, Herrick was driven from his post to London where, in 1648, he published a volume of over 1,400 poems with two titles, *Hesperides* for the secular poems and *Noble Numbers* for those with sacred subjects. Though they did not survive the harsh atmosphere of Puritanism and were virtually forgotten until the 19th century, Herrick was eventually restored to his post in Devonshire where he lived out his last years quietly.

SPENCER HOLST (b. 1926)

Well known in the literary underground, Holst has published his short stories and poetry in numerous periodicals such as *Mademoiselle* and *Oui*. He has translated the work of German poet Vera Lachmann and published several volumes of his own writing, including two volumes of short stories, *The Language of Cats and Other Stories* (1971) and *Spencer Holst Stories* (1976), a collection of imaginative and humorous fables which play with reality and fantasy.

GERARD MANLEY HOPKINS (1844–1889)

Hopkins's verse, in all its superbly controlled tension, strong rhythm, and sheer exuberance, has been championed by a number of modern poets—yet he made few attempts to publish what many of his contemporaries found nearly incomprehensible, and he was all but unknown until long after his death. Born the eldest of eight children of a marine-insurance adjuster (shipwrecks later figured in his poetry, particularly *The Wreck of the Deutschland*) Hopkins attended Oxford, where his ambition was to become a painter—until he was converted to Catholicism. He taught for a time, decided to become a Jesuit, burnt all his early poetry as too worldly, and was ordained in 1877. Near the end of his life Hopkins was appointed professor of Greek at University College, Dublin. Out of place and miserable, he died there of typhoid at the age of 44.

A. E. HOUSMAN (1859–1936)

After failing his finals at Oxford, perhaps because of unrequited love, Alfred Edward Housman became a clerk in the Patent Office in London, where he began publishing studies of classical authors. Recognized as a leading interpreter of classical literature, Housman was eventually appointed professor of Latin at Cambridge University. His first volume of poetry, *A Shropshire Lad*, was published in 1896. A nostalgic collection of ballads that was little noticed at the time, its popularity grew immensely in the years of assurance and stability before England entered World War I. In 1922, Housman published another volume, *Last Poems*, but perhaps the most notable event of his later years was a highly influential lecture, "The Name and Nature of Poetry" (1933), in which he insisted that poetry should be "more physical than intellectual."

DAVID HENRY HWANG (b. 1957)

The son of immigrant Chinese-American parents, Hwang grew up in California and attended Stanford University where his first play, *FOB*, was produced during his senior year ("FOB" is short for "fresh off the boat"—an immigrant). It was later performed at the New York Shakespeare Festival's Public Theatre and won an Obie Award in 1981. Hwang's plays, which have been produced world-wide, include *Family Devotions* (1981), *The House of Sleeping Beauties* (1983), and *The Sound of a Voice* (1983). *M. Butterfly* won the Outer Critics Circle Award for best Broadway play, the Drama Desk Award for best new play, and the Tony Award for best play of the year.

HENRIK IBSEN (1828–1906)

Ibsen was the foremost playwright of his time; his work is both a culmination of nineteenth-century "bourgeois" drama and a precursor of social realist and symbolist theatre. Born in Skien, Norway, Ibsen was apprenticed to an apothecary until 1850, when he left for Oslo and published his first play, *Catilina*, under a pseudonym. Two of his early works, written in Rome, were in verse—*Brand* (1866) and *Peer Gynt* (1867). During the course of his career, he turned to more realistic plays—including *Ghosts* (1881) and *An Enemy of the People* (1882)—which explored contemporary social problems; they won him a reputation throughout Europe as a controversial and outspoken advocate of moral and social reform. Near the end of his life, Ibsen explored the human condition in the symbolic terms of *The Master Builder* (1892) and *When We Dead Awaken* (1899), plays that anticipated many of the concerns of twentieth-century drama.

HENRY JAMES (1843–1916)

Son of a writer and religious philosopher, brother of the philosopher William James, Henry James was born in New York and entered Harvard Law School in 1862, after private study, art school, and study and residence abroad. Thereafter his American home was in Cambridge, Massachusetts, but he lived in England from 1876 until his death forty years later, having become a British subject in 1915. James's fiction often centers on the confrontation of Americans with Europe or Europeans; he treats the two as moral or value systems as much as geographical entities. His practice and theory of fiction, set forth mainly in the prefaces to his novels, dominated fiction criticism for generations. Among his works are *The American* (1877), *Daisy Miller* (1879), *Portrait of a Lady* (1881), *The Turn of the Screw* (1898), *The Wings of the Dove* (1902), *The Ambassadors* (1903), and *The Golden Bowl* (1904).

BEN JONSON (1572?–1637)

Poet, playwright, actor, scholar, critic, translator, and leader, for the first time in English, of a literary "school" (the "Cavalier" poets), Jonson was born the posthumous son of a clergyman and stepson to a master bricklayer of Westminster. He had an eventful early career, going to war against the Spanish, working as an actor and killing an associate in a duel, and converting to Catholicism (which made him an object of deep suspicion after the Gunpowder Plot of Guy Fawkes in 1605). Jonson wrote a number of plays in the midst of all this, including *Every Man in His Humor* (in which Shakespeare acted a leading role). *Volpone* (1606), and *The Alchemist* (1610). He spent the latter part of his life at the center of a vast literary circle. When in 1616 he published his collected works, *The Works of Benjamin Jonson*, it was the first time an English author had been so presumptuous as to consider writing a profession.

JAMES JOYCE (1882–1941)

In 1902, after graduating from University College, Dublin, Joyce left his native city for Paris, only to return in April 1903 to teach school. In the spring of 1904 he lived at the Martello Tower, Sandycove, a site made famous by his great novel, *Ulysses* (1921). In October 1904 he eloped with Nora Barnacle and left Ireland again, this time for Trieste where he taught English for the Berlitz school. Though he lived abroad the rest of his life, that first abortive trip proved symbolic: in his fiction the expatriate could never leave Dublin. Joyce had more than his share of difficulties with publication and censorship.

His volume of short stories, *Dubliners* (in which "Araby" appears), completed in 1905, was not published until 1914. His *Portrait of the Artist as a Young Man*, dated "Dublin 1904, Trieste 1914," appeared first in America, in 1916. *Ulysses* was banned for a dozen years in the United States and as long or longer elsewhere. Though he published a play, *Exiles*, and poetry, the three works mentioned and the monumental, experimental, and puzzling *Finnegans Wake* (1939) are the basis of his reputation.

FRANZ KAFKA (1883–1924)

Born in Prague of a middle-class Jewish family, Kafka earned a doctorate in law from the German University in that city and held an inconspicuous position in the civil service for many years. Emotionally and physically ill for the last seven or eight years of his short life, he died of tuberculosis in Vienna, never having married (though he was twice engaged to the same woman and lived with an actress in Berlin for some time before he died) and not having published his three major novels, *The Trial* (1925), *The Castle* (1926), and *Amerika* (1927). Indeed, he ordered his friend Max Brod to destroy them and other works he had left in manuscript. Fortunately, Brod did not, and not long after his death, Kafka's work was world famous and widely influential. His stories in English translation can be found in *The Great Wall of China* (1933), *The Penal Colony* (1948), and *The Complete Stories* (1976).

X. J. KENNEDY (b. 1929)

Kennedy's *Nude Descending a Staircase* (1961) is a *tour de force* performance, one of the most remarkable first volumes of poetry written in this century. Its range, from elegy to lyric to song to light verse, encompasses a great variety of tones and poetic kinds. Born Joseph Charles Kennedy in Dover, New Jersey, he was educated at Seton Hall College in New Jersey, Columbia University, and the Sorbonne in Paris. After serving in the U.S. Navy, he taught at several colleges and universities, was Poetry Editor of *Paris Review*, and edited anthologies of poetry, fiction, and essays. At present he works as a free-lance writer.

JAMAICA KINCAID (b. 1949)

Born in St. John's, Antigua (an island in the West Indies north of Guadeloupe), Jamaica Kincaid now lives in New York, where she is a staff writer for the *New Yorker*. She is the author of a volume of short stories, *At the Bottom of the River* (1984), and two novels, *Annie John* (1985) and *Lucy* (1990). Although Kincaid left her native island as a teenager, a deeply-felt—and richly-evocative—sense of place pervades her work.

D. H. LAWRENCE (1885–1930)

Son of a coal miner and a middle-class schoolteacher, Lawrence won a scholarship to Nottingham High School at thirteen but had to leave a few years later when his elder brother died. He worked for a surgical appliance manufacturer, attended Nottingham University College, and taught school in Croydon, near London. In 1911, when his first novel, *The White Peacock*, was published, he left teaching to devote his time to writing, though it was not until the publication of *Sons and Lovers* (1913) that he was established as a major literary figure. In 1912 he eloped to the Continent with Frieda von Richthofen, and in 1914, after her divorce, they were married. During World War I, both his novels and the fact that his wife was German gave him trouble: *The Rainbow* was published in September 1915 and suppressed in November. In November 1919 the Lawrences left England and their years of wandering began: first Italy, then Ceylon and Australia, Mexico and New Mexico, then back to England and Italy. *Women in Love* was published in New York in 1920, and *Lady Chatterley's Lover*, his most sexually explicit and controversial novel, eight years later. Through it all he suffered from tuberculosis, the disease from which he finally died, in France. Lawrence's stories are available in a three-volume edition, first published in 1961.

URSULA K. LE GUIN (b. 1929)

A writer of short stories, poetry, science fiction novels, novels of fantasy, and works increasingly difficult to categorize, Le Guin was born in Berkeley, California, and educated at Radcliffe and Columbia. She studied in Paris and taught creative writing before his first novel, *Rocannon's World*, was published in 1964. Since then, she has gone on to publish, among others, *The Left Hand of Darkness* (1969), which won the Hugo and Nebula Awards; *The Lathe of Heaven* (1970); *The Farthest Shore* (1973), winner of the National Book Award; *The Dispossessed* (1974); *Malafrena* (1979); *The Eye of the Heron* (1983); *Always Coming Home* (1985) and *Tehanu* (1990). Her volumes of short fiction include *The Wind's Twelve Quarters* (1975), *Orsinian Tales* (1976), and *The Compass Rose* (1982). She has also published a volume of essays, *The Language of the Night: Essays on Fantasy and Science Fiction*, which appeared in 1979. She says of her books, "I write science fiction because that is what publishers call my books. Left to myself, I should call them novels."

DORIS LESSING (b. 1919)

Born in Persia, Lessing lived for twenty-five years in Southern Rhodesia (now Zimbabwe) before moving to England, where soon thereafter her first novel, *The Grass Is Singing* (1950), was published. She has since published voluminously. Her books include *The Golden Notebook* (1962), the five Martha Quest novels, *Children of Violence*, published between 1952 and 1969, *Briefing for a Descent into Hell* (1971), *The Summer Before the Dark* (1973), and *The Good Terrorist* (1985). She has also published eight volumes of short fiction, including *A Man and Two Women* (1963) and *The Memoirs of a Survivor* (1975), and has written plays, television plays, poetry, and essays. Her work is known for its range and variety, some of it set in Africa, a significant portion of it political (she was once a Communist), much of it examining inner lives of women in modern society, and some of it lately reflecting her interest in extrasensory perception. Several of Lessing's recent novels, beginning with *Shikasta* (1979), are part of a visionary, futuristic work called *Canopus in Argos: Archives*.

HEATHER MCHUGH (b. 1948)

McHugh took Browning's line, "Our interest's on the dangerous edge of things," as the epigraph of her first book—and indeed her poems are violent with contrast and contradiction. Born in San Diego, California, she received her B.A. from Radcliffe. Since then she has worked in a number of academic settings, as Poet- and Writer-in-Residence at Stephen College (Missouri) and the University of Washington, and as visiting professor at Warren Wilson College, Columbia University, and the University of California. Her books include *Dangers* (1977), and *A World of Difference* (1981).

CLAUDE MCKAY (1890–1948)

Born in Sunny Ville, Jamaica, McKay became one of the most prominent figures of the Harlem Renaissance—the oldest as well as the first to publish. Always politically active, he was attracted to Communism and in 1922 met Lenin and Trotsky in Moscow, though he later repudiated this commitment with his 1942 conversion to Catholicism. "[To] have a religion," he wrote, "is very much like falling in love with a woman. You love her for her . . . beauty, which cannot be defined." McKay's conception of Black experience, infused with social reform and a consciousness of ethnic vitality, made him a catalytic poet for his generation. His works include *If We Must Die* (1919), *Home to Harlem* (1928), and A *Long Way from Home* (1937).

KATHERINE MANSFIELD (1888–1923)

Born in New Zealand, Mansfield studied music at Queen's College, London, and was an accomplished cellist. She published three major volumes of short stories during her short life: *Bliss* (1920), which established her reputation, *The Garden Party* (1922), and *The Dove's Nest* (1923). With John Middleton Murry and D. H. Lawrence she founded an influential literary review, *The Signature*. She died of tuberculosis in France, and a final volume of stories, *Something Childish* (1924), appeared shortly after her death. Her *Collected Stories* were published in 1945.

BOBBIE ANN MASON (b. 1940)

Mason, who grew up on a farm near Mayfield, Kentucky, has written for *Movie Stars*, *Movie Life*, and *T.V. Star Parade*. *The New Yorker* published her first story in 1980. Since then, she has been awarded a Guggenheim Foundation fellowship, has had stories in *Best American Short Stories* in 1981 and 1983, and won the Pushcart Prize for fiction in 1983. *Shiloh and Other Stories* (1982), her first collection, won the Ernest Hemingway Foundation Award. She has also written a novel, *In Country* (1985), a short novel, *Spence and Lila* (1988), and a second collection of stories, *Love Life* (1989). "The people I write about," she says "either want to get away from home, get away from town, see the world, or they want to stay home, and they're afraid to leave, so they accommodate. . . . I'm interested in that tension between longing to stay and longing to go."

GUY DE MAUPASSANT (1850–1893)

Born Henri René Albert in Normandy, France, at sixteen Maupassant was expelled from a Rouen seminary and finished his education in a public high school. After serving in the Franco-Prussian War, he was for ten years a government clerk in Paris. A protégé of Flaubert, during the 1880s he published some three hundred stories, a half-dozen novels, and plays. The short stories, which appeared regularly in popular periodicals, sampled military and peasant life, the decadent world of politics and journalism, prostitution, the supernatural, and the hypocrisies of solid citizens. With Chekhov, he may be said to have created the modern short story; his reliance on plot, plot twists, and sometimes heavy irony became facile in the hands of his followers and has somewhat diminished his own reputation the past quarter-century and more. His life ended somewhat like one of his own stories: he died in an asylum, of syphilis. His novels include *Une Vie* (*A Life*, 1883), *Bel Ami* (*Handsome Friend*, 1885), and *Pierre et Jean* (1888). His stories are most readily available in his *Collected Works*.

ARTHUR MILLER (b. 1915)

Born and raised in New York City, Miller studied journalism at the University of Michigan, began writing plays, and went to work—in the middle of the Depression—with the Federal Theatre Project, a fertile proving ground for some of the best playwrights of the period. He had his first Broadway success, *All My Sons*, in 1947, followed only two years later by his masterpiece, *Death of a Salesman*. With McCarthy's Communist "witch-hunts" in the early 1950s as his inspiration, Miller fashioned another modern parable, basing *The Crucible* (1953) on the seventeenth-century Salem witch trials. His work has provoked much theoretical discussion over whether real tragedy is possible in a modern context.

JOHN MILTON (1608–1674)

Born in London, the elder son of a self-made businessman, Milton exhibited unusual literary and scholarly gifts at an early age; before entering Cambridge University, he was already adept at Latin and Greek and was well on his way to mastering Hebrew and most of the European languages. After graduation, he spent six more years reading, day and night, just about everything of importance written in English, Italian, Latin, and Greek—after which his father sent him abroad for another year of travel and study. Returning to England, Milton immediately embroiled himself in political controversy, writing pamphlets defending everything from free speech to the execution of Charles I by Cromwell and his followers. In the midst of this feverish activity, the monarchy was restored, and Milton was imprisoned and his property confiscated—but worst of all he lost his sight. Blind, impoverished, and isolated, he set about writing the great works of his later years: *Paradise Lost* (1667), *Paradise Regained* (1671), and *Samson Agonistes* (1671).

MOLIÈRE (1622–1673)

The son of a prosperous Paris furniture maker, Molière studied the classics, philosophy, and law, but decided at an early age to devote his life to the theater. He joined a dramatic troupe at the age of twenty-one and took a stage name (his real name was Jean-Baptiste Poquelin), perhaps to avoid embarrassing his family by pursuing a profession that was then perceived as corruptive and disreputable. In 1658, after years of touring the country while Molière perfected his acting and writing skills, his company performed before the court of Louis XIV, who was so favorably impressed that he gave the troupe a theater in Paris. Molière's plays, performed at this theater (which developed into the Comédie Française) include *Tartuffe* (1664), *The Misanthrope* (1666), and *The Miser* (1670). He died only a few hours after performing the lead role of his last play, *The Imaginary Invalid*.

BHARATI MUKHERJEE (b. 1940)

Brought up in an upper-class Bengali family of the Brahmin caste, Mukherjee attended private schools in India, London, and Switzerland before a business disaster wiped out the family fortune. She won a scholarship in 1961 to the University of Iowa Writer's Workshop, and has since lived with her husband (also a writer) and two children in Canada, India, and the United States, supporting herself through teaching and other jobs, and writing in the small hours of the morning. In 1971 her critically acclaimed first novel, *The Tiger's Daughter*, appeared; her other novels are *Wife* (1975) and *Jasmine* (1989). Mukherjee's short fiction collections are *Darkness* (1985), stories of South Asian immigrants, and *The Middleman* (1988), which includes characters and voices from various countries and social strata: "Mine is not minimalism, which strips away, but compression, which reflects many layers of meaning."

ALICE MUNRO (b. 1931)

Munro grew up on a farm near Lake Huron in Ontario and attended the University of Western Ontario, where she began publishing short stories. Much of her fiction grows out of her childhood memories of rural family life: "I write about places where your roots are and most people don't live that kind of life anymore at all." Her first book, a collection of stories entitled *Dance of the Happy Shades* (1968) in which "Boys and Girls" appears, won a Governor General's Award. Munro has written a novel, *Lives of Girls and Women* (1971), and five other short-story collections, *Something I've Been Meaning to Tell You* (1974), *Who Do You Think You Are?* (1978, published in the United States as *The Beggar Maid* in 1979), *The Moons of Jupiter* (1983), *The Progress of Love* (1986), and *Friend of My Youth* (1990).

HOWARD NEMEROV (1920–1991)

Nemerov called his poems "bad jokes, and even terrible jokes, emerging from the nature of things as well as from my propensity for coming at things a touch subversively, and from the blind side, or the dark side, the side everyone concerned with 'values' would just as soon forget." The resonance of his poetry may lie in his ability to balance this subversive, wayward imagination with lucid, precise language and traditional verse forms. Born in New York City, Nemerov graduated from Harvard University, served in the Air Force during World War II, and returned to New York to complete his first book, *The Image and the Law* (1948). He taught at a number of colleges and universities and published books of poetry, plays, short stories, novels, and essays. His *Collected Poems* won the Pulitzer Prize in 1978.

FLANNERY O'CONNOR (1925–1964)

O'Connor was born in Savannah, Georgia, studied at the Georgia State College for Women, and won a fellowship to the Writer's Workshop of the University of Iowa, where she received an M.F.A. degree. Her first novel, *Wise Blood*, was published in 1952, and her first collection of stories, *A Good Man Is Hard to Find*, in 1955. She was able to complete only one more novel, *The Violent Bear It Away* (1960), and a second collection of stories, *Everything That Rises Must Converge* (1965), before dying of an incurable illness in Milledgeville, Georgia. Her reputation has grown steadily since her untimely death. A collection of letters, edited by Sally Fitzgerald under the title *The Habit of Being*, appeared in 1979.

SHARON OLDS (b. 1942)

Olds's poems might well be compared with those of the "confessional" poets (particularly Plath and Sexton) in their intense focus on and preoccupation with sexual and family relationships. Born in San Francisco, Olds studied at Stanford and Columbia Universities, settling afterwards in New York City, where she teaches creative writing at New York University and the Goldwater Hospital (a public facility for the severely physically disabled). Olds's books include *Satan Says* (1980), *The Dead and the Living* (1983; National Book Critics Circle Award), and *The Gold Cell* (1987).

GRACE PALEY (b. 1922)

A native New Yorker, Paley studied at Hunter College and New York University. She currently teaches literature at Sarah Lawrence College and gives frequent readings from her work. Her short stories have appeared in leading magazines as well as in three collections, *The Little Disturbances of Man* (1959), *Enormous Changes at the Last Minute* (1974), and *Later the Same Day* (1985). Though few, her stories have been admired for their stylistic liveliness and for their fusion of sardonic observation with spare, expressive form.

DOROTHY PARKER (1893–1967)

Parker satirized the literary, social, and sexual pieties of her time with a sharp eye and sardonic exuberance. If "Brevity is the soul of Lingerie," as she announced in a *Vogue* advertisement, it is also the heart of her wit. There are a number of "Parkerisms"—brief, witty aphorisms—still in circulation. Parker was born in New York City and was friendly with several other prominent writers and humorists of the 20s and 30s, including Harold Ross, founder of *The New Yorker*. Author of poetry, criticism, screenplays, and short stories, she published a number of collections, including *Enough Rope* (1926), *Sunset Gun* (1928), *Death and Taxes* (1931), and *Not So Deep as a Well* (1936).

LINDA PASTAN (b. 1932)

Author of more than half a dozen volumes of poetry, Pastan was born in New York City and attended Radcliffe College and Brandeis University before settling in suburban Washington, DC. Her books include *A Perfect Circle of Sun* (1971), *The Five Stages of Grief* (1978), *A Fraction of Darkness* (1985), and *The Imperfect Paradise* (1988). *PM / AM: New and Selected Poems* (1982) was nominated for the American Book Award.

MARGE PIERCY (b. 1936)

Piercy's earlier poetry examined the complex interplay between personal relationships and political forces, at the same time voicing the rage of women who have for so long been dominated and overwhelmed by men ("I imagine that I speak for a constituency, living and dead," she writes). Her later work, particularly the poems in *Stone, Paper, Knife* (1983), expresses also a sense of inclusiveness, of interconnection with all living things. Born in Detroit, Piercy studied at the University of Michigan and Northwestern University and taught for some time before the success of her novels allowed her to live a semi-rural life on Cape Cod. Her books of poetry include *Living in the Open* (1976), *The Moon Is Always Female* (1980), and *Available Light* (1988).

HAROLD PINTER (b. 1930)

Born and educated in East London, Pinter acted in a repertory company under the stage name of David Baron until his first play, *The Room*, was produced in 1957. This was followed immediately by *The Dumb Waiter*, *The Birthday Party*, and in 1960, *The Caretaker*, which established his reputation as a writer of disturbing and often absurd "realist" drama, as well as a master of pauses, double-entendres, and silences that communicate a secondary level of meaning beneath the surface textures of everyday speech. More recently, Pinter has worked on screenplays for filmed versions of John Fowles' *The French Lieutenant's Woman*, F. Scott Fitzgerald's *The Last Tycoon*, and Marcel Proust's *A la Recherche du Temps Perdu*.

SYLVIA PLATH (1932–1963)

Plath has attained the status of a cult figure as much for the splendid and beautiful agony of her poems as for her "martyrdom" to art. Her life, in all its outer banality and inner tragedy, might be seen as a confirmation that poetry is a dangerous vocation. Born the daughter of a Polish immigrant who died in 1940, Plath's early years were a vision of conventional success, including poetry prizes, scholarships at Smith College, and a *summa cum laude* graduation. She won a Fulbright Scholarship to Cambridge University, where she met and married the English poet, Ted Hughes, with whom she had two children. Yet beneath it all was a woman whose acute perceptions and intolerable pain led her to produce a novel, *The Bell Jar* (1963), and three volumes of poetry—and to commit suicide at the age of thirty.

EDGAR ALLAN POE (1809–1849)

Poe's actor father deserted his wife and son when Edgar was less than a year old. His mother died before he was three, and he and his younger sister were separated and taken into different families. The Allans (who gave Poe his middle name) moved, in 1815, to England, where Edgar had his early schooling. He studied briefly at the University of Virginia and in 1827 paid to have a volume of poems published in Boston (his birthplace); a second volume appeared in 1829 in Baltimore (where he was to die twenty years later). Having served for two years in the army, he was appointed to West Point in 1830 but apparently managed to have himself expelled within the year for cutting classes. Living in Baltimore with his grandmother, aunt, and cousin Virginia (whom he married in 1835 when she was thirteen), Poe began to attract critical attention but made very little money. For the twelve years of his bizarre marriage, he wrote, worked as journalist and editor, and drank. Not long after his wife died in 1847 he seemed to be straightening himself out when, on election day—October 3—he was found semiconscious near a polling place and died four days later without fully regaining consciousness. It is testimony to the continuing fame of his works that they need not be named here.

SHARON POLLOCK (b. 1936)

Pollock began her association with the theater as an actor and director in the mid-1960s, first in her native New Brunswick and then in Calgary as a member of Prairie Players, a touring company. Her first works for radio and theater date from the early 1970s; since then she has written several major stage plays and a number of children's works and radio scripts. She has taught at the University of Alberta, was playwright-in-residence at A.T.P., Calgary, and has been head of the Playwright's Colony at Banff. Her plays include *The Komagata Maru Incident* (1976), *One Tiger to a Hill* (1980), and *Generations* (1980).

ALEXANDER POPE (1688–1744)

Born near London, Pope was delicate as a child and deformed early on by tuberculosis of the spine. He nevertheless was encouraged to read widely and exhibited a precocious talent for poetry; his first successes were the *Essay on Criticism* (1711) and *The Rape of the Lock* (1712 and 1714). Pope's Catholicism, which precluded him from attending a university, voting, holding public office, or receiving the sort of patronage commonly bestowed on writers of his generation, led him to embark on translations of Homer's *Iliad* and *Odyssey* in 1713, the success of which would eventually make him the only important writer of his generation to make his living solely by his craft. Pope's extraordinary career resulted in works as diverse as the *Dunciad* (1728 and 1743), his great verse satire, and the *Essay on Man* (1733–34), his exploration of ethics and philosophy.

KATHERINE ANNE PORTER (1890–1980)

Porter was born Callie Russell Porter in Indian Creek, Texas. Her writing career was remarkable for its brilliance as well as its brevity. Her first volume, *Flowering Judas* (1930), was made up of stories that appeared in magazines in the previous decade. Her last (except for her *Collected Stories*, 1965, which included only earlier works) was *The Leaning Tower* (1944). She published a book of essays *The Days Before* (1952), and one long novel, *Ship of Fools* (1962), twenty-five years in the making, but is at her best in shorter forms, where her concision and precision of diction and style enable her brilliantly to capture a character, a culture, or chaos. A warning about reading "The Fig Tree" or her other stories: "Reviewers are much mistaken," she said, "when they insist on identifying me with any and every woman that appears in my stories. . . . I am a considerably more complicated person than they. They were not writers."

EZRA POUND (1885–1972)

Pound's tremendous ambition—to succeed in his own work and to influence the development of poetry and Western culture in general—led him to found the Imagist school of poetry, to advise and assist a galaxy of great writers (Eliot, Joyce, Williams, Frost, and Hemingway, to name a few), and to write a number of highly influential critical works. It also led him to a charge of treason (Pound served as a propagandist for Mussolini during World War II), a diagnosis of insanity, and twelve years at St. Elizabeth's, an institution for the criminally insane. Born in Hailey, Idaho, Ezra Loomis Pound studied at the University of Pennsylvania and Hamilton College before travelling to Europe in 1908. He remained there, living in Ireland, England, France, and Italy, for much of his life. Pound's verse is collected in *Personae: The Collected Poems* (1949) and *The Cantos* (1976).

MORDECAI RICHLER (b. 1931)

Richler was born in Montreal, the son of working-class Jewish parents; *The Street* (1975) is a loosely autobiographical depiction of his childhood. Richler attended Sir George Williams University for two years and worked as a freelance writer in Paris and London from 1952, returning to live in his native Quebec only in 1980. His writing is varied and includes short stories, essays, screenplays, and novels. His *Cocksure* (1968) and *St. Urbain's Horseman* (1971) won the Governor General's Award, and his own screen adaptation of his novel *The Apprenticeship of Duddy Kravitz* (1959) was nominated for an Academy Award in 1974. His novels include *Joshua Then and Now* (1980) and *Solomon Gursky Was Here* (1990).

THEODORE ROETHKE (1908–1963)

Born in Saginaw, Michigan, Roethke grew up around his father's 25-acre greenhouse complex—its associations with nurture and growth became an important subject in his later poetry. He worked for a time at Lafayette College, where he was professor of English and tennis coach, and later at the University of Washington, which appointed him poet-in-residence one year before he died. Roethke was an unhappy man, suffering from periodic mental breakdowns, yet the best of his poetry, with its reverence for and fear of the physical world, its quest for an ecstatic union with nature, seems destined to last. Roethke's books include *Open House* (1942), *Praise to the End!* (1951), and *The Far Field* (1964), which received a posthumous National Book Award.

ANNE SEXTON (1928–1974)

Poetry, Sexton once said, "should be a shock to the senses. It should almost hurt." Beginning with her early "confessional" poetry, Sexton's work remained physically and emotionally close to the bone. Born in Newton, Massachusetts, she attended Garland Junior College, married, worked at various times as a fashion model, teacher, and professor, and wrote poetry that by the time of her suicide in 1974 had won her a wide and attentive audience. Her books include *To Bedlam and Part Way Back* (1960), *All My Pretty Ones* (1962), *Live or Die* (1967), *Love Poems* (1969), *Transformations* (1972), and *The Death Notebooks* (1974).

WILLIAM SHAKESPEARE (1554–1616)

Considering the great and deserved fame of his work, surprisingly little is known of Shakespeare's life. We do know that between 1585 and 1592 he left his birthplace of Stratford for London to begin a career as playwright and actor. No dates of his professional career are recorded, however, nor can we be certain of the order in which he composed his plays and poetry. By 1594 he had established himself as a poet with two long works—*Venus and Adonis* and *The Rape of Lucrece*—but it was in the theatre that he made his strongest reputation. Shakespeare produced perhaps 35 plays in 25 years, proving himself a master of many genres in works such as *Macbeth*, *King Lear*, *Othello*, and *Antony and Cleopatra* (tragedy); *Richard III* and *Henry IV* (historical drama); *Twelfth Night* and *As You Like It* (comedy); and *The Tempest* (romance). His more than 150 sonnets are supreme expressions of the form.

SOPHOCLES (496?–406? B.C.)

Sophocles lived at a time when Athens and Greek Civilization had reached the peak of their power and influence. He not only served as a general under Pericles and played a prominent role in the city's affairs but was also arguably the greatest of the Greek tragic playwrights, an innovator who fundamentally changed the form of dramatic performance and the model Aristotle turned to when he discussed the nature of tragedy in his *Poetics*. Today only seven of Sopohocles' tragedies survive—the Oedipus Trilogy (*Oedipus the King*, *Oedipus at Colonus*, and *Antigone*), *Philoctetes*, *Ajax*, *Trachiniae*, and *Electra*—though records suggest that his output may have amounted to over 120 plays.

WALLACE STEVENS (1879–1955)

"I believe that with a bucket of sand and a wishing lamp I could create a world in half a second that would make this one look like a hunk of mud," Stevens once remarked to his wife. One of the great imaginative forces of this century, he was nevertheless an extraordinarily self-effacing public man, working for much of his adult life as an executive of the Hartford Accident and Indemnity Company while recreating the world at night in the "supreme fiction" of poetry. Born in Reading, Pennsylvania, Stevens attended Harvard University and New York Law School; his first book of poems, *Harmonium*, appeared in 1923. Stevens's poetry and prose can be found in *The Palm at the End of the Mind* (1971) and *The Necessary Angel: Essays on Reality and Imagination* (1951).

ELIZABETH TALLENT (b. 1954)

Tallent studied anthropology at the University of Illinois before turning to writing. Best known for her stories, she has won the Pushcart Prize and has had work published in *The New Yorker*, the *Paris Review*, *Esquire*, and *Grand Street*. Although she makes her home in Santa Fe, New Mexico, she teaches at the University of California at Davis in the winter and the University of Iowa in the summer. Her published books include the story collections *In Constant Flight* (1983) and *Time with Children* (1987), and the novel *Museum Pieces* (1985).

AMY TAN (b. 1952)

Tan was born in Oakland, California, just two and a half years after her parents immigrated there from China. She has worked as a consultant to programs for disabled children and as a freelance writer. In 1987 she visited China for the first time—"As soon as my feet touched China, I became Chinese"—and returned to write her first book, *The Joy Luck Club* (1989).

ALFRED, LORD TENNYSON (1809–1892)

Perhaps the most important and certainly the most popular of the Victorian poets, Tennyson demonstrated his talents at an early age; he published his first volume in 1827. Encouraged to devote his life to poetry by a group of undergraduates at Cambridge University known as the "Apostles," Tennyson was particularly close to Arthur Hallam, whose sudden death in 1833 inspired the long elegy, *In Memoriam* (1850). With that poem he achieved lasting fame and recognition; he was appointed poet laureate the year of its publication. Whatever the popularity of his "journalistic" poetry—"The Charge of the Light Brigade" (1854) is perhaps his best known—Tennyson's great theme was always the past, both personal (*In the Valley of Cauteretz*, 1864) and national (*Idylls of the King*, 1869).

DYLAN THOMAS (1914–1953)

In a Note to his *Collected Poems* (1952), Thomas wrote: "These poems, with all their crudities, doubts, and confusions, are written for the love of Man and in praise of God, and I'd be a damn fool if they weren't." Given their somber undertones and often wrenching awareness of death, his poems are also rich verbal and visual celebrations of life and its sweetness. Born in Swansea, Wales, into what he called "the smug darkness of a provincial town," Thomas published his first book, *18 Poems* (1934), at the age of twenty. Thereafter he had a successful, though turbulent, career publishing poetry, short stories, and plays, including the highly successful *Under Milk Wood* (1954). In his last years he supported himself with lecture tours and poetry readings in the United States, but his extravagent drinking caught up with him and he died in New York City of chronic alcoholism.

LEO TOLSTOY (1828–1910)

Tolstoy's life would have made a fitting subject for one of his novels. Born into a noble Russian family, orphaned before he was ten, he studied Oriental languages, then law, then settled on the family estate where he tried to improve the lot of his serfs though they treated him with suspicion. He served in the army, returned home to found a school, married, and wrote two monumental novels, his masterpieces *War and Peace* (1863–69) and *Anna Karenina* (1873–76). But he wasn't satisfied; he found his life, in his own words, "absurd . . . a stupid and spiteful joke," and was converted, first to his national religion, then to a kind of "primitive" Christianity. He opposed the military, capital punishment, persecution of the Jews; he gave up alcohol, meat, and as much of his property as his family would allow. In the end he fled from home—where his wife was trying to have him declared incompetent—intending to enter a monastery, but died in a railway station en route. His works, after his conversion, include *The Death of Iván Ilyich* (1886), "How Much Land Does a Man Need," and many other stories, parables, and novels.

WILLIAM TREVOR (b. 1928)

Born William Coxin in County Cork, Ireland, Trevor moved to Devon, England, in 1960. He was been a teacher—chiefly in England but including a stint in Armagh, Northern Ireland, 1950–52—advertising copywriter, sculptor, novelist—his novels include *The Old Boys* (1964), *Lovers of Their Time* (1979), *Other People's Worlds* (1980), and *Fools of Fortune* (1983)—and short-story writer. Many of his stories have been adapted for BBC radio. His volumes of short stories include *The Day We Got Drunk on Cake* (1972), *Angels at the Ritz* (1975), and *Beyond the Pale* (1982); *The Stories of William Trevor* was published in 1983. Trevor was named Commander, Order of the British Empire, in 1979.

LUISA VALENZUELA (b. 1938)

Valenzuela grew up in the thriving literary atmosphere of Buenos Aires, Argentina (her mother was a novelist and friend of Jorge Luis Borges). After attending the University of Buenos Aires, she began writing for magazines and newspapers, traveling widely in the United States, Europe, and Latin America. Her first story collection, *Hay que sonreir* (1966), was published in the United States as *Clara* (1979). Another collection, *Strange Things Happen Here* (1976, translated 1979), reflected some of the horrors of the military regime of the late 1970s. In 1979, Valenzuela moved to New York, where she now lives. She has published another novel, *The Lizard's Tale* (1983), and three collections of stories, *Other Weapons* (1985), *He Who Searches* (1987), and *Open Door* (1988).

OSCAR WILDE (1854–1900)

Oscar Fingal O'Flaherty Wills Wilde was born in Dublin, his father a leading surgeon, his mother a poet of the Free Ireland movement. Educated at Trinity College, Dublin and Oxford University, Wilde quickly established himself at the center of England's Aesthetic movement, attracting as much attention with his dress, conversation, and strong opinions as with his writing. His novel, *The Picture of Dorian Gray,* created a sensation when it was published in 1891, but his real success was as a writer of comedies, including *Lady Windermere's Fan* (1892), *A Woman of No Importance* (1893), *An Ideal Husband* (1895), and *The Importance of Being Earnest* (1895). By the spring of 1895, however, the events of Wilde's private life conspired to shatter his brilliant career. His relationship with the poet Lord Alfred Douglas led to a trial for homosexual "offences"; Wilde was found guilty and sentenced to two years' hard labor. He died in France a few years later, ignored by all but a few close friends.

TENNESSEE WILLIAMS (1911–1983)

The elements of Williams' dramatic voice—the instability of emotion, the shadows of violence, the imminence of death, guilty yet powerful sexuality, nostalgia for the past and hope for the future, the conviction that "we're all of us sentenced to solitary confinement inside our skins"—combine to make it one of this century's most distinctive. Born in Columbus, Mississippi, Thomas Lanier Williams wrote a number of plays while holding various jobs before *The Glass Menagerie* (1945) made his name and allowed him to devote himself exclusively to writing. Thereafter he had a remarkably prolific and successful career; two of his plays, *A Streetcar Named Desire* and *Cat on a Hot Tin Roof* (1955), won Pulitzer Prizes.

AUGUST WILSON (b. 1945)

Born in Pittsburgh, Wilson grew up in poverty and dropped out of school at sixteen. It was then, while working at low-paying jobs, that he started to write poetry. In 1968 he founded the Black Horizons Theatre Company of St. Paul, Minnesota, but he began writing plays only in the 1980s. His first play, *Jitney* (1982), was produced in Pittsburgh. Since then he has crafted several major works chronicling the Black experience in America, all of which have opened on Broadway after initial productions at the Yale Repertory Theatre and on tour. Two of them, *Fences* and *The Piano Lesson* (1990), have won Pulitzer Prizes.

WILLIAM CARLOS WILLIAMS (1883–1963)

Williams influenced a generation of American poets—many of them still living—by bringing to poetry the sense that "life is above all things else at any moment subversive of life as it was the moment before—always new, irregular." Born in Rutherford, New Jersey, Williams attended school in Switzerland and New York, and studied medicine at the University of Pennsylvania, where he met Hilda Doolittle (H.D.) and Ezra Pound. Thereafter he spent most of his life in Rutherford, practicing medicine and crafting a poetry of palpable immediacy, written in vital, local language. His long poem, *Paterson* (completed in 1963), vividly expresses what lies at the heart of his work: "No ideas but in things."

WILLIAM WORDSWORTH (1770–1850)

Born in Cockermouth in the sparsely populated English Lake District (which Coleridge and he would immortalize), Wordsworth spent his early years "drinking in" (to use a favorite metaphor) a rural environment which would provide material for much of his later poetry. After study at Cambridge University, he spent a year in France, hoping to witness first-hand the French Revolution's "glorious renovation." Remarkably, he was able to establish "a saving intercourse with my true self"—and to write some of his finest poetry—after a love affair with a French woman whose sympathies were Royalist, his own disillusionment at the Revolution, a forced return to England, and near emotional collapse. Perhaps because he was, above all, a poet of remembrance (of "emotion recollected in tranquility"), and his own early experience was not an inexhaustible resource, Wordsworth had written most of his great work—including his masterpiece, *The Prelude*—by the time he was forty.

WILLIAM BUTLER YEATS (1865–1939)

Perhaps the greatest twentieth-century poet in English, Yeats was born in Dublin, attended art school for a time, and left to devote himself to poetry (at the start of his career, a self-consciously romantic poetry, dreamy and ethereal). Yeats's reading of Nietzsche, his involvement with the Nationalist cause, and his desperate love for the actress (and Nationalist) Maud Gonne, led to a tighter, more actively passionate verse and a number of innovative dramatic works. Bitter and disillusioned at the results of revolution and the rise of the Irish middle class, Yeats later withdrew from contemporary events to "Thoor Ballylee," his Norman Tower in the country, there to construct an elaborate mythology and to write poetry, at once realist, symbolist, and metaphysical, which explored what were, for Yeats, fundamental questions of history and identity. Of the progress of his life, Yeats once said: "Man can embody truth but cannot know it."

WOODY ALLEN: "The Kugelmass Episode" from *Side Effects*. Copyright © 1977 by Woody Allen. Reprinted by permission of Random House, Inc.

MARGARET ATWOOD: "The Whirlpool Rapids" from *Bluebeard's Egg*. Copyright © 1983, 1986 by O. W. Toad, Ltd. Reprinted by permission of Houghton Mifflin Co. and the Canadian Publishers, McLelland and Stewart, Toronto.

JAMES BALDWIN: "Sonny's Blues" from *Going to Meet the Man*. Copyright © 1948, 1951, 1957, 1958, 1960, 1965 by James Baldwin. Reprinted by permission of Doubleday, a Division of Bantam, Doubleday, Dell Publishing Group, Inc.

TONI CADE BAMBARA: "My Man Bovanne" from *Gorilla, My Love*. Copyright © 1972 by Toni Cade Bambara. Reprinted by permission of Random House, Inc.

ANN BEATTIE: "Janus" from *Where You'll Find Me*. Copyright © 1986 by Irony and Pity, Inc. Reprinted by permission of Linden Press, a division of Simon & Schuster, Inc.

JORGE LUIS BORGES: "The Garden of Forking Paths" from *Labyrinths*. Copyright © 1962, 1964 by New Directions Publishing Corporation. Reprinted by permission of New Directions Publishing Corporation.

JOHN CHEEVER: "The Country Husband" from *The Stories of John Cheever*. Copyright 1954 by John Cheever. Reprinted by permission of Alfred A. Knopf, Inc.

RICHARD CONNELL: "The Most Dangerous Game." Copyright 1924 by Richard Connell; copyright renewed 1952 by Louise Fox Connell. Reprinted by permission of Brandt & Brandt Literary Agents, Inc.

LOUISE ERDRICH: "Love Medicine" from *Love Medicine*. Copyright © 1984 by Louise Erdrich. Reprinted by permission of Henry Holt and Company, Inc.

WILLIAM FAULKNER: "Barn Burning" and "The Old People" from *The Collected Stories of William Faulkner*. Copyright 1939 and renewed 1967 by Estelle Faulkner and Jill Faulkner Summers. Copyright 1930 and renewed 1958 by William Faulkner. "The Old People" from *Go Down, Moses*. Copyright 1940, 1942 and renewed 1968, 1970 by Estelle Faulkner and Jill Faulkner Summers. Reprinted by permission of Random House, Inc.

RICHARD FORD: "Great Falls" from *Rock Springs*. Copyright © 1987 by Richard Ford. Reprinted by permission of Atlantic Monthly Press.

GABRIEL GARCÍA MÁRQUEZ: "A Very Old Man With Enormous Wings" from *Collected Stories*. Copyright 1971 by Gabriel García Márquez. Reprinted by permission of Harper & Row, Publishers, Inc.

NADINE GORDIMER: "The Termitary" from *A Soldier's Embrace*. Copyright © 1975, 1977, 1980 by Nadine Gordimer. Reprinted by permission of the publisher, Viking Penguin, a division of Penguin Books USA, Inc.

ERNEST HEMINGWAY: "A Clean Well-Lighted Place" from *Winner Take Nothing*. Copyright 1933 by Charles Scribner's Sons; renewal copyright © 1961 by Mary Hemingway. Reprinted by permission of Charles Scribner's Sons, an imprint of Macmillan Publishing Company.

SPENCER HOLST: "The Zebra Storyteller" from *The Language of Cats and Other Stories*. Copyright © 1971 by Spencer Holst. Reprinted by permission of the author.

FRANZ KAFKA: "A Hunger Artist" from *The Penal Colony*, translated by Willa and Edwin Muir. Translation copyright 1948 and renewed 1976 by Schocken Books, Inc. Reprinted by permission of Schocken Books; published by Pantheon Books, a Division of Random House, Inc.

JAMAICA KINCAID: "Girl" from *At the Bottom of the River*. Copyright © 1978, 1979, 1981, 1982, 1983 by Jamaica Kincaid. Reprinted by permission of Farrar, Straus and Giroux, Inc.

D. H. LAWRENCE: "Odour of Chrysanthemums" from *The Complete Short Stories of D. H. Lawrence, Volume II*. Copyright 1922 by Thomas Seltzer, Inc.; copyright renewed 1950 by Frieda Lawrence; copyright renewed © 1962 by Angelo Ravagli and C. M. Weekley, Executors of the Estate of Frieda Lawrence Ravagli. "The Rocking-Horse Winner" from *The Complete Short Stories of D. H. Lawrence, Volume III*. Copyright 1922 by Thomas Seltzer, Inc.; copyright renewed 1950 by Frieda Lawrence; copyright renewed © 1961 by Angelo Ravagli and C. M. Weekley, Executors of the Estate of Frieda Lawrence Ravagli. Excerpts from "Auto biographical sketch," "Morality and the Novel," "Why the Novel Matters," and five letters from *Selected Literary Criticism*, edited by Anthony Beal. Copyright 1936 by Frieda Lawrence. Excerpts from "Art and Morality," "Love," "Nottingham and the Mining Countryside," and "Women are so

Cocksure" from *Phoenix I: The Posthumous Papers of D. H. Lawrence,* edited by Edward O. McDonald. Copyright 1936 by Frieda Lawrence, copyright renewed © 1964 by Frieda Lawrence Ravagli. All rights reserved. All selections reprinted by permission of the publisher, Viking Penguin, a division of Penguin Books USA, Inc.

URSULA K. LE GUIN: "The Eye Altering" from *The Compass Rose.* Copyright © 1982 by Ursula K. Le Guin. Reprinted by permission of Harper & Row, Publishers, Inc.

DORIS LESSING: "Our Friend Judith" from *A Man and Two Women.* Copyright © 1958, 1962, 1963 by Doris Lessing. Reprinted by permission of Simon & Schuster, Inc. and Jonathan Clowes Ltd., London, on behalf of Doris Lessing.

KATHERINE MANSFIELD: "Her First Ball" from *The Short Stories of Katherine Mansfield.* Copyright 1922 by Alfred A. Knopf, Inc., renewed 1950 by John Middleton Murry. Reprinted by permission of Alfred A. Knopf, Inc.

BOBBIE ANN MASON: "Shiloh" from *Shiloh and Other Stories.* Copyright © 1982 by Bobbie Ann Mason. Reprinted by permission of Harper & Row, Publishers, Inc.

BHARATI MUKHERJEE: "The Management of Grief" from *The Middleman and Other Stories.* Copyright © 1988 by Bharati Mukherjee. Reprinted by permission of Grove Weidenfeld.

ALICE MUNRO: "Boys and Girls" from *Dance of the Happy Shades.* Copyright 1968 by Alice Munro; published by Penguin Books. Reprinted by permission of McGraw-Hill Ryerson Limited, Toronto and Virginia Barber Literary Agency, Inc.

FLANNERY O'CONNOR: "Everything that Rises Must Converge" and "The Lame Shall Enter First" from *The Complete Stories.* Copyright © 1961, 1965 by the Estate of Mary Flannery O'Connor. Copyright © 1962, 1965 by the Estate of Mary Flannery O'Connor. Excerpts from *Mystery and Manners.* Copyright © 1969 by the Estate of Mary Flannery O'Connor. Reprinted by permission of Farrar, Straus and Giroux, Inc.

GRACE PALEY: "A Conversation with My Father" from *Enormous Changes at the Last Minute.* Reprinted by permission of Farrar, Straus and Giroux, Inc.

KATHERINE ANNE PORTER: "The Fig Tree." Copyright © 1960 by Katherine Anne Porter; copyright renewed 1988 by Isabel Bayley, Literary Trustee for the Estate of Katherine Anne Porter. Reprinted by permission of Isabel Bayley.

MORDECHAI RICHLER: "The Summer My Grandmother Was Supposed to Die" from *The Street: A Memoir.* Copyright © 1969 by Mordecai Richler. Reprinted by permission of International Creative Management, Inc. Originally appeared in *The New Republic.*

ELIZABETH TALLENT: "No One's a Mystery." Copyright © 1986, 1987 by Elizabeth Tallent. Reprinted by permission of Wylie, Aitken & Stone, Inc.

AMY TAN: "A Pair of Tickets" from *The Joy Luck Club.* Copyright © 1989 by Amy Tan. Reprinted by permission of the Putnam Publishing Group.

WILLIAM TREVOR: "Beyond the Pale" from *Beyond the Pale and Other Stories.* Copyright © 1981 by William Trevor. All rights reserved. Reprinted by permission of the publisher, Viking Penguin, a division of Penguin Books USA, Inc. and Peters Fraser & Dunlop Group, Ltd. Originally appeared in *The New Yorker.*

LUISA VALENZUELA: "The Redtown Chronicles" from *Open Door.* Copyright © 1988 by Luisa Valenzuela. Published by North Point Press and reprinted by permission.

DANNIE ABSE: "Breughel in Naples." Copyright © 1990 by Dannie Abse. "Pathology of Colours." Copyright © 1968 by Dannie Abse. Reprinted by permission of Anthony Sheil Associates, Ltd.

DIANE ACKERMAN: "Driving Through Farm Country at Sunset" and "Sweep Me Through Your Many-Chambered Heart" from *Wife of Light.* Reprinted by permission of the author. "Beija-Flor" from *Jaguar of Sweet Laughter.* Copyright © 1990 by Diane Ackerman. Reprinted by permission of Random House, Inc.

AGHA SHAHID ALI: "Houses" from *The Half-Inch Himalayas.* Copyright © 1987 by Agha Shahid Ali. Reprinted by permission of the University Press of New England.

DICK ALLEN: "Lost Love" from *Flight and Pursuit.* Reprinted by permission of Louisiana State University Press. Copyright 1976, 1982, 1983, 1984, 1985, 1986, 1987 by Dick Allen. Originally appeared in *The New Yorker.*

A. R. AMMONS: "Needs" from *Collected Poems, 1951–1971*. Copyright © 1972 by A. R. Ammons. Reprinted by permission of W. W. Norton & Company, Inc.

MAYA ANGELOU: "Africa" from *Oh Pray My Wings Are Gonna Fit Me Well*. Copyright © 1975 by Maya Angelou. Reprinted by permission of Random House, Inc.

RICHARD ARMOUR: "Hiding Place" from *Light Armour*. Copyright © 1954. Reprinted by permission of John Hawkins & Associates, Inc.

JOHN ASHBERY: "City Afternoon" from *Self-Portrait in a Convex Mirror*. Copyright © 1975 by John Ashbery. Reprinted by permission of Viking Penguin, a division of Penguin Books USA, Inc.

MARGARET ATWOOD: "Landcrab I," "Landcrab II," "Rat Song," "Siren Song," and "Tricks with Mirrors" from *Selected Poems 1966–1984*. Copyright © 1987, 1990 by Margaret Atwood. Reprinted by permission of Houghton Mifflin Co. and Oxford University Press Canada. "Variations on the Word *Sleep*" from *Selected Poems II: Poems Selected and New 1976–1986*. © Margaret Atwood (Toronto: Oxford University Press Canada, 1986). Reprinted by permission of the publisher. "Death of a Young Son by Drowning" from *Selected Poems*. Selection © Margaret Atwood (Toronto: Oxford University Press Canada, 1976). Reprinted by permission of the publisher.

W. H. AUDEN: "In Memory of W. B. Yeats" and "Musée des Beaux Arts" from *Collected Poems*, edited by Edward Mendelson. Copyright © 1940, renewed 1968 by W. H. Auden. Reprinted by permission of Alfred A. Knopf, Inc. and Faber and Faber Ltd.

CAROL JANE BANGS: "Touching Each Other's Surfaces" from *The Bones of the Earth*. Copyright © 1983 by Carol Jane Bangs. Reprinted by permission of New Directions Publishing Corporation.

JOHN BETJEMAN: "In Westminster Abbey" from *Collected Poems*. Reprinted by permission of John Murray (Publishers) Ltd.

ROO BORSON: "Talk." Reprinted by permission of the author.

ROBERT BRINGHURST: "For the Bones of Joseph Mengele, Disinterred June 1985" from *Pieces of Map, Pieces of Music*. Reprinted by permission of the Canadian Publishers, McClelland and Stewart, Toronto.

GWENDOLYN BROOKS: "First Fight. Then Fiddle" from *Blacks*. Copyright © 1987. Reprinted by permission of the author.

HELEN CHASIN: "The Word *Plum*" from *Coming Close and Other Poems*. Reprinted by permission of Yale University Press.

MARILYN CHIN: "Aubade" from *Dwarf Bamboo*, The Greenfield Review Press. Reprinted by permission of the author.

AMY CLAMPITT: "Beethoven, Opus 111" from *The Kingfisher*. Copyright © 1983 by Amy Clampitt. Reprinted by permission of Alfred A. Knopf, Inc.

FRANCES CORNFORD: "Parting in Wartime" from *Collected Poems*, the Cresset Press. Reprinted by kind permission of Hutchinson Publishing Group.

HART CRANE: "To Emily Dickinson" from *The Complete Poems and Selected Letters and Prose of Hart Crane*, edited by Brom Weber. Copyright 1933, © 1958, 1966 by Liveright Publishing Corporation. Reprinted by permission of Liveright Publishing Corporation.

ROBERT CREELEY: "I Know a Man" from *The Collected Poems of Robert Creeley, 1945–1975*. Copyright © 1983. Reprinted by permission of the University of California Press.

COUNTEE CULLEN: "For a Lady I Know" from *On These I Stand*. Copyright 1925 by Harper and Brothers; copyright renewed 1953 by Ida M. Cullen. Reprinted by permission of GRM Associates, Inc., agents for the Estate of Ida M. Cullen.

E. E. CUMMINGS: "[l(a]," "[anyone lived in a pretty how town]," and "[a salesman is an it that stinks Excuse]" from *Complete Poems, 1913–1962*. Copyright © 1923, 1925, 1931, 1935, 1938, 1939, 1940, 1944, 1945, 1946, 1947, 1948, 1949, 1950, 1951, 1952, 1953, 1954, 1955, 1956, 1957, 1958, 1959, 1960, 1961, 1962 by the Trustees for the E. E. Cummings Trust. Copyright © 1961, 1963, 1968 by Marion Morehouse Cummings. "[in Just-]" and "[Buffalo Bill 's]" from *Tulips and Chimneys*, edited by George James Firmage. Copyright 1923, 1925 and renewed 1951, 1953 by E. E. Cummings. Copyright © 1973, 1976 by the Trustees for the E. E. Cummings Trust. Copyright © 1973, 1976 by George James Firmage. "[ponder,darling,these busted statues]" from *Is 5*, edited by George James Firmage. Copyright © 1985 by E. E. Cummings Trust. Copyright 1926 by Horace Liveright. Copyright © 1954 by E. E. Cummings. Copyright © 1985 by George James Firmage. All selections reprinted by permission of Liveright Publishing Corporation.

J. V. CUNNINGHAM: "All In Due Time," "Here Lies My Wife," and "History of Ideas" from *Collected Poems and Epigrams of J. V. Cunningham.* Reprinted by permission of Ohio University Press / Swallow Press.

NORA DAUENHAUER: "Tlingit Concrete Poem" from *The Droning Shaman.* Copyright © 1988 by the Black Current Press. Reprinted by permission of the author.

WALTER DE LA MARE: "Slim Cunning Hands." Reprinted by permission of the Trustees of Walter de la Mare and the Society of Authors as their representatives.

PETER DE VRIES: "To His Importunate Mistress." Copyright © 1986 by Peter De Vries. Originally appeared in *The New Yorker.* Reprinted by permission.

JAMES DICKEY: "Cherrylog Road" and "The Leap" from *Poems, 1957–1967.* Copyright © 1963 by James Dickey. Reprinted by permission of the University Press of New England.

EMILY DICKINSON: Poems 249, 341, 467, 569, 632, 657, 712, 754, 986, 1434, and 1732 from *The Poems of Emily Dickinson,* edited by Thomas H. Johnson. Copyright 1951, © 1955, 1979, 1983 by The President and Fellows of Harvard College. Reprinted by permission of Harvard University Press. Poems 341, 569, 657, and 754 from *The Complete Poems of Emily Dickinson* edited by Thomas H. Johnson. Copyright 1929 by Martha Dickinson Bianchi. Copyright © renewed 1957 by Mary L. Hampson. Reprinted by permission of Little, Brown and Company.

DAVID DONNELL: "Potatoes" from *Settlements.* Reprinted by permission of the Canadian Publishers, McClelland and Stewart, Toronto.

RITA DOVE: "Daystar." Reprinted by permission of the author. "Fifth Grade Autobiography" from *Grace Notes, Poems.* Copyright © 1989 by Rita Dove. Reprinted by permission of W. W. Norton & Company, Inc.

ALAN DUGAN: "Elegy" from *New and Collected Poems, 1961–1983.* Reprinted by permission of the Ecco Press.

STEPHEN DUNN: "Dancing With God," "The Man Who Closed Shop," "Men Talk," and "Tenderness" from *Between Angels, Poems.* Copyright © 1989 by Stephen Dunn. Reprinted by permission of W. W. Norton & Company, Inc.

RICHARD EBERHARDT: "The Fury of Aerial Bombardment" from *Collected Poems 1930–1976.* Copyright © 1960, 1976 by Richard Eberhardt. Reprinted by permission of Oxford University Press, Inc.

T. S. ELIOT: "Journey of the Magi" from *Collected Poems 1909–1962.* Copyright 1936 by Harcourt Brace Jovanovich, Inc., copyright © 1964, 1963 by T. S. Eliot. Reprinted by permission of Harcourt, Brace Jovanovich, Inc. and Faber and Faber Ltd.

JAMES A. EMANUEL: "Emmett Till" from *The Treehouse and Other Poems.* Reprinted by permission of Broadside Press.

KENNETH FEARING: "Dirge" from *New and Selected Poems.* Reprinted by permission of Indiana University Press.

DAVID FERRY: "The Guest Ellen at the Supper for Street People" from *Raritan,* Volume VII, no. 1, Summer 1987. Reprinted by permission of the author.

ROBERT FRANCIS: "Hogwash" from *Collected Poems, 1936–1976.* Copyright © 1938, 1965, 1966 by Robert Francis. Reprinted by permission of the University of Massachusetts Press.

ROBERT FROST: "Design," "Never Again Would Birds' Song Be the Same," "Range Finding," "The Road Not Taken," "Stopping By Woods on a Snowy Evening," and "U.S. 1946 King's X" from *The Poetry of Robert Frost,* edited by Edward Connery Latham. Copyright 1916, © 1969 by Holt Rinehart and Winston. Copyright 1936, 1942, 1944, © 1962 by Robert Frost. Copyright © 1964, 1970, 1975 by Lesley Frost Ballantine. Reprinted by permission of Henry Holt and Company, Inc.

TESS GALLAGHER: "Sudden Journey," "Unanswered Letter," and "Not There" from *Willingly.* Reprinted by permission of the author.

SANDRA M. GILBERT: "Sonnet: The Ladies' Home Journal" from *Emily's Bread, Poems.* Copyright © 1984 by Sandra M. Gilbert. Reprinted by permission of W. W. Norton & Company, Inc.

ARTHUR GUITERMAN: "On the Vanity of Earthly Greatness" from *Gaily the Troubadour.* Reprinted by permission of Louise H. Sclove.

MICHAEL HARPER: "Dear John, Dear Coltrane" from *Dear John, Dear Coltrane.* Reprinted by permission of the author.

JAMES HARRISON: "Penelope" from *Flying Dutchman*. Reprinted by permission of Sono Nis Press.

ROBERT HASS: "Privilege of Being" from *Human Wishes*. Reprinted by permission of the Ecco Press.

ROBERT HAYDEN: "Frederick Douglass" and "Those Winter Sundays" from *Angle of Ascent, New and Selected Poems*. Copyright © 1975, 1972, 1970, 1966 by Robert Hayden. Reprinted by permission of Liveright Publishing Corporation.

SEAMUS HEANEY: "The Outlaw" from *Poems, 1965–1975*. Copyright © 1966, 1969, 1972, 1975 by Seamus Heaney. Reprinted by permission of Farrar, Straus & Giroux, Inc. and Faber and Faber Ltd.

ANTHONY HECHT: "The Dover Bitch" from *The Hard Hours*. Copyright © 1959, 1967 by Anthony Hecht. Reprinted by permission of Atheneum Publishers, an imprint of Macmillan Publishing Company.

DAVID HELWIG: "Lot" from *The Sign of the Gunman*. Reprinted by permission of Oberon Press.

JOHN HOLLANDER: "Adam's Task" from *The Night Mirror*. Copyright © 1970, 1971, by John Hollander. Reprinted by permission of the author and Atheneum Publishers, an imprint of Macmillan Publishing Company.

ROBERT HOLLANDER: "You Too? Me Too—Why not? Soda Pop" from The Massachusetts Review, Vol. 9, no. 3. © 1968. Reprinted by permission of the Massachusetts Review, Inc.

A. D. HOPE: "Imperial Adam" from *Collected Poems 1930–1970*. Reprinted by kind permission of Angus & Robertson Publishers.

A. E. HOUSMAN: "To an Athlete Dying Young" from *The Collected Poems of A. E. Housman*. Copyright © 1967, 1968 by Robert E. Symons. Reprinted by permission of Henry Holt and Company, Inc.

LANGSTON HUGHES: "Theme for English B" from *Montage of a Dream Deferred*. Copyright 1951 by Langston Hughes. Copyright renewed 1979 by George Houston Bass. Reprinted by permission of Harold Ober Associates Inc. "The Negro Speaks of Rivers" from *Selected Poems of Langston Hughes*. Copyright 1926 by Alfred A. Knopf, Inc. and renewed in 1954 by Langston Hughes. Reprinted by permission of Alfred A. Knopf, Inc. "Harlem (A Dream Deferred)" from *The Panther and the Lash*. Copyright 1951 by Langston Hughes. Reprinted by permission of Alfred A. Knopf, Inc.

RICHARD HUGO: "To Women" and "Places and Ways to Live" *from Making Certain It Goes On, the Collected Poems of Richard Hugo*. Copyright © 1984 by the estate of Richard Hugo. Reprinted by permission of W. W. Norton & Company, Inc.

RANDALL JARRELL: "The Death of the Ball Turrett Gunner" from *The Complete Poems*. Copyright © 1945, 1972 by Mrs. Randall Jarrell. Reprinted by permission of Farrar, Straus & Giroux, Inc.

ELIZABETH JENNINGS: "Delay" from *Collected Poems*. Reprinted by permission of David Higham Associates.

PAULETTE JILES: "Paper Matches." Reprinted by permission of the author.

HELENE JOHNSON: "Sonnet to a Negro in Harlem." Reprinted by permission of the author.

D. G. JONES: "Summer Is a Poem by Ovid" from *A Throw of Particles*. Reprinted by permission of Stoddart Publishing Co., Ltd. 34 Lesmill Road., Don Mills, Ontario, Canada.

DONALD JUSTICE: "Children Walking Home from School Through Good Neighborhood" from *The Sunset Maker*. Copyright © 1987 by Donald Justice. Reprinted by permission of Atheneum Publishers, an imprint of Macmillan Publishing Company. "Counting the Mad" from *The Summer Anniversaries*. Copyright © 1960 by Donald Justice. Reprinted by permission of the University Press of New England.

X. J. KENNEDY: "Epitaph for a Postal Clerk," "Nude Descending a Staircase," and "In a Prominent Bar in Secaucus One Day" from *Nude Descending a Staircase*. Copyright © 1961 by the author. Reprinted by permission of Curtis Brown, Limited.

GALWAY KINNELL: "After Making Love We Hear Footsteps" and "Blackberry Eating" from *Mortal Acts, Mortal Words*. Copyright © 1980 by Galway Kinnell. Reprinted by permission of Houghton Mifflin Company.

ETHERIDGE KNIGHT: "Hard Rock Returns from the Hospital for the Criminal Insane" and "The Idea of Ancestry" from *Poems from Prison*. Copyright © 1968 by Etheridge Knight. Reprinted by permission of Broadside Press.

KENNETH KOCH: "Variations on a Theme by William Carlos Williams" from *Thank You and Other Poems*. Copyright © 1962 by Kenneth Koch. Reprinted by permission of the author.

MAXINE KUMIN: "Woodchucks" from *Our Ground Time Here Will Be Brief.* Copyright © 1971 by Maxine Kumin. All rights reserved. Reprinted by permission of Viking Penguin, a division of Penguin Books USA, Inc.

PHILIP LARKIN: "Annus Mirabilis" from *High Windows.* Copyright © 1974 by Philip Larkin. Reprinted by permission of Farrar, Straus & Giroux, Inc. and Faber and Faber Ltd. "Church Going" from *The Less Deceived.* Reprinted by permission of the Marvell Press.

IRVING LAYTON: "Berry Picking" from *A Wild Peculiar Joy.* "Keine Lazarovitch, 1870–1959" from *Selected Poems.* Reprinted by permission of the Canadian Publishers, McClelland and Stewart, Toronto.

LI-YOUNG LEE: "Persimmons" and "Visions and Interpretations" from *Rose.* Copyright © 1986 by Li-Young Lee. Reprinted by permission of BOA Editions, Ltd. 92 Park Ave., Brockport, NY 14420.

DENISE LEVERTOV: "What Were They Like?" from *Poems: 1960–1967.* Copyright 1964 by Denise Levertov Goodman. Reprinted by permission of New Directions Publishing Corporation.

C. DAY LEWIS: "Song" from *Collected Poems.* Reprinted by permission of Jonathan Cape Ltd., Peters Fraser & Dunlop Group, Ltd., and the executors of the estate of the author.

DOROTHY LIVESAY: "Green Rain." Copyright 1977. Reprinted by permission of the author.

DOUGLAS LOCHHEAD: "Winter Landscape—Halifax." Reprinted by permission of the author.

AUDRE LORDE: "Recreation" and "Hanging Fire" from *The Black Unicorn, Poems.* Copyright © 1978 by Audre Lorde. Reprinted by permission of W. W. Norton & Company, Inc.

ROBERT LOWELL: "Skunk Hour" from *Life Studies.* Copyright 1956, 1959 by Robert Lowell, Sheridan Lowell, and Caroline Lowell. Reprinted by permission of Farrar, Straus & Giroux, Inc.

DAVID MCCORD: "Epitaph on a Waiter" from *Bay Window Ballads.* Copyright 1935 by Charles Scribner's Sons, renewed 1963 by David McCord. Reprinted by permission of Charles Scribner's Sons, an imprint of Macmillan Publishing Company.

CYNTHIA MACDONALD: "Two Brothers in a Field of Absence" from *Alternate Means of Transport.* Copyright © 1980, 1981, 1982, 1983, 1985 by Cynthia MacDonald. Reprinted by permission of Alfred A. Knopf, Inc.

HEATHER MCHUGH: "What Could Hold Us," "To the Quick," and "A Physics" from *To the Quick.* Copyright © 1987 by Heather McHugh. Reprinted by permission of the University Press of New England. "20–200 on 737" first published in *The Threepenny Review.* Reprinted by permission.

CLAUDE MCKAY: "America," "The Harlem Dancer," and "The White House" from *Selected Poems of Claude McKay.* Copyright © 1981. Reprinted with the permission of Twayne Publishers, a division of G. K. Hall & Co.

ARCHIBALD MACLEISH: "Ars Poetica" from *New and Collected Poems 1917–1982.* Copyright © 1985 by the Estate of Archibald MacLeish. Reprinted by permission of Houghton Mifflin Co.

LOUIS MACNEICE: "Sunday Morning" from *The Collected Poems of Louis MacNeice.* Reprinted by permission of Faber and Faber Ltd.

ELI MANDEL: "Houdini." Reprinted by permission of the author.

HARRY MATHEWS: "Histoire" from *Armenian Papers: Poems 1954–1984.* Copyright © 1987 by Harry Mathews. Reprinted by permission of Princeton University Press.

WILLIAM MATTHEWS: "The Psychopathology of Everyday Life" from *A Happy Childhood.* Copyright © 1982 by William Matthews. Reprinted by permission of Little, Brown and Company.

JAMES MERRILL: "Casual Wear" from *Late Settings.* Copyright © 1985 by James Merrill. "Watching the Dance" from *Nights and Days.* Copyright © 1966 by James Merrill. All selections reprinted by permission of Atheneum Publishers, an imprint of Macmillan Publishing Company.

W. S. MERWIN: "Burning the Cat" from *Green With Beasts.* Copyright © 1955 by W. S. Merwin. Reprinted by permission of Georges Borchardt, Inc. for the author.

SUSAN MITCHELL: "From the Journals of the Frog Prince" from *The Water Inside the Water.* Copyright © 1983 by Susan Mitchell. Reprinted by Permission of the University Press of New England.

EDNA ST. VINCENT MILLAY: "[I, being born a woman and distressed]," and "[What my lips have kissed, and where, and why]" from *Collected Sonnets,* Revised and Expanded Edition, Harper & Row, 1988. Copyright 1923, 1951 by Edna St. Vincent Millay and Norma Millay Ellis. Reprinted by permission.

ARTHUR W. MONKS: "Twilight's Last Gleaming" from *Jiggery-Pokery,* edited by Anthony Hecht and

John Hollander. Copyright © 1966 by Anthony Hecht and John Hollander. Reprinted by permission of Atheneum Publishers, an imprint of Macmillan Publishing Company.

MARIANNE MOORE: "Poetry" from *Collected Poems.* Copyright © 1935 by Marianne Moore, renewed 1963 by Marianne Moore and T. S. Eliot. Reprinted by permission of Macmillan Publishing Company. "Poetry" (shorter version) from *Selected Poems.* Reprinted by permission of Marianne Craig Moore, Literary Executor for the estate of Marianne Moore. All rights reserved.

PAT MORA: "Sonrisas" from *Borders.* Reprinted by permission of Arte Publico Press. "Gentle Communion." Reprinted by permission of the author.

SUSAN MUSGRAVE: "The Judas Goat" from *A Man to Marry A Man to Bury.* Reprinted by permission of the author.

HOWARD NEMEROV: "Boom!", "Epigram: Political Reflexion," "The Goose Fish," "The Vacuum," and "A Way of Life" from *The Collected Poems of Howard Nemerov,* the University of Chicago Press, 1977. Reprinted by permission of the author.

GABRIEL OKARA: "Piano and Drums" (originally appeared in *Black Orpheus*). Reprinted by permission of the author.

SHARON OLDS: "Leningrad Cemetary: Winter of 1941." Copyright © 1979, *The New Yorker Magazine,* Inc. Reprinted by permission. "May, 1968" from *Poetry* (May 1987). Copyright © 1987 by The Modern Poetry Association. Reprinted by permission of the author and the Editor of *Poetry.* "The Elder Sister," "Sex Without Love," and "The Victim" from *The Dead and the Living.* Copyright © 1975, 1978, 1980, 1981, 1982, 1983 by Sharon Olds. Reprinted by permission of Alfred A. Knopf, Inc. "The Glass," "In the Hospital Near the End," "Last Acts," and "The Moment of My Father's Death." Copyright © 1990 by Sharon Olds. Reprinted by permission of the author.

MICHAEL ONDAATJE: "Light" from *There's a Trick with a Knife I'm Learning to Do, Poems 1963–1978.* Copyright © 1979 by Michael Ondaatje. Reprinted by permission of the Ellen Levine Literary Agency and the Canadian Publishers, McLelland and Stewart, Toronto.

ERIC ORMSBY: "My Mother In Old Age." Copyright © 1989 Eric Ormsby. Reprinted by permission. Originally appeared in *The New Yorker.*

WILFRED OWEN: "Dulce et Decorum Est" from *Collected Poems.* Copyright © 1963 by Chatto and Windus. Reprinted by permission of New Directions Publishing Corporation.

P. K. PAGE: "Photos of a Salt Mine." Reprinted by permission of the author.

DOROTHY PARKER: "A Certain Lady," "Comment," "Indian Summer," and "One Perfect Rose" from *The Portable Dorothy Parker.* Copyright 1929, renewed 1957 by Dorothy Parker. All rights reserved. Reprinted by permission of Viking Penguin, a division of Penguin Books USA, Inc.

LINDA PASTAN: "Ars Poetica," "Erosion," "Turnabout," "love poem," and "To a Daughter Leaving Home" from *The Imperfect Paradise, Poems.* Copyright © 1988 by Linda Pastan. "Marks" from *AM/PM, New and Selected Poems.* Copyright © 1982 by Linda Pastan. All selections reprinted by permission of W. W. Norton & Company, Inc.

RAYMOND PATTERSON: "You Are the Brave" from *26 Ways of Looking at a Black Man.* Reprinted by permission of Universal Award House, Inc.

MARGE PIERCY: "Barbie Doll" from *Circles on the Water.* Copyright © 1982 by Marge Piercy. "To Have Without Holding" and "September Afternoon at Four O'clock" from *The Moon Is Always Female.* Copyright © 1980 by Marge Piercy. "What's That Smell In the Kitchen?" from *Stone, Paper, Knife.* Copyright © 1980 by Marge Piercy. All selections reprinted by permission of Alfred A. Knopf, Inc.

SYLVIA PLATH: "Daddy," copyright © 1963 by Ted Hughes, "Black Rook in Rainy Weather," copyright © 1960 by the Estate of Sylvia Plath, "Lady Lazarus," copyright © 1963 by Ted Hughes, "Mirror," copyright © 1963 by Ted Hughes, and "Morning Song," copyright © 1961 by Ted Hughes, from *The Collected Poems of Sylvia Plath.* Copyright © 1971, 1981 by Ted Hughes. Reprinted by permission of Harper & Row Publishers, Inc. and Olwyn Hughes. "Point Shirley" from *The Colossus and Other Poems.* Copyright © 1959 by Sylvia Plath. Reprinted by permission of Alfred A. Knopf, Inc. and Olwyn Hughes.

KATHA POLLITT: "Two Fish" from *Antarctic Traveller.* Copyright © 1972, 1973, 1974, 1975, 1977, 1978, 1979, 1980, 1981 by Katha Pollitt. Reprinted by permission of Alfred A. Knopf, Inc.

EZRA POUND: "The Bathtub," "The Garden," "The River-Merchant's Wife: A Letter," "In a Station of the Metro," "There Died a Myriad," and "A Virginal" from *Personae.* Copyright © 1926 by Ezra Pound. Reprinted by permission of New Directions Publishing Corporation.

JIM POWELL: "It Was Fever that Made the World." Copyright © The Paris Review, Inc. Reprinted by permission.

JAROLD RAMSEY: "Hand Shadows" and "The Tally Stick." Reprinted by permission of the author.

DUDLEY RANDALL: "Ballad of Birmingham" from *Poem Counter Poem.* Reprinted by permission of the Broadside Press.

JOHN CROWE RANSOM: "Bells for John Whiteside's Daughter" from *Selected Poems,* Third Edition, Revised and Enlarged. Copyright © 1924 by Alfred A. Knopf, Inc. and renewed 1952 by John Crowe Ransom. Reprinted by permission of Alfred A. Knopf, Inc.

ISHMAEL REED: "beware : do not read this poem" and "I Am a Cowboy in the Boat of Ra." Copyright © 1972 by Ishmael Reed. Reprinted by permission of the author.

ADRIENNE RICH: "At a Bach Concert," "Aunt Jennifer's Tigers," "Diving Into the Wreck," "For the Record," "Living In Sin," "Orion," "Planetarium," "Snapshots of A Daughter-In-Law," "Storm Warnings," and "Two Songs" from *The Fact of A Doorframe, Poems Old and New, 1950–1984.* Copyright © 1984 by Adrienne Rich. Copyright © 1975, 1978 by W. W. Norton & Company, Inc. Copyright © 1981 by Adrienne Rich. Reprinted by permission of W. W. Norton & Company, Inc. "Origins and History of Consciousness" from *The Dream of a Common Language, Poems 1974–1977.* Copyright © 1978 by W. W. Norton & Company, Inc. Reprinted by permission of W. W. Norton & Company, Inc. "Delta," "Letters in the Family," "Love Poem," and "Walking Down the Road" from *Time's Power, Poems 1985–1988.* Copyright © 1989 by Adrienne Rich. Reprinted by permission of W. W. Norton & Company, Inc. "When We Dead Awaken: Writing as Re-Vision" from *On Lies, Secrets, and Silence, Selected Prose 1966–1978.* Copyright © 1979 by W. W. Norton & Company, Inc. Reprinted by permission of W. W. Norton & Company, Inc. "An Interview with Adrienne Rich" by David Kalstone. Copyright © 1972 by Saturday Review, Inc. Reprinted by permission of Omni Publications International, Ltd. "Talking with Adrienne Rich," an interview with Wayne Dodd and Stanley Plumly, from *The Ohio Review,* No. 1. Reprinted by permission.

ALBERTO RÍOS: "Incident at Imuris" from *The Lime Orchard Woman.* Reprinted by permission of the author.

EDWIN ARLINGTON ROBINSON: "Mr. Flood's Party" from *Collected Poems.* Copyright 1921 by Edwin Arlington Robinson, renewed 1949 by Ruth Nivison. Reprinted by permission of Macmillan Publishing Company.

THEODORE ROETHKE: "My Papa's Waltz," "The Dream," and "The Waking" from *The Collected Poems of Theodore Roethke.* Copyright 1942 by Hearst Magazines, Inc., © 1948, 1954, 1955 by Theodore Roethke. Reprinted by permission of Doubleday, a division of Bantam, Doubleday, Dell Publishing Group, Inc.

PATTIANN ROGERS: "The Family Is All There Is" from *Splitting and Bending.* Copyright © 1989 by Pattiann Rogers. Reprinted by permission of the University Press of New England.

LIZ ROSENBERG: "Married Love" from *The Fire Music.* Copyright © 1986 by Liz Rosenberg. Reprinted by permission of the University of Pittsburgh Press.

LARRY RUBIN: "The Houses of Emily Dickinson," first published by the University of the South in the Sewanee Review, 91, 2 (Spring 1983). Copyright 1983 by Larry Rubin. Reprinted by permission of the author and the editor of the Sewanee Review.

MARY JO SALTER: "Welcome to Hiroshima" from *Henry Purcell in Japan.* Copyright © 1984 by Mary Jo Salter. Reprinted by permission of Random House, Inc.

ANNE SEXTON: "The Fury of Overshoes" from *The Death Notebooks.* Copyright © 1974 by Anne Sexton. Reprinted by permission of Houghton Mifflin Co.

ALAN SHAPIRO: "Familiar Story." Reprinted by permission of the author.

KARL SHAPIRO: "Auto Wreck" from *Selected Poems.* Copyright © 1978 by Karl Shapiro. Reprinted by permission of Wieser & Weiser, 118 East 25th Street, New York, New York 10010.

LOUIS SIMPSON: "To The Western World" from *A Dream of Governors.* Copyright © 1959 by Louis Simpson. Reprinted by permission of the University Press of New England.

DESMOND SKIRROW: "Ode on a Grecian Urn Summarized." Reprinted from *The New Statesman,* London, by permission.

KAY SMITH: "Annunciation." Reprinted by permission of the author.

STEVIE SMITH: "The Jungle Husband" from *Collected Poems of Stevie Smith*. Copyright © 1972 by Stevie Smith. Reprinted by permission of New Directions Publishing Corporation.

W. D. SNODGRASS: "Leaving the Motel." Reprinted by permission of the author.

STEPHEN SPENDER: "Judas Iscariot" from *The Edge of Being*. Reprinted by permission of Sterling Lord Literistic, Inc. and Faber and Faber Ltd. "The Express" from *Collected Poems*. Copyright © 1934 and renewed 1962 by Stephen Spender. Reprinted by permission of Alfred A. Knopf, Inc. and Faber and Faber Ltd.

WILLIAM STAFFORD: "At the Bomb Testing Sight." Copyright © 1960 by William Stafford. Reprinted by permission of Harper & Row Publishers, Inc.

WALLACE STEVENS: "The Emperor of Ice Cream," "Anecdote of the Jar," and "Sunday Morning" from *The Collected Poems of Wallace Stevens*. Copyright 1923 and renewed 1951 by Wallace Stevens. Reprinted by permission of Alfred A. Knopf, Inc.

RUTH STONE: "Second-Hand Coat" from *Second-Hand Coat*. Copyright © 1987 by Ruth Stone. Reprinted by permission of David R. Godine, Publisher.

NANCY SULLIVAN. "Burial in the Sand" from *Telling It*. Copyright © 1975 by Nancy Sullivan. Reprinted by permission of David R. Godine, Publisher.

DYLAN THOMAS: "Fern Hill," "In My Craft or Sullen Art," and "Do Not Go Gentle Into That Good Night" from *Poems of Dylan Thomas*. Copyright 1939, 1945 by New Directions Publishing Corporation, 1952, 1945 by the Trustees for the Copyrights of Dylan Thomas. Reprinted by permission of New Directions Publishing Corporation and David Higham Associates.

JEAN TOOMER: "Song of the Son" from *Cane*. Copyright 1923 by Boni & Liveright Publishing Corporation. Copyright renewed 1951 by Jean Toomer. Reprinted by permission of Liveright Publishing Corporation.

MONA VAN DUYN: "What the Motorcycle Said" from *Merciful Disguises*. Copyright © 1973 by Mona Van Duyn. Reprinted by permission of Atheneum Publishers, an imprint of Macmillan Publishing Company.

ELLEN BRYANT VOIGT: "For My Mother" from *The Forces of Plenty*. Copyright © 1983 by Ellen Bryant Voigt. Reprinted by permission of W. W. Norton & Company, Inc.

MIRIAM WADDINGTON: "Advice to the Young" and "Old Women of Toronto" from *Collected Poems*. Copyright © 1986 by Miriam Waddington. Reprinted by permission of Oxford University Press Canada.

DAVID WAGONER: "My Father's Garden" from *Through the Forest*. Copyright © 1987 by David Wagoner. Reprinted by permission of Atlantic Monthly Press.

DIANE WAKOWSKI: "The Photos" from *The Man Who Shook Hands*. Copyright © 1972, 1975, 1976, 1978 by Diane Wakowski. Reprinted by permission of Doubleday, a division of Bantam, Doubleday, Dell Publishing Group, Inc. "A Poet Recognizing the Echo of the Voice." © 1970 by Diane Wakowski. Reprinted by permission of the author.

TOM WAYMAN: "Picketing Supermarkets" and "Wayman in Love." Reprinted by permission of the author.

RICHARD WILBUR: "Love Calls Us to the Things of This World" from *Things of This World*. Copyright © 1956 and renewed 1984 by Richard Wilbur. All selections reprinted by permission of Harcourt Brace Jovanovich, Inc.

WILLIAM CARLOS WILLIAMS: "The Red Wheelbarrow" and "This Is Just to Say" from *Collected Poems: Vol. I 1909–1939*. Copyright 1938 by New Directions Publishing Corporation. "Poem," "The Dance," and "Raleigh Was Right" from *Collected Poems, Vol. II 1939–1962*. Copyright 1944, 1962 by New Directions Publishing Corporation. All selections reprinted by permission of New Directions Publishing Corporation.

YVOR WINTERS: "At the San Francisco Airport" from *The Collected Poems of Yvor Winters*, 1978, Swallow Press. Reprinted by permission of Ohio University Press / Swallow Press.

JAMES WRIGHT: "Arrangements with Earth for Three Dead Friends" from *Collected Poems*. Copyright © 1971 by James Wright. Reprinted by permission of the University Press of New England. First appeared in *The Green Wall*, published by Yale University Press.

JUDITH WRIGHT: "Dove-Love" from *Collected Poems 1942–1970*. Reprinted by kind permission of Angus & Robertson Publishers.

W. B. YEATS: "Among School Children," "Byzantium," "Easter, 1916," "A Last Confession," "Leda and the Swan," "On Being Asked for a War Poem," "Sailing to Byzantium," and "The Second Coming" from *The Poems of W. B. Yeats: A New Edition*, edited by Richard J. Finneran. Copyright 1933 by Macmillan Publishing Company, renewed 1961 by Bertha Georgie Yeats. Reprinted by permission of Macmillan Publishing Company.

ARISTOPHANES: *Lysistrata*, translated by Charles T. Murphy, from *Greek Literature in Translation*, edited by W. J. Oates and C. T. Murphy. Copyright 1944, © renewed 1971 by W. J. Oates and C. T. Murphy. Reprinted with permission of Longman Publishing Group.

SAMUEL BECKETT: *Krapp's Last Tape*. Copyright © 1958 by Grove Press, Inc. Reprinted by permission of Grove Weidenfeld and Faber and Faber Ltd.

ANTON CHEKHOV: "The Brute" from *The Brute and Other Farces*, ed. Eric Bentley. Copyright © 1958 by Eric Bentley. Reprinted by permission of Applause Theatre Book Publishers, 211 West 71st Street, New York, NY 10023.

MARGUERITE DURAS: *Hiroshima Mon Amour*. Copyright © 1961 by Grove Press, Inc. Reprinted by permission of Grove Weidenfeld.

SUSAN GLASPELL: *Trifles*. Copyright © 1951 by Walter H. Baker Company. This edition published by arrangement with Baker's Plays, 100 Chauncy Street, Boston, Massachusetts 02111. *Trifles* is the sole property of the author and is fully protected under the copyright laws of the United States, the British Empire including the dominion of Canada, and all other countries of the Copyright Union, and is subject to royalty. The play may not be acted by professionals or amateurs without formal permission in writing and the payment of royalty. All rights, including professional, amateur, stock, radio and television broadcasting, motion picture, recitation, lecturing, public reading and the rights of translation in foreign languages are reserved. All inquiries should be directed to Baker's Plays.

LILLIAN HELLMAN: *The Little Foxes*. Copyright 1939 and renewed 1967 by Lillian Hellman. Reprinted by permission of Random House, Inc.

DAVID HENRY HWANG: *M. Butterfly*. Copyright © 1986, 1987, 1988 by David Hwang. Reprinted by arrangement with New American Library, a division of Penguin Books USA, Inc.

HENRIK IBSEN: *Hedda Gabler*, translated by Michael Meyer. Copyright © 1962, 1974 by Michael Meyer. Reprinted by permission of Harold Ober Associates Incorporated. Caution: This play is fully protected, in whole, in part or in any form under the copyright laws of the United States of America, the British Empire including the Dominion of Canada, and all other countries of the Copyright Union, and is subject to royalty. All rights including motion picture, radio, television, recitation, public reading, are strictly reserved. For professional rights and amateur rights all inquiries should be addressed to the Author's Agent: Robert A. Freedman Dramatic Agency Inc., 1501 Broadway, New York, N.Y. 10036.

ARTHUR MILLER: *Death of a Salesman*. Copyright 1949, renewed © 1977 by Arthur Miller. All rights reserved. Reprinted by permission of Viking Penguin, a division of Penguin Books USA, Inc.

MOLIÈRE: *The Doctor in Spite of Himself*, translated by Donald Frame. Copyright © 1968 by Donald Frame. Reprinted by permission of New American Library, a division of Penguin Books USA, Inc.

HAROLD PINTER: "The Black and White" from *Complete Works, Volume 2: Revue Sketches*. Copyright © 1961 by Harold Pinter. Reprinted by permission of Grove Weidenfeld and Methuen.

SHARON POLLOCK: *Blood Relations* from *Blood Relations and Other Plays*, 1981. Reprinted by permission of NeWest Publishers, Ltd., Edmonton.

WILLIAM SHAKESPEARE: Notes to accompany *Hamlet* from the Norton Critical Edition, edited by Cyrus Hoy. Reprinted by permission of W. W. Norton & Company, Inc. Text and footnotes to accompany *A Midsummer Night's Dream* from *Complete Works of Shakespeare* by David Bevington. Copyright © 1980, 1973 by Scott, Foresman and Company. Reprinted by permission.

SOPHOCLES: *Oedipus the King* from *Three Theban Plays*, translated by Robert Fagles. Copyright ©

1982 by Robert Fagles. All rights reserved. Reprinted by permission of Viking Penguin, a division of Penguin Books USA, Inc.

TENNESSEE WILLIAMS: *A Streetcar Named Desire.* Copyright 1947 by Tennessee Williams. Excerpts from *Where I Live.* Copyright © 1978 by Tennessee Williams. Reprinted by permission of New Directions Publishing Corporation.

AUGUST WILSON: *Fences.* Copyright © 1986 by August Wilson. Reprinted by permission of New American Library, a division of Penguin Books USA, Inc.

INDEX OF AUTHORS

INDEX OF TITLES AND FIRST LINES

INDEX OF LITERARY TERMS